W. WAYNE TRITT   10-12-06

W. WAYNE TRITT   10-12-06

THE BRETHREN
ENCYCLOPEDIA

Volume 4

THE BRETHREN ENCYCLOPEDIA

Philadelphia, PA, and Bridgewater, VA: The Brethren Encyclopedia, Inc., 2005

Library of Congress Cataloging in Publication Data
Main entry under title:

The Brethren Enyclopedia
           Includes bibliographies
Church of the Brethren—Dictionaries
Old German Baptist Brethren—Dictionaries
The Brethren Church—Dictionaries
Fellowship of Grace Brethren Churches—Dictionaries
Dunkard Brethren—Dictionaries
Conservative Grace Brethren Churches International—Dictionaries

Library of Congress Number: 84-2003
ISBN Number: 0-936693-04-5

ACKNOWLEDGMENTS

References to specific books and articles follow each quoted passage. Many individuals and institutions provided photographs for use as illustrations in this encyclopedia. Their contributions are acknowledged as part of the photographic captions. Specific mention, however, should be made of the Brethren Historical Library and Archives (BHLA) from which a large number of photographs were secured.

Formatted by Dale V. Ulrich. Printed by The Lakeside Press, R. R. Donnelley & Sons Company, Willard, OH.

TABLE OF CONTENTS

Dedication to the Memory of Donald F. Durnbaugh ix

Introduction xi

Authors xiii

Abbreviations xvii

Articles 2127

List of Ordained Ministers and Elders (ca. 1981–2000) 2271

Necrology of Brethren Ministers and Elders (ca. 1981–2000) 2299

Supplement to Bibliography of the Brethren (ca. 1981–2000) 2309

List of Donors to the *Volume 4* Project of Brethren Encyclopedia, Inc. 2367

Additions and Corrections to *The Brethren Encyclopedia, Volumes 1–3* 2371

Index 2391

Donald F. Durnbaugh. BHLA collection.

DEDICATION TO THE MEMORY OF DONALD F. DURNBAUGH

Donald Floyd Durnbaugh (1927–2005) was born on November 16 in Detroit, MI, and passed away unexpectedly on August 27 in Newark, NJ, following a very brief illness. In recognition of his dedication to Christ and the church, his magnificent historical scholarship, and his wonderful leadership of the effort leading to the creation of *The Brethren Encyclopedia,* the Board of Directors of Brethren Encyclopedia, Inc., dedicates this volume to his memory.

In 1977 when the Brethren bodies were deciding to produce an encyclopedia to describe the Brethren movement, Durnbaugh was the unanimous choice to serve as editor. At that time he was professor of church history at Bethany Theological Seminary, IL, and an outstanding Brethren historian. He served as editor-in-chief supported by a paid office staff; he himself worked on a voluntary basis while continuing with his teaching responsibilities at the Seminary. In addition to his arduous role as editor-in-chief, Durnbaugh personally authored 827 and co-authored 301 of the ca. 6,000 articles in *Volumes 1-2,* published in 1983. *Volume 3,* published in 1984, contained valuable maps, a time-line of events shaping the Brethren

bodies, information on ministers ordained by each of the Brethren bodies from 1708 to 1980, and an exhaustive bibliography of the Brethren which he compiled. Durnbaugh's crucial and extensive work as co-editor of *Volume 4* is detailed in the introduction (pp. xi–xii).

Durnbaugh was educated at Manchester College (BA), the University of Michigan (MA), the University of Pennsylvania (PhD), and Philipps Universität, Marburg, Germany. He served in Brethren Volunteer Service in Europe (1949–51), and as Director of Brethren Service in Austria (1953–56). There he directed resettling of many refugees and developed a project to renovate the Karls-schule in Vienna which had been destroyed during the war.

While he was in Europe in the 1950s, Durnbaugh began researching the early history of the Brethren. He and his wife, Hedda, discovered original documents pertaining to the early Brethren and the Pietists and Anabaptists who helped shape the Brethren movement.

Durnbaugh taught at Juniata College, PA, for four years before joining the faculty of Bethany Theological Seminary in 1962. In 1988 he became the J. Omar Good

Distinguished Visiting Professor at Juniata, and in 1989 the Carl W. Ziegler Professor of History and Religion at Elizabethtown College. At Elizabethtown he was affiliated with the Young Center for the Study of Anabaptist and Pietist Groups. In recognition of his outstanding achievements, honorary doctorates were awarded to Durnbaugh by Manchester College (LHD, 1980) and Juniata College (LHD, 2003).

Throughout his career Durnbaugh was widely recognized as the foremost Brethren historian. Among his numerous books and articles are: *European Origins of the Brethren; Brethren Beginnings: The Origin of the Church of the Brethren in Early Eighteenth-Century Europe; The Brethren in Colonial America; The Believers' Church: The History and Character of Radical Protestantism; Pragmatic Prophet: The Life of Michael Robert Zigler; and Fruit of the Vine: A History of the Brethren, 1708–1995.* (For a list of Durnbaugh's publications, see *The Brethren Encyclopedia,* pp. 1920 – 22 and 2325–27.)

Durnbaugh served the Church of the Brethren in numerous capacities. His responsibilities included moderator in 1985–86, director of the Brethren Colleges Abroad program in Marburg, Germany, in 1964–65; leadership of the 1971 Brethren-Russian Orthodox Exchange; membership on an annual conference study committee on church and state; the Brethren Historical Committee; and the Germantown Trust. At the time of his death, he was a member of the committee planning the 300th anniversary of the beginning of the Brethren movement.

Thus, the Board of Directors of Brethren Encyclopedia, Inc. gives thanks for the life and achievements of Donald F. Durnbaugh and dedicates this volume to his memory. DVU

INTRODUCTION

The lengthy introduction included on pages v-xi of *Volume 1* of *The Brethren Encyclopedia* (1983-84) provides the background for this reference work. At the time of the incorporation of the encyclopedia project (1978), the board of directors, then established, was authorized to produce not only the first three volumes of the work but also to publish related items. Among these have been monographs, source books, and videotapes.

It was not long after the release of *Volumes 1-3* that the suggestion was made to plan in due course for a fourth volume. This was intended to provide: (1) articles on events and initiatives that took place after the general cut-off date for the original set, that is 1980, (2) additions and corrections, and, importantly, (3) a comprehensive index to make readily available the mass of factual information spread throughout the volumes.

The Brethren Encyclopedia Board began serious discussion of the suggestion to produce a fourth volume in its regular fall meeting in November 1994. D. F. Durnbaugh, editor of the first volumes, was asked to draft a prospectus of a potential *Volume 4,* which was presented to the board in the spring meeting, March 1995. At the subsequent fall board meeting, November 1995, members voted to authorize the creation and publication of a fourth volume.

A smaller meeting held in Bridgewater, VA, in the summer of 1996, as well as the fall meeting of the board in November 1996, continued the planning. Finally, on April 14-15, 1997, a meeting of a newly-selected Editorial Board met at Ashland, OH, to organize itself, settle editorial policies, establish deadlines, agree upon articles, and assign writers. This body decided to follow generally the method and style used in the first three volumes.

Members of the original Editorial Board, and their respective denominations, were:

Dale R. Stoffer (The Brethren Church)
Bradley E. Weidenhamer (The Brethren Church)
Donald E. Miller (Church of the Brethren)
Robert S. Lehigh (Dunkard Brethren)
Jacob C. Ness (Dunkard Brethren) (dec.)
Ronald T. Clutter (Fellowship of Grace Brethren Churches)
Jerry R. Young (Fellowship of Grace Brethren Churches)
Fred W. Benedict (Old German Baptist Brethren)
Glen L. Landes (Old German Baptist Brethren)

To this number were added in the course of time:

Kenneth M. Shaffer, Jr. (Church of the Brethren)
John E. Bryant (Conservative Grace Brethren Churches International)

D. F. Durnbaugh and Carl F. Bowman were named co-editors for the project, and Bridgewater College, Bridgewater, VA, was selected as the site of the editorial office. By agreement, Durnbaugh was to compile the necessary additions and corrections for the first three volumes and a supplement updating the extensive bibliography found in Volume 3 (pp. 1857-2111), while Bowman was to organize the acquisition and editing of new articles and arrange for the comprehensive index. Members of the Brethren Encyclopedia Board approved these persons and the projected plans in its meeting of April 16, 1997, which immediately followed that of the Editorial Board. The Brethren Encyclopedia Board took on the heavy responsibility for raising needed funds for *Volume 4*.

In the fall of 1998 a recent graduate of Bridgewater College, Darin Keith Bowman, was employed on a part-time basis to implement publishing plans as an assistant for Carl F. Bowman, in office space made available by the Sociology Department of the College. These two men sent out assignments, received most of the draft articles, reassigned articles where necessary, followed up extensively on tardy articles, and began the process of creating an index. By the autumn of 2000, it became evident that the indexing task was too great for the small office, and Darin Keith Bowman resigned his position. A professional indexer was sought, and a contract was signed early in 2001 with Kate Mertes, Alexandria, VA.

About this same time, because of his involvement in a major and demanding research program at the University of Virginia, which required a leave of absence from Bridgewater College, Carl F. Bowman found that he was unable to continue the tasks of following up on tardy articles, editing articles, re-assigning articles as needed, and compiling necessary lists. Dale V. Ulrich stepped into the breach, functioning first as managing editor of the project and then as co-editor with D. F. Durnbaugh. The successful completion of the manuscript is largely owing to his dedication, perseverance, and hundreds of hours of work. Both Ulrich and Durnbaugh edited the submitted articles, with the latter paying special attention to bibliographical citations. The former had major responsibility for securing tardy articles, facilitating reviews of edited articles by the authors and the editorial board, and compiling the list of newly ordained ministers, as well as the necrology of deceased ministers. Both men worked on the acquisition of appropriate illustrations, and Ulrich formatted the entire document in preparation for printing.

Numerous persons were exceedingly helpful as the *Volume 4* project progressed. In the Alexander Mack Memorial Library at Bridgewater College, Ruth E. Greenawalt, Director, and Terrell W. Barkley, Archivist, provided excellent help with resources. Emmert and Esther Bittinger provided funding for the purchase of a computer for the Brethren Encyclopedia office. Also, in the summer of 2004, Joshua T. Randall, student assistant in the library, double checked bibliographic references. Early in the work leading up to the *Volume 4* effort, Jennifer T. Sappington (summer, 1996), Sean S. North (summers, 1997-98), Sherri N. Simpson (part-time 1998), and Sara Lynn Crummett (part-time during the 1998-99 academic year) scanned the pages of *Volumes 1-2* to convert them to a computer file. David L. Brightbill and Haripriya I. Spreekumaran volunteered briefly in the spring of 2004 to phone ordained ministers who had not returned their questionnaires.

Several persons served as proofreaders. Reading all of the articles were Stanley J. Gilbert and Fred W. Benedict. In addition, the following worked as two teams to proofread the articles: Esther L. Bittinger, Naoma R. Clague, Jesse D. Robertson, LeVerle H. Sappington, Miriam R.

Smith, and Lucile H. Vaughn. In addition, helpful suggestions were made by Fred W. Benedict, Hedwig T. Durnbaugh, Marlin L. Heckman, and Claire M. Ulrich.

Those connected with this ambitious project, almost all contributing their time on a voluntary basis, are convinced that *Volume 4* will be considered a capstone of the entire Brethren Encyclopedia effort. The articles contained within it will serve to bring the general Brethren story up through the year 2000, that is to the cusp of the new century; additions and corrections will aid readers and researchers to receive more adequate and accurate information; and finally, of especial significance, the comprehensive index will open up all four volumes, revealing connections previously unseen. Though quite conscious of the limitations of this work, the editors and others involved are confident that their labors will prove useful to a large number of persons, including those of future generations.

D. F. Durnbaugh	Dale V. Ulrich	Carl F. Bowman
Co-Editor	Co-Editor	Contributing Editor

AUTHORS

This list of authors of articles in *Volume 4* is organized in accord with the policy followed in listing authors in *Volume 1*. In order that contributors may be identified, initials and names are provided along with brief locations of authors. Where possible, maiden names of married women who contributed articles have been used to help establish the initials. Although many authors possess them, neither titles nor academic degrees have been appended. Some contributors, we regret to report, died before the publication of this volume; they are designated by the abbreviation "dec." following their names. The listing is arranged by alphabetical order of initials within each letter grouping. Thus, all last names beginning with the letter "A" are listed first, alphabetized by initials, then all last names beginning with "B" and so on. It has not been possible, in this listing, to indicate which articles have been written by which authors.

HRA H. Raymond Aspinall
Orrville, OH

REA Richard E. Allison
Ashland, OH

CAB Christina A. Bucher
Elizabethtown, PA

CFB Carl F. Bowman
Grottoes, VA

CWBo Carl W. Bowman
Covington, OH

DKB Darrin Keith Bowman
Bridgewater, VA

DLB David L. Brumbaugh
Camden, IN

DWBr Dale W. Brown
Elizabethtown, PA

EFB Emmert F. Bittinger
Bridgewater, VA

FEB Floyd E. Bantz
Lancaster, PA

FMBo Fred M. Bowman
Bridgewater, VA

FMBow Freda M. Bowser
Arcanum, OH

FWB Fred W. Benedict
Union City, OH

GAB Gerald A. Barr
Hagerstown, MD

HZB Harold Z. Bomberger
Palmyra, PA

JAB Jeffrey Alan Bach
Richmond, IN

JBB Janice B. Burkholder
Ephrata, PA

JEB John E. Bryant
Mount Vernon, OH

JMBe James M. Beckwith
Dayton, VA

LABa Linetta A. Ballew
Harrisonburg, VA

LBB Louise Baugher Black
Lancaster, PA

MLBo Mary Louise Boyd
Venice, FL

MPB Myrna P. Baer
Friedens, PA

MPBr Margery P. Brubaker
Frederick, MD

REBo Ronald E. Boehm
Macedonia, OH

RGB Robert G. Byers
Bradenton, FL

SB SueZann Bosler
Hollandale, FL

SPB Shantilal Premchand Bhagat
La Verne, CA

ANC Alan N. Clingan
Greencastle, PA

BBC Brenda B. Colijn
Dublin, OH

BMC B. Merle Crouse
St. Cloud, FL

DAC Dale A. Claes
Marion, OH

DEC David E. Cooksey
Ashland, OH

DWC Donald W. Curry
Durbin, WV

GPBC Gerald P. Baile Crouse
Warrensburg, MO

KIC Kenneth I. Cosgrove
Pottstown, PA

LEC Leslie E. Cover
Tuohumne, CA

LNC Larry N. Chamberlain
Winona Lake, IN

OAC Olivia Ann Chapman
Inwood, WV

RBCr Rebecca Baile Crouse
Warrensburg, MO

RGC Robert G. Clouse
Terre Haute, IN

RTC Ronald T. Clutter
Newburgh, IN

TWC Thomas W. Conrad
Dillingham, AK

ACD Allen C. Deeter
North Manchester, IN

AVD Alma V. Dean
Romney, WV

DFD Donald F. Durnbaugh
James Creek, PA

DMD D. Miller Davis
Westminster, MD

EHD Edna H. Denlinger
Brookville, OH

GCD G. Calvin Durham
Eaton, OH

GED Gerald E. Deffenbaugh
Friedens, PA

JADa Jerry A. Davis
La Verne, CA

JGD Joan G. Deeter
North Manchester, IN

JJD John J. Davis
Warsaw, IN

KLD Kirby L. Dubble
Lebanon, PA

MED Mary Ellen Drushal
Ashland, OH

RLD Ralph L. Detrick
Elizabethtown, PA

DBE David B. Eller
Elizabethtown, PA

EEE Eldon E. Eller
San Marcos, CA

EPE Enten Pfaltzgraff Eller
La Verne, CA

GBE Guillermo B. Encarnación
Lancaster, PA

JOE James O. Eikenberry
Wilmington, DE

KPE Kathryn Pfaltzgraff Eller
La Verne, CA

TLE Thomas L. Eller
Cleveland, GA

WRE William R. Eberly
North Manchester, IN

CCF Clyde C. Fry
Mansfield, OH

DRF Donald R. Fitzkee
Manheim, PA

EWF, Jr. Earle W. Fike, Jr.
Bridgewater, VA

FJFi Fred J. Finks
Ashland, OH

GCF Galen C. Filbrun
Modesto, CA

LAF Lowell A. Flory
McPherson, KS

NPF Nadine Pence Frantz
Richmond, IN

NRF Nancy Rosenberger Faus
Richmond, IN

RRF Ronald R. Fleming
Powell, OH

SF Stephanie Farrier
Winona Lake, IN

WPF Wendell P. Flory (dec.)
Bridgewater, VA

AEG Arden E. Gilmer
Ashland, OH

DEG Duane E. Grady
Andersen, IN

EQG Elmer Q. Gleim
York, PA

FJG Fred J. Gerber
Lakeland, FL

GWG G. Wayne Grumbling
Indianapolis, IN

HLG H. Lamar Gibble
St. Charles, IL

JAGib June A. Gibble
Elgin, IL

JEGi Jay E. Gibble
Elgin, IL

JHGi John H. Gingrich
Claremont, CA

JLG Julie L. Garber
North Manchester, IN

PEG Paul E. Grout
Putney, VT

RAGr Robert A. Gross
North Manchester, IN

RBG Richard B. Gardner
Richmond, IN

RDGr R. Dallas Greene
Frederick, MD

SSG Sonja Sherfy Griffith
Kansas City, KS

WFGr Warren F. Groff
Bartlett, IL

WKG Warren K. Garner
North Manchester, IN

ARH Amy R. Heckert
Elgin, IL

ATH Allan T. Hansell
Mountville, PA

DMHo Debbie M. Hofecker
Dublin, OH

EBH Estella Boggs Horning
Goshen, IN

ELH Ervin L. Huston
Westerport, MD

GGH Gregory G. Harvey
Columbia, MO

JEHo James E. Hollinger
Goshen, IN

MEH Mildred Etter Heckert (dec.)
Elgin, IL

MWH Matthew W. Hamel
Montoursville, PA

RDH Reuben D. Hess
Greencastle, PA

DKJ Debra K. Johnson
Dublin, OH

RJ Renee Jenks
Island Pond, VT

RKJ Ruthann Knechel Johansen
Granger, IN

SMJ Stephen M. Jerrell
Lexington, KY

TTJ Thomas T. Julien
Warsaw, IN

AKK Arnold K. Kriegbaum
Ocala, FL

DBK Donald B. Kraybill
Elizabethtown, PA

EMK Edith Mae Kiester
Cuba, NM

HDK Herman D. Kauffman
Nappanee, IN

HSK Harvey S. Kline
New Oxford, PA

JGK Judith G. Kipp
Harrisburg, PA

JKK J. Kenneth Kreider
Elizabethtown, PA

KLK Karen L. Keller
Wales, ME

JMKe J. Mervin Keller
Wales, ME

MBK Mervin B. Keeney
Elgin, IL

REKe Robert E. Keim
Tucson, AZ

RGK Ronald G. Kreider
Stevens, PA

RLK Robert L. Keplinger
Ashland, OH

RWKi Russel W. Kiester
Cuba, NM

SBK Stewart B. Kauffman
Lancaster, PA

WHK William H. Kerner
Ashland, OH

DLL Dan L. Lawson
Ashland, OH

EAL Edward A. Lewis
Winona Lake, IN

JHL James H. Lehman
Elgin, IL

JKL Janice K. Long
Fort Wayne, IN

JWL, Jr. John W. Lowe, Jr.
Roanoke, VA

LELo Lois E. Long
Rossville, IN

OBL Olen B. Landes
Harrisonburg, VA

RGL Ronald G. Lutz
Ambler, PA

RSL Robert S. Lehigh
Spring Grove, PA

SLL Stephen L. Longenecker
Harrisonburg, VA

TLL Thomas L. Longenecker
Castaic, CA

WWL William W. Longenecker
Mt. Joy, PA

BMMe Benjamin Matthew Merrill
Wheaton, IL

DEM Donald E. Miller
Richmond, IN

DEMa David E. Marksbury
Maple Valley, WA

DEMi Dale E. Minnich
Moundridge, KS

DRM Donna Ritchey Martin
Myersville, MD

EWM E. William Male
Warsaw, IN

HSMa Harold S. Martin
Lititz, PA

JCM James C. McKinnell
Midlothian, VA

JCMi Juan Carlos Miranda
Pasadena, CA

JDM John D. Meyers
Moselle, MS

KMM Kathleen M. Metzger
Waynesboro, PA

MAM Melanie A. May
Rochester, NY

MAMi Melanie A. Miller
Carrboro, NC

MAMu M. Andew Murray
Huntingdon, PA

MFM Maria F. Miranda
Pasadena, CA

MM Marcus Miller
Pleasant Hill, OH

PM Paul Mundey
Frederick, MD

RLMa Ronald L. Marks
Hart, MI

RMM Rex M. Miller
Milford, IN

RRM Ronald R. Maust
Millersburg, OH

SAM Sara A. Miller
Greenville, OH

TAM Timothy A. McElwee
North Manchester, IN

WHM William H. Marling
New Albany, OH

DLN Debbie L. Noffsinger
Union Bridge, MD

DRN Dean R. Neher
Bridgewater, VA

FCN Fran Clemens Nyce
Westminster, MD

FDN Ferrell D. Nachatelo
Mauston, WI

FMN Frederick M. Nuzum
Powell, OH

LCN Leon C. Neher
Quinter, KS

WEN Wilfred E. Nolan
Elgin, IL

DRP David R. Plaster
Winona Lake, IN

JKP Jeffrey Kyle Peeler
Everett, PA

MP Mykel Pamperin
Grove City, OH

RJP Robert J. Pearson
Philadelphia, PA

DKRo Deborah K. Roberts
La Verne, CA

DLRo David L. Rogers
North Manchester, IN

DSMR Debra S. Michael Ritchey
Ashland, OH

ERR Emily R. Remillard
Eagle River, AK

HER Howard E. Royer
Elgin, IL

JER Jobie E. Riley
Elizabethtown, PA

MRR Martin R. Rock
Washington, DC

MSR Mary Sue Rosenberger
Greenville, OH

OR Orlando Redekopp
Chicago, IL

SBR Stephen B. Reid
Richmond, IN

SFRe Shawn Flory Replogle
McPherson, KS

TJR Timothy J. Ruesch
London, OH

BCS Brian C. Smith
Riverside, CA

CBS Carol B. Strickler
Gerardstown, WV

CSu Chris Suitt
Menefee, CA

DKS David K. Shumate
Roanoke, VA

DLSh David L. Shuman
Pendleton, IN

DLSt David L. Stone
Sarasota, FL

DPS Donald P. Shoemaker
Long Beach, CA

DRS Dale R. Stoffer
Ashland, OH

EMS Elaine Mock Sollenberger
Everette, PA

GFS Graydon F. Snyder
Chicago, IL

HSS Helen S. Stonesifer
New Windsor, MD

JLS Julie Lynn Smith
Pennsburg, PA

JMS Janet M. Smith
Blain, PA

JPS James P. Sluss
Krypton, KY

JRS Joseph R. Shultz (dec.)
Ashland, OH

KKS Kenneth Kline Smeltzer
Boalsburg, PA

KLSol Kenneth L. Solomon
Bradenton, FL

KMS, Jr. Kenneth M. Shaffer, Jr.
Elgin, IL

LAS Leroy A. Solomon
Ashland, OH

LSt Ludovic St. Fleur
Miami, FL

MJSw Mary Jane Swihart
Quinter, KS

PCS Phillip C. Stone
Bridgewater, VA

PLS Paul L. Stump
Englewood, OH

RASm Ronald A. Smals
Ocala, FL

RASo Robert A. Soto
McAllen, TZ

ROS Roger O. Stogsdill
Tucson, AZ

RRSm Reilly R. Smith
Ashland, OH

SESp Sara E. Speicher
Lancaster, United Kingdom

SRS Shyrl R. Smith
Franklin, WV

TES Thomas E. Sprowls
Berlin, PA

TLS Timothy L. Solomon
Sarasota, FL

WDSt W. Dean St. John
Ephrata, PA

CWT Charles W. Turner (dec.)
Winona Lake, IN

DET Daniel E. Thorton
Saldotna, AK

DGT Darrel G. Taylor
Stevens City, VA

JHT J Hudson Thayer
Mansfield, OH

RET Ronald E. Thompson
Mesa, Az

DVU Dale V. Ulrich
Bridgewater, VA

DEW Don E. White
Bradenton, FL

DLW Dennis L. Wray
Ellensburg, WA

GCW Gerald C. Wagoner
Bradford, OH

GEW, Jr. Guy E. Wampler, Jr.
Lancaster, PA

JDW Jeffrey D. Weidenhamer
Ashland, OH

JSW Jena S. Wells
Ashland, OH

LHW Lydia H. Walker
New Windsor, MD

MLW, Jr. Murray L. Wagner, Jr.
Richmond, IN

MLWo Michael L. Woods
Winchester, VA

RCWi Richard C. Winfield
Ashland, OH

RWW Ronald W. Waters
Waterloo, IA

WJW Walter J. Wiltschek
Elgin, IL

JRY Jerry R. Young
Manheim, PA

KEY Kathryn E. Yelinek
Boulder, CO

MDY M. Dwayne Yost
Manchester, KY

IRZ Irma R. Zayas
San Sebastian, P.R.

PNZ Philip N. Zinn
Bridgewater, VA

ABBREVIATIONS

General Abbreviations

Most abbreviations used in the encyclopedia are those in common currency and should thus be readily understood. These include academic degrees, directional designations, months of the year, books of the Bible, and the like. The two authorities employed by the editors in determining abbreviations were *Webster's Third New International Dictionary* (1976) and the University of Chicago *Manual of Style* (12th, revised edition, 1969). The two-letter codes established by the United States Postal Service ZIP Code were used for the fifty states. Provincial names in Canada follow this usage: Alberta – Alta., British Columbia – BC, Ontario – Ont., and Saskatchewan – Sask.

Organizational and institutional names are given in full upon first mention within each article, along with the abbreviations or acronyms to be used henceforth. The following list includes those abbreviations appearing most often in the encyclopedia, with special reference to denominational usages not well known to the broader reading public.

* Symbol used for cross references.

abr. abridged.

ATS Ashland Theological Seminary.

ave att. average Sunday morning worship service attendance.

b. born.

BC The Brethren Church (Progressive Brethren), 1883-.

BHLA Brethren Historical Library and Archives, Church of the Brethren General Offices, Elgin, IL.

bibliog. bibliography; bibliographical.

biog. biography; biographical.

BSC Brethren Service Committee (1939-47) or Brethren Service Commission (1947-69).

BTS Bethany Theological Seminary.

BVS Brethren Volunteer Service.

ca. circa.

CB Church of the Brethren, 1908-.

cf. compare.

ch. chapter(s).

Co. county.

CO conscientious objector.

comp. compiler; compiled by.

CGBCI Conservative Grace Brethren Churches International, 1992-.

CPS Civilian Public Service.

d. died.

DB Dunkard Brethren, 1926-.

diss. dissertation.

ed. editor(s); edition.

ff. and following.

FGBC Fellowship of Grace Brethren Churches (formerly National Fellowship of Brethren Churches), 1939-.

fl. flourished.

GBB German Baptist Brethren.

GTS Grace Theological Seminary.

illus. illustrated.

KJV King James or Authorized Version (1611).

m. married.

MS manuscript.

n.d. no date [of publication] known.

NEB New English Bible (1961, 1970).

no. number(s).

n.p. no place [of publication] known.

ns. new series.

OB Old Brethren, 1913-

OGBB Old German Baptist Brethren, 1881-.

p., pp. page; pages.

passim scattered references.

repr. reprinted; reprint edition.

rev. revised.

RSV Revised Standard Version (1946, 1952, 1971).

trans. translator; translated; translation.

Twp. township.

U. University.

vol. volume(s).

Inasmuch as extensive bibliographical citations follow all articles, titles of books, periodicals, and other sources are given in abbreviated form. Those titles used most often are most sharply abbreviated. These include district histories, standard histories, source books, and denominational periodicals. Titles of non-Brethren periodicals are also abbreviated if they are cited several times or more. Books used less often in the citations are listed with somewhat shortened, yet still recognizable, titles. Full bibliographical citations—with authors' names, complete titles, and publication data—are found in volume three of the encyclopedia. In those cases where reference is made in article bibliographies to publications not included in volume three, full names of authors are provided in the initial listing to enable easier library location.

The following list identifies those materials with very brief titles. Many periodicals are listed by initials. In many cases names of authors or editors have been omitted. By use of these techniques a great deal of space has been saved.

AAS *Proceedings Proceedings* of the American Antiquarian Society, Worcester, MA (New Series, 1880-).

AGR *American German Review* (1934-).

AJS *American Journal of Sociology* (1895-).

Almanac *The Pilgrim Almanac* (1873-74); *The Brethren's Family Almanac* (1875-1902); *Brethren Family Almanac* (1902-17).

Almanac (BW) *The Brethren at Work Almanac and Annual Register for All the People* (1881-?).

Almanac (Holsinger) *The Brethren's Almanac for the United States* (1871-74).

F. Ankrum, *Sidelights (1962)* Freeman Ankrum, *Sidelights on Brethren History* (Elgin, IL: 1962).

Annals *The Annals of the American Academy of Political and Social Science* (1890.).

Annual (BC) *The Brethren [Brethren's] Annual* (1884-); also known as *Brethren Evangelist, Annual Conference Number,* since 1976 as *General Conference Annual.*

Annual (FGBC) *Grace Brethren Annual* (1940-); also titled *Brethren Annual* (1940-77).

ATB *Ashland Theological Bulletin,* published by Ashland Theological Seminary, 1968-80; after 1981 called *Ashland Theological Journal.*

ATS, Ronk files, "N.N." Ashland Theological Seminary, A. T. Ronk files by name of subject or person.

Bb *Der Brüderbote* (1875-77).

Bb *Der Brüderbote* (1880-92).

BB (1964) Donald F. Durnbaugh and Lawrence W. Shultz, comps., "A Brethren Bibliography, 1713-1963," *BLT* 9 (Winter-Spring, 1964) 3-177.

BB (1966) Donald F. Durnbaugh, "Supplement and Index to the Brethren Bibliography," *BLT* 11 (Spring, 1966) 37-54.

BB (1970) Donald F. Durnbaugh, "Second Supplement to the Brethren Bibliography," *BLT* (Autumn, 1970) 187-204.

BBS Bulletin *Bethany Bible School Bulletin* (1912-30); *Bethany Biblical Seminary Bulletin* (1931-62).

BBS Evangel *Bethany Bible School Evangel* (published 1921, 1925, 1929); copies at Bethany Theological Seminary library/archives.

BE *The Brethren Evangelist* (BC) (1883-).

W. M. Beahm, *Christian Belief (1958)* William A. Beahm, *Studies in Christian Belief* (Elgin, IL: 1958).

F. W. Benedict, *Dunkers (OGBB) (1973)* Fred W. Benedict, *History, Belief, and Practice of the Dunkers (Old German Baptist Brethren),* rev. ed. (Covington, OH: 1973).

BHLA, biog. file Brethren Historical Library and Archives, biographical file.

BHLA, inactive ministers' file Brethren Historical Library and Archives, "deceased ministers" file.

BHLA, WMC pers./corr. file Brethren Historical Library and Archives, World Ministries Commission personnel/correspondence file (includes index to *Gospel Messenger* and *Missionary Visitor* articles about or by the subject of the file).

E. F. Bittinger, *Heritage (1970)* Emmert F. Bittinger, *Heritage and Promise: Perspectives on the Church of the Brethren* (Elgin, IL: 1970); rev. ed., 1983.

BLT *Brethren Life and Thought* (1955-).

Blue Book (1923) W. Arthur Cable and Homer F. Sanger, eds., *Educational Blue Book and Directory of the Church of the Brethren. 1708-1923* (Elgin, IL: 1923).

BM *The Brethren Missionary* (BC) (1917-35); merged with *BE* in 1935.

BMH *The Brethren Missionary Herald (FGBC)* (1939-).

P. H. Bowman, *Brethren Education SE (1955)* Paul H. Bowman, *Brethren Education in the Southeast* (Bridgewater,VA: 1955).

R. D. Bowman, *Brethren and War (1944)* Rufus D. Bowman, *The Church of the Brethren and War, 1708-1941* (Elgin, IL: 1944); reprinted 1971.

BQ *The Brethren [Brethren's] Quarterly* (1888-).

"Brethren Social Issues," BTS library "Brethren Social issues: Collected Papers." bound volume of typescript and mimeographed papers submitted to F. E. Mallott, Bethany Biblical Seminary, 1943-59.

Brethren's Tracts (1892) *The Brethren's Tracts and Pamphlets; Setting Forth the Claims of Primitive Christianity* (Elgin, IL: 1892).

BRF Witness *B[rethren] R[evival] F[ellowship] Witness* (1966-).

Bridgewater-Daleville (1930) John W. Wayland, ed., *Fifty Years of Educational Endeavor, Bridgewater College, 1880-1930; Daleville College, 1890-1930* (Staunton, VA: 1930).

H. B. Brumbaugh, Church Manual (1887) Henry B. Brumbaugh, *The Brethren's Church Manual Containing the Declaration of Faith, Rules of Order, How to Conduct Religious Meetings, etc.* (Huntingdon, PA; Mt. Morris, IL: 1887).

M. G. Brumbaugh, History GBB (1899) Martin G. Brumbaugh, *A History of the German Baptist Brethren in Europe and America* (Elgin, IL: 1899).

BTM *Brethren Teacher's Monthly* (CB) (1907-58).

Builders (1952) *Brethren Builders in Our Century* (Elgin, IL: 1952).

BW *Brethren at Work* (1876-83).

BWK *Blätter für württembergische Kirchengeschichte* (1886-).

California (1917) Matthew Mays Eshelman, ed., *History of the Church of the Brethren [Southern California and Arizona]* (Los Angeles. CA: 1917).

Carolinas (1971) Roger F. Sappington, *The Brethren in the Carolinas: The History of the Church of the Brethren in the District of North and South Carolina* (Kingsport, TN: [1971]).

CC *Christian Century* (1884-).

CFC *Christian Family Companion* (1864-74) and *Christian Family Companion and Gospel Visitor* (1874-76).

CH *Church History* (1932-).

Chronicon Ephratense (1786, 1889) Lamech and Agrippa, *Chronicon Ephratense, Enthaltend den Lebens-Lauf des ehrwürdigen Vaters in Christo Friedsam Gottrecht . . .* (Ephrata, PA: 1786); English trans. by J. Max Hark (Lancaster, PA: 1889).

Class. Min. (1778-1885) [Samuel S. Mohler, comp.], *Classified Minutes of the Annual Meetings of the Brethren* (Mt. Morris, IL; Huntingdon, PA: 1886).

Class. Min. (OGBB) (1944) Old German Baptist Brethren, *Minutes of The Annual Meetings of the Old German Baptist Church (Classified). From 1778 to 1943 and Appendix* (Ashland, OH: 1944).

Class Min. See also *Minutes; Rev. Min.; Brethren's Encyclopedia* (1867).

Colonial America (1967) Donald F. Durnbaugh, ed., *The Brethren in Colonial America* (Elgin, IL: 1967).

"Colorado" (1963) Blanche B. Frantz, "A History of the Church of the Brethren in Colorado, 1874-1957" (n.p.: ([1963]); mimeographed.

CT *Christianity Today* (1956-).

DAB *Dictionary of American Biography,* 21 vols. (New York: 1928-37); reprinted (1943); supplements (1944-74).

Deacon *The Deacon* (1878-79).

DNB *Dictionary of National Biography,* 22 vols. (London: 1885-1901); reprinted (1938); supplements (1901-81).

Doctrinal Treatise (OGBB) (1954, 1970) H. M. Fisher and others, *Doctrinal Treatise, Old German Baptist Brethren* (Covington, OH: 1954; rev. 1970).

Doctrine and Devotion (1919) D. W. Kurtz, S. S. Blough, and C. C. Ellis, *Studies in Doctrine and Devotion* (Elgin, IL: 1919).

Dunkard Brethren Polity (1980) *Dunkard Brethren Church Polity,* rev. ed. (n.p., 1980).

D. F. Durnbaugh, Brethren Beginnings (1962) Donald F. Durnbaugh, *Brethren Beginnings: The Origin of the Church of the Brethren in Early Eighteenth-Century Europe* (Philadelphia: Brethren Encyclopedia, Inc., 1962.

D. F. Durnbaugh, ed., Past and Present (1971) Donald F. Durnbaugh, ed., *The Church of the Brethren: Past and Present* (Elgin, IL: 1971).

D. F. Durnbaugh, ed., Present Age (1975) Donald F. Durnbaugh, ed., *To Serve the Present Age: The Brethren Service Story* by M. R. Zigler and Other Former Participants (Elgin, IL: 1975).

E. Pennsylvania (1915) S. R. Zug and others, *History of the Church of the Brethren of the Eastern District of Pennsylvania* (Lancaster, PA: 1915).

E. Pennsylvania (1965) Guy K. Saylor and others, *History of the Church of the Brethren, Eastern Pennsylvania. 1915-1963* (Lancaster, PA: 1965).

EB *Der evangelische Besuch* (1852-61).

"Elkhart Co." (1942) Paul C. Lantis, "A History of the Church of the Brethren in Elkhart County, Indiana" (BD thesis, Bethany Biblical Seminary, 1942).

D. B. Eller, "Ohio Valley" (1976) David B. Eller, "The Brethren in the Western Ohio Valley, 1790-1850: German Baptist Settlement and Frontier Accommodation" (PhD diss., Miami University, OH, 1976).

European Origins (1958) Donald F. Durnbaugh, ed., *European Origins of the Brethren* (Elgin, IL: 1958).

G. N. Falkenstein, *History GBB (1900)* George N. Falkenstein, *A History of the German Baptist Brethren Church* (Lancaster, PA: 1900).

"Florida" (1941) M. Margaret Parker, "A History of the Church of the Brethren in Florida" (BD thesis, Bethany Biblical Seminary. 1941).

Florida, Georgia (1953) James H. Morris, *Twenty-Five Years of Organized Work in Florida and Georgia by the Church of the Brethren from 1925 to 1950* (Hartville, MO: 1953).

Florida, Puerto Rico (1975) Elgin S. Moyer and others, *Brethren in Florida and Puerto Rico* (Elgin, IL: 1975).

J. S. Flory, *Literary Activity (1908)* John S. Flory, *Literary Activity of the German Baptist Brethren in the Eighteenth Century* (Elgin. IL: 1908).

FoBG *Newsletter Newsletter, Fellowship of Brethren Genealogists* (1969-).

Foreign Mission Echoes Foreign Mission Echoes, published monthly since ca. 1958 by the Foreign Missionary Society of the Fellowship of Grace Brethren Churches.

Full Report Report of the Proceedings of the Annual Meeting of the Brethren (Huntingdon, PA; Mt. Morris, IL: 1876-1930); later, *Full Report of the Proceedings of the Annual Conference of the Church of the Brethren,* reprinted in 9 vols. (Elgin, IL:1930).

A. M. Funke, "Ephrata Bibliography" (1944) Anneliese Marckwald Funke, "Ephrata: The Printing Press of the Brotherhood," in *The Ephrata Cloisters, An Annotated Bibliography* (Philadelphia, PA: 1944).

General Conference Annual (BC) See *Annual (BC).*

GM *The Gospel Messenger* (Mt. Morris, IL; Elgin, IL:1883-1965); became *Messenger* (1965).

GP *The Gospel Preacher* (1879-82).

GT *The Gospel Trumpet* (1873-76).

GV *The (Monthly) Gospel-Visitor* (1851-74).

R. V. Hanle, "Higher Education" (1974) Robert V. Hanle, "A History of Higher Education Among the German Baptist Brethren, 1708-1908" (PhD diss., University of Pennsylvania, 1974).

C. R. Hildeburn, *Pennsylvania Press (1885)* Charles R. Hildeburn, *A Century of Printing. The Issues of the Press of Pennsylvania, 1685-1784,* 2 vols. (Philadelphia, PA: 1885-86).

H. R. Holsinger, *Tunkers (1901)* Henry R. Holsinger, *Holsinger's History of the Tunkers and the Brethren Church* (Latbrop, CA: 1901); reprinted 1962.

Idaho, Montana (1914) [Aaron I. Mow, ed.], *A Brief History of Idaho and Western Montana As Settled and District Organized by the Church of the Brethren* (n.p.: 1914).

IMH *Indiana Magazine of History* (1905-).

Indiana (1917) Otho Winger, *History of the Church of the Brethren in Indiana* (Elgin, IL: 1917).

Indiana (1952) District Conferences of the Church of the Brethren in Indiana, *History of the Church of the Brethren in Indiana* (Winona Lake, IN: 1952).

Inglenook The Inglenook (1900-13).

Insight Insight into Brethren Missions (published monthly by the Missionary Board of the Brethren Church, ca. 1970-).

ISHS *Journal Illinois State Historical Society Journal* (1908-).

ISHS *Transactions Illinois State Historical Society Transactions* (1900-).

JHSCV *Journal of the Historical Society of the Cocalico Valley* (1976-).

JSSR *Journal for the Scientific Study of Religion* (1961-).

JUHS *Journal of the Universalist Historical Society* (1959-).

Kansas (1922) Elmer L. Craik, *A History of the Church of the Brethren in Kansas* (McPherson, KS: 1922).

H. A. Kent, Sr., *Frontiers (1958)* Homer A. Kent, Sr., *250 Years . . . Conquering Frontiers: A History of the Brethren Church* (Winona Lake, IN: 1958).

H. A. Kent, Sr., *Frontiers, 2nd ed. (1972)* Homer A. Kent, Sr., *Conquering Frontiers: A History of the Brethren Church (The National Fellowship of Brethren Churches)* (Winona Lake, IN: 1972).

J. M. Kimmel, *Chronicles (1951)* John M. Kimmel, *Chronicles of the Brethren. Comprising a Concise History of the Brethren or Dunker Church . . . and the . . . History of the Old German Baptist Church to . . . A.D. 1900* (Covington, OH: 1951).

H. Kurtz, ed. *Encyclopedia (1867)* Henry Kurtz, ed., *The Brethren's Encyclopedia* (Columbiana, OH: 1867).

LCHS *Papers Papers and Addresses* of the Lancaster County [PA] Historical Society (1896-).

J. H. Lehman, *Old Brethren (1976)* James H. Lehman, *The Old Brethren* (Elgin, IL: 1976).

LMHSLA Lancaster Mennonite Historical Society Library and Archives, Lancaster, PA.

I. G. Long, *Faces (1962)* lnez G. Long, *Faces Among the Faithful* (Elgin, IL: 1962).

M. *Pennsylvania (1925)* [Galen B. Royer and others], *A History of the Church of the Brethren in the Middle District of Pennsylvania* (n.p.: [1925]).

M. Pennsylvania (1981) Earl C. Kaylor, Jr., *Out of the Wilderness, 1780-1980: The Brethren and Two Centuries of Life in Central Pennsylvania* (New York, NY: 1981).

F. E. Mallot, *Studies (1954)* Floyd E. Mallott, *Studies in Brethren History* (Elgin, IL: 1954).

Manchester College (1964) Russell V. Bolinger and others, *Manchester College: The First Seventy-Five Years* (Elgin, IL: 1964).

D. D. Martin, "Grace" (1973) Dennis D. Martin, "Law and Grace: The Progressive Brethren and Fundamentalism" (Independent study, Wheaton College, IL, 1973).

Maryland (1936) J. Maurice Henry, *History of the Church of the Brethren in Maryland* (Elgin, IL: 1936).

ME Harold S. Bender and others, eds., *The Mennonite Encyclopedia,* 4 vols. (Scottdale, PA: 1955-59).

F. S. Mead, *Denominations* Frank S. Mead, *Handbook of Denominations in the United States,* 7th ed. (New York; Nashville, TN: 1980).

Messenger *Messenger* (1965-).

MfrKg Monatshefte für rheinische Kirchengeschichte (1907-).

MFH Mennonite Family History (1983-).

MHB Mennonite Historical Bulletin (Scottdale, PA; Goshen, IN: 1940-).

*MHS **Transactions*** *Transactions* of the Moravian Historical Society (1857-).

"Michigan" (1941) Walter M. Young, "The History of the Church of the Brethren in Michigan" (BD thesis, Bethany Biblical Seminary, 1941).

"Michigan" (1945) Robert Ebey, "Pioneering of the Brethren in Michigan" (BD thesis, Bethany Biblical Seminary, 1945).

Michigan (1946) Walter M. Young, *The History of the Church of the Brethren in Michigan* (Elgin, IL: 1946).

H. Miller, *Record (1882)* Howard Miller, *The Record of the Faithful; For the Use of the Brethren. Being a Statistical Record and a Complete Directory of the Brethren Church, for the Years 1881-1882* (Lewisburgh, PA: 1882).

J. E. Miller, *Stories (1942)* John E. Miller, *Stories from Brethren Life* (Elgin, IL: 1942).

J. E. Miller, *Story of Our Church* John E. Miller, *The Story of Our Church for Young People of the Church of the Brethren* (Elgin, IL: 1941).

Minister's Handbook (FGBC) (1945) *The Brethren Minister's Handbook* (Winona Lake, IN: 1945).

Minister's Manual (CB) (1940) Merlin C. Shull and John E. Miller, *Minister's Manual, Church of the Brethren* (Elgin, IL: 1940).

Minister's Manual (CB) (1946) Harvey L. Hartsough, Raymond R. Peters, M. R. Zigler, and Foster Statler, comps., *Minister's Manual, Authorized by the General Ministerial Board* (Elgin, IL: 1946).

Minutes (Brethren) *Minutes of the Annual Meetings of the Brethren* (Dayton, OH: 1876).

Minutes (CB) *Minutes of the Annual Meetings of the Church of the Brethren, 1778-1909* (Elgin, IL: 1909).

Minutes (DB) (1927-75) *Minutes of the General Conference of the Dunkard Brethren Church, 1927 to 1975* (Wauseon, OH: 1976).

Minutes index (1980) James D. Zaiger, *An Index to the Minutes of the Annual Meetings of the Old German Baptist Brethren, 1778 to 1980* (1980).

Minutes (OGBB) *Minutes of the Annual Meetings of the Old German Baptist Brethren, 1778-1955* (Winona Lake, IN: 1981).

Minutes See also *Rev. Min., Class. Min., Brethren's Encyclopedia (1867).*

Monatshefte *Monatshefte* (1899-).

Monitor *Bible Monitor (DB)* (1922-).

J. H. Moore, *Pathfinders (1929)* John Henry Moore, *Some Brethren Pathfinders* (Elgin, IL: 1929).

E. S. Moyer, *Missions (1931)* Elgin S. Moyer, *Missions in the Church of the Brethren: Their Development and Effect Upon the Denomination* (Elgin, IL: 1931).

MQR Mennonite Quarterly Review (1927-).

MRJ Mennonite Research Journal (1960-77).

G. E. Muir, *Pacific Slope (1939)* Gladdys E. Muir, *Settlement of the Brethren on the Pacific Slope: A Study in Colonization* (Elgin, IL: 1939).

MV The Brethren's Missionary Visitor (CB) (1894-97; 1902-31).

N. Atlantic (1975) Elmer Q. Gleim, *From These Roots: A History of the North Atlantic District, Church of the Brethren, 1911-1970* (Lancaster, PA: 1975).

"N. Dakota, E. Montana" (1940) Ralph R. Petry, "A Study of the Trends and Forces in the History of the District of North Dakota and Eastern Montana . . ." (BD thesis, Bethany Biblical Seminary, 1940).

"N. Illinois" (1933) Walter C. Sell, "A Brief History of the Founding and Development of the Churches of Northern Illinois and Wisconsin" (BD thesis, Bethany Biblical Seminary, 1933).

N. Illinois (1941) John Heckman and John E. Miller, *Brethren in Northern Illinois and Wisconsin* (Elgin, IL: 1941).

"N. Missouri" (1945) Ernest R. Vanderau, "A Historical Compilation of the District of Northern Missouri" (BD thesis, Bethany Biblical Seminary, 1945).

N. Plains (1977) Maryanna Hamer, Glenn J. Fruth, and Berwyn L. Oltman, comps., *History of the Church of the Brethren on the Northern Plains, 1844-1977* (n.p.: 1977).

NBHS *Collections* New Brunswick Historical Society *Collections* (1894-; suspended 1931-54).

NE. Ohio (1914) Tully S. Moherman and others, *A History of the Church of the Brethren, Northeastern Ohio* (Elgin, IL: 1914).

NE. Ohio (1963) Edgar 0. Diehm, ed., *The Church of the Brethren in Northeastern Ohio* (Elgin, IL: 1963).

New Nation (1976) Roger E. Sappington, ed., *The Brethren in the New Nation: A Source Book on the Development of the Church of the Brethren, 1785-1865* (Elgin, IL: 1976).

NGSQ National Genealogical Society Quarterly (1912-).

NJHS *Proceedings* *Proceedings* of the New Jersey Historical Society (1845-).

NQ Notes and Queries: Historical, Biographical, and Genealogical, Relating Chiefly to Interior Pennsylvania (Harrisburg, PA: 1880-1900).

"NW. Ohio" (1945) J. Dale Kyser, "The Brethren in Northwestern Ohio" (BD thesis, Bethany Biblical Seminary, 1945).

NW. Ohio (1982) William R. Eberly, *The History of the Church of the Brethren in Northwestern Ohio, 1827-1963* (Hartville, OH: [1982]).

G. B. Ogden, "Bibliography of Brethren Publications" (1941) Galen B. Ogden, "A Bibliography of Brethren Publications" (BD thesis, Bethany Biblical Seminary, 1941).

OON Old Order Notes (1978-2003).

"Oregon" (1944) Stanley O. Keller, "A Survey of the Church of the Brethren in Oregon" (BD thesis, Bethany Biblical Seminary, 1944).

Our Almanac Our Almanac and Annual Register (1880-ca. 1888).

Our Faith (BC) (1960) Albert T. Ronk, Smith F. Rose, Robert L. Keplinger, Donald E. Rowser, and L. E. Lindower, *Our Faith: A Manual of Brethren History, Bible Doctrine, and Christian Commitment* (Ashland, OH: 1960).

OYP Our Young People (CB) (1906-49).

Pastor's Handbook (BC) (1974) The Brethren Pastor's Handbook (Ashland, OH: 1974).

Pastor's Manual (CB) (1923) Albert Cassel Wieand, Joseph J. Yoder, and Edward Frantz, comps., *Pastor's Manual* (Elgin, IL: 1923).

Pastor's Manual (CB) (1978) Pastor's Manual, Church of the Brethren (Elgin, IL: 1978).

PC The Progressive Christian (1879-82).

PD The Pennsylvania Dutchman (1949-54); *The Dutchman* (1954-57); *Pennsylvania Folklife* (1958-).

PF Pennsylvania Folklife, 1958-. See also *PD.*

PG The Pennsylvania German (1900-14).

PGS *Proceedings* Pennsylvania German Society, *Proceedings and Addresses* (1891-1966).

PGS *Publications* Pennsylvania German Society *Publications* (1967-).

PH Pennsylvania History (1934-).

Pilgrim The Pilgrim, (1870-72); see also *The Weekly-Pilgrim* (1872-75).

PMH Pennsylvania Mennonite Heritage (1978-).

PMHB Pennsylvania Magazine of History and Biography (1877-).

PMLA Publications of the Modern Language Association (1884-).

PvC Primitive Christian (1876, 1878-83).

PvCP Primitive Christian and Pilgrim (1876-77).

F. Reichmann, *Sower Bibliography (1943)* Felix Reichmann, *Christopher Sower, Sr. 1694-1758: Printer in Germantown, An Annotated Bibliography* (Philadelphia, PA: 1943).

Rev. Min. (1882) German Baptist Brethren, *Minutes of the Annual Meetings of the Brethren Revised from Former Editions by a Committee authorized by Annual Meeting of May 30th 1882* (Huntingdon, PA; Mt. Morris, IL: 1883).

Rev. Min. (1898) German Baptist Brethren, *Revised Minutes of the Annual Meetings of the German Baptist Brethren* (Mt. Morris, IL: 1899).

Rev. Mm. (1922) Church of the Brethren, *Revised Minutes of the Annual Meetings of the Church of the Brethren from 1778 to 1922* (Elgin, IL: 1922).

Rev. Min. See also *Class. Min.; Minutes; Brethren's Encyclopedia* (1867).

RGG Die Religion in Geschichte und Gegenwart: Handworterbuch für Theologie und Religionswissenschaft, 3d ed. (1957-62).

A. T. Ronk, *History BC (1968)* Albert T. Ronk, *History of the Brethren Church: Its Life, Thought, Mission* (Ashland, OH: 1968).

G. B. Royer, *Thirty-three Years (1913)* Galen B. Royer, *Thirty-three Years of Missions in the Church of the Brethren* (Elgin, IL:1913).

E. F. Rupel, "Dress" (1971) Esther F. Rupel, "An investigation of the Origin, Significance, and Demise of the Prescribed Dress Worn by Members of the Church of the Brethren" (PhD diss., University of Minnesota, 1971).

S. Illinois [ca. 1908] [Daniel B. Gibson and others, comps.] *Compiled Minutes and History of the Church of the Brethren of the Southern District of Illinois* (Elgin, IL: [ca. 1908]).

S. Illinois (1950) Minnie S. Buckingham, ed., *Church of the Brethren in Southern Illinois* (Elgin, IL: 1950).

S. Iowa (1924) Willis P. Rodabaugh and A. H. Brower, *History of the Church of the Brethren in Southern Iowa* (Elgin, IL: 1924).

S. Missouri, Arkansas (1964) Earl Harvey, comp., *A History of the Church of the Brethren in the District of Southern Missouri and Arkansas* (n.p., 1964).

S. Ohio (1920) Jesse O. Garst and others, *History of the Church of the Brethren of the Southern District of Ohio* (Dayton, OH: 1921).

S. Ohio (1955) Harley H. Helman, ed., *Church of the Brethren in Southern Ohio* (Elgin, IL: 1955).

S. Ohio (FGBC) (1975) Everett Deubner and others, *History of the Southern Ohio District Fellowship of Brethren Churches, 1954-1974* (n.p., 1975).

S. Pennsylvania (1941) J. Linwood Eisenberg, ed., *A History of the Church of the Brethren in [the] Southern District of Pennsylvania* (Quincy, PA: 1941).

S. Pennsylvania (1973) Elmer Q. Gleim, *Change and Challenge: A History of the Church of the Brethren in the Southern District of Pennsylvania, 1940-1972* (Harrisburg, PA: 1973).

S. Plains (1976) Ethel S. Harris, ed., *Brethren on the Southern Plains* (Jennings, LA: 1976).

S. Plains (1979) Ethel S. Harris, ed., *Brethren on the Southern Plains, Update, 1972-1979* (1979).

J. F. Sachse, *German Sectarians (1899-1900)* Julius F. Sachse, *The German Sectarians of Pennsylvania, 1708-1800: A Critical and Legendary History of the Ephrata Cloister and the Dunkers*, 2 vols. (Philadelphia, PA: 1899-1900).

R. E. Sappington, *Social Policy (1961)* Roger E. Sappington, *Brethren Social Policy. 1908-1938* (Elgin, IL: 1961).

O. Seidensticker, *Printing (1893)* Oswald Seidensticker, *The First Century of German Printing in America, 1728-1830* (Philadelphia, PA: 1893).

S. Z. Sharp, *Ed. History (1923)* Solomon Z. Sharp, *The Educational History of the Church of the Brethren* (Elgin, IL: 1923).

Snake River (1966) Roger E. Sappington, *The Brethren Along the Snake River: A History of the Church of the Brethren in Idaho and Western Montana* (Elgin, IL: 1966).

Some Who Led (1912) Daniel L. Miller and Galen B. Royer, *Some Who Led, Or Fathers in the Church of the Brethren Who Have Passed Over* (Elgin, IL: 1912).

D. R. Stoffer, *Background and Development (1989)* Dale R. Stoffer, *Background and Development of Brethren Doctrines, 1650-1987* (Philadelphia: Brethren Encyclopedia, Inc., 1989).

R. B. Strassburger and W. J. Hinke, eds., *Pioneers (1934)* Ralph B. Strassburger and William J. Hinke, eds., *Pennsylvania German Pioneers* (Norristown, PA: 1934).

Texas (1922) James H. Morris and others, *Thirty-one Years of Organized Work in Oklahoma, Texas, New Mexico and Louisiana by the Church of the Brethren from 1891 to 1922* (Butler, IN: 1922).

"Texas-Louisiana" [ca. 1946] Lucile J. Homer, "An Introduction to the District of Texas-Louisiana" (Bethany Theological Seminary library, ca. 1946).

TRE Gerhard Krause and Gerhard Muller, eds., *Theologische Realenzyklopädie* (New York and Berlin: 1977-).

Trail Blazers (1960) Mary Garber and others, *Brethren Trail Blazers,* (Elgin, 1L: 1960).

Two Centuries (1908) *Two Centuries of the Church of the Brethren, Or The Beginnings of the Brotherhood: Bicentennial Addresses at the Annual Conference, Held at Des Moines, Iowa, June 3-11, 1908* (Elgin, IL: 1908).

Vindicator *The Vindicator* (OGGB) (1870-).

Virginia (1908) Daniel H. Zigler, *A History of the Brethren in Virginia* (Elgin, IL: 1908).

Virginia (1914) Daniel H. Zigler, *History of the Brethren in Virginia* (Elgin, IL: 1914).

Virginia (1973) Roger E. Sappington, *The Brethren in Virginia: The History of the Church of the Brethren in Virginia* (Harrisonburg, VA: 1973).

"W. Canada" (1943) Albert Hollinger, "A History of the Church of the Brethren in Western Canada" (BD thesis, Bethany Biblical Seminary, 1943).

W. Pennsylvania (1916) Jerome E. Blough, *History of the Church of the Brethren of the Western District of Pennsylvania* (Elgin, IL: 1916).

W. Pennsylvania (1953) Walter J. Hamilton and others, *Two Centuries of the Church of the Brethren in Western Pennsylvania, 1751-1950* (Elgin, IL: 1953).

W. Virginia (1945) Foster M. Bittinger, *A History of the Church of the Brethren in the First District of West Virginia* (Elgin, IL: 1945).

O. Winger, *Doctrines (1919)* Otho Winger, *History and Doctrines of the Church of the Brethren* (Elgin, IL: 1919).

WP *The Weekly-Pilgrim* (1872-75); see also *Pilgrim* (1870-72).

Wittgenstein *Wittgenstein: Blätter des Wittgensteiner Heimatvereins E. V.*; also *Des Schone Wittgenstein* (1913-31; 1937-43; 1956-).

Yearbook *Church of the Brethren Yearbook* (Elgin, IL: 1918-).

J. D. Zaiger, *Vindicator index (1978)* James D. Zaiger, Index to *The Vindicator, 1870-1977* (1978).

ZHT *Zeitschrift für historische Theologie* (1832-1875).

A-B

Abortion. The 1984 *Church of the Brethren *Statement on Abortion* represents in its opening words how the various Brethren groups regard this debated issue. "The Church of the Brethren opposes abortion because the rejection of unborn children violates the love by which God creates and nurtures human life." The CB's position is nuanced by concern over what contributes to unwanted pregnancies and calls the church to offer several responses. A report (not adopted) to the 1997 *Annual Conference supported the use of fetal tissue therapy but with several cautions.

Since 1982 the *Fellowship of Grace Brethren Churches has reaffirmed this resolution: "Human life is worthy of respect and protection at all stages from the time of conception." A 1996 FGBC resolution opposed fertilization techniques which disregard the worth of each newly conceived life. The *Conservative Grace Brethren Churches International has issued no statement on abortion since its separation from the FGBC in 1992, but it would affirm the latter's 1982 statement and mentions "the sanctity of human life" in clarifications of its Statement of Faith.

*The Brethren Church's 1991 statement denies that abortion is simply an issue of reproductive freedom: "It is rather a question of those circumstances under which a human being may be permitted to take the life of another." Abortion is opposed for personal or sociological purposes but may be necessary if the life of the mother is endangered.

In 1985 the General Conference of the *Dunkard Brethren Church issued a statement opposing abortion as murder. Human life from conception is a sacred creation of God and non-spontaneous abortion violates the sanctity of human life and the commandment of God. *Old German Baptist Brethren have not issued a position on abortion. DPS

Minutes (CB) (1984) 706; *Minutes* (CB) (1997) 548–56; *Annual* (FGBC) (1997) 16; *Annual* (BC) (1991) 19; *Dunkard Brethren Church Policy* (1993) 20; *Minutes* (DB) (1985) 5–6; *Statement of Faith* (CGBCI); *Messenger* (Sept., 1982) 21, (May, 1984) 5, (Dec., 1991) 9; *BLT* 32 (Summer, 1987) 178–79.

Aeby, John Milton (FGBC), 1916–97, pastor, educator. Born in Howe, IN, John Aeby attended *Ashland and *Manchester Colleges, and received a theological diploma from *Grace Theol. Sem. (1939).

Married to Joan Rosalie Hoover in 1939, he pastored the *Middlebranch, OH, First Brethren Church, and the *Fort Wayne, IN, First Brethren Church, from which he took leave to serve as a professor at Grace Seminary (1941–45), returning as pastor until 1952. Aeby then served at *Philadelphia, PA, First Brethren Church (1952–54), *Temple City, CA, Brethren Church, (1954–57), and *Waterloo, IA, Grace Brethren Church (1957–74). He hosted the *Gems of Grace* weekly *radio program in Waterloo (1957–72) and helped establish *Friendship Village Retirement Center; he was chosen as the first chair of the Center's board of directors (1965). Aeby was moderator of the *FGBC in 1961–62.

John Aeby moved to what came to be known as *Arvada, CO, Hackberry Hill Grace Brethren Church (1974–80) and then conducted a pulpit supply and Bible conference ministry until retirement in 1984. RTC
Denominational records; *Annual* (FGBC) (1939–84).

Brethren Couple Recognized for World's Longest Marriage

Harley Dewey Utz (1898–2001) and Sylvia Booker Utz (b. 1899) of Darke County, OH, were celebrated by *Guinness World Records* upon their 82nd wedding anniversary (June 15, 2000) as having the longest authenticated marriage world-wide. The couple surpassed that record one year later when they observed their 83rd anniversary. They had married in 1918 in Pitsburg, OH.

Harley and Sylvia Utz were members of the *Pitsburg, OH, Church of the Brethren. They attributed their longevity to their church attendance, "good, clean life," and abstinence from alcohol and tobacco. The Utz's had three children, four grandchildren, seven great-grandchildren, and two great-great-grandchildren. Harley Utz died on Nov. 12, 2001, at the age of 103. DFD

[Greenville, OH] Daily Advocate (Nov. 14, 2001); information supplied by Emerson B. Utz.

Africa Mission Project (DB). The call to "come to Kenya and help us" was answered in Jan. 1995 when the *Dunkard Brethren Church sent Paul L. Stump (b. 1928) and Mary Beery Stump (b. 1929) from Englewood, OH, as their first missionaries to Africa. Theresa Okello, who learned in Kenya about the Dunkard Brethren through the

Bible Monitor, had been pleading through letters for 10 years for the Dunkard Brethren to send someone to Kenya.

The Stumps arrived at Nairobi, Kenya, on Jan. 10, 1995, and made their home with Theresa for six weeks. They visited 14 mostly Pentecostal churches and many pastors, taught and preached the Word of God, and found many people who were willing to learn. A bond of love that was molded between Stumps and the people of Kenya was very evident as the Stumps departed for America on Feb. 22, 1995.

The Stumps returned to Kenya in Sept. 1995 along with Dale A. Jamison (b. 1920) and Doris Pease Jamison (b. 1923). After visiting in Kenya, they traveled into Uganda, where the first Dunkard Brethren congregation at Kampala was established in the fall of 1995. Twenty-three Africans were baptized. The first love feast was held on Oct. 1, 1995, in a home with nine brothers and six sisters present.

On subsequent visits, Rudy E. Shaffer (b. 1947) accompanied the Stumps as they preached the word, did administrative work, and conducted seminars on doctrinal teaching. This work resulted in more nationals requesting baptism at Kakumiro, Uganda, and Kapenguri, Kenya.

The Dunkard Brethren Church in Africa continued to grow in spirit and number, spreading to other areas in Kenya. As a result, Tim E. and Terry L. Scofield along with their two sons, William and Matthew, moved to Kapenguri, Kenya, in Jan. 1998 to administer the work for nine months. PLS

Bible Monitor (Feb. 15, 1995) 4–5, (March 15, 1995) 4–5, (Nov. 15, 1995) 4, (Jan. 1, 1997) 4–5, (Feb. 1, 1997) 4–5; personal information.

African Americans. Before there were Africans on the continent of North America there was the racial, political, and theological justification of enslavement of Africans. However, even before that, Africa was a continent with significant empires. One of the excesses of those empires was participation in the ancient institution of *slavery of conquered peoples. One finds parallels in Greece and western Asia. All of these factors came together to make possible the largest forced migration in world history.

Africans came to the North American continent early in the history of colonial settlement. The Jamestown settlers included a number of slaves (1619). Already in the 1660s *Virginia and *Maryland enacted laws making enslavement of Africans a life-sentence, contrasted with the limited period of indentured servitude for European immigrants.

The colonial period produced a group of freed slaves and so-called free Negroes who participated in the American Revolution, such as Crispus Attucks, who was killed in 1770 by British troops. The same period was a time of cultural activity for Africans in America. African slaves started churches in the earliest time of slavery. However, in some places religious tradition took a different turn. For instance, the African-American contribution to the religious landscape during this era includes the work of Richard Allen (1760–1831), who founded the African Methodist Episcopal Church; this took place after he was forcibly removed from a Methodist congregation in Philadelphia when he attempted to partake in communion with the white Methodists.

The antebellum period saw a diverse African population representing a number of tribes and regions in Africa who, however, were welded into a new people. During this time African-American literature began with the poetry of Philiss Wheatley (1753–84) and the oratory of Frederick Douglass (1818–95). The slave trade was consolidated into a way of life. The antebellum period was one of violence. Denmark Vesey (1767?–1822) and Nat Turner (1800–31) both staged abortive slave rebellions. John Brown (1800–59) tried to incite slaves to revolt and abolitionists to action by his raid on *Harpers Ferry.

While other denominations including Baptists, Presbyterians, and Methodists split over the issue of slavery, Brethren did not. Several times the *Annual Meeting made pronouncements against slavery and forbade its members to own slaves. During this period two African Americans were aided by Brethren to win their freedom. One such person was John Lewis (1835–1906) who later saved the life of the niece of Samuel Clemens (Mark Twain), who befriended him. *Samuel Weir (1812–84) was released by his Brethren owners and because the law at the time made it unlawful for freed slaves to continue their residence in Virginia, he migrated to Ohio, a free state. While there he continued his relationship with the Brethren and later was ordained to ministry and then to the eldership. Despite Brethren opposition to slavery, this does not mean that African American Brethren avoided all discrimination from their brothers and sisters in the faith.

The *Civil War and reconstruction shaped the American tradition. African-Americans were affected by these events. During the struggles of the war, President Lincoln and the Union Congress passed the Emancipation Proclamation on Jan. 1, 1863, which freed the slaves in the Confederacy. However, it was not made known to slaves until much later; for instance, not until June 19 in Texas. This gave rise to the name of the holiday "Juneteenth."

Reconstruction meant that an unprecedented number of opportunities opened up for African-Americans, including those among the Brethren. Reconstruction was unpopular in the old Confederacy. The excesses of the northern "carpet baggers" and new opportunities for African-Americans angered many. The backlash instigated creation of the Ku Klux Klan in 1867 by Nathan Bedford Forrest (1821–77), who was the Confederate commander of the Fort Pillow Massacre.

"Jim Crow" discrimination and black exodus from the South characterize the next stage in African-American experience. The Ku Klux Klan and racial repression returned with the end of reconstruction. Race laws were instituted and laws of racial discrimination ruled in the South. During the Jim Crow era, African-Americans moved from being slaves to becoming indentured servants under the model of sharecropping that provided cheap labor for the agricultural needs of the South. This context led many African Americans to immigrate to the Northern urban centers of New York, Boston, and Chicago. This gave rise to the present stereotype of African-Americans as being urban dwellers.

During this period, the Brethren started missions to African-Americans in *Colorado and *Arkansas. This work was supervised by *Mattie Cunningham Dolby (1878–1956), an African-American woman from Indiana who was a graduate of the early classes of the then new *Bethany Bible School. More recent decades saw the cause of Civil Rights come to the attention of the nation. With it, came greater participation by African-American rights initiatives in the 1960s. SBR

D. F. Durnbaugh, Fruit of the Vine (1997) 554–60.

*W. Harold Row, Ruth Early, and Polish agricultural exchangees confer with *Andrew W. Cordier at the United Nations. BHLA collection.*

Agricultural Exchange (China, Poland, Russia) (CB). The year 1997 marked the 50th anniversary of the *Polish Agricultural Exchange Program, having hosted over 1,250 agricultural specialists from Poland since its inception. Over 250 *Brethren Volunteer Service persons also served in Poland as exchangees, largely teaching English to these agricultural scientists in language preparation for their assignments. Today many former Polish exchange scientists hold influential positions in their nation, as ministers and vice ministers of agriculture, university rectors, directors of research institutes, senators, state governors, etc. To honor the exchange program, the Polish government in 1977 conferred Silver Medals of Honor of the Polish People's Republic on its current and former directors: H. Lamar Gibble, Paul W. Kinsel, and *John H. Eberly. On its 40th anniversary (1987), Poland again honored the exchange by conferring the highest state medal (the Gold Medal of Honor) on its director, Gibble. Motivated by a *General Board budget crisis and reductions in staff and programs in 1997, the Polish Exchange Program was terminated at its half-century mark.

In the late 1970s conversations were begun with officials of the Chinese Academy of Sciences and the Ministry of Agriculture regarding an agricultural exchange with China, assisted greatly by Polish professors Pieniazek and Zagaja, through their contacts with and visits to China. Negotiations from 1979 to 1982 concluded in an agreement with Chinese Ministry of Agriculture officials, and the first Chinese agricultural scientist was placed by the Brethren at Pennsylvania State U. in 1983. The first Brethren volunteer to teach English at the Jiangsu Academy of Sciences arrived in Nanjing during the spring of 1985. To date over 60 Chinese scholars have engaged in university research assignments in the U.S., 22 U.S. volunteers have taught at the Nanjing English Language Institute, and seven agricultural science professors (including two Brethren) have lectured in Chinese universities as a part of this exchange. CB grants to the Institute have assisted in building a library (the Sino-Brethren Library), provided library materials, and equipped a language laboratory. On its 10th anniversary in 1992, to honor and affirm this successful exchange program, the Gold Prize for International Cooperation in Agriculture was conferred on director H. Lamar Gibble by the Chinese Minister of Agriculture, Liu Zhongyi.

In 1991 as the USSR was dissolving and serious food shortages faced the newly independent states, friends of the Brethren in the *Russian Orthodox and Baptist churches of Russia appealed to the CB for food and agricultural assistance. From this appeal emerged an ecumenical endeavor through the *National Council of Churches and *Church World Service (CWS) to use the expertise of the Brethren's agricultural exchange experience in responding to this request. Gibble, the World Ministries staff person, was engaged by CWS as its consultant for Russian agricultural development programs. Through this ecumenical endeavor over a half million dollars was provided for the initiation and development of four Russian Orthodox and one Baptist agricultural projects in various parts of Russia: Moscow region, Ryazan region, Novosibirsk, Smolensk, and Valaam Island. HLG

D. F. Durnbaugh, *Fruit of the Vine* (1997), 482–83, 489–90; H. Lamar Gibble, "Twenty Plus One," and S. A. Pieniazek, "Reminiscences," *Seedtime and Harvest* (WMC Publication— Dec., 1977), 1, 14; *Messenger* (July, 1977) 10, (July, 1977) 4, (Dec., 1987) 10–15, (Dec., 1992) 8.

AIDS, Response to (CB). By 1986 Acquired Immune Deficiency Syndrome (AIDS) was becoming a national epidemic and spreading worldwide. A Brethren response to this epidemic was initiated through the Brethren Health and Welfare Association (BHWA), the predecessor organization to the *Association of Brethren Caregivers (ABC). At its meeting on Nov. 21, 1986, the BHWA board voted to develop a position statement on AIDS for the denomination. A committee chaired by James Kipp wrote the statement, *A Call to Compassion,* which was approved by the *General Board and adopted by the 1987 *Annual Conference.

Subsequently, BHWA formed a task group, chaired by

Ralph G. McFadden, to implement the ministry directives identified in the statement and to provide resources for ministry to persons with AIDS. Since 1990, ministry issues related to AIDS have been addressed by ABC. JEGi
BHWA Board Minutes (Nov. 21, 1986), (Sept. 25–26, 1987); CB Annual Conference Statement, *A Call to Compassion* (1987); *ABC Board Minutes* (Sept. 10–11, 1994); ABC, *What Your Family Needs to Know About HIV/AIDS* (1995); *Messenger* (1987–2000) indexes.

Akron, OH, Firestone Park Brethren Church (BC). The church was organized in 1946 with James Gilbert Dodds serving as its first pastor. The congregation purchased a parsonage in 1946 and built a modest chapel for its Sunday services in 1948. In 1960 the church built a larger addition which included a new worship area, auditorium, and classrooms. Other pastors who served the congregation were James R. Black and R. Glen Traver. The congregation reached its peak average worship attendance of 131 in 1962 but fell on hard times in the 1970s and closed in 1979. DRS
Congregational records; *Annual* (BC) (1948–79).

Alexander Mack Museum. *Schwarzenau/Eder, Germany, was the birthplace of the *Brethren movement. Since the 1930s thousands of members of the several Brethren denominations have made the pilgrimage to this scenic village. Local residents have graciously received these visitors and shown them sites of historic interest, in particular houses in the *Hüttental* area. An Historical and Tourist Association (*Heimats- und Verkehrsverein*) encourages visitation.

Members of a 1986 Brethren Heritage Tour (and others) raised nearly $30,000 as an endowment. Interest from this fund pays the rent of three rooms in the oldest structure in *Hüttental*, the so-called Kassel/Milde house. The rooms, decorated by volunteer labor, constitute the Alexander Mack Museum, dedicated in 1992. It features a library of Brethren literature (originated by Elder *J. William Miller, OGBB), displays, and objects of historical interest. Hundreds of visitors each year, both from the U.S. and from Germany, visit the Museum, which is listed in official guide books. DFD
Messenger (Nov., 1992) 4, (May/June, 1994) 8; *Wittgenstein* 80/56 (Sept., 1992) 3; *Museen und Heimatstuben: Siegerland/Wittgenstein* (1991) 39.

Andrew Center, The (1992–97), a multi-denominational resource agency for evangelism, rooted in the Brethren/Anabaptist tradition. The Center introduced a new paradigm for delivering denominational programming, and provided a platform for cooperation between Brethren and *Mennonite bodies in the area of evangelism and church growth. The Center was organized around four core functions: resourcing, consulting, training, and networking; the mission of the Center was "to multiply the number of persons turning to Jesus Christ, by multiplying the number of leaders and congregations that are spiritually alive and evangelistically effective."

The Andrew Center featured personalized consultation to churches through a parish or congregational advisor. Accessed through a toll-free telephone number, this individual developed customized solutions to congregational needs related to evangelism and effective outreach. The Center also developed and implemented numerous training or networking events across the U.S. and Canada; Steve Clapp, senior consultant for the Center, conducted many of these events. Clapp also provided editorial leadership to the Center's publishing initiative, best represented in The Andrew Center Growth and Vitality Series and the Center's journal, *New Beginnings*.

Paul Mundey served as the first director of The Andrew Center; in 1996, Mundey resigned to accept the pastorate of the *Frederick, MD, Church of the Brethren. Robert D. Kettering succeeded Mundey, serving until the Center closed in December 1997. The Andrew Center was closed by the *General Board of the *Church of the Brethren, its principal financial sponsor, as part of the General Board redesign process. The intent and methodology of The Andrew Center, however, was incorporated into the General Board's Congregational Life Teams, a key component of the Board's redesign. In Jan. 1998 The Andrew Center was succeeded by a new Brethren and Mennonite joint effort called New Life Ministries. PM
See also RESTRUCTURING, ORGANIZATIONAL.
Messenger (July, 1993) 8, (Aug./Sept., 1993) 20, (Sept., 1995) 8, (Feb., 1996) 8, (Dec., 1996) 10, (Feb., 1997) 8, (Aug./Sept., 1997) 7; personal information; D. F. Durnbaugh, *Fruit of the Vine* (1997), 477–78.

*Anointing continues to be practiced by all Brethren bodies with minimal changes from the interpretation in *The Brethren Encyclopedia, Vol. 1*. The recently formed *Conservative Grace Brethren Churches International perpetuates the practice of its parent body, the *Fellowship of Grace Brethren Churches, among which there may be a slight decrease from the other groups in its teaching and practice. The *Church of the Brethren is experiencing an increase in practice and a wider interpretation of usage. This includes moving beyond private to some public anointings and from specifically physical to emotional and spiritual healings. Restoring relationships, assuaging stress and guilt, and consecrating leadership for mission and service are often sealed by the imposition of oil. Commissioning of a new CB denominational executive director in 1998 included anointing. An "Anointing Packet" and an instructional video, *Is Any Among You Suffering?*, merchandised by *Brethren Press, are widely used. HZB
H. Z. Bomberger, "The Biblical Basis for the Anointing - Part 1," *Brethren Leader* (July/Aug., 1961) 2 and "The Anointing and the Church of the Brethren - Part 2," *Brethren Leader* (Sept., 1961) 3; *Anointing: A Biblical Teaching as Practiced by the Church of the Brethren* (1987); *Anointing Packet* (CB) (1987); D. M. Miller, *Anointing - The Congregation's Use of Anointing for Healing and Reconciliation* (1987); K. M. Shaffer, Jr. and G. F. Snyder, *Anointing - A Bible Study* (1992). *For All Who Minister: A Worship Manual* (CB) (1993) 253–68; *Messenger* (June, 1987) 26, (Aug./Sept., 1987) 24, (Jan., 1994) 24, (March, 1994) 20–23, (Nov., 1994) 11, (May/June, 1995) 1, (Aug., 1998) 20.

Appalachian Ministries (CB). In the fall of 1943 the *Flat Creek Church of the Brethren was organized as a home mission project in Southeastern *Kentucky, supported by the *General Brotherhood Board and the District of Southern Ohio. In 1950 Mud Lick fellowship was formed and has been part of the congregation along with the fellowship at Flat Creek. Ongoing growth and maturity was recognized at the congregation's 60th anniversary, celebrated in 2003. In 2001, 163 members were reported.

In 1973 the Church of the Brethren, along with United Methodist Red Bird Mission, started Kentucky Mountain Housing Development Corporation (KMHDC). This proj-

ect, providing low-income families with safe, decent, and affordable housing, is an independent organization with a controlling board. In the first 30 years, more than 600 new houses were built and more than 350 others were repaired, replacing substandard housing. KMHDC celebrated its 30th anniversary in 2003. MDY

S. Ohio (1955), 149–53; *Messenger* (Jan., 1973) 6, (March, 1981) 13–20, (July, 1986) 14–18, (May, 1987) 18–20, (Nov., 1992) 12–13, (Oct., 1993) 20–23, (Jan./Feb., 1994) 4.

*Architecture. Church building construction among the Brethren groups is currently focused on newly planted congregations. This has taken place as the Brethren have moved from rural to urban and suburban areas.

In addition, the house church is experiencing a small revival among the Brethren. The early Brethren believed this to be the biblical approach. In the New Testament, the word *ecclesia* is translated *church* and usually designates a local congregation and never a church building. Eventually the Brethren built plain *meetinghouses serving well the community focus of the gathering. In many present-day congregations the interest remains on fellowship and, therefore, there are only a few "mega" congregations. "Seeker" congregations designed not to look like a "church" are rare, but "seeker sensitive" congregations are on the rise. However, most Brethren congregations remain more traditional and "plain" in their approach to architecture.

Several trends are noticeable. There is an increasing use of chairs, first in the choir and then for seating in the worship space. Where pews are still being used the trend is toward upholstered instead of wooden ones. There is an increase in the construction of family education centers and gymnasiums. These are usually multi-purpose structures that are flexible and adaptable for several uses. Additional educational space, apart from the multi-purpose building, is not in the picture, but there is an improvement in the quality of this space. Less chancel furniture is used in an attempt to emphasize the priesthood of all believers. The *CB continues to prefer the divided chancel while the *OGBB maintains use of the elder's table. The remaining Brethren groups are usually pulpit-centered. REA

C. F. Bowman, *Brethren Society* (1995) 64–67, 164–66; D. F. Durnbaugh, ed., *Church of the Brethren: Yesterday and Today* (1986) 14, 16, 75–76; L. L. Fry, "A Study of Architecture and Worship in the Church of the Brethren," MATh thesis, Bethany Theol. Sem. (1986); D. R. Fitzkee, *Moving Toward the Mainstream* (1995) 270–79, passim; N. K. Frye, "The Meetinghouse Connection: Plain Living in the Gilded Age," *PF* 41.2 (Winter, 1991–92): 50–78; D. F. Durnbaugh, *Fruit of the Vine* (1997) 104–08, 512–14; K. I. Morse, *Move in Our Midst* (1977) 106–14; *BLT* 31 (Winter, 1986): 17–23; 36 (Summer, 1991) 227–38; T. Greenawalt, "Traditional Brethren Meetinghouses," Bridgewater College (2002); *Messenger* (April, 1980) 16–18, (April, 1980) 27–29, (April, 1982) 20–22, (April, 1982) 23–25, (Dec., 1982) 22–23, (Dec., 1983) 21–22, (Dec., 1983) 23–24, (May, 1988) 20–23; F. U. Groff, *By Faith I Will Overcome* (2002).

Arizona Brethren Camp (BC), the camp of the Southwest District Conference of *The Brethren Church. In March 1968, 25 acres of land were purchased for the camp in the Patagonia Mountains, 75 miles southwest of Tucson. The 1968–69 Brethren Youth Crusader project, "Camp for Cash," aided in the purchase and development of the land. Seven campers attended the inaugural summer camp in 1969. The camp program has expanded to three weeks during the summer, one for juniors, one for junior

high youth, and one for senior high youth. A family camp is held each Labor Day weekend as well as a women's retreat in the fall and a New Year's camp for high school and college youth. DRS/ROS

BE (Jan. 4, 1969) 4; (March 1, 1969) 31; (May 24, 1969) 22; (Aug. 16, 1969) 23–24.

Ashland Theological Seminary. ATS collection.

*Ashland Theological Seminary, OH, (BC) continues to serve the growing needs of *The Brethren Church in preparing men and women for Christian leadership positions throughout the world. The enrollment in 1998 was 683 students representing over 70 denominations and para-church organizations. Twenty-nine international students represented over 14 countries.

Frederick J. Finks assumed leadership of the seminary in 1982, being named vice president and chief executive officer after *Joseph R. Shultz became president of *Ashland University. In 1993, the University Board of Trustees named Finks president of the seminary.

Ashland Seminary strengthened its position among evangelical seminaries and in 2003 was the 12th largest seminary in North America. Twenty full-time faculty members with international credentials brought high visibility and academic credibility to the seminary. Forty-nine adjunct faculty members also served the educational needs of the seminary.

The seminary focused on academic, spiritual, and fiscal integrity in all of its programs. The average grade point average (GPA) of incoming students was 3.2 on a scale of 4.0. Spiritual formation is at the center of the academic community as well as the faith community of the seminary. Endowment grew from $172,000 in 1982 to $6,500,000 in 1997. The seminary engaged in several building projects in 1982–2001. In 1989, the 10,000 square foot Shultz Academic Center with five classrooms and a student center was completed. The *George Solomon Memorial Library addition was completed in 1991. The 10,000 square foot Gerber Academic Center with three classrooms, a 162 seat auditorium, a student lounge, computer center, and office complex was completed in 1997. The 16,000 square foot Sandberg Leadership Center, completed in Oct. 2001, houses faculty offices, classrooms, and a counseling center. FJFi

BE (Jan., 1989) 12–15, (Jan., 1983) 11–14, (Jan., 1999) 8–9, (Oct., 2000) 9.

*Ashland University (BC). *Ashland College was designated a university in May 1988 because of its large grad-

uate programs. Almost from its inception, the school has been a center of training for ministers and missionaries. *Ashland Theol. Sem. became a graduate division in 1930. The enrollment remained small until it was accredited in 1969, after which it grew to nearly 800 students in 2003 from over 60 denominations and about a dozen countries. The school offers seven degrees and is considered a conservative biblical seminary.

The College of Education has always been a strong unit of the College/University. Master's degree studies reached an enrollment of ca. 1,500 by 1998. The continuing education program enrolled thousands of students, and the Board of Regents of Ohio approved a doctoral program for the College of Education.

The College of Business also has been a leader in the University and the region. The Master of Business Administration degree program, beginning in 1978, had an enrollment of ca. 500 in 1999. Perhaps its most significant contribution was its teaching of the moral value of private enterprise, which gives the freedom for individuals to become the best they were divinely created to be.

Ashland U. has never had a large endowment, and the supporting church membership is relatively small. Money was often borrowed to build buildings and support special projects. In 1979 the debt was 1.7 times the annual budget. This was reversed in 1979–92 when the debt was eliminated. During this period the total enrollment, graduate and undergraduate, grew from ca. 2,000 to 6,000; in 1992 there were 34 buildings on campus.

"The Liberal Arts" is the foundation of all academic programs at Ashland University. Since its founding in 1878, Ashland has continuously emphasized the values of the liberal arts. Ashland believes in principle that the Christian message and faith is expressed in the liberal arts. This education is the basis for professions and careers: law, government, medicine, art, humanities, science, music, and theology. JRS

J. R. Shultz, *Ashland–from College to University* (1992); J. R. Shultz, *"Final Report—1962–1992"* (1992); *BE* (June, 1989) 18, (Oct., 1994) 12–13, (Nov., 1990) 12, (Dec., 1998) 11.

Ashland, OH, University Church (BC). The University Church was founded in 1991 on the campus of *Ashland University. The congregation meets in the remodeled worship center of Memorial Chapel. The church was begun with a vision to reach university students, faculty, and staff who were currently not attending any local congregation. Members of the *Ashland, OH, Park Street Brethren Church formed the core group of founding members. These included David W. and Morven Baker, J. Michael and Mary Ellen W. Drushal, Fred J. and Holly H. Finks, Michael F. and Sheila K. Gleason, and Richard D. and Dorothy A. Leidy. The first worship service was held on Nov. 3, 1991, with 175 in attendance. A shared ministry model is used with members and students dividing the leadership roles. *Ashland Theol. Sem. has provided student interns to assist a part-time ministerial staff. Part-time pastors have included Ken E. Cutrer, Eric J. Bargerhuff, and Leroy A. Solomon. FJFi

BE (Jan., 1994) 16, (July/Aug., 2001) 8.

Ashman, Charles Henry, Jr. (FGBC), b. 1924, pastor, teacher, administrator. Born to a Johnstown, PA, *Brethren Church pastor's family, Charles Ashman followed in the footsteps of his father and two brothers, entering the pastorate after graduation from Westmont

College (1947) and *Grace Theol. Sem. (1950). He served first at the *Rittman, OH, Grace Brethren Church. He then pastored the *Phoenix, AZ, Northwest Grace Brethren Church in 1955 where he and his wife, Frances, helped begin the Phoenix Brethren Christian School. In the fall of 1962, the Ashmans moved to Winona Lake, IN, where he became pastor of the *Winona Lake, IN, Grace Brethren Church. Under his leadership, the church moved out of a college facility into a new church building in 1969. In 1983, the church expanded its space through the purchase of an adjacent property owned by the Winona School of Photography. The congregation grew to a membership of over 700 at the time of his retirement in 1989, after almost 27 years in the pulpit.

While in Winona Lake, Ashman also served as professor at *Grace Theol. Sem. and College. He was FGBC moderator in 1973–74. After retirement he continued to serve as Fellowship Coordinator for the FGBC. RTC

BMH (Aug. 15, 1989) 29, (Dec. 15, 1993) 11, 13; *Annual (FGBC)* (1950–89).

Association of Brethren Caregivers (ABC) (CB). The birth of ABC represents the coming together of varied health and caring interests within the denomination under one umbrella organization. Those varied interests include Brethren homes, *Bethany Brethren Hospital, *Castañer Hospital, health education and research fund, *deacons, older adults, *Lafiya, *chaplains, nurses, persons with disabilities, mental health/illness, HIV/*AIDS, addictions, and conditions of childhood. The list of health and caring ministries concerns addressed by ABC continues to grow.

The guiding mission statement of ABC is: "Believing that the ministry of giving and receiving care is integral to Christian faith, the Association of Brethren Caregivers will develop resources, leadership, and programs within the *Church of the Brethren and the wider community that connect and undergird persons and communities in their lifelong journeys toward healing and wholeness."

As a legal entity, ABC came into being in 1990 as a nonprofit tax-exempt corporation in Illinois through the consolidation of *Brethren Health and Welfare Association (BHWA) and *Brethren Health Foundation (BHF). Initially, ABC assumed responsibility for the health and caring ministries within the denomination in an accountable programming relationship with the *General Board. From its inception, ABC depended on the General Board for staffing and financial support services. Additionally, up through 1998, *Annual Conference invited ABC to make verbal and written reports of its ministries.

In March 1997, the General Board took action to separate ABC from its standing as a dependent organization, effective Jan. 1, 1998. ABC now operates as an independent agency, with a stated desire to be in collaborative relationships with other denominational agencies, including the General Board and Annual Conference. JEGi

Minutes, ABC Board (1990ff.) passim; *Minutes, CB* (1990ff.) passim; M. S. H. Rosenberger, *That They Might Have Life* (1987), *Caring: A History of Brethren Homes* (1989), *Light of the Spirit* (1992), and *The Gift of Life: The Brethren and Bethany Hospital*, (1995); [K. I. Morse, ed.], *Communities That Care: Brethren Homes and Hospitals* (1984).

Aukerman, Dale H. (CB), peace activist, author, pastor. Born in 1930 into an *OGBB family, Dale Aukerman soon evidenced qualities of character and intellectual

attainment that marked his adult life. At age 16, he entered the U. of Chicago at a time when academic credits could be achieved by passing tests; this enabled him to secure a bachelor's degree within one year, earning him national attention in *Life Magazine*. He performed alternative service in *Germany and *Austria with the *Brethren Service Commission (1953–56), working primarily on refugee resettlement. Later he was the secretary of the European *Puidoux peace conferences. In the U.S. he was a pastor in *Indiana, *Michigan, and *Maryland, but his largely self-supported vocation was as a peace activist and writer. He published two noted books, *Darkening Valley: A Biblical Perspective on Nuclear War* (1981) and *Reckoning with Apocalypse: Terminal Politics and Christian Hope* (1993), as well as numerous articles and tracts. His moving book, *Hope Beyond Healing: A Cancer Journal* (2000), chronicled the last years of his life; he died in Sept. 1999. His family consists of his wife, the artist and teacher Ruth Seebass Aukerman, and their three children: Miriam, Daniel, and Maren. DFD

TBE 3 (1984) 1544; *S. Ohio* (1955) 260; J. K. Kreider, *A Cup of Cold Water: The Story of Brethren Service* (2001) index; *Bulletin of the [Manchester College] Peace Institute* 20.1–2 (1990) 17–19, 24.1–2 (1994) 3–6; *Messenger* (Nov., 1979) 24, (Jan./Feb., 1998) 4, (April, 1998) 16–19, (July, 1999), cover, 10–14; *CB Newsline* (Sept. 17, 1999); *Baltimore [MD] Sun* (Sept. 11, 1999); *Carroll County [MD] Times* (Fall, 1998) (special supplement), (Sept. 12, 1999): A1, 6–7; Christian Peacemaker Teams, *Signs of the Times* (Fall, 1999) [3]; *Sojourners* (Nov./Dec., 1999) 6; *Christian Living Magazine* (Dec., 1999) 13.

Baltimore Pilot House Project. BHLA collection.

Baltimore, MD, Pilot House Project

Baltimore, MD, Pilot House Project (CB). In 1950 the Baltimore City Housing Bureau designated a 27 square block area as a pilot project in east Baltimore in its fight against inner city blight. The Men's Work of the *Baltimore First Church of the Brethren, led by Chester Strayer, assisted the city by forming Brotherhood Service, Inc. With Frank C. Rittenhouse as president, Brotherhood Service purchased a dilapidated row house and renovated it. The building was named "Pilot House" and served as a referral center to assist neighborhood residents. Pilot House was staffed by *Brethren Volunteer Service (BVS) workers with Vern and Elsie Hoffman serving as the first directors.

By 1955 the city of Baltimore declared the Pilot Project completed and moved its urban renewal emphasis to a 50 square block area on the west side, where a Harlem

Park Urban Renewal Project was conducted with the support of the federal government. Brotherhood Service sold the Pilot House on the east side and once again purchased and fixed up a run-down row house as a second Pilot House on the edge of the Harlem Park Urban Renewal area. This project continued until 1972 with staffing by BVS. Serving as directors on the west side were Ralph and Joy Dull (1955–57), Dale V. and Claire Gilbert Ulrich (1957–58), Vernon and Jacqueline Stern (1958–59), Richard M. and Alice Edwards (1959–60), Porter and Lenora Bechtel, Sr. (1961–62), Robert D. and Dorothy Cain (1962–65), Arthur and Janet Shive (1966), and Warren E. and June Adams Miller (1966–72).

In both Baltimore locations, the Brethren volunteers assisted poor homeowners in repairing their homes, helped staff local community centers, led recreation for children in community playlots, helped poor people move, organized opportunities for inner city youth to spend time in the summer with rural families, organized block cleanup and rat poisoning campaigns, planned and conducted weekend work camps, worked with the federal government on urban renewal and the War on Poverty, and worked with the National Association for the Advancement of Colored People and the Congress on Racial Equality. In the latter years of the project, the attitude of Black people across America changed so that it was difficult for white volunteers to work in Black communities, even in helpful ways. The project closed in 1972. DVU

GM (Feb. 17, 1951) 20–21, (Dec. 29, 1951) 14–15, (Nov. 9, 1957) 10–12; *Horizons* (Dec. 11, 1955) 11–15; *Messenger* (Aug., 2001) 32; J. K. Kreider, *A Cup of Cold Water: The Brethren Service Story* (2001) 413–21; *Baltimore [MD] Sun* (June 30, 2001) 12A, (July 1, 2001) 3B.

Baptism, Eucharist, and Ministry, CB response to

Baptism, Eucharist, and Ministry, CB response to. The "Baptism, Eucharist, and Ministry" (BEM) text, adopted by the Faith and Order Commission of the *World Council of Churches at its plenary meeting in Lima, Peru, in 1982, is among the most significant ecumenical documents of the 20th century. The roots of this text can be traced to the early beginnings of the *ecumenical movement, particularly the Faith and Order movement itself. Differences among the churches having to do with doctrinal understanding and practice of *baptism, *eucharist, and *ministry continued to be central to ecumenical discussions throughout the following decades. Finally, in 1982, this text was considered "to have been brought to such a stage of maturity that it is now ready for transmission to the [member] churches [of the World Council of Churches] . . . for consideration and comment," and for "an official response . . . at the highest appropriate level of authority."

This request for response came to the Church of the Brethren *Committee on Interchurch Relations via *Robert W. Neff, then ecumenical officer as well as general secretary of the *General Board. A theological taskforce, whose members were Robert C. Bowman, *Dale W. Brown, Dena Pence Frantz, Estella B. Horning, Melanie A. May, and Lauree Hersch Meyer, was appointed to prepare a draft to be brought before "the highest appropriate level of authority," namely the *Annual Conference. In preparing the draft, the task force responded neither to the document as such nor out of Brethren life and thought as such. The focus of the response was, as requested, how "the faith of the Church through the cen-

turies" is recognizable in the document to the Brethren, given their particular manifestation of that faith.

While much was affirmed in the "BEM" text, the *Church of the Brethren response, adopted by the delegate body at the 1987 Annual Conference, also makes it clear that many Brethren were "alienated by the language and life of the sacramental ontology that characterizes" the text. Affirming the Brethren belief in the sacramentality of all life, the response states: "We find it inappropriate that Christians reduce to one understanding of sacrament states intended to speak to our shared confessions regarding baptism, eucharist, and ministry." The CB response was one of hundreds sent by member churches. MAM

Baptism, Eucharist, and Ministry (1982); *Baptism and Eucharist: Ecumenical Convergence in Celebration*, eds. M. Thurian and G. Wainwright (1986); *Churches Respond to BEM: Official Responses to the "Baptism, Eucharist, and Ministry" Text, Vol VI*, ed. M. Thurian (1988); *Baptism, Eucharist & Ministry, 1982–1990: Report on the Process and Responses* (1990); *Baptism & Church: A Believers' Church Vision*, ed. M. D. Strege (1986); D. B. Eller, ed., *Servants of the Word: Ministry in the Believers' Church* (1990); D. R. Stoffer, ed., *The Lord's Supper: Believers Church Perspectives* (1997); J. H. Yoder, *The Fullness of Christ: Paul's Vision of Universal Ministry* (1987).

Barnes, Edith Catherine Bonsack (CB), 1894–1990, editor, genealogist. Born near Westminster, MD, Edith was the daughter of *Charles D. and Ida Trostle Bonsack. She graduated from *Blue Ridge College in 1916 and in 1921 began 38 years of service at Elgin, IL, for the *Church of the Brethren. She was secretary in the editorial offices, assistant editor of church school publications, and the author of *Finding the Way*, a church *membership manual for young people. Active in the Elgin congregation, she assisted the YWCA, gave invaluable volunteer service for 29 years to the *Brethren Historical Library and Archives, and helped to revise the interdenominational *Sunday school literature, all after her retirement in 1959. MEH/DFD

I. G. Long, *Faces* (1962), 162–68; *Blue Book* (1923), 124; D. M. Bonsack and E. B. Barnes, *Bonsack Family History* (1974), 148; *Messenger* (Aug., 1979) 3, (May, 1984) 5, (Aug./Sept., 1990) cover 2, 2; *Highland Avenue CB* (1999) 18.

Beaver, Samuel Wayne (FGBC), b. 1918, pastor, missionary, educator. Born in Ganges, OH, Wayne Beaver received his bachelor's degree from Kent State U. (1940) and an MDiv degree from *Grace Theol. Sem. (1943). During his last semester at GTS, he pastored the *Osceola, IN, congregation. Beaver served with his wife, Dorothy, as a missionary in the *Central African Republic (1944–71), starting the first full-time Bible Institute in the CAR in Bellevue (1946). He started the mission station at Bata and the Bible Institute moved there in 1946. In 1963, the School of Theology was started on the station. From 1950 to 1959, Beaver worked on translating the Old Testament into the Sango language.

On extended leave from the mission, Wayne Beaver served as assistant pastor of the *Long Beach, CA, congregation (1963–67) and later pastored the *Los Alamitos, CA, congregation (1969–70). In 1972–74, he directed the *GROW '73 program for *Grace Brethren Foreign Missions. In 1974, he received an honorary DD degree from Grace Theol. Seminary.

Beaver taught missions at GTS (1974–89) and started a summer graduate program for missionaries. This work included an extension program at the *Chateau of Saint Albain, *France, for missionaries on the European and African fields. He was moderator of the FGBC (1972–73). RTC

Personal information; T. T. Julien, *Seize the Moment: Stories of an Awesome God Empowering Ordinary People* (2000) 45–52; *Annual (FGBC)* (1943ff.); denominational records.

Beeghley, John W. (OGBB), b. 1921, minister, farmer. Beeghley has been a lifelong resident of the *Willow Springs congregation, Douglas County, KS. He is the son of Daniel and Christena Beeghley and great-grandson of early Kansas pioneer, Jacob Ulrich, who had suffered at the hands of Quantrill's Raiders during the *Civil War. Baptized in 1942, he was elected to the ministry in 1957 and ordained elder in 1972. He served on *Standing Committee (1979–95) and for some years as nonresident elder in two adjoining congregations. He married Ethel Kinzie in 1943; they had two children: Marian Fife and Charles W. Beeghley. Ethel Kinzie died in 1996. In 2000, John Beeghly married Anna M. Hirt, widow of Clyde Hirt (1928–75), a minister of the *Cedar Creek congregation, Anderson Co., KS. John and Anna Beeghly reside in Douglas County, KS, where he served as presiding elder for 18 years. A man of moderate views, Beeghley enjoys poetry and writing. GCW

Vindicator (1958) 27, (1978) 346, (1996) 284–85; *Old Order Notes* No. 4 (Spring, 1981) 19.

Believers Church Commentary Series. In 1982 the Editorial Council for the Believers Church Commentary was established, with representation from the *Brethren in Christ, *Church of the Brethren, *Mennonite Brethren, *General Conference Mennonite Church, and the *Mennonite Church, plus representatives of Herald Press. This group was later joined by *The Brethren Church.

The dream of those gathered was to collaborate in the publication of a biblical commentary series oriented to an *Anabaptist perspective. Unique to this understanding of scripture is the importance of the ongoing conversation of the faith community. Thus, the commentary gives special attention to sections entitled the "Text in the Biblical Context," an intra-canonical discussion, and the "Text in the Life of the Church." The last named includes ways in which a text has been understood and applied historically in the life of the church, as well as continuing social, ethical, and theological issues. The commentary aims to make available scholarly information, at the same time remaining accessible to the reader who, although biblically literate, may not be conversant with technical scholarly language. Its intention is to be a resource for Sunday school teachers and pastors.

The first New Testament editor, Howard Charles (1982–89) was succeeded by Willard M. Swartley (1989–2002), both of the Associated Mennonite Biblical Seminary. Gordon Zerke was named New Testament editor in 2002. The Old Testament editor, Elmer A. Martens from Brethren Mennonite Biblical Seminary was replaced by Douglas Miller of Tabor College in 2003. As of Sept. 1998, ten volumes were published (Genesis, Jeremiah, Ezekiel, Daniel, Hosea/Amos, Matthew, Acts, Colossians/Philemon, Thessalonians, and 2 Corinthians). At the press for 1999 are Judges, and 1 and 2 Peter/Jude. In process for the year 2000 are Exodus, Mark, and Ephesians. EBH

Minutes and Correspondence of the Editorial Council, BCBC

(1982–1998); *Messenger* (Aug./Sept., 1987) 38, (May, 1991) 8; *BLT* 36 (Winter, 1991) 54–55, 38 (Winter, 1993) 61–63, 40 (Spring, 1995) 119–21; D. F. Durnbaugh, *Fruit of the Vine* (1997) 583.

The Witty William M. Beahm

One does not usually think of *Pietists or *Anabaptists as boisterous, jolly people. In those traditions, laughter and humor have needed to keep their proper place, have acceptable content, and be moderate in character. Still, *annual conferences, in addition to taking care of serious business, were full of visiting, story telling, and laughter. In the tradition of the *Church of the Brethren, one man comes to mind when thinking of persons who have combined the seriousness of faith study and the gift of humor. *William McKinley Beahm, teacher, dean, annual conference secretary, and twice moderator was a much admired and appreciated churchman. People respected his wisdom. But they also eagerly listened for his witty sayings and puns. His humor was sometimes carefully planned. Other times his quick wit emerged out of an immediate situation. Following are some samples of each.

PLANNED SAYINGS. On the contagious quality of Christ, he said, "He was a rash and not an eruption, if I may speak in measly terms."

"Sin is central," he said, "not peripheral in the experience of man. You can't clean up the water by painting the town pump."

He also said, "Sin is like a raspberry seed under God's denture."

"When I was a child," he said, "we moved every two years. In the church, three moves are equal to one firing."

On elders, he said, "An elder is an overseer and a supervisor according to the New Testament. What that means is that a good elder knows what to oversee and what to overlook."

Commenting on the wisdom of Solomon, he said, "Solomon is supposed to be so wise, but can you imagine day after day walking into the bathroom and getting tangled up in a thousand pair of nylons!"

Observing a reckless driver on the highway, he said, "If he continues driving like that, most likely down the road a ways one of his friends will have to come along and scrape up an old acquaintance."

QUICK RESPONSES TO IMMEDIATE SITUATIONS. The minister leading the opening of a district conference in Illinois and Wisconsin misread the text. When he came to "sexual immorality" he read "sexual immortality". The reader had hardly gone to the next word before William said softly under his breath, "That's more than I hoped for."

William returned to the *Akron, OH, City Church of the Brethren, where he was ordained, for a special service. There were elaborate decorations of ferns and floral pieces around the pulpit. Being short of stature, as he stood to speak he couldn't see the congregation for the ferns. Leaning forward, he parted the greenery and began his sermon with, "The voice of one crying in the wilderness."

After having been told before a morning class that Robert Roller's wife, Goldie, had given birth to twins during the night, William interrupted his routine roll-call when he came to Bob's name and said, "Boys, we are one of the few classes in theological education in the country with a student who has a roller-bearing wife."

As moderator of Annual Conference at Ocean Grove, NJ, William led the delegates down through the agenda; A,B,C,D,E, and F. After caring for F, he went on to item G. He announced it as, "Gee! Women in the ministry!" As item G was finished and they prepared to move on to the next item, William announced, "Now we can go to H!"

On a trip to the African Mission Field, *Leland Brubaker and William were together at a meeting in which Leland had been asked to speak. The people were delighted that "Malam" Beahm would assist in interpreting. Leland began by saying, "There comes a time in the destiny of human affairs when the whole history of mankind is in the crucible of change." William translated with a very short sentence in Bura. Leland looked at William and said, "What did you say?" William replied, "I said, He greets you in the name of Jesus Christ. Now, from here on take it easy!"

An alternative service worker shared a relatively unknown story which took place at the *Chicago, IL, First Church of the Brethren during a Chinese worship service on Sunday afternoon. Interested in the Chinese church, a Chicago newspaper sent a religious writer out to photograph and do a story about the service. William was preaching and an older Chinese member was translating. Seated in one of the iron and wood theater-type folding seats in the balcony, the writer, camera in hand, leaned out over the rail to take a picture. His foot slipped and caught between the seat and the seat back. There he hung, unable to both hold on to the camera and reach back to recover his balance. The congregation was unaware of the predicament, but the Chinese interpreter said to William, "Brother Beahm, what shall we do?" William responded, "Send an usher up to help him to safety and bring him down. We'll see if he wants to be baptized. Before the usher comes down, have him reset the trap."

Bevel Jones said, "Humor and faith are cousins; both deal with the incongruities of life. The aim of life is wholeness, and faith without humor is incomplete." If that be true, William Beahm helped several generations of Brethren toward wholeness. EWF, Jr.

Benedict, Harry G. (OGBB), 1918–98, was born July 19 near Duffield, Franklin Co., PA. Harry Benedict was the son of Elder Ezra G. and Lizzie Wingert Benedict. He was baptized in 1938, married Evelyn Hess in 1941, and they became the parents of nine children. They made their home in the *Antietam, PA, congregation where Benedict was elected to the ministry in 1948 and advanced to the eldership in 1961. Evelyn Benedict died in 1974 and Benedict then married Julia Bayer in 1975. Harry Benedict served on the Annual Meeting *Standing Committee (1968–92) and as nonresident elder of the *Beaver Dam, MD, congregation for 19 years. He enjoyed traveling across the brotherhood and could easily communicate with people from all walks of life. He spoke, closing the meeting at *Wolf Creek, OH, less than two months before his death. He died at home on Aug. 24. EHD

Vindicator (1948) 154, (1978) 352, (1998) 318; *Old Order Notes* No. 4 (Spring, 1981) 19.

*Bethany Hospital. Following the merger in 1982 of Bethany Hospital with the Evangelical Hospital Association, the primary residual involvement of the *Church of the Brethren is continuing representation on the hospital Governing Council. Three council members are to be selected by the *Association of Brethren Caregivers (ABC). In its outreach program Advocate Bethany Hospital assisted in the construction of Bethany Brethren Community Center, a part of *Chicago First CB. Bethany Hospital has one member on the BBCC Board.

In Jan. 1995 the Evangelical Health System negotiated a merger with Lutheran General Hospital System. As a key member of this large system, Advocate Health Care, the situation of Bethany Hospital became more secure. Despite the disproportionately large number of Medicaid patients at Bethany Hospital, improvements were made. New labor/delivery/recovery suites were constructed and in 1996 the Emergency Department was upgraded. The hospital continues to promote many *wellness programs and clinics (e.g., immunization, asthma treatment) in the East Garfield Park area of Chicago. GFS

M. S. H. Rosenberger, *The Gift of Life: The Brethren and Bethany Hospital* (1995); *Minutes (CB)*, (1983–94); *Messenger* (June, 1984) 12, (March, 1987) 6, (Jan., 1988) 6, (Dec., 1990) 7, (Jan., 1991) 7.

Bethany Theological Seminary, Richmond, IN.

*Bethany Theological Seminary (CB). Under the leadership (after 1975) of *Warren F. Groff as president and Graydon F. Snyder as dean, important curricular developments took shape at Bethany Theol. Seminary. A Doctor of Ministry (DMin) degree program reached its highest enrollment in 1977 with 30 students. Also inaugurated during Groff's tenure was a new program of seminary financing. In 1978, the *General Board reduced its budgetary support of the seminary, with all subsidies ending in 1983. Bethany became a self-supporting institution.

Bethany located in Oak Brook, IL, during years of high ecumenical optimism. Planners anticipated a future of cooperative theological education in the hope that other denominational seminaries would build on the same campus. They designed a 40-acre facility for nearly three times the highest student enrollment. Meanwhile, Brethren membership went into decline. Student enrollment dropped from a high in 1985 of 104 students to a low of 60 in 1995. For reasons of cost effectiveness, the board discontinued the DMin degree program in 1989. Unable to maintain the property out of its operating budget, the seminary began to borrow from endowment funds in 1978.

Fumitaka Matsuoka followed Snyder as dean in 1987, stressing cross-cultural education. A Peace Studies program headed by *Dale W. Brown attracted MATh students. In 1989 Wayne L. Miller succeeded Groff as president.

Under Miller, the Bethany board concluded that the Oak Brook campus was no longer financially viable. The seminary would either have to downsize and relocate or close. After exploring several partnership options, including affiliations with Brethren colleges, the board chose to move the seminary to Richmond, IN, to form a partnership with the Earlham School of Religion (ESR), a graduate school of the Religious *Society of Friends.

Succeeding Miller as president in 1992, Eugene F. Roop presided over Bethany's transition from Oak Brook to Richmond. With the appointment of Richard B. Gardner as dean during that same year, revisions in the Bethany curriculum made ministry formation basic to seminary education. In partnership with the many local Brethren congregations of the region, in close affiliation with the denominational staff, and in association with the Earlham School of Religion, Bethany's educational programs underwent a reorientation. An academy program to take up the mission of the discontinued *Bible Training School and courses offered at the Susquehanna Valley Satellite (located at *Elizabethtown College) were important new features. Shared resources with ESR allowed necessary reduction in the cost of seminary operations.

By the turn of the century, Bethany could report renewed congregational connections, a revitalized program of ministerial preparation, a vigorous association with a seminary from a kindred tradition, near equality of gender numbers in both faculty and student body, and a balanced budget. Bethany, in its fourth incarnation, had made its home in Indiana for the foreseeable future. MLW, Jr.

Messenger (April, 1990) 17–19, (June, 1990) 9, (May, 1992) 24–27, (June, 1992) 6, 9, (July, 1992) 7, (Jan., 1993) 11–15, (Aug./Sept., 1993) 35–36, (Nov., 1994) 6–7, (April, 1995) 9, (Jan., 1995) 6; (Aug., 1995) 8, (Nov., 1995) 16, (June, 1997) 11, (Aug./Sept., 1996) 7, (Nov., 1997) 6; *BLT* 28 (Winter, 1983) 49–56, 39 (Winter, 1994): 1–72, special issue.

Bethesda Church of the Brethren, MD, is located six and one-half miles south of Grantsville. Organized in 1975, the congregation was originally a meeting point of the *Maple Grove congregation. There were 36 founding members led by Preston J. Miller, who served as the minister until 1979. Evelyn M. Bowman was the first moderator. Other pastoral leadership included Walter Otto (1981–83), Connel T. Chaney (1985–87), and Joseph Lewis (1988–91). The current minister, Edwin E. Moore, Jr., began in 1993. Membership and attendance remained strong through the early 1980s with a peak average attendance of 65 in 1983. In 2000 there were 39 members and an average attendance of 38. DKB

Congregational records; *Yearbook (CB)*(1975–2000).

Beulah Beach I and II (BC). *General Conference of *The Brethren Church in August 1988 voted to support a denominational reorganization that would foster and support ministry rather than maintain organizational life. This initiated a year of structural transition which moderator Kenneth Sullivan felt would be better accomplished if the denomination developed a mission statement. Over the next year, moderator-elect Mary Ellen Drushal led the

General Conference Executive Council in writing this mission statement and underscoring its biblical basis.

With the new mission statement completed, Drushal led an ad hoc committee composed of Jerry R. Flora, Michael Gleason, William and Trudy Boardman Kerner, Vanessa Oburn, Debra Ritchey, Joan Ronk, Joann Seaman, and Richard C. Winfield in a process to identify goals. The committee developed the initial purpose statement and a list of goals for each new ministry commission prior to beginning its work after elections in Aug. 1989. This gave rise to a felt need to involve representation from congregations throughout the denomination in a process of planning and goal setting for the next decade.

Beulah Beach I. Each congregation was invited to send its pastor and one key lay person to Beulah Beach on Lake Erie in Vermilion, OH, for this first attempt at broad, participative denominational planning. The 165 Brethren who gathered at Beulah Beach on Nov. 27–29, 1989, represented every region of the denomination. The participants identified 11 denominational priorities for the next decade: spiritual formation, developing lay ministry, church planting, denominational interaction, unified vision, communication, pastoral care, leadership development, evangelism, stewardship, and regional focus. The accomplishments emerging from this time together had considerable impact upon denominational emphases and programming in the 1990s. The General Conference Executive Council distilled the 11 priorities identified at Beulah Beach into four Priorities for the Nineties: "Becoming Like Christ" (Spiritual Formation); "Sharing our Faith" (Passing on the Promise); "Training Growth Leaders" (Leadership Development for Outreach); and "Forming New Churches" (Church Planting). In 1992 General Conference adopted these priorities and authorized the formation of four commissions to give leadership to their implementation within the denomination.

Beulah Beach II. The BC Mission Board commissioned Mary Ellen Drushal to lead a planning session for church planting on Oct. 26–28, 1992. Using a planning process similar to that of Beulah Beach I, participants were asked to select one of four interest groups: Personnel and Training for Church Planters; Site Selection and Models for Church Planting; Financing Church Planting Opportunities; and Cooperation and Roles of Local, District, and National Boards in Church Planting. The groups were led by Dale R. Stoffer, Ronald W. Waters, Arden Gilmer, and Russell Gordon, respectively. In each interest group, the participants developed a purpose statement, goals, and strategy for planting churches. The results of Beulah Beach II became a greater urgency for church planting within the denomination and commitment by at least ten people to church planting within the next decade. Both Beulah Beach experiences contributed to a greater sense of unity, vision, and purpose for the denomination during the 1990s. MED

BE (Jan. 1990) 4–6, (Nov. 1992) 6–7.

*Bible Translations. Several new or revised translations have appeared since 1980. Revisions of earlier works include the New Jerusalem Bible (NJB), New Living Translation (NLT), New Revised Standard Version (NRSV), and Revised English Bible (REB). New translations include the Contemporary English Version (CEV), a common language translation prepared by the American Bible Society, and The Message, a paraphrase by Eugene Peterson distinguished by its vigorous street language.

A new issue that has emerged for translators since 1980 is that of gender and language. The NRSV and CEV reflect special sensitivity to this issue, using inclusive *language to refer to human subjects where the original text supports that usage.

The Brethren response to the growing number of available translations is mixed. For the *Dunkard Brethren and *Old German Baptist Brethren, the KJV continues to be the translation used in public worship, while other versions may be used for individual study. Among the other Brethren groups, acceptable translations for worship range more widely, with the NRSV and NIV receiving the most widespread use. In the *Church of the Brethren, the NRSV has essentially replaced the older RSV as a preferred translation for curricular publications.

Brethren have also contributed to the creation of new translations for at least three projects since 1980. David W. Baker (BC), a faculty member at *Ashland Theol. Sem., was one of three persons who developed the translation of Leviticus for the NLT. Lester E. and Esther Marie Frantz Boleyn, CB field staff working with the United Bible Societies, coordinated the translation of the Bible into Nuer, a language spoken by inhabitants of southern *Sudan. With the leadership of *John Guli, the New Testament was translated into the Kamwe language in *Nigeria. RBG

S. M. Sheeley and R. N. Nash, Jr., *The Bible in English Translation. An Essential Guide* (1997); *Messenger* (May, 1997) 17.

Bieber, Charles M. (CB), b. 1919, pastor, nurse, missionary, administrator. Charles Bieber was born on Sept. 11 to George Albert and Edith Seriff Bieber in Williamsport, PA. He received his undergraduate education at *Juniata College (BS, 1941), his nursing education at Pennsylvania Hospital School of Nursing for Men (RN, 1944), and his theological education at *Bethany Theol. Sem. (BD, 1949). Bieber married Mary Beth High (1922–2004) on June 24, 1944; they had five children: Larry, Dale, Bonnie, Marla, and Doreen.

Charles Bieber, accompanied by his family, served as a missionary in *Nigeria (1950–63) where he engaged in *evangelism, nursing, and church administration. He served as the district secretary for the Nigerian Church (1955–63), as a member of the *Hillcrest School Board of Governors, as a member of the board of trustees of the *Theol. College of Northern Nigeria, and as a member of the Northern Missions Council. He was especially diligent in writing articles about the work in Nigeria for the denominational periodical, *The Gospel Messenger.

During his career, Bieber pastored several congregations: *Fairview, IN (1948); *Lincoln, NE (1950); *Pottstown, PA (1960); *Big Swatara, PA (1963–70); *Black Rock, PA (1970–77); *Mingo, PA (1986–92); *Ephrata, PA (1992–96); and *Mt. Zion Road, PA (1996–97). During 1978–86 he served as the executive of the Northern Indiana District. He was a member of the *General Board (1966–74) and moderator of the denomination (1976–77). He served as a trustee of *Juniata College (1988–91) and of *Elizabethtown College (1996–97). He wrote two books, *Keeping the Embers Aglow: 100 Years of the Ephrata Church of the Brethren* (1999), and an autobiography, *Around God's World for Eighty Years* (2002). DVU

BLT 18 (Autumn, 1973) 189–98; *GM* (April 7, 1951) 22–23; *Messenger* (June, 1973) 12–15, (June, 1977) cover, 19–21, (Dec., 1985) 7, (Oct., 1998) 14–16; *E. Pennsylvania* (1965) 10; *S.*

BIEBER, CHARLES M.

Pennsylvania (1973) 303; *N. Atlantic* (1975) 47–48, 261, 341; K.
Thomasson, *The Old, Old Story Anew: The Church of the Brethren in
Nigeria* (1983).

Black, James R. (BC), pastor, denominational executive.
Born May 29, 1929, in Akron, OH, son of Robert and
Edith Black, James Black served in the U.S. military, then
entered civilian work. In 1954 he committed his life to
Christ and soon thereafter experienced God's call to min-
istry. He attended *Ashland College. (BS Ed, 1963),
International Theol. Sem. (ThM, 1981), and *Ashland
Theol. Sem. (MA, 1983).

Black pastored Brethren churches in *Akron, OH,
(Firestone Park, 1960–64); *Waterloo, IA, (1964–70);
*Milledgeville, IL, (1970–79); *Dayton, OH, (Hillcrest,
1979–81); *Canton, OH, (Trinity, 1996–2002); and Ashland, OH, (Garber, 2002). He served *The Brethren
Church as director of Home Missions and Evangelism
(1981–84), executive director of the Missionary Board
(1985–95), and director of stewardship and planned giving (part-time, 1995–96).

In 1955 he married Shirley L. Andrick. Two of their
five children (James F. and Glenn) entered pastoral ministry. Shirley Black served as national president (1992) of
the *Women's Missionary Society. RCWi

J. R. Black, *Predestined to be Conformed to His Image* (1992), autobiography; *BE* (June, 1981) 23, (July/Aug., 1995) 18, (March, 1996)
10.

**Blacksburg, VA, Good Shepherd Church of the
Brethren.** Blacksburg, Montgomery County, VA, is the
site of Virginia Polytechnic Institute and State University,
a land grant university. The church site was dedicated on
May 17, 1981. Norman L. Harsh began as pastor/develop-
er on Feb. 1, 1981. Subsequent pastors were Marianne
Rhoades Pittman (1986–94), Richard and Janice Kulp
Long (1995–2001), and Merilyn E. Lerch (2001–). Worship services were initiated Sept. 13, 1981. After using
leased space, the congregation dedicated a new building
on Nov. 5, 1989. Volunteers provided over 14,000 work
hours toward completion of the structure, now valued in
excess of one million dollars. Beginning with 11 charter
members, Good Shepherd's membership has averaged 40.
However, over 230 persons affiliated with the congregation during the period of 1982–94. A strong voice for
peace and justice concerns, Good Shepherd provides a
convenient ministry to many Brethren students and serves
a diverse local population. DKS

Records of the Virlina District Church Extension Committee; cong.
records; *Yearbook* (CB) (1982–2000); *Messenger* (Jan., 1983) 16.

**Blain, PA, Grace Brethren Church of Sherman's
Valley.** Several families associated with the *Three
Springs Church of the Brethren, PA, were unhappy with
their denomination because of its affiliation with the
*World and *National Councils of Churches. They met
with Michael J. Rockafellow, pastor of the *Elizabethtown Grace Brethren Church, to learn more about the
*Fellowship of Grace Brethren Churches. Meetings for
Bible study and prayer were initiated in the fall of 1981.
Beginning with Jan. 1982, Sunday evening services were
held in the Loysville post office. Sunday morning services were not held until the following year, first in a home
and then in the post office. A building on So. Main St. in
Blain was purchased in 1986 to provide a home for the
church. Pastors serving the congregation were George F.

Wilhelm (1982–84), Stephen Harold Blake (1984–85),
Edward P. Fleming, Sr. (1985), Brad Lee Lambright
(1986–88), Dennis D. Huratiak (1988–94), and James D.
Link (1995–). John Harold Hollinger and Steve Lee
Klinedienst also assisted with Bible teaching and preaching. Through the years, the Grace Brethren congregation
in Elizabethtown has been a constant encouragement to
the congregation in Blain. JMS/JRY

Congregational records; *Annual* (FGBC) (1982–2000).

**Blue Ridge Old German Baptist Brethren Church,
GA,** is located six miles north of Cleveland, White Co.,
GA. Brethren first settled permanently in the area in 1985.
More moved in quickly, and worship services were held in
the old Corinth Baptist meetinghouse until 1993. Prior to
that time, members were faithful in attending services at
*Fraternity OGBB, NC, where Georgia membership was
held. Early official leadership included Elder Russell D.
Knaus and deacons Thomas L. Eller and Danny W. Lynch.
With Georgia thriving, members (with Fraternity District
approval) called for help in forming a district. Aided by
elders from *Virginia, *West Virginia, and *Florida,
organization was effected, and 19 members signed the
charter on April 21, 1993. The present meetinghouse was
erected in Nov. 1993. As of June 1998 the district had 40
members including ministers Danny W. Lynch and
Wesley A. Killingsworth and deacons Thomas L. Eller,
Ronald C. Kinzie, and Harold R. Frantz. TLE

Vindicator (May, 1993) 153, (April, 1994) 122.

Bomberger, Harold Zug (CB), pastor, denominational
executive. He was born in Lebanon County, PA, on May
13, 1918, to Howard B. and Venona Zug Bomberger, was
ordained by the Eastern Pennsylvania District in 1940,
and was married to Margaret E. Mann in 1944.

Bomberger was educated at *Elizabethtown College
(BA, 1943), *Bethany Theol. Sem. (BD, 1946), and
Lutheran Theol. Sem., Gettysburg, PA (STM 1960). His
ministry included pastorates at *Allentown, PA (1946–
48), *Westminster, MD (1948–56), and *McPher-son, KS
(1960–71). He was the executive secretary of the Eastern
Region (1956–60), district executive of the Atlantic
Northeast District (1971–83), and moderator of the 1971
Annual Conference. Bomberger has been a district conference moderator, was a member of the *General Board,
and served on significant Annual Conference committees;
he also authored articles for *Church of the Brethren publications. His ecumenical activity included two terms as
president of the Kansas Council of Churches. FEB

S. Pennsylvania (1973) 304–05; *N. Atlantic* (1975), index.

Bowman, Carl W. (OGBB), b. 1925, minister, accountant, travel agent. The son of Elder Levi and Elizabeth
Holfinger Bowman, Carl Bowman was born near
Covington, Miami Co., OH. He was baptized in early
1944, and in Sept. 1944 he married Mildred Wagoner,
daughter of Floyd and Cecil Denlinger Wagoner. Bowman
was called to the ministry in the *Covington District in
1951 and ordained in 1964. Chosen to the Brotherhood
Service Committee in 1966, he was writing clerk for a
number of years until his term was completed in 1988. He
began serving on the *Standing Committee in 1980, was
again writing clerk for ten years, retiring in 1999 due to
illness. Other responsibilities included nonresident oversight for the *West Modesto congregation, CA, three
years; *Oak Grove congregation, OH, six years;

*Covington congregation, OH, (before reorganization) one year; and *Sugar Grove congregation, OH, ten years. Carl and Mildred Bowman have four children. In later years, he organized a travel agency and enjoys helping with arrangements for travelers. GCW

Vindicator (1951) 250–51, (1964) 57; *Minutes (OGBB)* (1966–99); *Old Order Notes* No. 4 (Spring, 1981) 20.

Boycott (CB). An economic boycott represents a combined effort to encourage persons to abstain from the purchase or use of products or services provided by a targeted firm, government, or other agency. The purpose of a boycott is to persuade the targeted body to cease from certain practices judged to be unjust or to perform certain practices deemed to be just.

Faith and ethics have traditionally guided Brethren economic boycotts. *Church of the Brethren boycott endorsements include a boycott of Nestlé Company because of its marketing policies and practices related to infant formula in poor countries, a boycott of Shell products because of apartheid concerns in South Africa, and a boycott of Salvadoran coffee. When the goals were accomplished, economic sanctions and boycotts were terminated. SPB

See also CHURCH AND STATE RELATIONS; LOBBYING; SOCIAL ACTION.

CB Annual Conference Resolution on Project Equality (1971); *CB Annual Conference Resolution on Suspension of Economic Sanctions, Boycott, and Divestiture Positions on South Africa* (1994); *CB General Board Resolutions on Infant Formula Concerns* (*1979,* 1982); *CB General Board actions: Nestlé Boycott* (1983), *Shell Boycott* (1988), *Salvadoran Coffee Boycott* (1990); *Messenger* (Dec., 1988) 4–5, (April/May, 1989) 4.

Boyer, James L. (FGBC, CGBCI), (1911–2003), educator. Born in Ashland, OH, and a graduate of *Ashland College, James Boyer attended *Ashland Theol. Sem., Bonebrake Theol. Sem. (BD), and Oberlin School of Theology (STM, 1942). He pastored *Evangelical United Brethren congregations in Warren and Mansfield, OH, before enrolling at *Grace Theol. Sem. where he earned a ThD degree (1952).

Upon graduation, Boyer entered a teaching ministry, focusing on Greek and New Testament studies, at *Grace College and Theol. Sem. until his retirement in 1976. He published *For a World Like Ours: Studies in 1 Corinthians and Prophecy: Things To Come.* He also produced chronological charts on the intertestamental period and on the New Testament. This work was published by *Brethren Missionary Herald and produced in laminated form by Moody Press.

During his teaching years, Boyer began developing *GRAMCORD,* a grammar concordance, which gave the user the ability to search different grammatical constructions found in the Greek New Testament. This work continued into his retirement years, during which he wrote articles on grammatical issues for *Grace Theological Journal.* Boyer was involved in the development of *Conservative Grace Brethren Churches International in the 1990s. RTC

Personal information; *Annual (FGBC)* (1953ff.).

Bradenton, FL, Grace Brethren Church started in 1986 as a mission church under the leadership of *Lester E. Pifer. Several people began to meet in the home of one of the initial participants. The group moved a short time later to the Red Cross facility in Bradenton. After much prayer,

the congregation agreed to purchase its present property at 5535 33rd St. East in Bradenton. The two buildings on the property were completely renovated and a parking area constructed. Following Pifer's ministry, Charles Barnhill served as pastor for a brief time. An interim ministry team formed by Ralph Hall, Ernie Bearinger, and Lynn Schrock served the church until Robert Byers became the pastor in Jan. 1992. RGB/JRY

Congregational records; *Annual (FGBC)* (1986ff.).

Brandon, FL, Good Samaritan Church of the Brethren. Fred M. Cline was installed as pastor of the Brandon CB on May 18, 1986. On July 13, 1986, the congregation voted to adopt the name "Good Samaritan Church of the Brethren." From July 20, 1986, through Jan. 14, 1990, services were held in a Seventh Day Adventist Church building, located in the northwest area of Brandon, five miles east of Tampa. The first worship service was held in the first unit of the new church, located at 1317 Providence Rd., in the southwest area of Brandon, on Jan. 21, 1990. The new building was dedicated on Feb. 25, 1990. Cline served as pastor until Oct. 2000; Richard Spears began Mar. 1, 2001, as interim pastor for one year. PNZ

Congregational records; *Yearbook (CB)* (1986ff.); *Messenger* (July, 1983) 39; *BLT* 36 (Summer, 1991) 172.

Brazil (CB). Inspired by his reading, Onaldo Alves Pereira (b. 1959) contacted various Brethren denominations in the U.S. during 1982. Stephen Newcomer, representing the *Church of the Brethren *World Ministries Commission, visited Pereira during 1983–84. Pereira studied at *Bethany Theol. Sem. during 1984–85 and was ordained in 1987 by the Virlina District.

With the help of Newcomer, an *Anabaptist congregation, the Christian Pacifist Community (Tunker), was incorporated in Fortaleza in 1988, but owing to difficulties it was dissolved later that year. By 1991 Pereira had organized a church located approximately 750 miles northwest of Sao Paulo, in Rio Verde, Goias State. With aid from the CB, a home for Pereira was constructed in March 1991.

The Rio Verde Brethren were accepted as a part of the CB by the 1992 *Annual Conference. The Virlina District accepted responsibility for the Igreja da Irmandade - Communidade Pacificista Christa - Tunker later the same year. These "Tunkers" called six of their 32 members to the plural ministry during 1993 and completed a meetinghouse in May 1994. During 1994–95, issues related to ownership of the property and ministerial discipline caused division in the congregation. Pereira and two other ministers lost their ministerial standing. The portion of the congregation remaining loyal to the CB was reorganized. They are now known as the Evangelical Anabaptist Church. The congregation in Rio Verde had dwindled to a very small number in 1999.

More recently another church planting effort was launched in Brazil, led by Marcos Inhauser, based in Sao Paulo. Early achievements seem to hold promise. DKS

Virlina District records; *Messenger* (June, 1986) 26–29, (April, 1987) 1, (July, 1987) 23–26, (April, 1993) 17–21, (May, 1993) 7, (March, 1995) 7.

Brethren Academy for Ministerial Leadership (CB), a program in *ministry education that incorporated and reconfigured several earlier programs. Launched in 1997,

the Academy is jointly sponsored by *Bethany Theol. Sem. and the *General Board of the *Church of the Brethren, with administrative offices at the seminary campus in Richmond, IN. It replaced the former Bethany Academy for Ministry Training, begun in 1992, as well as the Ministry Training program of the General Board.

The program of the Academy has three foci: (1) certificate programs in ministry training designed for persons unable to pursue graduate level theological training; (2) continuing education for pastors and other church leaders; (3) leadership development at all levels of the church, with the goal of strengthening and transforming the life of congregations.

Among its program initiatives, the Academy sponsors training institutes and workshops, facilitates the participation of Academy students in seminary courses, administers denominational training programs, and certifies a network of district and regional programs called Academy Certified Training Systems (ACTS). Oversight of Academy programs rests with the CB Ministry Advisory Council, which includes representatives from several denominational agencies working with ministry issues.

One of two certificate programs administered by the Academy is *Education For a Shared Ministry (EFSM). From 1977 to 1997, 70 small-membership churches completed the program, which provides ministry education for a leadership team that includes pastoral and lay leaders. Eleven congregations were enrolled in EFSM in 1998.

A second certificate program provided through the Academy goes by the acronym TRIM, for TRaining In Ministry. Launched in 1987, TRIM features a flexible training model that utilizes locally accessible educational opportunities provided by colleges and church agencies as well as graduate courses at the Seminary and/or Academy-sponsored training events. Under the direction of a seminary-trained district coordinator, TRIM students pursue curricular units in general education, Bible and theology, and ministry and ministry skills, and participate in an ongoing Ministry Formation Group. Graduates of TRIM through the end of 1997 numbered 151. Sixty-one students were enrolled in 1998.

Together, the programs of the Brethren Academy continue the heritage of the earlier *Bethany Training School. They provide opportunities for ministry education that are not limited to those pursuing a graduate degree, but rather accessible to the wider membership of the church. RBG
L. Glick, "Shared Blessings—The Story of EFSM," MATh thesis, Bethany Theol. Sem. (1989); *Minutes* (*CB*) (1985–89) 106–16; *Messenger* (Dec., 1997) 19–20.

Brethren Benefit Trust (CB) is the financial services agency of the *Church of the Brethren. Operating as the church's *Pension Board in 1943–88, its initial function was as trustee and administrator of the *Pension Plan adopted by the 1943 *Annual Conference. The Pension Board also administered the Ministerial and Missionaries Service Fund, Supplemental Pension Fund, and Ministers Group Insurance Fund. Beginning in 1981, the Pension Board assumed the funding and administrative responsibility for the Brethren Medical Plan and the group life and long-term disability plans.

During 1943–48, administrators of the Pension Board were also administrators of the *General Ministerial Board and included H. L. Hartsough (1943–45) and *Leland S. Brubaker (1945–47). From 1948 to 1980 the Pension Board administrators also had administrative

duties for the *General Board. Carrying these dual functions were *Harl L. Russell (1947–53, 1959–69), *H. Spenser Minnich (1953–59), *Galen B. Ogden (1969–77), and *Joel K. Thompson (1977–80). Beginning in 1980, Anne Myers (1980–82) became the first full-time Pension Board executive followed by Wilfred E. Nolen (1983–).

In 1988 Annual Conference approved a name change from the Pension Board to Brethren Benefit Trust (BBT) and a separate board of directors comprised of 12 members. New board members brought expertise in finance, investing, law, planned giving, and information systems. BBT employee benefit services continued to focus on pensions, insurance, and grants for retired church workers. In 1990 responsibilities were expanded to include the newly organized Brethren Foundation, Inc. The foundation is not a fund-raising entity but provides asset management, deferred gifts management, and technical assistance for development officers.

By 1990 BBT held the largest pool of financial assets in the CB. Because of large volume and related fiduciary functions, it was essential that a good investment system be devised that generated competitive returns while upholding the social and ethical values of the CB. The success of BBT's investment system generated strong interest by the general membership in using BBT services. In 1998, Annual Conference authorized BBT to expand services beyond church employees and agencies to include the total membership. These services will be built around a denominational credit union and a credit union service organization offering financial and estate planning, investment management, and insurance products. Additional financial services planned for local churches and districts are accounting and financial reporting software packages that are connected on-line with BBT through its virtual private network. To uphold the BBT objective to operate on fees instead of donations, all of these services are designed to generate fees to pay for costs. BBT is the only denominational agency with this objective. WEN
Agency records; personal information; *Messenger* (Aug./Sept., 1988) 22, (1989–2000), indexes.

*Brethren Church, The. The period since 1980 has been significant for the progress of The Brethren Church, specifically in the areas of *denominational reorganization, theological definition and discussion, development of denominational vision, church planting, and the growth of *Ashland Theol. Seminary. Denominational reorganization dominated the national life of the church from 1976 to 1996. Several concerns motivated this reorganization process: the need for a more unified vision for national ministry, more efficient use of personnel and financial resources, and a more streamlined structure that could be easily modified as necessary. Though there were many facets to restructuring, the main elements were: (1) consolidating the work of all cooperating boards under the direct oversight of a single executive board (the Benevolent, Christian Education, Publishing, and World Relief Boards were dissolved by action of *General Conference in 1988; the *Missionary Board merged with The Brethren Church, Inc. in 1996); (2) developing the position of an executive director of The Brethren Church who would give visionary leadership to all aspects of denominational ministry; and (3) keeping the focus of the denomination on missions and ministry to local churches. The final step of reorganization occurred in 1996 when

the position of executive director was adopted by General Conference together with a single executive board that was charged with overseeing the work of two ministry councils, the Congregational Ministries Council and the Missionary Ministries Council, each with its own director. Reflecting a shift in the responsibilities of the two boards, in 2002 they were renamed the United States Ministries Council and the International Ministries Council. The first executive director, Emanuel W. Sandberg, was affirmed by General Conference in 1997. He was followed by Kenneth D. Hunn in 2003.

The 1980s and 1990s were marked by concerted efforts to reacquaint the church with its historical and theological heritage. Noteworthy were the publication in 1984 of *A Centennial Statement, a pamphlet explicating the basic beliefs of the church in honor of its centenary in 1983; Jerry R. Flora's exposition of the first half of A Centennial Statement in a book entitled The Message of Faith, published in 1996; the creation in 1989 of a BC Doctrine, Research, and Publication Committee to "articulate clearly its faith and practice and pass on its heritage to succeeding generations"; the publication by this committee of a pamphlet entitled How Brethren Understand God's Word, detailing the Brethren understanding and use of scripture; and a series of articles in *The Brethren Evangelist on doctrine by Dale R. Stoffer during 1982–83 and by the Doctrine, Research, and Publication Committee from 1993 to 1996. This doctrinal work has created a greater sense of unity within the denomination on the major aspects of Brethren thought and practice.

The Brethren Church gave focused attention during the late 1980s and early 1990s to developing a unified denominational vision and mission as well as ministries that could carry out this mission. In 1988–89 the General Conference Executive Council (GCEC) formulated a mission statement for the denomination. Crucial to developing a unified vision for the denomination was a gathering of pastors and lay leaders from across the denomination at *Beulah Beach, OH, on Nov. 27–29, 1989. Led by the first woman moderator of General Conference, Mary Ellen Waters Drushal, the Denominational Planning Retreat developed a list of priorities for the denomination that became the focal point of ministry during the 1990s.

In 1991 GCEC identified four areas for denominational focus: becoming like Christ (spiritual formation), sharing our faith (passing on the promise), training growth leaders (leadership development for outreach), and forming new churches (church planting). These emphases were adopted by the 1992 General Conference as the Priorities for the 1990s. GCEC formed commissions for each of these priorities, and much of the denomination's energy and resources were invested into advancing each of them.

The Brethren Church has maintained its historic emphasis on *missions. Two new foreign mission fields have been opened since 1980: *Paraguay in 1987 and *Peru in 1992, the former work an outreach of the *Argentine Brethren Church. Since the late 1970s The Brethren Church has given special emphasis to the planting of new churches. Between 1980 and 2003 this emphasis resulted in the beginning of 41 new congregations, though 22 of these new works had closed by the end of 2003.

Renewed impetus for church planting resulted from the second denomination-wide gathering at Beulah Beach, OH, on Oct. 26–28, 1992. The Church Planting Planning Retreat established goals in the areas of identify-

ing and training church planters; site selection and models for church planting; financing church planting opportunities; and cooperation among local, district, and national entities in the work of planting new churches.

*Ashland Theol. Sem. has played a key role in the life of the church since the 1980s. Under the capable leadership of dean/vice president *Joseph R. Shultz (1963–80) and vice president/president Frederick J. Finks (1982–), the seminary grew from the smallest such institution in Ohio (22 students in 1963) to the 14th largest seminary in the U.S. (770 students in 2002). Though Brethren Church students number only about 30 to 50 in any given year, the size of the seminary makes possible not only a well-balanced educational and training program for all students but the offering of specialized courses for Brethren students in such fields as Brethren history, doctrine, polity, and *Anabaptist and *Pietist studies. The seminary works closely with the denomination in such areas as missions, church planting, church growth consultation, and examination of candidates for ordination.

Several prominent issues have been discussed in the church since 1980:

(1) The *elders (ordained ministers) discussed the ordination of *women during the early and mid-1980s and again between 1999 and 2002. Brethren *polity places responsibility for deciding matters relating to ordination in the hands of the elders. In the 1980s the elders could reach no consensus on the issue and, as a result, district boards tended to make decisions on a case-by-case basis. In 2002 the elders agreed that people duly called to ministry by a local congregation should be examined by the district examining board and the *National Ordination Council without regard to "sex, color, and nationality."

(2) The elders discussed the ordination of divorced persons in the early 1990s. The National Association of Brethren Church Elders (NABCE) agreed that ordination of *divorced persons would be considered on a case-by-case basis.

(3) In the mid-1990s the elders and the church at large discussed whether the church should recognize the *baptism of people previously baptized by any form of believer's baptism. (The practice since 1978 has been to recognize any form of believer immersion.) Because no consensus was reached on the issue, NABCE decided in 1996 to discontinue discussion and maintain the existing practice. In 2002, however, renewed interest in this issue caused NABCE to begin to discuss it once again. The 2003 General Conference encouraged broader discussion at the local and district levels. In 2004 General Conference adopted the proposal "to allow individual churches to accept as members those who have been baptised as believers by any form of water baptism.

Two important study papers were also received by the church during the 1980s. In 1987 the National Ministerial Association (renamed in 1988 the National Association of Brethren Church Elders) adopted a report by an Ordination Study Committee. There were several important features of this report; (1) Ordination should be viewed as functional, that is, for pastoral service; (2) The term elder should continue to be used to refer to the ordained leadership of the church; (3) Though the primary sense of the term elder should be reserved for those who have been ordained to pastoral work, the title can also appropriately be retained by ordained individuals who are retired, serving at the denominational level, Ashland Theol. Sem., and the religion department at *Ashland U., and those who

continue to serve the church in positions recognized by the Director of Pastoral Ministries (chaplaincies, for example); and (4) Those elders who no longer are serving the church in any capacity will, after a three-year period of inactivity, have their ordination lapse.

In 1988 General Conference adopted a Polity Committee study of the concept of church membership. This study recommended that churches hold people more accountable for their membership vows and that they discontinue the practice of an inactive membership list. It also suggested a format for receiving new members. Though most local Brethren congregations have not adopted all of these recommendations, some have incorporated features of the report into their membership practices.

Statistics for the denomination during the period from 1980 to 2002 provide a mixed picture. While membership in The Brethren Church declined from 15,485 to 10,287, average worship attendance grew from 10,466 to 11,133. DRS

A Centennial Statement (1984); J. R. Flora, *The Message of Faith* (1996); *How Brethren Understand God's Word* (1993). *BE* (Oct. 1987) 7–8, (Nov. 1987) 6–7, (June, 1988) 10–12, 13–14; (Sept. 1989) 6, (Jan. 1990) 5–6, (Nov., 1992) 6–7, (Dec. 1992) 12–13, (July/Aug., 1997) 9; (Jan.-Mar., 2003) 6; *Ashland Theological Seminary* (Fall, 1984) 4–21; *Journal of the Evangelical Theological Society* (Dec., 1987) 427–440; *Denominational Reorganization Proposal for the Brethren Church* (1996).

*Brethren Colleges Abroad (BCA) (CB) was founded in 1962 by the presidents of the six Church of the Brethren-related colleges to provide international opportunities only available earlier through the *Brethren Service Commission. A primary goal was to "further international understanding and promote world peace." BCA was to be an "in-depth educational experience" integrated as fully as possible in the overseas host university. Professors from Brethren and *Mennonite colleges have often mentored students as resident directors.

Philipps University, Marburg, Germany, hosted the first BCA program. Marburg's location near *Schwarzenau, where the first Brethren came together, and near the areas where the *Brethren Service Commission worked, made it a natural first site. In 1963 Brethren Colleges Abroad was extended to Strasbourg U. in France. Since then, nine more programs have been added: Barcelona, Spain; Cheltenham, England; Dalian, China; Sapporo, Japan; Athens, Greece; Nancy, France; Quito, Ecuador; Xalapa, Mexico; and Kochi, India. The program has grown from 25 in 1962–63 to over 300 U.S. students going abroad and 65 international students coming to U.S. colleges through BCA in 1997–98. In 36 years, over 4,800 students have participated. Allen C. Deeter served as executive director of BCA (1975–98); following his retirement Karen Jenkins was appointed president. ACD

Brethren Colleges Abroad: In Celebration of 30 Years of International Studies (1992); *BCA Alumni, 1962–1992; Juniata College Bulletin* (Spring, 1993) 14; *BCA News* 1/1 (Spring, 1996ff.); T. K. Jones, *Manchester College* (1989) 157-58.

Mack Seal

A seal used on some deeds related to the Germantown congregation was first discovered by Julius F. Sachse in the late 19th century. He believed it was Alexander Mack, Sr.'s personal seal because of the initials "A. M." Contrary to theories by Sachse, G. F.

Germantown Brethren congregational seal.

Falkenstein, Vernard Eller, Patricia Kennedy Helman, and others, the seal is not an original creation expressing the faith of Alexander Mack, senior or junior. It is probably not a personal seal, but one used on behalf of the Germantown congregation. The seal is an adaptation of an emblematic illustration created by a Dutch engraver, Jan Sommerfeld, for the first printing of the works of Jacob Boehme in 1682 in Amsterdam, edited and published by Johann Georg Gichtel, a Radical Pietist separatist.

The emblem originally illustrated Boehme's short work of 1623, *De testamentis Christi,* or by the German title, *Von Christi Testamenten* (Concerning the Testaments of Christ). The work presented Boehme's mystical interpretation of the two Lutheran sacraments, baptism and Eucharist. Gichtel provided a devotional commentary to go with Sommerfeld's copper engraving.

The seal is greatly simplified from the original emblem, due in part to the limitations of size and medium, and perhaps out of theological concern for some distance from Boehme's thought. The seal retains the cross with one heart imposed upon it, from which two separate clusters of grapes, leaves, and tendrils emerge. Additional elements from the emblem have disappeared from the seal.

Gichtel's commentary interpreted some of the illustration. He suggested that eating the Eucharist in faith reverses the poisonous effect of Adam's sin of eating the forbidden fruit in Paradise. The fiery effect of sin must also be extinguished by water, which flows from the heart in the emblem, but is lacking in the Germantown seal. According to Gichtel, through this water, and the flesh and blood of Jesus given on the cross, the fiery wrath of God is transmuted into God's love and light. Baptism and the Eucharist portray this love and grace.

The seal adds "A" and "M" on either side of the cross. Sachse believed they stood for Alexander Mack, Sr. The seal's earliest known use was in 1753. It was used by various members at Germantown on land

transactions. More likely the letters stand for Abendmahl, or supper, referring to the Lord's Supper, or love feast. The love feast is central to Brethren understandings of Christ's redemptive death and the nature of the Church. The "great supper" of the Lamb (Rev. 14), a common motif among Brethren and Radical Pietists, expressed hope for Christ's return and the Church's readiness.

The Brethren at Germantown may have designed a congregational seal to portray baptism and the Lord's Supper as "seals" of God's covenant with the Church through Christ. The seal suggests that the Germantown Brethren likely still found Boehme's literature meaningful. The alterations from the original emblem, perhaps that of the Germantown Brethren, also altered influences from Radical Pietism to a new commitment to a visible, disciplined Church. JAB

Jacob Boehme, *Von Christi Testamenten* (v. 6 in the complete Schriften) (1682, 1730, repr. 1957); Werner Buddecke, *Die Jakob Boehme-Ausgaben,* v. 1 (1937, 1957); Julius F. Sachse, *The German Sectarians of Pennsylvania,* v.1 (1899, repr. 1970):173; G. N. Falkenstein, *History of the Berman Baptist Brethren Church* (1901): 173; V. M. Eller, *Past and Present,* ed. D. F. Durnbaugh (1971): 40–41, and in *BLT* 10 (Winter 1965): 25–30, 12 (Summer 1967): 54–57; Patricia Kennedy Helman, *Sign and Symbol in the Church of the Brethren* (1991); 25–29.

Brethren Encyclopedia, Inc. grew out of the dreams of *M. R. Zigler and Brethren historians and writers for a comprehensive record of the five largest Brethren groups: The *Church of the Brethren, *The Brethren Church, *Fellowship of Grace Brethren Churches, *Old German Baptist Brethren, and *Dunkard Brethren Church. Zigler, encouraged by *W. Newton Long of Baltimore, MD, called an historic first assembly of Brethren at the Tunker House, Broadway, VA, in June 1973, which was followed by further meetings of writers and historians at Ashland, OH; Oak Brook, IL; New Windsor, MD; and Philadelphia, PA. On Dec. 17, 1977, seven persons met at New Windsor, MD, for incorporation under the laws of the State of Pennsylvania and formed a board of directors with Fred W. Benedict (OGBB) president, *Charles W. Turner (FGBC) vice-president, Dale V. Ulrich (CB) secretary, *Joseph R. Shultz (BC) treasurer, and *Howard J. Surbey (DB) board member. *Jacob C. Ness succeeded Surbey upon the latter's death in 1982, Robert S. Lehigh succeeded Ness upon his death in 2001, and Dale R. Stoffer succeeded Shultz upon his death in 2003. Ronald G. Lutz, *Germantown CB, was elected assistant treasurer and meets with the board. Donald F. Durnbaugh was appointed editor of *The Brethren Encyclopedia* (*TBE*).

In preparation for the huge project, Durnbaugh organized an enlarged board of editors from members of the five Brethren groups. Over one thousand people contributed articles to the first two volumes (published in 1983), with the third volume being published in 1984.

Following publication of the encyclopedia, several conferences of historians and writers were held. Brethren Encyclopedia, Inc. Board of Directors, desiring to continue work in the spirit of the encyclopedia, considered how they might continue to work together in the interests of the entire Brethren family of churches. Projects were desired which could be undertaken in the same spirit of cooperation which characterized the production of *Volumes 1–3* of *TBE*.

In Dec. 1984, publishing of a series of scholarly monographs and dissertations was approved, with William R. Eberly chosen as editor of the series. In the next ten years, six volumes appeared in this order: The *German Hymnody of the Brethren 1720–1903* by Hedwig T. Durnbaugh; *Background and Development of Brethren Doctrines 1650–1987* by Dale R. Stoffer; *Brethren Beginnings: The Origin of the Church of the Brethren in Early Eighteenth-Century Europe* by Donald F. Durnbaugh; *Hochmann von Hochenau 1670–1721* by Heinz Renkewitz, translated by William G. Willoughby; *Brethren Dress: A Testimony to Faith* by Esther Fern Rupel; and *The Beliefs of the Early Brethren 1706–1735* by William G. Willoughby. Further volumes were planned for publication following the appearance of the fourth volume of *TBE*.

In 1984 articles on the five major Brethren bodies along with an article by Durnbaugh on "Brethren, 1708–1883," all taken from *TBE,* were published as a 120-page paperback entitled *Meet the Brethren.* The popular volume was reprinted in 1995. In 1991 Brethren Encyclopedia along with *Brethren Missionary Herald Books sponsored *The Complete Writings of Alexander Mack,* a small attractive volume edited by William R. Eberly, which for the first time gathered together all known writings of the first Brethren leader.

In 1986, 1990, 1992, 1995, 1997, and 2000, D. F. and Hedda Durnbaugh led "Brethren Heritage Tours" to European centers of Brethren origins and activity–the last four tours being sponsored by the Brethren Encyclopedia, Inc. Board of Directors.

In Dec. 1986, the board considered a proposal to restore the central portion of an old house in the *Hüttental* area of Schwarzenau for a museum, library, and visitors center. The combined interests of Schwarzenau citizens and of tour participants (and friends) who pledged $30,000 toward the project, encouraged the board to establish an endowment to provide perpetual rent for the *Alexander Mack Museum.

Members of the BE board have consistently supported study conferences that have developed from the magnanimous spirit of M. R. Zigler. At a meeting on "Mission" at *Ashland, OH, in 1987, William R. Eberly proposed a celebration of the 250th anniversary of the first Annual Meeting of the Brethren in 1742. A *Brethren World Assembly was planned and conducted in July 1992. The Assembly, held at Elizabethtown, PA, had as its theme: *Christ Is Lord: Affirming Our Faith Heritage.* The theme of the second Brethren World Assembly held in July 1998 at Bridgewater, VA, was *Faith and Family: Challenges and Commitments.* The theme of the third Brethren World Assembly held in July 2003 at Winona Lake, IN, was *Brethren Presence Around the World.*

In the fall of 1999, the BE Board of Directors welcomed a sixth participating denomination, the newly-formed *Conservative Grace Brethren Churches International.

The intent of the board for the future of the corporation is to continue initiatives already begun, following now-established guidelines. The work should be scholarly; it should be historical; it should be in the interests of all the Brethren bodies; and it should contribute to understanding and conciliation among Brethren. The experience of members of the board testify that shared study and work contribute to an enlargement of the spirit which teaches that it is time for Brethren to learn from and to speak kindly to each other. FWB

BLT 30 (Summer, 1985) 131–88 (special issue); *TBE* (1983–84) vi-

xi; D. F. Durnbaugh, *Fruit of the Vine* (1997) 585–86; *Messenger* (Aug., 1998) 9, (Sept., 1999) 4.

Cooking Awards at Age 104:
Lou Anna River Shively

When Lou Anna River Shively (CB) died on June 7, 1992, she was 112 years old and fêted as one of the oldest persons in the world. Born on May 14, 1880, she noted that one of her first memories was running into the streets as a four-year-old girl to celebrate the election of Grover Cleveland as U.S. president. She lived through 23 presidential administrations and witnessed innumerable changes in society.

When she was a girl of ten, her mother died; during her mother's illness, she had primary care of her family. When the family members were dispersed, it was decided that Lou Anna should live in the home of an aunt in Mansfield, OH. Young Lou Anna traveled by herself on the train from Indiana to Ohio. The relative had just received a letter informing her of the plan when Lou Anna walked into her home.

Lou Anna River married Charles S. Shively (1875–1958) in 1904 and four days later learned that her husband had been given a position teaching mathematics in the recently conquered nation of the Philippines in Southeast Asia. Following the term of service there, the return to the United States in 1906 was eventful. While near Honolulu, their ship ran aground and they, along with other passengers, had to be rescued and remain three weeks in Hawaii until they secured other transportation. When they reached San Francisco, their ship could not dock because of the earthquake that had ravaged the port city and had to be diverted to another location.

After living in Colorado for 14 years, where Charles Shively taught and earned graduate degrees, and one year at *La Verne College, CA, the Shivelys moved to Huntingdon, PA. It was there at *Juniata College that Dr. Shively pursued a long career as a highly respected professor of mathematics and physics from 1920 to 1943 and again from 1945 to 1950. He died in 1958 at the age of 83.

After living for a time with a daughter in Shippensburg, PA, Lou Anna Shively moved to the *Brethren Village, Lititz, PA. She was noted for her activities while a resident. At the age of 104 she won two first-place awards in a local cooking contest and her photograph appeared in a local newspaper showing her leaving a polling place after voting.

Following her 100th birthday anniversary in 1980, each later anniversary was marked by publicity and letters from those in high places. Presidents Ronald Reagan and George H. W. Bush sent her congratulations. Often she was featured with her son, Arthur Shively, who was born on the same day of the month as his mother; when she was 109, he was 82. She remarked: "I thought that my life had come to an end when I became 100. But you know, I think that I have really done some living since I've been 100." DFD

E. C. Kaylor, Jr., *Truth Sets Free* (1977), 11, 182, 183; *[Huntingdon, PA] Daily News* (Sept. 16, 1958); *[Lancaster, PA] New Era* (April 28, 1980), (May 14, 1990), (June 9, 1992); *[Lancaster, PA] Intelligencer-Journal* (Feb. 10, 1988), (May 11, 1989), (May 14, 1991); *Messenger* (Oct., 1992) 3.

Sue Peterson and Ellie Halfhill of Elkart Valley Church of the Brethren. BHLA collection.

Brethren Family, The. The American family has continued to change since 1980. The size of the family is slowly decreasing. Premarital sexual relations along with pregnancies remain high but have stabilized or declined slightly. Age at first marriage has increased to 25 for women and to 27 for men as singles have greater freedom of cohabitation and greater gender equality, and seek to establish careers before marriage. This affects the age at which couples begin childbearing, and more couples are choosing to have no children. About half of couples marrying now have lived together before marriage. Single parent households now make up 27 percent of all families with children under age 18.

Greater diversity exists as more interracial and interethnic marriages occur. Traditional sex roles are less binding as more women work and husbands share more household tasks. Divorce rates are high but now are declining slightly. Socialization influences from nonparental sources, including peer groups, school culture, and electronic media are strong; men and women are now living longer and are able to be independent in their own homes or in retirement complexes. The use of assisted living facilities is increasing. More elderly persons are living together without marrying.

At the conceptual level, Americans are seeing marriage, family, divorce, and childrearing in more individualistic terms and less in accord with traditional religious definitions. Accordingly, moral assessments are based more upon personal concerns and situational circumstances rather than upon universally applicable standards.

Brethren families may be considered in relation to the degree to which they have been enmeshed in and affected by these broad social trends, or the degree to which they and the church have sought to counter those trends they oppose. Careful studies of family life of the Brethren are

lacking. Descriptions of change from 1980 to 2000 are impressionistic and based on statements of informants from the various groups.

The *Old German Baptist Brethren and *Dunkard Brethren have worked actively to resist some of the trends named above. They continue to draw a strong distinction between biblical and mainstream family practices. Ministers among the OGBB and DB preach strongly about the evils of mass media. Both groups encourage discipline and control over their children's exposure to societal influences which they believe would corrupt biblical understandings of appropriate sexual and family practices. Radios, television, tape players, and Internet entertainment are forbidden by the OGBB and discouraged by the DB. They restrict association with non-Brethren peer groups. These are all privileges that *Church of the Brethren, *The Brethren Church, and *Fellowship of Grace Brethren youth take for granted.

A larger proportion of OGBB and DB children are in parochial *schools. OGBB people operate 17 parochial schools that serve around half of their population. The DB have seven. In addition, many OGBB and DB families do *home schooling, a trend that is increasing among the CB, BC, and FGBC.

Most CB, BC, and FGBC families make use of the public school system and allow greater freedom to use technological and commercial media. Strong families, local church youth groups, and *National Youth Conferences are moderately successful in nurturing the youth of the CB and BC. Many experience a hiatus in their church relations while at college and thereafter. They often become active again when their own families are being established. In the CB, new biblical and church-centered Sunday school curricula have been helpful.

Marriage is seen as an important life decision by all Brethren groups. Diversity exists, however, in the meaning of marriage. OGBB, DB, and BC people define marriage as a life-long covenant not only between the married couple but between them and God, and therefore sacred. Among many youth today in the CB, the meaning of marriage has changed. It tends to be seen less as a sacred institution and more as a personal covenant. In addition to fulfilling commitments, personal growth and fulfillment become an important part of the expectation. Seen in this way, marriages that cease to be fulfilling and satisfactory to either or both persons may be broken. In many states this logic has been fully established in divorce law and community mores. CB, BC, and the FGBC believe premarital counseling, conflict resolution, and marriage nurture classes offer hope for strengthening the foundations of marriage, but effective preventative and remedial programs have yet to be adequately developed in most local churches. Some crisis counseling occurs among the OGBB and DB groups.

Spousal roles have evolved variably among the different Brethren groups. As increased gender equality and two-career families become more common, husbands have increased the time they spend in childcare and household duties, but such duties are not yet shared equally. Young families tend to follow a democratic model, with men giving the views and feelings of their wives more influence on family decisions.

Divorce and remarriage remain relatively uncommon and have unfavorable stigma among the OGBB and the DB. Both divorce and remarriage have increased in the CB and BC but still remain at a low level compared with national rates. Approximately 13 percent of CB married couples in the 1980s had experienced divorce, as compared with 35 percent nationally. Nevertheless, the stigma of divorce has declined. Divorce is widely viewed as sometimes necessary and a better choice than staying in a bad marriage. Pastoral counseling varies widely according to church policy and the particular views of the pastor.

The old view, still held by OGBB and DB, that remarriage should bring the same sanctions as adultery, would today be resisted in many CB and some BC congregations. Instead, many see the church as a community of believers that should support persons in troubled marriages and help those whose marriages have failed. Such couples are seen as needing encouragement, prayers, and aid in overcoming a difficult personal problem.

Care of the elderly at home is declining, though still somewhat prevalent among the OGBB and DB. Among all Brethren, the general trend is toward aging persons moving into retirement homes. The CB has 24 such homes, the DB one, the FGBC one, and the BC two. Brethren lacking access to their own denominational homes often use those of other denominations. Increased affluence of Brethren families has allowed greater independence and freedom in old age. EFB

S. M. Bianchi and L. M. Casper, *American Families,* 2000 (2001); R. J. Gelles, *Contemporary Families* (1995); Paul C. Glick, "American Families," Sociology and Social Research, 74 (April, 1990); D. B. Kraybill and C. F. Bowman, *On the Back Road to Heaven* (2001) 137–78; *Faith and Family: Challenges and Commitments: Report of the 1998 Brethren World Assembly* (1999); interviews with Fred W. Benedict (OGBB), W. C. Hess (OGBB), Robert S. Lehigh (DB), and Dale R. Stoffer (BC).

Brethren Folk Medicine. Like other aspects of Brethren folklife in 18th and 19th century America, the medical and healthcare practices of the Brethren reflected their German ethnic background. Brethren medical practices were a combination of *Pennsylvania German medical treatments, mainstream medical practices, remedies from printed sources, and popular medical systems. Brethren beliefs and medical treatments changed as the Brethren were assimilated into American society and as many Brethren moved from farm to urban lifestyles.

In the Pennsylvania German belief system, disease could have a natural origin (e.g., inheritance or contagion), or it could be caused by supernatural powers. Pennsylvania Germans treated diseases with natural herbal and botanical cures, sympathy, or *Brauche* (*Braucherei*). Sympathy involved treating the ailment through transference; for example, a widespread treatment for warts involved rubbing them with a rag, which was then buried. *Brauche,* also known as *powwowing,* consisted of a ritual with words or motions. Some *brauchers* were understood to have special power as a result of the circumstances of their birth, like being born with a *caul* (a membrane covering the head). Other *Brauch* practitioners gained the power by learning the ritual, which was usually handed down within families, to a person of the opposite sex. The Pennsylvania German influence was evident in Brethren in some parts of the eastern U.S. well into the 20th century.

Brethren used medical treatments from the Pennsylvania German oral tradition along with home remedies from printed sources, including *almanacs, newspapers, and broadsides. In the 18th and 19th centuries, the *Sauers published a series of almanacs, which included herbal and sympathy treatments. Popular (and

sometimes controversial) medical systems were used by the Brethren. *John Kline was trained in the Thomsonian System of Medical Practice, which was popular during most of the 19th century. Thomson's treatments called for large quantities of herbal tea, steaming, and sweating to remove impurities from the body.

In the 19th and 20th centuries, *Brauch* and sympathy treatments declined as professional doctors became more prevalent in medical treatment. Rural Brethren families had little access to professionally trained physicians, so they had to use home treatments, even for serious problems such as broken bones. Doctors became more accessible as the medical profession expanded and transportation improved, so that home remedies were limited to treating common, mild ailments like diarrhea and summer complaint, an intestinal ailment.

The *Inglenook Doctor Book,* a collection of Brethren home remedies from the early 20th century, contains treatments for common, mild conditions, with the admonition that a doctor should see serious illnesses. The remedies are mainly herbal, drug, or heat treatments, and are compatible with contemporary theories of the medical profession, which attribute the cause of illness to germs, not to supernatural forces. MAMi

See also: ACCULTURATION; MEDICINE; BRETHREN FOLKLORE.

The Inglenook Doctor Book (1903; reprint 1975); R. A. Neff, *Valley of the Shadow* (1987) 5–21; R. E. Sappington, *Courageous Prophet: Chapters from the Life of John Kline* (1964) 24–27; G. F. Snyder, *Health and Medicine in the Anabaptist Tradition* (1998), passim; E. L. Smith and others, *The Pennsylvania Germans of the Shenandoah Valley* (1964); T. R. Brendle and C. W. Unger, *Folk Medicine of the Pennsylvania Germans* (1935); Richard E. Wentz, *Pennsylvania Dutch: Folk Spirituality* (1993), passim; J. A. Hostetler, "Folk and Scientific Medicine in Amish Society," *Human Organization* 22 (1963–64) 269–75; G. C. Studer, "Powwowing: Folk Medicine or White Magic?" *Pennsylvania Mennonite Heritage* 3 (July, 1980) 17–23; B. L. Reimensnyder, *Powwowing in Union County: A Study of Pennsylvania German Folk Medicine in Context* (1989); P. P. McKegney, *Charm for Me, Mr. Eby . . .* (1989); David W. Kriebel, "Belief, Power, and Identity in Pennsylvania-Dutch Brauche, or Powwowing," PhD diss., U. of Pennsylvania (2000).

Brethren Logos

Use of logos by the Brethren bodies is as diverse as the people that call those churches home. Several Brethren groups use logos as an important part of their ministry while others find different ways to express their beliefs and values.

*The Brethren Church has made some use of logos since the latter 1950s. In ca. 1958 the denomination developed an adaptation of the *Mack seal which was accepted as a corporate seal, and continues to be used today. A logo was also adapted from the logo used by The Brethren Church in Florencio Varela, Buenos Aires Province, Argentina. This logo did not replace the corporate seal, and both of them are used for different purposes.

The three elements of the corporate seal represent early Brethren thinking about the word of God. First, the open Bible represents the outer word that is the objective foundation of Brethren Church faith. The motto adopted by The Brethren Church at the end of the 19th century was "The Bible, the whole Bible, and nothing but the Bible," and it continues to be the Church's motto. It reflects the early Brethren commitment to be people of the book. They wanted to pattern

their lives after the gospel, trusting God, and obeying his word. Second, the dove represents the Holy Spirit, the inner word that both inspired and illuminates the scriptures. The early Brethren believed that the Holy Spirit was always present with them to lead and to guide them as they read God's word and lived in obedience to it. They were very steadfast in their commitment to live as Christ's representatives in this fallen world, but they were also open to new light as the Holy Spirit led them. Third, the cross represents the Lord Jesus Christ who is the Living Word. The early Brethren believed that Christians must have a living relationship with the Lord Jesus Christ to whom the scriptures point and about whom the Holy Spirit teaches. The Bible and the dove point to the cross just as our Lord Jesus said the scriptures and the Holy Spirit point to him (John 5:39–40; 14:26; 15:26–27; 16:13–14). Brethren still see the Lord Jesus Christ as the center of their faith, not merely the object of their faith, but the living reality of trusting in relationship. He brings us to God and God to us through his active presence in our lives.

The Fellowship of Grace Brethren Churches is using a logo featuring a cross that touches the edge at three points, signifying a commitment to the core values of Biblical Truth, Biblical Relationships and Biblical Mission. The by-line "Knowing Jesus . . . Making Him Known" is an update of the phrase "To know Christ and to Make Him Known", used by Alva J. McClain in the

founding of Grace Theological Seminary.

The *Church of the Brethren *General Board and its staff have given much attention to logos, especially in the past two decades. An important change was the shift from General Brotherhood Board logos to abstract logos which can represent many things, e.g., the world in need, the presence of the Holy Spirit, the basin and the towel. This was controversial at the time, but is now widely accepted. The official Church of the Brethren logo, adopted in 1987, upholds the images of the life in Jesus Christ. The cross recalls our baptism into Christ's death and resurrection (Rom. 6:4) and testifies to God's plan to bring all in heaven and earth . . . into a unity in Christ (Eph. 1:10 NEB). The circle, partially defined, represents the world into which we are sent by Christ (Matt. 28:19). The circle also affirms that as members of Christ's body we are members one of another (Rom. 12:5), a people who confess one Lord, one faith, one baptism (Eph. 4:5). The wave connotes new life in Christ, born of water and the Spirit (John 3:5). The wave further evokes the waters of justice (Amos 5:24),

the cup of water offered in Christ's name (Mark 9:41), the basin and towel (John 13:5), and springs of living water (Rev. 7:17). Images central to life in Jesus Christ thus are lifted up as images for Brethren to live by. Many of the CB denominational staff have developed logos for their programs or publications. These logos help identify the program and its mission. Various agencies in the church have sought symbols that give those agencies a unique and recognizable identity while simultaneously evoking our faith. For more than 30 years the Church of the Brethren Annual Conference has featured a unique symbol each year that embodies the theme for that year. These logos have become an important part of the conference. Just as words, logos and printed symbols can have tremendous power when they genuinely touch us, moving our spirit closer to God.

The *Old German Baptist Brethren have felt little need for symbols, because they have little official organization. There is, however, increasing unofficial activity in mutual aid and material aid to the needy, here and abroad. These groups frequently use acronyms which may come nearest to the use of symbols for the OGBB.

Generally, members of the *Dunkard Brethren Church tend to shun the use of symbols and logos. There is nothing written about this issue in Dunkard Brethren publications. DLN
Church of the Brethren logo packet, Sept., 1987.

Brethren Folklore. The best-known forms of folklore are songs and stories, but folklore encompasses a wide variety of creative expression, including customs, folk medicine, games, and jokes. Folklife includes all aspects of life: language, architecture, crafts, foodways, dress, holidays, and all the other cultural expressions interwoven into the pattern of life.

Folklore defines group identity and binds a community together by expressing and validating community beliefs and values. Any group of people who share a common culture and interests is a folk group, including occupational, religious, socio-economic, and regional groups. The Brethren were initially an ethnic group of Germans who immigrated to North America, but they are also members of a religious group who are united by their common beliefs and customs.

The Brethren who migrated to North America from several German states had folkways similar to other groups of German immigrants. Groups with German heritage developed several distinctive *art forms, including *Fraktur (illuminated writing), decorated chests and barns, quilting, and carved gravestones. The Brethren desire for the *simple life caused their decorative arts to develop in a different direction from that of other German immigrant groups. In contrast to the *Pennsylvania Germans who elaborately decorated tools, furniture, textiles, dishes, and other objects, Brethren practiced simplicity in furnishings, dress, and other aspects of life.

As Brethren moved west, they lost German characteristics more quickly than those who remained in the East. The German influence survived the longest in Brethren communities in *Pennsylvania, *Maryland, and *Virginia, where elements of German culture, including dialect, food, holidays, sayings, and games, were still evident in the 20th century. The cohesiveness of German communities allowed their folkways to be preserved longer than that of other immigrant groups, which were assimilated into mainstream American life more quickly.

The development of folklife of the Brethren groups was influenced by multiple factors, including dispersion of German immigrants, assimilation of German groups into mainstream American culture, and the advent of the industrial age. As Brethren accepted formal education and began to move from farming to professional and industrial occupations, the shift from a rural lifestyle to a more urbanized one resulted in the loss of traditional farming lore, foods, and crafts. As the Brethren have grown more diverse culturally, elements from the folklore of other ethnic, occupational, and regional groups have been incorporated into Brethren life.

In the history of the Brethren bodies, members have been recognizable by distinctive practices, some of which are shared by other Anabaptist churches. Many visitors to Brethren churches commented on the scripturally-based holy kiss, or kiss of peace. Plain dress was an outwardly visible symbol of Brethren identity and separation from the world. The most common elements of dress which are distinctively Brethren are the prayer covering (prayer veil) for women and the *beard for men.

Food (*cooking) is an important part of Brethren life, where church social activities often include meals. The German influence is still evident in the Brethren tradition of the *love feast, which has a standard menu of beef, broth, and bread. Unleavened bread for the *communion service is made from traditional recipes, and some Brethren congregations continue the tradition of making apple butter using large copper kettles over an open fire.

Quilting is an important form of aesthetic expression in Brethren churches. Many congregations have quilting circles, which make quilts for fundraisers and to commemorate important events such as births, weddings, and the retirement of church leaders.

Folk narrative takes many forms, including legends and jokes. Brethren narrative is found mainly in stories about the church founders and leaders, and in stories which emphasize the virtuous qualities of the Brethren, including their good reputation, thrift, honesty, and generosity. In Brethren communities with a strong German heritage, folktales include stories of the trickster figure *Ilish Schpiegel,* also known as *Til Eulenspiegel.* Folk narrative also includes personal experience narratives, family stories, and place legends, which are found locally in many Brethren churches and families. Brethren jokes target the religious deficiencies of non-Brethren neighbors as well as those which are self-deprecating.

The holidays celebrated by the Brethren have been mainly Christian, but other special days were observed during the year. *Faschnachts* (fried cakes) were traditionally served on Shrove Tuesday, the day preceding Ash Wednesday. On Ash Wednesday, ashes were sprinkled on animals, on the garden, or around the house. Maundy Thursday, or Green Thursday, was the day to pick the season's first greens. Good Friday was a religious holy day, usually with special church services. It was a good day to plant potatoes or flax, but a day to avoid unnecessary hard labor. Eggs were central to the Brethren *Easter celebrations. Egg hunts and egg picking (egg fighting) were pop-

ular Easter activities. Children gathered and hid eggs before Easter, competing to see who would have the most on Easter morning. Some children set their caps for the Easter Rabbit, and many families celebrated Easter morning with a special egg feast. Hard labor was avoided on Ascension Day (the 40th day after Easter).

Shared customs and traditions have helped sustain the Brethren through the transition from the self-sufficient rural communities of German immigrants to the culturally and occupationally diverse churches of the late 20th century. Folklore plays an important role in the development and socialization of children, and it provides continuity from past to present, enabling a community to create the future from their shared traditions. MAMi

See also ACCULTURATION.

Esther P. Garber, *Button Shoes* (1975); J. E. Miller, *Stories from Brethren Life* (1942); Fredric Klees, *The Pennsylvania Dutch* (1951); Richard M. Dorson, *Folklore and Folklife: An Introduction* (1972); Julia W. Oxrieder, *Kiss the Doorknob: Folkways and Folklore of Floyd County, Virginia* (1996); Don Yoder, *Discovering American Folklife* (2001); Elmer L. Smith and others, *The Pennsylvania Germans of the Shenandoah Valley* (1964); Frederick S. Weiser and Howell J. Heaney, *The Pennsylvania German Fraktur of the Free Library of Philadelphia* (1976); Rupel, Esther F., *Brethren Dress: A Testimony to Faith* (1994).

Brethren Heritage Center, located at Brookside Plaza, just off I-70 in Brookville, OH; it began in March 2001 as a cooperative project of individuals from six Brethren bodies. Since the late 1970s Donald R. Bowman of Brookville has accumulated many books, historical records, and artifacts from the numerous congregations of the *Church of the Brethren in the Miami Valley, OH. After one of their members circulated letters in July and Dec. 1999 and Nov. 2000, *Old German Baptist Brethren became concerned about preserving their historical books and documents, and a joint project was born. In early Jan. 2001, a meeting brought together 31 persons from several Brethren bodies who concluded that a joint venture was needed. The Center became a tax-exempt organization in 2002. Members of a Planning Committee of 17, along with other interested persons, meet regularly to further the work. By the summer of 2002, a location was being prepared for the display, study, preservation, and interpretation of Brethren heritage. Provision for future growth has been pledged. FWB

Minutes, Brethren Heritage Center (2001–); *Old Order Notes* No. 24 (Fall/Winter, 2001) 114.

Brethren Hour, The (BC), a *radio program featuring Joseph D. *Hamel as the founder and speaker. The program began in 1967 on the Sarasota, FL, Christian station, WKZM. The format for the half-hour program primarily consisted of evangelistic preaching by J. D. Hamel. Special music was a common addition. At its peak, the program was aired weekly on 32 AM and FM stations in the United States. It was also broadcast by shortwave stations to Europe, Africa, South America, and Central America. The total coverage included over 100 countries and 14 time zones. Hamel continued as the speaker for the Brethren Hour until his death in 1997. That year David L. Stone, pastor of the Sarasota First Brethren Church, became the speaker. DLSt

BE (Sept. 25, 1971) 14, (Jan. 12, 1974) 25, (Mar. 1978) 20.

Brethren Identity. What are the benchmarks, the indicators that identify Brethren in a day when neither language accent nor dress may be a distinguishing characteristic? How are the core beliefs that motivate and differentiate a faith group transmitted both within its own community and to people outside?

Each of the Brethren bodies recognizes that the power of identity comes from within, from being and doing what its members believe in. Beyond that, identity-defining measures enacted by the respective bodies have taken varied forms.

Since the early 1980s, The Brethren Church has developed a range of materials to communicate its uniqueness to others, among them *A Centennial Statement* (1984), the pamphlet *How Brethren Understand God's Word* (1993); Jerry Flora's exposition of the first half of *A Centennial Statement* in the book *The Message of Faith* (1996); and a 13-part video, *Pilgrimage of Faith: The Witness of the Brethren Church,* (2000). A 105-word mission statement adopted by the General Conference Executive Council in 1989 lifted up the BC as "a priesthood of believers steadfast in commitment to its Lord and Savior Jesus Christ and obedient to the New Testament as the guide for faith and practice."

In the *Church of the Brethren the *General Board has initiated a series of resources on identity formation: a logo with a packet of suggested applications and guidelines offered in 1987 as a unifying emblem for church-wide use; a tagline and graphic, "Continuing the work of Jesus. Peacefully. Simply. Together," capsulizing pivotal elements of CB belief, developed in the mid 1990s; and a General Board mission statement and graphic, "Of God, for God, with God," developed in 2000–01 as a corollary to the tagline. Focus groups involving hundreds of members throughout the country had input into the tagline, which is regarded by some as a vision statement. Other approaches to identity formation include four theological conferences conducted between 1960 and 1981; membership study resources published in 1978–80 and in 2000; videos, books, tracts, and hymns that reflect group values; and scripturally-based themes that guide worship at Annual Conference, district conferences, youth events, General Board and other agency meetings, and historical observances.

For the *Conservative Grace Brethren Churches International, the primary vehicle for identity is a mission statement. The statement of 108 words points to "the Bible, the whole Bible, and nothing but the Bible" as "the infallible rule of faith and practice." To fulfill the great commission of Matthew 28, the statement calls on local churches "to perpetuate His Church by committing these biblical truths" to the faithful "who will teach others also until He comes for us."

While Dunkard Brethren traditionally have turned to church polity to provide guidance on matters of identity, two recent statements of leaders provide more detailed interpretation. One is the Mission and Vision Statement released by the Leadership Conference in 1999, addressing such topics as unity, tradition, outreach, relationships, and families. In 2001 the Leadership Conference issued the statement "Seeking a Biblical View of Church Government" that deals with the source, delegation, and application of authority within the church and provides counsel on matters of personal appearance and conduct.

The *Fellowship of Grace Brethren Churches has through a cooperating organization, *CE National, pro-

duced educational resources for children, youth, and adults on the topic *What does it mean to be Grace Brethren?* A pamphlet series speaks to the question and a video interview with *Thomas T. Julien and David L. Plaster details six identifying characteristics of a Grace Brethren church. The Fellowship's mission statement reads in full, "Grace Brethren churches work together to love and honor Jesus Christ by: Seeking God, Proclaiming the Word, Planting Churches, Developing Leaders, Reaching the Lost, and Nurturing Relationships."

The *Old German Baptist Brethren have no formal summation of beliefs, but the booklet *Doctrinal Treatise* produced by *The Vindicator* Committee at the request of *Annual Meeting sets forth the scriptural basis of faith and practice in the church. As a living testimony to faith, unofficial groups within the church have for 40 years organized mutual aid and disaster response locally and afar within and beyond the church.

The Brethren bodies are richly diverse, but a common thread is long-cherished rituals and practices that continue to inspire and shape life in community. The challenge of identity is to renew and communicate the church's vision in ways that remain faithful to God, credible, and energizing to succeeding generations. HER

See also IDENTITY STATEMENTS.

C. F. Bowman, *Brethren Society* (1995) 385–92, 414–17; D. F. Durnbaugh, *Fruit of the Vine* (1997) 591–93; C. F. Bowman, "Who are the Brethren of 1986?" *Messenger* (Jan./Dec., 1986); "Reflections on Brethren Image and Identity" (1995); J. Deeter, *Who Are These Brethren?* (1991); D. F. Fitzkee, *Moving Toward the Mainstream* (1995), 250–53, 309–11; E. F. Bittinger, *Heritage and Promise* (1970) 132–38; Communicorp, Reflections on Brethren Images and Identity (1995).

Identity Statements

The erosion of distinctive *Church of the Brethren *beliefs and practices during the 20th century has raised questions about the church's identity. A 1960 *Annual Conference study on declining membership linked blurred identity with diminishing membership. Emmert F. Bittinger (1970) cited lack of identity as one result of rapid change in the Church of the Brethren. A 1981 *Annual Conference study of diminishing membership listed "a sense of identity, clarity of purpose, and strong leadership" as necessary ingredients to reverse membership decline. Carl F. Bowman's year-long *Messenger* series, "Who are the Brethren of 1986?" placed the issue of identity before the entire church.

In response to a perceived need for a "sense of corporate identity" the 1975 Annual Conference approved a denominational goal-setting process, whereby Conference would approve goals and objectives each decade (and revise them at mid-decade). The Goals for the 1980s, approved by the 1979 Conference, centered on the prophet Micah's instruction to "do justice, love tenderly, and walk humbly with God." The Goals for the 1990s statement, approved by the 1988 Conference, highlighted five goal areas that represented a shift from *peace and justice ministries toward more emphasis on *evangelism and congregational concerns.

Citing the difficulty of saying who the Brethren are, a 1991 *query from the Atlantic Northeast District asked Annual Conference to "define the essential nature of the Church of the Brethren." Delegates returned the query without answer, some fearing such a definition would result in a *creed.

Who Are These Brethren? a 1991 *Brethren Press publication written by Joan G. Deeter, described the Brethren as a people of conviction, covenant, compassion, and conversation and named "love in the midst of diversity" a distinguishing characteristic of 20th century Brethren.

The phrases "Another way of living" and "Continuing the work of Jesus. Peacefully. Simply. Together." were the result of a study commissioned by the *General Board to sharpen Brethren image and identity. A packet of resources related to the study conducted by the Atlanta-based firm Communicorp was published by Brethren Press in 1995. DRF

Brethren Men of Mission (BC) is a successor organizational name for *National Laymen's Organization in order to more accurately reflect the purpose of the organization. A new constitution and bylaws were proposed in Aug. 1988 and adopted Aug. 10, 1989. Men of Mission helps coordinate some local and district men's activities, but the primary focus is on men's activities during *General Conference week. It has helped to coordinate work teams for home *mission church building projects and raised funds for students at *Ashland Theol. Sem. and *Riverside Christian Training School. Some local organizations also participate in Promise Keepers, *Habitat for Humanity, district camps, church planting, and international mission projects. JEHo
Annual (*BC*) 1989.

*Brethren Press (CB), the publishing and communications arm of the *Church of the Brethren. In the early 1980s the parts of Brethren Press that had been distributed among several *General Board departments were brought back together giving the Press a more visible identity. In 1986, because it was no longer feasible to maintain printing facilities and because the Press did not want to continue commercial printing, the plant was closed. In 1989 a new imprint, *faithQuest,* was established for the Christian book market.

Brethren Press was again separated into parts in 1990 and distributed throughout the General Board structure. Within two years, editing, production, and marketing were gathered back into one unit. A new *hymnal was published in 1992, the first since 1951, in a joint venture with the *Mennonite Church and the *General Conference Mennonite Church. Brethren Press published a new worship manual in 1993, *For All Who Minister*, the first since 1964. In 1994 it launched a new children's curriculum, *Jubilee: God's Good News,* published cooperatively with Mennonites and the Brethren in Christ.

In 1997 customer service was pulled back into Brethren Press, and, more significantly, all General Board communications were put under the Press, including *Messenger,* news services, *Yearbook,* interpretation (which has evolved into identity and relations), and the CB Web site. In a remarkable symmetry, at the end of the 20th century Brethren Press resumed the shape and role the *Brethren Publishing House had at the end of the 19th century.

Since 1980, directors of Brethren Press (exact title has varied) have been James S. Replogle (1979–84), Robert N. Durnbaugh (1984–91), and Wendy Chamberlain

McFadden (1992–). JHL

J. H. Lehman, *For This Day: 100 Years of Publishing in the Church of the Brethren, 1897–1997* (1997), 16–17; Annual Reports of Brethren Press in General Board reports to Annual Conference, *Minutes* (CB) (1980–98).

Just Like in the Movies

On the night of Sept. 25, 1991, the four-story brick building which housed the Brethren Publishing House in Elgin, IL, for 60 years was gutted by fire. The blaze was first spotted about 10:00 p.m. and could not be brought under control for nearly six hours. Five fire departments were called to battle the flames. Several hundred spectators lined the streets to see the spectacular blaze. The Sept. 26 Elgin *Courier-News* quoted one spectator as saying: "It was just like in the movies." The cause of the fire was not determined.

The first section of the State Street building was constructed during the summer of 1899, and in Sept. the Brethren Publishing House moved from Mt. Morris, IL, into the new building. Several additions were added during the first decade of the 20th century. Originally, the building housed only the printing operations and the offices of the General Missionary and Tract Committee (later known as the General Mission Board). But as new denominational programs developed, their offices were located in the State Street building. By 1930 there were offices for the Council of Boards, the General Mission Board, the Board of Religious Education, Women's Work, Children's Work, and Men's Work, as well as editorial offices and the printing plant.

In 1959 the State Street building was sold and the offices and the printing plant moved to a newly constructed building at 1451 Dundee Avenue in Elgin. New facilities were needed because the State Street building was inadequate for new printing technologies and did not have enough space for offices. After being sold by the Brethren, the old State Street building provided space for several businesses. At the time of the fire, it was being renovated into upscale apartments. In 1993 the remaining brick walls were demolished, and a small strip mall was constructed on the site. The center stone arch entrance was donated to the Church of the Brethren General Board. KMS, Jr.

See also BRETHREN PRESS.

The [Elgin, IL] *Courier-News* (Sept. 26, 1991), (Oct. 20, 1993); *Messenger* (Jan., 1992) 10–11; G. B. Royer, *Thirty-three Years* (1913): 217–19.

Brethren Profile Study (CB), conducted by Carl F. Bowman in 1985, was the first general study of *Church of the Brethren values, beliefs, and practices to be based upon a nationally representative sample of the entire denominational membership. With the support of the Society for the Scientific Study of Religion and the *Parish Ministries Commission (CB), the survey was administered to a sample of 1,411 members from 64 different congregations. Of these, 990 completed a lengthy mail survey. Their responses were analyzed and reported in monthly installments in *Messenger during 1986. The reports examined the extent of support in the church at large for historic Brethren teachings and *ordinances. CFB

C. F. Bowman, *Brethren Society,* (1995) 382–91, *A Profile of the Church of the Brethren* (1987), "Brethren Today" in D. F. Durnbaugh, ed., *Church of the Brethren Yesterday and Today* (1986) 201–25, and "Beyond Plainness: Cultural Transformation in the Church of the Brethren from 1850 to the Present," unpubl. dissertation, U. of Virginia (1989) 713–96; D. F. Durnbaugh, *Fruit of the Vine* (1997) 572–73.

Brethren Renewal Service (CB). In 1974 a group desired to have a site at the Roanoke (VA) *Annual Conference where voluntary *charismatic worship could be held. They secured an area in the basement concourse of the Civic Center, and during the group's first meeting, a committee was formed. In the 1980s its name was changed from *Holy Spirit Renewal Group to Brethren Renewal Service (BRS).

The committee wanted to foster relationship with the denomination on spiritual renewal issues. The committee was eventually granted permission by Annual Conference Program and Arrangements Committee to have a booth and to distribute literature on renewal as well as to conduct insight sessions at Annual Conference. In conjunction with *Brethren Revival Fellowship, the committee was instrumental in planning and carrying out a Day of Intercession before each Annual Conference. *Parish Ministries liaison staff met with the committee, and the committee held dialogue with representatives of Bethany Theol. Seminary. BRS officially disbanded in Nov. 1995, having concluded that their mission was fulfilled. CBS

Personal information.

Brethren Way of Christ. Inspired by their attendance at a Lutheran *via di cristo* retreat, two laymen, one from *The Brethren Church, the other from the *Church of the Brethren, used that model to develop the Brethren Way of Christ. It is a three-day school which takes a New Testament look at Christianity as a lifestyle. Brethren Way of Christ is a highly structured, 72-hour weekend designed to strengthen and renew the faith of Christian people and through them, their families, their congregations, and the environment in which they live and work. The leadership rests with the laity, with significant assistance from *ministers. It is intended to aid congregations in developing Christian leaders who will renew the church.

Brethren Way of Christ deals with the basics of Christianity, concentrating on the person and teachings of Jesus Christ. The focus of Brethren Way of Christ is not on the weekend but on the local congregation. It proposes no new type of spirituality—only a simple method through which one's grace-filled life may be lived and shared with others in a natural, loving way.

Candidates are expected to use this renewal experience as a basis for the rest of their lives. This period after the weekend is known as *The Fourth Day@.* Two things are expected during one's *Fourth Day@:* to expand one's spiritual life through study and church participation, and to become a more active Christian in daily living. The *Fourth Day@* offers two means of perseverance: group reunion—a small group of two to five friends who meet weekly to reflect on their spiritual growth and to encourage each other in discipleship and ultreya—a regular meeting of the larger Brethren Way of Christ community. WKG

BE (Oct., 1991) 10.

Brethren World Assemblies. The proposal for a meeting of Brethren from various denominations and countries emerged at a meeting on Brethren missions held at Ashland, OH, in March 1987. William R. Eberly suggested holding such a gathering on the 250th anniversary of the first known Brethren Yearly Meeting, that is in 1992. The board of *Brethren Encyclopedia, Inc. endorsed the plan and asked D. F. Durnbaugh to make arrangements. The intent, approved by the board, was to "bring together sisters and brothers from the Brethren bodies for information, inspiration, and formation, demonstrating that there are common ties despite some differences."

The First Brethren World Assembly was held at *Elizabethtown College, Elizabethtown, PA, not far from the early Brethren meeting held in 1742, from July 15 to 18, 1992. Its theme was: *Christ Is Lord: Affirming Our Faith Heritage.* The Assembly had two parts: one was a smaller, academic-style conference with formal presentations and panel discussions. The other consisted of larger meetings, open to the interested public. These featured speakers and missionaries from several foreign countries, culminating in a Saturday "Large Assembly" with preachers from the five cooperating Brethren bodies. The consensus was that another assembly should be held, perhaps in five or six years.

The Second Brethren World Assembly was held on July 15–18, 1998, at *Bridgewater College, Bridgewater, VA, with Dale R. Stoffer responsible for the program. It was again sponsored by the board of Brethren Encyclopedia, Inc. The theme of the assembly was *Faith and Family: Challenges and Commitments.* Worship experiences during the assembly featured Brethren from ethnic congregations in the U.S. and from congregations in other parts of the world. Other highlights of the gathering were a panel discussion on women's and men's roles in the five main Brethren groups, a tour of historical sites in the Shenandoah Valley, and workshops related to Brethren family life.

By 2000, the Encyclopedia Board had projected a third assembly to be held in Winona Lake, IN, in July 2003 and a fourth to be held in Schwarzenau, Germany, in August 2008 to commemorate the 300th anniversary of the founding of the Brethren movement. DRS/DFD

D. F. Durnbaugh, ed., *Report of the Proceedings of the Brethren World Assembly . . .* July 15–July 18, 1992 (1994); D. R. Stoffer, ed., *Report of the Proceedings of the 1998 Brethren World Assembly . . .* July 15–18, 1998 (1999) *BE* (Sept., 1992) 4–5, (Nov., 1998) 13–14; *Messenger* (Oct., 1991) 11, (Oct., 1992) 11–14, (Feb., 1993) 27, (Sept. 1998) 6–7; *Brethren Encyclopedia News* (Summer, 1998): 1–2; D. F. Durnbaugh, *Fruit of the Vine* (1997), 586.

Brethren Youth Crusader Program (BC). During the 1970s, the *Board of Christian Education (BCE) revived the *Summer Crusader* program which had been active from the 1940s through the mid-1960s. The BCE trained youth to travel on educational, music, and *camp teams which provided leadership at summer church camps and offered musical programs and *daily vacation Bible schools in congregations. Also, youth were given opportunities to serve as interns in congregations and summer camps where they received hands-on experience in Christian *ministry.

In 1992, *District Crusader* teams were added to the roster. Teams of three to five youths, who had completed their sophomore through senior years in high school, served in vacation Bible schools and camps within their own district instead of traveling throughout the denomination. Then in 1995, the name of the program was changed to *Brethren Church Summer Ministries* to encompass the whole aspect of the program. Also, due to the lack of youth interested in serving on educational and music teams which traveled throughout the denomination, the Summer Crusader teams were discontinued. However, the internship program continued and was renamed *Young Adult Ministries* to allow for older "young adults" to participate in the hands-on ministry program. Short-term *mission teams, aimed at educating youth on the importance of missions at home and overseas and giving them an opportunity to serve in these areas, were added to the program. In 1995, the first short-term mission teams traveled to Juarez, *Mexico. Since then, teams have traveled to Washington, DC; a *Native American reservation in *South Dakota; the *Appalachian area in *Kentucky; Jamaica; Mexico City; and *Tennessee. DSMR

See also NATIONAL BRETHREN YOUTH (BC); YOUTH.

Evangelist (BC) (May, 1992); *Evangelist* (BC) (May, 1995)

Brethren Youth in Christ (BC). In 1990 the *National Brethren Youth reorganized by electing a National Steering Committee, instead of officers, and changed their name from *Brethren Youth Crusaders* (BYC) to *Brethren Youth in Christ* (BYIC) to emphasize their desire to become more Christ-like. The seven-member youth Steering Committee, elected by their denominational peers, are trained in leadership and public speaking. They chair committees of the National Youth Council, which is composed of two youth from each of the nine districts. The council meets once a year to provide guidance on youth-related issues within the denomination. Steering Committee members also attend district functions such as rallies and retreats and help plan the National BYIC Convention. The BYIC Convention, held for one week annually, brings youth together from all over *The Brethren Church where they experience fellowship and spiritual growth. DSMR

BYC Convention Minutes (BC) (Aug., 1990); *Steering Committee Minutes* (BC) (Sept., 1990); *Morning Star* (BC) (Fall/Winter, 1990).

Brethren/Mennonite Council for Lesbian and Gay Concerns (BMC). BMC was founded in Oct. 1976 by Martin R. Rock to provide support for Brethren and Mennonite gay, lesbian, and bisexual people and their parents, spouses, relatives, and friends; to foster dialogue between gay and non-gay church people; and to provide accurate information about *homosexuality from the social sciences, biblical studies, and theology. It seeks to form community, nurture spirituality, and be prophetic within the context of the *Anabaptist heritage. BMC supports all persons seeking to know God's will for their lives—those open to same-sex covenanted relationships, seeking a life of celibacy, or exploring questions of sexual orientation. As of Jan. 1998 over 4,300 households were associated with BMC.

Supportive Congregations Network, formed in 1991, is a grassroots group of congregations which welcomes lesbian, gay, and bisexual members; builds closer links between congregations discussing homosexuality issues; and encourages other congregations to consider dialogue. As of Jan. 1998, 19 congregations have publicly declared their welcome to gay, lesbian, and bisexual members. SCN also encourages individuals to declare their welcoming support. The network holds international conferences

periodically. There is also a parental support group called Brethren/Mennonite Parents of Lesbian and Gay Children, which holds annual retreats.

A BMC international convention is held biennially in even years; on odd years national and regional retreats take place. There are local chapters across the U.S., Canada, and Europe. The main office is in Minneapolis, MN; its newsletter is *Dialogue*. MRR

Dialogue 1/1 (May, 1978ff.); *Messenger* (Sept. 28, 1978) 28–29, (Jan., 1987) 7, (Jan., 1988) 8, (Aug./Sept., 1993) 11–14, (Aug., 1994) 17, (Sept., 1994) 37–38, (July, 2002) 10–11; *BLT* 36 (Winter, 1991) 9–51 (special issue); C. F. Bowman, *Brethren Society* (1995), 405, 410; D. F. Durnbaugh, *Fruit of the Vine* (1997), 548–52.

*Brethren's Card, a concise summary of Brethren faith, differing notably in its two best-known versions. The card that circulated before the 1910s (beginning ca. 1887) was simpler in both tone and content than the one considered by *Annual Conference (CB) in 1923. The earlier version described the Brethren as "a people" who accepted the word of the New Testament "as little children." This depiction contrasted notably with the more formalized "body of Christians" and "denomination" language that predominated by the 1920s. The early card also omitted reference to evangelical doctrines such as the virgin birth, the power of the atonement, Christ's visible return, and the personality of the Holy Spirit. Instead, the distinctive Brethren *ordinances were highlighted; nonswearing, anti-secretism, and opposition to war were cited; and Brethren *theology was summarized by the simple assertion that Brethren "teach all the doctrines of Christ, peace, love, unity, both faith and works." The early card closed by asking the reader to accept Brethren teachings as "the word, which began to be spoken by the Lord," suggesting that they were neither final nor complete.

Compared to the earlier form, the 1923 version was 40 percent longer, more formal in tone, and reflected the fundamentalist-modernist debates of the 1910s. It added emphases such as proper appearance in *worship, *stewardship, and daily devotions at home; it also expanded the list of things to which Brethren were opposed to include violence in industrial controversy, going to *law, intemperance, *divorce and remarriage, games of chance, and immodest *dress. The 1923 card concluded by calling for the evangelization of the world, the conversion of people to Jesus Christ, and the realization of the life of Jesus in every believer.

During the first two decades of the 20th century, the *Gospel Messenger regularly printed a statement of faith that highlighted evangelical theology (the infallibility of the New Testament, the doctrine of the Trinity, final judgment, and the conditions of eternal life) and can thus be read as a precursor to the 1923 card. In addition to the two widely circulated versions of the card, others have appeared in print in *OGBB and *CB publications. An OGBB variant of the early CB card, entitled "The Doctrine of the Old German Baptist Church" dropped reference to *evangelism, while adding the practice of covering heads during worship and opposition to divorce, *musical instruments, and lawsuits. For many years after 1920, delegates to Annual Conference (CB) were required to sign a "Declaration of Principles and Purposes" that, while similar in some respects, was distinct from all versions of the Brethren's Card and from the *Gospel Messenger* faith statement.

Though the *Brethren's Card* originated as a tool for introducing non-Brethren to the faith, conservative Brethren often invoked it within church circles as a yardstick for measuring "drifting" from the faith. CFB

See also CHRISTOLOGY, GAMBLING, LABOR UNIONS, OATHS, TEMPERANCE.

Full Report (*CB*) (1923) 28–31; C. F. Bowman, *Brethren Society* (1995) 186–87; *BLT* 13 (Summer, 1968) 170–83; D. F. Durnbaugh, *Fruit of the Vine* (1997) 353, 412.

Brown, Dale Weaver (CB), b. 1926, seminary professor, church leader, theologian. A native of Wichita, KS, Dale Brown was the fourth child in a family of five sons born to Harlow and Cora Weaver Brown. Brown graduated from *McPherson College (AB, 1946) and *Bethany Bibl. Sem. (BD, 1949). In 1947, he married the former Lois Kauffmann, with whom he has three children: Deanna, Dennis, and Kevin. Brown served as pastor of the *Des Moines, IA, congregation (1949–57) before returning to teach at Bethany (1956–58) and to begin graduate studies at Northwestern University. After completing his doctorate (PhD, Northwestern U., 1962), Brown returned to Bethany Seminary, where he taught Christian theology from 1962 until his retirement in 1994. An active church leader, Brown served as moderator of the 1972 *Annual Conference, as a member of the *General Board, and on important denominational study committees. He participated in the first Brethren/*Russian Orthodox exchange in 1963.

As a teacher, Brown was known for his challenging but supportive probing of theological positions. Former students recall Brown's passion for peace and justice and his openness to persons on the left, right, and center. Popular courses that he taught at Bethany included "Brethren in Theological Perspective," "Luther, Calvin, and Wesley," and a seminar on Dietrich Bonhoeffer. For many years he directed the seminary's peace studies program.

Recognized as one of the leading scholars of *Pietism, Brown worked to overcome negative characterizations of Pietism that view it as narrowly subjective, moralistic, and quietistic. His book *Understanding Pietism* (1978, rev. ed. 1996), a reworking of his dissertation, is widely accepted as a solid introduction to Pietism.

As a theologian who refused to separate theological reflection from action, Brown counseled *conscientious objectors and marched on the Pentagon, as well as taught, preached, and wrote about peacemaking; see especially, *Brethren and Pacifism* (1970) and its major revision, *Biblical Pacifism: A Peace Church Perspective* (1986, 2nd ed. 2003). He helped found the *Brethren Action Movement and has been an active leader in *New Call to Peacemaking and *On Earth Peace Assembly.

In addition to numerous popular and scholarly articles and essays, Brown's other major publications are: *In Christ Jesus: The Significance of Jesus as The Christ* (1965), *Four Words for World* (1968), *So Send I You* (1969), *The Christian Revolutionary* (1971), *Simulations in Brethren History* (1976), *Flamed by the Spirit* (1978), *Berea College* (1982), *Led by Word and Spirit* (1983), *What About the Russians?* (1984), and *Anabaptism and Pietism* (1990). In 1996 the Atlantic Northeast District (CB) honored Dale Brown for 50 years of distinguished ministry. CAB

Messenger (Jan. 1, 1972) 10–12, 26; *N. Plains* (1977) 136; M. E. Marty, ed., *Where the Spirit Leads: American Denominations Today* (1980); *Who's Who in Religion*, 2nd ed. (1977) 81.

Browns Mill Old German Baptist Church, PA, located seven miles southeast of Chambersburg in Franklin Co., was initiated when the *Falling Spring OGBB Church was divided into two districts by vote of the congregation in response to the growth of the original district. There were 104 charter members with 147 remaining in Falling Spring. The Browns Mill congregation took possession of the old Browns Mill meetinghouse (one of two previously used by the Falling Spring congregation) and began to function as a separate district in Jan. 1989. A new, larger meetinghouse was built three miles to the east with provisions for *love feasts; it was occupied in June 1995. Browns Mill ministers have been Ray L. Strike, Ray M. Garber, Harold Slothour, Richard Hess, Mark D. Garber, Eldon Hess, and Matthew Hess. Membership in 2003 was 160. RDH

Vindicator 120 (1989) 2: 54; 126 (1995) 9: 281; D. R. Hess, Sr., comp., *Historical Materials on the Falling Spring District of the Old German Baptist Brethren* (n.d.); *Directory of Officials: The Old German Baptist Brethren Church* (2003).

Brubaker, Harold A. (OGBB), 1923–98, minister. Born near Eaton, OH, Harold Brubaker was the son of Omer and Runella Deaton Brubaker. He married Margaret Jean Bowser in 1944; a daughter was born to them in 1946 and a second daughter in 1948. Harold Brubaker lived and farmed in Preble County, OH, all his life; he was a member of the *Upper Twin congregation, being called as a deacon in 1948, as a minister in 1951, and was ordained as elder in 1964. He served in various capacities for the brotherhood: The *Vindicator* committee for 24 years, *Standing Committee for 23 years, and as nonresident elder at *Painter Creek, OH, congregation for 12 years. GCD

Vindicator (1951) 281, (1978) 347, (1998) 254; *Old Order Notes* No. 4 (Spring, 1981) 20.

Brunswick, ME, Church of the Brethren. The Brunswick church is the second congregation in the state of *Maine established through the efforts of *Brethren Revival Fellowship. It was organized in 1986 after a building on coastal U.S. Highway 1 was purchased. Several families from *Pennsylvania and the James Gould family from *North Carolina moved to southeastern Maine. Donald E. Miller (1924–89) served as pastor. James L. Gould and Mark K. Bucher have served in the *free ministry at Brunswick following Donald E. Miller's death.

Worship services are held each Sunday. A five-day revival series, the three-part *love feast, and teaching seminars are held on a regular basis. A few people from the area have been baptized. By 1997, a number of families which fit the conservative, independent, home-schooling model have been attracted to the congregation HSMa

Beams From Brunswick (1987–95), newsletters; *Minutes,* BRF Committee (May 12, 1986); personal information; *BLT* 36 (Summer, 1991) 173; *BRF Witness* 28.3 (1988) 11, 30.1 (1995) 14, 31.1 (1996) 14, 32.4 (1997) 14; J. H. Lehman, *Thank God for New Churches!* (1984), 36–45.

Byler, Robert Oliver (BC), 1921–97, was born on June 24 in a pastoral and musical family. Robert Byler married Jane King in 1945; they had five children. He studied at Goshen College and prepared for missionary service at *Moody Bible Institute. The Bylers sailed with their young daughter, Susan, to *Argentina in Oct. 1948 and served there until 1967. Byler first ministered in Cordoba, where he worked with the local church and aided in establishing a young people's camp. In 1950 the Byler family moved to Buenos Aires where he taught at the Buenos Aires Bible Institute. They opened their home to students from the Institute and established a congregation in their living room. As a musician, Robert Byler was involved in many citywide projects. Together with Harold Stacy, an Anglo-Argentine businessman, they began a radio program called *Adelante Juventud* (Onward Youth). Inspired by Byler, construction of a building was begun in 1956 to house a church, studio, offices, and apartments. When finished, the recording studio was the most modern of its kind in Argentina. A new radio program, *Platicas Cristianas* (Christian Chats), was recorded and broadcast in prime time over the most popular network in Argentina. His involvement in the Bible Institute, the radio programs, and his outgoing personality made Byler a well-known figure in evangelical circles in Argentina. He organized and directed the mass choir for the Billy Graham Evangelistic Crusade in Buenos Aires in 1962. The Byler family resigned from Argentina in 1967 and settled in New Jersey and later in Brooklyn, NY, where he ministered in a Baptist congregation while supporting his family by secular work. Byler retired to Missionary Village, Bradenton, FL, where he continued to minister as chaplain in a retirement home. He died August 15. HRA

H. R. Aspinal, "The Brethren Church in Argentina," MA thesis, Fuller Theol. Sem. (1973); A. T. Ronk, *History of Brethren Missionary Movements* (1971) 92, 94–96, 98, 100; *BE* (April 2, 1949) 8, Dec. 13, 1952) 10, (June 19, 1954) 7, (Aug. 7, 1954) 7, (Sept. 11, 1954) 6, (July 7, 1956) 6, (Jan. 11, 1964) 18, (July 10, 1965) 14, (Aug. 6, 1987) 27–28, and (Sept. 1997) 11.

C

William H. Cable. BHLA file.

Cable, William H. (CB), 1919–95, farmer, businessman, philanthropist. Cable was born in Redcliff, Alberta, Canada, and lived in Yakima, WA, and Southern California until he married to Miriam Weybright in 1942. Following *Civilian Public Service years in Washington State and Illinois, Cable moved his young family to the Weybright family farm in Syracuse, IN. Later the Cables added acreage to the farm to establish a flourishing seed corn business. This enterprise plus banking interests created significant wealth from which the Cables contributed financial support to numerous *Church of the Brethren agencies, Rotary International (which awarded him their

highest service award), and Trees for Life. Cable distinguished himself as a long-time chair of the *Bethany Hospital Board and as a board member of Brethren Health Foundation, *Association of Brethren Caregivers, CB *General Board, CB *Pension Board, *Bethany Theol. Sem., *Timbercrest (CB) Home, and *Manchester College. The Cables had five sons: Charles, Alan, Bruce, Lowell, and Edwin; all active in the *Church of the Brethren. Bill Cable is best remembered for hard work, simple living, and abundant giving. WEN

Messenger (Sept., 1989) 8, (Aug./Sept., 1990) 3, (July, 1993) 3; (Feb., 1996) 26–27; *Memorial Bulletin* (1995); *The Rotarian* (Feb., 1987) 42–43; *[Warsaw, IN] Times-Union* (Aug. 24, 1991).

Camp Canaqua (CB), near Water Valley, *Alberta, Canada. The District of Western Canada began its camping movement in 1934 when it established Camp Blackfoot with permission on part of a Blackfoot reservation near Arrowwood, Alberta. The 20-acre site for Camp Canaqua was purchased in 1950–51 at a cost of $400. Facilities included an assembly hall, kitchen, and sleeping quarters for leaders. Campers slept in tents. Each summer the camp offered one junior camp and one teen camp, plus a one-day family camp. These programs were ongoing in 1968 when the congregations of the District of Western Canada joined the United Church of Canada. KEY

Western Canada District Conference *Minutes* (1921–68); BHLA Camp Records (1935–68); A. Hollinger, "CB in Western Canada" (1943).

Carol Stream, IL, Christ Church of the Brethren. In 1980 the Illinois/Wisconsin District selected the community of Carol Stream in DuPage Co., at that time the fastest growing county in the state, as the site for new church development. Donald E. Leiter was called as pastor in 1981 and spent six months visiting homes in the area. The first worship service was held on Feb. 28, 1982, in the Evergreen School; and the first *love feast was held during Holy Week, 1983.

Leiter concluded his ministry in Aug. 1984. Later pastors serving the congregation were Olden D. Mitchell (interim 1984), Dean M. Miller (1985–90), Richard C. Witmer (interim 1990), Galen H. Brumbaugh (1990–93), Willard E. Dulabaum (interim 1993–94), William J. Christiansen (interim 1994), and Timothy Sollenberger Morphew (1995–96).

Construction of a building began in 1987 on property

at the corner of County Farm Road and Lies Road. The first worship service was held in the new building on May 15, 1988. Christ Church was recognized by the district as a fellowship in 1982 and as a full congregation in 1991. Membership peaked in 1991 with 81 members and declined thereafter due to differences over theology and Brethren practices. The congregation was disorganized in 1997. KMS,, Jr.

BHLA cong. file; *Yearbook* (*CB*) (1983–97); *Messenger* (Jan., 1983) 16.

Cascade Valley, WA, Old German Baptist Brethren Church, located six miles southeast of Ellensburg, Kittitas County. Members began moving into the Kittitas Valley area in 1988. The district was organized on March 14, 1992, from the *Columbia River district. Benjamin E. Root was the first oversight elder. The 29 charter members included ministers Dennis L. Wray and John D. Rumble. Other ministers who have served in the district were Galen R. Flory, Vince Tye, Joseph A. Root, and Merle D. Flory. The first worship services were regularly held in Kittitas Hall, and the first communion was held in May 1993 in a local school building. Construction of the meetinghouse began in 1994 and, with generous support from the OGBB brotherhood, was completed in 1996. The first services in the auditorium were held on July 28, 1996. Membership in Dec. 2003 was 135. DLW

Vindicator (April, 1992) 118, (Feb., 1996) 56.

Cashman, Edwin E. (FGBC), 1930–97, pastor. Born in South Gate, CA, into the family of Arthur Cashman, a Brethren pastor, Edwin Cashman graduated from Bob Jones U. (1952) and married Bettie Taber. He enrolled at *Grace Theol. Sem. from which he graduated in 1955. The Cashmans moved to Ashland, OH, where Cashman served as associate pastor under his father-in-law, Miles Taber.

In 1961 the Cashmans moved to California where he became pastor of the *Compton, CA, First Brethren Church and continued as pastor when that church merged with the *Bellflower, CA, Brethren Church in 1966, a position he held for almost 30 years. Three years after the death of his wife (1989), Cashman married Connie Becker. Upon retirement from duties as senior pastor, he became minister of pastoral care at Bellflower.

Cashman was FGBC moderator (1983–84) and was recognized as pastor of the year at the 1996 National Conference. He served on the board of Grace Brethren Foreign Missions (later, *Grace Brethren International Missions) and the *Board of Christian Education. RTC

Personal information; *Annual* (*FGBC*) (1956ff.).

CE National, Inc. (FGBC), formerly GBC Christian Education, strives to impact the church by serving as a catalyst for biblically accurate and culturally relevant ministries to children, youth, and adults. They do this by providing training opportunities, ministry expenses, and resources.

A strong emphasis on *youth is demonstrated through many youth-oriented ministries. Brethren National Youth Conferences, held at different locations for one week each year, challenge young people to grow and share their faith. About 2,500 youth and their leaders participate. Operation Barnabas provides intense ministry training to about 100 high-school-age young people for six weeks each summer. Numerous short-term weekends offer youth

and their leaders ministry opportunities in a number of cross-cultural environments. Students, under the supervision of CE National, also participate in Bible Quizzing and NAC (Nurturing Abilities for Christ) programs to increase Bible knowledge and ministry experiences.

The National Institute for the Development of Ministries to Youth, initiated in 1997 in cooperation with *Grace College, offers bachelor's and master's degree programs for those preparing to work with youth. This program also operates at Washington Bible College, Lanham, MD. In 1998 the Urban Hope Training Center was opened in Philadelphia, PA, to minister to inner-city families and to provide cross-cultural training opportunities for students associated with The National Institute.

Children are also an important focus of CE National. The Children's Cabinet provides direction for the children's ministries, which include SMM (Serving My Master), a girls' club curriculum, and the One-on-One curriculum for boys' discipleship. The Promising Always to Love and Serve (PALS) program offers training for kindergartners.

Ministries to adults include various training experiences for young, middle, and senior adults. Resources provided by CE National include study materials especially related to Grace Brethren distinctives and a lending library for churches. Edward A. Lewis has served as executive director of CE National since 1985. EAL

Personal information.

Cedar Falls, IA, Cedar Heights Brethren Church. The church was begun in 1967 by the Central District Mission Board with a nucleus of families from the *Waterloo First and *Mulvane, KS, congregations. It was organized June 29, 1968, with Gene R. Hollinger as pastor. A parsonage/worship center was built in 1967 and a church building in 1970. Though the church was built in a promising location, new housing developments were stymied when the city failed to extend utilities to the area. The congregation reached a peak average worship attendance of 41 in 1976 but disband in 1984. DRS

Congregational records; *Annual* (*BC*) (1970ff.).

Centennial Statement, A (BC). At the 1981 General Conference of *The Brethren Church, moderator Brian H. Moore recommended "that a formal and thorough statement of the beliefs and practices of The Brethren Church be developed for adoption and dissemination at the 1983 General Conference." The conference adopted this recommendation and Jerry R. Flora and Dale R. Stoffer were appointed co-chairpersons of a task force charged with developing such a statement.

The task force was composed of volunteers who worked on the statement for two years. The finished product was named *A Centennial Statement*, in honor of the denomination's founding in 1883. It was accepted at the 1983 General Conference, not as a *creedal statement but as "a testimony of the faith and life of The Brethren Church at this milestone in our history." The statement is composed of two parts, *The Message of Faith* and *The Life of Faith*, reflecting the historic Brethren conviction that faith must be evidenced in life.

The *Brethren Publishing Company published the statement in pamphlet form in 1984. Flora prepared an exposition of the first part of the Centennial Statement; it was published in 1996 with the title *The Message of Faith*. DRS

A Centennial Statement (1984); J. R. Flora, *The Message of Faith: An Exposition on the First Half of A Centennial Statement* (1996); *BE* (June, 1988) 12–15.

Central America. The *Central American region drew increased attention from Brethren bodies in 1980–2000. Seeking to support efforts toward peacemaking, reconciliation, and development during and after the civil wars that erupted there, the *General Board (CB) formed partnerships with churches and ecumenical groups throughout the region. These ecumenical partnerships included Misión Cristiana (Christian Mission) in Nicaragua, Iglesia Bautista de Emmanuel (Emmanuel Baptist Church) in El Salvador, and the Comisión Cristiana de Desarrollo (Christian Development Commission) in Honduras. A four-way partnership was begun between the General Board (CB), the *Disciples of Christ, Mision Cristiana (Christian Mission) in Nicaragua, and Iglesia Cristiana Pentecosal de Cuba (Christian Pentecostal Church of Cuba). This style of walking with the people, called "accompaniment," also included a number of service worker placements in development projects and advocacy roles, as well as short-term *disaster response. Ecumenical partnerships also included active participation in *Church World Service ministries in the region.

Close proximity of the region and increased international travel options as well as the requests from these partners prompted increased short-term mission opportunities in the region. Delegations and work groups (CB) constructed church buildings, clinics, and other structures, or visited and worshiped with these partners, sometimes in isolated areas. A sister church/community program (CB) partnered U.S. congregations with a church or community in *Guatemala, El Salvador, or Nicaragua. This linkage between churches and communities became a source of mutual encouragement and learning.

*Brethren Church mission work to *Mexico was begun in 1982 under the direction of Juan Carlos Miranda, who was, at the time, "on loan" from The Brethren Church to the Fuller Evangelistic Institute in Pasadena, CA. (Miranda is a product of the *Argentine BC work.) When an earlier work in Tijuana closed in 1984, the Brethren focused their work exclusively on Mexico City. There are currently six congregations in the Mexico City area with an average total worship attendance of about 300. The churches meet once a year at a General Conference which is devoted to fellowship and worship. A governing Board composed of elders, pastors, and lay representatives provides leadership and direction for the churches. Brethren missionaries to Mexico have included Juan Carlos and Maria Miranda, Thomas James Saunders, Timothy Ray and Jan Elaine (Zimmerly) Eagle, Todd William and Tracy Ann Clawson Ruggles, and Jennifer Ellen Thomas, who went to Mexico initially with the mission agency, Spearhead, but who joined the Brethren mission in Mexico City in 1999.

Work in Mexico by *Grace Brethren International Missions began in 1951 along the Mexico-U.S. border. In 1963 work began in Mexico City with university students and established a church there. Under the auspices of Equipo International, a fellowship of Mexican leaders inspired by the Dublin, OH, GBC, several branch churches have been organized in Mexico and Guatamala. Teams of Mexicans were sent to Cuba, where a GBC has been established. Since 1980, GBIM workers in Mexico included Jack and Rosa Churchill (1983–), Tom and Suzy

Sharp (1982–89), James and Elizabeth Schaefer (1984 –87), Brenda Welling (1985–), Martin and Kristy Guerena (1989–96), Bess Farrell (1989–), John and Tracey Pieters (1993–96), and Ron and Sue Schemmer (1995–97). MBK

General Board (CB) files; *Messenger* (Dec., 1980) 12–15, (June, 1981) 27–31, (March, 1983) 18–20, (March, 1984) 16–17, (March, 1984) 10–13, (Dec., 1984) 10–13, (Jan., 1988) 14–16, (Aug., 1989) 10, (Oct., 1990) 26–28, (March, 1993) 16–18, (Oct., 1993) 16–18, (May, 1986) 22–23, (Oct., 1986) 4, (Aug., 1998) 22–25, (March, 1999) 23–26, (Dec., 1999) 14–18; T. R. Eagle, *A History of Brethren Foreign Missions: 1972–1990;* A. T. Ronk, Independent Study (unpubl.), Ashland Theo. Sem. (1989); *BE* 122 (July-Aug., 2000) 1–5; T. T. Julien, *Sieze the Moment: Stories of an Awesome God Empowering Ordinary People,* (2000) 39–40.

*Chaplaincy is a specialized ministry, either voluntary or reimbursed, which is based in a social institution rather than a congregation. The chaplain, a called-out minister, serves primarily the population of the sponsoring agency rather than a congregation. Specialized education beyond seminary is often required for employment.

Brethren have long been active in special ministries to persons who are hospitalized or imprisoned, in obedience to Jesus' words: "I was sick and you cared for me; in prison and you visited me. . . ." (Matt. 25:36). Some Brethren bodies support the work of prison chaplaincy, either on a voluntary or employed basis. Some of the Brethren (*BC, *CB) encourage the ministry of *hospital chaplains, either as volunteers or as employed staff. Two Brethren branches (BC, *FGBC) support *military chaplains. In 2000, for example, FGBC had seven on active duty, one in the reserves, two with the Department of Veterans Affairs, and two with the Civil Air Patrol.

Since 1980, changes within church and society have resulted in new developments in chaplaincy which have affected Brethren. For example, the emergence of hospice care for the terminally ill, increased mobility of the population, and extensive new leisure-time activities have all impacted opportunities for ministry outside of traditional church settings. Longer life-expectancy, often involving a period of infirmity, has resulted in a Brethren ministry through long-term care facilities (*DB, CB, BC, FGBC) and new challenges for chaplains.

Within the church, changes in attendance patterns have resulted from the competing demands of employment, family, social obligations, and need for self-care. Also, the ordination of women (CB) in churches not entirely comfortable with female pastoral leadership has had a profound impact upon chaplaincy.

Current research in health care and social sciences has demonstrated the value of spiritual care in partnership with medical treatment, substance abuse rehabilitation, and correctional programs. Modern science is re-discovering what the Brethren have always known; body, mind, and spirit have been created by God as a wonderful unity. The abundant life Christ offers extends to every aspect of our being. These and other emerging trends in church and society have created new opportunities for chaplaincy among the Brethren. Six are notable:

1. *Retirement communities and/or long-term care facilities.* In 2000, there were 24 retirement communities/nursing facilities related to the Church of the Brethren. Thirteen of these homes employed chaplains and five had pastoral care staff of two or more. In long-term care facilities sponsored by other Brethren bodies (DB, BC, FGBC), pastoral care is provided by pastors of neighboring congregations who volunteer.

2. *Educational institutions.* The institutions of higher education related to the Brethren (CB, BC, FGBC) all have chaplains or ministers on staff.

3. *Hospice organizations.* This specialized, family-centered approach to care of the terminally ill requires that a chaplain be a member of the care team. Some Brethren currently serve in this way in various locations as volunteers or employed staff.

4. *Industrial chaplaincy.* Some industries have created staff positions within their organizations for chaplains. Offering pastoral care in the workplace is a developing approach to the spiritual nurture of a work force which spends more time at work than at church. A few Brethren serve in such settings.

5. *State and national parks.* Chaplain ministry to vacationers in state and national parks is another new opportunity. The majority of park chaplains, including a small number of Brethren, serve as volunteers.

6. *Community service and safety agencies.* Police departments, fire departments, and emergency medical services are increasingly calling chaplains. This ministry, also, is usually provided on a volunteer basis.

The Church of the Brethren Yearbook annually lists members who are employed as chaplains. The following comparison of statistics for 1990 and 2000 illustrates the changes described above:

	1990		2000	
	#	%	#	%
Total Chaplains	42		51	
Men	35	83	32	63
Women	7	17	19	37
Service Locations:				
Correctional systems	2	5	3	6
Counseling	1	2	2	4
Higher education	5	12	8	16
Hospices	0	0	3	6
Hospitals	17	40	11	21
Industry	2	5	0	0
Long term care	10	24	22	43
Mental health	1	2	1	2
Other	3	7	1	2

As ordained leaders, chaplains are accountable to the larger church for their ministries. Reports are made annually to governing conferences and in denominational directories (CB, BC). In 1999, the CB *Annual Conference recognized chaplaincy as one of nine approved areas of service for ordained leadership. The Brethren Chaplains Network, organized in 1993, relates to the larger church through the *Association of Brethren Caregivers (ABC). In the year 2000, the network had compiled a roster of more than 90 ordained chaplains within the denomination. ABC and Brethren Homes (CB) annually offer scholarships in support of summer chaplaincy training internships.

In 2000, the membership of the Association of Professional Chaplains, a national professional organization, included 12 Brethren (11 CB, 1 FGBC), three of them women. Their ministry settings were long-term care (5), hospitals (2), hospice (1), and other (2). Two were retired.

For Brethren, Jesus' command to "Go therefore and make disciples of all nations. . . ." (Matt. 28:19) has served as the charter for seeking to bring in the Kingdom of God on earth. Chaplaincy is one of many ways Brethren can respond obediently. MSR

Yearbook (CB) (1990–2000); *Association of Professional Chaplains, Annual Membership Directory* (2000); "Report of the Association of Brethren Caregivers," *214th Annual Conference (CB)* (2000) 90; interviews with Fred W. Benedict, Ronald T. Clutter, Roger A. Golden, Robert S. Lehigh, John Schumacher, Dale R. Stoffer, and members of Brethren Chaplains Network (July/Aug., 2000).

Chateau of Saint Albain, The (FGBC). Located 50 miles north of Lyons, *France, the Chateau of Saint Albain is a 14th century property serving the *Fellowship of Grace Brethren missionary work in Europe. Acquired in 1964 as an effort to bridge the gulf between the church and France's secular society, it has been a tool for creating an identity for evangelical Christians through encounters and discussions.

Initial ministries of the chateau focused on reaching youth through weekend activities, camps, and evangelistic efforts in the area. As the ministry developed, they were extended to entire families. Converts from these ministries were gathered together to create local congregations in neighboring cities. A decentralized Bible Institute was developed at the chateau to provide Bible training.

In the 1970s the chateau became a center for encounters on a national scale involving workers from mission groups serving in France. Yearly work-study conferences were held endeavoring to develop approaches to more effectively reach the French people with the message of Christ. These were extended into encounters involving both mission agencies and French denominations.

The chateau played a leading role in the development of Grace Brethren *missions throughout Europe. In the early 1980s it hosted a yearly EuroMissions Institute, initiating American youth to missions in Europe. It also became the center of a European extension of *Grace Theol. Seminary. During those years the Grace Brethren missionary team saw considerable growth. In addition to France, Grace Brethren missionaries now serve in *Germany, the *United Kingdom, *Ireland, the Czech Republic, *Spain, and Portugal. In 2000, the chateau served mainly as a conference center both for Grace Brethren churches and other evangelical organizations serving in France. TTJ

T. T. Julien, *Seize the Moment* (2000) 53–61.

Children. The intention of most Brethren groups (*BC, *CB, *DB, *FGBC) is to prepare children to participate in and influence the surrounding culture from a basic commitment to Christ and to Christian values such as community, simplicity, service, generosity, tolerance, and non-violence. Such Brethren accept children's activities in the church, including the *Sunday school, as a way of supplementing and strengthening the religious education that comes through the family.

For most congregations, children are present in some part of the *worship service, but children may also receive some care in the nursery, the preschool, the Sunday school, or children's church. Children's stories are widely used in worship. Newborn infants may be dedicated in a congregational service. "Church parents" may help the family to instruct the children. Worship often includes special attention to children such as gifts of Bibles, chil-

Chateau of Saint Albain, France. FGBC collection.

dren's choir, recognition for achievements, service as ushers, and children leading portions of the service. An adult mentor may be teamed with a child for intergenerational learning and preparation for baptism.

Some Brethren, particularly in the BC, do not have unbaptized children present at love feast/communion; childcare is provided for younger children. Other Brethren have the children sit with their parents during communion. Men and women may be divided because of the *feetwashing service. Parents decide how children will participate. Some parents allow fuller participation; some do not. Children may be given some substitute for the bread and the cup, e.g. juice and a cookie. When communion is a part of Sunday morning worship, families sit together. Many children become members of the church by 12 years of age, which is generally considered the beginning of the age of accountability.

The Sunday school, *daily vacation Bible schools, *camping, and service experiences are widely used by the church to guide children. In Sunday school, children are taught Bible stories and denominational beliefs. The denomination develops and/or recommends curriculum that is used by the majority of the congregations. Some BC congregations provide Sunday evening children's program in addition to their *youth program. For the CB and other Brethren bodies, camping provides an environment wherein children from families with similar religious and social values can be with leaders who embody those values.

Although the church offers some guidance to them, parents have great latitude as to how they train their chil-

dren. Families tend to be small. Couples who want children sometimes adopt them from other cultures out of concern for homelessness. Most children watch television and use other media such as, for example, computers. The problem of limits arises relative to what can be watched and whether other children are doing it. Monetary allowances and discipline in using money is important. Parents often seek to cultivate in children the habit of giving to the church.

Brethren groups generally support public schools. They encourage children to achieve in school in anticipation of high school and college. Children often take part in extra-curricular school activities, as well as in community activities. Learning social skills and performing well academically are both important values. Nevertheless, most DB parents and some from other Brethren groups withdraw their children from the public schools and choose Christian schools or *home education. Perhaps 30–40 percent of Brethren children remain within the church as adults.

By way of contrast, perhaps 80–90 percent of OGBB children remain within the church as adults. The OGBB differ from other Brethren groups in that their intention is to preserve a faithful way of life that is separated from the world, i.e. insulated at significant points from unwanted influence of the surrounding culture. They do not accept the Sunday school because it takes the religious instruction of children away from parents. Children are taught by instruction, by the example of parents, and by participation of the family in the life of the church.

In the OGBB, mothers hold their babies during the

worship service. Boys of one, two, or three years begin to sit with their fathers, while girls usually stay with their mothers. This is part of a seating pattern in which men and boys sit at one side of the *meetinghouse and women and girls at the other. Children are expected to sit quietly and pay attention throughout the two-hour service. Preachers often address the children. When the people kneel for prayer, the children who are old enough also kneel. During love feast young children sit with their parents. Children can help prepare for the service, observe the ceremony, receive leftover communion bread, and be part of the accompanying meals and other events over the weekend. They remain observers until their later teen years or early twenties, the age of accountability, when they become members. Occasionally membership comes earlier.

OGBB children are expected to be modest. Girls are to wear dresses. Television sets are banned from homes (also true for DB). Children are taught to respond nonviolently. Reading and other basic skills, particularly those that are essential to making a living, are much encouraged. Children are expected to have chores and to help with the family enterprise. Much time is spent in church and family gatherings such as love feasts, *weddings, *funerals, and reunions, which events are the heart of the social life. Such events allow children to become acquainted with children in other families, and thereby to form a bond to the wider church community.

OGBB find some public elementary schools particularly objectionable because of issues of modesty, sex education, drugs, and violence. The overwhelmingly secular interpretation of life in subjects such as biology and science may be offensive. Such issues have led some to practice home schooling, establish elementary schools of their own, or to enroll their children in Christian schools. DEM
See also EDUCATION; MASS MEDIA, MEMBERSHIP TRENDS.

D. M. Rhodes, *Little Stories for Little Children* (1995), *More Little Stories for Little Children* (1996), and *Even More Little Stories for Little Children* (2000); H. D. Moore and P. S. Moore, *The Mysterious Marvelous Snowflake* (1981); M. L. Anderson, *The Brown Bag* (1978); D. C. Benson and S. J. Stewart, *The Ministry of the Child* (1979); D. Ng and V. Thomas, *Children in the Worshiping Community* (1973); W. A. Smith, *Children Belong in Worship* (1984); D. E. Miller, *The Gospel and Mother Goose* (1987) and *Story and Context* (1987).

*Christian Day School Movement. The Christian school movement has shown only modest growth in Brethren circles from the mid-1980s through the end of the century. The primary reason for the lack of greater numerical growth is probably the popularity of home schooling as another viable alternative to public education. In addition, the availability of other private and church-sponsored Christian schools has met the needs of many families. Also, some schools originally sponsored by a single congregation merged with other schools or developed some type of cooperative sponsorship with other churches.

Although there are a few church-based schools in other Brethren groups, those that are most active in the Christian school movement are *Dunkard Brethren, *Grace Brethren, and *Old German Baptist Brethren.

In 1981 the DB organized a School Advisory Board of five elders to assist congregations in establishing Christian schools. As of 1998, five congregations sponsored such schools, in addition to the Torreon Navajo Mission school, which was established in 1977.

Although there has been a slight decline in the number of schools in the Grace Brethren Fellowship, their average size has grown. In 1999 there were 24 schools in eight states with a total enrollment of more than 7,700 students.

Among the OGBB, a June 1999 report indicated the operation of 16 schools in seven states with a total enrollment of 633.

It should be noted that, in many of these schools, the majority of students are from outside the school's sponsoring churches. The ministry of the schools in these cases is frequently viewed as outreach ministry to the communities in which they are located. Many Christian schools have also developed programs to assist parents who are home-schooling their children. EWM
See also HOME EDUCATION.
Directory of the Assoc. of Christian Schools International (1999).

*Christian Education. In the period 1980–98 the *Church of the Brethren continued to publish curricular materials for children, youth, and adults. The Foundation Series for Children was published in 1977 by the CB, the *Mennonite Church, the *General Conference Mennonite Church, and the *Brethren in Christ Church. In 1989 the four denominations just named decided to publish a new children's curriculum, later to be known as the *Jubilee Curriculum*. In 1993 the four were joined by Friends United Meeting and the *Mennonite Brethren Church as co-publishers. The *Jubilee Curriculum* used innovative methods of weaving together story telling, worship, lived experience, and was presented in an attractive, interesting format. Accompanied by a strong program of information and teacher training, *Jubilee* was widely used among the six denominations that published it.

A new youth curriculum entitled *Generation Why* was introduced in 1993. Co-published by CB, Brethren in Christ, and General Conference Mennonites, *Generation Why* focused upon questions youth ask. *Guide to Biblical Studies*, a resource for adult Sunday school classes celebrated its centennial in 1984, and continued to be widely used.

Sunday school attendance in the 1980s and 1990s continued a decline that began in the 1960s. However, junior high and senior high participation in denominational conferences, work camps, and other programs increased dramatically. Peace education for youth was carried on by both the *General Board (CB) and *On Earth Peace. The CB Association of Christian Educators (*CoBACE) was organized in 1980 to train and support Christian education workers in CB congregations.

Four major congregational training programs were introduced in the CB during the 1980s. The first was *People of the Covenant (PotC), a program designed to bring small groups together in a covenant of study, worship, sensitivity to one another, and engagement in outreach. Initiated in 1983, it picked up themes from the earlier *Mission Twelve program by aiming that participants be biblically informed, globally aware, and relationally sensitive. In 1990 the *Disciples of Christ became a partner denomination in the PotC program. Together the two denominations produced the Covenant Bible Series, which was widely used interdenominationally.

A second congregational training program was Passing on the Promise (PotP). Introduced in 1985, it was a three-year program designed to stimulate congregational evangelism and outreach. The same year a third program, Adventure in Mission, was introduced with the purpose of training persons for stewardship of time and

resources as well as financial management. Some 600 CB congregations became engaged in Adventure in Mission. A fourth program was addressed to the training of deacons, and was built around a resource entitled, *Call to Caregiving*. After 1990 The *Association of Brethren Caregivers picked up the concern for the training of deacons.

The *BC, *DB, and *FGBC used Sunday school resources produced by other publishers. Members of all Brethren groups, but particularly the OGBB, turned toward *home schooling. The OGBB increased the number of their private schools as well as their participation in the Christian school movement. In general, each of the Brethren groups responded in its own way to the increasing influence of the public media, the widening cultural options, and the expanded threat of drugs and violence in the public schools. DEM

"General Board Reports," *Minutes* (*CB*) (1980–98); "Christian Education Goals," *Minutes* (*CB*) (1988) 662–68; *CoBACE Newsletter* (1981–2000); V. A. Hostetter and L. Martin, eds., *Foundation Series Handbook* (1966); R. W. Geiger, *Jubilee Guidebook* (1987); *Called to Caregiving* (1987).

Billy M. Bosler. BHLA collection.

Let There Be Peace

Billy M. Bosler was born on Nov. 25, 1933, in Louisville, OH, where he attended the *Center Church of the Brethren. He graduated from *Manchester College in 1955 and studied two years at *Bethany Theol. Seminary.

In 1978 when he accepted the responsibility to be the pastor of the Miami, FL, First CB, Bosler was fully aware of the risks of locating there, but he felt a strong sense of God's calling to minister to that community. The crime rate was high, violence was not uncommon, and every day sounds of police or rescue squad sirens rang in the background. Bill knew that it was a rough and dangerous neighborhood.

On one occasion when Donald R. Booz, was visiting the Boslers, he asked Bill, "How do you handle living here?" and received the reply, "These are God's people and I love them." He was not afraid because he saw people as God's people, and if God loved them, so did he. Frequently Bill visited a local convenience store to converse with unemployed men and women loitering there. He would call them by name and stop to listen to their concerns. At other times the front doorbell would ring with someone at the door who was in need of food, wasthat person turned away, and he or she usually left

with counseling, a place to stay, money, or work. Never more than requested and always given in love. Bill never judged those persons and never expected anything in return.

On Dec. 22, 1986, Bill and his middle daughter, SueZann, were stabbed at the church parsonage. Bill died from 24 stab wounds; SueZann survived. It is ironic that someone took Bill's life. Had that man only asked for money, Bill would have given it to him with no questions asked. If Bill had survived, SueZann knows that he would have been the first to visit the assailant in prison, and he would have said, "I forgive you, and God loves you, too."

Eight years before he was killed, Bill and SueZann had a conversation about forgiveness and the death penalty. He said, "This is how I feel: If I were murdered, I would not want the murderer to receive the death penalty. The taking of a life is sacred, no matter what that person has done. It is not for us to handle, but rather it is for God and God alone." Since 1988 with her father's example in her heart, SueZann has gone around the world sharing Bill's belief regarding the death penalty, and letting people know how to move from anger to forgiveness. His favorite hymn was *Let There Be Peace on Earth, And Let It Begin With Me*. Bill lived the example that Jesus set for us: Love and forgiveness are the only way to peace. SB

The Miami [FL] Herald (Dec. 29, 1986); *Messenger* (Oct., 1997) 2, (Nov., 1997) 9, 12, (June, 1999) 3.

Christian Peacemaker Teams (CPT) (CB). A unique initiative in Christian peacemaking among cooperating *Church of the Brethren and *Mennonite congregations and *Friends meetings, CPT began following a visionary address to the 1984 Mennonite World Conference. Speaker Ronald J. Sider radically challenged Christians to confront actively the powers of injustice and violence with Jesus' way of nonviolent love and to accept any personal risks involved. CPT was officially established at a Dec. 1986 conference of Mennonite leaders, with Charles L. Boyer and *Donald E. Miller attending as CB observers. The CB is linked to CPT through On Earth Peace, and CB individuals and congregations claim the vision by actively participating and supporting CPT's work.

A ministry of biblically-based and spiritually-centered peacemaking, CPT emphasizes public nonviolent direct action and accompaniment as tools for protection of human rights and unmasking of injustice. Part of a growing global vision of nonviolence as a better way to resolve conflicts, CPT offers an organized alternative to war-making through trained teams that seek to bring the redemptive love of God into situations of militarization and violent inter-group confrontation.

A quarterly newsletter, *Signs of the Times*, informs several thousand subscribers of CPT's work. In 1993 CPT initiated annual training for its peacemaker corps and in 1997 added regional training for local groups of reservists. By 1998 regional CPT teams organized in Indiana, Ohio, Colorado, Ontario (Canada), and Manitoba (Canada). CB individuals are active at all levels of involvement; as delegation participants, as reservists working two to eight weeks annually, as full-time corps members, and as members of the support team and the steering committee. Through the 1990's, CPT teams

worked in Haiti, Mexico, Colombia, Israel-Palestine, Iraq, Bosnia, Chechnya, Afghanistan, Vieques Island (Puerto Rico), urban U.S. communities, and native communities in the U.S. and Canada. JKL

Signs of the Times (1993–); Gordon Houser, ed., "The First 10 Years of Christian Peacemaker Teams," *The Mennonite* (Feb. 11, 1997); *Messenger* (1987–2000), indexes; R. Herr and J. Z. Herr, *Transforming Violence: Linking Local and Global Peacemaking* (1998), index; P. Bush, *Two Kingdoms, Two Loyalties: Mennonite Pacifism in Modern America* (1998), 267–68; L. Driedger and D. B. Kraybill, *Mennonite Peacemaking: From Quietism to Activism* (1994), index; Ronald J. Sider, "God's People Reconciling" (unpubl. paper, 1984); Cliff Kindy, "What If. . . ? What If We Took Peacemaking Seriously?" *BPF Newsletter* (1995); Kathleen Kern, "Hebron's Theater of the Absurd," *The Link* (1996); D. F. Durnbaugh, *Fruit of the Vine* (1997) 584.

*Church and State. The differing positions on relationships between church and state among the several Brethren bodies identified in the article on Church-State Relations remain. Only the *Church of the Brethren persists in formulating pronouncements on current issues, ordinarily by statements from delegates at its *Annual Conferences. A listing of some of the relevant statements issued since 1980 include: "A Call to Halt the Nuclear Arms Race from the Church of the Brethren" (1982); "Reaffirmation of Opposition to War and Conscription for Military Training" (1982), and statements on "War Tax Consultation" (1983), "Position on Gambling" (1986); "Quest for Order" (1987), and "Covert Operations and Covert War" (1988). In 1989 the Conference accepted a foundational paper that sought to delineate the biblical basis, to describe typical ways that church and state have related historically, to understand these relations in the perspective of Brethren history, and to outline implications for approaching decisions facing the denomination based on these considerations. DFD

D. Aukerman, *Darkening Valley: A Biblical Perspective on Nuclear War* (1981); S. L. Bowman, *Power and Polity Among the Brethren* (1987); V. Eller, *Christian Anarchy: Jesus' Primacy Over the Powers* (1987); L. Griffith, *The War on Terrorism and the Terror of God* (2002); *BLT*, [special issue] 37 (Autumn, 1987) 196–255.

*Church of the Brethren. Relationships between the branches of Brethren who separated in 1881–83 remained cordial. The Church of the Brethren and *The Brethren Church cooperated formally with *evangelism programs, and informally through service programs and the spiritual renewal program, "The *Brethren Way of Christ." An Annual Conference (1988) invitation for a closer formal relationship was not accepted by The Brethren Church.

EVANGELISM AND MISSIONS. A 30-year decline in CB membership beginning in the 1960s was a matter of increasing concern and led to establishing successive evangelism programs, *Passing on the Promise* and *The *Andrew Center*. In spite of the fact that these programs were effective in many participating congregations, the overall denominational membership decline continued. Both urban and rural churches received attention. Predominantly black, Hispanic, or Korean churches were initiated in urban centers, primarily in Philadelphia, Chicago, Miami, and Los Angeles. Despite denominational efforts to support them, rural churches suffered under the declining number of family farms and the rural economic crisis of the 1980s. *Education for Shared Ministry (EFSM) was the program most effective in helping revitalize small rural congregations, insofar as they opted to participate in the program.

*Mission philosophy provoked intense controversy as queries came repeatedly to *Annual Conference. The primary issue was the extent to which overseas mission churches should be independent under their own leadership, or to what extent they should be related to the North American Brethren through missionary leadership. The division in mission philosophy was apparent in *India, *Nigeria, *Sudan, *Dominican Republic, *Central America, *Brazil, and South Korea. A century of mission activity was celebrated in India (1995), as well as 25 years of the *Church of North India (CNI). However, a group that separated itself from CNI sought affiliation with the Church of the Brethren.

The *Church of the Brethren in Nigeria (EYN) grew dramatically even as direct *General Board leadership was withdrawn. Work in Sudan was entered into with the *Presbyterian Church USA and the *Reformed Church of America to support the New Sudan Council of Churches. In the Dominican Republic a new church initiative was taken by Brethren from *Puerto Rico and later confirmed by Annual Conference action (1990). In Central America mutual solidarity relationships were developed with churches in *Cuba, El Salvador, Nicaragua, and Honduras. A new church start was initiated in Brazil (1992), but ran into difficulty. An effort to establish the CB in South Korea received mixed support by Brethren and was withdrawn in 1997. Annual Conference sought to bring overseas mission activity closer to the congregations by developing a cooperative administrative relationship between the General Board and the districts.

PUBLISHING AND EDUCATION. Two widely used productions of the publishing house stand out: *The Hymnal: A *Worship Book* (1992) and Jubilee Curriculum for children. *Messenger continued as the primary denominational periodical with ca. 20,000 subscriptions. An important publishing event was the closing of printing activity in 1986 due to increased cost of printing technology.

The six CB-related colleges thrived with increased attention to their Brethren origins. College enrollments generally contained between five and fifteen percent Brethren students. The growth of *Brethren Colleges Abroad was a major cooperative achievement of the colleges. In 1994 *Bethany Theol. Sem. relocated from Oak Brook, IL,, to Richmond, IN, drawn by a commitment to be closer to the congregations and driven by financial problems. In Richmond the seminary was adjacent to and in a cooperative relationship with Earlham School of Religion, administered on behalf of the Religious *Society of Friends.

Sunday school attendance declined continually beginning about 1960. The CB Association of Christian Educators (*CoBACE) was organized to support teachers in the church. Outdoor education flourished with the improvement of facilities at church *camps by districts. The trend was toward year-round facilities with use extended to non-Brethren groups. *Youth showed increased interest in the church, evident in attendance at the *National Youth Conference (NYC) held every four years. The 1994 NYC held in Fort Collins, CO, was attended by more than 4,000 young people and advisors, a dramatic increase over earlier years. National Young Adult Conferences also grew in attendance. District and regional youth conferences as well as summer work camps were increasingly well attended.

MILITARY SERVICE AND THE STATE. Although no mili-

tary draft was in effect following the *Vietnamese War, Brethren adopted statements at Annual Conference urging members to take a *pacifist position, even though other positions were tolerated. A 1995 statement challenged the use of the military for humanitarian assistance. The *Historic Peace Churches committee updated statements regarding the common peace commitment of Friends, *Mennonites, and Brethren.

Through its Peace Academies, *On Earth Peace (OEP) trained some 200 youth in *non-violence and conscientious objection each year. OEP also took on the *Ministry of Reconciliation (MOR), the purpose of which was to seek reconciliation in intra-church conflicts. The General Board supported *NISBCO and advocated a national peace tax fund, the latter as an alternative to tax money for support of the military. A number of Brethren were active with *Christian Peacemaker Teams (CPT), dedicated to dramatic action in areas of conflict, as, for example, in the Middle East. Brethren maintained an office in Washington, DC, to influence legislators and keep the church informed about legislation. Brethren were divided about whether the church should be engaged in such activity, and consequently scaled down the office in 1996.

SERVICE AND CARE GIVING. The *Brethren Service Center at New Windsor, MD, was a primary focus of service and care-giving activities. Each year Brethren assisted some 700 refugees from various parts of the world to resettle in the United States. Annually Brethren contributed well over $500,000 to world-wide *disaster relief from floods, storms, droughts, natural disasters, and warfare. Disaster contributions came from appeals and auctions, the largest of which was jointly sponsored by the Atlantic Northeast and S. Pennsylvania districts. In 1990 ca. 1,000 volunteers worked at disaster sites, and another 50 trained volunteers cared for 600 children of victimized families.

By selling handicrafts produced in low income areas around the world, *SERRV was able in a typical year to contribute as much as $2,500,000 to some 20,000 artisans in 40 countries, from a total sales approaching $5 million. In 1989 the Brethren Service Center, working with *Church World Service (CWS), processed and shipped $34,000,000 worth of clothing and medicines for worldwide relief. This amount was reduced sharply in the early 1990s as CWS reviewed its material aid philosophy.

As many as 200 *Brethren Volunteer Service (BVS) workers, primarily young adults, served annually in the U.S., *Europe, the Middle East, Africa, and Central America on projects relating to peace, justice, the environment, and care of neglected and oppressed victims. Sponsorship of training for agricultural researchers from *Poland and *China was highly regarded by both countries, but the programs were terminated in 1997.

Brethren *homes for the elderly grew dramatically in size and number to more than 30. Beginning as an association of homes and hospitals, the *Association of Brethren Caregivers (ABC) grew to include training and resources for traditional *deacons and other congregational caregivers. ABC also initiated the *National Older Adult Conferences (NOAC). Congregations increasingly took on the task of local care-giving with support for the homeless, soup kitchens, and prison ministries.

THEOLOGICAL CONTROVERSY. The General Board sought unity of direction through the *Goals for the 80s, the *Goals for the 90s, a new logo, and the *identity statement: "Another way of living. Continuing the work of Jesus Simply, Peacefully, Together." Nevertheless, the period was marked by theological controversy often reflecting controversy in the society at large. One point of controversy was whether pastors were required to subscribe to a statement about the Lordship of Christ as the only Savior. Annual Conference (1995) adopted such a statement, but in deference to the *non-creedalism of the denomination, did not make it a requirement for *ordination.

The women's movement pressed for a redefinition of women's roles in the church and for more women in leadership. Women constituted a third of the seminary student body. Yet many congregations continued to resist the ordination and leadership of women in the church. Nevertheless, *Elaine Mock Sollenberger was the first woman elected to serve as Annual Conference moderator in 1989, followed by Phyllis Carter in 1992, Judy Mills Reimer in 1995, and Sollenberger again (appointed to fill a resignation) in 1998.

Issues of sexuality, particularly *homosexuality, became a focus of controversy in the 1990s. The CB human sexuality statement of 1982 had not permitted a homosexual life style, but some congregations advocated for open, inclusive membership. After heated debate at the 1994 conference, Standing Committee asked for a moratorium of discussion and queries for a five-year cooling off period. Thereafter the intensity of the conflict diminished somewhat.

The period saw the growth of caucuses and special cause groups representing *women, Hispanics, Koreans, *African-Americans, *Native Americans, the handicapped, *urban ministry, and others. Minority groups sought special status at Annual Conference, but this was resisted as divisive. Nevertheless, the first Afro-American moderator, *William A. Hayes, was elected to serve in 1988. The *Brethren Revival Fellowship defended a conservative approach to the Bible, evangelism, and earlier church traditions. They established their own voluntary service programs and initiated two congregations in Maine.

CHURCH STRUCTURE. Questions of church structure dominated the period. Whereas the General Board was created in 1948 by bringing together various church boards into five commissions, simplified into three commissions in 1968, the direction was reversed thereafter. The seminary separated from the General Board ca. 1970. *Brethren Benefit Trust was separated from the General Board in 1987. ABC and OEP became accountable to their own boards. The Annual Conference took responsibility for its own administration from the General Board. The colleges became stronger and more self-sufficient. An independent Council of District Executives (CODE) was increasingly influential.

An Annual Conference *restructuring committee proposed a plan for a dramatically reduced General Board staff, but the plan was rejected (1989). Several years later a more modest plan was accepted. However, faced with declining resources, the General Board developed a redesign plan that focused upon greater support for congregational life and fewer staff. This plan was adopted by the 1997 Annual Conference. The conference and its officers also initiated meetings of the Inter-Agency Forum to

Nigerian Choir celebrates 250th anniversary of the Church of the Brethren. BHLA collection.

resolve structural conflicts.

Much attention was given to pastoral ministry. Education for Shared Ministry (EFSM) and *Training in Ministry (TRIM) were designed for ministers who did not have access to seminary education. CODE worked at establishing clearer and more consistent standards among districts for ministerial placement. Pastoral compensation and benefits improved dramatically. The Brethren Benefit Trust made noteworthy gains in managing retirement funds for ministers. A code of ministerial ethics was adopted by Annual Conference. A denominational procedure was set up for processing ministerial misconduct. At the same time, Annual Conference established a code of *ethics for congregations (1996). DEM

Minutes (CB) (1980–97); C. F. Bowman, *Brethren Society* (1995) 382–417; D. F. Durnbaugh, *Fruit of the Vine* (1997) 531–93; S. L. Bowman, *Power and Polity Among the Brethren* (1987); *Messenger* (July, 1992) 14–15, (Aug., 1995) 16–18.

*Church of the Brethren in Nigeria (*Ekklesiyar 'Yan' uwa a Nigeria* [EYN]). A key characteristic of the EYN church in *Nigeria, 1980–98, has been its remarkable growth. In 1980 membership was less than 40,000 with 10 districts and 44 ordained ministers. Statistics for 1990 showed nearly 60,000 members in 14 districts. By 1998, EYN reported ca. 140,000 members, 36 districts, 339 organized congregations, and 220 ordained ministers.

EYN members point to several reasons for this membership growth. The strong educational base provided by mission schools enabled many individuals to rise to high positions. EYN members in key positions of government and society gave the church stature and credibility.

Another factor named is the church's service ministries (rural health [*Lafiya], *agriculture, and wells program) which reach out to communicate God's love and touch many lives. An additional aspect mentioned is the dynamic fellowship and witness activity of many groups within the church, including Women's Fellowship (Zumuntar Matan Ekklesiyar [ZME]), Boys' Brigade, Girls' Brigade, and choirs.

Background societal factors possibly impacting EYN growth include the ongoing competition between *Islam and Christianity and the decreasing credibility of traditional religion. It must also be acknowledged that EYN's growth followed major investment of CB resources and personnel at mid-century which resulted in a strong foundation prior to the transition to Nigerian leadership in the 1970s. Since then, visitors have observed that EYN views extending the church as a central function of its existence.

Given the rapid expansion of the church, a primary challenge has been to prepare sufficient leadership. Kulp Bible College (formerly *Kulp Bible School) remains the main teaching institution, but persons also study at the *Theological College of Northern Nigeria (TCNN) and many other schools. In addition, some districts have started Bible schools. A program of theological education by extension (TEE) involves more than 1,400 persons and is the broadest educational program for lay and potential ordained leaders.

Growth in urban areas was significant during 1980–98. This has occurred as members moved to the city for employment opportunities and then formed congregations, typically comprising many tribes. Such urban movement has resulted in new congregations at

Maiduguri, Jos, Kano, Kaduna, Abuja, Minna, and Lagos.

A wider role for women in the church is emerging. The Women's Fellowship (ZME) has always been an energetic and significant group in the life of the church. Women have begun responding to God's call and encouragement from the faith community to serve the church beyond traditional women's roles. Polity restrictions previously excluding women from ordination have been removed.

A new venture is the Mason (EYN) Technical School at Garkida, begun in 1991 by mission staff Carol E. O. and Ralph I. Mason. The purpose of this school is to enable self-sufficiency by providing marketable skills, specifically programs in auto mechanics and office management. After Ralph Mason was killed in a vehicle accident in 1994, EYN renamed the school to honor its founders.

As the nation's school systems languished through neglect, EYN members demanded that the church reclaim its former educational role. In 1995 the church acquired over 62 acres adjacent to EYN headquarters near Mubi with the intent of building a secondary school. The EYN Comprehensive Secondary School opened in borrowed rooms of the new ZME women's center in 1996. Annual *workcamps, begun in 1985, have been a meaningful part of the ongoing relationship between the CB, *Basel Mission, and EYN. MBK

Personal information; General Board (CB) files; C. Cayford and M. Keeney, *The Church of the Brethren in Nigeria: Vital and Growing* (1995), Mission in Context Series; J. L. Musa, *50 Years of Christian Missionary Activities in Kibakuland (1941–1991)* (1991); T. H. Ragnjiya, "Toward Establishing a Continuing Education Program for Ekklesiyar Yanuwa a Nigeria," MA thesis, Ashland Theol. Sem. (1991); H. R. Boer, *A History of the Theological College of Northern Nigeria, 1950–1971,* (Christian Reformed World Missions) (1983); A. F. Baldwin, "The Impact of American Missionary Activities on the Bura People of Nigeria," PhD diss., Ball State U. (1973); K. Thomasson, *The Old, Old Story. . . Anew: The Church of the Brethren in Nigeria* (1983); B. A. Bdlia, "Principles of Administration: Management and Planning for Church Growth," MA thesis, Bethany Theol. Sem. (1993); S. D. Dali, "A Historical Development and Vision for the Future Growth of the Ekklesiyar ?Yan'uwa a Nigeria (E.Y.N.)(The Church of the Brethren in Nigeria)," MA thesis, Beth. Theol. Sem. (1994); "Mission in Christ's Way," CB General Board (1991), video-tape; *Messenger* (1983–2000) indexes.

*Church World Service (CWS) has served as the relief and rehabilitation arm of the *National Council of Christian Churches (NCCC) since its inception in 1946. The *Church of the Brethren has been a full partner with CWS since its beginning. CWS relies on the facilities and staff at the *Brethren Service Center, New Windsor, MD, to prepare and ship tons of material aid to more than 100 countries each year. The CB also supports CWS in planning annually for appropriate responses to dozens of disasters throughout the world. In addition to serving on the CWS Committee, CB staff have served on the CWS Disaster Response Committee, the CWS Immigration and Refugee Committee, and the Material Resource Committee. DMD

R. E. Stenning, *Church World Service, Fifty Years of Help and Hope* (1996); H. E. Fey, *Cooperation in Compassion* (1966); J. K. Kreider, *A Cup of Cold Water: The Story of Brethren Service* (2001) *passim; Messenger* (Nov., 2002) 6–7.

Cleveland, OH, Mt. Zion Fellowship of the Brethren (BC). The pastor, C. Ronald Williams, II, established the congregation in Jan. 1983. Fifteen persons attended the first service of worship. In 1998 the membership was approximately 2,000 with a weekly attendance of 1,800. The congregation met in various church buildings, Lutheran and Catholic, for 10 years. In 1993 Mt. Zion purchased 14 acres and began to build a large church complex. The first worship service was held in the new sanctuary in Jan. 1995.

Ronald Williams is gifted in both preaching and music. He has produced a number of recordings featuring his piano playing and the church choir which also sang with the Cleveland Orchestra. Williams attended Livingston College (AB, 1974) and *Ashland Theol. Sem. (MDiv, 1980) and received an honorary degree from China Christian College in Taiwan (DD, 1990). He joined *The Brethren Church in 1980. JRS

Personal information; congregational records.

CoBACE (Church of the Brethren Association of Christian Educators) was formed on Oct. 28–30, 1980, when 26 professional Christian educators met at New Windsor, MD, with the purpose: "To call out, support, encourage, and challenge those who are responsible for... Christian education activities at all levels of the Church of the Brethren." During 1980–99, Donna F. Steiner, Julie M. Hostetter, Alice E. Geiman, Doris Quarles, Jean Moyer, Larry M. Dentler, and Mark V. Herr have chaired Co-BACE Steering Committees.

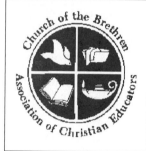

In Feb. 1982 a Co-BACE logo was developed—a circle intersected by a cross, and in the quadrants a dove, a basin and towel, a lamp, and a Bible. May 1982 saw the first issue of *CoBACE Newsletter,* with Donna Kensinger as editor. First published three times a year, it became a quarterly publication in 1991. Other editors have been Sharon Gehman, Cindy Booz, Ronald D. Finney, Juanita Deardorff, Martha E. Beahm, Doris Walbridge, June A. Gibble, and Donna McKee Rhodes. In 2001, it was replaced by the quarterly newsletter, *The Seed Packet,* published by Brethren Press.

CoBACE sponsored an annual professional growth event for teachers, pastors, and other educators, and planned an *Annual Conference luncheon and insight session each year. Membership in CoBACE was open to both individuals and congregations; annual membership grew from 30 in its early years to about 120. The association terminated its existence in Sept. 2001. JAGib

Messenger (Jan., 1981); BHLA files; CoBACE Historical Notebooks; *CoBACE History; CoBACE Newsletters, CoBACE Minutes.*

Colburn, Ralph J. (FGBC), 1916–96, pastor, youth leader. Born in Wheatland, ND, Ralph Colburn moved with his family to Pomona, CA, in 1923. Converted in 1928, he and his family moved to Long Beach in Sept. and became members of the *First Brethren Church there.

Colburn graduated from Long Beach City College (1936), *Bible Institute of Los Angeles (BIOLA) (ThB, 1940), and Westmont College (BA, 1941). He served as interim pastor at the *Whittier, CA, First BC (1942) and as pastor of the *Compton, CA, First BC (1942–47). In

1948 he was called to be the first conference national youth director, a post he held until 1954. In that year he married Julia Rowland, who also served as pianist for evangelistic crusades in which Colburn was the song leader (Sept.-Dec. 1954). He pastored the *Fort Lauderdale, FL, GBC (1955–68); then returned to California to pastor *Long Beach, CA, Community GBC (1968–78). He was called to serve as associate pastor to seniors at the *North Long Beach, CA, BC and continued in that position after the merger that created the *Los Alamitos, CA, Rossmoor GBC 10 years later. Colburn served as FGBC moderator (1960–61) and as executive secretary of the National Ministerium for 20 years. RTC

BMH (Aug. 15, 1989) 6–7, (Nov. 15, 1993) 5; personal information; Annual (FGBC) (1942ff.).

Collitt, Robert B. (FGBC), 1923–83, youth leader, pastor, administrator. Born in Wilkes-Barre, PA, Robert Collitt attended Bryan College (Dayton, TN), and completed degrees in education and psychology at *Ashland College. He married Flo Mellick in 1946, served as overseas deputation director for Youth for Christ, International, and pastored the Church of Christ in Greenwich, OH (1950–59).

After a successful ministry as national evangelist for the *FGBC Board of *Evangelism, Collitt was the pastor of the *Hagerstown, MD, GBC (1963–78), which became the third largest congregation in the fellowship under his leadership. During this pastorate, he served as chaplain to the Hagerstown Police Dept. for five years, had a significant *radio ministry, and was involved with the Hagerstown Rescue Mission and the Cedar Ridge Children's Home. He served as moderator of the FGBC (1971–72). Collitt pastored the *Roanoke, VA, Ghent GBC, (1978–79) before becoming stewardship counselor for Grace Brethren Stewardship Services (1979–83). RTC

See also CHAPLAINCY.

BMH (Sept., 1979) 18–19, (June, 1983) 10; Annual (FGBC) (1963ff.).

Columbia, MO, Fellowship (CB) began in March 1989 with a meeting of Brethren, Mennonites, and district representatives from both denominations. The group began meeting on Sunday evenings for Bible study, and then, in response to a felt need to worship together, monthly worship services were added. Charles Grove, pastor of both the *Shelby Co. CB and the Mt. Pisgah *Mennonite Church, volunteered to lead worship one Sunday evening each month. In Aug. 1990 weekly worship services were held with members of Columbia Fellowship leading the service, and a children's Bible study was added.

A series of retreats, begun in Jan. 1991, resulted in creation of a *free ministry style Shepherding Committee, which assumed responsibility for leadership, preaching, administration, and other pastoral duties. On Jan. 5, 1992, the Columbia Fellowship changed from an evening format to Sunday morning Bible study, worship, and a weekly carry-in dinner. Two rooms were rented from the Tiger-Kensington Retirement Home on Sunday mornings. Semiannual *communion, Women's Fellowship, and children's Bible school are held in homes. Preaching is provided by Darren Gabbert, John Brejda, and Gregory G. Harvey; Gabbert is responsible for administration. Janet Freisen Brejda is treasurer and music director, and Denise Gabbert is secretary and director of children's programming. In 2000, 16 members were reported; in August,

2002, Columbia Fellowship decided to cease meeting. GGH

Congregational records; Yearbook (CB) (2001) 128; BLT 36 (Summer, 1991) 175.

Columbus, OH, New Covenant Church of the Brethren began in partnership with the *General Board and Southern Ohio District which invested $438,000 to purchase four acres of land, to call Fred M. Bowman as pastor to start the church, and to rent a meeting place. The first Easter service was held on March 30, 1986.

In Oct. 1989 Ronald R. Fleming's ministry started. In 1990 the church purchased four more acres and built a new sanctuary. This congregation has initiated the endowment of a peace studies chair for Ohio State U., sponsored refugees from Vietnam and Bosnia, built *Habitat for Humanity houses, chartered scout troops, housed the Northside Montessori School and summer camps for children with severe behavioral disorders, piloted a whole person health ministry called *Lafiya, and started its own daycare program. A new 11,000 sq. ft. facility is soon to be built. RRF

Congregational records; personal information.

Columbus, OH, Smoky Row Brethren Church. The church was begun in 1980 as a joint mission project of the Ohio District and *National Mission Board. Members of the Deardurff, Graves, Shultz, and Stoffer families formed the initial core group, with Dale R. Stoffer serving as the founding pastor. The first service was held on Sept. 21, 1980. The congregation focused its efforts in northwest Franklin Co., meeting in several different facilities before moving into its own building on Easter Sunday 1983. A second unit, providing educational and administrative space, was built in 1990. Stoffer served the congregation until 1992 when Thomas E. Schiefer became the senior pastor and Jeffrey L. Whiteside the associate pastor. In 1997 a second worship service was added, providing a contemporary format. Reilly R. Smith became the senior pastor in 2003. There were 107 members in 2002. DRS

BE (Oct., 1980) 23, (Nov., 1981) 13, 23, (June, 1982) 16, (Nov., 1982) 12–13, (July, 1983) 19, (May, 1984) 21, (Nov., 1984) 12–13, (June, 1985) 11, (Nov., 1985) 13, (Nov., 1986), 14, (Nov., 1987), 15, (Nov., 1988) 12–13, (July/Aug., 1989) 20, (Nov., 1989) 13–14, (June, 1990) 16, (Oct., 1990) 18, (May, 1991) 20, (Oct., 1992) 17, 18, (Nov., 1993) 15, (June, 1995) 16, (Oct., 1997) 15.

*Committee on Interchurch Relations (CB). The CIR pursues relationships with other denominations and encourages congregations and districts to participate in ecumenical activities. The committee is staffed by the office of the general secretary.

The CIR sends representatives annually to meetings of other Brethren bodies (BC, OGBB, DB, FGBC, and CGBCI). Special consultations with *Brethren Church leaders (1987–88) were sparked by BC moderator Warren K. Garner's interest in greater cooperation, but concluded that joint projects must begin at the local level. Interest was re-kindled by BC Executive Director Emanuel "Buzz" Sandberg's impromptu speech at the Ecumenical Luncheon of the 2000 CB Annual Conference. A resolution drafted by the CIR was adopted by the 2002 Annual Conference, repenting of past divisiveness and calling for renewed CB-BC cooperative ministries. Conversations with *German Seventh Day Baptists began in 1985 and

led to CIR-facilitated negotiations in 1997 between that group's *Snow Hill Nunnery and the Southern Pennsylvania District (CB) regarding possible reunification. Those efforts ended when Snow Hill affiliated with the Salemville German Seventh Day Baptist congregation in Bedford County, PA.

Cooperative ventures with *Mennonites and denominations from the *Believers Church tradition are encouraged. An associated relationship established in 1972–73 with the *American Baptist Churches USA continues in 2003: consultations since 1984 have endorsed the exchange of *General Board observer-consultants and explored possibilities for cooperative programming. Contacts with the Progressive National Baptist Convention were sought after the 1988 Annual Conference recommended establishing relationships with a black denomination. Those efforts, however, did not bear fruit.

Global ecumenical efforts have been pursued primarily via the *World and *National Councils of Churches. Interfaith dialogues have been included. Efforts to also maintain contact with the *National Association of Evangelicals include the CIR's 1988 recommendation to the Standing Committee of Annual Conference (CB) that the CB send an observer to the NAE. Standing Committee asked the CIR to pursue relationships with churches related to NAE instead of relating directly to the NAE.

Local ecumenical efforts of individuals or congregations have been highlighted through annual Ecumenical Awards presented at *Annual Conferences since 1980. Scholarships were awarded annually in 1981–88 for ecumenical studies. A *Handbook on Christian Unity* was published in 1988 and re-issued a decade later. More recent ecumenical awards have highlighted cross-cultural, peacemaking, and young adult ecumenical efforts. A survey of congregations in 1996 documented extensive cooperation of local CB congregations with neighboring churches. JMBe

See also FRATERNAL RELATIONS COMMITTEE (BC); AMERICAN BAPTIST CHURCHES USA; CONSULTATION ON CHURCH UNION; FRATERNAL RELATIONS COMMITTEE (CB); ECUMENISM.

"Committee Reports," *Minutes* (CB) (1980–2000); "A Vision of Unity for the Church of the Brethren in the 1980s," *Minutes* (CB) (1982); L. L. Wright, *CB Handbook on Church Unity* (1988); E. K. Ziegler, "Ecumenical Relations" in D. F. Durnbaugh, ed., *Church of the Brethren: Yesterday and Today* (1986), 181–200; D. F. Durnbaugh, *Fruit of the Vine* (1997), 578–86; K. M. Shaffer, Jr. and G. F. Snyder, *Texts in Transit II* (1997); C. F. Bowman, *Brethren Society* (1995); "2002 Resolution on the Brethren Church," including background material by K.M. Shaffer, Jr., *Minutes* (CB) (2002).

Conservative Baptist Brethren Church. In 1986 a number of Brethren from several congregations felt the need to withdraw from the *Dunkard Brethren Church because of the development of what was considered to be undesirable and dangerous trends. These included the promotion of youth retreats, attendance at various seminars, and a general departure from the conservative standards of the denomination. Throughout the summer of 1986, a number of meetings were held which resulted in a consensus favoring withdrawal.

On Sept. 20, 1986, a public meeting was held at the meetinghouse in Frystown, PA, with all interested parties invited to attend. With Laverne E. Keeney (1928–94) and W. Dean St. John (b. 1931) in charge of the meeting, an organization was effected with 120 members. The name chosen for this group was the *Conservative Baptist Brethren Church*. Keeney was chosen to be the presiding elder. This appeared to be a strong movement, and in the first three years substantial growth was realized, including organizing a second congregation in Lititz, PA; election of several officials; and ordaining an additional elder. However, this growth was short-lived. An element of strong dissension developed, primarily within the official body. This situation ultimately resulted in the three elders, along with those who supported their position, forming the *Conservative Brethren Church. The remainder of the group, led by Jack L. Snyder (1938–93), continued worshipping together. In 1998, the group was led by George T. Longenecker, Jr. (1941–98), and elected several officials to continue the work of the church. WDSt

Personal information; D. B. Kraybill and C. N. Hostetter, *Anabaptist World USA* (2001) 153, 200.

Conservative Brethren Church. This fellowship originated in 1986 when a number of Brethren in different congregations felt the need to withdraw from the *Dunkard Brethren Church because of development of what was perceived by some to be undesirable and dangerous trends. This group became the *Conservative Baptist Brethren Church and flourished for about three years. However, dissension developed, primarily within the official body, that ultimately resulted in disciplinary action being taken against one official. After this, the church divided into two factions—those supporting the action taken by the elders and those rejecting it. Since the opposition held a large majority of the membership, it soon became apparent to the three elders that it would be more expedient to withdraw from the group than to oppose it.

On July 30, 1990, a meeting was held at the home of Laverne E. Keeney (1928–94). At this meeting, the three elders, Laverne Keeney, W. Dean St. John (b. 1931), and David H. Kegerreis (b. 1939), announced their intention to withdraw and invited any who desired to join them. On Aug. 18, 1990, another meeting was held at the Keeney home that resulted in organizing The Conservative Brethren Church with 42 charter members. Dean St. John was chosen as presiding elder. Membership in 1997 numbered 57. The church building is located near Millbach, PA, one mile north of Kleinfeltersville in Lebanon Co. The group also has a *meetinghouse in York Co., one mile north of Winterstown, PA, where in 1997 two services were held each month. WDSt

Personal information; D. B. Kraybill and C. N. Hostetter, *Anabaptist World USA* (2001) 153, 200.

Conservative Grace Brethren Churches International Fellowship. John R. Zielasko, former director of Grace Brethren Foreign Missions, was an early leader in forming a Brethren Association to represent the concerns of many Grace Brethren pastors and church members to the leaders of the *Fellowship of Grace Brethren Churches. Pastors John Fahrbach, Keith Merriman, and J Hudson Thayer invited other Grace Brethren pastors and theologians to join in forming a new fellowship. *John C. Whitcomb headed a committee to rewrite the *Brethren Statement of Faith* to give it precise clarity. The organizational meeting for a new fellowship which would become the sixth branch of the Brethren movement was held in Oct. 1992 at the *Eagle Creek Grace Brethren Church, Indianapolis, IN. The name, *Conservative Grace Brethren Churches International*, was adopted at the meeting, as

Logo of the Conservative Grace Brethren Churches International.

was the revised *Brethren Statement of Faith*.

Thayer proposed a *New Testament order for the polity of the new Fellowship that allowed for order without formal incorporation of the Fellowship. Working papers, entitled *Protocols of the Conservative Grace Brethren Churches International*, were adopted. The key concepts of these papers are that only congregations may belong to the Fellowship and that there would be no incorporated boards or agencies affiliated with CGBCI.

The first Fellowship conference was set for July 1993 at Toledo, OH, with John Fahrbach elected president and J Hudson Thayer, vice-president. In accordance with the *Protocols*, Thayer became president for the July 1994 conference also held at Toledo.

The Fellowship, originally established with 24 churches and 70 pastors, by 2000 had grown to nearly 50 churches and more than 80 pastors. In the Fellowship and College of Pastors there is a Home Missions Panel that has responsibility to endorse mission points and pastors. Delegates of the Fellowship are made up of members in good standing from each of the member congregations. They elect each year the vice-president of the Fellowship, who subsequently becomes the president and then the conference coordinator, thus serving on the President's Panel for three years.

The College of Pastors is composed of ordained Conservative Grace Brethren pastors who are recognized by the Pastoral Recognition Panel. The pastors elect each year a vice-president, who also serves for three years on the President's Panel, the second year as president and the third year as assistant to the president. The President's Panel is constituted of both the Fellowship president and the College of Pastors president along with the Youth Conference planners. The President's Panel plans the annual adult and youth conferences.

The Conservative Grace Brethren Churches International has endorsed the *Theological Practorium as its educational system for training pastors. The Fellowship polity invests in local congregations the true "headship" of Christ and views the Fellowship as a voluntary association of autonomous local congregations.

Voice Newsletter is a monthly communication among the congregations, published through the *Mansfield, OH, Grace Brethren Church, with pastor Les Vnasdale as editor. The journal *The Conservative Grace Brethren Publications* is issued by the Lakeland Conservative Grace Brethren Church, Warsaw, IN. *John C. Whitcomb, *James L. Boyer, and *John R. Zielasko comprise the editorial committee. This publication presents technical theological studies, which are intended to stimulate continuing research by pastors. The Conservative Grace Brethren Archives and Permanent Records are in the care of *Mount Vernon, OH, Conservative Grace Brethren Church. JHT

Personal knowledge; D. B. Kraybill and C. N. Hostetter, *Anabaptist World USA* (2001) 86–87, 145, 154.

D-F

*Deacons (CB). The office and ministry of deacons have been important in the histories of the denominations rising from the early *Brethren movement. The practices and responsibilities of deacons have remained rather constant within these bodies, with the exception of their roles in the *Church of the Brethren, which have been challenged and altered. The denomination has often been faced with difficult questions related to the office. Are deacons consecrated as ordained or lay leaders? Are they called for life or for set terms? Are they considered a congregational or a denominational office? Are women and divorced persons called? How do deacons relate to pastors? How are they included in polity and organizational structure? Over time these issues have been appropriately resolved.

Currently, the deacon office is congregationally based, considered a lay ministry, generally open to women and divorced persons, and called for an indefinite period, which may include a call for life. Further, relationship issues between pastors and deacons are resolved, and congregational structures usually include deacon ministry.

Historically, the ministry of deacons included service and caregiving functions, such as visitation (including the annual deacon visit); overseeing benevolent ministries; making preparations for *love feasts and *baptisms; assisting in *anointing and *worship services; dealing with congregational conflicts, and maintaining unity. The 1997 Annual Conference statement named four deacon functions: advocacy and support, discipleship and hospitality, health and healing, and unity and reconciliation.

There is continuing evidence that the office and ministry of deacons are important to the denomination. Annual Conference approved defining statements in 1983 and 1997; a training handbook was published in 1987; a deacon cabinet was formed in 1991; a quarterly newsletter was initiated in 1994; a deacon manual and video were produced in 1998. Also, deacons are included as a core ministry of the *Association of Brethren Caregivers (ABC), which provides a denominational home for supporting deacons and developing deacon ministry resources. JEGi

D. F. Durnbaugh, *Deacons in Historical Perspective* (1996); G. R. Hackman, *Deacons in Biblical Perspective* (1996); ABC, *Deacon Ministry in the Church of the Brethren* (1997), Annual Conference Statement, see also the statements (1983, 1987); *Caregiving* (1999ff.), a newsletter; June A. Gibble and Fred W. Swartz, eds., *Called to Caregiving: A Resource to Equip Deacons in the Believers Church,* (1987); *Minutes of First National Deacon Cabinet* (Nov. 23, 1991ff.); *ABC Board Minutes* (Sept. 20–21, 1995ff.).

Denominational Reorganization (BC). Following the 1881–83 division, *The Brethren Church spent 32 years forming an organizational plan that would combine the desire for congregational government and the need for denominational unity and direction. During that period, however, a variety of auxiliaries and cooperating boards were created with no coordinating agency.

In 1955, a *Central Council was formed to coordinate denominational ministries, but by the 1970s it was widely agreed that this council could not provide the unifying leadership needed to identify priorities and implement strategies for denominational ministry. This dissatisfaction led to three significant reorganizations.

In 1976, "Board Group," an *ad hoc* committee of denominational executives and cooperating board presidents, proposed a denominational reorganization to General Conference. Authored by Frederick T. Burkey, the proposal would have merged all cooperating boards into a single Board of Brethren Church Ministries with one director and several subordinate executives directing specific ministries. The proposal received a mixed response and was referred to the General Conference *Polity Committee.

The 1977 conference referred the Polity Committee's report back to that committee for further study. In 1978, Conference approved a Polity Committee proposal to replace Central Council with a reconstituted General Conference Executive Committee (name changed to Executive Council in 1984) composed of the conference officers. However, there was no consensus on how to change the cooperating board structure.

*Charles R. Munson then formed an *ad hoc* "Committee of 13" to discuss possible resolutions to the impasse. The committee designed a proposal that was approved by the 1979 General Conference, to be implemented as funds became available. The plan called for appointment of three denominational executives who would be equals: a director of pastoral ministries to work with pastoral placement and congregational relations; a director of denominational business to coordinate the national office and provide central services for the various ministries; and a director of denominational ministries to coordinate and give direction to the work of the cooperating boards. A director of pastoral ministries was employed in 1980, joined by a director of denominational business in 1982. Several proposals to implement the third posi-

tion, director of denominational ministries, failed to generate support from the cooperating boards. By 1987, financial shortfalls led to discontinuing the position of director of denominational business.

1988 REORGANIZATION. Though the 1979 re-organizational plan was never fully implemented, desire for greater coordination of denominational ministries persisted. Dale R. Stoffer, 1988 General Conference moderator, and the Polity Committee devised a plan to merge the cooperating boards into one organization. The merged organization would have one *director of Brethren Church ministries, with the General Conference Executive Council serving as the corporate board. The proposal received enthusiastic support from the 1988 General Conference, and all cooperating boards, except the *Missionary Board, joined the merger. The first director of Brethren Church ministries was employed in 1989, and the boards were merged on Jan. 1, 1990.

In anticipation of the merger, 1990 General Conference moderator Mary Ellen Drushal organized a denominational planning retreat on Nov. 27–29, 1989, at *Beulah Beach Conference Center, Vermilion, OH. Local church representatives learned to do strategic planning by using the denomination as a test case. Eleven denominational priorities identified were later consolidated into four "Priorities for the Nineties" adopted by the 1992 General Conference.

1996 REORGANIZATION. By the end of 1992, projections of future financial losses for the Brethren Church National Office raised serious doubts as to the viability of the new organization. The Moderator Track, composed of the present and past General Conference moderators and the moderator-elect, proposed to the General Conference Executive Council a reduction in the number of employees in the national office and downsizing the scope of denominational ministries. The proposal received mixed response when presented to the 1993 General Conference. Delegates adopted an alternate proposal to employ an outside facilitator to work with a self-study committee.

The committee developed a plan to address three issues: the need for (1) a unified vision, (2) a mission-focused organization, and (3) responsible stewardship. The plan went through several significant modifications that resulted from discussions at district gatherings and General Conference. A 1996 proposal to General Conference was approved, with implementation beginning immediately.

The reorganization created one Executive Board of 11 members to serve as the corporate board for both The Brethren Church and the Missionary Board. The board includes three staff members—an executive director, a *director of congregational ministries, and a *director of missionary ministries; six members representing two ministries councils and chosen by them from among their membership; the General Conference moderator; and the president of *Ashland Theol. Seminary. Each ministries council includes 13 members, with one member elected by each of the nine districts, three members elected by General Conference, and the director of that ministry. One council focuses on congregational issues and ministries in the U.S. while the other advises staff on international ministries, including world missions and relief.

The 1997 General Conference affirmed Emanuel W. Sandberg as the first executive director. The Executive Board selected David West as the first director of congregational ministries and Reilly R. Smith as the first direc-

tor of missionary ministries.

The resulting organization approved in 1996 resembles very closely the 1976 proposal in the way it structures the national office staff and denominational ministries. For the first time, however, the 1996 reorganization gave districts direct representation in developing denominational ministries. RWW

D. R. Stoffer, *Background and Development of Brethren Doctrines, 1650–1987* (1989), 235–36; *BE* (Oct., 1979) 2, (Nov., 1979) 6–8, (June, 1988) 13–14, (Jan., 1990) 5–6, (June, 1996) insert, (July/Aug., 1997) 9, (Sept., 1997) 9, 11, *BC General Conference Annual* (1976) 17–19, (1977) 15–17, 24, (1978) 11–13, (1979) 15–17, (1988) 7–9, 12–13, 17–19, (1990) 3–7, (1993) 9–13, (1994) 1–2, 11, (1995) 1, 15–17, (1996) 8–18; F. T. Burkey, "Organizing for Growth" (1976).

Director of Brethren Church Ministries (DBCM) (BC), 1989–96, was an executive position created in *The Brethren Church *denominational reorganization approved by the 1988 General Conference. The DBCM was responsible to give visionary leadership to the BC by guiding, coordinating, and implementing the priorities and ministries established by General Conference and its Executive Council. Though the DBCM served essentially as the chief executive officer for the BC, the position was considered on par with that of the director of pastoral ministries.

Ronald W. Waters served as the first director of Brethren Church ministries from July 1, 1989, until Dec. 31, 1995. J. Michael Drushal was part-time interim DBCM during much of 1996. The position was replaced by the 1996 General Conference with the similar but expanded position of executive director. RWW

BE (June, 1988) 13–14, (March, 1989) 20, (Dec., 1995) 10, (Jan., 1996) 12; *BC General Conference Annual* (1988) 7–9, 17–19, (1995) 5–11.

Director of Denominational Business (DDB) (BC), 1982–87, was an executive position created in *The Brethren Church *denominational reorganization approved by the 1979 General Conference. The DDB was employed to serve The Brethren Church National Office by the General Conference Executive Committee. Responsibilities included coordinating the day-to-day business interests of the denominational office and making arrangements for the annual General Conference. When created, the position was projected to be one of three equal offices (along with a *director of pastoral ministries and a *director of denominational ministries).

The position was first filled by Ronald W. Waters from 1982–84 through a joint employment arrangement with *Brethren Publishing Company. Sterling Ward served as DDB in 1984-87, after which the position was discontinued because of lack of funds. RWW

D. R. Stoffer, *Background and Development of Brethren Doctrines 1650–1987* (1989), 236; *BE* (July/Aug., 1984) 20, (May, 1987) 19; *BC General Conference Annual* (1979) 15–17.

Director of Pastoral Ministries (DPM) (BC). Recognizing the stress of pastoral work and the need for a "pastor's pastor," *The Brethren Church established a cooperative network of pastoral care and created a new position, a Director of Pastoral Ministries (DPM). Qualifications for the DPM include understanding the Brethren, their heritage and *polity, experience in management and organization, a high degree of personal integrity and confidentiality, a proven ability to relate to people, the skill to assess and intervene in difficult situa-

tions, direct involvement in ministerial examining procedures, and the ability to build a relationship of shepherding trust.

The work of the DPM falls into four general areas: (1) pastoral care—to help avoid pastoral crisis and burn-out, to insure that each pastor has a friend and confidant, to counsel pastors individually and at district conferences, to work with pastoral and congregational problems, and to serve as chair of the *National Ordination Council; (2) pastoral training—to promote ministerial recruitment in the denomination, to consult with those led by the Lord to realize their calling, and to work with *Ashland Theol. Sem. to know and counsel students; (3) pastoral problems—to provide help on the General Conference level for pastoral and church relations, to assist a pastor and a congregation in finding a common meeting ground for solutions to be worked out; (4) pastoral placement—to work with churches seeking pastors and pastors seeking churches, to encourage churches who are without pastors, to provide church evaluation programs and helps toward fitting the right pastor to the right church, and to make personal visits to churches seeking pastors. The DPM fills a critical and otherwise neglected need in the church. WHK

General Conference Minutes (BC) (1979, 1980); *BE* (Oct., 1979) 2, (April, 1987) 17, (Sept., 1991) 4–5.

R. Jan Thompson working in World Trade Center disaster child care (2001). Disaster Child Care file. Photo by Jean Bauer.

Disaster Child Care (CB) was initiated in 1980 under R. Jan Thompson, director of Brethren Disaster Response (1978–86). Karen Doudt, of *Manchester College, wrote the first training curriculum to prepare volunteers to provide specialized care for children suffering the effects of disaster. One of the first programs to acknowledge the psychological needs of children after disasters, it became recognized nationally for high standards of child care and expertise of its volunteers.

Renamed *Cooperative Disaster Child Care* in 1984, the program expanded to include participation by several denominations. A nationwide network of over 1,200 certified volunteers was developed under Lydia H. Walker. Renamed *Disaster Child Care* in 1997, the program was reincorporated into the Emergency Response/Service Ministries unit of the *Church of the Brethren. This ministry, in collaboration with the American Red Cross and the Federal Emergency Management Agency, continues in 2004 to provide children with safe space, caring adults,

and appropriate therapeutic play activities while their parents handle the tasks of recovery from floods, earthquakes, and other disasters.

In 1998 a Child Care in Aviation Incident Response team was established as another arm of the Disaster Child Care program. This team responds to aviation incidents and other mass casualty events when requested by the American Red Cross. In 2003, the name CAIR was changed to Critical Response Child Care (CRC) due to its role expanding with the ARC to include responding to weapons of mass destriction and terrorist incidents.

Directors or coordinators of the Disaster Child Care program have been R. Jan Thompson (1980–83), Roma Jo Thompson (1983–87), Donna Derr (1987–88), Lydia H. Walker (1988–2001), Roy Winter (2001–03) and Helen S. Stonesifer (2003–). LHW/HSS
See also DISASTER RESPONSE PROGRAM.
Messenger (March, 1985) 7, (April, 1986) 9–14; *CB Minutes* (1981–2003).

Disaster response to Wilkes-Barre (PA) flood (1972). BHLA collection.

Disaster Response Program (CB). In 1977 the General Board staff members responsible for the administration of the Disaster Response Program of the *Church of the Brethren proposed to the *General Board that a full-time director be employed to manage the Disaster Response Program. Permission was granted for a three-year trial period, and R. Jan Thompson was called to be the first full-time director. Improved training of district disaster coordinators and project directors was initiated, enabling the CB to operate in more areas of the country and on a larger number of simultaneous projects.

The needs and care of children in disaster sites

became an area of concern. An ecumenical program known as the Cooperative Disaster Child Care Program was created. Volunteers were given special training and equipment to assist children to deal better with the trauma caused by the disaster. Initially, child care volunteers were given space in One Stop Assistance Centers, and they cared for children while parents filled out the many needed forms. In more recent years, child care centers have been established in schools, churches, or other available facilities. This program proved to be of great assistance both to parents and children impacted by disasters.

In 1998 the CB signed an agreement with the American Red Cross to provide care for children following major transportation accidents. Child care volunteers were selected and given special training to become part of the Childcare in Aviation Incident Response (CAW) team. These volunteers are on call 24 hours a day to respond to major accidents. The children or families of victims are taken to a safe place and provided care while families deal with all that is required of them at such a time.

By endeavoring to meet emotional, spiritual, and physical needs of disaster survivors, the CB has become known even where no congregations exist. One such location is Orangeburg, SC, where the CB provided volunteers to rebuild the Butler Chapel AME Church that was burned down by arsonists. Glenn Kinsel, a volunteer who insured that volunteers were always available, presented one of the major addresses during the dedication weekend in Jan. 1998.

The CB also responds to international disasters by giving financial grants to ecumenical agencies that are better equipped to respond; *Heifer International, *Interchurch Medical Assistance, and *Church World Service have received grants from the Emergency Disaster Fund in recent years. DMD

See also DISASTER CHILD CARE.

Messenger (Feb., 1986) 10–13, (April, 1986) 9–12, (Dec., 1990) 8–9, (Jan., 1991) 8, (Nov., 1991) 12–15, (June, 1992) 11–12, (May 26, 1996) 25–29, (March, 1998) 18–21, (April, 1998) 9, (Nov. 1998) 7–8, (Jan./Feb. 1999) 7, (April, 1999) 8–9, (June, 1999) 6–7, (July, 1999) 7, (Aug., 1999) 23–25, (Dec., 1999) 11–12, (Sept., 2001) 22–23, (March, 2003) 18–19, (Aug., 2003) 7; see also these continuing features in *Messenger* (1990–2003), "In Brief," "In Touch," "News," "Outlook," "Update," "Worldwide," and "Worldwatch."

Discipleship and Reconciliation Committees (D&R) (CB) have been formed at the district level in the *Church of the Brethren to assist individuals or groups in resolving problems or reconciling broken relationships. While D&R Committees most often work with situations within congregations, requests for assistance may originate from either congregational or district leadership. D&R Committees were instituted in most districts in the late 1970s in response to a recommendation by the 1976 *Annual Conference. Organization, size, manner of appointment, and working patterns differ among D&R Committees in the districts, but most work closely with the district executive. Although D&R Committees have no formal connection to the *Ministry of Reconciliation (MoR), MoR published a *Discipleship and Reconciliation Committee Handbook* in 1995 and continues to serve as the primary source of training for D&R Committee members. In 2002 Annual Conference recommended that districts change from the Discipleship and Reconciliation model to a new model called Shalom Teams for responding to denominational conflicts. RAGr

AC Statement: Discipleship and Reconciliation (1976, rev. 1977);

Discipleship and Reconciliation Committee Handbook, MoR (1995); *Messenger* (Dec., 1995) 24, (May, 1998) 9.

Doctrine, Research, and Publication Committee (BC) is a committee of the General Conference Executive Committee and later of the Congregational Ministries Council. It was formed by *General Conference in 1989 on the recommendation of moderator Kenneth L. Sullivan (1942–97), who also served as its first chair. Its purpose was to help *The Brethren Church "articulate clearly its faith and practice and pass on its heritage to succeeding generations." The committee engaged in educational efforts through presentations at denominational pastors' conferences, articles in The *Brethren Evangelist*, and a 13-part video series on Brethren distinctives (*Pilgrimage of Faith: The Witness of the Brethren Church*). It also produced a consensus statement on the Brethren approach to Scripture, *How Brethren Understand God's Word*, which was accepted by the 1993 General Conference and thereafter printed and distributed by the denomination. BBC

"Understanding the Bible Series," *BE* (Sept., 1993/Sept., 1996).

Dominican Republic, Mission in the (CB). Following great destruction in the Domincan Republic by hurricane David in 1979, Jorge Toledo, a CB member from *Puerto Rico, traveled to the island seeking to help. In 1981 and 1982 he conducted preaching missions in the Dominican Republic. Enthusiastic response to his message led to worshiping groups in several villages in the province of Azua. Responding to Toledo's request, Latin America/Caribbean Area Representative, Karen Calderón (b. 1945), visited in 1983, affirmed the potential for new church development, and arranged for her office to contribute financially to the *Puerto Rican church efforts at outreach.

Simple structures were built. There were failed attempts to place personnel. Puerto Rican preaching and teaching missions continued as Puerto Rican leaders, Pedro Brull and Jorge Rivera joined Toledo. Brethren in the U.S., primarily from Atlantic Northeast District, with Earl K. Ziegler's leadership, began their significant support.

Conversations with Yvonne Dilling, new Latin America/Caribbean staff worker in 1987, led to a staff visit with Puerto Rican leaders in 1989. The 1990 *Annual Conference adopted the *General Board recommendation that the *World Ministries Commission accept the invitation of the Puerto Rico Board to enter into partnership for the development of CB ministry in the Dominican Republic. Atlantic Southeast District, with District Executive Berwyn L. Oltman, was a designated partner.

Despite difficulties implementing the partnership, in 1991 the church in the Dominican Republic was incorporated under Dominican law. The first Assembly of Brethren in the Dominican Republic held in Jan. 1992 elected a Dominican, Guillermo Encarnación, a CB pastor from Lancaster, PA, as moderator. Through his periodic visits, and advisory and educational roles, he became a defining presence for the Dominican church. A Dominican board was elected and the development and support of strong indigenous Dominican leadership was a priority. Dilling initiated a strong leadership training program, designed by Estella Horning and Marcos Inhauser. In contrast to local custom, women were trained and served in pastoral roles. Beginning in 1994, Miliciades Mendez

Baptisms in the Dominican Republic. BHLA collection.

provided local supervision. Following the service of Encarnación as moderator/advisor, local members assumed all leadership positions, beginning with Luis Ogando as moderator-elect in 1996.

As the church expanded, Haitian immigrants joined. The first mission coordinators, Gerald Crouse and Rebecca Baile Crouse, were placed in 1999. Work camp groups of U.S. Brethren helped Dominicans increase the number of church buildings. By 2000, there were 13 congregations, three fellowships, and six preaching points, with ca. 500 members. In that year the first ten pastors were ordained. JGD/MBK

Messenger (July, 1990) 16–20, (Dec., 1990) 18–20, (April, 1991) 12–13, 14–17, (Oct., 1991) 6, (Dec., 1991) 7, (April, 1992) 8, (Dec., 1992) 12, (April, 1993) 7, (April, 1994) 6, (April, 1996) 12, (Dec., 1996) 16, (July, 1997) 19, (Nov., 1998) 18–19, (Sept., 1999) 13–20, (Sept., 1999) 11–12, 21–23, (April, 2000) 6–7, 14–18, 18, (June, 2000 14–17; K. Wolford, *Dominican Republic* (*Mission in Context Series*) (1990); CB General Board files.

Dublin, OH, Northwest Chapel Grace Brethren Church. A daughter congregation of the *Columbus (Worthington), OH, Grace Brethren Church, Northwest Chapel was initiated in order to minister to the growing northwest suburbs of Columbus. Worship services began on June 23, 1985, in the basement of a Mid-America Bank building. Rapid growth caused the congregation to move its services three months later to the Dublin High School. It relocated to its permanent home on Rings Road in Amlin by April 1990. The church has a strong mission outreach to such locations as London, OH; Hartford, CT;

Lexington, KY; *Mexico; *Cuba; and *Chad (Africa).

Pastors who have served this congregation include Terry A. Hofecker (1985–), Louis M. Huesmann II (1985–86), Martin P. Guerena (1986–89, 1995–), J. Brad Gibson (1987–90), Don A. Buckingham (1989–2001), Clancy C. Cruise (1990–92), Roy E. Glass (1990–98), Robert Bolton (1992–95), Daron K. Butler (1993–94), Timothy J. Ruesch (1993–94), Kyle Beasley (1994–97), Jay G. McKinley (1995–2000), Shannon I. Hollinger (1998–2002), Kevin B. Harris (1998–), and Brian J. Etheridge (1999–). DKJ/-DMHo/JRY

Congregational records; *Annual* (*FGBC*) (1986ff.).

*Dunkard Brethren Church. Members of the Dunkard Brethren Church continue to see their purpose as being a light to the world. They maintain an earnest desire to please God, attempting to take scriptures literally and apply them to their daily lives. Very little in the *Declaration of Principles (DB) statement has changed since the denomination's formation in 1926. Issues that have not changed include the forbidding of *divorce and *remarriage while the former partner is still living and opposition to affiliation with lodges and *secret societies. They continue to uphold the doctrines of the *prayer veil, *holy kiss, *feetwashing, *nonconformity, *nonresistance, and *baptism by trine immersion.

During the 1960s, there was a major movement in American society in which the young people questioned the values and viewpoints of the generations before them. The Dunkard Brethren Church has not entirely escaped this influence. Dunkard Brethren *youth questioned why

Dunkards were different from other Christians around them. There was a growing trend which demanded biblical explanations for General Conference rulings as well as for existing church practice.

In an effort to guide the activities of the young people while at General Conference, the *Decorum Committee was established in 1960. It designed activities and outreach projects for young people for the duration of General Conference each year. These activities have included group singing, the election of a minister to speak at the following year's General Conference, and visits to local natural or historical attractions. This involvement has expanded to include singing at nursing homes, witnessing on the streets by a cappella singing and handing out tracts, and having panel discussions with ministers using questions originating from the young people.

Youth Retreat was established by Leonard Wertz (b. 1940) in 1975. Although it was never officially recognized by General Conference, the concept of more aggressively reaching out to the denomination's young people has gained wider acceptance since 1980. This event has been held annually in the Rocky Mountains of Colorado and is patterned on a four-to-five-day spiritually challenging, physically rigorous model. The lectures have been designed to assist young people in understanding how to interpret and apply biblical standards to life's daily decisions at their level. Many who attended Youth Retreat are now ministers and elders.

Dunkard Brethren have been affected by various outside influences since 1980. Christian *radio messages have made their way into many homes on a daily basis. The continual barrage of teaching from fundamentalist and evangelical broadcasters has made some impact on Dunkard Brethren life and thought. Possibly the biggest challenge Dunkard Brethren have encountered from Christian radio was the exhortation toward involvement in politics. While most fundamentalists and evangelicals strongly advocate aggressive political activism, Dunkard Brethren have traditionally limited their political involvement to praying for the leaders of the land, paying their taxes, and occasionally proffering their viewpoint by way of a letter with the intent of influence or appeal. The official policy continues to "advise all our members not to take part in politics or political matters."

Pro-life beliefs are strongly supported by Dunkard Brethren. A query opposing *abortion was brought to General Conference in 1985 where it was adopted. This issue, along with a statement opposing *homosexual practices, passed in 1992, following the precedent set in earlier conferences on addressing social and moral issues, such as *divorce and remarriage, which had been repeatedly considered in previous General Conference statements.

Another example of outside influence since 1980 has been the religious seminars conducted by Bill Gothard of the Institute in Basic Life Principles. More than a few of the membership have attended the week-long seminars and have been influenced by these teachings. For many, attending these seminars provided clarification of the basic issues about *salvation, the how's and why's of living out the teachings of Scripture in everyday life, and a challenge to be "salt and light" to their neighbors. Some viewed these outside influences as an aid to better understanding the Bible. Others saw these and other trends as a threat to the faith of the church. The progression of these trends was a factor in the development of a church division in 1986.

Dunkard Brethren church government can best be described as a theocratic democracy, which is interpreted as regenerated individuals teaming with the direction of the Holy Spirit under God in making decisions. The elders meet together on the District and General Conference levels to discuss the practical application of General Conference rulings. However, only the delegate body of General Conference sets policy. The denomination continues to maintain a congregation-centered model of church government rather than a pastor-centered one. They also continue the practice of a non-salaried, plural *free ministry, although many of the smaller congregations have only one minister. In addition to holding down regular jobs or running their own businesses, the ministers fulfill the role of pastor/shepherd in their congregations. A number of ministers have attended seminars for pastors, Bible institutes, or evening classes at local Bible colleges.

There have been a small but steady stream of changes to Dunkard Brethren church *polity since 1980. The Polity Revision Committee of the 1993 edition felt that the guidelines about the style and manner of dress had been modified sufficiently that the title "Dress Decision of 1911" no longer applied, so that title was discontinued. By action of the delegate body of General Conference, the length of the sisters' dresses was changed in 1987 from "not more than 10 inches from the floor with the shoes on" to "at least mid-calf or longer." The counsel of the church against taking out life *insurance policies was repealed in 1990, and the prohibition against wearing wrist watches was deleted in 1993. Members were asked, in 1995, to conscientiously guard their homes from the detrimental spiritual effects of commercial entertainment videos. In 1997, the dangers of the types of obscene material which are available and easily accessible through the Internet and other computer technology were recognized, and the use of such technology by the membership was discouraged.

These rulings by the delegate body of General Conference represented changes in the wording of the polity booklet. In previous versions of Dunkard Brethren Church Polity, much stronger language was used to "forbid" certain items or practices. In the changes made since 1980, the rulings were much more likely, for example, to "conscientiously guard" against videos and "discourage" the use of the Internet. These decisions are not to be construed as giving permission by the church for its membership to have television, videos, or computers connected to the Internet, cyberspace, or future similar services in their homes. But they do show a progression in the method of governing by the Dunkard Brethren Church over the years. Most Dunkard Brethren leaders of the 1990s were concerned that the use of such devices represented trends leading the membership away from a simple faith in God and from a practical, literal obedience to the teachings of the New Testament to abstain from all appearance of evil.

Concerning *education, the advent of the church-based Christian day school enjoyed widespread acceptance across the church during the 1980s. In 1981, a query was passed by General Conference to encourage the establishment of Christian schools in all congregations where feasible. At that time, a School Advisory Board consisting of five elders was also organized. Their responsibility was to assist the congregations in establishing Christian schools. As of 1998, five congregations sponsored Christian schools, along with one at the *Torreon Navajo Mission. In the congregations where no Christian day school was established, many members sent their

children to parochial schools in their communities which were run by *Mennonites or other conservative groups. The home school movement followed in the late 1980s and also gained acceptance. More than 40 families were directly involved in schooling their children at home in 1998.

There is a growing interest in *missions among the Dunkard Brethren. They continue to support the *Torreon Navajo Mission* in *New Mexico and have begun a new outreach in Africa. A considerable amount of money is given by individuals in support of various non-Dunkard mission and relief organizations. Individual members have been involved in *disaster relief work in the U.S. as well as working in Romania, Haiti, and other countries with organizations such as Christian Aid Ministries of Berlin, OH.

The *Bible Monitor* continues to be published and distributed throughout the membership as well as to several who are not members of the Dunkard Brethren Church. Milton C. Cook (b. 1943) has served as the editor since 1975. While the *Bible Monitor* had been published twice monthly since 1922, the General Conference delegates in 1997 decided to publish it monthly. This began in Sept. 1997.

Dunkard Brethren emphasize the worth and importance of the *family. Throughout the 1980s and 1990s, most Dunkard families continued to have a sit-down evening meal with all the members of the family present who are still living at home. This stands in contrast to the faster-paced lifestyles of their neighbors who rarely eat together as a family unit. Attending a General Conference is much like attending a family reunion. The group is small enough so that it is possible for most members to know one another on at least a last name basis. There have been intermarriages within the denomination across congregational and state lines, which have helped the group maintain strong ties throughout the brotherhood.

The members continue to enjoy *revival meetings which are traditionally a time for more focused periods of *evangelism and renewal. Some congregations have also begun sponsoring special evenings for married couples, or weekend meetings with an emphasis on a designated topic. Dunkard Brethren have been instrumental in founding and participating in an annual "Brethren Bible Conference" held in *California since 1991. In 1997, the first "Dunkard Brethren Men's Retreat" was held in *Michigan for the purpose of motivating and challenging men ages 14 and older to be better fathers and role models. It should be noted, however, that there has been a measure of concern about these innovations, because many of these activities have begun without the express approval of the delegate body of General Conference.

After 72 years of existence, the Dunkard Brethren numbered ca. 900 members in 24 congregations (1998). While members do not agree on the specifics of end-time events, they would generally agree that the coming of the Lord is near and that it is imperative to be faithful laborers in Christ's Kingdom. RSL

See also AFRICA MISSION PROJECT; CONSERVATIVE BAPTIST BRETHREN CHURCH; THE CONSERVATIVE BRETHREN CHURCH; ESCHATOLOGY; EVANGELICALISM; FUNDAMENTALISM; HOME EDUCATION; INFORMATION TECHNOLOGY, CHURCH USE OF; MASS MEDIA.

Conference Minutes (DB) (1927–75); *Minutes of General Conference* (1976–97); *Dunkard Brethren Church Polity* (1980, 1993 eds.); *Dunkard Brethren Church Manual* (1971 ed.); *Messenger* (April, 1992) 22–23, (May, 1992) 22; personal information.

Durbin, WV, Church of the Brethren, formerly part of the *Pocahontas congregation, became a separate congregation in 1989. Donald W. Curry, a 1981 graduate of *EFSM through the Pocahontas congregation, serves as full-time pastor. Key leaders during the transition to congregational status were Boyd Wright and Asa Wilfong. In 1990, the church participated in the "Passing On The Promise" program with Wesley and Joretta Coleman providing leadership.

In May 1997 the congregation began building an addition to the church, providing a sanctuary and larger *Sunday school rooms. Boyd Wright supervised the project, with church members contributing 2,265 hours of labor; construction costs totaled ca. $40,000. The first service in the new sanctuary was held on Aug. 9, 1998.

The congregation entered the EFSM program in 1998 by calling Richard Walther and John Riffe, Jr. to the ministry. In 2000 average worship attendance was ca. 60 including many new members in the previous five years. DWC

Congregational records; *Yearbook* (CB) (1990ff.).

Eagle River, AK, Grace Brethren Church. Organized in Aug. 1982, it was a mission point of the *Anchorage, AK, Grace Brethren Church. The Heatwoles and three other families from the Anchorage congregation were the first 12 active members. Members met in the Eagle River Elementary School for one year and later met in the Homestead and Birchwood Elementary Schools. The congregation purchased property in 1984, and constructed its church building in 1985 in northern Eagle River. Congregational pastors have been Eldred John Gillis II, Christopher Hay, and Mark William Roberts. In 1995, member Clifford F. Johnson founded Sagrada Scholarship Bible Camp in *Missouri. In 2000 the congregation added a youth pastor, James Alfred Dompier, and they developed an AWANA program for children and a thriving youth group. (AWANA stands for "approved workmen are not ashamed" and is an international program with headquarters in Streamwood, IL.) ERR

Congregational records; personal information.

Eberly, Allen B. (DB), 1932–93, elder, church leader. The son of Marvin and Elsie Eberly, Allen Eberly was born Aug. 19 in Lebanon, PA. Baptized into the *Dunkard Brethren Church at *Lititz, PA, in 1946, he married Martha Stauffer of Ephrata, PA, on Oct. 25, 1952. Eberly was installed into the ministry on March 15, 1961, and ordained an elder on June 5, 1972, at Lititz. He served as presiding elder in his home congregation from 1984 until his sudden death on Nov. 5, as well as in the neighboring congregations of *Bethel and *Shrewsbury, PA. Eberly was concerned that the church should remain faithful to the teachings of Christ. He served as reading clerk of General Conference in 1987, and was a member of the *Publication Board for several years. A mild-mannered, humble man, Eberly greatly desired peace. RSL

Bible Monitor (April 1, 1994) 13.

Eller, Vernard M. (CB), professor, author, churchman. Eller was born on July 11, 1927, the son of *Jay V. and Geraldine Crill Eller of Wenatchee, WA. He married

Vernard Eller. BHLA collection.

Phyllis Kulp; they have three children: Sander, Enten, and Rosanna. Vernard Eller holds degrees from *La Verne College (BA, 1949), *Bethany Theol. Sem. (BD, 1955), Northwestern U. (MA, 1958), and Pacific School of Religion (ThD, 1964).

As the author of over 20 books and scores of articles, Eller is one of the most prolific writers of the *Church of the Brethren. His life and work are rooted in his understanding of the radical *discipleship demanded by the gospel. Eller has spent most of his career teaching and writing at the U. of *La Verne, CA, an institution related to the CB. In addition to his work at La Verne, Eller has been active at all levels of the life of the denomination.

Two books stand out in Eller's scholarly impact. His reinterpretation of Soren Kierkegaard—*Kierkegaard and Radical Discipleship* (1968), in which he compares and parallels the Christian faith stance of Kierkegaard and the early Brethren, is a radical departure from most scholarly studies of Kierkegaard. Eller's last significant book, *Christian Anarchy: Jesus' Primacy Over Powers* (1987), is an attempt to communicate some of the themes of Jacques Ellul, one of Eller's theological colleagues and a personal friend, to a wide audience.

Eller's best selling book is *The Mad Morality* (1971), in which he used the popular *MAD Magazine* as a vehicle for communicating serious theological themes. Indeed, Eller's generous use of humor in dealing with serious religious issues is characteristic of his writings, which makes reading Eller a pleasure as well as a serious endeavor. JHGi

Who's Who in Religion, 2nd ed. (1977) 184; *Contemporary Authors: Vols. 21–24* (1977) 264–65; *Messenger* (1980–2000) indexes; *BLT* (1956–2000) indexes; H. Hogan and G. E. Muir, *The University of La Verne: A Centennial History, 1891–1991* (1991) *passim*; D. F. Durnbaugh, *Fruit of the Vine* (1997) 523, 527, 576; G. C. Eller, "Eller Chronicles" (1988).

Enten Eller: God Would Not Have Me Register

"The Courage of One Conscientious Objector" was the headline of a nationally-circulated column, first appearing in *The Washington Post* in August, 1982. A headline in the newsmagazine *Time* dealing with the same incident provided further information: "Uncle Sam Convicts No. 1: Trials begin for men refusing to register for the draft." Wire service reports spread the news widely.

Enten Eller, at this point 20 years old and a student at *Bridgewater College, was the first man brought to trial by the federal government for refusing to comply with regulations promulgated in 1980. Although the military draft was not in effect, Pres. Jimmy Carter had persuaded the U.S. Congress to fund a registration effort. The stated purpose was to enable any subsequent draft to proceed quickly, but observers agreed that the true reason for the action was "to send a signal" to the Soviet Union, which had shortly before invaded Afghanistan. Under the law, every young man had to report to the government within thirty days after his 18th birthday.

The prosecution of 160 men, of whom Eller was the first tried, was intended to motivate non-registrants to meet the law's requirement. Critics accused the Selective Service System of coercion of conscience and "selective prosecution." Most of the 160 were those who had informed the government of their conscientious grounds for non-cooperation. This was the pattern of Enten Eller, who had made a point of informing Selective Service offices of his changes of address.

Eller explained his actions in these words: "I have not registered simply because the U.S. government has asked me to do something God would not have me do. I am a non-registrant in order to be faithful to God, my conscience, and my church. Christ's way, the way of love, the way of concern for all peoples, the way of nonviolent peace, cannot be reconciled to involvement with the military, which uses killing and destruction, or the threat of such, to achieve its end."

"I am sad that I have to disobey an order of the United States government, but in my striving to be faithful I have no choice except to obey the higher authority of God. I view my action as constructive and positive, demonstrating in the best way I know the love and peace of God for everyone, even those threatening me with imprisonment. For this reason I have chosen to be open and to cooperate with the government and the U.S. attorney as much as I conscientiously can, for I do not have hatred of authority."

Commentators opined that the government was not wise in picking a clean-cut, articulate, straight-A student as the first non-registrant to be tried. Wrote one: "If the federal government wants to subvert draft registration, it couldn't have found a better way to begin than by picking Enten Eller as the first person to haul into court for failing to sign up." Why? "Intelligent, thoughtful, and personable, Eller is the son, grandson, and great grandson of preachers of the Church of the Brethren, whose members have sought conscientious objector status and alternative service for three centuries. There's no reason to expect him to change his mind regardless of the judge's deadline. 'I am obeying God,' he says."

Both the prosecutor and the judge at Eller's trial

conceded that he was sincere in his beliefs, but that did not hinder them in convicting him of breaking the law. The initial sentence was three years on probation and 250 hours of community service. He was given ninety days in which to register, failing in which he faced a possible prison term of five years and a fine of $10,000. Eventually, the harshest penalties were not levied. His communications with Selective Service were judged to have been tantamount to registration, although he never voluntarily registered. The final sentence, pronounced in Dec. 1982, was to perform public service for two years.

In a remarkable way, the quiet testimony of Enten Eller called forth a torrent of attention to the peace testimony of the Brethren. As the editor of *Messenger* put it: "[H]is brave public stand, his faithful Christian witness, his gift to be simple, and his exemplary Dunker honesty put him among a select group in our denomination, in the company of *John Naas, *John Kline, and *Ted Studebaker." DFD

The Washington Post (July 31, 1982), (Aug. 12, 1982); *Time* (August 30, 1982): 57; *Chicago Tribune* (Aug. 18, 1982), (Aug. 21, 1982); *Christianity and Crisis* (Nov. 15, 1982): 347; *Christian Century* (Aug. 18–25, 1982): 848–9; *Messenger* (Oct. 1982): 24, (Jan. 1983): 5, 18–20.

Enon, VA, New Covenant Church of the Brethren is located five miles east of Chester in the village of Enon, Chesterfield County. The New Covenant congregation was organized on Jan. 7, 1990, as a division from the *Hopewell congregation with William R. Faw as organizing pastor. The congregation met in the Enon Baptist Church for a year before purchasing property with a *meetinghouse in Enon. The congregation is characterized by strong loyalty to Brethren heritage, to *Annual Conference, the *General Board, and district ministries. It also has vital ministries of prayer, music, and local benevolence. Forty members were reported in 2000. New Covenant has been served by pastors Michael A. Clark (1992–97) and James C. and Letha M. McKinnell. (1998–). JCM

Yearbook (CB) (2001).

Environmental Issues. The biblical foundation of Christian environmental concern is found in Gen. 2:15, when God "took the man and put him in the Garden of Eden to till it and keep it." As evidence of human abuse of God's creation has multiplied in the latter half of the 20th century, environmental stewardship, or "earthkeeping," has become a vitally important concern. *The Brethren Church, *Dunkard Brethren, *Old German Baptist Brethren, and *Fellowship of Grace Brethren Churches have not dealt with environmental issues in a formal way. However, in rural congregations, many work in *agriculture-related vocations and practice a personal ethic of environmental *stewardship.

The *Church of the Brethren has worked actively on environmental issues since 1974. Concern for environmental stewardship grew from work on issues about the *simple life. Environmental stewardship falls under the responsibilities of the director of the Office of Witness. An environmental working group, which includes a youth representative, promotes environmental stewardship within the church. This group works cooperatively with the *World Council of Churches eco-justice working group.

Specific programs include creation care congregations, which offer congregations the opportunity to make an intentional commitment to education and action for environmental stewardship; the appointment of creation stewardship advocates for individual districts to raise awareness of creation stewardship issues among their congregations; and sponsorship of a national youth Christian citizenship seminar on environmental issues in 1999.

Publication of a quarterly newsletter, *The Third Day*, began in 1998. Growing concern for environmental issues is reflected by the fact that several Brethren colleges (*Ashland University, *Bridgewater College, *Elizabethtown College, *Manchester College, and *McPherson College) offer Environmental Science or Environmental Studies programs. JDW

L. Wilkinson, ed., *Earthkeeping in the '90s: Stewardship of Creation* (1991); C. B. DeWitt, (1998); S. P. Bratton, *Six Billion and More: Human Population Regulation and Christian Ethics* (1992); S. Bhagat, *Creation in Crisis* (1990) and *Your Health and the Government* (1998); D. Radcliff, *Messenger* (Nov., 1998) 22–23; J. Weidenhamer, *BE* (July/Aug., 1994) 4–6, (Jan., 1986) 4–5.

Ephrata Area, PA, Grace Brethren Church. A group of believers interested in forming a congregation in the Ephrata area met on March 27, 1980, at the Akron Borough Hall. The group consisted of members and pastors from the *Lititz, *Myerstown, *New Holland, and *Lancaster Grace Brethren churches. Several people from non-Brethren churches also attended the meeting. Luke E. Kauffman, representing the mission board of the Northern Atlantic District of Grace Brethren Churches, discussed steps to be taken to form a GBC. On May 28, the group met again, and 34 persons signed a charter and formally requested membership in the Northern Atlantic District. In July, Edward Gross of Goleta, CA, was called to be the first pastor. The first Sunday service was held on Sept. 7, 1980, in the former Kemper Church of the Brethren at 62 Hahnstown Road. The building was leased for one year before the congregation purchased it. Although the church began as a mission point, it became self-supporting within four months. In May 1982, Gross resigned his post. Mark E. Saunders served the congregation as senior pastor from Sept. 1982 through July 2000, and William J. Stonebraker served from July 2000 through March 2003. Other ministers who have served as members of the pastoral staff are Allen D. Edgington (associate pastor, May 1981–Jan. 1982), Robert D. Kern (co-pastor, May 1988–March 1994), and Aaron K. Wolfe (associate pastor, May 2000–June 2001). Rick G. Fairman (2003–) serves as interim pastor. Church membership in 2003 was 57 and average Sunday morning attendance was 94. JBB/JRY
Congregational records; *Annual* (FGBC) (1981ff.).

*Ethics. Brethren seek to live in communities guided by the living Spirit of Jesus Christ as witnessed in the New Testament. This faith has often led to an ethic of gracious obedience to Christ's way of love, humility, and simplicity. However, sometimes it resulted in a series of contradictions and paradoxes. Such contradictions between an ethic of prescription, of summary rules, of context, and of virtue were intensely evident from 1980 to 1998. Some Church of the Brethren members advocated that biblical prescriptions should be enforced by *Annual Conference. Others promoted summary rules, virtue, or contextual approaches as advisory and not obligatory.

Strong cultural influences such as gender, sexuality,

biological sciences, and violence raised ethical issues. For example, the activity of *women in leadership raised questions of biblical interpretation and of *ordination. The CB generally held to the equality of all believers in Christ, but other Brethren groups did not support the leadership of women. The issue was also debated in terms of the use of inclusive *language. With regard to sexual orientation, the CB Annual Conference (1983) stated that a homosexual lifestyle is not acceptable. Some Brethren sought to use scriptural texts to develop prescriptions. Others followed a non-prescriptive "Mind-of-Christ" approach.

The CB declared *abortion unacceptable. This was understood as a summary rule, which allowed for the exception of those who conscientiously acted otherwise. The CB was cautious about genetic engineering and was not willing to accept the use of fetal tissue for medical research. A number of CB Annual Conference statements counseled members to *conscientious objection and nonviolence. They advocated reduction of military budgets, a peace tax fund, and limitation of the use of the military, including the case of humanitarian assistance. The CB also lobbied against the death penalty.

Questions about community life and belief also demanded attention. The CB sought to include *minorities, but expected considerable conformity to tradition, and were reluctant to bend to minority pressure groups. The paradox of how minorities achieve equal status within such limitations remained. The CB debated a worldwide denominational *mission versus an ecumenical indigenous approach to mission. Members sought to work out a structure for an identifiable global body while respecting the interests of churches in other countries. Church growth versus traditional *discipleship was much debated. The specter of legal suits led to a procedure for handling ethical misconduct by ministers, as well as a ministerial code of ethics. This in turn led to a code of ethics for congregations.

The degree of controversy on all such issues raised the problem of how controversy is best handled. The redesign of the CB *General Board, with diminished mission and service budgets and increased focus upon congregational life, raised the issue of the relationship of the local and the global. A similar question for stewardship became evident in the movement away from unified giving toward project giving.

Between 1985 and 1991 The Brethren Church adopted position statements on a number of social issues. The denomination's Social Responsibilities Commission developed drafts for several of these statements. In 1985 General Conference went on record as opposing gambling and lotteries. Such activities were viewed as destructive socially, morally, and economically. In the same year The Brethren Church adopted a statement on homosexuality. The statement noted that Scripture consistently reserves sexuality for the marriage relationship between a man and a woman. Homosexuality is a sin that is condemned in Scripture, though Christians need to remember that all human beings have sinned. God's mercy and forgiveness are available for all who repent and believe the gospel. Homosexuals are entitled to equal protection under the law, but the statement opposes legislation that would extend them special consideration based on "sexual orientation." A third statement adopted by the 1985 General Conference was a strong condemnation of pornography. The proliferation of pornographic material in the media and the epidemic growth of the pornography industry have left a human toll of broken individuals and families. The destructive and dehumanizing effects of pornography are an insidious evil that the Brethren Church must prophetically speak against.

In 1986, in a "Brethren Resolve for Peace," The Brethren Church adopted a statement that reflected the differing views on the issue of peacemaking. Some within the church continue to affirm the historic stance of the church regarding nonresistance, but others uphold the role of the state in maintaining peace and deterring aggression through a strong military. The statement supported those who felt called to serve as chaplains in the armed forces. The statement called for continuing dialogue on the issues of peace as well as mutual understanding of the various positions found in the church.

In 1991 the General Conference of The Brethren Church issued statements on both AIDS and abortion. The conference sought to be sensitive to the multi-faceted issues raised by AIDS. This worldwide health crisis has complex moral, legislative, medical, and educational aspects. The conference called for compassionate ministry to those with AIDS or who were HIV-positive. But it also reinforced that the most realistic approach to curbing the spread of this tragic disease was to reaffirm the Christian values of chastity before marriage, fidelity in marriage, and rejection of the homosexual lifestyle.

Rejecting the argument that abortion is a matter of a woman controlling the reproductive functions of her own body, the conference held that the basic issue of abortion is under what circumstances a human being may be permitted to take the life of another. The conference affirmed that all human life has value and that life begins at conception. For this reason, abortion is opposed for personal or sociological purposes but may be necessary when pregnancy endangers the life of the mother.

The Fellowship of Grace Brethren Churches divided over the issue of whether *baptism could be only by trine immersion. The Old German Baptist Brethren experienced increasing affluence and higher standards of living. More comfortably furnished homes were accepted as compatible with simplicity, but use of the Internet was not permitted. Unacceptable influences in the public schools led many OGBB to *home schooling and establishing their own private schools. DEM

See also BIBLE; DISCIPLINE; EDUCATION; NONCONFORMITY; NONRESISTANCE; PEACE; SCIENCE; SEXUALITY, HUMAN; SIMPLE LIFE.

Minutes (BC) (1980–2000); Minutes (CB) (1980–2000); Minutes (DB) (1980–2000); Minutes (FGBC) (1980–2000); Minutes (OGBB) (1980–2000); Minutes (BC) (1980–2000); The Social Responsibilities Committee, comp., Brethren Positions of Social Issues (1991)..

Evangelicalism. The term *evangelical* has had long usage in Protestant circles. It was used originally to distinguish the *Lutheran Church, in its emphasis on the gospel, from the *Roman Catholic Church. However, it became more broadly applied during the 19th century in Europe and America to both individual denominations and associations of like-minded denominations. In some cases the term was used to continue the earlier emphasis on the gospel, vis-à-vis Roman Catholicism, but in other cases it enlarged its significance to include stress on *evangelism and a concern for cooperation among biblically-based denominations.

The term *Evangelicalism* came into common use only

during the 20th century, and, in the American setting, needs to be understood within the context of the liberal-fundamentalist controversy of the first decades of the century. Though fundamentalists had shown intellectual respectability in the publication of *The Fundamentals*, a 12-volume statement of conservative theology (1910–15), during the 1920s and 1930s they increasingly developed a militant and separatistic attitude and became quite critical of *higher education. This perspective eventually alienated many who otherwise were still committed to a conservative theological position.

Evangelicalism, as a self-conscious movement in America, had its origin in the early 1940s. The early leaders of evangelicalism sought to be identified not by their opposition to liberalism but by their commitment to a theologically conservative form of Christianity that would be intellectually respectable, evangelistically oriented, socially concerned, and cooperative in spirit. This vision led to the founding of the *National Association of Evangelicals (NAE) in 1942, Fuller Theol. Sem. in 1947, and the periodical *Christianity Today* in 1956. Important early leaders were Harold John Ockenga, Charles E. Fuller, Carl F. H. Henry, George Eldon Ladd, and Billy Graham. Reflective of the broad spectrum of churches that are aligned with evangelicalism is the composition of NAE. It includes denominations that, among others, are *Reformed, *Baptist, Wesleyan *Holiness, *Anabaptist, and *Pentecostal as well as groups influenced by the *charismatic movement.

*The Brethren Church was the first Brethren group to develop formal ties to Evangelicalism. This point is due to historical factors within the church that caused it to be wary of both liberalism and *fundamentalism. Church leaders around 1960 felt that the denomination, due to its limited resources, needed to develop associations with like-minded conservatives. These pragmatic, methodological, and theological concerns led the church to develop closer association with evangelicals in general and the NAE in particular. As a result, the *Brethren Evangelist* began carrying items from the Evangelical Press Association in 1960; the church in 1961 adopted the graded Sunday school curriculum of the evangelically-oriented Gospel Light Publication; by 1966 the *Missionary Board and Conference Peace Committee had become members of the corresponding agencies of the NAE; in 1967 General Conference voted to establish regular participating membership in NAE and urged individuals and congregations to do likewise; and in 1971 General Conference adopted a goal for local churches to become annual members of NAE. Many Brethren Church pastors and lay people receive *Christianity Today*; numerous pastors attend conferences and highlight social issues connected with evangelicalism; many members of the church listen to evangelical *radio programming. In addition, many leading evangelicals have spoken at General Conference and at *Ashland Theol. Seminary. The seminary identifies itself with the evangelical movement.

The *Fellowship of Grace Brethren Churches at its inception had close ties with the fundamentalist movement. However, by the late 1960s some leaders in the church began to associate more closely with evangelicalism. Since that time the denomination has come to view itself increasingly as evangelical in perspective. Though the denomination has never formally joined the NAE, some local congregations and individual members have. Openness to evangelicalism is reflected in the large number of pastors who read *Christianity Today* and the broad appeal among the membership of evangelical radio, literature, and conferences. Many members of the denomination identify with social issues that have been a priority for evangelicals, especially the pro-life movement and the *family. Speakers at the National Conference have frequently been identified with evangelicalism.

Reflective of the pluralistic nature of the *Church of the Brethren that has developed during the 20th century, evangelicalism, particularly since the mid-1970s, is one of several movements that has impacted the denomination. The sources of evangelical influence on the denomination are varied: the spiritual renewal connected with the charismatic movement; the desire to uphold a conservative, biblical theological perspective; and the commitment to *evangelism, church planting, church renewal, and church growth. Organizations and groups within the CB which have ties to evangelicalism are *Brethren Renewal Services, *Brethren Revival Fellowship, Brethren Evangelical Ministry Training Committee, Brethren Evangelical Leadership Foundation, *Concerns of the Grass Roots, and The Church's One Foundation. The short lived (1991–93) periodical, *Evangel 21*, published by Terry Hatfield, provided a voice and rallying point for evangelicals in the denomination. Some CB congregations are members of NAE, as are some individuals. The CB has also had observer status at the annual NAE convention, and the 1997 Annual Conference authorized the exploration of renewing observer status with NAE.

The *Dunkard Brethren have no formal affiliation with NAE, but the church has been influenced by evangelicalism, nonetheless, since the 1970s. This influence has come through some pastors reading *Christianity Today* and especially the impact of evangelical Christian radio on the members of the church. Both pastors and members would identify with issues such as the family and the pro-life movement that have been given high priority by the evangelical press.

The *Old German Baptist Brethren have no formal relationship with the evangelical movement. While some members would be in sympathy with certain emphases of evangelicalism, others have been critical of the movement because of its ties to politics, its general militaristic position, and its failure to take seriously separation from the world.

In summary, Brethren groups and individuals have been drawn to evangelicalism because of its strong commitment to Scripture, its evangelistic thrust, its concern for church planting and renewal, and its conservative perspective on social issues. Brethren who have reservations about the movement have noted its political overtones, its uncritical materialism, and its support of militarism. DRS

D. W. Dayton, *Discovering an Evangelical Heritage* (1976); G. M. Marsden, ed., *Evangelicalism and Modern America* (1984); L. I. Sweet, *The Evangelical Tradition in* America (1984); *Messenger* (Feb., 1992) 18–20; D. R. Stoffer, *Background and Development of Brethren Doctrines, 1650–1987* (1989), 237–38; D. F. Durnbaugh, *Fruit of the Vine* (1997), 575–78; C. F. Bowman, *Brethren Society* (1995), 411; *BLT* 32 (Summer, 1987) 148–53.

Evangelism. Most Brethren bodies demonstrated heightened interest in evangelism in the last two decades of the 20th century. In part, this stemmed from the influence of larger church culture (*Anabaptist, *evangelical, and mainline) which accented the need for renewed congregational outreach and vitality. Brethren impetus was evident,

as well. In 1987, Brethren theologian *Vernard Eller declared in *Proclaim Good Tidings* that: "Historically understood," evangelism "might even rate as the first and prior among traditional Brethren emphasis." Writing in this monograph, Eller pointed out that the Brethren movement was born as an evangelistic movement, coinciding with the birth of Protestant evangelism itself. In fact, Eller argued, ". . . the sixteenth-century forerunners of 'evangelism' and the sixteenth-century forerunners of [the Brethren] are the very same forerunners. . . ." Eller's research and bold assertion added new vigor to Brethren outreach efforts, along with inserting evangelism into a listing of Brethren core values.

New vigor was especially evident in efforts initiated by *The Brethren Church and *Church of the Brethren. In 1984, the CB launched a major new program entitled *Passing On the Promise*. Impacting over 200 congregations, the program was designed around a three-year covenantal process which encouraged congregations: to reach out in word and deed; to invite, welcome, and involve new people; and to grow in Christian *discipleship. Numerous program components were required, including: study curricula, study/action units, and a major training conference, the *Evangelism Leader's Academy (ELA). The ELA was a high visibility aspect of Passing On the Promise, involving over 10,000 persons in a ten-year period.

Shortly after the program's inception, The Brethren Church adopted the process, customizing it to fit its needs. The *General Conference Mennonite Church and *Mennonite Church took similar action, launching their efforts under the banner of "L.I.F.E." ("Living in Faithful Evangelism"). Emerging out of these joint efforts came the *Andrew Center in 1994, and its successor, *New Life Ministries, in 1998.

The *Dunkard Brethren also demonstrated renewed interest in evangelism over the last two decades. Particularly noteworthy was the *Africa Mission Project, a new thrust in foreign *mission. Initiated in 1995, this project grew out of interest from indigenous persons in Kenya, after reading The *Bible Monitor, the Dunkard Brethren periodical; in due time, the project also spread to Uganda. In the U.S., DB congregations expressed new interest in outreach as well. This was demonstrated in varied ways, as DB congregations reached out to neighbors through personal invitations and signs on church lawns promoting *revival meetings.

The *Fellowship of Grace Brethren Churches experienced major shifts in evangelism philosophy over the last two decades. A notable expression of this trend occurred as local churches were both encouraged and empowered to initiate new congregations. Prior to 1993, mission agencies had primary responsibility for starting new churches; when impetus shifted to congregations, new church starts nearly doubled in number. Another noteworthy trend among Grace Brethren included emphasis on cross-cultural church planting which brought new vigor to outreach efforts.

The *Old German Baptist Brethren continued their historic aversion to structured efforts in mission or evangelism. Though the denomination grew over the last two decades, there was no intentional growth effort. Rather, continued emphasis on life- style witness as the most valued expression of faith took place. PM

Personal interviews; personal information; S. Clapp, *Promising Results* (1993); V. Eller, *Proclaim Good Tidings* (1987); J. C. McKinnel, *Church Growth and the Brethren* (1979); C. W. Zunkel,

Church Growth Under Fire (1987) and *Dare To Grow: Building Healthy Churches* (1993); J. H. Lehman, *Thank God for New Churches!* (1984); B. M. Crouse, *Developing New Congregations in the Church of the Brethren* (1983) and *Releasing the Power* (1986); Andrew Center, *Evangelism: Good News or Bad News?* (1995); *Alive . . . '85! Program Guide: Evangelism and Church Growth in Action* (1985); *BLT* 35 (Summer, 1990) 186–232 (special issue), 36 (Summer, 1991) 135–238 (special issue), 39 (Summer, 1994) 210–21; *Evangel 21* (1991–93); *New Beginnings* (Jan., 1983ff.); *Messenger* (Nov., 1992) 14–17.

Everett, PA, Community Grace Brethren Church. In Dec. 1983, a group of 75 Grace Brethren gathered at the Everett Sportsmen's Club to discuss organizing a new Grace Brethren congregation in the Everett area. The group met again on Jan. 12, 1984, to vote on the question. The result was positive, and on Jan. 26, the new congregation chose to be called The Community Grace Brethren Church of Everett, PA. For the first month of its existence, the congregation gathered in the Raystown Ambulance Hall in Everett. Through much prayer and searching, church members eventually found a meeting hall owned by the Sani-Dairy Milk Company. After renting the facility for about 10 months, the church purchased the complex.

In Oct. 1984, Timothy Boal became the first pastor. In April 1987, ground was broken for a new facility. The building was completed and dedicated in March 1988. In Sept. 1990, the church called its first (and current) youth pastor, Lee Seese. Boal resigned in Feb. 1992 to accept the position of senior pastor at the *Penn Valley GBC in Telford, PA. Steven Jarrell served the congregation from 1992–95. In 1999 the pastor was Jeffrey Kyle Peeler, who came to the congregation from Portis, KS, in the summer of 1996. Membership in 2003 stood at 226, with Sunday worship services numbering ca. 250. JKP/JRY

Congregational records; *Annual (FGBC)* (1995ff.).

Faith Assembly, a small charismatic sect/cult located in Northern Indiana, founded in 1963 by Hobart Freeman (1920–84), who taught at *Grace Theol. Seminary. It began as "The New Testament Church at Winona." Freeman joined forces in 1972 with Mel Greider, a converted ex-convict and alcoholic, at the *Glory Barn* located east of North Webster, IN. Their meetings attracted a large number, including students from *Manchester College. In April 1978, conflict arose between Freeman and Greider, which led to their separation and the establishment of a fully independent ministry by Freeman, which became known as *Faith Assembly*.

The group met at several sites until completing a building at Wilmot, IN, that could seat 2,000. Its doctrines were basically evangelical and *charismatic, but with a very strong position on faith *healing that forbade its members to utilize medical care. Some reports claimed that as many as 100 children and adults died because of this restriction. The group was largely secluded from outside influences, and outsiders were not generally welcomed at its services. The ministry at Wilmot continued to operate into the 1990s, but then ceased activity. Small Faith Assembly groups still exist in the U.S. and England and are supported largely by the sale of audiotapes and books by Freeman. JJD

J. J. Davis, *Warsaw [IN] Times* (Sept., 1983) [a four-part series]; *The Goshen [IN] News* (Nov. 29, 2000); B. Barron, *The Health and Wealth Gospel* (1987); R. Nathan, *Charismatic Chaos* (1992) *passim*; D. F. Durnbaugh, "Freeman, Hobart (1920–1984)," *Dictionary*

of Christianity in America (1990) 453, and *Fruit of the Vine* (1997) 545–46; *Messenger* (April, 1987) 4; www.churches.kcon line.com/faithassembly (Oct., 2003) (contains address in Warsaw, IN, and a list of Freeman's audiotapes and publications).

*Farming in the year 2000 is rapidly becoming an occupation in which few Brethren can afford to engage. Economic depression in the *agricultural sector during the early 1980s forced many out of farming. Even so, many Brethren remain at least emotionally close to their rural heritage, and some remain actively involved in farming or related occupations. The *Old German Baptist Brethren probably retain closer "ties to the soil" than most other Brethren.

Farming as a full-time occupation in the year 2000 requires larger capital investments than most can afford. Depressed commodity prices have added to the difficulties. Even so, some Brethren have been ingenious in marketing their produce for a profit and live profitable, good lives on the farm. Some market seed, popcorn, meat, and other products nationwide, even worldwide.

Even as the trend toward larger farms continues, forcing many out of farming, there is a quiet undertow in the opposite direction. More persons in the past 20 years have chosen to live on small acreages, selling their produce in specialty organic food and other markets. They may subsidize their monetary needs with off-farm jobs.

What the future holds for Brethren engaged in farming, nobody knows. New biotechnologies may change the future in ways never even imagined in the year 2000. Some will still farm, some will continue to look back on farming nostalgically as a "good old days" way of life, but most Brethren will likely continue to find their occupations in areas other than farming. Even churches in rural areas may have few, if any, members who are farmers. LCN

P. L. Godwin, *Hope for the Family Farm* (1987); *Messenger* (July, 1984) 14–18, (July, 1985) 18–22, (July, 1986) 10–11, (March, 1990) 10.

Fellowship Church of the Brethren, WV, located five miles south of Martinsburg. The following pastors have served since Robert E. Alley left to become the pastor of the *Everett, PA, CB in October 1981: Mark B. Bowser (1982–83), Daniel S. Ringgold (1983–85), Jerry L. Wickline (1986–89), and Duane L. and Carol B. Strickler (1990–). The congregation built a parsonage in 1986; it was debt free by 1992. The present church note-burning was celebrated in 1995 on the 25th anniversary; an addition to the church was completed in 1993 to answer the need for Sunday school classes and office space. An Allen organ was purchased in May 1995, and a concert by the organist, Betty G. Miller, was held on May 5, 1996, to celebrate the retirement of the organ debt. Julie Sausser Miller from the congregation served as *BVS volunteer in Indianapolis, IN. Since it was founded in 1970, the congregation has never missed sending delegates to *Annual Conference, mid-Atlantic District Conference, and *National Youth Conference; and each year it has held Vacation Bible School as summer outreach. OAC
Congregational records.

*Fellowship of Grace Brethren Churches. The last two decades have been a period of unrest for the Fellowship of Grace Brethren Churches. Some years ago it was possible to write in extremely optimistic terms that the "FGBC appears to be the only Brethren group that is growing"

(*TBE* [1983], 488). However, by the end of the millennium its membership shrank from 42,023 (1981) in 19 districts to 28,446 (2000) in 24 districts. The problems that caused this decline were vaguely on the horizon over 20 years ago. Their genesis was found in the retirement of *Alva J. McClain and the leaders who had guided the movement since its inception in the 1930s. Most of these individuals were McClain's students and had gone through the troubled times at *Ashland Theol. Sem. and the early years of establishing *Grace Theol. Seminary.

During the same period that these men were lost to the church, new challenges had to be faced. One of these was caused by the success of the Fellowship in winning members from other evangelical traditions. A major problem with which the new generation of leadership was forced to struggle was what to do when individuals from non-Brethren groups who were satisfied with their own form of baptism and content with their observance of communion wished to join a Grace Brethren congregation. The solution was found in a revised method of accepting individuals into church membership. Passed at the National Conference in 1964, it indicated that all Grace Brethren congregations should continue to baptize by trine immersion but that "churches which receive members without triune immersion shall have their delegates seated in national conference with voting privileges on all matters except those involving the subject of water baptism in relation to church membership" (H. A. Kent, Sr., *Frontiers* [1972] 221).

Although there was continuing discussion about this decision, it was not until the 1980s that the subject was reopened with particular vigor. By 1989 an attempt was made to rescind the action of the 1964 national meeting, but it was defeated. By then there were two major positions advocated within the Fellowship. One of them was referred to as the "open" position which supported the 1964 decision, and the other as the "closed" view which wished to exclude non-triune immersed individuals from membership and to stop the practice of observing just the bread and the cup as the *communion service.

Some of the unrest within the Fellowship involved a revised set of bylaws which were brought to the National Conference in 1984. They included a statement of faith, a definition of membership, and provision for a 15-member Council or Board of Directors who would conduct the churches' business between the meetings of the National Conference. The Council was to consist of the moderator, moderator-elect, and the retiring moderator in addition to 12 members selected from the Western, Central, and Eastern geographical regions of the Fellowship. A report of a three-year study committee was also included to bring a resolution to the arguments between the two major factions in the church. They concluded: "that the words threefold communion only [would] be retained in our constitution as this clause best protects the perpetuation of the symbolic actions required by the New Treatment. (But) that the use of any part of the communion services for the purpose of teaching its doctrinal content is not in itself a violation of the FGBC constitution."

The committee also recommended that in FGBC churches the word "communion" be reserved exclusively for the threefold service, because it is our understanding that when the communion of the bread and cup is separated from the meal, it does not carry the same spiritual and symbolic impact as when it is joined together with the meal, and, therefore, is not that which fulfills what Christ

commanded to be perpetuated. If a church practices the Eucharist (the Bread and Cup) separately from the three-fold communion service, it must clearly teach that this does not fulfill the obligation of the believer to do what Jesus instituted and what the New Testament church practiced as communion. The motion to accept the study group's report was overwhelmingly accepted. Those who advocated a closed membership were not satisfied with this situation, and they found new targets for their discontent.

In 1986 there was also a change of leadership in the major incorporated bodies of the Brethren. John J. Davis became president of *Grace Schools, Larry N. Chamberlain took over as director of Home Missions, and *Thomas T. Julien assumed the role of director of Foreign Missions. In a memorable moderator's address at the 1987 conference, Julien, citing Alva McClain's remarks to the national meeting of 1930, challenged the group to move on from the argument over triune immersion and the ordinances, so that the Fellowship might focus on reaching a lost and needy world with the Word of God. Already suspect by conservatives, his message did little to calm their fears. What he argued for was a more open "evangelical" approach to others in contrast to the fundamentalist outlook of the conservatives. As the earlier struggles with liberals and modernists were won by the fundamentalists, many of them became more self-confident and abandoned their extreme rigidity. These individuals usually took the open view of church membership, but they were resisted by those who insisted on methods and a spiritual outlook more suitable for an earlier era. Julien called for the Fellowship Council of the church to present to the National Conference a fully developed outreach strategy for the FGBC that would give it direction for the last decade of the 20th century. It was to include a clear statement of Brethren identity, purpose, and goals. The majority of those in attendance were pleased with his presentation, because years of rather sterile debate over *baptism and communion had overshadowed the devotional agenda of the conferences. Julien's challenge was answered at the National Conference of 1989 when the so-called "Master Plan of the FGBC" was presented. John J. Davis was the moderator that year.

The controversy over the membership issue came to an open debate on the conference floor. The motion was made that the 1964 decision be rewritten to state that no congregation could belong to the FGBC unless it required triune immersion of all its members except for those with medical problems. A substitute motion softened the first motion and allowed those baptized by immersion and received into membership prior to 1989 to continue as church members. This motion was defeated by a three-to-one vote. Further study was recommended.

Perhaps a compromise might have been reached except for the leadership of some older Brethren including *John C. Whitcomb, *James L. Boyer and *John W. Zielasko. Of these three, the most important was Whitcomb, who had been professor of Old Testament, Hebrew, and Apologetics at Grace Theol. Sem. for almost four decades. Although he seized upon the issue of triune immersion baptism, there were deeper problems bothering Whitcomb. His emphasis on apologetics and flood geology led him to stress the idea of separation from the world. This included not only separation from liberals or those with ties to the *ecumenical movement but also from conservatives who cooperated with them. Often

called "second-degree separation," the teaching was too extreme for many Grace Brethren. Due to his insistence on issues such as this, his colleagues at Grace Sem. found it increasingly difficult to work with him. Consequently, in 1990 Whitcomb was suspended from his duties at the seminary and was given early retirement. The ensuing turmoil in the denomination also had its impact on the seminary, which underwent drastic reorganization in the early 1990s.

FORMATION OF THE CONSERVATIVE GRACE BRETHREN CHURCHES INTERNATIONAL. During the same year (1990) the Conservative Grace Brethren Association was formed. The group included several older FGBC pastors as well as younger individuals. When the 1992 National Conference voted to reaffirm the open church membership policy, the conservatives withdrew from the conference and announced a meeting at the Winona Lake Presbyterian Church to form a new denomination. The new group stated that the issues dividing them from the main body went deeper than the baptism-membership controversy. They included the tendencies towards denominationalism as expressed by a Fellowship Council of representatives of the church that met more frequently than the national conference. They also condemned the toleration of open membership churches by both Foreign and Home Missionary Councils. Developments at Grace Schools also troubled them, especially the acceptance of those on the faculty and board who did not insist on triune immersion. However, their most serious accusation against the Brethren was "a new way of interpreting Scripture [which] looks at truth with a subjective eye and seeks to divide God's Word into levels of certainty or clarity."

The new group set up an organization, elected several committees, and agreed to a three-year transition period during which conservative congregations could belong to both the FGBC and the new *Conservative Grace Brethren Churches International. They needed time to complete their organization and to convince their congregations to leave the Winona Lake group. They also expressed problems over finances and the debt owed by many churches to the Grace Brethren Investment Foundation. (This group was organized by the *Brethren Home Missions Council to finance churches which experienced difficulty obtaining commercial loans. If such churches left the brotherhood before they had paid their loans, they would forfeit their buildings.)

The conservatives have continued their existence in a loose association of congregations which functions through a series of "protocols." In common with other Brethren groups, they have *national conferences. Because their churches are mostly located in the Middle West and Pennsylvania, these conferences have met in Indianapolis, Toledo, Knoxville, and Pittsburgh. In addition to the conference officers, there are unincorporated bodies including a College of Pastors, a Foreign Mission Association, and a U.S. Home Mission Society. It is difficult to estimate how many congregations will eventually leave the Winona Lake group to join the conservatives, although it seems that their initial success has begun to wane. In addition to those lost to the Conservative Grace Brethren, several important church leaders and churches left the Fellowship to become independent or to join other denominations.

Reorganization of the FGBC occurred to deal with these losses and to establish a new sense of vision and "belonging" for the Grace Brethren. The leaders of the

national organizations such as Home Missions, Foreign Missions, and Grace Schools organized a series of "Focus" (Regional) retreats for church pastors. They were first held in 1993. During 1994 when the moderator, *Robert D. Fetterhoff, had the opportunity to travel throughout the country and visit most of the retreats, more than half of the pastors of the Fellowship attended. The comments that they made about the retreats were very enthusiastic. The *love feasts that were held and the extensive periods devoted to programs based upon the letter to the Ephesians were especially helpful. They felt that they had shared a vision of what the church could be, that is to see it from God's standpoint rather than the "underside" with which they were usually forced to deal.

Another encouraging development during the 1990s was the growth of *Christian education or *youth ministries under the leadership of Edward A. Lewis. By 1999 there were over 2,000 young people in attendance at their summer rallies held at the same time as the national conferences. In another development, also in the 1990s, the church periodical, *Brethren Missionary Herald*, was discontinued and, somewhat later, *FGBC: The Electronic Newsletter of the Fellowship of Grace Brethren Churches* was introduced as an online resource.

Other successful innovations included the GO (Global Opportunities) teams consisting of short term groups (usually two weeks) working in a cross-cultural setting. Adults of all ages and backgrounds provided strategic assistance in beginning new congregations in areas where the Grace Brethren had been active for a long time. In 1993 two teams went out, but the number grew rapidly, until by the end of the decade 20 teams consisting of 626 people participated in short-term missions. By 1994 Charis International, a global network of Grace Brethren leaders working together to encourage the creation and development of indigenous missionary initiatives, was founded. The first meeting was held at the *Chateau de Saint Albain in France. It was agreed that these encounters should be held every three years and, to signify this internationalization of the Fellowship, the Missionary Society was renamed *Grace Brethren International Missions* (GBIM). To accompany this change, the home mission work was renamed *Grace Brethren North American Missions* (GBNAM) and began to focus on evangelizing inner cities and *minority groups in America.

In 1994 the new evangelical and ecumenical outreach of the Fellowship was further demonstrated when the FGBC became a part of *AD 2000 and Beyond,* a collaborative effort by a number of Christian denominations and mission organizations to make disciples of every human community on earth. This took Brethren missionaries to some of the most culturally unique places on earth such as Cambodia, Thailand, Viet Nam, Kyrgyzstan, and *Turkey, as well as to groups such as the Pygmies and Fulani in *Africa.

By 1999 a full-time Fellowship coordinator was hired to work with the officers of the conference and the leaders of the principal national organizations. During the National Conference in 2000 at Winona Lake, IN, the 100th anniversary celebration of GBIM was held. An emphasis was placed upon representatives of indigenous churches who were in attendance at the meeting. Three Pygmies attended to represent the newest group reached with the gospel. Hispanic, African American, and Asiatic Brethren from North America were also represented.

It seemed to be the fulfillment of a previous moderator's address as the Fellowship was on the threshold of a new day of achievement. Julien commented on the great diversity that he had seen in the church and then he stated rather prophetically (in 1987): "Diversity and disunity are not to be confused. Scriptures do not demand uniformity of opinion in order to have a Fellowship. I for one do not fear diversity within our Fellowship" (T. T. Julien, *Annual (FGBC)* [1988] 9–10). In the 21st century, the challenge for the FGBC is to resume the pattern of growth that seemed to be characteristic of the Fellowship two decades ago. RGC

See also BAPTISM; EVOLUTION; POLITY.

Annual (FGBC) (1981–98); *Handbook (FGBC)* (1999ff.); R. G. Clouse, "Changes and Partings: Division in the Progressive/Grace Brethren Church," *BLT* 42 (Summer/Fall, 1992) 180–98; H. A. Kent, Sr., *Frontiers* (1972); D. Plaster, *Finding our Focus: A History of the Grace Brethren Church* (2004).

Feminism, Impact of. Most Brethren bodies support traditional views of the role of *women in church organizations, so that feminism has had its greatest impact within the *Church of the Brethren. Hints of feminism within the German Baptist Brethren (after 1908 known as the Church of the Brethren) appeared in 1885 with *Annual Meeting's authorization of organized *women's work. But women's commitment to their own empowerment began earlier than that. In 1835, *Sarah Righter Major (1808–84), responding to a 1834 Annual Meeting concern regarding "a sister's preaching," questioned the inconsistency in the church of lauding the apostle Paul for laying hands on both men and women, then quenching the gift of the Holy Spirit to preach if received by a woman. Grounded in this earlier spirit of empowerment, the *Womaen's (*a* for each wom*a*n and *e* for all wom*e*n) Caucus (CB) is considered to be the starting point of an active, committed, and ongoing feminist movement within the denomination.

At the 1970 Annual Conference in Lincoln, NE, a group of women caucused over their concern that the CB had not acted on its doctrine of equal dignity and rights. Carole Zeigler and Nancy J. Peters (Lamia) subsequently presented a resolution to *Standing Committee requesting the formation of a committee on women's equality in the church, which Annual Conference approved. (Members of the study committee were: Donna F. Forbes (Steiner), Ruth S. Hogan, Eldon L. Morehouse (replaced by *Paul W. Keller), Nancy J. Peters, and *Duane H. Ramsey.) In 1971 at Annual Conference in St. Petersburg, FL, feminist theologian Nell Morton led an inspirational and empowering all-day meeting regarding women's historical and potential role in the church, giving needed impetus for further work. The *Equality for Women* paper was presented and approved at the *General Board meeting in the spring of 1972. The following year, another all-day event at Annual Conference in Fresno, CA, concluded with the formal establishment of the Womaen's Caucus. Mary Cline Detrick and Mary Blocher Smeltzer were the first conveners of the caucus. In 1976 a half-time position on "person awareness" was created on the Elgin staff, with Beth Glick-Reiman (until 1978) and then Mary Cline Detrick and Ralph Detrick filling the position. Beginning in 1977 a series of conferences focusing on women's issues was held by the CB.

The mission of Womaen's Caucus calls for the naming and elimination of the inequalities derived from sexism, racism, homophobia, and other oppressive structures that compromise the dignity of persons; they also asked for

opportunities for women to claim their authority as theologians and church leaders. This has been met with various responses, from gratitude to hostility, the latter sometimes leading to silencing (by the refusal to ordain, appoint to leadership, or, in some cases, acknowledge the prophetic vision of congregations or church-related groups). The Caucus advocated the securing of child care facilities at Annual Conference, lobbied for the adoption of the *Equality for Women* paper," called for the use of inclusive *language, and pushed for the consideration of a *name change for the CB, among many other concerns. In the late 1990s, the commitment to collaborate with others dedicated to social transformation and justice led Womaen's Caucus to form liaison relationships with the CB *Global Women's Project and the *Brethren/Mennonite Council for Gay and Lesbian Concerns.

At many levels, the feminist movement within the church has encouraged church leaders to seriously consider the above issues. The results of feminism have slowly become visible as more women are placed in positions of leadership in business, worship, and other settings, and consequently are speaking with a sense of authority and self-confidence. The backlash is equally visible, instigated by those in the denomination who do not feel called to struggle deeply with the questions of mutuality and equality, and who are threatened by those who do. Despite this backlash, as more women and men feel the call of the Spirit toward wholeness and full potential, the movement continues to grow and to flourish. DKRo

P. Brubaker, *She Hath Done What She Could* (1985), index; *Minutes* (CB) (1970–74), 72–73; *Womaen's Caucus Brochure* (1997); *Femailings* (1971ff., newsletter of the Womaen's Caucus); D. F. Durnbaugh, *Fruit of the Vine* (1997) 546–48; C. F. Bowman, *Brethren Society* 1995), 405, 410; *BLT* 30 (Fall, 1996) 231–36.

Fetterhoff, Dean (FGBC), b. 1930, evangelist, pastor, administrator. Born in Lafayette, IN, Fetterhoff was converted to Christianity in his teens and graduated from Bob Jones U. (1952) and *Grace Theol. Sem. (1955). He then entered full-time evangelistic ministry with the National Board of Evangelism until 1960. During 1960–63, he was involved in mission work in Chicago.

Fetterhoff served as pastor of the *Wheaton, IL, GBC (1963–67) and then as business administrator of Wheaton Christian Grammar School (1967–73) with permission to take time from his administrative activities to lead evangelistic meetings. In 1973 Fetterhoff began an extended ministry at the *Marietta, GA, GBC of Greater Atlanta, serving as pastor until 1996 and then continuing as pastor of missions and seniors. Fetterhoff began a long term of service on the GBFMB in 1962 and was moderator of the *FGBC in 1987–88. RTC

Personal information; *Annual* (*FGBC*) (1964ff.).

Fike, Earle William, Jr. (CB), b. 1930, pastor, denominational executive, teacher, author. Son of Earle W. and Hannah Myers Fike, Earle Fike was raised in the home of Joseph and Dove Miller following his mother's death in 1938. He married Jean F. Kiser in 1949; they are the parents of three children: Joseph, Dwynn, and Jon. Fike was licensed to the ministry in 1948 in the *Linville Creek (VA) congregation and ordained an elder in 1955 at Meyersdale, PA.

Fike attended *Bridgewater College (BA, 1951) and *Bethany Theol. Sem. (BD, 1954; ThM, 1964). Bridgewater College awarded him an honorary degree (DHL,

1972) in recognition of his life devoted to ministry and further honored him by naming him as a distinguished alumnus (1982) and to the Athletic Hall of Fame (1997).

Earle Fike pastored several congregations: *Meyersdale, PA, CB (1954–57); *Chicago, IL, First CB (1957–63); *Elizabethtown, PA, CB (1978–87); and *Huntingdon, PA, Stone CB (1987–92). He also served as associate general secretary of the CB *General Board (1969–78). His creativity and special interest in *preaching and *worship found unique expression in teaching homiletics at Bethany Theol. Sem. (1964–69) and as writer and preacher for the nationally-broadcast radio series *Think About It* (1979–82). He was president of the Brethren Journal Association (1965–68).

In addition to acting as moderator of Annual Conference (1982), Fike served as a member of several boards, including the General Board, *Bethany Hospital, *Juniata College, and Bethany Theol. Sem. (chair, 1996–99). He was staff editor for the *Pastor's Manual* (1977) and chair of the committees for the 1964 and 1992 denominational manuals. Fike authored *A Raspberry Seed Under God's Dentures*, *Please Pray With Me*, and *A Month of Sundays* as well as numerous articles for periodicals. FMBo

Messenger (Feb., 1982) 19–23; *CB Yearbook* (1951–2002); F. F. Wayland, *Bridgewater College* (1993) index; personal interview.

Fike, Paul Henry (CB), pastor, churchman, chaplain. Born in 1918, a son of Albert J. and Sallie Fike, Paul Fike graduated from *Manchester College (BS, 1947) and *Bethany Theol. Sem. (BD, 1950). He served at the *Wabash, IN, CB (1945–47), and the *Edgewood, *Sams Creek, and *Beaver Dam congregations in Maryland (1950–53) where he was ordained as elder in 1952; he also pastored at *Cloverdale, VA, (1953–62); *Pleasant Valley, VA, (1962–73); and *East Chippewa, OH, (1973–85). He worked with youth in church *camps at the local, district, and national levels, and served as moderator of the First Virginia (1956), Second Virginia (1966), and Northern Ohio (1979) districts. Fike was a member of the *General Board and was moderator of *Annual Conference in 1984. After retirement, he served as chaplain at the *Bridgewater Home, VA, (1985–2001). He married Ella Mae Forney of Pennsylvania; they had two children: Jo Ellen Fike Bowman and David A. Fike. EFB

Messenger (May, 1984) 16–19; *Virginia* (1973) 258, 263, 279, 307, 316.

Filbrun, Stanley Clarence (OGBB), b. 1924, minister. A direct descendant of Johann Peter Filbrun who immigrated to North America in 1818, Stanley Filbrun was born near Fullerton, CA, within the bounds of the *New River district. His parents, Clarence and Bertha Churchbaugh Filbrun, moved with their family to Modesto, CA, in 1936. During *World War II he served as a *conscientious objector in *Civilian Public Service as a timber surveyor and fire fighter under the auspices of the U.S. Forest Service. He was called to the ministry on April 5, 1956, in the OGBB *Modesto district and to the eldership in 1964. He became a charter member of the *Tuolumne district in 1957 and served 28 years there as elder-in-charge, as well as five years (1971–76) as a nonresident elder of the *Olive Grove congregation, Ripon, CA. He has served on the *Standing Committee of Annual Meeting since 1978. He and his wife, Wilma Lucille Kinzie Filbrun, have three children, one living in Pennsylvania and two in

California. GCF

Vindicator (May, 1956) 154; *Minutes* (*OGBB*) (1956–2000); *Old Order Notes* No. 4 (Spring, 1981) 23.

Flora, Joseph E. (DB), 1922–93, minister, farmer, implement dealer. The son of Josiah and Sarah Jamison Flora, Joseph Flora was born on July 14 in Quinter, KS. He was baptized into the *Dunkard Brethren Church in 1936, and married Arlene Surbey of Stark County, OH, on March 3, 1942. Flora was called into the deacon's office at Quinter in 1943 and moved to Dallas County, IA, in 1944. He was installed into the ministry at Dallas Center, IA, in Sept. 1947 and ordained into the eldership on April 14, 1969. He became the presiding elder of the Dallas Center Congregation in 1970 and served in that capacity until his death.

Flora held numerous *revival meetings throughout the brotherhood, served on the *General Mission Board, and served three terms as moderator of *General Conference. He was instrumental in helping to establish the Dallas Center Christian School, and served as its administrator until his sudden death due to heart failure on Nov. 4, 1993. RSL

Bible Monitor (Jan. 15, 1994) 11–12.

Wendell and Marie Flory. Marie Flory collection.

Flory, Wendell Phillips and Marie Sarah Mason (CB) were married on June 5, 1945. Wendell Flory (1920–2003) was born in Pingding, Shanxi Province, *China, where his parents, Byron Morton and Nora Almira Phillips Flory, were *Church of the Brethren missionaries. The Flory family returned to the U.S. in 1932. Wendell Flory graduated from *Bridgewater College (BA, 1940) and *Bethany Bibl. Sem. (BD, 1943; DMin, 1977). Flory served in 1943–44 as the founding pastor of the *Dundalk, MD, CB. He studied Chinese language at Yale U. (MA, 1946) and after *World War II served as a missionary in China (1946–49). Marie Mason was born in 1922, the daughter of Russell and Mary Zigler Mason; she graduated from Bridgewater College (BA, 1945), married Wendell Flory, and studied Chinese language at Yale U.

(1945–46). She then joined her husband, who had preceded her to China by one year. Their first child, Theodore Wendell, was born in China.

When the China mission field closed in 1949 because of the Communist takeover of the country, the Flory family returned to the U.S. where Wendell served with the CB *Foreign Mission Office in Elgin, IL, (1949–52). The Florys' second son, Philip Earl, was born during this time. In 1952–58 the Florys served as missionaries in Gujarat, *India; two daughters, Janet Ruth and Mary Joann, were born there. The family was forced to return to the U.S. due to illness, particularly that of Marie.

Wendell Flory held CB pastorates in *Charlottesville, VA (1958–63), *Waynesboro, VA (1963–72), *Flower Hill in Gaithersburg, MD (1972–78), and *Easton, MD (1978–85). Marie Flory obtained special education certification and taught public school at the elementary and intermediate levels. In retirement, the Florys resided in Bridgewater, VA, where he served as half-time director of church relations at Bridgewater College. He also held interim pastorates at Flower Hill, MD; Easton, MD; *Middle River, VA; and *Mt. Vernon, VA. Wendell served the church in many capacities at the brotherhood, district, and local levels. He was a member of the *General Board, of the Annual Conference committee on mission philosophy, and of the committee to review the relationship between the India Brethren and the CB. The Florys also conducted travel tours to China in 1983, 1986, 1988, 1989, and 1992. DVU

See also INDIA, CHURCH OF NORTH.

W. Flory, "My Life from China to Heaven: An Autobiography" (unpubl.), *Brethren Missions in India* (1955), (with H. E. Sollenberger), "History of the UNRRA Brethren Service Unit [in China]" (1948) mimeographed; *Prayer for Missions* (1949) 68–69; *Missionary Visitor* (Oct., 1917) 272–73 (on parents); *BLT* 11 (Autumn, 1966) 33–48; *GM* (March 2, 1946) 19; *Messenger* (Jan. 15, 1970) 10–11; E. M. Wampler, *China Suffers, Or My Six Years of Work During the Incident* (1945) passim, and *Seeking God's Will for Me: An Autobiography* (1969) passim; *Virginia* (1973) 262, 273, 346, 382, 400; F. F. Wayland, *Bridgewater College* (1993) index; A. D. Satvedi, "History of the Church of the Brethren in India, 1894–1993," DMin thesis, Bethany Theol. Sem. (1993) 146.

Fort Seybert, WV, Bethlehem Fellowship (CB), Pendleton Co., was one of eight meetinghouses in the *South Fork congregation. In 1983, Bethlehem and Mount Carmel, the last remaining meetinghouses, disorganized the South Fork congregation and became separate fellowships. Bethlehem reported 32 members in 2000 and retained fellowship status. SRS

See also MOUNT CARMEL (CB).

Forum for Religious Studies, sponsored by *Bridgewater College, VA, promotes the study of historical and contemporary *Anabaptism with an emphasis on Brethren issues. Events organized by the Forum typically mix scholarly papers by professional historians, theologians, and sociologists with contemporary applications by pastors and laypersons. The Forum's conferences attract academics, pastors, and laity and include representatives from wider Anabaptism in addition to the six Brethren bodies. The Forum's first major conference, "Brethren in Transition" (1991), provided Brethren scholars with an opportunity to consider the *Church of the Brethren's crisis over declining *membership. Later conferences examined the relevance of traditional Anabaptism for the 21st century (1993), *spirituality among Anabaptists (1995), and

Brethren nonviolence (2003). The Forum also hosted a *Festschrift* in honor of D. F. Durnbaugh (1997), co-sponsored with **Brethren Life and Thought*. Bridgewater College faculty members comprise the Forum's membership. SLL

E. F. Bittinger, ed., *Brethren in Transition: 20th Century Directions and Dilemmas* (1992); C. F. Bowman and S. L. Longenecker, eds., *Anabaptist Currents: History in Conversation with the Present* (1995); S. L. Longenecker, ed., *The Dilemma of Anabaptist Piety: Strengthening or Straining the Bond of Community* (1997); D. B. Eller, ed., "From Age to Age: Historians and the Modern Church," *BLT* 42 [42] (Summer/Fall, 1997) iii–xiii, 1–296; S. L. Longenecker, "Brethren and the End Times," *BLT* 46 (Winter/Spring, 2001).

*Fraktur. Since the earlier article on *Fraktur* was written, new information has come to light concerning direct Brethren involvement in the art. (All scholars agree that the work of the related *Ephrata Society marked a high point of *Fraktur* artistry.) Examples from *Pennsylvania to *Virginia have been identified, for example the handsome bookplate (1816) in the hymnal of Dunker leader *John Kline and the religious rhyme of Anna Singer (1805) produced in a Brethren school in Shenandoah Co.: "Dunkers or German Baptist Brethren, who migrated to Virginia after the Revolutionary War, perpetuated *Fraktur* through their simple schools" (Wust). The 19th-century leader *Christian Hervey Balsbaugh produced many *Fraktur* drawings in a variety of formats. A number of *Fraktur* pieces have been preserved from the Brethren side of the extensive *Langeneker/Longenecker family of Pennsylvania, as well as from the extended *Kassel/Cassel family. Printers related to the Brethren such as the *Sala family of Ohio produced broadside *Fraktur* for completion by itinerant scribes. Quite recently, the work of Isaac Clarence Kulp, Jr., of Harleysville, PA, has received attention. The topic continues to be one requiring extensive research. DFD

K. Wust, *Virginia Fraktur: Penmanship as Folk Art* (1972), 4–5, 9; R. Cryer, ed., *Longenecker Family Newsletter* 2 (March/April, 2000); K. Stopp, *The Printed Birth and Baptismal Certificates of the German Americans* (1995–1999), 2: 98–107, 5: 114–25, 200; B. B. Garvan, *The Pennsylvania German Collection* (1982, repr. 1999); B. B. Garvan and C. F. Hummel, *The Pennsylvania Germans: A Celebration of Their Arts, 1683–1850* (1982); P. Conner and J. Roberts, *Pennsylvania German Fraktur and Printed Broadsides* (1988); R. Earnest and C. Earnest, ". . . A New Look at Motifs on American Fraktur," *Folkart* 25 (Winter, 2000/01) 44–53.

Frederick, MD, Grace Brethren Church. In Dec. 1978, the Frederick congregation began as a Bible study meeting in private homes. In the fall of 1980, the group acquired the use of the Gambril Park Church for Sunday services. The congregation grew to more than 40 persons and decided to move its services to the Holiday Inn in Frederick. Jeffrey Thornley, associate pastor at the *Temple Hills GBC, led the group from 1979 until 1981. Larry Humberd, associate pastor at the *Hagerstown GBC, served 1981–83. Warren E. Tamkin became the first full-time pastor in 1983. A five-acre plot of ground was

Fraktur bookplate in Elder John Kline's hymnal. Collection of the Alexander Mack Memorial Library, Bridgewater College.

during his tenure. R. Dallas Greene became the pastor in June 1985, and plans progressed for the construction of a church building. The facility was completed and the first services were held on Easter Sunday morning 1988. Several part-time associate pastors have served the congregation: Thomas Mahaffey, Duke Jeffries, and Aaron Wolfe. In 1995 Michael P. Brubaker became the first full-time associate pastor. On its 10th anniversary in 1988, the congregation liquidated its initial debt of $500,000. It is currently looking forward to building a larger facility in order to accommodate its growing ministries. RDGr/MPBr/JRY

Congregational records; *Annual* (*FGBC*) (1980–98).

G-H

Zella J. Galagen. Photo by Stewart B. Kauffman.

Gahagen, Zella Johns (CB), 1899–1984. The daughter of Ord and Ida Wechtenhiser Johns, Zella Gahagen lived in Somerset Co., PA. She attended the Brethren Normal College, Huntingdon, PA (*Juniata College) for one year, taught in a one-room school, and then became a bookkeeper for a coal mining company in the area. In 1923 she married Clarence (Kern) Gahagen, the owner of several mines. Clarence Gehagen died in 1951, after which his widow owned and operated the mines, selling them in 1981. Zella Gahagen, a member of the *Scalp Level congregation, Windber, had a strong stewardship perspective. Through her will she made gifts to individuals, but the bulk of her estate of ca. $7,400,000 went into the Gahagen Charitable Foundation, which benefitted the CB *General Board, Brethren Homes for the Aging, *Elizabethtown and Juniata Colleges, and New Day Incorporated of Johnstown. SBK

S. B. Kauffman, *Zella's Mountain* (1999).

Garver, Earl Simeon (CB), educator. Born in 1911 in Youngstown, OH, he was the son of David Newton and Martha Longenecker Garver. Earl S. Garver graduated from *Manchester College (BA, 1933) and Yale U. (PhD, 1943), with later graduate study at Harvard U. and the U. of Chicago. He taught American history at the Boardman School in Youngstown (1933–38) and economics at Trinity College, CT (1941–42). During *World War II, he participated in *Civilian Public Service (1943–46), assigned to four different camps in Pennsylvania, Virginia, and Michigan, in three of which he was the director. In 1946 he became an associate professor of economics at Manchester College, rising to full professor and academic dean in 1950 and serving until his death in March 1968. In the next year the college named a residence hall in his honor.

Garver coauthored a book, *Puerto Rico: Unsolved Problem* (1945) and contributed chapters to the text *An Introduction to Modern Economics* (1952). In the summer of 1950 he directed a peace seminar in Vienna for the *Brethren Service Commission. He was a member of the *General Brotherhood Board (CB), a trustee of *Bethany Brethren Hospital, and a commissioner on labor/management relations for the *National Council of Churches. Garver drafted the proposal that led to the inception of the *Brethren Colleges Abroad program, of which he was the first administrative coordinator. His wife was Winifred Sheppard Garver; they had three children. DFD

NSBRO, *Directory of Civilian Public Service, May, 1941 to March, 1947* (1947) x–xi, xiv–xv, 47; T. K. Jones, *Manchester College: A Century of Faith, Learning, and Service* (1989) 121, 122, 127, 128, 158, 177; *[Manchester College] Alumni Directory 2000* (2000) 128; J. K. Kreider, *A Cup of Cold Water: The Story of Brethren Service* (2001) 125; *GM* (Dec. 9, 1950) 18–19; *Messenger* (April 11, 1968) 30; L. Eisan, *Pathways of Peace* (1948) 107; H. Hogan, *Gladdys E. Muir* (1998) 47; biographical materials, Manchester College Archives.

Geisert, Wayne F. (CB), b. 1921, educator, churchman. Son of Fred J. and Martha Lauer Geisert, Wayne Geisert was born near Abilene, KS, on Dec. 20. He married Ellen Maurine Gish in 1944; they are the parents of three sons: Gregory Wayne, Bradley Kent, and Todd Wilfred. A graduate of *McPherson College (AB, 1944) and Northwestern U. (PhD, 1951), Geisert taught at Kendall College (1948–50), *Manchester College (1951–57), and he was academic dean and professor of economics at McPherson College (1957–64). From 1964 to 1994, Geisert served as president of *Bridgewater College. He was *Annual Conference moderator (1973–74), member of the *General

Wayne F. Geisert. Bridgewater College collection.

Board (1977–82), chair of the *Pension Board (1979–82) of the *General Services Commission (1979–82). Geisert holds honorary doctorates from Manchester College (1987), Bridgewater College (1993), and James Madison U. (1992), and a residence hall at Bridgewater College was named in his honor. PCS

See also HIGHER EDUCATION.

Who's Who in America (1988–89), 1104; F. F. Wayland, *Bridgewater College: The First Hundred Years, 1880–1980* (1993), esp. 569–71; T. K. Jones, *Manchester College* (1989), 237; *Messenger* (May, 1974) 20–22.

*Genealogy. Growing interest in geneology in general as well as in Brethren genealogy has produced many new resources and developments since 1980. These include publishing numerous new Brethren genealogies, new family-inclusive district church histories, a broad range of genealogy resource materials, and continuing publication of a quarterly newsletter of the *Fellowship of Brethren Genealogists (FOBG), which took a new name, *Brethren Roots,* in 1998. *Old Order Notes* (OGBB) continued to include a genealogical forum in its format. An earlier Brethren newsletter, *Brethren Roots and Branches,* published (1976–88) in southern Pennsylvania, has been discontinued. The most significant recent development is the explosion of genealogical information on the Internet.

While Brethren and *Mennonite college libraries, along with county libraries and archives, have continued rapidly to accumulate materials relating to genealogy, certain more specialized libraries are being recognized. The *Brethren Library and Archives (BHLA) at Elgin, IL, and the Lancaster, PA, Mennonite Historical Society Library are now primary resources for published family histories, resource books, and archival materials about families of German origin. Many county historical libraries are increasingly accumulating localized family history materials and resources. Both the BHLA (600 genealogies) and the Lancaster Mennonite Library (several thousand genealogies) periodically publish lists of family history holdings which they have acquired.

Older congregational and district histories by *J. E. Blough, H. A. Cooper, *J. M. Henry, and *R. E. Sappington, along with *Pennsylvania district histories, continue to be consulted as major source materials. More recently, genealogical studies have contributed to church history. Incorporating a genealogical method, *Allegheny Passage* by E. F. Bittinger, a book about the congregations of *West Virginia and Western *Maryland, identified early Brethren communities in West Virginia by tracing the *migration of their settlers from established older Brethren congregations in Pennsylvania and Maryland. Their continuing Brethren identity was confirmed by tracing their migrations on westward from West Virginia into Brethren communities in *Ohio, *Kentucky, *Indiana, and *Illinois. The CB history of southern Ohio (in preparation) utilizes a similar focus on migrating Brethren families. The study of the patterns of Brethren migration continues.

The indexing of *cemetery records by concerned individuals has begun, and some have already been published in the FOBG Newsletter, the *Roots and Branches* newsletters, and other periodicals. Indexing of obituaries published in The *Vindicator* (OGBB), in The *Gospel Visitor* (GBB), in The *Gospel Messenger* (GBB/CB), and in The *Christian Family Companion* (GBB) has been completed. Some obituaries from The *Primitive Christian* (GBB) have been published in the *FOBG Newsletter.* The *Mennonite Family History* quarterly welcomes and frequently publishes articles on Brethren families.

The number of genealogical data bases and family Web sites has grown astronomically in recent years. A few are devoted principally to Brethren genealogical interests, but thousands of family Web sites and data bases are now accessible. Census data, courthouse records, tax lists, etc. are rapidly coming on line. The family historian, whether amateur or professional, now has easy access to valuable data that was previously available only through much effort and expense. EFB

E. F. Bittinger, *Allegheny Passage* (1990); *W. Pennsylvania* (1916); H. A. Cooper, *Two Centuries of Brothersvalley* (1962), *The Church [Brownsville, MD] in the Valley* (1993), and *The Church [Locust Grove CB] of the Singing Hills* (1988); *S. Pennsylvania* (1941); *Maryland* (1936); *E. Pennsylvania* (1915); *Snake River* (1966); *Virginia* (1973); *Carolinas* (1971); Southern Ohio District Historical Committee, *History of the Church of the Brethren in Southern Ohio* (forthcoming); *BLT* 34 (Summer, 1989) 131–89 (special issue).

Germantown Trust was formed in 1982 by the *General Board (CB), and trustees were appointed to maintain the property of the *Philadelphia, PA, Germantown CB as a Brethren *historic site and a place of *worship. Earlier in 1964 ownership of the property had been transferred to the General Board because the congregation was no longer able to care for the meetinghouse and cemetery. Trustees are designated by the General Board, the Atlantic Northeast District (CB), the Germantown congregation, and other Brethren bodies that consider Germantown a historic site. Funds are provided by Brethren groups and individuals and by other interested groups and individuals. Examples of major projects include a new heating system, roof work, masonry repair of the cemetery wall, and a historical display. KMS, Jr.

General Board (CB) (1982ff.)

Germantown Church of the Brethren and pastor Richard Kyerematen. BHLA collection.

The Germantown Historical Museum

Germantown, the first congregation of the Brethren in the New World, is the Mother Church for the six Brethren bodies. Many of the early leaders of the Brethren movement are buried in the cemetery near the meetinghouse.

For many years there was a strong, self-sufficient congregation in Germantown, which cared for the historic property and sponsored a small museum in its basement. As the neighborhood began to change in its racial and ethnic composition, congregational size declined. In the 1970s the original congregation was closed as a result of sociological change. After a few years of hiatus, the Atlantic Northeast District and the *General Board of the *Church of the Brethren joined forces to sponsor a new congregation to serve the predominately black neighborhood near the church. By the turn of the century a relatively vigorous new congregation was in place. However, it remains financially weak, and depends on support from the district for some program needs and provides only a small portion of the property expenses.

In 1982 the General Services Commission of the General Board established the Germantown Trust to care for the deteriorating property and the church's historic interest in the site. The Trust, while led primarily by Church of the Brethren denominational, district, and local volunteers, has intentionally opened board membership to representatives of the other Brethren bodies. During the 1990s the Old German Baptist Brethren and The Brethren Church were regularly represented on the Trust board. While the Trust was limited initially by the lack of funds, first the district and later the General Board supported the renovation and development of the historic site through fund-raising efforts that provided over $300,000 for project use during the 1990s.

Members of the Germantown Trust carried a strong concern to improve the exhibits on display in the meetinghouse's musty basement. Through the leadership of a committee convened by Brethren historian Donald Durnbaugh and with the design services of John Bruckhart, a new museum exhibit was developed on the main floor of the 1770 meetinghouse. The museum room was designed to feature wall exhibits, so that the space could continue to be utilized for program activities of the present congregation.

Four panels or shadow boxes were developed with text and photographs to tell the story of the development of the Germantown congregation. Display boxes were inserted into window openings to the adjacent sanctuary. A partial loft was constructed in the original meetinghouse, modeled to suggest the loft housing of church visitors for such occasions as *Love Feast, and to provide an additional location for exhibiting artifacts. Benches long in use in the congregation have been renovated and provide the basic seating in the museum. A preachers' table similar to that which would have been used in the late 18th century is on display. To further serve visiting groups, a video relating both the history of the congregation and information about its present-day ministries is shown.

Persons interested in visiting the site, either individually or as a group, may contact the Germantown Church of the Brethren or the Germantown Trust for information. DEMi

Minutes (Germantown Trust); BHLA collection.

Martha Rupel Gilbert. BHLA collection.

Gilbert, Martha Rupel (CB), 1901–95, relief worker, nurse. A woman of great ability and humanitarian spirit, Martha Rupel was born in Indiana; while she was still a child, her family moved to Plaine, Washington, a frontier area. When she and two siblings reached secondary school age, they moved to Wenatchee, WA, where they supported and housed themselves to attend high school. Rupel graduated from *Manchester College (BA, 1929) and, after teaching in *Appalachia, studied nursing at Pasadena Junior College (RN, 1932). In 1936 she was seconded to the *American Friends Service Committee in Spain to aid those suffering in the *Spanish Civil War.

During *World War II she worked in *Civilian Public Service camps and soon after war's end went to Europe to help in reconstruction efforts under the *Brethren Service Committee. She later served in public health programs in *Puerto Rico, Iraq, and Laos. In all of these assignments, she was noted for her courage, compassion, and ability to overcome seemingly insuperable obstacles. In 1966, Martha Rupel married Walter P. Gilbert in Pasadena, CA. She was honored by Wenatchee High School (1973), Manchester College (1974), the government of The Netherlands, *International Voluntary Service, and *On Earth Peace Assembly. She died in 1995 at the age of 94. DFD

J. K. Kreider, *A Cup of Cold Water: The Story of Brethren Service* (2001) index; R. E. Sappington, *Social Policy* (1961) 77, 123, 126; D. F. Durnbaugh, *Fruit of the Vine* (1997) 463; *La Verne [CA] Daily Bulletin* (Oct. 25, 1995); Claire M. Ulrich, "Into All the World. . ." (unpubl. art.).

Gingrich, Raymond Eugene (FGBC), 1905–95 pastor, educator. Born in Mifflintown, PA, Gingrich graduated from *Ashland College (AB, 1928), *Ashland Theol. Sem. (ThB, 1932), and *Grace Theol. Sem. (ThM, 1941; ThD, 1946). He married Edith Garber in 1927 and was ordained to the ministry in the *Church of the Brethren in 1928. Gingrich pastored the *Fair Haven Brethren Church, OH (1931–35), the *Akron, OH, First BC, (1935–48) and the *Akron, OH, Fairlawn BC, (1948–62). While at the Akron First BC, he invited the founders of *Grace Theol. Sem. to begin their school in the church facilities, where classes were held until the school moved to *Winona Lake, IN (1939). Gingrich also taught in the seminary in those early years. In 1939, he began the Akron Bible Institute.

In 1962, the Gingrichs moved to Longview, TX, where he served at LeTourneau College (1962–77) as academic dean and professor of Bible. During the years in Longview, Gingrich led in establishing the *Longview Grace BC, which he pastored (1968–77). Raymond E. Gingrich also wrote *Outline and Analysis of the First Epistle of John* (1946). RTC

H. A. Kent, *Frontiers* (1972), 71, 154, 167; *GTS Journal* 10 (Spring, 1989) 51–66; A. J. McClain, "Background and Origin of Grace Theological Seminary," *Charis* [yearbook] (1951); personal information; *Annual* (FGBC) (1939ff.).

Global Women's Project (CB). Established in 1978, the Global Women's Project has challenged *Church of the Brethren members and other North American Christians to examine in the light of the Christian gospel overconsumption and the misuse of resources that contribute to global poverty and injustice. Using a self-imposed luxury tax, participants in the Global Women's Project have reassessed their own lifestyle choices as they have redistributed their taxes for the empowerment of poor women anywhere in the world. A self-governing, semi-autonomous body within the Brethren Witness Office, the Global Women's Project has made grants ranging from $1,000 to $15,000 since 1980 to support development for women in Kenya, Costa Rica, Chile, the Solomon Islands, the Philippines, El Salvador, Nicaragua, *Nigeria, *India, Korea, and in the U.S. (Kansas City, Grand Rapids). Since its beginning, the Global Women's Project has dispersed nearly $200,000 to benefit the lives of women. In 1997 the Global Women's Project established a liaison relationship with the *Womaen's Caucus. *Globalink* is a quarter-

ly newsletter of the Global Women's Project. RKJ

Messenger (May, 1979) 6, (Sept., 1985) 6; D. F. Durnbaugh, *Fruit of the Vine* (1997) 547.

Good Samaritan Church of the Brethren, PA. The W. Pennsylvania District Witness Commission began researching the possibility of developing a new church project in Nov. 1980. The commission brought a recommendation to a special district conference held on April 12, 1982. The conference approved the recommendation to develop a new congregation in Cranberry Twp., with the name *Cranberry Community Church*. With a dream of a new church in W. Pennsylvania in his mind, Lester Shaffer willed over $93,000 for the new church development. A task force was developed to guide the process. Isaac Baldeo, called as the first pastor, began work on Jan. 1, 1985. The group met in a community center while funds were raised jointly by the district, the Shaffer estate, and the local congregation. A church building was erected on Franklin Rd., Cranberry Township. Ground-breaking was conducted on Oct. 20, 1991, and the dedication service was held on Aug. 16, 1992. The congregation reported 92 members in 2000. GED/MPB

Congregational records; *Yearbook* (CB) (1985–2000); *BLT* 36 (Summer, 1991) 172.

Good Shepherd Church of the Brethren, FL, located midway between Bradenton and Sarasota. It began on Jan. 23, 1977, as a community congregation. Don E. White was organizing pastor and still pastor in 1998. With the help of B. Merle Crouse and other leaders of the Florida-Puerto Rico District, the body was adopted into the denomination at the Oct. 1977 District Conference. Good Shepherd Church was one of the first congregations in the new church development program. These new Brethren came as a self-supporting group. On March 30, 1980, the new church building was dedicated. Two other additions have been dedicated and the million dollar project is debt free. In 1998 the membership was 304. DEW

J. H. Lehman, *Thank God for New Churches!* (1984), 8–16; *BLT* 36 (Summer, 1991) 167.

Gotha, FL, New Covenant Church of the Brethren is located one-half mile from Gotha, Orange Co., west of Orlando. The new congregation began Sept. 12, 1987, at the initiative of six persons from the *Winter Park First Church of the Brethren: Robert E., Colleen, and Michelle Smith; and Joel, Nancy, and Richard Knepper meeting in the chapel of *Camp Ithiel. There were 14 charter members. Their goals were: to establish a Brethren presence in West Orange Co.; to enrich the camp's ministry with congregational life; to use broad participation of those attending in leadership roles; to be self-supporting from the beginning; and to use half of the giving for outreach. Commuting from Sebring, Olin J. Mason served as pastor for the first year. Robert E. Smith, who then served as part-time pastor until 1997, was followed by Guy R. Buch and then by Berwyn L. Oltman. The church sent out Nancy F. Knepper, David Smalley, Judy M. McGlothlin, and Peter M. Crouse to set-apart ministry. In 1999 there were 34 members with an average attendance of 29 and outreach giving of 30 percent of total giving. BMC

Congregational records; *Yearbook* (CB) (1988ff.); *BLT* 36 (Summer, 1991) 174.

Grace Brethren International Missions (FGBC). At the beginning of the 1980s the *Central African Republic continued as the main focus of Grace Brethren *Foreign Missions, both with respect to the missionary staff and the developing national church. The evangelism ministries of the 1970s made the western half of the country the most successfully evangelized area of the world, according to missiologists. By 1997 the African congregations numbered 837 with 191,360 members. Political upheavals in 1996 resulted in two evacuations of the missionary staff, resulting in further strengthening of indigenous leadership of the churches and institutions.

Europe, largely neglected as a mission field, moved to the forefront of Grace Brethren missions in the 1980s, when more than 60 missionaries were added to the small staff serving there. The *Chateau of Saint Albain, a castle in Burgundy, France, became the center of European-wide outreach through prayer, the establishment of a branch of *Grace Theol. Sem., and publications. In the 1990s the focus moved to world-class cities and a more simplified strategy of church planting. Church planting efforts were also undertaken in Novosibirsk, Siberia, and Kyrgestan.

Though *Argentina is the oldest field of Grace Brethren Missions, the congregations there suffered a period of stagnation and an attrition of the missionary staff until 1988, when a new and dynamic team joined hands with the Argentinians and spawned a movement of rapid church-planting called *Total Mobilization.* The effects of this have spilled over to *Brazil and *Mexico and have opened other Latin American countries to Grace Brethren church planting, such as in Uruguay, Paraguay, Chile, *Cuba, and Guatemala.

A "vision team" from the *Long Beach, CA, GBC visited several Asian countries, resulting in the beginning of church-planting ministries in *Japan and the Philippines. Since then church planting has begun in Cambodia through Cambodian evangelists, and short-term teams have been sent to Thailand and Vietnam.

In 1986 the executive director of Grace Brethren Foreign Missions, *John W. Zielasko, retired and was replaced by *Thomas T. Julien, who had served as a missionary in France and was the director in Europe. The mission later changed its name to *Grace Brethren International Missions (GBIM). Adopting the slogan, "Missions is not what the church does *for* the missionary; missions is what the church does *through* the missionary," the mission gradually shifted its emphasis from being a "missionary" society, to a "mission" society, with its stated purpose being to serve Grace Brethren congregations in *their* Great Commission ministries.

Though the past two decades have seen a decline in career missionaries, local churches have become alive in initiating many creative ministries throughout the world, such as establishing the first Christian radio transmitter in Phnom Penh. Global Opportunities teams have literally gone throughout the world in intensive prayer, evangelism, and discipleship ministries. Many churches have formally adopted people groups. Cooperative efforts with other Grace Brethren agencies, such as *Grace College and Seminary, *CE National, and Grace Brethren *Home Missions, have extended the vision and influence of the Grace Brethren Fellowship.

The vision of GBIM is to see a global movement of world mission churches faithful to the Brethren heritage, who are aware of the significance of the times and thrust into the mainstream of the movement of the Spirit of God in the fulfillment of their mission. Sensing the particular moving of the Spirit in these significant times, GBIM has cooperated in *AD 2000 and Beyond,* the global movement of evangelism seeking to reach the unreached people groups of the world by the end of the decade. As the mission program moved toward its 100th anniversary on Sept. 4, 2000, it sought to be a part of God's global team. TTJ

T. T. Julien, *Seize the Moment: Stories of an Awesome God Empowering Ordinary People* (2000); personal information.

Grace Brethren Investment Foundation (GBIF) was founded in 1955 as a ministry arm of Grace Brethren North American Missions (formerly Grace Brethren Home Missions Council). Its purpose is to provide competitive financing for Grace Brethren churches and Christian schools, offering passbook savings accounts to depositors across the nation. Growth of deposits and loans has been consistent over the years. Operating margins, combined with low overhead costs, allow for respectable rates of return for depositors and affordable mortgage rates for churches and schools.

The GBIF is registered under the securities laws of the various states where depositors reside. The director and officer of operations, Kenneth A. Seyfert, has a 25-year history in the fields of banking and investments. Conservative investment policies and sound lending practices have contributed to the remarkable success of this organization. LNC

Personal information.

Grace Brethren North American Missions (GBNAM), formerly known as Grace Brethren Home Missions Council, is the U.S. and Canadian church-planting arm of the *Fellowship of Grace Brethren Churches. Its mission statement is "to glorify God by providing strategic resources for the advancement of the Great Commission, church-planting ministries in North America, in cooperation with Grace Brethren Churches and Districts of Churches."

New churches are supported for three to five years, often with the cooperation of a sponsoring mother church and district of churches. The majority of the existing FGBC congregations received assistance from North American Missions in their formative years. Church-planting strategy includes a commitment to major cities, ethnic initiatives, training systems, and churches planting churches.

GBNAM also sponsors a ministry to Native Americans. Grace American Indian Ministries includes a church-planting and leadership-training center in Albuquerque, NM. The mission is to reach Native Americans for Christ through community outreach, church-planting, and leadership development.

Additionally, GBNAM oversees the military *chaplaincy ministry for the FGBC, providing funds for the office of the Endorsing Agent, underwriting expenses for chaplains to attend the FGBC National Conference, and sharing news and prayer requests of the chaplains with the Eagle Commission, a constituency of partners who pray and give financial support to underwrite this specialized ministry. LNC

Personal information.

McClain Hall, Grace Theological Seminary. GTS collection.

Grace Schools (Grace Theological Seminary and Grace College). The increase in the number of students enrolled at *Grace Theol. Sem. reflected the boom in evangelical seminary enrollments during the 1980s. This growth peaked with enrollments of over 400 for several years. In the midst of some decline in enrollment, the seminary was affected by tensions that developed within the *Fellowship of Grace Brethren Churches in the early 1990s. In 1993 the seminary was reorganized, with many faculty members released, and the MDiv curriculum was revised. The MA in Christian School Administration was discontinued. A DMin program was instituted in place of the ThD program. In 1996 a distance education network began linking classes in Winona Lake, IN, with church learning centers in Maryland, Ohio, and Pennsylvania, using two-way video conferencing equipment. Plans to expand the network into more states were put into place, with additional sites already operational in Alabama and Michigan by 1998. In the same year, a new intercultural ministries program replaced the curriculum in the previous missions department. Also in 1998, on-campus seminary enrollment was 89 with an additional 50 students in the DMin degree program and 30 students in distance education.

Grace Seminary has provided education for ministerial students from all evangelical groups, and this cross section of conservative Christianity in the student body has created a healthy climate for learning and has gained wide respect for the seminary. In 1999 it offered MDiv, MA, and DMin degrees. Special focus areas in pastoral ministries, youth and family ministries, and intercultural ministry are available. In the 1980s and 1990s the seminary published a substantial semiannual periodical, *Grace Seminary Journal*. In 1999 there were over 4,400 seminary alumni active in church ministries throughout the nation and in over 50 foreign countries.

A two-year collegiate division, which eventually became *Grace College, was added in 1948. It expanded to include the third and fourth years in 1953–54. In 1999 the college and seminary operated as a single institution under the original charter and covenant of faith, with the same board of trustees, the same president, and the same

senior administrators. Originally envisioned largely as a pre-seminary program, the college quickly grew to meet the educational needs of young people in many fields. After a period of declining numbers, enrollment in Grace College grew to 812 in 1998. In that year it offered BA and BS degrees with a variety of programs, as well as the BM and the BSW degrees. Library holdings in 1998 totaled 140,000 volumes, as well as an extensive collection of periodicals and microform units. Teacher education, behavioral science, and business have been the largest majors in recent years. Since 1985 the college has conducted classes in Indiana state prisons. By 1998 there were three prison locations involved with ca. 90 students enrolled in BA and associate degree programs. Many of the classes are taught from the campus using distance education equipment. In 1996 the college enrolled its first graduate students in an MA in counseling program. By 1999 there were over 8,900 college alumni.

The original college campus was constructed between 1958 and 1977. A general classroom building (Philathea Hall) and the gymnasium were completed in 1958, the Morgan Library (used by both college and seminary) in 1969, and the Cooley Science Center in 1977. Dormitories were completed in 1964 (Alpha Hall) and 1966 (Beta Hall). Other properties on the campus perimeter were also acquired for college and seminary use. With renewed enrollment growth, a second wave of expansion began in 1997 with the renovation of the historic Westminster Hotel into a new dormitory, student union, and community meeting rooms. In 1998 the renovated Mount Memorial building (previously the international headquarters of the Free Methodist Church) became a leased classroom building. In 1999 construction began on a new dormitory (Kent Hall) and a new student services office center combined with dormitory wings (Indiana Hall).

Administration of the seminary and college has preceded under five presidents: *Alva J. McClain (1937–62), *Herman A. Hoyt (1962–76), *Homer A. Kent, Jr. (1976–86), John J. Davis (1986–93), and Ronald E. Manahan (1993–). Assets of Grace Schools in 1999 totaled over $20 million. Grace Schools received a ten-year renewed accreditation from the North Central Association of Colleges and Schools in 1999. DRP
Personal information.

Grace Village Retirement Complex (GVRC)(FGBC) is a new name for *Grace Brethren Village. Late in 1990, new board members and administrators realized that GVRC had serious financial problems. With the assistance of administrators from a Mennonite institution, the Greencroft Retirement Community of Goshen, IN, a series of meetings began in an attempt to solve a growing financial crisis. Ultimately, the decision was reached to file for Chapter 11 bankruptcy. However, the board decided that an ethical course of action required restructuring the debt rather than canceling it; so they changed directions and established a plan which included repaying all investors. During 1993–96, administration of GVRC was provided under contract with Greencroft. In 1997, after a period of training, Jeffrey A. Carroll was appointed administrator. After restructuring, GVRC successfully maintained all its payments and enjoyed renewed financial stability. By 1999 the facility had a high occupancy rate in all its various services, and a number of remodeling projects were undertaken at that time.

Administrators of GVRC have been Kenneth A. Rucker (1971–72), Robert A. Ashman (1972–76), Sherwood Durkee (1976–90), R. Scott Puckett (1990–93), and Jeffrey A. Carroll (1997–). DRP

Annual (*FGBC*) (1981–1998); *Handbook* (1999–2000); personal information.

Grant, Richard E. (FGBC), (1921–2003), pastor, editor, administrator. Richard Grant was born in Akron, OH, and graduated from the U. of Akron (BA, 1949) and *Grace Theol. Sem. (BD, 1952). He married Mildred E. Turner.

While in seminary, Grant pastored the Masillon Grace Brethren Mission (1949–53). He left there to pastor the *Cedar Rapids, IA, GBC (1953–57) and then the *Martinsburg, PA, GBC (1957–61). There he witnessed the construction of a $110,000 church building and educational unit prior to his becoming general manager of *The Brethren Missionary Herald Co. and editor of the *Brethren Missionary Herald* (1961–66). Under his leadership, the building debt was liquidated and the *Herald* reached new heights in subscriptions. He served as moderator of the FGBC in 1965–66.

Grant returned to his first love, the pastorate, serving the *Alexandria, VA, Commonwealth Avenue BC (1966–69), *Mansfield, OH, GBC (1969–72), *Canton, OH, GBC (1972–77), and the *Canal Fulton, OH, Grace Brethren Chapel (1977–79). Due to his wife's illness, Grant left the pastorate in 1979, but in 1999 he was serving on the pastoral staff of the *Worthington, OH, Columbus GBC. RTC

BMH (June 17, 1961) 397, (Dec. 10, 1966) 20; personal information; *Annual* (*FGBC*) (1950ff.).

Grassroots, Concerns of the (CB). Organized at the *Greenmount Church of the Brethren, Rockingham Co., VA, in April 1993, Concerns of the Grassroots was a loosely-organized network of Brethren bothered by progressive tendencies in the denomination. The emotional issue of homosexuals serving in church leadership positions was the group's initial concern, yet the list of grievances quickly expanded to include the *ordination of ministers who embraced a low *Christology, an *Annual Conference paper on *Native Americans that was considered syncretistic, and participation by CB leaders in the ecumenical, feminist *"Re-Imagining God . . ." Conference (Nov., 1993).

To raise awareness about such issues, the Grassroots network published a newsletter, convened occasional meetings, and wrote letters to denominational leaders during the 1990s. A 1993 meeting on the issue of *homosexuality, widely referred to as the "Greenmount meeting," drew a large attendance and generated controversy across the denomination. A 1994 newsletter identified "New Age pantheism" as the broad threat underlying the group's specific concerns. Grassroots supporters were bothered by the proliferation of what they viewed as "feel good, new age buzz words," including diversity, inclusion, justice, tolerance, and unity, all of which they thought progressives used to dilute the authority of traditional Biblical teachings.

Concerns of the Grassroots was not the only evangelical effort to counter progressive tendencies in the CB during the 1990s. Other notable initiatives were: *Evangel 21*, a conservative periodical; the Brethren Evangelical Ministry Training Committee; and continuing activities of the *Brethren Revival Fellowship. In an attempt to build bridges between progressive and conservative wings of the denomination, the CB General Office staff invited Grassroots and BRF leaders to Elgin, IL, in May 1995 to dialogue with progressive leaders in a "Denominational Vision Gathering" weekend. CFB

See also FEMINISM.

Messenger (June, 1993) 6–7; D. F. Durnbaugh, *Fruit of the Vine* (1997) 550–52.

Greencastle, PA, Conococheague Grace Brethren Church was organized by a core group of four families as a daughter church of the *Waynesboro, PA, GBC. Alan N. Clingan was called to serve as pastor, and the first service was held on May 27, 1990. Grace Brethren North American Missions and the Mid-Atlantic District Mission Board subsidized the church for a period of five years. After meeting in various locations, including a train station and a funeral home, the congregation purchased 3.3 acres of land on the south side of town. There were 49 members in Jan. 1999. ANC/JRY

Congregational records; *Annual* (*FGBC*) (1991ff.).

Greenmount Meeting. *See* **Grassroots, Concerns of the**

Greenwood, IN, Christ Our Shepherd Church of the Brethren. The South Central Indiana District of the *Church of the Brethren decided to establish a congregation in Greenwood, IN (Indianapolis area). In 1986 the district bought six acres at 857 North State Road 135 and called pastors C. Wendell and Joan Bohrer to be church planters. Meetings began in their garage that fall. On Easter 1987 the congregation began meeting in the chapel of the Wilson St. Pierre funeral home. Two years later, construction began on the church building; and in 1991 worship started there. The church building was dedicated on May 3, 1991, and congregational status was granted later that year. Wendell Bohrer retired in 1994, and the congregation called Wayne and Jayne Grumbling as pastors. In Sept. 1997 the congregation hosted its first district conference, and the district completed payment of its share of the mortgage that weekend. GWG

Congregational records; *BLT* 36 (Summer, 1991) 173.

Greiner, Robert G. (CB), church official. A native of Manheim, PA, Greiner was born on June 11, 1918; his

Robert G. Greiner. BHLA collection.

home congregation was the *Chiques CB. He attended *Elizabethtown College before his assignment in 1941 as a *conscientious objector to the *Civilian Public Service (CPS) program. Following service at the Lagro, IN, camp, he was assigned to the CB treasurer's office in Elgin, IL, to oversee CPS finances. Greiner remained at the church offices as assistant treasurer of the denomination after discharge from the CPS program in 1945. While in Elgin he continued his education at Northwestern U., graduating with a degree in business administration. In 1952 he became treasurer of the *General Brotherhood Board, maintaining that position until his retirement in June 1981. During this same period, he managed the finances of the *Brethren Publishing House (Brethren Press) and the *Pension Board, and was the executive of the Finance Commission. He married Edna Mosemann in 1942; they had two daughters, Donna and Beverly. DFD

GM (April 12, 1952) 13; *Messenger* (April 1981) 5.

Grieve, Jerry Allen (BC), 1941–97, missionary, pastor. Grieve was born in Portis, KS, the son of Marion and Mary Elizabeth Pierson Grieve, and became a member of the *Mulvane, KS, Brethren Church. He attended *Ashland College (BA, 1964), *Ashland Theol. Sem. (BD, 1969), and took additional studies at Wycliffe Translators' Summer Institute of Linguistics and at Michigan State U. He married Cheryl Robinson of Mulvane in 1966, and they were the parents of three children: Dawn, Nicole, and Seth. The Grieves served as BC missionaries in Nigeria with Wycliffe Translators in 1971–76. They worked among the Kilba people in language training, linguistic analysis, translations, and literature preparation. After returning to the U.S., Grieve pastored churches in the Independence, KS, area. He was also an agent for the Farm Bureau and owned his own business. RCWi

BE (Sept. 13, 1969) 9, (Oct., 1976) 26, (Oct., 1997) 13; A. T. Ronk, *History of Brethren Mission Movements* (1971) 124, 126; *Annual* (*BC*) (1972ff.).

Groff, Warren Frederick (CB), b. 1924, educator, author. Groff was born near Harleysville, PA; he received there his early education. Although a high-school dropout, he went on to graduate with high honors from *Juniata College (BA, 1949) and attended *Bethany Bibl. Sem. before receiving a degree at Yale Divinity School (BD, 1952) and doctoral degree at Yale U. (PhD, 1956). His home congregation was the *Pottstown, PA, CB, where he was ordained; he was advanced to elder in Chicago, IL (1959). He held brief pastorates in Pennsylvania and in Connecticut while a student. Groff taught religion at *Bridgewater College (1954–58) before being called to Bethany Theol. Sem., where he taught *theology and *ethics, served as dean (1962–75) and as president (1975–89). He was CB moderator in 1979. In 1976 he received an honorary doctorate from Juniata College, which he also served as a longtime member of the board of trustees. Groff was active in the *ecumenical movement, with especial interest in Faith and Order discussions. Besides many scholarly articles, he wrote books, including: (coauthor) *The Shaping of Modern Christian Thought* (1968); *Christ the Hope of the Future: Signals of a Promised Humanity* (1971); *Story Time: God's Story and Ours* (1974); and *Prayer: God's Time and Ours!* (1988). He married Ruth Davidheiser in 1947; they have one son, David. DFD

Messenger (June, 1979) cover, 16–19, (April, 1988) 7; *TBE* 3 (1984) 1640; *GM* (Feb. 10, 1962) 19; *BLT* 39 (Winter, 1994) 12–15; F. F. Wayland, *Bridgewater College* (1993), index; Earl C. Kaylor, Jr., *Truth Sets Free* (1977) 403, and Juniata College: *Uncommon Vision, Uncommon Loyalty* (2001) 275; Juniata College: "The Centennial Convocation." *[Huntingdon, PA] Daily News* (April 29, 1976) 14, 23; *Juniata College Bulletin* (May, 1976) [1].

D. Ernst Wolf and Warren F. Groff. BHLA collection.

GROW '73. In deciding not to participate in Key '73, an interdenominational evangelistic outreach in the U.S., the *Fellowship of Grace Brethren Churches determined to coordinate a nationwide evangelistic outreach of its own. Led by *S. Wayne Beaver, GROW (an acronym for "God Reaching Our World") began with pastors' seminars in Philadelphia, PA; Columbus, OH; Portland, OR; Los Angeles, CA; and in Florida. A 16-lesson GROW Training Course was written to be used with *Explosive Evangelism* (1972) by G. R. Jaffray, Jr. The result was that the Fellowship realized the highest number of professions of faith (10,174) ever reported for a year. The GROW committee set goals for 1974. The number of reported professions dropped to 8,808 that year but rose to 10,082 in 1975. The total number of professions of faith for 1973 –75 is unequaled by any other similar period in the FGBC. The Fellowship also reported a growth in membership of 5,162 during this period. RTC

S. W. Beaver and D. Beaver, *God at Work in the Central African Republic, Africa, and GROW 1973, USA* (1999)

Guli, John (CB), 1942–92, Nigerian church leader, minister. Guli was born at Yabali in Michika district, Adamawa (then Gongola) State, *Nigeria. He attended *Kulp Bible School, the *Theological College of Northern

John Guli. BHLA collection.

Nigeria, and Ahmadu Bello U. He earned an MA (1980) and a PhD in missiology (1986) at Fuller Theol. Sem., CA. In Nige-ria his considerable gifts and energy led to leadership roles in both the church and government. Guli served the *Church of the Brethren in Nigeria (EYN) as an evangelist, district secretary, translator, principal at Kulp Bible School (1979–82), and as general secretary (1989–92). A member of the Kamwe (Higi) people, Guli led the translation of the New Testament into the Kamwe language. He chaired Michika local government (1982–83) and led the state delegation in pilgrimage to Jerusalem. John and Elizabeth Guli had seven children. He was killed by a passing vehicle while assisting with a disabled car near EYN headquarters. MBK
Messenger (Dec., 1972) 7.

Habitat for Humanity International, a non-denominational Christian organization headquartered in Americus, GA, is dedicated to the elimination of substandard housing. It was founded by Linda and Millard Fuller, a millionaire couple who gave their wealth to the poor in order to live a life of Christian service. In the 1960s, Millard Fuller and Clarence Jordan of *Koinonia Farm(s), a Christian community near Americus, developed the concept of partnership housing. This led the Fullers to organize Habitat for Humanity in Sept. 1976. This organization grew rapidly. By the end of 1997, Habitat volunteers had built or rehabilitated 20,793 houses in the U.S. and nearly 40,000 more houses in 57 countries around the world.

Habitat houses are built by volunteers working in partnership with the people who will live in those houses. The houses are simple, decent, and affordable. Each partner family or individual is required to work a certain number of "sweat equity" hours. When the house is completed, it

is sold to the family or individual at a price approximately equal to the cost of the materials. It is financed with a no-interest loan. Funds to build houses come from donations, fund-raising activities, and house payments.

The work of Habitat is carried out by local affiliates. Using guidelines established by Habitat for Humanity International, each affiliate creates its own organization, raises funds, selects partner families to receive homes, and builds houses. By the end of 1997 there were 1,400 local affiliates in the United States. Tithes from American affiliates fund houses in developing nations.

Brethren from several denominations have participated in the work of Habitat in various ways as members and leaders of local affiliates, as volunteers, and in Habitat work projects at annual meetings. Robert Gemmer (CB) was particularly active in the Habitat organization. RCWi M. Fuller and D. Scott, *Love in the Mortar Joints* (1980) and *No More Shacks* (1986); D. Lee, *The Cotton Patch Evidence: The Story of Clarence Jordan and the Koinonia Farm Experiment* (1971); T. E. K'Meyer, *Interracialism and Christian Community in the Postwar South: The Story of Koinonia Farms* (1997); A. L. Coble, *Cotton Patch for the Kingdom* (2002); *Messenger* (July, 1986) 2–3, (Dec., 1995) 6, (June, 1996) 6, (July, 1996) 16, (Aug./Sept., 1996) 24; *Communal Societies* 10 (1990) 114–232.

Hagerstown, MD, Gateway Brethren Fellowship (BC) was born out of a vision of eight people from the *Hagerstown, MD, First Brethren Church to reach out to people of the area who were not being served by the "traditional" churches of the community. The core group of eight persons met to pray for direction; they were led to an apartment complex on the south side of Hagerstown, where no ministry of any kind then existed. In 1998 the congregation met in the community room of the complex for worship, emphasizing praise and practical Bible teaching. Attendance currently averages 20 per week. Cell groups, community activities on holidays, and special events are the primary form of outreach. Special interest meetings and seminars are also planned as outreach tools, along with activities for the children and youth of the community. Gerald A. Barr serves as pastor. GAB
Congregational records.

Haller, Wesley (FGBC), 1923–91, pastor. Born in Dayton, OH, and converted as a ten-year-old, Wesley Haller graduated from Bob Jones College (BA, 1947) and *Grace Theol. Sem. (MDiv, 1951). He pastored *Ankenytown, OH, GBC (1951–54); and *Middlebranch, OH, GBC (1954–69); in the latter he witnessed the growth in Sunday morning worship attendance to an average of 300. He then pastored First BC of *Johnstown, PA (1969 –76); *Lancaster GBC, *Rohrerstown GBC (1976–82), a new home mission work in Milroy, PA (1982–83); and returned to pastor Middlebranch, OH, GBC (1984–91).

Haller served on the board of Grace Brethren *Foreign Missions (1967–91), as secretary of the board (1981–91), and on the *Brethren Missionary Herald Board (1964–67). He was moderator of the *FGBC (1969–70). RTC
Personal information; *Annual* (BC) (1952ff.).

Hamel, Joseph Donat (BC), 1923–97, minister. J. D. Hamel was born in Rumford, MA, and raised in Johnstown, PA, where he was a member of the *Johnstown Second Brethren Church. He served in the South Pacific during *World War II. He graduated from *Ashland College (BA, 1949) and *Ashland Theol. Sem.

(BD, 1951). Ashland College awarded him an honorary degree (DD, 1972). He married Jean Rowsey in 1949; they had three children: John, JoAnne, and Janet. While a student, Hamel pastored *Fair Haven Brethren Church of Lattasburg, OH, and subsequently served the *Lanark, IL, and *South Bend, IN, First Brethren Churches in 1951 and 1953 respectively. In 1960 he moved to Sarasota, FL, to lead a mission congregation until his retirement from pastoral ministry 28 years later. During his tenure, Hamel baptized 996 converts, and *Sarasota First Brethren congregation grew from 70 members to over 700. An educational building was added in 1964, and a new worship facility with seating for 700 was completed in 1970.

Pastor Hamel was also involved in outreach beyond the local congregation. He served as chaplain of the Sarasota City police and fire departments, Sarasota Co. sheriff's department, and the Florida Firemen's Association. In 1967 Hamel began producing a *radio program, The *Brethren Hour, which was broadcast internationally. The Sarasota First BC started two new congregations, the *Bradenton, FL, BC and a Spanish ministry that grew into a separate congregation, Iglesia de los Hermanos. Hamel is fondly remembered for his tireless ministry, his energetic preaching style, and his evident love for God and for others, from the least to the greatest. A Sarasota waterfront park was named in his honor in 1996. DLSt

BE (March, 1997) 11, (Oct., 1993) 17; *Sarasota [FL] Herald Tribune* (Feb. 23, 1997); congregational records.

Hylton Harmon with the judge of the court. BHLA collection.

Harman, Hylton (CB), lawyer, pastor, churchman. Born in 1910 in Kansas, Harman was ordained in Kansas City in 1932. After training in a number of colleges and universities (where he was known for his skill in debate and athletics), he earned the DJur legal degree from the U. of Missouri/Kansas City. Because of the church's position against law as a vocation, he secured a special dispensation from the district leadership. As a "temporary pastor" of the First Central City CB, Kansas City, he built up a strong congregation over 16 years, at the same time pursuing his legal career while also active in church work on a national level. When the church reorganized its polity in 1946, Harman became a member of the *General Brotherhood Board, assigned to the *Brethren Service Commission, serving until 1953. After 1971 he was co-pastor of the *Plattsburg, MO, congregation. Known as a peace advocate, in his law practice Harman specialized in reconciling estranged couples who sought his counsel in divorce proceedings. For his efforts in peacemaking, he was honored by *McPherson College (LLD, 1952) and by *On Earth Peace (posthumously, 1992). He was active in and honored by a host of community organizations, for which he performed many legal services without cost. Harman and his wife Maxine had three children. He died on Feb. 10, 1992. DFD

Yearbook (1932–40), (1948–89); *Messenger* (May 1992) 3; unpubl. OEPA citation by Paul Jewell, July 9, 1992; *BE* 3 (1984) 1645.

Hart, MI, Dunkard Brethren Congregation. The first meeting took place in March 1954 in the home of Lee Flory. It was a mission point of the *Pleasant Ridge (DB), OH, congregation for 39 years, during which time the ministry of that congregation served also at Hart. Between 1954 and 1966, the group met in the Vermontville, MI, firehouse and in the Lake Odessa OGBB meetinghouse. Eldon Flory (b. 1935) was called to the ministry in Nov. 1954 and served until 1968. The present building at 56th Street and Deer Road was dedicated in May 1964, with the first *love feast occurring in Sept. 1964. Ronald Lee Marks (b. 1949), a minister from the Shrewsbury (DB), PA, congregation, relocated to Hart in 1990. The congregation was organized with 29 members on March 6, 1993. A deacon, Timothy Eugene Kasza (b. 1959), was called in the organizational council meeting; and a minister, Jeremiah Lee Johnson (b. 1976), was called on May 30, 1998. On July 23, 2000, a new auditorium was dedicated. For many years, ministers from Ohio and Indiana conducted monthly preaching services for the Hart Brethren, and they continue to minister to the congregation occasionally. RLMa

Bible Monitor (Feb., 1998) 16; congregational records.

William A. Hayes. BHLA collection. Photo by Richard Keeler.

Hayes, William (Bill) A. (CB), 1928–93, minister, denominational leader. He grew up in South Bend, IN, graduated from the U. of Indianapolis, and received a master's degree from Colgate-Rochester Divinity School.

Hayes was ordained and served pastorates in the *United Church of Christ (UCC). In Kansas City, MO, he served as administrative director at St. Marks (UCC), the nation's first church to unite Protestants and Roman Catholics in a single congregation. In 1977, he accepted the call to become pastor of the First Church of the Brethren in *Baltimore, MD, retiring from there in 1992. Hayes was *Annual Conference moderator in 1988, the first African American to hold that office. He served on the *General Board, chairing the *Parish Ministries Commission and providing key leadership for the Urban Network Steering Committee and the Committee on Interchurch Relations. Bill Hayes consistently advocated on behalf of marginalized people and urged the denomination to make *urban ministry a priority. EMS

Messenger (May, 1987) 7, (Nov., 1987) back cover, (June, 1988) 10–13, (Aug./Sept., 1988) 1, 17, (Oct., 1993) 9, (Nov., 1993) 17; The (Baltimore) Sun (Aug. 22, 1993).

Heckert, Mildred Mae Etter (CB), 1913–93, educator, musician, editor. Born in Ft. McKinley, OH, the daughter of Ralph A. and Lydia M. Etter, Mildred Etter joined the *Dayton, OH, Ft. McKinley congregation in 1923 and later graduated from *Manchester College (AB, 1931) and Wittenberg College (MA in Ed, 1942). She taught in Ohio public schools from 1936 to 1952, at which time she moved to Elgin, IL, to work for the *Christian Education Commission of the *General Brotherhood Board. When she married Clinton I. Heckert in 1964, she left the Christian Education Commission and became a copy editor with *Brethren Press, where she worked until her retirement in 1975. She then volunteered for 17 years in the *Brethren Historical Library and Archives and continued her work as copy editor of BLT (last issue she edited, Autumn, 1990). Throughout her life, Mildred Heckert taught violin, played in several city orchestras, directed church youth choirs and ensembles, and participated in a rock and mineral society. ARH

BHLA files; Messenger (Feb., 1984) 2–3; BLT 39 (Spring, 1994) 134; Highland Ave CB (1999) 69–70.

A. Blair and Patricia K. Helman host students. Manchester College collection.

Helman, Alfred Blair (CB), minister, educator, college president. A. Blair Helman was born in 1920 in Windber, PA, the son of Henry E. and Luie Pritt Helman. In 1947 he married *Patricia Ann Kennedy; they have two daughters: Harriet Ann and Patricia Dawn. He graduated from *Bethany Training School (1944), *McPherson College (AB, 1946), U. of Kansas (MA, 1947), with further studies at the U. of Kansas. Helman received five honorary degrees, along with other honors, including the Sagamore of the Wabash, given by the governor of Indiana. In 1998 Manchester students created an endowment in his honor with *Heifer Project International, and a college dormitory was named Helman Hall.

He was pastor of congregations in *Newton, *Ottawa, and *Wichita, KS, and taught at Ottawa U., U. of Kansas, and Friends U. in Kansas. In 1956, Helman went to *Manchester College as president, serving until his retirement in 1986. He occupied many positions of leadership within the *Church of the Brethren, including moderator of *Annual Conference in 1976. He authored articles on religion and higher education and served on boards and committees dealing with higher education within the state and nation. WRE

See also HIGHER EDUCATION.

Manchester College files; Who's Who in Religion, 2nd ed. (1977); Who's Who in America (1988–89), 1: 1379; The Blue Book: Leaders of the English-Speaking World (1976) 743; T. K. Jones, Manchester College (1989) 136–93; Messenger (July, 1976) 12–14, (May, 1981) 7, (Sept., 1985) 6, (May, 1991), 24, (Nov., 1992) 5; personal information.

Helman, Patricia Kennedy (CB), artist, author, minister. Patricia Helman was born in 1925 in Marshalltown, IA, the daughter of Roy and Julia Plum Kennedy. In 1947 she married *A. Blair Helman; they have two daughters: Harriet Ann and Patricia Dawn. She graduated from *McPherson College (AB, 1947) and studied at *Bethany Biblical Sem., Associated Mennonite Sem., and Iliff School of Theology. She received two honorary degrees. An ordained minister, she served for a time as chaplain at *Timbercrest Retirement Home. In addition to many speaking engagements, she was a regular contributor to *Messenger and a number of other religious journals. She authored four books: *Free to Be a Woman* (1971), *In League with the Stones* (1976), *At Home in the World* (1980), and *Sign and Symbol in the Church of the Brethren* (1991). She was a member of the board of governors of the *National Council of Churches of Christ for six years. She was the founder of Art for Hunger, as well as founder and president of The Joyful Scribes Corporation (a religious greeting card company now owned by Abbey Press). WRE

Manchester College files; P. K. Helman, "Pilgrim's Pen," Messenger (monthly column, Jan., 1979/Dec., 1982); T. K. Jones, Manchester College (1989) 155, 159.

Herndon, VA, Chandon Brethren Church. The congregation began in 1963 in Chandon village, a subdivision of Herndon. Located ca. 40 miles from Washington, DC, Herndon was chosen because of its great potential for growth. The congregation held its initial worship service on Nov. 24, 1963, with Richard R. Kuns serving as pastor. It met initially in the church parsonage; the garage had been constructed as a meeting area. A church building was completed in 1966. Other pastors who served the congregation were Carl Barber and *Glenn "Doc" Shank. The highest average worship attendance of 81 occurred in 1968. The congregation experienced a divisive *charismatic controversy and eventually closed in 1978. DRS

Congregational records; Annual (BC) (1964ff.).

HESS, JAMES ARTHUR

Hess, James Arthur (OGBB), 1922–98, farmer, church leader. The son of elder Willis A. Hess and Elizabeth Miller Hess, James Hess was born near Waynesboro, PA. He lived his early life in Winchester, VA, moving at the age of 15 back to Waynesboro where he lived the remainder of his life. He was baptized into the *Old German Baptist Church on April 30, 1944, in the *Antietam District. He married Lois V. Benshoff in 1945. They were married for 53 years and had five children; he farmed all his life. James Hess was called to the ministry in 1961 and as elder in 1969. He was elected to serve as nonresident elder at *Pigg River, VA (1973–78) and Lancaster, PA (1994–98); and he served on a committee sent to *Columbia River, WA (1991). Hess was a member of *Standing Committee of *Annual Meeting (1993–98), and he was elder-in-charge of his home congregation from Oct. 2, 1996, until his death on Nov. 9. His widow died one year later on Nov. 5, 1999. KMM

Vindicator (1961) 153, (1998) 379; *Old Order Notes* No. 4 (Spring, 1981) 26.

Hispanic Ministries (BC). During 1976 the *Missionary Board of *The Brethren Church entered into a partnership that in time encompassed the inception of Hispanic Brethren Church work in the U.S., its spread into other Spanish-speaking countries, and an international radio ministry. Upon return from missionary service in *Argentina (1976), Juan Carlos and María Fiorenza Miranda were seconded by the Missionary Board to initiate the Hispanic Church Growth Department under the Fuller Evangelistic Association in Pasadena, CA. Their participation involved The Brethren Church from the very beginning.

In conjunction with those responsibilities, Miranda was very active in Hispanic ministries for a number of evangelical groups, including Campus Crusade for Christ, Church Growth Seminars, and Billy Graham Crusades. Nevertheless, during these years, the concept of planting Brethren congregations was constantly in focus. Late in 1978 the Mirandas began visiting Tijuana, *Mexico, every other week for several months. They knocked on doors in different areas until host homes were found for Bible study and a core group formed. The following year a married couple was brought from Mexico City to pastor the group. The work began to flourish. Four years later that effort was turned over to another denomination.

In 1978 Cirilo Ruiz was called to begin visitation in two new areas in Mexico City. By 1979 outreach was started in two homes in Santa Teresa, CA. Brethren *Youth Summer Crusaders worked two weeks that July, strengthening the church's ministry. In 1998 a missionary couple and several Mexican workers and congregations carried on the work in Mexico City.

The birth of Brethren congregations in Mexico and the U.S. occurred almost simultaneously during the first quarter of 1979. However, church planting in Pasadena required a special strategy. Without money, a building, or people, the Mirandas had only their call from God for church planting and a desire to discover principles of church growth. And that call was stronger than the obstacles.

In Feb. 1979 the Mirandas rented a small room for evangelistic services. Young people from another denomination distributed 5,000 flyers publicizing the meetings with a well-known evangelist and two excellent musical groups. Within three years this 110-member congregation

averaged 175 in attendance and was completely self-supported. As a missionary-minded congregation, the church contributed toward construction and work in Mexico, and also supported other Brethren fields.

While pastoring the church, Miranda became the Brethren Missionary Board Hispanic Director in conjunction with his duties at Fuller Evangelistic Association. The *Maranatha Bible Institute was begun for training lay-workers in Oct. 1982. He brought in two associate pastors, Manuel Rojas from Colombia (1981) and Vidal Juarez from Bolivia (1982) to assist him in meeting the heavy demands of this multifaceted work. The Pasadena congregation gave birth to a daughter congregation on Nov. 12, 1982, in Monrovia, CA, led by pastor Vidal Juarez. Later, this congregation moved to *Baldwin Park, CA.

Like the work in Mexico and the U.S., a mission in Bolivia was started in 1983 through family contacts of Vidal Juarez's father. Two congregations, led by young men, met in Cochabamba and Hasa Rancho. However, after two years these efforts encountered difficulties. Non-Brethren doctrines began to flourish, and very little could be done from a distance and with lack of Brethren missionary personnel in the field. A rather comparable possibility in Guatemala also failed to flourish.

The Mirandas have done extensive English-to-Spanish translation. The new churches—particularly those at a distance—needed training materials in church history, doctrine, discipleship, and pastoral and lay leadership. Their translations include parts of *C. F. Yoder's well-known doctrinal books, *God's Means of Grace* and *Faith of the Gospel;* additional material translated was *Our Faith, A Centennial Declaration, Manual of Procedures,* and *The Pastor's Handbook* written by denominational leaders; and *Follow Him Gladly* by Brenda B. Colijn and Dale R. Stoffer.

By 1991 the work in California came under Russell Gordon, director of Home Missions for The Brethren Church. The position of Hispanic Director was eliminated and Miranda was named director for Latin American Ministries for The Brethren Church.

During 1994, in conjunction with his other duties, Miranda accepted the call to be the Director of the Church Planting Program at Colombia Biblical Sem., Columbia, SC. In 1999, the Mirandas retired and returned to Pasadena, CA. Soon they started a cell group which met in their home. By Easter 2000, the group had outgrown their home; so they rented a sanctuary. In 2003, the group numbers ca. 100 people from 16 different countries. JCMi
See also HISPANIC RADIO MINISTRY.

BE (Sept., 1987) 21, (Mar., 1995) 13, (Mar., 2000) 6–7, (June, 2000) 8; Personal files.

Hispanic Ministries (CB). Conscientious objector volunteers serving in *Puerto Rico and *Ecuador during the 1940s led to Hispanic church beginnings in the United States. The Castañer congregation was organized in 1948, an outgrowth of the health and education ministries of the *Civilian Public Service (CPS) unit stationed in the village. By 2003, Spanish-speaking congregations have developed in California, Texas, Illinois, Indiana, Pennsylvania, New York, and Florida, as well as Puerto Rico. La Iglesia de los Hermanos (Church of the Brethren) in the *Dominican Republic was founded by an itinerant lay preacher, Jorge Toledo, from the *Vega Baja congregation in Puerto Rico. The Atlantic Southeast District has one Hispanic congregation in *Winter Park,

New Hispanic church plant (BC). Pasadena, CA. Juan Carlos Miranda collection.

FL, and six in Puerto Rico. Elsa Groff, from Castañer, has been district moderator. There have been associate district executives for the congregations in PR since 1985 (Stephen Newcomer, Rene Calderón, Pedro Brull, Jaime Rivera, Jorge Rivera, Milton García, and Irma Zayas). Guillermo

Encarnación, from the Dominican Republic, joined the CB denomination in 1972 when he was called to the pastorate in Castañer. Later he led in establishing Spanish-speaking congregations in Lancaster, Reading, and Bethlehem, PA. In recent years he has directed the ministerial training program for the Dominican church as a commuting missionary.

Quito was the site of beginning CB work in Ecuador in 1942 with CPS men serving in the Brethren Club, an inner city project. In 1946, a rural mission began among highland Indians. This work immersed non-Hispanic U.S. Brethren in Hispanic culture, an effort that produced Spanish-speaking leadership, both Ecuadorian and North American, for the Church in the U.S. and PR. Donald and Shirley Fike, René and Karen Calderón, David and Laura Jean Rittenhouse, and Mario and Olga Serrano eventually ministered in PR and the U.S. after serving in Ecuador. Dale E. Minnich assisted Hospital Castañer in receiving long-term government contracts that made the hospital economically secure. Estella Boggs Horning taught biblical studies in Spanish in both countries as well as in the Dominican Republic. B. Merle Crouse was involved in Hispanic church development in the U.S. and PR and represented the General Board during the transfer of Hospital Castañer from the denomination to a community board.

The CB began to provide support for the Hispanic congregations by providing staffing for Hispanic ministries from the early 1980s until the redesign of the General Board curtailed the program. Portfolio responsibilities included economic and social justice projects with the Puerto Rican Council of Churches and the National Farm Worker Ministry. Persons who served in the staff position were B. Merle Crouse, René Calderón, Roy Jiménez, and Guillermo Encarnación. From 1998 to 2003, the Congregational Life Team related to Hispanic churches through cross cultural events and congregational consultations, with Carol Yeazell and Duane E. Grady giving leadership. In 1980 the first denominational Hispanic assembly took place, establishing an annual forum and organization for Hispanic identity and a voice in the church. The assembly ceased to meet after 1998.

Phil Carlos Archbold, originally from Panama, co-pastor of the *Brooklyn, NY, CB, led the Church during 2001 as the first Hispanic moderator of Annual Conference. BMC

J. K. Kreider, *A Cup of Cold Water, The Story of Brethren Service* (2001); M. S. Helstern Rosenberger, *Light of the Spirit: The Brethren in Puerto Rico, 1942–1992* (1992); O. B. G. Serrano, *Un Canto Al Señor en la Isla del Encanto* (1992) and [K. Richie, tr.], "A History of the Church of the Brethren in Puerto Rico, 1942–1989," MTh thesis, Bethany Theol. Sem.

Hispanic Radio Ministry (BC). Juan Carlos and Maria Fiorenza Miranda returned from missionary service in *Argentina early in 1976. The *Missionary Board of *The Brethren Church seconded them to Fuller Evangelistic Association in Pasadena, CA, to establish the Hispanic Church Growth Department.

They quickly discovered that few ministries dealt with the unique problems faced by Hispanic women. Maria Miranda was challenged to step out in faith into that venue. In 1979, a five-minute, Monday-through-Friday

Maria Florenza Miranda broadcasting. Juan Carlos Miranda collection.

radio program, *Para Ti Mujer* (*For You My Dear Lady*) was launched. The program's dual purpose was to minister to Hispanic women and to start a Spanish-speaking Brethren congregation in Pasadena. While the program targets women, many men are also regular listeners. Over half of the response mail is from young adults.

Shared in a relational style without "churchy" jargon, this unique program exposed nonbelievers to biblical truth and counsel over secular radio stations. Many asked to broadcast the program since international radio programs for Hispanic women are so rare. In 2002 this five-minute, weekly program aired over 1,700 times a day in more than 1,200 stations in 26 countries including Latin American countries, the U.S., Spain, and Sweden. Individual stations donated broadcast radio time. Gifts from The Missionary Board of The Brethren Church, congregations, foundations, and individuals support the limited operating budget.

After Maria Miranda writes and records her messages in Pasadena, CA, the programs are duplicated and mailed out quarterly. Letters are answered monthly, and literature is provided upon request.

Para Ti Mujer has received much recognition for its impact on the Spanish-speaking world. *World Vision* magazine called Maria Miranda "the most listened-to woman in Latin America." In 1997 Southern Baptist's U.S. Home Missions Board honored *Para Ti Mujer* with its "Covenant Award."

Since 1999, a new 15-minute weekly radio program *Desde Mi Hogar Al Suyo* (*From My Home to Yours*) was started and is aired over 148 stations via satellite by the Bible Broadcasting Network in Charlotte, NC. The program has also received the Silver Angel Award from the Excellence in Media secular organization in 1999, 2000, and 2001. In 2002, the most coveted award, the Gold Angel Award, was received. Also in 2002, From *My Home to Yours* received a Silver Angel Award. In 2001, National Religious Broadcasters granted Maria Miranda and her

radio ministry the Milestone Award for over 20 years of Spanish radio production. MFM
See also HISPANIC MINISTRIES.
BE (May, 2001) 12.

*Historic Peace Churches. Following the 1968 *World Council of Churches (WCC) Uppsala Assembly, a seven-member Historic Peace Church/*Fellowship of Reconciliation (FOR) Consultative Committee (HPC/FOR CC) was formed by Brethren, *Friends, *Mennonites, and the FOR to affirm and encourage efforts within the WCC to fulfill the mandate of the Assembly's "Martin Luther King, Jr. Resolution." Two major consultations were initiated by this committee to provide an HPC/FOR point of view as the WCC study, "Violence, Nonviolence and the Struggle for Social Justice" was being prepared for WCC approval. Following this initiative the committee continued to meet several times a year, giving primary attention to issues of peace/war, nonviolence, militarism, and disarmament concerns within the WCC. The committee was represented at selected WCC Central Committee meetings and all subsequent WCC Assemblies.

The Nairobi Assembly (1975) requested that special attention be given to "the experience of the Historic Peace Churches," in the council's peace work. Subsequently, H. Lamar Gibble was named to the WCC's Commission of the Churches on International Affairs (CCIA), where he represented HPC/FOR interests for 15 years, helping to initiate or chair major WCC conferences on militarism, disarmament, peaceful resolution of conflict, and the negative effects of militarism on human rights and development. In 1988 Gibble prepared and presented the WCC's position paper on disarmament to the UN Special Session on Disarmament III.

In the tradition of earlier HPC/FOR statements (*The Church, The Christian, and War* [1947] and *Peace Is the Will of God* [1953]) the committee in 1991 published *A Declaration on Peace* in English, Spanish, and Russian to engage the wider ecumenical community in a dialogue for peace leading up to the Canberra WCC Assembly (1991). In more recent years the HPC/FOR CC has worked to initiate and support the WCC's Program to Overcome Violence and published a book, *Overcoming Violence: Linking Local and Global Peacemaking,* to complement this program in advance of the 1998 WCC Assembly. HLG

D. Gwyn and others, *A Declaration on Peace: In God's People the World's Renewal Has Begun* (1991); D. F. Durnbaugh, ed., *On Earth Peace* (1978), 229–393, and "Why They Call Them the Peace Churches," *[WCC] One World* (Dec., 1977) 18–20; H. L. Gibble, "Die Kirche der Bruder: Ueber den Pazifismus Historischer Friedenskirchen," *Zumutungen des Friedens,* ed. V. Deile (1982), 123–33, and "Reflections on a Brethren Peace Pilgrimage," unpubl. paper, OEPA Assembly (1996); M. Miller and B. N. Gingerich, eds., *The Church's Peace Witness* (1994) esp. 182–95; WCC, *A Programme to Overcome Violence* (1997); A. van der Bent, *Commitment to God's World: A Concise Critical Survey of Ecumenical Social Thought* (1995) 107–19; A. Lange, "Die Gestalt der Friedenskirchen," Heidelberg U. (1985); *Messenger* (Jan., 1986) 14–17, (Nov., 1988) 5, (July, 1989) 7, (Feb., 1994) 8, (April, 1994) 8, 22, (Sept., 1994) 7.

Historiography. Since the article on *Historical Writing was completed, using 1980 as the cutoff date, a substantial number of books have been published dealing with Brethren history, teaching, and practice. The most exten-

sive overall survey of Brethren historiography appearing during this period was compiled by a German seminarian, R. W. Burkart, as a MATh thesis at the U. of Erlangen-Nürnberg – *Die Kirche der Bruder* (1986). This was translated into English by Dennis L. Slabaugh, and published as a special issue of *Brethren Life and Thought* (2000), with an update of material from the 1980s and 1990s by D. F. Durnbaugh. Many of the publications mentioned in the following, as well, contain lengthy bibliographies; these can be consulted with profit.

*ANABAPTISM AND *PIETISM. As might be expected, the two formative movements for the Brethren, Anabaptism and Pietism, have been intensively researched in the nearly two decades since 1980. Only a few publications can be mentioned here. Besides the fifth volume of *The Mennonite Encyclopedia* (1990), there are: C. J. Dyck, *An Introduction to Anabaptism,* 3rd ed. (1993); W. R. Estep, *The Anabaptist Story,* 3rd rev. ed. (1996); J. D. Weaver, *Becoming Anabaptist* (1987); and C. A. Snyder, *Anabaptist History and Thought: An Introduction* (1995). The monumental monograph by G. H. Williams, *The Radical Reformation,* is now available in a third, revised edition (1992).

A definitive four-volume *Geschichte des Pietismus* is underway; thus far three volumes have been published (1993, 1995, 2000). The chapters of most direct interest for Brethren history were both written by H. Schneider, dealing with Radical Pietism in the 17th and 18th centuries; his research report on Radical Pietist historiography, published in the journal *Pietismus und Neuzeit* 8 (1982) and 9 (1983), also deals extensively with the early Brethren. (These three essays are in the process of English translation for publication in the U.S.) The masterful study of Radical Pietist publishing by H. J. Schrader (1989) contains helpful data. A brief history of Pietism paying attention to Brethren developments, that of J. Wallmann, *Der Pietismus* (1990), is part of a multivolume handbook on church history.

Several regional publications provide useful information; they include: *Chronik Düdelsheim, 792–1992* (1991), with the family history of Peter Becker; a revised edition of H. Brunn's study, *Schriesheimer Mühlen* (1989); and a special issue of *Wittgenstein* (Fall, 1997), focused on Radical Pietism.

English language studies of Pietism can be named: W. R. Ward, *The Protestant Evangelical Awakening* (1992); T. A. Campbell, *The Religion of the Heart* (1991); and the revision of D. Brown's book, *Understanding Pietism* (1996). The first named has only limited reference to the Brethren; the second none at all. S. L. Longenecker's book, *Piety and Tolerance: Pennsylvania German Religion, 1700–1850* (1994), treats Pietist influences upon American church-life.

GENERAL BRETHREN HISTORIES. Two comprehensive histories of Brethren development are *Brethren Society: The Cultural Transformation of a "Peculiar People"* (1995) by C. F. Bowman and *Fruit of the Vine: A History of the Brethren, 1708–1995* (1997) by D. F. Durnbaugh. Both of substantial size, they present the story of Brethren change over time. Bowman's book combines historical and sociological analysis, Durnbaugh's employs social history. Both draw on the series of source books, initiated in 1958, including the fourth in the series, that was edited by R. E. Sappington, *The Brethren in Industrial America* (1985). *The Brethren Historical Committee* (CB) has authorized S. L. Longenecker to compile a fifth source-

book. A revision of an earlier introduction, edited by D. F. Durnbaugh, is *Church of the Brethren: Yesterday and Today* (1986).

DISTRICT HISTORIES. The genre of district histories continues; four may be mentioned. The first, by E. C. Kaylor, Jr., dealing with the Middle District of Pennsylvania, is *Out of the Wilderness* (1981); it breaks with the older model of district history by employing a narrative style. The second follows the same path in describing the Brethren in Indiana; authored by Steve Bowers, it is *Planting the Faith in a New Land* (1992). The third, *Moving Toward the Mainstream* (1995), authored by D. R. Fitzkee, can be considered a case study of C. F. Bowman's approach applied to the Atlantic Northeast District of Pennsylvania. E. F. Bittinger's book, *Allegheny Passage* (1990) is a voluminous study of the West Marva District (West Virginia, Maryland). Building extensively on detailed family histories, Bittinger was able to locate early congregations hitherto undocumented.

EPHRATA SOCIETY. E. G. Alderfer, *The Ephrata Commune* (1985) is a general overview of the society resulting from the first division among the Brethren in North America. In the same year P. C. Erb edited a useful, if marred, anthology of Ephrata writings in translation, *Johann [sic] Conrad Beissel and the Ephrata Community: Mystical and Historical Texts* (1985). A dissertation by J. A. Bach (1997) provides the best available study of the roots of Ephrata religious understandings.

PERSONALITIES. A number of biographies and autobiographies have appeared since 1980. Among the longer and more substantive entries are: S. L. Longenecker, *The Christopher Sauers* (1981); D. G. Murray, *Sister Anna [Mow]* (1983); J. W. Miller, *Sammeln und Wieder Sammeln: Collections and Recollections* ([1986]), by an elder of the Old German Baptist Church; N. B. Rohrer, *A Saint in Glory Stands* (1986), the biography of Grace Brethren leader *Alva J. McClain; R. A. Neff, *Valley of the Shadow* (1987), a story of *John Kline based on sources only accessible to the author; S. L. Longenecker, *Selma's Peacemaker: Ralph Smeltzer and Civil Rights Mediation* (1987); D. F. Durnbaugh, *Pragmatic Prophet: The Life of Michael Robert Zigler* (1989), placed within the context of his church leadership; Inez G. Long, *Lord's Day Morning: Work and Worship the Brethren Way* (1989), a beautifully-written memoir by a teacher, author, and pastor's wife; R. R. Peters, *Foothills to Mountaintops: My Pilgrimage to Wholeness* (1990), by a church executive; R. H. Mason, *The Inimitable George Mason* (1991), a biography told largely in letters written by the loving widow of an ingenious missionary; E. C. Kaylor, Jr., *Martin Grove Brumbaugh* (1996), the biography of a noted educator and public servant; and C. M. Bieber, *Around the World for Eighty Years* (2002).

PEACE. D. W. Brown, *Biblical Pacifism: A Peace Church Perspective* (1986) is an updating and expansion of his earlier *Brethren Pacifism*. A. N. Keim and G. M. Stoltzfus, *The Politics of Conscience: The Historic Peace Churches and America at War, 1917–1955* (1988) expands on the work by R. D. Bowman for the Brethren. Much material on the Brethren peace witness is found in P. Brock, *Freedom from Violence: Sectarian Nonresistance from the Middle Ages to the Great War* (1991). See also C. Eller, *Conscientious Objection and the Second World War* (1991).

INSTITUTIONAL HISTORIES. M. S. H. Rosenberger has written several studies of Brethren institutions; these

include: *That They Might Have Life: A History of the Brethren Health and Welfare Association* ([1987]) and *Caring: A History of Brethren Homes, 1889–1989* (1989). S. L. Bowman wrote a thorough study of Brethren polity, *Power and Polity Among the Brethren* (1987); this can be matched, on the side of the Fellowship of Grace Brethren Churches, by J. R. Young's dissertation, *The Relationship Between Local Grace Brethren Churches and Their Denominational Leadership: Case Studies* (1996).

*BRETHREN ENCYCLOPEDIA MONOGRAPHS AND SPECIAL PUBLICATIONS. Although incorporated for the primary purpose of publishing the reference work, the board of Brethren Encyclopedia, Inc. also anticipated other publications. The first was a collection of articles from the encyclopedia (plus a bibliography) on the five sponsoring Brethren-related bodies. Called *Meet the Brethren* (1984) and intended to promote mutual understanding among the separate Brethren, it proved popular enough to be reprinted in 1995.

A major breakthrough came about in 1986 with the initiation of a monograph series on Brethren life and thought. Its rationale was to make available books worthy of publication but unlikely (because of their technical nature) to find acceptance by denominational publishers. The authors and titles of the series (edited by William R. Eberly) are: H. T. Durnbaugh, *The German Hymnody of the Brethren, 1720–1903* (1986); D. R. Stoffer, *The Background and Development of Brethren Doctrines, 1650–1987* (1989); D. F. Durnbaugh, *Brethren Beginnings* (1992); H. Renkewitz, *Hochmann von Hochenau (1670–1721),* trans. W. G. Willoughby (1993); E. F. Rupel, *Brethren Dress: A Testimony to Faith* (1994); and W. G. Willoughby, *The Beliefs of the Early Brethren 1706–1735* (1999). There are three additional Brethren Encyclopedia publications: *The Complete Writings of Alexander Mack* (1991), ed. W. R. Eberly; *Report of the Proceedings of the Brethren World Assembly, Elizabethtown College, Elizabethtown, Pennsylvania, July 15–July 18, 1992 (1994),* ed. D. F. Durnbaugh; and *Report of the Proceedings of the 1998 Brethren World Assembly, Bridgewater College, Bridgewater, Virginia, July 15–18, 1998* (1999), ed. D. R. Stoffer.

*FORUM FOR RELIGIOUS STUDIES. Since 1990 an interdisciplinary Forum for Religious Studies based at *Bridgewater College, VA, has sponsored a series of well-planned symposia on topics related to Brethren heritage, bringing together leading Brethren and Mennonite scholars. Presentations at their conferences were later published; the resulting books, with their editors (themselves active in the Bridgewater Forum), are: E. F. Bittinger, ed., *Brethren in Transition: 20th Century Directions and Dilemmas* (1992); C. F. Bowman and S. L. Longenecker, eds., *Anabaptist Currents: History in Conversation with the Present* (1995); and S. L. Longenecker, ed., *The Dilemma of Anabaptist Piety: Strengthening or Straining the Bonds of Community?* (1997). DFD

Rainer W. Burkhart, "History of Research on the Church of the Brethren," *BLT* 45 (Winter/Spring 2000) 1–71, 84–88; D. F. Durnbaugh, "Bibliographical Note for Publications Issued in the 1980s and 1990s," 72–83.

Hoffman, Paul W. (CB), b. 1932, pastor, educator, college president. The son of Ralph W. and Tessie M. Heeter Hoffman in Macy, IN, Paul Hoffman married Joanna Begerow of Woodland, MI, in 1954. They had four children: Deborah, Daniel, John, and James.

Paul W. Hoffman. McPheson College collection.

Hoffman's education included degrees from *Manchester College (BS, 1954), *Bethany Theol. Sem. (MDiv, 1957), U. of Michigan (MA, 1964), and Purdue U. (PhD in psychology, 1971). He was ordained at Roann, IN (1955). His career included a pastorate at the *Detroit, MI, Trinity congregation (1957–62), service at Manchester College as professor, coach, and dean of students (1962–76), and a long tenure as president of *McPherson College (1976–96). As president he was especially attentive to the nexus between college and church. Known as an exceptional fundraiser, Hoffman completed three capital campaigns and significantly increased the college's endowment.

During Paul Hoffman's educational career, part-time pursuits included being moderator of seven congregations, two districts, and the 1983 *Annual Conference. He served on numerous study committees and special consultations for Annual Conference and its agencies, including a genetic engineering study, oversight committee for *EFSM and TRIM programs, and a study of ministry. He received an honorary degree from Manchester College (DHum, 1997). LAF

See also HIGHER EDUCATION.

TBE (1983–84) 781, 1657; *Messenger* (May, 1976) 5, (Feb., 1983) 4, 12–14, (Sept., 1983) 13, 17, (April, 1996) 9, (June, 1996) 5; *McPherson College Bulletin* (April, 1976) 2, (Jan., 1977) 2, (July, 1977) 2; *McPherson College Review* (Fall, 1982) 1, (Summer, 1983) 1, (Summer, 1985) 6–7, (Winter, 1987) 11–13, (Spring, 1991) 10–11, (Winter, 1993) 3–5, (Summer, 1996) 2–4; *McPherson [KS] Sentinel* (Feb. 3, 1996) 1, (May 7, 1998) 1, 3; *Salina [KS] Journal* (Feb. 15, 1996); *Manchester College: The First Seventy-Five Years* (1964) 223; T. K. Jones, *Manchester College* (1989) 160, 238; C. Mines, *McPherson College: The First Century, 1887–1987* (1987) 26–27.

Holy Spirit Conference (CB). *Brethren Renewal Service sponsored the first Holy Spirit Conference in the spring of 1976 at Valparaiso, IN, with 1,400 persons

attending; the second conference was held in 1977 in Bowling Green, OH, with over 1,000 in attendance. In 1978, to afford more opportunities for people to attend, regional conferences planned by local committees were held in Fresno, CA; McPherson, KS; North Manchester, IN; and Elizabethtown, PA. Since 1978, a Holy Spirit Conference has been organized each July by a planning committee composed of *Church of the Brethren members, as well as non-Brethren, at Eastern Mennonite U., Harrisonburg, VA. Beginning in June 2004, the yearly conference will be held at *Bridgewater College. CBS
Personal information.

Home Education (OGBB). Home education or homeschooling among the *Old German Baptist Brethren is best understood by tracing the history of education in American society. During the 17th and 18th centuries, American education was centered in the home, with parental involvement and transmission of family values, emphases on community life and academic and vocational pursuits. In the late 19th and early 20th centuries, educational responsibility shifted from parents to the state. Compulsory school attendance, with trained professionals teaching children, became what is known as public education.

Alternative schooling rose to popularity in the 1960s and early 1970s. Some studies have shown a connection between this era and the present homeschooling movement. In a 2002 study, National Home Education Research Institute (NHERI) estimated that as many as two million U.S. students in grades K-12 were being homeschooled.

OGBB parents, disenchanted with the environment of the public school system, sent a query to their 1976 *Annual Meeting asking permission for individuals to withdraw their children from public schools in order to teach them in private schools. This appeal was denied; however, parents were given the liberty to teach them at home according to local and state laws. A four-part query came to conference in 1979, asking permission for OGBB children to attend private schools. The request was granted, with a three-part statement that began with "according to scripture, the instruction of children is the responsibility of parents . . . ." An important point in the homeschooling issue is that parents recognize their own responsibility to direct the education and the raising of their children. Homeschooling has been referred to as a "family restoration movement" (G. Sarris).

At the end of the 2001–02 school year, a comparison study showed 31 percent of OGBB students were attending public schools, 35 percent were attending private schools, and 34 percent were receiving their education at home. A small number of homeschooled students have received further vocational or college education.

Motivations for homeschooling vary. The responsibility to teach religious and cultural values, concern for individual growth and development, a desire for strong family relationships, an avoidance of peer pressure in an institutional environment, and perhaps financial reasons are contributing factors for OGBB members to decide to teach their children at home. In some areas, where the private school goes to the eighth grade, those students usually finish high school in the home.

There are a number of curricular approaches available for homeschooling. OGBB members use a variety of approaches, depending upon the individual, family needs,

and learning styles. Homeschooling laws vary from state to state. Documentation from a Homeschool Legal Defense Fund shows that 11 states and territories ask nothing from parents, 34 states and U.S. territories require low to moderate regulation, while 11 other states require records and test scores. All states provide information on homeschooling and sponsor a yearly state convention. There are many local support groups as well. SAM

Stewardship *Minutes* (*OGBB*) (1976, 1979); B. D. Ray, *2002–2003 Worldwide Guide to Homeschooling; Facts And Stats* (2003); *On The Benefits Of Homeschool* (2002); C. J. Klicka, *The Right Choice: The Incredible Failure Of Public Education and The Rising Hope Of Homeschooling* (1992); C. Clarkson and S. Clarkson, *Educating The Whole-Hearted Child* (1996); J. T. Gatto, *The Underground History of American Education* (2001); D. Guterson, *Family Matters: Why Homeschooling Makes Sense* (1992).

Home Schooling. *See* **Home Education.**

Homelessness. During the 1980s, the nation's homeless population grew and Brethren responded in a variety of ways. The problem of homelessness was evident in both rural communities and urban centers when economic policies increased the gap between the rich and the poor. As the economy made dramatic shifts from an industrial base to a service and technology-driven system, poverty and homelessness increased. The farm economy also suffered greatly during this time.

Church of the Brethren congregations were active in numerous ways. The *Washington City CB congregation opened a lunch-time soup kitchen to feed the homeless only a few blocks from the nation's capitol building. The soup kitchen was staffed by *Brethren Volunteer Service (BVS) workers and by volunteers from neighboring CB congregations. Other BVS projects were opened in Fremont, CA; San Antonio, TX; and Des Moines, IA.

Several congregations were involved in more long-term housing issues such as transitional housing ventures in Ambler, Harrisburg, and Lancaster, PA. After their church building burned down, the *Springfield, OR, congregation purchased a motel and used it as a place of worship and a shelter for homeless families. Others in the denomination became active in *Habitat for Humanity and shared their financial resources through the Global Food Crisis Fund.

In Chicago, Duane E. Grady, a *Bethany Theol. Sem. student, became the first executive director of the Interfaith Council for the Homeless and developed a warming center program, one of the most innovative and cost-effective emergency shelter programs of its time.

While the issue of homelessness has not been addressed by the *Dunkard Brethren Church in an official way, many individual members of several congregations have assisted the homeless. In some cases, young people from a congregation assisted at a homeless shelter by caring for the meal and giving gifts or care packages to those being served. One congregation conducts a service at the Bowery Mission in New York City each year. Members of other Brethren bodies assist the homeless in less structured ways. DEG

D. Grady, *Helping the Homeless: God's Word in Action* (1988); P. B. Wezeman, *Benjamin Brody's Backyard Bag,* illus. C. Raschka (1999), a children's book; "A Place to Call Home," video (1988); *Messenger* (Sept., 1988) 4, (Oct., 1988) 16, (May, 1990) 2–3.

Homosexuality existed as a silent reality among Brethren, dealt with privately rather than openly, until

well into the 20th century. Then in the 1970s, in the context of the sexual revolution in America, a controversy about homosexuality erupted in several large Protestant denominations, spreading to some Brethren congregations but missing others. Suddenly this issue, hidden for centuries, became divisive.

Four Brethren bodies remain remarkably free of contention over homosexuality. In the *Fellowship of Grace Brethren Churches and the *Old German Baptist Brethren, opposition to homosexual behavior is so widely accepted and uniformly understood that no written statement has been considered necessary. Homosexual members are required to be celibate.

The *Dunkard Brethren and *The Brethren Church have adopted official statements prohibiting homosexual conduct. At their 1992 General Conference, Dunkard Brethren opposed all homosexual practices unequivocally, refusing membership to persons who continued such practices. Scriptural passages (1 Cor. 6:9–10, Rom. 1:22–8, and Gen. 19:1–14) were listed without comment to substantiate the church's position. Dunkard Brethren rarely address social issues during General Conference; doctrinal and non-conformity items dominate their business agenda. The fact that homosexuality is one of only two social issues singled out for official action (abortion being the other) indicates strong conviction.

The Brethren Church at General Conference in 1986 linked homosexual activity with adulterous relationships as violations of the institution of marriage established by God, citing Lev. 18:22, Rom. 1:26–27, and 1 Cor. 6:9–10 as scriptures condemning homosexual relations. The Brethren Church ruled that homosexuality is not an inherited condition in a way that would remove choice and free individuals of moral responsibility, yet the church called for research on the causes of homosexuality in order to improve treatment of "a deviation" from the Creator's plan.

The *Church of the Brethren statement differs in tone and complexity from other Brethren positions. An Annual Conference statement adopted in 1983 (reaffirmed in 1995) declared that heterosexuality, not homosexuality, is "God's intention for creation." However, the Church of the Brethren cautioned against over generalization in the interpretation of scriptures. For example, Gen. 19 and Judges 19 decry assault and gang rape but not necessarily other forms of homosexual relationships. 1 Cor. 6:9–11, 1 Tim. 1:9–11, and Rom. 1:26–27 disallow male prostitution, lust, and cultic promiscuity but may not apply to enduring and loving relationships. Neither Jesus nor the prophets mention homosexuality. Although the Bible deals candidly with homosexuality, it is not a major theme.

The 1983 statement listed two acceptable lifestyle options for homosexual persons. *Celibacy* (Matt. 19:11–12; 1 Cor. 7:6–7) was advocated for those who are able to abstain from sexual activity and voluntarily choose to do so. *Conversion to heterosexuality* was commended with the admission that this alternative is "complex and difficult and for some impossible." Practical questions remain unanswered for those for whom celibacy is not a gift and conversion is impossible. *Covenantal relationships*, i.e., close-coupled, monogamous relationships for homosexual persons, although included as an option by the study committee, were ruled unacceptable.

Although homosexual acts were rejected, "open, forthright conversations" with homosexual persons were encouraged. From 1986 through 1996 Conference officers designated a room at the Annual Conference center for personal dialogue and scheduled panel discussions for public debate. Most of these events were organized by the *Brethren/Mennonite Council for Gay Concerns (established in 1976) or the *Parish Ministries Commission. GEW, Jr.

Minutes (CB) (1983, 1995); Minutes (DB) (1992); Minutes (BC) (1986); BLT 36 (Winter, 1991) 3–51 (special issue); 39 (Spring, 1994): 74–114 (special issue); Messenger (Sept., 1983) 14–16, (Feb., 1984) 20, 22, (April, 1984) 1, 24, 26, 28, 30–31, (Dec., 1987) 1, 7, 30, (June, 1993) 6–7; interviews.

Hope Brethren Fellowship (BC) was a multicultural church ministering in Stockton, CA. Pastor Bernie Tuazon began this ministry in 1990 under the direction of the Nazarene Church. *The Brethren Church assumed this ministry in 1995. The primary focus began in the Filipino community; however, the cultural demographics of the congregation were constantly changing. A main premise of this ministry was: "The Bible cuts across cultural boundaries." This was evident in that the church attracted members from the American, Mexican-American, Portuguese, and Vietnamese cultures, as well as several others. Hope Brethren Fellowship was a cell church with several home Bible studies based in apartment buildings throughout the Stockton area. Worship services were conducted in the *Stockton, CA, BC building as a shared facility and music was promoted as an integral part of worship. In Dec. 1998, this work was closed by the Northern California District Mission Board. DLL
BE (June, 1996) 10.

Nelson T. Huffman. BHLA collection.

The Rockingham Male Chorus

Some persons seem almost larger than life, and musician *Nelson T. Huffman was such a man. Vigorous, jovial, with a shock of wavy hair, and a solo voice whose timbre and range could have been the envy of many professionals, he contributed greatly to the spirit of Brethren singing in the *Shenandoah Valley of Virginia and beyond. Whether as a voice

teacher, a choral director, or in leading congregational singing, he inspired participants to sing old and new songs to the Lord "better than they could." When he retired as professor of music from *Bridgewater College in 1965, he immediately began work on the long held dream of organizing an all male chorus to sing religious music. While his Brethren roots and loyalty were deep, it was a mark of the man that, in those he recruited for the chorus, their ability to sing and their love of music was far more important than their individual church affiliation. By button-holing some, writing letters to others, Huffman persuaded 48 men, Brethren and non-Brethren, to show up for the first practice held in the *Bridgewater (VA) CB, on Nov. 8, 1966, and The Rockingham Male Chorus was born.

Membership in the chorus has varied from that number to as high as 60 or more, with over 170 different persons from all walks of life having participated over the years. The ages of the singers ranged from teenagers to nonagenarians. Practicing weekly on Tuesdays from 7:30 to 9:00 p.m. from mid-Sept. through early Dec., and from mid-Jan. to May, the participants have, across the years, continued to pay for their own personal expenses, including travel to rehearsals, board, and lodging for concerts. Offerings have helped pay for music, publicity, and additional expenses for bus transportation on extended trips.

With but a few concerts their first year, the Rockingham Male Chorus grew in their ministry of religious music, so that by the time of their 500th program at the Bridgewater CB, on Nov. 29, 1987, they had averaged over 25 concerts a year. Sometimes billed as the "Singing Evangelists," the members not only had a strong sense of fellowship and camaraderie, but as one member said, "We felt a common sense of mission and ministry to our Lord." Their program often included a testimony by a member which emphasized the importance of commitment to God, Christ, and the church. Through those first 500 performances, the charisma and the vitality of "Nelson T" kept the quality and vitality of the work of the chorus high, so that it held its reputation as an exceptional and inspirational singing group.

After Huffman's retirement following the 500th performance, the chorus voted to continue, and in a short time, called David MacMillan as director. Under his leadership the chorus has continued its ministry in travels ranging from Canada to Florida, from Iowa to the East Coast. And so the dream of a unique Brethren musician reared in the Brethren love of singing and skilled in classics, hymns, and gospel music, has continued to carry the message of the Good News through the voices of committed male singers. On Sept. 16, 2001, they presented their 1000th concert in the Bridgewater CB. EWF, Jr.

Bridgewater College (1993) passim; *Virginia* (1973) 411; materials in the Rockingham (VA) Historical Society.

Huffman, Nelson Thomas (CB), 1901–92, professor, music director, businessman, leading citizen. A son of William H. and Ella Mae Sours Huffman, Nelson Huffman was born at Rileyville, VA, and obtained degrees from *Bridgewater College (1925), Peabody Conservatory of Music (Voice Certificate), Cincinnati Conser-

vatory of Music (BMus), and Northwestern University (MMus, 1937). He was honored with a degree by Bridgewater College (DMus, 1976).

Huffman chaired the Department of Music at Bridgewater College (1925–65) and was granted the Alumnus of the Year Award (1965). He was music director for the Massanetta Bible Conference for 25 years, *Annual Conference several years, and the Bridgewater congregational choir 50 years. He organized and directed (1966–87) the *Rockingham Male Chorus and gave 500 programs from *Pennsylvania to *Florida. His performances, always featuring his outstanding solo voice, included several at Constitution Hall in Washington, DC.

An agent for Investors Diversified Services, Huffman also was active in business, owning companies in Rainelle, WV, Lynchburg, VA, and Bridgewater, VA. He served on the town council and as mayor of Bridgewater for three-and-a-half terms. He and Bertha Barbara Thomas were married in 1922; their children are Eleanor Christine Myers and Nelson Thomas. EFB

Messenger (May, 1992) 3, 39; *Virginia* (1973), 411; F. F. Wayland, *Bridgewater College: The First Hundred Years, 1880–1980* (1993) passim.

Hymnal: A Worship Book (CB). In 1992, *Hymnal: A Worship Book* was published jointly by the *Church of the Brethren, the *General Conference Mennonite Church, and the *Mennonite Church in North America, after ten years of work together. The CB's 1951 *Brethren Hymnal* was becoming dated, with many congregations purchasing other hymnals and songbooks; so the Brethren initiated preparation for a new hymnal. The two Mennonite bodies joined, with the understanding that the Brethren would provide 50 percent of the operating budget. Soon after the project began, *The Brethren Church sent two representatives to one meeting, but they decided not to participate. The Freewill *Baptists attended several meetings but pulled out because of doctrinal differences. The *Churches of God General Conference (Findlay, OH) and the *Mennonite Brethren participated for several years but did not continue through actual publication.

The work of the hymnal was shared by four committees: Music, Text, Worship, and Publishers. By the time of publication, 658 hymns and responses and over 200 worship resources, including scripture readings, had been selected for inclusion. Over 200 texts from the 1951 hymnal also were included. More than 100 texts, tunes, or translations are by Brethren and Mennonite writers and composers. The hymnal encompasses all musical eras and styles, from chants to chorales to contemporary texts and tunes, including *African-American spirituals and black gospel, Taizé "sung prayers," gospel songs, and songs from Asian, Hispanic, Native American, and African sources (most including their native language). Over 80 chorale-like selections represent the German roots of the participating denominations. Two hundred hymns and songs were written since the mid-1960's, influenced by inclusive *language concerns.

The format of the hymnal follows the structure of worship, an innovation for denominational hymnals: Gathering, Praising/Adoring, Confessing/Reconciling, Proclaiming, Affirming Faith, Praying, Offering, Witnessing, Sending. Also included are hymns on *baptism, *feetwashing, *love feast and communion, *weddings, child blessings, *anointings, *ordination, and *funerals, as well as a more devotional section reflecting

the faith journey. Traditional Brethren themes include peace and justice, service, nurture, evangelism, health, and healing.

The reception of *Hymnal: A Worship Book* by the participating denominations, congregations, and ecumenical hymnologists was more enthusiastic than expected; 120,000 copies were sold by 1994. By Jan. 1996 the hymnal was in its fifth printing, which included updated information and corrections. These three denominations, who identify themselves as *Anabaptists and *Pietists, produced a book, deemed quite eclectic, that reflects an eagerness to sustain denominational and historical tradition and to include recent hymns and songs from around the globe.

In addition to the hymnal, there are two important supplementary books. *Hymnal Accompaniment Handbook* (1993) contains accompaniments for over 70 melodies, essays on different musical styles, supplemental instrumental and choral parts, and performance suggestions for song leaders. *Hymnal Companion* (1996) gives anecdotal and historical information on hymns, tunes, and resources as well as biographies of the writers. NRF

"Reviews of *Hymnal: A Worship Book*," by Paul Westermeyer, Hedwig T. Durnbaugh, Glenn M. Lehman, and Stephen Jacoby, *Pennsylvania Mennonite Heritage* 17 (April, 1994) 2–16; D. J. Rempel-Smucker, "An Index of Hymn Texts in Hymnal: A Worship Book and Their Prior Usage in All Major English-Language Hymnals of the Church of the Brethren, (Old) Mennonite Church, and General Conference Mennonite Church in North America," *Pennsylvania Mennonite Heritage* 17 (April, 1994) 17–28; *Messenger* (May, 1988) 16, (Feb., 1989) 7, (March, 1992) 8, (June, 1992) 10, (Aug./Sept., 1992) 22, 28.

I-K

Iglesia Cristiana Pentecostal de Cuba (ICP) (CB). The Christian Pentecostal Church of *Cuba was a partner denomination with the *Church of the Brethren in the program, *Misión Mutua en las Américas, beginning in 1980. Chosen because it grew out of an indigenous movement after the revolution and was not conditioned by dependency on non-Cuban Christian groups, the ICP gave the CB an inside perspective on life for Christians under the Fidel Castro Ruz regime. The ICP favored many of the revolution's goals, even though they experienced personal restrictions because of their faith. ICP membership came from the poorer, less-educated segment of pre-revolutionary society. Women and African-Cubans have equal opportunity for leadership in the church, a result of new thinking in the Christian community encouraged by the revolution. Brethren "Mutualistas" stayed in Cuban homes and spoke in their *meetinghouses. ICP representatives attended *Annual Conferences to bring greetings and visited U.S. congregations. Activities with ICP were curtailed because of the U.S. embargo against Cuba and limited communication between the two nations. In later years, ICP joined the CB in relating to a church in Nicaragua. BMC

Messenger (Aug., 1979) 6, (Dec., 1980) 13–15, (June, 1981) 27–31, (Dec., 1981) 4, (Sept., 1982) 6–7, (Nov., 1982) 6–7, (Feb., 1986) 7, (April, 1986) 4, (July, 1988) 4, (Nov., 1990) 22, Feb., 1991) 9, (July, 1991) 8, (March, 1992) 6; *Christianity and Crisis* (Aug. 26, 1985) 329–33; D. F. Durnbaugh, *Fruit of the Vine* (1997) 365–66.

*India, Church of North (CNI) was inaugurated in 1970 following initiatives beginning as early as 1929. In 1957 the *Church of the Brethren and the *Disciples of Christ joined the negotiations begun in 1951 among the United Church of North India, the Anglican Church of India, the British and Australian Methodist Churches, and the Council of the Baptist Churches of North India. A plan for church union agreed upon in 1965 became the basis for inaugurating the CNI at Nagpur in 1970.

The 25 congregations of the First and Second Districts of the CB in India voted overwhelmingly to enter the united church. Brethren leaders from these two districts immediately assumed significant positions at diocesan and synod levels, including the first bishop of the Diocese of Gujarat, *Ishwarlal Christachari.

In the late 1970s, dissent arose in the former Brethren mission areas. A small schismatic group emerged, who called themselves Brethren and proceeded to initiate court suits in Gujarat State to claim ownership of mission properties held in the name of the Church of the Brethren *General Board. In response the *Annual Conference and General Board passed clarifying resolutions in 1988, reiterating support for the CNI and restating that these mission properties were meant for the use and ownership of the CNI. This notwithstanding, the controversy continued to emerge in India and in the U.S. in 2000.

Denominational participation continues in the CNI Partners in Mission Commission which brings together representatives from the various bodies which formed the united church. In 1994 and 1995 the CNI and the CB held special celebrations on the 100th anniversary of the Brethren mission in India and the 25th anniversary of the CNI. Financial support by the CB to the CNI and the Gujarat United School of Theology continued through 1997. CB financial support for the *Rural Service Center has continued to the present time. HLG

Minutes (CB) (1988) 649–60; General Board Minutes (CB), (Oct., 1988) 4; S. Bhagat, *Church Union in India: The Church of the Brethren Experience* (2001); "India Covenant (Some History, Some Concerns" (2001); D. F. Durnbaugh, ed., *Yesterday and Today* (1986), 146–47, and *Fruit of the Vine* (1997) 566; *Messenger* (Oct. 22, 1970) 14, (March 1, 1971) 2–7, (Oct., 1983) 13–22, (Jan., 1984) 26–28; (March, 1984) 26–29, (July, 1984) 5, (Dec., 1986) 6, (Feb., 1988) 10–11, (Oct., 1988) 43–44, (March, 1996) 22–23, (Feb., 1997) 23–25.

Information Technology, Church Use of. In the 1980s a computer small enough to fit on a desk became a cost-effective tool for individuals, small businesses, and organizations such as churches. In a church office, the desktop computer facilitated writing, editing, and filing manuscripts and correspondence; and preparing bulletins, newsletters, and minutes of meetings became convenient and efficient.

In the mid 1990s the Internet developed to the stage that it enabled computers to communicate easily with other computers. Thus, correspondence could be transmitted as electronic mail (e-mail) instantly without the delay and postage that was required for physical transmission of paper documents. In combination with the World Wide Web (WWW), the Internet provided a means of storing documents, photographs, and movies that could be addressed by a computer from anywhere in the world, and it opened the commercial world to online purchasing, banking, and transactions.

Most of the Brethren bodies made extensive use of the computer, the Internet, e-mail, and the WWW. *The Brethren Church, the *Church of the Brethren, the *Fellowship of Grace Brethren Churches, and the *Conservative Grace Brethren Churches International developed colorful and attractive official Web sites that enabled any interested person to learn about the denominations' beliefs, programs, and personnel. Many of these Web sites also functioned as repositories of information and as places of interaction, through downloading forms to registering for events and purchasing Brethren-related resources. Some dedicated persons also developed unofficial Web sites and e-mail discussion groups called listserves. The combination of the computer and e-mail transmitted over the Internet enabled rapid announcement of meetings, efficient dissemination of minutes and reports, and easy communication among individuals separated even by long distances allowing them to share ideas and to work cooperatively in drafting reports and documents.

Church of the Brethren Network (COB-NET) went online in 1996 as the first national Brethren Web site. It was a venture of Ronald J. Gordon to offer Brethren online identity and to provide an opportunity for members to express themselves and to reach out to the world for Jesus Christ. This unofficial voluntary ministry offers modest homepages without cost to CB congregations, districts, agencies, camps, and distinctively Brethren organizations such as the *Fellowship of Brethren Genealogists. COB-NET has a wealth of interpretative and historical documents, plus numerous articles submitted by the membership.

Because information available on the WWW is uncontrolled, inappropriate statements, pornographic images, and advertisements appear there. *Old German Baptist Brethren and *Dunkard Brethren caution their members concerning its use. While the OGBB have never taken an irrevocable stand on matters of modern technology, the Internet, being a blend of usefulness and perversion, posed a problem of control. It was held that news and useful information was available in less damaging ways, and permissive parents were admonished to preserve the sanctity of the home. While OGBB forbade use of the World Wide Web by OGBB families, by 2003 OGBB members increasingly used the Internet in connection with their employment. Recognizing the efficiency and economy of the Internet, Dunkard Brethren used the computer and e-mail, but they cautioned members concerning use of the WWW. DB families and many families of other Brethren bodies use electronic filters to prevent unwanted invasion of undesirable material.

To make a Web site available on the Internet, it was necessary for the information to be recorded on a host computer that was always turned on and connected to the Internet. In the CB, Brethren Benefit Trust established a subsidiary in 1998 called eMountain Communications to provide Internet-related and technology-related services to Brethren and others who affirm Brethren values; it hosted Web sites for congregations and other Brethren organizations, and makes available technical assistance to persons developing Web sites. eMountain also co-produced with *Brethren Press an outstanding Brethren history resource on CD-ROM entitled *Without Fear or Hesitation*.

In response to a need for some ministerial candidates to acquire a seminary education while residing at a distance from campus, *Bethany Theol. Sem. developed a graduate theological program called "Connections." In 2002, Daniel W. Ulrich was appointed Associate Dean and Director of Distributed Education to lead the implementation of this program. Beginning in 2003, a student could earn an MDiv degree by combining courses taught using the Internet and intensive courses on campus. Intensive courses involve either a two-week stay on campus or a series of weekend meetings. Courses taught over the Internet involve students communicating electronically with the professor and other students to achieve the desired learning objectives. *Ashland Theol. Sem. began Internet online courses in 2002 with a course entitled *Technology in Ministry* and in 2003, *Old Testament I.* Both seminaries use information technology to enhance learning by resident students.

Because of its tremendous advantages and in spite of its threats, use of the Internet by Brethren bodies, congregations, and related agencies increased spectacularly in the 1990s and the beginning of the 21st century. DVU

See also MASS MEDIA, USES OF.

www.cob-net.org (May 15, 2003); www.brethrenchurch.org (May 15, 2003); www.brethren.org (May 15, 2003); www.fgbci.org (May 15, 2003); www.dunkardbrethrenchurch.com (May 15, 2003); www.bright.net/~dmoeller/cgbci (May 15, 2003); www.eMountain.net (May 15, 2003); www.bethanyseminary.edu (May 15, 2003); D. B. Kraybill and C. F. Bowman, *On the Backroad to Heaven,* (2001): 167–69; correspondence, Fred W. Benedict (Jan. 12, 2002) and Dale R. Stoffer (May 22, 2003).

Ingraham, M. Virgil (BC), businessman, pastor, missions executive. Virgil Ingraham (1916–2003) was born on Oct. 30 near Merrill, OR, and was raised in Manteca, CA, where he completed education for a business career. He married Alice Larsen on June 14, 1941. During naval service in *World War II, he conducted many Bible studies on his transport ship. After the war he pursued a business career, eventually becoming the comptroller of Stockton (CA) Iron Works (1946–53).

Ordained in 1945, Ingraham was the self-supported pastor of churches in *Manteca, *Stockton, and *Thornton, CA. He pastored a large, growing congregation in *Nappanee, IN, (1956–63) and moderated the 1962 Brethren Church General Conference. Elected in 1961 to the *Missionary Board of The Brethren Church, he later served as its executive (1963–84). He initiated the establishment of 31 new congregations, missionary conferences, evangelism/church growth training for laity, and new mission fields in *India, *Colombia, *Malaysia, and *Mexico. In 1985 Ashland Theol. Sem. recognized his dedicated service by awarding an honorary degree (DHum). AEG

BE (Sept., 1984) 20, (July/Aug., 1985) 19; personal information.

International Fellowship of Grace Brethren Churches, a group of evangelical congregations whose heritage stems from the Brethren movement (influenced by *Pietism and *Anabaptism) that began in 1708 in *Schwarzenau, Germany. The *Fellowship of Grace Brethren Churches de-emphasizes denominational structure and emphasizes autonomy of the local church in congregational affairs and as a legal entity. The Grace Brethren heritage is evangelical in its understanding of the priesthood of believers as missional in nature. The Grace Brethren Fellowship is also progressive in its commitment to cultivate the essence of the church, rather than cultural or traditional practices, as an indigenous expression of the body of Christ.

Grace Brethren mission agencies, a seminary, and other institutions exist to equip Grace Brethren congregations in their local and international ministries. Member churches send delegates to an *annual meeting of the Grace Brethren corporation, whose affairs are governed by a 12-member board of directors. Member churches subscribe to a common statement of doctrine (the FGBC *Statement of Faith) based on an acceptance of the Bible as the sole authority in all matters of faith, doctrine, and practice.

In 2001, 28,446 people are members of 270 Grace Brethren congregations throughout the United States. A cell church movement is resulting in the rapid growth of new local congregations, particularly in the southwestern United States. In 2001 Grace Brethren congregations and church-planting ministries also exist in 19 countries outside the United States. The majority of Grace Brethren church members worldwide live in the *Central African Republic, where ca. 250,000 members in 2001 comprise 800 congregations. SF

See also FELLOWSHIP OF GRACE BRETHREN CHURCHES; GRACE BRETHREN INTERNATIONAL MISSIONS; POLITY.

Personal information; D. B. Kraybill and C. N. Hostetter, *Anabaptist World USA* (2001) 86–87, 154–55.

Island Pond, VT, Grace Brethren Church. Organized in 1978, the congregation began meeting in the Brighton School gymnasium. Charter members were Ronald B. and Jane Snay Maxwell, Daniel and Cindy Wright Pierce, Glen and Gunda Poehlmann Gray, William and Barbara Trudeau Hilliker, Claude and Mary Jane Marcoux, Tom and Trudy Lyon Leigh, and Michael and Judy Matteau Phoenix. A church building, located one-half mile west of Island Pond on Route 105, was completed in Dec. 1980. Pastors who served the congregation are James Hunt (1978), Warren E. Tamkin (1980–82), Dale Jenks (1982–89), Robert Kulp (1990–95), John Simpson (1995–96), William Stonebraker (1999–2002), and Jacob P. Kocis (2003–). There were 37 members in 1999. RJ/JRY

Congregational records; *Annual (FGBC)* (1979ff.).

Jackson, Edward A. (FGBC), b. 1925, missionary, pastor. Born in Lodi, OH, Ed Jackson served in the U.S. Marine Corps (1943–46) and then with the Ohio State Highway Patrol (1948–70). He married Pauline Shook. Jackson became president of the FGBC *National Layman's Organization (1968) and was founder and executive director of Grace Brethren Men (1970–74) and founder of Grace Brethren Boys (1972) associations. In 1975 he founded *Men in Missions (Yokefellows). Licensed for ministry in 1974, Jackson was ordained to the pastorate in 1981.

Jackson served Grace Brethren Home Mission in *Kenai, AK (1974–79), *Orlando, FL (1979–81), *Homer, AK (1981–83), *North Pole, AK (1983–84), and *Findlay, OH (1984–85), where he assisted in planting eight other churches, before becoming director of church planting and development for *Grace Brethren Home Missions (1985–90). Retired from the Home Missions agency, Jackson became executive director of Men in Missions (1990–97). He then served as elder/overseer of missions at the *Columbus, OH, GBC and elder/overseer of missions and prayer at the *Powell, OH, GBC. RTC

BMH (Aug. 15, 1990) 6–8, (Oct. 15, 1990) 3.

Jenkins, Charles Lee (FGBC) (1922–2000), pastor, chaplain. Born in Dayton, OH, Lee Jenkins was converted at *Camp Bethany and, sensing a call to ministry, attended Bob Jones College (1940–42). He took classes at Miami U., Oxford, OH, as part of the U.S. Marine Corp V-12 program (1943). He served for nine years in the marines (1942–51), spending time in the South Pacific during World War II. Jenkins married Janis Pleasant in 1946; he studied at *Grace Theol. Sem. (MDiv 1950), and pastored *Lake Odessa, MI, GBC (1950–53).

Jenkins left the pastorate for the *chaplaincy in the U.S. Navy (1953–70). He then served as chaplain at *Grace College and Theol. Sem. (1970–81). While there, he completed his undergraduate and seminary degrees (1975). In 1976, he was awarded an MS degree in guidance and counseling from St. Francis College, Fort Wayne, IN.

Upon leaving *Grace Schools, Jenkins joined the staff of *Grace Village Retirement Complex and, in 1987, began service with Grace Brethren Home Missions as an endorsing agent for military chaplains, a position he held until 1995. RTC

BMH (Sept. 12, 1953) 591, (July 3, 1954) 429, (Feb. 23, 1957) 118–19, (Jan. 3, 1959) 12–13, (Jan. 31, 1959) 71; *Annual (FGBC)* (1951ff.).

Jewell, Jesse Paul (CB), 1922–2003, educator, churchman, community leader. J. Paul Jewell was born in Arcadia, KS, fifth of eight children of Franklin A. and Maude E. Taylor Jewell. In 1947 he married Fern Irene Watkins.

Jewell attended Kansas State Teachers College (1940–47) with interruption for military service (1942–46) during *World War II. He completed both BA and MS degrees in 1947. From 1947 to 1988, he served as faculty member, coach, and dean of student activities at Kansas City, KS, Community College. As a professor of economics and history, he was revered and respected by students of widely diverse backgrounds and perspectives. In retirement he published a history of the college, and in 1996 a new student union building was named in his honor.

As a pillar of the *Kansas City First Central Church for 40 years, Jewell served in every position on the ballot. Active in civic affairs of Kansas City, KS, he served on 11 different community committees on taxation, budget, governmental structure and efficiency, and ethics; he drafted a new plan of city government for Kansas City. Jewell received numerous local and state awards for teaching and civic service, and he was a member of the Board of Trustees of *McPherson College (1966–96) and chair (1975–95). In 2001 he was inducted into the Mid-America Education Hall of Fame. LAF

Personal information; *Messenger* (May/June, 1994) 2–3, (July, 1996) 3.

Jubilee: God's Good News Curriculum (CB). In 1989 Christian educators from the *Church of the Brethren and the *Mennonite Church developed a proposal for a children's Bible-based curriculum. Four *Believers Church publishers entered the cooperative publishing venture (Brethren Press, Faith & Life Press, Mennonite Publishing House, and Evangel Press) and two denominations (Friends United Meeting and Mennonite Brethren Church) joined the Anabaptist Curriculum Publishing Council as partners but not publishers. The curriculum was published in 1994–97 and reused in three-year cycles.

Bible storytelling was the hallmark of Jubilee. In an era of decline in biblical literacy, Jubilee ensured that children through the eighth grade learned a large collection of Old and New Testament texts. Jubilee also emphasized the distinctive theology of the Believers Church tradition unavailable in other curricula, including themes of believer's baptism, discipleship, life in the faith community, and biblical peace and justice. JLG

Personal information; R. W. Regier, *Jubilee Guidebook* (1994).

Julien, Thomas T. (FGBC), b. 1931, missionary, administrator. Born in Arcanum, OH, Tom Julien was baptized in a *United Brethren congregation and simultaneously made a commitment to missionary service. He attended Bob Jones U. (BA, 1953) where he became acquainted with the *Grace Brethren fellowship through the influence of students, including Doris Briner, whom he married in 1953. After a year of teaching graduate studies, Julien enrolled at *Grace Theol. Sem. (MDiv, 1957). While in seminary, Julien was associate pastor of the *Fort Wayne, IN, First Brethren Church and assisted the Brethren Home Missions Council in establishing a sister congregation.

In 1958, the Juliens sailed for *France under the *Grace Brethren Foreign Mission Society. They spent four years in traditional evangelistic ministries, camps, and preaching in the Brethren chapel in Lyon. Sensing the gulf between Christians and non-Christians and the sectarian image of evangelical Christians in France, the Juliens sought a different approach to outreach. In 1964, they were able to secure the 14th century *Chateau of St. Albain, which became an encounter center serving as a bridge between believers and non-believers.

After serving as field superintendent in France, Julien became the European coordinator of Grace Brethren Missions. In 1986 he accepted the responsibility of executive director of Grace Brethren Foreign Missions, which changed its name to *Grace Brethren International Missions in 1995. Under his leadership several new ministries developed, including The World Mission Church, The ACT Strategy, People Adoption, Global Opportunities, the GTS International Institute, and Charis International. Church planting ministries extended into Portugal, the Czech Republic, *Turkey, Russia, Kyrgyzstan, Uruguay, Chile, Paraguay, *Cuba, Thailand, and Cambodia.

Julien served as moderator of the FGBC (1986–87), was made an *Officier de la Republique Centrafricaine* in 1991, and was awarded the honorary DD degree by Grace Theol. Sem. in 1996. In addition to Bible study guides, he authored four books: *Handbook for Young Christians* (1976), *Inherited Wealth: Studies in Ephesians* (1976), *Spiritual Greatness: Studies in Exodus* (1979), and *Seize the Moment* (2000). He also served as visiting professor in the School of Intercultural Studies at Grace Theol. Seminary. RTC

Personal information: *Annual* (*FGBC*) (1956ff.); T. T. Julien, *Seize the Moment: Stories of an Awesome God Empowering Ordinary People* (2000, repr. 2002); *Frontiers* (1972) 183–84.

Keller, Paul W., (CB), educator. Paul Keller (1913–2003) was born in Chicago, the son of J. Edwin and Myrtle Watson Keller. In 1944 he married Hazel Wright; they have four daughters: Judith, Barbara, Carol, and Virginia. He graduated from *Manchester College (AB, 1935), U. of Wisconsin (PhM, 1940), and Northwestern U. (PhD,

Paul W. Keller. BHLA collection.

1955), with other studies at Stanford U. and the U. of London. In 1942, he served his *Civilian Public Service assignment in Elgin, IL, after which he continued for a short time on the staff at the denominational headquarters. After five years of high school teaching, Keller taught at *Bridgewater College and Pennsylvania State U. before moving to Manchester College, where he taught from 1948 to 1983. He served three terms on the *Bethany Theol. Sem. Board, being chair for about ten years. He has authored one book (with Charles T. Brown), *Monologue to Dialogue: An Exploration of Interpersonal Communication* (1973). WRE

See also KELLER FAMILY.

Manchester College files; *Bulletin of the [Manchester College] Peace Studies Institute* 8.1 (July, 1978) cover 2, 13.1–2 (1983) cover 2, 1–2; T. K. Jones, *Manchester College* (1989) 240; L. Eisan, *Pathways of Peace* (1948) 129, 403; personal information.

Kent, Homer Austin, Jr. (FGBC), b. 1926, educator, administrator, author. Born into a pastor's home in Washington, DC, Homer Kent, Jr. made a public profession of faith in Christ on Easter Sunday, 1934. In 1940, his family moved to *Winona Lake, IN. Kent attended grades 9–11 in Warsaw, IN, and then attended and graduated from the academy associated with Bob Jones College, remaining at Bob Jones for his college training (BA, 1947); after this he studied at *Grace Theol. Sem. (BD, 1950; ThM, 1952; ThD, 1956). He began teaching Greek at *Grace College in 1950 and joined the New Testament department of the seminary in 1951. In 1953, he married Beverly Page.

Kent served as assistant dean of the seminary (1961) and was elevated to dean the next year. He became the third president of *Grace Theol. Sem. and College (1976–86). During his presidency, endowment grew from $300,000 to $1,767,000, the library holdings grew from 72,736 to 125,000 volumes, and the highest enrollment totals for both the Seminary and the College were achieved. An extension ministry began at the *Chateau de St. Albain, France, allowing missionaries and European

Homer A. Kent, Jr. Grace schools collection.

nationals opportunity for graduate education in Bible, theology, and missions.

Kent returned to full-time classroom teaching (1986–91) and then offered to retire, allowing the administration to renew his contract as they wished. He remained in the classroom on a part-time basis through the spring of 1999. A member of the *Winona Lake (IN) GBC, he served as FGBC moderator in 1982–83.

Kent's writings include *The Pastoral Epistles* (1958), an exposition of the Gospel of Matthew in the *Wycliffe Bible Commentary* (1962), *Ephesians: The Glory of the Church* (1971), *Jerusalem to Rome* (a commentary on Acts) and *The Epistle to the Hebrews* (1972), an exposition of the Gospel of John titled *Light in Darkness* (1974), a commentary on Galatians called *The Freedom of God's Sons* (1976), *Treasures of Wisdom*, which is a study of Colossians and Philemon (1978), *Studies in the Gospel of Mark* (1981), and commentaries on 2 Corinthians (*A Heart Open Wide*, 1982) and James (*Faith That Works*, 1986). *The Pastoral Epistles* has been translated into French, *Ephesians* into Spanish, and *From Jerusalem to Rome* into Russian. RTC

R. T. Clutter, "Homer A. Kent, Jr.: A Biographical Sketch," in *New Testament Essays in Honor of Homer A. Kent, Jr.*, ed. G. T. Meadors (1991) 9–15; personal information; *Annual* (*FGBC*) (1952ff.).

Kent, Wendell E. (FGBC), b. 1932, pastor, missions executive. The second son of *Homer A. Kent, Sr., Wendell Kent was born in Washington, DC, in 1932. After majoring in Greek at Wheaton College (BA, 1954), he attended *Grace Theol. Sem., earning an MDiv degree in 1957, the same year that he married Patricia Griffith.

Kent pastored *Beaumont, CA, Cherry Valley GBC (1957–62); *Roanoke, VA, Washington Heights GBC (1962–66); and *Waynesboro, PA, GBC (1966–78). He was personnel coordinator at the United Methodist Home for the Aging in Quincy, PA (1978–82). While in Quincy, he earned an MS degree in Human Relations at Shippensburg U. (1980).

In 1982, Kent took the post of church relations direc-

tor for Grace Brethren Foreign Missions, a position he held until 1991. He served on the board of the *Brethren Missionary Herald Co. (1970–79) and *Grace Retirement Village (1988–95). RTC

Personal information; *Annual* (*FGBC*) (1958ff.).

Kerner, William Hoff, Sr. (BC), b. 1918, pastor, denominational executive. William Kerner was born in Philadelphia, PA, on March 11 to Frank and Maude Kerner. After 23 years in the auto parts business, he entered *Ashland Theol. Sem., graduating in 1971. Kerner was ordained at *Ashland, OH, on May 23, 1971. He pastored Little Washington Congregational Church, Mansfield, OH, (1968–71); and Brethren congregations at *Roann, IN (1971–79), and *Fort Wayne, IN, Meadow Crest (1979–80). He was General Conference moderator in 1980.

In 1980, Kerner became the first *director of pastoral ministries for *The Brethren Church, serving until his retirement in 1987. He was a part-time supervisor of home missions for the *Missionary Board of the BC (1987–89) and held interim pastorates at several congregations. Kerner married Gertrude Mary Boardman on June 14, 1947; they had four children: Charlotte, Virginia, William, Jr., and David. RWW

BE (June 19, 1971) 18, (July, 1980) 19, (Sept., 1980) 4–7, (Sept., 1986) 21; Ashland Theol. Sem. Archives files; *BC General Conference Annual* (1980) 2–6.

Korean Mission (CB). In April 1984, responding to Korean members and others, the Pacific Southwest District Ministry and Church Extension Committee (CB) authorized Ick Won Kim (b. 1932) to explore possibilities for planting the denomination in his homeland. Moving beyond the district body's instruction and the counsel of *General Board staff, Kim began a congregation in Seoul. Lacking denominational support, the work was not sustained.

In the late 1980s, additional voices called for carrying the denomination to Korea. Citing concern about *ecumenical commitments and the number of different Christian groups already active in Korea, the General Board proposed to the 1990 *Annual Conference that a ministry partnership be developed with the Korean Evangelical Church. The conference affirmed the proposal, but also responded to a *query from the Northern Indiana District Board by instructing the General Board "to begin with intention to plant the Church of the Brethren in Korea." Atlantic Northeast was named the district connection, with Allen T. Hansell, then district executive, carrying the related responsibility.

David R. Radcliff was assigned General Board staff responsibility for Korea, and in Sept. 1992 the General Board sent Kwang Suk (Dan) Kim (b. 1940) as field staff to Korea. Kim developed relationships and conducted training sessions for pastors and others interested in ministry, using translations of key Brethren resources. He identified possible facilities for a seminary and held worship services for a small congregation in Seoul. Four years after he began, in Oct. 1996, the position occupied by Kim was among those eliminated by the General Board as part of a new design for denominational program.

Although the General Board closed the mission because of concerns relating to the board's funding and supervision of staff, Kim continued his work for a time with encouragement from a group of personal supporters. The degree of financial assistance provided was insuffi-

cient for long-term viability. JGD
See also RESTRUCTURING (CB).
Messenger (May, 1985) 18, (1985–2000) indexes; BLT 35 (Autumn, 1990) 291–97, 36 (Summer, 1991) 177.

Krypton, KY, Brethren Church. *Brethren Church activity in this *Appalachian community began in 1913. The Krypton work, though never claiming many congregants, was maintained by a series of faithful workers, most recently *Margaret E. Lowery. The Krypton Bible Center, as the ministry was called, was not considered a fully organized Brethren congregation. Following Lowery's retirement in 1990, several families committed to continuing the Brethren work began meeting with a desire to form a recognized Brethren church. In 1992, James P. Sluss, who had assisted Lowery in the ministry from 1966 to 1969, became the pastor of the congregation. It was officially recognized as a Brethren class in 1991 and upgraded to full congregational status by the 1994 *General Conference. In 2002 it had a membership of 42. DRS

Congregational records; *Annual* (BC) (1914ff.).

Jackpot, NV, Community Church. BHLA collection.

Jackpot Church

In the fall of 1985 the Idaho District (CB) became involved in establishing a church in Jackpot, NV, a small gambling mecca, located on the Nevada-Idaho border. This adventure in faith began for the Idaho Brethren when Robin Boies, who attended the *Fruitland Church of the Brethren as a youth, approached the Twin Falls County Association of Churches about the possibility of establishing a new church in Jackpot. The Boies family ranches were located about 25 miles south of Jackpot.

Ervin Huston, pastor of the Twin Falls, ID, Church of the Brethren and Idaho District Executive, was appointed to a committee that was to survey Jackpot and report back to the Association of Churches about how to approach such a ministry. This committee recommended pursuing an interdenominational community church. The participating denominations were the *Church of the Brethren, American Lutheran, Christian Church, Presbyterian Church, United Methodist Church, and Roman Catholic Church. With the belief that Jackpot was not large enough to support more than one church, the committee recommended that there be two worship services, one Catholic and one Protestant. The Association of Churches accepted this recommendation, and a Jackpot Ministry Committee was established with Huston being the Church of the Brethren representative.

The Jackpot Ministry Committee was composed of at least one representative from each sponsoring denomination plus interested citizens from the town of Jackpot. The committee felt that it was important to determine how much interest there was in a community church; so it decided to hold a Vacation Bible School in June 1986, co-directed by Huston and Sister Rosemary Boessen, from Our Lady of Guadalupe Catholic Center. Located in the Jackpot Elementary School, the school was attended by over 40 children, with teachers coming from the sponsoring churches in Jackpot.

In the fall of 1986, the Catholic Diocese donated to the Jackpot Community Ministry a church building, but it was located in Eden, ID. The steering committee needed to raise funds for moving and remodeling the building. It was to be placed on land that had been secured from the Bureau of Land Management. Over the next few years, funds were raised, incorporation was secured, constitution and by-laws were written, and the church building was moved from Eden to Jackpot. During the move, the rear dolly broke and the rear of the building was severely damaged, but it was repaired and finally placed on the basement foundation that had been built in Jackpot. In the fall of 1990 the first Protestant service was held under the guidance of Peggi Boyce, a Presbyterian minister.

In 2000, the Catholic Ministry is an active, vibrant ministry under the leadership of Sister Rosemary Boessen. It attracts many of its members from the Hispanic community in Jackpot. The Protestant ministry struggles from a lack of leadership. It rents space to the Missouri Synod Lutherans, who hold a weekly service of worship. The Protestant representatives to the steering committee hope that a counseling ministry can become the basis for developing a viable interdenominational protestant ministry in Jackpot. ELH
Messenger (March, 1990) 4; *BLT* 36 (Summer, 1991) 172.

L-O

Lakeland, FL, Grace Brethren Church. A Bible study in the Lakeland area was organized in 1979 under the leadership of John and Barbara Fretz, Willard and Esther Yothers, and Fred and Lorrie Gerber. The first teacher of the class was *Raymond E. Gingrich. Other teachers who served the class were Daryl Emsch and *Edward A. Jackson. The first Sunday morning worship service was held Oct. 12, 1980, in the Yothers' residence. Men who led the congregation in worship during its earliest days included Jim Jackson, Andy Anderson, John Chapman, Ray Sturgill, Arnold Kreigbaum, and Russell Betz. The congregation officially joined the *Fellowship of Grace Brethren Churches in 1981 and came under the administration of *Grace Brethren North American Missions. Randy Weekly, a recent graduate of *Grace Seminary, served as pastor (1982–94). Other pastors who served the congregation were Jack Peters (1984–87), Bill Smith (1987–88), James Taylor (1988–92), and David Kennedy (1992–). Services moved from the Yothers' residence to a variety of locations after July 1982. Property on Lunn Road was purchased in 1986, and a building was constructed in 1989. The church became fully self-supporting on Dec. 31, 1991. FJG/JRY

Congregational records; *Annual* (*FGBC*) (1982ff.).

Lancaster, PA, Acts Covenant Fellowship (ACTS) (CB) is a contemporary outworking of traditional Brethren values as a cell-based, elder-led, *charismatic, covenant congregation (i.e., membership must be renewed annually) with apostolic oversight, and committed to *urban ministry. At its founding, ACTS was dually affiliated with the *Church of the Brethren and the *Mennonite Church. In Dec. 1985, the Church Development Commission, Atlantic Northeast District, asked Douglas L. Fike to study the feasibility of starting a *charismatic congregation. Fike outlined specifics as described above. By July 1986, prayer meetings began in the John and Ann Gibbel home. Communion Fellowship, Goshen, IN, sent four people to help. Henry and Millie Buckwalter became the pastoral couple. In Jan. 1987, Sunday services began at the YWCA. By June 1999 the congregation had six elders led by James O. Eikenberry, 20 house churches and Sunday worship at the Lancaster Recreation Center. An average attendance of 161 was reported for the year 2000. In 2003, ACTS chose to affiliate with the Hopewell Network of Anabaptist congregations. Therefore, ACTS

requested and was granted release from its denominational affiliation with the Lancaster Conference of the Mennonite Church and the Atlantic Northeast District of the CB. JOE

Congregational records; *Yearbook* (*CB*) (1988–2000); *Messenger* (Jan./Feb., 1999) 12–13; *BLT* 36 (Summer, 1991) 174; *Minutes, Atlantic Northeast District CB* (October 10–11, 2003).

Lancaster, PA, Alfa y Omega (Alpha and Omega) Church of the Brethren (CB). In Aug. 1986 Guillermo B. Encarnación went to Lancaster as pastor to start a new Hispanic ministry sponsored by the Atlantic Northeast District. On April 17, 1988, a charter ceremony celebrated the installation of the Alpha and Omega Fellowship. The District Board acquired physical facilities located at 708 Wabank St. in Lancaster, formerly known as the Ascension Lutheran Church. The Fellowship has developed a Family Life Center, a special ministry to serve the Hispanic community. Through this program the following

Guillermo B. Encarnación (middle) at Annual Conference. BHLA collection.

services are offered to the community: individual and family counseling, food bank, prison ministry, alcohol and drug use prevention, weekly educational *radio program, and assistance in finding employment.

As a community of faith, Alpha and Omega Fellowship serves as a therapeutic aid to people constantly arriving from *Puerto Rico, *The Dominican Republic, *Cuba, and large cities in the United States. It continues to provide a testimony and a vision of ministry to the city

with the theme: "We come to church to worship God, we come out from Church to serve our brothers and sisters." GBE

Messenger (Dec., 1987) 7; *BLT* 36 (Summer, 1991) 173, 199–200; congregational records.

Language, Inclusive. Language, by its very nature, is always changing. Since the 1970s in the *Church of the Brethren, there has been a new awareness of the power and effectiveness of language. The church has sought direction on how language witnesses clearly to the inclusiveness and unity we experience together in Christ. Individuals have different understandings and interpretations of the word *inclusive*. In 1975 the *Parish Ministries Commission of the *General Board passed a paper that recommended the use of language which reflects human equality in scripture, worship materials, and all publications, including the *polity manual and *hymnals. In 1985 the Hymnal Project decided that *Hymnal: A Worship Book*, then under construction, would decrease the number of masculine images for God and increase feminine images, no longer use *man* as a word inclusive of all human beings, change archaic pronouns where feasible, and replace all racially biased or stereotyped words for people according to gender, race, age, and nationality.

Inclusive language has become more common and accepted throughout the church. Many church leaders in their speaking and writing attempt to model sensitivity to all people without drawing attention to the issue. The New Revised Standard Version (NRSV) of the Bible uses inclusive language and is the primary version used by *Brethren Press. Inclusive language is not a factor among *Dunkard Brethren, *Fellowship of Grace Brethren Churches, or *Old German Baptist Brethren. *The Brethren Church has not publicly addressed the issue, but *Ashland Theol. Sem. has a policy statement reflecting inclusive language that some pastors follow. NRF

Harriet Ziegler, ed., *Handbook of Style and Usage,* Church of the Brethren General Board, rev. ed. (1981); V. Eller, *The Language of Canaan and the Grammar of Feminism* (1982), critical; *Messenger* (Feb., 1987) 8, (April, 1988) 28.

Laughlin Church of the Brethren, MD, located some six miles southwest of Grantsville. The congregation was organized in 1974 with a founding membership of 37 and an average worship attendance of 40. Membership and attendance remained constant under the leadership of Evelyn M. Bowman, the congregation's first minister. Preston J. Miller, pastor of the neighboring *Bethesda congregation, served as the first moderator. Laughlin enjoyed an increase in membership under the leadership of James L. Deremer (1980–86). A peak membership of 61 was reported in 1987. Worship attendance, strongest in the congregation's early years, averaged 25 during the 1980s and 1990s. Two other ministers served the Laughlin congregation during that time, Joseph Lewis (1988) and Curtis G. Ketterman (1994–97). The congregation reported 41 members in 2000. DKB

Yearbook (CB) (1974–2001); congregational records.

Lenexa, KS, Fellowship (CB). The Lenexa Fellowship began in 1983–84 as a dream of the *Kansas City, KS, First Central Church of the Brethren; the Western Plains District adopted the project in 1984. The *General Board (CB) also supported the fellowship with Home Mission funds. Abraham Omman was the first pastor, holding worship in his home. As the group expanded, worship was moved to various schools in Lenexa. In 1994, the pastor was called away, and in that same year, financial aid from the district was discontinued. At the end of 1997, denominational funding also ceased. After an interim without pastoral leadership and with declining membership, Sonja Sherfy Griffith was called as part-time pastor in Oct. 1996. In 2000, ten members continue as a New Testament-style house fellowship. SSG

Congregational records; *Yearbook (CB)* (1985ff.).

Lersch, E. Phillip, Jr. (BC, CB). Lersch served as the National Brethren Youth Director (1956–60), *Ashland, OH, First (Park St.) Brethren Church (1960–66), and for many years in the innovative community work of the Brethren House (1967–97) in St. Petersburg, FL. After 30 years, his ministry concluded at the *St. Petersburg, FL, congregation (CB) (1992–). Lersch functioned as the Florida representative for the National Ordination Council of the Brethren Church. His wife, Jean Lindower Lersch, is an organist and writer. Phil and Jean Lersch were known for their dedication to world peace, and participated in an international *work camp in Austria in the 1950s. RLK

Personal information; *Annual (BC)* (1960ff.); *Yearbook (CB)* 1993ff.).

Lewiston, ME, Church of the Brethren. The *Brethren Revival Fellowship (BRF) envisioned a Brethren witness in New England. Ground work was laid for this congregation when *Brethren Volunteer Service was accepted by the Lewiston Housing Authority (LHA). J. Mervin Keller, a minister from the *White Oak, PA, congregation was asked to provide spiritual leadership. In May 1981 six Pennsylvania families were commissioned to build a congregation in Lewiston. The families were J. Marlin and Carol Fahnestock, pastor J. Mervin and Karen Keller, James H. and Lois Ann Minnich, Dennis J. and Mary Jane Myer, Shannon and Marian Negley, and John L. and June Stauffer, a group of 12 adults 18 children.

The first service was held on Aug. 2, 1981. Meetings were held in the Hillview Community Building in the LHA complex, and then in a fish market basement until May 1982, when the Beth-Jacob Synagogue in Lewiston was lease-purchased. A year later, the building was purchased by BRF for the Lewiston Fellowship. Congregational status was granted by the Atlantic Northeast District on Oct. 13, 1989. A church school was begun in Sept. 1994. Forty-six members were reported in 2000. JMKe/KLK

Congregational records; *Church of the Brethren Maine Newsletter* (1997ff.); Atlantic NE District *Newsletter* (April 16, 1982), (Jan. 23, 1986); *BRF Witness* 16.2 (1981) 10, 17.2 (1982) 10, 17.5 (1982) 11, 18.2 (1983) 11, 20.1 (1985) 11, 23.3 (1988) 11, 25.2 (1990) 14–15, 28.3 (1993) 14–15, 30.1 (1995) 14–15, 31.1 (1996) 14–15, 32.4 (1997) 14, 35.2 (2000) 14; *Lewiston [ME] Daily Sun* (Dec. 21, 1981); *New Beginnings* (Jan., 1983) [3], (June, 1984) [7]; *Yearbook (CB)* (1982–2000).

Lexington, KY, Grace Bible Church (FGBC) was organized in May 1980 under the leadership of Clyde K. Landrum, pastor of the *Clayhole, KY, congregation. The Lexington congregation began as a Bible study group in the home of David and Sandy Landrum. The group later moved its meeting place to the Continental Inn because it then numbered about 30 persons. Pastors who have served the congregation are Clyde K. Landrum (1980), Joseph E.

Nass (1981–84), Aloysius C. Riley (1985–89), Paul H. Michaels (1989–92), and Scott B. Taylor (1993–94). Various laymen led the congregation from Jan. 1995 until June 1996 when Stephen M. Jarrell became the pastor. The congregation currently worships in a day-care center and owns five acres of land in anticipation of a future building project. SMJ/JRY

Congregational records; *Grace Brethren Annual* (1981–2000).

London, OH, Grace Brethren Church started in 1982 as a Bible study in the home of Phillip B. Detwiler. The study was led by John Willet from the *Worthington, OH, Columbus GBC. As the group grew, it began to meet at another church in the London community under the leadership of Louis M. Huesmann II, an intern pastor with the Worthington, OH, Columbus GBC. In 1988 a facility located at 715 SR 42 SW of London was purchased and renovated. At that time the congregation affiliated with Grace Brethren Home Missions and called a full-time pastor. Over the next two years the church experienced some growth under the leadership of several pastors, but over the next four years, it declined. In April 1994 the *Dublin, OH, Northwest Chapel Grace Brethren Church adopted the congregation as a daughter church for redevelopment. At this time Timothy J. Ruesch became the full-time pastor. Since then the congregation has experienced growth and stability, adopting the following mission statement: "The mission of the London Grace Brethren Church is to reach out to people, bringing them into a relationship with Jesus Christ, building them up through relevant Bible learning and application, and beginning culturally relevant churches in Ohio and throughout the world." TJR

Congregational records; *Grace Brethren Annual* (1983–2000).

Long, John Daniel and Inez Goughnour (CB, pastor and teacher/author) were married Mar. 6, 1943. John Long (1914–98), the eldest child of D. W. and Susie Gnagy Long, was born Aug. 14 on a family farm near Myersdale, PA, baptized in the *Myersdale, PA, congregation in 1929, licensed to the ministry in 1933, ordained in 1936, and advanced to elder in 1942. He studied at *Juniata College (BA, 1936), *Bethany Biblical Seminary (BD, 1941) and Yale U. (STM, 1945). His outstanding pastoral expertise was recognized by *Elizabethtown College (DD, 1964). Long's pastoral experience began with a circuit ministry in Western Pennsylvania (1936–38) and as a student weekend pastor in the *Liberty Mills, IN, congregation (1939–40). Full-time pastorates were held in *University Park, MD, congregation (1941–44), *Dayton, OH, Mack Memorial congregation (1945–55), and *Lancaster, PA, congregation (1955–79). The latter two pastorates involved major building and relocation experiences. In retirement years, Long pastored congregations in five districts and served 12 interim pastorates.

Inez Goughnour Long was born on Nov. 19, 1917, in Elkhart, IA, to Earl and Mary Goughnour. She was baptized in the *Des Moines Valley, IA, CB (1925), studied at *Manchester College (AB, 1939) and at Millersville U. (MA, 1976). In 1974–75 she was a Fulbright Scholar in India through Indiana U. of Pennsylvania. In addition to a distinguished teaching career (including the 1975 Lancaster Teacher of the Year Award), Long authored 15 articles in *Messenger*, wrote or edited seven books, and wrote several other articles as requested by church organizations.

John and Inez Long were the parents of two children:

David (b. 1946) and Kathy Long Missildine (b. 1949). HSK/DVU

Inez Long, *Lord's Day Morning: Work and Worship the Brethren Way* (1989); *Messenger* (Dec., 1998) 5, 30; BLT 29 (Summer, 1984) 177–82; Yearbook (*CB*) (1940ff.).

Los Angeles, CA, Hermanos Unidos en Cristo (CB). The congregation was begun by pastor Jose Jimenez as *Jesucristo Es La Verdad*. In 1992, Jimenez moved away and took the name of the congregation with him. The remaining group reorganized in 1995 as *Hermanos Unidos en Cristo*, and became a *Church of the Brethren fellowship in East Los Angeles in the Pacific Southwest District. Leadership was provided by Salvador Rosales, pastor; Juan Garcia, chair; and Olga Reyes, clerk. The congregation then entered the *Education for Shared Ministry training program with several lay members participating. In 1995, there were 29 members. JADa

Pacific Southwest District files; personal information; *Yearbook* (*CB*) (1992ff.).

Los Angeles, CA, Central Evangelical Church of the Brethren (Korean) began as a Bible study group under the leadership of pastor Jang-kyun (John) Park in 1979. In 1981 the congregation purchased property in the ethnic commercial center of Koreatown and organized as a congregation of the Korean Evangelical Church in the USA. After leaving this denomination, in 1985 Park began relating to the *Church of the Brethren. In 1989, the congregation joined the denomination. In the early 1990s the congregation housed a Brethren Korean ministry training school. At this time, the congregation benefited from *Brethren Volunteer Service workers and denominational aid in purchasing additional property. In 1998 the congregation dedicated a new building. The economic crisis in the aftermath of the Los Angeles riots (1992) and several internal schisms found the congregation in 2002 as a worshipping community of about 30 people considering options for its future ministry. TLL

Congregational records.

Los Guaricanos, DR, Fuente de Vida (CB). The Fuente de Vida (Fountain of Life) Church of the Brethren was founded on Jan. 18, 1990, as a CB congregation from 14 days of evangelistic revival. The first worship service was held with 15 persons in a small house near the current church building in Los Guaricanos (a Santo Domingo suburb). The congregation met in this location six years and then two years in a slightly larger wooden house. The current church building was constructed in 1998. Each week there are 80 members, 50 new believers studying for baptism, 203 in Sunday school, and 125 in worship. Members established a new fellowship in Bonao and have been preaching in the town of Yamasa since April 19, 2000. The only pastor has been Angelica Beriguete. RBCr/GPBC

Congregational records

Los Toros, DR, Nuevo Renacer (CB). New Rebirth Church of the Brethren, located near Azua, was founded in 1980 as an independent congregation. It affiliated with the *Church of the Brethren in 1990. The congregation started in the home of Eliodora Mendenz and met there for four years before moving to the home of former pastor Santos Mota. Construction of the current church building was completed on Nov. 24, 1990. In 2000 the congre-

gation had 52 members, 36 new believers studying for baptism, 191 attending Sunday school, and 70 attending worship. Pastors who have served the congregation include Santos Mota (1980–94), Danilo Jimenez (1995–96), and David Reyes (1996–). RBCr/GPBC
Congregational records.

Lowery, Margaret E. (BC), 1910–92, missionary, educator, nurse. Born on Jan. 30 near Dam #4 on the Potomac River in Maryland, Margaret Lowery attended the *St. James Brethren Church, MD, where she accepted Christ and was baptized. She graduated from Hagerstown High School and pursued at Towson Normal School her lifelong ambition to be a teacher. She taught 14 years in Washington Co. public schools while continuing her education at Western Maryland and Madison Colleges, receiving a degree in elementary education (BS, 1939). During her residence in the Maryland area, Margaret Lowery served in children's ministries, *Christian Endeavor, *WCTU, 4-H, vacation Bible school (VBS), scouting, and the Brethren National Youth Board. In 1943 she entered the Washington Co. School of Nursing, graduating as a registered nurse (RN, 1946), and the same year became an instructor of nurses at Samaritan Hospital School of Nursing in Ashland, OH. In 1953, Lowery went to Eastern *Kentucky as a mission worker, where she spent 37 years teaching and training persons of all ages in the *Krypton, KY, area. Her main emphasis was in youth development through Sunday schools, VBS, *camping, 4-H, and Extension Homemakers. Margaret Lowery received state and national recognition for her work in 4-H and the church. In 1983 she received the Hazard/Perry County Woman of the Year Award. In 1990 Margaret retired and returned to her home area of St. James, MD. JPS
Gloria Dahlhammer, *A History of the St. James Brethren Church 1886–1986* (1986), 29–31; *BE* (Jan., 1993) 19.

Tók'ahookaadí Church of the Brethren under construction largely by volunteer native Americans. Keister collection.

Lybrook, NM, Tók'ahookaadí Church of the Brethren. Founding of the Tók'ahookaadí CB took place in two settings: The organization was at the Western Plains District Conference on Aug. 11, 1984, and chartering and ground breaking was at Lybrook on Oct. 28, 1984. The church building is located on mission property. Arviso, Chavez, Chiquito, Largo, and Thompson were key families who formed the fellowship, made decisions on location, selected the type of building, and did most of the construction. Many who received Christian training at Lybrook Mission are now serving as church, community, and professional leaders. The membership increased until late 1986. No records were kept from Apr. 1987 to Nov. 1995. Attendance was low from Nov. 1995 through Jan. 2000. Three pastors have served the congregation: Russell W. Kiester, CB; Cathrine Dell, Wesleyan Holyness; Leola Allen, United Church of Christ. Russell and Edith M. Kiester, who reside on the property as *Brethren Volunteer Service caretakers, conduct Sunday worship services and give help to Navajos in other ways. RWKi/EMK
See also LYBROOK NAVAJO COMMUNITY MINISTRY
Personal knowledge.

Macedonia, OH, Western Reserve Grace Brethren Church was organized in the fall of 1985 as a joint project of the Northeastern Ohio District Mission Board and *Grace Brethren North American Missions. Services began on Nov. 24, 1985, in the Dodge Middle School of Twinsburg, OH. Within the first year, the church grew from three leading couples (Boehms, Gillespies, and Allisons) to 34 charter members. In 1989 the church purchased 10 acres in a prime location in Macedonia on State Route 82. Significant funding for this purchase became available through the closing and sale of the *Lyndhurst GBC. A church building was completed in Dec. 1991 and a Christian education unit was added in 1995. The founding pastor, Ronald E. Boehm, continues to be a member of the congregation and serves GBNAM full time as the Midwest Career Missionary. Associate pastors who have served the congregation are Steve Winey (1993–96) and Jason Haymaker. Pastor Haymaker was called as associate and youth pastor in 1996 and became senior pastor in 2001. There were 114 members in 2003. REBo/JRY
Congregational records; *Annual* (*FGBC*) (1986–99).

*Mai Sule Biu (CB), 1922–92, churchman, song writer. A highly-regarded leader in the *Church of the Brethren in *Nigeria (EYN), Mai Sule held many offices in the Nigerian church and ecumenical church bodies, such as *TEKAS. He was also a well-known singer and songwriter, drawing upon traditional music styles and adding Scripture or a Christian message.

Mai Sule's personal story is remarkable. A member of the Pabur tribe, and of royal family, his grandfather, Mai Ali Dogo I, was the Emir of the Biu. He had leprosy as a child but was cured at the hospital of the Church of the Brethren Mission (CBM) at *Garkida. This beginning inspired a lifelong commitment to Christ.

Mai Sule and Gana had nine children who survived: Ritkatu, Lahadi Yatchanum, Arziki, Maina Ari, Bosler, Gamaliya, Sara Shisler, Gideon, and Ada. He died on Dec. 20 from injuries sustained in a car accident on the road to Maiduguri, which also claimed the life of EYN leader, Boaz Maina. MBK
A. Hieber, *Servant of Christ. A Leader of the Church: The Life of Rev. A. P. Mai Sule Biu* (1994); *Messenger* (March, 1993) 6–7, (Oct., 1998) 19; *Fifty Years in Lardin Gabas, 1923–1973* ([1973]) *passim*; C. E. Faw, ed., *Lardin Gabas: A Land, a People, a Church* (1973), 127; General Board (CB) files.

Male, E. William (FGBC), b. 1927, pastor, educator, administrator. Born in Streator, IL, William Male attended Western Michigan U. (AB, 1952), *Grace Theol. Sem. (BD, 1955), Temple U. (EdM, 1959), and Indiana U. (PhD, 1968). He was married in 1950 to Ella Beth Kauffman.

Mai Sule Biu. Photo by J. B. Grimley.

Male's pastoral experience includes Edwards Corner Methodist Church, Marcellus, MI (1951–53); Hepton Union Church, Nappanee, IN (1953–55); and *Philadelphia, PA, First Brethren Church, (1955–59). He also served interim pastorates at *Warsaw, IN, Community Grace Brethren Church; Berne, IN, Grace Bible Church; *Fort Wayne, IN, GBC; *Goshen, IN, GBC; and *Berne, IN, Bethel BC.

Male served at Grace Theol. Sem. and College (1959–93) as seminary instructor, assistant dean and dean of the College, academic dean of the College, dean of the Seminary, director of graduate school programs in Christian School Administration, assistant to the president and acting dean of the West Campus, and planned giving officer. He served for 39 years as a member of the *Brethren Missionary Herald Co. (1957–96). He also founded the National Institute of Christian Education, developed summer school programs for teachers and administrators of Christian schools, and he was a founding member of the Association of Christian Schools International. RTC

Personal information; *Annual (FGBC)* (1951ff.).

Malles, Mark Ellsworth (FGBC), 1918–96, pastor. Born in Waynesboro, PA, the seventh of eight children, Mark Malles felt the call to preach early, pastoring at age 19 a small Presbyterian church in Olena, OH. There he met and married Phyllis Coffey.

Malles enrolled at *Grace Theol. Sem. (Diploma in Theology, 1945) and, while a student, pastored the *Sterling, OH, Grace Brethren Church (1941–46). Mark and Phyllis Malles became missionaries to Spanish-speaking people of the *Taos, NM, First Brethren Church (1946–47). They moved to Indiana, where Mark pastored the *Flora, IN, GBC (1947–51). Other pastoral ministries followed at *Altoona, PA, First BC (1951–54); *Fort Wayne, IN, First BC (1955–66); *Warsaw, IN, Community GBC (1966–72); *Arvada, CO, Hackberry Hill GBC (1972–74); and the *Phoenix, AZ, GBC (1974–90). Malles served as moderator of the *FGBC (1962–63). RTC

Personal information; *Annual (FGBC)* (1940–90).

Manatí, PR, Pueblo de Dios (CB). The Pueblo de Dios (People of God Fellowship) was established in Manatí on the north coast of Puerto Rico as an independent congregation. Pastor Arcadio Natal and his wife, Millie, formed the group, mostly of older persons with roots in the Christian and Missionary Alliance (C&MA) denomination. Arcadio Natal had served as a pastor with the C&MA for 40 years. He came to know the *Church of the Brethren through associate executive Pedro Brull (who also had been in the C&MA) and developed a relationship with the Puerto Rico board and the congregations in *Castañer and *Río Prieto. The group joined the CB in 1990. Most of the original families have died or moved away. In 1999 there were 25 members, and Arcadio Natal continues as pastor. The congregation hopes soon to have their own property for worship and service. IRZ/BMC

Congregational records; *CB Yearbook* (2000) 115.

Mansfield, OH, Conservative Grace Brethren Church. *Arnold R. Kriegbaum, pastor of the *Ankenytown Grace Brethren Church, felt a call to found a new church in Mansfield. In 1939 he persuaded *John M. Aeby to start a Bible class there. As a result, a congregation was established which, on July 9, 1944, called Bernard N. Schneider as full-time pastor. There were 49 charter members.

The new church grew and erected buildings to house this active congregation of Brethren Christians. The sanctuary was dedicated on May 4, 1947, with *Alva J. McClain giving the dedicatory message to 556 persons. Attendance grew so that by the early 1960s the church was the largest Grace Brethren congregation in Ohio with over 500 worshipers each week.

Schneider, who resigned on March 22, 1960, was followed by R. Paul Miller, Jr. on April 17, 1960. Under Miller's leadership a Christian day school was proposed, and by Sept. 1961 the Mansfield Christian School was organized and operated by the congregation. Miller was followed by Richard E. Grant on April 20, 1969. During Grant's ministry the sanctuary was remodeled and dedicated on May 16, 1971. Grant's last Sunday with the congregation was Aug. 26, 1973.

In 2000 the pastor was J Hudson Thayer, who began his ministry in Sept. 1973. Under Thayer's guidance, in 1980 the congregation established a post-graduate school of theology for training students for ministry. The school is known as *The Theological Practorium, and this concept has spread to other churches in the Fellowship in the U.S. and other nations. The Mansfield Theol. Practorium has trained many graduates who are currently pastoring churches and working in missions.

The early characteristics of the Mansfield GBC are still present in the congregation. Bible preaching and teaching are emphasized with personal evangelism as the key to church growth. The Mansfield congregation has been the "Mother Church" for seven other Grace Brethren churches.

In 1993 as a result of its unhappiness with the doctrinal positions of the *FGBC, the Mansfield congregation joined the newly established *Conservative Grace Brethren Churches International. J Hudson Thayer was active in the foundation of the new denomination and authored the organizational document, *The Protocols*, which formed the denomination's *polity according to the model of a voluntary association of churches.

The Mansfield congregation began construction on a new site on Park Avenue West to relocate its facilities. The current full-time pastoral staff is composed of J Hudson Thayer, senior pastor and president of The Theological Practorium; Lester Vnasdale, pastor of evangelism and professor in The Theological Practorium; John Picard, youth pastor; Curtis Evans, assistant pastor and dean of the Theological Practorium. JHT

Personal information; *S. Ohio* (*FGBC*) (1975) 148.

Maple Valley, WA, Grace Brethren Church. Supported by the Grace Brethren Church of *Kent, WA, and its pastor, Jack V. Rants, a group of six families were sent out from the congregation to start a new work ten miles east of Maple Valley. They were led by pastor Robert Gentzel, and a Grace Bible Fellowship was formed in Oct. 1989. The core group included the Van Burskirk, Sanchez, Paul, Catlett, Sutief, and Miller families. They met in the Miller's home until April 1990 when they moved to the Lake Wilderness elementary school building for their first public worship service on Easter. On June 13, 1993, the church moved to its present facility in the Wilderness Business Park. Pastor Gentzel resigned in Oct. 1993, and the church was without a pastor for just over two years until David E. Marksbury accepted the call on Jan. 1, 1996. The church changed its name to "The Grace Brethren Church of Maple Valley" in 1997 to better reflect its affiliation. The facilities have been expanded twice by leasing adjacent space. The goal of the church body is to purchase land and erect its own building; in 2001–03 over $80,000 was raised through the Steps of Faith capital fund-raising program. DEMa

Congregational records; personal knowledge.

Marion, OH, Grace Brethren Church is an outgrowth of two separate Bible study groups, one in the southern part of Marion County (Prospect/Pleasant) and the other in the eastern part (Claridon). In 1983, both groups were recognized as congregations in the *Fellowship of Grace Brethren Churches. The two congregations merged in July 1985 and gathered for worship at the Pleasant Middle School. In Nov. 1987 the congregation constructed a building on six acres of land south of Marion. Pastors who have served the congregation are C. Dean Risser (1985–87), Stephan J. Edmonds (1985–86), David W. Kennedy (1988–92), and John Jones (1992–). DAC/JRY

Congregational records; *Annual* (*FGBC*) (1983–98).

Mason, George Edward (CB), 1916–83, engineer, missionary. Called by his wife and biographer "The Inimitable George Mason," he became a missionary first in *China (1947–49) and then in *India (1951–78) after learning to know the CB in *Puerto Rico. Born in Gardena, CA, into a *Methodist family, he took degrees in pre-medicine and engineering at UCLA and in chemical engineering from the U. of Washington. As a *conscientious objector to military participation, he was assigned to the Brethren hospital in *Castaner, PR, in 1942, where he used his mechanical genius to outfit and maintain a complex medical program with simple materials. In China he taught engineering students until foreigners were forced to leave China in 1949. During his long service in India, he was instrumental in establishing the ecumenical *Rural Service Center at Anklesvar, which trained teams to go into the villages to teach agriculture, public health, and nutrition. Mason married Rae Hungerford in 1945 while

George Mason uses lathe at the Rural Service Center, India, ca. 1955. BLHA collection.

in Puerto Rico; they had three children. After retirement in late 1978, the Masons returned to Washington State where George Mason died in 1983. DFD

Rae Hungerford Mason, *The Inimitable George Mason* (1991); *TBE 3* (1984) 1841; *Prayer for* Missions (1949) 70–71; *Meet Your Missionaries* (1955) 33, 121–22; *Messenger* (June, 1983) 6, (Oct., 1983) 7; M.S. H. Rosenberger, *Light of the Soul: The Brethren in Puerto Rico, 1942 to 1992* (1992) 3, 21, 88; J. H. Dasenbrock, *To the Beat of a Different Drummer* (1989), 100–01, 109, 128, 135; Anet Satvedi, "History of the Church of the Brethren in India, 1894–1993," DMin thesis, Bethany Theol. Seminary (1993) 86–88, 146; NSBRO, *Directory of Civilian Public Service, May, 1941 to March, 1947* (1947) 93.

Mass Media, Uses of. Brethren varied widely in their use of mass media during the rapidly changing technological years of the late 20th century. Some, like the *Dunkard Brethren and *Old German Baptist Brethren, had little or no involvement, tending to shun the mass media and to make official statements against its use by their members. Other Brethren bodies, however, had significant engagement. Radio ministry, video-tape and CD resources, electronic news releases, and telephone campaigns have all been part of denominational programs.

Media advocacy and literacy have also been emphasized, including *Church of the Brethren involvement with the *National Council of Churches Communication Commission and the National Interfaith Cable Coalition. By 2000, *The Brethren Church, Church of the Brethren, *Conservative Grace Brethren Churches International, and *Fellowship of Grace Brethren Churches had all established Web sites on the Internet offering a variety of information and resources. Numerous congregations had radio broadcasts of worship services, and a few had television broadcasts. WJW

See also INFORMATION TECHNOLOGY, CHURCH USE OF.

Personal information; S. M. Hoover, *The Electronic Giant* (1982).

McAllen, TX, Grace Brethren Church was founded by pastor Robert A. Soto (b. April 28, 1952) and his wife Iris A. Gully Soto (b. Sept. 13, 1956), as a new church plant of the Grace Brethren *Home Missions Council. The groundwork was first laid beginning in Aug. 1988 with a home Bible study group consisting mostly of new believers who came to know the Lord through Bible study outreach. On Jan. 8, 1989, the church was officially established, meeting first in a small office suite in a professional complex.

The year 1995 was a pivotal time in the congregational ministry. Since the majority of the church family came from *Native American heritage, as did its founding pastor (Lipan Apache), it became more and more evident that there was a need to further their evangelistic efforts in a culturally relevant way; so the Native American New Life Center was born—a ministry of McAllen Grace Brethren Church which is committed to reaching the Native American community both locally and beyond its borders.

As the ministry of the Native American New Life Center developed, the congregation's outreach opportunities expanded in four areas: a local church service geared to Native American cultural expressions; extending worship services by invitations to Native American celebrations such as powwows; a music ministry which, by May 2002, included two CDs of Native American powwow-style praise music (scriptures and biblical principles set to drum songs); and a traveling dancing and speaking ministry which presented the gospel and brought ministry encouragement through Native American culture in schools, camps, conferences, churches, reservations, and Native American communities locally and abroad.

In the past 14 years the congregation has established various ministries that have reached out to teenagers who were becoming involved with gangs; a Spanish language church body led by a lay leader; a ministry to meet the physical and spiritual needs of the many Central American refugees who found their way to this area in the early 1990s; a men's fellowship, a women's Bible-study group, and various ministries to children and by children. RASo

Congregational records; personal knowledge.

Medina, OH, Brethren Church. Larry L. Bolinger, chair of the Ohio District Mission Board, provided the initial vision for the church in 1977. A Bible study began that year with worship services commencing in 1978 in the facilities of the Medina YM-YWCA. Arden E. Gilmer and Richard E. Allison served the congregation together with volunteers from the *Ashland, OH, Park Street BC. In 1978 Terry Lodico was called as the first on-site pastor. The church purchased a large home for meeting space in 1980 and grew to an average worship attendance of 116 by 1985. The church was beset by internal conflicts and was closed temporarily in 1990. A restart with Terry Colley as pastor was short-lived. The congregation disbanded in 1991. DRS

Congregational records; *Annual* (*BC*) (1978–91).

Medina, OH, Church of the Brethren. The "Christ Our Joy" congregation began on Sept. 1, 1984, with Donald R. Flory as organizing pastor. A building site was purchased on Wadsworth Road. On April 7, 1985, 45 persons gathered at Heritage Christian School for their first worship service. In spite of a noble effort, attendance declined to 20 persons by the end of 1987, and the project was closed on Jan. 17, 1988.

On Sept. 1, 1989, a new start and a new name, "The Medina Congregation," began with Melvin Menker as pastor. A parsonage was purchased, and, in 1991 a church building was constructed. The congregation launched a day care center for children and worship attendance grew to over 90 persons but then began to decline. In 1996 Menker resigned, and the parsonage was sold. Joe Routh was appointed interim pastor.

On Nov. 3, 1996, the church disfellowshipped a member whose life-style violated church doctrine. The national media gave major coverage to the event. As a result, attendance dropped, but the remaining members committed themselves to a renewed effort. On Jan. 15, 1997, Mark Teal, former pastor of the *Black River congregation, accepted the call to Medina. Under his leadership a period of spiritual renewal and growth began. A new vision led to the sale of the church property and the congregation found temporary meeting space in a funeral home. Because a majority of its members lived within a reasonable distance of the Black River (CB) meetinghouse, the Northern Ohio District Conference (Aug. 5, 2000) approved the request of the two congregations to merge. In the spring of 2001, the parsonage and church building were damaged by a tornado. A major renovation of both buildings and grounds was dedicated on Oct. 21, 2001. CCF

"Summary of Task-Team and Church Activity" (April 14, 1988); "Medina Growth Pattern," "Information Update: Medina Events," (Nov. 27, 1996); "Medina Consultation Workshop," (Nov. 29, 1999); all documents in the Northern Ohio District Office Archives; BLT 36 (Summer, 1991) 170; *Yearbook* (*CB*) (1990ff.).

Medina, OH, Living Hope Brethren Church was founded by Thomas E. Sprowls, Jr. in Nov. 1994. Living Hope was a cooperative church planting project between *Ashland Theol. Sem., the Ohio District Missions Board and the *National Missionary Board of *The Brethren Church. A Brethren Church planning committee laid the ground work for the congregation. The root of the church came from a Fall 1994 Church Planting class at Ashland Theol. Seminary. Students in the class were given an opportunity to participate in various stages of the congregation's start in order to gain church planting experience. Thomas E. Sprowls, one of the students in that class, was called by the Brethren Church Planning Committee to serve as pastor of the church. In 1998 this work was closed. TES

BE (Dec., 1994) 16, (Nov., 1995) 7, (Dec., 1995) 10; congregational records.

Medina, OH, Shepherd's Grace Church (FGBC). The earliest vision for this church developed in the heart of the family of Jon and Karen Sommer. The vision was united with a growing friendship between the Sommers and another family, Will and Maria Lohnes. The Lohneses were serving a church in Kauai, HI. However, Willard Lohnes believed that God was leading him back to the mainland. The Sommers informed the Lohneses of a group of people in the Medina area who were interested in starting a new church. They asked them to consider the opportunity. A preliminary meeting with several families was held on Nov. 12, 1996, in the Sommer residence. Interest was high, and the group asked Lohnes to conduct a worship service the very next Sunday in the Lafayette Town Hall. Expecting only 20 or 30 people to be present, the pastor found to his surprise that approximately 125 persons had gathered to hear him preach. A core group of 27 persons called a business meeting and voted to call Will Lohnes to a church-planting ministry among them. He agreed, and the Lohnes family moved to Ohio in Jan. 1997.

Space in a factory was rented, and the first worship service of the new church welcomed 150 people to worship. The owners of the factory, John and Bonnie Semmelroth, have since joined the church. Membership

Sunday on April 27, 1997, produced a charter signed by 89 members. The congregation has purchased the factory and 18 acres of land from the Semmelroths with the intent of transforming the factory into a church facility. Renovations were completed in 2000. JSW/JRY

Congregational records; *Annual (FGBC)* (1997–98).

Membership Trends. A majority of Brethren bodies declined in membership during the last two decades of the 20th century. Specific statistics for Brethren denominations follow: *The Brethren Church (1980), 15,485 / (2000), 13,096, a net decline of 15.4 percent; *Church of the Brethren (1980), 170,884 / (2000), 135,879, a net decline of 20.5 percent; *Dunkard Brethren Church (1980), 1,035 / (2000), 937, a net decline of 9.5 percent; *Fellowship of Grace Brethren Churches (1980), 41,983 / (2000), 28,446, a net decline of 32.2 percent; *Old German Baptist Brethren (1980), 5,049 / (2000), 6,092, a net growth of 20.7 percent; *Conservative Grace Brethren Churches International (2000), 2220; combined Brethren bodies (1980), 234,436 / (2000), 186,670, a net decline of 20.4 percent.

Membership trends stemmed from factors both generic and particular to the Brethren. Generic factors included: (1) The rise of pluralism. Neither Protestants, Roman Catholics, nor Jews could claim religious dominance; a new wave of pluralism impacted culture, disturbing equilibrium in traditional churches. In addition, non-Anglo groups increased in population, complicating outreach strategies and growth possibilities for predominantly Anglo-Saxon congregations. (2) Decline of denominational significance. In large measure, persons no longer sought denominational distinctives; rather they sought vitality and attractive programming aimed at life enhancement; (3) Centrality of choice. Most persons no longer identified with a church out of loyalty or family tradition. Rather, pluralist society endorsed a smorgasbord of legitimate options for both belief and discretionary activity.

In addition to generic elements, factors within Brethren culture contributed to membership trends:

(1) Tension between sectarian identity and wider culture. Most Brethren bodies continued to struggle with appropriate connection with the larger society; i.e., it was difficult to preserve Brethren identity if non-Brethren practices or people were actively included in church life or formation. In 1986, for example, a split occurred in the First District of the Dunkard Brethren Church resulting in a loss of approximately 150 persons, when they began attending non-Dunkard Brethren seminars. A similar phenomenon occurred in the Grace Brethren Church in the early 1990s resulting in a loss of over 25 congregations when some Grace Brethren leaders began identifying with non-Brethren movements such as AD 2000. In both instances, those remaining feared loss of denominational distinctives, such as believers *baptism or qualifications for church *membership unique to Brethren tradition.

(2) Tendency toward church as a closed system. Brethren culture continued to define church as a particular, set-apart people; such a mindset resulted in experiences of the church as a closed system, focusing on existing members and their discipleship. Though understandable, this approach did not encourage the inclusion of outsiders and subsequent growth.

(3) Low corporate self-esteem. Given a heritage of persecution and small numerical size, Brethren continued to struggle with low corporate self-esteem. In the early 1990s, the Church of the Brethren addressed this reality through a major study/action project, coordinated by Communicorp, a major communications/marketing firm, located in Atlanta, GA. Communicorp's research and analysis confirmed the Brethren tendency toward low self-esteem, and recommended strategies for intervention. A major intervention was the adoption of a denominational "tag-line": "Continuing the Work of Jesus. Peacefully. Simply. Together." This theme was widely adopted across the denomination, resulting in new clarity regarding self-definition and identity.

Membership trends sparked varied responses among Brethren. Some expressed alarm, noting failure to evangelize in line with biblical command; others, however, accented faithfulness, noting the need to preserve denominational identity as a peculiar, even radical people, inherently unattractive to large numbers of individuals. PM

See also BRETHREN IDENTITY.

K. Bedell and A. M. Jones, *Yearbook of American and Canadian Churches* (1982, 1997); M. Coalter and others, *Vital Signs—The Promise of Mainstream Protestantism* (1996); *Reflections on Brethren Image and Identity* (1995); A. L. Gray, Jr., "Membership and Financial Contributions, Church of the Brethren, 1960–1998," *BLT* 45 (Summer, 2000) 133–43; personal interviews: Reva Benedict (OGBB), Robert S. Lehigh (DB), Kurt A. Miller (FGBC); personal information.

Menifee, CA, New Hope Community Church of the Valley (FGBC). The church was planted as a joint effort between the *Long Beach, CA, Grace Brethren Church and *Grace Brethren North American Missions. Pastors Mikal Smith and Chris Suitt moved with their families to Moreno Valley in 1988 to initiate the work. The David and Cathy Cornell family also moved with them to complete the core group. After several months of effort without success, the group moved down the road to Menifee and started again. A public worship service was held in Menifee on Easter Sunday 1989. The congregation eventually grew to over 200 in attendance and started another congregation in the area. In 2000 Chris Suitt remained as the pastor. Services are held in a commercial center in Canyon Lake, CA, located in Menifee Valley. CSu/JRY

Congregational records; *Annual (FGBC)* (1988–98).

***Mennonites.** In the beginning of the 21st century, Mennonites in the U.S. claimed about 232,000 baptized members and an estimated total population of 360,000 including children. Mennonites were organized into some 2,200 congregations and more than 30 distinctive subgroups. The three largest groups in 2000 included the *Mennonite Church (92,000), the *General Conference Mennonite Church (28,000), and the *Mennonite Brethren (23,000). In 2002 the General Conference Mennonite Church and the Mennonite Church merged into a new body, Mennonite Church USA. *The Mennonite* serves as the official bi-monthly publication of the new body.

Mennonites embody significant cultural and religious diversity, from horse-driving groups to those who have assimilated into mainstream American culture. Mennonites can be roughly divided into three types: Old Order groups, plain-dressing groups that use automobiles and other modern technologies, and assimilated groups. Assimilated groups account for about 65 percent of the Mennonite world; plain dressing ones 25 percent, and Old Order groups 10 percent. Old Order Mennonites share similarities with the *Amish, capping education at the

eighth grade and limiting technology. Many members of assimilated groups participate in professional occupations, support higher education, and attend congregations that vary greatly in language, ethnicity, and worship styles.

Seven institutions of higher education and three seminaries are affiliated with Mennonite bodies. *Mennonite Central Committee (MCC), with headquarters in Akron, PA, serves as the major relief and service agency for many North American Mennonite groups. MCC supports 1,400 staff members and volunteers in 60 countries with an annual budget of $60 million. Various denominational and regional mission boards and service agencies express Mennonite commitments to global mission and service. The Mennonite World Conference, which meets every five years, counts approximately 1.3 million Mennonites in 63 countries including the United States. A major trend is the rapidly growing number of Mennonite-related congregations in the non-western world, some of whom, however, do not use the Mennonite name. DBK

D. B. Kraybill and C. N. Hostetter, *Anabaptist World USA* (2001); D. B. Kraybill and C. F. Bowman, *On the Backroad to Heaven: Old Order Hutterites, Mennonites, Amish and Brethren* (2001); C. J. Dyck, *An Introduction to Mennonite History*, 3rd ed. (1993); T. Miller, ed., *America's Alternative Religions* (1995) 13–22; *The Mennonite Encyclopedia*, 5 vols. (1955–59, 1990); *Mennonite and Brethren in Christ World Directory*, 2000; *The Mennonite; Courier* (a quarterly, Mennonite World Conference, Strasbourg, France) (2000).

Men's Movements. The activity of men in the various Brethren bodies in the last two decades of the 20th century found expression in several areas. In the early 1980s, staff leadership in the *Church of the Brethren encouraged men to gather in small groups and retreats for the purpose of exploring the meaning of Christ-like masculinity in light of cultural values and pressures. This was seen as a complement to the "Women's Movement" and not a reaction to it. "For Men Only" retreats were sponsored and led by national staff. Resources were suggested and congregations were encouraged to facilitate men's support groups.

In 1990, Bill McCartney began Promise Keepers, a non-denominational program for men. By the mid-1990s, thousands of men attended weekend rallies in stadiums across the country. The mission statement of Promise Keepers is: "Promise Keepers encourages men to find support in bonding with one another for the purpose of holding one another accountable to keep promises as husbands and fathers and followers of Christ."

This movement had an impact on many men in the various Brethren bodies. It fostered the rise of local men's support and prayer groups. Following the example of Promise Keepers, these groups encouraged a deep level of intimacy that included personal sharing, confession, prayer, and holding one another accountable.

In *The Brethren Church, organized men's work ceased to exist in 1999. Called for many years the *National Laymen Organization, it was renamed *Brethren Men of Mission* in 1989 and in 1997 renamed *Brethren Laymen,* then disbanded in 1999. However, on a local level many activities continued, including efforts for home and foreign *mission and involvement in Promise Keepers.

In 1997, the first *Dunkard Brethren Men's Retreat was held in Michigan for the purpose of challenging men 14 years of age and older to be better men, fathers, and role models. This continued as an annual retreat, although without official sanction of the *General Conference. Promise Keepers also had an impact on many men in the denomination. RLD

J. A. Mathisen, "The Strange Decade of the Promise Keepers," *Books & Culture* (Sept./Oct., 2001) 36–39.

Mentoring (CB) is a practice used throughout Brethren history, but that word is not found in relevant history books. Brethren historians have used other words such as "eldering" or "admonishing" to describe what has been called "weighty counsel" given by an experienced or "seasoned" minister to a beginning or an unseasoned one. The long-time practice among Brethren has been that those senior in *ministry would provide counseling and advice to those new in ministry. The article on *Free Ministry ends with the sentence: "Younger and less experienced ministers receive counsel from those who are older."

The word "mentor" has become familiar in the *Church of the Brethren only in recent years. Synonyms or related terms include *elder, advisor, supervisor, nurturer, spiritual director, spiritual guide, support group, clergy group, ministerial meeting group. The word "mentor" comes from a Greek legend which referred to the loyal friend and wise adviser of Odysseus. Since then, a mentor has been considered a teacher or guardian, a wise and loyal advisor or elder.

Mentoring or eldering between two persons has gone on from the beginning of the Brethren movement. The relationship of *Alexander Mack, Sr. with *E. C. Hochmann von Hochenau could be understood as mentoring. Similar accounts have been told of such leading figures as *Peter Nead and *Henry Kurtz.

Not only have older, wiser, more experienced ministers mentored younger, beginning pastors on a one-to-one basis, mentoring also has gone on at ministerial meetings and elders' bodies, and, more recently, in ministerial support groups. In a "Synoptical Report" of a Brethren ministerial meeting held Nov. 26–28, 1895, the importance of ministers getting together in order to "qualify [them] to do better work" was spelled out in detail. Thirteen pastors were quoted in the report, providing down-to-earth advice on preaching and counseling.

For decades in the CB, the *Ministerial Association met prior to *Annual Conference. In the association's minutes of 1931, its purpose was stated as follows: to encourage growth and development, to provide opportunities for fellowship, and to initiate actions that will improve the relationship between ministers and [the] congregations they serve. The focus originally was on growth and support for ministry in a parish setting, although in recent years that has been broadened beyond the pastorate.

CB districts vary widely in their practice of mentoring, ranging from formal and structured programs to no program at all. Women pursuing ministry within the CB also report a wide variation of the extent to which they have been supplied with mentors.

In 2000, whatever name is used to describe support, encouragement, and guidance given to women and men as they begin various forms of ministry in and in behalf of the church, mentoring provides spiritual, theological, and personal support for those who seek growth in ministerial leadership and personal faith. NRF

Personal interviews; W. G. Willoughby, *Counting the Cost* (1979) 34;

Almanac (1909) 27; *BLT* 16 (Spring, 1971) 110; "Synoptical Report of the Proceedings of the Brethren's Second Ministerial Meeting of Eastern Pennsylvania" (Nov. 26–28, 1895) 1–6; Rebecca Slough and Debra Eisenbise, "The Significance of Theological Education in the Career Development of Women in Ministry: A Case Study from the Church of the Brethren," (unpubl. paper, 1996).

Mesa, AZ, Community Church of the Brethren. Members of the *Phoenix, AZ, CB who lived in East Mesa began holding Bible study sessions in their homes in the 1970s. Becker, Heitinger, and Vorhees were a few of the early family names. Paul R. Becker, a member of *Phoenix First CB, became one of the leaders. After several years the group decided, with the support of members of First Church and its pastor, Robert E. Keim, to begin holding services on Jan. 6, 1985. They soon found additional interest and turned to the Seventh Day Adventists for use of their sanctuary on Sundays. J. Calvin Hill and O. Magee Wilkes, retired ministers, served as part-time pastors. Lillian T. Brumbaugh was called to serve as the first full-time pastor. Claude Burlew served as pastor from 1998 to present. In 2000 the group had fellowship status in the Pacific Southwest District. REKe

Congregational records; *BLT* 36 (Summer, 1991) 172.

Metzger, Thurl D. (CB), service worker and administrator. Born in 1916 near Sidney, IN, Metzger is the son of Howard M. and Iva Leckrone Metzger. He graduated from Sidney High School (1934) and *Manchester College (BA, 1938), and received an honorary degree from Manchester (DHL, 1972). In 1941, he married Ruth Landis; they have four children: Kathleen, Robert, Richard, and Barbara. Metzger taught school for four years and in 1942 entered *Civilian Public Service, working first at Walhalla, MI, and later in an agricultural unit in Northern Minnesota. In 1946, he began working with *Heifer Project. His first major assignment was in *Poland as the representative of the *Brethren Service Committee with financial support from the *United Nations Relief and Rehabilitation Administration. In 1947 he initiated the *Polish Agricultural Exchange Program. Thurl Metzger became the executive director of Heifer Project International (HPI) in 1951 and two years later was instrumental in incorporating HPI as an independent agency with a number of supporting denominations. HPI's executive office was located at various places, and in 1971 it was moved to Little Rock, AR. Metzger retired in 1981. WRE

S. Bowers, *Planting the Faith in a New Land* (1992) 158; *Indiana* (1952) 359; D. F. Durnbaugh, ed., *To Serve the Present Age* (1975) 144–47; R. E. Sappington, *Social Policy* (1961) 130, 153; C. T. Johnson, *Milk for the World: The Heifer Project on the West Coast* (1981) *passim*; G. Yoder, *Passing on the Gift* (1978) 110, 131–34; B. Beck and M. West, eds., *Cowboy Memories...1944–1994* (1994); J. K. Kreider, *A Cup of Cold Water* (2001) index; D. F. Durnbaugh, *Fruit of the Vine* (1997) 464, 483; *Sharing Life* (HPI newsletter).

Mexico City, Mexico, Brethren Mission (BC). In 1998 Todd and Tracy Ruggles lived and worked in Mexico City's Jesus de Monte neighborhood. They coordinated outreach among The Brethren Churches in Mexico where in 2000 there were six Brethren congregations or mission points. The Ruggles, who assist with administration and work to develop leaders for the churches, hosted the first annual Mexico City Brethren pastors' retreat in 1997.

Missionary work in Mexico City is very difficult. The size of the population is overwhelming. Tremendous ethnic, cultural, and economic contrasts complicate spreading the gospel. Most of *The Brethren Church effort is among poor working people. Jennifer Thomas spent one year working with Spearhead, part of Latin America Mission. She also worked with the Ruggles and the Mexico City Brethren for five months during her year of service. RRSm

T. R. Eagle, *A History of Brethren Foreign Missions: 1972–1990;* A. T. Ronk, Unpublished Independent Study, Ashland Theo. Sem. (1989); *BE* (Oct., 1999) 9, (March, 2000) 7–8, (July-Aug., 2000) 1–5, (April 2002) 6, 8.

Miami, FL, Eglise des Frères Haitians (Haitian Church of the Brethren) began as a preaching point of the *Miami First CB. It was organized with four people, during the Haitian refugee influx into South *Florida in the early 1980s. Members met in various places until they were able to rent a storefront. Ludovic St. Fleur was the first pastor to be ordained in this congregation.

In 1995 the congregation was divided and some members withdrew because of the purchase of a church building and parsonage at 520 North West 103rd Street. Despite opposition and problems, the remaining congregation persevered, and the building was dedicated on Feb. 14, 1996. Worship services are conducted in French/Creole, and several activities are held each week. The congregation hosted the annual District Conference on Oct. 9, 1999. In 2000, reported membership was 176 and average worship attendance was 308. LSt

Cong. records; *Messenger* (July, 1994) 22–24, (Dec., 1999) 20–23; *BLT* 36 (Summer, 1991) 169; *Yearbook* (CB) (2001) 107.

Milam, WV, Mount Carmel Church of the Brethren, Hardy Co., was organized as a fellowship in 1983. Mount Carmel was first organized in 1892 as one of eight preaching points of the *South Fork congregation. Originally it was the only meeting place for regular services in the South Fork congregation in the area later to be called South Congregation. The other meeting houses of the South Fork congregation later included Bethlehem and South Mill Creek (1929), Sweedlin Valley School House (1935), Sycamore (1941), Hinkle Mountain, Mitchel Mountain, and Main Mountain (1959). South Mill Creek is now a *meetinghouse in the West Marva District. In 1983, Bethlehem and Mount Carmel disorganized the South Fork Congregation and became separate fellowships. Mount Carmel became a congregation in 1984. The remaining five meetinghouses had been closed earlier. SRS

Virginia (1973); *Mount Carmel: 100th Anniversary Celebration Booklet* (1992).

Miller, Donald Eugene (CB), b. 1929, teacher, social worker, minister, seminary professor, administrator. The son of Daniel and Eliza Coning Miller (OGBB), Donald Miller was born Dec. 2 in Dayton, OH. Following his studies at *Manchester College (1947–49) and the U. of Chicago (MA, 1952) he fulfilled *Brethren Volunteer Service assignments in Kassel, Germany, and Linz, Austria (1952–54) and then taught social studies at the Madison Township High School in Trotwood, OH (1954–55). Called to the ministry by the *Bear Creek CB in the S. Ohio district (1957), he continued his education at United Theol. Sem. (1955–56), *Bethany Theol. Sem. (MDiv, 1958), and Harvard U. (PhD, 1962), with further advanced study at Yale U. (1968–69) and Cambridge U.

Donald E. Miller and B. Merle Crouse confer at Panama Canal Treaty hearings of the U.S. Senate Committee on Foreign Relations Committee on Oct, 12, 1977. BHLA collection.

(1975–76). In 1956 Miller married Phyllis Gibbel; they are the parents of three children: Bryan, Lisa, and Bruce.

While teaching at Bethany (1961–86) Miller was advanced to a tenured position as professor of *Christian education and *ethics (1970). He was appointed director of graduate studies (1973) with responsibility for the design and implementation of the Doctor of Ministry program. His educational vision and skills were drawn upon during the development of the denominational *Education for a Shared Ministry (EFSM) and Training in Ministry (TRIM) programs. He directed a comprehensive 1981 self-study of the Chicago Cluster of Theological Schools. In 1982 he was designated the Alvin F. Brightbill Professor of Ministerial Studies.

Donald Miller served as general secretary of the CB *General Board (1986–96), providing leadership during a time of budgetary constraints, controversy over *ordination and *homosexuality, and urgent questions relating to *restructuring. He represented the denomination on the General Board of the *National Council of Churches and of the Central Committee of the *World Council of Churches. He introduced a resolution to the Central Committee to establish a "Program to Overcome Violence" (1994) and steadily persisted in that effort until it was adopted in renamed and expanded form in 1998 by the ecumenical council as the "Decade to Overcome Violence."

Through the years Miller has published a large number of articles and books, including: "The Theological Basis of Personal Ethics," adopted by the CB Annual Conference (1966); co-author with *W. F. Groff, *The Shaping of Modern Christian Thought* (1968); *The Wing-Footed Wanderer: Conscience and Transcendence* (1977); *Making Choices* (1981); co-author with J. L. Seymour, *Contemporary Approaches to Christian Education* (1982); "How My Mind Has Changed Over Ten Years (and Longer)," *Religious Education* 79 (Winter, 1984); *The Gospel and Mother Goose* (1987); and co-author with J. L. Seymour, *Theological Approaches to Christian Education,* (1990). Several of these works have been published in translation in other nations.

Since retirement as general secretary, Miller has taught occasional courses at BTS as professor emeritus of Christian education and ethics. His many contributions to denominational and ecumenical leadership received recognition in the awarding of an honorary degree by *Bridgewater College (DD, 1988). WFGr

Who's Who in Religion, 2nd ed. (1977) 451; *Contemporary Authors* (1982) 106: 356; *Who's Who in America* (1997); *TBE* (1983–84) 1710; D. F. Durnbaugh, *Fruit of the Vine* (1997) index; J. K. Kreider, *A Cup of Cold Water* (2001) 194, 332; F. F. Wayland, *Bridgewater College* (1993) 601; Panama Canal Treaties: Hearing Before the Committee on Foreign Relations, U.S. Senate, 95th Congress, Part 3, Public Witnesses, U.S. Government Printing Office, Washington, DC, 1977, pp. 381–91 (including biography of Donald E. Miller); personal information.

Miller, John William ("Willie") (OGBB), 1911–97, church leader, author. The son of John Perry Miller and Mary Ann Gearhart Miller, J. William Miller was born in Montgomery Co., OH. In 1930 he married Dora Evelyn Stoner; they lived at New Lebanon, OH, where they raised six children. They farmed and marketed in Dayton. In March 1950, Miller was elected to the ministry at the *Bear Creek congregation where he served for 47 years;

he was advanced to the eldership in 1959. He was a member of The *Vindicator Committee (1964–92).

J. William Miller grew up in a home where Pennsylvania German was spoken and over the years he became proficient in German and Danish because of his association with friends in *Germany and *Denmark. In 1951 he went to *Europe and Palestine with Joseph Rumble, Hubert Rumble, and Paul Balsbaugh. Following that, he and his wife traveled to Europe six more times, on five of which trips the Millers served as tour directors. They fell in love with *Schwarzenau, Germany, and its people, spending 39 days there in 1980. The friends of the Millers in Europe and the U.S. were numerous and varied.

William Miller collected a library of old books and historical materials, reprinted older Brethren books, and in 1975 he, with the help of his wife, translated into English *Jeremias Felbinger's Christian Handbook (1651). This book, along with the work of *Gottfried Arnold, was an important historical source for the early Brethren. He also authored Collections and Recollections (1986) in which he shared much of his life and travels.

Having served his congregation as elder-in-charge for 30 years, J. William Miller died on June 2 and was buried in the nearby Trissel Cemetery. Dora Miller died in 2000 and is buried beside her husband. FWB

Vindicator (1950) 122, (1978) 350, (1997) 222; Messenger (April, 1976) 3; D. F. Durnbaugh, "Old German Baptist Brethren and the Media: An Analysis," Old Order Notes No. 24 (Fall/Winter, 2001) 7–28 (15); Old Order Notes No. 4 (Spring, 1981) 30.

Millersburg, OH, Grace Brethren Church. In Oct. 1986 George Johnson began teaching a Bible class in Holmes County. Johnson had been a missionary to *Brazil from the *Wooster, OH, Grace Brethren congregation. Public worship services were conducted in Jan. 1987 at the Farm Credit Building in Millersburg and in other locations. Charles G. Thornton, the first full-time pastor, began his ministry on Aug. 30, 1987. He challenged the congregation to find more suitable accommodations. On Nov. 1, 1987, the congregation relocated to the Calvary Building on Route 39 between Millersburg and Berlin. In the spring of 1989, 13 acres of land were purchased along TR 305. A ground-breaking service was held on May 1, 1994, and the building was completed by July 1995. Pastor Thornton concluded his ministry a year later, and Roland R. Maust was called to be the pastor. He began his ministry on Sept. 1, 1996. RRM/JRY

Congregational records.

*Ministry. The only reported changes on ministry policy since 1980 were from *The Brethren Church and the *Church of the Brethren. The BC identified three significant changes: (1) During the mid-1980s and again between 1999 and 2002 the *elders (ordained ministers) discussed the ordination of women. In 2002 the elders agreed that people duly called to ministry by a local congregation should be examined by their district examining board and the *National Ordination Council without regard to "sex, color, and nationality." In 2003 and 2004 four women were ordained; the last ordinations of any women had been in the mid-1980s. (2) Divorce does not automatically exclude an individual from *ordination and pastoral leadership. (3) Ordination is viewed as functional, but the title is also used for non-pastoral leaders and retired persons. Ordination lapses for those who do not

serve the church in any capacity for three consecutive years.

The CB identified several major changes: (1) To address a shortage of pastors, major efforts have been made to call persons to the set-apart ministry in recent years. (2) While the Master of Divinity degree continues to hold a high priority in the CB, *Bethany Theol. Sem. and the denomination's General Board are now working together to provide three certificate-level training programs, through the *Bethany Academy for Ministerial Leadership, for more than two-thirds of those in training today. (3) The denomination continues to challenge congregations to call women and non-white pastoral leaders. (4) *Annual Conference approved an Ethics in Ministry Relations paper in 1996, and an Ethics for Congregations paper in 1998. (5) The *Council of District Executives, formed in the early 1970s, gained significant strength and denominational influence in the 1980s and 1990s. (6) The Ministerial Leadership paper, passed by Annual Conference in 1999, established uniform guidelines in all 23 districts for licensing, ordaining, and receiving non-Brethren pastors into the denomination. ATH

Minutes (BC) (1980ff.); Minutes (CB) (1980ff.).

Ministry of Reconciliation (MoR) (CB) is the conflict transformation program of the *Church of the Brethren. It provides conflict intervention, group facilitation, and training in conflict resolution and communication at all levels of the denomination. MoR was formed in the early 1980s under the supervision of Charles L. Boyer, then denominational peace consultant, by a committee of seven persons with interest and experience in the field. In 1990 the program was moved from the *General Board's Peace Consultant Office to *On Earth Peace Assembly. Barbara Daté served as coordinator of MoR in the late 1980s, and Robert A. Gross has served in that role since 1995. Primary program areas have included support and training for *Discipleship and Reconciliation Committees and others who assist in handling conflict in the church, facilitation of major events and discussions in the denomination, and educational workshops such as the Matthew 18 Workshop, a resource for congregations. RAGr

Messenger (Jan., 1993) 9, (Dec., 1995) 22–24; Crossroads: Ministry of Reconciliation Newsletter (1992ff.); Discipleship and Reconciliation Handbook (1995); D. F. Durnbaugh, Fruit of the Vine (1997) 588.

*Missions. In 1998, called by the *Great Commission (Matt. 28:19–20) to make disciples among all peoples, *The Brethren Church, through its *Missionary Ministries Council, was striving to encourage and equip Brethren to evangelize, establish new churches, and develop ministries among all peoples. Internationally the denomination works in Asia, Latin America, and Africa. Specifically there are Brethren churches in *Argentina, Colombia, *Mexico, *Peru, *India, *Malaysia, and *Paraguay. There is also a cooperative project with Eastern Mennonite Missions in Djibouti.

The most extensive mission work is in *India where there are 255 preaching points and more than 200 pastors and evangelists. They operate boys' and girls' orphanages, medical clinics, typing and sewing schools, and Bible training institutes. An emerging venture is the partnership between the *Argentine Brethren Church and *Ashland Theol. Sem. to create *South American Theol. Seminary. It is hoped that the Seminary will also train Brethren from

Peru, Paraguay, and Colombia. In Malaysia they have been able to build the first legal worship center in a business park in Penang.

At the beginning of the 1980s the *Central African Republic continued to be the main focus of *Grace Brethren Foreign Missions. By 1997 there were 837 churches, 191,360 members, and strong African leadership of churches and institutions.

Efforts in Europe moved to the forefront in the 1980s with 60 missionaries added to the small staff there. Publications were produced and a branch of *Grace Theol. Sem. was established in the *Chateau of Saint Albain, Burgundy, France, the center for European operations.

In *Argentina, the oldest field of Grace Brethren Missions, a new team joined hands with Argentinians to spawn a movement of rapid church planting called *Total Mobilization*. This has led to new developments in Brazil, *Mexico, Uruguay, Paraguay, Chile, *Cuba, and Guatemala.

Under the slogan, "Missions is not what the church does for the missionary; missions is what the church does through the missionary," the renamed *Grace Brethren International Missions (GBIM) shifted its emphasis from being a missionary society to a mission society, with the stated purpose of serving Grace Brethren churches in their Great Commission ministries.

Local churches have become alive in initiating many creative ministries throughout the world. The first radio transmitter was established in Phnom Penh. The visits of a vision team from the *Long Beach, CA, GBC led to developments in *Japan, the Philippines, Cambodia, Thailand, and Vietnam.

Cooperating with AD 2000 and Beyond, GBIM seeks to participate in reaching the unreached people groups of the world by the end of this decade.

The *Dunkard Brethren continue their work with the *Torreon Navajo Mission (NM) and have begun an *Africa Mission Project in Kenya and Uganda, with longer term mission personnel sent in 1997, following four missionary trips during the period from Jan. 1995 to Dec. 1996.

Mission in an *ecumenical context and mutuality with independent national churches were priorities for the *Church of the Brethren, supported by the statement of mission philosophy adopted by *Annual Conference in 1981. The largest of these national churches, the CB in *Nigeria (*Ekklesiyar 'Yan'uwa a Nigeria [EYN]), continues to grow rapidly with ca. 140,000 members by 1998. The last fraternal worker from the U.S. returned from India in 1988 as the Church of North India relied on local leadership. Support was also gradually eliminated from the church in *Ecuador.

New projects emerged, led by beginning work in the *Sudan in Jan. 1980. In *Haiti there was a covenantal relationship with Eglise Baptiste des Cites Haiti. With *Iglesia Christiana Pentecostal of Cuba and Mission Christiana de Nicaragua there were models for mutual mission (Missión Mutua) that included the development of pastoral training.

Mission philosophy was continually debated. A new statement was adopted by Annual Conference in 1989. It emphasized the planting of the church in new places and at the same time reaffirmed the denomination's established mission principles of indigenization, mutuality, and independence, as well as nurturing ecumenical relationships.

The Reeds excaping from China. Mary Jane Swihart collection.

Escaping the Communists

Little did Kyle and Mary Reed suspect when they arrived in Loho, China, that before long Communists would arrive to "liberate" the people. The Communists blew up the railroad station and bridge, demolished miles of track on both sides of town, and burned the hospital. When Communist soldiers came to the tractor depot, Mary Reed hid in a grease pit while Kyle Reed and the other men were taken away and interrogated.

The workers realized they had to leave quickly. The Communists had "borrowed" all of the trucks and jeeps, so they loaded two small two-wheeled trailers and hooked them behind Allis-Chalmers tractors. Unsure whether to escape Christmas night or the next day, they held a special prayer meeting and felt peace about waiting. The next morning heavy snow fell. Thankful for bad weather because bombing would lessen, Kyle and Mary Reed and the other men set out for Kaifeng, where they would board a transport plane to Shanghai. Mary, riding in one of the trailers, wore six dresses at once because their belongings could be taken from them at any time.

White flags made from sheets fastened to the trailers indicated that they were neutral. While traveling they still listened for Nationalist planes which would randomly strafe the roadways. When they heard a plane, they drove into the ditch and jack-knifed the trailers to simulate abandoned junk piles, then hid under the tractors. One time the tractors and trailers got stuck in a river. Civilians pulled them out with a long rope. Along the way they feared young boys who pointed guns at them almost more than the adult soldiers.

The escape to Kaifeng took three days. They felt great comfort the evening before flying out when Chinese Christians came to sing Christmas carols. This comfort accompanied them on to safety in Shanghai. MJS

The 1990 Annual Conference called for beginning with intention to plant the CB in *Korea and gave official status to the development of CB ministry in the *Dominican Republic. Emerging church groups in *Brazil were recognized in 1992 and 2001.

A new design for denominational program, adopted in 1997, sought to strengthen local congregations' connection to missions. It created the Mission and Ministries Planning Council to make future recommendations for new mission projects. JGD

BC: A. T. Ronk, *History of Brethren Missionary Movements* (1977); *A Centennial Statement* (1984); *How Brethren Understand God's Word* (1993). CB: E. F. Bittinger, ed., *Brethren in Transition* (1992); D. F. Durnbaugh, *Fruit of the Vine* (1997); F. Matsuoka, *Out of Silence: Emerging Themes in Asian-American Churches* (1995); M. S. Rosenberger, *Light of the Spirit: The Brethren in Puerto Rico, 1942 to 1992* (1992); O. Serrano, *Un Canot al Señor en la Isla del Encanto* (1992); L. Wilson, *Mission Factor: A Study Guide for the Church of the Brethren Goals for the '80s* (1980); *BLT* 29 [special issue on missions (Spring, 1984) 69–127; 30 (Winter, 1985) 47–49; 35 (Fall, 1990) 291–97; 36 (Summer, 1991) 139–41; 37 (Summer, 1992) 179–93; *Messenger* (Jan., 1980) 21, (Dec., 1980) 11–13, (March, 1981) 22, (June, 1981) 15, (Aug., 1981) 10, (Sept., 1981) 16, (Sept., 1984) 8, (June, 1986) 10–11, (Nov., 1986) 27–28, (June, 1981) 15, (Oct., 1988) 35–37, (May/June, 1989) 40–41, (Oct., 1989) 10–13, (Dec., 1990) 18–20, (May, 1998) 10–12, 15, (Aug., 1989) 28; (Jan./Feb., 2001) 14–21, (May, 2001) 6, 10; (Oct., 2002) 10–23; interviews, D. Radcliff, M. Keeney. FGBC: T. T. Julien, *Seize the Moment: Stories of an Awesome God Empowering Ordinary People* (2000); R. Snyder, *Estella Myers: Pioneer Missionary in Central Africa* (1984); *Brethren Missionary Herald* (1980) *passim*; *Significant Times* D. R. Plaster, *Finding Our Focus* (1983); W. Beaver, *God at Work in the Central African Republic* (2000); B. A. Hamilton, *Gibble's Dream...God's Design* (1987); www.gbim.org; interviews, T. T. Julien, Reilly Smith.

Missions, Short-Term, began in the later part of the 20th century within several Brethren bodies. These trips allowed for greater participation among members and responded to the changing needs of global mission. Most notable was the desire for more hands-on participation by church members and their growing unwillingness to commit to long-term mission assignments. Short-term experiences often focus on building relationships, completing work projects, and raising awareness of global issues.

Participation in short-term mission varies among Brethren bodies. The *Old German Baptist Brethren do not sponsor short-term mission trips. The *Dunkard Brethren Church has growing numbers of youth participating in short-term missions with other agencies because their denomination does not have a structured approach to short-term missions. The *Conservative Grace Brethren Churches International has a limited approach, which includes door-to-door evangelism within the U.S. and networking among congregations to form teams that travel abroad for short-term projects. Denominations that take a more expansive approach to short-term missions include the *Fellowship of Grace Brethren Churches, *The Brethren Church, and the *Church of the Brethren.

The FGBC began short-term mission trips in 1993 and sent out 152 teams over the next ten years. Teams were deployed to fields where long-term missionaries were stationed, including *Argentina, Uruguay, *Brazil, *Central African Republic, Cambodia, *Chad, *Chile, Czech Republic, *England, *France, *Germany, *Ireland, *Japan, Kyrgyzstan, *Mexico, *Niger, Philippines, Portugal, Russia, South Korea, *Spain, Thailand, *Turkey, and *Vietnam, as well as other sites in Europe and Southeast Asia. As of April 30, 2003, a total of 1,182 persons have participated in short-term missions through the FGBC.

The International Ministries Council organizes short-term missions in the BC. It provides opportunities for personal spiritual growth and development of ministry skills and an attitude of servanthood. Mission trips are coordinated for youth, adults, and families. Teams focus on work, service, and witness projects. Opportunities available in 2003 include working with long-term missionaries stationed in *Mexico, *India, Peru, and *China. Addi-

tional short-term mission experiences are offered within the United States to work with Native Americans, in *Appalachia, and in urban settings.

CB short-term missions developed in the 1980s as support and advocacy groups traveled to war-torn nations in Central America. A decade later the focus changed as church-planting efforts allowed for more interchurch relations. The concept of a global church beyond the borders of the U.S. developed in 1989 as changes were made in the denomination's mission philosophy, which further expanded mission efforts. Several congregations have developed sister church relationships across international borders, creating opportunities for short-term mission experiences.

An annual workcamp in *Nigeria, typically held for a month in Jan. or Feb., is the longest-running short-term mission experience sponsored by the Global Mission Partnerships of the CB. Philip W. and Louise Baldwin Rieman led the first workcamp in 1985 as an effort to strengthen relations between the denominations and to work alongside Nigerians on a variety of work projects.

Short-term CB mission trips are offered through several different denominational and local offices. The Youth and Young Adult Ministry office sponsors about two dozen workcamps each summer at numerous domestic and international locations. Faith Expeditions to countries in South and Central America, *Africa, the Middle East, Asia, and within the U.S. are coordinated through the Brethren Witness Office. Local congregations and districts also organize short-term mission trips. LABa

Messenger (June, 1981) 27–31, (Dec., 1984) 10–13, (Nov., 1992) 7, (March, 1993) 16–18, (May, 1993) 18–20, (Dec., 1994) 10–13, (March, 1996) 24–26, (March, 1999) 23–26, (Oct., 2002) 20–23; www.gbim.org, May 14, 2003; www.-brethrenchurch.org, May 14, 2003; www.brethren.-org, May 14, 2003; correspondence: Ted Rondeau (April 30, 2003) and Mervin B. Keeney (May 7, 2003); personal information.

Mount Vernon, OH, Conservative Grace Brethren Church. For 35 years prior to formation of the GBC in Mount Vernon, there were numerous attempts by various pastors to begin a work in the community. In 1981 Roger F. Bartlett (1951–98) of the *Mansfield, OH, GBC, in conjunction with his theological studies in the *Theological Practorium at Mansfield, held a weekly Bible study at Cooper Industries. He then enlisted the help of a fellow theological student, John E. Bryant, who assumed the vision and founded a new church on Sept. 19, 1982, with a charter membership of 17.

The fledgling church met the first year in rented school facilities before moving its location to the Senior Citizens Center in the heart of town. In June 1990 the Dan Emmett Grange Hall at the northern edge of town became available and was purchased on a faith basis; the 35 people comprising the congregation voted to purchase the building without using a bank loan. Ten weeks later, with offerings totaling over $40,000, the sale was completed. Remodeling took place during the next year as offerings continued to flow in for each successive phase. The building was dedicated on Oct. 20, 1991. Additional property in excess of seven acres adjoining the building was purchased in 1992.

In 1993 a Theological Practorium was established to train men for the ministry. The church celebrated the commencement of its first two graduates on July 25, 1999. This growing church is strongly committed to the Lord's *Great Commission of carrying the gospel into the com-

munity as well as training young men for pastoral leadership. The congregation has a strong emphasis in its program on marriage, family, children, and youth. In 2000 more than 120 regular worshippers of all ages attend weekly services.

The church staff includes John E. Bryant, senior pastor and president of the Theological Practorium, and Gordy A. Harmon, assistant pastor. JEB

Congregational records.

Mountain View Old German Baptist Brethren, VA, was the name chosen for a new district on June 1, 1994, which resulted from the reorganization of the large *Pigg River Church, Rocky Mount, VA. The new district has five ministers: Elwood C. Bowman, C. Abram Rutrough, Eugene W. Jamison, Dan L. Long, and I. Stephen Rutrough. Membership in December 2000 was 129. FWB

The Vindicator (July, 1944) 213; *Director of Officials* (Jan., 2001) 13.

Muncie, IN, Cornerstone Brethren Church and Ministries (BC) began from a building program for the *Oakville, IN, First Brethren Church. When it was realized that relocation was necessary, a group of parishioners asked that they be allowed to remain with the old building and retain the name. The result was the birth of two new congregations. The moving congregation began worshiping Oct. 1, 1995, in the nearby Cowan Elementary School and took the name "Cornerstone Brethren Church and Ministries," emphasizing the desire for members to be involved in the ministries of the congregation. On Oct. 5, 1997, a new multipurpose building was dedicated as phase one of a four-phase master plan. In 1998 Pastor Tim Dwyer led Cornerstone Brethren Church and Ministries with an average attendance of 100 for Sunday morning worship. The mission statement of the church is "Building lives with Jesus as our Cornerstone." DLL/BMMe

BE (Feb., 1996) 10, (Nov., 1997) 9, (Feb. 1998) 9; congregational records.

Munson, Charles Robert (BC), seminary professor and elder. Charles Munson (b. 1919) was born in Johnstown, PA, and confessed his faith in Christ at the First Brethren Church. He received a call to minister the gospel while working in the steel mills. He pursued his preparation for ministry by first graduating from *Ashland College (BA, 1947) and then *Ashland Theol. Sem. (BD, 1952). Following studies at Pittsburgh Theol. Sem. (ThM, 1954), he pursued further study at Case Western University (PhD, 1971).

Munson was appointed professor of practical theology at Ashland Theol. Sem. in 1954 and continued his teaching for 36 years. He was a popular teacher, filling his lectures with practical applications, humor, and wit. Munson served the church in many capacities while fulfilling his role as professor. He served as moderator of both General and District Conference and as president of the Brethren National Ministerial Association. The *Board of Christian Education was always grateful for his membership. He served on the Brethren Central Council and Brethren Central Planning and Coordination Committee. For his lifetime ministry to the church, the seminary awarded him an honorary doctorate in 1989.

Munson also served a number of congregations in several states in an interim ministerial capacity. These churches include *Williamstown (OH), *Gretna (OH),

Lexington (OH), Savannah (OH), *New Lebanon (OH), *Smithville (OH), Winding Waters (IN), *Flora (IN), Johnstown Second (PA), *Bradenton (FL), Goshen (IN), and Jefferson (Goshen, IN). He brought love, peace, and oneness in the church. JRS

BE (June, 1984) 17, (July/Aug., 1989) 20, 22, (June, 2001) 8–9.

*Music, always central to Brethren *worship, originally consisted only of unaccompanied (*a cappella*) singing. Today's worship music may be instrumental or vocal. When sung, it may be *a cappella* or with musical accompaniment. Musical styles among the various Brethren bodies include classical hymns, German chorales, gospel songs, folk songs, African-American spirituals, multicultural songs, Taizé-sung prayers, and contemporary gospel.

The organ and piano were the main accompanying *musical instruments of the 20th century (CB, FGBC, BC), but by the 1990s the synthesizer and electronic piano began to replace the organ and piano in some congregations. Rhythm instruments accompany African and Hispanic hymns. Solo instruments such as guitar, banjo, dulcimer, or drums, trumpets, and saxophones often are used. Handbell or chime choirs continue to appear. Some congregations have an instrumental ensemble or a praise band. Some use taped accompaniment for soloists or choirs, or when there is no church musician.

*Dunkard Brethren and *Old German Baptist Brethren continue to sing exclusively without accompaniment. Some Dunkard Brethren song leaders use a pitch pipe to determine the pitch. Special music is heard and sung only in homes or at social gatherings not connected with formal worship. At these events, popular gospel songbooks, conservative Mennonite books, or the *Brethren Hymnal* (1901) may be used.

Publication of **Hymnal: A Worship Book* (1992) and *Hymnal: Accompaniment Handbook* (1993) helped to introduce new hymns of various styles and cultures to the *Church of the Brethren. Since the church does not mandate the use of any particular hymnal, some congregations might use older Brethren hymnals. A significant number of congregations (BC, CB, FGBC) use non-denominational hymnals that have old gospel favorites or modern choruses. Dunkard Brethren use either the 1901 *Brethren Hymnal* (which the Dunkard *Board of Publications has kept in print) or a variety of non-Brethren hymnals. Old German Baptist Brethren only use their hymnal of 558 hymn texts edited in 1882, now nearing its 30th printing. A select number of texts have been slightly altered by editors. Song leaders choose tunes from memory, including a small number of contemporary tunes which tend to have a faster tempo.

An increasing number of CB, BC, DB, and FGBC congregations buy a copyright license such as CCLI (Christian Copyright License) to photocopy hymns and songs not in their hymnal, resulting in congregations singing medleys of hymns and choruses. Sometimes there are overhead projectors that feature words only, an uncomfortable approach for Brethren who enjoy singing four-part harmony or who resist modern technology in worship.

Praise choruses, often led by worship teams, involve physical movement, such as hand clapping, raising of arms, and stomping of feet; this causes contention in some congregations. Choirs for all ages are common. Some groups wear choir robes; others choose another unified

outfit or individual dress. Some choirs sing regularly in worship; others only on occasion or at hymn festivals.

Music will survive in Brethren worship, but culture and modern technology are testing the traditional way Brethren have sung. Some congregations have been influenced by popular music trends and styles; others resist. However music is sung, played, or listened to by Brethren, it will continue to play a crucial role in Brethren worship. NRF

K. I. Morse, *Move in Our Midst* (1977) 86–94; C. F. Bowman, *Brethren Society* (1995) *passim*; D. F. Durnbaugh, *Fruit of the Vine* (1997) *passim*; *Messenger* (Oct., 2001) 10–15; interviews.

*Musical Instruments. Between 1980 and 2000 there was a significant change in the kinds of musical instruments used in worship in the *Church of the Brethren, *The Brethren Church, the *Conservative Grace Brethren Churches International, and the *Fellowship of Grace Brethren Churches. Pianos and organs continue to be the primary instruments, but not the only ones. The guitar also may accompany congregational singing or small ensembles.

A praise band is increasingly used to accompany a new style of song, praise or Scripture songs. It is built around the guitar, in a primary role; keyboard, in a secondary role; and background strings, if available. Supplemental instruments are saxophone, trumpet, electric guitar, bass guitar, and percussion. Other instruments used in worship may include banjo, autoharp, flute, brass, and strings. A small number of congregations have handbell choirs. The aesthetics of worship changes when instrumentalists and their equipment sit in the front of the sanctuary, taking up considerable space, and when words of a hymn or a praise song are projected on the wall. Sound systems with expensive microphones have the ability to sufficiently amplify all instruments and voices. Small churches may use music recorded on computer disks or audio tapes to accompany singing. Larger churches may have live music, using small orchestras or praise bands. The *Accompaniment Book* to **Hymnal: A Worship Book*, published by the CB, *Mennonite Church, and *General Conference Mennonite Church, has guitar chords and instrumental settings for a considerable number of hymns and songs.

*Old German Baptist Brethren and *Dunkard Brethren continue to use no musical instruments in worship. Singing is *a capella* solely. Some Dunkard Brethren use musical instruments outside church, either at home or when singing for nursing homes. NRF

H. M. Best, *Music Through the Eyes of Faith* (1993) 117–41; D. F. Hustad, *True Worship* (1998) 160–88; B. Wren, *Praying Twice* (2000) 127ff.; *Messenger* (Oct., 2001) 10–15.

Name Change Discussion (CB). In the late 19th century the *German Baptist Brethren discussed the wisdom of choosing a name that indicated the denomination was no longer German-speaking. In 1908 they adopted the name *Church of the Brethren.

Nearly one hundred years later a similar discussion was held in the church. As English language usage changed, the word *brethren* came to signify to some people an exclusively male group. Some have urged that a name be sought to indicate a church where both men and women participate in all levels of the church's life. This discussion began in the 1970s as the church confronted issues of equality for women. Although there was no official consideration of the name of the church, letters to

*Messenger reflected a lively debate between those calling for a name that included women and those questioning the advisability of change.

After a query requesting a study of the name of the church was rejected by the Mid-Atlantic District Conference in 1990, individuals and groups petitioned *Standing Committee of *Annual Conference to consider the issue. In 1992 Standing Committee authorized a "pre-committee" to identify issues and discern the timing of a possible study. Its report was received in 1993 and no further action was taken "with the knowledge that the discussion will continue."

While many suggestions for a changed denominational name have surfaced (including Church of Reconciliation, Church of Believers, Servant Church of Christ) none has attracted wide-spread support. Those who encourage a change of name call for one that signals welcome for all persons and encourages the mission of the church. Others affirm that the content of the name will be determined by the witness of those who carry it. DRM

See also NAMES, BRETHREN.

C. F. Bowman, *Brethren Society* (1995) 396–99; *BLT* 44 (Summer, 1999) 55–73; *BRF Witness* 37 (March/April, 2002) 2–12; *Messenger* (Jan., 1973) 10, (Feb., 1979) 40, (Aug., 1980) 36, (Aug./Sept., 1992) 20–21, (March, 1993) 28–29, (April, 1993) 26, (June, 1993) 26, (July, 1993) 27, (Jan., 1994) 9, (July, 1994) 28, (Sept., 1994) 35, 36–37, (July, 1999) 32, (July, 2002) 2, (Aug., 2002) 28, 30; *Agenda* (Jan./Feb., 1994) 3; *Femailings* 21/ 3 (1992ff.); "Continuing the Conversation" (Womaen's Caucus portfolio on name change (2001); *Christianity Today* (Dec. 13, 1993) 65; personal files.

*National Council of Churches of Christ in the USA (NCCC) and *World Council of Churches (WCC), Support for (CB). Alone among Brethren bodies, the *Church of the Brethren has maintained strong ties with the NCCC and the WCC. The NCCC increased in membership to 35 denominations during the 1980s and 1990s, and during the same time the voice of the Black churches became increasingly important to the council. Members of the CB General Board staff actively participated, in particular with the governing board, the heads of communion groups, the executive committee, *Church World Service, Christian education, communication, political issues, Hispanic ministry, and stewardship education. CB staff often gave leadership, as for example, the work of *Robert W. Neff in chairing the search committee to find a new General Secretary (ca. 1984).

By 1997 the WCC increased its membership to 335 denominations, adding younger churches from Asia and Africa. Neff and *Donald E. Miller consecutively represented the CB on the council's Central Committee. At a meeting of the Central Committee in Johannesburg, South Africa, in Jan. 1994 church leaders of that country gave the WCC much credit for its influence in bringing apartheid to an end. During the same meeting representatives of the Brethren and the *Society of Friends introduced the *Program to Overcome Violence (POV), whose purpose is to change the world culture of violence to a culture of peace and justice.

Conservative voices in the media and changes within member denominations have led to declining resources and consequent structural revisions within both the NCCC and the WCC. The *Brethren Revival Fellowship and other CB members have been among those critics who object that the councils are religiously and politically too liberal. The CB *Annual Conference regularly supported membership in the councils, but allowed dissenting con-

gregations annually to allocate their contributions to programs not related to the councils. Perhaps 20 congregations did so. DEM

D. F. Durnbaugh, *Fruit of the Vine* (1997) 447–55, 532–34; *BRF Witness* 19 (July/Aug., 1984) 2–14, 35, (May/June, 2000) 2–11.

National Older Adult Conferences (NOAC) (CB). The 1985 Annual Conference approved a Statement on Aging which was developed by a committee appointed by the *Brethren Health and Welfare Association (BHWA). Committee members were Leah Musser Zuck, chair, Warren M. Eshbach, Dorothy Keller, Lois Horning Snyder, Harvey S. Kline, Raymond R. Peters, Hazel M. Peters, and Jay E. Gibble, staff. The concluding sentence in the statement authorized BHWA to implement the 16 recommended goals. Adoption of that statement provided an impetus for older adult ministries in the *Church of the Brethren for the last two decades of the 20th century.

The first National Older Adult Conference at Lake Junaluska, NC, Oct. 5–9, 1992, represented one concrete outcome from that Annual Conference paper. This new venture was planned by a committee appointed by the Homes and Older Adult Board of the *Association of Brethren Caregivers (ABC), successor organization to BHWA. Committee members were Hubert and Alice Newcomer (volunteer coordinators), Paul and Evelyn Bowman, James K. and Anne Winger Garber, Helen Goodwin, Dorothy Keller, and Jay E. Gibble, staff; Tana Hinson Durnbaugh and Lona Beabes Norris, served as ex-officio members. The conference was an instant success in terms of enthusiasm and denominational response. The 635 conference attendees, by an overwhelming vote, requested a biannual conference. Succeeding conferences were held in 1994, 1996, 1998, 2000, and 2002 at Lake Junaluska. The attendance increased to over 1000 by 1996. ABC, in close cooperation with the *General Board, was the sponsor for the first three conferences. After being separated from the General Board in 1997, ABC assumed exclusive sponsorship for the conference as one of its ministries through the Older Adult Ministries Cabinet. JEGi

Annual Conference Statement on Aging (1985); *Minutes, Brethren Homes and Older Adult Ministries* (July 1–2, 1990); ABC Board *Minutes* (Sept. 9–10, 1995), (March 21–23, 1997); *Messenger* (Jan., 1993) 18–20, (Nov., 1994) 8, (Dec., 1994) 15–21, (May, 1996) 8, (Oct., 1996) 10, (Oct., 1998) 10–13, (April, 2000) 8, (Nov., 2000) 28–31, (Nov., 2002) 22–25; *Transcripts of Sermons and General Sessions: Church of the Brethren National Older Adult Conference (NOAC II)* (1994).

National Ordination Council (BC). In the 1970s problems within the *Brethren Church from pressures to license and ordain those not fully qualified for ministry brought about an awareness that a better method of licensing and ordination of pastors was necessary. A recommendation in 1979 considered the possibility of forming a ministerial accreditation procedure on a national level. The *National Association of Brethren Church Elders presented a proposal to form a National Ordination Council. This proposal received the approval of the various districts of the church.

In the interest of congregational governance, facilitating of interviews, and convenience, the district examining boards remained intact. The call, licensing, and progress of candidates involve the local church and district. The board also evaluates their progress annually during the ordination process as they prepare the candidate for a written and oral examination and examine the tape of a sermon.

Once a district examining board feels a licensed minister is prepared for ordination, the board forwards the candidate's credentials to the national ordination council. The national ordination council is comprised of the chairperson of each district examining board, a representative of *Ashland Theol. Sem., and the director of pastoral ministries who serves as chair of the council. The purpose of the national ordination council is to set the standards for ordination in the church and to insure a thorough and uniform examination of all candidates. The ordination council meets annually to carry out the examination process. All districts and the candidates involved must send their papers and a sermon to the director of pastoral ministries well ahead of the examination date. The results of examinations are communicated to the candidate and the appropriate district and local church. The district board supervises any additional work required of the candidate. This system is efficient and works well. WHK

See also POLITY.

Minutes, General Conference, BC (1979, 1980).

Native Americans. Believing that all people are children of God, the Brethren have shown respect for Native Americans (Indians) since their first encounter with them when Brethren immigrated to North America. The first Brethren in the American colonies were neighbors to various tribes in *Pennsylvania, *Virginia, and *North Carolina. The *Sauer press addressed exploitation and mistreatment of Native Americans, several times publishing articles by Conrad Weiser, the Indian agent for the colonial government of Pennsylvania. The Sauers advocated hospitality and friendship to Native Americans.

It is said that *John Price (Preisz) of Eastern Pennsylvania married a Delaware tribe woman who was found ill and nursed back to health in the Price home. Soon after his death, she returned to her Delaware people, leaving two sons with the grandparents. Brethren faced the hostility of those tribes who were urged by the French to attack them. Several members of the Hochstetler family of Berks County, PA, were taken captive and then released several years later. Brethren in Western Virginia and the *Morrisons Cove area of Pennsylvania were attacked and many killed during the *French and Indian War and *Revolutionary War. Jacob Neff, who was a miller near Roaring Springs, PA, killed two Indians near the mill. He was called before the church and confessed it was wrong to take a human life.

In the early 1800's, *Adam Paine (Payne) moved among the Sauk and Fox tribes in the Illinois Territory, preaching the gospel and counseling peace between those tribes and whites that were settling in the territory. He was present at a war council following the Indian Removal Act of 1830. Payne's talk of peace angered Black Hawk, a war chief, but averted an immediate war. Later Black Hawk led the Sauk, Fox, Winnebago, Potawatomi, and Kickapoo in a war that bears his name.

With the rise of Brethren *publishing following the *Civil War, individual Brethren and their publications again addressed Native American problems and concerns. *The Brethren's Advocate* reprinted several articles from other sources seeking to create an awareness of these problems among the Brethren. *The Pilot,* a weekly paper for young readers, also reprinted an article on Native Americans from *The North American Review.* One

Brethren journalist who addressed the issue was *J. H. Moore, who wrote an editorial on "Indian Education" for *The Brethren at Work* in 1882. After the division of the Brethren in 1881–82, little was done or said about Indians.

Two Brethren ministers took special interest in the history of American Indians. *Landon West published a pamphlet with an explanation of the Serpent Mound near Peebles, OH. *Otho Winger wrote four small books on the history of the Miami nation; earlier, he had written the story of Frances Slocum, a white woman taken captive by the Miami. Yet another Winger book is the history of the Potawatomi nation. Several of Winger's books on Indians were reprinted by *Lawrence W. Shultz.

In 1896 an anonymous brother from Pennsylvania challenged the German Baptist Brethren (later Church of the Brethren) by sending one dollar to be used to start a Native American mission. The *General Mission Board did nothing with this request. Then in 1916 the General Mission Board again considered an Indian mission and in 1917 discussed providing scholarships for them to attend Brethren colleges. Financial concerns ended the discussions. This same reason was given in 1908 for denying a request from the Home Missions Council, an ecumenical agency, which asked the Brethren to work with the Hopi in New Mexico.

Given intermarriage between whites and Native Americans, it is likely that members of some local congregations could claim Indian ancestry. An obituary on March 14, 1924, noted that Betty Rathburn had died in Los Angeles; editorials called her the only Brethren member of Indian ancestry. Whether or not she was the only Native American member among the Brethren churches is not really known.

The first mission work among Native Americans was begun by the *Fellowship of Grace Brethren Churches in 1947. The Brethren Navajo Mission and Boarding School was located near Counselor, NM. The mission expanded from the school into home visitation, camps, vacation Bible schools, and medical work. A high school was added in 1981.

In 1976, the first Navajo congregation was accepted into the FGBC and another was accepted in 1978. There are currently three Native American Churches among the Grace Brethren. All have Native American pastors. In 2000 a new church start in Albuquerque, NM, seeks to minister to urban Indians. The ministry to Native Americans is organized as Grace American Indian Ministries, Inc. The director of this ministry is Steve Galegor.

The *Church of the Brethren began work with the Navajo in 1952, and it continues as the *Lybrook Navajo Community Ministry. Education, medical assistance, material aid, and establishment of a congregation were the four goals for this work. Staffed often by *Brethren Volunteer Service workers, the mission work grew. Through the mission the Lybrook Water Users Association was begun, as were job training programs. Indigenous leadership was also trained for the church. Although the church has struggled, a renewal of the congregation began in 2000 through the Western Plains District. The congregation is named the *Tok'ahookaadi' Church.

The *Dunkard Brethren became active among the Navajo in 1956. Contact with Ray Martindale of the FGBC gave the opportunity for the Dunkard Brethren to take over the work at *Torreon, NM, started by

Martindale. From the beginning, worship has been held with a Navajo interpreter. A medical clinic was also active (1958–74) with the establishment of a new medical clinic in Cuba, NM. In recent years, the work has expanded with many self-help programs and a Christian school that began in 1977.

Although the Brethren groups have passed few statements about Native Americans and their problems, the Church of the Brethren had conversations with members of the American Indian Movement (AIM) and sought to bring a peaceful solution to the crisis at Wounded Knee, SD. Dialogue continues in the Church of the Brethren with passage of the Community: A Tribe of Many Feathers, a 1993 statement whose impetus was the 1992 Christian Citizen Seminar. JWL, Jr.

See also MINORITIES, ETHNIC AND RACIAL; MCALLEN, TX, GBC; LYBROOK, NM, TÓK'AHOOKAADÍ CB

J. W. Lowe, "Racial Attitudes of the CB" (1970); *M. Pennsylvania* (1981) 49–50, 56–7; D. F. Durnbaugh, *Fruit of the Vine* (1997) 567–69.

Robert W. Neff. BHLA collection.

Neff, Robert Wilbur (CB), b. 1936, seminary teacher, denominational executive, ecumenical leader, college president. The son of Wilbur H. Neff and Hazel Martin Neff, he was born on June 16 in Lancaster, PA. He graduated from Pennsylvania State U. (BS, 1958) and earned further degrees (BD, 1961), (MA, 1963), and (PhD, 1969) all from Yale U. He received three honorary degrees from CB-related colleges: *Juniata (DD, 1978), *Manchester (DHL, 1979), and *Bridgewater (DHL, 1979). In 1959 he married Dorothy M. Rosewarne; the couple had two children: Charles Scott and Heather.

Ordained in 1960 at the *Pottsdown, PA, CB, Neff taught philosophy and religion at *Bridgewater College (1964–65) before becoming a professor of Old Testament at Bethany Theol. Sem. (1965–77). He assisted *Annual Conference in producing statements on a range of subjects, biblical authority, human sexuality, and mission

among them. As general secretary of the *General Board (1978–86), Neff engaged the denomination and districts in joint planning. During this period the General Board launched the "People of the Covenant" program of discipleship education, opened work in *Sudan, and extended its presence in Central America, spurred new church development, closed the in-house printing plant, inaugurated a human resources office, and intensified its work in interpretation and *stewardship.

Neff served on the Governing Board and Executive Committee of the *National Council of Churches of Christ, chaired its Presidential Panel (1982–84), and was a member of the Central Committee of the *World Council of Churches.

From 1986 to 1998 Neff was president of *Juniata College. His presidency was marked by increasing internationalizing of the student body and a quadrupling of the annual fund and endowment. Strides were also taken in *peace, through peace and conflict studies and United Nations seminars on arms control; in science, through the innovative Science in Motion project in area schools; in campus development, through refurbishment of five dormitories and the creation of the Peace Chapel designed by Maya Lin; and in environmental studies, through a new interdisciplinary department.

As educator, administrator, speaker, and writer, Neff approached envisioning, scholarship, and relationships in ways that imparted to students, coworkers, and audiences a zest for faith and the future. HER

Messenger (Jan., 1978) 12–16, (Oct., 1978) 21–23, (Feb., 1986) 6–7, (July, 1986) 12–13; E. C. Kaylor, Jr., *Juniata College: Uncommon Vision, Uncommon Loyalty* (2001) 303–53; *N. Atlantic* (1975) 144–45, 344; F. F. Wayland, *Bridgewater College* (1993) index; *Who's Who in America* (1988–89) 2266; D. F. Durnbaugh, *Fruit of the Vine* (1997) 450; *BLT* 39 (Winter, 1994) 3; BHLA files.

Jacob and Fern Ness. Robert and Sharon Lehigh collection.

Ness, Jacob C. (DB), 1928–2001, minister, warehouse manager. The son of John and Mabel Ness, Jacob Ness was born on Nov. 22 in York County, PA. He was baptized into the *Dunkard Brethren Church at *Shrewsbury, PA, in Aug. 1941 and married Fern Fahnestock of Lititz, PA, on June 26, 1954. Ness was installed into the ministry on

March 17, 1958, and ordained into the eldership in Sept. 1965 at Shrewsbury. He served as presiding elder in his home congregation from 1985 to 1997 when he resigned due to declining health. He also served as presiding elder in several neighboring congregations, including *Waynesboro, PA, and *Mechanicsburg, PA, as well as *Walnut Grove, MD, and *Swallow Falls, MD.

Ness was very active at district and denominational levels. He served three times as moderator of *General Conference and as reading clerk for six years. Ness served on many boards and committees, including the *Mount Hope Dunkard Brethren Church Home Board of Trustees, *Publication Board, *Mission Board, and the *Civilian Public Service Board. He held numerous *revival meetings throughout the brotherhood. He loved the Dunkard Brethren Church and made church work a high priority in his life.

One of the highlights of his life was serving on the Board of Directors of *Brethren Encyclopedia, Inc. for more than 15 years. He eagerly anticipated the rich fellowship which the board enjoyed during their biannual meetings. Ness loved peace and avoided controversy whenever possible. He has been referred to as "gentle Jake," which is a fitting summary of his life. RSL

Bible Monitor (July, 2001) 24–25; *BLT* 30 (Summer, 1985) 153–54.

New Albany, OH, Rocky Ridge Grace Brethren Church. Located in northeast Columbus, this congregation is a daughter church of the *Dublin, OH, Northwest Chapel GBC. Northwest Chapel retained William H. Marling to plant a church in a Columbus suburb. A core group began meeting in Oct. 1989 to prepare for public services scheduled to begin on March 25, 1990. Meeting facilities were rented until ground was purchased (Oct., 1993) and a building constructed (March, 1999). In 2001 Marling was sent by the Rocky Ridge GBC as a missionary in the Republic of Ireland, and Scott (Buzz) Imboden became the pastor. WHM/JRY

Congregational records.

New Life Ministries (CB). *See* **Andrew Center, The.**

Nicarry, Wayne A. (CB), b. 1912, churchman, educator, businessman, philanthropist. Married to Frances Oberholzer in 1939, they had two sons: Ronald and Wayne. Called to the ministry in 1944 and ordained in 1946 by the *Falling Spring, PA, congregation, Nicarry pastored the *Chambersburg, PA, congregation (1947–54). He served on the boards of the *Children's Aid Society and *The Brethren Home, New Oxford, PA. His tenure on the board of trustees of *Elizabethtown College from 1960 culminated in the chairmanship (1990–96) and then the vice-chairmanship. The college awarded him an honorary degree (DS, 1986) in recognition of his achievements and service.

Nicarry cofounded and served as president of the Grove Manufacturing Company, an international corporation with annual sales of more than a half-billion dollars. Among his many accomplishments was his work as civil engineer for the Jefferson Memorial in Washington, DC. Nicarry is known for his generous gifts to church agencies, including *Bethany Theol. Sem. where the chapel is named in his honor. LBB

S. Pennsylvania (1973) passim; Elizabethtown *Magazine* (Summer, 1994) 2–4, (Summer, 2000) 17.

Northview, OH, Brethren Life Church/Vineyard Community Church (BC). Archie L. Nevins started Northview Brethren Life Church at the beginning of 1989 using "The Phone's for You" telemarketing plan. The new congregation held its first worship service on March 5, 1989, in Springboro, OH, with 102 people attending.

In 1993 Northview relocated to Franklin, OH, to erect a building on 27 acres. These facilities were part of the congregation's outreach strategy. The church used sports ministry to serve the community and to build its cell group ministry. Nevins served Northview until 1995 when he left to start another church. Michael F. Sove, who became pastor of Northview in 1995, focused on building cell groups. Northview merged with Vineyard Fellowship of Franklin in 1997. In 2000, Sove and Charles W. Wolfinbarger copastored ca. 200 people at Vineyard Community Church (BC). RRSm

Congregational records; *Annual* (*BC*) (1989–2000).

Nuclear Arms Race. Following the advent of the nuclear age in 1945, many Brethren imbibed the following cultural responses to the bomb: "It provides deterrence to keep the peace." "God won't let it be used." "Wake up or blow up." "Nuclear holocaust is part of God's plan for the end times." Nevertheless, official CB positions transcended these views; *Annual Conference passed resolutions to halt the nuclear arms race. In addition, many Brethren joined nuclear freeze movements in the 1970s and 1980s.

Brethren authors responded to the issue. Donald B. Kraybill's Christ-centered analysis appealed to Christians to apply their faith to the nuclear threat as a witness to God's care for the entirety of creation. Dale H. Aukerman's award-winning book, *Darkening Valley,* was the fruit of a lifetime bond with Christian *discipleship and offered biblical perspectives on nuclear war. With Kraybill, he shared both biblical realism and biblical hope. Aukerman's book was widely appropriated in ecumenical circles; Roman Catholic bishops used it for daily devotions. Gen. George Lee Butler, head of the U.S. Strategic Command for 30 years, in a letter to Aukerman (1997) affirmed a common Christian basis for rejecting reliance on deterrence and advocating the elimination of nuclear weapons. Robert C. Johansen wrote prolifically on the dangers of unrestrained security programs.

Following the end of the Cold War (1989), Brethren reflected prevailing complacency. By the end of the century, however, resuscitated concerns emerged because of growing proliferation of nuclear and other weapons of mass destruction. DWBr

See also PEACE, BRETHREN POLITICAL WITNESS, ETHICS.

Minutes, CB (1982), 418–22; D. B. Kraybill, *Facing Nuclear War* (1982); D. H. Aukerman, *Darkening Valley: A Biblical Perspective on Nuclear War* (1981) and *Reckoning with Apocalypse: Terminal Politics and Christian Hope* (1993); R. C. Johansen, *Toward a Dependable Peace: A Proposal for an Appropriate Security System* (1978).

Ocala, FL, Grace Brethren Church originated in 1981 as a Bible class in the home of Russell and Viola Snavely. The core group consisted of seven families: the Kriegbaums, Snavelys, Johnsons, Christensens, Maxsons, Roberts, and Secaurs. While incorporated as a church in 1984, the congregation actually held its first worship services during 1983 in the Kriegbaums' home. The residence was located in the Lynne area of Marion County, east of Ocala. Later, the congregation met in three different store-front locations in Ocala before building a permanent facility at 6474 N.E. Seventh Street. The building was dedicated on March 31, 1990. Pastors who have served the congregation include Arnold R. Kriegbaum (1981–87), Charles Davis (1987–94), and Ronald A. Smals (1994–). AKK/RASm/JRY

Congregational records; *Annual* (*FGBC*) (1984–98).

Old Brethren Christian Schools. The *Old Brethren Church was the first of old order Brethren to operate their own schools. The school in Nappanee, IN, began in 1967 with 40 students as a joint effort of Old Brethren and conservative Mennonite churches. As the school grew, the Old Brethren, with faithful Mennonite help, built a separate school for their children on the property of Kenneth Martin. A school near Bradford, OH, was established in 1977 and operated in the church basement until 1994. The California school began in 1979 in the basement of the MiWuk Church and continued there until 2000 when the congregation built a new building (renamed Mountain View) with two classrooms near Tuolumne. Old Brethren Christian Schools are open to other families of conservative Christian belief. Supported by tuitions and donations, they are directed by school boards comprised of parents and church leaders. In 2003, 25 students attended in California and 80 in Indiana. LEC

Personal information; D. B. Kraybill and C. N. Hostetter, *Anabaptist World USA* (2001) 155, 179, 185, 198.

*Old Brethren Church. By 2004 the Old Brethren Church had grown to 250 members besides children, young people, and regular visitors. Main congregations center in *Wakarusa, IN, and Tuolumne, CA, with meetinghouses also in Bradford, OH, *Salida, CA, and Warren County, IN. Since 1980, the Canadian members have moved or passed away. Two active schools are maintained to teach children in the concentrated areas of membership. The Brethren conduct a tract ministry and continue monthly publication of The *Pilgrim. Each month the sisters sew comforts for charity. *Annual Meetings at Pentecost alternate between East and West. *Love feasts are enjoyed twice a year in each congregation, with the exception of Ohio which meets once a year. Outreach meetings have begun in Camden, IN.

New ministers since 1980 are Thomas L. Royer, Neil D. Martin, Joe L. Royer, and Daniel M. Beery in Indiana; Lloyd E. Wagner and Benjamin A. Cover in California; and Larry D. Cable in Ohio. Deacons serving in 2004 were Marvin B. Crawmer, Joseph E. Wagner, William S. Crawmer, and Peter D. Cover in California; Harold G. Royer, David W. Royer, and Jonathan R. Martin in Indiana; and Daniel S. Wagner in Ohio. Members reside in Mississippi, Arkansas, and Alaska in addition to the main centers in Indiana, Ohio, and California. LEC

See also OLD BRETHREN CHRISTIAN SCHOOLS.

Personal information; D. B. Kraybill and C. N. Hostetter, *Anabaptist World USA* (2001) 155, 179, 185, 198.

*Old Brethren German Baptist Church has one district, Camden, IN. Ministers Daniel P. Graybill, Glen Dale Oswalt, and Henry H. Brumbaugh are deceased. Ministers in 2003 are Steven L. Royer, David L. Brumbaugh, Denver D. Brumbaugh, and Virgil D. Graybill. Membership has steadily increased the last several years to 65 members in 25 households. Services are held every Sunday at the Deer Creek meeting house, 2 -

1/2 miles south of Camden. DLB

Minutes, Annual Meetings of the Old Order German Baptist Church (1778–1999); *The Vindicator* (1987) 60, (1996) 157; D. B. Kraybill and C. N. Hostetter, *Anabaptist World USA* (2001) 156, 198; S. Scott, *Plain Buggies* (1981) 86, and *Why Do They Dress That Way?* (1986) 136–37.

*Old German Baptist Brethren (OGBB). If there is a single motivating theme among the Old German Baptist Brethren, it would be one of harmony—endeavoring to keep the unity of the Spirit in the bond of peace (Eph. 4:3,13), with one mind and one mouth glorifying God, even the Father of our Lord Jesus Christ (Rom. 15:5–7). When the Brethren have been able to attain unity, peace has prevailed. Without unity, that peace has been disturbed. A growing diversity of thought and practice was one of the influences which led to the Old Order, Progressive, and Conservative factions prior to the three-way split among the Brethren in the late 19th century. Over a century later the Old German Baptist Brethren still strive with more or less success for unity of thought and practice among themselves.

The last two decades of the 20th century have been characterized by peace among the Brethren concerning biblical *doctrine. The Brethren embrace the doctrine of the trinity and the virgin birth of Jesus, the Son of God. They hold to the saving power of the shed blood of Jesus and to the work of the Holy Spirit in the lives of the converted. They believe that *baptism must be preceded by faith and repentance, accompanied by a confession of faith, a renunciation of sinful ways, and be followed by a covenant life faithful to God and the teachings of Jesus. Baptismal applicants are instructed in *non-conformity, *non-resistance, non-swearing of *oaths, and against using legal action to force one's purpose. After the reading of Matt. 18:10–22 and suitable instruction, the applicant is led into flowing water and is asked three questions: "Dost thou believe that Jesus Christ is the Son of God and that he brought from heaven a saving gospel?" "Dost thou willingly renounce Satan and his pernicious ways and the sinful pleasures of this world?" "Dost thou covenant with God through Christ Jesus to live faithful unto death?" This is followed by a triple immersion in the name of the Father, of the Son, and of the Holy Ghost. There follows in the water the laying on of hands and a prayer for the infilling of the Holy Spirit. The new brother or sister is then received by the church with the salutation of the hand of fellowship and the holy kiss.

The Brethren practice three-fold *communion preceded by the *deacons' visit at which time members renew their covenant and the congregation confirms its peace. After soul-searching self-examinations the brothers wash feet by the double mode and the sisters do likewise. *Feetwashing is followed by a simple agape meal shared in silence looking forward to the second coming of the Lord and to the everlasting presence of the church-bride with Christ in his kingdom. The communion is preceded by the binding of communicants in covenant with a *kiss of Christian love (a salutation which is shared among the brethren and also among the sisters on most occasions of meeting). The communion itself consists of unleavened bread and fermented wine with deep appreciation for the broken body and shed blood of the Lord. *Anointing with oil is for the assurance of sins forgiven and, if the Lord wills, for the healing of the body. The Brethren still instruct their youth in non-participation in war even in times of relative peace.

The Brethren strive to clothe themselves modestly through a characteristic uniformity of *dress. The sisters wear a *prayer covering. Most of the brethren wear *beards. While there is some variation in dress from individual to individual and from one geographic area to another, the Brethren are still united in the teaching of modesty and non-conformity by uniformity.

The Brethren form of government helps to maintain the unity and peace for which they strive. Each member is responsible to and responsible for the Brotherhood. Personal issues are to be settled between the brethren and the sisters, as the case may be (Matt. 18:10–22). These issues need not be brought to the attention of the congregation. It is recognized, however, that certain matters are the responsibility of the local congregation or even of the brotherhood as a whole. Congregations meet quarterly or as necessary to consider matters of local interest. The brotherhood meets annually for fellowship, spiritual strength, and consideration of matters of general interest to the fraternity. It is here that the most controversial matters surface because individuals and congregations have been unable to arrive at a satisfactory solution. Issues which have most commonly come before the brotherhood in the past two decades include: technological matters (computers for home use, business, or entertainment, VCRs, Internet, and public address systems); insurance (use of life insurance, Social Security); legal matters (using the law, victims of suits, legal council, appeals); and *dress (definition, compliance).

While issues of practice have frequently disturbed the church, issues of basic Christian doctrine have seldom surfaced. The 1984 *Annual Meeting reaffirmed the ancient Brethren teaching that the "New Testament is our only creed and doctrine . . . ." In 1988 the Meeting reaffirmed the doctrine of salvation by grace through faith leading to works of righteousness, in opposition to secular humanism and its emphasis on human effort versus the work of the Holy Spirit. The paucity of doctrinal issues and the predominance of matters of practice and interpretation indicate that the Brethren are solidly united on biblical teachings but are frequently disturbed by mode and application.

It is not surprising that external forces are impacting the Old German Baptist Brethren and perhaps more intensely in the complex social milieu of the late 20th century. Almost every innovation which appears in the greater society seems eventually to affect the Brethren in some way. Their response has been one of cautious consideration in the light of Scripture. If there is no direct scripture applicable, Brethren have considered the matter according to the tenor of the Scripture and the practice of the Brethren as they considered similar issues in the past. Issues without precedent sometimes arise, leading to serious consideration and possibly much discussion. There is much exhortation prior to the Annual Meeting, and many prayers are offered seeking the guidance of the Holy Spirit in the work of the Meeting.

The broader society ("the world") continues to disturb the church as it always has and especially so for a tradition such as that found in the Old German Baptist Brethren. Brethren have been influenced by affluence. While the church forbids the use of *radio, television, musical instruments, computer games, and video entertainment, many Brethren enjoy vacationing, traveling, fishing, tours to Europe and Israel, etc. Entertainment is to

Old German Baptist Annual Meeting 1990. BHLA collection.

be tempered by modesty and consistency with the Christian life. Vacation to many families consists of a yearly trip to the Annual Meeting or to a love feast with Brethren in some distant congregation.

Individualism, as an expression of secular humanism, has had its impact on Brethren thought. While Brethren have appreciated personal thought and expression, they have discouraged private interpretation. Brethren have sought the greatest possible consensus in coming to a decision followed by the greatest possible compliance through submission of every individual to brotherhood consensus. Where private opinion has been pressed too far, the peace of the Brotherhood has sometimes suffered.

Brethren are often influenced competitively in their occupations. They have moved away from *agriculture in metropolitan areas, but in the rural areas agriculture has sometimes become a major business enterprise. Some Brethren in construction employ large crews. Other Brethren prefer a farm with modest acreage for raising produce, work in construction alone or as independent contractors, or to provide some other service such as working as an electrician, plumber, cabinetmaker, accountant, or in a "cottage industry." Other members hire out to industry or enter the service professions. The choice of a profession is to be consistent with the Christian life as defined by the Brethren, avoiding professions where non-resistant and non-conforming principles may be compromised.

Some OGBB members have recently left the fellowship. While they do not differ in basic Brethren doctrine, their "Reasons" cite insurance and Social Security, the use of computers and VCRs for business, speaker systems in the meetinghouses, the social activities of youth, and other reasons for leaving the larger fellowship. They cite, as reasons for their stand, a departure by Annual Meeting from the "Reasons" of the Old Order Brethren in 1881

and from the "Reconsidered Minutes" of 1883 and 1884. This stand is in response to a perceived loss of traditional Old Order values. In their perception of an inclination toward loss of seminal values among the Brethren, this movement itself, ironically, has tended to erode the traditional unity of the church and its teachings of brotherhood. A positive result of this movement has been a self examination by many of the Brethren and a search for deeper spiritual values.

Brethren have approached most innovations with caution, rejecting some technological advances as superfluous or threatening to the Brethren life style but accepting others as beneficial. Brethren have, in general, been open to forms of technology which will enhance their lives but are wary of innovations which may detract from its spirituality.

Members of the OGBB have recently re-evaluated their stand on *mission in the light of Brethren tradition, the division of Brethren thought which arose over foreign missionary work in the late 19th century, and the needs of the church in the late 20th century. Annual Meeting recently reaffirmed its stand that Brethren should not participate in any organizational missionary work. Humanitarian response and *disaster aid alone or in conjunction with other Christian organizations is held to be consistent with Gal. 6:10. Brethren reaffirmed their traditional provision for the distribution of charities through the *deacons' office. Personal charities should be distributed according to Mark 14:7 and Matt. 6:3. The gospel should be spread according to 1 Pet. 3:15, both by word and by exemplary life.

The last quarter of the 20th century has seen significant growth in membership among the Brethren. Three established congregations have grown to a point where partition has occurred, forming new congregations in *Ohio, *Pennsylvania, and *Virginia. New congregations

have been established in *Washington, *Georgia, and *Wisconsin, and isolated members are testing the waters in *Alaska, *Arkansas, upstate *New York, and elsewhere. The beginning of 2003 records 55 congregations and over 6,200 members.

Parallel to their growing popularity in the larger society, private and *home schooling have also grown steadily among the OGBB in the last quarter of the 20th century. Teaching materials are largely borrowed from conservative *Mennonite publishers. While these materials are adapted to Brethren needs, it seems too early to assess the influence of this literature on Brethren thought and practice.

The *Vindicator, official publication of the OGBB, passed its 130th year at the turn of the century. Its editorial committee consists of seven elders from Ohio. Appointed by the Annual Meeting, they meet monthly to publish the 32-page paper with the help of an office editor. MM

Minutes (OGBB) (1980–98); Messenger (April, 1992) 10–11; Old Order Notes Nos. 1–22 (1978–2000); D. B. Kraybill and C. F. Bowman, On the Backroad to Heaven (2001) esp. 137–78; D. B. Kraybill and C. N. Hostetter, Anabaptist World USA (2001) passim; S. Scott, Why Do They Dress That Way? (1986) 133, 136–37.

*Old Order German Baptist Church, the first of two Old Order Brethren horse-and-buggy groups, originated from the *Old German Baptist Brethren in 1921 at Covington, Ohio. These folk are popularly called "Petitioners" because they promoted their cause with petitions. Many of the first generation have died, and a new generation of leaders cope with the problems of modernity. *Farming is largely a thing of the past. Rubber tired tractors provide acceptable transportation to job sites as members follow occupations in construction, building repair, lawn services, and the like. One brother is in the printing trade. Sisters are keepers-at-home, and the horse and buggy is much used. Use of the bicycle is popular. A couple of lawn mower sales and service companies are owned by members. Most recently, ownership of the telephone has been accepted, however, with the restriction that it be used only for business and located separately from both home and business.

In the last two decades, charter members and ministers Joseph Calvin Lavy and David Franklin Grim and minister David Paul Garber have died. In 2003 the ministers were: Charles M. Diehl II. Donald H. Burns, Robert G. Douglas, Michael D. Grim, Robert E. Jamison, William P. Diehl II, Gary W. Burns, and Mark D. Burns.

Since 1980 more youthful congregations and a modest increase in membership accounts for about 125 members and a total population of 281. Regular services are held by rotation in four locations: Covington, OH, meetinghouse, Painter Creek meetinghouse (near Arcanum, OH), and in homes in the Bradford area, OH. There is a recently organized district named "Salem" in Mississippi, and a few members are located in Wisconsin. FWB

Minutes, Annual Meetings of the Old Order German Baptist Church (1921–99); The Vindicator (1987) 60, (1996) 157; D. B. Kraybill and C. N. Hostetter, Anabaptist World USA (2001) 156, 198; S. Scott, Plain Buggies (1981) 86, and Why Do They Dress That Way? (1986) 136–37; Brethren Heritage Center, Recorder, July 2004; personal knowledge.

On Earth Peace Assembly (OEPA) (CB) developed in the mid-1970s under the leadership of *M. R. Zigler at the *Brethren Service Center in New Windsor, MD.

Organizationally, OEPA related to the *Church of the Brethren as a consultative body to the *World Ministries Commission (WMC). Its programs included assemblies devoted to addressing concerns for world *peace as well as assemblies of special interest to physicians, farmers, lawyers, and military veterans.

Because OEPA solicited funds independently from the *General Board (CB), it needed to organize as a separate entity. On Aug. 4, 1981, it was incorporated by the State of Maryland, and on May 19, 1982, it received tax-exempt status from the U.S. Internal Revenue Service. In 1982 OEPA asked *Standing Committee (CB) for recognition as an organization related to the church with the privilege of soliciting funds within the denomination. Standing Committee responded by asking that dialog occur between representatives of the General Board and OEPA. In 1983 agreement was reached that OEPA would become an officially recognized program of the General Board with the executive director jointly appointed by OEPA and the WMC. This relationship continued through 1997.

In 1981 OEPA opened a Brethren World Peace Bookstore at the New Windsor center. A Brethren World Peace Academy was inaugurated in 1982 for the purpose of promoting world citizenship for peace by holding weekend seminars to assist 17-year-olds in making conscientious choices concerning military service and other obligations of citizenship.

Harold D. Smith served as the OEPA executive director (1983–89). During this period, an M. R. Zigler Endowment was established which grew to $910,000 by 1999. The Brethren World Peace Academy's programs were expanded and held at locations beyond New Windsor, and a winter interterm program was initiated for college students.

Thomas A. Hurst was appointed executive director in 1990. Under his leadership, OEPA adopted several initiatives in addition to continuing peace academies (renamed Peace Retreats) and expanding the bookstore (renamed Peace Place). Responsibility for the General Board's *Ministry of Reconciliation (MoR) program was assumed by OEPA in 1991 and continued to train individuals in conflict transformation skills and to provide conflict transformation asssistance to congregations. Youth Peace Travel Teams, training for *Outdoor Ministries staff, and Journey of Young Adults (JOYA) teams were organized each summer to lead *youth in thinking about peace, meeting with them in church camps and in local congregations. Endowment funds were also established to recognize Hazel M. Peters (former staff member of the *Brethren Service Commission and longtime OEPA volunteer) and to support the MoR program and the youth travel teams.

As a result of organizational restructuring within the CB, on Jan. 1, 1998, OEPA became an independent agency. Later that year delegates at *Annual Conference voted for OEPA to relate to the denomination as an agency reporting to Annual Conference, with the director responsible solely to the OEPA Board of Directors, one third of whom are chosen by Annual Conference. In 2000, Barbara Sayler and Robert A. Gross became coexecutive directors of OEPA. DVU

TBE (1983–84) 198, 974, 1369, 1398; Messenger (Feb., 1981) 8, (June, 1982) 33, (July, 1982) 5, (Sept., 1982) 28, (Sept., 1983) 8–9, 20; D. F. Durnbaugh, Pragmatic Prophet: The Life of Michael Robert Zigler (1989) 274–88, and Fruit of the Vine (1997) 586–88; Messenger (1981–2000) indexes; On Earth Peace [newsletter]

M. Andrew Murray speaks to Brethren World Peace Accademy. BHLA collection.

(1981–2000), esp. 23 (Nov., 1999), celebration of the 25th anniversary; *OPEA Annual Report* (1998).

O'Neal, Glenn. (FGBC), 1919–85, pastor, educator. A native of Sunnyside, WA, Glenn O'Neal was converted under the ministry of *Louis S. Bauman. He graduated from Moody Bible Institute (1939) and *Grace Theol. Sem. (1942).

O'Neal pastored in *Canton, OH, (1941–44) and the *Ashland, OH, West Tenth Street Brethren Church (1944–47). In 1947, he became pastor of a mission church in Santa Barbara, the First Brethren Church, *Los Angeles, later named First Brethren Church, Inglewood

(1949–61). While in Ohio and California, he continued his education at Kent State U., *Ashland College, Santa Barbara College, and the U. of California at Santa Barbara.

O'Neal served as president of the national youth fellowship, as a member of the board of *Grace Brethren Foreign Missions (1952–84) and as moderator of the FGBC (1966–67). He received a PhD degree in speech from the U. of Southern California (1957) and served as professor of practical theology at Talbot Theol. Sem. (1961–85). RTC

Personal information; *Annual* (*FGBC*) (1947–85).

P-R

Paraguay, Brethren Church in. *The Brethren Church has been in Paraguay since 1988 when Juan Antonio Anzulovich and his family relocated to that country from *Argentina. This was and continues to be a cooperative effort of The Brethren Church in North America and The Brethren Church in Argentina. In 1998 Claudio and Karina Castelli worked in Asuncion, Paraguay. Claudio Castelli was the pastor of Iglesia de Esperanza (Hope Church) of The Brethren Church in Paraguay, assisted by Kafina Castelli as worship leader. Hope Church meets in a well-equipped facility, originally built for secular purposes. The Castellis and other Brethren in Paraguay are working to redeem the people in the neighborhood. About 40 worship together on Sundays. RRSm

BE (March, 1988) 14, (March, 1992) 1314, (Oct., 1997) 4, (April, 2002) 4.

Pasadena, CA, Centro Cristiano para la Familia (BC). This first Hispanic congregation in *The Brethren Church in the U.S. was started in 1979 by Juan Carlos Miranda while serving as the Latin American director for the Fuller Evangelistic Association. The congregation met initially in the facilities of the *Pasadena Church of the Brethren but later relocated to the facilities of the Immanuel Baptist Church. Other pastors who shared in the ministry were Manuel Rojas and Vidal Juarez. The church attained its highest average worship attendance of 142 in 1990. In 1991 a smaller Brethren Hispanic work at Monrovia/Baldwin Park merged with the congregation. The church disbanded in 1995 due to internal conflict. DRS

Congregational records; *Annual* (BC) (1979–95).

People of the Covenant (POC) (CB)**,** a small-group ministry program of "transformational education," was adopted by the *Church of the Brethren *General Board in Oct. 1982. The mission statement says, "people committed to Christ will intentionally live out their faith as they become more biblically informed so they understand better God's revelation, more globally aware so they know themselves connected with all of God's world, and more relationally sensitive to God, self, and others."

People of the Covenant centered around small groups meeting weekly for Bible study, sharing, and prayer. Group leaders were introduced to Bible studies and other small group helps through district training events. A denominational planning team worked with General Board staff, Shirley Heckman and June A. Gibble, who gave oversight to POC (1982–97).

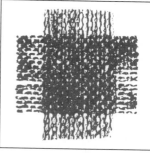

Following the pilot program in 1983–84 in the Southern Ohio, Pacific Southwest, and West Marva districts, other districts entered until there were Covenant groups in all 23 CB districts. The symbol of the burlap cross, the POC song, "Weave" by Rosemary Crow, the 1988 video, "Woven Together in Love," and Covenant breakfasts at Annual Conference helped tell the POC story.

In 1989–90, the Christian Church (*Disciples of Christ) adopted POC and by 1996 had Covenant groups throughout the denomination. Since 1988, *Covenant Bible Studies*, published by *Brethren Press, have been widely used by many denominations in the U.S. and Canada. JAGib

"Minutes, CB Administrative Council" (Jan., 1982); "Minutes, CB Goals and Budget" (March, 1982; July, 1982); "Minutes, CB General Board" (Oct., 1982); BHLA. POC files.

Peru, Brethren Church Miguel and Sonia Antunez started *Brethren Church mission work in Peru in 1988 with Bible studies in their home. They received a congregational charter in 1992, and in May 1995 the Peruvian government officially granted incorporation to The Brethren Church in Peru. The church is growing and maturing. The building purchased for them some years ago by the *National Women's Missionary Society already needs an addition.

The Antunez family live and work in Lima, the largest city (ca. six million) and the capital of Peru. In 1998 Miguel Antunez served as pastor of a congregation, attended seminary, and handled the administrative work of the national church. He also teaches English at an academy. Sonia Antunez taught in a Christian school.

In 2002 Italo and Rebecca (daughters of Richard and Dane Byler) Abuid arrived in Lima to assist in the work. They presently lead the minsitry after the Antunez family came to the United States in 2003. Miguel finished his seminary training at Ashland Theol. Sem. and is currently assisting the Brethren churches in Bradenton and Sarasota, FL, with hispanic ministry. RRSm

BE (July/Aug., 1991) 4–5, (Feb., 1997) 7, (Jan., 1998) 9, (April, 2002) 8.

Philadelphia, PA, Crossroads Grace Brethren Church. Located in Northeast Philadelphia, Crossroads was conceived in the heart and mind of James Brown while he was a student at *Grace Theol. Seminary. His love for the Lord and his concern for the people of his hometown led him to plant another Grace Brethren congregation in Philadelphia. Upon returning there from seminary, Brown and his wife, Lisa, gathered a group of believers from their home church, *Philadelphia First Grace Brethren, to help plant the new church. The core group consisted of Jack and Christine Brown, Robert J. and Sharon Pearson, and Joe and Theresa Wexler. The first worship service was held on Nov. 3, 1991, at the Tender Loving Childcare Center. Thirty-six persons attended this service. In June 1993 the Crossroads congregation purchased its own building in the Wissinoming section of Philadelphia. RJP/JRY

Congregational records; *Annual* (*FGBC*) (1991–98).

Pifer, Lester Elden (FGBC), b. 1920, pastor, missions administrator. Born in Wadsworth, OH, Lester Pifer married Genevene Edna Walter in 1941. He studied at Bryan College (1941–44) and received a ThB degree from *Grace Theol. Sem. (1947). GTS conferred upon him the DD degree in 1974.

As pastor, he served Dayton, IN, Christian Service Chapel (1941–44), *South Bend, IN, Ireland Road GBC, (1944–45), and the *Fremont, OH, Grace Brethren Chapel (1947–53) where he had a radio program, led Bible classes in other communities, and assisted in Child Evangelism Fellowship work.

As field secretary of *Grace Brethren Home Missions Council (1953–65), he was involved in promotions, speaking, and some administrative duties; he became executive secretary (1965–85). In his 33 years with Home Missions, over 200 churches were assisted, a new office building for Home and Foreign Missions was built, and the *Brethren Investment Foundation was established. He was FGBC moderator in 1984–85.

Upon retirement from home missions, The Pifers moved to Florida where he was founding pastor of the *Bradenton and North Port Grace Brethren Churches. After the death of Genevene, Pifer relocated, joining the pastoral staff at the *Worthington, OH, Columbus GBC to minister to seniors, and there he married Bonnie Howard in 1999. RTC

BMH (July, 1985) 4–7; *Frontiers* (1972) 189–90; *Annual* (*FGBC*) (1944–98).

Pine Ridge Church of the Brethren, VA, located three miles north of Earleysville in Albemarle Co., formerly part of the *Eastern Mount Carmel CB. The congregation was started in 1937 by community members on land donated by Nathaniel T. Knight, Mollie M. Knight, Charles R. Herring, and Etha K. Herring. Community members donated all labor and materials. Dedication of the new building in July 1939 was conducted by *I. N. H. Beahm and Henry Knight. Additions to the building were made in 1958, 1973, 1975, and 1980. In 1976 central heating and later air conditioning were donated and installed by Olen B. Landes. Serving the church as pastors have been Henry S. Knight, Daniel B. Garber, Isaac L. Bennett, Andrew L. Yelton, Olen B. Landes, Virgil Kover, and Richard Keller. In 2000, 134 members were reported. OBL

Virginia (1973) 375; congregational records; *Yearbook* (*CB*) 2001.

Pine Ridge Dunkard Brethren Congregation, MS. In the late 1980s, a few families from various Brethren backgrounds living in Covington Co., MS, began meeting together for services. On Sunday, Mar. 3, 1991, three families of the *Dunkard Brethren Church began to hold regular services in a former *Old Brethren *meetinghouse near Collins, MS, as a mission point of the *Pleasant Ridge (DB), OH, congregation. The first *love feast was held on the first weekend of May 1991. On Sept. 1, 1991, the Pine Ridge congregation was organized with 15 charter members. The presiding elder was Robert E. Carpenter (b. 1947) of Peru, IN. John Meyers (b. 1949) was ordained as deacon in the organizational meeting. Membership peaked at 17 in 1993. By 1996, all but seven members had moved away or left the fellowship; so regular services were curtailed. Services have since been held occasionally with visiting ministers. JDM

Monitor (Feb., 1998) 17.

Poland, Frank Jacob. (FGBC, CGBC), b. 1912, administrator. Born in Mt. Gilead, OH, Frank Poland was converted to the *United Brethren in Christ Church and discipled by *James L. Boyer. He held many positions in the *Fellowship of Grace Brethren Churches. He was involved with *Grace Brethren Home Missions (1949–81) as assistant secretary, office manager, business manager, and administrative coordinator. While in these offices, 150 churches were planted, of which 130 survived. He was statistician for the Indiana district, district missions secretary for 25 years, and the first lay moderator of the district (1975).

Poland also served as national statistician and treasurer and was a board member of the *Ministerial Relief and Retirement Board. He was a church Sunday school superintendent for 35 years and, with his wife, Alta Elizabeth Dawson Poland, served on the deacon board at *Winona Lake GBC. He was involved with establishing the *CGBCI as a charter member of *Lakeland Conservative GBC (1991). RTC

B. Skiles, *BMH* (Jan., 1981) 4–6; personal interview; *Annals* (*FGBC*) (1940–91).

Powell, OH, Grace Brethren Church. Two couples joined Pastor Jeff and Pam Carroll to initiate this church in the fall of 1991. It was first known as Sunrise Grace Brethren Church. The congregation began meeting in the Village Academy in Aug. 1992 about the time Lyle Sweeney became the pastor. The name was changed to Grace Chapel. In 1994, the church became a campus ministry of the *Worthington, OH, Columbus Grace Brethren Church. Frederick M. (Rick) Nuzum was elected pastor in 1995, and the church was re-incorporated in 1996. After a two-year search for a building site, the congregation selected the Charles Morrison property. A ministry center and a new discipleship building were constructed. In 2004 the Sunday morning worship attendance was in the 800s. Men, women, boys, and girls are being discipled appropriately to their needs through small groups and focused programs. RMN/JRY

Congregational records.

Prague Conferences. Between 1986 and 2000 six ecumenical conferences were held in Europe involving members of the *Historic Peace Churches and members of the "First Reformation." The latter are defined as those church bodies derived from the *Waldensian, Hussite, and *Czech Brethren movements, all originating before the Protestant *Reformation. The consultations grew out of contacts between *Mennonites and the Comenius Faculty (Czech Brethren) of Prague. The first three conferences (1986, 1987, and 1989) were held in Prague, hence the designation. The fourth (1984) and fifth (1998) meetings were held in *Geneva, Switzerland, hosted by the World Alliance of Reformed Churches. They broadened the theological and ethical discussions by including *Lutheran and *Reformed representatives. This also characterized the sixth conference, held in Strasbourg, France. A seventh concluding conference is slated for late 2003.

Brethren participants have included Jeffrey A. Bach, Shantilal P. Bhagat, D. F. Durnbaugh, David B. Eller, H. Lamar Gibble, Lauree Hersch Meyer, Dennis L. Slabaugh, and Murray L. Wagner. DFD

"Papers from the [First and] Second Consultation[s] on the Heritage of the First and Radical Reformations," *BLT* 35 (Winter, 1990) 4–113 (special issue), 36 (Winter, 1991) 92–101; *Reformed World* 43 (Sept., 1993) 77–124; Milan Opocensky, ed., *Towards a Renewed Dialogue: The First and Second Reformations* (1996) and *Justification and Sanctification: In the Traditions of the Reformation: Prague V* (1999); D. F. Durnbaugh, "A New Church Family?" *One World* (April, 1988) 10-11 and "First and Radical Reformations," *Dictionary of the Ecumenical Movement* (rev. ed., 2002); *Messenger* (April, 1986) 7, (Oct., 1987) 8, (Feb., 1995) 8, (April, 1998) 4; L. L. Johns, ed., *Apocalypticism and Millennialism* (2000) 309–25.

Putney, VT, Genesis Church of the Brethren. In late summer of 1981, three families moved to southeastern Vermont to establish a congregation of the *Church of the Brethren. They purchased a large New England farmhouse in Putney, which they renovated into three separate apartments. The families had met several years before at *Bethany Theol. Seminary. Through their three years of study they formed a house church. It was during that time that the idea of planting a congregation and sharing a common ministry was born. They envisioned going into an area where the Brethren had never been. They hoped to establish a congregation based on their best understanding of the New Testament and historic Brethren values, yet do it as far away as possible from the reach of modern cultural Brethrenism.

Following seminary the three families spent the next six years in separate pastorates in *Pennsylvania, *West Virginia, and *Michigan. It was through this time, working with the denominational representative for New Church Development, that the vision took form. The Southern Pennsylvania District became the sponsoring district. The plan called for the district and the denomination to provide support for the next several years. A single salary was divided among the three families. Finding work within the community was part of the ministry plan. The name Genesis was adopted on the basis of the New Testament application of beginning found in the first chapter of the Gospel of John. In the early years worship was held in the Putney Central Elementary School. In 1984, a large house in the village of Putney was purchased, and in 1991 a room for worship was added to the house. Genesis adopted a traditional board structure and established a membership covenant. No votes were taken in any decision-making matters. All major decisions were made in unity (by consensus). An elders' body was formed to oversee the spiritual life of the congregation and a salaried pastorate maintained. Three licensed ministers have been called from the membership. An informal, often quoted tenet has remained since the beginning: "Take God more seriously, take yourself less seriously." PEG

Messenger (May, 1991) 5; J. H. Lehman, *Thank God for New Churches!* (1984), 53–63; *BLT* 36 (Summer, 1991) 168, 196–99.

Ramsey, Duane H. (CB), b. 1924, pastor. Duane Ramsey was born and raised in Wichita, KS; he graduated from *McPherson College (1949) and *Bethany Theol. Sem. (1952). He was married in 1952 to Jane Krupenbach; they had five children: Kathy, Barbara, Michael, Nancy, and Brian. His first and only pastorate was the *Washington, DC, City Church of the Brethren. He served as moderator of *Annual Conference in 1981 and retired from the pastorate on Aug. 30, 1997.

Duane Ramsey was active in the *ecumenical church and hosted *Metropolitan Nikodim of the *Russian Orthodox Church, initiated the Capital Hill Group Ministry, and served on the board of the Metropolitan Christian Council of Washington, D.C.

His commitment to the community led him and the Washington City congregation to start a soup kitchen for street people in 1981, which still continued in 2003. Over the years the congregation ministered to preschoolers, did language tutoring, had a teen center, a senior citizen ministry, and sought communication with the community through ice cream socials and visiting door to door. During Ramsey's long tenure as pastor, the community experienced many changes in its socio-economic and racial character. RGL

Personal information; *Messenger* (Oct., 1997) 3, (March, 1998) 5, (Aug., 1998) 14.

Reamstown, PA, East Cocalico Church of the Brethren was organized in 1991 as a church planting by the Ephrata congregation. In Jan. 1989 the Ephrata congregation established "planting a new church" as one of six goals to be accomplished in the 1990s. In Oct. 1990 James H. Rhen was called to help organize a telephone solicitation of the target area and eventually to pastor the new congregation (effective Jan. 15, 1991). Volunteers made ca. ten thousand phone calls inviting persons to attend the first worship service. On Feb. 2, 1991, a building was purchased and the first service was held on Easter Sunday, March 31, 1991, with ca. 265 persons attending.

The new congregation developed rapidly and Charter Sunday was celebrated on Oct. 13, 1991, with 54 members transferring letters and six persons being baptized. In 2000, East Cocalico enjoyed full congregational status with a membership and average attendance of ca. 130. RGK

Messenger (July, 1999) 8–9, (May, 2002) 5; congregational records.

Redstone Valley Old German Baptist Brethren Church, WI. On April 24, 1995, the Ferrell D. Nachatelo family moved to the Elroy, WI, area. By Oct. 15, 1997, 53 members resided in the surrounding area and were organized as a congregation. Ministers were Roger Knaus, James Reed, and Dean Wrightsman, with Jay Brubaker of the *North Fork, IN, district having the oversight. Names of the charter families include Nachatelo, Brovont, Beachler, Riffey, Wolf, Knaus, Reed, Wrightsman,

Kyle and Mary Reed. Mary Jane Swihart collection.

Bowman, Culp, Deaton, Miller, Shankster, Anderson, Holgerson, and Witmer. Membership in Feb. 1998 was 57. FDN

Vindicator (Nov., 1997) 341.

Reed, Kyle Thayer (DB), 1918–85, missionary, deacon. The eldest son of William Sherman and Mary Jane Jameson Reed was born Feb. 9 in Carthage, IL. Reed was baptized into the *Dunkard Brethren Church in *Astoria, IL, as a teenager and was called to be a deacon in 1953. He married Mary Naomi Light in Dallas Center, IA, on May 26, 1946.

Kyle and Mary Reed served as missionaries to *China (1946–49) under the auspices of the *Mennonite Central Committee. While in Loho in the Hunan province, Kyle helped set up the first combine to operate in China. He worked at the tractor repair depot, assigned the task of returning the flooded land along the Yellow River to cultivation, following the Chinese blasting of its dikes to halt an advance of the Japanese in 1938. Mary, a registered nurse, worked in the hospital in Loho.

After escaping the Communists in Dec. 1947, Reed supervised the building and operation of 13 of 25 kitchens set up to feed over 100,000 refugees in Tsingtao. It took 550 people to cook and serve over 25 tons of rice each day.

After the closing of China to missionaries, Reed and a friend, Newton Jamison of Quinter, KS, searched for a new mission field in the southwestern U.S. during the 1950s. Seeing the great need among the Navajo people, Kyle Reed became instrumental in starting the *Torreon Navajo Mission southwest of Cuba, NM. He served on its board from 1956 until his death in 1985. MJSw

Bible Monitor (Sept. 1, 1944) 17–18, (Nov. 15, 1945) 9–12.

Refugee Resettlement. The number of people uprooted by war and other violence continued to increase during the last part of the 20th century to around 35 million in the year 2000. The *Church of the Brethren was the most active of the Brethren groups in resettling refugees in the United States. The church worked primarily through the *World Council of Churches, which selected the families to be resettled and assigned them to sponsoring churches and individuals. Several districts and congregations estab-

lished refugee committees to facilitate the transition. In 1980 most of the refugees being resettled came from Southeast Asia, particularly *Vietnam. By the early 1990s the place of origin had shifted to the former USSR and by the late 1990s to Southeast Europe. As the new millennium began, large numbers were coming from Africa. DRN

J. Graber, ed., *Monday* 19 (July 2000); *Refugee Reports:* (Dec., 2000); J. R. Mummert and J. A. Bach, *Refugee Ministry in the Local Congregation* (Scottsdale, PA: Herald Press, 1992).

Re-imagining Conference (1993) (CB). Called by the staffs of several main-line Protestant denominations, the conference was designed to mark the midpoint of the "Decade of Solidarity with Women" sponsored by the *World Council of Churches. Held in Minneapolis, MN, in early Nov., it created controversy because of its aggressive orientation toward *feminism. Presenters encouraged worship of female deities, such as the Heavenly Sophia (Wisdom). Conservative commentators accused conference planners, presenters, and participants of leaving the foundation of orthodox Protestant belief to pursue syncretistic, New Age, and neo-pagan beliefs.

Among the ca. 2,000 participants were 20 women and one man from the *Church of the Brethren. They drew considerable publicity when they announced in public that they were changing the denominational name to *Church of the Reconciliation*. One national religious publication titled its article about the event, "Don't Call These Women Brethren." According to one report, the renaming action resulted in public censure by denominational leadership.

The resolution presented to the conference stated, in part: "This name was conceived by the Holy Spirit in an incredible meeting last evening. It reflects our heritage as one of the *historic peace churches. It speaks of an ongoing process that is necessary for justice as well as peace. It proclaims the vision toward which men and women have worked in our denomination since our beginnings in Germany."

The initiative by these CB members was one of the irritants leading to the development of the conservative *"Concerns of the Grassroots" movement centering in Virginia. DFD

See also: GRASSROOTS, CONCERNS OF.

Christianity Today (Dec. 13, 1993) 65; *Messenger* (Jan., 1994) 9, (July, 1994) 28; *BLT* 44 (Summer, 1997) 55–73 (70–71); D. F. Durnbaugh, *Fruit of the Vine* (1997) 551–52.

From Janitor to Professor

One of the most moving personal stories emerging from the refugee resettlement efforts of the *Brethren Service Commission after *World War II involved a "Displaced Person" from the Soviet Union, George Dolnikowski. Brought to the U.S. by the Brethren just before Christmas Day in 1949, he was soon placed as a janitor at *Juniata College in Huntingdon, PA. Such was his progress in mastering the English language that four years later he was invited to join the faculty, following graduation from Juniata (BA 1952) and the U. of Pennsylvania (MA 1954).

George Dolnikowski was born in the heartland of Russia in 1918, and thus his early years were marked by the bloody tumults of the Bolshevik Revolution and Civil War. Childhood memories vacillated from pleas-

ant recollections of village life and early school years to the terrors of his father's imprisonment as an opponent of coerced collectivization and a staunch member of the Russian Orthodox Church. When the state tore down the village church, the father, a horticulturalist, led efforts to rebuild the structure. In 1936 while George was visiting an older brother, his father and mother were seized by the Communist authorities and exiled to Siberian forced labor camps. The son returned to his home to find it boarded up and used to house pigs and his parents gone. He never saw his parents again nor learned of their eventual fate, though he did receive one indirect communication about his father from Siberia telling of sixteen-hour workdays in terrible conditions.

After advanced studies at Voronezh and Moscow to prepare him as a teacher of German, he taught for one year before he was drafted into the Russian army in June 1941, four days after the Nazi army invaded the Soviet Union. Because of his language abilities, he was sent on intelligence missions behind the German lines until October when he was wounded by a landmine and captured. His knowledge of the German language saved his life, but also brought with it suspicion of being a spy. He was able to persuade his captors that he was, indeed, a teacher. Following his partial recovery from his wounds, he was sent from Smolensk to Germany (north of Berlin) as a forced laborer for more than three years. The worst tasks were cleaning up cities after bombing raids. When the end of the war came in the early summer of 1945, he made his way from the Berlin area to Bavaria and then to Austria in order to evade forced repatriation to the Soviet Union.

George Dolnikowski found employment on an Austrian farm near Salzburg, later in a theater, and finally as an assistant cook in a U.S. Army camp. It was here that he applied for and received resettlement aid from the *Brethren Service Commission, through its representative Joseph B. Mow. Following a brief reception time at the Service Center at *New Windsor, MD, he was sent early in January 1950 to Huntingdon, PA. The 32-year old was befriended by several faculty members at *Juniata College, who welcomed him to their homes, taught him English, and guided his sometimes humorous and sometimes awkward readjustment to a new life.

After teaching summer school at Juniata in 1952, he undertook graduate studies in Germanic language and literature at the U. of Pennsylvania, graduating with distinction in 1954. While working that summer as a sandwich maker at Ocean City, NJ, just before joining the college faculty, his story and photograph were distributed by a wire service and published across the country. In 1956 he married Joanne Phillips, an artist and native of nearby Alexandria; they have one son, Gregory. By 1960, his story was featured as a success story for Brethren efforts at refugee resettlement. Later, he also pursued further graduate work at Harvard U., receiving a second MA degree in Slavic languages and literature and shifting his teaching career at Juniata to that area.

On campus he was active in promoting peace and international understanding. He introduced a course on the Historic Peace Churches, served as translator for the Church of the Brethren-Russian Orthodox Exchange of 1963, and directed the *Brethren Colleges Abroad Program in Marburg, Germany, from 1970 to 1972. He received an award for distinguished teaching in 1987.

Following his retirement in 1988 after teaching German and Russian for 34 years, he translated the writings of the Peace Pilgrim into the Russian language, making possible wide distribution of that material in the Soviet Union. He was instrumental in bringing to the Juniata campus on several occasions the noted Russian poet, Yevgeny Yevtushenko, who was granted an honorary degree by the college in 1991. He also founded an emeriti association for retired teachers at Juniata College.

One of his noted accomplishments was his initiative (aided by other colleagues) in organizing a touring exhibit of Russian Ikons in 1988. The exhibit, featuring ikons from the golden age (1400–1700) was shown in the National Cathedral (Washington, DC); New York City; Lafayette College (Easton, PA); College of the Holy Cross (Worcester, MA); and the Frick Art Museum (Pittsburgh, PA).

George Dolnikowski was once asked by a student, "What is your greatest wish?" He responded, "My greatest wish is to see Americans and Russians joined by other people of the world in living and working together, enjoying the fruits of their labor, and playing and singing, rejoicing in celebration of the greatest gift from God, the gift of life." This quotation is found in his memoirs, published by Brethren Press in 1994. DFD

George Dolnikowski, *This I Remember: From War to Peace* (1994), excerpts published as "This I Remember," *Messenger* (July, 1994) 14–16. Erwin S. Koval, "Russian D.P. Advances from Janitor to College Faculty," *Huntingdon Daily News* (July 28, 1952); "Janitor to Prof," *Christian Science Monitor* (Aug. 24, 1954) 3; Ruth Early, "Ten Years After," *GM* (Nov. 5, 1960) 10–11; Howard E. Royer, "Encounter [Brethren/Orthodox Exchange]," *GM* (Oct. 12, 1963) 15–17; "Dolnikowski to Serve as Director of Program of Studies at Marburg," *Juniatian* (Dec. 16, 1969) 1; David Gildea, "Retiring Professor George Dolnikowski Recognized at Annual Trustee Dinner," *Juniata College News* (May 5, 1988) 1–2; "Dolnikowski Writes: *This I Remember: From War to Peace*," *Huntingdon Daily News* (July 30, 1994) 1, 3.

Restructuring, Organizational (CB). The 1946 *Annual Conference approved a recommendation to form a single *General Brotherhood Board, uniting the functions of various cause-oriented boards and committees that had emerged in earlier decades.

About 20 years later, organizational concerns resurfaced. The 1968 Annual Conference reduced the number of General Brotherhood Board commissions from five to three and shortened the board's name to *General Board. The 1988 *Annual Conference relieved the General Board of its responsibility as a *Pension Board through the creation of the *Brethren Benefit Trust.

Organizational concerns were re-examined in the latter half of the 1980s. The 1987 Annual Conference assigned four queries—the most significant of which asked for an overarching review of *polity relationships—to a five-member denominational structure-review committee. This committee sought to strengthen the authority of Annual Conference, to eliminate areas "of overlap, conflict, and competition" among General Board staff, to coordinate efforts of various denominational

agencies, and to make denominational structures more responsive to local congregations. To effect this, the committee recommended a total revamping of denominational structure to the 1989 Conference. Their proposals included: strengthening the role of the *moderator and secretary of Annual Conference by increasing the moderator's term of service to three years and making the secretary a full-time salaried position; reducing the size of the elected General Board and the employed staff; creating a Council of Cooperative and Emerging Missions to explore new mission and ministry opportunities; and merging smaller districts.

Delegates to the 1989 Annual Conference decisively rejected the committee's report, some suggesting that the committee had overstepped its mandate. Delegates appointed a new committee to restudy the issue. The new committee's report, approved by the 1991 Conference, recommended relatively minor changes, among them that *Standing Committee assume an envisioning role for the denomination; that congregations consider appointing Annual Conference delegates to two-year terms; renaming *Central Committee as the Program and Arrangements Committee; and convening a biennial Consultation of Denominational Agencies (which was discontinued after one meeting). In addition, the General Board was instructed to address areas of conflict and overlap in its functions, the excessive size of its staff, disproportionate ecumenical involvements, and the need for more flexible staff portfolios.

In response to projected budget shortfalls, in March 1995 the General Board initiated a process of redesign. A Redesign Steering Committee elected by the board spearheaded a two-year process of restructuring, which culminated with the 1997 Annual Conference approval by a large majority. Among significant changes were: replacing the board's three commissions with a single program arm; replacing the Administrative Council with a Leadership Team of directors; creation of a Mission and Ministries Planning Council (MMPC) to serve as a multiorganizational planning body; the addition of five Congregational Life Teams, with area field staff to assist congregations (reminiscent of *regions of earlier eras); and reduction of the board from 25 to 20 members. Delegates rejected a proposal that the board appoint five of its members. Functions of the eliminated *Goals and Budget Committee and *Planning Coordinating Committee were absorbed by the Executive Committee and MMPC.

In addition to these polity changes, the redesign resulted in reduction of denominational staff by 30 percent and budget by 16 percent from 1996 to 1998. The *Association of Brethren Caregivers, *On Earth Peace, the *Outdoor Ministries Association, and *SERRV International—groups with organizational ties to the board—were spun off as independent bodies. Relocation of the denominational offices was considered but rejected. In some ways, the new structure, with a variety of independent agencies, resembled earlier decentralized eras. DRF

Minutes, Annual Conference (1989, 1991, 1997); D. F. Durnbaugh, *Fruit of the Vine* (1997), 497–510; S. L. Bowman, *Power and Polity Among the Brethren* (1987); *Messenger* (March, 1987) 12–14, (May/June, 1989) 17, (Sept., 1989) 16–17, (Aug., 1995) 16, 18, (April, 1997) 6–9; (April, 1997), 8–9; (Aug./Sept., 1997) 20–21, (March, 1987) 12–14, (Aug./Sept, 1991) 19.

J. Benton Rhoades. BHLA collection. Photo by Kermon Thomasson.

Rhoades, J. Benton and Ruby June Frantz (CB). J. Benton Rhoades (1920–2003) was born in Astoria, IL, the son of Paul J. and Orpha Benton Rhoades. He studied at *Manchester College (BA, 1942), *Bethany Bibl. Sem. (BD, 1945), the U. of Chicago Divinity School, and the Bethel (ME) Institute of Behavioral Science. He married Ruby Frantz in 1943. Their children were Robert, Jeanne, Janet, and Rebecca.

Benton and Ruby Rhoades served as founding missionaries of the Brethren Rural Mission in *Ecuador (1946–56). He then worked for USAID for two years, strengthening the 4-H program in Ecuador.

Benton was director of leadership development for two years at the Church of the Brethren *General Board in Elgin, IL, and then moved to the New York area to direct *Agricultural Missions, Inc. for 30 years. He succeeded *I. W. Moomaw, who founded the agency to serve rural people worldwide. Benton Rhoades' work came to focus on issues of structural injustice affecting agriculturalists in over 50 countries. His published work dealt with Christian *mission in rural communities, emphasizing development and empowerment. Following the death of Ruby Frantz Rhoades, in 1988 he married Doris Caldwell, who had served the *Presbyterian Church in Hong Kong and China for three decades.

Ruby June Frantz Rhoades (1923–85) was born in Beattie, KS, the daughter of *Ira H. and Hattie Sellers Frantz. She studied at Manchester College, Bethany Bible Training School, and *Bethany Bibl. Seminary. In Ecuador with the Brethren Rural Mission, Ruby taught many classes related to the young church and school in Llano Grande. When her husband worked for USAID, the Rhoades family moved to Quito where Ruby provided hospitality for missionaries of various groups serving in the jungle. In Elgin, IL, she helped establish an English as a Second Language program in the public school system. While living in the New York City area, she was director of advertising and promotion for Fleming Revell Publishers (NJ). She became director of promotion for *Messenger* (CB, 1973–74), was director of the Washington Office (1976-79), and was then named executive of the *World Ministries Commission (1980-85), serving until her death from cancer. BMC

Prayer for Missions (1949) 128-9; B. M. Crouse, *Bread Upon the Waters* ([1976]) 20-22, revised and expanded from D. F. Durnbaugh, ed., *Yesterday and Today* (1986) 151–52; GM (Oct. 12, 1946) 18–19; *Messenger* (April, 1979), 8, (Jan., 1980) 10–12, 33, (Dec., 1982) 11,

Ruby Frantz Rhoades. BHLA collection.

(Aug., 1983) 10, (Jan., 1985) 5, (Feb., 1985) 9, (Jan., 1991) 25, (May/June, 1994) 13; I. W. Moomaw, *Crusade Against Hunger* (1966) viii, 198.

Rieman, Timothy Wayne (CB), 1912–94, educator, preacher, writer. T. Wayne Rieman was born in Berlin, Somerset Co., PA, the son of George S. and Emma Walker Rieman. In 1937 he married Gwen Radebach; they had three children: Sylvia (Houser), Philip, and Timothy. Rieman graduated from *Juniata College (BS, 1933); Pennsylvania State U. (MEd, 1942); *Bethany Theol. Sem. (BD, 1945); Northwestern U. (PhD, 1959); with

T. Wayne Reiman. BHLA collection.

special studies at several other institutions.

Rieman taught high school biology in Pennsylvania for nine years, was assistant pastor of the *Elgin, IL, CB 1948–49, and was pastor of the *York Center, IL, CB, (1942–48) and the *Waynesboro, VA, CB (1945–48). He was professor of religion and philosophy at *Manchester College. (1949–78), serving as student pastor much of this time. In retirement he served interim pastorates in *Pennsylvania, *Illinois, and *Indiana, and conducted 185 workshops across the nation. He was a popular speaker and writer, publishing many articles, several booklets, and one book, *Spirituality, God's Order of Being.* WRE

Manchester College files; H. A. Cooper, *Two Centuries of Brothersvalley CB* (1962); *W. Pennsylvania* (1953) 597; *Virginia* (1973) 273; *Messenger* (Sept., 1978) 2-3, (Jan./Dec., 1990) (series of 11 articles), (Dec., 1994) 3, (June, 1997) 13; *Manchester College Bulletin* (Spring, 1995) 15; *Bulletin of the [Manchester College] Peace Studies Institute* 25.1–2 (1995) 2, 26 (1996) 2–42 (special issue); T. K. Jones, *Manchester College* (1989) 121, 164, 180–81, 205, 244.

Rio Piedras, PR, Segunda Iglesia Cristo Misionera Fellowship (CB) (Second Christian Missionary Fellowship) is located in Caimito, Rio Piedras, in the metropolitan San Juan area. Juan Figueroa and Isabel Martinez Figueroa, husband and wife, are co-pastors. They pastored an independent Pentecostal church of some 50 members beginning in the 1970s. At the same time they were founding directors of the Christian Community Center (CCC), which has its own legal status but uses the same facilities. The Figueroas became acquainted with the *Church of the Brethren in the U.S. when disaster workers went to *Puerto Rico in 1989 to help in the reconstruction of homes damaged by Hurricane Hugo. The CCC was their base of work. Later, the Figueroas met Pedro Brull, associate executive for the Atlantic Southeast District (CB), and other members of the Puerto Rican sub-district board. They sought affiliation with the CB in 1990. The congregation had a membership of ca. 25 in 1999. The CCC continues its work of humanitarian service under the direction of both Juan and Isabel Figueroa and a community-based board. IRZ/BMC

Congregational records; *Yearbook* (CB) (2002) 114.

Rio Prieto, PR, Iglesia de los Hermanos (CB). The Río Prieto Church of the Brethren is located in rural Río Prieto near the city of Lares, west central *Puerto Rico. In the late 1950s, the *Presbyterian Church closed its service in rural areas, leaving a remnant group of families meeting in homes led by elder Luis (Luiche) Pérez. They were acquainted with the *Church of the Brethren through health services offered in the community. Early in the 1960s, Brethren from *Castañer began to visit. In coordination with pastor Donald L. Fike who ably guided evangelistic efforts in Río Prieto (1960–72), the group grew and sought a place for worship. The project continued vigorously during the pastorate of Guillermo B. Encarnación at Castañer. A building formerly used by a spiritualist movement was leased in 1973. Beth and Keith A. Nonemaker gave pastoral service as volunteers (1978–80), the group growing to 18 persons. Olga Serrano of Ecuador then pastored (1980–87), emphasizing education and leadership development. Río Prieto was recognized as a fellowship in 1985 with a membership of 30. Irma R. Zayas, a member of the congregation, pastored in

1988–92. Thirteen acres of land with a building were dedicated in 1990 with Phyllis Carter, former district executive, participating. The Río Prieto Fellowship served as laboratory for pastoral internships for Kurt R. Ritchie, Milton García, and Amy Gall, each supervised by Irma Zayas. Olga Serrano, Milton Garcia, and Irma Zayas went on to seminary studies. Membership in 1999 was 48 and average attendance was 55. The pastor in 2000 was Fausto Carrasco from the CB in the *Dominican Republic. The original pastor, Luis Pérez, and family continue to serve the congregation. IRZ/BMC

M. S. H. Rosenberger, *Light of the Spirit: The Brethren in Puerto Rico, 1942 to 1992* ([1992]), 70–73; O. Serrano, *Un Canto al Señor en la Isla del Encanto* (1992), *passim*; *Messenger* (Jan., 1983) 17; *BLT* 36 (Summer, 1991) 168.

Riverside, CA, Grace Community Church (FGBC) was initiated by four families who relocated to Riverside, a bedroom community 50 miles east of Los Angeles. Two of the families came from *North Long Beach GBC (the Swifts and Inlows), one from the *Long Beach GBC (the Jahns), and one from the *Bellflower BC (the Selmansons). On Jan. 1, 1980, they called Brian C. Smith to serve as the founding pastor. He had been the associate pastor at North Long Beach GBC where he was the Sunday school teacher for the Swifts and Inlows.

For 13 years, the congregation rented a *Seventh Day Adventist Church building in which to hold its services. In 1992, the church purchased and renovated an abandoned strip mall, which now serves as its permanent location. Only one of the founding members, the Swifts, remains in the church. Tim Inlow died three weeks after the church's inaugural service in 1980, the Selmansons moved to North Dakota, and the Jahns to Michigan. In 2003, the congregation had 203 active families. BCS/JRY

Congregational records; *Annual* (FGBC) (1981–98).

Romney, WV, Church of the Brethren began in the 1940s when Philip Stein Hochman held services in a small building with attendance of ca. 20. The congregation was discontinued in the 1950s and 1960s, but in 1969 two small groups of Brethren began meeting again; in 1975 they merged. In 1989 the congregation purchased a church building on Parsons Ave. and since then enlarged the fellowship room and kitchen and added classrooms. Adjacent lots were purchased, including a house that was renovated to provide an office, extra classrooms, and storage space. Pastors serving the congregation since 1980 have been India L. Hockman (1980), William T. Preston (1981–86), Leonard Dean (1986), Roger D. Leatherman (1986–94), and Brian D. Moreland (1994–). In 2000, Sunday worship attendance averaged ca. 60. AVD

E. F. Bittinger, *Allegheny Passage* (1990) 388–90; congregational records.

Rose, Smith Fuller (BC), 1915–99, pastor, denominational executive. Smith Rose was born on Dec. 7 in Hadden-ville, PA, the son of Charles and Mary Rose, and was ordained Aug. 25, 1940, at Mansfield, OH. Rose served as executive secretary for the *Central Council (1968-78) and the General Conference (1978–80) during a formative time in the development of the denominational organization.

A graduate of *Ashland College (BA, 1939) and *Ashland Theol. Sem. (BD, 1942), he pastored Brethren congregations in *Cameron, WV (student, 1938); *Roann, IN (1942–45); *Oak Hill and *Gatewood, WV (1945–51); *West Alexandria, OH (1951-53); Brighton Chapel, Howe, IN (1953–57); *Bryan, OH (1957–67); and, in his retirement, *Fort Scott, KS (1980–84). Several of his pastorates were bi-vocational ministries. He was General Conference moderator in 1957. Smith Rose married Florence Vincent on June 8, 1939; they had two daughters: Mary and Martha. Rose died on April 17 and was followed in death four days later by his wife. RWW

BE (Sept. 7, 1940) 19, (Aug. 24, 1957) 4ff., (Jan., 1980) 6; Ashland Theol. Sem. archives file; A. T. Ronk, *History BC* (1968), 465, 477.

S-V

San Luis, DR, Principe de Paz (Prince of Peace, CB), was founded on Oct. 2, 1988, and affiliated with the *Church of the Brethren in Nov. 1989. In 2000 this congregation had 90 members, 55 new believers studying for baptism, 130 attending Sunday school, and 150 attending worship services. The church started with 13 meeting under an avocado tree. During the first two years, the congregation met in a small wooden house; in 1990 the CB bought a small home, and congregational members remodeled it. The first baptisms were held in 1993. On March 18, 2000, the denomination bought a lot for 90,000 pesos ($5,600) where the congregation built a new sanctuary in 2002. The pastor during this entire time has been Isaías Santos Teña; his wife, Anastasia Bueno, is also a licensed minister. RBCr/GPBC

Congregational records.

San Marcos, CA, North County Church of the Brethren started as a dream of the *San Diego, CA, First Church of the Brethren. After a year of preliminary study by Glenn R. Stanford, the Pacific Southwest District hired Glenn J. Frazier in 1983. He organized the North County Church of the Brethren in San Marcos, CA.

At the same time the congregation started a gift store staffed by volunteers, Loving Hands Gifts International, selling *SERRV products and a few other items. In 1990 construction was started on a new *meetinghouse on land purchased with a grant from the *General Board and a loan from the district; construction was completed in 1992. Frazier left in 1997 to pursue interests in Hawaii. That same year, the church called Valentina Satvedi as their pastor. EEE

Congregational records; *Messenger* (Jan., 1983) 16; *BLT* 36 (Summer, 1991) 168; *Yearbook (CB)* (1983–2000).

Sanctuary Movement (CB). "The refugees are here at our door pleading for help to avoid capture." Churches across the U.S. declared sanctuary to aid refugees in Central America fleeing from oppressive regimes. The U.S. government did not honor the Immigration Act of 1980, allowing political and religious asylum. Following biblical actions of "cities of refuge" and Jesus' "liberty to the captives," sanctuary provided a safe haven for undocumented persons (an "Underground Railroad") giving cultural adjustment, physical and emotional solace, education, and assistance in securing legal documents. Churches began declaring sanctuary in 1982 as thousands

Olivares family, sanctuary refugees from El Salvador, with Edward and Martha Miller. Martha Miller collection.

of Central Americans swarmed across the U.S. border. By the mid-1980s 13 congregations of the *Church of the Brethren declared sanctuary, and 10 others were hosting documented ("Overground Railroad") refugees. "The crucified Christ comes to us in the poor, homeless refugee. Through the eyes of these refugees we have seen God!" DLRo

Personal information; *Minutes* General Board (CB); *Messenger* (May, 1983) 4, (March, 1984) 4–5, (June, 1984) 4, (April, 1985) 4–5, (Aug., 1985) 28; quotations are from Jim Corbett, Texas Quaker, and Jon Sobrino, Jesuit priest from El Salvador.

Santa Ana, CA, Principe de Paz Fellowship, (CB). The Pacific Southwest District and the *Santa Ana Church of the Brethren called Mario and Olga Serrano to begin a new Hispanic congregation in Jan. 1990. The Serranos served in Santa Ana throughout the 1990s. From over 250 home visits made in the neighborhood, five families began a core fellowship, using the facilities of the Santa Ana CB. In May 1995 the Santa Ana CB closed. The

property reverted to the district which then leased it to Principe de Paz. The meeting was received as a Fellowship in 1993. At that time, Edmundo Hildago was board chair, Margarita Salinas was treasurer, and Gaudencio Cruz, Jr., was youth adviser. In 2000, the Fellowship reported a membership of 39. On Oct. 5, 2002, the Fellowship was granted congregational status in the Pacific Southwest District CB. JADa

Pacific Southwest District files; personal information; *Yearbook* (*CB*) (1990–2000).

Roger E. Sappington. BHLA collection.

Sappington, Roger E. (CB), 1929–89, educator, historian, minister. A son of Ross F. and Beulah Snader Sappington, Roger Sappington was born March 6 in Avon Park, FL. He was educated at *Manchester College (BA, 1951), *Bethany Theol. Sem. (BD, 1954), and Duke U. (MA, 1954; PhD, 1959). He married LeVerle Hochstetler in 1949; they had four children.

Ordained to the ministry at *Sebring, FL, in 1951, Sappington pastored the *Pleasant View CB near Lima, OH, (1955–58). He joined the history faculty at *Bridgewater College in 1958, where he taught for the next 31 years. Following the publication of a revision of his doctoral dissertation, *Brethren Social Policy, 1908–1958* (1961), Sappington authored a biograpical study of John Kline, *Courageous Prophet* (1964) and histories of the Brethren in several states, including Idaho (1966), the Carolinas (1972), Virginia (1973), and Tennessee (1988). He also produced for Brethren Press two carefully researched documentary source volumes, *Brethren in the New Nation* (1976) and *Brethren in Industrial America* (1985).

In addition to his teaching, research, and writing, Sappington was coach of the college debate team. He served two terms on the CB Historical Committee, and was also active in local and district church work, as well as Boy Scouts of America. He died of congestive heart failure on March 19. Bridgewater College honored Sappington by creating an award for Anabaptist and Pietist scholarship in his name in the late 1990s. DBE

F. F. Wayland, *Bridgewater College: The First Hundred Years, 1880–1980* (1993), index; *[Harrisonburg, VA] Daily News Record* (March 21, 1989); *Directory of American Scholars, 7th* ed. (1978); *Who's Who in Religion,* 3rd ed. (1985) 338; *Contemporary Authors* (1975) 13–16; *Virginia* (1973) 206; *NW. Ohio* (1982) 99; *CBMF; Messenger* (May/June, 1989) 6, (July, 1989): 31; BHLA files.

Sarasota, FL, Iglesia de los Hermanos (BC). This Hispanic ministry was begun in 1979 by Janet Hamel Solomon, initially as an outreach to the children of migrant workers. When adults began attending, the local Brethren congregation, the *Sarasota First Brethren Church, decided to call the *Kenneth L. Solomon family in mid-1981 to lead this missionary endeavor. To aid the outreach, Solomon began a *radio ministry in Spanish. In 1988 the Daniel Rosales family assumed leadership of the work with Daniel Rosales continuing the radio ministry. Rosales, who is a product of the Brethren mission work in *Argentina, has also conducted evangelistic campaigns in other countries as invitations have come from radio listeners. In 1993 the congregation moved into its own facility. Membership at the end of 1998 was 59 with pastor Italo Abuid. In 2004 the congregation is pastored by Timothy Solomon who co-founded this ministry with his wife Janet. Attendance is ca. 100. KLSol

Congregational records; *Annual* (*BC*) 1981–98).

Bitrus P. Sawa of Nigeria. BHLA collection.

Sawa, Bitrus Pilasar (CB), 1934–89, Nigerian educator, churchman. Sawa was born in Lassa; his father, Pilasar (also Pilesar, Pilesaw) K. Sawa, was one of the first four persons baptized in the *Nigeria CB mission. Among the first to gain an English teaching certificate, Sawa taught at several schools and became the first Nigerian principal at *Waka Teachers College. With support from the *Lititz, PA, congregation and the *Foreign Mission Commission, Sawa received an MA in education at Millersville State College (1968) and spoke at *Annual Conference (CB) that year. His advanced education for the time and his ability to articulate issues led to senior government appointments and prominent roles in the church. In 1985

he earned a PhD from Ahmadu Bello U. at Zaria. He was recognized nationally by appointment as registrar for the Federal U. of Technology at Minna. Bitrus and Nkwarfaku Sawa had four children: Sunday, Markus, Joshua, and Olive. MBK

Messenger (Oct., 1989) 7, (March, 1993) 3; C. E. Faw, ed. *Lardin Gabas* (1973) 4, 74–87, 121–26.

Tom and Marilyn Ryan and Eula Brumbaugh at SERRV outlet. BHLA collection.

*SERRV International (CB). Organized in post-*World War II years and nurtured in succeeding decades by the *Church of the Brethren, SERRV continues its mission of promoting social and economic progress of people in developing areas of the world by purchasing and marketing their handcrafts in a just and direct manner. SERRV, for many years a *General Board (CB) agency, was headquartered at the *Brethren Service Center, New Windsor, MD; in 2001 its administrative office moved to Madison, WI, while processing and warehousing remained at New Windsor. An ecumenical Christian ministry, SERRV has partnered with many other groups, notably the *Presbyterian and *United Methodist churches and the *United Church of Christ. In the 1990s, the Christian Children's Fund, Catholic Relief Services, and Luthern World Relief became its most significant partners in terms of sales volume.

By 1997, SERRV was importing handcrafts and some staple food products from 110 producer groups in 37 countries and marketing them through 3,500 churches, Fair Trade stores, and community groups throughout the United States. Sales in 1997 totaled $4,992,000. The 1980s were a period of substantial growth for SERRV as interest grew in the world-wide alternative trade movement, of which SERRV is one of the oldest and largest members. This movement seeks to reflect values other than the profit motive and to ensure a fair wage for producers.

The major area of sales growth by 1997 was from the SERRV retail sales catalog. Two retail stores were located at the Brethren Service Center in New Windsor and in a shopping mall in Westminster, MD. In 1998, SERRV

was poised to expand its program of educating U.S. customers to the need for greater economic justice for people of the developing world.

In 1998, explorations were underway on the feasibility of SERRV severing ties with the General Board and becoming an independent, not-for-profit agency. While the continuing viability of SERRV's ministry was affirmed, such a potential move was seen as a way to provide more flexibility, to enter new markets, and to attract new funding sources not available to church groups as such. On Feb. 1, 1999, SERRV became an independent non-profit organization, incorporated in the state of *Maryland as SERRV International, Inc. The continuation of Brethren influence was assured by a by-laws requirement that the majority of the seven-member Board of Directors be members of the Church of the Brethren. FCN

K. I. Morse, *New Windsor Center* (1979) 86–93; *Messenger* (Nov., 1983) 4, (July, 1985) 11–13, (Aug./Sept., 1988) 24, (June, 1990) 5, (Oct., 1991) 7, (Nov., 1991) 9, (April, 1993) 7, (Dec., 1994) 10, (Aug., 1995) 7, (March, 1996) 8, (Aug./Sept., 1996) 19, (Dec., 1997) 6, (March, 2001) 8; J. K. Kreider, *A Cup of Cold* Water (2001), index; *Partnerships: Fair Trade for the Developing World* (SERRV International Newsletter); *The Wall Street Journal* (Dec. 14, 1995) B-1; *World View* (Peace Corps magazine) (Summer, 1996) 31–37; *USA Today* (April 3, 1996) 11A; *Sky* (U.S. Air magazine) (March, 1995) 106–15; *Catholic Review* (Dec. 11, 1997) B-2; D. F. Durnbaugh, *Fruit of the Vine* (1997) 491.

Sewell, Laura A. (CB), missionary. Born in 1920 in Spokane, WA, she was the daughter of Charles H. and Alice Powell Sewell. Her home congregation was *Clearwater CB, Teakean, ID. She attended Simpson Institute, Seattle, WA, (1939–41), *Bethany Theol. Sem. (BSL, 1944), *McPherson College (BS, 1954), and U. of Denver (MA in Library Science, 1968). Sewell was a missionary in *India (1948–84), serving in the Girls' Boarding School, *Anklesvar, in work with churches and pastors, in Women's Fellowship for Christian Service, and in literature work with Libraries and Literacy. After formation of the *Church of North India in 1971, she was a member of the Gujarat Diocesan Council Executive and Synod Executive Committee, and Secretary of the Women's Fellowship for Church of North India (1976–79). She was the last CB missionary in India, retiring in 1984. Sewell received the CB Outstanding Ecumenical Award (1989), McPherson College Citation of Merit (1994), and Oregon Community Colleges' license as tutor for Oregon State in 1991. WPF

GM (April 10, 1948) 19; *Messenger* (Oct., 1978) 2, (Nov., 1981) 8, (Jan., 1985) 7, (May, 1985) 4, (Oct., 1985) 3, (March, 1996) 23; *Prayer for Missions* (1949) 37; A. C. Mow, ed., *Meet Your Missionaries* (1955); Laura A. Sewell notes (1997).

Shank, Glenn H. ("Doc") and Catherine Jean Heck (BC), pastor, nurse, missionaries. Born in Mason and Dixon, PA, Doc Shank (1921–2003) was the son of Harvey and Rose Shank. He attended *Ashland College (BA, 1948) and *Ashland Theol. Sem. (BD, 1962; MDiv, 1973). While in Ashland, he pastored the *Glenford, OH, BC (1945–50). He was ordained in 1953 at the *Hagerstown, MD, First BC.

Born on Dec. 14, 1926, in Hagerstown, Jean Heck was the daughter of Vernon and Roberta Heck. She attended nurses training at Union Memorial Hospital School of Nursing in Baltimore, MD (RN, 1948), then attended Ashland College, serving as school nurse while earning both BS and BA degrees (1952). The Shanks were mar-

ried in 1952 and then did graduate work at the School of Missions at Concordia Theol. Sem. in St. Louis, MO.

From 1955 to 1966 the Shanks served as missionaries on the *Church of the Brethren mission field in *Nigeria. They taught at Waka, but later were given oversight of the mission work first in the Wandali area, then in the Marama area. They spent their last four years in Jos, Nigeria, where they served as house parents at *Hillcrest School, and Doc was purchasing agent for the mission.

After returning to the U.S., Jean Shank became a full-time nurse and Doc Shank returned to the pastoral ministry. Brethren churches served included *Maurertown, VA (1966–73); *St. Luke, Woodstock, VA, (1967–73); *Liberty, Quicksburg, VA (1967–73, 1979–99); *Gretna, Bellefontaine, OH (1973–77); Chandron, Herndon, VA, (1977–79); and *Mathias, WV (1979–87). During his years of pastoral service, Shank also had an active ministry as a volunteer hospital *chaplain and participated in the work of *On Earth Peace. The Shanks were parents of two children: Dennis Glenn and Donna Jean. RCWi
BE (March 21, 1953) 10, (Oct. 17, 1953) 14, (Nov. 14, 1953) 7, (Nov., 1985) 8–9; *Annual* (*BC*) (1953–87).

Owen and Celia Shankster. BHLA collection.

Shankster, Owen L., Jr., and Celia Smith (CB), missionaries. Owen Shankster (1927–2000) was born May 28 at Alvordton, OH, the son of a *Church of the Brethren pastor. He entered *Civilian Public Service after high school, serving two years in the *China Tractor Unit. Celia Smith was born in 1929 in Ellingson, SD. She graduated from *Manchester College in 1949, where she and Owen met. He completed his college work in 1959.

The Shanksters were married in May 1950, and, because of their eagerness to serve in *mission, they left for *Nigeria that September. This experience confirmed their commitment to missionary service. In 1954, they went to Waka, where Owen Shankster managed the building of the campus of *Waka Teachers College and related schools. Celia Shankster served as treasurer and kept student records. They served at Waka for 17 years.

In 1971 they moved to *Garkida, where Owen Shankster became the builder and workshop manager for the *Lafiya Rural Health Program, while Celia Shankster kept the program's financial records. Contaminated water was identified by Lafiya staff as a major source of illness; for that reason in 1978 Owen was assigned to start a program to construct wells. Eventually the effort was named the Self-Help Well-Digging Project, recognizing the participatory style which involved village labor and decisions. By 1991 the project had completed 2,700 wells.

In 1981 Celia Shankster began teaching Christian religious knowledge at the local government school. She also ran the mission guest house, was active in the Women's Fellowship, and being fluent in Bura and Hausa languages, she served as the local church secretary for many years.

Owen Shankster researched and built the first wooden truss constructions required to span the long diagonals across the center of the cross-shaped church buildings. He also led building projects at *Kulp Bible College, *Hillcrest School, and many mission compounds. In the Nigerian church he served as an elder and evangelist.

The Shanksters served 41 years in Nigeria, retiring in 1991. They had five surviving children: Donald, Edwin, Carl, Susan, and Janice. Twin daughters died at birth and are buried at Garkida. Owen Shankster died in 2000. MBK.
W. Snavely, "Meet Your Missionary," *GM* (Nov. 13, 1954) 25, (Dec. 4, 1954) 25; *Messenger* (May, 1978) 34–35, (Sept., 1978) 18, (Oct., 1984) 18–21, (Mar., 1991) 8, (Nov., 2000) 4; A. Mow, ed., *Meet Your Missionaries* (1955) 108–09; *Fifty Years in Lardin Gabas, 1923–1973* [1973] 36; C. E. Faw, ed., *Lardin Gabas: A Land, A People, A Church* (1973) 116; General Board (CB) files.

Shaver, Emanuel Bydler (GBB, BC), 1843–1927, minister, farmer, businessman. The son of German Baptist Brethren elder George Shaver of the *Woodstock, VA, congregation, E. B. Shaver was called to the ministry in his home congregation along with his brother Samuel A. The conservative/progressive discord divided the congregation early in 1885, and E. B. Shaver invited progressive evangelist *Stephen H. Bashor to lead services nearby. The *Maurertown, VA, Round Hill (Strasburg, VA), Mt. Zion (*Reliance, VA), and Mt. Pleasant, VA, congregations grew out of this work. A staunch defender of the progressive movement, he served *The Brethren Church for 55 years in the *Shenandoah Valley, organized 22 churches, and served as district moderator. As "Moses of the Valley," he baptized an estimated 2,000 persons, officiated at 500 marriages, and at many funerals. MWH
Virginia (1914) 177; *Virginia* (1973) 107; *W. Virginia* (1945) 99; *BE* (Oct. 29, 1927) 14–15, (Dec. 3, 1927) 14–15, (April 26, 1930) 15, (March 7, 1931) 6, (April 19, 1952) 8–10, (March 15, 1954) 4–5, 8–9, (June 19, 1954) 4–5, 8–9; Maurertown Brethren Church, *Local History of Maurertown Brethren Church* (dedication booklet, 1978).

Shepherd's Spring Outdoor Ministries Center (CB), near Sharpsburg, MD. In 1989 the Mid-Atlantic District purchased land on the Potomac River to develop a year-round retreat center and summer camp to replace *Camp Woodbrook, which had been sold to Carroll County, MD, for a future reservoir, and *Camp Shiloh which was sold to the Baltimore *Society of Friends. The 220 acres of land was located in the rolling hills of the Potomac Highlands of Central Maryland, overlooking the Chesapeake and Ohio Canal National Park. Initial development included a summer camp village with cabins and pavilion, a swimming pool and bath house, a lodge for year-round use, and a maintenance center. The administrator during the development and operation of the center was Rex M. Miller (1991–2002). RMM
Messenger (Oct., 1990) 5, (June, 1991) 4, (May, 1992) 9, (Jan./Feb., 2000) 22–23, (May, 2001) 10–11, (Aug., 2001) 9, (Sept., 2001) 3, (Jan./Feb., 2002) 10, (Nov., 2002) 7; personal information.

Sherfy, Robert Livingston (CB), 1913–94, pastor and descendant of a long line of Brethren ministers in the *Scherffig/Sherfy family. Robert Sherfy was born in

Kansas as the only son of Ernest F. and Effie Strohm Sherfy and the grandson of John Sherfy of Tennessee. Educated at *Bridgewater College (BA, 1934) and *Bethany Theol. Sem. (BD, 1940), he received an honorary degree from Bridgewater College (DD, 1955).

Sherfy was ordained by *John S. Flory at the *Bridgewater CB congregation in 1934. His pastorates were at *Frederick, MD; *Kokomo, IN; *New Carlisle, OH; *Harrisonburg, VA; and *Bridgewater, VA. Sherfy served a five-year term on the *General Board and on the Board of Bethany seminary, was chosen as Ohio's outstanding pastor of the year in 1948, and retired in 1978. He married Evelyn S. Clark in 1935; they had two children: Robert and Ellen. EFB

GM (May 16, 1936), cover; *Messenger* (Sept. 29, 1962) 8, 9, 14, (Feb. 1995) 31; W. E. Sherfey, *Sherfey Family in the United States* (1921), rev. by H. E. Sherfey (1948); *Virginia* (1973) index; F. F. Wayland, *Bridgewater College* (1993) index; *Bridgewater Brethren* (1978) 197; *NE. Ohio* (1963) 350.

Joseph R. Shultz. Ashland University collection.

Shultz, Joseph R. (BC), 1927–2003, denominational executive, pastor, seminary vice-president, university president. Joseph Shultz was born in Berlin, PA, the son of Harry and Ruth Shultz, and was raised in the *Berlin Brethren Church. He was a graduate of *Ashland College (BA, 1950), *Ashland Theol. Sem. (MRE, 1952), and Southwestern Baptist Theol. Sem. (EdD, 1954, upgrade to PhD, 1994). In 1962–63 he was an honors scholar at New College, U. of Edinburgh. He married Doris Virginia Hart in 1950; they are the parents of four children.

Shultz was ordained as an elder in *The Brethren Church in 1948 and pastored Brethren congregations in *Williamstown, OH (1948–52) and *Washington, DC (1956–62). He served as the executive secretary of the *Board of Christian Education (1954–56).

In 1963 Shultz began a long educational career with Ashland Theol. Sem., serving as dean and vice-president (1963–79), and then with Ashland U. as president (1979 –92). At both institutions he began his service at critical times, due, in both cases, to enrollment and financial con-

cerns. At both schools he instituted innovative ideas and programs that enabled those institutions to flourish under his leadership. With his guidance, Ashland seminary became one of the nation's largest, with enrollment exceeding 400 students when Frederick J. Finks assumed leadership on the seminary in 1992. ca. 800 students.

Shultz was active both in his denomination and in the church at large. He served as moderator of *General Conference in 1960 and as a member of the Board of Christian Education. He was a director on the boards of Jerusalem University College; EMERGE Counseling Center in Akron, OH; International Institute for Christian Studies; Friends World Ministries; and Ashland Theol. Sem. Foundation. He served on the Theology and Higher Education Commission of the *National Association of Evangelicals and was a founding director and treasurer of *Brethren Encyclopedia, Inc.

Joseph R. Shultz contributed articles to journals and reference works, and authored two books, *The Soul of the Symbols* (1966), a theological study of *communion, and *Ashland, From College to University* (1997). DRS

J. R. Shultz, *Ashland, From College to University* (1997); J. R. Shultz, *Final Report—1962–1992*, (1992); *Who's Who in America* (1988–89), 2: 2841; A. T. Ronk, *History BC* (1968) 462, 265, 478, 490; *BLT* 30 (Summer, 1985) 145–47.

Shuman, L. Herman (OGBB), b. 1916, farmer, minister, author. The son of Luther and Florence Miller Shuman, Herman Shuman resided near Pendleton, Madison Co., IN, his entire life. He was baptized Aug. 25, 1935, near the *Beech Grove OGBB meetinghouse. United in marriage on March 28, 1937, to Ruby Reavis, daughter of Henry and Mary Long Reavis, they raised four children. Ruby Shuman died in 1994. Shuman was called to the office of deacon (1942), to the ministry (1943), and to the eldership (1951). While he was yet in his 30s, just as church responsibilities were increasing, his father's blindness caused full responsibility for the family farm to pass to him. He was frequently called away to preach and was tireless in his ministry. He said he soon determined that if he wanted to keep the weeds out of his ministry, he must let some weeds grow in his fence rows.

Herman Shuman was chosen to Standing Committee (1972–92) and named assistant reading clerk (1973–74) and reading clerk (1975–92). He had nonresident oversight of two congregations: Don River, Maple, Ontario (1955–81) and *Painter Creek, OH (1961–76) and resident oversight of his home congregation, *Beech Grove, IN (1987–2001). Shuman authored *Highlights and Heartaches of Brethren Pioneers* (1981), *The Passover, The Lord's Supper, The Communion* (1986), and *The Country Preacher: The Life and Ministry of Elder Solomon Stoner* (1992). He wrote numerous articles for *Vindicator* and other church publications, including *The Brethren Encyclopedia. Being very interested in church history, in 2003 he was gathering material on central Indiana and the origin of the Beech Grove congregation. DLSh

Vindicator (1943) 122, (1944) 157, (1978) 351; *Old Order Notes* No. 4 (Spring, 1981) 32.

Skiles, Clement S. (OGBB), b. 1917, the son of David A. and Hettie Milyard Skiles, was born at Rossville, IN. In 1940 Skiles married Esther (Hettie) Marie, daughter of Ezra and Anna Myer Flora; they had three children. Skiles farmed at Flora, IN, where he was elected to the ministry in 1948 and ordained to the eldership in 1958. Clement

and Esther Skiles experienced double grief by losing their 19-year-old son, Gary, by accident (1960) and a 19-year-old grandson, David, also by accident (2000). Clement Skiles began serving on the Standing Committee in 1967 and was foreman in 1975–96. His companion, Esther, died in 1986. He then married Virginia Frantz Blocher in 1988. It is significant that Skiles is numbered among the few elders whose counsel is much sought. He served as nonresident oversight at *Eight Mile, KS, for ten years; at *Beech Grove, IN, for ten years; at *Mud Valley, IL, for three years; and at *Pigg River, VA, for six years. He also served on special committees sent to four congregations. Skiles has served as oversight elder of his home congregation, *Bachelor Run, IN, since 1978. FWB

Vindicator (1948) 252, (1960) 286, (1986) 316, (2000) 254; *Minutes of Annual Meeting (OGBB)* (1967–2000); *Old Order Notes* No. 4 (Spring, 1981) 33.

Smeltzer, Mary Blocher (CB), b. 1915, advocate for women and oppressed peoples. The daughter of H. D. and Evalena Porter Blocher, Mary Blocher was born Oct. 17 in Taft, TX, but grew up in La Verne, CA. After graduating from *La Verne College (BA, 1937) and Claremont Graduate School (MA, 1939), she married *Ralph Emerson Smeltzer (1916–76) in 1940. They taught in California public high schools, then at the *Manzanar Relocation Center for *Americans of Japanese ancestry (1942–43). The Smeltzers directed work for the *Brethren Service Committee to resettle Japanese-Americans in Chicago, IL, and Brooklyn, NY, (1943–44). From 1944 to 1971, Mary Smeltzer raised a family; their children were Janet Marilyn Smeltzer (1944–53), Martha Smeltzer West (b. 1946), Kenneth Kline Smeltzer (b. 1951), and Patricia Smeltzer Himes (b. 1952); she taught school and was active in race relations, local politics, and the *Elgin, IL, Highland Avenue CB.

One of the first coordinators of the *Womaen's Caucus (1972–76), she became active in raising consciousness and promoting the leadership of women in the church. She served as the first female moderator for the Mid-Atlantic District (1976) and was chair of the board of the *Washington, DC, CB (1975–76). After Ralph Smeltzer's death in 1976, she served in the *Peace Corps (1977–79) in Botswana and as director of the *World Friendship Center (1981–82) in Hiroshima, Japan. In 2000 she remains active in peace and justice efforts in Southern California as a member of the *La Verne CB and edits the newsletter of the Peace With Justice Center of Pomona Valley, CA. KKS

Messenger (Dec., 1981) 10–11, 13–14, (Nov., 1988) 9–12, (April, 1996) 3, (June, 1997) 14; D. F. Durnbaugh, ed., *Present Age* (1975) 123–30; J. K. Kreider, *A Cup of Cold Water: The Story of Brethren Service* (2001) 183, 399; P. Smith, *Democracy on Trial: The Japanese-American Evacuation in World War II* (1995); S. L. Longenecker, *Selma's Peacemaker* (1987).

Snell, William Harrison (FGBC), b. 1932, pastor, administrator. Born in Arkport, NY, William Snell graduated from Moody Bible Inst. (1954), *Grace College (BA, 1955), and *Grace Theol. Sem. (MDiv, 1958). He married Helen Jean Swallen of Alliance, OH, in 1954.

Snell served the *Grace Brethren Home Mission Council in Needham, MA (1958–60). He pastored the *Meyersdale, PA, GBC (1960–68) and the *Martinsburg, PA, GBC (1968–90). In Oct. 1990, he became Eastern Field Director of Church Planting and Development for Grace Brethren Home Missions, where he served until March 1997. He joined the pastoral staff of the *Worthington, OH, Columbus GBC, in 1998.

William Snell served as president of the National Ministerium (1979–80) and as moderator of the Fellowship of Grace Brethren Churches (1992–93). He sat on the Christian Education National Board (1982–90) and on the Grace Brethren Home Missions Council Board of Directors (1982–90). RTC

Personal knowledge; *Annual (FGBC)* (1968–98).

Pfaltzgraff Pottery and the Brethren

Is there a connection between the Pfaltzgraff pottery company and the Pfaltzgraff family in the Church of the Brethren? Actually. . . yes!

The Pfaltzgraff potters document their beginning with Johann George Pfaltzgraff, born on May 5, 1808, in Frielendorf, a village in the Schwalm Valley in the German state of Hessen-Kassel. While Johann George was listed as a potter in church records at the time of his marriage in 1833, prospects for potters in that area of Germany were bleak, so within months the newly married couple immigrated to the United States. Birth records for their second child, in Oct. 1835, show that they had moved to Conewago Township, York County, PA, had joined the German Baptist Brethren, and Johann George was operating a pottery business. As Conewago Twp. records indicate that a certain George Falsgraff had begun a pottery business there in 1811, it is presumed that there must have been some family connection that brought Johann George Pfaltzgraff to the same area in the same trade.

The pottery business passed from Johann George to his three eldest sons, John B., George B., and Henry B. Pfaltzgraff. John diversified, beginning successful coal and tobacco businesses, in addition to pottery. John married Susan Keeney, and they were evidently active in Brethren congregations, helping to found the missionary church later called the *York, PA, Second CB. It is through John that the current *Church of the Brethren Pfaltzgraffs trace their roots. *Roy E. Pfaltzgraff, Sr., who with his wife, Violet Hackman Pfaltzgraff, served as life-long missionaries in *Nigeria, is John's great-grandson. Roy, retired from the mission field, is a minister at *Middle Creek CB (PA), and two of his children are ministers in the Church of the Brethren, Roy Pfaltzgraff, Jr. in *Haxtun, CO, and Kathryn Pfaltzgraff Eller in *La Verne, CA.

The pottery business did not stay with John B. Pfaltzgraff, but eventually passed on to his brother George's grandson-in-law, Louis Appell. It was then transferred to Louis Appell, Jr., who is the current (2004) chair of the Pfaltzgraff Company. The Appells still recognize the Pfaltzgraffs as cousins. EPE/KPE

D. A. Walsh and P. Stetler, Pfaltzgraff: *America's Potter* (1989); information from Roy E. Pfaltzgraff, Sr.; oral Pfaltzgraff family history.

Soldotna, AK, Peninsula Grace Brethren Church was organized in May 1983 with ca. 60 people from the *Kenai GBC. The first building was constructed later that fall, and a multi-purpose gymnasium/classroom building was constructed in 1988. Known for its children, youth, and music ministries, the church grew to an average attendance of 275 in 1998. Pastors who served the congregation were Howard M. Snively (1983–88) and Daniel E.

Thornton (1989–). Associate pastors were Theodore Scott Franchino (1985–88, 1991–97), Daniel E. Thornton (1986–88 and interim), Gary E. Leiter (1989–94), Jeremy Foster (1996–97), Donald C. Nagle (1996–98) and Charles Gash Thornton (1996–). DET/JRY

Congregational records; *Annual* (*FGBC*) (1984–98).

Sollenberger, Dorcas Elaine Mock (CB), b. 1931, churchwoman, dairy farmer, educator, columnist, county commissioner, homemaker. A native of Pittsburgh, PA, Elaine Mock was baptized and nurtured in the *Dunnings Creek CB congregation, and was graduated from *Juniata College (AB, 1951). She married Ray A. Sollenberger in 1954; they have three children: Beth, Lori, and Leon. She served as chair of the *General Board and as *Annual Conference moderator in 1989 and in 1998 (appointed because of a resignation). Under her strong and stable leadership, the Church of the Brethren was challenged to recommit itself to open communication, unity, graciousness, and Christian friendship. Making her home in Bedford Co., PA, and an active member of the *Everett congregation, she served as district moderator, helped run the family dairy business, served as chair of the school board, as a county commissioner, and on a number of other community boards. MAMu

M. Pennsylvania (1981) 13, 299; *Messenger* (Aug., 1988) 14–17, (May, 1989) 12–15, (Sept., 1989) 12–15, (May, 1991) 21–23, (Oct., 1996) 22–24, (Aug., 1997) 24–25, (Jan., 1998) 14–17, (Aug., 1998) 14; P. Brubaker, *She Hath Done What She Could* (1985) 166; D. F. Durnbaugh, *Fruit of the Vine* (1997) 548; *Juniata College: The Alumni Record* (1958) 206.

Solomon, George Walton (BC), 1920–85, pastor, church leader. George Solomon served as a pastor in *The Brethren Church from 1951 to 1985. He graduated from *Ashland College (BA, 1954) and *Ashland Theol. Sem. (BD, 1957). Ordained at the *Ashland BC in 1955, he was a dedicated and hard working pastor whose ministry had a tremendous impact on the lives of many people, young and old.

Solomon was strongly committed to The Brethren Church. He served as moderator of the *General Conference in 1957 and again in 1985. Pastorates included congregations at *Gretna, OH (1951–57); *Hagerstown, MD (1957–63); *Louisville, OH (1963–67); *Ashland Park Street, OH (1967–73); *Derby, KS (1973–79); and *Milledgeville, IL (1979–85).

Solomon also served on many church boards and committees at district and national levels. He was active in recruiting students for Ashland Theol. Seminary. In 1991 the seminary dedicated a new library addition to honor his leadership. A George Solomon Memorial Scholarship Fund was established by Brethren and family members at Ashland Theol. Seminary.

George Solomon was married on Sept. 6, 1942, to Jessie Mae Words; they were the parents of eight children, five daughters and three sons. One son is a Brethren elder and one daughter is married to a Brethren elder. LAS

BE (Dec. 17, 1955) 9–10, (May 13, 1961) 5, (Aug. 4, 1962) 23, (Dec., 1985) 11, 22, (May, 1986) 17, (Feb., 1992) 15; *TBE* 3 (1984) 1778.

Solomon, Kenneth LeRoy and Jeannette Ruth DeLozier Solomon (BC), missionaries. Born Sept. 11, 1926, in Chadville, PA, Kenneth Solomon was the fourth of eight children of LeRoy Quinter and Grace Marie Bryson Solomon. He received degrees from *Ashland

College (BA, 1952; BS, 1955), *Ashland Theol. Sem. (BD, 1957), and Hartford Sem. Foundation (MA, 1958). In 1951 he married Jeannette Ruth DeLozier (1928–87), the youngest daughter of *Arthur Lee and Margaret Alice Himes DeLozier. Born July 17 in *Ashland, OH, Jeannette Solomon graduated from Ashland College in 1950.

Kenneth Solomon served *Ashland, OH, Garber Memorial Church as a student pastor (1949–52), and pastored the *Williamstown (OH) First BC (1952) and the *Fremont (OH) First BC (1955–57), prior to leaving for *Argentina in Oct. 1958. In 1965, he co-founded (with H. Raymond Aspinall) *Eden Bible Institute in Soldini, near Rosario, Argentina. Taking a lengthy sabbatical leave, Solomon studied at Southern Baptist Theol. Sem. in Louisville, KY, earning a Graduate Specialist in Religious Education degree in 1969.

The Solomons served in Argentina (1958–72), then began preparations for starting a new Brethren mission work in Medellin, *Colombia, in Nov. 1973. They returned to the U.S. in 1981, due in part to Jeannette Solomon's poor health, settling in Sarasota, FL, where they provided much needed leadership to the young Hispanic Brethren work, *Iglesia Hispana de los Hermanos, which was started by the *Sarasota First Brethren Church. Solomon served Iglesia Hispana as pastor (1981–88), then joined the staff of the Sarasota First BC as associate pastor (1988–91).

The Solomons had four children: Timothy, Rebecca (Abbott), Joel, and Margaret (Dodds). Jeannette Solomon died unexpectedly on Dec. 29, 1987, in Sarasota, and in 1988, Kenneth married Carolyn Elaine Bearinger Dowdy. He returned to Colombia with his wife, where they served in Medellin (1991–95). Returning to Sarasota, FL, they actively serve both the Sarasota First BC and the Hispanic congregation, Iglesia Hispana de los Hermanos with Solomon as mentor to the Hispanic pastor. He also served as a prison chaplain in Manatee Co., FL. TLS

Interview of K. L. Solomon; A. T. Ronk, *History of Brethren Missionary Movements* (1971), index, and *History of the Brethren Church* (1968), 495–97; *My Missionary Partners* (1976); *Ashland [OH] Times Gazette* (Jan. 19, 1970); *Annual* (*BC*) (1981–2000).

South America Theological Seminary. ATS collection.

South America Theological Seminary (BC) has its roots in the *Eden Bible Institute which served The Iglesia de Los Hermanos en la Argentina (BC) until it closed in the mid 1980s. In 1995, Eduardo and Mariela Rodrigeuz, from the *Colon Church (BC), enrolled in *Ashland Theol. Sem. and in 1996 were commissioned by the Iglesia de los Hermanos to reopen the institute and be-

come its directors. A commissioning service was conducted at the 1997 General Conference in South Bend, IN.

A delegation from Ashland, OH, including Frederick J. Finks and Harley Gerber from Ashland Theol. Sem., along with Emanuel W. Sandberg and Reilly R. Smith from the National Office (BC), arrived in Argentina in Oct. 1997. Formational meetings were held in Rosario with leadership from the Iglesia de los Hermanos, including José Rivero, president of the Executive Board and president of the Argentine Brethren Church; Hector Labanca, pastor of the Rosario congregation; Victor Alesandroni, president of the Missionary Committee; Billy Romanengui, pastor of Corral De Bustos; Guillermo Rojas, secretary to the Board of Elders; Malva de Rivero, president of the Women's Committee; and Allen Baer, Brethren missionary.

South America Theol. Sem. (STS) was created by a joint Board of Trustees with the model of education patterned after the theological education by extension (TEE) design. Eduardo and Mariela Rodriguez were named directors of STS, and the school officially opened on Nov. 5, 1998. In 1997 the Brethren Conference (BC) provided an offering exceeding $25,000 to support the founding of STS. In Estes Park, CO, in 2000 a conference offering of $53,000 was given to support the STS classroom project. In addition, $26,000 was given for the development of the library.

The dedication of the STS headquarters in Colon, Argentina, was held on May 19, 2001. Marcela Rivero and Monica Santiago completed their seminary degrees at Ashland Theol. Sem. and joined the STS faculty in 2001. Student enrollment in 2002 was 73.

Two meetings of South American leaders were held at Estes Park, CO, in Aug. 2000 and at Colon, Argentina, in Oct. 2001 resulting in the establishment of extensions of STS in *Peru, *Colombia, *Paraguay, and *Mexico. FJFi
BE (March, 1997) 7, (Sept., 1997) 6, (Feb., 2000) 11, (July/Aug., 2000) 6–7, (Sept., 2000) 6, (July/Aug., 2001) 6, (Sept., 2001) 8; A. T. Ronk, *History of Brethren Missionary Movements* (1971) 96, 98–103.

South Bend, IN, Iglesia Evangelica Emanuel (CB). Iglesia Evangelica Emanuel began as a joint project of the *Church of the Brethren, *General Conference Mennonite Church, and the *Mennonite Church to plant an Anabaptist congregation in the Hispanic community of South Bend, IN. During the summer of 1984, several Goshen College students, under the supervision of Fabricio Guzman, visited the Hispanic community to determine interest in a new church. One of the students, Gilberto Gaytan, became the first pastor in May 1985. The congregation was chartered on March 16, 1986. In 1993 the congregation divided, with Iglesia Evangelica Emanuel continuing as a Spanish-speaking congregation and Manos de Cristo became an English-speaking house church devoted to teaching English as a second language to the Hispanic community. Manos de Cristo was granted fellowship status in 1998. Iglesia Evangelic Emanuel remained small and met in rented facilities until it closed in the fall 2000. It was formally disorganized in Sept. 2001. HDK
Congregational records; CB district records; *South Bend [IN] Tribune* (Jan. 11, 1986) A 13; *BLT* 36 (Summer, 1991) 170; interviews with R. Finney (CB), R. Larue (GCMC), and W. Fahrer (MC).

STAKE (BC), an acronym for Saturation of the Target Area for Kingdom Extension, was an attempt to plant multiple Brethren Churches in the Orlando, FL, area in the mid-1990s. The Florida District proposed planting five small groups that would each be the seedbed for a new congregation. The scale of the vision and the small size of the Florida District led them to use volunteer workers exclusively.

Kerry Scott arrived in 1994 with his family to provide leadership to a group of six other workers. The difficulty of beginning a new church while working full time soon became evident, and Scott resigned from the project. Others resigned due to various circumstances. Although three remaining workers continued the ministry for three years, they were unable to assimilate new members, and they closed the work in 1998. DLSt
Personal information.

Stevens Hill Community Church of the Brethren, PA. In Jan. 1989 the *Stevens Hill Church near Elizabethtown, PA, was closed at the suggestion of the District Church Development Commission. In Oct. 1989 it was reopened by several people who felt led to begin a new fellowship. The old congregation was dissolved and a new congregation, now called Stevens Hill Community, was begun. By visiting homes in the community, the church grew to 92 members in 1999 and an average weekly attendance of 125. Eighty percent of those now attending were not active in another place of worship before coming to Stevens Hill Community. Members continue to reach out to others in the community who do not presently attend a place of worship. In 2000, William W. Longenecker was serving as part-time pastor. WWL
Congregational records; *Yearbook (CB)* (1900–2000).

***Stewardship** is an important concept for the Brethren bodies. *The Brethren Church adopted a stewardship section as part of its 1983 *Centennial Statement affirming that God has entrusted us with resources to manage during our lifetimes and instructs believers to entrust all back to God, to be rich in good deeds, generous, and willing to share. It comments, "Because our culture has clouded the difference between real and perceived needs, the believer must learn to be content with what God has provided and renounce selfish materialism."

The 1985 *Annual Conference of the *Church of the Brethren adopted a paper, *Christian Stewardship: Responsible Freedom*. It outlines God's creation and ultimate ownership of all of our resources and gifts and uses the biblical metaphor of the steward to illustrate the individual's responsibility and accountability before God for their use. Believers are to be wise and faithful stewards of each day, of their physical bodies, of their energies, and of the earth and its resources. Christians are stewards of the gospel of Jesus Christ.

While not limiting Christian stewardship to financial resources, the stewardship of material resources is emphasized as an important area. Believers are called to share their material possessions and money as an act of gratitude for the blessings they have received, as a ministry of love in sharing with others, and out of a personal journey of *discipline and maturity in faith. The biblical model of tithing is affirmed, not as a law, but as a proven and useful spiritual discipline out of Brethren heritage.

The CB stewardship paper formed the conceptual basis for five years of high-profile efforts at stewardship education in the denomination in (1985–89). Using the name *Adventure in Mission*, a broad network of national, regional, district, and congregational volunteers was

Beyond the rivers of Sudan. BHLA collection. Photograph by Kermon Thomasson.

formed and an in-depth program of congregational training instituted. At its peak over 600 congregations participated in the Adventure in Mission emphasis.

Other Brethren bodies also taught stewardship principles to their members in comparable ways, while not using the above-mentioned programs. DEMi

Personal information; Eugene F. Roop, *Let the Rivers Run: Stewardship and the Biblical Story* (1991); *The Centennial Statement of the Brethren Church* (1983); *Christian Stewardship: Responsible Freedom* (1985).

Sudan (CB). The Church of the Brethren mission entered Sudan at the request of the Sudan Council of Churches (SCC) in 1980. The CB committed itself to strengthen the ability of existing Sudanese churches to be faithful and to spread the gospel in their own context. This approach sought to avoid creating additional divisions between ethnic groups and churches.

Joining J. Roger Schrock (b. 1945) and Carolyn Pieratt Schrock (b. 1945) in the community health program at Mayom, Upper Nile, Steven P. Metzler (b. 1954) and Karen Glick Metzler (b. 1955) developed wells and Ruth Goehle (b. 1944) served as medical consultant. By 1983, fighting in the area prompted withdrawal of staff from Mayom. The CB refocused on theological education by extension (TEE), led by Kenneth O. Holderread (b. 1938) and Elsie Lucore Holderread (b. 1936). During the severe droughts of the mid-1980s, Mervin Keeney (b. 1951) and Gwen Brumbaugh Keeney (b. 1959) managed relief and development assistance for displaced Sudanese and Ethiopian/Eritrean refugees. R. Jan Thompson (b. 1935) and Roma Jo Mickey Thompson (b. 1935) followed in relief and TEE work.

As Sudan became increasingly divided into territory controlled by the Sudanese government and ground held by southern forces, the southern churches formed New Sudan Council of Churches (NSCC). In 1991, Roger and Carolyn Schrock became the first NSCC executive secretary and communications staff. By May 1992, government military overran Torit, Eastern Equatoria, forcing the relocation of NSCC to Nairobi, Kenya.

Because of continuing war, displacement of peoples, and a revived slave trade, the CB responded with peacemaking and advocacy activities for the people and churches caught in this crisis. Many CB congregations prepared emergency relief kits for distribution among southern Sudanese. Philip W. Rieman (b. 1944) and Louise Baldwin Rieman (b. 1946) established the first NSCC peace staff. Their peacemaking training stirred local initiative for regional peacemaking conferences. Merlyn Kettering (b. 1942) also served as a NSCC consultant.

Lester Boleyn (b. 1937) and Esther Frantz Boleyn (b. 1936) accepted leadership for a Nuer *Bible translation effort in 1988. CB staff felt a special kinship with the Nuer people from working together at Mayom. In Jan. 2000, the plane carrying the CB delegation and the first complete Nuer Bibles into southern Sudan crashed upon landing, but miraculously no one was injured. Praise and worshipful celebrations were offered, consistent with the vibrant faith of the severely challenged, but growing Sudanese churches. MBK

CB General Board files; personal experience; "Church of the Brethren in Mission: Special Interpretive Report on Sudan" (1990); C. Cayford and M. Keeney, "Sudan: Hunger for Peace" (1995); *Messenger* (1981–2000) indexes.

Sugar Grove Old German Baptist Brethren Church, OH, located southeast of Covington, Miami County. Because of the continued growth of the *Covington OGBB congregation and to better care for all members, the congregation decided to reorganize into two separate districts. This change was effected on Jan. 7, 1989, with each district agreeing to use on alternating Sundays the brick building that was constructed in 1950. This arrange-

ment has continued in a very satisfactory manner, with maintenance expenses shared equally by the two congregations. The membership of the new Sugar Grove congregation when organized was 180. Elder-in-charge has been Carl W. Bowman, with Roger K. Rapp, Gerald G. Stull, Brian K. Stull, and Rodney D. Sprenkel active in the ministry. Membership in 2000 was 202. CWBo

Vindicator 120.2 (1989) 54; congregational records.

Theological Practorium, The (CGBCI) provides theological education within *Conservative Grace Brethren Churches International. The Theological Practorium is a learning concept for preparing pastors in both scholarly studies and pastoral practice. This approach was employed by Jesus with his disciples while he conducted his ministry with the multitudes. The apostle Paul also followed the same plan with his theological students in Ephesus (Acts 19:8–10).

The Theological Practorium is a two-dimensional educational plan. All theology courses are presented following the plan of *Alva J. McClain, founder of *Grace Theol. Seminary. Biblical theology is understood as the study of God as revealed solely from the Scriptures. In Hebrews 11:3 is found the model for this "Bible, the whole Bible, and nothing but the Bible" approach.

The Practorium focuses on biblical theology, with one course presented in full concentration before moving on to the next course. The classes are presented in the evenings to men who qualify according to the requirements found in the pastoral epistles. The core courses range over historical theology and biblical studies, emphasizing Christology, soteriology, ecclesiology, homiletics, exegesis, and related topics. Special studies include "Brethren Beliefs and Practices," and "Principles and Concerns in African Missions."

The other dimension of the Practorium is the field experience or practice of ministry. Each student is responsible for earning his education by his weekly church work. In reality, the Practorium is a barter system in operation; no tuition is required of the students, but they are responsible for purchasing their books and materials. Students are required to use their education in the church, which is also the teaching institution. They serve in every area of church ministry. This program is an exchange of service for service.

Pastor J Hudson Thayer was the architect of the original Theological Practorium. He presented the idea to his congregation, the *Mansfield, OH, GBC in 1979. The congregation approved the plan for fall 1980. The first graduating class in 1982 produced four Grace Brethren pastors: John E. Bryant, Roger Bartlett, David Blevins, and Jeffrey Smith. Many more graduates have since joined the ranks of pastors and missionaries prepared by the Theological Practorium. A *Manual of Procedure* was prepared so that other Conservative Grace Brethren Churches would have a model for establishing an "in church" training of "faithful men, who shall be able to teach others also" (2 Tim. 2:2). JHT

Personal knowledge.

*Theology. In the last decades of the 20th century, some Brethren appeared to be tossed to and fro by winds of doctrine. They encountered a climate of pluralism, media-acclaimed issues, and life-styles propelled by consumerism. The growing presence of other world religions and manifestations of New Age phenomena surfaced fears of compromised faith. Members of Brethren bodies generally maintained a stance of *noncreedalism, but they anchored it by reclaiming the New Testament as their guide for faith and life. An *Annual Conference of the *Church of the Brethren (1998) rejected both boundless tolerance and judgmental exclusiveness.

The paper strongly reaffirmed the New Testament as the "rule of faith and practice" and explained that this did not imply a rejection of the Old Testament. In 1984 a *Centennial Statement of *The Brethren Church summarized the faith and life of the church. This ten-page statement was not meant to be a creed but rather a milepost in the spiritual journey of the BC. This revealed a different mood than the CB Annual Conference (1994), which respectfully rejected a query calling for a statement of basic beliefs.

Those concerned about correct doctrine focused on *Christology as a defense against alien intrusions. Consultants hired by the CB produced a widely-used phrase for use as a motto: "Continuing the work of Jesus. Peacefully. Simply. Together." However, Annual Conferences (1994, 1995) adopted statements naming Jesus as head of the church, the Son of God, and affirming the uniqueness of Jesus Christ as the only divine Lord and Savior. Differences in emphases led to doctrinal variations. Is the focus on the exclusive or inclusive Christ? Is the gospel primarily about relationships with God, Jesus, his way, and others, or does it consist of propositions about Christ, acceptance of which are required for salvation?

Similar polarities sought doctrinal agreement about the *Bible. The CB conference paper (1979) represented a strong consensus that the Bible is a trustworthy guide for faith and practice. The paper also revealed a lack of agreement on whether "trustworthy" means "inerrant." All CB branches espoused the authority of the Bible in matters of faith and practice. Differences remained, however, between those who appropriated higher criticism to better understand texts and others who treasured more literal interpretations and applications.

Leaders of The Brethren Church defined their denomination as evangelical, emphasizing a generally conservative theology, whereas the *Fellowship of Grace Brethren Churches and the *Conservative Grace Brethren Churches International espoused frankly fundamentalistic doctrines, especially in the earlier years of their fellowship. In more recent years, some Grace Brethren have aligned themselves with the *Evangelical movement. Although the *Dunkard Brethren and the *Old German Baptist Brethren are reluctant to codify theological beliefs, following the traditionally Brethren noncreedal stance, their teachings reject theological liberalism. Some aspects of *dispensationalism can be found among the latter.

As *charismatic and *Holy Spirit movements became less divisive, revivals of the doctrine of the Holy Spirit meshed with the quest for the *spiritual life. Mystical currents joined emphases on the fruit and gifts of the Spirit in prayer groups, retreat centers, and wider participation in congregational worship and life. A DB conference (1993), revising its statement about election and voluntary choice in salvation, placed a greater emphasis on the work of the Holy Spirit. The OGBB experienced divisiveness between some who stressed grace-only themes in salvation and those who held to obedience beliefs in faith and works.

In spite of the above tensions, most doctrinal positions

endured without fundamental shifts from the article on "Theology" in *TBE 2*. A renewed interest in Brethren *identity accompanied studies that confirmed *acculturation. *M. R. Zigler's inspired gathering of representatives of five Brethren bodies at *Tunker House in 1973 led to joint efforts to recover the heritage: a three-volume *Brethren Encyclopedia (1983–84), three *Brethren World Assemblies (1992, 1998, 2003), subsequent gatherings of historians, and a Brethren Encyclopedia board which published additional volumes including a Monograph Series. The recovery appropriated sources and historical writings by D. F. Durnbaugh, Dale R. Stoffer, and others. The 1989 BC General Conference appointed a committee to articulate clearly its faith and practice and pass on its heritage to succeeding generations.

Anabaptist ecclesiology abetted affirmations of the church as an extended caring community amidst damaging influences on the *family. Consistent with early Brethren practice, *baptism increasingly implied *ordination for ministries. Concepts of the *Believers Church led to concerns about the age of baptism, addressed by a CB conference committee (1980) but whose findings were generally ignored. Efforts to recover ordered *discipline by requiring triune immersion of new members contributed to a division of the Fellowship of Grace Brethren Churches, resulting in the formation of the Conservative Grace Brethren Churches International.

A major theological voice entered the Brethren ranks when James Wm. McClendon (1924–2000), a professor at Fuller Theol. Sem. of Southern Baptist background, joined the CB in the 1990s. Shortly before his death, the last of his three volumes of *Systematic Theology* (1986–2000) was published. In it he acknowledged his indebtedness to the work of Mennonite theologian and ethicist, John Howard Yoder (1927–97). McClendon's Anabaptist orientation is revealed by his weighting of themes in his comprehensive study; he assigned the first volume to "Ethics" ("How must the church live now to be really the church?"), the second to "Doctrine" ("What must the church teach now to be really the church?"), and the third to "Witness" ("How must the church testify now to be really the church?").

Service theology continued to bear fruit. An OGBB member acclaimed the *Habitat for Humanity program as designed for Old Order Brethren. The CB experienced the revival of *work camps, traveling peace teams, and *peace education programs. Anabaptist motifs of *discipleship continued to nurture biblical obedience to the way of suffering love. Pietist faith in the restoration of the entire creation bequeathed motifs for witness in movements for reconciliation and peace on earth. Both nonresisters and nonviolent resisters to evil imbibed an Anabaptist doctrine of *nonconformity in espousing faith in redemptive love instead of the culture's faith in redemptive violence. Discipleship themes influenced most Brethren, whether pre-millennial or not, to avoid dispensationalist interpretations which delay obedience to teachings of the *Sermon on the Mount until Jesus returns.

Brethren espoused theological identities such as fundamentalist, liberal, evangelical, and neo-orthodox. Some preferred such to being Brethren. Unapologetic members believed that being Brethren theologically does not easily coalesce with the other labels. Most could point to unique theological ingredients of the heritage.

Increasing affluence may help explain why Brethren were less concerned about sins of mammon such as greed and gluttony than sins related to *sexuality. They often were influenced by cultural preoccupations in dealing with issues such as *abortion and *homosexuality. However, the CB Annual Conference of 1997 adopted a paper on the *simple life and many Brethren shared with others concerns for health and the environment.

Along with honest and often heated differences, Brethren modeled a Pietist love theology with emphases on reconciliation and unity. During the *1998 Brethren World Assembly representatives of the Brethren groups testified to a greater sense of openness to other Brethren and fellow Christians. Gathering to explore common issues, the meeting experienced a foretaste of the unity of the Spirit in a bond of peace. DWBr

See also BIBLE; CHRISTOLOGY; EVANGELISM; HOLY SPIRIT; LIBERALISM; NEO-ORTHODOXY; PREMILLENIALISM.

E. F. Bittinger, ed., *Brethren in Transition* (1992); C. F. Bowman, *Brethren Society* (1995); C. F. Bowman and Stephen L. Longenecker, eds., *Anabaptist Currents* (1995); *BE* [series on "Understanding the Bible" (Sept., 1993–Sept., 1996); *BLT* [special issues], 35 (Winter, 1990), 36 (Fall, 1991), 39 (Summer 1994), 40 (Summer/Fall, 1995), 41 (Winter, 1996); 42 (Summer/Fall, 1997); 43 (Summer/Fall, 1998, 44 (Summer, 1999), 46 (Winter/Spring, 2001; Brethren Church, *A Centennial Statement* (1984); D. W. Brown, *Led by Word and Spirit* (1983), *Biblical Pacifism: A Peace Church Perspective* (1986), *Understanding Pietism,* rev. ed. (1996), and *Brethren Interactions with Twentieth Century Theologies* (forthcoming); B. Colijn and D. R. Stoffer, *Follow Him Gladly: A Brethren Course in Discipleship* (1991); J. Deeter, *Biblical Inspiration and Authority* (1980); D. F. Durnbaugh, *Fruit of the Vine* (1997); D. F. Durnbaugh, ed., *Church of the Brethren: Yesterday and Today* (1986) and *Report of the Proceedings of the [1992] Brethren World Assembly* (1994); D. R. Fitzkee, *Moving Toward the Mainstream* (1995); J. R. Flora, *The Message of Faith: An Exposition on the First Half of A Centennial Statement* (1996); Stephen L. Longenecker, ed., *The Dilemma of Anabaptist Piety* (1997); Harold S. Martin, *New Testament Beliefs and Practices: A Brethren Understanding* (1989); J. W. McClendon, Jr., *Systematic Theology,* three vols. (1986–2000) – interpretations of his theology are found in Mennonite Quarterly Review 74 (Oct., 2000) 503–10 (autobiographical) and 76 (Jan., 2002) 120–32; G. F. Snyder and K. M. Shaffer, Jr., *Texts in Transit II* (1991); D. R. Stoffer, *Background and Development of Brethren Doctrines* (1989); D. R. Stoffer, ed., *The Lord's Supper: Believers Church Perspectives* (1997) and *Report of the Proceedings of the 1998 Brethren World Assembly* (1999).

Thompson, Joel Kent (CB), 1933–94, missionary, ecumenist, church and hospital administrator. Born Aug. 10, the son of George and Lois Thompson of Ludlow Falls, OH, Joel Thompson died in the crash of USAir flight 427 near Pittsburgh, Sept. 8.

Thompson graduated from *Manchester College (1955) and *Bethany Biblical Sem. (1959). He was an ordained (1955) minister who served as pastor in Roann, IN (1954–56). He married Phyllis Yount in 1954; they had three children: Kevin, Renee, and Kraig. They were later divorced. On Dec. 18, 1982, he married Janine Katonah.

From 1959 to 1980, Thompson was called by the *CB General Board to various positions: interim director of *Brethren Volunteer Service; theological teacher in Ambon, *Indonesia; director of mission education and recruitment; executive of *World Ministries Commission; and executive of *General Services Commission and Brethren Pension Plan. He also served a term as vice-president of the *National Council of Churches and chair of its Division of Overseas Ministries.

Joel Thompson teaching in Indonesia (1961). BHLA collection.

In 1991, after 11 years as a hospital administrator in the Chicago area, Thompson became director of benefits for the *Brethren Benefit Trust. His mentoring skills and gifts of executive leadership were widely acknowledged by employees and colleagues. A Joel K. Thompson Memorial Endowment for Peace and Service has been established with the General Board. HER

Messenger (Dec., 1980) 1, (Oct., 1984) 8, (Dec., 1991) 8, (Dec., 1994) 18; BHLA, biog. Files; D. F. Durnbaugh, ed., *Church of the Brethren: Yesterday and Today* (1986), 152, 154, and *Fruit of the Vine* (1997), 565; *Who's Who in Religion,* 2nd ed. (1977) 662.

Thompson, Robert W. (FGBC), 1924–93, pastor, home missions leader. Born in Colorado, Robert Thompson served as an Army Air Force pilot, flying B-29 bombers during World War II. While in military service, he married his high-school sweetheart, Betty Carter. After the war he worked for Proctor and Gamble Co. for 15 years. When he and his wife were converted, they joined the *Long Beach, CA, First BC. Thompson attended the *Bible Institute of Los Angeles (BIOLA) and graduated from Talbot Theol. Sem. in 1962. He planted the *Westminster, CA, GBC in 1959 while a student and continued there as pastor after graduation.

After seven years as a pastor, Thompson became Western field director for *Grace Brethren Home Missions (GBHM). In 1985, after 19 years as field director, he was appointed executive director of GBHM, serving until his retirement in 1989. He served as the moderator of *FGBC (1976–77). RTC

BMH (July 15, 1993) 13; Annual (FGBC) (1959–89).

Tók'ahookaadí Church. *See* **Lybrook, NM, Tók'a-hookaadí CB**.

Trappe, PA, Tri-County Grace Brethren Church. Following the combined efforts of the *New Holland and *Penn Valley *FGBC congregations in 1983, the congregation was organized by a core group of 12 persons. The church first met in the Humane Fire Company facilities in Royersford. In 1984 the congregation relocated to rented quarters at Caroline T. Moorehead's Catering in Trappe. Pastors who have served the congregation are Thomas Carlson (1983), Gene DeJongh (1984–86), and Kenneth I. Cosgrove (1986–). In 1999, the church had 20 members. KIC/JRY

Congregational records; *Annual (FGBC)* (1999).

Turner, Charles W. (FGBC), (1926–2004), pastor, administrator. Born in Akron, OH, Charles Turner graduated from Bob Jones U. (BA, 1948) and from *Grace Theol. Sem. (MDiv, 1951).

Turner pastored Grace Brethren Churches in *Flora, IN, (1952–56) and *Rittman, OH, (1956–70). He served as assistant secretary to the *FGBC National Conference (1960), president of the National Ministerial Association (1975), and FGBC moderator (1975–76). He also held memberships on the Ministers Retirement Board and *Brethren Missionary Herald Board (1964–70).

In 1970, Turner became executive director and general manager of Brethren Missionary Herald, Inc., a position he held until retirement in 1993. The BMH Book Division began under his leadership, publishing or co-publishing over 150 books, including three that he wrote: *Wise Words in a Wicked World* (1977), *Pulpit Words for Pew People* (1978), and *My Favorite Reflections* ([1979]). The bookstore ministry expanded from Winona Lake, IN, to the opening of stores in Indianapolis, IN, and Columbus, OH. He was editor of *Herald Magazine,* contributing editorials for 23 years (1970–93).

Charles W. Turner. Brethren Encyclopedia collection.

Turner was vice president of the *Brethren Encyclopedia, Inc. Board of Directors from its beginning and has also been a member of its Editorial Board. In retirement, Turner continued as consultant to the Board of the Brethren Missionary Herald and as secretary of the Board of GBC Media. RTC

Personal information; *Frontiers* (1972) 201; *Annual (FGBC)* (1952–98); *Who's Who in Religion* 2nd ed. (1977) 675.

*Urban Ministry. The *Church of the Brethren's urban ministry moved back and forth in the last years of the 20th century. The early 1980s saw several urban developments: two consultations, the merger of the urban and the Hispanic portfolios, and the loss of the CB's first African-American urban ministry staff person. The mid-decade witnessed the creation of an urban education program, Education for Urban Ministry (EFUM). EFUM trained ca.

Urban Ministries Consultation 1996. BHLA collection.

12 congregations for urban ministry, between 1984 and the early 1990s. In 1990, *Annual Conference approved a major paper on Brethren and Black Americans; little of the paper was ever implemented. The Urban Ministry portfolio sat dormant (1992–94). In the next two years the faces of urban and ethnic congregations were apparent in several urban peace tours, the growth of sister-church relationships, musical concerts at *Annual Conferences, and another major urban consultation. The staff position was eliminated again, along with other ethnic-related ministries, in the General Board's redesign of 1996–97. At the 1998 Annual Conference, leaders from diverse urban congregations gathered to rebuild, and the Cross Cultural Ministries Team (CCMT) was born, a grouping of multicultural and urban congregations intent on leadership development, financial stability, and new church development. The CCMT, informally sanctioned but without formal CB status, expresses the programmatic and mission arm of the CB in the beginning of the 21st century.

Most of the urban churches in *The Brethren Church have continued their existence during this period. New Hispanic congregations have been planted in Sarasota, FL; Tucson, AZ; and Pasadena, CA. Nearly all of the established urban churches have experienced major demographic shifts in the last four decades, with middle-class white families moving to the suburbs. Responses to this development have been varied. In a few cases new church complexes were built in suburban locations and the urban buildings were sold. In others, the congregations chose to remain in their urban settings, though this frequently led to only minimal success in reaching the new residents in the area. In one case (*Washington, DC, Southeast Christian Fellowship) the congregation committed itself to minister to the surrounding African-American population. Here, an African-American pastor was brought in and the church made a very successful transition from a small, struggling white congregation to a thriving Black congregation. In addition, the denominational leadership has, as part of its vision for the new century, committed itself to a more concerted urban ministry to Hispanics and African-Americans.

The experiences of the *Fellowship of Grace Brethren Churches and the *Conservative Grace Brethren Churches International are similar to those of The Brethren Church. *Dunkard Brethren and *Old German Baptist Brethren remain in their largely rural configurations, although metropolitan sprawl has increasingly encroached on their once isolated settings. OR/DRS

Minutes (*CB*) (1980–84) 32, 155–157, 473–74, 488, 634 (1985–89) 38, 228–29, 377, 565, 728, (1990–94) 37, 124, 193, 312–19, 376, 523, 671, (1995–98) 30, 32, 199, 454; [BC] *Centennial Statement* (1984); D. F. Durnbaugh, *Fruit of the Vine* (1997) 518–19.

Valley Brethren-Mennonite Heritage Center, The. Brethren and Mennonites have lived in the Shenandoah Valley (VA) for over 200 years. During that time, they created a rich heritage and a major center of religious, educational, and commercial life. They currently comprise ca. one-fourth of the population of Rockingham County.

In 1998 Shenandoah Mennonite Historians, seeing the need to celebrate the vital life and faith of Anabaptists in the Valley, proposed that Brethren and Mennonites work together to create a heritage center. The following year, The Valley Brethren-Mennonite Heritage Center Board was organized with its 18 members equally divided among the two groups. Its first two chairpersons were Calvin W. Redekop and Robert E. Alley.

In 2001, 11 acres were purchased on the west side of Garbers Church Road at the south edge of Harrisonburg, a quarter mile equidistant from Garbers Church and Weavers Church in the heart of the two faith communities. The 1854 house of Mennonite Bishop Martin Burkholder

was donated by the Brethren Daniel Myers family. Other gifts were the Turner Mill which had both Mennonite and Brethren owners during its nearly 200-year history, the 1829 Weaver log house, and a one-room schoolhouse. Except for the mill, these buildings together with a meetinghouse and barn will represent a traditional farm and a religious community. The plan includes a field museum guided tour of selected historic sites in the nearby Route 42 corridor. The center has been named CrossRoads (Jer. 6:16) to signify the crucial decisions Anabaptists make in order to be faithful to their calling. EFB

[Harrisonburg, VA] Daily News-Record (Aug. 26, 2000) 19, (July 16, 2002) 9–10, (July 24, 2002) 9; The Valley Brethren-Mennonite Heritage Center publications: Journeys of Faith/Battles of Conscience (May, 2001), CrossRoads, Journeys of Faith and Conscience (2002), Keeping the Legacy Alive (2002), P. C. Stone, Transforming History into Legacy—The Valley-Mennonite Story (2002), Jordan's Stormy Banks (Aug., 2002); Chronicles (Spring, 2003), quarterly-newsletter.

Vega Baja, PR, Iglesia de los Hermanos Cristo El Señor (CB) (Christ the Lord). This church is located in the El Rosario subdivision of Vega Baja on the north coast of *Puerto Rico. The congregation began in the early 1980s as a partnership of the Atlantic Southeast (then Florida-Puerto Rico) and Shenandoah Districts and the *Castañer congregation. The Shenandoah District provided primary funding for the building and the volunteer services of Donald R. Horn, architect. Key to the project was the presence of Jaime Luis Rivera, a resident of the community, who grew up in Castañer. Rivera sensed a call to start a congregation and turned to the *Church of the Brethren when the denomination with which he was affiliated showed no interest in the project.

Christ the Lord Church was received as an organized fellowship in 1982. Jorge Toledo and Pedro Brull, gifted leaders who served the CB in unusual ways, came into the church in Vega Baja, their hometown. Toledo did evangelistic and disaster work in the *Dominican Republic on his own initiative, which led to the founding of the CB in that country. Brull became the associate executive for Puerto Rico and brought a number of congregations into the Brethren family. Both men were non-salaried servants of the church.

The building in Vega Baja was dedicated in 1986 with 40 members. After leaving the position for several years, Jaime Rivera was again pastor in 1999, with Nydia Valdes as a licensed minister. In 2001 there were 74 members and an average attendance of 78. IRZ/BMC

M. S. H. Rosenberger, Light of the Spirit: The Brethren in Puerto Rico, 1942 to 1992 (1992) 73–75; O. Serrano, Un Canto al Señor en la Isla del Encanto (1992) passim; congregational records; Yearbook (CB) (1982–99); Messenger (Jan., 1983) 17, (Feb., 1988) 3, (Dec., 1990) 18–20,; BLT 36 (Summer, 1991) 172.

Venice, FL, Church of the Brethren is located in Sarasota Co., and is also known as the Venice Community Church of the Brethren. Brethren in Venice began worshiping together in Nov. 1986 under the direction of retired pastor, Harold C. Miller. In 1986, the group was granted fellowship status and called Frank W. Herbert to be licensed and installed as pastor. The new congregation was a mission of the *Brandenton, FL, Good Shepherd congregation.

Among the several retired pastors who served the congregation were Charles F. Stouder, Elmer I. Brumbauqh, and Harold C. Miller. Peter Crouse served part time for several months and Judy McGlothlin was the first full-time pastor for seven months. James R. Graybill served as a free minister for two years, and in 1996 Mary L. Boyd was called to serve part-time as pastor for four months; she was then called to serve the church on a full-time basis for an indefinite time. In Feb. 1999 the congregation was invited to share worship facilities with the Venice *Society of Friends. Thirty-two members were reported in 2000. MLBo

Congregational records; Yearbook (CB) (2001); BLT 36 (Summer, 1991) 170.

Villa Prades, PR, Iglesia Cristiana Getsemani (CB) (Christian Gethsemane Church). The church is located in Río Piedras, in the greater San Juan area. It was an independent, Pentecostal church organized in the 1970s and pastored by Oscar and Carmen M. López Villanueva, husband and wife. They obtained a small building with a capacity of about 100. The group became acquainted with the *Church of the Brethren when disaster workers gave service after Hurricane Hugo in 1989 in Caimito. The church had fellowship with the Brethren early in the 1990s through Pedro Brull and the Puerto Rico Board, and by attending the Atlantic Southeast District Conference. The congregation was received into the CB in 1995 and was recognized by the 1996 Annual Conference in Long Beach, CA. In 1999 the congregation reported a membership of 93 and had begun a ministry of evangelization in nearby communities but closed in 2001. IRZ/BMC

Congregational records; Yearbook (CB) (2002) 114.

W-Z

Wagoner, Gerald C., Sr. (OGBB), b. 1932, layman in the Sugar Grove congregation, Covington, OH. The son of Elder Floyd and Cecil Denlinger Wagoner, Gerald was stricken with polio in 1954 while in *Alternative Service. Perhaps this experience initiated a willingness to serve, as he and his wife, Ruby Miller Wagoner, along with four other couples, founded the Brethren Charity Fund (BCF) in Jan. 1963. Traditionally arising from individual initiative, charitable endeavors find ready acceptance. In 1975, a local disaster response program was formed, at first as a subsidiary of BCF. Today, BCF also operates a clothing distribution center in Brookville, OH, where used clothing is collected, processed, and placed in containers for shipment to poor people, here and abroad. Comforters are also made at the center. Food is distributed in *Haiti through the channel of Christian Aid Ministries, Berlin, OH.

Gerald and Ruby Wagoner had an interest in *Christian education and helped found one of the first OGBB-related schools in Southern Ohio. Gerald Wagoner wrote a family history (1978), developed a detailed chart of Brethren history, and served as genealogical editor of *Old Order Notes* since 1979. In 2000 he continues to teach part time and enjoys history, genealogy, volunteer work, and sitting on the front porch. Wagoner would say, "In the Lord's work, names and faces are not important . . . only the end results."

Gerald and Ruby Miller Wagoner have four children. In 1987 more than 110 craftsmen—carpenters, contractors, electricians, and roofers—all church members and friends, completed an extensive ranch house in one day as a gift of love to the Wagoners. Initiators of the "house-raising" project stated that their motivation came in response to the couple's activity in helping others. FWB

G. C. Wagoner, *Biography and Family History of Floyd R. Wagoner [1898–1977]* (1978); *The Piqua [OH] Daily Call* (June 22, 1987); *The Stillwater [OH] Valley Advertiser* (Oct. 14, 1987) 5; D. F. Durnbaugh, "Old German Baptist Brethren and the Media: An Analysis," *Old Order Notes*, No. 24 (Fall/Winter, 2001) 7–28 (18).

Wagoner, Raymond K. (OGBB) was born on Oct. 8, 1916, to Jesse A. and Elizabeth Hufford Wagoner in Surrey, ND. The family moved to Camden, IN, in 1936; soon after moving Raymond met Fern Miller. On March 11, 1937, both were baptized into the *Old German Baptist Brethren Church and on June 1, 1938, they were married by Morris Wagoner. Raymond and Fern Wagoner started their married life in the little town of Camden, but in 1942 moved to a rural area near the *Deer Creek meetinghouse. Three children were born to them: Lois (b. 1940), Gordon (b. 1944), and Shirley (b. 1949). Wagoner was a carpenter, who built and remodeled houses along with other carpentry jobs. He had always been interested in farming, even though that was not his occupation. After his retirement, he enjoyed spending several winter months in Florida each year, helping with the small *Lakeland congregation.

Wagoner was called to the ministry in June 1949 and ordained to the eldership in 1962. He was a member of the committee of arrangements for the *Annual Meetings of 1953 and 1959, and served on its *Standing Committee (1977–96). He was the elder-in-charge of his home congregation at Deer Creek (1980–98) and was the non-resident elder at *Eight Mile, KS, (1984–93). LELo

Vindicator (July, 1949) 218; *Minutes* (*OGBB*) (1977–96); *Old Order Notes* No. 4 (Spring, 1981) 34.

Wampler, Charles W., Sr. (CB), 1885–76, businessman, churchman. Born April 16 in Rockingham Co., VA, Charles Wampler was the son of John and Catherine Miller Wampler. He was married to: (1) Sadie Zigler, who died in 1922; (2) Zola Huffman, who died in 1962; and (3) Mae Wine who died in 2002. Wampler was the father of nine children.

An active churchman and civic leader, Wampler was considered to be the "Father of the Turkey Industry" and held national leadership positions in that industry. He was a state leader in agriculture, a member of the Virginia Board of Agriculture, a trustee of Virginia Polytechnic Institute, and was board chair at *Bridgewater College where he once taught agriculture (1920–21) while also acting as a county agent. A founder of WLR, Inc., and other agri-businesses, Wampler was active in the *Dayton, VA, congregation (CB). PCS

C. W. Wampler, *My Grandfather, My Grandchildren, and Me: An Autobiography* (1968); F. F. Wayland, *Bridgewater College* (1993) index; *Virginia* (1973), 413, 414, 419; C. W. Bowers and R. W. Bryan, eds., *100th Anniversary of [the] John Wampler Family* (1971), 75ff.; J. B. Yount III, ed. *Tunker House Proceedings, 1972* (1973) 44.

Washington, DC, Southeast Christian Fellowship (BC). In 1992 the *Washington, DC, Brethren Church had declined to less than ten in attendance. For some time the neighborhood in the vicinity of the church had been in

transition from a predominantly white to a predominantly African-American population. Rather than close the church, the congregation in 1992 decided to call an African-American pastor, Rickey Bolden. Bolden, who had played with the Cleveland Browns of the National Football League, helped to expand the ministry of the church in many new directions. He is involved in various sports ministries and has been a catalyst for The House, an inner city ministry that serves youth and their families through the arts, academics, and athletics and models the transforming love and power of Jesus Christ. In order to reflect the community outreach of the congregation, the church name was changed to Southeast Christian Fellowship. Attendance in 2000 averaged 150. DEC

Congregational records; *Annual* (*BC*) (1980–2000).

Washington Office (CB). Whereas previously church leaders appealed directly to national governmental officials only on rare occasions, during *World War II, *Church of the Brethren representatives met far more frequently with federal policy makers as they endeavored to attain legal status for conscientious objectors. During the years 1946–47, for approximately 12 months, *Paul Haynes Bowman served as the first Washington representative. However, the current Washington Office was established by an act of the 1962 Annual Conference.

Rooted in the prophetic tradition, the dual purpose of this ministry is that of expressing concerns of the church to the government, while seeking to engage the church in public policy advocacy for peace, justice, and environmental stewardship. A distinctive Brethren witness based on Annual Conference and *General Board policy statements shapes the character of the office. Yet from the beginning, Brethren have engaged in cooperative public policy advocacy.

In Jan. 1962, Ruth E. Early began her one-year tenure as director of the Washington Office. Other notable leaders who followed Early include *W. Harold Row (1969–71), *Ralph E. Smeltzer (1971–79), and *Ruby F. Rhoades (1977–79). Only during the years 1976–97 has the director served on a full-time basis. Under the 1996 General Board reorganization, supervision of the Washington Office was transferred to the director of Brethren Witness. In 2003 the positions of director of the Washington Office and the director of Brethren Witness were combined. Staff members serve the church by coordinating the annual Youth Christian Citizenship Seminars, providing testimonies for congressional hearings, drafting denominational position papers, providing congregational and district-level briefings and by producing a variety of publications including the *Index of Church of the Brethren Annual Conference and General Board Statements and Resolutions* and the newsletter *Witness to Washington.* TAM

BLT 32 (Autumn, 1987) 198–255 (special issue); L. E. Ebersole, *Church Lobbying in the Nation's Capital* (1951) esp., 40–41; A. N. Keim and G. M. Stoltzfus, *The Politics of Conscience* (1988) *passim.*

Waterbrook, VA, Brethren Church was organized in the spring of 1982 when 29 members of the *Maurertown, VA, Brethren Church withdrew to form a new congregation. These members met initially in various homes and then temporarily moved to a building on the north side of Woodstock, VA.

In 1985 land was purchased on the southeast side of Edinburg, VA. In Oct. of that year, ground was broken and construction begun in a beautiful pastoral setting. The building, the exterior design of which gives the effect of a small village, was dedicated on Sept. 25, 1988. The basement was later completed to provide classrooms. Pastors of the congregation include P. Kent Bennett (founding pastor), Michael L. Woods, John Swope, and Jonathan Dowdy. MLWo

Congregational records; *Annual* (*BC*) 1986–2000.

Waterloo, IA, Hammond Avenue Brethren Church (BC, CB). On Jan. 1, 1993, *Waterloo, IA, First Brethren Church and *City Church of the Brethren merged to become one congregation. The two churches shared a common origin dating to 1856 in the German Baptist Brethren at Orange Center. In 1992 the First Brethren congregation was hampered by limited off-street parking and inaccessibility to the disabled. City Church of the Brethren was accessible but had declined due to an economic downturn in the 1980s. Through the efforts of pastors Eugene Burry and Ronald L. Waters, the congregations began conversations that led to the merger. The new congregation occupies the former City Church building. Since the merger, the congregation has built a Family Life Center. The church remains affiliated with both *The Brethren Church and the *Church of the Brethren. In 2003, the membership was 159. RWW

Congregational records; personal knowledge.

Clyde Weaver in Russia. BHLA collection.

Weaver, Clyde E. (CB), 1924–94, minister, entrepreneur, and marketer. Clyde Weaver was born on Sept. 26 in East Petersburg, PA, a son of Samuel Clyde and Emma Weaver. After graduating from *Elizabethtown College (BA, 1949) he prepared for the ministry through studies at *Bethany Theol. Sem. (BD, 1953) and the U. of Chicago Divinity School. He was ordained to the eldership in 1957. He married Katherine A. Linscheid on June 24, 1951; they had three children.

Weaver served as chaplain at *Bethany Brethren Hospital (1951–55), the Chicago Parental School (1955–58), and worked in social services for the Church Federation of Greater Chicago (1958–60). Before joining the *General Board staff of the *Church of the Brethren in 1969, he was part owner of Weaver-Young Dodge in Elmhurst, IL, and in 1970 helped establish, with his children, the Inglenook Pantry restaurant in St. Charles, IL.

Weaver became marketing director for *Brethren Press in 1973. His folksy wit, pithy advice, sharp sense of business, and Anabaptist piety endeared him to the entire denomination, and beyond. He had an especially strong interest in promoting peace concerns and U.S.-Russia friendship.

Following his retirement in 1986, Weaver remained active in numerous civic-minded organizations. He was a volunteer chaplain for the Fox Valley Hospice, and he served on the boards of the Bethany Hospital Foundation and the Gail Borden Public Library, Elgin, IL. For more than ten years he was an arbitrator for the Better Business Bureau. Weaver died of a heart attack on March 2. DBE

The {Elgin, IL] Courier News (March 4, 1994); *Messenger* (Jan., 1984) 7, (March, 1986) 7, (Dec., 1987) 6, (Dec., 1990) 22, (Dec., 1991) 10, (April, 1994) 3; *Chicago Tribune* (June 28, 1992); *Highland Ave. CB* (1999) 118–19; BHLA files.

Weaver, Scott L. (FGBC, CGBCI) b. 1919, pastor, evangelist. A native of Kokomo, IN, Scott Weaver married Betty Parker in 1939 and worked at Chrysler Corp. in Kokomo, IN, at General Electric Corp. in Fort Wayne, IN, and finally at Delco Radio Co. in Kokomo. Having made a profession of faith in Christ, he entered *Grace College and was a member of the first graduating class (AA, 1950). He received a ThB degree from Grace Theol. Sem. (1953).

Weaver pastored the *Osceola, IN, Bethel Brethren Church (1953–66), and started a Christian day school that reached an enrollment of 400. With a passion for *evangelism, he held evangelistic meetings for the Grace Brethren *Board of Evangelism twice a year during his pastorate at Bethel. In 1964, he went to *Africa for three months, preaching at evangelistic services (2,500 decisions were recorded) and teaching courses on evangelism. In 1966, he left the Osceola congregation to return to Africa, spending 10 weeks in 13 countries and witnessing 5,000 professions of faith. He continued evangelistic work in Israel, South America, and *Mexico until accepting a call to pastor the *South Bend, IN, Ireland Road Grace Brethren Church (1969–86). He was FGBC moderator (1974–75) and served for 17 years on the board of *Grace Brethren Foreign Missions.

Unable to remain retired, Weaver planted and pastored the *Mishawaka, IN, (Conservative) Grace Brethren Church (1987–97). Upon retirement he continued to preach for another year until the church called a new pastor. RTC

Personal information; *Annual* (FGBC) (1954–93).

Weldy, Allen (CB), 1899–1989, educator and administrator. Weldy was born near Wakarusa, IN, the son of Levi and Alice Weldy. In 1922 he married Nina Roose (1900–77), daughter of Eli and Ellen Culp Roose; they had three sons: Winfred, Gilbert, and Edgar. Nina Roose Weldy died in 1977, and in 1980 he married Mary Loucks. He graduated from *Manchester College (AB, 1930) and Indiana U. (1939). He served 33 years as a public school teacher, 25 of those as principal of Lincoln School in Elkhart, IN. In 1951 he was ordained to the ministry and became director of the *Flat Creek Mission, KY (1951–57). He also was active in N. Indiana district work and with *Camp Mack. He was president of the *National Men's Work cabinet (1938–40) and recording secretary for several years after that. Weldy served in *Germany as a volunteer (1957–59); he later pastored several churches

in Northern Indiana. WRE

S. Ohio (1955), 431–32; *Indiana* (1952) index, esp. 425; J. K. Kreider, *A Cup of Cold Water* (2001) 241, 445; *Messenger* (Sept., 1980) 2–3, (April, 1985) 2–3, (March, 1990) 27, (April, 1990) 31.

Wellness is a concern for the health of the whole person. It marks a shift from treatment of health problems to a concern for prevention. A development of the last half of the 20th century, wellness has been known by other rubrics such as "wholistic health," or simply as "wholeness." Wellness is defined as a way of life designed to enjoy the highest level of health and well-being. It combines concerns for physical, emotional, spiritual, intellectual, and social dimensions. Using more biblical terms, Christian programs often describe wellness as a concern for the whole person—body, mind, and spirit (Matt. 22:37; 1 Thess. 5:23)—in a faith community context.

While all the various Brethren groups are concerned about health and the healing ministry, only the *Church of the Brethren has established a wellness program. The concern of the Brethren for wholistic health is rooted in the belief that ill health results from the human *environment rather than as divine punishment for *sin. This belief took specific form in 1930, when *Bethany Hospital and Sanitarium was constructed to encourage health programs similar to the sanitaria of the *Seventh Day Adventists in Battle Creek, MI. Brethren doctors in *Nigeria followed the same understanding of health when they developed a program entitled *Lafiya* (a word in the Hausa language that means wholeness and well being). *Lafiya* was an effort to train village health workers in primary health care and disease prevention.

The wellness program in North America was initiated by the *Association of Brethren Caregivers (ABC), an organization formed in 1990 by the union of the *Brethren Health Foundation (created in 1987 by the consolidation of the *Brethren Health Education Foundation and the *Bethany Hospital Foundation) with the *Brethren Health and Welfare Association. When, in 1991, ABC sought a model for its wellness program, it turned to the Nigerian initiative. The U.S. counterpart of *Lafiya* has encouraged congregations to form *Lafiya* committees which assess the wellness needs of the congregation and make congregationally-specific suggestions for wellness programs and procedures. In some congregations this assessment has led to the formation of wellness or care groups that meet on a regular basis. Care groups usually involve *worship, exercise, diet suggestions, support, stress control, and reflection on personal decision-making. It is the goal of *Lafiya* to create congregations where personal needs are heard (listening), persons are encouraged to make their own choices (empowering), and support and services are offered (resourcing). A faith community so rooted would result in the promotion of personal health as well as involvement in broader programs of healing. GFS

The Lafiya Guide: A Congregational Handbook for Whole-Person Health Ministry (1993); M. S. H. Rosenberger, *That They Might Have Life: A History of the Brethren Health and Welfare Association* (1987), and *The Gift of Life: The Brethren and Bethany Hospital* (1995); G. F. Snyder, *Health and Medicine in the Anabaptist Tradition: Care in Community* (1995), 124–36; *The Mennonite Mutual Aid Wellness Program* (1987); *Minutes* (CB), 1992–97.

West, Murray Guy (CB), 1901–91, pastor, church leader. Guy West was the son of Andrew Eldridge and Exonie Elizabeth Akers West of Vesta, VA. West was baptized at the Patrick Springs, VA, CB on May 18, 1919. Called to

the ministry in Feb. 1922, he prepared for a career as pastor-evangelist at *Hebron Sem., VA, *Bridgewater College (BA, 1926), *Bethany Bibl. Sem. (BD, 1931), and Yale Divinity School (BST, 1935), with special training in psychology in several New Jersey hospitals and in the Federal Detention Prison in New York City. In his senior year at Bridgewater College, he pastored the *Bridgewater, VA, congregation, where he continued as pastor for two years after college graduation. While a student at Bethany, he served the *North Liberty congregation, IN (1928–31). He was granted honorary degrees from *Elizabethtown (DD, 1959) and Bridgewater (DHL, 1982) Colleges.

West was married on June 30, 1937, to Naomi E. Miller (b. 1907), who graduated from Bridgewater College (1929) and studied at the U. of Virginia. Naomi West promoted programs of *Brethren Service and social justice along with her husband in the various congregations they served in PA, VA, and CA. Twin sons were born to this family. Through the 30 years they ministered together in various congregations, they promoted interests in evangelistic, ecumenical, and peace and social justice concerns. A visit to Europe in 1958 stirred interests in world hunger and refugee resettlement programs.

Guy West served the denomination in various capacities as district moderator, *Brotherhood Board member, and *Annual Conference moderator. His Annual Conference message in 1968 summarized a basic interest of his life when he spoke of "Diatribe or Dialogue." This was done in a period when the church was disturbed by many sub-groups and the theme in the nation was "Crisis in the Nation." The Wests retired from the *San Diego, CA, First CB in 1974, after which he served as chaplain and as chaplain emeritus of the *Bridgewater Retirement Community. EQG

S. Pennsylvania (1973); Atlantic (1975), 73; Indiana (1952); Virginia (1973); W. Pennsylvania (953); GM (June 13, 1942) 9–10; (March 12, 1960) 2–3; (Aug. 25, 1962) 18; (June 8, 1967) 18–21; Messenger (Mar. 28, 1968) 15; (Aug. 1, 1968) 13; (Sept. 26, 1968) 24–26; (Apr., 1980) 23–26; (Feb. 1987) 2–3.

Whitcomb, John Clement, Jr. (FGBC, CGBCI), b. 1924, educator, writer. Born in Washington, DC, into the family of a military father, John Whitcomb spent three years of his childhood in northern *China. He enrolled at Princeton U. for a year and was converted under the ministry of Donald B. Fullerton (1943). He then spent three years in the U.S. Army (1944–46). While in the military, Whitcomb furthered his education with studies at Virginia Polytechnic Institute and Shrivenham American U. in England. He returned to complete his undergraduate education at Princeton U. (BA, 1948) and enrolled at *Grace Theol. Sem. (BD, 1951; ThM, 1953; ThD, 1957).

While at Grace Seminary, Whitcomb left the *Presbyterian Church to become a member of the *Winona Lake, IN, Grace Brethren Church. Upon his graduation in 1951 from the seminary, he joined the Old Testament department. His service there continued into 1990. During this time he was also chair of the dept. of theology (1968–85), director of doctoral studies for 20 years, and editor of Grace Theological Journal (1980 –89).

With a passion for *missions, Whitcomb was president of the Board of *Grace Brethren Foreign Missions (1972–79) and of the Board of Spanish World Gospel Mission (1962–90). He helped to establish a church in *Puerto Rico (1957–58) and was a leader in creating the

Grace Seminary Extension program in the *Chateau of Saint Albain, *France.

He became widely-known in evangelical circles through his defense of creationism and of flood geology; he contended that the doctrine of biblical inerrancy required interpretation of the Genesis flood as worldwide and the creation account as occurring in six literal 24 hour days. Recognizing the need for a qualified scientist to write the scientific portions of a book on the flood based on his dissertation, he joined with Henry M. Morris to publish The Genesis Flood (1963); this work sold more than 200,000 copies over 25 years. He also wrote many other books, including Darius the Mede (1959), The Nature of Biblical Creation (1966), The Early Earth (1986), and The World That Perished (1988). He contributed commentaries on Ezra, Nehemiah, and Esther to the Wycliffe Bible Commentary (1962), and on Esther (1979) and Daniel (1985) to the Everyman's Bible Commentary series, as well as Solomon to the Exile: Studies in Kings and Chronicles, later incorporated into Israel: A Commentary on Joshua to 2 Kings (1989), co-authored with John J. Davis. He collaborated with Donald DeYoung to write The Moon: Its Creation, Form and Significance (1978). There are over 300,000 copies in print of his chart on Old Testament chronology.

Through Whitcomb Ministries, he has distributed his books, audio cassettes, and video tapes and held lectures in churches and schools throughout the world. Because of differences with the administration of Grace Theol. Sem., he was asked to leave the faculty shortly before he was due to retire. Whitcomb led in the development of the *Conservative Grace Brethren Association, serving as president of its first board of directors. RTC

R. L. Numbers, The Creationists (1992), 184–213; Internet Web site, Answers in Genesis Ministries; personal information.

Winchester, VA, Blue Ridge Grace Brethren Church was organized in 1981 as an offshoot of the *Winchester Grace Brethren Church. Wayne Strickland filled the pulpit in its formative days. The congregation started with ten charter members: Roy and Bertha Duncan, Ken and Virginia Unger, Herbert and Geraldine Yost, Perry and Linda Duvall, and Donald and Constance Gregory.

At first, the members met in the Conference Center of the Lee-Jackson Motel in Winchester. In 1983 they purchased land on the western edge of Winchester on Cedar Creek Grade. They erected a new brick building and moved in the same year. In 1999 the church dedicated a new auditorium with classrooms. Pastors Lee Myers (1982–85), Ronald Welsh (1986–89), Kim G. Robertson (1989–2000), and Darrel G. Taylor (2001–) have served the congregation. In 2001 the membership was ca. 110. DGT

Congregational records; Annual (FGBC) (1982–2001).

Winning the Race Ministries (WTRM) (BC) began in Sept. 1992 as a joint church planting effort of the Indiana Missions Ministry and the *National Missionary Board of *The Brethren Church. Thomas W. and Tiona Conrad moved to Greenwood, IN, to begin the ministry. Greenwood is a suburb of the greater Indianapolis, IN, area. The vision of WTRM was to plant "Cell Base Congregations" in the Indianapolis area and beyond. Every congregation created was to intentionally found new congregations as part of its vision. The plan was to target major urban centers in the Midwest and beyond.

Cell Base Congregations are balanced ministries that

International Women's Conference (1985). Deanna Brown and Linnea Halverson give leadership. BHLA collection.

have both *Community* and *Corporate* dimensions. The *Community* dimension is the life of the church in which believers are edified and equipped for ministry, and leader interns are made ready to lead as growth occurs. This all happens in small groups no larger than 15 people called "cells." Members of these cells pledge to evangelize together and multiply into new cells every nine to twelve months. The *Corporate* dimension is evidenced when the cells come together for *worship, celebration, *missions, and special events. All in Cell Based Congregations are called upon to "count the cost" (Luke 14:28) and live their lives in obedience to Jesus Christ. In July 1998 this ministry was closed by the Indiana District and the National Missionary Board. TWC

BE (Nov., 1995) 7, (Feb., 1997) 12.

*Women. The family lives of women have been changing in recent decades as society has changed. In all Brethren groups, more women are working outside the home. The *Old German Baptist Brethren have a small but growing number of single women who work as nurses, secretaries, or founders of small businesses; some women continue to work after *marriage, either part-time or after the children are grown. The trend toward smaller families allows time for other activities. By contrast, some *Dunkard Brethren are having larger families because of the teachings of Bill Gothard, a popular seminar leader in some conservative circles.

The home schooling movement has also had a significant impact on the lives of women, especially among the more conservative Brethren. Some changes in *dress are taking place: a few *Grace Brethren women are choosing to wear the *prayer covering (veil), while some *Old German Baptist Brethren women have begun to adopt more casual dress outside of religions occasions.

In local congregations, women's commitment to *hospitality is still important (especially OGBB, DB). In *The Brethren Church and the *Church of the Brethren, women generally perform the same church functions that men do, although some congregations restrict women from some offices on theological grounds. Among other Brethren groups, women do not preach or lead worship, although some women may lead singing or pray in worship (DB). Women teach other women and children (DB, FGBC), and they *mentor younger women and minister through sewing circles (DB). Women also serve as *deaconesses (BC, CB, FGBC), having the same responsibilities as male deacons, or as the wives of deacons (OGBB, DB), assisting their husbands' ministry, especially in dealing with women and girls. The widows of ministers and deacons continue to assist the married officials' wives (OGBB).

Women's participation in decision-making and office-holding differs among Brethren groups. Old German Baptist Brethren women participate and vote in congregational council meetings but may not serve as *messengers (delegates) to *Annual Meeting or participate in business discussions there. Dunkard Brethren women vote in congregational council meetings and district conference but do not serve as delegates to the business meeting of their *General Conference. While they serve on some congregational committees, they do not serve on the official boards of congregations or on the *Standing Committee of General Conference. Grace Brethren women participate and vote in congregational meetings but may not serve as *elders in those congregations governed by lay elder boards. A few female deaconesses serve on congregational ministry commissions. Women seldom serve as district officials but may serve on district committees. They may serve as delegates to district conferences and

General Conference but may not serve as national moderator. By 1998, no women had served on the national Fellowship Council.

In The Brethren Church and Church of the Brethren, women have made up a significant percentage of the membership of national committees, councils, and boards. Women have chaired the General Conference *Executive Council (BC) (Mary Ellen Waters Drushal); the Congregational Ministries Council (BC) (Brenda Barnett Colijn); and the *General Board (CB) (Elaine Mock Sollenberger, Judy Mills Reimer, Kathy Hess). They have served as CB General Board commission executives (Ruby Frantz *Rhoades, Connie Andes, Joan George Deeter), Interim General Secretary/Executive Director (Karen Peterson Miller, 1997), and Executive Director (CB) (Judy Mills Reimer, 1998). They have also served as national moderator: Elaine Mock Sollenberger (CB, 1989, 1998), Mary Ellen Drushal (BC, 1990), Phyllis Nolan Carter (CB, 1992), and Judy Mills Reimer (CB, 1995).

The Church of the Brethren officially endorses the *ordination of women, although some segments of the denomination are still opposed to it. Some women who have trained for the ministry have difficulty finding pastorates, since calling pastors is a congregational decision. In 1977, according to ministerial listings in the CB Yearbook, ca. 11 percent of ordained ministers (ca. 225) were women, as were ca. 29 percent of licensed ministers. Some 48 percent of ordained women were serving congregations. Conversely, about 12 percent of congregations were served by an ordained or licensed woman.

In The Brethren Church, the 1980s saw a reawakening of interest in calling women to the ordained ministry. The denomination has taken no official position on the issue, although the 1974 General Conference adopted a motion in favor of joint ministry. Women's ordination was discussed by the *Ministerial Association in 1983–84 without reaching consensus. Two women (Kathryn Rinehart Mitchell and Jennifer Ray) were ordained between 1980 and 1998, but a third was refused ordination at the district level because of her gender. By 1998, Jennifer Ray still retained ordination but was not serving in the pastorate. The 1997 Pennsylvania District Conference defeated a motion to bar women from ordination. In 2002, the National Association of Brethren Church Elders approved a resolution that left the decision whether to call or ordain women in the hands of local congregations. District and national boards were to be neutral on the issue. In 2003 and 2004 four women were ordained to ministry in The Brethren Church. Other Brethren groups continue their practice of calling only men to the ministry, although the wives of ministers continue to have an important function in supporting their husbands' ministry.

The *Program for Women (CB) was formed in the mid-1980s in order to "nurture women and enable women to be co-partners in the ministry and mission of the whole church." It focused on improving communication among women, developing a national resource center, and planning conferences. Melanie A. May was employed by the denomination in 1985 to focus on women's issues. The Program for Women was eliminated at the end of the 1997 budget year during denominational restructuring. Other perspectives have been voiced by groups not sponsored by the denomination, including the *Womaen's Caucus (a feminist perspective) and the *Brethren/Mennonite Council for Lesbian and Gay Concerns. While the Women's Missionary Society is the primary denominational women's program in The Brethren Church, there has been increasing interest in the diversity and importance of women's ministries.

Women are active in *education and *missions. They teach in private church-affiliated primary and secondary schools (especially DB, FGBC, OGBB). They serve on the faculties and administrative staffs of denominational colleges (BC, CB, FGBC) and on the faculties of both *Bethany Theol. Sem. (CB) and Ashland Theol. Sem. (BC). In all groups, women write for denominational publications. Women have served in editorial capacity for *Messenger (CB) and as publisher of *Brethren Press (Wendy Chamberlain McFadden) and as editor of *Brethren Life and Thought (Christina Bucher).

The *Women's Missionary Society (BC) and *Women's Missionary Council (FGBC) raise funds for missions as well as provide fellowship and spiritual nurture. The *Global Women's Project (CB) has funded international projects that benefit women and children. Since 1980, women have taken on more of a partnership and leadership role in missions (CB, BC). Women have directed missions programs (Ruby Frantz Rhoades, Joan G. Deeter), and women missionaries have ministries in their own right. For example, María Miranda (BC) has an *Hispanic radio program for women that is heard throughout Latin America and in the United States. BBC

P. Brubaker, She Hath Done What She Could (1985); B. J. Buckingham, ed., Women at the Well (1987); D. F. Durnbaugh, Fruit of the Vine (1997) 546–48; C. F. Bowman, Brethren Society (1995) index; Yearbook (CB) (1997); J. Flora and J. Flora, Faith and Fortitude: Lives of W. M. S. Presidents (1987); A. T. Ronk, History BC (1968) index; BE (June, 1983) 18–19, (Sept., 1983) 20–21, (June, 1984) 18, (Sept., 1984) 16–17, (Dec., 1988) 5–7, (Oct., 1995) 4–5; Reports of National Ministerial Association (BC) (1983–84) discussion of women's ordination; J. R. Flora, "Ordination of Women in The Brethren Church: A Case Study from the Anabaptist-Pietist Tradition" Journal of the Evangelical Theological Society, 30 (Dec., 1987) 427–440; BRF Witness, 17 (May/June, 1982) 3–9, (Nov./Dec., 1982) 2–10; CB Parish Ministries Commission. "Proposal for Women's Program" (March, 1987); BLT 30 (Winter, 1984) 4–61 (special issue).

Women's Conferences (CB) made their first official appearance in the 1970s under the auspices of the *Parish Ministries Commission. After inception of *Womaen's Caucus in 1970 and appointment of Beth Glick-Reiman to the half-time national staff position for person awareness in 1975, the idea of conferences for women soon developed into reality.

The first was held at *Elizabethtown College in May 1977 with the theme The Role and Status of Church of the Brethren Women. The four-day event included over 30 workshops focused on women as persons, women in the church, and church women in the world. The 250 women from 24 districts and other countries also participated in a business session modeled after *Annual Conference. This was an effort to provide experience in parliamentary procedure as well as to discuss items for the upcoming conference.

The gathering held in July 1978 at *Manchester College focused on the theme Break Forth, Go Forth. The daily schedule for 300 women included plenary sessions, dialogue groups, workshops, and special interest groups. An address by Ruthann Knechel Johansen challenged women to aid global sisters through the means of a self-imposed luxury tax. During the business session, the women approved a resolution, which led to formation of

the *Global Women's Project by the *General Board that same year. Another recommendation called for a five-year, full-time staff position in person awareness. Ralph L. and Mary Cline Detrick received the assignment to become the denominational staff for life-cycle ministries. In all, ten resolutions were approved for further action.

As the anniversary of 100 years of CB women's organizations approached, a series of celebrative events and projects were developed for 1985. The culmination of the anniversary year was the conference, *Empowered by Our Birthright*, held at *Bridgewater College, August 1–4. According to Melanie A. May, General Board staff person for women's programs, this was the first attempt to bring together the entire spectrum of women in the *Church of the Brethren, from conservative to feminist. Over 900 women attended, including 14 international participants from *India, *Nigeria, *Puerto Rico, *Cuba, *Guatemala, and Costa Rica. Approximately 15 men were also in attendance.

In addition to the usual conference sessions and informal activities, an open-air *love feast was held. Gathered in circles across the lawn, small groups participated in washing one another's feet, a brown-bag meal, and communion. The bread of *communion, prepared according to the traditions of congregations from across the denomination, symbolized the diversity and unity of the participants and women's organizations.

Following the anniversary celebration a new design for women's programs evolved at the national level and was officially recognized in March 1987. Integral to this new creation were annual women's conferences beginning in 1988. One per year was to be held in a different region, ending with a second international conference in 1993 on *Story-Telling and Bridge-Building*. Conferences were held at the U. of *La Verne in Aug. 1988; *Needs and Support* at Estes Park, CO, in 1989; *Wounds and Healing* at *Manchester College in 1990; and *Gifts and Giving* at Elizabethtown College in 1991. Because of denominational program shifts, the 1991 conference was the last one. The cycle of women's conferences thus ended in the same location it had begun 14 years earlier. JGK

Personal information; P. Brubaker, *She Hath Done What She Could* (1985) 163–65; *Messenger* (Sept., 1977) 26–27; (Nov., 1985), 11–15; D. F. Durnbaugh, *Fruit of the Vine* (1997) 547–48.

Program to Overcome Violence

In 1994, South African Methodist Bishop Stanley Mogoba, preaching at the opening worship of the *World Council of Churches Central Committee meeting in Johannesburg, called on the WCC to establish a program to combat violence. In his sermon he noted that violence is found all over the world—and so are Christian congregations; the WCC could play a critical role in linking global and local experience and action. Some participants immediately saw these words as a program possibility, including two representatives of the *Historic Peace Churches (HPC), who were members of the Central Committee; these were *Donald E. Miller, then general secretary of the *Church of the Brethren, and Barbara Bazett of the Canadian Yearly Meeting of the Religious *Society of Friends. Along with a WCC staff member, Elizabeth Salter, herself a Quaker, they lobbied delegates and staff and proposed this project to the Unit Committee on Justice, Peace, and Creation. With the strong support of WCC general secretary Konrad Raiser and the moderator of the Unit

Committee, Margot Kässmann, the Central Committee unanimously approved the establishment of a Program to Overcome Violence (POV), with the purpose of challenging and transforming the global culture of violence in the direction of a culture of just peace.

Part of the recommendation from the Central Committee in January 1994 that established the program included a call for a consultation to define it more fully. This was held at Corrymeela, Northern Ireland, in June 1994 and moderated by H. Lamar Gibble. Participants decided that the focus of the POV would be the networking of churches and other agencies which have had some success in addressing the problem of violence. This recommendation was further refined by a consultation in Rio de Janeiro in April 1996 which called for a "Peace to the City" Campaign to give the POV further focus.

However, it became very clear that with only one staff member to coordinate the Campaign and the POV, little progress could be made. Thus, HPC representatives offered to send a volunteer to the WCC for two years. The position, financially supported by Dutch and German *Mennonites and the European office of the *Mennonite Central Committee, was itself a statement of the strong practical support the HPC could offer this program of the WCC. The person selected to serve was Sara E. Speicher, from the CB and formerly associate director of the *Association of Brethren Caregivers. Speicher joined the WCC program in Jan. 1997. The Peace to the City Campaign highlighted local peacemaking initiatives in seven cities around the world and shared stories and ideas through Web and e-mail communication, newsletters, and a video series. The Campaign culminated in the Eighth Assembly of the WCC, meeting in Harare, Zimbabwe, in Dec. 1998. There, inspired by the work of the partners in the Campaign along with other initiatives and needs and voting on a motion made by Fernando Enns, a representative of the German Mennonites, delegates called for a "Decade to Overcome Violence" for the years 2001–2010, ensuring that the HPC will continue to challenge, and be challenged by, the global fellowship of churches. SESp

Minutes of the 45th Meeting, WCC (1994) 113; M. Kaessmann, *Overcoming Violence: The Challenge to the Churches in All Places* (1998); *Overcome Violence: A Programme of the World Council of Churches* (1997); *Messenger* (Dec., 1998) 11–16.

World Hunger Issues (CB). Caring for the physical needs of people is a characteristic of the Brethren from the inception of the movement. For the *Church of the Brethren, food is a human rights issue and production and distribution of food is a response to basic human need. Justice, at the very least, implies a situation where gross economic inequalities do not exist between persons and where basic physical needs such as food are satisfied for all. The withholding of food as a method of coercion or retaliation in national foreign policy is inconsistent with Brethren understanding of the proper use of food, and the proper response in terms of conflict, even with those who would be our adversaries.

Hunger never seems to go away from the global scene. Growing out of its New Testament heritage of ministry in service to others, the CB has maintained a commitment to

feeding the hungry, helping the impoverished, healing the broken, and promoting freedom, justice, and reconciliation. This commitment, particularly as related to food and hunger issues, has been actively expressed in programs such as *Heifer Project, *Christian Rural Overseas Program (CROP), *Church World Service (CWS), One Great Hour of Sharing, Emergency Disaster Fund, and Global Food Crisis Fund of the CB.

Historically, relief and service efforts were undertaken for refugees, immigrants, and poor members by early Brethren congregations in *Germany and in *Germantown, PA. CB missionaries in *India and *China undertook extensive relief activities during drought, famine, and war as early as 1897. In the years following World War I, *Armenian refugees were given sizeable aid and Brethren relief expanded to a worldwide scope during the years following *World War II. SPB

See also AGRICULTURAL MISSIONS; AGRICULTURAL MISSIONS, INC.; AGRICULTURE; ARMENIANS, BRETHREN RELIEF TO; CHURCH-STATE RELATIONS; FAMINE RELIEF; LOBBYING; POOR, CARING FOR THE; POOR BOX; RELIEF AND SERVICE; RURAL SERVICE CENTER; SOCIAL ACTION.

J. K. Kreider, A Cup of Cold Water (2001) index; D. F. Durnbaugh, Fruit of the Vine (1997) index, esp. 477–96; CB Annual Conference statements: Family Planning and Population Growth (1964), World Hunger Concern (1975), Christian Ethics, Law and Order (1977), and Justice and Nonviolence (1977).

*Worship. Brethren worship has never had a mandated structure. However, in the second half of the 20th century worship practices in the *Church of the Brethren have been influenced by the liturgical structure of major protestant denominations. Liturgy (Greek, leiturgia) is the work of the people in worship and in service to the world. Brethren do liturgy as they plan and participate in the drama of worship, giving God the worth (Old English, weorthscipe) due God. How that is done varies from congregation to congregation, from Sunday to Sunday, and from region to region.

The worship structure of *Hymnal: A Worship Book (1992) by churches in the Believers Church tradition, loosely follows the biblical model of Isa. 6:1–9 including Gathering, Praising, and Adoring; Confessing and Reconciling, Proclaiming, Affirming Faith, Praying, Offering, Witnessing, Sending. Brethren also follow Eph. 5:15–20, an exemplary worship model showing how early Christians met together for a sense of community, mutual support, study, prayer, and singing. For All Who Minister (1993), a CB worship manual, also suggests a worship format that respects the church's tradition and Brethren theology patterned after New Testament teachings. Worship seeks to balance structure and freedom, tradition and innovation, while listening to the leading of the Holy Spirit.

Some *Church of the Brethren congregations have a formal worship style. A few follow the traditional plain style of worship similar to that practiced by the *Old German Baptist Brethren. Some are very informal, bordering on a *charismatic style of worship. A small number of congregations (CB, *The Brethren Church, *Fellowship of Grace Brethren Churches) follow the "seekers service structure" (a late 20th century philosophy of worship aimed at the unchurched or disenfranchised who seek a comfortable place to worship in an informal, contemporary setting). Such a service emphasizes music by a "praise band" and a worship team which leads con-

gregational singing and may provide dramatization of scripture or the day's theme. There is a growing concern about a widening gap between those who want to preserve a more traditional style of worship and those who favor new styles. Some churches provide two different worship styles in separate services, while others blend several styles into one service.

The pastor, worship leader, and musicians often work cooperatively to plan and lead worship. Some churches have a worship committee, including various ages and theological stances, which may try new forms of worship and new hymns, while being sensitive to the various needs of the congregation. Church bulletins provide the order of worship and church announcements, although the newer form of worship may project on the wall an order of worship and song texts, or use computer-generated programs.

Brethren believe that the congregation should actively participate in worship. CB and BC members share personal joys and concerns during the service of worship, as well as concerns for the larger church of Jesus Christ and of the world. These are then lifted to God in prayer. The congregation also participates in singing hymns, reading litanies, and praying together. In some congregations, worshippers "pass the peace" by shaking hands or embracing, and serve as ushers and greeters. A dramatic interpretation of scripture or interpretive dance may be offered in more liberal congregations. The *love feast (the remembrance of Jesus's life and suffering) usually is celebrated twice a year by the CB and BC, inviting those present to prepare themselves, practice *feetwashing, share a simple meal together, break bread and drink the cup. In doing so, Brethren renew their sense of community and discipleship.

Children are ministered to and minister to others in worship. They may offer their musical gifts, usher, share in joys and concerns, read scripture, and lead in prayer. Many congregations have a special time with children in worship, affirming them as an important part of the congregation and connecting the sermon message to their lives through stories and object lessons.

Various biblical *translations are used in worship. An increasing number of CB congregations follow the Revised Common Lectionary readings, although usually not on a regular basis. While freedom to read from biblical texts that seem appropriate for a given Sunday still takes priority, lectionary readings provide a discipline for preaching on a variety of topics that challenge pastors to go beyond comfortable and familiar texts. For all Brethren bodies, the sermon is highly significant, even though theologically everything that is done to praise God is equally important. CB sermon styles may be expository, topical, and narrative. A well-crafted sermon delivered in a conversational manner is replacing a more formal and rhetorical style. More important than style or delivery is the *exegesis of the scriptural passage, understanding its significance in its original community and interpreting it for today's world.

*Prayers are spontaneous or prepared, often concluding with the *Lord's Prayer. DB, OGBB, and some traditional CB congregations kneel during prayer. A growing number of CB congregations include a time for silent reflection. Congregations may have altar calls or prayers of re-commitment after the sermon. There may be *anointing, *laying on of hands and prayer for *healing from physical illness or emotional pain, and for reconciliation, critical decisions, spiritual renewal, commission-

ing, dedication, or blessing.

Since 1980 the BC and the CB have been influenced by the modern *church growth movement, charismatic renewal, and the seeker-service model, resulting in new styles of worship. FGBC worship services are very structured and evangelistic, with expository or topical preaching and spontaneous prayers. Some worship practices are changing, influenced by contemporary Christian authors, speakers, and musicians.

*Old German Baptist Brethren and *Dunkard Brethren continue to worship in their traditional ways. A typical service includes unaccompanied singing, spontaneous prayers in a kneeling position and the Lord's Prayer. Scripture and sermon are followed by one or more sermonic testimonies. There is no formal benediction. The *holy kiss, preceding and following worship, is often accompanied by an embrace. The fine arts are suspect. Suggestions of any change in worship would appear to many members as a threat to gospel simplicity, although a few OGBB congregations have accepted voice-amplifcation systems because of ambient noise. NRF

GENERAL: C. F. Bowman, *Brethren Society* (1995) *passim*; D. F. Durnbaugh, *Fruit of the Vine* (1997) *passim*; CB: *For All Who Minister* (1993); W. F. Groff, *Prayer: God's Time and Ours* (1984); *We Gather Together: Worship Resources for the Church of the Brethren* (1979); D. R. Fitzkee, *Moving Toward the Mainstream* (1995); I. G. Long, *Lord's Day Morning* (1989); H. S. Martin, *New Testament Beliefs and Practices* (1989); K. I. Morse, *Move in Our Midst* (1977) and *Preaching in a Tavern* (1997); *BLT* 31 (Winter, 1986) 7–60 (special issue); BC: *The Brethren: Growth in Life and Thought* (1975); OGBB: M. Miller, *"Roots by the River"* (1973); F. W. Benedict, ed., *Old Order Notes*, Nos. 1–22 (1978–2000); FGBC: H. H. Etting, *Our Heritage: Brethren Beliefs and Practices* (1975); D. R. Plaster, *Ordinances: What Are They?* (1985); DB: *Dunkard Brethren Church Manual* (1951).

Yahuecas, PR, Iglesia de los Hermanos Cristo Nuestra Paz (CB) (Christ Our Peace). The church is located in Yahuecas, part of the city of Adjuntas in the hills of south central *Puerto Rico. The work began as an outreach of the *Castañer CB in 1962 under the leadership of Donald L. Fike and his wife, Shirley. Meetings were held in the homes of Francisco González and Ruiz Sedeño, who later joined the Castañer congregation, thus interrupting the continuation of the project. In 1988 evangelization in the area was initiated again by Alberto and Doris Rivera González with Castañer's interim pastor, David B. Rittenhouse. The work was continued with energy and effectiveness by pastor Mario Serrano and Olga Serrano (1981–87), who focused on leadership development. By 1989 there was a group of 15 persons pastored by leaders who rose up from Mario Serrano's teaching, Jorge and Norma Medina Rivera. A property was dedicated in 1990 with the participation of CB representatives from the United States. In 1999 there was a membership of 43 and average attendance of 55. Jorge and Norma Medina Rivera serve as co-pastors. IRZ/BMC

Congregational records; *BLT* 36 (Summer, 1991) 174; *Yearbook (CB)* (1989–99).

Yoder, D. Willard (OGBB), 1913–97, farmer, minister, clockmaker. The son of Daniel and Lizzie Garber Yoder, Willard Yoder was born on Nov. 19 near New Lebanon, Montgomery Co., OH, where he lived and farmed the same 80 acres which his grandfather, Henry Garber (1842–1920), also tilled. In 1968, he and his wife, Dorothy Bowman Yoder, moved to Brookville, OH, where they spent their remaining years. They were the parents of two daughters. Willard Yoder was a well known craftsman, specializing in building grandfather clocks and pillar-and-scroll shelf clocks. Fashioning barometers and wooden letter openers were also notable skills.

Elected to the ministry in 1950, and to the eldership in 1960, he soon became well respected and influential in those services. His obligations included much traveling across the nation, and he especially enjoyed many visits to the West Coast and fellowship with Brethren there. He was a member of The *Vindicator Committee (1962–92) and contributed many articles and poems to that publication. Yoder was also a member of the Hymn Book Committee (1958–81). He served on the *Standing Committee of Annual Meeting (1976–90) where he fulfilled the duties of writing clerk. He also presided as oversight elder of his home congregation, *Wolf Creek, OH, for many years. Yoder died on March 5, and was buried in the Eversole Cemetery near New Lebanon, OH. FMBow

Vindicator (1997) 126; *Minutes (OGBB)* (1976ff.); *Old Order Notes* No. 4 (Spring, 1981) 35.

Young Center, The. In 1986 *Elizabethtown College (PA) established the Young Center for the Study of Anabaptist and Pietist Groups. The threefold mission of the academic research center includes: (1) public programs to interpret the culture and religious heritage of groups related to *Anabaptism and *Pietism, (2) undergraduate courses related to such groups, and (3) scholarly research on Anabaptist and Pietist communities. A new facility, constructed in 1988, houses the Young Center and the Bucher Meetinghouse, an auditorium seating 150 persons. The academic center was named for *Galen S. Young, alumnus and trustee of the college, and his wife, Jessie M. Young. The meetinghouse carries the name of *Rufus P. Bucher (1883–1956), chairman of the college board of trustees (1939–54) and long-time regional and national Brethren (CB) leader.

John A. Hostetler served as the founding director of the center for three years, followed by Donald B. Kraybill who served seven years (1989–96). David B. Eller was appointed director in 1997. The center has organized and supported a variety of regional, national, and international programs including major conferences, a center fellows program, a senior fellow, the annual Durnbaugh Lectures (1993–), an annual banquet, as well as various lectures, exhibits, dramas, and musical programs. By 2000 more than 30 scholars had served as fellows for a summer or semester. Presentations and publications of the center have enjoyed wide dissemination in both church and academic presses and in the public media. In 2000 the center's name was changed to "The Young Center for Anabaptist and Pietist Studies" to better reflect the religious and theological topics in its activities. The Center has played a key role in fostering dialogue and understanding between many groups who share common Anabaptist-Pietist themes in their religious history. DBK

The Young Center: Interpreting a Distinctive Heritage, 1986–1996 (1996); C. Williamson, *Uniting Work and Spirit: A Centennial History of Elizabethtown College* (2001) 294, 311, 334; D. F. Durnbaugh, *Fruit of the Vine* (1997) 583; *Messenger* (Aug./Sept., 1987) 10–11; *The Etownian* (Sept. 15, 1989) 3; *[Lancaster, PA] Intelligencer Journal* (Feb. 13, 1987) 14, (April 29, 1993) C-6; *Elizabethtown Magazine* (Winter, 1987) 20, (Summer, 1993) 31, (Fall, 1990) 26; "The Young Center Report," *President's Report [Elizabethtown College]* (1996–97) 16–17; *Media Ethics 2001* 13.1 (Fall, 2001) 15–26.

The Young Center, Elizabethtown College, PA. Elizabethtown College collection.

Young, Galen S. (CB), b. 1912, surgeon, teacher, churchman. Galen Young was born on Jan. 6 near Mount Joy in Lancaster County, PA, and graduated from *Elizabethtown College and the Philadelphia College of Osteopathic Medicine (PCOM). He married Jessie Magnin; the couple had three children: Galen D., Jeffrey R., and Sandra JoAnn (Male).

Young trained successive generations of PCOM graduates, interns, and surgical residents, and was professor and chairman of the department of surgery. He also was chair of the department of surgery at Riverside Hospital in Wilmington, DE. After 52 years of working as a nationally-known surgeon, serving on many medical boards, acting as president of the American Osteopathic Association, and receiving numerous awards, Young was named chancellor of PCOM; he still continued seeing patients at his general surgical practice.

As a devoted and supportive churchman, Galen Young was instrumental in founding congregations in *Drexel Hill and *Paoli, both suburbs of Philadelphia. He served for many years as a trustee of Elizabethtown College, where he endowed the Young Center for Anabaptist and Pietist Studies. He was also moderator of the Drexel Hill CB and the North Atlantic District conference. JKK

Elizabethtown Magazine (Spring, 1989) 2–5; *PCOM Digest* (Winter, 1994) 12; *N. Atlantic* (1973) index; *The Young Center for the Study of Anabaptist and Pietist Groups: Interpreting a Distinctive Heritage, 1986–1996* (1996) *passim.*

*Youth. In 1926, one issue of the *Dunkard Brethren/*Church of the Brethren division concerned youth. The Dunkard Brethren believed the church of the 1920s limited youth involvement in the church by separating them from the wisdom of their elders through conducting age-specific activities. They also believed that these activities were more about entertainment than truth and could compromise the central aim of the church.

Congregations have been the focus for youth ministries within the Dunkard Brethren Church. Interest in youth nationally has grown since the 1960s. At the *General Conference held each year, youth are involved in leading singing during the services. The *Decorum Committee (established in 1960) guides youth activities at General Conference. The youth also select a minister (or elder) to speak at the next year's Conference. In addition, Leonard Wertz holds an annual Youth Retreat that attracts an average of 70 youth and advisors for lectures and fellowship. Although the denomination does not sponsor these retreats, half the Dunkard Brethren congregations support the program.

Similarly, the *Old German Baptist Brethren focus youth ministry within the congregation. The goal of youth ministry is to help youth avoid the temptations of society and the entertainment offered by the world. Special service activities for widows, the poor, the elderly, and the handicapped are encouraged to provide assistance to the underprivileged and to stimulate a deeper sense of responsibility among young people. Since 1979, the denomination has sponsored private Christian schools. Congregations organize youth activities much more loosely. *Love feast is an important time of gathering for youth, both for worship and fellowship with peers. At OGBB *Annual Meetings, the church holds activities for youth, including recreational sports such as volleyball, baseball, and group games. Attendance at these activities has consistently been high, with ca. 1,000 youth involved.

Youth programs in the *Fellowship of Grace Brethren Churches, *The Brethren Church, and the Church of the Brethren have focused on leadership development. In the FGBC, *Brethren National Youth Conference (BNYC) has been the focus of youth ministry. Held every year since 1938, BNYC hosts two thousand youth and advisors. BNYC includes speakers, musicians, training programs for youth workers, leadership development for young people, and service activities in the communities where the conference is held. Conference staff gives particular attention to strengthening local youth groups. Another part of the program is Nurturing Abilities for Christ (NAC), a talent competition for youth, and Bible quizzing.

Through its partnership with *Grace College, in 1997 the denomination developed a youth ministry course of study, the National Institute for Development of Ministries to Youth. *CE National, the office of youth ministry in the FGBC, coordinates the youth ministry major as an accredited part of the college program. CE National also organizes: *Operation Barnabas, a ministry training experience begun in 1974 for youth during summers; *Training in Ministry Experiences (TIME), a three-week, cross-cultural experience where youth are trained how to work with others in the spirit of servanthood; and the Big Retreat, an annual gathering to help local youth ministers become more effective.

During the 1970s, The Brethren Church revived the "Summer Crusader" program which was active in the 1940s through the 1960s. The program is now called the "Summer Ministry Program." The denomination trains youth to travel on educational, music, and camp teams providing leadership at Bible and music camps and in vacation Bible schools in congregations. Youth were also given opportunities for experiences as ministry interns. Many Summer Crusader and Intern participants went on to serve in ministry in their local churches and a large percentage became pastors. The Summer Ministry Program continues in 1998 to provide opportunities for youth to serve in internships, on district crusader teams serving within their own district, and on short-term mission teams educating youth on the importance of missions both at home and overseas.

Throughout the 1980s, a BC National Youth Council was composed of two youth from each of the nine districts. The members met once a year to provide guidance on youth-related issues within the BC. In the 1990s, the youth reorganized at the national level by changing their name from BYC (Brethren Youth Crusaders) to *BYIC (Brethren Youth in Christ) to emphasize the desire to become more Christ-like. Young people also elected a National Steering Committee which supplemented the National Youth Council's work. The seven youth elected by their denominational peers to this committee are trained in leadership and public speaking. They chair committees of the National Youth Council and attend district functions such as rallies and retreats; they also help to plan the National BYIC Convention. Held for one week every year, BYIC brings youth together from all over The Brethren Church.

The 1940s and 1950s were "glory years" of youth ministry in the Church of the Brethren. The establishment of *Brethren Volunteer Service (BVS) in 1948 represented decades of successful youth work in *camp settings. Held every four years, *National Youth Conferences (NYC) began in 1954, hosting several thousand youth and advisors. The denomination also offered *work camps. In the late 1960s the CB entered a period of organizational restructuring, which de-emphasized age-specific ministries. A multiple-staff youth ministry team in 1968 became a one-sixth position by 1975. NYC continued during the 1970s as did several smaller, issues-oriented conferences known as Study Action Conferences (SAC).

In 1980, Annual Conference (CB) was petitioned to provide for a more vigorous program that would speak to youth. The *General Board carried out this recommendation in 1985, and since then the Youth Ministry Office has expanded to include young adult and junior high ministries. Instead of recruiting one BVS worker to assist every four years, the Office uses two full-time BVSers,

and in NYC years, three. The Office offers a *Christian Citizenship Seminar each spring in New York and Washington, DC. A workcamp program begun in 1987 grew from four to 22 camps by 1996. The Office has organized youth leadership training events in 13 districts, and youth-led programs such as Youth-to-Youth have been equally successful. NYC attendance has shown growth, with more than 4,000 youth and advisors attending the event in 1994. SFRe

Messenger (Nov., 1982) 12–16, (Nov., 1986) 14–20, (Nov., 1990) 15–23, (Nov., 1994) 10–23; BHLA (CB) files; Minutes (DB) (1927 –75); BLT 32 (Winter, 1992) 5–63 (special issue); personal interviews.

Zeigler, Carl Wenger (CB), 1910–87, churchman, scholar, educator, writer. Born in Annville, PA, Carl Zeigler graduated from *Elizabethtown College and United Theol. Sem., studied at many other institutions, and was proficient in Latin, Greek, French, German, and Pennsylvania German. He was a high-school teacher, pastor, and a faculty member at Elizabethtown College for 25 years, teaching religion and sociology. He was much beloved and admired by his students and colleagues, acknowledged by the creation of the Carl W. Zeigler Chair of Religion and Philosophy in 1989.

Zeigler was moderator of the Eastern District CB and of many congregations; a member of the *General Brotherhood Board and of the Bethany Theol. Sem. board; a trustee of Elizabethtown College, and recipient of an honorary doctorate (DD, 1951) and the Steinman teaching award at Elizabethtown College. He wrote church history, curriculum, tracts, and journal articles; pursued genealogical research; and wrote letters to such diverse persons as church workers, former students, and death-row inmates. Among his publications were: a tract Baneful Effects of Worldly Amusements (n.d.); Our Brethren Heritage: Student Manual for Adults (1973); A Genealogy of John Ziegler [sic] and His Wife Kathryn Kline Ziegler (1978); and 15 articles for The Gospel Messenger and Messenger, dating from 1949.

In 1936 Carl Zeigler married Naomi Weaver (who died in 1971); they had three children: Carl W., Jr., George W., and Linda D. (Loser). JER

Messenger (Dec., 1983) 2, (Dec., 1987) 9; D. R. Fitzkee, Moving Toward the Mainstream: 20th Century Change Among the Brethren of Eastern Pennsylvania (1995) index; N. Atlantic (1975) 106; S. Pennsylvania (1972) 98, 229, 232; R. W. Schlosser, History of Elizabethtown College, 1899–1970 (1971) 346; C. Williamson, Uniting Work and Spirit: A Centennial History of Elizabethtown College (2001) 276; Outstanding Educators of America (1971).

Zielasko, John Warlow (FGBC, CGBCI), b. 1921, pastor, missionary, administrator. Born in Minersville, PA, John ("Jack") Zielasko served in the U.S. Navy (1942–45), during which time he married Jean Beveridge (1944). After leaving the service he graduated from Millersville State College (BS, 1947) and *Grace Theol. Sem. (BD, 1950; ThM, 1979).

Raised in the Methodist Church and for a time attended a *Baptist congregation, John Zielasko joined the *Winona Lake, IN, Grace Brethren Church just prior to his graduation from seminary. He served as pastor of the *South Bend, IN, Sunnymeade Brethren Church (1950–52) and then served three terms as a missionary in *Brazil. In 1966 he became foreign secretary of *Grace Brethren Foreign Missions (GBFM) and then general director (1967–86). Under his leadership, over 350 congregations were planted and the baptized membership of

the overseas churches grew to over 125,000. Offerings to the mission rose from less than $500,000 in 1965 to more than $2,500,000 in 1985.

Upon his retirement from leadership in GBFM, the Zielaskos returned to Brazil to assist in the work for a year. In Feb. 1988, Zielasko went to Portugal in pioneering efforts to establish a church there. He returned in June 1988 and fully retired from GBFM that fall. He served as a leader in the development of *Conservative Grace Brethren Churches International. RTC

BMH (Dec. 9, 1950) 835, (Aug., 1986) 24–27; Historical Committee, *A History of Grace Brethren Churches, Northern Atlantic District, 1956–1986* (1991) 59.

LIST OF ORDAINED MINISTERS AND ELDERS
(ca. 1981–2000)

Compiled by Dale V. Ulrich.

Names of ministers and elders ordained by any of the Brethren bodies (ca. 1981–2000) were provided by several persons: Fred W. Benedict (OGBB), John E. Bryant (CGBCI), Leslie E. Cover (OB), Lee H. Dice (FGBC), Robert S. Lehigh (DB), Margaret A. Paris and Edward R. Leiter (CB), and Bradley E. Weidenhamer (BC). To obtain the information presented here, questionnaires were mailed three times to individuals, and attempts were made to phone those not responding. In some cases, the partial information that is included was provided by the denominational source. Because ordination practices vary among the Brethren bodies, some ministers listed here have not yet been ordained.

The information given for each entry is in the form: Name (Brethren body); birth date / death date; ordination date, ordination city, state; other ordination information.

Abshire, William Everett (CB); 4–24–1962 / ; ord. 3–10–1991, Charlottesville, VA.

Ackerman, Steve J. (CB); 8–6–1941 / ; ord. 2–21–1988, Richmond, MO.

Airesman, Royden E. (CB); 2–6–1948 / ; ord. 9–29–1996, Windber, PA.

Aldinger, Steven Glen (DB); 1–7–1965 / ; ord. 4–8–2000, Mechanicsburg, PA.

Alejado, John Arthur (FGBC); 10–23–1951 / ; lic. 1997, Honolulu, HI.

Allan, Daniel W. (FGBC); 12–8–1956 / ; ord. 4–16–1989, Ashland, OH.

Allem, David B. (FGBC); 12–20–1960 / ; ord. 10–14–1991, Telford, PA.

Amundson, Louis A. (FGBC); 7–18–1951 / ; ord. April 1989, Anchorage, AK.

Andrews, Mark R. (DB); 4–19–1962 / ; ord. 4–28–1989, Grandview, MO; eld. 7–19–2001, Grandview, MO.

Andrews, Roy A. (BC); 1–5–1964 / ; ord. 9–14–1997, Nappanee, IN.

Anpaugh, Eric C. (CB); 9–28–1949 / ; ord. 9–5–1989, Arcanum, OH.

Anutunez, Miguel (BC); ord. 1999, Lima, Peru.

Archbold, Phill Carlos (CB); 3–22–1936 / ; ord. 7–11–1982, Brooklyn, NY.

Arenobine, Robert D. (FGBC); 8–2–1952 / ; ord. 11–28–1982, Johnstown, PA.

Arregin, Juan L. (BC); 2–8–1936 / ; ord. 11–14–1999, Tuscon, AZ.

Arthur, Randall J. (FGBC).

Ashman, Charles (FGBC); 6–1–1924 / ; ord. 2–17–1950, Winona Lake, IN.

Atkins, David C. (FGBC); 4–9–1953 / ; ord. 4–12–1992, Freemont, OH.

Auker, Kevin L. (CB); 9–18–1955 / ; ord. 8–8–1998, Blue Ball, PA.

Aungst, David S. (DB); 3–6–1957 / ; ord. 11–1–1986, Bethel, PA; eld. 5–9–2002, Bethel, PA.

Aungst, Jeffrey Lynn (DB); 2–12–1962 / ; ord. 5–12–2001, Bethel, PA.

Austin, Gary L. (FGBC); 2–7–1944 / ; ord. 5–16–1982, Warsaw, IN.

Avey, Thomas D. (FGBC); 5–8–1953 / ; ord. 1985, Orlando, FL.

Bach, Jeffrey Alan (CB); 1–19–1958 / ; ord. 7–24–1983, Middletown, OH.

Baer, Samuel S. (FGBC); 8–5–1944 / ; lic. 9–12–1971, Myerstown, PA.

Baker, Allen J., Jr. (CB); 12–16–1947 / ; ord. 8–20–1995, Flutstone, MD.

Baker, George E. (CB); 4–3–1941 / ; ord. 10–31–1993, Berlin, PA.

Baker, Jimmy Lee (CB); 10–6–1958 / ; ord. 3–24–1991, Peru, IN.

Baker, Paul (Tony) A. (CB); 9–19–1966 / ; ord 4–2–1995, Stanley, VA.

Baldwin, Charles F. (CB); 8–20–1954 / ; ord. 8–10–1997, Syracuse, IN.

Baldwin, Terry Lee (CB); 11–25–1955 / ; ord. 7–20–1986, Pioneer, OH.

Baliles, Mark E. (CB); 4–15–1963 / ; ord. 11–18–1990, Hagerstown, IN.

Ball, Christopher A. (FGBC); 3–3–1952 / ; ord. 6–19–1991, Arvada, CO.

Ballinger, John A. (CB); 4–5–1951 / ; ord. 6–25–1995, Akron, OH.

Ball-Miller, Rebecca L. (CB); 5–11–1960 / ; ord. 6–10–1990, Milford, IN.

Balmer, Richard H. (CB); 3–2–1954 / ; ord. 9–20–1998, Manheim, PA.

Banaszak, David Francis (CB); 1–30–1956 / ; ord. 5–16–1993, Martinsburg, PA.

Barber, Howard (CB); 11–4–1954 / ; ord. 5–18–2000, Kettering, OH.

Barger, Raymond J., Jr. (FGBC); 7–20–1948 / ; lic. 5–6–1996, Waynesboro, PA.

Bargerhuff, Eric (BC); 10–19–1970 / ; ord. 5–26–1996, Ashland, OH.

Barkey, Ray W. (CB); 8–4–1955 / ; ord. 9–10–1985, Rockford, IL.

Barley, Shirley M. (CB); 8–8–1942 / ; ord. 3–26–2002, Reisterstown, MD.

Barlow, Bruce S. W. (FGBC); 8–29–1956 / ; ord. 5–15–1994, Winona Lake, IN.

Barlow, Robert William (FGBC); 1–24–1966 / ; lic. Sept. 1985, Waterloo, IA.

Barnhill, Charles William (FGBC); 12–5–1939 / ; eld. 4–1–1985, Mifflin, OH.

Barnum-Steggerda, Daniel S. (CB); 8–31–1957 / ; ord. 10–28–1989, Virginia Beach, VA.

Barnum-Steggerda, Lucinda Kay (CB); 2–9–1959 / ; ord. 7–12–1987, Midland, MI.

Bartholomew, Paul Harmon (CB); 5–24–1965 / ; ord. 6–7–1998, West Salem, OH.

Bartlett, Roger F. (CGBCI); 6–23–1951 / ; ord. April 1987, Mansfield, OH.

Bartley, Richard John (FGBC); 5–17–1951 / ; ord. 6–1–1997, Cleveland, OH.

Barton, Max (OGBB); 4–9–1952 / ; 1st deg. 3–19–1988; 2nd deg 2–7–1995; eld. 3–18–2000.

Barton, Paul William (OGBB); 2–2–1962 / ; 1st deg. 4–3–1998, Modesto, CA.

Baskin, Carl (CB); 7–29–1927 / ; ord. May 1960, Philadelphia, PA.

Basler, Lucy Hollinger (CB); 1–5–1941 / ; ord. 5–4–1996, Rice Lake, WI.

Bauer, Gary W. (CB); 11–22–1950 / ; ord. 10–26–1980, Elkhart, IN.

Bauer, James R. (CB); 6–23–1950 / ; ord. Dec. 1990, Newport, PA.

Bauman, Abraham (OGBB); 7–14–1959 / ; 1st deg. 6–29–1985; 2nd deg. 11–8–1993; eld. 2–13–1999; Athens, WI.

Bauman, Glenn (OGBB); 11–30–1938 / ; 1st deg. 11–28–1970; 2nd deg. 11–19–1977; eld. 1–6–1984; Garnett, KS.

Bauman, James H. (OGBB); 3–8–1964 / ; 1st deg. 8–26–1995; Delphi, IN.

Bauman, Joseph H. (OGBB); 7–12–1961 / ; 1st deg. 8–18–1990, Westphalia, KS.

Bauman, Wesley Allen (OGBB); 4–25–1962 / ; 1st deg. 4–22–1991; 2nd deg. 8–6–1999, Ripon, CA.

Bayer, Lloyd (OGBB); 12–4–1951 / ; 1st deg, 6–28–1982; 2nd deg. 3–28–1987; eld. 6–26–1993, Brookville, OH.

Bayles, Gordon C. (CB); 10–26–1937 / ; ord. 2–7–1982, Toms Brook, VA.

Bayne, David (FGBC).

Beach, Gregory Allen (CB); 9–16–1952 / ; ord. 1996.

Beahm, Martha Ellen (CB); 9–27–1959 / ; ord. 6–12–1988, Bridgewater, VA.

Beam, Nicholas E. (CB); 6–12–1956 / ; ord. 2000.

Beck, Justin G. (DB); 2–22–1959 / ; ord. 5–10–2001, Bethel, PA.

Becker, Christian J. (FGBC); 5–23–1951 / ; lic. 6–10–1979, Berrien Springs, MI.

Beeghley, Charles W. (OGBB); 8–15–1953 / ; 1st deg. 3–27–1993; 2nd deg. 3–20–1998, Baldwin City, KS.

Beeman, Steven Edward (DB); 6–26–1951 / ; ord. 4–8–2001, Mechanicsburg, PA.

Beery, Daniel M. (OB); 2–12–1967 / ; 1st deg. 5–24–1996.

Beery, Helen H. (CB); 8–3–1936 / ; ord. 11–19–1989, North Manchester, IN.

Beery, John H. (OGGB); 3–19–1955 / ; 1st deg. 4–9–1982; 2nd deg. 10–23–1986; eld. 10–26–1989, Athens, WI.

Beery, Matthew Lee (OGBB); 10–21–1962 / ; 1st deg. OGBB, 10–25–1990, Collins, MS; 2nd deg. 10–30–1995; min. term. 9–19–1998; ord. German Baptist Brethren 9–23–1999, Jamesport, MO; eld. German Baptist Brethren, 10–6–2000, Jamesport, MO.

Beeson, Joseph (FGBC).

Bell, David Owen (CB); 10–9–1947 / ; ord. 5–18–1986, Norton, KS.

Bell, Eugene G. (BC); 9–29–1939 / ; eld. 6–18–1997, Muncie, IN.

Belohlavek, Robert A. (FGBC); 11–24–1953 / ; eld. 7–19–1981, Warsaw, IN.

Belsterling, Donald Lee (BC); 6–12–1963 / ; ord. 10–10–1999, Ashland, OH.

Benedict, James L. (CB); 2–27–1959 / ; ord. 8–12–1986, Royersford, PA.

Benesh, Gary L. (CB); 8–14–1953 / ; ord. Oct. 1984, North Wilkesboro, NC.

Benner, Michael S. (CB); 10–4–1963 / ; ord. 10–7–1995, Mifflintown, PA.

Benshoff, David E. (BC); 5–20–1950 / ; ord. June 1990, Louisville, OH.

Bentzel, Paul W. (CB); 10–6–1948 / ; ord. 10–11–1998, York, PA.

Berkey, Corey A. (CB); 3–31–1970 / ; ord. Feb. 2000, Dry Run, PA; min. term. Jan. 2002.

Berkley, Richard Wayne (CB); 9–3–1953 / ; ord. 2–6–2000, Danville, VA.

Betoney, Arnold (FGBC).

Beutler, Kelly J. (CB); 9–1–1954 / ; ord. 11–21–1999, Liberty Mills, IN.

Bhagat, Shantilal P. (CB); 10–13–1923 / ; ord. 4–1–1990, Elgin, IL.

Bibbee, David M. (CB); 7–3–1953 / ; ord. 4–14–1983, South Bend, IN.

Bickel, Kenneth E. (FGBC); 6–27–1947 / ; ord. April 1982, Goshen, IN.

Biddle, William R. (CB); 1–16–1934 / ; ord. 7–12–1985, Peterstown, WV.

Bidgood Enders, Elizabeth Lynn (CB); 8–20–1974 / ; ord. 2–24–2001, Dayton, OH.

Bidgood Enders, Gregory S. (CB); 2–4–1974 / ; ord. 2–24–2001, Dayton, OH.

Biedebach, Brian R. (FGBC); 11–7–1969 / ; ord. 5–19–1999, Seal Beach, CA.

Binkley, Timothy Scott Grimm (CB); 4–15–1963 / ; ord. 9–10–1995, Onekama, MI.

Binns, Gordon F. (CB); 8–18–1928 / ; ord. 10–6–1985, Sunfield, MI.

Bitner, Robert L. (CB); 7–12–1946 / ; ord. 10–12–1997, Union City, OH.

Black, Brian S. (CB); 11–14–1961 / ; ord. 2–25–2001, Lititz, PA.

Black, James F. (BC); 11–23–1956 / ; ord. July 1985, Bellefontaine, OH.

Black, Larry G. (CB); 4–2–1947 / ; ord. 1–10–1993, Salix, PA.

Blevins, Dave (CGBCI); 5–13–1905 / ; ord. 12–7–1982, New Philadelphia, OH.

Blevins, Monte L. (CB); 10–21–1932 / ; ord. 4–17–1988, Arrington, VA.

Boal, Timothy E. (FGBC); 1–15–1957 / ; ord. 4–5–1987, Everett, PA.

Bohrer, Bradley C. (CB); 3–23–1954 / ; ord. 1–15–1984, Brook Park, OH.

Bolden, Rickey (BC); ord. 1995, Washington, DC.

Bollinger, Dale L. (CB); 4–20–1966 / ; ord. 9–5–1995, Denver, PA.

Bollinger, Glenn Edwin (CB); 10–27–1964 / ; ord. 10–3–1993, Bridgewater, VA.

Bollinger, Steven Wayne (CB); 9–20–1969 / ; ord. 4–25–1999, Englewood, OH.

Booker, Ted J. (FGBC).

Boone, Billy W. (OGBB); 1–8–1949 / ; 1st deg. 3–19–1983; 2nd deg. 11–19–1988; eld. 6–18–1996, Ferrum, VA.

Boone, Randy (OGBB); 7–9–1945 / ; 1st deg. 11–12–1983; 2nd deg. 11–11–1989; eld. 7–22–1997; Boones Mill, VA.

Booth, Marilou Genereaux (CB); 2–11–1936 / ; ord. 7–19–1998, San Marcos, CA.

Boothe, Fannie (CB); 3–7–1923 / ; ord. 1989.

Boothe, Rodger L. (CB); 8–12–1942 / ; ord. 8–9–1990, Lindside, WV.

Booz, Donald R. (CB); 12–9–1949 / ; ord. 1981.

Borgmann, Robert Kurt (CB); 5–11–1966 / ; ord. 6–23–1991, Wilmington, DE.

Bosserman, Sandra L. (CB); 11–8–1949 / ; ord. 9–27–1997, Peace Valley, MO.

Bower, Darryl E. (OGBB); 5–24–1943 / ; 1st deg, 4–30–1983; 2nd deg. 8–12–1989; eld. 8–3–1996; Roanoke, VA.

Bower, Larry A. (OGBB); 9–3–1958 / ; 1st deg. 11–14–1992; 2nd deg. 3–28–1998, West Alexandria, OH.

Bowers, George A. (CB); 8–2–1963 / ; ord. 12–1–1996, Woodstock, VA.

Bowland, Ron (CGBCI); 4–29–1905 / ; ord. 11–19–1996, Peru, IN.

Bowman, Christopher D. (CB); 19–1962 / ; ord. 5–31–1987, Elgin, IL.

Bowman, Dale (OGBB); 4–14–1953 / ; 1st deg. 8–2–1991; 2nd deg. 8–7–1998; Modesto, CA.

Bowman, Daniel Ray (OGBB); 7–22–1968 / ; 1st deg. 12–13–1997, Pendleton, IN.

Bowman, Gerald Lee (OGBB); 4–4–1961 / ; 1st deg. 1–4–1997, New Carlisle, OH.

Bowman, Mark A. (CB); 6–12–1953 / ; ord. 6–22–1997, New Lebanon, OH.

Bowman, Trent L. (OGBB); 3–20–1967 / ; 1st deg. 4–5–1997, Covington, OH.

Bowser, Mark B. (CB); 4–22–1955 / ; ord. 4–18–1982, Gettysburg, PA.

Bowser, Paula Picard (CB); 10–26–1951 / ; ord. 6–5–1994, Ankeny, IA.

Boyd, Mary L. (CB); 5–9–1937 / ; ord. 3–21–1999, Venice, FL.

Boyer, Susan Stern (CB); 10–14–1960 / ; ord. 6–23–1985, La Verne, CA.

Bradley, E. Arnold (CB); 7–11–1952 / ; ord. April 1991, Amherst County, VA.

Brandon, Fred, Jr. (BC); 12–20–1934 / ; eld. 1–13–1991, Bryan, OH.

Breiner, Sue R. (CB); 3–11–1945 / ; ord. 3–28–1982, South English, IA.

Brenneman, Jerry Dean (CB); 11–10–1957 / ; ord. 1983.

Brinkmeier, Kathleen Diane (CB); 1–28–1944 / ; ord. 8–27–2000, Lima, OH.

Britton, Mark Allen (BC); 12–12–1959 / ; ord. 6–5–1988, Bryan, OH.

Broadwater, Howard (CB); 4–29–1917 / ; ord. 1982.

Brockway, Wayne E. (CB); 4–1–1955 / ; ord. 5–6–1990, Lima, OH.

Brooks, Daniel (OGBB); 1–19–1958 / ; 1st deg. 10–13–1986; Ottawa, KS; 2nd deg. 10–12–1992; ord. 11–17–1998.

Bross, Scott J. (DB); 9–21–1962 / ; ord. 2–28–1987, Bethel, PA.; min. term. 3–15–98.

Brotherton, Bobbi Alie (CB); 6–18–1934 / ; ord. 12–29–1991, Surgoinsville, TN.

Brovont, Richard A. (OGBB); 7–2–1964 / ; 1st deg. 1–29–2000, North Manchester, IN.

Brown, C. James (FGBC); 1–4–1962 / ; ord. May 2002, Goshen, IN.

Brown, Deanna G. (CB); 8–13–1955 / ; ord. 4–28–1985, Kalamazoo, MI.

Brown, Edward Martin (CB); 9–16–1945 / ; ord. 5–29–1983, Fruitdale, AL.

Brown, James A. (FGBC); 10–26–1961 / ; ord. 10–15–1995, Philadephia, PA.

Brown, Jeffrey H. (CGBCI); 5–1–1961 / ; ord. 8–17–92, Elyria, OH.

Brown, Kenneth James (FGBC); 8–8–1953 / ; ord. 11–22–1981, Akron, OH.

Brown, Philip D. (CB); 1–27–1938 / ; ord. 1987.

Broyles, Dewey V. (CB); 3–17–1970 / ; ord. 7–13–1996, Lindside, WV.

Brubaker, Alfred D. (OGBB); 3–10–1962 / ; 1st deg. 11–21–1988, Homestead, FL; 2nd deg. 3–7–1994, Homestead, FL; eld. 3–17–1999, Waynesboro, PA.

Brubaker, J. Eric (CB); 8–25–1966 / ; ord. 6–12–1994, Lititz, PA.

Brubaker, Michael Phares (FGBC); 1–9–1952 / ; ord. 4–1–1984, Philadephia, PA.

Brubaker, Randy (OGBB); 7–2–1953 / ; 1st deg. 3–12–1983; 2nd deg. 9–12–1987; eld. 9–18–1993, Sawyer, KS.

Brumbaugh, Alan E. (CB); 4–1–1963 / ; ord. 8–16–1998, Bellwood, PA.

Brumbaugh, Lillian Frances Trageser (CB); 4–4–1931 / ; ord. 3–25–1984, Hyattsville, MD.

Brumbaugh-Cayford, Cheryl A. (CB); 6–24–1963 / ; ord. 8–22–1999, Windsor, CO.

Brunk, Gene (OGBB); 5–16–1955 / ; 1st deg. 8–22–1989, Union City, OH; 2nd deg. 3–25–1995; eld. 3–18–2000, Union City, OH.

Bryant, James Emory, Jr. (OGBB); 6–7–1960 / ; 1st deg. 6–11–1991, Roanoke, VA; 2nd deg. 3–5–1997; eld. 10–30–2002, Roanoke, VA.

Bryant, John E. (CGBCI); 3–30–1951 / ; ord. 2–24–1985, Mount Vernon, OH.

Bryant, Thomas Thaxton (CB); 9–26–1962 / ; ord. 1986, Roanoke, VA.

Bucher, Mark K. (CB); 3–8–1959 / ; ord. 10–25–1992, Brunswick, ME.

Buckingham, Don (FGBC).

Buckwalter, Anita Smith (CB); 1–23–1946 / ; ord. 6–3–1984, Lansing, MI.

Buford, Robert (BC); 1–15–1954 / ; ord. 1997.

Burgess, Wayne (DB); 8–30–1953 / ; ord. 1989, McCave, CO.

Burk, Kelly J. (CB); 8–24–1973 / ; ord. 10–8–2000, Westminster, MD.

Burns, Ronald R. (BC); 5–1–1954 / ; ord. 4–27–1997, Roanoke, IN.

Burns, Stephen J. (CGBCI); 10–12–1952 / ; ord. 5–6–1990, Dalas Center, IA.

Burtz, Ronald G. (CB); 4–4–1960 / ; ord. 9–12–1999, Virden, IL.

Butler, Tully (FGBC).

Butters, Terry D. (CB); 10–16–1947 / ; ord. 8–18–1988, Flint, MI.

Button-Harrison, Mary Jane (CB); 9–15–1962 / ; ord. 6–13–1993, Ankeny, IA.

Button-Harrison, Timothy Glen (CB); 11–5–1959 / ; ord. 9–23–1990, Grundy Center, IA.

Byers, William A. (FGBC); 4–2–1931 / ; ord. 6–15–1967, Hollins, VA.

Byrd, Randall (FGBC).

Calderon, Karen Irene (CB); 11–4–1945 / ; ord. 5–12–1982, Elgin, IL.

Caldwell, Rodney R. (CB); 6–23–1960 / ; ord. 1990.

Campbell, Harold (Pete) Wray (CB); 5–5–1946 / ; ord. 4–23–1996, Staunton, VA.

Caplinger, Robert (CB); 6–17–1931 / ; ord. 1–15–1996, Gratis, OH.

Card, Charles David (FGBC); 12–7–1954 / ; ord. 6–27–1982, Wahiawa, HI.

Carey, Art (FGBC); 9–7–07 / .

Carey, Jonathan Paul (FGBC); 10–26–1967 / ; ord. 9–30–2001, Akron, OH.

Carlson, Melinda K. (CB); 12–2–1940 / ; ord. 5–13–2000, Baltimore, MD.

Carmichael, Paula S. (CB); 6–27–1952 / ; ord. 6–9–1999, Middletown, IN.

Carnevali, Ronald P. (FGBC); 5–9–1939 / ; ord. 11–22–1992, Johnstown, PA.

Carr, Arthur C. (BC); 4–17–1970 / ; eld. 11–18–2001, Smithville, OH.

Carroll, Jeffrey A. (FGBC); 7–10–1950 / ; ord. 6–23–1993, Dublin, OH.

Carroll, Robert B. (FGBC); 8–1–1953 / ; ord. 5–23–1995, Atlanta, GA; eld. 1–5–1999, Atlanta, GA.

Carter, Jeffrey W. (CB); 4–19–1970 / ; ord. 5–28–1998, Manassas, VA.

Carter, Karen Spohr (CB); 6–25–1935 / ; ord. 11–15–1981, Roanoke, VA.

Cary, Jack L. (CB); 8–2–1936 / ; ord. 9–17–2000, Osceola, IN.

Chae, David Indu (CB); 3–11–1941 / ; ord. 5–18–1988, Phoenix, AZ.

Chappell, James I. (CB); 3–24–1943 / ; ord. 1989, Stuarts Draft, VA.

Charlton, Burl Eugene (CB); 8–3–1956 / ; ord. 3–14–1998, Augusta, WV.

Chinworth, James H. (CB); 4–6–1957 / ; ord. 12–8–1996, Mountville, PA.

Christiansen, William J. (CB); 6–2–1950 / ; ord. Sept. 1996, Franklin Grove, IL.

Christner, Jay Lewis (CB); 10–21–1929 / ; ord. 5–23–1982, Somerset, PA.

Chronister, James E. (CB); 9–21–1952 / ; ord. 6–6–1976, York, PA.

Clapper, Donald L. (CB); 11–30–39 / ; ord. 8–15–1981, Greencastle, PA; eld. 8–21–1983.

Clark, Michael A. (CB); 2–21–1960 / ; ord. 3–31–1985, Beaverton, MI.

Clark, Rick A. (FGBC); 8–17–1957 / ; ord. 4–21–1985, Ankenytown, OH; eld. 4–21–1985, Ankenytown, OH.

Clark, Thomas J. (CB); 3–25–1938 / ; ord. 6–6–1987, Goshen, IN.

Clark, Wanda Mills (CB); 4–25–1954 / ; ord. 11–12–1995, Linwood, MD.

Clasper-Torch, Lee (CB); 1–8–1958 / ; ord. 1987.

Coates, Earl Edward (CB); 9–23–1923 / ; ord. 10–7–1997, Dunkirk, IN.

Coffin, Joseph H. (CB); 3–3–1947 / ; ord. 2–20–2000, Windfall, IN.

Coffman, Dennis E. (CB); 6–3–1947 / ; ord. 2–5–2000, Hershey, PA; min. term. 11–2–02.

Coffman, Eldon Henry (CB); 11–3–1931 / ; ord. May 1985, Cabool, MO; min. term. 12–31–1996.

Cohen, Ronald Nathan (FGBC); 3–6–1941 / ; ord. 1983, Lancaster, PA.

Cole, Neil (FGBC); 9–10–1960 / ; ord. 10–1–1989, Alta Loma, CA.

Cole, Wallace Glenn (CB); 9–12–1950 / ; ord. 8–23–1992, Lexington, NC.

Collins, Benjamin F., III (FGBC); 9–29–1952 / ; ord. April 1987, Simi Valley, CA.

Collins, John W. (CB); 8–2–1963 / ; ord. 9–24–2000, Pulaski, VA.

Combs, Daniel O. (CB); 9–23–1949 / ; ord. 3–14–1998, Levels, WV.

Combs, Harold P. (FGBC).

Combs, Robert P. (FGBC); 10–14–1939 / ; ord. 11–14–1965, Sterling, OH.

Combs, Rosella J. (CB); 3–27–1931 / ; ord. 11–15–1992, Tipp City, OH.

Conn, Barry L. (CB); 11–14–1965 / ; ord. 1994.

Conrad, Thomas W. (BC); 11–22–1953 / ; ord. 3–17–1994, New Lebanon, OH.

Cook, Glen A. (OGBB); 9–20–1967 / ; 1st deg. 4–6–1998, Cleveland, GA.

Cooper, Leslie Ernest (CB); 4–3–1948 / ; ord. Church of God-Anderson, 3–14–1984, Wiley, CO; tran, CB 9–22–1985, Sabetha, KS.

Cooper, Scott (CB); 6–2–1957 / ; ord. 6–13–1982, Rockwood, PA.

Coppernoll, Sue (CB); 12–31–1933 / ; ord. 4–26–1994, Mt. Morris, IL.

Corbitt, Jim C. (BC); 10–3–1951 / ; ord. 1999, Mathias, WV.

Cordrey, Mark Edward (DB); 12–29–1965 / ; ord. 7–30–1989, Modesto, CA; eld. 2004, Modesto, CA.

Cory, Martha E. (CB); 6–14–1935 / ; ord. 7–13–1986, Kokomo, IN.

Cosentino, Joseph M. (FGBC); 11–11–1956 / ; eld. 1–31–1993, Cleveland, OH.

Cosgrove, Jonathan C. (FGBC); 7–14–1972 / ; lic. 11–8–1998, Buena Vista, VA.

Cosner, Elmer Richard (CB); 9–10–1928 / ; ord. 11–6–1998, Dryfork, WV.

Cosner, Randy Wayne (CB); 7–3–1958 / ; ord. 6–25–1989, Rawlings, MD.

Cottrell, Richard (OGBB); 3–13–1974 / ; 1st deg. 10–7–1999, Camden, IN.

Coulter, Carol R. (CB); 1–25–1946 / ; ord. 11–6–1999, Waka, TX.

Coulter, Nina R. (CB); 2–10–1941 / ; ord. 10–14–2000, Waka, TX.

Coursen, Robert A. (CB); 7–18–1970 / ; ord. 9–20–1998, Youngstown, OH.

Courter, Douglas A. (FGBC); 1–16–1957 / ; ord. 5–29–1988, Winchester, VA.

Cover, Benjamin A. (OB); 8–29–1967 / ; 1st deg. 5–16–1997.

Cover, Dwight E. (FGBC); 7–9–1957 / ; ord. 9–23–1984, Anchorage, AK.

Cover, Leslie (OB); 1–21–1934 / : first deg. 10–29–1971; eld. 4–19–1980.

Covington, Charles L. (FGBC); 4–23–1933 / ; ord. 1973, El Toro, CA.

Cox, Mary Margaret (CB); 6–14–1931 / ; ord. 11–15–1997, Petersburg, WV.

Crago, Florence M. (CB); 5–15–1927 / ; ord. 8–24–1986, Toledo, OH.

Cragun, Rodger Lawson (CB); 2–13–1941 / ; ord.United Presbyterian Church USA, 5–28–1970, Lewiston, NY; tran. CB, May 1981.

Crain, Marion Keith (CB); 8–28–1951 / ; ord. 9–8–1990, Tryon, NC.

Cripe, Carl E. (FGBC); 4–3–1933 / ; lic. 1979, Modesto, CA.

Cripe, Larry L. (OGBB); 9–20–1954 / ; 1st deg. 1–31–1987, North Manchester, IN; 2nd deg. 1–30–1993; eld. 1–29–2000, North Manchester, IN.

Crissman, Darrell L (BC); 10–6–1960 / ; ord. 6–30–1989, Gratis, OH.

Crouse, Gerald Paul Baile (CB); 7–7–1957 / ; ord. 9–16–1988, Rocky Mount, VA.

Crouse, Rebecca Baile (CB); 9–30–1959 / ; ord. 9–16–1988, Rocky Mount, VA.

Cruise, Clancy Calvin (FGBC); 9–8–1961 / ; eld. 3–15–1998, Wooster, OH.

CRULL, WALTER L.

Crull, Walter L. (CB); 12–15–1937 / ; ord. 4–28–1996, Rockingham County, VA.

Crumley, John B. (CB); 2–15–1946 / ; ord. July 1988, Knoxville, TN.

Crumrine, Duane E. (CB); 1–4–1958 / ; ord. 12–5–1999, Fredericksburg, PA.

Cruz, William R., Jr. (BC); 11–8–1960 / ; ord. 1994, Valrico, FL.

Cullers, Eston L. (CB); 7–25–1933 / ; ord. 7–26–1992, Moorefield, WV.

Cullers, Harold Glenn (CB); 4–26–1948 / ; ord. 10–16–1988, Brandywine, WV.

Culp, Ray D. (OGBB); 10–23–1955 / ; 1st deg. 4–8–1989, Wakarusa, IN; 2nd deg. 3–16–1996; eld. 3–16–2002, Wakarusa, IN.

Cunningham, Amos V. (CB); 4–29–1930 / ; ord. 4–5–1987, Coopersburg, PA.

Cunningham, Mark A. (CB); 6–20–1964 / ; ord. 7–11–1993, Quarryville, PA.

Curry, Donald W. (CB); 5–15–1954 / ; ord. 5–17–1981, Arbovale, WV.

Custer, Janice E. (CB); 3–2–1949 / ; ord. 8–18–1991, Mechanicsburg, PA.

Daam, Rick (FGBC).

Daggett, Joan Lawrence (CB); 7–24–1961 / ; ord. 5–31–1998, Tryon, NC.

Daggett, Kevin Wayne (CB); 8–21–1962 / ; ord. 6–3–1990, Daleville, VA.

Dahlberg, Nancy (CB); 3–21–1946 / ; ord. 1996.

Daniels, Terry L. (FGBC); 10–9–1953 / ; ord. 10–15–1990, South Pasadena, CA.

Daughtery, David S. (FGBC); 3–18–1947 / ; lic. 1982, Worthington, OH.

Davidson, Jeffrey A. (CB); / ; ord. 1991.

Davidson, Kenneth W. (CB); 6–26–1943 / ; ord. 6–13–1983, Anderson County, KS.

Davis, Clarence (Chuck) R., Jr. (CB); 1–11–1948 / ; ord. Nov. 1982, Arbovale, WV.

Davis, James A. (CB); 12–17–1957 / ; ord. 1984, McFarland, CA.

Davis, James H. (CB); 1–21–1945 / ; ord. 12–4–1994, North Liberty, IN.

Davis, John J. (FGBC); 10–13–1936 / ; eld. 6–6–1963, Winona Lake, IN

Davis, Linda E. S. (CB); 3–14–1958 / ; ord. 11–28–1999, McFarland, CA.

Davis, Raymond Harry (FGBC); 6–7–1937 / ; ord. 9–22–1979, Meyersdale, PA.

Davis, Vernita Jane Neher (CB); 11–5–1937 / ; ord. 5–6–1984, Enders, NE.

De Oleo, Ruben (CB); ord. 1990.

Dean, Vernon F. (CB); 7–7–1928 / ; ord. 6–22–1988, Lowpoint, IL.

Dearth, Thomas Eugene (CB); 2–21–1942 / ; ord. 11–12–1994, Forest, OH.

Deaton, Dean (OGBB); 5–18–1944 / ; 1st deg. 6–21–1980; 2nd deg. 12–20–1986; eld. 9–17–1994, Rossville, IN.

Deaton, Kenneth A. (OGBB); 2–11–1956 / ; 1st deg. 4–9–1988, Palestine, OH; 2nd deg. 4–3–1993; eld. 3–27–1999, Palestine, OH.

DeBolt, Robert Lynn (CB); 9–25–1949 / ; ord. 7–18–1999, Lowpoint, IL.

Deeter, Jeanne (CB); 11–9–1948 / ; ord. 1996.

Deeter, Joan George (CB); 11–2–1930 / ; ord. 6–27–1982, North Manchester, IN.

Deetscreek, Bradley J. (FGBC); 5–11–1973 / ; ord. May 2001, Johnstown, PA.

Deffenbaugh, Barron K. (CB); 2–2–1958 / ; ord. 12–31–1994, Johnstown, PA.

Dell, Phillip C. (CB); 11–22–1951 / ; ord. 7–18–1982, Ottawa, KS.

Denlinger, Danny L. (OGBB); 2–2–1967 / ; 1st deg. 9–27–1997, Dayton, OH.

Denlinger, Gary W. (OGBB); 8–23–1952 / ; 1st deg. 3–25–1989, Brookville, OH; 2nd deg. 9–9–1995; eld. 12–9–2000, Brookville, OH.

Denlinger, Ned Martin (FGBC); 2–13–1957 / ; ord. 11–16–2003, Loveland, OH.

Dentler, Larry M. (CB); 7–13–1951 / ; ord. 7–21–1985, North Liberty, IN.

Derr, H. Kevin (CB); 7–19–1969 / ; ord. 5–10–1998, Hollansburg, OH.

Derr, Horace E. (CB); 2–6–1947 / ; ord. 1987, Sommerset, PA.

DeSilva, Mark (FGBC).

Detwiler, Samuel K. (CB); 4–26–1951 / ; ord. 1–23–1983, Wiley, CO.

DeVeny, Daniel Judson (BC); 10–19–1946 / ; ord. 6–7–1981, Ashland, OH.

Deyerle, Gordon Ernest (CB); 9–17–1947 / ; ord. Feb. 1986, Troutville, VA.

DeZago, Edmund K. (FGBC).

Diaz, Manuel A. (CB); 9–5–1955 / ; ord. 1984.

Dietz, Arnold (CB); 8–3–1935 / ; ord. 6–2–1996, Wakarusa, IN.

Dietz, Paul Ernest (CB); 9–27–1955 / ; ord. 7–10–1983, Richland Township, PA.

Dinkins-Curling, Jeffrey (Rusty) (CB); 10–26–1956 / ; ord. 1–15–1995, Arcanum, OH.

DiSalvio, Robert S. (CB); 2–24–1945 / ; ord. 8–8–1998, Stockton, NJ.

Distler, Scott K. (FGBC); 2–24–1965 / ; ord. 2–3–1991, West Milton, OH.

Dobos, William (CB); 9–8–1959 / ; ord. 1988.

Doerr, Robert (FGBC).

Donohoo, Byron Douglas (CB); 2–29–1944 / ; ord. 5–21–2000, West Milton, OH.

Dorsey, Janice Welch (CB); 3–21–1928 / ; ord. 1997.

Doss, Martin C. (CB); 8–16–1966 / ; ord. 7–30–2000, Blue Ridge, VA.

Douglas, Lucinda M. E. (CB); 9–23–1954 / ; ord. 1–29–1989, Pomona, CA.

Doutrich, Stephen D. (FGBC); 3–29–1959 / ; ord. 11–12–1989, Lancaster, PA.

Dowdy, Christy L. (CB); 1–9–1954 / ; ord. June 1990, Lincoln, NE.

Dowdy, Dale W. (CB); 8–24–1949 / ; ord. 6–14–1981, Carleton, NE.

Downing, Howard L. (FGBC); 11–7–1947 / ; ord. 1999, Columbus, OH.

Driver, Brent K. (CB); 3–10–1951 / ; ord. 6–2–1985, Columbus City, IN.

Dubble, Carol Cave (CB); 5–26–1945 / ; ord. 8–10–1984, Lebanon, PA.

Dubel, William F., Jr. (CB); 10–25–1943 / ; ord. 1989.

Dueck, Stanley B. (CB); 6–22–1958 / ; ord. 5–17–1998, Pottstown, PA.

Duncan, Ralph M. (CB); 10–30–1931 / ; ord. 10–2–1988, Floyd, VA.

Durr, Marilyn Jeanne (CB); 1–23–1957 / ; ord. 10–14–1990, Grantsville, MD.

Durr, Stephen George (CB); 10–15–1952 / ; ord. 11–21–1982, LaVale, MD.

Eady, Kevin (FGBC).

Earlenbaugh, Donald G. (CB); 5–13–1937 / ; ord. 1982.

Eberly, James D. (DB); 5–3–1954 / ; ord. 3–28–1989, Lititz, PA; eld. 2003, Lititz, PA.

Ebersole, George D. (CB); 12–30–1940 / ; ord. 5–21–1972, Denver, CO.

Echard, Alan R. (CGBCI); 9–6–1968 / ; ord. 5–6–1990, Harrisburg, PA.

Edgecomb, Glen (OGBB); 3–1–1949 / ; 1st deg. 12–12–1981; 2nd deg. 3–15–1986; eld. 10–12–1992, Ottawa, KS.

Edgington, Allen (FGBC).

Edmonds, Edwin Hill (CB); 3–18–1952 / ; ord. 1–7–1996, Martinsburg, WV.

Edmonds, Stephan J. (FGBC); 2–14–1950 / ; ord. 1998, Ft. Lauderdale, FL.

Edwards, Kenneth L. (CB); 12–26–1943 / ; ord. 1991, Rogersville, TN.

Edwards, Larry David (FGBC); 5–30–1950 / ; ord. 12–4–1983, Berne, IN.

Ehrhardt, Roddy C. (FGBC); 10–7–1954 / ; ord. 10–25–1998, Dallas Center, IA.

Eickhoff, Eric L. (FGBC); 10–30–1959 / ; ord. 10–25–1999, Longview, TX; eld. 10–17–2002, Portis, TX.

Eikenberry, Susan Lynn (CB); 5–1–1950 / ; ord. 10–10–1993, Elizabethtown, PA.

Eisenbise, Debra L. (CB); 8–10–1960 / ; ord. May 1989, Fremont, CA.

Eldredge, Charles McGreger (CB); 12–5–1956 / ; ord. 5–20–1988, Lebanon, PA.

Elgin, Richard Glenn (CB); 10–18–1931 / ; ord. 11–21–1999, Lynchburg, VA.

Eller, David B. (CB); 4–30–1945 / ; ord. 9–19–1978, Lima, OH.

Eller, Janice M. (CB); 6–11–1946 / ; ord. 11–8–1992, Wenatchee, WA.

Elliott, Christian W. (CB); 8–3–1956 / ; ord. 10–7–1989, McConnellsburg, PA.

Elmore, Carolyn Stone (CB); 5–16–1945 / ; ord. 10–9–1999, Midland, VA.

Elsea, Henry Dearmont, Jr. (CB); 8–21–1947 / ; ord. 2–6–2000, Augusta, WV.

Emmons, Anthony E. (CB); 10–4–1952 / ; ord. 1997.

Eno, Jeffrey C. (CGBCI); 9–30–1948 / ; ord. 10–22–1995, Mansfield, OH.

Erisman Valeta, Gail E. (CB); 4–13–1959 / ; ord. April 1993, Abilene, KS.

Ernst, Steve (FGBC).

Eshelman, Donald E. (FGBC); 5–16–1951 / ; ord. 12–13–1981, Wichita, KS.

Estep, John Robert (CB); 10–25–1934 / ; ord. 5–17–1987, Edinburg, VA.

Evans, Curtis Garret (CGBCI); 3–11–1962 / ; ord. 10–15–1995, Mansfield, OH.

Ewert, Jeanine L. (CB); 6–9–1960 / ; ord. Sept. 1989, Modesto, CA.

Ewert, Milton H. (CB); 6–3–1933 / ; ord. 5–21–1961, Kingman, KS.

Fahnestock, Lloyd Roy (CB); 1–1–1940 / ; ord. 8–17–1986, Dry Run, PA.

Fairman, Richard Gary (FGBC); 11–7–1948 / ; eld. 7–20–1986, Winona Lake, IN.

Fall, John C. (OGBB); 9–8–1945 / ; 1st deg. 11–5–1990, Modesto, CA; 2nd deg. 11–5–1996; eld. 11–9–2001, Modesto, CA.

Farque, Joan (CB); ord. 2000.

Farquharson, J. Keith (CB); 3–3–1940 / ; ord. 6–1–2000, Peace Valley, MO.

Faus, Nancy Rosenberger (CB); 4–6–1934 / ; ord. 10–25–1981, Lombard, IL.

Faus, Ronald E. H. (CB); 2–11–1960 / ; ord. 9–21–1986, Manheim, PA.

Feisel, Keith (FGBC).

Ferreri, Marcelo (BC); 4–10–1963 / ; ord. 1997, Argentina, SA.

Fether, Eric J. (CB); 4–2–1954 / ; ord. 4–17–1983, Lewistown, PA.

Fetterhoff, Robert D. (FGBC); 9–8–1954 / ; eld. 11–10–1981, Wooster, OH.

Fields, Damon Wagner (CB); 11–29–1954 / ; ord. 7–12–1987, Decatur, IL.

Fields, Susan Wagner (CB); 7–24–1955 / ; ord. 1–3–1988, Bethel, PA.

Figueroa, Morales Juan A. (CB); 6–23–1937 / ; ord. Oct. 1990, Lorida, FL.

Fike, Douglas L. (CB); 3–8–1959 / ; ord. Sept. 1987, Goshen, IN.

Fike, J. Melvin (CB); 9–4–1957 / ; ord. 7–24–1983, Eglon, WV.

Fike, Jerry Lee (BC); 8–16–1953 / ; ord. 6–9–1985, Denver, IN.

Fike, John Michael (CB); 5–26–1950 / ; ord. 10–17–1982, Eglon, WV.

Fike, Lisa Jayne (CB); 11–1–1958 / ; ord. 8–9–1995, Westminster, MD.

Fike, Matthew P. (CB); 8–4–1968 / ; ord. 11–13–1992, Blue Ridge, VA.

Fike, Valeria J. (CB); ord. 9–19–1988, Knoxville, TN.

Filbrun, Roger (OGBB); 1–16–1973 / ; 1st deg. 4–28–1998, Harris, KS.

Finkbiner, Audrey J. (CB); 3–20–1955 / ; ord. 1–6–1985, Quarryville, PA.

Finkbiner, Jeffrey L. (CB); 9–28–1956 / ; ord. 1–6–1985, Mountville, PA.

Finley, Donald C. (CB); 6–24–1919 / ; ord. 5–7–1995, Wheatland, MO.

Finney, Ronald Dean (CB); 3–21–1941 / ; ord. 8–26–1990, Plymouth, IN.

Finster, Robert D. (FGBC); 8–31–1956 / ; ord. 12–14–1997, South Bend, IN; eld. 6–1–1990, South Bend, IN.

Firestone, Reid A. (CB); 2–24–1958 / ; ord. 9–12–1999, North Canton, OH.

Firstbrook, Clinton Fisk, III (CB); 5–20–1947 / ; ord. July 1981, Astoria, IL.

Fisher, Neil R. (CB); 7–1–1946 / ; ord. 9–10–1995, Mohrsville, PA.

Fiske, Randall C. (CB); 2–20–1955 / ; ord. 4–14–1991, Mifflinburg, PA.

Fitchett, William R. (CB); 2–11–1950 / ; ord. 5–19–1996, Edinburg, VA.

Fitzkee, Donald R. (CB); 12–25–1963 / ; ord. 2–6–1994, Manheim, PA.

Fitzsimons, Walter G. (CB); 8–30–1950 / ; ord. 5–6–1989, Sesmont, CA.

Fix, Eleanor A. (CB); 10–20–1946 / ; ord. 7–2–2000, Everett, PA.

Flick, Thomas E. (OGBB); 1–8–1943 / ; 1st deg. 5–8–1982; 2nd deg, 4–4–1987; eld. 4–7–1993, West Manchester, OH.

Flora, Gerald Alan (OGBB); 5–31–1962 / ; 1st deg. 2–1–1997, Gettysburg, OH; 2nd deg. 8–17–2002, Gettysburg, OH.

Flora-Swick, Jane Ellen (CB); 10–27–1954 / ; ord. 7–30–1987, Quinter, KS.

Flora-Swick, Mark John (CB); 10–29–1960 / ; ord. 11–19–1989, Liberty Mills, IN.

Flory, Brian T. (CB); 11–12–1973 / ; ord. 11–7–1999, Bridgewater, VA.

Flory, Denton (OGBB); 12–14–1961 / ; 1st deg. 5–11–1985, Harris, KS; 2nd deg. 4–27–92; eld. 4–26–1999, Westphalia, KS.

Flory, Eldon (GBB); 6–20–1935 / ; 1st deg. 7–25–1972; 2nd deg. 4–28–1973; eld. 4–24–1976; with GBB 9–23–1999, Jamesport, MO.

Flory, Galen R. (OGBB); 6–11–1958 / ; 1st deg. 2–24–1986, Modesto, CA; 2nd deg. 4–4–1992; eld. 12–11–1998, Ellensburg, WA.

Flory, Lester M. (OGGB); 10–27–1943 / ; 1st deg. 2–27–1982; 2nd deg. 3–26–1988; eld. 3–25–1995, Chilhowee, MO.

Flory-Steury, Mary Jo (CB); 3–16–1956 / ; ord. 6–17–1984, Easton, MD.

Fogle, Lerry W. (CB); 8–15–1947 / ; ord. 11–16–1997, Frederick, MD.

Folden, Don (FGBC).

Foote, Robert L. (FGBC); 8–2–1952 / ; ord. May 1986, Davenport, IA.

Ford, Charles Wesley (CB); 1–25–1958 / ; ord. 10–29–1983, Columbus, NC.

Ford, Hollace A. (CB); 10–14–1934 / ; ord. 1–1–1984, Jonesborough, TN.

Forsythe, Douglas Miller (FGBC); 1–9–1952 / ; eld. May 1996, Columbus, OH.

Foster, Chris C. (CB); 12–11–1961 / ; ord. 1994.

Frantz, Nadine Pence (CB); 5–29–1953 / ; ord. 11–18–1984, La Verne, CA.

Frederick, Stafford C. (CB); 2–5–1949 / ; ord. 2–10–1985, Olathe, KS.

Freeman, Wendell Lee (CB); 8–23–1936 / ; ord. 6–1–1958, Indianapolis, IN.

Frey, William Ray, Sr. (CB); 5–13–1956 / ; ord. 8–6–1999, Wiley, CO.

Friddle, Stephen R. (FGBC); 1–3–1959 / ; ord. 4–27–1997, Martinsburg, PA.

Funk, Keith Alan (CB); 12–26–1956 / ; ord. 6–16–1991, Lincoln, NE.

Funk, Kevin Neal (DB); 9–2–1952 / ; ord. 4–7–1994, Dallas Center, IA.

Funkhouse, Mitchell W. (BC); 10–20–1960 / ; ord. 1991, Warsaw, IN.

Galegor, Stephen Stuart, Sr. (FGBC); 11–17–1946 / ; ord. 2–2–1995, Counselor, NM.

Garber, Aaron W. (OGBB); 8–13–1966 / ; 1st deg. 9–12–1992; 2nd deg. 4–4–1998, Flora, IN.

Garber, Alan R. (OGBB); 12–22–1964 / ; 1st deg. 11–13–1999, West Alexandria, OH.

Garber, Clair E. (OGBB); 11–24–1966 / ; 1st deg. 3–24–1995, Chambersburg, PA.

Garber, Harold D. (CB); 3–17–1941 / ; ord. 1–4–1981, Petersburg, WV.

Garber, Kent (OGBB); 6–29–1953 / ; 1st deg. 5–8–1982; 2nd deg. 4–1–1995, New Paris, OH.

Garber, L. Randy (OGBB); 9–21–1958 / ; 1st deg. 9–7–1991, Covington, OH; 2nd deg. 4–5–1997; eld. 4–6–2002, Covington, OH.

Garber, Mark D. (OGBB); 8–19–1962 / ; 1st deg. 1–6–1990, Chambersburg, PA; 2nd deg. 8–30–1995; eld. 3–8–2000, Chambersburg, PA.

Garber, Steven (OGBB); 9–15–1965 / ; 1st deg. 3–27–1999, Palestine, OH.

Garber, William H. (CB); 9–24–1936 / ; ord. 6–14–1984, Craigsville, VA.

Garner, Timothy P. (BC); 4–12–1957 / ; eld. 6–27–1982, North Manchester, IN.

Garrett, Dean Alan (CB); 12–8–1962 / ; ord. 9–18–1994, Popular Grove, OH.

Garrison, Dennis W. (CB); 6–13–1950 / ; ord. 1–14–1990, Hershey, PA.

Gass, Harold Lee (CB); 7–23–1929 / ; ord. 12–12–1989, Essex, MO.

Gatliff, Michael R. (FGBC); 8–26–1963 / ; ord. Oct. 1996, Indianapolis, IN.

Gauby, Sidney F. (CB); 1–20–1961 / ; ord. Aug. 1987, McPherson, KS.

Gault, Mary (CB); ord. 1997.

Gaver, B. Joanne (CB); 11–2–1933 / ; ord. 9–11–1999, Ellicott City, MD.

Gehr, George Douglas (CB); 5–10–1955 / ; ord. 4–29–1984, Ephrata, PA.

Geisewite, Kenneth E. (CB); 4–11–1949 / ; ord. 7–8–1984, Loganton, PA.

George, Charles S. (CB); 3–20–1919 / ; ord. 2–21–1993, Canton, OH.

Georges, Judith L. (CB); 6–7–1955 / ; ord. Aug. 1984, Fremont, CA.

Gerardo, Lefton (FGBC).

Gibble Kipp, Judith (CB); 12–13–1945 / ; ord. 9–16–1984, Elizabethtown, PA.

Gibble, June Adams (CB); 6–28–1937 / ; ord. 9–21–1986, Elgin, IL.

Gibson, James Howard (CB); 6–23–1943 / ; ord. Sept. 1989, Buchanan, VA.

Gilbert, Martha Waas (CB); 2–27–1949 / ; ord. 5–19–1991, Indianapolis, IN.

Giles, Jerry W. (FGBC); 8–29–1946 / ; ord. 1989, Long Beach, CA.

Gill, Jeffrey A. (FGBC); 5–30–1956 / ; eld. 6–1–1985, Delaware, OH.

Gillette, Dan L. (FGBC); 1–18–1953 / ; ord. 11–16–1986, Covington, VA.

Gilley, William Daniel (CB); 7–27–1942 / ; ord. 11–28–1999, Floyd County, VA.

Gingrich, Kathleen A. (CB); 8–17–1955 / ; ord. 1981, Harrisburg, PA.

Gish, Philip B. (DB); 10–18–1946 / ; ord. OGBB Aug. 1979, New Carlisle, OH; min. term. July 1990; ord. DB 2–23–1991, Englewood, OH; eld. 2003, Englewood, OH.

Glass, Roy E. (FGBC); 4–28–1928 / ; eld. 10–29–1961, Altoona, PA.

Glass, Roy E., III (FGBC); 5–23–1955 / ; ord. Feb. 1991, Troy, OH.

Glass, William Robert (FGBC); 12–13–1955 / ; ord. Sept. 1987, Silver Springs, MD.

Glover, Clara C. (CB); 11–25–1938 / ; ord. 10–24–1999, New Carlisle, OH.

Godfrey, Geraldine M. (CB); 6–16–1950 / ; ord. 9–8–1996, Loganville, PA.

Godfrey, Richard E. (CB); 5–29–1947 / ; ord. 8–30–1998, York, PA.

Godfrey, Stanley L., Jr. (CB); 3–22–1953 / ; ord. 7–19–1998, Loganville, PA.

Gohn, Greg (CB); 10–4–1952 / ; ord. 1984.

Golden, Roger Alton (CB); 12–25–1943 / ; ord. 8–4–1996, Wawaka, IN.

Good, Barry L. (CB); 7–8–1955 / ; ord. 1990.

Good, Ronald E. (CB); 2–28–1942 / ; ord. 1981, Blue Ball, PA.

Goodson, Barry (FGBC).

Gorrell, James J. (CB); 4–14–1955 / ; ord. 6–12–1999, Toledo, OH.

Gould, James L. (CB); 6–13–1952 / ; ord. 1–12–1992, Brunswick, ME.

Grady, Duane E. (CB); 11–25–1957 / ; ord. 12–5–1989, Indianapolis, IN.

Graetz, David E. (BC); 1–1–1957 / ; eld. 11–16–1987, Marianna, PA.

Graham, Douglas Lyle (CB); 4–8–1956 / ; ord. 6–22–1986, Collegeville, PA.

Graham, Issac V. (CGBCI); 1–9–1953 / ; ord. June 1983, Homerville, OH.

Grandusky, Robert (CB); 12–12–1948 / ; ord. 8–24–1981, Elkins, WV.

Green, Daniel B. (FGBC); 6–16–1952 / ; ord. 5–11–1986, Columbus, OH.

Green, John D., Jr. (CB); 3–20–1942 / ; ord. 9–24–1989, Monrovia, MD.

Greene, R. Dallas (FGBC); 12–4–1957 / ; ord. 6–15–1986, Temple Hills, MD; eld. 9–22–1986, Temple Hills, MD.

Gregersen, Joseph Paul (CB); 1–29–1949 / ; ord. 10–15–1995, Lombard, IL.

Gregory, Dan (FGBC).

Greiser, Terence E. (CB); 2–23–1959 / ; ord. 6–22–1997, Elizabethtown, PA.

Gresh, Kenneth P. (CB); 8–27–1957 / ; ord. Sept. 1996, Arcadia, IN.

Griffin, Kathi D. (CB); 6–24–1945 / ; ord. May 1983, LaPorte, IN.

Griffin, W. LeRoy (CB); 10–6–1944 / ; ord. 5–30–1982, Lombard, IL.

Griffith, Charles Randy (CB); 6–28–1957 / ; ord. 10–24–1982, Erwin, TN.

Griffith, Jim (CB); ord. 1982.

Griffith, Sonja Pauline (CB); 4–19–1942 / ; ord. 4–18–1999.

Grimes, David L. (CB); 7–25–1969 / ; ord. 4–30–2000, Dunmore, WV.

Groff, Carl R. (CB); 7–20–1949 / ; ord. 12–6–1987, Manheim, PA.

Groff, Mervin C. (CB); 8–11–1954 / ; ord. 4–23–1995, Manheim, PA.

Groth, Harold J. (CB); 6–11–1946 / ; ord. 8–7–1999, Independence, KS.

Grove, Charles (CB); 11–26–1923 / ; ord. 6–1–1986, Cherry Box, MO.

Grubb, Eldon (FGBC).

Grumbling, G. Wayne (CB); 10–18–1955 / ; ord. 8–9–1991, West Salem, OH.

Guay, Paul T. (FGBC); 6–6–1942 / ; eld. 3–25–2001, Mabton, WA.

Guerena, Martin Paul (FGBC); 10–31–1960 / ; ord. 1987, Dublin, OH.

Guiles, David A. (FGBC); 6–25–1960 / ; ord. 1987, Warsaw, IN.

Gumble, Herman F. (CB); 7–29–1920 / ; ord. March 1971, Congregational Christian, Fairfield, IL.

Gunderman, Terry D. (DB); 4–13–1947 / ; ord. 1983, Goshen, IN; eld. 1989, Goshen, IN; eld. 1998, Goshen, IN.

Guthrie, Donald Lee (CB); 2–22–1952 / ; ord. 1996.

Hagenberger, Gene M., Jr. (CB); 12–1–1956 / ; ord. 4–7–1983, Union Bridge, MD.

Halberg, Roy D. (FGBC); 3–16–1950 / ; ord. 1973, Long Beach, CA.

Haldeman, William C. (CB); 12–25–1947 / ; ord. 1986.

Haldeman-Scarr, Sara (CB); 4–19–1956 / ; ord. June 1987, Oak Brook, IL.

Haldeman-Scarr, William L. (CB); 12–8–1953 / ; ord. 6–5–1987, Oak Brook, IL.

Hale, Arthur Chester, Jr. (CB); 6–26–1942 / ; ord. 6–4–1995, Laura, KY.

Hall, Charles W. (FGBC); 4–14–1961 / ; ord. 3–16–1998, Meyersdale, PA.

Hall, Johnathan N. (FGBC); 5–30–1951 / ; ord. 4–29–1984, Westminster, CA.

Hall, Mary Lou T. (CB); 7–24–1935 / ; ord. 10–26–1980, Curryville, PA.

Hall, Richard Joseph (CB); 12–25–1941 / ; ord. 8–28–1983, York, PA.

Hall, Wayne A. (CB); 12–24–1948 / ; ord. 11–15–1998, Taneytown, MD.

Halverson, Dorothy (CB); 4–4–1950 / ; ord. 1944.

Hammel, Daniel A. (CB); 10–18–1952 / ; ord. 6–1–1986, Roaring Spring, PA.

Hammond, Barbara K. (CB); 12–9–1949 / ; ord. 5–18–1997, Orbisonia, PA.

Hammond, Todd R. (CB); 10–23–1961 / ; ord. 6–7–1988, Troutwood, OH.

Hankins, Steve A. (CB); 12–16–1949 / ; ord. Nov. 1980, Hebron, KY.

Hanks, Thomas Patrick-Joseph (CB); 8–29–1957 / ; ord. 12–12–1999, Winston-Salem, NC.

Hanley, Richard Morgan (CB); 12–13–1945 / ; ord. 1984.

Hanna, Raymond C. (CB); 3–5–1932 / ; ord. 9–18–1988, Phildelphia, PA.

Hannah, Wayne Lee (FGBC); 5–14–1949 / ; ord. Oct. 1983, Richmond, VA; eld. Oct. 1983, Richmond, VA.

Hanson, Larry (BC); 10–13–1957 / ; ord. 7–13–1997, New Paris, IN.

Hardesty, Bradley A. (BC); 11–7–1956 / ; eld. 6–29–1986, Milledgeville, IL.

Hare, Barbara J. (CB); 6–13–1934 / ; ord. 4–25–1993, Tacoma, WA.

Harkins, Joseph L. (FGBC); 10–4–1946 / ; lic. 1995, Martinsburg, PA.

Harmon, Gordon A. (CGBCI); 7–2–1961 / ; ord. June 1983, Mount Vernon, OH.

Harness, Charles B. (CB); 2–16–1954 / ; ord. 2–1–1992, Morgantown, WV.

Harness, Leah Oxley (CB); 7–9–1949 / ; ord. 5–18–1988, Richmond, IN.

Harris, Earl Lafayette (CB); 6–5–1939 / ; ord. 6–2–1992, Fredonia, KS.

Hartman, Charles L., Jr. (CB); 8–16–1960 / ; ord. 3–26–2000, York, PA.

Hartman, Wayne (CB); 7–24–1956 / ; ord. 10–11–1998, York, PA.

Harvey, Timothy Paul (CB); 5–27–1970 / ; ord. 5–30–1999, Dayton, VA.

Haulk, Randy Lee (FGBC); 5–2–1956 / ; ord. 6–18–2000, Meyersdale, PA.

Hawbaker, Duane L. (CB); 7–31–1945 / ; ord. 8–5–1971, Upton, PA.

Hawkins, Stanley Harold (CB); 9–16–1951 / ; ord. Dec. 1981, Floyd, VA.

Hay, Christopher A. (FGBC); 2–5–1958 / ; ord. 1989, Eagle River, AK.

Haymaker, Jason Craig (FGBC); 9–20–1970 / ; lic. 2000, Macedonia, OH.

Haynes, Peter Lawrence (CB); 8–13–1955 / ; ord. 6–16–1985, Nappanee, IN.

Hazen, Lisa Lynn (CB); 12–28–1965 / ; ord. 1–17–2004, Beavercreek, OH.

Heffner, Richard Allen (CB); 1–14–1927 / ; ord. 5–19–1985, Woodbridge, VA.

Heilman, Edwin C. (CB); 9–13–1958 / ; ord. 1–18–1987, Middleton, PA.

Heim, Jeffrey D. (FGBC); 7–10–1954 / ; ord. 12–5–1985, Blacklick, OH.

Heisey, Jan L. (DB); 1–13–1951 / ; ord. Feb. 1982, Lititz, PA; min. term. 1984.

Heisey, Walter K. (CB); 9–21–1949 / ; ord. 11–21–1978, Myerstown, PA.

Heishman, Irvin Russell (CB); 4–6–1960 / ; ord. 6–22–1986, Manassas, VA.

Heishman, Nancy S. (CB); 5–11–1955 / ; ord. 6–16–1985, Annville, PA.

Helfer, Phil (FGBC).

Heller, Jack B. (CB); 4–30–1931 / ; ord. 1–18–1998, Johnstown, PA.

Helman, Patricia Kennedy (CB); 9–15–1925 / ; ord. 3–15–1981, North Manchester, IN.

Hendricks, David K. (CB); 8–9–1951 / ; ord. 4–12–1981, Reading, MN.

Hendricks, Joseph C. (CB); 6–21–1956 / ; ord. 3–28–1982, Cloris, NM.

Henman, Kirk L. (FGBC).

Henry, Barry Kenneth (CB); 10–22–1953 / ; ord. 4–10–1983, Custer, MI.

Henry, Kenneth E. (CB); 12–5–1936 / ; ord. 1987.

Hensley, Raymond Keith (BC); 1–10–1956 / ; ord. 6–6–1982, Ashland, OH.

Herbert, Frank William (CB); 9–20–1937 / ; ord. 4–22–1990, Venice, FL.

Hershberger, Ronald D. (CB); 11–29–1933 / ; ord. 9–1–1956, Johnstown, PA.

Hesketh, Raymond C. (BC); 1–22–63 / ; ord. 10–26–91, Vandergrift, PA; min. term. March 1994.

Hesketh, William (Billy) Alan (BC); 8–13–1961 / ; ord. 8–9–1997, Milford, IN.

Hess, Alan W. (FGBC).

Hess, Eldon H. (OGBB); 11–18–1960 / ; 1st deg. 8–19–1992; 2nd deg, 8–5–1998, Greencastle, PA.

Hess, Howard Robert (OGBB); 9–8–1964 / ; 1st deg. 6–23–1998, Ephrata, PA.

Hess, John F. (CB); 9–13–1961 / ; ord. Nov. 1988, Collegeville, PA.

Hess, John M. (CB); 4–24–1956 / ; ord. 3–15–1998, Lititz, PA.

Hess, Matthew Henry (OGBB); 5–2–1971 / ; 1st deg. 3–8–2000, Chambersburg, PA.

Hess, Nancy Heisey (CB); 10–1–1969 / ; ord. 9–21–1997, Palmyra, PA.

Hess, Roland R. (OGBB); 1–8–1957 / ; 1st deg. 3–22–1989, Waynesboro, PA; 2nd deg. 3–24–1995; eld. 3–17–1998, Waynesboro, PA.

Hess, Stephen R. (CB); 4–5–1957 / ; ord. 6–1–1986, Pottstown, PA.

Hewitt, Nancy Marie (CB); 8–25–1935 / ; ord. 6–5–1994, Hanover, PA.

Hicks, William F. (CB); 12–27–1929 / ; ord. 12–4–1983, Greenville, TN.

Hildebrand, Brian C. (CB); 5–1–1938 / ; ord. 1985, Mt. Clinton, VA.

Hildreth, Janet (CB); 5–3–1941 / ; ord. 4–25–1993, Burnettsville, IN.

Hilton, Donald H. (CB); 4–5–1954 / ; ord. 10–13–1981, Johnson City, TN.

Hinton, George David (CB); 11–18–1957 / ; ord. 1995, Salkum, WA.

Hironimus, Bertha Marie (CB); 10–4–1938 / ; ord. 11–18–1990, Ligonier, PA.

Hisey Pierson, Anna Lee (CB); 7–13–1957 / ; ord. 6–27–1992, Baltimore, MD.

Hoblit, Bart L. (OGBB); 9–23–1960 / ; 1st deg. 3–19–1994, Arcanum, OH; 2nd deg. 3–13–1999.

Hocking, Thomas G. (FGBC); 12–15–1959 / ; ord. 1985, Bellflower, CA.

Hockley, Albert E. (FGBC); 9–12–1930 / .

Hodges, Kathleen L. (CB); 12–2–1952 / ; ord. 1986.

Hofecker, Terry A. (FGBC); 10–20–1955 / ; ord. 4–1–1984, Worthington, OH.

Hoffard, R. Jeffrey (FGBC); 6–3–1954 / ; ord. 5–1–1988, Warsaw, IN.

Hoffert, Gordon R. (CB); 6–19–1948 / ; ord. 2–18–1990, Lewiston, MN; min. term. 1–31–2001.

Hoffman, John Michael (CB); 4–18–1958 / ; ord. 8–8–1986, Wiley, CO.

Hollenberg, Keith Earl (CB); 2–1–1964 / ; ord. 10–6–1990, Mifflintown, PA.

Hollinger, Donald E. (CB); 2–14–1945 / ; ord. 6–9–1985, Quarryville, PA.

Holsinger, Robert (BC).

Hooks, Eric Lee (CB); 2–5–1961 / ; ord. 9–26–1999, Robinson, PA.

Hoover, James L. (CB); 8–20–1943 / ; ord. 1–16–1988, York, PA.

Hornbacker, Tara Lea (CB); 10–15–1951 / ; ord. 5–31–1989, Pleasant Hill, OH.

Horner, J. Richard (FGBC); 10–8–1950 / ; ord. 1–16–1983, Leamersville, PA.

Horning, Estella Boggs (CB); 3–18–1929 / ; ord. 6–10–1984, Lombard, IL.

Hosler, Wilbur H. (CB); 3–5–1942 / ; ord. 8–18–1991, Penn Run, PA.

Hostetler, Bruce (CB); 4–25–1954 / ; ord. 1994.

Hostetter, John D. (CB); 9–22–1955 / ; ord. Sept. 1982, Mifflenburg, PA.

Hostetter, Julie Mader (CB); 3–31–1951 / ; ord. 9–12–1982, Dayton, OH.

Hostetter, Rick E. (CB); 5–17–1954 / ; ord. 1997.

Houff, Marlin Dean (CB); 6–24–1951 / ; ord. 12–29–1996, Palmyra, PA.

Houff, Mary Ziegler (CB); 4–12–1922 / ; ord. 1987, Champaign, IL.

Houghton, James E. (CB); 8–30–1935 / ; ord. 11–9–1997, Johnstown, PA.

Howard, Courtland David (CB); 2–16–1955 / ; ord. 2–27–1994, Red Lion, PA.

Howard, Craig Alan (CB); 12–20–1958 / ; ord. 1984.

Howell, Gregory M. (FGBC); 3–24–1954 / ; ord. 10–19–1981, Warsaw, IN.

Hubbell, Donald George (CB); 7–6–1956 / ; ord. 11–28–1982, Frederick, MD.

Hubble, James W. (CB); 7–28–1932 / ; ord. 2–15–1998, Carleton, NE.

Hudson, Elliott Anderson (FGBC); 11–14–1940 / ; ord. 1982, Baltimore, MD.

Huesmann, Lou M. (FGBC); 3–28–1957 / ; ord. 1–6–1991, Long Beach, CA.

Huffman, Bruce Edward (CB); 11–14–1952 / ; ord. 9–5–1982, Roanoke, VA.

Huffman, Reuben Ephraim (OGBB); 5–1–1975 / ; 1st deg. 12–6–1996, New Lebanon, OH.

Hufford, Craig D. (OGBB); 4–15–1960 / ; 1st deg. 1–26–1991, North Manchester, IN; 2nd deg. 1–25–1997, North Manchester, IN.

Hufford, Lisa M. (CB); 12–30–1955 / ; ord. 10–12–1997, Nappanee, IN.

Huggett, John B. (CB); 5–15–1945 / ; ord. 1984.

Huh, Ben Un (CB); 10–21–1939 / ; ord. 8–1–1993, Los Angeles, CA.

Humberd, Larry T. (FGBC); 6–3–1954 / ; ord. 11–18–1984, Hagerstown, MD.

Hurd, G. Emery (BC); 2–4–1957 / ; eld. 9–16–1984, Cheyenne, WY.

Hurlbut, Phil (FGBC).

Huskins, James C. (CB); 6–10–1905 / ; ord. 1988.

Hutchison, Martin Earl (CB); 5–31–1965 / ; ord. Aug. 1990, Cordova, MD.

Hutchison, Sharon Cobb (CB); 1–30–1961 / ; ord. Aug. 1990, Manassas, VA.

Hyre, Greg Allen (CB); 5–14–1961 / ; ord. 5–22–1997, Eaton, OH.

Ilyes, Charles L. (CB); 3–4–1957 / ; ord. Jan. 1994, York, PA.

Ilyes, John Samuel (CB); 10–11–1961 / ; ord. 6–11–2000, York, PA.

Inhauser, Marcos (CB); ord. 1993.

Inhauser, Suely (CB); ord. 1993.

Jackson, Daniel J. (FGBC); 11–20–1956 / ; ord. 8–10–1986, Osceola, IN.

Jackson, James E. (FGBC); 3–27–1954 / ; lic. 4–23–1983, Yakima, WA.

Jackson, John Jullian (CB); 2–14–1958 / ; ord. June 1986, Centreville, MI.

Jacobsen, Bruce A. (CB); 5–25–1962 / ; ord. 8–20–2000, New Middletown, OH.

Jacobson, Jon Richard (FGBC); 7–10–1942 / ; ord. May 1974, Santa Barbara, CA.

Jamison, Dennis R. (OGBB); 12–23–1965 / ; 1st deg. 11–15–1997, Rocky Mount, VA.

Jamison, Eugene W. (OGBB); 9–7–1960 / ; 1st deg. 7–13–1994, Rocky Mount, VA; 2nd deg. 1–25–2000.

Jamison, R. Glen (OGBB); 9–24–1955 / ; 1st deg. 3–21–1991, Chambersburg, PA; 2nd deg. 3–17–1998.

Jarrell, Stephen M. (FGBC); 5–31–1949 / ; ord. 5–15–1984, Atlanta, GA.

Jenks, Dale D. (CGBCI); 1–28–1943 / ; ord. Oct. 1983, Island Pond, VT.

Jensen, Douglas S. (FGBC); 11–6–1952 / ; ord. May 1985, Cuyahoga Falls, OH.

Jensen, Russell James (CB); 4–3–1953 / ; ord. 6–25–2000, Middlebury, IN.

Jentes, Michael A. (FGBC); 9–28–1973 / ; ord. May 2000, Columbus, OH.

Jinks, James Paul (CB); 3–13–1940 / ; ord. 4–20–1986, Dyke, VA.

Jodry, David L. (CGBCI); 6–23–1956 / ; eld April 1990,Peru, IN.

Johnson, Daniel M. (CB); 2–21–1964 / ; ord. 3–26–2000, Pine Grove, PA.

Johnson, Elwood (Woody) O. (CB); 9–30–1952 / ; ord. 11–15–1987, Front Royal, VA.

Johnson, Fred A. (DB); 2–23–1947 / ; ord. 5–27–1989, Wauseon, OH.

Johnson, Guy (FGBC); 5–14–1961 / ; ord. 11–25–2001, Bellflower, CA.

Johnson, Howard P. (FGBC); 1–12–1948 / ; ord. 9–20–1992, Seal Beach, CA.

Johnson, Jeremiah Lee (DB); 7–29–1976 / ; ord. 5–30–1998, Hart, MI.

Johnson, Paul D. (CB); 6–1–1937 / ; ord. 2–12–1989, Claysburg, PA.

Johnson, Raymond L. CB); 7–30–1931 / ; ord. June 1985, Surrey, ND.

Johnson, Robert Clyde (CB); 1–11–1945 / ; ord. 1994.

Jones, Daren (OGBB); 9–22–1968 / ; 1st deg. 3–17–1999, Waynesboro, PA.

Jones, Eugene W. (CB); 8–28–1952 / ; ord. 6–20–1999, Newport, PA.

Jones, Evan (Chip) Luther (CGBCI); 8–30–1954 / ; ord. 9–10–1999, Trout Lake, MI.

Jones, Gregory L. (CB); 2–6–1960 / ; ord. 7–23–2000, Shippensburg, PA.

Jones, John W. (FGBC); 6–2–1953 / ; eld. 3–24–1996, Marion, OH.

Jones, Nancy M. (CB); 4–11–1950 / ; ord. 9–23–1995, York, PA.

Jones, Phillip L. (CB); 10–14–1954 / ; ord. 11–14–1992, Rocky Mount, VA.

Jones, Ralph Douglas (CB); 4–24–1956 / ; ord. June 1982, Roanoke, VA.

Joo, Andre (CB); 2–26–1933 / ; ord. 4–23–1995, Brooklyn, NY.

Joseph, Elysee (FGBC).

Juday, Robert (FGBC).

Julian, Don W. (FGBC); 11–10–1954 / .

Kahler, Allen R. (CB); 10–26–1959 / ; ord. 5–11–1997, Marion, IN.

Kallberg, Ethan (CGBCI); 3–23–1972 / ; ord. 8–29–1999, Orrville, OH.

Karchner, Bryan G. (BC); 12–8–1961 / ; ord. 7–28–1991, Goshen, IN.

Kaufman-Frey, Cameron Blake (CB); 8–5–1968 / ; ord. 2–13–2000, Morgantown, WV.

Keck, Lorie (BC); 6–5–1951 / ; ord. 2000, Peru, IN.

Keegan, Gerald P. (CB); 10–2–1950 / ; ord. 11–7–1982, Danville, VA.

Keeling, Calvin Montgomery (Monty) (CB); 3–10–1951 / ; ord. 5–2–1986, Bakersfield, CA.

Keener, Frederick Mark (CB); 6–26–1957 / ; ord. 10–17–1982, Martin, WV.

Keith, Jean E. (CB); 10–24–1946 / ; ord. 7–23–1995, Chicago, IL.

Kelley, Bradley A. (FGBC); 10–24–1962 / ; ord. Oct. 1994, Roanoke, VA.

Kennedy, Dale (OGBB); 1–26–1967 / ; 1st deg. 9–18–1993, Sawyer, KS; 2nd deg. 3–18–2000.

Kennedy, David W. (FGBC); 4–1–1952 / ; ord. July 1989, Marion, OH.

Kennedy, Lester Washington, Jr. (FGBC); 7–4–1926 / ; ord. 2–11–1952, Winona Lake, IN.

Kent, W. David (CB); 8–20–1950 / ; ord. 9–18–1988, Welsh Run, PA.

Kerkove, David (CB); 7–18–1971 / ; ord. 11–21–1999, South English, IA.

Kern, Robert D. (FGBC); 6–15–1933 / ; ord. 10–8–1960, Philadephia, PA.

Kern, Steve B. (FGBC); 7–10–1962 / ; ord. May 1989, Mansfield, OH.

Kerner, David Christian (BC); 5–14–1958 / ; ord. June 1985, Goshen, IN.

Kessler, Clinton E. (CB); 10–17–1942 / ; ord. 6–19–1994, Liberty Mills, IL.

Kessler, Kevin L. (CB); 10–22–1958 / ; ord. 6–22–1997, Canton, IL.

Ketterman, Curtis G. (CB); 11–1–1946 / ; ord. 11–20–1993, Grantsville, MD.

Ketterman, Richard Eugene (CB); 11–9–1948 / ; ord. 10–5–1997, Flintstone, MD.

Kidder, Shawn (FGBC).

Kiester, Edith Mae (CB); 9–19–1925 / ; ord. 4–30–2000, Lybrook, NM.

Killingsworth, Wesley (OGBB); 4–16–1963 / ; 1st deg. 3–16–1996, Cleveland, GA.

Kim, Kwang (Dan) Suk (CB); 5–2–1941 / ; ord. 7–10–1982, Panorama City, CA.

Kimmel, Jo (CB); 2–11–1931 / ; ord. 7–8–1984, Live Oak, CA.

Kimmel, Lois E. (CB); 6–4–1922 / ; ord. 1988, Petersburg, WV.

Kimmel, Myers P. (CB); 11–14–1915 / ; ord. 1981, Rocky Mount, VA.

King, Alvin R. (OGBB); 7–16–1956 / ; 1st deg. 4–7–1984, Elida, OH; 2nd deg. 4–7–1990; eld. 4–6–1996, Elida, OH.

King, Keith Daniel (OGBB); 9–26–1964 / ; 1st deg. 4–7–1990, Elida, OH; 2nd deg. 4–6–1996; eld. 4–13–2002, Elida, OH.

King, Kevin Daniel (CB); 5–3–1964 / ; ord. 1998, Orlando, FL.

King, Lavern O. (OGBB); 1–30–1955 / ; 1st deg. 12–7–1996, Silver Lake, IN.

King, Russell C. (BC); 5–11–1957 / ; eld. 1986, Ashland, OH.

Kingsbury, Robert D. (FGBC); 8–2–1931 / ; lic. 4–1–1980, Long Beach, CA.

Kinsley, Dean R. (OGBB); 3–2–1950 / ; 1st deg. 1–11–1992, Maple Grove District, OH; 2nd deg. 1–4–1997; eld. 4–6–2002, Maple Grove District, OH.

Kipp, John Snyder (CB); 12–1–1940 / ; ord. 11–28–1982, Newport, PA.

Kirkendall, James E. (BC); 9–12–1946 / ; eld. 7–18–1993, Adrian, PA.

Kirnbauer, Ted J. (FGBC); 7–6–1956 / ; ord. 1997, Long Beach, CA.

Kitzel, Sandra R. (CB); 1–28–1943 / ; ord. 3–3–1996, Conway, KS.

Klaus, Gerald E. (CB); 1–28–1937 / ; ord. 2–23–1992, Billings, OK.

Klinger, Gene A. (FGBC); 10–19–1933 / .

Knaus, Merl W. (OGBB); 4–4–1956 / ; 1st deg. 12–9–1989, Flora, IN; 2nd deg. 9–9–1995; eld. 6–14–2001, Flora, IN.

Knaus, Roger D. (OGBB); 10–17–1954 / ; 1st deg. 3–2–1991, Quinter, KS; 2nd deg. 9–20–1997; eld. 4–16–2001, Hillsboro, WI.

Knepper, Nancy F. (CB); 2–5–1948 / ; ord. 9–15–1997, Gotha, FL.

Knight, David Wilhelm (FGBC); 12–13–1951 / ; lic. 11–21–1995.

Knotts, Donald Raymond (CB); 8–16–1961 / ; ord. 7–17–1999, Aurora, WV.

Koch, Richard A. (CB); 4–21–1957 / ; ord. 6–12–1988, Lawrenceville, IL.

Kochheiser, Gary Melvin (FGBC); 6–15–1951 / ; ord. 8–9–1992, Cedar Rapids, IA.

Koehn, Elise M. (CB); 12–23–1938 / ; ord. 4–30–1995, Aline, OK.

Kohler, Paul S. (CB); 6–14–1941 / ; ord. 2–5–1993, Champaign, IL.

Kontra, Peter Joseph (CB); 4–2–1970 / ; ord. 5–9–1999, Bradford, OH.

Koontz, James C. (BC); 5–24–1954 / ; ord. 7–19–1981, Waynesboro, PA.

Koontz, Kenneth David (FGBC); 3–27–1937 / ; ord. 1963, Leesburg, IN.

Koontz, Steve L. (FGBC); 10–14–1962 / ; lic. June 1992, Murrysville, PA.

Kostlevy, William C. (CB); 5–19–1952 / ; ord. Nov. 1985, Constentine, MI.

Kover, Virgil K. (CB); 12–3–1930 / ; ord. 1–30–1983, Lititz, PA.

Krape, J. David (CB); 6–10–1952 / ; ord. 9–29–1985, York, PA; eld. 1992, York, PA.

Kuns, Marlin E. (OGBB); 7–3–1942 / ; 1st deg. 8–14–1982; 2nd deg. 3–19–1988; eld. 2–7–1995, Twelve Mile, IN.

Kunselman, Dorothy (CB); 11–13–1941 / ; ord. 2–7–1993, Distant, PA.

Kurt, Victor A. (FGBC); 6–23–1966 / ; eld. Jan. 1993, Long Beach, CA.

Kyerematen, Richard (CB); 11–28–1959 / ; ord. 6–7–1991, Philadelphia, PA.

Laird, James S., Sr. (FGBC); 7–29–1948 / ; ord. 1992, Martinsburg, PA.

Lake, Leslie (CB); 6–16–1953 / ; ord. 1998.

Lambert, Linda Rae (CB); 1–16–1947 / ; ord. 7–19–1998, Thurmont, MD.

Landes, Bruce E. (OGBB); 4–13–1963 / ; 1st deg. 4–1–1989, Covington, OH; 2nd deg. 12–31–1994; eld. 6–26–1999, Covington, OH.

Landis, Henry (CB); 7–8–1941 / ; ord. 1982.

Langdon, Kenneth J. (CB); 3–9–1952 / ; ord. 1982.

Lare, Dawn Larue (CB); 8–8–1947 / ; ord. 6–3–1989, Ruckersville, VA.

Lawson, Dan L. (BC); 9–21–1957 / ; eld. 6–8–1986, Wabash, IN.

Lawson, David Ronald (FGBC); 9–6–1961 / ; eld. 9–9–2001, Wooster, OH.

Laycook, Catherine L. (CB); 10–27–1954 / ; ord. 4–17–1983, Tonasket, WA.

Layman, Norman R. (OGBB); 9–13–1941 / ; 1st deg. 7–1–1986, Modesto, CA; 2nd deg. 11–20–1990; eld. 8–7–1998, Modesto, CA.

Lease, Anna Leiter (CB); 1–13–1934 / ; ord. 1–4–1987, Monrovia, MD.

Leatherman, Paul N., Jr. (CB); 12–1–1956 / ; ord. 4–7–1983, Union Bridge, MD.

Leatherman, Roger D. (CB); 6–19–1950 / ; ord. 1990.

Ledington, John D. (DB); 6–28–1960 / ; ord. 2–4–2000, Englewood, OH.

Lee, Douglas Montgomery (FGBC); 11–10–1957 / ; ord. Sept. 1998, Long Beach, CA.

Leftwich, Danny Robert (CB); 3–18–1946 / ; ord. 10–18–1998, Mt. Airy, NC.

Lehigh, Daniel Grant (CB); 8–8–1941 / ; ord. 4–4–1998, East Berlin, PA.

Lehigh, Robert S. (DB); 12–12–1954 / ; ord. 7–20–1991, Shrewsbury, PA; eld. 5–18–1996, Shrewsbury, PA.

Lehman, Randall S. M. (CB); 3–12–1924 / ; ord. 8–2–1981, Muskegon,.

Leidy, J. Brant (FGBC); 10–29–1969 / ; ord. 8–12–2001, Martinsburg, PA.

Leininger, Kenneth G. (CB); 6–15–1960 / ; ord. 2–16–1986, Denver, PA.

Leiter, David A. (CB); 10–16–1958 / ; ord. 8–23–1987, Smithsburg, MD.

Leiton, Gerardo (FGBC); 1–18–1973 / ; ord. 8–29–2000, Tampa, FL.

Lengel, Dean Michael (CB); 10–27–1952 / ; ord. Nov. 1982, Pine Grove, PA.

LePage, Richard (CB); 1–6–1945 / ; ord. 1985.

Lerch, Marilyn E. (CB); 11–10–1949 / ; ord. 6–4–1994, Naperville, IL.

Lesher, Dana K. (OGBB); 10–5–1965 / ; 1st deg. 3–17–1998, Chambersburg, PA.

Lewis, Warren K. (CB); 4–12–1916 / ; ord. 5–18–1991, Windber, PA.

Libby, Scott M. (CGBCI); 4–28–1958 / ; ord. 4–28–1992, Irasburg, VT.

Lifer, James E. (CB); 1–2–1940 / ; ord. 1988.

Liggett, Julie (CB); 8–6–1939 / ; ord. Jan. 1991, Windsor, CO.

Liller, Mark Wesley (CB); 6–10–1960 / ; ord. 9–26–1993, Carlisle, OH.

Lingenfelter, Rodney (FGBC).

Little, Douglas (BC); ord. 1992, Ashland, OH.

Littman, Elsa Carter (CB); 7–29–1931 / ; ord. 8–22–1999, LaPorte, IN.

Logan, Mark A. (BC); 12–21–1943 / ; ord. 4–9–1989, Bogotá, Colombia.

Lohnes, William E., Jr. (FGBC); 6–11–1956 / ; ord. 10–5–1999, Medina, OH.

Lohr, Dennis Michael (CB); 8–19–1961 / ; ord. 11–8–1987, Harrisonburg, VA.

Long, Dan (OGBB); 11–17–1958 / ; 1st deg. 7–13–1994, 2nd deg. 1–25–2000; Rocky Mount, VA.

Long, Duane C. (OGBB); 1–24–1965 / ; 1st deg. 2–23–1999, Mexico, IN.

Long, Janice Kulp (CB); 4–20–1949 / ; ord. 4–28–1991, Louisville, OH.

Long, John Richard (CB); 3–15–1949 / ; ord. 4–28–1991, Louisville, OH.

Longenecker, David L. (CB); 3–7–1953 / ; ord. 2–22–1998, Lititz, PA.

Longenecker, Jerre L. (OGBB); 2–13–1948 / ; 1st deg. 3–7–1981; 2nd deg. 12–7–1985; eld. 3–9–1991, Bernville, PA.

Longenecker, Thomas William (CB); 12–18–1965 / ; ord. 3–5–2000, Glendale, CA.

Longwell, Eric Matthew (CB); 9–20–1970 / ; ord. 9–28–1997, Hagerstown, IN.

Lorenz, Lloyd (DB); 10–6–1960 / ; ord. 1988; Plevna, IN; eld. 2000, Plevna, IN .

Lovett, Diana L. (CB); 9–16–1956 / ; ord. 12–13–1998, Pleasant Hill, OH.

Lowry, Alys Joan (CB); 1–27–1937 / ; ord. 9–22–1996, Thomas, OK.

Lowry, James L. (CB); 1–31–1929 / ; ord. 11–22–1998, Thomas, OK.

Lucore, Donald L. (CB); 7–9–1948 / ; ord. 2–26–1984, Newton, KS.

Ludwick, G. Daniel (CB); 1–24–1952 / ; ord. 12–6–1981, Burlington, WV.

Lynch, Danny W. (OGBB); 11–12–1960 / ; 1st deg. 12–4–1993, Cleveland, GA; eld. 3–8–1997, Cleveland, GA.

Lynn, Thomas P. (FGBC); 3–15–1952 / ; eld. 1981, Long Beach, CA.

MacMillan, Robert, Jr. (FGBC); 6–23–1946 / ; ord. 1–16–1983, Ventura, CA.

Madison, Kenneth J. (BC); 12–8–1953 / ; ord. 12–6–1987, Kokomo, IN.

Mahaffey, Thomas (FGBC).

Makofka, Stephen E. (FGBC); 1–30–1961 / ; ord. 11–26–1995, Marietta, GA.

Malenke, Elizabeth A. (CB); 6–11–1927 / ; ord. 10–25–1987, Pottstown, PA.

Malick, Walker L. (FGBC); 10–16–1948 / ; eld. 10–21–1995, Norton, OH.

Mallon, Henry Clemente (FGBC); 4–15–1949 / ; ord. 5–10–70 Iwakuni, Japan; eld. 4–24–1988, Brookville, OH.

Malone, Sarah Quinter (CB); 3–26–1955 / ; ord. 3–16–1997, State College, PA.

Manges, Craig D. (FGBC); 5–26–1956 / ; ord. June 1991, Everett, PA.

Manges, David L. (FGBC); 8–9–1952 / ; ord. 3–29–1987, Chambersburg, PA.

Manthos, Michael Charles (CB); 1–16–1950 / ; ord. 8–27–2000, Oakland, MD.

Mantz, Elmo V. (CB); 10–15–1937 / ; ord. 11–24–1991, Stephens City, VA.

Mantz, Shelvie J. (CB); 5–6–1944 / ; ord. 11–24–1991, Stephens City, VA.

Marang, Timothy Ryan (CGBCI); 2–15–1971 / ; ord. 8–13–2000, Mansfield, OH.

Markey, Dale E. (CB); 8–25–1932 / ; ord. 1–15–1994, York, PA.

Marks, Marlin D. (DB); 8–18–1949 / ; ord. 7–20–1991, Shrewsbury, PA; eld. 5–18–1996, Shrewsbury, PA.

Marling, William H. (FGBC); 3–31–1964 / ; ord. 4–15–1992, Columbus, OH.

Marshall, Dick A. (CB); 7–24–1943 / ; ord. 7–27–2000, Sugarcreek, OH.

Marston, Bruce S. (CB); 2–7–1950 / ; ord. 6–24–1984, Lewiston, MA.

Martin, Aaron L., Jr. (CB); 3–27–1935 / ; ord. 11–9–1989, Lebanon, PA.

Martin, Donna Ritchey (CB); 2–27–1955 / ; ord. 3–21–1982, Franklin Grove, IL.

Martin, George H. (CB); 6–30–1946 / ; ord. 8–16–1998, Waynesboro, PA.

Martin, H. Stanley (CB); 2–19–1955 / ; ord. 2–18–1988, Lebanon, PA.

Martin, Helen L. (CB); 10–2–1928 / ; ord. 5–16–1982, Millbury, OH.

Martin, Kenneth L. (OB); 12–27–1930 / ; 1st deg. 5–19–72; eld. 5–23–1980.

Martin, Neal D. (OB); 8–15–1961 / ; 1st deg, 6–5–1992.

Martin, Paul M. (CB); 10–28–1921 / ; ord. 5–16–1982, Millbury, OH.

Martin, Tim Ritchey (CB); 3–7–1955 / ; ord. 3–21–1982, Franklin Grove, IL.

Martinez, De Figueroa Isabel (CB); 11–14–1938 / ; ord. 2–22–68 Church Dios Pentecostal, San Juan, Puerto Rico; ord. Oct. 1990, Church of the Brethren, Lorida, FL.

Mason, Cynthia Gail (CB); 3–26–1964 / ; ord. 10–31–1993, Dayton, OH.

Mason, Dorotha Fry (CB); 12–21–1926 / ; ord. 6–5–1983, Nappanee, IN.

Mason, George E. (OGBB); 4–8–1948 / ; 1st deg. 3–28–1981, Waynesboro, PA; 2nd deg. 3–29–1986, Waynesboro, PA; eld. 7–20–1994, Waynesboro, PA.

Mason, Nathan (OGBB); 9–21–1960 / ; 1st deg. 6–18–1996, Rocky Mount, VA.

Mason, Norris (FGBC).

Mason, Steven Watts (CB); 4–27–1950 / ; ord. 4–30–1989, Bolar, VA.

Mathis, Terry Richard (CB); 11–14–1947 / ; ord. 4–17–1994, Whittier, CA.

Matteson, Erin A. (CB); 10–10–1966 / ; ord. 7–31–1993, Fremont, CA.

Matteson, Russell Leon (CB); 11–30–1965 / ; ord. 9–12–1993, Fremont, CA.

Matthews, W. Eugene (CB); 10–7–1926 / 9–30–04; ord. June 1955.

Maust, Roland R. (FGBC).

May, Sharon Nearhoof (CB); 12–5–1969 / ; ord. 5–10–1998, Warriors Mark, PA.

Mayer, J. Norman (FGBC).

Mayer, Robin Wentworth (CB); 10–6–1955 / ; ord. Dec. 1990, Nappanee, IN.

McAdams, Ronald Lee (CB); 11–18–1937 / ord. 1–19–1997, Tipp, OH.

McCauliff, Linda L. (CB); 5–31–1952 / ; ord. 5–18–1997, Johnstown, PA.

McClung, Kevin (CB); ord. 1987.

McClure, Dennis H. (CB); 7–21–1943 / ; ord. Feb. 2001, Oakley, IL.

McCombs, Earl W. (CB); 7–6–1927 / ; ord. 4–29–1985, Hollansburg, OH.

McCoy, Ray (FGBC).

McCrickard, Glenn Anthony (CB); 10–11–1964 / ; ord. 6–23–1991, Penhook, VA.

McDonald, Richard A. (CB); 1–31–1954 / ; ord.1988, Wardensville, WV.

McDowell, Kimberly Anne (CB); 8–30–1954 / ; ord. 8–11–1985, Lombard, IL.

McGann, Elaine Hartman (CB); 12–2–1945 / ; ord. 6–15–1986, Harrisonburg, VA.

McGlothlin, Judith Mohler (CB); 5–8–1950 / ; ord. 1996.

McGuckin, Charles J. (CB); ord. 1994.

McKinley, Jay Gordon (FGBC); 4–17–1960 / ; ord. 4–26–1998, Dublin, OH.

McKinnell, Letha M. (CB); 5–21–1929 / ; ord. 6–14–1998, Chester, VA.

McLaughlin, Thomas John (BC); 10–13–1963 / ; eld. 6–15–1997, Vandergrift, PA.

Mclearn-Montz, Alan Lee (CB); 11–14–1957 / ; ord. 7–18–1999, Columbia City, IN.

McPherson, Steven Robert (CB); 2–24–1959 / ; ord. 7–19–1987, Bellefontaine, OH.

Meeks, Gary M. (CB); 1–22–1946 / ; ord. 3–15–1997, Deshler, OH.

Mellen, Chuck (FGBC).

Mellott, Dorothy A. (CB); 10–3–1941 / ; ord. March 1996, Free Union, VA.

Mellott, Patrick L. (CB); 3–17–1939 / ; ord. June 1985, Ruckersville, VA.

Mendez, Miliciades (CB); 4–27–1992 / ; ord. 2000.

Menker, Harmon Remmel (CB); 12–23–1949 / ; ord. 11–22–1981, Springfield, OH.

Mercer, Lynn W. (BC); 12–26–1954 / ; ord. 8–8–1982, North Georgetown, OH.

Merriman, Keith Andrew (CGBCI); 7–16–1952 / ; ord. 6–29–1986, Orrville, OH.

Metzger, Melvin Lynn (OGBB); 7–2–1957 / 1–19–90; 1st deg. 1–31–1987, North Manchester, IN;

Metzger, Robert D. (OGBB); 5–20–1948 / ; 1st deg. 6–21–1980; 2nd deg. 12–20–1986; eld. 9–17–1994, Mulberry, IN.

Meyer, Lauree Hersch (CB); 7–15–1934 / ; ord. 1983, Lombard, IL.

Meyers, Darlene C. (CB); 9–11–1948 / ; ord. 3–1–1992, Hyattsville, MD.

Meyers, James W. (DB); 6–21–1955 / ; ord. 10–24–1986, Dallas Center, IA; eld. 5–28–1996, Dallas Center, IA.

Meyers, Leon E. (CB); 6–3–1960 / ; ord. 4–20–1997, Upton, PA.

Michael, Michael Lynn (CB); 12–4–1953 / ; ord. 8–14–1998, Johnstown, PA.

Miller, Bruce Alan (OGBB); 10–3–1957 / ; 1st deg. 6–2–1984, Pyrmont, IN; 2nd deg. 12–7–1991; eld. 12–4–1999, Pyrmont, IN.

Miller, Christen A. (CB); 12–8–1971 / ; ord. 9–27–1998, North Manchester, IN.

Miller, Daniel E. (CB); 3–2–1957 / ; eld. 8–4–1991, Abbottstown, PA.

Miller, Darrell E. (BC); 2–25–1960 / ; ord. 1998, Gremont, OH.

Miller, David E. (OGBB); 1–12–1962 / ; 1st deg. 3–11–1989, Pendleton, IN; 2nd deg. 3–11–1995; eld. 3–10–2001, Pendleton, IN.

Miller, David L. (CB); 1–25–1948 / ; ord. 5–14–1988, Grants Pass, OR.

Miller, David Lloyd (CB); 5–27–1946 / ; ord. 3–19–2000, Bryan, OH.

Miller, David Racy (CB); 4–25–1960 / ; ord. Jan. 1990, Harrisonburg, VA.

Miller, David W. (CB); 5–7–1959 / ; ord. 1–3–1999, Richmond, VA.

Miller, DeLane F. (CGBCI); 12–2–1955 / ; ord. 1995, Albany, OR.

Miller, Duane L. (OGBB); 9–9–1955 / ; 1st deg. 11–14–1981; 2nd deg. 11–12–1988; eld. 3–25–1995, West Alexandria, OH.

Miller, Ervin (OGBB); 9–9–1960 / ; 1st deg. 12–16–1989; 2nd deg. 9–20–1997, Abbotsford, WI.

Miller, Fredric Geary (BC); 4–19–1958 / ; ord. CB, 1986, Danville, OH; eld. BC, 1990, Danville, OH.

Miller, Jerry Lee (CB); 6–13–1948 / ; ord. 11–13–1983, West Grove, PA.

Miller, Karen Peterson (CB); 2–11–1945 / ; ord. 3–8–1987, Carol Stream, IL.

Miller, Kenneth L. (OGBB); 3–20–1962 / ; 1st deg. 2–6–1993, Modesto,CA; 2nd deg. 4–23–1999, Modesto, CA.

Miller, Lowell Edward (OGBB); 2–11–1955 / ; 1st deg. 2–22–1993, Modesto, CA; 2nd deg. 4–4–1992; eld. 7–11–1998, New Paris, OH,

Miller, Lynn Hayes (DB); 1–21–1953 / ; ord. 4–8–2001, Mechanicsburg, PA.

Miller, Michael (OGBB); 1–31–1947 / ; 1st deg. 12–12–1981; 2nd deg. 4–5–1985; eld. 4–10–1992, Brookville, OH.

Miller, Norma Jean (CB); 4–4–1947 / ; ord. 2–27–1991, New Paris, IN.

Miller, Orla E. (GBB); 4–18–1953 / ; 1st deg. 9–28–1985, Union Bridge, MD; 2nd deg. 3–21–1991; eld. 3–24–1995, Chambersburg, PA; 9–23–1999, Athens, WI.

Miller, Phillip W. (OGBB); 7–6–1954 / ; 1st deg. 2–6–1982; 2nd deg. 2–4–1989; eld. 2–3–1996, Bradford, OH.

Miller, R. Eugene (OGBB); 1–4–1950 / ; 1st deg. 4–4–1980; 2nd deg. 4–7–1984; eld. 4–7–1990, Lima, OH.

Miller, Robert R. (CB); 10–10–1956 / ; ord. 1983, Bridgewater, VA.

Miller, Rodney W. (FGBC); 3–23–1972 / ; ord. 8–18–2002, Kittaning, PA.

Miller, Ronald Eugene, Sr. (BC); 4–25–1955 / ; eld. 7–25–1999, Linwood, MD.

Miller, Stephen A., Sr. (FGBC); 3–13–1953 / ; ord. 7–21–1989, Pataskala, OH.

Miller, Wesley L. (DB); 9–4–1971 / ; ord. 6–23–2001, Quinter, KA.

Miller, Wilbert Ray (FGBC); 8–14–1953 / ; ord. 1–27–1985, Toledo, OH.

Min, Young Son (CB); 7–5–1955 / ; ord. 1997.

Miner, Blaine Allan (CB); 10–28–1955 / ; ord. 6–10–1996, Elgin, IL.

Minor, Floyd Earl (BC); 10–9–1963 / ; eld. 6–22–1997, Fort Scott, KS.

Mitchell, David A. (FGBC); 1–29–1943 / ; ord. 10–15–1980, Limestone, TN.

Moeller, Daniel Paul (FGBC); 1–1–1954 / ; ord. 8–16–1984, Winona Lake, IN; min. term. 4–15–01.

Moellering, Christopher Paul (BC); 2–21–1971 / ; ord. 1998, Huntington, IN; eld. 7–12–1998, Huntington, IN.

Mohler, Marlan Ray (OGBB); 3–2–1957 / ; 1st deg. 9–9–1995; 2nd deg. 12–9–2000, Brookville, OH.

Molyneux, Ralph (FGBC).

Montauban, Verel (CB); 2–27–1950 / ; ord. 6–20–1992, Brooklyn, NY.

Montgomery, Calvin L. (OGBB); 5–27–1964 / ; 1st deg. 7–22–1997, Wirtz, VA.

Montgomery, Joseph A. (OGBB); 6–28–1965 / ; 1st deg. 6–28–1997, Greenville, OH.

Moore, Rodney (CB); ord. 6–27–1982, Waterloo, IA.

Morningstar, M. Albert (CB); 11–15–1946 / ; ord. 4–30–1987, Thurmont, MD.

Morphew, Timothy Sollenberger (CB); 5–20–1953 / ; ord. 6–19–1983, Kokomo, IN.

Morris, Robert Lee, III (CB); 12–14–1958 / ; ord. June 1985, Naperville, IL.

Morrison, David E. (BC); 10–5–1947 / ; ord. 1993, Mt. Pleasant, IN.

Morrow, Michael R. (CB); 9–8–1949 / ; ord. 7–4–1982, Ephrata, PA.

Moser, Gregg A. (BC); 2–2–1946 / ; ord. 1983, Elkhart, IN.

Mosorjak, Gary Nicholas (CB); 9–15–1951 / ; ord. 1–23–2000, Mt. Airy, MD.

Mouk, Curtiss Dean (CB); 8–8–1943 / ; ord. 11–29–1981, Sidney, OH.

Moyer, John Martin (CB); 6–28–1958 / ; ord. 2–15–1992, Shelocta, PA.

Mumma, Emily Metzger (CB); 4–1–1933 / ; ord. 10–24–1993, St. Petersburg, FL.

Mummert, John Ronald (CB); 11–9–1941 / ; ord. 6–5–1966, York, PA.

Munoz, Jesus G. (FGBC); 10–26–1954 / ; ord. June 1994, Tampa, FL.

Murphy, Nancey Claire (CB); 6–12–1951 / ; ord. 4–4–1993, Pasadena, CA.

Myer, Mary Jane (CB); 5–26–1931 / ; ord. 6–26–1988, Mountville, PA.

Myers, Charles R. (CB); ord. 1993.

Myers, Craig Alan (CB); 7–18–1964 / ; ord. 1–6–1991, Friendsville, MD.

Myers, Dennis D. (DB); 12–8–1956 / ; ord. 4–7–1994, Dallas Center, IA.

Myers, Donald E. (CB); 7–13–1945 / ; ord. 10–6–1985, York, PA; eld. 10–4–92, York, PA.

Myers, Guy L. (CB); 10–25–1953 / ; ord. 1–13–1991, Johnstown, PA.

Myers, Jacob Lincoln (CB); 3–2–1963 / ; ord. 2–22–1994, Red Lion, PA.

Myers, Partick Henry. (CB); 9–15–1997 / ; ord. Jan. 1983, Red Lion, PA`.

Myers, Roger K. (FGBC); 10–23–1959 / ; lic. 4–11–1988, Hagerstown, MD; ord. 5–16–1993, Waynesboro, PA.

Naff, Elbert Lee, Jr. (CB); 7–15–1959 / ; ord. 7–21–1996, Boones Mill, VA.

Naff, Robin Collins (CB); 6–9–1962 / ; ord. 8–25–1996, Boones Mill, VA.

Nalley, John A. (CB); 11–30–1953 / ; ord. 7–21–1990, Delphi, IN.

Napp, John M. (CB); 11–5–1945 / ; ord. 8–11–1985, York, PA.

Nass, Joseph E. (FGBC); 11–12–1951 / ; ord. Sept. 1996, Grofton, WV; eld. Aug. 1981, Grafton, WV.

Natal, Arcadio (CB); 10–5–1927 / ; ord. 1990.

Nealis, Louise Maxine (CB); 10–25–1939 / ; ord. 8–29–1999, Danville, MD.

Nealis, Robert Gerald (CB); 5–2–1938 / ; ord. 8–29–1999, Danville, MD.

Nell, Allen L. (CB); 11–22–1953 / ; ord. 11–24–1985, Abbotstown, PA; eld. 6–3–1995, Abbotstown, PA.

Nell, Kenneth Eugene (CB); 8–7–1952 / ; eld. 9–21–1985, Spring Grove, PA.

Nell, Paul L. (DB); 7–27–1925 / ; ord. 9–28–1991, Taneytown, MD; eld. 1996, Taneytown, MD.

Nelson, John E. (FGBC); 1–15–1951 / ; ord. 12–16–2001, North Lauderdale, FL.

Nesbitt, Leslie B. (FGBC); 4–25–1969 / ; lic. 7–14–2002, Long Beach, CA.

Nettleton, G. Stephen (CB); 5–7–1946 / ; ord. 1981, Middlebury, IN.

Neubauer, Frank R., III (CB); 6–3–1954 / ; ord. 1995.

Neuman-Lee, Jeff (CB); 2–20–1953 / ; ord. 1981, Chicago, IL.

Neuwirth, Richard K. (CB); 3–24–1942 / ; ord. 2000, Delta, OH.

Newlin, Stuart Gordon (FGBC); 4–13–1953 / ; lic. 1977, Whittier, CA.

Nichols, Mark Wayne (CB); ord. 1995.

Nies, Curt D. (BC); 6–6–1953 / ; eld. 6–9–1991, Falls City, NE.

Nix, Dayne (FGBC).

Nixon, Tim (FGBC).

Noffsinger, Bruce Adams (CB); 7–15–1952 / ; ord. May 1981, Warren, IN.

Nogle, Joel F. (CB); 9–5–1957 / ; ord. 6–23–1985, East Petersburg, PA.

Nolen, Wilfred E. (CB); 12–3–1940 / ; ord. 5–2–1982, Elgin, IL.

Norman, Shirley (CB); 10–29–1937 / ; ord. 1991.

Norris, Esther L. (CB); 4–4–1933 / ; ord. 8–5–1995, Graden City, KS; min. term. 3–31–2002.

Norris, Mark M. (FGBC); 7–4–1963 / ; lic. July 1999, York, PA.

Norsworthy, Rolan (CB); 7–2–1955 / ; ord. 6–16–1985, Peace Valley, MO.

Numrich, Paul David (CB); 12–30–1952 / ; ord. 3–15–1987, Montgomery, IL.

Nuzum, Frederick M. (FGBC); 6–30–1952 / ; ord. June 1996, Worthington, OH.

Nye, Paul E. (CB); 7–9–1936 / ; ord. 8–29–1999, Plymouth, IN.

Ober, Janet Lee (CB); 7–10–1963 / ; ord. 4–25–1993, Redondo Beach, CA.

Ober Miller, David (Skip) Charles (CB); 2–23–1966 / ; ord. 2–27–1993, Redondo Beach, CA.

Ober, Barbara F. (CB); 6–1–1939 / ; ord. 2000.

Oberbrunner, Kary (FGBC).

Oburn, L. E. (BC); 4–15–1941 / ; ord. 1995, Pleasant Hill, OH.

Ocealis, Michael A. (FGBC); 4–4–1954 / ; ord. 9–10–1989, Windber, PA.

O'Deens, Daniel P. (FGBC); 11–10–1962 / ; lic. 5–22–1989, Osceola, IN; ord. 3–3–1993, Osceola, IN.

O'Dell, Cecil G., II (FGBC); 10–1–1954 / ; eld. 10–10–1989, Long Beach, CA.

Oessenich, Frank (CB); 3–21–1934 / ; ord. 6–7–1992, Altoona, PA.

Ogden, David Edward (FGBC); 1–17–1952 / ; eld. 1–5–1994, Sebring, FL.

Oke, Festus E. (CB); 12–23–1938 / ; ord. 8–6–1994, North Liberty, IN.

Oligee, David S. (BC); 1–26–1948 / ; eld. 4–10–1987, West Alexandria, OH; min. term. 4–10–1999.

Oliver, Gordon V. (CB); 12–24–1929 / ; ord. 5–20–1990, Batavia, IA.

Olszewski, Bud (FGBC); 10–12–1952 / ; ord. March 1980, Wooster, OH.

Omman, Abraham (CB); 3–14–1948 / ; ord. 2–2–1986, Kansas City, MO.

Oren, Kenneth W. (CB); 6–6–1954 / ; ord. 4–9–2000, Clayton, OH.

Orme, Lawrence S. (FGBC); 8–8–1961 / ; ord. Oct. 1998, Telford, PA.

Orndorff, Jan M. R. (CB); 1–29–1963 / ; ord. 10–8–2000, Wardensville, WV.

Ort, David Allen (CB); 5–28–1945 / ; ord. 11–29–1998, Mapleton Depot, PA.

Ortega, Frank (CB); ord. 1992.

Osborne, Helen L. (CB); 11–2–1948 / ; ord. 4–2–2000, Glenville, PA.

Oskin, Michael D. (CB); 6–17–1959 / ; ord. 10–22–1989, Danville, OH.

Ott, Clifford W. (CB); 8–19–1941 / ; ord. 1984.

Ours, Randall D. (CB); 9–24–1955 / ; ord. 1988, Moorfield, WV.

Overly, Ronald H. (CB); 10–17–1946 / ; ord. 10–20–1985, Natrona Heights, PA.

Overpeck, Michael J. (CB); 1–30–1959 / ; ord. 9–27–1990, New Paris, IN.

Owens , Arnold L. (BC); 12–23–1953 / ; ord. 6–27–1999, Vandergrift, PA.

Page, Ronald E. (CB); 8–13–1944 / ; ord. 3–29–1987.

Park, John Jang-Kyun (CB); 8–12–1942 / ; ord. 5–3–1973, Seoul, Korea.

Parker, Jonathan Fred (CB); 10–10–1941 / ; ord. 5–27–1984, Taylors Valley, PA.

Patrick, John (FGBC).

Peel, Cynthia Ann (CB); 12–10–1956 / ; ord. 10–27–1991, Kent, OH.

Peeler, Jeffrey K. (FGBC); 6–22–1963 / ; ord. 7–1–2001, Everett, PA.

Peer, Peter Paul (CGBCI); 11–29–1949 / ; ord. 11–29–1981, Berne, IN.

Pegg, Wyatt E. (OGBB); 5–28–1961 / ; 1st deg. 8–7–1998, Dallas, OR.

Penrod, Robert R. (CB); 7–20–1927 / ; ord. 1995, Huber Heights, OH.

Perkins, Scott Eugene (FGBC); 3–11–1961 / ; lic. Long Beach, CA.

Person, Frances Joyce (CB); 9–19–1936 / ; ord. 8–14–1994, Polo, IL.

Petcher, Richard L. (CB); ord. 1999.

Petcher, Steven P. (CB); 6–10–1958 / ; ord. 9–8–1990, Citronell, AL.

Peter, Timothy H. (CB); 2–2–1965 / ; ord. 6–16–1991, Boulder Hill, IL.

Peters, Donald B. (CB); 2–24–1957 / ; ord. 7–14–1985, Rochester, IN.

Peters, Donald E., Jr. (CB); 12–11–1957 / ; ord. 9–14–1991, Johnstown, PA.

Peters, Gary L. (OGBB); 10–31–1962 / ; 1st deg. 6–24–1989; 2nd deg. 6–28–1995; eld. 3–25–2000, Brookville, OH.

Peters, Keith A. (OGBB); 6–25–1970 / ; 1st deg. 3–5–1997, Roanoke, VA.

Peters, Stephen Paul (FGBC); 5–25–1953 / ; ord. Dec. 1984, Hagerstown, MD.

Peters, Thomas A. (FGBC); 4–28–1959 / ; ord. 12–19–1993, Wooster, OH.

Peterson, Deborah D. (CB); 3–28–1950 / ; ord. 8–7–1999, North Webster, IN.

Peterson-Karlan, Cheryl Lynn (CB); 1–24–1957 / ; ord. 5–30–1993, Ft. Wayne, IN.

Petry, Daniel Mark (CB); 5–23–1955 / ; ord. 5–31–1981, Akron, IN.

Petry, Joyce E. (CB); 11–12–1951 / ; ord. 7–19–1987, Thornville, OH.

Peyton, James Madison (CB); 3–4–1943 / ; ord. 7–11–1999, Myersville, MD.

Pfaltzgraff Eller, Enten Vernard (CB); 9–29–1961 / ; ord. 2–19–1994, Preston, MN.

Pfaltzgraff Eller, Kathryn Joyce (CB); 10–22–1953 / ; ord. 1–15–1984, Arcedia, FL.

Pfaltzgraff, Roy E., Jr. (CB); 9–8–1943 / ; ord. 4–25–1982, Haxtun, CO.

Pfeiffer, Carol Marie Stiverson (CB); 3–17–1945 / ; ord. 11–9–1997, Englewood, OH.

Pfeiffer, Robert A. (CB); 1–5–1944 / ; ord. 6–8–1997, Arcanum, OH.

Phillips, Carl M. (BC); 9–28–1961 / ; ord. 7–13–1989, Vinco, PA.

Picard, John Stuart (CGBCI); 9–6–1967 / ; ord. 8–31–1997, Mansfield, OH.

Pinkerton, Kevin W. (FGBC); 9–16–1959 / ; ord. 5–3–1998, Fremont, OH.

Pinkham, David W. (CB); 10–27–1963 / ; ord. 5–24–1992, Laporte, IN.

Pittman, Marianne Rhoades (CB); 7–12–1930 / ; ord. 8–21–1988, Blacksburg, VA.

Placeway, Timothy (FGBC); 9–13–1955 / ; lic. 9–30–1985, Winona Lake, IN.

Pohlhaus, Karl (Charlie) A. (CB); 1–18–1939 / ; ord. Lutheran Church in America, Sept. 1967, Philadelphia, PA; ord. CB, 1987.

Poling, Larry R. (CB); 8–25–1955 / ; ord. 12–4–1994, Montrose, WV.

Poole, Daniel Lee (CB); 5–24–1965 / ; ord. 10–12–1991, Wabash, IN.

Pote, Edwina C. (CB); 2–14–1936 / ; ord. 1989, Wichita, KS.

Powell, Lewis Eugene (CB); 2–10–1935 / ; ord. 3–28–1999, Orbisonia, PA.

Powers, James J. (CB); 7–1–1937 / ; ord. 2–13–1999, Osceola, MO.

Powers, Thomas Samuel. (CB); 11–9–1956 / ; ord. 5–13–1982, Mt. Morris, IL.

Preston, Thomas William (CB); 3–31–1925 / ; ord. 11–14–1982, Romney, WV.

Price, Anthony M. (BC); 3–21–1972 / ; eld. 7–1–2000, New Lebanon, OH.

Price, Douglas E. (CB); 11–18–1959 / ; ord. 6–4–1994, Dupont, OH.

Price, Maurice E. (CB); 11–29–1949 / ; ord. 1993, Fruitdale, AL.

Princell, Pamela Sue (CB); 12–11–1968 / ; ord. 5–7–2000, Mexico, IN.

Pritchett, Daniel J. (FGBC); 1–29–1954 / ; ord. 1981, Winona Lake, IN.

Pugh, Michael Lynn (CB); 9–12–1950 / ; ord. 1988, Selma, VA.

Quesenberry, James Hebron (CB); 8–19–1942 / ; ord. 8–28–1994, Floyd, VA.

Quinn, Jack W. (CB); 4–14–1947 / ; ord. 1997, Sidney, OH.

Quintrell, Gregory Scott (CB); 1–28–1965 / ; ord. 12–13–1992, Middletown, VA.

Ragoonath, Ancil (FGBC).

Ramirez, Tomas M. (CB); 11–9–1965 / ; ord. 1–9–1999, Lancaster, PA.

Ramsey, Dwight K. (CB); 5–12–1949 / ; ord. 10–31–1998, Lebanon, PA.

Rants, Jack V. (FGBC); 11–12–1950 / ; ord. 10–29–1995, Kent, WA.

Rath, Michael J. (CB); 10–10–1954 / ; ord. 3–17–1985, Mt. Pleasant, MI.

Ratliff, Paul (FGBC).

Ray , Jennifer Kathryn (BC); 5–10–1955 / ; ord. 12–11–1983, Roann, IN.

Ray, James A. (BC); 2–5–1952 / ; eld. 12–11–1983, Roann, IN.

Ray, Mark A. (CB); 10–14–1969 / ; ord. 6–4–2000, Columbia City, IN.

Raymor, William Elwood, Jr. (CB); 7–17–1937 / ; ord. 5–17–1981, Crystal, MI.

Redekopp, Orlando (CB); 8–7–1946 / ; ord. 11–29–1982, Chicago, IL.

Reece, Richard L. (OGBB); 11–12–1945 / ; 1st deg. 11–6–1999, Lindside, WV; 2nd deg. 11–16–2002, Lindside, WV.

Reed, Douglas E. (CB); 7–22–1922 / ; ord. 10–30–1988, Floyd, VA.

Reed, James (OGBB); 3–7–1951 / ; 1st deg. 12–7–1991, Rocky Mount, VA; 2nd deg. 9–20–1997, Hillsboro, WI.

Reed, Jason L. (DB); 7–4–1949 / ; ord. 12–16–1989, Bethel, PA.

Reed, Lester Galen (CB); 4–30–1931 / ; ord. 9–16–1989, Roanoke, VA.

Reed, Robert William (CB); 4–7–1955 / ; ord. 5–22–1994, Laurel Springs, NC.

Reid, Kathryn Goering (CB); 5–20–1951 / ; ord. 2–21–1988, Fremont, CA.

Reid, Stephen Breck (CB); 10–21–1952 / ; ord. 6–14–1981, North Manchester, IN.

Reiff, Opal G. (CB); 4–9–1934 / ; ord. 1–16–1988, Camden, IN.

Reimer, Judy Mills (CB); 9–5–1940 / ; ord. May 1994, Roanoke, VA.

Reininger, Linda L. (CB); 1–28–1948 / ; ord. 11–10–1996, Nanty Glo, PA.

Renicker, Rodney Duane (DB); 11–29–1955 / ; ord. Aug. 1989, Modesto, CA; min. term. 2004.

Renken, Charles George (FGBC); 3–26–1936 / ; ord. 11–18–1964, North Plainfield, NJ.

Replogle, Norman L. (CB); 3–1–1955 / ; ord. 6–19–1983, New Paris, IN.

Replogle, Shawn Flory (CB); 2–10–1970 / ; ord. 1998, Bridgewater, VA.

Resh, Timothy E. (CB); 8–26–1953 / ; ord. 6–20–1993, Brotherton, PA.

Ressler, Willard David (CB); 8–13–1932 / ; ord. 1–15–1989, La Verne, CA.

Reynolds, Philip B. (CB); 5–28–1957 / ; ord. 5–7–1995, Pendleton, IN.

Rhen, James H. (CB); 10–3–1951 / ; ord. Sept. 1985, Elizabethtown, PA.

Rhodes, Donna McKee (CB); 10–12–1962 / ; ord. 4–6–1997, Huntingdon, PA.

Rhodes, Rebecca O. (CB); 1–10–1952 / ; ord. 3–26–2000, Roanoke, VA.

Riccius, Daniel E. (CB); 9–10–1954 / ; ord. 6–12–1985, Pyrmont, IN.

Rice, David L. (DB); 12–16–1952 / ; ord. 2–26–1994, Englewood, OH.

Rice, Robert E., Jr. (CB); 1–11–1949 / ; ord. 1995.

Richard, Sue C. (CB); 5–21–1940 / ; ord. 6–13–1987, Lima, OH.

Richard, Wesley D. (CB); 12–7–1939 / ; ord. 6–13–1987, Lima, OH.

Richards, Joel E. (FGBC); 5–12–1950 / ; ord. Sept. 1979, Modesto, CA.

Richardson, Lonnie L. (CB); 10–29–1929 / ; ord. Associate Reformed Presbyerian, 6–8–1965, Flat Rock, NC; tran. CB 7–10–1982.

Richardson, Rex W. (CB); 4–27–1954 / ; ord. 4–29–2001, Champaign, IL.

Richeson, Larry (FGBC).

Riege, Yvonne Renee Priser (CB); 7–27–1961 / ; ord. 6–20– 1999, Troy, OH.

Rieman, Kenneth Martin (CB); 3–19–1970 / ; ord. 3–5–2000, Huntington, IN.

Rieman, Louise Baldwin (CB); 6–23–1946 / ; ord. 6–15–1980, Fort Wayne, IN.

Rieman, Phillip Wayne (CB); 8–27–1944 / ; ord. 9–8–1985, South Bend, IN.

Riffey, Mark A. (OGBB); 4–13–1957 / ; 1st deg. 3–9–1991, Lancaster, PA; 2nd deg. 3–12–1998; eld. 6–26–2002, Lancaster, PA.

Riley, Bobby A., Sr. (CB); 5–9–1936 / ; ord. 5–20–1984, Buchanan, VA.

Riley, Richard David (CB); 7–29–1965 / ; ord. 7–11–1999, Frostburg, MD.

Rill, Jeffrey B. (CB); 9–16–1961 / ; ord. 6–18–1989, Glenville, PA.

Rininger, Glenn W., Jr. (FGBC); 11–9–1948 / ; ord. 1–22–1995, Sebring, FL.

Ritchey Moore, Dorothy L. (CB); 10–28–1958 / ; ord. 10–18–1987, Bryan, OH.

Ritchey, Lucretia M. (CB); 3–18–1934 / 12–20–2002; ord. 1987, Mt. Joy, PA.

Ritchie, Amy S. Gall (CB); 10–15–1963 / ; ord. March 1992, Constantine, MI.

Ritchie, Kurt R. (CB); 4–11–1961 / ; ord. May 1998, Constantine, MI.

Ritchie, Ricky Lee (CB); 11–8–1954 / ; ord. 1992, Stafford, VA.

Rittenhouse, D. Julian (CB); 5–4–1961 / ; ord. 10–20–1991, Dunmore, WV.

Rivera , Jorge A. (CB); 9–20–1938 / ; ord. 12–12–2000, Castaner, PR.

Rivera, Jaime Luis (CB); 4–12–1940 / ; ord. 5–29–1993, Vega Baja, PR.

Roberts, Deborah K. (CB); 3–15–1953 / ; ord. 4–1–1990, North Manchester, IN.

Roberts, Mark William (FGBC); 12–30–1959 / ; ord. 12–15–1992, Ankorage, AK

Robertson, Kim G. (FGBC); 8–30–1954 / ; eld. 9–14–1991, Winchester, VA.

Robinson, Patricia Roop (CB); 2–28–1939 / ; ord. 9–19–1987, Union Bridge, MD.

Rodabaugh, Stanley E. (CB); 3–21–1946 / ; ord. 5–24–1981, Hartford City, IN.

Rogers, Clifford B. (CB); 7–13–1937 / ; ord. 11–29–1981, Knoxville, TN.

Rogers, H. Kendall (CB); 4–30–1950 / ; ord. 11–11–1984, North Manchester, IN.

Rogers, Ingrid H. L. (CB); 5–3–1951 / ; ord. 10–20–1985, Akron, IN.

Rohrer, Wilbur G. (CB); 5–8–1944 / ; ord. 11–6–1988, Lititz, PA.

Roland, Jimm A. (CB); 10–2–1959 / ; ord. 8–20–1995, Chambersburg, PA.

Romero, Gilbert, Jr. (CB); 1–16–1952 / ; ord. 5–8–1993, Los Angeles, CA.

Roop, Calvin Mark (CB); 12–26–1958 / ; ord. 9–16–1990, York, PA.

Root, Joseph A. (OGBB); 11–4–1964 / ; 1st deg. 11–14–1997, Ellensburg, WA.

Rosales, Daniel (BC).

Rose, Harold W. (CB); 5–18–1943 / ; ord. 9–12–1999, Clintwood, VA.

Rose, James K. (CGBCI); 1–15–1957 / ; ord. 12–2–2001, Mansfield, OH.

Rosenberger, Mary Sue Helstern (CB); 3–10–1940 / ; ord. 9–26–1993, Greenville, OH.

Rotruck, Gregory A. (CB); 2–9–1957 / ; ord. 11–18–1984, Petersburg, WV.

Routh, Joseph D. (CB); 10–19–1955 / ; ord. 5–31–1998, Orrville, OH.

Rowe, Barry L. (FGBC); 6–20–1948 / ; eld. 4–2–1995, Altoona, PA.

Rowe, Twyla D. (CB); 2–2–1958 / ; ord. 2–22–1998, Lititz, PA.

Rowland, Curtis Glenn (CB); 8–3–1956 / ; ord. 9–17–1989, McVeytown, PA.

Royer, Allen (OGBB); 10–5–1954 / ; 1st deg. 6–20–1981; 2nd deg. 1–16–1988; eld. 12–17–1994, Goshen, IN.

Royer, Joe L. (OB); 12–2–1960 / ; 1st deg. 5–24–1996.

Royer, Thomas L. (OB); 6–11–1958 / ; 1st deg. 9–29–1989; eld. 5–24–1996.

Rumble, David L. (OGBB); 6–18–1950 / ; 1st deg. 4–5–1989, Modesto, CA; 2nd deg. 5–16–1995; eld. 1–28–2000, Modesto, CA.

Rumble, John D. (OGBB); 10–11–1955 / ; 1st deg. 2–23–1981; 2nd deg. 5–19–1987; eld. 9–15–1995, Zillah, WA.

Rumble, Joseph Mark (OGBB); 7–14–1954 / ; 1st deg. 1–3–1994; 2nd deg. 8–6–1999, Modesto, CA.

Rumble, Russell Lee (OGBB); 12–18–1958 / ; 1st deg. 3–5–1998, Modesto, CA.

Runkle, Dwayne A. (CB); 1–8–1960 / ; ord. 4–17–1999, Red Lion, PA.

Rupert, Edward Jack (CB); 10–12–1946 / ; ord. 11–21–1992, Tire Hill, PA.

Rush, David (FGBC).

Rusmisel, Dan David (CB); 10–28–1949 / ; ord. 5–18–1986, Lombard, IL.

Russell, Robert A. (FGBC); 1–20–1938 / ; ord. 1969, Altoona, PA.

Rust, C. Timothy (CB); 10–2–1942 / ; ord. 1968.

Ruth, Brian Curtis (CB); 3–30–1961 / ; ord. 1997.

Rutrough, Stephen (OGBB); 5–15–1963 / ; 1st deg. 1–25–2000, Rocky Mount, VA.

Sabin, Douglas Dean (FGBC); 8–1–1953 / ; ord. 10–1–1986, Reedsville, PA.

Sadd, Tracy Wenger (CB); 5–15–1964 / ; ord. 9–3–1989, Quarryville, PA.

Salsgiver, Robert (FGBC).

Salyards, Harry H. (CB); 7–25–1933 / ; ord. 4–25–1982, Duncansville, PA.

Sanders, Cynthia Sue (CB); 8–25–1958 / ; ord. 5–6–1995, Cabool, MO.

Sandy, D. Brent (FGBC); 3–19–1947 / ; ord. 7–8–1984, Winona Lake, IN.

Sarver, David (FGBC).

Satvedi, Anet D. (CB); 8–28–1936 / ; ord. 1989.

Satvedi, Valentina F. (CB); 8–6–1964 / ; ord. 11–8–1998, San Marcos, CA.

Sauder, Steven E. (CB); 12–8–1958 / ; ord. 11–22–1998, Gortner, MD.

Saunders, James C. (BC); 4–25–1934 / ; ord. 1–25–1987, Bakersfield, CA; eld. 6–23–1989, Billings, OK.

Saunders, Mark E. (FGBC); 3–30–1950 / ; ord. Sept. 1985, Ephrata, PA.

Savage, Donald E. (CB); 9–28–1953 / ; ord. 5–12–1995, Oakland, MD.

Scarbro, Roger L. (FGBC); 5–4–1953 / ; ord. 6–7–1987, Bolingbrook, IL.

Schaadt-Patterson, J. Michael (CB); 1–6–1967 / ; ord. 1999.

Schaefer, James E. (FGBC); 7–29–1956 / ; ord. March 1984, Temple Hills, MD.

Schaffer, Robert P. (FGBC); 9–25–1956 / ; ord. 5–23–1999, Beaver City, NE.

Schemmer, Ronald A. (FGBC); 9–17–1957 / ; ord. 5–7–1999, Columbus, OH.

Scheppard, Carol A. (CB); 2–13–1957 / ; ord. 6–20–1999, Putney, VT.

Schiefer, Thomas E. (BC); 9–7–1957 / ; ord. 5–28–1989, Lanark, IL.

Schildt, Dwane E. (CB); 1–9–1964 / ; ord. 10–29–2000, Spring Grove, PA.

Schildt, Paul E. (CB); 1–30–1956 / ; ord. 12–6–1992, East Berlin, PA.

Schload, Jess L. (CB); 6–1–1953 / ; ord. 6–22–1986, Lititz, PA.

Schneiders, Francis A., II (CB); 8–30–1953 / ; ord. June 1998, Lititz, PA.

Schnieders, Richard G. (FGBC); 5–11–1958 / ; eld. Nov. 1987, Ft. Myers, FL.

Scholl, Emory F. (CB); 5–20–1945 / ; ord. 2–4–1990, New Enterprise, PA.

Schrock, James Roger (CB); 4–16–1945 / ; ord. Nov. 1985, Elgin, IL.

Schuler, Rodney (BC); 12–6–1959 / ; ord. 1998, Corinth, IN.

Schultz, Gary L. (CB); 1–24–1958 / ; ord. 6–13–1998, Astoria, IL.

Schwarze, Robert M. (CB); 3–14–1957 / ; ord. 8–8–1982, Mathow, IN.

Scoles, Todd Stephen (FGBC); 11–15–1961 / ; ord. 10–7–1987, Worthington, OH; eld. 6–14–1992, Worthington, OH.

Seese, Leland D. (FGBC); 1–3–1963 / ; ord. 7–13–1997, Everett, PA.

Self, Don Stuart (CB); 2–22–1966 / ; ord. 11–6–1997, Lake Charles, LA.

Sellers, Nada B. (CB); 5–14–1964 / ; ord. 9–24–1995, Pasadena, CA.

Serrano, Mario Edwardo E. (CB); 10–6–1941 / ; ord. Oct. 1980, Quito, Ecuador.

Serrano, Olga B. (CB); 11–2–1941 / ; ord. April 1984, Rio Prieto, PR.

Shaffer, Dean E. (DB); 9–12–1967 / ; ord. 10–12–1996, Waynesboro, PA; min. term. 4–15–2002.

Shaffer, Frank E. (DB); 7–7–1946 / ; ord. 1991 Waynesboro, PA; eld. 1995, Waynesboro, PA.

Shaffer, John B. (CB); 3–2–1948 / ; ord. 11–5–1988, Drexel Hill, PA.

Shaffer, Rudy A. (DB); 11–14–1947 / ; ord. 2–23–1982, Lititz, PA; eld. 5–24–1989, Lititz, PA; min. term. 1998.

Shank, I. David (CB); 12–15–1948 / ; ord. 6–1–1986, Upton, PA.

Shank, Ronald L. (FGBC); 6–13–1959 / ; ord. 6–12–1994, Hagerstown, MD.

Shattuck, Lois Marie (CB); 8–1–1954 / ; ord. 10–31–1982, Ashland, OH.

Shattuck, William Everett (CB); 4–17–1956 / ; ord. 10–24–1982, Marion, IN.

Shaw, James Russell (CB); 5–18–1945 / ; ord. 2–28–1999, Ambler, PA.

Sheaffer, Charles A. (CB); 12–24–1931 / ; ord. 11–6–1983, Port Royal, PA.

Sheaffer, Timothy E. (FGBC); 5–18–1967 / ; ord. June 1996, Johnstown, PA.

Shearer, Clark C. (CB); 12–30–1953 / ; ord. 6–14–1981, Monticello, IN.

Shearer, Keith A. (FGBC); 10–5–1954 / ; ord. 11–16–1983, Osceola, IN.

Shearer, Velma Miller (CB); 1–2–1921 / ; ord. 1–25–1987, Englewood, OH.

Sheller, Gayle Hunter (CB); 4–28–1949 / ; ord. 6–12–1983, Springfield, OR; ord. Mennonite Church USA, 1997.

Shelly, Galen Scott (DB); 5–26–1967 / ; ord. 1991, Tannytown, MD; min. term. 1999..

Shelly, John A. (CB); 8–26–1953 / ; ord. 5–24–1992, Greencastle, PA; eld. 1–31–1999, Greencastle, PA.

Shelton, Harry W. (CB); 11–10–1940 / ; ord. 8–15–1999, Rocky Mount, VA.

Shenk, J. Marvin (CB); 5–3–1945 / ; ord. 1982, Manheim, PA.

Sheppard, Daniel J., Jr. (CB); 1–25–1942 / ; ord. 1–8–2000, Ft. Myers, FL.

Sherck, Ronald G., II (CB); 3–29–1961 / ; ord. Aug. 1986, Middlebury, IN.

Sherlock, Douglas D., Jr. (CB); 2–18–1970 / ; ord. 4–9–2000, Lewistown, PA.

Shipley, Greg (FGBC).

Shipman, William (Bill) J. (BC); 12–30–1951 / ; eld. 8–14–1988, Milledgeville, IL.

Shirk, Glen W. (FGBC); 6–11–1943 / ; ord. 7–10–1983, Ripon, CA.

Shively, Donald E. (OGBB); 9–16–1961 / ; 1st deg. 12–3–1994, Prymont, IN; 2nd deg. 12–2–2000, Rossville, IN.

Shively, Jonathan Adin (CB); 11–13–1967 / ; ord. 6–13–1993, Lancaster, PA.

Shook, Gregory Paul (CB); 2–16–1956 / ; ord. 1–29–2000, Hagerstown, IN.

Shrope, Francis (CB); 2–27–1922 / ; ord. 1990.

Shumaker, Sheila D. (CB); 8–27–1947 / ; ord. 5–18–1997, Dayton, OH.

Shumaker, Terry L. (CB); 9–1–1944 / ; ord. 9–12–1982, Hagerstown, IN.

Shuman, David E. (CB); ord. 1988.

Shumate, David K. (CB); 9–27–1957 / ; ord. 7–14–1985, Crab Orchard, WV.

Shutt, Barry L. (CB); 10–14–1947 / ; ord. 7–8–1984, Harrisburg, PA.

Siders, Donald O. (BC); 11–10–2024 / ; ord. 6–24–1990, Wabash, IN.

Siebert, Alvin V. (FGBC); 7–31–1948 / ; lic., Bellflower, CA.

Sigle , Dennis E. (BC); 9–12–1948 / ; ord. May 1977, Derby, KS; eld. April 1989, Derby, KS.

Simmons, Brian (CB); 4–10–1955 / ; ord. 1985.

Simmons, Keith Walter (CB); 12–10–1956 / ; ord. Aug. 1987, Winber, PA.

Simmons, Randall V. (CB); 8–9–1952 / ; ord. 1992.

Simpson, Russ (CGBCI); 5–3–1950 / ; ord. 12–2–2001, New Albany, IN.

Simpson, Russell Edwards (FGBC); 10–27–1950 / ; ord. 2–20–1982, New Albany, IN.

Sincock, David (FGBC).

Singo, Tom (CB); ord. 1989.

Sink, Barry Dean (CB); 3–29–1955 / ; ord. 7–8–1982, Roanoke, VA.

Sinteff, Michael David (FGBC); 2–10–1959 / ; ord. 10–8–1997, Marietta, GA.

Sisco, Richard (CB); 6–9–1951 / ; ord. Brethren In Christ 7–8–1984, Stowe, PA; tran. CB, Aug. 1989.

Skeen, Robert A. (CGBCI); 10–31–1946 / ; eld. 7–11–1982, Worthington, OH.

Skiles, Leland (OGBB); 10–27–1966 / ; 1st deg. 9–29–1997, Rossville, IN.

Skiles, Paul David (DB); 1–15–1963 / ; ord. 12–7–1997, Plevna, IN.

Slothour, Wilbur M. (CB); 8–18–1950 / ; ord. 12–31–1978, East Berlin, PA; 8–19–1983, East Berlin, PA.

Sloughfy, JuliAnne Bowser (CB); 5–5–1949 / ; ord. 6–7–1981, Chicago, IL.

Sluss, Paul Timothy (BC); 4–14–1971 / ; eld. 8–8–1999, Smithville, OH.

Smalley, David L. (CB); 2–20–1957 / ; ord. 2–22–1987, Williamsburg (Fairview), PA.

Smalley, Marjorie Mae (CB); 3–29–1938 / ; ord. 6–4–1989, Beaver, IA.

Smals, Ronald Alvin (FGBC); 7–19–1955 / ; ord. 5–2–1985, Warsaw, IN.

Smeltzer, Bonnie Kline (CB); 6–22–1954 / ; ord. Nov. 1981, Dundalk, MD.

Smeltzer, Kenneth Kline (CB); 4–28–1951 / ; ord. 9–18–1983, Elgin, IL.

Smith, Arthur Eugene (CB); 2–27–1956 / ; ord. 1989.

Smith, Christian (FGBC).

Smith, Craig H. (CB); 2–17–1949 / ; ord. 6–7–1981, Forrest, OH.

Smith, John F. (FGBC); 3–12–1956 / ; ord. 10–10–1983, Hatboro, PA.

Smith, Leonard William (CB); 6–15–1951 / ; ord. 2–28–1999, Rouzerville, PA.

Smith, Michael E. (CB); 6–7–1955 / ; ord. BC, 11–4–1984, Oakville, IN; tran. CB, April 1987, Garrett, IN.

Smith, Peter (FGBC).

Smith, Reilly Richard (BC); 3–28–1953 / ; ord. July 1986, Mulvane, KS.

Smith, Robert E. (CB); 1–12–1941 / ; ord. 9–17–1992, Orlando, FL.

Smith, Shyrl R. (CB); 11–5–1937 / ; ord. 6–19–1983, Milam, WV.

Smith, Thomas H. (CB); ord. 1999.

Smitley, Lester Olin (FGBC); 4–2–1928 / ; ord. 1954, Berne, IN.

Snavely, James E. (FGBC); 12–16–1946 / ; ord. 3–14–1982, Lititz, PA.

Snell, Timothy A. (CB); 6–2–1952 / ; ord. 6–30–1985, La Verne, CA.

Snider, R. Wayne (FGBC); 12–16–1928 / ; ord. 12–29–1957, Martinsburg, PA.

Snyder, Carl Harrison (FGBC); 5–16–1946 / ; ord. General Association of Regular Baptist, 4–15–1979, Ft. Washington, MD; ord. FGBC, 4–20–1999, Waldorf, MD.

Snyder, David James (DB); 8–16–1956 / ; ord. 8–27–1996, McClave, CO.

Snyder, Ernest M. (CB); 11–14–1935 / ; ord. 5–31–1998, Tucson, AZ.

Snyder, Sue Cushen (CB); 1–23–1937 / ; ord. 12–4–1996, Elgin, IL.

Snyder, R. Wayne (FGBC); 12–16–1928 / ; ord. 12–29–1957, Martinsburg, PA

Solano, Abner Aldero (FGBC); 7–12–1954 / ; ord. 1989, Mabton, WA.

Sollenberger, Dennis L. (CB); 8–31–1952 / ; ord. 11–15–1992, Upton, PA; eld. 3–6–1994.

Sollenberger-Morphew, Beth Eileen (CB); 10–12–1956 / ; ord. July 1981, Everett, PA.

Sollenberger-Morphew, Timothy (CB); 5–20–53 / ; ord. 6–9–1983, Kokomo, IN.

Soto, Robert (FGBC); 4–28–1952 / ; ord. Oct. 1990, Waterloo, IA.

Soule, Donald James (FGBC); 11–17–1955 / ; ord. 6–1–1980, Anderson, SC.

Sove, Mike (BC).

Sowers, Daniel B. (OGBB); 12–16–1948 / ; 1st deg. 9–4–1982; 2nd deg. 10–24–1987; eld. 5–6–1995, Petersburg, WV

Sowers, Joe (FGBC).

Spaid, Darrel Robert (CB); 3–7–1958 / ; ord. 8–29–1999, Maysville, WV.

Spangler, Joyce Gayle Horton (CB); 1–20–1955 / ; ord. 5–26–1996, Sparta, NC.

Spangler, Keith Allen (CB); 8–5–1951 / ; ord. 12–15–1985, Mt. Airy, NC.

Sparling, Philip J. (FGBC); 8–20–1963 / ; eld. 8–16–1986, Sacramento, CA.

Sparzak, Chet J. (FGBC); 12–27–1946 / ; ord. 4–5–1992, Ivywood, PA.

Speicher, Timothy D. (CB); 8–8–1953 / ; ord. 7–8–1984, Washington, DC.

Spence, Phillip E. (FGBC); 5–3–1955 / ; ord. 10–7–1989, Mishuaka, IN.

Spire, Catherine Brill (CB); 1–4–1967 / ; ord. 11–19–1994, Mexico, IN.

Spire, Samuel Glenn (CB); 5–15–1967 / ; ord. 5–16–1999, Everett, PA.

Spire, Steven Ronald (CB); 7–7–1970 / ; ord. 8–17–1997, Dandridge, TN.

Sprenkel, Rodney D. (OGBB); 8–31–1963 / ; 1st deg. 1–11–1997, Covington, OH; 2nd deg. 10–12–2002, Covington, OH.

Sprowls, Thomas E., Jr. (BC); 2–12–1961 / ; ord. 9–29–1996, Medina, OH.

Spry, Charles G. (CB); 10–11–1954 / ; ord. 9–10–2000, Culver, IN.

St. Clair, Ronald J. (CB); 12–4–1952 / ; ord. 12–12–1982, Connellsville, PA.

St. Fluer, Ludovic (CB); 4–30–1949 / ; ord. 6–24–1990, Miami, FL.

St. John, Thomas M. (DB); 7–2–1955 / ; ord. 6–4–1989, West Unity, OH; eld. 5–15–2000, West Unity, OH.

Stafford, Robert (BC); 5–20–1951 / ; ord. 9–17–1989, Teegarden, IN.

Stallter, Thomas M. (FGBC); 7–26–1951 / ; ord. 10–30–1983, Osceola, IN.

Stamm, Gregory Alan (FGBC); 1–11–1956 / ; ord. April 1985, Findlay, OH.

Statler, Dana Eugene (CB); 5–3–1971 / ; ord. 6–7–1998, Lancaster, PA.

Steele, David A. (CB); 3–19–1963 / ; ord. 5–24–1992, Warrensburg, MO.

Steele, Dorothy Greenloaf (CB); 6–8–1941 / ; ord. 11–20–1994, Martinsburg, PA.

Steele, Jay H. (CB); 10–2–1958 / ; ord. 1985.

Stern, Michael S. (FGBC); 7–14–1964 / ; eld. 4–16–1998, Colombus, OH.

Stern, Pattie L. (CB); 12–25–1930 / ; ord. 11–23–1985, La Verne, CA.

Steury, Mark Flory (CB); 9–27–1953 / ; ord. 7–29–1984, Decatur, IN.

Stevens, Carson Berkley (CB); 11–25–1930 / ; ord. June 1980, Hardy, VA.

Stevens, Glenn Douglas (CB); 8–27–1947 / ; ord. 11–17–1991, Elkhart, IN.

Stewart, William B., Jr. (CB); 11–25–1945 / ; ord. 1993.

Stoever, Greg E. C. (FGBC); 12–15–1959 / ; ord. 3–21–1993, Simi Valley, CA.

Stogsdill, Roger O. (BC); 11–9–1955 / ; eld. 6–2–1985, Tucson, AZ.

Stone, David L. (BC); 11–19–1961 / ; eld. 6–26–1988, Roann, IN.

Stonebraker, William J. (FGBC); 3–13–1970 / ; ord. 11–17–2002, Ephrata, PA.

Stoner, Peggy J. (CB); 12–6–1941 / ; ord. 4–22–1996, Mechanicsburg, PA.

Storaci, David (FGBC).

Stouffer, Clarence D. (CB); 5–30–1949 / ; ord. 6–21–1992, Rouzerville, PA.

Stouffer, Darlene W. (CB); 6–21–1949 / ; ord. 4–13–1997, Dallas Center, IA.

Stout, Kurtis Allen (BC); 8–28–1969 / ; ord. 10–12–1997, North Manchester, IN.

Stovall, Earl F. (CB); 4–4–1954 / ; ord. 1984.

Strickler, Carol Brake (CB); 2–9–1943 / ; ord. 10–20–1985, Reisterstown, MD.

Strickler, Ronald A. (CB); 12–25–1949 / ; ord. 6–21–1992, Manheim, PA; eld. 2–12–1995, Manheim, PA.

Strite, Harry E. (CB); 8–22–1954 / ; ord. 6–4–1989, Hancock, MD.

Strite, Stephen C. (CB); 4–24–1949 / ; ord. 7–22–1990, Waynesboro, PA.

Stroede, Oscar F. (FGBC); 11–5–1959 / ; ord. 5–5–1996, Bowling Green, OH.

Stroup, Donald W. (CB); 9–6–1934 / ; ord. 5–23–1999, Brethren, MI.

Stuber, Ray Lamar (DB); 7–13–1951 / ; ord. 11–17–1990, Shrewsbury, PA; eld. 5–13–1995, Shrewsbury, PA.

Studebaker, Guy Mack (CB); 3–11–1955 / ; ord. Sept. 1988, Pyrmont, IN.

Stull, Brian K. (OGBB); 10–8–1963 / ; 1st deg. 1–14–1989, Covington, OH; 2nd deg. 7–9–1994; eld. 7–10–1999, Covington, OH.

Stull, Gerald (OGBB); 1–11–1955 / ; 1st deg. 7–3–1982; 2nd deg. 7–11–1987; eld. 1–9–1993, Covington, OH.

Suitt, Chris (FGBC); 3–1–1960 / ; ord. May 1989, Long Beach, CA.

Sumpter, Lynette Marie (CB); 2–6–1955 / ; ord. 11–3–1996, North Liberty, IN.

Surin, Joseph Philip (CB); 12–14–1962 / ; ord. Nov. 1999, Grand Canyon National Park, AZ.

Sutton, David Corliss (CB); 9–16–1939 / ; ord. 11–20–1993, Ridgeley, WV.

Swick, Michael R. (CB); 10–9–1970 / ; ord. 7–19–1998, Meyersdale, PA.

Swihart, Ellen Marie (CB); 7–1–1931 / ; ord. 10–3–1993, Goshen, IN.

Swope, John (BC); 3–13–1962 / ; ord. 1998, Waterbrook, VA.

Sykes, Clarence (CB); 11–15–1920 / ; ord. 6–26–1982, Clintwood, VA.

Taylor, Cynthia B. (CB); 6–23–1948 / ; ord. 1995.

Taylor, Darrel Glen (FGBC); 9–24–1949 / ; ord. 12–13–1984, Sidney, IN.

Taylor, Jack (CB); 9–2–1938 / ; ord. 5–11–1996, Clintwood, VA.

Taylor, James O. (FGBC); 10–10–1940 / ; eld. 11–11–1989, Lakeland, FL.

Taylor, Michael C. (FGBC); 5–5–1957 / ; ord. 1988, Anderson, SC.

Taylor, Steve W. (FGBC); 2–8–1949 / ; ord. April 1978, Aiken, SC.

Teal, Mark A. (CB); 7–9–1960 / ; ord. 1–26–1997, Medina, OH.

Teeter, Allene Mae (CB); 5–11–1938 / ; ord. 12–10–1995, Amaranth, PA.

Teeter, Chester Frank (CB); 2–14–1937 / ; ord. 4–5–1992, Amaranth, PA.

Thacker, Robert M. (CB); 8–23–1950 / ; ord. 8–17–1996, Jennersville, PA.

Thomas, James L. (BC); 1–24–1950 / ; ord. 6–23–1984, Falls City, NE.

Thomas, Richard Wood, Sr. (CB); 4–3–1940 / ; ord. 8–23–1992, Floyd, VA.

Thomas, Ricky Lane (CB); 7–15–1961 / ; ord. 5–30–1999, Laurel Springs, NC.

Thomas, Rodger Jay (CB); 3–23–1936 / ; ord. 3–23–1996, Windber, PA.

Thompson, Daniel W. (FGBC); 1–30–1949 / ; ord. 12–30–1990, Naples, FL.

Thompson, Margaret May Sherman (CB); 12–21–1923 / ; ord. 11–20–1993, Kansas City, MO.

Thompson, R. Jan (CB); 9–13–1935 / ; ord. 2–6–1983, Union Bridge, MD.

Thompson, Ron E. (FGBC); 2–4–1935 / ; ord. CB 1957, Buena Vista (CB), VA; ord. FGBC 1964, Virginia Beach, VA.

Thornley, Jeffrey Mark (FGBC); 5–10–1955 / ; ord. 4–20–1986, Waldorf, MD.

Thornton, Daniel E. (FGBC); 11–14–1958 / ; ord. 6–16–1991, Soldotna, AK.

Thornton, Wile Frank (CB); 5–26–1942 / ; ord. 4–16–1989, Fruitdale, AL.

Titus, Michael R. (CB); 8–27–1951 / ; ord. 8–28–1983, Wenatchee, WA.

Todd, Richard E. (FGBC); 6–10–1953 / ; lic. 1982, Long Beach, CA.

Tompkins, Jonathan (FGBC); 1–4–1935 / ; ord. 1–15–1944, Lancaster, PA.

Townsend, France R. (CB); 8–28–1956 / ; ord. 9–22–1996, North Manchester, IN.

Townsend, George D. (CB); 10–21–1933 / ; ord. Mennonite Church 9–16–62, Cunberland, MD; tran. CB 1987, Altoona, PA.

Townsend, Kenneth G. (FGBC); 1–3–1954 / ; ord. 5–31–1981, Norwalk, CA.

Traub, George (FGBC).

Travis, Daniel D. (FGBC); 3–12–1953 / ; ord. 6–8–1995, Columbus, OH.

Trefry, Robert A. (FGBC); 3–15–1942 / ; ord. 1992, Temple Hills, MD.

Trenner, Ed A. (FGBC); 12–23–1941 / ; ord. 6–18–1989, Orange, CA.

Trindale, Ivanildo C. (FGBC); 11–10–1958 / ; ord. 8–18–2002, Wooster, OH.

Triplehorn, Bruce W. (FGBC); 11–21–1957 / ; ord. Aug. 1993, Wooster, OH.

Troxel, Davy (FGBC).

Tschetter, John (CB); ord. 1996.

Tubbs, John L. (CB); 4–1–1941 / ; ord. Baptist Church 11–17–1968, Cone, TX; tran. CB, 1982.

Turley, Charles Eugene (CB); ord. 1998.

Turley, John R. (CB); 10–4–1953 / ; ord. BC 1–1–1981, Kokomo, IN; tran. CB 1–1–81.

Turner, Charles Russell (CB); 11–14–1940 / ; ord. 9–11–1994, Luray, VA.

Turner, Gale L. (OGBB); 6–8–1954 / ; 1st deg. 4–7–1984, Arcanum, OH; 2nd deg. 3–31–1990; eld. 3–16–1996, Arcanum, OH.

Turpin, Roy Uriah (CB); 3–12–1945 / ; ord. 4–13–1975, Willis, VA.

Tye, Vincent (OGBB); 8–1–1956 / ; 1st deg. 11–20–1990, Modesto, CA; 2nd deg. 4–4–1998; eld. 6–13–2002, Flora, IN.

Tyner, Ira L. (CB); 4–9–1955 / ; ord. 8–3–1986, Bridgewater, VA.

Ullery, Howard E., Jr. (CB); 9–16–1948 / ; ord. 6–15–1997, Pleasant Hill, OH.

Ullery, Victoria Lynn (CB); 1–22–1961 / ; ord. 5–16–1999, Dayton, OH.

Ulrich, Daniel Warren (CB); 5–8–1959 / ; ord. 10–27–1985, Easton, MD.

Urban, Louis Michael (FGBC); 2–23–1964 / ; ord. 1–12–2002, Roanoke, VA.

Valentine, Albert George II (FGBC); 11–12–1948 / ; ord. 3–5–1984, Meyersdale, PA.

Valentine, Donald G. (DB); 2–10–1951 / ; ord. 10–6–2001, Waynesboro, PA.

Van Hoose, Robert (BC); ord. 9–5–1982, Williamstown, OH.

Van Houten, Steven Wayne (CB); 1–1–1956 / ; ord. 6–19–1983, Columbia City, IN.

Van Vleet, Daniel (CB); ord. 1989.

Vance, Harvey Jason (CB); 9–1–1933 / ; ord. May 1983, Onego, WV.

Vance, Paul R. (FGBC); 9–20–1968 / ; commissioned Jan. 1998, Wooster, OH.

Vandermark, James Curtis (CB); 4–4–1952 / ; ord. BC 7–3–1981, South Bend, IN; tran. CB 1985, Winston-Salem, NC.

Varner, James Michael (CB); 7–8–1950 / ; ord. 1989, Stuart, VA.

Vaught, Sherry Reese (CB); 11–15–1961 / ; ord. 1996, Fort Wayne, IN.

Vaught, Terry L. (CB); 2–1–1957 / ; ord. 1993, Hartford City, IN.

Veal, Russell E. (CB); 10–6–1945 / ; ord. June 1987, Roanoke, VA.

Vecchio, Joseph Vincent (CB); 5–5–1952 / ; ord. 5–2–1987, Pasadena, CA.

Velanzon, Patrick Richard (BC); 8–24–1947 / ; ord. 5–9–1982, Maurertown, VA.

Victor, Kurt A. (FGBC); 6–23–1966 / ; ord. 7–24–1997, Long Beach, CA.

Vnasdale, Lester Arl (CGBCI); 6–11–1945 / ; ord. 7–19–1981, Mansfield, OH.

Wade, Marvin D. (CB); 4–11–1959 / ; ord. 3–21–1999, Mount Airy, NC.

Waggoner, Timothy L. (FGBC); 5–15–1950 / ; ord. 12–10–1983, Fremont, OH.

Wagner, Kenneth Charles (CB); 1–28–1933 / ; ord. 3–3–1991, Lewistown, PA.

Wagner, Liane E. (CB); 11–24–1929 / ; ord. 6–1–1980, Burnham, PA.

Wagner, Lloyd E. (OB); 5–12–1962 / ; 1st deg. 5–20–1983; eld. 5–16–1997.

Wagoner, Curtis H. (OGBB); 12–16–1953 / ; 1st deg. 6–15–1985, Camden, OH; 2nd deg. 12–15–1990; eld. 3–16–1996, Camden, OH.

Wagoner, Eric Floyd (OGBB); 10–3–1964 / ; 1st deg. 10–7–2000, Covington, OH.

Wagoner, Gene (OGBB, GBB); 7–23–1951 / ; 1st deg. 8–28–1982; 2nd deg. 4–8–1989; GBB 9–23–1999, Athens, WI.

Wagoner, Stephen Eugene (CB); 5–2–1952 / ; ord. 10–28–1984, Canton, OH.

Wagoner, Zandra Lynnae (CB); 7–4–1967 / ; ord. 10–29–1994, La Verne, CA.

Waits, Timothy O. (CB); 2–24–1955 / ; ord. 6–6–1993, North Webster, IN.

Waken, Edward W. (FGBC); 5–16–1957 / ; ord. June 1998, Peoria, AZ; eld. May 1984, Long Beach, CA.

Walker, Cort I. (FGBC); 4–3–1976 / ; lic. 7–20–2000, Johnstown, PA.

Walker, Glennis Simmons (CB); 7–30–1921 / ; ord. 9–15–1991, Reading, MN.

Walker, John Earl (CB); 8–11–1939 / ; ord. 9–23–1988, Mount Storm, WV.

Wallace, Mike (FGBC).

Waltersdorff, Christy Jo (CB); 4–16–1959 / ; ord. 9–30–1990, York, PA.

Wantz, Douglas Edward (CB); 9–19–1956 / ; ord. 1–24–1988, Middleton, MI.

Wardlaw, Gretchen Diane Davis (CB); 12–22–1953 / ; ord. 1993.

Waters, Ronald Wayne (BC); 7–23–1951 / ; ord. 7–6–1986, McGaheysville, VA; eld. 7–6–1986, McGaheysville, VA.

Waugh, William Albert (CB); 3–29–1957 / ; ord. 7–28–1985, Johnstown, PA.

Waybright, Stanley Milton (CB); 5–17–1946 / ; ord. 4–23–1972, Eglon, WV.

Weatherholt, Otis S., Jr. (CB); 3–24–1940 / ; ord. 5–3–1998, Moorefield, WV.

Weaver, Beverly G. (CB); 6–18–1955 / ; ord. Feb. 1988, Elgin, IL.

Weaver, Garnet E. (CB); 9–9–1949 / ; ord. 4–20–1986, Levels, WV.

Weaver, Herbert G. (CB); 3–26–1930 / ; ord. 7–2–2000, Jacksonville, FL.

Webb, Tony F. (FGBC); 12–11–1959 / ; ord. 10–1–1989, Warsaw, IN.

Weber, Linda F. (CB); 3–11–1926 / ; ord. 9–9–1995, Lombard, IL.

Weekley, Rendal A., Jr. (FGBC); 6–21–1949 / ; ord. 6–24–1986, Pinellas Park, FL.

Weigand, Martha Creager Bonine (CB); 12–26–1948 / ; ord. 12–14–1986, Naperville, IL.

Welsh, Ronald Nevin (CGBCI); 11–22–1948 / ; ord. 6–1–1984, Englewood, OH; 5–24–1987, Winchester, VA.

Wenger, William Warren (CB); 3–6–1960 / ; ord. Feb. 1999, Lebanon, PA.

Wenzel, Ronald L. (CB); 11–24–1961 / ; ord. 8–11–1991, Roanoke, LA.

West, C. Edward, Jr. (CB); 9–3–1940 / ; ord. June 1967, Masontown, PA.

Westfall, Robert Dennis (BC); 3–9–1956 / ; ord. 6–23–1985, Pleasant Hill, OH.

Weyant, John S. (CB); 3–8–1955 / ; ord. 1995, Shrewsbury, PA.

Wheeland, Frank Elliott (CB); 8–26–1942 / ; ord. 8–15–1993, Everett, PA.

Whetzel, Bobby W. (CB); 10–20–1949 / ; ord. 10–26–1993, Woodstock, VA.

Whetzel, J. Diann (CB); 6–13–1951 / ; ord. 6–10–1997, Front Royal, VA.

Whitacre Samland, Vickie Lynn (CB); 7–23–1950 / ; ord. Jan. 1998, Littleton, CO.

Whitacre, Christopher J. (CB); 9–10–1958 / ; ord. 8–5–1995, Littleton, CO.

White, Brian L. (FGBC); 6–3–1951 / ; ord. 3–20–1988, Dayton, OH.

Whitehead, Brad (BC); 4–15–1964 / .

Whiteside, Jeffrey Lynn (BC); 7–22–1957 / ; eld. 8–6–1995, Columbus, OH.

Whitmore, Kevin B. (BC); 2–8–1954 / ; ord. Aug. 1984, Ashland, OH.

Whitten, David A. (CB); 5–18–1955 / ; ord. 12–10–2000, Mt. Solon, VA.

Wilhelm, Dawn Ottoni (CB); 9–22–1961 / ; ord. 8–8–1987, Ambler, PA.

Wilkerson, Kenneth Eugene (DB); 3–30–1952 / ; ord. 2–28–1987, Bethel, PA.

Wilkins, Kevin A. (CB); 1–2–1950 / ; ord. 1987.

Wilkinson, Bruce Gerald (BC); 8–14–1957 / ; eld. 7–19–2000, Linwood, MD.

Williams, Brian L. (FGBC); 8–17–1962 / ; ord. 3–16–1997, Delaware, OH.

Williams, Dorman L. (CB); 5–16–1937 / ; ord. 1985, Fairmont, WV.

Williams, E. Thomas (CB); 7–6–1955 / ; ord. June 2000, Midland, VA.

Williams, Larry E. (CGBCI); 1–26–1943 / ; ord. Aug. 1984, Elkhart, IN.

Williams, Steven E. (FGBC); 2–19–1949 / ; ord. 6–1–1997, Seal Beach, CA.

Willoughby, Carolyn S. (CB); 6–22–1965 / ; ord. 2–21–1993, Copernish, MI.

Willoughby, Marie Hoover (CB); 9–9–1935 / ; ord. 5–22–1988, Copernish, MI.

Wilson, Henry E., Sr. (BC); 6–1–1940 / ; eld. 5–7–1983, Lost Creek, KY.

Wilson, Ralph H. (CB); 2–23–1933 / ; ord. 6–8–1997, Lewistown, PA.

Wiltschek, Walter J. (CB); 11–5–1969 / ; ord. 3–21–1999, Logansville, PA.

Wine, John Michael (CB); 10–8–1952 / ; ord. Oct. 1982, Carthage, MO.

Winkler, Golan James (CB); 10–31–1917 / ; ord. 8–11–2002, Nocona, TX.

Wirt, Andrew Lowell (FGBC); 9–26–1971 / ; lic. 1998, Colorado Springs, CO.

Wise, Carol A. (CB); 10–14–1958 / ; ord. 1986, Denver, CO.

Wiser, Tracy Lee (CB); 7–3–1959 / ; ord. 2–6–2000, Myersville, MD.

Witkovsky, Lowell David (CB); 7–22–1956 / ; ord. 10–30–1983, Williamsburg, PA.

Witmer, Nelson H. (CB); 12–19–1968 / ; ord. 8–23–1998, Greencastle, PA; eld. 5–26–2002, Greencastle, PA.

Witzky, Gene E. (FGBC); 9–20–1926 / ; ord. Aug. 1955, Mansfield, OH.

Wolf, Arlan (OGBB); 8–12–1961 / ; 1st deg. 12–14–1996, Quniter, KS; 2nd deg. 2–28–2003, Quinter, KS.

Wolf, Gregory (OGBB); 11–23–1967 / ; 1st deg. 12–12–1998, Sawyer, KS.

Wolf, Steven D. (OGBB); 9–10–1972 / ; 1st deg. 11–19–2000, Pasco, WA.

Wolfe, Tracey Vaughn (OGBB); 5–31–1953 / ; 1st deg. 2–25–1985, Ripon, CA; Brethren Community Fellowship; eld. 1–16–1998, Modesto, CA.

Wolfe, Verling H. (DB); 1–14–1934 / ; ord. 5–12–2001, Bethel, PA.; eld. 2003, Bethel, PA.

Woodard, Emma Jean (CB); 2–12–1950 / ; ord. 2–6–2000, Roanoke, VA.

Woodin, Ataloa Snell (CB); 9–9–1961 / ; ord. 8–15–1997, Fresno, CA.

Woods, Michael L. (BC); 12–29–1955 / ; eld. 6–28–1992, Edinburg, VA.

Wooten, Eddie (CB); 1–1–1973 / ; ord. 1999.

Workman, Dale (FGBC).

Worley, Ken (FGBC).

Worline, James R. (CB); 3–20–1941 / ; ord. 2–7–1988, Roanoke, VA.

Wray, Everett Wayne (OGBB); 4–19–1952 / ; 1st deg. 8–12–1989, Pasco, WA; 2nd deg. 11–4–1996; eld. 8–17–2001, Pasco, WA.

Wray, Harry W. (CB); 6–27–1928 / ; ord. 2–3–2000, Kokomo, IN.

Wray, John H. (OGBB); 11–24–1950 / ; 1st deg. 12–12–1981; 2nd deg. 4–2–1988; eld. 4–10–1993, New Carlisle, OH.

Wray, Marshall L. (OGBB); 10–9–1954 / ; 1st deg. 8–12–1992; 2nd deg. 1–13–1999, Twain Harte, CA.

Wray, Michael A. (DB); 2–25–1950 / ; ord. OGBB Jan. 1973, Rippon, CA; ord. DB Jan. 1987 DB, Modesto, CA; eld. 1990, Modesto, CA; min. term. Feb. 1998.

Wright, Andrew James Omar (CB); 1–23–1954 / ; ord. 9–29–1985, Springfield, OH.

Wright, Lee-Lani (CB); 2–17–1959 / ; ord. April 1995, Lombard, IL.

Wurzburger, Kenneth D. (CB); 6–28–1953 / ; ord. 8–28–1994, Floyd, VA.

Wyman, Victor R. (FGBC); 10–29–1957 / ; ord. 6–15–1997, Aira, HI.

Yaussy Albright, Kim A. (CB); 3–8–1961 / ; ord. 7–13–1989, Beavercreek, OH.

Yeager, Harold E. (CB); 7–1–1942 / ; ord. 8–16–1992, Dry Run, PA.

Yeater, Norman David (CB); 6–10–1963 / ; ord. 12–10–1989, McAlisterville, PA.

Yeazell, Carol L. (CB); 10–2–1938 / ; ord. 5–26–1991, Winter Park, FL.

Yelinek, Prudence B. (CB); 5–10–1946 / ; ord. 10–28–1984, Waynesboro, PA.

Yenser, Herald E. (CB); 12–24–1942 / ; ord. 10–14–1990, Defiance, OH.

Yerkey, Berma (CB); 12–26–1917 / ; ord. 1989.

Yi, Tae Ho (CB); 4–22–1948 / ; ord. 1999.

Yocum, George C. (CB); 11–3–1945 / ; ord. 7–9–1991, Orbisonia, PA.

Yoder, Gary Dean (CB); 2–27–1955 / ; ord. 1996.

Yoder, Leon Ray (CB); 9–2–1953 / ; ord. 7–6–1986, Myersville, MD.

Yohe, Robert G. (CB); 3–25–1933 / ; ord. Sept. 1980, Pigeon Hills, PA.

Young, Charles L. (FGBC); 9–2–1934 / ; ord. 10–23–1994, Troutville, VA.

Young, Jerry R. (FGBC); 7–3–1939 / ; ord. 7–21–1965, Kittanning, PA.

Young, Sarah M. Leatherman (CB); 8–8–1956 / ; ord. 7–29–1990, Bellafontaine, OH.

Young, Victor (FGBC); 1–9–54 / ; ord. CB 10–28–79, Johnson City,, TN; ord. FGBC 3–14–2000, Roanoke, VA.

Younkins, Gale Harley (CB); 1–10–1947 / ; ord. 5–27–1984, Brownsville, MD.

Youstra, George Thomas (BC); 4–27–1960 / ; ord. 1993, Ashland, OH.

Zakahi, Nathan M. (FGBC); 3–20–1959 / ; ord. July 1988, Aiea, HI.

Zuercher, Tom L. (CB); 6–27–1953 / ; ord. 10–28–1982, North Canton, OH.

Zumbrun, Melvin J. (CB); 5–6–1964 / ; ord. 5–6–1990, Nappanee, IN.

NECROLOGY OF BRETHREN MINISTERS AND ELDERS (ca. 1981–2000)

Lists of deceased ministers (ca. 1981–2000) were provided by the following: Fred W. Benedict (OGBB), John E. Bryant (CGBCI), Milton Cook (DB), Leslie E. Cover (OB), Kenneth M. Shaffer, Jr., and Mary T. Beliveau (CB), Bradley E. Weidenhamer (BC), and Jerry R. Young (FGBC). Using the information provided, Dale V. Ulrich compiled the following list.

Each entry is in the form: Name (Brethren body) date of death.

Adams, Evan M. (FGBC) 5–9–1998

Aeby, John M. (FGBC) 6–30–1997

Ahern, Jerry (FGBC) 3–27–1996

Albin, Charles A. (CB) 10–23–1997

Allison, Roy (FGBC) 6–6–1986

Arndt, Christian R., Jr. (CB) 3–24–2002

Arnold, Levi J. (CB) 1–1–1993

Ashman, Kenneth B. (FGBC) 7–10–1981

Ashman, Robert A. (FGBC) 2–8–1997

Atherton, Willard I. (CB) 10–8–1992

Aukerman, Dale H. (CB) 9–4–1999

Austin, Alfred L. (OGBB) 10–28–1999

Ayres, J. Samuel (CB) 1–3–1993

Bailey, Danny Ray (CB) 5–25–2002

Baird, Chester N. (CB) 3–12–2000

Baker, W. Wayne (FGBC) 6–22–1989

Baldwin, Arthur M. (CB) 4–20–1997

Barnard, Russell D. (FGBC) 3–10–1986

Barnes, Robert W., Sr. (CB) 3–25–1995

Bartlett, Roger (CGBCI) March 1998

Bashor, William E. (DB) 2–4–1983

Bashore, Paul Minnich (CB) 1–7–1989

Baugher, Milton M. (CB) 10–13–1993

Beahm, Eugene Russell (CB) 1–9–1997

Bearinger, Earnest H. (FGBC) 7–27–1995

Beatty, Charles A. (FGBC) 12–8–1980

Beckner, Clyde S. (OGBB) 3–24–1995

Beckner, Josiah L. (OGBB) 4–17–1990

Beery, Neil L. (FGBC) 2–28–1996

Bendsen, Victor C. (CB) 11–18–1996

Benedict, Harry (OGBB) 8–24–1998

Bennett, Leonard S. (FGBC, BC) 3–1–1985

Benzie, Mark J. (FGBC) 5–17–1994

Bess, S. Herbert (FGBC) 1–22–1998

Bingaman, Carroll J. (CGBCI) 5–27–1997

Bird, Walter (DB) 12–7–1984

Bittner, Galen M. (CB) 3–30–1994

Black, Thornton 0. (CB) 8–3–1998

Blickenstaff, Orlando M. (OGBB) 4–13–1984

Blocher, Paul (DB) 10–1–1994

Blough, Lester, Jr. (CB) 5–28–2002

Bontrager, Andrew S. (CB) 5–14–1992

Bowers, Norman L. (CB) 12–17–2000

Bowman, Edward D. (FGBC) 4–11–1996

Bowman, Ernest Everett (CB) 1–12–2000

Bowman, Ezra S. (CB) 6–17–1995

Bowman, Joel H. (OGBB) 9–28–1986

Bowman, Luther D. (CB) 10–13–1996

Boyer, James (CGBCI) 7–22–2003

Boyer, John W. (CB) 1–9–1997

Bracker, Gordon W. (FGBC) 2–18–1987

Braham, Chester N. (FGBC) 8–26–1985

Brandt, Ira D. (CB) 12–26–1993

Brenneman, Maxwell H. (FGBC) 5–2–1987

Bright, J. Calvin (CB) 1–9–1997

Broadwater, Carl (DB) 8–6–1994

Brooks, Harlan J. (CB) 7–7–1996

Brovant, Elmer A. (OB) 9–8–1987

Brovont, Ray O. (OGBB) 12–17–1983

Brubaker, Amos T. (OGBB) 4–21–1984

Brubaker, Clarence O. (CB) 5–12–1997

Brubaker, Crawford F. (CB) 11–11–1992

Brubaker, Harold (OGBB) 7–5–1998

Brubaker, Harry L., Sr. (CB) 4–28–2001

Brubaker, Ira H. (OGBB) 3–18–1987

Brubaker, Jacob J. (OGBB) 4–17–1994

Brumbaugh, Daniel M. (CB) 1-18-1996

Brumbaugh, Elmer L. (CB) 6–29–2001

Brunk, William C. (OGBB) 10–1–1997

Bucher, Caleb W. (CB) 12–8–1992

Bucher, Cyrus G. (CB) 8–23–1996

Buntain, Paul (CB) 8–30–1998

Burgess, William (CB) 9–21–1998

Burke, Eldon R. (CB) 11–30–1993

Burton, D. Conrad (CB) 3–31–1999

Byerly, Robert A. (CB) 6–19–2000

Callender, Mervyn J. (FGBC) 4–8–1982

Campbell, Joseph E. (CB) 5–11–1998

Carpenter, Julian 0. (CB) 10–29–2001

Carr, A. Wayne (CB) 1–18–2002

Carter, Donald F. (FGBC) 10–3–1993

Cashman, Edwin E. (FGBC) 1–22–1997

Cessna, Robert S. (FGBC) 2–19–1983

Chesney, Robert (CB) 8–22–1994

Clapper, Horace G. (CB) 4–6–1992

Clark, Edward (FGBC) 11–1–1986

Clark, Paul H. (OGBB) 11–8–1987

Clay, Donald 0. (CB) 10–5–1997

Clingenpeel, George (FGBC) 3–11–1989

Clouse, Raymond E. (FGBC) 9–30–1983

Coffman, Walter S. (CB) 1–9–1995

Colburn, Ralph J. (FGBC) 1–13–1996

Collins, Arthur F. (FGBC) 2–7–1989

Collitt, Robert B. (FGBC) 4–10–1983

Cone, George E., Sr. (FGBC) 11–12–1983

Coning, Raymond (OGBB) 2–11–1996

Cook, Harry (OGBB) 7–12–1996

Cook, O. Wayne (CB) 4–3–1997

Cool, Omer S. (OGBB) 1–4–1983

Cooper, H. Austin (CB) 1–22–1999

Copenhaver, William A. (CB) 4–1–1994

Couser, Mable M. (CB) 12–31–1996

Cover, Christie R. (OB) 11–27–1965

Cover, Joseph I. (OB) 11–13–1975

Cox, Alvin S. (CB) 3–30–1998

Crago, Glen W. (CB) 12–21–2000

Crees, Robert D. (FGBC) 12–31–1986

Cripe, George R. (FGBC) 12–17–1985

Crist, Galen B. (CB) 5–3–1994

Cron, Richard (FGBC) 3–8–1999

Crouse, Charles (CB) 4–23–1994

Crouse, W. Dean (CB) 3–3–1997

Cruz, Roger E. (CB) 12–18–1999

Curry, A. Stauffer (CB) 1–15–1994

Custer, Leonard M. (CB) 3–10–1996

Davis, Gary W. (CB) 8–26–1994

Davis, Thomas C. (CB) 1–30–1995

Davison, Alpha L. (OGBB) 4–16–1995

Day, Stanley (CB) 9–29–1995

Deardorff, Noble E. (CB) 11–11–1990

DeArmey, Richard P. (FGBC) 9–14–1995

Deaton, Glen D. (OGBB) 5–20–1987

DeBolt, Edgar C. (CB) 6–17–1994

Dilley, Oliver C. (CB) 11–22–1996

Dixon, James G., Jr. (FGBC) 12–6–1994

Dixon, Robert H. (CB) 10–2–1999

Dodds, Alfred (FGBC) 8–19–1987

Dotterer, Stanley S. (CB) 8–20–1993

Dowdy, J. Paul, Sr. (FGBC) 12–23–1992

Dunbar, Dorothy (FGBC) 3–1–1982

Dunning, Harold L. (FGBC) 1–31–1997

Durand, Frank B. (CB) 7–18–1999

Eberly, Allen (DB) 11–5–1993

Ebling, David (DB) 6–2–1990

Edgecomb, George A. (OGBB) 3–19–2000

Eikenberry, Ivan L. (CB) 4–14–1993

Eiselstein, Paul (FGBC) 4–5–1985

Eller, Paul C. (CB) 3–18–1996

Eller, Ralph C. (OGBB) 11–7–1982

Ellis, Calvert N. (CB) 4–7–1995

Ellis, John D. (CB) 4–1–1995

Emerson, David C. (CB) 3–11–1992

Enders, J. Harry (CB) 1–28–1997

Engle, Louis D. (FGBC) 4–23–1989

Engle, Roy G. (CB) 5–20–1993

Ensign, C. David (CB) 1–25–2000

Esbensen, Edwin (CB) 3–21–2000

Fasnacht, Harold D. (CB) 5–17–1994

Faus, Robert E. (CB) 4–28–2001

Faw, Chalmer E. (CB) 3–13–2002

Faw, Mary Platt (CB) 3–26–1996

Fells, H. William (CB) 11–19–1995

Fesler, Wayne L. (CB) 6–18–1993

Fetterman, Ivan C. (CB) 10–18–1994

Fike, Clarence B. (CB) 7–1--998

Fike, Lester E. (CB) 12–19–1996

Finnell, Ralph T. (CB) 7–8–1992

Fisher, Lester R. (OGBB) 6–24–1995

Fisher, Ross B. (OGBB) 12–9–1986

Flora, Bruce H. (CB) 7–19–1994

Flora, John H. (OGBB) 12–1–1989

Flora, John H. (OGBB) 3–5–1999

Flora, Joseph Eugene (DB) 11–4–1993

Flora, Myrl J. (OGBB) 5–13–1989

Flora, Reuben (OB) 5–16–1953

Flory, Lester M. (OGBB) 5–9–1997

Flory, Riley W. (OGBB) 11–23--1992

Flory, Thomas H. (OGBB) 7–15–1986

Flowers, Charles (FGBC) 4–2–1999

Forney, Paul (CB) 1–13–1998

Forney, Samuel M. (CB) 4–11–1995

Foster, Harold S. (CB) 3–17–1994

Frantz, Jacob (OGBB) 10–30–1985

Frantz, Royal H. (CB) 12–19–1992

Fry, Ivan L. (CB) 4–14–1996

Fryman, Darrell Calvin (CB) 5–14–1997

Frysinger, Hiram J. (CB) 8–20–1997

Fulk, Beidler Jennings (DB) 10–26–1989

Fulk, Roy Walter (CB) 8–23–1995

Fullmer, Everett (OGBB) 8–21–1998

Funderburg, Earl O. (FGBC) 9–24–1980

Garber, David Paul (OOGBC)

Garber, Elmer D. (OGBB) 10–15–1982

Garber, Isaac J. (CB) 4–14–1996

Garber, Leroy C. (OGBB) 7–7–1985

Garland, Clair W. (FGBC) 6–25–1995

Garrett, Edwin A. (CB) 11–7–1993

Garst, Lawrence (CB) 11–30–1994

Gearhart, C. Lowell (CB) 8–30–2000

Gehman, Ord (FGBC) 7–20–1983

Gibbel, Harry B. (CB) 10-25-1993

Gibbel, Ira W. (CB) 6–21–1993

Gibble, Ann E. (CB) 5–10–1999

Gibbs, Charles (CB) 1–10–1997

Gilbert, Ralph W. (FGBC) 2–9–1992

Giles, William W. (CB) 2–6–2001

Gingrich, Raymond E., Sr. (FGBC) 3–30–1995

Girtman, Mary M. (CB) 12–19–1997

Godwin, Kenneth O. (FGBC) 12–27–1992

Good, Lester E. (CB) 9–8–1994

Gorden, Israel C. (CB) 8–2–2001

Gosnell, John W. (CB) 1–28–1997

Gould, William L. (CB) 6–24–2000

Gray, Reed Edward (CB) 12–24–1995

Grim, David Franklin (OOGBC) 1966

Grim, John E. (CB) 12–17–2000

Grimley, John B. (CB) 9–18–1997

Grubb, Harlan C. (CB) 5–26–1995

Grumbling, Richard A. (CB) 8–1–1997

Gunderman, Harry M. (DB) 4–11–1982

Guthrie, Ellis G. (CB) 3–30–1990

Haag, Walter (CGBCI) 1–3–2002

Hackman, Chalres M. (OGBB) 6–8–1981

Hackman, Richard H. (CB) 3–26–1996

Haldeman, Millard Sidney (DB) 2–9–1995

Hall, Claude E. (CB) 12–21–1997

Hall, Elmer Cassidy (CB) 9–10–1993

Hall, George W. (FGBC) 3–14–1985

Hall, Jesse K. (FGBC) 8–5–1983

Hall, Warren E. (FGBC) 6–20–1992

Haller, Wesley (FGBC) 6–5–1991

Hamilton, Benjamin A. (FGBC) 5–1–1986

Hammer, James D. (FGBC) 5–7–1996

Hammers, Thomas E. (FGBC) 3–27–1991

Haney, Robert A. (CB) 9–1–1994

Hanna, Homer M. (FGBC) 2–20–1985

Hare, Jack Denis ?? (CB) 5–1–2001

Harlacher, Galen (DB) 5–30–1986

Harley, Chester I. (CB) 11–13–1995

Harman, Alvin T. (CB) 7–15–1996

Harris, Glenn (CB) 2–26–1997

Harshbarger, Albert E. (CB) 1–14–1994

Harvey, John W. (FGBC) 7–10–1981

Haught, Albert M. (CB) 3–27–1995

Hawbaker, John (DB) 4–23–1995

Hay, William N. (CB) 10–31–1995

Hayes, William A. (CB) 8–21–1993

Heatwole, Merle E. (CB) 3–1–2000

Heckman, Galen A. (CB) 5–3–1995

Heckman, Glenn A. (CB) 8–8–1997

Heeter, Robert L. (CB) 11–16–1994

Heinrich, Walter A. (OGBB) 11–25–1985

Hess, Abram M. (CB) 6–17–1994

Hess, Daniel M. (OGBB) 5–10–1992

Hess, Homer C. (CB) 10–18–1992

Hess, James (OGBB) 11–9–1998

Hess, Robert O. (CB) 8–28–1994

Hess, Willis A. (OGBB) 10–11–1981

Higgins, Robert K. (CB) 10–24–1989

Hill, Robert W. (FGBC) 8–31–1986

Hinegardner, B. D. (CB) 3–19–1996

Hinegardner, C. H. (FGBC) 11–9–1980

Hines, J. W. (CB) 12–28–1989

Hochman, N. A. (OGBB) 10–11–1983

Hodgdon, Earle (FGBC) 3–7–1999

Holder, James (CGBCI) 2003

Hollinger, Allen B. (CB) 1–14–1994

Hollinger, Kenneth W. (CB) 9–19–1992

Hood, John H. (FGBC) 5–11–1994

Hoover, William (CB) 10–7–1999

Houff, Robert E. (CB) 2–7–1999

Howard, William E. (FGBC) 8–5–1995

Hoyt, Herman (CGBCI) 8–29–2000

Hubbard, F. Bryce (CB) 7–3–1994

Humphreys, Elwood F. (CB) 3–1–2002

Hunt, True L. (FGBC) 12–10–1993

Hurst, Wilmer R. (CB) 5–24–1998

Ilyes, Charles Edward (CB) 8–6–2000

Jackson, Richard J., Jr. (FGBC) 11–6–1986

Jehnsen, Ernest R. (CB) 1–25–1995

Jenkins, Charles Lee (FGBC) 4–12–2000

Johnson, John W. (CB) 9–29–2001

Johnson, Ralph W. (CB) 10–27–1998

Jones, Robert R. (CB) 6–14–2001

Jordan, Fred A., Sr. (CB) 2–11–2001

Karns, Lon (FGBC) 5–23–1989

Kaser, James D. (CB) 2–22–1997

Keeney, Laverne (DB) 3–19–1994

Keeny, Eli S. (CB) 11–9–1992

Kegerreis, James M. (DB) 5–11–2004

Keim, Howard H. (CB) 1–18–1999

Keiper, D. Howard (CB) 9–11–1991

Keller, Samuel E. (CB) 10–12–1994

Kent, Homer A., Sr. (FGBC) 3–5–1981

Kessler, D. Marion (OGBB) 1–22–1994

Kessler, Frank E. (OGBB) 1–5–1995

Kettell, Raymond H. (FGBC) 9–14–1980

Kilmer, Orvil R. (CB) 10–29–1995

King, Rufus B. (CB) 11–21–1994

Kinsel, Paul W. (CB) 1–25–1998

Kinzie, Fred V. (FGBC) 9–16–1982

Kipp, Earl S. (CB) 2–9–1998

Kiracofe, Homer N. (CB) 12–7–1994

Kliever, Jacob P. (FGBC) 8–21–1989

Klotz, Alvin F. (CB) 2–25–1996

Klotz, Lyle M. (CB) 7–22–1998

Knaus, Jess (OGBB) 5–5–1993

Knife, Wayne D. (FGBC) 12–20–1991

Kolb, William M. (FGBC) 7–6–1998

Koontz, Herman W. (FGBC) 11–27–1983

Krall, Clarence N. (CB) 1–17–1998

Kreider, Caleb A. (CB) 1–9–2002

Kreimes, Roy E. (FGBC) 2–18–1988

Kurtz, Ray A. (CB) 8–20–1997

Kyser, Gerald P. (FGBC) 8–14–1993

Lackey, Clarence (FGBC) 6–23–2000

Lance, Forest F. (FGBC) 5–14–1986

Lance, Robert (FGBC) 11–7–1984

Landes, Daniel E. (OGBB) 12–5–1989

Landis, George W. (CB) 1–25–1998

Landrum, Clyde K. (FGBC) 1–25–1998

Landrum, Sewell S. (FGBC) 5–19–1984

Lavy, Joseph Calvin (OOGBC) 1966

Lawlor, G. Lawrence (FGBC) 6–23–1983

Layman, Ezra (OGBB) 11–30–1998

Leatherman, Charles (DB) 8–10–2003

Leatherman, Virgil (DB) 4–20–2002

Leavenworth, Marie B. (CB) 2–24–2001

Leckrone, Elmer F. (CB) 7–25–1994

Lehman, Wilmer M. (CB) 2–19–1999

Leistner, Lowell J. (FGBC) 9–8–1984

Leppke, Harold (FGBC) 3–25–2003

Lesher, Harry A. (OGBB) 2–13–1985

Lewellen, Duane A. (CB) 1–26–1996

Lewis, Howard B. (OGBB) 5–9–1984

Lewis, Joseph A. (CB) 4–17–1997

Lipscomb, William C. (CB) 9–18–1994

Liskey, Perry B. (CB) 8–28–1993

Litten, John (CB) 5–24–1995

Locker, William F. (OGBB) 7–10–1983

Long, John D. (CB) 11–6–1998

Longenecker, Samuel W. (CB) 6–19–1993

Lorenz, Orville A. (FGBC) 4–29–1993

Loshbaugh, Ralph E. (CB) 1–6–1994

Loucks, William H. (CB) 7–15–1994

Lowdermilk, Donald L. (CB) 5–2–1995

Lyons, Edward E. (CB) 2–2–2002

Maconaghy, Hill (FGBC) 6–9–1996

Malaimare, Theodore (FGBC) 6–22–1996

Malles, Mark E. (FGBC) 8–16–1996

Margush, Stephen G. (CB) 7–1–2002

Martin, Charles M. (FGBC) 8–3–1989

Martin, Noah W. (CB) 2–8–1994

Marvin, Lyle W., Sr. (FGBC) 8–23–1984

Mathis, Jefferson (CB) 8–20–1992

Matthews, W. Eugene (CB) 9–30–04

Mauzy, Carl (CB) 7–27–1996

Mays, Robert G. (CB) 6–2–2001

McBernie, Robert S. (FGBC) August 1993

McCain, Wilbur A. (FGBC) 11–9–1980

McCartt, Arlie L. (FGBC) 1–6–1988

McDonald, Grant (FGBC) 11–17–1981

McKillen, J. C. (FGBC) 4–17–1995

Mease, Gerald R. (CB) 5–7–1992

Mellott, Brethred (CB) 5–23–1997

Mellott, Homer (DB) 6–16–2000

Messner, Richard G. (FGBC) 7–9–1991

Metzger, Glenn L. (OGBB) 10–6–1986

Metzger, Lester C. (CB) 4–4–2000

Metzger, Melvin Lynn (CB) 1–19–1990

Metzler, John D., Sr. (CB) 12–20–1993

Meyer, Nathan M. (FGBC) 5–29–2000

Meyers, J. Frank (FGBC) 1–1–1987

Miller, DeWitt L. (CB) 5–22–1997

Miller, Donald F. (FGBC) 12–3–1991

Miller, Irvin B. (FGBC) 11–23–1988

Miller, J. William (OGBB) 6–2–1997

Miller, R. Eugene (CB) 3–15–1999

Miller, Walter R. (OGBB) 10–4–1988

Million, Floyd Blake (CB) 9–18–1993

Mohler, Daniel W. (OGBB) 1–18–1996

Mohler, Horce H. (FGBC) 10–4–1987

Mohler, Paul (CGBCI) 1–21–2002

Mohler, Paul (CB) 10–1–1995

Monroe, Kenneth M. (FGBC) 4–1–1987

Montgomery, Charles O. (OGBB) 5–11–1984

Montgomery, Joel A. (OGBB) 2–18–1992

Moore, Roland J. (OGBB) 4–17–1987

Morse, Kenneth I. (CB) 3–23–1999

Morton, Robert (FGBC) 8–23–1990

Mow, Baxter M. (CB) 7–31–1994

Myers, Cletus S. (CB) 11–3–1997

Myers, Howard (DB) 9–18–1991

Myers, Jay G. (CB) 12–6–1994

Myers, Leon M. (FGBC) 10–1–1993

Myers, Paul R. (DB) 5–18–1995

Nance, Ward (CB) 2–27–1993

Nelson, Leland A. (CB) 12–21–1993

Ness, Jacob C. (DB) 3–27–2001

Nickel, Arthur T. (FGBC) 8–10–1988

Nielson, Johanna (FGBC) 7–17–1981

Norris, Glen E. (CB) 6–1–2001

North, Shelby (CB) 9–19–1997

Nyce, William P. (CB) 2–25–1996

Ockerman, David E. (CB) 9–29–1991

Ogden, Galen B. (CB) 12–3–2000

O'Neal, Glenn F. (FGBC) 2–8–1985

Overly, Richard C., Sr. (CB) 7–20–1999

Oyler, Joseph L. (OGBB) 4–22–1986

Pandya, James A. (CB) 2–3–1998

Parr, Alvery Bowman (CB) 2–18–2001

Patrick, John A. (CB) 1–8–1995

Patrick, Norman W. (CB) 2–25–2002

Pease, Walter (DB) 1–14–1988

Peek, George (FGBC) 2–9–2000

Peer, Earle E. (FGBC) 3–12–1992

Penny, Orville C. (CB) 12–6–1993

Perdieu, C. P. (OGBB) 12–22–1982

Persons, Helen E. (CB) 7–12–2002

Peters, Charles W. (OGBB) 10–27–1986

Peters, Fred (FGBC) 8–19–1989

Peters, William J. (OGBB) 3–25–1982

Petry, Elden M. (CB) 4–17–2000

Pfeffer, Mary Lou (CB) 12–2–1998

Phennicie, William F. (CB) 7–25–1995

Pluck, David W. (FGBC) 3–19–1996

Poff, Roy A. (CB) 1–23–1993

Poling, Newton L. (CB) 2–16–2002

Porter, Nolan (CB) 11–18–1992

Powell, Vernon S. (CB) 12–13–1996

Presley, Guy C. (CB) 2–27–1993

Radcliffe, Carl D. (FGBC) 9–15–1997

Radford, Henry L. (FGBC) 5–4–1982

Rager, Adam H. (FGBC) 4–18–1980

Reber, Norman F. (CB) 9–26–1998

Reed, Doris Paul (DB) 10–23–1990

Reed, Paul, Jr. (CB) 11–13–2000

Reed, Ray Rolland (DB) 4–8–2004

Reed, William Sherman (DB) 5–28–1985

Replogle, George (DB) 6–8–1993

Ricard, Ronald J. (FGBC) 1–8–1986

Rich, Norville J. (FGBC) 6–28–1990

Richardson, Kesler E. (FGBC) 8–31–1990

Rieman, T. Wayne (CB) 11–9–1994

Ritchey, Arthur W. (CB) 9–1–1996

Ritchey, George H. (FGBC) 11–10–1991

Ritchey, Lucretia M. (CB) 12–20–2002

Ritchey, John W. (FGBC) 12–14–1988

Rittle, John David (CB) 6–22–1996

Roesch, Melvin (DB) 1–24–1986

Rohrer, Ferdie C. (FGBC) 1–27–1984

Roller, John M. (CB) 4–15–1996

Root, Isaac William (DB) 8–15–1982

Rosenberger, Clarence H. (CB) 5–29–2002

Rotenberger, Lindford (CB) 9–10–1996

Rotruck, Dorsey (CB) 10–1–2000

Royer, Edward (OB) 11–12–1964

Ruhl, Donald E. (CB) 6–29–1997

Rumble, C. J. (OGBB) 3–15–1984

Rummel, Arthur L. (CB) 6-7-1997

Rummel, Paul Z. (CB) 7–21–1993

Ruthrauff, Herbert L. (CB) 6–15–994

Sachs, Elmer B. (FGBC) 1–24–1985

Sampson, Lloyd (FGBC) 7–27–1998

Sandy, A. Rollin (FGBC) 6–1–1981

Sansom, John E. (FGBC) 5–21–1988

Schneider, Bernard N. (FGBC) 4–2–1983

Seese, Herald V. (CB) 4–21–1996

Shaffer, Foster (DB) 6–2–1998

Shanaman, Frederick L., Jr. (CB) 2–22–1997

Shank, Ray (DB) 11–22–1981

Shankster, Owen L. (CB) 9–5–2000

Sharp, Thomas L. (FGBC) 8–24–1989

Sheets, Antoinette H. (CB) 9–17–1997

Shelton, Susan Jane (CB) 5–20–2000

Sherfy, Robert D. (CB) 1–1–1995

Sherfy, Robert L. (CB) 10–20–1994

Shiery, Floyd W. (FGBC) 8–29–1984

Shober, Emil E. (CB) 1–25–2000

Show, James R. (CB) 8–29–1996

Showalter, Russell K. (CB) 3–18–1992

Shull, Ernest M. (CB) 5–18–2002

Shultz, Clyde (DB) 1–29–1988

Shultz, Joseph R. (BC) 9–23–2003

Shumake, Lawrence A. (DB) 8–13–1990

Shuman, John A. (CB) 2–25–1998

Simmons, Carl, Jr. (CB) 10–9–1998

Simmons, James W. (CB) 4–19–1992

Simmons, Phillip J. (FGBC) 9–18–1986

Sines, Jonas W. (CB) 6–23–1991

Sines, Oscar (CB) 12–31–1995

Skaggs, Ralph E. (CB) 5–14–1995

Skiles, Daniel V. (OB) 9–22–1969

Skiles, David A. (OB) 8–13–1969

Skiles, Joseph D. (OGBB) 8–26–1983

Skiles, Joseph D., Jr. (OGBB) 6–26–1995

Skiles, M. Keith (OGBB) 7–24–1997

Skiles, Ora Samuel (DB) 7–17–1989

Skiles, Roy D. (OGBB) 8–18–1981

Skinner, Harry (FGBC) 11–8–1981

Smith, Arthur Morris (CB) 7–4–1999

Smith, Charles R. (FGBC) 8–29–1990

Smith, Edwin W. (CB) 1–6–1998

Smith, Emory C. (CB) 1–6–1996

Smith, George V. (FGBC) 8–6–1983

Smith, Jasper E. (CB) 6–10–1991

Smith, Raymond R. (CB) 9–24–1993

Smith, Willie D., Sr. (CB) 4–17–2002

Snelling, William J. (CB) 3–16–1993

Snider, Daniel J. (CB) 3–21–2001

Snyder, Blain (FGBC) 5–20–1998

Snyder, Jack (DB) 8–30–1993

Sowers, Charles (OGBB) 1–28–1998

Sowers, Graham B. (CB) 10–14–1997

Stamy, Daniel W. (OGBB) 4–10–1993

Steele, Randy L. (CB) 7–16–1994

Stewart, H. H. (FGBC) 2–2–1995

Strietzel, P. Herbert (CB) 1–14–1993

Strike, Ray L. (OGBB) 8–2–1992

Stroman, Curtis W. (FGBC) 4–8–1994

Stuber, Vern (FGBC) 2–11–1990

Stufflebeam, L. C. (CB) 2–10–1998

Sturz, Harry A. (FGBC) 4–25–1989

Surbey, Howard (DB) 10–14–1982

Suttle, Bernard H. (CB) 10–15–1993

Swigart, Paul E. (CB) 1–5–1995

Swihart, Floyd (DB) 3–9–1987

Swihart, Merle (DB) 5–26–1981

Swihart, Roy J. (DB) 6–18–1997

Tay, Herbert H. (FGBC) 8–27–1981

Taylor, Frank T. (FGBC) 8–13–1985

Taylor, William L. (FGBC) 6–10–1985

Teegarden, Robert A. (CB) 1–8–2000

Teeter, Gerald W. (FGBC) 4–5–1983

Thomas, Harry E. (CB) 5–22–2002

Thomas, Herbert R. (CB) 4–1–1993

Thompson, Joel K. (CB) 9–8–1994

Thompson, Raymond W. (FGBC) 9–26–1993

Thompson, Robert W. (FGBC) 5–4–1993

Toroian, Simon T. (FGBC) 5–22–1994

Truax, Floyd A. (CB) 6–15–1996

Trujillo, Lee (FGBC) 4–16–1981

Turman, Frank K. (FGBC) 5–1–1988

Turner, Alva (OGBB) 5–12–1991

Turner, Charles W. (FGBC) 11–27–2004

Turner, Robert R. (CB) 3–1–1996

Uphouse, Norman H. (FGBC) 2–1–1985

Uplinger, Wilbur (DB) 1–15–1998

Vaughn, Leonard E. (CB) 11–29–1999

Wagaman, B. Franklin (CB) 11–4–1992

Wagner, John Otto (CB) 4–10–1993

Wagner, Murray L., Sr. (CB) 3–21–1999

Wagoner, Eldo (OGBB) 5–6–1989

Wagoner, Harvey L. (OGBB) 12–25–1984

Wagoner, John R. (CB) 2–14–1997

Walker, Ivan B. (CB) 1–13–1997

Walter, Dean I. (FGBC) 7–25–1998

Wampler, David B. (CB) 2–6–1993

Wareham, C. Roscoe (CB) 11–8–1995

Wastler, Leroy E. (CB) 10–15–1994

Weaver, Clyde E. (CB) 3–2–1994

Weaver, James Norman (CB) 10–22–1994

Weaver, L. John (CB) 8–29–1997

Weber, Russell H. (FGBC) 12–12–1981

Welborn, Glen H. (FGBC) 5–17–1991

Wells, Gratton E. (OGBB) 10–23–1981

Wertz, David L. (CB) 5–5–1997

Wertz, Emery (DB) 7–16–1995

West, C. Elmer (CB) 11–11–1999

West, Murray Guy (CB) 12–16–1991

Weyant, E. Myrl (CB) 2–16–1993

Wheeler, Arthur (CB) 6–6–1995

Whipple, Lee (CB) 10–7–1997

Whitacre, Alan L. (CB) 1–24–1998

Whitacre, Howard A. (CB) 11–9–1993

Whitacre, Jesse W. (CB) 3–15–1995

Whitacre, Ruth (CB) 1–11–1999

White, Thomas L. (CB) 6–13–1997

Wiley, James Allen (CB) 7–27–2000

Wilhelm, George (CGBCI) 3–8–1996

Wilhelm, George F. (FGBC) 3-6-1997

Williams, Max (FGBC) 4–19–1990

Williams, Roger (CGBCI) 4–6–1998

Williams, Russel L. (FGBC) 4–6–1998

Wilson, Robin Dawn (CB) 4–11–1993

Wilt, Kenneth E. (FGBC) 1–27–1988

Wisler, Claude H. (CB) 6–14–1996

Witmer, Richard (CB) 12–20–2000

Wolf, Daniel F. (OB) 10–11–1985

Wolf, Paul B. (OGBB) 10–29–1993

Wolfe, Mark W. (CB) 8–12–1995

Wolgemuth, Herbert 0. (CB) 5–15–1993

Wood, Bruce K. (CB) 9–18–2001

Wood, Clara (CB) 10–20–1999

Wray, Jesse A. (OGBB) 2–2–1989

Yoder, D. Willard (OGBB) 3–5–1997

Yoder, Daniel J. (OGBB) 5–12–1987

Yoder, Rufus (OGBB) 10–28–1987

Young, David G. (CB) 11–8–1995

Young, Mary E. (CB) 11–23–2000

Young, Robert S. (CB) 7–27–1996

Young, Walter M. (CB) 12–26–1996

Ziegler, Dale T. (CB) 6–27–1994

Ziegler, Jesse H. (CB) 3–7–2001

Zimmerman, Caleb S. (FGBC) 10–30–1995

Zook, Carl E. (CB) 10–11–1992

Zook, J. Herbert (CB) 1–4–1997

Zook, Keith L. (FGBC) 9–5–1984

Zunkel, Charles E. (CB) 11–21–1992

SUPPLEMENT TO
BIBLIOGRAPHY OF THE BRETHREN

Compiled by Donald F. Durnbaugh

This list is an update of the extensive bibliography featured in *Volume 3* of *The Brethren Encyclopedia* (1983–84), pp. 1857–2111. Its intent is to list books and articles, as well as unpublished theses and dissertations, relevant to the history of the several Brethren movements, including the Ephrata Society (often known as the Ephrata Cloister), issued after 1983. A few citations appear that were published prior to 1983, if they were not included in the earlier listing.

Items listed were derived from a wide number of sources, ranging from the Internet to bibliographies appended to published monographs. Many genealogical references were gleaned from the pages of the journal

Fellowship of Brethren Genealogists Newsletter, known beginning with *Volume 30* as *Brethren Roots*, Homer G. Benton, editor.

A number of Ephrata references were found in the recent bibliography compiled by Jobie E. Riley, "Ephrata Cloister: A Bibliography, 1945–2000," designed to update the work by Eugene E. Doll and Anneliese M. Funke, comps., *The Ephrata Cloister: An Annotated Bibliography* (Philadelphia: Carl Schurz Memorial Foundation, 1944). Ruth Greenawalt, librarian of Bridgewater College (VA), identified a number of Brethren-related imprints not listed in the original bibliography. Assistance was also provided by Kenneth M. Shaffer, Jr., and Rosalita Leonard of the staff of the Brethren Historical Library and Archives (Elgin, IL).

Bibliographical Entries

Arndt, Karl J. R., 1903–1991, and Eck, Reimer C., eds.
The First Century of German Language Printing in the United States of America: A Bibliography Based on the Studies of Oswald Seidensticker and Wilbur H. Oda. Volume 1 (1728–1807); Volume 2 (1808–1830). Göttingen: Niedersächsische Staats- und Universitätsbibliothek, 1989. xxx, 1245pp., illus.
Gerd-J. Bötte, Werner Tannhof, and Annelies Müller, compilers, co-published with the Pennsylvania German Society. The definitive bibliography of German-American imprints, with many references to the productions of the Sauer press in Germantown and the Society press in Ephrata.

Benjamin, Steven M., 1942–, and Benjamin, Renate L., comps.
"Annual Bibliography of German-Americana: Articles, Books, and Dissertations." Yearbook of German-American Studies, 19 (1984): 175–211; 20 (1985): 173–203; 21 (1986): 215–45; 22 (1987): 199–219.

Benjamin, Steven M., 1942–, Kauffman, Donna C., and Benjamin, Renate L., comps.
"Annual Bibliography of German-Americana. Articles, Books, and Dissertations." Yearbook of German-American Studies, 23 (1988): 201–18.

Bonta, Bruce D.
Peaceful Peoples: An Annotated Bibliography. Metuchen, NJ: Scarecrow Press, 1993. 288pp.
Includes the Brethren (pp. 34–37).

Burkart, Rainer W.
"History of Research on the Church of the Brethren from the Eighteenth Century to the Present." BLT, 45 (Winter/Spring, 2000): i–viii, 1–88.
Translated by Dennis L. Slabaugh from "Die Kirche der Brüder (Church of the Brethren, Schwarzenauer Täufer, Neutäufer, Dompelaars, German Baptist Brethren, Dunkers, etc.): Geschichte ihrer Erforschung vom 18.

Jahrhundert bis zur Gegenwart," MATh thesis (Friedrich-Alexander-Universität Erlangen-Nürnberg, 1986), 94pp.
It also contains a "Bibliographical Note for Publications Issued in the 1980s and 1990s" by D. F. Durnbaugh (pp. 72–83).

Durnbaugh, Donald F., 1927–2005
"A Cumulative Bibliography of Publications by Donald F. Durnbaugh." BLT, 42 (Spring/Summer, 1997): 276–96.

Hoyt, Giles R. and Hoyt, Dolores J., comps.
"Annual Bibliography of German-Americana: Articles, Books, and Dissertations." Yearbook of German-American Studies, 24 (1989): 183–206; 25 (1990): 245–79; 26 (1991): 311–52; 27 (1992): 191–240; 28 (1993): 195–236; 29 (1994): 173–231; 30 (1995): 183–236; 31 (1996): 237–91; 32 (1997): 219–69; 33 (1998): 205–67; 34 (1999): 225–90; 35 (2000): 203–303; 36 (2001): 243–315; 37 (2002): 183–232.

Ibach, Robert D., Jr.
"The Writings of Herman A. Hoyt: A Select Bibliography, 1934–1984." Grace Theological Journal, 6/2 (Fall, 1985): 187–99.

Kutz, Sara K.
"A History and Index of the Pennsylvania German Magazine." MA thesis, Pennsylvania State University, 1975.

Lippy, Charles H., ed., 1943–
Bibliography of Religion in the South. Macon, GA: Mercer Press, 1985.
"Church of the Brethren" (p. 318); "Church of the Brethren (Dunkers) in the South" (p. 327); "Germanna and German Mystics [Ephrata] in the South" (p. 328).

Riemer, Shirley J.
The German Research Companion. Sacramento, CA: Lorelei Press, 1997. 672pp.
Contains a section on the Church of the Brethren (Dunkers).

Riley, Jobie E., 1928–
"Ephrata Cloister: A Bibliography, 1945–2000." Young Center for the Study of Anabaptist and Pietist Groups, Elizabethtown College, Elizabethtown, PA, 2000. [vii], 46, [ii]pp.

Rudolph, L[avere] C., 1921–, and Endelman, Judith E., eds.
Religion in Indiana. Bloomington, IN: Indiana University Press, 1984.
Many Brethren entries.

Shaffer, Kenneth M., Jr., 1945–, comp.
"A Third Supplement to the Brethren Bibliography, 1970–1983." BLT, 31 (Spring, 1986): 70–110.

"Brethren Historical Library and Archives: Genealogical Resources and Services." Illinois Libraries, 74/5 (November, 1992): 459–60.

Strom, Jonathan
"Problems and Promises of Pietism Research." Church History, 71 (September, 2002): 536–54.

Trussell, John B. B., Jr., comp.
Pennsylvania Historical Bibliography. VI. Additions Through 1985. Harrisburg, PA: Pennsylvania Historical and Museum Commission, 1989. 136pp.

Votaw, John M.
Index to Monographs, Theses, and Dissertations at Grace Theological Seminary, 1937–1984. Winona Lake, IN: Grace Theological Seminary, 1984.

Wilsdorf, Heinz G. F., 1917–
Early German-American Imprints. New York: Peter Lang, 1999. xvi, 269pp.
New German-American Studies, Vol. 17.
Includes detailed, but quite inaccurate, bibliographical information on the Sauer and Ephrata presses.

Zaiger, James D., comp.
1995 Vindicator & Minute Book Index. [n.p.: 1995]. 612pp.
Old German Baptist Brethren. The *Vindicator* index (including obituaries) covers the years 1870–1995, the minutes index covers 1778–1995.

The Vindicator Titles Index. [n.p.: n.d.] 232pp.

General Entries

Acrelius, Israel, 1714–1800
The Visit to Ephrata Cloister as Written by Israel Acrelius, September 7 and 8, 1753. Ephrata, PA: Science Press, for Pennsylvania Historical and Museum Commission/Ephrata Cloister Associates, 1985. [40pp.]. illus.

Adams, Margaret E., 1938–
George Long and Margaret Rebecca Keefer: Their Ancestors and Descendants. New Carlisle, IN: author, [1996]. 471pp.
Originally of Somerset Co., PA, the family moved to Ohio in the 1840s and then to Indiana.

Adams, Willi Paul, 1940–
"Amerikanische Verfassungdiskussion in deutscher Sprache: Politische Begriffe in Texten der deutsch-amerikanischen Aufklärung, 1761–88." Yearbook of German-American Studies, 32 (1997): 1–20.
Mentions Christoph Sauer.

Ainlay, Steven C.
"Ministry in the Anabaptist Tradition." In: Anabaptist Currents: History in Conversation with the Present, eds. Carl F. Bowman and Stephen L. Longenecker. Camden, ME: Penobscot Press, 1995, 237–58.

Alderfer, E. Gordon, 1915–1996
The Ephrata Commune: An Early American Counter Culture. Pittsburgh: University of Pittsburgh Press, 1985. xiii, 273pp.
A well-informed general survey of the origin and development of Ephrata and Snow Hill, although it has some inaccuracies.

"Conrad Beissel: Colonial Visionary." In: Pennsylvania Religious Leaders, eds. John M. Coleman and others. University Park: Pennsylvania Historical Association, 1986, 22–33.

Alexander, James
"Universalism Among the Early Brethren." BLT, 32 (Winter, 1987): 25–32.

Alley, Robert E., 1947–
"A History of the Joseph Alley Family." Barren Ridge, VA: author, 1968. 57pp., typescript.

"The Life and Mission Work of Howard L. Alley." Barren Ridge, VA: author, 1970. 47pp., typescript.

Althouse, Richard and others, comps.
. . . And the Improvements upon the Land. Pictorial Book 4. Ephrata, PA: Historical Society of the Cocalico Valley, 1988. 135pp.
Rare views of the Ephrata Cloister (pp. 4–14), Union Station meetinghouse, Denver, used by "German Baptist and Reformed Mennonite congregations" (p. 69), Daniel Eicher residence (p. 77).

American Red Cross
Report of the China Famine Relief. [n.p.]: American Red Cross, [1921]. 236pp.
Includes CB efforts.

American Stores Company
"'Cloister Town,' Ephrata, Pa." The Trumpeter 41 (April, 1960): 1–2, 7–15.

Amsler, Gary M., ed.
Bucks County Fraktur. Kutztown, PA: Pennsylvania German Society, 1999. x, 387pp.
Contains a section on Jacob Brecht (c.1784–1850), a Dunker Fraktur artist/schoolteacher in Bucks and Northampton Counties (pp. 288–91).

Anderson, Gerald H., ed., 1930–
Biographical Dictionary of Christian Missions. New York: Simon and Schuster, 1998.
Contains articles by D. F. Durnbaugh on "Kulp, H. Stover" and on "Stover, Wilbur." Reprinted: Grand Rapids, MI: Eerdmans, 1999.

Anderson, Richard C., 1934–
Peace Was in Their Hearts: Conscientious Objectors in

World War II. Watsonville, CA: Correlan Publications, 1994. 318pp.
Narrative of the Civilian Public Service program, based on a survey of 1,000 COs.

Andrews, George W., 1929–
Descendants of Valentine and Christina Becker of Warwick Township, Lancaster County, Pennsylvania. [Akron, PA]: author, 1991. 59pp.

Becker and Stumpf Families of Lancaster County, Pennsylvania." Mennonite Family History, 14 (October, 1995): 161–66.

Schäublin and Thommen Emigrants from the Canton of Basel, Switzerland. Akron, PA: author, 1996. 47pp.
Genealogy of families connected with the Ephrata Society.

Angle, Carolyn
Plowing New Ground: A History of the Troy Church of the Brethren, Prepared for the 75th Anniversary, 1909–1984. Troy, OH: Troy Church of the Brethren, 1984.

Annual Conference Committee
Church and State: Statement of the Church of the Brethren, 1989 Annual Conference. Elgin, IL: BP, 1991. 28pp.

Annual Conference Office, comp.
Minutes of the Annual Conference of the Church of the Brethren, 1985–1989. Elgin, IL: BP, 1990. 909pp.

Minutes of the Annual Conference of the Church of the Brethren, 1990–1994. Elgin, IL: BP, 1995. 778pp.

Minutes of the Annual Conference of the Church of the Brethren, 1995–1999. Elgin, IL: BP, 2000.

Armstrong, Jean Bowman
Homage to the Past. [Vero Beach, FL]: Ironside Press, 1992. iii, 81pp.
About Virginia Brethren.

Arnett, Ronald C., 1952–
Dialogic Education: Conversation About Ideas and Between Persons. Carbondale, IL: Southern Illinois University Press, 1992. 266pp.

"Language of the Faith and Every Day Life." In: Anabaptist Currents: History in Conversation with the Present, eds. Carl F. Bowman and Stephen L. Longenecker. Camden, ME: Penobscot Press, 1995, 171–80.

"Therapeutic Communication: A Moral *Cul de Sac*." In: The Dilemma of Anabaptist Piety: Strengthening or Straining the Bonds of Community?, ed. Stephen L. Longenecker. Camden, ME: Penobscot Press, 1997, 149–59.

Arnoldshainer Protokolle
Friedensauftrag und Friedensgestalt der Kirche: Die Herausforderung der Volkskirche durch die historischen Friedenskirchen (Pazifisten). Arnoldshain: Evangelische Akademie Arnoldshain, 1981. 78pp.

Aronson, Karl E.
"The Love Feast of the Old German Baptist Brethren in Kansas." MA thesis, University of Kansas, [1982?]. 127pp.
Partly published in *Old Order Notes*, no. 14 (Fall, 1996): 7–54.

Ash, Rodney, 1930–
"The Colorful Chorales from 'The Hill of Incense.'" Ars Musica Denver 1 (Spring, 1989): 14–19.
On an Ephrata hymnal.

Association of Brethren Caregivers
The Lafiya Guide: A Congregational Handbook for the Whole-Person Health Ministry. Elgin, IL: Association of Brethren Caregivers, 1993.

Health Missions Update. Spring, 1990.
A newsletter for the combined work of the Brethren Health Foundation and the Brethren Health and Welfare Association, renamed as the Association of Brethren Caregivers. By 1994 the title was changed to *Caregiving Missions Update*, then by 1996 to *Caregiving Ministries Update*. The last issue was published in Winter, 1999.

Caregiving. Volume 1, Winter 1999.
A quarterly publication, combining the former newsletter *Caregiving Ministries Update*, *The Caregiver, A Newsletter for Deacons in the Church of the Brethren*, and the *Older Adult Ministries Newsletter*.

Aukerman, Dale, 1930–1999
Darkening Valley: A Biblical Perspective on Nuclear War. Scottdale, PA: Herald Press, 1989. xiii, 236pp.
Reprint of 1981 original.

Reckoning with Apocalypse: Terminal Politics and Christian Hope. New York: Crossroad Publishing Company, 1993. 250pp.

"Anabaptist Peacemaking for a New Century." BLT, 39 (Summer 1994): 203–09.

"Apprenticeship in Peacemaking." Bulletin of the [Manchester College] Peace Studies Institute 24.1/2 (1994): 3–6.

"The Biblical and Theological Basis of Reconciliation." BLT 41 (Spring/Summer, 1996): 10–18.

Hope Beyond Healing: A Cancer Journal. Elgin, IL: BP, 2000. viii, 238, [1]pp.
Excerpts from the intimate journal of a Brethren writer, pastor, and peace activist, during the last three years of his life (1996–99).

Austin, Joan
To the Ends of the Earth: Prayers for a College Community in a Global Society. Elizabethtown, PA: Elizabethtown College Press, 2000. xi, 108pp.
Written by the chaplain of Elizabethtown College.

Bach, Jeffrey A., 1958–
"Incorporation into Christ and the Brethren: The Lord's Supper and Feetwashing in Anabaptist Groups." In: Anabaptist Currents: History in Conversation with the Present, eds. Carl F. Bowman and Stephen L. Longenecker. Camden, ME: Penobscot Press, 1995, 129–52.

BACH, JEFFREY, A.

"Voices of the Turtledoves: The Mystical Language of the Ephrata Cloister," PhD dissertation, Duke University, 1997.

Published as *Voices of the Turtledoves: The Sacred World of Ephrata* (University Park: Pennsylvania German Society/Pennsylvania State University Press, 2003), xix, 282pp.

"Maria Eicher of Ephrata: A Case Study of Religion and Gender in Radical Pietism." In: From Age to Age: Historians and the Modern Church, BLT, 42 (Summer/Fall, 1997): 117–57.

"The Agape in the Brethren Tradition." In: The Lord's Supper: Believers Church Perspectives, ed. Dale R. Stoffer. Scottdale, PA/Waterloo, ON: Herald Press, 1997, pp. 161–68.

"A Lily Sprouting: Origins of Snow Hill from the Ephrata Community." Old Order Notes, no. 17 (Spring/Summer, 1998): 59–72.

"'Our Conscience Is Bound': A Survey of the Brethren Peace Witness." BLT, 45 (Fall, 2000): 137–97.

Bach, Jeffrey, A., 1958–, trans.
"The Death Registers of the Ephrata Cloister," Journal of the Historical Society of the Cocalico Valley, 21 (1996): 1–62.
Index prepared by Clarence E. Spohn.

[Bachman, David J.]
Woodberry Church of the Brethren. Baltimore, MD: Woodberry Church of the Brethren, 1987. [14pp.]

Baker, Ardelta Delores Wolfe
Descendants of Leonard Wolf, Sr., and Catharine Cripe, 1755–1984. Wichita, KS: author, 1984. 450pp.
Addendum - corrections and additions (1989), 53pp.

Baker, John C., ed., 1896–1999
Her Words. Writings of Elizabeth Evans Baker [1902–1990]. [n.p.]: privately printed, [ca. 1996]. 83pp.
On benefactors of Bethany Theological Seminary and Juniata College.

Baldwin, Alma F. Strohm, 1919–
"The Impact of American Missionary Activities on the Bura People of Nigeria." PhD thesis, Ball State University, 1973, 153pp.

"The Roots of the Mission Program in the Church of the Brethren." In: The Brethren Presence in the World…: Proceedings of the 3rd Brethren World Assembly, July 23–26, 2003, ed. William R. Eberly. Philadelphia, PA: Brethren Encyclopedia, Inc., 2004, 9–18.

Balmer, Randall H.
A Perfect Babel of Confusion: Dutch Religion and English Culture in the Middle Colonies. New York: Oxford University Press, 1989. xi, 258pp.
Mentions Dunkers (pp. 64, 154).

Barkley, Terry
One Who Served: Elder Charles Nesselrodt of Shenandoah County, Virginia. [Bridgewater, VA]: author, 1996. 85pp.
Second, revised and enlarged edition (1998), 109pp.

Barrett, Lois
"The Anabaptist Vision and Modern Mission." In: Anabaptist Currents: History in Conversation with the Present, eds. Carl F. Bowman and Stephen L. Longenecker. Camden, ME: Penobscot Press, 1995, 303–10.

"Spirituality and Discernment: or How Do You Know if This Spirituality is Christian?" In: The Dilemma of Anabaptist Piety: Strengthening or Straining the Bonds of Community?, ed. Stephen L. Longenecker. Camden, ME: Penobscot Press, 1997, 173–81.

Barrow, Zelma D.
Danner [Family]. St. Petersburg, FL: author, 1986. 28pp.

Bartolosch, Thomas A. and others, eds.
Siegerländer und Wittgensteiner in der Neuen Welt: Auswanderung im 18. und 19. Jahrhundert. Siegen: Universität Siegen, 1999.
Articles on the emigration of the Schwarzenau Brethren and on Christoph Sauer.

Bashor, Lee T. and Bashore, Melvin L.
Perry Calvin Bashore, A Family History. [n.p.: authors], 1989. 48pp.

Bauer, Eberhard
"Christoph Sauers Tätigkeit als Drucker in Germantown: Erweiteres Referat einer amerikanischen Dissertation." Wittgenstein, 81 (1993): 62–76.

Bauman, Elizabeth Hershberger
Coals of Fire: A Christian Peace Shelf Selection. Scottdale, PA: Herald Press, 1995. 127pp.
True stores of nonresistance among Mennonites, Brethren, Quakers, and others.

Bauman, Louis S., 1875–1950
"The Louis S. Bauman Papers." 1999.
Microfiche of 1401 sheets of MSS from the Grace Brethren leader; from the Morgan Library, Grace Theological Seminary, and from BIOLA University.

Bible Prophecy in an Apocalyptic Age. NY: Garland Publishing, [ca. 1986].
Collected writings of Louis S. Baumann.

Bauman, Wesley
"Rethinking the Great Commission." Old Order Notes, no. 13 (Fall, 1995): 36–46.

Bayer, Frank
Harmon Dick Family, 1756–1985. New Enterprise, PA: author, [1986]. 91pp.

Bdlia, Bitrus A.
"Principles of Administration: Management and Planning for Church Growth." MATh thesis, Bethany Theological Seminary, 1993, 80pp.

Bdlia, Bitrus and others
Progressive History of the Ekklesiyar 'Yan'uwa a Nigeria (EYN): Church of the Brethren in Nigeria: 75th Anniversary Celebration, 17th March, 1998. Jos, Nigeria: Midland Press, 1998. 111pp.

Beachler, Lowell H.
My Grandma's 1887 Diary. [Modesto, CA: author], 1982. [16], 38, [2]pp.

New River District: Old German Baptist Brethren Church, Whittier, Los Angeles County, California. Records Researched and Compiled in the Years of 1982, 1983, 1984. [Modesto, CA: author], 1985. 176pp., illus.

Wood Colony District. [Modesto, CA: author], 2002. Illus.
Deals with Brethren in California, and in particular with the OGBB in the Modesto area; it contains some 750 photos.

Beachler, Lowell H. and Binnie, Lester H., 1907–1998
Renicker Cemetery, Lagro Township, Wabash County, Indiana. [North Manchester, IN: L. H. Binnie], 1979. 6pp.

Beaver, (Samuel) Wayne, 1918–
God at Work in the Central African Republic. [n.p.: ca. 1990]. v, 185pp.
FGBC missionary memoirs.

Beck, Bill and West, Mel, eds.
Cowboy Memories: Published in Honor of the Seagoing Cowboys, Air Attendants, and Truckers of the HPI Animals – On the Fiftieth Anniversary of Heifer Project International (1944–1994). [n.p.]: Florida United Methodist Conference Print Shop, 1994. 179pp.

Beeghly, W. G.
Descendants of Michael Beeghly and Barro Inken, Book I. Listie, PA: author, 1983. 174pp.

Descendants of Michael Beeghly and Barbara Zook, Book IX. Listie, PA: author, 1984. 320pp.

Beissel, James D., Sr., 1927–
The Wedge: Beisel/Beissel International Genealogy. Ephrata, PA: Science Press for Crystal Educational Counselors, 1990. xx, 462.
Much data on family history but not always accurate.

Benad, Matthias
"Ekstatische Religiosität und gesellschaftliche Wirklichkeit: Eine Untersuchung zu den Motiven der Inspirationserweckung unter den separatistischen Pietisten in der Wetterau, 1714/15." Pietismus und Neuzeit, 8 (1882): 119–61.

Toleranz und Oekonomie. Das Patent des Grafen Ernst Casimir von 1712 und die Grundung der Büdinger Vorstadt. Büdingen: Büdinger Geschichtsblätter, 1983. 272pp.
Mentions the Brethren in the Marienborn area of Germany.

Bender, Carrie
Beachwood Acres. Morgantown, PA: Masthof Press, 2003. 136pp.
Fiction, including a segment on Ephrata.

Bender, Courtney
"Place, Process, and Practice: Perspectives on Changes in the Character of Mennonite Spirituality." In: The Dilemma of Anabaptist Piety: Strengthening or Straining the Bonds of Community?, ed. Stephen L. Longenecker. Camden, ME: Penobscot Press, 1997, 123–29.

Bender, Wilbur J., 1903–1969
Nonresistance in Colonial Pennsylvania. Ephrata, PA: Eastern Mennonite Publications, 1985. 31pp.
A reprint of a classic article, first published in the Mennonite Quarterly Review 1/3 (1927): 23–40.

Benedict, Fred W.
"A Plain Wedding in a Plain Meetinghouse." Old Order Notes, no. 8 (Spring, 1985): 37–39.

"The Significance of Old German Baptist Plain Dress in the 1980s." BLT, 31 (Summer, 1986): 162–74.
Also published: Old Order Notes, no. 9 (Fall, 1986): 7–21. See response by Emmert F. Bittinger: BLT, 31 (1986): 175–79; Old Order Notes, no. 9 (Fall, 1986): 23–27.

"The Old Order Brethren in Transition." In: Brethren in Transition: 20th Century Directions and Dilemmas, ed. Emmert F. Bittinger. Camden, ME: Penobscot Press, 1992, 91–100.

"Yieldedness and Accountability: Contemporary Applications and Prospects." In: Anabaptist Currents: History in Conversation with the Present, eds. Carl F. Bowman and Stephen L. Longenecker. Camden, ME: Penobscot Press, 1995, 281–86.

"The Plain Meeting House." Old Order Notes, no. 16 (Fall/Winter, 1997): 85–96.

"Old Order Attitudes to Scholarly Research." Old Order Notes, no. 19 (Spring/Summer, 1999): 43–45.

"Worship in the Meetinghouse." In: Papers from the Elder John Kline Bicentennial Celebration, ed. William R. Eberly. Ambler, PA: Brethren Encyclopedia, Inc., 2002, 25–35.

"Nonconformity Among German Baptists." In: Papers from the Elder John Kline Bicentennial Celebration, ed. William R. Eberly. Ambler, PA: Brethren Encyclopedia, Inc., 2002, 69–81.

Benedict, Fred W., ed.
[Special issue on plain dress]. BLT, 31 (Summer, 1986): 132–91.
Contributors include: Esther F. Rupel, Dale R. Stoffer, Marcus Miller, Fred W. Benedict, Emmert F. Bittinger, William F. Rushby, and D. F. Durnbaugh.

[Special issue on Brethren missions]. Old Order Notes, no. 10 (Spring, 1988): 1–64.
Contains presentations by: Dale W. Brown, D. F. Durnbaugh, Joseph R. Shultz, Thomas Julien, Harley T. Flory, Robert S. Lehigh, Marcus Miller, Charles M. Bieber, and Dale R. Stoffer. They were given at a conference at Ashland, OH, March 27–28, 1987, sponsored by the Brethren Encyclopedia, Inc.

"The [Maurice] Hess Letters." Old Order Notes, no. 6 (Autumn, 1982): 7–32; no. 7 (Autumn, 1983): 29–47; no.

8 (Spring, 1985): 11–24; no. 9 (Fall, 1986): 30–51; no. 11 (Spring, 1990): 7–53; no. 12 (Summer, 1993): 7–43.
An important source for conscientious objection during World War I. Many letters are quoted extensively, others are described concisely. Maurice A. Hess (1888–1967), a member of the OGBB, was an educated and articulate teacher. The testimony he prepared for his court-martial was published many times.

[Special issue, Snow Hill Society]. Old Order Notes, no. 17 (Spring/Summer, 1998): 1–104.
With articles by D. F. Durnbaugh, Crist M. King, Denise A. Seachrist, Jeffrey A. Bach, and Larry Dean Calimer.

"Three Letters of F. E. Mallott to Maurice A. Hess." Old Order Notes, no. 19 (Spring-Summer, 1999): 39–41.

Benevento, Tom
Inwardly Rich, Outwardly Simple: Reflections of a Volunteer in Guatemala. Elgin, IL: Brethren Volunteer Service, 1998.

Benson, Cynda L.
Early American Illuminated Manuscripts from the Ephrata Cloister. Chicopee, MA: AM Lithography Corporation, [1994]. 24pp.
Smith College Museum of Art.

"Early American Illuminated Manuscripts from the Ephrata Cloister." PhD dissertation, University of Kansas, 1994. xxi, 313pp.

Benz, Ernst, 1907–1978
"Littérature du Désert chez les Evangéligues allemands et les Piétistes de Pennsylvanie." Irénikon, 51/3 (1978): 338–57.

Bergsten, Gunilla
Thomas Mann's Doctor Faustus: The Sources and Structures of the Novel. Chicago: University of Chicago Press, 1969.
Translated from the original version (Stockholm: 1963). Mann based the musical theories of his protagonist on those of Conrad Beissel.

Berkey, William Albert and Reichly, Ruth Berkey
The Berkey Book. Arlington, VA: R. B. Reichley, 1984. 527pp.

Berry, Brian J. L., 1934–
America's Utopian Experiments: Communal Havens from Long Wave Crises. Hanover, NH: University Press of New England, 1992.
Ephrata and Snow Hill, pp. 4–5.

Best, Jane Evans
"Turmoil in Conestoga." Pennsylvania Mennonite Heritage, 17 (January, 1993): 2–27.
Religious unrest leading to affiliation with Ephrata.

The Groff Book: Volume 2: A Continuing Saga. Ronks, PA: Groff History Associates, 1997.
See also Groff, C. L., Groff, W. B., and Best, Jane Evans, eds., The Groff Book, Volume 1 (1995).

Bethany Theological Seminary
Seminarian. Vol. 41, no. 3, Fall, 1998.
Ordinarily published three times a year.

Bhagat, Shantilal, 1923–
The Family Farm: Can It Be Saved? Elgin, IL: BP, 1985. [iv], 74pp.

What Does It Profit? Christian Dialogue with the U. S. Economy. Elgin, IL: BP, 1983.
With A Teacher's Guide . . . by Shirley J. Heckman (1983).

Bhagat, Shantilal, 1923–, ed.
Between the Flood and the Rainbow. Vol. 1 [1993].
A newsletter on ecological concerns, by the CB staffperson.

Church Union in India: The Church of the Brethren Experience. Elgin, IL: BP for the Global Missionary Partnerships Office, 2001. v, 117pp.

Bicentennial Committee
Two Hundreth Anniversary of the Lost Creek Church of the Brethren. [n.p.: 1990].
The Bunkertown, Free Spring, and Lost Creek meetinghouses in Pennsylvania.

Bieber, Charles M., 1919–
"Mission: The Church of the Brethren." Old Order Notes, no. 10 (Spring, 1988): 43–48.

Keeping the Embers Aglow: 100 Years of the Ephrata Church of the Brethren. Morgantown, PA: Masthof Press for the Ephrata Church of the Brethren, 1999. vii, 200 pp.

Around God's World for Eighty Years. Morgantown, PA: Masthof Press for the author, 2002. 338pp.
Candid memoirs of a CB nurse, missionary, and pastor.

Biechler, Doris E. Mylin
Mylin [Family History]. [Lancaster, PA: Doris E. Beichler], 1988. 95pp.

Binnie, Lester H., 1907–1998
Brethren Cemeteries in Kosciusko and Northern Wabash Counties, Indiana. [North Manchester, IN]: author, 1983. 4pp.

Cemetery Records for Paw Paw and Pleasant Townships, Wabash County, Indiana, revised edition. [North Manchester, IN]: author, 1983. 196pp.

Abraham Abshire of Virginia and Some of His Indiana Descendants. North Manchester, IN: author, 1985. 98pp.

A Century of Service, 1889–1989. North Manchester, IN: Church of the Brethren Homes, Inc., 1989.
The Mexico and Timbercrest Homes.

The German Baptist Arnolds. [North Manchester, IN]: author, 1990. 114pp.

The Arnold and Wertenberger Family Letters. North Manchester, IN: author, 1990.

Bird, Michael S., 1941–
Ontario Fraktur: A Pennsylvania German Folk Tradition in Early Canada. Toronto: M. F. Feheley Publishers, 1977.
Ephrata (pp. 17, 32–33, 36.)

O Noble Heart/O Edel Hertz: Fraktur and Spirituality in Pennsylvania German Folk Art. Lancaster, PA: Heritage Center Museum of Lancaster County, 2002.

Bister, Ulrich, 1948–
"Gerhard Tersteegen – Die Rezeption seiner Schriften in Nordamerika und sein dortiger Freundeskreis." In: Gerhard Tersteegen – Evangelische Mystik inmitten der Aufklärung, ed. Manfred Kock. Köln: Rheinland-Verlag, 1997, 123–34.

Gerhard Tersteegen: Für dich sei ganz mein Herz und Leben: Eine Auswahl seiner Lieder und Briefe an Erweckte im Bergischen Land. Giessen: Brunnen Verlag, 1997. xviii, 251pp.
Co-editor: Michael Knieriem.
References to Johann Lobach and E. C. Hochmann von Hochenau.

"Beziehungen zwischen amerikanischen und rheinischen Erweckten des innerkirchlichen und radikal-täuferischen Pietismus." Schöne Neue Welt: Rheinländer erobern Amerika, ed. Komelia Panek. Kommern/Mechernich: Landesmuseum für Volkskunde, 2001. Bd. 2. Führer und Schriften des Rheinischen Freilichtsmuseum und Landesmuseum fur Volkskunde, Nr. 60.
With references to colonial Brethren (pp. 343–48).

"The Pietism of Johann Lobach," BLT, 47 (Winter/Spring 2002): 89–94.
Translated by Hedwig T. Durnbaugh

Bittinger, Desmond W., 1905–1991
The Song of the Drums: African Life and Love Under the Monkey Bread Tree. Elgin, IL: BP, 1978.

Bittinger, Emmert F., 1925–
Heritage and Promise: Perspectives on the Church of the Brethren. Elgin, IL: BP, 1983. 158pp.
Revised edition, first published (1970); a sociologically-based learning guide to Brethren history, practice, and belief.

"Response to 'The Significance [of Old German Baptist Plain Dress in the 1980s].'" Old Order Notes, no. 9 (Fall, 1986): 23–27.

"Valentine and Martin Powers Families." BLT, 34 (Autumn, 1989): 229–36.

Allegheny Passage: Churches and Families, West Marva District, Church of the Brethren, 1752–1990. Camden, ME: Penobscot Press, 1990. 856pp.
A thoroughly detailed district history, based on extensive research, with many family histories. Second, revised printing (1991).

"The Organizational Imperative and its Implications: The West Marva Example." In: Brethren in Transition: 20th Century Directions and Dilemmas, ed. Emmert F. Bittinger. Camden, ME: Penobscot Press, 1992, 141–65.

"Coventry Henry Landis of Schuylkill and Coventry." Mennonite Family History, 12/3 (1993): 118–21.
First of three articles sorting out Brethren-related Landis/Landes families.

"John 'Hannesli' Landis, Jr., and Wife Anna Good of Earl Township, Lancaster County, Pennsylvania." Mennonite Family History, 12/4 (1993): 148–51.

"Ephrata John 'Hannes' Landes of Lancaster County, Pennsylvania, Part I." Mennonite Family History, 13/1 (1994): 28–33.

"Elder Peter Bowman of Virginia: Defender of Brethren Beliefs." Mennonite Family History, 14/2 (1995): 7–24.

"The Jacob and Varena Bowman Family, Brethren Pioneers of Maryland and Virginia." Mennonite Family History, 16/1–2 (1997): 119–26, 156–67.

"Tips [on Peter Bowman (1762–1823)]." Pennsylvania Mennonite Heritage, 24/1 (2001): 38.

"A Brother Named Albertus . . . : A Brethren Hendricks Family." Mennonite Family History, 20/2 (2001): 122–25.

"The Brethren and the Civil War." In: Papers from the Elder John Kline Bicentennial Celebration, ed. William R. Eberly. Ambler, PA: Brethren Encyclopedia, Inc., 2002, 50–57.

"Elder John Kline: His Family and His Missionary Spirit." In: Papers from the Elder John Kline Bicentennial Celebration, ed. William R. Eberly. Ambler, PA: Brethren Encyclopedia, Inc., 2002, 154–59.

Bittinger, Emmert F., ed., 1925–
Brethren in Transition: 20th century Directions and Dilemmas. Camden, ME: Penobscot Press for the Forum for Religious Studies, Bridgewater College, 1992. vii, 245pp.
Proceedings of a conference (September, 1992); those presenting papers included: Stephen L. Longenecker, Carl F. Bowman, Allen C. Deeter, Vernard Eller, Warren S. Kissinger, Fred W. Benedict, Dale R. Stoffer, James C. Juhnke, Thomas D. Hamm, Donald B. Kraybill, Emmert F. Bittinger, Donald R. Fitzkee, Donald E. Miller, Hedwig T. Durnbaugh, Dale W. Brown, Christina Bucher, Melanie A. May, D. F. Durnbaugh, and David G. Metzler.

Unionists and the Civil War Experience in the Shenandoah Valley. Volume 1: Mt. Crawford and Cross Keys, Rockingham County, Virginia. Harrisonburg, VA: Valley Brethren-Mennonite Heritage Center/The Valley Research Associates, 2003. 741pp.
Introduction by Bittinger, compiled by David S. Rodes and Norman R. Wenger, with documents submitted to the US Claims Commission by Brethren and Mennonites following the Civil War.

Bittinger, Lucy Forney, 1859–1907
The Germans in Colonial Times. Bowie, MD: Heritage Books, 1992. 314pp.
Reprint of 1901 original.

Bittinger, Wayne
The Bittinger, Bittner, Biddinger, and Bidinger Families and Their Kin of Garrett County, Maryland. Parsons, WV: McClain Printing Co., 1986. 836pp.

Bittle, Debbie A.
"The Ephrata Cloister." BLT, 30 (Autumn, 1985): 242–48.

Bixler, R. Russell, 1927–2000
The Spirit Is A'Movin'. Carol Stream, IL: Creation House, 1974. 197pp.
Teaching lectures.

Learning to Know God as Provider. Springdale, PA: Whitaker House, 1982. 90pp.

The Bible, Creation Science, and the Age of the Earth. Wall, PA: Cornerstone TeleVision, Inc., 1984. 104pp.
Revised and enlarged edition (1985).

Earth, Fire and Sea: The Untold Drama of Creation. Pittsburgh: Baldwin Manor Press, 1986. 214pp., illus.
Written with Waltraud Hendel; later published in a revised and enlarged edition.

Unbreakable Promises: How to Know – and Receive – All That God Has Given You. Pittsburg, PA: Baldwin Manor Press, 1987. 192pp.
On biblical covenants.

Faith Works. Shippensburg, PA: Treasure House/Destiny Image, 1999. x, 286pp., illus.
The story of Cornerstone TeleVision, founded by Bixler.

Bixler, R. Russell, 1927–2000, and Gaydon, Michael
Eyes to Behold Him. Carol Stream, IL: Creation House, 1973. 139pp.

Bixler, R. Russell, 1927–2000, and Jarman, Ray Charles
Sunrise at Evening. Monroeville, PA: Whitaker House, 1975. 157pp.

Bixler, R. Russell, 1927–2000, and Kelton, David F.
Chosen to Live. [Springdale, PA: Whitaker House], 1983. 169pp.

Blanchard, Scott
"Living with Dying." Carroll County [MD] Times, 1999.
A special illustrated supplement about Dale Aukerman.

Black, James R., 1929–
Predestined To Be Conformed to His Image. [n.p.]: author, 1992.
Autobiography of a Brethren Church pastor.

Blatt, Genevieve
"Katherine Mary Drexel of Philadelphia." In Quest for Faith, Quest for Freedom, ed. Otto Remiherr. Selingrove, PA: 1987, 180–92.

Blom, Bouke
"Excerpts from a Court Martial of Officers at Camp Cody, New Mexico." Old Order Notes, no. 8 (Spring, 1985): 25–28.

Bloomfield, Donna J.
"Arrowhead [Alberta]: A Dunkard Community, 1911–1936." MA thesis, University of Calgary, 1978. vi, 113pp.

Blooming Grove Historical Society
The Journal of the Blooming Grove Historical Society. Volume I, no. 1 (Spring, 1980).
Articles on the history and descendants of the semi-communal Dunker congregation near Williamsport, PA. Thirteen issues of Volume 1 were published between 1980 and 1992, following which the annual issues were simply numbered 14ff.

Boecken, Charlotte
"Early Brethren in Krefeld – Lists and Documents: Some Supplements to Previous Research, Part I." BLT, 35 (Spring, 1990): 122–39.

"Early Brethren in Krefeld – Lists and Documents: Some Supplements to Previous Research, Part II." BLT, 36 (Spring, 1991): 102–13.

"The Krefeld Congregation of the Brethren – Some New Archival Finds." BLT, 37 (Fall, 1992): 231–36.

Boer, Harry R.
History of the Theological Seminary of Northern Nigeria, 1950–1971. Grand Rapids, MI: Christian Reformed World Missions, 1983.

Bohlman, Philip V.
"Religious Music/Secular Music: The Press of the German-American Church and Aesthetic Mediation." In: The German-American Press, ed. Henry Geitz. Madison, WI: Max Kade Institute for German-American Studies, University of Wisconsin-Madison, 1992, 69–90.
References to compositions by Christopher Sauer II and the Brethren.

Boise Valley Church of the Brethren
Boise Valley Church of the Brethren: 50th Anniversary Recorded History. [n.p.]: 1996. 139pp.

Bollinger, Amsey F., 1898–
Christian Farmers in the Making: Anklesvar Vocational Training College. 1940.
A slide set.

Bomberger, Lloyd Huber
Bomberger: Lancaster County Roots, 1722–1986, ed. Barbara Nissley Miller. Lancaster, PA: Barbara N. Miller, 1986. 224pp.

Bonomi, Patricia Updegraff, 1928–
Under the Cope of Heaven: Religion, Society, and Politics in Colonial America. New York: Oxford University Press, 1986. xii, 291pp.
References to the Dunkers, Ephrata, and the Sauer family.

Boor, James D.
Soloman S. Baker (1850–1920) Family. New Enterprise, PA: author, [1986]. 78pp.

Botetourt Church of the Brethren
Historical Sketches of Botetourt Congregation, 1851–1912, and Daleville Congregation, 1912–1949. [Daleville, VA]: 1949. 14pp.

Bowden, Henry W.
"Beissel, Johann Conrad." Dictionary of American Religious Biography. Westport, CT: Greenwood Press, 1977, pp. 39–40.
Rev. ed. (1993), pp. 42–43.

Bowers, Steve
Planting the Faith in a New Land: The History of the Church of the Brethren in Indiana. Nappanee, IN: Evangel Press, 1992. 403pp.
A district history.

Bowman, Carl F. 1957–
"The Brethren Today." In: Church of the Brethren: Yesterday and Today, ed. D. F. Durnbaugh. Elgin, IL: BP, 1986, 201–25.

A Profile of the Church of the Brethren. Elgin, IL: BP, 1987, 40pp.

"Beyond Plainness: Cultural Transformation in the Church of the Brethren from 1850 to the Present," PhD dissertation, University of Virginia, 1989, 920pp.
Published as Brethren Society: The Cultural Transformation of a "Peculiar People." Baltimore: Johns Hopkins University Press, 1995. xii, 491pp.
Adds several chapters to dissertation in a definitive treatment of Brethren change.

"The Therapeutic Transformation of Brethren Tradition." In: Brethren in Transition: 20th Century Directions and Dilemmas, ed. E. F. Bittinger. Camden, ME: Penobscot Press, 1992, 39–57.

"The Reconstruction of Brethren Culture." In: Report of the Proceedings of the Brethren World Assembly, July 15–18, 1992, . . . , ed. D. F. Durnbaugh, Elizabethtown, PA: Elizabethtown College/Brethren Encyclopedia, Inc., 1994, [156–86].

"Reflections on Brethren History and Society." BLT, 40 (1995): 139–45.

"Keynote Address: The Impact of Modern Culture on the Brethren Family." In: Report of the Proceedings of the 1998 Brethren World Assembly, Bridgewater College . . . , ed. Dale R. Stoffer. Ashland, OH: Ashland Theological Seminary/Brethren Encyclopedia, Inc., 1999, 53–96.

"John Kline: One of Us?" In: Papers From the Elder John Kline Bicentennial Celebration, ed. William R. Eberly. Ambler, PA: Brethren Encyclopedia, Inc., 2002, 93–101.

Bowman, Carl F. and Kraybill, Donald B., 1945–
On the Backroad to Heaven: Old Order Hutterites, Mennonites, Amish, and Brethren. Baltimore: Johns Hopkins University Press, 2001. xvi, 331pp.
Chapter 5: "The [Old German Baptist] Brethren" (pp. 137–78).

Bowman, Carl F. and Longenecker, Stephen L., eds.
Anabaptist Currents: History in Conversation with the Present. Camden, ME: Penobscot Press for Forum for Religious Studies, Bridgewater College, 1995. 319, [ii]pp.
Proceedings of a conference (Fall, 1993), with papers by Mennonite and Brethren scholars. Presenters included: Dale W. Brown, Dawn Ottoni Wilhelm, J. Denny Weaver, Virginia Wiles, John D. Roth, Willard Swartley, John L. Ruth, Robert R. Miller, Jeffrey Bach, Nadine Pence Frants, Gerald Shenk, Ronald C. Arnett, Steven M. Nolt, Dale R. Stoffer, D. F. Durnbaugh, John David Bowman, Steven C. Ainlay, E. Morris Sider, Donald B. Kraybill, Fred W. Benedict, Wilbert R. Shenk, and Lois Barrett.

Bowman, Christopher, 1962–
Wisdom. Elgin, IL: BP, 1995. x, 71pp.
Covenant Bible Studies Series.

Bowman, John David, 1945–
Psalms. Elgin, IL: BP, 1989. 39pp.
Covenant Bible Studies Series.

Invitation to the Journey: Membership in the Church of the Brethren. Elgin, IL: BP, 1990.

"Membership Expectations." In: Anabaptist Currents: History in Conversation with the Present, eds. Carl F. Bowman and Stephen L. Longenecker. Camden, ME: Penobscot Press, 1995, 225–33.

Bowman, Lewis S., 1867–
From Hesse to Hagerstown in Fifty Years. Indianapolis, IN: author, [n.d.]. 15pp.
Benjamin Bowman family.

Bowman, Robert C., 1934–
A Light for My Path: Six Biblical Themes from A Believers Church Point of View. Elgin, IL: BP, 1988. 172, [52]pp.
Foundation Series, with Linea Geiser.

Sermon on the Mount. Elgin, IL: BP, 1988. 40pp.
Covenant Bible Studies Series.

Bowman, S. Loren, 1912–
Power and Polity Among the Brethren: A Study of Church Governance. Elgin, IL: BP, 1987. xi, 158pp.

Bowser, Paula
Jonah: God's Global Reach. Elgin, IL: BP, 1992. 48pp.
Covenant Bible Studies Series.

Bowser, Thomas L.
"The Search for a Brethren Model of the Office of Deacon" BLT, 29 (Summer, 1984): 137–44.

"A Vision for a Renewed Office of Deacons in the Church of the Brethren." DMin thesis, Bethany Theological Seminary, 1984. ii, 101pp.

Bowyer, James
"The Soul's Desire: An Exploration of the Language and God-Image in 'Hymnal: A Worship Book.'" MATh thesis, Bethany Theological Seminary, 1998. vii, 88pp.

Boyd, Kimberly R.
"The Age of Lilies and Roses: The Song of Songs and the New Zion in the Watercolor and Ink Illuminations of the Eighteenth-Century Ephrata Cloister Manuscripts." MA thesis, East Tennessee State University, 1996. iii, 100pp.

Boyer, Bryan
"The Current Philosophy and Situation of Missions in the Church of the Brethren." Paper, History of the Church of the Brethren, Bethany Theological Seminary, 1985. 13, [3]pp.

Boyer, Carol Constance Younker
Boyer Family in Maryland-Ohio-Indiana. Denver, CO: author, 1985. 58pp.

Barnhiser/Bernheisel Family. Denver, CO: author, 1985. 263pp.

Some Cripe Lines from Immigrant Jacob Cripe Through His Son Samuel. Denver, CO: author, 1988. 69pp.
Also includes Smith lines in Pennsylvania and Indiana.

Grossnickle Descendants in Maryland and Indiana and Other States. Rev. ed. Denver, CO: author, 1990. 387pp.

Barnhysle/Barnhisel and Hisle/Hysell Families of Virginia. Rev. ed. Denver, CO: author, 1991. 713pp.

Boyer, Donald Arthur
American Boyers, Volume One, 7th ed. Gettysburg, PA: Association of American Boyers, 1984. 646pp.

Boyer, James I., 1911–
For a World Like Ours: Studies in I Corinthians. Winona Lake, IN: BMH Books, [n.d.]

Prophecy: Things to Come. Winona Lake, IN: BHM Books, [n.d.].

Boyers, Auburn A., 1932–
"The Brethren's Educational Stance: The Early Roots." BLT, 35 (1990): 140–47.

Brackney, William H., ed., 1948–
The Believers Church: A Voluntary Church. Kitchener, Ontario: Pandora Press, 1998. v, 237pp.
Proceedings of the Twelfth Believers Church Conference, McMaster Divinity College, October 17–19, 1996; includes papers by A. Scott Holland and D. F. Durnbaugh.

Bradley, Earlene Y.
Blakely Family History. Adelphi, MD: author, 1986. 88pp.

Bradley, John L.
Ephrata Cloister: Pennsylvania Trail of History Guide. Mechanicsburg: Pennsylvania Historical and Museum Commission, 2000. 48pp.

[Branagan, Thomas, 1774–1843]
A Concise View of the Principal Religious Denominations. Philadelphia: John Cline, 1811.
Dunkers (pp. 232–34), mostly on Ephrata.

Brandt, Armin M.
Bau deinen Altar auf fremder Erde: Die Deutschen in Amerika – 300 Jahre Germantown. Stuttgart-Degerloch: Seewald Verlag, 1983.
Chap. XII: "Dunkers und Drucker" (pp. 151–75).

Brandt, Harry A., 1885–1974
Our Brethren Publishing House. Elgin, IL: BPH, 1941.

The Narrow Land: An Interpretation of the Life and Destiny of Pioneers. The First of Three Related Presentations of Southwestern History, the Two Others Being Five Southwestern Plaza and The Southwestern Troubador. La Verne, CA: author, 1968.

Breidenstine, John S., 1937–
A History of the Spring Creek [PA] Church of the Brethren, 1848–1988. [n.p.]: 1988. 89pp.

Brekus, Catherine A., 1963–
"Harriet Livermore, The Pilgim Stranger: Female Preaching and Biblical Feminism in Early Nineteenth-Century America." Church History, 65 (September, 1996): 389–404.

Strangers & Pilgrims: Female Preaching in America, 1740–1845. Durham: University of North Carolina Press, 1998.
Based on "'Let Your Women Keep Silence in the Churches': Female Preaching and Evangelical Religion in America, 1740–1845," PhD dissertation, Yale University, 1993. Extensive coverage of Harriet Livermore and several references to Sarah Righter Major.

Brethren Church
A History of the St. James [MD] Brethren Church, 1886–1986. [n.p.]: St. James Brethren Church, 1986.

Bright, C. Emmert
The Life Adventures of Aldeba Klepinger Bright and Hamilton Garver Bright. Clemmons, NC: author, 1988.

Brinck, Andreas
Die deutsche Auswanderungswelle in die britischen Kolonien Nordamerikas um die Mitte des 18. Jahrhunderts. Stuttgart: Franz Steiner Verlag, 1993. 295pp.
Many citations and quotations about Christoph Sauer I.

Brock, Peter, 1920–
Freedom from Violence. Sectarian Nonresistance from the Middle Ages to the Great War. Toronto: University of Toronto Press, 1991. 385pp.
Many references to the Brethren.

"Accounting for Difference: The Problem of Pacifism in Early Upper Canada." Ontario History, 90 (Spring, 1998): 19–30.
Also published separately.

Pacifism in the Twentieth Century. Syracuse, NY: Syracuse University Press, 1999. liv, 436pp. illus.
Revised and enlarged edition of Twentieth-Century Pacifism (1970).

Brock, Peter, ed., 1920–
Liberty and Conscience: A Documentary History of the Experiences of Conscientious Objectors in America Through the Civil War. New York: Oxford University Press, 2002. xi, 194pp.

Brock, Peter, 1920–, and Socknat, Thomas P., eds.
Challenge to Mars: Essays on Pacifism from 1918 to 1945. Toronto: University of Toronto Press, 1998.
Has an article by D. F. Durnbaugh, "The Fight Against War by the Historic Peace Churches in the United States, 1919–1941" (pp. 218–39).

Brock, Robert L.
47 Pioneer Families of Rockingham County, Virginia, Who Migrated Through Ohio, Indiana, and Illinois to Missouri. Baltimore, MD: Gateway Press, 1997. xvii, 434pp.
Includes the following Brethren family names — Beery, Bowman, Clemens, Dove, Mason, Miller, Minnich, Myers/Moyers, Shirky, Showalter; as well as information on the Brethren in Ray County, MO, and the obituary of Brethren minister George W. Clemens.

Brockwell, Charles, and Durnbaugh, Donald F.
"The Historic Peace Churches: From Sectarian Origins to Ecumenical Witnesss." In: The Church's Peace Witness, eds. Marlin E. Miller and Barbara Nelson Gingerich. Grand Rapids, MI: Eerdmans, 1994, pp. 182–95.

Brooke, John L., 1953–
The Refiner's Fire: The Making of Mormon Cosmology, 1644–1844. New York: Cambridge University Press, 1994.
Many references to Ephrata.

Brooks, Edythe L.
"A Re-Evaluation of the Significance of Johannes Kelpius and 'The Woman of the Wilderness.'" MA thesis, University of South Florida, 1996.

Brooks, Harlan J., 1898–1996
Call to India: The Missionary Journey of Harlan and Ruth Forney Brooks, [Sterling, VA]: H. J. Brooks, 1991. xii, 155pp.
Autobiography of a CB missionary to India.

Brown, Dale W., 1926–
What About the Russians? Elgin, IL: BP, 1984. 159pp.
An anthology of essays on international relations and peace.

Biblical Pacifism: A Peace Church Perspective. Elgin, IL: BP, 1986. 204pp.
A revision of Brethren and Pacifism (1970); second, rev. edition (2003).

"A People Without a Liturgy? An Essay on Brethren Worship, Past and Present." BLT, 31 (Winter, 1986): 24–32.

"Mission: Biblical Considerations." Old Order Notes, no. 10 (Spring, 1988): 7–14.

"What Has Happened To Our Peace Witness?" In: Brethren in Transition: 20th Century Directions and Dilemmas, ed. Emmert F. Bittinger. Camden, ME: Penobscot Press, 1992, 205–13.

"Nonresistance and Nonviolent Resistance: Tensions and Accomodations." BLT, 39 (Spring, 1994): 180–89.

Brethren in Historical and Theological Perspectives. Office of Institutional Advancement of Bethany Theological Seminary and the Bethany Academy for Ministry Training, 1995.
Twenty sessions on fifteen videotapes; produced by David Sollenberger.

"Understandings of Sin: Original Blessedness and the Second Adam." In: Anabaptist Currents: History in Conversation with the Present, eds. Carl F. Bowman and Stephen L. Longenecker. Camden, ME: Penobscot Press, 1995, 7–13.

Understanding Pietism, rev. ed. Nappanee, IN: Evangel Press, 1996. 125pp.
Chapter 1 ("Pietism: What Is It?" was republished in Old Order Notes, no. 19 (Spring/Summer, 1999): 43–60.

"John Kline: Martyr in Pursuit of Peace." In: Papers From the Elder John Kline Bicentennial Celebration, ed.

William R. Eberly. Ambler, PA: Brethren Encyclopedia, Inc., 2002, 146–50.

Brown, Dorothy Noffsinger and McNeil, Cathy Brown, eds.
Sadie Brallier Noffsinger: A Collection of Poems, Short Stories, and Articles Written by Sadie Brallier Noffsinger and Printed in Church of the Brethren Publications. Johnstown, Pennsylvania, May 13, 1869–February 8, 1922. Elgin, IL: Cathy McNeil, [1983]. 137pp.

Brown, Kenneth Lee, 1933–
Ethics of Prophetic Nonviolence. [n.p.]: 1981.

Brubaker, John W.
Old German Baptists in Civilian Public Service. Dayton, OH: author, 1989. v, 288pp.

Brubaker, Marcus
"Old German Baptist Brethren Church." In: The Brethren Presence in the World…: Proceedings of the 3rd Brethren World Assembly, July 23–26, 2003, ed. William R. Eberly. Philadelphia, PA: Brethren Encyclopedia, Inc., 2004, 117–18.

Brubaker, Marvin E. and Brubaker, Margaret Brubaker Eller
Descendants of John and Anna Myers Brubaker, 1750–1995. [n.p.]: authors, 1995. 808pp.

Brubaker, Naomi E.
Yesterday, Today, and Tomorrow: The Boone Family. New Carlisle, OH: author, 1968.

Brubaker, Pamela, 1946–
She Hath Done What She Could. A History of Women's Participation in the Church of the Brethren. Elgin, IL: BP, 1985. xvii, 222pp.
Monograph on women in the Brethren movement.

Brumbaugh, G. Edwin, 1890–1983
"Medieval Construction at Ephrata." Antiques (July 1944): 18–20.

Brumbaugh, Pam and Dunmire, Ruth, eds.
"Rooms with a View: The Kishacoquillas Seminary." Common Ground 13/3 (Spring 2002): 52–55.
On S. Z. Sharp's involvement in the leadership of the seminary until 1866.

Brumbaugh-Cayford, Cheryl Ann, 1963–, and Eisenbise, Debra Lee, 1960–
BVS Stories: 50 Years Through the Eyes of Volunteers. Elgin, IL: Brethren Volunteer Service, 1998. 131pp.

Brunn, Hermann, 1919–
Schriesheimer Mühlen, 2nd rev. ed. Schriesheim: Stadt Schriesheim, [1989]. xxvii, 204pp.

Bryant, John E.
"Conservative Grace Brethren Churches International." In: The Brethren Presence in the World…: Proceedings of the 3rd Brethren World Assembly, July 23–26, 2003, ed. William R. Eberly. Philadelphia, PA: Brethren Encyclopedia, Inc., 2004, 110–12.

Bryer, John Baugher
"Abraham Harley Cassel's Letters to His Family." BLT, 48 (Winter/Spring, 2003): 39–65.

Bucher, Caleb, 1908–1992
From Where I Stand, ed. Inez Long. Lititz, PA: author, 1988. 127pp.
The autobiography of a churchman and educator.

Bucher, Christina
Biblical Imagery for God. Elgin, IL: BP, 1995. x, 62pp.
Covenant Bible Studies Series.

The Prophecy of Amos and Hosea. Elgin, IL: BP, 1997. viii, 69pp.
Covenant Bible Studies Series.

"Eschatology in Selected Brethren Doctrinal Texts, 1876–1919." BLT, 46 (Winter/Spring, 2001): 92–103.

Bucher, Christina, ed.
[Special issue, youth ministry in the Church of the Brethren]. BLT, 37 (Winter, 1992): 2–63.
Essays by Chris Michael, William R. Myers, Don Richter, Don Jordan, and Sharon Cobb Hutchinson.

[Special issue, "The Cultural Transformation of the Brethren: Understanding the 20th Century"]. BLT 40 (Summer-Fall, 1995): 135–260.
Papers from a conference at Elizabethtown College, summer 1995, based on the book Brethren Society by Carl F. Bowman. Contributors include: Carl F. Bowman, Murray L. Wagner, Jr., Wallace B. Landes, Jr., Donald R. Fitzkee, Nadine Pence Frantz. Frank Ramirez, Christina Bucher, Dale W. Brown, Stephen Breck Reid, David B. Eller, D. F. Durnbaugh, Christopher D. Bowman, Paul Grout, Donald E. Miller, Jeffrey A. Bach, Dawn Ottoni Wilhelm, and Judy Mills Reimer.

Bucher, Gordon W., 1926–
The David Family Genealogy. [n.p.: author], 1984. 74pp.

Bucher, Marie K.
A Century of Service at the Grove: Mechanic Grove [PA] Church of the Brethren: 100th Anniversary, 1897–1997. [n.p.]: 1997. 138pp.

Buckingham, Betty Jo and Hendricks, Jean Lichty, eds.
Women at the Well: Expressions of Faith, Life, and Worship Drawn from Our Own Wisdom. Elgin, IL: Womaen's Caucus of the Church of the Brethren, 1987. 214pp.
Anthology of devotional materials from a feminist perspective.

Bunnell, Paul J., 1946–
The New Loyalist Index. Volume 1. Bowie, MD: Heritage Books, Inc., 1989. Volumes 1–3. 525pp.
References to the Sauer (Sower) family during the Revolutionary War.

Bunners, Christian
"The Birth of Freedom Out of Bondage: Thomas Mann and the German-American Poet-Composer, Johann Conrad Beissel." The Hymn, 36 (July, 1985): 7–10.
Translated by Hedwig T. Durnbaugh.

Burdge, Edsel, Jr., and Horst, Samuel L., 1919–
Building on the Gospel Foundation: The Mennonites of Franklin County, Pennsylvania and Washington County, Maryland. Scottdale, PA: Herald Press, 2004.
Vol. 42, Studies in Anabaptist and Mennonite History Series; many references to their Brethren neighbors.

Burgert, Annette K.
Eighteenth Century Emigrants from German-Speaking Lands to North America. Volume II: The Western Palatinate. Birdsboro, PA: Pennsylvania German Society, 1985. xvi, 405pp. illus.
Brethren and Ephrata references: "Müller, Joh. Peter" (pp. 240–43).

Brethren from Gimbsheim in the Palatinate to Ephrata and Bermudian in Pennsylvania. Myerstown, PA: AKB Publications, 1994. 37pp.

Burkett, Jerri Lynn
The Huber-Hoover Family History Index. Elverson, PA: Olde Springfield Shoppe, 1993.
Compiled for the 1992 reprint of the Huber/Hoover family history by Harry M. Hoover.

Burkhart, William H.
"Snow Hill Nunnery." [Shippensburg, PA] News-Chronicle, 1967.
A series of newspaper installments.

Burkholder, Paul Z.
Family Record of Christian Burkholder, 1746–1990. [n.p.: author], 1990. 537pp.

Bush, Perry, 1957–
Two Kingdoms, Two Loyalties: Mennonite Pacifism in Modern America. Baltimore, MD: Johns Hopkins University Press, 1998. xii, 362pp.
Many references to the Brethren, in particular to the Civilian Public Service program.

Bynum, LaTaunya
Paul's Prison Letters. Elgin, IL: BP, ca. 1998.
Covenant Bible Studies.

Cable, William A., 1919–1995
The Golden Pen: The Inscriptions of Motherhood on the Tablets of the Heart. Elgin, IL: BPH, 1927. 57pp.

Calimer, Larry Dean, comp.
"Snow Hill Nunnery Graveyard." Old Order Notes, no. 17 (Spring-Summer, 1998): 88–101.

Callahan, Wanda L.
Straight Talk from a Brethren Sister. Scottdale, PA: Herald Press, 2000. 112pp.
Essays on social activism, including ministry to prisoners on death row.

Callen, Barry L., ed.
A Time to Remember: Teachings. Anderson, IN: Warner Press, 1977, 37–42.

Radical Christianity: The Believers Church Tradition in Christianity's History and Future. Nappanee, IN: Evangel Publishing House, 1999. xv, 221pp.
Many references to the Brethren.

Campbell, Ted A.
The Religion of the Heart: A Study of European Religious Life in the Seventeenth and Eighteenth Centuries. Columbia, SC: University of South Carolina Press, 1991.
Chapter Four: Pietism (pp. 70–98).

Carlson, Charles Howard
"The Ephrata Cloister's Music of Yesteryear." Music Journal 27 (1964): 52, 118–20.

Carroll, Lucy Ellen
"Three Centuries of Song: Pennsylvania's Choral Composers, 1681–1981." DMA dissertation, Combs College of Music, 1982.
Includes much material on Ephrata music.

"Selected Music from the Eighteenth-Century Ephrata Cloister: New Editions Prepared for Concerts and Recordings of the Ephrata Cloister Chorus." Ephrata, PA: Ephrata Cloister, 1999.

"Transcription Manual: A Guide to Preparing Accurate Transcriptions and Editions of the Original Music from the 18th Century Community of the Solitary, Ephrata, PA." Ephrata, PA: Ephrata Cloister, 1999.

Selected Music from the Eighteenth-Century Community of the Solitary at Ephrata. Ann Arbor: University of Michigan, 2003.
MUSA 13.

Carter, Karen
"The Birth of Misión Mutua en las Américas." MATh thesis, Bethany Theological Seminary, 1985. vi, 113pp.

Carter, Phyllis
"Quiet Place: A Contemplative Prayer Center and a Ministry for Spiritual Growth." In: Report of the Proceedings of the 1998 Brethren World Assembly, Bridgewater College . . ., ed. Dale R. Stoffer. Ashland, OH: Ashland Theological Seminary/Brethren Encyclopedia, Inc., 1999, 185–92.

Carter, Phyllis and Marlene Kropf
"Contemporary Forms of Spirituality." In: The Dilemma of Anabaptist Piety: Strengthening or Straining the Bonds of Community?, ed. Stephen L. Longenecker. Camden, ME: Penobscot Press, 1997, 145–48.

Cassel, Daniel Kolb, 1820–1898
A Genealogical History of the Cassel Family. Reprint. [n.p.]: 1989. 463pp.

A Genealogical History of the Kolb, Kulp, Culp Family. Reprint. [n.p.:] 1990. 584pp.

Cassel, Franklin K., 1914–
Flowers for Peggy: One Couple's Experience with Alzheimers. [Lititz, PA]: author, 1994. 25pp.
Written by a Brethren physician about his wife's illness.

Jonas Meyer Cassel Family Tree: Sequel to The Cassel Family in America by Daniel Kolb Cassel, 1896. Lancaster, PA: author, 1998. 34pp.
Includes family of Katie Nyce Cassel.

Cassel, Joseph Nyce, 1877–1963
Joseph N. Cassel, 1877–1963: Reflections on a Life. [Lancaster, PA:] C. M. Forry, 1998.
Biography of a CB pastor.

Castor Association
The Descendants of Paulus and Gertrude Kusters of Kaldenkirchen, Germany and Germantown, Pennsylvania: The First Four Generations.

Christian Peacemaker Teams
Signs of the Times. [Volume 1, no. 1, 1991].
Quarterly publication of the activist Christian Peacemaker Teams, sponsored by Mennonite, Brethren, and Friends congregations.

Church of the Brethren
A Strategy for Denominational Growth. Elgin, IL: Church of the Brethren General Board, 1984.

Church and Health Conference. Bridgewater, Va., Feb. 7–9, 1984. Elgin, IL: Church and Welfare Office, Church of the Brethren, 1984.

Heralds of a New Age. Elgin, IL: BP, 1985.
For All Who Minister. Elgin, IL: BP, 1993. xiii, 454pp.

Church of the Brethren: General Board
Manual of Organization and Polity. Elgin, IL: Church of the Brethren General Board, 1992. 145pp.

"Journey in Jesus' Way." Elgin, IL: Church of the Brethren General Board, n.d. Video.
Thirteen sessions preparing for church membership; produced by David Sollenberger.

Church of the Brethren: Ministry and Home Mission Commission
Brethren Churches in the City. Elgin, IL: General Brotherhood Board, [1955]. 232pp.

Church of the Brethren: Office of Brethren Witness
People of God's Peace. Vol. 1, 1988.
A quarterly newsletter providing "A Resource for Brethren Peacemakers"; David Radcliff and others, editors.

Church of the Brethren: Parish Ministries Commission
New Beginnings. [Volume 1, no. 1], January, 1983.
Publication designed to encourage evangelism and church extension. Editors: Paul E. R. Mundey, Merle Crouse, Rene Calderon. Published three times a year. After 1995 it was sponsored by the Andrew Center.

Church of the Brethren: Refugee Resettlement, Diaster Response, and Cooperative Disaster Child Care
Bridges. Spring, 1996ff.
Newsletter.

Church of the Brethren: Urban Ministries
Church of the Brethren Urban Network Newsletter. [Volume 1], June, 1980.

Church of the Brethren: Washington [DC] Office
Witness to Washington. [Volume 1, 1983].
Quarterly newsletter of the CB office in Washington that follows legislative activity and registers CB concerns.

Church of the Brethren and others
Hymnal: A Worship Book. Prepared by Churches in the Believers Church Tradition. Elgin, IL: BP/Newton, KS: Faith and Life Press/Scottdale, PA: Herald Press, 1992. vi, 904pp.

Clancy, Jane
"Simple Joys." Colonial Homes 19 (Dec. 1993): 6, 76–81.
On Christmas time at Ephrata.

Clapp, Steve
Promising Results. Elgin, IL: BP, 1993. 96pp., illus.
On methods of evangelism.

Preaching, Planning, and Plumbing: The Implications of Bivocational Ministry for the Church and for You. Fort Wayne, IN: Christian Community, 1999. 128pp.

Clark, Glenn William
The Woman in the Wilderness: Reflections on a Mormon Family's Dunkard Roots Which Put Forth Shoots Through Margaret Harley Randall (1823–1919). McLean, VA: author, 1986. [iv], 142, [2].

Clark, Ruth
"Brethren in Montana." In: Religion in Montana: Pathways to the Present, ed. Lawrence F. Small. Billings, MT: Rocky Mountain College, 1991, 337–51, 473–74 (notes).

Clouse, Bonnidell
Moral Development: Perspectives in Psychology and Christian Belief. Grand Rapids, MI: Baker Book House, 1985.

Clouse, Bonnidell and Clouse, Robert G., 1931–, eds.
Women in Ministry: Four Views. Downers Grove, IL: InterVarsity Press, 1989. 250pp.
With contributions from Robert D. Culver, Susan Foh, Walter Liefeld, and Alvera Mickelsen.

Clouse, Robert G., 1931–
Millennialism and America. Portland, OR: Western Baptist Press, 1977. 71pp.

"The Brethren – 1780–1860, Reconsidered." Old Order Notes, no. 7 (Autumn, 1983): 23–27.

"The Church of the Brethren and World War I." Mennonite Life, 45/4 (1990): 29–34.

"Nonresistance, Nationalism, and the New World Order." In: Report of the Proceedings of the Brethren World Assembly, July 15–18, 1992, . . . , ed. D. F. Durnbaugh, Elizabethtown, PA: Elizabethtown College/Brethren Encyclopedia, Inc., 1994, [192–208].

"Hope for the Triumph of God's Reign." In: The Lord's Supper: Believers Church Perspectives, ed. Dale R. Stoffer. Scottdale, PA/Waterloo, ON: Herald Press, 1997, 129–39.

The New Millennium Manual: A Once and Future Guide. Grand Rapids, MI: Baker Books, 1999. 222pp.
Co-authors: Robert N. Hosack, Richard V. Pierard.

"Fundamentalism, Modernism, and Brethren Millennialism." BLT, 46 (Winter/Spring, 2001): 112–23.

Clouse, Robert G., ed., 1931–
Ch'onnyon wangguk. Seoul: Songgwang Munhwasa, 1980. 283, 4pp.
Translation of The Meaning of the Millennium (1977).

Milénio: Signicado e Interpetaçoes. Campenas, SP: Luz para o caminho, 1977. 202pp.
Translation of The Meaning of the Millennium (1977).

Der Christ und der Krieg: [4 Standpunkte]. Marburg/Lahn: Francke-Buchhandlung, 1982. 164pp.
Translation of War: Four Christian Views (1981).

Das Tausendjährige Reich: Bedeutung und Wirklichkeit. Marburg/Lahn: Francke-Buchhandlung, 1983. 172pp.
Translation of The Meaning of the Millennium (1977).

Wealth & Poverty: Four Christian Views of Economics. Downers Grove, IL: InterVarsity Press, 1984. 228pp.
With contributions from Gary North, William E. Diehl, Art Gish, and John Gladwin.

"Premillennialist Christology, Nonresistance, and the Believers Church." Restoration Quarterly, 28 (1985/96): 215–29.

War: Four Christian Views. Winona Lake, IN: BMH Books, 1986. 210pp.
Reprint of 1981 original.

"Brethren and Modernity: Change and Development in the Progressive/Grace Church." BLT, 33 (Summer, 1988): 205–17.

War: Four Christian Views. Downers Grove, IL: InterVarsity Press, 1991. 212pp.
Reprint of 1981 original.

Que Es El Milenio?: Querto Enfoques Pava una Respuesta. El Paso, TX: Casa Bautista de Publicaciones, 1991. 206pp.
Translation of The Meaning of the Millennium (1977).

Clover Creek [PA] Church of the Brethren
Clover Creek 200th Anniversary: Commemorative Booklet. [n.p.]: 1991.

Clutter, Ronald T.
"Herman A. Hoyt: A Biographical Sketch." Grace Theological Journal, 6/2 (Fall, 1985): 181–86.

"A Background History of Grace Theological Seminary." Grace Theological Journal 9/2 (Fall, 1988): 204–32.

"The Development of Grace Theological Seminary and the Division of the Brethren Church." Grace Theological Journal, 10/1 (Spring, 1989): 51–66.

"Homer A. Kent, Jr.: A Biographical Sketch." In: New Testament Essays in Honor of Homer A. Kent, Jr., ed.

Gary T. Meadors. Winona Lake, IN: BMH Books, 1991, 9–15.

"Law and Gospel in the Brethren Tradition." Grace Theological Journal, 12/2 (Fall, 1991): 215–32.

"The Historical Place of the Family in Brethren Heritage." In: Report of the Proceedings of the 1998 Brethren World Assembly, Bridgewater College. . . , ed. Dale R. Stoffer. Ashland, OH: Ashland Theological Seminary/Brethren Encyclopedia, Inc., 1999, 3–32.

"The Roots of the Progressive Brethren Mission." In: The Brethren Presence in the World…: Proceedings of the 3rd Brethren World Assembly, July 23–26, 2003, ed. William R. Eberly. Philadelphia, PA: Brethren Encyclopedia, Inc., 2004, 19–35.

Cole, Daryl L.
Kensinger Families of Central Pennsylvania. Altoona, PA: Blair County Genealogical Society, 1987. 206pp.

Colijn, Brenda B.
"Incarnational Hermeneutics: The Brethren Approach to Scriptures." BLT, 36 (Fall, 1991): 246–70.

"The Vine and The Branches: Biblical Interpretation Among the Brethren." In: Report of the Proceedings of the Brethren World Assembly, July 15–18, 1992, . . . , ed. D. F. Durnbaugh, Elizabethtown, PA: Elizabethtown College/Brethren Encyclopedia, Inc., 1994, [98–124].

"The Faith of Family and the Family of Faith." In: Report of the Proceedings of the 1998 Brethren World Assembly, Bridgewater College. . . , ed. Dale R. Stoffer. Ashland, OH: Ashland Theological Seminary/Brethren Encyclopedia, Inc., 1999, 97–130.

"The End Times among Evangelical Brethren Today." BLT, 46 (Winter/Spring, 2001): 124–33.

Communicorp
Reflections on Brethren Image and Identity. Elgin, IL: BP, 1995. 64pp.

Conner, Alvin E., 1927–
Sectarian Childrearing: The Dunkers, 1708–1900. Gettysburg, PA: Brethren Heritage Press, 1987. 247pp.

"Patterns of Rearing Children Among the Brethren." In: Report of the Proceedings of the 1998 Brethren World Assembly, Bridgewater College . . . , ed. Dale R. Stoffer. Ashland, OH: Ashland Theological Seminary/Brethren Encyclopedia, Inc., 1999, 159–82.

Conner, Paul and Roberts, Jill, comps.
Pennsylvania German Fraktur and Printed Broadsides: A Guide to the Collections in the Library of Congress. Washington, DC: Library of Congress, 1988. 48pp., illus.
Introduction by Don Yoder (pp. 8–19); Ephrata (pp. 21, 23).

Cool, Omer S., 1900–1983
Darke County Footprints: A Brief History of the German Baptist Church in Darke County, Ohio. Arcanum, OH: Lew Williams. 1978. 60pp.

Cooper, H. Austin, 1911–1998
The Church of the Singing Hills: A History of the Locust Grove Church of the Brethren, at Linganore Creek, Mt. Airy, Maryland, 1760–1988. Mt. Airy. MD: Locust Grove Church of the Brethren, 1988. 437pp.
Extensive congregational history.

Two Centuries of Brothersvalley Church of the Brethren, 1762–1962: An Account of the Old Colonial Church, the Stony Creek German Baptist Church. [Brotherton, PA]: Committee, 1992. 544pp.
Reprint of 1962 edition, with added index.

The Church in the Valley: Brownsville Church of the Brethren, 1760–1993, Brownsville Heights, Maryland. Brownsville, MD: Brownsville Church of the Brethren, 1993. 542pp.

A Pleasant View: Pleasant View Church of the Brethren, Burkittsville, Maryland. [Burkittsville, MD: Church of the Brethren, 1998]. [xvii], 505pp.

Cossee, E. H.
"De Rotterdamse Familie De Koker." Doopsgezinde Bijdragen, NS 22 (1996): 233–37.
Detailed information on the important Dutch family of Collegiants who had many connections with the Brethren, unknown to this author.

Coyle, J. Timothy
"The Agape/Eucharist Relationship in I Corinthians 11." Grace Theological Journal, 6/2 (Fall, 1985): 411–24.

Cramer, Peggy C., comp.
Early Records of the Ambler Church of the Brethren, Ambler, Montgomery Co., PA. Apollo, PA: Closson Press, 1990.
Contains index of 1,900 names.

Cremer, Estelle, and Shenk, Pamela
Coventry: The Skool Kill District: A Basic History of the Three Coventry Towships. Morgantown: Masthof Press for the authors, 2003. 186pp.
Describes Brethren as early settlers.

Crouse, B. Merle, 1931–
Developing New Congregations in the Church of the Brethren: A Manual for Church Planters. Elgin, IL: BP, 1983.

Crutchfield, James
"German-American Yesteryears." German Life (March 31, 1996):
On Ephrata.

Cryer, Richard
Anabaptist Chronology (Chart). [n.p.]: author, 2000.
Includes Brethren data.

Culp, C. Richard
Nonresistance vs. Political Pacifism. [n.p.: author, n.d.].

Custer, James
"When Is Communion Communion?" Grace Theological Journal, 6/2 (Fall, 1985): 403–10.

Custer/Kusters Family
The Descendants of Paulus and Gertrude Kusters of Kaldenkirchen, Germany, and Germantown, Pennsylvania: The First Four Generations. Richmond, TX: Castor Association of America, 1991. 303pp.
Information on Christian Custer (d.1879), pastor in Germantown.

Dali, S. D.
"A Historical Development and Vision for the Future Growth of the Ekklesiyar 'Yan'uwa a Nigeria (E.Y.N.) (The Church of the Brethren in Nigeria)." MATh thesis, Bethany Theological Seminary, 1994, 170pp.

Daniels, Marta
Peace is Everybody's Business: Half a Century of Peace Education with Elizabeth Evans Baker. Huntingdon, PA: Juniata College Press, 1999. xviii, 253pp.
Biographies of Elizabeth Evans Baker (1902–1990) and John Calhoun Baker (1895–1999) and their efforts at peacemaking and peace education. Includes information on the peace studies programs at Manchester and Juniata Colleges and Bethany Theological Seminary.

Daniels, Roger, 1928–
Concentration Camps, North America: Japanese in the United States and Canada during World War II., rev. ed. Malabar, FL: R. E. Krieger, 1981.
Mentions Brethren efforts on behalf of Japanese-Americans.

Dasenbrock, J. Henry, 1920–
Brethren Serve in Puerto Rico. Elgin, IL: BPH, 1946.

To the Beat of a Different Drummer: A Decade in the Life of a World War II Conscientious Objector. Winona, MN: Northland Press, 1989. vii, 247pp., illus.
Has information on the Civilian Public Service Camp in Castañer, Puerto Rico.

David, Hans
"Litterae ab musica." Quarterly Journal of the Riemenschneider Bach Institute, USA, 2 (Jan. 1971): 33–34
On Ephrata.

Davis, Daniel, Sr.
Parables of Matthew. Elgin, IL: BP, 1998. x, 106pp.
Covenant Bible Study Series.

Davis, Richard Warren
Emigrants, Refugees, and Prisoners (An Aid to Mennonite Family Research). Volumes 1 and 2. Provo, UT: author, 1995, 1997. 429pp., 450+pp.
Detailed and documented genealogy with references to families that became Brethren.

Davison, Mary
My Mother Etta: A True Story of the German Baptist Brethren People. Dallas, OR: author, 1986. 279pp., illus.

Davison, Mary and Garber, Sherda
And They Twain . . .. [n.p.: n.d.]. 320pp.
An account of the lives of OGBB elder Alpha L. Davison (b. 1917) and his wife Mary Davison in Kansas, California, and Oregon.

Deardorf, Noble E., 1902–1990
Noble Stories: An Assortment of Recollections. [Wenatchee, WA]: Author, [1987]. 63pp., illus.

Dechert, Michael S. A.
"The Ephrata Community: An American Utopian Experiment of Anabaptist and Rosicrucian Inspiration." Spazio e Società, 14, no. 54 (April/June, 1991): 70–81.

Deeter, Allen C.
"Recent Developments Within the Church of the Brethren: Their Influence on the Future." In: Brethren in Transition: 20th Century Directions and Dilemmas, ed. Emmert F. Bittinger. Camden, ME: Penobscot Press, 1992, 59–72.

Deeter, Joan George
Who Are These Brethren? Elgin, IL: BP, 1991. 32pp.
Second edition (1995).

Dell, Robert W., 1939–
Presence and Power. Elgin, IL: BP, 1991. 48pp.
Covenant Bible Studies Series.

Including and Involving New People. Elgin, IL: BP, 1992. 94pp.

Denlinger, Carolyn Teach, ed.
Every Name Index for the History of the Church of the Brethren of the Southern District of Ohio [1920, 1921]. [n.p.]: Southern Ohio District Church of the Brethren Historical Committee, 1982.

[Special issue, Brethren genealogy]. BLT, 34 (Summer, 1989): 133–89.
Articles by David B. Eller, Gwendolyn F. Bobb, James R. Lynch, David J. Rempel Smucker, Gerald C. Wagoner, Sr., Fred W. Benedict, Carolyn Teach Denlinger, Emmert F. Bittinger, and Paul H. Bowman.

Barnhart Family Record. The Family of Daniel Barnhart II (c1765–1802) and Elizabeth Naff (c1767–1805), by Josephus Edward Barnhart. Rev. ed. [n.p.: author], 1990. 282pp.

Dew, Charles B., 1937–
Bond of Iron: Master and Slave at Buffalo Forge. New York: W. W. Norton, 1994. xviii, 429pp.
The slavemaster, William Weaver (1781–1863), was the grandson of Alexander Mack, Jr.

Dewhurst, C. Kurt; MacDowell, Betty; and MacDowell, Marsha
Religious Folk Art in America: Reflections of Faith. New York: E. P. Dutton/Museum of American Folk Art, 1983.
Includes Ephrata Fraktur.

Dilling, Yvonne, 1955–
In Search of Refuge. Scottdale, PA: Herald Press, 1984. 288pp.

Doerksen, Victor G.
"Pietism, Revivalism, and the Early Mennonite Brethren." In: The Dilemma of Anabaptist Piety: Strengthening or Straining the Bonds of Community?, ed. Stephen L. Longenecker. Camden, ME: Penobscot Press, 1997, 69–84.

Doll, Eugene E., 1915
"Rebirth at Ephrata." Reading Times (Nov. 16, 18, 1942). The Ephrata Cloister: An Introduction. Ephrata, PA: Ephrata Cloister Associates, 1990. 32pp.
Reprint of a brief and well-illustrated survey of the Ephrata Society; originally published in 1958.

Dolnikowski, George, 1917–
This I Remember: From War to Peace. Elgin, IL: BP, 1994), ix, 59pp.
Memoirs of a former displaced person resettled by the Brethren Service Commission. Beginning as a janitor at Juniata College, he became a respected professor and advocate for peace. With illustrations by Christopher Raschka.

Dorfman, Mark H.
"The Ephrata Cloister." Early American Life 10/1 (1979): 338–41, 64–65.

Drechsler, Wolfgang
"The Church of the Brethren." Newsletter, Society for German-American Studies, 7 (1986): 12–13.

Driedger, Leo, 1928–, and Kraybill, Donald B., 1945–
Mennonite Peacemaking: From Quietism to Activism. Scottdale, PA: Herald Press, 1994. 344pp.

Driedger, Michael D.
"Mennonites? Heretics? Obedient Citizens?" Categorizing People in Hamburg and Altona, 1648–1713." PhD dissertation, Queen's University, Kingston, ON, 1996. 156pp.
Includes materials on the Dompelaars.

Drudge, Casey
Appropriate Response: The Centennial History of the Church of the Brethren in Fort Wayne, Indiana, 1894–1994. Nappanee, IN: Evangel Press, 1994. vi, 136, xxxi-iipp.

Dubble, Curtis W., 1922–
Real Families: From Patriarchs to Prime Time. Elgin, IL: BP, 1995. x, 85pp.
Covenant Bible Studies Series.

Duck, Dorothy Hampton
"Ludwig Blum, Ephrata's First Music Teacher." Historic Schaefferstown Record, 22 (1988): 1–2, 3–33.

"The Art and Artists of the Ephrata Cloister." Journal of the Lancaster County Historical Society, 97 (Winter, 1995): 134–51.

Dueck, Al
"Anabaptists, Pietism, and the Therapeutic Culture." In: The Dilemma of Anabaptist Piety: Strengthening or Straining the Bonds of Community?, ed. Stephen L. Longenecker. Camden, ME: Penobscot Press, 1997, 161–72.

Dull, Christine and Dull, Ralph
Soviet Laughter, Soviet Tears. Englewood, OH: Stillmore Press, 1991. 372pp.
Based upon a CB farm couple's many and extended visits to the Soviet Union.

Dunkard Brethren
Dunkard Brethren Church Polity – 1993 Edition. [n.p.]: Dunkard Brethren Church, 1993.

[Program booklet] Welcome . . . to the 75th Anniversary of the Founding of the Dunkard Brethren Church, 1926–2001, Dunkard Brethren Church, Plevna, Indiana, June 8–10, 2001. [n.p.: 2001]. 12pp.
Program committee: Frank Reed, Milton Cook, Robert Lehigh.

[Dunkers]
"Many Peculiarities of the Dunker and Amish Sects." Chicago Tribune (January 22, 1893).

Dunn County, WI
"Small White Church That Served Dunkard Congregation Is Vacant." Dunn County News (Menomonie, WI: August 3, 1960).

Durnbaugh, Donald F., 1927– 2005
"M. R. Zigler at Ninety: Still Chafing at the Status Quo." Messenger (November, 1981): 13–15.

"Brüderkirchen." Taschenlexikon Religion und Theologie, ed. E. Fahlbusch, 4th rev. ed. Göttingen: Vandenhoeck & Ruprecht, 1983, 1: 196–98.

The Believers' Church: The History and Character of Radical Protestantism. Scottdale, PA: Herald Press, 1985. xii, 315pp.
Slightly revised reprint of 1968 original.

"Bowman, Rufus David." In: Biographical Dictionary of Modern Peace Leaders. Westport, CT: Greenwood Press, 1985, 104–05.

Counting the Cost of Peace. Elgin, IL: BP, 1985. [16pp.].
Also published in BLT 32, (Winter, 1987): 53–62, and New Call to Peacemaking, 7 (March, 1987): 16–21.

"Women as Heroes: Gladdys E. Muir." Messenger (January, 1985): 10.

"Brethren and Moravians in Colonial America." Unitas Fratrum, no. 22 (1986): 16–30.

"The Flowering of Pietism in the Garden of America." Christian History, 5/2 (1986): 23–27.

"The First Washington Representative of the Church of the Brethren: A Little-Known Story." BLT, 32 (Autumn, 1987): 217–24.

"Brethren Missions: Historical Considerations, 1708–1880." Old Order Notes, no. 10 (Spring, 1988): 15–25.

"The Blooming Grove Colony. Journal of the Blooming Grove Historical Society, 1 (Spring, 1989): 12–17.
Reprint (in shortened form) from Pennsylvania Folklife, 25 (Spring, 1976): 18–23.

"Mutual Aid in Ministry to God's World." BLT, 33 (Spring, 1988): 87–98.

"Gladdys Muir as Educator." Bulletin of the [Manchester College] Peace Studies Institute, 19 (Summer, 1989): 34–35.

DURNBAUGH, DONALD F.

Pragmatic Prophet: The Life of Michael Robert Zigler. Elgin, IL: BP, 1989. xii, 415pp.
Biography of a noted CB leader and peace activist.

"Civilian Public Service: An Experiment in Church-State Relations." Messenger (October, 1990): 11, 14.

"New Understandings of Anabaptism and Pietism." BLT, 35 (Fall, 1990): 250–61.

"Peter Becker (1687–1758)." In: Chronik Düdelsheim 792–1992, eds. Werner Wagner and others. Büdingen: Magistrat der Stadt Büdingen, 1991, 62–67.

Brethren Beginnings: The Origin of the Church of the Brethren in Early Eighteenth-Century Europe. Philadelphia: Brethren Encyclopedia, Inc., 1992. 99pp.
Publication of a 1960 doctoral dissertation with an additional section on newer literature (pp. v–x).

"Closing the Circle: Germantown and Philadelphia Revisited." In: Brethren in Transition: 20th Century Directions and Dilemmas, ed. Emmert F. Bittinger. Camden, ME: Penobscot Press, 1992, 229–240.

"The Legacy of Suffering and Persecution in the Church of the Brethren." BLT, 37 (Spring, 1992): 73–86.

"Studebaker and Stutz: The Evolution of Dunker Entrepreneurs." Pennsylvania Folklife, 41 (Spring, 1992): 110–26.

"The Brethren World Assembly: Background and Basis." In: Report of the Proceedings of the Brethren World Assembly, July 15–18, 1992, . . ., ed. D. F. Durnbaugh, Elizabethtown, PA: Elizabethtown College/Brethren Encyclopedia, Inc., 1994, [1–15].

"Nineteenth-Century Dunker Views of the River Brethren." Mennonite Quarterly Review, 67 (April, 1993): 133–57.

"Samuel Saur (1767–1820): German-American Printer and Typefounder," The Report: A Journal of German-American History, 43 (1993): 68–79.

"Research Note: Ernst H. Correll and Juniata College." Mennonite Quarterly Review, 77 (October, 1993): 481–88.

"Membership and Indoctrination in Anabaptist Churches." In: Anabaptist Currents: History in Conversation with the Present, eds. Carl F. Bowman and Stephen L. Longenecker. Camden, ME: Penobscot Press, 1995, 211–223.

"Brethren and Friends in a New Land: A Shared History." BLT, 39 (Fall, 1994): 227–40.

"A Letter from Blooming Grove." Der Reggeboge/The Rainbow: Journal of the Pennsylvania German Society, 28/2 (1994): 16–19.

"Radical Pietist Involvement in Early German Emigration to Pennsylvania." Yearbook of German-American Studies, 29 (1994): 29–48.

"Research Note: The Hylkema-Cassel-Taylor Correspondence." Mennonite Quarterly Review, 69 (April, 1994): 247–52.

"Radical Pietism as the Foundation of German-American Communitarian Settlements." In: Emigration and Settlement Patterns of German Communities in North America, eds. Eberhard Reichmann and others. Indianapolis: Max Kade German-American Center, Indiana University-Purdue University at Indianapolis, 1995, 31–55.

Deacons in Historical Perspective. Elgin, IL: Association of Brethren Caregivers, 1996. 16pp.

"Henry Kurtz: Renewal Architect." Messenger (July, 1996): 14.

"The Brethren and Non-Resistance." In: The Pacifist Impulse in Historical Perspective, ed. Harvey L. Dyck. Toronto: University of Toronto Press, 1996), 125–44.

"Knepper/Martin Discoveries." Der Reggeboge/The Rainbow: Journal of the Pennsylvania German Society, 31/1&2 (1997): 35–36.

"Receiving a Priceless Legacy: Snow Hill Artifacts Come to Juniata College." Messenger (July, 1997): 10–11.

"Stalwart for Peace: John C. Baker." Messenger (June, 1997): 10–15.

"Believers Church Perspectives on the Lord's Supper." In: The Lord's Supper: Believers Church Perspectives, ed. Dale R. Stoffer. Scottdale, PA/Waterloo, ON: Herald Press, 1997, pp. 63–78.

Fruit of the Vine: A History of the Brethren, 1708–1995. Elgin, IL: BP, 1997. 675pp.
Comprehensive history of the Brethren movement, with primary attention to the CB after the 1880s, with endnotes.

"Sustainers or Seducers? The Rise and Meaning of Church-Related Institutions." Mennonite Quarterly Review, 71 (1997): 345–64.

"Harmony and Blooming Grove: A Study in Contrasts." The Journal of the Blooming Grove Historical Society, 19 (1998): 18–24.

"Snow Hill Society: Past and Present." Old Order Notes, no. 17 (Spring-Summer 1998): 7–15.

"The Struggle Against War by the Historic Peace Churches." In: Challenge to Mars: Essays on Pacifism from 1918 to 1945, eds. Peter Brock and Thomas F. Socknat. Toronto: University of Toronto Press, 1999, 218–39.

"Brethren Churches," "Free Church Ecclesiology." In: The Encyclopedia of Christianity. Grand Rapids, MI/London: Eerdmans, 1999, 297–98, 495–97.

"Tribute to M. R. Zigler." In: Report of the Proceedings of the 1998 Brethren World Assembly, Bridgewater College, Bridgewater, Virginia. Ashland, OH: Ashland Theological Seminary/Brethren Encyclopedia, Inc., 1999, 273–74.

"Christopher Sauer, Pennsylvania-Deutchen Drucker: Seine Jugend in Deutschland und seine späteren Beziehungen zu Europa," in Deutschsprachige Kolonialpublizistik am Vorabend der Amerikanischen Revolution, ed. Winfried B. Lerg. Münster: LIT, 1999.
Translation of 1958 article.

"Brethren Missions." In: The Evangelical Dictionary of World Missions, ed. A. Scott Moreau. Grand Rapids, MI: Baker Book house, 2000.

"Advice to Prospective Immigrants: Two Communications from Pennsylvania in the 1730s." Yearbook of German-American Studies, 35 (2000): 57–71.
Letter of Andreas Bohni and also open letter signed by Christoph Sauer, Lorentz Schweizer, Johann Heinrich Kalcklößer, and others.

"The Brethren Peace Witness in Ecumenical Perspective." In: The Fragmentation of the Church and Its Unity, eds. Jeffrey Gros and John D. Rempel. Grand Rapids, MI: Eerdmans, 2001, 59–86.

"Pennsylvania's Crazy Quilt of German Religious Groups." Pennsylvania History, 68 (Winter, 2001): 8–30.

"The Fundamentalist-Modernist Struggle Within the Church of the Brethren, 1910–1950." BLT, 47 (Winter/-Spring 2002): 54–88.

"M. R. Zigler: A Spiritual Descendant of John Kline." In: Papers From the Elder John Kline Bicentennial Celebration, ed. William R. Eberly. Ambler, PA: Brethren Encyclopedia, Inc., 2002, 118–129.

"John Kline as Annual Conference Moderator." In: Papers From the Elder John Kline Bicentennial Celebration, ed. William R. Eberly. Ambler, PA: Brethren Encyclopedia, Inc., 2002, 130–145.

"Pietism: A Millennial View from an American Perspective." Pietismus und Neuzeit, 28 (2002): 11–29.

"First and Radical Reformations." Dictionary of the Ecumenical Movement, rev. ed. Geneva: WCC Publications, 2002, 475–76.

"Historic Peace Churches" (with Sara Speicher). Dictionary of the Ecumenical Movement, rev. ed. Geneva: WCC Publications, 2002, 521–22.

"Martin Grove Brumbaugh, the 'Pionner Brethren Historian' and His Rivals." BLT, 48 (Winter/Spring, 2003): 66–90.

Durnbaugh, Donald F., ed., 1927– 2005
The Brethren Encyclopedia. Three volumes. Philadelphia and Oak Brook, IL: Brethren Encyclopedia, Inc., 1983–84. xlii, 2126pp.
The most complete reference work on the several Brethren bodies stemming from the Schwarzenau movement in 1708; Dennis D. Martin was assistant editor.

[Special issue on The Brethren Encyclopedia]. BLT, 30 (Summer, 1985): 131–88.
With major contributions by: M. R. Zigler, Fred W. Benedict, Kenneth I. Morse, Cynthia Mason and Ronald G. Lutz, D. F. Durnbaugh, and J. C. Wenger.

Church of the Brethren: Yesterday and Today. Elgin, IL: BP, 1986. xiv, 246pp.
A revision of Church of the Brethren: Past and Present (1971). Authors include D. F. Durnbaugh, Dale R. Stoffer, Dale W. Brown, S. Loren Bowman, Allen C. Deeter, David B. Eller, B. Merle Crouse, Karen S. Carter, Pamela Brubaker, Edward K. Ziegler, and Carl F. Bowman.

Meet the Brethren. Elgin, IL: BP, 1984. 120pp.
Reprint articles on Brethren origins and the five major Brethren bodies from The Brethren Encyclopedia, with additional photography and a bibliographical note. Reprinted: 1995.

Report of the Proceedings of the Brethren World Assembly: Elizabethtown College, Elizabethtown, Pennsylvania, July 15–July 18, 1992. Elizabethtown, PA, Young Center for the Study of Anabaptist and Pietist Groups/Brethren Encyclopedia, Inc., 1994. iii, separate pagination.
Authors of major presentations include: D. F. Durnbaugh, Dale R. Stoffer, Hedwig T. Durnbaugh, Donald R. Hinks, Brenda B. Colijn, William R. Eberly, Carl F. Bowman, Robert G. Clouse, Joseph R. Shultz.

Durnbaugh, Donald F., 1927–2005, and Brockwell, Charles W., Jr.
"The Historic Peace Churches: From Sectarian Origins to Ecumenical Witness." In: The Church's Peace Witness, eds. Marlin E. Miller and Barbara Nelson Gingerich. Grand Rapids, MI: Eerdmans Press, 1994, 182–95.

Durnbaugh, Hedwig T., 1929–
"Hymnody in the Church of the Brethren." Messenger (October, 1977): 30.
Correction of title in earlier bibliography.

"Hymnody in the Church of the Brethren." The American Organist, 15 (June, 1981): 30

The German Hymnody of the Brethren, 1702–1903. Philadelphia: Brethren Encyclopedia, Inc., 1986. 322pp. Brethren Encyclopedia Monographs, 1.
A detailed analysis of German-language hymns and hymnals used by the Brethren.

"Music in Worship, 1708–1850." BLT, 33 (Autumn, 1988): 270–78.

"Geistreiches Gesang-Buch, 1720: The First Brethren Hymnal." The Hymn, 42/4 (October, 1991): 20–23.

"Changes Reflected in Brethren Hymnody: Trends and Implications." In: Brethren in Transition: 20th Century Directions & Dilemmas, ed. Emmert F. Bittinger. Camden, ME: Penobscot Press, 1992, 193–203.

"Hymnal: A Worship Book: Its Place in the Brethren Singing Tradition." Pennsylvania Mennonite Heritage, 17/2 (April, 1994): 5–12.

"The Lost Hymns of the Brethren, 1720–1880." In: Report of the Proceedings of the Brethren World Assembly, July 15–18, 1992, . . . , ed. D. F. Durnbaugh, Elizabethtown, PA: Elizabethtown College/Brethren Encyclopedia, Inc., 1994, [54–86].

"Ephrata, Amana, Harmonie: Drei christliche kommunistische Gemeinschaften in Amerika: Beispiele kirchlicher Identität im Kirchenlied." I.A.H. Bulletin, 24 (October, 1996): 203–18.

"1791: A Watershed Year in Brethren Hymnody." BLT, 45/3 (Summer, 2000): 89–119.

"The End Times in German Brethren Hymnody." BLT, 46/1–2 (Winter/Spring, 2001): 29–42.

Dvorak, Eileen K.
"Barnhart Family." [n.p.: author], 1990. 128pp. typescript.
Descendants of Daniel Barnhart, 1749 immigrant.

Dyck, C[ornelius] J., 1921–, and Martin, Dennis D., 1952–, eds.
Mennonite Encyclopedia, Volume 5. Scottdale, PA: Herald Press, 1990.
Includes articles on "Believers Church;" "West, Daniel;" "Zigler, Michael Robert" by D. F. Durnbaugh.

Dyck, Harvey L., ed., 1934–
The Pacifist Impulse in Historical Perspective. Toronto: University of Toronto Press, 1996.
Contains article by D. F. Durnbaugh, "The Brethren and Non-Resistance" (pp. 125–44).

Earnest, Russell and Earnest, Corrine Pattie
Papers for Birth Dayes: Guide to the Fraktur Artists and Scriveners. Albuquerque, NM: R. D. Earnest Associates, 1989. 496pp., illus.
Includes Ephrata; second ed. (East Berlin, PA: R. D. Earnest Associates, 1998).

Fraktur: Folk Art and Family. Altglen, PA: Shifffer Publishing Co., 1999. 192pp., illus.

"Where's the Cow? A New Look at the Motifs on American Fraktur." Folk Art, 25/4 (Winter, 2000/2001): 44–53.
Fraktur from the Cassel family, Juniata College Special Collections (p. 52).

Earnest, Corinne Pattie and Hoch, Beverly Repass
The Genealogist's Guide to Fraktur for Genealogists Researching German-American Families. Albuquerque, NM: Russell D. Earnest Associates, 1999.

Ebenhack, Mary Jeanette
Bless This Camp: The Story of Camp Peaceful Pines [Northern California]. [La Verne, CA]: author, 1986, viii, 195pp.

Eberly, Charles H.
"The Eberly and Ecklerin Controversy." Pennsylvania Mennonite Heritage, 12/2 (1989): 7–12.
Demonstrates that these are two distinct families, despite previous claims to the contrary.

Eberly, William R., 1926–
Church of the Brethren History. Academy for Church Leadership, South Central/Central Indiana District of the Church of the Brethren, 1990.
Seven videotapes of thirty class sessions, augmented by visual materials; produced by David Sollenberger.

"The Brethren and Education." In: Report of the Proceedings of the Brethren World Assembly, July 15–18, 1992, . . . , ed. D. F. Durnbaugh, Elizabethtown, PA: Elizabethtown College/Brethren Encyclopedia, Inc., 1994, [136–50].

Manchester Church of the Brethren, 1983–2000. North Manchester, IN: Manchester Church of the Brethren, 2000. 128pp.

"Brethren Ecumenism: The Faith and the Works." BLT, 47 (Summer/Fall, 2002): 147–163.

"The Camp Mack Murals." In: The Brethren Presence in the World…: Proceedings of the 3rd Brethren World Assembly, July 23–26, 2003, ed. William R. Eberly. Philadelphia, PA: Brethren Encyclopedia, Inc., 2004, 126–28.

"Memorials at Camp Alexander Mack." In: The Brethren Presence in the World…: Proceedings of the 3rd Brethren World Assembly, July 23–26, 2003, ed. William R. Eberly. Philadelphia, PA: Brethren Encyclopedia, Inc., 2004, 129–32.

Eberly, William R., ed., 1926–
Papers from the Elder John Kline Bicentennial Celebration. Ambler, PA: Brethren Encyclopedia, Inc., 2002. x, 173pp.
Authors include: William Kostlevy, Fred W. Benedict, Stephen L. Longenecker, John L. Heatwole, Emmert F. Bittinger, Philip C. Stone, Dale R. Stoffer, Carl F. Bowman, James O. Lehman, Klaus Wust, D. F. Durnbaugh, and Dale W. Brown.

The Brethren Presence in the World, Including World Directory of Brethren Bodies: Proceedings of the 3rd Brethren World Assembly, July 23–26, 2003, Grace College, Winona Lake, Indiana. Philadelphia, PA: The Brethren Encyclopedia, Inc., 2004. [iv], 166pp., illus.

Eberly, William R., 1926–, and Eberly, Eloise Whitehead
The Story of a Family, Argus and Myrtle Whitehead. North Manchester, IN: authors, 1986. 118pp.

Ebersole, Mark C., 1921–
Hail to Thee, Okobohi U! A Humor Anthology on Higher Education. New York: Fordham University Press, 1992. xiii, 322pp.

Ebey, Robert D., 1914–
Preacher Bob. [n.p.]: author, 1990. vi, 242pp.
Memoirs of a CB pastor in the Midwest.

Eby, Lela, comp.
Index; Record of the Faithful, 1881, by Howard Miller. [n.p.]: author, 1970.

Edington, Allen
"Footwashing as an Ordinance." Grace Theological Journal, 6/2 (Fall, 11985): 425–34.

Edwards, Lorraine Frantz
"Faith of My Forefathers." Mennonite Family History, 10/1 (1991): 9.
Description of an OGBB annual meeting.

"Thanksgiving in Modesto [CA]." Mennonite Family History, 10/4 (1991): 126.
Visit to an OGBB congregation.

Frantz Families – Kith & Kin. Three Volumes. Lancaster, CA: author, 1996]. 3,180pp.
A genealogy of 17,500 descendants of the immigrant Michael Frantz (1687–1748) of Pennsylvania.

Edwards, Lorraine Frantz and Larick, Ellen Louise, eds.
La Verne Evergreen Cemetery Tombstone Inscriptions. La Verne, CA: authors, [1994]. 270pp.

Egan, Eileen, 1911–
Peace Be With You: Justified Warfare or the Way of Non-violence. Maryknoll, NY: Orbis Books, 1999. xiii, 337pp.
Mentions the CB and the other Historic Peace Churches.

Egge, Doris Cline, ed.
[Special issue on human sexuality]. BLT, 36 (Winter, 1991): 3–50.
Contributors include: Deanna Brown, Beverly Brubaker, Anita Smith Buchwalter, Janice M. Eller, Everett Fisher, Richard A. Livingston, Harold S. Martin, Ralph G. McFadden, Dean L. Miller, Duane H. Ramsey, Gerald W. Roller, Mary Sue Rosenberger, Guy Wampler.

Eisenbise, Debra Lee, 1960–
"Brethren Values in Action." BLT, 36 (Fall, 1991): 284–87.

Elam, Fern M.
"The Musical History of the Church of the Brethren." Senior research project, University of Maryland, Baltimore County, 1986. [iv], 134pp.

Elam, Jennifer and Fager, Charles E., 1942–
"Renewing Our Peace Witness: What Can Quakers Learn from Mennonites, Brethren, and Buddhist Activists?" In: Sustaining Peace Witness in the Twenty-First Century. Wallingford, PA: Pendle Hill Press, 1997. 157pp.
Bibliography, pp. 153–55.

Elizabethtown College
The Brethren Heritage. Elizabethtown, PA: Elizabethtown College, 1993). 12pp.

"Making Our Mark on the World: The Elizabethtown College Story." Elizabethtown College, Elizabethtown, PA, 1999. Video.
Produced for the 1999 centennial observance of the college: Jeff Lynch, producer; Chet Williamson, writer.

Eller, Cynthia Lorraine
Conscientious Objectors and the Second World War: Moral and Religious Arguments in Support of Pacifism. New York: Praeger Publishers, 1991. 218pp.
Based on her PhD dissertation: "Moral and Religious Arguments in Support of Pacifism: Conscientious Objectors and the Second World War," Univ. of Southern California, 1988.

Eller, David B., 1945–
"The Pietist Origins of Sectarian Universalism in the Midwest." The Old Northwest 12 (Spring, 1986): 41–64.
"Stories by and about Brethren." BLT, 39 (Fall, 1994): 266–73.

Eller, David B., ed., 1945–
Servants of the Word: Ministry in the Believers Churches. Elgin, IL: BP, 1990). 252pp.
Papers from the eighth conference on the Believers Churches, Bethany Theological Seminary, Sept. 2–4, 1987.

[Special issue] "From Age to Age: Historians and the Modern Church. A Festschrift for Donald F. Durnbaugh." BLT, 43 [42] (Summer-Fall, 1997): i–xiii, 1–296.
Contributors included: Jeffrey Bach, Dale W. Brown, Robert G. Clouse, David B. Eller, William Kostlevy, Franklin H. Littell, Marcus Meier, Donald E. Miller, Hans Schneider, Dennis L. Slabaugh, Dale R. Stoffer, Murray L. Wagner, John Howard Yoder. A cumulative bibliography lists the writings of D F. Durnbaugh (pp. 276–96).

The Brethren Heritage of Elizabethtown College. Elizabethtown, PA: Young Center for Anabaptist and Pietist Studies, 2003. 24, [1]pp.

Eller, Geraldine Crill, 1905–2001
Along the Snake, ed. Cynthia Eller. La Verne, CA: University of La Verne Press for the author, 1986. [v], 96, [1]pp.
Family history.

Jay Vernard Eller, 1899–1978: Master Teacher, Minister, Civic Leader, Humanitatian. Wenatchee, WA: Wenatchee World, [1987]. 43pp., illus.

A Potpourri of People. [n.p.: author], 1991.

"G[reat] N[orthern] – A Catalyzer: Wenatchee Valley – The Brethren – Great Northern Railway." Confluence (Spring, 2001): 3–15 (illus.)

Eller, Henry C., comp.
This I Remember: Memories of Christian "Crist" Emory Eller and Rebecca "Becky" Eller Martha by Relatives and Friends. [Bridgewater, VA]: author], 1984. 45pp.

Eller, Vernard, 1927–
The Language of Canaan and the Grammar of Feminism. Grand Rapids, MI: W. E. Eerdmans, 1982. xiv, 56pp.

Pearl of Christian Counsel for the Brokenhearted. Washington, DC: University Press of America, 1983. 142pp.
With Roaanna Eller McFadden.

Peace as Stewardship (or Vice Versa). New York: Commission on Stewardship, National Council of Churches of Christ in the U.S.A., 1984.

Christian Anarchy: Jesus' Primacy Over the Powers. Grand Rapids, MI: Eerdmans, 1987. 267pp.

The Beloved Disciple – His Name, His Story, His Thought: Two Studies from the Gospel of John. Grand Rapids, MI: Eerdmans, 1987. xi, 124pp.

Proclaim Good Tidings: Evangelism for the Faith Community. Elgin, IL: BP, 1987. ix, 52pp.

Eller's Ethical Elucidations: Collected Readings on Christian Ethics (1970–89). La Verne, CA: University of La Verne, 1989. Various paginations.
Contains his 1979 Doubleday book (*The Promise: Ethics in the Kingdom of God*) and 16 more recent essays.

Apocalipsis, el libro más revelador de la Biblia. Ciudad de Gutatemale, Guatemale: Semilla-Santaté de Bogotá, Columbia: Clara, Editorial Buena Semilla. 280, [2]pp., illus.

"Recent Trends From the Long Term Perspective." In: Brethren in Transition: 20th Century Directions and Dilemmas, ed. Emmert F. Bittinger. Camden, ME: Penobscot Press, 1992, 73–83.

History of the Decline and Fall of Biblical Brethrenism (Done After the Pattern Though Certainly Not on the Scale of Gibbon's Massive History of the Roman Empire): A Personal History. Lancaster, PA: Brethren Evangelical Leadership Foundation, 1995. 24pp.
Originally published in BLT, 40 (Winter, 1995): 23–45.

Eller, Vernard, ed., 1927–
In the United States District Court for the Western District of Virginia, Roanoke Division: United States of America, Plaintiff vs. Enten V. Eller, Defendant; Before Honorable James C. Turk, Chief Judge. [n.p.]: 1983. 96pp.

Enns, Fernando
Friedenskirche in der Ökumene: Mennonitische Wurzeln einer Ethik der Gewaltfreiheit. Göttingen: Vandenhoeck & Ruprecht, 2003. 364pp.
A thorough theological and historical study by a German Mennonite of the initiatives taken since 1935 by the Historic Peace Churches to place their peace testimony into the heart of ecumenical dialogue, especially within the World Council of Churches. It emphasizes the ecclesiological importance of the Believers Church stance of the HPC.

Enns, Fernando; Holland, Scott; and Riggs, Ann K., eds.
Seeking Cultures of Peace: A Peace Church Conversation. Telford, PA: Cascadia Publishing House, in cooperation with the World Council of Churches and Herald Press, 2004. 260pp.
Provides documentation from the June, 2001, conference of the Historic Peace Churches at Bienenberg, Switzerland. The foreword was written by Samuel Kobia, WCC general secretary, and the first chapter is by Konrad Raiser, immediate past WCC general secretary. Essays by Brethren writers are by Patrick K. Buga (pp. 124–31), Scott Holland (pp. 132–46), Daniel W. Ulrich (pp. 157–70), and Debbie Roberts (pp. 182–93).

Ephrata Cloister]
A Triad of Lancaster County History: Ephrata Cloister, Pennsylvania Farm Museum of Landis Valley, Railroad Museum. Ephrata, PA: Science Press, 1985. 120pp.

Works of Patience: Being a Description of the Texts Found on the Wall Charts of the Ephrata Cloister . . .. Ephrata, PA: Ephrata Cloister, 2001.

Erb, Peter C., 1943–
"Eschatology at Ephrata." In: The Coming Kingdom: Essays in American Millennialism and Eschatology, eds. M. Darrol Bryant and Donald W. Dayton. Barryton, NY: New Era Books, 1983, 19–44.

"Pietist Spirituality: Some Aspects of Present Research." In: The Roots of the Modern Christian Tradition, ed. E. Rozanne Elder. Kalamazoo, MI: Cistercian Publications, Inc., 1984.
The Spirituality of Western Christendom, Vol. 2.

"Anabaptist Spirituality." In: Protestant Spiritual Traditions, ed. Frank C. Senn. New York: Paulist Press, 1986.

Pietists, Protestants, and Mysticism: The Use of Late Medieval Spiritual Texts in the Work of Gottfried Arnold (1666–1714). Metuchen, NJ: Scarecrow Press, 1989. viii, 329pp.
Pietist and Wesleyan Studies, No. 2.

Erb, Peter C., ed., 1943–
Johann Conrad Beissel and the Ephrata Community: Mystical and Historical Texts. Lewistown, ME: Edwin Mellen Press, 1985. iv, 393pp.

Eshelman, Mathew M., 1844–1921
True Vital Piety. [Arcanum, OH]: J. W. Miller, 1989. 215pp.
Originally published (ca. 1876).

Everham, Wendy
"The Recovery of the Feminine in an Early American Pietist Community: The Interpretive Challenge of the Theology of Conrad Beissel." Pennsylvania Folklife, 39 (Winter, 1989–90): 50–56.
Published in German as "Johann Conrad Beissels Leben und Theologie: Versuch eines Grundverständnisses," 90 (April, 1991): 55–67.

Fahlbusch, Ervin and others, eds.
The Encyclopedia of Christianity. Grand Rapids, MI: Eerdmans/Leiden: Brill, 1998.
"Brethren Churches" (pp. 297–298), by D. F. Durnbaugh.

Fahrney, Walter, 1877–1966, and Long, Omer
The Descendants of Dr. Peter Fahrney (1767–1837). [n.p.]: authors, [n.d.]. 199pp.

Fairhurst, Janet
"Ephrata Cloister." Early American Life, 4 (June, 1973): 16–19, 87.

Farner, Donald
"The Lord's Supper Until He Comes." Grace Theological Journal." Grace Theological Journal, 6/2 (Fall, 1985): 391–401.

Faus, Nancy Rosenberger
"Spirituality and Worship in the Church of the Brethren." BLT, 39 (Fall, 1994): 241–50.

"Spiritual Nurture of the Family: A Heritage and a Challenge for the Brethren." In: Report of the Proceedings of the 1998 Brethren World Assembly, Bridgewater College . . . , ed. Dale R. Stoffer. Ashland, OH: Ashland Theological Seminary/Brethren Encyclopedia, Inc., 1999, 131–58.

Faus, Nancy Rosenberger, ed.
[Special issue on Brethren worship]. BLT, 31 Winter, 1986): 3–60.
Essays by Warren F. Groff, Nancy Rosenberger Faus, Dale W.

Brown, Jimmy R. Ross, Donald E. Miller, Ronald C. Arnett, and Vicki S. Dill.

[Special issue on Brethren hymnody]. BLT, 33 (Autumn, 1988): 261–318.
Contributors are J. Douglas Archer, Hedwig T. Durnbaugh, Phyllis J. Warner. Rebecca Slough, Brian Wren, Lee-Lani Wright, Mary K. Oyer, and Kenneth I. Morse.

Faw, Chalmer E., 1909–96
Our Heritage, 1886–1986: A Centennial Project of the Church of the Brethren, Quinter, Kansas. Osborne, KS: Osborne Publishing Company for the Quinter, KS, Church of the Brethren, 1986. ix, 306pp.
Extensive congregational history.

Acts. Scottdale, PA: Herald Press, 1993. 335pp.
Believers Church Bible Commentary Series.

Faw, William R., 1940–
"Simple Life: Concepts in Brethren History." BLT, 29 (Summer, 1984): 152–57.

Fellowship of Brethren Genealogists
Brethren Roots. Spring, 1998.
The new name of the *Fellowship of Brethren Genealogists Newsletter*, beginning with Volume 30, no. 1; editor, Homer G. Benton.

Fellowship of Grace Brethren Churches
[The] 1999 Ministry Handbook. Winona Lake, IN: Fellowship of Grace Brethren Churches, 1999.

Fike, Earle W., Jr., 1930–
A Month of Sundays: Making Sense of Things. Scottdale, PA: Herald Press, 2001. 256pp.
Selected sermons; foreword by D. F. Durnbaugh.

Please Pray With Me: Prayers for People at Worship. Elgin, IL: BP, 1990. 113pp.

Fike, Ezra Edwin, 1884–1949, and Fike, Faye Davidson
Direct Line History and Genealogy of the Children of John T. Fike and Olivia Rogers Fike: Children, Reva Espage Fike Findley, John Rogers Fike, Ezra Edwin Fike. Flemington, WV: authors, 1987. 183pp.

Fike, Mary Antes
The Centennial History of the Peach Blossom [MD] Congregation of the Church of the Brethren, 1881–1981: As Gleaned from the Records of the Nine Books of Records of the Council Meetings of These 100 Years of the Work of Peach Blossom Church. [n.p.]: 1982.

Finney, Harriet and Martin, Suzanne DeMoss
A Spirituality of Compassion. Elgin, IL: BP, 1996. x, 76pp.
Covenant Bible Studies Series.

Fitzkee, Donald R.
The Transformation of the Lititz Church of the Brethren, 1914–1989. [Lebanon, PA]: Forry and Hacker, 1990. [iii], 45pp.

"Congregational Transformation: A Case Study of the Lititz Church." In: Brethren in Transition: 20th Century Directions and Dilemmas, ed. Emmert F. Bittinger.

Camden, ME: Penobscot Press, 1992, 167–83.
Moving Toward the Mainstream: 20th Century Change Among the Brethren of Eastern Pennsylvania. Intercourse, PA: Good Books, 1995. 347pp.
Well-documented study of changes in the Atlantic Northeast District of the Church of the Brethren.

Fleischman, Dewey Denton, 1899/1900?–
A Witness to Three Centuries: The Memoirs of Dewey Denton Fleishman. [Bridgewater, VA]: author, 2003. 88pp., illus.

Flora, Jerry, 1933–, and Flora Julie
Faith and Fortitude: Lives of W[omen's] M[issionary] S[ociety] Presidents. Ashland, OH: Brethren Publishing Company, 1987. 85pp.
On The Brethren Church.

Flory, Harley T., 1928–
"The Dunkard Brethren Church on Missions." Old Order Notes, no. 10 (Spring, 1988): 31–32.

Flory, Raymond L., 1915–
Curtis Elmer Flory and Carrie Sarah (Bird) Niswander Flory. [McPherson, KS]: author, 1993. [iii], 41pp.

Flory, Wendell P., 1920–2003
My Life From China to Heaven. [Bridgewater, VA: author, n.p.], unpubl. computer printout.

Fogleman, Aaron S.
Hopeful Journeys: German Immigration, Settlement, and Political Culture in Colonial America, 1717–1775. Philadelphia: University of Pennsylvania Press, 1996. 288pp.
Careful study of German immigrants with many references to the Brethren and to Ephrata. co-published with the Pennsylvania German Society. Revised from "Hopeful Journeys: German Immigration and Settlement in Greater Pennsylvania, 1717–1775," PhD dissertation, University of Michigan, 1991.

Foreman, Harry E.
History of Little Cove, Franklin County, Pennsylvania. [Chambersburg, PA: author, 1967. 192pp.

Foster, Venia Hurr; Galassini, Florence Kuhn; and Wonso, Jacqueline Kuhn, eds.
A Kuhn Hunter's Guide. The Families of John and Susannah Mock Kuhn. [n.p.: authors], 1991.

Fourman, Larry D., 1942–
"The Holy Spirit in the New Testament: Directions for Renewing the Local Congregation." DMin thesis, Bethany Theological Seminary, 1979. 111, 129pp.

The Life of David. Elgin, IL: BP, 1990. 40pp.
Covenant Bible Studies Series.

Fox, Karen M.
"The Pennsylvania Germans' Gentle Art [Fraktur]." Pennsylvania Heritage (Winter, 1987): 24–31.
Ephrata (pp. 28–30).

Frame, Randy
"Grace Brethren Split Over 'Doctrinal Drift.'" Christianity Today, 36 (Sept. 14, 1992): 64.

Francis, Lillie
"Brethren (Dunkards). In: Plains Folk: North Dakota's Ethnic History, eds. William C. Sherman and Playford V. Thorson. [n.p.]: authors, 1988, pp. 104–10.

Frantz, John B.
"Franklin and the Pennsylvania Germans." Pennsylvania History, 65 (Spring 1998): 21–34.
On the Sauers.

"Beissel, Johann Conrad." American National Biography. New York: Oxford University Press, 1999. 484–86.

Frantz, Nadine Pence
"The Lord's Supper: Contemporary Reflections." In: Anabaptist Currents: History in Conversation with the Present, eds. Carl F. Bowman and Stephen L. Longenecker. Camden, ME: Penobscot Press, 1995, 153–61.

"Theological Reflections on Nineteenth-Century Forms of Piety: Humility, Yieldedness, and Denial." In: The Dilemma of Anabaptist Piety: Strengthening or Straining the Bonds of Community?, ed. Stephen L. Longenecker. Camden, ME: Penobscot Press, 1997, 131–40.

Frantz, Nadine Pence and Meyer, Lauree Hersch, eds.
[Special issue on women]. BLT, 30 (Winter, 1985): 3–63.
Major contributions by: Pamela Brubaker, Lauree Hersch Meyer, Fran Clemens Nyce, Theresa Cocklin Eshbach, Harriet A. Ziegler, Paula J. Stanley, Nadine Pence Frantz and Deborah L. Silver, Jean Lichty Hendricks, Mary Eikenberry, Ruthann Knechel Johansen, Mary E. Jessup, and Melanie A. May.

Women in Ministry and Mission. Elgin, IL: BP, 1985. 63pp.

Frasca, Ralph
"'To Rescue the Germans Out of Sauer's Hands': Benjamin Franklin's German-Language Printing Partnerships." Pennsylvania Magazine of History and Biography, 121 (October, 1997): 329–50.

Frazer, Heather T. and O'Sullivan, John
"We Have Just Begun to Not Fight": An Oral History of Conscientious Objectors in Civilian Public Service During World War II. New York: Twayne Publishers/London: Prentice Hall International, 1996. xxv, 268pp.

Free Gift, The
Edited by J. W. Beers. Meyersdale, PA: October, 1875.

French Broad Church of the Brethren
Centennial Book: 100 Years of Christian Service, 1875–1975. [Dandridge, TN: French Broad Church of the Brethren, 1975]. [114pp.]

Frick, Paul Sumner
The Hans Grumbacher Family of Coventry Township, 1733–1814: A German Baptist Brethren Farm Family. Arizona City, AZ: author, 1993. vii, 103pp.

Friedland, Michael B.
Lift Up Your Voice Like a Trumpet: White Clergy and the Civil Rights and Antiwar Movements, 1954–1973. Chapel Hill: University of North Carolina Press, 1998. 336pp.
Many references to the work of Ralph E. Smeltzer in Selma, AL.

Froese, Wolfang, ed.
Sie kamen als Fremde: Die Mennoniten in Krefeld von den Anfängen bis zur Gegenwart. Krefeld: Stadtarchiv Krefeld, 1995. 387pp.
With references to the Brethren (pp. 85–88).

Fromm, Roger W.
"The Migration and Settlement of Pennsylvania Germans in Maryland, Virginia, and North Carolina, and Their Effects on the Landscape." Pennsylvania Folklife, 37 (Autumn, 1987): 33–42.

Fry, Dorotha Winger. *See* **Mason, Dorotha Winger Fry**

Fry, Linda L.
"A Study of Architecture and Worship in the Church of the Brethren." MATh thesis, Bethany Theological Seminary, 1986. xi, 183pp., illus.

Fry, Pauline Frade De Lauter
De Lauter Families in America: De Lauder, De Lawd(t)er, De Laughter: A Genealogy. Elgin, IL: BP, [n.d.]. xxviii, 402pp.

Frye, Nancy Kettering
"The [Brethren] Meetinghouse Connection: Plain Living in the Gilded Age." Pennsylvania Folklife, 41 (Winter, 1991–92): 50–82.
With many illustrations.

"'An Uncommon Woman' in the Age of the Common Man: The Life and Times of Sarah Righter Major." Pennsylvania Folklife, 46 (1996–97): 54–70.

An Uncommon Woman: The Life and Times of Sarah Righter Major. Elgin, IL: BP, 2000. 60pp.
Reprinting of the above article, with an appendix of Major's communication to Jacob Sala of April 1, 1835, defending women's right to ministry.

Fyock, Joan and Wright, Lani, eds.
Hymnal Companion. Elgin, IL: BP, 1996. 768pp.
Information on poets and composers of hymns contained in Hymnal: A Worship Book.

Garber, Julie, 1956–
Many Cultures, One in Christ. Elgin, IL: BP, 1993. 76pp.
Covenant Bible Studies Series.

For Crying Out Loud: Studies in Exodus. Elgin, IL: BP, 1998. 35pp.

Garber, Julie, ed., 1956–
Ministry with Young Adults. Elgin, IL: BP, 1992, 1998. 14pp.
Handbook for youth ministry.

Shoes of Peace: Letters to Youth from Peacemakers. Elgin, IL: BP, 2002. [vi], separate pagination.
Thirty-six letters, mostly of two-to-three pages, from Brethren peace activists and writers.

Garber, Merlin E., 1912–2001
Karlsschule. Salem, VA: Salem Printing Co. for the author, 1983. 66pp.
Reconstruction of the famous Protestant school in the heart of Vienna by Brethren and Mennonite COs.

Tilted Halo: An Autobiography. Radford, VA: Commonwealth Press for the author, 1983. iv, 180pp.
Memoirs of a pastor in the Church of the Brethren.

Pearls of Lesser Price. Roanoke, VA: Toler and Co. for the author, 1984. [v], 81pp.
A book of essays and memoirs of a pastor.

Gardner, Richard B., 1940–
Matthew. Scottdale, PA: Herald Press, 446pp.
Believers Church Commentary Series.

Gardner, Richard B., 1940, ed.
[Special issue, Bethany Theological Seminary]. BLT 39 (Winter, 1994): 1–72.
Contributors are: Paul M. Robinson, Warren F. Groff, John Eichelberger, Gerald Harley, E. Floyd McDowell, Eugene F. Roop, Nadine Pence Frantz, Dale W. Brown, David S. Young, and D. F. Durnbaugh.

[Special issue, Brethren and Quakers]. BLT 39 (Fall, 1994): 224–77.
Essays by D. F. Durnbaugh, Nancy Rosenberger Faus, Alan Kolp, Wilmer A. Cooper, David B. Eller, and John Punshon.

Garner, Warren
"The Brethren Way of Christ." In: Report of the Proceedings of the 1998 Brethren World Assembly, Bridgewater College . . . , ed. Dale R. Stoffer. Ashland, OH: Ashland Theological Seminary/Brethren Encyclopedia, Inc., 1999, 193–202.

Gardner, Richard B., 1940–, and Shaffer, Kenneth M. Jr., 1945–
Let Our Joys Be Known: A Brethren Heritage Curriculum for Adults. Elgin, IL: BP, 1998. [v], 164pp.
Contains biblical and historical exposition on Brethren history and beliefs.

Garrett, Dean
The Annals of the Upper Twin [OH] Church of the Brethren: A History of the Eaton Congregation. [n.p.: author, ca. 1985]. 86, [4]pp.
Also contains doctrinal articles by Dean Garrett, Harold S. Martin, and James F. Myer.

Garvan, Beatrice B.
The Pennsylvania German Collection. Philadelphia: Philadelphia Museum of Art, 1982 (reprinted 1999). xiv, 372pp., illus.
A handbook of the museum's collections: Jacob Gorgas, clockmaker (p. 42), Ephrata (pp. 292–93, 319, 324), Bloomng Grove (p. 294), C. Sauer (pp. 324–25).

Garvan, Beatrice B. and Hummel, Charles F.
The Pennsylvania Germans: A Celebration of Their Arts, 1683–1850. Philadelphia: Philadelphia Museum of Art, 1982.
An extensive catalog of the exhibit at the Philadelphia Museum of Art and the Winterthur Museum.

Gibbel, Ira W., 1924–1993, comp.
A Family of Eckerts: The Story of William J. Eckert, His Eckert Ancestors and Descendants. Palmyra, PA: author, 1991.

The Descendants of Henry Gibbel [1717–1789]. Palmyra, PA: author, 1995. 12, 596pp.

Gibble, June Adams
Stories of Covenant. Elgin, IL: BP, 1993. 48pp.

Gibble, June Adams and Swartz, Fred W., 1938–, eds.
Called to Caregiving: A Resource for Equipping Deacons in the Believers Church. Elgin, IL: BP, 1987. 175pp.
Also published for the Mennonite Church, General Conference Mennonite Church, and the Brethren in Christ.

Gibble, Kenneth L., 1941–
"Brethren Preaching: Law or Gospel?" BLT, 38 (Fall, 199): 197–208.

Gilbert, Audrey
West Alexandria First Brethren Church, 1885–1985. West Alexandria, OH: Women's Missionary Society, [1985]. 35pp.

The Family of Thomas and Elizabeth Gilbert of Frederick County, Maryland. West Alexandria, OH: author, 1991. 363, [xv]pp.

Gill, David W., ed., 1946–
Does God Have Tenure? Essays on Religion and Higher Education. Grand Rapids, MI: Eerdmans, 1997.
Contains articles by Robert G. Clouse on diversity, by Earl C. Kaylor, Jr. on J. Omar Good (1877–1969), and by D. F. Durnbaugh on Brethren higher education.

Gillett, Rachel E. Kuns
History and Records of the Gillett Family. [n.p.]: author, 1936. 78pp.

Gingerich, Owen, 1930–
"The Return of the Seagoing Cowboy: Horses Afloat and Books Astray." The American Scholar 68 (Autumn 1999): 71–81.
Memoir of a young Mennonite scholar who participated in a BSC-sponsored delivery of horses to Poland in 1946.

Gingrich, Rhonda Pittman
Heart, Soul, and Mind: Becoming a Member of the Church of the Brethren. Elgin, IL: BP, 2000. vii, [1], 143pp., illus.
Membership guide based on Brethren heritage, belief, and practice.

Heart, Soul, and Mind: Becoming a Member of the Church of the Brethren. Leader's Guide. Elgin, IL: BP, 2000. viii, 210pp., illus.

Gingrich, Raymond E., 1905–1995
Outline and Analysis of the First Epistle of John. Winona Lake, IN: BMH Books, 1946.

Gish, Arthur G., 1939–
Hebron Journal: Stories of Nonviolent Peacemakers. Scottdale, PA: Herald Press, 2001. 301pp., illus.
On the work of Christian Peacemaker Teams in the Middle East.

Glatfelter, Charles H.
Pennsylvania Germans: A Brief Account of Their Influence on Pennsylvania. Harrisburg, PA: Pennsylvania Historical and Museum Commission, 1990).
Mentions Brethren and Ephrata.

The Churches of Adams County, Pennsylvania: A Brief Review and Summary. Biglerville, PA: St. Paul's Lutheran Church, 1981. 32pp.
"The Church of the Brethren" (p. 8) includes four congregations.

Gleim, Elmer Q., 1917–
The History of the Gleim Family in America. [n.p.: author], 1985. 230pp.

A Child in Their Midst: A History of the Children's Aid Society, Southern Pennsylvania District, Church of the Brethren, 1913–1988. [New Oxford, PA]: Southern Pennsylvania District, 1988. 189pp.

The History and Families of the Black Rock Church of the Brethren (1738–1988): Anniversary Volume. [Brodbrecks, PA]: Black Rock Church of the Brethren, [1988]. x, 278pp.

The Huntsdale Church of the Brethren, 1864–1989. [Carlisle, PA]: Huntsdale Church of the Brethren, 1989. v, 182pp.

Brethren Heritage Along the Big Conewago: Anniversary Volume, 1741–1991. Mechanicsburg, PA: Center Square Press for the Upper Conewago Church of the Brethren, 1991. vi, 237pp.
Includes information on Ephrata and Snow Hill.

Hanover, PA, Church of the Brethren: 100th Anniversary Book. Hanover, PA: Church of the Brethren, 2002.

Glick, Allen R.
Glicks in America. [Mifflintown, PA]: author, 1989. 62pp.

Glick, Joseph Paul
"The Trail I've Followed: Ancestral Biographies; A Series of Brief Genealogical Sketches for My Four Grandchildren." [n.p.]: 1977, typescript, 300pp.

Goosen, Rachel Waltner, 1960–
Women Against the Good War: Conscientious Objection and Gender on the American Home Front, 1941–1947. Chapel Hill, NC: University of North Carolina Press, 1997. 180pp.
Includes CB women in CPS camps.

Gordon, Ronald
Two Hundredth Anniversary of the Lost Creek [PA] Church of the Brethren, 1790–1990. [n.p.]: Lost Creek Church of the Brethren, 1990. 32pp.

Grace Brethren
"Grace Brethren Split." Christianity Today, 36 (Sept. 14, 1992): 64.

Graffius, Charles
Ephrata Cloisters and German Seventh Day Baptists: Then and Now. Martinsburg, PA: Morrisons Cove Herald, [n.d.]. [36pp.].
Many illustrations; includes Snow Hill.

Grant, Mary F.
"Our Heinrich": The Ancestry, Life, and Some Descendants of Heinrich/Henry Fox (1818–1898) of Earl and Ephrata Townships, Lancaster County. Morgantown, PA: Masthof Press, 1995.

Green, Ernest
"The Labadists of Colonial Maryland (1683–1722)." Communal Societies, 8 (1988): 103–21.
Mentions Ephrata.

Greiner, Alyson Lee
"Geography, Humanism, and 'Plain People' in Missouri: The Case of the Dunkard Brethren." MA thesis, University of Missouri-Columbia, 1991.

Griffith, Lee
The Fall of the Prison: Biblical Perspectives on Prison Abolition. Grand Rapids, MI: Eerdmans, 1993. 258pp.

The War on Terrorism and the Terror of God. Grand Rapids, MI: Eerdmans, 2002. xv, 399pp.
A theology of peace.

Groff, Clyde L., Groff, Walter B., 1923–, and Best, Jane Evans, 1926–
The Groff Book, Vol. 1: A Good Life in a New Land. [Ronks, PA]: Groff Family Association, 1985. 432pp.

Groff, Everett R., 1916–
Fulfillment in the Way of Christ: An Adventure into the 21st Century With Only Jesus Christ As Our Guide in the Way, the Truth, and the Life: Meditations in the Garden of Light Where Jesus Christ Is Reality. [n.p.]: ca. 1990. 196pp.

Groff, Forrest U., 1914–
By Faith I Will Overcome: A Poor Boy's Most Amazing True Adventure Through the Twentieth Century. Springfield, OR: author, 2002. 417pp.

Groff, Warren F., 1924–
Prayer: God's Time and Ours. Elgin, IL: BP, 1984.

Grossnickle, Edwin
Grandpa Jonas [Grossnickle], 1852–1944. Kalamazoo, MI: author, 1983. 110pp.

Grubb, Michael R.
"Rulers, Armor, Swords, and the Anabaptist Perspective: A Study of Ephesians 6: 10–20." MATh thesis, Bethany Theological Seminary, 1998, v, 120pp.

Grutschnig-Kieser, Konstanze-Mirjam
"'Auf, auf mein Herz und sing': Zwei Homburger Gesangbücher des 18. Jahrhinderts." Alt Homburg, 44/6 (June, 2001): 3–8
A Radical Pietist hymnal incorporates Ephrata material.

Guenther, Karen
"'A Garden for the Friends of God': Religious Diversity in the Oley Valley to 1750." Pennsylvania Folklife, 33 (Spring, 1984): 138–44.

Guiles, Dave, and Teevan, John
"The Ministries of the Fellowship of Grace Brethren Churches in the World." In: The Brethren Presence in the World...: Proceedings of the 3rd Brethren World Assembly, July 23–26, 2003, ed. William R. Eberly. Philadelphia, PA: Brethren Encyclopedia, Inc., 2004, 76–80.

Guimond, Anice Joseph, 1907–
One Word Blue, One Word Red: A Memoir. Austin, TX: Firefly Group, 1997. 88, [4]pp.
North Dakota biography.

Gump, Arlo K.
The Gump Family in America, 1732–1983. Fort Wayne, IN: author, 1983. 250pp.

Gutek, Gerald, 1935–, and Gutek, Patricia
Experiencing America's Past: A Travel Guide to Museum Villages, second ed. Columbia, SC: University of South Carolina Press, 1994.
Ephrata Cloister (pp. 113–21).

Visiting Utopian Communities. Columbia: University of South Carolina Press, 1998.
Includes the Ephrata Cloister.

Guth, Hermann, 1912–
The Amish-Mennonites of Waldeck and Wittgenstein, trans. Gertrud Guth. Elverson, PA: Mennonite Family History, 1986. iii, 58pp.
Refers to the Schwarzenau Baptists.

Hacker, Werner
Auswanderung aus Rheinpfalz und Saarland. Stuttgart/-Aalen: Konrad Theiss, 1987.
Background of some Ephrata members.

Hackett, Lucile Eleanor
"Johann Conrad Beissel: Early German-American Mystic and Musician." MA thesis, University of Alaska, Fairbanks, 1996. 78pp.
See also in Studies in Puritan-American Spirituality, 5 (1995): 95–121.

Hackman, Galen R., 1953–
Brethren Beliefs and Practices. Mubi, Adamawa State, Nigeria: TEE Programme, EYN, 1993. 185pp.

"The Influence of James 2:14–26 on Brethren Theology." BLT, 41 (Spring/Summer, 1996): 39–55.

Bible Peace and Nonresistance. (York, PA: Brethren Bible Institute, n.d.)

Hackman, Walter N. Jr., ed.
100th Anniversary, 1899–1999: Mohler [PA] Church of the Brethren. [n.p.]: 1999. 12pp.

Haldeman, Myrtle Long, 1924–
Cassie: The Girl with the Hero's Heart. Hagerstown, MD:

Review and Herald Publishing, 1997. 108pp.
A "fact-based reconstruction" of Brethren during the Civil War, dealing with the family of Elder David Long.

Thy Kingdom Come: A Journey of Faith. Morgantown, PA: Masthof Press, 1999. vii, 132pp.
Autobiographical memoir.

Haller, Charles R.
Distinguished German-Americans. Bowie, MD: Heritage Books, 1995. xii, 303pp.
Lists: Ephrata (pp. 27ff.); Conrad Beissel (pp. 65ff.); W. H. Rinehart (p. 33); German Baptist Brethren (p. 55); Peter Becker, Alexander Mack, Sr., Alexander Mack, Jr. (p. 67); the Studebaker family (pp. 97, 101); Harry Stutz (pp. 97, 97, 101); the Sower family (pp. 201, 212).

Hallowell, Marvin E.
"Jacob Duché, D. D., 1737–1798." STM thesis, University of the South, 1968.
Penned description of Ephrata.

Hamilton, Benjamin A., 1913–1986
Gribble's Dream – God's Design. Winona Lake, IN: BMH Books, 1987. 300pp.
FGBC missionary in Central Africa.

Hamm, Thomas D.
"Separation, Discipline, and Nineteenth Century Quakers." In: Brethren in Transition: 20th Century Directions and Dilemmas, ed. Emmert F. Bittinger. Camden, ME: Penobscot Press, 1992, 123–32.

Hanover Church of the Brethren
Hanover, PA, Church of the Brethren: 100th Anniversary Book. Hanover, PA: Church of the Brethren, 2001. ca. 300pp., illus.

Hanson, Phyllis Brechbiel, 1921–
The Brechbiel/Dilling Ancestry of Harry K. Brechbiel. Reprint. Decorah, IA: author., 1982. 256pp.

The Dilling/Puterbaugh Family Chronicle. Decorah, IA: Amundsen Pub. Co., 1991. 632pp.

Harper, Douglas
"The Witman Incident: Revolutionary Revisions to an Ephrata Tale." Journal of the Lancaster County Historical Society, 97/3 (1995): 90–97.

Harper, Glenn
"The Test of Time: Ohio German Baptists and the Development of the Meetinghouse." BA paper, Antioch College, 1985. 70pp.

Harris, C[larence] D.
The Invisible Hand on My Shoulders. La Verne, CA: University of La Verne Press, 1983. xvi, 398pp.
Memoirs of a CB family in Indiana, North Dakota, and California.

Hartzler, H. Harold
King Family History: Vol. I–II. Mankato, MN: author, 1984. 1400pp.

Only One Life: My Autobiography. Elverson, PA: Olde Springfield Shoppe, 1992. [6], 167pp., illus.
On Juniata College (pp. 26–30, 113–18).

Hatfield, Terry, 1947–, ed.
Evangel 21. Vol. 1, No. 1, Fall, 1990.
"Proclaiming Christ's Good News through the Church of the Brethren in the 21st. Century." A modest-sized newsletter designed to provide a network for evangelical CB members; it soon expanded to a slick-paper journal but ceased publication after several issues.

Hawkley, Louise and Juhnke, James C., eds.
Nonviolent America: History through the Eyes of Peace. Newton, KS: Bethel College, 1993. xiii, 279pp.
With articles by Robert G. Clouse (pp. 82–87), Ken Brown (pp. 88–103), D. F. Durnbaugh (pp. 165–96), and Stephen L. Longenecker (pp. 227–43); second edition (2004).

Heatwole, John L.
"The Impact of the Civil War on the Local Community." In: Papers from the Elder John Kline Bicentennial Celebration, ed. William R. Eberly. Ambler, PA: Brethren Encyclopedia, Inc., 2002, 40–49.

Heckler, Jas. Y., 1829–1901
"History of Harleysville and Historical Sketches of Lower Salford Township." Bulletin of the Historical Society of Montgomery Co., 23 (1982): 3: 199–249, 4: 279–353; 24 (1987): 1: 3–60; 2: 135–181; 3: 267–317; 4: 349–406. Reprint: Bedminster, PA: Adams Apple Press, 1993, with added index.

Heckman, Marlin L., 1937–
The Gem of Lordsburg: The Lordsburg Hotel/College Building, 1887–1927. La Verne, CA: University of La Verne Press, 1987. xxii, 89pp.

Heckman, Shirley J., 1938–
Visions of Peace. New York: Friendship Press, 1984. vi, 75pp.

Vision and Ministry for the 1990s: A Guide for Congregational Planning. Elgin, IL: BP, 1988. 40, [2]pp.

Heckman, Shirley J., 1938–, and Gibble, June Adams
Covenant People. Elgin, IL: BP, 1993. x, 61pp.
Covenant Bible Studies Series.

Heiges, George L.
"Letters Relating to Colonial Military Hospitals in Lancaster County." Lancaster County Historical Society Papers, 52/4 (1948): 73–96.

Heiss, Heide-Inge and others, eds.
125 Jahre Evangelische Schule am Karlsplatz, 1861–1986. Vienna: Evangelischen Schule am Karlsplatz, 1986. 143pp.
Reconstructed with the aid of Brethren and Mennonite COs.

Helman, Patricia Kennedy
Sign and Symbol in the Church of the Brethren. Elgin, IL: BP, 1991. 112pp.

Henning, Elma Snyder
The Ulrich Rinehart Family and Descendants, 1704–1985. Dayton, OH: author, 1986. 400+pp.

Herr, Donald M.
Pewter in Pennsylvania German Churches. Birdsboro, PA: Pennsylvania German Society, 1995. xvi, 214pp.
General discussion of CB (pp. 21–23); refers to pewterware in several CB congregations, Black Rock (Fig. 26, p. 23; Fig. 97, p. 61); Chiques congregation (p. 60), Codorus (Fig. 25, p. 22; Fig. 95, p. 60, p. 185); Middle Creek (p. 60). See also Ephrata (Fig. 242, pp. 117, 163).

Herr, Robert, 1948–, and Herr, Judy Zimmerman, 1952–, eds.
Transforming Violence: Linking Local and Global Peacemaking. Scottdale, PA: Herald Press, 1998. 255pp.
Written by members of the Historic Peace Churches and the Fellowship of Reconciliation to further ecumenical dialogue. Dedicated to M. R. Zigler, with a concluding theological essay by Lauree Hersch Meyer (pp. 219–230).

Hershey, Mary Jane Lederach
This Teaching I Present: Fraktur from the Skippack and Salford Mennonite Meetinghouse Schools, 1747–1836. (Intercourse, PA: Good Books), 2003. 356pp., illus.
Contains pieces from the Kassel/Cassel family, Juniata College Special Collections.

Hershey, Milton C., 1895–
A Time to Every Purpose: The Memoirs of Milton C. Hershey. [n.p.]: author, 1983. xii, 236pp.
Deals among other things with the Heifer Project and the free ministry.

Hess, Maurice A., comp., 1888–1987
"Old German Baptists Called to Camp." Old Order Notes, no. 8 (Spring, 1985): 9–10.
OGBB conscientious objectors in World War I. See also his correspondence, listed under Benedict, Fred W., ed.

Hess, Robert A., 1928–
"Wholeness and Health in Contemporary Nigeria." Missiology, 11 (April, 1983): 185–200.
CB mission activity focusing on the Lafiya program.

Hieber, Albrecht and others
Servant of Christ, a Leader of the Church: The Life of Rev. A. P. Mai Sule Biu [1919–1992]. Mubi, Adamawa State, Nigeria: TEE College, Ekklesiyar 'Yan'uwa a Nigeria, 1994. 76, [16]pp.

Hildebrand, Jacob R., 1819–1908
A Mennonite Journal, 1862–1865: A Father's Account of the Civil War in the Shenandoah Valley, ed. John R. Hildebrand. Shipppensburg, PA: Burd Street Press, 1996. xv, 100pp.
Also refers to Brethren.

Hill, Samuel S., ed., 1927–
Encyclopedia of Religions in the South. Macon, GA: Mercer Press, 1984.
"Church of the Brethren" (pp. 163–64).

Hills, Julian, ed.
Common Life in the Early Church. Harrisburg, PA: Trinity Press International, 1999. 449pp.
A Festscrift for Graydon F. Snyder, former dean of Bethany Theological Seminary, with chapters by Richard B. Gardner, Donald E. Miller, Robert W. Neff, Kenneth M. Shaffer, Jr., Robert E. Wagoner, and Virginia Wiles, among others.

Hiner Church of the Brethren
The Bread of Life: A Collection of Recipes from Hiner Church of the Brethren. Collierville, TN: Fundcraft

Publishing, 1996. 124, 16pp.
Contains a photograph and brief history of the congregation.

Hinks, Donald R.
Brethren Hymnbooks and Hymnals, 1720–1884. Gettysburg, PA: Brethren Heritage Press, 1986. 205pp.
A bibliographical study.

"A consise History of Brethren Hymn Books and Hymnals 1720–1884." In: Report of the Proceedings of the Brethren World Assembly, July 15–18, 1992, . . . , ed. D. F. Durnbaugh, Elizabethtown, PA: Elizabethtown College/Brethren Encyclopedia, Inc., 1994, [88–96].

Hinson, E. Glenn, 1931–
Love at the Heart of Things: A Biography of Douglas V. Steere. Wallingford, PA: Pendle Hill Publications, 1998. xvi, 391pp.
Biography of an outstanding Quaker leader, with mention of Brethren, including aid to Finland (p. 154) and the Prague Peace Conference with Dale Aukerman (p. 223).

[Historical Committee]
History of the Stone Bridge Church of the Brethren. Hagerstown, MD: Dixie Press, 1971. 85pp., illus.
Also contains the history of the Licking Creek, Pleasant Ridge, Welsh Run, and Damascus Christian congregations.

Everett [PA] Church of the Brethren: 100th Anniversary, 1893–1993. Everett, PA: Shoppers Guide, 1993. [ii], 62pp.

Historical Committee, FGBC
A History of Grace Brethren Churches, Northern Atlantic District, 1956–1986. Gettysburg, PA: Brethren Heritage Press, 1991. 244pp.
Members of the committee were: Donald Hinks, Jeremiah Kauffman, James Knepper, Warren Tamkin, Roger Wambold, and Jerry Young.

Hochmann von Hochenau, Ernst Christoph, 1670–1721
"Confession of Faith," trans. William G. Willoughby. BLT, 48 (Winter/Spring, 2003: 1–17.

Hocker, Edward W., ed., 1873–
Genealogical Data Relating to the German Settlers of Pennsylvania . . . from Advertisements in German Newspapers published in Philadelphia and Germantown, 1743–1800. Baltimore: Genealogical Publishing Co., 1989. 242pp.

Hoecker, Ludwig, 1708–1791
Ephrata Cloister School Booklet: An 18th Century Textbook for Children, ed. Nadine A. Steinmetz; trans. Tamara S. Groff. Ephrata, PA: Ephrata Cloister Associates/Pennsylvania Historical and Museum Commission, 1988.

Hoff, Ernest G., 1890–1953, and Minnich, H. Spenser, 1893–1982
In My Name: The Church of the Brethren at Work in America. Elgin, IL: BP, [n.d.]. Video.
Re-release of 1937 film.

Hoffman, Vern, comp.
Reverend George Tarvin, 1742–1813, Virginia – Kentucky. [n.p.]: author, 1988.

Hoffmann, Barbara
Radikal-pietismus um 1700: Der Streit um das Recht auf eine neue Gesellschaft. Frankfurt/New York: Campus Verlag, 1996. 318pp.
Much detail on Wittgenstein developments, especially on "Mother" Eva von Buttlar and her group.

Hogan, Herbert, 1921–
Gladdys E. Muir: Professor, Peacemaker, Mystic. La Verne, CA: University of La Verne Press, 1998. vi, 116pp.
Biography of an outstanding CB teacher and peace educator.

Hogan, Jan
Gladdys Makes Peace. Elgin, IL: BP, 1985.
Children's book about Gladdys E. Muir.

Hogan-Albach, Susan
"Don't Call These Women Brethren." Christianity Today, 37 (Dec. 13, 1993): 65.

Höhn, Eberhard
"'Die Bittre Suse – oder das Gesäng der einsamen Turteltaube.' Konrad Beisel [sic] und seine Musik." Eberbacher Geschichtsblatt, 90 (April, 1991): 68–83.

Holl, David L.
The Holl Family, Including the Schrantz, Murray, and Daily Families. [n.p.: author], 1988. 60pp.

Hollinger, James E.
"Brethren Church Service in the World." In: The Brethren Presence in the World...: Proceedings of the 3rd Brethren World Assembly, July 23–26, 2003, ed. William R. Eberly. Philadelphia, PA: Brethren Encyclopedia, Inc., 2004, 108–09.

Holmes, Carl T.
"A Study of the Music of the 1747 Edition of Conrad Beissel's Das Gesäng der Einsamen and Verlassenen Turtel Taube . . . ." MA thesis, University of Southern California, 1959, v, 258pp.

Holmes, Shirley F.
The Switzer Family, Ancestors and Descendants of Benjamin Bowman Switzer. Midland, VA: author, 1983. 47pp.

Homan, Gerlof D., 1929–
American Mennonites and the Great War, 1914–1918. Scottdale, PA: Herald Press, 1994. 237pp.
Many references to Brethren.

Honeyman, Gale E. S. and McDaniel, Linda Kay Stephens
Descendants of John & Susanna (Ulrich) Deeter. Morgantown, PA: Masthof Press, 1998. 782pp.
Morrison's Cove, Bedford County, PA, family (citations lacking).

Hoover, Paul
Saigon, Illinois. New York: Vintage Contemporaries, 1988.
Poetry, experiences of a C.O.

Hoover, Susan Bame
Faith the Cow. Elgin, IL: BP, 1995. Unpaginated.
Illustrated by Maggie Sykora; a children's book about the Heifer Project.

Hopping, Carol Flora, comp.
The Family of Eli and Elizabeth Flora's Son, Henry Franklin Flora. [n.p.: author], 1985. Various pagination.

Horst, Paul D.
The Brethren Mutual Fire Insurance Company: The First Fifty Years of Service, 1897–1947. Hagerstown, MD: The Company, [1947]. 28pp.

Hostetler, Beulah Stauffer, 1926–
American Mennonites and Protestant Movements: A Community Paradigm. Scottdale, PA: Herald Press, 1987. 366pp.
Has references to the Brethren.

Hostetler, Harvey R., 1857–1939
Descendants of Barbara Hochstedler and Christian Stutzman. Scottdale, PA: Mennonite Publishing House, 1988.
Reprint of 1938 publication.

Hostetter, Richard L. and Bachman, David J.
Descendants of Jacob and Anna Hostetter of Engleside, Lancaster County, Pennsylvania, the Immigrants of 1712; Descendants of Oswald and Maria Hostetter of Warwick Township, Lancaster County, Pennsylvania, the Immigrants of 1732. Baltimore: Gateway Press, 1984. 222pp.

Hoy, Virginia Senseman
What Beautiful People! The Story of the Family of Samuel and Nancy Studebaker. Hamilton, GA: author, 1984. 167pp.

Hoyt, Herman A., 1909–
"James I. Boyer." Grace Theological Journal, 2/2 (Fall, 1981): 167–70.

"The Purpose and Program of the Prophetic Word." Grace Theological Journal, 4/2 (Fall, 1983): 163–71,

Studies in 2 Peter. Winona Lake, IN: BMH Books, 1983. 133pp.

"Alva J. McClain: Faithful, Honorable, Diligent." Fundamentalist Journal, 3/4 (Fall, 1984): 44–46.

The End Times. Winona Lake, IN: BMH Books, 1987. 256pp.
Originally published in 1969.

[special issue honoring Herman A. Hoyt]. Grace Theological Journal, 6/2 (Fall, 1985): 161–480.

Hubbard, Marilyn
A People of Living Faith: History and Memoirs of the Washington Creek [KS] Church of the Brethren. [n.p.]: 1985. vii, 167pp.

Huelsbergen, Helmut E.
"Stephen Koch (1695–1765), Brethren and Ephrata Leader: A Link Between the Pennsylvania Brethren and the Pietists Along the Lower Rhine." Unpubl. paper, Society of German-American Studies symposium, 1985.

Huffaker, John L., 1937–
Here Am I, Send Me: Monologues on Callings of Old Testament Leaders. Bloomington, IN: 1st Books, 2003. viii, 92pp.

Huffaker, Josephine Costello
Christian Gish of Virginia. [Baltimore, MD]: Gateway Press, 1989.

Huffman, Cathy Simmons
The Hagerstown Brethren: The First Hundred Years of the Hagerstown Church of the Brethren. Hagerstown, MD: Hagerstown Bookbinding and Printing Co., 1983. 198pp.

Huffman, Glenn
Wampler: The Descendants of Ben Wampler and Elizabeth Beery of August County, Virginia, 1701–1982. Washington, DC: author, 1982. 42pp.

Humphrey, Elwood F., 1908–
As I Remember. Craigsville, VA: author, ca.1990. 78pp.
The autobiography of a CB pastor.

Hunter, William A.
"German Settlers and Indian Warriors." Der Reggeboge/The Rainbow: Journal of the Pennsylvania-German Society, 3/3 (Sept. 1969): 12.

Hurd, Fred
"The Theology of Ephrata: The Roots and Unfoldment of Conrad Beissel's Creed." MA thesis, Mansfield University, 1981.

Hurt, Frank B.
The Heritage of the German Pioneers in Franklin County, Virginia. Roanoke, VA: Stone Printing Co., 1982. 47pp.

Inhauser, Marcos R.
1 Corinthians: The Community Struggles. Elgin, IL: BP, 1994. x, 83pp.
Covenant Bible Studies Series.

"Historical Highlights for the Igreja Da Irmandade Brazil." In: The Brethren Presence in the World...: Proceedings of the 3rd Brethren World Assembly, July 23–26, 2003, ed. William R. Eberly. Philadelphia, PA: Brethren Encyclopedia, Inc., 2004, 70–75.

Isherwood, Christopher, 1904–1986
Diaries: Volume One, 1939–1960. London: Methuen, 1996.
Also published in the U.S. by HarperCollins. Has information on an AFSC seminar held in La Verne College (sponsored by "Dunkards," pp. 161ff.) and on Rachel Garner, who aided at a Friends center for refugees in Haverford, PA (pp. 184, 194, 199–200, 211, 222, 225).

Jackson, Dave
Dial 911: Peaceful Christians and Urban Violence. Scottdale, PA: Herald Press, 1982. 47pp.
A leader's guide for group study.

Jackson, Dave and Jackson, Neta
Glimpses of Glory: Thirty Years of Community: The Story of Reba Place Fellowship. Elgin, IL: BP, 1987. 323pp., illus.
Co-affiliation with the Church of the Brethren and the Mennonite Church.

Jacob, Rebekah Leigh
"A Study of Pennsylvania German Iconography: A Common Language and Its Ephrata Variant." MA thesis, University of Mississippi, 2001.
Depends on the work and theses of John Joseph Stoudt.

Jagger, Bruce A.
Wigle and Wolf [Families]. [n.p.: author], 1984. 32pp.

Jamison, Ethel R.
"The Gascho Tour." Old Order Notes, no. 11 (Spring, 1990): 54–57.
Descendants (primarily OGBB) of John Gascho, Sr. (1784–1867), settler in Indiana.

Janzen, David and others
Fire, Salt, and Peace: Intentional Christian Communities Alive in North America. Evanston, IL: Shalom Mission Communities, 1996.
Contains chapters on the Plow Creek Community (pp. 122–25) and Reba Place Fellowship (pp. 128–33).

Jecker, Hanspeter
Ketzer, Rebellen, Heilige: Das Basler Täufertum von 1580–1700. Basel: Verlag des Kantons Basel-Landschaft, 1998. 664pp.
Material on the Bohni/Boni family (pp. 518, 532, 576), and announcement of research plans for further investigation of the role of Andreas Bohni in Swiss Pietism.

Jessup, Mary, 1950–
When God Calls. Elgin, IL: BP, 1997. x, 59pp.
Covenant Bible Studies Series.

Johansen, Ruthann Knechel
Listening in the Silence, Seeing in the Dark. Berkeley: University of California Press, 2002. 236pp.
On the brain injuries of her teenage son.

Johns, Loren, ed., 1955–
Apocalyticism and Millennialism: Shaping a Believers Church Eschatology for the Twenty-First Century. Kitchener, Ontario: Pandora Press, 2000.
Papers of the thirteenth conference on the Believers Church, Bluffton, OH, August 8–10, 1999, including one by D. F. Durnbaugh, "Anti-Modernism, Dispensationalism, and the Origins of Fundamentalism: A Response to [William V.] Trollinger" (pp. 282–89) and by Walter Sawatsky, "Eschatology and Social Ethics in Ecumenical Perspective: Reflections on the Prague Consultations" (pp. 309–25), in which Brethren have participated since 1986.

Johnson, Clara T.
Volunteer Service in Greece. Modesto, CA: Southern Mines Press, 1989. v, 143pp.
Work with the Greek Team, 1957–1961.

Johnstone, Mary Ann
A Pattern of Love: Brethren Village, 1897–1997. Morgantown, PA: Masthof Press, 1997. viii, 184pp., illus.

Jones, Timothy K., 1955–
Manchester College: A Century of Faith, Learning, and Service. No. Manchester, IN: Manchester College, 1989. viii, 271pp., illus.
Edited by William R. Eberly.

Juhnke, James C.
"Recent Trends Among Mennonites." In: Brethren in Transition: 20th Century Directions and Dilemmas, ed. Emmert F. Bittinger. Camden, ME: Penobscot Press, 1992, 113–21.

Juhnke, James C. and Hunter, Carol M.
The Missing Peace: The Search for Nonviolent Alternatives in United States History. Scottdale, PA: Herald Press, 2001. 321pp.
Second edition (2004).

Julien, Thomas, 1931–
"Brethrenism and Creeds." Grace Theological Journal, 6/2 (Fall, 1985): 373–81.

"The Grace Brethren Church in Missions." Old Order Notes, no. 10 (Spring, 1988): 28–30.
Seize the Moment: Stories of an Awesome God Empowering Ordinary People. Winona Lake, IN: Grace Brethren International Missions, 2000. 131pp.
Appendix: "Missionaries, 1900–2000, includes BC and GB personnel by nation served, with dates of service."

Juniata College
"Brethren in Deed." Huntingdon, PA: Juniata College, ca. 1990. Video.
Brethren involvement, past and present, in the college.

Jurisson, Cynthia Ann
"Federalist, Feminist, Revivalist: Harriet Livermore (1788–1868) and the Limits of Democratization in the Early Republic." PhD dissertation, Princeton Theological Seminary, 1994, ix, 338pp.

Karst, Theodor
"Johann Conrad Beissel in Thomas Manns 'Doktor Faustus.'" Jahrbuch der Deutschen Schillergesellschaft, 121 (1968): 543–85

Kasdorf, Julia, 1962–
Fixing Tradition: Joseph W. Yoder, Amish American. Telford, PA: Pandora Press, U.S., 2002. 280pp., illus.
Revised from "Fixing Tradition: The Cultural Work of Joseph W. Yoder and His Relationship with the Amish Community of Mifflin County, Pennsylvania," PhD dissertation, New York University, 1997, vi, 324pp., illus. Yoder (1872–1956), author of Rosanna of the Amish and other books, was associated for many years with Juniata College, the archives of which contain his papers (p. 87ff.).

Kates, Alberta
Danuel U. Stutzman, His Ancestors and Descendants. Livingston, TX; author, 1982. 77pp.

Kauffman, Henry J.
"Aunt Lydia." Pennsylvania Folklife, 34 (1984–85): 114–32.
Daughter of a "Dunkard bishop."

Kauffman, Jeremiah and others
A History of the Grace Brethren Church, Northern Atlantic District, 1956–1986. Gettysburg, PA: Brethren Heritage Press, 1991. 244pp.

Kauffman, Sandra
The Merkey Family of Bethel and Tulpehocken Townships [PA]. [n.p.: author], 1990. 285pp.

Kauffman, Stewart B., 1919–
Zella's Mountain. Elgin, IL: BP, 1999. [iii], 123pp., illus.
Biography of Zella Johns Gahagen (1899–1984), mine-owner and CB philanthropist.

Kaufman, Stanley A.
German Baptist Brethren in Eastern Ohio. Walnut Creek, OH: German Culture Museum, 1989. 82pp., illus.
Catalog of an exhibition.

Kaylor, Earl C., Jr., 1927–
"Church of the Brethren," in Penn's Example to the Nations: 300 Years of the Holy Experiment, ed. Robert G. Crist. Harrisburg, PA: Pennsylvania Council of Churches, 1987, pp. 45–53.

Martin Grove Brumbaugh: A Pennsylvanian's Odyssey from Sainted Schoolman to Bedeviled World War I Governor, 1862–1930. Madison, NJ: Fairleigh Dickinson University Press for Juniata College, 1996. 382pp.
The definitive biography of the CB educator and politician.

Juniata College, Uncommon Vision, Uncommon Loyalty: The History of an Independent College in Pennsylvania Founded by the Brethren, 1876–2001. Huntingdon, PA: Juniata College Press, 2001. xi, 403pp., illus.
A revision and expansion of his book, Truth Sets Free (1977), the centennial history.

Kaylor, Earl C., Jr., 1927–, and Kaylor, Harriet Beahm
From Home to Village: A Centennial History of the Village at Morrisons Cove. Martinsburg, PA: Village at Morrisons Cove, 2003.

Keeney, Mervin B.
"Church of the Brethren Presence in the World: 1953–2002." In: The Brethren Presence in the World…: Proceedings of the 3rd Brethren World Assembly, July 23–26, 2003, ed. William R. Eberly. Philadelphia, PA: Brethren Encyclopedia, Inc., 2004, 54–69.

Keim, Albert N., 1935–
The CPS Story: An Illustrated History of Civilian Public Service. Intercourse, PA: Good Books, 1990. 128pp.
A well-illustrated account of CPS during World War II.

Harold S. Bender, 1897–1962. Scottdale, PA: Herald Press, 1998. 590pp., illus.
Refers to the CB, M. R. Zigler, and the Brethren Service Committee.

Keim, Albert N., 1935–, and Stoltzfus, Grant M., 1916–1974
The Politics of Conscience: The Historic Peace Churches and America at War, 1917–1955. Scottdale, PA: Herald Press, 1988. 170pp.
Thorough study of conscientious objectors, including the Brethren.

Kent, Homer Austin, Jr., 1926–
The Pastoral Epistles: Studies in 1 and 2 Timothy and Titus. Chicago: Moody Press, 1958. 313pp.
Revised editions (Winona Lake, IN: BMH Books, 1982); (Chicago: Moody Press, 1982); (Chicago: Moody Press, 1986); (Salem, WI: Sheffield, 1993); also translated into French.

Gospel of Matthew, Wycliffe Bible Commentary. [n.p:] 1962.

Ephesians: The Glory of the Church. Chicago: Moody Press, 1971.
Also published (Winona Lake, IN: BMH Books, 1971). 128pp.
Also translated into Spanish.

Jerusalem to Rome: Studies in the Book of Acts. Grand Rapids, MI: Baker Book House, 1972. 202pp., illus.
Also published (Winona Lake, IN: BMH Books, 1972); translated into Russian.

The Epistle to the Hebrews: A Commentary. Grand Rapids, MI: Baker Book House, 1972. 303pp., illus.
Fourth edition (Winona Lake, IN: BMH Books, 1995).

Light in the Darkness: Gospel of John. Grand Rapids. MI: Baker Book House, 1974. 239pp., illus.
Also published (Winona Lake, IN: BMH Books, 1974).

The Freedom of God's Sons: Studies in Galatians. Grand Rapids, MI: W. B. Eerdmans, 1976. 191pp., illus.
Also published (Winona Lake, IN: BMH Books, 1976).

Treasures of Wisdom: Studies in Colossians and Philemon. Grand Rapids, MI: Baker Book House, 1978. 184pp., illus.
Also published (Winona Lake, IN: BMH Books, 1978).

A History of the Early Church – Studies in Acts. Winona Lake, IN: BMH Books, 1978. 168pp.
Efesios: La Gloria de la Iglesia. Spain: Publicaciones Portavoz Evangelico, 1981. 141pp.

Studies in the Gospel of Mark. Winona Lake, IN: BMH Books, 1981. 151pp.

A Heart Opened Wide: Studies on II Corinthians. Grand Rapids, MI: Baker Book House, 1982. 205pp., illus.
Also published (Winona Lake, IN: BMH Books, 1982).

Faith That Works: Studies in the Epistle of James. Grand Rapids, MI: W. B. Eerdmans, 1986. 203pp., illus.
Also published (Winona Lake, IN: BMH Books, 1986).

"Philippians, Colossians, Philemon." In: The Expositor's Bible Commentary, eds. Frank E. Gaebelein and others. Grand Rapids, MI: Zondervan, 1995, vol. 11.

Kennedy, Stephen J.
The Ancestors of Albina Johnson (Hoover) Lehr, rev. ed. [n.p.]: author, 1986. 178pp.
Revision of 1980 edition.

Kilian, Oskar
"Konrad Beissel (1691–1768): Gründer des Klosters Ephrata in Pennsylvanien." Eberbacher Geschichtsblatt, 56 (July 1957).

King, Bernard Nathan, 1906–
A Dunker Boy Becomes Ecumenical. Mechanicsburg, PA: Center Square Press for the author, [n.d.]. 204pp.
Autobiography of a CB pastor and executive.

Heritage and Promise. Mechanicsburg, PA: Center Square Press for the author, 1997.
Further memoirs.

Kinsey, Marjorie Blocher
Blough Family History. [n.p.: author], 1989. 264pp.

[Kinsey, Samuel, 1832–1883]
The Complete Editorial Writings of Samuel Kinsey, comp. James Zaiger. [n.p.: n.d.]. 262pp.
Taken from editorials in *The Vindicator*.

Kinsley, Bob
Alexander Mack: His Greatest Legacy. Nappanee, IN: Evangel Press for the author, 1996. 95pp.
Subtitle: "The Dilemma of the 19th Century Brethren; An Inquiry into the Challenges Encountered by the Church During the Century Past."
A combination of historical reflections and personal critical comment, with many inaccuracies.

Kintner, Elgin Perry, 1917–
A Family History and Tour Guide of Reuel B. Pritchett and Ella Poff, The Parents of Ethel Pritchett Kintner. A Memento on the Occasion of Ethel's Eightieth Birthday, 28 Aug. 1993. [Marysville, TN]: author, 1993. 310pp., illus.

Edward Kintner and Glada Snyder: An Ancestral Genealogy and Tour Guide. Marysville, TN: author, 1994. 320pp.

Events in the Life of Elgin Perry Kintner: A Personal Journey. [Marysville, TN]: author, 1997. 106pp.

Kinzie, Thomas A.
Jeremiah. Elgin, IL: BP, 1999. x, 72pp.
Covenant Bible Studies Series.

Kiracofe, Kathryn
A Dream–A Reality: Memoirs of 35 Years in India. Bridgewater, VA: author, 1988. 132pp.

Kirkpatrick, Truman
History of York Center [IL] Cooperative. [n.p.]: author, 1976. 75pp.
Co-founded by Brethren.

Kirschner, Ann
"From Hebron to Saron: The Religious Transformation of an Ephrata Convent." Winterthur Portfolio, 32 (1997): 39–63.
Derived from her like-titled MA thesis, University of Delaware, 1995.

Kline, Paul G., comp., 1901–
Cline-Kline Family History. Salem, MA: Higginson Book Co., 1997. xii, 484pp.
A reprint by Floyd R. and Kathryn Garst Mason of the 1971 original, with some additions by the Masons.

Kleiner, John W. and Lehmann, Helmut T., eds.
The Correspondence of Heinrich Melchior Mühlenberg. Volume 1, 1740–1747; Volume 2, 1748–1752. Camden, ME: Picton Press, 1993, 1997.
Translated from Kurt Aland, ed., *Die Korrespondenz Heinrich Melchior Mühlenbergs . . .* Band I: 1740–1752 (1986); many references to the Sauers.

Knauss, David C.
A Century of Servanthood at Midway [PA] Church of the Brethren, 1895–1995. Lancaster, PA: Brenneman Printing Co. for Midway Church of the Brethren, Lebanon, PA, 1995.

Knepper, Wayne F.
Wilhelm Knepper (1691–1755): His Life . . .His Faith . . . His Legacy. Ca. 1703. CD-ROM.

Kochheiser, Gary M.
"The Doctrine of Nonresistance: A Historical Survey with Special Attention Being Given to the Fellowship of Grace Brethren Churches and the Grace Brethren Church of Longview, Texas." DMin project, Trinity International University, Deerfield, IL. vii, 279pp.
Large portions of this thesis were published in *Old Order Notes*, nos. 26 (pp. 45–88) and 27 (pp. 7–48).

Kostlevy, William
"A Persistant Sectarian Community: James Quinter and the Nineteenth Century Reformulation of Brethren Identity." In: The Dilemma of Anabaptist Piety: Strengthening or Straining the Bonds of Community?, ed. Stephen L. Longenecker. Camden, ME: Penobscot Press, 1997, 85–91.

"Eschatology, Mission and American Destiny: Brethren and the Moral Equivalent of Imperialism." BLT, 46 (Winter/Spring, 2001): 103–111.

"The Spirituality of John Kline." In: Papers From the Elder John Kline Bicentennial Celebration, ed. William R. Eberly. Ambler, PA: Brethren Encyclopedia, Inc., 2002, 1–6.

Kraft, John L.
Ephrata Cloister: An Eighteenth-Century Religious Commune. Harrisburg, PA: Pennsylvania Historical and Museum Commission, 1980.
A booklet written by a site manager of the Cloister.

Kraybill, Donald B.
"Yieldedness and Accountability in Traditional Anabaptist Communities." In: Anabaptist Currents: History in Conversation with the Present, eds. Carl F. Bowman and Stephen L. Longenecker. Camden, ME: Penobscot Press, 1995, 269–80.

The Riddle of Amish Culture, revised ed. Baltimore: Johns Hopkins University Press, 2001, 397pp.

Kraybill, Donald B., 1945–, and Bowman, Carl F.
On the Backroad to Heaven: Old Order Hutterites, Mennonites, Amish, and Brethren. Baltimore: Johns Hopkins University Press, 2001. xvii, 331pp.
Comparative discussions show which values and practices unite these groups and also wherein they differ. Chapter V (pp. 137–78) describes the Brethren.

Kraybill, Donald B., 1945–, and Hostetter, C. Nelson
Anabaptist World USA. Scottdale, PA: Herald Press, 2001. 296pp., illus.
Contains an essay on "The Brethren" (pp. 79–91); provides detailed information on membership, locations of congregations, addresses, and resource materials for all Brethren bodies.

Kraybill, Donald B., 1945–, and Peachey, Linda Gehman, eds.
Where Was God on Sept. 11? Seeds of Faith and Hope. Scottdale, PA: Herald Press, 2002. 215pp.
Anthology of responses to the attacks on the World Trade Towers and the Pentagon, from members of the Historic Peace Churches and others.

Kreider, J. Kenneth
A Cup of Cold Water: The Story of Brethren Service. Elgin, IL: BP, 2001. xv, 588pp., illus.
A thorough recounting of BSC activity around the world, from its beginnings through 1969. Appendix VI contains a list of "BVS Personnel, Units 1–81, 1948–1968" (pp. 491–567).

Kreider, Robert S., 1919–
Looking Back into the Future. North Newton, KS: Mennonite Press, 1998. xx, 302pp.
Memoirs of a General Conference Mennonite leader with many contacts with the Brethren, especially in post-World War II Germany.

Kroh, Andreas and Lückel, Ulf
Wittgensteiner Pietismus in Portraits: Ein Beitrag zur Geschichte des radikalen Pietismus in Wittgenstein. Bruchsal: Horn-Verlag, 2003. 189pp., illus.
Thirty-three documented biographical sketches of the leading actors among Radical Pietists in Wittgenstein during the first half of the eighteenth century, including E. C. Hochmann von Hochenau (pp. 73–77), Alexander Mack (pp. 83–87), Christoph Sauer (pp. 171–72).

[Krupp, Abraham]
Watchman of the Night and Millennial Morning: A Voice from the Land Shadowed with Wings, to the Church in the Wilderness . . . the Church of Philadelphia, whether in Palestine or America, etc. . . . . Philadelphia: author, 1833.
Designated as No. 1, Vol. 1. Authorship attributed by A. H. Cassel (PHuJ).

Kuhn, Gertrud
USA – Deutschland – Baden und Württemberg: Eine Auswahl von Titeln zur Auswanderung und zur Geschichte der Deutsch-Amerikaner vor allem aus Baden und Württemberg, von den Anfängen bis zum Ende des Zweiten Weltkrieges. Stuttgart: Institut für Auslandsbeziehungen, 1976.
Conrad Beissel (pp. 46–47).

Kulp, Isaac Clarence, Jr.
"The Order." Der Reggeboge/The Rainbow, 29/1 (1995): 1–12.
Traditions of the "Plain People," including Brethren.

Kulp, Philip M. ed.
[Special issue on Church of the Brethren missions]. BLT, 29 (Spring, 1984): 67–127.
Essays by: Ivan Eikenberry, Desmond W. Bittinger, Shantilal P. Bhagat, Nywa D. Balami, Karen and Rene Calderon, Wendell Flory, and Robert A. Hess.

Kult, G. D.
"Friends, Brothers, and Some Sisters: Using Cultural Research to Guide the Merger of Two Seminaries." Review of Higher Education, 19 (1996): 71–95.

Kuroiwa, Wallace Ryan
In the Beginning. Elgin, IL: BP, 1993. ix, 65pp.
Covenant Bible Studies Series.

"Events in the Internment of the Japanese in America During World War II: An Interpretation According to the Ethics of Character." 420pp.
PhD dissertation, Emory University, 1983.

Kurtz, Henry, 1796–1874
Zeugnisse der Alten von der christlichen Taufe, wie Dieselbe von der Apostel Zeit an Geübt Werden Sey. [n.p.: n.d.] 12pp.

Lair, Bonnie Layman
Lair Family of Ohio, ed. Carol Constance Younger Boyer. Troy, OH: author, 1988. 20, [vii]pp.

Lamb, Ardis Krieg
The True Identity of Christina (Mack) Gorgas, Wife of Jacob Gorgas, Clockmaker, Germantown, Philadelphia County, PA, and Ephrata, Lancaster County, PA, Time Period, 1734–1763. Marcellus, MI: author, 1990. 21pp.

Landes, Alva D.
The William and Lucinda Landes Family of Montgomery County, Ohio. [n.p.: author], 1987. 83pp.

Landes, Wallace B., 1952–
"Radical Pietism and Contemporary Religious Experience." DMin thesis, Princeton Theological Seminary, 1998.
Much of its content was published in a special issue of BLT, 45 (Winter/Spring, 1998): 1–116. Includes contributions by Wallace B. Landes, Jr., Dale W. Brown, Christina Bucher, Donald E. Miller, Robert W. Neff, and Edward L. Poling.

Landis, James E.
Landis/Landes Family (John Landis of Colalico [Cocalico] Township, Lancaster, PA, and Descendants. Salt Lake City, UT: Church of Jesus Christ of Latter-Day Saints, 1997. Microfilm.

Lane, Elizabeth Miller
A Genealogical Index of Martin Weybright III [1756–1827] of Montgomery County, Ohio. Trotwood, OH: author, 1999. 16pp.

Lange, Andrea
"Die Gestalt der Friedenskirche: Offentliche Verantwortung und Kirchenverständnis in der neueren mennonitischen Diskussion." Paper, Theologische Fakultät, Heidelberg University, 1985.
With references to the Brethren.
Well-illustrated 32-page journal featuring folksongs and stories.

The Highland Avenue [Elgin, IL] Church of the Brethren Centennial Encyclopedia: An Abcedarium Celebrating 100 Years of Faith, Life, and History, 1899–1999. Elgin, IL: Highland Avenue Church of the Brethren, 1999. 145pp.
Because of the location of the central church offices at Elgin, this congregational record has broader significance for Brethren history.

Lehman, James H., and others, eds.
Without Fear or Hesitation. An Interactive Encounter with the Early Brethren. CD-ROM, ca. 2002.

Lehmann, Hartmut
"Transatlantic Migration, Transatlantic Networks, Transatlantic Transfer." In: In Search of Peace and Prosperity, eds. Hartmut Lehmann and others. University Park, PA: Pennsylvania State University Press, 2000, pp. 307–30.
Compares Benjamin Franklin and Christoph Sauer I.

Lehmann, Hartmut and others, eds.
In Search of Peace and Prosperity: New German Settlements in Eighteenth-Century Europe and America. University Park, PA: Pennsylvania State University Press, 2000. xii, 332pp.
Many of the essays included in this volume refer to Dunkers and the Sauer family of printers in Germantown.

Leibungutt, Peter
The Peter Leibungutt Journal, ed. Lois Mast. Elverson, PA: Mennonite Family History, 1991. 118pp.
About an Amish family that became Brethren.

Leonard, Rosalita J., 1944–
"Write On, Sisters: An Analysis of the Writings of Women in the Church of the Brethren, 1851–1950." MA thesis, Northern Illinois University, 1994, 143pp.

Leonard, Rosalita J., 1944– and others, eds.
Gospel Messenger Obituary Index. Elgin, IL: Brethren Historical Library and Archives, 2000. CD-Rom disk.

Lerg, Winfried B., ed.
Deutschsprachige Kolonialpublizistik am Vorabend der Amerikanischen Revolution: Fünf Beiträge zur Funktion deutscher Drucker und ihrer Periodika. Münster: LIT Verlag, 1999. 216pp.
Focuses on J. C. Sauer and J. H. Müller in Pennsylvania.

Lewellen, Clifford Peters
Genealogy and Family History of Peters-Lewellen Families in America. [n.p.]: 1951.

Lewis, Ed, ed.,
Biblical Beliefs: A Study in Grace Brethren Doctrine. Book 2. Winona Lake, IN: CE National, 1988.
Also published in a youth version.

Linder, Wilbur
The Families of John Peter Butterbaugh. Portland, IN: author, [n.d.].

Puterbaugh: History of the George Puterbaugh (1737–1800), Wife Christina Adams, Family Through His Eldest Son, Jacob Puterbaugh (1757–1822), Wife Susanna Ulerich (1759–1830) . . . . Portland, IN: author, [n.d.]. 69pp.

Link, Donald M.
The Wine Family in America – Section IV: The Descendants of Daniel Wine (1777–1863), Son of Michael Wine (1774–1822). [Mt. Sydney, VA:] author, 2000. xvii, 1010pp.

Little Swatara Church of the Brethren
225th Anniversary of Little Swatara [PA] Church of the Brethren, 1757–1982. Bethel, PA: Little Swatara Church of the Brethren, 1982. 28pp.

Logan, Linda
Fruit of the Vine: A Study Guide. Elgin, IL: BP, 1998. 56pp.

"Christian Education of Children: Passing Our Faith on to Our Children." In: Report of the Proceedings of the 1998 Brethren World Assembly, Bridgewater College . . . , ed. Dale R. Stoffer. Ashland, OH: Ashland Theological Seminary/Brethren Encyclopedia, Inc., 1999, 203–18.

Long, Inez Goughnour, 1917–
Pastor and People. Lancaster, PA: author, 1974.
Sermons by John D. Long.

Lord's Day Morning. Work and Worship the Brethren Way. Lititz, PA: Forry and Hacker, 1989. vii, 246pp.
Autobiography, with account of the pastoral ministry of John D. Long.

Exiles from Home. [New Oxford, PA: author], 2003. ii, 139pp.

Longenecker, Stephen L.
Selma's Peacemaker: Ralph Smeltzer and Civil Rights Mediation. Philadelphia: Temple University Press, 1987. xii, 273pp.

"The Church of the Brethren Washington Office: Twenty-Five Years." BLT, 32 (Autumn, 1987): 225–36.
Co-written with Kenneth L. Gibble.

"Democracy's Pulpit: Egalitarianism Among Pennsylvania German Sectarians in the 18th Century." BLT, 33 (Summer, 1988): 191–99.

"Modern, Non-Brethren Historians and the Early Dunkards." BLT, 35 (Fall, 1990): 298–301.

"From Urban Village to Urban Society: The Church of the Brethren and Modern America." In: Brethren in Transition: 20th Century Directions and Dilemmas, ed. Emmert F. Bittinger. Camden, ME: Penobscot Press, 1992, 29–37.

"*Wachet Auf*: Awakening, Diversity and Tolerance among Early Pennsylvania Germans." In: Nonviolent America: History through the Eyes of Peace, eds. Louise Hawkley and James C. Juhnke. North Newton, KS: Bethel College, 1993, 227–43.

Piety and Tolerance: Pennsylvania German Religion, 1700–1850. Metuchen, NJ: Scarecrow Press, 1994. 195pp.

Pietist and Wesleyan Studies, No. 6.
A view of the pietistic sub-culture of German immigrant religion, with much on the Brethren.

"Emotionalism Among Early American Anabaptists." In: The Dilemma of Anabaptist Piety: Strengthening or Straining the Bonds of Community?, ed. Stephen L. Longenecker. Camden, ME: Penobscot Press, 1997, 61–67.

"John Kline's Preaching." In: Papers From the Elder John Kline Bicentennial Celebration, ed. William R. Eberly. Ambler, PA: Brethren Encyclopedia, Inc., 2002, 36–39.

"Slavery in John Kline's Virginia and Shenandoah Valley." In: Papers From the Elder John Kline Bicentennial Celebration, ed. William R. Eberly. Ambler, PA: Brethren Encyclopedia, Inc., 2002, 58–63.

Shenandoah Religion: Outsiders and the Mainstream, 1716–1785. Waco, TX: Baylor University Press, 2002. xiv, 247pp.
Includes Brethren.

Longenecker, Stephen L., ed.
The Dilemma of Anabaptist Piety: Strengthening or Straining the Bonds of Community? Camden, ME: Penobscott Press for Forum for Religious Studies, Bridgewater College, 1997. 237pp.
Proceedings of the symposium held in September, 1995; those presenting papers included: John D. Roth, Dale R. Stoffer, Hans Schneider, Stephen L. Longenecker, Victor G. Doerksen, William Kostlevy, Susan Fisher Miller, Robert Wuthnow, Courtney Bender, Nadine Pence Frantz, Phyllis Carter and Marlene Kropf, Ronald C. Arnett, Al Dueck, Lois Barrett, and Lauree Hersch Meyer.

Special issue "Brethren and the End Times." BLT, 46 (Winter/Spring, 2001): 1–138.

With essays by: Stephen L. Longenecker, Carol A. Scheppard, Marcus Meier, Hedwig T. Durnbaugh, D. F. Durnbaugh, Michael Hodson, Dale R. Stoffer, Christina Bucher, William Kostlevy, Robert G. Clouse, Brenda B. Colijn, and Murray L. Wagner, Jr.

Longenecker Family
Longenecker Family Newsletter. Volume 1, No. 1 (January/February, 1999).

Published six times a year by Richard Cryer, Greenwich, CT, on behalf of the Langenegger/Langenecker/Longenecker/Longacker and related families.

Lord, Charles R.
"The Response of the Historic Peace Churches to the Internment of the Japanese Americans during World War II." MATh thesis, Associated Mennonite Biblical Seminaries, [n.d.], v, 115pp.

Lorsong, Gernot G., 1940–
Taufe Uns, Alexander. Kurpfälzer Geschichte der Dunker (German Baptist Brethren). Karlsruhe: INFO Verlagsgesellschaft, 1990. 299pp.
Contains many inaccuracies.

Ladenburg: Von den Steinzeiten bis Heute. Karlsruhe: INFO Verlagsgesellschaft, 1994. 235pp.
Birthplace of J. C. Sauer I.

Louis, Jeanne Henriette, ed.
Separation from the World for American Peace Churches: Asset or Handicap? York, UK: Sessions Book Trust, 1997. x, 62pp.
Derived from a workshop at the conference of the European Association for American Studies, Luxembourg, 1994.

Lovejoy, David S.
Religious Enthusiasm in the New World: Heresy to Revolution. Cambridge, MA/London: Harvard University Press, 1985.
Ephrata (pp. 161, 168).

Lowe, John W., Jr., 1944–
"Brethren and Native Americans: An Unfilled History." BLT, 38 (Summer, 1993): 137–50.

Lowery, Richard H.
Revelation: Hope for the World in Troubled Times. Elgin, IL: BP, 1994. x, 85pp.
Covenant Bible Studies Series.

Lowry, James W., 1934–
The *Martys' Mirror* Made Plain: A Study Guide and Further Studies. Aylmer, ON/Lagrange, IN: Pathway Publishers, 1997.
On the early translation by A. Mack, Jr. and the complete translation by Peter Miller, with final publication by the Ephrata Society, 1748–49 (pp. 80–81).

Luthy, David
"The German Psalter: A Popular Pennsylvania Book." Pennsylvania Mennonite Heritage, 8/2 (1985): 2–5.
C. Sauer imprints.

"The Ephrata Martyrs' Mirror: Shot from Patriots' Muskets." Pennsylvania Mennonite Heritage, 9/1 (1986): 44.

"The First Century of German Bibles Printed in North America." Pennsylvania Mennonite Heritage, 13/4 (1990): 32–37.

McCann, Samuel N., 1858–1917
Outline and Exegetical Study of Hebrews. Lititz, PA: Express Printing Co., [n.d.]. 16pp.

Mack, Alexander, Sr., 1679–1735
The Complete Writings of Alexander Mack, ed. William R. Eberly. Winona Lake, IN: BMH Books/Brethren Encyclopedia, Inc., 1993. 120pp.
Translations taken from *European Origins of the Brethren* (1958) and *Brethren in Colonial America* (1967).

McClendon, James William, 1924–2000
Systematic Theology. Nashville, TN: Abingdon Press, 1988–2000.
In three volumes: Ethics, Doctrine, and Witness.

McDaniel, Jewel N., ed.
Autobiography of Grace Courtney Beam McDaniel and Genealogy of the Beam and McDaniel Families. [n.p.]: author, 1983. 81pp.

McFadden, Dan
"Brethren Volunteer Service." In: The Brethren Presence in the World…: Proceedings of the 3rd Brethren World Assembly, July 23–26, 2003, ed. William R. Eberly. Philadelphia, PA: Brethren Encyclopedia, Inc., 2004, 102–07.

McFadden, Joyce S.
"[The] Church of the Brethren's Stance on Alcohol, Tobacco, Drugs and Recovery." Journal of Ministry in Addiction & Recovery, 4/2 (1997): 39–51.

McFadden, Wendy Chamberlain
The Story Behind The Touch of the Master's Hand. Elgin, IL: Brethren Press, 1997. Unpaginated, illus.
Describes the origin and wide circulation of the poem by Myra Brooks Welch (1877–1959).

MacMaster, Richard K., 1935–
Land, Piety, Peoplehood: The Establishment of Mennonite Communities in America, 1683–1790. Scottdale, PA: Herald Press, 1985. 343pp., illus.
The Mennonite Experience in America Series, Volume 1, with many references to the Brethren.

Elizabethtown: The First Three Centuries. Elizabethtown, PA: Elizabethtown Historical Society, 1999. xii, 323pp.
Elizabethtown College (pp. 163–65) and Elizabethtown CB (pp. 234–35).

Main, Kari M.
"Illuminated Hymnals of the Ephrata Cloister." Winterthur Portfolio, 12 (1997): 65–78.

Mallett, Manley W.
All Those Newcomer Families in Maryland. Decorah, IA: author, 1982. 48pp.

[Mannhardt, Jacob]
"Ein Sommer unter der Tunkers." Mennonitische Blätter, 13 (May, 1866): 43–45.
Reprints an article from the Volksblatt für Stadt und Land on an annual meeting and love feast in (West) Virginia.

Maple Press Company
The Cloister in Ephrata. York, PA: Maple Press Company, [n.d.]. 16pp.
The Printed Page Series, No. 9.

Marquet, Cynthia
"A Brief History of the Ephrata Cloister Lower Mill." Journal of the Historical Society of the Cocalico Valley, 27 (2002): 2–13.

Marsden, Parker G., ed.
Special issue, BLT, on "Theological Reflections on Vocations." BLT, 46 (Summer/Fall, 2001): 139–255.
By twenty authors, predominantly from the Church of the Brethren.

Martin, Donna Ritchey
Ephesians: Reconciled in Christ. Elgin, IL: BP, 1994. viii, 62pp.
Covenant Bible Studies Series.

Martin, Harold S., 1930–
Let's See Your Tongue! An Explanation of James 3: 1–12. Hanover, PA: Bible Helps, 1970–79?. [8]pp.

The Scriptural Headveiling. Minerva, OH: A-M Publications, 1981. 11pp.

Glimpses from the Book of Revelation. Elgin, IL: BP, 1981.

Biblical Reliability. Harrisonburg, VA: Sword and Trumpet, 1983. [8]pp.

Biblical Inerrancy and Reliability. Harrisonburg, VA: Fellowship of Concerned Mennonites, 1985. 44pp.

Expository Studies in Colossians. York, PA: Brethren Revival Fellowship, 1985. 39pp.

What Every New Christian Ought to Know. Hanover, PA: Bible Helps, 1980–1986?. 24pp.

New Testament Beliefs and Practices (A Brethren Understanding). Elgin, IL: BP, 1989. 123pp.

Glimpses of the Past: A Study of Brethren Heritage (A Series of 13 Lessons): The History and Beliefs of the Church of the Brethren. [Lititz, PA]: author, 2001. 103, [i]pp.

Colossians and Philemon. Ephrata, PA: Brethren Revival Fellowship, 2003. 136pp.
Brethren New Testament Commentary Series.

James and Jude. Ephrata, PA: Brethren Revival Fellowship, 2003. 148pp.
Brethren New Testament Commentary Series..

Mason, Dorotha Wenger Fry, 1926–
Mystery and Glory in John's Gospel. Elgin, IL: BP, 1992. 86pp.
Covenant Bible Studies Series.

J. O. [Winger] (1891–1947); Another Real One. No. Manchester, IN; author, 1998. viii, 110pp.

Mason, Floyd R.
John Zigler and Elizabeth Kline of Virginia. [Alexandria, VA]: author, 1984. 20pp.

Michael Miller of 1692. [Alexandria, VA]; author, 1986. 20pp.
A genealogy of the immigrant Michael Miller.

Eld. John P. Zigler [1875–1907] of Maryland, Virginia: Diaries 1880, 1881, 1891, 1907. Bridgewater, VA: author, 1998. 32, 109pp.

Mason, Floyd R. and Mason, Kathryn Garst, 1921–
John Mason [1802–1870] & Mary Ann Miller of Virginia. Bridgewater, VA: authors, 1986. 367pp.
A genealogy of a Virginia family and its descendants in Indiana, Missouri, and Ohio.

Ziegler, Zeigler, Zigler Family Records, Revised. [Alexandria, VA]: authors, 1990. 672pp.
A genealogy of Philip Ziegler and Regina Requel Ziegler of Berks Co., PA, and their descendants in Virginia, Indiana, and Ohio.

Shank Family Record. Bridgewater, VA: authors, 1992.
A genealogy of Michael Shank of Pennsylvania and Virginia.

The Michael Miller [1652–1771] and Susanna Bechtel Family Record, 2nd ed. Bridgewater, VA: authors, 1993. iii, 1008pp.
A genealogy of Michael Miller and Susannah Bechtl Miller of Pennsylvania and Maryland and their descendants in Virginia, Ohio, and farther west.

MASON, FLOYD R.

Mathias Miller [1743–1805] & His 17 Children, 2nd ed. Bridgewater, VA; authors, 1996. 137pp.

A genealogy of a Berks Co., PA, family and descendants in Virginia, Indiana, Ohio, and farther west.

George Klein Sr. Family Record. Bridgewater, VA: authors, 1997. 143pp.

A genealogy of George Klein and Dorothy Rebman Klein and their sons Philip and David, in Pennsylvania, Virginia, Texas, and Oklahoma.

Also published: Salem, MA: Higginson Book Co., 1994.

A Wampler Family Record. Bridgewater, VA: authors, 1996. 483pp.

A genealogy of Hans Peter Wampler of Pennsylvania and Maryland and his descendants in Virginia and the West.

Niclous Garber [d. 1748] Family Record. Bridgewater, VA: authors, [1997]. 310pp.

A genealogy of Niclous and Elizabeth Garber of Pennsylvania, Maryland, and Virginia, and their descendants.

John H. Garber and Barbara Miller of Pennsylvania, Maryland, and Oregon. [Bridgewater, VA]: authors, 1998. 153pp.

Mason, Rae Hungerford
The Inimitable George Mason. [n.p.]: author, 1991. xvii, 376pp., illus.

A biography based largely on correspondence.

Mathis, Jefferson, 1897–
Jeff's Stories: Told by Jefferson Mathis in His Eighty-Eighth Year, 1986, ed. Inez Goughnour Long. [La Verne, CA.]: author, 1987. vi, 116pp.

May, Melanie A.
"Now Is The Time So Urgent: Called Into God's Future." In: Brethren in Transition: 20th Century Directions and Dilemmas, ed. Emmert F. Bittinger. Camden, ME: Penobscot Press, 1992, 221–28.

Mayer, Robin Wentworth, 1955–
Stepping Stones for Stumbling Saints. Elgin, IL: BP, 2001.

Meador, Michael L.
"Overview of Home Schooling." In: Report of the Proceedings of the 1998 Brethren World Assembly, Bridgewater College . . . , ed. Dale R. Stoffer. Ashland, OH: Ashland Theological Seminary/Brethren Encyclopedia, Inc., 1999, 219–25.

Meadors, Gary T., ed.
New Testament Essays in Honor of Homer A. Kent, Jr. Winona Lake, IN: BMH Books, 1991. 294pp.

"Biographical Sketch" by Ronald T. Clutter (pp. 9–15); "Bibliography of Articles, Books, and Reviews by Homer A. Kent, Jr." (pp. 289–94).

Mease, Gladys Price (Nyce), ed.
The Abraham and Susan (Alderfer) Price Family, Their Ancestors and Descendants. Harleysville, PA: Nyce Manufacturing Company, Inc., 1991. 121pp.

Mease, Gladys Price (Nyce) and Hartzel, Gwendolyn Price (Nyce).
The Abraham and Leanna (Goshall) Nyce Family. Harleysville, PA: Nyce Manufacturing Company, 1986. 109pp.

Memoirs of a teacher, writer, and pastor's wife.

Meier, Marcus
"Eberhard Ludwig Grüber's Basic Questions: Report of a Discovery." BLT, 42 (Summer/Fall, 1997): 64–67.

An unique copy of Gruber's Grundforschende Fragen (1713), answered by A. Mack, Sr., in MS form. It had previously been thought that both questions and answers were published together in 1713.

"Mack, Alexander." In: Biographisch-Bibliographisches Kirchenlexikon, ed. Friedrich Wilhelm Bautz. Hamm: Verlag Traugott Bautz, 2001.

"Early Brethren Eschatology: A Contribution to Brethren Beginnings." BLT, 46 (Winter/Spring, 2001): 17–28.

"Die Anfange der Schwarzenauer Neutäufer: Genese einer radikalpietistischen Gemeinschaftsgründung." PhD dissertation, Philipps-Universität Marburg, 2003, [iv], 365pp.

Meinicke, Elka and Fillbrunn, Günter
"Ueber eine amerikanische Kirche Schriesheimer Ursprungs, Teil 1." Schriesheimer Jahrbuch 1998, 2 (1998): 58–91.

"Ueber eine amerikanische Kirche Schriesheimer Ursprungs, Teil 2." Schriesheimer Jahrbuch 1999, 3 (1999): 107–31.

"Ueber eine amerikanische Kirche Schriesheimer Ursprungs, Teil 3." Schriesheimer Jahrbuch, 4 (2000): 130–59.

All three articles describe the OGBB.

Melton, J. Gordon, ed., 1942–
Biographical Dictionary of American Cult and Sect Leaders. New York: Garland Publishing, Inc., 1986.

Contains: "Beissel, Johann Conrad" (pp. 27–29); "Mack, Alexander, Sr." (pp. 167–68).

The Encyclopedia of American Religions: Religious Creeds. First Edition. Detroit, MI: Gale Research Company, 1987.

Chapter 9, European Free-Church Family, Brethren: "We Believe (Association of Fundamental Gospel Churches)" (p. 437); "Affirmation of Faith (Ashland Theological Seminary, Brethren Church [Ashland, Ohio])" (pp. 437–38); "A Declaration of Faith (Church of the Brethren)" (pp. 440–41); "A Statement of Belief and Purpose (Church of the Brethren)" (p. 441); "Bible Teachings (Dunkard Brethren)" (pp. 441–43); "The Message of the Brethren Ministry (Fellowship of Grace Brethren Churches)" (pp. 444–46); "Doctrinal Statement of the Old German Baptist Brethren" (446–48).

The Encylopdia of American Religions. Second Edition. Detroit, MI: Gale Research Company, 1987.

Chapter Eight, European Free-Church Family, The Brethren (p. 53).

Metsker, Shirley and Metsker, Gary
Metsker Recollections. [Brighton, CO]: authors, 1983. 107pp.

Meyer, Lauree Hersch
"Reflections on Pneumatology in the Church of the Brethren Tradition." Greek Orthodox Theological Review, 31/3–4 (Fall/Winter, 1986): 389–400.

"Liturgy, Tradition, and Ministry in the Church of the Brethren." BLT, 34 (Autumn, 1989): 198–211.

"Fencerow Theology: Spiritual Openness to the Cosmic God." In: The Dilemma of Anabaptist Piety: Strengthening or Straining the Bonds of Community?, ed. Stephen L. Longenecker. Camden, ME: Penobscot Press, 1997, 183–98.

Miller, Daniel
"Conrad Weiser as a Monk." Transactions of the Historical Society of Berks County, 3 (1921): 169–81.

Miller, Donald E., 1929–
"The Influence of Gottfried Arnold on the Brethren." Old Order Notes, no. 19 (Spring-Summer, 1999): 61–71.
Reprinted from BLT 5 (Summer, 1960).

"The Historic Peace Churches and the Origin of 'The Decade to Overcome Violence.'" BLT, 48 (Summer/Fall, 2003): 148–58.

Miller, Gene Edwin
As A Good Soldier of King Immanuel: A History and a Genealogy of David Y. Miller (1809–1898). Irvine, CA: author, 1937. xvi, 666

The History and Genealogy of David Y. Miller, 1809–1898. [n.p.: author], 1989. 666pp.

Miller, J. William, 1911–1997
Sammeln und Wiedersammeln/Collections and Recollections. Arcanum, OH: Lew Williams Printing for the author, 1989. 352pp., illus.
By an OGBB elder and historian.

Doctrinal Reproductions. [Arcanum, OH]: author, 1989. 585pp.
Contains: Jeremias Felbinger's *Christian Handbook* (1651, 1975), Alexander Mack's *Ground Searching Questions and Rites and Ordinances* (1715), Peter Nead's *Primitive Christianity* (1834), and Samuel Kinsey's *Pious Companion* (1865).

Miller, Jacob L., Jr. and Miller, Arlene Thomas, eds.
A Market Family: The David and Ella Markey Freindschaft. York, PA: York Graphic Services, Inc., 1991. 136pp. illus.

Miller, James F.
Our Michael Krousz's Line. [n.p.: author, 1987]. 74pp.

Miller, Karen Peterson
Disciplines for Spiritual Growth. Elgin, IL: BP, [n.d.].

Miller, Leslie, ed.
Lest We Forget. [n.p.: n.d.]. 66pp.
Notes of OGBB meetings dealing with conscription during World War II, including communications with government officials.

Miller, Marcus
"Marriage in the Meetinghouse." Old Order Notes, no. 9 (Fall, 1986): 52–53.
Practices among the OGBB.

"Mission: Old German Baptist Brethren." Old Order Notes, no. 10 (Spring, 1988): 37–42.

"The Annual Meeting of the Brethren: Its Development and Operation." Old Order Notes, no. 16 (Fall/Winter, 1997): 7–34.

Miller, Randall M. and Pencak, William, eds.
Pennsylvania: A History of the Commonwealth. Harrisburg: Pennsylvania Museum and Historical Commission, 2002. 688pp., illus.
Dunkards (pp. 373, 547); Ephrata (pp. 79, 80, 366, 373, 432, 517, 547); German Baptist Brethren (p. 79); Juniata College (;. 432); C. Saur (p. 110); Snow Hill (p. 79). Has some inaccuracies.

Miller, Robert R.
"Concerning Coming Together." In: Anabaptist Currents: History in Conversation with the Present, eds. Carl F. Bowman and Stephen L. Longenecker. Camden, ME: Penobscot Press, 1995, 101–25.

Miller, Susan Fisher
"John S. Coffman's Mennonite Revivalism." In: The Dilemma of Anabaptist Piety: Strengthening or Straining the Bonds of Community?, ed. Stephen L. Longenecker. Camden, ME: Penobscot Press, 1997, 93–104.

Miller, Timothy, ed., 1944–
America's Alternative Religions. Albany: State University of New York Press, 1995.
The chapter on "The Anabaptists" by D. F. Durnbaugh includes the Brethren (pp. 13–22).

Mines, Cynthia
McPherson College: The First Century, 1887–1987. McPherson, KS: McPherson College, 1987. 26pp., illus.

Ministry of Reconciliation
Crossroads: Ministry of Reconciliation Newsletter. 1995ff.
Administered by the On Earth Peace Assembly, Inc., New Windsor, MD, for the Church of the Brethren; published three times a year.

Mitchell, Olden D., 1912–
"A Brief History of Brethren Evangelism." BLT, 35 (1990): 199–204.

"Some Glimpses of Brethren Preaching in Years Past." BLT, 38 (Fall, 1993): 231–32.

Mittelberger, Gottlieb, 1715–ca.1779
Reise nach Pennsylvanien im Jahr 1750 und Rückreise nach Deutschland im Jahr 1754, ed. Jürgen Charnitzky. Sigmaringen: Jan Thorbecke Verlag, 1997. 214pp., illus.
A reprint of Mittelberger's travel account (originally published in 1756), with an extensive introduction by the editor; references to the Brethren, the Sauer press, and Ephrata.

Mohn, Kerry
"The Ephrata Cloister: Enigmatic Oasis." In: Preserving America's Utopian Dream. Washington, DC: National Park Service, 1991.

Moomaw, I[ra] W., 1894–1990, and Moomaw, Mabel E.
Family Memories and Reflections. Sebring, FL: authors, ca.1985.
Memoirs of a famous CB agricultural missionary.

Moomaw, Robert A., comp.
Moomaw – Mumma – Mumaw – Mumaugh Genealogy. [n.p.: author], 1990. 541pp.
Second printing (1992).

Moore, Joy Hofacker
Ted Studebaker: A Man Who Loved Joy. Scottdale, PA: Herald Press, 1987.
Children's story of CB volunteer killed in Southeast Asia in 1971.

Moore, Richard and Barnes, Jay
Faces from the Flood: Hurricane Floyd Remembered. Chapel Hill, NC: University of North Carolina Press, 2004. xiii, 225pp., illus.
Many references to Brethren involved in disaster aid.

Morrellville Church of the Brethren
Morrellville Church of the Brethren, 1898–1998: Celebrating 100 Years. [Johnstown, PA: 1998]. Unpaginated.

Morris, Barry
Evergreen [Greene County, VA]: A Look Back. [n.p.]: 1996. 35, [xxv]pp.

Morse, Kenneth I., 1913–1999
Preaching in a Tavern and 129 Other Surprising Stories from Brethren Life. Elgin, IL: BP, 1997. Unpaginated.
Many taken from "sidebars" in The Brethren Encyclopedia, vols. 1–2.

Mount Olivet Church of the Brethren
A Century for Christ, 1872–1972. Timberville, VA: Mount Olivet Church of the Brethren, 1972. 29pp.

Mow, D. Merrill
Torches Rekindled: The Bruderhof's Struggle for Renewal. Ulster Park, NY: Plough Publishing House, 1989. 332pp., illus.
A continuation of the history of the Bruderhof, Torches Together (1964, 1971) by Emmy Arnold, written by a church leader and former CB member; second, enlarged edition (1990).

Moyer, Dennis K.
Fraktur Writings and Folk Art Drawings of the Schwenkfelder Library Collection. Kutztown, PA: Pennsylvania German Society, 1997. xviii, 301pp.
"Early collectors such as Abraham Harley Cassel ... were among the first to bring a more general awareness of the Pennsylvania German arts to the public. Cassel, a grammar school teacher who taught fraktur in the 18th century manner, organized the first public exhibit of the art form in 1884 at Norristown [PA]" (p. xii).

Moyer, Walton Z.
"Conrad Beissel im Lichte der innerkirchlichen Kritik des achtzehnten Jahrhunderts." MA thesis, Millersville State College, 1973, 88pp.

Mullen, Lena Belle Ohlwin
Johann Werner Ohlwein, 1756–1829, and His Descendants: Genealogy of the Olwine/Olwin Families in America. [n.p.: author], 1987. 429pp.

Müller [-Bahlke], Thomas
Kirche zwischen Zwei Welten: Die Obrigkeitsproblematik bei Heinrich Melchior Mühlenberg und die Kirchengründung der deutschen Lutheraner in Pennsylvanien. Stuttgart: Franz Steiner Verlag, 1994. 302pp.
Extensive references to the Sauers.

Mummert, J. Ronald, 1941–, and Bach, Jeffrey A., 1958–
Refugee Ministry in the Local Congregation. Scottdale, PA: Herald Press, 1992. 128pp

Murray, Dorothy Garst, 1915–2000
Sister Anna. Elgin, IL: BP, 1983. 175pp.
Biography of Anna Beahm Mow (1893–1985).

Murray, John F.
Neff Families and Their Descendants in the 1700s and Early 1800s. [n.p.]: author, 1991.

Musa, J. L.
50 Years of Christian Missionary Activities in Kibakuland (1941–1991). Maidugur, Nigeria: Ellyon Communications, 1991. 57pp.

Nampa Church of the Brethren
Centennial History of the Nampa Church of the Brethren, 1899–1999. Nampa, ID: Nampa Church of the Brethren, 1999. 80, 50pp., illus.

Nead, Peter, 1796–1877
Theological Writings on Various Subjects. Poland, OH: Dunker Reprints, 1985. 486pp.
Reprint of the 1866 original edition; reissued in 1998.

The Restoration of Primitive Christianity, comp. James Zaiger. [n.p.: n.d.]. 76pp.
Reprints 34 articles written by Nead for The Vindicator.

Neff, Ray A.
Valley of the Shadow. Terre Haute, IN: Rana Publications, 1987. vi, 313pp.
Detailed history of Elder John Kline during the Civil War, based on private papers unavailable to other researchers. Second ed. (1989), viii, 315pp.

Negley, Betty Jane
Divine Legacy: God's Riches for the Servant Heart. Shippensburg, PA: Treasure House, 1996. [xi], 236, [iv]pp.

Neher, Bertha Miller, 1873–1948
My Biblical Tour – Egypt, Palestine, Italy. [No. Manchester, IN: Viola Whitehead, 1993]. ii, 71pp.
Written in 1927.

Nolt, Stephen M., 1968–
"The CPS Frozen Fund: The Beginning of Peace-Time Interaction Between Historic Peace Churches and the United States Government." Mennonite Quarterly Review, 67 (April, 1993): 201–24.

"Reinterpreting Nonconformity: Mennonite and Brethren Thought and Practice." In: Anabaptist Currents: History in Conversation with the Present, eds. Carl F. Bowman and Stephen L. Longenecker. Camden, ME: Penobscot Press, 1995, 183–97.

Formal Mutual Aid Structures Among American Mennonites and Brethren: Assimilation and Reconstructed Ethnicity. [New Brunswick, NJ]: Transaction Periodicals Consortium, 1998.
Taken from *Journal of American Ethnic History*, 17 (Spring, 1998): 71–86.

"Plain People and the Refinement of America." Mennonite Historical Bulletin, 40 (October 1999): 1–11.
Includes OGBB.

Ober, Mary Velma, 1903–
A Laborer Was Sent to the Field. [North Manchester, IN]: author, 1985. 69pp.
CB missionary to China.

O'Diam, Eva
Love and Justice. Elgin, IL: BP, 1990. 40pp.
Covenant Bible Studies Series.

Old Order German Baptist Church, C.O. Committee
The Witness of a Conscientious Objector. [n.p.] Old German Baptist Church, 1996, 1997.
A revision of an earlier document.

Olds, Doris R.
Walnut Grove [CB] Cemetery of Bonpas Township, Richland County, Illinois. Leesburg, FL: author, 1983.

O'Malley, Steven, 1942–
Early German-American Evangelicalism; Pietist Sources on Discipleship and Sanctification. Lanham, MD: Scarecrow Press, 1995. vii, 350pp.
Contains material on Radical Pietists in the Wittgenstein area.

Opocenský, Milan, ed., 1931–
Towards a Renewed Dialogue: Consultation on the First and Second Reformations, Geneva, 28 November to 1 December 1994. Geneva: World Alliance of Reformed Churches, 1996). 199pp.
Includes paper by D. F. Durnbaugh, "The First and Radical Reformations and Their Relations with the Magisterial Reformation" (pp. 8–29).

Opocenský, Milan and Réamonn, Páraic, eds.
Justification and Sanctification in the Traditions of the Reformation: Prague V, The Fifth Consultation on the First and Second Reformations, Geneva, 13 to 17 February 1998. Geneva: World Alliance of Reformed Churches, 1999. 280pp.

Oswinski, Thomas E.
"Jeremia from the Paradiesisches Wunder-Spiel: A Critical Edition and Study of a Musical Document of the Eighteenth-Century Ephrata Cloister." MA thesis, West Chester University, 1997, 245pp.

Ottoni-Wilhelm, Dawn
"Understandings of Sin: Contemporary Applications and Prospects." In: Anabaptist Currents: History in Conversation with the Present, eds. Carl F. Bowman and Stephen

L. Longenecker. Camden, ME: Penobscot Press, 1995, 15–24.

Oved, Yaacov, 1929–
Two Hundred Years of American Communities. New Brunswick, NJ: Transaction Books, 1988. xxvi, 500pp.
Chap. 2: "Ephrata and the First Communes in North America" (pp. 19–37).

Overholt, James J.
From Tiny Beginnings: Elgin, IL: BP, 1987. 70pp.

[Overholtzer, Durand, ed., 1945–]
Brethren History Lectures. Ripon, CA: 1990. Unpaginated.
Lectures by William G. Willoughby, Myron Dietz, Fred W. Benedict, and Marcus Miller.

Pardoe, Elizabeth Lewis
"The Many Worlds of Conrad Weiser: Mystic Diplomat." Explorations in Early American Culture, 4 (2000): 113–47.
Many details on his connections with Ephrata.

Parker, Don
"Life Is Great. Yea!" [West Salem, OH: author, 2000]
A play celebrating the life of Ted Studebaker who died in Vietnam in 1971.

Parmer, John A.
"Notes on the Geography of the Cloister Lower Mill Tract." Journal of the Historical Society of the Cocalico Valley, 27 (2002): 14–21.

Parrott, Mary Anne, 1943–
Hymns and Songs of the Bible. Elgin, IL: BP, 1998. xii, 57pp.
Covenant Bible Studies Series.

Parsons, William T., 1923–
"The Pernicious Effects of *Witness* upon Plain-Worldly Relations." Pennsylvania Folklife, 36 (Spring, 11987): 128–35.
Includes materials on singings with Brethren participation.

Peachey, Paul, ed.
Peace, Politics, and the People of God. Philadelphia: Fortress Press, 1984. vii, 184pp.
Essay by Donald E. Miller (pp. 163–75).

Peer, Marie Jean Smith
John Rudy and Mary Garman, Their Ancestors and Descendants, Including the Barth/Bard, Grossman, Leib, and Long Surnames. Craig, CO: author, 1990. 587pp.

Peer, Marie Jean Smith and Hull, Judith Maxine Yarger
A History of the George Jurger/Yarger Family in America. Craig, CO: authors, 1987. 87pp.
With an addition by Frederick Noah Smith, Jr.

Pegler, Westbrook, 1894–1969
"Dunkers." Chicago Daily News (February 15, 1937).
Reference in *GM* (March 3, 1934): 46.

Pendleton, Philip E., 1934–
Oley Valley Heritage: The Colonial Years, 1700–1775. Birdsboro, PA: Pennsylvania German Society, 1994. 232pp., illus.
Mentions German Baptist Brethren in the Oley Valley region under the rubric "Other German Sectarian Groups" (pp. 109, 149) and Ephrata (p. 107).

Petcher, Rhett R. and Quimby, Dorothy Petcher
"The Knot Hole." Bridgewater, VA: Beacon Press, [1988]. 100pp.
Memoirs and poetry.

Peters, Edward L.
Some Descendants of Michael Peters. Manson, WA: Peters Publishing, 1993. 593pp.

Peters, Mildred Hull, ed.
Every Name Index for the History of the Church of the Brethren of the Southern District of Ohio [1955]. [n.p.]: Southern Ohio District Church of the Brethren Historical Committee, 1985.

Peters, Raymond R.
Foothills to Mountaintops: My Pilgrimage to Wholeness. Elgin, IL: Brethren Press, 1990. 387pp.

Peterson, Jerry, ed.
[Special issue], "Called to Make Disciples: New Church Development in the 1990s and Beyond". BLT, 36 (Summer, 1991): 131–238.
Major contributors included are: Joan George Deeter, Duane Ramsey, Paul E. R. Mundey, B. Merle Crouse, Irven Stern, Patty Stern, Norman Harsh, Roy Johnson, and Gary Martin.

Petty, Donald B.
"An Investigation of Printing at the Ephrata Cloister During the Period 1743–1793." MA thesis, Millersville State College, 1976.

Pflug, Günther
"Ephrata (Pennsylvania." Lexikon des gesamten Buchwesens, 2nd. rev. ed. Stuttgart: Anton Hiersemann, 1989, 2:473.

Pippenger, Wesley E.
Pippenger and Pittenger Families: A Genealogical History of the Descendants of William Pippenger of New Jersey, and Allied Families. Alexandria, VA: author, 1988.

Pister, Grace Rodabaugh
The Rodabaugh Family: A Genealogy with Allied Families. Sequim, WA: author, [1988]. 250pp.

Pitzer, Donald E., ed., 1936–
America's Communal Utopias. Raleigh: University of North Carolina Press, 1997. xxxi, 537pp., illus.
Contains article by D. F. Durnbaugh, "Communitarian Societies in Colonial America" (pp. 14–36), with information on the Ephrata Society.

Plagge, Andreas and Bautz, Friedrich Wilhelm
"Beissel, Johann Konrad." Biographiscche-Bibliographisches Kirchenlexikon, eds. Traugott Bautz and others. Herzberg: Verlag Trautgott Bautz, 1990, 1:467.

Plaster, David R.
Ordinances: What Are They? Winona Lake, IN: BMH Books, 1985. 144pp.
FGBC publication.

"The Christian and War: A Matter of Personal Conscience." Grace Theological Journal, 6/2 (Fall, 1985): 435–55.
Favors non-combatant service in the military.

"Baptism by Triune Immersion." Grace Theological Journal, 6/2 (Fall, 1985): 383–90.

Finding Our Focus: A History of the Grace Brethren Church. Winona Lake, IN: BMH Books, 2003. 189pp.
"A Revision and Continuation of Conquering Frontiers, by Homer A. Kent, Sr."

Platou, Arnold S.
After the Dunker Church – A Century of Faithful Service: The Sharpsburg Church [MD] of the Brethren, 1899–1999. [Sharpsburg, MD]: author, 1999. 68pp.

Plunkett, N. Geraldine
Nathan's Secret. Elgin, IL: BP, 2000. 87pp.
Beth Gallo, illustrator. Fiction, based on fact, of Virginia Brethren during the Civil War.

Sarah Beth's Problem. Elgin, IL: BP, 2003. 88pp.
Fictional story for juveniles.

Poling, James, ed., 1942–
[Special issue on health and welfare]. BLT, 33 (Winter, 1988): 5–67.
Articles by James Poling, Joseph Schechter, Steve Tuttle, Graydon Snyder, Mary Sue Rosenberger, Clyde Shallenberger, James E. Kipp, Curtis Dubble, and Karen S. Carter.

Poling, Virginia, 1911–, and Poling, Newton L., 1914–2002
The Story of Solomon and Lydia Smith Miller and Their Children, 1797–1988. [Hagerstown, MD]: authors, 1988. 162pp.

Hans Crumbacker Family, 1733–1800. [Hagerstown, MD]: authors, 1996. 32pp.

The Ulrich Crumpacker Family. [Hagerstown, MD]: authors, 1997. 115pp.

Poling, Virginia, ed., 1911–
Letters from Lydia, and Other Members of the Family. Hagerstown, MD: author, 1988. 37pp.
Letters from Lydia Smith Miller (1808–1879) and Solomon Miller (1797–1864).

Poling, Virginia, 1911–, and Meyerding, Esther Smith, 1915–
Memories – Memories. Hagerstown, MD: authors, 1993. 43pp.
Correspondence.

Polos, Nicholas C.
"A Historian's Vignette of Jesse Christian Brandt: A Christian Gentleman of La Verne." BLT, 32 (Spring, 1987): 93–103.

Pullen, Elizabeth
"The Virgin Sophia and the Spiritual Bridegroom: Eros and Androgeny in the Mysticism of Georg Conrad Beissel." unpubl. paper, American Academy of Religion meeting, 2001.

Quinn, D. Michael, 1944–
Early Mormonism and the Magic World View. Salt Lake City, UT: Signature Books, 1987.
Ephrata connections, pp. 14ff.; second, enlarged ed. (1998).

Quinter, James, 1816–1888
The Origin of Single Immersion. Urbana, IL: G. W. Flynn & Co., 1874. 15, [1]pp. BHLA
An earlier edition than previously known.

Raabe, Paul, comp.
Separatisten, Pietisten, Herrnhuter: Goethe und die Stillen im Lande. Leipzig: Fliegenkopf Verlag, 1999. 232pp., illus.
Richly-illustrated catalog of an exhibition in the Franckeschen Stiftungen, Halle, May-October, 1999.

Raabe, Paul and others, comps.
Pietatis Hallensis Universalis: Weltweite Beziehungen der Franckeschen Stiftungen im 18. Jahrhundert. Halle: Verlag der Franckeschen Stiftung, 1995. 99pp., illus.
Connections with North America (pp. 85–96).

Ragnjiya, T. H.
"Toward Establishing a Continuing Education Program for Ekklesiyar 'Yan'uwa a Nigeria, West Africa." MA thesis, Ashland Theological Seminary, 1991. 59pp

Ramirez, Frank, 1954–
The Gospel of Mark. Elgin, IL: BP, 1996.
Covenant Bible Studies Series.

Coming Home: Advent/Christmas Sermons from the Book of Haggai. Lima, OH: C.S.S. Publishing Company, 1998. 65pp.

Daniel. Elgin, IL: BP, 1998. x, 101pp.
Covenant Bible Study Series.

Apocalypse When: Daniel and Revelation: Bible-Based Exploration of Issues Facing Youth. Elgin, IL: BP, 1998. 40pp.

Choosing Sides: Faithfulness in the Book of Joshua. Elgin, IL: BP, 1998. 53pp.
Covenant Bible Studies Series.

Universal Restoration, An Essay. Elgin, IL: BP, 2001. 43pp.
From the Perspectives series.

Ramirez, Frank, ed., 1954–
[Special issue], "Essays by Pastors in Honor of Graydon F. Snyder." BLT, 43 (Winter-Spring, 1998): i–viii, 1–112.
Papers by David A. Leiter, Joan George Deeter, Frank Ramirez, David S. Young, A. Lee Kinsey, James Benedict, and Ronald Petry.

The Love Feast. Elgin, IL: Brethren Press, 2000. 165pp. illus.
A treasury and anthology.

Rarick, Ron
"The Baroque Organ at Elgin [IL]: A Saga." The Diapason (September, 1998): 14–16.
Detailed article on the Henry Kurtz organ, "one of the oldest organs now to be found in the United States" (p. 14).

Rarick, Vinna C., 1891–
Vinna's Fourscore and Seven Years. [n.p.]: author, 1980. xiii, 367pp.
Revised edition of memoirs of the wife of a CB evangelist and pastor, Ralph Glen Rarick (1893–1975).

Raymond, Edith Madeline Replogle and Replogle, Paul Hudson
Replogle-Replogle Genealogy, second edition. Battle Creek, MI: authors, 1995. 824pp.
Originally published (1984).

Redekop, Calvin W., 1925–
The Pax Story: Service in the Name of Christ, 1951–1976. Telford, PA: Pandora Press, 2001. 160pp., illus.
Includes description of the BSC/PAX reconstruction of the Karlsschule in Vienna (pp. 65–66, 80–85).

Reed, Frank L. and Renno, John R.
The Capitalistic Communist: A Story of Israel Eckerlin and the Ephrata Community. Danville, PA: J. R. Renno, 1986. 14, [2]pp.

Reed, John Ford, 1911–
Campaign to Valley Forge. Philadelphia: University of Pennsylvania Press, 1965.
About the role of the Ephrata Cloister members in carrying for American troops following the battle of Brandywine.

Reichel, Joseph J.
The Genealogy of Minne Lee Jones. [n.p.: author], 1987.
Includes also Funk, Brubaker, Harshbarger, and Gish families.

Reichmann, Eberhard and others, eds.
Emigration and Settlement Patterns of German Communities in North America. Indianapolis, IN: Max Kade German-American Center, 1995.
Has article by D. F. Durnbaugh, "Radical Pietism as the Foundation of German-American Communitarian Settlements" (pp.31–54).

Reid, Daniel G., ed., 1949–
Dictionary of Christianity in America. Downers Grove, IL: InterVarsity Press, 1990. xxix, 1305pp.
Articles on "Becker, Peter," "Beissel, Johann Konrad," "Church of the Brethren," "Free Church Tradition in America," "Mack, Alexander," "Major, Sarah Righter," by D. F. Durnbaugh; "Ephrata Society," by David B. Eller; "Fellowship of Grace Brethren Churches," by Robert G. Clouse; ""Bauman, Louis Sylvester," "McClain, Alva J." by Ronald T. Clutter.

Reid, Stephen Breck and Reid, Kathy Goering
Uncovering Racism. Elgin, IL: BP, 1999.
Covenant Bible Studies.

Reidy, Miriam
"Brethren Volunteers for Peace." [World Council of Churches] One World, No. 100 (November, 1994): 10.

Renkewitz, Heinz, 1902–1974
Hochmann von Hochenau (1670–1721), trans. William G.

Willoughby. Philadelphia: Brethren Encyclopedia, 1993. 148pp.
Based on the definitive monograph on the Radical Pietist leader, but excludes the scholarly apparatus.

Rentmeister, Jean R., with Wine, Clyde C.
The Descendants of Christian and Susanna Moyers Wine. [n.p.: author], 1988. 171pp.

Replogle, Edith Madeline
The Replogle-Reprogle Genealogy. Pullman, WA: author, 1984. 519pp.

Replogle, Jacob F., 1910–
"Called To Be a Minister": Looking Back on Life. [n.p.: author], 1984.

Replogle, Justin
Ancestors on the Frontier: Genealogical Narrative Spanning Three Centuries. [Cedarburg, WI: author, ca. 1999].
Follows the Miller, Cripe, Ulrich, Replogle, Shively, and Metzger families of Brethren.

Reynolds, Clarence L.
Elder George Philip Rothenberger and His Descendants. [n.p.: author], 1986. 25pp.

Reynolds, Margaret C., –1999
Plain Women: Gender and Ritual in the Old Order River Brethren, ed. Simon J. Bronner. University Park, PA: Pennsylvania German Society/Pennsylvania State University Press, 2001. xii, 192pp.
Many references to the Brethren/Dunkers.

Rhodes, Donna McKee, 1962–
Little Stories for Little People: A Worship Resource. Scottdale, PA: Herald Press, 1995. 128pp.

More Little Stories for Little People: A Worship Resource. Scottdale, PA: Herald Press, 1996. 128pp.

Even More Stories for Little Children: A Worship Resource. Scottdale, PA: Herald Press, 2000. 128pp.

Richter, Helmut
Bilder aus Wittgenstein: Zeichnungen aus vier Jahrzehnten. Bad Berleburg: Wittgensteiner Heimatverein, 1986. 204pp., illus.

Richman, Irwin
"Johann Conrad Beissel (1690–1768)." American Writers Before 1800: A Biographical and Critical Dictionary. Westport, CT: Greenwood Press, 1983, 1: 126–28.

Riffle, Conrad
German Baptist Brethren (Dunker) of the Lion Hill Church … [VA]. Clinton, OH: author, 1995. 59pp.

Riley, Jobie E., 1928–
"The Solitary Sisters of Saron." Pennsylvania Folklife, 44 (1994/95): 89–97.

Rineer, A[mos] Hunter, Jr., –1985
Churches and Cemeteries of Lancaster County, Pennsylvania: A Complete Guide. Lancaster, PA: Lancaster County Historical Society, 1993. 560pp.

Risser, Audrey Gates
The Mattias Hoffer Family, 1743–1986. Baltimore: Gateway Press, 1986. 724pp.

Ritter, David R.
"Four Kendig Brothers Move to Augusta County, Virginia." Pennsylvania Mennonite Heritage, 18/4 (October 1999): 15–24.
Some members of this Mennonite family were converted to the Brethren by James R. Gish in 1866.

Roberson, Holly
"Surrounded by Family and Close to God." Roanoke [VA] Times, Nov 8, 1998, p. A1.

"Feast for Body and Soul." Roanoke [VA] Times, Nov 9, 1998, p. A1.

"In the World, Not of it." Roanoke [VA] Times, Nov 10, 1998, p. A1.
A three-part overview of the Old German Baptist Brethren with photos.

Roberts, Nancy L., ed., 1954–
American Peace Writers, Editors, and Periodicals. New York: Greenwood Press, 1991. 362pp.
Many references to Brethren leaders.

Roberts, Warren E.
"Ananias Hensel and His Furniture: Cabinetmaking in Southern Indiana." Midwestern Journal of Languages and Folklore, 9 (Fall, 1983): 69–122.
An elder in the Lick Creek OGBB congregation, near Clay City, IN.

Robinson, Mitchell
"Civilian Public Service During World War II: The Dilemmas of Conscience and Conscription in a Free Society." PhD dissertation, Cornell University, 1990.

Robinson, Yvonne
"The Ephrata Cloister and the Lititz Moravian Settlement, 1732–1820, and a Comparative Study of Their Musical Cultures." DMA dissertation, Juillard School, 1986. viii, 93pp.

Roeber, A. G[regg], 1949–
"'The Origin of Whatever Is Not English Among Us': The Dutch-speaking and the German-speaking People of Colonial British America." In: Strangers within the Realm: Cultural Margins of the First British Empire, eds. Bernard Bailyn and Philip D. Morgan. Chapel Hill, NC: University of North Carolina Press for the Institute of Early American History and Culture, 1991, 220–83.
References to the Brethren.

Palatines, Liberty, and Property: German Lutherans in Colonial British America. Baltimore: Johns Hopkins University Press, 1993. xiii, 432pp.
Many references to the Sauer family of printers.

"Der Pietismus in Nordamerika im 18. Jahrhundert." In: Geschichte des Pietismus, Band 2: Der Pietismus im achtzehnten Jahrhundert, eds. Martin Brecht and Klaus Deppermann. Göttingen: Vandenhoek & Ruprecht, 1995, pp. 666–99.
On Brethren, Ephrata, and the Sauer press.

"German and Dutch Books and Printing." In: A History of the Book in America, eds. Hugh Amory and David D. Hall. New York: Cambridge University Press, 2000, 298–313.

Rogers, Ingrid, comp.
Swords into Plowshares. Elgin, IL: BP, 1983. 281pp.
Collectio of dramas on peace.

Peace Be Unto You: A Folk Songbook for Christian Peacemaking. North Manchester, IN: author, 1983.

Rohrer, Norman B., 1929–
A Saint in Glory Stands: The Story of Alva J. McClain, Founder of Grace Theological Seminary. Winona Lake, IN: BMH Books, 1986. 136, 2pp.

Roop, Eugene F., 1942–
Genesis. Scottdale, PA: Herald Press, 1987. 350pp.
Believers Church Bible Commentary Series.

Heard In Our Land. Elgin, IL: BP, 1991. 112pp.
A collection of prayers.

Let the Rivers Run: Stewardship and the Biblical Story. Grand Rapids, MI: Eerdmans, 1991. xii, 108pp.
Esther. Elgin, IL: BP, 1997. x, 76pp.
Covenant Bible Studies Series.

Ruth, Jonah, Esther. Scottdale, PA: Herald Press, 2002. 304pp.
Believers Church Bible Commentary Series.

Roop, Eugene F., 1942–, and others
A Declaration of Peace: In God's People the World's Renewal Has Begun. Scottdale, PA: Herald Press, 1991. 109pp.
Statement of the Historic Peace Churches and the Fellowship of Reconciliation to the wider church; Authors are: Douglas Gwynn, George Hunsinger, Eugene F. Roop, and John Howard Yoder. Appendix C, compiled by John Howard Yoder, is a chronology of the ecumenical activities of the Historic Peace Churches, 1948–1986 (pp. 93–105).

Roop, Wendell
American Branches of the Family Roop (Rupp, etc.). [n.p.: author], 1988.

Rosenberger, Mary Sue Helstern, 1940–
Journey of Faith, Eighty-Five Years and Beyond: A History of the Brethren's Home, Greenville, Ohio, 1902–1987. Greenville, OH: Brethren's Home, 1987. 434pp. illus.

That They Might Have Life: A History of the Brethren Health and Welfare Association. Elgin, IL: Brethren Health and Welfare Association, [1988]. x, 127pp.

Harmless as Doves: Witnessing for Peace in Vietnam. Elgin, IL: BP, 1988. 188pp.

Caring: A History of Brethren Homes, 1889–1989. Elgin, IL: Brethren Homes and Hospital Association, 1989. 208pp., illus.

The Lord's Prayer. Elgin, IL: BP, 1989. 48pp.
Covenant Bible Studies Series.

Abundant Living: Wellness from a Biblical Perspective. Elgin, IL: BP, 1991. 48pp.
Covenant Bible Study Series.

Light of the Spirit: The Brethren in Puerto Rico, 1942 to 1992. Elgin, IL: Association of Brethren Caregivers, 1992. 92pp., illus.

La Luz del Espiritu: Los Hermanos en Puerto Rico, 1942 to 1992. Gotha, FL: Atlantic Southeast District, Church of the Brethren, 1992. [iv], 104pp.
Translation into Spanish of the above.

"Indigenization of Missions: Closing a Door on the Sisters." BLT, 37 (Summer, 1992): 179–93.

The Gift of Life: The Brethren and Bethany Hospital. Elgin, IL: Association of Brethren Caregivers, 1995. 88pp.

Ross, Keith E.
Ancestors and Descendants, George Ross and Hannah Heckman. North Manchester, IN: author, 1983. 58pp.

Ross, Keith E. and Ross, Helen M., 1913–
Ancestors and Descendants, John Eikenberry and Mary Clingenpeel. [North Manchester, IN: authors], 1987. 32pp.

Roth, John D.
"Community as Conversation: A New Model of Anabaptist Hermeneutics." In: Anabaptist Currents: History in Conversation with the Present, eds. Carl F. Bowman and Stephen L. Longenecker. Camden, ME: Penobscot Press, 1995, 51–64.

"Pietism and the Anabaptist Soul." In: The Dilemma of Anabaptist Piety: Strengthening or Straining the Bonds of Community?, ed. Stephen L. Longenecker. Camden, ME: Penobscot Press, 1997, 17–33.

Rowdabaugh, J. W.
"Annual Conference of 1882." In: The Brethren Presence in the World…: Proceedings of the 3rd Brethren World Assembly, July 23–26, 2003, ed. William R. Eberly. Philadelphia, PA: Brethren Encyclopedia, Inc., 2004, 122–125.

Royer, Harry K.
Addendum to History of the Royer Family in America, [by] J. G. Francis. Altavista, VA: Altavista Printing Co., 1983. 117pp.

Ruff, Phyllis Kingery, comp.
Minutes of the Annual Conference of the Church of the Brethren, 1980–1984. Elgin, IL: BP, 727pp.

Rummel, Merle C., 1934–
Four Mile [IN] Community. Richmond, IN: author, 1998.
Portions of this work are available online (cob-net.org).

Rupel, Esther Fern, 1924–
"The Dress of the Brethren (and Church of the Brethren)." BLT, 31 (Summer, 1986): 135–50.

Brethren Dress; A Testimony to Faith. Philadelphia: Brethren Encyclopedia, Inc., 1994. xviii, 183pp., illus. Brethren Encyclopedia Monograph, No. 5.

The published version of "An Investigation of the Origin, Significance, and Demise of the Prescribed Dress Worn by Members of the Church of the Brethren," PhD dissertation, University of Minnesota, 1971, xix, 344pp.

"Plain Dress from a Church of the Brethren Perspective." In: Report of the Proceedings of the 1998 Brethren World Assembly, Bridgewater College . . . , ed. Dale R. Stoffer. Ashland, OH: Ashland Theological Seminary/Brethren Encyclopedia, Inc., 1999, 227–42.

Ruth, John L., 1930–
Maintaining the Right Fellowship: A Narrative Account of Life in the Oldest Mennonite Community in North America. Scottdale, PA: Herald Press, 1984.

Franconia Conference; many references to the Brethren.

"'Not Only Tradition But Truth': Legend and Myth Fragments among Pennsylvania Mennonites." Pennsylvania Folklife, 46 (Autumn, 1996): 20–37.

Includes Dunker stories.

The Earth Is the Lord's: A Narrative History of the Lancaster Mennonite Conference. Scottdale, PA: Herald Press, 2001. 1390pp.

Contains many references to the Brethren and to Ephrata as Mennonite neighbors, with both cooperative and competitive relations.

"Glimpses of 'Swiss' Anabaptist-Mennonite Worship." In: Anabaptist Currents: History in Conversation with the Present, eds. Carl F. Bowman and Stephen L. Longenecker. Camden, ME: Penobscot Press, 1995, 83–100.

Sanford, Don A.
A Choosing People: The History of the Seventh Day Baptists. Nashville, TN: Broadman Press, 1992. 448pp.
References to the Ephrata Society.

Sanger, S[amuel] F., 1849–1927, and Hays, D[aniel], 1839–1916
The Olive Branch of Peace and Good Will to Men. [n.p.]: Linville Creek [VA] Church of the Brethren and Shenandoah District, Church of the Brethren, 1997. 232pp.

Reprint of the original 1907 edition, by Dunker Springhaus Ministries, Youngstown, OH.

Sangmeister, Ezechiel, 1723–1784
"The Life and Conduct of the Late Brother Ezechiel Sangmeister . . . Consisting of Six Parts . . .," trans. Barbara M. Schindler. Journal of the Historical Society of the Cocalico Valley, Vols. 4–10 (1979–1985).

Translation of Sangmeister's Leben und Wandel (1825–27); also published as a unit (1986).

Sappington, Roger E., 1929–1989
"John H. Reviewed." BLT, 30 (Spring, 1985): 105–10.

The Brethren in Tennessee and Alabama. [n.p.]: 1988. 178, [xxv]pp.

"Brethren Certificates of Membership from Virginia." The Rockingham Recorder, 31/4 (April, 1988): 31–33.

Sappington, Roger E., 1929–1989, ed.
The Brethren in Industiral America: A Surce Bood on the Development of the Church of the Brethren, 1865–1915. Elgin, IL: BP. 1985. 504pp.
Fourth in a series of documentary source books.

"Brethren Family Life in America, 1768–1868." BLT, 34 (Winter, 1989): 6–15.

Bareyan, Alex, 1913–
The Turning Point: How Men of Conscience Brought About Major Change in the Care of America's Mentally Ill. Washington, DC: American Psychiatric Press, 1994. xviii, 309pp.
CPS men in mental hospitals and the reforms they brought.

Sattler, Gary R.
God's Glory, Neighbor's Good: A Brief Introduction to the Life and Writings of August Hermann Francke. Chicago: Covenant Press, 1982. x, 262pp.
Pietist leader.

Nobler Than Angels, Lower Than a Worm: The Pietist View of the Individual in the Writings of Heinrich Müller and August Hermann Francke. Lanthan, MD: University Press of America, 1989.

Satvedi, Anet Daniel
"History of the Church of the Brethren in India. 1894–1993." DMin thesis, Bethany Theological Seminary, 1993, ix, 151pp.

Saxby, Trevor J., 1954–
Pilgrims of a Common Life: Christian Communities of Goods Through the Centuries. Scottdale, PA: Herald Press, 1987. 207pp.
On Ephrata (pp. 134–35); foreward by D. F. Durnbaugh (pp. 9–11).

The Quest for the New Jerusalem: Jean de Labadie and the Labadists, 1610–1744. Dordrecht: Martinus Nijhoff, 1987.

Schechter, D[avid] O., 1918–
Yordy: A Snyoptic Geneology of Amos and Jessie Yordy. [n.p.: author], 1986. 23pp.

Schelbert, Leo, 1929–
Die Stimme eines Einsamen in Zion: Ein unbekanntern Brief von Brüder Jaebez [Johann Peter Müller] aus Ephrata, Pennsylvanien, aus dem Jahre 1743." Zeitschrift für Kirchengeschichte, 85 (1974): 77–92.

"Von der Macht des Pietismus: Dokumentarbericht zur Auswanderung einer Basler Familie im Jahre 1736."

Basler Zeitschrift für Geschichte und Alterumsforschung, 75 (1975): 89–119.
Ephrata connections.

"From Reformed Preacher in the Palatinate to Pietist Monk in Pennsylvania: The Spiritual Path of Johann Peter Müller (1709–1796)." In: Germany and America: Essays on Problems of International Relations and Immigration,

ed. Hans Trefousse. New York: Brooklyn College Press, 1980, 139–49.

"On the Power of Pietism: A Documentary on the Thommens of Schaefferstown." The Historic Schaefferstown Record, 18 (October, 1984): 42–77.
Ephrata connections.

"People of Choice: Decision Making in an Eighteenth Century Swiss-German Family." The Report: A Journal of German-American History, 40 (1986): 77–93.
On the Thommens, a family connected with Ephrata.

"Die Ausformung von Konrad Beissels Ephrata Gemeinschaft im Widerstreit geistlicher Traditionen, 1743–1745." Eberbacher Geschichtsblatt, 90 (April, 1991): 41–54.

Schelbert, Leo, ed., 1929–
"'A Modest Sketch of God's Work': John Peter Miller's Letter of 1743 about Ephrata's Spiritual Evolution." Historic Schaefferstown Record, 19 (1975): 1–15.

America Experienced: Eighteenth and Nineteenth Century Accounts of Swiss Immigrants to the United States. Camden, ME: Picton Press, 1996. 453pp.
Refers to the Ephrata Society.

Schelbert, Leo, 1929–, and Rappolt, Hedwig, eds.
"Alles ist ganz anders hier": Auswanderschicksale in Briefen aus zwei Jahrhunderten. Freiburg I. Breisgau: 1977.

Schifflet, Anne Frysinger
Pennsylvania German Ancestors: Frysinger, Schaffner, Royer, Keller, and Related Families. Frederick, MD: author, [n.d.]
Many Brethren among the sixty families listed.

Schildknecht, C. E. and others. eds.
Monocacy and Catoctin: A Source Book for Early Western Maryland History and Genealogy. Shippensburg, PA: Beidel Printing House, 1986. 465pp.
Completed in three volumes (1985–89).

Schlabach, Theron F., 1933–
Peace, Faith, Nation: Mennonite and Amish in Nineteenth Century America. Scottdale, PA: Herald Press, 1980. 352pp.
The Mennonite Experience in America Series, Volume 2; with references to Brethren.

Schmoe, Floyd
"Seattle's Peace Churches and Relocation." In: Japanese Americans: From Relocation to Redress, eds. Roger Daniel and others. Salt Lake City, UT: 1986, pp. 117–22.

Schneider, Hans, 1941–
"Der radikale Pietismus im 17. Jahrhundert." Geschichte des Pietismus, Band 1: Das 17. und frühe 18. Jahrhundert, ed. Martin Brecht. Göttingen: Vandenhoeck & Ruprecht, 1993, pp. 391–437.
Along with the following, the best summary of Radical Pietism.

"The Attitude of Pietists toward Anabaptism." In: The Dilemma of Anabaptist Piety: Strengthening or Straining the Bonds of Community?, ed. Stephen L. Longenecker. Camden, ME: Penobscot Press, 1997, 47–55.

"'Basic Questions on Water Baptism': An Early Anti-Brethren Pamphlet." BLT, 42 (Spring/Summer, 1997): 31–63.

"Beissel, Georg Conrad." Religion in Geschichte und Gegenwart, 4th ed. 1998, 1:1228.

"Alexander Mack's Notes about Immersion Baptism in His Personal Bible." BLT, 48 (Winter/Spring, 2003): 18–28.

Schneider, Ulf-Michael
Propheten der Goethezeit: Sprache, Literatur und Wirkung der Inspirierten. Göttingen: Vandenhoeck & Ruprecht, 1995. 248pp.
Basic monograph on the Community of True Inspiration, the movement contemporary with and rivalling the early Brethren.

Schrader, Hans-Jürgen, 1943–
Literaturproduktion und Büchermarkt des radikalen Pietismus. Göttingen: Vandenboeck & Ruprecht, 1989. 635pp.
Masterly survey of the publication of Radical Pietist works, with references to Sauer and the Brethren.

Schrock, Janet West
"Brethren Volunteer Service: A Look at the Coming Decade." BLT, 36 (Fall, 1991): 288–93.

Schwalm, E. J.
Nonresistants Under Test: A Compilation of Experiences of Conscientious Objectors as Encountered in Two World Wars. Nappanee, IN: E. V. Publishing House, 1949. 276pp.

Scott, Stephen, 1948–
Why Do They Dress That Way? Intercourse, PA: Good Books, 1986. 160pp.
Dress of the "Plain People," including the conservative Brethren.

Seachrist, Denise Ann
"Snow Hill and the Seventh-Day Baptists: Heirs to the Musical Traditions of Conrad Beissel's Ephrata Cloister." PhD dissertation, Kent State University, 1993.

"The Snow Hill Cloister and Its Music Traditions." Der Reggeboge/The Rainbow, 28/1 (1994): 1–7.

"A Baptismal Service at Snow Hill: An Affirmation of Faith and Tribute to the Past." Der Reggeboge/The Rainbow, 31/1–2 (1997): 27–34

"Snow Hill and the German Seventh-Day Baptists: Heirs to the Musical Tradition of Conrad Beissel's Ephrata Cloister." Old Order Notes, no. 17 (Spring/Summer, 1998): 17–53, 56–57.

"The Snow Hill Auction: Change and Dissolution." Old Order Notes, no. 17 (Spring-Summer, 1998): 73–87.

"Musical Treasures of the Snow Hill Cloister: Manuscripts, Monographs, and Monastical Mysticism." Communal Societies, 18 (1998): 53–61.

"The Sisters of Saron: Continuing the Musical Traditions of Ephrata and Snow Hill." Der Reggeboge/The Rainbow: Journal of the Pennsylvania German Society, 33/1–2 (1999): 26–35

Seese, Nelson M.
Nelson: A Childhood Remembered. Falls Church, VA: Lizmar Press, 1992. [iv], 95, [i]pp.

Seilhamer, Chester Whitmore
Seilhamer History and Genealogy. Hagerstown, MD: author, 1984.
Descendants of Nicholas Johann and Marsilla Elizabeth Pohl Seilhamer.

Seilhamer, Larry
"A Letter to Peter Nead." BLT, 30 (Spring, 1985): 111–12.

"Peter Nead: Pioneer Dunker Theologian." Old Order Notes, no. 13 (Fall, 1995): 7–35.

Sell, Jeanne Lyle
The Miller Family of Knob Creek, Washington Co., Tennessee. Utica, NY: McDowell Publishing, 1985. 257pp.

Serrano, Olga.
Un Canto al Señor en la Isla del Encanto. Elgin, IL: BP, 1992. 95pp.
History of the Brethren in Puerto Rico.

Shaffer, Kenneth M., Jr, 1945–
"The Brethren Service Explosion." In: The Brethren Presence in the World…: Proceedings of the 3rd Brethren World Assembly, July 23–26, 2003, ed. William R. Eberly. Philadelphia, PA: Brethren Encyclopedia, Inc., 2004, 81–101.

Shenk, Gerald
"The Lines Have Fallen in Pleasant Places." In: Anabaptist Currents: History in Conversation with the Present, eds. Carl F. Bowman and Stephen L. Longenecker. Camden, ME: Penobscot Press, 1995, 165–70.

Shenk, Wilbert R.
"Mission and Outreach: The Anabaptist Heritage." In: Anabaptist Currents: History in Conversation with the Present, eds. Carl F. Bowman and Stephen L. Longenecker. Camden, ME: Penobscot Press, 1995, 289–301.

Shirk, Willis L., Jr.
"The European Roots of the Ephrata Commune." Journal of the Lancaster County Historical Society, 98 (Fall, 1996): 130–60.

Shoemaker, Benjamin H., III, 1901–
Supplement to Shoemaker Pioneers. [Philadelphia]: author, 1982. 24pp.
Additions and corrections to his 1975 book.

Showalter, Michael S.
"Carved in Stone: A Study of the Tombstones in Cocalico." Journal of the Historical Society of the Cocalico Valley, 11 (1986): 25–44.

"'And We, the Fathers of Families . . .': A Study of the Householders of the Ephrata Cloister." Journal of the Historical Society of the Cocalico Valley, 13 (1988): 1–54.

"The Good Samaritan Reconsidered: The Revolutionary War Hospital at Ephrata Cloister." Der Reggeboge/The Rainbow: Journal of the Pennsylvania German Society, 36/1 (2002): 28–40.

Shull, Arthur G., comp.
Ancestors and Descendants of William Harrison Shull and Clara Elizabeth Gibson. [n.p.: author], 1985. 35pp.

Shull, Lois Netzley
Women in India Who Kept the Faith. Bourbon, IN: Harmony Press, 1985. 73pp.
CB missions.

Shultz, Joseph R., 1927–2003
"Mission: The Brethren Church – Ashland." Old Order Notes, no. 10 (Spring, 1988): 26–27.

"Brethren Ordinances." In: Report of the Proceedings of the Brethren World Assembly, July 15–18, 1992, . . . , ed. D. F. Durnbaugh, Elizabethtown, PA: Elizabethtown College/Brethren Encyclopedia, Inc., 1994, [234–55].

Shultz, Lawrence W., 1890–1982, and others
A Mural History of the Church of the Brethren, Spanning Three Centuries, ed. Phyllis E. Leininger. Milford, IN: Camp Alexander Mack, 2000. 36pp., illus.
Reprint and updating of the 1953 book of historical panels painted by Medford Neher, with a new panel covering the years 1950–2000, painted by Margaret James Petry.

Shuman, L. Herman, 1916–
The Passover, the Lord's Supper, the Communion. [Pendleton, IN]: author, 1986. 59pp.
Discussion of church ordinances by an OGBB minister.

The Country Preacher: The Life and Ministry of Elder Solomon Stoner. Anderson, IN: Hudson Printing Co., 1992. viii, 206pp.
The biography of an OGBB minister.

Sider, E. Morris
"Anabaptist Ministry." In: Anabaptist Currents: History in Conversation with the Present, eds. Carl F. Bowman and Stephen L. Longenecker. Camden, ME: Penobscot Press, 1995, 259–66.

"Conversion Narratives in Anabaptist and Pietist Groups." BLT, 47 (Winter/Spring, 2002): 40–53.

Siegel, Nancy
Juniata College: Uncommon Visions of Juniata's Past. Charleston, SC: Arcadia Publishing, 2000. 128pp. illus.
A volume of photographs dating from the earlier years of Juniata College, with captions derived from contemporary publications. Dedicated to the memory of Harold Bennett Brumbaugh, who collected many of the illustrations; part of the College History Series, the Images of America.

Sisters and Brothers, Inc.
"Conchies: An American Story of Commitment and

Courage." Harrisonburg, VA: Sisters and Brothers, Inc., [n.d.]. Video.
On conscientious objectors during World War II.

Sittser, Gerald L.
A Cautious Patriotism: The American Churches and the Second World War. Chapel Hill: University of North Carolina press, 1997. 320pp.
Deals with the Historic Peace Churches among others.

Skinner, Charles
The American Communes . . .. Brooklyn Daily Eagle (1901). 38pp.
Includes "The Dunkards of Ephrata."

Slabaugh, Dennis L., ed.
[Special issue, First and Second Prague Consultations]. BLT, 35 (Winter, 1990): 3–113.
Essays on the First and Radical Reformations by: Marlin E. Miller, Amedo Molnár, D. F. Durnbaugh, Giovanni Gonnet, Hans Meier, Milan Opocenský, Bertold Klappert, and Harry M. de Lange.

"Dunkers and Dompelaars." BLT, 42 (Spring/Summer, 1997): 68–116.

Slough, Rebecca and Eisenbise, Debra Lee, 1960–, eds.
[Special issue on ministry]. BLT, 42 (Winter/Spring, 1997): i–viii, 1–122.
Contributors included: Rebecca Slough and Debbie Eisenbise, Warren M. Eshbach, Shawn Flory Replogle, Cheryl Brumbaugh-Cayford, Frances R. Townsend, and Karen Woody Hoover.

Smith, Catherine E., comp.
Christian Kuntz (?–1774), Born Near Thun, Switzerland. A Genealogy of the Kinsey-Kinzie Families in America, rev. ed. [n.p.: author], 1985. 483pp.

Smith, Larry
150th Anniversary History of Blair County, Pennsylvania. Apollo, PA: Closson Press, 1997. 926pp.
Many references to Brethren families.

Smith, Timothy L., 1924–
"A Shared Evangelical Heritage." TSF Bulletin (November/December, 1986): 12.
Mentions Brethren.

[Snowberger Family]
"The Snowberger Family." Antietam Ancestors, 3 (Winter, 1989): 10–19.

Snuffer, Thomas Earl
The Snuffers, A History of the Forebearers [sic] and Descendants of Isaac and Malinda (Rakes) Snuffer of Raleigh County, West Virginia. Beckley, WV: author, 1989.

Snyder, Graydon F., 1930–
Tough Choices. Elgin, IL: BP, 1988. xiv, 129pp.
Medical decision-making in moral perspective.

Health and Medicine in the Anabaptist Tradition: Care in Community. Valley Forge, PA: Trinity Press International, 1995. 160pp.

Snyder, Graydon F., 1930–, and Shaffer, Kenneth M., Jr., 1945–
Texts in Transit II. Elgin, IL: BP, 1991. 255pp.

Snyder, Ruth
Estella Myers: Pioneer Missionary in Central Africa. Winona Lake, IN: BMH Books, 1984. 167pp.
FGBC missionary.

Sollenberger, David,
"M. R. Zigler: Profile of a Peace-Maker." New Windsor, MD: On Earth Peace, [n.d.]. Video.

"Celebration of Service: Fifty Years of the Brethren Service Center." New Windsor, MD: Brethren Service Center, 1994. Video.

"Brethren Heritage Tour: Switzerland, France, Germany, the Netherlands, October 9–20, 1995." Ambler, PA: Brethren Encyclopedia, Inc., 1995. Video.
Coverage of the tour conducted by D. F. and Hedda Durnbaugh.

"By Water and the Word: The Birth of the Brethren." Elgin, IL: BP, 1996. Video.
Portrayal of the beginning history of the Brethren movement.

The Work of Jesus. Elgin, IL: Church of the Brethren General Board, ca. 1998. Video.

Somerset Church of the Brethren
Seventy-Fifth Anniversary, 1922–1997: Somerset [PA] Church of the Brethren. [Somerset, PA: 1997]. 48pp.

Southern Plains District
Brethren on the Southern Plains: Update, 1972–1979. [n.p.]: 1979.

Spease, Rachel Keller
A Keller History: Descendants of Hans Jacob Keller and Elizabeth Keller of the Cocalico Valley, Lancaster County, Pennsylvania. Lewistown, PA: author, 1995, two vols.

Splitter, Wolfgang
Pastors, People, Politics: German Lutherans in Pennsylvania, 1740–1790. Trier: Wissenschaftlicher Verlag, 1998. xii, 401pp.

"'Von allerhand merkwürdigen Sachen': Die deutschsprachige Presse in Pennsylvania und ihre politischen Bedeutung im 18. Jahrhundert." Schöne Neue Welt: Rheinländer erobern Amerika, ed. Komelia Panek. Kommern/Mechernich: Landesmuseum für Volkskunde in Kommern, 2001.
Bd. 2: Führer und Schriften des Rheinischen Freilichtsmuseums und Landesmuseums für Volkskunde in Kommern, Nr. 60. Deals significantly with the Sauers (pp. 71–111).

Spohn, Clarence E.
"The Historical Significance of the Writings of Ezechiel Sangmeister." Journal of the Historical Society of the Cocalico Valley, 13 (1988): 41–54.
Defends the historical importance and basic accuracy of the Sangmeister account, over against the article by Felix Reichmann of 1944.

"The Konigmacher Family of the Cocalico Valley." Journal of the Historical Society of the Cocalico Valley, 14 (1989): 1–43.

"The Zerfass Family of the Cocalico Valley." Journal of the Historical Society of the Cocalico Valley, 15 (1990): 1–56.

"The Kimmel Family of the Cocalico Valley." Journal of the Historical Society of the Cocalico Valley, 17 (1992): 1–43.

"The Kelp/Kölb Family of the Cocalico Valley." Journal of the Historical Society of the Cocalico Valley, 18 (1993): 1–48.

"The Bauman/Bowman Family of the Cocalico Valley: Printers, Papermakers, and Tavernkeepers." Journal of the Historical Society of the Cocalico Valley, 19 (1994): 1–93.
An important monograph; translations by Amos B. Hoover.

The Eicher Family and Their Homestead. Lititz, PA: Miller Printing for the Eicher Arts Center, 1995. 16pp.

"The Myths Surrounding the Ephrata Cloister and the Revolutionary War." Journal of the Historical Society of the Cocalico Valley, 27 (2002): 22–48.

"The Establishment of the Ephrata-Eberbach Sister City Relationship." Journal of the Historical Society of the Cocalico Valley, 27 (2002): 50–68.

Spohn, Clarence E., ed.
"Michael Müller/Miller of Cocalico Township, Lancaster County and His 'Debt Book' (1748–1786)," trans. Alan G.

Keyser. Journal of the Historical Society of the Cocalico Valley, 22 (1995): 1–76.
With assistance from Amos B. Hoover; information on the Ephrata Society.

Unreserved Public Auction of the Contents of the "Snow Hill Nunnery" Property of the German Seventh Day Baptist Church of Snow Hill. Ephrata, PA: Horst Auctioneers, 1997. [ii], 92, [ii]pp.
Contains "Auction Introduction" (p. 2) and "Historical Background of The Snow Hill 'Nunnery' and The German Seventh Day Baptist Church of Snow Hill" (pp.3–5), as well as many illustrations, some in color.

Important Unreserved Public Auction . . . [of] 18th, 19th, and 20th Century Brethren Books from the Collection of Donald R. Hinks of Gettysburg, Penna . . . . [December 18, 1999]. Ephrata, PA: Horst Auctioneers, 1999.

Spohn, Clarence E., and Marquet, Cynthia, eds.
"Pencillings About Ephrata, by a Visitor." Journal of the Historical Society of the Cocalico Valley, 23 (1998).
Facsimile reprint of the 1856 original.

Spring Run [PA] Church of the Brethren
The Brethren Trail of History and the Spring Run Church of the Brethren: 1708–1858–1983. [McVeytown, PA]: Spring Run Church of the Brethren, 1983.

Stafford, William E., 1914–1993
Down in My Heart. Elgin, IL: BPH, 1947. 95pp.
Memoirs of CPS experience; reprinted (Elgin, IL: BP, ca. 1998); (Corvallis: Oregon State University Press, 1998).

A Scripture of Leaves. Elgin, IL: Brethren Press, 1989. 78p.
Poetry.

Stall, Velma Hufford and Clark, Doris Hufford
Trials and Triumphs of John and Frances. [n.p.: n.d.]. 242pp.
The life of the OGBB Hufford family recorded by their daughters.

Stauffer, Ezra Nelson (1878–1968)
Stauffer Genealogy of America. History of the Descendants of Jacob Stauffer from the Earliest Available Records to the Present Time. [n.p.]: 1982. 901pp.
Supplements earlier genealogy (1917).

Stayer, Jonathan R.
"An Interpretation of Some Ritual and Food Elements of the Brethren Love Feast." Pennsylvania Folklife, 34 (1984–85): 61–70.
Also printed in BLT, 30 (1985): 199–208.

Stein, K. James
Philipp Jakob Spener: Pietist Patriarch. Chicago: Covenant Press, 1986. xiii, 352pp.
Well-documented biography of the Pietist leader.

Stenning, R. E.
Church World Service: Fifty Years of Help and Hope. New York: 1996.
Many references to the Brethren.

Stentz, Howard W.
Invisible Forces in the Great Awakening. Coos Bay, OR: author, 1989. xiv, 724pp.
Contains scattered material on the Brethren, including excerpts from European Origins of the Brethren (pp. 98–147), Brethren in Colonial America (pp.274–89), a reproduction of A True and Authentic Account of Andrew Frey . . . (pp. 434–504), family information on Alexander Mack (pp. 509–25), etc.

Andreas Frey, "The Prediger from Falkner Schwalm." Coos Bay, OR: Stentz Library, 1992. 300pp

Stern, Mary Ellen, 1888–1972
God's Ground. [n.p.: n.d.]. [ii], 132pp.

Stevens, Glenn D.
Leap of Faith: A History of the Saunders Grove [VA] Church of the Brethren. [n.p.]: Goose Creek Press, 1993. [xi], 125pp.

Stitzel, Quinter and Stitzel, Iva May
The Descendants of Daniel R. and Isabelle Price. [n.p.]: authors, 1982. 65pp.

Stockwell, Foster
Encyclopedia of American Communes, 1663–1963. Jefferson, NC: McFarland & Company, 1998.
Contains material on Ephrata (pp. 67–71) and related colonies: the Bermudian Settlement (p. 27), Cheat River (pp. 49–50, Mahanaim (p. 129), Nantmel (pp. 138–39), Shenandoah (p. 190), Snow Hill (p. 194), and Women [sic] of the Wilderness (pp. 222–44).

Stoffer, Dale R., 1950–
"The Progressive Position on Plain Dress." BLT, 31 (Summer, 1986): 151–57.
See response by Marcus Miller (pp. 158–61).

"Thoughts on Brethren Missions." Old Order Notes, no. 10 (Spring, 1988): 49–59.

Background and Development of Brethren Doctrines, 1650–1987. Philadelphia: Brethren Encyclopedia, Inc., 1989. 327pp.
Brethren Encyclopedia Monograph Series, No. 2; a thorough treatment of basic Brethren doctrinal positions, based on "The Background and Development of Thought and Practice in the German Baptist Brethren (Dunkers) and the Brethren (Progressive) Churches (c.1650–1979), PhD dissertation, Fuller Theological Seminary, 1980," ix, 804pp.

"Count Well the Cost: The Brethren Pilgrimage in Discipleship." In: Report of the Proceedings of the Brethren World Assembly, July 15–18, 1992, . . . , ed. D. F. Durnbaugh, Elizabethtown, PA: Elizabethtown College/Brethren Encyclopedia, Inc., 1994, [19–44].

"Brethren Heritage of the Lord's Supper: Introduction." In: The Lord's Supper: Believers Church Perspectives, ed. Dale R. Stoffer. Scottdale, PA/Waterloo, ON: Herald Press, 1997, pp. 157–60.

"In Search of a Past and a Future: The Brethren Church." In: Brethren in Transition: 20th Century Directions and Dilemmas, ed. Emmert F. Bittinger. Camden, ME: Penobscot Press, 1992, 101–11.

"Nonconformity: Archaic Ideal or Timeless Essential?" In: Anabaptist Currents: History in Conversation with the Present, eds. Carl F. Bowman and Stephen L. Longenecker. Camden, ME: Penobscot Press, 1995, 199–208.

"Anabaptized Pietism: The Schwarzenau Brethren." In: The Dilemma of Anabaptist Piety: Strengthening or Straining the Bonds of Community?, ed. Stephen L. Longenecker. Camden, ME: Penobscot Press, 1997, 35–45.

"Brethren Heritage of the Lord's Supper: Eucharist." In: The Lord's Supper: Believers Church Perspectives, ed. Dale R. Stoffer. Scottdale, PA/Waterloo, ON: Herald Press, 1997, pp. 185–192.

"The Eschatological Thought of Peter Nead." BLT, 46 (Winter/Spring, 2001): 80–91.

"Peter Nead and John Kline as Spiritual Friends." In: Papers from the Elder John Kline Bicentennial Celebration, ed. William R. Eberly. Ambler, PA: Brethren Encyclopedia, Inc., 2002, 82–92.

"Innovative John Kline: Education, Evangelism, and Church Government Reform." In: Papers from the Elder John Kline Bicentennial Celebration, ed. William R. Eberly. Ambler, PA: Brethren Encyclopedia, Inc., 2002, 160–72.

"A Swiss Brethren (Anabaptist) Source for the Beliefs of Alexander Mack and the Early Brethren." BLT, 48 (Winter/Spring, 2003): 29–38.

"Brethren Missions Since 1939." In: The Brethren Presence in the World...: Proceedings of the 3rd Brethren World Assembly, July 23–26, 2003, ed. William R. Eberly. Philadelphia, PA: Brethren Encyclopedia, Inc., 2004, 36–53.

Stoffer, Dale R., ed., 1950–
The Lord's Supper. Believers Church Perspectives. Scottdale, PA: Herald Press, 1997. 336pp.
Papers from the 11th conference on the Believers Churches, with many Brethren references. Essays by Brethren writers include those by D. F. Durnbaugh, Robert G. Clouse, Dale R. Stoffer, and Jeff Bach.

Report of the Proceedings of the 1998 Brethren World Assembly, Bridgewater College, Bridgewater, Virginia, July 15–18, 1998. Ashland, OH: Ashland Theological Seminary/Brethren Encyclopedia, Inc., (1999). v, 289, [viii]pp.
With major contributions from Ronald T. Clutter, John C. Shultz, Carl F. Bowman, Brenda B. Colijn, Nancy Rosenberger Faus, Alvin Conner, Phyllis Carter, Warren Garner, Linda Logan, Mike Meador, Esther F. Rupel, and Jerry R. Young.

Stokes, Ruth R.
Ruthie, Brethren Girl. [n.p.]: Wine Press Publishing, 1996. 240pp.
Autobiographical account of the background of the author's parents in Bedford County, PA, and her childhood in Montgomery County, PA, with emphasis upon the 1940s and 1950s.

Stone, Philip C.
"Recounting Kline's Last Days." In: Papers From the Elder John Kline Bicentennial Celebration, ed. William R. Eberly. Ambler, PA: Brethren Encyclopedia, Inc., 2002, 64–68.

"John Kline: The Community Man." In: Papers From the Elder John Kline Bicentennial Celebration, ed. William R. Eberly. Ambler, PA: Brethren Encyclopedia, Inc., 2002, 151–153.

Stoner, Norris Eugene, ed.
Our Stoner Family, 1932–1991. The Family of Jacob Stoner "II" (1781–1836) of Botetourt County, Virginia, and Some Other Descendants of His Grandfather Jacob Stoner "I" (1731/32–1804) of the Spring Garden Farm, Frederick County, Maryland, 2nd ed. [n.p.: author], 1991. 392pp.

Stopp, Klaus
The Printed Birth and Baptismal Certificates of the German Americans. Mainz, Germany/East Berlin, PA: author, 1997–2001. Illus.
A six-volume publication describing artists and publishers of *Fraktur* certificates. Volume II contains material on those produced at the Ephrata Cloister (pp. 98–219); Volume V contains materials on the Jacob, Johann, and Solomon Sala family of printers; Volume VI contains additional Ephrata material.

Stowe, David
"From Ephrata (F-Ra-Ta) to Arkestra." Esoterica, 5 (2004).

Strege, Merle D., ed.
Baptism and Church: A Believers' Church Vision. Grand Rapids, MI: Sagamore Books, 1986. 221pp.
Papers from the 7th Believers Church conference, Anderson School of Theology, June 5–8, 1984, including "The Brethren," by Dale W. Brown (pp. 29–37) and "Teaching and Preaching Issues Arising from the B.E.M. Document," by Lauree Hersch Meyer (pp. 157–72).

Stryz, Jan
"The Alchemy of the Voice at Ephrata Cloister."
Esoterica 1 (1999): 133–59.

Stuckey, Clara Mabel
Stuckey, 7 Generations of the Descendants of Christian
Stuckey and Maria Richer. Also Associated Ziegler and
Conrad Families, ed. Ellen L. Svejda. [n.p.: author],
1984. 19pp.

Studebaker, David H., 1919-
A Biographical Sketch of the Life of Paul Basinger
Studebaker [1896–1968]. Burlingame, CA: 1996. Various
pagination.

Studebaker, Florence S.
My Stories, ed. Gwen Miller. Modesto, CA: author, [n.d.]
288pp.
Autobiography and biography of a Church of the Brethren writer and
editor, wife of pastor Paul B. Studebaker. It is about life in the
Northwest, with illustrations by Kevin Miller.

**Studebaker, Ruth Epler, 1928–, and Studebaker, David
Emmert, 1925–, eds.**
The Studebaker Family in America, 1736–1986. Volume
II. Tipp City, OH: Studebaker Family National Associ-
ation, 1986. xvi, 877pp., illus.
Detailed genealogical study.

**Studebaker, Ruth Epler, 1928–, and Merritt, Didra,
eds.**
The Studebaker Family in America, 1739–1996. Volume
III. Tipp City, OH: Studebaker Family National Association, 1996. xviii, 767pp., illus.

Stump, Paul
"Dunkard Brethren Mission in Africa." In: The Brethren
Presence in the World...: Proceedings of the 3rd Brethren
World Assembly, July 23–26, 2003, ed. William R.
Eberly. Philadelphia, PA: Brethren Encyclopedia, Inc.,
2004, 113–16.

Stutesman, John Hale, 1930–
Jacob Stutzman (?–1775), His Children and Grandchild-
ren. Baltimore: Gateway Press, 1982. 308pp.
With many related Brethren families.

"A Revolutionary War Company of Maryland Which
Included Members of the Dunker Community." Mennonite Family History, 15 (1996): 39–41.

"A 1782 North Carolina Petition Pertaining to the
Dunkers." Mennonite Family History, 16 (1997): 153.

Sutton, Robert P.
Communal Utopias and the American Experience:
Religious Communities. Westport, CT: Prager, 2003, 1:
1–16.
On the Ephrata Society.

Svejda, Ellen, comp.
Stuckey: Descendants of Christian Stuckey and Maria
Richer. [n.p.: author], 1984.
Also Ziegler and Conrad families.

Swank, Scott T., 1941–, and others, eds.
Arts of the Pennsylvania Germans. Philadelphia: W. W.
Norton for the Winterthur Museum, 1983.

Swartley, Willard
"The Anabaptist Use of Scripture: Contemporary
Applications and Prospects." In: Anabaptist Currents:
History in Conversation with the Present, eds. Carl F.
Bowman and Stephen L. Longenecker. Camden, ME:
Penobscot Press, 1995, 65–79.

Swartz, Joseph and Swartz, George
Descendants of George William Swartz and Rebecca
Snell Swartz. [n.p.]: authors, 1983. 28pp.

Sweet, Leonard I.
The Minister's Wife: Her Role in Nineteenth-Century
American Evangelicalism. Philadelphia: Temple Univer-
sity Press, 1983.
Refers to Harriet Livermore.

Taylor, Eugene
Shadow Culture: Psychology and Spirituality in America.
Washington, DC: Counterpoint, 1999.
Includes Conrad Beissel as a counterpart to Jonathan Edwards.

Temme, Willi
"Die Buttlarsche Rotte – Ein Forschungsbericht."
Pietismus und Neuzeit, 16 (1990): 53–75.

Krise der Leiblichkeit: Die Sozietät der Mutter Eva
(Buttlarsche Rotte) und der radikale Pietismus um 1700.
Göttingen: Vandenhoeck & Rupprecht, 1998. 486pp.
Arbeiten zur Geschichte des Pietismus, 35; a detailed study of
"Mother" Eva von Buttlar, her society, and the Wittgenstein Pietists.
Many references to E. C. Hochmann von Hochenau and also to
Georg Grebe (p. 150) and the Brethren (p. 418).

[Thalitzer, Johannes Hansen]
Vor Menigheds Historie. [Copenhagen: Rolff. Dupl., ca.
1958]. 52pp.
A history of the Brethren in Europe, America, and Scandinavia, written by leaders of the Christ's Assembly. An English translation in
manuscript by Kenneth D. Whitehead (completed Dec. 1, 1998) is
located in the Young Center, Elizabethtown PA.

Thomas, Richard, 1940–
Simple Answers to Faith Questions. Columbus, GA:
Brentwood Christian Press, 1994. 70pp.
Includes: "God's plan of salvation" and "Tell me about the Church of
the Brethren."

Thomas, Susie M.
More Than Conquerors Through Him Who Loved Us.
[n.p.]: author, 1970. 104pp.

Thomasson, Kermon, 1936–
The Old, Old Story . . . Anew: The Church of the Brethren
in Nigeria. Elgin, IL: BP, 1983. 32pp.
Reflections on a visit to Nigeria for a 60th anniversary celebration.

"The Saga of Snow Hill (Nunnery)." Messenger (July,
1997): 10–12.

Thompson, Charles Dillard
"'You Must Not Idle Stand': A Labor Theory of Religion;
A Study of the Old German Baptist Brethren in the Pigg

River District [VA]." MA thesis, University of North Carolina, Chapel Hill, 1994, v, 121pp.

Thurian, Max, ed., 1921–1996
Churches Respond to BEM: Official Responses to the "Baptism, Eucharist, and Ministry" Text. Geneva: World Council of Churches, 1988.
Contains CB response.

Trahair, Richard C. S.
Utopians and Utopias: An Historical Dictionary. Westport, CT: Greenwood, 1999.
Articles on "Ephratans" (p. 117–18) and Conrad Beissel (p. 32).

Tussing, Ann K. U.
"The Hungry Orphan, Conrad Beissel." Communal Societies, 10 (1990): 87–101.
A somewhat-tortured explanation of Beissel's character and behavior as caused by his orphan status.

Ulrich, Daniel, 1959–, and Fairchild, Janice, 1947–
Caring Like Jesus: The Mathew 18 Project. Elgin, IL: Brethren Press, 2002. 157pp.

Van Dyck, Harry R.
Exercise of Conscience: A WW II Objector Remembers. Buffalo, NY: Prometheus Books, 1990. 250pp.
On CPS.

Versluis, Arthur, 1959–
Wisdom's Children: A Christian Esoteric Tradition. Albany: State University of New York Press, 1999). xiv, 370pp.
On the Brethren and Ephrata (pp. 100–11).

Viehmeyer, L. Allen, 1942–
"Anna of Ephrata." Historic Schaefferstown Record, 8 (March, 1974): 22–30.

"The *Bruderlied* and the *Schwesterlied* of the Ephrata Cloister." Yearbook of German-American Studies, 31 (1996): 121–36.

Viehmeyer, L. Allen, ed., 1942–
An Index to Hymns and Hymn Tunes of the Ephrata Cloister, 1730–1766. Including All Printed and Manuscript Hymnals and Hymnal Fragments and Representative Music Manuscript. Ephrata, PA: Ephrata Cloister Associates, 1995. Various pagination.

Virginia Council of Churches
Watchers of the Springs: A Collection of Rural Life Sermons and Addresses. Richmond, VA: Virginia Council of Churches, [1950]. 132pp.
Contains sermons by CB pastors.

Vogt, Esther Loewen
The Splendid Vista. Scottdale, PA; Herald Press, 1984. 192pp.
Fictional account of Kirsten Weber, a young Brethren woman, during the Battle of Antietam in the Civil War.

Vogt, Peter
"Zinzendorf und die Pennsylvanischen Synoden 1742." Unitas Fratrum, 36 (1994): 5–60.

Vogt, Peter, ed.
Authentische Relation von dem Anlass, Fortgang und Schlusse der am 1sten und 2ten Januarii Anno 1741/2 in Germantown gealtenen Versammlung einiger Arbeiter derer meisten Christlichen Religionen und Vieler vor sich selbst Gott-dienenden Christen-Menschen in Pennsylvania. An Authentic Relation of the Occasion, Continuance, and Conclusion of the First Assembly of Some Labourers out of Most of the Christian Religions and Other Private Religious People in Pensilvania, Kept in Germantown 1st and 2nd Jan. 1741/2. Hildesheim: G. Olms, 1998. lxx, 195pp.
Well-annotated and introduced edition of the first of the Pennsylvania Synods held under the leadership of the Moravian Count Zinzendorf, with Brethren participation.

Von Flue, Eleanor Grace
Ancestral Charts of Hazel Hannah Sayer, Wife of George Maxwell von Flue. [n.p.: author], 1987.

Voorheis, Grace Schock, comp.
Shock Work Book, Volume I: Memories of Elmer (1890–1970) and Bessie (1888–1986) Shock. [n.p.: author], 1988. 96pp.

Waas, Benaiah Frank, 1894–
One Life. [n.p.: 1980]. 181pp.
Autobiography of a Brethren settler in Indiana, Kansas, Idaho, and California.

Wagner, Murray L., Jr., 1937–
A Centennial History: First Church of the Brethren, Harrisburg, PA, 1896–1996. Kearney, NE: Morris Publishing Company, 1996. 79pp.

"Social Gospel Liberalism: Postmillennial Views among the Brethren." BLT, 46 (Winter/Spring, 2001): 134–38.

Wagner, Murray L., Sr., 1905–
To Heal the Broken. Elgin, IL: General Brotherhood Board, 1965. 65pp.

Wagner, Walter H.
The Zinzendorf-Muhlenberg Encounter: A Controversy in Search of Understanding. Nazareth, PA: Moravian Historical Society, 2002.
On Beissel and Ephrata, A. Mack and the Brethren (pp. 19–21).

Wagoner, Bob, 1930–, and Wagoner, Shirley
Community in Paraguay. Farmington, PA: Plough Publishing House, 1992. 282pp.
The account of a visit to the Society of Brothers (Bruderhof) in Paraguay in 1953. The original account was instrumental in motivating several young CB ministerial families to join the Bruderhof.

Wallmann, Johannes, 1930–
Der Pietismus. Band 4/O 1, Die Kirche in ihrer Geschichte. Göttingen: Vandenhoeck & Ruprecht, 1990. 143pp.
"Die Schwarzenauer Neutäufer" (pp. 105–06).

Wallower, Lucille, 1910–
Chooky. Philadelphia: David McKay Company, [1942]. 91pp.
A children's book dealing with a Dunker family.

Walter, Hugo G., 1959–
True Christianity: Twelve Lives of True Christians. New York: Vantage Press, 1988. ix, 209pp.
Includes August Hermann Francke (pp. 146–58).

Walters, Jonathan S., comp.
Genealogical Records of Some Early Fayette County [PA] Brethren. Birmingham, MI: author, 1979. 228pp.

Wampler, Joseph D.
That All May See in Comfort. Bridgewater, VA: author, [1955]. 27pp.

Wangman, Andrew
"Translation of Peter Miller's letter to Peter Lehman." Chronicon, 11 (February, 1993): [4].

Ward, W. R[eginald], 1925–
The Protestant Evangelical Awakening. Cambridge, UK: Cambridge University Press, 1992. xv, 370pp.
References to the Brethren.

Warfel, Stephen G.
Historical and Archaeological Investigations Associated with the Ephrata Cloister Fire Detection and Suppression System Project. Harrisburg: State Museum of Pennsylvania, 1990.

Historical Archaeology at Ephrata Cloister: A Report on 1993 Investigations. Harrisburg: State Museum of Pennsylvania, 1993.
The series was continued annually through 2001 (2002).

Wayland, Francis Fry
Bridgewater College: The First Hundred Years, 1880–1980. Bridgewater, VA: Bridgewater College, 1993. xxv, 979pp., illus.

Weaver, E. Paul, 1912–2001
Journey into Faith. Jos, Nigeria: Midland Press, 1994. 208pp.
Reflections on ministry as a pastor, missionary, and church executive, active in witnessing to governments.

Weaver, J. Denny
"Understandings of Salvation: The Church, Pietistic Experience, and Nonresistance." In: Anabaptist Currents: History in Conversation with the Present, eds. Carl F. Bowman and Stephen L. Longenecker. Camden, ME: Penobscot Press, 1995, 27–39.

Weaver, William Woys, trans. and ed., 1947–
Sauer's Herbal Cures: America's First Book of Botanic Healing, 1762–1778. New York/London: Routledge, 2001. xii, 400pp.
Taken from the almanacs of Christoph Sauer II.

Weber, Barbara Ohler
Fleeing to the Enemy. Post Falls, ID: author, 1996. iv, 222pp.
With Vera-Fern Holland. Autobiographical account of a Volksdeutsche refugee family resettled by the Wenatchee, WA, Sunnyslope CB congregation following World War II.

Weber, Richard R.
Stoner Brethren. Columbia, MD: author, 1993. 638pp.
Detailed and documented genealogy of the descendants of John Stoner (1705–69), largely in Pennsylvania and Maryland, with 6,000 indexed names.

Stover Brethren: The Family of Elder William Stover of Antietam. Morgantown, PA: Masthof Press for the author, 2001. 702pp.
Detailed genealogical study of the 13,000 plus descendants of Elder J. W. Stober (1726–1800), including references to the Barnhart, Flora, Good, Naff, Royer, Shank, and Welty families, among others.

Weddle, Ethel Harshbarger
Pleasant Hill. Girard, IL: Girard History Book Committee, 2002. 377pp., illus.
A reprint of 1956 story based on the Southern Illinois CB congregation, it also contains a 92-page pictorial section, an every-name index, and a cemetery listing of the 1970s.

Weidner, Marilyn Kemp
"The Repair of the Wall Charts from the Cloister at Ephrata, Pennsylvania." In: Conservation and Restoration of Pictorial Arts. London/Boston: Butterworths, 1976.

Weiser, Frederick S.
The Gift Is Small, The Love Is Great: Pennsylvania German Small Presentation Frakturs. York, PA: York Graphic Services, Inc., 1994. 119, [1]pp., illus.
Ephrata (pp. 9, 26).

Weitzel, Louise A.
A Quiver of Arrows. Lititz, PA: Express Printing Co., 1908.
Contains "The Old Cloister at Ephrata, Pa.," a poem.

Welch, Gladys Snavely, 1913–
The Nebraska Wines. [n.p.: author], 1984. 42pp.

Keeping the Promise. [n.p.: author], 1987. 198pp.
Pioneer life in Kansas.

Wellenreuther, Hermann
"Image and Counterimage, Tradition and Expectation: The German Immigrants in English Colonial Society in Pennsylvania, 1700–1765." In: America and the Germans: An Assessment of a Three-Hundred Year History. Volume One, eds. Frank Trommler and Joseph McVeigh. Philadelphia: University of Pennsylvania Press, 1985, pp. 84–105.
Many references to Christoph Sauer I.

"Contexts for Migration in the Early Modern World: Public Policy, European Migrating Experiences, Transatlantic Migration, and the Genesis of American Culture." In: In Search of Peace and Prosperity, eds. Hartmut Lehmann and others. University Park, PA: Pennsylvania State University Press, 2000, pp. 3–35.
Discusses Christoph Sauer I and his use of language.

Wells, (Mrs.) Cecil F. and others
"The Snowberger Family." Old Order Notes, no. 19 (Spring/Summer, 1999): 99–111.

Wenger, Samuel S., Wenger, Earl K., Sr., and Wenger, Helen L.
The Wenger Book. Lancaster, PA: Pennsylvania German Heritage Association, 1997.
Reprint.

[Wenger Family]
The Wenger Book Index. Lancaster, PA: Wenger Family, 1989. 340pp.

Wentz, James E.
Cove Giants of the 20th Century. [New York]: Krause Publ., 1999. 224pp.
Biographies of ca. 100 men and women of Morrison's Cove, Central Pennsylvania.

Wentz, Richard E., ed.
Pennsylvania Dutch Folk Spirituality. New York: Paulist Press, 1993. vii, 329pp.
Ephrata texts (pp. 87–105).

Western Plains District, Church of the Brethren
Western Plains District Directory, Church of the Brethren. McPherson, KS: Western Plains District, 1998. 40pp.

Whisler, William
Grand Old [Manchester] College Daze. [Bremen, IN]: author, 1993. 185, [2]pp.

What Happened, Grandpa? [Bremen, IN]: author, 1981. [iii], 199pp.
Memoirs of life in Indiana, North Dakota, New Mexico, and Kansas.

Whitcomb, John C., Jr., 1924–
The Nature of Biblical Creation. Grand Rapids, MI: Reformed Fellowship, 1966. 29pp.

Bible and Astronomy. Winona Lake, IN: BMH Books, 1984.

"Grace Brethren Divide." The Biblical Evangelist, 26 (Sept. 1, 1992): 8, 17.

World That Perished. Grand Rapids, MI: Baker Books, 1984.
Also published (Winona Lake, IN: BMH Books, 1984).

Mundo Que Perecio. [n.p.]: Kreger Publications, 1991.

Terra Primitiva. [n.p.]: Kreger Publications, 1993.

Whitcomb, John C., Jr., 1924–, and Davis, John J., 1936–
History of Israel. Winona Lake, IN: BMH Books, [n.d.] Israel: From Conquest to Exile: A Commentary on Joshua-2 Kings. Winona Lake, IN: BMH Books, 1989. 542pp., illus.

Whitcomb, John C., Jr., 1924, and Masters, Peter
The Charismatic Phenomenon. London: Metrolitan Tabernacle, 1982. 23pp.

White, Janet R.
"The Ephrata Cloister: Intersection of Architecture and Culture in an Eighteenth-Century Utopia." Utopian Studies, 11/2 (2000): 57–76.

Whitney, Mary E.
Bring Me a Windmill: The Gibbel Family of Hemet [CA]. Hemet, CA: Curry Copy Center, 1985. [4], 39pp.
Mentions the families of Isaac Markey Gibbel, Isaac Brubaker Gibbel, and Owen Walmer Gibbel.

Wiles, Virginia
"Gentle Strength: Contemporary Prospects for an Understanding of Salvation." In: Anabaptist Currents: History in Conversation with the Present, eds. Carl F. Bowman and Stephen L. Longenecker. Camden, ME: Penobscot Press, 1995, 41–48.

Wilhelm, Paul A.
Civilian Public Servants: A Report on 210 World War II Conscientious Objectors, rev. ed. Washington, DC: NISBCO, 1994. x, 85pp.
First published in 1990.

Williams, Anna Blough
The Family of Jesse Conner of Montgomery County, Pennsylvania. Bridgewater, VA: author, 1985. 70pp.

Williamson, Chet, 1948–
Uniting Work and Spirit: A Centennial History of Elizabethtown College. Elizabethtown, PA: Elizabethtown College, 2001. v, 352pp., illus.

Willoughby, William G., 1917–
"Meet the Brethren Church." Messenger (March, 1992): 10–11.

"Meet the Old German Baptist Brethren." Messenger (April, 1992): 10–11.
Published as "The Other Brethren: The Old German Baptist Brethren," BE (April, 1992): 8–9.

"Meet the Dunkard Brethren." Messenger (May, 1992): 22–23.
Published as "The Other Brethren: The Dunkard Brethren," BE (May, 1992): 6–7.

"Meet the Grace Brethren." Messenger (June, 1992): 18–19.
Published as "The Other Brethren: The Fellowship of Grace Brethren Churches""BE (June, 1992): 10–11.

"The Other Brethren: The Church of the Brethren." BE (July-Aug., 1992): 10–12.

The Beliefs of the Early Brethren, 1706–1735. Ambler, PA: Brethren Encyclopedia, Inc., 1999. x, 108pp.
A revision of the author's like-titled 1951 doctoral dissertation, Boston University.

"Honors to Alexander Mack." www.cob-net.org/mack/-honors.

Wilmann, Christa M.
"A Small Herbal of Little Cost, 1762–1778: A Case Study of a Colonial Herbal as a Social and Cultural Document." PhD dissertation, University of Pennsylvania, 1980.
On the publication by Sauer II, Kurzgefasstes Kräuter-Buch, issued serially in his almanac.

Wilson, Leland, 1930–
Silver City. Elgin, IL: BP, 1980. 96pp.

Living with Beauty. York, PA: Memory Lane Publishers, 1984. 147pp.

Wilson, Leland, ed., 1930–
[Special issue on church-state relationships]. BLT, 32 (Autumn, 1987): 196–255.
Articles by Robert W. Neff, Susan I. Boyer, D. F. Durnbaugh, Stephen L. Longenecker, Kenneth L. Gibble, Duane H. Ramsey, Ralph E. Watkins, and Leland Wilson.

Wilson, Renate
Pious Traders in Medicine: A German Pharmaceutical Network in Eighteenth Century North America. University Park, PA: Pennsylvania State University Press, 2000. xiv, 258pp., illus.
Includes material on C. Sauer (pp. 6, 53, 117, 135).

Wittler, Catherine
The Bungalow. [Sebring, FL:] author, ca. 1984.
A novel.

Wittman, Bruce C.
Lancaster Inspiring: Steeples of Lancaster County. Lancaster, PA: author, 1992. Poster.
Includes Mountville Church of the Brethren.

Wittschiebe, Charles E.
"Prophetism among German-American Sects in the United States." MA thesis, Seventh-Day Adventist Theological Seminary, 1946. 99pp.

Wokeck. Marianne Sophia
"The Flow and Composition of German Immigrants to Philadelphia, 1727–1775." Pennsylvania Magazine of History and Biography, 105 (July, 1981): 245–78.

"Tide of Alien Tongues: The Flow and Ebb of German Immigration to Pennsylvania, 1683–1775." PhD dissertation, Temple University, 1983.

"Harnessing the Lure of 'The Best Poor Man's Country': The Dynamics of German-Speaking Immigration to British North America, 1683–1783." In: To Make America: European Emigration in the Early Modern Period, eds. Ida Altman and James Horn. Berkeley, CA: 1991, pp. 104–43.

Trade in Strangers: The Beginnings of Mass Migration to North America. University Park, PA: Pennsylvania State University Press, 1999. xxx, 319pp.
Detailed study of the emigration, primarily of Germans and Irish, to the American colonies, with many references to C. Sauer's involvement in encouraging migration and alleviating its hardships.

Wolf, Dorothy K., comp.
"Indian Creek Church of the Brethren Cemetery, Vernfield, PA." [n.p.]: 1991.

Womelsdorf, Josef
"Womelsdorf and Wittgensteiners." Die Shilgrut fun der Tulpehock 15 (November, 1983): 1–88.
On C. Sauer (pp. 27–33).

Wood, Stacy B. C., Jr.
Clockmakers and Watchmakers of Lancaster County, Pennsylvania. Lancaster: Lancaster County Historical Society, 1995.
Includes Gorgas from Ephrata.

World Friendship Center
The Unforgettable Fire. [n.p.: n.d.].
About the atomic bomb damage at Hiroshima, Japan; contains an English text by Leona Zigler Row.

Worstner, Betty Miller
"A Short History of the Daniel Miller/Susannah Bowman Family." Old Order Notes, no. 14 (Fall, 1996): 61–68.

Wright, E. Edward
18th Century Church Records of Lancaster County. Volume 5. Lancaster, PA: Willow Bend, 2002.
Contains records from these Brethren congregations: Cocalico/Conestoga German Baptists, White Oak German Baptists (Warwick Township), East Conewago German Baptists, Ephrata Seventh-Day German Baptist.

Wright, Lee-Lani
The Church of the Brethren Handbook on Church Unity. Elgin, IL: BP, 1988. 60, [2]pp.

Wust, Klaus, 1926–2003
"Feeding the Palatines: Shipboard Diet in the Eighteenth Century." The Report: A Journal of German-American History, 39 (1984): 32–42.

"The Emigration Season of 1738 – Year of the Destroying Angel." The Report: A Journal of German-American History 40 (1986): 21–56.
On Sauer's involvement with emigration.

"Dunkers on the Move: Brethren Migrations to Virginia, 1745–1800." In: Papers from the Elder John Kline Bicentennial Celebration, ed. William R. Eberly. Ambler, PA: Brethren Encyclopedia, Inc., 2002, 113–17.

Yoder, Don, ed., 1921–
Pennsylvania German Fraktur and Color Drawings. Lancaster, PA: Acorn Press, Inc., 1989.
Reprint of 1969 edition; with Ephrata Fraktur.

Wuthnow, Robert
"The Changing Character of American Spirituality." In: The Dilemma of Anabaptist Piety: Strengthening or Straining the Bonds of Community?, ed. Stephen L. Longenecker. Camden, ME: Penobscot Press, 1997, 109–21.

Yoder, Don, 1921, and others, eds.
Pennsylvania German Fraktur and Color Drawings. [Lancaster, PA]: Landis Valley Associates, 1969. Unpaginated, illus.
Ephrata (plates and descriptions, 1–20).

Yoder, Rosa L.
Old German Baptist Brethren Obituary Summaries from The Vindicator, 1870–1988: Volume 1. Goshen, IN: author, 1988. 345pp. (loose-leaf).
Lists names from A to C.

Yoder, Russell
Confidential Writings of Conrad Beissel, Colonial Mystic, 1691–1768: Selected and Translated from the Original German with Notes. [Waynesboro, PA]: Snow Hill Press, [1994]. 26pp.

Yothers, Richard J., Jr.
Descendants of Jacob Yothers, Bucks County, PA. Baltimore: Gateway Press, 1984. 210pp.

York Center Church of the Brethren
By God's Grace, We Have Flourished, 50 Years (1951–2001). York Center, IL; 2001. Unpaginated.

Young, Andrew (J.), 1932–
An Easy Burden: The Civil Rights Movement and the Transformation of America. New York: Harper Collins, 1996.
Mention of CB (p. 57), Manchester College (pp. 70–72), and Brethren Service workcamps (pp. 72–73).

Young, David S., 1944–
James: Faith in Action. Elgin, IL: BP, 1992. 79pp.
Covenant Bible Studies Series.

Servant Leadership for Church Renewal: Shepherds Try the Living Springs. Scottdale, PA: Herald Press, 1999. 176pp.

Young, Jerry R., 1939–
"The Relationship Between Local Grace Brethren Churches and Their Denominational Leadership: Case Studies." DMin dissertation, Dallas Theological Seminary, 1996. iv, 393pp.

"The Christian School Movement in the Fellowship of Grace Brethren Churches." In: Report of the Proceedings of the 1998 Brethren World Assembly, Bridgewater College . . . , ed. Dale R. Stoffer. Ashland, OH: Ashland Theological Seminary/Brethren Encyclopedia, Inc., 1999, 243–50.

Yount, Joseph B., III
"The Tunker House at Broadway, Rockingham County, Virginia." BLT, 33/2 (1988): 12–21.

Zeiser, Samuel R.
"Ecclesiolae in Ecclesia and Ecclesia Plantanda: Conflicting Approaches in Mission among the German Protestants in Colonial Pennsylvania." MDiv thesis, Lutheran Theological Seminary, Philadelphia, 1989.

Ziegler, Edward Krusen, 1903–1989
Joyful Noises: Poems, Hymns, and Meditations. Bridgewater, VA: author, 1985. 70pp.
Collection of poetry and readings.

Prayers for Public Worship. Elgin, IL: BP, 1986. 72pp.

Ziegler, John L., comp.
The Ziegler Family Record, Elder Jesse Ziegler and Daniel P. Ziegler, compilers. 1906, 118pp. Levi C. Ziegler Family Record, 1865–1981, Lois Rienhard, compiler, 1981, 39pp. Compiled and Reprinted by John L. Ziegler. Elgin, IL: BP, 1983.

Zikmund, Barbara Brown; Lummis, Adair T., and Chang, Patricia M., eds.
Clergy Women: An Uphill Calling. Louisville, KY: Westminster/John Knox Press, 1998.
Includes CB ministers in its survey.

Zook, Harry D.
Zug/Zuck/Zook Genealogy. Baltimore, MD: Gateway Press, 1983. 428pp.

Zook, Lois Martin
A Bit of Heaven on the Conestoga. Morgantown, PA: Masthof Press for the author, 2001. 162pp., illus.
Fictionalized account supposedly based on fact, with reference to Alexander Mack, Conrad Beissel, and the Eberly, Wenger, and Sauer families.

Zunkel, C. Wayne, 1931–
To Follow in Jesus' Steps. Elgin, IL: BP, 1985. 106pp.
Reprinted: Elgin, IL: BP, 1991; translated into Korean, Spanish, and Creole.

Church Growth Under Fire. Scottdale, PA: Herald Press, 1987. 250pp.

Dare to Grow: Building Healthy Churches. Elgin, IL: David C. Cook Press, 1993.

Zunkel, C. Wayne, ed., 1931–
[Special issue, Brethren evangelism]. BLT, 35 (Summer, 1990): 183–232.
Essays by: Paul E. R. Mundey, Olden D. Mitchell, Harold S. Martin, Floyd E. Bantz, Harold Z. Bomberger, Earl K. Ziegler, and William P. Robinson.

Zunkel, Cleda Shull, 1903–
A Faith That Sings. Elgin, IL: BP, 1981. 111pp.

Trimming the Wicks. Bourbon, IN: Harmony Press, 1982. 192pp.
Memoirs of the William H. and Clara Gibson Shull family.

LIST OF DONORS TO THE VOLUME 4 PROJECT OF BRETHREN ENCYCLOPEDIA, INC.

Compiled by Ronald G. Lutz and Dale V. Ulrich.

Fund raising to support preparation of *Volume 4* of *The Brethren Encyclopedia* began at the 1998 Brethren World Assembly in Bridgewater, VA. Prior to that, the Board of Directors approved following the pattern for financing *Volume 4* that had been used in the late 1970s to support publication of *Volumes 1-3*. That was, contributions would be sought to support preparing the manuscript, and pre-publication sales would provide for the cost of printing.

Dale V. Ulrich, provost and professor of physics emeritus at Bridgewater College, prepared and distributed *Brethren Encyclopedia News* describing the *Volume 4* project and other programs sponsored by Brethren Encyclopedia, Inc. Ronald G. Lutz, pastor of the Ambler Church of the Brethren, received and deposited contributed funds. During the course of this project, Lutz retired from full-time pastoral ministry. Both Lutz and Ulrich served voluntarily without remuneration for their work on this project.

Records of sales and contributions for the *Volume 4* project were maintained by Ronald G. Lutz, and financial statements were prepared by Claire M. Ulrich. A total of $95,134.58 was contributed, and $28,086.00 was received through pre-publication sales. The cost of preparation of the manuscript was $80,117.38.

Volume 4 was made possible by the generosity of the following plus some anonymous donors:

Anderson Church of the Brethren (IN)

Annville Church of the Brethren (PA)

Ferne Baldwin

Floyd and Alta Bantz

Baugo Church of the Brethren (IN)

Harlan J. and Betty L. Bayer

Ronald D. and Linda E. Beachley

Fred W. and Reva Benedict

Bermudian Church of the Brethren (PA)

Charles M. and Mary Beth (dec.) Bieber

Emmert F. and Esther L. Bittinger

Black Rock Church of the Brethren (PA)

Harold Z. and Betty Bomberger

Aretas C. and Edna E. Boone

Carl W. Bowman

Darin Keith Bowman

Auburn A. Boyers

Brethren Village Chapel (PA)

Brethren World Assembly (1998)

Brethren World Assembly (2003)

Bridgewater Church of the Brethren,
Altruistic Class (VA)

Bridgewater College

Dale W. Brown

Paul W. and Evelyn M. Brubaker

Lillian T. Brumbaugh

John E. and Janie T. Bryant

Betty Jo Buckingham

J. Mark and Martha M. Bushong

L. Clyde Carter, Jr.

Champaign Church of the Brethren (IL)

Christian Fellowhip Dunkard Brethren Church

Church of the Brethren General Board

Clay County Church of the Brethren (FL)

Robert G. and Bonnidell A. Clouse

Craig Coble

Alvin E. Conner

Conservative Baptist Brethren Church (PA)

Lawrence Crist

James L. Custer

Margaret Glick Davis

Allen C. and Joan G. Deeter

Sophia V. Dilling (dec.)

DONORS

Dixon Church of the Brethren (IL)

Scott L. and Rebecca Duffey

Dunkard Brethren Church

Donald F. and Hedda T. Durnbaugh

William R. and Eloise W. Eberly

Charles and Cynthia Ebersole

Linda W. Effinger in honor of Margaret Ella Longenecker Wagner

Eikenberry-Langdon Family in memory of Lorrel and Nelda Rhoades Eikenberry

David L. and Ruth H. Eiler

Eldon and Margaret Eller

John C. and Elizabeth Eller

Vernard and Phyllis Eller

English River Church of the Brethren (IA)

Warren and Theresa Eshbach

Grace W. Evans

Larry and Sonia Ewald

Fletcher Farrar and Mary Jessup

Ronald J. Filbrun

Donald R. Fitzkee

Jerry Flora

Lowell and Barbara Flory

Pauline G. Flory

Clyde and Elsie Fry

Roy D. and Doris Frysinger

David E. Fuchs

Paul E. Garber

Wayne F. and Maurine G. Geisert

James C. and Elaine Gibbel

Stanley J. and Barbara J. Gilbert

John T. Glick, Jr.

G. Wayne and Barbara Z. Glick in honor of John T. Glick, Jr.

Judith L. Glick-Smith in memory of M. R. Zigler, Geraldine Zigler Glick, and Amy Glick Hill

Clara Glover

Green Tree Church of the Brethren (PA)

Greenville Church of the Brethren (OH)

LeRoy and Kathi Griffin

Lavonne I. Grubb

Wayne and Lynette Guyer

Lowell D. and Kathryn L. Hackman

Norman and Lois Eby Harsh

Jim and Bonnie Haughn

Marlin L. and Shirley L. Heckman

A. Blair and Patricia Helman

D. Robert Hess

Robert L. Hoffman

James Hollinger

Holmesville Church of the Brethren (NE)

John and Janet Hoover

Huntsdale Church of the Brethren (PA)

Thomas E. and Janice Hurst

Ervin L. and Joan Bucher Huston

John Earl and Mary Ellen Hutchison

Mike and Mindi Jentes

Robert and Ruthann Johansen

Roy Johnson

Robert and Sybil Keim

Robert and Dolores Keplinger

Anna M. Kepner

Robert (dec.) and Mary Kintner

Warren S. and Jean Kissinger

Harold R. and Dawn M. Kulp

Dennis Landes

Glen Landes

John David Lefever

Robert S. and Sharon Lehigh

Thomas Liby and Carol Smith

D. Eugene and Eloise Lichty

Linville Creek Church of the Brethren (VA)

Lititz Church of the Brethren (PA)

Stephen L. Longenecker

Ronald G. and Ila Lutz

Harold S. and Priscilla Martin

Mary Margaret Longaker Foundation

Joseph M. and Dorotha Fry Mason

Marion E. and Joan M. Mason

Louise McFadden

J. Jack and Mary Melhorn

Michigan City Church of the Brethren (IN)

Middle Creek Church of the Brethren (PA)

Middlebury Church of the Brethren (IN)

Glen and Linda Miller

Jacob and Arlene Miller

John M. and Mary M. Miller

John M. Miller in memory of Sunday school teachers
Emma Ludwick, Luella Bailey, and Bessie Holsinger of
the Beaver Run Church (WV)

Lowell A. and Peggy W. Miller

Marcus and Emily Miller

Richard R. and Joyce D. Miller

Wayne L. and Gwendolyn Miller

Elma L. Moss

Mountville Church of the Brethren (PA)

Charles Munson

James F. and Faye Myer

Beatrice M. Myers

Myerstown Church of the Brethren
Home Builders Class (PA)

Phyllis Honaker Needleman

Dean R. and Betty Y. Neher

Jacob C. and Fern Ness

Keith A. and Beth H. Nonemaker

North Manchester First Brethren Church (IN)

North Winona Church of the Brethren (IN) in honor of
William R. Eberly

Alfred and Betty Lou Nyce

Frances C. Nyce

Phoebe M. Orebaugh

Osceola Church of the Brethren (IN)

Palmyra Church of the Brethren (PA)

Dorothy Patterson

N. Ivan and Clara Patterson

Jean Petre

Roy E. and Violet H. Pfaltzgraff

Philip and Gena Phenix

Plevna Dunkard Brethren Church (IN)

Prymont Church of the Brethren (IN)

George and Judy Mills Reimer

Maris T. Rice

Thomas and Mary Lou Riethof

Jesse D. and Wilma Robertson

Alpheus and Alice Rohrer

Glenn N. Rohrer

Jimmy Ross

Donald E. (dec.) and Eleanor Rowe

Douglas and Sally Ruby

Janice L. Ruhl

Esther Fern Rupel

Rupert and Kinsel Families

Viola R. Sager (dec.) in memory of Preston L. Sager

Sangerville Church of the Brethren in honor of William
and Elsie Eicher

LeVerle H. Sappington

Dean Shaffer

Kenneth M. Shaffer, Jr.

Ralph and Catherine Shively

Merlin G. Shull

Joseph (dec.) and Doris Shultz

DONORS

Ron and Janice Sink

Harold D. and Miriam R. Smith

Armon and Lucille Snowden

Benjamin and Nelda W. Sollenberger

South Bay Community Church of the Brethren (CA)

St. Petersburg First Church of the Brethren (FL)

Staunton Church of the Brethren (VA)

Paul and Donna Steiner

Dale R. and Marcia Stoffer

Claude (dec.) and Barbara (dec.) Stone

Phillip C. and Cherrill K. Stone

Stuart and Lorraine Suter

J Hudson and Cheryl D. Thayer

Marvin W. Thill

Ellen Thomason

R. Jan and Roma Jo Thompson

Charles W. Turner (dec.)

Dale V. and Claire M. Ulrich

Daniel W. and Paula Z. Ulrich

David L. and Robyn T. Wampler

Fred F. and Dorris B. Wampler

Fred W. and Josephine S. Wampler

J. Paul and Priscilla W. Wampler

Wayne Heights Brethren Church (PA)

Waynesboro Church of the Brethren (PA)

Max E. and Pauline S. Webb

J. Calvin and Shirley Wenger

White Oak Church of the Brethren (PA)

Mark and Dawn O. Wilhelm

Dewey M. and Melissa Williard

J. C. and Jean Wine

David and Joy Wolf

Jerry R. and Loreen Young

Joseph B. Yount III

Earl K. Ziegler

Levi J. and Helen R. Ziegler

Eugene and Mary Zimmerman

ADDITIONS AND CORRECTIONS
TO THE BRETHREN ENCYCLOPEDIA VOLUMES 1–3

Compiled by D. F. Durnbaugh.

In volumes containing as many details as *The Brethren Encyclopedia,* with limited time and staff, it was inevitable an unfortunate number of errors were published in it. Already with the publication of volume three of the reference work, errata were printed at the end of the volume (pp. 2125-26). Included with this were eleven articles inadvertently dropped in the composition process— **Alexandria, VA, Grace Brethren Church** through **Allison Prairie Church of the Brethren, IL.** Because of their location, these entries have often been overlooked by those consulting the encyclopedia.

Since 1983-84 errors and omissions have been called to our attention by helpful readers, some of whom had personal information unavailable to the encyclopedia staff. We are grateful to all of those who took the trouble to inform us of these problems. In particular, past and present staff members of the Brethren Historical Library and Archives, Elgin, IL—Gwendolyn F. Bobb, James R. Lynch, Rosalita Leonard, and Kenneth M. Shaffer, Jr.—

have been diligent in noting and reporting needed improvements. Bradley F. Weidenhamer corrected the list of ministers of The Brethren Church. The present editors also made numerous corrections and additions. We have made no effort to update bibliographical references where no additions or corrections were entered.

In the case of men and women who were allocated biographical sketches in volumes one and two, we have attempted to ascertain and list death dates where these have occurred since 1983. Similarly, we have included elsewhere lists of deceased ministers and missionaries from the several Brethren bodies previously noted in volume three. Regrettably, because of the numbers involved, it is possible that some names have been missed, for which we apologize.

In the following, corrections and additions are listed in concise fashion. Some readers may wish to transfer these changes to the first three volumes. Our concern is to create an encyclopedia as accurate as humanly possible, recognizing that even near perfection is unattainable.

Volume 1:

[page number, line (of relevant article, caption, or notation), and action to be taken]

-xx, 2: **ERG**, *delete* 4

-xxxvii, 5: **DB** Dunkard Brethren, 1927-; *replace* 1927 *with* 1926

-xxxviii, 5: **W. M. Beahm,** *for* William A. Beahm *read* William M. Beahm

-xxxix, 4: **Full Report**, *delete* reprinted in 9 vols. (Elgin, IL: 1930)

-7, 1: **Africa**, *delete* **Cameroon** from the cross-reference.

-20, 2: **Altig, Jerome Keith and Vivian Carroll Force**, *for* Feb. 27, 1911 *read* Feb. 26, 1911

-78, 1, 7: **Baker, John Calhoun**, *replace* b. 1895 *with* 12-21-1895 / 6-9-1999; *add for* Elizabeth Evans Baker *this text*: d. 6-21, 1990; *add* (obit.) *New York Times* (June 12, 1999), (June 13, 1999): *Juniata* (Fall, 1999) 31; *Messenger* (Dec., 1990) 3, (June, 1997) 10-15

-105, 3-4: **Beaver Creek Church of the Brethren**, *replace the text* "was first organized ca. 1828" *with this text* "was first organized in 1806"

-112, 1: **Beissel, Johann Conrad**, *replace* Johann *with* Georg

-118, 1: **Benshoff, William St. Clair**, *replace* b. 1914 *with* 4-24-1914 / 8-5-1991

-139, 13-14: **Bible Translations, Brethren**, *for* William M. Beahm (CB) translated the gospel of John into the Bura language *read* William M. Beahm translated *The New Testament* into the Bura language, revising earlier partial translations; it was published as *Alkawal Na Bilia.*

-143, 1ff., 20: **Bittinger, Desmond Wright**, *replace* b. *1905 with* 1-14-1905 / 11-5-1991; *for* pacificism *read* pacifism; *add Messenger* (Dec., 1985) 20-22, (Jan., 1992) 22, (June, 1998) 3; *Elizabethtown Magazine* (Summer, 1992) 75; *Bulletin of the Peace Studies Institute* 6/1 (Feb., 1976) 1-8

-145: *for* Carrol Co., MD *read* Carroll Co., MD.

-147, 1-6: **Blocher Family**, *replace first sentences with* – Matthias (1723-1803), son of Andreas and Anna Catharine Wegenast Blocher, was born at Holzhausen, Sulz, Württemberg. He arrived on the ship *Brothers* in Sept., 1753. Matthias (m. Barbara Schwab) settled in Manheim Twp., York Co., PA, near Hanover and reared eleven children.

-157, 7: **Bollinger, Florence Moyer**, *add* 12-16-1896 / 5-2-1993; *add Messenger* (July, 1993) 3

-158, 1: *****Bollinger, Russell V.**, *replace* b. 1901 *with* 10-5-1901 / 12-11-1985; *add Messenger* (March, 1986) 9

-165, 3, 5: **Bowman, Curtis Buford**, *for* Miranda *read* Maranda; *for* Baugher, *read* Baucher.

-167, 12: **Bowman, James Brubaker and Merle Allen**, *for* 1937 *read* 1946

-167, 3: **Bowman, Joseph B.**, *for* Christian *read* Christina

-168, 6: **Bowman, Rufus David**, *add* Northwestern U. (PhD, 1944)

-169, 1: **Bowman, Warren Daniel**, *replace* b. 1894 *with* 4-9-1894 / 4-23-1987; 27: *add* LLD degree by Bridgewater College, 1966; *add Messenger* (Aug./Sept., 1987), 48; F. W. Wayland, *Bridgewater College: The First Hundred Years, 1880–1980* (1993), esp. 467–567

-172, 1: **Brandt, Lucille Long Strayer**, *replace* b. 1900 *with* 7-22-1900 / 8-20-1994; *add Messenger* (Dec., 1994) 3

-174, 8-9: **Bremen, OH, Rush Creek Church of the Brethren**, *replace the text* until 1902 *with* until 1898

-178, 49: **Brethren, 1708-1883**, *for* sobor *read* sober

-193, 10-11: **Brethren Placement Service**, *replace present sentence with* Through Dec., 1964, 1,673 numbered listings included ads of job openings, persons seeking jobs, homes and land for sale, and church furnishings for sale or wanted.

-208, bibliography: **Bridgewater College**, *replace first sentence with* F. F. Wayland, *Bridgewater College: The First Hundred Years, 1880-1980* (1993)

-210, 8: **Broadfording Bible Brethren Church**, *for* offic *read* office

-210/11, 17-18: **Broadwater Chapel Dunkard Brethren Congregation, MD**, *delete the last sentence of the article*

-212, 7: **Brooks, Harlan Jesse and Ruth Elizabeth Forney**, *replace* b. 1896 *with* 10-5-1896 / 2-11-1989; *add Messenger* (April, 1989) 7, (April, 1991) 3

-219, 1: **Brumbaugh, Aaron John**, *add* d. Feb. 25, 1983; *add*, [obit.] *St. Petersburg Times* (Feb., 27, 1983): 23b and editorial.

-220, 1: **Brumbaugh, G. Edwin**, *replace* b. 1890 *with* 1890 / 11-29-1983; *add Messenger* (Feb., 1984) 8

-225, 1: **Buchele (Beachley, Beeghly) Family**, *for* (Beachley, Beeghly) Family, *read* (Buechley, Buechly, Beachley, Beeghly) Family

-225, photo caption: **Bucher, Rufus Pfautz**, *replace with* – Rufus P. Bucher, at the entrance to the chapel of Bethany Biblical Seminary, Oct. 1, 1946. Photo by J. Henry Long.

-225, bibliography: **Bucher, Rufus Pfautz**, *add GM* (Sept. 13, 1958) 6-10; *Elizabethtown* (Winter, 1988) 2-3; Caleb Bucher, *From Where I Stand* (1988).

-230, 1: **Burke, Cecile Davis**, *replace* b. 1899 *with* 1899 / by 1989; *add [Manchester College] Alumni Directory, Centennial Edition* (1989) 34

-230, 1: **Burke, Eldon R.**, *replace* b. 1898 *with* 1898 / 11-

30-1993; *add Messenger* (Nov., 1993) 2; *Manchester College Bulletin* (June, 1988) 3, (March, 1994) 2; *Bulletin of the Peace Studies Institute* (1988); Steve Bowers, *Planting the Faith in a New Land: The History of the Church of the Brethren in Indiana* (1992) 151-52; *[Manchester College] Alumni Directory, Centennial Edition* (1989) 34

-230, bibliography: **Burke, Homer Lionel and Marguerite Schrock**, *add Messenger* (June, 1983) 1, 7; Steve Bowers, *Planting the Faith in a New Land: The History of the Church of the Brethren in Indiana* (1992) 152-53

-254, photo caption: *replace with* -- Members of the Evergreen, VA, Church of the Brethren at love feast, wearing prayer veils or caps.

-272, 61, 63: **Charismatic Movement**, *for* converences *read* conferences; *for* memebers *read* members

-280, 1: **Christachari, Ishwarlal L.**, *replace* b. 1906 *with* 1906 / 3-22-1990; *add Messenger* (June, 1990) 8

-299, 6-8: **Church of the Brethren**, *replace with* was created n 1880 when some $500 was transferred to it from an evangelism fund; after four years its receipts were less than $6,000.

-326: *after* **Columbia City, IN, Church of the Brethren** *add cross reference* -- **Columbia Furnace, VA, Church of the Brethren.** *See* **Woodstock Church of the Brethren, VA**

-317, 15: **Clapper (Cloppert) Family**, *for* six years *read* twenty-six years

-326, after 3: *add new entry* **Columbus, OH, Church of the Brethren.** Organized in 1957 as the Columbus Brethren Student Fellowship, the congregation was active under the leadership of Edward H. Lander, Jr., Kenneth B. Byerly, and Donald N. Crusius until it was disorganized by the S. Ohio district in 1968. Membership varied from 26 in 1959 to a high of 106 in 1964. DFD

-329, photo caption: *replace with Fellowship meal during communion at the Evergreen Church of the Brethren, VA, ca. 1955. BHLA, Local Church File; J. Henry Long photo.*

-342, 1: *for* **Coon River Church of the Brethren, IA.** *See* **Panora, IL, Church of the Brethren** *read* **Coon River Church of the Brethren, IA.** *See* **Panora, IA, Church of the Brethren.**

-343/4, 1ff.: **Cordier, Andrew Wellington**, *replace* 1901-1975 *with* 3-3-1901 / 7-11-1975; *add Messenger* (Sept., 1995), inside cover, 14-15; Steve Bowers, *Planting the Faith in a New Land: The History of the Church of the Brethren in Indiana* (1992) 153-6

-356/7, 1: **Curry, Abram Stauffer**, *replace* b. 1913 *with* 4-6-1913 / 1-14-1994; *add Messenger* (March, 1994) 3

-361, 2: **Danner (Donner), Henry**, *for* Amy, *read* Anna

-362, 12: **Danner (Tanner, Donner), Michael**, *for* Amy, *read* Anna

-395, 12: Don River Old German Baptist Brethren Church, ONT., *add this sentence* The congregation was dissolved in 1981. *Add Vindicator* (1981) 216

-409, 59: Dunkard Brethren, *for* triune *read* trine

-410, 11: Dunkard Brethren, *replace* They serve at communion *with* They serve in preparing for communion

-410, 40-42: Dunkard Brethren, *replace this sentence* The congregations separately support other local or worldwide missionary or relief effort not organized by the church *with* The congregations sometimes separately support other local or worldwide relief efforts not organized by the church

-411, following Durst Family: *add new entry* **Dutch Bethel, German Baptist Brethren Church**, Owen Co., IN, located in Jefferson Twp., one mile north of Arney. The Arney, Fiscus, Inman, and Hauser families moved into this area shortly after 1820, many of them from *North Carolina. About 1825, *Abraham Kern of nearby Lawrence Co. organized a *Hostetler Brethren congregation with Obadiah Winters and John Arney as ministers, Charles Inman and Andrew Arney, deacons. Members built a log meetinghouse ca. 1830. In the early 1830s, after Kern joined the *Restoration movement, he persuaded the Dutch Bethel church to abandon trine immersion *baptism and eventually, under other leadership, the *love feast was dropped as well. It is thought that a minority faction withdrew over these changes and moved to Iowa, where they continued the Brethren ordinances. Frederick Hauser was an important preacher at Dutch Bethel in the 1840s. The membership in 1830 was said to number 200 and to be the largest Restoration congregation in the county. DBE
Millennial Harbinger (August, 1839) 355; Charles Blanchard, ed., *Counties of Clay and Owen, Indiana* (1994) 726, 731-33; A. T. DeGroot, *The Churches of Christ in Owen County, Indiana* ([1935]) 47-49, 102-10.

-413, 7-8: Early, Henry Clay (CB), *for* Shenandoah Valley Normal School *read* Virginia Normal School.

-417, 2: Eberbach, *replace* Johann *with* Georg

-417, 1: Eberly, John H., *replace* b. 1904 *with* 4-30-1904 / 10-13, 1985; *add Messenger* (Jan., 1986) 7; Steve Bowers, *Planting the Faith in a New Land: The History of the Church of the Brethren in Indiana* (1992) 156-7

-425, following Edict of 1712: *insert new article* – **Edison German Baptist Brethren Church, NE**. The Edison congregeation was organized in 1914 in Furnas Co., NE. Some of the members had been earlier part of the *Sappa Creek congregation. The Edison congregation represented the last effort of the District of Nebraska to establish new churches within its boundaries. Elder J. B. Moore and Elder H. D. Michael served the congregation, which neither built nor purchased a building for its services. These were held either in area school houses or in tents. In 1917 a membership of thirty-six was recorded. Edison was hampered by a lack of consistent and strong leadership. On Nov. 11, 1930, a meeting was held in which members voted to disband the congregation. Elder David G. Wine and Elder Paul K. Brandt represented the district at this final meeting. JND

District Meeting Minutes, NE (1914-30); Sappa Creek Minutes; personal correspondence with the John Fetters family.

-431, 1: Eikenberry, Ivan Leon, *replace* b. 1913 *with* 1-11-1913 / 4-14-1993; *add Messenger* (June, 1993) inside cover

-432, 6: Eiler (Eilar, Oyler) Family, *for* son Jacob *read* grandson Jacob.

-441, 1: Ellis, Calvert Nice, *replace* b. 1904 *with* 4-16-1904 / 4-7-1995; *add Messenger* (May/June, 1995) 3

-443, 19: Emigration, *following* not all were Brethren *add* Some scholars assert that Mack had also chartered the ship *Mortonhouse*, which arrived in Philadelphia on Aug. 17, 1729, prior to the *Allen*. Among Brethren-related family names on the earlier ship were Peffley (Pfäffli), Grebil (*Graybill, Krehbiel), Wedel, Keiser (*Keyser), Mohr, Shamback (Shambaugh), Sligloff (Slingluff), Fetter (Vetter), Bowman (*Baumann), and Langenecker (*Longenecker).

-448, 3-4: Ephrata Community, *replace* Johann *with* Georg

-461: "Are You Saved?," *add* K. I. Morse, *Preaching in a Tavern* (1997), No. 53; *Context* (Jan. 15, 1986) 5; *GM* (June 23, 1945) 15.

-463, 2: Ewing Church of the Brethren, VA, *add following the phrase* in 1915 *this text*: In the mid-1880s Lewis Jones, a resident of Bell Co., KY, "came under conviction" in a revival meeting and prayed fervently for enlightenment. Inspired by a dream, he traveled into Kentucky where he met a Brethren minister named David Derrick (one source says Abraham Molsbee). The Kentucky Brethren sent ministers to visit Jones at his home, where a small congregation was formed under the ministry of a man named Billie Miracle, aided by traveling ministry from Tennessee. The gathering became known as Black Snake; it expanded into Virginia where the work was known as White Shoals. Following a period of little activity, members of the Black Snake and White Shoals meetings were reorganized at Ewing in 1915.
Add Norman E. Jones, "Church of the Brethren, Ewing Congregation" (1964); R. E. Sappington, *The Brethren in Tennessee and Alabama* (1988) 145-47

-479-80, 1: Fasnacht, Everett Merlin, *replace* b. 1912 *with* 4-19-1912 / 4-10-1991; *add Messenger* (June, 1991) 3

-480, 1: Fasnacht, Harold Dale, *replace* b. 1908 *with* 2-8-1908 / 5-17-1994; *add Messenger* (July, 1994) 3

-480, 1: Fast, Henry A., *replace* b. 1894 *with* 10-12-1894 / 1-3-1990; *add Mennonite Encyclopedia V* (1990) 295

-480, 5: Faw, Chalmer Ernest, *replace* b. 1909 *with* 1909 / 3-26-1996; *add Messenger* (June, 1996) 3. 31

-489, photo caption: *replace with -* A reunion of the family of Moses Fike and Sophia Rudolph Fike, Eglon, WV, 1908. Galen E. Fike Collection.

-490, following **Filbrun Family** *insert new article*: **Filley German Baptist Brethren Church, NE.** The Filley congregation of Gage Co., NE, was organized ca. 1884, probably as a sufficient number of Brethren settled in the Filley and Virginia areas of the county to organize themselves into a church fellowship. Members of this congregation included W. H. Miller, John S. Stutzman, A. C. Peters, Joel Flory, Aaron Deardorff, Fred Kohler, and Elder Perry Beckner. The 1893 district survey lists fourteen members but no minister. The year 1894 was the last time that this congregation was listed in district records. Its members most likely united with the (*Holmesville) South Beatrice congregation, which was located some ten miles away, as the population shifted during the 1890s. JND
District Meeting Minutes, NE (1883-1965); Minutes, Bethel German Baptist Brethren Church (1891); South Beatrice Council Meeting Minutes (1890, 1892, 1893).

-492, 1: **Fisher, Nevin Wishard**, *replace* b. 1900 *with* 1900 / 2-12-1984; *add Messenger* (April, 1984) 7

-492, 1: **Fisher, Virginia Showalter**, *replace* b. 1908 *with* 1908 / 5-2-1991; *add Messenger* (Aug./Sept., 1991) 3

-493, 8: **Flat Creek Church of the Brethren, KY**, *for* (1896-1944) *read* (1896-1984); a*dd Messenger* (Oct., 1993) 20-23.

-495, 1: ***Flora, Delbert Benjamin**, *replace* b. 1901 *with* 6-27-1901 / 8-31-1995

-496, 1: **Florence, MI, Church of the Brethren**, *replace* **Florence, MI, Church of the Brethren** *with* **Florence Church of the Brethren, MI**

-499-1: ***Flory, Paul John**, *replace* b. 1910 *with* 6-10-1910 / 9-9-1985; *add* (obit.) *Chicago Tribune* (Sept. 12, 1985); *Messenger* (March, 1986) 9; *Manchester College Bulletin* (Sept., 1982) 5, (Sept., 1984) 6, (Sept., 1985) 5, 11, (June, 1988) 1; *Manchester Magazine* (Summer, 1998) 43-5

-500, 2-3: *Flying Eagle, The, for* The first (and possibly only) issue contained *read* The first of the three known issues contained ... .

-534, 53: **Genealogy**, *for* Mennonite *read* Mennonite-related

-535, 17, 58: **General Board**, *for* committe's *read* committee's; *replace* In 1965 Annual Conference appointed a committee of seven to study the needs *with* This committee was appointed by the General Board at the 1965 Annual Conference.

-538, 8: **General Ministerial Board**, *for* *M. R. Zigler *read* *D[avid] H. Zigler

-546, bibliography: *for* W. E. Sherfy, *Sherfy Family read* W. E. Sherfey, *Sherfey Family*

-556, *following* **Golden Gate Church of the Brethren, CA** cross-reference: *insert new article –* **Golden Spring German Baptist Brethren Church, NE.** The congregation, located in Burt Co., NE, first appears in the district minutes in 1888. During the ten years of its recorded dis-

trict history, it was only represented twice at district meetings. The district survey taken in 1893 lists George W. Stambaugh as elder-in-charge, three ministers, and forty members. By 1897 there were only twenty-two members and two ministers listed. There is no record of the congregation after 1898. The nearby Decatur congregation appears in the district minutes the following year, which could possibly indicate that members from the Golden Spring congregation combined to form the short-lived Decatur fellowship. Names of members known to have been active in the Golden Springs congregation include Joseph Hintler, Joseph Imler, John Bear, C. Light, and L. J. Hedding. JND
District Meeting Minutes (1888-1898).

-564, 1: **Grahe, Jakob**, *replace* 1695-1747 *with* 1677-1747

-564, 1: **Grahe, Wilhelm**, *replace* 1693-1763 *with* 1693-1774

-575, 1-13: ***Grundforschende Fragen*** (*Basic Questions*, 1713), *replace entire article with this text following topic listing*: ... long understood as the first Brethren publication, authored by *Alexander Mack, Sr., it is now known that it must have only circulated in manuscript form in Germany and found first publication in America. The "ground-searching questions" to which Mack provided answers appeared in a 1713 publication authored by *E. L. Gruber (*Grundforschene Fragen welche ... denen neuen Täuffern in dem Wittgensteinischen insonderheit so die Wasser-Tauffe zur Seeligkeit absolut-nothwendig machen ... wohlmeynend vorgeleget worden ...*, along with a discussion of the tract on immersion baptism written by the separatist *Christoph Seebach. Mack's answers to the questions posed by Gruber remain the first extant public writing of the Brethren and defense of their beliefs and practices. DFD
Hans Schneider, "*Basic Questions on Water Baptism*: An Early Anti-Brethren Pamphlet," *BLT* 42 (Summer/Fall, 1997) 31-63; Marcus Meier, "Eberhard Ludwig Gruber's *Basic Questions*: Report of a Discovery, *BLT* 42 (Summer/Fall, 1997) 64-67.

-585, 1ff.: **Harper, Clara Belle (CB)**, *replace* b. 1895 *with* 9-15-1895 / 1-25-1986; *add Messenger* (Jan., 1985) 11, (April 1986) 7

-587, 1: **Harshbarger, Luther H.**, *replace* b. 1914 *with* 12-4-1914 / 9-14-1986; *add Messenger* (Jan., 1987) 27

-588, 6-8: **Hartsough Family**, *replace with this*: was executive secretary of the General Ministerial Board (1943-7), secretary of the Ministry and Home Missions Commission (1947-8), and field man for the Middle Indiana District (1948-53).

-589, 1: **Haug, Johann Friedrich**, *replace* d. 1753 *with* 1680-1753; *add* M. Brecht and others, eds., *Geschichte des Pietismus, Band 2* (1995) 160-2

-596, 1ff.: **Helser, Lola Bechtel**, *add Messenger* (July, 1986) 1

-596, 1: **Henckels, Johann Friedrich**, *replace* b. 1686 *with* 1686-1752

-598, 1: **Herring, Friedrich**, *replace* b. 1812 / *with* 10-30-1812 / 10-1-1898; *add* Herring Papers, Elkhart County [IN] Historical Society

-616, 1-2: **Hoff, Emanuel Buechley**, *for* **Buechley** *read* **Buechly**

-617, 29: **Hoff, Ernest Gockley**, *replace* written by Ernestine Hoff Emrick *with* poetry by Ernestine Hoff Emrick

-622, 22: **Holsinger, Henry Ritz**, a*dd following the sentence ending* Johnstown, PA. *the following text*: Holsinger died on March 12, 1905.

-623, bibliography: **Holsinger, Henry Ritz**, *add* [obit.] *Altoona [PA] Tribune* (March 14, 1905).

-629, following **Hope Church of the Brethren, MI**: *add new article*: **Hope Memorial Church (German Baptist Brethren), NE**. Named in memory of the pioneer Brethren missionary, *Christian Hope, who died in 1899, the history of this congregation is obscure. A deed is extant, executed by William Scully, of Washington, DC, granting land in Gage Co., NE, to the "Legal Trustees of the German Baptist Brethren Church" with the "express condition" that it was "to be used only as a church site..." The deed was notarized in Gage County on June 29, 1904. Further, a program of the dedication of the church building on June 26, 1904, has been preserved. It locates the structure as "ten miles northeast of Pickrell and seven miles west of Adams." Elder Aaron D. Sollenberger (1869-1963) of Pickrell, gave the dedicatory sermon. Family names of those taking part in the service included: Groff, Netzley, Frantz, Miller, and Kline. It is not included in the *Brethren Family Almanac for 1916,* when congregations were first listed, so its existence may have been of relatively short duration. DFD

-671, 5: **Johansen, Martin (CB)**, *for* 1855 *read* 1885

-675: **Johnsontown Church of the Brethren, WV**, *relocate to p. 673 following* **Johnson City, TN, Knob Creek Church of the Brethren**

-676, 5: **Jordan Mines, VA, Rich Patch Brethren Church**, *for* Jacob S. Bowman *read* John S. Bowman

Volume 2

-687, photo caption, 2: *for* Sarah Keller *read* Lanah Keller

-694, 1: **King, Lester Vernon**, *replace* b. 1894 *with* 1894 / 1989

-699, bibliography: **Klein(e), Georg**, *add* Annette K. Burgert, *Eighteenth Century Emigrants from German-Speaking Lands to North America: Vol. 2, The Western Palatinate* (1985) 202-03

-703, 1: **Klingensmith, J. Ray**, *replace* b. 1907 / *with* 10-8-1907 / 6-24-1996

-703, 1: **Knepper, Wilhelm**, *replace* 1691-ca.1743 *with* 1691-1767

-704, bibliography: **Knouff, Hannah Pfouts**, *for* 1917 *read* 1914

-708, 11-12: **Krumrein (Crumrine, Grumrine) Family**, *replace* Two of his sons, Noah and Jacob, and a great-great-grandson, Gail D., were Brethren ministers *with* Two of his sons, Noah and Jacob, were Brethren ministers, and a great-great-grandson, Gale D., is a Brethren minister.

-710, 26b: **Kurtz, Daniel Webster**, *for* 1924 *read* 1914.

-721, 4: **Lancaster, PA, Church of the Brethren**, *for* twenty-three years *read* twenty-five years

-721, 15, 18: **Lancaster Old German Baptist Brethren Church**, *delete* and *following* Harry G. Benedict, *add* and Robert Matthews, Jr. *following* Charles M. Hackman, and *replace* Robert Matthews, Jr. *with* Jerre Longenecker *following* Eldon Flory and

-743, 1: **Lindower, Leslie E.**, *replace* b. 1903 *with* 12-16-1903 / 10-29-1993

-741, 1: **Lichty, Anna Eby**, *replace* b. 1886 *with* 9-16-1886 / 1-9-1987; *add Messenger* (June, 1987) 8

-744, 1: **Lindsay, Samuel David**, *replace* b. 1907 *with* 2-10-1907 / 3-2-1991; *add Messenger* (May, 1991) 3

-747, 48: **Literature, Brethren and**, *delete* J. *from* *J. Conrad Beissel

-747, 53: **Literature, Brethren and**, *for* Dubble *read* Dubbel

-756, 2: **Longenecker Family**, *add following* *Palatinate, Germany *this sentence*: A Christian Longinacre (Langen Ekker) arrived in Philadelphia in August, 1729, on the ship *Mortonhouse*, accompanied by other passengers with Brethren-related names. Ulrich Longenecker (1681-1757) and his brother Daniel Longenecker (1686-1756) were born near Langnau in the Swiss Emmental. *Add following* Lancaster Co., PA. *this sentence*: Ulrich Longenecker was baptized by *Martin Urner on Nov. 7, 1724, as one of the nine constituent members of the [*Pottstown, PA] Coventry congregation, Chester Co.; he is not identical with the Ulrich Longenecker active in Rapho Twp., Lancaster Co. *Add to bibliography* R. B. Strassburger and W. J. Hinke, eds., *Pioneers* (1934), 1:24, 27, and [Richard Cryer], "Ulrich Longenecker Found!" *Longenecker Family Newsletter*, 6/1 (Jan./March 2004): 1

-764, General Bibliography, 4-5: **Love Feast**, *after* J. S. Flora *replace* 1945 *with* 1973; delete J. S. Fora, "Brethren Love Feast" (1973).

-765, bibliography: **Lower Conewago Church of the Brethren**, *add* Glenn Julius, *From the Beginning: Bermudian Church of the Brethren [sic], 225th Anniversary* (1983); *Messenger* (Dec., 1982) 22-23

-769, 2: **Lyon, Quinter Marcellus**, *for* Fannie Stover Lyon *read* Fannie Stoner Lyon

-769, 2-3, 5: **Lyon, William Marcellus**, *replace* Presumably the son of Michael and Singly Lyon *with* The son of

Hiram Lyon and Margaret Cassady Lyon; *for* Fannie Stover *read* Fannie Stoner

-770, 5: **Lyon, Thoburn C.**, *for* Fannie Stover Lyon *read* Fannie Stoner Lyon

-786, 8-9: **Mandatory Decisions**, *following* came in 1842 *insert* (although Art. 2 of the Annual Meeting of 1805 dealt with the question of response to those members "who would not heed" its conclusions)

-791, following **Maple Spring Church of the Brethren PA**, *add this article*: **Maple Valley Church of the Brethren, MN**, located in Cherokee Co. Some time after 1880 some Brethren moved to the vicinity of Aurelia, were soon organized, and erected a "large, substantial church-house." John Early was the first minister, was ordained, and advanced to the eldership. The thriving congregation was badly split by the Progressive/Conservative schism of 1883. Those holding to the *Progressives (organized as The *Brethren Church) began a new congregation and built a meetinghouse two miles east of the original one. Neither faction flourished following the division and were unable to "maintain regular preaching services," and in 1912 were "both on the verge of disorganization." DFD
Compiled District Meeting Minutes of the Church of the Brethren of Northern Iowa, Minnesota, and South Dakota (1912) 11, reprinted in *N. Plains* (1977), 194; H. R. Holsinger, *Tunkers* (1901), 561-2.

-797, bibliography: *for* ch. 21 *read* ch. 31

-798, 10-11: **Martinsburg, WV, Moler Avenue Church of the Brethren**, *replace the text* and in the Stewart building, 1926-28. A meetinghouse was constructed on High St. in 1928. *with* in the Stewart building, 1926-8, and in the Yeakley church building on High Street, 1926-40. *Add this text before the final sentence*: In the 1950s a group of members left the congregation to form the *Martinsburg Rosemount Grace Brethren Church.

-804, 1: **Mays, Morley Josiah**, *add* d. July 4, 1998 and [obit.] *Lancaster [PA] Intelligencer-Journal* (July 6, 1998)

-816, 5-7, 15, 16: **Men's Work**, *replace lines with this text*: organization of a denominational Men's Work Committee (1926), confirmed (1927); *insert* General *between* Fellowship *and* Council; *replace* Men's Work program *with* Men's Work movement

-820, 1, 3: **Metzler, Burton**, replace b. 1894 *with* 1-20-1894 / 2-15-1988; *add following* at Nappanee, IN *the text* He married Alma Stump in 1921; their three children are Anne Metzler Albright, Mary Metzler Wagoner, and David G. Metzler; *add Messenger* (June, 1988) 7

-820, 4: **Metzler, John D., Sr. (CB)**, *add* Margaret E. Metzler (d. Jan. 13, 1983) aged 79; *add Messenger* (March, 1983) 7

-821, 22: **Mexico, IN, Church of the Brethren**, *for* Donald Ritchey, 1959-80 *read* Donald Ritchey, 1959-; *add* "A Brief History of the Mexico Church of the Brethren," *Dedication Sunday, Church of the Brethren, Mexico, Indiana, January 232, 1977* (1977).

-821, 10-11: **Mexico Old German Baptist Brethren Church, IN**, *replace* Elders-in-charge have been George Balsbaugh, Howard Flora, and L. D. Wolf *with* Elders-in-charge have been George Balsbaugh, Howard Flora, Lester Kinzie, Glen Metzger (non-resident), L. D. Wolf, and Willis Benedict (non-resident) since July, 1991

-825-26, 11-12: **Middlebury, IN, Church of the Brethren**, *insert following* as pastor *this sentence*: Later the congregations again operated independently.

-826, 14: **Midland, MI, Church of the Brethren**, *add text* Lucinda K. Barnum was ordained on July 12, 1987, and on Sept. 28, 1999, the congregation celebrated its 75th anniversary.

-827, 34: **Migration of Brethren**, *for* Huntington *read* Huntingdon

-828, top photo caption: *for* Brethren Voluntary Service *read Brethren Volunteer Service*

-839, 21-22: **Miller, John Allen**, *replace the phrase* the newly elected head, died a month after assuming office *with* the newly elected head was forced to resign a month after assuming office.

-852, 5: **Mission Boards**, *for* **Mission Board, The (BC)** *read* **Missionary Board, The (BC)**

-864, 2: **Missouri**, *for* Spain *read* France

-874, 1, 13-14: **Moomaw, Ira Wilbur**, *replace* b. 1894 *with* 7-8-1894 / 10-2-1990; *add Messenger* (Oct., 1988) 9, (Jan. 1991) 25

-878, 1: **Morse, Kenneth I.**, *re[ace* b. 1913 *with* 5-30-1913 / 3-23, 1999; *add to bibliography* H. Royer, *Agenda* (May, 1999) 5

-878, following **Morse, Kenneth I.**: *add this article*: ***Mortonhouse***, a ship which brought Brethren-related families to Pennsylvania in the August, 1729. Some scholars believe that Alexander Mack, Sr., chartered two ships to bring Brethren to the New World, the better-known **Allen*, and the *Mortonhouse*. The latter arrived in the port of Philadelphia on Aug. 17, 1729, with about 180 passengers. Among the names of those registering their arrival were Peffell (Pfäffli), Grebil (Graybill, Krehbiel), Wedel, Keiser (*Keyser), Schlaback (*Schlabach), Moor, Bowman (*Baumann), Fetter (Vetter), Sligloff (Schlingluff), and Langen Ekker (*Longenecker).
R. B. Strassburger and W. J. Hinke, eds., *Pioneers* (1934), 23-27; E. E. Reeves-Graybill, correspondence.

-890, 9: **Mountaindale Dunkard Brethren Congregation, MD**, *add after the final sentence* In 1980 Joshua Rice was made presiding elder; he served many years in the ministry after losing both hands in a farm accident. JCN

-890, 1: **Mow, Anetta Cordula**, *replace* b. 1889 *with* 10-2-1889 / 10-18, 1987; *add Messenger* (Jan., 1988)

-890, 1: **Mow, Anna Beahm (CB)**, *replace* b. 1893 *with* 7-31-1893 / 7-7- 1985; *add to bibliography*: *Messenger*

(July, 1983) 28-29, (Aug., 1985) 11, (Nov., 1985) 11, 32b; Anna Mow, *Two of Ninety-Two: For Youngsters and Oldsters and Those Who Care for Them* (1997, 2001).

-890-91, 1: **Mow, Baxter Merrill (CB)**, *replace* b. 1892 *with* 3-30-1892 / 3-31-1994; *add to bibliography*: *Messenger* (May, 1986) 2-3. (March, 1992) 3, (Sept., 1994) 2; *Roanoke Times and World News* (Feb. 9, 1986); *Myrtle Beach [SC] Sun News* (Aug. 4, 1994) 10; *Loris Times* (Aug. 2, 1994)

-892, 1; **Moyer, Laura Emma**, *replace* b. 1899 *with* 1899 / 5-29-1899; *add Messenger* (Aug., 1989) 8

-892, 14: **Mud Valley Old German Baptist Brethren Church, IL**, *add this sentence*: The congregation was dissolved in 1997. *Add Vindicator* (1997) 57

-893, 1ff.: **Muir, Gladdys Esther (CB)**, *add* Herbert Hogan, *Gladdys E. Muir: Professor, Peacemaker, Mystic* (1998); *Messenger* (Jan., 1985) 10-11

-897, 1: **Murphy, Sara Florence Fogelsanger**, *for* 1886?-1967 *read* 3-15- 1885 / 3-11-1967; *add Messenger* (April 13, 1967) 30

-912, 27-29b: **What's in a Name?**, *add following* *Civil War neared its end *this text*: Another reason for the naming was that the Grant and Stiverson families were neighbors.

-921, 11: **Neckties**, *replace the phrase* "most Dunkard Brethren" *with* "the Dunkard Brethren"

-938, 1: **Nininger, Harvey Harlow**, *replace* b. 1887 *with* 1887 / 3-1-1986; *add Messenger* (May, 1986) 7

-962, photo captions: *delete in both captions the phrase* Logan Co., 1876, or

-973, 17: **Olive Grove German Baptist Brethren Church, CA**, *add this sentence*: The congregation was dissolved in 1995. *Add Directory of Officials* (1996)

-986, 10: **Overholtzer, Samuel A.**, *add following* College in 1891 *this text*: A son, Jesse Irvin Overholtzer, was an active Church of the Brethren pastor in the Covina, CA, area, but left to found the Child Evangelism Fellowship. *Add to bibliography*: Norman Rohrer, *The Indomitable Mr. O.* (1970).

-1012, 9: **Petersburg, WV, Memorial Church of the Brethren**, *for* Earle N. Fike *read* Earl W. Fike, Sr.

-1013, following **Petry Family**. *See* **Petri Family**: *insert new article*: **Pettikoffer (Pettighofer, Pethkoffer) Family**, a Brethren family active in Germantown. Four members of the family – Anna Elizabeth, Gertrud, John, and Martha Lina – arrived in Philadelphia with *Alexander Mack, Sr., on the ship *Allen* in 1729. Early meetings of the Germantown Brethren were held in a log house that John Pettikoffer built in 1732. Older historians claimed that he had raised money for its construction in by begging money (thus supplying the basis for calling Germantown "Beggarstown") but historian G. N. Falken-

stein published legal documents disproving that story. After the Germantown members erected their stone meetinghouse behind the Pettikoffer house in 1770, it was used as a home for aged persons, where they "were sheltered, clothed, and fed at the expense of the congregation." Several members of the family joined the *Ephrata Society. DFD

G. N. Falkenstein, *History GBB* (1900) 79, 81, 112-26; M. G. Brumbaugh, *History GBB* (1899), 166; *European Origins* (1958) 297-8; *Brethren in Colonial America* (1967) index.

-1013, 1ff.: **Pfaltzgraff, Roy Edward and Violet Hackman (CB)**, *add Messenger* (March, 1983) 9

-1022, 39: **Pietism**, *for* EFS *read* FES

-1025, following **Pine Orchard, MD, Church of the Brethren**: *insert new article*: **Pine Run German Baptist Brethren**, originated as a mission point of the *Hatfield and (*Harleysville) Indian Creek congregations. In 1850 the congregation constructed its meetinghouse in New Britain Twp., Bucks Co., not far from Fountainville. Its fortunes waxed and waned over the decades and the meetinghouse came into non-Brethren hands. It is currently the headquarters of the Bucks Co. Genealogical Society, which applied in 1987 for listing of the building under the National Register of Historic Places.
E. Pennsylvania (1965); Joseph H. Hackman, correspondence.

-1035, following **Pleasant Valley Church of the Brethren, ND**: *insert new article*: **Pleasant Valley German Baptist Brethren Church, NE**. Little is known about the Pleasant Valley congregation in Nehama Co., NE. It appears in the 1884 records of the district with Elder Benjamin F. Flory as its delegate to district meeting. It presented a query to district meeting in 1884 urging the brothers of the district to organize a *mutual aid society to help Brethren with losses from fire, lightning, and cyclones. Joseph Lapp served on the committee which helped to formulate the *Brethren Mutual Aid Society in Nebraska. Other names mentioned from this congregation were C. H. Sharp (1888) and Tirlla Roush (1892), both delegates to district meeting. A survey taken of the Nebraska churches in 1893 lists Owen Peters as elder but only five members. Pleasant Valley does not appear in the district records after this time. JND
District Meeting Minutes, NE (1893-1965).

-1036, 1-10: **Pleasant View Brethren Church, IN**, *replace present article with* **Pleasant View Brethren Church, IN**. The original meetinghouse was located at the NE corner of what is now SR 15 and US 20. The property was deeded to the Indian Creek Congregational Church by Richard and Nancy Lake, Oct. 19, 1881. The original trustees were *George Neff, Andrew Sigerfoos, and Benjamin Gardner. The first building was sold to the United Brethren on Mar. 20, 1891. The second churchhouse was dedicated in Oct., 1891, at what is now the SW corner of CR 20 and CR 23, and was known as Pleasant View. The last board of trustees – Jacob Swihart, George Snyder, and Lewis Barthel – were elected ca. 1932. In 1936 these trustees granted use of the empty building to the Pleasant View Mennonite Church and in 1942 transferred the deed to this congregation. DFD/J. Hollinger.
H. R. Holsinger, *Tunkers* (1901) 586-624; Elkhart Co. deeds.

-1040, 1, 6: **Pokogan, MI, Church of the Brethren**, *for* Pokogan *read* **Pokagon**

-1057, 13: **Prices Creek Old German Baptist Brethren Church, OH**, *insert* Harvey Coning, *before* Raymond Coning

-1069, 27: **Bowman, Warren Daniel**, *add following* Seminary in 1960 and a LLD from *Bridgewater College in 1966; *add* F. F. Wayland, *Bridgewater College: The First Hundred Years, 1880-1980* (1993) index

-1071, 1-2: **Pulaski, VA, Church of the Brethren**, *for* Montgomery Co. *read* Pulaski Co.

-1072, 1: **Puterbaugh, Milton P.**, *replace* b. 1900 *with* 9-17-1900 / 4-13-1991

-1077, 4: **Quinter, James**, *for* Triune *read* Trine

-1117, 3: **Rock Run Church of the Brethren, IN**, *replace* Elkhart (*West Goshen) congregation *with* Elkhart (*Goshen, IN, West Goshen) congregation

-1122, following **Roosevelt, Franklin Delano**: *insert new article*: **Root, Isaac William (DB)**, 1908-82. He was born on Nov. 4, 1893, the son of Joseph and Emma Root, and was married on Feb. 8, 1914, to Ethel L. Booze. Root was baptized in Sept., 1908, installed as a minister in 1933, and ordained an elder in 1943. In 1927 he was a charter member of the *(Cloverleaf) McClave, CO, Dunkard Brethren congregation and lived at Great Bend, KS, while a member of the *Quinter (DB) congregation. Elder Root was a frequent contributor to The *Bible Monitor. He died on Aug. 15, 1982. JCN/W. Smith

-1125, 10: **Row, W. Harold**, *add* Row, Leona Eller, d. 6-30-1993, aged 83; *add Messenger* (Oct., 1993) 3

-1127, 1: **Royer, Byron P.**, *replace* b. 1915 *with* 2-15-1915 / 1-1-1986; *add Messsenger* (March, 1986) 9

-1128, 10: **Royer, Gladys Violet Hawbaker**, *add* Gladys Royer died at N. Manchester, IN, on Aug. 27, 1999.

-1131, 1: **Russell, Harl L.**, *replace* b. 1903 *with* 1904 / 4-26-1992; *add Messenger* (July, 1992) 3

-1146, photo caption: *replace 4445-53 with 5253*

-1166, 15: **Seneca Church of the Brethren, OH**, *for* disorganized about 1912 *read* disorganized in 1912

-1171, **Shafer, Joseph**: *delete this cross reference*

-1171, 1: **Shamberger, Chauncey Howard**, *replace* b. 1894 *with* 4-27-1894 / 10-3-1997; *add Messenger* (Dec., 1997) 2

-1180-81, 1ff.: **Shumaker, Ida cora (CB)**, *add Messenger* (Jan., 1985) 10

-1186, photo caption: *replace caption with: Feetwashing at the Evergreen Church of the Brethren, VA. Harry Graybill is washing the feet of Gilmer Shifflet. BHLA, Local Church File; J. Henry Long photo.*

-1189: *replace* **Skyridge, MI, Church of the Brethren** [cross-reference] *with* **Skyridge Church of the Brethren, MI**

-1189, 15: **Slabaugh, Warren William**, *for* Emma Gensinger *read* Anna Gensinger; *add* [A. Stauffer Curry], "Warren William Slabaugh, 1879-1954," *Brethren Bible Study Monthly* (Jan. 1957) 2; Frank S. Durand, "A Claim in the Kingdom: A Biographical Sketch of Dr. Warren W. Slabaugh," paper, BBS (1946); Dennis L. Slabaugh, "Between Two Eras: The Acting Presidency of W. W. Slabaugh," paper, BTS (1975).

-1189, **Slabaugh Family**: *delete cross reference*

-1194, 1: **Snider, Harold**, *replace* b. 1900 *with* 7-4-1900 / 8-9-1993; *add Messenger* (Nov., 1993) 3

-1205, 4: **South Fork Church of the Brethren, WV**, *for* Grant Co. *read* Hardy Co.

-1216, 1: **Stafford, William Edgar**, *replace* b. 1914 *with* 1914 / 8-28-1993; *add Messenger* (Nov., 1993) 3

-1219, 1: **Stauffer, John N.**, *replace* b. 1915 *with* 1915 / 9-28-1983; *add Juniata College Bulletin* (Jan., 1984) 13

-1221, **Steiner (Stoner) Family**: *replace article with*: **Steiner (Stoner) Family**. Many Steiner immigrants were Mennonites from Switzerland, some having lived in the *Palatinate before coming to America. Others were Lutheran and Reformed. *Morgan Edwards listed Steiner and Stohner members in several Brethren congregations of eastern Pennsylvania in 1770. Peter Royer and Michael Frantz were executors of the estate of John Stoner of Heidelberg Twp., Berks Co., who died in 1777; his son John Stoner evidently joined the Reformed church.

John Stoner (c.1705-1769), the ancestor of most Brethren Stoners, moved beside *Martin Urner in Chester Co., PA, in 1728. About 1743 John Stoner moved to *Antietam, near present-day Waynesboro, PA, and acquired land in both Pennsylvania and Maryland. He lived in Anne Arundel Co., MD, during the *French and Indian War, returning afterward to Antietam. He appears in the *Chronicon Ephratense in assocation with *George Adam Martin. The children of Stoner were Catherine (m. Andrew Arnold), Mary Ann (m. John Price), John (m. Anna Light), Jacob (m. Lenah Ferguson, Autrian (Adrian?) Ferguson), David (m. Margaret ?), Agnes (m. Daniel Arnold), and Abraham (m. Mary Ann Miller, Mary Holmes). These sons and daughters were members of several Brethren congregations in Franklin Co., PA, and Frederick Co., MD. By the early 1800s some Stoner descendants lived in the Shenandoah Valley, Kentucky, and Ohio. Descendants include *Jacob F. Oller, both wives of *Daniel P. Saylor, *Ephraim W. Stoner, and *Solomon Stoner. Related families include *Arnold, *Crumpacker, *Flory, *Garber, *Long, *Myers, *Royer, *Ulrey, and *Wine. RRW

R. R. Weber, *Stoner* (1993); L. H. Steiner and B. C. Steiner, *Genealogy of the Steiner Family* (1896); S. S. Wenger, "Essay on the Stoner/Steiner Families of Pennsylvania," *PMH* (Jan. 1988); R. R. Weber, "Jacob Stoner and the Seven Siblings," *PMH* (Jan. 1998); H. Shuman, *Country Preacher: The Life and Ministry of Elder Solomon Stoner* (1992); *European Origins* (1958) index; *Colonial America* (1967) index; R. T. Stoner, *Genealogical Study of the Antecedents of Calvin C. Stoner* (1972); V. B. Stoner, *Our Stoner Family* (1965); N.

E. Stoner, *Our Stoner Family* (1991); *Some Who Led* (19112) 173-74; *New Nation* (1976) index; *Steiner Memoir: Sketch of the Steiner Family, 1311-1878* (1880); *W. Pennsylvania* (1916) 593; *Indiana* (1952) 410-11; *S. Ohio* (1920) index; *Maryland* (1936) index; *ME* (1959) 4:626.

-1222, 1: **Stetius, Gottfried Luther**, *replace* ca.1689-1758 *with* 1691-1758

-1223, 13: **Stillwater Old German Baptist Brethren Church, OH**, *insert following* Eldon Denlinger *the name* L. Dean Denlinger,

-1227, 1-18: **Stover, William**, *replace the present article with this new article*: **Stover, William**, 1726-1800. Johann Wilhelm Stober, pioneer minister and ancestor of many Brethren descendants, was born on Sept. 15, 1726, in Staffort, Baden, and baptized in the Evangelical Lutheran church. He reached North America on Sept. 10, 1737, with his father, Valentine Stober. Following William's marriage to Margaret Süss he became a founder of the Bindnagel Lutheran church in present Lebanon Co., PA. In 1754 he removed to present Franklin Co., PA. His second wife was Elizabeth Süss and his third wife was Judith End, the widow of Philip Snell of Washington Co., MD. In his 1772 MS, "Materials Towards a History of the Baptists in the Province of Maryland," Morgan Edwards identifies William Stober as the minister of the "Tunker-baptists" at "Antitum" (Antietam, Price's). Stober's children are Dr. George, Rev. William, Michael, Elder Daniel (who succeeded his father at Antietam), Jacob, Emanuel, Margaret Britz, Elizabeth Stoner, Susannah Gish, Catharine Gish, Hannah Landis, and Esther Feaster; they scattered to five states. Twenty-two ancestors of Stover's children have been identified. Missionary *Wilbur B. Stover is a descendant of Emanuel. Related families include *Barnhart, *Bowman, *Deardorff, *Flora, *Gish, *Good, *Landis, *Long, *Miller, Montgomery, *Moomaw, *Naff/Neff, Noffsinger, *Price, *Royer, *Shank, *Stoner, *Wampler, and *Welty. RRW.

R. R. Weber, *Stover Brethren* (2001); *Colonial aAmerica* (1967), index; B. F. Royer, "William Stober, A Pioneer on Antitum" (1949); *S. Pennsylvania* (1941), esp. 417-9, 431; *N. Illinois* (1941), index; B. E. R. Hughey, *Stover Genealogy* (1936); R. B. Strassburger and W. J. Hinke, *Pioneers* (1934), 1:173; G. Wanger, *Descendants of Rev. Jacob Price* (1926); A. J. Fretz, *Descendants of Henry Stauffer and Other Stauffer Pioneers* (1899); M. G. Brumbaugh, *History GBB* (1899); I. H. M'Cauley, *Historical Sketch of Franklin Co., PA* (1878).

-1235, following **Sugar Grove Brethren Church, PA**: *insert a new cross reference*: **Sugar Grove Church of the Brethren, OH**. *See* **Covington, OH, Church of the Brethren**; **Camp Sugar Grove**

-1246, running head: *for* SWIHART FANILY *read* SWIHART FAMILY

-1253, photo caption: *replace with this text*: *A group of Tennessee and Virginia elders and deacons, on the occasion of the 50th wedding anniversary of Daniel Frederick Bowman and Suzanne Pence Bowman, Knob Creek community, near Johnson City, TN*

-1253, **Ten Mile Brethren Church, PA**: *delete cross reference*

-1285-6, 14-17: **Ulrich (Ullery, Ulery) Family**, *delete the sentence beginning* In 1767 *Stephen Ulrich *and ending in* 1772.

-1299, 1: **Utz, Ruth Earl**, *replace* b. 1892 *with* 6-20-1892 / 6-3-1985; *add Messenger* (Aug., 1985) 7

-1302, 1: **Van Dyke, Joe**, *replace* b. 1903 / *with* 9-17-1903 / 5-10-1992; *add Messenger* (July, 1992) 3

-1306, **Viewpoint Church of the Brethren, PA**: *replace with* **Viewmont Church of the Brethren, PA**

-1309, 1: **Visser 't Hooft, Willem Adolph**, *replace* b. 1900 *with* 1900 / 7-5-1985; *add One World* (Aug./Sept., 1985) 6-7, (Aug./Sept., 1988) 31

-1326, 8, 10-11: **Weddle Family**, *for* Anna Eller *read* Anna Maria Eiler; *delete following* Elizabeth Boone *this text*: niece of Daniel Boone *so that the text reads* (m. Elizabeth Boone)

-1330-31; **West, Daniel**, *add Messenger* (Oct., 1986) 5

-1332-1: **West, Murray Guy**, *replace* b. 1901 *with* 7-25-1901 / 12-16- 1991; *add Messenger* (March, 1992) 31, (April, 1992) 3

-1338, following **Westward Expansion**: *insert new article*: **Wetonka, SD, Willow Creek Church of the Brethren**, formed in 1883 near Frederick (now Delhi), SD, by the families of W. W. Horning, James Evans, and J. M. Mansfield, all recent settlers. At the organization, Horning was made an elder, and Evans and Mansfield, ministers. Early meetings were held in tents during the summer and in the Horning home during the winter. Members gathered for *love feasts under the trees, in homes, or in barns, attracting many onlookers. The congregation was known for its hearty singing, derived from singing schools conducted by W. W. Horning. As the congregation grew, the necessity of a meeting place became acute; a churchhouse was dedicated, free of debt, in June, 1901.

Ministers elected from the congregation included Samuel Horning, J. M. Mansfield, Grant Tooker, George Heagley, John Moore, and O. E. Stern. Three missionaries went from Willow Creek to China: *Mary Emma Horning, D. L. Horning, and Ferne Heagley Coffman. Though church rolls numbered at one time over 100 persons, many members and ministers moved away and the congregation dwindled. During the 1940s and 1950s the district mission board supplied summer pastors but by 1959 the church had been disorganized. DFD

N. Plains (1977), 173-74; *Yearbook* (1959) 37 (last listing).

-1339, 1: **White, Roy Irvin**, *replace* b. 1901 *with* 1901/2; *add Manchester College Alumni Directory* (1994) 392

-1344-45, 1: **Wieand, David John**, *replace* b. 1914 *with* 9-4-1914 / 4-14-1986; *add Messenger* (June, 1986) 7

-1359, 1: **White, David Clark**, *replace* b. 1884 *with* 7-22-1885 / 7-1-1990

-1366, upper photo caption: *add* Lower row (L-R), William Willoughby, Leon Kurtz, Edward Lander, Wilbur Mullen; upper row (L-R), Ruth Lawrence, L. John Weaver

-1391, 1, 3: **Yount, Daniel**, *replace* (fl. 1840s/1850s) *with* August 1, 1785 / July 29, 1860; *delete words* and wife; *add* Joseph B. Yount III, unpublished genealogical records, Yount family.

-1391, **Yount Family**, *add* Joseph B. Yount III, unpublished genealogical records, Yount family.

-1395, 4, 6: **Zeller, Harry Knode**, *for* Union (NY) *read* Union (VA); *add following* pastor at *this text* Hopewell, VA (1936-7),

-1395, 1: **Ziegler, Edward Krusen**, *replace* b. 1903 *with* 1-3-1903 / 10-31-1989; *add Messenger* (Dec., 1989) 1

-1398, 1: ***Zigler, Michael Robert**, *replace* b. 1891 *with* 1-9-1891 / 10-25-1985; *add Messenger* (Dec., 1985) cover, 12-13, (March, 1989) cover, 14-17; D. F. Durnbaugh, *Pragmatic Prophet: The Life of Michael Robert Zigler* (1989)

-1402, 1: ***Zunkel, Charles Edward**, *replace* b. 1905 *with* 2-25-1905 / 11-21-1992; *add Messenger* (Feb., 1993) 3

Volume 3:

-1404, **Chart of Brethren Bodies**: *insert* on line marked 1728 following Ephrata Community *this text* (German Seventh-Day Baptists)

-1419, 47-8: [Mount Morris College], *replace* Melchior S. Newcomer, president *with* John W. Stein, president

-1435, Chronology, 9b: *replace* 1977, Jan. *with* 1976, Jan. *and reposition*

-1435, Chronology, 43: *replace* Brethren Evist *with* Brethren Evangelist

-1481, under **VIRGINIA**: *insert in appropriate alphabetical order the following*: ***Harrisonburg: Bethlehem** (1898-); ***Maurertown** (1885-); ***Pineville: Mount Olive** (1884-)

-1483, 38: **Patterson**, *for* (1905-) *read* (1911-41)

-1487, 2: **KENTUCKY**, *add* Black Snake, (ca.1899-ca.1908)

-1491, 27: **Seneca**, *for* (1828-1912?) *read* (1828-1912)

-1495, 43: **Cumberland**, *replace* (Dickinson County) *with* (Dickenson County)

-1495, 44: **Cumberland** (Wise County), *replace* (?-1916?) *with* (?-1915)

-1496, 59: **VIRGINIA**, *following* White Rock *insert* xWhite Shoals, ca. 1900-15)

-1489, 61: **Smith**, *replace with* **Smith Grove,** (1894-1912)

-1501, under **VIRGINIA**: *delete the following* – **Harrisonburg: Bethlehem**; **Maurertown**; **Pineville: Mount Olive**

-1506, 17: *for* Washington Co., IN *read* Washington Co., TN

-1515, 10, 22: *replace* Southeast *with* Southeastern

-1541, 1: **Anderson, Anders (CB)**, *replace* /1939/40? *with* 5-2-1856 / 1-5-1940; *GM* (March 5, 1940) 13

-1544, 1-2: **Aspinall, Ray (BC)**, *merge* with the preceding entry, **Aspinall, H. Raymond (BC)**

-1549, *following* **Barringer, Henry S.(OGBB)**: *insert new entry* – **Bartholomew, John H. (CB)**; ord. 1969; Zion Hill, Columbiana, OH (p. (1971-82); Peru, IN (1983-ca.93); Zion Hill, Columbiana, OH (ca.1994-)

-1552, 1-2: **Beckner, Clyde S. (OGBB)**, *replace* 9-2-1896 / *with* 9-2-1896 / 3-24-1995; *add Vindicator* (1991) 156

-1552, 1-2: **Beckner, Josiah (OGBB)**, *replace* 1-14-1901 / *with* 1-14-1901 / 4-17-1990; *add Vindicator* (1990) 188

-1554, 1-2: ***Benshoff, William St. Clair (BC)**, *replace* 4-21-1914 / *with* 4-21-1914 / 8-5-1991

-1556, 1: **Bittinger, Desmond Wright (CB)**, *replace* 12-16-1905 / *with* 12-14-1905 / 11-5-1991; *add Messenger* (Jan., 1992) 22

-1557, 1-2: **Blickenstaff, Orlando M. (OGBB)**, *replace* 7-25-1901 / *with* 7-25-1901 / 4-13-1984: *add Vindicator* (1984) 189

-1560, 1: **Bollinger, Larry L. (BC)**, *should be listed as* **Bolinger, Larry L. (BC)**, on page 1559 following **Boleyn, Lester E. (CB)**

-1560, 1-2: ***Bollinger, Russell V. (CB)**, *replace* 10-5-1901 / *with* 10-5-1901 / 12-11-1985; *add Messenger* (March, 1986) 9

-1560, 2, 7, 9: **Bomberger, Harold Zug (CB)**, *add* ord. 9-10-1940, Annville, PA; *for* (exec. secy. 1955/56?-60) *read* (exec. secy. 1956-60; *for* (exec. secy. 1971-) *read* (exec. secy. 1971-83); *add* moderator, Annual Conference (1971); *add* seven interim pastorates (1984-96)

-1561: *combine* **Boone, Samuel (CB)** *and* **Boone, Samuel Ludwick (CB/OGBB)**

-1561, 1-2: **Bosler, William Monroe (CB)**, *replace* 11-25-1933 / *with* 11-25-1933 / 12-22-1986

-1562, 1-2, 4: **Bowlby, Glenn Horner**, *replace* 4-2-1918 / *with* 4-2-1918 / 2-24-1987; *add* exec. secy. W.PA (1958-64), PSWC (1964-69)

-1562, 2-3: **Bowman, Benjamin H. (OGBB)**, *delete* min. term. 1923

-1563, 1-2: **Bowman, Daniel**, *for* (10-7-1795 / 17-30-1833 *read* (10-7-1795 / 9-23-1883

-1564: *combine these entries* – **Bowman, J. Price (CB)** *and* **Bowman, Joseph Price (CB)**

-1564, 2: **Bowman, Joseph Cline (CB)**, *replace* 6-7-1908 / *with* 6-7-1908 / 10-6-1992

-1564 (1565): *combine these entries –* **Bowman, Loren (CB)** *and* ***Bowman, Samuel Loren (CB)**

-1564, 1-2: **Bowman, Joel H. (OGBB)**, *replace* 10-1-1903 / *with* 10-1-1903 / 9-28-1986; *add Vindicator* (1986) 346

-1565: **Bowman, Paul Hoover (CB)**, the son of **Bowman, Paul Haynes (CB)**, is sometimes referred to as **Bowman, Paul H., Jr.**

-1565, 1: ***Bowman, Warren Daniel, Sr. (CB)**, *replace* 4-9-1894 / *with* 4-9-1894 / 4-23-1987; *add Messenger* (Aug./Sept., 1987) 48; F. W. Wayland, *Bridgewater College: The First Hundred Years, 1880-1980* (1993), esp. 467-567

-1565, 1: **Bowser, George (OGBB)**, *replace* 110-29-1865 / *with* 11-29-1865

-1568, 1-2: **Bright, John Calvin (CB)**, *replace* 9-9-1915 / *with* 9-19-1915 / 1-9-1997; *add Messenger* (March, 1997) 3

-1569, 1: ***Brooks, Harlan Jesse (CB)**, *replace* 5-5-1898 *with* 5-5-1898 / 2-11-1989; *add Messenger* (April, 1989) 7

-1569, 1-2: **Brovont, Ray O. (OGBB)**, *replace* 2-25-1925 / *with* 2-25-1925 / 12-17-1983; *add Vindicator* (1984) 61

-1571, 1-2: **Brubaker, Amos T. (OGBB)**, *replace* 1-30-1899 / *with* 1-30-1899 / 4-21-1984; *add Vindicator* (1984) 190

-1572, 1-2: **Brubaker, Ira H. (OGBB)**, *replace* 7-15-1904 / *with* 7-15-1904 / 3-18-1987; *add Vindicator* (1987) 157

-1572, 1-2: **Brubaker, Jacob J. (OGBB)**, *replace* 1-16-1916 / *with* 1-19-1916 / 4-17-1994; *add Vindicator* (1994) 217

-1574, 1-2: **Brumbaugh, James William (CB)**, *replace* 8-25-1924 / *with* 8-25-1924 / 8-2-1997; *add Seminarian,* 40/3 (1997)

-1574, 1-2: **Brunk, William C. (OGBB)**, *replace* 6-22-1909 / *with* 6-22-1909 / 10-1-1997; *add Vindicator* (1997) 345

- 1578, 1-2" **Byerly, Robert Allen (CB)**, *replacle* 2-27-1915 / *with* 2-27-1915 / 6-19-2000; *add Elizabethtown Magazine* (Winter, 2001) 31

-1581, 1: **Carter, Donald F. (BC)**, *replace* **(BC)** *with* **(BC/FGBC)**

-1581, 4: **Carter, Leonard Clyde, Jr. (CB)**, *replace* Mt. Bethel, VA (p. 1979-) *with* (p. 1979-95); *add* district moderator (1966, 1993)

-1581, 1: **Cashman, Arthur D. (BC)**, *replace* **(BC)** *with* **(BC/FGBC)**

-1584, 1-2: **Clark, Paul H. (OGBB)**, *replace* 1895 / *with* 1895 / 11-8-1987; *add Vindicator* (1987) 379

-1586: **Cober, Ephraim (CB)**, *add* "Cober Genealogy," (MS), Berlin [PA] Historical Society

-1587, 2: **Coffman, John Isaac (CB)**, *for* 1-27-1896 / *read* 1-27-1896 / 2-22-1983; *for* Laton, CO *read* Laton, CA

-1588, 1-2: **Coning, Raymond (OGBB)**, *replace* 2-9-1904 / *with* 2-9-1904 / 2-11-1996; *add Vindicator* (1996) 94

-1589, 1-2: **Cool, Omer S. (OGBB)**, *replace* 9-25-1900 / *with* 9-25-1900 / 1-4-1983; *add Vindicator* (1983) 62

-1588, 1-2: **Cook, Harry (OGBB)**, *replace* 2-8-1946 / *with* 2-8-1946 / 7-12-1996; *add Vindicator* (1996) 225

-1589, 1: ***Cordier, Andrew Wellington (CB)**, *add Messenger* (Sept., 1995) inside cover, 14-15

-1592, 1: **Cripe, Mervin A. (CB)**, *replace* 5-3-1919 / *with* 5-3-1919 / 9-5-2003; *add* interim min. in 14 congs. following retirement in 1981; *add Bridgewater* (Winer, 2003) 39

-1593, 1: **Crist, Lee Jacob (BC)**, *replace* **(BC)** *with* **(BC/FGBC)**

-1593, 1: **Crummett, Wilmer Quentin (CB)**, *replace* 2-28-1919 / *with* 2-28-1919 / 9-14-2003; *add Bridgewater* (Winter, 2003) 39

-1595, 1: ***Curry, Abram Stauffer (CB)**, *replace* 4-6-1913 / *with* 4-6-1913 / 1-14-1994; *add Messenger* (March, 1994) 3

-1596, 1: **Davis, Joseph Marion (BC)**, *replace* **(BC)** *with* **(BC/FGBC)**

-1597, 1-2: **Davison, Alpha L. (OGBB)**, *replace* 11-19-1917 / *with* 11-19-1917; *add Vindicator* (1995) 188

-1597, 1-2: **Deaton, Glen (OGBB)**, *replace* 8-19-1917 / *with* 8-19-1917; *add Vindicator* (1987) 222

-1601, 4-5: **Ditmars, John G. (CB)**, *for* (1957-61) *read* (1957-66); *for* (1961-66) *read* (1957-66); *for* (1966-73) *read* (1973-6)

-1605, 1-2: ***Eberly, John H. (CB)**, *replace* 4-30-1904 / *with* 4-30-1904 / 1985

-1606, before **Eby, John**: *insert new entry:* **Eby, Jacob Allen (CB)**; 12-3-1877 / 12-23-1950; ord. 1905, Sunnyside, WA; Sunnyside, WA (free min. 1907-20, p. 1920-4); Tacoma, WA (p. 1924-8); Mound City, MO (p. 1928-37); Marshalltown, IA (1937-45); Fernald, IA (1945-9); Nocona, TX (1949-50; *GM (*May 5, 1951) 26; Eby family information.

-1607, 1: ***Eikenberry, Ivan Leon (CB)**, *replace* 1-11-1913 / *with* 1-11-1913 / 4-14-1993; *add Messenger* (June 1993) inside cover

-1609, 1-2: **Eller, Ralph C. (OGBB)**, *replace* 12-22-1896 / *with* 12-22-1896 / 11-7-1982; *add Vindicator* (1983) 28

-1609, 1: ***Ellis, Calvert Nice**, *replace* 4-16-1904 *with* 4-16-1904 / 4-7-1995; *add Messenger* (May/June, 1995) 3

-1609, 1: **Ellis, John Dwight (CB)**, *replace* 9-30-1907 *with* 9-30-1907 / 4-1-1995; *add Messenger* (May/June, 1995) 3; *Juniata Magazine* (Fall, 1995) 27

-1612, 1: **Eyman, Peter**, *replace* ca. 1905 / *with* 1794 / 1852

-1613, 1: ***Fasnacht, Everett Merlin (CB)**, *replace* 4-19-1912 / *with* 4-19-1912 / 4-10-1991; *add Messenger* (June, 1991) 3

-1613, 1: **Fairbanks, Clarence Sylvester (BC)**, *replace* **(BC)** *with* **(GC/FGBC)**

-1613, 1: ***Fasnacht, Harold Dale (CB)**, *replace* 2-8-1908 *with* 2-8-1908 / 5-17-1994; *add Messenger* (July, 1994) 3

-1614-1: **Fells, H. William (BC)**, *replace* **(BC)** *with* **(BC/CB)**

-1616, 2ff.: **Fike, Lester Earl (CB)**, *add* ord. 4-6-1918; *add* South Bend, IN (student p. 1926-8); Pleasant Chapel, IN (1962-9); Little Pine, IN (1969-72); West Goshen, IN (1976 interim); *delete* WV listings; *add W. Virginia* (1950) 50, 136

-1616, following **Fike, Lester Earl (CB)**: *add new entry*: **Fike, Lorenzo H. (CB)**; 5-20-1875 / ; ord. 12-2-1905; Canaan Valley, WV: Harness Run, WV; Terra Alta, WV; Knobley, WV (p. 1946-9); *W. Virginia* (1950) 50, 136

-1617, 1-2: **Fisher, Lester R. (OGBB)**, *replace* 8-18-1903 / *with* 6-24-1995; *add Vindicator* (1995) 254

-1617, 1-2: **Fisher, Ross B. (OGBB)**, *replace* 1-20-1895 / *with* 1-20-1895 / 12-9-1986; *add Vindicator* (1987) 30

-1619, 1-2: ***Flora, Delbert Benjamin (BC)**, *replace* 6-27-1901 / *with* 6-27-1901 / 8-31-1995

-1619, 5: **Flora, Earl L. (CB)**, *for* Guthrie, OK *read* Guthrie, MN

-1619, 1-2: **Flora, John H. (OGBB)**, *replace* 1-18-1907/ *with* 1-18-1907 / 12-1-1989; *add Vindicator* (1990) 89

-1619, 1-2: **Flora, Myrl (OGBB)**, *replace* 10-11-1919 / *with* 10-11-1919 /5-13-1989; *add Vindicator* (1989) 221

-1621: *combine these entries*: **Flory, Johannes (Yohnones)** *and* **Flory, Johannes** [in third column]

-1621, 1-2: **Flory, Lester (OGBB)**, *replace* 10-27-1943 / *with* 10-27-1943 / 5-9-1997; *add Vindicator* (1997) 220

-1621, 1-2: **Flory, Riley W. (OGBB)**, *replace* 8-5-1896 / *with* 8-5-1896 / 11-23-1992; *add Vindicator* (1993) 25

-1621, 1-2: **Flory, Thomas H. (OGBB)**, *replace* 1-6-1898 / *with* 1-6-1898 / 7-15-1986; *add Vindicator* (1986) 254

-1624, 1-3: **Frantz, Joseph H. (CB)**, *delete entire entry*

-1624, 1-2: **Frantz, Jacob (OGBB)**, *replace* 3-19-1894 / *with* 3-19-1894 / 10-30-1985; *add Vindicator* (1985) 377

-1627, 1: **Fry, Ivan Lowell (CB)**, *replace* 7-22-1924 / *with* 7-22-1924 / 4-14-1996; *add Messenger (*June, 1996) 3`

-1627, following ***Funk, Jacob (CB)**: *insert new entry*: **Funk, John;** 5-23-1790 / 4-18-1851; *add [Hagerstown, MD] Herald of Freedom* (April 23, 1851)

-1628, 1-6: **Garber, Daniel Benjamin (CB)**, *replace with this text*: **Garber, Daniel Benjamin (CB);** 3-2-1879 / 7-15-1957; eld. 1917/18? At Headwaters, Highland Co., VA (1916-20); Bridgewater, VA, District Mission Board (1920-1); Waynesboro, VA (1922-45); Barboursville, VA serving mission churches in E. VA (1945-50

-1628, 1-2: **Garber, Elmer D. (OGBB)**, *replace* 7-20-1905 / *with* 7-20-1905 / 10-30-1985; *add Vindicator* (1982) 346

-1629, 4: **Garber, John**: 7-14-1792 / 7-16-1854, *for GM read GV*

-1629, 1: **Garber, John Fair (BC)**, *replace* **(BC)** *with* **(BC/FGBC)**

-1629, 1-2: **Garber, Leroy C. (OGBB)**, *replace* 9-5-1895 / *with* 9-5-1895 / 7-7-1985; *add Vindicator* (1985) 254

-1632, 1: **Gemmer, Hiram Robert (CB)**, *replace* 4-4-1923 / *with* 4-4-1923 / 12-21-1992; *add Messenger* (May, 1993) 3

-1633, 1-2, 7: **Gibbel, Ira William (CB)**, *replace* 12-25-1924 / *with* 12-25-1924 / 6-21-1993; *for KS read MO*

-1634, 1: **Gibson, Ota E. (CB)**, *replace* 7-5-1888 / *with* 7-5-1888 / 6-25-1990; *add Messenger* (Oct., 1990) 3

-1634, *folllowing* **Gillan, Harvey**, *insert new article*: ***Gillin, John Lewis (BC)**; 10-12-1871/12-8-1958; ord. 1894; Brooklyn, IA (p.); Waterloo, IA (p.); Ashland, OH (p. and college president, 1907-11); university professor (IA, WI); *see bibliography after article, BE* 1:549.

-1637, 1: **Goodman, Marvin L. (BC)**, *replace* **(BC)** *with* **(BC/FGBC)**

-1637, 1: **Goodman, Marvin L., Jr. (BC)**, *replace* **(BC)** *with* **(BC/FGBC)**

-1638, 1: **Gould, William Lewis (CB)**, *replace* 5-21-1917 / *with* 5-21-1917 / 7-x-2000; *add Elizabethtown Magazine*(Winter, 2001), 31

-1639, following **Graybill, A. K. (OBGB)**: *insert new entry*: **Graybill, Daniel Perry;** 3-25-1898 / 4-30-1985; minister for 55 years in the OGBC; *add Pilgrim* (July, 1985) 11

-1640, 1-2: **Grimley, John B. (CB)**, *replace* 8-23-1915 / *with* 8-23-1915 / 9-18-1997; *add Seminarian,* 40/3 (1997)

-1641, 1-10: **Grumbling, Richard A. (CB)**, *replace entire article*: **Grumbling, Richard A. (CB)**; 1-1-1908 / ; ord. Conemaugh, PA (1949); Grantsville, MD, and Maple Grove, PA (p. 1948-53); Smith Creek, Franklin, WV (p. 1953-6); Bellwood, PA (p. 1956-62); Yellow Creek/ Bethel, PA (1962-69); Newville, PA (1969-77); Ridge, PA (int. p. 1977-79, 1981-82); *S. Pennsylvania* (1973) 31; *W. Pennsylvania* (1953) 526; CBMF; personal correspondence

-1642, 1-2: **Hackman, Charles M. (OGBB)**, *replace* 1-30-1901 / *with* 1-30-1901 / 6-8-1981; *add Vindicator* (1981) 251

-1642, 6: **Hahn, Martin Luther (CB)**, *for* Guthrie, OK *read* Guthrie, MN

-1643, 1: **Hall, Jesse Keeney (BC)**, *replace* **(BC)** *with* **(BC/FGBC)**

-1644, 1: **Hammond, Herbert C. (BC)**, *replace* **(BC)**, *with* **(BC/FGBC)**

-1647, 1: ***Harshbarger, Luther H. (CB)**, *replace* 12-4-1914 / *with* 12-4-1914 / 9-14-1986; *add Messenger* (Jan. 1987) 27

-1648, 1: **Hartman, Anthony**; *for* Middle Brook *read* Middle Creek

-1648, 3: **Hartong, Dana**, *add* Florence, MI (1970-9)

-1648, 1-2: **Haught, Albert M. (CB)**, *replace* 8-10-1906 / *with* 8-10-1906 / 3-27-1995; *add Juniata Magazine* (Fall, 1995) 28

-1649, 1-2: **Hayes, William A. (CB)**, *replace* 6-15-1928 / *with* 6-15-1928 / 7-21-1991; *add Messenger* (Oct., 1991) 3, (Nov. 1991)

-1650, 1-2: **Heckman, Galen Andrew (CB)**, *replace* 1-11-1939 / *with* 1-11-1939 / 5-3-1995; *add Juniata Magazine* (Fall, 1995) 28

-1651, 1-2: **Heinrich, Walter A. (OGBB)**, *replace* 1-25-1906 / *with* 1-25-1906 / 11-25-1985; *add Vindicator* (1986) 28

-1653, 1: **Hershey, Graybill (CB)**, *replace* 11-19-1896 / *with* 11-19-1896 / 6-4-1984: *add Messenger* (Sept., 1984) 7

-1654, 1-2: **Hess, Daniel M.**, *replace* 2-23-1919 / *with* 2-23-1919 / 5-10-1992; *add Vindicator* (1992) 190

-1654, 1-2: **Hess, Robert O. (CB)**, *replace* 1-13-1919 / *with* 1-13-1919 / 7-28-1994; *add ANE Newsletter* (Oct., 1994) 4

-1654, 1-2: **Hess, Willis A. (OGBB)**, *replace* 10-5-1884 / *with* 10-5-1884 /10-11-1981; *add Vindicator* (1981) 344

-1656, 5: **Hiser, Escil I. (CB)**, *for* Bedford, OR *read* Medford, OR

-1656, 1-2: **Hockman, Noah A. (OGBB)**, *replace* 6-1-1892 / *with* 6-1-1892 / 10-11-1983; *add Vindicator* (1983) 346

-1656, 2-3: **Hodgden, Dorsey CB)**, *add* 1894-9 *following* eld. 1882; *add* Dorsey Hodgden, "Family History" (MS), BHLA, Individuals File

-1656, 2, 6-7: **Hodgden, Sidney (CB)**, *for* eld. 1850s at Neosho, KS *read* eld. 1870, Greene Co., MO; *for* Moscow, ID (1890-?) *read* Moscow, ID (1890-4); *add* Dorsey Hodgden, "Family History" (MS), BHLA, Individuals File

-1658, 1: **Hollenberg, Frederick Michael (CB)**, *replace* 7-8-1893 / *with* 7-8-1893 / 6-7-1986; *add Messenger* (Aug./Sept., 1986) 9

-1666, 1: **Hutchinson, Samuel J. (CB)**, *add* - /5-19-1880

-1668, 1: **Ingraham, M. Virgil (FGBC)**, *replace* **(FGBC)** *with* **((BC)**

-1670, 1: **Johnson, Cecil (FGBC)**, *replace* **(FGBC)** *with* **(FGBC/BC)**

-1674, 1-2: **Kegarise, Percy R. (CB)**, *replace* 12-29-1917 / *with* 12-29-1917 / 8-22-1995

-1674, 1-2: **Keil, Samuel (BC)**, *delete listing and merge under correct spelling*, **Keihl, Samuel (BC)**, p. 1677

-1677, 1-2: **Kessler, Frank E. (OGBB)**, *replace* 8-29-1900 / *with* 8-20-1900 / 1-5-1995; *add Vindicator* (1995) 62

-1677, 1-2-: **Kessler, D. Marion (OGBB)**, *replace* 12-25-1925 / *with* 12-25-1925 / 1-22-1994; *add Vindicator* (1994) 92

-1677, following **Kessler, Raymond (OGBB)**: *insert new entry*: **Kessler, Ulrich**; eld.; migrated from Rockingham Co., VA, to Wilkes (Ashe) Co., NC in late 1780s; *Carolinas* (1971) 89

-1677, 1: **Kidwell, W. M. (CB)**, *for* W. M. *read* E. M.; *combine with* **Kidwell, Ezra M.**

-1677, 3: **Kidwell, William (CB)**, *add* Bethany, Madison Heights, MI (p. 1955-3)

-1677, 1: **Keiffaber, Alan George (CB)**, *replace* **Keiffaber** *with* **Kieffaber**

-1677, 1: **Keiffaber, George Washington (CB)**, *replace* **Keiffaber** *with* **Kieffaber**

-1678, 1-2: **Kimmel, Michael (CB)**, *replace with* **Kimmel, Michael (CB)**, 1821 / 1888; ord. Middle Creek, PA (1850); to Lanark, IL; *W. Pennsylvania* (1916); *N. Illinois* (1941) 44

-1678, 1: **Kindley, Clarence R. (CB)**, *replace* **(CB)** *with* **(BC)**

-1679, 1-2: **King, Lester Vernon (BC)**, *replace* 8-12-1894 / *with* 8-12-1894 / 3-19-1989

-1679, 2ff.: **Kinsel, Paul Wilbur (CB)**, *add* ord. Brookville, OH (1932); University Park, MD (p. 1969-77)

-1681, 1-2: ***Klingensmith, J. Ray (BC)**, *replace* 10-8-1907 / *with* 10-8-1907 / 6-24-1996

-1681, 1-2: **Knaus, Jesse A. (OGBB)**, *replace* 5-20-1901 / *with* 5-20-1901 / 5-5-1993; *add Vindicator* (1993) 191

-1682, 1: **Knechel, Robert, W. Sr. (CB)**, *replace* 7-9-1920 / *with* 7-9-1920 /10-15-1987; *add Messenger* (Jan., 1988) 9

-1683, 2-3: **Krabill, John William**, *replace* Denton, OH *with* Denton, MD and Green Hill, VA *with* Green Hill, MD

-1685, 1: **Landes, Daniel E. (OGBB)**, *replace* 6-17-1898 / *with* 6-17-1898 / 12-5-1989; *add Vindicator* (1990) 29

-1685, 1: **Lance, Forrest E. (BC)**, *replace* **(BC)** *with* **(BC/FGBC)**

-1686, 1: **Landis, Herman Benjamin (CB)**, *replace* 7-18-1898 / *with* 7-18-1898 / 12-13-1990; *add Messenger* (March, 1991) 3

-1686, 1: **Lantz, Albert L. (BC)**, *replace* **(BC)** *with* **(BC/FGBC)**

-1687, 1: **larimore, David (BC)**, *replace* **(BC)** *with* **(BC/FGBC)**

-1688, 1-2: **Leatherman, John**, *following* eld. before 1836 *insert* during ca. 30 years ministry in Tusacarawas Co., OH; *add The History of Tuscarawas County, Ohio* (1884) 667

-1691, 1: **Lesher, Harry A. (OGBB)**, *replace* 9-5-1893 / *with* 9-5-1893 / 2-13-1985; *add Vindicator* (1985) 124

-1692, 1: **Lewis, Howard B. (OGBB)**, *replace* 4-7-1911 / *with* 4-7-1911 / 5-8-1984; *add Vindicator* (1984) 220

-1692, 1: **Lichty, Solomon (CB)**, *replace* **Lichty, Solomon (CB)**; Middle Creek, PA (eld.) *with* **Lichty, Solomon (CB)** 1821 / 1879; ord. ca. 1850; Carroll Co., IL; *W. Pennsylvania* (1916) 585; *N. Illinois* (1941) 44.

-1693, 1-2: **Lindower, Leslie E.**, *replace* 12-16-1903 / *with* 12-16-1903 / 10-29-1993

-1693, 1: **Locker, William F. (OGBB)**, *replace* 7-1-1928 / *with 7-1-1928 / 7-10-1983;* add *Vindicator* (1983) 286

-1693, 1: ***Lindsay, Samuel David (CB)**, *replace* 2-10-1907 / *with* 2-10-1907 / 3-2-1991; *add Messenger* (May, 1991) 3

-1693: **Livengood, David**, *add W. Pennsylvania* (1916) 465; H. Austin Cooper, *Two Centuries of Brothersvalley [CB]* (1962) 223

-1694: *combine these entries –* **Long, Joseph A. (CB)**; /12-10-1923 *and* **Long, Joseph A. (CB)**; 5-8-1853 /

-1695, 1-2: **Long, Orville Valentine (CB)**, *for* 12-5-1880 *read* 12-5-1860

-1696, 1: **Lorenz, Orville A. (BC)**, *replace* **(BC)** *with* **(BC/FGBC)**

-1696, 1-2: **Lowdermilk, Donald Lee (CB)**, *replace* 6-24-1935 / *with* 6-24-1935 / 4-2-1995; *add Juniata Magazine* (Fall, 1995) 28

-1696, 1: **Lucero, Rubel V. (BC)**, *replace* **(BC)** *with* **(BC/FGBC)**

-1700, 1: **Maconaghy, Hill (BC)**, *replace* **(BC)** *with* **(BC/FGBC)**

-1704, 2: **Matsuoka, Fumitaka (CB)**, *for* ord. 9-28-1943 *read* 9-28-1973

-1706, 1: **Metzger, Glenn L. (OGBB)**, *replace* 2-5-1906 / *with* 2-5-1906 / 10-6-1986; *add Vindicator* (1987) 28

-1707, 1: **Meyers (Myer), Joseph (CB)**, *replace* **Meyers** *with* **Myer**; *replace* 1807 / 1892 *with* 5-12-1806 / 3-18-1891; *add* ord. 1844; Myer family genealogy

-1708, 1: **Middlekauff, John Claude (CB)**, *replace* 9-20-1911 / *with* 9-20-1911 / 10-18-1999

-1708, 1: **Miller, Abram (CB)**, *replace* **(CB)** *with* **(BC?)**

-1709 (1713): *combine these entries*: **Miller, Curtis (CB)** *and* **Miller, John Curtis (CB)**

-1710, 1-2: **Miller, David, Sr. (CB)**, *delete* 4-6-1844 / ; adv. After 1883;

-1711, 1: **Miller, Donald E.**, *replace* 1-14-1924 *with* 1-14-1924 / 1-31-1989; *add Messenger* (May/June, 1989) 6

-1712, 1: **Miller, J. William (OGBB)**, *replace* 3-26-1911 / *with* 11-26-1911 / 6-2-1997; *add Vindicator* (1997) 222

-1713 (1716): *combine these entries –* **Miller, William (CB)**; / 1912 *with* **Miller, John William (CB)**; *delete* / 1912 *from former entry*

-1713, 1: **Miller, Oscar S. (CB)**, *replace* 3-7-1883 / *with* 3-7-1883 / 10-14-1986; *add Messenger* (Jan., 1989) 8

-1715, 1: **Miller, Roy Eugene (CB)**, *replace* 2-3-1930 *with* 2-3-1930 / 3-15-1989; *Messenger* (Oct., 1999) 5

-1716, 2-3: **Miller, Walter A. (CB)**, *replace* Stanley, WI (1949-56) *with* Stanley, WI (1949-51)

-1716, 1: **Minderman, Daniel L. (BC)**, *replace* **(BC)** *with* **(BC/FGBC)**

-1717, 1-2: **Modoski, Robert (BC)**, *replace* **Modoski** *with* **Modaski**

-1718, 1: **Mohler, Daniel W. (OGBB)**, *replace* 2-1-1925 / *with* 2-1-11925 / 1-18-1986; *add Vindicator* (1996) 89

-1719, 1: **Montgomery, Charles O. (OGBB)**, *replace* 10-5-1890 / *with* 10-5-1890 / 5-11-1984; *add Vindicator* (1984) 220

-1719, 1: **Montgomery, Joel A. (OGBB)**, *replace* 7-20-1895 / *with* 7-20-1895 / 2-18-1992; *add Vindicator* (1992) 123

-1719, 1: *****Moomaw, Ira Wilbur**, *replace* 7-8-1894 / *with* 7-8-1894 / 10-2-1990; *add Messenger* (Jan., 1991) 25

-1720, 1: **Moore, Roland J. (OGBB)**, *replace* 7-28-1924 / *with* 7-28-1904 / 4-17-1987; *add Vindicator* (1987) 190

-1720, 1-2: **Morgan, Terry (BC)**, *delete entry*

-1724, following **Myer, John W.,Sr. (CB)**: *insert article on* **Meyers (Myer) Joseph** *from 1707 under* **Myer, Joseph (CB)**

-1725, 1: **Myers, Henry**, *replace* 11-9-1797 / *with* 11-9-1797 / 1877

-1725, 1: **Myers, John B. (CB)**, *insert* 1810-1866

-1725, 1: **Myers, Michael**, *replace* **Myers, Michael**; /3-14-1836 *with* **Myers (Meyers), Michael**; 1762 / 3-14-1836; *add* H. R. Holsinger, *Tunkers* (1901), 202; H. Austin Cooper, *Two Centuries of Brothers Valley [CB]* (1962) 189-90

-1725, following **Myers, Michael**: *insert new entry –* **Myers, Michael**; 9-18-1804 / 4-1-1855; ord. ca. 1840; migrated to Wisconsin; *add W. Pennsylvania* (1953) 582

-1731, 1-2: **Norris, Glen Elvin**, *replace* 11-21-1899 *with* 11-21-1899 / 6-1-2001; *add Altoona [PA] Mirror* (June 3, 2001), A-9

-1732, 1: **Northup, R. Truman (CB)**, *replace* 8-25-1920 / *with* 8-25-1920 / 4-18, 1991; *add Messenger* (June, 1991) 3

-1732, 1: **Nowag, H. Walter (BC)**, *replace* **(BC)** *with* **(BC/FGBC)**

-1734, 1: **Oyler, Joseph L. (OGBB)**, *replace* 12-30-1910 / *with* 12-30-1910 / 4-22-1986; *add Vindicator* (1986) 190

-1736,3: **Perdieu, Charles P. (OGBB)**, *add Vindicator* (1983) 60

-1737, 1: **Petcher, Ralph Rhett (CB)**, *replace* 12-5-1915 / *with* 12-5-1915 / 3-4-2002; *add Bridgewater* (Spring, 2002) 37

-1737, 1; **Peters, Charles W. (OGBB)**, *replace* 1-26-1900 / *with* 1-26-1900 / 10-27-1986; *add Vindicator* (1986) 378

-1737, 1: **Peters, William J. (OGBB)**, *add Vindicator* (1982) 189

-1739, 1; **Phillips, George W.**, *replace* 12-29-1893 *with* 12-29-1893 / 3-22-1989; *add Messenger* (May/June, 1989) 6

-1739: *add between the entries for* **Pippen, Everett (CB)**, *and* **Pippinger, John (CB)**, *the following:* **Pittinger, C. Frank (OGBB)**, 12-10-1862 / 12-26-1941; ord. 1906; Brookville, OH; *add Vindicator* (1942) 62

-1740, 1: **Plew, Thomas H. (CB)**, *replace* **(CB)** *with* **(BC)**

-1740, 1: **Poling, Newton Lyon (CB)**, *replace* 3-25-1914 *with* 3-25-1914 / 2-16-2002; *add Bridgewater* (Spring, 2002) 37

-1743, 1-2: *replace* **Pritchett, John R. (CB)** *with* **Pritchett, John Alfred, Sr. (CB)**

-1749, 1: **Richardson, Bert Gay (CB)**, *replace* 3-31-1921 / *with* 3-31-1921 / 7-30-1991; *add Messenger* (Oct., 1991) 3

-1749, 1: **Rieman, Timothy Wayne (CB)**, *replace* 5-14-1912 / *with* 5-14-1912 / 11-9, 1994; *add Messenger* (Dec., 1994) 3; spec. issue *Bulletin of the Peace Studies Institute* (1996) 2-42; *Juniata Magazine* (Fall, 1995) 27

-1750, following **Riley, Forrest (CB)**: *insert new entry*: **Riley, Jobie E. (CB)**; ord. Chicago, IL (1958); *Yearbook* (1997) 176

-1750, 1: **Riley, J. H. (CB)**, *replace* **J. H.** *with* **Jobie Hamilton (CB)**; 3-4-1889 / 12-23-1981

-1750, 1: **Rinehart, Joseph Paul (CB)**, *add* b. 1951 / 7-19-2003; *add Bridgewater* (Winter, 2003) 39

-1751, *following* **Ritzens, Henry (CB)**: *insert new entry*: **Ritzius, Henry**, 2-x-1832 / 2-x-1905; minister, IN; [obit.] *GM* (March, 18, 1905) 175. = **Ritzens, Henry (CB)?**

-1754, following **Root, Benjamin (OGBB)**: *insert new entry*: **Root, C. C., (CB)**; 6-10-1839 / 5-22-1909; lived in Indiana and Colorado; *"Colorado"* 1963; *GM* (June 26, 1909)415.

-1757, 1: *****Royer, Byron Paul (CB)**, *replace* 2-15-1915 / *with* 2-15-1915 / 1-1-1986; *add Messenger* (March, 1986) 9

-1758, 1: **Rulon, Dale Paul (BC)**, *replace* 1-30-1945 / *with* 1-30-1935

-1758, 1: **Rumble, C. Joseph (OGBB)**, *replace* 11-23-1899 / *with* 11-23-1899 / 3-15-1984; *add Vindicator* (1984) 154

-1760, 1: **Sappington, Roger Edwin**, *replace* 3-6-1929 *with* 3-6-1929 / 3-19-1989; *add Messenger* (May/June, 1989) 6

-1762, following **Secrist, Isaac (CB)**: *insert new entry*: **Secrist, Jacob S. (CB)**; b. 1861? / ; Eugene, IN (1898-1901); Ladoga, IN (1902); Myrtle Point, OR (1903-06); Olympia, WA (1907-13, 1915); *Indiana* (1952) 188; G. E. Muir, *Pacific Slope* (1939) index

-1764, 1: *****Shamberger, Chauncey Howard (CB)**, *replace* 4-27-1894 / *with* 4-27-1894 / 10-3-1997; *add Messenger* (Dec., 1997) 2

-1767: *combine these entries*: **Sherfy, Joel (CB)** *and* **Sherfy, Joel (CB);** *add GM* (April 6, 1929)

1767, following entry for **Sherfy, John Samuel (CB)**: *insert new entry*: **Sherfy, Joseph (GBB)**, 6-12-1812 / 10-4-1882; deacon, 10-4-1851, Marsh Creek, Gettysburg, PA; ord. 5-29-1853; eld., 11-8-1881; W. E. Sherfey, *The Sherfey Family in the United States* (1949), 204-07; *S. Pennsylvania* (1941), 150-2.

-1771, 4: **Sifrit, Robert L. (CB)**, *for* Waka, TX (p. 1971-76) *read* Waka, TX (1971-7); *add* Fairview, Udell, IA (1980-8); Milledgeville, IL (1988-9); Peace Valley, MO (1989-92)

-1771: *combine these entries* – **Simmons, C. Reynolds, Jr. (CB)** *and* **Simmons, Claude Reynolds, Jr. (CB)**

-1771, 1-2: **Simmons, Carl, Jr. (CB)**, *replace* 3-13-1927 / *with* 3-13-1927 / 10-9-1998

-1772, 3: **Sizemore, Joseph I. (CB)**, *for* WV *read* VA

-1773, 1: **Skiles, Joseph D., Sr. (OGBB)**, 12-6-19-896/7? / 8-26-1983; *add Vindicator* (1983) 317

-1773, 1: **Skiles, M. Keith (OGBB)**, *replace* 8-13-1930 / *with* 8-13-1930 / 7-24-1997; *add Vindicator* (1997) 284

-1773, 1-2: **Smell, Donald G. (BC)**, *delete entry and merge with correct spelling* **Snell, Donald G. (BC)**, p. 1776

-1774: *combine* **Smith, Beverly (CB)** *and* **Smith, Beverly Albert (CB)**

-1777: *combine* **Snider, Chester (CB)** *and* **Chester, D. C. (CB)**

-1777, 1: ***Snider, Harold (CB)**, *replace* 7-4-1900 / *with* 7-4-1900 / 8-9-1993; *add Messenger* (Nov., 1993) 3

-1778, 1: **Sollenberger, Oliver Clark (CB)**, *replace* 3-19-1889 / *with* 3-19-1889 / 11-20-1987; *add Manchester College Bulletin* (March, 1988) 7

-1781, 1: **Stamy, Daniel W. (OGBB)**, *replace* 9-8-1899 *with* 9-8-1899 / 4-10-1993; *add Vindicator* (1993) 159

-1781, 2: **Stauffer, Wilfred N. (CB)**, *for* ord. 1930/36? *read* ord. 1930

-1782, 5: **Stern, Oscar Evert (CB)**, *for* Guthrie, OK *read* Guthrie, MN

-1783, 9-10: **Stogsdill, Clarence A. (BC)**, *delete* Warsaw, IN (p. 1970s) *and See also* Stogsdill, Claude?

-1783, 7-8: **Stogsdill, Claude (BC)**, *delete See also* Stogsdill, Clarence?

-1785, 1: **Strike, Ray L. (OGBB)**, *replace* 12-16-1916 / *with* 12-16-1916 / 8-2-1993; *add Vindicator* (1992) 286

-1790-1, 1: **Tay, Herbert H. (BC)**, *replace* **(BC)** *with* **(BC/FGBC)**

-1793, 1-2: **Thompson, Joel Kent (CB)**, *replace* 8-10-1933 / *with* 8-10-1933 / 9-8-1994; *add Messenger* (Oct., 1994) 8

-1794, 1: **Tinkle, Arthur H. (BC)**, *replace* **Tinkle** *with* **Tinkel**

-1796, 1: **Turner, Alvah (OGBB)**, *replace* 9-3-1895 / *with* 9-3-1895 / 5-12-1991; *add Vindicator* (1991) 221

-1796: *combine these entries* – **Ulery, John (CB)** *and* **Ulery, John C. (CB)**; *add* 6-10-1841 / 8-21-1924; ord. ca. 1867-68; active, Edna Mill and Lancaster, MO; *add* [obit.], *Delphi [Carroll Co.] Journal* (Aug. 21, 1924)

-1798, 6: **Van den Doel, Anthonie (CB)**, *for* Aniba, Netherlands (p. 1966-9) *read* Aruba (p. 1966-69, 1983-; *add* Indonesia (p. 1970-80); Surinam (p. 1980-3)

-1798, 1-2: **Van Duyne, Kenneth (BC)**, *delete entry*

-1799: *add between* **Wagoner, A. Paul (CB)** *and* **Wagoner, David** *a new entry*: **Wagoner, Charles (GBB)**, licensed to marry in Allen Co.,OH, Aug., 1857; *see The Report* 23/2 (Summer, 1983): 67.

-1799, 1: **Wagoner, Eldo (OGBB)**, *replace* 2-2-1897 / *with* 2-2-1897 / 5-6-1989; *add Vindicator* (1989) 220

-1799, 1: **Wagoner, Harvey L. (OGBB)**, *replace* 8-2-1903 / *with* 8-2-1902 / 12-25-1984; *add Vindicator* (1985) 60

-1800, 1-2: **Wagoner, John Robert (CB)**, *replace* 5-28-1918 / *with* 5-28-1918 / 2-14-1997; *add* [obit.] *Manchester College Bulletin* (Spring, 1997) 30

-1801, 1-2: **Wampler, Guy Edgar, Sr. (CB)**, *replace* 2-16-1902 / *with* 2-16-1902 / 1-22-1985; *add Messenger* (March, 1985) 9

-1803, 1-2: **Weaver, Clyde E. (CB)**, *replace* 9-7-1924 / *with* 9-7-1924 / 3-2-1994; *add* J. Lehman, ed. *The Highland Avenue [CB] Centennial Encyclopedia* (1999) 118-9; *Messenger* (April, 1994) 3

-1803, **Weaver, D. F. (CB)**, **Weaver, D. H. (CB)**: *combine entries to read* **Weaver, David H. (GBB/CB)**; 8-15-1844 / 3-2-1915; Hygiene, CO; Covina, CA; "Colorado" (1963) 186; *Almanac* (1915) 56; *California* (1917) 17; family correspondence

-1806, 1: **Wells, Gratton E. (OGBB)**, *replace* 7-20-1900 / *with* 7-20-1900 / 7-23-1981; *add Vindicator* (1981) 377

-1807, 1: ***West, Murray Guy (CB)**, *replace* 7-25-1901 / *with* 7-25-1901 /12-16-1991; *add Messenger* (March, 1992) 31, (April 1992) 3

-1809, 1-2: ***White, David Clark (BC)**, *replace* 7-22-1885 / *with* 7-22-1885 / 7-1-1990

-1809, 1: ***White, Roy Irvin (CB)**, *replace* 12-23-1901 / *with* 12-23-1901 / 1992; *add Manchester College Alumni Directory* (1994) 392

-1810, 1: ***Wieand, David John**, *replace* 9-4-1914 / *with* 9-4-1914 / 4-14-1986; *add Messenger* (June, 1986) 7

-1812, 2: **Wine, Daniel David (CB)**, ord. ca. 1872

-1815, 1: **Wolf, Paul B. (OGBB)**, *replace* 9-20-1902 / *with* 9-20-1902 / 10-29-1993; *add Vindicator* (1993) 379

-1817, 1: **Wray, Jesse A. (OGBB)**, *replace* 12-26-1898 / *with* 12-26-1898 / 2-2-1989; *add Vindicator* (125

-1818, 1: **Yearout, William**, *replace* -/1954/55? *with* - / 9-x-1954; ord. 7-4, 1917; eld. 11-11-1922; min. at branches of the Red Oak Grove cong., VA.

-1818, 1: **Yearout, Willie**, *combine with* **Yearout, William**.

-1819, 1: **Yoder, D. Willard (OGBB)**, *replace* 11-14-1913 / *with* 11-14-1913 / 33-5-1997; *add Vindicator* (1997) 126

-1819, 1: **Yoder, Daniel J. (OGBB)**, *replace* 4-3-1897 / *with* 4-3-1897 / 5-12-1987; *add Vindicator* (1987) 190

-1819, 1: **Yoder, Rufus R. (OGBB)**, *replace* 10-15-1900 / *with* 10-15-1900 / 10-28-1987; *add Vindicator* (1987) 378

-1821, 1: **Ziegler, Carl Wenger, Sr.**, *replace* 2-1-1910 / *with* 2-1-1910 / 10-1-1987; *add Messenger* (Dec., 1987) 9

-1821, 1: ***Ziegler, Edward Krusen**, *replace* 1-3-1903 / *with* 1-3-1903 / 10-31-1989; *add Messenger* (Dec., 1989) 1

-1822, 1: ***Zigler, Michael Robert (CB)**, *replace* 11-9-1891 / *with* 11-91-1891 / 10-25-1985; *add Messenger* (Dec., 1985) 12-13

-1823, 1: ***Zunkel, Charles Edward**, *replace* 2-26-1905 *with* 2-26-1925 / 11-21, 1992; *add Messenger* (Feb., 1993) 3

List of Institutions

-1825, 8a: **Burnetts Creek Normal School**, *for* Elderton, PA *read* Burnettsville, IN

Lists of Missionaries

-1833, 1: **Baldwin, Elmer Rufus**, *replace* 4-2-1916 / *with* 4-2-1916 / 3-24-1985; *add Messenger* (June, 1985) 7

-1834, 1: ***Bittinger, Desmond Wright**, *replace* 12-14-1905 *with* 12-14-1905 / 11-5-1991; *add Messenger* (Jan., 1992) 22

-1834, 1: **Blickenstaff, Leonard Ellis**, *replace* 1-11-1913 *with* 1-11-1913 / 10-28-1995; *add Messenger* (Dec., 1995) 3

-1834, 1: **Bosler, Edith Mae Gump**, *replace* 7-3-1904 / *with* 7-30-1904 / 1-1-1985; *add Messenger* (March, 1985) 9

-1834, 1: ***Brandt, Lucille Long Strayer**, *replace* 7-22-1900 *with* 7-22-1900 / 8-20-1994; *add Messenger* (Dec., 1994) 3

-1835, 1: **Bright, John Calvin**, *replace* 9-19-1915 *with* 9-19-1915 / 1-9-1997; *add Messenger* (March, 1997) 3

-1835, 1-2: ***Brooks, Harlan Jesse**, *replace* 5-5-1898 / *with* 5-5-1898 / 7-7-1996; *Messenger* (Sept., 1996) 2

-1835, 1: ***Brooks, Ruth Elizabeth Forney**, *replace* 10-5-1896 *with* 10-5-1896 / 2-11-1989; *add Messenger* (April, 1989) 7

-1835, 1: **Brubaker, Marie Hannah Woody**, *replace* 6-30-1899 *with* 6-30-1899 / 6-14-1991; *add Messenger* (Oct., 1991) 3

-1837, 1: **Crim, Bessie Mae**, *replace* 10-4-1914 *with* 10-4-1914 / 4-x-1990; *add Messenger* (June, 1990) 8

-1837, 1: ***Eikenberry, Ivan Leon**, *replace* 1-11-1912 *with* 1-11-1912 / 4-14-1993; *add Messenger* (June, 1993) inside cover

-1837, 1: ***Esbensen, Maren Christine Bendsen**, *replace* 7-10-1891 *with* 7-10-1891 / 7-23-1991; *add Messenger* (Nov., 1991) 3

-1837, 1: ***Fasnacht, Everett Merlin**, *replace* 4-19-1912 *with* 4-19-1912 / 4-10-1991; *add Messenger* (June, 1991) 3

-1837, 1: **Faw, Mary Platt**, *replace* 5-14-1909 *with* 5-14-1909 / 3-26-1996; *add Messenger* (June, 1996) 3

-1838, 1-2: **Grimley, *John* Bechtel**, *replace* 8-23-1915 / *with* 8-23-1915 / 9-18-1997; *add Seminarian*, 40/3 (1997)

-1838, 1: **Hall, Von Lee**, *replace* 12-6-1928 *with* 12-6-1928 / 10-25-1993; *add Messenger* (Jan., 1994) 3

-1838, 1-2: ***Harper, Clara Belle**, *replace* 9-15-1895 / *with* 9-15-1895 / 1-25-1986; *Messenger* (April, 1986) 7

-1838, 1: ***Heckman, Lucille Gibson**, *replace* 8-10-1902 *with* 8-10-1902 / 8-20-1991; *add Messenger* (Nov., 1991) 3

-1839, 1: **Hollenberg, Frederick Mitchel (CB)**, *replace* 7-8-1893 / *with* 7-8-1893 / 6-7-1986; *add Messenger* (Aug./Sept., 1986) 9

-1839, 1: **Holsopple, Kathren M. Royer (CB)**, *replace* 4-1-1892 *with* 4-1-1892 / 6-27-1986; *add Messenger* (Aug./Sept., 1986) 9

-1839, following **Horning, Martha A. Daggett:** *insert new entry*: ***Horning, Mary Emma**; 9-9-1876 / 2-11-1937; China (1908-37); *GM* (Feb. 20, 1937) 16, (May 1, 1937) 1, 14-15, 20; F. H. Crumpacker and others, *Brethren in China* (1937), 9-14, 50

-1840, 1: **Kulp, Philip Masterton**, *replace* 10-29-1929 *with* 10-29-1929 / 8-10-1994; *add Messenger* (Oct., 1994) 3

-1840, 1: **Landis, Hazel Minnich**, *replace* 9-14-1899 / *with* 9-14-1899 / 4-13-1985; *add Messenger* (June, 1985) 7

-1840, 1: **Landis, Herman Benjamin**, *replace* 7-18-1898 *with* 7-18-1898 / 12-13-1990; *add Messenger* (March, 1991) 3

-1840, 1: ***Lichty, Anna Eby**, *replace* 9-16-1896 / *with* 9-16-1896 / 1-9-1987; *add Messenger* (June, 1987) 8

-1841, 1: ***Moomaw, Ira Wilbur**, *replace* 7-8-1894 *with* 7-8-1894 / 10-2-1990; *add Messenger* (Jan., 1991) 25

-1841-42, 1: **Moomaw, Mabel Ellen Winger**, *replace* 2-8-1899 *with* 2-8-1899 / 7-8-1988; *add Messenger* (Oct., 1988) 9

-1842, 1: **Moss, Hazel Elvina Messer**, *replace* 7-2-1906 *with* 7-2-1906 / 3-4-1987 *add Messenger* (June, 1987) 8

-1842, 1: ***Mow, Anetta Cordula**, *replace* 10-22-1899 *with* 10-22-1899 / 10-18-1987; *add Messenger* (Jan., 1988

-1842, 1: ***Mow, Anna Beahm**, *replace* 7-31-1893 *with* 7-31-1893 / 7-7-1985; *add Messenger* (July, 1983) 28-9; (Aug., 1985) 11, (Nov. 1985) 11, 32b

-1842, 1: ***Mow, Baxter Merrill**, *replace* 3-30-1892 *with* 3-30-1892 / 7-31-1994; *add Messenger* (Sept., 1994) 2

-1842, 1: **Myer, Clara B.**, *replace* 6-26-1909 / *with* 6-26-1909 / 12-16-1996; *add Messenger* (March, 1997) 3

-1842, following ***Neher, Minneva Josephine**: *insert new entry*: ***Nickey, Barbara Marie**; 1886-1979; Dahanu, India (1915-52); *Fifty Years, India* (1945); *Messenger* (Sept., 1979) 7

-1842, 1: **Ober, Mary Velma**, *replace* 2-13-1903 *with* 2-13-1903 / 6-20-1991; *add Messenger* (Oct., 1991) 3

-1842, 1: **Oberholtzer [Overholtzer?], Margaret Elizabeth Weybright**, *replace* 5-31-1885 *with* 5-31-1885 / 11-13-1986; *add Messenger* (June, 1987) 8

-1842, 1: ***Oiness, Sylvia Marie**, *replace* 11-17-1912 *with* 11-17-1912 / 7-9-1991; *add Messenger* (Nov., 1991) 3

-1842, 1: **Parker, Daryl M.**, *replace* 3-17-1904 *with* 3-17-1904 / 11-17-1989; *add Messenger* (Jan., 1990) 8

-1842, 1-2: **Parker, Martha Neiderhiser**, *replace* 1-31-1907 *with* 1-31-1907 / 2-25-1997; *add Messenger* (April, 1997) 3

-1843, 1: ***Royer, Gladys Violet Hawbaker**, *replace* 4-1-1902 / *with* 4-1-1907 / 8-27-1999

-1844, 1: ***Schaeffer, Mary Ann**, *replace* 12-16-1890 *with* 12-16-1890 / 8-13-1991; *add Messenger* (Oct., 1991) 3

-1844, 4: **Sewell, Laura**, *for* (1948-80) *read* (1948-84)

-1845, 1: **Shull, Susan Lavinia Stoner**, *replace* 10-26-1898 *with* 10-28-1898 / June 20, 1991; *add Messenger* (Oct., 1991) 3

-1845, 1-2: **Sollenberger, Oliver Clark**, *replace* 3-19-1889 / *with* 3-29-1889 / 11-20-1987; *Manchester College Bulletin* (March, 1988) 7

-1845, 1: **Stayer, Raymond**, *add* 1905 / 7-18-1999; *Messenger* (Aug., 1999) 5

-1845, 1: **Studebaker, Modena Elizabeth Minnich**, *replace* 10-17-1902 *with* 10-17-1902 / 8-7-1991; *add Messenger* (Oct., 1991) 3

-1845, 1: **Thompson, Joel**, *replace* 8-10-1933 *with* 8-10-1933 / 9-8-1994; *add Messenger* (Oct., 1994) 8

-1845, 1-2: ***Utz, Ruth Earl**, *replace* 6-20-1892 / *with* 6-20-1892 / 6-3-1985; *Messenger* (Aug., 1985) 7

-1845, following ***Vaniman, Susie Cordelia Neher**: *insert new entry*: **Van den Doel, Anthonie**; 2-13-1931 / ; Kulp Bible School, 1963-5, Nigeria; *Lardin Gabas, 1923-1973* (1973) 72.

-1846, 1: **Weaver, Paul M.**, *replace* 5-16-1918 *with* 5-16-1918 / 7-2-1999; *Messenger* (Aug., 1999) 5

-1846, 1: ***Ziegler, Edward Krusen**, *replace* 1-3-1903 *with* 1-3-1903 / 10-31-1989; *add Messenger* (Dec., 1989) 1

-1846, 1: **Ziegler, Emma King**, *replace* 7-7-1895 *with* 7-7-1895 / 1-1-1987; *add Messenger* (June, 1987) 8

-1847, 1: ***Zigler, Rachel Myers**, *replace* 7-20-1905 *with* 7-20-1905 / 1-15-1996; *add Messenger* (March, 1996) 3

-1854, 1: **Byler, Jane King**, *replace* 12-2-1922 *with* 12-2-1922 / 10-16-1996

-1855, 1: **Byler, Robert Oliver**, *replace* 6-24-1921 / *with* 6-24-1921 / 8-15-1997

-1855, 1: **Palaci, June Byler**, *replace* 6-27-1916 *with* 6-27-1916 / 9-14-1994

-1861, 3: **Reichmann, Felix**, "German Printing," *transfer* Samuel Sauer *from line 2 to line 3*

-1861, 4: **Sower, Charles G.**, Publications, *for* 1871 *read* 1876

-1883, 1: **Bowman, Donald R., 1926-**, *replace* **1926** *with* **1925**

-1908, 1: **Coffman, Roxanne, 1894-**, *for* **Roxanne** *read* **Roxanna**; *for* **1894**, *read* **1895-1983**

-1919, 1: **Dubble, S. Earl**, *for* **Dubble** *read* **Dubbel**

-1930, 3: **Emrick, Ernestine Hoff**, *replace* By father-daughter team. *with* Poetry, with photographic illustrations by Hoff. Following *Look to the Light* entry: *add the following titles*: *His Kingdom in My Kitchen* (Elgin, IL: Women's Work Department, Christian Education Commission, ca.1957), originally published in *Messenger* (Nov. 26, Dec. 3, Dec. 10, 1955); *Tall Thoughts: Poems for God* (La Verne, CA: ULV Graphics, University of La

Verne, 1997), 74pp., with photographs by Ernest G. Hoff; *Heaven Along the Way: Collected Poems* (La Verne, CA: ULV Graphics, University of La Verne, 1997), 124pp., with phtographs by Ernest G. Hoff.

-1951, 1: **Gould, William L., 1917-,** *replace* **1917-** *with* **1917-2002**

-1973, 1: **Hostetler, Harvey R.,** *for* **1894-1965** *read* **1857-1939**

-2006, 1: **Marani, Stephen A.,** *for* **Marani** *read* **Marini**

-2111, 1: **Zunkel, Charles E., 1905-,** *replace* **1905-** *with* **1905-1992**

INDEX

Providing an index for *The Brethren Encyclopedia* was the initial impetus for producing *Volume 4*. The Board of Directors decided that *Volume 4* should also include up-date information for the period 1980–2000. Darin Keith Bowman, part-time staff assistant, began working on an index, but after he had processed about 150 pages of *Volume 1*, it became obvious that too much time would be required for part-time staff to complete the huge job. The professional indexing services of Kate Mertes were employed which resulted in a first draft of the index of *Volumes 1–3*. After the up-date portion of *Volume 4* was complete, Mertes merged index items for *Volume 4* into the index for *Volumes 1–3*. During the last few weeks of his life, Donald F. Durnbaugh made invaluable editorial notes on the Mertes draft copy. Dale V. Ulrich followed Durnbaugh's notes, made additional editorial changes and corrections, and formatted the following index for *Volumes 1–4*.

In the index, a bold page number designates an article and an italicized number designates a photograph.

A. C. Baugher Student Center, Elizabethtown College, 438
A. H. Cassel Library, *See* Cassel Library
Aa, A. J. van der, 1862
AACB, *See* Association for the Arts in the Church of the Brethren
AAMFT, *See* American Association of Marriage and Family Therapists
Abbot, Rebecca, 2251
Abbotstown, PA, 136
Abbott, Charles D., 1862
Abbott family, 1142
Abbott, Stephen, 1142
Abbott, Z. E., 1539
ABC, *See* Association of Brethren Caregivers
Abe, Mr. and Mrs. Clarence, 171
Abe family, 1345
Abe, Lacy Ann (later Whitacre), 1339
Abe, Leroy James, Jr., 1539
Abe, Mr. and Mrs. Merle, 171
Abe, Stephen, 1539
Abee family, *See* Eby family
Abel, Bertha May, 1847
Abendmahl (Mack seal), 2142
Abernathy family, 430, 468
Abernathy, Isaac W., 468, 1539
Abernathy, James W., 1539
Abernathy, John, 468
Abernathy, Mary Isabell, 468
Abey, John M., 1322, 1539
Abie, Thomas, 279
Abilene, KS, Church of the Brethren, **1**
    Buckeye, KS, Church of the Brethren, 226
    Cottonwood Church of the Brethren, KS, members of, 345
    Herington, KS, Church of the Brethren, 598
    Holland Church of the Brethren, KS, 619
    Saline Valley, KS, Church of the Brethren, organized from, 1139
    Washington Creek Church of the Brethren, KS, boundary with, 1321
    Wrightsman, P. R. and Navarre, KS, Church of the Brethren, 918
Abilene Old German Baptist Brethren Church, KS, **1**
abolition of slavery, **1**, *See also* slavery
    American and Foreign Anti-Slavery Society, **22**, 1190

American Anti-Slavery Society, **22**, 1190
American Colonization Society, **22**
    Benezet, Anthony, 2077
    Cedar Co., MO, Church of the Brethren, 263
    emancipation, 443
    Knouff, Hannah Pfouts, 704
    Price, Isaac, advocate, 1056
    societies for, 1189–1190
    Sunday school movement, 283
    underground railroad, 1286
    United Brethren in Christ, 1290
abortion, **2**, **2127**
    Brethren Church, 2127, 2178
    Church of the Brethren, 2127, 2178
    Dunkard Brethren Church, 2127, 2174
    FBGC beliefs and practices, 486
    theology and, 2255
Aboud, Emma, **2**, 933, 1539
Abraham Lincoln Friendship Train, 286
Abrams, Ray H., 1862
Abrat family, 1302
ABS, *See* American Bible Society
Abshire, Abraham, 2314
Abshire, Donald, Sr., 163
Abshire, J. Donald, 1539
Abshire, W. Randolph, 1539
Abshire, William David, 1539
Abshire, William Everett, 2271
abstinence, *See* entries at temperance
Abuhl, Oma Marie (later Ogden), 961
Abuid, Italo, 2237
Abuid, Rebecca, 2237
Aby family, *See* Eby family
Aby, Franklin Stanton, 1862
academies, **2**
    Brethren movement and, 178
    Christian Day School movement, 282–283
    Church of the Brethren, 300
    secondary education, 1162–1163
Academy Certified Training Systems (ACTS), 2140
ACC, *See* American Council of Churches
Accident, MD
    Bear Creek Church of the Brethren, **2**
    Grace Brethren Church, **2**
accountability, age of, 2159, 2160
accounting packages offered by Brethren Benefit Trust (BBT), 2140
accreditation

    elementary education, 435
    Elizabethtown College, 437
    Manchester College, 786
acculturation, **2–3**
    Amish in Europe, 26
    Amish in the United States, 26
    automobiles, 74–75
    bibliographical sources, 2050, 2064
    Brethren movement, evolution of, 314, 355
    Canada, Brethren in, 15
    Church of the Brethren, 300–301, 1000
    discipline of children, 389
    Easter, 416
    Eby, Kermit, 420
    education, 426
    Eshelman, Matthew Mays, 455
    ethics, 458
    family, 474
    Fast Element, 480
    fellowship, 482
    FGBC on, 487
    frontier, 519
    funerals, 524
    furniture, 525
    German Seventh-Day Baptists, 542
    Germantown, 544
    gravestones, 567
    Gribble, Florence Alma Newberry, 573
    higher education, 603
    historical writing, 612
    Holsinger, Henry Ritz, 621–622
    Industrial Revolution, 655
    Kesler, Benjamin Elias, on, 690
    Mallott, Floyd Ellwood, 784
    mixed marriage, 865
    naming conventions, 912–913
    nonconformity, 940
    noncreedalism, 942
    Old Order Fellowships, 972
    peace position of Church of the Brethren, 1000
    religious liberty and military service, 1098
    schisms, 298
    sources on, 2317, 2320, 2322
    theology and, 2255
Acevedo, Lita Helen, 1849
Ache (Aughey), John Ludwig, 322, 1539
Achiras, Argentina, 53
Ackerman family, 2088
Ackerman, George, 2088

Ackerman, John, 1539
Ackerman, Stephen, 2088
Ackerman, Steve J., 2271
acknowledgment, doctrine of, **3**
    Church of God (New Dunkers), 297
    confession, public, 333
    disfellowship, doctrine of, 390
    Far Western Brethren, 476
    restoration of disciplined members,
        1102
Acme School, North Manchester, IN, *1334*,
    1350
ACPA *See* All-Christian Peace Assembly
Acquired Immune Deficiency Syndrome
    (AIDS) and HIV, **2129–2130,** 2178
Acrelius, Israel, 840, 1863, 2310
Acts
    Kent, Homer Austin, Jr. on, 2340
ACTS, *See* Academy Certified Training
    Systems
Acts of the Apostles
    1:4–8, 85
    1:5, 85, 86
    1:8, 86
    2, 36
    2:1, 37
    2:4, 86
    2:17–18, 85
    2:38, 84, 85, 86
    2:38–39, 56
    7:51, 55
    8:14–16, 86
    8:17, 85
    9:17–19, 85
    10:43, 55
    10:47–48, 83
    13:46–48, 56
    15:1–35, 33
    17:30, 55
    19:1–7, 85
    19:5–6, 85
    22:16, 84
AD 2000 and Beyond, 2183, 2191, 2220,
    2225
Ada Co., ID, 157
Adair, Denise Elaine, 1853
Adam family, 512
Adam and Eve and doctrine of human
    nature, 635
"Adam and Eve Broadsides," *2064*
Adam, Ernst Max, 148, 1948–1949
Adam, Johann, 1863
Adamawa local government, Nigeria, 3
Adamawa Provincial Leprosarium, Garkida,
    Nigeria, **3–4,** *4*
    Bowman, James Brubaker and Merle
        Allen, 167
    Church of the Brethren mission,
        opened by, 306
    Garkida General Hospital, 531
    hospitals, 630
    Mai Sule Biu, 782
    medical care, 810
    medical missions, 807
    nurse missionaries in, 952
    Pfaltzgraff, Roy Edward, superinten--
        dent, 1013
    Robertson, Russell L., 1115
Adams Co., IA, 881, 1137
Adams Co., IL, 177, 251, 298, 321, 331,
    476, 740, 757, 829, 1288, 1356,
    1357
Adams Co., IN, 152, 1030, 1316

Adams Co., NE, 678, 1182
Adams Co., OH, 247, 364, 791, 804, 961,
    1231, 1332, 2096
Adams Co., PA, 141, 145, 147, 163, 170,
    215, 338, 546, 1004, 1005, 1230,
    1285, 1294, 1950
Adams, B. E., 1863
Adams, C. D., 1863
Adams, Christina (later Putterbach), 1070,
    2343
Adams, Daniel M., 1539
Adams, David M., 1539, 1863
Adams, Dorothy, 758
Adams, E. Bryding, 1863
Adams, Elizabeth (later Flory), 499
Adams, Emmit, 758
Adams, Evan, 192
Adams, Evan M., 192, 1539, 2299
Adams family, 740, 1866
Adams, Hannah, 1863
Adams, James Truslow, 1946
Adams, June (later Gibble), 2279
Adams, June (later Miller), 2133
Adams, Margaret E., works by, 2310
Adams, Mary Joan, 192
Adams, Myrtle Snell, 233
Adams, Ruth Ann, 1848
Adams, S. J., 503
Adams, Samuel, 699
Adams, Samuel S., 1539
Adams, W. A., 673, 675
Adams, Wesley A., 1539–1540
Adams, Willi Paul, 1863, 2310
Adamsboro Church of the Brethren, IN, **4,**
    752, 821
Adamson, Ione (later Nolan), 2031
Adamson, James, 1142
Adamson, Jason Rainey, 1863
Adamson, Lorena Blanche, 1863
Addison family, 1341
Addison, Robert, 1540
"additional elder" position created by
    Mooreites, 875
Adel, IA, Panther Creek Church of the
    Brethren, 753, 803, **992**
Ades, Linna (later Whitacre), 1956
adjoining elders, **4–5**
    Brethren movement, 176
    Brethren polity, 1042
    call to ministry, 845
    degrees of ministry, 374
    district organization, 391
    election of church officers, 434
    election of new elders, 432
    installation of ministers, 656
    Mooreites, 875
    voting for ministers, 844
Adkins, Arthur William, 72, 237, 244, 263,
    479, 1540
Adkins family, 956
Adkins, J. M., 1540
Adkins, Jesse, 1540
Adkins, Josie, 244
Adler, Cyrus, 223
Administrative Council, 536, 555
administrators
    Brethren Church ministry, 846
    Grace Brethren Church ministry, 847
admission into the church, **5**
adolescents, church membership of, 813
Adolph family, 1038
adoption of children, **5–6**
Adrian, MI, Church of the Brethren, **6**

Adrian, MO, Church of the Brethren, **6**
Adrian, PA, Brush Valley Brethren Church,
    224, 268
adult baptism, 5, 776, *See also* baptism
adultery, **6**
    discipline and, 388
    divorce and remarriage, 795, 1099
    homosexuality, 2204
advancement in the ministry, **4, 6,**
        432, **656,** *See also* ministry;
        ordination
Advent, *See* Christmas/Advent
Adventism, **6,** *See also* Seventh-Day
        Adventists
    bibliographical sources, 2023
    Church of Jesus Christ of Latter-day
        Saints, 298
    Greenmount Church of the Brethren,
        VA, 571
    Maine, debate held in, 783
    millennialism, 834
    missionaries, 990
    The Morning Watch, 876
    Schuler, Lydia, 990
    Thurman, William C. favored by,
        1264
Adventure in Mission, 2160–2161,
    2252–2253
Adventurer (ship), Heisey family, 595
The Adventurous Future (Paul H. Bowman,
    Sr.), 168, 1282
The Adversary (Satan), 462, 486
advertisements and advertising, **6–7**
    almanacs, 7, 1948
    clothing, 7
    mass media concerns, 801
    nonconformity, 940
    patent medicines, 995
advocacy, public policy, 2260
Advocate Bethany Hospital, 2136
Advocate Health Care, 2136
*The Advocate of the Doctrines of Christ as
    Believed by the Ancient Brethren
    and Primitive Dunkards,* 7
Aebi family, *See* Eby family
Aeby, Joan Rosalie Hoover, 2127
Aeby, John Minton, 62, 377, 503, 564,
        1365, 1540, **2127,** 2217, 2299
Aellig, Francine Andrae Polo, 1847
Aellig, Gilbert, 1847
Aellig, Jerome Kelth, 1847
Aesch, Switzerland, and Huber-Hoover
        family, 2073
Aeschlimann family, *See* Eshelman
        (Eshleman) family
affirmation, **7,** 959, 2126
Afflick family, 2087
AFOR (American Fellowship of Reconcil-
    iation), *See* Fellowship of
    Reconciliation (USA)
Africa, 2024, *See also* specific countries
    and locations
    Adamawa Leprosarium, *See* Adamawa
        Provincial Leprosarium, Garkida,
        Nigeria, 2371
    ALM involvement in, 24
    Basel Mission work in, 92
    Bickel, Florence Marguerite, 141
    Church of the Brethren, 303
    community development, 23
    education programs of Brethren
        Church, 185
    Foreign Missionary Society, 501,

1930
Foster, Joseph Henry and Rose Alverda Brosius, 504
Grimley, John, 1026
Hamilton, Benjamin A. on FGBC mission, 2335
Heifer Project International, 594
literacy, thesis on, 1956
Mai Sule Biu, first Nigerian elder, 782
Mamza, Ngamariju Keliri, 784
medical care, 810
medical missions, 807
Mennonites, 815
missions and missionaries, 160, 853, 854, *857*, 862, 985, 985, 2091
Oiness, Sylvia Marie, 963
physicians' volunteer service in, 2073
relief and rehabilitation work, 236, 931
resettling freed slaves in, 22
Rollier, Antoine E. and Mary Ganshorn, 1119
Snyder, Myrtle Mae, 1196
sources on, 2315
stories of, 1962
Stump, Paul on Dunkard mission in, 2360
travel by Brethren to, 1273
Weaver, Scott L. (FGBC, CGBCI) and, 2261
Williams, John Henry Bashor, 1346
World Council of Churches, 1368
Africa Inland Mission, 573
Africa, J. Simpson, 1863
Africa Mission Project, **2127–2128**, 2225
evangelism, 2180
African American spirituals, 2205
African Americans, **2128**
Baltimore, MD, Pilot House Project, 2133
Baptists and, 88
Carter, Harvey, 1327
Chicago, IL, First Church of the Brethren, 275
church members and congregations, 1209
Circleville, OH, Church of the Brethren, 313
Colorado, 377
education for, 405
Emmings, Jacob, 1327
Frankfort, OH, Church of the Brethren, 506
Fremont, OH, Grace Brethren Chapel, 515
Fremont, OH, Grace Brethren Church, 515
Garden City, KS, Church of the Brethren, 530
Hayes, William A., 2163
identities and liberation for, 304
Jordan Run Church of the Brethren, WV, 677
Lewis, John T., 738
ministry to minority groups, 1297
mission work among, 1332
Palestine, AR, Ministry to Blacks, 991
Scioto Valley, OH, Church of the Brethren, 256
slavery, opposition to, 1307–1308, 1357, 1391
Smeltzer, Ralph E., 302–303
Spencer, C. C., 1209
spirituals, 1211, 1279

underground railroad, 1286
urban ministry and, 2257
Washington, DC, Southeast Christian Fellowship (BC) and, 2259–2260
Weir, Samuel, 1327–1328, 1332
African Colonization Society, 873
African-Cubans and Iglesia Cristiana Pentecostal de Cuba, 2207
African Methodist Episcopal Church, 2128
AFSC, *See* American Friends Service Committee
Afton Church of the Brethren, NE, 7
Agabus, Brother, *See* Koch, Stephan
Agadez, Niger, 220
Agape Acres, 7, 790
Agape Church of the Brethren, IN, **7**
agape meal, *See* love feasts
Agape retreat center, Prali, Italy, 1365
Age Group Consultative Committee, General Council of Children's Work (CB), 537
age of accountability, 2159, 2160
Aged, Infirm, and Orphans' Home, Darlow, KS, **8**, 266, 410, 419, 682, 1354
Aged Ministers' Fund, 1007
aged persons, 8, 116–117
aid for elderly Brethren, 1198
bibliographical sources, 1987, 2024
Imler, Tobias F., 648
Indiana, 652
medical care, 810
minorities, ethnic and racial, 850
motion pictures publicizing care for, 879
pensions, *See* pensions
Relief Board (DB), 1097
respect for, 8
retirement homes and communities, *See* retirement homes and communities
trends in care of, 2145
Agee, J. Willard, 934, 1540
Agenda
Church of the Brethren Leader and, 308
General Services Commission (CB), 539
Agilla, Bitrus F., 1540
Agonius, Brother, *See* Wohlfahrt (Welfare), Michael
Agricola, Ludwig, and Alexander Mack, Sr., 775
Agricultural College Units, **9**, 316, 380
agricultural depressions
Kansas, 682
Surrey Old German Baptist Brethren Church, ND, 1242
Agricultural Exchange Program, **2129**
Japan, 1330
Poland, 1330
agricultural missions, 9
bibliographical sources, 2044
Nigeria, by Church of the Brethren Mission, 937
relief and rehabilitation work, 167, 186, 198, 200
Agricultural Missions, Inc. (Agricultural Missions Foundation), **9**, 12
bibliographical sources, 2021, 2044
Moomaw, Ira Wilbur, 874
Rhoades, J. Benton and, 2242
Rural Missions Cooperating Committee (RMCC), 1131

Rural Service Center (CB), 1131
agriculture and farming, **9–12**, 17, 89, 477, **477–479**, 478, 2181, *See also* headings at rural
American Farm School, Greece, 569
American Revolution, 477
barn raisings, 89, 902, 1046
Brethren congregations as rural churches, 1130
Bucher, William P., 2072
business beliefs and, 234
conservation movement, 337
cooperatives, 342–343
crop failures, Maple Grove Church of the Brethren, KS, aiding affected families, 789
crop subsidies and nonconformity, 941
Emergency Farm Labor, *See* Emergency Farm Labor
Ephrata, 2015
Ethiopia, 458
Fahrney, Samuel, 466
farm machinery, 476, 478, 479
Friendship Trains, 286, 518
General Investment Council (CB), 537
Greece, 569
Greenwood Church of the Brethren, WA, 572
Heifer Project International, 593–594
Hispanic Ministries (CB), 2199
homesteading, 626
Hostetler, Joseph, 631
Houser, Daniel, 633
Idaho, 645
Interchurch Service to Greek Villages, 658
irrigation, 645, 663–664
Israel, 664
machinery, 18
Marion, OH, First Church of the Brethren, query concerning, 793
McPherson College, offering curriculum in, 780
migration of Brethren, 829, 830, 831
minorities, ethnic and racial, 850
mission schools, 853
missions, 861
Modesto, CA, Church of the Brethren, 866, 867
Moomaw, Ira Wilbur, 874
Mount Morris College students, 883
Old German Baptist Brethren, 969, 970, 2234
Old Order German Baptist Church, 2235
Pennsylvania Germans, 1006–1007
Pleasant Valley Church of the Brethren, ND, source of income, 1035
Poland, exchange program, 1041
Prairie City Church of the Brethren, IA, ownership of, 1050
Puerto Rico, projects in, 1070
Reber, Norman Franklin, 1085
relief and rehabilitation work, 167, 186, 198, 200, 1097
Rolston, Frances Fitz Simon and William Wendell, **1120**
Ronk, Albert T., 660
Royer, Gladys Violet Hawbaker and Harold Albertus ("Red"), **1128**

settlement patterns and, 186
shift away from, 2147
sources on, 2314
subsistence, 12
Agrippa, Brother, *See* Miller, John Peter
Ahard, Mary, 383
Ahern, Gerald, 1540
Ahern, Jerry, 2299
Ahl family, 503
Ahlstrom, Sydney E., 612, 1863
Ahmedabad, India, 229, 576
Ahner, Jacob, 504, 1540
Ahwa, India, 417, 649
aid societies
    children's aid, *See* Children's Aid
        Societies
    mutual aid, *See* mutual aid
    Potsdam, OH, Church of the Brethren,
        1049
Aide aux Enfants (Aid for Children), Haiti,
    579–580
Aidin, 1280
AIDS/HIV, **2129–2130**, 2178
Aiea, HI, Waimalu Grace Brethren Church,
    12
Aiken Grace Brethren Church, SC, **12,**
    1205
Aikey, A. Elmer, 1540
Ainlay, Steven C., 2310
Air Point, VA, Mount Union Church of the
    Brethren, **887**
Airesman, Royden E., 2271
Ajlune (Richland Valley) Church of the
    Brethren, WA, **1108,** 1139, 1338,
    2097
Ake family, 2084
Akers, A. J., 1540
Akers, Alonzo Edwin, 1863
Akers, Exonie Elizabeth (later West), 1332,
    2261
Akers family, 1341, 1863
Akers, Floyd, 613, 1540
Akers, G. W., 1540
Akers, J. H., 958, 1216
Akers, Joseph H., 1540
Akers, Lawrence, 124
Akers, Newton, 1540
Akers, Roley Tazewell, 1540
Akers, Waddie Hosie, 407, 1341, 1540
Akers, Wallace, 1341, 1540
Akers, Washington, 1341, 1540
Akron Bible Institute, Cuyahoga Falls, OH,
    Grace Brethren Church, 357, 2190
Akron Cooperative, Akron, IN, Church of
    the Brethren, 12
Akron, dirigible explosion, 1303
Akron, IN, Church of the Brethren, **12**
Akron, OH, 13
    Chippewa, OH, Church of the
        Brethren, 279
    City Church of the Brethren,
        2135
    Eastwood Church of the Brethren, **12,**
        13
    Ellet Grace Brethren Church, **12–13,**
        563
    Fairlawn Brethren Church, 2190
    Fairlawn Grace Brethren Church, **13**
    Firestone Park Brethren Church, **2130**
    First Brethren Church, 2190
    First Brethren Church (Ellet Grace
        Brethren Church), **12–13,** 563
    First Church of the Brethren, 12, **13,**

    13
    Grace Schools (Grace Theological
        Seminary, Grace College), 563
    Springfield Church of the Brethren,
        13–14, 688
Akron, PA, Church of the Brethren, **14**
    Middle Creek Church of the Brethren,
        PA, 825
    Mohler Church of the Brethren, PA,
        868
Alabama, Brethren in, **14,** 324, 831, 2354
Alafuerte, Argentina, 53
Alameda Co., CA, Oakland Church of the
    Brethren, 957
Aland, Kurt, 1021
Alaska
    Brethren in, **14**
    Old German Baptist Brethren in, 2235
Alazraki, Marcos, 975
Albanese, Catherine L., 612, 1863
Albania, 23
Albany, OR (formerly Lebanon), 14, 1138
    Grace Brethren Church, 14
    Mabel, OR, Church of the Brethren,
        771
    Oregon Territory, 734
    Sunrise Community Church (CB), 14
Albaugh, Catharine (later Stoner), 1221
Albaugh, Clyde S., 1540
Albaugh, David, 256, 407, 1540
Albaugh, David Z., 1540
Albaugh family, 740, 1115, 1138
Albaugh, Henry Preston, **14,** 786, 1540
Albaugh, Jacob P., 14
Albaugh, John E., 1540
Albaugh, John S., 1540
Albaugh, Rebecca Petry, 14
Albaugh, Zachariah, 1119, 1540
Albemarle Co., VA, 272
    Free Union, VA, Church of the Breth-
        ren, 513
    Pleasant Valley Church of the Brethren,
        VA, preaching points, 1035
Albert, Charles William, 1540
Albert, Ethel Evans, 1863
Albert, Leon Brewnell, 1540
Alberta, Canada, **15,** 1893
    Arrowwood, Bow Valley Church of
        the Brethren, 15, **59,** 817, 1034,
        1172, 1893
    Calgary, 15, 250, 251
    Church of the Brethren Annual
        Conference, 250
    Irricana (First) Church of the Brethren,
        15, 59
    Legislature, 15
    Medicine Hat, 15
    migration of Brethren to, 830
    Old German Baptist Brethren, 250
    Pleasant Ridge Church of the
        Brethren, 59
    Pleasant Valley congregation, 250
    Redcliff, 250
    Second Irricana Church of the Breth-
        ren, 15, 59
    Sharon Church of the Brethren, 59
Albertini, Valentine, 1863–1864
Albi, Languedoc, 15
Albigensians (Cathari), **15,** 315, 998, 1098
Albin, Charles, 985, 1323
Albin, Charles A., 1540, 2299
Albin family, 142
Albrecht (Albright) family, **16,** 1289, 1864,

    2085, 2088
Albrecht, August, 1355
Albrecht, Christian, 1879
Albrecht, Daniel, 1864
Albrecht, Harriet Martin, 1864, 1879
Albrecht, John, 1917
Albrecht, Lena I., 1864
Albrecht (Albright), Lena Waltner, 2088
Albrecht, Louis, 1206
Albrecht, Louis M., 1540
Albrecht, Waltraud, 2073
Albright, A., 622
Albright, Alda, 16
Albright, Anne Metzler, 1864, 2376
Albright, Barbara Elizabeth Delp, 16
Albright, Catherine, 16
Albright, Clarence, 1540
Albright, Claribel, 1864
Albright, Clayton Monroe, 1864
Albright, Elizabeth, 16, 317
Albright family, See Albrecht (Albright)
    family
Albright, Galen W., 1540
Albright, George, 2061
Albright, H. C., 1540
Albright, Ida, 16
Albright, Jacob (1759–1808), **16,** 459, 1867
Albright, Jacob (1827–1908), 16
Albright, Jacob, Jr., 16
Albright, James David, 1540
Albright, John, 16, 1540
Albright, John M., 1540
Albright, Julia, 16
Albright (Albrecht), Lena Waltner, *See*
    Albrecht, Lena Waltner
Albright, Lyle C., 752, 1285, 1540
Albright, Mae, 16
Albright, Noah, 16
Albright, Peter, 16
Albright, Raymond W., 1864
Albright, Rowena, 752
Albright, Samuel B., 16
Albright, W. David, 7, 503
Albright, William, 16, 974
Albright, William Burgess, 2085
Albright, William David, 1540
Albright, William F., 688
Albright, William Henry, 1540
Albright, William P., 1540
Albright Church of the Brethren, Roaring
    Spring, PA, 513, **1114**
Albright meetinghouse, Blair Co., PA, 16
Albright's People, *See* Evangelical Associa-
    tion
Albryoca (Allegheny Brethren Youth
    Camp), PA, 242
Albuquerque, NM
    Heights Grace Brethren Church, **16**
    Hispanic congregations in, 931
    Mission Viejo, CA, Saddleback Valley
        Grace Brethren Church, 855
    Native Americans, 2230
Alcatraz Island, CA, imprisonment of con-
    scientious objectors on, 1370
alchemy and Jakob Boehme, 156
alcoholic beverages, **16,** 203, *See also* grape
    juice, entries at; temperance, and
    wine
    auctions, prohibited at, 1251
    brewing and distilling, 206, 1251
    Christian education, 1999
    Church of the Brethren, 301
    discipline, doctrine of, 388

Dunkard Brethren, 409
Fahrney, Jacob, 465
Fellowship of Grace Brethren
    Churches (FGBC), 486
Hess, Maurice Abram, 601
Lancaster, PA, Alfa y Omega (Alpha
    and Omega) Church of the
    Brethren, 2213
Lybrook Navajo Community Ministry
    to alcoholics, 768
McFadden, Joyce on stance of CB
    on, 2344
nonconformity, 941
sale of, 1251
use of, 16
wedding receptions, 1326
Woodbridge, VA, Church of the
    Brethren; ministry to alcoholics
    at, 1364
Alder, Barbara Ann Moyer, 822
Alder, Garfield, 1864
Alder, Marcus, 822
Alderfer, Alvin Slotter, 1540
Alderfer, David, 1864
Alderfer, E. Gordon, 1864, 2201, 2310
Alderfer, Owen, H., 1864
Alderfer, Susan, 2346
Alderman, Clarence, 1540
Alderman, J. T., 1864
Alderman, Marcus B., 1540
Alderman, Martha B., 515
Alderman, Rupert E., 1540
Alderman, S. D., 1540
Alderman, Simon Benton, 1540
Alderman, Wesley, 515
Aldinger, Harry Elias, 1540
Aldinger, J. B., 1540
Aldinger, Jacob A., 1389, 1540
Aldinger, Joseph, 1540
Aldinger, Steven Glen, 2271
Aldis, Stedman, 1540
Aldrich, Pearl, 1864
Aleasar, Brother *See* Jakob Christian Eicher
Alejado, John Arthur, 2271
Aleppo, PA
    Grace Brethren Church, **16**
    Quiet Dell Brethren Church, **1076**
Aleppo, WV, Brethren Church, 241
Alesandroni, Victor, 2252
Alexander, Arthur J., 1864
Alexander family, 749, 2016
Alexander, J. W., 1540
Alexander, James, 2310
Alexander, Jane (later Miller), 837
Alexander, Jon, 1864
Alexander Mack Historical Society, 190,
    610, 1158
Alexander Mack Museum, **2130**, 2143
Alexander Mack School, **16–17**, 17, 609,
    1158, 1283, 1355
Alexandria, VA
    Commonwealth Avenue Brethren
        Church, 2193
    Grace Brethren Church, 1308, **2125**
Alexian Brothers Hospital, Chicago, 808
Alfalfa Co., OK, Hoyle Creek Church of
    the Brethren, 633
Alford, Herbert, 1540–1541
Alger, Lonnie L., 1541
Algeria, 23
Algles (Angle), Ellis T., 1215, 1542
Alivisatos, Hamilcar, 422
Alkire, Marie Jane (later Million), 843

All-Christian Peace Assembly (ACPA), 286
All Things Whatsoever I Have Commanded
    (Hoyt), 634
Allan, Daniel W., 951, 2271
Allan, Thomas, 1035
Allan (Allen), Thomas J., 1541
Allbaugh, Malisse I. (later Flora), 495
Allbeck, Willard D., 1864
Alldredge, John S., 1541, 1864
Alldredge, Leathy, 1864
Alldredge, Nila, 245
Allebach, Gerald, 674, 1348
Allegany Co., MD, 363, 713
    Flintstone, MD, Glendale Church of
        the Brethren, 494
    Frostburg, MD, First Church of the
        Brethren, 519
    Mill Run Grace Brethren Church,
        MD, 833
Alleghany Co., NC, 946
    Little Pine Church of the Brethren,
        749
    Mount Carmel Church of the
        Brethren, 880
    New Bethel Church of the Brethren,
        925
    New Haven Church of the Brethren,
        928
    White Rock Church of the Brethren,
        1341
Alleghany Co., VA
    Alleghany Church of the Brethren,
        2125
    Jordan Mines, VA, Rich Patch Brethren
        Church, 676
    mission point, Botetourt Co., VA,
        Church of the Brethren, 164, 2125
    Selma, VA, Church of the Brethren,
        1166
Allegheny Brethren Youth Camp
    (Albryoca), PA, 242
Allegheny College, 693
Allegheny Mountains, 150–152
Allegheny Tableland Community, 1935
Allegheny, VA, Brethren Church, 25, **2125**
Allegheny Valley Church of the Brethren,
    PA, *See* Natrona Heights, PA,
    Church of the Brethren
Allegheny Valley, PA, congregation, 918
Allegheny, WV
    Church of the Brethren (Durbin, Poca-
        hontas Co.), **2125–2126**
    Church of the Brethren (Mount Storm,
        Grant Co.), **2125**
    Jordan Run Church of the Brethren,
        676
    Old German Baptist Brethren Church,
        16
    Pocahontas Church of the Brethren,
        WV, mission point of, 1039
allegiance, oath of, *See* oaths
allegory, 2052
Allegri, John (Giovanni), 212, 1541
Allem, David B, 2271
Alleman family, 2040
Allen, Asa W., 1864
Allen Co., OH, 2386
Allen, Devere, 1864
Allen family, 227, 1309, 1864, 2060
    Hanawalt family, 582
    records, 1957
Allen, Frank K., 872, 1541
Allen, Fred, 1321

Allen, George L., 1865
Allen, George M., 1541
Allen, H. C., 1541
Allen, Harold Boughton, 1864
Allen Harry Raymond, 1864
Allen, Harvey W., 167, 1541
Allen, Ira Mason, 1865
Allen, J. D., 1865
Allen, James, 1864, 1865
Allen, Jean Gray, 1865
Allen, Joseph Rothrock, 1541
Allen, Leola, 2216
Allen, Mary Moore, 167
Allen, Merle (later Bowman), 167, 2372
Allen, Paul Wayne, 1541, 1865
Allen, Richard, 2128
Allen (ship), 159, 350, 697, **2126**
    Eiler (Eilar, Oyler) family, 432
    emigration, 443, 2373
    Kalcklöser, Johann Heinrich, 681
    Kipping, Johanna and Johannes, 697
    Knepper, Veronica Bloom, 703
    Knepper, Wilhelm Knepper, 703
    Mack family and Brethren voyage to
        America on, 777, 778
    migration augmented by arrival of
        Brethren on, 827
    Pettikoffer (Pettighofer, Pethkoffer)
        family, 2377
    Surhuisterveen Brethren, 1241
    voyage to America by Christian,
        Jacob, and Mathias Schneider,
        1154
    Weiss, Jacob, 1354
Allen, T. Darley, 1541
Allen, Thomas (BC, FGBC), 1541
Allen (Allan), Thomas J., 1541
Allen Bethel, IN
    Church of God (New Dunkers), 297
    New Dunkard News, 927
Allen Co., IN
    bibliographical sources, 2099
    Cedar Creek Church of the Brethren,
        264
    Flat Rock Church of the Brethren, **493**
Allen Co., KS, Mount Zion Church of the
    Brethren, 888
Allen Co., KY (originally Warren Co.), 398,
    688, 689
Allen Co., OH, 142, 215, 236, 742, 1234
    Bower, Daniel, 961
    descendants of Sanger family helping
        to build congregations, 1144
    Dunkard Brethren Church, 2086
    Mennonite Church, 2086
    Pleasant View Church of the Brethren,
        OH, 1037
    Sugar Creek, OH, congregation, 961
Allenbach, Gerald, 1541
Allenbaugh, Lincoln, 1541
Allensville, WV
    Church of the Brethren, **2126**
    Johnsontown Church of the Brethren,
        675
Allentown, PA
    Bethlehem, PA, Lehigh Valley Grace
        Brethren Church, **130**
    Church of the Brethren, **2126**
    First Brethren Church, 1247
    Gingrich, Joseph L., 550
    Harleysville, PA, Indian Creek Church
        of the Brethren, **583–584**
Allenworth, J. B., 561, 1541

Allerheiligan, Ronald, 104
Alley family, 2310
Alley, Hattie Zelma Miller, 1833
Alley, Howard Lee, 251, 511, 1541, 1833, 1938
Alley, Mary Bruins, 1833
Alley, Robert Earl, 482, 1541, 1865, 2181, 2257–2258, 2310
Alliance, OH, Church of the Brethren, 514, 1865, **2126**
Allisbaugh, Mr. and Mrs., 949
Allison, David W., 1177, 1541
Allison family, 270, 1108, 2216
Allison, John, 1541
Allison, Mary Bruins, 1833
Allison, Richard E., 670, 1541, 1865, 2219
Allison, Roy, 1541, 2299
Allison, William, 1857
Allison Prairie Church of the Brethren, IL, 1979, **2126**
ALM *See* American Leprosy Missions; Adamawa Provincial Leprosarium, Garkida, Nigeria; leprosy
Alm Bruderhof, Hutterian Society of Brothers, 640
Alma, MI, 1302
Almafuerte, Argentina, 180, 854, 535, 1181
    Almanac, 18
    bibliography, 1889
    Fly Creek Church of the Brethren, KS, 500
    genealogy, 535
    Harrison, OK, Church of the Brethren, 586
    Miami, NM, Church of the Brethren, advertised in, 823
    published lists of ministers, 1218
    publishing, 1068
almanacs, 7, **17–18**, *See also* specific almanac
    advertisements and announcements, 7, 1948
    Brethren Almanac of 1874, 1962
    Brethren Family Almanac, 7, 18, 194, 404, 696, 1384, 1889–1890
    Christian education movement, 283
    education, 426
    English language, 18
    first in America (German), 17
    folk medicine, 2145–2146
    historical writing, 611
    Kurtz, Henry J., 712
    medicine, 809
    Pennsylvania German astronomy and astrology, 2102
    publication of, 712, 1063
    Sauer family, 1160, 1948, 1965, 2102
    Sauer, Christoph (Christopher II), 1146
    Sauer, Johann Christoph (Christopher I), 1147
    Sauer, Samuel, 1149
    scientific activities, 1160, 2102
    yearbooks as adaptations, 1384
Almena, MI, 824
    Brethren Church, **18**
    Church of the Brethren, **18**
alms, **18–19**
Almstedt, Louise Arlene Snyder, 1865
Alpena, SD, congregation, 1205
Alpha Hall
    Elizabethtown College, 437
    Grace Schools (Grace Theological

Seminary, Grace College), 564
Alquire, John, 755
Alsace, France (formerly Germany), **19**, 25, 545
    Eckerlin, Samuel, 422
    Näff family, 909
    Pennsylvania Germans from, 1006
    Rhine River Valley, Brethren origins in, 1106
    Schweitzer, Albert, 1159
    Urner family driven to by persecution, 1298
Alspaugh, Clair H., 19, 135, 1541
Alspaugh, Clara M., 19
Alspaugh, Cora M. Williamson, 19
Alspaugh, Ruth (later Rohrer), 1119
Alspaugh, Thomas H., **19**
Alta Loma, CA, Grace Brethren Church, 19, 755, 1111
Altaffer, Elizabeth (later Klein), 699
Altamont, KS, Church of the Brethren, 19, 716
altar calls, 460, 930–931
altars (communion tables), 328, 474
Alter, Donald, 1541
Alterffer, Frederick, 1166, 1541
Altermatt, Lester William, Jr., 1541
alternative service, **19–20**, 23–24, 202, 1268, 2028, *See also* conscientious objection; historic peace churches
    bibliographical sources, 1864, 1879
    chaplaincy, 271
    Civilian Public Service and National Service Board for Religious Objectors (NSBRO), 917
    Germans serving in, 202
    International Voluntary Services Agency (IVS), 660
    Karlsschule group, 684
    Korean War, 707
    medical missions and projects, 807, 808
    Mennonite-Brethren cooperation, 1963–1964
    Murray, Don, 625
    Old German Baptist Brethren peace position, 1000
    Peace Corps, 1002
    religious liberty and military service, 1098
    sociological study of men in, 2100
    suitable work projects for, 19
    Vietnamese War, 1305
    Wagoner, Gerald C., Sr. (OGBB) and, 2259
    work camps as, 1367
    World War I, 1370
    World War II, 316, 1372
Alternatives (film, 1958), 20
Althouse, Richard, 2310
Altick, Elizabeth, 157
Altick, Richard D., 1865
Altig, Howard K., 754, 1541
Altig, Jerome Keith, **20**, 30, 136, 503, 758, 1343, 1541, 2371
Altig, Vivian Carroll Force, 20, 136, 172, 1847, 2371
Altizer, Bertie W. (later Reed), 1090
Altizer, R. E., and Mountain Normal School, 889
Altizer, Thomas, 1541
Altland, Charles H., 1541

Altland (Aultland), Daniel, 1541
Altland union house, Lower Conewago Church of the Brethren, PA, 765
Altman family and David Shoemaker, 1157
Alto, MI
    Calvary Grace Brethren Church, 239
    Hope Church of the Brethren, 629
Altona, Germany, *See* Hamburg-Altona, Germany
Altona, populations of, 2325
Altoona, KS, Church of the Brethren, **20**
Altoona, PA, 20, 1213, 1316
    Bible Church, 21, 709
    conservative theology and schism, 1005
    First Brethren Church, 2217
    First Church of the Brethren, **20**, 21, 407
    Grace Brethren Church, **20–21**
    Grace Brethren congregations, 1005
    Juniata Church of the Brethren, 20, **21**
    Juniata Grace Brethren Church, **21**
    Sisters' Aid Society, 1187
    Twenty-Eighth Street Church of the Brethren, 20, **21**, 303, 709, 729, 1347
Alum Ridge, VA, Pleasant Valley Church of the Brethren, **21**, 1341
Alumni Physical Education Center, Elizabethtown College, 438
Alva, OK, missions, *858*
Alvin F. Brightbill Speech Laboratory, 209
Alvin, TX, Church of the Brethren, *See* Manvel, TX, Church of the Brethren
Alvo, NE, Church of the Brethren, 21, 743
Alwine, Paul Eugene, 1541
Alyea family, New Rockford, ND, Church of the Brethren, 932
Alzheimers' disease, 2321
Amana, *See* Community of True Inspiration
Amapá territory, Brazil, 172
Amaranth Church of the Brethren, PA, **21**, 62
Amazon River mouth, missions and missionaries at, 172
Amberg, WI, 1341
Ambler, PA
    Church of the Brethren, **21–22**, 455, 587, 2323
    homelessness in, 2203
Amdavadi, Jacob V., 1541
Amendments to Constitution, *See* Constitution, US
Ament, James, 596
Ament, James D., 1141
America, *See* colonial America; United States of America (USA)
America, Sylvanus, 1541
American Advice and Help Book (Kurtz), 1992
American Advisory Committee for China Relief, 277
American Almanack (1747), 18
American and Foreign Anti-Slavery Society, **22**, 1190
American Anti-Slavery Society, **22**, 1190
American Armenian International College, 715, 716
American Association for Jewish Evangelism, 634, 772
American Association of Marriage and Family Therapists (AAMFT), 796

American Baptist Building Services, 51
American Baptist Churches, **22**, *See also* Baptists
Big Sky Church of the Brethren/American Baptist Church, MT, **142**, 1301
Church of the Brethren, 304
Committee on Interchurch Relations, 2167
fraternal relations, 510
Garden Terrace Retirement Home, 530
graded Sunday school lessons, 1236
Harper Woods, MI, Detroit First Church of the Brethren, 585
"Principles for a Plan of Union," 22
Sacramento, CA, Prince of Peace joint congregation, 1134
American Bible Society (ABS), **22**, 1865
"American Bottom" near St. Louis, MO, 1358
American Centennial fairs and public shows, 467
American Christian Missionary Society, 385
American Civil War, *See* Civil War
American Colonization Society, **22**, *See also* abolition of slavery; slavery
American Committee for Relief in the Near East, **22–23**, 55, 1096
American Council of Churches (ACC), **23**
American Council of Voluntary Agencies for Foreign Service, 23
American Encyclopedia (Schaff), 379
American Farm School, Greece, 569
American Fellowship of Reconciliation (AFOR), *See* Fellowship of Reconciliation (USA)
American Field Service student exchange program, 1231
American Friends Service Committee (AFSC), 19, **23–24**, 146, 200
Ambulance Unit, 23
Community Relations programs, 23
CPS camps, 23
Gilbert, Martha Rupel, 2189
Heifer Project International, 593
Historic Peace Churches, 609
Murphy, Sara Florence Fogelsanger, liason to, 897
Peace Education work, 23
Pickett, Clarence Evan, 1021
refugee resettlement, 1092, 1093
Russia, funds raised for relief work, 1288
Smeltzer, Ralph E., 302
social welfare, 1198
Society of Friends (Quakers), 1199
Spain, 23, 517–518, 1207, 1208
Wilson, Edward Raymond, 1347
work camp, Westmoreland Co., PA, 1367
American German Review, 1857
American Indian Movement (AIM), 2230
American Indians, *See* Native Americans
American Institute of Family Relations, marriage counseling by, 796
American Institute of Holy Land Studies, 46
American Legion, **24**, 241
American Leprosy Missions (ALM), 4, **24**, 432, 807, *See also* Adamawa Provincial Leprosarium, Garkida, Nigeria; leprosy
American Lutheran Church, *See* Lutheran

Church
Jackpot Church, NV, 2212
mass media cooperative effort, 801
American Medical Missionary College, MI, 936
American Missionary Fellowship, Vermont, 1304
American Philosophical Society, 840, 1865
American Protestant Hospital Association College of Chaplains, 1332
American Red Cross, *See* Red Cross
American Revolution, 16, 18, 42, 1100, 1105, **1105–1106**
agriculture and farming, 477
allegiances, 176
authorities, 18
bibliographical sources, 1863, 1864, 1868, 1875, 1892, 1895, 1898, 1907, 1908, 2019, 2021, 2030, 2031, 2034, 2041, 2045, 2087
Brandywine Creek, Battle of, 172, 686
Brethren movement and, 250
Brethren participation in, 989, 1922
Bromback (Brumbach), Jacob, 516
Catawba, NC, German Baptist Brethren Church, and effects of, 262
church-state relations, 310
churches with significant history from, 80
Committee of Observation, 327
confiscation of property, 334
Continental money, 338
Dilling family, 384
dress, 400
Dutchman's Creek German Baptist Brethren Church, NC, 411
education, 426
Edwards, Morgan, 429
Ephrata, 2008
ethics, 458
field hospitals and, 172
Frederick Tory Plot, 2100
Frederick treason trial, 1918
frontier, 519
Garber (Gerber), John H., 529, 534
German-Americans and, 2095
German language newspapers pulished during, 2088
Germantown, Battle of, 544
Hesse, 601
higher education, 603
historic peace churches, 607
historic sites, 609
historical writing, 613, 1873
Kedar at Ephrata Community used as hospital during, 686
Kern, Conrad; Rowan Co., NC militia records regarding, 689–690
Lancaster Co., PA, 2074
Loyalists during, *See* Loyalists
Maryland, 2056
medical care at Ephrata, 809
Mennonites, 2052
Metzler family, 820
Meyer family, 822
migration of Brethren and, 170, 829
military service, 176, 387
military substitutes, 1233–1234
militia organization and development in North Carolina, 2097
Miller, John Peter, 2015

ministerial exemption, 844
Morrisons Cove, 877
Muhlenberg, John Peter Gabriel, serving with American army, 893
Müller, Johann Heinrich, 893
Murray, Samuel M., 897
Musselman, Christian, 901
Native Americans, 2229
Nead, Peter, as spokesman for post-war Brethren world view after, 918–920, 919
non-associators in, 939
nonresistance and, 176
nursing, 952
oaths, 959, 1233, 1299, 2126
Ontario, Brethren moving to, 975
pacifism, doctrine of, 2074
pacifist groups, 1990
peace movement and peace churches, 999, 2005, 2074
Pennsylvania Brethren, 1004
Pennsylvania Germans, 2106
Powers, Valentine, 1204
printing industry, 2088
prisons and prisoners, 1059, 2074
publications and, 154
Quakers, 1190, 1916
records, 2104
Reed, John Ford on Ephrata Cloister and, 2351
religious freedom and persecution, 1009
Rowland, Gasper, noncombatant posture during, 1126
Sauer family and publications, 925, 1067, 1146, 1147, 1149, 2055
A Short and Sincere Declaration, 176, 310, 312, 1178–1179, 1993, 2064
Showalter, Michael S. on hospital at Ephrata Cloister during, 2356
slaves in, 2128
social action, 1196
Spohn, Clarence E. on Ephrata Cloister during, 2358
Stutesman, John Hale on Dunkers and, 2360
Stutzman, Jacob, refusal of oath of allegiance, 1233
Urner, Martin, fined for feeding American soldiers, 1298
Uwharrie German Baptist Brethren Church, NC, 1299
Widman incident, 2074
Yadkin German Baptist Brethren Church, NC, 1383
American Scientific Affiliation and Alva J. McClain, 773
American Standard Version (ASV) of the Bible, 138
American Stores Company, 2310
American Sunday School Union (ASSU), **24**, 283, *See also* entries at Sunday school; International Sunday School Association
Covington, WA, Community Church of the Brethren, sponsorship by, 350
Fort Scott, KS, Brethren Church, 503
Ohio, 272
Americanism, 24
Americus, GA; Koinonia Farms, 705
Ames, IA, Church of the Brethren, **25**
Ames, OK, Hoyle Creek Church of the

Brethren, **633–634**
Amherst Co., VA, Oronoco Church of the Brethren, 982
Amherst, VA, Brethren Church, **25**
Amick, Elizabeth Reiff, 58
Amick, Elizabeth Rothrock, 25
Amick family, 232
Amick, Hannah Reiff, 25
Amick, Irena (later Arnold), 58
Amick, Jonathan, 25
Amick, Joseph M., **25**, *25*, 58, 195, 818, 836, 872, 1541
Amick, Susanna Mertz, 25
amillennialism, 833, 834
Amish, **25–26**, 28, 122, 2098
  affiliation with Brethren and Mennonites, 26
  baptism, doctrine of, 2107
  barnraising, 89
  beards, 103
  bibliographical sources, 2325, 2341
  Brethren family names of Amish orgin, 26
  fiction, references in, 2106–2107
  Frantsville, MD, 2014
  Garber (Garver, Gerber) family, 529
  genealogies, index of, 1912
  Graybill (Grabill, Krehbiel) family, 567
  growth rate, 26
  Hershberger (Harshbarger) family, 598
  Hertzler (Hartzler) family, 601
  Hochstetler (Hostetler) family, 615
  Keim, Johannes, 686
  Kraybill, Donald B. on, 2341
  Lantz (Lentz) family, 725
  Lehman, Peter, 736
  medicine, 809
  Mennonite Central Committee (MCC), 814
  Mennonites, 2220
  migration to Brethren congregations, 175
  musical instruments, 900
  nonconformity, 940
  Old Order Amish, 26
  plain people, 1029
  relationships with Dunkers, 1974
  Stutzman, Jacob, 1233
  Yoder, Eli Lorenzo, 1386
  Yoder, Joseph J., 1386
  Yoder, Joseph Warren, 1386–1387
  Yoder, Rosanna McGonegal, 1387
  Zug family, 1401
Amish Mennonites
  affiliation of Amish with Brethren and Mennonites, 26
  Fahrney, Peter, 466
  Gnagey (Gnaegi) family, 554
  Mennonite Central Committee (MCC), 814
Ammann group, *See* Amish
Ammann, Jakob, 25, 26
Ammermann, Ernest Gifford, 1541
Ammi–My People (William J. Shoup), 1179
amnesty for conscientious objectors, **26**
Among the Giants (Neher), 748
Amos, Brother, *See* Jan Mäyle
Amos, William, 605
Amsler, Gary M., 2310
Amstutz family, 1221, 2074
Amstutz, Gladys Mary Lehman, 2074

Amstutz, Roy, 1541
Amthabhai, Mitalal, 1541
Amundson, Louis A., 2271
Amundson, Louis A., Sr., 532
amusements, worldly, 3, **26**, *See also* specific types
  acculturation and, 3
  art, 59
  athletics, 69–70, 70, 557, 1087, 2045, 2232
  Church of the Brethren, 2110
  drama, 398–399
  East Fairview Church of the Brethren, PA, 415
  Fellowship of Grace Brethren Churches (FGBC), 486
  lyceums, 768
  mass media, 800–801
  motion pictures, 879
  nonconformity, 940
  radio, *See* radio
  recreation, 1087
  television, 1251
Amwell Church of the Brethren, NJ, **27–28**
  Bethel German Baptist Brethren Church, NJ, 129
  Dierdorff, Anthony, 383
  Eckerlin, Emmanuel, 421
  graveyards, 267
  Harley family, 583
  Harley (Herli, Harli), Hans Rudolf, 583
  history of, 1926
  Howe, William Mohler, 633
  Klein family, 699
  Kline, John, 701
  Laschet, Abraham van, 726
  Mooreites, 875
  Naas, Jakob Wilhelm residence, 909
  Naas, Johannes, buried, 909
  Nicholson, John, minister in, 935
  origin of, 929
  Poulson, Israel, 1049
  San Brook Church of the Brethren, NJ, 1142
  Union Church of New Jersey (CB), 1287
  Wise, John, and Mooreite dispute, 1354
Amwell, East, 2070
Anabaptism and Anabaptists, 5, 19, 25–26, **28–29**, 121–122, 1933, 1953, *See also Bernese Anabaptists*
  accused of works righteousness, 1368
  alternative names for, 28, 82
  The Andrew Center, **2130**, 2162, 2180
  Apocrypha, use of, 43
  Apostolic Christian Church, 43, 1246
  Apostolic Church, viewed as link to, 43
  Arminianism and, 56
  art, attitude toward, 59
  Believers Church Commentary Series, 2134
  Bernese, *See* Bernese Anabaptists
  Bible and, 183
  biblical commands, 132
  bibliographical sources, 1949, 2032, 2051, 2326, 2330, 2332, 2334, 2341, 2344, 2347, 2353, 2356, 2357, 2359, 2360
  Brethren Church, 184
  Brethren movement and, 29, 174, 291, 292, 294, 355, 1080, 1259–1260, 2075
  church membership, 813

Church of the Brethren, 303
Churches of God (CG), 309
communitarianism, 328
community, 329
congregational polity, 1041
conversion, doctrine of, 339
COs, 335
  definition of, 292
  Dueck, Al on community and, 2325
  eschatological community, 293
  essence of, 29
  ethics, 457
  family, 472
  Felbinger, Jeremias, 482
  fellowship, need for, 1373
  Fellowship of Hope, 488
  Forum for Religious Studies, 2185–2186
  Frantz, Michael, 508
  Frederick Co., PA, 146
  free ministry, 513
  Frenkendorf, 516
  Froelich (Fröhlich), Samuel Heinrich, 518, 1246
  fundamentalism, 522, 523
  Gingerich (Kingery) family, 549
  Hess family, 601
  historic peace churches, 607
  historical writing, 612
  historiography, 2201, 2202
  Holderman (Haldeman) family, 618
  honorific titles, 1266
  house churches, 632
  human nature, doctrine of, 635
  Hutterian Brethren, 639, 640
  Hymnal: A Worship Book, 2206
  hymnals of, 72
  infant baptism, 655
  intercession with authorities by Treytorren, Nicolas Samuel de, 1274
  interest-taking, 658
  International Fellowship of Grace Brethren Churches, 2208
  Karl Ludwig, count of Sayn-Wittgenstein-Sayn, denunciation of Anabaptists by, 683
  Kurtz, Henry, preached to, 1246
    Lancaster, PA, Acts Covenant Fellowship, 2213
  Landes, Hans, 722
  Landes, Johann Heinrich, 722
  Liebe, Christian, 527, 741, 1246
  Longenecker, Stephen L. on emotionalism among, 2343
  Lutheran criticism of, 71
  Mallott, Floyd Ellwood, 784
  martyrology, 154
  Marxist view of, 28
  Mehrning, Jacob, 811
  membership and indoctrination in churches of, 2326
  Mennonites and, 814, 815, 816, *See also* Anabaptist-Mennonites
  Mishler family, 852
  Müller, Joseph, parents of, 893–894
  musical instruments, 900
  names of Brethren fellowships, 910
  oaths, taking of, 959, 2126
  opponents of, 28
  original sin, 981
  Palatinate, 146, 159
  peace, 998, 999

persecution of, 28
Pietism, 1022
Pleickersdorffer, Hans Jacob, 146
poor, caring for the, 1046
premillenialism, 833
Priesthood of All Believers, 1057
primitivism and, 1058
prisons, 1059
prophecy, 1062
Radical German Pietism, 1079
Reba Place Fellowship, 1084
redemption, 1090
Reformation, Protestant, 1091, 1092
religious liberty, 1098
restitutionism and restitutionist com-
    munity, 293
resurrection, 1101
roots of, 28–29
salvation, Brethren doctrine of, 1140
Schwarzenau Brethren, 292
sect-church typology, 1275
    sin, 1184
Sojourners Fellowship, 1200
sources on, 2310, 2311, 2312, 2317,
    2323
spiritual life, 1209
Surhuisterveen as possible settlement
    place, 1241
Surhuisterveen refugees, 1976
Swiss Anabaptist-Mennonites, 29
theology/doctrine of, 29
threat to society, viewed as, 28
toleration of, 28–29
trinity, doctrine of, 1275
Wenger family, 1330
writings, 28, 29
The Young Center and, 2267
Anabaptist Curriculum Publishing Council,
    2209
Anabaptist-Mennonites
    Graybill (Grabill, Krehbiel) family, 567
    preservation of heritage, 171
    Ruth, John L. on Swiss worship among,
        2354
    Swiss, 29
Anabaptist-Socinians, 288
Anburey, Thomas, 1865
Anchorage, AK, Grace Brethren Church,
    14, 30, 687
"Ancient Documents," 30, 511, See also
    Far Western Brethren
Ancient Order of Free and Accepted
    Masons, See Freemasonry
Andean Indians, service to, 1289
Andel, Cornelius Pieter van, 1865
Anders, Coy, 749, 1541
Anders, Daniel M., 1865
Anders, David L., 1542
Anderson Co., KS, 682
    Cedar Creek Old German Baptist
        Church, 264
    Mont Ida, KS, Church of the Brethren,
        870
    Olathe Old German Baptist Brethren
        Church, KS, 964
Anderson, IN
    Church of God, 1394
    First Church of the Brethren, 30
        youth conference, 989, 2050
Anderson, SC, Grace Brethren Church, 30,
    1205
Anderson, A. S. M., 679
Anderson, Alvin Lee, 1865

Anderson, Anders, 1541, 2380
Anderson, Andreas, 1541
Anderson, Andy, 2213
Anderson, Barbara (later Metzger), 1944
Anderson, Bart, 1865
Anderson, Bruce E., 1541
Anderson, Charles Ernest, 320, 1541
Anderson, Darrell, 1541
Anderson, Elsie Nelson, 322
Anderson, Ernest W., 1541
Anderson, Frances, 220
Anderson, George, 1541
Anderson, Gerald H., 2310
Anderson, Homer, 318, 1031, 1541
Anderson, James I., 1541
Anderson, John, 1541
Anderson, Mildred Marie Forney, 1865
Anderson, R. Darrell, 1028
    Modesto, CA, La Loma Grace Brethren
        Church, pastor, 867
Anderson, Ralph Werner, 713, 825, 1242,
    1541
Anderson, Richard C., 2310–2311
Anderson, Russell H., 1865
Anderson, Thelma Chidester, 1865
Anderson, Victor, 1541–1542
Anderson, Willard I., 1930
Anderson, William H., 1542
Anderson, William L., 1865
Anderson, Z. W., 1542
Anderson family, 322, 1348, 1927, 2087
    Placerville, CA, Sierra View Grace
        Brethren Church, 1028
    Redstone Valley Old German Baptist
        Brethren Church, WI and, 2240
    Reliance, VA, Mount Zion Brethren
        Church, 1096
    Salem Church of the Brethren, ND,
        1137
Andes, Connie, 2264
Andes, David L., 668, 733, 1542
Andes family, 733, 1318
    Glück (Glick, Click) family, 553
    Good (Guth) family, 556
    North Bethel Church of the Brethren,
        MO, 945
    South Bethel German Baptist Brethren,
        MO, 1204
Andes, Ivie (later Frank), 1940
Andes, Levi, 1542
Andes, Norman W., 1542
Andes, Ray Clifford, 1542
Andrae, Johann Valentin, 1123
The Andrew Center, 2130, 2162, 2180
Andrew Co., MO, 1342
Andrew, Fred, 1542
Andrews, IN, Church of the Brethren, 30
    Ogan's Creek, IN, Church of the
        Brethren, 960
    Salamonie congregation, organized
        from, 1136
    Shull, Chalmer George, pastor, 1180
Andrews, Claire M., 169
Andrews, E. E., 275
Andrews, Earl (W.), 1542
Andrews family, 828
Andrews, George W., 1865, 2311
Andrews, Harry Eugene, 30, 1542
Andrews, J. Fred, 1542
Andrews, Jedidiah, 1865
Andrews, Kenneth Wilbur, 1542, 1865
Andrews, Levi, 1542
Andrews, M. E., 520

Andrews, Marion E., 1542
Andrews, Mark R., 2271
Andrews, Roy A., 2271
Andrews, Therman Leroy, 1542
Andrick, Shirley (later Black), 2138
androgyny, 2351
Anaheim, CA, Grace Brethren Church,
    29–30
Angel Brethren (Engel-Brüder), 30
    Gichtel, Johann Georg, 548
    letters from, 1948
    Universalism, 1080
Angel's Rest Church of the Brethren, VA,
    30, 1267
The Angelus, 77, 1237
Angeny, Edward Thomas, 1542, 1833
Angeny, Helen Frances Buehl, 1833
Angevine, Erma Beatrice Miller, 1865
Angle (Algles), Ellis T., 1215, 1542
Angle, Anna, 579
Angle, Benjamin D., 1542
Angle, Carolyn, 2311
Angle, Daniel, 446
Angle, David, 446
Angle, Earla Ferguson, 1865
Angle, Elizabeth, 446
Angle (Engle) family, 446, 1911
Angle, Henry, 446
Angle, Henry, Jr., 446
Angle, Jacob, 446
Angle, Jacob Martin, 446
Angle, John, 446
Angle, Lee, 1542
Angle, Mary E., 211
Angle, Peter, 1865
Angle, Roseann Elizabeth Zeller, 446
Angle, William Lee, 1542
Anglemeyer, David H., 1542
Anglemeyer, Jesse J., 1542
Anglemeyer (Anglemeyer), John, 1287,
    1542
Anglican (Episcopal) Church
    charismatic movement, 272
    Church of North India, 298
    communion table, 328
    Ephrata Press, 452
    episcopal polity, 1042
    Fellowship of Reconciliation (USA),
        488
    International Christian Youth
        Exchange (ICYE), 658–659
    pietism, 1022
    religious liberty, suppression of, 1098
    Smith, William, 1191, 1914, 2069
    Sunday school lessons, 1237
    Sunday school movement, 283
    Van Nuys, CA, 272
Angtada, Roman, 1248
Anhang zum Widerlegten Wiedertäufer
    (Appendix to the Refuted
    Anabaptist; 1788, Alexander
    Mack, Jr.), 31, 43, 774, 2004
animal life, congregational names derived
    from, 911
animism, 31
    Hinduism, 607
    Indonesia, 655
    missions to animistic tribes, 861
    Nigeria, 305
Anjou, Gustave, 1865–1866
Ankenman, Guy, 1542
Ankeny, Charles F., 1542
Ankeny, E. Eugene, 1542

Ankeny, Frank, 1542
Ankeny, IA, Church of the Brethren (Des
    Moines Valley), 31
Ames, IA, Church of the Brethren, 25
    Farnhamville, IA, Church of the
        Brethren, 479
    First Church of the Brethren, **31**
    Gochenour (Goughnour) family, 555
    Maxwell, IA, Church of the Brethren,
        803
Ankeny, Isaac, 424, 1542
Ankenytown, OH, Grace Brethren Church,
    31
    Bowman, Isaac Daniel, 166
    Butler, OH, North Liberty Brethren
        Church, 235
    Christner, David C., 289
    Haller, Wesley, 2195
    Klingensmith, J. Ray, 703
    Lindower, Leslie E., 744
    Lynn, Archibald L., 768
    Mansfield, OH, Conservative Grace
        Brethren Church, 2217
Ankenytown, OH, Owl Creek Church of
    the Brethren, **31–32**
    Davy, Henry Dorsey, 364
    Delaware, OH, Church of the
        Brethren, 374
    Leedy family and Leedy Brethren,
        734
    Long, John (1728–91), 724
Anklesvar, India, 229, 649, *650*
    Bhagat, Premchand Ganeshji, 131
    Girls' School, 1319
    Lichty, Anna Eby, 741
    Lichty, Daniel John, 741
    Lichty, Nora S. Arnold, 741
    Long, Effie Virginia Showalter, 753
    Long, Isaac Samuel, 753
    McCann, Samuel Napoleon, 772
    Miller, Eliza Belle, missionary, 837
    mission schools, 131, 853, 1319
    missions and missionaries, 212
    orphanages, 651
    Rural Service Center (CB), 1131,
        1131
    Sewell, Laura A. (CB) in, 2247
    Sheldon Church of the Brethren, IA,
        provided building for, 1175
    Shickel, Elsie Naomi, missionary,
        1176–1177
    Vocational Training College, 2316
    Vocational Training School, 131
    Warstler, Anna Margaret, 1319
Ankn1ey, Charles F., 1542
Ankrom, J. V., 1542
Ankrum, Armstrong L., 32
Ankrum, Esther McAvoy, 32
Ankrum, Freeman, **32**
    bibliographical sources, 1866
    Garwin, IA, Carlton Brethren Church,
        532
    genealogical writings of, 535
    Hamlin, KS, Brethren Church, 581
    historical writings of, 535, 612
    Mount Zion Brethren Church, OH, 888
Ankrum, Lucinda Mack, 32
Ankrum, Viola Myers, 32
Ann Galley (Philip Ziegler), 1397
Ann Maria Moser meetinghouse, Harmony
    Church of the Brethren, MD, 584
Anna Elizabeth (Long), 748
Anna, IL, 1288

Anna, Sister, *See* Anna Eicher
Annihilationism and Brethren Church, 185
anniversary celebrations
    Centennial fairs and public shows, 467
    publications, 1282–1283
    *Two Centuries of the Church of the
        Brethren* conference, 1282
    two-hundred-fiftieth anniversary at
        Schwarzenau, 1274, 1282, 1283,
        1355
Annon, Benjamin F., 880, 1542
Annon, George W., 124, 1542
Annon, Sylvannus M., 1542
Annon, Zechariah (Zachariah), 124, 1033,
    1177, 1542
Annoni, Pfarrer H., 2056
Annual Conference, *See* Annual Meeting
Annual Meeting, **32–39**, *483, 589, 652,*
    696, 1505, 2022, 2033, 2045,
    See also queries; specific conven-
    tion
    1783, 16
    1788, 18
    1804, 103
    1812, 1
    1825, 75
    1839, 71
    1840, 115
    1848, 77
    1851, 22
    1854, 22
    1855, 48, 71
    1864, 87
    1875, 87
    1876, 26
    1880, 39
    1881, 63, 121
    1882, 58, 67, 121
    1883, 7, 67
    1890, 81
    1893, 30, 94
    1901 (Lincoln, NE), 35
    1906, 69
    1908, 7
    1911, 3
    1920, 22
    1920s, ca. (Hershey, PA), 32
    1921, 123
    1923 (Calgary, Canada), 15
    1925, 126
    adjoining elders, responsibilities of, 4
    advertising, restraint in, 7
    alcoholic beverages, 16, 1251
    American Revolution, Brethren non-
        participation in, 1105, 1106
    American Revolution, celebrating the
        centennial of, 26
    amusements, worldly, 26
    anointing, 39
    appeal to, **44**
    arrangements for, 178
    Association of Brethren Caregivers
        (ABC), 2132
    authority of, *See* authority of Annual
        Meeting
    authorization of annual statistical
        reports (1921), 1218–1219
    automobile, use of, 74, 75
    avoidance, complete and partial, 75
    banking business, participation in, 81
    Baptism, Eucharist, and Ministry
        (BEM) text (1987), 2133–2134
    baptism, indoor ("pools"), 87

beards, 103
bells, use of, 115
Bethany Hospital, 123
Bethany Seminary, 125, 126
Bible Institute, followed by (1906),
    1215
bibliography, 1866, 1889, 1900, 1903,
    1905
Brethren Church, *See* Brethren
    Church General Conference
Brethren music, 899
Brethren service, address about, 1925
    California, migration of Brethren
        to, 830
A Call to Compassion (1987), 2129
carpets, use of, 256
chaplaincy, 271
chartered trains, 273
Children's Aid Societies, 276
choice of name for denomination, 910
Christian Day School movement, 282
Christian education movement, 284
Christian Science, 287
chronological list of, 1505–1511
church discipline, 942
Church of God (New Dunkers), 297
Church of the Brethren, *See* Church of
    the Brethren Annual Conference
    Committee, 2311
committees to investigate congrega-
    tions, 44, 121
conscientious objector inter-denomi-
    national cooperation, 917
controversial ideas, 285
credentials committee, 409
criticism of sale of spirits (1804),
    1251
Davy, Henry Dorsey, 364
decisions at, 5, 33, 36, *See also*
    mandatory decisions
defellowship of Bowman, John A.,
    170
defense industries, 373
delegates to, 33
denomination, listed by, 1505–1511
Des Moines, IA, *194, 378*
development from "Great Assembly,"
    1298
dining hall, 257
divorce issues, 393
drama, position on, 398
dramatic performances at, 399
dress decisions, 59, 160, 301, 400–403,
    921
Dunkard Brethren, *See* Dunkard
    Brethren General Conference
education, 426–428, 435
Eighteenth Amendment, endorsement
    of, 1251, 1252
election of church officers, 434
electricity, 434
emancipation, 443
engagement, 446
ethics, 457
evangelism, 460, 461
evolution, 463
Eyman, Peter, 464
Eyman schism, 77, 78
fairs and public shows, 467
Far Western Brethren, 475, 476
farming, 477
fasting, 480
feetwashing, 481, 1186

fellowship at, 482

Fellowship of Grace Brethren Churches (FGBC), *See* Grace Brethren National Conference

fetal tissue therapy (1997), 2127

Filbrun family, 490

first (1742), 33

First Petition, 491

first west of the Allegheny Mountains, 177

Fisher, Elias, 491

Flat Rock Church of the Brethren, VA, 494

Flora, John F., 495

foreman, 502

Forward Movement, 504

Franklin Grove, IL, Church of the Brethren, 507

Frantz, Aaron, 508

Frantz, Ira Henry, 508

fraternal relations, 510

Fraternity of German Baptists, 511

Fredericksburg, PA, Clover Creek Church of the Brethren, 512

Freemasonry, 514

Fresno, CA, First Church of the Brethren, 517

frontier, 519

Fulk, George, 521

functions of, 176

fundamentalism, 522

funerals, 524

furniture, 525

gambling, 528

Garber (Gerber), Daniel, 528

Garber (Gerber), John H., 529

Garber, Ora W., 529

Garver, Daniel M., 532

Geisert, Wayne F., 2187

genealogy, 534

German Baptist Brethren, *See* German Baptist Brethren Annual Meeting

Gibson, Isham, 548

Gilbert Julia A., 548

Girard, IL (1874), 1234

Gish, Barbara Kindig and James Rufus, 550

Goals and Budget Committee, 554

Goshen Conference, 559

Gospel Messenger Advisory Committee, 559

The Gospel Visitor, 561, 712

grape juice, 566

grassroots concerns, 2193

"Great Assembly," development from, 1298

H., John, 577

hairstyles, 579

Ham, John, 580

Hamilton, Hiel, 580

Harris Creek Church of the Brethren, OH, 585

Hayes, William (Bill) A., 2197

head coverings, 160

Heaven, 591

Helman, Alfred Blair, 2197

Hendricks, Franklin A., 597

Hendricks, James, 597

Hendricks, John, 597

Herring, Friedrich, 598

Hershey family, 600

Hertzler, Samuel Hoffer, 600

historic sites, 609

historical societies, 610

historical writing, 611

history of, 1917

Hoffman, Paul W., 2202

Hoke, George, 618

Holsinger, Henry Ritz, 621, 622

Holsinger, Levi Teeter, 623

houses, furnishings and decorations of, 59

Huffaker, Perry Lee, 635

Huffman, Nelson Thomas, 2205

humility, 636

Hummer, Catherine, 636

Huntingdon, PA, Stone Church of the Brethren, 637

Hutchison, Andrew, 639

hymnals, 641, 642

Iglesia Cristiana Pentecostal de Cuba, 2207

imposters among the Brethren, 648

incorporation, 649

Independence Day, 649

Indiana, 652

installation of pastors, 657

insurance, 192, 657

Interchurch World Movement (IWM), 658

International Fellowship of Grace Brethren Churches, 2209

inventions and scientific discoveries, 660

Iowa, 661

Irricana (First) Church of the Brethren, Alberta, Canada, 663

Israel, 664

jewelry, 671

Johnson City, TN, Knob Creek Church of the Brethren, 673

Juniata Church of the Brethren, NE, 678

Juniata College, 678

kneeling at prayer, 1052

Korean Mission, 2211

Lanark, IL, *721*

lawsuits and legal issues, 728–729

laying on of hands, 730

leadership for, choosing, 8

letters of membership, 738

list of, 1505–1511

location of, 33, 42, 1271

Logan Co., OH (1876), 1225

Lord's supper, food at, 757–758

lyceums, participation in, 768

"Magnetic Healing," 287

Mahoning Church of the Brethren, OH, dispute query, 782

Major, Sarah Righter, and women preaching, 783

mandatory decisions at, *See* mandatory decisions

manuals, 788

Markey family, held on farm of, 793

marriage, rulings on, 795

Martin, George Adam, on regular conferences, 797

Maryland Brethren activity, 798

material possession, questions of, 3

Maundy Thursday, 416

meeting time of year, 178

meetinghouses

furnishings of, 48, 59

propriety of, 48

mentoring, 2221

Mexican War noted, 820

Miami Valley Petition presented to, 823

military substitutes (1780, 1781, 1865), 1233–1234, 1248

ministry, 2224

ministry system, 844–845

minorities, ethnic and racial, 849

minutes, *See* minutes of Annual Meeting

minutes of, 2311

missionary conferences paralleling, 856

missions, 858, 2225

Missouri, 865

moderators, *See* moderators

Mohican Church of the Brethren, OH, 867

Mohler family, 869

Mooreites, 875

motion pictures, position on, 398

musical instruments, 900

name change discussion, 2228

Naperville, IL, Church of the Brethren, 913

National Cabinet of Children's Work establishment, 915

National Council of Churches of Christ in the USA and World Council of Churches, 2228–2229

National Council of Churches of Christ (NCCC) representative elections, 915

National Youth Cabinet, 917

Neff, Robert Wilbur, 2230

Nettle Creek meetinghouse, 432

North Manchester, IN, 949

nuclear arms race, 2232

oaths, on taking of, 2126

Office, 2311

Ohio, held in, 961, 962

Old Brethren Church, 970, 2232

Old German Baptist Brethren, *See* Old German Baptist Brethren Annual Meeting

Old Order Fellowships, 972

On Earth Peace Assembly, 2235

"Order of the Brethren," reference to, 976

organizational restructuring and, 2241–2242

origins of, 33

orphans, care for, 6

Ottawa, KS, Church of the Brethren, held at, 984

patent medicine advertisement elimination, 995

peace education, 1002

peace position, 998, 999, 1000

Pennsylvania Brethren settlement, 1004

pensions, military, 1008

Pentecost, 1008

Pfautz family, 1014

photography, 1019, 1020

police, Brethren as, 1041

polity, 1042–1043, 1044, *See also* polity

poor, caring for, 986, 1046

prayer, 1051, 1052

prayer meetings, 1053

prohibition, 1061–1062

property insurance, 192

publications for announcements and

reports, 1069
queries, 1076, *See also* queries
Quinter, James, 1077
race relations, social action in, 1172
radio, 1080
railroads, 1081
raised pulpits, 48
"Reconsidered Petition," 1086
Reconstruction Committee, 1086
recreation, 1087
relief and service efforts, 1096
remarriage, 389, 1099
repentance, doctrine of, 1100
reports, publishing of, 1068
restructuring plan, 2163
Rowdabaugh, J. W. on 1882 confer-
    ence, 2353
salaried preachers, 1053
Sawa, Bitrus Pilasar (CB) at, 2246
Sayler, Daniel P., defense of Anual
    Meeting by, 1151
schedule of, 33
schisms, 334
Schumacher, Daniel, held in home of,
    1157
science discussed at, 1160
secondary schools, debate over, 1165
secret societies, Brethren opposition to,
    1164
sexuality, 1170
"simple life" discussed at, 1183
singing discussed at, 1185
singing schools, 1185
slavery, 22, 838, 1190, 2128
Society of Friends, 24
soliciting, house-to-house, 18
Sollenberger, Dorcas Elaine Mock
    (CB) and, 2251
spiritualism, denouncing of, 1211
Springfield, IL (1906), 1215
Standing Committee, *See* Standing
    Committee
stewardship and, 2252–2253
study guide to 1979 conference, 1916
Sunday schools
    Advisory Committee, 1239
    approval of (1857, 1870), 1239
    movement regarding, 283
tax refusal (1775, 1781, 1815, 1973,
    1978), 1248–1249
theology and, 2254
Tipp City, OH, West Charleston
    Church of the Brethren, 1265
traditions, status of, 133–134
traveling to, 1080, 1081
urban ministry and, 2256–2257
West, Murray Guy (CB) and, 2262
women delegates, 1151
women preaching, 783
youth and, 2269
Zinzendorf, Count, effect of visits of,
    33
annual reaffirmations of faith, 5
Annual Visits, *See* deacons' visit
Annuals, *See* Yearbooks
Annville, PA, Church of the Brethren,
    38, **39**
Conewago Church of the Brethren,
    PA, 332
Hershey, PA, Spring Creek Church of
    the Brethren, 599
meetinghouse, 39
Mount Wilson Church of the Brethren,

PA, 887
anointing, **2130**
    Hymnal: A Worship Book, 2205
    Old German Baptist Brethren, 2233
    worship and, 2266
anointing the sick, **39–40**, 169, 2044
    bibliographical sources, 1881, 1885
    Declaration of Principles, 372
    degrees of ministry, 374
    Dunkard Brethren, 410
    early 20th century sermon on, 1168
    Fellowship of Grace Brethren
        Churches (FGBC), 486
    German Seventh-Day Baptists, 542
    God's Means of Grace (Yoder), 555
    healing, 39–40, 591, 980
    laying on of hands, 730–731
    Mack, Alexander, Sr., and New
        Baptists of Schwarzenau, 776
    "Message of the Brethren Ministry,"
        818
    ministry, 845
    oil and, 185
    Old German Baptist Brethren, 967
    ordinances, 976, 977, 979
    ordination, 980
    other religious groups, as used in, 68
    prayer, 1052
    Primitivism, 1058
    procedure for, 39
    public services, 39
    public worship ritual, 1375
    purposes of, 39, 40
    Radical Pietists, 293
    restitution, 1100
    Schwarzenau Brethren, 1079
    sriptural references for, 39
    thesis on, 1958
    tracts about, 1269
    Weiand, Albert Cassel, 1344
Anpaugh, Eric C., 2271
Anspach, Amanda Loose, 40
Anspach, Charles L., **40**
Anspach, Elizabeth Wheeler, 40
Anspach family, *See* Reinhardt (Reinhard,
    Rinehart, Rhinehart) family
Anspach, Mary Fisher, 40
Anspach, Philip N., 40
Anstine, Ida May, 343
Antelope Park Community Church of the
    Brethren, Lincoln, NE, 743
Antelope Valley (Black Bear) Church of the
    Brethren, OK, **40**, 448, 869
Antes, John Henry, **40**, 334, 423, 510, 2052
Anthony, Annie M. Friedly, 40
Anthony, David, 40
Anthony family, 588
Anthony, Frederick Dorsey, 40, 433, 628,
    1542
Anthony, Nancy Boward, 40
Anthony, Susie C. Shriner, 40
Anthony, William A., **40–41**, 270, 1542
anti-Communism, *See* Communism
Anti-Saloon League, 623, 1251
Anti-Secrecy Monthly, 1866
Antichrist, Roman Catholic pope seen as,
    1209
anticlericalism and Freemasonry, 514
Antietam, battle of, **41–42**, 912
    Bible removed from Dunker meeting
        house during, 738
    bibliographical sources, 1866, 1919,
        2060, 2083

field hospital, meetinghouse used as,
    810
historic sites related to Brethren, 609
"Little Dunker Church," *See* Mumma
    meetinghouse
Maryland Brethren, effect on, 798
McClellan, General George B., 475,
    912
meetinghouse as field hospital, 810
Monrovia, MD, Bush Creek Church
    of the Brethren meetinghouse
    used by officers, 870
photo of, 41
Sharpsburg, MD, Church of the
    Brethren meetinghouse center
    of, 1174
Antietam (Conococheague, Prices) congre-
    gations, MD/PA,
    bibliographical sources, 1910
    Blässer, Herman, 149
    Church of the Brethren, *See* Antietam
        (Conococheague, Prices) Church
        of the Brethren
    Fahrney, Jacob, 465, 809, *1019*
    German Seventh-Day Baptist congre-
        gation, *See* Snow Hill Community
    Independent Brethren, 649
    Long, David, 724, 753
    Martin, Nicholas, 797
    Maryland, Brethren activity in, 798
    migration of Brethren, 827
    Miller, Jacob, 838
    Old German Baptist Brethren Church,
        See Antietam Old German
        Baptist Brethren Church
    Oller, Jacob Franklin, 974
    Pfautz family, 1014
    Preiß (Price) family, 1055
    Snowberger family, 1153
    Stauffer, Abram, 1220
    Stover, Wilbur Brenner, 1225, 1227
    Stover, William, 1219, 1227
    Studebaker, Peter, 1230
    Stutzman, Jacob, 1233
    Ulrich, Stephen, 1285
Antietam (Conococheague, Prices) Church
    of the Brethren, MD/PA, **42**
    Back Creek Church of the Brethren,
        PA, 77
    Beaver Creek Church of the Brethren,
        MD, 104
    Fahrney-Keedy Chapel Fellowship
        Church of the Brethren, MD,
        467
    Falling Spring Church of the Brethren,
        PA, 471
    Longmeadow Church of the Brethren,
        MD, 756
    Ridge Church of the Brethren, PA,
        1108
    Rouzerville Church of the Brethren,
        PA, 1125
    Waynesboro, PA, Church of the Breth-
        ren, 1323
    Welty Church of the Brethren, MD,
        1330
Antietam Old German Baptist Brethren
    Church, MD/PA, **42**, 967
    Beaver Dam Old German Baptist
        Brethren Church, MD, 106
    Falling Spring Old German Baptist
        Brethren Church, PA, 471
    Hess, James Arthur, 2198

members living in Maryland, 798
Price, Jacob, 1057
Antietam, PA
Steiner family, 2378
Stover, William, 2379
antiintellectualism, 1258–1259
Antinomianism, **42**, 193, *See also* eternal
security; legalism
Brethren Church doctrine on, 183
communes, 236
Fellowship of Grace Brethren
Churches accused of teaching, 42
Frey, Andreas, 517
Antioch Church of the Brethren, CO, **42**
Antioch Church of the Brethren, IN, *See*
Andrews, IN, Church of the
Brethren
Antioch Church of the Brethren, KS,
42–43, 1304
Antioch Church of the Brethren, VA
(Bedford Co.), 43
Antioch Church of the Brethren, VA (Rocky
Mount, Franklin Co.), 43
Bethany Church of the Brethren, VA,
124
biographies of ministers, 1873–1973,
1938
Boones Chapel Church of the Brethren,
VA, 162
Botetourt Co., VA, Church of the
Brethren, 164
Faiview-Rocky Mount Church of the
Brethren, VA, 470
Ferrum, VA, First Church of the
Brethren, 488
Franklin Co. Church of the Brethren,
VA, 507
Germantown Brick Church of the
Brethren, VA, 43, 544
Henry Fork Church of the Brethren,
VA, 598
Oak Grove-South Church of the
Brethren, VA, 956
Pigg River Old German Baptist
Brethren Church, VA, 1023
Antioch congregation, Woodstock Church
of the Brethren, VA (Shenandoah
Co.), 1364
Antioch, WV, 1337
antitheological beliefs, 1258–1259
antiwar movement, *See* peace movement
Antoine, Carrie and Richard, 843
Anton, José, 53
Antonius, Brother, *See* Everson, William
Antrim Twp., Franklin Co., PA, 1219
Antunez, Miguel, 2237
Antunez, Sonia, 2237
Anutunez, Miguel, 2271
Anvil family, Mount Cassell Old German
Baptist Brethren Church, WV, 880
anxious bench, **930–931**
Anzulovich, Juan Antonio, 2237
Apache, Lipan, 2219
apartheid and World Council of Churches,
2228
Apikian, Stephen, 1542
apocalypticism, *See* eschatology/millennial-
ism
Apocrypha, **43**
Berleburg Bible, 120
translations, 138
use by Brethren, 133
apologetics, *See* debates

Apologia, or *Scriptural Vindication*
(*Apologie, Oder schriftmasige
Verantwortung,* 1788), Mack Jr.,
43, 370
bibliographical information, 2004
Christology of, 290
doctrine, 774
Kunze, Johann Christoph, response to,
710, 1991
Mehrning, Jacob, writings of, 811
"Apologia Pro Vita Sua" (Mallott), 2005
Apology for the True Christian Divinity
(Robert Barclay), 1199
apostolic church
Bowman on, 166
apostasy, *See* sin
bibliographical sources, 2048
Roman Catholic Church, 1120
apostles
dress of, 403
inner Word and outer Word, 656
Apostles' Creed, 184, *See* noncreedalism
The Apostolic Banner, **43**, 1866
Apostolic Baptist Church, 598
Apostolic Brethren, *See* Waldenses
Apostolic Christian Church, **43**, 122, 1864,
See also Bernese Anabaptists;
Mennonites
developed from Anabaptists, 1246
Froelich (Fröhlich), Samuel Heinrich,
518
Kurtz, Henry, preached to, 1246
musical instruments, 900
Rothenberger, George Philip, 1124
apostolic church, 28, 29, **43–44**, *See also*
restitutionism and restitutionist
community; Restoration movement
authority, as source of, 73
Doctrinal Treatise, 394
interest-taking, 658
noncreedalism, 942
Orthodox Church, 983
practices of, 698
Primitivism, 1058
restitution, 1100
Apostolic Constitutions, 698
apostolic principles and practices
Brethren movement, 293
Herring, Friedrich, 598
Holdeman, John, 618
Reformation, Protestant, 1091
Schwarzenau Brethren and Radical
Pietists, 1079
apostolic succession, **44**
Brethren, lineage of, 613
episcopal polity, 1042
apothecaries, 1136, 1148
Appalachia, 23, **44**
Brethren roots in, 44
Church of the Brethren, 304
Gilbert, Martha Rupel, 2189
Krypton, KY, Brethren Church, 2212
minorities, ethnic and racial, 850
missions, short-term, 2226
Appalachian Ministries, **2130–2131**
Appanoose Co., IA, 661, 1212
Brethren Church, 1285
Fairview Church of the Brethren, IA,
468
Fairview, IA, congregation, 1157
migration of Brethren, 830
Pleasant Valley German Baptist
Brethren, IA, 1036

Appanoose, KS, Church of the Brethren
(Eight Mile), **44**, 1321
Appanoose, KS Old German Baptist
Brethren Church (Eight Mile), 431
apparel, *See* dress
Appell, Louis, 2250
Appell, Louis, Jr., 2250
Appendix to the Refuted Anabaptist
(*Anhang zum Widerlegten Wieder-
täufer;* 1788), 31, 43, 774
Appleby, Mildred, 687
Appleby, Terry, 687
Applegate family, 1302
Appleman, Adam, 1542
Appleman family, 141
Appleman, Jacob F., **44**
Big Creek Church of the Brethren,
OK, 141
Cherokee Church of the Brethren, KS,
273
Guthrie, OK, Church of the Brethren,
576
migration of Brethren, 830
ministers and elders, list of, 1542
Paradise Prairie Church of the Breth-
ren, OK, 964, 992
Appleman, John F., 1038, 1542
Appleman, John F., 1542
appointment of church services, **44–45**, 965
aprons, Church of the Brethren, 300
Arab states, relief and rehabilitation work
by youth from, 200
Arakaki family, 1312
Arble, L. W., 124
Arbogast, James M., 1542
Arbor Hill Church of the Brethren, VA, **45**,
1220
Arbutus Church of the Brethren, Johns-
town, PA, **673**, 675, 752
Arcadia, FL, Church of the Brethren, **45**
Arcadia, IN, Church of the Brethren
(Cicero), **45**, 109
Arcadia, NE, Church of the Brethren
(Muddy Valley), 45–46, 46
Arcadia Hotel, Staunton, VA, 1219, 1220
Arcanum, OH, Old Order German Baptist
Church, 972
archaeology, **46**
Brethren interest in, 46
debates and support from, 371
definition of, 46
Ephrata Community, 451
Flora, Delbert Benjamin, 495
Great Serpent Mound, OH, 1332
Kent, Homer Austin, 688
Robert Huston Smith collection of
archaeological artifacts, 46
Archbold, Phill Carlos, 2199, 2271
Archer, KY, 406
Archer family, 1062
Archer, J. Douglas, 1542
architecture, 2131, *See also* church archi-
tecture
barns, 89
Brethren Architectural Services, 188,
575
Brethren Building Ministries, 51, **180**,
188, 575
Fry, Linda L. on CB, 2332
Kurtz, Henry, and renewal, 2326
plain people, 1029
White, Janet R. on Ephrata Cloister's
culture and, 2363

archives, **52**
    BHLA, *See* Brethren Historical Library and Archives (BHLA)
    Cassel Library, *See* Cassel Library
    historical libraries and historical societies, 230, **610**
Archubta, Felix, 1248
Arden, Maud (later Eddy), 424
Ardenheim Church of the Brethren, PA, **52**
Ardinger, Elsie Baker, 1866
Ardmore, IN, Brethren Church, *See* South Bend, IN, Ardmore Brethren Church
"Are We Ready to Enter the Foreign Field?" (Cassel), 500
Arenobine, Robert D., 2271
Areopagitica (Milton), 1098
Arey/Earrey, Mary (later Moyer), 822
Argabright, John Henry, 468, 1024, 1542
Argabright, Joseph Oscar, 468, 1542
Argabright, W. A., 1280
Argabright, William Robert, 141, 468, 582, 1542–1543
Argentina, **52–54**
    Bell, Bertha May, 1386
    Bible Coach ministry, 53
    bibliographical sources, 1867
    Boardman, Edwin E., Jr., 155
    Brethren Bible Institute, 180
    Brethren Church in, **53–54**, 183, 250, 324, 861–862
    Byler, Jane King, 2153
    Byler, Robert Oliver, 2153
    CAVEA (Centro Audio-Visual Evangélico Argentina), 54
    Consejo Nacional de La Iglesia de Los Hermanos de la Argentina, 53
    Di Nardo, Juan, 382
    Dowdy, Dortha Mae Frank and James Paul, 398
    Eden Bible Institute, 424
    effect of 1939 division on, 53
    evangelism, 182
    Fellowship of Grace Brethren Churches, 250
    field council, 398
    Foreign Missionary Society, 501
    Grace Brethren in, 53, 250, 501
    Grace Brethren International Missions, 2191
    Hispanic Ministries (BC), 2198
    Hispanic Radio Ministry (BC), 2199
    Hollins, VA, Patterson Memorial Grace Brethren Church, 620
    Maconaghy, Dorothy Helen Lewis and Hill, 779
    mass media use by Brethren, 801
    mission schools, 854
    The Missionary Board (BC), 855, 856
    missions, 2224, 2225
    missions, short-term, 2226
    Nielsen, Johanna, 362, 936
    Reina, Domingo, 1094
    Roman Catholic Church and Brethren in, 1120
    Sarasota, FL, Iglesia de los Hermanos (BC) and, 2246
    Siccardi, Luis, pastor, 1181
    Sickel, Clarence Leroy and Loree Cutright, 1181
    Solomon, Kenneth LeRoy and Jeannette Ruth DeLozier Solomon

    (BC) in, 2251
    Testigo Fiel (*Faithful Witness*) magazine, 53–54, 1255
    Wagner, Ricardo, 1312
    Webb, Maude Cripe, 1325
    Yoder, Charles Francis and Pearl Lutz, 1386
Argentine Brethren Church (*Iglesia de los Hermanos en La Argentina*), 54, 2141, 2224
Argos, IN, 1315
arid land, farmers immigrating to, 1145
Arius, 289
Arizona, **54**
    Church of the Brethren, 1932
    Gillett, Charles Edwin, 549
    migration of Brethren to, 830
    minorities, ethnic and racial, 850
Arizona Brethren Camp, 2131
Arizona Improvement Agency and B. A. Hadsell, 577
Arizona State University and Nininger meteorites, 781
Arkadelphia congregation, AR (CB), 54
Arkansas, **54**
    African American mission, 2128
    Brethren movement in, 217
    Church of the Brethren, 2068
    congregations in Missouri district, 864
    debates on doctrines, 370
    Forney, Daniel L., 502
    Old German Baptist Brethren, 2235
Arkansas City, KS, Church of the Brethren (Silver Creek), 54
Arkton, VA, Brethren Church, **54**
Arlington congregation, Silver Springs, MD, Good Shepherd Church of the Brethren, 182, 1320
Arlington, OH, Church of the Brethren, 413, 1138, 1355
Arlington, VA, Church of the Brethren, **54–55**, 1320
Armacost, David Livingstone, 1543
Armagh, PA, Valley Grace Brethren Church, **55**, 674
armed forces, *See* entries at military
Armenia and Armenian relief work, **55**
    American Armenian International College, 715
    Culler, Arthur Jerome, 355
    General Mission Board (CB), 539
    Miller, John Ezra, surveying relief needs, 840
    Near East Foundation, 920
    orphans, care for, 982
    refugees, social welfare for, 1198
    Relief and Reconstruction Committee, 1096
    relief and rehabilitation work, 303, 920, 1096, 1198
    world hunger issues (CB) and, 2266
Arment, Alan, 749, 1543
Arment, James D., 1543
Armentrout, George W., 1543
Armentrout, Jacob, 887
Armentrout, Susan (later McNett), 1923
Armey, Douglas Richard, 1543
Armey family, 1137
Arminianism, **55–56**
    Brethren in America, Arminian theology of, 923
    Calvinism and, 240
    Collegiants, 324

    free will, 514
    scriptural references for, 55, 56
Arminius, James/Jacob (Jacob Hermandszoon), 55, 56
Armocast, David, 704
Armorials and surname origins, 2078
Armourdale Mission Church of the Brethren, KS, *See* Kansas City, KS, Calvary Church of the Brethren
arms, bearing of, *See* entries at military
Armsberger, Jacob, 944, 1543
Armstrong Co., PA
    Bowser family, 170
    Brethren Church congregations, 1005
    Brethren in Christ (Shoemakerites), 189–190
    Brush Valley Brethren Church, 224
    Center Hill Church of the Brethren, 268, 350
    Cowanshannock Brethren Church and Cowanshannock Church of the Brethren, 350
    Glade Run Brethren Church, 551
    North Buffalo Grace Brethren Church, 945
    Oakdale Church of the Brethren, 957
    Plum Creek Normal School, 1038
Armstrong family, 233, 1902, 1958
Armstrong, Helen, 739
Armstrong, Herbert W., 210
Armstrong, Jacob, 1143
Armstrong, Jacob D., 264
Armstrong, Jean Bowman, 2311
Armstrong, John, 739
Armstrong, John H., 264
Armstrong, Nancy, 1143
Armstrong, Sherry, 739
Armstrong, Tom, 739
Armstrong, William C., 1866
Armudgee (Ocmulgee) congregation, GA, 540
army, *See* entries at military
Armytage, Walter Henry Green, 1866
Arndt, Bernhard, 1866
Arndt, Christian R., Jr., 1543, 2299
Arndt family, 1866
Arndt, Johann, **56**
    Morgen und Abend-Gebethe, advertisement for, 1917
    prayer and prayer books, 1051, 1052
    sermons of, Pia Desideria as introduction, 1209
    theology of love, 761
    Wahres Christentun (*True Christianity*), 381
Arndt, John Stover, 1866
Arndt, Karl J. R., 140, 1857, 1866, 2309
Arnet, Charles Albert, 990, 1543
Arnett, Betty, 1838
Arnett, Ronald C., 1866, 2311
Arney, Andrew, 2373
Arney family, 2373
Arnold, A. C., 1543
Arnold, Abbie (later Garber), 529
Arnold, Abigail Miller, 58
Arnold, Agnes Stoner, 2378
Arnold, Albert S., 1012, 1543
Arnold, Amy (later Zigler), **1397**, 1398, 1398–1399
Arnold, Arthur W., 1543
Arnold, Benjamin, 56, 1543
Arnold, Benjamin F., 1866

Arnold, Catherine, 1265
Arnold, Catherine Stoner, 2378
Arnold, Charles A., 508
Arnold, Charles Edward, **56**, 58, 164, 781, 1543
Arnold, Charles M., 931, 1543
Arnold, Christian, 1543
Arnold, D. E., 1543
Arnold, Daniel (of Redstone, MD, and Beaver Run, WV; fl.1787), 58, 1543
   Beaver Run Church of the Brethren, WV, 106
   Nead, Peter, baptism of, 58, 918
   Pleasant View Church of the Brethren, MD, minister, 1037
Arnold, Daniel (m. Elizabeth Thomas, Elizabeth Wise; fl.1785–1824), 58
Arnold, Daniel (1792–1864), 58
Arnold, Daniel (son-in-law of Henry Herschberger; fl. 1830), 599, 1265
Arnold, Daniel (m. Elizabeth Price; fl. 1840), 58, 59
Arnold, Daniel (Dayton, OH homestead; fl. mid-1800s), 609, 1265
Arnold, Daniel B. (of Beaver Run, WV; fl. 1828), 1543
Arnold, Daniel B. (1842–1914), 56, 58, 1543
Arnold, Daniel T., 1543
Arnold, Eberhard, 56, 639–640
Arnold, Elizabeth, 1833
Arnold, Elizabeth E. Bartholow, 1833
Arnold, Elizabeth Thomas, 58
Arnold, Elizabeth Wise, 58
Arnold, Ella Beahm, 56
Arnold, Emmy von Hollander, 56, 639
Arnold, Etta M., 1866
Arnold family, 58, 353, 1253, 1336, 1365, 1866, 1920, 2029, 2314
   Fairview Church of the Brethren, MD, 468
   family history, 1980
   Fike family, 490
   geneaology, Arnold-Flickinger family, 1934
   Preiß (Price) family, related to, 1055
   Salem Church of the Brethren, OH, 1138
Arnold-Flickinger family, 1934
Arnold, Frank W., 1543
Arnold, George, 632
Arnold, George S., 1397, 1543
Arnold, Gottfried, **57**
   apostolic church, 43
   Beissel, influence on, 113
   bibliographical sources, 1866, 2075, 2086
   Brethren movement, influence on, 73, 288, 293, 296
   celibacy, 266
   church, doctrine of, 293
   church fathers, writings on, 296
   Church of the Brethren, influence on, 2013
   devotional literature, 381
   Die Erste Liebe (The First Love, 1696), 43, 453
   Dippel, Johann Konrad, 385
   ethics, 457
   Hochmann von Hochenau, Ernst Christoph, 614
   hymns by, 700

Miller, Donald E. on, 2347
Miller, John William, 2224
mysticism, 907
noncreedalism, 942
Parsons, Johanna Christina Zeidig, raising of, 994
restitution, 1100
Schwarzenau Brethren, 1079
sexuality, human, 1170
Troeltsch, Ernst, influence on, 1275
Unparteiische Kirchen- und Ketzer-Historie (A Nonpartisan History of Church and Heresy, 1699–1700), 57, 1275, 1294, 1866, 2086
Arnold, Hannah Catherine Simpson, 1397
Arnold, Harvey E., 1543
Arnold, Henry Harley, 583, 1543
Arnold, Ira, 1543
Arnold, Irena (Amick), 58
Arnold, Jacob, 58
Arnold, Janis Kerr, 1866
Arnold, John (d. 1790), 58
Arnold, John (d. 1798), 58
Arnold, John (1813–1863), 1047, 1543
Arnold, John (1846–1929, of Illinois), 58, 1543
Arnold, John (Annual Meeting 1882 held at farm of), 124
Arnold, John (father of Nora Arnold Lichty, 1880–1918), 741
Arnold, John A., 1543
Arnold, Joseph, 57, 791, 1543, 1866
Arnold, Levi J., 1543, 2299
Arnold, Libbie, 1866
Arnold, Lois (later Puterbaugh), 58, 1072
Arnold, Magdalena (later Fike), 489
Arnold, Margaret, 56
Arnold, Martha A. Kelly, 57
Arnold, Mary B. Ludwig, 56
Arnold, Mary Hendricks, 741
Arnold, Mary Ludwig, 58
Arnold, Nora Susannah (later Lichty), **741,** 1840
Arnold, Perry A., 106, 1543
Arnold, Peter, **57,** 1543
Arnold, Ralph, 58
Arnold, Robert E., 58, 195, 1866
Arnold, Samuel (ca. 1760–1831), **58,** 1543
   Beaver Run Church of the Brethren, WV, 106
   Chestnut Grove Old German Baptist Church, WV, 274
   Eglon, WV, Church of the Brethren, 430
   Far Western Brethren, 475
Arnold, Samuel Ira, 667, 717, 1543, 1833, 1866, 2020
Arnold, Silas, 791, 1543
Arnold, Silas J., 1543
Arnold, Sol G., 1543
Arnold, Solomon, 167
Arnold, Susannah, 167
Arnold, Whitmore (Whitmer), 1543
Arnold, Yearl, 244
Arnold, Zachariah, 58, 106
Arnold, Zelmah, 945
Arnold's Grove, IL, Church of the Brethren, **58–59**
   Cherry Grove Church of the Brethren, IL, 273
   Emmert family, 444
   first congregation in, 647

Hickory Grove Church of the Brethren, IL, 602
Indiana, 652
Long, Christian, 753
migration of Brethren, 829
Milledgeville Church of the Brethren, IL, 833
Mount Carroll, IL, Church of the Brethren, 880
Rock Creek Church of the Brethren, IL, 1116
Strickler, Henry W., 647, 1228–1229
Yellow Creek Church of the Brethren, IL, 1384
Arnoldshainer Protokolle, 2311
Arnsbarger (Armsberger), Jacob, 1543
Arnsbarger, Jacob, 1543
Arnsberg cloister, Community of True Inspiration, 330
Aronson, Karl E., 2311
Arregin, Juan L., 2271
Arrington, A. Harold, 558, 578, 1079, 1309, 1543
Arritt Brethren Church (Jordan Mines, VA, Rich Patch Brethren Church), **676**
Arritt, F. M., 1543
Arrow Rock, MO, 320
Arrowood, Samuel, 1012, 1543
Arrowood, Theodore R., 1543
Arrowwood, Alberta, Canada, Bow Valley Church of the Brethren, 15, **59,** 817, 1034, 1172, 1893
Arroyo Hondo Brethren Church, 1248
art, **59–62,** *See also* architecture; church architecture; folk art; Fraktur; Pyle, Howard; quilting
   AACB (Association for the Arts in the Church of the Brethren), 61–62, 69, 1867
   Blosser, Merrill, 149
   Brandywine School, 61
   Brethren negativism toward, 59–60
   Brethren openness to, 61
   Brumbaugh, Wilbur Eugene, 223, 1574, 1895
   Church of the Brethren Annual Conference, use at, 61
   drama, *See* drama
   Dunkard Brethren and Old German Baptist Brethren attitudes toward, 62
   education, 60, 61
   iconoclastic period, 59
   Illuminative writing, 2010
   illustration, 59, 61
   modern, controversies over, 61
   Mural Paintings, Camp Mack, 61
   NAC (National Achievement Competition), 203, 533, 934
   Neher, Medford D. illustrations, 922
   Old German Baptist Brethren, 971
   painting, 2032
   photography, 1020
   spirituality in, 2315
   Sunday bulletins, 61
   Swank, Scott T. on PA Germans and, 2360
   the Waldport group, OR, 61, 317
"Art for Hunger" exhibit, AACB, 61, 2197
Artemas, PA, Church of the Brethren, 21, **62,** 494, 1192
Artesia, CA, Carson Avenue Grace Brethren Church (Lakewood, CA, Grace Brethren Church), **720**

Arthur family, 332
Arthur, Lynn, 1850
Arthur, Randall J., 2271
articles of faith, *See* noncreedalism
Artz family, Mabton, WA, Grace Brethren
  Church, 771
Artz, Samuel, 1543
Arvada, CO, Hackberry Hill Grace Brethren
  Church, **62**, 377, 2127
Arviso family, 2216
Asbury, VA meetinghouse and mission
  point, 164
Ascension Day, observance of, 2148
asceticism, *See* celibacy; monasticism
  Ephrata Community, 452
  nonconformity, 940
  Society of the Woman in the Wilder-
    ness, 686
Aschenbrenner, George, 162, 1543
Ash, Anna, 2013, 2016, 2059
Ash, Rodney, 2311
Ash family, Martinsburg, WV, Rosemont
  Grace Brethren Church, 798
Ash Grove, OH
  Church of the Brethren, **62**, 950
  Old German Baptist Brethren Church,
    62–63
    (Big) Oak Grove Old German
      Baptist Brethren Church, OH,
      142
    Custer, O. Adolphus, 357
    Genesee Old German Baptist
      Brethren Church, MI, 540
    Owl Creek Old German Baptist
      Brethren Church, OH, 986
    Sugar Creek Church of the
      Brethren, OH, 1235
    White Oak Grove Old German
      Baptist Brethren Church, OH,
      1341
Ash Ridge Church of the Brethren, WI, **63**,
  829, 1354
Ash Wednesday, observamce of, 737, 2147
Ashby, Bernice M., 1866
Ashe Co., NC
  Brethren settlement, 946
  Flat Rock Church of the Brethren, 493
  Golden Church of the Brethren, NC,
    555
  Lewis, James G., and Walnut Grove
    Church of the Brethren, VA, 1315
  Long Hope Church of the Brethren,
    755
  Peak Creek Church of the Brethren,
    1003
  Pleasant Valley Church of the Brethren,
    1035
  Weber (Weaver) family, 1325
  White Rock Church of the Brethren,
    1341
Asher Glade Church of the Brethren, PA,
  See Markleysburg, PA, Church of
  the Brethren
Ashland Academy
  academies, 2
  Christian day school movement, 282
  secondary school, 1163
Ashland Brethren, *See* Brethren Church
Ashland College, **65–67, 2131–2132**
  Aeby, John Milton, 2127
  Ashland Academy opened by, *See*
    Ashland Academy
  Ashland Convention (1882) and, 67,

368
Ashland, OH (city), located in, 63
bankruptcy, saved from, 166
Bickel, Florence Marguerite, 141
Black, James R., 2138
Boardman, Edwin E., Jr., 155
Bollinger, Russell V., 158
Bowman, Isaac Daniel, 166
Boyer, James L., 2139
Brethren Church and, 182, 961, 963
Brethren Church General Conference,
  site of, 37, 63
Brethren Publishing Company, 195
Burnworth, Benjamin Taylor, 232
Cambodia, demonstrations protesting
  invasion of, 1305
The Card with a Red Border (Hum-
  berd), 748
Carpenter, A. Glenn, 256
Carpenter, George C., 256
Cassel, Jacob C., 259
Cassel Library, 260
charter statement of 1888, 67
Christian Day School movement, 282
Christner, David C., 289
Clayton, Glenn Lowell, 319
Collitt, Robert B., 2166
DeLauter, Ora Dale, 374
Detwiler, Vianna, 381
division of 1881–83, effect of, 66
division of 1939, effect of, 66
Dodds, Gilbert, 394
Dowdy, Dortha Mae Frank and James
  Paul, 398
drama at, 399
Drushal, Ada Louella Garber and
  George Emery, 405
Drushal, John Garber, 406
Duker, William Irvin, 407
England, William Ferdinand, 446
evolution, 463
Ewing, John Cook, 463
Fellowship of Grace Brethren
  Churches (FGBC), 484, 485
Flora, Benjamin H., 495
Flora, Delbert Benjamin, 495
Furry, William Davies, 526
Garber, Aaron Leedy, 528
Garber, Levi Leedy, 529
Garst, Samuel Sherfy, 531
Gehman, Frank, 417
genealogy, 535
Gillin, John Lewis, 549
Gingrich, Joseph L., 550
Gingrich, Raymond Eugene, 2190
God's Means of Grace (Yoder), 555
Grace Brethren and, 484, 485
Grace Schools (Grace Theological
  Seminary, Grace College), 563
Gretna, OH, Brethren Church, 573
Grieve, Jerry Allen, 2194
Hamel, Joseph Donat, 2195, 2196
Hammers, Thomas E., 581
Harper, Clara Belle, 585
higher education, 605
history, 1978, 2012
Holsinger, Henry Ritz, 622
Hoyt, Herman Arthur, 634
Humberd, Russell I., 636, 1976
Interchurch World Movement (IWM),
  658
investigation of, 1151
Jacobs, Edwin Elmore, 667–668

Kem, George Frederick, 687
Kem, Myron S., 687
Kent, Homer Austin, 688
Kilhefner, Isaac, 693
Kimmel, Joseph L., 693
King, Lester Vernon, 694
Klingensmith, J. Ray, 703
Kolb, William, Jr., 706
Kriegbaum, Arnold R., 708
Leatherman, N. Victor, 733
Lindower, Leslie E., 744
Locke, John Funk, 751
Lynn, Archibald L., 768
Lyon, Quinter Marcellus, 768
Mackey, John Crawford, 779
Maple Grove Church of the Brethren,
  OH, 790
Marlin, High Crist, 794
Mason, Edward Glenn, 800
Mayes, Charles W., 804
McClain, Alva J., Board of Trustees,
  772
medical technologist degree, 952
Memorial Chapel, funded by
  Woman's Missionary Society, 1360
"Message of the Brethren Ministry,"
  817
Miller, Clara Worst, 834
Miller, Edward Lewis, 837
Miller, John Allen, 182. 839
Miller, Robert Henry, 842
ministry training, 67–68, 428
missions, 861
Moherman, Tully S., 867
Mount Morris College, 883
Munson, Charles Robert, 2227
Nielson, Johanna, 936
noncreedalism and statement of faith,
  943
nursing degree, 952
Oberholtzer, Harvey, 787
Old Founders Hall (ca. 1881), 65
O'Neal, Glenn, 2236
Perry, William, 1009
persons attending, 32, 40
pharmacology degree, 952
photos, *66, 603*
Porte, Robert Fowler, 1047
Progressive Brethren, 1044–1045, 1192
Puterbaugh, Milton P., 1072
Rench, George W., 1099
Riddle, Earl M., 1108
Ronk, Albert Teller, 660, 1121
Ronk, George Teller, 1121
Ronk, Willis E., 1121
Rowsey, Herbert H., 1127
Sandy, Conrad Keller, 1143
schism, 2006
scholarships from National Laymen's
  Organization, 917
secondary school on campus, 1163
Sharp, Solomon Zook, president of,
  1174
Sheldon, Hattie Louise Cope, mission-
  ary, 1175
Shively, Martin, bursar, 1178
Shultz, Joseph R., 183, 2249
Sisters' Society of Christian Endeavor
  (BC), 1188
Sterling, Mary Malinda, 1221
Stuckey, Melvin Atwood, 1229
Studebaker, Claud, 1229
Swartz, Goldie Elizabeth, 1243

Taber, Ada Zellner, 1247
Taber, Floyd W., 1247
Taber, Miles, 1247
Teeter, Roy R., 1250
theological education at, 1257
Tombaugh, James M., 1267
Weimer, Glen Emerson, 1327
Wilson, Emmert R., 1347
Worst, John H., 1379
Yoder, Charles Francis, 1385
Yoder, Eli Lorenzo, 1386
Young, Emanuel Sprankle, 1389
Ashland Convention (1882), **67**
    Ashland College and, 67, 368
    Ashland, OH (city), 63
    Beer, Joseph Wampler, 110
    Brethren Church, organization of, 37, 961
    church extension, 295
    Congregational Brethren attending, 335
    Committee of Reconstruction, 67, 110
    Declaration of Principles, 372
    Fraternal Relations Committees (BC), 511
    Hendricks, Franklin A., 597
    Leedy Brethren, 734
    Reconstruction Committee, 1086
    Swihart, Jonathan H., 335
Ashland Dickey Church of the Brethren, OH, 63, 64, **67**, 760
Ashland Co., IL, 1234
Ashland Co., OH
    bibliography, 1870
    Dickey family, 383
    history of Brethren in, 2356
    Kerner, William Hoff, Sr., 2211
    Kilhefner, Isaac, 693
    Loudonville Church of the Brethren, 760
    Maple Grove Church of the Brethren, OH, 790
    Studebaker family, 1231
Ashland, OH (city), **63**
    Agape Acres, 7
    Ashland College students, 1902 photo of, *603*
    Foreign Missionary Society (BC, FGBC), 501
    Garber, Aaron Leedy, 528
    Glenford, OH, Brethren Church, 553
    Gnagey, Abraham Daniel, 554
    gospel music, 559
    Gospel Preacher, The, 559
    Harrison, Stephen J., 586
    historic sites, 609
    historical writing, 613
    Holsinger, Henry Ritz, 622
    Investigator, The, 660
    Kilhefner, Isaac, 693
    The Missionary Board (BC), 855
    Parker, Isaac Dillon, as pastor in, 993
    Studebaker blacksmith shop, 1230
    Taber, Miles, ministry of, 1247
    Yoder, Charles Francis, 1385
    The Young Disciple published out of, 1389
Ashland, OH, First Brethren Church (Park Street), **63–64**
    Anspach, Charles Leroy, 40
    Copp, Zed H., 343
    Gillin, John Lewis, 549
    King, Lester Vernon, 694

Medina, OH, Brethren Church, 2219
Miller, John Allen, pastor, 839
Ohio, Brethren Church in, 961, 963
Perry, William, 1009
Ronk, Willis E., pastor, 1121
University Church and, 2132
Ashland, OH, First Church of the Brethren, 63, **64**, 67, 2214
Ashland, OH, Garber Memorial Brethren Church, **64**
Ashland, OH, Grace Brethren Church (West Tenth St.), **64–65**, 804, 963, 1995, 2236
Ashland, OH, South View Grace Brethren Church, 64, 65
Ashland, OH, University Church, **2132**
Ashland, OR, Brethren Church, **65**
Ashland, OR, Church of the Brethren, **65**, 633, 806, 1346
Ashland Theological Seminary, **67–68**, 605, 1257, **2131**, *2131.,* 2132
    archaeology, interest in, 46
    bibliographical sources, 1866–1867
    Black, James R., 2138
    Boardman, Edwin E., Jr., 155
    Boyer, James L., 2139
    Brethren Church and, 182, 963
    Christian education movement, 284
    Director of Pastoral Ministries, 2171
    Dowdy, James Paul, 398
    Flora, Delbert Benjamin, 495
    Gingrich, Raymond Eugene, 2190
    Grace Schools (Grace Theological Seminary, Grace College), 563
    Gretna, OH, Brethren Church, 573
    Grieve, Jerry Allen, 2194
    group dynamics, 575
    Grubb, Luther L., 575
    Hamel, Joseph Donat, 2195
    Hammers, Thomas E., 581
    historical collections at, 52
    historical libraries, 610
    Hoyt, Herman Arthur, 634
    India, 651
    information technology, church use of, 2208
    Ingraham, M. Virgil, 2208
    Kerner, William Hoff, Sr., 2211
    Kliever, Freda Neufeld, 701
    Kliever, Jacob Paul, 701
    Klingensmith, J. Ray, 703
    language, inclusive, 2214
    library photo, 622
    Lindower, Leslie E., 744
    Locke, John Funk, 751
    Maconaghy, Hill, 779
    marriage counseling, 796
    McClain, Alva J., 183, 772
    Medina, OH, Living Hope Brethren Church, 2219
    Methodist Theological School, OH, consortium with, 1291
    Miller, John Allen, dean, 839
    ministers, education issues, 428
    missions, 862, 2224
    Mount Zion Brethren Church, OH, providing student pastors for, 888
    Munson, Charles Robert, 2227
    National Laymen's Organization, funds from, 917
    National Ordination Council, 2229
    Robert Houston Smith Archaeological

    Collection, article about, 1938
    role in Brethren Church, 2141
    Ronk, Albert Teller, teacher, 1121
    Ronk, Willis E., dean, 1121
    Schneider, Bernard N., 1154
    Shultz, Joseph R., 183
    Shultz, Joseph R. (BC) and, 2249
    Solomon, George Walton (BC) and, 2251
    South America Theological Seminary (BC) and, 2251–2252
    Stuckey, Melvin Atwood, 1229
    Williams, C. Ronald, II, 2165
    women and, 2264
Ashland University, **2131–2132**, *See also* Ashland College
Ashman, Charles, 2271
Ashman, Charles Henry, Jr., 1111, 1543, 2132
Ashman, Charles Henry, Sr., **68**, 1543–1544
    The Brethren Minister's Handbook, 788
    Covina Church of the Brethren, CA, 348
    Fair Haven Brethren Church, OH, 467
    Grace Village Retirement Complex, 564
    Hammers, Thomas E., son-in-law, 581
    Johnstown, PA, First Brethren Church, 673
    New Lebanon, OH, First Brethren Church, 930
    Phoenix, AZ, Grace Brethren Church, pastor, 1019
    prophecy conferences, 1062
    South Pasadena, CA, Grace Brethren Church, pastor, 1206
    Sunnyside, WA, Grace Brethren Church, 1240
    Whittier, CA, Grace Brethren Church, 1343
    Winona Lake, IN, Grace Brethren Church, 1353
Ashman family, 348
Ashman, Flora B. Canfield, 68, 581
Ashman, Frances, 2132
Ashman, Judy K. (later Fairman), 1169
Ashman, Karl, 1303
Ashman, Kenneth B., **68**, 382, 674, 1365, 1544, 2299
Ashman, Mary Louise (later Hammers), 581
Ashman, Patti, 1303
Ashman, Robert A., 587, 674, 1010, 1544, 2193, 2299
Ashtabula Co. Church of the Brethren, OH, 68
Asia, *See* specific countries
    ALM involvement in, 24
    Church of the Brethren, 303
    Heifer Project International, 594
    Mennonites, 815
    mission schools, 853
    missions, short-term, 2226
    travelogues, 2101
    World Council of Churches, 1368
Asia Minor, 860, 2012, *See also* Turkey
Askins, Ralph W., 348, 1544
Asper, Mr. and Mrs. Joseph, 1048
Aspinall, H. Raymond (Ray), 1544, 2251, **2380**
Aspinall, Harrison Raymond, Jr., 1544, 1854, 1867

Aspinall, Marilyn Jean Murray, 1854, 2026
Asplund, John, 1867
Asquith, Charles, 1544
Assemblies of God and Pentecostalism, 1009
Assemblies of Yahweh, **68,** *See also* entries at Sacred Name
    chart of Brethren bodies, place on, 1403–1405
    pork, eating of, 1047
    similarities to Brethren, 68
Assembly of Christ, *See* Christ's Assembly
Assiniboia District, Canada, *See* Saskatchewan, Canada
associate elders, 848
Associated Brethren of the Skippack, **68–69,** 1189
    Antes, John Henry, 40, 334, 423, 510, 2052
    Frey, Andreas, 517
    Frey, Wilhelm, 517
    Gruber, Johann Adam, 575
    Moravian Church, 875
    Pennsylvania Synods, 1007
Associated Chicago Theological Schools, 1116
Associated Churches of Fort Wayne and Allen Co., 503
Associated Gospel Churches, 190
Associated Mennonite Biblical Seminaries and Fellowship of Hope, 488
Association for the Arts in the Church of the Brethren (AACB), 61–62, **69,** 1377, 1867
Association of American Colleges, 441, 480
Association of Brethren Caregivers (ABC), **2132,** 2242
    AIDS, **2129–2130**
    Bethany Hospital Governing Council, 2136
    Brethren Chaplains Network, 2158
    Cable, William H., 2155
    deacons in, 2169
    National Older Adult Conferences, 2229
    training of deacons, 2161, 2163
    violence and, 2265
    wellness and, 2261
    works by, 2311
Association of Brethren Church Teachers, **69**
Association of Christian Schools International, 804, 2217
Association of Council Secretaries, 1218
Association of Fundamental Gospel Churches, **69**
    chart of Brethren bodies, place on, 1403–1405
    Free Brethren, 513
Association of Professional Chaplains, 2158
Association of Theological Schools, 1397
associators and non-associators, American Revolution, 939
ASSU, *See* American Sunday School Union
assurance, *See* eternal security
Asthabula Co., OH, 719
Astoria, IL
    Black Rock Church of the Brethren, PA, 145
    Bucher family, 226
    Church of the Brethren, **69,** 151
    Dunkard Brethren Church, 2240
    Mound Brethren Church, **69**

South Fulton Dunkard Brethren congregation, IL, 69, 911, 1205, 1364
    Woodland Church of the Brethren, IL, 1364
astrology and Pennsylvania Germans, 2102
Astronomical Diary and Almanack (1780ff), 18
astronomy
    moon, creation, form and significance of, 2097
    Pennsylvania Germans, 2102
    Whitcomb, John C., Jr. on Bible and, 2363
ASV *See* American Standard Version of the Bible
Atcheson (Atchison), Robert, 1544
Atchison, Topeka, and Santa Fe, *See* Santa Fe Railroad (Atchison, Topeka, and Santa Fe)
Athanasian Creed, Brethren Church, 184
Athanasius, 290
atheism and religious liberty, 1098
Atherton schoolhouse, Zion Church of the Brethren, MI, 1400
Atherton, Willard I., 1544, 2299
athletics, **69–70,** 70, 557, 1087, 2045, 2232, *See also* amusements, wordly; recreation
Atkins, David, 787
Atkins, David C., 2271
Atkins, Joseph M., 1544
Atkinson, Bertha Perrin, 1847
Atkinson, E. G., 1544
Atkinson, Earl A., Jr., 1544, 1867
Atkinson, Edward, 1181, 1847
Atkinson, Robert, 1544
Atland meetinghouse, York Co., PA, 48
Atland, Daniel, 1544
Atlanta, GA, Grace Brethren Church (Marietta, GA, Grace Brethren Church of Greater Atlanta), 540, **793**
Atlantic Northeast district, Church of the Brethren in New Jersey, 929
atlases of German settlement in U. S., 1988
atomic weapons, *See* entries at nuclear
Attaway, John Frances, 676, 1544
Atterbury, Ella Hazel, 2072
attestation, *See* oaths
attire, *See* dress
attorneys, *See* law
Atwood, A. F., 1544
Au Soo Ping, wife of Moy Gwong Han, 891
Auburn, CA, Gold Rush Community Grace Brethren Church, **70,** 1134
Auburn, IN, Church of the Brethren, **70–71,** 265
Auburn Junction, IN, Brethren Church, **71**
auctions, prohibition of alcoholic beverages at, 1251
audio recordings of annual meetings, Church of the Brethren, 1303
Aufrichtige Nachricht (*Sincere Account,* 1763), Wilhelm Grahe, 71
    author, information about, 564
    Jülich, Brethren imprisonment in, 677
    Solingen Brethren, 1201
Aufrichtiges Mitglied (Artless Member=Alexander Mack, Sr.) in *Grundforschende Fragen* (*Basic Questions,* 1713, E. L. Gruber), 575

Augé, Friedrich, 1867
Auge, Moses, 1867
Aughey (Ache), John, 322
Aughey (Ache), John Ludwig, 1539
Aughwick Church of the Brethren, PA, **71**
Ardenheim Church of the Brethren, PA, **52**
    Beech Run Church of the Brethren, PA, 109
    bibliography, 1863
    Black Log, Valley Point Church of the Brethren, PA, 144
    Burkholder, Wealthy Agnes Clark(e), 231
    Eby, Enoch, 419
    Kishacoquillas Valley branch, 406
    Long, Christian, 753
    Lutz family, 767
    Myers, Graybill, minister, 903
    Rockhill Furnace, PA, Rockhill Church of the Brethren, 1117
    Scholten, Marian and Martin Scholten, pastors, 1155
    Spanogle, William L., 1208
Auglaize Chapel, OH, 71, 410
Auglaize Church of the Brethren, OH, 71, 78
Augsburg, 456, 545
Augsburg Confession, **71–72,** 942, 1368
August David, count of Sayn-Wittgenstein-Hohenstein, 72, 597
Augusta, KS, Church of the Brethren, 72
Augusta Co., VA
    bibliographical sources, 2077, 2088
    Blue Ridge Chapel Church of the Brethren, 152
    Brethren in Shenandoah Valley, VA, 1176
    Brower, David, 214
    Crist family, 352
    Elk Run Church of the Brethren, VA, 439
    Forest Chapel Church of the Brethren, VA, 502
    Garber (Garver, Gerber) family, 530
    Grottoes, VA, Church of the Brethren, 574
    Little River Church of the Brethren, 749
    Middle River Church of the Brethren, VA, 825
    Moscow Church of the Brethren, VA, 878
    Mount Vernon Church of the Brethren, VA, 887
    Pleasant Hill Church of the Brethren, VA, 1033
    Pleasant Valley Church of the Brethren, VA, 1035
    Sangerville Church of the Brethren, VA, 1144
    Staunton, VA, Church of the Brethren, 1220
    Summit Church of the Brethren, 1235
    Thomas, Jacob, 1263
    Waynesboro, VA, Church of the Brethren, 1324
    White Hill Church of the Brethren, 1340
    Yount, Daniel, 1391
Augusta, WV, Tear Coat Church of the Brethren, 1249
Augusta Co., WV, Thurmanites in, 1264
Augustine, David, 855, 1203, 1544

Augustine of Hippo
  amillennialism of, 833
  Arminianism reflecting church fathers prior to, 55
  church father, regarded as, 296
  Donatism, 396
  oaths, taking of, 959
  peace in Christian church history, 998
Aukeny, Isaac, 1544
Auker, J. C., 1544
Auker, Joseph, 1544
Auker, Kevin L., 2271
Auker, Thomas Earl, 888, 1544
Aukerman, Dale H., 1544, **2132–2133**, 2299, 2311
  bibliographical sources, 1867, 2039
  Brethren Action Movement (BAM), 179, 302
  Brethren Peace Fellowship, 193
  Eaton, OH, Church of the Brethren, 417
  nuclear arms race, 2232
  Pritchett, Reuel Bowman, sayings of, 1061
Aukerman, Daniel, 2133
Aukerman family, 708
Aukerman, Maren, 2133
Aukerman, Miriam, 2133
Aukerman, Ruth Seebass, 193, 2133
Auld, Pam, 566
Auldinger, Jacob, 1544
Ault, Elizabeth, 217
Ault, James E., 1544
Aultland (Altland), Daniel, 1541
Aultman, D., 668
Aumbrum, Maggie (later Parker), 993
Aungst, David S., 2271
Aungst, Jeffrey Lynn, 2271
Auraham, Yonan Y., 72, 501, 662, 1386, 1544, 1847
Aurand, Ammon Monroe, Jr., 1867
Aurand, Muriel Boardman, 155
Aurandt family, 1876
Aurbacher, Kilian, 292
Aurelia, IA, Mount Zion Brethren Church, **72**, 661, 773
Aurora (*Day-Dawning*) (Boehme), 156
Aurora Mission Church of the Brethren (Spring River Church of the Brethren,, MO), 257, 334, **1214**
Aurora, MO, 1214
Ausbund (*Paragon*), **72**
Ausherman, Charles F., 1544
Ausherman, David, 540, 1544
Ausherman family, 216
Austin, AR, Church of the Brethren, **72–73**
Austin, A. William, 72, 141, 956, 1544
Austin, Alfred, 1023, 1544
Austin, Alfred L., 2299
Austin, Carola Jean Fluke, 1847
Austin, Charles LaVerne, 1544
Austin, Charlotte Irene, 1142, 1847
Austin, Donald Glenn, 1544
Austin, Gary Lloyd, 1847, 2271
Austin, Gordon Lee, 53, 1142, 1544, 1847
Austin, Hazel (Quear), **72**, 461
Austin, Joan, 2311
Austin, Malinda Barnhizer, 72
Austin, Maynard, 826, 1544
Austin, Oliver Henry, **72**, 461, 1544
Austin, Paul R., 1544
Austin, Richard A., 1544
Australia

Church of the Brethren, 324
  Old German Baptist Brethren, 324
Austria, **73**
  Aukerman, Dale H., 2133
  Brethren Haus at Linz, *746*
  Brethren service in, 2068
  BSC, 2066, 2100
  Church of the Brethren, 303
  Evangelical Church in Austria, 459
  International Refugee Organization (IRO), 659
  Kruger, Helena, 708
  medical projects, 809
  Peters, Woodford W., 1011
  relief and rehabilitation work, 23, 73, 200, 1097
  relief work in, 23, 73
  religious liberty, former suppression of, 1098
  Smeltzer, Ralph Emerson, 1190
  Thalham Tubercular Sanitorium, 1255–1256
  United Nations Relief and Rehabilitation Administration (UNRRA), 1291
  Vienna, 684, 1367
  work camps, 1367
authority, **73–74**, 2059, *See also* polity
  American Revolution and Brethren neutrality, 1105–1106
  Annual Meeting, *See* authority of Annual Meeting
  Biblical, *See* authority of the Bible
  Brethren movement, 291
  Church of God (New Dunkers), 297
  Congregational Brethren, 334
  Declaration of Principles, 372
  definition of, 386
  Fundamental Brethren Church, 522
  Holy Spirit, doctrine of, 624
  minutes, 852
  moderator, 866
  Modernism, 866
  noncreedalism and doctrine, 942
  Old German Baptist Brethren, 967
  "Order of the Brethren," 976
  Plow Creek Fellowship, 1038
  Reformation, Protestant, 1091
  schism and church authority, 1152
  scriptures, *See* authority of the Bible
  six sources of for early Brethren, 73
authority of Annual Meeting, 33, 73, 334
  Brethren Church, 182
  Brethren polity and, 1042–1043, 1044
  Miami Valley Elders, 823
  nonconformity, 941
  Old Brethren, 971
  Old German Baptist Brethren, 970
  Old Order Movement, 973
  scriptural basis (authority) for, 33
  Swihart, Jonathan H., questioned authority of, 1245
authority of the Bible, 131, 132–133
  Anabaptism, 1260
  Brethren committed to, 135
  creeds and statements of belief, replacing, 1258
  Pietism, 1260
  source of Brethren theology, as, 1259
Authorized version of the Bible, 138
authors, Brethren children named for, 912
autobiographies
  Cartwright, Peter, 647

Franklin, Benjamin, 506
Gribble, Florence Alma Newberry, 573
historiography, 2201
Miller, Minor C., 2017
Moyer, Elgin S., 2025
Murray, Samuel, 2026
Myer, Anna Balmer, 2027
Neumann, Friedrich C., 2030
Pritchett, Reuel B. and Dale Aukerman, 2039
Ronk, Albert T., 2047
Root, Jacob, 2048
Schwalm, Vernon F., 2060
automobiles, **74–75**
  "Auto Days," 74
  business beliefs and, 234
  family, 474
  farming, 477
  impact on the Brethren, 3, 74–75
  nonconformity and, 74, 941
  Old Brethren, 964, 970, 971
  Old Brethren German Baptists, 965, 972
  Old German Baptist Brethren, 969, 1271
  Old Order German Baptists, 972
  photos, *27, 74*
  Shoup, William J., 1179
  Skiles, Jacob W., 1189
  Studebaker Company, 75, 1230, 1231
  Stutz, Harry Clayton, 1232–1233
  Stutz Motor Car Co., 75
  use by Brethren, 1271
autonomy of the congregation, *See* polity
Auvil, Andrew Coleman, 1544
  Bethany Church of the Brethren, WV, 124
  Goshen Church of the Brethren, WV, 558
  Mount Hebron Church of the Brethren, WV, 881
  Pleasant Valley Church of the Brethren, WV, elder, 1036
  Union Chapel Church of the Brethren, WV, 1287
Auvil, C., 1544
Auvil, Elias, 1177, 1544
Auvil, William, 1544
Auxt,, Mr. and Mrs. Andrew, 579
Avery family, 241
Avey, Thomas; Orlando, FL, Grace Brethren Church, 982, 2271
avoidance, **75**
  acknowledgment and, 3
  Amish, as practiced by, 25
  Anabaptists, 29
  ban synonmymous with, 81
  Brethren movement, 292
  Christian Brethren and, 281
  complete, 75
  disfellowship, 390
  fellowship, 482
  Holdeman, John, 618
  marital avoidance, 390, 793
  partial, 75
  Rechte und Ordungen, 1086
Avon Park, FL, mission of Sebring, FL, J. H. Moore Memorial Church of the Brethren, 1162
AWANA program, 2175
Ayers (Ayres), J. Samuel, 1544, 2299
Ayers, John H., 1544
Ayers, George Bucher, 1867

Ayres, S. G., 1867

B-1 bomber, opposition to, 23
B. Mary Royer Hall, Elizabethtown
  College, 438
Babcock, William Emerson, 1867
Babylon and Christ (Gish), 550, 1950
Babylon, Emmanuel, 1032, 1544
Baca Co., CO, 313, 324
Bach, Jeffrey Alan, 826, 2201, 2239, 2271,
  2311, 2312, 2348
Bachelor Run, IN, congregations, 463, 652,
  766
  Church of the Brethren, **77**
  Flora, IN, Bachelor Run Old German
    Baptist Brethren Church, 495, 496
  Flora, IN, Church of the Brethren, 496
    German Baptist Brethren, 996
  Hart, John, 587
  Howard Co. Old German Baptist
    Brethren Church, IN, 633
  Howard, IN, Church of the Brethren,
    633
  Lower Deer Creek, 297
  Monticello/Pike Creek Church of the
    Brethren, IN, 872
  Replogle, Peter, 1100
Bacher, Rhoda Hochstetler, 1867
Bachman (Backman/Baughman) families,
  1887, 2089
Bachman, Barbara (later Eby), 420
Bachman, Barbara (later Zug), 509, 1401
Bachman, David J., 2312
Bachman, Emma Krehbiel, 1867
Bachman, Mae Graybill, 748, 1867
Bachtel family, 2070
Bachtel, Kenneth, 1544
Bachtel, Samuel, 2070
Back Creek, PA, Church of the Brethren,
  42, **77**, 172, 570, 686, 736, 1295
Back Creek, VA
  meetinghouse, 164
  mission point, Botetourt Co., VA,
    Church of the Brethren, 164
Backus, Isaac, 429, 1867
Bacon family, 377
Bacon, Henry, 1544
Bacon, Theodore D., 1867
Bacon, William, 793, 1544
Baden, Duchy of, 362
Bader, Charles, 1544
Badgeley, Lause Moore, 1919
Badger, Robert, 1544
Badger, Samuel, 1544
Baehr, Ann Eby, 420
Baehr, Barbara Eby, 420
Baehr, Heinrich, 420
Baehr, Johannes, 420
Baensch, Emil, 1867
Baer and related families, 216, 712, 1867,
  1887, 1892
Baer (Bare), Abraham, 1, 226, 1544
Baer, Allen, 2252
Baer, Arthur R., 1544
Baer, Carrie (later Hoff), 77
Baer, Ella S. Martin, 1867
Baer, George F., 779
Baer, George S., **77**, 186
Baer, George Stanley, 1544
Baer, Henry, 1867
Baer, Hiram, 439
Baer, John (Bär, Johann), **77**, 1067
Baer, Judith (later Loehr), 752

Baer, Maria, 219
Baer, Michael, 1
Baer, Moses Tousaint, 1036, 1212, 1280,
  1544–1545, 1867
Baer, Samuel, 406, 1545
Baer, Samuel A., 1867
Baer, Samuel S., 2271
Baer, Solomon J., 1545
Baer, Willis Nissley, 1867
Baerg, Herman Jonathon, 104, 140, 585,
  814, 1240, 1545
Bager family, *See* entries at Baugher
Bagley, Bob, 713
Bagley, Ruby, 713
Bagwell, David Burton, 1545
Bagwell, Elihu Burton, 1545
Bagwell, Olive, *248*
Bahr el Arab River, 1234
Bahr el Gazel River, 1234
Bahr, Jacob, 14, 771, 1545
Baier family, 1955
bail, **77–78**
Bail, Arthur, 1545
Bail, Craig Kenneth, 1545
Bail, Garrett D., 1545
Bail, Gurney E., 244
Bail, Gurney Simpson, 1867
Bail, Maggie Berkley, 1545
Bail, Samuel Wishert, 45, 719, 963, 1545
Baile, Rebecca (later Crouse), 2173, 2275
Baile, Sarah L., 1315
Bailer, Sophi Leininger, 1867
Bailey, NC, Church of the Brethren, **78,**
  224
Bailey, NC, Fundamental Brethren Church,
  522
Bailey, Danny Ray, 2299
Bailey, David, **78**, 186, 799
Bailey, Esther S., 401, *554*
Bailey family, 1026, 1062
Bailey Grove Church of the Brethren, TN,
  78, 453
Bailey, Guy, 365
Bailey, Hiram F., 1545
Bailey, James, 1867
Bailey, James (John) M., 1545
Bailey, John, 78
Bailey, John P., 1137, 1545
Bailey, Keith, 1545
Bailey, Kenneth P., 1868
Bailey, M. J., 1545
Bailey, Mary, 318
Bailey, Maxine, 365
Bailey, Sarah (Kinzer), 78
Bailey, Thomas, 1545
Bailey, Thomas A., 31, 515, 982
Bailey, William H., 1545
Bain, Paris E., 343, 973
Bain, Paris Elbert, 1545
Bainton, Roland H., 998, 1868
Bair, Barbara, 163
Bair family, 503, 950
Bair, Jacob A., 1545
Baird, Chester, 1235
Baird, Chester N., 1545, 2299
Baird, Glen, 504
Baird, Glen M., 674, 1287
Baird, Glen Marshall, 1545
Baisinger, Lovina (later Studebaker), 1157
Bakeless, John E., 1868
Bakener, Fred, 1545
Baker Co., FL, Church of the Brethren at
  Glen St. Mary, 552

Baker Church of the Brethren, Lafayette,
  OH, 71, **78**
Baker congregation, PA, 1294
Baker house (Boiling Springs, PA, Church
  of the Brethren), **157**, 255, 765
Baker meetinghouse, Lower Cumberland
  Church of the Brethren, PA, 765
Baker, Abraham, 395
Baker, Adam, 1545
Baker, Addison, 1214
Baker, Admiral Dewey, 912
Baker, Allen J., Jr., 2271
Baker, Amelia Bear, 547
Baker, Anna (later Cover), 606
Baker, Ardelta Delores Wolfe, 2312
Baker (Becker) family, **78–79**, 142, 479,
  686, 1154, 1342, 1929, 2060,
  2316, *See also* Becker family
Baker, Bruce B., 1545
Baker, Carl A., Jr., 164, 798, 1545
Baker, Carmie LeRoy, 1545
Baker, Charles L., 1545
Baker, Conrad, 1868
Baker, D., 1545
Baker, Daniel, 790, 1026, 1138, 1545
Baker, Daniel M., 1545
Baker, Daryl Paul, 1545
Baker, David, 1868
Baker, David (Daniel), 1545
Baker, David H., 1545
Baker, David W., 2132, 2137
Baker, Dwight, 1545
Baker, Elisabeth Ziegler, 1870
Baker, Elizabeth Evans, 78, 2312
Baker, Elizabeth (later Long), 753
Baker, Elizabeth (later Wampler), 1316,
  1846, 1866
Baker, Elizabeth Miller, 1980
Baker, Ezra, 1545
Baker, Florence, 1843
Baker, Florence (later Gibbel), **547**
Baker, Florence (later Pittenger),
  1026–1027, 1843
Baker, Francis, 78
Baker, Frank L., 1545, 1868
Baker, Frank S, 1868
Baker, Frederick Mervin, 1545
Baker, free minister at Snake Spring Valley
  Church of the Brethren, PA, 1192
Baker, G. Landis, 500, 605, 1135
Baker, George E., 2271
Baker, George Landis, 1545
Baker, George R., 1545
Baker, George S., 1545
Baker, George W., 1545
Baker, H. Jesse, 1545
Baker, Henry (BC), 1545
Baker, Henry (CB), 1545
Baker, Henry C., 90, 1545
Baker, Henry M., 78
Baker, Henry Miller, 1545–1546
Baker, Henry S., 1546
Baker, Isaac C., 470, 817, 1546
Baker, Isaac Newton, 912
Baker, J. A., 417, 1546
Baker, J. Hiram, 972
Baker, J. M., 1546
Baker, Jacob, 1546
Baker, Jacob L., 78, 1546
Baker, Jacob M., 547, 1546
Baker, James L., 1546
Baker, Jennie Calhoun, 78
Baker, Jimmy Lee, 2271

Baker, John, 584, 723
Baker, John Calhoun, **78, 2371**
   Durnbaugh, Donald F. on peace move-
      ment and, 2326
   works by, 2312
Baker, John H., 1546
Baker, John K., 1546
Baker, John M., 1546
Baker, John N., 1868
Baker, John S., 1192, 1546
Baker, John Snider, 1546
Baker, John, Sr., 1980
Baker, Jonas D., 1546
Baker, Joshua, 990, 991, 1546
Baker, Joyce Wilma, 1852
Baker, Larry Robert, 1546
Baker, Lawrence, 1546
Baker, Levi, 1546
Baker, Lydia Kempf, 790, 1026
Baker, Mark Edward, 1546
Baker, Mary Snyder, 1882
Baker, May Allread, 1868
Baker, Mervin, 759
Baker, Morven, 2132
Baker, N. E., 377, 758
Baker, Naaman R., 14, 15, 1546, 1868
Baker, Nathaniel, 1976
Baker, Newton D., **78,** 559
Baker, Nicholas, 1868
Baker, Noah Emory, 1546
Baker, Paul (Tony) A., 2271
Baker, Peter, 1868, 1882, 1923
Baker, Raphael, 1546
Baker, Robert Helsley, 1868
Baker, Roscoe Perry, 1546
Baker, Ruth Matilda Good, 1868
Baker, S. H., 1021
Baker, Samuel, 1546
Baker, Samuel H., 791, 1546
Baker, Samuel S., 1882
Baker, Simeon, 1870
Baker, Thoreau Butler, 1868
Baker, W. S., 360, 637, 674, 746, 1122
Baker, W. Wayne, 16, 670, 699, 700, 1221,
      1365, 1546, 2299
Baker, Walter, 1546
Baker, Ward Neville, 1868
Baker, Wayne W., 265
Baker, Wendell, 78
Baker, William, 752
Baker, William Henry, 1546
Baker, William, Jr., 1546
Baker, William Sherman, 1546
Baker's Cross Roads Church of the
      Brethren, TN, **79**
Bakersfield, CA, Church of the Brethren,
      79, 244, 774
Bakker, Johannes de, 1868
Balami, Ali Yerima, 1546
Balami, Nvwa Dzarma, 306, 307, 1546,
      1868
Balami, Yusufu M. B., 1546
Baldeo, Isaac, 2190
Balderston, Robert W., 339
Baldner, Karl Wayne, 1546
Baldner, Phyllis Ann Burkholder, 1897
Baldwin Park, CA, Hispanic ministries in,
      2198
Baldwin, Alma Ferne Strohm, 1213, 1833,
      2312
Baldwin, C. Harry, 1546

Baldwin, C. Howard, 1546
Baldwin, Charles Franklin, Jr., 1546, 2271
Baldwin, Charles Luther, 1546, 1833
Baldwin, Elmer Rufus, 1213, 1546, 1833,
      1868, **2387**
Baldwin family, 164
Baldwin, Jacob Franklin, 743, 866, 1009,
      1206, 1546
Baldwin, John B., 315
Baldwin, Lelland Marion, 1546
Baldwin, Louise (later Rieman), 2226,
      2253, 2291
Baldwin, Naomi Roller, 1833
Baldwin, Otto, 1546
Baldwin, Richard, 1546
Baldwin, Terry Lee, 2271
Baliles, Mark E., 2271
Balilies, Herman Lee, 1546
Ball, Alma (later Williams), 1345
Ball, Arden Keith, 242, 1546
Ball, Christopher A., 2271
Ball, David K., 1245
Ball family, 987
Ball, G. M., 1546
Ball, Harold Richard, 1847
Ball, Isaac, 880, 1033, 1546
Ball, Janice Marilyn MacConnick, 1847
Ball, John M., 1546
Ball-Miller, Rebecca L., 2271
Ballinger, Bob, 145
Ballinger, Floyd S., 1546
Ballinger, John A., 2271
Ballou, Hosea, **79,** 1292
Balmer, Anna (later Myers), 747, 2027
Balmer, Randall H., 2312
Balmer, Richard H., 2271
Balph family, 1958
Balph, Marguerite (later Harrison), 1958
Balsbaugh, A. H., 1546
Balsbaugh, Albert, 540, 867, 990, 1356,
      1546
Balsbaugh, Catherine (later Reichard), 753
Balsbaugh, Charles H., 1547
Balsbaugh, Christian Hervey, **79,** *79,* 80,
      381, 907, 930, 1051, 1210, 1868,
      2027, 2186
Balsbaugh, Daniel, 821, 1547
Balsbaugh, Elizabeth (Longenecker), 79
Balsbaugh, Elizabeth Miller, 79, 894
Balsbaugh, Elnora (later Grisso), 574
Balsbaugh, Eva (Minich), 79, 80
Balsbaugh family, 142, 1868, 1927
Balsbaugh, George, 79, 80, 821, 826, 887
Balsbaugh, George (Beaver Creek OGBB
      congregation, WI), 105
Balsbaugh, George W. (Beech Grove
      OGBB congregation, IN), 109,
      1547
Balsbaugh, Harry K., 1547
Balsbaugh, Henry, 1039, 1868
Balsbaugh, J. Henry, 821, 1547
Balsbaugh, Lizzie (later Hollinger), 620
Balsbaugh, Paul, 867, 973, 1547, 2224
Balsbaugh, Peter, 79
Balsbaugh (Pfaltzbach, Baltzbach) family,
      79–80
Balsbaugh, Valentine, 79, 894, 1547
Balsbaugh, Vernon, 360
Balsbaugh, Walter, 1547
Balster, Kenneth, 1547
Baltic congregation, 1235
Baltic, OH, 345
Baltic, OH, Church of the Brethren (Sugar-

creek), 80
Baltimore Co., MD, 755, 1095
Baltimore, MD, 175
   Dundalk Church of the Brethren, **80**
   First Church of the Brethren (Fulton
      Ave.), **80,** 745, 753, 805, 2133,
      2197
   Friendship Church of the Brethren
      (Linthicum Heights), **745**
   Liberty Heights congregation, 963
   Pilot House Project, *2133,* **2133**
   publishing industry, 2067
   Sauer, Samuel, printer, 1149
   South Paca Church of the Brethren, **80**
   Trinity Church of the Brethren (North
      Baltimore), **80**
   urban ministry, 299
   urban mission, 1296
   Woodberry Church of the Brethren, 40,
      80, **80–81,** 805, 2312, 2099
Baltimore, Aaron H., 14, 1547
Baltimore family, 14
Baltimore, Lord, 800
Baltzbach family, *See* Balsbaugh family
Balyo, Clyde, 367
Balyo, Clyde G., 1547
Balzer, Albert William, 814, 1847
Balzer, Elsie Clam Kersting, 117, 1847
Bamberger family, *See* Bomberger family
Bame, Caroline M. (Myers), 81
Bame, Charles A., 64, **81,** 366, 505, 1015,
      1254, 1372, 1547
Bame, Donald, 1547
Bame, Lucina (Bosserman), 81
Bame, Samuel M. F., 81
Banaszak, David Francis, 2271
Bandon, OR, Church of the Brethren, **81**
Bane, William W., 1547
Baneful Effects of Worldly Amusements
      (Zeigler), 2269
Baney, Ernest, 1547
Bangalore, India, Theological College,
      1319
Banger (Bangor), Timothy, 81, 1015, 1292,
      1547
Bangor, CA
   Fruitvale Church of the Brethren, 520
   Gillett, Charles Edwin, 549
Bangor, MI, 144
Bangor, Timothy, *See* Banger, Timothy
Bangui, Africa
   Evangelical School of Theology, 854
   Grace Brethren Church in, 268
   banks, Brethren attitudes toward, **81**
   Banks, Martin C., 1547
   Bannerville, PA, Church of the
      Brethren, **81–82,** 406, 739, 783
   bans and banning, *See* avoidance
      Brethren movement, 292
      Brethren opposition to secret
         societies, 1163–1164
      Brethren polity, 1042
      discipline, doctrine of, 387
      Häcker (Höcker), Wilhelm, 577
      Mack, Alexander, Sr., and New
         Baptists of Schwarzenau, 776
      Rechte und Ordungen, 1086
Banshaff, Christopher, 118
Banta, Richard E., 1857
Bantz, Cyrus M., 1547
Bantz, Floyd Eugene, 683, 1114, 1547,
      1868
Bantz, Kathy, 587

Bantz, Leslie, 587
Bantz, Wilbur Monroe, 504, 1547
Banu, Babi T., 306
baptism, **82–86**, *84, 213, 552, See also* baptismal instruction; immersion; rebaptism
  as an act of obedience, 83
  admission, as means of, 5
  adult, 5, 776
  apostolic, 2021
  applicants, instruction of, **5**, 86, *See also* catechism
  Arnold, Gottfried, by, 2013
  article about, 1952
  Basic Questions (*Grundforschende Fragen*), 2374
  Beissel, Conrad, 910
  Beissel, Conrad, giving back, 804
  believer's, *See* believer's baptism
  bibliographical sources, 1866, 1868, 1869–1870, 1871, 1876, 1882, 1884, 1886, 1891, 1932, 2028
    of blacks, 395
  book by Longenecker, Christian L., 756
  Brethren Doctrine of Salvation and, 1140
  Brethren, first, 159
  Brethren in Christ, 189
  Brethren movement, 292
  Brethren movement and, 168, 174
  Brethren music, 898
  Brethren witness on, 83, 84, 85–86
  camp meetings, 246
  capital punishment, 292
  Catechism on, 1985–1986
  celibacy and, 266
  charismatic movement, 271, 272
  charters/charter membership, 273
  Christian Brethren and, 281
  Christian Catholic (Apostolic) Church, 282
  Christliches Hand-Büchlein (Christian Handbook), 288
  Christmas, celebration of, 288
  Christology and, 290
  church membership, 812–813
  Church of God (New Dunkers), 296, 297
  Church of the Brethren, 305
  church parents, 308
  church-state relations and, 309
  Churches of God (GC), 309
  as civil disobedience, 1260
  Clear Creek, 1357
  Community of the True Inspiration, 330
  confession of faith, 333
  confirmation, 333–334
  Congregational Brethren of Pleasant Hill, OH, differing qualifications for, 335
  controversies about, Samuel König's involvement in, 706
  controversy regarding, 1969
  conversion, doctrine of, 339–340
  Covenant Theology, 348
    as criminal act, 1058
  Dayton, OH, Patterson Park Grace Brethren Church, 367
  debates, 168, 370, 371
  Declaration of Principles, 372
  defense of, 1987

degrees of ministry, 374
Doctrinal Treatise, 394
doctrine of, *See* baptism, doctrine of
Dominican Republic, *2173*
Dowie, John Alexander, 398
dress symbol of, 401
Drexel, Hannah Jane Langstroth, of, 405
Düdelsheim, baptisms performed by Mack, A., Sr. near, 407
Dunkard Brethren Church, 298, 409, 2173
Dunker baptism, article about, 1920
Dutch Bethel, German Baptist Brethren Church, 2373
early 20th century sermon, 1168
early Christianity, 296
early polemic context of, 83
Ebey home, revival in, 399
Ecuador, Tasiguano family, 1248
Eder River, 424
Edisto German Baptist Brethren Church, SC, 425
educational materials, 284
Eicher, Daniel, 431
elders presiding at, 432
Faw, Jacob, 1013
feetwashing, 481
Fellowship of Grace Brethren Churches, 2178, 2181, 2182
Fellowship of Grace Brethren Churches (FGBC), 486
first among Swiss Brethren, 28
first among the Brethren
  in America, **82**, 175, 704, 1270
  in Europe, **82**
  in Germantown, PA, 704
form of, and names of Brethren fellowships, 910
Fostoria, OH, West Independence Brethren Church, 505
Frankfort, OH, Church of the Brethren, 506
Frantz, Michael, 508
Fraternity Church of the Brethren, NC, 511
Frey, Andreas, 517
Froelich (Fröhlich), Samuel Heinrich, 518
Frostburg, MD, First Church of the Brethren, 519
Funk, Joseph, 525
Gantz (Gans), Georg Balthasar, 528
Garden City, KS, Church of the Brethren, 530
Gass (Gast), Jakob, 532
Geiger, Henry, 533
Geiger, Mary Schwenk, 533
General Church Erection and Missionary Committee (CB), 536
Geringer Schein, Ein (*A Humble Gleam*), 540
German Baptist Brethren, 2046
German Seventh-Day Baptists, 542
Gibson, Daniel B., 547
"giving back" baptism, 175
God's Means of Grace (Yoder), 555
Grace Brethren and creeds, 943
grace, doctrine of, 562
Grahe, Jakob, 564
Grahe, Wilhelm, 564
Great Commission, 568
Great Swamp Church of the Brethren,

PA, 569
Grebe (Grebi), Georg, 569
Guice (Geist Guß, Guss, Güß), Christopher, 576
handclasp, 582
Harlan Church of the Brethren, IA, 583
Harrison, Stephen J., 586
Heidelberg Catechism, 593
Henckels, Johann Friedrich, 596
Henry Fork Church of the Brethren, VA, 598
Henry, J. M., performing, at Selma, VA, Church of the Brethren, 1166
Hesse, 602
Hilton, George William, 607
Himbach, 607
historic sites, 609
historical survey of, 1971
history and exegesis, 1992, 1996
Hiwasse, VA, Church of the Brethren, 613
Hochmann von Hochenau, Ernst Christoph, 615, 1967
Hoening, Johann Georg, 616
Hoffmann, Eva Elizabeth, 617
Holdeman, John, 618
Holsinger, Henry Ritz, 621
Holtzapfel (Holsapple, Holsopple), Johann Heinrich, 623
holy kiss used at, 698
of the Holy Spirit, 85, **86**, 271, 272, 624
Hon, Peter Keithly, 627
Honites, 628
Hope, Christian, 628
Hostetler Brethren, 631
Hostetler, Joseph, 631
Hoyle Creek Church of the Brethren, OK, 633
Huffman, Edward N., performing at South Saint Joseph Church of the Brethren, MO, 1135
Hutterian Society of Brothers, 639, 640
hymns, 643, 2205
Hyndman, PA, Church of the Brethren, 643
illustrations of
  1887, *82*
  Dominican Republic, *2173*
  in Kortwolde, *1241*
  ordinances, *978*
  Stony Creek, VA (1905), *84*
  Sumner, NE (1913), *87*
immersion, *See* immersion
India, 649
Indian converts, 176
infant baptism, 174, 443
infants, *See* infant baptism
inner Word and outer Word, 656
instruction, 5, 86, *See also* catechism
instruction about tobacco to candidates, 1266
instruction in, 262
Irricana (First) Church of the Brethren, Alberta, Canada, 663
Jarboe, John Edwin, 669
Johnsontown Church of the Brethren, WV, 675
Judaism, 677
Kakumiro, Uganda, 2128
Kampala, Uganda, 2128
Kämpfer, Johannes, attendee at first baptisms in Germantown, 682

Kapenguri, Kenya, 2128
Klein(e), Georg(e), 699
Kline, John, 701
Kortwolde, 707, *1241*
Kurtz, Henry, 711
laying on of hands during, 730, 731
letters of membership in lieu of rebaptism, 738
Longenecker, Christian, performing at Conestoga, 1177
Mack, Alexander, Jr., 134, 774
Mack, Alexander, Sr., 776
Mack, Anna Margaretha Kling, in the Eder River, 778
Mack, Johann Valentin, rebaptism, 778
Mack, Johannes, 778
maintenance of statistics, 1219
Manteca, CA, Northgate Community Brethren Church, 788
Manvel, TX, Church of the Brethren, 789
Marienborn, 792
Marienborn area, public baptism not permitted in, 683
Markey family, 793
Mehrning, Jacob, writings on, 811
membership trends 1980 to 2000, 2220
Menno Simons, 814
Mennonites, 83, 87, 815, 816
  disagreement with, 701, 707
  General Conference of Mennonite Brethren Churches, 814
  immersion, sermon on, 1912
"Message of the Brethren Ministry," 818
method, 1985, 2003
military service, renouncing, 831
mode of, 82, 85
  affusion (pouring), 87
  earliest identifiable, 83
  immersion, *See* immersion
  sprinkling, 1007
Mooreites, 875
Moravian Church, 876
Murray, Don, 625
Naas, Johannes, performance by, 909
Nägele, Hans Rudolph and Elizabeth, 910
Nead, Peter, 918
New Testament, 2063
New Testament theology of, 82, 83, 84–85
oaths, taking of, 959
Olathe Old German Baptist Brethren Church, KS, 964
Old German Baptist Brethren, 967, 2233
"Order of the Brethren," 976
ordinances, 976, *978,* 980
ordination and, 719, 980
orphans, care for, 982
Orthodox Churches, 983
Patton, George, disagreement with, 996
Pennsylvania Brethren, by, 1004
Petersen, Barthold Jurgen, 1012
Philadelphia, PA, Germantown Church of the Brethren, 1016
Piney Creek Church of the Brethren, MD, 1025
plain coat, 1029
Plate, Lewis (Ludwig) A., 1030
Pleasant Dale Church of the Brethren, IN, 1030

Pleasant Hill Church of the Brethren, WV, 1033
Pleasant Valley Church of the Brethren, Alberta, Canada, 1034
Pleasant Valley Church of the Brethren, NC, 1035
Plow Creek Fellowship, 1038
postadolescent, 1227
prayer, 1052
preaching about, 1053
Preiß, Johannes Jakob, present at first in America, 1055
Preiß (Price), Johannes, 1055
public worship ritual, 1375, 1378
Radical Pietists, 293
rebaptism, *See* rebaptism
Rechte und Ordungen, 1086
Reformation, Protestant, 1091
regeneration, 84
Reitz, Johann Heinrich, defense by, 1095
repentance, doctrine of, 1099
reply to an essay on, 1958
Ritter, Daniel, participating in, 1111
River Wupper, 1222
robes, 1115
Rodney Church of the Brethren, MI, 1119
role of, for FGBC, 42
Roman Catholic Church, 1120
sacramental view of, 83, 84
salvation through, 1368
Sauer, David, performing incorrectly, 1147
Schneider, Hans
  on Alexander Mack and, 2355
  on water, 2355
Schroyer, David, first baptism at Sugar Valley Church of the Brethren, PA, 1235
Schwarzenau Brethren, 1079
Schwarzenau Brethren movement, 298
Seachrist, Denise Ann on Snow Hill Nunnery and, 2355
second degree of ministry, 845
Seebach, Christoph, views on, 1165
separatism and, 1167
sermon on, 2021
Seventh-Day Adventists, 1169
Smith Chapel Church of the Brethren, WV, pool at, 1191
"spiritual," 83
by sprinkling, 1007
Stauffer, Christian, 1220
Stetius, Gottfried Luther, 1222
Stoll, Jacob, 1224
Stone Bridge Church of the Brethren, MD, first in 1867, 1224
Stoner, Ephraim Winfield, 1225
Stopp, Klaus on fraktur certificates for, 2359
Strege, Merle D. on, 2359
Sturgis, Daniel B., by Isham Gibson, 1232
Sugar Creek Church of the Brethren, IN, 1234
Sunday schools influencing, 1239
Surbey, Howard J., 1241
Swedeland Valley Old German Baptist Brethren Church, WV, 1243
by Swigart, William Joseph, 1245
symbolism of, 85
Taylor family by David Martin, 1249

Texas, by Spencer, C. C., 1209
thesis about, 1938
Thomas, Jeremiah, 1263
Thurian, Max on CB and, 2361
tracts about, 1269
Traut, Georg Balthasar, 1270
trine immersion, *See* trine immersion
validity of, and rebaptism, 1085
values of, 1997
Wassam, J. J., 1213
water symbol, 1246
Weimer, Glen Emerson, 1327
wife of Julian Stumpf by Alexander Mack, Sr., 1232
Wimmer, S. D., performing, 959
Wingert, Mrs. Peter N., 1311
Wissahickon Creek, baptism of Urner family, 1298
Wissihickon Creek, near Germantown, PA, 1354
Wohlfahrt (Welfare), Michael, 1355
Wolfe, David, 1356
Wolfe family, 1357
women
  roles in, 1361
  Schwarzenau, 1360
Wood, Julia A., 1363
Yin, Han Chang, 1385
York Co. Old German Baptist Brethren Church, 1389
Zuck, John, 1401
Zug, Johannes, 1401
baptism, doctrine of, **82–86,** 2082
  Amish Church, 2107
  Brethren Church, 2089
  Brethren movement and Mennonites, 231
  Germantown, PA, 2079
  history of, 2067
  importance of, 2096
  Mountville, PA, 2100
  New Testament, 2080
  order of the Brethren evaluation, 237
  Progressive movement, 2089
  theology and, 2255
  treatise on, 2071
  trine immersions, 2071, 2079, 2080, 2102
Baptism, Eucharist, and Ministry (BEM), CB response to, **2133–2134**
Baptism for the Remission of Sins; The Faith Alone and Prayerless Doctrine Considered (Nead, P.), 919
Baptism in the Schuykill River, Phildelphia, PA, in the 18th century, 1006
"Baptism of Repentance" (Bowman), 166
Baptist World Alliance, 88
baptistries, 48, **86–87**
  indoor, and Philadelphia, PA, First Church of the Brethren, 1015
  San Ponziano, 2003
  Sarasota, FL, Brethren Church, 1145
  Smith River Church of the Brethren, VA, 1192
Baptists, **87–88,** 395, *See also* American Baptist Churches
  and Arminianism, 56, 87
  bibliography, 1861, 1862, 1864, 1867, 1875
  Big Sky Brethren Church/American Baptist Church, MT, 142
  camp meetings, 245

China, 296
Church of North India, 298
congregational polity, 1041
debates regarding, 370
Edwards, Morgan, 429, 1218, 1285, 1292, 1299
Fairview, MO, Shoal Creek Church of the Brethren, 468
family rules and regulations, 2073
Fellowship of Reconciliation (USA), 488
First Baptist Church, MT, 1301
Flat Rock Church of the Brethren, NC, 493
Fleming Co., KY, German Baptist Brethren Church, 494
frontier, 519
frontier era, 1783–1830, 2079
Funk, Benjamin, 525
Garden Terrace Retirement Home, 530
German Baptist Brethren, See German Baptist Brethren
German Seventh Day Baptists, See German Seventh Day Baptists
Germantown, PA, 2087
Germany, 545
Hamilton, Hiel, 580
higher education, 603
historical writing, 611
history of, 2083
Hope, Christian, 628
Hope, Mary Katherine Neilsen, 629
Hostetler, Joseph, 631
Keithian, See Keithian Baptists
Kentucky, 2072
King, Frank, 694
King, Martin Luther, Jr., 695
Landmark movement, 44
Log Creek Church of the Brethren, MO, 752
Materials Towards a History of the Baptists, 803
McCabe Baptist Church, 142
New Testament Baptist Church, CA, 726
Penn, William, and settlement of Pennsylvania, 1004
Pietism, 1022
Ray, D. B., 1220
Russian Agricultural Exchange Program, 2129
Schwarzenau Brethren, 1079
Seventh-Day, See Seventh-Day Baptists
slavery, 2128
South Carolina, 2083
Southern Baptists, See Southern Baptists
Stein and Ray Debate, 2074
Stein, John William, 1220
Sunnyside, WA, Grace Brethren Church, 1240
"Tunker Baptists," 2011
union church with Terrace View Church of the Brethren, VA, 1254
Urner, Isaac Newton, Parkerford Baptist Church member, 1298
Wright, John, 1380
Yadkin German Baptist Brethren Church, NC, 1383
Yin, Han Chang, 1385
baptizers, See Dompelaars (Dompelaers)
Bär, Johann (Baer, John), **77,** 1067

Barba, Eleanor, 1868
Barba, Preston A., 1868
Barber Co., KS, Elm Creek Church of the Brethren, 442
Barber, Carl, 1547, 2197
Barber, Darrell W., 275, 1547
Barber, Douglas Howard, 1380, 1547. 2271
Barber, Erret G., 236. 1547
Barber family, 1206
Barber, Stephen J., 1547
Barberton OH, 951
Barbour Co., VA, 315
Barbour Co., WV, 244, 888, 1177
Bardman, Edward, 1547
Bardwell schoolhouse, Black Valley Federated Church of the Brethren and Christian Church, PA, 145
Bare, Abraham J., 1547
Bare, Abram, 1177
Bare, Daniel M., 1868
Bare, Daniel Matthias, 1868
Bare, David, 1547
Bare, Edward, 1547
Bare family, 889, 996, 2086
Bare, Henry W., 1547
Bare, Howard C., 1868–1869
Bare, James Jerold, 1869
Bare, John, 889, 1547, 1868–1869
Bare, Lee, 152
Bare, Magdalena, 2086
Bareville meetinghouse, Leola, PA, Conestoga Church of the Brethren, 737
Bareyan, Alex, 2354
Barg, Elizabeth Kagey, 2079
Barge, Hermann, 1869
Barger, Raymond J., Jr., 2271
Bargerhuff, Eric J., 2132, 2272
Barick, Isaac, 1547
Baringer family, 922
Baringer, Henry S., 1385, 1547
Barkdoll, Evelyn M. (later Frantz), 1941
Barkdoll, Galen Erb, 45, 1206, 1547, 1869
Barkdoll, Harvey Mathias, 1547
Barkdoll, Kathryn E. (later Garner), 531, 1838
Barkdoll, Stanley Galen, 242, 1547
Barker, Frank, 1547
Barker, Isaac, 654
Barker, Norma, 654
Barkett family, 228
Barkey, Ray W., 2272
Barkley, Margaret (later Shideler), See Shideler, Margaret Barkley
Barkley, Terry, 2312
Barklow, Annah, 88
Barklow, Benjamin Franklin, 1547
Barklow, Charles H., 81, 1547
Barklow, David, **88,** 906, 1547
Barklow family, 295, 1869
  Myrtle Point, OR, 980
  Myrtle Point, OR, Church of the Brethren, 906
Barklow, James, 88
Barklow, John Y., **88**
Barklow, Ronald S., 1869
Barklow, Samuel S., **88,** 906, 986, 1547
Barklow, Thomas, 81, 906, 1547
Barley, Myrtle J., 25, 1547
Barley, Shirley M., 2272
Barlow, Bruce S. W., 798, 2272
Barlow, Robert William, 2272
barn raisings, **89,** 89, 902, 1046

Barnard, Ferne (Hartzler), 88
Barnard, Jessie (Bennett), 88
Barnard, John F., 88
Barnard, Lydia (later Fisher), 491
Barnard, Russell D., **88,** 366, 501, 629, 914, 1141, 1547, 1869, 2299
Barndt, Sarah, 150, 151
Barnes, Edith Catherine Bonsack, 285, 1881, **2134**
Barnes, Fleming C., 1547
Barnes, J. W., 1547
Barnes, James A., 21
Barnes, Jay, 2348
Barnes, John, 1547
Barnes, Lee, 1547
Barnes, Robert, 1869
Barnes, Robert W., Sr., 1547, 2299
Barnes, Ruth Lucille Glessner, 1833
Barnes, Timothy M., 1858
Barnes, William E., 432, 1547–1548,
Barnet family, 1866
Barnett, Brenda (later Colijn), 2264
Barnett, Calvin, 78, 118, 522, 1012, 1023, 1294, 1548
Barnett, Doris, 1111
Barnett family, 1023
Barnett, Garther, 1548
Barnett, Harold, 1548
Barnett, Harold E., 1111, 1126
Barnett, James William Seybert (J. W.), 81, 793, 1548
Barnett, Jesse A., 933, 1548
Barnett, Joseph W., 1012, 1023, 1548
Barnett, P. N., 1548
Barney's Run congregation, PA, (BC), 16
Barnhard family, 165
Barnhard, John, 1548
Barnhart, A. B., 1946
Barnhart, Abraham, 1548
Barnhart, Abraham (CB), 1548
Barnhart, Abram Baker, **88–89,** 1548
Barnhart, Amos Arthur, 1548
Barnhart, Amos B., 431
Barnhart, Christian, 1548
Barnhart, Clifford, 360, 1548
Barnhart, Daniel, 1548
Barnhart, Daniel B., 264, 431, 984, 1112, 44, 89, 1548
Barnhart, Daniel III, 1869
Barnhart, Daniel L., 1548
Barnhart, Daniel (m. Elizabeth Naff), 89
Barnhart, Daniel (m. Eva Bowman, Catherine Brubaker), 89
Barnhart, Elizabeth (Baker), 88
Barnhart, Elizabeth (Naff), 89
Barnhart, Ezra Earl, 236, 878, 1045, 1548
Barnhart family, **89,** 241, 396, 1893
  Dvorak, Eileen K. on, 2328
  Hertzler (Hartzler) family, 601
  Jamison family, 668
  Peters family related by marriage, 1012
  Root family related by marriage, 1122
  sources on, 2324
Barnhart, Florence, 236
Barnhart, George, 257, 468, 733, 924, 1125
Barnhart, George A., 1548
Barnhart, Hannah May (Kuhnes), 88
Barnhart, Henry, 88
Barnhart, Henry T., 691, 1548
Barnhart, Henry Tazewell, 1548
Barnhart, J. H., 445
Barnhart, J. N., 1548
Barnhart, J. O., 1548

Barnhart, Jacob, 1548
Barnhart, Jeremiah, 1548
Barnhart, Joel, 791, 1548
Barnhart, John, 152, 1298, 1548
Barnhart, John W., 1548
Barnhart, Joseph O., 1869
Barnhart, Josephus Edward, 1548, 1869, 1916
Barnhart, Lawrence, 445
Barnhart, Lee Elmer, 142, 431, 972, 1346, 1548
Barnhart, Levi, 566, 1023, 1548
Barnhart, Miles Goodwin, 1869
Barnhart, Owen, 345, 1548
Barnhart, P. B., 1548
Barnhart, Rebecca Susan, 321
Barnhart, Riley, 350, 1335, 1346
Barnhart, Samuel Lawrence, 552, 1548
Barnhart, Virgil, 1390
Barnhart, Walter J., 417, 848, 1869
Barnhart, Walter J. (FGBC), 1548
Barnhart, Walter J. (OGBB), 1548
Barnhart, William Riley, 431, 1548
Barnhart, William W., 1548
Barnhill, Charles William, 2139, 2272
Barnhiser/Bernheisel/Barnhysle/Barnhisel family, 2318
Barnhizer, Isaac, 373, 1548
Barnhizer, Malinda (later Austin), 72
barns, **89–90,** *90*
barns, as meeting places
   Big Creek Old German Baptist Brethren Church, KS, 142
   Big Swatara Church of the Brethren, PA, 142
   Black River Church of the Brethren, OH, 144
   Greenville Creek congregation, OH, 1288
   La Porte, IN, Church of the Brethren, 713
   Liberty, IL, Church of the Brethren, 740
   Limestone Old German Baptist Brethren Church, KS, 743
   Loree, IN, Brethren Church, 758
   Loudonville Church of the Brethren, OH, 760
   Lower Conewago Church of the Brethren, PA, 765
   Lower Twin Old German Baptist Brethren Church, OH, 766
   Old Brethren German Baptist Church, 965
   Sugar Creek Church of the Brethren, IN, 1234
   Sunfield Church of the Brethren, MI, 1239
   Swan Creek Church of the Brethren, OH, 1243
   Three Springs Church of the Brethren, PA, 1263
   Upper Conwego Church of the Brethren, PA, 1294
   Upper Deer Creek Church of the Brethren, IN, 1294
   Walnut Church of the Brethren, IN, 1315
   West Branch Church of the Brethren, IL, 1333
   Wildcat Territory, IN, 1345
   Wolf Creek Church of the Brethren, OH, 1355

   Wolf Creek Old German Baptist Brethren Church, OH, 1356
   Wood Colony Old German Baptist Brethren Church, CA, 1363
   Yellow Creek Church of the Brethren, IL, 1384
   Zimmerman, OH, Beaver Creek Old German Baptist Brethren Church, 1399
Barnthouse, Jasper, 1289, 1548–1549
Barnum Church of the Brethren, MN (Deer Park, Nemadji), **90,** 848
Barnum/Deer Park, MN, congregation, 848
Barnum-Steggerda, Daniel S., 2272
Barnum Steggerda, Lucinda (Linda) Kay, 2272, 2376
Baroda Union Bible School or Gujarat United School of Theology (GUST), India, 576, 1145
Baron Co., KS, 1315
Barr family, 805
Barr, Francis Henry, 14, 906, 1549
Barr, George R., 2084
Barr, Gerald A., 2195
Barr, Gerald Alan, 1549
Barr, John G., 1833
Barr, Martin, family, 1963
Barren Ridge Church of the Brethren, VA, **90,** 413, 502, 825, 887, 1220, 1865, 1908–1909
Barrett, David B., 1869
Barrett, Lois, 2312
Barrett, Steven, 1033
Barrette, P. N., 1549
Barringer, Henry S., 1549
Barron, Carrie M., 1869
Barron Church of the Brethren, WI, **90–91**
Barron Co., WI, Rice Lake Church of the Brethren, 322, 1107
Barrow, Zelma D., 2312
Barry Co., MI, 318, 1363
   Hope Church of the Brethren, 629
   migration of Brethren to, 829
Barry Co., MO, 334, 864
Barry, IL, Church of the Brethren (Hadley Creek Church of the Brethren), **577**
Barryville, OH, Nimishillen Church of the Brethren, 937
Barsop family, 228
Bartbolow, Elizabeth E., 1833
Barten, Lloyd, 1869
Barth, Karl, on neoorthodoxy, 922
Barthel, John, 439
Barthel, Lewis, 2377
Barthold, Friedrich W., 1869
Bartholomew, H. S. K., 1869
Bartholomew, John H., *1167, 2380*
Bartholomew, Paul Harmon, 2272
Bartholomew, Timothy Lee, 1549
Bartholow, Elizabeth E. (later Arnold), 1833
Bartle, Duane, 871, 1046, 1549
Bartlesville, OK
   Church of the Brethren, 91
   First Congregation, 142
Bartlett, Clara, 705
Bartlett, Donald, 496, 705, 1549
Bartlett, Hannah (later Sturgis), 1232
Bartlett, Roger, 2299, 2254
Bartlett, Roger F., 2226, 2272, 2299
Bartlett, Walter, 826
Bartley, Richard John, 2272

Barto (Barton), Isaac, 791, 1549
Barto, Katie (later Kegerreis), 686
Bartolosch, Thomas A., 2312
Barton Co., KS, 424, 682
Barton family, 1038, 2104
Barton, George William, 743, 1549
Barton, James, 265, 1549
Barton, James Edward, 973, 676, 1549
Barton, John W., 973, 1549
Barton, Max, 2272
Barton, Paul William, 2272
Barton, Thomas, 2104
Barton, Will, 1335
Barton, William E., 747, 1869
Barwick, Edith (Workman), 91
Barwick, Henry Milton, **91,** 656, 842, 1549
Barwick, J. W., 912, 1290
Barwick, James, 912
Barwick, James E., 91
Barwick, John, 912, 1914
Barwick, John Workman, **91,** 545, 579, 912, 1549, 1869
   War Prisoner's Aid program, 1058
   World War II relief work, 1373
   Young Men's Christian Associations (YMCA), 1390
Barwick, Laura Hershey, 91, 912, 2039
Barwick, Milton B., 1549
Barwick, Peter, 912
Barwick, Rebecca Hixson, 91
base camps, **91–92**
   agricultural college units, 316
   CPS camps, 316
   dairy farm work, 316
   detached programs, 316, 380
   Emergency Farm Labor, 443
   emergency farm labor, 316
   forest service, 316, 502
   medical projects, 316
   mental hospital service, 316
   military service, 301
   Minnesota Starvation Project, 316
   National Park Service, 316
   relief training units, 316
   soil conservation, 316
Basehoar family, 356, *See* Basehoar family
Basel Mission, 861, 937
Basel, Switzerland, **92,** 296, 516, 545, 1246
   Boni, Andreas, persecution of, 1010
   EYN and, 307
   Keller family immigrating from, 686
   Lafiya program, 718
   Mai Sule Biu, visiting, 782
   religious persecution in, 159
Basermann, Appolonia, 163
Basermann, Johann Daniel, 163
Bashor Chapel, IN, 557
Bashor, Amos M., 354, 372, 1549
Bashor (Bashore, Beashore), Andrew, 1549
Bashor, B. J., 416, 1549
Bashor (Bashore, Basore, Beashore, Besher) family, **93–94,** 144, 232, 532, 753, 906, 1035, 2072
Bashor, Benjamin, 92, 1549
Bashor, Christina (later Taylor), 1249
Bashor, Conrad, 1033, 1035, 1549
Bashor, Corda Weller, 93
Bashor, Daniel G., 590, 1340, 1549
Bashor, Ed, 1549
Bashor, Elizabeth, 92
Bashor, George H., 553, 758, 1549
Bashor (Besher, Basehore, Beashor, Beasher, Baszhaar, Bäßhaar), Hans

Georg (1745–1780), 93, 122, 1555
Bashor (Beshor), Hans George (1775–1841), 123
Bashor (Besher, Beshor, Basehore, Beashor, Baszhaar), Hans Jacob, 123, 1555
Bashor, Hattie P. (later Montgomery), 872
Bashor, Henry, 92
Bashor, Isaac, 1178
Bashor, J. B., 92
Bashor, Jacob, 1549
Bashor, Jacob H., 1549
Bashor, James D., 1340, 1549
Bashor, John C., 1549
Bashor (Beashore), John R., 1549
Bashor, Joseph, 1342
Bashor, Joseph Bowman, 1549
Bashor, L. D., 1549
Bashor, Lee T., 2312
Bashor, Louisa (later Williams), 1345
Bashor, Margaret (later Dove), 397, 398
Bashor, Martin, 348
Bashor, Michael M. (Martin), 14, 92, 771, 1549
Bashor, Samuel C., 1549
Bashor, Stephen H., 63, 92, 92, 114, 150, 178, 182, 186, 255, 289, 345, 355, 370, 372, 461, 559, 720, 1345, 1549, 1869–1870, 1952
    Iowa, 661
    Mexico, IN, Brethren Church, pastor, 821
    Milledgeville, IL, Brethren Church, pastor, 833
    missions, 860
    Pineville, VA, Mount Olive Brethren Church, evangelism meetings, 1025
    The Progressive Christian, 1061
    Rosenberger, Isaac J., evangelist with, 1123
    Shaver, Emanuel Bydler (GBB, BC) and, 2248
    train travel, 1271
Bashor, Susan (Garst), 92
Bashor, Walter A., 931, 1223, 1340, 1549
Bashor, William E., 2299, 1549
Bashore, Anna (later Miller), 895
Bashore, Benjamin, 1870
Bashore, Catherine (later Hoover), 628
Bashore, Elias B., 1870
Bashore family, See Bashor family
Bashore, Isaac H., 1213, 1549
Bashore, Jacob, 248, 743
Bashore, Jacob (1802–1878), 93
Bashore, Jacob G. (1827–1895), 93
Bashore, Jacob H., 323, 997, 1549
Bashore, John R., 1192
Bashore (Bashor), Joseph D., 1549
Bashore, Melvin L., 2312
Bashore, Michael, 93
Bashore, Paul Minnich, 670, 1549, 2299
Bashore, Perry Calvin, 2312
Bashore, S. H., 1321
Bashore, Sallie (Miller), 94
Bashore, Sally (Noffsinger), 93
Basic Belief (Frantz), 508
Basic Questions, See Grundforschende Fragen
    Mack, Alexander, Sr., debate with Gruber, 776
    Mack, 998–999, 2374
Basket, Barton Severe, 1549
Baskin, Carl, 2272

Basler, Lucy Hollinger, 2272
Basore, Almira Kinsey, 696
Basore family, See Bashor family
Basore, John, 696
Bass family, 559
Bass, Max, 94, 251, 273, 569, 1242, 2082
    North Dakota Brethren settlement, 946
    Peters, Amos B., 1011
    railroad immigration agent, 1082
Bassai, Central African Republic, 501, 688
    Deeter, Minnie, 373
    Gribble, Florence Alma Newberry, 573
    medical missions, 807
    mission schools, 854
    Noatemo, Jean, missionary and pastoral work in, 938
    Sheldon, Hattie Louise Cope, missionary, 1175
Bassermann, Michael, 163
Bassett, Harry William, 628, 1549
Bassett, Josephine Risser, 1870
Bassett, VA, Church of the Brethren, 94, 324, 544
Bassey, Comfort Minso, 306
Bas(s)inger, FL, congregations, 94, 963, 1162
Bastin, Fred G. (C.), 1003, 1549
Bata, Central African Republic, 854, 2134
Batavia, IL, congregations and mission point, 94, 151, 736, 740, 913, 1959, 2096
Bateman, Dr., 296
Bateman family, 1113
Bateman, Newton, 1870
Bateman, Thomas H., 1870
Bates Co., MO, 334
    Gibson, Isham, 548
    Happy Hill Church of the Brethren, MO, 582
    Missouri, 864
Bates, Clyde E., 94
Bates, David, 1399, 1549
Bates, Elizabeth "Bess" (Royer), 94, 748, 836, 1870
Bates, Henry, 1549
Bates, Robert L., 720, 1549–1550
Bath Co., KY, 935
Bath Co., VA, 277
Batson, Jesse Norman, 1274, 1550
Battis, Richard, 1550
Battle Creek Church of the Brethren, Vidora, Sasketchewan, Canada, 1305
Battle Creek, MI
    American Medical Missionary College at, 936
    Church of the Brethren, 94
battlefields, See specific sites, e.g. Antietam
Battorf, Permilla (later Kline), 702
Baty family, 143
Batzel, George Steward, 1550
Baucher, John, 1550
Bauer (Bower, Bowers) family, 95, 384, 413, 493, 1212, 1216, 1224, 1883, 1911, 2077, 2094, 2105
    Muhlenberg Co., KY, German Baptist Brethren, 893
    Olive Branch German Baptist Brethren Church, IN, 973
    Prosperity congregation, Oak Hill Old German Baptist Brethren Church, WV, 957
    Root family related by marriage, 1122

Salem Church of the Brethren, OH, 1138
Bauer, Eberhard, 1870, 2312
Bauer, Gary W., 1550, 2272
Bauer, Hans, 1882, 2094
Bauer, James R., 2272
Bauermeister, Lydia, 2107
Baugher, A. C. (Charles Abba), 95, 437, 1550, 1870, 1927–1928
Baugher, Aaron, 96, 1550
Baugher, Aaron S., 95, 1550, 1927–1928
Baugher, Anna Maria Moyer, 822
Baugher (Bager) family, 96
Baugher, Catharine (Sweitzer), 96
Baugher, Charles Abba See Baugher, A. C.
Baugher, Christiana (Miller), 96
Baugher, Daniel, 822
Baugher, Edward E., 1550
Baugher, Ella Cassel Booz, 95
Baugher, George M., 1550
Baugher, Henry M., 1550
Baugher, Jacob Ira, 95, 95, 208, 1550
Baugher, Joseph M., 1179, 1550
Baugher, Lillian Stermer, 95
Baugher, Lydia Buser, 95
Baugher, Mary, 165
Baugher, Mary Bowman, 165
Baugher, Milton M., 1550, 2299
Baugher, Norman J., 22, 95–96, 96, 304, 600, 695, 754, 1132, 1369, 1550, 1870
Baugher, Raymond R., 1550
Baugher, Ruth Crist, 95
Baugher, Stanley B., 1870
Baughman, Abraham J., 1870
Baughman, Andrew J., 1346, 1550
Baughman, Barbara (later Huston), 638
Baughman, Carl Leon, 1550
Baughman, Christian, 1863
Baughman, E. A., 1346
Baughman, Elizabeth, 1863
Baughman family, 1908
Baughman, J. W. H., 1550
Baughman, Loreeta Houser, 1833
Baughman, Max David, 1833
Baughman, William, 251
Baugo, IN, congregations, 96, 749, 820, 984, 1313, 1925
Baum, Archer F., 1141, 1550
Baum family, 566
Baum, Henry L., 1550
Bauman, Abraham, 2272
Bauman, Amelia Leckington, 96, 98
Bauman, Angus Spaeth, 1870
Bauman, Anna (later Tombaugh), 1267
Bauman, Arthur, 1181
Bauman(n) (Bowman), Benjamin (1732–1809), 98
Bauman, Elizabeth Hershberger, 2312
Bauman, Esther, 2110
Bauman family, See Bowman family
Bauman, Glenn, 264, 2272
Bauman, Hans Dietrick, 2081
Bauman, Heinrich, 1971
Bauman, Henry, 1195
Bauman, James H., 2272
Bauman(n), Johann (Bowman, John, 1765–1809), 98, 98, 99
Bauman(n) (Bowman), Joseph (1790–1862), 98
Bauman, Joseph H., 2272
Bauman, Louis S. (L. S.), 53, 72, 75, 96,

96–97, 98, 136, 166, 183, 259, 260, 288, 360, 362, 461, 485, 501, 561–562, 688, 694, 725, 754, 1261, 1273, 1324, 1385, 1550, 1870
biographical information, 1918
Interchurch World Movement (IWM), 658
Iowa, 661
Iran (Persia), 662
Jews, 671
Mayes, Charles W., 804
McClain, Alva J., 772, 773
"Message of the Brethren Ministry," 817
Mexico, IN, Brethren Church, pastor, 821
Miller, John Allen, 839
missions, 861
Moody Bible Institute, 872
Morrill, KS, (First) Brethren Church, 876
O'Neal, Glenn, 2236
papers of, 2312
Philadelphia, PA, First Brethren Church, pastor, 1015
Portis, KS, Grace Brethren Church, pastor, 1048
prophecy conferences, 1062
Roann, IN, (First) Brethren Church, pastor, 1112
Seal Beach, CA, Grace Brethren Church, 1161
Bauman, Lydia (later Yearout), 1384
Bauman, Martin H., 1870
Bauman, Mary Melissa Wageman, **97–98,** 1187, 1360, 1550
Bauman, Nancy Carol Landes, 1870
Bauman, Paul R., **98,** 136, 137, 757, 1221, 1255, 1550
Bauman, Retta Virginia Stover, 97
Bauman, Roy Groff, 1870, 1924
Bauman, Salome, 1870
Bauman(n), Samuel (1788–1820), **99,** 2064
Bauman, Sarah, 1870
Bauman, Sarah I, 98
Bauman, William J. H., 96, 98, **98,** 209, 425, 581, 682, 1550
McLouth, KS, Brethren Church, elder, 779
Morrill, KS, Church of the Brethren, 876
Morrill, KS, (First) Brethren Church, 876
Mulvane, KS, Brethren Church, pastor, 896
South Haven Brethren Church, KS, elder, 1205
Bauman, Wesley, 2312
Bauman, Wesley Allen, 2272
Baumann, Christian (1755–1815), 98
Baumann family, *See* Bowman family
Baumann, Hans, 99
Baumann, Joseph, 595, 1067
Baumann, Kathaina Kühlwein, 925
Baumann, Margaret (Fahnestock), 98, 99
Baumann, Mary (Pitzer), 98
Baumann, Mattheis, 720
New Born, 925
prophecy, 1062
Baumann, Mattheis (Matthias), **98–99**
Baumann, Roland M., 1858
Baumann, Sarah Fahnestock, 98

Baumann, Susannah Eckstein Weaver, 99
Baumann, Wendel, 99, 2058
Baumbaugh, J. S., 1550
Baumberger family, *See* Bomberger family
Baumgardner family, 262
Baumgarten, Siegmund Jacob, 1871
Baumgartner, Samuel Henry, 1871
Bauserman, Elizabeth (later Glick), 553
Bausman, Lottie M., 1858
Bausser, Esther, 170
Bausser, Mathias, 170
Baustian (Bastjan), Joachim, 1871
Baustian, Doris Jean, 1871
Bautts, Paul, 867
Bautz, C. M., 1550
Bautz, Friedrich Wilhelm, 2350
Baxter, Mary L. (later Mow), 890, 891
Baxter, S. S., 2086
Bay Creek Old German Baptist Brethren Church, MO, **99**
Bay, Jacob, 1146
Bayer, Archie S., 42, 1139, 1550
Bayer (Boyer), Christian, 170
Bayer family, 1955, *See also* Boyer family
Bayer, Frank, 2312
Bayer, John N., 42, 1550
Bayer, Julia (later Benedict), 2135
Bayer, Lloyd, 1139, 1550, 2272
Bayer, Michael C., 720, 1550
Bayer (Boyer), Samuel, 170
Bayer (Boyer), Solomon, 170
Bayles, Gordon C., 2272
Baynard, C. M., 1003
Bayne, David, 2272
Baynes, Melissa, 1871
Bayview Church of the Brethren, Portland, TX, 1948
Bazett, Barbara, 2265
Bazza, Nigeria, 306
BBT, *See* Brethren Benefit Trust
BCA, *See* Brethren Colleges Abroad
BCF, *See* Brethren Charity Fund
BCS, *See* Brethren Community Service
Bdlia, Bitrus A., 2312, 2313
Bdliya, Ishaku Borama, 1550
Beabes, Lona (later Norris), 2299
Beabes, Newton E., 1550
Beach, Dennis, 720, 754, 843, 1550
Beach, Gregory Allen, 2272
Beach, Guy K., 1550
Beach, Richard C., 1871
Beachdale Church of the Brethren, Berlin, PA, **99,** 121, 531, 791, 1139, 1314
Beachdale meetinghouse, Schmaltz Thal, PA, 99
Beachey, Joel C., 1871
Beachey, Jonas, 1550
Beachler, Albert, 281
Beachler family, 2239
Beachler, Lowell H., *509,* 1871, 2313
Beachler, Mable (Garber), 99
Beachler, William A., 476, 823
Beachler, William H., **99–100,** 102, 366, 505, 823, 1550
Beachley (Buchele, Beeghley, Beeghly) family, **225,** 1234, 1873, 2313
Beachley, H. J., 1550
Beachley, Jacob, 1550
Beachley, Ronald DeVon, 1550
Beachy, Albert D., 1871
Beachy, Anna Helmuth, 1871
Beachy, Catherine, 2078
Beachy, David Jacob, 2106

Beachy, Elizabeth Yoder, 1923
Beachy, Ida, 1923
Beachy, Marie Agnes (later Miller), 2016
Beachy, Nettie (later Gingerich), 1871, 1949
Beachy, Noah Edward, 2106
Beachy, Rosa Bontrager, 1871
Beachy, Samuel J., 1923
Beachy, Tillie M., 1871
Beacon Heights Church of the Brethren, Fort Wayne, IN, **503,** 504, 1917–1918
Beagle family, 1172
Beagle, Eli, 347, 1550
Beagle, Howard J., 1551
Beagle, John P., 1551
Beahm, Abraham (1788–1847), 101
Beahm, Anna (later Mow) *See Mow,* Anna Beahm
Beahm, Anne Elizabeth Showalter, 100, 101
Beahm, Annie Ruth (later Whitacre), 1339
Beahm, B. C., 1551
Beahm, Barbara (later Wine), 1349
Beahm, C. Isaiah, 101
Beahm, Christian, 167
Beahm, E. Russell, 733
Beahm, Ella (later Arnold), 56
Beahm, Esther Mae Eisenbise, 100, 1833, 1871
Beahm, Eugene Russell, 1551, 2299
Beahm family, **101,** 226, 411
Rittenhouse family, related to, 1111
Scherffig family, related to, 1152
Beahm, George W., 1551
Beahm, Henry Abraham, 43, 100, 101, 1551
Beahm, Isaac Newton Harvey, 100, *100,* 101, 140, 164, *207,* 269, 299, 360, 462, 471, 591, 731, 768, 912, 1336, 1551, 1871, 1915
Elizabethtown College, 437
Hebron Seminary founder, 939
The Little Man (Davis family), 748
Montebello Church of the Brethren, VA, moderator, 871
Mount Horeb Church of the Brethren, VA, 882
Mow, Anna Beahm, father of, 890
Pine Ridge Church of the Brethren, VA and, 2238
sermons on Jubilee Journey, **1168**
train travel, 1271
Beahm, Jacob, 1551
Beahm, Jacob (John), 101, 2025
Beahm, James Henry, 737, 793, 1551, 1871
Beahm, James (Joseph) Charles, 164, 1551
Beahm, Kate (Kagy), 101
Beahm, Martha Ellen, 2165, 2272
Beahm, Mary Bucher, 100, 890
Beahm, Mary Elizabeth Baughman, 101
Beahm, Samuel P., 43, 1551
Beahm, Sister Anna (later Mow), 2201
Beahm, Wilbur Isaac, 1551
Beahm, William Edward, 226, 548, 1551
Beahm, William McKinley, 13, **100–101,** 101 box, 126, 139, 190, 226, 912, 1389, 1551, 1833, 1871, 1917, 1936, 2062, **2135**
prayer, writings on, 1051
spelling changed from William A., **2371**
student volunteer movement, 1231

Beahm's Chapel, VA, Mount Zion Church of the Brethren, 888
Beal, Asa, 101
Beal family, 994, 1929
Beal, Ida, 101
Beal, Jesse, 1551
Beal, John Calvin, **101**, 192, 490, 562, 563, 585, 912, 1062, 1212, 1240, 1322, 1365, 1551
Beal, Mary (Trapp), 101
Beal, Pearl (Miller), 101
Beal, Stewart, 1551
Bealman, George W., 1551
Beals, Samuel West, 1035, 1551
Beam, Aaron Rudolph, 1871
Beam, Annette Huffaker, 1335
Beam, Bill, 1311
Beam, Christopher Isaiah, 1551
Beam, Clark Stanley, 1551
Beam, E. G., 1551
Beam family, 280, 700, 2100
Beam, Fred David, 1551
Beam, J. T., 1871
Beam, J. W. C., 1551
Beam, James W., 1551
Beam, Joseph C., 1551
Beam, Lucinda (later Swihart), 1245
Beam, Nicholas E., 2272
Beam, Stan, 1019
Beamsville mission point, Oakland Church of the Brethren, OH, 957
Bean, Clark S., 102, 558
Bean, E. G., 558, 881
Bean, Eartha, 102
Bean, Eugene H., 1871
Bean, Nathan, 101
Bean Settlement, WV, congregations, **101**, 106, 1397
Bean, William John, 1551
Bean, William M., 1551
Beanblossom, D. W., 1551
Beanblossom, George, 638, 1551
Beanblossom, Ira, 1551
Beans Chapel Church of the Brethren, WV (Indian Camp), **101–102**
Bear, Amelia (later Baker), 547
Bear, David, 1551
Bear, George, 1551
Bear, John
    Golden Spring German Baptist Brethren Church, NE, 2374
    Revolutionary War, 1994
Bear (Bare), John, 1551
Bear, Robert Bruce, 1868
Bear, Sam, 1135
Bear, Walter Scott, 1871–1872
Bear Creek, IL, 1234, 1288
    Brethren Church, **102**
    Church of the Brethren, **102**
    Miller, John William, 2223
Bear Creek, IN, Portland Church of the Brethren, 1048
Bear Creek, MD
    Accident, MD, Bear Creek Church of the Brethren, **2**
    Pine Grove Church of the Brethren, 1024
Bear Creek, OH, 165, 208, 220, 283, 367, 491, 1267, 1276, 1303, 1320, 1355
    Brethren Church, 78, 98, 930, 995
    Church of the Brethren, **102**, 2222
    Garver, Daniel M., 532

Miamisburg, OH, Brethren Church, 823
Miller, Donald Eugene, 2222
Miller, Jacob, organizing, 838
Old German Baptist Brethren, **102**, 967
Patterson, Roy A, 995
Scheublein, Isaac and Christian, 1178
Bear Creek, OK, Antelope Valley (Black Bear) Church of the Brethren, **40**, 448, 869
Bear Creek, PA, 1295
Bear family, 1871–1872
Bear Lake, MI, congregations, 317, 1389
Bear Meadow, PA, 1215
Bear Run Church of the Brethren, PA, **102**
Beard, Catherine (later Pfoutz), 1015
Beard, David R., 1551
Beard family, 663
Beard, Jonathan, 793, 1551
Beard, T. K., 1321
Bearden, A. Edith, 1351
Bearden, Evert, 1351
beards, **102–103**, 400, 2075, *See also* hair and hairstyles
    Bible Brethren, 135
    Brethren in Christ, 189
    Dunkard Brethren and nonconformity, 940
    hairstyle, 579
    Old German Baptist Brethren, 2233
    Old German Baptist Brethren and nonconformity, 941
    Old German Baptist Brethren men, 967
    personal appearance, 1010
    simple life, 1183
    symbolism of, 2147
Bearinger, Carolyn (later Dowdy), 820, 1848
Bearinger, Charles, 1551, 1872
Bearinger, Elaine de Fontes, 1319, 1847
Bearinger, Ernest Harry, 114, 1551, 1847, 1319, 2139, 2299
Bearinger, Eunice Marie, 1851
Bearinger, N. M., 2007
Beasher family, *See* Bashor family
Beashor, Mary (later Rothrock), 1124
Beashore family, *See* Bashor family
Beasley, Kyle, 2173
Beatitudes, 2002, *See also* Sermon on the Mount
Beatrice, NE, Church of the Brethren, **103–104**, 248, 268, 920
Beatty, Charles A., 1551, 2299
Beatty family, 1927
Beatty, James C., 758, 1551
Beauman, J. H., 1551
Beaumont, CA, 1247
    Cherry Valley Grace Brethren Church, 104
    Grace Brethren Church, 2211
Beaver, Adam, 1551
Beaver, Anna Baker, 104
Beaver, C. J., 1551
Beaver, IA, Church of the Brethren, **104**
Beaver City, NE
    Brethren Church, history of, 1913
    Grace Brethren congregation, **107**, 921
    Somerset Grace Brethren Church, **104**
Beaver Co., PA, Harmony Society, 584
Beaver Creek, IN, congregations, 228, **228**
Beaver Creek, MD, 756
    Church of the Brethren, 40, 42, **104**, 2371

Fahrney-Keedy Chapel Fellowship Church of the Brethren, MD, 467
fiction, references in, 2083
Hagerstown, MD, Church of the Brethren, 578
Katy of Catoctin: Or, the Chain-Breakers (Townsend), 747
Scheublein, Uhli and Elizabeth (probably), 1178
Beaver Creek, NE, Church of the Brethren, **104–105**
Beaver Creek, OH, congregations, 363, 365, 1255, 1277, 1399
Beaver Creek, SC, congregations, **105**, 210, 797, 1204, 1312
Beaver Creek, TN, Church of the Brethren, 79, **105**, 704
Beaver Creek, VA, congregations, 206, 208, 341, 354, 1301, 1318, 1262, 1263
    125 year anniversary, 1974
    Elk Run Church of the Brethren, 439
    Floyd Co. Church of the Brethren, 21, **105**
    Glick, Jacob Daniel, 553
    Highland Co. Mission Church of the Brethren, VA, 605
    Hiner Church of the Brethren, VA, 607
    Montezuma Church of the Brethren, VA, 871
    Moscow Church of the Brethren, VA, 878
    Mount Bethel Church of the Brethren, VA, 880
    North Fork Church of the Brethren, WV, 947
    Rockingham Co. Church of the Brethren, **105**
Beaver Creek, WI, Old German Baptist Brethren Church, **105**, 321
Beaver Creek, WV, congregation, 354
Beaver Dam, IN, Church of the Brethren, **106**, 821
Beaver Dam, MD, congregations, 362, 383, 752, 1221, 1298, 1389, 2135
    Church of the Brethren, **105–106**
    Garber (Garver, Gerber) family, 530
    Garber (Gerber), John H., 529
    historical materials, 1872
    Maryland Brethren, 798
    migration of Brethren, 829
    Monrovia, MD, Bush Creek Church of the Brethren, 870
    Old German Baptist Brethren, 967
    Old German Baptist Brethren Church, **106**
    Pfoutz, Isaac, elder-in-charge, 1015
    Rocky Ridge, MD, Monocacy Church of the Brethren, 1119
    Rupp (Roop) family, 1130
Beaver, Dorothy Mae Wolf, 1847, 2134
Beaver family, 1872, 1972
    Schultz, Martin, related to, 1156
Beaver, Frederick Philip, 1872
Beaver, IA, Church of the Brethren, **104**
Beaver, Irvin M., 1872
Beaver, Isaiah, 1551
Beaver, John, 104
Beaver, John Lawshe, 1551
Beaver, Mary (Royer), 104
Beaver, Oliver J., 582, 1551
    Morrill Church of the Brethren, MN, elder, 877
Beaver, Peter Horlacher, **104**, 369,

1551–1552, 1872, 1915
Beaver, R. Pierce, 1872
Beaver Run Church of the Brethren, WV
(Tunker Society), 57, 58, 101, **106,**
1249
Harness Run Church of the Brethren,
WV, 585
Old Furnace Church of the Brethren,
WV, 966
Beaver Run, WV, congregation (GBB, CB),
274, 1336
Beaver, Samuel Wayne, 755, 1552, 1847,
2134
GROW '73, 2194
works by, 2313
Beaver, Spencer S., 1552
Beaver, Will H., 1552
Beavercreek, OH, Church of the Brethren,
See Xenia, OH, Beaver Creek
Church of the Brethren
Beavers family, 2077
Beaverton, MI, congregations, **106–107,**
323, 826
Beaverton, OR, Walker Road Grace
Brethren Church, **106**
Beazley, George G., Jr., 1872
Bebb, Lillie, 1091
Bebb, Perry, 1091
Beble, James W., 1552
Bechner, Clyde S., 2299
Bechtel (Bechtol, Bechtold) family, **107,**
1882, 1957
encyclopedia, 1914
Minerva, OH, Grace Brethren Church,
843
Bechtel, Jackson, 596
Bechtel, Jacob (1765-1844), 107
Bechtel, Jacob (m. Susan Rhoads), 107
Bechtel, Jacob (son of Samuel), 107
Bechtel, John George, 1948
Bechtel, Kenneth Clyde, 1552
Bechtel, Lenora, 2133
Bechtel, Lois, 1839
Bechtel, Lola (later Helser), 305, 596, 2374
Bechtel, Martha Hess, 596
Bechtel, Martin, 107
Bechtel, Oscar H., 1552
Bechtel, Polly Sickman, 107
Bechtel, Porter, Sr., 2133
Bechtel, Samuel, 107
Bechtel, Veronica Casimir, 107
Bechtelheimer (Bechtelhimer), Boyd, 1552
Bechtelheimer, David, 106, 1552
Bechtelheimer, Samuel H., 1552
Bechtelsheimer (Beckleshammer), Johann,
107, 1552
Bechtelsheimer, John, 726
Bechtelsheimer (Bechleshammer), Margaret
(later Laschet), 726
Bechtl, Susannah, 2345
Bechtle, Bertha B. (later Flory), 499
Bechtol, Enos, 347
Bechtol, Mrs. Enos, 347
Bechtol family, *See* Bechtel family
Bechtol, John Leroy, 1552
Bechtold family, *See* Bechtel family
Bechtold, Paul F., 7, 1552, 1872
Beck, August, 1552, 1872
Beck, Bill, 2313
Beck, Daniel, 1872
Beck, David, 1872
Beck family, 572, 1872
Beck, Frank, 1552

Beck, Imogene Zook, 1872
Beck, Jacob, 1213, 1552
Beck, Jesse McFall, 1872
Beck, John, 1872
Beck, Jonas, 1552
Beck, Justin G., 2272
Beck, Katherine, 1872
Beck, Margaret L., 1872
Beck, Thaddeus Stevens, 235, 912
Beck, William M., 1552
Beckel, Kenneth E., 2272
Becker, Albert, 1872
Becker, Allan (Allen), 1552
Becker, Anna Dorothea Partmann, 107, **107,**
108
Becker, Augustine Peter, 553, 1242, 1552
Becker, Christian J., 122, 948, 2272
Becker, Connie (later Cashman), 2156
Becker, Elizabeth (later Stump), 1232
Becker family, 1872, 1952, 2097, *See also*
Baker family
Mesa, AZ, Community Church of the
Brethren, 2222
sources on, 2311
tombstone inscriptions, 1937
Becker, Henry, Sr., 882
Becker, Henry T., 1552
Becker, J. G. Burman, 1872
Becker, John H., 1552
Becker, Leah B., 1872
Becker, Mary (later Harly), 583
Becker, Paul R., 2222
Becker, Peter, 78, 82, 107, **107–108,** 112,
175, 225, 242, 258, 381, 383, 392,
407, 443, 477, 508, 528, 569, 576,
583, 611, 618, 704, 707, 1552,
1872, 2097
article about, 1921
baptisms by, 722
biography, 1938
contacted by Urner, Martin, 1298
descendants, 1232
Durnbaugh, Donald F. on, 2326
grave, *107*
historiography, 2201
Holtzapfel (Holsapple, Holsopple),
Johann Heinrich, 623
hymns by, 1933
Leola, PA, Conestoga Church of the
Brethren, 737
Mack, Alexander, Sr., 776, 777
Mack, Johann Valentin, 778
Marienborn, and religious freedom,
792
Martin, George Adam, 1194
migration to America, 1232
ministry, 844
missions, 857
Mohrsville Church of the Brethren, PA,
869
ordination of Christopher Sauer II and
Alexander Mack Jr., 1146
In Our Own Strength (Eller), 748
Pennsylvania settlement, 1004
Peter Becker Community, 1010
Philadelphia, PA, Germantown Church
of the Brethren, elder, 1016
play about, 1928
poetry and hymns, 1039
Preiß (Price) family, 1055
publishing, 1063
Quakertown, PA, First Church of the
Brethren, 1075

Reiff family, 1094
Ritter, Daniel, migrating to Pennsyl-
vania with, 1111
Skippack area, PA, 1189
Stauffer, Abram, ordained by, 1220
Traut family, 1270–1271
Becker, Ruth S., 1872
Becker, Wendell, 228
Beckerath, Gerhard von, 1872
Beckham Co., OK, Elk City Church of the
Brethren, 438
Beckler family, 2078
Beckler, Mary Ann, 2078
Beckleshammer (Bechtelsheimer), Johann,
107, 1552
Beckley family, 515
Beckman, Abraham, 1552
Beckman, Everett Gladstone, 1552
Beckman, Vernon R., 1552
Becknell, Harriett E. (later Rowsey), 1127
Beckner, Benjamin Elias, 990, 991, 1552
Beckner, Bessie Flory, 108
Beckner, Clyde S., 511, 1025, 1552, 2299,
2380
Beckner, Edward L., 1552
Beckner, Edwin L., 1552
Beckner, Eleanor, 157
Beckner family
Botetourt Co., VA, 1872
Howard Co. Old German Baptist
Brethren Church, IN, 633
Beckner, G. S., 1552
Beckner, Henry, 264
Beckner, Mrs. Henry, 264
Beckner, John E., 511, 1033, 1552
Beckner, Josiah L., 990, 1552, 2299, 2380
Beckner, Laurence (Lorenz), 1552
Beckner, Lucinda Bashor, 108
Beckner, Mary (later Hess), 601
Beckner, Mary (later Slabaugh), 1189
Beckner, Perry, 108, 1340, 1552, 2374
Beckner, Samuel O., 676, 1012, 1552
Beckner School, Lakeview, MI, 179
Beckner, Silva (Miller), 108
Beckner, William Abram, 511, 1552
Beckner, William Everett, 1872
Beckner, William Oliver, **108,** 1552
Beckwith, Carl Clinton, 198, 1552, 1833
Beckwith, Carrie Belle Lewis, 1833
Beckwith family, 996
Beckwith, James Merle, 1552
Beckwith, T. Judson, **108–109,** *109,* 251,
946
Bedächtliches Antwortschreiben, 1872
Bedel, Luther, 1552
Bedford Co., PA, 145, 146, 170, 216, 229,
274, 380, 410, 461, 685, 697, 706,
724, 740, 1294, 1347, 1384, 2084
bibliographical sources, 1878
Brethren Church congregations, 1005
Church of the Brethren, **109**
Church of the Brethren history, thesis
on, 1917
Diehl family, 1917
Fairview Brethren Church, PA, 468
German Seventh-Day Baptists, 542
history, 1967
history and genealogy, 1989
Holsinger Church of the Brethren, PA,
623
Hopewell Grace Brethren Church, PA,
629
Jeters Chapel Church of the Brethren,

VA, 670
migration of Brethren, 827
Paul family in, 996
Pennsylvania Brethren settlement, 1004
Raven Run Church of the Brethren,
PA, 1083
Replogle family, 1100
Snake Spring Valley Church of the
Brethren, PA, 1192
Snake Valley Old German Baptist
Brethren Church, PA, 1192
Sollenberger family, 1202
Bedford Co., VA, 237
Antioch Church of the Brethren, **43**
Gillaspie, VA, Oak Grove Brethren
Church, 548
National Park Service projects, 917
Saunders Grove Church of the
Brethren, VA, 1150
Bedillion family, 1320
Bedinger family, 1878
Bedminster Twp., Bucks Co., PA, 1911
Beebe family, 871
Beeber family, 1872
Beech Grove, IN, congregations
Church of the Brethren, 2031
Church of the Brethren at Stony Creek,
45, **109**
becomes Noblesville, IN, Church of the
Brethren, 938
Sugar Creek congregation formed out
of, 1234
Old German Baptist Brethren, **109,**
2249
Beech Grove, OH, Church of the Brethren,
109, 1295, 1333
historical materials, 1873
Paradise Church of the Brethren,
divided from, 992
West Branch Church of the Brethren,
OH, 1333
Beech Run, PA, Church of the Brethren, 71,
109–110
Beecher City, IL, Kaskaskia Church of the
Brethren near, 684
Beecher, Henry Ward, 1151
Beechley, H., 1552
beef as food at Lord's Supper, 757–758, 764
Beeghley, Anna M. Hirt, 2134
Beeghley, Benjamin, 274
Beeghley, Charles W., 2134, 2272
Beeghley, Christena, 2134
Beeghley, Daniel, 2134
Beeghley, Dorothy (Graham), 110
Beeghley, Emanuel, 1143
Beeghley, Ethel Kinzie, 2134
Beeghley, Ezra J., 110
Beeghley (Beeghly, Buchele, Beachly)
family, **225**, 1234, 1873, 2313
Beeghley, Ida Jane (Foft), 110
Beeghley (Buchley), Jeremiah, 1552
Beeghley, John, 1346, 1552
Beeghley, John A., 1552
Beeghley, John W., 1552, **2134**
Beeghley, Marian Fife, 2134
Beeghley, Martin, 1552
Beeghley, Mary, 1143
Beeghley, Milford, **110**
Beeghley, Morris E., 1552
Beeghly, Ananias J., 519, 1219, 1337, 1552
Beeghly, Benjamin, 430, 1552
Beeghly Church, OH, mission point, 790
Beeghly, Cora Gnagy, 1219

Beeghly, Elizabeth, 375
Beeghly, Elizabeth (later Fleure), 495
Beeghly (Beeghley, Buchele, Beachly)
family, **225**, 1234, 1873, 2313
Beeghly, Floyd F., 1552
Beeghly, Gladys (later Klotz), 1681
Beeghly, Jacob, Jr., 2, 1552
Beeghly, Jacob, Sr., 1552
Beeghly, James W., 1552
Beeghly, Jeremiah, 2, 273, 790
Beeghly, John, 2, 7, 495, 1552
Beeghly (Buechly), John, 1080
Beeghly, John W., 1552
Beeghly, Leon, 7
Beeghly (Buechley), Michael Joshua, 1553
Beeghly, Ruth (later Statler), 748, 1219
Beeghly, S. A., 1553
Beeghly (Beeghley), Samuel Boyd, 1553
Beeghly, Susanna (later Forney), 466, 1873
Beeghly, Susannah Fleure, 495
Beeghly, Wilbert G., 1873, 2313
Beegle, Mary Myers, 1873
Beegley, Morris, 874
Beeker (Becker), G(eorge) S., 1553
Beekley, Charles E., 269, 1553
Beekley, Eugene J., 252, 1553
Beekley, Ruth (later Lyon), 768
Beekly, Ezra, 1553
Beelman, Adam, 1553
Beelman, Adam B., 1553
Beelman, D. E., 1553
Beelman, George W., 1553
Beelman, Henry, 1553
Beeman, Steven Edward, 2272
beer, *See* alcoholic beverages
Beer, Abraham, 1873
Beer, Catherine Wampler, 110
Beer, Christian, 1907
Beer, Eliza (later Wampler), 1317, 1381
Beer family, 411, 1036
Beer, Hanna Elizabeth Henegan, 110
Beer, J. Harvey, 137, 129, 376, 1118, 1359
Beer, J. W., 215, 720, 1265, 2039
Holsinger, Henry Ritz, 622
Mulvane, KS, Brethren Church, pastor,
896
The Pious Youth, editor, 1025
Reconstruction Committee, 1086
Beer, Jacob Harvey, 110, 1553
Beer, Jacob Wampler, 110, 1138, 1205,
1553
Beer, Joseph W., 67, 102, **110**, *110,* 186,
350, 469, 1553, 1873
Nickerson, KS, Church of the Brethren,
elder in, 936
The Progressive Christian, 1061
publishing, 1068
Salem (Community) Church of the
Brethren, elder in, 936
Beer, Peter, 274, 872, 1118, 1553
Beer, Solomon, 350
Beers, Ernie, 1134
Beers, J. W., 2332
Beers, John Landis, 1994
Beers, Pearl, 1134
Beers, William, 793
Beery, Abraham, 2095
Beery, Adaline Hohf, **110–111**, 111, 556,
643, 1361, 1873
Beery, C. O., 513
Beery, Catherine or Cassie (later Van
Dyke), 630, 952, 1302, 1361, 1798
Beery, Charles O., 21, 798, 1108, 1553

Beery, Cleo C., 1553
Beery, Daniel, 111, 1953
Beery, Daniel M., 2232, 2272
Beery, Elizabeth, 380
Beery, Elizabeth (Bucher), 110
Beery, Elizabeth (later Snell), 1193
Beery, Ella (later Wagoner), 1312
Beery, Emma Jane (later Gregg), 1953
Beery, Enoch, 111, 1302
Beery (Bieri) family, **112**, 149, 731, 1221,
1873, 1943, 2095
Beery, Fanny Good, 111
Beery, George S. M., 1553
Beery, Harvey D., 111
Beery, Helen H., 2272
Beery, Hiram, 269
Beery, Ida Heisey, 111
Beery, Isaac R., 1553
Beery, Jacob D., 1553
Beery, Jesse C., **111**, 1553, 1873
Beery, John H., 1553, 2272
Beery, Joseph E., 1953
Beery, Judith (later Garber), 1873
Beery, Karen Diane, 1836
Beery, Lawrence W., **111**, 137, 626, 1553,
1873
Beery, Magdalena (later Hunsaker), 637
Beery, Margaret Ganger, 111
Beery, Mary Hatfield, 111, 1302
Beery, Mary (later Stump), 2127–2128
Beery, Matthew Lee, 2272
Beery, Meda Coppock, 111
Beery, Michael, 110
Beery, Neil L., 106, 585, 1048, 1553, 2299
Beery, Nettie Mary (later Jackson), 1953
Beery, Nicholas, 1873, 2095
Beery, Noah V., 24, 1553
Beery, Paul H., 1181
Beery, Perry Hunsicker, 445, 654, 722,
1553
Beery, Robert, 949
Beery, Salem, 1553
Beery, Solomon, 1873
Beery, William, *111,* **111–112**, 112, 560,
1858, 1873, 1945
Brethren music, 899
hymnals, 642
hymns, 643
singing schools, 1185
Beery, William A., 1553
Beeson, Joseph, 2272
Begerow, Joanna (later Hoffman), 2202
"Beggarstown," PA, 2377
Beghtol, Catherine Bruner, 1957
Beghtol, Peter, 1957
Beghtol, Polly Bruner, 1957
Beghtol, Sarah Ann Evans, 1957
Behmenism, 2082
Behmer, Clara Mae (later Frantz), 1940
Behrendt, Eleanore Friederika, 1846
Beidelman, William, 1873
Beidler, Emmanuel, 1553
Beidler, Paul, 280
Beier family, Pennsylvania records of, 1955
Beiler family, 1276
Beiler, Joseph B., 1873
Beisel/Beissel family, 2313
Beissel, James D., Sr., 2313
Beissel, Johann (Georg) Conrad (Konrad),
88, 98, 107, 108, **112–113**, 121,
156, 175, 266, 291, 332, 379, 381,
417, 421, 422, 686, 687, 704, 722,
736, 910, 1232, 1292, 1553, 1874,

1879, 1880, 1882, 1891, 1939, 1947, 1952, 1986, 2029, 2035, 2081, 2090, 2102, 2111, 2371
article about, 1913
Baumann, Mattheis and, 925
Bautz, Friedrich Wilhelm on, 2350
biography of, 290, 2093, 2105
birthplace, *112*
Doktor Faustus (Mann), 747
Eicher, Anna and Maria, 431
Eicher, Daniel, 431
Eicher, Jakob Christian, 431
encyclopedia entry for, 1874
Ephrata Cloister, 1977
Ephrata Community, 448, 451
Erb, Peter C. on, 2330
Fahnestock, William M., 465
Falckner's Swamp, 470
fictional character influenced by, 2006
Frantz, Michael, 508
French Creek, 516
Frey, Andreas, 517
frontier, 519
funeral, description of, 2103
Gass (Gast), Jakob, 532
German Seventh-Day Baptists, 542
Gesäng der einsamen und verlassenen Turtel-Taube, Das (*The Songs of the Lonely and Forsaken Turtledove*), 546
Grove's Dictionary of Music and Musicians, entry for, 1948
Hackett, Lucile Eleanor on, 2335
Heidelberg, 593
Hildebrand, Johannes, 606
historiography, 2201
Höhn, Heinrich, 618
hymnals, 1874
Judaism, 677
Karst, Theodor on, 2339
Kilian, Oskar on, 2340
Kuhn, Gertrud on, 2342
Leola, PA, Conestoga Church of the Brethren, 737
list of works, 1957
Mack, Alexander, Sr., leadership disputes, 777
marriage, 795
Martin, George Adam, 797
Mäyle, Johann, 804
Melton, J. Gordon on, 2346
Miller, John Peter, 840
Mohr, Jacob, Sr., 869
Moyer, Walton Z. on, 2348
music, 1874, 1970, 1974
mystic poet, 2003
Old German Baptist Brethren and charismatic movement, 970
Pennsylvania Brethren settlement, 1004
Plagge, Andreas on, 2350
prayer, 1051
prophecy, 1062
publishing, 1067
Pullen, Elizabeth on Eros and androgyny in mysticism of, 2351
Radical German Pietism, 1080
references to, 1913, 1919, 1956
research regarding, 1970
Richman, Irwin on, 2352
Sabbath observance, influenced by Seventh-Day Baptists, 1133
Sangmeister, Heinrich (Ezechiel), conflict with, 1144

Sauer, Maria Christina Gross, follower of, 1147, 1148
Schneider, Hans on, 2355
Seventh-Day Baptists, 1170
singing at Ephrata, 1184
Snow Hill Community, 1194, 1195
Society of the Woman in the Wilderness, 1200
sources for his ideas, 113
sources on, 2316, 2320
Taylor, Eugene on, 2360
theology of love, 761
Tussing, Ann K. U. on, 2361
Wohlfahrt (Welfare), Michael, supported by, 1355
works by, 2310
writings of, 1873
Yoder, Russell on confidential writings of, 2364
Zionitischer Weyrauchs Hügel (*Zionitic Hill of Incense*), 1400
Belair, MD, 755
Belcher, David B., 715
Belcher family, 1134
Belcher, Hazel Irene, 1847
Belcher, Joseph, 1874
Belcher, Willis G., 1553
Belém, Brazil, 172
Belgian Congo, 573
Belgic Confession (1561), 55
Belgium, **113**
    Kruger, Helena, 708
    prisoner of war camps, 199
    relief and rehabilitation work in, 200
    relief and social work, 303
Belida, Patricia Ann Reber, 1085
The Beliefs of the Early Brethren 1706–1735 (Willoughby), 2143
believer's baptism, 31, 87, 107
    Ephrata Community, 448
Believers' Church, 5, **113–114**, 304, 1259, 2063, *See also* Anabaptism and Anabaptists; sects
    Brethren, and Roman Catholic Church, 1120
    Brethren movement, 292
    Canada, 2108
    Christian education movement, 284
    Commentary Series, **2134–2135**
    Committee on Interchurch Relations, 2167
    conference, 1970, 2006
    Durnbaugh, Donald F. on perspectives of Lord's Supper by, 2325, 2326
    education, 425
    Eller, David B. on, 2329
    infant baptism, 655
    Johns, Loren on eschatology of, 2339
    Jubilee: God's Good News Curriculum, 2209, 2210
    Lutheran-Believers' Church dialogue, 71
    Mennonites, 816
    millenialism, 834
    ministry, 845
    mutual aid, 901
    nonconformity, 940
    pluralistic society, in, 1998
    prophecy, 1062
    Reformation, Protestant, and Brethren doctrine, 1092
    religious liberty, 1098
    Restoration Movement, 1101

sect-church typology, 1275
sermons, 1168
Sojourners Fellowship, 1200
sources on, 2318, 2322
theology and, 2255
trinity, doctrine of, 1275
worship and, 2266
worship patterns derived from, 1373
Belknap, The Reverend, *See* Oiness, Sylvia Marie
Bell, Albert D., 1874
Bell, Bertha May, 52, **114,** 501, 1847
Bell, C. C., 1553
Bell, CA, Brethren Church (FGBC, Gage Avenue), **114**
Bell Co., KY, Ewing Church of the Brethrn, VA, 2373
Bell Creek Church of the Brethren, NE, **115**
Bell Creek, NE, congregations
    migration of Brethren, 830
    origins of, 920
Bell, David Owen, 2272
Bell, Eliza Ann, 114
Bell, Eugene G., 2272
Bell family, 1215, 1885
    North English, IA, Church of the Brethren, 947
    Prosser, WA, Community Grace Brethren Church, 1062
Bell, Fanny (Walker), 114
Bell, G. K. A., 422
Bell, Helen, 2093
Bell, J., 1553
Bell, Leah K. (Sprinkel), 114
Bell, P. G., 1874
Bell, Raymond Martin, 1874
Bell, Richard E., 360, 948, 1553
Bell, William Spencer, 65, **114,** 241, 366, 1240, 1321, 1348, 1553
    Johnstown, PA, First Brethren Church, 673
    Mount Pleasant, PA, Brethren Church, 886
    prophecy conferences, 1062
Bell Whifield J., Jr., 1874
Bell, William G., 114
Bella Vista Church of the Brethren, Los Angeles, CA, **758**
Bellah, Robert N., 314
Bellefontaine, OH, congregations, 287, 693
    Church of the Brethren, **115**
    Gretna Brethren Church, 693, 694
    request for Temperance and Purity Committee, 1252
Belleville, KS, congregations, **115,** 727, 765, 1305, 1345
Belleville, OH, 286
Bellevue mission, Central African Republic Bible Institute, 2134
    Sheldon, Chauncey Burt, missionary, 1175
    Sheldon, Hattie Louise Cope, missionary, 1175
Bellevue, Oubangui-Chari, 141
Bellflower, CA, Brethren Church, 110, **115,** 2244
bells
    Church of the Brethren, 301
    discouraged at annual meeting, 1376
    East Fairview Church of the Brethren, PA, 415
    on horses, 60, **115**
    on meetinghouses, 48, 59, **115**

simple life, 1183
Bellville, OH, Ankenytown Grace Brethren Church, *See* Ankenytown, OH, Grace Brethren Church
Bellwood, PA, congregations, 20, **115**, 1347
Belmont Co., OH, 935
Belmont, VA, Church of the Brethren, **115–116**
Belohlavek, Robert A., 2272
Belote, Dyoll, **116**, 186, 195, 562, 746, 1289, 1346, 1553
The Brethren Pastor's Handbook, 788
Rosedale, PA, Brethren Church, pastor, 1122
Belser, Julius Harry, Jr., 1553
Belser, Vernon, 1553
Belsterling, Donald Lee, 2272
Belvedere, CA, congregations, 758, 759
Belvidere Church of the Brethren, York, PA, **1387–1388**
Belz, Helga, 1874
BEM (Baptism, Eucharist, and Ministry), CB response to, **2133–2134**
Bemenderfer (Bemendorfer), A. R., 410, 439, 931, 1036, 1553
Bemenderfer (Bemendorfer) family, 1893
Bement, IL, Church of the Brethren, **116**
Bemis mission point, Glady, WV, Church of the Brethren, 551
Ben Co., AR, 1215
Benad, Matthias, 2313
Benalcazar, Leanna Fay Koontz, 1833
Bend Chapel, VA, Green Hill Church of the Brethren, **569–570**, 1011
Bender, Carrie, 2313
Bender, Courtney, 2313
Bender family, 547
Bender, Fannie, 2107
Bender, Gertrude Mae Gingerich, 1874
Bender, Harold S., 29, **116**, 1275, 1858, 1874, 1961
Keim, Albert N. on, 2340
Mennonites, 816
Reba Place Fellowship, 1084
Bender, Henry, 1554
Bender, Laura (later Fisher), 492
Bender, Magdelena, 151
Bender, Wilbur J., 1874, 2313
Bender, Wilhelm, 1874
Bendes, Mark Steven, 1554
Bendon, MI, 179
Bendsen, Maren Christine (later Esbensen), 1837, 2387
Bendsen, N. P., 1875
Bendson, Victor Chresten, 157, 505, 1162, 1342, 1554, 2299
Benedict, Daniel M., 471, 1554
Benedict, David, 106, 577, 1875
Benedict, David G., 471, 1554
Benedict, Elwyn Ellsworth, 1875
Benedict, Evelyn Hess, 2135
Benedict, Ezra G., 1554, 2135
Benedict family, 778, 1875
Benedict, Fred W., 612, 973, 1875, 2143, 2313
Benedict, Harry Good., 42, 106, 721, 1554, 2299, **2135**
Benedict, Henry Marvin, 1875
Benedict, Irvin P., 1554
Benedict, James L., 2272
Benedict, John Dunkel, 396, 471, 1554
Benedict, Julia Bayer, 2135
Benedict, Lee H., 142, 1385, 1554

Benedict, Lizzie Wingert, 2135
Benedict, Mark H., 42, 731, 1554
Benedict, Reva C., 1875
Benedict, Willis P., 109, 826, 1554, 2376
Benedict, Zella, 161
Benedictine monks, 28
benefits, emergency and retirement, 155, *See also* pensions
Benesh, Gary L., 2272
Benevento, Tom, 2314
Benevolent Board of the Brethren Church, **116**, 181, 182, 693
Kimmel, Joseph L., 693
King, Lester Vernon, 695
Retirement Board, 1102
Benezet, Anthony, **117**, 1875, 2077
Bengel, Johann Albrecht, 348
Bengtson, Eugene Harold, 1554
Benjamin, Renate L., 1858, 2309
Benjamin, Steven M., 1858, 2309
Benner family, 1939
Benner, Levi B., 257, 1554
Benner, Michael S., 2272
Bennet, J(ames) M., 1554
Bennetch, Paul Crouse, 1875
Bennett, Allen Lee, **117**, 136, 1554, 1847
Bennett, Bruce Earl, 1554
Bennett, Conway E., 1554
Bennett, David H., 1554
Bennett, David I., 1554
Bennett, Dennis, 272
Bennett, Eliza (later Trout), 1276
Bennett family, 886
Bennett, Isaac Lee, 272, 1554
Bennett, James A., 676
Bennett, James Y., 1554
Bennett, John, 62, 1554
Bennett, Joseph, 62
Bennett, Keith, 171
Bennett, Leonard S., 1084, 1554, 2299
Bennett, Orpha (later Whitacre), 1339
Bennett, Phillip Keith, 1554
Bennett, Philo Kent, 1554, 1875
Bennett, Rachel, 62
Bennett, Sadie (later Morse), 878
Bennett, Salley, 1345
Bennett, Sylvester, 1034
Bennett, Vernon Lester, 1554
Benneville, George de, **117**, 1292, 1874, 1875, 1979, 2081, 2100
Benshof, Barbara (Wisehart), 118
Benshof, Paul, 118
Benshoff, Barbara (Wisehart), 117
Benshoff, Benjamin, 117, **117**
Benshoff, Catherine (Snyder), 117
Benshoff, David E., 2272
Benshoff, Eli, 118, 1554
Benshoff family, **118**
Benshoff, Floyd S., 190
Benshoff Hill, PA, 1944
Benshoff, Kenneth, 1875
Benshoff, Lois V. (later Hess), 2198
Benshoff, Paul, 117
Benshoff, Sara Blanche (St. Clair), 117, 118
Benshoff, Solomon, **117**, 118, 675, 843, 1554
Benshoff, William Crofford, 20, 102, **117**, 118, 319, 759, 1324, 1554
Miamisburg, OH, Brethren Church, pastor, 823
Mount Zion Brethren Church, OH, minister, 888
New Lebanon, OH, First Brethren

Church, pastor in, 930
Benshoff, William St. Clair, **118**, 186, 1554, 2371, 2380
Benshoof family, 1875
Benson Co., ND
Flora Church of the Brethren, 496
Pleasant Valley Church of the Brethren, 1035
Benson, Cynda L., 2314
Benson, Evelyn Abraham, 1875
Benson, Horace, 1875
Benson, Jane, 1875
Benson, Max Eugene, 1554
Bent Co., CO, 322, 1345
Benton Co., IA
Garrison, IA, Church of the Brethren, 531
Garrison Old German Baptist Brethren Church, IA, 531
Benton Co., MO, 1212, 1280
Benton, George, 1554
Benton, Homer S., 1554
Benton, Orpha (later Rhoades), 2242
Bentz, Fred, 674
Bentz, John (Mr. and Mrs.), 578
Bentzel, Paul W., 2272
Benz, Ernst, 1875, 2314
Benzie Co., MI, Homestead Church of the Brethren, 626
Benzie, Mark, 739
Benzie, Mark J., 2299
Beougher family, 2067
Berachah meetinghouse, Glenford, OH, 553
Berchtol (Becktel), Susanna (later Miller), 895
Berea, NC, congregations, 224
Church of the Brethren, **118**
Fundamental Brethren Church, 522
Berea, VA congregation, 1305, 1308
Berean Bible School, **118**, 137
Eshelman, Matthew Mays, 455
Lehmer, Solomon G., 736
mission point for Los Angeles, CA, First Church of the Brethren, 759
training for mission work, 1297
Berean Dunkard Brethren congregation, Dayton, VA, **367–368**, 553
Berg, Elsie (later Matula), 1554, 1704
Berg, Elton, 1554
Berg, Jakob, 720
Berg, Ralph F., 1554
Bergen, John J., 1554
Berger, A., 1554
Berger family, 515, 700
Berger, Jacob, 632
Berger, Joseph, 347, 1554
Berger, Matthias, 1554
Bergerson, Charles Byron, 496, 1554
Bergey, Lorna L., 1875
Bergin, George, 1554
Bergson, Henri, and Modernism, 866
Bergsten, Gunilla, 2314
Bergstresser, P., 1869
Bergyold, Esther Snavely, 2094
Bergyold, Michael, 2094
Beriguete, Angelica, 2215
Berka family, 1304
Berke, Merlin, 974
Berkebile, Aaron J., 1243, 1554
Berkebile, Adam, 1554
Berkebile, Andrew, 119
Berkebile, Andrew II, 119
Berkebile, C. E., 1555

Berkebile, David, 118, 1243, 1555
Berkebile, David Garfield, 109, 558, *795,* 1243, 1555
Berkebile (Berkeybile), David J., 1555
Berkebile, Effie, *795*
Berkebile family (Berkeybile, Berkebill, Perkepile), **118,** 332, 708, 752, 1193, 1243
Berkebile, Jacob II, 119
Berkebile, James M., 1555
Berkebile, Nora E. Flory, 118, *119,* 1833, 1875
Berkebile, Paul, 588
Berkebile, R. K., 1555
Berkebile, Roberta Hartsough, 588
Berkebile, Sarah (Stutzman), 118
Berkebile, Stephen, 505
Berkebile, Stephen Peter, 118, *119,* 1225, 1555, 1833
Berkebile, Walter F., 267, 1118, 1555
Berkebill, *See* entries at Berkebile
Berkeley Co., SC, 321, 425
Berkeley Co., VA, 1154
Berkeley Co., WV, Church of the Brethren, **119,** 735
   Allensville, WV, Church of the Brethren, 2126
   Fellowship Church of the Brethren, WV, 482
   Johnsontown Church of the Brethren, WV, 675, 2126
   Martinsburg, WV, Moler Avenue Church of the Brethren, 798
   Mountain View Church of the Brethren, WV, 889
Berkeley's Mills meetinghouse, PA, 1139
Berkemer, C. Fred, 1206, 1554
Berkey, Andrew S., 1876
Berkey, Byron Jay, 1555
Berkey Church of the Brethren, PA, **119**
Berkey congregation, PA, 1348
Berkey, Corey A., 2272
Berkey, D. R., 1555
Berkey, Daniel, 119, 1170
Berkey, David, 955
Berkey, Earl, 496
Berkey, Elizabeth Poorman, 119
Berkey, Elsie, 496
Berkey family (Birkey, Burki), **119,** 152, 1170, 1875, 1878
   Howard Co. Old German Baptist Brethren Church, IN, 633
   Peabody Old German Baptist Brethren Church, KS, 997
   sources on, 2314
Berkey, Foster, 558, 1555
Berkey, Isaac L., 265, 1555
Berkey, Jacob, **119,** 447, 1255, 1267, 1346, 1555
   migration of Brethren, 830
   Pleasant Valley Church of the Brethren, IN, 1034
   Rock Run Church of the Brethren, IN, minister, 1117
Berkey, John, 119, 1555
Berkey, Joseph, 119, 1555
Berkey, Lennie Martin, 1875
Berkey, Merlin D., 13, 119, 503, 1555
Berkey, Peter, 558
Berkey, Randy, 1875
Berkey, Ruth (later Reichly), 2314
Berkey, S. J., 1555
Berkey, Samuel, 1555

Berkey, Sarah Lint, 119
Berkey, William Albert, 2314
Berkeybile, Aaron, 1280, 1555
Berkeybile family, *See* Berkebile family
Berkeybile, Richard E., 1280, 1555
Berkeybile, W. C., 1555
Berkin (Birkin), Leonard, 79, 1559
Berkley, Albert U., 1555
Berkley Co., VA, 1192
Berkley, Cornelius, 1555
Berkley, Eliza (later Myers), 905
Berkley family, 267, 490
Berkley, John, 347, 1322
Berkley, John, Jr., 1139, 1555
Berkley, Jonathan, 1555
Berkley, Josiah, 1555
Berkley, Norman William, 1555
Berkley, Peter, 1555
Berkley, Richard Wayne, 2272
Berkley, Samuel J., 632, 1555
Berkman, D. G., 1281, 1555
Berkman, Hiram, 870, 1555
Berks Co., PA, 144, 170, 247, 456, 697, 699, 700, 737, 750, 1233, 1237, 1293, 1320, 1328, 1397, 1401, 2074
   Baumann, Mattheis, residence, 925
   Dietrich family, 1917
   Frantz family, 1940
   Frystown, PA, Bethel Dunkard Brethren Congregation, 521
   Gaube (Gaby), Martin, 532
   Heckman family, 593
   Hertzler (Hartzler) family, 601
   Mohrsville Church of the Brethren, PA, 869
   Oley Valley annals, 1912
   Pennsylvania Dunkard Brethren, 1005
   Pennsylvania settlement, 1004
   Reading, PA, First Church of the Brethren, 1084
Berkshire, Charles, 1555
Berkshire, H. Francis, 1251, 1285, 1555
Berkshire, J. Edgar, 1555
Berkshire, W. Clayton, 801, 856, 1251
Berkshire, William Clayton, 1555
Berleberg castle, 1354
Berleberg, Ernst Casimir, count of, 1354
Berleburg Bible, 19, 57, **120–121,** 138, 1354, 2100
   article about, 1942
   Haug, Johann Friedrich, 589
   Philadelphian Society, 1019
   Sauer, Christopher I, 1148
   Sauer German Bibles, 1149
   Seebach, Christoph, 1165
Berleburg, Casimir, count of, 1274
Berleburg, Germany, **120,** 385, 684
   court printer, 706
   Geistliche Fama (Spritiual Report), 533
   Haug, Johann Friedrich, 589
   history (trans), 1966
   Hochmann von Hochenau, Ernst Christoph, 614
   publishing in, 1063
   refuge for separatists, 1158
   separatism in, 2100
Berlin College (Brethren High School, Berlin, PA), **187**
Berlin Committee, 67, 121
   Holsinger, disfellowship of, 1151
   Holsinger, Henry Ritz, 622

   Miller, Howard, 838
   Wise, John, 1354
Berlin, Germany
   Christliches Hand-Büchlein (Christian Handbook), 288
   Spener, Philipp Jakob, 1209
Berlin (Kitchener), Canada, 250
Berlin, PA, 144, 151, 214, 703, 733, 1276, 1338, 1339, 2059
   Beachdale Church of the Brethren, **99,** 121, 531, 791, 1139, 1314
   Berlin meetinghouse, 99
   Brethren Church, **121,** 2249
   Brethren High School, **187**
   Holsinger, H. R., elder, 1005
   Holsinger, Henry Ritz, 621
   large congregations in Pennsylvania, 1005
   Meyersdale, PA, Main Street Brethren Church, 823
Berlin Wall, 546
Berlincourt, Catharine, 2078
Bermudian congregations, PA, 736
   cemetery, 2084
   German Seventh-Day Baptist Brethren, **121,** 141, 1403–1405
   Lower Conewago Church of the Brethren, PA, 765
   Martin, George Adam, 141, 797, 1194
Bern, Switzerland, 151, 231, 697
   galley slaves, 253
   Liebe, Christian, 741
   religions, suppression of, 2084
   Wenger family, 1330
   Ziegler, Philip, 2109
Bernard, Claude, 1555
Bernard of Clairvaux, 1259
Berne, IN
   Bethel Brethren Church, **121,** 2217
   Christ's Assembly and, 280
   Grace Bible Church, 2217
   Holsinger, Henry Ritz, 622
Bernese Anabaptists, **121–122**
   Brethren movement condemnation of, 174
   Estates General or States General, 456
   galleys, 527
Bernhard family, 348
Bernhard, H. Fred, *547,* 1555
Bernhard, Howard W., 670, 882, 1555
Bernhart, John N., 1555
Berrien Co., IN, Portage Prairie Church of the Brethren, 1047
Berrien Springs, MI, congregations
   Church of the Brethren, **122**
   Michigan Brethren settlement, 824
Berry, Brian J. L., 2314
Berry, Cleon, 264
Berry, Emma, 298, 1299
Berry family, 1213
Berry, George, 298, 1299
Berry, I. R., 1124
Berry, June Carol, 1850
Berry, N. V., 1555
Berry, Thomas, 1340, 1555
Bert, Norman A., 1876
Berthelsdorf, Oberlausitz, 1399
Berthold, Arthur Benedict, 1876
Berthold Church of the Brethren, ND, 122
Bertolet, Daniel, 1211
Berwyn, PA, Paoli Immanuel Church of the Brethren, **122**
Besher, Beshor, Beshore, Beshoar, *See*

entries at Bashor
Besher, George, 93
Besher, Jacob, 93
Beshor (Beasore), J. R., 1555–1556
Beshor, Christine (Alderfer), 123
Beshore, Sarah (later Myers), 903
Der Besiegte Wiedertäufer (*The Conquered Anabaptist;* 1788), 31
Bess, S. Herbert, 275, 1010, 1270, 1556, 2299
Bessao, Chad
    Harrell, Richard, 270
    Kliever, Freda, 270
    Kliever, Jacob, 270
Besse, Clair, 69
Besse, G. Henry, 69, 1556
Besse, Lynn, 69
Bessler, Andrew, 1556
Bessler family, 1277
Best, David, 914
Best, Jane Evans, 2314, 2334
Best, Randall A., 1556, 1876
Best, William T., family of, 1347
Bestor, Arthur E., 1876
Bet Emet (House of Truth), 191
Beta Hall, Grace Theological Seminary, Grace College, 564
Bethabara settlement, NC, 1311
Bethania, Ephrata Community, *122, 123,* 1004
Bethania, NC, 946, 1311
Bethany Academy for Ministerial Leadership, 2224
Bethany Academy for Ministry Training, 2140
Bethany Bible School, *See* Bethany Theological Seminary
Bethany Bible Seminary, *See* Bethany Theological Seminary
Bethany Bible Training School, *See* Bethany Training School
Bethany Biblical Seminary, *See* Bethany Theological Seminary
Bethany Brethren Church, Hamlin, KS, 32, 98, **581**, 773
Bethany Brethren Church, VA, **123**
Bethany Brethren Community Center, construction of, 2136
Bethany Brethren Hospital, **123–124**, 275, 305, 1876, **2136**
    article about, 1944–1945
    Association of Brethren Caregivers (ABC), 2132
    Bowman, Curtis Buford, 165
    Cable, William H., 2155
    fellowship houses, 482
    Fike, Earle William, Jr., 2184
    Frantz, Ira Henry, 508
    Garver, Earl S., 532
    Garver, Earl Simeon, 2187
    Helstern, Mary Sue on, 2353
    hospitals, 630
    Long, Harvey Lawrence, 754
    Neher, Minneva Josephine at, 922
    Nickey, Barbara Marie, as physician missionary, 936
    Nurses' Training School, 220, 359, 952, 1230, 1276
    Rosenberger, Mary Sue Helstern on, 2353
    social welfare, 1198
    Weaver, Clyde E. (CB) and, 2260
    Weiand, Albert Cassel, 1344

wellness, concept of, 2261
    Wine, Laura M., 1349
Bethany Church of the Brethren, CO, 124
Bethany Church of the Brethren, DE (Farmington), 374, 1957
Bethany Church of the Brethren, Detroit, MI, **380**
Bethany Church of the Brethren, IN, **124**
Bethany Church of the Brethren, MO (Pleasant View), **124**
Bethany Church of the Brethren, ND, **124**
Bethany Church of the Brethren, OH, **124**
Bethany Church of the Brethren, OK (Jennings), **670**
Bethany Church of the Brethren, PA (Philadelphia), 91, **1015**
Bethany Church of the Brethren, VA, 43, **124**, 130
Bethany Church of the Brethren, WV
    Greenbrier Co., **125**
    Taylor Co., **124–125**
Bethany College
    Campbell, Alexander, 247
    Christner, David C., 289
Bethany congregation, IN, 1338
Bethany congregations as example of biblically inspired name, 911
Bethany Hospital, *See* Bethany Brethren Hospital
Bethany, IL, 713
Bethany, IN, 1246, 1280
    Dunkard Brethren Church, 2097
    Milford, IN, Bethel Church of the Brethren, 831
    pioneer boyhood in, 2097
    Pleasant View Chapel Church of the Brethren, IN, 1036
Bethany meetinghouse, Greenmount Church of the Brethren, VA, 571
Bethany meetinghouse, Ladoga, IN, Church of the Brethren, 717
Bethany mission, Philadelphia, PA, 1296
Bethany, MO, congregations, 1118, 1314
Bethany Seminary, *See* Bethany Theological Seminary
Bethany Theological Seminary, 24, 25, 123, **125–127**, 399, 428, 535, 693, 696, 697, 1155, 1876, 2036, 2042, 2056, 2060, **2136**, *2136*
    affiliation with Mennonite Biblical Seminary, 126
    area surrounding, medical care for, 952
    article about, 1954
    assistance to prisoners, 78
    Bethany Brethren Hospital, 810
    Bieber, Charles M., 2137
    Blough, Anna Viola, 149
    Blough, Silas S., 151
    board membership, and regions, 1094
    Bomberger, Harold Zug, 2138
    Bosler, Billy M., 2161
    Bowman, Curtis Buford, 165
    Bowman, James Brubaker, 167
    Bowman, Merle Allen, 167
    Bowman, Rufus David, 168–169
    Bowman, Samuel Loren, 169
    Bowman, Warren Daniel, 169
    Brandt, Harry Alonzo, 171
    Breidenstine, Aaron Gibble, 173
    Brethren Academy for Ministerial Leadership, 2139–2140
    Brethren archives at, 52
    Brethren Life and Thought, 190, 191

Bright, Jacob Homer, 208
Bright, Minnie Flory, 209
Brightbill, Alvin Franz, 209
Brooks, Harlan, 212
Brown, Dale Weaver, 2152
Brown, Kenneth L., 179
Brubaker, Leland Stanford, 217–218
Brumbaugh, Wilbur Eugene, 223
Buchanan, MI, Church of the Brethren, leadership from, 225
Bucher, Rufus Pfautz, 225, 2372
Buckingham, Minnie Susan, 226
Butterbaugh, Andrew G., 236
Butterbaugh, Bertha Belle Lehman, 236
Cable, William H., 2155
camping movement, 248
Cassel Library, PA, 260
and Chicago Cluster of Theolgocial Schools, 126
Chicago, IL, Douglas Park Church of the Brethren, 275
Chinese immigrants, 278
Christian Catholic (Apostolic) Church, ministers and, 282
Christian Education Commission (CB), 285
Christian education movement, 284
Church of the Brethren, 300, 303
Committee on Higher Education (CB), 327–328
Cooper, Herbert Austin, 342
Cottrell, Asher Raymond, 345
Cripe, Winifred E., 352
CROP, offices and, 286
Crystal, MI, Church of the Brethren, 355
D. W. Kurtz, *710*
development of, 137
Dolby, Mattie Cunningham, 2128
East Chippewa Church of the Brethren, OH, 415
Ebbert, Ella, 417
Education for a Shared Ministry (EFSM), 429, 993
Eisenbise, Forest Sard, 432
Eller, Vernard M., 2176
Ellis, Charles Calvert, 441
Elrod, James H., 442
Evangelical Covenant Church, 460
faculty of (ca. 1920s), *127*
faith and order, 470
Faw, Chalmer Ernest, 480
fellowship houses, 482
field education, 251
Fike, Earle William, Jr., 2184
Fike, Paul Henry, 2184
Flory, Ezra, 498
Flory, John Samuel, 499
Flory, Lizzie Mae Neher and Raymond Chester, 499
Flory, Wendell Phillips, 2185
founding of, 275
Frantz, Ira Henry, 508
fraternal relations, 510
fundamentalism, 522
Funderburg, Drue Dresher, 523
Germany, 546
Gibbel, Henry Royer, 547
Grisso, Lillian Etna, 574
Groff (Grove) family, 574
Groff, Warren Frederick, 2194
group dynamics, 575

Hanawalt, David Kirk, 581
Hanover, PA, Church of the Brethren, 582
Harley, Samuel Abraham, 583
Harper, Clara Belle, 585
Harsh, Alva Carlton, 587
at Hastings St., *125,* 127
Heckman, Benjamin Franklin, 591
Heckman, Clarence C., 592
Heckman, Jacob Hugh, 592
Heckman, Minna Mote, 592
Helman, Patricia Kennedy, 2197
higher education, 605
Hilton, Blanche Cover, 606
Hilton, George William, 607
historical libraries, 610
historical societies, 610
history, 1996
Hoff, Emanuel Buechley, 616
Hoff, Ernest Gockley, 617
Hoff, Ida Wagner, 1361
Hoffman, Paul W., 2202
homelessness, 2203
hospitals, 630
Huston Memorial Peace Lectures, 638
Huston, Ora Ivan, 638
Hutchison, Anna Martha, 639
Illinois, 647
influence of New York Theological Seminary on, 138
information technology, church use of, 2208
interest in archaeology, 46
Jarboe, John Edwin, 669, *1257*
Jewish evangelism, 671
Keller, Harvey and J. E., 686
Keller, Paul W., 2210
Kimmel, Theodore Acroyd, 693
Kinsey, William, 696
Kiracofe, Anna Kathryn, 697
Kurtz, Daniel Webster, 711
Lauver, George Myers, 728
Lear, John Wallace, 732
Leatherman, Irvin D., 732
Lehman, Galen T., 736
library, history of, 1961
Lichty, Anna Eby, 741
Long, John Daniel, 2215
Long, W. Newton, 754
Mallott, Floyd Ellwood, 784
marriage counseling, 796
mass media, 801
Mathis, Jefferson H., 803
Metzger, Minerva, 819
Metzler, Burton, 820
Michigan City, IN, Church of the Brethren, students serving, 824
Miller, Daniel Long, 836
Miller, DeWitt L., 836
Miller, Donald Eugene, 2222
ministry in the Church of the Brethren, 2224
Minnich, Herbert Spenser, 848
minorities, ethnic and racial, 850
missions, 859
Montgomery, IL, Boulder Hill Neighborhood Church of the Brethren, 872
Moody Bible Institute, 872
Moomaw, Ira Wilbur, 874
Moore, James Milton, 874
Morrill, KS, Church of the Brethren, 876–877

Morris, James Henry, 877
Morse, Kenneth Ivan, 878
Moss, Loring Isaac, 878
motion pictures, courses on, 879
Mow, Anetta Cordula, 890, 891
Mow, Anna Beahm, 890
Mow, Baxter Merrill, 891
Moy Gwong Han, 891
Moyer, Elgin Sylvester, 872, 892
Moyer, Naomi Ann Holderread, 892
Mshelbila, Mamadu K., 307
Neff, Robert Wilbur, 2230
Neher, Medford D. at, 922
Neher, Minneva Josephine at, 922
Nicarry, Wayne A., 2231
Nickey, Barbara Marie, as student in, 936
Baptist Seminary, cooperation with, 304
Oak Brook, IL, 51, 126
Ogden, Galen Brown, 139, 961
peace education, 1002
peace witness, 2008
Pereira, Onaldo Alves, 2139
Peters, Raymond Russell, 1011
Pfaltzgraff, Roy Edward, 1013
Prather, John Perry, 1051
prison ministries, *1059,* 1060
prison worship service, *1059*
professional ministry for Church of the Brethren, 1136
Putney, VT, Genesis Church of the Brethren and, 2239
Rainey, Nellie Morgan, 1083
relocation of, 305, 2162
Rieman, T. Wayne, 1388
Robertson, Russell L., 1114
Robinson, John Amos, 1115
Robinson, Paul Minnich, president, 1115
Rohrer, Perry Lawrence, 1088, 1119
Roman Catholic seminaries, cooperation with, 1120
Roop, Eugene F., 1130
Rothrock, Edgar Eli, 1124
Royer, Byron P., 1127
Royer, Harold Albertus ("Red"), 1128
Rufus D. Bowman Chapel (1950), 51
Satvedi, Govindji, 1145
Schaeffer, Mary Ann, 1152
Scholten, Marian Aetna Rinehart, 1154–1155
Schrock, Mark Y., 1156
Schwalm, Vernon Franklin, 1157
Shamberger, Chauncey, 1171
Sherfy, Robert Livingston (CB) and, 2249
Shickel, Elsie Naomi, 1176
Shisler, Sara Cassel, 1177
Shull, Chalmer George, 1180
Shull, Mary Ruth Speicher, 1180
Shull, Susan Lavinia Stoner, 1180
Slabaugh, Warren William, 1189
Smeltzer, Ralph Emerson, 1190
Snider, Donald Mitchell, 1193
sources on, 2314
Stahly, Cora Miller as head of music department, 1216
Statler, Foster Boyd, 1219
Steele, Lafayette, 1220
Stover, Wilbur Brenner, 1226
Studebaker, Ellis M., 1230
students working as train conductors,

717
Sunday school teacher training, 1239
supplied mission workers in Chicago, IL, 1296
Swartz, Goldie Elizabeth, 1243
theological education, 1257
theological study conference (1964), 1258
ties with Chicago Theological Seminary, 1290
Trostle, Eva Alora, 1276
Utz, Ruth Earl, 1299
Van Buren St., 125, *126*
Van Dyke, Catherine Beery, 1302
Van Dyke, George Henry, 1302
Wampler, Elizabeth Baker, 1316
Wampler, Guy Edgar, Sr., 1317
Warstler, Anna Margaret, 1319
Weaver, Mahlon J., 1324
Weiss, Edgar Lorell, 1328
West, Daniel, 1330
West, Murray Guy, 1332
Whisler, Ezra Leroy, 1338
White, Ralph Emerson, 1339
White, Roy Irvin, 1339
Wieand, Albert Cassel, 279, 1344
Wieand, David John, 1344
Will, Harper S., 1345
women and, 2264
women students, *1360*
York Center, IL, Church of the Brethren, students active in, 1389
Zeigler, Carl Wenger (CB) and, 2269
Zeller, Harry Knode, Jr., 1395
Ziegler, Edward Krusen, 1395
Ziegler, Jesse H., 1395, 1397
Zigler, Earl Myers, 1397
Zigler, Michael Robert, 1398
Zunkel, Charles Edward, 1402
Zunkel, Cleda Pearl Shull, 1402
Bethany Training School, 126, **127–128**
Bollinger, Russell V., 158
Brethren Academy for Ministerial Leadership, **2139–2140**
Brightbill, Alvin Franz, 209
Helman, Alfred Blair, 2197
Mow, Anna Beahm, 890
Pfaltzgraff, Violet Hackman, 1013
Bethany, WV, 1033, 1136
Bethaus (chapel) at Kedar, Ephrata Community, 686
Bethel Brethren Church, AR (Pennington), 54, 1004
Bethel Brethren Church, IN (Berne) (FGBC), **121**
Bethel Brethren Church, IN (Osceola), 983
Bethel Brethren Church, KS (Mulvane), 2, 377, **895–896**, 2194
Bethel Brethren Church, MI (Cassopolis), 260
Bethel Brethren Church, OH (Glenford), 553
Bethel, CA, congregation, 280
Bethel Center Church of the Brethren, IN, 124, **128**, 587
Bethel Church of the Brethren, CO, **128**
Bethel Church of the Brethren, IL (Naperville), 517, 736, 913, 1339, 1867, 2036
Bethel Church of the Brethren, IN (Milford), **831**, 1036, 1099
Bethel Church of the Brethren, KS, **128**
Bethel Church of the Brethren, MO, 945,

1204
Bethel Church of the Brethren, NC, **128**
Bethel Church of the Brethren, NE, **128,**
1865, 1919
Bethel Church of the Brethren, OH (New
Middleton), 782, 931
Bethel Church of the Brethren, OK
(Griggs), **573**
Bethel Church of the Brethren, PA, **129**
Bethel Church of the Brethren, TX (San
Antonio), 1141
Bethel Church of the Brethren, VA
Fairview-Endless Caverns, 470
Ferrum, **488**
Mayland, 2028
Nelson Co., **129,** 768
Rockingham Co., **129,** 1291
Bethel Church of the Brethren, WV
Grant Co., **129**
Hardy Co., 106, **129**
Bethel Church, shared building for Seneca
Church of the Brethren, OH, 1166
Bethel College, 1278
Bethel congregation, IN, 1280
Bethel congregation, MN (Guthrie), 576,
848
Bethel congregation, NJ, 1142, 1287
Bethel congregation, OH, 1400
Bethel congregations as example of bibli-
cally inspired name, 911
Bethel Dunkard Brethren congregation,
Frystown PA, **521**
Bethel Fellowship, Pleasant Valley Church
of the Brethren, TN, 1035
Bethel German Baptist Brethren Church,
IN, **129**
Bethel German Baptist Brethren Church,
NJ, 28, **129**
Bethel Grace Brethren Church, Osceola, IN,
948, 983–984
Bethel Hódum, Denmark, *376,* 456
Bethel, IL, congregation, 151
Bethel, IN, congregation, 373, 932
Bethel, KS, mission point, 1078
Bethel Mahoning congegation, New
Middleton, OH, 931
Bethel, MD, congregation, 376, 1025
Bethel meetinghouse
Glenford, OH, Brethren Church, 553
Greenmount Church of the Brethren,
VA, 571
Ladoga, IN, Church of the Brethren,
717
Linville Creek Church of the Brethren,
VA, 746
Yellow Creek Church of the Brethren,
PA, 384
Bethel, MN, 576, 848
Bethel, MO, North Bethel Church of the
Brethren, 945
Bethel, NE, congregation
Fillmore Co., origins of, 920
migration of Brethren, 830
Thayer Co., origins of, 920
Bethel, NJ, congregation, origins of, 929
Bethel, PA
Dunkard Brethren Church, 418
Rockton, Church of the Brethren,
preaching point of, 1118
Bethel, VA, 164, 321
Bethel, WV, congregations, 949, 1341
Bethesda Brethren Church, OH, **129–130**
Bethesda Church of the Brethren, VA, 152

Bethesda. MD, Church of the Brethren,
2136
Laughlin Church, 2214
Maple Grove Church, mission point of,
790
Bethesda, VA, 164, 321
Bethlehem Brethren Church, Harrisonburg,
VA, **586**
Bethlehem Brethren Church, IL (Milledge-
ville), 833
Bethlehem Brethren Church, VA, 751
Bethlehem Church of the Brethren, VA,
124, **130**
Franklin Co. Church of the Brethren,
VA, 507
history of, 2103
Bethlehem meetinghouse, Germantown
Brick Church of the Brethren, VA,
544
Bethlehem, PA, congregations, 1216, 1243
Harleysville, PA, Indian Creek Church
of the Brethren, 584
Hispanic Ministries (CB), 2199
Lehigh Valley Grace Brethren Church,
130
Bethlehem, VA, congregations, 163,
Monte Vista Church of the Brethren,
VA, 871
New Bethel Church of the Brethren,
ministers for, 925
Red Hill Church of the Brethren, VA,
1088
Betoney, Arnold, 2272
Betoney, Nelson, 1267, 1556
Betsy (ship), 741
Betts, David, 1556
Betts family, 951
Betts, Issac F., 1556
Oak Grove Church of the Brethren,
OK, minister, 956
Reedley, CA, Church of the Brethren,
elder, 1091
Betts, Jacob F., 956, 1556
Betts, Minnie, 1091
Betts, Nannie, Hammer, 1876
Betz family, 1137
Betz, Israel H., 1876
Betz, Robert W., 1556
Betz, Russell W., 104, 1046, 1556, 2213
Beulah Beach I and II, **2136–2137**
denominational reorganization, 2170
development of Brethren Church vision
and mission, 2141
Beuningen, Conrad von, 1988
Beutler, Kelly J., 2272
Beverage, Josiah, 1263
Beverage, Josiah W., 1556
Beverage, Levi, 1556
Beverage, William, 1263
Beveridge, Jean (later Zielasko), 2269
Beverlin, Ronald Arthur, 672, 1117–1118,
1556
Bey, Jacob, 521
Beydler, Crafton J., 263, 1556
Beyer (Beer), Abraham, 1873, 1988
Beyer family, Pennsylvania records of,
1955
Beyer-Miller family, 2012
Beyerly, Caspar, 2034
Beyreuther, Erich, 1021, 1876
Beza, Theodore, 55
Bhagat, Francis, 1833
Bhagat, Kalidas B., 1556

Bhagat, Nagarji D., 1556
Bhagat, Premchand Ganeshji, *130,* **131,**
650, 853, 1556
Bhagat, Shantilal Premchand, 9, *1131,*
1833, 1876, 1916, 2239, 2272,
2314
Bhagat, Surjanial, 1556
Bhagat, Tsun-Hsien Kwan, 1833
Bhagat, Vahalibai, 131
BHF, *See* Brethren Health Foundation
(BHF)
BHLA, *See* Brethren Historical Library and
Archives
Bhoir, Prabhakar S., 1556
Bhone family, 2097
Bhoney, Andreas, *See* Boni, Andreas
Bhonsale, Doulatrao J., 1556
Bhonsale (Bhousle), Jivanrao, 1556
BHWA, *See* Brethren Health and Welfare
Association
Biancheri, Paul, 1847
Bianchi, Lawrence, 1556
Bibbee, David M., 2272
Bible, **131–135,** 2024, 2029, 2048, 2371,
See also New Testament; Old
Testament; Sauer Bible; specific
gospels and books
archeological mounds and Bible sto-
ries, 2096
authority of, 131, 132–133, 135, 1973,
See also authority of the Bible
Believers Church Commentary Series,
2134
Berleburg Bible, *See* Berleburg Bible
biography of printer of first Bible produced in America, 2055
Brethren Church doctrine on, 183
Brethren movement, 289
canon, Brethren, 133
charismatic movement, 272
children's stories, 150
corporate logo of the Brethren Church,
2146, *2146*
debates, 371
dispensationalism, doctrine of, 390
distribution of, 22
divine inspiration, 132
doctrine of, 2068
Fellowship of Grace Brethren Churches
(FGBC), 486, 487
first Saur Bible, 2051
German concordance, 2036–2037
German language publication,
2097–2098
Germantown Bible of 1743, 2098
God's Means of Grace (Yoder), 555
Grace Schools (Grace Theological
Seminary, Grace College), 563
graveclothes, 566
Great Commission, 568
Halle on the Saale River, 580
Hell, doctrine of, 595
Hertzler, Samuel Hoffer, 600
Hoff, Emanuel Buechley, 616
Hoff, Ernest Gockley, 617
Holy Spirit, doctrine of, 624
Horst, Melvin Clyde, 630
Hoyt, Herman Arthur, 634
Huston, Ora Ivan, 638
Hutchison, Andrew, 639
Indian Bible, Asian, 2104
inerrancy, *See* inerrency of Scripture
inner Word and outer Word, 656

interdenominational study of, 415
interpretations, 134–135
introduction to, 1968
Jews, 671
Jubilee: God's Good News Curriculum, 2210
language, inclusive, 2214
as literature, 435, 1913
Luthy, David on history of North American German, 2344
Martin, Harold S.
    on inerrancy of, 2345
    on reliability of, 2345
meditations on passages from, 2075
message of, 188
"Message of the Brethren Ministry," 817
Miller, John Allen, 839
ministry, 845
Modernism, 866
nuclear arms race, 2232
Parrot, Mary Anne on hymns and songs of, 2349
peace movement, and sanctions for war, 2070
Pietism, basis for, 1021
prescribed dress and, 401
prophecy in, 2312
The Prophetic Age, 2039–2040
publications about, 2108
publications, German language, 2097–2098
Revelation, Book of, 2061
science and, 2022
Sharp, Solomon Z., 2063
sources on, 2317, 2318, 2320, 2323, 2324
study by adults, 1979
study, Rosenberger, Isaac J. writing about, 1123
Theological Practorium, The (CGBCI) and, 2254
theology and, 2254
tradition, devaluation of, 133–134
translations of, 22, 120
truth in Scriptures, 2012
twelve "Apostle" Bibles, 2104
views on, 197
Whitcomb, John C., Jr. on astronomy and, 2363
as the Word of God, 29
worship and, 2266
worship services, 1378
Bible and Prophecy Conferences, *See* prophecy conferences
Bible Brethren Fellowship (Broadfording Bible Brethren Church), 19, **135–136**, 1891, **2372**, *See also* entries at Broadfording
    chart of Brethren bodies, place on, 1403–1405
    Glendora, CA, Church of the Brethren, 553
    Hagerstown, MD, elementary and high schools, 1163
Bible Christian Church, OH, 272
Bible Coach ministry (Argentina), 53
Bible colleges, Church of the Brethren, 300
Bible conferences, **136**
    Evangelistic and Bible Study League (BC), 461
    missionary conferences, 856
    National Brethren Bible Conference,

Winona Lake, IN, 914
    Sebring, FL, J. H. Moore Memorial Church of the Brethren, 1162
Bible Helps, **136**, 1032
Bible Institute, Canton, OH, *252*
Bible Institute of G. W. Kieffaber, *131*
Bible Institute of Los Angeles (BIOLA), 20, 97, 98, **136**, 236, 688
    Altig, Jerome Keith, 136
    Altig, Vivian Carroll Force, 136
    Bauman, Paul R., 136
    Bennett, Allen Lee, 136
    Colborn, Ralph J., 2165
    Fellowship of Grace Brethren Churches (FGBC), 488
    Kent, H. A., Sr., 136
    Kliever, Freda Neufeld, 136, 701
    Kliever, Jacob Paul, 136, 701
    Landrum, Clyde Kermit, 136, 724
    Mayes, Charles W., 804
    McClain, Alva J., 136, 772
    Miller, Robert Paul, 842
    Monroe, Kenneth, 136
    O'Neal, Glenn F., 136
    Overholtzer, J. Irwin, 136
    Penrose, Harold, 136
    Polman, Leo, 1045
    Sheldon, Chauncey Burt, 136, 1175
    Sheldon, Hattie Louise Cope, 136, 1175
    Sickel, Clarence Leroy, 136, 1181
    Sickel, Loree Cutright, 136, 1181
    Stewart, Lyman, 136
    Talbot, Louis T., 136
    Thompson, Robert W. (FGBC) and, 2256
    Torrey, Reuben A., 136
Bible Institute of Pennsylvania, 688, 1220, 1339
Bible Institute of the Chicago Evangelistic Society, 872
Bible institutes, **136–137**
    dispensationalism, 390
    Eden Bible Institute, 424
    Goshen, IN, Grace Brethren Church, *558*
    Mennonite Brethren Churches, General Conference of, 814
    mission schools, 854
    missions, 860
    prophecy conferences, 1062
    Shrewsbury, PA, Church of the Brethren, 1179
    as source of education for ministers, 1257
    Springfield, IL (1906), 1215
Bible, James William, 1556
Bible, John Calvin, 912
Bible lands, travel to, *1272, 1273,* 1274, 2012, *See also* Israel; Middle East; Palestine
    travelogues, 2101
    Weiand, Albert Cassel, 1344
    Winger, Otho and Ida Miller Winger, 1351
The Bible Monitor, **137**, 210, 409, 690, 1384, 1976
    Africa Mission Project, 2128
    Click, Daniel Medford, 321
    Cripe, Glenn A., activities in movement, 352
    Declaration of Principles (DB), 372
    Eshelman, Matthew Mays, 455

historical libraries, 610
Hostetler, Daniel W., 631
Indiana, 653
Kesler, B. E. (publisher and editor), 300, 301
Kreiner (Kriner), Samuel A., 708
Masterson, Benjamin Franklin, writing for, 802
Missouri, 865
Moss, Loring Isaac, 878
Ohio, printed in, 963
publication of, 2175
Root, Isaac William, 2378
Shroyer, Reuben, ariticles written for, 1180
Wallick, Cyrus B., 1314
The Bible Monitor (Dunkard Brethren)
    capital stock provided for promotion, 1289
    poetry, 1039
    Pratt, Eugene W., 1051
    Publication Board, 1063
    published lists of ministers, 1218
    Surbey, Howard J., 1241
    Underhill, Nancy D. Blain, 1286
Bible Monitor Publishing Co., 137
    Moss, Loring Isaac, 878
    official church publishing, 1069
    organization and incorporation, 1289
Bible personages, Brethren children named for, 912
Bible quiz programs
    CE National, Inc., 2156
    National Achievement Competition (NAC), 914
Bible Sabbath (Fahnestock, William M.), 465
Bible schools and training, *See* Bible Teacher Training School
    Bethany Theological Seminary, 2136
    colleges, **137**
    Kulp Bible School, Nigeria, 709–710
    mission schools, 853, 854
Bible societies and ecumenism, 422
The Bible Student, **137**, 1876
    Puterbaugh, Amsey Hascall, articles in, 1072
Bible study
    Brethren Church in Peru and, 2237
    Donnels Creek Church of the Brethren, OH, Bible reading society, 396
    Elyria, OH, Grace Brethren Church, 443
    Men's Work (CB), 816
    People of the Covenant (POC) (BC), 2237
Bible Study Board (DB), **137**, 284, 700, 1237
Bible Study Monthly, 933
Bible Teacher Training School, **137–138**
    Blough, Silas S., 151
    Graybill, Jacob Franklin, 567
    India, *See* Bulsar Bible School
    prayer, 1051
    Wieand, Albert Cassel, 1344
    White, David Clark, 1339
    Widdowson, Sadie Olive, 1343
Bible translations, **138, 139, 2137**, 2253, *See also* language shift
    Authorized King James, 1378
    Kennedy, Matilda Wilhelmina Schwab, 688
    Revised Standard, 1378

worship and, 2266

Bible Truths (McClain), 773, 2002

Bible versions, *See* Bible translations

Bibles
Berleburg, *See* Berleburg Bible
bibliography, 1860
Brethren, 1966
European languages, 1991
gilt edges discouraged, 1376
Mack, Alexander, Sr., belonging to, 777
Nyce, William Godshall, collection of, 952
Sauer, Christopher I, 1148, *1149*
Sauer German Bibles, 1146, 1149, *1149*
Scofield, 1160
Seebach, Christoph, 1165

La Biblia Abierta, 801

biblical interpretation, 55–56, 68

Biblical Review, 773

Biblical Seminary of New York, *See* Bible Teacher Training School

biblically inspired, congregational names, 911

biblicism, 29

Bibliotheca Sacra, 773

Bice, Blair Miller, 1876

Bice family, 1876

Bice, Lucille Bonebreak, 1876

bicentennial celebration, *140,* **140–141,** *141*
Annual Conference, Des Moines IA, *140, 141*
Bicentennial Committee, sources on, 2314
Schwarzenau Brethren movement, 298
Two Centuries of the Church of the Brethren conference, 1282

Bichsel, Johannes, 1878

Bichseler (Bixler, Bicksler) family, 1998

Bickel, Clair E., 768

Bickel, Florence Marguerite N., **141,** 807, 938, 1847

Bickel, Kenneth E., 558

Bicket family, 727

Bickford, Carl, 1556

Bicknell, I. J., 831, 1556

Bicksler, Barbara Peffley, 144

Bicksler (Bichseler, Bixler) family, 1998

Bicksler, Jacob L., 1955

Bicksler, Peter, 144

bicycle, Henry Spickler's travel around the world by, 1273

Biddix, Floyd Nick, 1556

Biddle, William R., 2272

Bidgood Enders, Elizabeth Lynn, 2273

Bidgood Enders, Gregory S., 2273

Bieber, Bonnie, 2137

Bieber, Charles McClellan., 706, 1556, 1876, **2137,** 2201, 2314

Bieber, Dale, 2137

Bieber, Doreen, 2137

Bieber, Edith Seriff, 2137

Bieber family, 1872, 1916, 2074

Bieber, George Albert, 2137

Bieber, Larry, 2137

Bieber-Lescer family, 2074

Bieber, Marla, 2137

Bieber, Mary Elizabeth High, 706, 1834, 2137

Biechler, Doris E. Mylin, 2314

Biedebach, Brian R., 2273

Biederwolf, William E., 1353

Biehl, 148

Bieri, Barbara (Miller), 112

Bieri (Beery) family, **112,** 149, 731, 1221, 1873, 1943, 2095

Bieri, Nicholas, 112, 637, 800

Bievenour, Merle Emory, 1032, 1556

Biever, Dale E., 1876

Biever family, 1872

Big Branch, KY, preaching point, 405

Big Conewago, PA, Church of the Brethren, 121, **141,** 163, 384, 732, 765, 1294
Brethren peace position, 999
Rowland, Gasper, minister, 1126

Big Creek, IL, Church of the Brethren, 1315, 2126, *See also* Walnut Grove Church of the Brethren, IL

Big Creek, KS, congregations
Old German Baptist Brethren Church, **142,** 682
Sheridan Lake Old German Baptist Brethren Church, CO, 1176

Big Creek, OK, Church of the Brethren, **141–142,** 670, 723, 964

Big Dam, PA, congregation organized from Little Swatara congregation, 1157

Big Grove, IA, Church of the Brethren, 531

Big Lake, MN, Church of the Brethren, 872

Big Meeting, *See* Annual Meetings

(Big) Oak Grove Old German Baptist Brethren Church, OH, **142,** 494

Big Raccoon Creek, IN, 717

Big Retreat (FGBC), 2269

Big Run Old German Baptist Brethren Church, OH, **142,** 494

Big Sky Church of the Brethren/American Baptist Church, MT, **142,** 1301

Big Spring, OH, German Baptist Brethren Church, 956

Big Swatara, PA, 458, 737
Church of the Brethren, **142–143**
Dunkard preacher at, reference to, 1956
Etter family, 459
as example of place name, 911
Harrisburg, PA, First Church of the Brethren, 586
Hershey, PA, Spring Creek Church of the Brethren, 599
Hollinger family, 620
Miller, George, preacher, 837
Müller (Miller) family, 894

Bigham, Elva, 275

Bigler, Andrew, 288, 1556

Bigler family, 924, 1897

Bigler, Lydia (later Fahnestock), 465

Bigler, Mark, 1897

Bigler, W. Frank, 1556, 1897

Bigsby, Nina Kagarise, 1876

Bihar, India, work camp at, 1367

Bilatum, Nigeria, 306

Bilderback, Rose, 1854

bilingualism, 471

Bill of Rights, 88

Billheimer family, 520

Billheimer, Isaac, 743, 1556

Billhimer family, 453

Billigmeier, Robert H., 1876

Billman, Mary Maud, 1360, 1876

Billman, Maud, 1187

Billmeyer, Michael, 18, 736, 809, 1067

Billow family, *11*

Bills family, 983

Billy Graham Crusades, *See* Graham, Billy

Billy Sunday Tabernacle, Winona Lake, IN, 1353

Binder, Frederick M., 678

Bindnagel Lutheran church, 2379

Bingaman, Adam L., 1556

Bingaman, Carroll J., 906, 2299

Bingaman, George H., 1556

Bingaman, William, 1556

Bingeman, Hannah, 2070

Biniatoglon, Prodromos, 1556

Bining, Arthur C., 1858

Binkele, Christine (later Frey), 1942

Binkley, Daniel Franklin, 1876

Binkley family, 1224, 1876

Binkley, Newton W., 1556

Binkley, R. K., 1556

Binkley, Timothy Scott Grimm, 2273

Binkley, Walter V., 1556

Binnie, Lester H., 1877, 2314

Binns, Gordon F., 2273

Binns, John, 1067

biographies, 2022
historiography, 2201
Hoff, Ernest G., 1968
Old Order Notes, 973
publishing, 1069
Quinter, James, 2040

BIOLA, *See* Bible Institute of Los Angeles

Birch Tree, MO, Old German Baptist Brethren Church, **99**

Birchfield, E. W., 1556

Birchfield, Ray, 590

Bird-in-Hand meetinghouse, Leola, PA, Conestoga Church of the Brethren, 737

Bird, Lucy (later Weir), 1327

Bird, Michael S., 2314

Bird, Walter, E., 137, 2299

Birdling, Bulama, 1556

Birdville Church of the Brethren, Natrona Heights, PA, 415, **918,** 1027

Birkey, Berneice Barbara (later Naffziger), 2028

Birkey family, *See* Berkey family

Birkey, Margaret (later Oyer), 2034

Birkhead, James A., 1556

Birkhead, James I., 929

Birkin (Berkin), Leonard, 79, 1556

Birmingham, AL, 14, 415
Sun Valley Church of the Brethren, **143**

Birmingham, England, 1290

Birstein Community of the True Inspiration, 330

birth certificates, 2359

birth control, 795

birth rate, trends in, **143**

Bischof, Beatrice Mae King, 204, 1854

Bischof, Robert Paul, 204, 1556, 1854

Biser family, 58

Biser, Jacob, 1556

Biser, M. M., 1556

Biser, Solomon, 1556

Bishard, Dwight, 377

Bishard, Mrs. Dwight, 377

Bishop, Donald Eugene, 688, 1556, 1847

Bishop family, 566

Bishop, Hazel Irene Belcher, 1847

Bishop, James L., 1877

Bishop, Joseph, 749

Bishop, Mary S. (later Moore), 874

Bishop, Nathan, 1556

Bishop, Olga Bernice, 1858, 1877

Bishop, Philip R., 1877

Bishop, Roger, 515

Bishop schoolhouse, OH, used as meeting

house for Sand Ridge Church of the Brethren, 1143
Bishop, Shirley Leigh, 1854
bishops, *See* elders; ministers
   degrees of ministry, 374
   episcopal polity
      government of church, 1041, 1042
      Roman Catholic Church, 1120
   Hertzler (Hartzler) family, 601
   as title, **143**, 432–433
Bismark Grove, KS, 682
Bismark, Otto von, 545
Bissel, Asa E., 1556
Bister, Ulrich, 2315
Bitner, Galen, 1556
Bitner, Robert L., 2273
Bittinger, Barbara Bowser, 144
Bittinger, Beau Stanley, 261, 1556
Bittinger, D. B., 1556
Bittinger, David, 144
Bittinger, Desmond Wright, **143**, 190, 430, 748, 1556, 1834, 1877, **2371, 2380, 2387**
   historical writing, 613
   McPherson College, president, 781
   Messenger, editor, 818
   mission schools, 854
   Morse, Kenneth Ivan, 878
   photography, 1020
   works by, 2315
Bittinger, Elizabeth Durst, 144
Bittinger, Emmert F., 2, 1858, 1877, 2149, 2188
   district histories, 2201
   Forum for Religious Studies, 2202
Bittinger, Emmert Foster, 1556
Bittinger, Esther Bair Sellers, 143–144
Bittinger, Etta Fike, 143
Bittinger family, **144**, 1878
   Fike family, 490
   sources on, 2315
Bittinger, Foster Melvin, **143–144**, 1557, 1878
Bittinger, Henry, 144
Bittinger, Ilda M. (later Ziegler), 1395, 1846
Bittinger, Irene Frantz, 143, 1834, 1877
Bittinger, John, 144
Bittinger, Jonas H., 143, 144
Bittinger, Joseph, 144
Bittinger, Juliana, 144
Bittinger, Lucy (Lucie) Forney, 1878, 2315
Bittinger, Lydia Boger, 144
Bittinger, Mary Boger, 144
Bittinger, Patricia L., 1845, 1878
Bittinger, Philip, 144
Bittinger, Richard D., 179, 1834
Bittinger, Sara Ann Coffman, 1834
Bittinger, Wayne, 1878, 2315
Bittinger, Wilma Erma, 1557, 1803
Bittle, Debbie A., 2316
Bittner, Galen Milton, 1557, 2299
Bitzer, Hannah, 1155
Biu, Mai Sule, 307
Biundo, Georg K. J., 1878
bivocational ministry, 2322
Bixel, David C., 1878
Bixler (Bicksler, Bichseler) family, 1998
Bixler, E. C., 1119
Bixler, Edward Clinton, **144**, 786, 1026, 1119, 1557
Bixler, Elma Bertha Nussbaum, 1878
Bixler family, **144**

Bixler, Margaret B. Englar, 144
Bixler, Marguerite Arthelda (later Garrett), 111, **531**, 643, 1050, 1945
Bixler, Paul, 1878
Bixler, Roy Russell, 625, 304, 1557, 1878, 2316
Bixler, Sarah Myers, 144
Bixler, Sarah Worster, 531
Bixler, Uriah, 144, 1337, 1557
Bixler, Virginia, 1878
Bixler, William D., 531, 1557
Bjorklund, Flora Mae Nickey Ross, 678, **1123–1124**, 1834
Bjorklund, John, 1123, 1557
Black, A. G., 243, 1205, 1214, 1557
Black, A. J., 1557
Black Americans, *See* African Americans
Black, Anne, 1557
Black, Arthur G., 1878
Black Bear (Antelope Valley) Church of the Brethren, OK, **40**, 448, 869
Black, Brian S., 2273
Black, Cora Jean, 1557
Black, Edith, 2138
Black, Everett J., 1557
Black family, 1299
Black Fork, WV, 440
Black, Frederick, 946
Black, Glenn, 2138
Black, Grace, 1878
Black Hawk Co., IA, 149, 1322, 1878
   Hudson, IA, First Brethren Church, 635
   migration of Brethren, 830
Black Hawk (Native Americans), 2299
Black Hawk War (1832), 258, 989, 1357, 2074
Black, Helen Kuhn Jackson, 1878
Black, Jacob, 1299
Black, James F., 2138, 2273
Black, James R., 856, 1557, 2130, **2138**
Black, Larry G., 2273
Black Log, Valley Point Church of the Brethren, PA, 71, **144**
Black, Mrs. Merle, 1046
Black, N. P., 1878
Black Oak Ridge Church of the Brethren, MD, *See* Beaver Creek, MD
Black River, MI
   Church of the Brethren, **144**
   Michigan Brethren settlement, 823
   migration of Brethren, 829
Black River, OH, Church of the Brethren, **144–145**, 446, 1175
   Medina, 2219
   Mohican Church of the Brethren, 867
   Rittenhouse, Joseph, 1111
Black River, OH, Old German Baptist Brethren Church, **145**
Black, Robert, 2138
Black Rock Church of the Brethren, PA, **145**, 732, 1032, 1870
Black, Ruth Anne Heisey, 1878
Black Sea, 55
Black, Shirley Andrick, 2138
Black Snake gathering, Ewing Church of the Brethern, VA, 2373
Black Swamp, OH, Church of the Brethren, **720**
Black, Thornton Orville, 1557, 2299
Black Tower, NM, 719
Black Valley Federated Church of the Brethren, PA, **145**, 274, 911

Black Water German Baptist Brethren Church, VA, **145**
Blackboard Bulletin, 26
Blackburn, E. Howard, 1878
Blackburn family, 1923
Blackburn, Rebecca (later Holsinger), 621
Blackfoot Reservation, Alberta, Canada, 1034
Blacklick, OH, East Side Grace Brethren Church of Columbus, **145**, 1380
Blacklog, PA, Valley Point congregation, 1117
Blackquell, John, 1557
Blacksburg, VA
   Good Shepherd Church of the Brethren, **2138**
   Summerdean Church of the Brethren, Roanoke, 1114
Blackwater Chapel Church of the Brethren, VA, 130, 871
Blackwater German Baptist Brethren Church, MO, **145**
Blackwater River settlement, VA, 1307
Blackwell, Leonard Wetzel, 399, 663, 880, 934, 1247, 1308, 1557
Blades, Mary (later Miller), 841
Blain, Clarissa, 1286
Blain, Elam, 1286
Blain, Nancy D. (later Underhill), 1286, 1797
Blain, PA, 1263, **2138**
Blaine, Harry S., 1878
Blaine, Robert K., 1557
Blainsport, PA, congregation, 322
Blair, Albert, 1878
Blair, B. H., 1879
Blair Co., PA, 256, 317, 353, 357, 380, 384, 407, 731, 765, 1294, 1304, 1878, 2080, 2084
   Fairview Church of the Brethren, PA, 469
   Fredericksburg, PA, Brethren Church, 512
   migration of Brethren, 827
   Pennsylvania Brethren settlement, 1004
   Raystown Brethren Church, PA, 1084
   Roaring Spring
      Albright Church of the Brethren, 513, **1114**
      First Church of the Brethren, 896, **1114**
   Native Americans of, 2229
   Smith, Larry on Brethren of, 2357
   Smithfield Church of the Brethren, PA, 1192
   Snake Valley Old German Baptist Brethren Church, PA, 1192
Blair family, 1879, 2016
Blair, J. C., 235
Blair, John Alvin, 748, 1557, 1879
Blair, Robert B., 3, 357, 612, 1879
Blair, Virginia E., 1557
Blair, William T., 1879
Blake, Clara Anna Zierlein, 1879
Blake, Eugene Carson, 338
Blake, James, 1557
Blake, Robert Paul, 825, 1557
Blake, Stephen Harold, 2138
Blakely, Don, 1286
Blakely family, 1302, 2318
Blakely, Lloyd G., 1879
Blakely, Michael S., 1557
Blanchard-Anglaize congregation, OH, 142

Blanchard, Charles A., 259
Blanchard, OH, 410–411, 2083
    Church of the Brethren, 71
    preaching provided for Sand Ridge
        Church of the Brethren, OH, 1143
Blanchard, Scott, 2316
Blankenbaker, Robert, 602
Blankenship family, 1863
Blankenship, Fay Boitnott, 157
Blankenship, Gertrude May (later Stude-
    baker), 1229
Blankenship, Obediah, 157
Blaser, Anneliese, 1879
Blässer family, *See* entries at Blosser
Blässer, Herman, 149
Blatt family, 700
Blatt, Genevieve, 2316
Blauch, Annie Kauffman, 151
Blauch, Christian, 151
Blauch, Christian, Jr., 151
Blauch, D. D., 1879
Blauch family, 585, 1879
Blauch, Hans, 151
Blauch, Jacob, 151
Blauch, Magdelena Bender, 151
Blaugh, Thomas, 1557
Blessed Sacrament Sisters for Indians and
    Colored People, 405
Blessing family, 701
Blessing, S. A., 262
Blessing, Sidney Alpheus, 109, 262, 691,
    1557
Blevan family, 880
Blevins, David, 2254, 2273
Blevins family, 1315
Blevins, J. C., 1557
Blevins Monte L., 2273
Blickensderfer family, 1879
Blickensderfer, Jacob, 1879
Blickensdörfer family, *See* entries at
    Blickenstaff
Blickenstaff, Andrew, 79, 774, 1557
Blickenstaff, Annie, 1879
Blickenstaff, Betty Rogers, 752, 924
Blickenstaff, Catherine Brubaker, *146*
Blickenstaff, Daniel Levi, 141, 1312, 1557
Blickenstaff, David Emerson, **146**, 261, 518
    medical projects, 808
    Spain, relief work in, 1207, 1208
    World War II relief work, 1373
Blickenstaff, David J., 893, 1557, 1879
Blickenstaff, Delaney, 343
Blickenstaff, Eli, 375
Blickenstaff, Elia Elizabeth Rogers, 1834
Blickenstaff, Elizabeth Ochs, 146
Blickenstaff, Ermal T. McGaffey, 1834,
    1912
Blickenstaff family, **146**, 226, 405, 574
Blickenstaff, Hannah, 146
Blickenstaff, Jacob, *146, 343*
Blickenstaff, Jacob J., 1557
Blickenstaff, Janine, 261
Blickenstaff, Jesse, 1335, 1363, 1557
Blickenstaff, Jesse E., 1557
Blickenstaff, Joseph, Sr., 146
Blickenstaff, Leah (later Shively), 1177
Blickenstaff, Leo, 1557
Blickenstaff, Leonard Ellis, 931, 1834,
    2387
Blickenstaff, Lloyd Curtis, 1557
Blickenstaff, Lynn A., **146**, 148, 1834, 1943
Blickenstaff, M. G., 1383
Blickenstaff, Margaret Fuller, 146

Blickenstaff, Martha (later Bowman), 748
Blickenstaff, Mary Brubaker, **146**, 1834,
    1893
Blickenstaff, Mary Crull, 343
Blickenstaff, Maxine L., 2104
Blickenstaff, Miles G., 7, 906, 1557, 1834,
    1884
Blickenstaff, Orlando M., 1335, 1557, 2299,
    2380
Blickenstaff, Rosemary, 1837
Blickenstaff, Solomon, 1557
Blickenstaff, Ulrich, 146
Blickenstaff, Verna Mabel, 1834
Blickenstaff, Yost, 146
Bliss, Nina (later Fraser), 1941
Bliss, W. D. P., 1197
Blissville Church of the Brethren, IN, **147**,
    267, 1024
Blocher, Amos H., 1035, 1281, 1557, 1558
Blocher, Andreas, 2371
Blocher, Andrew, family of, 1035
Blocher, Anna Catharine Wegnast, 2371
Blocher, Anna Marie, 147
Blocher, Barbara, 147
Blocher, Daniel J., 147, 1242, 1557
Blocher, David, 147, 1557
Blocher, Elizabeth Leedy, 147
Blocher, Elizabeth Roberts, 147
Blocher, Evalena Porter, 2250
Blocher family, **147**, 1281, **2371**
    Pleasant Hill Old German Baptist
        Brethren Church, IL, 1033
    Rio Linda, CA, congregation, 1134
Blocher, Frederick, 147
Blocher, H. D., 2250
Blocher, Henry, 147
Blocher, Ira Glunt, 1557
Blocher, Isaac, 1242
Blocher, Jacob, 147
Blocher, John, 147
Blocher, Joseph, 147
Blocher, Leah, 147
Blocher, Malinda, *147, 1242*
Blocher, Mary (later Smeltzer), 147,
    200–201, *See* Smeltzer, Mary
    Blocher
Blocher, Matthias, 147, 2371
Blocher, Michael, 1557
Blocher, Mrs. Floyd, 1879
Blocher, Paul, 2299
Blocher, Paul D., 1557
Blocher, Peter, 147
Blocher, Ruth, 1841, 2089
Blocher, Samuel Wyland, 109, 147, 1046,
    1557–1558
Blocher, Sara, 147
Blocher, Sarah Hollinger, 1038
Blocher, Sarah (later Hoff), 617
Blocher, Virginia Frantz (later Skiles), 2250
Block, Daniel, 1348
Block, Ervin Frederick, 695, 1558
Block, Rosemary (later Rose), 2048
Blocker, Barbara (later Peters), 1011
Blocker, H. D., 1048
Blocker, Ruth (later Mallott), 784
Bloesch, Donald G., 1879
Blois, G. de, 147
Blom, Bouke, 2316
blood
    strangled animals and, **147**
    symbolized by grape juice in commun-
        ion, 1252
Blood, Louie (later Grubb), 575

Blood, Raymond, 16, 21, 104, 515, 532,
    1251, 1558
Bloody Tenet of Persecution (Williams),
    1098
The Bloody Theater, 154, 171
Bloom, KS, Church of the Brethren, **147**,
    726
Bloom, Louis D., 1558
Bloom, Merle E., 768
Bloom, Vernonica (later Knepper), 703
Bloomfield, Donna J., 2316
Bloomfield, IN, 696, 1010
Blooming Grove Colony, **147–149**
    articles about, 1922, 1949
    bibliography, 1863, 1866
    choristers, **279–280**
    communitarianism of, 329
    defection of, 1922
    Dunkers, 148–149
    Durnbaugh, Donald F. on, 2325, 2326
    Garvan, Beatrice B. on, 2333
    German Baptists, 542
    in Germany, 545
    Haller, Friedrich Conrad, 580
    Harman (Harmon) family, 584
    Harmony Society, 584
    meetinghouse, *148*
    meetinghouse (Williamsport, PA), 48,
        609
    in Pennsylvania, 542, 2085
Blooming Grove Historical Society, 2316
Bloomville, OH, 1166
Bloss, Barbara (later Moyer), 822
Bloss, Catherine (later Moyer), 822
Blosser, Amanda, 149
Blosser, Edith R. Lewis, 1879
Blosser, Elizabeth Ellen (later Showalter),
    See Showalter family
Blosser family, **149**, 1229, 1879
Blosser, Merrill, **149**
Blosser, Mrs. Eli, 1879
Blosser, Peter, 149, 1954
Blosser, S. H., 1879
Blossers family, 2077
Blough, Albert Perry, **149**, 1322, 1323,
    1558
Blough, Amy Mangus, 150
Blough, Anna, 2363
Blough, Anna Viola, **149**, 1834, 1866
Blough, Anna Zook Detweiler, **149**, *150,*
    150, 380, 1834
Blough, Carman George, 149, **151**
Blough, Charles Wilbur, 628, 1558
Blough, Detweiler Anna, 380
Blough, Dinah Walker, 149
Blough, Dorris Murdock, 748, 1879
Blough, E. J., 1558
Blough, E. Percy, 1558
Blough, Elijah E., 785, 1558, 1879
Blough, Eliza (later Hamer), 580
Blough, Elizabeth Delp Rosenberger, **150**,
    1879
Blough, Emanuel J., 150, 151, 1558
Blough, F. E., 1879
Blough family, **151–152**, 164, 2087
    Fike family, 490
    Kinsey, Marjorie Blocker on, 2341
Blough, Galen Roy, 1202, 1558
Blough, Helene (later Crill), 1911
Blough, Homer Earl, 1343, 1558, 1879
Blough house, *See* Blough, PA, Sugar
    Grove Church of the Brethren
Blough, Jacob, 1879

Blough, Jacob B., 151
Blough, Jacob, Jr., 1558
Blough, Jacob M., 139, **149**, *150,* **150,** 151, 229, 1558, 1834
Blough, Jacob Roy, **150**
Blough, Jeannette (later Miller), 839
Blough, Jennie (later Miller), 1841, 1942
Blough, Jerome E., **150–151,** 1176, 1558, 1879–1880, 2188
Blough, John, 1558
Blough, John Glenn, 1558
Blough, John H., 1321, 1558, 1880
Blough, John J., 149
Blough, Jonathan W., 151, 628, 1558
Blough, Joseph W., 1558
Blough, Kenneth Ray, 628, 1558
Blough, Leslie E., 1558, 1880
Blough, Lester, Jr., 2299
Blough, Martha Dorris Murdoch, 1834
Blough, Marvin Earl, 1558, 1834
Blough, Mary Alice Wertz, 149, 150, 151
Blough, Mary Miller, 149
Blough, Mollie M. Dietz, 150
Blough, Noah, 1558
Blough, Norman H., 1558
Blough, P. P., *538*
Blough, PA
    Maple Spring Church of the Brethren, PA, 791
    Sugar Grove Church of the Brethren, **151**
Blough, Perry J., 150, 151, 1202, 1558
    Hooversville, PA, Church of the Brethren, 628
    store of, *151*
Blough, Richard, 320
Blough, Sarah Barndt, 150, 151
Blough, Silas S., 149, **150,** 151, 504, 949, 1027, 1388, 1558, 1879, 1880
Blough, Susan Boger, 151
Blough, Telford B., 1558
Blough, Tobias, 1558
Blough, Urias S., 149, 1121, 1558
Blough, Valentine, 1558
Blough, Warren Wilbert, 551, 1558, 1880
    Omaha, NE, Church of the Brethren, minister, 974
    Rockingham Church of the Brethren, MO, pastor, 1118
Blough, Walter H., 714, 1558–1559
Blough, William M., 1559
Blough work camp, *1366*
Blougher, Samuel, 1030
Blount, B. M., 2017
Blount Co., AL, 415, 975
Blount Co., TN, Maryville, Oakland German Baptist Brethren Church, 799
Blue Ball, PA, 1213
Blue, Blair, 1559
Blue Creek, IN, Church of the Brethren, **152,** 411, 1048, 1316
Blue Creek, OH, Church of the Brethren, **152,** 1320
Blue, Elmer, 1559
Blue Hill, KS, 1048
Blue Mound, TX, Church of the Brethren, *See* Fort Worth, TX, Church of the Brethren
Blue Ridge Chapel, VA, 1324
Blue Ridge College, **152–153**
    Barnes, Edith Catherine Bonsack, 2134
    Bixler, Edward Clinton, 144

Blosser, Merrill, 149
Blough, Elizabeth Delp Rosenberger, 150
Bonsack, Charles Daniel, 160
Bowman, Paul Haynes, 168
Bowman, Samuel Loren, 169
    Brethren Service Commission and, 200
    Bridgewater College and, 208
    Church of the Brethren and, 198
    Fisher, Nevin Wishard, 492
    Henry, Jerry Maurice, 598
    Holl, Carl Waldo, 619
    Holsopple, Frank Ferry, 623
    Hoover, William I. T., 628
    Hutchison, Anna Martha, 639
    John, John Jay, 671
    Kettering, Joseph W., 691
    Kinsey, William, 696
    Lindsay, Samuel David, 744
    Long, Isaac Samuel, 753
    Mallott, Floyd Ellwood, teaching, 784
    Maryland Brethren, 799
    McCann, Elizabeth Gibbel, 771
    Miller, Blanche Bonsack and Harold Clayton, 834
    Morris, Charles Stephen, 877
    Murphy, Ross Dale, president, 897
    Murphy, Sara Florence Fogelsanger, 897
    Parker, Isaac Dillon, fund raising by, 993
    Rowland, Charles Luther, 1126
    students of, *153*
    Wine, William M., 1350
    Yount, Walter Bowman, 1391
Blue Ridge congregation, 1264
Blue Ridge, GA, Old German Baptist Brethren Church, **2138**
Blue Ridge, IL, 270
    Champaign, IL, Church of the Brethren, mission point of, 270
    Church of the Brethren, **152**
Blue Ridge, NC
    Church of the Brethren, **152**
    Peak Creek Church of the Brethren, NC, 1003
    Blue Ridge Parkway as National Park Service project, 917
Blue Ridge, VA, 164
    Chapel Church of the Brethren, **152**
    Church of the Brethren, 152
    Cloverdale, VA, Church of the Brethren, preaching point for, 321
Blue River, IN, 326
    Baptist Association and Restoration Movement, 1101
    Baptist Church, 1380
    Church of the Brethren, **153**
    Hostetler Brethren and Blue River Baptist churches, 632
    Old German Baptist Brethren Church, **153**
Blue River Valley Church of the Brethren, NE, 960
Blue Rock congregation, PA, Independent Brethren, 649
Blue Springs, KY, congregation, 689
Blu(e)baugh, Ida E. (later Miller), 839
Bluefield, WV
    Church of the Brethren, **154**
    minorities, ethnic and racial, 850
    Sunday schools, 278
Bluffton College historical libraries, 610

Blume, Friedrich, 1880
Blumen-Gärtlein (Little Flower Garden) (Tersteegen), 1051
Blunston, Samuel, 800
Blunt, Richard, 87
Der Blutige Schau-Platz oder Martyrer Spiegel der Tauffs Gesinnten (The Bloody Theater or Martyrs' Mirror of the Baptist-Minded) (J. Böhme), **154,** 171, 309, 923
    bicentary, 1994
    destruction, 1978
    Ephrata Community, 451
    Ephrata Press, 452
    Ephrata publishing, 1067
    frontispiece of, *154*
    Hess family, 601
    Miller, John Peter, translating, 840
    restitution, 1100
    title page of, *154*
BMH Books, 192
BMH/College Bookstore, 161
BNYC (Brethren National Youth Conference), 2268
Boal, Timothy E., 2180, 2273
Boali, Africa, 1309
Boan, Lydia, 1559
board buildings, *34*
Board family, Prosperity Brethren Church, WV, 1062
Board of Christian Education, 285, 915, 1392, *See also* Christian Education Commission
    alcohol education, 1252
    Brethren Youth Council and National Sunday School Board merger, 917
    Church of the Brethren, 304
    General Sunday School Board (CB), 540
    General Welfare Board (CB), 540
    Music Committee (CB), 899
    National Cabinet of Children's Work, 915
    Peters, Raymond Russell, 1011
    recognition of Twenty Thousand Dunkers for Peace movement, 1281
    Shultz, Lawrence W., 1180
    Sunday school movement, 1239
    West, Daniel, 1331
    Zigler, Rachel E. Myers, 1397
Board of Christian Education (BC), **154–155,** 182
    Brethren Youth Crusader Program, 2151
    historical writing, 612
    Munson, Charles Robert, 2227
Board of Christian Education (CB), **155,** 1903, *See also* Brethren Service Commission (BSC)
    Council of Women's Work (CB), 347
    youth department, 248
Board of Christian Education (FGBC), 155, 2156
Board of Evangelism (FGBC), 155, 460
    Weaver, Scott L. (FGBC, CGBCI) and, 2261
Board of Ministerial Emergency and Retirement Benefits, 155
    Grace Brethren pension funds, 1008
    Schaffer, William Herbert, treasurer, 1152
Board of Ministerial Relief and Grace

Brethren pension funds, 1008
Board of Publications (DB), 2227
Board of Religious Education, *See* entries at
    Board of Christian Education;
    General Board (CB); General
    Sunday School Board (CB);
    General Welfare Board (CB)
Board of Trustees of the Retirement Fund
    (BC), 182, 1008
Boardman, Clara Smith, 155
Boardman, Edwin E., Jr., **155**, 1559, 1847,
    1880
Boardman, Edwin, Jr., 635
Boardman, Edwin (Ted), 155
Boardman, Edwin W., 155
Boardman, Elizabeth, 155
Boardman, Gertrude Mary (later Kerner),
    155, 2211, 2137
Boardman, Muriel (later Aurand), 155
Boardman, Muriel Welstead, 155, 1847
boards (BC), 182
Boathe, Raymond, 958
Boaz, Jacob Moyer, 1559
Boaz Maina, 2216
Boaz, Roy A., 1277
Boaz, Roy Delp 1559, 1880
    North Manchester, IN, Church of the
        Brethren, pastor, 949
    Roanoke, VA, Williamson Road
        Church of the Brethren, moderator,
        1114
Bob Jones University, 212
    Cashman, Edwin E., 2156
    Fellowship of Grace Brethren Churches
        (FGBC), 488
    Fetterhoff, Dean, 2184
    McClain, Alva J., honorary LLD, 772
Bock, Catherine Hoover, 155
Bock, Daniel, 633, 1559
Bock, David, 471, 1559
Bock, Edna Polk, 1847
Bock, Elizabeth Gable, 155
Bock family, 1219
Bock, Samuel (I), **155**, 1559
    Oregon Short Line Railroad, 981
    railroads and Brethren settlement, 1082
Bock, Samuel (II), 1559
Bock, W. H., 1559
Bock, William H., 1847
Bodano, Gualtero, 1880
Bodkin, Berlin, 1559
Bodnar family, Mission Viejo, CA, Saddle-
    back Valley Grace Brethren
    Church, 855
Body of Christ and house churches, 632
Boe, Jorgen, 851, 1559
Boecken, Charlotte, 2316
Boehm family, Macedonia, OH, Western
    Reserve Grace Brethren Church,
    2216
Boehm, Johann (John) Philip, **156**, 378,
    1880, 1941, 1966
Boehm, Martin, 188, 1289
Boehm, Ronald E., 165, 439, 1559, 2216
Boehme, Jakob (Jacob), 30, 57, 98, 148,
    156–157, 266, 381, 548, 923,
    1019, 2124
    Hochmann von Hochenau, Ernst
        Christoph, 614
    influence of, 120
    reference to, 1919
    Society of the Woman in the Wilder-
        ness, 1199

as source for Beissel's ideas, 113
Boehmists, 606
    celibacy, views on, 266
    theology, 148, 156
    writings of, 30
Boepple, Rolland, 1559
Boer, Hans de, 638, 1880
Boer, Harry R., *1256,* 2316
Boessen, Sister Rosemary, 2212
Boganreif, John, 1559
Bogart, Charles Ortain, 1559
Boger, Barbara (later Thomas), 1263
Boger, Christian, 157
Boger family, Sandy Creek Old German
    Baptist Brethren Church, WV,
    1143
Boger, John, 144, **157**, 1559, 1880
    Jehovah's Witnesses, 670
    millennialism, 834
    publishing works of, 1067
Boger, Lydia (later Bittinger), 144
Boger, Mary (later Bittinger), 144
Boger, Susan, 151
Boggess, Frank, 1559
Boggs, Bertha, 104, 1559
Boggs, Calvin H., 1559
Boggs, E.
    Portland, OR, Peace Church of the
        Brethren, 1048
Boggs, Elsie Byrd, 1880
Boggs, Estella Ruth, *See* Horning, Estella
    Ruth Boggs
Boggs family, Nevada, MO, Church of the
    Brethren, 924
Boggs, Lydia Bright, 209
Boggs, Richard, 318, 1559
Boggs, Richard T., 1559
Boggs, William Hitt, 1559
Bogue, Frank M., 1348, 1559
Boguila, Africa, 268
Bohemia Manor, MD, Labadist colony, 869
Bohemian Brethren, *See* Moravian Church
Böhler, Eliseba, 1880
Bohlman, Philip V., 2316
Böhme, *See* entries at Boehme
Bohn, D. Richard, 1559
Bohn family, 2097
Bohn, J. S., 1559
Bohne, *See* entries at Boone
Bohne, Johannes Diel, 162, 2097
Bohni, Andreas, 1954, 2096, *See also* Boni,
    Andreas
    Durnbaugh, Donald F. on, 2327
    reference to, 1955, 1956
Bohni family, 2083, *See also* entries at Boni
Bohr, Mary Louise Ronk, 1121
Bohrer, Anthony P., 1559
Bohrer, Bradley C., 2273
Bohrer, Bruce, 1559
Bohrer, Charles Wendell, 1559, 1880
    Greenwood, IN, Christ Our Shepherd
        Church of the Brethren, 2193
Bohrer, Joan, Greenwood, IN, Christ Our
    Shepherd Church of the Brethren,
    2193
Bohrer, Lydia J. (later Zuck), 1401
Bohrer, Roscoe, 1559
Boice, Samuel, 1559
Boies, Robin, Jackpot Church, NV, 2212
Boiling Springs, PA, Church of the Breth-
    ren, **157**, 255, 765
Boise, ID
    Mountain View Church of the

    Brethren, **157**
    preaching point maintained by Nampa,
        ID, Church of the Brethren, 913
Boise Valley, ID, 170, 913
    Church of the Brethren, **157**, 2316
    preaching point maintained by Nampa,
        ID, Church of the Brethren, 913
Boitnott, Adaline Goode, 157
Boitnott, Daisy Bell Berkebile, 1559
Boitnott, David, 157
Boitnott, Eleanor Beckner, 157
Boitnott, Elizabeth Altick, 157
Boitnott, Elizabeth Donahue, 157
Boitnott family, **157**, 1880
    Jamison family, 668
Boitnott, Fay, 157
Boitnott, Ferdinand, 157
Boitnott, George, 157
Boitnott, Henry, 157
Boitnott, James C., 343, 1202, 1559
Boitnott, John Wesley, 1559, 1880
Boitnott, Julia Sink, 157
Boitnott, Justus, 157, 1880
Boitnott, Peter, 157
Boitnott, Polly Hambrick, 157
Boitnott, Sarah Hodges, 157
Boitnott, Susannah Dishong, 157, 1880
Bolar Springs, VA, 1301
Bolar, VA, 1301
Bole, D. J., 215
Bole, Daniel J., 1027, 1559
Bole, David K., Pittsburgh, PA, First
    Brethren Church, 1027
Bole, Mrs. David K., Pittsburgh, PA, First
    Brethren Church, 1027
Bolen family, 1341
Bolenius, R. M., 1880
Boles, D. B., 1880
Boles, Harold W., 1880
Boleyn, Esther Marie Frantz, 1834, 2137,
    2253
Boleyn, Lester E., 516, 1559, 1834, 2137,
    2253
Bolinger family, *See* entries at Bollinger
Bolinger, John B., Paint Creek Church of
    the Brethren, KS, 989
Bolinger, Larry Lee., 1854
    Medina, OH, Brethren Church, 2219
Bolinger, Noble, 1559
Bolinger, Rose Bilderback, 1854
Bolinger, Solomon, 157
Bolinger, Sophia, Paint Creek Church of the
    Brethren, KS, 989
Bolivar, PA
    Church of the Brethren, 1116
    Waterford, PA, Ligonier First Church
        of the Brethren, Bolivar meeting
        house, 1321
Bolivia, Mennonites migrating to, 815
Boll, Paul Henry, 733, 1177, 1559
Bolle, Simon, **157**
    Assembly of Christ, 376
    Krefeld, Brethren of, 375–376
Bolle, Soren, **157**
    Assembly of Christ, 376
    Krefeld, Brethren of, 375–376
Bolling Conference Grounds and camping
    movement, 247
Bolling, Ernest, 247
Bollinger, Amsey Floyd, **157–158**, 462,
    1559, 1834, 2316
Bollinger, Andrew, 1559

Bollinger, Benjamin B., 1559
Bollinger, Benjamin J., 1880
Bollinger, Dale L., 2273
Bollinger, Daniel, 356
Bollinger, Daniel (1), 1559
Bollinger, Daniel (2), 1559
Bollinger, Daniel D., 157, 1559
Bollinger, Elizabeth Moyer, 157
Bollinger family, 256, 1338, 1881
  Fahnestock family, 465
  Royer family related to, 1128
  Shoemaker, David, related to, 1157
Bollinger, Florence T. Moyer, **157–158**,
  1834, 1880, 2371
Bollinger, Floyd S., 1559–1560
Bollinger, Gideon, 1560
Bollinger, Glenn Edwin, 2273
Bollinger, Isaac M., 1560
Bollinger, John, 158
Bollinger, LaMar, 1560
Bollinger, Larry L., 1560
  spelling changed to Bolinger, **2380**
Bollinger, Martha Cripe, 158
Bollinger, Mary (later Kurtz), 710
Bollinger, Matilda, 256
Bollinger, Michael, 1560
Bollinger, Milton M., 1560
Bollinger, Noah M., 1881
Bollinger, Nora Cripe, 158
Bollinger, Richard A., 1881
Bollinger, Richard Amsey, 1560, 1881
Bollinger, Rudolph B., 158, 534, 1560,
  1880
Bollinger, Russell V., **158**, 1560, 1880,
  2371, 2380
  North Manchester, IN, Church of the
    Brethren, elder (moderator), 949
Bollinger, Samuel, 355, 725
Bollinger, Samuel (1), 1560
Bollinger, Samuel (2), 1560
Bollinger, Steven Wayne, 2273
Bollinger, Virginia Moyer, 1844
Bollinger, Wendell LaMar, 1560
Bollman, Jesse G., 1560
Bolten, J. A., 1881
Bolton, Catherine (later Wrightsman), 1380
Bolton, Cecil R., Jr., 1560
Bolton, James, 1881
Bolton, Robert, 2173
Bolyard, Dorothy Hartsough, 588
Bolyard, John, 588
Bolz, Ernest J., 758, 1560
Bombastus von Hohenheim, Theophrastus,
  See Paracelsus
Bombay Christian Council, 131, 150
Bombay, India, 146, 191
Bomberger (Bamberger) family, 1881, 1927,
  1939, 2316
  Fahnestock family, 465
Bomberger, Charles D., 1560
Bomberger, Christian (1801–1880), **158**,
  825, 1560
Bomberger, Christian (d. 1742), 158
Bomberger, Christian Martin Hess, 1881
Bomberger, Cyrus S., 158, 1560
Bomberger, David Roy, 1560
Bomberger, Harold Zug, 1560, 1881, **2138,
  2380**
Bomberger, Henry Hess, 1881
Bomberger, Howard B., 2138
Bomberger, Jacob Cauffman, 1881
Bomberger, John M., 1560
Bomberger, Kenneth Eugene, 1560

Bomberger, Lloyd Huber, works by, 2316
Bomberger, Margaret E. Mann, 2138
Bomberger, Maria, 158
Bomberger, Venona Zug, 2138
Bon Meade, PA, Grace Brethren Church,
  See Coraopolis, PA, Bon Meade
  Grace Brethren Church
Bonao, Dominican Republic, 2215
Bonar, Elaine Hahn, 1881
Bonar, Hugh, 1560
Bonbrook mission point, Germantown
  Brick Church of the Brethren, VA,
  544
Bond Co., IL, 1232
  Hurricane Creek Church of the
    Brethren, IL, 638
  Hurricane Creek Old German Baptist
    Brethren Church, IL, 638
Bond, Elizabeth Blocher Leedy, 147
Bond family, 342, 2076
Bond, John A., 1560
Bond, Shadrach, (Illinois governor), 1357
Bond, Thomas, 1560
Bond, William N., 432, 1560
bonds, *See* War Bonds
Bonebrake, David H., 471, 1560
Bonebrake, Donna, 754
Bonebrake, Elizabeth (later Oller), 974
Bonebrake family, 348
Bonebrake, Mel, 754
Bonebrake, Simon, North Manchester, IN,
  (First) Brethren Church, pastor,
  949
Bonebrake Theological Seminary, 1121,
  2139
Bonebreak family, 1876
Bonewitz, John Z., 906, 1338, 1560
Boney, Andreas, *See* Boni, Andreas
Bonham, Bob, 366
Bonham, Norma, 366
Boni, *See* entries at Bohni
Boni, Andreas, **159**, 174, 443, 516, 593
  historic sites, 609
  Pieter de Koker recommended to emi
    grants, 705
  prisons, 1058
  religious freedom and persecution,
    1010
Boni, Andreas (father), 159
Boni, Anna Hämer, 159
Boni family, as passengers on *Allen*, 2126
Boni, Johanna Noethiger, **159**, 174
Boni, Martin, **159**, 516
Bonis family, 1920
A Bonnet for Virginia (Frantz), 748
bonnets, *159*, **160**, 300, 401, *See also* caps;
  hats
  Church of the Brethren, 254, 300
  Old German Baptist Brethren women,
    967
  plain people, 1029
  prayer veil, 1053
  Rinehart, Mary Snader, worn by, *1109*
Bonney, Don, 1560
Bonney, Willard Donald, 1560
Bonomi, Patricia Updegraff, works by,
  2316
Bonsack, Blanche (later Miller), physician,
  160, **834**
Bonsack, Charles Daniel, **160–161**, 201,
  435, 538, 1026, 1273, 1386, 1560,
  1881, 2019, 2134
  Interchurch World Movement (IWM),

658
Miller, Blanche Bonsack, father of, 834
Minnich, Herbert Spenser, 849
Bonsack, Catharine Roop Royer, 160
Bonsack, Daniel Malcolm, 1881
Bonsack, David D., 160, 1337, 1560
Bonsack, Edith Catherine (later Barnes),
  160, **2134**
Bonsack, Elizabeth, 161
Bonsack family, **161**, 1881
Bonsack, Franz Heinrich, 1881
Bonsack, Ida A. Trostle, 160, 834, 2134
Bonsack, J. Ralph, 160
Bonsack, Jacob, 161
Bonsack, Johann Georg, 161
Bonsack, Johann Jacob, 161
Bonsack, John, 161
Bonsack, Katharina Gebhart, 161
Bonsack, Mary Rinehart, 161
Bonsack, Marya Hackman, 161
Bonsack, Nathaniel, 161
Bonsack, Olga, 160
Bonsack, Paul, 160
Bonsack, Susannah Harshbarger, 161
Bonta, Bruce D., works by, 2309
Bontrager, A. A., 1322
Bontrager, Alvin William, 1882
Bontrager, Amanda M. Hershberger, 1881
Bontrager, Ammon E., 1881
Bontrager, Amos D., 1881
Bontrager, Andrew, Paradise, CA, Church
  of the Brethren, 992
Bontrager, Andrew S., 2299
Bontrager, Anna (later Schrock), 2059,
  2078, 2106
Bontrager, Clement Elam, 350, 445, 1341,
  1560, 1881
  Mount Hope Church of the Brethren,
    WA, 882
  Omak, WA, Church of the Brethren,
    leadership by, 974
Bontrager, David R., 1881
Bontrager, Delcie Beulah Mishler, 1881
Bontrager, Ella Moses Schrock, 1882
Bontrager, Elva Ellen Miller, 1881
Bontrager, Emma, 1341
Bontrager, G. Edwin, 1560
Bontrager, H. A., 1881
Bontrager, L. M., 1341
Bontrager, Levi J., 1881
Bontrager, Lydia Mae Yoder, 1881
Bontrager, Mary (later Fry), 1943
Bontrager, Ora W., 1881
Bontrager, Susan Maye Miller, 1882
Bontrager, Susie J. Hochstetler, 1882
Bony family, *See* Boni entries
Boocher family, 2067
  Genesee Old German Baptist Brethren
    Church, MI, 540
Boogher family, 2067
Booher, David Lehman, *See* Booher family
Booher, Elizabeth Nutts, *See* Booher family
Booher family, 1882, 2037, 2067
Booher, Lora N., 1882
Book and Tract Committee, *See* Brethren's
  Book and Tract Committee
Book, Edmund D., 161, 1264, 1560
Book, Elizabeth Long, 161
Book family bibliography, 1882
Book, Isaac, 1560
Book, Isaac Bruce, 1560
The Book of Mormon, 298
Book of Worship, 51, 1377

Book, Samuel, 1263
The Book to Live By (Hoff), 617
Book, William I., Philadelphia, PA, First Church of the Brethren, providing leadership, 1015
Book, William Ira, 161, 1560
Book, Zella Benedict, 161
Booker, Sylvia (later Utz), 2127
Booker, Ted J., 2273
Booker, TX, 1312
Bookout, Gary Dean, 1560
books, *See* almanacs; atlases; printing business; publishing
    Berleburg church book (trans), 1966
    school books (trans), 1968
Books family, 2082
bookstore ministries, 779
bookstores, 161, 539
Bookwalter, Catherine Ann Shock, 161
Bookwalter, Jesse Eugene, 1560
Bookwalter, Joseph, 161
Bookwalter, Levi Asbury, **161**, 1560, 1945
Bookwalter, Susan Brumbaugh, 161
Bookwalter, Sylvan, 109, 264, 1560
    Potsdam, OH, Church of the Brethren, elder, 1048
Boomer, John F., 103
Boomershine family, Hurricane Creek Old German Baptist Brethren Church, IL, 638
Boomershine, Reuben, 1560–1561
Boon family, 717, 1927, 2097
Boone, Alice, 654, 1361
    Brooklyn, NY, urban ministry in, 933
Boone, Alice Brubaker, *162*
Boone, Alice H., 1882
Boone, Alice J., 212, 685, 1296
Boone, Amos, 1561
Boone, Billy W., 1561, 2273
Boone, C. Benjamin, 1561
Boone, C. D., 1561
Boone, Catherine (later Jamison), 668
Boone, Cephas R., 268, 142, 1561
    North Fork Old German Baptist Brethren Church, IN, minister, 947
    Sand Creek Old German Baptist Brethren Church, KS, minister in, 1143
    Sheridan Lake Old German Baptist Brethren Church, CO, ministers travelling to, 1176
Boone, Claude D., 965, 1356, 1561
Boone Co., AR, Pilot Knob Church of the Brethren, AR, 1024
Boone Co., IN, 717
Boone Co., KY, 338, 689
Boone, Daniel, **161–162**, 236, 609, 1326
Boone, Dave, 705, 948
Boone, Elizabeth, 668
Boone, Elizabeth (later Weddle), 1326
Boone, Eve (later Funderburgh), 523, 1943
Boone family, 142, 162, 2033, 2046, 2072, 2097
    bibliography, 1863, 1882, 1893, 1907
    family history, 1979
    sources on, 2319
Boone, Gary, 142, 1561
Boone, George, 162, 2072
Boone, George, III, 162
Boone, Hannah, 1960
Boone, Henry E., *162,* 1561
    Pigg River Old German Baptist Brethren Church, VA, elder-in-

charge, 1023
Boone, Israel, 1882
Boone, J. B., Maple Grove Old German Baptist Brethren Church, OH, minister, 791
Boone, Jacob Chelsey., 162, 1561
    Pigg River Old German Baptist Brethren Church, VA, elder-in-charge,1023
Boone, John, 162
Boone, John, 668, 1561
    Pigg River Old German Baptist Brethren Church, VA, minister, 1023
Boone, John Dempsey, 1561
Boone, John O., 162, 470, 1561
Boone, Joseph Benjamin, 544, ,1561
    North Hampton, OH, Donnels Creek Old German Baptist Brethren Church, minister, 948
Boone, Marcy, 705
    North Kokomo Grace Brethren Church, IN, 948
Boone, Mary, 2072
Boone, Ralph M., 102, 1561
    Oak Grove Old German Baptist Brethren Church, OH, minister, 956
    Shady Grove Old German Baptist Brethren Church, OH, minister in, 1171
    Pine Grove Old German Baptist Brethren Church, FL, resident minister, 1025
Boone, Randy, 1561, 2273
Boone River, IA, Church of the Brethren, **162**, 754
Boone, Robert C., 1561
    Maple Grove Old German Baptist Brethren Church, OH, minister, 791
Boon(e), Samuel, 1561
Boone, Samuel Ludwick, 1561, **2380**
Boone, Sarah Morgan, 161
Boone, Squire, **161–162**
Boone, Squire, Sr., 161
Boone, Stephen, 1561
    Oak Hill Old German Baptist Brethren Church, VA, elder, 957
Boone, Thomas Cabel, 1561, 1882
    Shady Grove Old German Baptist Brethren Church, OH, elder in, 1171
Boones Chapel, VA, *See* entries at Boones Mill, VA
    Boones Chapel Community Church, 162
    Church of the Brethren, 130, **162**, 163
    Jones Chapel Church of the Brethren, VA, 676
Boones Creek Seminary, 168
Boone's Creek, TN
    Johnson City, Knob Creek Church of the Brethren, 672
    Boones Creek, TN, 166
Boones Mill, VA, 162, 163, 262, 1317
    Church of the Brethren, 130, **163**
    Grace Brethren Church, **163**
    meetinghouse dedication, Church of the Brethren, *163*
    Red Hill Church of the Brethren, VA, 1088
Boonsboro, MD, 1350
Boor, James D., 1882

works by, 2316
Boor, Pearl(e) Merrill, 1561
Boorse, Isaiah S., 1249
Boorse, Josephine Rahn, 1249
Boorse, Madolin (later Taylor), 1249, 1791
Boose, Raymond Richard, 654, 1561
Boose, Ronald Ray, 1561
Booten, Mr. and Mrs. Stephen, 503
Booth, Jesse, 1561
Booth, KS, *See* Darlow, KS
Booth, Marilou Genereaux, 2273
Booth, Orville, 1561
Booth, Raymond Elbert, 744, 1561
    Olean Church of the Brethren, VA, leadership by, 973
Booth, Sherman Edward, 1561
    Olean Church of the Brethren, VA, 973
Booth, Sherman Edward, 1561
Boothe, Fannie, 2273
Boothe, Joel P., 1216, 1561
    Old Order German Baptist Church minister, 972
Boothe, N. Taylor, 1561
Boothe, Noah A., 105
Boothe, Noah R., 1561
Boothe, Peter, 1561
Boothe, Rodger L., 2273
Boots, Lizzie Brubaker, Sand Creek Old German Baptist Brethren Church, KS, 1143
Boots, Louis, 264
Boots, Mrs. Louis, 264
Booz, Ben, *1393*
Booz, Cindy, 2165
Booz, Donald R., 2161, 2273
Booz, Jacob, 1561
Booz, Jacob M., 1561
Booze, Ethel L. (later Root), 2378
Booze, Hezekiah, 1561
Booze, Jacob, 1561
Borden family, 1391
Borden, Garland Bauman, 1561
Border, David Arnold, 1561
Border, Sarah Agnes, 275, 1561
Borders building, Windber, PA, Rummel Church of the Brethren, 1348
Borgmann, Robert Kurt, 2273
Borkholder, John J. and Anna Schmucker, 1967
Bornemann, Henry S., 1882
Borntrager, Daniel Moses, 1882
Borntrager, Hannah (later Grebil), 567
Borntrager, Katie, 1882
Borntrager, Martin, 1561
Borntrager, Mary Ellen Bontrager, 1882
Borntrager, Salome D. Borntrager, 1882
Borntrager, Samuel, 1882
Borough, Samuel, 1561
Borough, William, 45, 1561
Borst, Evelyn Horst, 630
Bosely, David, 172, 1561
Bosely, J. F., 1561
Boshor, John Jacob, 1340
Bosler, Edith Mae Gump, 7, 931, 1834, 2387
Bosler, Howard A., 7, 1156, 1561, 1834
Bosler, Howard E., 807
Bosler, SueZann, 2161
Bosler, William Monroe, 1561, 2161, *2161,* 2380
    Rossville, IN, Church of the Brethren, minister, 1124
Bosley, Mary (later Good), descendants of,

1951
Bossangoa mission, Africa, 1175
Bosse, George von, 1882
Bossembele, Africa, 1309
Bosserman, Abraham, 163
Bosserman, Amanda, 2098
Bosserman, Anna Marie Bushey, 163
Bosserman, Barbara Bair, 163, 1882
Bosserman, Beulah Williams, 163
Bosserman, Catharine, 163
Bosserman, Christina, 163
Bosserman, Daniel, 163, 1561, 1882
Bosserman, David, 1561, 1882
Bosserman, Eleazer (Eleazor), 413, 1561
Bosserman, Elisabeth J. Rodabaugh, 163
Bosserman family, 163–164, 413, 752
    Monitor Church of the Brethren, KS,
        869
    Scherffig family, related to, 1152
Bosserman, Hannah, 163
Bosserman, Hannah Graybill, 163
Bosserman, J. H., 1561
Bosserman, Jesse, 1882
Bosserman, John, 163
Bosserman, Joseph Ellis, 1882
Bosserman, Joseph H., 1882
Bosserman, Levi D., 103, 278, 1561
    San Bernardino, CA, Church of the
        Brethren, 1141
Bosserman, M. Grace, See Miller, M. Grace
    (wife of L. D. Bosserman)
Bosserman, Margretha, 163
Bosserman, Mary, 163
Bosserman, Michael, 163, 1561, 1882
Bosserman, Peter, 163
Bosserman, Philip, 163
Bosserman, Ronald Dee, 1834
Bosserman, Roy E., 1882
Bosserman, Samuel T., 163, 1561, 2098
Bosserman, Sandra L., 2273
Bosserman, Susannah, 163
Bosserman, William Otto, 1561
    Peace Valley Church of the Brethren,
        MO, 1003
Bosserman, William Phillip, 651, 1287,
        1561
    Monitor Church of the Brethren, OK,
        elder, 869
    Pleasant Plains Church of the Brethren,
        OK, pastor, 1034
Bosserman, Willis Orlo, 1312, 1561–1562
Bosserman(n), Christiana Dierdorff, 163,
        1882
Bossert family as passengers on Allen, 2126
Bossert, Jakob, 720
Bostater, Elizabeth (later Leedy), 734
Bostater, Nancy (later Leedy), 734
Bosteter, Catherine, 364
Boston Mountain, AR, 1215
    Round Mountain Church of the
        Brethren, AR, mission point, 1125
Boston University School of Theology
    Miller, J. Quinter, 1326
    Miller, Minor C., 1326
Boswell, PA, Laurel Mountain Grace
    Brethren Church, 164, 670
Botany, IA, Church of the Brethren, 992
Der Bote, General Conference Mennonite
    Church, 536
Botetourt Co., VA, 152, 161, 164, 262, 321,
        352, 359, 360, 700, 1212, 1221,
        1275, 1277, 1327
    Good (Guth) family, 556

Graybill (Grabill, Krehbiel) family, 567
    migration of Brethren, 829
    Noffsinger, Peter, in, 939
    Old Valley congregation, 321
    Peters family, 1012
    Reiff (Rife) family, 1094
    Schneider family, 1154
Botetourt Co., VA, Brethren Church,
        Oriskany, 981
Botetourt Co., VA, Church of the Brethren,
        164, 262, 359
    Graybill, Jonas, 567
    Greenbrier Church of the Brethren,
        WV, 570
    historical sketches, 1977
    Jeters Chapel Church of the Brethren,
        670
    mission points, 164, 2125
    Mount Bethel Church of the Brethren,
        880
    Mount Joy Church of the Brethren, 882
    Pleasant Dale Church of the Brethren,
        1031
    Roanoke, VA, First Church of the
        Brethren, 1113
    Saunders Grove Church of the
        Brethren, 1150
    works by, 2316
Botetourt Co., VA, 216
    Botetourt Co., VA, Old German Baptist
Brethren Church, 164
Botetourt Co., VA, Rockbridge German
        Baptist Brethren Church, VA, 1117
Botetourt Normal School, 164, 360
    Eller, David Newton, 440
    Ikenberry, Levi Daniel, 646
Bothgef, Martin, 1562
Bottorff, Jerry, 1562
Boucher, Glenn, 1562
Boucher, Rufus, 1562
Boudinot, Elias, 22
Bougainville, Louis Antoine de, 1882
Bough, John H., 1343
Bough, Kenneth, 1265
Bough, S. S., 1388
Bougher family, 2067
Boulding, Kenneth E., 638
Boulton, J. Dan, 1380, 1562
    "A Bountiful Harvest/40th Anniversary
        Church Planting Campaign," 188
    Pataskala, OH, Grace Brethren Church
        of Licking Co., 995
Bouquet, Colonel Henry, 1882
Bourbon Co., KS, Paint Creek Church of
        the Brethren, 989
Bourbon Co., KY, 245, 688, 1224
    migration of Brethren, 829
    Nicholas Co. German Baptist Brethren
        Church, 935
    Restoration Movement, 1101
Bourbon College, See Salem College
Bourbon, IN, 1245
    Gospel Messenger, The (1881–1883),
        559
    Salem College, 1138
Bourignon, Antoinette, 120
Boville, Robert G., 359
Bow Valley Church of the Brethren,
    Arrowwood, Alberta, Canada, 15, 59,
        817, 1034, 1172, 1893
Boward, Bud (Mr. and Mrs.), 579
Bowbells, ND, Church of the Brethren,
    164, 251, 688

Bowden/ Golden Willow, ND, congrega-
        tion, 256
Bowden, Henry Warner, 1882
    works by, 2316
Bowden mission point, Glady, WV, Church
    of the Brethren, 551
Bowden Valley, ND, Church of the Breth-
        ren, 164–165, 165
Bowden, WV, Church of the Brethren, 164
Bowe, John, 1562
Bowen, Cora Price, 1562
Bowen, Francis B., 1562
Bowen, Rachel Senger, See Sanger family
Bower, Clarence Elsworth, 244, 719, 1353,
        1562
Bower, Daniel, 165
    Brethren settlement in Ohio, 961
Bower, Darryl E., 1562, 2273
Bower, Evelyn, Pompano Beach, FL, Grace
    Brethren Church, 1046
Bower family, See Bauer family
Bower, Fred, Pompano Beach, FL, Grace
    Brethren Church, 1046
Bower, Hannah Cable, 165
Bower, Harman Jay, Jr., 1562
Bower, Henry Stauffer, 1882
Bower, Isaac, 1562
    Palestine Old German Baptist Brethren
        Church, OH, 991
Bower, Jacob, 165, 1882, 1941, 2079
Bower, Jacob (b. 1786), 95
Bower, Jacob Samuel, 95
Bower, John (b. 1763), 95
Bower, John D., 1562
Bower, John, Jr., 95, 1562
Bower, Larry A., 2273
Bower, Oscar S., 1883
Bower, Phoebe, 215
Bowerman family, 731
Bowers, Abner, 1562
Bowers, Abraham, 1562
Bowers, Adam, 95
Bowers, Adonijah J., 1562
Bowers, Beatrix Adella Kuntz, 1883
Bowers, Birnie L., 1562
Bowers, David, 416, 1562
Bowers family, See Bauer family
Bowers, Floy, 1883
Bowers, George, 1562
Bowers, George A., 2273
Bowers, Harold Richard, 1854
Bowers, Harvey S., 1562
Bowers, J. F., 374, 1562
Bowers, J. P., 288
Bowers, James, 1562
Bowers, Joe W., 1834
Bowers, John, 1562
    Mount Olivet Brethren Church, DE,
        pastor, 886
Bowers, John D., 1562
    Flat Rock, NC, congregation, 95
Bowers, Martin, 1562
Bowers, Mary Brown, 2033
Bowers, Norman L., 1562, 2299
    Salunga, PA, Church of the Brethren,
        minister in, 1140
Bowers, Peter, 1562, 2033
Bowers, Philander, 1562
Bowers, Robert W., 430, 1562
    Nimishillen Old German Baptist
        Brethren Church, OH, minister in,
        937–938
Bowers, Shirley Leigh Bishop, 1854

Bowers, Steve, 2201, 2317
Bowers, Vina (later Helstern), 596
Bowers, W. A., 1562
Bowers, W. O., 1562
Bowers, William, Massillon, OH, Jackson
  Bible Church (BC), 801
Bowersox, J. H., 1562
Bowie, J. B., 1562
Bowland, Ron, 2273
Bowlby, Glenn Horner, 1562, 2380
Bowlby, Helen Hackman, 1883
Bowlen, Edward Caldwell, 1562
Bowles, Lee, Mount Union (Airpoint)
  Church of the Brethren, VA,
  trustee, 887
Bowlin, Donald, 265, 343, 1562
  North Kokomo Grace Brethren Church,
    IN, pastor, 948
Bowling Green, OH, Grace Brethren
  Church, **165**
Bowlus, John Stephen, 1562
Bowman (Bauman, Baumann) family, 18,
  26, **99,** 142, 1224, 1277, 1280,
  1927, 2028, 2060, 2068, 2081,
  2091, 2094
  bibliographical sources, 1870, 1883,
    1884, 1885, 1893, 2358
  Fahnestock family, 465
  Filbrun family, 490
  Germantown Old German Baptist
    Brethren Church, VA, 544
  Hylton family, 641
  Jamison family, 668
  Jasper, MO, Church of the Brethren,
    669
  Johnson City, TN, Knob Creek Church
    of the Brethren, 672
  McFarland, CA, Church of the Breth-
    ren, 774
  Modesto, CA, La Loma Grace Brethren
    Church, 867
  Mortonhouse (ship), 2373, 2376
  Myerstown, PA, Grace Brethren
    Church, 906
  Nevada, MO, Church of the Brethren,
    924
  *Out of the Melting Pot, Being a Search
    into the History of Some Early
    American Families,* 2016
  Pennsylvania Brethren settlement, 1004
  Peters family related by marriage, 1012
  Pleasant Valley Church of the Brethren,
    TN, 1035
  Redstone Valley Old German Baptist
    Brethren Church, WI and, 2240
  Rockingham and Shenandoah Counties
    Old German Baptist Brethren
    Church, VA, 1118
  Schowalter family, related to, 1155
  Shady Grove Old German Baptist
    Brethren Church, OH, 1171
  sources on, 2315, 2317
Bowman, A. D., 516, 552
Bowman, Abraham, 1562, 2091
Bowman, Abraham, III, 2035
Bowman, Abraham L., 1562
Bowman, Abram (Abraham) D., 1562
Bowman, Addie Bell Showalter, 166
Bowman, Alfred S., 1883
Bowman, Anna, 1844
Bowman, Anna Hylton, 166
Bowman, Anna (later Weber), 1325
Bowman, Anna Mae Harman, 1883

Bowman, Annie Zigler, 1883
Bowman, Asa, 1562
Bowman, B. Floyd, 1562
Bowman, B. O., 1562
Bowman, Barbara Bowser, 165
Bowman, Barbara Jane, 169
Bowman (Bauman[n]), Benjamin (1732–
  1809), **98**
Bowman, Benjamin, **165,** 404, 923, 1264,
  1562, 1883, *See also* Bowman,
  Peter Nead, Peter, influence on,
  918
  publishing works of, 1067
  Shady Grove Old German Baptist
    Brethren Church, OH, elder in,
    1171
Bowman, Benjamin (CB), 1562
Bowman, Benjamin F., 168, 169
Bowman, Benjamin H., 1562, **2380**
  Oak Hill Old German Baptist Brethren
    Church, VA, minister, 957
  Pigg River Old German Baptist
    Brethren Church, VA, elder -in-
    charge, 1023
Bowman, Benjamin J., 1562
Bowman, Benjamin, Jr., 99, 1562
Bowman, Benjamin, Sr., 99, 1562
Bowman, Berkeley Owen, 1562
  Pipe Creek Church of the Brethren,
    MD, minister, 1026
Bowman, Beverly (later Good), 1637
Bowman, Blanche, 2103
Bowman Brethren, 167, **169–170,** 177, 334
  chart of Brethren bodies, place on,
    1403–1405
  dispute involving administration of an
    estate, 728
  named after leader, 910
  Old German Baptist Brethren, 364
  schism, 531
Bowman, Bryon Whitener, 1883
Bowman, C. A., 1562
Bowman, C. D., 1562
Bowman, Calvin, 1562
Bowman, Carl, 350
Bowman, Carl F., 2149, 2150
  on Amish, 2341
  brethren history, 2201
  district histories, 2201
  Forum for Religious Studies, 2202
  on Hutterites, 2341
  on Mennonites, 2341
  works by, 2317
Bowman, Carl W., 1562, **2138–2139**
Bowman, Carole Sue, 169
Bowman, Charles D., 1562
  Oak Hill Old German Baptist Brethren
    Church, VA, minister, 957
Bowman, Charles Wesley, 1883
Bowman, Chrisley (Christian), 1562
Bowman, Christian, 350, 1562–1563
  Red Oak Grove Church of the
    Brethren, VA, 1089
Bowman, Christian Beahm, 167
Bowman, Christopher D., 2273
Bowman, Christopher, works by, 2317
Bowman, Claire M. Andrews, 169
Bowman, Clarence Rufus, 1563
Bowman, Clinton, 167
Bowman, Cora Anna, 168
Bowman, Cornelluis D., 169
Bowman, Curtis Buford, **165,** 355, 1563,
  1883, **2371**

Bowman, D. B., 1563
Bowman, D. F., 590
  Piney Flats, TN, Church of the Breth-
    ren, minister, 1025
Bowman, Dale, 731, 2273
Bowman, Dale Eldon, 1563
Bowman, Daniel, 672, 727, **2380**
  Palestine Old German Baptist Brethren
    Church, OH, 991
  Pigg River Old German Baptist
    Brethren Church, VA, 1023
Bowman, Daniel (1), 1563
Bowman, Daniel (2), 1563
Bowman, Daniel A., family, Franklin Co.,
  VA, *971*
Bowman, Daniel (CB-1), 1563
Bowman, Daniel (CB-2), 1563
Bowman, Daniel (CB-3), 1563
Bowman, Daniel E., 1339, 1563
Bowman, Daniel Frederick, 673, 1563
  anniversary (photo caption), *2379*
Bowman, Daniel Ray, 2273
Bowman, Daniel W. (CB), 1563
Bowman, Daniel W. (OGBB), 1563
Bowman, Daniel W., related to Shultz and
  Paul families, 1157
Bowman, Daniel Webster, 1563
Bowman, David, **165,** 445, 923, 1265, 2083
  Maple Grove Old German Baptist
    Brethren Church, OH, elder-in-
    charge, 791
  Prairie View Church of the Brethren,
    MO, elder, 1050
Bowman, David (CB-1), 1563
Bowman, David (CB-2), 1563
Bowman, David (CB-3), 1563
Bowman, David (CB-4), 1563
Bowman, David (CB-5), 1563
Bowman, David (CB-6), 1563
Bowman, David, Jr., 165, 1563
Bowman, David L., 1563
Bowman, David Lee, 1563
Bowman, David, Sr., 99, 102, 220, 1563
  Miami, OH, congregation, minister,
    961
Bowman, Donald R., 1883, 2148, **2388**
Bowman, Dorothy (later Yoder), 2267
Bowman, E. F., Monte Vista Church of the
  Brethren, VA, trustee, 871
Bowman, Earl McKinley, **165,** 733, 912,
  913, 1563, 1883
Bowman, Edward D., 227, 318, 532, 620,
  1563, 2299
Bowman, Edythe Elizabeth, 1841
Bowman, Effie (later Hershey), 599
Bowman, Eli Harvey, 90, 1563, 1883
Bowman, Elizabeth, 220
Bowman, Elizabeth Eichenberg, 430
Bowman, Elizabeth Holfinger, 2138
Bowman, Elizabeth (Ikenberry), 99
Bowman, Elizabeth (later Moomaw), 874
Bowman, Elizabeth (later Thomas), 1262
Bowman, Elizabeth (later Yount), 1391
Bowman, Ellen, 169
Bowman, Elwood, 1563
  Mountain View Old German Baptist
    Brethren, VA, 2227
  Pigg River Old German Baptist
    Brethren Church, VA, minister,
    1023
Bowman, Emaline, 320
Bowman, Enoch Eby, 1563
Bowman, Ernest Everett, 1563, 2299

Bowman, Esther Miller, 1834
Bowman, Etta Tennessee Garst, 165, 913
Bowman, Etta Warvel, 1360, 1563
Bowman, Eva M. Craun, 168
Bowman, Evelyn Mae, 1563, 2136
    Laughlin Church of the Brethren, MD, 2214
    National Older Adult Conference, 2229
Bowman, Ezra S., 1563, 2299
    Pigg River Old German Baptist Brethren Church, VA, minister, 1023
Bowman, Flora Etta Hoover, 168
Bowman, Floyd Melancht(h)on, 912
Bowman, Fred M., 239, 692, 1563, 2166
    New Hope Church of the Brethren, TN, 929
Bowman, G. C., 672
Bowman, Galen, 1563
Bowman, George, C. 165, **166,** *166,* 354, 355, 1563, 1883
Bowman, George L., 1883
Bowman, George William, Jr., 1563
Bowman, Gerald Lee, 2273
Bowman, Hannah, Red Oak Grove Church of the Brethren, VA, 1089
Bowman, Harold I., 1563
Bowman, Harvey
    Old Order German Baptist Church minister, 972
    Sheridan Lake Old German Baptist Brethren Church, CO, ministers travelling to, 1176
Bowman, Henry, 315
Bowman, Henry Brubacher, 1883
Bowman, Henry D., 1563
Bowman, Hervey M., 1883
Bowman, Hezekiah, 1883
Bowman, Isaac Daniel, 31, 97, 130, **166–167,** 168, 239, 374, 381, 468, 567, 760, 1563–1564, 1883, 2091
    contact with Dowie, 1957
    Jews, 671
    Jordan Mines, VA, Rich Patch Brethren Church, 676
    Louisville Middlebranch Brethren Church, pastor, 948
    Mansfield, OH, Walcrest Brethren Church, preaching, 787
    missions, 860
    Mount Olivet Brethren Church, DE, pastor, 886
    Philadelphia, PA, First Brethren Church, pastor, 1015
    Pineville, VA, Mount Olive Brethren Church, 1025
    prophecy conferences, 1062
    St. James Brethren Church, MD, pastor in, 1134
    Sergeantsville, NJ, Brethren Church, 1167
Bowman, Isabell Campbell, 168
Bowman, J., **170**
Bowman, J. L., 323, 674, 1225, 1884
Bowman, J. M., 362, 2065
    Miamisburg, OH, Brethren Church, pastor, 823
    Roann, IN, (First) Brethren Church, pastor, 1112
Bowman, J. M. (BC-1), 1564
Bowman, J. M. (BC-2), 1564
Bowman, J. M. (CB), 1564
Bowman, J. Milton, 1564

Bowman, J. Price, 1564
    merged with Bowman, Joseph Price, **2380**
Bowman, J. R., 672
Bowman, J. S., 2125
    Roanoke, VA, First Brethren Church, pastor, 1113
Bowman, J. W., 1564
Bowman, J. Willard, 124, 1564
Bowman, Jacob, 1564
Bowman, Jacob C., 1564
Bowman, Jacob S.
    Jordan Mines, VA, Rich Patch Brethren Church, 2375
    Oriskany, VA, Brethren Church, pastor, 981
Bowman, Jacob, Sr. (1781–1848), 99
Bowman, Jacob, Sr. (d. ca. 1783), 99
Bowman, James Brubaker, **167,** 1564, 1834, **2372**
Bowman, James Ezra, 1564
Bowman, Jane Wray, *971*
Bowman, Jesse Brubacher, 1883
Bowman, Jesse Emmert, 1564
Bowman, Jesse, Sr., 1883
Bowman, Jo Ellen Fike, 2184
Bowman, Joel H., 511, 1564, 2299, **2381**
    Modesto, CA, Old German Baptist Brethren Church, minister, 867
Bowman, John, 167, 226, 315, 430, 1961, 2091
Bowman, John (1), 1564
Bowman, John (2), 1564
Bowman, John (1765–1809), *See* Bauman(n), Johann
Bowman, John A., *167,* **167,** 169, 672, 1354, 1564, 1883
    temperance sermon, 1168
Bowman, John (CB-1), 1564
Bowman, John (CB-2), 1564
Bowman, John David, 1314, 1564
    works by, 2317
Bowman, John E., 540
Bowman, John E. (CB-1), 1564
Bowman, John E. (CB-2), 1564
Bowman, John J., 1564
Bowman, John L., 1564
Bowman, John M., 553, 1564
Bowman, John Michael, 1564
Bowman, John Price, 913, 1564
Bowman, John S., 1564
    Jordan Mines, VA, Rich Patch Brethren Church, 676, 2375
Bowman, John, Sr., 165
Bowman, John, Sr. (d. 1804), 99
Bowman, John, Sr. (d. in Indiana), 99
Bowman, John W., 166, 1264, 1564
Bowman, Joseph, 673, 1264, 2091
Bowman, Joseph (1757–1830), 99
Bowman, Joseph (1790–1862), *See* Bauman(n), Joseph
Bowman, Joseph B., **167,** *168,* **2372**
Bowman, Joseph (BC), 1564
Bowman, Joseph Beahm, 1564
Bowman, Joseph Benjamin, 1564
Bowman, Joseph (CB-1), 1564
Bowman, Joseph (CB-2), 1564
Bowman, Joseph Cline, 1564, **2381**
Bowman, Joseph (father) (TN), 167
Bowman, Joseph Henry, 1564
Bowman, Joseph James, 1884
Bowman, Joseph Price, 1564
    merged with Bowman, J. Price, **2380**

Bowman, Joseph (VA), 209
Bowman, Josephus, 1883
Bowman, L. A., 676
Bowman, Lawrence Gerald, 1884
Bowman, Leah Francis Miller, 165
Bowman, Lee, New Enterprise, PA, Church of the Brethren, minister, 927
Bowman, Levi, 350, 511, 1335, 2138, *See also* Old German Baptist Brethren
Bowman, Levi Abraham, 363, **168,** 1564
Bowman, Levi E., 1564
Bowman, Levi Elbert, 1564
Bowman, Levi H., 1564
Bowman, Lewis S., 1884
    works by, 2317
Bowman, Loren, *See* Bowman, S. Loren
Bowman, Lula Nolen, 168
Bowman, Luther D., 1564, 2299
Bowman, Madison M., **168,** 1564
Bowman, Magdalene, 209
Bowman, Margaret (later Yount), 1391
Bowman, Maria L. Worthington, 167
Bowman, Mark A., 2273
Bowman, Martha, 417
Bowman, Martha Anne Yoder, 1834
Bowman, Martha Blickenstaff, 748, 1884
Bowman, Martha (later Ulrich, Teeter), *1250*
Bowman, Mary Baugher, 165
Bowman, Mary E. Miller, 168, 169
Bowman, Mary Elizabeth (later Jamison), *See* Jamison family
Bowman, Mary Ellen, 1884
Bowman, Mary Jo, 1884
Bowman, Mary (later Garst), 531
Bowman, Mary (later Vaniman), 1302
Bowman, Mary Petry, 166
Bowman, Merle Allen, 167, **167,** 1834, **2372**
Bowman, Michael, 1564
Bowman, Mildred Wagoner, 2138, 2139
Bowman, Miranda Brubaker, 165
Bowman, N. R., 1564
Bowman, Nancy Ellen (later Teeter), 1250
Bowman, Nancy Peters, 166
Bowman, Noah Marvin, 14, 1564
Bowman, Noble Orla, 1564
Bowman, Nora (later Ebbert), 1923
Bowman, Odell, 1564
    Oak Hill Old German Baptist Brethren Church, VA, minister, 957
Bowman, Olive Murann Smith, 169
Bowman, Orion E., 204
Bowman, Oscar Franklin, 1564–1565, 1884
    Salem Church of the Brethren, VA, pastor in, 1138
Bowman, P. D., 350
Bowman, Parker, 1286
Bowman, Paul Haynes, 160, **168,** *199,* 208, 242, 312, 316, 1565, 1884, 1955
    The Adventurous Future, 1282
    as historic peace church representatives to F. Roosevelt, 917
    Philadelphia, PA, Bethany Church of the Brethren, pastor, 1015
    Roosevelt, Franklin Delano, 1122
    Washington Office (CB) and, 2260
    World War II, 1372
Bowman, Paul Hoover, 518, 1565, **2381**
    medical projects, 808
    National Older Adult Conferences, 2229
    Spain, relief work in, 1207, 1208

Bowman, Paul S., 1565
Bowman, Pearl Charlotte Stauffer, 165, 1834, 2084
Bowman, Peter, 99, 138, **168**, 1565, 1884, 2104
  publishing works of, 1067
  Simons, Menno, 814
  sources on, 2315
Bowman, Peter (CB-1), 1565
Bowman, Peter (CB-2), 1565
Bowman, Peter D., 1565
  Nimishillen Old German Baptist Brethren Church, OH, elder in, 937–938
  Old Order German Baptist Church minister, 972
Bowman, Price E., 1565
  Mount Hermon Church of the Brethren, VA, pastor, 881
Bowman, Ralph, 430, 590
  McFarland, CA, Church of the Brethren, pastor, 774
Bowman, Ralph D., 1884
Bowman, Ralph Dulaney, 1565
Bowman, Randy, 1565
Bowman, Raymond A., 1565
Bowman, Rebecca A. (later Pritchett), 1060, 1060
Bowman, Rhea Miller, 165
Bowman, Richard A., 467
Bowman Ridge, WV, Ryerson Station Church of the Brethren, PA, preaching point, 1132
Bowman, Robert Cover, 417, 1565, 1834, 1884, 2133
  works by, 2317
Bowman, Robert F., 676, 1565
Bowman, Ronald, 350, 1565
Bowman, Rufus David, 51, 126, **168–169**, 242, 309, 912, 1234, 1565, 1877, 1884, 2025, **2372**
  Bible interpretation, 134
  Brethren peace position, 999
  Durnbaugh, Donald F. on, 2325
  as historic peace church representatives to F. Roosevelt, 917
  historical writing, 612
  historiography of peace, 2201
  review of Seventy Times Seven, 1958
  Roosevelt, Franklin Delano, 1122
  Sanger, Conrad, descendant of, 1144
  World War I, 1371
  World War II, 1372
Bowman, Ruth B., 1884
Bowman, S. J., 269
Bowman, S(amuel). Loren, **169**, 190, 305, 754, 1330, 1884–1885, 1913, **2381**
  Marion, IN, Church of the Brethren, pastor, 793
  Melvin Hill Church of the Brethren, NC, pastor, 812
  works by, 2317
Bowman, S. Randy, 145
Bowman, Samuel B., 1565
Bowman, Samuel Joseph, 1565
Bowman, Samuel, 169, 1923
Bowman, Samuel Benjamin, 1834
Bowman, Samuel J., 673
Bowman, Samuel Joseph, 168
Bowman schoolhouse, Labette Church of the Brethren, KS, 716
Bowman, Shadrach Laycock, 1885
Bowman, Sidney L., 1565

Bowman, Solomon Isaac, 1565
Bowman, Stover Daniel, 1565, 2103
Bowman, Susan V., 168
Bowman, Susanna (Millhouse), 99
Bowman, Susannah
  Miller, Betty on descendants of, 2364
  Worstner, Betty Miller on descendants of, 2364
Bowman, Susannah Arnold, 167
Bowman, Suzanne Pence, anniversary (photo caption), 2379
Bowman, Thomas Isaac, 1565
Bowman, Trent L., 2273
Bowman, Vinna Brubaker, 167
Bowman, W. J. H., 1565
  Rock Grove German Baptist Brethren Church, IA, minister, 1117
Bowman, Walter Dean, 247, 249, 1365, 1565, 1885
Bowman, Warren, 602
Bowman, Warren Daniel, Sr., **169**, 208, 733, 749, 1565, 1885, **2372, 2378, 2381**
Bowman, Warren (R.), 1565
Bowman, Wayne Fosdick, 1834
Bowman, William, 531, 1565
Bowman, Z., 1565
Bowmansville, PA, 934
Bowmont, ID
  Church of the Brethren, **170**
  preaching point maintained by Nampa, ID, Church of the Brethren, 913
Bowmont, ND, congregation, 170
Bowser, Addison Bartholomew, 1885
Bowser, Barbara, 165
Bowser, Barbara (later Bittinger), 144
Bowser, Benjamin F., 1565
Bowser, Caroline Williams, 170
Bowser, D. Luke, Jr. 1565
  Michigan City, IN, Church of the Brethren, part-time pastor, 825
  Rouzerville Church of the Brethren, PA, pastor, 1125
Bowser, D. M., 65
Bowser, Daniel (CB-1), 1565
Bowser, Daniel (CB-2), 1565
Bowser, David, 170
Bowser, Earl C., 21, 1565
Bowser family, **170**, 1885, 2043
Bowser, George, 1356, 1565, **2381**
  Salem Old German Baptist Brethren Church, OH, elder-in-charge in, 1139
  Shoal Creek Old German Baptist Brethren Church, Newton Co., MO, minister, 1178
Bowser, George W., 1565
Bowser, H. G., 1565
Bowser, Harold C., 1565
Bowser, Harold Lloyd, 513, 1287, 1565
Bowser, Harry C., 1565
Bowser, Henry, 1295, 1565
Bowser House, New Freedom, PA, Church of the Brethren, 927
Bowser, Israel M., 1565
Bowser, Israel, New Fairview Church of the Brethren, PA, as minister, 927
Bowser, J. J., 1565
Bowser, Jacob Jerome, 1565–1566
Bowser, Jeremiah, See Bowser family
Bowser, Jesse E., 1885
Bowser, John K., 1566
Bowser, Joseph J., 1566

Bowser, JuliAnne (later Sloughfy), 2293
Bowser, Kermit R., 204
Bowser, Margaret Jean (later Brubaker), 2153
Bowser, Mark B., 2181
Bowser, Mary Razor, 170
Bowser, Paula Picard, 2273
  work by, 2317
Bowser, Robert, 224, 1566
Bowser, Robert B., 1556
  Robinson, PA, Church of the Brethren, minister, 1116
Bowser, Samuel, 1566
  Maxwell, IA, Church of the Brethren, minister, 803
Bowser, Stanley K., 1566
Bowser, Thomas L., 1566
  works by, 2317
Bowser, William H., 1566
Bowshe, Benjamin, 1566
Bowyer, James, works by, 2317
Boxer, James, 705
  the boy preacher (Joseph Hostetler), 631
Boy Scouts, 190, 439
Boyce, Peggi, Jackpot Church, NV, 2212
  boycotts, economic, **2139**
Boyd, Abraham Lincoln, 173, 912, 1566
Boyd, Allen, 1566
Boyd, Anna, 142
Boyd, Arthur Sumner, 1885
Boyd, Auburn Archie, 1566
Boyd, C. L., 1566
Boyd, Charles F., 1566
Boyd, Charles Lowell, 1566
Boyd, Charles R., 1566
Boyd, Christian, 1566
Boyd, Daniel, 1566
Boyd, Darrell L., 1566
Boyd, Darrell, North Fork Old German Baptist Brethren Church, IN, minister, 948
Boyd, Donald, 1307
Boyd family, 1280, 1885
  Pleasant Hill Old German Baptist Brethren Church, IL, 1033
  Salem Church of the Brethren, ND, 1137
Boyd, Henry, 1566
Boyd, Ira, 373, 496, 1566
Boyd, J. Robert, 1566
Boyd, James L., 1566
Boyd, James P., 54
Boyd, John, 406, 1566
Boyd, John L., 1566
Boyd, John William, 1566
Boyd, Joseph E., 1566
Boyd, Kimberly R., works by, 2317
Boyd, L. W., 689
Boyd, Margarette, 236
Boyd, Martin, 268, 406, 494, 1213, 1566
  Old Brethren minister, 965
Boyd, Mary, 2103
Boyd, Mary L, 2273
Boyd, Mercelia Louise, 1885
Boyd, Norman L., 1566
  Sierra Pines Old German Baptist Brethren Church, CA, elder-in-charge, 1181
Boyd, Ralph, 1566
Boyd, Richard, 1566
Boyd, S. J., 1566
Boyd, Scott Lee, 1885

Boyd, Simon, 1566
Boyd, Susannah C., 1885
Boyd, Thomas H. S., 1885
Boyd, W. L., 1566
Boyd, Will, 142
Boyd, William, 268, 1566
Boyd, William E., 1566
Boyer, Anna Rice, 170
Boyer, Barbara, 170
Boyer, Brian, works by, 2317
Boyer, Carl, 1885
Boyer, Carol Constance Younker, 1885
    works by, 2317
Boyer, Catherine, 220, 221
Boyer, Charles Clinton, 1885
Boyer, Charles L., 1885, 2108, 2161
    Ministry of Reconciliation, 2224
Boyer, Donald Arthur, works by, 2318
Boyer, Elias, 170
Boyer, Elizabeth, 170
Boyer, Elizabeth (later Leckrone), 733
Boyer family, **170**, *See also* entries at Bayer
    bibliography, 1885, 1890
    Honey Creek Church of the Brethren,
      MO, 627
    Pennsylvania records, 1955
    sources on, 2317, 2318
Boyer, Henry, 170
    sale of personal property, 1993
Boyer, Irene Lindsey, 170
Boyer, James, 2299
Boyer, James I., works by, 2318
Boyer, James L., 1353, 1885, 2069, **2139,**
    2168, 2182
    biographical sketch, 1975
    Poland, Frank Jacob and, 2238
Boyer, John W., 749, 2299
Boyer, Oda Mitchel, 1885
Boyer, Rachel, 219, 221
Boyer, Robert, 1243
Boyer, Samuel, 170
Boyer, Sarah, 170
Boyer, Susan Spitler, 170
Boyer, Susan Stern, 2273
Boyer, Susannah, 170
Boyer, WV, mission point of Pocahontas
    Church of the Brethren, WV, 1039
Boyers, Auburn A., 613, 1885–1886, 2318
Boyle Heights Mission, CA, 758
Boyle, P., 611
Boyle, Philip M., 22, 170–171, 258, 424,
    577, 580, 1566, 1886
    Pipe Creek Church of the Brethren,
      MD, minister, 1026
Boyle, Rachel Zimmerman, 170
Boys' Brotherhood Advisory Board, 1390
Boys' Brotherhood (BC), *See* Young Men
    and Boys' Brotherhood
Boys' Camp, IN, **171**
Boy's Clubs, **180,** 203, 915, 1251, 2032,
    See also Grace Brethren Boys;
    scouting programs
Boy's Congress, 676
Boy's work (National Fellowship of Breth-
    ren Laymen), 915
Bozoum, French Equatorial Africa
    Gribble, Florence N., 268
    Gribble, James, 268
    Myers, Estella C., 268
    Noatemo, Jean, missionary and pastoral
      work in, 938
Brackbill (Brechbull) family, 1943, 2040
Bracken Co., KY, German Baptist Brethren

Church, **171**
Bracken family, 1885
Bracken, Nora (later Davis), 689, 1360
Bracker, Gordon W., 439, 515, 699, 1566,
    2299
    Osceola, IN, Grace Brethren Church,
      intern and associate pastor, 984
    West Kittanning, PA, Grace Brethren
      Church, pastor, 945
Bracker, J. E., 1566
Brackney, William H., works by, 2318
Bradbury, William, 1185
Braddock, Edward, 211, 516
Bradenton, FL
    Brethren Church, **171**
    Hamel, Joseph Donat, 2196
    Munson, Charles Robert, 2227
    Brethren Church in Peru and, 2237
    Good Shepherd Church of the Brethren
      and Venice, FL, Church of the
      Brethren, 2258
    Grace Brethren Church, **2139**
    organization of new congregation by
    Sarasota, FL, Brethren Church,
      1145
Bradfield, Landis R., 1566
Bradford, Andrew, 17, 451
Bradford, OH
    Church of the Brethren, **171**
    Harris Creek Church of the Brethren,
      585
    Old Brethren Christian Schools, 2232
    Old Brethren Church, 2232
Bradford (West Branch) mission point,
    Fredericksburg, IA, Hillcrest Baptist
      and Brethren Church, 512
Bradford, William S., 1566
Bradley Co., TN, 1340
Bradley, David, 1566
Bradley, E. Arnold, 2273
Bradley, E. J., 1566
Bradley, Earlene Y., works by, 2318
Bradley, Eli J., 570
Bradley, F. A., 1566
Bradley family, 1341
Bradley, Frank H., 415, 1242, 1566
Bradley, George W., Sr., 1216
Bradley, George William, Jr., 1566
Bradley, George William, Sr., 1566
Bradley, Hezekiah F., 1566
Bradley, John L., works by, 2318
Bradley, Phillip Keith, 1566, 1886
    Root River Church of the Brethren,
      MN, pastor, 1122
Bradley, Steve B., 357
Bradley, VA, preaching point of Manassas,
    VA, Church of the Brethren, 785
Bradley, William H., 1566
Bradshaw, Delvis F., 1566
Bradshaw family, 224
Bradshaw, John W., 1566
Bradshaw, M. E., 224, 1294
Bradshaw, Marcus E., 1566
Bradt, William, 384, 572
Bradway, Dorotha, 1339
Brady family, 1958
Brady, George W., 1243, 1566–1567
Brady, Isaac, 1567
Brady, Matthew, 41
Brady, Roy M., 1567
Brady, William W. III, 1567
Braght, Tieleman Jans van, **171,** 1886
Braham, Chester N., 2299

Braillier, George, 356
Brake, Carol (later Strickler), 2295
Brake Church of the Brethren, WV, **171**
Brake family, 171
Brake, VA schoolhouse, 211
Brake, WV, congregation, North Mill Creek
    Church of the Brethren, 949
Braker, J. Elwood, 72, 1567
    Philadelphia, PA, Third Brethren
      Church, pastor, 1019
Brallier, Arthur G., 1567
Brallier (Brailler), Chester A., 1567
Brallier (Brailler), Daniel, 1567
Brallier (Brailler), Eva M. Whitmer, 1567
Brallier family, South Keokuk Church of
    the Brethren, IA, 1205
Brallier (Brailler), George H., 1567
Brallier, Hannah (later Strayer), 1228
Brallier, Henry Harrison, 1567
Brallier, Sadie (later Noffsinger), 747, 2031
    sources on, 2319
Brallier, Samuel, 1567
Brallier, Virgil V., 1324, 1567, 1886
Brallier, W. A., 1567
Brallier, W. H., 1567
Brammell, Guy H., 1567
Brammell, Harvey Leander, 1567
    Ozawkie, KS, Church of the Brethren,
      elder, 987
Brammell, Ira N. H., 1567
Brammell, P. Roy, 748, 1886
Brammell, Willard, 1567
Branagan, Thomas, works by, 2318
Branch congregation, WV, *See* Hevener
    Church of the Brethren, WV
Brand, Millen, 747, 1886
Brandal, Rebecca (later Sherrick), *See*
    Sherrick, Rebecca Brandal
Brandenburg family and Grossnickle family,
    574
Brandenburg, Helen (later Ronk), 1121
Brandon, Dorotha, 1886
Brandon, FL, Brethren Church, **171**
Brandon, FL, Good Samaritan Church of
    the Brethren, **2139**
Brandon, Fred, Jr., 2273
Brandonville, WV
    Salem Church of the Brethren, WV,
      located near, 1138, 1143
    Sandy Creek Church of the Brethren,
      WV, near, 1143
Brandt, Armin M., works by, 2318
Brandt, C. J., 331, 596
Brandt, Daryl, 432
Brandt, J. David, 172, 1567
Brandt, Dorothy (later Davis), 748
Brandt family, **172,** 356, 1936
Brandt, Francis Burke, 1886
Brandt, Harry Alonzo., **171–172,** 381, 748,
    1567, 1886
    Social Gospel Movement, 1197
    Messenger, assistant editor, 818
    works by, 2318
Brandt, Henry, 696
Brandt House meetinghouse (PA), 77
Brandt house, Upton, PA, Church of the
    Brethren, 1295
Brandt, Ira D., 1567, 2299
Brandt, Isaac, 1936
Brandt, Jacob S., 1567
Brandt, Jesse Christian, 2350
Brandt, Lucile Long Strayer, **172,** 748,
    1834, 1886–1887, **2372, 2387**

Brandt, Luke Hoffer, 1567
Brandt, Lydia Kinsey, 696
Brandt, Mary D., 1887
Brandt, Mary Ellen Daggett, 171
Brandt, Nancy, 432
Brandt, Paul K., 445
    Edison German Baptist Brethren
        Church, NE, 2373
Brandt, Paul Kenneth, 1567
    Paradise, CA, Church of the Brethren,
        992
Brandt, Sarah F. Yoder, 171
Brandt, William, 1567
Brandt's Church of the Brethren, PA, 77,
    172
Brandywine Creek, battle of, **172**, 1400
    Brethren aid to wounded, 1106
    Kedar at Ephrata Community used as
        hospital for casualties of, 686
    medical care at Ephrata, 809
    medical care at Ephrata and, 809
Brandywine Creek, PA
    Ephrata Community, 451
    Höcker, Ludwig, 616
Brandywine School (of art), 61
Branham, Chet, 654
Branham family, 1385
Branscom, George A., Sr., 45, 152, 555,
    570, 1567
    Melvin Hill Church of the Brethren,
        NC, pastor and elder, 812
    Mill Creek Church of the Brethren,
        NC, 832
    Peak Creek Church of the Brethren,
        NC, 1003
    Pleasant Valley Church of the Brethren,
        NC, providing leadership, 1035
    Reddies River, NC, Riverside Church
        of the Brethren, elder, 1089
Branscom, George A., Jr., 1567
Branscom, Herman (Hermon) C., 1567
Branscom, R. H., 1567
Branscomb, G. A., 353
Branson, Hiram, 1567
Branson, Isaac E., 1567
Branson, Merrill C., 268, 1567
Brant family, 1908
Brant, Fred W., 1103, 1390
Brant, Woodrow Beachley, 467, 1567
Brant, Woodrow W., 1567
Brashear family, Mill Run Grace Brethren
    Church, MD, 833
Brass Ring (Blough), 748
Braswell, W. J., 1567
Bratt, William, 1567
Brattleboro, VT, 1304
Bratton, Purcel Ray, 1567
Brattser, Enoch L., 1567
Brauche, folk medicine, 2145–2146
Braucher, Dwight, 357
Braucher, Emma, 357
Braucher, Urias D., 1567
Brauer, Anna Barbara (later Stuckey), 1229
Braun, George, 1567
Braun, Helena (later Kruger), **708**
Braxton Co., WV, 172, 2079
Braxton, WV, German Baptist Brethren
    Church, **172**
Bray, Clara Lucille, 993
Bray, Douglas, 1337, 1567
    South Pasadena, CA, Grace Brethren
        Church, pastor, 1206
Bray, Talbert, 373

Bray, W. H., 1567
Bray, William T., 445, 1567
Brazil, **2139**
    Church of the Brethren, 324, 2162
    Foreign Missionary Society (BC,
        FGBC), 501
    General Conference Mennonite
        Church, 536
    Grace Brethren International Missions,
        2191
    Millersburg, OH, Grace Brethren
        Church
    Johnson, George, 2224
    mission schools, 854
    missions and missionaries in, 20, 155,
        172–173, 862, 2225, 2226
    Old Brethren, 970
    Old German Baptist Brethren, 324, 967
    Zielasko, John Warlow (FGBC,
        CGBCI) in, 2269–2270
Brazil, Igreja Da Irmandade, 2338
Brazilian, KS, Neosho Valley Old German
    Baptist Brethren Church, 923
Brazilton, KS
    Church of the Brethren, **173**
    Osage Church of the Brethren, 983
    Brazoria Co., TX, Manvel Church of
        the Brethren, 788
    Brazzaville, French Equatorial Africa,
        857
bread, communion, *See* unleavened bread
"Breathe Upon Us, Holy Spirit," 643
Breathitt Co., KY, 318, 689
    Riverside Christian Training School,
        1111
Brechbiel (Brechbill, Brechbeil) family,
    1943
    Poplar Valley Church of the Brethren,
        MT, 1047
Brechbill, Earl D., 1887
Brechbill, Henrietta Davidson, 1887
Brechbill, John, 1887
Brechbuhl, Benedict, 1897
Brechbull (Brackbill) family, 1943, 2040
Brecht, Elinor, 924
Brecht, Jacob, works by, 2310
Brecht, Margareta Simone, 209
Brecht, Martin, 1887
Brecht, Michael, 209, 1953
Brecht, Samuel Kriebel, 1887
Breckbill, Anna (later Doner), 1918
Breckenridge Co., KS, 682, 1286
Breckenridge Co., OH, 347
Breidenbaugh, Martha (later Reed), 2042
Breidenstine, Aaron Gibble, **173,** 720–721,
    1887
Breidenstine, Ella Elizabeth Steffy, 173
Breidenstine, John S., 600, 1567
    works by, 2318
Breiner, Sue R., 2273
Breininger, Herman P., 1567
Breitbard, Gail Ann Jones, 1887
Breitenbach, Edgar, 1887
Brejda, Janet Freisen, 2166
Brejda, John, 2166
Brekus, Catherine A., works by, 2318
Bremen, 545
    Christopher Sauer Workshops, 290
Bremen, Germany, **173**
    medical projects, 808–809
    relief and rehabilitation work, 230
Bremen, IN,
    Church of the Brethren, **173–174**

Mount Pleasant Church of the Breth-
    ren, 886
Bremen, OH
    Meracle congregation, Olivet Church
        of the Brethren, 973
    Mount Zion Brethren Church, *See*
        Mount Zion Brethren Church, OH
    Rush Creek Church of the Brethren,
        174, 2372
        Beery, Jesse C., **111,** 1553, 1873
        Parker, Isaac Dillon, as pastor in,
            993
Brendle, Thomas Royce, 1887, 2051
Brendlinger, Chalmer D., 274, 1567
    Mohican Church of the Brethren, OH,
        pastor, 868
    Natrona Heights Church of the
        Brethren, as minister, 918
Brendlinger, Charles D., 1567
Brendlinger, W. J., 1567
Breneiser, Elizabeth (later Klein), 700
Breneman, Floyd P., 1568
Breneman, Howard D., 1568
Brenemen family, Rittman, OH, First
    Brethren Church, 1111
Breniser, Barbara (later Kimmel), 693
Brennecker, John Henry, 1568
Brenneman, Barbara Schrock, 2016
Brenneman, Catherine (later Miller), 2059
Brenneman, Daniel, Mud Valley Old
    German Baptist Brethren Church,
    IL, deacon, 892
Brenneman, Elaine Polman, 1353
Brenneman, Eli G., 1887
Brenneman, Elizabeth (later Gingerich),
    549
Brenneman, Emanuel P., 2016
Brenneman, Hannah (later Wenger),
    descendants of, 1940
Brenneman, Jacob, 1568
Brenneman, Jerry Dean, 2273
Brenneman, Lois Hershberger, 1887
Brenneman, Maxwell H., 1070, 1568, 2299
Brenneman, Melchior, 901, 1887
Brenneman, Merna Ruth (later Shank),
    2063
Brenneman, Paul Emanuel, 1887
Brenneman, Richard, 1568
Brenneman, Willaim J., 1568
Brenner, Catherine (later Krumrein), 708
Brenner, Scott Francis, 1887
Brennerman, Arlie, Pine Grove Old German
    Baptist Brethren Church, FL,
    deacon, 1024
Brent, Charles E., 470
Brent, Charles H., 422
Breon, William Earl, 157, 520, 1330, 1568,
    1887
    Pomona, CA, Church of the Brethren,
        pastor, 1045
Breshear, B. E., family of, Myers Creek
    Church of the Brethren, WA, 905
Breshears, Asro, 1212, 1568
Breshears, B. E., Omak, WA, Church of the
    Brethren, minister, 974
Breshears, Burr Emerson, 1212, 1568
Breshears, Florence, Omak, WA, Church of
    the Brethren, leadership by, 974
Breshears, H. T., 1212
Brethren's Sunday School Song Book, 642
Brethren, **174–179,** 2143, 2310, **2372**
    affiliation with Amish, 26
    affiliation with Mennonites, 29

Alexander Mack Museum, 2130
Apostolic Succession and, 43–44
Arminianism and, 55, 56
Ashland and, 2356
Barnes, Jay on Hurricane Floyd and
    disaster aid from, 2348
bearing of arms and, 56
Blair County and, 2357
chart of Brethren bodies, 1403–1405
chronology, 1407–1436
Civil War and, 2350
Civil War experiences of women, 2361
colonial America and, 2325, 2352
criticism of, 16, 40
culture, 3, 59–62
as denominational name, 910
development and operation of, 2347
doctrines of, 2346, 2347, 2359
early (European), *See* European
    Brethren; Schwarzenau Brethren
early (US), 2343, 2357
alcohol and, 16
anointing and, 39
Apocrypha, use of, 43
Apostolic Church, view of, 43–44
attitude toward art, 59–61
doctrine of, 2347
eschatology in, 2346
fictionalized accounts of, 2365
first baptism, 82
influence of Gottfried Arnold on, 57
rejection of church buildings and fur-
    nishings, 46, 48
sources of authority for, 73
Eberly, William R., and world directory
    of, 2328
ecumenism and, 2328
education and, 2328
end times and, 2344
in Europe, *See* European Brethren
evangelism and, 2347, 2357, 2365
Fayette County, PA and, 2362
Fraktur type and, 61
Friends and, 2326
Germantown and, 2326
Great Northern Railway and, 2329
heritage of, 2345
Hinks collection on, 2358
histories of, 2326, 2333, 2349, 2358,
    2359, 2360
Hurricane Floyd and disaster aid from,
    2348
Hutterites, Mennonites and Amish
    compared with, 2341
hymns of 1720–1880, 2327
industrial America and, 2354
Mennonites, contact with, 815
missions of, 2359
modern, admission into the church, 5
modern directions and dilemmas of,
    2346
Native Americans and, 2344
The New Encyclopedia Britannica,
    entry for, 1922
non-resistance and, 2326
ordinances and, 2356
origins of movement, 17, 29, 57
peace leaders of, 2352
persecution of, 1009
pilgrimage in discipleship and, 2359
polity, *See* polity, Brethren
postmillennial views and, 2361
preaching and, 2347

Schwarzenau, *See* Schwarzenau
    Brethren
service and, 2358
Shenandoah Valley and, 2344
slavery and, 1, 22
as source for Beissel's ideas, 113
Southern Plains District and, 2357
theology, 55–56
three phases of history of, 425
women and, 2337
Brethren Academy for Ministerial
    Leadership, **2139–2140**
Brethren Action Movement (BAM), **179,**
    See also Brethren Peace Fellow-
    ship; New Left; peace
bibliography, 1887
Brown, Dale Weaver, 2152
Church of the Brethren, 301
One Hundred Dunkers for Peace, 975
Van Dyke, Joe, 1302
West, Daniel, 1331
Brethren Advisory Committee for Con-
    scientious Objectors, **179–180**
Committee on Counsel for Conscien-
    tious Objectors, 327
Peace Committee, 1001
Zigler, Michael Robert, 1398
Brethren Almanac, See Almanac
Brethren and United Foundations
    ministry in Ecuador, 1289
The Brethren Annual, 18, 495, 1384, *See
    also* yearbooks
Brethren Architectural Services, 188, 575,
    See also Brethren Building
    Ministries
Brethren Argentina, 180
The Brethren at Work, 18, 25, **180,** 193,
    218, 720, 1327
bibliography, 1887
Burkholder, Wealthy Agnes Clark(e),
    231
Children at Work and, 276
Church of the Brethren, 300
Eshelman, Matthew Mays, 455
Gospel Tract Association, 561
Harrison, Stephen J., 586
Lanark, IL, congregation, 273
Messenger, 818
Miller, Daniel Long, publisher, 836
minorities, ethnic and racial, 849
Mount Morris College, 884
Native Americans, 2230
Pfautz, John Eby, 1014
Plate, Lewis (Ludwig) A., 1030
publishing, 1068
Quinter, James, 1077
Brethren-Baptist Church United, Wenatchee
    Valley congregation, WA, 1240
*Brethren Beginnings: The Origin of the
    Church of the Brethren in Early
    Eighteenth-Century Europe*
    (Durnbaugh), 2143
Brethren Benefit Trust (BBT), **2140,** 2163
information technology, church use of,
    2208
organizational restructuring and, 2241
Thompson, Joel Kent and, 2256
The Brethren Bible Class Quarterly (BC),
    182
Brethren Bible Conference, *See* National
    Brethren Bible Conference
Brethren Bible congregations
example of place name, 911

Brethren Bible Institute, **180,** 398, *See also*
    Eden Bible Institute
Argentina, 53
mission schools, 854
Brethren Bible Study Monthly, 308
Brethren Biblical Seminary, 918
Brethren Biblical Seminary Association,
    180, 694
Brethren bodies
description, 2009, 2010
Durnbaugh, Donald F. on Schwarzenau
    movement and, 2327
Eberly, William R. on world directory
    of, 2328
Hostetter, C. Nelson on information
    about, 2342
Kraybill, Donald B. on information
    about, 2342
overview, 1994
Brethren Book and Pamphlet Commission,
    180, 1269
Brethren Boys' Brotherhood, *See* Young
    Men and Boys' Brotherhood
Brethren Boy's Clubs, **180,** 203, 915, 1251,
    2032
Brethren Building Ministries, 51, **180,** 188,
    575, *See also* Brethren Architect-
    ural Services
Brethren Camp of the Ozarks, *See* Camp
    Hamm Mill; Camp Hammond's
    Mill, MO
Brethren Camps Committee (CB), 249, *See
    also* Outdoor Ministries Associa-
    tion
Brethren Care, 116, **181,** 319
Brethren Central Council (BC), 2227
Brethren Central Planning and Coordination
    Committee (BC), 2227
Brethren Chaplains Network, 2158
Brethren Charity Fund (BCF), 2259
Brethren children's papers, 149
Brethren Chinese Fellowship (Church of
    the Brethren), *See* Chinese
    Brethren Church
Brethren Christian School, Osceola, IN,
    Grace Brethren Church, 984
Brethren Church, **181–185, 2140–2142,**
    See also Progressive Brethren
abortion, 2127, 2178
advertising, 7
agricultural missions, 9
AIDS, response to, 2178
alcohol abstinence, 1252
Annual Conference, *See* Brethren
    Church General Conference
and anointing, 39
archival policy, 52
in Argentina, 2251–2252
in Arizona, 54
Arizona Brethren Camp, 2131
Armenians, relief to, 55
Ashland Convention, 368
Ashland, OH, 366
Ashland Theological Seminary, 1257,
    2131, *2131,* 2141
Ashland University, 2131–2132
authority of scripture, 133
baptism, 2089
basic principles of, 182–183
Believers Church Commentary Series,
    2134
Beulah Beach I and II, 2136–2137,
    2141, 2170

Bible translations and versions, 138
bibliography, 1888
bicentennial celebration, 141
Brethren Encyclopedia, Inc., 2143
The Brethren Evangelist, official publication of, 286
Brethren identity, 2141
Brethren music, 899
Brethren Tract Society, 1269
Brethren Way of Christ, 2150
burial customs and, 230
business doctrine, 235
in California, 97
camp meetings, 246
camping movement, 249–250
Cassel, Henry C., 259
Cassel, Jacob C., 259
A Centennial Statement, 2141, 2156
Central Council, 2169
Chad, 270
chaplaincy, 271, 2178
chart of Brethren bodies, place on, 1403–1405
charters/charter membership, 273
choristers and, 280
Christian Day School movement, 282
Christian education movement, 283
Christ's Assembly and, 280
church extensions, 295
church membership, 813
Church of God, Anderson, IN, 296
Church of God (New Dunkers), 297
Church of Jesus Christ of Latter-day Saints, 298
church-state relations, 312
in Colombia, 2251
Columbus, OH, Co-operative Brethren (BC/CB), 326
Committee on Interchurch Relations, 2166–2167
communion table, 328
Conemaugh, PA, Grace Brethren Church, 332
confirmation, 333–334
congregational autonomy and Brethren polity, 1043
cooperation with Church of the Brethren, 2162, 2166
courts of law, attitudes toward use of, 728–729
Credential(s) Committee, 351
Daily Vacation Bible Schools, 359
Dayton, OH convention, 368
Dedication of Infants, 372
as denominational name, 910
denominational offices (Ashland, OH), 37–38, 63
denominational reorganization, 2169–2170
description of, 2095
devotional literature, 381
Director of Brethren Church Ministries (DBCM), 2170
Director of Denominational Business (DDB), 2170
Director of Pastoral Ministries (DPM), 2170–2171
disaster relief, 385
discipline, 389
disfellowship, 365
dispensational eschatology, 293
District of Columbia, 391
district organization, 391

division of congregations, 392
divisions of 1883 and 1939, *See under* divisions
divorce and remarriage, 1099, 2145
divorce issues, 393
doctrines of, 2075
dress, 388
dress, style of, 404
Driver family, 405
On Earth Peace, 974
ecumenism, 423
education, 428
educational materials, 284
elder, 433
elections, electioneering, 434
Encyclopedia of Modern Christian Missions, 1950
environmental issues, 2177
eschatological community, 293
Eshelman, Matthew Mays, 455
ethics, 2178
evangelicalism, 2179
evangelism, 460, 461, 2180
evolution, 463
executive director, development of position, 2140–2141, 2170
family, 2145
Far Western Brethren, 476
feetwashing mode, 1186
Fike family, 490
flags, 493
Flora, Benjamin H., 495
Flora, Clara Myers, 495
Florida, 497
formation of, 31
founding of, 368
fraternal relations, 510
Fraternal Relations Committees (BC), 511
free ministry, 513
Freemasonry, 515
Fremont, OH, Grace Brethren Church, 515
French Equatorial Africa, 270
funerals, 524
Gaiwaka, Noel, 527
gambling and lotteries, 2178
Garber, Aaron Leedy, 528
Garber (Garver, Gerber) family, 530
Garner family, 531
General Conference, *See* Brethren Church General Conference
George's Creek Old German Baptist Brethren Church, PA, 540
German Baptist Brethren, 298
Germantown Trust, 2189
Germany. 546
Gochenour (Goughnour) family, 555
Gospel Messenger, The (1881–1883), 559
gospel music, 559, 561
Grace Brethren Church of Canton, OH, 563
grace, doctrine of, 562
Grace Schools (Grace Theological Seminary, Grace College), 563
Gribble, Florence Alma Newberry, 573
hairstyle, 579
Hendricks, Franklin A., 597
higher education, 283
Hispanic Radio Ministry, 2199
historical writing, 612
history of, 1952

Holsinger, Henry Ritz, 622
Holsinger (Holtzinger) family, 623
holy kiss, 699
homosexuality, 2178, 2204
honorific titles, 1266
Hope Brethren Fellowship, 2204
hospital chaplaincy, 2157
Hymnal: A Worship Book, 2205
hymnals, 642
hymns, 643
impact of Liberalism and Fundamentalism on, 74
Indiana, 653
information technology, church use of, 2208
Kansas, 682
Kentucky, 689
Kerner, William Hoff, Sr., 2211
language, inclusive, 2214
laying on of hands, 731
Leedy Brethren, 734
logo, 2146, *2146*
maintenance of statistics, 1219
Maple Valley Church of the Brethren, MN, 2376
marriage, 389, 796, 2145
mass media, 800–801
mass media, uses of, 2218
medical missions, 807–808, 810
Medina, OH, Living Hope Brethren Church, 2219
membership trends 1980 to 2000, 2220
men's movements, 2221
Mexico City, Mexico, Brethren Mission, 2222
Mexico, missionaries to, 820
Meyersdale, PA, Grace Brethren and Main Street Brethren Churches, 822, 823
military chaplaincy, 2157
military service, 831–832
millennialism, 834
ministry, 846–847, 2224
minorities, ethnic and racial, 850, 851
mission schools, 854
mission statement, 2136–2137, 2148
The Missionary Board (BC), 856
missionary conferences, 856
Missionary Convocation, 856
missions, 860, 2224
in Appalachia, 44
in Argentina, 52, 53–54
missions, short-term, 2226
motion pictures, 879
Murray family, 898
musical instruments, 900, 2228
National Ordination Council, 2171, 2229
Nebraska congregation emergence, 921
neoorthodox influence, 923
and nonconformity, 3
noncreedalism, 942
"Order of the Brethren," 976
ordination, 980
Oregon, 981
Oubangui-Chari, Africa, 270
in Paraguay, 2237
peace position, 1000
peacemaking, 2178
Pennsylvania, 1005
Pennsylvania membership, 1005
pension funds, 1007
Peru, 2141, 2237

Philadelphian Society, providing theological background for, 1019
placement of pastors, 1028
polity, 294, 1044–1045
Polity Committee, 2169
prayer veil, 1053
Priorities for the Nineties, 2137, 2141, 2170
programs for the destitute, 250
restoration, 365
retirement homes, 8, 1102
salaried, trained ministers, 1136–1137
salary for ministers, 1137
Saskatchewan, Canada, 250
Shenandoah Valley, VA, congregations in, 1176
Society of Friends and, 255
sources on, 2318
Spanogle, William L., a founder, 1208
stand on Vietnamese War, 1305
stewardship and, 2252
Swihart, Jonathan H., 1245
Tancacha, Argentina, 382
theology, 1259, 1261, 2254
tobacco use, 1266
tract distribution, 1269
urban ministry, 1297, 2257
Virginia, 1308
vision and mission, 2141
wedding customs, 1326
West Virginia, 1336–1337
Willoughby, William G. on, 2363
wine, in communion services, 1349
women and, 2263–2264
women, ordination of, 2141
women, roles of, 1360
World War I, 1370
World War II, 1372
worship and, 2266
worship, public, 1377
Wyoming, 1381
youth and, 2268–2269
youth programs, 250, 285, 1391–1392
Brethren Church General Conference, 37–38, **37–38**, 180–181, 1351, *1352, See also* Annual Meeting
  1892 (Warsaw, IN), 37
  1897 (Johnstown, PA), 37
  1910–11 (Ashland, OH), *63*
  1978, 37
  bibliographical sources, 1940
  bicentennial anniversary, 141
  committees
    Central Council (1955), 38
    Committee of Ten, 37
    Committee of Twenty-Five, 37
    Executive Committee (1978), 38
    National Executive Committee (1883), 37
  first conventions at Ahland and Dayton, 37, 63
  Four-Year Program, 505
  fraternal relations committee, 510
  Gingrich, Joseph L., 550
  Holsinger, Henry Ritz, 622
  incorporation, 649
  Iran (Persia), 662
  issues
    examination of Wolfe, George, III, 1358
    military pensions, 1304
    prohibiting house-warmings and wedding receptions, 1325

public worship, 1376
voting in political elections, 1318
wallpaper advised against, 1314
widows, care for, 1344
wine, in communion services, 1349
women, roles of, 1360, 1361
Jacobs, Edwin Elmore, 667
Krypton, KY, Brethren Church, 2212
location of, 37, 63
  West Manchester, IN, shelter for, *1335*
  Winona Lake, IN, 1351, *1352, 1353*
Manual of Procedure for the Brethren Church, 788
minutes, 1306, 1351
moderators
  Drushal, John Garber, 406
  Duker, William Irvin, 407
  Flora, Delbert Benjamin, 495
  Gillin, J. L., 817
  Gillin, John Lewis, 549
  Kimmell, Arthur Vance, 694
  King, Lester Vernon, 695
  Lindower, Leslie E., 744
  Mackey, John Crawford, 779
  Mason, Edward Glenn, 800
  McClain, Alva J., 772
  Miller, Edward Lewis, 837
  Miller, John Allen, 839
  office of, 38, 865–866
  Perry, William, 1009
  Rench, George W., 1099
  Riddle, Earl M., 1108
  Ronk, Willis E., 1121
National Brethren Youth, recognition of, 915
National Laymen's Organization, recognition of, 917
offices of
  Director of Board Ministries, 38
  Director of Business, 38
  Director of Pastoral Ministries, 38
  executive secretary (field secretary), 38
  moderator, 38, 865–866
  Peace Committee, 1001
  polity, 1044
  quilting project, 62
  Reconstruction Committee, 1086
  Rose, Smith Fuller (BC) and, 2244
  Shultz, Joseph R. (BC) and, 2249
  Solomon, George Walton (BC) and, 2251
  "The Manual of Procedure for the Brethren Church," 37
Brethren Church, Nanty Glo, PA, *See* Pike Grace Brethren Church, Johnston, PA
Brethren Church Properties, Inc., **185**
Brethren churches
  future, 2013
  history, 1992, 1996, 2004, 2013
  Lutheran Cyclopedia, 2001
  middle American colonies, 1720–1750, 1999
  US religions and, 1994
  in USA, 2010
The Brethren Church's Manual (Brumbaugh), 788
Brethren Civilian Public Service
  bibliography, 1888

camps, 1216
Brethren Clear Lake Camp, WA, 234, 243
Brethren Cloverleaf (McClave), CO, congregation, 324
Brethren colleges, *See* colleges and universities, and also specific institutions
Brethren Colleges Abroad (BCA), **185,** 1207, **2142,** 2162
  branch in Strasbourg, 1228
  Breidenstine, Aaron Gibble, 173
  Committee on Higher Education (CB), 328
  Dolnikowski, George and, 2241
  foreign travel, 1273
  Garver, Earl Simeon, 532, 2187
  Germany, 546
  Hesse, 602
Brethren Community Service (BCS), 2096
Brethren Construction Co., 180, 188, *See also* Brethren Building Ministries
Brethren denomination names, 1922
Brethren Disaster Service Network, 385, 2171
  Johnstown flood, 673
  relief and service efforts, 1097
  work camps, 1367
Brethren Dress: A Testimony to Faith (Rupel), 2143
Brethren Education in the Southeast (Bowman), 168
Brethren Elementary School, Warsaw, IN, 1319
Brethren Encyclopedia, **204,** 535, 1992, 2143, **2143–2144**
  article about proposal for, 1922
  Brethren World Assemblies, 2151
  church government, 1044
  Church of the Brethren, 349
  Covington, OH, Church of the Brethren, 349
  description of order of worship service (1867), 1375
  donors, list of, 2113–2123
  On Earth Peace, 974
  fraternal relations, 510
  Henry Kurtz, publisher, 712
  historiography, 2202
  Kurtz on, 294
  manuals, 788
  meeting at Tunker House led to publication, 1279
  monographs and special publications, 2202
  Ness, Jacob C., 2231
  Old Brethren German Baptist Church, 965
  Old German Baptist Brethren, 349
  pensions, military, 1008
  publishing of, 1068
  Shultz, Joseph R. (BC) and, 2249
  Shuman, L. Herman (OGBB) and, 2249
  Surbey, Howard J., 1241
  theology and, 2255
  Turner, Charles W. (FGBC) and, 2256
  Zigler, Michael Robert, 1399
Brethren Evangelical Ministry Training Committee, 2179
The Brethren Evangelist, 32, 55, 63, 77, **185–186,** 186, 693, 1319, 1360,

1384, 1888, *See also* Progressive Brethren
articles on doctrine, 2141, 2171, 2172
Baer, George, 1250
Bible translations and versions, controversy about, 138
Brethren Church call to ministry, 846
Brethren Church ministry, 847
Brethren Church, official publication, 286
Brethren Church peace position, 1000
Carpenter, George C., 256
Christian Endeavor movement, 285
Evangelical Press Association, 2179
Flora, Delbert Benjamin, 495
Foreign Missionary Society (BC, FGBC), 501
Garber, Aaron Leedy, 528
Gnagey, A. D., 772
Gnagey, Abraham Daniel, 554
Gospel Preacher, The, 560
Goughenour, Herbert L., 562
Grace Schools (Grace Theological Seminary, Grace College), 563
Harrison, Stephen J., 586
historical writing, 612
Holsinger, Henry Ritz, 622
Home Pulpit, The, 625
Iowa, 661
Jordan Mines, VA, Rich Patch Brethren Church, 676
Judaism, 677
Kimmel, Joseph L., 693
Kolb, William, Jr., 706
Mayes, Charles W., editor, 804
McClain, Alva J., contributing writer, 773
"Message of the Brethren Ministry," 817
missions education, 864
Moomaw, B. C., 873
Norcatur, KS, Maple Grove Brethren Church, 945
peace articles during World War II, 1371
peace education, 1002
poetry, 1039
The Progressive Christian, 286, 1061
prohibition, 1062
publishing, 1068
Ronk, Albert Teller, 660
writer for, 1121
Shively, Martin, articles in, written by, 1178
Sisters' Society of Christian Endeavor, 1361
Spanish-American War, editorial position on, 1208
Teeter, Roy R., 1250
women as ministers, support of, 1362
Worst, John H., 1379
Yoder, Charles Francis, 1385, 1386
Yoder, Eli Lorenzo, 1386
Brethren family, *See* family
Brethren Family Almanac, 7, 18, 194, 404, 696, 1384, 1889–1890
Brethren Financial Planning Service, 1045
Brethren folk medicine, **2145–2146**
Brethren folklore, **2147–2148**
Brethren Food Preservation Systems (CB), **186**
Brethren Foreign Missionary Society (FGBC), *See* Foreign Missionary

Society of the Grace Brethren Church
Brethren Foundation, **186–187,** 2140
Ecuador, 422, 1248
The Brethren Fundamentalist, **187,** 1888–1889
Gospel Trumpet, The, 561
Snider, Harold, publisher, 1194
Brethren Haus, 200, *746*
Brethren Health and Welfare Association (BHWA), 2132
Helstern on, 2353
historiography, 2202
Long, Harvey Lawrence, 754
National Older Adult Conferences, 2229
Rosenberger, Mary Sue Helstern on, 2353
wellness and, 2261
Brethren Health Education Foundation
scholarships and loans, 952
wellness and, 2261
Brethren Health Foundation (BHF)
Association of Brethren Caregivers (ABC), formation of, 2132
Cable, William H., 2155
The Brethren Herald, 192, *See also The Brethren Missionary Herald*
Brethren Heritage Center, **2148**
Brethren Heritage Tours, **202,** 2130, 2143, 2357
first (1949), 16–17
Germany, 545
Schwarzenau, 1158
Shultz, Lawrence W., 1180
Brethren High School, Berlin, PA, **187**
Brethren Hillcrest Homes, **187,** 714
Brethren Hispanic Caucus, 850
Brethren Historical Committee, research guide, 140
Brethren Historical Library and Archives (BHLA), 52, **187,** 191
Barnes, Edith Catherine Bonsack, 535, 1857, 2134, 2188
General Offices (CB), 535, 539
General Services Commission (CB), 539
Heckert, Mildred Mae Etter, 2197
Historical Committee (CB), 610
historical writing, 612
Moore, John Henry, 874
museums, 898
statistical reports, 1218–1219
Brethren Historical Society, 1190
Brethren histories
collection of Julius F. Sachse, 1133, 1170
historiography, 2201
Renkewitz, Heinz Gottfried, 1099
Brethren History Newsletter, 1889
Brethren Home and Benevolent Board, 1178
Brethren Home Department Quarterly, 1236
Brethren Home Missions Council (FGBC), 14, 16, 19, 187, **187,** 188, 191, 192, 1353
adoption of Taos, NM, First Brethren Church, 1248
Brethren Building Ministries (FGBC), 180
Cheyenne, WY, First Brethren Church, 274

church extensions, 295
Colorado Springs, CO, 325
Coraopolis, PA, Bon Meade Grace Brethren Church, 343
Cumberland, MD, Grace Brethren Church, 356
Denver, CO, 325
division of congregations, 393
evangelism, 460
Grace Brethren church government, 1045
Grace Brethren International Missions, 2191
Grace Brethren North American Missions, 2191
Grubb, Luther L., 575
Indiana, 653
Indianapolis, IN, Eagle Creek Grace Brethren Church, 654
Irasburg Grace Brethren Church, VT, 662
Jackson, Edward A., 2209
Jenkins, Charles Lee, 2209
Johnstown, PA, Geistown Grace Brethren Church, 674
Lakeland, FL, Grace Brethren Church, 720
The Missionary Board (BC), 855
missions, 860
North Saint Joseph Church of the Brethren, MO, 1134
Patterson, Roy A., board member, 995
Riverside Christian Training School, 1111
Schaffer, William Herbert, treasurer, 1152
shift of focus away from inner-city missions, 1297
Snell, William Harrison (FGBC) and, 2250
Thompson, Robert W. (FGBC) and, 2256
Training in Missionary Endeavor (TIME), 1270
Wyoming, 1380–1381
Brethren Homes for the Aged, 810, *See also* specific locations and names
Brethren Retirement Homes, Inc., 564
chaplaincy scholarships, 2158
Flora, IN, 116, **204,** *205,* 839, 1198
Gahagen Charitable Foundation, 2187
Girard, IL, 1033
Good Shepherd Home, 340, *557,* **557**
Greenville, OH, **204–205,** 574
historiography, 2202
Huntsdale Church of the Brethren, PA, 638
Neffsville/Lancaster, PA, 421
New Oxford, PA, **187,** 2231
Ohio homes, bibliographical sources, 2353
Pinecrest Manor, 1025
Pleasant Hill Village, IL, 1033
Rosenberger, Mary Sue Helstern on, 2353
Timberville, VA, 1265
Brethren Hospital and Sanitarium (CB), **188**
"The Brethren Hour," **2148**
Hamel, Joseph Donat, 2196
mass media, 801
radio ministry by Sarasota, FL, Brethren Church, 1145
Brethren House Ministries (BC), **188**

Brethren House, Washington, DC, 1320
The Brethren Hymnal, 194, 209, 1211, 1279, 1378, 1889
 1901 *Brethren Hymnal*
  gospel songs, 560
  music, 2227
  Music Committee (DB), 900
 1951 *Brethren Hymnal*
  Hymnal: A Worship Book, 2205
  Morse, Kenneth Ivan, 878
 Christian Education Commission (CB), 285
 Church of the Brethren, 300, 301
 Fisher, Nevin Wishard, 492
 Garber, Ora W., 529
 Garrett, Marguerite Arthelda Bixler, 531
 gospel songs, 561
 Holsinger, George Blackburn, 621
 Huffaker, Perry Lee, 635
 hymnals, 642
 hymns, 643
 poetry in 1951 ed., 1039
 Robinson, Paul Minnich, 1115
 Wine, Mary Stoner, 1350
The Brethren Hymnbook, 1889
The Brethren Hymnody, 642
 Ewing, John Cook, 463
 gospel songs, 560
The Brethren Hymnody with Tunes, 642, 1279
Brethren identity, **2148–2149**
 Brethren Church, 2141
 Church of the Brethren, 2163
 Fellowship of the Grace Brethren Churches, 2182
 identity statements, **2149,** 2163
 membership trends 1980 to 2000, 2220
 sources on, 2323
 theology and, 2255
Brethren in Christ Fellowship, 190
Brethren in Christ (River Brethren), **188– 189,** 753, 1900
 American revivalism, 1104
 article about, 1933
 Believers Church Commentary Series, 2134
 Canada, 2067
 Christian education curricula, 2160
 Dunkard Brethren Church relationship to, 2074
 Dunkard influence, 1994
 Durnbaugh, Donald F. on Dunkers' views of, 2326
 establishment, 1974
 Mennonite Central Committee (MCC), 814
 Merrington Church of the Brethren, Sask., 817
 Miller, George, refusing to baptize, 837
 Ontario, 975
 origin of, 2074
 Reynolds, Margaret C. on Plain Women in, 2352
 Stump, Daniel, 1232
 Woodstock Church of the Brethren, VA, 1364
 Yorkers, 189
Brethren in Christ (Shoemakerites), 158, 177, **189–190,** 753
 American revivalism, 1104
 chart of Brethren bodies, place on, 1403–1405

educational materials, 284
Foundation series publications, 1237
Glendale, AZ, Church of the Brethren, 552
Hadsell, B. A., 577
Heisey family, 595
Holiness Movement, American, 619
independents, 190
Longenecker, Christian L., approached by, 756
Mount Joy Church of the Brethren, PA, 882
named after leader, 910
Oakdale Church of the Brethren, PA, 957
Ontario, 975
plain people, 1029
Stump, Daniel, 1232
Thomas, OK, Church of the Brethren, 1263
Waynesboro, PA, church used as meeting place, 1324
Wengerites (Pentecostal Brethren in Christ), 1008
Wise, John, explored union with, 1354
Woodstock Church of the Brethren, VA, 1364
Brethren in Colonial America (Durnbaugh) 612
Brethren in Industrial America (Sappington), 2246
Brethren in Northern Illinois and Wisconsin (Miller), 840
Brethren in the New Nation (Sappington), 2246
Brethren Industrial School for Mexicans, **190,** 201, 202
 Falfurrias, TX, Church of the Brethren, 471
 mission schools, 853
 relief and service efforts, 1097
 Stump, John and Mary J. Keehn, 1232
Brethren Intermediate and Senior Quarterly, 1236
Brethren Intermediate Quarterly, 1236
Brethren Investment Foundation, 188, **190**
 camping movement, 247
 Grubb, Luther L., 575
Brethren Journal Association, 190
 Fike, Earle William, Jr., 2184
 publications, 2109
Brethren Junior Quarterly, 1236
The Brethren Layman, **190,** 917
Brethren Laymen (BC) and men's movements, 2221
Brethren leaders, Brethren children named for, 912
Brethren Life and Thought, 139–140, **190–191,** 1395, 1889, 2186
 historical writing, 612
 historiography, 2201
 poetry, 1039, 1040
 publishing, 1069
 women and, 2264
Brethren life, stories from, 2015
Brethren loan library, Christian Education Commission, 155
Brethren logos, *2146,* **2146–2147,** *2147*
Brethren Media Project, 801
Brethren Men of Mission, **2149,** 2221
Brethren/Mennonite Council for Lesbian and Gay Concerns, **2151–2152,** 2184, 2204

Brethren/Mennonite Council for Lesbian and Gay Concerns (CB), 2264
Brethren/Mennonite Parents of Lesbian and Gay Children, 2152
Brethren Messianic Testimony, 188, **191**
 Grubb, Luther L., 575
 Jewish evangelism, 671
 Judaism, 677
 minorities, ethnic and racial, 850
Brethren, MI
 Lakeview Church of the Brethren, **179**
 Marilla Church of the Brethren, 793
 Michigan Brethren settlement, 824
 place-names, Brethren, 1028
Brethren Minister's Handbook, 2028
The Brethren Minister's Handbook, 788, 1377
Brethren Mission Free Clinic and Maternity Center, India, 808
Brethren Mission Hospital
 bibliography, 1889
 Dahanu, India, 1078
Brethren Mission Hospital, Dahanu, India, **191,** 807
 hospitals, 630
 Nickey, Barbara Marie, as physician missionary, 936
The Brethren Missionary, **191–192,** 203, 694, 1889, *See also* Gribble, F. N.; Gribble, J.
 Foreign Missionary Society (BC, FGBC), 501
 Kimmell, Arthur Vance, 694
 missions education, 864
The Brethren Missionary Herald, **192,** 1384
 Bible translations and versions, controversy about, 138
 bibliography, 1889
 Boyer, James L., 2139
 Christian Day School movement, 282
 The Complete Writings of Alexander Mack (Eberly), 2143
 discontinuance of, 2183
 Grant, Richard E., 2193
 Indiana, 653
 Kriegbaum, Arnold R., 708
 Landrum, Clyde Kermit, 724
 Mayes, Charles W., editor, 804
 McClain, Alva J., contributing writer, 773
 missions education, 864
 National Brethren Bible Conference as alternate annual meeting for Grace Brethren, 914
 photography and visual art, 1020
 poetry, 1039
 Polman, Leo, 1045
 Sandy, Conrad, 1143
 Taber, Miles, 1247
Brethren Missionary Herald Co., 38, **192,** 1237, 1353
 Fort Wayne, IN, First Brethren Church, 504
 Grant, Richard E., 2193
 Hoyt, Herman Arthur, 634
 Male, E. William, 2217
 mission tours, 855
 official church publishing, 1069
Brethren Missionary Herald Co. board
 Haller, Wesley, 2195
 Kent, Wendell E., 2211
 Turner, Charles W., on board of, 2256
Brethren Mutual Aid Societies, **192,**

903, *See also* insurance
Northeast Kansas, 192
Northeastern Kansas, 682
Pleasant Valley German Baptist
    Brethren Church, NE, 2377
Brethren Mutual Fire Insurance
    Company, 2338
Brethren Mutual Insurance Company,
    See German Baptist Brethren
    Mutual Protective Association of
    Western Maryland
Brethren National Christian Endeavor
    Union (FGBC), **192,** 203
Brethren National Ministerial Association,
    2227
Brethren National Youth Conference,
    See National Youth Conference
Brethren Navajo Mission and Boarding
    School, 188, **192–193,** 931, 2230
  bibliography, 1888
  Grubb, Luther L., 575
  medical missions, 808
  mission schools, 853
  secondary school, 1163
  Trujillo, Grace Sandoval, 1277
  Trujillo, Lee, 1277
Brethren Normal College, *See* Brethren's
    Normal College; Juniata College
Brethren of the Common Life, 28, **193,** *See
    also* Brethren (Sisters) of the
    Common Life
"Brethren of the Free Spirit," **193**
Brethren old folks' homes, *See* Brethren
    Homes for the Aged
The Brethren Pastor's Handbook, 788, 1377
Brethren Peace Action, 1281
The Brethren Peace Fellowship, 193, **193,**
    301, 1889
Brethren Peace Witness, 2327
Brethren Peacemaker of the Year Award,
    193
Brethren Placement Service, **193, 2372**
Brethren Press (Brethren Publishing
    House), 7, 18, 25, 58, 150, 161,
    171–172, 190, **193–195,** *195,* 203,
    656, *1064, 1065, 1066,* **2149–2150**
  bibliography, 1866
  Christian Workers' Meetings (CB), 287
  Church of the Brethren, 300, 304
  cookbooks, 340
  Cottrell, Asher Raymond, 345
  Daily Vacation Bible Schools, 359
  Elgin, IL, 435
    Highland Avenue Church of the
        Brethren, 436
  exhibit at bicentennial annual confer-
    ence, *140*
  fire, 2150
  General Board (CB), 535
  General Mission Board (CB), 538
  General Offices (CB), 539
  General Services Commission (CB),
    539
  Greiner, Robert G., 2194,
  Heckert, Mildred Mae Etter, 2197
  Hersch, Elmer Myron, 598
  Holsinger, George Blackburn, 621
  Holsinger (Holtzinger) family, 623
  Imler, Tobias F., 647–648
  information technology, church use of,
    2208
  Investigator, The, 660
  Is Any Among You Suffering?, 2130

  Jubilee: God's Good News
    Curriculum, 2209
  language, inclusive, 2214
  Long, W. Newton, 754
  Messenger, 818
  Miller, Daniel Long, 836
  Miller, John Ezra, literary and research
    editor, 840
  Miller, Mary Grace Hileman, 841
  missions, 859
  Newcomer, Maud Odessa as assistant
    editor, 933
  official church publishing, 1069
  Royer, Galen Brown, bookkeeper, 1127
  Senger, Ray W., 1144
  Weaver, Clyde E. (CB) and, 2261
  Who Are These Brethren?, 2149
  women and, 2264
Brethren Primary Quarterly, 1236
Brethren Profile Study, **2150**
Brethren Publishing Co., 63, 77, 180, 182,
    186, **195–197,** *197,* 256
  A Centennial Statement, 2156
  Dodds, James Gilbert, 395
  Kolb, William, Jr., 706
  Mason, Edward Glenn, board of
    trustees, 800
  Miller, John Allen, board member, 839
  official church publishing, 1069
  Rench, George W., board president,
    1099
The Brethren Quarterly, **197,** 905, 1237,
    1889
Brethren Recreation Fellowship, *See*
    Recreational Fellowship (CB)
Brethren Relocation Service, *See* Brethren
    Placement Service (CB)
Brethren Renewal Service (BRS), **2150**
  evangelicalism and, 2179
  Holy Spirit Conference, 2202
"Brethren Resolve for Peace," 2178
Brethren Retirement Homes, Inc., 38, 564
Brethren Revival Fellowship (BRF), **197,**
    202, 206, 303, 1262, 1889
  Bible institutes, 428
  Bible schools and institutes, 137
  BRF Witness, 197, 206
  Brunswick, ME, Church of the
    Brethren, 2153
  Day of Intercession, 2150
  evangelicalism and, 2179
  Grassroots, Concerns of the, 2193
  inerrancy of scripture, 133
  Lewiston, ME, Church of the Brethren,
    783, 2214
  millennialism, 834
  National Council of Churches of Christ
    in the USA and World Council of
    Churches, 2229
  voluntary service programs, 2163
Brethren Revolving Tract Fund Plan, 2047
Brethren Roots, 2188
Brethren Roots and Branches, 1889, 2188
  Southern Pennsylvania, 535
Brethren Rural Mission Foundation, *See*
    Brethren Foundation
Brethren-Russian Orthodox Exchange of
    1963, 2241
Brethren School Company
  Fruitdale Academy, 520
  Neff, Earl, 313
Brethren service
  Brethren Doctrine of Salvation, 1140

  Central Service Committee, *See*
    Central Service Committee
  Church of the Brethren, 2162–2163
  commissioning services, 327
  Durnbaugh, Donald F. on church-state
    relations and, 2326
  EIRENE, 432
  Geneva, 540
  Helstern, Russell Fred, 596
  National Park Service projects, 917
  Naylor, Jurtis Friend and, 918
  Near East Foundation, 920
  New Paris, IN, Church of the Brethren,
    931
  in Niger, 936
  Nigerian civil war, 937
  Oakland Church of the Brethren, OH,
    957–958
  Panora, IA, Church of the Brethren,
    involvement in, 992
  Plow Creek Fellowship, 1038
  Poages Mill Church of the Brethren,
    VA, 1039
  Poland, 1041
  Roanoke, VA, Central Church of the
    Brethren, 1112
  Rolston, Frances Fitz Simon and
    William Wendell, 1120
  Stenning, R. E. on Brethren, 2358
  theology of, 2255
Brethren Service Centers, 153
  bookstores and, 161
  Brethren Food Preservation Systems
    (CB), 186
  Church World Service (CWS), joint
    activities, 2163, 2165
  On Earth Peace, 974
  On Earth Peace Assembly, 2235
  Eberly, John H., 417
  Funderburg, Drue Dresher, 523
  illustration, *608*
  Indiana, 653
  Interchurch Medical Assistance, Inc.
    (IMA), 658
  International Christian Youth Exchange
    (ICYE), 659
  Long, W. Newton, 754
  Maryland Brethren activity, 799
  medical projects, 809
  Modesto, CA, 197–198
  Nappanee, IN, 198
  New Windsor, MD, 198–199, 200, 202,
    385
    Bushong, Benjamin G., 233
    CARE, meeting at, 286
    Kyle, W. Ray, 712
    relief and service efforts, 1097
    SERRV (Sales Exchange for
        Refugee Rehabilitation Voca-
        tions), 1139
    Zigler Hall, 685
    Zigler, Michael Robert, 1399
  SERRV International (CB) and, 2247
  Sollenberger, David on, 2357
Brethren Service Commission (BSC), 9, 19,
    20, 23, 24, 91, 198, 199, **199,** 233,
    2032, 2037, 2044, 2047, *See also*
    service
  American Relief for Korea, 1291
  Aukerman, Dale H., 2133
  Austria, 2066
  bibliography, 1889
  Bittinger, Desmond Wright, 143

Blue Ridge College and, 153
books about, 1922, 1944
CARE, 342
China, 261, 277
Christopher Sauer Workshops, 290
Church of the Brethren, 301, 2094
Commission of Fifteen (CB), 327
CWS and, 308
displaced persons, 390
Dolnikowski, George on displaced person resettlement by, 2325
On Earth Peace Assembly, 2235
Eberly, John H., 417
Ecuador, 422
Emergency Farm Labor, 443
Encyclopedia of Modern Christian Missions, 1950
Ethiopia, 458
Evangelical Church in Austria, 459
Falfurrias, TX, Church of the Brethren, 471
fellowship houses, 482
Florida, 496–497
foreign travel, 1273
Forest Service, 502
Garver, Earl Simeon, 2187
General Mission Board (CB), 539
Germany, 546
Gilbert, Martha Rupel, 2190
Gingerich, Owen, delivery of horses to Poland sponsored by, 2333
Greek Orthodox Church, 569
Haiti, 579
Harman, Hylton, 2196
Hartzler, Russell M., 588
Heifer Project International, 594
Hesse, 602
High Commissioner for the Occupation of Germany, 603
Historic Peace Churches, 610
historical writing, 612
Homeless European Land Program, 625
hospitals, 631
humanitarianism, 636
Huston, Ora Ivan, 638
Inter-Church Aid and Service to Refugees, 657
International Refugee Organization (IRO), 659
Italy, 665
Japan, 669
Kaltenstein Castle's conversion to first German YMCA model youth village, 681
Karlsschule rebuilding project, 684–685
Kreider, J. Kenneth on, 2342
Leopold, Nathan, 738
Linz, Austria, 746
medical care, 810
medical projects, 808–809
Mennonite Church, 2086
Metzger, Thurl D., 2222
migrant labor, 827
missions, 861
Moravian Church, contact wirh, 876
Murphy, Ross Dale, 897
Murphy, Sara Florence Fogelsanger, 897
mutual aid, 903
National Park Service projects, 917
Near East Foundation and, 920

Peace Committee (BC), 1001
Peace Corps, 1002
Polish Agricultural Exchange, 1041
polity, 1043
post-World War II relief efforts in Russia, 1288
post-WWII aid to Netherlands, 923
prisoners of war, Brethren service to, 1058
prisoners of war programs, World War II, 2110
Puerto Rico, 261
Quito, Ecuador, 1290
recommendation to give twice the amount invested in war bonds to, 1318
Redekop, Calvin W. on BSC/PAX reconstruction of Karlsschule, 2351
references to, 1922
refugee resettlement, 1092–1093
refugee resettlement and, 2240–2241
relief work in Austria, 73
relief and service efforts, *1096,* 1097
relief training units, 1097
relief work in Korea, 707
Row, W. Harold, 1126
Royer, Byron P., 1127
Schwalm, Vernon Franklin, 1157
Schwarzenau, 1158
seagoing cowboys, 1161, *1161*
Shultz, Lawrence W., 1180
Smeltzer, Mary Blocher (CB) and, 2250
Smeltzer, Ralph Emerson, 1190
Snider, Donald Mitchell and Martha Keever, 1194
social action, 1196
Social Gospel Movement, 1197
social welfare, 1198
Sollenberger, David video on, 2357
Spain, relief work in, as basis for, 1207
student exchange program, 1231
support of fine art, 61
Thalham Tubercular Sanitorium, Austria, 1255–1256
Volksdeutsche, 1309
Washington, D.C., 391
West, Naomi E. Miller and, 2262
work camps, 1367
Kansas, 2103
World Health Organization (WHO), 1369
World War II, 286, 1372
Young, Andrew (J.) on workcamps and, 2365
Young Men's Christian Association (YMCA), 2110
Young Men's Christian Associations (YMCA), 1390
Zigler, Michael Robert, 1246, 1398
Brethren Service Committee, *See* Brethren Service Commission
Brethren Service Cowboys
Panther Creek, IA, Church of the Brethren, anniversary party at, 992
Brethren Service Cup, 201
Brethren Service stamps, 201
Brethren (Sisters) of the Common Life, 28, **193**
Brethren Social Policy (Sappington), 2246
The Brethren Songbook, 223, 642, 900,

1378, 1889
Brethren South American Field Council (BC), 53
Brethren South China Mission, **201–202,** 277
Flory, Martha Belle Shick, 499
Lehmer, Solomon G., 736
minorities, ethnic and racial, 850
mission schools, 853
Moy Gwong Han, pastor, 891
Brethren State Mission Board, IN, Dutchtown Brethren Church, IN, 411
Brethren Statement of Faith, 2167–2168
Brethren Student Life Volunteers, 1231
developed into training in Missionary Endeavor (TIME), 1231
Brethren Sunday School Quarterly
Sharp, Solomon Zook, 1174
Teeter, Lewis Wallace, 1250
Brethren Teacher's Quarterly, 1889
Church of the Brethren, 300
Flory, John Samuel, 499
Frantz, Ira Henry, 508
Murphy, Ross Dale, 897
Stine, Bertha Miller Neher, 1223
Brethren tours, *See* Brethren Heritage Tours
Brethren Tract Society, 205, 773, 1269, *See also* Brethren's Book and Tract Committee
Brethren Universalists, *See* Universalist Brethren
Brethren Village
Home for Orphan and Friendless Children (CB), 625
Lancaster, PA, **202,** 225
Shively, Lou Anna River, 2144
Brethren Volunteer Service (BVS), 12, 19, 20, 95, 190, 197, 198, 199, **202–203,** 993, 1968, 1978, 2026, 2096
article about, 1915
bibliography, 1867, 1885, 1889
Chinese Sunday Schools (CB), 278
Church of the Brethren peace position, 1000
COs, 336
Dayton, OH, Emmanuael Church of the Brethren, 365
East Fairview Church of the Brethren, PA, 415
Edwards, Chandler S., 429
Enders, NE, Church of the Brethren, 446
Europe, article about, 1917
Evangelical Church in Germany, 459
Flat Creek Church of the Brethren, KY, 493
foreign travel, 1273
future, 1999
Guatemala, 576
Harrisburg, PA, First Church of the Brethren, 586
Historic Peace Churches, 608
homelessness, 2203
Honduras, 627
hospitals, 631
Huntsdale Church of the Brethren, PA, 638
Ireland, 662
Ivester Church of the Brethren, IA, 665
Kassel as headquarters in Europe, 684, 685

Korean War, 707

Lewiston, ME, Church of the Brethren, 2214

Linz, Austria, 746

Los Angeles, CA, Central Evangelical Church of the Brethren (Korean), 2215

Lybrook, NM, Tók'ahookaadí Church of the Brethren, 2216

Maine, 783

Maryland Brethren activity, 799

McFadden, Dan on, 2344

Mechanicsburg, PA, Church of the Brethren, 806

medical care, 810

migrant labor, 827, 828

military service, 301

Miller, Donald Eugene, 2222

minorities, ethnic and racial, 850

mission schools, 854

Modesto, CA, South Modesto Community Church of the Brethren, 867

Montgomery, IL, Boulder Hill Neighborhood Church of the Brethren, 872

Morocco, 876

Morrill, KS, Church of the Brethren, 877

Mountain Grove Fellowship Church of the Brethren, VA, 889

Native Americans, 2230

nature, extent, and accomplishments, 1977

One Hundred Dunkers for Peace, 975

Osage Church of the Brethren, KS, 983

peace caravans, 1001

peace education, 1002

Pilot House Project, Baltimore, MD, 2133

Polish Agricultural Exchange, 2129 programs, 2163

relief and service efforts, 1097

religious liberty, 1098

Salem Church of the Brethren, OH, 1138

Schrock, Janet West on, 2355

Shaffer, Kenneth M., Jr. on, 2356 social action, 1196

Social Gospel Movement, 1197

sources on, 2319

Springfield, OH, First Church of the Brethren, 1215

Studebaker, Ted Allen, 1230

Sunnyslope Church of the Brethren, WA, 1240

Thompson, Joel Kent and, 2255

Torreon Navajo Mission, 1268

Turkey, 1280

twenty fifth year statistics, 2007

West, Daniel, 1331

West, Janet on, 2355

work camps, 1367

York, PA, Second Church of the Brethren, 1388

youth and, 2269

youth in, 1391

Zigler, Amy Arnold, 1397

Zigler, Michael Robert, 1398

Brethren Way of Christ, **2150**

The Brethren Witness, 191–192, **203**

Brethren Witness Office and short-term missions, 2226

Brethren World Assemblies, **2151**

Brethren Encyclopedia, Inc, support for, 2143

Durnbaugh, Donald F. on background and basis of, 2326

Durnbaugh, Donald F. on report of proceedings of July 15–18, 1992 meeting, 2327

historiography, 2202

sources on, 2321, 2323

Stoffer, Dale R. on 1998 meeting, 2359

theology and, 2255

Brethren World Peace Academy, On Earth Peace Assembly, 2235, *2236*

Brethren Yearbook (1918), 18, *See also* yearbooks

Brethren Young People's Department (BYPD), **203,** 218, 917, 1088, 1394

Brethren Youth, **203,** 915

Brethren Youth Board, *See* entries at National Brethren Youth

Brethren Youth Council, 155, 192, **203,** 1889, *See also* Brethren Youth Fellowship

GBC Christian Education (Department), 533

National Sunday School Board merger, 917

Brethren Youth Crusaders (BYC), 182, **2151**

Arizona Brethren Camp, purchase of land for, 2131

Brethren Youth Fellowship (BYF), **203**

Brethren Youth in Christ (BYIC), **2151,** 2269

Brethren Youth, Inc., 915

Brethren Youth Quarterly, 1236

The Brethren's Advocate, **203,** 1889

Native Americans, 2229

The Brethren's Almanac, See Almanac

The Brethren's Annual, 1889

Brethren's Book and Tract Committee, 155, **203,** 203–204, 1268, 1269

General Church Erection and Missionary Committee (CB), 536

General Missionary and Tract Committee (GBB), 539

Gospel Tract Association, 561

Hays, Daniel, 590

incorporation, 649

National Book and Tract Committee (BC), **205,** 1269

Vaniman, Daniel, 1303

Brethren's Card, 133, **204,** 528, 942, 1262, **2152**

Brethren's Church Extension Union, **204,** 206, 295

Miller, Howard, 837

missions education, 863

Moomaw, Daniel Crouse, 873

Sisters' Aid Society, 1187

urban ministry, 1296

women, roles in, 1361

Wood, Julia A., 1363

Yoder, Eli Lorenzo, 1386

Brethren's Church Manual, 133, 220

Brethren's Hymn Book, 1890

poetry, 1039

Quinter, James, 1077

The Brethren's Hymnal, 1890

Ewing, John Cook, 463

gospel music, 559

The Brethren's Hymnbook, 641, 642

Brethren's Illustrated Teacher's Quarterly, 1236

Brethren's Juvenile Quarterly, 1236

Brethren's Messenger, **180,** *See also Der Brüderbote,* under B

The Brethren's Messenger, 218, 1068

The Brethren's Missionary Visitor, **205,** 1218, 1890

missions, 859

missions education, 864

Pittenger, John Milton, indexer of, 1026

Vaniman, Daniel, 1303

Williams, John Henry Bashor, 1345

Brethren's National Book and Tract Committee, **205,** 1269, *See also* Brethren's Book and Tract Committee

Brethren's Normal College, *See* Juniata College

Brumbaugh, Isaac Harvey, 220

Brumbaugh, Jacob H., 221

Brumbaugh, Martin Grove, 222

Burkholder, Wealthy Agnes Clark(e), 231

Gahagen, Zella Johns, 2187

Quinter, James, 1077

School Visiting Committees, 1155

Brethren's Orphan Home (CB), 276

The Brethren's Pastor's Handbook, 1377

Brethren's Publishing Company, 193, *195,* *See also* Brethren Press

The Brethren's Quarterly, **205,** 1890

Brethren's Quarterly (*Advanced Quarterly*), 236

The Brethren's Reasons, **205–206,** 696

Kinsey, Samuel, 696

Murray, Samuel M., 898

Old German Baptist Brethren, 967

Siler, George V., helped edit, 1181–1182

Brethren's Teacher's Monthly, 1236

Brethren's Tracts and Pamphlets, 371, 1269, *See also* tracts

Hays, Daniel, 590

Rosenberger, Isaac J., writing for, 1123

The Brethren's Tune and Hymn Book, 642, 899, 1211, 1278–1279

Brethren's Work of Evangelism, 204, **206**

Bretz family, 1890

Brewbacher family, 1948

Brewbaker family, *See* Brubaker family

Brewer family, Mount Pleasant Brethren Church, VA, 886

Brewer, M. D., 1568

Brewer, Mary Angle, 446

Brewer, W. H., 267

Brewer, Mrs. W. H., 267

brewing and distilling, **206**

BRF, *See* Brethren Revival Fellowship

Briceton (Briston) schoolhouse, preaching point of Blue Creek, OH, congregation, 152

Brick Church, Augusta Co., VA, congregation, Middle River Church of the Brethren, 825

Brick House, Nettle Creek, IN, 923

Brick House, Union Center Church of the Brethren, IN, 1287

Brick House, White Branch Church of the Brethren, IN, 1339

Brick Union, VA

meetinghouse, 164
mission point, Botetourt Co., VA,
    Church of the Brethren, 164
Brick, VA, congregation, 345
    Floyd Co. Church of the Brethren, **500,**
    1267
    New Bethel Church of the Brethren,
        ministers for, 925
    Ninevah mission point, 938
Brickel, Clair E., 213, 319, 1568
    Sinking Spring, OH, Grace Brethren
        Church, pastor, 1186
Bricker, George W., 1568
Bricker, Jacob A., 1568
Bricker, James, Mabel, OR, Church of the
        Brethren, deacons, 771
Bricker, Marion Leroy, 1834
Bricker, Marlin Glen, 1568
Brickey, J. Allen, 241, 1568
Bricktown congregation, Oak Grove
        Church of the Brethren, IL, 955
Bridenbaugh, Carl, 1890
Bridge, Albert Rizer, 576, 1568
    Monticello/Pike Creek Church of the
        Brethren, IN, pastor, 872
Bridge, George O., 1333, 1568
Bridge, Jacob, 1568
Bridges family, Prosperity Brethren Church,
        WV, 1062
Bridgewater Academy, 208, 360, 1299
Bridgewater College, 105, **206–208,** 535,
        2021, **2372,** 2378
    Alexander Mack's Bible, 777
    appraisal, 2009
    Baugher, Jacob I., president, 208
    Bhagat, Premchand Ganeshji, 131
    Bittinger, Foster Melvin, 143
    Bixler, Edward Clinton, 144
    Blough, Carman George, 149
    Blough, Elizabeth Delp Rosenberger,
        150
    Blue Ridge College and, 153
    Bonsack, Charles Daniel, 160
    Bowman, Paul Haynes, president, 168,
        208
    Bowman, Rufus David, 168
    Bowman, Samuel Loren, 169
    Bowman Warren Daniel, president,
        169, 208
    Brandt, Lucile Long Strayer, 172
    Brethren World Assembly, 2151
    Cassel Library, PA, 260
    Church of the Brethren, 300
    Cooper, Herbert Austin, 342
    Copp, Zed H., 343
    crest design, 61
    Crouch, Eugene Morgan, 353
    Daleville College, consolidation with,
        360
    difficulties, 1978
    Dove family, 398
    Dove, John Adams, 397
    Early, Henry Clay, 413
    Eller, David Newton, 440
    Eller, Enten, 301
    establishment of, 1308
    evolution, 463
    Fike, Earle William, Jr., 2184
    Fisher, Nevin Wishard, 492
    Fisher, Virginia Showalter, 492
    Fitzwater, Perry Braxton, 492
    Flory, Daniel Christian, founder, 206,
        207, *497,* 497–498

Flory, George W., 498
Flory, John Samuel, president, 207,
        498–499, *499*
Flory, Marie Sarah Mason, 2185
Flory, Wendell Phillips, 2185
Forum for Religious Studies,
        2185–2186, 2202
Frantz, Edward, 508
Fry, Francis on, 2362
Garber, David Benjamin, 528
Geisert, Wayne F., president, 208,
        2187–2188
German Baptist Brethren and, 227
Groff, Warren Frederick, 2194
Harley, Samuel Abraham, 583
Hays, Daniel, 590
Hebron Seminary, 591
Henry, Jerry Maurice, 598
Hershey, John Willard, 599
higher education, 605
historic sites, 609
historical libraries, 610
history of, 2090, 2091
Holsinger, George Blackburn, 621
Holy Spirit Conference, 2203
Hoover, William I. T., 628
Huffman, Nelson Thomas, 2205
Keller, Paul W., 2210
library photo, *472, 493, 495, 508, 537*
Lindsay, Samuel David, 744
Little River Church of the Brethren,
        VA, 749
Locke, John Funk, 751
Long, Effie Virginia Showalter, 753
Long, Isaac Samuel, 753
Mays, Morley Josiah, professor and
        administrator, 804
McCann, Elizabeth Gibbel, 771
McCann, Samuel Napoleon, 772
Miller, DeWitt L., 836
Miller, Donald Eugene, 2223
Miller, Joseph Quinter, 841
Miller, Minor Cline, 841
Moherman, Tully S., 867
Moomaw, Benjamin Franklin, 873
Moomaw, Daniel Crouse, 873
Morris, James Henry, 877
museums, 898
Myers, Minor Morton, 904
Neff, Robert Wilbur, 2230
opened as Spring Creek Normal
        School, 1213
Peters, Raymond Russell, 1011
Pritchett, Reuel Bowman, Museum,
        1060
Robinson, Paul Minnich, 1115
The Rockingham Male Chorus, 2204
Row, Harold W., 1125
Sanger, Samuel F., trustee of, 1143
Sappington, Roger E. (CB) at, 2246
School Visiting Committees, 1155
Shively, Levi Stephen, 1178
Strayer, Ord Lee, 1228
Summit Church of the Brethren, VA,
        1236
teacher education programs, 2089
Wampler, Ernest Michael, 1316
Wampler, Frederick Jacob, 1316
Wampler, Guy Edgar, Sr., 1316
Wampler, Nelie Florence, 1317
Wampler, Vida Eunice Miller, 1316
Wayland, Francis Fry on, 2362
Wayland, John Walter, 1323

West, Murray Guy, 1332
Will, Harper S., 1345
Wine, Joe A., 246
Wine, William M., 1350
Women's Conferences (CB) and, 2265
Wright, Charles C., acting president,
        208
Yount, Walter Bowman, president,
        206–208, 207, 1391
Zeller, Harry Knode, Jr., 1395
Ziegler, Jesse H., 1395
Zigler, Amy Arnold, 1397
Zigler, David H., 1397
Zigler, Earl Myers, 1397
Zigler, Michael Robert, 1398, 1399
Zigler, Rachel E. Myers, 1397
Bridgewater-Daleville College, 208,
        360, 1890
    Blue Ridge College and, 153
Bridgewater Home, **208**
    Fike, Paul Henry, 2184
    West, Murray Guy, 1332
Bridgewater Retirement Community, 2262
    Bridgewater, VA, 613, 697, 1213,
        1235, 1308
Bridgewater, VA, congregations
    Church of the Brethren, **206,** *207,* 341,
        342
    Flory, John Samuel, 499
    history of, 2055
    The Rockingham Male Chorus, Church
        of the Brethren, 2204
    Sherfy, Robert Livingston (CB) and,
        2249
*A Brief and Simple Exhibition from the
        Word of God* (Bowman), 165
*Brief and Simple Presentation of the
        Outward But Sacred Rights and
        Ordinances of the House of God,*
        147, 175
Brien, Lindsay Decker Metcalfe, 1890
Briery Branch Church of the Brethren, VA,
        105, **208,** 1144
Briggs, Emmer, 204
Briggs, John, 204
Brigham, Clarence S., 1858
Bright, Aldeba Klepinger, 2318
Bright, Anna Denlinger, 209, 375
Bright, C. Emmert, works by, 2318
Bright, Daniel, 1891
Bright, Edith McBaffey, 209
Bright family, **209,** 396, 701, 1953
Bright, Grace Hollenberg, 209
Bright, Hamilton Garver, 2318
Bright, Harriet Howard, 209, 1138, 1568,
        1834
Bright, Isaac B., 208, 209, 375, 1568
Bright, J. F., 417, 1568
Bright, Jacob Homer, **208,** 209, 462, 1568,
        1838, 1891, *See also* Bright,
        Minnie Flory missionary supplied
        by Salem Church of the Brethren,
        OH, 1138
Bright, J. Russell, 209
Bright, John Calvin (1881–1919), **208–209,**
        912, 1568, 1835, 1891, **2381, 2387**
Bright, John Calvin (1915–1996), 209, 912,
        913, 1568, 1945, 2299
    missionary supplied by Salem Church
        of the Brethren, OH, 1138
    Peoria IL, (First) Church of the
        Brethren, pastor, 1009

Bright, John Daniel, 209, 1568
Bright, Lydia, 209
Bright, Magdalene Bowman, 209
Bright, Minnie, 1138
Bright, Minnie Flory, 208, **209**, 1835, 1891
Bright, Peter L., 209
Bright, Richard, 1568
Bright, Richard G., 21
Bright, Sara Rife, 208
Bright, Sarah Rive, 209
Bright Star, OK, Church of the Brethren,
    See Harrison, OK, Church of the
    Brethren
Brightbill, Alvin Franz, *111,* **209**, 242, 248,
    248, 399, 1331, 1389, 1568, 2020,
    See also camping programs
Brightbill, David C., 209
Brightbill family, 1943
    Myerstown, PA, Grace Brethren
      Church, 906
Brightbill, John Frantz, 1185
Brightbill, Katie Frantz, 209
Brightbill, Mae Esther Good, 209
Brightbill, Marlin S., 1568
Brightbill, Martha (later Fulk), 1943
Brightbill, Olive Yoder, 1891
Brighton Chapel Cemetery, IN, 167
    Brighton, IN, 167
Brighton, IN, Brighton Chapel Brethren
    Church, **209**
Brights Hollow, WV, 254
Brigner, Charles W., 20, 1568
Brilhart, John A., 1568
    Rockton, PA, Church of the Brethren,
      elder and minister, 1118
Brill, Catherine (later Spire), 2294
Brill, Francis, 1277, 1568
Brill, Frank, 674
Brillhart, Barbara (later Yount), 1391
Brillhart, David Y., 1568
    New Fairview Church of the Brethren,
      PA, elder in, 927
Brillhart, John, 424, 1568
    Seneca Church of the Brethren, OH,
      elder in, 1166
Brillhart, Peter, 800
Brillhart, Riley, 1568
Brillhart, Uriah S., 1568
Brillinger, Anna (later Sanger), *See* Sanger,
    Anna Brillinger
Brinck, Andreas, works by, 2318
Brindle, Cyrus, 1568
Brindle, John, 1568
Brindle, John Henry, 1568
Brindle, Josiah, 1568
Brindle, Marvin C., 1891
Briner, Andres, 1891
Briner, Doris (later Julien), 2210
Briner, Doris Mardella, 1850
Brinkmeier, Kathleen Diane, 2273
Brinkworth, Henry P., 1568
Brinson, M. L., 1568
    Bristol congregation, TN, Johnson City,
      Knob Creek Church of the Breth-
      ren, 673
Bristol, Roger Pattrell, 1858
Bristol, TN, 1339
    First Church of the Brethren, **209**
Bristol Twp., OH
    Dunkard Brethren Church, 2079
    Mennonite Church, 2079
Bristol Twp., Trumbull Co., VA, 209
Bristolville, OH

Brethren Church, 2079
    Church of the Brethren, **209–210**
Britain, *See* United Kingdom
Britannia (ship)
    Holsinger (Holtzinger) family, 623
    Holtzapfel (Holsapple, Holsopple)
      family, 624
    Horst family, 630
British Columbia, Canada, 19
British East Africa, 573
British-Israelism movement, **210**, 349, 455
British Museum (London), Nininger mete-
    orites in, 781
Briton, WV, 254
Britt, Benjamin F., 1568–1569
Britton, Edna (later DeLong), 1916
Britton, Joseph Ferdinand, **210**, 1305, 1569
Britton, Mark Allen, 2273
Britz, Margaret Stober, 2379
Broache, Stephen, 1891
Broad, Raymond, Penn Run Church of the
    Brethren, PA, pastor, 1004
Broad River, SC
    French Creek, 516
    German Baptist Brethren Church, **210**
Broad, Thomas A., 715
Broad, Thomas H., 490, 1212, 1569
broadbrims, *See* hats
broadcasting, *See* mass media
The Broadfording Beacon, 210
Broadfording Bible Brethren Church, *See*
    Bible Brethren Fellowship
    (Broadfording Bible Brethren
    Church)
Broadfording Bible Seminary, 210
Broadfording Christian College, 210
Broadfording, MD, 1329
    Bible Brethren Church, 210, **210**
    Church of the Brethren, 42, **210**, 232
    Harsh, Mary Lou Hykes, 587
    Pfautz family, 1014
Broadhurst, Stephen, 271, 1569
Broadwater, Carl, 1569, 2299
Broadwater Chapel, MD
    Dunkard Brethren congregation,
      210–211, 2372
    Green, John Thomas, 569
    Georges Creek Church of the Brethren,
      540
Broadwater, Clyde, 1569
Broadwater, Edith M., 211
Broadwater, Eliza Ellen (later Green), 569
Broadwater family, Root River Church of
    the Brethren, MN, 1122
Broadwater, Howard, 211, 1569, 2273
Broadwater, Jonas, 211, 1569
Broadwater, Jonathan, 1569
Broadwater, Katherine G. (later Weiand),
    1344
Broadwater, MO
    Church of the Brethren, **211**
    Farrenburg Church of the Brethren, 479
    Fisher, E. R., from, 929
Broadway, VA, 699, 701, 745, 1291, 1391,
    1397
    fraternal relations, 510
    historic sites, 609
    historical writing, 613
    Tunker House, 2108, 2109
Brock, John Dale, 1569
    Prosser, WA, Community Grace
      Brethren Church, pastor, 1062
Brock, M. J., 726

Brock, Peter, 1891, 2318
Brock, Peter de B., 613, 638, 2201
Brock, Robert L., works by, 2318
Brock's Gap, VA, congregations, 351, 397,
    725, 746
    Church of the Brethren, **211**
    Mountain Grove Church of the
      Brethren, VA, 889
    Ritchey (Ritchie) family, 1110
Brockway, Wayne E., 2273
Brockwell, Charles W., Jr., 2319, 2327
Brockwell, George W. A., 1297, 1569
Brodbeck, A. M., 1569
Broederen movement, 2087
Broken Sword, OH, Church of the Breth-
    ren, **211**
Broken Sword territory, OH, 424
Bromback (Brumbach), Johann Jacob, **211,**
    516
Bromback, Jacob, 211
Bromback, Mary E. Angle, 211
Bromley, Thomas, 120
Brons, Anna, 1891
Brook family, Farmers Grove Fellowship
    (BC), PA, 476
Brooke, John L., works by, 2319
Brookens, Henry, 1569
Brooklyn First Church of the Brethren,
    Brooklyn, NY, 1296
Brooklyn, IA, congregations, 372
    Brethren Church, **211**
    Church of the Brethren, **211**
    English River Church of the Brethren,
      IA, 447
    Gillin, John Lewis, 549
    Snyder, Jacob S., 1195
Brooklyn Mission, *See* Urban Ministry
    Brooklyn, NY, 25
    Calvary Church of the Brethren,
      211–212, *212*
    Caruso, John G., 258
    Church of the Brethren, 299
    congregations, 709, 710
    First Church of the Brethren, **212,**
      932–933
    Hispanic Ministries (CB), 2199
    Howe, William Mohler, 633
    Italian mission, 1285
    Second Church of the Brethren, 212
    urban ministry in, 932–933, 1296
Brooklyn, SC, congregations
    Church of the Brethren, **212**
    Mill Creek Church of the Brethren,
      NC, 832
Brookpark, OH, Community Church of
    the Brethren, **320–321**
Brooks, Betty Jeanne, 1835
Brooks, Daniel, 2273
Brooks, Donald W., 1891
Brooks, Edythe L., works by, 2319
Brooks, Ella Maude (later Dulany), 1920
Brooks, Emma Martin, 212
Brooks family
    Fremont, OH, Grace Brethren Church,
      515
    Meadow Branch Church of the Breth-
      ren, TN, 805
    Outlook, WA, Church of the Brethren,
      986
    Patterson, CA, Church of the Brethren,
      995
    Salem Church of the Brethren, ND,
      1137

Sandy Creek Old German Baptist Brethren Church, WV, 1143
Brooks, George, 212
Brooks, H. F., 1569
Brooks, Harlan Jesse, **212**, 505, 1235, 1240, 1569, 1835, 2299, **2372, 2381, 2387**
works by, 2319
Brooks, J. W., 1569
Brooks, James Chester, 1569
Brooks, James, Shoal Creek Old German Baptist Brethren Church, Newton Co., MO, minister, 1178
Brooks, John D., 1891
Brooks, John, Meadow Branch Church of the Brethen, TN, 805
Brooks, Myra (later Welch), 1329, 2094
MacMaster, Richard K. on poem by, 2345
Brooks, Ruth Elizabeth Forney, **212**, 1835, **2372, 2387**
Brooks, Ruth Forney, 1969
Brooks, W. Oscar, 264
Brookside meetinghouse, Eglon, WV, Church of the Brethren, 430
Brooksville, FL
Church of the Brethren, **212–213**
as example of place name, 911
Grace Brethren Church, **213**
Brookville, OH, 213, 693, 1355, 1356
baptisms, *213*
Church of the Brethren, **213**, 462
Englewood, OH, Grace Brethren Church, 447
as example of place name, 911
Grace Brethren Church, **213–214**, 319
Brosius, Rose Alverda (later Foster), **504**, 1849
Bross, Harvey E., 1891
Bross, Scott J., 2273
Brossmand, Schuyler C., 1891
Brother Agabus, *See* Koch, Stephan
Brother Agnonius, *See* Wohlfahrt (Welfare), Michael
Brother Amos, *See* Mäyle, Johann
Brother Bonsack, *See* Bonsack, Charles D.
Brother Enoch, *See* Weiser, Johann Conrad, 1328
Brother Harvey (Brammell), 748
Brother Hoheim, Hamburg-Altona, 580
Brother Jethro, *See* Gass (Gast), Jakob
Brother Jojoda (Jehoiada), *See* Nägele, Hans Rudolph
Brother Jonadab, *See* Höcker, Heinrich
Brother Lamech, 840
Brother Obed, *See* Höcker, Ludwig
Brother Puterbaugh, Osceola Church of the Brethren, IN, elder, 984
Brother Sealthiel, *See* Landert, Sigmund
Brother Stein, *See* Stein, John W.
Brotherhood Board (CB), 2262
brotherhood, doctrine of, 996, 2096
Brotherhood Fund, 1218
Brotherhood Service, Inc., 2133
Brotherhood (ship), 151, 1155
Brothers and Sisters of the Common Life, 193
Brothers (ship), 147, 380, 2371
Brothers, Society of, *See* Hutterian Society of Brothers
Brothers Valley (Brothersvalley), PA, 225, 1338
Church of the Brethren, *See* Brother-

ton, PA, Brothersvalley Church of the Brethren
congregation, 736, 1225
Forney, Roy S., 503
history of, 1918
place-names, Brethren, 1027
Rayman Fellowship Church of the Brethren, PA, as preaching point of, 1084
sources on, 2323
Brotherton, Bobbi Alie, 2273
Brotherton, Don, 363, 705, 1569
Brotherton, PA, 1225
Brotherton, PA, Brothersvalley Church of the Brethren, 99, 121, **214**
Geiger Church of the Brethren, PA, 533
Middle Creek Church of the Brethren, PA, 825
Brough, Andrew, 1569
Brough family, 1886
Brough, J. A., 1569
Brough, Jacob A., 1569
Brough, John, 1569
Broughand, H., 1569
Brougher family, 267
Brougher, Madison, 214
Brougher, Maggie Meyers, 214
Brougher, Mahlon J., **214**, 244, 415, 571, 1569, 1891, 1918, 2072
Brougher, Mary Kathryn Wolford, 214
Brougher, Uriah D., 1569
Broughman, Elizabeth Jennings, 670, 1569
Mount Bethel Church of the Brethren, VA, pastor, 880
Brouhard, Harvey (Henry), 1569
Brouse, W. P., 1569
Brovant, Elmer A., 2300
Brovant, Gail, 588
Brovant, Henry, *See* Browand, Henry
Brovant, Linda, 588
Brovant, Ray O., 1569
Brovont, Anna (later Wolf), *See* Wolf, Anna Brovont
Brovont, Daniel, Scottville Old German Baptist Brethren Church, MI, 1161
Brovont, David, 1569
Brovont, Elmer, Old Brethren minister, 965
Brovont, Emma, Scottville Old German Baptist Brethren Church, MI, 1161
Brovont family
Genesee Old German Baptist Brethren Church, MI, 540
Redstone Valley Old German Baptist Brethren Church, WI and, 2239
Brovont, Henry Ephraim, 248, 1385, 1569
Pine Grove Old German Baptist Brethren Church, FL, elder-in-charge, 1025
Scottville Old German Baptist Brethren Church, MI, elder-in-charge, 1161
Brovont, Joseph, 248
Scottville Old German Baptist Brethren Church, MI, minister in, 1161
Brovont, Joseph W., 1569
Brovont, Ray O., 248, 1385, 2300, **2381**
Scottville Old German Baptist Brethren Church, MI, elder-in-charge, 1161
Brovont, Richard A., 2273
Brovont, Susanne, Scottville Old German Baptist Brethren Church, MI, 1161
Browand family, Nimishillen Old German Baptist Brethren Church, OH,

937–938
Browand, Henry, 1569
Nimishillen Old German Baptist Brethren Church, OH, elder in, 937–938
West Nimishillen, OH, congregation, 945
Browder, KY, settlers from western Pennsylvania in, 1232
Brower, A. H., 2046
Brower, Alfred, 1569
Brower, Ann (later Umstad), 1286
Brower, Ben, 377
Brower, Mrs. Ben, 377
Brower, C. M., 447
Brower, Cecil J., 1569
Brower, Christian M., 1569
Brower, Clarence E., 1569
Brower, Daniel, 215, 980, 1286, 1319, 2087
Brower, Daniel (1815–93), 62, 78
Brower, Daniel (CB), 1569
Brower, Daniel (Elder), 214
Brower, Daniel M., 1569
Brower, Daniel (minister), **214**
Brower, Daniel (OGBB), 1569
Brower, David, 14, **214**, 215, 447, 519, 1223, 1569
Maquoketa German Baptist Brethren, IA, preaching, 791
migration of Brethren, 830
Oysterville, WA, German Baptist Brethren Church, 986
Powelis Valley Church of the Brethren, OR, elder, 1049–1050
Salem and Lebanon German Baptist Brethren Churches, OR, elder in, 1138
Brower, David Martin, 65, 1569
Brower, Elizabeth (later Fischer), 491
Brower, Elizabeth Leedy, 214
Brower, Enoch, 430, 1569
Marion Co. German Baptist Brethren, IA, minister, 793
Brower, Enoch, (Elder), 214
Brower, Enoch L., 1569
Brower family, **214–215**, 1391, 1950
English River Church of the Brethren, IA, 447
Howard, IN, Church of the Brethren, 633
Mayville, ND, Red River Valley Church of the Brethren, 805
Preiß (Price) family related to, 1055
Brower, Frances Ikenberry (Fanny Eichenberg), 214, 430
Brower, Francis, 1286
Brower, Frank Early, 1277, 1569
Brower, George, 1569
Brower, Hannah Miller, 214
Brower, Henry, 214
Brower, Hubert, 214
Brower, I. A., 1569
Salem Church of the Brethren, ND, 1138
Brower, Isaac Urner, 1569
Brower, Isaac W., 1569
Brower, Israel, 1569
Brower, J. C., Peru, IN, First Brethren Church, pastor, 1010
Brower, J. H., 1569
Brower, J. J.
Oak Grove Church of the Brethren, IA, district meeting delegate, 955

Reedley, CA, Church of the Brethren, elder, 1091
Brower, J. R., 1569
Brower, J. W., 637
Brower, Jacob, 447
Replogle, Peter, election as minister, 1100
Brower, Jacob A., 1569–1570
Brower, Jacob (CB-1), 1569
Brower, Jacob (CB-2), 1569
Brower, Jacob Henry, 345,1570
Brower, Jacob J., 1570
Brower, Jane Yoder, 214
Brower, Jay, 1891
Brower, Joel, 633, 1570
Brower, John, 214, 1235, 1570
Barren Ridge congregation, VA, 90
Beaver Creek congregation, VA, 105
Brower, John (CB-1), 1570
Brower, John (CB-3), 1570
Brower, John D., 1570
Brower, John (Elder) (VA), 214, 215, 1570
Brower, John (PA), 214
Brower, Jonas W., 1570
Brower, Joseph, 1570
Brower, Lottie Keyser, 345
Brower, Lydia Miller, 214
Brower, Magadalena (later Snell), *See* Snell, Magadalena Brower
Brower, Mark, 1570
Brower, Mary Cupp, 214
Brower, Mrs. M. L., 1305
Brower, Nancy Landes, 214
Brower, Peter, 447, 1570
Monroe Co. Church of the Brethren, IA, elder, 870
Brower, Phoebe (later Moore), 874
Brower, Samuel F., 157, 1570
Brower, Susan Noffsinger Root, 214
Brower, Susannah Miller, 214
Brower, Wilbur I., 1570
Brower, William Henry, 1570
Brown, Adam, **215**, 1294, 1570
Brown, Albert, 245
Brown, Anna Amy Hoover, *See* Brown family
Brown, Barbara, on clergy women, 2365
Brown, Beulah, 45
Brown, C. Glennon, 264
Brown, C. James, 2273
Brown, Catherine, 216
Brown, Cathy (later McNeil), works by, 2319
Brown, Charles, 1341
Brown, Charles C. (CB-1), 1570
Brown, Charles C. (CB-2), 1570
Brown, Charles H., 322, 719, 1215, 1570
Brown, Charles Henry, 1312, 1570
Brown, Charles M., 1570
Brown, Charles T., 1983
Brown, Christine, Philadelphia, PA, Crossroads Grace Brethren Church, 2238
Brown, Claron, 1570
Shelby Co. Church of the Brethren, MO, leadership in, 1175
Brown Co., KS, 682
Morrill, KS, Church of the Brethren, 876
Brown Co., SD, Willow Creek congregation, 1205
Brown, Cora Weaver, 2152
Brown, Craig Robert, 1570

Brown, Dale Weaver, 378, 998, 1343, 1570, 1891, **2152,** 2201
Bethany Theological Seminary, 2136
books and essays by, 2152
Brethren peace teaching, 999
historical writing, 612, 613, 2201, 2319
Mallott, Floyd Ellwood, essay on, 784
theological task force, "Baptism, Eucharist, and Ministry," 2133
Brown, Daniel, 163, 326, 1570
Brown, David, 1570
Brown, Deanna G., 2152, 2273
Brown, Dee A., 2057
Brown, Dennis, 2152
Brown, Dennis Lee, 1570,
Brown, Dorothy Mae, 1836
Brown, Dorothy Noffsinger, works by, 2319
Brown, Edward Martin, 2274
Brown, Elizabeth, 216
Brown, Elizabeth Eby, 1924
Brown, Elizabeth Ulrich, 216
Brown, Everett, 1892
Brown, Ezra C., 1570
Brown family, 153, 216, **216**, 262, 348, 446, 1240, 1359, 1911, 1989, 2010, 2061
Fremont, OH, Grace Brethren Chapel, 515
Poplar Valley Church of the Brethren, MT, 1047
Brown, George, 215, 216, 1570
Brown, George C., 1570
Brown, Glea (later Richer), 2045
Brown, Glennon (Glenon, Glendon) C., 1340, 1570
Meadow Branch Church of the Brethren, TN, 806
Mountain Valley Church of the Brethren, TN, free minister, 889
Brown, Hannah (later Furry), 526
Brown, Harlow, 2152
Brown, Henry, 216
Brown, Ira A., 1892
Brown, Isaac, 45
Brown, J. D., Poplar Valley Church of the Brethren, MT, minister, 1047
Brown, Jack, Philadelphia, PA, Crossroads Grace Brethren Church and, 2238
Brown, Jacob, 216, 741
Ozawkie, KS, Church of the Brethren, 987
Brown, Jacob (CB-1), 1570
Brown, Jacob (CB-2), 1570
Brown, Jacob Kifer, 1570
Brown, Jacob U., *See* Brown family
Brown, James A., 1346, 2274
Philadelphia, PA, Crossroads Grace Brethren Church and, 2238
Brown, Jeffrey H., 2274
Brown, Jeremiah, 216, 961, 1570, 2032
Brown, Jesse D., 1570
Brown, Joe
Pigeon River Church of the Brethren, NC, minister, 1023
Brown, John, 585, 741, 1286, 1570, 1910, 2090, 2091, 2128
Brown, John, Jr., 1570
Brown, John T., 1892
Brown, Kenneth H., 1570
Brown, Kenneth James, 13, 2274
Brown, Kenneth Lee, 179, 638, 1570, 1892
works by, 2319
Brown, Kevin, 2152

Brown, Landis, 1346
Brown, Leah Jacobs, 215
Brown, Lisa, Philadelphia, PA, Crossroads Grace Brethren Church, 2238
Brown, Lois Kauffman, 2152
Brown, Lois (later Miller), 1943
Brown, Margaret King, 215
Brown, Marrietta (later Studebaker), 1229
Brown, Mary Blocher, 147
Brown, Mary Duncan, 215
Brown, Mary (later Bowers), 2033
Brown, Myrtle, 45
Brown, Nettie Pearl, 1835, 1845, 2044
Brown, Nettie Summer, 226
Brown, Newton J., 2019
Brown, O. L., 1570
Norcatur, KS, Mount Zion Church, 945
Brown, P. J., *182, 215,* 353, 467, 760, 1333, 1386
Homerville, OH, Grace Brethren Church, 626
Miamisburg, OH, Brethren Church, pastor, 823
Mohican Church of the Brethren, OH, 867
Brown, Peter, 1570
Brown, Philip Donald, 1570. 2274
Brown, Phillip J., 102, **215–216,** 1570
Brown, Richard, 21
Brown, Robert
Mishawaka, IN, Brethren Church, 852
Brown, Mrs. Robert,
Mishawaka, IN, Brethren Church, 852
Brown, Rosa (later Seitz), 2061
Brown, Rudolph, 216
Brown, Ruth (later Ogden), 961
Brown, S. H., 1570–1571
Brown, S. M., 1343
Brown, Samuel, 526
Brown, Susannah Bosserman, 163
Brown, Susannah Thomas, 163
Brown, Susannah Wolf, 216
Brown, Thomas and Susan, 1988
Brown, Wallace, 1892
Brown, William, 1571
Brown, Woodrow, 1571
Brownback, Garret E., 1892
Brownback, Oscar B., 1892
Brownback, Stephen S., Philadelphia, PA, Geiger Memorial Church of the Brethren, 1016
Browne, Samuel (Dr.), 216
Brownfield, Rex Newlon, 1892
Brownfield, Robert Long, 1892
Browning, Vernard Branson, 1571
Brownists, and congregational polity, 1041
Brownlee, William C., 1892
Brownlow, Donald G., 1892
Brown's Mill meetinghouse, Falling Spring Church of the Brethren, PA, 471
Browns Mill, PA, Old German Baptist Church, **2153**
Brownsberger, John A., 439, 1571
Brownsville, MD, Church of the Brethren, **216,** 475, 1037, 2323
Brownsville, MO, 145, 320
Broyles, Dewey V., 2274
Broyles, Jack, 30
BRS, *See* Brethren Renewal Service
Brubacher, Aden H., 1892
Brubacher, Ammon H., 1185, 1571
Brubacher, Anna Myers, 216
Brubacher, Anson Beeshy, 1893

Brubacher, Barbara Martin, 1893
Brubacher, Benjamin, 1893
Brubacher, Daniel M., 2051
Brubacher family, *See* Brubaker family
Brubacher, Hans, 216
Brubacher, Henry Martin, 1883
Brubacher, Jacob B.
    family history, 2005
Brubacher, Jacob N., 1893
Brubacher, John Hess, 1893
Brubacher, John (Prupecker), 216
Brubacher, John Sherk, "Cooper," 1893
Brubacher, Lovina Horst, 1893
Brubacher, Susanna Martin Sittler, 1893
Brubaker, A. C., 1571
Brubaker, A. O., 1571
    Pomona, CA, Church of the Brethren,
        pastor, 1045
Brubaker, A. W., 1571
Brubaker, Aaron, 417, 566, 1571
Brubaker, Abraham, 43, 217
    Olathe Old German Baptist Brethren
        Church, KS, deacon, 964
Brubaker, Abraham Kurtz, 1893
Brubaker, Abraham Z., 1571
Brubaker, Albert, 1571
    Pleasant Valley Church of the Brethren,
        Alberta, Canada, providing pastoral
        care, 1034
Brubaker, Albert J., 1571
Brubaker, Albert S., 1571
Brubaker, Alfred D., 2274
Brubaker, Alice, *162*
Brubaker, Alice Mae Stitzel, 217
Brubaker, Amos, 1295, 1571, 2300, **2381**
    North Fork Old German Baptist
        Brethren Church, IN, minister, 948
Brubaker, Amos A., 1571
Brubaker, Amos Oscar, 1571
Brubaker, Anna Myers, 217
Brubaker, Arthur, 1571
Brubaker, B., 1571
Brubaker, Barbara, 217
Brubaker, Barbara Crist, 352, 353
Brubaker, Benjamin, 431, 1571
    Olathe Old German Baptist Brethren
        Church, KS, minister, 964
Brubaker, Benjamin F., 1571
    Protection Church of the Brethren, KS,
        1062
Brubaker, C. A., 1571
Brubaker, C. C., 1571
Brubaker, Calvin Bowman, 1893
Brubaker, Carl Luke, 1571
Brubaker, Catherine, *146,* 217
Brubaker, Charity Himes, 654
Brubaker, Charles Henry, **217,** 1571, 1835
Brubaker, Christena, 217
Brubaker, Christian, 1571
Brubaker, Clair D., 1571
Brubaker, Clarence, 759, 1394
Brubaker, Clarence Edward, 759, 1394,
    1571
Brubaker, Clarence O., 264, 1571, 2300
Brubaker, Claude A., 641
Brubaker, Core Mae Cripe, **217,** 1835, 1977
Brubaker, Crawford E., 2300
Brubaker, Crawford F., 1571
Brubaker, D. E., Maxwell, IA, Church of
    the Brethren, minister, 803
Brubaker, D. G.
    Nocona Church of the Brethren, TX,
        elder in, 939

Portland, TX, Bayview Church of the
    Brethren, pastor, 1048
Brubaker, D. M., 740
Brubaker, Dale
    Muncie, IN, Church of the Brethren,
        pastor, 896
Brubaker, Daniel, 742, 1571
Brubaker, Daniel B., 1893
Brubaker, Daniel E., 1571
Brubaker, Daniel G., 1571
Brubaker, Daniel M., 1571
Brubaker, Daniel R., 1571
Brubaker, Daniel Sherk, 1892–1893
Brubaker, David, 626, 1354
Brubaker, David (CB), 1571
Brubaker, David (DB), 1571
Brubaker, Dean M., 1893
Brubaker, Diana (later Vaniman), 1303
Brubaker, Donald W., 1571
    North Manchester Old German Baptist
        Brethren Church, IN, minister, 949
Brubaker, Donald W., 1571
Brubaker, Dwayne, 244
Brubaker, E. H., 1307, 1571
Brubaker, E. S., 1978
Brubaker, Earl C., 1571
    Salunga, PA, Church of the Brethren,
        minister in, 1140
Brubaker, Edith, 1893
Brubaker, Edwin B., 1571
Brubaker, Elias, 1571
Brubaker, Elizabeth Ault, 217
Brubaker, Elizabeth Howe, **217,** 1296,
    1344, 1361
    Moody Bible Institute, 872
Brubaker, Elizabeth (later Shull), 502
Brubaker, Elizabeth Miller, 217
Brubaker, Elizabeth Myers, *See* Brubaker
    family
Brubaker, Elizabeth, Sand Creek Old
    German Baptist Brethren Church,
    KS, 1143
Brubaker, Ella Miller, **217,** 1835, 1893
Brubaker, Ellis S., 146. 1571
Brubaker, Emma Fisher, 217
Brubaker, Emma J. (later Knepper), 703
Brubaker, Emory
    Peters Creek Old German Baptist
        Brethren Church, VA, 1012
Brubaker, Ezra Howard, 1571
Brubaker (Brubacher) family, 157, 158,
    701, 750, 1229, 1311, 1326, 1872,
    1893, 1948, 1958, 2037, 2068,
    2077, 2082, 2093, 2111, *See also*
        entries at Brubacher
history of, 1939
Jamison family, 668
Monitor Church of the Brethren, KS,
    869
Neher family, related to, 922
Peters family related by marriage, 1012
Pipe Creek Old German Baptist
    Brethren Church, IN, 1026
Royer family, related to, 1128
Shull family, related to, 1156
Snavely family, related to, 1193
sources on, 2319
Brubaker (Brubachker) family, 150,
    216–217
Brubaker, Frank Edward, 1571
Brubaker, Frederic Leon, 1893
Brubaker, George, 217
Brubaker, Gilbert H., 1571

Brubaker, Gorden Lynn, 1571
Brubaker, Grace M., 1571
Brubaker, H., 438
Brubaker, H. A.
    Pasadena, CA, Church of the Brethren,
        pastor in, 994
Brubaker, H. Dale, 245
Brubaker, H. Elmer, 1571
Brubaker, H. M., 553
    Raisin City, CA, Church of the
        Brethren, pastor, 1083
Brubaker, Harold A., 1295, 1571, 2300,
    2153
    Painter Creek Old German Baptist
        Brethren Church, OH, 990
Brubaker, Harry L., 383, 1571–1572, 2300
    Penn Run Church of the Brethren, PA,
        pastor, 1004
Brubaker, Harvey A., 1572
Brubaker, Harvey Melvin, 1572
Brubaker, Henry, 217, **217,** 264, 620, 1281,
    1893, 2068, 2093
    Nocona Church of the Brethren, TX,
        elder in, 938–939
    Poplar Bluff Church of the Brethren,
        AR, 1046
    St. Francis Church of the Brethren, AR,
        minister in, 1134
    Shoal Creek Old German Baptist
        Brethren Church, Newton Co.,
        MO, minister, 1178
Brubaker, Henry (CB-1), 1572
Brubaker, Henry (CB-2), 1572
Brubaker, Henry (CB-3), 1572
Brubaker, Henry D., 268
    Richland Center Church of the
        Brethren, KS, elder-in-charge,
        1107
Brubaker, Henry D. (CB), 1572
Brubaker, Henry D. (OGBB), 1572
Brubaker, Henry T., 1572
Brubaker, Henry Strickler, 1893
Brubaker house, near Gratis, OH, 1235
Brubaker, Howard Dale, 1572
Brubaker, I. E., 1572
Brubaker, I. W., 665
Brubaker, Ira H., 1295, 1572, 2300
Brubaker, Isaac, 1572
Brubaker, Isaac S., 1572
Brubaker, Isaac William, 1572
Brubaker, J. A., 1572
Brubaker, J. E. (CB), 1572
Brubaker, J. E. (OGBB), 1572
Brubaker, J. Eric, 2274
Brubaker, J. Franklin, 1572
Brubaker, J. H., 442, 1281, 1307, 1572,
    1948
    Monticello, MN, Church of the
        Brethren, elder, 872
Brubaker, J. J., 1572
Brubaker, J. O., 415
Brubaker, J. S., 553
Brubaker, J. S. (CB-1), 1572
Brubaker, J. S. (CB-2), 1572
Brubaker, Jacob, 217, 2111
    Peters Creek Old German Baptist
        Brethren Church, VA, minister,
        1012
Brubaker, Jacob David, 1893
Brubaker, Jacob J., 1572, 2300, **2381**
Brubaker, Jacob O., 1572
Brubaker, Jacob Sherk, 1892–1893, 1893
Brubaker, James A., 1572

Brubaker, James
  Maple Grove Old German Baptist
    Brethren Church, OH, minister,
    791
Brubaker, Jay, 1572
  North Fork Old German Baptist Breth-
    ren Church, IN, minister, 948
Brubaker, Joan Bake, 1893
Brubaker, John, 216–217, 217, 496, 1242,
    1879
  Modesto, CA, Old German Baptist
    Brethren Church, minister, 867
  Mountain Valley Church of the
    Brethren, TN, elder, 889
Brubaker, John Alexander, 1970
Brubaker, John B., 1572
Brubaker, John (CB), 1572
Brubaker, John Eckerd, 1893
Brubaker, John G., 766, 1572
Brubaker, John H., 217, 1572, 1893
Brubaker, John Henry, 124, 1572
Brubaker, John Morgan, 1572
Brubaker, John (OGBB), 1572
Brubaker, John S., 217, 1572
Brubaker, John W., 1572
  works by, 2319
Brubaker, Jonas, 633
Brubaker, Jonathan, 352, 353, 1307
  Mountain Valley Church of the Breth-
    ren, TN, 889
Brubaker, Jonathan (CB-1), 1572
Brubaker, Jonathan (CB-2), 1572
Brubaker, Jonathan H., 1572
Brubaker, Jonathon, 596
Brubaker, Joseph, 431, 463, 1295
Brubaker, Joseph C., 1572
Brubaker, Joseph (CB), 105
Brubaker, Joseph (CB-1), 1572
Brubaker, Joseph (CB-2), 1572
Brubaker, Joseph S., 1213, 1572
  New River Old German Baptist
    Brethren Church, ministers for,
    931
Brubaker, Josiah E., 676, 1572
  Peters Creek Old German Baptist
    Brethren Church, VA, elder-in-
    charge, 1012
Brubaker, L. S., 335
Brubaker, Lanis H., 1893
Brubaker, Leland Stanford, **160**, 217, *538*,
    248, 912, 1572–1573, 1835, 1893,
    2018, 2135, 2140
  Japan, 669
  Rural Missions Cooperating Committee
    (RMCC), vice chairman, 1131
Brubaker, Lena Heiny, 217
Brubaker, Lewis Edward, 1573
Brubaker, Lila C., 1893
Brubaker, Lizzie (later Boots)
  Sand Creek Old German Baptist
    Brethren Church, KS, 1143
Brubaker, Lydia (later Flora), 495
Brubaker, Mabel E. (later Reist), 2043
Brubaker, Marcus, 1573
  Salem Old German Baptist Brethren
    Church, OH, minister in, 1139
  works by, 2319
Brubaker, Margaret Brubaker Eller, works
    by, 2319
Brubaker, Margaret Jean Bowser, 2153
Brubaker, Maria G. Horning, 1893
Brubaker, Marie Hannah Woody, 218, 1835,
    1893, **2387**

Brubaker, Marvin E., works by, 2319
Brubaker, Mary, 2074
Brubaker, Mary Catherine Deputy, 1893
Brubaker, Mary D., 146, 1834
Brubaker, Mary Hamilton, 217
Brubaker, Mary Neff (Naff), 217
Brubaker, Mary S., 146
Brubaker, Merlin, family, missionaries to
    Nigeria, 1144
Brubaker, Michael Phares, 1573, 2186,
    2274
Brubaker, Miranda, 165
Brubaker, Moses E., 683, 1573
Brubaker, Mrs. Noah, 264
Brubaker, Noah Franklin, 128, 633, 651,
    1573
Brubaker Naomi E., works by, 2319
Brubaker, Nicholas, 1573
Brubaker, Nicholas J., 1573
Brubaker, Noah, 264, 268, 1573
  Olathe Old German Baptist Brethren
    Church, KS, minister, 964
  Sand Creek Old German Baptist
    Brethren Church, KS, elder-in-
    charge, 1143
Brubaker, O. A., Raisin City, CA, Church
    of the Brethren, pastor, 1083
Brubaker, O. G., medical missions of, 807
Brubaker, Omer, 2153
Brubaker, Ora George, 217, 1835, 1977
Brubaker, Otis, 1311
Brubaker, Pamela, works by, 2319
Brubaker, Paul W., 1573
Brubaker, Peter (CB), 1573
  Minneapolis, MN, Golden Valley
    Community Church of the
    Brethren, minister, 848
  Pleasant Valley Church of the Brethren,
    Alberta, Canada, providing pas-
    toral care, 1034
Brubaker, Peter (OGBB), 1573
Brubaker, Randy, 1573, 2274
Brubaker, Robert L., 1893
Brubaker, Runella Deaton, 1893, 2153
Brubaker, Ruth Marie Brown, 1893
Brubaker, S. S., 2093
Brubaker, Samuel, 1573
Brubaker, Samuel F., 1573
  Macoupin Creek Church of the
    Brethren, IL, minister, 779
Brubaker, Sarah, 352
  Sand Creek Old German Baptist
    Brethren Church, KS, 1143
Brubaker, Sarah Mohler, 217
Brubaker, Stanley K., Old Brethren minis-
    ter, 965
Brubaker, Susannah, 217
Brubaker, Tobias, 2043
Brubaker, Uriah F., 496, 633, 1573
  North Fork Old German Baptist
    Brethren Church, IN, minister, 947
Brubaker, Vinna, 167
Brubaker, W. R., 438
Brubaker, W. U. (N.), 1573
Brubaker, Walter, 129
Brubaker, Walter N.
  Rockton, PA, Church of the Brethren,
    elder and minister, 1118
Brubaker, Warine, 1573
Brubaker, Warren I., 1948
Brubaker, Wesley Hart, 1573, 1894
Brubaker, William, 217
Brubaker, William H., 1573

Brubaker, William R., 1573
Brubaker, Wilmer E., 1573
Bruce, Eugene, 1573
Bruce, Herbert R., 1573
Bruce, MT, 142
  Pioneer congregation and Montana
    Brethren settlement, 870
Bruceton Mills, WV, and Sandy Creek
    Old German Baptist Brethren
    Church, 1143
Bruch Run, PA, congregation, 247
Bruchey, Charles E., 106, 1573
  Old Order German Baptist Church
    minister, 972
Bruchfield, Erva Wilfred, 1576
Bruck, Engelbert von, 1894
Bruck, M. H., 267
Bruck, Mrs. M. H., 267
Brucker, Benjamin, *216*
Brucker, Susannah Denlinger, *216*
Bruckhart, John, and Germantown
    Historical Museum, 2189
Brüder as name of Brethren fellowships,
    910
Der Brüderbote (*Brethren's Messenger*),
    180, 218, **218**, 1890, 1894
  example of use of German language,
    725
  General Church Erection and
    Missionary Committee (CB), 536
  Iowa, 218
  Myers, Jacob Tobias, publisher, 904
  Pennsylvania, 218
  Plate, Lewis (Ludwig) A., 1030
  publishing, 1068
  Snyder, John Martin, editor, 1196
Brüdergemeine, *See* Moravian Brethren;
    Moravian Church
Bruderhof, *See* Hutterian Society of
    Brothers
Brüderkirchen, 2325
Bruderthal, PA, 1027
Bruere, Harvey, 1573
Brugh family, 1953
Brugh, Jacob, 415
Bruins, Mary, 1833
Bruist, ___, early minister at Ten Mile
    Church of the Brethren, PA, 1253
Brull, Pedro
  Hispanic Ministries (CB), 2199
  Manatí, PR, Pueblo de Dios, 2217
  Rio Piedras, PR, Segunda Iglesia Cristo
    Misionera Fellowship (CB) and,
    2243
  Vega Baja, PR, Iglesia de los
    Hermanos Cristo El Señor (CB)
    and, 2258
  Villa Prades, PR, Iglesia Cristiana
    Getsemani (CB) and, 2258
Brumagen, Mike, 739
Brumagen, Nancy, 739
Brumbach family, 149, 516, 2077
Brumbach, Gerald, 1892
Brumback, Andrew B., *219*
Brumback, Elizabeth, 2087
Brumback family, *See* Brumbaugh family
Brumback, George Boyer, *218*
Brumback-Hotsinpiller family, 2087
Brumback, Melchoir, 2087
Brumbaugh, A. B., 220, 1863
Brumbaugh, Aaron John, **219**, 343–344,
    912, 1573, **2372**
Brumbaugh, Abraham, 1573

Brumbaugh, Alan E., 2274
Brumbaugh, Alice M., 397
Brumbaugh, Andrew Boelus, **219**.
 Huntingdon, PA, Stone Church of the
  Brethren, 637
 Juniata College, 678
 medical practice, 810
Brumbaugh, Anna Belle, 1835
Brumbaugh, Anna Konigmacher, 220, 223
Brumbaugh, Baius Marcus, **220**
Brumbaugh, Bertha L., 1573
Brumbaugh, Catherine Boyer, 220, 221
Brumbaugh-Cayford, Cheryl Ann, 2274,
 2319
Brumbaugh, Charles, 1573
 Painter Creek Old German Baptist
  Brethren Church, OH, 990
Brumbaugh, Christiana Metzger, 220
Brumbaugh Church of the Brethren, ND,
 223–224
 Ellison Church of the Brethren, ND,
  442
 place-names, Brethren, 1028
Brumbaugh, Conrad, 153, 220, 1356, 1573
Brumbaugh, Daniel
 Maquoketa German Baptist Brethren,
  IA, 791
Brumbaugh, Daniel M., 2300
Brumbaugh, Daniel Martin, 1573
Brumbaugh, David, 102, **219–220**, 1573
 Old Brethren German Baptist Church,
  minister, 965
Brumbaugh, David L.
 Old Brethren German Baptist Church,
  2232
Brumbaugh, David O., 1573
 Portis, KS, Grace Brethren Church,
  pastor, 1047–1048
 Portis, KS, North Solomon Church of
  the Brethren, 1048
Brumbaugh, David (OGBB), 1573
Brumbaugh, Denver D.
 Old Brethren German Baptist Church,
  2232
Brumbaugh, Donald, 1573
Brumbaugh, Eleanor J. Van Dyke, **220**, *221,*
 222, 1301
Brumbaugh, Eli, 424
Brumbaugh, Elizabeth Bowman, 220
Brumbaugh, Elizabeth (later Kinsey), 696
Brumbaugh, Elmer, 1573
Brumbaugh, Elmer Isaac, 1573
Brumbaugh, Elmer L., 2300
Brumbaugh, Elnora E. Eichinger, 1894
Brumbaugh, Emma Kurtz, 220
Brumbaugh, Emma (later Flory), 498
Brumbaugh, Emma (later Showalter), *See*
 Showalter, Emma Brumbaugh
Brumbaugh, Enos E., 1573
Brumbaugh, Ephraim, 153, 1243, 1385,
 1573
 South Haven Old German Baptist
  Brethren Church, MI, elder, 1205
Brumbaugh, Eral Dean, 1894
Brumbaugh, Erma L, 223
Brumbaugh, Ernest Acker, 1573
Brumbaugh, Eula
 SERRV International (CB) and, *2247*
Brumbaugh (Brumback) family, 149, **219,**
 1338, 1868, 1894, 1911, 2108, *See*
 also Brumback entries
 Engle/Angle family, 446
 Hyattsville, MD, University Park

Church of the Brethren, 641
Marklesburg, PA, James Creek Church
 of the Brethren, 794
Paul family relations, 996
Pennsylvania and Brethren publishing,
 1004
Reliance, VA, Mount Zion Brethren
 Church, 1096
Salem Church of the Brethren, OH,
 1138
Snider, Jacob, descendants of, 1154
Brumbaugh, Flora Belle Parks, 223
Brumbaugh, Frances Anderson, 220
Brumbaugh, Frances Gehman, 219
Brumbaugh, Francis, 219
Brumbaugh, G. Edwin, **220**, 1894, **2372**
 historic sites, 609
 works by, 2319
Brumbaugh, Gaius Marcus, **220,** 534, 1894
Brumbaugh, Galen
 Skippack Church of the Brethren, PA,
  minister, 1189
Brumbaugh, Galen H., 596, 2155
Brumbaugh, George, 621, 1573
Brumbaugh, George B., *10,* 222, 1573
Brumbaugh, George, Sr., 512, 513, 1573
Brumbaugh, George W., 461
 Raven Run Church of the Brethren,
  PA, elder, 1083
Brumbaugh, George Wineland, 1573
Brumbaugh, Glen Henry, 1573
Brumbaugh, Grayce, **220,** 588, 1835
 medical missions, 807
Brumbaugh, Gwen (later Keeney)
 Sudan (CB) and, 2253
Brumbaugh, Henry Boyer, 18, 140, 219,
 220, *221,* 556, 747, 573, 1574,
 1858, 1894, 1951, 1982, 2039,
 2079, 2105
 The Brethren Church's Manual, 788
 Brethren's Church Manual, 133
 Huntingdon, PA, Stone Church of the
  Brethren, 637
 interpretation of the Bible, 134
 Juniata College, 678
 manuals describing order and polity,
  1377
 The Pilgrim, 1058
 The Pilgrim (published 1870–1880),
  editor, 1023
 *The Primitive Christian and the
  Pilgrim,*1058
 Quinter, James, and merger of papers,
  1077
 publishing, 1068
 publishing reports of Annual Meeting,
  1069
 The Young Disciple, 1389
Brumbaugh, H. J., 818
Brumbaugh, Hannah (later Heckman), 593
Brumbaugh, Henry, 416, 1573
 Old Brethren German Baptist Church,
  minister, 965, 2232
Brumbaugh, Henry Holsinger, 1574
Brumbaugh, I. Harvey
 Juniata College, 678
Brumbaugh, Irvin B., 1574
Brumbaugh, Isaac Harvey, 220, **220–221,**
 637, 1574
 Marklesburg, PA, James Creek Church
  of the Brethren, elder-in-charge,
  794
Brumbaugh, J. C., 1574

Brumbaugh, J. H., *679*
Brumbaugh, Jacob, 211, 219, 221, 1280
Brumbaugh, Jacob H., 221
Brumbaugh, Jacob R., 1574
Brumbaugh, James
 Markle, IN, Church of the Brethren,
  ordination, 794
 Salkum, WA, Community Church of
  the Brethren, pastor in, 1139
 Seattle, WA, Lakewood Community
  Church, pastor in, 1162
Brumbaugh, James Dougherty, 1574
Brumbaugh, James William, 1574, 2381
Brumbaugh, Jesse K., 1335, 1574
Brumbaugh, Johann Jacob, 446
Brumbaugh, John, 220, 221
Brumbaugh, John A., 1574, 1894
 Milk River Valley Church of the
  Brethren, MT, resident minister,
  832
Brumbaugh, John Boyer, 178, 219, 220,
 221, *221,* 556, 698, 1574, 1911,
 1951, 2039
 Huntingdon, PA, Stone Church of the
  Brethren, 637
 Juniata College, 678
 The Pilgrim, 1058
 The Pilgrim (published 1870–1880),
  editor, 1023
 *The Primitive Christian and the
  Pilgrim,* 1058
 Quinter, James, and merger of papers,
  1077
 Riddlesburg, PA, Church of the Breth-
  ren, elder, 1108
 The Young Disciple, 1389
Brumbaugh, John Calvin, 912, 1574, 1894
Brumbaugh, John D., 1574
Brumbaugh, John H., 1574
Brumbaugh, John Hoover, 1574
Brumbaugh, John W., 469, 1574
Brumbaugh, John Willard, 1574
Brumbaugh, Josiah B., 1574
Brumbaugh, Justin C., 220
Brumbaugh, Levi Replogle, 1574
Brumbaugh, Lewis Henry, 1574, 1894
Brumbaugh, Lillian Fances Trageser, 1894,
 2274
 Mesa, AZ, Community Church of the
  Brethren, 2222
Brumbaugh, M. G., 140, 427, 458, 481,
 545, 613, 1273–1274, 2033, 2093,
 2103
 Cassel library, 260
 challenged by Daniel Webster Kurtz,
  711
 description of first baptism and communion in the colonies, 1375
 historical writing, 611
 *History of the German Baptist
  Brethren,* 258, 259, 300
 Howe, Roland Levi, 633
 medical projects, 808
 migration of Brethren, 827
 noncreedalism, 942
 place-names, Brethren, 1028
 poetry, 1039
 prohibition, local, 1061
 publishing, 1069
 Puerto Rico, education commissioner,
  1208
 social action, and elections, 1196
 Sontag, Jakob, 1203

Sunday school movement, 283
World War I, 1370
Brumbaugh, Maria Baer Frank, 219,
220
Brumbaugh, Martha Peightal Grove, *218,*
222
Brumbaugh, Martha V. (later Flory), 498,
499
Brumbaugh, Martha Washington, 912
Brumbaugh, Martin Grove, 120, 140, 220,
222, **222–223,** 261, 301, 311, 427,
458, 481, 534, 545, 1273–1274,
1574, 1894, 1895, 1906, 1942,
2033, 2093, 2103
article about, 1940
bio-bibliography, 2002
biography of, 2072
Cassel library, 260
challenged by Daniel Webster Kurtz,
711
description of first baptism and com--
munion in the colonies, 1375
discussion of writings by, 1939
Durnbaugh, Donald F. on, 2327
educator, 2010
historical writing, 611
historiography
biography of, 2201
history, review of, 1917
*History of the German Baptist
Brethren,* 258, 259, 300
Howe, Roland Levi, 633
Juniata College, 678, 1981
Kaylor, Earl C., Jr. on, 2340
medical projects, 808
migration of Brethren, 827
Oakley, Annie, related to, 958
noncreedalism, 942
place-names, Brethren, 1028
poetry, 1039
prohibition, local, 1061
publishing, 1069
Puerto Rico, education commissioner,
1208
Reconstruction Unit, 1985
reference to, 1953
reminiscences of, 1938
social action, and elections, 1196
Sontag, Jakob, 1203
Sunday school movement, 283
World War I, 1370
Brumbaugh, Mary Elizabeth Engle, 446
Brumbaugh meetinghouse, KS, 1311
Brumbaugh, Milton S., 1574
Brumbaugh, Moses, 912
Brumbaugh, Moses Robert, 1574
Brumbaugh, ND, 1281
Church of the Brethren, **223–224,** 251
Brumbaugh, Pam, works by, 2319
Brumbaugh, Paul, 1574
Brumbaugh, Phillip, 1574
Brumbaugh publishing interests (Hunting-
don, PA), 25
Brumbaugh, Rachel Boyer, 219, 221
Brumbaugh, Rachel Edith Jodon, 221
Brumbaugh, Ralph L, 223
Brumbaugh, Ralph Whittier, 1574
Brumbaugh, Reuben H., 1574
Brumbaugh-Rinehart Reunion Associates,
1895
Brumbaugh, Roy, 567, 1574
Portis, KS, Grace Brethren Church,
pastor, 1048

Brumbaugh, S. H.
Portis, KS, Grace Brethren Church,
1048
Brumbaugh, Samuel I., 1574
Raven Run Church of the Brethren,
PA, pastor, 1083–1084
Brumbaugh, Samuel L., 1574
Brumbaugh, Susan, 161
Portis, KS, Grace Brethren Church,
1048
Brumbaugh, Susan Peightal, 220, *221*
Brumbaugh, Susannah, 996
Brumbaugh, Theodore A., 1574
Brumbaugh, W. L., 1574
Brumbaugh, Wilbur, 308, *677,* 2023
photographs in *Messenger,* 1020
Brumbaugh, Wilbur Eugene, **223,** 1574,
1895
Brumfield, Dacke
Olean Church of the Brethren, VA, 973
Brumfield, John
Olean Church of the Brethren, VA, 973
Brummetts Creek, NC, Church of the
Brethren, 78, 79, **224,** 1294,
Hollow Poplar Church of the Brethren,
NC, 620
Pleasant Grove Church of the Brethren,
NC, 1031
Brundage family, 739
Brundage, Rick, 739
Bruner, Catherine (later Beghtol)
descendants, 1957
Bruner, John, 297
Bruner, Polly (later Beghtol)
descendants, 1957
Brunhouse, Robert L., 1858
Brunk, Artie, 275
Brunk, Chester, 275
Brunk, David Lee, 1574
Brunk, Dennis, 1356, 1574
Brunk, E. E., 124, 1574
Brunk family, 211
Brunk, Fred J., 1574
Brunk, Gene, 2274
Brunk, Gerald R., 1895, 1990
Brunk, Harry Anthony, 1895
Brunk, Henry, 1574
Brunk, Joseph, 1574
Brunk, Marvin, 1295, 1574
Brunk, Perry, 1574
Brunk, William C., 676, 1574, 2300, **2381**
Brunn, Hermann, 1895.
historical writing, 611
historiography, 2201
works by, 2319
Brunner, Anna M. Reiff, 22
Brunner, Edward A., 511
Brunner, Edward C., 1574
Brunner, Emil
on neoorthodoxy, 922
Bruns, Mark D.
Old Order German Baptist Church,
2235
Brunswick, ME, Church of the Brethren,
2153
Brunton, Walter, 1574
Brush Creek, MO
Log Creek Church of the Brethren,
752, 1118, 1313
Old German Baptist Brethren Church,
224
Osceola Church of the Brethren, 984
Brush Creek, OH, congregations, 347,

1332, 1335, 1389
Church of the Brethren, **224,** 240, 1227
early Ohio settlement, 961
Honites, 628
May Hill Church of the Brethren, 804
migration of Brethren, 829
Painter Creek Church of the Brethren,
990
Painter Creek Old German Baptist
Brethren Church, 990
Pitsburg Church of the Brethren, 1026,
1100
Potsdam Church of the Brethren, 1048
Ridge Church of the Brethren, 1108,
1227
Brush meetinghouse, Greenmount Church
of the Brethren, VA, 571
Brush Ridge, PA, 1215
Brush Run, PA, congregation, 248
Restoration Movement, 1101
Brush Run, WV, mission point for
Pocahontas Church of the
Brethren, 1039
Brush Valley Brethren Church, PA, **224,**
268
Bryan Brethren Church, **224**
Bryan, Carroll Guy, 1895
Bryan, Charles Arthur, 1574
Bryan, J. D., 1895
Bryan, OH, 741
Brethren Church, 961
Riddle, Earl M., pastor, 1108
Pleasant Ridge Dunkard Brethren
Congregation, 1034
Bryan, Otey Lee, 1574
Mount Bethel Church of the Brethren,
VA, pastor, 880
Bryan Run Chapel
Black Log, Valley Point Church of the
Brethren, PA, 144
Bryan, William Jennings
Winona Lake Auditorium, IN, 1353
Bryant, Betty, 243
Bryant, J. E., family
North Beatrice Church of the Brethren,
NE, 945
Bryant, James Emory, Jr., 2274
Bryant, James Milton, 1574–1575
Bryant, John, 1380
Bryant, John E., 2274
Mount Vernon, OH, Conservative
Grace Brethren Church, 2226,
2227
Theological Practorium, The (CBBCI)
and, 2254
works by, 2320
Bryant, John Edward, 1575
Bryant, L. J., 1575
Bryant, MO
Fairview Church of the Brethren, MO,
469
Bryant, S. S., 1575
Petersons Chapel Church of the
Brethren, NC, 1012
Pigeon River Church of the Brethren,
NC, minister, 1023
Bryant, Thomas Thaxton, 2274
Bryant, William, 1327, 1575
Brydon, Carl C., 1575
Bryer, John Baugher
works by, 2320
Bryson, Grace Marie (later Solomon)
Solomon, Kenneth LeRoy (BC) and,

2251

BSC, *See* Brethren Service Commission
Bubb, Grace (later Eisenbise), 432
bubonic plague and famine relief, 475
Bucer, Martin, 292
    Reformed Church, 1092
Buch, Edwin, 1575
Buch, Guy R., 415, 695, 1324, 1575
    Gotha, FL, New Covenent Church of
        the Brethren, 2190
Buch, Ira, *507*
Buchanan Co., MO
    South Saint Joseph Church of the
        Brethren, 1134
Buchanan, James, 521
Buchanan, MI, Church of the Brethren,
    224–225
Buchanan, NM, Sunshine congregation, 931
Buchele, Barbara Zug, 225
Buchele, Barro Inken, 225
Buchele (Beachley, Beeghley, Beeghly)
    family, **225**, 1234, 1873, 2313
Buchele, Cathrina Hirtzler, 225
Buchele, Johann Adam, 225
Bucher, A. Lester, 623
Bucher, Allen D., 1575
Bucher, Alton P., 1575
Bucher, Anna Pfautz, 225
Bucher, Barbara Dohner, 226
Bucher, Benedict, Jr., 226
Bucher, Caleb White, 1575, 1895, 2300,
    2372
    Mechanic Grove Church of the
        Brethren, PA, free minister, 806
    works by, 2320
Bucher, Capt. John Conrad, 1867
Bucher, Catherine Petry, 1013
Bucher, Christian, 1575
    Midway Church of the Brethren, PA,
        elder, 827
    Mohrsville Church of the Brethren, PA,
        elder, 869
Bucher, Christina, 226
    Brethren Life and Thought and, 2264
    works by, 2320
Bucher, Clayton F., 1575
Bucher, Cyrus, 226, 1575, 1896, 1993
Bucher, Cyrus G., 2300
Bucher, Daniel N., 1575
Bucher, David, 226
Bucher, Dianna, 1895
Bucher, Elizabeth (later Ikenberry), 646
Bucher family, **226**, 461, 721, 1221, 1896,
    1927, 2038, 2067
Bucher, Fianna Pfautz Philippy, 225
Bucher, George, 225, **225**, 721, 1575, 1896
    Mechanic Grove Church of the
        Brethren, PA, elder and minister,
        806
Bucher, Glenn R., 1896
Bucher, Gordon Wayne, 1575, 2320
Bucher, Hans, 226
Bucher, Hazel B., *592*
Bucher, Hazel E., *414*
Bucher, Henry G., 1575
Bucher, Henry P., 1575
Bucher, Hobart H., 1896
Bucher, James, 226
Bucher, John, 1575
Bucher, John Conrad, 1919
Bucher, John Jacob, 1867
Bucher, Joseph, 1575
Bucher, K. Ezra, 1575

Bucher, L. Gene, 588, 1308–1309, 1575
Bucher, Leah, 1896, 1993
Bucher, Leah Gibble, 226
Bucher, Leroy, Mount Wilson Church of the
    Brethren, PA, 887
Bucher, Lester A., 1575
Bucher, Louise, 226
Bucher, Luke Beaver, 1575
Bucher, Mabel Weaver, 225–226
Bucher, Marie K., works by, 2320
Bucher, Mark K., 2153, 2274
Bucher, Mary (later Beahm)
    Mow, Anna Beahm, mother of, 890
Bucher, N. G., 1575
Bucher, Peter, **225**
Bucher, Raymond Baugher, 1575
Bucher, Rufus P., 461, 1273
    Jennersville, PA, Church of the Breth-
        ren, 670
    Mechanic Grove Church of the
        Brethren, PA, minister and pastor,
        806
    The Young Center and, 2267
Bucher, Rufus Pfautz, *225*, **225**, 226, 1575,
    2372
Bucher, Sadie (later John), 671
Bucher, Samuel G., 1575
Bucher, Sara, Mount Wilson Church of the
    Brethren, PA, 887
Bucher, Simon G., 1575
Bucher, Susan H. (later Hoffer), 617
Bucher, Susanna Mohler, 226
Bucher, Walter Eugene, 738, 1575
Bucher, William, Jr., 226
Bucher, William P., 2072
Bucher, William Pfautz, Sr., **225–226**
Bucher, Willis Herbert, 1896
Bucherthal (Denver), Lancaster Co., PA,
    226
Büchlein vom Sabbath (*Booklet on the
    Sabbath*), *451*
Buchley, Louis, 1240
Buchman, Laura Alice (later Reichelderfer),
    2042
Buchman, William H., 1575
Buchwalter family, 1882
Buck, Abraham, 469, 1575, 2085
Buck Catherine, 2085
Buck, Catherine, descendants of, 1937
Buck, Charles, 1896
Buck, Charles L., 1575
Buck, Christian, 2085
    descendants of, 1937
Buck Creek Church of the Brethren, IN, 42
    Buck Creek, IN, Church of the
        Brethren, **226**
Buck Creek, IN, congregation, organized
    from Nettle Creek Church of
    Brethren, 923
Buck, Edith (later Fisher), 1937, 2085
Buck, Edwin, 1575
Buck, Eliza, 1285
Buck family, 2085
    North Solomon Old German Baptist
        Brethren Church, KS, 950
Buck, Henry, 1285
Buck, Hiram, North Solomon Old German
    Baptist Brethren Church, KS, 950
Buck, Jacob, 1304, 1575
Buck, Johannes, 1937, 2085
Buck, John S., 1575
Buck, Minnie Mae (later Sherrick), *See*
    Sherrick, Minnie Mae Buck

Buck, Miriam (later Ulrey), 1285, 1937
Buck, Oliver D., 1575
Buck, Solon J., 1896
Buck, W. J., 1896
Buckalew family, 319
Buckalew, William, Mount Cassell Old
    German Baptist Brethren Church,
    WV, 880
Bückeburg, (West) Germany,
    Freundschaftsheim (Friendship
    House), 517
Buckey, John, 746
Buckeye Apartments, 181
Buckeye Church of the Brethren, KS
    (Chapman Creek), 1, **226**
Buckeye City, OH, Brethren Church, *See*
    Danville, OH, Grace Brethren
    Church
Buckeye, KS, Church of the Brethren, **226**
Buckeye, OH, Brethren Church, 362
Buckingham, Ben, 246
Buckingham, Benjamin Frederick, 1575
Buckingham, Betty Jo, works by, 2320
Buckingham, David C., 226
Buckingham, Don A., 2173, 2274
Buckingham family, 731
Buckingham, Flossie, 246
Buckingham, Ida, 1243, 1835, 1896, 2012
Buckingham, Minnie Susan, **226,** 1261,
    1896
Buckingham, Susan Wagoner, 226
Buckingham, William Irwin, 1575
Bucklew, A. D., 1575
Bucklew, A. R., 1575
Bucklew, Albertus H., 1575
Bucklew, Catherine Miller, 226
Bucklew, Dan, 1575
Bucklew, Daniel William, 1575
Bucklew, David, 1575
Bucklew, Elias, 1254
Bucklew, Elizabeth Strawser, 226
Bucklew, George, 1254, 1575–1576
Bucklew, J. S., 1576
Bucklew, James B., 1576
Bucklew, Laportie R., 1576
Bucklew, Lettie, 1254
Bucklew, Marcellus, 1576
Bucklew, Philip, 226
Bucklew, Solomon, **226,** 1576
    Markleysburg, PA, Church of the
        Brethren, presiding elder, 794
Bucklew, William, 101
    Red Creek Church of the Brethren,
        WV, 1088
    Salem Old German Baptist Brethren
        Church, OH, minister in, 1139
Buckley Chapel mission point, Oakton, VA,
    Church of the Brethren, 958
Buckley, William J., 1576
Buckman, Mary (later White), 1339
Buckmaster, G. W., 1576
Buckmaster, Nicodemus, 1576
Buckner, Gerolean Marshal, 2037
Buckner, Hampton, 613
Bucks Co., PA, 383, 734, 1216, 1911, 2077
    Genealogical Society, and Pine Run
        German Baptist Brethren, 2377
    Great Swamp Church of the Brethren,
        PA, 569
    Lutheran Church, 2088
    Mennonite Church, 2088
    migration of Brethren, 827
    Pennsylvania settlement, 1004

Quakertown, PA, First Church of the Brethren, 1075
Buckwalter, Anita Smith, 2274
Buckwalter, Barbara (later Weber), 1325
Buckwalter, Ella, 758
Buckwalter, Henry, Lancaster, PA, Acts Covenant Fellowship, 2213
Buckwalter, Isaac Newton, 912
Buckwalter, J. Lester, 1576
Buckwalter, Millie, Lancaster, PA, Acts Covenant Fellowship, 2213
Buckwalter, Richard Owen, 1576
Bucyrus, OH, 148
Budd, Amos S., 1576
Budd, J. A., 152
Buddhism, **226**, 2062
Buddhist refugees, 198, 227
Buddhists
    Fellowship of Reconciliation (USA), 488
    Büdingen, **227**, 545
    castle, *227*
    historic sites, 609
    Hoffmann, Eva Elizabeth, 617
    Marienborn administrative center, 792, *792*
Büdingsche Sammlung, 611
Buechley, Elias K., 1323, 1576
Buechley family, **225**, 1234, 1322, 1873, 2313
Buechley, Martin, 1322
Buechley, Mary (later Hoff), 616
Buechley, Sarah Anna (later Seiler), *See* Seiler, Sarah Anna Buechley
Buechly (Bueghly), Martin, 1576
Buechly, David, 1576
Buechly family, 152, **225**, 1234, 1873, 2313
Buehl, Helen Frances, 1833
Buehler, Allan Moyer, 1896
Buel, Eli, 1576
Buen Pastor Church, Tijuana, Mexcio, 1142
Buena Vista, VA, congregations
    First Brethren Church, **227–228**
    Mount Vernon Church of the Brethren, VA, 887
    Stone Church of the Brethren, **228**
Buenos Aires, Argentina, 52–54
    The Missionary Board (BC), 856
    missions, 862
Buenos Aires Bible Institute, 2153
Buffalo Co., NE, 685
Buffalo Co., WI, 1354
Buffalo Hills preaching point, Smith Creek Fellowship Church of the Brethren, WV, 1191
Buffalo, IN, Church of the Brethren, **228**
Buffalo Mills, PA, Select School, 1165
Buffalo, NY
    Bonsack family, 161
    Community of True Inspiration, 330
Buffalo, PA
    Church of the Brethren, **228**
Buffalo Run Valley, PA, 1347
Buffalo Valley, PA, 228, 369, 1235
    Old German Baptist Brethren Church, **228**
    Royer, John Grove, 1128
    Scheublein, Christian and Esther Neff, children of, 1178
Buffalo, WV, German Baptist Brethren Church, **228**
Buffaloe Creek, VA (later Bethany, WV), 1136

Buffenmyer, John A., 760, 1576, 1896
Buffenmyer, John Hoffer, 494, 1576
Buffenmyer, Luke H., 1576
Buffenmyer, Stella Hoffer, 1576
Buffenmyer, Stella (later Markley), 1702
Buffington family, 2105
Buford, Robert, 2274
buggies, horsedrawn, 75, **228**, *229*
    Old Brethren German Baptist Church, 965, 970
    Old Order Fellowships, 971
    Old Order German Baptist Church, 972
Bugher family, 2067
Bühaar, Hans Georg, *See* Bashor, Hans Georg
Bühl, 148
Buhl, ID, 1282
Buikema, Lois Evelyn, 1853
building campaigns
    Chicago, IL, Douglas Park Church of the Brethren, 275
    Chimney Run, VA, Church of the Brethren, 277
building maintenance, 180
buildings generally, *See* architecture; church architecture
Buker, Raymond S., Sr., 1896
Bukowski, John, 19
Bukuru Theological College of Northern Nigeria, 1256, *1257*
Bulgaria, 23
Bull Run mission point, Oakton, VA, Church of the Brethren, 958
Bull, Zane, 566, 1576
Bulletin of the Peace Studies Institute, 1003
bulletins, church, *See* worship, public
Bullinger, Heinrich, 56
Bullion, Earl, 1576
Bull's Gap, TN, 1340
Bulsar Bible School, India, **229**, 651, *See also* Gujarat United School of Theology; mission schools
Blough, Jacob M., **150**
    Long, Effie Virginia Showalter, 753
    Long, Isaac Samuel, 753
    mission schools, 853
    Satvedi, Govindji, 1145
Bulsar, India, 229, 649, 651
    Cottrell, Asher Raymond, 345
    Cottrell, Laura Murphy, 345
    Eby, Emma Ada Horner and Enoch Howe, 418
    India orphanages, 651
    medical missions, 807
    Miller, Eliza Belle, missionary, 837
    mission schools, 853
    missions, 861
    orphanage, 131
    orphans, care for, 982
    Quinter, Mary, missionary, 1077, 1078
    Quinter Memorial Hospital, 1078
    Ross, Amos Walter and Flora Mae Nickey (Bjorklund), missionaries to, 1123
    Yeremian (Yereman), O. H., 1385
Bulsari, Benjamin J., 1576
Bulsari, Gershom J., 1576
Bulsari, Maganial J., 1576
Bulsari, Naomibai Raghevji, 229
Bulsari, Theophil G., **229**
Bulsaria, Joseph A., 1896
Bultmann, Rudolph, 454
Bunch family, South Bend, IN, Ireland

Road Grace Brethren Church, 1203
Bunch, John Franklin, 1576
    Marion, IN, Church of the Brethren, pastor, 793
Bunche, Ralph J., 344
Bunderman, Walter Q., 1896
Bungalow, The (Wittler), 2364
Bunger family, 2087
Bunker Brethren Church, Hill, IN, *See* Loree, IN, Brethren Church
Bunker Hill, IN
    Brethren Church, 758
    Santa Fe Church of the Brethren, 1144
Bunker Hill, OH, meetinghouse, 80
Bunker Hill, PA
    Brethren Church, **229**, 740
    Raystown Brethren Church, PA, 1084
Bunkertown, PA, 760, *See also* Lost Creek Church of the Brethren, PA
Bunn, Catharine (later Good), 1951
Bunnell, Paul J., works by, 2320
Bunners, Christian, works by, 2320
Buntain, Arnold Paul, 1576
Buntain family, 1330
Buntain, George W., 1576
Buntain, John C., 1576
Buntain, Paul, 2300
    Richland Valley Church of the Brethren, WA, pastor, 1108
Buntain, Webster Ellsworth, 360, 1576
Burch, Richard Leslie, 357, 367, 1576
Burcham, William, 1576
    Noblesville, IN, Church of the Brethren, elder in, 938
Burchfield, Donald, 731
Burchinell building, Juniata College, *678*
Burckett family
    Hurricane Creek Old German Baptist Brethren Church, IL, 638
Burckhardt, P., historical writings, 611
Burckhardt, Paul, 1896
Burdge, Edsel, Jr., works by, 2320
bureaucracies, individual freedom in, 2110
Burg, Walther von der, and Funderburgh family, 523
Burgard, Jacob, 1576
Burgard, Peter, 1576
Burger, Anna Mae Witmore, 1835
Burger, Ella (later Funk), 525
Burger family, 216, 360, 743
    North Solomon Old German Baptist Brethren Church, KS, 950
Burger, G. W., 1576
Burger, John, 685
Burger, John and Leah, 927
Burger, Joseph, 1576
Burger, Melba Marie, 1842
Burger, Richard Allen, 1285, 1576, 1835, 1896
Burger, Robert Eugene, 1576
Burger, Samuel J. (CB-1), 602, 1576
Burger, Samuel J. (CB-2), 1576
Burger schoolhouse, Fly Creek Church of the Brethren, KS, 500
Burgers, Robert, 109
Burgert, Annette K., 2375
    works by, 2320
Burgess, Albert D., 1576
Burgess, Ellis Beaver, 1896
Burgess, Evelyn, 725
Burgess family
    Ozark Grace Brethren Church, MI, 987

Burgess, Raymond, 725
Burgess, Wayne, 2274
Burgess, William, 2300
Burget, Andrew Bolger, 1576
Burget, Isaac, 383
Burghardt family, 148
Burgin, George W., 1576
    Ottumwa, IA, Church of the Brethren, pastor, 985
Burgundy, France, 505
burial customs and funerals, **229–230, 523–525,** *See also* cemeteries; death and dying; tombstones
    coffins, 229, 323
    death notices in Pennsylvania communities, 2005
    graveclothes, 566–567
    Hochmann von Hochenau, Ernst Christoph, 615
    Hymnal: A Worship Book, 2205
    memorial services, 814
    processions, 229
    stewardship, Christian, 230
burial grounds, *See* cemeteries
Burk, Arthur A., 30, 750
Burk, Bill A., 1576
Burk, Carl, family of, North Beatrice Church of the Brethren, NE, 945
Burk, Charles, 1576
Burk family, 173
    Mount Pleasant Brethren Church, VA, 886
    Poplar Valley Church of the Brethren, MT, 1047
Burk, Kelly J., 2274
Burk, Luella, 758
Burk, Roxie Imogene Westan, 1847
Burk, William Allen, 173, 1847
Burkart, Rainer W., 2201
    works by, 2309
Burke, Albert, 230
Burke, Ann, 1303
Burke, Arthur, 1303
Burke, Cecile Davis,25, **230, 2372**
Burke, Eldon Ray, 173, 230, **230,** 347, 506, 545, 1576, 2300, **2372**
    medical projects, 808–809
    Young Men's Christian Associations (YMCA), 1390
Burke, Homer Lionel, **230,** 261, 306, 530, 726, 1576, 1835, 1871, **2372**
    medical missions, 807
Burke, John P., 12, 1322, 1577
Burke, Lucy Mae Freed, 230
Burke, Marguerite Schrock, **230,** *248,* 306, 530, 726, 1835, 2009, **2372**
Burke, Orie Manuel, 1577
Burke-Wadsworth Bill for Selective Compulsory Military Training and Service, 312
Burket, Ben, North Manchester Old German Baptist Brethren Church, IN, elder-in-charge, 949
Burket family, 1389
Burket, Jehu, 602, *See* Burkhart, Jehu
Burket, Samuel E., 1577
Burkett, A. A., 1896
Burkett, Adam, 1070
Burkett, Benjamin, 1384, 1385, 1577
Burkett, Clinton, 1577
Burkett, Elizabeth (later Hardin), 643
Burkett family, 753
    Flat Rock Church of the Brethren, NC,

493
Burkett, Jerri Lynn, works by, 2320
Burkett, Margaret, Riverside Church of the Brethren, MI, 1111
Burkett, Mary Putterbach, 1070
Burkett, Moses, 323
    Riverside Church of the Brethren, MI, 1111
Burkett, Paul, 1577
Burkey, Frederick T., 1577, 1896, 2169
Burkey, Hershel R., 1577
Burkey, Margaret E. (later Myers), 904
Burkhalter family, 142
Burkhardt, Jehu (mother), 230
Burkhardt, Magdalena Kroll, 230
Burkhardt, Ul(l)rich, 230
Burkhart, Anna R. Miller, 231
Burkhart, Barbara, 405
Burkhart (Burket, Byrkett), Jehu, 1577
Burkhart family, 752, 2083
Burkhart, Jacob S., 1577
Burkhart, Jehu, **230–231,** 511, 1013, 1383
    elder, North Carolina Brethren, 946
    Miami, OH, congregation, minister, 961
Burkhart, Joseph S., 1577
Burkhart, Joseph U., 1577
Burkhart, Magdalena (later Faw), 480, 481, 1013
Burkhart, Magdalene (later Faw), 1013
Burkhart, Peter, 1577
Burkhart, Samuel W., **231,** 251, 1896
Burkhart, William H., works by, 2320
Burkholder, Abraham Reiff, 1965
Burkholder, Albert North, 1896, 1897
Burkholder, Anna, 216
Burkholder, Anna Mary, 1896–1897
Burkholder, Barbara, 1896
Burkholder, C. K., 1577
    Octavia, NE, Church of the Brethren, minister, 960
Burkholder, Catherine, 2090
Burkholder, Catherine A., 1897
Burkholder, Catherine Stump, 1232
Burkholder, Christian, 2320
Burkholder, Daniel C., 231
Burkholder, Daniel S. and Anna W., 1971
Burkholder, David H., 1959
Burkholder, Edgar Frey, 1897
Burkholder, Elizabeth W. (later Weaver), *See* Weaver family
Burkholder, Elmer John, 1897
Burkholder, Emma W. Hess, 1897
Burkholder, Ernest Jacob, 1577
Burkholder family, **231,** 2080, 2090
    family history, 2008
    Jamison family, 668
    Rittman, OH, First Brethren Church, 1111
    Rotruck (Rothrock, Roderick) family, related to, 1124
    Royer family, related to, 1128
Burkholder, Hans, 231, 1897
Burkholder, Harry Lehman, 1897
Burkholder, Henry L., 1897
Burkholder, J. C., 1897
Burkholder, J. Lawrence, 1897
Burkholder, Jacob Emanuel, 1577
Burkholder, John, 231, 1232, 1287
Burkholder, John H., 1577
Burkholder, John Richard, 1897
Burkholder, John S., 1897
Burkholder, Joseph, 231, 1577

Burkholder, Joseph C., 1897
Burkholder, June, 2092
Burkholder, Lawrence J., 1897
Burkholder, Lizzie *See* Overholtzer, Lissie Burkholder Weaver, 2032
Burkholder, Maggie, 2080
Burkholder, Martin, Valley Brethren-Mennonite Heritage Center, 2257–2258
Burkholder, Mrs. Bill R., 1897
Burkholder, Muriel, Phoenix, AZ, Grace Brethren Church, 1019
Burkholder-Newcomer controversy, Historic Peace Churches, 608
Burkholder, Paul Herbert, 1897
Burkholder, Paul Z., works by, 2320
Burkholder, Peter, 231
Burkholder, Ruth Leanna (later Hartman), 1959
Burkholder, Wealthy Agnes Clark(e), **231,** 1389, 1897
Burkholder, William A., 1577
Burkholder, William H., 1577
Burki, Elizabeth (Blough), 119
Burki family, *See* Berkey family
Burki, Jacob, 119
Burkittsville, MD, 216
Burkman, D. G., 1577
Burks Fork, VA, Church of the Brethren, 231, **231,** 1267
    Parkway Church of the Brethren, preaching for, 994
burlap cross and People of the Covenant (POC) (BC), 2237
Burlew, Claude, Mesa, AZ, Community Church of the Brethren, 2222
Burley, D. E., and Oregon Short Line Railroad, 981
Burlingame, Evelyn E., 1897
Burlington, IN, 1338
    Brethren Church, **231**
    example of place name, 911
Burlington, KS, Scott Valley Church of the Brethren, 1160
Burn, John, 106
Burner, J. Mark, 1577
    Root River Church of the Brethren, MN, pastor, 1122
Burner, Ralph J., Meadow Mills Church of the Brethren, VA, minister, 806
Burner, Ralph Junior, Sr., 1577
Burner, Walter Elwood, 1577
Burners family, 2077
Burnes, Charles H., 1577
Burnes, J. W., 1577
Burnes, John, 1577
Burnes, John J., 1577
Burnes, Ralph S., 1577
Burnes, Robert L., 1577
Burnes, William H., 1577
Burnet, Isabella Neff, 1897
Burnet, John, 1577
Burnett family, 1341
Burnett, J. D., 1577
Burnett, J. G., 1577
Burnett, Jeff, 1577
    New Hope Church of the Brethren, AR, elder in, 929
Burnett, John, 1577
Burnett, Luke, 72, 1577
    New Hope Church of the Brethren, AR, elder in, 929
Burnett, Oliver P., 1577

New Hope Church of the Brethren, AR, elder in, 929
Burnett, P. R., 1577
Burnett, Samuel Garfield, 1577
Burnett schoolhouse, White Rock Church of the Brethren, VA, 1341
Burnette family, Outlook, WA, Church of the Brethren, 986
Burnett's Creek
    Normal School, 231
    Mount Morris College, 884
    Royer, John Grove, 1128
Burnett's Creek, IN, 232
    Monticello/Pike Creek Church of the Brethren, 872
Burnettsville, IN, Church of the Brethren, 232
Burnham, PA, 406
    Church of the Brethren, 232, 994
    Maitland Church of the Brethren, PA, 783
    Parkview Church of the Brethren, 994
Burns, Donald H.
    Old Order German Baptist Church minister, 972, 2235
Burns, Earl D., 540, 1385, 1577
Burns family, 384, 1881, 2087
Burns, Gary W.
    Old Order German Baptist Church, 2235
Burns, Irvin S., 1577
Burns, J. W.
    Mount Hope, OK, congregation, 964
    Sand Ridge Church of the Brethren, OH, minister in, 1143
Burns, John
    Old Order German Baptist Church minister, 972
Burns, John J., 746
    Reading Grace Brethren Church, PA, pastor, 1084
Burns, Michael, 1385
Burns, Norman Ray, 1897
Burns, Ralph, 318
Burns, Ralph S., 30, 674
Burns, Robert, 16, 21
Burns, Robert L., 705
    Meyersdale, PA, Grace Brethren Church, pastor, 822
    North Buffalo Grace Brethren Church, PA, pastor, 945
    Norton, OH, Grace Brethren Church, minister, 951
Burns, Ronald R., 2274
Burns, Stephen J., 2274
Burnside, General Ambrose E., 475
Burnworth, B. T., 720, 1289
    Morrill, KS, (First) Brethren Church, 876
Burnworth, Benjamin Taylor, 232, 1577
Burnworth, E. D., 232, 438, 553, 558, 1577
Burnworth, J. H., 211., 1320
Burnworth, J. T., 581
Burnworth, John H., 232, 1577
Burough, S., 1577
Burr, Aaron, 1897, 1915
Burr, Nelson R., 1858
    Burr Oak, KS, congregations, 157, 665, 742, 765, 1305
    Church of the Brethren, 232
    Portis, KS, North Solomon Church of the Brethren, 1048
    South Red Cloud Church of the

Brethren, NE, 1206
Bur(r)all, Jesse M., 1577
Burrass, W. P., 1577
Burrell, Percy Jewett, 1897
Burress, W. P., 676
Burris, Lee D., 14, 515, 1577
    River City Grace Community Church, associate pastor of, 1134
Burris, Russell, 21, 246, 1577
Burrous family, 2094
Burrow, G. Pearl, 573
Burrow, George P., 1577
Burrows, Pearl, 1577
Burrs, W. H., 1577
Burry, Eugene Allen, 1577
    Waterloo, IA, Hammond Avenue Brethren Church, 2260
Burson, Rubye Harris, 1897
Burt Co., NE, Golden Spring German Baptist Brethren Church, 2374
Burt, J., 296
Burtner, Roger, 1577
Burton, Conrad, 759
Burton, Cordelia (later Mathis), 803
Burton, Dewey Conrad, 1577, 2300
Burton, J. E., Oakvale Church of the Brethren, WV, 958
Burton, Jan, Ripon, CA, Grace Brethren Church, 1110
Burton, John Franklin, 31, 1577–1578
Burton, John T., 1578
Burton, Katherine Kurz, 1897
Burton, Ken, Ripon, CA, Grace Brethren Church, 1110
Burton, Molly, 90
Burtz, Ronald G., 2274
Bury, Peter H., 332, 1578
    Modesto, CA, La Loma Grace Brethren Church, pastor, 867
bus ministry, 232
    East Fairview Church of the Brethren, PA, 415
    Geiger Church of the Brethren, PA, 533
    Greensburg, PA, Church of the Brethren, 571
    Redondo Beach, CA, South Bay Community Church of the Brethren, 1090
Busch, Julius Hermann Moritz, 232–233, 232, 233, 379, 1897, 1921
    description of love feast, 1376
Buschbell, Gottfried, 1897
Busey family, Martinsburg, WV, Rosemont Grace Brethren Church, 798
Bush Creek, IN, congregations, 1288, 1299
    Fisher, Elias, 491
    German Baptist Brethren Church, 233
    Old German Baptist Brethren Church, 233
Bush Creek, MD, congregations, 752
    Church of the Brethren, See Monrovia, MD, Bush Creek Church of the Brethren
Bush Creek, OH, German Baptist Brethren, 237
Bush family, Mabton, WA, Grace Brethren Church, 771
Bush meetinghouse, Paint Creek congregation, OH, 1327
bush-meetings, 2106
Bush, Orvile Clyde, 145, 1578
    Riddlesburg, PA, Church of the Breth-

ren, minister, 1108
Bush, Perry, works by, 2320
Bushey, Anna Marie, 163
Bushman, Michael, 1578
Bushnell, IL, Church of the Brethren, 233, 243, 1214
Bushong, Benjamin G., 594, 233
    refugee resettlement, 1093
Bushong family, 413
Bushong, M. Rebecca, 1897
business and business ventures, 233–235
    capitalism, 253
    Eckerlin, Israel, 421
    Ephrata Community, 451
    farming, 477, 479
    interest-taking, 658
    inventions and scientific discoveries, 660
    Miller, Daniel Long, 836
    postcard production, 235
Buskirk, Esther Whyella, 1897
Buss, Dale, 565
Bussard family, Middletown Valley Church of the Brethren, MD, 826
Bussard, John M., 1578
Bussard, Raymond Earl, 1578
Bussard, William, 1578
Bussear, Z. L., 1578
Bussert, Clarence, 1578
bustles, See hoops
Butcher, E. C., 1578
Butcher, N. F., 1578
Butcher, William, 1578
Buterbaugh, Martin, 1578
Butler Chapel AME Church, 2172
Butler Co., AR, Poplar Bluff Church of the Brethren, 1046
Butler Co., IA, Greene, IA, Church of the Brethren, 570
Butler Co., KS
    Augusta, KS, Church of the Brethren, 72
    Lone Star Old German Brethren Baptist Church, 753
Butler Co., MO, 865
Butler Co., NE, 1349
    Octavia, NE, Church of the Brethren, 960
    Platte Valley German Baptist Brethren Church, NE, 1030
Butler Co., OH, 1281
    Middletown, OH, Church of the Brethren, 826
Butler Co., PA, 317
    Brethren Church congregations, 1005
    Harmony Society, 584
Butler, D. L., 1578
Butler, Daron K., 2173
Butler, George Lee, and nuclear arms race, 2232
Butler, Henry Newton, 1578
Butler, J. L., 1578
Butler, OH, North Liberty Brethren Church, 235–236
Butler, Tully, 2274
Butt, Garry, 1578
Butte Co., CA, 275
    Fruitvale Church of the Brethren, CA, 520
    Paradise Church of the Brethren, 992
Butte Valley, CA, Church of the Brethren, 236
    Haynes, W. F. and Etta, move from,

995

Butte Valley, ID, migration from Tekoa, WA, 1250

Butterbaugh, ___, (son-in-law of Jacob Long), 724

Butterbaugh, Alta Mae, 1835

Butterbaugh, Andrew G., **236,** 1333, 1578, 1835, 2016

Butterbaugh, Bertha Belle Lehman, **236,** 1835

Butterbaugh, Daniel, 236

Butterbaugh, Dorothy, 344

Butterbaugh, Dorsey F., 1578

Butterbaugh family, 1951, *See* Puderbaugh family

    Salem Church of the Brethren, OH, 1138

Butterbaugh (Buterbaugh) family, 1214, 1276

Butterbaugh, Fred W., 275, 1578, 1835, 1898

Butterbaugh, George, 1578, *See* Pooderback, George

    children of, 1951

Butterbaugh, Hannah Ulrich, 1070

Butterbaugh, Henry, 1070

Butterbaugh, I. W., 1578

Butterbaugh, Isaiah, 1578

    North Manchester Old German Baptist Brethren Church, IN, elder-in-charge, 949

Butterbaugh, (Buterbaugh), J. O., 1578

Butterbaugh, J. W., 356, 1578

Butterbaugh, Jacob, 1578

Butterbaugh, John Peter

    children of, 1951

    descendants, 1943

    family history, 1996

    Linder, Wilbur on descendants of, 2343

Butterbaugh, Margarette Boyd, 236

Butterbaugh, Mary (later Metzger)

    Metzger, John, mother of, 819

Butterbaugh, Noah W., 1578

Butterbaugh, Samuel, 1578

Butterbaugh, Susan Stallsmith, 1070

Butterbaugh, Theron D., 1333, 1578

Butters, Terry D., 2274

Butterworth, Hezekiah, 747, 1898

Butterworth, James S., 1307, 1578

Buttlar, Eva von, **236,** 239, 1903

    Hochmann von Hochenau, Ernst Christoph, 615

Button, Bruce L., 14, 188, 191, 318, 1578

Button, Frances, 1898

Button, Francis Everet, 20, 1578

Button-Harrison, Mary Jane, 2274

Button-Harrison, Timothy Glen, 2274

Button, Lenora, 318

Button, Leonore, 188, 191

Button, Orville Orland, 1578

Butts, E. O., 1578

Butts, Ira, 1578

Butts, J. Elmer, 1578

Butts, Marcus, 250, 1578

    Palestine Old German Baptist Brethren Church, OH, 991

    Shady Grove Old German Baptist Brethren Church, OH, minister in, 1171

Buzard, Samuel H., 689

Buzinda, Jilasari K., 1578

Buzzard (Buzard), Samuel H., 1578

BVS, *See* Brethren Volunteer Service

BYC, *See* Brethren Youth Crusaders

Byer, Franklin J. , 1578, 1930

Byer, R. D., 1578

Byer, W. D., 1578

Byer, W. H., 1578

    Selma, VA, Church of the Brethren, minister in, 1166

Byer, William H., Mount Bethel Church of the Brethren, VA, pastor, 880

Byerley, Benjamin, 742

Byerly, Andrew, 2006

Byerly, Benjamin, 672, 1578

Byerly, Daniel, 236

    Pleasant Dale Church of the Brethren, IN, minister, 1030

Byerly, Daniel Miller, 602, 1578

Byerly, David E., 236, 1578

    Pleasant View Church of the Brethren, OH, elder, 1037

    Sand Ridge Church of the Brethren, OH, 1143

Byerly family, **236,** 1898, 2084

    Sanger family, related to, 1144

Byerly, George, 236

Byerly, George Strather, 236, 1898

Byerly, Jacob, 236

Byerly, Jesse, 236

Byerly, Jesse S., 1578

Byerly, John Jacob, 2084

Byerly, Kenneth Brandt, 1578

    Columbus, OH, Church of the Brethren, 2372

Byerly, LeRoy, 1898

Byerly, Martin, 236

Byerly, Robert Allen, 141, 247, 713, 1578, 1898, 2300, **2381**

    Michigan City, IN, Church of the Brethren, pastor, 825

Byerly, Sarah Miller, 236

Byerly, Wesley Grimes, Jr., 1898

Byers, Alonzo, 1578

Byers, Alvin, 236, 1579

    North Georgetown, OH, Brethren Church, pastor, 948

Byers, Calvin S., 1579

Byers, Charles, 236

Byers, David, 236, 1579

Byers, E. Forest, 635, 1289, 1348, 1579

Byers, Earl, 236

Byers, Edward E., 229, 629, 740, 1579

Byers family, **236,** 384, 1330

    Grace Brethren Church of Canton, OH, 562

    Marietta, GA, Grace Brethren Church of Greater Atlanta, 793

    Martinsburg, WV, Rosemont Grace Brethren Church, 798

Byers, Forrest, 236, 332, 674

Byers, Glenn, 236, 332, 1579

Byers, Howard, Jr., 236

Byers, Howard, Sr., 236

Byers, J. Donald, Jr., 1579

    Orange, CA, Grace Brethren Church, pastor, 975

Byers, John, 1348

Byers, John Dean, 273, 674, 1579

Byers, John (Jack), 453

Byers, Lillian Carney, 236

Byers, Lindy, 236

Byers, Robert, 2139

Byers, Roy, 236

Byers, W. D., 1579

Byers, William A., 188, 215, 236, 620, 674, 1579, 2274

Mineral Point, PA, Vinco Brethren Church, pastor, 843

    Marietta, GA, Grace Brethren Church of Greater Atlanta, pastor, 793

BYF (Brethren Youth Fellowship), **203**

Byfield, Paul, 1579

BYIC (Brethren Youth in Christ), 2269

Byler, Amanda J., 1898

Byler, Christian, 1898

Byler, Dane, and Brethren Church in Peru, 2237

Byler, Dorothy Ann, 2087

Byler, Eli, 2097

Byler, Elizabeth M. Miller, 1898

Byler family, 2087, 2097

Byler, J. I., 1391

Byler, Jacob, 2079

Byler, Jacob and Nancy Kauffman, 2008

Byler, Jane Eileen King, 1854–1855, 2153, **2388**

Byler, John Ira, Sr., 1579

Byler, John, Jr., 1579

Byler, John T., 1579

Byler, June (later Palaci), **2388**

Byler, Mary Kaufman, 1898

Byler, Nancy Kauffman, 2079

Byler, Phoebe A., 1898

Byler, Richard, and Brethren Church in Peru, 2237

Byler, Robert O., 54, 1579

    The Missionary Board (BC), 856

Byler, Robert Oliver, 1855, **2153, 2388**

Byler, Saloma J. Oni, 1898

Byler, Susan, 2153

Bynum, La Taunya, works by, 2320

BYPD, *See* Brethren Young People's Department

Byram, Thomas L., 1898

Byrd, Cecil K., 1858

Byrd, Doris Wade Hartley, 1579

Byrd family, 244

Byrd, George R., 244

Byrd, I. D., 1579

Byrd, Randall, 2274

Byrd, Robert Lee, 244, 558, 663, 679, 1579, 1898

Byrd, Rosemary, 204

Byrket, Darrel (Mr. and Mrs.), 439

Byrket, Margaret (later Younce), 1389

Byrkett, Jehu, *See* Burkhart, Jehu

Byroads, Susannah Woodling, Oak Grove, IN, Church of the Brethren, 955

Byron, Brace, 236

Byron, Ethel, 236

Byron, Grace

    medical missions, 807

    ship sinking en route to Africa, 863

Byron, Lee-Anna Grace, **236,** 1847

Cabaniss, Julius E., 1295, 1579

    Peters Creek Old German Baptist Brethren Church, VA, minister, 1012

Cabinet of Children's Work (CB), *See* National Cabinet of Children's Work

cabinetmaking

    Roberts, Warren E. on Hensel, Ananias and, 2352

Cable, Alan, 2155

Cable, Annie Lula Moore, 237

Cable, Bruce, 2155

Cable, Cecil R.

Mud Valley Old German Baptist Brethren Church, IL, deacon, 892

Cable, Charles, 2155

Cable, Edwin, 2155

Cable family, 1234, 1338
Genesee Old German Baptist Brethren Church, MI, 540
Hurricane Creek Old German Baptist Brethren Church, IL, 638

Cable(?), Hannah (later Brower), 165

Cable, Isaac
Mud Valley Old German Baptist Brethren Church, IL, minister, 892
Sand Creek Old German Baptist Brethren Church, KS, minister in, 1143

Cable, Jeremiah M., 237

Cable, John, 753, 1579

Cable, Larry D.
Old Brethren Church, 2232

Cable, Lowell, 2155

Cable, Martin, 1579

Cable, Miriam Weybright, 2155

Cable, William Arthur, 237, 1278, 1579, 1898, 1938
Mothers' Day, 879
works by, 2320

Cable, William H., 2155, 2155

Cabool congregation, MO, 1324
Greenwood Church of the Brethren, MO, 572

Cabool, MO, 397
Cabool, MO, Church of the Brethren, 237

Cabool, MO, congregation
Mountain Grove Church of the Brethren, MO, 888

Cabrera, Argentina, 53
Cabrera congregation, Argentina
Siccardi, Luis, pastor, 53

Caddo Co., OK
Harrison, OK, Church of the Brethren, 586

Cadwallader Brethren, See Congregational Brethren of Pleasant Hill, OH

Cadwallader, Harald E., 1898

Cadwallader, John, 237, 335, 349, 364, 1579
Pleasant Hill, OH, Church of the Brethren, 1031
Pleasant Hill, OH, First Brethren Church, elder, 1032

Cady, John F., 1898

Caes, Clyde, 1579
North Lauderdale, FL, Grace Brethren Church, pastor, 948
Omaha, NE, Grace Brethren Bible Church, pastor, 974

Caes, Everett N., 366, 439, 1579
Peru, IN, Grace Brethren Church, pastor, 1010

Cafferata, Zona Goshorn, 1898

Cain, Dorothy, 2133

Cain, Norman Richard, 232, 1330, 1579
Newville, PA, Church of the Brethren, pastor in, 935

Cain, Robert D., 2133

CAIR, See Child Care in Aviation Incident Response

Cajon Valley, CA, See El Cajon, CA, Valley Church of the Brethren

Cakerice, John Henry, 1579

Calamus, IA

Maquoketa German Baptist Brethren, IA, mission point, 791

Calane family
Howard Co. Old German Baptist Brethren Church, IN, 633

Calaveras Co., CA, 1358

Calderón, Karen, 2172
Hispanic Ministries (CB), 2199

Calderón, René Alfonse, 1579
Hispanic Ministries (CB), 2199

Calderon Valley, Ecuador, 1290

Caldwell Co., KY, 157

Caldwell Co., MO, 692, 752, 1313

Caldwell, Doris (later Rhoades)
Rhoades, J. Benton and, 2242

Caldwell, Jesse, 1579

Caldwell, Lorenzo O., 1579

Caldwell Parish, LA, 760
Oak Grove Church of the Brethren, LA, 955

Caldwell Parish, LA, Oak Grove Church of the Brethren, See Oak Grove Church of the Brethren, LA

Caldwell, Rodney R., 2274

Caledonia, MI
Hope Church of the Brethren, MI, 629

calendar of appointments, 45, 237–238

calendars
inclusion of Christian festivals and saints' days, 1376

Calgary, Alberta, Canada, 15, 250, 251

Calhoun, Allen, 1579

Calhoun, Charles L., 1579

California
Brethren from, and Oregon, 981
Brethren in 1956, 1970
Brethren migration to, 1143, 1145
Brethren movement in, 324
Church of the Brethren, 299
colonization and, 238–239
colonization in, 455
debates, 370
Far Western Brethren, 476
frontier, 519
Indiana, 653
irrigation, 663
migrant labor camps, 827
migration of Brethren, 830
missions, 860
North Dakota Brethren relocating to, 946
Old Brethren, 971
Old German Baptist Brethren, 967, 970
Old German Baptist Brethren Church in, 2313
Old Order German Baptists, 972
railroads and Brethren settlement, 1082
southern California history, Church of the Brethren, 1932

California Association of Christian Schools, 282

California Development Company "Big Ditch," 432

Calimer, Larry Dean
works by, 2320

Calkins family, 753

Call to Caregiving, 2161

A Call to Compassion, 2129

call to minister, 845

Callahan, North, 1898

Callahan, Wanda L.
work by, 2320

Callahan, Wanda S., 1579

"called-out community," 291–292

Callen, Barry L.
works by, 2320

Callenberg, Clara Elizabeth von, 239
Marsay, Charles Hector de St. Georges, Marquis de, 796

Callender, Mervyn J., 1579, 2300

Calley, Ephraim, 1579

Callihan, Enos, 1579

Calvary Bible Church, PA, 240

Calvary Brethren Church, MD, 239

Calvary Brethren Church, MI, 239
Hastings, MI, Grace Brethren Church, 588

Calvary Brethren Church, NJ, 239, 929, 1200

Calvary Brethren Church, OH, 365

Calvary Chapel, Hartville, OH, 69

Calvary Church of the Brethren, CA, See Los Angeles, CA, Ladera Church of the Brethren.

Calvary Church of the Brethren, KS, See Kansas City, KS, Calvary Church of the Brethren.

Calvary Church of the Brethren, PA, See Philadelphia, PA, Calvary Church of the Brethren.

Calvary Church of the Brethren, VA, 239, 2101

Calvary congregations, as example of biblically inspired name, 911

Calvary Creek school, OK, 1321

Calvary (formerly Jubilee) congregation, VA, 1138

Calvary Grace Brethren Church, Kettering, OH, 691

Calvary Grace Brethren Church, MD, See Hagerstown, MD, Calvary Grace Brethren Church

Calvary Grace Brethren Church, MI, 239–240

Calvary Grace Brethren Church, OH, See Kettering, OH, Calvary Grace Brethren Church

Calvary Independent Church of the Brethren, PA, 240, 729
Snider, Harold, 1194

Calvary, NJ, congregation, 929

Calvary Pentecostal Church, 1009

Calvert, Ed
Simi Valley, CA, Grace Brethren Church, 1182

Calvert family, 323
May Hill Church of the Brethren, OH, 804

Calvert, Grace
Simi Valley, CA, Grace Brethren Church, 1182

Calvert, H. Noah, 263

Calvert, Ira, 320, 1234, 1579, 2126

Calvert, J. C., 1579

Calvert, James, 1579

Calvert, Jesse, 235, 1319, 1898
Mansfield, OH, Walcrest Brethren Church, preaching, 787
South Bend, IN, First Brethren Church, pastor, 1203

Calvert, Jesse (1832–1902, BC), 71, 1579

Calvert, Jesse (CB, FGBC), 31, 1579

Calvert, Joseph G., 1579

Calvert, Mills, 1579

Calvert, Noah
May Hill Church of the Brethren, OH,

minister, 804
Calvert, Noah H., 1579
Calvert, Robert, 240, 1579
    Paint Creek Church of the Brethren, OH, 990
    Ridge Church of the Brethren, OH, minister, 1108
Calvert, Sarah Stretch, 240
Calvert, T. M., 1579
Calvert, William Quinter, 1340, 1579–1580
    May Hill Church of the Brethren, OH, minister, 804
Calverton, Victor F., 1898
Calvin, John, 240
    and Geneva, 540
    interest-taking, 658
    musical instruments, 900
    prophecy, 1062
    Reformation, Protestant, 1091
    Reformed Church, 1092
Calvin, Moses F., 1580
Calvinism, 28, 55, **240–241**, *See also* Reformed (Calvinist) Church
    business beliefs and, 234
    Christmas, celebration of, 288
    Covenant Theology, 347
    Eternal Security and Calvinistic Fundamentalism, 456
    Fellowship of Grace Brethren Churches (FGBC), 486
    free will, 514
    in German Palatinate, 990
    Indonesia, 655
    influence on antitheological views, 1258
    justification, doctrine of, 679–680
    peace, 998
    Peace of Westphalia, 1338
    plain people, 1029
    predestination, 1055
    premillennialism, 833
    Reformation, Protestant, 1091
    religious liberty, suppression of, 1098
    Restoration Movement, 1101
    Social Gospel Movement, 1197
    trinity, doctrine, 1275
Calvinist leaders, Brethren children named for, 912
Calvo, Gabriel
    marriage enrichment, 796
Calvocoressi, Roy, 357
Camber family, 313
Cambodia, 23
    Julien, Thomas T., 2210
    missions, 2225
    missions, short-term, 2226
    relief and service efforts, 1097
Cambria Co., PA, 150, 332, 752
    Brethren Church congregations, 1005
    Maple Grove Church of the Brethren, PA, 790
    Pleasant Hill Church of the Brethren, PA, 1032
    Singer Hill Grace Brethren Church, PA, 1184
    Snake Valley Old German Baptist Brethren Church, PA, 1192
Cambria, IN
    Mount Pleasant Brethren Church, 241, 425
    Teeter, Roy R., 1250
Cambridge, NE, 7
Cambridge, Ontario, German Baptist

Brethren, 975
Camden, AR, Saint Francis Church of the Brethren preaching point, 1134
Camden, IN, 766, *See also* Hickory Grove Church of the Brethren, IN
    Deer Creek Old Brethren congregation, 971
    Old Brethren German Baptist Church, 2232, 2233
    Old Brethren German Baptists, 970
    Old German Baptist Brethren divisions, 969
    Old Order German Baptist Church, 972
Camden, OH, Grace Brethren Church, **241**
cameras, motion-picture, *See* drama; motion pictures
Camerer family, 1304
Camerer, Inez (later Riddle), 1108
Camerer, James
    Martinsburg, PA, Memorial Church of the Brethren, 798
Camerer, John
    Martinsburg, PA, Memorial Church of the Brethren, 798
Camerer, Mary (later Fahrney), 1361
Cameron, AR
    Round Mountain Church of the Brethren, AR, mission point, 1125
Cameron, Charles H., 21, 574, 692
    Grossnickle and Myersville, MD, congregations, 826
    Myersville, MD, Church of the Brethren, pastor, 906
Cameron, Charles Homer, 1580
Cameron, Craig D., 1580
Cameron, OK, Church of the Brethren, **241**
Cameron, WV, Brethren Church, **241**
Cameroon
    Lassa General Hospital, 727
Camisards, **241–242**
    Community of True Inspiration, and roots in, 330–331
Camp Albryoca (FGBC), PA, 242
Camp Alexander Mack, 61, 242, 245, 248, 249, 1898, 2067
    Indiana, 653
    mural paintings, 896
    Neher, Medford D. murals for, 922
    Pleasant View Chapel Church of the Brethren, IN, meetinghouse given to, 1036
    Shultz, Lawrence W., 1180
    Wakarusa, IN, Church of the Brethren, 1313
    Weldy, Allen (CB) and, 2261
    Young, Andrew, 1367
Camp Bethany
    Brethren Church, Holmes Co., OH, 242
    Church of the Brethren, *See* Camp Emmanuel (CB)
    Indiana, 250
    Jenkins, Charles Lee, 2209
    Camp Bethel, 2037
    Church of the Brethren, VA, 242, 248, 567
    Ikenberry, Charles Samuel, 646
Camp Blue Diamond (CB), PA, 242, *See also* Maple Grove Child Rescue Home
Camp Brethren Heights, MI, 242
    Hartzler, Russell M., 588
    Rodney Church of the Brethren, 1119
Camp Brethren Woods (CB), VA, 242–243

Camp Canaqua, **2155**
Camp Carmel (CB), NC, 243
Camp Carolina (CB), 243
Camp Clear Lake (FGBC), WA, 243
Camp Cody, NM, 2316
Camp Colorado (CB), CO, 243
Camp Conewago, 693
    Church of the Brethren, *See* Camp Swatara.
    Kilhefner, Galen C., 693
Camp Conewago, PA, 247
Camp Conquest (FGBC), PA, 243
Camp Creek congregation, WI (CB), 63
Camp Creek, IL, Church of the Brethren, 233, 243
Camp Creek, IN, Church of the Brethren, 243, 886
Camp Diquecito, Argentina (BC), 54, 243, 250
Camp Eder (CB), PA, 243
Camp Emmanuel, IL (CB), 243, 647
Camp Emmaus (CB), IL, 243–244, 647, 1219
Camp Fire Girls, *See* scouting programs
Camp Funston, KS
    conscientious objectors confined in, 921
    Hess, Maurice Abram, 601
Camp Galilee (CB), WV, 244
    Maple Grove Child Rescue Home (CB), 789
Camp Grace (FGBC), *See* Camp Tuk-a-Way (FGBC)
Camp Greenhorn Mountain Park (CB), CA, 244
Camp Hammond's Mill (CB), MO, 244
Camp Harmony (CB), PA, 202, 244, 248
    Assembly, 214
    Bushong, Benjamin G., 233
    Hamilton, Walter J., 581
    Statler, Foster Boyd, 1219
Camp Hilltop, PA, 233
Camp Hope (CB), WV, 244
Camp Inspiration Hills (CB), OH, 244
Camp Ithiel, FL, 244
Gotha, New Covenent Church of the Brethren, 2190
    meetinghouse from Seneca Church of the Brethren, 1166
    Sebring, J. H. Moore Memorial Church of the Brethren, 1162
Camp Juniata, PA, 246
Camp Kane, PA, 1397
Camp Keystone (FGBC), *See* Camp Albryoca (FGBC), PA; Camp Mantowagan (FGBC), PA
Camp Keystone, PA, 242, 315
Camp Koinonia (CB), WA, 244
Camp La Verne (CB), CA, **244–245**, 248, 714
    Rothrock, Edgar Eli, 1124
Camp Lewiston, IL, 243
Camp Living Waters (CB), IN, 245
Camp Mack, *See* Camp Alexander Mack
Camp Mantowagan (FGBC), PA, 245, 315
Camp Mardela (CB), MD, 245, *245*
camp meetings, 245–246, **245–246**, *See also* gospel songs; revival meetings; spirituals
    Brethren movement, 245–246
    evangelism, 460
    frontier, 519
    gospel songs, 560

Holiness Movement, American, 619
hymns, 642–643
revival meetings, 1103
Second Awakening and American
revivalism, 1104
spiritual songs and hymns, 1211, 1279
Wolfe, John P., converted at, 1359
Camp Mon-Dak, 1242
Camp Mount Hermon, KS (CB), **246**
Camp Mount Heron, 682
Camp Mountain Lake, OH (CB), **246**
Camp Myrtlewood, OR (CB), **246**
Camp of the Ozarks, MO (BC), *See* Camp
Hammond's Mill, MO
Camp Peaceful Pines (CB), CA, **246**, 2328
Camp Peniel (BC), PA, **246**, 1005
Camp Peniel (CB), MD, 246, **246**
Camp Pine Lake (CB), IA, **246**
Camp Placid (CB), TN, **246**
Camp Schwarzenau (CB), Kearney, NE,
246–247, 920–921
Camp Shiloh (CB), VA, **247**
Shepherd's Spring Outdoor Ministries
Center, 2248
Camp Shipshewana, IN, 249, *See also*
Indiana Brethren Retreat
Camp Spring Lake (CB), OK, **247**, 1321
Camp Stover, Fruitland, ID, Church of the
Brethren, 520
Camp Sugar Grove (CB), OH, **247**, 248,
349
Helstern, Russell Fred, 596
Camp Swatara (CB), PA, **247**, 248, 693
Carper, Frank Stauffer, 256
Kilhefner, Galen C., 693
Camp Tuk-a-Way, VA (FGBC), **247**
Camp Verde Indian Reserve, 54
Camp Verde mission point, Glendale, AZ,
Church of the Brethren, 552
Camp Wait-Some-More, French Equatorial
Africa, *985*
Camp Wilbur Stover, ID (CB), **247**
Camp Woodbrook (CB), MD, **247**
Shepherd's Spring Outdoor Ministries
Center, 2248
Camp Woodland Altars (CB), OH, **247**,
1227
Camp Wyandotte (BC), KS, **247–248**, 682
Camp Zion, OH (CB), 244, 888, *See also*
Camp Inspiration Hills
Campbell, Alexander, 177, 247, **248**, 281,
385, 1224, 1380, 1898
Disciples of Christ leader, 1136
Hon, Peter, in Restoration movement,
935
Hostetler Brethren, 632
Hostetler, Joseph, 631
Indiana, 652
letter to, 1974
in "New Lights" revivalism, 930
Restoration Movement, 1101
Campbell, Alfred H., 1580
Campbell, Betty Jeanne Brooks, 1835
Campbell Brethren Church, MI, *See*
Clarksville, MI, Grace Brethren
Church
Campbell, C. A., 1580
Campbell Co., KY, 1225
Campbell, David, 246
Campbell, David Charles, 1580
Campbell family, 241, 248, 320, 768, 2087
Haddix, KY, Brethren Church, 577
Meadow Branch Church of the

Brethen, TN, 805
Roanoke, VA, Washington Heights
Grace Brethren Church, 1114
Campbell, Florence, 735
Campbell, Glen, 740
Campbell, Glen Alfred, 740, 576, 1580,
1835
Campbell, Glenn, 1394
Campbell, Harold (Pete) Wray, 2274
Campbell, Hugh, 1580
Campbell, Isabell, 168
Campbell, J. F., 1580
Campbell, James A., 1280, 1580
Campbell, James Warren, 1580
Campbell, John Alonzo, 1580
Campbell, John F., 1580
Campbell, Joseph
Paradise, CA, Church of the Brethren,
992
Reedley, CA, Church of the Brethren,
pastor, 1091
Romine Church of the Brethren, IL,
providing leadership, 1121
Campbell, Joseph Elmer, 1580, 2300
Campbell, MI, congregations
Brethren Church (Progressive
Brethren), 318
Michigan Brethren settlement, 824
Old German Baptist Brethren Church,
248
Campbell-Stone Restoration Movement,
See Restoration Movement
Campbell, Ted A.
historiography, 2201
works by, 2321
Campbell, Thomas, 248
Restoration Movement, 1101
Campbell, Ulysses Simpson, 1580
Campbell, Warren, 1280
Campbellism, 2022
Campbellites, *See* Disciples of Christ
Hon, Peter Keithly, 627
Hostetler Brethren, 632
Hostetler, Joseph, 631
Campbellsville, KY, congregation, 689
Campbelltown, PA, 136
Bible Brethren congregation, 280
campground ministry, 2019, 2036,
2044, 2060
Camping in Southern Ohio (Helstern), 596
camping movement, 248–250, 1898, 1903,
See also conservation; leisure;
scouting; work camps
Argentina, 382
and automobiles, 74
Bethany Biblical Seminary, 248
Bible conferences as forerunners to,
136
Bolling Conference Grounds, 247
Brethren Church, 249–250
Brethren Investment Foundation, 247
Brethren movement, 248–250, 2084
Church of the Brethren, 246, 248, 300
Crumpacker, Franklin Henry, 354
devotional literature, 381
Dunkard Brethren, 250
evangelism and, 250
Fellowship of Grace Brethren
Churches, 250
gifted children, 247
Hanawalt, David Kirk, 581
Helstern, Russell Fred, 596
Indiana, 652

Indiana Brethren Retreat (BC), 654
Jones, George H., 676
learning-disabled children, 247
Lowery, Margaret E., 2216
McFarland, CA, Church of the
Brethren, 774
missions, 859
missions education, 864
mural paintings, 896
National Park Service projects, 917
nature studies in, 2066
Nebraska Church of the Brethren
youth, 920
Ohio Church of the Brethren, 963
orphans, care for, 983
Parish Ministries Commission involve-
ment in, 993
Pennsylvania, located in, 1005
Petersime, Ray, 1012
polity concerning, 1043
recreation, 1087–1088
Redford, MI, Trinity Church of the
Brethren, 1090
Rohrer, Perry Lawrence, 1119
Rothrock, Edgar Eli, 1124
Russell, Harl L., 1132
songs for camps, 2084
Southern Ohio, in, 1962
camping programs, 408, *See also* scouting
programs
Boys' Camp, IN, 171
Brightbill, Alvin Franz, 209
Brougher, Mahlon J., 214
Bushong, Benjamin G., 233
Butterbaugh, Bertha Belle Lehman,
236
Camp Bethan (BC), OH, 242
Camp Blue Diamond (CB), PA, 242
Camp Harmony Assembly, 214
Leatherman, N. Victor, 733
relief and rehabilitation work and, 202
Seneca Church of the Brethren, FL,
1166
Shamberger, Chauncey, 1171
Van Dyke, Joe, 1302
Wagner, Ricardo, 1312
West, Daniel, 1331
youth and, 192
youth in, 1391
camps, *See* individual camps, e.g. Camp
Emmaus
analysis of resident camping program,
Church of the Brethren, 1957
Brethren Civilian Public Service camps,
1216
children and, 2159
Church of the Brethren, 2162
Civilian Public Service, 1372
CPS, 316
historic sites, 609
Kansas, 682
Shepherd's Spring Outdoor Ministries
Center (CB), 2248
work camps, *See* Work camps
World War I, 1370
World War II, 1372
Young Men's Christian Association,
prisoner-of-war camps, England,
1290
youth and, 2269
Campus Crusade for Christ
evangelism, 461
Hispanic Ministries (BC), 2198

Camrin, Bette, 1394
Camrin, Roy, 1394
Camrine, Joseph, 424
Cana, KS, Church of the Brethren, *See*
    Grenola, KS, Church of the
    Brethren
Cana, VA, Saint Paul Church of the
    Brethren, 1135
Canaan, PA
    Church of the Brethren, *See* Sandy
        Creek, WV, Church of the
        Brethren
Canada, **15**, 59, 176, 202, 250, 2037, 2042,
    2043, *See also* specific provinces
    and locations, e.g. Alberta
    Believers' Church, 2108
    bibliography, 1858, 1870, 1893
    Brethren from North Dakota home-
        steaded in, 1305
    Brethren in Christ Church, 2067
    Brethren migration after Revolutionary
        War, 1106
    Brethren movement, 250
    Church of the Brethren history in
        Western Canada, 1969
    colonization and Brethren movement,
        250
    Community of True Inspiration, 330
    Conference of Historic Peace Churches,
        333
    COs, and refuge in, 337
    credit unions, 351
    Dunkard Brethren, 250
    farming, 477
    Fellowship of Grace Brethren
        Churches, 250
    Flora, Delbert Benjamin, 495
    General Church Erection and
        Missionary Committee (CB), 536
    migration of Brethren, 830
    migration of Brethren to, 827
    missions and missionaries in, 250, 858
    North Dakota Brethren relocating to,
        946
    Old Brethren, 971
    railroads and Brethren settlement, 1082
    Winger family, 2101
Canadian Pacific Railway, 15, **250–251**
Canal Fulton, OH
    Grace Brethren Chapel, 2193
    Grace Brethren Church, 251, 1111
    Rittman, OH, First Brethren Church,
        1111
Candler, Emma Leatherman, 1998
Cando, ND, congregations, 109, 231, 251,
    251, 256
    Church of the Brethren, **251**
    Ellison Church of the Brethren, ND,
        442
    migration of Brethren, 830
    Pleasant Valley Church of the Brethren,
        ND, 1035
    Salem Church of the Brethren, offshoot
        of, 1137
    Towner Co., ND, 946
Cane Ridge, KY
    camp meeting, 245
    Presbyterian Church and Restoration
        Movement, 1101
    Second Awakening and American
        revivalism, 1104
Canfield, Flora B. (later Ashman), 68, 581
Canfield, George Grant, 461, 1580

Cannaday family, 1863
Cannaday, Jimmy
    New Hope Church of the Brethren, VA,
        pastor in, 929
Cannaday, Jimmy Odell, 1580
Cannell, D. H., 1580
canning food projects, Codorus, PA, Church
    of the Brethren, 323
Cannon, E. B., 1898
Cannon, Jay Donald, 1580
Canomore, Jacob, 105
    South Carolina, 1204
canon, Brethren, 133
Canon Brethren Church, Taos, NM, 1248
Canon City, CO, 1286
Cañon, NM, Grace Brethren Church, *See*
    Taos, NM, First Brethren Church
    (FGBC)
canonization, 405
Canright, Dudley M.
    Seventh-Day Adventists, writings on,
        1169
Canstein Bible Institution, Halle
    Luther translation of Bible, use of, 138
Canton Bible Institute
    Young, Emanuel S., 251
Canton Center, OH, 251, 267, *See also*
    Center, OH, Church of the
    Brethren
Canton Co., OH, landmarks, 1914
Canton College and Bible Institute, **252**
    Bible Institute of G. W. Kieffaber, *131*
    established by E. S. Young, 137
    Moherman, Tully S., 867
    Young, Emanuel Sprankle, 252, 1389
Canton, IL, 233, 251
    Church of the Brethren, **251**
    Church of the Brethren (Upper Fulton),
        69, 233,
Canton, OH, congregations, 251, 744, 761,
    See also Center, OH, Church of
    the Brethren
    First Church of the Brethren, 251, **251**,
        267
    Grace Brethren Church of Canton, OH,
        101, 251, 252, **562–563**
    Maple Avenue Church of the Brethren,
        251, **251**
    Minerva, OH, Grace Brethren Church,
        843
    Trinity Brethren Church, **251–252**, 563
Capanema, Brazil, 172, 173
Cape Coral, FL, Christ the Servant Church
    of the Brethren, **252**
    Cape family, 318
    Cape Girardeau Co., MO, 321, 1342
    census of early settlers, 1944
    Far Western Brethren, 475, 476
    German Baptist Brethren Church, *See*
        White Water, MO, German Baptist
        Brethren Church
    Missouri Brethren settlement, 864
    Niswanger, Joseph with, 924
    Whitewater Creek congregation, 597
capes
    Old German Baptist Brethren women,
        967
    women, cape and neckerchief for, 921,
        1175
Capilla de la Iglesia de Los Hermanos
    (Chapel of the Church of the Brethren),
    261
capital punishment, 24, 252–253

    attitude of Billy M. Bosler toward,
        2161
    baptism, 292
    Brethren movement, 252–253
    Fellowship of Grace Brethren Churches
        (FGBC), 487
    galley slaves, 253
    religious liberty and, 253
    Solingen Brethren, 253
    U.S. Supreme Court rulings, 253
capitalism, 253–254
    Brethren movement, 253–254
    business beliefs and, 233–234
    labor unions, 253
    Vietnam War and CPC, 286
Capitol Hill Group Ministry (CHGM),
    1320, 2239
Capler family, Grand River German Baptist
    Brethren Church, MO, 565
Caplinger, Robert, 2274
Capon Chapel Church of the Brethren, WV,
    254
    Little Capon, 57, 106
    Oak Grove Church of the Brethren,
        WV, 956
    preaching points
        Brights Hollow, WV, 254
        Briton, WV, 254
        Emboden, WV, 254
        Mission Chapel, WV, 254
        Mountain Dale, WV, 254
        Oak Grove, WV, 254
        Road Ridge, WV, 254
        Taylor, WV, 254
        Tear Coat, WV, congregation, 254
caps, 160, 254, 400, 404, *See also* bonnets;
    hats; prayer veils
    Brethren movement, 254
    Church of the Brethren, *254*
    communion and, 254
    Dunkard Brethren, 409
    graveclothes, 567
    hairstyle, 579
    Old German Baptist Brethren women,
        967
    plain people, 1029
    prayer veil, 1053
    Rinehart, Mary Snader, worn by, *1109*
Capwell's Hall, meetingplace for Waterloo,
    IA, City Church of the Brethren,
    1322
CAR, *See* Central African Republic
Carbon Co., PA, 756
Carbon Co., WY, 1213, 1380
Carbone, Louis, 212, 1580
Card, Charles David, 2274
card playing, 254–255
    Brethren movement, 254–255
    nonconformity, 940
The Card With a Red Border (Humbred),
    636, 748
Carder, John, 142, 1580
Cardinal Krol of Philadelphia, 405
Cardington, Sciota Church of the Brethen,
    OH, preaching point, 1160
Cardoso, Raimundo, 172
Cards, Fred, 566
CARE, *See* Cooperative for American
    Remittances to Europe; Coopera-
    tive for Remittances to Europe;
    relief work
care giving and Church of the Brethren,
    2162–2163

Carey Act and irrigation, 663
Carey, Charles, 1580
Carey, Eli, **255,** 1580
   minorities, ethnic and racial, 850
Carey, George Arthur, 318, 319, 566, 674,
   1277, 1580, 1847, 2274
   New Troy, MI, Grace Brethren Church,
     visiting pastor in, 932
   Rittman, OH, First Brethren Church,
     pastor, 1111
Carey, George W., 1580
Carey, Jonathan Paul, 2274
Carey, Leah Belle Carter, 1847–1848
Carey, Ross Allen, 1580
Carger, Harry V., 1580
Caricofe, A. Joseph, 1580
   Meadow Branch Church of the
     Brethren, MD. pastor, 805
   Mountville, PA, Church of the
     Brethren, pastor, 890
   Roanoke, VA, Hollins Road Church of
     the Brethren, pastor, 1113
Carini, John, 213
Caritas, Honduras, 627
Carl, August, 255
Carl, Edward Lee, 1580
Carl, Ernest, 244
Carl family, 255
   Payette Valley Church of the Brethren,
     ID, 996
Carl, George Clinton, **255,** 269, 276, 295,
   461, 552, 1223, 1319, 1364, 1580,
   1898, 2026,
   missions, 858
   Newberg, OR, Church of the Brethren,
     support for, 933
   Oregon, 981
   orphans, care for, 982
   Oysterville, WA, German Baptist
     Brethren Church, 986
   Portland, OR, Peace Church of the
     Brethren, 1048
   Powelis Valley Church of the Brethren,
     OR, elder, 1050
   Redondo Beach, CA, South Bay
     Community Church of the Breth-
     ren, pastor, 1090
Carl, Johann Samuel, 120, 255, 2058
   Geistliche Fama (Spritiual Report),
     533
Carl (Karl), Johann (fl.), **255**
Carl (Karl) Ludwig, count of Sayn-
   Wittgenstein-Sayn, 683–684
   Graf zu Sayn-Wittgenstein, 1898
Carl, O. S., 1580
Carl, Walter George, 1580
Carleton, NE, Brethren Church, **255,** 921
Carlisle, AR, Church of the Brethren, **255,**
   354
Carlisle congregation, PA, 1294
Carlisle, Leonard, 1277
   Peoria IL, (First) Church of the
     Brethren, pastor, 1009
Carlisle, Leonard Bay, 1580
Carlisle, PA, 157, **255–256,** 765, 1388
   Church of the Brethren, 1898
   First Church of the Brethren, 255–256
   Home of the Children's Aid Society,
     625
Carlisle Springs, PA, 135
Carlock, Walter, 1899
Carlson, Charles Howard, 1899
   works by, 2321

Carlson, John Jacob, 1580
Carlson, Melinda K., 2274
Carlson, Tom, 1251
Carlton, Alva, 1838
Carlton Brethren Church, IA, Brethren
   Church (FGBC), Garwin, IA
Carlton, NE, congregation
   Brethren Church, 2
   McFaden, John Duke, 773
Carman, A. J., 1580
Carmean, Robert, 251
Carmichael, Mark Joseph, 1240, 1338,
   1580
Carmichael, Paula S., 2274
Carmichael, Wendell Paul, 1580
Carnegie, Andrew, 253
   Huntingdon, PA, Stone Church of the
     Brethren, 637
Carnevali, Ronald P., 2274
Carney, James S., 1580
Carney, Joseph
   Shelby Co. Church of the Brethren,
     MO, leadership in, 1175
Carney, Lilliam, 236
Carol Co., IL, 1870
Carol Stream, IL, Christ Church of the
   Brethren, **2155–2156**
Caroline Co., MD
   Ridgely, MD, Church of the Brethren,
     1109
Carpe, Thomas, 1580
Carpenter, A. F., 1580
Carpenter, Carnie Acil, 1580
Carpenter, Chauncy, 256
Carpenter, Delburn, 1899
Carpenter, Eliza (later Long), 753
Carpenter family
   Fruitdale, AL, Church of the Brethren,
     520
Carpenter, George C., **256,** 1580
   Peru, IN, First Brethren Church, pastor,
     1010
Carpenter, Jerry L., 398, 1581
Carpenter, Joseph, 1581
Carpenter, Julian O., 2300
Carpenter, Mary Greiner, 256
Carpenter, Robert E., 1581
Carpenter, S. T., 1581
Carpenter Shop, 161
Carpenter, Susan (later Frazer), 1941
Carpenter, William, 1581
Carpenter-Zimmerman family, 1974
Carpenter's Hall
   Santa Maria, CA, Grace Brethren
     Church, used as meetinghouse,
     1145
Carpenters house, Leola, PA, Conestoga
   Church of the Brethren, 737
Carper, Albert B., 256
Carper, Arthur G., 1581
   Meadow Mills Church of the Brethren,
     VA, 806
   Salem Church of the Brethren, VA,
     pastor in, 1138
Carper, E. P., 749, 1581
Carper, Eugene G., 1581, 1899
Carper family, 256, 1390
Carper, Fannie Stauffer, 256
Carper, Frank Stauffer, **256,** 1581, 1899
   Palmyra, PA, Church of the Brethren,
     991
Carper, George, 1581
carpets, 3, 48, 59, **256**

Old Brethren German Baptist Church,
   965
simple life, 1183
use of, 256
Carr, Alva Glenn, 1581
Carr, Alva Wayne, 1581, 2300
   Rossville, IN, Church of the Brethren,
     minister, 1124
Carr, Arthur C., 2274
Carr, Charles E., 1581
Carr, John, 1581
   New Hope Church of the Brethren,
     OK, minister to, 929
Carrara, Italy, 200
Carriage Hill (historical park), OH, 1265
carriages, *See* buggies
Carribean and Heifer Project International,
   594
Carrier, Joseph F., 1581
Carrier, Joseph J., 1581
Carrier, W. H., 1315
Carrier, William H., 224, 1581
Carrington, ND, 164, 251
   Brethren settlement, 946
   Church of the Brethren, **256**
   James River Church of the Brethren,
     ND, 668
   New Rockford, ND, Church of the
     Brethren, 932
   North Dakota Brethren settlement, 946
   Northern Pacific Railroad and Brethren
     colonists, 951
Carrithers, Elmer R., 1581
Carrithers, Loretta, 1581
Carrithers, Mrs. Elmer, Mansfield, OH,
   Grace Brethren Church, pastor,
   787
Carrol Co., IN, 373
Carrol Co., MD, 145
Carroll (Carrell), George, 1581
Carroll Co., IL, 720, 753, 1228, 1899
   Falls City, NE, Brethren Church, 472
   Hickory Grove Church of the Brethren,
     IL, 602
   history, 1967
   Maryland Brethren immigrating to, 798
   Milledgeville Church of the Brethren,
     IL, 833
   Naperville Church of the Brethren, 913
   Preiß (Price) family, 1055
   Rittenhouse family, 1111
   Rock Creek Church of the Brethren,
     IL, 1116
   Shannon, IL, Church of the Brethren,
     1172
Carroll Co., IN, 231, 297, 352, 362, 363,
   463, 1312, 1345
   Church of God (New Dunkers), 297
   Flora, IN, Church of the Brethren, 496
   Hamilton, Hiel, 580
   North Fork Old German Baptist
     Brethren Church, IN, 947
   Old Brethren, 964
   Patton, George and Magdaline, 996
   Patton, Uriah, 996
   Replogle family, 1100
   Replogle, Peter, 1100
Carroll Co., MD, 162, 247, 425, 708
   Maryland Progressive Brethren activi-
     ty, 799
   Meadow Branch Church of the
     Brethren, MD, 805
   Piney Creek Church of the Brethren,

MD, 1025
Pipe Creek Church of the Brethren,
MD, 1025
Sams Creek Church of the Brethren,
MD, 1141
Carroll Co., MO, Grand River German
Baptist Brethren Church, MO, 565
Carroll Co., TN, 354
Carroll Co., VA, 345, 352
Fremont Church of the Brethren, VA,
515
St. Paul Church of the Brethren, VA,
1135
Carroll, Donald R., 1215, 1581
Carroll family, 740
Carroll, Henry K, 379, 1899
Carroll, Jeffrey A., 1267, 2274
Grace Village Retirement Complex,
2192, 2193
Carroll, Lucy Ellen
works by, 2321
Carroll, Robert B., 2274
Carruthers, S. W., 1899
Carson City, MI, congregations, 323
Michigan Brethren settlement, 824
Old German Baptist Brethren Church,
256
Carson, Delpha Crook, 345
Carson family, 320
Carson Valley Church of the Brethren, PA,
256–257, 407, 732, 1899
Carson Valley house, 407
Hollidaysburg, PA, Church of the
Brethren, 619
Carstetter, Daniel, 1581
Cart Creek, IN, Church of the Brethren,
257, 1202, 1245
Carter, Betty (later Thompson)
Thompson, Robert W. (FGBC) and,
2256
Carter, Clyde, See Carter, Leonard Clyde,
Jr.
Carter, Clyde LeRoy, 1581, 1835
Carter, D. L., Sr., family
Selma, VA, Church of the Brethren,
1166
Carter, Daniel, 1581
Carter, Donald F., 29, 552, 553, 715, 755,
1581, 2300, 2381
Carter, E. James, 1581, 1899
Carter, Earl F., 1581
Carter, Ethelmae Eylar, 1899
Carter family, 265
McFarland, CA, Church of the
Brethren, 774
Outlook, WA, Church of the Brethren,
986
Carter, Forest Alonzo, Jr., 1581
Carter, Harvey, 257, 506, 1327, 1581
minorities, ethnic and racial, 849
Carter, Jeffrey W., 2274
Carter, Joseph, 1581
Oak Grove Church of the Brethren,
OK, minister, 956
Carter, Karen Spohr, 2274
works by, 2321
Carter, Leah Belle, 1847–1848
Carter, Leonard Clyde, Jr., 1581, 1899,
2381
Mount Bethel Church of the Brethren,
VA, pastor, 880
Carter, Lois Eleanor Snare, 1846
Carter, Lydia, 708

Carter, Martha, 257, 506, 1327
minorities, ethnic and racial, 849
Carter, Phyllis Nolan, 1581, 2111, 2163
church governance and, 2264
Rio Prieto, PR, Iglesia de los
Hermanos (CB) and, 2244
works by, 2321
Carter, William C., 1899
Carter, William Robert, 1581
Carthage, MO, Church of the Brethren, 7,
257, 1214
75th anniversary of, 1959
Jasper, 670
Joplin, MO, 676
Missouri, 865
Nevada, 924
Carthage, VA, 1341
Cartland, Fernando G., 1899
Cartmell, Thomas K., 1899
cartographers, 768–769
cartoonists, 149
Cartwright, Peter, 257–258, 647, 1899
Caruso, Giovanni, 258
Caruso, John (Giovanni) G., 212, 1296,
1581
Brooklyn, NY, urban ministry in, 933
Italian Sunday School (CB), 664
Carver, Christian, 1914
Carver family, 411
Carver, Mahlon, 1581
Carver, Mary (later Landis), 722
Cary, Cletus Clayton, 1581
Cary, Evelyn S., 1899
Cary, Jack L., 2274
Casa de Modesto
Modesto, CA, Church of the Brethren,
866
Retirement Center, CA, 258
Cascade Locks, OR, 1156
Cascade Valley, WA, Old German Baptist
Brethren Church, 2156
Casebeer, Rufus D., 1581
Casement, Nathan D., 367, 1581
Cases, Everett N., 1302
Cashman, Arthur D., 319, 360, 366, 552,
626, 629, 1581, 2156, 2381
Rittman, OH, First Brethren Church,
pastor, 1111
Cashman, Bettie Taber, 2156
Cashman, Connie Becker, 2156
Cashman, Edwin E., 65, 115, 1581, 2156,
2300
Casimir, Ernst, count of Berleberg, 227,
1274, 1354, 1394
Casimir, Johann (Count), 119
Caskey family, Salem Church of the
Brethren, IA, 1137
Caskey, Homer F., 345, 447, 1581
Omaha, NE, Church of the Brethren,
minister, 974
Red Cloud, NE, Church of the Breth-
ren, providing leadership, 1088
Caskey, Metta, 345
Caskey, Olaf C., 345, 377, 1581
Caslow, Mrs. E. F., 1080
Caslow, Ellis F., 1080, 1581
Casner, Anna Elizabeth (later Harshbarger),
587
Caspian Sea, 55
Cass Co., IN, 297, 344, 345, 352, 463, 700
Church of God (New Dunkers), 297
Hamilton, Hiel, 580
Mexico Old German Baptist Brethren

Church, IN, 821
Cass Co., MI, 260, 288
Newton Grove Church of the Brethren,
934
Pokogan, MI, Church of the Brethren,
1040
Portage Prairie, IN, Church of the
Brethren, 1047
Cass Co., MO, Mound Valley Church of the
Brethren, 879
Cassaday, John H., 1899
Cassady, J. B., 1254
Cassady, J. Harry, 637
Cassady, John A., 675
Cassady, John Henry, 461, 641, 675, 695,
1581
Philadelphia, PA, Calvary Church of
the Brethren, 1015
Cassady, Margaret (later Lyon), 2376
Cassady, Maynard L., 1581, 1899
Cassady, Meribah V., 1581
Cassel, Abraham Harley, 52, 61, 108, 120,
258, 258–259, 424, 541, 577, 580,
583, 613, 751, 1581
acrostic sonnet, 258, 259, 260
articles about, 1921, 1943
bibliographical material, 1875, 1879,
1894, 1899
bibliographical sources, 1938, 1967,
2036, 2039, 2044, 2048, 2070,
2083, 2093
collection at Juniata College, article
about, 1942
Das Wochenblatt, 2103
Dunkard bibliophile, 1991
historic sites, 609
historical writing, 611
Holdeman, John, 618
letters from, 2087
on Harley family, 2102
Library, See Cassel Library
Miller, Daniel Long, 836
Menno, Simons, 814
plagiarism, 2017
references to, 1933
Seidensticker, Oswald, friend of, 1165
single mode feetwashing, 1186
sources on, 2320
thesis on, 1961
The Thunderstorm (Rhoades), 747
writings of, 1899–1900
Cassel, C. W., 1900
Cassel (Cassell), Henry, 1582
Cassel, Catherine (later Rittenhouse), 1111
Cassel, Catherine M. Nyce, 260
Cassel, Charles D., 1340, 1581–1582
Cassel, Daniel Kolb, 1901
works by, 2321
Cassel, David, 1338
Cassel, David N., 1582
Cassel, Elizabeth (later Wieand), 1344
Cassel family, 1229, 1901
Fraktur artistry, 2186
Preiß (Price) family related to, 1055
sources on, 2321
Cassel, Franklin J., 707
Cassel, Franklin Kulp, 1291, 1582, 1901
works by, 2321
Cassel, Franklin P., 1582
Cassel, George, 64
Cassel, Hannah (later Shisler), See Shisler,
Hannah Cassel
Cassel, Henry, 1582

Mingo Church of the Brethren, PA, elder, 843

Cassel, Henry C., 97, **259**

Cassel, Hupert, 260

Cassel, Isaac Y., 1582

Cassel, J. B., 1582

Cassel, J. J.
missions, 861

Cassel, Jacob C., 97, 250, 259, **259–260,** 381, 500–501, 691, 1210, 1582, 1901
Holiness Movement, American, 619
Kolb, William, Jr., business partner of, 706
missions, 861
Quebec, 1075
Ridgely, MD, Brethren Church, pastor, 1109

Cassel, Jere H., 1340

Cassel, Jeremiah H., 1582

Cassel, Johannes, 260

Cassel, John, 349

Cassel, John Joseph, 357, 1582

Cassel, Jonas M., 260

Cassel, Joseph Nyce, **260,** 1582, 1901
Skippack Church of the Brethren, PA, minister, 1189
sources on, 2321

Cassel, Laura (later Moyer)
Moyer, Laura Emma, mother of, 892

Cassel Library, 52, 258, **260,** 1220, 2073
bibliographies, Brethren, 139
historical writing, 611
The History of the German Baptist Brethren in Europe and America, 613
Holdeman, John, 618

Cassel, Margaret "Peggy," 2034

Cassel, Mary Brown (later Jacobs), 667

Cassel, Mary Harley, 258

Cassel, Merlin Emerson, 1582

Cassel, Russell N., 1901

Cassel, Samuel M., 1582

Cassel, Samuel W., 1340

Cassel, Sara, 1844

Cassel, Wilbur, Skippack Church of the Brethren, PA, moderator and deacon, 1189

Cassel, William, Painter Creek Old German Baptist Brethren Church, OH, 990

Cassel, Yelles, 258, 260

Cassell, Leonard, 260

Cassell, Maria, 260

Cassell, William, **260,** 1582
Mount Cassell Old German Baptist Brethren Church, WV, 880

Cassidente, Ronald B., 1582

Cassidy, J. H., *See* Cassady, John Henry

Cassopolis, MI, Bethel Brethren Church, **260**

Casstown, OH,
Church of the Brethren, **261**
congregation, 363, 396

Castañer Hospital, Puerto Rico, 230, *261,* **261–262**
Association of Brethren Caregivers (ABC), 2132
medical care, 810
reconstruction project for, 344
relief and service efforts, 1097

Castañer, Puerto Rico, 146, 199, 202
Brethren presence, 1070
Church of the Brethren, **261**

CPS, 316

Hispanic Ministries (CB), 2198, 2199
hospitals, 631
Manatí, PR, Pueblo de Dios, 2217
Mason, George Edward, 2218
medical projects, 808
relief training units, use of outside the USA, 1097
Rio Prieto, PR, Iglesia de los Hermanos (CB), 2243
Vega Baja, PR, Iglesia de los Hermanos Cristo El Señor (CB) and, 2258
Yahuecas, PR, Iglesia de los Hermanos Cristo Nuestra Paz (CB) and, 2267

Castelli, Claudio
Brethren Church in Paraguay and, 2237

Castelli, Karina
Brethren Church in Paraguay and, 2237

Caster, Samuel Edgar, 740, 1582

Castine, OH, Church of the Brethren, 262, **262**
Prices Creek Church of the Brethren, OH, 1057

Castle, A. H., 1582

Castle, Cornelius W., 1582

Castle family, 216

Castle, Ira, 1582

Castle, Noah Phillip, 1582

Castle Thunder, **261,** *See also* Confederate States of America; military service

Castor Association
works by, 2321

Castors congregation, Central African Republic
Gaiwaka, Noel, 527

Castro, Fidel
Iglesia Cristiana Pentecostal de Cuba, 2207

Catawba Co., NC
Brethren settlement, 946
German Baptist Brethren Church, **262**
Revolutionary War, 946

Cate, Steven Blaupot ten, 1901

catechism, 5, 86, **262,** *See also* Heidelberg Catechism
Christian education movement, 283
church membership, 813
Spener, Philipp Jakob, reinstated by, 1209
A Summary of Religious Faith and Practice or Doctrine and Duties, Beer, 1873
Sunday school movement, 1237

Cathari, *See* Albigensians

Cathcart, William, 1901

Catholic Church, *See* Roman Catholic Church

Catholic Relief Services and SERRV International (CB), 2247

Catlett family
Maple Valley, WA, Grace Brethren Church, 2218

Catlins, William N., 1582

Catoctin, MD, congregation
Martin, Nicholas, 797

Cattell, William C., 379, 1901

Cattepoel, Dirk, 1901

Caub, Jacob, 630

Cauble, Comm. Wesley, 1901

Caudill, Ted Ellis, 209, 1582
Pleasant Hill Church of the Brethren, TN, pastor/elder, 1032

Cauffiel, D. Edward, 752, 1582

Rockwood Church of the Brethren, PA, supply pastor, 1118

Cavanaugh, Gerald (Mr. and Mrs.), 579

Cave, Carol (later Dubble), 2277

Cave, David Earl, 1582

Cave, Dewey B., 740, 1582

Cave, Ernest Lee, 1582

Cave, Herman E., 1582

Cave Rock, VA, Church of the Brethren, 262, **262,** 1277

Cave Springs, VA
mission point, Peters Creek Church of the Brethren, VA, 1011
Poages Mill Church of the Brethren, VA, 1039

Cave, William W., 1582

CAVEA *See* Centro Audio-Visual Evangélico Argentina

Cavell, Jean Moore, 1901

Cavert, Samuel McCrea, 422, 1901

Cawley, Ernest Clarence, 1582

Cawley family
Irricana (First) Church of the Brethren, Alberta, Canada, 663

Cawood, Carl Berry, 1582

Cayford, Betty Lou Hershberger, 13, 1835

Cayford, Cheryl Ann (later Brumbaugh-Cayford)
works by, 2319

Cayford, Elvis Clarence, 1582, 1835

Caylor, Abraham, 1582

Caylor, Abraham (CB), 1582

Caylor, Alice (later Shank), *See* Shank, Alice Caylor

Caylor, Amos, 1582

Caylor, David Samuel, 1582

Caylor, Elias, 45, 109, 1582

Caylor, John H., 1582

Caylor, Oliver, 1582

Caylor, William, 1582

Cayoga Co., NY, Kings Ferry congregation, 933

Cazden, Robert E., 1901

Cazenove, Theophile, 1901

Cazes, Eric, 1848

Cazier, Stanford O., 1901

CBYF Bible Studies, 1236

CCC (Christian Community Center) and Rio Piedras, PR, Segunda Iglesia Cristo Misionera Fellowship (CB), 2243

CCC *See* Civilian Conservation Corps

CCMT *See* Cross Cultural Ministries Team

CE National
Brethren identity, publications about, 2148–2149
Grace Brethren International Missions, 2191
youth and, 2269

Cecil, Bertha Idell (later Robertson), 1114, 1843

Cecil Co., MD
Elkton Immanuel Church of the Brethren, MD, 440

Cecil family, 1914

Cedar Bluff Community Church, VA, 130, 163, **262**

Cedar Co., IA, 263, 661, 1401
Cedar Church of the Brethren, **263,** 1401
Old German Baptist Brethren Church, **263**

Cedar Co., MO, 263, 734

Church of the Brethren, **263,**
Missouri Brethren settlement, 864
Cedar Creek, AL, Church of the Brethren,
263, **263–264**
Fruitdale, AL, Church of the Brethren,
520
Cedar Creek Grove, TN, Old German
Baptist Brethren Church, **264**
Cedar Creek, IN, Church of the
Brethren, 70, **264,** 749
Cedar Creek, IN, congregation, 264, 265
Cedar Creek, KS, 410, 2134
Mont Ida Church of the Brethren, **870,**
1161
Old German Baptist Brethren Church,
264, 682, 731
Cedar Creek schoolhouse, Liberty Church
of the Brethren, TN, 740
Cedar Falls, IA, 1321, *See also* Waterloo,
IA, Cedar Heights Community
Brethren Church
Cedar Heights Brethren Church, **2156**
Cedar Grove Academy of Virginia, *See*
Cedar Grove Seminary (Academy)
Cedar Grove Academy (Seminary), 701,
1308
Cedar Grove, IA, 263
Cedar Grove, OH, 264
Church of the Brethren, **264**
Prices Creek Church of the Brethren,
OH, 1057
Cedar Grove Seminary (Academy), 2,
265, 701, 1308
Cedar Grove, TN, Church of the Brethren,
264
Meadow Branch Church of the Breth-
ren, TN, 805
migration of Brethren, 829
Cedar Grove, VA, 265, 342, 416, *See also*
Flat Rock Church of the Brethren,
VA
Cedar Grove-Ruckersville Fellowship
Church of the Brethren, **265**
Mount Carmel Church of the Brethren
and Cedar Grove-Ruckersville
congregation, 880
Cedar Grove, WV, Church of the Brethren,
264–265
Cedar House, MI, Church of the Brethren,
265
Cedar Lake, IN, Church of the Brethren,
70, **265,** 1030, 1298, 1901
Cedar Rapids, IA, 736
Church of the Brethren/First Baptist
Church, **265**
German Baptist Brethren, 265
Grace Brethren Church, **265**
Grant, Richard E., 2193
Waterloo, IA, Grace Brethren
Church mission point for, 265
Miller, Jacob Kurtz, 838–839
Robins, IA, Church of the
Brethren, 1115
Cedar Run Church of the Brethren, VA ,
265, 746
meetinghouse, Linville Creek Church
of the Brethren, 746
The Cedars Retirement Home, KS, 8,
265–266, 682, 780
celibacy, 113, **266**
Amana Church Society, 330
Beissel, Conrad on, 2045
Christ's Assembly and, 280

Community of True Inspiration, 330
continence and sexual relations, 338
discipline, 388
doctrine on, 175
Eicher, Daniel, 431
Eicher, Maria, 431
Ephrata Community, 448, 451, 1147
family, 474
German Seventh-Day Baptists, 542
Hebron, 591
Hildebrand, Maria (later Mack), 606
Höcker, Heinrich, 615
Höcker, Ludwig, 616
homosexuality, 2204
Kalcklöser, Johann Heinrich, 681
Koch, Stephan, 704
Lehman, Peter, 736
marriage, 795
monasticism, 869
Nägele, Hans Rudolph and Elizabeth,
910
Radical German Pietism, 1080
sexuality, human, 1170
Zion, Ephrata Community, 1399–1400
Cell Base Congregations
Winning the Race Ministries and,
2262–2263
Cement, OK, Church of the Brethren, **266**
cemeteries, *524,* 2034, 2038–2039, 2188,
See also burial customs and funer
als; death and dying; tombstones
Bieber-Lescer family, 2074
Bomberger family, 158
College Hill Church, 1
Coventry congregation, PA, 1298
Ephrata Community, 2057
Germantown, PA, *266,* 1984
Great Swamp Church of the Brethren,
PA, 569
Happy Corner cemetery, OH, 696
Harleysville, PA, Indian Creek Church
of the Brethren, 583
Heitler, Martin P., 595
Heitler, Richard R., 595
Huntsdale Church of the Brethren, PA,
638
Indian Creek Church of the Brethren
Cemetery, 2364
Influenza Pandemic, 655
inscriptions, 1969, 2000, 2008
inscriptions, tombstone
Bermudian Church of the Brethren
Cemetery, 2084
Keim family, 2074
Stump family, 2074
La Verne Evergreen Cemetery tomb-
stone inscriptions, 2329
of Lancaster County, 2352
Long family, 2000
Mennonite Cemetery, Coventry, PA,
709
Mount Zion, near Ephrata, PA, 2007
Oak Lawn Memorial Gardens, near
Gettysburg, PA, 1241
Omaja, Cuba, 355
Sauer, Christopher, grave of, 2090
Snow Hill, 2320
sources on, 2314
Surrey Old German Baptist Brethren
Church, ND, 1242
tombstones, 2090
union churches, 1287
Urner, Martin, 1298

Walnut Grove CB Cemetery, 2349
cemetery associations, 149
censorship of drama, 398
censure, *See* discipline
census
death records, Somerset Co., PA, 2104
Miller, Howard, 838
Montgomery Co., IN, 2089
obituaries, Fort Wayne, Co., IN, 2099
The Record of the Faithful, 1086
Rockingham Co., VA, 2077
statistics, US, 2086
US Department of Census, 1086, 2086
West Earl Twp., PA, 2092
Centennial fairs and public shows, 467
Centennial meetinghouse, La Place, IL,
Church of the Brethren, 713
Centennial, OH, 1265
A Centennial Statement, 2141, 2148, **2156,**
2252
Center Chapel Brethren Church, IN, **267,**
821
Center Chapel Church of the Brethren, MD,
See Accident, MD, Bear Creek
Church of the Brethren
Center Church of the Brethren, IN, **267**
Center Church of the Brethren, OH, **267,**
1306
Center Church of the Brethren, PA,
267–268
Center for Community Education, Eliza-
bethtown College, 438
Center for Theological Studies (CB),
Ecuador, 854
Center Hill Church of the Brethren, PA,
170, **268,** 433, 699
Glade Run Brethren Church, PA, 551
Center House meetingplace, Yellow Creek
Church of the Brethren, IL, 1384
Center House of Pine Creek, IN, congrega-
tion, 267
Center, IN, congregation, 267
Center of Theological Studies/Centro
de Estudios Teológicos (CET),
Ecuador, **268,** 1290
Center of Theological Studies, Evangelical
Covenant Church, 460
Center, OH, Church of the Brethren, 251,
2049
Nimishillen Church of the Brethren,
organized from, 937
Center Point, AL, 143
Centerview, IA, congregation, 901
Centerview, MO, Church of the Brethren,
268, 1318
Centerview, NE, Old German Baptist
Brethren Church of the Brethren,
268
Centerville, OH, Grace Brethren Church,
268, 366
Centerville, VA, 1235
Central Africa, *See* Africa
Central African Republic
Beaver, Dorothy, 2134
Beaver, Samuel Wayne, 2134
Bible Institute, 2134
CSB, 287
education, 2010
Foreign Missionary Society (BC,
FGBC), 501
France, 506
Gaiwaka, Noel, 527
Grace Brethren International Missions,

2191
Hull, Margaret, missionary to, 1019
International Fellowship of Grace
    Brethren Churches, 2209
Islam, 664
James Gribble Memorial High School,
    668, 1246
medical care, 810
medical evangelists, Grace Brethren,
    952
medical missions, 807–808
mission schools, 854
missions, 862
missions and missionaries in, 250, 862,
    2225, 2226
Oubangui-Chari mission, 268–269, 270
Oubangui-Chari (Ubangi-Shari), 985
Sheely, Lila, missionary to, 1019
Taber, Ada Zellner, 1247
Central America, 2157
    Church of the Brethren, 2162
    Mennonites, 815
    missions, short-term, 2226
Central Bible School, Bozoum, Central
    African Republic, 854
Central Church of the Brethren, VA, See
    Roanoke, VA, Central Church of
    the Brethren
Central Committee, See under Church of
    the Brethren Annual Conference
Central Council (BC), 154, 183, 2169
    placement of pastors, 1028
    Rose, Smith Fuller (BC) and, 2244
Central Pacific Railroad, building of,
    1288–1289
Central Plains, VA, Church of the Brethren,
    269
Central Planning and Coordinating Com-
    mittee (BC), 269
Central Point, TN, Church of the Brethren,
    269
    Pleasant View Church of the Brethren,
    TN, daughter congregation of,
    1037
Central Region Board, 1902
Central Regional Council of Women's
    Work, 1157
Central Service Committee, 269, 1370
    conscientious objector inter-denomina-
    tional cooperation, 917
    Goshen Conference, 559
    Henry, Jerry Maurice, 598
    social action, 1196
    Swigart, William Joseph, 1245
Centralia congregation, WA, 1319, 1364
Centralia, WA, 255, 1338
    Church of the Brethren, 269, 1319,
    1364
Centro Audio-Visual Evangélico Argentina
    (CAVEA), 54, 856
Centro de Estudios Teológicos (Center of
    Theological Studies) (CET), 268
Ceres, CA, 161, 239
Cérésole, Pierre, 1365, 1367
Cerro Gordo, IL, congregations, 270, 713,
    732, 1863, 1949
    Brethren Church, 269
    Church of the Brethren, 270
    Flora, Benjamin H., 495
    Flora, Delbert Benjamin, 495
    Heckman, Benjamin Franklin, 591
    Metzger, John, providing nonresident
    oversight, 819

Oakley Brick Church of the Brethren,
    IL, 958
Old German Baptist Brethren Church,
    270
certificates
    membership, See letters of membership
    Sappington, Roger E. membership,
    2354
    Stopp, Klaus on fraktur, 2359
Cessna, Robert S., 1582, 2300
CET (Center of Theological Studies/Centro
    de Estudios Teológicos), Ecuador,
    1290
Chad, Republic of
    Brethren Church, 270
    Foreign Missionary Society (BC,
    FGBC), 501
    Islam, 664
    Kliever, Freda Neufeld, 701
    Kliever, Jacob Paul, 701
    medical care, 810
    mission schools, 854
    missions, 862, 2226
    Oubangui-Chari (Ubangi-Shari), 985
Chaddock, Robert E., 1902
Chae, David Indu, 2274
Chaffin, Patrick, 1582
Chafin family
    Riner Grace Brethren Church, VA,
    1110
chairs, replacing pews, 2131
Chalcedon, decisions of, 289
Chalcedonian Creed (BC), 184
Chalkley, Lyman, 1902
Chalon-sur-Saône, France, 506
Chaloupka, Clara Rebecca, 1816
Chamber Memorial Church, Harlem, NY,
    inter-racial exchange program
    with, 1218
Chamberlain, Larry N., 2182
Chamberlain, Wendy (later McFadden),
    2149–2150
    Brethren Press and, 2264
Chamberlin, Maggie D. (later Haughtelin),
    589
Chambers, Andrew, 1582
Chambers, Daniel, 106, 211, 1582
    New Haven Church of the Brethren,
    leadership in, 928
Chambers, George Washington, 586, 1209,
    1582
Chambers, Harold S., 1582
Chambers, John W., 1582
Chambers schoolhouse
    Washington, PA, Grace Brethren
    Church, 1320
Chambers, Theodore F., 1902
Chambers, William, 211, 1582
Chambersburg, PA
    Church of the Brethren, 40–41, 42,
    270, 1220
    Grace Brethren Church, 270
    New Testament Brethren, 932
Chamblissburg, VA, Saunders Grove
    Church of the Brethren, 1150
CHAMP, inter-racial exchange program
    State College, PA, University Baptist
    and Brethren Church, 1218
Champaign Co., IL, 152, 1297–1298
Champaign Co., OH, 261
Champaign, IL, Church of the Brethren,
    270, 2089
    Blue Ridge, IL, congregation, mission

point for, 270
    work in Champaign, 1986
Champaign, MI, First congregation, 270
Champion, John, Orlando, FL, Grace
    Brethren Church, 982
Chance, Hilda Snowberger, 1902
Chance, James and Chris, 16
chancel, arrangement of for worship, 1377
Chandler, Catherine Voigt Soleman, 1902
Chandler, Edgar H. S., 1902
Chandler, Elizabeth (later Poff), 1060
Chandler family, 1917
Chandler, James, 1582
Chandler, Joseph R., 1902
Chandler, William, 1582
Chaners, J. E., 1583
Chaney, Charles, 1224
Chaney, Connell Thomas, 129, 1583, 2136
Chaney, Drusilla (later Stouffer), 1225
Chang, Patricia M., on clergy women, 2365
change
    experienced unevenly, and schism,
    1152–1153
    Progressive Brethren and polity,
    1042–1043
Channer, Frances Mildred, 1835
Channing St. Mission, CA, 758
Chanute, KS, Church of the Brethren, 270
Chao, F. L., 1583
Chaparral congregation, CA, 1358
chapel, Ephrate Community, See Saal,
    Ephrata Community
Chapel of the Church of the Brethren
    (Capilla de la Iglesia de Los
    Hermanos), 261
chaplains and chaplaincies, 270–271,
    2157–2158
    Association of Brethren Caregivers
    (ABC), 2132
    Brethren Church, 312, 2178
    Copp, Zed H., 343
    Fellowship of Grace Brethren Churches
    (FGBC), 486
    Grace Brethren Church, 312
    Grace Brethren North American
    Missions, 2191
    Hamel, Joseph Donat, 2196
    hospital chaplaincy of Glenn H.
    ("Doc") Shank, 2248
    hospital service, 2072
    Jenkins, Charles Lee, 2209
    military chaplaincy, 100, 832, 1305,
    1372–1373, 2157
    prison ministries, 1060
    vocations, Christian, 2091
Chapman College, CA, 143
Chapman Creek, KS, Church of the
    Brethren, 226, See also Buckeye,
    KS, Church of the Brethren
Chapman, Everett R., 1583
Chapman, Giles, 271, 511, 768, 1292, 1583,
    2078
    South Carolina minister, 1204
Chapman, J. Wilbur
    Winona Lake Auditorium, IN, 1353
Chapman, John
    Lakeland, FL, Grace Brethren Church,
    2213
Chapman, William, 1583
Chapparal, CA, Jenny Lind Brethren
    Church, 238, 271
Chappel, Julianne (later Elliott), 1928
Chappelear, George W., 1982

Chappell, Edward A., 1902
Chappell, James I., 2274
Charis International, 2183
charismatic congregations
    Lancaster, PA, Acts Covenant Fellowship, 2213
charismatic controversy at Herndon, VA, Chandon Brethren Church, 2197
charismatic movements, **271–272**, 1210, 1903, 2040, *See also* prophecy
    Argentina, 53, 180
    Brethren Doctrine of Salvation, 1140
    Brethren heritage, 1986
    Brethren movement, 280
    Brethren prayer, 1051
    Camisards, 242
    Christ's Assembly and, 280
    Christ's Assembly and Old German Baptist Brethren, 970
    Church of the Brethren, 304
    Covington, OH, First Brethren Church (FGBC), 349
    Dayton, OH, Patterson Park Grace Brethren Church, 367
    Faith Assembly, 2180
    Fellowship of Grace Brethren Churches (FGBC), 486, 487
    healing, 591
    Holy Spirit, doctrine of, 624
    Holy Spirit Renewal Group, 625
    house churches, 632
    Masters, Peter, Jr. on, 2363
    Old German Baptist Brethren, 967
    Pittsburgh, PA, Church of the Brethren, 1027
    prophecy, 1062
    Reba Place Fellowship, 1084
    schisms and, 175, 177
    Siccardi, Luis, pastor, 1181
    Sojourners Fellowship, 1200
    theology and, 2254
    Whitcomb, John C., Jr. on, 2363
    worship and, 2266
charitable organizations, 19
charity
    Ephrata Community, 451
    income tax law regarding, 405
Charity School Movement, 1874, 1895
    article about, 1952
    colonial era, 2092–2093
    Pennsylvania, 2092–2093, 2098
    Sauer I's opposition to, 1147–1148, 1153, 1957
Charles August, count, *See* Karl August, count of Ysenburg-Büdingen-Marienborn
Charles family
    Neher family, related to, 922
Charles Hector St. Georges, Marquis de Marsay, 239
Charles, Howard, 2134
Charles II (King of England) and Society of Friends (Quakers), 1199
Charles, Warren, 1583
Charleston, OH, Church of the Brethren, **272**
Charleston, WV, Church of the Brethren, **272**
Charley Newcomer (Stover), 747
Charlotte, NC, Grace Brethren Church, **272**, 946
Charlottesville, VA, Church of the Brethren, **272–273**, 273, 1308

Free Union, VA, Church of the Brethren, 514
Charlton, Burl Eugene, 2274
Charlton family, 1914
Charming Nancy (ship)
    Hochstetler (Hostetler) family, 615
    Strickler, Ulrich, 1229
chart of Brethren bodies, 1403–1405, **2380**
chartered trains, **273**, *See also* railroad committees and immigration agents
charters/charter membership, **273**
Chase Co., NE
    Enders, NE, Church of the Brethren, 445
Chase family
    Garwin, IA, Carlton Brethren Church, 532
Chase, Orville Earl, 1583
Chase, Sandra L., 1902
    Modesto, CA, Big Valley Grace Community Church (FGBC), 866
Chase, Vince
    Modesto, CA, Big Valley Grace Community Church (FGBC), 866
chastity, *See* continence
Chatauqua movement, 441, 733, 1389
"Chatauqua salute," 327
Chateau de St. Albain, Burgundy, France, **2158**, *2159*
    Beaver, Samuel Wayne, 2134
    Grace Brethren International Missions, 2191
    Julien, Thomas T., 2210
    Kent, Homer Austin, Jr., 2210
    missions, 2225
    Whitcomb, John Clement, Jr. (FGBC, CGBCI) and, 2262
Chatfield, Charles, 1902
Chatham, OH, 144, 145
Chaudhari, J. J., 1583
Chauhan, Daulat Daniel, 2019
Chaves Co., NM, 719
    Lake Arthur congregation, 931
Chavez, Cesar, 659
Chavez family
    Lybrook, NM, Tók'ahookaadí Church of the Brethren, 2216
Cheat River, WV, 164, 1254, 1336, *See also* Terra Alta, WV, Cooperative Brethren Church
Cheek, Calvin E., 262
Cheek, Calvin Edgar, 1583
The Cheerful Messenger, 822
Cheering Words, 1237
Chelan Co., WA, 1240
    Greenwood Church of the Brethren, WA, 572
Chelcicky, Petr, 357
Chelsea meetinghouse, Lena, IL, Church of the Brethren, 737
Chemberlen, Fred, 1583
Chemberlen, George F., 331, 348, 759, 1583
Chenoa, IL, Church of the Brethren, *See* Pike Creek, IL, Church of the Brethren
Cherian, Sam, 1583
Cherokee Church of the Brethren, KS, 44
Cherokee Co., KS, Church of the Brethren, 273, **273**
    Fly Creek Church of the Brethren, 500
    New Hope Church of the Brethren, 929
    organization of, 929

Osage Church of the Brethren, 983
Cherokee Co., MN, Maple Valley Church of the Brethren, 2376
Cherokee Strip, 273
Cherokee War, 576
Cherry, Charles F., 1583
Cherry Grove, IL, Church of the Brethren, 59, **273**, 361, 693
    Hope, Christian, 628
    Rockford, IL, First Church of the Brethren, 1117
    Shannon, IL, Church of the Brethren, 1172
Cherry Grove, MD, Church of the Brethren, **273**
Cherry Hill, PA, Brethren Church, **273–274**
Cherry Lane, PA, Church of the Brethren, 145, 274, **274**, 1192
Cherry Valley, CA, Grace Brethren Church, **104**, 1354
Cherry, Vivian Evelene, 1841
Cherry, William, 264
    Sand Creek Old German Baptist Brethren Church, KS, elder-in-charge, 1143
Cherry, William C., 1583
Chesney, Robert, 2300
Chess Creek, PA, Church of the Brethren, **274**
Chester Co., PA, 210, 214, 355, 686, 1233, 1298, 1401, 1865, 2086
    anonymous minister of, 1318
    Crumpacker, Peter, 1013
    French Creek, 516
    Jennersville, PA, Church of the Brethren, 670
    migration of Brethren, 827
    Pennsylvania settlement, 1004
Chesterfield, IN
    Church of God (New Dunkers), 297
    New Dunkard News, 927
Chestnut Grove, WV
    Church of the Brethren, *See* Pleasant View, WV, Church of the Brethren
    Old German Baptist Brethren Church, **274**
    Persinger, George, family of, 1134
Chestnut Hill, OH, Church of the Brethren, 272
Chestnut, Paul I., 1902
Chestnut Ridge schoolhouse, Washington, PA, Grace Brethren Church, 1320
Chewelah, WA, 1212
chewing tobacco, *See* tobacco
Cheyene Co., NE, Grand Prairie Church of the Brethren, 565
Cheyenne Co., CO
    Sheridan Lake Old German Baptist Brethren Church, CO, ministers travelling to, 1176
Cheyenne, KS, Church of the Brethren, 274, **274**, 396
Cheyenne, WY, First Brethren Church, **274**, 1380–1381
Cheyenne, WY, First Brethren Church (FGBC), **274**
CHGM (Capitol Hill Group Ministry), 1320
Chibuk, Nigeria, 306
    Brumbaugh, Grayce, 220
    Mshelia, Madu B., 892
    school for pastors in, 892, 936
Chicago, Burlington and Quincy Railroad, Annual Meetings on property of,

1081
Chicago Cluster of Theolgocial Schools, 126
Chicago Corner, IN, Church of God (New Dunkers), 297
Chicago, IL, 732, 1345, 1361
    Bethany Brethren Hospital, 936
    Brethren Chinese Sunday School and Church, 275, 278, 850, 891, 892
    Church of the Brethren, 299, 1940, 1998
    Douglas Park Church of the Brethren, **274–275**, 638, 850
    Douglas Park Mission, 275, 1296
    fellowship houses, 482
    First Church of the Brethren, **275**, 466, 732, 1296, 1388, 1936, 2135
        Bethany Brethren Community Center, 2136
        fellowship houses, 482
        Hadsell, B. A., 577
        minorities, ethnic and racial, 850
    Flora, Benjamin H., 495
    Hastings Street Mission, *1296,* 1302
    Hilton, George William, 607
    hospitals, 630
    Huston, Ora Ivan, 638
    hymns, 2096
    McFaden, John Duke, 773
    minorities, ethnic and racial, 850
    missions and missionaries, 859, 860, 2103
    relocation of Japanese-Americans to, 1373
    Royer, John Grove, 1128
    Scholten, Marian Aetna Rinehart, 1155
    Shull, Chalmer George, pastor, 1180
    urban missions, 1296, 1297
Chicago Theological Seminary, 114
    ties with Bethany Theological Seminary, 1290
Chicago United Ministry to Evacuees, 25
Chicao, CA, Church of the Brethren, 992
Chickies, PA, Church of the Brethren, *See* Chiques, PA, Church of the Brethren
Chico, CA, congregations, 323
    Church of the Brethren, **275**
    Grace Brethren Church, **275**
Chiefly, Johann, 1583
Chilcote, T. J., 1583
Child Care in Aviation Incident Response (CAIR), 2171, 2172
Child Evangelism Fellowship
    Bible Institute of Los Angeles (BIOLA), 136
    evangelism, 461
    Overholtzer, Samuel A., 2377
child labor laws, 222
child rescue, **276**, *See also* orphans and orphanages
    Martinsburg, PA, *See* Home of the Child Rescue Work, Martinsburg, PA
    pamphlet issued by Homeless Children Committee, 276
    Pleasant Hill Village, **1033**
    relief and service efforts, 1097
Child Rescue and Orphan Society, 410, 682
Child Rescue Committee, *See* Homeless Children Committee (CB)
Child Rescue Home, 31, **275**
Child Rescue Services, Inc., 91, **276**, 579

Child Rescue Work, **276**
Child Saving Mission of Oklahoma (German Baptist Brethren's Home Society), Enid, OK, Church of the Brethren, 448
Childers family, 2016
Childers, Robert, 1583
Childers, W. H., 1583
childrearing
    Brethren attitudes toward, 2158–2160
    demographic trends, 2144
children, 155, 177–178, 188, 200, **2158–2160**
    age of accountability, 2159, 2160
    Christian homes, living in, 1985
    church membership, 813
    Committee on Saving our Children to the Church (CB), 328
    Disaster Child Care, 2171–2172
    Dunker girl, sketch of, 1996
    family and, 472
    gifted, 247
    health clinics, 270
    homeless, ministry to, 410
    learning disabled, 247
    Logan, Linda on education of Christian, 2343
    McKee, Donna on worship for, 2352
    missions and missionaries, and stories about, 2078
    orphaned, *See* orphans and orphanages
        Rhodes, Donna McKee on worship for, 2352
    rights of, 2032
    sources on, 2323
    underprivileged, 5–6, 8, 18
    Wallower, Lucille, and Dunkard books for, 2361
    working with, 2013
    worship and, 2266
Children at Work, 1236, 1394
    Lanark, IL, **276**, 277
    Mount Morris, IL, **276**
    Our Children at Work, 985
    Sharp, Solomon Zook, associated with, 1174
Children of the Bush Country (Grimley), 748
Children's Aid Societies, **276**
    Aide aux Enfants (Aid for Children), Haiti, 579–580
    Gibbel, Henry Royer, 547
    Home for Orphan and Friendless Children (CB), 625
    Huntsdale Church of the Brethren, PA, 638
    Nicarry, Wayne A., 2231
Children's Cabinet, CE National, Inc., 2156
The Children's Friend
    Duncan, N. A. (editor), 277
German Baptist Brethren's Home Society, 276, **277**, 541
children's literature, 149, 150, 747, 1236–1237, 2038
    African bush country, book about, 1954
    Brethren history, 1937
    Ephrata and J. C. Sauer, 1957
    Kline, John, picture book about, 1915
    Naas, John, picture book about, 1915
    thesis on, 1957
The Children's Paper, 277, 712, 1236, 1902
The Children's Society of the Church of the Brethren, 276

Children's Work, *See* General Council of Children's Work; National Cabinet of Children's Work
Childres, W. H., 1341
Childs, Jean (later Young), 1367
Childs, Lewis, 1583
Chile
    Julien, Thomas T., 2210
    missions, 2225
    missions, short-term, 2226
chiliasm, *See* eschatology/millennialism
Chilton, Mary (later Pritchett), 1060
Chimney Run, VA, Church of the Brethren, **277**
China, 2016, 2019, 2024, 2025, 2027, 2032
    Agricultural Exchange, **2129**
    agricultural missions, 9, 12
    bibliography, 1904, 1905
    Brethren South China Mission, *See* Brethren South China Mission
    Chinese Sunday school, 736
    Christian education, 1963
    Church of the Brethren, **277–278,** 299–300
    Church of the Brethren mission work, study course on, 1913
    Coffman, Lulu Ullom, 1345
    Communist Revolution, 861
    Communists and Kuomintang, 23
    Confucianism, 334
    Cottrell, Asher Raymond, 345
    Cottrell, Laura Murphy, 345
    Crim, Bessie, 1215
    Cripe, Winifred E., 352, 1024
    Crumpacker, Anna L. Newland, 354
    Crumpacker, Frank Henry, 354
        missionary to, 779
    Crumpacker, Franklin Henry, 354
    Early, Henry Clay, 413
    Eisenbise, Forest Sard, 432
    Ethiopia, 458
    evangelistic work in, 149
    famine relief, 475, 2310
    Flory, Lizzie Mae Neher and Raymond Chester, 499
    Flory, Marie Sarah Mason, 2185
    Flory, Martha Belle Shick, 499
    Flory, Wendell Phillips, 2185
    Freeburg Church of the Brethren, OH, 514
    General Mission Board (CB), 539
    Harsh, Alva, and Mary Lou Hykes, 1012
    Harsh, Alva Carlton, 587
    Harsh, Mary Lou Hykes, 587
    Heckman, Benjamin Franklin, 591
    Heckman, Minna Mote, 592
    Heisey family, 595
    Hilton, Blanche Cover, 606
    Hilton, George William, 607
    Horning, Mary Emma, 630
    hospitals, 630
    Hutchison, Anna Martha, 639
    Ikenberry, Ernest Leroy and Olivia Dickens, 646
    Kreps, Esther, missionary to, 1049
    Krieger, Corda Wertz, 145
    Lehmer, Solomon G., 736
    Mason, George Edward, 2218
    medical care, 810
    medical missionaries to, 806, 807
    Metzger, Minerva, missionary to, 819
    Mill Creek Church of the Brethren,

VA, sending missionaries to, 832
mission schools, 853, 854
missions and missionaries, 160,
       201–202, 208, 209, 859, 860,
       861, 862, 1152, 1939, 2225,
       2225
   Brubaker, Leland Stanford, 218
   Brubaker, Marie Hannah Woody,
       218
   Brubaker, Ora George, 217
   conferences, 856
   Salem Church of the Brethren,
       OH, 1138
   Senger, Nettie, 2077
   short-term missions, 2226
   Sino-Japanese War, 2089
   UNRRA, 2071
Moy brothers, missionaries to, 850
Moy Gwong Han, 891
Moyer, Elgin Sylvester, 892
Myers, Minor Morton, missionary to,
       904
Myers, Valley Miller, 724
nurse missionaries, 952
Ober, Mary Velma on CB missions to,
       2349
Oberholtzer, Elizabeth Weybright, 1276
order of dress in, 403
orphans, care for, 982
Parker, Martha Neiderhiser, 2034
people of, 1977
Ping Ting hospital, 1316
Pollock, Myrtle Ferris, missionary to,
       869
Protestant missions in, 296
reconstruction in, thesis on, 1945
Reed, Kyle and Mary and, 2225, 2225,
       2240
Reed, Kyle, missionary to, 1091
Relief and Reconstruction Committee,
       aided by, 1096
relief and rehabilitation work in, 200,
       209
   Brubaker, Leland Stanford, 218
   Buddhists, 227
relief and service efforts, 1097
relief and social work, 295
religious education in villages, 1973
rural areas, mission work in, 1130
rural reconstruction movement, 9
Senger, Nettie, 2077
Sollenberger, Hazel, 1265
Sollenberger, Howard Edwin, 1202
Sollenberger, O. C., 1265
   missionary to, 1202
Student Volunteer Movement, 1231
tractor boys, 2005
tractor unit, 1268, 1269
travel to by Brethren, 1273
UNRRA Brethren Service Unit, history
       of, 1939
Vaniman, Ernest David, 1303
Vaniman, Susie Cordelia Neher, 1303
Wampler, Elizabeth Baker, 1316
Wampler, Ernest Michael, 1316
Wampler, Frederick Jacob, 1316
Wampler, Rebecca C. Skeggs, 1316
Wampler, Vida Eunice Miller, 724,
       1316
war with Japan, 23
Waterloo, IA, South Waterloo Church
       of the Brethren, 1323
Whitcomb, John Clement, Jr. (FGBC,

CGBCI) in, 2262
Women's Missionary Societies, 1363
world hunger issues (CB) and, 2266
World War II relief work, 1373
Yin, Han Chang, 1385
China Suffers (Wampler, Ernest Michael),
       1316
China Tractor Unit, 2248
Chinese Brethren Church, 278, 1888
   Chicago, IL, 278, 1296
   in Illinois, 278
   Oak Park, IL, 278
Chinese Fellowship, 278
Chinese immigrants
   Berean Bible School, 278
   La Verne College, 278
   minorities, ethnic and racial, 850
   mission to, and San Bernardino, CA,
       Church of the Brethren, 1141
   missions, 859
Chinese Sunday School, 201, 391, 850,
       891, 892
   Chicago, IL, 499, 1296
   Church of the Brethren, 275
   Detroit, 2100
   District of Columbia, 391
   Harper Woods, MI, Detroit First
       Church of the Brethren, 585
   Hilton, Blanche Cover, 606
   Hilton, George William, 607
   minorities, ethnic and racial, 850
   Moy Gwong Han, 891
   Moy Way, 891
   Moy Wing Lum, 891
   Moyer, Elgin Sylvester, 892
Chinworth, James H., 2274
Chippewa Church of the Brethren, OH, 13,
       415
Chippewa Co., MI, Ozark Grace Brethren
       Church, 987
Chippewa Co., WI, 1354, 1365
   Maple Grove Church of the Brethren,
       WI, 791
Chippewa congregation, OH
   Hiestand (Heistand, Heestand,
       Heaston) family, 602
Chippewa congregation, PA, 1386
Chippewa Creek, MI, congregation
   Rodney Church of the Brethren, MI,
       1119
Chippewa, OH, Church of the Brethren,
       279, 799, 1344
   Paradise Church of the Brethren, divid-
       ed from, 992
Chippewa Valley, WI
   Church of the Brethren, 279
   Irvin Creek Church of the Brethren,
       664
Chiques Church of the Brethren, PA, 279,
       279, 456, 1334, 1340, 1397, 1401,
       See also East Fairview Church of
       the Brethren, PA
   Elizabethtown, PA, Church of the
       Brethren, 436
Chiquito family
   Lybrook, NM, Tók'ahookaadí Church
       of the Brethren, 2216
Chirighotis, Demetrius, 1583
Chittick, Adelaide, 754
Choice Collection of Hymns (Winchester),
       288
Choice of Ministers, See Election of Church
       Officers

A Choice Selection of Hymns, 171, 642
   publishing of, 1068
choirs, 279, See also music ministry
   Brethren music, 899
   choir stalls, 51
choristers, 279–280
   Palmyra, PA, Church of the Brethren,
       991
   Panther Creek, IA, Church of the
       Brethren, 992
   robes, 1376
   singing, 1185
   worship services, 1378
Chollet, Cecilia (later Sower), See Sower,
       Cecilia Chollet
choral music
   Church of the Brethren, 300, 301
   Codorus, PA, Church of the Brethren,
       323
Chowchilla, CA, Church of the Brethren,
       280
Chrisco, Frank L., 30, 1583
Chrisinger, Irene Pearl Roth, 1902
The Christian's Duty
   publishing of, 1067
Chrisman family
   Fleming Co., KY, German Baptist
       Brethren Church, 494
Chrissie (Rolston), 1120
Christ, See Jesus Christ
Christ Church of the Brethren, OH, See
       Wooster, OH, Christ Church of the
       Brethren
Christ, Jacob, 1583
Christ Life magazine
   Humberd, Russell I., 636
Christ-likeness
   Brethren Doctrine of Salvation, 1140
   sin and, 1184
Christ Parish, Rockhill Furnace, PA,
       Rockhill Church of the Brethren,
       in ecumenical federation, 1118
"Christ the Lord is Risen Today"
   hymns, 643
Christ the Servant Church of the Brethren,
       FL, See Cape Coral, FL, Christ the
       Servant Church of the Brethren
Christ the Servant congregations
   example of biblically inspired name,
       911
Christachari, Dhankorbai, 280
Christachari, Ishwarlal Laraji, 280, 1583,
       2372
   India, Church of North, 2207
Christendom, See established churches
Christensen family
   Ocala, FL, Grace Brethren Church,
       2232
Christensen, Sigurd E., 1583
Christi Menighed, 280, 375, 1256, See also
       Christ's Assembly
   Old German Baptist Brethren, 970
Christian Academy of Learning
   Ormond Beach, FL, Grace Brethren
       Church, 982
Christian Aid Ministries
   Brethren Charity Fund (BCF) and,
       2259
Christian, Amos D., 1583
Christian Anarchy: Jesus' Primacy Over
       Powers (Eller), 2176
Christian and Missionary Alliance, 1261
   Bauman, L. S., 260

Cassel, Jacob C., 259
  devotional literature, 381
  Manatí, PR, Pueblo de Dios, 2217
Christian, Anna Mary (later Erbach), 453
The Christian Baptist, 247
  Campbell, Alexander, 247, **281,** 1101
  Hostetler, Joseph, 631
  Sala, Solomon, printer, 1136
The Christian Beacon, See Fundamentalism
  McIntire, Carl, 774
  McIntire, Carl (publisher), **281**
Christian Book Depot
  Humberd, Russell I., 636
Christian Brethren Church, IN, 233
Christian Brethren (Landisites), 177, **281,**
    722, 1225, *See also* Plymouth
    Brethren
  chart of Brethren bodies, place on,
    1403–1405
  Congregational Brethren, 335
  feetwashing mode, 1186
  Landisites and Christian Brethren, 281
  Lord's supper, food at, 757
  Okeechobee, FL, Grace Brethren
    Church, 963
  Salem Church of the Brethren, OH,
    1138
  Studebaker, John, 1327
  Weimer, Peter, 1327
  Wolf Creek Church of the Brethren,
    OH, 1355
Christian Brethren (OH), 334
Christian (Campbellite) Church
  Mendon, T. M., 757
Christian Catholic Apostolic Church,
    281–282
  Dowie, John Alexander, 398
Christian Catholic Church, Zion City, IL,
    1400
Christian Children's Fund
  SERRV International (CB) and, 2247
Christian Church, *See* Disciples of Christ
  Black Valley Federated Church of the
    Brethren and Christian Church,
    PA, 145
  Church of God (New Dunkers), 297
  Jackpot Church, NV, 2212
  Slifer, IA, church of the Brethren, 1190
  Stone, Barton Warren, 1224
  Sunnyside, WA, Grace Brethren
    Church, 1240
  Uniting Church of the Brethren, VA,
    See Virginia Beach, VA, Christian
  Church Uniting (CB/UCC)
Christian Church of the Brethren, IN, **282**
Christian Citizenship Seminar (CB)
  youth and, 2269
Christian communities, congregational
  names derived from, 911
Christian community
  Mission Twelve (CB), 855
Christian Community Center (CCC) and
    Rio Piedras, PR, Segunda Iglesia
    Cristo Misionera Fellowship (CB),
    2243
Christian Council of Nigeria.
    Ekklesiyar 'Yan'uwa a Nigeria (EYN),
    member church, 937
Christian day schools, 14, **282–283,** 284,
    2160, **2160,** *See also* Christian
    schools; elementary education;
    weekday religious education
  bus ministries and, 232

Dunkard Brethren Church, 2174–2175
  La Mirada, CA, 1342
  in local congregations, 30
  Long Beach, CA, Grace Brethren
    Church, 754–755
  Long Beach, CA, Los Altos Brethren
    Church, 755
  Marietta, GA, Grace Brethren Church
    of Greater Atlanta, 793
  Mayes, Charles W., 804
  mission schools, 854
  Old German Baptist Brethren, 969
  Phoenix, AZ, Grace Brethren Church,
    1019
  St. Petersburg, FL, Grace Brethren
    Church, 1136
  Whittier, CA, Community Grace
    Brethren Church, 1342
Christian Dental Society, 197
Christian education, **283–285,** 427, 2019,
    2022, 2028, 2038, 2041, 2047,
    2160–2161, *See also* Bible confer-
    ences; Bible schools; Board of
    Christian Education (BC); camp-
    ing; Christian Education
    Commission (CB); Christian work-
    ers's societies; Daily Vacation
    Bible Schools; daily vacation Bible
    schools; discipline of children;
    education; education, Christian;
    elementary education; family;
    GBC Christian Education (FGBC);
    mass media; men's work; mission
    schools; missions education;
    prophecy conferences; secondary
    education; theological education;
    weekly religious education;
    women's work; youth organiza-
    tions
  Board of Christian Education, 155
  Brethren Church, 154, 182
  Brumbaugh, Martin Grove and, 223
  Camp La Verne (CB), CA, 244
  camping movement and, 249
  of children, 2024
  Church of the Brethren, 300
  colleges, 2100
  Connecticut Church of the Brethren,
    335
  Davis, Charles Ernest, 364
  day school movement, 426
  drama in, 399
  Dunkard Brethren, 408
  Elgin, IL, Highland Avenue Church of
    the Brethren, 436
  Fellowship of Grace Brethren Churches
    (FGBC), 484, 487, 2183
  Fisher, Virginia Showalter, 492
  Flory, Ezra, 498
  Forney, Roy S., 503
  Fresno, CA, First Church of the
    Brethren, 516–517
  GBC Christian Education (Depart-
    ment), 533
  General Council of Children's Work
    (CB), 537
  Glendale, CA, First Brethren Church,
    552
  Grace Schools (Grace Theological
    Seminary, Grace College), 563
  Heckman, Jacob Hugh, 592
  Heckman, Minna Mote, 592
  Huntingdon, PA, Stone Church of the

Brethren, 637
  Ikenberry, Charles Samuel, 646
  International Council of Religious
    Education, 659
  International Sunday School Conven-
    tion, 659
  International Sunday School Lessons
    (Uniform Lessons), 659
  Miller, Donald Eugene, 2223
  Mission Twelve (CB), 855
  missions, 859
  Rohrer, Perry, and recreation, 1088
  Shultz, Lawrence W., 1180
  sources on, 2311, 2318
  Wagoner, Gerald C., Sr. (OGBB) and,
    2259
  women and, 2264
Christian Education Board
  FGBC, *See* Board of Christian Educa-
    tion (FGBC)
  National Brethren Young People's
    Department Cabinet, 917
Christian Education Commission (CB),
    155, 169, **285,** *See also* Brethren
    Service Commission (BSC)
  camping movement and, 249
  Commission of Fifteen, 327
  Committee on Higher Education, 327
  Fleming, Lenoir Avery, 494
  National Cabinet of Children's Work as
    advisory body, 915
  Parish Ministries Commission, reorga-
    nization by, 993
  Recreational Fellowship, 1088
  Shriver, Ruth Marie, 1180
  Warstler, Anna Margaret, 1319
  West, Daniel, 1331
Christian Education Commission of the
    General Brotherhood Board
  Heckert, Mildred Mae Etter, 2197
Christian Education Department, 155, **533,**
    1392
  Etling, Harold Hartz, 458
  National Achievement Competition
    (NAC), 914
  Serving My Master, 1169
Christian Education: Shared Approaches
    program, 1237
Christian Endeavor, 192, 285
  Carpenter, George C., 256
  devotional literature, 381
  Lowery, Margaret E., 2216
  Young People's Society of, 53, **285,**
    695, 1391–1392
  Riverside Christian Training School,
    1111
Christian family, *See* families
The Christian Family Companion, 18, 178,
    221, **285–286,** 295, 1902
  Brethren, lineage of, 613
  Cumberland Co., IL, Church of the
    Brethren, 356
  Davy, Henry Dorsey, 365
  genealogy, 535, 2188
  Gospel Visitor, The, 561
  Holsinger, Henry Ritz, 621, 1283
    letter to, 1999
  Mercer Co., MO, love feast, 1202
  Messenger, 818
  Meyersdale, PA, 822
  Myers, Graybill, 903
  Pfautz, John Eby, 1014
  The Pilgrim (published 1870–1880),

1023
The Pious Youth, 1025
publishing, 1068
Quinter, James, purchased by, 1077
Sell, James Arnold, 1165
*The Christian Family Companion and
Gospel Visitor,* **286,** 818, 1058
bibliography, 1902
The Christian Field, 1902
Christian, Govindji C., 1583
The Christian Guide, **286,** 1902
*Christian Handbook (Christliches Hand-
Büchlein)* (Felbinger, J.), 77, **288,**
482, 923, 2014–2015
Miller, John William, 2224
Christian Heimreich, A Religious Dialogue
(Kurtz), 1992
Christian Herald
publication of statistics, 1218
Christian Holiness Associations
Brethren of Christ, 189
Holiness Movement, American, 619
Christian home, *See* families
Christian Hope ministry, 212
Eby, Enoch, 419
missions, 858
Nielson, Johanna, joined through, 936
Christian humanism, 28
Christian, Jivanji K., 1583
Christian, John H., 585
Christian, John H. (CB-1), 1583
Christian, John H. (CB-2), 1583
Christian League for the Handicapped
Hoyt, Herman Arthur, 634
Christian Life, 210
Christian Light
Christian Day School movement, 282
Christian, Madhavial G., 1583
Christian Mission
State College, PA, University Baptist
and Brethren Church, 1218
Christian, Naranji K., 1583
Christian Peace Conference (CPC), **286**
Germany (German Democratic
Republic), 546
international exchange with Russia,
1288
Nikodim, Metropolitan, president of,
937
Prague, Czechoslovakia, 357
Christian Peacemaker Teams (CPT),
2161–2162, 2163
works by, 2321
Christian, Punaji M., 1583
Christian Quakers, *See* Keithian Baptists
Christian Reformed Church of Nigeria
(CRCN), *See* Fellowship of Churches
of Christ in Nigeria
Christian Reformed Church of the Brethren,
Nigeria (CRCN), 296
Christian Reformed World Relief Commis-
sion, 197
Christian Rural Overseas Program (CROP),
12, 23, 198, **286–287**
book about, 1912
Brethren Church, 423
East Chippewa Church of the Brethren,
OH, 415
Friendship Trains, 518
Hartzler, Russell M., 588
Holmesville Church of the Brethren,
NE, 620
Ivester Church of the Brethren, IA, 665

Metzler, John D., Sr., 820
Nebraska Brethren contributions to
post-WWII efforts, 921
reference to, 1956
relief and service efforts, 1097
relief and social work, 303
Rolston, William Wendell, 1120
Row, W. Harold, 1126
Springfield, OH, First Church of the
Brethren, 1215
world hunger issues (CB) and, 2266
Zigler, Michael Robert, 1398
Christian, Samuel D., 1583
Christian schools, 2159, 2160, 2175, *See
also* Christian day schools
Dunkard Brethren Church, penmanship
as folk art, 2105
Grace Brethren Church, 2088
mission, *See* mission schools
organization and administration, 1977
Temple Hills, MD, Grace Brethren
Church of Greater Washington,
1253
Torreon Navajo Mission, 1268
Tracy, CA, Grace Brethren Church,
1270
Yucca Valley, CA, Grace Brethren
Church, 1394
Christian Science, **287**
Brumbaugh, G. Edwin, 220
Christian Service Brigade, 203, **287,**
915, 1161
devotional literature, 381
Christian Service Commission, *See* Breth-
ren Service Commission
*Christian Stewardship: Responsible
Freedom* (CB)
stewardship and, 2252
Christian Times (Kristelig Tidende), **708**
Christian Unity, *See* entries at ecumenical,
ecumenism
Christian Workers' Board (CB), *See* General
Christian Workers' Board
Christian Workers' Meetings (later Christian
Workers' Societies), 13, **287–288**
General Christian Workers' Board
(CB), 536
Hopewell, VA, Church of the Brethren,
629
Christiania, MI, German Baptist Brethren
(CB), **288**
Christianity
cross-cultural perspective, 1989
disciples *vs.* Christians, 385
history, 1991
influence of Brethren on other denomi-
nations, 2055
Martin, Harold S. on information for
new Christians, 2345
Nead, Peter on restoration of primitive,
2348
primitive, 247
Christianity and Social Crisis (Rauschen-
busch)
"Message of the Brethren Ministry,"
817
Christianity at the Fountain
Hays, Daniel, 590
Christianity Today, 2179
Christians Associated for Relationships
with Eastern Europe (CAREE)
CPC and, 286
The Christian's Duty, 175, **288,** 736, 1902,

See also language shifts
Brethren music, 899
hymnals, 642
hymns, 643, 1279
Christian's Secret of a Happy Life (Smith),
1051
Christiansburg, VA congregations, 288
Church of the Brethren, **288**
example of possessive place name, 911
Red Oak Grove Church of the
Brethren, VA, 1089
Christiansen, Ethel, 1351
Christiansen, Lloyd, 1583
Christiansen, S. E., 130, 235, 467
Mount Olivet Brethren Church, DE,
pastor, 886
Roanoke, VA, First Brethren Church,
pastor, 1113
Christiansen, William J., 2155, 2274
Christiansy, Ludwig, 1903
Christie, George R., 556, 566, 1383, 1583
Mabton, WA, Grace Brethren Church,
pastor, 771
Prosser, WA, Community Grace
Brethren Church, pastor, 1062
Christie, Randy
Prosser, WA, Community Grace
Brethren Church, pastor, 1062
Christliche Bibliothek (Martin), 797,
2006–2007
*Der Christliche Calender (The Christian
Calender),* 18
Das Christliche Gesang-buch, 1903
*Ein christliches Gesang-Buch (A Christian
Hymnal)*
hymnals, 641
*Christliches Hand-Büchlein, See Christian
Handbook*
Christliches Jugenddorfwerk Deutschlands,
681
Christlieb, Alice S., 269
Christmas/Advent, **288–289**
Holtzapfel (Holsapple, Holsopple),
Johann Heinrich, 623
observance of, 288, 2351
Ramirez, Frank on sermons from Book
of Haggai, 2351
Christner, Amos, 1583
Christner, Craig D., 13, 1583
Christner, David C., 31, 255, **289,** 1319,
1583
North Manchester, IN, (First) Brethren
Church, pastor, 949
Christner, Jay Lewis, 2274
Christner, N. B., 1583
Christocentricism
peace movement, 2098
Christoffessen, C. S., 708
Christology
Brethren Church and, 184
Brethren movement, **289–290**
definition of, 386
Grassroots, Concerns of the, 2193
Martin, George Adam, differences over,
797
Reformation, Protestant, and Brethren
doctrine, 1092, *See also* Jesus
Christ
theology and, 2254
Christophel, Alta Kurtz, 1902
Christophel, Sandford Jay, 1583
Christopher, Mary Ann Saylor, 1835
Christopher Sauer Workshops, 173, **290,**

809

Christ's Ambassadors, **280**
  chart of Brethren bodies, place on, 1403–1405
Christ's Assembly, 157, **280**, 375, 1875, *See also* Bolle, Simon; Bolle, Soren
  Bolle, Simon, 376
  Bolle, Soren, 376
  Brethren remnants in Europe, 1099
  charismatic movement, 272
  chart of Brethren bodies, place on, 1403–1405
  Community of the True Inspiration, 280
  Dunkard Brethren Church, 376
  Germany (Federal Republic of Germany), 546
  Germany, witnesses in, 376
  Holy Spirit, doctrine of, 624
  missions, 862
  Myers, Paul R., 904
  Norway, witnesses in, 376
  Old German Baptist Brethren, 970
  prophecy, 1062
  Sweden, witnesses in, 376
  USA, witnesses in, 376
Christy family, 165
The Chronic Loafer (Lloyd), 747
Chroniccon Ephratense, See historic writing
The Chronicles of the Brethren (John M. Kimmel), **290**, 693
  historical writing, 612
  manuals, 788
Chronicon Ephratense, 33, 113, 175, **290**, 925, 1355, 1992, 1993
  Brethren movement, descriptions of, 379
  community, 329
  continence, and sexual relations, 338
  Ephrata Community, 451
  Ephrata publishing, 1067
  historical writing, 611
  Hoening, Johann Georg, 616
  Martin, George Adam, autobiography in, 797
  Miller, John Peter, collaborating on, 840
  Naas, Johannes, church discipline dispute, 909
  poor, caring for the, 1046
  South Carolina, correspondence with, 1204
  Steiner family, 2378
Chronister, James E., 1388, 2275
chronologies
  Annual Meetings/Conferences, 1505–1511
  Brethren history, 1407–1436
Chumney, Charles E., 1583
Chupp, Alvin, 1583
Chupp family, 1881
church
  anti-church positions, 22
  doctrine of, 28–29, 43, 73
  Gemeinde, Gemeinschaft, 534
  God's Means of Grace (Yoder), 555
  hymns, 643
  nature of, 28–29, 48
church administration
  social action, service, and education programs, 1996
  Church and Peace movement

Historic Peace Churches, 610
church and state, 28–29, 88, 113–114, **309–313**, 2023, 2029, 2090, 2100, **2162**
  Church of the Brethren, 301, 2162–2163
  Durnbaugh, Donald F. on service and, 2326
  established churches, 456
  flags, 492
  Haddix, KY, Brethren Church, 577
  Historic Peace Churches, 607–610
  historical writing, 610
  Illinois, 647
  jury service, 679
  millennialism, 833
  Old German Baptist Brethren peace position, 1000
  sources on, 2311
  taxes, refusal to pay, 1248–1249
church architecture, **46–52**, *47, 49–50*
  "Akron" plan, 51, 270
  auditoriums/sanctuaries, 51
  Baptist Church, 301
  bell, 301
  building counselors and services, 51
  chancel designs, pulpit-centered *vs.* alter-centered, 51
  changes in, 19th-20th century, 51
  choir stalls, 51
  combining traditional and contemporary styles, 51
  communion table, 328
  ecumenical movement, influence of, 51
  ethics, 458
  furnishings, 48, 51, 59
  love feasts, location of, 301
  meetinghouses, **2131**
  Methodist Church, 301
  Old German Baptist Brethren meetinghouses, 967
  Oxford movement, influence of, 51
  pulpits, *See* pulpits
  rejection of established church style, 46, 48
  revivalism, influence of, 51
  "theater" plan, 51
  United Methodist Church, 301
  worship influences, 301
church bulletins, *See* worship, public
church charters, *See* charters
Church Chatter, 296
Church Committee for China Relief, **295**, *See also* Church of Christ in China; ecumenism; Sollenberger, H.
Church Committee on Overseas Relief and Rehabilitation of the Federal Council, 308
Church Committee on Relief in Asia, 308
  church, concept of, 1260
Church [congregation] of Southern California, CA, 238
church council meetings, *See* council meetings
Church, D. G., 1583
church discipline, *See* discipline (church)
church, doctrine of, **291–294**, *See also* ecclesiology
church, early, *See* early church
church endowments
  opposition to, 724
Church Extension Fund (CB), **295–296**

church extension programs, **295**, *See also* comity; evangelism; Ministry and Home Mission Commission (CB); Parish Ministries Commission; urban ministry
  automobiles and, 74
  Church of the Brethren, 305
  colonization, 324
  comity agreements, 326
  evangelism, 460
  General Board (CB), 535
  home missions, 203
  Hutchison, Andrew, 639
  meetinghouses, financial assistance for, 295
  The Missionary Board (BC), 855
  missions, 857, 860
  Ogden, Galen Brown, 961
  Parish Ministries Commission involvement in, 993
  sources on, 2323
Church Extension Union, *See* Brethren's Church Extension Union
church fathers, 55, 56, **296**
Church Federation of Greater Chicago, 25
  Robinson, Paul Minnich, president, 1115–1116
Church Federation of Greater Dayton, OH
  Peters, Raymond Russell, 1011
church governance, *See* governance, church; polity
church growth movement
  evangelism, 461
  Fellowship of Grace Brethren Churches (FGBC), 485–486
  sources on, 2312, 2321
  worship and, 2267
Church Growth Seminars
  Hispanic Ministries (BC), 2198
Church Guidebook (BC)(1964), 51
  church history, 2023
  Brethren children names from, 912
Church Investment Committee (CB), General Investment Council, 537
church law and noncreedalism, 942
church letters, *See* letters of membership
church lobbying, *See* lobbying
church manuals, *See* manuals
church membership, *See* membership
church names, *See* membership; names, Brethren
Church News, 296, 927
Church of Ashe Co., NC, Church of the Brethren, *See* Flat Rock, NC, Church of the Brethren
Church of Burma (Anglican)
Church of North India, 298
Church of California, CA, 238
Church of California, near Gilroy, CA, 1358
Church of Ceylon (Anglican)
Church of North India, 298
Church of Christ, 201
  debate with Church of the Brethren, 1984
  White Oak Church of the Brethren, OH, 1340
Church of Christ in China (CCC), 296, **296**
Church of Christ in Nigeria (COCIN), 296, 307, *See also* Fellowship of Churches of Christ in Nigeria
Church of Christ in the Sudan, **296**
  Fellowship of Churches of Christ

in Nigeria, 484
Church of Christ, Scientist, 287
Church of Crete
    Orthodox Church, 983
Church of Cyprus
    Orthodox Church, 983
Church of England, 87
Church of God, 1903
Church of God, Anderson, IN, **296–297**
    fraternal relations, 510
Church of God, General Eldership
Church of God, Anderson, IN, 296
Church of God in Christ, Mennonite
    Holdeman, John, 618
Church of God in Christ (Pentecost)
    Pentecostalism, 1009
Church of God in Columbia City, IN, 326
Church of God (New Dunkards), 77, 78,
        177, **297–298**, 700, 766, *See also*
        Dunker Brethren movement; law
    Brethren opposition to secret societies,
        1164
    chart of Brethren bodies, place on,
        1403–1405
    Church News, 296, 297
    Church of God in North America, 297
    Churches of God (GC) and, 309
    Columbia City, IN, Church of the
        Brethren , 326
    Cooperative Curriculum Project, 1236
    debate with Church of the Brethren,
        1984
    as denominational name, 910
    Dolby, Martha Cunningham, 395
    Eyman, Peter, 464
    feetwashing mode, 1186
    Fraternal Relations Committees (BC),
        511
    Indiana, 652
    jury service, 679
    Million, Robert, elder, 843
    Monticello/Pike Creek Church of the
        Brethren, IN, members from, 872
    New Dunkard Church of God, IN, 297
    New Dunkard News publication, 927
    origin, doctrine, constitution, and by-
        laws, 1969
    Patton, George, founder of, 996
    Patton, George, organization by, 996
    Patton, George, preaching at first meet-
        inghouse, 996
    Patton, Uriah, elder and evangelist, 996
    Replogle, Peter, 1100
    secret societies, Brethren opposition to,
        1164
    Yuba City, CA, Queens Avenue
        Community Church, 1394
Church of God, PA, 309
Church of God (Seventh Day), 68
Church of God (Winebrennerian), *See*
        Churches of God, General
        Conference
Church of India (Anglican)
    Church of North India, 298
Church of Jesus Christ of Latter-day Saints,
        298, *See also* British-Israelism
    debates on doctrine, 371
Church of North India (CNI), 280, 298,
        300, 651, **2207**, *See also* India
    Christachari, Ishwarlal Laraji, 280
    Church of the Brethren, 2162
    ecumenism, 423
    Fasnacht, Everett Merlin 480

Hinduism, 607
    missions, 861, 2225
    Presbyterian relationships with
        Brethren, 1056
    Sewell, Laura A. (CB) and, 2247
Church of Pakistan (Anglican)
    Church of North India, 298
Church of South India
    ecumenism, 423
    Hinduism, 607
Church of Southern California, 348, *See
        also* Covina, CA, Church of the
        Brethren
    Conejo, CA, Church of the Brethren,
        preaching point for, 331
Church of the Brethren, **298–305,
        2162–2164, 2372**
    *Abingdon Dictionary of Living
        Religions,* entry for, 1922
    abortion, 2127, 2178
    AIDS, response to, 2129–2130
    alternative service
        sociological study of men in, 2100
    American Baptists, possible merger
        with, 22
    in America, 307
    amusements, 2110
    The Andrew Center, 2130
    anniversary committee, sponsored pub-
        lications, 1282–1283
    Annual Conference, *See* Church of the
        Brethren Annual Conference
    anointing, 39, 2130
    architecture, 328
    archival policy, 52
    in Arizona, 54
    Arkansas, 2068
    Armenians, relief to, 55
    Association of Brethren Caregivers
        (ABC), 2132
    audio recordings of annual meetings,
        1303
    authority of scripture, 133
    Baptism, Eucharist, and Ministry
        (BEM), **2133–2134**
    BCS, 2096
    and beards, 103
    Believers Church Commentary Series,
        2134
    Bethany Hospital Governing Council,
        2136
    Bible translations and versions, 138
    bibliography, 1877, 1878, 1879,
        1903–1906
    bicentennial celebration, 140, *140, 141*
    blacks in Scioto Valley, OH, 256
    Board of Religious (later Christian)
        Education (Church of the Breth-
        ren), 1252
    bonnets and, 254
    boycott endorsements, 2139
    Brethren Academy for Ministerial
        Leadership, 2139–2140
    Brethren Benefit Trust, 2140
    Brethren Encyclopedia, Inc., 2143
    Brethren Heritage Center, 2148
    Brethren identity, 2149
    Brethren Press, 2149–2150
    Brethren profile study, 2150
    Brethren Service Committee, 2094
    Brethren Way of Christ, 2150
    building of meetinghouses, 295
    burial customs and, 230

bus ministries and, 232
    business doctrine, 235
    California, 238
    in California, 238
    camping movement and, 246, 248
    Canada, 250
    in Canada, 15
    capital punishment and, 253
    capitalism and, 253
    caps and, 254
    Casa de Modesto Retirement Center,
        CA, 258
    Central America, 2157
    chaplaincy, 271
    charismatic movement, 272
    charters/charter membership, 273
    Chiliasm, 2068
    China missions, 277, 283, 296
    China, study course on, 1913
    Chinese Agricultural Exchange, 2129
    The Christian Beacon, 281
    Christian education curricula, 2160
    Christian Peacemaker Teams (CPT),
        2161
    Christ's Assembly and, 280
    church and state, 2162
    church extensions, 295
    Church of God, Anderson, IN, 296
    Church of North India, 298
    church-state relations, 310
    Church World Service (CWS), 1936,
        2165
    Colorado, 320
    Columbia, MD, Oakland Mills Uniting
        Church (CB, UCC), 326
    Columbus, OH, Brethren Church, 326
    Columbus, OH, Co-operative Brethren
        (BC/CB), 326
    comity agreements, 326
    Commission of Fifteen (CB), 326–327
    commissioning services, 327
    Committee on Interchurch Relations
        (CB), 328, 2166–2167
    Committee on Saving our Children to
        the Church (CB), 328
    communion, 328
    confession of faith, 333
    Connecticut, Christian education in,
        335
    conscientious objection, 269, 2178
        World War II, 1371–1372
    conscientious objectors
        religious issues, and statements on,
            2107
    conservation movement, 338
    Consultation on church Union
        (COCU), 338
    conversions, handbook of religious,
        2084
    cooperation with outside agencies, *See*
        Brethren Service Commission
        American Committee for Relief in
            the Near East, 22–23
        American Leprosy Missions
            (ALM), 24
    cooperation with The Brethren Church,
        2162, 2166
    council meetings, 346
    and Council of Churches of Christ
        (NCCC), 915
    courts of law, attitudes toward use of,
        728, 729
    covenant of purposes and, 252

CPS, 315
credit unions, 351
cultural changes, dissertation on, 1919
Daily Vacation Bible Schools, 359
deacon/deaconess role, 369
deacons, 2169
debts, 371
decline in membership, 2185
dedication of infants, 372
defense industries, 373
as denominational name, 911
description of, 2095, 2108, 2109
devotional literature, 381
Disaster Child Care, 2171
disaster relief, 385
Disaster Response Program,
    2171–2172
discipleship, 2178
discipline, 388, 389
District of Columbia, 390–391
district organization, 391
divided chancel, 2131
division of congregations, 392
divorce and remarriage, 1099, 2145
divorce issues, 389, 393
doctrines of, 2077, 2101
discipline, 2103
divorce for ministers, 2109
dress, 2080
ecumenicism, 2109
fundraising, 2075
    in the Dominican Republic, 2258
    Drechsler, Wolfgang on, 2325
dress, 388
dress reform in, 402–403
Driver family, 405
Drudge, Casey on history of, 2325
Durnbaugh, Donald F. on origins of,
    2326
Durnbaugh, Donald F. on revision of,
    2327
Durnbaugh, Donald F. on suffering and
persecution in, 2326
Durnbaugh, Donald F. on Washington
    representative of, 2325
Durnbaugh, Hedwig T. on hymnody of,
    2327, 2328
On Earth Peace, 974
On Earth Peace Assembly, 2235
Easter, 416
Eberly, William R. on (video tapes)
    history of, 2328
ecumenism, 328, 422–423
education, 428, 2162
educational materials, 284
Elam, Fern M. on musical history of,
    2329
elections, electioneering, 434
elementary education, 435
Encyclopedia of Modern Christian
    Missions, 1950
environmental issues, **2177**
eschatology, 454
Eternal Security, 457
ethics, 457, **2177–2178**
European origins, documents about,
    1920, 1921
Evangelical Church in Germany, 459
Evangelical Covenant Church, 459,
    460
evangelicalism, **2179**
evangelism, 460, 461, **2180**
evangelism in China, 277

evolution, 463
family, 2145
famine relief, 475
farming, 479
Fast Henry A., 480
feetwashing, 481
feetwashing mode, 1186
fellowship houses, 482–484
Fellowship of Reconciliation (USA),
    488
feminism, impact of, 2183–2184
fetal tissue, use of, 2178
Fike family, 490
flags, 493
Flat Creek Church of the Brethren, KY,
    493
Florida, 496–497
foreign mission office in India, 913
Forum for Religious Studies,
    2185–2186
Forward Movement, 504
Foundation series publications, 1237
fraternal relations, 510
Fraternal Relations Committees (BC),
    511
free ministry, 513
Freemasonry, 515
Freundschaftsheim (Friendship House),
    517
Friends Committee on Spain, 518
Fry, Linda L. on architecture and, 2332
Fundamental Brethren Church, 522
fundamentalism, 303, 522, 523
funerals, 524
Gandhi, Mohandas Karamchand, 528
Garber (Garver, Gerber) family, 530
Garden Terrace Retirement Home, 530
Garkida General Hospital, 530
Garner family, 531
genealogy, 534
General Board (CB), 535–536
General Offices (Elgin, IL), 36, 51
    chapel at, 51
    construction of, 95
    use of building counselors, 51
genetic engineering, 2178
Geneva, 540
Georgia, 540
German Baptist Brethren, 540
Germany (Federal Republic of
    Germany), 546
Germany (German Democratic
    Republic), 546
Gibbel (Gibble) family, 547
Gibson family, 548
Gingerich (Kingery) family, 549
Gingrich, Raymond Eugene, 2190
Global Women's Project, 2190
Glück (Glick, Click) family, 553
Goals for the 1980s, 2163
Goals for the 1990s, 2149, 2163
Goshen Conference, 559
The Gospel Messenger, official publica-
    tion of, 286
gospel music, 559, 560
Greece, 569
hairstyle, 579
Haiti, 579
hats and, 254
headquarters staff, *435*
healing, 591
help for Americans of Japanese ances-
    try, 24–25

higher education, 283, 605
historic peace churches, 316
historical writing, 612
history of, 1915, 1938, 1944, 2020,
    2036, 2087, 2325, 2328, 2340,
    2356
    Indiana, 2101
    Michigan, 2108
    Pennsylvania, 2111
Holtzapfel (Holsapple, Holsopple)
    family, 624
holy kiss, 699
Holy Spirit Conference, 2202, 2203
Holy Spirit Renewal Group, 625
homosexuality, 2163, 2204
honorific titles, 1266
Horst family, 630
hospital chaplaincy, 2157
Hostetler, Quincy Vern, 631
Hull, Mildred on name index of
    Southern District of Ohio, 2350
Hymnal: A Worship Book, 2205
ideals, 1992
identity formation, 2148
identity statement, 2163
Iglesia Cristiana Pentecostal (Christian
    Pentecostal Church), 355
Iglesia Cristiana Pentecostal de Cuba,
    2207
Illinois, 647
impact of Liberalism and Neoortho-
    doxy on, 74
India, 649, *650*
in India, 2247, 2314
India, Church of North, 2207
Indiana, 653
in Indiana, 319–320
Indonesia, 655
in Indonesia, 2255
industrial cooperatives in China, 277
influence of, 2099
information technology, church use of,
    2208
integration, article about, 1912
issues, *See* Annual Conference (CB);
    Annual Meeting
Jackpot Church, NV, 2212
Jubilee: God's Good News Curriculum,
    2209
Kansas, 682
Kassel headquarters, funds for build-
    ing, 684
Kaylor, Earl C., Jr. on, 2340
Keeney, Mervin B. on history of, 2340
Kentucky Mountain Housing
    Development Corporation
    (KMHDC), 2130–2131
Kulp, Philip M. on missions of, 2342
Lancaster, PA, Acts Covenant
    Fellowship, 2213
language, inclusive, 2214
lay preachers, 730
laying on of hands, 730, 731
Leonard, Rosalita J. on women's writ-
    ings and, 2343
logo, *2146–2147,* 2148, 2163
Longenecker, Stephen L.
    on history of Washington office,
        2343
    on urbanism and, 2343
Los Angeles, CA, Central Evangelical
    Church of the Brethren (Korean),
    2215

Los Angeles, CA, Hermanos Unidos en Cristo, 2215
love feast, 763
Mahan, Grant on, 305
Manatí, PR, Pueblo de Dios, 2217
marriage, 389, 2145
Marsden, Parker G. on vocations in, 2345
mass media, uses of, 2218
McFadden, Joyce on stance on alcohol, tobacco, drugs and recovery, 2344
media issues, 2099
membership decline, 2162
membership trends 1980 to 2000, 2220
men's movements, 2221
mentoring, 2221
Mexico, missionaries to, 821
Meyer, Lauree Hersch
    on liturgy, tradition and ministry of, 2347
    on pneumatology of, 2347
migrant workers programs and, 252
military service, 387, 831–832, 2162–2163
minister of music position, 843–844
ministers
    recreational activities, 2097
    self-perceptions of, 2096
ministry, 845–846, 2224
Ministry Advisory Council, 2140
Ministry of Reconciliation, 2224
minorities, 2163, 2178
minorities, ethnic and racial, 850, 851
minutes of annual conferences, 1303
misconduct, 2178
mission versus ecumenical approach, 2178
missionary conferences, 856
missions, 1912, 2225
    to African Americans at Palestine, AR, 54
    agricultural, 9
    at Camp Verde Indian Reserve, 54
    in Nigeria, 3–4
missions and missionaries, 2100
    stories about children, 2078
missions, short-term, 2226
Missouri, 2068
modernism, 2070
Morrill, KS, 2100
motion pictures, 879
Murray, Don, 626
Murray family, 898
music, 2227
musical instruments, 900, 2228
name change discussion, 2228
name change to, 140
National Council of Churches of Christ in the USA and World Council of Churches, 2228–2229
National Interreligious Service Board for Conscientious Objectors (NISBCO), 916–917
National Ministry Board (CB), 2262
National Older Adult Conferences, 2229
National Service Board for Religious Objectors (NSBRO) cooperation, 917
Native Americans, 2230
neoorthodox influence, 923
New Call to Peacemaking, 925–926,

926
in New Jersey, 929–930
newsletter about, 2325
in Nigeria, 2246–2247, 2248, 2261, 2313
nonconformity and, 3
North Manchester, IN, congregation, 2101
Ober, Mary Velma, missionary to China, 2349
opposition to labor unions, 716
"Order of the Brethren," 976
origin, 1991
Orthodox Churches, 983
pacifism, doctrine of
    World War II, 2094
Page, Kirby, 989
Palestine, 990
peace issues, 316
peace movement, 1911, 2097, 2108
peace position, 1000
People of the Covenant (POC) (BC) and, 2237
Peters family, 1012
Peters, Mildred Hull on name index of Southern District of Ohio of, 2350
Pfaltzgraff pottery and, 2250
placement of pastors, 1028
political issues, 2094
polity, 294, 1043–1044
position on alcoholic beverages, 1252
practice of responsible television viewing, 1251
preferred Bible translations, 2137
present and future, 1975
prounoucements on current issues, 2162
publications of, 2321
publishing, 2162
in Puerto Rico, 2243–2244, 2258, 2267
racial issues, 2094
Re-imagining Conference and, 2240
reconciliation, doctrine of, 2108
reference to, 1956
refugee resettlement and, 2240
relief and service projects with the Waldensian Church, 1314
research on, 2309
responsible television viewing encouraged, 1251
restructuring, 2163–2164
retirement homes, 1102
retirement homes, support for, 8
sack coats, 1029
salaried ministry and, 3
salary issue for ministers, 1137
Sanctuary Movement and, 2245
Schelbert, Leo on dress and, 2355
separation from Brethren Church, 2162
separatism, 2094
SERRV International (CB) and, 2247
service, 2162–2163
service, and Mennonite Church, 2086
Shenandoah Valley, VA, congregations in, 1176
Shull, Lois Netzley on India and missions of, 2356
Shultz, Lawrence W. on murals and history of, 2356
silver centennial jubilee, 1939
social development of, 2094
social issues, contemporary, 2111
sources on, 2315, 2317, 2324

stand on Vietnamese War, 1305
statistical review, 1953
stewardship and, 2252–2253
study of declining membership, 2149
in Sudan, 2253
Sunday school movement, history of, 2082
tagline, 2148
tax refusal, 1248–1249
Temperance and Purity Committee, 1252
Temperance Committee, 1252
Tennessee, 1253
tents used by, 1254
Texas, 1255
theological study conferences, 1257–1258
theology, 1259, 1261–1262
theology and, 2254
Thomasson, Kermon on Nigeria and, 2360
Thurian, Max
    on baptism and, 2361
    on eucharist and, 2361
    on ministry and, 2361
tobacco use, 1266
Twenty Thousand Dunkers for Peace, 1281
250th Anniversary of Church of the Brethren, 1141, 2075
United Church of the Brethren of Canada and, 250
urban ministry, 1295–1297, 2256–2257
Vietnamese War, 1306
views on communism and arms race, 1288
violence and, 2265
Virginia, 1308
Virginia Council of Churches, and sermons of pastors of, 2361
Vocational Training College, 1309
Washington, 269
Washington Office (CB), 2260
Web site, 2149
wedding customs, 1326
wellness and, 2261
West Virginia, 1336
Westminster Dictionary of Christian Education, entry for, 1913
Willoughby, William G. on, 2363
wine, in communion services, 1349
Wisconsin, 1354
women and, 2263–2264
women, roles of, 1360, 1361, 1362, 2178
women's issues, 2109
work camps, 1366, 1367
works by, 2322
World Council of Churches, 2087
world hunger issues (CB) and, 2265–2266
World War I, 1370
World War II, 1372
worship and, 2266–2267
worship, public, 1377, 1378
Wright, Lee-Lani on church unity and, 2364
Yearbook, 1218, 1219
youth and, 2268–2269
youth programs, 1391, 1392
Church of the Brethren Annual Conference, 33, 36, See also Financial Secretary of Annual Meeting (CB)

1946, 26
1952, 51
1955, 17
1957, 32
1958, *36*
1960, 32
1963, 39
1964, 61
1973, 26
1975, 123
1978, 123
1980, 123
"Art for Hunger" exhibit, 61
art, use at, 61
authority of scripture, 133
biblical view of human body, organ
    transplants and medical research,
    230
bibliography, 1905
bicentennial celebration, 140, *140, 141*
boards and committees, 36, *See also*
        General Board (CB)
    Brethren Service Commission, 36
    Central Committee, **32**
    Committee on Health and Welfare,
        327
    General Education Board, 36
    General Mission Board (Domestic
        and Foreign Mission Board),
        36
    Peace Committee, 36
    Standing Committee, *See* Standing
        Committee
Calgary, Alberta, Canada, 250
capital punishment, 253
caps, 254
Central Committee, **32**, 333, 535,
    2242
Christian Workers' Meetings, 287
Committee on Counsel for
    Conscientious Objectors, 327
Committee on Dress Reform, 327
delegates to, 36
Eberly, William R., 417
ecumenism, 423
elementary education, 435
Ellis, Calvert Nice, 441
Ellis, Charles Calvert, 441
fasting, 480
Faw, Chalmer Ernest, 480
Fellowship of Brethren Genealogists
    (FOBG), 484
Finance Commission, 490
Financial Secretary, **490**
Foreign Mission Commission, 500
Fraternal Relations Committee, 510
General Board (CB), 535, 536
General Christian Workers' Board
    (CB), 536
General Church Erection and
    Missionary Committee (CB), 536
General Council of Children's Work
    (CB), 537
General Education Board (CB), 537
General Investment Council (CB), 537
General Ministerial Board (CB),
    537–538
General Mission Board (CB), 538, 539
General Offices (CB), 539
General Sunday School Board (CB),
    539
General Welfare Board (CB), 540
Health and Welfare committee, *See*

Committee on Health and Welfare
Hospital Committee (CB), 630
issues
    abortion, stance on, 2
    American Bible Society, endorse-
        ment of, 22
    amnesty for conscientious objec-
        tors, 26
    anointing, significance and admin-
        istration of, 39
    chancel, arrangement of for wor-
        ship, 1377
    intercollegiate football and base-
        ball at Brethren schools, 69
    public worship, 1376
    pulpit-centered *vs.* alter-centered
        chancel designs, 51
    Sisters' Aid Societies forbidden,
        1361
    war bonds, 1318
    women, roles of, 1360, 1361
    World War II, 1372
    youth petition for church involve-
        ment, 1391
leadership at, 36
location, 1351, *1352,* 1353
location of, 33, 36
locations of, and Church of the Breth-
    ren regions, 1093, 1094
marriage, 795
mass media, 801
Milledgeville Church of the Brethren,
    IL, query on dress, 833
Miller, Jacob Kurtz, purchasing agent,
    838
minutes, 1306, 1351
moderators, 36
    laying on of hands during installa-
        tion, 731
    Mays, Morley Josiah, 804
    Miller, DeWitt L., 836
    Miller, Robert Henry, 842
    Mohler, Samuel Sayler, 868
    Moore, James Milton, 874
    Ober, Henry Kulp, 960
        office of, 865–866
    Peters, Raymond Russell, 1011
    Peters, Woodford W., 1011
    Price, David E., 1056
    Schlosser, Ralph Wiest, 1153
    Schwalm, Vernon Franklin, 1157
opposition to labor unions, 716
Peace Committee, 1002
peace position, 1000
peace vigil in Louisville, KY, following
    1969 meeting, 1305
Pension Board, 1007
Peters Creek Church of the Brethren,
    VA, 1011
Pipe Creek Church of the Brethren,
    MD, hosting, 1026
prison reform, 1060
public office holding issues, 311
quilting at, 61–62
refugee resettlement, 1093
Standing Committee, 36, 37, 1182,
    1216–1217
    Early, Henry Clay, 413, 414
    Eby, Enoch, 419
    Flory, John Samuel, 499
    Furry, Leonard, 526
    Graybill, Jonas, 567
    Koontz, Henry, 706

Kurtz, Henry, 711
Pfoutz, Isaac, 1015
Sell, James Arnold, 1165–1166
verbatim reports, 1303
voting issues, 311
Church of the Brethren Association of
    Christian Educators (COBACE),
    284, 2160, 2162, 2165
Church of the Brethren at Garfield, CO
    Mount Garfield, CO, Church of the
        Brethren, previous name of, 881
Church of the Brethren Directory, 18, *See
    also* yearbooks
Church of the Brethren Ecumenical Award
    Zigler, Michael Robert, 1399
Church of the Brethren/First Baptist
    Church, Cedar Rapids, IA, 265
Church of the Brethren Foreign Mission
    Commission
    Ecuador, 422
Church of the Brethren General Boards, *See*
    entries at General Parish Ministries
    Commission, organization of, 993
    works by, 2321
Church of the Brethren General Offices,
    See General Offices
Church of the Brethren Heritage Learning
    Program, 1237
Church of the Brethren Home, Windber,
    PA, 305
Church of the Brethren Homes and Hospi-
    tals Association
    Committee on Health and Welfare
        (CB), 327
Church of the Brethren Hymnal
    hymnals, 642
    hymns, 643
Church of the Brethren in India, 280
Church of the Brethren in Nigeria
        (*Ekklesiyar 'Yan'ura a Nigeria*
        [EYN]), 92, 250, 296, 299, 300,
        305–308, **305–308,** 307, 937,
        1914, 1927, 2162, **2164–2165,**
        2324
    evangelism, 461
    Fellowship of Churches of Christ in
        Nigeria, 484
    Guli, John, 2194, 2195
    Mai Sule Biu, first Nigerian elder, 782,
        2216
    Mamza, Ngamariju Keliri, secretary,
        784
    mission schools, 854
    missions, 861, 2225
    Mshelia, Madu B., 892
    Ragnijiya, T. H. on continuing educa-
        tion program for, 2351
    Sawa, Bitrus Pilasar (CB) and,
        2246–2247
    Shank, Glenn H. ("Doc") and Catherine
        Jean Heck (BC) in, 2248
    Shankster, Owen L., Jr., and Celia
        Smith (CB) in, 2248
Church of the Brethren Industrial School,
    158, **308,** 413, *See also* Bollinger,
    Amsey; Early, H. C.; Wampler,
    Nelie
    mission schools, 853
    Mount Carmel Church of the Brethren,
        VA, 880
    Wampler, Nelie Florence, 1317
Church of the Brethren Leader, 223, **308**
    Music Committee (CB), 899

Church of the Brethren Men's Fellowship, *See* Men's Work

Church of the Brethren: Ministry and Home Mission Commission
works by, 2321

Church of the Brethren Mission
Helser, Albert David, 596

Church of the Brethren Network (COB-NET)
information technology, church use of, 2208

Church of the Brethren of N.E. Ohio, 252

Church of the Brethren: Office of Brethren Witness
works by, 2321

Church of the Brethren Pacific Southwest District Conference
Fasnacht, Harold Dale, 480

Church of the Brethren Parish Ministries Commission
works by, 2321

Church of the Brethren Recreation Leaders' Fellowship, *See* Recreational Fellowship (CB)

Church of the Brethren Refugee Resettlement, Disaster Response, and Cooperative Disaster Child-Care
works by, 2321

Church of the Brethren Trust, 191

Church of the Brethren Urban Ministries
works by, 2321

Church of the Brethren Washington [DC] Office
works by, 2322

Church of the Brethren Women's Fellowship, *See* Women's Fellowship (CB)

The Church of the Brethren Yearbook, 1384
statistics on chaplaincy, 2158

Church of the Brethren Youth Fellowship (CBYF), 1394

Church of the Brethren Youth Site
Mount Zion Church of the Brethren, OH, 888

Church of the Good Shepherd, Bradenton, FL
example of possessive place name, 911

Church of the Good Shepherd congregations
example of biblically inspired name, 911

Church of the Nazarene
Holiness Movement, American, 619

Church of the Open Door, Los Angeles, CA, 136

Church of the Reconciliation, *See* Re-imagining Conference

church offices, *See* ministers; ministry
dress for, 402
Dunkard Brethren, 409–410

church officials, election of, 189

church on earth
amillennialism, 833

church order, *See* polity

church ordinances, *See* ordinances

church papers, *See* publishers and publishing

church parents, **308**, *See also* Christian education; Dedication of Infants; dedication of infants

Church Peace Mission
Historic Peace Churches, 610

Row, W. Harold, 1126

church planting, *See* church extension programs

church property
congregational names derived from ownership of, 911
disputes over, 739
lawsuits regarding, 729
legal name for denomination and, 910
Trustees of the General Conference, ownership of, 1278

church, purpose of, 407–408
Eby, Kermit, 420

Church, Ralph, 1903

church-related institutions
Durnbaugh, Donald F. on, 2326
rise and meaning of, 2326

church renewal, Young, David S. on leadership and, 2365

Church reunion, *See* ecumenism

church school leaders
training programs for, in Church of the Brethren, 2066

church schools, *See* Christian schools

church-sect typology, *See* sect-church typology

church-state relations, *See* church and state

church statistical reports, *See* statistics

church structure
Church of the Brethren, 304–305

church trials, *See* discipline; trials, church

church union, *See* ecumenism

church unity
dress and, 402–403
Wright, Lee-Lani on CB, 2364

church visits, *See* deacons' visits

Church World Service Center (New Windsor, MD), 22

Church World Service (CWS), 146, 197, 198, **308–309, 2165**
Brethren Church, 423
Brethren Service Center, joint activities, 2163
Bushong, Benjamin G., 233
Central America, 2157
Church of the Brethren Emergency Disaster Fund, 2172
Cleveland, OH, Brookpark Community Church of the Brethren, 320
CROP, 286
Greece, 569
Guatemala, 576
Haiti, 579
material aid, 802
Metzler, John D., Sr., 820
Murphy, Sara Florence Fogelsanger, 897
National Council of Churches of Christ in the USA and World Council of Churches, 2228
refugee resettlement, 1093
relief and service efforts, 1097
relief and social work, 303, 308, 309, 312
Row, W. Harold, 1126
Russian Agricultural Exchange Program, 2129
Sales Exchange for Refugee Rehabilitation Vocations (SERRV), 1139
Springfield, OH, First Church of the Brethren, 1215
Vietnam, 1305

world hunger issues (CB) and, 2266
Zigler, Michael Robert, 1398

Churchbaugh, Bertha (later Filbrun), 2184

Churches of Christ, 1892
Disciples of Christ, 385

Churches of Christ Uniting
Consultation on Church Union (COCU), 338

Churches of God, General Conference (Winebrennerians), 189, **309**, *See also* Fraternal Relations Committee (CB)
American revivalism, 1104
Church of God, Anderson, IN, 296
fraternal relations, 510
Hymnal: A Worship Book, 2205
Piney Creek Church of the Brethren, MD, 1025
Robinson, PA, Church of the Brethren, 1116

Churches of God, General Eldership, 177

Churches of God in North America, 309, *See also* Churches of God, General Conference

churches, Old German Baptist, 2018

Churchfield, George C., 1583

Churchhill, Kenneth, 1583

Churchill, Jack Butler, 53, 1583, 1848, 2157
Mexico, missionary to, 820

Churchill, Kenneth, 19, 553

Churchill, Miriam Aileen Sickel, 1181, 1848
Mexico, missionary to, 820

Churchill, Rosa, 2157

The Church's One Foundation
evangelicalism and, 2179

Churchtown, PA, 765

Churchwell, James, 448

Chustner, A. D., 1583

Ciampa, Valentine Anthony, 1906

Cicero, IN, Church of the Brethren (Arcadia), **45**, 109

Cider, Jacob, 1583

Ciferd, Peter, 1583

cigarettes, *See* tobacco

Cimarron River, CO, congregation, 324

Cimarron River, CO, Old German Baptist Brethren Church, **313**

Cimmaron Co., OK
Griggs, OK, Bethel Church of the Brethren, 573

Cincinnati, NE, 1280

Cincinnati, OH, 689
Church of the Brethren, **313**
Grace Brethren Church, 1380, *See also* Sharonville, OH, Cincinnati Grace Brethren Church
Grace Brethren Church, Sharonville, OH, 1172, 1174
thesis on opinions of church members, 1933–1934

Cinco de Mayo, Argentina, 53

circle
logo of Church of the Brethren, 2146, *2147*

Circle, Thomas, 1311

Circleville, OH, Church of the Brethren, 272, **313**
May, James, minister, 804

circulation
publishing, 1069

Circulo OK Club

Italy, 665
Cisney, Charles E., 1583
Cissna, A. H., 1583
Cissner family
    Salem Church of the Brethren, ND, 1137
cities
    fellowship houses in, 482
    missions in, *See* urban ministry
citizenship, *See* church-state relations; lobbying; voting issues
    Illinois, 647
    kingdom of God and, **313**
Citronelle, AL, 1339
    Church of the Brethren, *See* Cedar Creek, AL, Church of the Brethren
Citronelle College, 14, 263, **313**, *See also* education; higher education; secondary education
    Fruitdale Academy, 520
    Neff, James Monroe at, 922
Citronelle Seminary, AL, 1350
City Church of the Brethren, Waterloo, IA
    Waterloo, IA, Hammond Avenue Brethren Church and, 2260
City Church, Warrensburg, MO, 1318
civic affairs
    Eshelman, Matthew Mays, 455
    Fasnacht, Harold Dale, 480
civil disobedience, 292, **313**, *See also* conscientious objection; peace
    COs, 336
    General Conference Mennonite Church, 536
    Old German Baptist Brethren peace position, 1000
civil elections, *See* elections, electioneering
civil law and noncreedalism, 942
civil lawsuits, *See* lawsuits
civil office, holding
    oaths, taking of, 959
    overseer of the poor, 986
civil religion, **314**
    flags, 492
civil rights, 2128
    demonstrations and incarceration of Brethren, 1060
    Gandhi, Mohandas Karamchand, 528
    historiography, 2201
    mediation
        Longenecker, Stephen L. on, 2343
    Messenger, 819
    Miller, Mary Grace Hileman, 841
    minorities, ethnic and racial, 850
    Mississippi, 864
Civil Rights Act of 1965 and Christian Day School movement, 282
Civil War, 1, 41, 41 (sidebar), **314–315,** 403, 1151, 2021, 2026
    African Americans, 2128
    Annual meeting, disruption of, 169
    Antietam, *See* Antietam, battle of
    Brethren movement, 314–315
    Brethren victims of, 167
    capitalism and, 253
    Cedar Co., MO, Church of the Brethren, 263
    Cedar Grove Seminary (Academy), and effects of, 265
    chaplaincy, 271
    commutation tax, 149, 314, 331
    Confederate States of America, 167, 333

conscientious objectors, 2104
Davy, Henry Dorsey, 364–365
description of church service in Cumberland valley, 1939
Dunkard Brethren and, 148–147, 2086
Dunker church at Antietam, 1919
effects of, 178
Eshelman, Matthew Mays, 455
ethics, 458
family worship, 475
fugitives
    Mennonite Church, 2086
funerals, 524
Garst, Henry, 531
Geiger, Henry, 533
Gettysburg, Battle of, 546
gospel songs, 560
Graybill, Jonas, 567
Greenland Church of the Brethren, WV, 571
Harmony Church of the Brethren, MD, 584
Harpers Ferry, 585
Hays, Daniel, 590
higher education, 603
Hillery, Lemuel, 606
Historic Peace Churches, 608
Hixson, Armanus Jefferson, 613
Holsinger, Henry Ritz, 621
Hutchison, Andrew, 639
illustration of Dunkers and Mennonites receiving passes, 1959
Indiana conscientious objectors, 1966
Jackson, Thomas Jonathan "Stonewall," 667
Kansas, Brethren escape to, 987
Kansas, settlement of Brethren in, 682
Katy of Catoctin: Or, the Chain-Breakers (Townsend), 747
Kentucky as mission field, interest in, 689
Kline, John, 701
Kline, John, questioned by Confederate military authorities, 1349
Letcher, John, 738
Limestone Church of the Brethren, TN, 742
Maryland Brethren, effect on, 798
medicine, 809–810
meetinghouse as field hospital, 810
migration of Brethren, 829, 830
migration to Nebraska, 920
migrations after, 206
military service, 311, 333
military service required, 831
military substitutes, 1233–1234
minorities, ethnic and racial, 849, 851
missions, 858
Missouri Brethren settlement, 864
Monrovia, MD, Bush Creek Church of the Brethren, 870
Montgomery, Michael, 872
Moomaw, Benjamin Franklin, 873
Moomaw, John Crouse, 874
Native Americans, 2229
Nead, Peter, and, 918–920, *919*
New Vienna Academy, OH, 961
noncombatants in the Shenandoah Valley, 1923
nonresistance and, 148–149
nonresistance movement, 2082, 2107
Osceola Church of the Brethren, MO, 984

Ozawkie, KS, Church of the Brethren, 987
pacifism, 1973
peace advocacy and, 228
peace position, 999
Pennsylvania Brethren and military service, 1004
Peters, Amos B., 1011
Petersburg, WV, Memorial Church of the Brethren, 1012
Pine Glen Church of the Brethren, PA, 1024
    Church of the Brethren, MO, 1030
Pleasant Ridge Church of the Brethren, Alberta, Canada, 1034
Plunkett, N. Geraldine on Brethren movement and, 2350
prisons, 261, 1059
railroads, 1081–1082
Reconstruction Era, 1086
relief and service efforts, 1096
religious freedom and persecution, 1009
Rowland, Ann Gilbert, 1126
Rummel, Isaiah, 1129–1130
secession, 1162
Sharpsburg, MD, Church of the Brethren, 1174
slavery, 1190
social action, 1196
social issues, 2085
social welfare, 1198
sources on, 2315
Studebaker, Jacob, discouraged from serving, 1230
Sunday school movement, 283
Thurman, William C., treatise on nonresistance, 1264
Ulrich, Jacob, 2134
Union and, 148
veterans received in church, 1304
Virginia, 1307–1308, 2110
Vogt, Esther Loewen on Brethren woman during, 2361
Walnut Creek Church of the Brethren, MO, 1315
Weimer family, 1327
Wine, Jacob, questioned by Confederate military authorities, 1349
Wine, Joseph, ministered to both armies, 1349
Wolf River Church of the Brethren, KS, 1356
Wrightsman, Peter R., petition for military exemption, 1380
Yoder, Eli Lorenzo, 1386
Zigler, Samuel, 1399
Zollers, George DeHaven, 1400
Civilian Conservation Corps (CCC), 245, **315**
    Kosch, Lewis F., 707
Civilian Public Service (CPS), 146, 168, 197, 198, 199, **315–317**, 2028, 2067, *See also* conscientious objectors
    AFSC involvement with, 23
    agricultural college units, 9
    base camps, 91
    base camps for National Park Service, 917
    Cable, William H., 2155
    camp operations during World War II, 707

camps, 1216
Castañer, PR, 261, 316
Church of the Brethren, 301, 316
Civilian Conservation Corps (CCC), 315
conscientious objectors, 1169, 2097
conservation movement in WWII, 338
COs, 312, 315–316
criticism of, 24
Dairy Farm Assignments, 359
DeLauter, Ora Dale, 374
detached programs, 380
East Fairview Church of the Brethren, PA, 415
Elgin, IL, 436
Emergency Farm Labor, 443
Enders, NE, Church of the Brethren, 446
Evangelical Covenant Church, 459
fellowship houses, 482
Filbrun, Stanley Clarence, 2184
fire fighting, 491
Forest Service, 502
fraternal relations, 510
French, Paul Comly, 515
Funderburg, Drue Dresher, 523
Garver, Earl Simeon, 532, 2187
Gilbert, Martha Rupel, 2190
Greiner, Robert G., 2194
Harley, Samuel Abraham, 583
Hershey, Lewis Blaine, 599
Hispanic Ministries (CB), 2198
Historic Peace Churches, 608
history of, 1927
hospitals, 630–631
Huston, Ora Ivan, 638
Indiana, 653
Keim, Albert N. on, 2340
Keller, Paul W., 2210
Mathis, Jefferson H., 803
medical projects, 808
Mennonites and Brethren, 1949
mental hospital service, 816, *817*
Metzger, Thurl D., 2222
military service, 831
Minnesota Starvation Project, 848
    and National Service Board for
    Religious Objectors, 917
Ness, Jacob C., 2231
Norristown, PA, Church of the Brethren, 945
Old German Baptist Brethren peace position, 1000
poetry, 1039–1040
Puerto Rico, 1070, 1945
rejected as model for alternative service, 19, 20
relief and service efforts, 1097
relief training units, 1097
religious liberty and military service, 1098
Roosevelt, Franklin Delano, establishing, 1122
Row, W. Harold, Brethren director, 1126
Schrock, Mark Y., 1156
Shankster, Owen L., Jr., (CB) in, 2248
smokejumpers, 337
social action, 1196
soil conservation units, 1200
sources on, 2319
study of effects of hunger, University of Minnesota, 1955

thesis about, 1939
unit at Waldport, OR (1944–1945), 61
World War II, 336, 1372–1373
Ziegler, Levi King, 1397
Zigler, Michael Robert, 1398
civilian service, *See* alternative service
Civilian Service Board (DB), 317
    peace education, 1002
Claar, Abraham Ickes, 1583
    Queen, PA, Church of the Brethren, 1075
Claar, Christina Walter, 1294
Claar Church, PA, 1896
Claar Congregation, Lebanon Co., PA, 1863
Claar congregation, PA, 1347
Claar, Frederick, 1294
Claar, Jacob C., 1583
Claar meetinghouse, Woodbury, PA, Church of the Brethren, 1364
Claar, Michael M., 1583
Claar, PA, Church of the Brethren, *See* Upper Claar, PA, Church of the Brethren
Claasen, Arlin G., 1583, 1906
Claassen, Faye Birky, 1906
Clague, W. Donald, 1583
Clair, Aaron L., 317, 1345, 1583
Clair family, 1958
Clair, Mary, 317
Clair, Preston, 317
Clairvaux, Bernard of, 56
Clanahan, John, 1583
Clancy, Jane
    works by, 2322
Clannin, Velma
    Ozark Church of the Brethren, MI, vacation Bible school, 986
Clapham, Elizabeth
    Cincinnati Grace Brethren Church, Sharonville, OH, 1174
Clapham, Michael C.
    Cincinnati Grace Brethren Church, Sharonville, OH, pastor at, 1174
Clapp family, 2085
Clapp, Steve, 2130
    works by, 2322
Clapper, Cicero, 760
Clapper (Cloppert) family, 317, **2372**
Clapper, D. M., 1583
Clapper, D. Russell, 1583
Clapper, Daniel, 1583
Clapper, Daniel K., 1583–1584, 1906
Clapper, David, 674
Clapper, David K., 335, 674, 1584, 1907
Clapper, David Steele, 317, 461, 1584
    Scalp Level, PA, Church of the Brethren, elder in, 1151
Clapper, Donald L., 2275
Clapper, Eloise (later Hanawalt), 581
Clapper family, 1939
    Mount Hope Church of the Brethren, WA, 882
    Schultz, Martin, related to, 1156
    Snake Valley Old German Baptist Brethren Church, PA, 1193
Clapper, Frank, 252
Clapper, Mrs. Frank, 252
Clapper, George M., 1584
Clapper, Grace, 1907
Clapper, Harlan, 252
Clapper, Mrs. Harlan, 252
Clapper, Henry, 317, 1384, 1584
Clapper, Horace G., 1584, 2300

Riddlesburg, PA, Church of the Brethren, minister, 1108
Clapper, J. Henry, 317
Clapper, John, 1584
Clapper, Joseph H., 317, 1584
Clapper, Joseph H., Sr., 1384
Clapper, Josiah
    Roaring Spring, PA, First Church of the Brethren, interim pastor, 1114
Clapper, Levi, 1584
Clapper, Paul, 760
Clapper, S. M., 165
Clapper, Sherman, 1212
    Mount Hope Church of the Brethren, WA, 882
Clapper, Sherman H., 1584
Clapper, Viola Grace, 317, 1835, 2038
Clappert, John, Jr., 1584
Clappert, John, Sr., 1584
Clara Flora, 211
Clarence, IA, Church of the Brethren, *See* Cedar Church, IA, Church of the Brethren; Cedar, IA, Church of the Brethren
Clarion Co., PA, 317, 456
Clarion German Baptist Brethren, 925
Clarion, MI, 1389
    Bear Lake Church of the Brethren, **317**
Clarion, PA, Church of the Brethren, **317**
Clark, B. O., 1584
Clark, C. C.
    Oklahoma City, OK, Church of the Brethren, 964
Clark, Caroline E. (later Myers)
    Myers, Garry Cleveland, wife of, 903
Clark, Charles W., 1584
Clark Co., IN, 1292
    Indiana Territory, 1233
    migration of Brethren, 829
Clark Co., OH, 352, 1215, 1271
    Donnels Creek Church of the Brethren, 396
    New Carlisle, OH, Church of the Brethren, 926
Clark Co., WI, 317
Clark, Colgate, 280
Clark, Cynthia, 2093
Clark, D. C., 1584
    Palestine, AR, Ministry to Blacks, 991
Clark, D. H., 1584
Clark, D. Jesse, 264
Clark, Daniel, 264, 318
Clark, David, 318
Clark, Dennis, 1584
Clark, Diana Houch, 231
Clark, Doris Hufford
    on Hufford, Frances, 2358
Clark, E. Finlay, 1584
Clark, E. L., 379
Clark, Edward, 318, 1584, 2300
    Pleasant Grove Grace Brethren Church, IA, pastor, 1031
Clark, Elizabeth (later Hon), 626
Clark, Elizabeth (later Reiss), 1927
Clark, Ella, 662
Clark, Ellen, 318
Clark, Elmer T., 1907
Clark, Emanuel, 318
Clark, Esther Rinker, 318
Clark family, 1215, 1385, 1907
    Honey Creek Church of the Brethren, MO, 627
    Howard Co. Old German Baptist

Brethren Church, IN, 633
Niota, TN, Church of the Brethren, 938
Roanoke, VA, Garden City Grace
 Brethren Church, 1113
Clark, George, 662
Clark, George Rogers, 989
Clark, Glenn William
 works by, 2322
Clark, Hendricks, **318**, 1584
Clark, Hendricks, Jr., **318**, 1584
Clark, J. W.
 North Liberty, IN, Brethren Church,
  pastor, 948
Clark, James Ratcliffe, 1907
Clark, Jesse D., 78, 590, 740, 1584
 Midway Church of the Brethren, TN,
  providing leadership, 827
 Piney Flats, TN, Church of the
  Brethren, minister, 1025
Clark, John, 318
Clark, John S., 20, 1584
Clark, John Walter, 1584
Clark, Joshua, 318
Clark, Lawrence Albert, 1584, 1835, 1907
Clark, Lewis H., 1584
Clark, Martin, 318
Clark, Mary Bailey, 318
Clark, Meribah Eliza, 1907
Clark, Merlin Leroy, 236, 1584, 1907
Clark, Michael A., 2177, 2275
Clark, N. E., 1584
Clark, N. F., 1584
Clark, Nancy, 318
Clark, Noah J., 1584
Clark, Paul H., 540, 965, 1223, 1399, 1584,
 2300, **2381**
 Old Brethren minister, 965
Clark, Rebecca, 318
Clark, Rick A., 2275
Clark, Ronald L., 1584
Clark, Roy English, 672, 676, 1584
Clark, Ruth
 works by, 2322
Clark, Ruth E., *507*
Clark, Ruth Genevieve Clark, 1835
Clark, Sammy Dean, 1584
Clark, Thomas, 318, 430
Clark, Thomas J., 2275
Clark, Thomas, Jr., 1584
Clark, Thomas, Sr., 1584, 2125
Clark, Tom, 633
Clark, W. C., 1584
Clark, W. H., 627
Clark, Walter, 18, 260, 1584
 Newton Grove Church of the Brethren,
  elder in, 934
Clark, Wanda Mills, 2275
Clark, Wealthy A., *See* Burkholder, Wealthy
 Agnes Clark
Clark, William, 318
Clark, William (CB-1), 1584
Clark, William (CB-2), 1584
Clark, William (CB-3), 1584
Clark, William F., 231
Clark, William H., 1584
Clark, William S., 1584
Clark, William S., Jr., 105
Clark, William S., Sr., 105
Clarke, Blanche (later Stutz), 1233
Clarke Co., AR, 1281
Clarke Co., IA
 Osceola, IA, Church of the Brethren,
  983

Clarke Co., IN
 Olive Branch German Baptist Brethren
  Church, IN, 973
Clarke family
 Pleasant View Church of the Brethren,
  TN, 1037
Clarke, Grace Julian, 1907
Clarke, Roy E., 1907
 New Hope Church of the Brethren, TN,
  elder in, 929
 Pleasant Hill Church of the Brethren,
  TN, pastor/elder, 1032
Clarkson Cemetery Association
 Paradise Prairie Church of the
  Brethren, OH, land deed to, 992
Clarksville, MI
 Grace Brethren Church, **318**
  Michigan Brethren settlement, 824
 Hope Church of the Brethren, MI, 629
Clarkton, VA, 1243
Clasper-Torch, Lee, 2275
Classen, Jerry, 104, 1584
 Omaha, NE, Grace Brethren Bible
  Church, pastor, 974
classified minutes of annual meetings, **318**
 publication of, 6, 868
Claus, Nettie Young, 1907
Claussen, W. Edmunds, 1907
Clawson, John B., 1584
Clawson, John Harvey, 1584, 1907
 Penn Run Church of the Brethren, PA,
  pastor, 1004
 Philadelphia, PA, Calvary Church of
  the Brethren, pastor, 1015
Clawson, Tracy Ann (later Ruggles), 2157
Clay City, IN, 733
 First Brethren Church (FGBC), **318**
Clay Co. Church of the Brethren, FL
 Jacksonville, FL, Church of the
  Brethren, 667
 Glen St. Mary, FL, Glenside Church of
  the Brethren, 552
Clay Co., IA
 Gillett Grove, IA, German Baptist
  Brethren, 549
Clay Co., KY, 689
 Flat Creek Church of the Brethren, KY,
  493
Clay Co., TX
 Pleasant Valley Church of the Brethren,
  TX, 1035
Clay, Donald Owen, 1341, 1584, 2300
Clay family
 Riner Grace Brethren Church, VA,
  1110
Clay, Henry, 1584
Clay, John Wesly, 1907
Clay Twp., Montgomery Co., OH
 Salem Church of the Brethren, 1138
Claybaugh, Henry A., 1315, 1584–1585
 Pine Creek Church of the Brethren, IN,
  1024
Claybaugh, Nellie, 1907
Clayborn congregation, 1225
Clayhill, PA, 1228
Clayhole Grace Brethren Church, KY, 188,
 318, 689
 Lexington, KY, Grace Bible Church,
  2214
Claypool, H. S., 1585
Claypool, IN, Brethren Church, **318**
Claypool, Mabel Gertrude, 1835
Claysburg, PA, 765, 1294

Church of the Brethren, **318–319**, 732
Holsinger Church of the Brethren, PA,
 623
Clayton Brethren Church (FGBC), 213
Clayton, Fred R., 679, 1287, 1585
 Mount Zion Church of the Brethren,
  WV, 888
 Pleasant Hill Church of the Brethren,
  WV, 1033
Clayton, George B., 124, 1585
Clayton, Glenn L. (son), 319
Clayton, Glenn Lowell, 66, 67, 183, **319**
Clayton, J. Thomas, 265
Clayton, James Monroe, 1585
Clayton, John M., 319
Clayton, Lottie Erbaugh, 319
Clayton, OH, 1355
 First Brethren Church, 319
 Grace Brethren Church, **319**, 1277
 Happy Corner Church of the Brethren,
  102, **319**
 Englewood, OH, Grace Brethren
  Church, 447
 Salem Church of the Brethren
  organized from, 1138
 Salem Old German Baptist Brethren
  Church, OH, located near, 1139
Clayton, Sherman, 319
Clayton, Thomas Jacob, 1585
Clayton, William T., Jr., 1907
Claytons School (Schoolhouse No. 7,
 Ashland, OH), 67
Claytor Lake
 Eckerlin brothers and place-names,
  Brethren, 1027
cleanliness
 personal appearance, 1010
 cleansing the feet, *See* feetwashing
Clear, Catherine
 Scottville Old German Baptist Brethren
  Church, MI, 1161
Clear Creek, IL, congregation, 352, 1234,
 1358
 baptisms, 1357
 Far Western Brethren, 475
Clear Creek, IN, Church of the Brethren,
 319–320
 Huntington (Co.) Church of the
  Brethren, IN, 638
 Huntington, IN, City Church of the
  Brethren, 637
Clear Creek, MO, Church of the Brethren,
 320, 683
Clear, John Daniel, 264, 270, 638,
Clear, John W., 264, 270, 638, 540, 1242,
 1585
 Mount Pleasant Old German Baptist
  Brethren, IN, minister, 887
 North Fork Old German Baptist
  Brethren Church, IN, minister, 947
 Pleasant Hill Old German Baptist
  Brethren Church, IL, providing
  leadership, 1033
 Scottville Old German Baptist Brethren
  Church, MI, 1161
Clear Spring, MD, 1285
Clearbrook, VA, Grace Brethren Church,
 320
Clearfield Co., PA, 274
Clearfork, MO, Church of the Brethren, *See*
 Leeton, MO, Clearfork Church of
 the Brethren
Clearville, PA, 410

Dunkard Brethren congregation, *See*
Waynesboro, PA, Dunkard Brethren congregation
mission point for Waynesboro, PA,
Dunkard Brethren Congregation,
1324
Clearwater Church of the Brethren, ID, **320**
Sewell, Laura A. (CB) and, 2247
Clearwater Co., ID, 320
Clearwater, FL, Grace Brethren Church,
320
St. Petersburg, FL, Grace Brethren
Church, daughter congregation of,
1136
Cleary, Connie, 749, 1585
Cleary, David, 518, 749, 1585
Mount Airy, NC, First Church of the
Brethren, pastor, 880
Pleasant Valley Church of the Brethren,
NC, providing leadership, 1035
Cleaver, George D., 129, 1585
Rockton, PA, Church of the Brethren,
elder and minister, 1118
Cleaver, Urban L., 1585
Cleland, Jessie M., 1907
Clem, Amsey Ervin, 124, 1585
Clem family, Mount Pleasant Brethren
Church, VA, 886
Clem, Rilla (later Puterbaugh), 1072
Clemens, Catherine (later Keyser), 691
Clemens family, 2077
Clemens, Frances Z. (later Nyce), 190, 285,
1907, 2032
recreation, 1088
Clemens, Fred W., 1907
Clemens, George W., 124, 1585
Clemens, Samuel L. (Mark Twain), 2128
friendship with John T. Lewis, 738
minorities, ethnic and racial, 851, *851*
Clemens, William Montgomery, 1907
"Clement" as pen name of James Quinter,
1077
Clement, Clara C. Wheeler, 320
Clement, Emaline Bowman, 320
Clement family
Hollins, VA, Patterson Memorial Grace
Brethren Church, 620
Clement, John A. N., 320, 1585
Clement, John Addison (son), **320**
McPherson College, president, 781
Clement of Alexandria, 296
agape meals, 757
Clemes, Catharine (later Keyser), *692*
Clemmer, Sarah, 1897
Clepinger, Henry, *See* Klepinger, Henry
clergy, *See* ministers
Clermont Co., OH, 177, 1224, 1225
Stonelick congregation and Ohio settlement, 961
Cleveland Church Federation
Miller, J. Quinter, 1326
weekday religious education, 1326
Cleveland Heights, OH, First Church of the
Brethren, **320–321**
Cleveland, OH, congregations, 768, 1227
Brookpark Community Church of the
Brethren, **320**
Hammers, Thomas E., 581
Lyndhurst Grace Brethren Church, *See*
Lyndhurst, OH, Grace Brethren
Church
missions, 860
Mount Zion Fellowship of the

Brethren, **2165**
urban mission, 1297
Clewell, John H., 1907–1908
Click, Berryman F., 338, 1585
Click, Charles Andrew, 1585
Click, D. G.
Newberg, OR, Church of the Brethren,
pastor in, 933
Click, Daniel Medford, **321**, 1212, 1585,
1908
Click family, 396, 1318, *See* Glick family;
Glück (Click, Glick) family
Nevada, MO, Church of the Brethren,
924
at New Rockford, ND, Church of the
Brethren, 932
Click, Isa E., 1585
Click, J. A., 1585
Click, J. W., 1585
Click, Jacob Orville, 171, 668, 1585
Click, John, 1585
Click, Michael, 352
Click, Ralph Ernest, 79, 1585
Click, Rebecca Barnhart, 321
Click, Samuel, 263, 1585
Nevada, MO, Church of the Brethren,
elder in, 924
Pilot Knob Church of the Brethren,
AR, minister, 1024
Click, Susanna Crist, 352
Clifford, Elizabeth (later Neff), 2029
Clifford family
Garwin, IA, Carlton Brethren Church,
532
Clifford, L. A., 368, 1585
Clifford-Mayville, ND, Old German Baptist
Brethren Church, 105, **321**
Clifford, Paul, 1585
Clift family, 721
Clift, G. Glenn, 1908
Clifton Mills
Sandy Creek Church of the Brethren,
WV, meetinghouse, 1143
Clifton, V. C., 1585
Climax School, preaching point maintained by Kansas Center Church of
the Brethren, KS, at, 683
Cline, Ananias, 2102
Cline, Annie (later Flory), *495*
Cline, Attie, 1846
Cline, Bertha Ellen (later Miller), 1585
Miller, DeWitt L., mother of, 836
Cline, Charles A., 1585
Cline, Charles C., 1585
Cline, Charley Norton, 1908
Cline, Cyrus H., 1585
Cline, Doris (later Egge), 1927
Cline, E. H., 1908
Cline, Ernest J., 1585
Cline family, 733, 750, 1345, 1956, *See also*
Klein family
Prosperity Brethren Church, WV, 1062
Schowalter family, related to, 1155
Cline, Fred Milton, 143, 367, 2139, 1585
Cline, Frederick, 62, 1585
Rockingham and Shenandoah Counties
Old German Baptist Brethren
Church, VA, elder, 1118
Cline, George, 1585
Cline, J. W., 759
Raisin City, CA, Church of the Brethren, 1083
Cline, Jack, 562

Cline, Jacob, 1585
Cline, John, 1585
Cline, John A., 1585
Cline, John F., 468, 1585
Cline, John W., 733, 1585
Cline, Joseph M., 1585
Cline, Joseph W., 1585
Philadelphia, PA, Geiger Memorial
Church of the Brethren, 1016
Cline, Justus H., 1585
Cline-Kline family
Kline, Paul G. on, 2341
Cline, M. B.
Oak Grove Church of the Brethren, IA,
district meeting delegate, 955
Cline, Mary E.
biography of, 2110
Cline, Mary (later Detrick), 1359, 2183
marriage enrichment, 796
Women's Conferences (CB) and, 2265
Cline, Mary (later Richards), 714
Cline, Minnie L. (later Miller)
Miller, Joseph Quinter, mother of,
840–841
Miller, Minor Cline, mother of, 841
Cline, Minor Justus, 1585
Cline, M. J., 1277
Cline, P. F., 733
Cline, Paul Charles, 1908
Cline, Peter, 1585
Cline, Peter Frederick, 1585
Cline, Samuel (CB-1), 1585
Cline, Samuel (CB-2), 1585
Cline, W(ill) M., 1585
Cline, D.
Prairie View Church of the Brethren,
MO, 1050
Clingan, Alan N., 55, 1585
Greencastle, PA, Conococheague Grace
Brethren Church, 2193
Clingan, Elnora Schechter, 1835
Clingenpeel, George, 2300
Clingenpeel, George W., 1585–1586
Clingenpeel, John, 1586
Clingenpeel, Marvin E., 130, 1586
Clingenpeel, Mary
Ross, Helen M. Ross on, 2353
Ross, Keith E. on, 2353
Clingingsmith (Clingensmith), John, **321,**
577, 1586, 1908
Clingingsmith, Daniel, 321
Clingingsmith family, 1342
Clingingsmith, Lovina Hendricks, 321
Clinical Pastoral Education (CPE), 271
Cink (Sink?), Daniel, 1583
Clinton Co., IA
Maquoketa German Baptist Brethren,
IA, 791
Clinton Co., IN, 231, 425
Middlefork Old German Baptist
Brethren Church, IN, 826
Rossville, IN, Church of the Brethren,
1124
Skiles, Jacob W., 1188
Clinton Co., MI
Elsie Church of the Brethren, MI, 442
Clinton Co., MO
migration of Brethren, 830
Missouri Brethren settlement, 864
Plattsburg Church of the Brethren, MO,
1030
Sell, Daniel, elder, 1165
Clinton Co., OH, 237

Clinton Co., PA, 1235
Clinton family, 1277
Clinton, Robert G., 2, 21, 1586
Clippinger, Anthony, 701
Clippinger family, *See* Kleppinger family
Clippinger, Frederick, 701
Clive, J. F., 1586
Clive, John, 2019
clockmaking at Ephrata, 2005
cloister, *See* Ephrata Community
Cloppert family, 317, *See also* Clapper family
Cloppert, Hugh L., 317, 1586
Cloppert, John, 1586
Cloppert, John, Sr., 281
close communion, **321**
    Doctrinal Treatise, 394
Close Communion: Or, Plea for the Dunkard People (West, Edmund Landon), 1332
clothing, *See* dress
Clouds Creek, SC
    German Baptist Brethren Church, **321**
        Martin, David, minister, 797
Clough, Robert, 1586
Clough, William H., 1270, 1343, 1586
    South Bend, IN, Ireland Road Grace Brethren Church, pastor, 1203
Clouse, Bonnidell
    works by, 2322
Clouse, Paul, 1251
Clouse, Raymond, 1586
Clouse, Raymond E., 2300
Clouse, Robert G., 265, 318, 1586, 1908
    works by, 2322
Clover Creek, PA, Church of the Brethren, 383, 1364, *See also* Fredericks- burg, PA, Clover Creek Church of the Brethren
    Fairview Church of the Brethren, PA, 469
    Holsinger, Daniel Mack, 621
    Holsinger, Henry Ritz, 621
    Hüber (Hoover) family, 634
    Marklesburg, PA, James Creek Church of the Brethren, 794
    Smithfield Church of the Brethren, PA, 1192
    Snider, Donald Mitchell, pastor, 1194
    sources on, 2322
Cloverdale, VA, 152, 164, **321–322,** 397, 1308
    Church of the Brethren, history of, 1944
    Jeters Chapel Church of the Brethren, VA, 670
    mission point, Botetourt Co., VA, Church of the Brethren, 164
    Roanoke, VA, Summerdean Church of the Brethren, 1113
Cloverdale, WI, Church of the Brethren, **322**
Cloverleaf McCave, CO, Dunkard Brethren Congregation, **322,** 324–325
    Root, Isaac William, 2378
Clovis, NM, 831
    First Church of the Brethren, **322**
    migration of Brethren, 830–831
Clower, Elbert Lee, 1586
Clower, Lewis M., 1586
Cloyd, ___, 1586
Club Brethren
    Ecuador, 422

Cluecon, T. J., 1586
Clum, George, 1586
Clutter, Rice Morgan, 1586
    Mount Bethel Church of the Brethren, VA, pastor, 880
Clutter, Ronald T.
    works by, 2322
Clyde, Joseph, 1586
CO Committee (DB), *See* Civilian Service Board (DB)
Co-operative Brethren congregation, OH, 326
Co-Operative Colonization Company
    Empire, CA, Church of the Brethren, 445
Coal Creek (Canton), IA, congregation, 226
Coal Creek, IL, 1357
    congregation, 251, 647
Coal Creek, NC, 749
Coast Community, 19
Coate, Abitha David, 1586
Coate, Naida, 1335
Coates, Earl Edward, 2275
Coates, Harvia (later Shaffer-Faust), 2062
Coates, Mary E., 345
coats
    plain frock coats, 967, 1029
Coats, Glenn R., 1586
CoBACE *See* Church of the Brethren Association of Christian Educators
Cobaugh, Lewis, 1586
Cobaugh, Paul, 1321, 1586
Cobb, Edward M., 2, 204, 366, 656, 748, 1586, 1908
    railroads and Brethren settlement, 1082
Cobb, Sharon (later Hutchinson), 2282
Cober, Alvin Alonzo Brant, 121, 322, 914, 1225, 1333, 1586, 1908
    Milford, IN, Brethren Church, pastor, 831
Cober (Cover, Coover) family, **322**
Cober (Cover), Wesley, 1586
Cober, Ephraim, 322, 1586, **2381**
    Quinter, KS, Church of the Brethren, 1078
    Rock Creek Church of the Brethren, KS, 1117
Cober family, 152, 322, 1908
Cober, George, 1586
Cober, Jacob A., *238*
Cober, Jacob, family
    Ontario German Baptist Brethren, 975
Cober, John P., 322, 1586
Cober, N. P., family
    Ontario German Baptist Brethren, 975
Cober, Peter, 322, 632
Cober, Peter, Jr., 1586
Coblentz family
    Roher (Rohrer) family, 1119
Coblentz, Perry E., 1586
Coburn, Frank J., 758, 1586
Coburn, Richard Lyle, 1586, 1848
Coburn, Rolland, 348, 1586
    Santa Maria, CA, Grace Brethren Church, pastor in, 1145
Coburn, Sheryl Lynn Patterson, 1848
Cocalico Creek, Lancaster Co., PA
    Ephrata Community, 448
    Scheublein, Christian and Esther Neff, 1178
Cocalico (Flickinger's), PA, congregation, 280
Cocalico Mystics, 1989

Cocalico, PA, congregations, 158, 225
    Church of the Brethren, **322,** 620
    Mohler Church of the Brethren, PA, 868
Cocalico Valley, IL
    Showalter, Michael S. on tombstones in, 2356
Cocceius, Johannes
    Summa doctrinae de foedere et testa mento Dei (Comprehensive Theology of the Covenant and Testament of God), 347
Cochanower, E., 1586
Cochran, Charles L., 1586
Cochran, Clara Hymer, 91
Cochran, Martin, 1586
    Rock Camp German Baptist Bethren Church, WV, elder, 1116
Cochran, Rebecca, 743
Cochran, Rosella, 1848
Cochran, Thomas D., 743
Cochran, William, 725, 746, 1586
Cochrane, Pauline, 1908
Cockley, Anna Hunsecker, 1908
Cockley, Noah B., 1586
Cocklin, Clara Mohler, 322
Cocklin family, 356
Cocklin house
    Lower Cumberland Church of the Brethren, PA, 765
Cocklin, Lena Fay (later Shank), *See* Shank, Lena Fay Cocklin
Cocklin, Robert Levi, 157, 1586
Cocklin, Walter, 322, 1324, 1586
    Ray Shank, father-in-law of, 1172
Cocozzoli, Gary R., 1860
COCU, *See* Consultation on Church Union
Coder, Al, 755
Codora, CA, Church of the Brethren, **322–323,** 438
Codorus, PA, Church of the Brethren, 145, **323,** 362, 686, 1388, 1391, 1401, 1952
    example of place name, 911
    New Fairview Church of the Brethren, sponsorship of, 927
    New Freedom, PA, Church of the Brethren, sponsorship of, 927
    place-names, Brethren, and New York, PA, 1027
    Pleasant View Church of the Brethren, PA, 1037
    Shrewsbury, PA, Church of the Breth- ren, 1179
Coffee family, 227
Coffelt, E. B., 1586
Coffelt family, 1348
Coffey Co., KS
    Gravel Hill Church of the Brethren, KS, 567
    Scott Valley Church of the Brethren, KS, 1160
Coffey, F. C., 768
Coffey family, 1866
Coffey, Phyllis (later Ellsworth)
    Malles, Mark Ellsworth, 2217
Coffield, Glen, 317
Coffin, Joseph H., 2275
coffins, 229, 323, *See also* burial customs
Coffman, ___ (son-in-law of Jacob Long), 724
Coffman, Aubrey Reherd, 513, 1586, 1908
Coffman, Benjamin, 476, 685

Coffman, Carl Flory, 261, 1586, 1835, 1972
  medical projects, 808
Coffman, Christian, 2000
Coffman, Clifford Lee "Kip," 12, 463, 1586
Coffman, Curtis Paul, 209, 731, 1586
Coffman, Dennis Eugene, 1586, 2275
  Newton, KS, Church of the Brethren, pastor in, 934
Coffman, Eldon Henry, 2275
Coffman, Ernest S., 105, 1586
Coffman family, 319, 453, 1391, 1908, 2087, *See also* Kauffman family; Kauffmann family
  Good (Guth) family, 556
  Muhlenberg Co., KY, German Baptist Brethren, 893
Coffman, Ferne Heagley, 1835, 1908, 2102
  Wetonka, SD, Willow Creek Church of the Brethren, 2379
Coffman, Frances C. (later Ogden), 961
Coffman, H. McKinley, 912
  refugee resettlement, 1093
Coffman, Henry C. N., 447, 1586–1587
Coffman, J. B., 1587
Coffman, J. M., 1908
Coffman, Jacob, III, 685
Coffman, Jehu, 365
Coffman, John Isaac, 727, 759, 1587, **2381**
  McFarland, CA, Church of the Brethren, pastor, 774
Coffman, John M., 1587
Coffman, John S.
  Miller, Susan Fisher on Mennonite revivalism, 2347
Coffman, Joseph, 1587
Coffman, Joseph D., 1587
Coffman, L. C., 1254
Coffman, Letitia, 463
Coffman, Lucinda, 260
Coffman, Lulu Pearl Ullom, 1345, 1836
Coffman, Luther C., 1587
Coffman, Mary, 1908
Coffman, Mary Stemple, 1908
Coffman, McKinley, 244, 520, 574, 685, 1277, 1587
  Myersville, MD, Church of the Brethren, pastor, 906
Coffman, Noah Walter, 502, 1324, 1587
Coffman, Paul, 343
Coffman, Richard Allen, 1587
Coffman, Roxanne, 748, 1908
  spelling changed to Roxanna, **2388**
Coffman, Sara Ann, 1834
Coffman, Susanna (later Erbach), 453
Coffman, Thurston Rodney, 685, 1587
  Somerset, PA, Church of the Brethren, pastor, 1202
Coffman, W. Paul, 1908–1909
Coffman, W. W.
  Pleasant Dale Church of the Brethren, VA, 1031
Coffman, Walter Scott, 520, 685, 912, 1587, 2300
Coffman, William Paul, 1587
Cogan family, 1304
Coggins, Larry, 384
Cohen, Ronald Nathan, 2275
Coil, Abram L., 1587
  Ross Church of the Brethren, OH, leader, 1124
Coiner, Kitty, 2100
Cokeville congregation, PA, 1321
Colany family

at New Rockford, ND, Church of the Brethren, 932
Colb (Kolb), P. J., 1587
Colbert family
  Johnstown, PA, Geistown Grace Brethren Church, 674
Colbert, Frank, 1335
Colbert, George, 1587
Colbert, H. M., family
  Myers Creek Church of the Brethren, WA, 905
Colborn, Julia Rowland, 2166
Colburn, Ralph J., 115, 203, 250, 497, 503, 754, 1335, **2165–2166**, 2300
  North Lauderdale, FL, Grace Brethren Church, leadership by, 948
Colburn, Theda, 714
Colburn, Willard, 714
Colby, KS, congregation
  Menlo Church of the Brethren, KS, 814
Cold War, 23
  Germany (Federal Republic of Germany), 546
  nuclear arms race, 2232
Coldren, Walter E., 1243, 1587
Coldwater, IA, Church of the Brethren, *See* Greene, IA, Church of the Brethren
Cole, Charles William, 1587
Cole, Daryl L.
  works by, 2323
Cole, Don, 755
Cole, Earle, 357
Cole, G. Frederick, 2094
Cole, Gary M., 503, 1587
  Ormond Beach, FL, Grace Brethren Church, pastor, 982
Cole, James E., 1587
Cole, Jayne, 357
Cole, Neil, 2275
Cole, Stephen Samuel, 1587
Cole, Wallace Glenn, 2275
Cole, William E., 1587
Colebank, Evelyn Miller, 1909
Colebank, Frank G., Jr., 1587
Colebank, Frank G., Sr., 1587
Colebank, Marshall, 1587
Colebank, William J., 1587
  Shelby Co. Church of the Brethren, MO, elder in, 1175
Coleman, A. C., 768
Coleman, Donald, 1321
Coleman, Frank G., 130, 755
Coleman, Frank, Sr., 1240
Coleman, James Willard, 1587
Coleman, John P., 1587
Coleman, Joretta, 2175
Coleman, MI
  Church of the Brethren, **323**
  Michigan Brethren settlement, 824
  Old German Baptist Brethren Church, **323**
Coleman, Mildred Moomaw, 1909
Coleman, Wesley, 2175
Coler, Frank, 1587
Coler, S. A., 1390
Colfax Co., NM
  Brethren colonization in, 931
Colfax, IN, 1339
Colijn, Brenda Barnett
  church governance and, 2264
  Hispanic Ministries (BC), 2198
  works by, 2323

Colket, Meredith B., Jr., 1909
Collar, Jesse, 1587
collars on plain coats, 1028–1029
Collbran, CO, 1286
Collected Annual Meeting Minutes (1886)
  Old German Baptist Brethren, 967
A Collection of Hymns and Sacred Songs
  hymnals, 642
A Collection of Psalms, Hymns, and Spiritual Songs
  hymnals, 642
A College Algebra, (Levi Stephen Shively), 1178
College Corner, IN, 766, 1338
  Brethren Church, **323**
College Hill Church cemetery, 1
College of Agriculture and Forestry, Nanking, China, 9
College (Park St.) Brethren Church, OH
  Garber, Aaron Leedy, 528
colleges and universities, 2, 12, 399, 426, 427–428, *602, 603,* 603–605, **603–605,** 690, 2031, 2053, *See also* specific institutions
  Annual Meeting and Brethren polity, 1042
  art, openness to, 61
  article about, 1961
  and athletics, 69
  bibliography, 1870, 1877, 1904
  Brethren Church and, 182
  Brethren Colleges Abroad (BCA), **2142,** 2162
  Brethren movement and, 178
  Brethren of Christ, 189
  Brethren-related colleges, Church of the Brethren regions, 1093, 1094
  Brethren, student personnel services in, 1984
  changes in attitudes about, 1376
  Christian, 1995
  Christian Day School movement, 282–283
  Christian Education Commission (CB), 285
  church and, 2003
  church, and the Brethren family, 2010
  church colleges, 1968
  Church of the Brethren, 1944
  curriculum, pre-seminary, 2009
  drama, attitude toward, 398–399
  Early, Henry Clay, 414
  education, 426
  education, Christian, 2100
  Evangelical Association, 459
  Fast Element, 480
  fundamentalism and, 2179
  Geiger, Mary Schwenk, 533
  General Board (CB), 535
  General Education Board (CB), 537
  geographic location of insitutions, 1464
  German Baptist Brethren, 1957
  Girard, IL, Church of the Brethren, 550
  Grace Schools, 2192
  Grace Schools (Grace Theological Seminary, Grace College), 563
  Harshbarger, Luther H., 587
  Hess, Maurice Abram, 601
  historical writing, 613
  Holsinger, Henry Ritz, 621
  honorific titles, 1266
  Hoover, William I. T., 628
  Illinois, 2069

importance for spiritual life, 1210
incorporation, 649
Indiana, 2069
Influenza Pandemic, 655
information technology, church use of, 2208
Inglenook Nature Study Club (CB), 656
Jacobs, Edwin Elmore, 667–668
Juniata College, 1980–1981
language, inclusive, 2214
list of academies, colleges, and seminaries
    international, 1829
    USA, 1825
map of institutes of higher education in USA, 1464
Mennonite Brethren Churches, General Conference of, 814
Mennonite Church (MC), 815
mid-Western America, 2069
military recruitment on campus, 831
Miller, Daniel Long, supporting, 834
Miller, Oliver W., advancing, 841
ministers, and salary, 1136–1137
ministry in the Church of the Brethren, 2224
missionary children, 854
modern science, 1160
Moore, John Henry, 874
Mount Morris College, 883–885
Murphy, Sara Florence Fogelsanger, 897
museums, 898
Old German Baptist Brethren, 810, 969
peace education, 1002–1003
Pennsylvania, 1005
Petersime, Ray, 1012
philosophy of, article about, 1935
Pleasant Hill College, 1033
poetry, 1039
Polish students brought to USA, 1041
Progressive Brethren, 298, 972
Progressive Brethren support of, 67–68
reasons for attending, 2081
rejection of military training units, 1373
Salem College, 886
schism, 1152
seen as encouraged by Sunday schools, 1239
seminarians
self-perceptions of, 2096
students, study of, 2110
study abroad, 1274
survey of Brethren colleges, 1983
United Brethren in Christ, 1290
Zuck, Jacob Martin, 1400
collegia pietatis, 323
    Lutherans and Radical German Pietism, 1079
Collegiants, 82, 87, 175, **324**, 1865
    aid to Schwarzenau folk, 923
    Brethren recieving charity from, 777
    de Koker family, 1125
    Dutch, 2009
    Groningen, 1241, 1965, 1971
    Huizinga (Huisinga), Jacob Dircks, 635
    Koker family, 705
    Mack, Alexander, Sr., urged to perform adult baptism, 776
    monograph on, 2068
    Netherlands, 1229

Pauw, Adrian, 996
Polish Brethren, 1041
poor, caring for the, 1046
Colley, E. L., 1587
Colley, Ephraim family
    Ramey Flats Church of the Brethren, VA, 1083
Colley, Terry
    Medina, OH, Brethren Church, 2219
Collier, Glenn Forrest, Jr., 1587
Collier, Hudson
    Pineville, VA, Mount Olive Brethren Church, 1025
Collingridge, H. E., 1240
Collingridge, Herbert Edwin, Jr., 1587
Collings, Arthur, 1587
Collings, Arthur F., 1587
Collings, Benjamin, 1587
Collings, Bob, 1587
Collings, C. B., 1587
Collings, C. C., 1587
Collings, Edwin G., 1587
Collings, Henry, 1587
Collings, Jimmie, 1587
Collings, John C., 1587
Collings, S. S., 1587
Collings, William W., 1587
Collingsworth, Orrin, 1587
Collington family
    in Neosho Valley Old German Baptist Brethren Church near, 923
Collins, Arthur F., 362, 2300
    Reading Grace Brethren Church, PA, pastor, 1084
Collins, Benjamin F., III, 2275
Collins family
    French Broad Church of the Brethren, TN, 516
Collins, Floyd
    River City Grace Community Church, 1134
Collins, Garret
    Peach Blossom Colored Church of Rising Light (CB), MD, 1003
Collins, John A., 516
Collins, John W., 2275
Collins, Margaret, 2087
Collins, Ralph L., 305
Collins, Roberta
    River City Grace Community Church, 1134
Collins, Robin (later Naff), 2288
    Collinsville, VA, Church of the Brethren, 94, **324**
Collitt, Flo Mellick, 2166
Collitt, R. B.
    Roanoke, VA, First Brethren Church, pastor, 1113
Collitt, Robert B., 155, 579, 1587, **2166, 2300**
Collyer, Harry, 1587
Collyer, I. N.
    South Haven Brethren Church, KS, elder, 1205
Colman, Frank, 1322
Colombia, 182
    General Conference Mennonite Church, 536
    Ingraham, M. Virgil, 2208
    The Missionary Board (BC), 856
    missions, 862, 2224, 2225
    Peace Studies Institute, 1003
    Solomon, Kenneth LeRoy and

Jeannette Ruth DeLozier Solomon (BC) in, 2251
Colombia Co., WA
    migration of Brethren, 830
Colon, Argentina, Brethren Church
    South America Theological Seminary (BC) and, 2251
colonial America, *See under* specific states
    almanacs, 17–18
    bibliographical sources, 1860, 1926, 1981, 2005, 2026, 2325
    Brethren movement, 2066, 2100
    brotherhood issues, 2074
    charity school movements, 2092–2093
    church architecture in America during, 48
    devotional literature, 2074
    education issues, 2092–2093
    emigrants, German, 2106
    Ephrata Community, 2079
    German settlements, 2091
    Heiges, George L. on military hospitals in, 2336
    history of colonial Brethren in Pennsylvania, 1950
    Indian policies, 2089
    Indian policy in Pennsylvania during, 2089
    Mennonite Church, 2085
    Middle American colonies, 1999
    ministers of, 2093
    Moravians in, 2325
    music of Ephrata Community and, 2098
    mysticism in Pennsylvania during, 2074
    naturalization issues, 2105
    North Dakota Brethren settlement, 946
    Northern Pacific Railroad, 951
    printers, 2104
    Revolutionary War, *See* American Revolution
    Roeber, A. G[regg] on Brethren movement and, 2352
    social issues, 2085
    Zeiser, Samuel R. on mission of German Protestants in, 2365
colonization, 7, 14, 15, 54, 94, **324**, 2026, *See also* immigration agents; missions and missionaries
    Brethren movement, 324
    California, 238, 1143
    California Butte Valley Land Company, 236
    Canada, Brethren movement in, 250
    Church of the Brethren, 295, 299
    Church of the Brethren congregations, Canada, 250
    in Colfax Co., NM, 931
    Conejo, CA, Church of the Brethren, preaching point for, 331
    Cooperative Colonization Company, 342
    Cuba, 355
    Eshelman, Matthew Mays, 455
    Flory, Jacob S., 498
    frontier, 519
    Germany, 545
    Great Northern Railroad, 568–569
    Hadsell, B. A., 577
    Harrison, Stephen J., 586
    Hutchison, Andrew, 639
    McDonough, George L., 773

migration of Brethren, 829, 830
missions, 858
Montana Brethren settlement, 870
Mott, Charles W., 879
Neff, James Monroe as promotor of, 922
Nicholson, John, organization of Rosena, CA, 935
North Dakota, 251
Old German Baptist Brethren, 967
Oregon Short Line Railroad, 981
Peters, Amos B., 1011
place-names, Brethren, 1027–1028
Quinter, KS, 2014
railroads, 1082
railroads and, 177, 238
Santa Fe Railroad, 238
schisms, as cause for, 238
Southern Pacific Railroad, 238
Union Pacific Railroad, 238
Washington, 320
western U. S., 721–722, 2003
Colorado, *See* Camp Colorado
African American mission, 2128
blacks and Brethren movement, 377
Brethren movement in, 217
Church of the Brethren, 324
Church of the Brethren, history of, 1940
Frantz family, 1941
German Baptist Brethren, **324–325**
irrigation, 663
migration of Brethren, 830
"Mother of the Year" awards
Reyher, Mildred, 1345
Ullom, Rosalie, 1345
Old German Baptist Brethren congregations, 967
Colorado City, CO, Church of the Brethren, *See* Colorado Springs, CO, Church of the Brethren
Colorado Museum of Natural History
Nininger, Harvey Harlow, expert on meteorites, 938
Colorado Springs, CO, Church of the Brethren, **325**
Colorado Springs, CO, Grace Brethren Church, **325**, 377
Colossians
1:21–23, 55
2:12, 85
Kent, Homer Austin, Jr., 2211
Kent, Homer Austin, Jr. on, 2340
Martin, Harold S. on, 2345
Columbia (Brethren Church), **324**
Columbia City, IN, 153, 326
Church of the Brethren, **326** (2)
Columbia Furnace, VA, Church of the Brethren, *See* Woodstock Church of the Brethren, VA
Columbia Furnace, VA congregation, 1364
Columbia, MD, Oakland Mills Uniting Church (CB, UCC), **325–326**
Columbia, MO, Fellowship, **2166**
Columbia, NC, Church of the Brethren, *See* James River, ND, Church of the Brethren
Columbia River, WA
Hess, James Arthur, 2198
Columbia University
Brooklyn, NY, urban ministry, students from as pastors in, 933

Noffsinger, John Samuel, student in, 939
Columbiana (later Mahoning) Co., OH, 320, 712, 756, 1255, 1325, 1400
Brethren settlement in, 961
Evangelische Besuch, Der, 460
Friedensbote von Concordia, Der (The Peace Messenger of Concordia), 517
The Monthly Gospel Visiter (later *Visitor*), 961
Nicholson, John, minister in, 935
Reading Church of the Brethren, OH, 1084
Sandy German Baptist Brethren Church, OH, 1143
Zion Hill Church of the Brethren, *1167,* 2047
Columbus Brethren Student Fellowship
Columbus, OH, Church of the Brethren, 2372
Columbus Cooperative congregation, OH
example of Christian community place name, 911
Columbus, KS
New Hope Church of the Brethren, KS, 929
Columbus, OH, 145
Brethren Church, **326**
Church of the Brethren, **2372**
Co-operative Brethren (BC/CB), **326**
East Side Grace Brethren Church, *See* Blacklick, OH, East Side Grace Brethren Church of Columbus
Grace Brethren Church, 963, *See also* Worthington OH, Grace Brethren Church.
Jackson, Edward A., 2209
New Covenant Church of the Brethren, **2166**
Smoky Row Brethren Church, **2166**
Southwest Grace Brethren Church, **326**, 1380
Colusa Co., CA, 322
Elk Creek, CA, Church of the Brethren, 438
Colyn, Charles A. 1587
Salem Church of the Brethren, IA, 1137
Colyn, Esther Irving, 1909
Comanche Co., KS
Protection Church of the Brethren, KS, 1062
Comanche Co., OK
Harrison, OK, Church of the Brethren, 586
combat veterans, *See* veterans
combine harvester
Houser, Daniel, 633
Combs, Charles H, 1315, 1587–1588
Combs, Daniel O., 2275
Combs family, 318
Combs, Harold P., 553, 2275
Combs, J. W., 590, 1588
Piney Flats, TN, Church of the Brethren, providing leadership, 1025
Combs, Robert P., 145, 1221, 2275
Norton, OH, Grace Brethren Church, pastor, 951
Roanoke, VA, First Brethren Church, pastor, 1113
Combs, Roger Madison, 1588

Combs, Rosella J., 2275
Combs, Serena Belle (later Landrum), 724
Combs, T. W., 1588
Come and Worship, 2016
Comenius Faculty (Czech Brethren)
Prague Conferences and, 2239
Comenius, Johann Amos
Moravian Church, 875
religious liberty, 1098
Comer, Alfred C.
Newport Church of the Brethren, VA, pastor in, 934
Comer, Alfred Carleton, Jr., 1588
Comer, Charles Jennings, 1588
Comer, Joseph, 1588
Coming of Christ, *See* Second Coming
"The Coming of Jesus Christ" (Boger), 157
coming of the Holy Spirit, 695
Coming Together: Male and Female in a Renamed Garden (Johansen), 1979
Comisión Cristiana de Desarrollo (Christian Development Commission), Honduras, 2157
Comité Evangélico para Desarrollo y Emergencia Nacional (CEDEN)
Honduras, 627
comity agreements, **326**
Basel Mission, 296
India, 649
missions, 861
Portland, OR, Peace Church of the Brethren, 1048
Comly, J., 378
Comly, John, 1909
commandments, 2022
ethics, 457
Commentary on Romans (Barth), 922
commercialism and Easter, 416
Commission of Fifteen, 165, **326–327**
General Board, 535
Lear, John Wallace, 732
Commission of Stewardship
of National Council of Churches of Christ (NCCC), 915
Commission on Christian Education, 285
General Board (CB), 535
Commission on Christian Service (CB), *See* Brethren Service Commission
Commission on Christian Service (later Brethren Service Commission)
General Board (CB), 535
Commission on Christian Unity (American Baptist), 22
Commission on Faith and Order, National Council of Churches of Christ (NCCC), 915
Commission on Finance, *See* Finance Commission (CB)
Commission on Foreign Missions, 535, *See also* Foreign Mission Commission (CB)
Commission on Inter-Church Aid, Refugee and World Service of the WCC
Program Unit on Justice and Service
Inter-Church Aid and Service to Refugees, 657
Commission on International Understanding
Fasnacht, Harold Dale, 480
Commission on Ministry and Home Missions
General Board (CB), 535

Commission on Regional and Local Ecumenism, 1218
Council of Churches of Christ (NCCC), 915
commissioning of missionaries
    laying on of hands, 731
    commissioning services, **327**
    ordinances, 979
    ordination, 980
Committee for Relief and Reconstruction
    Goshen Conference, 559
Committee of Arrangements
    Eby, David Bowman, 418
    Financial Secretary of Annual Meeting (CB), 490
Committee of Observation, **327**, 1909
Committee of Reconstruction, *See* Ashland Convention
Committee of Twenty-Five (BC), *See Manual of Procedure* (BC); "Message of the Brethren Ministry" (BC)
    Kolb, William, Jr., 706
Committee on Civilian Service, 1372
Committee on Counsel for Conscientious Objectors, 169, **327**
Committee on District and Regional Organization and Realignment, *See* Continuing Committee on District and Regional Organization and Realignment (CB)
Committee on Dress Reform, **327**, 403
Committee on Education
    Gillin, John Lewis, 549
Committee on Evangelism and Organization
    General Mission Board (DB), 539
Committee on Fraternal Relations (CB), *See* Committee on Interchurch Relations (CB)
Committee on Health and Welfare, *See* Annual Conference (CB), Committee on Health and Welfare
    Peters, Raymond Russell, 1011
Committee on Health and Welfare (CB), **327**
Committee on Higher Education (CB), **327–328**
Committee on Homes for the Aging
    Grace Village Retirement Complex, 564
Committee on Interchurch Relations, **2166–2167**
    Baptism, Eucharist, and Ministry (BEM) text, 2133
    Row, W. Harold, 1126
Committee on Interchurch Relations (CB), **328**, *See also* Baptist Churches, USA; Consultation on Church Union; ecumenicism; fraternal relations
Committee on Interchurch Relations (Fraternal Relations, CB), 22
Committee on Pastorless Churches and Available Men
    placement of pastors in Grace Brethren, 1028
Committee on Resolutions (CB), **328**
Committee on Saving Our Children to the Church, **328**, 408
Committee on Understanding and Reconciliation, **328**
committees
    Brethren Church, 182

Fellowship of Grace Brethren Churches (FGBC), 484
common Brethren
    ministry, terminology, 848
common schools, *See* elementary education; elementary schools
Commonwealth of Independent States (CIS), *See* Russia
communal movements, 2031
    Amish Church, 2098
    Bruderhof movement, 2098
    Concordia community, 2099
    Doukhobors Church, 2098
    Ephrata Community, 1990, 2092, 2098
    Monteverde movement, 2098
    Oved, Yaacov on, 2349
    Pitzer, Donald E. on, 2350
    Shaker Church, 2098
    Stockwell, Foster on early, 2358
communication, *See* mass media
    Christian oration, 1992
    christian witness, 1990
    interpersonal, 1983
    publications facilitating, 1069
    radio, 1080, *1080*
Communication Commission
    of Council of Churches of Christ (NCCC), 915
communications
    Keller, Paul W., 2210
Communicorp
    works by, 2323
communion, **328**, 396, **459**, *See also* Lord's Supper; love feasts
    Baptism, Eucharist, and Ministry (BEM) text, 2133–2134
    bibliography, 1882, 1883
    Brethren Church doctrine on, 184–185
    Brethren Doctrine of Salvation, 1140
    Brush Creek, MO, Old German Baptist Brethren Church, 224
    Buffalo Valley, PA, Old German Baptist Brethren Church, 228
    caps and, 254
    Carson City, MI, congregation, 323
    Carson City, MI, Old German Baptist Brethren Church, 256
    Cedar Creek Grove, TN, Old German Baptist Brethren Church, 264
    children at, 2159
    church membership, 813
    Clifford-Mayville, ND, Old German Baptist Brethren Church, 321
    close communion, 297, 321, 394, 2103
    Coleman, MI, Old German Baptist Brethren Church, 323
    communion table, 328
    compared to love feast, 762, 764
    cooking, traditional, 341
    cups, *1095*
    Eucharist, 459
    Fairview Old German Baptist Brethren Church, KS, 470
    Far Western Brethren, 475
    feetwashing, 481
    Fellowship of Grace Brethren Churches (FGBC), 486, 2181–2182
    Flat Creek, KY, Church of the Brethren, *328*
    Flat Rock Old German Baptist Brethren Church, OH, 494
    Floyd Co., VA, 1326
    fraternity, 511

Freeling Settlement Old German Baptist Brethren Church, WV, 514
Gilbert Julia A., 548
God's Means of Grace (Yoder), 555
grape juice, 566
holy kiss in, 698
holy kiss used at, 698
Hoppingite Schism, 630
Howard Co. Old German Baptist Brethren Church, IN, 633
Iowa, 661
Leaf River Old German Baptist Brethren Church, 731
Limestone Old German Baptist Brethren Church, KS, 743
Lone Star Old German Baptist Brethren Church, KS, 753
Lord's supper, food at, 757–758
Mechanicsburg, PA, Dunkard Brethren Congregation, 806
North Solomon Old German Baptist Brethren Church, KS, 949–950
Old German Baptist Brethren, 967, 2233
ordinances, 976, *977,* 978–979, 979, 980
Peabody Old German Baptist Brethren Church, KS, held at, 997
Pleasant Hill Old German Baptist Brethren Church, IL, held at, 1033
Plum Creek Old German Baptist Brethren Church, KS, held at, 1038
Plymouth Brethren, 1038
preaching about, 1053
preparatory service for, 1056
Reformation, Protestant, and Brethren doctrine, 1092
Rockingham and Shenandoah Counties Old German Baptist Brethren Church, VA, held at, 1118
sacramentalism and, 28, 83, 84
St. Albany Old German Baptist Brethren Church, WV, 1134
Sandy Creek Old German Baptist Brethren Church, WV, 1143
second degree of ministry, 845
Shady Grove Old German Baptist Brethren Church, OH, 1170
Snake Valley Old German Baptist Brethren Church, PA, 1193
The Soul of Symbols (Shultz) and, 2249
sources on, 2311, 2323
South Solomon Old German Baptist Brethren Church, KS, 1206
Spring Creek, OK, Old German Baptist Brethren Church, 1213
Spring River, MO, Old German Baptist Brethren Church, 1214
Sugar Creek Old German Baptist Brethren Church, IL, 1234
Swedeland Valley Old German Baptist Brethren Church, WV, 1243
symbols in, 1246
tables, **328,** 474
tents used for, 1254
theology of, 2066
Thurian, Max on CB and, 2361
trine, and Leviticus, 1984
unleavened bread, 1293
Walnut Grove Dunkard Brethren Congregation, MD, 1316
weekly, and Restoration Movement,

1101

West Fulton Dunkard Brethren
Congregation, OH, 1334
Willow Springs Old German Baptist
Brethren Church, KS, 1346
wine, 16, 1251, 1252
women in, 1360
Women's Conferences (CB) and, 2265
Yellow River Old German Baptist
Brethren Church, IN, 1385
youth participation in, 1394
Communism, 1288
Brethren movement and, 2100
China, 277
The Christian Beacon and anti-
Communist movement, 281
Eby, Kermit, 420
fundamentalism, 522
mission work, 299–300
missions, 2225
Vietnam War, 286
communitarian socialism, 1198, 1876
communitarians and communitarian
societies, **328–329**, *See also*
Ephrata Community
Concordia, 1255
Harmony Society, 584
Hutterian Brethren, 639
Kelpius or Kelp, Johannes, 686–687
Kurtz, Henry, 711
New Harmony, IN, 928
Sala, Solomon, 1136
Teutonia (OH), 1255
Zimmerman, Johann Jakob, 686
community, **329–330**, 2025
American, 1965
Gemeinde, Gemeinschaft, 534
group life of the church, 2013
Miller, Robert R. on, 2347
redemptive, and Priesthood of All
Believers, 1057
religious, survey of, 1978
Community Alternatives in Criminal Justice
State College, PA, University
Baptist and Brethren Church, 1218
Community Church, IL, 2111
Community Grace Brethren Church, La
Mirada, CA, 713
Community Ministry Center
organized with help of Natrona Heights
Church of the Brethren, 918
Community Mission Church of the Breth-
ren, VA, **330**
community of believers
importance of Bible study, 134
Community of Goods, *See* communitarian-
ism
community of goods
Plow Creek Fellowship, 1038
Community of True Inspiration (Amana),
57, 68, 112, 132, 175, 280, 330,
330–331, 370, 1148, 2062, *See
also Grund Forschende Fragen*
(Basic Questions) (Gruber)
as a source for Beissel's ideas, 113
Brethren movement, 378
Camisards, 242
Christ's Assembly and, 280
Geistreiches Gesang-Buch (*Spiritual
Songbook*)*,* 534
Goebel, Max, 555
Gross, Andreas, 574
Gruber, Eberhard Ludwig, 575

Gruber, Johann Adam, 575
historical writing, 611
Holy Spirit, doctrine of, 624
hymns, 2328
Mack, Alexander, Sr., debating leader
of, 776
Marienborn, and religious freedom,
792
music of, 1935
Neumann, Gottfried at, 924
Old German Baptist Brethren and
charismatic movement, 970
Parsons, Johanna Christina Zeidig, 994
prayer, 1051
prophecy, 1062
Radical German Pietism, 1080
Rock, Johann Friedrich, 1116
Ronneburg Castle, use of, 1121
Schneider, Ulf-Michael on, 2355
theology of love, 761
community orientation
Seattle, WA, churches, 1162
community outreach
Elkhart, IN, City Church of the Breth-
ren, 439
Elkhart, IN, Southside Fellowship
(CB/Menn), 439
Elkton Immanuel Church of the
Brethren, MD, 440
Ephrata, PA, Church of the Brethren,
448
Fairview Church of the Brethren, MD,
469
Flat Creek Church of the Brethren, KY,
493
Fort Wayne, IN, Beacon Heights
Church of the Brethren, 503
Freeport, IL, Church of the Brethren,
515
Goshen, IN, City Church of the Breth-
ren, 557
Community Playthings
Hutterian Society of Brothers, 641
community programs
Philadelphia, PA, Bethany Church of
the Brethren, 1015
Portland, OR, Peace Church of the
Brethren, 1048
Redford, MI, Trinity Church of the
Brethren, 1090
Redondo Beach, CA, South Bay
Community Church of the Breth-
ren, 1090
Ridgeway Community Church of the
Brethren, PA, 1109
Roanoke, VA, Central Church of the
Brethren, 1112
Rocky Ford, CO, Church of the
Brethren, 1118
Community Relations programs (AFSC),
23
community service
Flower Hill Church of the Brethren,
MD, 500
Garbers Church of the Brethren, VA,
530
Germantown, 544
Lancaster, PA, Alfa y Omega (Alpha
and Omega) Church of the
Brethren, 2213–2214
Miller, Mary Grace Hileman, 841
Mission One (CB), 853
Montgomery, IL, Boulder Hill Neigh-

borhood Church of the Brethren,
872
mutual aid, 901
Community United Church of the Brethren,
PA, *See* Erie, Pennsylvania, Com-
munity United Church (CB/UCC)
commutation tax
Civil War, 311, 314, **331**
Civil War and, 149
peace position during Civil War, 999
WWI, 301
compensation for property lost during
the Revolutionary War, 1147
*The Complete Writings of Alexander
Mack* (Eberly), 2143
Compton, CA, Brethren Church, *See*
Bellflower, CA, Brethren Church
(FGBC)
Compton, Carol, 1845
Compton family
Pataskala, OH, Grace Brethren Church
of Licking Co., 995
Compton First Brethren Church, CA, 755
computers, 2188
Dunkard Brethren Church and, 2174
information technology, church use of,
2207–2208
mass media, uses of, 2218
Old German Baptist Brethren and,
2178
Comstock family
Mabton, WA, Grace Brethren Church,
771
Conaway, Mrs. Raymond
Mount Olivet Brethren Church, DE,
886
Conaway, Raymond
Mount Olivet Brethren Church, DE,
886
Concerns of the Grass Roots
evangelicalism and, 2179
"Concerns of the Grassroots" movement,
See Grassroots, Concerns of
conciliation/reconciliation/service
Bonsack, Charles Daniel, 160–161
Concord
Mennonites, 707
Concord, IL, Church of the Brethren, **331,**
331, 740
Concord, VA, Church of the Brethren, **331**
Mount Vernon Church of the Brethren,
VA, 887
concordances, 331, **331**
Concordia, **331**
communitarianism, 329
Friedensbote von Concordia, Der (The
Peace Messenger of Concordia),
517
Concordia (communitarian society), 1255
Concordia community, 2099
Condensed Lectures on Eschatology
(Myers), 905
conditional security, *See* Eternal Security
Condo, Marion, 1588
Condry, D. B., 1588
Cone, George, 360
Cone, George E., 1285
Portis, KS, Grace Brethren Church,
pastor, 1048
Cone, George Edward, Jr., 1588, 1848
Cone, George Edward, Sr., 1285, 1588,
2300
Cone, Ruth Ann Adams, 1848

Conejo, CA, Church of the Brethren, **331**, 348

Conemaugh, PA, congregations, 236, 331, 332, 466, 752, 1916
   Church of the Brethren, **331–332**
   First Brethren Church, 332
   Johnstown, PA, First Brethren Church, 673
   Johnstown, PA, Pike Grace Brethren Church, 674
   Grace Brethren Church, **332**
   Johnstown, PA, First Brethren Church, 674
   Johnstown, PA, Roxbury Church of the Brethren, 674
   Johnstown, PA, Walnut Grove Church of the Brethren, 675
   Mineral Point, PA, Vinco Brethren Church, 843
   Old Conemaugh, PA, congregation, 331
   Shade Creek Church of the Brethren, PA, organized from, 1170
   Singer Hill Grace Brethren Church, *See* Singer Hill, PA, Grace Brethren Church

Conestoga Creek, PA, 158

Conestoga Crosswoods, PA, 2103

Conestoga, PA, 108, 158, 175, 177, 225, 332, **332**, 383, 400, 430, 704, 722, 726, 737, 756, 767, 1224, 1278, 1340, 1355
   Church of the Brethren, 1909, 2095, *See also* Leola, PA, Conestoga Church of the Brethren
   Ephrata Community, 448
   Ephrata, PA, Church of the Brethren, 448
   German Seventh-Day Baptists, 542
   history, 2008
   Middle Creek Church of the Brethren, PA, 825
   Mohler Church of the Brethren, PA, 868
   Spring Grove Church of the Brethren organized from, 1213

Conestoga wagons
   Pennsylvania Germans, 1007

Conewago, PA, congregations, 216, 332, 362, 383, 1312
   Church of the Brethren, **332–333**
   Hershey, PA, Spring Creek Church of the Brethren, 599

Confederacy, **333**
   Jackson, Thomas Jonathan "Stonewall," 667
   peace position during Civil War, 999
   recognition by the British, 41

Confederate Congress
   petition for military exemption by Wrightsman, Peter R., 1380

conference centers
   Winona Lake, IN, 1351, *1352,* 1353

Conference News, 927

Conference of Historic Peace Churches, **333**

Conference Peace Committee (BC)
   National Associaton of Evangelicals (NAE), 2179

conference proceedings
   verbatim minutes, 1303

Conference Program Committee (CB), **333**

conferences, *See* Annual Meetings, 1903

songs for, 2084

Two Centuries of the Church of the Brethren, 1282

Conferences of Pacifist Churches
   Historic Peace Churches, 608

confession of faith, 5, **333**
   in anointing, 39
   Eyman, Peter, 464
   Gleim's treatise on, 464

confession of sins, 3, **333**
   Ephrata Community, 448
   German Seventh-Day Baptists, 542
   God's Means of Grace (Yoder), 555
   in anointing. 39
   preparatory service for communion, 1056
   public, and Old German Baptist Brethren, 967

The Confessions of Tom Harris, 626

confirmation, 5, **333–334**, *See also* confession of faith; "message of the Brethren ministry"
   in the Brethren Church, 85
   Declaration of Principles, 372
   doctrine on, 185
   Holy Spirit, doctrine of, 624
   "Message of the Brethren Ministry," 818

confiscation of goods, **334**, *See also* persecution
   Brethren and Revolutionary War, American, 1106
   Sauer, Christopher, II, for treason, 1146

conflict
   Brethren rural churches, 1130
   family, 474
   Historic Peace Churches, 608
   Holsinger, Henry Ritz, 621
   Homestead Church of the Brethren, MI, 626
   Hope Church of the Brethren, MI, 629
   Hoyt, Herman Arthur, 634

conflict resolution, Dunkard Brethren, 409

conformity to the world, *See* nonconformity; Order of the Brethren

Confucianism, **334**

Congregation of God in the Spirit, 309, **334**, *See also* Pennsylvania synods
   bibliography, 1909
   Frey, Andreas, 517

congregational autonomy, *See* polity

Congregational Baptist Brethren, *See* Congregational Brethren

Congregational Brethren, 67, **334–335**, 368, 1308, 1909
   Cadwallader, John, 237
   chart of Brethren bodies, place on, 1403–1405
   on choice of legal name for denomination, 910
   confirmation, 333–334
   as denominational name, 910
   Dieter (Deeter, Teeter) family, 384
   Dunlap(s), IN, Brethren Church, 410
   Far Western Brethren, 476
   feetwashing, 481
   feetwashing mode, 1186
   fellowships, Kansas, 682
   Fraternal Relations Committees (BC), 511
   Gibson, Isham, 548
   Gospel Messenger, The (1881–1883), 559

Gospel Trumpet, The, 561
   Hendricks, Franklin A., 596, 597
   Hoppingite Schism, 630
   Missouri, 864
   Myers, Jonathan, 904
   naming of, 910
   Philadelphian Society, 1019
   Pleasant Grove Grace Brethren Church, IA, 1031
   Pleasant Hill, OH, First Brethren Church, 1032
   Progressive Brethren joining with, 186
   Roann, IN, (First) Brethren Church, 1112
   Swihart, Jonathan H., 1245
   union with Thurmites, 1264
   Virginia, 166
   Wolfe, George, III, 1358

Congregational Brethren of Pleasant Hill, OH, **335**
   chart of Brethren bodies, place on, 1403–1405
   Church in Pleasant Hill, 237

Congregational Christian Church, La Motte Prairie Federated Church of the Brethren, IL, 713

Congregational Christian Churches, General Council
   United Church of Christ formed from, 1290

Congregational Church
   in Canada, 15
   Coolville, OH, 342
   missions in China, 296
   New Haven, CN, 710
   Pietism, 1022
   Pleasant Hill, OH, First Brethren Church, former name of, 1032
   Sunnyside, WA, Grace Brethren Church, 1240

congregational histories, bibliography of, 1857

congregational life-style of Brethren rural churches, 1130

Congregational Ministries Council (BC), 2141

congregational polity, *See* polity

congregational training programs, 2160

congregationalism, *See* polity
   Calvinism and, 240

Congregationalists, 87
   Dowie, John Alexander, 398

congregations
   church membership, 813
   code of ethics, 2178
   division of
      St. Joseph, MO, 1135
      Shiloh Church of the Brethren, WV, 1177
   geographical listings of, 1479–1503

Congress of Industrial Organizations (CIO)
   Eby, Kermit, 419

Congress, OH, 215

Congresses on Prophecy
   Hoyt, Herman Arthur, 634

Coning, Daniel M., 102, 1588

Coning, Eliza (later Miller)
   Miller, Donald Eugene, 2222

Coning, Harvey M., 1588

Coning, Jesse, 430
   North Manchester Old German Baptist Brethren Church, IN, elder-in-charge, 949

Coning, Jesse M., 1588
Coning, Melvin G.
    Old Brethren minister, 965
Coning, Raymond E., 1588, 2300, **2381**
    Prices Creek Old German Baptist
        Brethren Church, OH, elder or
        minister,1057
Coning, Walter A., 1909–1910
Coning, William H., 350, 1588, 1910
    Oak Grove Old German Baptist
        Brethren Church, OH, minister,
        956
    Pine Grove Old German Baptist
        Brethren Church, FL, minister,
        1024
    The Trumpet Call, 1277
Conkle, Peter, 1588
Conley, Dewey
    Sinking Spring, OH, Grace Brethren
        Church, pastor, 1186
Conley, Lafayette, 1588
Conn, Barry L., 2275
Connecticut, **335**
Connecticut Council of Churches
    Miller, Joseph Quinter, 841
Connell, A. J.
    North Georgetown, OH, Brethren
        Church, 948
Connell, B. F., 1588
Connell family, 211
Connell, Ivan A., 1588
Connell, J. C., 553
Connellsville, PA, 1364
    Church of the Brethren, **335**
Conner, Abraham L.
    Manassas, VA, Church of the Brethren,
        elder, 785
Conner, Alva L., 527, 586, 721, 1588
    Santa Maria, CA, Grace Brethren
        Church, pastor in, 1145
Conner, Alvin E., 1910
    works by, 2323
Conner (Connor), William Kinsel, 1588
Conner family, 740
    Roanoke, VA, Washington Heights
        Grace Brethren Church, 1114
Conner, Isaac L., 1588
Conner, Jacob L., 1588
Conner, Jesse
    Blough, Anna on descendants of, 2363
    Williams, Anna Blough on descen-
        dants of, 2363
Conner, Mary (later Ziegler), 1395
Conner, Paul
    works by, 2323
Conner, Robert
    Mount Union (Airpoint) Church of the
        Brethren, VA, trustee, 887
Conner, W. K., 553
Conneway family
    Fairview Church of the Brethren, MD,
        468
Connor, A., 1588
Connor, Abraham, 1588
Connor, Jacob L., 1588
Connor, William K., 1910
Conococheague, MD/PA
    Church of the Brethren, *See* Antietam
        (Prices) Church of the Brethren,
        PA
    German Seventh-Day Baptist congre-
        gation, *See* Snow Hill Community
Conover, Norman Alvin, 683, 1588

Conrad, 236
Conrad, Daniel, 2105
Conrad family, 2108
Conrad, John Stephen, Jr.
    Meyer family, 822
Conrad, Mary Margaret Moyer
    Meyer family, 822
Conrad, Thomas W., 2275
    Winning the Race Ministries and, 2262
Conrad, Tiona
    Winning the Race Ministries and, 2262
Conrad, W. P., 1910
Conradi, Ludwig Richard, 1910
Conry, Goldie, 1588
    conscience
        Miller, Donald Eugene, 2223
        Petersen, Barthold Jurgen, and career
            as soldier, 1012
        religious liberty, 1098
conscientious objection, **335–337,**
        1995, 2046, *See also* alternative
        service; conscription; nonresis
        tance; pacifism; peace
    "A Short and Sincere Declaration,"
        1178
    Advisory Committee, *See* Brethren
        Advisory Committee for Conscien-
        tious Objectors
    AFSC involvement with, 23–24
    and agricultural college units, 9
    alternate service, 202
    and alternative service, 19–20, 91
    alternative service due to, *See* alterna-
        tive service
    amnesty for, 26
    and Baker, Newton D., 78
    Bible sanctions for war, 2070
    bibliography, 1910
    book about, 1941
    Brown, Dale Weaver, 2152
    BSC projects, 199
    in Canada, 15
    census, 267
    Cérésole, Pierre, 1365, 1367
    chaplaincy, 271
    Chicago C. O. Conference of Nov. 15,
        1941, 2110
    China, 261
    Church of the Brethren, 269, 301, 2178
        religious issues, and statements on,
        2107
    Churches of God (GC), 309
    Civil War, 149, 261, 2104
    Civil War, military substitutes,
        1233–1234
    Civilian Conservation Corps (CCC),
        315
    Civilian Public Service (CPS), 312,
        315–316, 1372, 2097
    conservation movement, 338
    conservation work, 1372
    control patients in medical experi-
        ments, 1372
    CPS, *See* Civilian Public Service
    criticism of, 24
    Dairy Farm Assignments, 359
    detached programs, 380
    doctrine and, 2082
    dress of, 403
    Dunkard Brethren Church
        religious issues, and statements on,
        2107
    Dunkards, 2010

Edwards, Chandler S., 429
Eller, Cynthia Lorraine on World War
    II, 2329
Eller, Enten, 2176–2177
ethics, 458
Evangelical Covenant Church, 459
Fast Henry A., 480
Filbrun, Stanley Clarence, 2184
fraternal relations, 510
French, Paul Comly, 515
Freundschaftsheim (Friendship House),
    517
Germantown, 542
Goshen Conference, 559
Graybill, Jonas, 567
Greiner, Robert G., 2194
Hershey, Lewis Blaine, 599
Hess, Maurice Abram, 601
Historic Peace Churches (HPC), 301,
    608, 1371–1372, 1990
historiography, 2201
Hoover, Paul on, 2337
Illinois, 647
Indiana, 1966
International Voluntary Services
    Agency (IVS), 660
Kahler, Dean, 1306
Karlsschule group, *684*
Korean War, 707
lobbying by Church of the Brethren,
    391
Mason, George Edward, 2218
medical missions, 807
medical projects, 808
medicine as alternative, 810
Mennonite Church, 269, 316, 815
mental hospital service, 816, *817*
military service, 831, 2067
Minnesota Starvation Project, *849*
missions, 861
motion pictures, 879
Murphy, Ross Dale, 897
Murray, Don, 625
National Interreligious Service Board
    for Conscientious Objectors, 1290,
    1291
naturalization and refusal of loyalty
    oath, 918
non-associators in Revolutionary War,
    939
Old German Baptist Brethren, 1000,
    2107, 2349
origins of movement, 1262
other religious groups practicing, 68,
    69
Peace Corps, 1002
peace education, 1002
peace position during Civil War, 999
peace position during World War I,
    1000
Pennsylvania Brethren and military
    service, 1004
Petersburg, WV, Memorial Church of
    the Brethren, 1012
Plaster, David R. on, 2350
Puerto Rico, 1070
relief training units, 1097
religious freedom and persecution,
    1009
religious issues, and statements on
    Church of the Brethren, 2107
    Dunkard Brethren Church, 2107
    Old German Baptist Brethren

Church, 2107
religious liberty and military service, 1098
review board perspective, 1983
Revolutionary War, 176
Robinson, Mitchell on World War II and, 2352
Roosevelt, Franklin Delano, 1122
San Francisco, CA, 2089
schism and, 1153
schoolmaster from Vaud, 1365
Schwalm, E. J. on World War I and II and, 2355
Selective Service System, 1165
Service Committee, 1169
Seventh-Day Adventists, 1169–1170
A Short and Sincere Declaration, 176, 310, 312, 1178–1179, 1993, 2064
Sisters and Brother, Inc. and World War II, 2356–2357
Skiles, Jacob W., 1188–1189, 2068
social action, 1196
social backgrounds of, 2108
Society of Friends, 269, 316
sources on, 2313–2314, 2318, 2324
Stafford, William Edgar, 1216
Stein, John William, 1220
Studebaker, Ted Allen, 1230
substitutes and, 149
Swigart, William Joseph, 1245
taxes, refusal to pay, 1248–1249
Taylor, Isaac W., 1249
Torreon Navajo Mission, staff at, 1268
Twenty Thousand Dunkers for Peace, 1281
United Church of Christ, 1290
United Methodist Church, 1291
Van Dyck, Harry R. on World War II and, 2361
Vietnamese War, 1305
volunteers, Ecuador, 422
war bonds, recommendation not to purchase, 1318
War of 1812, 1318
Washington Office (CB) and, 2260
Weimer family, 1327
West, Daniel, 1331
Wilhelm, Paul A. on World War II and, 2363
Wilson, Edward Raymond, 1347
World War I, 1365, 1367, 1370, 2068
World War I, confined at Camp Funston, KS, 921
World War II, 312, 1371–1372, 2068, 2089, 2108, 2111
Wrightsman, Peter R., 1380
Zigler, Michael Robert, 1398
conscription, 19–20, 78, *See also* alternative service; conscientious objection
amnesty from, 26
avoidance of, and prisons, 1059
draft counseling, 22
ethics, 458
first peacetime, 19
military recruitment, 831
Miller Leslie on World War II and, 2347
ministerial exemption, 844
Moomaw, Benjamin Franklin, 873
noncooperation with, 19, 20
World War I, 1370
Consecration of Children, *See* Dedication of Infants

Consejo Nacional (National Council), Argentina
Di Naardo, Juan, 382
consensus, **337**
Annual Meeting, 1044
Annual Meetings and Brethren polity, 1042
Brethren movement, 294
building, and Brethren rural churches, 1130
changes from, 178
community, 329
Darst, John Charles, 363
election of church officers, 434
humility, 636
Hutterian Society of Brothers, 641
majority vote as replaced by, 401
Old Order Fellowships, 971
Plow Creek Fellowship, 1038
Reba Place Fellowship, 1084
consensus, decision by, 33, 37
conservation movement, **337–338**, *See also* environmental issues
conscientious objectors, 1372
conservatism, 2104
Conservative Baptist Brethren Church, **2167**
Brethren Encyclopedia, Inc., 2143
mission statement, 2148
Conservative Brethren Church, 1910, **2167**
Conservative Brethren Church, PA, **338**
Conservative Brethren Church, VA, **338**
conservative doctrine of Pennsylvania Dunkard and Old Order Brethren, 1005
Conservative German Baptist Brethren, **338**
chart of Brethren bodies, place on, 1403–1405
Conservative Grace Brethren Association
Whitcomb, John Clement, Jr. (FGBC, CGBCI) and, 2262
Conservative Grace Brethren Churches International Fellowship, **2167–2168**
abortion, 2127
annointing, 2130
Boyer, James L., 2139
formation of, 2182
information technology, church use of, 2208
logo, *2168*
Mansfield, OH, Conservative Grace Brethren Church, 2217
mass media, uses of, 2218
membership trends 1980 to 2000, 2220
missions, short-term, 2226
musical instruments, 2228
sources on, 2320
Theological Practorium, The (CBBCI), 2254
theology and, 2254, 2255
urban ministry and, 2257
Zielasko, John Warlow (FGBC, CGBCI) and, 2270
The Conservative Grace Brethren Publications, 2168
conservative movement, *See* Old Order movement
conservatives, *See* Church of the Brethren
consistories
Established Churches, 456
Reformed Church, *See* Reformed Church consistory

Consortium for Peace Research, Education, and Development
Peace Studies Institute, 1003
constables, *See* police
Constance, KY, Church of the Brethren, **338**
Constantine I (the Great), emperor, 292, 296
noncreedalism, 942
oaths, taking of, 959
Orthodox Church, 983
peace in Christian church history, 998
Constantinianism, 292
Constitution, U.S.
Amendments to, 1
anti-constitution positions, 22
Eighteenth Amendment, *See* Eighteenth Amendment
Equal Rights Amendment, *See* Equal Rights Amendment
Fifteenth Amendment, 1
First Amendment and conscientious objectors, 336
Fourteenth Amendment, 1
separation of church and state, 88, 113
Thirteenth Amendment, 1
construction, *See* architecture
Consultation on Church Union (COCU), 303–304, **338**, 1872, *See also* ecumenism; Interchurch Relations Committee
Consultative Council of the National Service Board for Religious Objectors, *See* National Interreligious Service Board for Conscientious Objectors
contemplation
Sojourners Fellowship, 1200
continence
Ephrata Community, 448
Mack, Alexander, Sr., on, 776
marital, 776
sexual relations and, **338**
Continental Congress
Ephrata Press, 452
Continental money, **338**
Continuation Committee of the Historic Peace Churches, **339**, 608, 610, *See also* historic peace churches
Continuing Committee on District and Regional Organization and Realignment (CB), 339, **339**
control patients, *See* Brethren Voluntary Service (BVS); Civilian Public Service (CPS); Medical Projects (BSC); Minnesota Starvation Project
research experiments, 810
controversy
division and, 183
feetwashing, 364
Hummer, Catherine, 636
conventicles, 48
Lutherans and Radical German Pietism, 1079
Pietism, 1021
conversion, **339–340**, 2020
Brethren Church, 184
Brethren doctrine of salvation and "flow" of, 1140
church membership, 813
Church of the Brethren, 328

Finney, Charles G.'s "New Measures" revivalism, 930–931
Fredonia, KS, Church of the Brethren, 513
handbook of religious, 2071
Holy Spirit, doctrine of, 624
Lincoln, Abraham, 2084
narratives
    Sider, E. Morris on Anabaptists and, 2356
    Sider, E. Morris on Pietists and, 2356
oaths, taking of, 959
order of dress for converts, 403
repentance, doctrine of, 1099
Conway, KS, 736
Conway Springs, KS, **340**, 1354
Conwell, Russell
    Brumbaugh, Martin Grove and, 223
Conyngham, Redmond, 1910
Cook, A. L., 705, 1588
Cook, Alvin Chester, 705, 1588
Cook, Amos, 705, 1588
Cook, Arthur L., 430, 705, 1588
Cook, Catherine, 340
Cook Co. Hospital, 123
Cook, Daniel Anthony, 62, 1588
    Old Order German Baptist Church minister, 972
Cook, Delbert J., 705, 1588
Cook, E. G., 1588
Cook, E. M., 521
Cook, Elizabeth, 357
Cook, Emery Elza, 430, 1588
Cook family, **704–705**, 2060, *See also* Koch family
    Nevada, MO, Church of the Brethren, 924
Cook, Glen A., 2275
Cook, H. M., 705, 1588
Cook, Harry D., 109, 1558, 2300, **2381**
Cook, Henry, 705, 1588
Cook, Henry (OGBB), 705
Cook, Hezekiah, 1588
Cook, J. Albert, 157, 1588
Cook, J. J., 1235
Cook, James, 319
Cook, James A., 360
Cook, James S., 705, 708, 1281, 1305, 1588
    Martinsburg, PA, Grace Brethren Church, pastor, 798
    Portis, KS, Grace Brethren Church, pastor, 1048
Cook, Jesse J., 705, 1588
Cook, John W., 340
Cook, Joseph Clay, 705, 1588
Cook, L. Arthur, 1588
Cook, Lester, 705, 1270, 1588
Cook, Marvin, 1588
Cook, Mary, 705
Cook, Mary L., 115, **340**, *340,* 399, 1588
Cook, Milton C., 137, 1354, 1588, 2175
Cook, Nicholas L., 1588
Cook, Oliver Wayne, 1588, 2300
Cook, Opal, 296
Cook, Philip Lee, 1910
Cook, Roy D., 1588
Cook, S. K., 705, 1588
Cook, Sampson G., 705, 1588
Cook, W. E., 1588
Cook, William G., 40, 705, 1588–1589
cookbooks in Pennsylvania German tradition, **340–341**

Cooke Co., TX, 1232, 1255, 1346
    migration of Brethren, 830
Cooke, Jay
    Northern Pacific Railroad, 951
Cooke, Margaret A., 274, 1589
cooking
    German influence, 2147
    The Inglenook Cook Book, 1978
Cooks Creek, VA, Church of the Brethren, 168, 206, 264, **341–342**, 367, 1236, 2044
    Flat Rock Church of the Brethren, VA, 493
    Flory, John, 498
    Garbers Church of the Brethren, VA, 530
    Harrisonburg, VA, First Church of the Brethren, 586
    Mill Creek Church of the Brethren, VA, 832
    Smith Creek Fellowship Church of the Brethren, WV, 1191
Cooksey, David, 1589
Cookson family, 142
Cool, A. S., 1589
    Mount Hebron Church of the Brethren, WV, pastor, 881
Cool, Edward, 1589
Cool, Ezra, 1223, 1589
    Modesto, CA, South Modesto Community Church of the Brethren, 867
    Shady Grove Old German Baptist Brethren Church, OH, minister in, 1171
Cool family, Rockingham and Shenandoah Counties, Old German Baptist Brethren Church, VA, 1118
Cool, Isaac B., 1589
    Painter Creek Old German Baptist Brethren Church, OH, 990
Cool, Isaac H., 1589
    Painter Creek Old German Baptist Brethren Church, OH, 990
Cool, J. L., 1589
Cool, Jonathan B., 1589
    Palestine Old German Baptist Brethren Church, OH, 991
Cool, Martin Van Buren, 1589
    Oak Grove Old German Baptist Brethren Church, OH, minister, 956
Cool, Mary
    Modesto, CA, South Modesto Community Church of the Brethren, 867
Cool, Newton David, 1589
Cool, Noah I., 1589
    Pleasant View Church of the Brethren, OH, minister, 1037
Cool, Omar S., 1589, 1910, 2300, **2381**
    Painter Creek Old German Baptist Brethren Church, OH, 990
    works by, 2323
Cool, P. N., 1589
Cool Spring meetinghouse
    Ladoga, IN, Church of the Brethren, 717
Cooley family, 1956
Coolville, OH, Grace Brethren Church, **342**
Coon Creek, IA, congregation
    Maxwell, IA, Church of the Brethren, 803
Coon, J. W., 1589

Coon River, IA
    Church of the Brethren, *See* Panora, IA, Church of the Brethren
    Dunkard Brethren congregation, **342**, 360
Coon River, LA, Church of the Brethren, *See* Panora, IL, Church of the Brethren
Coon, William, Jr.
    San Jose, CA, South Bay Community Church (FGBC), 1142
Cooney, Mae, family
    North Beatrice Church of the Brethren, NE, 945
Cooper family, 461
    Pataskala, OH, Grace Brethren Church of Licking Co., 995
Cooper, Gale
    Romine Church of the Brethren, IL, providing leadership, 1121
Cooper, Herbert Austin, **342**, 535, 1589, 1910, 1918, 2300, 2384
    historical writing, 612
    Pipe Creek Church of the Brethren, MD, minister, 1026
    Two Centuries of Brothersvalley, 342
    works by, 2323
Cooper, James Otes, 1589
Cooper, James "Otis," 1385
Cooper, Leslie Ernest, 2275
Cooper, Lillie Orrison, 342
Cooper, Mary Rohrbough, 584
Cooper, Mason, 65, 350, 1589
    Martinsburg, WV, Rosemont Grace Brethren Church, pastor, 798
Cooper, Scott, 2275
    Rockwood Church of the Brethren, PA, supply pastor (full-time), 1118
Cooperative Brethren Church, Terra Alta, WV, 1254
Cooperative Colonization Company, **342**, 722
Cooperative Curriculum Project, 284, 1236
Cooperative Disaster Child Care, 2171, 2172, *See also* Disaster Child Care
Cooperative for American Relief Everywhere (CARE), 342
Cooperative for American Remittances to Everywhere (CARE) 342
Cooperative for American Remittances to Europe (CARE), 23, **342**
    French, Paul Comly, 515
    relief and service efforts, 1097
    Zigler, Michael Robert, 1398
cooperatives, **342–343**, *See also* credit unions; missions and missionaries; mutual aid
    Chinese industrial cooperatives, 277
    ethics of, 458
    Wine, David Glick, 1349
Cooperider, Orpha P., 2088
Cooperrider, Mr. and Mrs. Irvin
    Newark, OH, Brethren Church, as minister, 933
Coopersburg, PA, 1216
Coos Co., OR
    Barklow family, 980
    Myrtle Point Old German Baptist Brethren Church, OR, 906
Coover, A. B., 1589
Coover family, 322, *See also* Cober family
Coover, J. C., 322, 1589

Coover, Mary (later Gipe), 2027
Coover, Melancthon, 1910
Coover, Paul Hartman, 1589
Cope family
    Haddix, KY, Brethren Church, 577
Cope, Hattie Louise (later Sheldon), 136,
    1853, See also Sheldon, Hattie
    Louise Cope
Cope, Paul R., 596
Copeland, C. E., 320
Copeland, Denzil F., 1589
Copeland family, 1866
Copenhagen, Denmark, 280, 1256
Copenhaver, William A., 1589, 2300
    Redford, MI, Trinity Church of the
        Brethren, pastoral leadership, 1090
Copp family
    Reliance, VA, Mount Zion Brethren
        Church, 1096
Copp, George A., 356, 1228, 1338, 1589
    Mount Pleasant Brethren Church, VA,
        minister, 886
    Maurertown, VA, Brethren Church, 803
    Reliance, VA, Mount Zion Brethren
        Church, pastor, 1096
Copp, Jeffrey O., 1589
Copp, Zed H., 271, **343**, 366, 578, 1281,
    1589
    Saturday worship, belief in, 1133
Copper Creek meetinghouse, Santa Fe
    Church of the Brethren, IN, 1144
Copper Hill, VA, congregations, 1224
    Church of the Brethren, **343**
    Mount Union (Airpoint) Church of the
        Brethren, VA, 887
    Old German Baptist Brethren Church,
        See Stonewall, VA, Old German
        Baptist Brethren Church
    Peters Creek Church of the Brethren,
        daughter congregation, 1011
Coppernoll, Sue, 2275
Coppert family
    Salem Church of the Brethren, OH,
        1138
Coppess, Josiah, 1589
Coppinger, Joe K., 1589
    Phoenix, AZ, Grace Brethren Church,
        pastor, 1019
Coppock, Claude V., 343, 1589
Coppock (Cobbs), Aaron, 1865
Coppock (Cobbs), Amy, 1865
Coppock, Delaney Blickenstaff, 343
Coppock, Elias, 343
Coppock, Elizabeth, 343
Coppock, Ethel Oaks, 343
Coppock family, **343**
Coppock, Fern E. (later Walker), 1314
Coppock, Gertrude Metzler, 343
Coppock, Harley M., 124, 343, 1589
    Pueblo, CO, Church of the Brethren,
        pastor and elder, 1070
Coppock, Hazel (later Sollenberger), 1845,
    See Sollenberger, Hazel Coppock
    article about, 1927
Coppock, Jacob, **343**, 365, 1589
Coppock, John W., 343
Coppock, Martha Evans, 343, *571*
Coppock, Mary Heikes, 343
Coppock, Mary Martindale, 343
Coppock, Moses, 343
Coppock, Nannie (later Flory), 499
Coppock, Olive Pearson, 343
Coppock, Samuel, 343, 1265, 1589

Coppock, Susan Studebaker, 343
Coppock, Xury Landon, 343, *571, 735*,
    1589
    biography, 1962
Copp's Chapel Brethren Church,
    Rappahannock, VA, See Sperryville,
    VA, Copp's Chapel Brethren
    Church
Copps Chapel Brethren Church, Sperry-
    ville, VA, 1209
Copps Church, VA, meetinghouse, 164
Copps Church, VA mission point, Botetourt
    Co., VA, Church of the Brethren,
    164
Coquille Valley, OR, 295
    Church of the Brethren, See Myrtle
        Point, OR, Church of the Brethren
Coquille River, 81
    Newberg, OR, Church of the Brethren
        as mission point, 933
    settlement in, 980
Coraopolis, PA, Bon Meade Grace Brethren
    Church, **343**
Coraopolis, PA, congregation, 343
Corbitt, Jim C., 2275
Corbridge, Ona Delwin, 1910
Cordell, OK, 1321
Corder family
    Pleasant Valley German Baptist
        Brethren, IA, 1036
Corder, J. H., 1589
Cordian, Joseph, 1589
Cordier, Andrew Wellington, *199*, 261, 302,
    343–344, *344*, 416, 358, 1291,
    1589, 1910, *2129, See also*
    Vietnam Christian Service, **2372,
    2381**
    love feast, comments about, 765
Cordier, C., 1589
Cordier, Dorothy Butterbaugh, 344
Cordier, F. P., 1589
Cordier family
    Rupp (Roop) family related to, 1130
Cordier, Frank, 1589
Cordier, Ida May Anstine, 343
Cordier, Joseph J., 1589
Cordier, Louise, 344
Cordier, Lowell, 344
Cordier, Wellington J., 343
Cordis, William, 1589
Córdoba, Argentina, 53, 54, 2153
Cordrey, Mark Edward, 2275
Cordula, Anetta (later Mow), 1842, **2376,
    2388**
Core, Earl I., 1910
Coriellena Brethren Church, 1248
Corinth, IN, Brethren Church, **344–345,**
    395
    Mexico, IN, Brethren Church, 821
1 Corinthians
    6:11, 84
    10:1–2, 85
    12:4–13, 85, 86
    12:13, 85
2 Corinthians, 1:21, 39
    Kent, Homer Austin, Jr., 2211
    Kent, Homer Austin, Jr. on, 2340
Corle, Oliver S., 1589
Corley, Ernest Loran, 1589
Corn, Emmett William, 1589
Cornell, Cathy
    Menifee, CA, New Hope Community
        Church of the Valley, 2220

Cornell, David
    Menifee, CA, New Hope Community
        Church of the Valley, 2220
Cornell, Harold G., 619
Cornell (Vermillion), IL, Church of the
    Brethren, 96, **345**
    Pike Creek (Chenoa), IL, Church of the
        Brethren, 1023
Cornerstone TeleVision
    sources on, 2316
Cornish, John, 1355, 1589–1590
Cornish, Vernon, 1590
Cornwall house, Tulpehocken Church of the
    Brethren, PA, 1278
Cornwall, PA
    Bucher family, 226
Cornwell family, 2087
Cornwell, Richard H., 318, 699, 1590
    Roanoke, VA, Washington Heights
        Grace Brethren Church, pastor,
        1114
corporate logos
    Brethren Church, *2146*
corpus Christi, 292
Corpus Christi, TX, congregation, 1255
corpus Christianum, 292
Corral de Bustos, Argentina, 53
    Maconaghy, Dorothy Helen Lewis and
        Hill, 779
correctional facilities
    chaplaincy, 2157, 2158
Correl, Caleb, 1590
Correll, A. J., 1590
    Mountain Valley Church of the
        Brethren, TN, elder, 889
    South Bethel German Baptist Brethren,
        MO, leadership, 1204
Correll, A. S., 1590
Correll, Ada P., 1590
Correll, Daniel, 279
Correll, Ernst H., 1910
    Durnbaugh, Donald F. on Juniata
        College and, 2326
Correll, Harold G., 1590
Correll, Peter Miller, 1590.
    Mountain Valley Church of the
        Brethren, TN, free minister, 889
Cory, Lee R., 1246, 1590
Cory, Martha E., 2275
Cosentino, Joseph M., 2275
Cosgrove, Jonathan C., 2275
Cosgrove, Kenneth I., 367, 1388, 1590
    Norton, OH, Grace Brethren Church,
        pastor, 951
Coshocton Co., OH, 345, 753
Coshocton, OH, Church of the Brethren,
    345
Cosner, Carol Virginia, 1315, 1590
Cosner, Daniel, 1590
Cosner, Earl C., 1590
Cosner, Elmer Richard, 2275
Cosner, Henry H., 1590
Cosner, J. P., 1590
Cosner, John Taylor, 1590
Cosner, Martin, 750, 1590
Cosner, Michael, 1590
Cosner, Newton D., 519, 1590
Cosner, Randy Wayne, 2275
Cosner, William H., 468, 1590
Cosner, Zina G., 1590
Cossee, E. H.
    works by, 2323
Cost, Andrew A., 1590

Costa Rica
Women's Conferences (CB) and, 2265
Costanzo, James T., 1590
Costello, John R., 1910
costumes, *See* dress
Cotsamire, Leslie I., 320
Cotsamire, Leslie J., 21
Cotterman, Francis, 367, 1590
Cotterman, Frank P., 1590
Cotterman, J., 1590
Cottonwood, KS, Church of the Brethren, **345**, 682, 1304
migration of Brethren, 830
Cottrell, Asher Raymond, **345**, 1836
medical missions, 807
Cottrell, Catherine Wagoner, 345
Cottrell, D. Owen, 1590
New Enterprise, PA, Church of the Brethren, as minister, 927
Cottrell, Eli M., 345
Cottrell, Laura M. Murphy, **345**, 807, 1836, 2017
Quinter Memorial Hospital, 1078
medical missions, 807
Cottrell Nursing Home, 345
Cottrell, Pete, 1590
Painter Creek Old German Baptist Brethren Church, OH, 990
Cottrell, Raymond, 2017
Quinter Memorial Hospital, 1078
Cottrell, Richard, 2275
Cottrill, Richard Dickson, 1590
Couch, Bill, 115
Cough, William, 1289
Coughenour, H. L.
Raystown Brethren Church, PA, pastor, 1084
Coughenour, Izora Sarah, 1910
Coughenour, Ralph Stauffer, 1910
Coulson congregation, 1267
Coulson, F. M., 1590
Coulson, VA, Church of the Brethren, **345**
Coulter, C. Brewster, 1910
Coulter, Carol R., 2275
Coulter, Nina R., 2275
Council Bluffs congregation, PA, 1294
Council Bluffs, IA, Peace Church of the Brethren, **345–346**, *346,* 974
Council for Relief Agencies Licensed for Operation in Germany, 545
council meetings, 4, **346**
camp meetings, 246
camp meetings and, 246
Church of God (New Dunkers), 297
Church of the Brethren, **346**
confession of faith, 333
degrees of ministry, 374
description of, 1375
disorderly observers, 729
doctrine on, 180
dress subject of, 401
Dunkard Brethren, 409
elders presiding at, 433
Fruita, CO, Church of the Brethren, 519
Hostetler Brethren, 631
humility, 636
hymnals, 642
Indian Creek Church of the Brethren, OK, 651
Ivester Church of the Brethren, IA, 665
ministry, terminology, 847
Old German Baptist Brethren, 967

"Order of the Brethren," 976
possible origin of, 33
Council of Boards, **346**
Dove, John Adams, 397
General Board, 535
Lear, John Wallace, 732
Yoder, Joseph J., 1386
Council of Churches, American (ACC), **23**
Council of Churches, Calgary, 15
Council of Churches, Canadian, 15
Council of Churches of Christ in the USA, National (NCCC), 23
Council of District Executives (CODE), 2163, 2164, 2224
council of elders, *See* elders
Council of Men's Work, *See* Men's Work
Council of Promotion, 346, **346**
General Board (CB), 535
Lear, John Wallace, 732
Council of Relief Agencies Licensed for Operation in Germany (CRA LOG), 23, 173, 200, 230, **346–347**
Council of Trent, 1120
Council of Women's Work, *See* Women's Work
council tents, 1254
councils, Christian Brethren and, 281
counseling
Church of the Brethren ministry, 846
Lancaster, PA, Alfa y Omega (Alpha and Omega) Church of the Brethren, 2213
marriage, 796
remarriage after divorce, 1099
Counselor, NM, 192
Brethren Navajo Mission and Boarding School, 1277
Native Americans, 2230
Counselor's Post, NM, 188
"Count Well the Cost"
Geistreiches Gesang-Buch (*Spiritual Songbook*)*,* 534
Counter-Reformation
Evangelical Church in Austria, 459
Hutterian Brethren, 639
Moravian Church, 875
Country Church, Warrensburg, MO, 1318
The Country Preacher: The Life and Ministry of Elder Solomon Stoner (Shuman)
Shuman, L. Herman (OGBB) and, 2249
Countryman, Annie Marie Ridenour, 347
Countryman, Christina Setty, 347
Countryman, Henry, 347
Countryman, John, **347**, 1590
Ohio minister, 961
Ridge Church of the Brethren, OH, 1108
County Line, IN, Brethren Church, **347**
County Line, OH, Church of the Brethren, 78, **347**
County Line, PA, Church of the Brethren, **347**, *See also* Elbethel Church of the Brethren, PA
Church of the Brethren (Indian Creek), 102
Couper, William, 1910
Courageous Prophet (Sappington)
Sappington, Roger E. (CB) and, 2246
Coursen, Robert A., 2275
Courter, Douglas A., 2275
Courter, IN, congregation

Mexico, IN, Church of the Brethren, 821
courts of law, *See* law
Brethren Church beliefs and, 169
Franklin Co., VA, 2102
Couser, David Gray, 21, 743, 1590
Couser, E. Friend, 1383, 1590
Couser family
Sinking Spring, OH, Grace Brethren Church, 1186
Couser, Jacob Wilber, 1590
Sinking Spring, OH, Grace Brethren Church, pastor, 1186
Couser, Joseph A. R., 1590
Couser, Mable Mote, 1590, 2300
Couser, Mary Catherine Miranda, 365, 1590
Couser, William, 365
Cove Echo, 1911
Covenant Bible Studies
People of the Covenant (POC) (BC) and, 2237
covenant of purposes
Church of the Brethren, 252
Covenant Theology, 56, **347–348**, *See also* church, doctrine of; membership; original sin
covenantal community
Brethren movement, 291–292
covenantal relationships
homosexuality, 2204
covenanting
church membership, 813
covenants
peace given by God, 997–998
sources on, 2316
Coventry Church of the Brethren (Brethren Church), PA, 33, 175, 267, 400, 709, 722, **1049**, 1298, 1312, 2036, 2086, *See also* Pottstown, PA, Coventry Church of the Brethren
250 year anniversary, 1991
cemetery restored and endowed by Isaac Newton Urner, 1298
Oaks, PA, Green Tree Church of the Brethren, 958
Pipe Creek Church of the Brethren, MD, 1025
Cover, Adam, 322
Cover, Albert Barnabas, 759, 1590
Cover, Anna Baker, 606
Cover, Benjamin A., 2275
Old Brethren Church, 2232
Cover, Blanche (later Hilton), **606,** 1839
Cover, Christie R., 2300
Old Brethren minister, 965
Cover (Coover), David, 1590
Maumee Church of the Brethren, OH, minister, 803
Cover, Dulcie Lovie Williams, 1836
Cover, Dwight E., 2275
Cover, Eliza Miller, 348, 540
Cover, Ephraim, 1590
Cover family, 322, 2089, *See also* Cober family
Cover, J. H., 606
Cover, J. P., 1590
Cover, Jack, 1590
Olive Grove Old German Baptist Brethren Church, CA, minister, 973
Cover, Jacob Austin, 1363, 1590, 1871
Modesto, CA, Old German Baptist

Brethren Church, presiding elder, 867
New River Old German Baptist Brethren Church, ministers for, 931
Cover, Joe
South Haven Old German Baptist Brethren Church, MI, deacon, 1205
Cover, Joene Toon, 1319, 1848
Cover, John, 322
Cover, John, Jr., 348
Cover, Joseph I., 322, 540, 1306, 1590, 2300
Old Brethren minister, 965
Cover, Joseph, Jr.
Old Brethren German Baptist Church, minister, 965
Cover, Joseph L.
Old Brethren minister, 965
Cover, Joseph Miller, 1363, 1590
Old Brethren minister, 965
South Haven Old German Baptist Brethren Church, MI, minister, 1205
Cover, Leslie E., 322, 2275
Old Brethren minister, 965
The Pilgrim, 965, 1023
Cover, Leslie S., 1590
Cover, Mary, 540, 1871
Cover, Mary Immel, 348
Cover, O. L.
Pleasant Hill Old German Baptist Brethren Church, IL, providing leadership, 1033
Cover, Oliver, 540
Cover, Oliver C.
Mud Valley Old German Baptist Brethren Church, IL, minister, 892
Cover, Oliver Lytton, 1363, 1590
Old Brethren minister, 965
South Haven Old German Baptist Brethren Church, MI, minister, 1205
Cover, Peter D.
Old Brethren Church, 2232
Cover, Robert, 53, 1590
Cover, Robert J., 1319, 1848
Cover, Rudolph, 1590
Cover, Samuel, 540
Cover, Samuel C., 1590–1591
Cover, Solomon Leslie, 322, 1591
Ottumwa, IA, Church of the Brethren, pastor, 985
coverlets, woven
William Leinbach, article about, 1915
Covert, KS, 1305
Portis, KS, North Solomon Church of the Brethren, preaching point of, 1048
Covina, CA, Church of the Brethren, 171, 218, **348**
Conejo, CA, Church of the Brethren, preaching point for, 331
Flory, Jacob S., 498
Fruitvale Church of the Brethren, CA, 520
Glendora, CA, Church of the Brethren, 553
migration of Brethren, 830
Overholtzer, Samuel A., 986
Covina, CA, congregation, 1275
Covina, CA, New Life Grace Brethren

Church, **348**
Covington, CA, Old German Baptist Brethren, *See* Covington, OH, Church of the Brethren
Covington, Charles L., 2275
Covington Co., MS, 731
Pine Ridge Dunkard Brethren Congregation, MS and, 2238
Covington, OH, 350, 696, 704, 757, 1306, 1307
Annual Meetings, *962*
Church of the Brethren, **348–349**
First Brethren Church, **349**
historical libraries, 610
Old Brethren, 964
Old German Baptist Brethren Church, **350**
Sugar Grove Old German Baptist Brethren Church, OH and, 2253
Old Order German Baptist Church, 971, 972, 2235
Owl Creek Old German Baptist Brethren Church, OH, 986
Piqua, OH, Church of the Brethren, 1026
Pleasant Hill, OH, Church of the Brethren, 1031
Spring St. Baptist Church, 349
Stillwater congregation
Harris Creek Church of the Brethren, OH, 585
Covington, VA, Grace Brethren Church, **349–350**
Covington, WA, Community Church of the Brethren, **350**
Cowan, Robert, 1591
Cowanshannock, PA, 1318
Brethren Church, **350**
Church of the Brethren, **350**, 433
German Baptist Brethren congregation, 350
Oakdale Church of the Brethren, 957
Cowel, J. A., 1591
Cowell, Amos, 1591
Philadelphia, PA, First Church of the Brethren, minister, 1015
Cowes, Isle of Wight
emigration, Brethren, 443
Cowles family
Grandview, WA, Grace Brethren Church, 566
Cowley, E. C., 1591
Cowley, Richard Charles, 1591
Philadelphia, PA, Calvary Church of the Brethren, pastor, 1015
Cowlitz Valley, WA, 1338
Cox, Alvin Spanogle, 1591, 2300
Parkview Church of the Brethren, PA, leadership by, 994
Cox, Charles L., 318, 1591
Cox, Elizabeth Spanogle, 1911
Cox, Everette Harold, 1591
Cox family, *See* Rinehart family
Nezperce, ID, Church of the Brethren, 935
Cox, Francis A., 1911
Cox, H. Paul, 115, 1591, 1911
Cox, Harold
Olean Church of the Brethren, VA, leadership by, 973
Cox, J. W., 1591
Cox, John Matthew, 1591
Cox, Joshua, 1911

Cox, Kenton M., 1911
Cox, Mary Margaret, 2275
Cox, Meral E., 1591
Cox, O. B., 1911
Cox, Ralph Herbert, 1591
Cox, Raymer David, 141, 1591
Cox, Robert, 1911
Cox, Samuel Marshal, 1591
Cox, Thomas, 1591
Cox, William Wise, 1591
Coxe family, *See* Sellers family
Coxill, H. Wakelin, 1911
Coy, Aaron, 1383, 1591
Coy family, 1383
Filbrun family, 490
Coyle, J. Timothy, 1380, 1591
Newark, DE, Grace Brethren Church, pastor in, 933
works by, 2323
Coyle, OK
Paradise Prairie Church of the Brethren, 992
Coyler family
Nevada, MO, Church of the Brethren, 924
CPS, *See* Civilian Public Service (CPS); Robinson, Jo Ann Ooiman
CPT, *See* Christian Peacemaker Teams
Crab Orchard, WV, Church of the Brethren, **350**, 1267
Crab River, WV, congregation
Mathias, WV, Church of the Brethren, 803
Crab Run Church of the Brethren (WV), **350**, 2078
Mathias, WV, Church of the Brethren, sister congregation of, 803
preaching point for Upper Lost River congregation, 1295
Crabb, Glen E., 504, 1591
Crabbs, William, 674, 742, 1591
Crabill, Joseph Milton, 1591
Craft, Conway, 1278
Craft, J., 438
Craft, Jacob, 1591
crafts, *See Fraktur*
Pennsylvania Germans, 1007
SERRV International (CB) and, 2247
Crafts, Wilbur F., 1911
Craghead, Thomas J., 1591
Riner Grace Brethren Church, VA, pastor, 1110
Crago, Florence M., 714, 2275
Crago, Glen William, 714, 1591, 1911, 2300
Pasadena, CA, Church of the Brethren, pastor in, 994
Crago, Janet Nadine, 1836
Crago, Thomas Glen, 1836
Cragun, Rodger Lawson, 1591, 2275
Craig Co., OK
Hollow Church of the Brethren, OK, 620
Craig, George, 2034
Craig, Herman Shaw, 1591
Craig, Marie Wolff, 1911
Craigie (Craigs, Craiges), James, **350–351**, 2126
Craigsville, VA, 749
Craik, Elmer Leroy, 351, 1911
Craik, Rink Frances Mary, 351
Crain, Marion Keith, 2275
Crall family

Salem Church of the Brethren, IA, 1137

CRALOG, *See* Council of Relief Agencies Licensed for Operation in Germany

Cramer, Edward R., 1591

Cramer, Emma Davis, 540

Cramer family, 165, 448

Cramer, Mrs. Vera, 252

Cramer, Peggy C.
  works by, 2323

Cramer, Samuel, 1911

Cramer, William, 540

Cranberry Community Church, Good Samaritan Church of the Brethren, PA, 2190

Crane Creek settlement, NC, 1383

Crane Creek (Yadkin), NC, congregation, 690

Cranesville, WV, 728

Crary, Catherine S., 1911

Craun, Benjamin Harrison, 1591

Craun, Ernest Brown, 1591

Craun, Eva M., 168

Craun, Marion Jefferson, 1591

Craver, Richard, 1591

Crawford Addition mission point, Grand Junction, CO, Koinonia Brethren-Baptist Church, 565

Crawford, B. Eldora, 1911

Crawford Co., IL, 713

Crawford Co., KS
  Neosho Valley Old German Baptist Brethren Church near, 923
  Osage Church of the Brethren, KS, 983
  Parsons Old German Baptist Brethren Church, KS, 994

Crawford Co., OH, 211
  Rome Old German Baptist Brethren Church, OH, 1121

Crawford Co., PA, 317

Crawford, D. Lee, 1591

Crawford, Daniel, 1591

Crawford family, 461, 1304
  South Bend, IN, Ireland Road Grace Brethren Church, 1203

Crawford, Frederick John, 1591

Crawford, Frederick, Jr., 2

Crawford, Howard S., 1591

Crawford, John, 1591

Crawford, Lee D., 264
  Pleasant View Church of the Brethren, TN, 1037

Crawford, Mabel Jeannette, 1848, 1849

Crawford, Ruth P., 1911

Crawmer family, 142
  South Haven Old German Baptist Brethren Church, MI, 1205

Crawmer, Marvin B.
  Old Brethren Church, 2232

Crawmer, Samuel
  Old Order German Baptist Church minister, 972

Crawmer, William S.
  Old Brethren Church, 2232

crazy quilts of German religious groups
  Durnbaugh, Donald F. on, 2327

creation, 2061
  doctrine of, **351**
  Nead, Peter, writings of, 919
  Whitcomb, John C., Jr. on, 2363
  creationism, 2076, 2083
  evolution, 463

Fellowship of Grace Brethren Churches (FGBC), 487
  scientific thought, 2097
  sources on, 2316
  Whitcomb, John Clement, Jr. (FGBC, CGBCI) and, 2262

Credential Committee, 37, **351**, 409, *See also* delegates; messengers
  Dunkard Brethren, 410
  Receiving Committee (OGBB), 1085

credit unions, **351**, *See also* cooperatives; missions and missionaries; mutual aid
  Brethren Benefit Trust (BBT), 2140
  Elgin, IL, Highland Avenue Church of the Brethren, 436

Cree family, 1281

creeds, 204, *See also* noncreedalism; specific confessions
  Apostles' Creed, 184
  Athanasian Creed, Brethren Church, 184
  Brethren Church, 183
  Brethren movement, 289
  Brethren polity, 1042
  Church of the Brethren polity, 1043
  doctrinal statements, 942
  Dunkard Brethren, 409
  Eby, Kermit, 420
  Gleim's treatise on, 464
  Hochmann von Hochenau, Ernst Christoph, 614
  Restoration Movement, 1101

Creek Hill churchhouse, MD, 1329

creeks, congregational names derived from, 911

Creekville, KY, *492*

Crees, Robert D., 439, 562, 558, 699, 731, 758, 768, 1324, 1591, 2300
  Martinsburg, WV, Rosemont Grace Brethren Church, pastor (interim), 798

Crefeld, *See* Krefeld

Creiger, Albert, 1591

Creighton family, 721, 2105

Cremer, C. W., 1911

Cremer, Estelle
  works by, 2323

Crenshaw, John Bacon
  biography, 1911

Crenshaw, Margaret E., 1911

Creps, B. F.
  Raystown Brethren Church, PA, pastor, 1084

Cresap, Thomas, 1868

Crescent Hill, MO, 6

Cress, George W., 1591

Crest Manor, IN, Church of the Brethren, *See* South Bend, IN, Crest Manor Church of the Brethren

Creswell, Nancy Carol, 1849

Crewdson, Samuel, 271

Crews family
  Gospel Grace Brethren Church, VA, 559

Creyfeld, Creyfeldt, *See* Krefeld

Creyfelt, Joseph, 1591

Crick, W. S., 368, 515, 1289
  Raystown Brethren Church, PA, pastor, 1084

Crick, William S., 16, 1591
  Newark, OH, Brethren Church, as minister, 933

Crider, Daniel, Sr.

descendants of, 1911

Crider, Jacob, 1591

Crider, Julian J., 1911

Crider, Lester E., 1911

Crider, Lester W., 1911

Crider, Mrs. Marion, 345

Criders, VA, Damascus Church of the Brethren, **351–352**

Crigger family
  Fremont, OH, Grace Brethren Church, 515

Crill, Edward, 248, 1907, 1911
  recreation, 1088

Crill, Geraldine (later Eller), 440, 1928, 2097, 2175

Crill, Helene Blough, 1911

Crill, Joseph, 913

Crim, Bessie Mae, 1215, 1836, **2387**

Crim, Charles, 482

Crim, Margaret, 482

crime, *See* bail; capital punishment; law, doctrine of; law enforcement; prisons

Criminal Justice Reform, *See* prisons

criminal justice system
  reform, 24

criminology
  Gillin, John Lewis, 549

Crimora, VA
  Forest Chapel Church of the Brethren, VA, 502

crinolines, *See* hoops

Cripe, Adam, 1912

Cripe, Alvin, 352

Cripe, Barbara, 217

Cripe, Calvin, 1591

Cripe, Carl E., 2275

Cripe, Charles C., 738, 1591, 1911

Cripe, Clyde C., 71, 1591

Cripe, Cora Mae, 217, 1835

Cripe (Creib, Greib, Gripe), John, 1592

Cripe, D. C., 1591–1592, 1592

Cripe, D. E., 277, 438

Cripe, Daniel, 352, 558, 1355, 1356
  Indiana, 652
  migration of Brethren, 829
  Müller (Miller) family, 895

Cripe, Daniel (1), 1592

Cripe, Daniel (2), 1592

Cripe, Daniel C., 1592

Cripe, Daniel P., 373, 1592

Cripe, Daniel S., 1592

Cripe, David, 1223, 1592

Cripe, David B., 1592

Cripe, David C., 1592

Cripe, David E., 541, 1592

Cripe, David S., 410, 439, 1592

Cripe, Edith S., 1911

Cripe, Elizabeth (later Hoover), 628

Cripe, Elizabeth (later Ulrich), 1285

Cripe, Elizabeth Ulrich, 352

Cripe, Elsie Long, 352

Cripe, Esther, 352, 1312

Cripe, Evelyn L., 1911

Cripe, F(red) Florian, 1592

Cripe, George, 1592

Cripe, George R., 2300

Cripe, George Washington, 217, 637, 1592

Cripe, Glenn A., **352**, 1592

Cripe (Gripe) family, 142, 146, **352–353**, 1213, 1312, 1342, 2078, 2094
  bibliography, 1883
  Mishler family, related to, 852

Root family related by marriage, 1122
Shively family, related to, 1178
sources on, 2318
Cripe, Hannah, 352
Cripe, Isaac, 1592
Cripe, Israel, 1592
Cripe, Israel and Malinda
family history, 2014
Cripe, J.
Newton Grove Church of the Brethren, elder in, 934
Cripe, J. C., 121, 410, 1592
Cripe, J. R., 396
Cripe, Jacob, 335, 352, 429, 440, 1294, 1365, 1592, 1912, 2050
Cripe, Jacob C., *See* divisions
Cripe, Jacob, Jr., 352
Cripe, James, 1592
Cripe, John, 352, 407, 1592
Cripe, John U., 1592
Cripe, Jonathan M., 352, 1592
Cripe, Joseph, 1592
Salem Church of the Brethren, IL, elder in, 1137
Cripe, Larry L., 2275
Cripe, Leona Huber, 352
Cripe, Linnea Joan, 1912
Cripe, Magdalena Miller, 352
Müller (Miller) family, 895
Cripe, Manfred L., 1836
Cripe, Mark L., 1592
Cripe, Martha, 158
Cripe, Mary Elizabeth, 1848
Cripe, Mary Maude, 1854
Cripe, Maude, 1804, *See* Webb, Maude Cripe
Cripe, Maude (later Webb), 1094, **1324–1325**
Cripe, Mervin A., 246, 1243, 1592, 1912, **2381**
Cripe, Nathaniel, 1592
Cripe, Nora, 158
Cripe, Owen, 105, 204, 1255
debate with F. M. Tidrick, 1912
Mud Valley Old German Baptist Brethren Church, IL, minister, 892
Old Brethren minister, 965
Cripe, Owen Clark, 1592
Cripe, Priscilla (later Neher), 922
Cripe, Richard, 1270, 1592
Ripon, CA, Grace Brethren Church, pastor, 1110
Cripe, Rinehart, 1338
Cripe, Rosa (later Hess), 601
Cripe, Rupel Ellen Mary, 352
Cripe, Samuel, 352
Cripe, Sarah Weybright, 1338
Cripe, Stephen
Pipe Creek Old German Baptist Brethren Church, IN, deacon, 1026
Cripe, Susannah, 352
Cripe, Una (later Steele), 1220
Cripe, Winifred E., **352,** 1836, 1912
Pine Creek Church of the Brethren, IN, sent to China by, 1024
"Crisis Theology," 922
Crisman, L. W.
Mulvane, KS, Brethren Church, 895
Crissman, Darrell, L., 2275
Crissman, Earl E., 1592
Crissman, G. W., 1592
Crissman, John, 1592
Crist, Asa D., 1247, 1592

Crist, Barbara, 353
Crist, Burton Wayne, 759, 1330, 1592
Pomona, CA, Church of the Brethren, pastor, 1045
Crist, Catherine, 352
Crist, Catherine Ohmart, 352
Crist, Charles
Old Order German Baptist Church minister, 972
Crist, C(harles) C., 1592
Crist, D. Floyd, 1592
Crist, Daniel Albert, **352,** 682, 1592
Crist, David W., 1592
Crist, Delbert, 1385, 1592
Crist, Edwin E., 1592
Crist, Elizabeth, 352
Crist, Evamae Barton, 1912
Crist family, 1318
Crist, Galen Benjamin, 209, 440, 672, 1308, 1592, 2300
Pleasant Hill Church of the Brethren, TN, pastor/elder, 1032
Mount Hermon Church of the Brethren, VA, pastor, 881
Crist, Genevieve, 285
Crist, H. F., Newton, KS, Church of the Brethren, pastor, 934
Crist, Harold H., 1592
Crist, Henry F., 415, 1592
Crist, Isaac H., **352,** 415, 682, 683, 1592, 1902
McLouth, KS, Church of the Brethren, pastor, 779
Olathe, KS, Church of the Brethren, elder, 964
Ottawa, KS, Church of the Brethren, elder, 985
South Saint Joseph Church of the Brethren, MO, 1135
Crist, Jacob, 352
Crist, Jacob, Jr., 1592–1593
North Hampton, OH, Donnels Creek Old German Baptist Brethren Church, elder, 948
Crist, Jacob, Sr., 1593
Crist, John, 102, 352, 1593
Crist, John E., 415, 1593
Olathe Old German Baptist Brethren Church, KS, minister, 964
Crist, Jonathan, 431, 1593
Crist, Lee, 350
Crist, Lee Jacob, 318, 546, 1593, **2381**
Crist, Magdalena Frantz, 352
Crist, Margarette Hob, 352
Crist, Myrtle (later Porter), 748, 2038
Crist, Nicholas, 142, 264, 431
North Hampton, OH, Donnels Creek Old German Baptist Brethren Church, minister, 948
Sheridan Lake Old German Baptist Brethren Church, CO, minister in, 1176
Crist, Nicolas, 1346
Crist, Nicolas J., 1593
Crist, Roesch Ellen Mary, 352
Crist, Roy A., 1593, 1912
Crist, Salome Frantz, 352
Crist, Samuel, 664, 1593
Crist, Sarah Brubaker, 352
Crist, Susanna, 352
Critchfield, Beatrice
Sipesville, PA, Church of the Brethren, Bible School director, 1187

Crites, Beulah
Manzanar Relocation Center, dietician, 789
Crites family, 262, 750
Crites, Marvin
Manzanar Relocation Center, teaching at, 789
Critical Response Child Care (CRC), 2171, *See also* Child Care in Aviation Incident Response (CAIR)
criticism
publishing, 1068
Crockett, E. R., 227
Crofford (Crawford), W. A., 1305
Crofford, Daniel, 673, 1593
Crofford, W. A., 746
Mount Pleasant, PA, Brethren Church, pastor, 886
Crofford, William A., 1593
Croft, Julia A., 1296, 1593
Philadelphia, PA, Bethany Church of the Brethren, 1015
Philadelphia, PA, Calvary Church of the Brethren, 1015
Croft, Samuel B., 1296
Philadelphia, PA, Bethany Church of the Brethren, 1015
Philadelphia, PA, Calvary Church of the Brethren, 1015
Croghan, C., 2080
Croghan, George, 1912
letters and journals, 1912
Croker, C. Wayne, 1593
South Bend, IN, Ireland Road Grace Brethren Church, pastor, 1203
Croker, Elsie Ruth, 1853
Croll family
articles about, 1912
Croll, Mary (later Hamilton), 580
Croll, Phillip C., 1912
Crompacker, Abraham, 355
Crompacker, Elias, 355
Crompacker, Hans, 355
Crompacker, John, 355
Crompacker, Mary Rife, 355
Crompacker, Peter, 355
Crompacker, Ulrich, 355
Cron, Richard, 1593, 2300
River City Grace Community Church, pastor of, 1134
Cron, Richard M., 713
Cronau, Rudolf, 1912
Crone family
history of, 1912
Crone, Frank Linden, 1912
Cronise, Jacob
railroad fares, 1081
traveling to Annual Meeting, and railroad committees and agents, 1080
Crooked Creek, IA, Church of the Brethren, **353**
English River Church of the Brethren, IA, 447
Oak Grove Church of the Brethren, IA, 955
CROP, *See* Christian Rural Overseas Program
crop failures
Maple Grove Church of the Brethren, KS, aiding affected families, 789
crop subsidies
nonconformity, 941
Crosby, Kenneth W., 1593

cross
 Brethren logos, *2146, 2147, 2168*
 Good Friday, 556
Cross, ___, 1912
Cross, A. Sherman, 1593
Cross, Benjamin R., 1593
Cross Co., AR
 New Hope Church of the Brethren, 929
Cross Cultural Ministries Team (CCMT), 2257
Cross, F. L., 1912
Cross, George G., 1923
Cross, Harold E., 1912
Cross, J. J., 1593
Cross, John, 1593
Cross Junior High School, Tucson, AZ, meetingplace for Northwest Brethren Chapel, 1278
Cross Keys retirement home, PA, 1388
Cross, Mollie (later Long), 754
Cross Roads meetinghouse, Summit Mills Church of the Brethren, PA, 1236
Cross Roads, TN, German Baptist Brethren Church, **353**
Cross Roads, VA, 1265
 meetinghouse, 164
 mission point, Botetourt Co., VA, Church of the Brethren, 164
Cross, Sherman, 1593
Crossroad Brethren Church. PA, **353**
Crossroad congregation, PA
 Fredericksburg, PA, Brethren Church, 512
CrossRoads, *See* Valley Brethren-Mennonite Heritage Center
Crossroads Emergency Food Aid Center
 Redford, MI, Trinity Church of the Brethren, 1090
Crosswhite, Albert Graham, 496, 1593
 Peru, IN, Church of the Brethren, pastor, 1010
 Roaring Spring, PA, First Church of the Brethren, pastor, 1114
Crosswhite, Jesse, 1593
 Maryville, TN, Oakland German Baptist Brethren Church, organizing, 799
 Pleasant View Church of the Brethren, TN, elder, 1037
Crosswhite, John M., 1593
Crosthwaite, Georgia E., 1912
Crothers, John B., 620
Crotsley, George A., 1593
Crouch, D. E., 1593
Crouch, Donald C., 1593
Crouch, Eugene Morgan, **353–354,** 1593
 Manchester College, President, 786
Crouch, Mary (later Robertson), 1114
Crouder, Waldo, 1278
Crous, Ernst, 1912, 1961
Crous, Jan, **354,** 1912
Crouse, Alma, 1215
Crouse, Bernard Merle, 1836, 1912
 Good Shepherd Church of the Brethren, FL, 2190
 Hispanic Ministries (CB), 2199
 Miller, Donald Eugene, *2223*
 missions, *860*
 works by, 2323
Crouse, Bernard Merle, 1593, 1836, 1912
 Good Shepherd Church of the Brethren, FL, 2190
 Hispanic Ministries (CB), 2199

Miller, Donald Eugene, *2223*
missions, *860*
works by, 2323
Crouse, Charles, 2300
Crouse family, 411
 history of, 1912
 Myerstown, PA, Grace Brethren Church, 906
 Nicholas Co. German Baptist Brethren Church, 935
Crouse, G. W., 1593
Crouse, Gerald Paul Baile, 2173, 2275
Crouse, J. H., 1912
Crouse, J. M., 1593
Crouse, Jacob Harrison, 1593
Crouse, John
 family history, 1912
Crouse, Joseph M., 1593
Crouse, Martha Jean Potter, 1836
Crouse, Mary Ann (later Moomaw)
 Moomaw, Benjamin Franklin, wife of, 873
 Moomaw, Daniel Crouse, mother of, 873
 Moomaw, John Crouse, mother of, 874
Crouse, Peter M.
 Gotha, FL, New Covenent Church of the Brethren, 2190
Crouse, Rebecca Baile, 2173, 2275
Crouse, William Dean, 1593, 2300
Crouthamel, Floy Souder (later Hoffer), 617
Crouthamel, Hillery (Hilary), 1593
Crow, Alexander
 medical practice, 810
Crow (Croe), Levi
 Portage Church of the Brethren, OH, minister, 1047
Crow, Joe Lynn, 1593
Crow, Rosemary
 People of the Covenant (POC) (BC) and, 2237
Crowe, William C., 482
Crowel, Mina (later Van Dyke), 1302
Crowell (Crowl), Devault, 1593
Crowell, J. A., 320
Crowell, Joseph A., 1593
Crowell, Larry, 1335
Crowell, Ruth, 1335
Crowl, Jane
 Plum Creek Old German Baptist Brethren Church, KS, 1038
Crowl, Samuel
 Plum Creek Old German Baptist Brethren Church, KS, 1038
Crown Chapel Brethren Church, Leon, IA, 737, *See also* Leon, IA, Brethren Church (FGBC)
Crownsville, MD, State Hospital
 medical projects, 808
Crowson, TN, Church of the Brethren, **354**
Croyle, Arthur L., 1593
 Rockton, PA, Church of the Brethren, pastor, 1118
Crozer Theological Seminary
 Myers, Tobias Timothy, 905
 Row, Harold W., 1125
 Walker, Galen Knepper, 1314
crucifixion, 556, 2048
Cruden, Alexander, 331
Cruea, Moses, 320, 1593
cruelty in marriage, 795
Cruise, Clancy C., 2173

Cruise, Clancy Calvin, 2275
Crull family, 1883
Crull, Mary, 343
Crull, Salome, 2080
Crull, Walter L., 2276
Crumba[c]ker family, *See* (Grumbacker, Grumbacher, Crumba[c]ker) family
Crumbacker, Hans
 Poling, Newton L. on descendants of, 2350
 Poling, Virginia on descendants of, 2350
Crume, John, 1593
Crumley, John B., 2276
Crumley, Paul David, 516, 1593
Crumley, William Carl, 105, 1593
Crummet Run, WV, Church of the Brethren, 105, **354**
Crummett Run, VA, 1301
 Highland Co. Mission Church of the Brethren, VA, 605
 Hiner Church of the Brethren, VA, 607
 Sangerville Church of the Brethren mission point, 1144
 Simmons family, 1182
Crummett, Wilmer Quentin, 1277, 1593, **2381**
 Pleasant Valley Church of the Brethren, VA, pastor, 1035
Crumpacker, ___ (later Miller)
 Miller, Robert Paul, mother of, 842
Crumpacker, A. H., 1593–1594
Crumpacker, A. J.
 Mound Valley Church of the Brethren, MO, 879
Crumpacker, Abraham, 1594
Crumpacker, Abraham (OGBB), 676, 1594
Crumpacker, Alden (Aldine) Hutchison, 1594
Crumpacker, Andrew J., 1594
Crumpacker, Anna L. Newland, 277, **354,** 1836, 1912
Crumpacker, Catherine Pfautz, 1013
Crumpacker, E. C., 676, 1254
Crumpacker, Edgar L., 1594
Crumpacker, Emory Cline, 1594
 Selma, VA, Church of the Brethren, minister in, 1166
Crumpacker, F. H., 1345
Crumpacker (Grumbacker, Grumbacher, Crumba[c]ker) family, 354, **354–355,** 1913
 Graybill (Grabill, Krehbiel) family, 567
 Jacob-Susan, 2052
 Sanger family, related to, 1144
Crumpacker, Frank Henry, 277, **354,** 1594, 1836, 1913
 McPherson, KS, First Church of the Brethren, pastor, 779
 Sanger, Conrad, descendant of, and missionary, 1144
Crumpacker, Grace (later Ruthrauff), 2052
Crumpacker, Harry C., 1594
Crumpacker, J. P., 373
Crumpacker, J. S., 152
Crumpacker, Jacob, 496
Crumpacker, Jacob Peter, 354
Crumpacker, James P., 1363, 1594
Crumpacker, Joel, 1594
Crumpacker, John Samuel 1594
 Selma, VA, Church of the Brethren, minister in, 1166

Crumpacker, Mary (later Garber), 676, 1944
Crumpacker, Mary (later Hutchison), 639
Crumpacker, Ned William, 152, 768, 1594, 1913
    Roanoke, VA, Ninth Street Church of the Brethren, pastor, 1113
Crumpacker, Pearl (later Murrey), 2052
Crumpacker, Peter, 676
    Pfautz, Johann (Hans) Michael, 1013
Crumpacker, Peter G., 1594
Crumpacker, Rebecca Ann (later Moomaw)
    Moomaw, Daniel Crouse, wife of, 873
    Mumma (Moomaw) family, 896
Crumpacker, Rebecca J., 1913
Crumpacker, S. C., See Bridgewater College
    Bridgewater College difficulties, 1978
Crumpacker, Samuel, 321, 670, 676, 1594
    Mumma (Moomaw) family, 896
Crumpacker, Sanger P., 173, 1594
Crumpacker, Sarah (later Graybill), 567
Crumpacker, Susan Sanger, 354
Crumpacker, Ulrich
    Poling, Newton L. on descendants of, 2350
    Poling, Virginia on descendants of, 2350
Crumpacker, Ulrich, family
    Pipe Creek Church of the Brethren, MD, 1026
Crumrine, Duane E., 2276
Crumrine family, See Krumrein family
    genealogy, 1913
Crumrine, Gale David, 708, 1277, 1594, 1913
Crumrine, Jacob, 335, 1594
Crumrine, Jacob R., 1594
Crumrine, John, 1311, 1594
Crumrine, Michael, 708
    descendants, 1913
Crumrine, Noah W., 1311, 1594
Crumrine, Peter
    descendants, 1913
Crumrine, Samuel, 708
Crumrine, Susannah Nyswaner, 708
Crusader teams
    funds from National Brethren Youth, 915
Crusades
    Orthodox Church, 983
    peace in Christian church history, 998
Crusea, Moses, 479
Crusius, Donald N.
    Columbus, OH, Church of the Brethren, 2372
Crustus, Donald, 1594
Crutchfield, James
    works by, 2323
Cruz, Gaudencio, Jr. (CB)
    Santa Ana, CA, Principe de Paz Fellowship (CB) and, 2246
Cruz, Roger E., 2300
Cruz, William R., Jr., 2276
Cryder family, 1911
Cryer, Richard, 2375
    works by, 2323
Crystal congregation, MI, 1304
Crystal, MI, Church of the Brethren, 355, 725
    New Haven Church of the Brethren, 928
Crystal Plains, KS

Portis, KS, North Solomon Church of the Brethren, preaching point of, 1048
Cuba, 189, 355
    Brethren Sunday school, 2005
    colonization, 324
    Grace Brethren International Missions, 2191
    Iglesia Cristiana Pentecosal de Cuba (Christian Pentecostal Church of Cuba), 2157
    Iglesia Cristiana Pentecosal de Cuba, 2207
    Julien, Thomas T., 2210
    Lancaster, PA, Alfa y Omega (Alpha and Omega) Church of the Brethren, 2213
    Mahan, Grant, 782
    Misión Mutua en las Américas, 852
    missions, 858, 2225
    Peace Studies Institute, 1003
    refugees from, 198
    Stump, John, 1232
    Women's Conferences (CB) and, 2265
Cuba, NM
    Native Americans, 2230
    Navajo congregations near, 931
    Cubbage, Ausby, 731, 1594
Cubbage, Saylor Casper, 1594
    Shelton Church of the Brethren, NC, pastor in, 1176
Cubbage, William S., 1594
Culbertson, Helen M., 1913
Culbertson, MT, 142
Cullar family, 1885
Cullen, Joy (later Fasnacht), 479–480, 1345, 1837
Cullen, Mark E., 480
Cullen, Ray R., 1594
Cullen, Virginia Skinner, 480
Culler, A. J.
    McPherson, KS, First Church of the Brethren, pastor, 779
    Temperance Bulletin, 1252
Culler, Amanda Kurtz, 355
Culler, Anna Harstine, 355
Culler, Arthur Jerome, 22, 55, 355, 1594, 1913
Culler, Clara (later Hartsough), 588
Culler, David D., 355, 1594, 1913
Culler, Edward Monroe, 1594
    Oneonta, AL, Church of the Brethren, free minister, 975
Culler, Elmer A., 1594
Culler family, 153
Culler, Farrell Alfred, 1594
Culler, George F., 565, 1364, 1594
Culler, John, 355
Culler, Mary Stover, 355
Culler, Mina Hoover, 355
Cullers, Eston L., 2276
Cullers, Harold Glenn, 2276
Cully, Kendig Brubaker, 1913
Culp, A. S., 551, 1594
Culp, Andrew C., 1594
    Monticello/Pike Creek Church of the Brethren, IN, minister, 872
Culp, Andrew S., 1594
Culp, C. Richard
    works by, 2323
Culp, Charles E., 1594
Culp, Clyde, 706
Culp, Clyde M., 435

Culp, Ellen (later Roose)
    Weldy, Allen (CB) and, 2261
Culp family, 164, 1913, See Kolb family
    Irricana (First) Church of the Brethren, Alberta, Canada, 663
    Redstone Valley Old German Baptist Brethren Church, WI and, 2240
Culp, Frederick, 164, 735, 1594
    Pleasant Valley Church of the Brethren, ND, elder, 1035
Culp, Ira, 1594
Culp, J. S., 1594
    Merrington Church of the Brethren, Sask., elder, 817
Culp, John, 1315
Culp, John C., 1594
Culp (Kulp), Isaac, 1594
Culp, Mary, 1913
Culp, Mary Ann (later Royer), 1128
Culp, Michael
    biography, 1913
Culp, Ray D., 2276
Culp, Susanna, 432
Cultural Changes in the Church of the Brethren (Dove), 397
cultural considerations
    Brethren folklore, 2147–2148
    ethics, 2177–2178
    German culture, importance of, 16
    Mennonites, 816
    Old German Baptist Brethren, 969
Culver family, Harrah, WA, Grace Brethren Church, 585
Culver, Robert Duncan, 515, 546, 585, 1270, 1594, 1913
Cumberland Co., IL, 356
    Church of the Brethren, 356
Cumberland Co., PA, 309, 322, 701, 765, 1294
    biographical annals, 1913
    German Baptist Brethren Church, 356
    Huntsdale Church of the Brethren, PA, 638
    Hyndman, PA, Church of the Brethren, 643
    later Franklin Co., 1233, 1294
    New Testament Brethren, 932
    Pennsylvania Dunkard Brethren, 1005
    records of deaths and marriages, 2005
    Ridge Church of the Brethren, PA, 1108
Cumberland Co., VA
    Mount Horeb Church of the Brethren, VA, 882
Cumberland Gap, migration of Brethren through, 829
Cumberland, MD, 713
    Brethren Church, 356
    Church of the Brethren (Dickenson Co.)
        Pound River, VA, congregation, preaching point of, 356
    Grace Brethren Church, 356
    Living Stone Church of the Brethren, 356
    Maryland Progressive Brethren activity in, 799
Cumberland River settlements, TN, 1253
    Guice (Geist Guß, Guss, Güß), Christopher, 576
Cumberland, VA
    Church of the Brethren (Dickenson

Co.), **356**
Church of the Brethren (Wise Co.), **356**
Pound River Church of the Brethren, 1049
Ramey Flats Church of the Brethren, 1083
Cumberland Valley, PA, 42, 1329
Snow Hill, 1918
Cumming, Mary Gauntz, 1594
Cummings, Chris, 1913
Cummings, Eric, 1343
Cummings, James Thomas, 1594
Cummings, Mary Elizabeth Gauntz, 1836
Cummins, Dester J., 1595
Cummins, Silver J., 1595
Cundiff, C. Dayton, 104, 1345, 1913
Roanoke, VA, Washington Heights Grace Brethren Church, pastor, 1114
Cundiff, Dayton F., 1595
Cundiff family, 1345
Cunningham, Amos, 670
Cunningham, Amos V., 2276
Cunningham, Carl, 1595
Cunningham, E. Lloyd, MD
medical missionary, 807, *807*
Cunningham, Ed, 1595
Cunningham, Ernest Lloyd, 1836, 1913
Cunningham family, 1885
Cunningham, J., 1595
Cunningham, James, 1315
Cunningham, Mark A., 2276
Cunningham, Martha (Mattie) (later Dolby), 395, 1361, 1602
May, James, home mission work with, 804
minorities, ethnic and racial, 850
Palestine, AR, Ministry to Blacks, 991
Cunningham, Orpha Ellen Edmister, 1836
Cunningham, Richard, 395
Cunningham, W. Elwood, 129, 1595
Montebello Church of the Brethren, VA, pastor, 871
Cunnington, G. A., 1595
Cuntz (Kuntz), Johann Frantz and Anna Elizabeth Kirsch
family history, 1991
Cunz, Dieter, 1913
Cupie, Mark, 1595
Cupp, Arthur, 1595
Cupp, Boyd E., 733, 1595
Cupp, Charles Sherman, 1595
Cupp family, 241, 411, 733, 2066
Cupp, Marion, 1338
Salkum, WA, Community Church of the Brethren, minister in, 1139
Cupp, Marion Earl, 1595
Cupp, Mary, 214
Cupp, P. F., 1595
Cupp, Sarah (later Miller), 1223, 1350
curative claims, patent medicine, 995
Curfman family, 1267
Curlew, IA, Church of the Brethren, **356**
curriculum, Brethren, 2044
Curry, Abram Stauffer, 190, 308, **356–357**, 1337, 1595, 1913, 2300, **2372**, **2381**
Curry, Amos K., 356–357
Curry, Annie Stauffer, 356–357
Curry, Donald W., 2175, 2276
Curry, Harriet E. (later Ziegler), 1395
Curry, Mitchell L., 1595
Curry, Neff Marguerite Eleanor, 357

Curry, Robert, 1595
Curryville, PA, Church of the Brethren, **357**, 1364
Curryville meetinghouse, Woodbury, PA, 1364
Curtis, Frances Rose Schneider, 1855
Curtis, Kenneth A., 1278, 1595
Curtis, William, 1278
Curtis, William Kean, 1595, 1855
Curtright, Albert O., 274, 1595
Curtwight, Mrs. Albert, 274
Curwin, Martha (later Harshbarger), *599*
Cushen, Sue (later Snyder), 2294
Cushing, OK, 141
Custer Brethren Church, Faihope, PA, *See* Fairhope, PA, Custer Brethren Church
Custer, Christian, 1595
Philadelphia, PA, First Church of the Brethren, minister, 1015
railroad committees and agents, 1080
reference to, 1913
Custer Co., NE
South Loup Church of the Brethren, NE, 1206
Custer, Edgar A., 1913
Custer, Elenore C., 2075
Custer, Elizabeth Cook, 357
Custer (Kuster[s]) family, 323, 2075
Martinsburg, WV, Rosemont Grace Brethren Church, 798
sources on, 2321, 2324
works by, 2324
Custer, Franklin C., 1595
Custer, G. Paul, 248, 357
Custer, George
Brethren relations, 2010
Custer, Grafton Paul, 1595
Custer, Isaiah, 1595
Marble Furnace, OH, Church of the Brethren, 791
Custer, Jacob, 1595
Custer, James L., 360, 1365, 1380, 1595, 1913–1914
works by, 2323
Custer, Janice E., 2276
Custer, Leonard M., 1333, 1595, 2300
Custer, MI, 1235
Custer, Oscar Adolphus, **357**, 1595
Middlefork Old German Baptist Brethren Church, IN, presiding elder, 826
North Manchester Old German Baptist Brethren Church, IN, elder-in-charge, 949
Custer, Paul, 62
Nimishillen Old German Baptist Brethren Church, OH, elder in, 937–938
Custer, Rodney, 733
Custer, Rodney L., 733, 1595
Custer, Viola Underwood, 357
Custer, Wyatt, 124
The Customs of Primitive Churches (Edwards), 429
customs, of the Church, 2104
cut-garment program, 198
Cutrer, Ken E., 2132
Cutright, Lois Loree, 1853
Cutright, Loree, *See* Sickel, Loree Cutright
Cuyahoga Falls, OH, Grace Brethren Church, **357**
CWS, *See* Church World Service

The Cyclopedia of Temperance and Prohibition, reference to German Baptists in, 1914
Cypress, CA, Grace Brethren Church, **357**, 720, 1337
Cyprian, 698
Cyprian of Carthage, 296
Cyprus, **357**
work camps, 1367
Czech Brethren, **357**
hymns, 642
pacifism in Christian church history, 998
Czech Republic
Julien, Thomas T., 2210
missions, short-term, 2226
Czechoslovakia
Brethren movement in, **357**
congregations sponsoring refugees from, 30
CPC, 286
Czigans (Cayigans), Milton G., 1595
Czigans, Milton C.
Pleasant Valley Church of the Brethren, WV, elder, 1036
Rock Camp German Baptist Bethren Church, WV, 1116
Czolgosz, Leon, 442

Daam, Rick, 2276
Dade Co., FL, Homestead Old German Baptist Brethren Church, 626
Dade, Susan (later May)
May, James, wife of, 804
Dadisman, Claude Franklin, 1595
Dadisman, Elmer Lee, 1595
Pleasant Hill Village, administrator, 1033
Dadisman, Lee, 359, 1595
San Antonio, TX, Church of the Brethren, minister in, 1141
Dadisman, Mary Nancy, **359**, 807, 1836, 1914
medical missions, 807
Dadisman, Minnie, 359
Dagen, Catherine (later Yount), 1391
Daggett, Albion Curtiss, 377, 1305, 1595
Rhodes, William, 1107
Daggett, Chester F., 1595
Daggett, Joan Lawrence, 2276
Daggett, John W., 1595
Daggett, Kevin Wayne, 2276
Daggett, Martha A., 1839
Daggett, Mary Ellen, 171
Daggett, Walter W., 1595
Dague family, 1235
Homerville, OH, Grace Brethren Church, 626
Dague, Levi, 1235, 1595
Dahanu congregation, India
Nickey, Barbara Marie, as physician missionary, 936
Dahanu, India, 649, 651
Brethren Mission Hospital, 1078
Ebbert, Ella, 417
Ebey, Adam, 418
medical missions, 807
Yeremian (Yereman), O. H., 1385
Dahanu Road Hospital, India, *See* Brethren Mission Hospital
Dahlberg, Nancy, 2276
Dahlinger, Charles W., 1914
Daiber, Richard, 1848

Dailey, Charles
  Mount Laurel, NJ, Grace Brethren
    Church, 883
Dailey, Ellen (later Quinlan), 1076
Dailey, Elmer E., 1595
Dailey family
  Pipe Creek Old German Baptist
    Brethren Church, IN, 1026
Daily Vacation Bible Schools, 192–193,
    359, See also Christian education
  Dowdy, Dortha Mae Frank and James
    Paul, 398
  history and organization, 1977
  Ikenberry, Charles Samuel, 646
  Johnstown, PA, Roxbury Church of the
    Brethren, 675
  Little Swatara Church of the Brethren,
    PA, 750
  Long Beach, CA, Community Grace
    Brethren Church, 754
  Meadow Branch Church of the
    Brethren, MD, 805
  missions education, 864
  Mount Wilson Church of the Brethren,
    PA, 887
  Palmyra, PA, Church of the Brethren,
    991
  Sipesville, PA, Church of the Brethren,
    1187
daily vacation Bible schools
  Weaver, Mahlon J., 1324
Dairy Farm Assignments, 316, **359**
  detached programs, 380
Dairy Testing Assignments, **359**
Dakotas, **627**
Dalby, Barbara N., 1914
Dale City, PA, See Meyersdale, PA
  Meyersdale, PA, Church of the
    Brethren, previous name of, 822
The Dale City Record, 1914
Dale, Elias, 1595
Dale, Noah S., 1595
Daleville College, 164, 208, **360**
  Bowman, Paul Haynes, 168
  Dove, John Adams, 397
  Gilbert, James Zacchaeus, 548
  Henry, Jerry Maurice, 598
  Ikenberry, Charles Samuel, 646
  Ikenberry, Levi Daniel, 646
  John, John Jay, 671
  Moherman, Tully S., 867
  Pritchett, Reuel Bowman, 1060
  Shickel, Elsie Naomi, missionary, 1176
Daleville, VA, Church of the Brethren, 164,
    359–360, 360, 1317
  Pleasant Dale Church of the Brethren,
    VA, 1031
  Pulaski, VA, Church of the Brethren,
    1071
Dali, S. D.
  works by, 2324
Dalke, Henry, 1383, 1595
  San Diego, CA, Grace Brethren
    Church, pastor in, 1141
Dall family
  Plum Creek Old German Baptist
    Brethren Church, KS, 1038
Dallas Center, IA, 1216, 1268
  Church of the Brethren, 104, 342, **360**,
    661, 662
  Maxwell, IA, Church of the
    Brethren, 803
  Panther Creek, IA, Church of the

Brethren, daughter church of,
    992
  Dunkard Brethren Church, 342, **360,**
    491
  First Brethren Church (FGBC), **360**
Dallas Co., IA, 360
Dallas, OR, 1319
  Old German Baptist Brethren Church,
    360–361, 1319
  Olive Grove Old German Baptist
    Brethren Church, CA, 973
  Oregon Brethren, 981
Dallas Theological Seminary
  Fellowship of Grace Brethren Churches
    (FGBC), 488
  Lindower, Leslie E., 744
  McClain, Alva J., lecturer, 772
Dalrymple, Edmund, 1595
Dalton, Clark
  Meadow Branch Church of the Breth-
    ren, TN, 806
Dalton, I., 1595
Daly family
  Montclair, CA, Grace Brethren Church,
    871
Dalzell, Isabelle, 345
Damascus congregation, VA, 746
Damascus, MD, 1224
Damascus, VA, 351, 1315
  Church of the Brethren, 746, See also
    Criders, VA, Damascus Church of
    the Brethren
  meetinghouse at, 211
  Mountain Grove Church of the Breth-
    ren, VA, 889
Damet, John E., 1595
D'Amico, James Vincent, 212, 1595
  Philadelphia, PA, Calvary Church of
    the Brethren, pastor, 1015
Damman, Ernst, 1914
Damodarbhai, Pochabhai, 1595
Damron, William B., 1595
  Salkum, WA, Community Church of
    the Brethren, minister in, 1139
dancing, 26, 27, See also amusements,
    worldly
  musical instruments, 900
Dancy, Fred Fulton, 749, 766, 1595
  Mount Carmel Church of the Brethren,
    NC, minister, 880
  New Haven Church of the Brethren,
    NC, pastor in, 928
  Peak Creek Church of the Brethren,
    NC, 1003
  Shelton Church of the Brethren, NC,
    pastor in, 1176
Dändliker, See Denlinger
Dandliker family, 375
Dandridge, TN, French Broad Church of
    the Brethren
  Pritchett, Reuel Bowman, 1060
Danes
  Herington, KS, Church of the Brethren,
    598
Danford, Edward M., 1595
Daniel
  Ramirez, Frank on, 2351
Daniel, Book of 2020–2021
Daniel family
  Mount Pleasant, PA, Brethren Church,
    886
Daniele, Joseph W., 1914
Daniels, Felton, 258

Daniels, Marta
  works by, 2324
Daniel's Prophecy of the Seventy Weeks
    (McClain), 773, 2002
Daniels, Roger
  works by, 2324
Daniels, Terry L., 2276
  South Pasadena, CA, Grace Brethren
    Church, associate pastor, 1206
Danish Mission, **361,** 629
  Eshelman, Matthew Mays, 455
  Eskildsen, Christen(?) Christensen,
    456
  Fry, Daniel, 521
  Hope, Mary Katherine Neilsen, 629
  Illinois, 647
  missions, 858–859, 860, 862
  missions education, 863
  Myers, Paul R., 904
  relief and service efforts, 1096
  Sisters' Aid Society, 1187
Dannenbaum, A. O., 1595
Danner, Anna (later Petry), 361, 362, 1013
Danner, Christian, 1595
Danner (Donner), Henry, **361, 2372**
Danner (Donner, Tanner), Jacob, **362,** 1596
Danner, Elizabeth, 361
Danner family, 145, 411
  history of, 1960
  sources on, 2312
Danner, Frederick
  history of, 1914
Danner, G. Howard, 1595
  Pleasant Hill Church of the Brethren,
    PA, presiding elder, 1032
Danner, H., See Schuricht, Hermann
Danner, Heinrich, 1914
Danner, Henry, **361,** 732, 1595–1596
  publishing, 1063
Danner, Henry (CB), 1596
Danner, J. D., 1914
Danner, J. E., 1596
Danner, Jacob, 106, 145, 323, 370, 732
  history of, 1914
  Maryland Brethren activity, 798
  Pipe Creek Church of the Brethren,
    MD, presiding elder, 1026
  publishing, 1063
Danner, Jacob, family
  Pipe Creek Church of the Brethren,
    MD, 1026
Danner, Jacob Monroe, 1596
Danner, Jesse, 1596
Danner, John, 1914
Danner, Rose Carver, 1914
Danner, Samuel, 689, 1596
  Muhlenberg Co., KY, German Baptist
    Brethren, 893
Danner (Tanner, Donner), Michael, 361,
    362, 2372
  former Mennonite, 1994
  Mason-Dixon Line, 800
Danner (Tanner), John
  Madison Church of the Brethren, VA,
    781
Danville, MD, Church of the Brethren, **363,**
    714
Danville, OH, 1340, 1367
  Church of the Brethren, **363,** 374
  Grace Brethren Church, 362
  North Bend Church of the Brethren,
    362
Danville, VA

Emmanuel Church of the Brethren, 105, **362–363**
First Church of the Brethren, **363**
Danzig (Gdansk)
  Felbinger, Jeremias, 482
Dapp, Charles Frederick, 1914
Darby, John N., 390
  Plymouth Brethren, 1039
Darbyites, *See* Plymouth Brethren movement
Darius the Mede (Whitcomb)
  Whitcomb, John Clement, Jr. (FGBC, CGBCI) and, 2262
Darke Co., OH, 147, 260, 262, 264, 281, 349, 707, 708, 729, 1231, 1281, 1288, 1324, 1333, 1910
  Greenville Church of the Brethren, 571
  North Star Church of the Brethren, 950
  Oak Grove Old German Baptist Brethren Church, 956
  Oakland Church of the Brethren, 957
  Oakley, Annie, 958
  Old German Baptist Brethren, 967
  Old Order German Baptist Brethren, 970
  Painter Creek Church of the Brethren, 990
  Painter Creek Old German Pabtist Brethren Church, 990
  Pitsburg, Church of the Brethren, 1026
  Pleasant Valley Church of the Brethren, 1035
  Poplar Grove, Church of the Brethren, 1046
  Shady Grove Old German Baptist Brethren Church (formerly Union City), 1170
  sources on, 2323
Darkening Valley: A Biblical Perspective on Nuclear War (Aukerman), 2133
Darling, Roger E., 1281, 1596
  Pittsburgh, PA, First Brethren Church, pastor, 1027
  Ripon, CA, Brethren Church, pastor, 1110
Darlington, Marwood, 1865
Darlington, MD, 755
Darlow, KS, 8, 410
  Aged, Infirm and Orphans' Home
    Wise, John, 1354
  Eby, Enoch, 419
  Old Folks Home, 1972
  unpublished historical materials, 1913
Darms, Anton, 1914
Darnell, Benjamin
  article about, 1914
Darnell, C. A., 1914
Darnell, Cansada (later Reed), 1091
Daron, Garman Harlow, 1914
Daron, Gulah Velma Hoover, 1914
Darr, John J., 1596
Darr, Shimer E., 1320, 1596
Darst, Abraham, 363, 912
Darst (Durst), Abraham, 363,
Darst, B. F., 1399
Darst, Benjamin F., 363, 1596
Darst (Durst) family, **363**, 1914
  children named for Bible personages, 912
  Reading Grace Brethren Church, PA, 1084

Darst, Henry Jackson, 1914
Darst, Isaac, 363, 912, 1596
Darst, J. Charles, 1399
Darst, Jacob, 363, 912
Darst, John, 261, 363, 912, 1265, 1596
Darst, John Charles, **363**, 1596
Darst, Katherine Markey, 363
Darst, Mary Miller, 363
  Müller (Miller) family, 894
Darst, Rebecca Shoup, 363
Darst, Samuel, 363
  Müller (Miller) family, 894
Darstites (OGBB), *See* Darst, John Charles
Darvell (Robertsbridge, Sussex, England)
  Hutterian Society of Brothers, 640
Darwin, Charles, 463
Darwin, IN, Brethren Church, **363**
Das, Gershom S., 1596
Dasenbrock, J. Henry
  works by, 2324
Daslow, W. H., 1581
Dassdorf, Richard, 1914
Dassel, H., Sr., 1914
Daté, Barbara
  Ministry of Reconciliation, 2224
  dative case in place name, 912
Daub, Elizabeth Amy Lick, 1998
Daubenspeck, George E., 1596
Da(u)ge, Jacob
  Morrill Church of the Brethren, MN, 877
Daugherty family
  Prosperity Brethren Church, WV, 1062
Daugherty, S. Paul, 1596
Daughter of the Plain Folk (Dubble), 747
Daughters of the American Revolution, 1914
Daughterty, Robert
  New Hope Church of the Brethren, AR, elder in, 929
Daughtery, David S., 1380, 2276
Daughtry, James Earl, 1596
Dauphin Co., PA, 383, 456, 737, 1401
  biographical encyclopedia, 1975
  Engle family history, 1930
  Hershey, PA, Spring Creek Church of the Brethren, 599
  history of, 1927
  Huber family, 1975–1976
  Ridgeway Community Church of the Brethren, PA, 1109
  Sanger family, 1144
Dauphin Co., VA, 236
Davalos, Jesus, 1596
  San Ysidro, CA, Grace Brethren Church, pastor in, 1142
Daveler, Harold, 1596
Davenport, IA, Grace Brethren Church, **363**
Davenport, John Scott, 1914–1915, 2037
Davey, Henry D., 170
David C. Cook (publisher), 1237
David, Christian
  Moravian Church, 875
David E. Brinser Residence for men
  Elizabethtown College, 438
David family
  sources on, 2320
David, Hans Theodore, 1915
  works by, 2324
David J. Craik, 351
David, John B. (or Davis), 2125
David, King, 267
David, Thomas C., 1596

Davidheiser, Ruth (later Groff)
  Groff, Warren Frederick, 2194
Davidic Psalter, See Das Kleine Davidische Psalterspiel, under K
Das Davidische Psalterspiel, See Das Kleine Davidische Psalterspiel, under K
  Community of the True Inspiration, 330
Davidisches Psalter-Spiel der Kinder Zions, 1915, *See also Das Kleine Davidische Psalterspiel der Kinder Zions,* under K
David's Children (Bates), 748
Davidson Co., NC, 230, 734, 1299, 1383
  Brethren settlement, 946
  Maple Grove Church of the Brethren, NC, 790
  Pfautz family, 1014
Davidson Co., TN, 1253
  Guice (Geist Guß, Guss, Güß), Christopher, 576
Davidson family, 721, 739, 749
Davidson, Goldie, 1915
Davidson, Jeffrey A., 2276
Davidson, Kenneth, W., 2276
Davidson, O. G., 1596
Davidson, Oliver L., 1596
Davidson, Philip, Jr., 1915
Davidson, Ross C., 1596
Davidson, Samuel, 1915
Davidson, William Dell, 1915
Davies Co., NC, 411, 1383
  Brethren settlement, 946
Davis, A. Tamar, 1915
Davis, Ada, 2038
Davis, C., 1596
Davis, Carl B., 1915
Davis, Charles, 1596
  Ocala, FL, Grace Brethren Church, 2232
  Okeechobee, FL, Grace Brethren Church, pastor, 963
Davis, Charles Ernest, 236, 285, **363–364,** *364,* 1330, 1596, 1915
  historical writing, 612
Davis, Charles Wesley, 354, 363, 1596
Davis, Christian, 1596
Davis, Christian Simeon, 1596
Davis, Clarence (Chuck) R., Jr., 503, 2276
Davis, D. C., 1596
Davis, Daniel, Sr.
  works by, 2324
Davis, Diana Dala, 1848
Davis, Dorcas A., 500
Davis, Dorothy Brandt, 748, 1915
Davis, E. L., 2060
Davis, Edward, 1596
Davis, Ella L., 2060
Davis, Elwood, 1596
Davis, Emma (later Cramer), 540
Davis, Ethel, 236
Davis family, **364,** 1312, 2060
  Faiview-Rocky Mount Church of the Brethren, VA, 470
  Martinsburg, WV, Rosemont Grace Brethren Church, 798
  McFarland, CA, Church of the Brethren, 774
  Mission Viejo, CA, Saddleback Valley Grace Brethren Church, 855
  Mount Etna, IA, Church of the Brethren, 881

Neher family, related to, 922
Pataskala, OH, Grace Brethren Church of Licking Co., 995
Pipe Creek Old German Baptist Brethren Church, IN, 1026
South Haven Old German Baptist Brethren Church, MI, 1205
Davis, Gary W., 2300
Davis, George, 1288, 1596
Davis, George A., 1915
Davis, Glen R., 446, 1596
Davis, Grace Heisel, 364, *364*
Davis, Gretchen Diane (later Wardlaw), 2296
Davis, Harrison, 1596
Davis, Hiram Ellsworth, 1596
Davis, J. K., 1596
Davis, J. Rodney, 1915
Davis, James, 1596
Davis, James A., 2276
Davis, James H., 2276
Davis, Jefferson, 1596
Davis, Jeffrey, 213
Davis, Jehu, 1315
Davis, Jerry, 1915
Davis, Joanne, 1915
Davis, Joe, 236
Davis, John, 1596
Davis, John B. (or David), 2125
Davis, John F., 1596
Davis, John G., 364
Davis, John J., Jr., 1915, 2182, 2276
    Grace Schools, 2192
    on Joshua-2 Kings and history of Israel, 2363
    Whitcomb, John Clement, Jr. (FGBC, CGBCI) and, 2262
Davis, John N., 1596
    Maple Glen Church of the Brethren, PA, minister, 789
Davis, Joseph Marion, 1596, **2381**
Davis, Kenneth A., 268, 1596
Davis, Linda E. S., 2276
Davis, Linna Worster, 363–364
Davis, Linnie Wersyer, 354
Davis, Martha E., 364
Davis, Mary, 377
Davis, Matthew, 1915
Davis, Maurice, 377
Davis, Miss, 1339
Davis, Nora Pearl Bracken, 1360, 1596
Davis, O. G., 1596
Davis, Oliver, 1315
Davis, P. Sherman, 1596
Davis, Paul Alvin, 318, 626, 738
    Portis, KS, Grace Brethren Church, pastor, 1048
Davis, Raymond Harry, 2276
    Meyersdale, PA, Grace Brethren Church, pastor, 822
Davis, Rebecca I., 1915
Davis, Richard Warren
    works by, 2324
Davis, Sara E., 1915
Davis, Stanley Lewis, Jr., 1596
Davis, Thomas Alvin, 1596
Davis, Thomas C., 1596, 2300
Davis, Thomas E., 1596
Davis, Vernita Jane Neher, 2276
Davis, W. H., 1596
Davis, William, 632, 689, 1596–1597
Davis, William Eugene, 1597
Davison, Alpha L., 264, 360, 1596, 2300,
    2381
Olive Grove Old German Baptist Brethren Church, CA, minister, 973
    sources on, 2324
Davison family, 1333
Davison, Fannie
    Reedley, CA, Church of the Brethren, 1091
Davison, Franklin
    Reedley, CA, Church of the Brethren, 1091
Davison, Mary
    works by, 2324
Davison, Oliver Landon, 1597
Davisson family, 1267
Davisson, Willard Dale, 1597
Davy, Catherine Bosteter, 364
Davy, Elizabeth Leatherman, 364
Davy family
    article about, 1915
Davy, Henry Dorsey, 31, 261, 350, **364–365**, 374, 419, 618, 728, 1265, 1597
    Annual Meeting moderator, 1151
    church trial, 1274
    medicine, 810
    Miami, OH, and Brethren settlement, 961
    minutes, 852
    Owl Creek Old German Baptist Brethren Church, OH, minister, 986
Davy, J. O., 1915
Davy, Jacob A., 728
Davy, John, 364
Davy, John, Jr., 364
Dawha, Thlama A., 306
Dawson, Alta Elizabeth (later Poland)
    Poland, Frank Jacob and, 2238
Dawson Co., MT
    Montana Brethren settlement, 870
Dawson, M. M., 241, 1597
Dawson, NE, 148
    day care centers
    Elgin, IL, Highland Avenue Church of the Brethren, 436
    Loon Creek Church of the Brethren, IN, 757
    Xenia, OH, Beavercreek Church of the Brethren, 1383
Day, Dorothy, 659
Day, Kelly M., 1597
Day, Neva Hope, *629*
day schools, See Christian day schools
Day, Sherman, 1915
Day, Stanley, 1597, 2300
Dayar, Nigeria, 306
Dayes, Birth
    Earnest, Corrine Pattie on, 2328
    Earnest, Russell on, 2328
Dayhoff, Guy W., 1597
Dayton congregation, VA, 1305
Dayton Convention (1883), 37, 110, 235, 692
    Brethren Church, 335, 368
    Brethren Church, organization of, 961
    Congregational Brethren, 335
    and denominational name, 910
    First Brethren Church of Pleasant Hill, OH, 335
    German Baptist Brethren controversy, 260
Leedy Brethren, 734
Mason, Edward, clerk, 799
Progressive Brethren, 335
Progressive Brethren movement, 368
Reconstruction Committee, 1086
Sisters' Society of Christian Endeavor (BC), 1188
Spanogle, William L., 1208
Dayton, James F., 1597
Dayton, NM, 719
Dayton, OH, 177, 313, 692, 693, 696, 1281, *1331,* 1335, 1338, 1355, 1376, 1915
    Basore Road Grace Brethren Church, **365,** 367
    Bear Creek congregation, 366, 652
    Brethren Church, 694
    East Dayton Church of the Brethren, **365,** 1523
    Emmanuel Church of the Brethren, **365**
    First Brethren congregation, 367, 1220
    First Brethren Church, 318, 365, 373, 687, 692, See also Dayton, OH, First Grace Brethren Church
    Fellowship of Grace Brethren Churches (FGBC), 485
    Gearhart, William A., 533
    First Grace Brethren Church, 2, 81, **365–366**
    Fort McKinley Church of the Brethren, **366,** 2197
    German Baptist Brethren, 692
    Grace Brethren Church, **366,** 406, 1276
    Grace Brethren Church of Huber Heights, **366,** 367
    Grace Brethren retirement home, 1198
    Hillcrest Brethren Church, **366**
    historic sites, 609
    Kettering, OH, Calvary Grace Brethren Church founded in, 691
    Lower Miami Church of the Brethren, 102, **366–367,** 367
    Lower Stillwater congregation, 1255
    Mack Memorial Church of the Brethren (West Dayton), 81, 102, **367,** 532, 628, 639, 1011, 2216
        25 year anniversary, 1995
        history, 1995
    Meyer family, 822
    Miller, Jacob, 838
    North Riverdale Grace Brethren Church, 366, **367,** 1277, 1302
    North Riverside Grace Brethren Church, **367**
    Patterson Park Grace Brethren Church, **367**
    Prince of Peace Church of the Brethren, **367**
    Stillwater Old German Baptist Brethren Church near, 1223
        First Petition, 491
Dayton, PA, Cowanshannock Brethren Church, See Cowanshannock, PA, Brethren Church
Dayton, VA, 342, 1308
    Church of the Brethren, **367**
    Dunkard Brethren Congregation, **367–368**
    Mount Zion Brethren Church, **368**
DBCM, See Director of Brethren Church Ministries

DDB, *See* Director of Denominational Business
De Baca Co., NM, 1240
de Boer, Hans, *See* Boer, Hans de
De Bolt, Elizabeth (later Sterling), 1221
De Bolt, George W.
Philadelphia, PA, First Brethren Church, pastor, 1015
"De Doopsgezinden to Leeuwarden in het begin des 18. Eeuw" (Hoop Scheffer) De Hass, Wills, 1916
De Koker family, *See* Koker, de, family
De La Plain, John
Peace Valley Church of the Brethren, MO, 1003
De Moines, IA
urban mission, 1297
De Oleo, Ruben, 2276
De peccato originali (*On Original Sin*) (Zwingli), 348
De Sherbinin, M. A., 1599
De Signatura rerum (*Concerning the Birth and Designation of All Being*) (Boehme), 156
De Soto Co., FL, Church of the Brethren, *See* Arcadia, FL, Church of the Brethren
De testamentis Christi (Boehme), 2142
De tribus principiis (*On the Three Principles of Divine Being*) (Boehme), 156
Deacon, 1915
The Deacon, 104, **369**, 1915
deaconesses, 177, **369**, *See also* unleavened bread
ordination, 980
women and, 2263
deacons, 165, 177, 189, **368–369, 369, 1884, 2169,** *See also* election of church officers
Association of Brethren Caregivers (ABC), 2132
commissioning services, 327
degrees of ministry, 374
Dilling family, 384
dress for, 402
Dunkard Brethren, 409–410
Durnbaugh, Donald F. on historical perspective of, 2326
Gibble, June Adams on resource for, 2333
Grace Brethren Church ministry, 847
hats, 589
Holsinger, Henry Ritz, 621
laying on of hands during consecration of, 730
manuals for, 788
marriage counseling, 796
medical care, 810
messenger selection, 819
ministry, 844, 845
Old German Baptist Brethren, 2233, 2234
at Old German Baptist Brethren love feast, 967
Old German Baptist Brethren, seating in meetinghouses, 969
ordination, 980
overseer of the poor, 986
poor box, 1046
poor, caring for, 1046
role in worship services, 1377
role of, 294

Swartz, Fred W. on resource for, 2333
sources on, 2317
training programs, 2161
widows, care for, 1344
deacon's visit, **369**, 763, *See also* home visitation
Dunkard Brethren, 410
ministry, 845
preparatory service for communion, 1056
Deaf Fellowships
Frederick, MD, Church of the Brethren, 511
Roanoke, VA, Central Church of the Brethren, 1112
Deal, Diane
Pomona, CA, Fellowship Church of the Brethren, 1045
Deal (Diehl), John E., 1597
Deal family, *See* Diehl
Garrett, PA, Church of the Brethren, 531
Harley family, 583
Deal, Grace, 1597
Deal, Hannah
Onekama, MI, Church of the Brethren, 975
Deal, Howard Walter, 1597
Deal, John, 124, 1213, 1281
Salem Church of the Brethren, ND, 1138
Deal, Noah
Onekama, MI, Church of the Brethren, 975
Deal, Thomas A.
Modesto, CA, Church of the Brethren, 866
Deal, Thomas W., 1597
Deal, W. W., 1917
Dean, Arthur, 51
Dean, Fred V., 1597
Dean, Vernon F., 2276
Deardorf family, 1219, *See also* Dierdorff family
Deardorf, George E., 257
Deardorf, Jacob, 430
Deardorf, Lewis
Shultz and Paul families, related to, 1157
Deardorf, Rebecca, 365
Deardorff, A. M., 1597
Deardorff, Aaron
Filley German Baptist Brethren Church, NE, 2374
Deardorff, Barbara Reber, 1085
Deardorff, Barry, 1597
Deardorff, Catherine (later Williams), 1916
Deardorff, Charles, 442
Deardorff, Charles H., 51, 64, 442, 1597
Deardorff, Cletus Owen, 1597
Deardorff, Daniel, 1597
Deardorff, Earl Fenton, 246, 1597
Deardorff family, 1281, 1953
history of, 1916
Deardorff, George Emmanuel, 1597
Deardorff, Henry, 1597
Deardorff, Hope L. (later Prather), 1051
Deardorff, Isaac, 257, 1597
Deardorff, Jacob Warren, 445, 1597
Patterson, CA, Church of the Brethren, 995
Deardorff, Jesse S., 1916
Deardorff, John Benton, 1597

Deardorff, John D. W., 1597
Deardorff, Juanita, 2165
Deardorff, Lewis, 1597
Deardorff, Lova, 246
Deardorff, Mattie (later Huffman)
South Saint Joseph Church of the Brethren, MO, 1135
Deardorff, Moses, 1597
Soldier River German Baptist Brethren, IA, 1201
Deardorff, Noble E., 1240, 1597, 2300
Mount Hope Church of the Brethren, WA, 882
Deardorff, William A., 668, 1330, 1597
Minot, ND, Church of the Brethren, elder, 851
Deardurff, family
Columbus, OH, Smoky Row Brethren Church, 2166
Dearing, James Oliver, 462, 1597
Dearing, Oliver J., 264
Romine Church of the Brethren, IL, providing leadership, 1121
DeArmey, Larry Allen, 1597, 1848
DeArmey, Max A., 670, 746, 1597
DeArmey, Richard P., 670, 1322, 1353, 1380, 1597, 2300
Orange, CA, Grace Brethren Church, pastor, 975
Osceola, IN, Grace Brethren Church, pastor, 984
Sidney, IN, Grace Brethren Church, pastor, 1181
DeArmey, Vicki Anne Shirey, 1848
Dearmond, Mary
Oakville, IN, Brethren Church, 959
Dearth, Thomas Eugene, 2276
Deary, James E., 1597
death and dying, **369–370,** 2079, 2316, *See also* burial customs and funerals; cemeteries; tombstones
death notices in Pennsylvania communities, 2005
death of Jesus Christ and Brethren Doctrine of Salvation, 1140
death penalty, *See* capital punishment
death records, Somerset Co., PA, 2104
Deaton, Dale, 142, 1597
Deaton, Dean, 1597, 2276
Deaton family, 142
Haddix, KY, Brethren Church, 577
Redstone Valley Old German Baptist Brethren Church, WI and, 2240
Deaton, George W., 1597
Deaton, Glen D., 1597, 2300, **2381**
Prices Creek Old German Baptist Brethren Church, OH, elder or minister, 1057
Deaton, Joseph Fletcher, 417, 1597
Deaton, Kenneth A., 2276
Deaton, Runella (later Brubaker), 2153
Deaton, William Monroe, 417, 1597
Deatrick, W. W., 1916
Deatwole, Daniel R., 1960
debates, 31, **370–371,** 2017
Brethren movement, 385
Brethren opposition to secret societies, 1164
Brethren-sponsored higher education, 1138
Campbell, Alexander, 247
Church of Jesus Christ of Latter-day Saints, 298

controversies over modern art, 61
Danner (Donner), Jacob, 362
devotional literature, 381
Disciples of Christ, 385
Disciples of Christ, with Strickler, William, 1157
Fairview, MO, Shoal Creek Church of the Brethren, 468
Gibson, Isham, 548
Gish, William R., 550
Great Commission, 568
Grebe (Grebi), Georg, 569
Hess, Maurice Abram, 601
Holsinger, Levi Teeter, 623
Hostetler, Joseph, 631
Kesler, Benjamin Elias, 409, 690
Liberal-Fundamendalist controversy, 1261
lyceums, 768
Miller, Robert H., Sr., and Sommer, Daniel, 1313
Miller, Robert Henry, 841–842
noncreedalism, 942
Pleasant Dale Church of the Brethren, IN, held at, 1030
Quinter, James, 1077
Quinter, James, and Harry Knepper, 1236
Rockingham Church of the Brethren, MO, 1118
Shamberger, George A., elder, 1171
Stein and Ray Debate, 2074
Stein, John William, and Ray, D. B., 1220
Sturgis, Daniel B., 1232
Thomas, Daniel, and Methodist minister, 1262
Thurman, William C., 1264
Wakenda Church of the Brethren, MO, 1313
with other denominations, 1210
Wolfe, George, II, and Catholic priest, 1357
DeBella, Mrs. Winifred
San Jose, CA, South Bay community Church (FGBC), 1142
DeBenedetti, Charles L., 1916
DeBerry, William Henry, 1597
Debiro, Nigeria, 306
Debo family
Roanoke, VA, Washington Heights Grace Brethren Church, 1114
DeBoer family
Minerva, OH, Grace Brethren Church, 843
DeBolt, Alpheus, 469, 1597
DeBolt, Edgar Charles, 1597, 2300
DeBolt family, 2089
DeBolt, G. W.
Masontown, PA, Brethren Church, pastor, 800
DeBolt, George W., 255, 1597–1598
South Bend, IN, First Brethren Church, pastor, 1203
DeBolt, Michael, 1973
DeBolt, Robert Lynn, 2276
debt
house churches, 632
debts, 371, See also businesses; ethics; interest-taking; law, doctrine of
collection of
attitudes toward, 728
law enforcement authorities and,

729
"Decade of Solidarity with Women"
Re-imagining Conference and, 2240
"Decade to Overcome Violence"
World Council of Churches and, 2265
Decatur Co., IA, Church of the Brethren,
See Franklin, IA, Church of the Brethren
Decatur congregation
Golden Spring German Baptist Brethren Church, NE, 2374
Decatur, IL, 151, 713, 732
Church of the Brethren, 58, 371, 1314
Decatur, TX
Fort Worth, TX, Church of the Brethren, 504
Dechert, Michael S. A.
works by, 2324
Decker, Donald
Monticello, MN, Church of the Brethren, minister, 872
Decker, Samuel E., 65, 1598
Declaration of Independence
Miller, Peter, translations of, 2104
Declaration of Principles, 67, 371–372, 409
Brethren Church and noncreedalism, 942
Dunkards, 2173
Progressive Brethren, 133
Declaration of Sentiments (1608), 55
Decorum Committee (DB), 372
establishment of, 2174
youth and, 2268
Dedication of infants, 372, See also church parents; infant baptisms
German Seventh-Day Baptists, 542
laying on of hands, 731
Prather, John Perry, 1051
dedication service
Dutchtown Brethren Church, IN, 411
Dee, Philip M., 1916
Deemy, Richard Lynn, 1598
Deener (Deaner, Deanor), Henry Clay, 1598
Deep River Church of the Brethren, IA, 211
English River Church of the Brethren, IA, 447
Deep River, IA, German Baptist Brethren congregation, 372–373
Deepwater, MO, Church of the Brethren, 373
Deer Creek, IN
congregation, 1294
example of place name, 911
Old Brethren, 964
Old German Baptist Brethren Church, 373
Deer Creek meetinghouse
Wagoner, Raymond K. (OGBB) and, 2259
Deer Creekers, See Old Brethren
Old Brethren, 964
Deer Park, MN, Church of the Brethren,
See Barnum, MN Church of the Brethren
Deer Spring (Norfolk, CT)
Hutterian Society of Brothers, 640
Dees family
Poplar Valley Church of the Brethren, MT, 1047
Deeter, A. F., 348, 1320
migration of Brethren, 830
Deeter, Abraham, 384
Deeter, Absalom, 1598

Deeter, Allen C., 669, 1598, 1916
Brethren Colleges Abroad, 2142
historical writing, 612
works by, 2324
World Friendship Center, 1369
Deeter, Daniel, 335
Deeter, David, 348, 384, 1598, 2085
Deeter, Effel, 1916
Deeter, Emerson, 759
Deeter family, 1389, See also Dieter family
Salem Church of the Brethren, ND, 1137
Deeter, Harold Isaac, 1598
Lake Breeze Church of the Brethren, Sheffield Village, OH, 1175
Deeter, Ida Hoover, 373
Deeter, J. W., 759
Deeter, Jeanne, 2276
Deeter, Joan George, 191, 1598, 1916, 2108, 2276
church governance and, 2264
Who Are These Brethren?, 2149
works by, 2324
Deeter, John Wilby, 373, 384, 1598
Honeyman, Gale E. S. on descendants of, 2337
Pomona, CA, Church of the Brethren, pastor, 1045
Deeter, Manly Huggins, 44, 373, 493, 1598
Milford, IN, Bethel Church of the Brethren, minister, 831
New Salem Church of the Brethren, Milford, IN, as minister, 932
Deeter, Mary Ann (later Mohler)
Mohler, Samuel Sayler, wife of, 868
Deeter, Mary (later Ives), 665
Deeter, Minnie, 373, 1848
and Noatemo, Jean in French Equatorial Africa, 938
Riverside Christian Training School, teacher and missionary, 1111
Deeter, Sarah Reed, 373
Deeter, Sarah Sipes, 373
Deeter, Shively Elizabeth, 384
Deeter, Susanna Ulrich 384
Honeyman, Gale E. S. on descendants of, 2337
Deeter, William Reed, 319, 373, 1285, 1598
Milford, IN, Bethel Church of the Brethren, minister, elder, 831
Norcatur, KS, Maple Grove Brethren Church, 945
Portis, KS, Grace Brethren Church, pastor, 1048
Deets, B. F., 1598
Deetscreek, Bradley J., 2276
DeEtt, Wilma (Prowant, Benson, Pugh), 2040
defellowship, 169, 179
defense industries, 373, See also peace movement
defense industry, WWI employment in, 301
Deffenbaugh, Barron K., 2276
Deffenbaugh, Charles, E., 1598
Mount Zion Brethren Church, OH, minister, 888
Deffenbaugh, Donald Wayne, 6, 632, 1598
Deffenbaugh, George, 553
Deffenbaugh, Gerald Edward, 267, 1598
Deffenbaugh, Mary Mack, 553
Defiance Co., OH
Hicksville, OH, Church of the Brethren, 602

Maumee Church of the Brethren, OH, 803

Poplar Ridge Church of the Brethren, OH, 1047

Poplar Ridge congregation, organization of, 939

Defiance Co., OH, 736

Defiance, OH
Church of the Brethren, **373–374**
Poplar Ridge Church of the Brethren, mission point, 1047
Maumee Church of the Brethren, OH, 803

Degoede, Ariaen, 2063

DeGraff, IN
Christian Brethren and, 281

DeGraff, OH, 1225
degrees of ministry, 177, **374**, *See also* ministry, degrees of; ministry, terminology; ordination
advancement, 845
elder, 432
handclasp, 582
Hoke, George, 618
Holsinger, Henry Ritz, 621
installation of ministers, 656
messenger selection, 819
Mooreites, 875
ordination, 980
Pennsylvania Church of the Brethren, 1005

DeGroot, Alfred T., 1945

DeHaan, M. R.
The Upper Room, Our Daily Bread, 382

DeHart family
Radford, VA, Fairlawn Grace Brethren Church, 1079

DeHart, Sylvia Mae (later Weiss), 1328

DeHaven, Hannah (later Sutter), 760

DeHaven, Jonas, 1598

Deheza, Argentina, 53

Deheza congregation, Argentina
Siccardi, Luis, pastor, 1181

Deihl, Catharine
descendants, 1917

Deihl, John Adam
descendants, 1917

Deile, Volkmar, 1948

Deisch, Susie Lenom, 1854

Deism
religious liberty, 1098
Freemasonry, 514

Deissinger, Catherine Moyer
Meyer family, 821

Deitz, Benjamin Franklin, Sr., 1598

Deitz, Harry, 1598

DeJean, John S., 1235, 1598

DeKalb Co., IN, 264, 265
Pleasant Chapel Church of the Brethren, IN, 1030

DeKoker family, *See* Koker, de, family

Del Paso Heights congregation, CA, 726

Del Rey, WV, 1249

Delaney, Terry, 1598

Delaney, W. D., 1598

Delany, Hazel Coppock, 1845

Delaplain (De La Plain), John, 1598

Delaplaine, Edward S., 1916

DeLauter, Aaron, 374

DeLauter, Ella Snell, 374

DeLauter, Eva Domer, 374

DeLauter, Ora Dale, **374**, 1598

Delaware, **374**
Church of the Brethren mission, 374
Materials Towards a History of the Baptists, 803
Pennsylvania district (BC), congregations in, 1005

Delaware Co. Church of the Brethren, 405

Delaware Co., IN, 233, 1156, 1288

Delaware Co., OH, 364, 374
Sciota Church of the Brethren, 1160

Delaware Co., PA, Church of the Brethren, *See* Drexel Hill, PA, Church of the Brethren

Delaware District German Baptist Brethren Church, OH, *See* Scoita, OH, Church of the Brethren

Delaware Indians, 2093

Delaware, OH, Church of the Brethren, 31, **374**
Sciota Church of the Brethen, OH, 1160

Delaware, OH, Grace Brethren Church, **375**, 1380

Delawder (Delauter?), Clerenda (later Fitzwater), 492

Delbert, J. H., 1598

Delcamp, Juanita, 377

delegates, **375**, *See also* Credential(s) Committee; polity

delegates to Annual Meeting
messengers, 819
women from Scalp Level, PA, Church of the Brethren, 1151

Delk, Ralph M.
Morrisons Cove Home, administrator, 877

Dell, Byron Earl, 448, 1598

Dell, Catherine
Lybrook, NM, Tók'ahookaadí Church of the Brethren, 2216

Dell, Isaac, 1598

Dell, Jacob, 1598

Dell, Jacob S., 1598

Dell, Phillip C., 2276

Dell, Robert L., 318, 579, 691, 1598
Martinsburg, WV, Rosemont Grace Brethren Church, pastor, 798
Ozark Grace Brethren Church, MI, pastor, 987

Dell, Robert W., 1598, 1916
works by, 2324

Dellenbaugh, Grant
North Georgetown, OH, Brethren Church, 948

Deloe, Jesse B., Jr., 367, 768, 1343, 1353, 1598

DeLong, Edna Britton, 1916

DeLong family, 1916

DeLong, Irwin Hoch, 1916

DeLozier, Arthur Lee, 130, 629, 740, **375**, 1598
Solomon, Jeannette Ruth DeLozier (BC) and, 2251

DeLozier, Austin Blair, 375

Delozier family, 731, 1304

DeLozier, Harry, 1598

DeLozier, Himes Alice Margaret, 375

DeLozier, Jeannette Ruth (later Solomon), 1855
biography of, **2251**

DeLozier, M. L., 229

DeLozier, Margaret Alice Himes
Solomon, Jeannette Ruth DeLozier (BC) and, 2251

Delozier, Mary C. (later Hileman)
Miller, Mary Grace Hileman, mother of, 841

DeLozier, States Mae Etta, 375

Delp, Barbara Elizabeth (later Albright), 16

Delp, Charles A. (family), *473*

Delp, Charles E., 72, 255, 1598

Delp, Elizabeth, 150

Delp, Elizabeth (later Rosenberger), 150, 1123, 2048

Delp family
in New Bethel Church of the Brethren, NC, 925

Delp, Godshall, 150

Delp, Jacob, 1598

Delp, Mary Heckler, 150

Delp, Sylvanus E., 1598

Delp, William M., 1598

Delph, Sheldon Glen, 1598

Delphi, IN, Church of the Brethren, **375**
Pittsburg, IN, Church of the Brethren, 1027

Delta, OH, 1243

DeMaio, Lorenzo, 1598

Demeunier, Jean N., 1916

democracy
creation of, 1992

Democratic Republic of the Sudan, *See* Sudan

Democrats
appeal to keep out of office, 1945
demographic trends in America, 2144
demographics, 2029

Demuth, David, 1598

Demuth, Henry, 1598

Demuth, Joseph H., 1598

Demuth, Philip Edwin, 1598

Demy (Demmy), John C., 1598–1599

Denair, CA
Empire, CA, Church of the Brethren, 445

Denbigh, ND, 1341

Denck, Hans, 28

Denlinger, A. L., 375
Old Order German Baptist Church minister, 972

Denlinger, Anna, 209, 375

Denlinger, Anna Wolf, 375

Denlinger, Carl Eugene, 1916

Denlinger, Carolyn Teach, 1916, 1945
works by, 2324

Denlinger, Cecil (later Wagoner), 2138
Wagoner, Gerald C., Sr. (OGBB) and, 2259

Denlinger, Christian, 375

Denlinger, Dale, 1286

Denlinger, Danny L., 2276

Denlinger, Dean, 1599

Denlinger, Don, 360

Denlinger, E. Howard, 1599

Denlinger, Edward, 1295

Denlinger, Edwin Jacob, 1599

Denlinger, Eldon, 1223, 1599

Denlinger, Elizabeth Beeghly, 375

Denlinger family, 142, 233, 353, **375**, 701, 1280, 1916, 2073

Denlinger, Forest Ethel (later Funderburg), 523

Denlinger, Henry, 375

Denlinger, Howard, 1223

Denlinger, Isaac, 1223, 1999

Denlinger, Israel, 1870

Denlinger, John, 375, 2005
Denlinger, L. Dean, 1599
Denlinger, Lawrence W., 1223, 1599
Denlinger, Marlin, 1399, 1599
Denlinger, Martin, 375
Denlinger, Mary, 375
Denlinger, Mary S., 2073
Denlinger, Michael, 375
Denlinger, Ned Martin, 2276
Denlinger, Sarah Funderburg, 375
Denlinger, Susannah, 216
Denlinger, Vernon, 1223
Denlinger, Vernon R., 1599
Denlinger, William H., 1599
    Prices Creek Old German Baptist
        Brethren Church, OH, presiding
        elder, 1057
Denmark, 157, 375–376, 629, 1256
    Brethren in tobacco industry, 1266
    conscientious objectors, 336
    Danish Brethren, article about, 1914
    Danish Mission, 361
    debates, 370
    Eby, Enoch, 419
    Eskildsen, Christen (?) Christensen,
        456
    evangelism, 299
    Frey (Fry) family, 517
    Fry, Daniel, 521, 1384
    General Church Erection and
        Missionary Committee (CB), 536
    German Baptist Brethren, 361
    Germany, 545
    Graybill, Alice Minora Hoffer and
        Jacob Franklin, 567
    Hickory Grove Church of the Brethren,
        IL, 602
    Hope, Christian, 361, 375, 628
    Hope, Mary Katherine Neilsen, 629
    Johansen, Martin, 671
    Kristelig Tidende (Christian Times),
        708
    Lena, IL, Church of the Brethren, 737
    Miller, John William, 2224
    mission, history of, 1932
    mission work, 273, 280
    missions, 858–859, 860, 862
    missions and missionaries in, 160, 178
    missions education, 863
    Myers, Paul R., missionary to, 904
    order of dress in, 403
    Thalitzer, Johannes, 1256
    visits to mission, 1273
Denmark, IN, congregation
    Maple Grove Church of the Brethren,
        IN, 789
Denner, Jacob, 395
Denney, John Burcham, 1599
Dennis, John
    Maine, Brethren activity in, 783
Dennison, Dorothy Mae Brown, 1836
Dennison family, 1380
Dennison, Melvin Paul, 1599, 1836
Denny family, 2087
Denny, John B., 1599
    Mulvane, KS, Brethren Church, pastor,
        896
Denny, Margaret Collins, 2087
denomination organization, study of,
    165
denominational differences
    membership trends 1980 to 2000, 2220
denominational exchanges

Nikodim, Metropolitan, promotion of,
    937
denominational leadership
    historiography, 2202
denominational offices
    Brethren Church, See Brethren Church,
        denominational offices (Ashland, OH)
    Church of the Brethren, See Church of
        the Brethren, General Offices
        (Elgin, IL)
denominational reorganization,
    2169–2170
    Beulah Beach I and II, 2136–2137
    Brethren Church, 2140–2141
"Denominational Vision Gathering" (May,
    1995)
    Grassroots, Concerns of the, 2193
denominations, 2019, 2036–2037, 2037,
    2051, 2056, 2057
    Annual Meetings/Conferences listed
        by, 1505–1511
    districts listed by, 1513–1538
    geographical listings of, 1479–1503
    regions listed by, 1513–1538
Densmore, William, 114, 1599
Dentler, Larry M., 2165, 2276
Dentler, William Norman, 1599
Denton, MD, 137, 409
    Church of the Brethren, 137, 376, 409,
        1397, 2079
        Farmington, DE, Bethany Church
            of the Brethren, 479
        Ridgely, MD, Church of the
            Brethren, 1109
    Elkton Immanuel Church of the
        Brethren, MD, 440
Denton, Theodore C., 360, 1599
    Pleasant Dale Church of the Brethren,
        VA, minister, 1031
Denver, CO
    Brethren movement, 325
    Church of the Brethren, 376, 377
    First Church of the Brethren, 72,
        376–377
    Grace Brethren Church, 62, 325, 377
    Prince of Peace Church of the
        Brethren, 72, 376, 377, 1348
    Second Church of the Brethren, 377,
        1209
    minorities, ethnic and racial, 850
    mission, 2063
Denver, IN, Brethren Church, 377
    Mexico, IN, Brethren Church, 821
Denver Omnibus & Cab Co., 325
Department of Agriculture
    Emergency Farm Labor, 443
Department of Family Life (CB)
    bibliography, 1903, 1904
Depression, See Great Depression
Der Feigling (Marx), 747
Der Friedensbote von Concordia
    Sala, Johann, printer, 1136
Der Fröhliche Botschafter, 1293
Der Hoch-Deutsch Americanische
        Calendar, 614
    Sauer, Johann Christoph, I, publisher
        of, 1147
Der Hoch-Deutsch Pennsylvanische
        Geschichts-Schreiber
    Sauer, Johann Christoph, I, publisher
        of, 1147
Der Pennsylvanische Staats-Courier, 1146,
    1149

Der Vaterlandsfreund
    Sala, Solomon, printer, 1136
Der Westliche Beobachter
    Sala, Johann and Solomon, printers,
        1136
Der Wöchentliche Philadelphische
        Staatsbote, 2103
Derby, KS, Brethren Church, 377, 682
Derdes, E. Wayne, 1632
Deremer, James Lee, 1599
    Laughlin Church of the Brethren, MD,
        2214
Derflinger, C. P., 1599
Derham family
    Mill Run Grace Brethren Church, MD,
        833
Derr, Donna, 2171
Derr, H. Kevin, 2276
Derr, Horace E., 2276
Derr, Lizzie, 269
Derrick, A., 1599
Derrick, C. C., 1599
Derrick, D. David, 264
Derrick, David, 264
    Ewing Church of the Brethren, VA,
        2373
Derrick, David D. (CB), 264, 1599
Derrick, David D. (OGBB), 1599
Derrick, F. D.
    Midway Church of the Brethren, TN,
        providing leadership, 827
Derrick, Marvel, 264, 1599
Derrick, Mrs. Marvel, 264
Derry, PA, 693
Des Lacs Valley, ND, Church of the
        Brethren, See Kenmare, ND,
        Church of the Brethren
Des Moines Co., IA, 1358
Des Moines, IA, 1370
    Annual Meetings, 378
    bicentennial celebration, 140, 141
    Church of the Brethren in, article
        about, 1955
    First Church of the Brethren, 377, 495,
        1115,
    First Grace Brethren Church, 377–378,
        804, 1121
    homelessness, 2203
    missions, 860
    Stover Memorial Church of the
        Brethren, 378
Des Moines Valley Church of the Brethren,
    IA, See Ankeny, IA, Church of the
    Brethren (Des Moines Valley)
    Long, Inez Goughnour, 2215
Desai, R. B., 576
Descendants of Jacob Hochstetler, the
        Immigrant of 1736 (Hostetler), 534
descriptions of the Brethren, 378–379, See
    also culture; historical writings
descriptive properties of place name, 911
desegregation
    of schools, 24
Desenberg (Dessenberg), William L., 1599
Deshler, OH, 1235
    Church of the Brethren, 380, 2102
DeShong family
    Mill Run Grace Brethren Church, MD,
        833
"The Design of Baptism" (Bowman), 166
DeSilva, Mark, 2276
Dester, John Wilby, 1599
detached programs, 380

Agricultural College Units, 380
Dairy Testing Assignments, 359
soil conservation units, 1200
Detar, George W., Jr., 1599
detention camps
Japanese-Americans, 2093
Deter, Eunice, 1916, 1979
Detmold
Hochmann von Hochenau, Ernst
Christoph, 614, 615
Detrich (Detrick) family, **380**
Detrick, Abraham, 380
Detrick, Andrew, 1599
Detrick, Andrew Jackson, 1599
Detrick, Anna Elizabeth Beard, 1599
Detrick, B. Ernest, 1599
Detrick, Beery Elizabeth, 380
Detrick (Deitrick, Deedrick), Abraham,
1599
Detrick family, *See* Detrich (Detrick)
family; Detrich family
Good (Guth) family, 556
Detrick, Goldie M. Wyatt, 1599
Detrick, Herbert J., 1599
Detrick, J. B., 1599
Detrick, John, 380, 1193, 2069
Detrick, John William, 1599, 1836
Detrick, Joseph, 1599
Detrick, Judith, 380
Detrick, Judy Snell, 1193
Detrick, Mahala, 380
Detrick, Mary Elaine Cline, 1359, 1599,
2183
marriage enrichment, 796
Women's Conferences (CB) and, 2265
Detrick, P. J., 573, 1225
Detrick, Peter, 734
Detrick Ralph Leroy, 1599, 2138
marriage enrichment, 796
Women's Conferences (CB) and, 2265
Detrick, Snell Judy, 380
Detrick, William C., 1311, 1599
Detroit First Church of the Brethren, MI
example of numerical place name, 911
Detroit, MI
Bethany Church of the Brethren, **380**
Chinese Sunday Schools (CB), 278,
2100
Harper Woods First Church of the
Brethren, 380, 585
Historic Peace Churches, 610
Hoffman, Paul W., 2202
minorities, ethnic and racial, 850
Moy Way, minister, 891
Trinity Church of the Brethren, 585
See Redford, MI, Detroit Trinity
Church of the Brethren
Detsch, Earl, 1599
Dettra, John Emmert, 1599
Dettra, Lewis A. (R.), 1599
Dettweiler family
family history (trans), 1988
Detweiler, Andrew S., 1599
Detweiler, Anna Detweiler
descendants, 1945
Detweiler, Anna Zook, 149, 1834
Detweiler, Christian F., 149, 2107
Detweiler (Detwiler) family, **380–381**
Detweiler, Elias L., 2088
Detweiler, Ezra H., 380, 1916
Detweiler family, 1887, 1994, 2088
family history, 2003
Harley family, 583

Maryville, TN, Oakland German
Baptist Brethren Church, 799
Detweiler, George Lowell, *199,* **380,** 1323
Huntingdon, PA, Stone Church of the
Brethren, 637
Somerset, PA, Church of the Brethren,
pastor, 1202
Detweiler, Gideon and Lydia Kanagy, 1974
Detweiler, Hans, 2088
Detweiler, Harrison Emma, 380
Detweiler, Lois Norris, 244
Detweiler, Meyers Zola, 380
Detweiler, Salome Zook, 149
Detweiler, Zola Meyers, 1599
Detwiler, A. J., 1599
Detwiler, Anthony John, 380
Detwiler, Christian Fisher, 1599
Detwiler, David Teeter, 1599, 1916
Detwiler, Edgar Marion, 1599
Detwiler family, 1998, *See also* Detweiler
family
Detwiler, George Lowell, 1599
Detwiler, Hans C. F., 1599
Detwiler, Jacob, 380
Detwiler, Jacob, Jr., 380
Detwiler, Lois Anna (later Norris), 1599,
1731, 1842
Detwiler, Merle C., 1599
Detwiler, Moyer Anna, 380
Detwiler, Philip B.
London, OH, Grace Brethren Church,
2215
Detwiler, Rachel (later Sell), *See* Sell,
Rachel Detwiler
Detwiler, Robert Warren, 1599–1600
Detwiler, Samuel K., 2276
Detwiler, Teeter David, 380
Detwiler, Vianna, 250, **381,** 501, 1297,
1361, 1600, 1848
missions, 860, 861
Quebec, 1075
Detwiler, Wenger Elizabeth, 380
Detwiler, Willis Oakley, 1600
Deubner, Everett, 1916
Deuteronomy, 28:40, 39
Deutschen Evangelisch Luterischen Synode,
1916
Devan, Fred W., 16
Devan, Fred W., Jr., 1600
Roanoke, VA, Washington Heights
Grace Brethren Church, pastor,
1114
Devault, James Frederick, 1600
DeVeny, Daniel Judson, 2276
Devil, The, *See* Satan
Devilbiss, Willis B., 1600
Devine, Janice (pseud.), 1916
DeVore, William O., 1337
devotional life
education, 427
devotional literature, **381–382,** 2039,
See also tracts
Brethren Publishing House, 300
colonial era
Pennsylvania, 2074
Grisso, Lillian Etna, 574
hymns read as poetry, 1039
Mack, Alexander, Jr., 774
Miller, Robert Henry, 842
Pennsylvania, colonial, 2074
photography as art, 1020
publishing, 1069
Dew, Charles B.

works by, 2324
Dewey Co., OK
place-names, Brethren, 1028
Dewey family, 1944
Dewey, Mary Imogene (later Stutsman),
1317
Dewhurst, C. Kurt
works by, 2324
Dexter, NM, 719
Dey, Mary L. MacManes, 1836
Deyerle, Gordon Ernest, 2276
Deymeir, Eileen, 1916
DeYoung, Donald, B., 2097
Whitcomb, John Clement, Jr. (FGBC,
CGBCI) and, 2262
DeZago, Edmund K., 2276
Dhanjibhai
saint of Taropa, 1998
Di Nardo, Juan, **382**
Dial, PA, Brush Valley Brethren Church,
See Brush Valley, PA, Brethren
Church
dialect, *See* Pennsylvania Germans
"Dialectical Theology," 922
Dialects
congregational name pronunciation,
911
Dialogue, 1916–1917
Diamond schoolhouse, KS, 1305
diaries
Hempstead, Joshua, 1962
The Diary, 26
Diaz, Bra D., 1600
Diaz, David, 714
Diaz, John L., 503, 749, 1600
Okeechobee, FL, Grace Brethren
Church, pastor, 963
Orlando, FL, Grace Brethren Church,
pastor, 982
Diaz, Manuel A., 2276
Diaz, Virginia, 714
DiBenedetto, Anthony, Jr., 1600
Dice, D. F.
North Manchester, IN, (First) Brethren
Church, 949
Dice, Lee H., 384, 496, 654, 1600
Dice, Mrs. D. F.
North Manchester, IN, (First) Brethren
Church, 949
Dice, N., 561
Dice, Philip, 468, 1600
Dice, Roy M. Jr., 265, 749, 1251, 1351,
1600
Dick, Bruce, 398
Dick, E. LeRoy, 1600
Dick, Ernestine, 629
Dick family, 262
Dick, Hostetler Esther, 382
Dick, Isaak, 2088
Dick, Jacob Trostle, 685, 1600, 1917
Dick, John, 689, 1234, 1600
Muhlenberg Co., KY, German Baptist
Brethren, 893
Rowland, Joseph, 1126
Dick, LeRoy, 576, 695
Dick, Margaret, 382
Dick, Paul E., **382,** 564, 1348, 1600
Dick, Phillip, 382
Dick, Rancy B., 382
Dick, Richard, 382
Dick, Stanley, 629
Dick, Trostle Perry, 1600
Dick, Velva Jane, 1836, 1917

Pottstown, PA, Coventry Church of the Brethren, missionary, 1049
Dick, Wayne Hollinger, 1600
New Enterprise, PA, Church of the Brethren, as minister, 927
Oaks, PA, Green Tree Church of the Brethren, pastor, 958
Dickens, Ethel Hubbard Morrill, 646
Dickens, John, 646
Dickens, Olivia (later Ikenberry), **646**, 1839
Dickenson Co., KS
Navarre Church of the Brethren, Navarre, KS, 918
Dickenson Co., VA, 356
Pound River Church of the Brethren, VA, 1049
Ramey Flats Church of the Brethren, VA, 1083
Dickerson, G. Fay, 1858–1859
Dickerson, Isaac, 264
Dickerson, Moses J., 30, 1600
Dickerson, Mrs. O. E., 296
Dickerson, W. George, 264
Dickerson, W. I., 1600
Dickey, A. L., 1600
Dickey, A. M., 383, 1217
Seattle, WA, Olympic View Community Church of the Brethren, elder in, 1162
Dickey, Abraham, 1600
Dickey, Alpheus M., 1316, 1600
Dickey (Ashland Co.) congregation
Hoke, George, 618
Dickey cemetery, 383
Dickey, Elias, 67, 382, 383, 1600
Dickey, Elias (CB), 1600
Dickey, Esther, 1600
Dickey family, **383**, 2083
Dickey, Florence, 590
Dickey German Baptist Brethren congregation, Ashland Co., OH, 693
Dickey, Hoke Elizabeth, 382, 383
Dickey, Howard, 1600
Dickey, Howard B., 1600
Dickey, Jane (later Jamison), 668
Dickey, John Priest, 118, 383, 1600, 1917
Dickey, John S., 1600
Dickey, Lavina (later Workman), 1367
Dickey, Levi Hoke, 244, **382–383**, 720, 1600
Oak Grove Church of the Brethren, OH, 956
Dickey, Michael, 383
Nimishillen Church of the Brethren, minister in, 937
Dickey, Nancy, 382
Dickey, O. I., 1878
Dickey, O. J., 1600
Dickey, OH, Church of the Brethren, 383
England, William Ferdinand, 446
Dickey, S. Boyd, 1600, 1917
Dickey, Sarah K.
Pike Run Church of the Brethren, PA, 1023
Dickey, Sol C., 1353
Dickinson Co., KS, 226
Holland Church of the Brethren, KS, 619
Dickinson, J. Merrill, 1600
Dickinson, Jonathan
Great Awakening and American revivalism, 1104
Dickinson, W. Harry, 1600

Dickson, Duane, 1600
Dickson, G. James, 1600
Dickson, H., 1600
Dickson, James, family
Puerto Rico, missionaries to, 1070
Dicky, James, 1315
Dictionary of American English (ed. Buckingham), 226
Dictionary of Christianity in America
Reid, Daniel G. and articles in, 2351
Didrikson, Babe, *See* athletics
Die Erste Liebe (The First Love, 1696), Gottfried Arnold, 43, **453**
Die Geistliche Viole (hymnal), 1211
Die Kleine Harfe (Naas, Johannes), 909
Die Kleine Perlen-Sammlung (hymnal), 1211, 1279
Diederich family, *See* Dieter (Deeter, Teeter) family
Diefenbacher, Elizabeth Frey, 2098
Diehl, A. O., 1600
Diehl, Abraham, 383
Diehl, Austin, 1600
Pleasant Valley Church of the Brethren, TN, 1035
Diehl, C. H.
Pleasant Valley Church of the Brethren, TN, 1035
Diehl, Charles M., II
Old Order German Baptist Church minister, 972, 2235
Diehl, Christian Henry, 383, 1600
Diehl, Christina Bosserman, 163
Diehl, D. A., 1600
Diehl, Elias Henry, 1917
Diehl, Eliza (later Haughtelin), 589
Diehl Eva Katherine, 1917
Diehl family, 211, **383**, 731, 1221, 1917, 2034
Diehl, Frederick
condensed record, 1960
Diehl, Frederick J., 383
Diehl, George West, 1917
Diehl, Harley Magdalena, 383
Diehl, Harry A., 1917
Diehl, J. B., 1600
Diehl, J. Frederick, 383
Diehl, Jacob, 163, 383
Diehl, James, 373, 1600
Diehl, Johann Georg, **383**
Diehl, John, 383
Oak Grove Church of the Brethren, IA, elder, 955
Diehl, John B., 1600
Diehl, John Irvin, 1600
Diehl, John W., 360, 1600
Panora, IA, Church of the Brethren, 992
Diehl, Lorena C. (later Lahman), 718
Diehl, Mary (later Pfoutz), 1015
Diehl, Merklin
Old Brethren German Baptist Church, minister, 965
Old Order German Baptist Church minister, 972
Diehl, Nicolaus, **383**
Diehl, Oscar W., 104, 1600–1601
Diehl, Paul, 1601
Diehl, Philip, 383
Diehl, Samuel
descendants, 1917
Mount Carmel Church of the Brethren, VA, 880

Diehl, Stanley Theron, 1601
Diehl, Susan (later Trostle), 1276
Diehl, Valley V. later Myers), 1842
Myers, Minor Morton, wife of, 904
Diehl, Wilhelm, 1917
Diehl, William, 731
Diehl, William P., II
Old Order German Baptist Church, 2235
Diehl's Crossroads, PA, Church of the Brethren, **383**
Fredericksburg, PA, Clover Creek Church of the Brethren, 513
Diehm, Edgar G., 1391, 1400, 1601, 1917
Diel, Johannes, 2097
Diener family, 1916
Dierdorff, Ahard Mary, 383
Dierdorff, Andrew, 384, 1601
Dierdorff, Andrew M.
descendants, 1917
Dierdorff, Ann (later Stoner)
Myers, Salome Stoner, mother of, 904
Dierdorff, Anthony, 27, 383, **383**
Dierdorff, Anthony, Jr., 383, 2036
Dierdorff, Christian, 383
Dierdorff, Christiana, 163
Dierdorff, Christina, 383
Dierdorff, Daniel T., 430, 447, 688, 1242, 1601
Minot, ND, Church of the Brethren, elder, 851
Salem Church of the Brethren, ND, 1138
Dierdorff, Daniel, 1221
Dierdorff (Deardorf) family, **383–384**
Dierdorff (Deardorff), Daniel, 1601
Dierdorff, Erhart Marie Anna, 383
Dierdorff, Fahnestock Catrina Anna, 383
Dierdorff, Falkenstein Magdalena, 384
Dierdorff family, 1276, 1892, 1902, 1917
family history, 2000
Dierdorff, Henry, 383
Dierdorff, J. W., 1601
Dierdorff, John, 383, 1601
Dierdorff, Kaufman Katherine, 384
Dierdorff, Lee Henry, 1917
Dierdorff, M., 1601
Dierdorff, March Margaret Mary, 384
Dierdorff, Moore Elizabeth, 383
Dierdorff, Peter, 334, 383, 384, 765, 1601
Dierdorff, Russell D., 1601
Dierdorff, Swyer Christine, 383
Dierdorff, Wolgamult Anna, 384
Dierdorff, Yager Marie Anna, 383
diet, *See* cooking
dietary laws, 68
pork, 68, 1047
dietary rules, 147
Dietrich, Earl R.
Martinsburg, PA, Grace Brethren Church, pastor, 798
Dietrich family, 1956
history of, 1916
third reunion, 1917
Dietrich, Mary (later Haight), 1956
Dietrick, Earl W., 629, 1601
diets
Wust, Klaus on shipboard, 2364
Dietz, Arnold, 2276
Dietz, B. F., 1276
Dietz, Clara (later Stutz), 1232
Dietz, Conrad, 31
Dietz, Earl D,, 516, 714, 1209, 1601

Dietz family, 377
Dietz, Harry A., 1276, 1601
Dietz, J. M., 1601
Dietz, John F., 585, 1601
Dietz, Mollie M., 150
Dietz, Paul Ernest, 2276
Diffenderfer family, 721
Diffenderffer, Frank Ried, 1917
Diffendorfer, Helen, 1380
Diffendorfer, Warren, 1380
Digges' Choice, PA, 733
Digman, Samuel P., 1601
Digman, T. B.
    Pine Grove Church of the Brethren,
        MD, minister and presiding elder,
        1024
Digman, Thomas B., 1601
Dilbert, Daniel Webster, 1600
Dilbert, Thomas F.
    Snake Valley Old German Baptist
        Brethren Church, PA, deacon,
        1192, 1193
Dill, Gary A., 1601
Dill, Philip, 1601
Dillard, P. H., 1601
Dillard, Robert D., Jr., 1601
Dille, Nigeria, 306
Diller, Aaron B., 1601
    Monitor Church of the Brethren, OK,
        minister, 869
Diller, Carol Barbara, 1917
Diller, NE, Church of the Brethren, **384**
Dilley, Oliver C., 90, 683, 1601, 2300
Dilley, Ruby Weimer, 1601
Dilling, Casper, 384, 1070
Dilling, Chalmer C., 674, 913, 1601
Dilling, Christina Putterbach, 1070
Dilling, David, 1601
Dilling, Edwin Paul, 1601
Dilling family, **384**, 2038, 2064
    Poplar Valley Church of the Brethren,
        MT, 1047
    Snider, Jacob, descendants of, 1154
    Snowberger family, related to, 1153
Dilling, George Elby, 1601
    Montgomery Church of the Brethren,
        PA, pastor, 872
    Rockton, PA, Church of the Brethren,
        pastor, 1118
Dilling, George S., 1601
Dilling, Herbert C., 1601, 1917–1918
Dilling, John R., 562, 1601
Dilling, Levi S., 1601
Dilling, Paul, 1601
Dilling, Puterbaugh Christina, 384
Dilling, Roy, 1601
Dilling, Yvonne, 627, 2172
    works by, 2324
Dillman, Augusta Annie, 2081
Dillman, Morris, 1601
Dillmon, Don, 705
Dillmon, Susan, 705
Dillon, Frank M., 1601
Dillon, Robert, 1601
Dillon, W., 1870
Dillsburg, PA, 765
    Harrisburg, PA, Melrose Gardens
        Grace Brethren Church, 586
    Hope Grace Brethren Church, **384**
Dilts, Elizabeth (later Herder), 593
Dilts, John C.
    Sergeantsville, NJ, Brethren Church,
        1167

Dilts, Mrs. John C.
    Sergeantsville, NJ, Brethren Church,
        1167
Dimm family, *See* Rinehart family
Dinger, Evan M., 1601
Dingfelder, Dorothy Rines, 1918
    dining tents, 1254
Dinkins-Curling, Jeffrey (Rusty), 2276
Dippel, Johann Konrad, 57, 72, 120, **385,**
        589, 1874, 1918
    Hochmann von Hochenau, Ernst
        Christoph, 614
dippers, *See* names, Brethren; Dompelaars
        (Dompelaers)
Director of Brethren Church Ministries
        (DBCM), **2170**
Director of Denominational Business
        (DDB), **2170**
Director of Pastoral Ministries (DPM),
        2170–2171
directories
    Juniata College, 1980–1981
directors of pastoral ministry (BC)
    Kerner, William Hoff, Sr., 2211
Directory
    General Services Commission (CB),
        539
    directory of churches
    The Record of the Faithful, 1086
Directory of Officials (Old German Baptist
        Brethren)
    published lists of ministers, 1218
dirigibles
    design of by Chester Melvin Vaniman,
        1303
disabled
    rehabilitation, 290
    vocational training for, 173
disaffiliation
    Philadelphia, PA, Calvary Church of
        the Brethren, 1015
DiSalvo, Robert S., 2276
disarmament, 23–24
    article on, 1919
disaster aid
    Barnes, Jay on Brethren Hurricane
        Floyd and, 2348
    Moore, Richard on Brethren Hurricane
        Floyd and, 2348
    Old German Baptist Brethren, 2234
Disaster Network
    mutual aid, 903
disaster relief, 182, 198, 200, **385**, *See also*
        KLM crash; relief and rehabilita-
        tion work; relief and social work
    Beam, Annette Huffaker, 1335
    Brethren Church cooperation with
        Church of the Brethren, 682
    Church of the Brethren contributions,
        2163
    Church World Service (CWS), **2165**
    Coate, Naida, 1335
    Disaster Child Care, 2171, *2171*
    Dunkard Brethren Church, 2175
    East Chippewa Church of the Brethren,
        OH, 415
    East Fairview Church of the Brethren,
        PA, 415
    Elizabethtown, PA, Church of the
        Brethren, 436
    famine relief, 475
    Guatemala, 576
    Honduras, 627

Huntsdale Church of the Brethren, PA,
        638
Ivester Church of the Brethren, IA, 665
Johnstown floods, 673
Mississippi, 864
Mount Joy, PA, Florin Church of the
        Brethren, 882
Niger, Brethren response to drought,
        936
Relief Agency Brethren (FGBC), 1096
relief and service efforts, 1096, 1097
Springfield, OH, First Church of the
        Brethren, 1215
Wakarusa, IN, Church of the Brethren,
        1313
Disaster Response Program, *2171,*
        2171–2172
disasters, *See* Johnstown floods
    social welfare, 1198
Disciples of Christ, 80, 129, 176, **385**, 1901,
        See also Believers' Church
    Alexander Campbell, leader, 1136
    Brethren movement and, 289
    Campbell, Alexander, 247
    Central America, 2157
    chart of Brethren bodies, place on,
        1403–1405
    Church of North India, 298
    Culler, Arthur Jerome, 355
    debates, 370
    Fairview Church of the Brethren, PA,
        469
    Free Union, VA, Church of the
        Brethren, 513, 514
    Gish, Barbara Kindig and James Rufus,
        550
    history of, 1945, 1960
    Hostetler Brethren, 632, 689
    Hostetler, Joseph, 631
    India, Church of North, 2207
    Indiana, 652
    International Christian Youth Exchange
        (ICYE), 659
    Jackson Co. German Baptist Brethren,
        IN, 667
    Kentucky-Indiana Brethren, 1014
    Kern family, 690
    Kesler, Benjamin Elias challenged by
        minister of, 690
    Liberty German Baptisit Brethren
        Church, IN, 740
    Maple Grove Church of the Brethren,
        WI, granting membership to, 791
    missions, 857
    Newport Church of the Brethren, VA,
        shared union church, 934
    noncreedalism, 942
    Olive Branch German Baptist Brethren
        Church, IN, 973
    People of the Covenant (POC) (BC)
        and, 2237
    People of the Covenant (PotC) pro-
        gram, 2160
    Pipe Creek Church of the Brethren, IN,
        1025
    Plattsburg College, 1030
    publications about, 1918
    references to, 1933
    Restoration Movement, 1101
    Robins, IA, Church of the Brethren,
        site of debate, 1115
    Slifer, IA, church of the Brethren, 1190
    Stone, Barton Warren, 1224

Strickler, William, debates with, 1157
Sunday school lessons, 1236, 1237
Wakenda Church of the Brethren, MO, 1313
White River German Baptist Brethren Church, 1341
Windsor, CO, Northern Colorado Church of the Brethren, 1348
Wood Grove Brethren-Christian Parish, MI, 1363
discipleship, 385, **386,** 695, 1876, *See also* ethics; spiritual life
article about, 1929
BAM, 179
in baptism, 84
Brethren Church, 183
Brethren doctrine of salvation, 1140
Brethren in Christ, 188
Brethren movement, 289, 292, 296, 2084
church membership, 813
community, 329
in confession of faith, 5
conversion, doctrine of, 339
early Christianity, 296
educational materials, 284
eschatology, 454
essence of Anabaptism, 29
ethical issues, 2178
feetwashing, 481
Fellowship of Reconciliation (USA), 488
Friedmann, Robert F., 1259
Grace Brethren Boys, 562
Heaven, 591
humility, 636
hymns, 643
influence of Anabaptists, 1209, 1260
justification, doctrine of, 679
law, doctrine of, 729
Mack, Alexander, Jr., 774, 775
Mack, Alexander, Sr., 1259
Mennonites, 816
and New Covenant Fellowship, 926
nonconformity, 940
nuclear arms race, 2232
Old Order Brethren, 1210
Old Order Fellowships, 971
ordination, 980
peace, 997
redemption, 1090
resurrection, and Radical Pietist teachings about, 1102
sanctification, 1142
Sermon on the Mount, 1169
simple life, 1183
Sojourners Fellowship, 1200
tax refusal as, 1249
theology and, 2255
Discipleship and Reconciliation Committee Handbook, 2172
Discipleship and Reconciliation Committees (D&R), **2172**
Discipleship Committee
Ministry of Reconciliation, 2224
discipline (church), 3, **386–389,** 1255, 2047
among early Anabaptists, 28, 29
Annual Meeting and, 176
Annual Meeting role in, 44
attitudes toward use of courts of law, 728
avoidance, *See* avoidance
and baptismal vows, 5

Brethren Doctrine of Salvation, 1140
Brethren movement, 291, 292
Brethren polity, 1042
Brethren rural churches, 1130
capitalism, 253
caps, 254
Christliches Hand-Büchlein (Christian Handbook), 288
church membership, 813
Church of the Brethren, 300, 2103
church trials, 1274
confession, public, **333**
congregational, and Old Order Movement, 973
Davy, Henry Dorsey, 365
deacons' visits, 369
debts, 371
Declaration of Principles, 372
devotional literature, 381
discipline of children, 389–390
district organization, 391
doctrinal statements, 942
dress and, 401–402
Dunkard Brethren Church, 292, 409
elections, electioneering, 434
Ephrata Community, 448
ethics, 457–458
by excommunication, 698
fairs and public shows, 467
fellowship, 482
Fuchs, Justus, 521
Gibson, Isham, 548
Grebe (Grebi), Georg, 569
handclasp, 582
Heidelberg Catechism, 593
Hendricks, James, 597
hiring military substitutes, 1233–1234
Holsinger, Henry Ritz, 622
holy kiss, denial of, 698
house churches, 632
Hutterian Society of Brothers, 640
hymnals, 642
inner Word and outer Word, 656
law enforcement, 729
Liebe, Christian, and Naas, Johannes, disagreement about, 741
Mack, Alexander, Sr., and New Baptists of Schwarzenau, 776
manuals for, 788
marital avoidance, 793
marriage concerns, 795
Martin, George Adam, differences over, 797
ministry, terminology, 848
mixed marriage, 865
motion pictures, 879
mutual aid, 902
Naas, Johannes, dispute over, 909
nonconformity, 940
Old Brethren, 970
Old German Baptist Brethren peace position, 1000
Old Order movement, 292
opposition to secret societies, 1164
"Order of the Brethren," 976
in other religious groups, 68
Pfoutz, Isaac, 1015
plain people, 1029
Plow Creek Fellowship, 1038
publications by Christopher Sauer II, 1146
radio, 1080
Reba Place Fellowship, 1084

Rechte und Ordungen, 1086
Reformation, Protestant, and radical reformers, 1092
restoration of disciplined members, 1101–1102
role of Standing Committee, 1217
Schwarzenau Brethren, 1079
stewardship and, 2252
The Testimony of Truth, 1255
theology and, 2255
tobacco use, 1266
discipline of children, 389–390, *See also* Dock, Christopher
discrimination
African Americans, 2128
minorities, ethnic and racial, 850, 851
disfellowship, **390,** *See also* avoidance; bans and banning; excommunication
avoidance, 390
Brethren polity, 1042
Cadwallader, John, 1031
Copp, Zed H., 343
Davy, Henry Dorsey, 365
discipline, 387
dress, due to, 402
Early, John B., from German Baptist Brethren, 414
Far Western Brethren, 476
feetwashing, 334
Garber (Gerber), Daniel, 528
Ham, John, 577, 580
handclasp, 582
Hendricks, Franklin A., 597
Holsinger, Henry Ritz, 622, 1970
Hon, Peter Keithly, 627
Honites, 628
Hoppingite Schism, 630
Hostetler, Adam, 631
Hostetler Brethren, 631
imposters among the Brethren, 648
Indiana, 652
Leedy, Isaac, 734
Mahoning Church of the Brethren, OH, dispute query resulting in, 782
Martin, George Adam, 1194
Medina, OH, Church of the Brethren, 2219
Miller, Howard, 838
minorities, ethnic and racial, 850
North Carolina Dunkers, 946
Reconstruction Committee, 1086
remarriage, 795
Restoration Movement, 1101
Rhodes, William, 1107
Sauer, David, 1067
Schwarzenau Brethren sectarian practices, 1079
South Carolina believers in universalism, 1204
Spring Creek, PA, congregation, 334
Dishong, Jackson, 1601
Dishong, Susan, 157
Dismos, Lowell, 1601
disobedience
Brethren Doctrine of Salvation, 1140
dispensationalism, **390,** 2021, *See also* Hoyt, H. A.; Humberd, R. L.; Jews: fundamentalism; Montgomery, M.
Bauman, L. S., 97
Brethren Church doctrine on, 184
eschatology, 454

Fellowship of Grace Brethren Churches (FGBC), 486
influence on Brethren theology, 1261
Jews, 671
millennialism, 834
missions and missionaries, 2110
Montgomery, Michael, 872
Plymouth Brethren, 1039
premillennialism, 1975
prophecy, 1062
rapture, 1083
Roman Catholic Church and Brethren, 1120
Scofield Bible, 1160
State of Israel and interpretation of Bible, 990–991
theology and, 2254
displaced persons, 200, **390**, *See also* refugee aid; refugee resettlement
Church World Service (CWS)
Bushong, Benjamin G., 233
Germany, 545
International Refugee Organization (IRO), 659
Lone Star Church of the Brethren, KS, 753
medical projects, 809
Petersime, Ray, 1012
refugee resettlement, 1093
dissent, *See* division
dissenters, *See* religious persecution; Separatists
Boni, Martin, 159
Ernst Casimir, 453
hats, 589
Historic Peace Churches, 607
historical writing, 611
dissenters, Palatinate, 990
Dissinger, Moses, 2051
Disslin, Catherine (later Pfau), 481
distance education
Grace Schools, 2192
information technology, church use of, 2208
distillers, *See* brewing and distilling
Distler, Scott K., 2277
District Mission Board
Realignment (CB), *See* Continuing District and Regional Organization and Realignment CB). *See* Continuing Committee on District and Regional Organization and Realignment (CB)
District Board of Evangelists (BC), **390**
district histories
historiography, 2201
district meetings
dress for delegate, 402
Dunkard Brethren, 410
tents used for, *1254*
District Mission Board (CB), 14
Dorrance, KS, Church of the Brethren, control of, 396
Dry Run, PA, Church of the Brethren, 406
missionary work, 270
organization of Church of the Brethren, Nanty Glo, PA, 913
District Mission Board, ND
Englevale Church of the Brethren, ND, 447
District Mission Board of Eastern Pennsylvania

Allentown, PA, Church of the Brethren, 2126
Hertzler, William, 601
District Mission Board of Middle Pennsylvania
Hollidaysburg, PA, Church of the Brethren, 619
district mission boards
Fort Wayne, IN, Lincolnshire Church of the Brethren, 504
Front Royal, VA, Church of the Brethren, 518
General Church Erection and Missionary Committee (CB), 536
District of Columbia, 160, 168, 169, **390–391,** 703, 725
Brethren Church, 391, **1319**
mission, 391
Washington, DC, Southeast Christian Fellowship (BC) and, 2259–2260
Chinese Sunday Schools (CB), 278
Church of the Brethren congregation, 390, 391
City Church of the Brethren, 55, **1319–1320,** 1970
fellowship houses, 484
homelessness, 2203
Early, Henry Clay, 413
fellowship houses, 484
First Brethren Church, 391, 688, 1252–1253
First Grace Brethren Church, *See* Lanham, MD, Grace Brethren Church
Greater Washington Grace Brethren Church, *See* Temple Hills, MD, Grace Brethren Church of Greater Washington
Henry, Jerry Maurice, 598
minorities, ethnic and racial, 850
mission congregation, 390, 769
The Missionary Board (BC), 855
missions, 391, 860, 1297
Ogden, William Augustus, pastor, 961
Silver Springs, MD, Good Shepherd Church of the Brethren, 1182
Southeast Christian Fellowship (BC)
history of, **2259–2260**
urban ministry and, 2257
suburbs of, and Maryland Grace Brethren activity, 799
Temple Hills, MD, Grace Brethren Church of Greater Washington, 1252–1253
urban mission, 1297
District of Southern Ohio
Appalachian ministries, 2130
District of Western Pennsylvania
history of, 1918
district organization
Dunkard Brethren, 409–410
Kansas, 682
Kentucky, 689
list of districts and regions by denomination, 1513–1538
Nebraska, 396
Tennessee, 1253–1254
Texas, 1255
Utah, 1298–1299
Virginia, 1308
district programs
polity, 1043

districts, 2023, 2024, 2031, *See also* bibliographies; historical writing
Atlantic Northeast conference, 1976, 1991
bibliography, 1904
Brethren Church, Southwest District (BC), 54
Christian Workers' Meetings (CB), 287
Church of the Brethren (German Baptist Brethren)
Antietam district (1752), 42
First District of Arkansas, 54
Northwestern Ohio, District of (CB), 6
Pacific Southwest District (CB), 54
Southeastern district (CB), 14
Southern Missouri and Arkansas, District of, 54
Western Canada, district of (CB), 15
Church of the Brethren, observations on, 1975
Church of the Brethren Pacific Southwest District Conference, 480
Church of the Brethren regions, within, 1093
Continuing Committee on District and Regional Organization and Realignment (CB), 339
discipline doctrine, 387
election of church officers, 434
evangelism, 460
Fellowship of Churches of Christ in Nigeria, 484
Fellowship of Grace Brethren Churches, 484
Northwest District (FGBC), 14
Southern California and Arizona District (FGBC), 54
Florida, 496
Fundamental Brethren Church, 522
Garden City, KS, Church of the Brethren, 530
Garver, Daniel M., 532
General Board (CB), 536
General Ministerial Board (CB), 538
General Mission Board (DB), 539
German Baptist Brethren's Home Society, 541
Good Shepherd Home (CB), 557
Grace Brethren Village, 563
Greencastle, PA, Church of the Brethren, 570
Hadley Creek Church of the Brethren, IL, 577
Hagerstown, MD, Valley Grace Brethren Church, 579
Hanover, PA, Church of the Brethren, 582
Hart, MI, Church of the Brethren, 587
Hartford City, IN, Grace Brethren Church, 587
historical writing, 612
Indiana, 652–653
Iowa, 661
mission work, 299
missions, 858
North Atlantic district, Church of the Brethren, 455
North Dakota and Eastern Montana, 2036
Ohio, 2064

organization in Kansas, 410
Pennsylvania Church of the Brethren, 1005
Pennsylvania Grace Brethren, 1005
post-conference travel, *391*
prerogatives of, 204
Ditch, L. W., 71, 104, 121, 235, 267, 318, 410, 417, 1318–1319, 1348, 1601
    Mexico, IN, Brethren Church, pastor, 821
    Oakville, IN, Brethren Church, pastor, 959
    Roann, IN, (First) Brethren Church, pastor, 1112
    South Bend, IN, First Brethren Church, pastor, 1203
Ditmars, Iva, 1601
Ditmars, John G., 1601, **2381**
Ditmars, Lloyd Gauby, 1601
Ditmer family
    Mishler family, related to, 852
Ditmer, Robert Lee, 76, 1281, 1286, 1601
Ditzler, Floyd
    Octavia, NE, Church of the Brethren, minister, 960
Ditzler, Floyd E., 1601
Divelbiss, Bill, 356
Divelbiss, Dianne, 356
Divelbiss, Nancy, 356
Dively, Frederic Claar, 1601
Dively, Taylor Lawrence, 1601
diversity
    schism due to, 427
divine legacy
    Negley, Betty Jane on, 2348
Divine, Robert, 1602
Divine, Robert E.
    New Holland, PA, Church of the Brethren, pastor in, 929
divinity, *See* eternity
divinity, studies of, 2076
Division of Church and Society
    of National Council of Churches of Christ (NCCC), 915
division of churches, *See* schism
    Sidney, OH, Trinity Church of the Brethren, 1882, 1181
    Silver Creek Church of the Brethren, OH, 1182
division of congregations
    Amwell congregation, NJ, 1142
    church membership, 813
    Glades and Elk Lick, PA, congregations, 1139
    St. Joseph, MO, 1135
    Salem Church of the Brethren, VA, 1138
    Sandy German Baptist Brethren Church, OH, 1143
    Willamette Valley (originally South Santaam), OR, 1138
Division of Education and Ministry
    of National Council of Churches of Christ (NCCC), 915
Division of Foreign Missions, *See* Foreign Missions Conference of North America
Division of Overseas Ministries, *See* Foreign Missions Conference of North America of National Council of Churches of Christ (NCCC), 915

divisions, **392–393**, 2052, *See also* Brethren movement; Old Order movement; Progressive Brethren movement; schisms
    1848, Eyman schism (Church of God-New Dunkers), 77, 78
    of 1881–1883, 3, 18, 63, 64, 73, 121
        differences at Annual Meeting, 33
        dress as contributing to, 402
        effect on Ashland College, 66
    of 1913 and 1921 (schism among OGBB), 75
    of 1939 (Brethren Church and Grace Brethren), 53, 63
        effect on Ashland College, 66
        and views of Church authority, 74
    chart of, 1403–1405
    Dunkard Brethren, leading to formation of, 3, 407
    Fairview Church of the Brethren, IA, 468
    Fellowship of Grace Brethren Churches (FGBC), 484–485
    Fernald, IA, Church of the Brethren, 488
    fraternal relations, 510
    George's Creek Old German Baptist Brethren Church, PA, 540
    German Seventh-Day Baptists, 542
    Glen St. Mary, FL, Glenside Church of the Brethren, 552
    Glendale, CA, First Brethren Church, 552–553
    Gnagey (Gnaegi) family, 554
    Goyen, Gossen, 562
    Grace Brethren Church of Canton, OH, 563
    grace, doctrine of, 562
    Grafton, WV, First Grace Brethren Church, 564
    Greenmount Church of the Brethren, VA, 571
    Greenwood Church of the Brethren, MO, 572
    Greenwood Church of the Brethren, OH, 572
    Häcker (Höcker), Wilhelm, 577
    Hamlin, KS, Brethren Church, 581
    Heckman family, 593
    Hempfield Church of the Brethren, PA, 596
    Hendricks, John, 597
    historical writing, 612
    Hixson, Armanus Jefferson, 613
    Höhn, Heinrich, 618
    Holsinger, Henry Ritz, 622
    Honites, 628
    Hostetler Church of the Brethren, PA, 632
    house churches, 632
    Huntington (Country) Church of the Brethren, IN, 638
    Indiana, 652
    insurance, 657
    Iowa River Church of the Brethren, IA, 662
    Johnstown, PA, First Brethren Church, 673–674
    Johnstown, PA, Pike Grace Brethren Church, 674
    Johnstown, PA, Westmont Church of the Brethren, 675
    jury service, 679

    list of, 1403–1405
    Old German Baptist Brethren, 969–970
divorce, 6, **393–394**, 1904, 2047, 2048, *See also* discipline, doctrine of; marriage counseling; remarriage
    Brethren Church, 2145
    Church of the Brethren, 389, 2145
    deacons, 2169
    demographic trends, 2144
    discipline, doctrine of, 388
    Doctrinal Treatise, 394
    Dunkard Brethren, 408, 409
    Dunkard Brethren and nonconformity, 941
    Dunkard Brethren Church, 2145, 2173, 2174
    family, 474
    Fellowship of Grace Brethren Churches, 2145
    Hutterian Society of Brothers, 640
    marriage concerns, 795
    ministry in the Brethren Church, 2224
    nonconformity, 940
    Old German Baptist Brethren, 2145
    Old German Baptist Brethren and nonconformity, 941
    Old German Baptist Brethren Church, 389
    ordination of divorced persons, 2141
    remarriage, 1099
    Rosenberger, Isaac J., writing about, 1123
divorce and remarriage
    Upper Marsh Creek Church of the Brethren, PA, 1295
    Wise, John, 1354
divorce, doctrine of
    ministers
        Church of the Brethren, 2109
The Divorce of Russell Hershey (Lehman), 748
Dixon, A. L., 1602
Dixon, Andrew Martin, 578, 1602
Dixon, IL
    article about, 1961
    Church of the Brethren, **394**
        Franklin Grove, IL, Church of the Brethren, 507
        Snider, Donald Mitchell, pastor, 1194
    urban mission, 1297
Dixon, J. C., 1602
Dixon, James G., Jr., 64, 725, 1253, 1602, 2300
    South Bend, IN, Ireland Road Grace Brethren Church, pastor, 1203
Dixon, Jeremiah
    Mason-Dixon Line surveyor, 800
Dixon, John M., 154, 1602
Dixon, Margaret Collins Denny, 2087
Dixon, MO, 1324
    Church of the Brethren, *See* Waynesville, MO, Church of the Brethren
Dixon, Paul
    Mabton, WA, Grace Brethren Church, pastor, 771
Dixon, Robert H., 2300
Dixon School, MI, 179
Dixon, William Hepworth, 1918
Djibouti
    missions, 2224
Dümpler, *See* Risler, Jeremias
Doane, W. Howard, 560

Dobbins, James T., 1602
Doberstein, John W., 2080
Dobos, William, 2277
Dobson, Ed, 1935
Dock, Catharine, 394
Dock, Christopher, 61, **394**, 1895
    biography of, 2078
    educator, 1986
    elementary education, 434
    progressive educational treatise, 1146
    published by Henry Kurtz, 712
    Skippack area, PA, 1189
Dock, Margarethe, 394
Dockstader, Gordon, 30, 1602
Docksteder, Charles
    Paradise, CA, Church of the Brethren, 992
Doctor Faustus, See Doktor Faustus
Doctor White's Teacher Training School, *See* Bible Teacher Training School
doctors, *See* physicians
Doctrinal Points, 1918
Doctrinal Treatise, **394**, 1261, 1306, 2149
    fermentation of grape juice, 1349
    Old German Baptist Brethren and non-creedalism, 943
Doctrinal Treatise (Lehr-Betrachtungen)
    mutual aid, 901–902
doctrine, 2017, 2028, 2033, *See also* Bible; Christology; church; discipleship; discipline; nonconformity; non-creedalism; nonresistance; ordinances; salvation; simple life; theology
    baptism, 2040
    bibliography, 1895, 1904
    Brethren, 2004
    community, 329–330
    conservative, and Pennsylvania Dunkard and Old Order Brethren, 1005
    debates of Brethren with leaders of other denominations, 1979
    Eshelman, Matthew Mays, 455
    faith, fundamentals of, 1991
    Historic Peace Churches, 608
    historiography, 2202
    Holdeman, John, 618
    hymns, 642
    lectures and sermons, 2014
    Martin, George Adam, differences over, 797
    Materials Towards a History of the Baptists, 803
    Menno Simons, 814
    Mennonites, 816
    "Message of the Brethren Ministry" (BC, FGBC), 817
    Nead, Peter, systematic study and publication of, 919
    New Testament, 1996
    noncreedalism, 942
    Old German Baptist Brethren, 969, 2233
    outline of practices, National Fellowship of Brethren Churches, 1954
    queries about, 1076
    Shoup, William J., 2064
    studies in, 1992
    verbal inspiration, 1983
doctrine and practices
    Grace Brethren Church, 1975

doctrine, church, *See* church doctrine
The Doctrine of the Brethren Defended (Miller), 842
Doctrine, Research, and Publication Committee (BC), **2172**
    creation of, 2141
doctrines, *See* specific doctrine
    treatises, 2105
Dodd, C. H.
    eschatology, 454
Dodds, Alfred, 1270, 1602, 2300
Dodds, Edna, 394
Dodds, Gilbert L., **394–395**, 1602
    National Brethren Youth organization by, 915
Dodds, James Allen, 1602
Dodds, James Gilbert, 195, 394, 395, 1602, 2130
    Massillon, OH, Jackson Bible Church (BC), pastor, 801
    Norcatur, KS, Maple Grove Brethren Church, 945
Dodds, James William, 395
Dodds, Margaret
    Solomon, Kenneth LeRoy and Jeannette Ruth DeLozier Solomon (BC) and, 2251
Dodds, Myron W., 377, 1602
Dodds, Robert C., 1918
Dodge, Arthur L., 1602
Dodge Co., NB
    Bell Creek congregation origins, 920
Dodge Co., NE, congregation
    migration of Brethren, 830
Dodge, John, 1254
Dodson, John William, 1602
Doel, Anthony van den, 1798, 1602, 2386, 2388
Doerksen, Victor G.
    works by, 2324
Doernenburg, Emil, 747, 1918
Doerr, Robert, 2277
Dogwood, MO
    Fairview Church of the Brethren, MO, 469
Dohner, A. R., 1918
Dohner, Barbara, 226
Dohner family, 1289, 1918
Dohner, Harry H., 1918
Dohner, Harry S., 14, 1602
Doktor Faustus (Mann), 747, 2314
Dolby, Martha (Mattie) Cunningham, 395, 506, 1361, 1602, 2128
    May, James, home mission work with, 804
    minorities, ethnic and racial, 850
Dolby, Newton, 395
Dolby, Wiley, 395, 1602
    minorities, ethnic and racial, 849
Dole, Esther Mohr, 1918
Doll, Eugene E., 140, 1857, 1859, 1918, 2043
    historical writing, 611
    on Ephrata Cloister, 2325
Doll family
    Osceola, IN, Grace Brethren Church, 983
Dollar, George W., 1918
Dollin, Norman W., 1918
Dolmetsch, Christopher L., 1918
Dolnikowski, George
    on BSC and resettlement of displaced person, 2325

refugee resettlement and, 2240–2241
Dolnikowski, Gregory, 2241
Dolnikowski, Joanne, 2241
Dolohan family, 164
Domer, Emma
    Okeechobee, FL, Grace Brethren Church, 963
Domer, Esther
    Okeechobee, FL, Grace Brethren Church, 963
Domer, Eva, 374
Domer, Henry, 439
Domer, Jacob, Sr., 1602
Domer, John
    North Manchester, IN, (First) Brethren Church, 949
Domer, Mrs. John
    North Manchester, IN, (First) Brethren Church, 949
Domer, Russell
    Okeechobee, FL, Grace Brethren Church, 963
Domer, Victor
    Okeechobee, FL, Grace Brethren Church, 963
Domestic and Foreign Mission Board (CB), 295, *See also* General Mission Board (CB)
    Eby, Enoch, 419
Domestic and Foreign Missionary Board (GBB, later CB)
    missions, 858
Dominic, JoAnn, 244
Dominican Republic, **2172–2173**
    baptisms, *2173*
    Church of the Brethren, 2162
    Church of the Brethren in, 2258
    Hispanic Ministries (CB), 2198, 2199
    Lancaster, PA, Alfa y Omega (Alpha and Omega) Church of the Brethren, 2213
    Los Guaricanos, DR, Fuente de Vida, 2215
    Los Toros, DR, Nuevo Renacer, 2215–2216
    missions (CB), 2225
Dompelaars (Dompelaers) 395, 707, 910, 1865, 2029, 2031
    article about, 1942
    Collegiants, 324
    Driedger, Michael D. on, 2325
    Hamburg-Altona, 580
    Lobach, Johann, 751
    Mehrning, Jacob, 811
    Riewald, J. G., 2045
    school of, 751
    Slabaugh, Dennis L. on, 2357
Dompier, James Alfred, 2175
Don River Old German Baptist Brethren Church, Ontario, 250, **395–396.** 975, **2373**
Donafrank, Mrs. Orville, 2036
Donahao, James D., 1602
Donahue, Elizabeth, 157
Donahue, George D., 320, 1602
Donatism, 396, *See also* Albigenses; Waldenses
    religious liberty, 1098
Donatus, Bishop of Carthage, 396
Donehoo, George P., 1918
Doner, Anna Breckbill, 1918
Doner, Elmina, 1602
Doner family, 1918

Doner, George, 1602
Doner, Harold, 1918
Doner, Harry, 1918
Doner, John, 1918
Doney, Patrick, 1602
Doney, Samuel, 1602
Doniphan Co., KS, 682, 1356
Donnell family, 1958
Donnels Creek, OH, 1215, 1265
    Church of the Brethren, 352, **396,** 926,
        1232, 1341
        example of place name, 911
        Frantz, Aaron, 508
        Frantz, Edward, 508
        Frantz family, 509
        Funderburg, Drue Dresher, 523
Donnels Creek, OH, district, 2064
Donnels Creek Old German Baptist
        Brethren Church, OH, *See* North
        Hampton, OH, Donnels Creek Old
        German Baptist Church
        Owl Creek Old German Baptist
        Brethren Church, OH, 986
Donner, *See* Danner
Donohoo, Byron Douglas, 2277
donors to Brethren Encyclopedia
    list of, 2113–2123
Donovan, Edith Harley, 1918–1919
Dooley, Mabel (later Myers)
    Myers, Oscar Reiff, wife of, 904
Doolittle, David, 297
Doopsgezinden
    baptism-minded, *See* Anabaptism
    Dutch Mennonites Collegiants, 324
Door Co., WI, 1354
Dorchester Church of the Brethren, NE,
    396
Dordrecht, 171
Dorer, Solomon E., 1602
Dorfman, Mark H.
    on Ephrata Cloister and early American
        life, 2325
Dornback, Mary (later Klein), 700
Dorpalen, Andreas, 1919
Dorrance, KS, Church of the Brethren, 396,
    See also North Solomon, KS, con-
        gregation
    Quinter, KS, Church of the Brethren,
        1078
    Russell Co. Church of the Brethren,
        KS, 1132
Dorsey, Anna Leola (later Hoyt), 634
Dorsey, Bruce, 758
Dorsey, Cleo, 758
Dorsey, George W., 211, 1602
Dorsey, J. S., 1602
Doss family, 1224
Doss, Martin C., 2277
Doteerer family, 2077
Dotson family, 2087
Dotterer, Henry S., 1919
Dotterer, John E., 1960
Dotterer, Stanley S., 1602, 2300
Doty, C. E., 271
Doty, Cecil LeRoy, Jr., 552, 754, 1602,
    1919
Doty, Clois E., 1602
Doty, V. A., 141, 1602
Dotzour, Boyer and Edna Price
    family history, 1998
Dotzour, Grover C., 1602
Double Creek mission point
    Flat Creek Church of the Brethren, KY,

493
double mode feetwashing, 396–397, 481,
    1186, *See also* feetwshing; single
    mode
    Far Western Brethren, 475, 476
    Old German Baptist Brethren, 967
    ordinances, *977*
Douds mission point, IA, 740
Doudt, David William, 1836
Doudt, Karen Diane Beery, 1836, 2171
Doughterly, Charles, 1358, 1602
Doughtry, Jane Allen, 1339
Douglas Co., KS, 334, 682, 753, 1311,
    1321, 1346, 1914
    Hoppingite Schism, 630
    migration of Brethren, 830
    Pleasant Grove Church of the Brethren,
        KS, 1031
    Root family, 1122
Douglas Co., MO
    Fairview Church of the Brethren, MO,
        469
    Mount Hermon Church of the Breth-
        ren, MO, 881
Douglas, Dorothy Lee, 406
Douglas, George, 662
Douglas, Henry Kyd, 41, 1919
Douglas, Lucinda M. E., 2277
Douglas, Maxine, 662
Douglas Park, Chicago, IL, Church of the
    Brethren, *See* Chicago, IL,
        Douglas Park Church of the
        Brethren
    Shull, Chalmer George, pastor, 1180
Douglas Park Mission, Chicago, IL, 171,
    1296, 1970, 2010, *See also* Urban
    Ministry
    founding of, 275
    White, Roy Irvin, 1339
Douglas, Robert G.
    Old Order German Baptist Church,
        2235
Douglas, Susan, 397, 1325
    elementary education, 434
Douglass, Frederick, 2128
Douglass, William, 1919
Doukhobors Church, 2098
Doutrich, Stephen D., 2277
Doutt family, 715
dove
    corporate logo of the Brethren Church,
        2146
Dove, Addison, 1602
Dove, F. W., 572
    Peace Valley Church of the Brethren,
        MO, 1003
    Pleasant Mound Church of the Breth-
        ren, TN, elder, 1033
    Pleasant View Church of the Brethren,
        TN, elder, 1037
Dove family, 397–398, 1313
    Pleasant Valley Church of the Brethren,
        TN, 1035, 1037
Dove, Frederick A., 397
Dove, Frederick Denton, 2, 397, 398, 1602,
    1919
    historical writing, 612
    migration of Brethren, writings on, 829
Dove, Frederick Washington, 237, 397,
    398, 1602
    Mount Hermon Church of the Breth-
        ren, MO, elder, 881
Dove, George A., 1602

Dove, George L., 1602
Dove, Henry, 397
Dove, J. Luther, 1602
Dove, John Adams, 312, 397, 398, 912,
    1602
Dove, Lula Huff, 397
Dove, Margaret Bashor, 397, 398
Dove, W. A., 351, 1602
Dovel, Peter S., 1602
Dowdy, Carolyn Elaine Bearinger (later
        Solomon), 1848
    Solomon, Kenneth LeRoy (BC) and,
        2251
    Mexico, missionary to, 820
Dowdy, Christy L., 2277
Dowdy, Dale W., 2277
Dowdy, Dortha Mae Frank, 53, 398, 1848
Dowdy, James Paul, Jr., 1602, 1848
    Mexico, missionary to, 820
Dowdy, James Paul, Sr., 53, 398, 620,
    1602, 1848, 2300
Dowdy, Ruth Hoffert, 1919
Dowie, John A.
    pork, eating of, 1047
Dowie, John Alexander, 281, 398, 586,
    1400
    biography, 1914, 1957
Dowieism Exposed (Bowman), 166
Dowis family
    Honey Creek Church of the Brethren,
        MO, 627
Dowling, Hannah Elizabeth Foster, 1919
Dowling, W. W., 1919
Down in My Heart (Stafford), 1216
Downer, Michael, Sr.
    descendants of, 1918
Downey Brethren Church, PA, *See* Stoney
    Creek Brethren Church, PA
Downey, Gregg, 1919
Downing, A. S., 1602
Downing, Howard L., 735, 1380, 2277
Downsville Church of the Brethren,
    MD, 398
    Manor Church of the Brethren, MD,
        daughter congregation of, 787
Doxie, OK, Beckham Co., OK
Doyai, Esther (later Gaiwaka), 527
Doyle, Catherine (later Pfautz), 1015
Doyle, James, 1919
DPM, *See* Director of Pastoral Ministries
D&R, *See* Discipleship and Reconciliation
    Committees
Dr. Fahrney's Blood Cleanser or Panacea,
    995, *See also* Fahrney, Peter
Dr. P. Fahrney's Health Messenger, 1918
draft, *See* military service
draft inductions
    suspention of, 337
draft (military), *See* conscription (military)
draft refusal, *See* conscientious objection;
    military service; peace
Draft resistance, *See* military service, non-
    resistance
Dragon
    Naff brothers immigration, 910
Drake, A. C., 1602
Drake, Harold, 1268
Drake, Nathaniel, 1602
Drake, Ruth, 1268
Drakes Creek, KY, 688
    German Baptist Brethren Church, 398
    Far Western Brethren, 475
    settlement, 1253

drama, 398–399
  Civil War, 2050
  Dunkard Brethren, 409
  Dunkard Brethren and nonconformity, 941
  Ephrata Community, 2030
  Frantz, Ira Henry, 508
  Hagerstown, MD, Church of the Brethren, 578
  religious, 2011
  Under the Shadow: A Two-Act Play, 1968
Drama in the Church (Eastman), 399
Drammen, Norway, 157
Dranesville mission point
  Oakton, VA, Church of the Brethren, 958
  Dranesville, VA, Church of the Brethren, **399**
Draper, Glen, 1836
Draper, NC, *See* Eden, NC, Church of the Brethren
drawing, 2035
Drayton Plains, MI, First Church of the Brethren, **399**
Drechsler, Wolfgang
  on CB, 2325
Dredge, David S., 1602
Dreibelbis, Lee
  Mishawaka, IN, Brethren Church, 852
Dreibelbis, Mrs. Lee
  Mishawaka, IN, Brethren Church, 852
Dreisbach, Johannes, 1211
Dreiser, Theodore, 747
Drennon, Kenneth T., 1343, 1602
Drescher, James, 193
Dresden, 156
  Spener, Philipp Jakob, 1209
Dresden
  missionaries voyaging to France on, 863
Dresher, Carrie (later Funderburg), 523
Dresher, J. N., 683
Dresher, Mollie (later Leatherman), 732
dress, 3, 26, 399–404, **399–404,** 405, 690, 1373, 1896, 2038, 2045, 2051, *See also* beards; bonnets; capes; caps; coats; hats; jewelry; neckties; prayer veils
  advertisements for, *7,* 18
  Annual Meeting decisions regarding, 59, 160, 301, 400–403, 921
  Annual Meeting rulings on, 59
  aprons, **45,** *45,* 300
  Bible Brethren, 135
  book about, 1945
  Brethren, 1996
  Brethren Church, 388
  Brethren in Christ, 189
  Brethren polity regarding, 1042
  Christian Brethren, 281
  Christ's Ambassadors, 280
  Church of the Brethren, 388
  collars on plain coats, 1028–1029
  Committee on Dress Reform (CB), 327
  contemporary, and Philadelphia, PA, First Church of the Brethren, 1015–1016
  description by Edwards, Morgan, 1375
  description of, 2080, 2105
  discipline, 388
  dress capes, 45
  dresses (OGBB), 45

Dunkard Brethren, 148, *159,* 301, 388, 408, 409, 940, 2174,
Early, Henry Clay, 414
East Fairview Church of the Brethren, PA, 415
Evangelical Association, 459
evangelism, 460
Fellowship of Grace Brethren Churches, 388
Free Brethren, 513
frontier, 519
frontier lifestyles, 283
Garb Law, 528, **528,** 1896
graveclothes, 566–567
Hadsell, B. A., 577
hats, 301, 589
head coverings, *159,* 160
Historic Peace Churches, 608
historical writing, 612
historiography, 2202
history of, 1923
Holsinger, Henry Ritz, 621
hoops, **628**
Hostetler Brethren, 631
Hygiene, CO, Church of the Brethren, 641
imposters among the Brethren, 648
Independent Brethren, 649
Indiana, 653
jewelry, 670
Kurtz, Daniel Webster, 710
late 19th century, *45*
Mennonites, 1949
men's costumes, 2106
Milledgeville Church of the Brethren, IL, query on, 833
ministry, 845
missions, 862
modesty, 1996
Müller, Joseph, wearing Brethren, 894
Muscatine, IA, First Church of the Brethren, 898
music, 2227–2228
neckerchief and neckties, 921
neckerchiefs for women, 921
objection to, in other religious groups, 69
Old Brethren, 964
Old German Baptist Brethren, *146,* 206, 941, 967, 971, 972, 2233
"Order of the Brethren," 976
in other religious groups, 68
plain, and Pennsylvania Church of the Brethren, 1005
plain, and photographs, 1020
plain coats, 189, 300, 400, 402, 921, **1028–1029**
plain people, 1029, 2013
prayer veil, 1053
prescribed dress, 400–401, 403
Progressive Brethren, 388, 1061
publications on, 7
question of, and prayer, 1052
reform, annual conference addresses about, 1911
regulations for, 178
Rupel, Esther Fern CB and, 2353–2354
Schelbert, Leo on CB and, 2355
Scott, Stephen on conservative Brethren and, 2355
sermon on temperance in, 1168
sexuality, human, 1170
shawls and capes, 1175

simple, and Brethren opposition to secret societies, 1164
simple life, 1183
sources on, 2313, 2315
Spring Creek, PA, congregation, 334
Stoffer, Dale R. on, 2358
Stover, Wilbur Brenner, 1226
symbolism of, 2147
Taylor, Lydia E., 1249
theological basis, 1261
Umstad, John Horning, 1286
Wolfe, George, II, 1357
women and, 2263
Dress Committee, 690
Dress Reform Committee, 1252
  General Welfare Board (CB), 540
  Lear, John Wallace, 732
  Peace Committee (CB), 1002
  Taylor, Lydia E., 1249
  Teeter, Lewis Wallace, 1250
Drexel, Elizabeth, 405
Drexel, Francis A., 405
Drexel, Hannah Jane Langstroth, 405
Drexel Hill, PA, Church of the Brethren, **404–405**
  Young, Galen S. and, 2268
Drexel, Mary Katharine, 405
  biography, 1920
  sources on, 2316
Driedger, Leo
  on Mennonite peacemaking, 2325
Driedger, Michael D.
  on Altona populations, 2325
  on Dompelaars, 2325
  on Hamburg populations, 2325
Driftwood congregation, IN, 667
Drips, Mary, 1243
Dritt family
  history of, 1912
Driver, Anna (later Wampler), 1316
Driver, Brent K., 2277
Driver, Carl Samuel, 1602, 1919
Driver, Casper M., 462, 1602
Driver, Catherine S. (later Flory), 498
Driver, Charles, 1603
Driver, F. Wise, 1603
Driver family, 236, 405, 700, 1318
  Sanger family, related to, 1144
Driver, Frederick Anthony, 1603
Driver, Jacob, 405, 410, 1603
Driver, Joe, 246
Driver, John F., *84,* 1265, 1603
Driver, John L., 1603
Driver, Lewis, *See* Treiber, Ludwig
Driver, Lewis, Jr., 405
Driver, Michael, 405
Driver, Peter, 405
Driver, Samuel I., 347, 410, 742, 1603
  drivers' licenses
  photographs on, 1020
drought
  Kansas, and social welfare, 1198
  Niger, Brethren response to, 936
  North Beatrice Church of the Brethren, NE, 945
  North Dakota Brethren relocating, 946
  Octavia, NE, Church of the Brethren, 960
  Rothrock, Abraham, 1124
  San Antonio, TX, Church of the Brethren, 1141
droughts
  Big Creek Old German Baptist

Brethren Church, KS, 142
Kansas, 682
Cheyenne, KS, Church of the Brethren, 274
New Mexico, 1240
Surrey Old German Baptist Brethren Church, ND, 1242
Drucker
sources on, 2318
Drudge, Casey
on CB, history of, 2325
drugs
McFadden, Joyce on stance of CB on, 2344
Druley, Rose R., 1919
Drummond, Henry
prayer, 1051
Drummond, Robert R., 1919
Drury, William, 1603
Drushal, Ada, 183, 282
Drushal, Ada G.
The Missionary Board (BC), 855
missions, 860
Drushal, Ada Irene, 405
Drushal, Ada Louella Garber, 44, 405, 406, 689, 760, 1361, 1603
Riverside Christian Training School, 1111
Rowdy, KY, Brethren Church, 1126
Drushal, Garbe, 190
Drushal, George, 183
Drushal, George E., 44, 282, 577, 689, 760
The Missionary Board (BC), 855
missions, 860
Rowdy, KY, Brethren Church, pastor, 1126
Drushal, George Emory, 405, 406, 1603
Riverside Christian Training School, 1111
Drushal, J. Michael, 2132, 2170
Drushal, John Garber, 405–406, 1603
Drushal, Mary Ellen Waters
Beulah Beach I and II, 2136–2137, 2141, 2170
church governance and, 2264
founding member of Ashland, OH, University Church, 2132
moderator of General Conference, 2141, 2170
Drushal Memorial Brethren Church, KY, 689, See also Lost Creek, KY, Drushal Memorial Brethren Church
Dry Creek congregation,
Dry Creek Old German Baptist Brethren Church, IA, 406, See also Robins, IA, Dry Creek congregation, IA, 661
Dry Fork Church of the Brethren, MO, See Jasper, MO, Church of the Brethren
Dry Fork (Jasper), MO, congregation, 257
Dry Fork territory
Harman Church of the Brethren, WV, 584
Dry Run, PA, Church of the Brethren, 406
Dry Run Union Church of the Brethren, VA, See Mount Bethel Church of the Brethren, VA
Dry Valley Church of the Brethren, PA, 25, 81, 217, 232, 406, 739, 1215
Maitland Church of the Brethren, PA, 783

Dry Wood, KS, congregation, 989
Dryhill, KY, 188
congregation, 689
Victory Mountain Grace Brethren Chapel, 406
dualism, spirit and flesh, 15
Dubbel, S. E.
patent medicine remedy business, 995
Dubbel, S. Earl
spelling changed from Dubbel, 2388
Dubbel, William, 1603
Dubble, Carol Cave, 2277
Dubble, Curtis William, 1603
on families, from patriarchs to real, 2325
Dubble, Earl W., 747
Dub(b)le family, 715
Dubble, Kirby Lynn, 1603
Dubbs, John, 1319
Dubbs, Joseph Henry, 1919
Dubel, William F., Jr., 2277
Dubes, Henry, 1603
Dublin, OH
Northwest Chapel Grace Brethren Church, 2173
London, OH, Grace Brethren Church, 2215
New Albany, OH, Rocky Ridge Grace Brethren Church, 2231
Sciota Church of the Brethen, OH, preaching point, 1160
Dubois, Abraham, 569
Eppstein, 452
Mack, Alexander, Sr., welcoming to America, 777
Dubois (Duboy), Abraham, 406, 1603
Dubois (Duboy), Anna, 406
Dubois (Duboy), Philip, 406
DuBois, NE, 1280
Duché, Jacob, 452
letters from, 1917, 1919–1920
Duck, Dorothy Hampton
on Ephrata Cloister, art and artists of, 2325
Düdelsheim, 545
historic sites, 609
Holtzapfel (Holsapple, Holsopple) family, 624
Holtzapfel (Holsapple, Holsopple), Johann Heinrich, 623
Marienborn, village belonging to, 792
Naas, Johannes as settler, 909
Ritter, Daniel, 1111
Stumpff family, 1232
Traut family, 1270
Traut, Georg Balthasar "Balser," 1270
Dudley, Lewis, 1315
Dudrow, LeRoy A., 1603
Dueck, Al
on Anabaptists, community and, 2325
on Pietism, community and, 2325
Dueck, Stanley B., 2277
Duerksen, Vernon D., 1920
Duffey, Scott Lee, 1603, 1920
Duffles (Eggleston), 747
Duffy, Consuela Marie, 1920
Dugan, Elaine K., 1859
Dugard, Andrew Peter, , 572, 1603
Duisburg, 407
Duke of Bedford
Scherffig, Kaspar, voyage to America, 1152
Duke University Library

Brethren historical collections at, 52
historical libraries, 610
Duke, William, 1920
Duker, Edgar A., 1603
Duker, William Irvin, 407, 1603
Dulabaum, Willard Elden, 1603, 2155
North Manchester, IN, Church of the Brethren, pastor, 949
Ridgeway Community Church of the Brethren, PA, pastor, 1109
Dulaney, A. O., 1603
Dulaney family, 1341
Dulaney, Ora E. (later Reed), 1090
Dulaney, William, 407, 1603
Dulany, Ella Maude Brooks, 1920
Dulheuer, Henry, 2064
Dull, Christine
on Soviet Union, visits to, 2325
Dull family, 1322
Dull, Joy, 2133
Dull, Ralph, 2133
on Soviet Union, visits to, 2325
Dumond, Charles Edward, Jr., 496, 1603, 1920
Dumond, Charles, Sr., 496, 1603
Newton, KS, Church of the Brethren, pastor in, 934
Dumplars, See names, Brethren
Dumplers, See Dunkard Brethren Church
Dunahoo, George D., See Donahue, George D.
Dunahue, George D., See Donahue, George D.
Dunbar, Dorothy, 188, 192, 2300
Dunbar, Elias Peter, 1603
Dunbar, Joseph E., 1603
Dunbar, Lute M., 1603
Dunbar, Peter, 1603
Dunbobbin, Christine, 1836
Duncan, A. J., 1603
Chestnut Grove German Baptist Brethren Church, pastor, 956
Duncan, Alfred H., 1603
Duncan, Andy, Mrs., 754
Duncan, Arthur B., 1603
Chestnut Grove German Baptist Brethren Church, pastor, 956
Duncan, Bertha
Winchester, VA, Blue Ridge Grace Brethren Church and, 2262
Duncan, Denis, 463
Duncan, Edward W., 90, 246, 740, 1603
Root River Church of the Brethren, MN, pastor, 1122
Duncan family
Mountain View Church of the Brethren, VA, 889
Duncan, Gayle, 463
Duncan, Henry, 1603
Duncan, John, 1603
Duncan, Leander, 1603
Duncan, Mary, 215
Duncan, Noah Anderson, 215, 277, 1603
Mount Hermon Church of the Brethren, MO, minister and elder, 881
Duncan, Presley, 1603
Duncan, Preston, 1603
Duncan, Ralph M., 2277
Duncan, Roy
Winchester, VA, Blue Ridge Grace Brethren Church and, 2262
Duncan, Samuel, 560, 1341
Duncan, U., 1603

Duncans Chapel Church of the Brethren, VA, 21, **407**
Duncanson, Harold W., 1603
Duncanson, Lloyd, 1603
Duncansville, PA, 731
  Church of the Brethren, **407**
    Fairview Church of the Brethren, PA, 469
  congregation, 256–257
  Fredericksburg, PA, Brethren Church, 512
Duncansville, PA, Grace Brethren Church, *See* Leamersville, PA, Grace Brethren Church
Dundalk, MD, Church of the Brethren, 2063
Dunigan, Frank, 1603
Dunkard Bottom, WV, 1336, *See also* Monroe Co., WV
  place-names, Brethren, 1027
Dunkard Brethren, 210, 407–410, 429, 1920, 2012, 2020, 2022, 2030, 2033, 2037, 2039, 2042, **2173–2175**
  The Dunkard-Dutch Cook Book, 1920
  "A Dunker girl in the fields," *1361*
  abortion, 2127, 2174, **2371, 2373**
  admission into the church, 5
  Africa Mission Project, **2127–2128**
  alcohol abstinence, 1252
  alcohol, use of, 16
  Allen Co., OH, 2086
  American Revolution, 1914, 1916, 2082, 2097, 2108
  Annual Meeting, *See* Dunkard Brethren General Conference
  Annual Meeting at Lanark (IL), 1975
  and anointing, 39
  Antietam, MD, 2083
  archival policy, 52
  Assemby of Christ, 376
  authority of scripture, 133
  baptism, 298, 2173
  and beards, 103
  Bethany, IN, 2097
  Bible Study Board, 137, 1237
  Bible translations and versions, 138
  Bible translations, response to, 2137
  bibliography, 1859, 1866, 1867, 1899
  Blooming Grove Colony, 148
  Brethren Encyclopedia, Inc., 2143
  Brethren in Christ, 2064
  Brethren in Christ and, 188
  Brethren in Christ Church relationship to, 2074
  Brethren in Christ, Ontario, 189
  Brethren music, 899
  Bristol Twp., OH, 2079
  Broederen (Tunkers) movement, 2087
  burial customs, 230
  business doctrine, 235
  California, 239
  camping movement, 250
  Canada, 250, 2067
  caps, 254
  Cassel Library, PA, 258
  chaplaincy, 271
  chart of Brethren bodies, place on, 1403–1405
  choirs, 279
  Chowchilla, CA, Church of the Brethren, 280
  Christian day school movement, 282,

2160, 2174–2175
  Christian sects, 2002
  Christ's Ambassadors, 280
  church extensions, 295
  church manual, 1920
  church membership, 813
  Church of the Brethren, withdrawal from, 403
  church polity, 1920
  Civil War, 148–149
    fugitives, 2086
  Colorado, 320
  communion table, 328
  computer technology, 2174
  concerns leading to founding of, 690
  conference, first, 408
  confession of faith, 333
  conscientious objectors, 336
  religious issues, and statements on, 2107
  Conservative German Baptist Brethren, 338
  conversions, handbook of religious, 2071
  cookbooks, traditional, 340–341
  courts of law, attitudes toward use of, 728
  Croghan, C., 2080
  Daily Vacation Bible Schools, 359
    DB, 317
  deacons, 369
  Declaration of Principles (DB), 372, 409
  Dedication of Infants, 372
  degrees of ministry, 374
  Denmark, 280
  description of, 1949, 2078, 2079, 2095, 2096, 2098, 2104, 2108
  devotional literature, 381
  discipline, 389
  disciplined community, 292
  district organization, 391
  division of 1926, *See under* divisions
    division of congregations, 392
  divorce, 393
  divorce and remarriage, 1099, 2145, 2173, 2174
  doctrines of, 2075
    love feasts, 2093, 2100
    worship services, 2106
  drama, position on, 399
  dress, 148, *159,* 301, 388
  dress, order of, 404
  Dunkard Reader, 1920
  Ebling, David F., 418
  ecumenism, 423
  education, 428
  education and schools, 2159, 2160, 2174–2175
  educational materials, 284
  elder, 433
  elections, electioneering, 434
  environmental issues, 2177
  eschatology, 454
  evangelicalism, 2179
  evangelism, 461, 2180
  evolution, 463
  exemptions
    American Revolution, 2097
    Fairfield Co., OH, 2086
  family, 474, 2145, 2174
  farming, 477, 479
  Farnhamville, IA, Church of the

Brethren, 479
  Farrenburg Church of the Brethren, MO, 479
  Faw, Jacob, 2084
  feetwashing, 481
  fellowship, 482
  First Day Dunkers, 210
  Fiscel, Emory (Emery) David, 491
  flags, 493
  Fleming Co., KY, German Baptist Brethren Church, 494
  Flohr, Lewis Benton, 494
  Flory, Harley T. on missions and, 2331
  formation of denomination, 137
  fraternal relations, 510
  Frederic Co., MD, 2100
  free ministry, 513
  free ministry system, 1137
  Free Will Dunkers, 177
  fundamentalism, 522
  funerals, 524
  Garst, Samuel Sherfy, 531
  General Conference, *See* Dunkard Brethren General Conference
  geographic history, 1972
  Georges Creek Church of the Brethren, MD, 540
  German Baptist Brethren, 540
  Germantown, *543, 544*
  Gibbel (Gibble) family, 547
  Glick, Jacob Daniel, 553
  Glück (Glick, Click) family, 553
  gospel music, 559, 561
  grape juice, in communion services, 1349
  hairstyle, 579
  Hampshire, Co., VA, 2078
  Hardy Co., VA, 2106
  hats, 254
  historical materials regarding, 1950
  history of, 2074, 2080, 2083, 2084–2085, 2086, 2109
  holy kiss, 699
  homelessness, 2203
  homosexuality, 2174, 2204
  honorific titles, 1266
  Hostetler, Daniel W., 631
  Hostetler, Quincy Vern, 631
  humanitarianism, 636
  Hygiene, CO, 2071
  hymnals, 642
  hymns, 2098
  Idaho, 157, 320
  Illinois, 647
  illustrations, *1361, 1374*
  Indiana, 653
  information technology, church use of, 2208
  insurance, 657
  Iowa, 662
  isolationism, 1297
  Jamison, Owen Thomas, 668
  jewelry, 671
  Johnson, H. Edward, 672
  Johnson, John L., 672
  Jung-Stilling, 2105
  Kansas, 682
  Kentucky, 171
  Kesler, B. E. as member, 910
  Kesler, Benjamin Elias, *690*
  language, inclusive, 2214
  lay preachers, 730
  laying on of hands, 731

lifestyle, 148
Lord's prayer, 757
love feast, 233, 763, 764
Lutheran Church, 2005
Maiden Creek, PA, 2078
maintenance of statistics, 1219
marriage, 796, 2145
Maryland Brethren activity, 799
mass media, 800, 2218
medical missions, 808, 810
meetinghouse, 159
membership trends 1980 to 2000, 2220
Mennonite Church, 2106
Michigan Brethren settlement, 824
migration to, 175
military service, 311–312, 388, 832
Miller, Robert J., journals of, 2099
ministers
    Maryland, 2105
ministry, 845
Minneapolis/St. Paul, MN, 2082
minorities, ethnic and racial, 850, 851
Mission and Vision Statement, 2148
missions, 860, 862, 2225
missions, short-term, 2226
Missouri, 865
Moravians and, 2093
motion pictures, 879
music, 2106, 2227
music of, 1920
musical instruments, 900, 2228
Myers, Paul R., 904
Myers, Theodore, 904
National Service Board for Religious
    Objectors (NSBRO) cooperation,
    917
Native Americans, 2230
neckties, avoidance of, 921
neoorthodox influence, 923
Ness, Jacob C., 2231
New Dunkards, See Church of God
    New York, 2100
Newberg, OR, congregation, 981
as nickname of Brethren fellowships,
    910
nonconformity, 3, 940–941
noncreedalism, 943
nonresistance movement
    Lancaster Co., PA, 2077
nonresistance position of, 148
North Carolina
    settlements in, 2104–2105
North Dakota, 2077, 2082
oaths, taking of, 959
Ohio congregations, effect on, 963
Oklahoma
    fiction, references in, 2099
One Hundred Dunkers for Peace, 179
Ontario, 975
opposition to labor unions, 716
opposition to television, 1251
ordination, 980
organizational meeting held at Plevna,
    IN, Church of the Brethren, 1037,
    1038
Orion Dunkard Brethren Congregation,
    OH, 981
Oxford Dictionary of the Christian
    Church, entry for, 1912
Ozark village, sociological study of,
    2102
Parker, William Herbert, as minister
    for, 993

peace education, 1002
peace position, 1000–1001
Pennsylvania, 322, 1981, 2069, 2103
pension system, lack of, 1008
Piney Creek Church of the Brethren,
    MD, 1025
placement of pastors, 1028
polity, 294, 1045
Pratt, Eugene W., 1051
prayer, posture in, 1052
prayer veil, 1053
Prices Creek Church of the Brethren,
    OH, 1057
publication about, 2068, 2069, 2070
Publication Board, 1063,
    Bible Monitor Publishing Com-
    pany, 137
Reed, Roscoe Quinter Evans, 1090
Reed, William Sherman, minister,
    1090, 1091
reference to, 1918, 1939, 1943, 1951,
    1955
Relief Board, 1097, 1268
restoration of disciplined members,
    1102
retirement homes, 8, 1102
River Brethren, article about, 1919
Robbins, Joseph P., elder, 1114
Rocky Ridge, MD, Monocacy Church
    of the Brethren, 1119
Roesch, Melvin C., 1119
Royer, Ira Roscho, elder, 1128
sack coats, 1029
schisms, 301, 303
schools
    penmanship as folk art, 2105
secret societies, opposition to, 1164
Seneca Co., OH, 2086
sermons, 1168
Seventh Day Dunkers, 210
Shenandoah Valley, VA, congregations
    in, 1176
Shroyer, Reuben, 1180
Silver Creek Church of the Brethren,
    OH, 1182
simple life, 1183
singing, unaccompanied, 1185
"singings," 1186
sources on, 2316
South Carolina, 1985
spiritual life, 1210
stand on Vietnamese War, 1305
Standing Committee, 1217
Strayer, Ord Lee, transfer to, 1228
Studebaker, John Clement, 1230
Studebaker, Rebecca Mohler, 1230
Sunday school movement, 1239
Swallow, James F., 1243
symbols and logos, attitudes about,
    2147
television viewing prohibited, 1251
theological education, 1256
theology, 1259, 2254
theology, expressions of, 1261
tobacco use, 1266
Torreon Navajo Mission (NM), 1268
tracts published by, 1920
Trustee Board, 1278
Tuolumne Old German Baptist
    Brethren Church, CA, shared
    meetinghouse with, 1280
universalism, 1292
unleavened bread, recipe, 1293

urban ministry and, 2257
Van Dyke, S. Perry, 1302
Virginia, 1308, 2068, 2090
Washington, 320
Washington Co., PA, 2106
wedding customs, 1326
West Nimishillen, OH, congregation,
    946
West Virginia, 1337
withdrawal of Conservative Baptist
    Brethren Church, 2167
withdrawal of Conservative Brethren
    Church, 2167
women and, 2263
women, roles of, 1361
World War II, 1372
worship and, 2266–2267
worship, public, 1376, 1378
youth and, 2268
youth in, 1392
Dunkard Brethren Church Manual, 409,
    788
Dunkard Brethren Church Polity, 133,
    1261, 1376, 2174
    booklet, 409
Dunkard Brethren peace position, 1000
    manuals, 788
Dunkard Brethren Civilian Service
    Committee, 1372
Dunkard Brethren General Conference, 37,
    298, 409–410
    1963, 37
    1979, 37
    appeal of decisions, 37
    boards and committees
        Credential Committee, 37
        Standing Committee, 37
        Trustee Board, 37
    Ebling, David F., 418
    Ecker, Thomas C., 421
    editorial policy, 137
    Flora, Joseph E., 2185
    General Mission Board (DB), 539
    Hostetler, Quincy Vern, 631
    Johnson, H. Edward, 672
    leadership at, 37
    location of, 37
    men's movements, 2221
    moderators, 30
        Fahnestock, Adam G., 465
        Flohr, Lewis Benton, 494
        Hostetler, Daniel W., 631
        Miller, Jacob A., 838
        Moss, Loring Isaac, **878**
        Myers, Paul R., 904
        office of, 865–866
        Reed, Roscoe Quinter Evans, 1090
        Roesch, Melvin C., 1119
        Shank, Ray (1971), 1172
    Ness, Jacob C., 2231
    polity, 1045
    Publication Board, authority over, 1063
    women and, 2263
    youth and, 2268
Dunkard Brethren Men's Retreat, 2221
"Dunkard Church," Antietam, MD, See
    Mumma meetinghouse ("Little
    Dunker Church," Antietam, MD)
Dunkard Congregation, WI, 2325
Dunkard Creek (West Fork River) congre-
    gation, See West Virginia
Dunkard Ridge Cemetery, OH, 240
Dunkard Township, PA

place-names, Brethren, 1027
Dunkard (village of)
place-names, Brethren, 1027
"Dunkard's Church" at Greene, IA, *570*
Dunkard's Corner (Tunker), IN, 1234
Dunkard('s) Creek, PA
place-names, Brethren, 1027
Dunkelberger, Ralph D., 1918
Dunker Bottom, PA, 407
place-names, Brethren, 1027
Dunker Brethren's Orphan Home Society,
Kansas, 8, **410,** 682
"Dunker Church," Antietam, MD, *See*
Mumma meetinghouse ("Little
Dunker Church," Antietam, MD)
Dunker (Dunkard) Bottom settlement, VA,
1307
Dunker-Dutch Cook Book, 340–341
Dunker Ham, *See* Ham, John
Dunker Hollow, PA
place-names, Brethren, 1027
Dunker Valley, PA
place-names, Brethren, and New York,
PA, 1027
Dunkers, 1999, 2022, 2043, 2046, 2059,
See also Dunkard Brethren;
Schmauk, Theodore E.
about, 2325
articles about, 1920
baptism, 1920
Benjamin Franklin, reference to, 1940
bibliography, 1860, 1871, 1875, 1910
books about, 747, 748
burial ground records, 1920
church polity and, 2325
in colonial America, 2042
conversion of Amish, 1973
*Cyclopedia of Temperance and
Prohibition,* entry for, 1914
denominations and, *See* Milner,
Vincent L.
The Dunkard-Dutch Cookbook, 1920
Durnbaugh, Donald F. on Dunkers'
views of River Brethren, 2326
Durnbaugh, Donald F. on entrepreneurs
and, 2326
Eastern Synod of the Reformed
Church, records about, 1923
eighteenth-century Pennsylvania
church music, 1914
Encyclopedia International, entry for,
1920
The Encyclopedia of Christianity, 1983
Encyclopedia Universal Sopena, entry
for, 1920
founding of, 2325
Georgia, 540
Germany, 545
historical writing, 612
history of, 1930, 2020
Hon, Peter Keithly, 626
Hostetler, Joseph, 631
Illinois, 647
in Iowa, 2020
Juniata River settlements, 1975
Lehmann, Hartmut on, 2343
Longenecker, Stephen L. on history of,
2343
Maryland, 1913, 1920
meetinghouse, description of, 1919
music, 1920
as nickname of Brethren fellowships,
910

North Carolina during the Revolution,
1914–1915
North Dakota, 2046
Ontario, 975
Pegler, Westbrook on, 2349
Pennsylvania, 2035
Pfautz family, 1014
reference to, 1933, 1957, 1960
Ruth, John L. on, 2354
St. Francis and, 2018
simple life, 1965
Slabaugh, Dennis L. on, 2357
sociological interpretation, thesis on,
1949
sources on, 2309, 2312, 2318, 2323
statistics for congregations near
Harrisburg, 1911
Stump, Paul on mission in Africa, 2360
Stutesman, John Hale on American
Revolution and, 2360
Universalist fiction, references to, 1919
Wallower, Lucille, and children's book
about, 2361
Willoughby, William G. on, 2363
Wust, Klaus on, 2364
The Dunkers: A Sociological Interpretation
(Gillin), 549
Dunkers (Hoefs), 1968
Dunkerstown, *See* Ephrata Community
Dunkerstown, PA, 1027
Dunkerton, IA
place-names, Brethren, 1028
Dunkertown, NJ, 1027
Dunkirk Chapel, OH, Church of the
Brethren, 413
Dunkirk, OH, 163
Dunkle, Jeffrey L., 579, 1603
Dunkle, Nancy (later Groff), 574
Dunlap, Carol Jean, 1845
Dunlap, John, 18
Dunlap, KS
Ozawkie, KS, Church of the Brethren,
preaching point, 987
Dunlap, Raymond L., 1920
Dunlap(s), IN, Brethren Church, **410**
Dunmire, Fern, 1604
Dunmire, Rebecca (later Swigart), 1245
Dunmire, Ruth
works by, 2319
Dunmore Co., VA, 363
Dunn Co., WI, 1354
Irvin Creek Church of the Brethren,
WI, 664
Dunn, Frederick W., 1604
Dunn, Phyllis Belle (later Fulk), 1943
Dunning, Ada Viola, 1839
article about, 1927
Dunning, Avery B. (P.), 1604
Dunning, Cora Garber Gregory, 1920
Dunning family, 1215
Dunning, Harold Leroy, 29, 114, 573, 626,
754, 1604, 1848, 2300
Dunning, L. P., 1341
Dunning, Marguerite Edna Gribble, 573,
1848
Moody Bible Institute, 873
Dunnings Creek, PA, 1027
Church of the Brethren, PA, **410**
Point Church of the Brethren, 1040
Dunson, W. C., 1604
DuPage Co., IL, 1226
Frey (Fry) family, 517
Naperville Church of the Brethren, 913

Sollenberger family, 1202
Dupler, Alphaeus William, 1604
Dupler, Dorothy, 1886
Dupler, E. Parker, 748, 1920
DuPont, OH, Church of the Brethren, 71,
410–411, 1985, 2083
duPont, Richard, 1604
Durand, Frank B., 1604, 2301
Durand, Frank S., 2378
Durand, MI, Church of the Brethren, *See*
Elsie Church of the Brethren, MI
Durand, Sylvester, 719, 1604
Durbin Run meetinghouse, OH, 112
Durbin, WV
Allegheny, WV, Church of the
Brethren, 2125
Church of the Brethren, **2175**
Hoover Brethren Church, **411**
Pocahontas Church of the Brethren,
WV, mission point of, 1039
Durkee, Harry, 1944, 2097
Durkee, Sherwood Verdan, 1302, 1604
Grace Village Retirement Complex,
2193
South Bend, IN, Ireland Road Grace
Brethren Church, pastor, 1203
Durkw, Nigeria, 306
Durnbaugh, Donald Floyd, 114, 139, 191,
423, 473, 483, 535, *541, 589, 608,
627, 640,* 1604, 1859, 1920–1922,
2074
bibliography of, 2309
on biography, 2201
Brethren Encyclopedia, role in creation
of, 2143
on Brethren history, 2201
Brethren World Assemblies, role in
organizing, 2151
Dyck, Harvey L. on, 2328
On Earth Peace, 974
Eller, David B. on bibliography list of
writings of, 2329
European Origins of the Brethren,
1282
Festschrift in honor of, 2186
Germantown Historical Museum, 2189
historical writing, 612
on historiography, 2201, 2202
Miller, Timothy on Anabaptists written
by, 2347
Prague Conferences and, 2239
theology and, 2255
writings of, 2319, 2325–2327
Durnbaugh, Eve/Eva (later Fahrney), 104,
465, 466
medicine, 809
Durnbaugh family
Fahrney-Keedy Chapel Fellowship
Church of the Brethren, MD, 467
Durnbaugh, Hedwig (Hedda) T., 1922,
2143,
on historiography, 2202
on hymnals and hymnody, 2327, 2328
Durnbaugh, Jacob, 104
Durnbaugh, Robert N., 2149
Durnbaugh, Tana Hinson
National Older Adult Conferences,
2229
Durr, Arthur A., 1604
Durr (Dorer), Solomon, 1604
Durr, Francis Fast, 552, 1604
Durr, Lawrence Ervin, 1604
Durr, Marilyn Jeanne, 2277

Durr, Raymond W., 1922
Durr, Samuel, 540
Durr, Stephen George, 714, 2277
Durst, Elizabeth (later Bittinger), 144
Durst family, See Darst family
Durst, John R., 1604
Durwangen, Württemberg
　Neher family immigration, 922
Duryea, Rhea (later Johnson), 1927
Dush family
　Pataskala, OH, Grace Brethren Church
　　of Licking Co., 995
Duss, John S., 1922
Düsseldorf, 545
　prison, 71
Dust Bowl
　Griggs, OK, Bethel Church of the
　　Brethren, 573
dust storms
　Big Creek Old German Baptist
　　Brethren Church, KS, 142
Dustin, Hannah (later French), 1941
Dutch Bethel, German Baptist Brethren
　Church, 2373
Dutch Collegiants, See Collegiants
Dutch East Indies, See Indonesia
Dutch immersionists, See Collegiants;
　Dompelaars (Dompelaers)
Dutch Mennonites, See Anabaptism;
　Mennonite Church
　Collegiants, 324
Dutch Reformed Church, 55
　members from Amwell, NJ, congrega-
　　tion, 929
　Remonstrant (Arminian) party, 324
Dutchess, William, 705
Dutchman's Creek German Baptist Brethren
　Church, NC, 411
Dutchtown Brethren Church, IN, 411
Dutchtown congregation, IL, 750, See also
　Milledgeville Church of the
　Brethren, IL
Dutchtown, IN, 1385
　Flora, Benjamin H., 495
Dutruc-Rosset, Daniel, 1848
Dutruc-Rosset, Julia, 1848
Dutter, Edna, 1242
Dutton, Jack, 1604
　Ramey Flats Church of the Brethren,
　　VA, minister, 1083
Duvall, Linda
　Winchester, VA, Blue Ridge Grace
　　Brethren Church and, 2262
Duvall, Perry
　Winchester, VA, Blue Ridge Grace
　　Brethren Church and, 2262
Dvorak, Eileen K.
　on Barnhart family, 2328
Dwyer, Tim
　Muncie, IN, Cornerstone Brethren
　　Church and Ministries, 2227
Dyck, C. J.
　historiography
　　Anabaptism, 2201
Dyck, Cornelius J., 1922
　on Mennonite Encyclopedia, Vol. 5,
　　2328
Dyck, Harvey L.
　on Durnbaugh, D. F., 2328
　on pacifism, 2328
Dyer, A. A., 1604
Dyer, Carole Sue Bowman, 169
Dyer, Donita, 1922

Dyer, Robert, 169
Dyess, David, 1604
dying, See burial customs and funerals;
　death and dying
Dyson, Violet, 496
Dyson, Wilbur, 496
Dzangola, Nigeria, 306

E., H. F., 1922–1923
E. Nimishillen congregation, OH, 710
Eaby family, See entries at Eby
Eady, G. Kevin, 251, 2277
Eagle, Ann Lindower, 744
Eagle, Charles, 1604
Eagle Creek, OH, Church of the Brethren,
　163, 413, 2016
Eagle, Jan Elaine Zimmerly, 2157
Eagle Park, IN, 1351
Eagle River, AK
　FGBC congregation, 30
　Grace Brethren Church, 2175
Eagleton, Fred K., 1604
Eaker, Ervin
　Pompano Beach, FL, Grace Brethren
　　Church, 1046
Eaker, Jean
　Pompano Beach, FL, Grace Brethren
　　Church, 1046
Eaker, Lorena Shell, 1923
Eames, W., 2104
Earhardt, Philip, 262
Earhart, Abraham, 262
Earhart, Elva Hunt, 2007
Earhart, J. Stanley, 210, 670, 1337, 1604,
　1923
Earhart, Robert Lee, 1604
　Pasadena, CA, Church of the Brethren,
　　pastor in, 994
Earheart, Philip, elder
　North Carolina Brethren settlement,
　　946
Earl Twp., PA, 2102
Earle, Alice Morse, 1923
Earle, Phebe (later Gibbons), 1948
Earlenbaugh, Donald G., 2277
Earlham School of Religion (ESR)
　partnership with Bethany Theological
　　Seminary, 2136
Earlville house
　Leola, PA, Conestoga Church of the
　　Brethren, 737
Early, A. B., 1604
Early, Anna Margaret Smith, 414
Early, B. F., 1604
early Brethren, See Brethren; European
　Brethren; Schwarzenau Brethren
Early, Christian, descendants of, 1923
Early, Christina Regina Sichele, 1923
early church
　feetwashing, 481
　free ministry, 513
　Kent, Homer Austin, Jr. on history of,
　　2340
Early, D. Oscar, 1604
Early Days of Vyara (Ross), 1123
The Early Earth (Whitcomb)
　Whitcomb, John Clement, Jr. (FGBC,
　　CGBCI) and, 2262
Early, Eliza Gilbert, 1178
Early, Emma Martin, 413
Early family, 144, 236, 414–415, 688,
　1330, 1342, 1383
　Sanger family, related to, 1144

Early, George A., 1337, 1604
Early, Goldie, 94
Early, Henry Clay, 132, 133, 299, 310,
　413–414, 461, 462, 538, 912,
　1273, 1604, 1923, 2373, See also
　missions; peace; polity
　biography, 1939
　conservation movement, 337
　early 20th century sermon, 1168
　Mill Creek Church of the Brethren,
　　VA, moderator, 832
　minorities, ethnic and racial, 850
　missions, 861
Early, Isaac, 1604
Early, J. W., 1923
Early, Jacob, 414
　Nokesville, VA, Church of the
　　Brethren, meetinghouse on farm
　　of, 939
Early, John, 356, 414, 549, 1342, 1604,
　1923, 2034
　descendants, 1957
　Maple Valley Church of the Brethren,
　　MN, 2376
Early, John B., 116, 204, 414, 1604, See
　also Benevolent Board (BC)
Early, John Cabell, 1923
　Civil War, 2000
Early (Wehrly?), Jonathan
　Pigeon River Church of the Brethren,
　　IN, minister, 1023
Early, Magdelene Wenger, 414
Early, Margaret V. (later Harshbarger), 278,
　587
Early, Mark D., 635, 1251, 1604
Early, Mattie Miller, 414
Early, Mervin F., 1604
Early, Michael G., 414, 1604
Early, Milton C., 1604, 1923
　Omaha, NE, Church of the Brethren,
　　minister, 974
Early, Mr. and Mrs. Perry, 914
Early, Noah, 413, 1604
Early, Nora (later Shively), See Shively,
　Nora Early
Early, Oscar, 1604
Early, Perry A., 1178, 1604
　Milford, IN, Brethren Church, 831
Early, Polly Yoder, 414
Early, Ruth, E. 660, 1923, 2129
　refugee resettlement, 1093
　Washington Office (CB) and, 2260
Early, S. C., 740
Early, Sarah Kidd, 413
Early, Simon Peter, 912, 1604
　Roaring Spring, PA, First Church of
　　the Brethren, pastor, 1114
Early, Thomas, 1923
Early, William, 1923
Early Yellow Creek, PA, Church of the
　Brethren, See New Enterprise, PA,
　Church of the Brethren
Earnest, Corrine Pattie
　on Dayes, Birth, 2328
　on fraktur art, 2328
　on Scriveners, 2328
Earnest family, 2044
Earnest, Russell
　on fraktur art, 2328
Earnheart, E. A., 582
Earnheart, Eugene O., 1604
Earrey/Arey, Mary (later Moyer), 822
Earth Peace, 198

earthquakes
Bihar, India, 1367
New Madrid, MO, 1357
Union Co. Church of the Brethren, IL, triggered a religious awakening, 1288
Earwood, Samuel, 1604
Eash, Barbara (later Yoder), 2016
Eash family, 1881
Eash, John Eugene, Jr., 673, 752, 1604
Eash, Lucy, 1923
Eash, Sam T., 1923
Easley, AL, Church of the Brethren, 143, **415**
East Amwell, NJ, Bicentennial Committee, 1923
East Arm, *See* Floyd Co. Church of the Brethren, VA
East Berlin, PA, 765, 1230, 1294
East Chippewa, OH, Church of the Brethren, 279, **415**, 963
Paradise Church of the Brethren, divided from, 992
East Fairview Church of the Brethren, Manheim, PA, 279, **415**
75th anniversary, 1923
East Garfield Park Hospital, IL (CB), *See* Bethany Brethren Hospital
East Gate Mission, CA, Church of the Brethren, *See* Oakland, CA, Church of the Brethren
East Good Hope congregation, CO, 1221, *See also* Haxtun, CO, Church of the Brethren
East Hanover house, Big Swatara Church of the Brethren, PA, 142
East House (Plunge Creek Chapel), IN
Eel River Church of the Brethren, 429
Yellow Creek Old German Baptist Brethren Church, 1385
East Huntington Twp, Westmoreland Co., PA
Alverton and Tarr cemeteries, 1937
East Los Angeles, CA, Church of the Brethren, 994, 1275
minorities, ethnic and racial, 850
East Maple Grove, KS, Church of the Brethren, **415–416**
Olathe, KS, Church of the Brethren, 964
East McKeesport, PA, Church of the Brethren, **415**
Greensburg, PA, Church of the Brethren, 571
Pittsburgh, PA, Church of the Brethren, 1027
East McPherson Church of the Brethren, KS, **415**
East Nimishillen Church of the Brethren, OH, **416**, 710, 937
Hartville, OH, Church of the Brethren, 588
Nimishillen Old German Baptist Brethren Church, OH, members from, 937
East Nodaway Church of the Brethren, IA, **416**
East Pasadena Grace Brethren Church, 1252
East Pennsylvania District Board, 693
District Mission Board, 695
Kilhefner, Galen, 693
New York (NY) mission work, 933

Standing Committee, 693
East Petersburg, PA
Church of the Brethren, **416**
Hempfield Church of the Brethren, PA, 596
Mountville, PA, Church of the Brethren, 890
East Pine congregation, WI (CB), 63
East Pittsburgh, PA, *See* East McKeesport, PA, Church of the Brethren
East Prairie Church of the Brethren, MO, **416**
East San Diego, CA, Church of the Brethren, *See* San Diego, CA, First Church of the Brethren
East Sugarcreek, OH, Church of the Brethren, *See* Sugarcreek, OH, Sugarcreek East Church of the Brethren
East Tampa, FL, Church of the Brethren, *See* Tampa, FL, Church of the Brethren
East Tampa Mission, FL, 1247
North Tampa, FL, Zion Church of the Brethren, 950
East Union "Dunkers" German Baptist Brethren, KY, 935
East Wenatchee, WA, congregation, 1240, 1330
Eastburn, Iola Kay, 1923
Easter, **416**
Good Friday, 556
Lent, 737
observation of, 2147–2148
Easter, Joseph, 1604
minister of Saint Paul Church of the Brethren, NC, 1135
Easterday, John, 106, 1604
Eastern Cookbook, 340
Eastern District of Pennsylvania (CB)
Elizabethtown College, 437
Eastern District or *Lardin Gabas* of TEKAS
Fellowship of Churches of Christ in Nigeria, 484
Eastern Mount Carmel Church of the Brethren, VA, 265, **416**, 880
Pine Ridge Church of the Brethren, 2238
Eastern Orthodox Church, **983**, *See also* Greek Orthodox Church; Russian Orthodox Church
beards, 102
canonical scripture, 43, 55
episcopal polity, 1042
Greek Orthodox Church, 569
international exchange with Russia, 1288
Pentecostalism, 1009
Reformation, Protestant, and Brethren doctrine, 1092
refugee resettlement, 1093
role in development of Brethren theology, 1259
Roman Catholic Church, 1120
trinity, doctrine of, 1275
Eastern Region
Kilhefner, Galen, 693
Eastern Synod of the Reformed Church in USA
minutes and letters, 1923
Eastman, Fred, 399
Easton, MD
Fairview Church of the Brethren, MD,

469
Hutchison, Anna Martha, 639
Rittenhouse family, 469
Easton, MD, Peach Blossom Church of the Brethren, **416–417**, 1111
Peach Blossom Colored Church of Rising Light (CB), MD, 1003
Easton, PA
Parsons, William, founder of, 994
Eastville, PA, 1235
Eastwood, Albert M., 1604
Eastwood, OH
Church of the Brethren, *See* Akron, OH, Eastwood Church of the Brethren
as example of place name, 911
Eaton Co., MI, 725, 1239
Hope Church of the Brethren, MI, 629
Eaton George E., 204
Eaton, IN, 1288
Maple Grove Brethren Church, **417**
Eaton, OH, 766, 1256, 1295, 2333
Church of the Brethren, **417**, 963
Eau Claire, WI, 1354
Brethren Church, **417**
Eavey, George W., 1604
Ebaugh, Thomas A., 1923
Ebbert, Elizabeth Schuman, 417
Ebbert, Ella, **417**, 1836
article about, 1923
Ebbert, Nora Bowman, 1923
Ebbert, Samuel S., 1604, 1923
Ebbert, William, 417, 519
Ebe, Jacob, 420
Ebeling, Christoph Daniel, 1923
Ebenhack, Mary Jeanette
on Camp Peaceful Pines, 2328
Eber family, 1863
Eberbach, *112,* **417,** 2373
Eberhardt family, 1956
Eberhart, A. D., 1923
Eberhart family
history of (1265–1890), 1923
Eberhart, John Adam, 1923
Eberhart, Uriah, 1923
Eberle (Eberly) family, **417,** 1923, 2090
bibliography, 1875
genealogy of Heinrich Eberly family, 1923–1924
genealogy of the Alsacian branch, 1924
Royer family related to, 1128
Snavely family, related to, 1193
Eberle, William H., 1923
Eberly, Allen, 1605, 2175, 2301
Shrewsbury, PA, Dunkard Brethren Congregation, presiding elder, 1180
Eberly, Alvin B., 1923–1924
Eberly, Charles H.
on Eberly/Ecklerin controversy, 2328
Eberly, Clayton, 1924
Eberly, Daniel, 2090
Eberly, Daniel S., 417
Eberly, David G., 1924
Eberly/Ecklerin controversy
Eberly, Charles H. on, 2328
Eberly, Elias, 417
Eberly, Eloise Whitehead
on Whitehead, Argus, 2328
on Whitehead, Myrtle, 2328
Eberly, Elsie, 2175
Eberly, Emma Snoke, 417
Eberly family, *See* Eberle (Eberly) family

Eberly, Harvey M., 1605
Eberly, Heinrich, 2062
Eberly, J. David, 1605
Eberly, Jacob, 417
Eberly, James D., 2277
Eberly, James William, 1605
Eberly, John H., *385,* 417, **417,** 1605, 1926, 2129, **2373, 2381,** *See also* Polish agricultural exchange; student exchange
    family history, 2007
    refugee resettlement, 1093
Eberly, Joseph S., 417
Eberly, Levi, 417
Eberly, Martha Stauffer, 2175
Eberly, Marvin, 2175
Eberly, Ollie Heaston, 417
Eberly, Roger W., 1605
Eberly, Susanna Hess, 417
Eberly, Veronica Ulrich, 417
Eberly, Wayne J., 119, 654, 1605
Eberly, William R., 417, *652,* 1605, 1859, 1924
    on Brethren and education, 2328
    on Brethren ecumenism, 2328
    Brethren World Assemblies, 2151
    on Brethren, world directory of, 2328
    on CB (video tapes), history of, 2328
    The Complete Writings of Alexander Mack, 2143
    on Elder John Kline Bicentennial Celebration, 2328
    historiography, 2202
    on Manchester CB, IN, 2328
    North Manchester, IN, Church of the Brethren, elder (moderator), 949
    Roann, IN, Church of the Brethren, student and part-time pastor, 1112
    sources on, 2319
    on Whitehead, Argus, 2328
    on Whitehead, Myrtle, 2328
Ebersol, Amos Moyer, 1924
Ebersol, Charles E., 1924
Ebersol family, 1924
Ebersol, William, 1605
Ebersole, Abraham, 1924
Ebersole, Abraham Burkholder, 2086
Ebersole, Anna, 2086
Ebersole, Benjamin W. S., 1605
Ebersole, Bess V., 1924
Ebersole, Chester Miles, 1605
Ebersole, Christian, 1320
Ebersole, Ella, 256
Ebersole, Elmer E., 513, 571, 1605
Ebersole family, 396, 1924, 1927, 2086
    Garwin, IA, Carlton Brethren Church, 532
Ebersole, George D., 2277
Ebersole, Henry, 2102
Ebersole, Isaiah E., *See* Oberholtzer, Terre Hill
Ebersole, Jacob, 396, 720, 1605
Ebersole, John, 670
    descendants of, 1924
Ebersole, John Diffenderfer, 1605
    Salunga, PA, Church of the Brethren, elder at, 1140
Ebersole, John F., 1235, 1605, 1924
Ebersole, John Peters, **418,** 1605, 2087
    Oak Grove Church of the Brethren, OH, 956
    Ohio Brethren settlement, 961
    patent medicine remedy business, 995

    Sand Ridge Church of the Brethren, OH, revival meeting at, 1143
    Seneca Church of the Brethren, OH, elder in, 1166
Ebersole, Luke E., 599–600, 1605, 1924
Ebersole, Margaret (later Rosenberger), 1123
Ebersole, Mark C., 1605
    Elizabethtown College, 438
    on humor anthology on higher education, 2328
Ebersole, Martha Yeager, 2102
Ebersole, Martin, 1605
Ebersole, Mary
    descendants of, 1924
Ebersole, Peter, 418
Ebersole, Rachel Peters, 418
Ebersole, Ralph Zug, 1605
Ebersole, Robert D.
    memoirs, 2328
Ebersole, Ruth, 2102
Ebersole, Sarah (later Frantz), 508
Ebersole, Silas N., 1605
Ebersole, Simon, 1605
Ebersole, Susan Green, 418
Ebersole, William H., 1385, 1605
Ebert, Christena (later Moyer)
    Meyer family, 822
Ebert family, 145
Ebert, John L., 1605
Ebert, Otis P., 1605
Ebey, Adam, 418, *418,* **418,** 706, 1605, 1836, 1924
Ebey, Alice King, 137, 418, *418,* **418,** 706, 1307, 1836, 2101
Ebey, Cornelius A., 418, 1924
Ebey, Enoch J., 399, 1924
Ebey family
    history of, 1924
Ebey, Leah Ruth, 1307
Ebey, Robert Daniel, 261, 1235, 1605, 1924
Ebey, Susan Huff, 418
Ebi-Eby, Nicholaus, 1863
Ebie (Eby), John L., 1605
Ebie family, 1214, 1390
    history of, 1924
Ebie, George, 1924
Ebie, J. A., 1605
Ebling, David F., **418,** 521, 1243, 1605, 2301
Ebling, Della Kleplinger, 418
Ebling, Franklin, 418
Ebling, Laura Gibble, 418
Ebling, Sarah Bashore, 418
Ebony Madonna (Bowman), 748
Ebstein, *See* Eppstein
Eby family (Aby, Aebi), **420,** 721, 1863, 1926, 2046
    Ephrata Area Grace Brethren Church, PA, 448
    Gibbel (Gibble) family, 547
    history of, 1924, 1925, 1958
    tombstone inscriptions, 1937
Eby, Ada, 313
Eby, Aden, 1924
Eby, Allan A., 1924
Eby, Amelia Erb, 1924
Eby, Andreas, 420, 1605
Eby, Ann (later Baehr), 420
Eby, Anna, 521, 1950, *See* Eby, Annie Lauver Gilfillen; Lichty, Anna Eby
Eby, Anna (later Lichty), **741, 2375**
Eby, Anna Meylin, 420

Eby, Anna Price, 418
Eby, Annie Lauver Gilfillen, 419
Eby, B. Z., 1340
Eby, Barbara Bachman, 420
Eby, Barbara Groff, 420
Eby, Barbara (later Baehr), 420
Eby, Benjamin, 721, 1926
Eby, Benjamin Zug, 1605
Eby, Betty Lou (later Robbins), 2046
Eby, C. W., 1924
Eby, Christian, 420, 2019
Eby, David Bowman, 269, **418,** 419, 717, 905, 1240, 1319, 1605
Eby, David Davis, 420
Eby, David E., *See* Eby family
Eby, David F., *420,* 1605, 1924
    Pleasant Grove Church of the Brethren, IL, minister, 1031
Eby, Durst, *See* Eby, Theodorus (Durst)
Eby, E.
    Richland Center Church of the Brethren, KS, preacher, 1107
Eby, E. H., 229
    socialism, 1198–1199
Eby (Eaby/Ebi/Ebe/Ebie) families
    bibliography, 1862–1863, 1887
Eby, Effie Eugenia (later Minnich), 2019
Eby, Elisabeth Mayer, 420
Eby, Elizabeth (later Brown), 1924
Eby, Elizabeth (later Pfautz), 1014
Eby, Elmer, 419, 1924
Eby, Emma Ada Horner, 128, **418,** 1836, *See also* socialism
Eby, Emma Landis, 741
Eby, Enoch, 205, 361, 418, *419,* 419, 521, 587, 618, 682, 737, 1273, 1605, 1946, *See also* Danish mission
    education, 427
    Germany, 545
    Hope, Christian, 628
Eby, Enoch Howe, 25, 71, **418,** 419, 1605, 1836 *See also* socialism
Eby, Ephraim, 1924
Eby, Ezra E., 1924, 2019
Eby, Frank, 1605
Eby, Franklin Stanton, 1862, 1924
Eby, George, 420
Eby, Hanna Studebaker, 418
Eby, Henry H., 1605
Eby, Hettie Howe, 418, 419, 1273
Eby, Ira P., 211, 355, 416, 479, 571, 1605, 1924
    Poplar Bluff Church of the Brethren, AR, 1046
    Poplar Bluff, MO, Church of the Brethren, 1046
Eby, J. A., 1240
Eby, J. H., 504
Eby, Jacob Allen, 246, 419, 420, 662, 1924–1925, 2381
Eby, James Brian, 1925
Eby, Johannes, 420
Eby, John, 1263, 1606
Eby, John C.
    Rock Grove German Baptist Brethren Church, IA, minister, 1117
Eby, John G., 418, 1606
Eby, Josiah, 741, 1606
Eby, Judy Kay, 2077
Eby, Kermit, 96, 190, 302, **419–420,** 1606, 1871, 1925, 2023
    Rural Life Association (RLA), 1131
    socialism, 1198–1199

Eby, Leah, *See* Eby family
Eby, Lela
    on Index: Record of the Faithful, 1881
        by Howard Miller, 2328
Eby, Levi H., 1606
    Manchester College, acquisition of and
        trustee, 785
Eby, Lizzie Schwalm, 419
Eby, Lois Ann, 2007
Eby, Margaret Hess, 1925
Eby, Marie, 246
Eby, Marie L., 1606
Eby, Martin E.
    descendants, 1925
Eby, Martin R., 1925
Eby, Mary, 420
Eby, Mary L. (later Garver), 532
Eby, Mary (later Heistand), 602
Eby meetinghouse
    Leola, PA, Conestoga Church of the
        Brethren, 737
Eby, Paul R., 571, 1606
Eby, Pauletta (later Johnson), 672
Eby, Peter, 420, 1925, 1994
The Eby Report, 420
Eby, Retha Fish, 419
Eby, Richard Amos, 1926
Eby, Ruth, 1924
Eby, Ruth L., 1926
Eby, Samuel M., 1606
    Santa Ana, CA, Church of the
        Brethren, ministerial leadership
        given to, 1144
Eby, Simon P., 1926
Eby, Susannah MacDonald, 2019
Eby, Susannah Myers, 419
Eby, Theodore, 1863
Eby, Theodorus (Durst), 420
    descendants, 1954
    family history, 2007
Eby, Vinnie (later Kiracofe), 697
Eccard, C. L., 1606
Ecclesianthem
    poetry, 1039
Ecclesiastes
    book of, exegesis of, 2005
ecclesiastical establishment, *See* estab-
        lished churches
ecclesiology
    Brethren Church, 183–184, 185
    Brethren Church doctrine on, 184
    Brethren movement, 174, **291–294**
    conflicts, 157
    definition of, 386
eccoesiolae ecclesia
    Lutherans and Radical German
        Pietism, 1079
Echard, Alan R., 2277
Echard family, 731
Eck, Reimer C.
    works by, 2309
Eckartshausen, **421**
Ecker, David, 1606
Ecker, David R., 1606
Ecker, Donald, 1354, 1606
Ecker family
    Sharpsburg, MD, Church of the
        Brethren, 1174
Ecker, Greenberry (Greenbury), 1606
Ecker, Jacob Aldene, 1606
Ecker, Levi, 421
Ecker, M. Ella Utz, 421
Ecker, Mary Giddings, 421

Ecker, Thomas C., **421,** 1315, 1606
Eckerle, Phillip Franklin, 1606
Eckerley family, 1956
Eckerley, Gene A., 1606
Eckerlin, Anna, 421, 422
Eckerlin, Anna Grimman, *See* Eckerlin,
        Anna
Eckerlin brothers, 1985
    Hebron, 591
    Miller, John Peter, 840
    New River settlement, 1982
Eckerlin Creek, WV
    place-names, Brethren, 1027
Eckerlin, Emmanuel (Brother Elimelech),
        113, **421**
    article about, 1957
    Eicher, Jakob Christian, 431
    Lancaster Co., SC, 1204
    Martin, David, baptizing, 797
Eckerlin family, 2078, 2088, 2089, 2104,
        2105
    article about, 1915
    captivity, reference to
        by Benjamin Franklin, 1940
Eckerlin brothers, Ephrata Community,
        1336
    frontier, 519
    history of, 1935
    Manahaim colony, VA, 1307
    reference to, 1956
    request for land in Virginia, 1912
    Virginia, 2102
    Western Virginia, 1916
Eckerlin, Gabriel, 113, **421**
Eicher, Jakob Christian, 431
    French and Indian War, 516
    place-names, Brethren, 1027
Eckerlin, Israel, 421, **421,** 422, 516, 1926
Eicher, Jakob Christian, 431
    Mason-Dixon Line, 800
    place-names, Brethren, 1027
    Reed, Frank L. on, 2351
    reference to, 1939
    Renno, John R. on, 2351
    Rhode Island, visiting, 1107
Eckerlin, Maria, 421
Eckerlin, Martha Linck, 421
Eckerlin massacre, 2001, 2045
Eckerlin, Michael, 19, **421,** 422, 505, 574,
        589, 1227–1228, 2108
    Solingen Brethren, 1201
Eckerlin, Samuel, 113, 421, **422,** 519
    letters to Benjamin Franklin, 1960
    Mason-Dixon Line, 800
    medicine, 809
    place-names, Brethren, 1027
    Rhode Island, visiting, 1107
Eckerlin settlement, 1910, 2068
Eckerly, Herbert, 1606
Eckerman, Daniel, 1606
Eckerman family, Ridge Church of the
        Brethren, PA, 1108
Eckerman, Jacob, 1606
Eckert, Dana Zug, 1606
Eckert, Lester E., 1606
Eckhardt, George H., 1926
Eckhardt, James, 1606
Eckhartshausen
    Marienborn, village belonging to, 792
Eckleberger, Mr. and Mrs. John
    New Paris, IN, Brethren Church, 931
Eckman, Daniel G., 2074
Eckman family, 2074

Eckman, Leah Hoak, 2074
Eckman, Pearl Jackson, 1606
Eckstein, Christian, *See* Ephrata
        Community, tombstone incriptions
Eckstein family, 1961
ecology, *See* environmental issues
economic justice
    SERRV International (CB) and, 2247
economics, 2050, 2066
    agriculture, settlement patterns deter-
        mined by, 177
    cooperatives, 342–343
    credit unions, 351
    ethics and, 458
    Garver, Earl Simeon, 2187
    lifestyles and, 2066
    mills
        grain, 161, 206
        inventions for, 168
        woolen, 161
    socialism and Christianity, 1199
    sources on, 2314, 2322
Economy, PA, and Harmony Society, 584
Ecuador, **422,** 2022, 2044
    4-F club movement, 9
    agricultural missions (CB), 9, 12
    Church of the Brethren Rural Mission
        in, 2242
    Ellis, Calvert Nice, 441
    Evangelical Covenant Church, 460
    foreign missions, 1912
    Hispanic Ministries (CB), 2198, 2199
    medical missions, 807
    ministry education, 268
    mission schools, 854
    mission tours, 855
    mission work, 299, 300
    missions, *860,* 861, 2225
    missions and missionaries in, 187
        Church of Brethren, 250
    pastoral ministry and theological edu-
        cation, 1973
    Presbyterian relationships with
        Brethren, 1056
    relief and rehabilitation work in, 200
    relief and service efforts, 1097
    Rhoades, J. Benton and Ruby June
        Frantz in, 2242
    rural areas, mission work in, 1130
    United Andean Indian Mission
        (UAIM), 1289
    United Evangelical Church of Ecuador,
        187, 1289, 1290
    Wolfe, Claude E., missionary to, 1145
    work camps, 1367
Ecuador Concerns Committee, 422
ecumenical activities
    Elgin, IL, Highland Avenue Church of
        the Brethren, 436
    meetings on Pentecost, 1008
    Portland, OR, Peace Church of the
        Brethren, 1048
    Prairie City Church of the Brethren,
        IA, 1050
    Presbyterian relationships with
        Brethren, 1056
Ecumenical Center, Geneva, 540
ecumenical church, Ramsey, Duane H., on,
        2239
ecumenical conferences (Prague Confer-
        ences), 2239
ecumenical councils of Orthodox Church,
        983

Ecumenical Institute (Chicago, IL)
Robinson, Paul Minnich, president, 1116
Ecumenical Ministries, Portland, OR, Peace Church of the Brethren, 1048
Ecumenical Patriarch of Constantinople, 983
ecumenism, **422–423**, 2035, 2036, 2049
Baptism, Eucharist, and Ministry (BEM) text, 2133–2134
bibliography, 1904
Brethren movement and, 2079
Brethren view of Roman Catholic Church, 1120
changes in attitudes about, 1376
Church of the Brethren, 301, 303–304, 2109
comity agreements, 326
Committee on Interchurch Relations (CB), 328, 2167
Committee on Understanding and Reconciliation (CB), 328
Durnbaugh, Donald F. on Brethren Peace Witness and, 2327
Eberly, William R. on Brethren movement and, 2328
Eller, Jay Vernard, 440
ethical issues, 2178
faith and order, 470
Fellowship of Grace Brethren Churches (FGBC), 486
Fellowship of Reconciliation (USA), 488
first efforts of in America, 68
Fraternal Relations Committee (CB), 328, 510
Groff, Warren Frederick, 2194
Historic Peace Churches, 607–610
Hochmann von Hochenau, Ernst Christoph, 2057
Horst, Melvin Clyde, 630
Interchurch World Movement (IWM), 658
International Christian Youth Exchange (ICYE), 659
Korean Mission, 2211
Materials Towards a History of the Baptists, promoting, 803
Mennonites, 816
Miller, J. Q., 335
missions, 2225
Moravian Church, 875
Mott, John Raleigh, 879
organizations, 150
Pietism, 1022
Smithfield Church of the Brethren, PA, opposition to, 1192
Spain, relief work in, 1207
Visser 't Hooft, W. A., 1368, *1368*
World Council of Churches, 1368–1369
Zigler, Michael Robert, 1368, *1368, 1369,* 1398
Eddy Co., ND
James River Church of the Brethren, ND, 668
New Rockford Church of the Brethren, 932
Eddy, [George] Sherwood, **423–424**
Eddy, George Simpson, 1926
Eddy, J. A., 738, 1380
Eddy, Jayson (Jason) Ackley, 1606
Eddy, Mary Baker, 287

Eddy, Maud Arden, 424
Eddy, Richard, **424,** 577, 580, 1926
Eddy, Rosemary Byrd, 204
Eddy, Ruth, 1351
Eddy, Sherwood, **423–424** See Eddy, [George] Sherwood
as teacher of Page, Kirby, 989
Edelblute, Clara L., 1926
Edelmann, J. Christian, 589
Edelmann, Johann Christian, 120, 1926
biography, 1954
Eden Bible Institute (BC), 54, **424,** *See also* theological education
mission schools, 854
missions, 862
Solomon, Kenneth LeRoy (BC) and, 2251
Eden Church of the Brethren, OH, 211, **424**
Eden, NC
Church of the Brethren, **424**
Germantown Brick Church of the Brethren, VA, 544
Eden, OH, congregation
Mount Zion Church of the Brethren, OH, 888
Eden Twp., OH, Brethren movement in, 2086
Eden Valley Church of the Brethren, KS, **424,** 726, 1316
Edens family
St. Albany Old German Baptist Brethren Church, WV, 1134
Eder, George
Eller family, 440
Eder River, Schwarzenau, 174, **424–425**
historic sites, 609
two-hundred-fiftieth anniversary celebration, 1274, *1282, 1283*
Edesto, SC, congregation
minorities, ethnic and racial, 849
Edgecomb, Albie L., 1606
Edgecomb family, 142
Edgecomb, George A., 431, 1606, 2301
Edgecomb, Glen, 2277
Edgecomb, Nancy
Parsons Old German Baptist Brethren Church, KS, 994
Edgecomb, Robert, 1606
at New Hope Church of the Brethren, KS, 929
Parsons Old German Baptist Brethren Church, KS, elder in, 994
Edgecomb, Samuel, 40, 141, 273, 670, 1606
New Hope Church of the Brethren, KS, elder in, 929
New Hope Church of the Brethren, OK, elder in, 929
Osage Church of the Brethren, KS, minister, 983
Edgecomb, William, 500, 923, 1606
at New Hope Church of the Brethren, KS, 929
New River Old German Baptist Brethren Church, ministers for, 931–932
Parsons Old German Baptist Brethren Church, KS, minister in, 994
Edgemoor Park, KS, 1343
Edgewood Church of the Brethren, MD, **425**
Sams Creek Church of the Brethren, MD, Edgewood meetinghouse,

1141
Edgington, Allen D., 448, 2177, 2277
Edict of 1712, **425**
Marienborn, religious freedom in, 792
edict of toleration issued by Ernst Casimir, 453
Edinburg, VA, 1313
Edinburgh
Krumrein, Georg Lenhart, 708
Edinburgh, Scotland, 470
Edington, Allen, 2328
Edison German Baptist Brethren Church, NE, **2373**
Edisto, SC, 1249
German Baptist Brethren Church, **425**
Martin, David, minister, 797
editors, anecdotal definition of, 195
Edminister, Worden (Warden), 374, 1606
Owl Creek Old German Baptist Brethren Church, OH, minister, 986
Edminston, Sibley, 1248
Edmister family
Nezperce, ID, Church of the Brethren, 935
Edmister, Joseph F., 531, 1606
Edmister, Lois Rupert, 1926
Edmister, Orpha Ellen, 1836
Edmiston, Dave
River City Grace Community Church, 1134
Edmiston, June
River City Grace Community Church, 1134
Edmiston, Sibley Marvin, 1606, 1848
Edmiston, Willetta Marie Hanson, 1848
Edmonds, Edwin Hill, 2277
Edmonds, Stephan J., 343, 1380, 1606, 2277
Marion, OH, Grace Brethren Church, 2218
Edmonson family
Reading Grace Brethren Church, PA, 1084
Edna Mills, IN, 693
Brethren Church, **425,** 693
Shively, Martin, 1178
Rossville, IN, Church of the Brethren, 1124
Edom, VA
Wenger family, 2092
Edris, Elias W., 1606
Mount Zion Road Church of the Brethren, PA, minister, 888
educated ministry
Brethren Church ministry, 846
Church of the Brethren, 846
Grace Brethren Church ministry, 847
Priesthood of All Believers, 1057
The Vindicator, 845
education, **425–428,** 2027, 2032, 2058, *See also* Christian education; Christian schools; colleges and universities; religious education; Sunday school; specific institutions
academies, *See* academies
African programs, 268
agricultural, 12
alcohol education, 1252
Argentine pastors and, 180
Ashland College, *See* Ashland College
BaKongo village, 1996
Bethany Bible School, 2063

Bible conferences, 136
Bible courses not offered initially, 1256
Bible Institutes, *See* Bible institutes
Biblical piety, 2010
bibliography, 1884, 1885–1886, 1894, 1901, 1903
Brethren Academy for Ministerial Leadership, 2139–2140
Brethren movement development, 355
Brethren publishing, 1067
Brumbaugh, Martin Grove and, 222
Bura animist folklore, 1962
chaplaincies at educational institutions, 2158
China, 277
Chinese Sunday School and Church of the Brethren (CB), 275
Christian, 24, *See also* Christian Day School Movement
art, use of in, 61
Christian education, **2160–2161**
Christian education, articles about, 1937
church colleges, article about, 1911
Church of the Brethren, 300, 2162
Church of the Brethren higher education, 1997
church-related colleges, 1911
classroom materials, 284, 285
colleges, Christian, 2069, 2100
colonial era, 2092–2093
CPE, 271
curricular materials, 2160
demise of Brethren nonconformity, as contributing to, 74
distance education
Grace Schools, 2192
information technology, church use of, 2208
Douglas(s), Susan, 397
dress and, 402, 403
Drushal, Ada Louella Garber and George Emery, 405
Dunkard Brethren, 408, 2159, 2160, 2174–2175
early Lutheran, in Pennsylvania, 2009
Eberly, William R. on Brethren movement and, 2328
Ebersole, Mark C. on humor anthology on higher education, 2328
Eby, Emma Ada Horner and Enoch Howe, 418
elementary, **434–435**
Eller, Vernard on feminism grammar, 2329
Ephrata Community, 451
evolution, 463
family, 474
Fellowship of Grace Brethren Churches, 2183
Finnell, Virgil Carl, 490
formal, need for, 166
formalized Christian education, emphasis on, 1210
Forward Movement, 504
Four-Year Program, 505
Fruitdale Community Church of the Brethren, OR, 520
Fundamentalism and, 428, 2179
Funderburg, Drue Dresher, 523
General Conference Mennonite Church, 536
General Education Board, 441

General Educational Board (CB), 414
Germantown, 544
Gill, David W. on higher, 2333
Golden Dawn, The, 556
Gospel Visitor, The, 561
Grace Schools (Grace Theological Seminary, Grace College), 563, 2192
Haddix, KY, Brethren Church, 577
Halle on the Saale River, 580
Hamer, Oliver Stuart, 580
Hebron Seminary, 591
Herr, John, 598
Hertzler, Samuel Hoffer, 601
Hess, Maurice Abram, 601
higher, *See* higher education
historical writing, 613
history of in Church of the Brethren, 1938
Holsinger, Henry Ritz, 621, 622
home education, 2203
home schooling, *See* home schooling
Hospital Committee (CB), 630
Howe, William Mohler, 633
Hoyt, Herman Arthur, 634
India, 229, 651
international programs, 185
James Gribble Memorial High School, 668
list of academies, colleges, and seminaries
international, 1829
USA, 1825
Logan, Linda on education of Christian children, 2343
map of institutes of higher education in USA, 1464
Mennonites, 2220–2221
message of the Church, 1992
Miller, Jacob, 1347
ministers, and salary, 1136–1137
minorities, ethnic and racial, 850
minorities, of, 405
mission schools, 853, *See* mission schools
missions, 861, 2224
missions, for, *See* missions education
modern science, 1160
Native Americans, 2230
New Vienna Academy, OH, 932
Nigeria, 306
Nigeria mission work, 936
nonconformity, 940
normal schools, 945
Old Brethren Christian Schools, 2232
Old Brethren Church, 2232
Old German Baptist Brethren, 969, 971, 2235
Osceola, IN, Grace Brethren Church, 984
peace education
in homes, 2096
Pennsylvania, 2098
post-high school, 231–232
Progressive Brethren, educational enterprises of, 1061
publications on, 7
publishers and publishing, 426–427
Ragnijiya, T. H. on continuing education program for Ekklesiyar 'Yan'uwa a Nigeria, 2351
religious, 1963, 1977, 1983, 2016, *See also* religious education

religious, at Miami, NM, Church of the Brethren, 1995
religious education
Sunday school movement, 2084
religious education curriculum, thesis on, 1961
Salem College, 1138
Sauer, J. C. on education, 2098
schools sponsored by other religions, 178
secondary, *See* secondary education
singing, 1970
teachers, *See* teacher training
theological, *See* theological education
theory of, 223
women, of, *436,* 438
women, roles in, 1361
work in, 167
education centers, 2131
Education for a Shared Ministry (EFSM), 226, **429**
Bethany Theological Seminary, involvement in, 993
Brethren Academy for Ministerial Leadership, 2140
Durbin, WV, Church of the Brethren, 2175
Fruitdale, AL, Church of the Brethren, 520
Hoffman, Paul W., 2202
Los Angeles, CA, Hermanos Unidos en Cristo, 2215
Miller, Donald Eugene, 2223
Mont Ida, KS, Church of the Brethren, 870
Olean Church of the Brethren, VA, 973
Parish Ministries Commission involvement in, 993
pastoral ministry, 2164
rural congregations, 2162
Smith, Rufus E., 1049
Education for Urban Ministry (EFUM), 2256–2257
Education of Primitive People (Helser), 596
Educational Association of the Schools (CB), **429**
Educational Bluebook and Directory, 234
Educational Board
Church of the Brethren, *See* General Education Board
School Visiting Committees, 1155
Educational History of the Church of the Brethren (Solomon Zook Sharp), 1174
educational movement, 3
The Educator and Companion, **429,** 1926
Snyder, John Martin, editor, 1196
educators
Brethren children named for, 912
Grace Brethren Church ministry, 847
Edward family
Sandy Creek Old German Baptist Brethren Church, WV, 1143
Edward, Robert M.
Pleasant View Church of the Brethren, TN, 1037
Edwards, Alice, 2133
Edwards, Chandler W., **429,** 726
International Voluntary Services Agency (IVS), 660
Edwards Corner Methodist Church, Marcellus, MI
Male, E. William, 2217

Edwards, Donald W.
Mount Bethel Church of the Brethren, VA, pastor, 880
Edwards, E. B., 1946
Edwards, Emmanuel Andrew, 1606
Edwards, Frank, 1312
Edwards, Frank G., 270, 1606
Edwards, (Gary) Wayne, 1606
Edwards, Hobart P., 1606
Edwards, John F., Jr., 1606
Edwards, Jonathan
Great Awakening and American revivalism, 1104
postmillenialism, 833–834
Edwards, Kenneth L. 2277
Pleasant View Church of the Brethren, TN, 1037
Edwards, Larry David, 121, 2277
Edwards, Leola Scott, 429
Edwards, Levi C., 1606
Pigeon River Church of the Brethren, NC, 1023
Edwards, Lorraine Frantz
on Frantz, Michael and descendants, 2329
on La Verne Evergreen Cemetery tombstone inscriptions, 2329
on OGBB, 2328, 2329
Edwards, M. Robert, 264
Edwards, Martin, 1606
Petersons Chapel Church of the Brethren, NC, 1012
Edwards, Mary Ann (later Gillett), 549
Edwards, Mary Nunn, 429
Edwards, Morgan, 39, 48, 98, 175, 379, **429**, 493, 534, 923, 1867, 1926,
See also historical writing
article about, 1927
description of Brethren worship, 1375
findings of, 105, 113
historical writing, 611
history of Germantown, 1935
house churches, 632
Hüber (Hoover) family, 634
Leatherman (Letterman), Daniel, statement about, 732
life and works, 2004
Martin, David, 797
Materials Towards a History of the Baptists, 379, 803
ministry, terminology, 848
preaching, 1053
Sontag, Jakob, 1203
South Carolina, 1204
statistics gathered by, 1218
Steiner family, 2378
Stover, William, 2379
universalism, 1292
Uwharrie German Baptist Brethren Church, NC, account of, 1299
Edwards, N. T., 1606
Edwards, Ova, 105, 429, 453, 516, 673, 1607
Meadow Branch Church of the Brethen, TN, 806
New Hope Church of the Brethren, TN, elder in, 929
Edwards, R. G., 78, 1607
Pleasant View Church of the Brethren, TN, 1037
Edwards, Richard M., 2133
Edwards, Robert M., 453, 673, 1607
Eel River Christian Temple, Winona Lake,

IN, 914
Eel River, IN, 352, 652, 740, 1213, 1334
bibliography, 1877
Church of the Brethren, **429–430**
example of place name, 911
North Manchester, IN, Church of the Brethren, 949
Old German Baptist Brethren Church, **430**
EFUM, *See* Education for Urban Ministry (EFUM)
egalitarian community
ministry education, 293–294
Egan, CA Church of the Brethren, *See* Hemet, CA, Church of the Brethren
Egan, Eileen, 1927
on nonviolence movement, 2329
on peace churches, historic, 2329
Egan, Elias J., 1607
Egealton, Fred K., 1607
Egeland, Janice A., 1927
Egeland, ND, 251
Church of the Brethren, **430**
Ellison Church of the Brethren, ND, 442
Egerton, Hugh Edward, 1927
Egge, Dean, 1607
Egge, Doris Cline, 191, 1927
on human sexuality, 2329
Egge, Lora Shatto Mainard, 1836
Eggleston, Edward, 747, 1927
eggs and Easter celebrations, 2147–2148
Egle family, genealogy, 1927
Egle, William Henry, 1919, 1927
Eglin, N. P., 1607
Eglise Baptiste des Cites Haiti, 2225
Eglon, WV, Church of the Brethren, 144, 274, 1336
Church of the Brethren, **430**
Fairview Church of the Brethren, MD, 468
history of, 1936, 1960
Jordan Run Church of the Brethren, 676–677
Oak Park Church of the Brethren, MD, 957
Pine Grove Church of the Brethren, MD, 1024
Egypt
relief and rehabilitation work by youth from, 200
tours of, 202
travel to with D. L. Miller, *1273*
Ehlers, Henry, 1607
Ehresman, Catherine (later Shively), *See* Shively, Catherine Ehresman
Ehrhardt, Roddy C., 2277
Ehrle (Early), Jacob, 414
Eichelberger, Abdiel Wirt, 1927
Eichelberger, Charles, 1607
Eichelberger, Christian, 2028
Eichelberger, John A., 190
Eichelberger, John E., 1927
Eichelberger, Mary Schantz, 2028
Eichelberger, Peter, 1340, 1607
Eichelberger, Philip Frederick descendants, 1927
Eichenberg, Anna Maria Dorn, 430
Eichenberg (Eikenberry, Ikenberry) family, **430**
Eichenberg, Elizabeth (later Bowman), 430
Eichenberg, Fanny (later Brower), 430

Eichenberg, Henry, 430
Eichenberg, John, 430
Eichenberg, Martin, 430
Eichenberg, Peter, 430, 722
family history and genealogy, 1977
Eichenberg, Peter, Jr., 430
Eichenberg, Susannah (later Myers), 430
Eichenberger, A., 1607
Eicher, Anna (Sister Anna), **430–431**
Eicher, Daniel, 431, **431**
Eicher family
Schultz, Martin, related to, 116
Spohn, Clarence E. on, 2358
Eicher, Jakob Christian (Brother Aleasar), **431**
Eicher, John K., 1607
Eicher, Maria, **430–431**
Sister Maria of the Roses of Sharon, 1172
Eicher, Naomi, 431
Eicher, William Clyde, 1236, 1607
Eichholtz, Lydia (later Miller)
Mont Ida, KS, Church of the Brethren, 870
Eichler family
Mission Viejo, CA, Saddleback Valley Grace Brethren Church, 855
Eichman, Larry, 264, 731, 1607
Eichoff, Sophia (later Kem), 687
Eichorn family
Garwin, IA, Carlton Brethren Church, 532
Eichorn, Floyd, *See* Hooley family
Eichorn, Marnetta, *See* Hooley family
Eickenberry, J., 470
Eickhoff, Anton, 1927
Eickhoff, Eric L., 2277
Eidemiller, Elizabeth Coppock, 343
Eidemiller, J. Howard, 1383, 1607, 1927
Eidemiller, Martin P., 343
Eidemiller, Sylvia Jean, 1842
Eight Mile, IN, Church of the Brethren, *See* Markle, IN, Church of the Brethren
Eight Mile, KS, 1321
Church of the Brethren, *See* Appanoose Church of the Brethren, KS
example of dative case in place name, 912
Old German Baptist Brethren Church, **431,** 682
Plum Creek Old German Baptist Brethren Church, 1038
Shoal Creek Old German Baptist Brethren Church, Newton Co., MO, 1178
Eighteenth Amendment, *See* Prohibition; temperance movement
Church of the Brethren, 301
endorsed by annual meeting, 1251, 1252
Eighteenth century
Alsace, France, 19
"Angel Brethren" (*Engel-Brüder*), 30
immigration of Germanic peoples, 26
religious supression, 19
Eighth-day Tumplers, *See* Names, Brethren
Eikenberry, Amos R., **431,** 1607, 1927
Eikenberry, Beulah Minnich, 431
Eikenberry, C. Wayne, 1607
Eikenberry, Christian, 496
Eikenberry, D. R., 1607
Eikenberry, David Franklin, 12, 20, 562, 635, 1607

Eikenberry, Della Filbrun, 1927
Eikenberry, E. Ralph, 1607
Eikenberry, Edward Harvey, 1607
Eikenberry, Elder
    Raisin City, CA, Church of the
        Brethren, elder, 1083
Eikenberry, Elizabeth Wagoner, 431
Eikenberry, Emma, 1265
Eikenberry, Ephraim, 1607
Eikenberry, Ervan, 105, 766, 1295, 1607,
    See also Old German Baptist
    Brethren
Eikenberry family, 142, 1383, *See also*
    Eichenberg (Eikenberry, Iken-
    berry) entries
    Four Mile Church of the Brethren, IN,
        505
    Greene, IA, Church of the Brethren,
        570
Eikenberry, Florence Shaw, 431
Eikenberry, Gletha Mae Hoffsinger, 431
Eikenberry, Harvey, 1607
Eikenberry, I. M., 1607
    Morrill Church of the Brethren, MN,
        resident minister, 877
Eikenberry, (Ikenberry), John F., 1607
Eikenberry, Isaac, 297, 464, 1607
Eikenberry, Ivan Leon, 306, **431**, 464, 1607,
    1836, 1607, **2373, 2381, 2387**
Eikenberry, J. E., 479, 1380, 1607
Eikenberry, J. Kernie, 1607
Eikenberry, Jacob H.
    Pipe Creek Old German Baptist
        Brethren Church, IN, deacon, 1026
Eikenberry, James Owen, 1607
    Lancaster, PA, Acts Covenant
        Fellowship, 2213
    Pomona, CA, Fellowship Church of the
        Brethren, 1045
Eikenberry, Jesse E., 241
Eikenberry, Joel W., 1607
Eikenberry, John, 431, 1607
    family of, 1927
    Middletown, OH, Church of the
        Brethren, pastor, 826
    Ross, Helen M. Ross on, 2353
    Ross, Keith E. on, 2353
Eikenberry, John A., 1607
Eikenberry, John E., 570, 1607
Eikenberry, John F.
    Rock Grove German Baptist Brethren
        Church, IA, minister, 1117
Eikenberry, Joseph, 1607
Eikenberry, Josiah, 1607
Eikenberry, Lester J.
    New Hope Church of the Brethren, TN,
        elder in, 929
Eikenberry, Lorrel Spencer, 515, 1607
    Peoria, IL, (First) Church of the
        Brethren, pastor, 1009
Eikenberry, M. K., 1927
Eikenberry, M. W., 104, 360
Eikenberry, Mary Clingenpeel, 306, 431
    Ross, Helen M. Ross on, 2353
    Ross, Keith E. on, 2353
Eikenberry, Mary Elizabeth Flora, **431,**
    1836
Eikenberry, Mary (later Lybrook, Moss)
    Moss family, 878
Eikenberry, Morris Walter, 1607
Eikenberry, Oren, 1927
Eikenberry, Peter, 1281, 1607
Eikenberry, Susan Berkley, 431

Eikenberry, Susan Lynn, 2277
Eikenberry, T. S., 431
Eikenberry, W. Lewis, 1977
Eikenberry, Wayne, 1607
Eikenberry, William H. (W. H.), 431, 90,
    1380, 1607
Eikenberry, William Lewis, **431,** 1607
Eikenberry, Wilmer, 1607
Eikens family
    South Haven Old German Baptist
        Brethren Church, MI, 1205
Eilar family, *See* Eiler family, 1927
Eilar, Frances, 296
Eilar, Jacob, 432
Eilar, Jesse H., 296
Eilar, John Sylbert, 1927
Eiler(?), Samuel, 432
Eiler(?), Susanna Snider, 432
Eiler, Austin, 1338, 1607
Eiler, C. F., 1333
Eiler, Calvin F., 1608
Eiler, David L., 1608
Eiler (Eilar, Oyler) family, 432, **2373**
Eiler, Emmert (Emmet), 1608
Eiler family, 1281, 1927
Eiler, Homer, 1927
Eiler, John, 269
Eiler, Noah Austin, 1608
Eiler, Samuel (1819–1905), 106, 1608
Eiler, William H., 142
    Rice Lake, WI, Church of the Brethren,
        minister, 1107
Eiler, William Henry, 1608
Eilles, John, 1608
    Rockingham and Shenandoah Counties
        Old German Baptist Brethren
        Church, VA, elder, 1118
Eilles, Mrs. John
    Rockingham and Shenandoah Counties
        Old German Baptist Brethren
        Church, VA, 1118
Ein geringer Schein (*A Humble Gleam*),
    176
Ein Prediger, 2039
Ein Schönes Lied (Mack)
    Pfautz, John Eby, publisher, 1014
Ein Zeugniß von der Taufe (Bowman) , 168
Eine Deutsche Concordanz
    Pfautz, John Eby, publisher, 1014
Einfältige Lehr-Betrachtungen, und kurze
    fabtes Glaubens-Bekäntnib
    (*Frantz*), 509
EIRENE, **432,** 876
    Historic Peace Churches, 610
    peace, 998
    relief and service efforts, 1097
    Row, W. Harold, 1126
Eis, David R., 1608
Eisan, Leslie, 316, 917, 1927
Eisele, George A., 1836
Eisele, L. Katherine Hamm, 1836
Eiselstein, Paul, 62, 1608, 2301
Eisenberg, J. Linwood, 1608, 1927–1928
    Shippensburg, PA, Church of the
        Brethren, pastor in, 1177
Eisenberg, J. T., 1608
Eisenberg, John Y., 1608
Eisenbise, Allie Stutzman, 432, 1608
Eisenbise, Charles W., 695, 1608
Eisenbise, Clinton S., 432, 1608
Eisenbise, Debra Lee, 2277
    on Brethren values, 2329
    on ministry, 2357

works by, 2319
Eisenbise, Esther Mae, 1833, 2103
Eisenbise family, 1928
Eisenbise, Forest Sard, **432,** 1608
    Pasadena, CA, Church of the Brethren,
        pastor in, 994
    World War II relief work, 1373
Eisenbise, George
    Owl Creek Old German Baptist
        Brethren Church, OH, 986
Eisenbise, Grace Bubb, 432
Eisenbise, Jane
    Owl Creek Old German Baptist
        Brethren Church, OH, 986
Eisenbise, John, 1608
Eisenbise, Julia Ann Elder (later Fry), 521
Eisenbise, Peter, 521
Eisenbise, Peter J., 1608
Eisenbise, Thomas A., 1608
Eisenbise, Viola, 1928
Eisenbise, William Gilbert, 1608
Eisenbise, William H., 1608
Eisenhour, Ira C., 1608
Eisler, Tobias, 120
Eje Ecuménico (Nicaragua)
    Misión Mutua en las Américas, 852
Ekklesiyar 'Yan'uwa a Nigeria (*EYN*), *See*
    Church of the Brethren in Nigeria
El Cajon, CA
    Cajon Valley Church of the Brethren,
        432
    San Diego, CA, First Church of the
        Brethren, 1141
El Centro Church of the Brethren, CA, **432**
El Dorado, MO, congregation, 263
El Salvador
    Church of the Brethren, 2157
    Honduras, 627
    Iglesia Bautista de Emmanuel
        (Emmanuel Baptist Church), 2157
Elam, Fern M.
    on CB musical history, 2329
Elam, Jennifer
    on peace witness movement, 2329
Elam, William, 638, 1608
    Mulberry Grove, IL, Church of the
        Brethren, elder, 893
Elbethel Church of the Brethren, PA, 347,
    432
Elbow Creek, TX
    congregations, 1255, 1346
    migration of Brethren to, 830
Elder family
    Hatboro, PA, Suburban Grace Brethren
        Church, 588
Elder, W. S., 1608
elderly persons, *See* aged persons
elders, 4, 6, **432–433,** *525,* 2034
    "additional elder" position created by
        Mooreites, 875
    adjoining elders, *See* adjoining elders
    associate elders, 848
    Brethren Church, 184, 846, 2224
    Church of the Brethren, 305, 846
    Churches of God, General Eldership,
        177
    commissioning services, 327
    degrees of ministry, 374
    dress for, 402
    Dunkard Brethren, 409–410
    election of church officers, 434
    farming, 477
    frontier, 519

Grace Brethren Church ministry, 847
hairstyle, 579
healing, 591
installation of ministers, 656
list of, 1539–1823
marriage counseling, 796
mentoring, 2221
ministry, terminology, 847
ordination, 980
ordination of, 185
ordination of women, discussion of, 2141
Pennsylvania Church of the Brethren, 1005
plan of ministry, 844
presiding, 45
role in Standing Committee, 1216–1217
role in worship services, 1377
role of, 294
women and, 2263
elders-in-charge, 847
elders' table, 1071, *1072*
Elderton, PA, 693
Oakdale Church of the Brethren, PA, 957
Plum Creek Church of the Brethren, 268, 350, **433**
Murphy, Ross Dale, minister, 896
Eldorado, KS, 753
Eldorado, OH, Dunkard Brethren Congregation, OH, **433**
Englewood, OH, Dunkard Brethren Congregation, 447
Eldredge, Charles McGreger, 2277
Eldrick family, *See* Ulrich family
Eldridge, Margaret (later Metzler)
Metzler, John D., Sr., wife of, 820
Eldridge, William, 1608
Eleazar, Brother, *See* Eicher, Jakob Christian
elections, 4, **434**, *See also* polity
Brethren in Christ, 189
Church of God (New Dunkers), 297
church officers, and
"Order of the Brethren," 976
church-state relations, 310
degrees of ministry, 374
Dunkard Brethren and nonconformity, 941
elder, 432
ethics, 458
General Board (CB), 535, 536
German Seventh-Day Baptists, 542
Plymouth Brethren, 1038–1039
U.S. national, 301
electricity, **434**
Industrial Revolution, 655
nonconformity, 941
nuclear power, 951
Old Brethren German Baptist Church, 965
Old Brethren's Reasons, 965
Old German Baptist Brethren, 969
Old Order German Baptists, 972
Skiles, Jacob W., 1189
elementary schools, 426, **434–435**, *See also* Christian day schools
Eler, Henry
Eller family, 440
Eley, Theodore R., 1608
Elgin, Buren A., 1608
Elgin, IL, 18, 25, 36, 168, 194, **435–436**, 647, 709, 1331, 1345, 1395, 1397,

1398, *See also* fellowship houses
Brethren Publishing House, 300
camping movement, 248
church structure, 304
fellowship houses, 482
genealogy, 535
General Brotherhood, 706
General Offices (CB), *See* General Offices
General Services Commission (CB), 539
Highland Avenue Church of the Brethren, **436,** 1965
historic sites, 609
historical libraries, 610
hymnals, 642
Messenger, 818
SERRV international gift shop, 1139
State Hospital, medical projects at, 808
Elgin, Richard Glenn, 2277
Elgin, William A., 1608
Elias, Johan E., 1928
Elimelech, Brother, *See* Eckerlin, Emmanuel
Elisha's Creek mission point
Flat Creek Church of the Brethren, KY, 493
elite, treatise on Brethren concept of, 2054
Elizabeth Myer Hall
Elizabethtown College, 399, **436, *437,*** **437–438,** 535, 693, 2057, 2103
Bieber, Charles M., 2137
Bittinger, Desmond Wright, 143
Bixler, Edward Clinton, 144
Bomberger, Harold Zug, 2138
Bonsack, Charles Daniel, 160
Breidenstine, Aaron Gibble, 173
Brethren heritage and, 2329
Brethren Heritage Room, *437*
Brethren World Assembly, 2151
Brightbill, Alvin Franz, 209
Bucher, George, 225
Bucher, Rufus Pfautz, 225
Carper, Frank Stauffer, 256
Cassel, Joseph Nyce, 260
Church of the Brethren, 300
Curry, Abram Stauffer, 357
Detweiler, George Lowell, 380
Elizabethtown, PA, Church of the Brethren and, 436
"Elizabethtown Plots Its Course" (EPIC), 438
Eller, David B. on, 2329
Eshelman, Walter Witmer, 455
Falkenstein, George Ness, 471
Fisher, Nevin Wishard, 492
Fisher, Virginia Showalter, 492
Forney, Roy S., 502
Francis, Jacob "Jay" Gottwals, 506
Gahagen Charitable Foundation, 2187
Graybill, Alice Minora Hoffer, 567
Graybill, Jacob Franklin, 567
Greiner, Robert G., 2194
Hamer, Oliver Stuart, 580
Harsh, Alva Carlton, 587
Harsh, Mary Lou Hykes, 587
Herr, John, 598
Hertzler, Samuel Hoffer, 601
higher education, 605
historical libraries, 610
history of, 2329
Hoffer, Irwin Seymour, 617
Horst, Melvin Clyde, 630

Imler, Tobias F., 648
Judaism, 677
Kettering, Joseph W., 691
Kilhefner, Galen, 693
Kilhefner, Galen C., 693
library photo, *525*
Long, John Daniel, 2215
Longenecker, Jacob Hollinger, 756
Mack University, 779
MacMaster, Richard K. on, 2345
Mays, Morley Josiah, president, 804
McCann, Elizabeth Gibbel, 771
Meyer, Jacob Gibble, 821
missions and missionaries, lectures on, 2076
Moyer, Laura Emma, 892
Myer, Elizabeth, 903
Neumann, Friedrich at, 924
Nicarry, Wayne A., 2231
Nye, Harry Hess, interim president, 953
Ober, Henry Kulp, president, 960
Pennsylvania, 1005
Peters, Woodford W., educator, 1011
Pfaltzgraff, Roy Edward and Violet Hackman, 1013
Pittenger, John Milton, teacher, 1026
Reber, Daniel Conrad, president, 1085
Reber, Norman Franklin, 1085
Robinson, John Amos, 1115
Shisler, Sara Cassel, 1177
students on sleigh, *27*
Waltz, Benjamin Franklin, 1316
Wenger Building, 1330
West, Murray Guy, 1332
Williamson, Chet on, 2363
Women's Conferences (CB) and, 2264, 2265
The Young Center and, 2267, *2268*
Young, Galen S. and, 2268
youth conferences, 247
Zeigler, Carl Wenger (CB) and, 2269
Ziegler, Edward Krusen, 1395
Ziegler, Jesse Conner, 1395
Ziegler, Levi King, 1397
Zigler, Michael Robert, 1399
Elizabethtown, PA, 279, 456, 1334, 1401
Church of the Brethren, **436,** *600*
Elizabethtown College and, 436
Grace Brethren Church, **436,** 2138
Middletown, PA, Swatara Hill Church of the Brethren, 826
New Call to Peacemaking conference, 926
Elk City, OK, Church of the Brethren, **438**
Elk Co., KS
Grenola Church of the Brethren, KS, 572
Elk Creek, CA, Church of the Brethren, 323, **438**
Elk Creek, NE, Church of the Brethren, **438**
Elk Lick, PA, 206, 214, 685, 1139, 1236
bibliography, 1869
Church of the Brethren, *See* Salisbury, PA, Church of the Brethren
Maple Glen Church of the Brethren, PA, 789
Salisbury Brethren Church, **438**
Elk River Church of the Brethren, WI, **438–439**
Elk Run, VA , Church of the Brethren, 105, **439,** 749, 2110, *See also* Luray, VA, Mount Zion Church of the

Brethren
Moscow Church of the Brethren, VA, 878
Rockbridge German Baptist Brethren Church, VA, 1117
Elk Shoal, NC, congregation, 224
Elkhart Co., IN, 153, 318, 334, 335, 352, 384, 407, 410, 652, 694, 703, 725, 749, 752, 1280, 1287, 1313, 1384, 1385, 1389, 2091, 2092
Brethren Church, **439**
Elkhart, IN, Winding Waters Brethren Church, 439
Fort Wayne, IN, Meadow Crest Brethren Church, 504
Jefferson Brethren Church, IN, 670
Pleasant View Brethren Church, IN, 1036
Winding Waters Brethren Church, 439, **439**
Church of the Brethren, 1995, 2095, *See also* Goshen, IN
Elkhart Valley Church of the Brethren, IN, **439–440**
Goshen, IN, City Church of the Brethren, **439,** 557
Osceola Church of the Brethren, IN, 984
South Bend, IN, Crest Manor Church of the Brethren, 1203
Fellowship of Hope, 488
Grace Brethren Church, 352, 439, **439,**
Osceola, IN, Grace Brethren Church, 984
Historical Society, Herring Papers, 2375
Miami, OH, Brethren settlement, 961
migration of Brethren, 829
Southside Fellowship (CB/Menn), **439**
West Goshen congregation, 1384
Elkhart, IA, *See* Ankeny, IA
Elkhart Valley, IN, Church of the Brethren, **439–440,** 1384, *2144*
Puterbaugh, Amsey Hascall, minister, 1072
Elkhorn, KY, 406
Elkin, V. L., 551
Elkins, VA, 410
Elkins, WV, 164
Church of the Brethren, **440**
Elkton Immanuel Church of the Brethren, MD, **440**
Ellen Lewis (Singmaster), 747
Ellenberger, Albert J., 65, 1608
Ellenberger family, 1345
Plattsburg Church of the Brethren, MO, 1030
Ellenberger, George William, 551, 1608
Ellenberger, Hervin R., 1608
Ellenberger, Josiah Evans, 692, 752, 1608
Ellenberger, Mary Polk, 1608
Ellenberger, Ruth (later Fasnacht), 480
Ellenberger, Samuel Albert, 1608
Ellenberger, William Sturgis, 1608
Eller, Abraham, 440
Eller, Adolphus Hill, 2035
Eller, Alice Kathryn (later Peters), 1011
Eller, Anna Belle, 1608
Eller, Anna Brubaker, 217
Eller, Anna (later Weddle), 1326
Eller, C., 2201

Eller, Christian, Emory (Emery), 343, 1608
Eller, Henry C. on, 2329
Oakvale Church of the Brethren, WV, elder, 958
Roanoke, VA, Oak Grove Church of the Brethren, free minister and elder, 1113
Selma, VA, Church of the Brethren, minister in, 1166
Eller, Catherine Brubaker, 217
Eller, Cynthia Lorraine
on conscientious objectors in World War II, 2329
on pacifism, 2329
Eller family, 440
Eller, David Barry, 1608, 1915, 1928, 2277
on Believers Churches, 2329
on Durnbaugh, D. F., bibliography list of writings of, 2329
on Elizabethtown College, 2329
historical writing, 612
on Pietism, 2329
Prague Conferences and, 2239
on sectarian universalism, 2329
The Young Center and, 2267
Eller, David Newton, 164, *207,* 359, 360, **440,** 1608
Eller, Eldon, 440
Eller, Elfreda, 440
Eller, Enten, 301, 302, 2176, **2176–2177**
Peters Creek Old German Baptist Brethren Church, VA, minister, 1012
Eller family, **440**
Ellison Church of the Brethren, ND, 442
Graybill (Grabill, Krehbiel) family, 567
Peters family related by marriage, 1012
Root family related by marriage, 1122
Salem Church of the Brethren, OH, 1138
Eller, Francis Asbury, 676, 766, 913, 1609
Eller, George Michael, 440, 1971
Eller, George Riley, 415, 1609
Eller, Geraldine Crill, 440, 1928, 2097, 2175
on Eller, Jay Vernard, 2329
family history of, 2329
on Great Northern Railway and Brethren, 2329
Eller, Henry Cline (Mr. and Mrs.), 130, 440, *440,* 1609, 1928
on Eller, Christin "Crist" Emory Eller, 2329
on Martha, Rebecca "Becky" Eller, 2329
Oakvale Church of the Brethren, WV, leadership by, 958
Olean Church of the Brethren, VA, leadership by, 973
Rossville, IN, Church of the Brethren, minister, 1124
Eller, J. F., 445
Eller, Jacob, 440, 1928
Eller, Janice M., 2277
Eller, Jay Vernard, **440,** 502, 1212, 1319, 1330, 1609, 2175
Eller, Geraldine Crill on, 2329
Eller, John, 1341, 1609
Eller family, 440
Smith Chapel Church of the Brethren, WV, 1191
Eller, John Clinton, 1609, 1928

Eller, John Flory, 1609
Eller, John Wirtz, 440, 1609
Eller, Leah Barnhart, 440
Eller, Leona Z. Row, 638, 669, 2378
World Friendship Center, 1369
Eller, Leonard, 440
Eller, Lydia Alice Graybill, 440
Eller, Mary C. (later Peters), 1011
Eller, Orien Dnton, 1609
Olean Church of the Brethren, VA, leadership by, 973
Eller, Paul Christian, 520, 1609, 2301
Red Hill Church of the Brethren, VA, pastor, 1088
Eller, Peter, 440
Eller, Phyllis Kulp, 706, 714, 2176
Eller, Ralph C., 142, 1609, 2301, **2382**
Middlefork Old German Baptist Brethren Church, IN, minister, 826
Modesto, CA, Old German Baptist Brethren Church, minister, 867
North Fork Old German Baptist Brethren Church, IN, minister, 948
Eller, Raymon Ernest, 1609, 1928
Eller, Rosanna, 2176
Eller, Russell, 766, 1609
Eller, Sander, 2176
Eller, Sylvia, 1928
Eller, Thomas L., 2138
Eller, Vernard Marion, 440, 706, 714, 748, 1260, 1609, 1886, 1928–1929, 2142, **2175–2176,** *2176,* 2180
on apocalypse, 2330
on Biblical Brethrenism, 2330
on Brethren, 20th century, 2330
on Christian anarchy of Jesus, 2329
eschatology, 454
on ethics, 2330
on evangelism, 2329
on feminism grammar, 2329
on Gospel of John, 2329
historical writing, 612
on peace as stewardship, 2329
on Pearl of Christian Counsel for the Brokenhearted, 2329
Pomona, CA, Fellowship Church of the Brethren, 1045
on U. S. A. *vs.* Enten V. Eller, 2330
Eller, Virginia, 1971
Eller, Wendell C., 1609
Eller, Willie Elias, 766, 1609
Ellet (Akron) congregation, OH, 744
Ellet Grace Brethren Church, OH, *See* Akron, OH, Ellet Grace Brethren Church
Ellicot City, MD, Pine Orchard Church of the Brethren, **441**
Elling, Edward H., 1929
Elling family, 1929
Elliot family, 251
Elliot, George
Seneca Church of the Brethren, OH, minister in, 1166
Elliot's Creek Church of the Brethren, VA, **441**
Elliott, Charles, 1394
Elliott, Christian W., 2277
Elliott, Delbert
Manteca, CA, Northgate Community Brethren Church, 788
Elliott, Donna Kaye McBride, 1836
Elliott, Eleanor E., 1848
Elliott, Ella Zerbey, 1929

Elliott, George W., 1316, 1609
Elliott, John, 691
Elliott, Joseph M., 1609
  Peabody Church of the Brethren, KS, 997
Elliott, Julianne Chappel, 1928
Elliott, Larry L., 306, 1836–1837
Elliott, Luther E., 1609
Elliott, Mrs. Delbert
  Manteca, CA, Northgate Community Brethren Church, 788
Elliott, Walter Scott, 1609, 1848
Ellis, Benjamin, 570, 1609
Ellis, Calvert Nice, 381, **441**, 578, 1609, 1929, 2301, **2373, 2382**
  article about, 1929
  Juniata College, 678
  Piqua, OH, Church of the Brethren, summer pastor, 1026
Ellis, Charles Calvert, 136, 137, 242, 282, 303, 381, 441, *441,* **441–442,** 1210, 1400, 1929, 1609
  Juniata College, 678
  millenialism, 834
  Philadelphia, PA, First Church of the Brethren, providing leadership, 1015
  prayer, 1052
  Quinlan, James T., 1076
Ellis, Elizabeth Oller Wertz, 441
Ellis, Emma Reed Nice, 441, 442
Ellis, Esta (later Kreiter), 1683
Ellis, Frances, 1278
Ellis, Franklin, 1929
Ellis, Henry James, 441
Ellis, Howard, 70
Ellis, J. J., 1609
Ellis, John, 1609
Ellis, John Dwight, 441, 674, 1609, 2301, **2382**
Ellis, John M., 1609
Ellis, Joseph J., 1929
Ellis, Kathryn Calvert, 441
Ellis, Oziah, 1609
Ellis, Weston F., 1609
Ellisforde Church of the Brethren, WA, **442**, 1342
Ellison Church of the Brethren, ND, 124, 224, 231, 430, **442**
Ellison, H., 1609
Ellison, Matthew, 1929
Ellisville, IL, 1214
Ellmore, William, 1984
Ellsworth, Phyllis Coffey
  Malles, Mark Ellsworth, 2217
Ellul, Jacques, 2176
Elm Creek, KS
  Church of the Brethren, KS, 128, **442**
  Portis, KS, North Solomon Church of the Brethren, preaching point of, 1048
Elm family
  Peabody Old German Baptist Brethren Church, KS, 997
Elm, PA, Graybill Church of the Brethren
  Graybill (Grabill, Krehbiel) family, 567
Elmdale, MI, Church of the Brthren, 239, **442**, 753, 1263
  Hope Church of the Brethren, MI, 629
  Scholten, Marian and Martin Scholten, pastors, 1155
Elmer Esbenshade Classroom Building
  Elizabethtown College, 438

Elmira, NY, 738
Elmore, Carolyn Stone, 2277
Elmore, George, 296
Elmore, Ken
  Red Hill Church of the Brethren, VA, pastor, 1088
Elmore, Kendal Wilson, 1609
Elmville, OH, 1227
elocution, *See* drama
Elpaso, IL, *550*
Elrod, Alpha L., 1609
Elrod, Bessie Franks, 442
Elrod, Henry, 1609
Elrod, James Henry, **442,** 619, 1609, 1929
Elrod, Samuel Luther, 1609
Elroy, WI
  Redstone Valley Old German Baptist Brethren Church, WI and, 2239
Elsea, Henry Dearmont, Jr., 2277
  Elsie Church of the Brethren, MI, **442–443**
  Flint, MI, Church of the Brethren, 494
Elsoff, **443**
Elson, C. E., 365
Elson, Harrison, 749
Elson, J. H., 1609
Elwell, James, 13, 1609
Ely, Warren S., 2046
Elyria, OH
  Grace Brethren Church, **443**
  Homerville, OH, Grace Brethren Church, 626
  YWCA, Lake Breeze Church of the Brethren, Sheffield Village, OH, 1175
emancipation, 1, 22, **443,** *See also* American Colonization Society
  slavery, 1190
Emancipation Proclamation, 41, 2128
Embaugh, John, 145
Embaugh, Millie, 145
emblems on Mack seal, 2142
Emboden, WV, 254
Emch, Daryl, 1380, *See* Emsch, Daryle
emergency and retirement benefits, 155
Emergency Conservation Work, 315
Emergency Farm Labor, 316, **443**
  military service, 301
Emergency Peace Campaign
  peace caravans, 1001
  West, Daniel, 1331
Emergency Response/Service Ministries
  Disaster Child Care, 2171
Emerich family, 1274
Emerick, Israel W., 1609
Emerson, David C., 1609, 2301
  Pleasant Valley Church of the Brethren, TN, minister, 1035
  Rockhill Furnace, PA, Rockhill Church of the Brethren, pastor, 1117
Emerson, Ralph Waldo, 1929
Emert, Johann Jorig (George) Fredrig, 444
Emery, Jane, 1929
Emick family
  Hurricane Creek Old German Baptist Brethren Church, IL, 638
Emig family, 142
Emig, Jesse, 1315
Emig, Jesse Brilhart, 1610
Emigh, Don, 505
emigrants and emigration, **1373, 1375,** *See also* immigration; transatlantic passage

colonial era, from Germany, 2106
  Dunkers, 1930
  fiction, references in
    crossing the Atlantic Ocean, 2097
    Indiana to Fruitdale, AL, 2097
  geographic history of Brethren, 1972
  Germans to America, 1978
  Germany, 2105, 2106
  Wust, Klaus on 1738, 2364
Emley, Benjamin Frank, 1610
Emley, Cora, 637
Emmanuel B. Hoff, Bible Teacher (Hoff), 617
Emmanuel Church of the Brethren, VA, *See* Danville, VA, Emmanuel Church of the Brethren
  Sangerville Church of the Brethren, VA, 1144
Emmanuel congregations as example of biblically inspired name, 911
Emmanuel, OH, 365
  Church of the Brethren, *See* Dayton, OH, Emmanuel Church of the Brethren
Emmert, Benjamin (Mr. and Mrs.), 578
Emmert, Catherine, 736
Emmert, Catherine Gunckle, 444
Emmert, Catherine Scheller, 444
Emmert, Catherine Wolfe, 444
Emmert, Catherine Zollers, 1225
Emmert, David, 61, 235, 276, 444, *444,* **444,** 595, *679,* 1389, 1610, 1930, *See also* business; inventions and science discoveries
  Home for Orphan and Friendless Children, 625
  inventions and scientific discoveries, 660
  orphans, care for, 982
Emmert, Dennis R., 1837
Emmert, Eliza Benedict, 444
Emmert, Elizabeth (later Lahman), 718
Emmert family, **444,** 1359
  Fahrney (Forney) family, 466
  Preiß (Price) family related to, 1055
Emmert, Gertrude Elvina Rowland, **444,** 1361, 1837, *See also* urban ministry
Emmert, Harvey Denton, 760, 1610
  Shippensburg, PA, Church of the Brethren, pastor in, 1177
Emmert House
  Franklin Grove, IL, Church of the Brethren, 507
Emmert, Jesse Benedict, 160, 444, **444,** 1610, 1837, 1930
  India orphanages, 651
Emmert, John H., 503
Emmert, John J., 1225, 1610
  diary excerpts, 1961
  Pierce Co. Church of the Brethren, WI, 1021
Emmert, John Leonard, 444, **444,** 1610
Emmert, Joseph, 444, 507, 577, 736, 753, 1225, 1610
Emmert, Joseph (Mr. and Mrs.), 578
Emmert, Lewis L., *444, 477*
Emmert, Magdalena (later Lehman), 736
Emmert, Marcia A. Yoder, 1837
Emmert, Mary, 1845
  Riverside Christian Training School, teacher and missionary, 1111
Emmert, Mary Elizabeth Myers, 444

Emmert, Mary L., 360, 1310, 1361
Emmert, Mary (later Stover), 1225–1227, *1226*
India, 649
Emmert, Mary Leora, **444**, 1848, 1930
Emmert, Michael, 1610
Emmert, Michael Wolf, 381, 444, **444,** 1610, 1930
prayer, 1052
Emmert, Sarah Beale, 444, *444*
Emmert, Susan (later Price), 1056
Emmert, Theodore, 444
Emmet Co., MI, 750
Emmett Church of the Brethren, ID, **445**
Emmings, Jacob, 1327
Emmons, Anthony E., 2277
Emmons, Esther Wagoner, 1930
Emory family
Modesto, CA, La Loma Grace Brethren Church, 867
eMountain Communications
information technology, church use of, 2208
Empire, CA, Church of the Brethren, **445,** 1217
50 year anniversary, 2014
Modesto, CA, Church of the Brethren, 866
Oakland, CA, Church of the Brethren, 957
employment
guidance and assistance, 193
photographs on name tags, 1020
Emporia, KS, Cottonwood congregation, 682
Emrick, Ernestine Hoff, 127, 381, 617, 1930, 2388
Emrick, Floyd C., 1610
Emrick, Leland Brinley, 1343, 1610
Emsch, Darryl, 1135, 1380
St. Petersburg, FL, Grace Brethren Church, pastor in, 1135
Lakeland, FL, Grace Brethren Church, 2213
Emswiler, Mark W., 142, 1610, 1930
Enberg, Craig, 1930
Enberg, Nels Dwight, 714, 1610
Encampment, WY, 1213
Encarnación, Guillermo B., 261, 1610, 2172
Hispanic Ministries (CB), 2199
Lancaster, PA, Alfa y Omega (Alpha and Omega) Church of the Brethren, 2213, *2213*
Rio Prieto, PR, Iglesia de los Hermanos (CB) and, 2243
Encyclopedia, Brethren, *See Brethren Encyclopedia, The*
Encyclopedia Britannica, German Baptist Brethren in, 1992
Encyclopedia of Modern Christian Missions, 1950
End, Judith (later Stober)
Stover, William, 2379
The End Times (Hoyt), 634, 1975
Endelman, Judith E.
works by, 2310
Enders, J. Harry, 1610, 2301
Enders John W., 1610
Enders, NB
sod house in, *920*
Enders, NE, *445, 1254*
Church of the Brethren, **445–446**

congregation, 1349
Endless Caverns, VA, 1291
Endress, Christian, 1930
Endt, Elizabeth Hirt Landes, 722
Endt, Heinrich, 722
Endt, Johann Theobald, **446**
engagements, **446,** *See also* wedding customs
announcement in newspapers, 1326
marriage banns, 1325, 1326
Engel, Belinda (later Stoner), 1225
Engel-Brüder, See Angel Brethren (*Engel-Brüder*)
Engel, Elizabeth, 1879
Engel, John R., 1610
Engel, Mary Alice, 1837, *See* Oiness, Sylvia
ship sinking en route to Africa, 863
Engel, Ulrich
descendants, 1930
Engelhage, John
Pineville, VA, Mount Olive Brethren Church, 1025
Engelhard, Helga, 1930
Engelsthal, cloister at, 330
England, *See* United Kingdom
England, John, 446
England, Luella Workman, 446
England, Susannah Moore, 446
England, Wendell H., 1610
England, William Ferdinand, 118, **446,** 714, 1610
Englar, Adam, 566
Englar, David E., 425, 1610
Pipe Creek Church of the Brethren, MD, minister, 1026
Englar, Elizabeth Bonsack, 161
Englar family
Reinhardt family, 1094
Englar, H. G., 1930
Englar, J. Walter, 1610
Englar, John, 161
Englar, Margaret B. (later Bixler), 144
Englar, Nathan, 746
Englar, William Philip, 1610
Engle (Angle) family, **446,** 1911
Engle, Barbara Yoder
descendants, 1930
Engle, E. B., 1610
Engle, Eldon, 1610
Engle, Elizabeth (later Masterson)
Masterson, Benjamin Franklin, wife of, 802
Engle family, 1930
Harrisburg, PA, Melrose Gardens Grace Brethren Church, 586
Jenners, PA, Grace Brethren Church, 670
Peace Valley Church of the Brethren, MO, 1003
Engle, Henry, 446
Engle, Herbert Clinton, 1930
Engle, J. M., 1930
Engle, Jacob S.
descendants, 1930
Engle, Joseph, 152
Engle, Louis D., 1610, 2301
Sidney, IN, Grace Brethren Church, pastor, 1181
Engle, Mary Elizabeth (later Brumbaugh), 446
Engle, Morris M., 1930
Engle, Prudence, 179

Engle, Reed Laurence, 1930
Engle, Roy G., 124, 1610, 2301
Engle, Ulrich
descendants, 1930
Engle, Winfield Scott Hancock, 1930
Englehart, Hannah (later Mack)
Mack family, 778
Engleman, Gilbert D., 1610
Engleman, James
San Diego, CA, Grace Brethren Church, pastor in, 1141
Engler, David *See* Englar, David
Engler (Englar), Daniel Edwin, 1610
Engler, Lloyd, 1610
Engler, Philip, 1610
Pipe Creek Church of the Brethren, MD, presiding elder, 1026
Engler, Samuel E., 1610
Englevale, ND, Church of the Brethren, 256, **447**
Englewood, OH, 161, 224, 700, 1265, 1355
Dunkard Brethren Congregation, **447**
Eldorado Dunkard Brethren Congregation, 433
Plainview Dunkard Brethren Congregation, 1029
Grace Brethren Church, **447,** 1276
Grace Brethren Village, 563
Salem Church of the Brethren
English Arm, VA, *See* Floyd Co. Church of the Brethren, VA
Franklin Co. Church of the Brethren, VA, 507
English Baptists, *See* Baptists
English congregation, Brooklyn, NY, 1296
English, John H., 260, 318, 1610
New Troy, MI, Grace Brethren Church, organized by, 932
English, John Virgil, 1930
English language, *See* language shift
Brethren and, 3
instruction in, 17
poetry, 1039
Smith, William, preaching in, 1191
transition to, and legal name of denomination, 911
English Prairie, IN, Church of the Brethren, **447**
Pigeon River Church of the Brethren, IN, 1023
Shipshewana, IN, Church of the Brethren, organized from, 1177
English, Raymond, 1610
English Revised Version (ERV) of the Bible, 138
English River, IA, **447,** 661, 1908
Church of the Brethren, 214, 372
Crooked Creek, IA, Church of the Brethren, preaching point of, 353
Keokuk Church of the Brethren, IA, 1205
Middle Creek Church of the Brethren, IA, 825
North English, IA, Church of the Brethren, 947
migration of Brethren to, 830
Pleasant Grove Grace Brethren Church, 1031
English Seventh-Day Baptists
French Creek, 516
South Carolina, 1204
English translations of the Bible, *See* Bible translations

Enid Mission, OK, congregation
    Monitor Church of the Brethren, OK,
        daughter congregation of, 869
Enid, OK
    Church of the Brethren, **447–448**
    German Baptist Brethren's Home
        Society, 541
Enlightenment (18th century), 74
enlightenment and noncreedalism, 943
Ennis, David E., 266, 1610
Ennis, M. Marshall, 266
Ennis, Marshall
    Round Mountain Church of the
        Brethren, AR, 1125
Ennis, Marshall M., 1610
    Pleasant Home Church of the Brethren,
        OK, elder, 1033
Enns, Fernando
    on historic peace churches, 2330
    violence and, 2265
Eno, Jeffrey C., 2277
Enon Brethren Church, IA, 1321, *See*
    Waterloo, IA, Brethren Church
Enon, IA (Waterloo), 661
    Gillin, John Lewis, 549
Enon, VA, New Covenant Church of the
    Brethren, **2177**
Enos, Irvin V., 6, 582, 683, 1610
Ens, Gerhard, 1930
Ensign, Chauncey David, 445, 502, 619,
    1212, 1610, 1930, 2301
    historical writing, 612
    Mount Hope Church of the Brethren,
        WA, 882
Enslow, E. N., 1610
Enslow, H. S., 1610
Enslow, H. S. (1845), 72
Ensminger, John, 1610
Ensor, Eli
    Pleasant View Church of the Brethren,
        TN, 1037
Ensor, Gertrude Peterson, 1610
Enterprise Church of the Brethren, ND, *See*
    Cando, ND, Church of the
    Brethren
Enterprise, ND, 251
    Enterprise schoolhouse, Whitestone
        Church of the Brethren, WA, 1342
entertainment, *See* amusements, worldly;
    drama
entire sanctification, 691
environmental issues, **2177**, *See also* con-
    servation movement; simple life
    camping movement and environmental
        interpretation programs, 249
    sources on, 2314
    symbol, 403
    wellness and, 2261
Enzor, Russell, 739
Ephesians
    1:3–13, 56
    1:4, 55
    2:1–3, 55
    5:26, 84
    5:27, 26
    book of, 1980
    Julien, Thomas T., 2210
    Kent, Homer Austin, Jr., 2211
    Kent, Homer Austin, Jr. on, 2340
    Martin, Donna Ritchey on, 2345
Ephrata Area, PA, Grace Brethren Church,
    448, 749, **2177**
Ephrata Chronicle, See Chronicon

Ephratense
Ephrata Cloister, *See* Ephrata Community
Ephrata Community, 19, 107, 108, 112,
    400, 422, 448, **448–452**, 534, 693,
    694, 1228, 1254, 1930–1931, 1965,
    1988, 2020, 2022, 2023, 2043,
    2057
    accounts of visions, 1309, **2373**
    American mystic communities, 1978
    American Revolution and, 2040
    antinomianism communes and, 236
    archaeological excavations at, 46
    architecture, 51
    archival collections from, 52
    articles about, 1916, 1930, 1934, 1943
    Battle of Brandywine and, 2038
    Baumann, Mattheis and, 925
    Beissel *vs.* Sower, 2035
    beliefs, 2015
    Benjamin Franklin, reference to, 1940
    in Berks and Lebanon county histories,
        2051
    Bethania, *122, 123,* 1004
    bibliography, 140, 1857, 1859, 1862,
        1863, 1865, 1867, 1876, 1879,
        1887, 1896, 1899, 1902, 1910,
        2310
    bicentennial celebration, 1966
    Blutige Schau-Platz oder Martyrer
        Spiegel der Tauffs Gesinnten, Der,
        154
    Boehme and, 156
    book about, 1940
    break from Leola, PA, Conestoga
        Church of the Brethren, 737
    Brethren, lineage of, 613
    Brethren music, 898–899
    Brotherton, PA, Brothersvalley Church
        of the Brethren, 214
    buildings, 1979
    celibacy and, 266
    cemeteries, 2057
    chart of Brethren bodies, 1403–1405
    Christian education movement, 283
    Christmas at, 2322
    Christ's Assembly and, 280
    Chronicles of the Brethren, 290
    Chronicon Ephratense, 379, 1993
    clock, 1984
    cloister, 2029, 2030, 2040, 2043
    colonial era, 2098
    colonial society and, 2035
    communal movements, 2092, 2098
    communitarianism, 328–329
    community, 329
    Continental money, 338
    cultural contributions, 175
    debates, 371
    decline of, 2050
    description, 1916, 1949, 1998, 2067,
        2078, 2084, 2103
    Doll, Eugene E. on, 2325
    Dorfman, Mark H. on early American
        life and, 2325
    drama, 2030
    Duché, Jacob, reprint of letters from,
        1917
    Duck, Dorothy Hampton on art and
        artists of, 2325
    "Dumplers" at "Euphrates," 2042
    early description of, 1923
    Eastern Synod of the Reformed
        Church, records about, 1923

Eberbach, 417
Eckerlin brothers, 1336
Eckerlin brothers and place-names,
    Brethren, 1027
Eckerlin, Emmanuel, 421
Eicher family, 430–431
Encyclopedia of Religious Knowledge,
    entry for (inaccurate), 1930
Ephrata Press, 452, 1986
    as experiment, 2008
    explanation of the "T" on the mile-
        stone, 1941
Fahnestock family, 465
Fahnestock, William M., 465
Falckner's Swamp, 470
fiction, 2027
fiction, references in, 2083, 2089
folk art, 2097
Fraktur, 60, 505, 2094, 2186
Franklin, Benjamin, 506
Frantz, Michael, 508
French Creek, 516
frontier, 519
Funck (Funk) family, 521
Gass (Gast), Jakob, 532
gazetteer, inclusion in, 1952
Geistliche Fama (Spritiual Report),
    533
German-American studies and, 2323
German language, use of by printing
    press, 724
German Sectarians of Pennsylvania,
    The, 542
German Seventh-Day Baptists, 542
Germantown Brethren, 2377
Gesäng der einsamen und verlassenen
    Turtel-Taube, Das (The Songs of
    the Lonely and Forsaken
    Turtledove), 546
Good (Guth) family, 556
Graybill (Grabill, Krehbiel) family, 567
Great Awakening, 568
hand work, 1995
Hebron, 591
Heitler, Martin P., 595
Heitler, Richard R., 595
Hildebrand, Johannes, 606
Hildebrand, Maria (later Mack), 606
historic building restoration, 220
historiography, 2201
history of, 611, 1872, 1915, 1918,
    1919, 1927, 1929, 1930, 1932,
    1934, 1950, 1952, 1961, 1977,
    1981, 1995, 1998, 1999, 2000,
    2001, 2072, 2074, 2086, 2088,
    2090, 2095, 2096, 2099, 2105,
    2108
Höcker, Heinrich, 615
Höcker, Ludwig, 615–616
Hoening, Johann Georg, 616
Höhn, Heinrich, 618
Holy Spirit, doctrine of, 624
Howard Pyle's visit to the remains of,
    61
Hüber (Hoover) family, 634
hymnals, 1947, 2088
hymns, 2085, 2328
immigration to, 175
influence of, 105
influences on, 156
    Gottfried Arnold, 57
    Sabbatarianism, 88
inner Word and outer Word, 656

Kalcklöser, Johann Heinrich, 681
Kedar, 685–686
Keller family, 686
Kelpius, Johannes, 2007
Kemp, Marilyn on wall charts of, 2362
Kimmel family, 693
Kirschner, Ann on, 2341
Koch, Stephan, 704
Koenig (König), Simon, 706
Kraft, John L. on, 2341
La Rochefoucauld-Liancourt, Francois
    A. F., Duc de, 1995
Lamb, Ardis Krieg on Gorgas, Christin
    (Mack) and, 2342
Lancaster Co., PA, records, 2009
on Lancaster County, history of, 2330
Landert, Sigmund, 722
Laschet, Johannes Peter van, 726
literature about, 747, 748
literature of, articles about, 1919
Lititz, 1999
Lovejoy, David S. on history of, 2344
Mack, Alexander, Jr., 774
Mack, Alexander, Sr., and Brethren
    leadership, 777
Mack, Elizabeth Neiß (Nice), 778
Mack, Johann Valentin, 1155
Mack, Johann Valentin, joining with
    family, 778
Main, Kari M. on hymnals of, 2345
Maple Press Company and, 2345
Marquet, Cynthia on, 2345, 2358
marriage, 795
Marsh, Witham, 2006
Marshall, Christopher, 2006
Martin, David, 797
Martin family, 797
Martin, George Adam, 141, 797
Mäyle, Johann, 804
medicine, 809
members from Amwell, NJ, congrega-
    tion, 929
members of, 98
migration of Brethren, 829
Miller, Hans Michael, 837
mission work of, 121
Mohn, Kerry on, 2347
Mohr, Jacob, Sr., 869
monasticism, 869
Müller, Johann Peter, 840, *840*, 1328,
    1981
Müller (Miller) family, 894
museums containing collections from,
    88
music, 2045, 2053, 2090, 2098
music of, 1915, 1919, 1948, 2321,
    2324
mutual aid, 902
Mylins, article about, 1954
mysticism, 907
Nägele, Hans Rudolph and Elizabeth,
    910
Native Americans, and Indian policy in
    Pennsylvania, 2089
North Carolina Brethren settlement,
    946
nursing, 952
oaths, taking of, 959
Old German Baptist Brethren and
    charismatic movement, 970
origin of, 175
Oswinski, Thomas E. on musical docu-
    ment of, 2349

Oved, Yaacov on, 2349
papermill, 2053
Parmer, John A. on geography of low
    mill tract of, 2349
Patriot's Day at, 2035
Peniel, 1003
Pennsylvania Brethren settlement, 1004
Pennsylvania Synods, 1007
Petty, Donald B. on printing at, 2350
Pfautz, John Eby, 1014
Pflug, Günther on, 2350
photographs of, 2072
pietism, 2036
Plain People, *See* Robertson, Archibald
    T.
poems about, 1918
poetry, 1039
pork, eating of, 1047
post-Reformation religion, 2040
prayer, 1051
prayer books, 1052
press, 18, 31, 43, 46, 98
printing industry, 2081, 2090, 2110
printing press, 694
prophecy, 1062
Protestant monks and nuns, 1998
publications, 1960, 2080
publications of, 171, 2075
publishing, 1067
Radical German Pietism and celibacy,
    1080
Reed, John Ford on American Revo-
    lution and, 2351
references to, 1911, 1912, 1933, 1939,
    1941, 1943, 1951, 1955, 1956,
    1957
referred to by Voltaire, François Marie
    Arouet de, 1310
Reformed Church and Brethren move-
    ment, 1092
registers of, 2053
religious Socialist colonies, 1976
restoration of, 1918
Revolutionary War, 172, 1106, 2010
Rhode Island, members visiting, 1107
Rittenhouse, David, 2046
Robinson, Yvonne on, 2352
Roeber, A. G[regg] on, 2352
Roher (Rohrer) family, 1119
Rosicrucian influence on, 1123
Roth, Heinrich and Catherine, 1124
[Rousselot] De S[urgy, Jacques] P.,
    2050
Russel, William A., 2052
sabbatarian, fellowship naming to dis-
    tinguish from, 910
Sagot, Francois, 2053
Sangmeister, Heinrich (Ezechiel), 1144,
    2054
Saturday as true Sabbath, 1133
Sauer, Maria Christina Gross, 1147,
    1148
Sauer's works describing, 2055
Saxby, Trevor J. on, 2354
Schelbert, Leo on, 2355
Schlechter, Edward W., 2057
school building constructed by, 1237
Seidensticker, Oswald, 2061
Separatism, 1989
Seventh-Day Baptists, 210, 1170, 2041,
    2062
sex and marriage in, 2026
sexuality, human, 1170

S(h)aron, 123
Sharon, sisterhouse, 1172
Shirk, Willis L., Jr. on, 2356
Showalter, Michael S. on, 2356
Showalter, Michael S. on American
    Revolution and hospital at, 2356
singing, 1184
Sister Anatasia, 1927
Skinner, Charles on, 2357
Snow Hill Community, 1194, 1195
social and economic organization of,
    1918
sources on, 2310, 2312, 2313, 2314,
    2316, 2317, 2318, 2319, 2324
South Carolina, 11204
spiritualism in, 1211
Spohn, Clarence E. on, 2358
    on American Revolution and, 2358
Stryz, Jan on, 2360
Sunday school movement, 1237
survey of, 2325
Sutton, Robert P. on, 2360
tests on wall charts of, 2330
Thoma, Anastasia(?), 2081
Tinkcom, Harry M., 2083
tombstone inscriptions, 2034–2035
Town and Country Magazine, 2039
Trahair, Richard C. S. on, 2361
Traut family, 1271
Turtle Taube, reference to, 1922
universal restoration, 1292
utopian comunities, 1970
Versluis, Arthur on, 2361
Viehmeyer, L. Allen on, 2361
visit to, 1984
Vorspiel, 747
Wagner, Walter H. on, 2361
Warfel, Stephen G. on, 2362
Weidner, Marilyn Kemp on wall charts
    of, 2362
Weiser, Frederick S. on, 2362
Weiser, Johann Conrad, 1328
Weiser, John Conrad, 2093
Weitzel, Louise A. on, 2362
Wentz, Richard E. on texts of, 2363
White, Janet R. on architecture and cul-
    ture of, 2363
Wohlfahrt, Michael, 943
Wohlfahrt (Welfare), Michael, 943,
    1355
women and, 2051
Wood, Stacy B. C., Jr. on Gorgas,
    Christin (Mack) and, 2364
worship, 2048
writing and, 2035
Zion, 123
Zionitic Brotherhood and Peter Bucher,
    225
Zionitischer Weyrauchs Hügel (*Zionitic
Hill of Incense*), 1400
Zizendorf visit, and religious condtions
    in, 2071
Ephrata congregation, 1931
Ephrata-Eberbach Sister Cities
    Spohn, Clarence E. on relationship of,
        2358
Ephrata Area Grace Brethren Church, PA,
    448
    New Holland, PA, Church of the
        Brethren, support to, 929
Ephrata Hospital, 1910
Ephrata Monument Association, 1931
Ephrata (Neusbaum and Popp), 748

Ephrata, PA, 158, 686, 721, 1213
  Church of the Brethren, **448**
    Robinson, John Amos, pastor, 1115
    Rupp, Christian, elder, 1130
  Ephrata Community, 448
  First Church of the Brethren, 322
  German Seventh-Day Baptists, *543*
  history, 1964
  Kilhefner, Galen C., 693
  Mohler Church of the Brethren, PA, 868
  Pennsylvania, large congregation, 1005
  Reamstown, PA, East Cocalico Church of the Brethren and, 2239
  Taylor, Isaac W., 1249
Ephrata Press, **452**, 2038, 2041, 2064, *See also Anhang zum Widerlegten Wiedertäufer*; *Apologia* (Mack); Baumann, Johann; Baumann, Joseph; Baumann, Samuel; *Chronicon Ephratense*; *Gesäng der Einsamen...Turtel-Taube, Das*; Heitler, Martin P.; Heitler, Richard R.; *Zionitischer Weyrauchs-Hügel*
  Ephrata Community, 451
  historical libraries, 610
Ephrata publications, 260
Ephrata Society, *See* Ephrata Community
epidemics and missions, 861
Episcopal Church, *See* Anglican (Episcopal) Church
episcopal issues, *See* bishops
Epistles, Biblical, *See* specific titles, e.g. *James*
Epler, Ruth
  on Studebaker family, 2360
Epp, Frank H., 1931
Epp, Maria (later Peters), *See* Peters family
Epperly, Dave, 1285
Epperly, I. H., 1285
Eppley, Henry Elmer, 269, 326, 417, 553, 1305, 1610
  Martinsburg, PA, Grace Brethren Church, pastor, 798
  Roanoke, VA, First Brethren Church, pastor, 1113
Eppstein, 174, **452–453**, 545, *See also* Palatinate
  Liebe, Christian, 741
  radical pietist dissension in, 990
Epstein, *See* Eppstein
Equal Rights Amendment
  attitudes toward, 1362
  Fellowship of Grace Brethren Churches (FGBC), 487
Equality for Women, 2183, 2184
Equipo International, 2157
Erasmus Roterodamus, Desiderius, 56
Erb, Amelia (later Eby), 1924
Erb, C. Henry, 342
Erb, Carl, 588
Erb, Christian, **453**
  Hochmann von Hochenau, Ernst Christoph, 615
Erb, Elizabeth J. Miller, 1931
Erb family, 2081
  Hertzler (Hartzler) family, 601
Erb, Fannie (later Miller), 2017
Erb, Jacob, 1610, 2081
Erb, Janet, 588
Erb, John, 1610
Erb, John D., 1610
Erb, Peter C., 1931

on Anabaptist spirituality, 2330
on Arnold, Gottfried, spiritual texts of, 2330
on Beissel, Johann Conrad/Konrad, 2330
on Ephrata Cloister, eschatology of, 2330
on Ephrata Society, 2201
on Pietist spirituality, 2330
Erb, Susan Funk, 2081
Erbach, Abraham, 453
Erbach, Anna Mary Christian, 453
Erbach, Esther Funk, 453
Erbach, Jacob, 453
Erbach, Lorentz, 453
Erbach, Sarah Gibler, 453
Erbach, Susanna Coffman, 453
Erbaugh, Abraham, 1610
Erbaugh, Bessie (later Helstern), 596
Erbaugh, Clarence G., 1610
Erbaugh family, **453**
Erbaugh, George W., 1611
Erbaugh, Howard F., 1280, 1611
Erbaugh, Ivan Leroy, 1611
Erbaugh, Lottie, 319
Erbaugh, Noah W., 1611
Erbaugh, Omy, 338
Erbaugh, Orion, 338, 1611
Erbaugh, Philip, 1611
  Pipe Creek Church of the Brethren, IN, elder, 1025
Erhart, Marie Anna, 383
Erickson, Elroy, 687
Erie Co., NY, 147
Erie Co., PA, 317
Erie, PA, Community United Church (CB/UCC), **453**
Erisman Valeta, Gail E., 2277
Erisman, Wilbert Austin, 1611
Erisman, Wilbert Ethmer, 31, 479, 1611
Ernest, William, 1611
Ernst Casimir, count of Ysenberg-Büdingen, 407, 453, **453**, 684, 924
  Eckartshausen, 421
  Edict of 1712, 425
  Marienborn, 792
Ernst, James E., 1932
  historical writing, 611
Ernst, John Jacob, 45, 1161
  Red Cloud, NE, Church of the Brethren, providing leadership, 1088
  South Red Cloud Church of the Brethren, NE, minister, 1206
Ernst, Joseph W., 1611
Ernst, Steve, 2277
Ernzen, Inez Hutton, 1932
Eros
  Pullen, Elizabeth on Beissel, Georg Conrad and, 2351
Ersery, Phyllis, 1929
Erskine, Albert Russel, 1932
Die Erste Liebe (*The First Love*, 1696), 43, 57, **453**
Ervin, Albert, 504
Erwin, George, 1611
Erwin, P., 439
Erwin, TN, Church of the Brethren, 78, **453**
  Pleasant View Church of the Brethren, TN, daughter congregation of, 1037
Esbensen, (Christian) Henry Williams, 759, 1611

Esbensen, Christine, 361, 714, 1243
Esbensen, Edwin, 2301
Esbensen, Edwin R., 1611
Esbensen, Henry, 553
Esbensen, J. K., 1611
Esbensen, Kresten N., 453
Esbensen, Maren Christine Bendsen, 1837, 1875, **2387**
Esbensen, Martine, 453
Esbensen, Niels, 361, 445, **453**, 714, 1611, 1837, 1932, 2060
  Paradise, CA, Church of the Brethren, 992
Esch, Jacob Daniel, 1932
Esch, Magdalene (later Oswald), *See* Oswald family
eschatology/millennialism, 148, 157, 185, **453–455**, 833–834, *See also* Second Coming
  amillennialism, 834
  bibliographical sources, 2027, 2322, 2351
  Brethren, and Roman Catholic Church, 1120
  Brethren Church and, 185
  Cassel, Jacob C., 260
  chiliasm, **833–834**
  Church of the Brethren, 2068
  debates, 371
  definition of, 386
  dispensationalism, 293, 390
  Eller family, 440
  eschatology, 454
  Eshelman, Matthew Mays, 455
  Fellowship of Grace Brethren Churches (FGBC), 486
  French Prophets, 2060
  fundamentalism, 522
  Grace Schools (Grace Theological Seminary, Grace College), 563
  Hoyt, Herman Arthur, 634
  Jews, 671
  Kelpius or Kelp, Johannes, 686–687
  millennialism, 833, 834
  Moomaw, B. C., 873
  Nead, Peter, writings on, 919
  prophecy, 1062
  rapture, **1083**
  resurrection, and Brethren teachings about, 1102
  second coming of Christ, 1985
  sources on, 2320, 2323
  thesis on, 1913
  thousand-year rule of Christ, 695
  Zimmerman, Johann Jakob, 686
Eschelmann family, *See* Eshelman family
Eschelmann, David, 456
Eschelmann, Elizabeth Groff, 456
Eschelmann, Esther Longanecker, 456
Eschelmann, Heinrich, 456
Eschelmann, Martin, 456
Eschelmann, Peter, 456
Esh, James, 42
Eshbach family, 2025
Eshbach, Theresa A., 1932
Eshbach, Warren Milton, 193, 745, 1337, 1611, 1932, 1987
  National Older Adult Conferences, 2229
Eshel, A. M., 1611
Eshelman, A. L. (M.), 1611
Eshelman family (Aeschlimann, Eschelmann, Eshleman), **455–456**,

1911, 1932, 2008, 2040
Eshelman, Abram N., 1611
Eshelman, Amanda Witmer, 455
Eshelman, Andrew, 455
Eshelman, Barbara Ann
    descendants, 1932
Eshelman, Bruce N., 1611
    Red Cloud, NE, Church of the
        Brethren, providing leadership,
        1088
Eshelman, Clair D.
    Southern Lancaster Grace Brethren
        Church, PA, 1207
Eshelman, Clair W.
    Southern Lancaster Grace Brethren
        Church, PA, 1207
Eshelman, Clarence A., 1611
    Red Cloud, NE, Church of the
        Brethren, providing leadership,
        1088
Eshelman, Daniel M., 1611
Eshelman, Daniel S., 620, 1309, 1611
    Mount Laurel, NJ, Grace Brethren
        Church, pastor, 883
Eshelman, David, 317, 1611
Eshelman, David D., 1611
Eshelman, David Emmert, 1214, 1611
Eshelman, David W., 1611
Eshelman, Donald E., 1343, 2277
Eshelman, E. J., 1611
Eshelman, Earl Emerson, 1611, 1932
    Ozark Church of the Brethren, MI,
        minister, 986
    Red Cloud, NE, Church of the
        Brethren, providing leadership,
        1088
    South Red Cloud Church of the
        Brethren, NE, resident pastor,
        1206
Eshelman, Earl G., 1611
Eshelman, Esther F., 1932
Eshelman, Frank E., 1932
Eshelman, Glenn Marlin, 1611
Eshelman, Grace Lucile, 1837, 1932
Eshelman, Harry Wolgemuth, 1611
Eshelman, Heinrich
    article about, 1911
Eshelman, Hiram S., 1611
Eshelman, I. James, 1611
Eshelman, J(acob) L., 1611
Eshelman, James Marlin, 1611
Eshelman, John, 455, 1611
    Ottawa, KS, Church of the Brethren,
        984
Eshelman, John H., 1611
Eshelman, John Ross, 1611
Eshelman, John William, descendants of,
    1932
Eshelman, Joseph C., 586
Eshelman, L. A., 857, 2019
Eshelman, Leah Aurand, 455
Eshelman, Margaret, 586
Eshelman, Mary, 1343
    Southern Lancaster Grace Brethren
        Church, PA, 1207
Eshelman, Mary Minnich, 455
Eshelman, Mathew M.
    on piety, true vital, 2330
Eshelman, Mathew Mays, 48, 137, 180,
    209, 218, 274, 276, 277, 299, **455,**
    455, 561, 682, 715, 720, 722, 743,
    1394, 1924, 1932, 2019, 2108, *See
    also* migration; *Our Children at*

Work; publishing; railways
    immigration agent for Santa Fe Rail-
        road, 1145
    McDonough, George L., 773
    millennialism, 834
    The Missionary Worker, 857
    missions, 858
    publishing, 1068
    Sand Creek Church of the Brethren,
        KS, elder in, 1143
    Santa Fe Railroad and Brethren settle-
        ment, 1082
    True Vital Piety, 381
Eshelman meetinghouse, Woodbury, PA,
    Church of the Brethren, 1364
Eshelman, Minnie Mae (later Hersch), 598
Eshelman, Nathan W., 1611
Eshelman, Peter
    descendants, 1932
Eshelman, Robert Forney, 2, 1932
    historical writing, 612
Eshelman, Samuel S., 1612
Eshelman, Shirley
    Southern Lancaster Grace Brethren
        Church, PA, 1207
Eshelman, Walter Witmer, **455**
    minorities, ethnic and racial, 850
Eshleman, Daniel S., 579
Eshleman family, *See* Eshelman family
Eshleman, Henry Frank, 1932, 1933
Eshleman, I. James, 206, 504, 1276, 1611
Eshleman, Ira, 1932
Eshleman, Jacob, 2062
Eshleman, Jacob, I
    genealogy and descendants, 1932
Eshleman, Martin, 1933
Eshleman, Mettha Katheryn Westfeldt,
    1932
Eshleman, Milton B., 1933
Eshleman, Robert F., 695, 1612
Eshleman, Wilmer J., 1933
Eskew, Harry Lee, 1933
Eskildsen, C. C., 361
Eskildsen, Christen Christensen, **456,** 1612
Eskildsen, Lillie Toft or Katrina (Trine)
    Jensen, 456
Espenshade, A. Howry, 1933
Espenshade, Edward Bowman, 1933
Espionage, *See* Sauer, Christopher III
espionage
    World War I, Brethren accused of,
        1370–1371
Espionage Act, 1917, *See* Sedition Act
essays, 2022
Essex Co., VT, 1304
Essex, Keith H., 563, 1612
Essick, Charles, 1612
established churches, 5, 15, 28, 107, **456**
    Brethren movement, 292
    Brethren movement evangelist work
        and, 174
    church membership, 813
    discipline, doctrine of, 386
    division of congregations, 392
    Edict of 1712, 425
    education, 428
    engagement, 446
    Ephrata Community, 451
    Europe, and Brethren in prison, 1058,
        1059
    flags, 492
    Germany, 241, 545
    historical writing, 610

    Hochmann von Hochenau, Ernst
        Christoph, 614, 615
    Hope, Christian, 628
    house churches, 632
    Hutterian Society of Brothers, 639
    missions in countries with, 861
    musical instruments, 900
    nonconformity, 940
    noncreedalism, 942
    oaths, taking of, 959
    opposition to, 159
    ordination, 980
    Pennsylvania, 309
    Philadelphian Society, 1019
    Radical German Pietism, 1079
    Reformation, Protestant, 1091
    rejection of their church buildings and
        furnishings, 46, 48
    religious liberty, 1098
    Roman Catholic Church, 1120
    separatism and, 1166–1167
estate executors
    attitudes toward role of, 728
Estates General, Dutch, 71, **456**
    Pauw, Adrian, in, 996
    Solingen Brethren release, 147
Estep, John Robert, 2277
Estep, William R., 1933, 2201
Esterling, Margaret (later Ikenberry), 646
Estes family, 1277
Estes Park, CO
    Women's Conferences (CB) and, 2265
Esther
    Roop, Eugene F. on, 2353
eternal security, **456–457,** *See also* Inner
        Word and Outer Word; justifica-
        tion, doctrine of
    Brethren Church doctrine on, 183
    Brethren doctrine of salvation, 1140
    doctrine on, 183
    Old German Baptist Brethren, 967
Eternal Verities (Miller), 836
eternity, **457,** *See also* Hell, doctrine of;
        universal restoration
Etheridge, Brian J., 2173
ethical creedalism, 457
ethics, **457–458, 2177–2178,** *See also* abor-
        tion; authority; nonresistance;
        polity
    article about, 1925
    capitalism, 253
    Church of the Brethren, 2164
    doctrine on, 185
    Groff, Warren Frederick, 2194
    limited war, 2003
    Miller, Donald Eugene, 2223
    ministerial, 2164
    plain people, 1029
    social, 6
Ethiopia, **458**
    ALM involvement in, 24
    refugees from, 198
    United Nations Relief and
        Rehabilitation Administration
        (UNRRA), 1291
ethnic and racial minorities, *See* entries
    at racial; specific groups, e.g.
        African Americans
    Church of the Brethren, 2094
    Church of the Brethren racial attitudes,
        2001
    May, James, 804
    migrant labor, 827

ministry to, 1297
Monrovia, MD, Bush Creek Church of the Brethren, 870
Peach Blossom Colored Church of Rising Light (CB), MD, 1003
racial conflicts in northern USA, 2072
religion and, 2069
religious liberty, 1098
Russell, Harl L., housing programs, 1132
Weir, Samuel, 2096
ethnic diversity, 166
Etliche Liebliche und Erbauliche Lieder . . , 1933
Etling, Harold Hartz, 12, 533, **458,** 1612, 1239, 1933
Etter, Charlotte (later Studebaker), 1230
Etter, Christian, 459
Etter, David K., Jr., 1612
Etter, David, Sr., 1612
Etter, Erma Prowant, 1612
Etter family, 142, **458–459,** 700
Ridge Church of the Brethren, PA, 1109
Etter, Georg Hans, 459
Etter, George, 459, 1612
Etter, Henry, 459, 1612
Shippensburg, PA, Church of the Brethren, elder in, 1177
Etter, Henry G., 1612
Etter, Jacob, 459
Etter, Jacob, Jr., 459, 1933
Etter, Jacob, Sr.
biography, 1933
Etter, John, 459, 1612
Etter, Lorenz, 1612
Etter, Lydia M.
Heckert, Mildred Mae Etter, 2197
Etter, Margaret Wine, 459
Etter, Michael, 348, 459, 1612
Pleasant Hill, OH, Church of the Brethren, elder, 1031
Etter, Mildred Mae (later Heckert), 191, **2197**
Etter, Ralph A.
Heckert, Mildred Mae Etter, 2197
Etter, Samuel, 1612
Etter, Susan Miller, 459
Etter, William, 459, 1612
Ettlein, Frederic
New Paris, IN, Brethren Church, 931
Ettleman family, 1939
Ettwein, John, 1933
Moravian Church and, 1956
euangelion, See evangelism
Eucharist, *See* communion
Eugene, OR, 1215
Euphrates, *See* Ephrata
Eureka, KS, 1213
Eureka schoolhouse, Larned Brethren Church, KS, 726
Europe, *See* individual cities and countries
Brethren Service in, 918
Chateau of Saint Albain, 2158, *2159*
historic sites, 1922
Mennonite Brethren Churches, General Conference of, 814
Mennonites, 815
Miller, John William, 2224
Minnesota Starvation Project, 848
missions, 2225
missions and missionaries in

Brubaker, Leland Stanford, 218
missions, short-term, 2226
Relief and Reconstruction Committee, aided by, 1096
relief and rehabilitation work in, 199–200
relief and service efforts, 1097
tours of, 202
travelogues, 2101
work camps, 1365, *1366*
European Brethren, *See* Schwarzenau Brethren
attitude toward art, 59
culture, 59, 60, 61
and hymnals, 72
places of worship, 48
rejection of church buildings and furnishings, 46, 48
sources of information on, 31
Eustis, FL, *497*
Seneca Church of the Brethren, FL, near, 1166
Eutingen, Baden, 225
Evalson, Sarah A. Freas Gibbons, 1612
Evangel 21, 2179
Grassroots, Concerns of the, 2193
Evangel Press
Jubilee: God's Good News Curriculum, 2209
Evangelical and Reformed Church, *See* United Church of Christ
Evangelical Association, 16, 177, 188, **459**
American revivalism, 1104
New Paris, IN, 931
Evangelical Audio-Visual Center, 801
Evangelical Church
Austria, 73, **459,** 684
bibliography, 1864
Ecuador, 1290
Etling, Harold Hartz, 458
medical projects, 809
participation in two-hundred-fiftieth anniversary convocation, Schwarzenau, 1282
United Brethren in Christ united with, 1290
Evangelical Church in Germany, **459**
Puidoux Conferences, 1071
Ronneburg Castle, purchase of, 1122
Evangelical Church of the Brethren in Ecuador, 422
Evangelical Covenant Church, Ecuador, 268, **459–460**
ministry education, 268
Evangelical Foreign Missions Associations, 914
Evangelical Health System
merger with Lutheran General Hospital System, 2136
Evangelical Hospital Association, 123
merger with Bethany Hospital, 2136
Evangelical Lutheran Church, 1896
Stover, William, 2379
Evangelical Missionary Society, *See* Basel Mission
evangelical movements
Plymouth Brethren, 1038
theology and, 2254
Evangelical Press Association, 2179
Evangelical services
New Haven Church of the Brethren, NC, 928
Evangelical Theological Society

Hoyt, Herman Arthur, 634
McClain, Alva J., 773
Evangelical United Brethren Church (EUB), 16, 94, 155, **460,** *See also* United Methodist Church
Boyer, James L., 2139
Evangelical Association, 459
Flat Creek Church of the Brethren, KY, 493
United Andean Indian Mission (UAIM), 1289
United Brethren in Christ, 1290
United Brethren in Christ united with Evangelical Church to form, 1290
United Methodist Church formed from, 1291
Evangelical Visitor
Hadsell, B. A., 577
Evangelii Büdbarare (Gospel Messenger), **460**
Der Evangelische Besuch, 288, **460,** 1933
example of use of German language, 725
Henry Kurtz, 712
publishing of, 1068
Evangelische Gemeinschaft, See Evangelical Association
Evangelische Kirche in Deutschland (EKD), *See* Evangelical Church in Germany
Evangelische Prediger, 1934
Evangelisches Hilfswerk
Evangelical Church in Austria, 459
Evangelisches Hilfswerk (protestant welfare agency), 73
Evangelisches Hilfwerk/Evangelical Reconstruction Work, 1933
Evangelisches Kirchenlexikon
Pietism subdivisions, 1021
Evangelisches Magazin
historical writing, 611
Evangelisches Staatslexikon
Pietist subdivisions, 1021
evangelism, **460–461,** 2026, 2046, **2179–2180,** *See also* bus ministry; Forward Movement; missions and missionaries
The Andrew Center, **2130**
Ashland Convention, 368
and the automobile, 74
Bashor, Stephen H., 150
Blanchard, Charles A., 259
Blough, Perry J., 149
Blough, Silas S., 149
Board of Evangelism (FGBC), 155
books about, 1936, 1938
bookstores, 161
Bosserman, Samuel T., 163
Bowman, George C., 166
Bowman, Isaac Daniel, 166
Bowman, James Brubaker, 167
Bowman, Merle Allen, 167
Brethren Church, 206
Brethren movement and, 174
churches, established, 174
Brethren Publishing House, 287
Brummetts Creek, NC, Church of the Brethren meeting, 224
camping movement, 250
China, 149, 277
Chinese Sunday Schools (CB), 278
Christian Education Commission, 155
Christian Workers' Meetings (CB), 287

church membership growth, 813
Church of Jesus Christ of Latter-day Saints, 298
Church of the Brethren, 298–299, 305, 2162
colonization, 295
confession of faith, 333
Declaration of Principles, 372
definition of, 386
Denmark, 299
dispensationalism, 390
dissenters and, 175
dress and, 402, 403
Dunkard Brethren Church, 2175
Eby, Emma Ada Horner and Enoch Howe, 418
educational materials, 284
Eller, Vernard on, 2329
Emmert, Gertrude Elvina Rowland and Jesse Benedict, 444
Ephrata Community, 451
eschatology, 454
ethics, 457
Evangelistic and Bible Study League (BC), 461
Fellowship of Grace Brethren Churches (FGBC), 484, 485–486
Fellowship of the Grace Brethren Churches, 2182
Flora, Clara Myers, 495
Flory, George W., 498
Foreign Mission Commission (CB), 500
Forney, Anna Marie Shull and Daniel L., 502
Forward Movement, 504
France, 505
frontier, 440
Gaiwaka, Noel, 527
General Board (CB), 535
General Christian Workers' Board (CB), 536
General Conference Mennonite Church, 536
Gibson, Daniel B., 547
gospel songs, 561
Great Commission, 568
Grisso, Clarence C., 574
Harsh, Mary Lou Hykes, 587
Hershberger (Harshbarger) family, 599
higher education, 603
Hochmann von Hochenau, Ernst Christoph, 614
Holiness Movement, American, 619
Holsinger, Levi Teeter, 623
Holy Spirit, doctrine of, 624
Hon, Peter Keithly, 626
Hoover, Samuel W., 628
Hostetler, Daniel W., 631
Hostetler, Joseph, 631
Hummer, Catherine, 636
Hutchison, Andrew, 638–639
Ikenberry, Ernest Leroy, 646
India, 150, 229, 299, 649, 651
India and China, 1973
Influenza Pandemic, 655
Jarboe, John Edwin, 669
Juniata Church of the Brethren, NE, 678
Mansfield, OH, Conservative Grace Brethren Church, 2217
meetings, 413
membership trends 1980 to 2000, 2220

Men's Work (CB), 816
methods and functions, 1996
migration as means of, 413
Miller, David Alfred, 836
Miller, Robert Paul, 842
ministry, 846
Ministry and Home Mission Commission (CB), 848
minorities, ethnic and racial, 849
The Missionary Board (BC), 855
missions, 858, 859, 861
Mitchell, Olden D. on Brethren and, 2347
Moyer, Laura Emma, 892
Neher, Minneva Josephine in China, 922
nonconformity, 940
orphans, care for, 982
Parish Ministries Commission involvement in, 993
Parker, Isaac Dillon, and, 993
Progressive Brethren, 298
prominent evangelists, 92
protracted meetings, 1063
protracted series of meetings, 178
publication on, 2109
Quinter, James, 1077
radio, 1080
Reina, Domingo, 1094
revival meetings, 299, 1103–1104
sermon, mid 20th century, 1168
Shrewsbury, PA, Church of the Brethren, 1179
Simpson, A. B., 259
Smith, Timothy L. on Brethren and, 2357
sources on, 2312, 2321, 2322
Sunday school movement, 283
thesis on, 1953
Ward, W. R[eginald] on Protestant Church and, 2362
Weaver, Scott L. (FGBC, CGBCI) and, 2261
Winning the Race Ministries and, 2262–2263
women and, 204
women involved in, 1361
Yearout, Charles Madison, 1384
Ziegler, Edward Krusen, 1395
Zunkel, C. Wayne on Brethren and, 2365
Evangelism Leader's Academy (ELA), 2180
Evangelistic and Bible Study League (BC), **461**
evangelism, 460
evangelistic meetings, See revival meetings
evangelists
    Early, Henry Clay, 413
    Kilhefner, Isaac, 693
evangelization of the world, See foreign missions
    student volunteer movement, 1231
Evans, A. J., 14
Evans, Albert Allen, 1612
Evans, Alexander, 1612
Evans, Alice, 1848
Evans, Amanda (later Myer)
    Myer, Elizabeth, mother of, 903
Evans, Charles, 140, 1859
Evans, Curtis Garret, 2277
    Mansfield, OH, Conservative Grace Brethren Church, 2218
Evans, Daniel, 1612

Evans, Dave, 739
Evans, Eldon, 1612
Evans, Elizabeth (later Baker)
    works by, 2312
Evans, Eytive Long, 1933
Evans family, 1863, 1957
    Placerville, CA, Sierra View Grace Brethren Church, 1028
Evans, Grace Radcliff, 1933
Evans, James, 43, 565, 1612, 1933
    Wetonka, SD, Willow Creek Church of the Brethren, 2379
Evans, John W., Jr., 366, 496, 1612, 1933
Evans, Lester S., 1612
Evans, Lewis, 1933
Evans, Lillian M., 1933
Evans, Lloyd E., 1612
Evans, Madison, 1933
Evans, Martha (later Coppock), 343, *571*
Evans, Richard M., 1612
Evans, Robert Lee, 1933
Evans, Robert M., 99, 1612
Evans, Samuel, 1929
Evans, Sarah Ann (later Beghtol)
    descendants, 1957
Evans, Stanley, 1612
Evans, Theodore Quentin, 1933–1934, 1612
Evans, W. H., 1612
Evanston, IL, 1359
    Reba Place Fellowship Church of the Brethren/Mennonite Church, See Reba Place Fellowship, Evanston, IL
Evarts, John D., 1612
Everett, PA, 145, 1384
    Church of the Brethren, **461**
    Communnity Grace Brethren Church, **2180**
    Grace Brethren Church, **461–462**
    Snake Spring Valley Church of the Brethren, PA, churchouse, 1192
Everett, Portia Showalter, 1934
Evergreen, **462**
    Sipesville, PA, Church of the Brethren, 1187
Evergreen, MD, Church of the Brethren, See Reisterstown, MD, Evergreen Church of the Brethren
Evergreen meetinghouse, Seneca Church of the Brethren, WV, 1166
Evergreen, VA, Church of the Brethren, **462**, 2372
    Mount Carmel Church of the Brethren, 880
Everham, Wendy
    Beissel, Conrad on feminism in early Pietist community, 2330
Everhart family
    history of, 1934
Everhart, Israel, 1934
Everhart, Maria Ropp, 1934
Everhart-Miller family
    family history, 2012
Everhart, O. T., 1934
Everhart, William D., 1934
Evers, Lizzie C. (later Glick), 553, 554
Eversole family
    Mayville, ND, Red River Valley Church of the Brethren, 805
Eversole, Hannah Maria (later Garst), 531
Eversole house, Wolf Creek Church of the Brethren, OH, 1355
Eversole, John P., 170

Eversole, OH, Church of the Brethren, 213, **462**, 1355
Eversole, Silas, 1612
Eversole, Simon P., 173, 1612
Everson, Thomas, 1612
Everson, William (Brother Antonius), 317
Everts, Eng(?) (later Henckels), 596
Everts, John D., 1612
Everybody's Friend
    Duncan, N. A. (editor), 277
    German Baptist Brethren's Home
        Society, 277
Everyman's Bible Commentary
    Whitcomb, John Clement, Jr. (FGBC,
        CGBCI) and, 2262
Evey, George, 1612
evil, **462–463**, 981, 1184
evolution, **463**
    Creation, Doctrine of, 351
    Fellowship of Grace Brethren Churches
        (FGBC), 486, 487
    fundamentalism, 522
    human, 1160
    Modernism, 866
    religious groups, and sect-church typol-
        ogy, 1164–1165
Ewa Beach, HI, Rainbow Grace Brethren
    Church, **463**
Ewarry congregation, NC, *See* Uwharrie
    German Baptist Brethren Church,
    NC
Ewers, D. W., 1934
Ewert, Jeanine L., 2277
Ewert, Milton H., 2277
Ewing Church of the Brethren, VA, **463**,
    2373
Ewing, James, 463
Ewing, John Cook, **463**, 560, *679*, 1612
    biography of, 1873
    Brethren music, 899
    hymnals, 642
    hymns, 643
    singing schools, 1185
Ewing, Ruth Richards, 463
Ewings family, 313
examination and Brethren Church ministry,
    846
exchange students, *See* student exchange
    programs
exclusion of members, *See* avoidance; dis-
    cipline
excommunication, *See* avoidance; dis-
    cipline; disfellowship
    discipline by, 698
    divorce, 393
    Guice (Geist, Guß, Guss, Güß),
        Christopher, 576
    Hoppingite Schism, 630
    Martin, George Adam, of, 797
    Moomaw, Daniel Crouse, 873
    Powers, Valentine, of, 1050
    Thurman, William C., 2082
Executive Committee
    Goals and Budget Committee, 555
Executive Council (BC)
    women and, 2264
executive structures
    Standing Committee, 1216–1217
exegesis and worship, 2266
exemption from military service, *See* mili-
    tary exemptions
exemption tax
    Dunkard Brethren Church, 2097

military service, 333
    Payne, Adam, 2083
An Exercise for Youth (Mack, Jr.), 283
Exeter Church of the Brethren, NE, **463**
exhorters
    ministry, terminology, 848
exile, 1222
    Treytorrens, Nicolas Samuel de, 1274
Exodus
    29:7, 39
    30:23–30, 39
    40:10, 39
    Julien, Thomas T., 2210
expelled members, *See* discipline
Experiment Station Units, CPS, *See*
    Agricultural College Units
Exploring the Bible (Hoff), 617
*An Exposition of Certain Evangelical
    Truths* (Nead, P.), 919
Expositions, *See* fairs
expulsion
    Boni, Andreas, from Switzerland, 1246
    Stein, John William, from Silver Creek,
        IL, congregation, 1220
    Thurmanites, 1264
Extension Committee of the Missionary
    Board
    Newark, OH, Brethren Church, organi-
        zation of, 933
Eyeman, Thomas, 1612
Eylar family, 1934
Eylar, Joseph
    descendants, 1934
Eylar, Mary A. Rosenmiller
    descendants, 1934
Eyler, Conrad, *See* Iller, Conrad
Eyler family, 1927, 1957
Eyman, Jacob, 297, 464
Eyman, Peter, 77, 177, 297, **463–464**, 700,
    766, 910, 1612, **2382**
    Indiana, 652
    Replogle, Peter, dipute with, 1100
Eymanites, *See* Church of God (New
    Dunkers)
Eymann-Eberle family, 2025
EYN, *See* Church of the Brethren in
    Nigeria
Eyster, Anita L., 1934
Eyster, Hosie (later Hershey), 599
Ezechiel, Brother, *See* Sangmeister,
    Heinrich
1 Ezra, 120
2 Ezra, 120
Ezra family, 228

F., A. S., 1934
F., I. N., 1934
Fabbro, Rebecca Lee, 1852
Faber du Faur, Kurt von, 1859
Faber, Gellius, 29
Fabian, Monroe H., 1934
Fackler, David, 1612
Fackler, George, 894
Fackler, Maria Miller, 894
faculties
    Bethany Theological Seminary, *127*
    Giessen faculty, 2074
    Grace Theological Seminary faculty
        statement on authority of scripture,
        133
    Juniata College directories, 1980–1981
    Mount Morris College, 884, *885*
Fadely, A. (H.) E., *See* Faidley, Hiram E.

Fadely, E. Stanley, 1612
Fadely, Henry L., 1612
Fadely, Turner, 586
Fadley, ___, 755
Fagan, Ada Correll, 1612
Fagan, Lester R., 1612
Fagar, Abraham, 743
Fager, Charles D., 471, 1312, 1612
    Paradise, CA, Church of the Brethren,
        992
    Santa Ana, CA, Church of the Breth-
        ren, ministerial leadership given
        to, 1144
Fager, Charles E.
    civil rights conflict, 1190
    on peace witness movement, 2329
Fages, Jacob, 1612
Faggart, Rua (later Wolfe), 1358, *1358,
    1359*
Fahlbusch, Ervin, 2330
Fahnestock, A. K., 1934
Fahnestock, Adam G., **465**, 749, 1612, 1920
Fahnestock, Amanda Kaufman, 465
Fahnestock, Andrew, 465, 1931, 1939
Fahnestock, Carol, 2214
Fahnestock, Catrina Anna, 383
Fahnestock, Cephas, 1612
Fahnestock, Conrad, 465
Fahnestock, Daniel, 373, 1138
Fahnestock, Dean Olin, 1612
Fahnestock, Ephraim, 373
Fahnestock family, 158, **465**, 1934, 1961
Fahnestock, Fern (later Ness), 2231, *2231*
Fahnestock, George Wolff, 1934
Fahnestock, Harold H., 1612
Fahnestock, Harry G., 1612
Fahnestock, J. Marlin, 2214
Fahnestock, Jacob, 373, 1613
Fahnestock, Jacob N., 1613
Fahnestock, Johann Diedrich, 465, 1934,
    2037
Fahnestock, John, 373
Fahnestock, Joseph, 465
Fahnestock-Kerlin-Worley families, history
    of, 1983–1984
Fahnestock, Lloyd Roy, 2277
Fahnestock, Lydia Bigler, 465
Fahnestock, Mary Harlacher, 465
Fahnestock, Nathan B., 1340, 1613
Fahnestock, Roy, 406, 1008
Fahnestock, Rufus G., 1340, 1613
Fahnestock, S. G., 719, 1613
Fahnestock, Samuel Bigler, **465**, 1613
Fahnestock, W. F., 1934
Fahnestock, William, 373
Fahnestock, William M., **465**, 1934
Fahrback, John, 2167, 2168
Fahrenstuck, Johann Diedrich, *See*
    Fahnestock, Dietrich
Fahrney, Ann Sartoris, 466
Fahrney, Callo, 1613
Fahrney, Catherine Welty, 465
Fahrney, Daniel, 1225
Fahrney, Daniel F., 809
Fahrney, Daniel H., 203, 1613
Fahrney, Daniel P., 809
Fahrney, Elizabeth Holsinger, 465
Fahrney, Eve Durnbaugh, 465, 466, 809
Fahrney family, 235
    Snowberger family, related to, 1153
Fahrney (Forney) family, **466**
Fahrney, J. T.
    St. James Brethren Church, 1134

Fahrney, J. Welty, 1613
Fahrney, Jacob, **465**, 466, *466,* 1613
  medical practice, 809
  photograph taken of, 1019
Fahrney, Josiah B., 42, 1613
Fahrney-Keedy Chapel Fellowship
    Church of the Brethren, MD, 104,
    467
Fahrney-Keedy Memorial Home, MD, **467,**
    1361
  Fahrney, Peter, 466
  Long, W. Newton, 754
Fahrney, Lewis E., 1613
  Nickerson, KS, Church of the Brethren,
    elder in, 936
Fahrney, Mary, 466
Fahrney, Mary Camerer, 1361
Fahrney Memorial Home, *See* Fahrney-
    Keedy Memorial Home
  Fahrney Memorial Home for the Aged,
    2097
Fahrney, Mrs. J. T.
  St. James Brethren Church, 1134
Fahrney, Mrs. Katie E.
  The Missionary Advocate, business
    manager and secretary, 855
Fahrney, Peter, 465, **466,** 1918, 1934, *See
    also* medicine
Fahrney-Keedy Memorial Home, 467
  medical practice, 809
  patent medicine remedy business, 995
Fahrney, Peter Dennis, 511, 1613
Fahrney, Peter, Jr., *See* Fahrney, Peter
Fahrney, Ralph, 1613
Fahrney, Samuel, 466
  inventions and scientific discoveries,
    660
Fahrney, Susan (later Stouffer), 1225
Fahrney, Walter
  on Fahrney, Peter and descendants,
    2330
Fahrney's Church, MD, *See* Mount Zion
    congregation, MD
Faidley, Hiram E., 1613
Faidley, Ira D., 1613
Fair, C. G., 1613
Fair, Ernest, 204
Fair, Fred L., 1613
Fair Haven Brethren Church, OH, **467**
  Gingrich, Raymond Eugene, 2190
Fair, Jerry Lee, 1613
Fair View Brethren Church, IN, *See* South
    Bend, IN, Ardmore Brethren
    Church
Fair-View (Georges Creek)
    Church of the Brethren, PA, 102, **469,**
    1289
  George's Creek Old German Baptist
    Brethren Church, PA, 540
Fairchance, PA, Church of the Brethren,
    467
Fair View meetinghouse
Fairbanks, Clarence Sylvester, 1319, 1613,
    2378, 2382
Fairchance mission, PA, 1289
Fairchance, PA, Church of the Brethren,
    467
Fairchild, Janice
  on Mathew 18 Project, 2361
Fairchild, M. H., Jr., 19
Fairchild, M. J., Jr., 19
Fairchild, Mrs. B. R., 1613
Fairfax Church of the Brethren, VA, *See*

Oakton, VA, Church of the
    Brethren
Fairfax Co., VA, 399
  Oakton, VA, Church of the Brethren,
    958
Fairfax, VA, congregation
  Manassas, VA, Church of the Brethren,
    785
Fairfield Co., OH, 237
  Dunkard Brethren Church, 2086
  Mennonite Church, 2086
Fairfield Co., SC, 210
  South Carolina, 1204
Fairfield schoolhouse
  Leetown, WV, Church of the Brethren,
    735
Fairhaven Brethren Church of Lattasburg,
    OH, 215, 744
  Hamel, Joseph Donat, 2196
Fairhope, PA, Custer Brethren Church, **467**
Fairhurst, Janet, 1934
  on Ephrata Cloister, 2330
Fairless Hills Community Center
  Fairless Hills-Levittown, PA, Brethren
    Church, **467**
Fairman, Judy K. Ashman, 1169
Fairman, Richard Gary, 2177, 2277
fairs and public shows, 26, 59, **467,** *See
    also* amusements; names; noncon-
    formity
  Old German Baptist Brethren and non-
    conformity, 941
  simple life, 1183
Fairview, ID, 157
Fairview congregations,
  Canada
    Church of the Brethren, 15, 250,
      469–470, 830, 2064
  Iowa
    Fairview Church of the Brethren,
      IA, **468,** 661, 1212, 1285,
    Fairview, IA, German Baptist
      Brethren congregation, 1212
    Grace Brethren congregation, 661
      Ogden, William Augusta, min-
        ister, 961
    migration of Brethren, 830
    Pleasant Valley German Baptist
      Brethren, IA, **1036**
    Schuyler German Baptist Brethren
      Church, MO, 1157
  Indiana
    Southbend, IN, Ardmore Brethren
      Church, 1203
    Fairview Church of the Brethren,
      IN, 256, **468,** 717, 1385
    Goshen, IN, Dunkard Brethren
      congregation, 352, **557–558**
    Hedrick, Laura E. N. Grossnickle,
      593
    Prymount, IN, Church of the
      Brethren, 1073
  Kansas
    Abilene, KS, Church of the Breth-
      ren, **1**
    Fairview Church of the Brethren,
      468
    Fairview Old German Baptist
      Brethren Church, **470**
    Lone Star, KS, Fairview Brethren
      Church, 753
    Neosho Church of the Brethren,
      KS, 923

Maryland
    Fairview Church of the Brethren,
      417, 430, **468, 469**
  Michigan
    Fairview Church of the Brethren,
      469
  Missouri
    Fairview Church of the Brethren,
      469
    Mount Herman Church of the
      Brethren, 881
    Shelby Co. Church of the Breth-
      ren, **1175,** 2011
    Shoal Creek Church of the Breth-
      ren, **467–468**
  Ohio
    Fairview Church of the Brethren,
      469
    Hixson, Armanus Jefferson, **613**
  Washington Court House, OH,
    Fairview Brethren Church, 1267,
      1320–1321
    Weir, Samuel, **1327**
  Pennsylvania
    East Fairview Church of the Breth-
      ren, Manheim, PA, 279, **415,**
      1923
    Fairview Brethren Church, PA,
      468
    Fairview, PA, Church of the Breth-
      ren, **469**
    Fairview-Sculton Church of the
      Brethren, PA, 469
    Fredericksburg, PA, Clover Creek
      Church of the Brethren,
      512–513
    Masontown, PA, Brethren Church,
      800
    Smithfield Church of the Brethren,
      PA, **1192**
  Virginia
    Fairview, VA, Church of the
      Brethren, 2047
    Fairview-Endless Caverns Church
      of the Brethren, VA, 129, **470**
    Fairview-Mount Clinton Church of
      the Brethren, VA, **470**
    Fairview-Rocky Mount Church of
      the Brethren, VA, **470**
    Greenmount Church of the
      Brethren, VA, **571**
    Unity Church of the Brethren, VA,
      1291
Fairview Hall
  Elizabethtown College, 437
Fairview meetinghouse
  Linville Creek Church of the Brethren,
    VA, 746
  Upper Twin Old German Baptist
    Church, OH, 1295
Fairview meetinghouse, PA, *See* Amarath
    meetinghouse (Fairview, PA)
faith, 2024
  articles of, 133
  Brethren Doctrine of Salvation, 1140
  church membership, 813
  Priesthood of All Believers, 1057
  psychology and, 2322
  Reformation, Protestant, 1091
  repentance, doctrine of, 1100
  sources on, 2311
  Thomas, Richard on answers to ques-
    tions about, 2360

Faith and Life Movement, 926
Faith and Life Press
    Jubilee: God's Good News Curriculum,
        2209
Faith and Order, **470**, *See also* ecumenism
    Baptism, Eucharist, and Ministry
        (BEM) text, 2133–2134
    Commission, World Council of
        Churches, 470
Faith and Order Conference
    ecumenism, 422
    life and work movement, 742
Faith Assembly, **2180**
Faith Expeditions
    missions, short-term, 2226
Faith Gospel Mission and the Second
        Brethren Church, Hagerstown,
        MD, *See* Hagerstown, MD, Grace
        Brethren Church
faith healing
    Dowie, John Alexander, 398
Faith, IL, Church of the Brethren, *See*
        Batavia, IL, Faith Church of the
        Brethren
Faith the cow, 594
faith-works debate, 1368
Faithful Account (Wilhelm Grahe)
    Solingen Brethren, 1201
faithfulness and membership trends,
        1980–2000, 2220
faithQuest, 2149
Fake, Elizabeth
    Mount Wilson Church of the Brethren,
        PA, 887
Fake, Harry
    Mount Wilson Church of the Brethren,
        PA, 887
Falckner, Daniel, 470
    Society of the Woman in the Wilder-
        ness, 1200
Frey (Fry) family, 517
Falckner's Swamp, PA, 175, **470**, 584
Falfurrias, TX, 202, 1255, *See also*
        Brethren Industrial School for
        Mexicans
    Church of the Brethren, **471**
    minorities, ethnic and racial, 850
    mission, 1232
Falkenstein, David, 471, 1613
Falkenstein, Eva Shellenberger, 471
Falkenstein, George Ness, 60, *103*, 140,
        471, 686, 1613. 1928, 1934–1935,
        2111, 2142, 2377
    Elizabethtown College, 437
    historical writing, 611
    Milk River Valley Church of the
        Brethren, MT, elder, 832
    Philadelphia, PA, Germantown Church
        of the Brethren, 1016
    publishing, 1069
Falkenstein, Jacob, 686, 1613
Falkenstein, Magdalena, 384
Falkenstein, Mary Ness, 471
Falkenstein, Samuel, 1364
Falkner family, 384
Falkner's Swamp congregation, PA, *See*
        Falkner's Swamp
Fall Creek, OH, Church of the Brethren
    Lexington Church of the Brethren, OH,
        739
Fall Creek, OH, congregation
    Major, Thomas, presiding elder, 784
    New Vienna Academy, 932

Fall family, 1213
Fall, John C., 2277
Fall River, KS, Church of the Brethren, *See*
        Fredonia, KS, Church of the
        Brethren; Greenwood Co. Church
        of the Brethren, KS
Falling Spring Church of the Brethren, PA,
        40, 42, **471**
Falling Spring Old German Baptist Breth-
        ren Church, PA, **471**, 2153
Falling Spring, PA, congregation
    history of, 1942
    Nicarry, Wayne A., 2231
Falling Springs, PA, congregation, 1256
    Greencastle, PA, Church of the
        Brethren, 570
Fallis, J. M., 1613
Falls City, NE, 1385
    Church of the Brethren, NE, **472**
    congregation, 921
    Brethren Church, 394, **472**, 921
Falsgraff family, *See* Pfaltzgraff family
Falsgraff, George
    Pfaltzgraff pottery and, 2250
Falter family
    Goldendale, WA, Community Grace
        Brethren Church, 556
Falwell, Jerry, 1935
Fame (ship)
    Hoffman (Huffman) family, 617
families, *472*, **472–474**, 2019, 2036,
        2144–2145, *See also* acculturation;
        birth rate; children; simple life
    Brethren Church, 2145
    church in new community, 1964
    Church of the Brethren, 2145
    demographic trends, 2144–2145
    devotional literature, 381
    discipline of children, 389–390
    distribution in U. S. (1619–1880), 1974
    Dubble, Curtis W. on patriarchs to real,
        2325
    Dunkard Brethren Church, 2145, 2175
    ethics, 457
    Faus, Nancy Rosenberger on spiritual
        nurture of, 2330
    Fellowship of Grace Brethren Churches
        (FGBC), 487, 2145
    frontier worship style, 283
    funerals, 523, 524
    genealogy, 534
    General Board (CB), 535
    General Investment Council (CB), 537
    Hutterian Society of Brothers, 641
    Mabton, WA, Grace Brethren Church,
        771
    marriage, 795–796
    Neher family, related to, 922
    nuclear, 294
    Old German Baptist Brethren, 2145
    Salem Church of the Brethren, OH,
        1138
    Sappington, Roger E. on Brethren and,
        2354
    sexuality, human, 1170
    size of, *See* birth rate, trends in
    theology and, 2255
    training children, 2159
family altar, *See* family worship
"The Family Altar"
    Hagerstown, MD, Grace Brethren
        Church, 579
The Family Companion, **474,** 1935

family, doctrine of, 2091
    rules and regulations, Baptist Church,
        2073
family education centers, 2131
family histories, 1857
    Brethren, 2016
Family Life, 26
family ministry
    Ephrata, PA, Church of the Brethren,
        448
A Family Record of John Michael Pfautz
    Pfautz, John Eby, publisher, 1014
family restoration movements
    home education, 2203
family reunions, **474**
family worship, **474–475**, *See also*
        Christian education; family; spiri-
        tual life
    Civil War, 475
    prayer, 1051
    publications on, 2076, 2109
    singing, 1184
famine
    China, 277
    Hilton, George William, 607
    humanitarianism, 636
    India, famine relief in, 651
    material aid, 802
    mission schools, 853
    missions, 861
    relief, **475**
Fancher, Donald Eugene, 1613, 1837
    missionary sponsored by Salamonie
        Church of the Brethren, IN, 1136
Fancher, Doris Elizabeth Thompson, 1837
Fanning, Arnold, 1613
Fansler, ___, 755
Fansler, Anna, 2090
Fansler, William Franklin, 1613
Far Western Brethren, 30, 58, 177, 321,
        475–476, 688
    chart of Brethren bodies, place on,
        1403–1405
    Congregational Brethren, 334
    Drakes Creek German Baptist Brethren
        Church, KY, 398
    feetwashing, 481
    feetwashing dispute, 1186
    Fraternity of Baptists, 511
    frontier, 519
    Gibson, Daniel B., 547
    Gibson, Isham, 548
    Hendricks, Franklin A., 597
    Hendricks, James, 597
    Hendricks, John, 597, 1292
    Hochstetler (Hostetler) family, 615
    Illinois, 646
    migration of Brethren, 829, 830
    Missouri Brethren settlement, 864
    Oregon, 980
    origin of, 1292
    protest of word "German" in Fraternity
        of German Baptists, 910
    Rowland, Gasper, 1292
    Rowland, Joseph, helping to establish,
        1126
    schisms, 334
    Sturgis, Daniel B., 1232
    Swihart, Jonathan H., 1245
    Weigle, Jacob W., 1327
    White Water German Baptist Brethren
        Church, MO, 1342
    Wolfe, George, II, 1292, 1357

Wolfe, George, III, 1358
fares, railroad, 1081
Fargo Valley, ID, mission, 157
Faris, Ellsworth, 2, 1935
Faris, John T., 1935
Farlee, Lloyd Winfield, 1935
Farm Bureau
    student exchange program, 1231
farm machinery, **476,** *478,* 479
farm scenes
    Defiance Co., OH, *11*
    Harleysville, PA, *11*
    Middle Pennsylvania, *10*
    North Webster, IN, *10*
Farmer family
    Myerstown, PA, Grace Brethren
      Church, 906
Farmers Development Co.
    Miami, NM, Church of the Brethren,
      823
Farmers Grove Fellowship (CB), PA, **476,**
    1281
The Farmer's Monthly, 1935
Farmersville, OH, 2074
    Home Pulpit, The, 625
Farmersville, OH, Brethren Church, **476**
    Mason, Edward, pastor, 799
farming, *See* agriculture and farming
Farmington, DE, Bethany Church of the
    Brethren, 374, **479,** 1957
Farmington, PA, Bethel Church of the
    Brethren, **479**
    Markleysburg, PA, Church of the
      Brethren, 794
Farneman, Frank, 1613
Farner, Donald, G., Jr., 65, 585, 1212, 1351,
    1613
Farner, Donald W., 699, 1267
Farner family, 1267
Farner, Sandra Carlene Simpson, 173, 1848
Farner, Timothy Hugh, 173, 1380, 1613,
    1848
Farnhamville, IA, Church of the Brethren,
    479
    Slifer, IA, church of the Brethren, 1190
Farque, Joan, 2277
Farquharson, J. Keith, 2277
Farrell, Bess, 2157
Farrell, Gene D., 1613
Farrell, Jack R., Sr., 1613
Farrenburg Church of the Brethren, MO,
    479
Farringer, Dean Leroy, 1277, 1613
Farringer, Leland Dwight, 1613
Farrington, Kermit B., 152, 518, 749,1613
Farry, Ed. G., *499*
Farsomlungs Briefli (Versammlungs Brief),
    1935
Farthing, Mildred Hoover, 1971
Faschnachts (fried cakes), 2147
fashion, *See* dress
Fasnacht, Earl, 1613
Fasnacht, Everett Merlin, **479–480,** 1345,
    1613, 1837, **2373, 2382, 2387**
    Peace Valley Church of the Brethren,
      MO, 1003
Fasnacht, Glenda (later Jimmink), 480
Fasnacht, H. E., 1613
Fasnacht, Harold Dale, **480,** 1613, 1935,
    2301, **2373, 2382**
Fasnacht, Jacob Clyde, 480
Fasnacht, Joy Cullen, **479–480,** 1345, 1837
Fasnacht, Lois Elaine (later Miles), 480

Fasnacht, Lorena May Frantz, 480
Fasnacht, Roger Elwood, 1613
Fasnacht, Ruth Ellenberger, 480
Fasnacht, Uriah C., 1613
    Mechanic Grove Church of the
      Brethren, PA, free minister, 806
Fasnacht, Viola Funk, 480
Fast, Allen, 1613
Fast Element, **480**
Fast, Ethel Schindler, 480
Fast for Hunger
    Sunnyslope Church of the Brethren,
      WA, 1240
Fast, Henry A., **480,** 608, *608,* **2373**
fasting, **480**
    Brethren prayer, 1051
    Lent, 737
    Quinter, James, emphasis on, 1210
Fatary, Fred, 1613
Fath, David K., 1613
    Palmyra, PA, Grace Brethren Church,
      991
    Pataskala, OH, Grace Brethren Church
      of Licking Co., pastoral intern in,
      995
Fathers and Sons' Meetings
    Conference Program Committee (CB),
      333
Faulkender family, 695
Faulkner, Leonard, 758
Fauquier Co., VA
    Midland, VA, Church of the Brethren,
      826–827
FAUS (Fund for the Americas in the United
    States), *See* SHARE
    minorities, ethnic and racial, 850
Faus, Glen Mervin, 1613
Faus, Nancy Rosenberger, 1123, 1613,
    1935, 2277
    on CB spirituality and worship, 2330
    on family, spiritual nurture of, 2330
    on hymnody, 2331
    on worship, 2330–2331
Faus, Robert Eugene, 1613, 2301
Faus, Ronald E. H., 2277
Fausler, W. F., 1613
Fausnight, Ivan J., 7, 1613
Fausnight, Lola Hershberger, 7
Fausnight, Samuel, 7
Faust, Albert Bernhardt, 1894, 1935
Faust, Alvin G., 2, 1348, 1899, 1918, 1935
    historical writing, 612
Faust family, 1935
Faust (Foust), Alvin Giraud, 1614
Faust (Foust), David A., 1614
Faust, Howard Macy, 1935
Faust, J. E., 1614
Faust, Judson E., 1614
Fauts family, *See* Pfautz family
Fautz family, *See* Pfautz family
Faw, Adam, 481
Faw, Amos, 511, 1614
    Maple Grove Church of the Brethren,
      NC, minister, 790
Faw, Anna Magdalena Yount, 480, 481
Faw, Birdie Nead, 480
Faw, C. R.
    Maple Grove Church of the Brethren,
      NC, co-moderator, 790
Faw, C. Rufus, 1614
Faw, Chalmer Ernest, 190, 304, 307, **480,**
    1013, 1614, 1837, 1935, 2301
    on acts, 2331

    on congregational history, 2331
Faw, Charles E.
    Raisin City, CA, Church of the Breth-
      ren, pastor, 1083
Faw, Enoch, 320, 1319, 1614
    Moscow, ID, Church of the Brethren,
      minister, 878
Faw family, 1215, *See* Pfau family
    Harrah, WA, Grace Brethren Church,
      585
    North Carolina, 1979
Faw, Isaac, **480,** 481, 511, 1013, 1614
Faw, Jacob, 480, **481,** 511, 1013, 1614, *See*
    also Wachovia, NC
    biography of, 2084
    Maple Grove Church of the Brethren,
      NC, minister, 790
Faw, Magdalena Burkhart, 480, 481, 1013
Faw, Mary Platt, 304, 480, 1614, 1837,
    2387
Faw, Robert E., 480
Faw, Sarah Martin, 481
Faw, Verda (later Gibble), 1633
Faw, William R., 275, 1013, 1614, 1935,
    2177
    on Brethren history, concepts in, 2331
Faw, Zalma, 1846
Fawl, Doris Jean, 1614
Fawley, Ralph Dean, 1614
Fawn River congregation, *See* English
    Prairie Church of the Brethren, IN
Fay, Edgar Nelson, 53, 1614, 1848
Fay, Marjorie Jean Hurlbut, 1848
Fayette Co., IL, 684
Fayette Co., OH
    Fairview Church of the Brethren, OH,
      469
    Nicholson, John, minister in, 935
Fayette Co. Old German Baptist Brethren
    Church, PA, *See* Georges Creek
    Old German Baptist Brethren
    Church, PA
Fayette Co., PA, 189, 322, 347, 348, 1229,
    1232, 1263, 1287, 1356, 1364,
    2089
    Brethren Church congregations, 1005
    Elbethel Church of the Brethren, PA,
      432
    Fair-View (Georges Creek) Church of
      the Brethren, PA, 469
    George's Creek Old German Baptist
      Brethren Church, PA, 540
    history and genealogy, 1980
    Markleysburg, PA, Church of the
      Brethren, 794
    Pennsylvania Old Order Brethren, 1005
    Walters, Jonathan S. on Brethren of,
      2362
Fayette Co., WV, 1336
    Gatewood Brethren Church, WV, 532
    Oak Hill Old German Baptist Brethren
      Church, WV, 957
    Pleasant View Church of the Brethren,
      WV, 1037
Feaster, Esther Stober
    Stover, William, 2379
Feather family, 731
Feather, Homer, *See* Fether, Homer A.
Feather, Raymond I., 30, 515, 1614
    Okeechobee, FL, Grace Brethren
      Church, pastor, 963
Federal Communications Commission
    mass media concerns, 801

Federal Council of Churches, 308, 915,
    2070, *See also* ecumenism;
    National Council of Churches;
    National Council of Churches of
    Christ in the USA (NCCC);
    National Council of Churches of
    Christ in the USA (NCCCUSA);
    National Council of Churches of
    Christ (NCCC)
  The Christian Beacon and, 281
  Committee on Understanding and
    Reconciliation (CB) , 328
  ecumenism, 422, 423
  fraternal relations, 510
  Friends Committee on Spain, 518
  fundamentalism, 522
  Interchurch World Movement (IWM),
    658
  Mow, Anna Beahm, 890
Federal government, US
  Civilian Public Service and National
    Service Board for Religious
    Objectors (NSBRO), 917
Federal (National) Council of Churches
    Preaching Mission
  Kurtz, Daniel Webster, 711
  Zigler, Michael Robert, 1398
Federal (National) Council of the Churches
    of Christ in America
  Bible Brethren, concern about, 135
Federal Republic of Germany, 545
Feece family
  Mount Etna, IA, Church of the Breth-
    ren, 881
Feece, Isaiah, 1614
Feece, Jacob, 1614
Feenstra, Chuck, 1614
feetwashing, 25–26, 397, **481–482**, 698, *See
    also* Church of God (New
    Dunkers); Communion; debates;
    double mode feetwashing; single
    mode feetwashing
  article about, 1924
  bibliography, 1868, 1882, 1900
  books about, 1938, 1939
  Brethren Church doctrine on, 184
  Brethren in Christ, 188
  children at, 2159
  Christian Brethren, 281
  Christliches Hand-Büchlein (Christian
    Handbook), 288
  Church of God, Anderson, IN, 296
  Church of God (New Dunkers), 297
  Churches of God (GC), 309
  communion, 328
  Congregational Brethren of Pleasant
    Hill, OH, differing views of, 335
  Dayton, OH, Patterson Park Grace
    Brethren Church, 367
  debates, 371
  Declaration of Principles, 372
  description of, 1375, 2082, 2096
  division of 1881–1883, 396
  double mode, 134, 763
    attacked by Thurman, William
      C., 1264
  Dunkard Brethren, 409, 2085, 2173
  East Union "Dunkers" German Baptist
    Brethren, KY, 935
  Easter, 416
  Ephrata Community, 448
  Evergreen Church of the Brethren, VA
    (photo caption), *2378*

Eyman, Peter, 464
Far Western Brethren, 475, 476, 1357
Fellowship of Grace Brethren Churches
    (FGBC), 486
Flory, John, 498
Fox, John, letter by, 1939
frontier, 519
German Seventh-Day Baptists, 542
Gibson, Daniel B., 547
God's Means of Grace (Yoder), 555
Greenmount Church of the Brethren,
    VA, 571
handclasp, 582
Hendricks, Franklin A., 597
Hendricks, John, 597
Hoppingite Schism, 630
Hostetler Brethren, 631
humility, 636
Hymnal: A Worship Book, 2205
Mack, Alexander, Jr., 134, 774, 1168
"Message of the Brethren Ministry,"
    818
Miami Valley Petition, 823
mutual aid, 901
Old German Baptist Brethren, 206,
    364, 967, 2233
"Order of the Brethren," 976
ordinances, 976, *977,* 978, 979, 980,
    1973
  Oregon, 980
  in other religious groups, 68
Pennsylvania Brethren Church and
    Grace Brethren, 1005
plain coat, 1029
preaching about, 1053
Primitivism, 1058
publications on, 7
Radical Pietists, 293
reason for, 2003
  as reason for schism, 1210
Reitz, Johann Heinrich, 1095
restitution, 1100
Restoration Movement, 1101
ritual of, 1379
Schwarzenau Brethren, 1079
Seventh-Day Adventists, 1169
single mode dispute, *See* single mode
    of feetwashing
Social Gospel Movement, 1197
Swihart, Jonathan H., 1245
  as symbol, 1246
woodcut by Isaac J. Sanger, *59*
worship and, 2266
Fehl, Caroline (later Stiverson), 1223
Fehnel, E. E., 1614
Feightner, I. Levi, 1614
Feiler, Otto Herman, 638, 1312, 1614
Feisel, Keith, 2278
Felb, Sharon Ruth, 1855
Felbinger, Jeremias, 77, 133, 138, 288, 296,
    482, 923, 1259, 1935–1936
  Miller, John William, 2224
  Polish Brethren, 1041
Feldkircher, Fred, 1614
Feldkirchner, Frank, family
  Rice Lake, WI, Church of the Brethren,
    1107
Fellers, Forest S., 1936
Fellers, Mary
  Mulvane, KS, Brethren Church, 895
fellowship, 5, **482,** *483*
  Brethren Church doctrine on, 184
  Brethren doctrine of salvation, 1140

Brethren, loyalty to, 5
Brethren rural churches, 1130
community, 329
cooking, meals in Pennsylvania
    German tradition, 341
Fellowship of Reconciliation (USA),
    488
handclasp, 582
National Fellowship of Brethren
    Laymen, 915
National Youth Conference, 917–918
Old German Baptist Brethren, 969
Pietism, 1021–1022
restoration to, 698
Ruth, John L. on Mennonites and right,
    2354
Fellowship Church of the Brethren,
    CA, *See* La Verne, CA, Fellowship
    Church of the Brethren
Fellowship Church of the Brethren, WV,
    482, 798, **2181**
Fellowship Homes, Inc., *See* Casa de
    Modesto Retirement Center
Fellowship House, Elgin, IL
  medical projects, 808
  Zigler, Amy Arnold, 1397
fellowship houses, **482–484,** *See also*
    Zigler, A. A.
fellowship meal, *See* Lord's Supper
Fellowship of Brethren Genealogists
    (FOBG), **484**
  on Brethren, history of, 2331
  genealogy, 535, 2188
  Long, Harvey Lawrence, 754
  newsletter of, 1936, 2188
Fellowship of Churches of Christ in Nigeria
    (Tarayyar Ekklesiyoyin Kristi a
    Nigeria or TEKAN), **484**
  Church of the Brethren, 296, 300, 307
  ecumenism, 423
  Ekklesiyar 'Yan'uwa a Nigeria (EYN),
    member church, 937
  Mai Sule Biu, 782, 2216
  mission schools, 854
  missions, 861
  Theological College of Northern
    Nigeria, *1256, 1257*
Fellowship of Churches of Christ in the
    Sudan (TEKAS), 307
Fellowship of Grace Brethren Churches
    (FGBC), 97, 161, 192, 193,
    484–488, 2181–2183
  abortion, 2127
  advertising, 7
  in Africa, 2261
  agricultural missions, 9
  alcohol abstinence, 1252
  American Council of Churches and, 23
  Annual Conference, *See* Grace Breth-
    ren National Conference
  anointing, 2130
  and anointing, 39
  archival policy, 52
  in Arizona, 54
  authority of scripture, 133
  and beards, 103
  Bible translations and versions, 138
  biblical numerology, 1915
  in Brazil, 2269–2270
  Brethren Encyclopedia, Inc., 2143
  Brethren identity, 2182
  Brethren music, 899
  Brethren Student Life Volunteers, 1231

building counselors and services, 51
burial customs and, 230
bus ministries and, 232
business doctrine, 235
California, 238
Calvinism and, 241
Camp Albryoca (FGBC), PA, 242
Camp Mantowagan (FGBC), PA, 245
camping movement, 250
Canada, 250
capital punishment, 253
chaplaincy, 271
charismatic movement, 272
chart of Brethren bodies, place on, 1403–1405
charters/charter membership, 273
Chateau of Saint Albain, 2158, *2159*
Christian day school movement, 282, 284, 2160, 2183
Christian Education Department, 1353
church extensions, 295
church membership, 813
church-state relations, 312
communion service, 2181–2182
congregations in, 2, 12, 20, 31
conservation movement, 338
courts of law, attitudes toward use of, 728–729
Creation, Doctrine of, 351
Credential(s) Committee, and role in, 351
Daily Vacation Bible Schools, 359
Dayton, OH, Patterson Park Grace Brethren Church, 367
deacons, 369
decline in membership, 2181
Dedication of Infants, 372
Delaware, settlements in, 374
as denominational name, 911
description of, 2095
devotional literature, 381
Di Naardo, Juan, 382
discipline, doctrine of, 388, 389
district organization, 391
division of congregations, 392
divorce and remarriage, 1099, 2145
divorce issues, 393
drama, position on, 399
dress, style of, 404
Driver family, 405
ecumenism, 423
education, 428
educational materials, 284
elder, 433
elementary education, 434–435
Encyclopedia of Modern Christian Missions, 1950
environmental issues, 2177
Eternal Security, 456–457
ethics, 2178
Eucharist, distiguished from communion service, 2181–2182
evangelicalism, 2179
evangelism, 460, 461, **2180**
evolution, 463
family, 2145
farming, 479
Fike family, 490
flags, 493
Florida, 497
formation of Conservative Grace Brethren Churches International Fellowship, 2167, 2182

formerly National Brethren Bible Conference, 914
Frame, Randy on split of, 2332
France, 250, 505, 506
in France, 2262
fraternal relations, 510
free ministry, 513
Freemasonry, 515
fundamentalism, 522
fundamentalist *versus* evangelical views, 2182
funerals, 524
Gaiwaka, Noel, 527
Georgia, 540
Germany (Federal Republic of Germany), 546
Gingerich (Kingery) family, 549
gospel music, 559
gospel songs, 561
Grace Brethren North American Missions, 2191
Grace Brethren Village, 563
grace, doctrine of, 562
Grace Schools, 2192
GROW '73, 2194
Guiles, Dave on, 2335
hairstyle, 579
Haller, Wesley, 2195
Hamilton, Benjamin A. on mission in Central Africa and, 2335
Hawaii, 590
Historical Committee, FGBC on, 2337
historical writing, 612
holy kiss, 699
homosexuality, 2204
honorific titles, 1266
hospitals, 630
Hoyt, Herman Arthur, 634
human nature, doctrine of, 635
humanitarianism, 636
hymnals, 642
impact of Fundamentalism on, 74
Indiana, 652–653
Indianapolis, IN, Eagle Creek Grace Brethren Church, 654
inerrancy of scripture, 133
information technology, church use of, 2208
International Fellowship of Grace Brethren Churches, 2208
Jewish evangelism, 671
Johnstown, PA, First Brethren Church, 674
Judaism, 677
Julien, Thomas on missions and missionaries, 2339
Julien, Thomas T., 2210
Kansas, 682
Kauffman, Jeremiah on, 2340
Kentucky, 689
Kochheiser, Gary M. on nonresistance 2341
Lakeland, FL, Grace Brethren Church, 2213
language, inclusive, 2214
laying on of hands, 731
Lewis, Ed on doctrine of, 2343
logo, *2146*
maintenance of statistics, 1219
Malles, Mark Ellsworth, 2217
Mansfield, OH, Conservative Grace Brethren Church, 2217
manual of procedure, 788

Marion, OH, Grace Brethren Church, 2218
marriage, 389, 796, 2145
Maryland, 391
Maryland Brethren activity, 799
mass media, 800–801, 2218
McClain, Alva J., 773
medical missions, 807–808, 810
membership trends 1980 to 2000, 2220
Mennonite Brethren Churches, General Conference of, 814
in Mexico, 2261
Mexico, missionaries to, 820
Michigan Brethren settlement, 824
military chaplaincy, 2157
military service, 831–832
millenialism, 834
minister of music position, 843–844
ministry, 847
Ministry Handbook of 1999, 2331
minorities, ethnic and racial, 850, 851
mission schools, 854
mission statement, 2148–2149
missionary conferences, 856
Missionary Convocation, 856
missions, 268, 280, 860, 862
    in Argentina, **53**
    in Brazil, 20
    short-term, 2226
motion pictures, 879
musical instruments, 900, 2228
naming based on church polity, 910–911
National Achievement Competition (NAC), 914
National Brethren Bible Conference as alternate annual meeting for, 914
National Conference, *See* Grace Brethren National Conference
National Fellowship of Grace Brethren Men affiliation, 915–916
Native Americans, 2230
neoorthodox influence, 923
in New Mexico, 931
and nonconformity, 3
noncreedalism and statement of faith, 943
Ohio, history of, 1916
ordination, 980
Oregon, 981
organization by Grace Brethren movement, 911
Ozark Church of the Brethren, MI, 986
Patterson, Roy A., legal consultant for, 995
peace education, 1002
peace position, 1000
Pennsylvania, 1005
pension funds, 1007
Peters family, 1012
Philadelphia, PA, Third Brethren Church, 1019
placement of pastors, 1028
Plaster, David R. on, 2350
polity, 1044–1045
prayer veil, 1053
predestination, 1055
Presbyterian seminaries, attended by some leaders, 1056
Progressive Brethren church government, 1044–1045
prophecy conferences, 1062
in Puerto Rico, 2262

rebaptism, 2178, 2181, 2182
reorganization, 2182–2183
retirement homes, 8, 1102
revivalism, 1210
Roman Catholic Church, view of, 1120
salaried ministry and, 3
salary for ministers, 1137
sanctification theology, 1210
schisms, 251, 287, 293, 294, 303, 332, 366
schools, Christian, 2088
secondary schools, 1163
sermons, 1168
Shenandoah Valley, VA, congregations in, 1176
split of, 2332, 2334, 2363
stand on Vietnamese War, 1305
statement of faith, 133
Sunday school program, 1239
Teevan, John on, 2335
Tennessee, 1253
Texas, 1255
theology, 1259
theology and, 2254, 2255
tobacco use, 1266
urban ministry and, 2257
views on communism, 1288
Virginia, 1308
Washington, D.C., 391
wedding customs, 1326
West Virginia, 1337
Whitcomb, John C., Jr. on schism in, 2363
Willoughby, William G. on, 2363
women and, 2263–2264
women, roles of, 1361, 1362
World War II, 1372
worship and, 2266, 2267
worship, public, 1377
Young, Jerry R. on leadership and, 2365
youth and, 2268–2269
youth ministries, 2183
youth programs, 1392
Fellowship of Hope, 329, 439, **488**, 1085, *See also* Shalom Covenant Communities
Fellowship of Reconciliation, 169, **488**, *See also* International Fellowship of Reconciliation
Bushong, Benjamin G., 233
Consultative Committee, 2200
Curry, Abram Stauffer, 356–357
Helstern, Russell Fred, 596
International Fellowship of Reconciliation, 659
Muste, Abraham Johannes, 901
Fells, H. William, 1614, 2301, **2382**
Massillon, OH, Jackson Bible Church (BC), pastor, 801
Felpel family, 749
Felthouse, John V., 439, 1614
North Tampa, FL, Zion Church of the Brethren, elder and presiding elder, 950
Felthouse, Mary, 439
Felton, Ralph, 1323
Felts, Pauline Alice (later Yoder), 1917
Femailings, Womaen's Caucus newsletter, 1359
feminism
denomination name, and exclusion of women in name "Brethren," 911

Fellowship of Grace Brethren Churches (FGBC), 486, 487
grammer of, Eller, Vernard on, 2329
impact of, **2183–2184**
Re-imagining Conference and, 2240
Smeltzer, Mary Blocher (CB) and, 2250
sources on, 2320
fencerow theology, Meyer, Lauree Hersch on, 2347
Feng Shang Pen, 201
Fenig, Bruce, 1614
Fenstermacher, J. Howard, 1936
Fercken, Gaston John, **488**, 505, 1246, 1385, 1614, 1837, 1936
prayer, writings on, 1051
Turkey, 1280
Fercken, Seline (Phebe) Roberdean Shober, **488**, 1837
Fergus, Morris F., 1936
Fergus, Walter M., 1614
Ferguson, Ashley, 1614
Ferguson, Autrain (later Stoner), 1221
Ferguson family, 2076
Ferguson, Horace, 1399
Ferguson, Isaiah B., 1614
Ferguson, John, 216, 1614
Fern, Guy Smiley, 1235, 1614
Rockton, PA, Church of the Brethren, pastor, 1118
Fern Ridge, British Columbia, Canada, 15
Fernald, IA, Church of the Brethren, **488**
Fernald, T. Herbert, 1614
Ferrell, Abraham, 1614
Ferreri, Marcelo, 2278
Ferris, Myrtle, 2107
Ferris, Robert Dale, 1338, 1614
Paradise, CA, Church of the Brethren, 992
Ferrum, VA, First Church of the Brethren, 43, **488**
Ferster, Barbara Ann, 1936
fertilization techniques, 2127
Ferverda, Irene Shock, 1936
Fesler, Frederic, 1614
Fesler, G., W., 2071
Rock Creek Church of the Brethren, CO, elder, 1116
Fesler, George, 641, 1614
Fesler, Wayne L., 6, 1614, 2301
Fess, Louisa Barbara (later Root), 1122
Fessler, George, 2071
Fessler, M. G.
Oak Grove Church of the Brethren, IA, district meeting delegate, 955
Fessler, Sam, 2071
Festschrifts
Durnbaugh, D. F., 2186
Snyder, Graydon F., 2351
fetal tissue therapy, 2127
fetal tissue, use of
Church of the Brethren, 2178
Fether, Eric J., 2278
Fether, Homer A., 1614
Fether, Wilbur Ellis, 1614, 1936
Maitland Church of the Brethren, PA, salaried minister, 783
Fetter family, *See* Vetter
Mortonhouse (ship), 2373, 2376
Fetter Hall, 211
Fetter, Lucas, *See* Vetter, Lukas
Fetterhoff, Dean, 1614, 1936, **2184**
Marietta, GA, Grace Brethren Church

of Greater Atlanta, pastor, 793
Fetterhoff, Robert D., 122, 1365, 2183, 2278
Fetterman, Ivan Clyde, 1614, 1936, 2301
Montgomery Church of the Brethren, PA, pastor, 872
Oaks, PA, Green Tree Church of the Brethren, pastor, 958
Penn Run Church of the Brethren, PA, pastor, 1004
Fetters, Enoch R., 130, 347, 503, 1614
Fetters, Grace Prudence, 1614
Fetzer, Edna M., 2094
Fetzer family
Reliance, VA, Mount Zion Brethren Church, 1096
Fetzer, John Earl, 1936
Fever! The Hunt for a New Killer (John Fuller)
nurse missionaries, 952
Fey, Harold E., 1936
FGBC: The Electronic Newsletter of the Fellowship of Grace Brethren Churches, 2183
Fiant, Isaiah
Mount Zion Church of the Brethren, KS, 888
Fiant, Rachel
Mount Zion Church of the Brethren, KS, 888
Fichte, Johann Gottlieb
Pietist background, 1022
fichu, *See* neckerchief
Ficke, Edith (later Leckrone), 733
fiction, 26, 2016, *See also* literature
for children, 2030
juvenile, 2047, 2052
Myer, Anna Balmer, 2027
Noffsinger, Sadie Brallier, 2031
Priddy, Mollie, 2039
Rhoads, John N., 2044
Richardson, W. H., 2045
Richter, Conrad M., 2045
fiction, references to Brethren in
Amish Church, 2106–2107
Beaver Creek, MD, congregation, 2083
Brethren movement, 2067
creative writers, dictionary of, 2090
Dunkard Brethren Church, 2083, 2099
emigration
crossing the Atlantic Ocean, 2097
from Indiana to Fruitdale, AL, 2097
Ephrata Community, 2083, 2089
Fruitdale, AL, 2097
Indiana, 2097
Oklahoma, 2099
racial issues, 2072
Seventh Day Baptist Church, 2076
Snow Hill Nunnery, 2083
Ticknor, Bessie (author), 2083
Fiddler, Abner, 1614
Fidler, Andrew, 1614
Fiddler, John W., 213, 313, 581, 1614
Field, Gregory, 436, 1615
Field, L. A., *497*
Field, Louis, 1615
field program, 2050
Fields, Damon Wagner, 2278
Fields, Fayette, 1615
Fields, Harry M., 713, 1615
Fields, James L., 1615
Fields, John Henry, 1615

Fields, Robert, 1615
    Ramey Flats Church of the Brethren,
        VA, minister, 1083
Fields, Susan Wagner, 2278
Fife, Angeline, 496
Fife, Don, 496
Fife, Gladys, 496
Fife, Ken, 496
Fife, Lester, 496
Fife, Marian (later Beeghley), 2134
Fife, Paul, 496
Fife, Peggy, 496
Fife, Rosanna, 496
Fifer, Barbara Ellen (Ella or Ellie) Kinsey,
    488
Fifer, Charles, 570
Fifer, Eli, 488
Fifer, Elizabeth Garber, 488
Fifer, Ella Kinsey, 696
Fifer, Jesse C., **488–489,** 696, 1306
Fifteenth Amendment, 1
fifteenth century revolutionary peasant
    movements, 28
Figarden Church of the Brethren , CA, **489**
    Fresno, CA, First Church of the
        Brethren, 516
Figdale, CA, Church of the Brethren, *See*
    Figarden Church of the Brethren,
    CA
Figgers, Frank H., 1615
    Oronoco Church of the Brethren, VA,
        pastor, 982
Figgers, Robert H., Jr., 1615
Figgers, Robert M., 228, 1615
    Oronoco Church of the Brethren, VA,
        pastor, 982
Figgers, Robert W.
    Oronoco Church of the Brethren, VA,
        982
Figley, Stephen
    Sebring, FL, Grace Brethren Church,
        pastor in, 1162
Figueroa, Isabel Martinez
    Rio Piedras, PR, Segunda Iglesia Cristo
        Misionera Fellowship (CB) and,
        2243
Figueroa, Morales Juan A., 2278
    Rio Piedras, PR, Segunda Iglesia Cristo
        Misionera Fellowship (CB) and,
        2243
Fike, Aaron, 468, 489, 912, 1615
Fike, Abraham R., 320, 1240, 1615
Fike, Albert J., 417, 1615, 2184
Fike, Albert S., 1615
Fike, Alva Clayton, 1615
    Peace Valley Church of the Brethren,
        MO, free minister, 1003
Fike, Bert J., 1240, 1615
Fike, Bertha (later Whitacre), 1339
Fike, Catherine (later Gnagey), 554
Fike, Cecil Wayne, 1615
Fike, Christian, 489, 1873
Fike, Christian, Jr., 489
Fike, Christian, Sr., 489
Fike, Christina, 913
Fike, Clarence Beachy, 243, 515, 557,
    1615, 2301
    Peace Valley Church of the Brethren,
        MO, 1003
Fike, Daniel, family
    Milledgeville, IL, Brethren Church,
        833
Fike, Daniel M., 1615

Fike, David A., 2184
Fike, Donald LeRoy, 261, 1243, 1615
    Hispanic Ministries (CB), 2199
    Peace Valley Church of the Brethren,
        MO, 1003
    Rio Prieto, PR, Iglesia de los
        Hermanos (CB) and, 2243
    Yahuecas, PR, Iglesia de los Hermanos
        Cristo Nuestra Paz (CB) and, 2267
Fike, Douglas Lee, 1615, 2278
    Lancaster, PA, Acts Covenant Fellow-
        ship, 2213
Fike, Dwynn, 2184
Fike, Earle W., Jr., 101, 191, 1615, 1936,
    2035, **2184**
    mass media, 801
    Parish Ministries Commission, execu-
        tive secretary in, 993
    on prayers for worship, 2331
    sermons, 2331
Fike, Earle W., Sr., 558, 1287, 1615
    Petersburg, WV, Memorial Church of
        the Brethren, pastor, 1012
    Roanoke, VA, Ninth Street Church of
        the Brethren, pastor, 1113
Fike, Effie (later Harsh), 587
Fike, Elizabeth (later Lichty), 741
Fike, Ella Mae Forney, 2184
Fike, Elna, 467
Fike, Elra, 1936
Fike, Emerson Samuel, 469, 1615
    Mount Hermon Church of the
        Brethren, VA, pastor, 881
    New Hope Church of the Brethren, VA,
        pastor, 929
Fike, Emma (later Neher), 2029
Fike, Emra Trenton, 728, 1615, 1936
    Oak Grove Church of the Brethren,
        MD, elder, 956
Fike, Ervin T., 1615
Fike, Etta (later Bittinger), 143
Fike, Ezra Edwin, 584, 1615, 1936
    on Fike, John T. and descendants, 2331
    on Fike, Olivia Rogers and descendants
        of, 2331
Fike, Ezra T., 425
Fike, F. W., 1615
Fike family, 58, 165, 430, *489,* **489–490,**
    1336, 1936
    children named for Bible personages,
        912
    descendants of Susanna Beeghly and
        Christian Fike, 430
    Garrett Co., MD, 1975
    Nezperce, ID, Church of the Brethren,
        935
    Peace Valley Church of the Brethren,
        MO, 1003
Fike, Faye Davidson
    Fike, John T., history and genealogy of,
        2331
    on Fike, Olivia Rogers, ascendants and
        descendants of, 2331
Fike, Galen Ezra, *489,* 584, 692, 1615
Fike, George Daws, 913, 1615
Fike, Hannah Myers, 2184
Fike, J. H., 442, 1615
    Middlebury, IN, Church of the
        Brethren, presiding elder, 826
Fike, J. J., 1615
Fike, J. Melvin, 2278
Fike, J. Rogers
    Mount Pleasant Church of the

Brethren, VA, pastor, 887
Fike, Jacob, 489
Fike, Jean Kiser
    mass media, 801
Fike, Jerry Lee, 2278
Fike, Jo Ellen (later Bowman), 2184
Fike, John, 489
Fike, John G., 1615
Fike, John Michael, 1615, 1936, 2278
Fike, John Rogers, 1615
Fike, John S., 1615
Fike, Jon, 2184
Fike, Jonas, 584, 1615
Fike, Joseph, 2184
Fike, Juanita, 1837
Fike, Lester Earl, 257, 467, 923, 1616,
    1936, 2301, **2382**
    Pleasant Chapel Church of the
        Brethren, IN, pastor, 1030
    Peace Valley Church of the Brethren,
        MO, 1003
Fike, Lisa Jayne, 2278
Fike, Lorenzo H., 2382
Fike, Lydia (later Gnagey), 554
Fike, Lydia (later Miller)
    Miller, Eliza Belle, mother of, 837
    Miller, Sadie Jane, mother of, 842
Fike, M. H., 1287
Fike, Magdalena Arnold, 489
Fike, Mary Antes
    Peace Blossom Congregation of CB,
        MD, 2331
Fike, Mary (later Thomas), 1262
Fike, Matthew P., 2278
Fike, Moses, 144, 468, 489, 912, 1616
    family reunion (photo caption), 2373
Fike, Noah H., 1287, 1616
    Mount Zion Church of the Brethren,
        WV, 888
Fike, Olivia Rogers
    Fike, Faye Davidson on ascendants and
        descendants of, 2331
Fike, Olonzo Paul, 1616
Fike, Oscar Ray, 130, 343, 567, 1616
    Rossville, IN, Church of the Brethren,
        minister, 1124
    Peace Valley Church of the Brethren,
        MO, 1003
Fike, Paul Henry, 415, 425, 1616, **2184**
    Michigan City, IN, Church of the
        Brethren, part-time pastor, 825
    Pleasant Valley Church of the Brethren,
        VA, pastor, 1035
Fike, Peter L., Sr., 489, 1616
Fike, Phineas Landis, 1616
    Peace Valley Church of the Brethren,
        MO, presiding elder, 1003
Fike, Rachael Snyder, 489
Fike, Sallie, 2184
Fike, Samuel A., 101, 430, **489,** 490, 1616
Fike, Samuel K., 417, 1337, 1616
Fike settlement, ND, 164
Fike, Shirley
    Hispanic Ministries (CB), 2199
    Yahuecas, PR, Iglesia de los Hermanos
        Cristo Nuestra Paz (CB) and, 2267
Fike, Silas Wesley, 1616
Fike, Sophia Rudolph, 144
    family reunion (photo caption), 2373
Fike, Tobias Snyder, 1264, 1616
    Rocky Ridge, MD, Monocacy Church
        of the Brethren, presiding elder,
        1119

Fike, Uriah J., 1616
Fike, Valeria J., 2278
Fike, Walter A., 1616
Filbrun, Bertha Churchbaugh, 2184
Filbrun, Christina, 490
Filbrun, Clarence, 2184
Filbrun, David S., 298, 1298
Filbrun, Della (later Eikenberry), 1927
Filbrun, Elisabeth Harshbarger, 490
Filbrun family, 142, **490**, 1280
Filbrun, Henry H., 1616
Filbrun, Henry Joseph, 264, 1223, 1616
Filbrun, J. J., 572, 1212
Filbrun, Jacob, 470
Filbrun, Johann Peter, 490, 2184
Filbrun, John
 Sand Creek Old German Baptist
  Brethren Church, KS, 1143
Filbrun, Jonas, 268
Filbrun, Joseph, 270, 490, 1223, 1616
 Pleasant Hill Old German Baptist
  Brethren Church, IL, deacon and
  minister, 1033
Filbrun, Joseph J., 1616
Filbrun, Lowell, 1616
 Maple Grove Old German Baptist
  Brethren Church, OH, minister,
  791
Filbrun, Lydia
 Sand Creek Old German Baptist
  Brethren Church, KS, 1143
Filbrun, Mohler, 1277
Filbrun, Parker Milton, 1616
Filbrun, Peter, 490, 599
Filbrun, Roger, 2278
Filbrun, Stanley Clarence, 1280, 1616,
 2184–2185
 Modesto, CA, Old German Baptist
  Brethren Church, minister, 867
 Olive Grove Old German Baptist
  Brethren Church, CA, presiding
  elder, 973
Filbrun, Stanley Clarence, **2184–2185**
Filbrun (Vielbrunn, Fillbrunn, Brunn, Brun)
 family
 family history, 2005
Filbrun, Wilma Lucille Kinzie, 2184
Fillbrun, Alexander
 Mack, Alexander, Sr., 775
Fillbrun, Christina (later Mack)
 Mack, Alexander, Sr., 775
 Mack, Johann Philipp, 778
Fillbrunn, Günter, 2346
Filless, Tony, 590
Filley German Baptist Brethren Church,
 NE, **2374**
Fillmore, A. Green, 1616
 Red River Church of the Brethren, OK,
  elder, 1089
Fillmore, CA, 238, 1247
Fillmore, CA, congregation
 Ogden, William Augustus, pastor, 961
Fillmore, CA, First Brethren Church
 (FGBC), 101, **490**
Fillmore Co., MN
 Minnesota Brethren settlement, 848
 Root River Church of the Brethren,
  MN, 1122
Fillmore Co., NB
 Bethel congregation, origins of, 920
Fillmore Co., NE, 463
Fillmore family, 141, 750, 1322
Fillmore (Filmore), John H., 1616

Fillmore, J. H.
 Pleasant Hill Church of the Brethren,
  IA, minister, 1032
Fillmore, John, 531, 1616
Fillmore, Oliver E., 1616
Fillmore, Walter A., 1616
film, *See* drama; motion pictures
Filmore family
 Greene, IA, Church of the Brethren,
  570
Filmore, John, 45
Filmore, John F., 570
Filson, John A., 232
final restoration, *See* universalism
finanacial services
 Brethren Benefit Trust, 2140
Finance Commission, **490**, 1278
 Commission of Fifteen, 327
 General Board, 535
 General Investment Council, 537
finances, *See* stewardship
financial associations
 credit unions, 351
financial management
 Trustee Board (Dunkard Brethren
  Church), 1278
Financial Secretary of Annual Conference
 (CB), **490**
financial statements
 published in *The Vindicator,* 1306
Finch, Samuel
 Pleasant Center Church of the
  Brethren, OH, minister, 1030
Finch, Thomas, 331
Finck, W. J., 1900
Finckh, Elsie E., 1616
Finding the Way (Barnes), 2134
Findlay, OH, congregation
 Jackson, Edward A., 2209
Findlay, OH, Grace Brethren Church, **490**
fines
 Brethren nonparticipation and
  Revolutionary War, American,
  1106
Finfrock, Elizabeth (later Snyder), *See*
 Snyder, Elizabeth Finfrock
Finfrock family
 Peace Valley Church of the Brethren,
  MO, 1003
Finfrock, Hubert
 Maitland, FL, Grace Brethren Church,
  783
Finfrock, Mildred
 Maitland, FL, Grace Brethren Church,
  783
Fingerle, John, 1213
Fingerly family
 Genesee Old German Baptist Brethren
  Church, MI, 540
Fingler, H., 1616
Finifrock, Lillie M., 1936
Fink, Christian, 531
Fink, Elizabeth, 531
Fink family, 1333
Fink, Mary A., 1936
Fink, Paul R., 755, 1616
Fink, Samuel, 152, 1616
Finkbiner, Audrey J., 2278
Finkbiner, Jeffrey L., 2278
Finkenbinder, George, 1616
 Prairie View Church of the Brethren,
  KS, minister, 1050
Finkenbinder, Katie (later Roesch), 1119

Finks, Frederick J., 1616, 2131, 2132, 2141
 Ashland Theological Seminary and,
  2249
 South America Theological Seminary
  (BC) and, 2252
Finks, Holly H., 2132
Finley, Donald C., 2278
Finley family, 1885
Finnell, Lucinda Alice Pugh, 490
Finnell, Ralph Theodore, 588, 2301, 1616
Finnell, Vera Hartsough, 588
Finnell, Virgil C., 248, 1936
Finnell, Virgil Carl, 248, **490**, 1616, 1936,
 See also tobacco
Finney, Beatrice, 1616
Finney, Charles G.
 American revivalism, 1104
 "New Measures" revivalism, 930–931
Finney Co., KS
 Fairview Old German Baptist Brethren
  Church, KS, 470
 Garden City, KS, Church of the
  Brethren, 530
 Prairie View Church of the Brethren,
  KS, members living in, 1050
Finney, Harriet Jane Wenger, 1616
 on compassion, spirituality of, 2331
Finney, Ronald Dean, 2165, 2278
Finney, William, 1616
Finney, William M., 1616
Finster, Robert D., 2278
Fipps, Elmer E., 1616
fire departments
 chaplaincy, 2158
fire fighters
 military service substitute, 301
fire fighting, **490–491**, *See also* conscien-
 tious objection (smokejumpers)
fire insurance, *See* insurance
fires, church
 Kelley Chapel, White Pine Church of
  the Brethren, WV, 1341
 Kittanning, PA, West Kittanning Grace
  Brethren Church, 699
 La Porte, IN, Church of the Brethren,
  713
 Landesville (Landess), IN, Church of
  the Brethren, 723
 Liberty Mills, IN, Church of the
  Brethren, 740
 Los Angeles, CA, Ladera Church of the
  Brethren, 759
 Louisville, OH, First Brethren Church,
  760
 Stiverson Church of the Brethren, WA,
  1223
 Summit Mills Grace Brethren Church,
  PA, 1236
 Sunnyslope Church of the Brethren,
  WA, 1240
 Surrey Old German Baptist Brethren
  Church, ND, 1242
 Timberville, VA, Church of the
  Brethren, 1265
 Vicksburg, PA, Grace Brethren Church,
  1305
 Walnut Church of the Brethren, IN,
  1315
 Walnut Grove Dunkard Brethren
  Congregation, MD, 1315
 White Church of the Brethren, IN,
  1339
 White Oak Church of the Brethren,

OH, 1340

Windber, PA, Rummel Church of the Brethren, 1348

Wood Colony Old German Baptist Brethren Church, CA, 1363

Worthington Church of the Brethren, MN, 1380

Firestone, E. C., 1617

Firestone family, 2077

Firestone, Joseph B., 1617

Rosepine, LA, Church of the Brethren, elder, 1123

Firestone, Leonard J., 1617

Firestone, Reid A., 2278

Firl, Robert L., 62, 1617

San Bernardino, CA, Grace Brethren Church, pastor, 1141

First Amendment

conscientious objectors, 336

First and Radical Reformations

Durnbaugh, Donald F. on, 2327

Opocensk, Milan on, 2349

Réamonn, Pàraic on, 2349

Slabaugh, Dennis L. on, 2357

First Baltimore Church, 1963

First Baptist Church, Cedar Rapids, IA, 265

First Baptist Church of Hammond, IN, 232

First Brethren Church (BC), Louisville, OH, 267

First Brethren Church, CA, 362

First Brethren Church, Chicago, IL, 1349

First Brethren Church, Dayton, OH, 241

Patterson, Roy A., in, 995

First Brethren Church, Hagerstown, MD, 155

First Brethren Church, Inglewood, CA

O'Neal, Glenn, 2236

First Brethren Church, Long Beach, CA

Nielson, Johanna, member of, 936

First Brethren Church, Nappanee, IN

Shively, Nora Early, 1178

First Brethren Church of Altoona, See Altoona, PA, Grace Brethren Church

bibliography, 1871

First Brethren Church of Ardmore, IN

South Bend, IN, Ardmore Brethren Church, 1203

First Brethren Church of Long Beach, CA, 282, See also Long Beach, CA, Grace Brethren Church

First Brethren Church of Martinsburg, PA

Martinsburg, PA, Grace Brethren Church, previous name of, 798

First Brethren Church of Middlebranch, OH

Middlebranch, OH, Grace Brethren Church, previous name of, 825

First Brethren Church of Modesto, CA

Modesto, CA, La Loma Grace Brethren Church, former name of, 867

First Brethren Church of New York, 933

First Brethren Church of Philadelphia, 1284

First Brethren Church of Philadelphia, PA

Ridgely, MD, Brethren Church, 1109

First Brethren Church of Pomona, CA

Pomona, CA, Church of the Brethren, 1045

First Brethren Church of Whittier, CA, 1342

First Brethren Church, OH, 241

First Brethren Church, Philadelphia, PA

McClain, Alva J., pastor, 772

First Brethren Church, Rittman, OH, 398

First Brethren Church, Udell, IA, 1285

First Brethren Church, VA, 349

First Brethren Church, WA, See Harrah, WA, Grace Brethren Church

First Brethren Church, Washington, D.C., 391

First Brethren Church, Waynesboro, PA, 1324

First Brethren Church, Whittier, CA

Sickel, Clarence Leroy, interim pastor, 1181

First Brethren Church, Winchester, VA, 1348

First Brethren Church, Wooster, OH, 1365

First Brethren congregation, CA, 192

First Brethren congregation, OH, 326

first Brethren (Europe), See European Brethren

first Brethren (Schwarzenau), See Schwarzenau Brethren

first Brethren (US), See Brethren, early (US)

First Central Church of the Brethren, Kansas City, KS, 683

The First Century of German Printing in America, 1728–1830

Seidensticker, Oswald, 1165

The First Christian Theology: Studies in Romans (Hoyt), 634

First Church congregation, VA, 1307

First Church congregation, Wichita, KS, 1343

First Church of the Brethren, Alliance, OH

bibliography, 1865

First Church of the Brethren, Altoona, PA, 204

First Church of the Brethren at Liberty Heights, MD, See Baltimore, MD, First Church of the Brethren

First Church of the Brethren, Brooklyn, NY, 932–933

Italian Sunday School (CB), 664

First Church of the Brethren, CA, 994

First Church of the Brethren, Kansas City, MO, 683

First Church of the Brethren, Lewistown, PA, 187, 240, 281

First Church of the Brethren, Los Angeles, CA

Chinese immigrants, 278

First Church of the Brethren of Dayton, OH, See Dayton, OH, Mack Memorial Church of the Brethren

First Church of the Brethren of Detroit, MI, See Harper Woods, MI, Detroit First Church of the Brethren

First Church of the Brethren of Hutchinson, See Hutchinson, KS, Community Church of the Brethren

First Church of the Brethren, OH, 367

First Church of the Brethren, PA

Wagner, Murray L., Jr. on, 2361

First Church of the Brethren, Philadelphia, PA, 161

First Church of the Brethren, Springfield, OH, 1215

First Church of the Brethren, York, PA, 1337, 1387–1388

First Church, Roanoke, VA

Peters Creek Church of the Brethren, VA, daughter congregation, 1011

First Day Baptist Church

Pennsylvania, 2077

First Day Baptists

Materials Towards a History of the Baptists, 803

names of Brethren fellowships, 910

First-Day Brethren

Sunday as Sabbath, 1133

First Day Dunkers, 210

First Day Society

Sunday school movement, 283

First Dry Creek Church of the German Baptist Brethren

Robins, IA, Church of the Brethren, 1115

First General Convention of the Brethren Church, See Ashland Convention

First Grace Brethren Church, Yakima, WA, 1383

First Grand Valley Church of the Brethren, CO, See Grand Junction, CO, Koinonia Brethren/Baptist Church

First Grand Valley congregation, CO, See Grand Junction, CO, Koinonia Brethren-Baptist Church

First Irricana Church of the Brethren, Canada, 1913

First Los Angeles congregation, 1275

The First Love (*Die Erste Liebe,* 1696), 43, 57

First Petition, 205, **491**, See also *Brethren's Reasons;* Miami Valley Petition; Reconsidered Petition

Miami Valley Petition, 823

Old Order Movement, 973

"First Reformation"

Prague Conferences and, 2239

First Reformed Presbyterian Church, Brooklyn, NY

Mackey, John Crawford, pastor, 779

First Spokane congregation, 1212

First Toledo Church of the Brethren, 1266–1267

Firstbrook, Clinton Fisk, III, 2278

Fiscel, David, 491

Fiscel, Emory (Emery) David, 360, **491**, 1617

Fiscel, Evelyn Henry, 491

Fiscel, Mary, 491

Fischer, Adam, 491

Fischer, Baron Adam von, 491

Fischer, Christian, 491

Fischer, Della Reagan, 1937

Fischer, Elizabeth Brower, 491

Fischer family

Musselman family related to by marriage, 901

Fischer (Fisher) family, **491**

Fischer, Johann, **491**, 580

prisons, 1059

Solingen Brethren, 1201

Fischer, 421

Fischer, Peter, 491

Fischer, Wilbur Ludwig, 1617

Fiscus family

Dutch Bethel, German Baptist Brethren Church, 2373

Fish, Amos

article about, 1925

fish, as symbol for the church, 1246

Fish, Leroy M., 1617

FISH program

Dayton, OH, Emmanuael Church of the Brethren, 365

Tacoma, WA, Larchmont Community

Church of the Brethren, 1247
Fish, Retha (later Eby), 419
Fishback family, 1937, 1983
Fishback, Harman
　descendants of, 1937
Fishback, Reuben DeWitt, 1937
Fishbauer family
　Root River Church of the Brethren,
　　MN, 1122
Fishbaugher, Harvey (E.), 1617
Fishbourn, Elizabeth (later Landis), 722
Fishburn, George A., 1617
　Overbrook, KS, Church of the
　　Brethren, elder, 986
Fishburn, Vera, 2092
Fishel, J. H., 1617
Fisher (later Neff), 922
Fisher, A. B., 503
Fisher, Abraham, 105
　South Haven Old German Baptist
　　Brethren Church, MI, minister,
　　1205
Fisher, Abram (Abraham), 248, 270, 373,
　1333, 1617
Fisher, Anna Belle Shoulders, 1617
Fisher, Ben, 1937
Fisher, Benjamin, 491, 1356
Fisher, Benjamin E., 1617
Fisher, Benjamin Lawrence, 1617
Fisher, C. Earl, 1617
Fisher, Calvin, 105, 373, 496, 1617
　North Fork Old German Baptist
　　Brethren Church, IN, minister, 947
Fisher, Charles Kenneth, 1617
Fisher, Chester Lynn, 1617
Fisher, Christian
　descendants of, 1927
　genealogy and descendants, 1937
　Southern Lancaster Grace Brethren
　　Church, PA, 1207
Fisher, David, 297, 464, 491
　Monticello/Pike Creek Church of the
　　Brethren, IN, 872
Fisher, E. R., 505
　New Hope Church of the Brethren, AR,
　　elder in, 929
Fisher, Earl, 79
Fisher, Edith Buck, 1937
Fisher, Elias, **491**, 1617
　minorities, ethnic and racial, 849
　Monrovia, MD, Bush Creek Church of
　　the Brethren, minister, 870
Fisher, Elizabeth Stoltzfus, 1937
Fisher, Emma, 217
Fisher, Enos, 1617
　Maple Grove Old German Baptist
　　Brethren Church, OH, minister,
　　791
　North Hampton, OH, Donnels Creek
　　Old German Baptist Brethren
　　Church, minister, 948
　South Haven Old German Baptist
　　Brethren Church, MI, minister,
　　1205
Fisher, Everett Russell, 1276, 1617
Fisher, Everett S., 1937
Fisher, F. A., 1617
Fisher family, 162, 215, 384, 700, 721, *See
　also* Fischer (Fisher) family
　Garrett, PA, Church of the Brethren,
　　531
　Honey Creek Church of the Brethren,
　　MO, 627

New Holland, PA, Church of the
　Brethren, 928
Poplar Valley Church of the Brethren,
　MT, 1047
Reiff family, 1094
Roanoke, VA, Washington Heights
　Grace Brethren Church, 1114
Fisher, Frank, 276, 491, **491**, 1617
　Mexico, IN, Church of the Brethren,
　　elder, 821
　orphans, care for, 982
Fisher, George
　South Bend, IN, Ardmore Brethren
　　Church, 1203
Fisher, Gideon, 1937
Fisher, Harley Medford, *See* Old German
　Baptist Brethren
Fisher, Harley Medford, 1617
Fisher, Harley U., 1617
Fisher, Harry Jacob, 1937
Fisher, Helen F.
　Massillon, OH, Trinity Church of the
　　Brethren, pastor, 801
Fisher, Henry
　Old Order German Baptist Church
　　minister, 972
Fisher, Herbert Allen, 367, 1245, 1617
　Massillon, OH, Trinity Church of the
　　Brethren, pastor, 801
Fisher, Herman
　article about, 1919
Fisher, Ira, 1617
Fisher, Irvin, 1617
Fisher, Isaac, 1617
Fisher, Jacob, 1617, 2077
　article about, 1919
Fisher, John Adam, 1335, 1617
　Olive Grove Old German Baptist
　　Brethren Church, CA, minister,
　　973
Fisher, John K., 1898
Fisher, John M., 1937
Fisher, John W., 492
Fisher, Joseph L., 633, 1617
Fisher, L. A., 1617
Fisher, Laura Bender, 492
Fisher, Lawrence, 496
Fisher, Lee M., 1617
　Slifer, IA, church of the Brethren, elder
　　and pastor, 1190
Fisher, Leo Jeard, 1617
Fisher, LeRoy, 1617
Fisher, Lester, 350, 1307, 1617, 2301, **2382**,
　See also Old German Baptist
　Brethren
Fisher, Levi, 1617
Fisher, Lillie Reiff, 491
Fisher, Lydia Barnard, 491
Fisher, Malinda, 627
Fisher, Mary, 496
Fisher, Mary (later Anspach), 40
Fisher, Max William, 1315, 1617
Fisher, Medford, 350
Fisher, Melvin, 496
Fisher, Mrs. Peter
　Mexico, IN, Brethren Church, 821
Fisher, Neil R., 2278
Fisher, Nevin Wishard, **492**, 1859, 1937,
　2073, **2374**, *See also* Fisher,
　Virginia Showalter
　historical writing, 612
　hymnals, 642
　McPherson, KS, First Church of the

Brethren, 780
Fisher, Virginia Showalter, 492
Fisher, Noah, 256, 637, 1617
Fisher, Norman Jerome, 1617
Fisher, Oscar, 1335
Fisher, P. M.
　New Enterprise Brethren Church, IN,
　　elder in, 927
　Peru, IN, First Brethren Church, 1010
Fisher, Perry A., 743, 1617
　St. Albany Old German Baptist
　　Brethren Church, WV, minister,
　　1134
Fisher, Peter M, 491, 1617
　family history, 1995
　Mexico, IN, Brethren Church, 821
Fisher, Ross B., 1617, 2301, **2382**
　Prices Creek Old German Baptist
　　Brethren Church, OH, presiding
　　elder, 1057
Fisher, Ruth
　Southern Lancaster Grace Brethren
　　Church, PA, 1207
Fisher, Silas Theodore, 1617
　Peru, IN, Church of the Brethren,
　　pastor, 1010
　Plevna, IN, Church of the Brethren,
　　minister, 1037
Fisher, Stanley, 1617
Fisher, Virginia Showalter, 492, **492**, 1937,
　2374
　historical writing, 612
Fisher, Walter G., 1618
Fisher, William Daniel, 1618
　family of, 1937
　Mexico Old German Baptist Brethren
　　Church, IN, minister, 821
Fishing Creek Valley house, Big Swatara
　Church of the Brethren, PA, 142
Fiske, Randall C., 2278
Fitchett, William R., 2278
Fitz, Conrad E., 7, 269, 1618
Fitz, Elizabeth (later Simon), 1120
Fitz family, 145
Fitz, Harriet L. (later Hoyt), 634
Fitz, John, 1356, 1364, 1618
Fitz, John, Sr., 69, 1618
Fitz Simon, Frances (later Rolston), 748,
　2047
Fitzgerald, J. F., 1265
Fitzgerald, John W., 102, 367, 758, 1618
　Roann, IN, (First) Brethren Church,
　　pastor, 1112
Fitzkee, Donald R., 2278
　on CB, Atlantic Northeast District of,
　　2331
　district histories, 2201
　on Lititz CB, 2331
Fitzsimmons family, 326
Fitzsimons, Walter G., 2278
Fitzwater, Andrew Johnson, 518, 1618
Fitzwater, Bella
　conversion of, and Oaks, PA, Green
　　Tree Church of the Brethren, 958
Fitzwater, Clerenda Delawder (Delauter?),
　492
Fitzwater, Cyprianus, 492
Fitzwater family
　Mount Cassell Old German Baptist
　　Brethren Church, WV, 880
Fitzwater, Isabella Umstad, 1286
Fitzwater, John W., 1618
Fitzwater, L. W., 1618

Saline Valley church of the Brethren, KS, minister, 1139
Fitzwater, Perry, Braxton, 118, 136, 137, **492,** 1618, 1937
Moody Bible Institute, 872
prophecy conferences, 1062
Sidney, OH, Trinity Church of the Brethren, minister, 1181
Fitzwater, S. W., 1618
Five Year Forward Movement (CB), *See* Forward Movement (CB)
Fix, Eleanor A., 2278
Fix, J. M., 496
Flack George, 1618
Flack, Lewis Hess, 345, 1618
flags, **492–493**
The Flaming Torch (Blair), 748
Flanagan, Robert, *See* Flannagan, Robert, Sr.
Flanigan family
Jenners, PA, Grace Brethren Church, 670
Flannagan, Robert, Sr., 551, 1618
Flanner, Jacob K., 1618
Flashlights from History (Flory), 407
Flat Creek Church of the Brethren (KY), 373, **493,** 689, 2130, **2374**
communion, *328*
Flat Creek, KY, Church of the Brethren mission , 44, *492*
Weldy, Allen (CB) and, 2261
flat-earth theory
Voliva, Wilbur Glenn, 282
Flat Rock Church of the Brethren, IN, **493**
Flat Rock Church of the Brethren, VA, 101, *493,* **493–494, 745,** 1265, 1276, 1307, 1313, 1314, 1323, 1349, 1350, 1364, 2101
Greenmount Church of the Brethren, VA, 571
history of, 2101
Mount Olivet Church of the Brethren, VA, 886
Pleasant View Church of the Brethren, VA, 1037
Flat Rock, NC, 1315
Church of the Brethren, **493,** 755, 946,
Mount Carmel Church of the Brethren, NC, 880
Pleasant Valley Church of the Brethren, NC, 1035
Flat Rock Old German Baptist Brethren Church, OH, 142, **494**
Flat Rock, PA, 1287
Flathead Valley Church of the Brethren, MT, *See* Whitefish, MT, Church of the Brethren
Flatin, Janet Flory, 417
Flaugherty Creek meetinghouse, PA, 1139
Fleischman, Dewey Denton, 130, 141, 744, 1618
memoirs, 2331
Fleischmann, Konrad A., 149, 542
Fleishman, D. W., 1618
Fleming, Anne Neiderhiser Royer, 494
Fleming, Avery, 1212
Fleming, Beverly, 1618
Fleming Co., KY, 171, 688
German Baptist Brethren Church, **494**
Fleming, Edward P., Sr., 2138
Fleming, James W., 1618
Fleming, John H., 1618
Fleming, Joseph H., 1618

Fleming, Lenoir Avery, **494,** 1618
Fleming, Martha Griffith, 494
Fleming, Ronald Ray, 1618, 2166
Fleming, W. F., 2088
Fleming, Wealthy Ihrig, 494
Fleming, William, 494
Flemming, J. W., 1618
Flenner, Jacob, 1618
Fleshman, Abraham, 744
Fleshman, Andrew L., 1618
Fleshman, Elijah P., 744, 1216, 1618
Red Oak Ridge German Baptist Brethren Church, WV, elder, 1089
Fletcher, Elbert, 1618
Fletcher family, 1348
Fleure, Abraham, 495
Fleure, Anna Kagy, 495
Fleure, Catherine Garber, 495
Fleure, Elizabeth Beeghly, 495
Fleure, Emmanuel, 495
Fleure family, *See* Flora (Flory) family
Fleure, Henry, 495
Fleure, Jacob, 495
Fleure, John, 495
Fleure, Joseph, 495
Fleure, Joseph, Jr., 495
Fleure, Katherine (later Neff), 495
Fleure, Mary, 495
Fleure, Sarah Kagy, 495
Fleure, Susannah (later Beeghly), 495
Fleury (Flory, Flora) family
family history, 2006
Fleury, Joseph J.
descendants, 1938
Flick, Clyde, 1618
Flick family
Reading Grace Brethren Church, PA, 1084
Flick, Thomas E., 1618, 2278
Flickinger, Andreas, 1937
Flickinger, Catherine (later Lint), 744
Flickinger, Daniel Kumler, 1937
Flickinger, Eli, 1934
Flickinger, family
history of, 1937
Flickinger, Johannes, 1937
Flickinger, Joseph, 1937
Flickinger, Peter, 1937
Flickinger, Robert Elliott, 1937
Flickinger, S. H., 1937
Flickinger, Ulrich, 1937
Flinn, John, 115
Flint, Donald K., 1618
Flint, MI, Church of the Brethren, **494**
Flint Daily Journal, 494
Flint, Timothy, 1937
Flintstone, MD, Glendale Church of the Brethren, 21, 62, **494**
Flohr, Anna E. Kipe, 494
Flohr, Charles G., 1618
Flohr, Daniel S., 1618
Flohr, Earl Wilbur, 1618, 1837
Flohr, Ella Miller, 1837
Flohr, Hilda (later Strayer), 1228
Flohr, Leonard J., 1618
Flohr, Lewis Benton, **494,** 1305, 1618, 1920
Service Committee for Conscientious Objectors, 1372
Flohr, Matthias Ryston, 1618
Flohr, Ryson M., 1618
floods
Brethren Haus, Linz, Austria, 746

Johnstown, and sharing of church buildings, 1151–1152
Johnstown, PA, 385
Lichtenstein, 1367
Summit Mills Grace Brethren Church, PA, 1236
Flora, A. W.
Maxwell, IA, Church of the Brethren, minister, 803
Oak Grove Church of the Brethren, IA, district meeting delegate, 955
Flora, Abraham, 495, 496, 1618
Flora, Abraham J., 496
Flora, Abraham Y., 1618
Flora, Alfred, 496, 1618
Flora, Amos K., 633, 1618
Old Brethren minister, 965
Flora, Anna Myer
Skiles, Clement S. (OGBB) and, 2249
Flora, Arlene Surbey, 2185
Flora, B. D.
Pigg River Old German Baptist Brethren Church, VA, minister, 1023
Flora, Mrs. Ben Clarence, 377
Flora, Benjamin D., 1618
Pigg River Old German Baptist Brethren Church, VA, elder-in-charge, 1023
Flora, Benjamin H., 15, 24, 231, 269, 318, 363, **494–495,** 495, 496, 567, 914, 1618
Dutchtown Brethren Church, IN, 411
Flora, Blanche, 494
Flora, Bruce H., 442, 759, 1247, 1618, 1937, 2301
Reedley, CA, Church of the Brethren, pastor, 1091
Okeechobee, FL, Grace Brethren Church, pastor, 963
Flora, C. A., 1619
Flora, C. O.
Monte Vista Church of the Brethren, VA, trustee, 871
Flora, Carl, 496
Flora Church of the Brethren, ND, **496**
Flora, Clara Myers, 211, **495,** 1285, 1360, 1619
Flora, Clarence, 377
Flora, Mrs. Clarence, 377
Flora, Damuel H., 1323
Flora, Daniel, 1217
Flora, Darrell E., 1619
Flora, David, 65, 318, 467, 1619
Flora, Delbert Benjamin, 68, **495,** 1619, 1938, **2374, 2382**
Flora, Duane, 1223, 1619
Flora, Earl, 576, 674, 1281
Flora, Earl L., 430, 1619, **2382**
Flora, Earl S., 20, 104, 1212, 1619
Flora, Earl W., 105, 1619
Flora, Elizabeth Garver, 431
Flora, Elmer R., 1619
Sand Creek Old German Baptist Brethren Church, KS, elder-in-charge, 1143
Flora, Emanuel, 1619
Flora, Emily Saul, 2103
Flora, Esther (Hettie) Marie (later Skiles)
Skiles, Clement S. (OGBB) and, 2249–2250
Flora, Ezra
Skiles, Clement S. (OGBB) and, 2249

Flora family, 142, 157, 165, 360, 384, 1281, 2088
    Graybill (Grabill, Krehbiel) family, 567
    Guthrie Church of the Brethren, MN, 576
    Jamison family, 668
    Peters family related by marriage, 1012
    Pipe Creek Old German Baptist Brethren Church, IN, 1026
    South Haven Old German Baptist Brethren Church, MI, 1205
Flora (Flory), Amos W., 1618
Flora (Flory) family, **495–496**
Flora (Flory, Fleury) family
    family history, 2006
Flora (Flory), Henry, 1619
Flora (Flory), Newton B., 1619
Flora, Fred A., 1619
Flora, George, 496
Flora, George B., 1619
Flora, Gerald Alan, 2278
Flora, Goldie (later Harter), 1958
Flora, Henry
    Maxwell, IA, Church of the Brethren, minister, 803
Flora, Hollis E., 1619
    Oak Grove Old German Baptist Brethren Church, OH, minister, 956
    Old Brethren minister, 965
Flora, Howard G., 1619
    Mexico Old German Baptist Brethren Church, IN, elder-in-charge, 821
Flora, IN, 1338
    Skiles, Clement S. (OGBB) and, 2249–2250
    Turner, Charles W. (FGBC) and, 2256
Flora, IN, Bachelor Run Old German Baptist Brethren Church, **496**
    Flora, John F., 495
Flora, IN, Church of the Brethren, 77, 232, **496**
Flora, IN, (First) Brethren Church, **496,** 232, 2227
Flora, IN, Grace Brethren Church, **496**
    Malles, Mark Ellsworth, 2217
Flora, J. Allen (Allan), 1619
Flora, J. B., 373
    Monte Vista Church of the Brethren, VA, trustee, 871
Flora, J. C., 431, 578, 674, 1277
Flora, J. Henry, 1223
Flora, J. Parker, 1619
Flora, Jacob, 496, 1619
Flora, Jacob B., 105, 321, 1619
Flora, Jacob Henry, 1619
Flora, Jacob, Jr., 43
    Pigg River Old German Baptist Brethren Church, VA, minister, 1023
Flora, Jacob, Sr., 1938
Flora, James S., 511, 1619, 1938
    Palmyra, PA, Church of the Brethren, 991
Flora, Jerry R., 494, 1619, 1938
    on Women's Missionary Society presidents, 2331
    The Message of Faith, 2141, 2148, 2156
    mission statement, ad hoc committee, 2137
Flora, Joel B.
    Pigg River Old German Baptist

Brethren Church, VA, elder-in-charge, 1023
    Pigg River Old German Baptist Brethren Church, VA, minister, 1023
Flora, Joel Cephas, 1619, 1938
Flora, John, 430
Flora, John F., **495,** 496, 1619
Flora, John H., 105, 248, 1385, 1619, **2382**
    Salem Old German Baptist Brethren Church, OH, elder-in-charge, 1139
Flora, John H. (2), 2301
Flora, John, Sr., 1958
Flora, John W., 633, 1619
Flora, Jonas, 496
Flora, Joseph Eugene, 360, 1619, **2185,** 2301
Flora, Josiah, 2185
Flora, Julie
    on Women's Missionary Society presidents, 2331
Flora, Katherina, *See* Flure, Katherina (later Naff)
Flora, Kermit P., 1619, 1938
Flora, L. W., 264
Flora, Levi W., 1346, 1619
Flora, Lloyd C.
    Old Brethren German Baptist Church, minister, 965
    Old Order German Baptist Church minister, 972
Flora, Lydia Brubaker, 495
Flora, Mable, 496
Flora, Malissa (later Jamison), 668
Flora, Malisse I. Allbaugh, 495
Flora, Marshall L., Sr., 1884
Flora, Martha, 1217
Flora, Mary
    "From Among Them," 2000
Flora, Mary Elizabeth, 1836
Flora, Mary Elizabeth (later Eikenberry), 431
Flora, Maurice R., 1837
Flora, Merit, 267
Flora, Mrs. Merit, 267
Flora, Myrl J., 1223, 1619, 2301, **2382**
Flora, ND, congregation, 256, **496**
    Pleasant Valley Church of the Brethren, ND, 1035
Flora, Noah A., 211, 360, 495, 1285, 1619
    Mulvane, KS, Brethren Church, pastor, 896
Flora, Opel, 1938
Flora, R. Franklin
    family history, 1972
Flora, Reis, 1837
Flora, Reuben, 2301
    Old Brethren minister, 965
Flora, Riley, 1619
Flora, Riley J., 1619
Flora, Robert, 1223, 1619
Flora, Rollo, 105, 1619
    Mexico Old German Baptist Brethren Church, IN, minister, 821
Flora, Romayne Keyes, 495
Flora, Rosemary Blickenstaff, 1837
Flora, Samuel Henry, Jr., 80, 94, 1619
    Pleasant Valley Church of the Brethren, VA, pastor, 1035
Flora, Samuel Henry, Sr., 1619
    Fraternity Church of the Brethren, NC, 511
    Mount Hermon Church of the

Brethren, VA, pastor, 881
Flora, Sarah Jamison, 2185
Flora, Sarah Trent, 494
Flora, Solomon, 496, 1619
Flora-Swick, Mark John, 2278
Flora, Sylvus Dean, 1619
Flora, Verne U., 1620
Florence, MI, Church of the Brethren, 496, **2374**
    Shipshewana, IN, Church of the Brethren, organized from, 1177
Florida, 496–497, 691, 2023, 2025, 2034, *See also* Brethren House Ministries (BC); Camp Ithiel (CB)
    colonization, 324
    Huffman, Nelson Thomas, 2205
    Miami, FL, Eglise des Frères Haitians, 2222
    migrant labor camps, 827, *828*
    migration of Brethren, 831
    The Missionary Board (BC), 856
    Old German Baptist Brethren, 967, 970, 2001
Florida Brethen Homes
    The Palms, 758
    Peters, Raymond Russell, 1011
    retirement community, 991
    Sebring, FL, J. H. Moore Memorial Church of the Brethren, 1162
    Weimer, Glen Emerson, 1327
Florida Fellowship of Grace Brethren Churches, 497
Florida Live Wires, 1938
Florin, PA, 1334
    Church of the Brethren, *See* Mounty Joy, PA, Florin Church of the Brethren
Flory, A. E.
    Plum Creek Old German Baptist Brethren Church, KS, minister, 1038
Flory, A. J., 1620
Flory, Abbie McCurry (McKinney?), 498
Flory, Abraham, **497,** 498, 1223, 1620, 2087
Flory, Abram
    North Fork Old German Baptist Brethren Church, IN, elder, 947
Flory, Abram E., 1620
Flory, Albert L., 64, 114, 755, 1221, 1620
    San Diego, CA, Grace Brethren Church, pastor, 1141
Flory, Anna
    Sand Creek Old German Baptist Brethren Church, KS, 1143
Flory, Annie Cline, *495*
Flory, Arthur Edmund, 246, 1346, 1620
Flory, Barbara Sites, *495*
Flory, Benjamin F., 743, 1280. 1620
    Nishney Valley German Baptist Brethren, IA, minister in, 938
    Pleasant Valley German Baptist Brethren Church, NE, 2377
Flory, Bertha B. Bechtle, 499
Flory, Brian T., 2278
Flory, Byron Morton, Jr., 1383, 1620
Flory, Byron Morton, Sr., 1620, 1383, 1938, 2185
    article about, 1939
    termpaper about, 1945
Flory, Byron S., 1620
Flory, Carol, 1938

Flory, Catherine S. Driver, 498
Flory, Charles David, 373, 1277, 1620
Flory, Charles Larkin, 1620
    Piqua, OH, Church of the Brethren,
        pastor, 1026
    Pleasant Hill, OH, Church of the
        Brethren, pastor, 1032
Flory, Christian, 1620
Flory, Christopher, 1346, 1620
    Plum Creek Old German Baptist
        Brethren Church, KS, elder, 1038
Flory, Claude R., 1938
Flory, D. H., 1620
Flory, Dan
    Peru, IN, Church of the Brethren, pas
        tor, 1010
Flory, Daniel Christian, 206, 207, 453, *472,
    497,* **497–498,** 1213, 1315, 1346,
    1391, 1620
    biography, 1938
    college founder, 1982
    Sanger, Conrad, descendant of, 1144
Flory, Daniel (Dee) Casper, 129, 494, 1620
Flory, David, 766, 1295, 1620
Flory, Denton, 2278
Flory, Donald Robert, 1620
    Medina, OH, Church of the Brethren,
        2219
Flory, Earl, 350, 1620
Flory, Edna Rosamond, 1837
    article about, 1939
Flory, Eldon, 721, 731, 1620, 2278
    Hart, MI, Dunkard Brethren Congrega-
        tion, 2196
Flory, Elihu K., 1620
    New River Old German Baptist
        Brethren Church, ministers for,
        931
Flory, Elizabeth Adams, 499
Flory, Elizabeth (later Sanger)
    Sanger, Samuel F., mother of, 1143
Flory, Elmer, 499
Flory, Emanuel, 1333, 1620
    Salem Church of the Brethren, OH,
        elder, 1138
Flory, Emily Tabor, 499
Flory, Emma Brumbaugh, 498
Flory, Etta Helman, 1620
Flory, Ezra Younce, **498,** 499, 1239, 1620,
    1938
Flory family, 153, 405, 447, *472,* 700, 753,
    1286, 1938, *See also* Flora family
    article about, 1919
    Good (Guth) family, 556
    Neher family, related to, 922
        North English, IA, Church of the
            Brethren, 947
    Salem Church of the Brethren, OH,
        1138
    Sanger family, related to, 1144
    Shady Grove Old German Baptist
        Brethren Church, OH, 1171
Flory (Flora, Fleury) family
    family history, 2006
Flory, Frances Garber, 498
Flory, Frank Herbert, 1346, 1620
Flory, Galen R., 2156, 2278
Flory, George B., 461, 1620
Flory, George W., **498,** 1620, 1938
    Rileyville, VA, Church of the Brethren,
        holding revival at, 1109
    Roanoke, VA, Central Church of the
        Brethren, 1112

Flory, Golda Kreider, 499, 1620
Flory, Harley Todd, 1620
    on Dunkard Brethren Church missions,
        2331
    Pleasant Ridge Dunkard Brethren
        Congregation, OH, presiding elder,
        1034
Flory, Harold Garber, 1620
Flory, Henry, 1620
Flory, Irvin H., 1939
Flory, Isaac, 497
Flory, J. B., 1620
Flory, J. T., 1620
Flory, Jacob
    Shoal Creek Old German Baptist
        Brethren Church, Newton Co.,
        MO, elder, 1178
Flory, Jacob F., 1938
Flory, Jacob S., 43, 54, 139, 324, 348, **498,**
    714, 747, 1620, *See also* literature,
    Brethren in
    historical writing, 611
    *The Home Mirror and The Home
        Mirror and Our Flag,* 625
    The Home Mirror and Our Flag, pub-
        lisher, 1971
    The Home Mirror, publisher, 1971
    Hygiene, CO, Church of the Brethren,
        641
    hymnals, 642
    migration of Brethren, 829, 830
    patent medicine remedy business, 995
    Root River Church of the Brethren,
        MN, pastor, 1122
Flory, Jacob S., 1938
Flory, James A., 128, 499
Flory, James Arthur, 1620
Flory, Janet Ruth, 1837, 2185
Flory, Jesse B., 1621
    Old Order German Baptist Church
        minister, 972
    Painter Creek Old German Baptist
        Brethren Church, OH, 990
Flory, Joel, 1621
    Filley German Baptist Brethren
        Church, NE, 2374
Flory, Johannes (Yohones), 1621
    merged with Flory, Yohnones, **2382**
Flory, John, 334, 335, **498,** 499, 525, 561,
    1264, 1621, 2106, *See also* Con-
    gregational Brethren
    Poplar Ridge Church of the Brethren,
        OH, 1047
    "Single Mode" Brethren, 1186
Flory, John and Mary (Schock), 118
Flory, John Calvin, 912
Flory, John H., 1234, 1621
    New River Old German Baptist
        Brethren Church, ministers for,
        931
Flory, John Michael, 498
Flory, John Michael, Jr., 1621
Flory, John 209
Flory, John Samuel, 207, 300, 407,
    498–499, *499, 537,* 1621, 1859,
    1929, 1938–1939, 1952
    Alexander Mack's Bible, 777
    poetry, 1039
    Sherfy, Robert Livingston (CB) and,
        2249
Flory, Joseph J., 497
Flory, Josephine Keever, 1837
Flory, Katherina, *See* Flure, Katherina (later

Naff)
Flory, Katie, 272
Flory, Kitty, *207*
Flory, Lee
    Hart, MI, Dunkard Brethren Congre-
        gation, 2196
Flory, Lester M., 350, 1621, 2278, 2301,
    2382
Flory, Lizzie Mae Neher, **499,** 1837, 1968
Flory, Lottie (later Neher), 922
Flory, Marie Sarah Mason, 1837, *2185*
Flory, Marillis (later Stoner), 1225
Flory, Martha Belle Shick, 201, 277, 278,
    499, 1621, 1837
Flory, Martha V. Brumbaugh, 498, 499
Flory, Martin, *495*
Flory, Mary A. (later Shoup), *See* Shoup,
    Mary A. Flory
Flory, Mary E., 1791
Flory, Mary Joann, 417, 2185
Flory, Mary (later Miller), 2016
    Miller, Sebastian Christian, wife of,
        842,
Flory, Mary Schock, 499
Flory, Merle D., 1347, 2156
Flory, Merle L., 1621
Flory, Michael, 498, 550, 1621
Flory, Millie Younce, 209, 498
Flory, Minnie, 208, 1835
Flory, Mirna Belle, 1846
Flory, Nannie Coppock, 499
Flory, Newton B., 1621
Flory, Noah, 264, 350, 531, 1315, 1621
    Sand Creek Old German Baptist
        Brethren Church, KS, elder-in-
        charge, 1143
    Shady Grove Old German Baptist
        Brethren Church, OH, minister,
        1171
Flory, Nora Almira Phillips, 1837, 2185,
    See also Berkebile, Nora (Flory)
    article about, 1923
Flory, Nora E., 1833
Flory, O. Blaine, 1621
Flory, Owen
    Old Order German Baptist Church
        minister, 972
Flory, Paul John, 496, 498, **499,** **2374**
    Holl, Carl Waldo, 619
    inventions and scientific discoveries,
        660
    Nobel Prize, 1160
Flory, Philip Earl, 2185
Flory, R. C.
    Mount Hope Church of the Brethren,
        WA, 882
Flory, R. F., 1922
    historical writing, 612
Flory, Ray H., 1939
Flory, Raymond Chester, 9, 128, **499,** 1621,
    1837, 2016
Flory, Raymond LeRoy, 246, 1621
    Flory, Carrie Sarah (Bird) Niswander,
        2331
    Flory, Curtis Elmer, 2331
    Newton, KS, Church of the Brethren,
        pastor in, 934
Flory, Raymond William, 1621
Flory, Riley W., 270, 1621, 2301, **2382**
    Prices Creek Old German Baptist
        Brethren Church, OH, elder or
        minister, 1057
Flory, Rolland Carol, 1837

Flory, Rolland Floyd, **499,** 535, 1621, 1939
Flory, S. I., 228
Flory, Samuel, 447, 1621
Flory, Samuel Henry, 1621
Flory, Samuel Isaac, 331, *495,* 1340, 1621
Flory, Sarah Hedrick, 498
Flory-Steury, Mary Jo, 2278
Flory, Susan Miller, 497
Flory, Susanna Wampler, 498
Flory, T. B., 1621
Flory, Theodore Wendell, 2185
Flory, Thomas H., 62, 1621, 2301, **2382**
   Painter Creek Old German Baptist
      Brethren Church, OH, 990
Flory, Vinnie Mikesell, 499
Flory, W. F., 367
Flory, W. Howard, 1621
Flory, Walter S., Jr., 1621
Flory, Wayne S., 755, 1342, 1621
   South Gate, CA, First Brethren Church,
      pastor, 1205
Flory, Weldon I., 1621
Flory, Wendell P., 272, 417, 1324, 1939,
   2071
   tractor unit, 1268
   memoirs, 2331
Flory, Wendell Phillips, 1621, 1837, *2185*
Flory, William Franklin, 1621
   Sand Creek Old German Baptist
      Brethren Church, KS, elder-in-
      charge, 1143
Flory, William R., 1621
Flory, Winfred Laverne, 431, 1621
Flory, Yohnones
   merged with Flory, Johannes, **2382**
Flower Hill Church of the Brethren, MD,
   500
   Silver Springs, MD, Good Shepherd
      Church of the Brethren, 1182
   Flower Hill congregation, MD, 1397
   Monrovia, MD, Bush Creek Church of
      the Brethren, 870
Flowers, Charles A., 239, 318, 320, 553,
   1621, 2301
Floyd, Clair and Bemma Sue, 30
Floyd Co., IA
   Rock Grove German Baptist Brethren
      Church, IA, 1117
Floyd Co., MO
   Fairview Church of the Brethren, MO,
      469
Floyd Co., VA, 21, 231, 343, 345, 350, 407,
   727, 737, 1224, 1267, 1307, 1341
   Church of the Brethren, VA, **500,** 1267
   Franklin Co. Church of the Brethren,
      VA, 507
   Free Will Dunkers, 514
   Fremont Church of the Brethren, VA,
      515
   Mountain Normal School, 889
   Parkway Church of the Brethren, VA,
      994
   place-names, Brethren, 1027
   Pleasant Hill Church of the Brethren,
      VA, 1033
   Red Oak Grove Church of the
      Brethren, VA, 1089, *1089*
   supplying preaching services to Saint
      Paul Churches of the Brethren,
      1135
   Topeco congregation, Smith River
      Church of the Brethren, VA, 1192
Fluck (Fluke), John B., 1621

Fluck, Susanna (later Imler), 647
Fluke
   Snake Spring Valley Church of the
      Brethren, PA, free minister, 1192
Fluke, Carola Jean (later Austin), 1847
Fluke, Doris J., 1838
Fluke, Max, 674, 1621
Flure, Katherina (later Naff), 910
Fluvanna Co., VA, 269, 338
Fly Creek, KS
   Church of the Brethren, **500**
   organization of, 929
   Osage Church of the Brethren, KS, 983
The Flying Eagle, **500,** 1939, **2374**
FMS (Foreign Missionary Society)
   The Missionary Board (BC), 855
Fockler, Mary Elisa
   Saxton, PA, Stonertown Church of the
      Brethren, 1150
Fodor, Steven, 1621
Foflins, Bernard M.
   Rockton, PA, Church of the Brethren,
      pastor, 1118
Fogarty, Robert S., 1939
Fogelsanger, David, 1621
   Ridge Church of the Brethren, PA,
      minister, 1108
Fogelsanger, David Minnich, 1621, 1939,
   2041
Fogelsanger, Donald Herbert, 21, 733, 1621
Fogelsanger family, 158, *See also* Rahn,
      Barbara Elizabeth Shearer
   history of, 1939
   Ridge Church of the Brethren, PA,
      1108
Fogelsanger, John M., 235
   New Ideas publication, 929
Fogelsanger, John Mervin, **500**
Fogelsanger, John R., 1621
   Shippensburg, PA, Church of the
      Brethren, elder, 1177
Fogelsanger, Samuel, 1621
Fogelsanger, Samuel E. L., 1621
Fogelsanger, Sara Florence (later Murphy),
   500, 1362, 1722–1723, **2377**
   Fogelsanger, Elizabeth Newcome,
      mother of, 897
   Murphy, Ross Dale, wife of, 897
Fogelsanger. Wendell M., 500
   Murphy, Sara Florence Fogelsanger,
      father of, 897
Fogle, Caleb John, 157, 913, 1622
Fogle, Elaine G., 1939
Fogle family, 319
   Garrett, PA, Church of the Brethren,
      531
   Good (Guth) family, 556
Fogle, Fred, 505
   Omaha, NE, Grace Brethren Bible
      Church, pastor, 974
Fogle, Kenneth E., 1939
Fogle, Lerry W., 2278
Fogle, Maurita Mae, 505, 1848
   Omaha, NE, Grace Brethren Bible
      Church, 974
Fogle, Paul Fredrick, 1622, 1848
Fogle, Simon Peter, 54, 740, 912, 1209,
   1622
   Reliance, VA, Mount Zion Brethren
      Church, pastor, 1096
Foglesanger, J. B., 1622
Fogleson, D., 1622
Fogleson, John, 1622

Folden, Don, 2278
Folden, Richard, 720
Foley family
   Gospel Grace Brethren Church, VA,
      559
Foley, Mary Margaret, 1850
   Fogleman, Aaron S.
      German immigration, 2331
Folger, Duane S., 720
Folger, Wyman Worth, 1622
   New Virginia, IA, Brethren Church, as
      minister, 932
   Osceola, IA, Church of the Brethren,
      minister, 983
folk art, 60, 61
   Ephrata Community, 2097
   Fraktur, See Fraktur
   penmanship, 2105
   Pennsylvania, 2076, 2097
   Pennsylvania Germans, 1007, 2094
   Virginia, 2105
folk medicine, 2145–2146, *See also*
      Brethren folk medicine; medicine,
      folk
Folker, Howard Oliver, 1939
folklore, 2147–2148, *See also* Brethren
      folklore
folklore societies
   Pennsylvania German Folklore Society,
      2074
Follis, John H., 1622
Follis, John M., 1622
   Ottumwa, IA, Church of the Brethren,
      elder, 985
Foltz, Samuel, 1622
Foltz, Samuel M., 1622
Foltz, Thomas, 1622
Fontana, CA, 715
Fontanelle Co., NB
   Bell Creek congregation origins, 920
Fontes, Elaine de, 1847
food, *See* cooking
foodbanks
   Tacoma, WA, Larchmont Community
      Church of the Brethren, 1247
footbinding, 403
Foote family, *See* Sellers family
Foote, Robert L., 363, 2278
Foote, Wilder, 1910
footwashing, *See* feetwashing
   Edington, Allen on ordinance, 2328
For a World Like Ours: Studies in I Corin-
      thians and Prophecy: Things To
      Come (Boyer), 2139
For All Who Minister, 2149
   worship and, 2266
Forbes, Donna Steiner, 193, 1287, 1837,
   1845, 2183,
Forbes, James Edward, 125, 1622
Forbes, John (General)
   Sauer, Johann Christoph, I, questioning
      of, 1148
force in religion, *See* religious liberty
Force, James H., 1622
Force, Vivian Carroll (later Altig), 20, 136,
   172, 1847, **2371**
Ford, Albert, 1622
   Portage Church of the Brethren, OH,
      minister, 1047
Ford, Charles Wesley, 2278
Ford Co., KS, 147
Ford, Darrell Leland, 1622
   Paradise, CA, Church of the Brethren,

992
Ford, Donald J., 1622
Ford family
    Hatboro, PA, Suburban Grace Brethren
      Church, 588
Ford Foundation
    grant for nursing school feasibility
      study, 952
Ford, Hollace A., 590, 2278
Ford, James, 1622
Ford, Norman F., 1622
Forehand, John T., 1212
Foreign and Domestic Missions Board
    (GBB), 163, 206, **500**
    Church of the Brethren, 299
    Church of the Brethren and polity,
      1043
    General Board (CB), 535
    General Church Erection and
      Missionary Committee (CB), 536
    Hamilton, Hiel, 580
Foreign Mission Commission (CB), **500,**
    See also missions and missionaries
    Commission of Fifteen (CB), 327
    Elgin, IL, 167
    Flory, Wendell Phillips, 2185
    General Brotherhood Board, 539
    mission tours, 855
    The Missionary Board (BC), 856
    Sawa, Bitrus Pilasar (CB) and, 2246
    Schwalm, Vernon Franklin, 1157
Foreign Missionary Society (FMS), 15, 38,
    52, 53, 88, 97, 172, 183, 188, 191,
    500–501, 1353
    Beaver, Samuel Wayne, 2134
    Bickel, Florence Marguerite, 141
    Cashman, Edwin E., 2156
    Cassel, Jacob C., 260
    England, 1290
    Evangelical Foreign Missions Associa-
      tions and, 914
    Fetterhoff, Dean, 2184
    First Brethren Church, CA, 362
    France, 505, 506
    Hathaway, Carrie E. and John Wesley,
      588
    Hawaii, 590
    historic sites, 609
    India, 651
    Indiana, 653
    Iran (Persia), 662
    Julien, Thomas T., 2210
    Kent, Homer Austin, 688
    Kent, Wendell E., 2211
    Kimmell, Arthur Vance, 694
    Landrum, Clyde Kermit, 724
    McClain, Alva J., 772
    Miller, John Allen, 839
    The Missionary Board (BC), 855
    missions, 861, 862
    missions in Central African Republic,
      2225
    Montreal, Quebec, 1297
    Ogden, William Augustus, 961
    O'Neal, Glenn, 2236
    publications, 1939
    Puerto Rico, 1070
    Quebec, 1075
    Relief Agency Brethren (FGBC), 1096
    Spain, missions to, 1207
    Studebaker, Claud, 1229
    Training in Missionary Endeavor
      (TIME), 1231, 1270

Waipio Acres, HI, Grace Brethren
    Church, 1312
Weaver, Scott L. (FGBC, CGBCI) and,
    2261
Webb, Maude Cripe, 1325
Whitcomb, John Clement, Jr. (FGBC,
    CGBCI) and, 2262
Yoder, Charles Francis, 1385–1386
Zielasko, John Warlow (FGBC,
    CGBCI) and, 2269–2270
foreign missions, *See* missions and
    missionaries
    Brethren introduced to travel through,
      1273–1274
    China, article about, 1939
    Ecuador, 1912
    India, book about, 1939
    La Verne, CA, Grace Brethren Church,
      715
    Lena, IL, Church of the Brethren, 737
    Long Beach, CA, First Church of the
      Brethren, 754
    Nigeria, 1954
    training for in Chicago missions, 1296
    translation of tracts, 1269
    Vandalia, OH, Grace Brethren Church,
      1302
    Whittier, CA, Grace Brethren Church,
      1343
    Williams, John Henry Bashor, 1345
    women, roles in, 1361, 1363
    World Ministries Commission, 1369
    Yoder, Charles Francis, 1385–1386
    Yoder, Joseph J., 1386
    Zug, Samuel Ruhl, 1401
Foreign Missions Conference, **501**
    ecumenism, 422
Foreign Missions (FGBC)
    Grace Brethren International Missions,
      2191
    Haller, Wesley, 2195
foreign travel, 1271–1274, *1272, 1273*
    fact-finding tour of post-World War II
      Europe, 1273
    foreman, **502**
    Davy, Henry Dorsey, 364
    Frantz, Aaron, 508
    ministry, terminology, 847
    moderator, 865
    moderator role in OGBB, 502, 865
Foreman, Donald L., 553, 1622
Foreman, Harry E., 1939
    on Little Cove, PA, 2331
Foreman, Hugh, 145
forensics, *See* debates
Foresinger, *See* chorister
Forest Center Church of the Brethren, WA,
    502
Forest Chapel Church of the Brethren, VA,
    502
    Cloverdale, VA, Church of the Breth-
      ren, preaching point for, 321
Forest Chapel, VA, congregation
    Middle River Church of the Brethren,
      VA, 825
Forest congregation, WI (CB), 63
forest fires, *See* fire fighting
Forest Service, 316, **502**
    fire fighting, 491
forestry programs
    detached programs, 380
Forestville Elementary School, Temple
    Hills, MD, 1253

Forestville, VA, 1350
forgiveness, 1871
    remarriage after divorce, 1099
Forks, MD, congregation
    Maple Grove Church of the Brethren,
      MD, mission point of, 790
Forks of the Yadkin settlement, NC, 411,
    1383
Forner, S. M.
    Silver Lake Church of the Brethren,
      NE, elder-in-charge, 1182
Forney, A. S., 1622
Forney, Abraham, 466
Forney, Adam E., 1622
Forney, Anna M.
    article about, 1915
Forney, Anna Marie Shull, 212, **502**, 1837,
    2076
Forney, Anne Smith
    descendants, 1939
Forney, Annie (later Yoder), 1386
Forney, Barbara Ellen Heckman Wagoner,
    502, 1837
Forney, Benjamin, 1622
Forney, C., 211
Forney, Catherine (later Shick), 499
Forney, Charles William, 1939
Forney, Christian, 72, 104, 438, 466, 472,
    1622
    Portis, KS, Grace Brethren Church,
      pastor, 1048
Forney, Clayborn, *See* Forney, John
    Clayborn
Forney, D. E., 438
Forney, Daniel L., 212, **502,** 1622, 1837,
    2076
    article about, 1915
    India orphanages, 651
    Pomona, CA, Church of the Brethren,
      pastor, 1045
    Reedley, CA, Church of the Brethren,
      elder, 1091
    St. Francis Church of the Brethren, AR,
      pastor, 1134
    Santa Ana, CA, Church of the
      Brethren, ministerial leadership
      given to, 1144
Forney, David H., 45, 1622
Forney, Earl E., 1622
Forney, Edmund, 502, 1622
Forney, Elizabeth Hershey, 502
Forney, Ella Mae (later Fike), 2184
Forney, Ellen Swarr, 502
Forney family, 216, 231, 721, 1315, 1939,
    2079, *See* Fahrney family
    bibliography, 1865, 1878
    Rotruck (Rothrock, Roderick) family,
      related to, 1124
    Shull family, related to, 1156
Forney, Helen
    Ozark Church of the Brethren, MI,
      vacation Bible school, 986
Forney, Henry J., 1622
Forney, Hiram Willard, 275, 504, 1622
Forney, Isaac, 1622
Forney, J. Clyde, 687, 1383
Forney, J. S., 1622
Forney, Johann Adam, 1878
Forney, John, 226, 424, 466, 472, **502,** 682,
    1320, 1622, 1939
    Peabody Church of the Brethren, KS,
      997
Forney, John Clayborn, 124, 1622

Forney, John Clyde, 1622
Forney, John, Jr., 466
Forney, John Keller, 1939
Forney, John, Sr., 1622
Forney, Joseph, 466
Forney, Michael, 226, 466, 1622, 2126
Forney, Milton G., 416, 502, 1622
Forney, Paul M., 1623, 2301
Forney, Peter, 466, 531, 552, 1623
    family history, 1939
Forney, Phares J(oseph), 1623
Forney, Roy S., **502–503**, 670, 1623
    Johnstown, PA, Morrellville Church of
        the Brethren, 674
    Mount Joy, PA, Florin Church of the
        Brethren, free minister, 882
Forney, Ruth Elizabeth (later Brooks), 212,
    1835 , **2372, 2387**
Forney, Samuel, 1623, 2126
Forney, Samuel L., 685
Forney, Samuel Michael, 45, 1623, 2301
Forney, Susanna Beeghly, 466
Forney, Susan(nah?) (later Rothrock), 1124
Forney, Susie, 1939
Forney, William, 638, 1623
fornication
    family, 474
    sanctions against, 1325–1326
Fornwalt, Donald, 1623
Forrer (Forror), Charles O., 1623
Forrer, Jacob, 1320
Forrer, John, 1623
Forrer, Samuel, 1623
Forrest, Dale Andrew, 375, 1622
Forrest family, 1302, 1380
Forrest, Marion, 1380
Forrest, Nathan Bedford, 2128
Forry, Elizabeth, 405
Forry (Forrey), William A., 1623
Forry, Nettie (later Rhoads), *See* Rhoads
    family
Forry, Roger Longenecker, 1623
    Somerset, PA, Church of the Brethren,
        pastor, 1202
Forster, Mitchell, 566, 1224
Forsyth Co., NC, 1311
Fraternity Church of the Brethren, NC, 511
Fraternity Old German Baptist Brethren
    Church, NC, 511
Forsythe, Douglas, 2278
Fort Collins, CO, 320
Fort Erie, PA
    Brethren movement, 2089
Fort Jefferson, OH, 1333
Fort Lauderdale, FL, Grace Brethren
    Church, **503**
    North Lauderdale, FL, Grace Brethren
        Church, 948
Fort Leavenworth, KS
    imprisonment of conscientious objec-
        tors, 1370, 1371
Fort McKinley, OH, Church of the
    Brethren, 319, 1243, *See also*
    Dayton, OH, Fort McKinley
        Church of the Brethren
Fort Myers, FL, Grace Brethren Bible
    Church, **503**
Fort Royal, VA, 150
Fort Scott, KS, 990
Fort Scott, KS, Brethren Church, **503**, 682
    Missouri, 864
Fort Scott, KS, Church of the Brethren, **503**
Fort Seybert, WV, Bethlehem Fellowship,

2185
Fort Wayne, Co., IN
    obituary records, 2099
Fort Wayne Co., IN, 2099
Fort Wayne, IN, 7, 151, 693, 1345
    Agape Church of the Brethren, *See*
        Agape Church of the Brethren, IN
    Beacon Heights Church of the Breth-
        ren, **503**, 504, 1917–1918
    First Brethren Church, **503–504**
    Fort Wayne, IN, Grace Brethren
        Church, **504**
    Lincolnshire Church of the Brethren,
        504, **504**
    Meadow Crest Brethren Church, **504**
        Elk Run Church of the Brethren,
            VA, 439
        Kerner, William Hoff, Sr., 2211
Fort Worth, TX, 1972–1973
    Church of the Brethren, **504**, *1238,*
        1255
Fortaleza, Brazil
    Christian Pacifist Community (Tunker),
        2139
Fortenbaugh, Robert, 1939
Fortna, Pat Stohl, 1959
Fortner, Charles, 1623
Fortune (ship)
    Hylton family, 641
Forum for Religious Studies, **2185–2186**
    historiography, 2202
The Forward and Backward Mode of
        Baptism Considered, 696
Forward Movement, 160, **504**
    Council of Promotion (CB), evolution
        from, 346
    Interchurch World Movement (IWM),
        658
    orphans, care for, 276
    Williams, John Henry Bashor, 1345
Fory (Flora/Fleury) families, 1896
Foss, Louis, 1623
Foster, Benjamin, 1319
Foster, Chris C., 2278
Foster Co., ND, 256
    James River Church of the Brethren,
        ND, 668
Foster, Frank, 620, 1623
Foster, Hannah Elizabeth (later Dowling),
    1919
Foster, Harold S., 2301
Foster, Joe
    Newport Church of the Brethren, VA,
        leadership in, 934
Foster, John Martin, 1623, 1939
    mutual aid, 902, *902*
Foster, Joseph F., 1623
Foster, Joseph Henry, **504**, 1623,
    1848–1849
Foster, Joseph Martin, Jr., 1623
Foster, Joseph Samuel, 1623
Foster, O. D., 1623
Foster, Rose Alverda Brosius, **504**, 1849
Foster, Venia Hurr
    on Kuhn, John, 2331
    on Kuhn, Susannah Mock, 2331
Foster, Virgil E., 1940
Fostoria, OH, *557,* 1334
    Church of the Brethren, 118, **505**, 1264
    Rome, OH, congregation, 956
    West Independence Brethren Church,
        505
Fouch Family, 2089

Fouch (Pfautz), James, 1623
Foucht, Michael, 566
Foulk, Hiram, 583, 1623
Foulk, Marian
    Ormond Beach, FL, Grace Brethren
        Church, 982
Foulke, Rose M., 1849
    Foundation of Independent Colleges of
        Pennsylvania
    Ellis, Calvert Nice, 441
Foundation Series
    educational materials, 284, 1237
Founders Hall, Juniata College, *426*
Fountain family
    Modesto, CA, La Loma Grace Brethren
        Church, 867
Fountain Rock school
    St. James Brethren Church Sunday
        School, 1134
Four Books of True Christianity (Arndt), 56
4-H Clubs
    American movement, 9
    Elkhart, IN, City Church of the
        Brethren, 439
Four Mile, IN, congregation, 652, 838, 924,
    2353,
    becomes New Bethel, IN, Church of
        the Brethren, 766, 924, 925
    Church of the Brethren, **505**
    migration of Brethren, 829
    Nettle Creek, ministers for, 923
    Richmond, IN, Church of the Brethren,
        1108
Four Year Program, 81, **505**, *See also*
    Forward Movement; Interchurch
        World Movement
    "Message of the Brethren Ministry,"
        817
Fourman, Arthur, 247
Fourman, Larry D., 1623
    on David, life of, 2331
    on Holy Spirit in New Testament, 2331
    Pipe Creek Church of the Brethren,
        MD, minister, 1026
Fourteenth Amendment, 1
Fourth Lateran Council
    Roman Catholic Church, 1120
Fourth of July, *See* Independence Day
"Fourth Principle of the Doctrine of Christ
        (Laying on of Hands)" (Bowman),
        166
Fourth St., PA, congregation (CB), 270
Fouse (Fauss), Theobald, 1894
Fouse, John G., 1894
Foust, Daniel, 1623
Foust family, 1935
Foust (Faust), Jeremiah E., 1623
Fouts, Annabelle Berg, 1837
Fouts, D. H., 1623
Fouts, David H., Jr., 269, 1014, 1623
Fouts, David, Sr., 1014
Fouts, David Wilson, 1837–1838
Fouts, Elmer S., 1623
Fouts, F. S.
    Prairie Lake Church of the Brethren,
        OK, pastor, 1050
Fouts family, 2044, *See also* Pfautz family
    article about, 1914
Fouts (Foutz, Pfoutz, Pfautz) family, 2016
Fouts, Frances (later Wilson), 2030
Fouts, Goldie (later Ronk), 377, 1121
Fouts, Jacob
    Ottawa, KS, Church of the Brethren,

984
Fouts, Michael, 1014
Fouts, Mrs. F. S.
    Prairie Lake Church of the Brethren,
      OK, pastor, 1050
Fouts (Pfoutz) family, 1299
Fouts, S. S.
    Romine Church of the Brethren, IL,
      minister, 1121
Fouts, Samuel S., 1623
Foutz, Annie (later Skeggs), 1316
Foutz, Conrad
    biography, 1915
Foutz family, *See* Fouts (Foutz, Pfoutz,
      Pfautz) family; Pfautz family
Foutz, Frederick, 1014
Foutz, Rebecca, 1940
Fowler, Clara (later Porte), 1047
Fowler family, *See* Shaffer, Andrew
Fowler, Marcus H., 512, 1623
    Maquoketa German Baptist Brethren,
      IA, minister, 791
Fox, A. P., 1623
Fox, Anna Mack
    Mack family, 778
Fox, Barry T., 417, 1623
Fox, Bessie Marie King, 1838
Fox, Blanche (later Weimer), 1327
Fox, Boice family
    Prosperity Brethren Church, WV, 1062
Fox, Dickie, 1623
Fox, Edna H., 2094
Fox, Edwin Stanton, 1623
Fox, Emanuel
    Mack family, 778
Fox family, 227
    Honey Creek Church of the Brethren,
      MO, 627
Fox, Franklin C., 106, 1623
Fox, George
    Society of Friends (Quakers), 1199
Fox, H. C., 1940
Fox, Harvey, 1623
Fox, Ira H., 1623
Fox, J., 2102
Fox, J. M., 241, 417, 425
Fox, Jacob, 1348
Fox, Jacob J., 1623
Fox, Janet Louise King, 1855
Fox, Jesse R., 106, 1623
Fox, John, 323, 1623
    Philadelphia, PA, First Church of the
      Brethren, minister, 1015
    single mode feetwashing, 1186
Fox, John M., 1623
Fox, John Wesley, 913, 1623, 1838
Fox, Justus, 2030, *See also* Fuchs, Justus
    reference to, 1956
Fox, Karen M.
    on PA Germans, 2331
Fox, Lemuel Royal, 1623
Fox, Levi, 1213
Fox, Lydia, 116, 204
Fox, Rebecca, 1348
Fox, Robert Earle, 106, 1623
Fox, William, 283
Fracassini, Mary Martha, 1883
Fradenburgh, Jesse M., 1623
Fradenburgh, John E., 1623
Frady, Martha Marie, 1853
Fraktur, 17, 60–61, 175, **505**, 2147, *2186*
    bibliographical sources, 2323, 2324
    certificates, 61, 99

definition of, 60
Dock, Christopher, 394
Earnest, Corrine Pattie on, 2328
Earnest, Russell on, 2328
Hershey, Mary Jan Lederach on, 2336
Hoch, Beverly Repass on, 2328
Moyer, Dennis K. on, 2348
museums containing, 898
penmanship, 2105
Pennsylvania Germans' handwriting,
    1007
publishing, 1067, 1998
Salford Mennonite Meetinghouse
    Schools and, 2336
Skippack Mennonite Meetinghouse
    Schools and, 2336
Stopp, Klaus on birth and baptismal
    certificates and, 2359
writings, 2063
Yoder, Don on, 2364
Fralin, George
    Mount Union (Airpoint) Church of the
      Brethren, VA, trustee, 887
Fralin, Riley Thomas, Jr., 1623
Fraling family
    Pipe Creek Old German Baptist
      Brethren Church, IN, 1026
Fram, Sebastian, 1623
Frame (Fraim), Sebastian, 741
Frame, Gabriel, 1623
Frame, Randy
    on GBC split, 2332
France, 15, 23, **505–506**, 2020
    Beaver, Samuel Wayne, 2134
    Bercken, Gaston J., 1246
    Brethren, and Roman Catholic Church,
      1120
    Brethren movement and, 174
    Chateau of Saint Albain, 2158, *2159*
    Community of the True Inspiration,
      330
    education programs, 185
    Fercken, Gaston John and Seline
      (Phebe), 488
    Foreign Missionary Society (BC,
      FGBC), 501
    French and Indian War, 516
    Friendship Trains, 518
    Germany, 545
    Grace Brethren Church, 280
    Julien, Thomas T., 2210
    missions, 860, 862, 2225
    missions and missionaries in, 160
    Fellowship of Grace Brethren
      Churches, 250
    missions, short-term, 2226
    Reformation, Protestant, 1091
    Reformed Church, 1092
    relief and rehabilitation work in, 200
    Revolutionary War, American, 1105
    Waldenses, 1314
Frances Slocum Trail
    history of, 2101
Francis and Elizabeth (ship)
    Gnagey (Gnaegi) family, 554
    Waidele, Johann Michael and family,
      1326
    Zug family, 1401
Francis family
    history of, 1940
Francis, Jacob "Jay" Gottwals, **506**, 534,
      540, 733, 1624, 1939, 1940, 2111,
      See also Flying Eagle, The

historical societies, 610
    Elizabethtown College, 437
    Mack University, 779
Francis, John Umstad, 506
Francis, Lillie
    on Dunkers, 2332
Francis, Mary Jane Gottwals, 506
Francis of Assisi
    mysticism, 1259
Francis, Thomas, [III?], 1940
Franciscan friars, 28
Francisco, Jose J., 1624
Franck, Ira S., 1940
Francke, A. H., 580, 614
Francke, August Hermann, **506**, 580, 614,
      1258, *See also* Muhlenberg, Henry
      Melchior
    noncreedalism, 942
    Pietism, 1021
    Sattler, Gary R. on, 2354
    Walter, Hugo G. on, 2362
Franconia Twp., Harleysville, PA, 2071
Frank, Art, 1624
Frank, D. R., 1624
Frank, Dortha Mae (later Dowdy), 398,
      1848
Frank, Evelyn Evangeline, 153, 1838
Frank, Ivie Andes, 1940
Frank, Maria Baer, 219
Franke, August Hermann, 1876
Frankenhausen, battle of (1525), 28
Frankenthal, **506**
    Germany, 545
    Kämpfer, Johannes, 682
    radical pietist dissension in, 990
    Traut family, 1270
    Traut, Georg Balthasar "Balser," 1270
Frankfort, KS
    Richland Center Church of the
      Brethren, KS, preaching point, 1107
Frankfort, OH, Church of the Brethren,
      257, 395, **506**
    May, James, minister and deacon, 804
    minorities, ethnic and racial, 849
Frankfurt (Germany)
    Hochmann von Hochenau, Ernst
      Christoph, 614
Frankfurt Land Company
    Falckner's Swamp, 470
Frankfurt/Main
    greeting for Sower bicentenary, 1940
    Spener, Philipp Jakob, 1209
Franklin, Benjamin, 117, **506**, 516, 912,
      1860, 1874, *See also* names
    anecdote about Wohlfahrt (Welfare),
      Michael, 1355
    Brethren and noncreedalism, 943
    Charity School proposal, 1147–1148
    letters to, from S. Eckerlin and Peter
      Miller, 1960
    Lehmann, Hartmut on Sauer,
      Christoph, I compared with, 2343
    lightning rods, 742
    Miller, John Peter, 2015
    Oley Conference, pamphlet on, 1912
    papers of, references to Brethren, 1940
    Pennsylvania Germans, 2091
    Pennsylvania Hospital, 1007
    printing of books for Ephrata
      Community, 1926
    Quaker Party, 2110
Franklin Boro, PA, 752
Franklin Co. Church of the Brethren, IA,

1289, *See also* Union Ridge
Church of the Brethren, IA
Franklin Co. Church of the Brethren, VA,
507
Franklin Co., KS, 682
Eight Mile Old German Baptist Brethren Church, KS, 431
Franklin Co., OH, 374
Sciota Church of the Brethen, OH, 1160
Franklin Co., PA, 172, 251, 298, 380, 384, 406, 724, 1219, 1227, 1228, 1229, 1243, 1329, 1877
Fahnestock family, 465
Falling Spring Church of the Brethren, PA, 471
Falling Spring Old German Baptist Brethren Church, PA, 471
history of, 1939
migration of Brethren, 827
Pennsylvania Brethren settlement, 1004
Pennsylvania Old German Baptist Brethren, 1005
Rouzerville Church of the Brethren, PA, 1125
Royer family, 1128
Snake Spring Valley Church of the Brethren, PA, members from, 1192
Snow Hill Community, 1194–1195
Steiner family, 2378
Studebaker, Heinrich, 1231
Franklin Co., VA, 157, **162**, 163, 216, 262, 350, 363, 424, 722, 737, 1271, 1307, 1863
Faiview-Rocky Mount Church of the Brethren, VA, 470
Ferrum, VA, First Church of the Brethren, 488
Floyd Co. Church of the Brethren, VA, 500, 507
Free Will Dunkers, 514
Germantown Brick Church of the Brethren, VA, 544
Germantown Old German Baptist Brethren Church, VA, 544
Henry Fork Church of the Brethren, VA, 598
migration of Brethren, 829
Monte Vista Church of the Brethren, VA, 871
New Bethel Church of the Brethren, ministers to, 925
Ninevah Church of the Brethren, VA, 938
Oak Grove-South Church of the Brethren, VA, 956
Oak Hill Old German Baptist Brethren Church, VA, 957
Old Order Fellowship family, *971*
Pigg River Old German Baptist Brethren Church, VA, 1023
Rocky Mount, VA, Church of the Brethren, 1118
Ruckers German Baptist Brethren Church, VA, 1129
Franklin German Baptist Brethren congregation, IA, 661
Franklin Grove, IL, 394, 718, 736, 741, 1343, 1357, 1384
Church of the Brethren, **507**, *507*, 1968
history, 1993
meetinghouse, 2062
Franklin, IA, Church of the Brethren, **507**

Franklin, Joseph, 1940
Franklin, Kenneth Lee, 228, 1624
Rouzerville Church of the Brethren, PA, part-time pastor, 1125
Franklin mission point
Greene, IA, Church of the Brethren, 570
Franklin publications, 260
Franklin, Ross, 1624
Franklin, William H., 1624
Franklin, Woodrow W., 1624
Peace Valley Church of the Brethren, MO, 1003
Franks, Bessie (later Elrod), 442
Franks, Dorothy Lee Shaffer
Serving My Master, 1169
Frankstown (Duncansville) congregation, PA, 731
Frankstown, PA, 1303
Church of the Brethren, *See* Duncansville Church of the Brethren, PA
Frankstown, PA, congregation, 407
Frantz, Aaron, **508**, 1624
North Hampton, OH, Donnels Creek Old German Baptist Brethren Church, elder-in-charge and minister, 948
Frantz, Abraham, 1225, 1624
Frantz, Abraham (Abram) Michael, 570, 1624
Frantz, Alan, 508
Frantz, Alta Williams, 508
Frantz, Anna, 509
Frantz, Anna Barbara (Hannah), 509
Frantz, Balser, 509
Frantz, Barbara Glick, 553
Frantz, Benjamin A., 1624
North Hampton, OH, Donnels Creek Old German Baptist Brethren Church, elder-in-charge and deacon, 948
Frantz, Bertha, 244
Frantz, Blanche B., 1940
Frantz, Catherine Crist, 352
Frantz, Charles, 1624
Frantz, Charles E., 669
Frantz, Christian, 396, 1624
Frantz, Christian, II, 509
Frantz, Christian, III, 509
Frantz, Christian, Sr., 509
Frantz, Clair Gordon, 1940
historical writing, 611
Frantz, Clara Mae Behmer, 1940
Frantz, Daniel, *509*
Frantz, Daniel, Jr.
North Hampton, OH, Donnels Creek Old German Baptist Brethren Church, deacon, 948
Frantz, Dave, 1327
Frantz, David, 1624
Frantz, David W., 1624, 1940
Frantz, Dean L., 25, 190, 191, 1624, 1940
Mount Morris, IL, Church of the Brethren, pastor, 883
Frantz, Dena Pence, 1327, 2133
Frantz, E. A., 1624
Frantz, Earl M., 565, 1624
Frantz, Early M.
Newton, KS, Church of the Brethren, pastor in, 934
Frantz, Edward, 118, *248*, **508**, *508*, 1259, 1386, 1624, 1911, 1940
McPherson College, president, 781

Messenger, editor, 818
North Fork Old German Baptist Brethren Church, IN, minister, 947
Frantz, Edward, wife of, 1391
Frantz, Effie B. Wine, 508, 1996
Frantz, Elias Harold, 1940
Frantz, Elias M., 1624
Frantz, Elizabeth Crist, 352
Frantz, Elizabeth Moyer
Meyer family, 822
Frantz, Elmer E., 1624, 1940
Pleasant Valley Church of the Brethren, Alberta, Canada, providing pastoral care, 1034
Frantz, Elvin D., 128, 243, 1624, 1941
Frantz, Esther Marie (later Boleyn), 1834, 2137
Sudan (CB) and, 2253
Frantz, Evelyn M. Barkdoll, 1941
Ridgeway Community Church of the Brethren, PA, moderator, 1109
Frantz, Ezra, 75
Frantz family, 260, 280, 396, **509**, 750, 1280, 1330, 1893, 2089
Hope Memorial Church (German Baptist Brethren), NE, 2375
Neher family, related to, 922
Royer family related to, 1128
Snider, Jacob, descendants of, 1154
Frantz, Galen, 508
Frantz, Harold R., 1624, 2138
Frantz, Harrison A., 552, 1624
North Beatrice Church of the Brethren, NE, elder, 945
Pomona, CA, Church of the Brethren, pastor, 1045
Red Cloud, NE, Church of the Brethren, providing leadership, 1088
Frantz, Harrison G., 1624
North Hampton, OH, Donnels Creek Old German Baptist Brethren Church, minister, 948
Frantz, Harvey W., 1624
Frantz, Hattie Netzley
home mission work, 945
Frantz, Hattie W. Sellers, 508
Frantz, Ruby June (later Rhoades) and, 2242
Frantz, Hazel (later Turner), 1941
Frantz, Henry, 272, 508, 1624
Frantz, Ida (later Lehmer), 736
Frantz, Ira Henry, **508**, 1624, 1941, 2044, 2101
Frantz, Ruby June (later Rhoades) and, 2242
Frantz, Irene, 1834
Frantz, Irene (later Bittinger), 143
Frantz, Isaac, 1624
Frantz, J. C., 1624
Frantz, J. Royal, 1624
Frantz, Jacob, 264, 396, 430, 496, 508, 1225, 2301, **2382**
North Manchester Old German Baptist Brethren Church, IN, elder-in-charge, 949
Frantz, Jacob H., 268, 1234, 1624
North Fork Old German Baptist Brethren Church, IN, overseer, 947
Olathe Old German Baptist Brethren Church, KS, minister, 964
Frantz, Jacob L., 1624
Frantz, Jacob R., 508, 1624

Frantz, Jesse Orlin, 1624
    North Hampton, OH, Donnels Creek
        Old German Baptist Brethren
        Church, minister, 948
Frantz, John, 360, 509, 1624
Frantz, John B., 1941
    on Beissel, Johann Conrad/Konrad,
        2332
    on Sauers family, 2332
Frantz, John F., 1624
Frantz, Joseph, 1356, 1624
    North Hampton, OH, Donnels Creek
        Old German Baptist Brethren
        Church, minister, 948
Frantz, Joseph H., 1624, **2382**
Frantz, Katie, 209
Frantz, Kenneth Sidney, 378, 1624
Frantz, Laura Susan (later Pfautz), 1940
Frantz, Lauren, 1625
Frantz, Loren Daniel, 1625
Frantz, Lorena May (later Fasnacht), 480
Frantz, Lydia (later Harshbarger), 490
Frantz, M., 1220
Frantz, M. S., 744, 1343, 1394
Frantz, Magdalena, 352
Frantz, Magdalena Zug, 509, 532
Frantz, Marilyn, 508
Frantz, Mary Murphy, 508
Frantz, Mary Ryman, 508
Frantz, Mathias, 1625
Frantz, Matthias, 1940
Frantz, Maurice Samuel, 445, 1625
Frantz, Merlin L., 1625
Frantz, Michael, 291, 352, 381, **508–509,**
        576, 924, 1260, 1625, 1941, *See*
        also barns
    Apocrypha, citation of, 133
    descendants, 1941
    Funderburgh family, 523
    Holy Spirit, doctrine of, 624
    interpretation of the Bible, 134
    Meyer family, 822
    mutual aid, 901–902
    mysticism, 907
    Pfautz, Johann (Hans) Michael, 1013
    poetry, 1039
    publishing, 1063
    sermons, 1167
    Steiner family, 2378
    theology of love, 761
    writing on spiritual life, 1209
Frantz, Michael, II, 532
Frantz, Michael, Jr., 459, 509
Frantz, Michael, Sr., 509
Frantz, Mrs. Jacob, 264
Frantz, Nadine Pence, 2278
    on Anabaptist community, bonds with-
        in, 2332
    on the Lord's Supper, 2332
    on women, 2332
Frantz, Nicholas, 352, 1625
    North Manchester, IN, Church of the
        Brethren, elder, 949
Frantz, Peter, 75, 553
Frantz, Rachel Hamm, 1941
Frantz, Ralph, 1625
Frantz, Roy A., 1625
Frantz, Royal Hoover, 508, 1625, 2301
Frantz, Ruby June (later Rhoades), 508,
        1843, 2044, **2242,** *2243*
Frantz, Salome, 352
Frantz, Sarah Ebersole, 508
Frantz, Sarah Leedy, 508

Frantz, Simeon, 1625
    Maple Grove Old German Baptist
        Brethren Church, OH, elder-in-
        charge, 791
Frantz, Sophia Ohmart, *509*
Franz, John C., 1625
Franz Joseph I, emperor of Austria, 684
Frasca, Ralph
    on printing partnership with Benjamin
        Franklin, 2332
Fraser, Isobel, 191
Fraser, Nina Bliss, 1941
fraternal relations, **510,** *See also* ecumenism
    between Brethren Church and Church
        of the Brethren
    opposition to, 97
    persons leading, 81
Fraternal Relations Committee, 328, **510,**
        511, *See also* Committee on
        Interchurch Relations (CB)
    Congregational and Progressive Breth-
        ren, 335
    Evangelical Covenant Church, 460
        Schwalm, Vernon Franklin, 1157
        Statler, Foster Boyd, 1219
        Will, Harper S., 1345
fraternity, **511,** *See also* names, Brethren
    Old Order Fellowships, 970–971
Fraternity, NC, 946, 1311
    Church of the Brethren, **511,** 2071
    Maple Grove Church of the Brethren,
        NC, 790
    Old German Baptist Brethren Church,
        2138
Fraternity of Baptists, **511,** *See also* names,
        Brethren
    as denominational name, 910
Fraternity of German Baptists, **511,** *See*
        also names, Brethren
    as denominational name, 910
Fraternity Old German Baptist Brethren
        Church, NC, **511**
Fratt, Nancy B., 1941
Fravel, George
    St. Luke, VA, Brethren Church, 1135
Frazee family
    Pipe Creek Old German Baptist Breth-
        ren Church, IN, 1026
Frazee, Minnie, 362
Frazer, Heather T.
    conscientious objectors in World War
        II, 2332
Frazer, Susan Carpenter, 1941
Frazier, Elizabeth, 914
Frazier family
    at New Rockford, ND, Church of the
        Brethren, 932
Frazier, Glenn Jay, 743, 1625
Frazier, Vernon, 1625
Fread family
    South Loup Church of the Brethren,
        NE, 1206
Freas, Sarah A. (later Gibbons, later
        Evalson), 1612
Freckles and His Friends (Blosser), 149
Frederick, Adam Em(m)ert, 1625
Frederick Church of the Brethren, MD,
    1314
Frederick Co., MD, 170, 216, 352, 355,
        362, 364, 383, 732, 733, 752,
        1221, 1285, 1318, 1350
    Brethren on the frontier, 1984
    cemetery inscriptions, 1969

    Grossnickle Church of the Brethren,
        MD, 574
    Harmony Church of the Brethren, MD,
        584
    Middletown Valley Church of the
        Brethren, MD, 826
    Monrovia, MD, Bush Creek Church of
        the Brethren, 870
    Mountaindale Dunkard Brethren
        Congregation, MD, 890
    Myersville, MD, Church of the
        Brethren, 906
    Pleasant View Church of the Brethren,
        MD, 1037
    Rocky Ridge, MD, Monocacy Church
        of the Brethren, 1119
    Snake Spring Valley Church of the
        Brethren, PA, members from, 1192
    Tory Plot, 2100
Frederick Co., PA, 146
Frederick Co., VA, 239, 2077, 2090
    Meadow Mills Church of the Brethren,
        VA, 806
    Nead family in, 918
Frederick, Cornelius, 1625
Frederick Co.,VA, 239
Frederick, Donald Ray, 1625
    McPherson, KS, First Church of the
        Brethren, 780
Frederick, Donald Ray, 1625
Frederick family, 1341
Frederick, Harvey, 1969
Frederick, Jacob Ezra, 1625
Frederick, John D., 1625
Frederick (later Carroll) Co., MD, 1233
Frederick (later Washington) Co., MD,
    1233
Frederick, Mabel (later Schrock), *See*
    Schrock, Mabel Frederick
Frederick, MD, *512,* 1339
    Church of the Brethren, **511–512,** 2130
    Grace Brethren Church, **2186**
    Hagerstown, MD, Grace Brethren
        Church, 579
    Maryland Brethren, 799
    Monrovia, MD, Bush Creek Church of
        the Brethren, 870
Frederick, Norman L., 1625
Frederick, Norman S., 588, 1625
Frederick (now Carroll) Co., MD
    Kaspar Scherffig family, 1152
Frederick, Stafford C., 2278
Fredericks, Jim
    Montclair, CA, Grace Brethren Church,
        pastor, 871
Fredericksburg congregation, PA, 750
Fredericksburg, IA
    First Baptist Church, 512
    Hillcrest Baptist and Brethren Church,
        512
Fredericksburg, PA, 1364
    Brethren Church, **512**
    Church of the Brethren, *See* Mount
        Zion Road Church of the Brethren,
        PA
    Clover Creek Church of the Brethren,
        16, **512–513**
Fredericksburg, PA, Brethren Church, 512
    Roaring Spring, PA, Albright Church
        of the Brethren, 1114
Fairview Church of the Brethren, PA, 469
    Martinsburg, PA, Grace Brethren
        Church, 798

Martinsburg, PA, Memorial Church of the Brethren, 798

Mount Zion Road Church of the Brethren, PA, previous name of, 888

Frederickstown, MD, 2061

Fredonia, KS, Church of the Brethren, 20, **513**

Greenwood Co. Church of the Brethren, KS, 572

Freds, Carl

Markle, IN, Church of the Brethren, trustee, 794

Freds, John, 1625

Free Brethren, PA, 338, **513**

chart of Brethren bodies, place on, 1403–1405

Free Church, See also Believers' Church

Brethren polity and, 1042

Durnbaugh, Donald F. on ecclesiology of, 2326

historical background, 1999

Melton, J. Gordon on doctrine of, 2326

Free Discussion, **513,** 1941

The Free Gift (Beers), 2332

"Free Grace" (Bowman), 166

Free, Joseph, 1625

Free, Lawrence, 105

South Carolina, 1204

The Free Man (Richter), 747

Free Masons, See Freemasonry

Free Methodist Publishing House

Grace Schools (Grace Theological Seminary, Grace College), 563

free ministry, 134, 403, **513,** 1137, 1870, 2007, 2027, See also ministry, free

Big Sky Church of the Brethren/American Baptist Church, MT, 142

Bradford, OH, Church of the Brethren, 171

Bradley, Frank, 1242

Brandt, David, 172

Brethren movement, 176

Brethren rural churches, 1130

Bridgewater, VA, Church of the Brethren, 206

Brownsville, MD, Church of the Brethren, 216

Brubaker, John, 1242

Brumbaugh, Henry Boyer, 220

Bucher, Rufus Pfautz, 225

Buckeye, KS, Church of the Brethren, 226

Cabool, MO, Church of the Brethren, 237

Carlisle, PA, First Church of the Brethren, 255

Carson Valley, PA, Church of the Brethren, 256–257

Cedar Lake, IN, Church of the Brethren, 265

Center Chapel Brethren Church, IN, 267

Center Church of the Brethren, IN, 267

Chiques, PA, Church of the Brethren, 279

church membership, 813

Church of the Brethren, 300

Codorus, PA, Church of the Brethren, 323

Columbia, MO, Fellowship, 2166

Conemaugh, PA, Grace Brethren Church, 332

Conewago, PA, Church of the Brethren, 333

Covington, WA, Community Church of the Brethren, 350

Dallas Center, IA, Church of the Brethren, 360

Deardorff, Noble, 1240

Dierdorff, Daniel T., 1242

Dunkard Brethren Church, 2174

Early, Henry Clay, 413

East Fairview Church of the Brethren, PA, 415

Easton, MD, Peach Blossom Church of the Brethren, 417

egalitarian community, 294

Eglon, WV, Church of the Brethren, 430

Eller, Jay Vernard, 440

Empire, CA, Church of the Brethren, 445

evangelism, 461

Falling Spring Church of the Brethren, PA, 471

farming, 477, 479

Flat Rock Church of the Brethren, VA, 494

Forney, Roy S., 502

Francis, Jacob "Jay" Gottwals, 506

Fraternity Church of the Brethren, NC, 511

Frederick, MD, Church of the Brethren, 511

Fredericksburg, IA, Hillcrest Baptist and Brethren Church, 512

Fredericksburg, PA, Clover Creek Church of the Brethren, 513

Free Union, VA, Church of the Brethren, 513

Freeburg Church of the Brethren, OH, 514

Fremont Church of the Brethren, VA, 515

frontier lifestyles, 283

Fruitdale Community Church of the Brethren, OR, 520

Fruitland, ID, Church of the Brethren, 520

Garrison, IA, Church of the Brethren, 531

Geiger Church of the Brethren, PA, 533

Gettysburg, PA, Marsh Creek Church of the Brethren, 547

Girard, IL, Church of the Brethren, 550

Glendora, CA, Church of the Brethren, 553

Goshen, IN, City Church of the Brethren, 557

Goshen, IN, West Goshen Church of the Brethren, 558

Greenhill Church of the Brethren, MD, 571

Greenwood Church of the Brethren, MO, 572

Haller, Friedrich Conrad, 148

Hancock, MN, Church of the Brethren, 582

Hanover, PA, Church of the Brethren, 582

Harman Church of the Brethren, WV, 584

Hartville, OH, Church of the Brethren, 588

Hatfield Church of the Brethren, PA, 588

Heim, Gottlieb, 148

Heisey family, 595

Hershey, PA, Spring Creek Church of the Brethren, 599

Holmesville Church of the Brethren, NE, 620

Holsinger Church of the Brethren, PA, 623

Horst family, 630

Huntingdon, PA, Stone Church of the Brethren, 637

Illinois, 647

installation of ministers, 656

Iowa River Church of the Brethren, IA, 662

Irricana (First) Church of the Brethren, Alberta, Canada, 663

Ivester Church of the Brethren, IA, 665

Johnstown, PA, Roxbury Church of the Brethren, 675

Jordan Mines, VA, Rich Patch Brethren Church, 676

La Porte, IN, Church of the Brethren, 713

La Verne, CA, Church of the Brethren, 714

Lansing, MI, First Church of the Brethren, 725

lay preachers, 730

Leeton, MO, Mineral Creek Church of the Brethren, 735

Lehman, Samuel, 172

Leola, PA, Conestoga Church of the Brethren, 737

Libertyville Church of the Brethren, IA, 740

Lititz, PA, Church of the Brethren, 748

Little Swatara Church of the Brethren, PA, 750

Locust Grove Church of the Brethren, MD, 752

Long Green Valley Church of the Brethren, MD, 755

Longmeadow Church of the Brethren, MD, 757

Los Angeles, CA, Imperial Heights Church of the Brethren, 759

Lower Conewago Church of the Brethren, PA, 765

Lower Cumberland Church of the Brethren, PA, 765

Luray, VA, Church of the Brethren, 767

Marklesburg, PA, Church of the Brethren, 794

Martinsburg, PA, Memorial Church of the Brethren, 798

Meadow Branch Church of the Brethen, TN, 806

Meadow Branch Church of the Brethren, MD, 805

Mechanic Grove Church of the Brethren, PA, 806

mentoring, 2221

Mexico, IN, Church of the Brethren, 821

Middle Creek Church of the Brethren, PA, 825

Middletown, IN, Church of the Brethren, 826

Midland, VA, Church of the Brethren, 827

Mill Creek Church of the Brethren, NC, 832

minister of music, 844

ministry, 844

ministry, terminology, 847

Monroe Co. Church of the Brethren, IA, 870

Monrovia, MD, Bush Creek Church of the Brethren, 870

Mount Etna, IA, Church of the Brethren, 881

Mount Joy, PA, Florin Church of the Brethren, 882

Mount Pleasant Church of the Brethren, IN, 887

Mount Zion Road Church of the Brethren, PA, 888

Myrtle Point, OR, Church of the Brethren, 906

Nokesville, VA, Church of the Brethren, service from, 939

North Dakota congregations, 251

North Saint Joseph Church of the Brethren, MO, 1134

Oak Grove Church of the Brethren, MO, leadership by, 956

Oakland Church of the Brethren, OH, 957

Onekama, MI, Church of the Brethren, 975

Oneonta, AL, Church of the Brethren, 975

Osceola Church of the Brethren, IN, 984

Overholser, J. E., 171

Peace Valley Church of the Brethren, MO, 1003

Pennsylvania Church of the Brethren, 1005

pension funds, 1007

pension system, lack of, 1008

Petre, David R., 210

Pine Creek Church of the Brethren, IN, 1024

Piney Flats, TN, Church of the Brethren, 1025

placement of pastors, 1028

Pleasant Chapel Church of the Brethren, IN, 1030

Pleasant Dale Church of the Brethren, IN, 1030

Pleasant Hill Church of the Brethren, TN, 1032

Pleasant Valley Church of the Brethren, IN, 1034

Pleasant Valley Church of the Brethren, TN, 1035

Pleasant Valley Church of the Brethren, WV, 1036

Porter, Samuel E., 171

Potsdam, OH, Church of the Brethren, 1048

preaching, 1137

priesthood of all believers, 1057

pulpits, 1071

Purchase Line Church of the Brethren, PA, 1072

railroad fares, 1081

Reedley, CA, Church of the Brethren, 1091

Reichard, John Rowland, 1094

Reisch, Christian, 148

Richland, PA, Church of the Brethren, 1107

Roanoke, VA, First Church of the Brethren, 1113

Roanoke, VA, Oak Grove Church of the Brethren, 1113

Rock Run Church of the Brethren, IN, 1117

Rockingham Church of the Brethren, MO, 1118

Rocky Ridge, MD, Monocacy Church of the Brethren, 1119

Root River Church of the Brethren, MN, 1122

Rouzerville Church of the Brethren, PA, 1125

St. Paul Church of the Brethren, NC, 1135

Salem Church of the Brethren, IA, 1137

services to New Fairview Church of the Brethren, PA, 927

The Shepherd of the Valley (Blair), 748

shift to salaried ministry, 1376

Shorb, David M., 1242

Skippack Church of the Brethren, PA, 1189

South Keokuk Church of the Brethren, IA, 1205

Spring Run, PA, Church of the Brethren, 1215

Stover, John M., 171

Strycker, George, 1242

Sugar Valley Church of the Brethren, PA, 1235

Tacoma, WA, Larchmont Community Church of the Brethren, 1247

theological basis, 1261

theological education, 1256

Thomas, J. Irvin, 1330

training of ministers at Bible conferences, 136

Union Bridge, MD, Church of the Brethren, 1287

Union Ridge Church of the Brethren, IA, 1289

Upper Conwego Church of the Brethren, PA, 1294

Upper Fall Creek Church of the Brethren, IN, 1294–1295

vs. salaried, 1136–1137

Wakenda Church of the Brethren, MO, 1314

Washington, KS, Church of the Brethren, 1320

Weinman, Friedrich, 148

Welsh Run Church of the Brethren, PA, 1329

West Green Tree Church of the Brethren, PA, 1334

West Milton, OH, Church of the Brethren, 1335

White Branch Church of the Brethren, IN, 1339

White Horn Church of the Brethren, TN, 1340

White Oak Church of the Brethren, PA, 1340

Whitestone Church of the Brethren, WA, 1342

Windfall Church of the Brethren, IN, 1348

Wine, David Glick, 1349

women, contributions of, 1361–1362

Woodland Church of the Brethren, IL, 1364

Worthington Church of the Brethren, MN, 1380

Yellow Creek Church of the Brethren, PA, 1384

York, PA, Belvidere Church of the Brethren, 1388

York, PA, First Church of the Brethren, 1388

Young, David, 148

Free Spring meetinghouse, Lost Creek Church of the Brethren, PA, 760

Free Union, VA, Church of the Brethren, 273, **513–514**

free will, **514**, *See also* Arminianism human nature, doctrine of, 635

Free Will Baptists, 189

Free Will Brethren Lemon, John H., 1129

Free Will Dunkers (Lemonites), 177, **514, 737**

chart of Brethren bodies, place on, 1403–1405

Fundamental Brethren Church, 522 naming of, 910

Freeburg, OH, Church of the Brethren, **514**

Alliance, OH, Church of the Brethren, 2126

Reading Church of the Brethren, OH, 1084, 2126

Sandy German Baptist Brethren Church, OH, division of, 1143

Freed, Allan Gale, 1625

Freed, Amos, 1625

Freed, Lucy Mae, 230

Freed, Peter, 1625

Freed, William Henry, Jr., 210, 1625

freedom of conscience, *See* religious liberty

freedom of religion, *See* religious liberty

Freeland, Charles H., 1625

Freeland Church of the Brethren, WV, *See* Terra Alta, WV, Cooperative Brethren Church (CB/BC)

Freeland, David, 1254

Freeland German Baptist Brethren Church, WV, 1254

Freeland, Herman, 1315

Freeland, John M., 1254, 1625

Freeland schoolhouse, WV, 1254

Freeland settlement, WV, 1254

Freeling Settlement Old German Baptist Brethren Church, WV, **514**

Freeman, D. R., 1625

Freeman, Daniel, 228

Freeman, Erna, 1870

Freeman, Harold L., 1625 Pleasant Hill Church of the Brethren, TN, pastor/elder, 1032

Freeman, Harrison, 1625

Freeman, Hobart, 1625, 2180

Freeman, I. N. Mulvane, KS, Brethren Church, 895

Freeman, Leonard B., 1941

Freeman, Lillian (later Reed), 496

Freeman, Mrs. I. N. Mulvane, KS, Brethren Church, 895

Freeman, Wendell Lee, 2278

Freemasonry, **514–515** Brethren opposition to secret societies, 1163, 1164 Christianity and, 2002 debates, 371

Rosicrucians, related to, 1123
schisms, 296
Freeport, IL, Church of the Brethren, **515,**
1316, 1983
Freeport, MI
Hope Church of the Brethren, MI, 629
Freewill Baptists
Hymnal: A Worship Book, 2205
Freidel, Frank, 1859
Der Freidensbote von Concordia, 1942
Freighter, Isaiah Levi, 438, 1625
Freindschaft, David
Miller, Arlene Thomas on, 2347
Miller Jacob L., Jr. on, 2347
Thomas, Arlene on, 2347
Freindschaft, Ella Markey
Miller, Arlene Thomas on, 2347
Miller Jacob L., Jr. on, 2347
Thomas, Arlene on, 2347
Freinsheim, Palatinate, 2091
Freisen, Janet (later Brejda), 2166
Frelinghuysen, Jacob
Pietism, 1022
Fremantle, Anne Jackson, 1941
Fremont Avenue Brethren Church
South Pasadena, CA, Grace Brethren
Church, 1206
Fremont, CA
homelessness, 2203
Fremont Church of the Brethren, VA, **515,**
1267
Fremont Co., IA
Nishney Valley German Baptist
Brethren, 938
Fremont, OH
(First) Brethren Church, **515**
Grace Brethren Chapel, **515**
Grace Brethren Church, **515**
Grace Brethren congregation
minorities, ethnic and racial, 850
French, Alice
Ripon, CA, Grace Brethren Church,
1110
French and Indian War, 42, **515–516**
Brethren movement, 309
destruction of Dunkard Bottom settle-
ment, WV, 1336
Ephrata Community, 451
Mennonite Church (MC), 815
frontier, 519
Germans and, 2091
Hochstetler, Christian, 615
Morrisons Cove, 877
Native Americans, 2229
Pennsylvania Brethren settlement, 1004
Steiner family, 2378
Studebaker, Heinrich and wife killed
by Indians, 1231
French Broad Church of the Brethren, TN,
516
history of, 2332
French Creek, **516**
French, Donald
Matteson, MI, Brethren Church, 803
French Equatorial Africa, *See* Central
African Republic
Brethren Church, 270
Foreign Missionary Society (BC,
FGBC), 501
France, 506
Grace Brethren Church, 268
Hathaway, Carrie E. and John Wesley,
588

medical missions, 807
mission schools, 853, 854
missionaries voyaging to, 862
missions, *857,* 862
missions, thesis about, 1956
Noatemo, Jean, 938
Oubangui-Chari district, *See* Oubangui-
Chari, French Equatorial Africa
Voloungou, Marc, 1309
French Evangelical Free Churches, 505
French family
at New Rockford, ND, Church of the
Brethren, 932
French, Hannah Dustin, 1941
French Huguenots
Community of True Inspiration, and
roots in, 330–331
French, Ivan H., 1319, 1625
French, John
Ripon, CA, Grace Brethren Church,
1110
French language
study of in Quebec, 1075
French Lick, IN
theological study conference (1981),
1258
French Loyalist refugees, 146
French, Mary Jane (later Miller), 2018
French, Mrs. Donald
Matteson, MI, Brethren Church, 803
French, Paul Comly, **515,** 1941
French Revolution
Ephrata Community, 451
millennialism, 834
French, Robert, 1625
Frenkendorf, **516**
Fresenius, Johann Philip, 611, 1941
historical writing, 611
Freshour, C. N., 1625
Fresno, CA, 255
Fresno, CA, First Church of the Brethren,
238, 244, **516–517**
Fresno Co., CA, 689, 727
Figarden Church of the Brethren, CA,
489
Reedley, CA, Church of the Brethren,
1091
Fresno Irrigated Farms Company, 689
Fretz, Abraham James, 534, 1941–1942
Fretz, Barbara
Lakeland, FL, Grace Brethren Church,
2213
Fretz, C. D., 1942
Fretz, Daniel, 1625
Fretz, J. Winfield, 1942
Fretz, Jay, 1625
North Kokomo Grace Brethren Church,
IN, pastor, 948
Fretz, John
Lakeland, FL, Grace Brethren Church,
2213
Fretz, Mable (later Kulp), 709
Fretz, Tobias L., 1625
Fretz, Walter R., 188
Fretz, William B., 1625
Freundschaftsheim (Friendship House),
517, *See also* World Friendship
Center
Frey, Adam, 1942
Frey, Andreas, 176, 517, **517,** 923, 1399,
1625, 1942, 2057
influence against the Moravians, 1957
Marienborn Moravian Church center,

staying in, 792
Moravian Church, 876
Stentz, Howard W. on, 2358
Frey, Charles C., 42, 1625
Frey, Christine Binkele, 1942
Frey, Daniel D., 1942
Frey, Elizabeth, 2098
Frey, Enoch, 1625
Frey, Eugene R., 1942
Frey family
family history, 1942,1980
Frey (Fry) family, **517**
Frey (Fry), Obed F., 1625
Frey, Gottfried, 1942
Frey, Jacob C., 2031
Frey, James E., 2063
Frey, John
descendants, 1942
Frey, Kenneth Harvey, 1625
Frey, L. M., 1942
Frey, Levi B., 1942
Frey, Martin, 1942
Frey, Mary Ann, 1942
Frey, Miriam Carper
Palmyra, PA, Church of the Brethren,
991
Frey, Orlin F., 1625
Frey, Ralph R., 1222, 1625
Frey, Samuel Challot, 1942
Frey, Samuel Clarence, 1942
Frey, Veronica (later Müller), 517
Müller, Joseph, wife of, 894
Frey, Wilhelm, **517**
Frey, William Ray, Sr., 2278
Frick, Elmer E., 1625
Frick, John, 569, 1625
"Dunker" of Great Swamp, 1974
Frick, Paul Sumner
on Grumbacher, Hans and descendants,
2332
Fricke, Elmer D., 114, 720, 758, 1625
Simi Valley, CA, Grace Brethren
Church, pastor, 1182
Fricke, Gloria
Simi Valley, CA, Grace Brethren
Church, 1182
Fricker, William, 503
Fricks family
Patterson, CA, Church of the Brethren,
995
Friddle, Stephen R., 2278
Fridley, Andrew, 1333
Fridley, Benjamin H., 1333
Fridley family, 1333
Fridley, John, 1333
Rock Camp German Baptist Bethren
Church, WV, elder, 1116
Fridley, Robert, 243
Der Friedensbote von Concordia, 1942
(The Peace Messenger of
Concordia), **517**
Concordia, 331
Friedensburg
Hochmann von Hochenau, Ernst
Christoph, 615
Friedenstal
Schwarzenau Brethren worship in, 911
Friedland, Michael B.
on antiwar movements, 2332
Friedly, Annie M. (later Anthony), 40
Friedly, John, 1626
Friedmann, Robert F., 1942
Theology of Anabaptism, 1259

Friedrich, Gerhard G., 1859, 1942
Friedrich I, King of Prussia, 72
Friedrich Wilhelm, king of Prussia
 Naas, Johannes, 1063
Friedsam, Father, *See* Beissel, Conrad
Friedsam Gottrecht, Father, See Beissel, Conrad
Friend, A., 1942
Friend family, 1302
Friend, George Henry, 1626
Friend, Louisa, 514
Friend, Mary Ann
 South Haven Old German Baptist Brethren Church, MI, 1205
Friend, Samuel M., 1626
Friend, Virginia, 918
The Friend of the Fatherland
 Sala, Solomon, printer, 1136
Friends, *See* Quakers
Friends Ambulance Unit (FAU, AFSC), 23
Friends Committee of Spain, **517–518**
Friends Committee on National Legislation
 Wilson, Edward Raymond, 1347
Friends Committee on Spain (AFSC), 23
Friends Grove meetinghouse
 Gettysburg, PA, Marsh Creek Church of the Brethren, 547
Friends Meeting, Clear Creek, OH
 Cadwallader, John, 237
Friends meetings
 Christian Peacemaker Teams (CPT), 2161
Friends Run Fellowship
 Smith Creek Fellowship Church of the Brethren, WV, 1191
Friends Service Council of London, 23, 1199
Friends, Society of, *See* Quakers
Friends United Meeting
 Jubilee: God's Good News Curriculum, 2209
Friends University
 Peters, Woodford W., educator, 1011
Friendship Church of the Brethren, MD,
 See Linthicum Heights, MD, Friendship Church of the Brethren
 example of Christian community place name, 911
Friendship Church of the Brethren, NC, **518**
 example of Christian community place name, 911
Friendship Manor, **518**
Friendship, NC, congregation
 Peak Creek Church of the Brethren, NC, 1003
Friendship Press
 Kimmel, Theodore Acroyd, 693
friendship, right hand of, 698
Friendship schoolhouse
 Sams Creek Church of the Brethren, MD, 1141
Friendship (ship), 260
 Bicksler, Peter, 144
 Rowland family voyage to America, 1127
 Strickler, Heinrich, 1229
Friendship Trains, 286, **518**
Friendship Village Retirement Center
 Aeby, John Milton, 2127
Fries, Adelaide L., 1942
Friesen, Gerhard Kurt, 1943
Friesen, Leland I., 357, 1626
Friesen, Leland J., 275, 515

Friesland, Netherlands, 1241, *See* Surhuisterveen, Friesland
 Brethren, lineage of, 613
 Brethren moving to, 1158
 Grebe (Grebi), Georg, 569
 immigration of Brethren and Mack family to, 776–777, 778
 Kalcklöser, Johann Heinrich, 681
Frietchie, Barbara
 Sauer Bible, 1994
Frisia, Dompelaars in, 395
Frisian village, 2083
Fristoe, MO, 1280
Fritsch, William A., 1943
Fritter, Robert Nolan, 1626
Fritz, Friedrich, 1943
Fritz, John, 1626
Fritz, Katie (later Wolf), 1359
Frizellburg, Carroll Co., MD, 162
frock coats, 967, 1029
Frodel, Jacob, 1626
Froehlich, Harry J., Jr., 725, 1626
Froelich (Fröhlich), Samuel Heinrich, 43, **518**, 1246, 1864, *See also* Bernese Anabaptists
 Rothenberger, George Philip, 1124
Froese, Wolfang, 2332
Der Fröhliche Botschafter, 1943
 Meyers, Jacob, 822
Fröhliche Botschafter, Der (*The Cheerful Messenger*), **518**
Froid, MT, 142
 Church of the Brethren, *See* Big Sky Church of the Brethren/American Baptist Church, MT
Frölich, S. H., 1246
From the Beginning; Bermudian Church of the Brethren (Julius), **2375**
Fromm, Roger W.
 on PA Germans, 2332
Froncek, Thomas, 1943
Front Royal, VA, Church of the Brethren, **518**
frontier, **518–519**
 Baptist Church, 1783–1830, 2079
 Christian education movement, 283
 congregational life and, 176
 culture of, 59
 migration of Brethren, 829
 railroads and settlement, 1082
Frontier Church of the Brethren, NE, *See* Highline Church of the Brethren, NE
Frontier churches
 and "New Lights" revivalism, 930
 Nezperce, ID, Church of the Brethren, 935, *935*
Frontier Co., NE
 Highline Church of the Brethren, NE, 606
Frost, Alexander (Elech), 749, 1626
Frost, Earl Clarence, 1943
Frost, May Miller, 1943
Frostburg, MD, First Church of the Brethren, **519**, 1339
Fruit, G. L., 1626
"Fruit of the Vine" (Logan), 2343
Fruita, CO, Church of the Brethren, **519–520**, 1299
 Glade Park, CO, Community Church of the Brethren, 551
 Grand Junction, CO, Koinonia Brethren-Baptist Church, 565

Fruitdale Academy, 14, **520**, 1350
Fruitdale, AL, Church of the Brethren, **520,** 1339
 Neff, James Monroe at, 922
 fiction, references in, 2097
Fruitdale Community Church of the Brethren, OR, **520**, 1346
Fruitland, ID, Church of the Brethren, 247, **520**
 Shamberger, Chauncey, 1171
 Jackpot Church, NV, 2212
 Emmett Church of the Brethren, ID, 445
 as mission point, 996
Fruitvale Church of the Brethren, (Bangor) CA, **520**
Frushnour, Charles N., 1626
Fruth, Glenn John, 1626, 1943, 1956
Fruth, Lois Marie, 1838
Fruth, Melchior
 family history, 1943
Fruth, Pearl Ann, 1841
Fry, 755
Fry, Andrew, *See* Frey, Andreas
Fry, Barbara Hochstetler, 1949
Fry, Carl, 245
Fry, Clyde Clifford, 517, 1626, 1312
Fry, Daniel, 361, 419, 517, **520–521**, 521, 545, 737, 1273, 1384, 1626, *See also* Fry, Julia Ann Elder
 Hope, Christian, 628
Fry, Daniel E., 1626
Fry, David, 1626
Fry, Dorotha Wenger (later Mason), 2286
 on Gospel of John, 2345
 on Winder, J. O., 2345
Fry, Earl S., 1626
Fry, Enoch, 109, 1626
 North Manchester Old German Baptist Brethren Church, IN, elder-in-charge, 949
Fry, Esther Kinsey, 517
Fry family, 1390, *See also* Frey family
Fry, Francis
 on Bridgewater College, 2362
Fry, Harold D., 1626
Fry, Henry, 1626
Fry, Isaac, 384
Fry, Ivan Lowell, 7, 1626, 2301, **2382**
Fry, Joseph D., 1949
Fry, Julia Ann Elder Eisenbise, 419, **521**, 1273
Fry, Levi, 1626
Fry, Linda L.
 on CB architecture, 2332
 on CB worship, 2332
Fry, Mary Bontrager, 1943
Fry, Mattie (later Gingerich), 1949
Fry, Mattie V. (later Wayland), 1323
Fry, Mattie Yoder, 1943
Fry, Nancy, 521
Fry, Noah Joseph, 1943
Fry, Pauline Frade De Lauter, 1943
 on De Lauter families, 2332
Fry, Ralph L., 517, 1626, 1943
Fry, Russell, 1626
Fry, Samuel, 517
Fry, Susane, 521
Fry, W. J., 1626
Fry, William H., 1626
Frybarger family, 1224
Frye, A. B., 1626
Frye family, 1348

Maryville, TN, Oakland German Baptist Brethren Church, 799
Frye, Nancy Kettering
on Brethren, life of, 2332
on Major, Sarah Righter, 2332
Frye, William H., 1626
Fryer, Judith E., 1859
Fryfogle, Addison, 1626
Fryfogle, Benjamin, 1239, 1626
Fryman, Calvin O., 1626
Fryman, Darrell Calvin, 1626, 2301
Michigan City, IN, Church of the Brethren, pastor, 825
Fryman, Robert Paul, 1235, 1626
Frymoyer, Cochran T., 1626
Frysinger, Anne on
on PA German families, 2355
Frysinger, Doris J. Fluke, 1838
Frysinger, Hiram J., 249, 1626, 2301
Frysinger, Roy Donald, 1838
Frystown house
Little Swatara Church of the Brethren, PA, 750
Frystown, PA, Bethel Dunkard Brethren Congregation, **521**
Fuchs, Emanuel, 521
Fuchs, Justus, **521,** 1626
moveable type, casting of, 1146
Fudge, Ira, 204
Fuerst family
Grandview, WA, Grace Brethren Church, 566
Fugate's Fork, KY, preaching point, 405
Fugett, John, 1243
Fugett, Mary (Molly), 1243
Fuhrman, George B., 1626
Fuhrmann, Otto W., 1943
Fulbright scholars
Bittinger, Desmond Wright, 143
Fulk, Beidler Jennings, 1626, 2301
Fulk, George H., **521,** 1626
Fulk, John, 521
Fulk, Martha Brightbill, 1943
Fulk, Murl E., 1626
Fulk, Phyllis Belle Dunn, 1943
Fulk, Roy Walter, 1626, 2301
Fulk, Sara Wine, 521
Fulker family, 735
Fulk's Run, VA, 1243
Mountain Grove Church of the Brethren, VA, 889
Full family
Prosperity Brethren Church, WV, 1062
Full Gospel Business Men's Fellowship International, **521**
full ministry, *See* elders
Full Report, **2371,** *See also* Verbatim Report
Fuller, Carlton J., 360, 1626
Fuller, Charles E., 2179
Fuller Evangelistic Asociation
Hispanic Ministries (BC), 2198, 2199
Mexico, missionaries to, 820
The Missionary Board (BC), 856
Fuller, Harry, 1626
Fuller, J. P., 1292
Fuller, John, 1626
Fever! The Hunt for a New Killer
nurse missionary, 952
Fuller, Linda
Habitat for Humanity International, 2195
Fuller, Margaret, 146

Fuller, Millard
Habitat for Humanity International, 2195
Fuller Theological Seminary
founding of, 2179
Fullerton, CA, 161
Fullmer, Everett, 102, 1626, 2301
Fult, A. H., 1626
Fulton, Calvin B., 559, 1626
Fulton Co., IL, 233, 251, 1214, 1357, 1364
Mud Valley Old German Baptist Brethren Church, IL, 892
South Fulton Dunkard Brethren Congregation, IL, 1205
Fulton Co., IN, 691
Fulton Co., OH, 1243, 1334
Good (Guth) family, 556
Fulton Co., PA, 338
history, 1967
New Testament Brethren, 932
Pentecostal Brethren, 1008
Pleasant Ridge Church of the Brethren, PA, 1034
Fulton, Eleanore J., 1943
Fultz family, 733
Fultz, Hazel, 102
Fultz, Samuel, 1626
Fulz, Jesse, 212
Funck, Abraham, 521
Funck, Bishop Henry, 1941
Funck, Christian, 521
Funck (Funk) family, **521**
Funck, Heinrich, 453, 521, 525
Funck, Henry, 521
Funck, Jacob, 521
Funck, John, 521
Fund for the Americas (CB), *See* SHARE
Fund for the Americas in the United States (FAUS)
minorities, ethnic and racial, 850
Fundaciones Brethren y Unida, *See* Brethren Foundation
Fundamental Brethren, 78, 118, 303, **522**
chart of Brethren bodies, place on, 1403–1405
"Message of the Brethren Ministry," 818
Pigeon River Church of the Brethren, NC, 1023
Upper Brummetts Creek Church of the Brethren, NC, 1294
Fundamentalism, 74, 187, **522–523,** 695
Brethren Church, 183, 185
Brethren in Christ Fellowship, 190
Brooklyn, SC, Church of the Brethren, 212
bus ministries and, 232
church membership, 812–813
Church of the Brethren, 1969
churches leaving the Brethren for, 21
education, 428
Emmett Church of the Brethren, ID, 445
evangelicalism and, 2179
evolution, 463
Fellowship of Grace Brethren Churches (FGBC), 484, 486, 2181
Frostburg, MD, First Church of the Brethren, 519
grace, doctrine of, 562
Grace Schools (Grace Theological Seminary, Grace College), 563
higher education and, 2179

impact on the Brethren, 73–74
influence on Brethren theology, 1261
Jewish evangelism, 671
Juniata College School of Theology, 1155
kingdom of God, position on, 695
McIntire, Carl, 774
Medford, OR, Church of the Brethren, 806
Mennonites, 816
"Message of the Brethren Ministry," 817
millennialism, 834
missions, 860
Modernism, 866
modernism, struggles with, 2327
noncreedalism, 942
Pennsylvania Brethren and schism, 1005
prophecy conferences, 1062
resurrection, and Brethren teachings about, 1102
schisms, 303
science, attitudes regarding, 1160
Scofield Bible, 1160
Snider, Harold, 1194
Social Gospel Movement, 1197
vs. liberalism and neoorthodoxy, 923
The Fundamentals, 2179
fundamentalism, 522
"Message of the Brethren Ministry," 817
Funderberg, Cyrus, 1626
Funderberg, Daniel, 523, 1277, 1626,
Funderberg, Drue Dresher, **523,** 1277, 1626
Funderberg, Earl Oren, 239, 240, 626, 1626, 2301
New Troy, MI, Grace Brethren Church, pastor in, 932
Ozark Grace Brethren Church, MI, pastor, 987
Funderberg, George K., 1627
Funderberg, George W., 1627
Funderberg, Harrie C., 1627
Funderberg, Michael D., 1627
Funderburg, Alvin K., 1943
Funderburg, Carrie Dresher, 523
Funderburg, David, 352
Funderburg, Mrs. Earl, 239
Funderburg family
Fahnestock family, 465
Filbrun family, 490
Funderburg, Forest Ethel Denlinger, 523
Funderburg, George, 375
Funderburg, Isaac Vaughn, **523,** 1627, 1943
Pasadena, CA, Church of the Brethren, pastor in, 994
Funderburg, Jacob C., 523
Seneca Church of the Brethren, FL, presiding elder, 1166
Funderburg, Mary Denlinger, 375
Funderburg, Michael D., 356
Mill Run Grace Brethren Church, MD, pastor, 833
Funderburg, Sarah D. Ratekin, 375, 523
Funderburg, Susanna Crist, 352
Funderburg, William, 523
Funderburg, Eve Boone, 523
descendants, 1783–1978, 1943
Funderburgh family, 236, **523**
Funderburgh, J. Truman, 1943
Funderburgh, Jacob, 523, 1627
descendants, 1783–1978, 1943

North Manchester, IN, Church of the Brethren, elder, 949

Funderburgh, Jacob C., 1627
    Rocky Ford, CO, Church of the Brethren, minister, 1118

Funderburk family
    history of, 1943

Funderburk, Guy B., 1943
    fundraising, 187, 188, *See also* stewardship
    Church of the Brethren, 2075

funerals, *See* burial customs and funerals

Fung, Timothy, 1627

Funk, Benjamin, **525,** 561, 1943, 1952
    hymnals, 642
    Life and Labors of Elder John Kline, 974
    Philadelphian Society, 1019

Funk, Benjamin H., 1627

Funk, Boyd (Boyte) Howell, 1627

Funk, Christian, 144

Funk, Cora Landis, 525

Funk, Dan, 144

Funk, Ella Burger, 525

Funk, Emma (later Platt), 758

Funk, Esther (later Erbach), 453

Funk family, 1307, 2090, *See also* Funck family
    genealogy and descendants, 1941
    Roanoke, LA, Church of the Brethren, 1112

Funk, Heinrich, *See* Funck, Heinrich

Funk, J. E., 1627

Funk, J. W.
    Smithville, OH, First Brethren Church, 1192

Funk, Jacob, **525,** 1343, 1345, 1627, 1943
    Pomona, CA, Church of the Brethren, pastor, 1045
    San Bernardino, CA, Church of the Brethren, pastor, 1141

Funk, John, 144, 1627, 2382

Funk, Jonathan, 1627

Funk, Joseph, 525, **525,** 1860, 1864, 1895, 1943, 1973, 2090

Funk, Katherine Wagner, 525

Funk, Keith Alan, 2278

Funk, Kevin Neal, 2279

Funk-Kline controversy
    Historic Peace Churches, 608

Funk, Levi, 525

Funk, Lloyd Victor, 1627

Funk, Mrs. J. W.
    Smithville, OH, First Brethren Church, 1192

Funk, Onnie (Mr. and Mrs.), 579

Funk, Peter, 1627

Funk, Polly, 405

Funk, Samuel William, 332, 553, 1627
    Santa Ana, CA, Church of the Brethren, 1144

Funk, Susan, 2081

Funk, Turah, 751

Funk, Viola (later Fasnacht), 480

Funk, William, 1627

Funke, Anneliese Marckwald, 140, 1859
    historical writing, 611

Funkhouse, Mitchell W., 2279

Funkhouser family, 1868

Funkhouser, Frances Virginia (later Locke), 751

Funkhouser, Madison
    Maurertown, VA, Brethren Church, 803

Funkhouser, Perry M., 239

Fuqua, Evelyn, 188, 406

Furer, Howard B., 1943–1944

Furgesen, Ashley, 1627

Furnace Co., NE
    Edison German Baptist Brethren Church, NE, 2373

Furnace, PA, 144

Furnas Co., NB
    Beaver City congregation, 921

Furnas Co., NE
    Sappa Creek Church of the Brethren, NE, 1145

furniture, 59, **525,** *525*
    in churches, 2131
    Ephrata, 1990
    stoves, Bible imprint on, 2010

Furrey, G. W., 1627

Furrow, Donald D., 1627
    Montclair, CA, Grace Brethren Church, pastor, 871

Furry family, 216

Furry, Hannah Brown, 526

Furry, John, 525

Furry, John B., 1627

Furry, John E., 1627

Furry, Leonard, **525–526,** 1627

Furry, Samuel B., 512, 1627
    Martinsburg, PA, Grace Brethren Church, pastor, 798

Furry, Samuel E., 259

Furry, William Davies, 501, **526,** 746, 1627,
    "Message of the Brethren Ministry," 817
    South Bend, IN, Ardmore Brethren Church, pastor, 1203

fusion reactors
    nuclear energy, 952

Fuska, Bernard Anthony, 1627

Fuson, Washington, 1627

Fuss, John Calvin, 912

Futch, Earl, 1627
    Orlando, FL, Grace Brethren Church, 982

Futch, Earl L., 1849

Futch, Lita
    Orlando, FL, Grace Brethren Church, 982

Futch, Lita Helen Acevedo, 1849

Fyoch, C. E., 1627

Fyock, Abraham, 1627

Fyock, Elizabeth (Zenobia or Senopie)
    Snow Hill Community, 1195

Fyock family
    Hoffman (Huffman) family, 618

Fyock, James W., 1627

Fyock, Joan
    on hymns, poets and composers, 2332

Fyock, John, family
    Shade Creek Church of the Brethren, PA, 1170

Fyock, John W., 1627

Fyock, Olan
    Montgomery Church of the Brethren, PA, pastor, 872

Fyock, Oran, 1627

Fyock, S. H., 675, 1627

Fyock, W. H., 1944

G., E. B., 1944

G. R. and I. Railroad, 317

G. W. Kieffaber
    Bible Institute, *131*

Gabas, Lardin, 307, 2056

Gabbert, Darren, 2166

Gabbert, Denise, 2166

Gable, Austin F., 705, 1627

Gable, Eli, 1627

Gable, Elizabeth, 155

Gable, J. S., 1211, 1627

Gable, John, 1627
    Maquoketa German Baptist Brethren, IA, 791
    Middle Creek Church of the Brethren, IA, elder, 825
    South Keokuk Church of the Brethren, IA, elder, 1205

Gable, Opal, 241

Gaby, Martin, *See* Gaube, Martin

Gaby, Samuel A., 1627

Gaby, Waldo E., 1627

Gaddis, M. E., 1944

Gaddis, V. H., 1944

Gaddis, Vincent H., 1944

Gads, John, 1627

Gadzama, Bubwa N., 1627

Gadzama, Karagama Apagu, 307, 1627

Gadzama, Margima N., 1627

Gadzama, Njida Madanda, 1627

Gadzama, Wambursa Y., 1627

Gaebelein, A. C., 390

Gaga, W. M., 1627

Gage Avenue Brethren Church, *See* Bell, CA, Brethren Church (FGBC, Gage Avenue)

Gage Co. Central Church of the Brethren, NE, 268

Gage Co., IA
    Centerview, IA, congregation, 901

Gage Co., NE
    Filley German Baptist Brethren Church, NE, 2374
    Holmesville Church of the Brethren, NE, 620
    Hope Memorial Church (German Baptist Brethren), NE, 2375
    migration of Brethren, 830
    North Beatrice Church of the Brethren, NE, 945
    (South) Beatrice congregation, origins of, 920

Gager, William Herbert, 1944

Gahagen Charitable Foundation, 2187

Gahagen, Clarence Kern, 2187

Gahagen, Zella Johns, **2187,** *2187,* 2340

Gahm, William Bernard, 1627
    Sheldon Church of the Brethren, IA, pastor in, 1175

Gailor, Henry, 1628

Gainer family
    Mount Zion Church of the Brethren, WV, 888

Gainer (Ganer), N. W., 1628

Gainer, Solomon
    Mount Cassell Old German Baptist Brethren Church, WV, 880

Gainesville, TX, 1346
    Gaiwaka, Esther Doyai, 527
    Gaiwaka, Noel, 268, **527**
    mission schools, 854
    and Noatemo, Jean in French Equatorial Africa, 938

Galassini, Florence Kuhn
    on Kuhn, John, 2331
    on Kuhn, Susannah Mock, 2331

Galatians

3:27, 85
3:27–28, 85
Kent, Homer Austin, Jr., 2211, 2340
Galbreath, Marie (later Good), 1951
Gale, Ethel L., 1628
Galegor, Stephen Stuart, Sr., 2279
Galentine, Homer P., 571
Galesburg Church of the Brethren, KS, **527**
Galey, Jack, 1278, 1628
Galion, OH, Grace Brethren Church, **527**
Gall, Amy (CB)
    Rio Prieto, PR, Iglesia de los Hermanos (CB) and, 2244
Gall, Amy S. (later Ritchie), 2291
Gallatin schoolhouse
    Fairchance, PA, Church of the Brethren, 467
Galle, Jack, 227
Galley family, 2089
Galley, Harriet
    Mechanicsburg, PA, Dunkard Brethren Congregation, 806
Galley, Jacob
    Mechanicsburg, PA, Dunkard Brethren Congregation, 806
galley slaves, 121, 159, **527**
    Bern, Switzerland, 253
    Brethren movement, 174
    capital punishment, 253
    Goyen, Gossen, 562
    Mennonites securing release of Christian Liebe from, 815
    persecution, 1009
    prisons, and Christian Liebe, 1058–1059
Galloway schoolhouse, Wood Grove Brethren-Christian Parish, MI, 1363
Galpin Union chapel, MT, 1301
Galveston Grace Brethren Church, IN
    North Kokomo Grace Brethren Church, IN, 948
Galveston Hurricane of 1900
    Manvel, TX, Church of the Brethren, destroying meetinghouse, 789
Galveston, IN, 1294
Gamadia, Reshamlal A., 1628
Gamble, Arlene, 755
gambling and lotteries, **528**, *See also* card playing
    Brethren Church, 2178
    United Brethren in Christ, 1290
Gameti, Chimanlal V., 1628
Gameti, Keshavlal, 1628
Gameti, Maganlal, 1628
Gameti, Manubhai B., 1628
Gameti, Rupsing M., 1628
Gammon, James Roger, 1944
Gammon, Jewell Josephine Neer, 1944
Gammon, W. C(lyde), 1628
Gammon, W. W., 738
Gammon, William J., 1944
"Gandastogues" tribe, Conestoga, 332
Gandhi, Mahatma (Mohandas Karamchand), 313, **528**, 874, 1003
Gandy, Ted Elwin, 1628
Ganer (Gainer), Solomon C., 1628
Ganer, Solomon C., 268, 679, 1213
Ganer, William A., 679
Ganeshiji, Ghagwandas, 1628
Ganns, Grey O., 1628
Gans, Albert, 1628
Gans family, 1215

Gans, John, 1628
    Nimishillen Church of the Brethren, minister in, 937
    Stark Co., OH, Brethren settlement, 961
Gans, John D., 1628
Gans, Lewis Albert, 1628
Gans, William G., 1628
    Masontown, PA, Brethren Church, pastor, 800
Ganshorn, Mary, 1852
Gantt, Charles E., 349, 366, 1628
Gantt, Frank L., 350, 1628
    North Hampton, OH, Donnels Creek Old German Baptist Brethren Church, minister, 948
    Old Order German Baptist Church minister, 972
Gantz, Agnes (later Mack)
    Mack family, 778
Gantz, Fred Barry, 1628
Gantz (Gans), Georg Balthasar, **528**
Gantz, J. D., 1289
Gantz, Johanna, 528
Gantz, John, 1628
Gap Fellowship
    Mechanic Grove Church of the Brethren, PA, 806
Gap, Greenland, WV, 16
Gapp, Samuel H., 2060
Garabel family, 2099
Garb Law, **528**, 1896
Garber, (son-in-law of Jacob Long), 724
Garber, A., 192
Garber, A. Z., *See The Prophetic Age*
Garber, Aaron Leedy, 64, 186, **528**, 734, 1628
    Mansfield, OH, Walcrest Brethren Church, preaching, 787
Garber, Aaron W., 2279
Garber, Abbie Arnold, 529
Garber, Abraham, **528**, 529, 1628, 1909
    Middle River Church of the Brethren, VA, minister, 825
    Mountain Valley Church of the Brethren, TN, 889
Garber, Abraham (1760-1846), 90
Garber, Abraham D., 1628
Garber, Abram, 1628
Garber, Ada Louella (later Drushal), 405, 689, 760, 1361, 1603
    Riverside Christian Training School, 1111
    Rowdy, KY, Brethren Church, 1126
Garber, Alice Stebbins, 529
    Mount Carroll, IL, Church of the Brethren, mission worker, 880
Garber, Anne Winger
    National Older Adult Conferences, 2229
Garber, B. B., 331, 502
Garber, B. F., 1628
Garber, Barbara (later Snowberger), *See* Snowberger, Barbara Karper
Garber, Barbara Miller, 529, 530
    Mason, Floyd R. on descendants of, 2346
    Mason, Kathryn Garst on descendants of, 2346
    Müller (Miller) family, 895
Garber, Benedict
    descendants, 1944
Garber, Benjamin Bowman, 1628

Garber, Beverly Jean Wooley, 1849
Garber, Brother
    Replogle, Peter, election as minister, 1100
Garber, C. S., 438
Garber, Catherine (later Fleure), 495
Garber, Charles Solivan (Sullivan), 1628
    Palestine Old German Baptist Brethren Church, OH, 991
    South Saint Joseph Church of the Brethren, MO, minister, 1135
Garber, Christian M., 528
Garber, Clair E., 2279
Garber, Clara, 1849
Garber, Clark M., 1944
Garber, Clem
    Ripon, CA, Grace Brethren Church, 1110
Garber, Cora
    Old Order German Baptist Church minister, 972
Garber, Cora Gregory (later Dunning), 1920
Garber, D. H., 1628
Garber, Daniel, 475, 529, 530, 1264, 1628
    Prices Creek Old German Baptist Brethren Church, OH, minister and presiding elder, 1057
Garber, Daniel Benjamin, 1628, **2382**
Garber, Daniel (Gerber), 58
Garber, David Benjamin, **528–529**, 1324, 1356, 1628, 1944
    Old Order German Baptist Church minister, 972
Garber, David H., 213, 1628
Garber, David Leedy, 528, 529
    Old Order German Baptist Church, 2235
Garber, David Paul, 2301
Garber, Dean Kenneth, 1944
Garber, Della Tinkel, 528, 529
Garber, Dennis, 1628
    Painter Creek Old German Baptist Brethren Church, OH, 990
Garber, Edith (later Gingrich)
    Gingrich, Raymond Eugene, 2190
Garber, Elizabeth
    Mason, Floyd R. on descendants of, 2346
    Mason, Kathryn Garst on descendants of, 2346
Garber, Elizabeth (later Fifer), 488
Garber, Elizabeth (later Myers)
    Myers, Minor Morton, mother of, 904
Garber, Elizabeth (later Wine), 1349
Garber, Elmer D., 1628, 2301, **2382**
    Oak Grove Old German Baptist Brethren Church, OH, minister, 956
Garber, Essie, 256
Garber, Esther M. Reiser, 1944
Garber, Esther Pence, 748, 1944
Garber family, 355, 700, 740, 1214, 1253, 1333, 1391, 1944
    Erbaugh family, 453
    Flat Rock Church of the Brethren, VA, 493
    history of, 1956
    Jasper, MO, Church of the Brethren, 669
    Johnson City, TN, Knob Creek Church of the Brethren, 672
    Modesto, CA, La Loma Grace Brethren Church, 867
    Parsons Old German Baptist Brethren

Church, KS, 994
Peabody Old German Baptist Brethren
    Church, KS, 997
Pleasant View Church of the Brethren,
    TN, 1037
Sanger family, related to, 1144
Scherffig family, related to, 1152
Garber, Floyd Hyre
    Palestine Old German Baptist Brethren
        Church, OH, 991
Garber, Frances (later Flory), 498
Garber, Frank, 274
Garber, Mrs. Frank, 274
Garber, Frank A., 1628
Garber, Frank W., 274, 1629
Garber, Frank Yount, 1628
Garber, Franklin Levi, 1628
Garber, Fred M., 471, 1628
Garber (Garver, Gerber) family, 58,
    529–530
Garber, George W., 106, 1628
Garber (Gerber), Daniel, **528**
Garber (Gerber), John H., 529, **529**, 530
Garber, Glenn M., 1628
Garber, H. P., 1628
Garber, Harold D., 1628, 2279
Garber, Helen, 1217
Garber, Henry, **529**, 1306, 1341, 1356, 1628
    Oak Grove Old German Baptist
        Brethren Church, OH, minister,
        956
    Yoder, D. Willard (OGBB) and, 2267
Garber, I. A., 208
Garber, IA, Church of the Brethren, **529**
Garber, Isaac J., 1628, 2101
    Melbeth, VA, congregation, 1024
    Sangerville Church of the Brethren,
        minister, 1144
Garber, J. A.
    Johnstown, PA, First Brethren Church,
        673
    National Laymen's Organization, lead-
        ership in, 917
    New Lebanon, OH, First Brethren
        Church, pastor in, 930
Garber, J. C., 1220
Garber, J. Ruskin, 1628
Garber, Jacob, 529, 530, 1628
    genealogy and descendants, 1944
Garber, Jacob A., *530, 1629*
Garber, Jacob C., 1629
Garber, James K.
    National Older Adult Conferences,
        2229
Garber, James William, 1629
Garber, Joel, 1214, 1629
Garber (Carver, Garver), John, 149, 396,
    410, 528, 529, 737, 738, 740,
    1276, 1306, 1307, 1356, 1383,
    1581, 1629, **2382**
    biography, 1938
    Middle River Church of the Brethren,
        VA, elder, 825
Garber, John A., 1944
Garber, John Absolom, 1629
Garber, John Adam, 1629
Garber, John Cline, 45, 1629
Garber, John Fair, 1629, **2382**
Garber, John, family
    Pipe Creek Church of the Brethren,
        MD, 1026
Garber, John H., 106, 1629
    Mason, Floyd R. on descendants of,

2346
    Mason, Kathryn Garst on descendants
        of, 2346
Garber, John H., elder
    Müller (Miller) family, 895
Garber, John (Johannes), 1629
Garber, John R., 1629
Garber, Joseph, 1629
    family history, 1944
Garber, Joseph D., 1629
Garber, Judith Beery, 112, 1873
Garber, Julie
    on Christ and Brethren beliefs, 2332
    on Exodus, 2332
    on youth ministry, 2332, 2333
Garber, Kent, 1629, 2279
Garber, L. Randy, 2279
Garber, Leroy C., 1356, 1629, 2301, **2382**
Garber, Levi Leedy, **529**, 1629, 1920
    Painter Creek Old German Baptist
        Brethren Church, OH, 990
    Pipe Creek Old German Baptist
        Brethren Church, IN, minister,
        1026
Garber, Lizzie (later Yoder)
    Yoder, D. Willard (OGBB) and, 2267
Garber, Louise Virginia, 1839
Garber, Lowell D., 1629
    Salem Old German Baptist Brethren
        Church, OH, minister, 1139
Garber, Lydia Heeter, 529
Garber, Magdalene (later Wampler), 1318
Garber, Magdaline Mohler, 1920
Garber, Mark D., 2153, 2279
Garber, Martin, 529, 1013, 1270, 1629,
    1920
Garber, Martin Murray, 1849
Garber, Mary Crumpacker, 676, 1944
Garber, Mary (later Wampler), 1317
Garber, Mary Long, 529
Garber, Mary Miller, 528
Garber, Mary Petry, 1013
Garber, Mathias, 1629
    Mountain Valley Church of the
        Brethren, TN, 889
Garber, Mel, 1286
Garber, Merlin Estes, 2, 70, 270, 511, 1314,
    1629, 1944
    on Karlsschule, VA, 2333
    memoirs, 2333
Garber, Michael, 529, 530, 1629
Garber, Niclous
    Mason, Floyd R. on descendants of,
        2346
    Mason, Kathryn Garst on descendants
        of, 2346
Garber, Noah W., 1629
    Sand Creek Old German Baptist
        Brethren Church, KS, minister,
        1143
Garber, Ora W., 191, **529**, 1629, 1944
Garber, Orval S., 676, 1629
Garber, Orville Leo, 1629
Garber, Paul E., 1629
    Prices Creek Old German Baptist
        Brethren Church, OH, elder or
        minister, 1057
Garber, Perry
    Pipe Creek Old German Baptist
        Brethren Church, IN, deacon, 1026
Garber, Peter, 1235–1236, 1629
Garber, Peter Isaac, 1629
Garber Printing Company

Garber, Aaron Leedy, 528
Garber, Priscilla (later Shumake), 1274
Garber, R. I., 1629
Garber, Ray M., 471, 1629, 2153
Garber, Raymond
    Old Order German Baptist Church
        minister, 972
Garber, Raymond H., 62, 1629
Garber, Richard O., 766, 1295, 1629
Garber, Robert E., 1629
    Painter Creek Old German Baptist
        Brethren Church, OH, 990
Garber, Robert B., 1629
Garber, Ruskin, 1212
Garber, S. D.
    Mountain Valley Church of the
        Brethren, TN, free minister, 889
Garber, S. H., 1629
Garber, S. W., 1629
Garber, Sam, 737, 738, 1285
Garber, Samuel, 1, 141, 448, 507, 529,
    529, 672, 1217, 1253, 1356, 1629,
    See also abolition
    migration of Brethren, 829
    minorities, ethnic and racial, 849
Garber, Samuel A., 1629
Garber, Samuel Allbaugh, 1630
Garber, Samuel L., 1630
Garber, Sara (later Holtzapfel), 624
Garber, Sherda
    works by, 2324
Garber, Silas D., 1630
Garber, Simon, 1630
Garber, Solomon, 342, 1630
Garber, Solomon, Jr., 672, 742
Garber, Solomon, Sr., 672, 742
Garber, Solomon Wine, 1630, 1944
Garber, Steven, 2279
Garber, Susan, 528, 529
Garber, Walter, 274
Garber, Mrs. Walter, 274
Garber, Wilbur F., 1630
Garber, William Allen, 1630
Garber, William Frank, 1630
Garber, William H., 2279
Garbers Church of the Brethren, VA, 342,
    530, 1317
Garber (Gerber), Daniel, 528
Garcia family
    Orange, CA, Grace Brethren Church,
        975
Garcia, Juan
    Los Angeles, CA, Hermanos Unidos en
        Cristo, 2215
García, Milton (CB)
    Hispanic Ministries (CB), 2199
    Rio Prieto, PR, Iglesia de los
        Hermanos (CB) and, 2244
Gardemna, Nigeria, 306
Garden City Brethren Church, VA, *See*
    Roanoke, VA, Garden City Grace
    Brethren Church
Garden City, KS, Church of the Brethren,
    530
    minorities, ethnic and racial, 850
Garden City, VA, Grace Brethren Church,
    163
Garden Grove, CA, 1337
The Garden in the Vale (Kinsey), 1985
Garden of Eden
    Great Serpent Mound, Adams Co., OH,
        believed to be site of by West,
        Edmund Landon, 1332

Garden Terrace Retirement Home, Wenatchee, WA, **530**, 1330
Gardener family
    Modesto, CA, La Loma Grace Brethren Church, 867
Gardner, Alexander, 41
Gardner, Benjamin
    Pleasant View Brethren Church, IN, 2377
Gardner family, 375
Gardner, Frank, 1380
Gardner, Frank H., 363, 1309
Gardner, Frank H., Jr., 241, 1630
    Pataskala, OH, Grace Brethren Church of Licking Co., pastor of, 995
Gardner, Guy H., 1341, 1630
Gardner, Harry Miller, 106, 1277, 1323, 1630
Gardner, Orville, 245
Gardner, Richard Bruce, 1630, 1945, 2136
    on Bethany Theological Seminary, 2333
    on Brethren, history and beliefs of, 2333
    on Gospel of Matthew, 2333
    on Quakers and Brethren, 2333
Gardner, Rose, 1266
Gardner, William
    Pataskala, OH, Grace Brethren Church of Licking Co., pastor of, 995
Gardner, William O., 1630
    Richmond, VA, Grace Brethren Church, pastor, 1108
Garfield Co., NE, 767
Garfield Community Church
    South Red Cloud Church of the Brethren, NE, 1206
Garfield Park Hospital, 123
    article about, 1944–1945
Garger, F. L., 1630
Garkida
    Dadisman, Mary Nancy, 359
    Utz, Ruth Earl, 1299
    Waka Teachers' Training College and Secondary School, 1312–1313
    Garkida General Hospital, Nigeria
        hospitals, 630
    Garkida leper colony, See Adamawa Provincial Leprosarium
    Garkida Leprosarium
        Mai Sule Biu, 782
Garkida, Nigeria, 3, 305, 306, 718
    Mai Sule Biu, 2216
    medical missions, 807
    missionary work in, 936
    missions and missionaries
        Brumbaugh, Grayce, 220
        Shankster, Owen L., Jr., and Celia Smith (CB) at, 2248
Garland, Charles C., 1630
Garland, Clair W., 2301
Garland, H. R., 1630
Garland, Harold, 1630
Garland, John Calvin, 1630
Garland, OH
    Christian Brethren and, 281
Garling, Karl, 65, 626, 1221, 1630
Garman family, 1216
    Gentry German Baptist Brethren Church, MO, 540
    Hiestand (Heistand, Heestand, Heaston) family, 602
Garman, Henry K., 22, 1630

Garman, J. H., 240, 1620
Garman, John, 676, 1227, 1630
Garman, Mary
    Peer, Marie Jean Smith on ancestors and descendants of, 2349
    Smith, Marie Jean on ancestors and descendants of, 2349
Garman, Peter, 1227
Garman, Peter S., 1281, 1630
Garman, Salome (later West), 1332
Garman, Susanna, 240
Garner, Charles C. (M.), 531, 1630
Garner, Charles Oren, 531, 1630
Garner family, **531,** 749
Garner, Florence E., 1945
Garner, George W., 531, 1630
Garner, Glenn S., 531, 1630
    Pleasant Valley Church of the Brethren, VA, pastor, 1035
Garner, Hannah Yon, 531
Garner, Harold W., 531
    Midland, VA, Church of the Brethren, pastor, 827
Garner, Holly Pearl, 531, 1630, 1838
    article about, 1945
    Okeechobee, FL, Grace Brethren Church, pastor, 963
Garner, Hugh Barrick, 531, 1630, 1945
Garner, Jacob
    Ontario German Baptist Brethren, 975
Garner, Jasper C., 531
Garner, Jesse, 746
Garner, Kathryn E. Barkdoll, 531, 1838, 2012
Garner, Timothy P., 531, 2279
Garner, Uriah, 531, 1630
Garner, Warren K., 2166
    on Christ and Brethren, 2333
Garner, William Harold, 827, 1090, 1630,
Garner, William, Sr., 720
Garnes family
    Ridge Church of the Brethren, PA, 1108
Garnes, John, 1630
    Shippensburg, PA, Church of the Brethren, minister in, 1177
Garnett, Robert, 198
Garnett, Ruth, 198
Garrard, Mary Margaret Kern, 1945
Garratt, John
    Muncie, IN, Brethren Church, 896
Garratt, Mrs. John
    Muncie, IN, Brethren Church, 896
Garret Co., MD
    Pine Grove Church of the Brethren, MD, 1024
Garrett Biblical Institute
    Miller, Robert Henry, 842
    Shull, Chalmer George, 1180
Garrett, Buck Dwain, 247, 1630
Garrett Co., MD, 144, 210–211, 273, 1243
    Fairview Church of the Brethren, MD, 468
    Georges Creek Church of the Brethren, MD, 540
    Maple Grove Church of the Brethren, MD, 790
    Oak Grove Church of the Brethren, MD, 956
    Oak Park Church of the Brethren, MD, 957
Garrett, Dean Alan, 2279
    on Eaton Congregation, OH, 2333

    on Upper Twin CB, OH, 2333
Garrett, Edwin A., 1630, 2301
Garrett, James Leo, Jr., 1945
Garrett, Joseph William, 1630
Garrett, Marguerite Arthelda Bixler, 111, **531,** 643, 1050, 1945
Garrett meetinghouse (PA), 99
Garrett, O. D., 531
Garrett, PA, Church of the Brethren, **531**
Garrison, Dennis W., 2279
Garrison, IA, Brethren Church, **531**
Garrison, IA, Church of the Brethren, **531**
Garrison, IA, congregation
    Robins, IA, Church of the Brethren, 1115
Garrison, Martin V., 1630
Garrison, Mary Elizabeth, 2038
Garrison Old German Baptist Brethren Church, IA, **531,** See Garrison, IA, Church of the Brethren
Garrison, William Loyd, 22
Garrison, Winfred E., 1945
Garst, Barbara (later Stoner), 1221
Garst, Dorothy (later Murray)
    on Mow, Anna Beahm, 2348
Garst, Elias, 531
Garst, Eliza Huffer, 531
Garst, Etta Tennessee, 165
Garst family, 280, 396, **532,** 701, 1945
    genealogy, 1943
    Pleasant Valley Church of the Brethren, TN, 1035
Garst, Frederick, 531
Garst, George, 1630
Garst, Grace, 531
Garst, Hannah Maria Eversole, 531
Garst, Henry, 170, 531, **531,** 1630
Garst, Henry M., 1630
Garst, Isaac B., 1630
Garst, Jeremiah, 1630
Garst, Jesse, 1630
Garst, Jesse O., **531,** 532, 1215, 1277, 1945
Garst, John Henry, 719, 1630, 1631
    Pleasant Hill Church of the Brethren, TN, free minister, 1032
    Sebring, FL, J. H. Moore Memorial Church of the Brethren, elder and pastor, 1162
Garst, John M., 531, 1631
Garst, John Nicholas, 509
    descendants, 1945
Garst, Lawrence A., 109, 531, 1631, 2301
Garst, Levi, 1631
    Roanoke, VA, Ninth Street Church of the Brethren, pastor, 1113
Garst, Mary Bowman, 531
Garst, Nathan H., 1631
Garst, Noah N., 1631
Garst, Pauline Elizabeth, 1840
Garst, Rebecca May, 531
Garst, Samuel, 672
Garst, Samuel H., 170, 676
Garst, Samuel Henry, 1631
    Meadow Branch Church of the Brethren, TN, 806
    New Hope Church of the Brethren, TN, elder in, 929
    Piney Flats, TN, Church of the Brethren, minister, 1025
    Pleasant Hill Church of the Brethren, TN, pastor/elder, 1032
Garst, Samuel Sherfy, 280, **531–532,** 1631
    medical practice, 810

Miller, John Allen, 839
Modesto, CA, Pleasant Home Dunkard Brethren Congregation, elder, 867
Garst, Theobald
    descendants, 1945
Garst, Thomas Chester, 1631
Garst, William Tell, 1945
Gartland, Clair W., 674, 731, 1631
Garvan, Beatrice B.
    writings of, 2333
Garver, Barbara, 430
Garver, Charles, 1631
Garver, Daniel Miller, 272, 109, 338, **532, 537,** 1276, 1631, 1945
Garver, David Newton, 532, 1390
Garver, Earl Simeon, 2187
Garver, Earl S., **532,** 1391, 1945
Garver, Earl Simeon
    educator, **2187**
Garver, Elizabeth Kauffman, 1923
Garver family, 11, 236, 396, See Garber family; Garber (Garver, Gerber) family
    Salem Church of the Brethren, ND, 1137
Garver (Garber), John, Sr., 1631
Garver, George, 532, 1631
Garver, George W., 1631
Garver, Ina (later Mayes)
    Mayes, Charles W., mother of, 804
Garver, J. B., 1631
Garver, Jacob, 628, 1340, 1631
Garver, Jesse A., 204
Garver, John, 1631, 1923
Garver, John E., 1631
Garver, John, Sr., 396
Garver, Joseph, 531, 1631
Garver, Lewis E., 1631
Garver, Lydia (later Lutz), 767
Garver, Lydia (later Miller), 2059
Garver, Margaret Miller, 532
Garver, Martha Longenecker, 532
    Garver, Earl Simeon, 2187
Garver, Mary L. Eby, 532
Garver, Rebecca (later Mason)
    Mason, Edward Glenn, mother of, 800
    Mason, Edward, wife of, 799
Garver, S. R., 2020
Garver, Samuel, 1631
Garver, Solomon, 170
Garver, Winifred Sheppard
    Garver, Earl Simeon, 2187
Garvey, Jesse Howard, 1631
Garwick, Darlene M., 104
Garwick, Howard, 1838
Garwick, Ruth Darlene Messamer, 1631
Garwin, IA, Carlton Brethren Church, **532**
Gary family
    Scherffig family, related to, 1152
Gary, IN
    weekday religious education initiated, 1326
Gary, Robert Daniel, 1631
gas lamps
    Old Order German Baptist Church, 972
Gascho, Christian, 1631
Gascho, Eli J., 1631
    New Haven Church of the Brethren, NC, pastor in, 928
Gascho, Ivan Duane, 319, 1631
Gascho, John B., 109, 1631
Gascho, Maria (later Smeltzer), See Smeltzer, Maria Gascho

Gascho, Mary, 1631
Gascho, Raymond, 1631
    Middlefork Old German Baptist Brethren Church, IN, minister, 826
Gascho, Seth K., 109, 1631
Gaselee, Judy, 658
Gashala, Nigeria, 306
Gass (Gast), Jakob, 290, **532**
Gass, Harold, 469
Gass, Harold Lee, 1631, 2279
Gass, Harold R., 1631
Gass, Harold S., 479
Gass, Ramie Lee, 469, 1631
    Mountain Grove Church of the Brethren, MO, pastor, 889
Gates, Audrey
    on Hoffer, Mattias and descendants, 2352
Gates, Elizabeth (later Gibson), 547, 548
Gates family
    Sharon Church of the Brethren, Alberta, Canada, 1172
Gates, Marion D., 319, 738, 1631
Gates, Nathan, family
    Pleasant Valley Church of the Brethren, ND, 1035
Gatewood Brethren Church, WV, **532**
Gathers, VA, congregation, 342
Gatliff, Michael, R., 2279
Gattein, John T., 1631
Gaube (Gaby), Martin, **532–533,** 1631
    Mohrsville Church of the Brethren, PA, elder, 869
    Pricetown Meetinghouse, 1057
Gaube, Susanna, 532
Gauby, John M., 1631
Gauby, Martin Allen, 157, 503, 1338, 1631
Gauby, Martin Deeter, 1631
Gauby, Samuel M., 1631
Gauby, Sidney F., 2279
Gaulk, John
    Prosperity Brethren Church, WV, minister, 1062
Gault, Esther Mary, 1631
Gault family, 1214
    Parkersburg, WV, Grace Brethren Church, 994
    Prosperity Brethren Church, WV, 1062
Gault, John, 1631
Gault, Mary, 2279
Gault, Samuel, 1631
Gaunt, Greg O., 1631
Gaunt, William Andrew, 1631
    Riddlesburg, PA, Church of the Brethren, minister, 1108
    Saxton, PA, Stonertown Church of the Brethren, pastor, 1150
Gauntz, Mary Elizabeth, 1632, 1836, 1838
Gauntz, William B., 1632
Gaustad, Edwin Scott, 1945
Gaut family, 1885
Gauver, B. Joanne, 2279
Gaw, Ka Tong, 1632
gay and lesbian issues, See homosexuality
    Brethren/Mennonite Council for Lesbian and Gay Concerns, 2151–2152
    Brethren/Mennonite Council newsletter, 1916–1917
    Fellowship of Grace Brethren Churches (FGBC), 487
Gaylor(d), N. M., 1277, 1292

Gaytan, Gilberto
    South Bend, IN, Iglesia Evangelica Emanuel (CB) and, 2252
GCMC, See General Conference Mennonite Church
Geake, Gold Collins, 1945
Gearhart, C. Lowell, 1632, 2301
Gearhart, Dean Eugene, 1632
Gearhart, Earl, 1632
Gearhart, Joseph A., 1632
Gearhart, Mary Ann (later Miller)
    Miller, John William, 2223
Gearhart, Samuel Barr, 1632
Gearhart, William A., **533,** 1632
    National Laymen's Organization, leadership in, 917
Gearheart, J. Stanley, 210
Geary, John M., 1632
Geaslen, Gene A., 204
Geaslen, Jeffrey L., 1632
Geaslen, Jimmie Rodger, 1632
Gebhart, Katharina, 161
Geedey family
    Farmers Grove Fellowship (BC), PA, 476
Geer, A., 462
Geer, Elijah S., 1632
Geer, VA, 1317
Gegenheimer, Albert F., 1945
Gegner, Larry K., 31, 239, 705, 1253, 1276, 1632
Gegner, Nancy Carol Creswell, 1849
Gegner, Philip Robert, 1632, 1849
Das Geheimnis der göttlichen Sophia (The Mystery of the Divine Sophia, 1700), 57
Gehenna, See Hell, doctrine of
Gehman, Clayton H., 654
    Penn Run Church of the Brethren, PA, pastor, 1004
Gehman, Clayton Hurst, 1632
Gehman, Edna Rickert, 1945
Gehman, Elizabeth, 2092
Gehman, Ernest G., 1945
Gehman, Frances, 219
Gehman, Frank, 417, 708, 1224, 1289, 1632
    Osceola, IN, Grace Brethren Church, pastor, 984
Gehman, Irwin Gehman, 1945
Gehman, John W., 2006
Gehman, Ord, 121, 490, 1303, 1632, 2301
    Rittman, OH, First Brethren Church, pastor, 1111
Gehman, Sharon, 2165
Gehman, Thelma, 1303
Gehr, George Douglas, 2279
Gehret, Ellen J., 1945
Geib, Amos Philip, 1632, 1945
Geibe, Clara
    Southern Lancaster Grace Brethren Church, PA, 1207
Geibe, Harvey
    Southern Lancaster Grace Brethren Church, PA, 1207
Geibe, Ken
    Southern Lancaster Grace Brethren Church, PA, 1207
Geibe, Margaret
    Southern Lancaster Grace Brethren Church, PA, 1207
Geiger Church of the Brethren, PA, **533**
Geiger, Henry, 533, **533,** 1239, 1632, 1945

medical practice, 809–810
Philadelphia, PA, First Church of the Brethren, minister, 1015
Geiger, Linwood, 1632
Geiger, Mary Schwenk, 533, **533**, 1361
Philadelphia, PA, Geiger Memorial Church of the Brethren, 1016
Rockhill Furnace, PA, Rockhill Church of the Brethren, 1117
Geiger Memorial, PA, Church of the Brethren, 1296, *See* Philadelphia, PA, Geiger Memorial Church of the Brethren
Middle Creek Church of the Brethren, PA, 825
Geiger, Sem, 1945
Geigley, A. W., 243
Geil family, 2095
Geil, J. Conrad, 2095
Geil, Jacob, 2095
Geiman, Alice E., 2165
Geiman, Christian, 1632
Geiman family, 145
Geiman, Thomas W., 273, 514, 1632
Geiny, Henry, 686
Geiny, John, 686
Geiny (Keeney/Keeny) family, 686
Geiser, John S., 142, 1632
Poplar Valley Church of the Brethren, MT, elder, 1047
Geiser, Jorg, 1849
Geiser, Max, 373, 1632
Geisert, Bradley K., 1945, 2187
Geisert, Ellen Maurine Gish, 2187
Geisert, Fred J., 2187
Geisert, Gregory Wayne, 2187
Geisert, Martha Lauer, 2187
Geisert, Todd Wilfred, 2187
Geisert, Wayne F., 208
educator, churchman, **2187–2188**, *2188*
Geisewite, Kenneth E., 2279
Geiss, Christopher, *See* Guice (Geist Guß, Guss, Güß), Christopher
Geistliche Fama (*Spiritual Report,* 1730–1744), 57, 120, 378, **533–534**, 925, 1946
Carl, Johann Samuel, 255
historical writing, 611
Die geistliche Gestalt eines evangelischen Lehrers (*The Spiritual Form of a Gospel Teacher,* 1704), 57
Geistliche und andächtige Lieder (Preiß), 1055
Ein Geistliches Magazien, **534**, 1146, 1946
Mack, Alexander, Jr., 774
Geistreiches Gesang-Buch (*Spiritual Songbook*), 60, 175, **534**, 700, 1946
humility, 636
hymnals, 641
printing of by Christoph Konert, 706
publishing of, 1063
Geisttown Grace Brethren Church, PA, *See* Johnstown, PA, Geisttown Grace Brethren Church
Gelassenheit (yieldedness, surrender), doctrine of, 29
Gelsinger family, 1274
Gelsinger, Howard H., 1274, 1632
Myerstown, PA, Grace Brethren Church, pastor, 906
Gemeinde
Brethren movement, 291
fraternity, 511

Mack, Alexander, Sr., and New Baptists of Schwarzenau, 776
Gemeinde, Gemeinschaft, **534**, 1209, 1260
Brethren movement, 291
community, 329
Gemeinschaft of the Holy Spirit (BC), 184
insurance, 657
nonconformity, 941
Old Order Fellowships, 970–971
ordination, 980
plain people, 1029
Gemmer, Hiram Robert, 1632, **2382**
Habitat for Humanity International, 2195
Gems of Grace, 2127
gender and gender roles, *See* feminism; men; sexuality; women
Bible translations, language use, 2137
dress symbol of, 401
ethics and, 2177–2178
family, 472, 474
family roles, 2145
feetwashing, 481
Fellowship of Grace Brethren Churches (FGBC), 487
General Board (CB), 535
marriage, 795
separation of in meetinghouses, 2160
genealogy, **534–535, 2374**
Church of Jesus Christ of Latter-day Saints, 298
Ephrata Press, 452
Fellowship of Brethren Genealogists (FOBG), 484
foreign genealogical records, 2089
Francis, Jacob "Jay" Gottwals, 506
information technology, church use of, 2208
Miller family, 2018
Ogden, Galen Brown, 961
Old Order Notes, 973
publication of, 158
sources for, 2324
A Genealogy of John Ziegler [sic] and His Wife Kathryn Kline Ziegler (Zeigler)
Zeigler, Carl Wenger (CB) and, 2269
Genealogy of the Brumbach Families (Brumbaugh), 534
General Baptists, 87
General Board (CB), 22, 36, 285, 295, 305, 346, **535–536**, 1904, **2374**, *See also* polity
The Andrew Center, 2130
Appalachian ministries, 2130
Association of Brethren Caregivers (ABC), 2132
Bethany Theological Seminary, 2136
Bittinger, Desmond Wright, 143
Brethren Academy for Ministerial Leadership, 2139–2140
Cable, William H., 2155
A Call to Compassion, 2129
Central America, 2157
church extensions, 295
Church of the Brethren, 304
Commission of Fifteen (CB), 327
Committee on Higher Education (CB), 328
On Earth Peace Assembly, 2235
Ellis, Calvert Nice, 441
Fasnacht, Harold Dale, 480
Fike, Earle William, Jr., 2184

Finance Commission (CB), 490
Foreign Mission Commission (CB), 500
Gahagen Charitable Foundation, 2187
Garver, Earl Simeon, 532, 2187
Geisert, Wayne F., 2187–2188
General Board (CB), 535
General Council of Children's Work (CB), 537
General Investment Council (CB), 537
General Offices (CB), 539
General Services Commission (CB), 539
Germantown Trust, 2188, 2189
Goals and Budget Committee, 554
Greiner, Robert G., 2194
Halladay, Sara Heebner, 580
Harman, Hylton, 2196
Hayes, William (Bill) A., 2197
Heckert, Mildred Mae Etter, 2197
Historical Committee (CB), 610
Israel, 664
Kettering, Joseph W., 691
Korean Mission, 2211
language, inclusive, 2214
Lenexa, KS, Fellowship, 2214
Long, W. Newton, 754
mass media concerns, 801
membership, and regions, 1094
Miller, Donald Eugene, 2223
Ministry of Reconciliation, 2224
Misión Mutua en las Américas, 852
National Council of Churches of Christ in the USA and World Council of Churches, 2228
National Older Adult Conferences, 2229
Neff, Robert Wilbur, 2231
organizational restructuring and, 2241–2242
Peace Corps, 1002
Pension Board, 1007
People of the Covenant (POC) (BC) and, 2237
Peters, Raymond Russell, 1011
Polish Agricultural Exchange, 2129
Rhoades, J. Benton and, 2242
San Marcos, CA, North Country Church of the Brethren and, 2245
Schwalm, Vernon Franklin, 1157
SERRV International (CB) and, 2247
Sherfy, Robert Livingston (CB) and, 2249
Sollenberger, Dorcas Elaine Mock (CB) and, 2251
urban ministry and, 2256–2257
Weaver, Clyde E. (CB) and, 2260
West, Daniel, 1331
West, Murray Guy, 1332
Will, Harper S., 1345
women and, 2264
Women's Conferences (CB) and, 2265
World Ministries Commission, 1369
youth and, 2269
Zeigler, Carl Wenger (CB) and, 2269
Zeller, Harry Knode, Jr., 1395
General Brotherhood Board (CB), *See* General Board (CB)
General Cabinet of Children's Work, *See* National Cabinet of Children's Work
General Child Rescue Committee, 276
General Christian Workers' Board, 287, **536**

Forward Movement, 504
General Sunday School Board (CB),
    539
General Church Erection and Missionary
    Board
    Stover, Wilbur Brenner, 1226
    urban ministry, 1296
General Church Erection and Missionary
    Committee, 204, **536**, *See also*
    church extension programs
    General Missionary and Tract
        Committee (GBB), 539
    incorporation, 649
    Ontario German Baptist Brethren, 975
    Plate, Lewis (Ludwig) A., 1030
General Church Missionary and Tract
    Committee, 204
General Committee, as precursor to Stand-
    ing Committee, 1216
General Conference, *See* Annual Meeting
    Brethren Church, *See* Brethren Church
        General Conference
    Dunkard Brethren, *See* Dunkard
        Brethren General Conference
General Conference Executive Council
    (GCEC)
    Brethren Church mission statement,
        2141, 2148
General Conference Mennonite Church
    (GCMC), **536**
    Believers Church Commentary Series,
        2134
    and Believers' Church study confer-
        ences, 114
    and Bethany Theological Seminary,
        126
    Christian education curricula, 2160
    Elkhart, IN, Southside Fellowship
        (CB/Menn), 439
    evangelism, 2180
    Foundation series publications, 1237
    Hymnal: A Worship Book, 2205
    joint ventures with Brethren Press,
        2149
    membership in 2000, 2220
    Mennonite Brethren Churches, General
        Conference of, 814
    Mennonite Church (MC), 815
    Mennonites, 815
    musical instruments, 2228
    Plow Creek Fellowship, 1038
    South Bend, IN, Iglesia Evangelica
        Emanuel (CB) and, 2252
General Conference of The Brethren Church
    ethics, 2178
General Council of Children's Work (CB),
    537, 915
General Council of Men's Work, *See* Men's
    Work
General Council of the Women's Fellow-
    ship, 1362
General Education Board (CB), 36, 428,
    537, **537**
Educational Association of the Schools
    (CB), 429
Ellis, Charles Calvert, 441
    first statistical reports, 1218
    Flory, John Samuel, 499
    Forward Movement, 504
    Frantz, Edward, 508
    fundamentalism, 522
    Garver, Daniel M., 532
    General Board (CB), 535

Hospital Committee (CB), 630
Kurtz, Daniel Webster, 711
Lear, John Wallace, 732
Mount Morris College, 885
Noffsinger, John Samuel, member of,
    939
Reber, Daniel Conrad, 1085
Taylor, Isaac W., 1249
Williams, John Henry Bashor, 1345
Winger, Otho, 1351
Yount, Walter Bowman, 1391
General Education Committee
    Schwalm, Vernon Franklin, 1157
General Investment Council (CB), **537**
General Ministerial Board (CB), **537–538**,
    1904, **2374**, *See* ministry; salaried
    ministry
    Early, Henry Clay, 414
    Pension Board, 1007
    White, Ralph Emerson, 1339
    Zigler, David H., 1397
General Ministry and Home Missions
    Board
    Hartsough family, 588
General Mission Board (BC), *See* Mission-
    ary Board
General Mission Board (CB), 36, 255, 295,
    299, 304, 395, *538*, **538–539**, *See
    also* Bonsack, C. D.; Brubaker, L.
    S.; Early, H. C.; General Offices;
    Miller, D. L.; Vaniman, D.;
    Williams, J. H. B.; Zigler, M. R.
    Alliance, OH, Church of the Brethren,
        2126
    Bhagat, Premchand Ganeshji, 131
    bibliography, 1904
    decentralized plan drafted by Daniel
        Vaniman, 1302–1303
    Dorrance, KS, Church of the Brethren,
        aid to, 396
    Early, Henry Clay, 413, 414
    farming, 479
    Flat Creek Church of the Brethren, KY,
        493
    Forward Movement, 504
    General Investment Council (CB), 537
    General Missionary and Tract Commit-
        tee, 1269
    Gospel Messenger Advisory Commit-
        tee, 559
    Grandview, MO, Dunkard Brethren
        Congregation, 566
    Gratis, OH, Church of the Brethren,
        566
    Hoover, Samuel W., 628
    Hope, Christian, 628
    Houser, Daniel, 633
    incorporation, 649
    Italian Sunday School (CB), 665
    Long, W. Newton, 754
    missions, 859, *859*
    Nigeria, mission in, 305
    Nye, Harry Hess, 953
    Parker, Isaac Dillon, fund raising by,
        993
    Pension Board, 1007
    Relief and Reconstruction Committee,
        1096
    Russia, 1288
    St. Francis Church of the Brethren, AR,
        1134
    Sanger, Samuel F., 1143
    Stover, Wilbur Brenner, 1226

Teeter, Lewis Wallace, 1250
Torreon Navajo Mission, 1268
Tract Examining Committee, 1268
Williams, John Henry Bashor, 1345
Winger, Otho, 1351
Women's Missionary Societies, freewill
    offering to, 1363
Yoder, Joseph J., 1386
Zigler, Michael Robert, 1398
Zuck, John, 1401
General Mission Board (DB), **539**, 1859
    Flora, Joseph E., 2185
    Ness, Jacob C., 2231
General Mission Board (GBB/CB)
    Native Americans, 2230
General Missionary and Tract Commit-
    tee, 54, 205, 295, **539**, 1269
    Church of Jesus Christ of Latter-day
        Saints, 298
    District of Columbia, 390
    France, 505
    General Church Erection and Mission-
        ary Committee, 536
    General Mission Board, 538
    Gish, Barbara Kindig and James Rufus,
        550
    Gish Fund Books, 551
    Helping Hand, The, 595
    Hoover, Samuel W., 628
    Iran (Persia), 662
    McCann, Samuel Napoleon, 772
    Messenger, 818
    Ministerial and Missionary Relief Fund
        (CB), 844
    Missionary Reading Circle, 857
    missions, 859
    Palestine, AR, Ministry to Blacks, 991
    publications, official, 1068
    Quebec, 1075
    Salt Lake City, UT, 1298
    urban ministry, 1296
    Washington, 1319
    Yeremian (Yereman), O. H., 1385
    Zuck, John, 1401
    Zug, Samuel Ruhl, 1401
General Missionary Committee of the
    German Baptist Brethren, 2019
General Music Committee, *See* Music
    Committee (CB)
General Offices (CB), 161, 187, 194, 304,
    539, **539**, *See also* Church of the
    Brethren, General Offices
    Elgin, IL, 435
    Garber, Ora W., 529
    historic sites, 609
    Minnich, Herbert Spenser, 848
General Peace Committee (CB)
    Howe, William Mohler, 633
General Railway Transportation Agent, *See*
    railroad committees and immigra-
    tion agents
General Relief Board (DB), *See* Relief
    Board (DB)
General Services Commission (CB), 305,
    539
    Geisert, Wayne F., 2188
    General Board, 536
    Historical Committee (CB), 610
    origin of, 36
    Parish Ministries Commission involve-
        ment in, 993
    Thompson, Joel Kent and, 2255
General Sunday School Board (CB), 155,

539–540, 1236, 1904
Flory, Ezra, 498
Forward Movement, 504
General Christian Workers' Board
(CB), 536
General Welfare Board (CB), 540
German Baptist Brethren, 1239
Mothers and Daughters' Association,
878
Steele, Lafayette, 1220
Zigler, David H., 1397
General Welfare Board (CB), 155, **540,**
1252, *See also* peace education
alcohol education, 1252
Committee on Dress Reform, 327
General Sunday School Board (CB),
540
Peace Committee (CB), 1002
Generation Why, 2160
Genereaux, Marilou (later Booth), 2273
Genesee, MI, congregation
Michigan Brethren settlement, 824
Genesee Old German Baptist Brethren
Church, MI, **540**
Genesis
31:13, 39
commentaries on, 156
Roop, Eugene F. on, 2353
The Genesis Flood (Whitcomb)
Whitcomb, John Clement, Jr. (FGBC,
CGBCI) and, 2262
Genet, Sandra, 760
genetic drift in religious isolates,
Bentley Glass' works on, 1950
genetic engineering
Church of the Brethren, 2178
Geneva, **540**, *See also* Fercken, G. J.
Fercken, Gaston J., relocated to, 1246
Geneva Psalter (Ambrosius Lobwasser)
singing, 1184
Geneva, Switzerland, 199
Inter-Church Aid and Service to
Refugees, 657
Prague Conferences and, 2239
Russian Orthodox Church, peace semi-
nar with, 1132
World Council of Churches, 2087
World Health Organization (WHO),
1369
Young Men's Christian Associations
(YMCA), 1390
Zigler, Amy Arnold, 1397
Zigler, Michael Robert, 1398
Gensinger, Emma (later Slabaugh), *See*
Slabaugh, Emma Gensinger
Gensinger family, 1330, 1341
Gentile Christians, 147
Gentle, Spencer, 186, 1632
Gentry Co., MO
Gentry German Baptist Brethren
Church, MO, 540
Gentry family, 1315
Gentry, G. F., 1632
Gentry, George T., 1632
Gentry German Baptist Brethren Church,
MO, **540**
Gentzel, Robert
Maple Valley, WA, Grace Brethren
Church, 2218
Gentzler, Lydia (later Lehmer), 736
Genzmer, George H., 1946
geographic identity
Church of the Brethren regions, 1093

Geographical area and congregational
names, 911
geographical expansion of Brethren, *See*
migration of Brethren
geographical listings of congregations by
denomination, nation, and state,
1479–1503
Geogres Creek Church of the Brethren,
MD, **540**
George and Margaret Tract, MD, 1246
George, Ard., 1632
George, C. Maynard, 1632
George, Charles S., 2279
George, D. Wiatt, 1632
George, David, 1343
George, Geneva, 1632
George, Gilbert W., 1632
George I (king of England)
Penn, William, and settlement of
Pennsylvania, 1004
George, Joan (later Deeter), 1916, 2276
church governance and, 2264
George (Kinzie), Geneva, 602
George, Maynard
Omaha, NE, Church of the Brethren,
minister, 974
George Solomon Memorial Library, 2131
George, Thomas Ezra, 557, 1632
North Manchester, IN, Church of the
Brethren, pastor, elder (modera-
tor), 949
George, Timothy
Myerstown, PA, Grace Brethren
Church, pastor, 906
George, William, 1632
Georges Creek Brethren Church, PA, *See*
Masontown, PA, Brethren Church
Georges Creek Church of the Brethren, PA,
See Fair-View (Georges Creek)
Church of the Brethren, PA
Georges Creek congregation, PA, 1356
George's Creek, MD, Church of the
Brethren, 211, **540**
George's Creek Old German Baptist
Brethren Church, PA, **540**
Georges Creek, PA, 1289
George's Creek, PA, congregation, 348
Quinter, James, pastor, part-time, 1077
Georges, Judith L., 2279
Georgetown, DE, Mount Olivet Brethren
Church, *See* Mount Olivet
Brethren Church, DE
Georgetown, OH, congregation
Potsdam, OH, Church of the Brethren,
1048
Georgia, **540**, 2023
Florida, 496
German settlement in, 2069
*Materials Towards a History of the
Baptists*, 803
migration of Brethren, 829, 831
Moravian Church, 875
Old German Baptist Brethren, 2235
Georgia mission
article about, 1961
Gephart, Dennis, 714
Gephart, Edith, 230
Gephart, Edith (later Schrock), *See*
Schrock, Edith Gephart
Gephart, Henry, 1632
Shipshewana, IN, Church of the
Brethren, minister in, 1177
Gephart, J. W., 1281

Gephart, Jacob, 1632
Gephart, John, 1281
Gephart, John W., 54, 1632
Gephart, Vera Mae Rupel, 714
Pomona, CA, Fellowship Church of the
Brethren, 1045
Gerardo, Lefton, 2279
Gerber, E. P., 1946
Gerber, Eli, 424
Gerber, Esther
genealogy and descendants, 1944
Gerber family, *See* Garber family
Gerber, Fred, 720
Lakeland, FL, Grace Brethren Church,
2213
Gerber, Harley
South America Theological Seminary
(BC) and, 2252
Gerber, Harry, 1946
Gerber, Johannes H., 529, *See* Garber
(Gerber), John H.
Gerber, Lorrie, 720
Lakeland, FL, Grace Brethren Church,
2213
Gerber, Michael, 529
descendants, 1946
Gerberich, Albert Horwell, 1894
Gerdes, David E., 1370–1371, 1632
Gerdes, E. Wayne
Paradise, CA, Church of the Brethren,
992
Gerdes, Galen G., 1632
Gerhart, Basil R., 1633
Gerhart, Daniel
family history, 1946
Gerhart family
history of, 1946
Gerhart (Gerhard) family, 1891
Gerhart, Jacob, 1633
Gerhart, Lyman S., 1946
Gerhart, Marguerite Elaine, 1855
Gerhart, R. R., 1633
Gerig, David, 1946
Gerig family
family history, 2011
Gerig, Mattie Gingerich, 1946
Ein Geringer Schein (*A Humble Gleam*),
132, 134, **540**, 541, 1946
Mack, Alexander, Jr., 774
Gerlach, David, 1340, 1633
German
language of worship, 396
German-American press, 2074
publications, 2074
German-American studies
bibliography, 1858, 1860, 1861, 1867,
1876, 2309, 2310
sources on, 2310, 2315
German-Americans
American Revolution, 2095
French and Indian War, 2091
genealogical research, 2069
Haller, Charles R. on distinguished,
2335
lifestyles, 2106
poems, 2085
printing industry
Virginia, 2104
Virginia, settlements in, 2105
German archives
research resources, 2069
German Arm Church of the Brethren,
VA, *See* Floyd Co. Church of the

Brethren, VA; Franklin Co. Church of the Brethren, VA
German Baptist Brethren (GBB), 3, 33, *180, 512*, **540**, 2045, 2098
  advertising, 7
  alcohol, use of, 16
  Annual Meeting, *See* German Baptist Brethren Annual Meeting
  baptism of Hannah Jane Langstroth Drexel, 405
  bibliography, 1859, 1869, 1895
  bicentennial celebration, 140
  Blocker family in Ohio, 147
  Blooming Grove congregation, 148, 149
  Blue Ridge College, 152
  Bomberger family, 158
  Brethren Church, 298
  Brethren in Christ, 188
  Brethren, lineage of, 613
  Brubaker family (PA), 216
  California, 238
  Canada, 250
  caps, 254
  Cedar Rapids, IA, 265
  Christian Brethren and, 281
  Christian education and, 283
  Church of God (New Dunkers), 297
  Church of the Brethren and, 149
  Civil War, 475
  Click family, 320
  Colorado, 320
  Congregational Brethren, 335
  courts of law, attitudes toward use of, 728
  Cyclopedia of Temperance and Prohibition, entry for, 1914
  Dayton Convention, and controversy with, 260
  Declaration of Principles, 372
  Denmark, *361*
  as denominational name, 910, 911
  Dictionary of American History, entry for, 1946
  doctrines of, 2075
  Eastern District of PA, minutes of district meetings, 1946
  eighteenth century, and history of, 2074
  Eiler (Eilar, Oyler) family, 432
  Elizabethtown College, 437
  Encyclopedia Americana, entry for, 1922
  Encyclopedia Brittanica, entry for, 1930
  Encyclopedia International, 1920
  environmental effects on, thesis on, 1919
  Eshelman, Matthew Mays, 455
  Eternal Security, 457
  ethics, 457
  Evangelii Büdbarare, 460
  expelled members, 7
  Fairview Church of the Brethren, OH, 469
  Falling Spring Old German Baptist Brethren Church, PA, 471
  Falls City, NE, Brethren Church, 472
  First happenings, discoveries, and inventions in U. S., 1981
  Fiscel, Emory (Emery) David, 491
  Flohr, Lewis Benton, 494
  Flora, Clara Myers, 495
  Flory, John, 498

foreign mission office in India, 912
Fraternal Relations Committees (BC), 511
Fraternity Church of the Brethren, NC, 511
fraternity of, 1992
Fraternity of Baptists, 511
Fraternity of German Baptists, 511
Geiger, Mary Schwenk, 533
General Church Erection and Missionary Committee, report to annual meeting, 1946
General Missionary and Tract Committee, hand-book, 1946
General Missionary and Tract Committee, tract tablet, 1946
General Missionary Committee, annual report, 1946
George's Creek Old German Baptist Brethren Church, PA, 540
German Baptists, 542
Gish family, 551
Glade Run Brethren Church, PA, 551
Glick, Jacob Daniel, 553
Gospel Trumpet, The, 561
group name modifications, 910
hairstyle, 579
hats, 589
Heisey family, 595
Helping Hand, The, 595
higher education, 283, 603, 605
history of, 1917
Holsinger, Henry Ritz, 621
Holsinger, Levi Teeter, 623
Hostetler, Daniel W., 631
Imler, Tobias F., 647
Industrial Revolution, 655
insurance, 657
Johnson, John L., 672
Kaufman, Stanley A. on, 2340
Kesler, Benjamin Elias, *690*
literary activity in the eighteenth century, thesis about, 1938
meeting list of 1905, 1982
missionaries, *690*
Missionary Committee, plan, 1947
missions and missionaries, 283, 375, *376*
name change discussion, 2228
name change to Church of the Brethren, 140
Native Americans, 2230
neckerchiefs and neckties, 921
New Virginia, IA, Brethren Church, 932
Old German Baptist Brethren, 966
Old Order Fellowships, 970
Old Order Movement, 973
Ontario, 975
opposition to labor unions, 716
"Order of the Brethren," 976
origins of, 179
Patton, George and Magdaline, minister in, 996
Pennsylvania, 149, 322, 2097
Peters Creek Old German Baptist Brethren Church, VA, 1012
Philadelphia congregation, salaried ministers, 1136
photography of Brethren, 1020
Pleasant Grove Grace Brethren Church, IA, 1031
position on alcoholic beverages,

1251–1252
publication of annual meeting proceedings, 1303
publishing, 18
references to in Universalist fiction, 1919
revivalism, 1210
Riffle, Conrad on, 2352
sanctification theology, 1210
schism, 298
schisms, 349, 362
Sidney, IN, Grace Brethren Church, 1181
Silver Creek (Mount Morris) congregation, 1226
Stony Creek Brethren Church, PA, 1225
Sunday school movement, 1237, 1239
Tennessee, 1253–1254
Theological Writings on Various Subjects (Nead, Peter), 1258
theology in Europe, 2074
tobacco use, 1266
tract distibution, 1269
United Brethren in Christ, 1289
urban ministry, 1297
use of German language, 725
Van Dyke, S. Perry, 1302
Virginia, 1308
wine, in communion services, 1349
German Baptist Brethren Annual Meeting, *512*, 540
  card playing, 254–255
  General Missionary and Tract Committee (GBB), 539
  minutes, 1946–1947
  proceedings, 1947
  verbatim reports, 1303
  women, right to vote in, 1361
  women, roles of, 1361
German Baptist Brethren Historical Association, **540**
Flying Eagle, The, 500
Francis, Jacob "Jay" Gottwals, 506
historical societies, 610
German Baptist Brethren, MI, congregation, 260
German Baptist Brethren Mutual Insurance Association (OH), 192, 903
German Baptist Brethren Mutual Protective Association of Western Maryland, **540**, *See also* insurance; mutual aid
German Baptist Brethren (songbook), 1890
German Baptist Brethren's Home Society, 276, 277, **540–541**
  Oklahoma district program, 964
German Baptist Church, Elkhart District, IN, *See* Goshen, IN, West Goshen Church of the Brethren
German Baptist Church of Cedar Lake, IN, 265
German Baptist Installation Service (Sayler)
  manuals, 788
German Baptist Sabbath School Association, 1239
German Baptists, **542**
  as colloquial name for denomination, 910
  Hiestand (Heistand, Heestand, Heaston) family, 602
  Materials Towards a History of the

Baptists, 803
German Baroque literature, bibliography of, 1859
German Bible, 26
German characterisitics of the Brethren, 3
German, Christian, 1633
"German Christian-Industrial Community" Concordia, 331
German Democratic Republic, 545
German dialect, *See under* Pennsylvania Germans
German, ethnic, refugees refugee resettlement, 1093
German hymnody of Brethren, 1702–1903 Durnbaugh, Hedwig T. on, 2327
German Hymnody of the Brethren 1720– 1903 (Durnbaugh), 2143
German immigrants cared for by Johann Christophe Sauer I, 1148
German language, *See* language shift; Pennsylvania German
Alexander Mack's Bible, 777
Brethren and, 3
New Testament, translated by Reitz, Johann Heinrich, 1095
poetry, 1039
Price, William Weidner, poetry and hymns, 1057
printing in, bibliography of, 2309
publications
Bible, 2097–2098
genealogical data, 1968
newspapers, 2088
publishing, 1063, 1067, 1068
Quaker peace policies, publications supporting, 999
transition from, and legal name of denomination, 911
German Lutherans, *See* Lutherans
German New River settlement book about, 1960
German New Testament Ephrata Press, 452
German Palatinate, *See* Palatinate (Electoral, Rhenish)
German Pietists
German Sectarians of Pennsylvania, The, 542
German pioneers
Hurt, Frank B. on Franklin County, VA and, 2338
German Reformed Church, *See* Presbyterians; Reformed (Calvinist) Church
American, 1966
Fraktur, 505
French and Indian War, 2091
Knepper, Harry, 1236
Philadelphia, PA, 1221
German refugees
Maple Grove Church of the Brethren, IN, helping, 789
German religious groups
Durnbaugh, Donald F. on crazy quilt of, 2327
German Sectarians of Pennsylvania (Julius F. Sachse), **542,** 1133
historical writing, 611
German separatists, migration of, 147
German Settlement Church of the Brethren, WV, *See* Eglon, WV, Church of the Brethren

German settlements
colonial era, 2091
Georgia, 2069
North Carolina, 2069, 2104–2105
South Carolina, 2069
Virginia, 2105
German Seventh-Day Baptists, **542,** *543,* 694, 2108, *See also* King, Frank
articles about, 1915
Bermudians, **121,** 1403–1405
Chart of Brethren Bodies, 2380
chart of Brethren bodies, 1403–1405
Committee on Interchurch Relations, 2166–2167
Ephrata Community, 451, 1170
Keller, Jacob, 686
King, Frank, 694
Miller, John Peter, 840
Sabbath observance, 1133
Snow Hill Community, 1194, 1195
Snowberger family, 1153
Stony Creek, PA, congregation, 214
writings about, 1934
German states
oaths, taking of, 959
German translations of the Bible, *See* Bible translations
German type, *See Fraktur* type
Germans
alternate service for, 202
chronology and fact book, 1607–1870, 1943–1944
ethnic refugees, 201
history of, in the United States, 1935
in Pennsylvania, *See* Pennsylvania Germans
Shenandoah Valley, PA, 2068
Germantauner Zeitung newspaper, 1146
Germantown Academy, **544,** 2032, 2084
bibliography, 1892
education, 426
founding years, 1978
Germantown, Battle of, **544**
Germantown (Beggarstown), PA
Good (Guth) family, 556
Germantown Bible
Geistliches Magazien, Ein (*A Spiritual Storehouse*), 534
Germantown Brethren
congregational seal, *2142*
Ephrata Society, 2377
Germantown Brick Church of the Brethren, VA, 43, **544,** 1243, 1884
Franklin Co. Church of the Brethren, VA, 507
Germantown Historical Museum
Philadelphia, PA, Germantown Church of the Brethren, **2189**
Germantown Historical Society, newspaper items, 1947
Germantown Old German Baptist Brethren Church, VA, **544**
Germantown, PA, 12, 17, 108, 139, 147, 159, 175, 209, 397, 400, **542–544,** *543,* 692, 722, 1347, 1397, 1892, 2011, 2035, 2036, 2053, 2064
article about, 1921
bicentennial anniversary, 141
Brethren congregations as rural churches, 1130
Brethren-related sites, 1979
cemeteries, *266,* 1984

Christmas, celebration of, 288
Church of the Brethren, *See* Philadelphia, PA, Germantown Church of the Brethren
description of, 2103
Durnbaugh, Donald F. on Brethren in, 2326
Eicher, Anna and Maria, 431
elementary education, 434
emigration, Brethren, 443
Endt, Johann Theobald, 446
evangelism, 460
Falckner's Swamp, 470
farming, 477
first meetinghouse, 48
German Baptist Brethren Church, 471
Germantown Bible of 1743, 2098
Goyen, Gossen, 562
Gruber, Johann Adam, 575
Gumre (Gomri, Gomorry, Gomry), Anna and Johann, 576
Gumre, Johnann, 684
Haller, Friedrich Conrad, 580
Harley (Herli, Harli), Hans Rudolf, 583
Hildebrand, Maria (later Mack), 606
Historic Peace Churches, 607
historic sites, 609
historical societies, 610
history, 1967, 1974, 1983
history of, 1935, 2075, 2083
Höcker, Heinrich, 615
Höcker, Ludwig, 616
Holtzapfel (Holsapple, Holsopple), Johann Heinrich, 623
Judaism, 677
Kalcklöser, Johann Heinrich, 681
Kämpfer, Johannes, 682
Käsebier, Johann Georg, 684
Keim, John, 686
Keyser, Peter, 691
Laschet family, 726
Lehman, Christian, historian, 735
Lehman family, 736
Leibert, Peter, 736
letters of 1738, 2096
Liebe, Christian, 742
Luther, Heinrich Ehrenfried, 767
Mack, Alexander, Sr., 777
Mack, Johann Valentin, 778
Mack, Johannes, and family, immigrating to, 778
meetinghouse built, 811
Mennonites, 707
Mennonites providing help for Brethren, 815
migration of Brethren from, 827
Mohrsville Church of the Brethren, PA, 869
museum in Brethren meetinghouse, 898
mutual aid, 902
Nägele, Hans Rudolph, hospitality offered on evangelistic trip from, 910
Neff brothers settlement, 910
New Ideas publication, 929
Pennsylvania Brethren settlement, 1004
Pennsylvania Synods, 1007
publishing, 1063
references to, translated letters, 1921
relief and service efforts, 1096
Roth, Heinrich, 1124
Sauer, Christopher, II, 1145–1146, *1146*

Sauer, Johann Christoph, I, 1147
Sauer Press and Dunker Church, 1984
Society of the Woman in the Wilderness, 686–687, 1199
Trinity Lutheran Church, 1967–1968, 1972
200th Anniversary of First Baptism and Love Feast, 2079
Universalist Restoration movement, 2087
Wissihickon Creek, 1354
world hunger issues (CB) and, 2266
Zimmerman mystics, 686
Germantown, PA, Battle of, Brethren aid to wounded in, 1106
Germantown press, *See* Seidensticker, Oswald
Germantown Trust
Philadelphia, PA, Germantown Church of the Brethren, **2188**
Germantown Union School, *See* Germantown Academy
Germany, **544–545**
Assembly of Christ, 376
Aukerman, Dale H., 2133
Community of the True Inspiration, 330
Eder River, 424
education programs, 185
established religions, 241
feeding children in, 23
Foreign Missionary Society (BC, FGBC), 501
General Church Erection and Missionary Committee (CB), 536
High Commissioner for the Occupation of Germany (HICOG), 603
immigrants from, 15
International Christian Youth Exchange (ICYE), 659
International Refugee Organization (IRO), 659
medical projects, 808–809
Miller, John William, 2224
mission schools, 854
missions, 857, 862
missions, short-term, 2226
Moravian Church, 875
Muhlenberg, Henry Melchior, 892
Naas, Johannes, ministering through, 909
Night of Broken Glass (Nov. 9–10, 1938), 23
Nordhausen, 30
Palatinate, 990
prisoner of war camps, 199
Prussia, 1063
reconstruction after the war, 23
Reformation, Protestant, and radical reformers, 1091, 1092
refugees resettled by Sugar Ridge Church of the Brethren, MI, 1235
relief and rehabilitation work in, 200, 303, 1097
relief and service efforts, 303, 1097
Snider, Donald Mitchell and Martha Keever, 1194
state churches of, 304
Traut, Georg Balthasar "Balser," 1270
world hunger issues (CB) and, 2266
Germany (Democratic Republic), **546**
Germany (Federal Republic), **546**
CRALOG, 230
Germany Twp., PA, 686

Germany Valley, PA, Church of the Brethren, 71, *71*
Gernand, Ernest J., 106, 1633
Gerner, Tobias, 531
Gerson, Robert A., 1947
Gerst family, 1958
Gerst, John Nicholas, I, 532
Gerst, Theobold, 532
Gerstenlauer, Catherine (later Kilhefner), 693
Gerster, Daniel G., 1633
Gesäng der einsamen und verlassenen Turtel-Taube, Das (*The Songs of the Lonely and Forsaken Turtledove*), **546,** 1947
Geschichte der neuern evangelischen Theologie (Hirsch)
Pietism subdivisions, 1021
Geschichte des Christentums (von Walter)
Pietism subdivisions, 1021
Geschichte des christlichen Lebens in der rheinisch-westphälischen evangelischen Kirche (*History of Christian Life in the Rhenish-Westphalian Protestant Church*)
Goebel, Max, 555, 611
Geska, Edith, 1849
Gespersen, Peter S., 1633
Ein Gespraech, 1947–1948
Gestapo, 23
Gettle, Samuel, 1633
Gettysburg, OH
Old Order German Baptist Church, 972
Gettysburg, OH, Oakland congregation
Petersime, Ray, 1012
Gettysburg, PA, 161, 1276, 1295
Marsh Creek Church of the Brethren, **546–547**
Gettysburg, Battle of, **546**
effect on Maryland Brethren of, 798
Independent Brethren, 649
Pfoutz, David, elder, 1015
Getz family, 1988
Getz, J. A., 1633
Getz, Jacob
Portis, KS, Grace Brethren Church, 1047
Getz, John, 516
Getz, John E., 1633
Getz, John H., 1633
Getz, Mary E., 1948
Getz, Paul
Poland, 1041
Getz, Russell P., 1948
Geyer, Alan F., 638
Geyer, Milo H., 1633
Geyer, Saylor, 228
Gheen, Ernest B., 1633
Ghent Grace Brethren Church, VA, *See* Roanoke, VA, Ghent Grace Brethren Church
Gibbel, Aaron R., 1633
Mohler Church of the Brethren, PA, free minister, 868
Gibbel, Abraham, 596
Gibbel, Ann
Lancaster, PA, Acts Covenant Fellowship, 2213
Gibbel, Christian Wenger, 1340, 1633
Gibbel, Cyrus R., 1633
Gibbel, Elizabeth (CB), 1841, *See also* McCann, Elizabeth Gibbel

McCann, Samuel Napoleon, 772
Gibbel, Elizabeth Hummer, 547
Gibbel, Elizabeth Royer, 547, 771
Gibbel family, 1330
Royer family related to, 1128
Whitney, Mary E. on, 2363
Gibbel, Fanny, 596
Gibbel, Florence Baker, **547**
Gibbel (Gibble) family, **547**
Gibbel, H. G., 235
Gibbel, Harry B., 1633, 2301
Gibbel, Henry, 1633
Gibbel, Henry Royer, 547, **547,** 1633
Gibbel, I. M., 596, 1633
Gibbel, Ira, 683
New Enterprise, PA, Church of the Brethren, as minister, 927
Gibbel, Ira D., 1633
Gibbel, Ira William, 1633, 2301, **2382**
on Eckert, William J. and descendants, 2333
on Gibbel, Henry and descendants, 2333
Gibbel, J. P.
medical missions, 807
Rural Life Association (RLA), 1131
Gibbel, James, 193
Gibbel, John
Lancaster, PA, Acts Covenant Fellowship, 2213
Gibbel, John B., 547, 748, 771, 1340, 1633
Gibbel, Jonathan Paul, 1838
Gibbel, Maria Longanecker, 547
Gibbel meetinghouse
Gibbel (Gibble) family, 547
Gibbel, Paul, 1307
Gibbel, Phyllis (later Miller)
Miller, Donald Eugene, 2223
Gibbel, Verda Elizabeth Hershberger, 1838
Gibble, Abraham D., 1633
Gibble, Amy, 686
Gibble, Ann E., 2301
Gibble, David G., 1633
Gibble family, *See* Gibbel family
Gibble, Harry, 322
Gibble, Henry, 1948
Gibble, Hiram, 415, 1340, 1633
Gibble, Hiram G., *547*
Gibble, Hiram Lamar, 1633, 1948, 2129
historic peace churches, 2200
Prague Conferences and, 2239
Silver Springs, MD, Good Shepherd Church of the Brethren, pastor, 1182
violence and, 2265
Gibble, Isaac M., 1633
Gibble, Isaac S., 1633
Gibble, J. B., 1633
Gibble, J. Paul, 1633
Gibble, Jacob, 1633
Gibble, Jay Emmert, 21, 1633
National Older Adult Conferences, 2229
Gibble, Jonas, 1237
Gibble, June Adams, 2165, 2279
on covenant people, 2336
on covenant, stories of, 2333
deacons, resource for, 2333
People of the Covenant (POC) (BC) and, 2237
Gibble, Kenneth L., 1633, 1948
on law *vs.* gospel, 2333
Ridgeway Community Church of the

Brethren, PA, pastor, 1109
Gibble Kipp, Judith, 2279
Gibble, Laura May (later Ebling), 418
Gibble, Leah (later Meyer), 226
    Meyer, Jacob Gibble, mother of, 821
Gibble, Lois Jean, 1842
Gibble, Mary Ann (later Longenecker), 756
Gibble, Phares Brubaker, 1948
Gibble, Pius Rohrbaugh, 109, 505, 923, 1633
Gibble, Sadie, *547*
Gibble, Samuel S., 1948
Gibble Science Building
    Elizabethtown College, 437
Gibble, Verda Faw, 1633
Gibbon, Daniel, 1633
Gibboney, Dale Edward, 1277, 1633
Gibbons, Daniel, 106, 1633
    New River Old German Baptist
        Brethren Church, ministers for, 931
Gibbons, Mr.
    Portis, KS, Grace Brethren Church, 1048
Gibbons, Mrs.
    Portis, KS, Grace Brethren Church, 1048
Gibbons, Phebe Earle, 379, 1948
Gibbons, Sadie
    Portis, KS, Grace Brethren Church, pastor, 1048
Gibbons, Sadie A., 1297
Gibbons, Sarah, 1633
Gibbony, Gerald C., 1633
Gibbs, Charles B., 1301, 1633
Gibbs, Charles Walter, 1400, 1633, 2301
Gibbs, Ezra, 1633
Gibbs, William, 1633
Gibler, Alexander, 1633
Gibler, Sarah (later Erbach), 453
Gibony, Joel, 1633
Gibson, Andrew P., 334, 335, 548, 561, 1633
    Mulvane, KS, Brethren Church, pastor, 895–896
    South Haven Brethren Church, KS, elder, 1205
Gibson, Anna Sturgis, 547
Gibson, Charles and Susan, 1977
Gibson, Charles C., 548, 550, 1633
Gibson, Clara Elizabeth (later Shull) 1402
    Shull, Arthur G. on descendants of, 2356
    Zunkel, Cleda Shull on descendants of, 2365
Gibson, Cullen C., 548, 550, 1633
Gibson, Daniel B., **547**, 548, 550, 1335, 1633, 1948
    Milmine Church of the Brethren, IL, elder, 843
    Plattsburg Church of the Brethren, MO, minister, 1030
Gibson, Elizabeth Gates, 547, 548
Gibson family, **548**
    Filbrun family, 490
    Neher family, related to, 922
    Shull family, related to, 1156
Gibson, Frank W., 1634
Gibson, G. W., 1634
Gibson, George, 548, 592
Gibson, H. P., 1634
Gibson, I. J., 1364
Gibson, I. M., 757, 1634

Gibson, Ira, 1634
Gibson, Irvin J., 1634
Gibson, Isham, 30, 334, 370, 460, 475, 476, 511, 547, **547–548**, 548, 910, 1232, 1234, 1356, 1357, 1634
    Hostetler, Joseph, 631
    Illinois, 646
    Rowland, Joseph, 1126
Gibson, J. Brad, 2173
Gibson, J. P., 1634
Gibson, James, 548
Gibson, James Howard, 2279
Gibson, Javan, 548, 1634
Gibson, John, 1948
Gibson, Lucille (later Heckman), **592**, 1838, **2387**
Gibson, Ota E., 1634, **2382**
Gibson, Ralph D., 1634
Gibson, Rebecca Harshbarger, 592
Gibson, Rebecca Robinson, 548
Gibson, Sadie, 1285
Gibson, Walter, 1634
    Osceola, IN, Grace Brethren Church, pastor, 984
Gibson, Walter W., 1217, 1634
Gibson, William A., 1634
Gichtel, Johann Georg, 30, 266, 481, **548**, 1948, 2142
    Angel Brethren and Universalism, 1080
    Holy Spirit, doctrine of, 624
Gichtelians, *See* Boehmists, Engel-Brüder
Gieseke, Franz, 1948
Giessen faculty
    Wittgenstein, Countesses, and findings by, 2074
Giffin, E. J., 1634
Giffin, Elias, 1634
Giffin family, 332
Giffin Hill Church of the Brethren, PA, *See*
    Locust Grove Church of the Brethren, PA
Gift, Aaron Kern, 1948
Gift family
    history of, 1948
The Gift of the Morningstar (Gordon), 747
gifted children
    camping movement, 247
Gigax, Godfrey, 1634
Gilbert, Ann (later Rowland), **1126**
Gilbert, Audrey
    on Gilbert, Elizabeth and descendants, 2333
    on Gilbert, Thomas and descendants, 2333
    on West Alexandria First Brethren Church, OH, 2333
Gilbert, C., 1301
Gilbert, Caleb, family of, 1332
Gilbert, Claire (later Ulrich), 2133
Gilbert, Eliza (later Early), *See* Early, Eliza Gilbert
Gilbert, Elmer H., 320, 1333, 1634
Gilbert, Ezra, 1634
Gilbert, F. B., 1948
Gilbert family, 2079
Gilbert, Frank, 1634
Gilbert, Greenberg B., 1634
Gilbert, Harriet Yoder, 548
    Mothers and Daughters' Association, 879
Gilbert, Harry, 1634
Gilbert, Israel, 548

Gilbert, J., 1634
Gilbert, J. O., 1634
Gilbert, Jacob, 1126
Gilbert, James G., 366
Gilbert, James Zacchaeus, **548**, 758, 759, 1634
Gilbert, John, 1634
Gilbert, Julia A., 304, **548**, *549*, 1360
Gilbert, Martha Rupel
    relief worker, nurse, **2189–2190**, *2189*
Gilbert, Martha Waas, 2279
Gilbert, Mary Horning, 548
Gilbert, N. R., 1634
Gilbert, Ralph Wilmer, 1255, 1634, 1948, 2301
Gilbert, Russell W., 1948–1949
Gilbert, S. D., 228
Gilbert, Sarah Slifer, 548
Gilbert, Silas, 1634
Gilbert, Solomon, 548
Gilbert, Walter P.
    Gilbert, Martha Rupel, 2190
Gilbert, William Hampton, 1634
Gilchrist, Joseph, 1634
Giles Co., VA
    Olean Church of the Brethren, VA, 973
Giles, Jerry W., 2279
Giles, William Ward, 1634, 2301
Gilfillen, Annie Lauver (later Eby), 419
Gilgan, Gilbert W., Jr., 265, 1634
Gill, David W.
    on higher education, 2333
Gill family
    Osceola, IN, Grace Brethren Church, 983
Gill, Jeffrey A., 375, 2279
Gill, Susan B. (later Lahman), 718
Gillan, Harvey, 1634
Gillaspie, VA, Oak Grove Brethren Church, **548**
Gillenwater, John B., 1224
Gillespie, 1634
Gillespie, A. G., 1634
Gillespie, Artie (later Lynn), 768
Gillespie family, 1267
    Macedonia, OH, Western Reserve
        Grace Brethren Church, 2216
    Roanoke, VA, First Brethren Church, 1113
Gillespie, Jesse, 1634
Gillespie, Robert P., 1267
Gillet, W. F., 432
Gillett (Gillette), Charles Edwin, 322, 520, **549**, 552, 572, 1312, 1324, 1634, 1949
Gillett Grove, IA, German Baptist Brethren (Church), **549**
Gillett, John A., 549
Gillett, Mary Ann Edwards, 549
Gillett, Rachel E. Kuns, 549
    on Gillet family, 2333
Gillett, W. B., 1949
Gillett, W. F., 552, 1634
Gillette, Charles Edwin, *See* Gillett, Charles Edwin
Gillette, Dan L., 2279
Gillette, Ola E., 1634
Gilley, William Daniel, 2279
Gilliam, Peter, 1997
Gilliam, William, 411
Gillin, Anna Louisa Straley, 549
Gillin, Etta Shaffner, 549
Gillin, J. H., 1321

Gillin, John Lewis, 2, 211, 239, 484, **549,** 1261, 1949, 2382
  divine inspiration of scripture, 132
  historical writing, 612
  Iowa, 661
  Liberal theology and noncreedalism, 943
  "Message of the Brethren Ministry," 817
Gillin, John Phillip, 549
Gillin, Mary McCutcheon, 549
Gillin, Richard Doyle, 1634
Gillin, Samuel Brallier, 549
Gillis, Eldred John, II, 1634, 2175
  Seal Beach, CA, Grace Brethren Church, pastor, 1161
  Simi Valley, CA, Grace Brethren Church, pastor, 1182
Gillis, Eldred John, II, 2175
Gillis, Jesse, 1634
Gillis, Robert, 347
Gillis, Mrs. Robert, 347
Gilmer, Arden E., 1634, 2137
  Medina, OH, Brethren Church, 2219
  The Missionary Board (BC), 856
Gilmer, Clarence, 1634
Gilmer, Clarence Y., 1634
Gilmer Co., WV, 172
Gilmer, Elmer, 1634
Gilmer, Herbert R., 1311, 1634
Gilmer, James Allen, 1634
Gilmore, Charles, 1634
Gilpin family, 313
Gilpin, Joshua, 1949
Gilroy, CA, 727, 1358
Gilroy, CA, Brethren Church, *See* Lathrop, CA, Brethren Church
Ginder, Ira Z., 1634
Ginder, John Becker, 1634
Gindlesberger, Herma, 377
Ginger, P. E., 277
Ginger, Perry E., 277, 1634
Gingerich, Abe, 1949
Gingerich, Benjamin George, 1949
Gingerich, Catharine Schlabaugh
  descendants, 1946
Gingerich, Catherine, 2068
Gingerich, Catherine Miller, 2107
Gingerich, Christian, 2107
Gingerich, Daniel J., 549, 1871
  genealogy and descendants, 1949
Gingerich, Elizabeth Brenneman, 549
Gingerich family, 1949, 2107
  records, 1949
Gingerich, Herman W., 1949
Gingerich, Jacob D., 1932
Gingerich, Jacob Wagner, 1949
Gingerich, Johannes
  descendants, 1946
Gingerich, John
  family history, 1967
Gingerich, John W., 1949
Gingerich (Kingery) family, **549**
Gingerich, Lydia, 1932
Gingerich, Magdalena, 2105
Gingerich, Malinda J. Yoder, 1949
Gingerich, Mattie Fry, 1949
Gingerich, Mattie (later Gerig), 1946
Gingerich, Mattie (later Miller), 2016
Gingerich, Melvin, 1949
Gingerich, [Mrs.] Val, 1949
Gingerich, Nettie Beachy Shetler, 1949
Gingerich, Noah, 1949

Gingerich, Owen
  on horses, and BSC-sponsored delivery to Poland, 2333
Gingerich, Sarah A., 1871
Gingerich, Sarah Kauffman, 1949
Gingerich, Veronica Litwiller, 1949
Gingery, James B., 758
Ginghamsburg, OH, 1265
Gingrich, Alfred B., 39, 1635
Gingrich, Alice Trostle, 550
Gingrich, Anna B. Martin, 1951
Gingrich, Beatrice P. Smith, 550
Gingrich, Christian, 549
Gingrich, David, 549
Gingrich, Edith Garber
  Gingrich, Raymond Eugene, 2190
Gingrich, Elias M.
  family history, 1951
Gingrich, Esther
  Mount Wilson Church of the Brethren, PA, 887
Gingrich family, 1949, 2089
  Harrisburg, PA, Melrose Gardens Grace Brethren Church, 586
  records, 1949
Gingrich, Glenn L., 1635
Gingrich, Hiram G., 670, 1635
  Mount Wilson Church of the Brethren, PA, part-time pastor, 887
Gingrich, I. F.
  Nickerson, KS, Church of the Brethren, elder in, 936
Gingrich, Isaac F., 549, 1635
Gingrich, J. L., 332, 1221
Gingrich, Jacob, 549
Gingrich, Jacob H., 1635
Gingrich, John H., 1635
Gingrich, John, II
  family history, 1978
Gingrich, Joseph L., 130, 443, **550,** 731, 755, 1635
Gingrich, Josephine (later McClain), 772
Gingrich, Kathleen A., 2279
Gingrich, Lucille M. (later Good), 1951
Gingrich, Raymond E., Jr., 1635
Gingrich, Raymond Eugene, 12, 13, 357, 563, 757, 1255, 1635, 1949, 2301
  John, first Epistle of, 2333
  Lakeland, FL, Grace Brethren Church, 2213
  pastor, educator, **2190**
Gingrich, Rhonda Pittman
  leader's guide, 2333
  membership guide, 2333
Gingrich, Samuel W., 550
Gingrich, Simon
  Mount Wilson Church of the Brethren, PA, 887
Gingrich, Ulysses L., 1635
  Manheim, PA, Grace Brethren Church, pastor, 787
  North Buffalo Grace Brethren Church, PA, pastor, 945
Gingrich, Yost (Joseph), 1949
Ginter family
  Harrisburg, PA, Melrose Gardens Grace Brethren Church, 586
Gipe, Andrew, 1635
Gipe, Harrison Smith, 1635
Gipe, Joseph, 471, 1635, 2027
Gipe, Joseph H., 1635
Gipe, Mary Coover, 2027
Gipe, Samuel, 1635

Gipple family, *See* Gibbel (Gibbel) family
Girard area, IL
Gibson family, 548
Girard congregation, IL, 1307
Girard, IL
  Pleasant Hill Village, 1033
Girard, IL, Church of the Brethren, **550**
  Macoupin Creek Church of the Brethren, IL, 779
  Pleasant Hill Church of the Brethren, IL, 1032
  Shull, William H., elder, 1156
Girl, Christian, 1949
Girl, John, 1635
Girtman, Mary M., 1635, 2301
Gish, Abraham, 1635
Gish, Addaline (later Robinson), 1115, *1115*
Gish, Anna Sell, 550
Gish, Arthur G., 302, 1949
  on Christian peacemaker teams in Middle East, 2334
Gish, Barbara Kindig, 54, 295, 479, **550,** *550,* 551, 1361
  McCann, Samuel Napoleon, 772
  missions, 858
Gish Book Fund
  founding of, 1361
Gish, Catherine Stober
  Stover, William, 2379
Gish, Charles C., 1635
Gish, Edward, 1335, 1635
Gish, Elender Hopkins, 743
Gish, Ellen Maurine (later Geisert)
  Geisert, Wayne F., 2187
Gish family, 164, 238, **550–551,** 743, 753, 1219, 1280
  Graybill (Grabill, Krehbiel) family, 567
  Muhlenberg Co., KY, German Baptist Brethren, 893
Gish Fund, 1950
  Books, **551**
  Committee
    Lear, John Wallace, 732
    Statler, Foster Boyd, 1219
    Williams, John Henry Bashor, 1345
  Gish, Barbara Kindig and James Rufus, 550
Gish, George W., 635, 1635
  Panther Creek, IL, Church of the Brethren, 992
Gish, Henry A., 373, 1635
Gish, Ira Montgomery, 1949–1950
Gish, J. R., 479
Gish, James, 295
Gish, James and Barbara, 461
Gish, James Rufus, 54, 72, 170, 255, 479, **550,** *550,* 551, 760, 1232, 1281, 1635, 1950
  Hudson, IL, Church of the Brethren, 635
  Hygiene, CO, Church of the Brethren, 641
  McCann, Samuel Napoleon, 772
  missions, 858
  Missouri Brethren settlement, 864
  Mount Vernon Church of the Brethren, VA, 887
  Panther Creek, IL, Church of the Brethren, 992
  Poplar Bluff Church of the Brethren, AR, 1046
  Poplar Bluff, MO, Church of the

Brethren, 1046
Roanoke, LA, Church of the Brethren, 1112
Round Mountain Church of the Brethren, AR, minister, 1125
St. Francis Church of the Brethren, AR, 1134
Gish, James W., 1635
Gish, John H., 1635
Gish, Katherine, 551
Gish, Matthias, 550
family history, 1956
Gish, Orval, 430
Mud Valley Old German Baptist Brethren Church, IL, presiding elder, 892
Gish, Orvel M., Jr., 1635
Gish, Peggy, 1949
Gish, Philip B., 1635, 2279
Maple Grove Old German Baptist Brethren Church, OH, minister, 791
Gish, R. William, 263
Gish, Roger L., 1635
Modesto, CA, Old German Baptist Brethren Church, minister, 867
Gish, Rufus G., 1635
Gish, Susannah Stober
Stover, William, 2379
Gish, Walter H., 1635
Gish, William, R., **550**, 1635
Miller, Robert Henry, 841
Gish, William Byrd, 1635
Missouri Brethren settlement, 864
Ozawkie, KS, Church of the Brethren, elder, 987
Gish, William Warren, 1635
Gitt, Charles William, 1635
Gittinger, Frank, 738
Giuseppe, Montague S., 1950
Given, Laura M., 1950
giving, doctrine of
poems, 2105
Gjerde, Wayne, 1635
G(K)reider, Michael and Elizabeth, 1990
Glad Songs, 642, 1950
Gladden, Washington
Social Gospel Movement, 1197
Glade Creek, VA, 152
Glade meetinghouse, Summit Church of the Brethren, VA, 1236
Glade Park, CO, Community Church of the Brethren, **551**
Fruita, CO, Church of the Brethren, 520
Grand Junction, CO, Koinonia Brethren-Baptist Church, 565
Glade Run Brethren Church, PA, **551**, 699
Glade Run, PA, Church of the Brethren, *See* Center Hill Church of the Brethren, PA
Glade Run, PA, congregation, 170, 268, 1314, *See also* Center Hill congregation
Glade Run, PA, German Baptist Brethren congregation, 224, 699
Glade Union
Sandy Creek Church of the Brethren, WV preaching point, 1143
Glade Valley Church of the Brethren, MD, *See* Walkersville, MD, Glade Valley Church of the Brethren
Glade View meetinghouse

Eglon, WV, Church of the Brethren, 430
Glades, PA, congregation, 348
Flora, (Flory) family, 495
Maple Spring Church of the Brethren, PA, 791
Glady, WV, Church of the Brethren, 164, **551**
Glady, WV, congregation, 164
Glaize family, 1868
Glaser, L. J. K., 1950
Glaser, Ruth Kulp, 1950
Glasgow (ship)
Klein(e), Georg(e), 699
Metzler, Yost, and family, voyage to America on, 820
Glasgow Church of the Brethren, MT, *See* Valley Church of the Brethren, MT
Glasgow, MT, 142, 1301
Glasgow, MT, Valley congregation
Montana Brethren settlement, 870
Glasmire, Leah Shaeffer, 361, 1838, 2026
Glasmire, William E., 361, 1635, 2057
Glass, Bentley, 1950
Glass, Jeffrey E., 1635
Glass, Lewis, 1635
Glass, Roy, E., 21, 1277, 2173, 2279
Radford, VA, Fairlawn Grace Brethren Church, pastor, 1079
Glass, Roy E., III, 2279
Glass, Roy E., Jr., 1635
Minerva, OH, Grace Brethren Church, pastor, 843
Glass, William Robert, 2279
Glatfelter, Charles H., 1950
on Adams County, PA churches, 2334
on PA Germans, 2334
Glaubhafftes Send-Schreiben aus Pennsylvania in America . . ., 1950
Glays family, 377
Gleason, Michael F., 1635, 2132, 2137
Gleason, Sheila K., 2132
Glee, Donna, 1837
Gleim, Elmer Quentin, 1950, 1635
on Black Rock CB, PA, 2334
on Children's Aid Society, 2334
on Gleim family and descendants, 2334
on Hanover, PA CB, 2334
on Huntsdale CB, PA, 2334
Philadelphia, PA, First Church of the Brethren, providing leadership, 1015
Philadelphia, PA, Germantown Church of the Brethren, 1016
Upper Conewago CB, PA, 2334
Glen Arm, MD, 755
Glen, C. E., 1254
Glen Hope, PA, congregation, 274
Glen, John, 1635
Glen Mary, Saskatchewan, Canada, 15
Glen Rock (Glenrock), NE, Church of the Brethren, **551**
Glen Rock, NE, *552*
Glen St. Mary, FL, Glenside Church of the Brethren, **552,** *920*
Glendale, AZ, Church of the Brethren, 54, **552**
migration of Brethren, 830
Phoenix, AZ, Lynnhaven Community Church of the Brethren, 1019
Glendale, CA, 255
urban mission, 1297
Glendale, CA, Church of the Brethren, **552,**

759, 768
Glendale, CA, First Brethren Church, **552–553**
Glendale Community Grace Brethren Church, *See* Glendale, CA, First Brethren Church
Glendale, CA, Church of the Brethren, 552
Glendale, MD, Church of the Brethren, *See* Flinstone, MD, Glendale Church of the Brethren; Flintstone, MD,
Glendora, CA, Bible Brethren Church, 19, **553**
Glendora, CA, Church of the Brethren, 217, 348, **553**, 732, 758, 1314
Glendora, MI, Brethren Church, *See* Clarksville, MI, Grace Brethren Church
Glenford, OH, Brethren Church, **553**
Miller, John Allen, pastor, 839
Glengy family, 1914
Glenhope congregation, PA, 1347
Glenn, Chalmers E., 564, 1635
Glenn Co., CA
Elk Creek, CA, Church of the Brethren, 438
Glenn, John, 1276
Glenside, FL, Church of the Brethren, *See* Glen St. Mary, FL, Glenside Church of the Brethren
Glenwood, NC, 749
Glenwood, OH, Grace Brethren Community Church, **553**
Glessner family, 165
Glessner, Philip H., 1635
Glessner, Ruth Lucille, 1833
Glick, Allen R.
on Glick family and descendants, 2334
Glick, Anna Harshbarger, 553
Glick, Anna (later Sherfy), 553
Glick, Barbara (later Frantz), 553
Glick, Benjamin Franklin, 1335, 1635
Glick, Carolyn
Southern Lancaster Grace Brethren Church, PA, 1207
Glick, Catharine (later Landes), 553
Glick, Catherine Teater, 553
Glick, Daniel, 540, 1342, 1635
Glick, Daniel (1824–1891), 92
Glick, Daniel M., 673, 1635
Glick, David C., 1635
Glick, Dawn (later Phibbs), 554
Glick, Donald, 554
Glick, Effie Evers, 554
Glick, Elizabeth Bauserman, 553
Glick, Elizabeth (later Wine), 553
Glick, Elizabeth Miller, 553
Glick family, 1950, 2098, *See also* Glück (Click, Glick) family; Glück (Glick, Click) family
Dutchman's Creek German Baptist Brethren Church, NC, 411
Flat Rock Church of the Brethren, VA, 493
history of, 1950
North Bethel Church of the Brethren, MO, 945
South Bethel German Baptist Brethren, MO, 1204
Glick, Garland Wayne, 554, 638, 1636, 1950
and neoorthodoxy, 923
Glick, George H., 1950
Glick, Harry Newton, 1636

Glick, J. A., 1636
Glick, Jacob Daniel, 368, **553**, 1636
Glick, Joel, 553, 1636
    South Bethel German Baptist Brethren,
        MO, minister, 1204
Glick, John, 1636
Glick, John D., 1277, 1636
Glick, John III, 553
Glick, John, Jr., 553, 1636
Glick, John K., 1871
Glick, John, Sr., 1636
Glick, John T., Jr., 554
Glick, John Titus, 554, 1636
Glick, John William, 1636
Glick, Joseph, 553, 1636, 1909
    South Bethel German Baptist Brethren,
        MO, minister, 1204
Glick, Joseph A., 128, 442, 1636
Glick, Joseph Livingstone, 554, 1636
Glick, Joseph Paul, 1636, 1950
    on ancestral biographies, 2334
Glick, Karen (later Metzler)
    Sudan (CB) and, 2253
Glick, Lizzie C. Evers, 553
Glick, Margaret (later Hunkins?), 554
Glick, Martha Anne, 1051
Glick, Mattie V., 1361
Glick, Paul E., 554
Glick-Reiman, Elizabeth G., 554, 1636,
    2183
    Women's Conferences (CB) and, 2264
Glick, Royal D., 1636
    Raisin City, CA, Church of the
        Brethren, pastor, 1083
    San Bernardino, CA, Church of the
        Brethren pastor, 1141
Glick, Ruth (later Welliver?), 554
Glick, Simon Daniel, 516, 1636
Glick, Stanley, 554
Glick, Susie Wampler, 553
Glick, Victor E., 554
Glick, Wendell P., 554, 1636
Global Food Crisis Fund
    homelessness, 2203
Global Mission Partnerships (CB)
    missions, short-term, 2226
Global Opportunities (GO) teams, 2183
Global Women's Project (CB)
    global poverty and injustice, **2190**
    women and, 2264
    Womaen's Caucus and, 2184
    Women's Conferences (CB) and, 2265
Globalink
    Global Women's Project, 2190
Glock, John G., 1636, 1863
The Glory of the Impossible (Helser), 596
glossolalia, 2011
    Pentecostalism, 1008
Glotfelty family, 740
Glotfelty, James, 1636
    Pleasant Hill Church of the Brethren,
        IA, 1032
Glotfelty, Michael, 1636
Glotfelty, William Nelson, 1636
Gloucester, England
    Sunday school movement, 283
Glover, Clara C., 2279
Glover, E. S., 246
Glover, Edwin Julius, 79, 1636
Glover, Henry Harrison, 1636
Glover, Irving Ray, 1636
    Shippensburg, PA, Church of the
        Brethren, pastor in, 1177

Glover, Murrell K., 1636
Glück (Click, Glick) family, 26
Glück (Glick, Click) family, **553–554**
Glück, Johannes, Sr. (Glick, John, Sr.), 553
Gnaegi, Christian, 554, 1950
Gnaga family, 153
Gnäge, Johannes, 554
Gnagey, A. D., 562, 1236
    hymnals, 642
    McClain, Alva J., 772
    "Message of the Brethren Ministry,"
        817
    Meyersdale, PA, Main Street Brethren
        Church, pastor, 823
    Sunday school literature, 1237, 1239
    support of women as ministers, 1362
Gnagey, Abraham Daniel, 20, 121, 186,
        205, **554**, 1636, *See also* hymnals
Gnagey, Abraham Lincoln, 1636
Gnagey, Catherine Fike, 554
Gnagey, Clarence H., 1636
Gnagey, Daniel, 554
Gnagey, Elias, 1950
Gnagey, Eliza Livengood, 401, *554*
Gnagey, Eugene, 717
Gnagey family, 152
    Fike family, 490
Gnagey, Gary P., 587
Gnagey (Gnaegi) family, **554**
Gnagey, J. Erwin, 1636
Gnagey, Joel, 273, 554, 1236, 1636
Gnagey, Lydia Fike, 554
Gnagey, Mary E.
    McClain, Walter Scott, 773
Gnagey, Mary Ellen (later McClain)
    McClain, Alva J., 772
Gnagey, Sevilla, 1874
Gnagey, William J., 1636
Gnagy, Cora (later Beeghly), 1219
Gnagy, Dillon Cecil, 582, 1280, 1636
    San Francisco, CA, Church of the
        Brethren pastor, 1142
Gnagy, Eugene, 236, 1330
    Newton, KS, Church of the Brethren,
        pastor in, 934
Gnagy, Eugene Edward, 1636
Gnagy, Eugene V., 504
Gnagy, Harvey Andrew, 531, 1323, 1636
Gnagy, Mary
    Pasadena, CA, Church of the Brethren,
        994
Gnagy, Sarah
    Pasadena, CA, Church of the Brethren,
        994
Gnagy, Susie (later Long)
    Long, John Daniel, 2215
Gnegy, Larry, 728, 1636
Goals and Budget Committee (CB),
    554–555
    General Board (CB), 536
    organizational restructuring and, 2242
Goals Discovery Experience
    Nampa, ID, Church of the Brethren,
        913
Gochenour, B., 1636
Gochenour, Christena (later Hofmann), 617
Gochenour, Emanuel, 555
Gochenour family, 1212
Gochenour, Frank, 676, 1636
Gochenour (Goughnour), Emanuel, 1636
Gochenour (Goughnour) family, 31, **555**
Gochenour, H. L., 1636, *See also* Goughen-
    our, H. L.

Gochenour, Jacob
    family history, 1933
Gochenour, James Harvey, 1863
Gochenour's Chapel Church of the
    Brethren, VA, *See* Trinity Church
    of the Brethren, VA
Gochnauer, Harry W., and Gochnauer
    family, 1950
Gochnour (Goughnour), Elizabeth (later
    Roberts), 1114
Gockley, Anna (later Hoff), 616, 617
    Mothers and Daughters' Association,
        879
God
    Kindom of, 5
    Nead, Peter, writings on, 919
    Neoorthodox view of, 922
    new covenant with, 5
    saving action in baptism, 83, 84
    as source of authority for the Church,
        73
God, doctrine of, *See* Trinity, doctrine of
The God in You (Eby), 420
Goddard, Burton, 1950
Goddard, Lloyd, 566
Goddard, Reginald N., 1636
Godfemality, 1865
Godfrey family, 686
Godfrey, Geraldine M., 2279
Godfrey, KS, Brethren Church, *See* Fort
    Scott, KS, Brethren Church
Godfrey, Richard E., 2279
Godfrey, S. C.
    Pleasant View Church of the Brethren,
        PA, elder-in-charge, 1037
Godfrey, Samuel C., 1636
Godfrey, Stanley L., Jr., 2279
Godparents, *See* church parents
God's Means of Grace (Yoder, C. F.), 184,
    555, 1349, 1385, 1386
Godshall, Horace, *477*
Godshall, Jacob, *477*
Godshall, Leanna (later Nyce), 952
Godwin, Kenneth O., 2301
Godwin, Richard, 1636
Goeb, Frederick, 2078
Goebel, Friedrich, 1951
Goebel, Julius, 1951
Goebel, Max, 379, **555**, 611, 1951, *See also*
    historical writing; Solingen
    Brethren
    Reformed Church and Pietism, 1021
Goehring, Harry D., 1636
Goelhe, Ruth
    Sudan (CB) and, 2253
Goens (Goers), Ernest G., 1637
Goering, Agnes Alice Wadel, 1972
Goering, Kathryn (later Reid), 2290
    on racism, 2351
Goghenour, Herbert Logan, 1638
Gohn, Greg, 2279
Goiffon, V., 1637
Goings, Darrell Dean, 1637
Golay, Kenneth, 399
Golbert, Dorothy, 2082
Gold Rush Community Grace Brethren
    Church, CA
    River City Grace Community Church,
        CA, 1134
gold, wearing of, *See* jewelry
Golden Church of the Brethren, NC, **555**
The Golden Dawn, **555–556**, 1236, 1951
Golden Gate Church of the Brethren, CA,

See Oakland, CA, Church of the Brethren

Golden Gate Mission

    Oakland, CA, Church of the Brethren, 957

golden jubilees

    Highland Avenue, Elgin, IL, Church of the Brethren, 1965

The Golden Pen (Cable)

    Mother's Day, 879

Golden, Roger Alton, 2279

Golden Spring German Baptist Brethren Church, NE, **2374**

Golden Valley Community Church of the Brethren, MN, *See* Minneapolis, MN, Golden Valley Community Church of the Brethren

Golden Valley, NC

    Golden Church of the Brethren, NC, 555

Golden Willow Church of the Brethren, ND, 165, *See also* Bowden Valley Church of the Brethren, ND

Goldendale, WA, Community Grace Brethren Church, **556**

Goldinger, David, 1637

Goldizen, John C., 1637

Goller family, *11*

Golly, Abraham, 211, 1637

Gomorry, *See* Gumre

Gonawein family

    Fremont, OH, Grace Brethren Church, 515

Gonderman, Mr. and Mrs. S. C.

    New Paris, IN, Brethren Church, 931

Gongwer family

    Osceola, IN, Grace Brethren Church, 983

Gonzales family, 1312

González, Alberto

    Yahuecas, PR, Iglesia de los Hermanos Cristo Nuestra Paz (CB) and, 2267

González, Doris Rivera

    Yahuecas, PR, Iglesia de los Hermanos Cristo Nuestra Paz (CB) and, 2267

Good, A. Hanson, 1637

Good, Aaron Zimmerman, 1951

Good, Ada Zeigler, 1397, 1838

Good, Barbara G., 2092

Good, Barbara (later Weber), 1325

Good, Barry L., 2279

Good, Becky, 503

Good, Benjamin F., 1637

Good, Beverly Bowman, 1637

Good, Catharine Bunn

    family history, 1951

Good, Catherine Statler, *See* Good family

Good, Charles T., 1637

Good, Christian, 556, 1951

Good, Conrad, 556

Good, D. L., 1637

Good, Daniel F., 42, 1637

Good, David B., 1637

Good, Elias Hosea, 1951

Good, Eliza (later Wine), 1350

Good, Emanuel, Sr.

    family history, 1951

Good family, 415, 1219, 1243, 1318, 1868, 1874, 1951, 2034, 2042

    Flat Rock Church of the Brethren, VA, 493

    Glück (Glick, Click) family, 553

    history of, 1944, 1945, 1951

Scherffig family, related to, 1152

Good, Fannie Vera Lehman, 1951

Good, Franie (later Schrag), *See* Schrag, Franie Good

Good Friday, **556**

    observation of, 2147

Good, George K., 1637

Good, George W., 1951

Good (Guth) family, **556**

Good Hall, Juniata College

    Good, J. Omar, 556

Good, Hanson, 1637

Good, Henry A., 42, 471, 1637

Good Hope (ship), 317

Good Hope, CO, Church of the Brethren, *See* Haxtun, CO, Church of the Brethren

Good, Howard E., 1945

Good, J. Omar, **556**

Good, Jacob, 556, 1951

Good, Jacob C., 556

Good, James Isaac, 1951

Good, John, 262, *See also* Good family

    family history, 1951

Good, John Harvey, 1637

Good, John S., 1637

Good, Joseph, *See* Good family

Good, Kent Carlton, 503, 1849

Good, Lester E., 2301

Good, Lewis Christian, 1951

Good, Lucille M. Gingrich, 1951

Good, Mae Esther, 209

Good, Maria Snavely, 556

Good, Marie Galbreath, 1951

Good, Mary, *See* Good family

    family history, 1951

Good, Mary Bosley, 556

    descendants, 1951

Good, Mary Christine (later Michael), 1708

Good, Mary Elizabeth, 1951

Good, Mary Ellen Sappington, 1951

Good, Michael J., 1637

Good, Milton R., 1951

Good, Monroe Crouse, 80, 1637, 1838

Good, Nelson Blosser, 1951

Good News Bible (Today's English Version), 138

Good News Brethren Church, OH, 165

Good, Rebecca Lynn Sheffer, 1849

Good, Ronald E., 2279

Good, Roy R., 1637

Good, Ruth Irene, 1951

Good, S. M., 1637

Good, Salome, 1637

Good Samaritan Church of the Brethren, PA, **2190**

Good Shepherd Church of the Brethren, FL, **556–557, 2190**

Good Shepherd congregation, Washington, DC, 1320

Good Shepherd Home, 340, *557,* **557**

Good Shepherd, MO, Church of the Brethren, *See* Springfield, MO, Good Shepherd Church of the Brethren

Good, T. D., 1637

Good, William, 556

    family history, 1976

Good, William Harvey, 556, 1400, 1637

    good works, *See* works, doctrine of salvation, 1140

    sanctification, 1142

    Social Gospel Movement, 1197

Goodbye, Still Night, 158

Goode, Adaline, 157

Goode, VA, 1254

Gooden, Alice Kinzie, 1637

Goodhart, Donald R., 1251, 1637

Goodman, David, 30, 165, 348, 1637

Goodman, Dorothy Ethel Hay, 1849

Goodman, John H., 1637

Goodman, John W., 1637

Goodman, Marvin Lester, Jr., 1637, 1849, **2382**

    Modesto, CA, La Loma Grace Brethren Church, pastor (interim), 867

Goodman, Ralph A., 1637

Goodmiller, Lawrence R., 1333, 1637

Goodson, Barry, 2279

Goodwill meetinghouse

    Lost Creek Church of the Brethren, PA, 760

Goodwill, VA, congregation

    becomes New Hope Church of the Brethren, 929

Goodwin, Cora Leah (later Hamilton), 580

Goodwin, Helen

    National Older Adult Conferences, 2229

Goodwin, Kenneth E., 1637

Goodyear, Charles

    business beliefs and, 234

Goosen, Rachel Waltner

    women conscientious objectors, 2334

Goossens, Thomas E., 350, 490, 1637

    North Buffalo Grace Brethren Church, PA, pastor, 945

Gorden, Daniel A., 1637

Gorden, Emmanuel, family

    Michigan City, IN, Church of the Brethren, 825

Gorden family, 1240

Gorden (Gordon), William L., 1637

Gorden, Israel C., 1637, 2301

Gorden, Israel, family

    Michigan City, IN, Church of the Brethren, 825

Gorden, Jacob H. (M.), 1637

Gorden, Mary Louise, 1845

Gorden, William Israel, 1637

Gordon, Armistead C., 747, 1951–1952

Gordon, B. L., 1637

Gordon, Clair (later Frantz), 1940

Gordon, Forest Benjamin, 760, 1637

Gordon, J. H.

    Minot, ND, Church of the Brethren, elder, 851

Gordon, Raymond P., 1637

    Point Church of the Brethren, PA, 1040

Gordon, Ronald J.

    information technology, church use of, 2208

    Lost Creek CB, PA, 2334

Gordon, Russell C., 171, 1637, 2137

    Hispanic Ministries (BC), 2198

Gordon, Thomas F., 1952

Gorgas, Christin (Mack)

    Lamb, Ardis Krieg on, 2342

    Wood, Stacy B. C., Jr. on, 2364

Gorgas family, 2063

Gorgas, Jacob, *See* Gorgas family

    Garvan, Beatrice B. on, 2333

Gorham, Adelbert Lawson, 1637

Gorham, C. W., 1637

Gorrell, Earl, 1637

Gorrell, James J., 2279

Gorrill, William Earl, 1637

Gorsuch, John, 1637
Gorum, B., 1637
Goschenhoppen Region
    Christmas customs, 1991
Goshall, Leanna
    Hartzel, Gwendolyn Price (Nyce) on descendants of, 2346
    Mease, Gladys Price (Nyce) on descendants of, 2346
    Nyce, Gwendolyn Price on descendants of, 2346
Goshen Brethren Church, IN, 2090
    Jefferson Brethren Church, IN, 670
Goshen Church of the Brethren, WV, **558–559**
    history of, 1929
Goshen College
    Byler, Robert Oliver, 2153
    Warstler, Anna Margaret, 1319
Goshen Conference of 1918 (CB), 269, 403, **559**
    Early, Henry Clay, 414
    "Goshen Statement," 559
    noncreedalism, 942
    Relief and Reconstruction Committee, 1096
    religious liberty and military service, 1098
    social action, 1196
Goshen congregations as example of biblically inspired name, 911
Goshen, IN, 690, 1338, 1385
    City Church of the Brethren, **557,** 1929
    Dunkard Brethren, 352, **557–558**
    First Brethren Church, **558**
    Goshen Conference, 559
    Grace Brethren Church, **558**
    Jefferson Brethren Church, *See* Jefferson Brethren Church, IN
    relief and service efforts, 1097
    special conference on noncombatant service in World War I, 1370
    West Goshen Church of the Brethren, 96, **558,** *558,* 749
    Elkhart Valley Church of the Brethren, IN, 440
Goshen meetinghouse, White Cottage, OH, Church of the Brethren, 1339
"Goshen Statement," 301, 559
Goshenhoppen Reformed Charge
    history, 1966
Goshorn, B. F., 1637
Goshorn, Ezra Nicholas, 1637
Goshorn, G. V., 1637
Goshorn, Glenn Gilbert, 588, 750, 1334, 1637
Goshorn, Martin, 1637
Goshorn, Robert R., 1637, 1898
    St. Petersburg, FL, First Church of the Brethren, leadership, 1135
Gosnell, Barbara Dove, 397
Gosnell, John W., 1637, 2301
Gosnell, William E, 1638
The Gospel According to Jesus (Mason), 799
Gospel Chimes
    hymnals, 642
Gospel Church Polity (Bowman), 166
Gospel Grace Brethren Church, VA **559**
The Gospel Herald
    Mennonite Church (MC) official paper, 815
Gospel Light Publications, 1237, 2179

The Gospel Messenger, 220, 403, 535, 689, 712, 1327, 1952, 2081, 2188
    1881–1883, **559**
    1883ff, *See Messenger*
    1965 redesign of, 61
    Advisory Committee, **559**
    Bible translations and versions, controversy about, 138
    Bittinger, Desmond Wright, 143
    Blough, Jerome E., 149, 151
    Brandt, Harry Alonzo, 172
    brass bands in religious services, 1377
    Brethren Church, 178
    Brethren Press and, 194
    Brethren relocation column, establishment of, 193
    Brethren's Card, 2152
    Brumbaugh, Wilbur Eugene, 223
    Christian Family Companion, 286
    Christian Science, and critical articles in, 287
    Christ's Assembly and, 280
    Church of Brethren doctrine publication in, 204
    Church of the Brethren, 300
    Church of the Brethren Leader and, 308
    Church of the Brethren, official publication, 286
    Congregational Brethren, 335
    Crumpacker, Franklin Henry, 354
    devotional literature, 381
    distribution of, 203
    Early, Henry Clay, 413
    editors of, 172
    establishment of, 180, 220
    Evangelii Büdbarare, 460
    Evangelische Besuch, Der, 460
    Figarden Church of the Brethren, CA, 489
    Flint, MI, Church of the Brethren, 494
    Flory, Jacob S., 498
    Flying Eagle, The, 500
    Frantz, Edward, 508
    fundamentalism, 522
    German Baptist Brethren publication of, 205
    Gospel Visitor, The, 286, 561
    Haughtelin, Jacob Diehl, 589
    Hendricks, Franklin A., 597
    Holsinger (Holtzinger) family, 623
    Huntingdon, PA, Stone Church of the Brethren, 637
    imposters among the Brethren, 648
    index (1923–1927), 1936
    index, (1932–1936), 1857
    Judaism, 677
    Mahan, Grant, editor, 782
    merger of, 186
    Messenger, 818–819
    Metzger, John, writing for, 819
    millennialism articles, 834
    Miller, Daniel Long, managing editor, 836
    ministry, 845
    missions, 859
    missions education, 864
    Mohler, Samuel Sayler, 868
    Moore, John Henry, editor, 874
    Morse, Kenneth Ivan, editor, 878
    North Tampa, FL, Zion Church of the Brethren, 950
    notice about Michigan settlement, 1400

Obituary Index, Leonard, Rosalita J. and, 2343
Oklahoma City, OK, Church of the Brethren, 964
Page, Kirby, 989
Peace Valley Church of the Brethren, MO, 1003
Peach Blossom Colored Church of Rising Light (CB), MD, 1003
photographs on cover, 1020
place-names, Brethren, 1028
Plate, Lewis (Ludwig) A., assistant editor, 1030
Pleasant Home Church of the Brethren, OK, 1033
poetry, 1039, 1040
Poor Fund, 767
Price, David E., writer for, 1056
The Primitive Christian and the Pilgrim, 1058
publication of statistics, 1218, 1219
publishing, 1068
Puterbaugh, Amsey Hascall, articles in, 1072
Quinter, James, editor, 1077
Recreational Fellowship, 1088
Rosenberger, Isaac J., writing for, 1123
Royer, Galen Brown, missions section editor, 1128
Sebring, FL, 1162
secret societies, 1164
smear campaign against, 187
Snider, Pastor, 187
Social Gospel Movement, 1197
Spanish-American War, editorial position on, 1208
Statler, Ruth Beeghly, 1219
Swihart, J. H., 186
Swihart, Jonathan H., 1245
Taylor, Lydia E., 1249
thesis about topical trends, 1928
Underhill, Nancy D. Blain, 1286
Van Dyke, Joe, 1302
Vaniman, Daniel, 1303
Weir, Samuel, biography, 1332
West, Edmund Landon, 1332
Winger, Otho, 1351
Zeigler, Carl Wenger (CB) and, 2269
gospel music, **559, 560–561,** 1378, *See also* camp meetings; hymns
    Brethren music, 899
    choirs and, 279
    Holsinger, George Blackburn, 621
    hymnals, 642
    hymns, 643
    publishing, 1069
    singing, 1184, 1185
Gospel of Nicodemus, 296
Gospel of Prayer (Wieand), 1051
"Gospel of Wealth," 253
The Gospel Preacher, 63, 78, 186, 195, **559–560,** 1952
    Holsinger, Henry Ritz, 622
    Mason, Edward, co-editor, 799
    The Progressive Christian, 1061
    Sharp, S. Z., question of authorship, 1174
    Worst, John H., 1379
Gospel Songs and Hymns
    hymnals, 642
Gospel teams
    funds from National Brethren Youth, 915

Gospel Tract Association, **561**, 1269
The Gospel Trumpet, 187, **561**, 1264, 1952
  Brethren movement, 334–335
  Congregational Brethren, 335
  Flory, John, 334, 498
  Funk, Benjamin, 525
  Hendricks, Franklin A., 597
  "Single Mode" Brethren, 1186
The Gospel Visiter (Visitor), 1, 2, 3, 148,
  165, 267, 426–427, 535, **561**, 932,
  1355, 1952, 2188, *See also*
  Evangelishe Besuch
  Advent, observance of, 288
  Annual Meetings at Pentecost, 1008
  Brethren and science, 1160
  Brethren movement, descriptions of,
  379
  Cassel, Abraham Harley, writer for,
  258
  Christian Brethren and, 281
  The Christian Family Companion, 822
  *Christian Family Companion and
  Gospel Visitor,* 286
  Church of Jesus Christ of Latter-day
  Saints, 298
  Davy, Henry Dorsey, 365
  description of Oregon Territory, 1327
  favorable mention of Thurman,
  William C., 1264
  Frantz, Michael, 509
  Furry, Leonard, 526
  Germany, 545
  Henry Kurtz, 712
  Herring, Friedrich, 598
  historic sites, 609
  historical writing, 611
  Hoke, George, 618
  Holsinger, Henry Ritz, 285, 621
  imposters among the Brethren, 648
  Juniata College, 678
  Knouff, Hannah Pfouts, 704
  Kurtz, Henry, 281, 285, 288, 294
  marital avoidance, 387
  Messenger, 818
  minorities, ethnic and racial, 849
  missions, 858, 859
  Palestine, 990
  Pfautz, John Eby, 1014
  The Pilgrim (published 1870–1880),
  1023
  The Primitive Chrisitan, 1058
  Progressive Brethren movement, 1061
  publishing of, 1067, 1068
  Quinter, James, 285, 349, 1077
  railroads, 1081
  sermons, publication of, 381
  Theophilus, writer for, 258
  universalism in Oregon, letters about,
  1293
Gospels, *See* individual Gospels; specific
  doctrine
  communication of, 1989–1990
  Good News, 1992
Goss, Charles E., 1638
Goss, David, 232
Goss, Kenneth A., 1638
Gossard, Harry A., 1638
Gossard School
  Locust Grove Church of the Brethren,
  PA, 752
Gossen, Eva (later Häcker), 562
Gossner Mission
  Germany (German Democratic

Republic), 546
Gotha, FL, New Covenent Church of the
  Brethren, **2190**
Gothard, Bill, 2174
  women and, 2263
Gotom, Musa D., 1256
Gotschall, R. E., 1638
Gotshall, R. E., 1638
"Gotswiltahns"
  Morrisons Cove, 877
Gotswold Bruderhof
  Hutterian Society of Brothers, 640
Gott family, 1917
*Göttliche Liebes-Funcken (Divine Sparks of
  Love,* 1701), 57, 1952
Gottman, Charles Lilburn, 1638
Gottshall, Jay Richard, 1638
  Pine Glen Church of the Brethren, PA,
  pastor, 1024
Gottshall, Wayne Z., 1638
Gottwalls (Gottwals), John, 1638
Gottwals, Jacob Z., 1638
Gottwals, Mary Jane (later Francis), 506
Goubeau, J. C., 1638
Goudy, Fred, 1638
Goughenour, Benjamin
  Rosedale, PA, Brethren Church, pastor,
  1122
Goughenour family, *See* Gochenour
  (Goughnour) family
Goughenour, H. L.
  hymnals, 642
Goughenour, Herbert L., **561–562**, *See also*
  hymnals; liberalism; Social Gospel
Goughnour, Ben, 675
Goughnour, Benjamin, 555, 1638
Goughnour, David, 555
Goughnour, Earl, 555
  Long, Inez Goughnour, 2215
Goughnour family, *See* Gochenour family;
Gochenour (Goughnour) family
  Engle/Angle family, 446
Goughnour, Glee (later Yoder), 555
Goughnour (Gochnour), Elizabeth (later
  Roberts), 1114
Goughnour, H. C., 1638
Goughnour, H. L., 438
Goughnour, Henry, 360, 1638
Goughnour, Inez (later Long), 555, **2215**
Goughnour, Jacob, 555
Goughnour, James L., 1638
Goughnour, James Quinter, 31, 555, 1638
  Slifer, IA, church of the Brethren,
  elder, 1190
Goughnour, Mary
  Long, Inez Goughnour, 2215
Goughnour, Mary Mathis, 555
Goughnour, Samuel M., 31, 555, 1638
Goughnour, T. Z., 1638
Gould family
  Harrah, WA, Grace Brethren Church,
  585
Gould, J. E., 260
Gould, James L., 2153, 2279
Gould, Nathaniel D.
  singing schools, 1185
Gould, Roxanne (later McCann), 771
Gould, William Lewis, 733, 1337, 1638,
  1952, 2301, **2382, 2388**
Goulder, Grace, 1952
Gourley, William R., 1638

New Hope Church of the Brethren, TN,
  elder in, 929
Gove Co., KS, 142
  place-names, Brethren, 1028
  Quinter, KS, Church of the Brethren,
  1077
governance, church, *See* polity
  sources on, 2317, 2321
  women and, 2263–2264
governing bodies
  responsibility for dress discipline, 401
government, *See* church and state
  Brethren and revolution, 1995
  church and state, 1992, 2015
  in Church of the Brethren, 1973
  disputes with, 728
  Fellowship of Grace Brethren Churches
  (FGBC), 487
  Frenkendorf, 516
  irrigation, 663
Goyen, Gossen, 527, **562**, 577, 909, 1865
  "Goyen, Gossen" (Krahn), 1990
Goyen, Maria (later Naas), 562
Goyen, Maria Margaret (later Naas), 909
Graber, Joseph Samuel, 1952
Graber-Miller family, 1989
Grabile, S. A., 605
Grabill, Abraham, 1638
Grabill, Dan, 673, 1638
Grabill, Daniel, family, *1029*
Grabill family, 731, 750, 2099, *See also*
  Graybill family
Grabill, Ida, 2070
Grabill, J. H., 1638
Grabill, John, 1638
Grabill, Peter T., 1638
  Silver Lake Church of the Brethren,
  NE, elder, 1182
Grabill, Susan Jacobs, and family, *1029*
Grable family, 1912, 2099
  Prosperity Brethren Church, WV, 1062
Grable, Nancy (later Wise), 1354
Grace American Indian Ministries, Inc.
  Native Americans, 2230
"Grace and Obedience" (Bowman), 166
Grace Bible Institute and Grace Graduate
  School (FGBC), Long Beach, CA,
  See Grace Graduate School and
  Bible Institute (FGBC), Long
  Beach, CA
Grace Brethren, *See* Fellowship of Grace
  Brethren Churches
Grace Brethren Academy
Grafton, WV, First Grace Brethren Church,
  564
Grace Brethren Annual, 1384
Grace Brethren Boys, **562**
  Board, 562
  Jackson, Edward A., 2209
  merged into National Fellowship of
  Grace Brethren Men and Boys,
  916
Grace Brethren Christian Endeavor, 192
Grace Brethren Church, Camden, OH, 241
Grace Brethren Church, IN, *See* Milford,
  IN, Brethren Church
Grace Brethren Church of Canton, OH,
  101, 251, **562–563**
Grace Brethren Church of Greater
  Washington, D.C., 391
Grace Brethren Church of Long Beach, CA,
  238
The Grace Brethren Church of Maple

Valley, 2218
Grace Brethren Church of San Jacinto
  Valley, CA, *See* Hemet, CA, Grace
  Brethren Church
Grace Brethren Churches Christian
  Education
  Training in Missionary Endeavor
    (TIME), 1231, 1270
Grace Brethren congregations in South
  Carolina, 1205
Grace Brethren Disaster Aid (FGBC), *See*
  Relief Agency Brethren (FGBC)
Grace Brethren Foreign Missions, *See*
  Foreign Missionary Society
Grace Brethren General Conference, 485
Grace Brethren Home Missions Council,
  See Brethren Home Missions
  Council (FGBC)
Grace Brethren International Missions
  (GBIM)
  Grace Brethren Foreign Missions, **2191**
  Julien, Thomas T., 2210
  Mexico, 2157
  missions, 2225
  name change, 2183
  Grace Brethren Investment Foundation,
    2191
Grace Brethren Men, *See* National Fellow-
  ship of Grace Brethren Men
Grace Brethren National Conference, **38,**
  634
  abortion, stance on, 2
  cooperating organizations
    Brethren Missionary Herald Co.,
      38
    Brethren Retirement Homes, Inc.,
      38
    Foreign Missionary Society, 38
    Grace Schools, 38
    National Fellowship of Grace
      Brethren Men and Boys, 38
    National Fellowship of Grace
      Brethren Ministers, 38
    Women's Missionary Council, 38
  delegates to, 38
  Etling, Harold Hartz, 458
  Fellowship of Grace Brethren Churches
    (FGBC), 484
  Gingrich, Joseph L., 550
  Grace Brethren Boys, 562
  Grace Village Retirement Complex,
    564
  Grubb, Luther L., 575
  Hammers, Thomas E., 581
  location, 38, 1351, *1352*, 1353
  Message of the Brethren Ministry
    adoption as Statement of Faith,
    916
  moderators
    Miller, Robert Paul, 842
    office of, 865–866
    Patterson, Roy A., 995
    Schneider, Bernard N., 1154
  National Achievement Competition
    (NAC), 914
  National Brethren Bible Conference as
    beginning of, 914
  National Fellowship of Grace Brethren
    Men, 915–916
  National Sunday School Association,
    917
  National Sunday School Board, 917
  Ogden, William Augustus, moderator,

961
Sandy, Conrad, moderator, 1143
Grace Brethren North American Missions,
  2183
Grace Brethren Investment Foundation,
  2191
  Lakeland, FL, Grace Brethren Church,
    2213
  Macedonia, OH, Western Reserve
    Grace Brethren Church, 2216
  Menifee, CA, New Hope Community
    Church of the Valley, 2220
Grace Brethren Relief Board (FGBC), *See*
  Relief Agency Brethren (FGBC)
Grace Brethren retirement homes, 1198
Grace Brethren Stewardship Services
  Collitt, Robert B., 2166
Grace Brethren Sunday School of the Year
  St. Petersburg, FL, Grace Brethren
    Church, 1136
Grace Brethren Village, **563,** 2192
Grace Chapel, *See* Powell, OH, Grace
  Brethren Church
Grace Christian School
  Irasburg Grace Brethren Church, VT,
    662
  Long Beach, CA, Grace Brethren
    Church, 755
  Myerstown, PA, Grace Brethren
    Church, 906
Grace College, *See* Grace Schools (Grace
  Theological Seminary, Grace
  College)
grace, doctrine of, **562,** 2002, *See also*
  antinomianism; discipleship; eter-
  nal security; human nature; inner
  and outer word; law; works
  Brethren Doctrine of Salvation, 1140
  conversion, doctrine of, 339
  Covenant Theology, 348
  Doctrinal Treatise, 394
  in FGBC, 42
  human nature, 635
  Montgomery, Michael, 872
  Old German Baptist Brethren, 967
  operation of, for sinners, 2004
  ordinances, 976
  original sin, 981
  Progressive Brethren and fundamental-
    ism, 2006
Grace, Dorothy Elaine Hackman, 1952
Grace Graduate School, *See* Grace Schools
  (Grace Theological Seminary,
  Grace College)
Grace Graduate School and Bible Institute,
  563, 755
Grace Schools (Grace Theological Semin-
  ary, Grace College), 38, 183, 192,
  399, 535, **563–564,** 1353, 2127
  article about, 1952
  Ashman, Charles Henry, Jr., 2132
  Beaver, Samuel Wayne, 2134
  Bible conferences, 136
  bibliography of, 2310
  Boyer, James L., 2139
  Cashman, Edwin E., 2156
  CE National, Inc., 2156
  charismatic movement, 272
  Christian Day School movement, 282
  Christian education movement, 284
  church extensions, techniques for, 295
  Cuyahoga Falls, OH, Grace Brethren
    Church, organized by, 357

Dowdy, James Paul, 398
Etling, Harold Hartz, 458
faculty statement on authority of scrip-
  ture, 133
Fellowship of Grace Brethren Churches
  (FGBC), 484, 485
Fetterhoff, Dean, 2184
Fort Lauderdale, FL, Grace Brethren
  Church, 503
founding, 1152
Freeman, Hobart, 2180
Gingrich, Raymond Eugene, 2190
Grace Brethren International Missions,
  2191
Grace Graduate School, persons attend-
  ing, 20
Grace Schools, 2192, *2192*
Grace Theological Seminary, 13, 66, 67
  founding of, 97
  historical collections at, 52
  interest in archaeology, 46
Grant, Richard E., 2193
Grubb, Luther L., 575
Haller, Wesley, 2195
Hammers, Thomas E., 581
higher education, 605
historical libraries, 610
Hoyt, Herman Arthur, 634
Indiana, 653
Jenkins, Charles Lee, 2209
Julien, Thomas T., 2210
Kent, Homer Austin, 688
Kent, Homer Austin, Jr., 2210
Kent, Wendell E., 2211
Kimmell, Arthur Vance, 694
Kliever, Jacob Paul, 701
Kriegbaum, Arnold R., 708
Landrum, Clyde Kermit, 724
Maconaghy, Hill, 779
Male, E. William, 2216, 2217
Malles, Mark Ellsworth, 2217
mass media, 801
Mayes, Charles W., board of trustees,
  804
McClain, Alva J., president, 772, 773
meetingplace for Winona Lake, IN,
  Grace Brethren Church, 1353
Miller, Robert Paul, 842
missions, 2225
motion pictures, 879
Ogden, William Augustus, serving on
  board of, 961
Ohio, and Grace Brethren movement,
  963
O'Neal, Glenn, 2236
Patterson, Roy A., board member, 995
prenursing program, 952
Progressive Brethren church govern-
  ment, 1045
publications, 1952
reorganization, **2192,** *2192*
revision of the Scofield Reference
  Bible and the New International
  Version, 139
Sandy, Conrad, teacher, 1143
Schneider, Bernard N., 1154
sermons, 1168
Sickel, Clarence Leroy, 1181
sources on, 2322
Steffler, William Arno, 1220
Taber, Miles, 1247
theological education, 1257
Theological Practorium, The (CBBCI)

and, 2254
Weaver, Scott L. (FGBC, CGBCI) and, 2261
Weekly, Randy, 2213
Whitcomb, John Clement, Jr. (FGBC, CGBCI) and, 2262
Winona Lake Christian Assembly, 1353
youth and, 2269
Grace Seminary Journal, 2192
Grace Theological Journal
Boyer, James L., 2139
Whitcomb, John Clement, Jr. (FGBC, CGBCI) and, 2262
Grace Theological Seminary, *See* Grace Schools (Grace Theological Seminary, Grace College)
Grace Village Retirement Complex, **564, 2192–2193**
board of, 2211
Jenkins, Charles Lee, 2209
Graceview Brethren Church, *See* North Lauderdale, FL, Grace Brethren Church
graded lessons, 284, 539, **564**
Grady, Duane E., 2279
Hispanic Ministries (CB), 2199
homelessness, 2203
Grady, George W., 1638
Grady, Isaac S., 1638
Graeber, Phillip John, 1638
Graebner, A. L., 1952
Graef, Eve op den (later Häcker (Höcker)), 577
Graeff, Arthur D., 1952
Graetz, David E., 2279
Graf, Hans, 1890
Graff, Andreas, 574
Graff, Catherine (later Landes), 722
Graff family
history of, 1952, 1954
Graff, George, 574
Graff, J. C., 1638
Graff, Jacob
history of, 1952
Graff, Kenneth R., 1638
Graff, Leroy, 1952
Graff, Paul, 1952
Graff, Ron, 1638
Graff, Ronald A., 758
Graffius, Charles
writings of, 2334
Grafton, ID, Church of the Brethren, 320, *See also* Clearwater Church of the Brethren, ID
Grafton, WV, 1337
Grafton, WV, Brethren Church, 382
Grafton, WV, congregation, 744
Grafton, WV, First Brethren Church, *See* Grafton, WV, First Grace Brethren Church
Grafton, WV, First Grace Brethren Church, **564**
Graham, Barry, 1952
Graham, Billy, 1103, 1104, 2179, 2198
Graham Co., KS
Sand Creek Church of the Brethren, KS, 1142
Graham, David, 1638
Graham, Douglas Lyle, 2279
Graham family, 211, 2087
Graham, Isaac V., 2279
Graham, J. H., 1638
Graham, Jim, 244

Graham, John Frederick, 228, 1953, 1638
Graham, Thomas, 1638
Grahe, Anna Margaretha Naas, 564
Grahe, Jakob, **564,** 2077, **2374**
Solingen Brethren, 1201
Grahe, Wilhelm, 71, 103, 132, 255, **564,** 909, 1953, 2077, **2374**
interpretation of the Bible, 134
medicine, 809
prisons, 1059
Solingen Brethren, 1201
Grain Valley, MO, 683
Grainger Co., TN
Meadow Branch Church of the Brethren, TN, 805
Gram Sevaks, **564–565**
missions, 861
Rural Service Center (CB), 1131
GRAMCORD (Boyer), 2139
Gramley, F., 1953
grammar schools, *See* elementary schools
grammatical properties of place name, 911
Granada Church of the Brethren, KS, **565**
Sabetha, KS, congregation, 1133
Grand Co., UT, 1299
Grand Junction, CO, 320, 1286
Church of the Brethren, **565**
Koinonia Brethren-Baptist Church, **565**
Fruita, CO, Church of the Brethren, 519
Glade Park, CO, Community Church of the Brethren, 551
Grand Junction, CO, Church of the Brethren, 565
Mount Garfield, CO, Church of the Brethren, 881
Grand Mound, IA
Maquoketa German Baptist Brethren, IA, mission point, 791
Grand Prairie Church of the Brethren, NE, **565**
Grand Rapids, MI, 1263
Hope Church of the Brethren, MI, 629
Grand Rapids, MI, Church of the Brethren, **565**
Grand River Church of the Brethren, IA, *See* Osceola, IA, Church of the Brethren
Grand River German Baptist Brethren Church, MO, **565**
Grand River, IA, congregation
Osceola, IA, Church of the Brethren, 983
Grand Valley, CO, Church of the Brethren, *See* Grand Junction, CO, Koinonia Brethren-Baptist Church
Granddaughters' Inglenook Cookbook, 340
Grandusky, Robert F., 679, 2280
Grandview Church, MT, 1930
Grandview congregation, MT, 142
Grandview, MO, Dunkard Brethren Congregation, **565–566**
Missouri, 865
Grandview, MT, Big Sky Church of the Brethren-First Baptist
Montana Brethren settlement, 870
Grandview, WA, Grace Brethren Church, **566,** 1240
Mabton, WA, Grace Brethren Church, mission point of, 771
Prosser, WA, Community Grace Brethren Church, 1062
the Grange

secret societies, opposition to, 1163
granges, *See* secret societies
Grangeville, MO
Fairview, MO, Shoal Creek Church of the Brethren, 468
Grant, Barbara Louise, 1638
Grant Co., IN, 1350, 2102
Somerset, IN, Church of the Brethren, 1202
Grant Co., OK
Monitor Church of the Brethren, OK, 869
North Star Church of the Brethren, OK, 950
Grant Co., WV, 171, 1336, 2079
Allegheny, WV, Church of the Brethren, 2125
Greenland Church of the Brethren, WV, 571
history, 1980
Jordan Run Church of the Brethren, WV, 676
Mennonite Church, 2079
North Mill Creek Church of the Brethren, WV, 949
Petersburg, WV, Memorial Church of the Brethren, 1012
South Fork Church of the Brethren, WV, 1205
Grant, Dixon, 347
Grant family
What's in a Name?, 2377
Grant (formerly Hampshire) county, WV
South Branch Church of the Brethren, WV, 1204
Grant, Mary F.
on Fox, Heinrich/Henry and descendants, 2334
Grant, Mildred E. Turner
Grant, Richard E., 2193
Grant, Richard E., 192, 251, 265, 562, 1638
Mansfield, OH, Conservative Grace Brethren Church, 2217
Martinsburg, PA, Grace Brethren Church, pastor, 798
pastor, editor, administrator, **2193**
Grant, Ruth
Mount Union (Airpoint) Church of the Brethren, VA, deaconess, 887
Grant, Vester
Mount Union (Airpoint) Church of the Brethren, VA, deacon, 887
Grant, W. A., 1638
Grant, Willard Leroy, 246, 1638
Rossville, IN, Church of the Brethren, minister, 1124
Grantham, Thomas, 87
Grants Pass, OR, 1346
Fruitdale Community Church of the Brethren, OR, 520
Grants Pass, OR, Church of the Brethren, *See* Fruitdale Community Church of the Brethren, OR
Oregon settlement, 981
Granville, Lord, 1311
Granville Manor, NC
difficulty securing land titles in, 1299
grape juice, 16, **566**
communion, 328
Dunkard Brethren, 409
love feasts, 764
Price, Isaac, advocating for communion service, 1056
grape juice, in communion, 1252

Grapes, Charles E., 760, 1638
Grasmick, Gary Kenneth, 1638
Grass Valley, CA, Community Brethren
    Church, **566**
Grasshopper Falls, KS, Church of the
    Brethren, *See* Ozawkie, KS,
    Church of the Brethren
    becomes Ozawkie, KS, Church of the
        Brethren, 987
Grasshopper Falls, KS, congregation, 682
    Ozawkie, KS, Church of the Brethren,
        987
grasshopper plagues
    Kansas, 682
    Kansas, and social welfare, 1198
Grassroots, Concerns of (CB)
    conservative concerns, **2193**
    Re-imagining Conference and, 2240
Grater, Abraham (Abram) L., 1638
Grater, Elizabeth, 1296
    Norristown, PA, Church of the
        Brethren, 945
Grater, Jacob W., 1638
Grater, Mildred, 1953
Grater, W. H., 1638
Gratiot Co., MI, 256
    New Haven Church of the Brethren,
        928
Gratis, OH, 697, 1235, 1295
Gratis, OH, Brethren Church, **566,** 703,
    1267
    Mackey, John Crawford, pastor, 779
    Mason, Edward, pastor, 799
Gratis, OH, Church of the Brethren, **566**
Gratz, Delbert, 1953
Grauman, Stephanie, 2103
graveclothes, **566–567,** *See also* primitive
    Christianity
    funerals, 523
Gravel Hill (Antioch) Christian Church,
    Craig Valley, VA
    history and membership, 1980
Gravel Hill Church of the Brethren, KS,
    567
Gravelton, IN, Brethren Church, **567**
Graves, family
    Columbus, OH, Smoky Row Brethren
        Church, 2166
Graves, Gershom, 723
gravestones
    Mack, Alexander, Sr., *775*
    simple life, 1183
Grawe, John C., 1953
Gray, Albert L., Jr., 1953
Gray, Alice Parker, 1953
Gray Co., TX, 1232
    Pampa Church of the Brethren, 991
Gray, Daniel Leslie, 1638
Gray, Elkanah Dulaney, 1639
Gray family, 1999
Gray, Glen
    Island Pond, VT, Grace Brethren
        Church, 2209
Gray, Gunda Poehlmann
    Island Pond, VT, Grace Brethren
        Church, 2209
Gray, Lilian Reaugh, 1953
Gray, Melvin, 1639
Gray, Reed Edward, 2301
Gray, Roberta, 713
Gray, Samuel S., 1283, 1639
Gray, Sandy, 713
Gray, Tazewell (Taswell), 1285, 1639

Middle Creek Church of the Brethren,
    IA, minister, 825
Schuyler German Baptist Brethren
    Church, MO, elder, 1157
Gray, Thomas, 1639
Gray, William, 16, 130, 318, 349, 1324,
    1639
Gray, William A., 1639
Gray, William R., 1639
Graybill, A. K., 1639
Graybill, Alice Minora Hoffer, **567,** 1243,
    1838
Graybill, Barbara Snavely, 567
Graybill, C.
    notes, 1936
Graybill, Catherine (later Moomaw)
    Moomaw, John Crouse, wife of, 874
Graybill, Catherine Snider, 567
Graybill, Christian, 158
Graybill congregation, PA
    Hollinger family, 620
Graybill, Daniel Perry, 2382
    Old Brethren German Baptist Church,
        2232
    Old Brethren German Baptist Church,
        minister, 965
Graybill, David, 1639
Graybill, Elizabeth (later Hollinger), 620
Graybill, Ervin
    Old Brethren German Baptist Church,
        minister, 965
    Old Order German Baptist Church
        minister, 972
Graybill, Eve (later Wenger), 1330
Graybill family, 142, 144, 158, 355, 721,
    1253, 1916, 1943, 2042, 2063
    Mortonhouse (ship), 2373, 2376
    in Neosho Valley Old German Baptist
        Brethren Church near, 923
    Royer family related to, 1128
Graybill, George Henry, 1639
Graybill (Grabill, Krehbiel) family, **567**
Graybill (Greybill), Paul J., 1639
Graybill, Hannah, 163
Graybill, Harry
    feetwashing (photo caption), 2378
Graybill, Henry, 567
Graybill, Henry Benner, 1953
Graybill House, White Oak Church of the
    Brethren, PA, 1340
Graybill, I. R., 1639
Graybill, Israel, 1340, 1639
Graybill, Israel B., 1340, 1639
Graybill, J. F., 567
Graybill, J. H., 155, 913, 1342
    Oregon Short Line Railroad, 981
Graybill, J. H. family, 913
Graybill, Jacob Franklin, 1243, 1639, 1838
Graybill, James Henry, 567, 1639
Graybill, John, 1953
    family history, 1990
Graybill, John G., 1639
Graybill, John W., 1213, 1639
Graybill, Jonas, 567, **567,** 1277, 1639
Graybill, Joseph
    biography, 1953
Graybill, Kathryn Ruth, 1982
Graybill, Larry Carper, 1639, 1953
Graybill, Lydia Alice (later Eller), 440
Graybill, Lydia (later Brubaker), 1893
Graybill, Paul, 1330
Graybill, Reuben S., 1340, 1639
Graybill, Riley L., 1639

North Fork Old German Baptist
    Brethren Church, IN, minister, 947
Graybill, Ruth Yoder, 1953
Graybill, Samuel, 1340, 1639
Graybill, Sarah Crumpacker, 567
Graybill, Susan
    biography, 1953
Graybill, Virgil D.
    Old Brethren German Baptist Church,
        2232
Graybill, William, 579
Graybill, William and Elizabeth Shelley
    family history, 1982
Graybille, Mae (later Bachman), 748
Grayson Co., TX, 1255, 1346
    migration of Brethren, 830
Grayson Co., VA
    Mountain View Church of the
        Brethren, VA, 889
Great Assembly, *See* Annual Meeting
Great Awakening, 87, **568**
    American revivalism, 1104
    "New Lights" revivalism, 930
    Second, 88
Great Bend, KS, 682
Great Britain, *See* United Kingdom
Great Commission, **568**
    evangelism, 460
    missions, 858, 860, 861
    Mount Vernon, OH, Conservative
        Grace Brethren Church,
        2226–2227
    revival meetings, 1103
    Schwarzenau Brethren, 1079
Great Depression
    Hamilton, OH, First Church of the
        Brethren, 581
    Hevener Church of the Brethren, WV,
        602
    Kansas, 682
    and publications, effects on, 191–192
    relief programs during, at South Saint
        Joseph Church of the Brethren,
        MO, 1135
"The Great Elgin Smear," 187
Great Essay (Francke)
    Pietism, 1022
Great Friday, *See* Good Friday
Great Kentucky Revival of 1800, 1224
    Restoration Movement, 1101
Great Northern Railroad, 94, *568,* **568–569,**
    See also migration
    chartered trains, 273
    Eller, Geraldine Crill on Brethren
        movement and, 2329
    land sales and, 231
    Mayville, ND, Red River Valley
        Church of the Brethren, 805
    McDonough, George L., 773
    migration of Brethren, 830
    Montana Brethren settlement, 870
    Montana settlements along, 1342
    Myers Creek Church of the Brethren,
        WA, 905
    North Dakota Brethren settlement, 946
    Northern Pacific Railroad, 951
    Omak, WA, Church of the Brethren,
        974
    Peters, Amos B., 1011
    promotion to Brethren, *1081*
    Wenatchee Valley, WA, 1319
Great Plains
    homesteading, 626

migration of Brethren, 830
Great Serpent Mound, Adams Co., OH
    believed to be site of Garden of Eden
      by West, Edmund Landon, 1332
Great Swamp, PA, 383
    Church of the Brethren, **569**
    Pennsylvania settlement, 1004
    Quakertown, PA, First Church of the
      Brethren, 1075
Greater Bay Area Fellowship
    Oakland, CA, Church of the Brethren,
      957
Greater Washington Grace Brethren
    Church, 391
Greathouse, John, 1303
Greathouse, Marie, 1303
The Greatness of the Kingdom (McClain),
    486, 773, 2002
Grebe family, 1920
Grebe, Georg (George), 174, 239, 684
    Hesse, 602
    Hochmann von Hochenau, Ernst
      Christoph, 615
    Marsay, Charles Hector de St. Georges,
      Marquis de, 796
    public dispute with Alexander Mack,
      Sr., 703
Grebe (Grebi), Georg, **569**, *See also*
    Callenberg, Clara Elizabeth Von
Grebe (Grebi), Juliana, 569
Grebel, Conrad, 28
    Reformation, Protestant, and radical
      reformers, 1092
Grebil, Christian, 567
Grebil family
    Mortonhouse (ship), 2373, 2376
Grebil, Hannah Borntrager, 567
Grebil, John, 567
Grebil, Maria, 567
Greece, **569**
    Interchurch Service to Greek Villages,
      658
      Zigler, Michael Robert, 1398
    Kruger, Helena, 708
    relief and rehabilitation work in, 200
    relief and service efforts, 1097
    relief and social work, 303
    relief from New Paris, IN, Church of
      the Brethren, 931
    University of La Verne degree pro-
      grams on military bases, 715–716
    work camps, 1367
Greek language, 160
Greek Orthodox Church, **569**
    Brethren contact, and Roman Catholic
      Church, 1120
Greece, 569
    Interchurch Service to Greek Villages,
      658
    Orthodox Church, 983
Greele, NE, 20
Green, A. G., 1953
Green, A. J., 1639
Green, Bonnie, 1852–1853
Green, Charles Walter, 1639
Green, Clarence O., 1639
Green Co., OH, 147
Green Co., TN, 1253
Green Co., VA, 158
Green, Daniel B., 2280
Green, Eliza Ellen Broadwater, 569
Green, Ernest
    on Labadists, 2334

Green family, 752, 1267, 2077
    Grandview, WA, Grace Brethren
      Church, 566
Green, Harold Perry, 1639
Green Hill, MD, congregation, 376
Green Hill, VA, Church of the Brethren,
    569–570, 1011
Green, Jack, 1639
Green, Jesse Richard, 1639
Green, John, 1849
Green, John D., Jr., 2280
Green, John Thomas, 211, **569**, 1243, 1639
    Ridge Dunkard Brethren Congregation,
      WV, elder, 1109
Green Lake, WI
    New Call to Peacemaking conference,
      926
Green, Louis (Lewis) F., 1639
Green, Mary G. McMillan, 569
Green, Minnie Ulery Lasley, 1953
Green, Olive M., 1639
Green, R. Dallas, 2186
Green River area, Muhlenburg Co., KY,
    1688
Green River Cove Church of the Brethren,
    NC, **570**
Green River Cove, NC, congregation
    Mill Creek Church of the Brethren,
      NC, 832
Green, Simeon Ward, 569
Green Spring congregation, PA, 1294
Green Springs, OH, Church of the Brethren,
    340
    Pleasant Center Church of the Brethren,
      OH, 1030
    Seneca Church of the Brethren, OH,
      1166
Green, Susan (later Ebersole), 418
Green Thursday
    observation of, 2147
Green Top, MO, congregation, *See*
    Schuyler German Baptist Brethren
    Church, MO
Green Township, OH
    Paradise Church of the Brethren, 992
Green Tree, PA, Church of the Brethren,
    See Oaks, PA, Green Tree Church
    of the Brethren
Green Tree, PA, congregation, 1286
    Elizabethtown College, 437
    German Baptist Brethren Historical
      Association, 540
    Myers, Jacob Tobias, pastor, 904
    Pottstown, PA, Coventry Church of the
      Brethren, 1049
    Preiß (Price) family, 1055
    Price, Isaac, 1056
    Rittenhouse, David, minister, 1110,
      1111
Greenawalt (Greenwalt), William Henry,
    1639
Greenback, TN, Mount Zion Brethren
    Church, **570**
Greenbriar Creek, KY
    Nicholas Co. German Baptist Brethren
      Church preaching point, 935
Greenbriar, WV
    meetinghouse, 164
    mission point, Botetourt Co., VA,
      Church of the Brethren, 164
    Church of the Brethren, WV, **570**
Greencastle-Antrim Community, 1910
Greencastle, PA, 151

Church of the Brethren, 42, **570**
Conococheague Grace Brethren
    Church, **2193**
historic sites, 609
Greene Co., OH, 363, 375, 1399
    Old German Baptist Brethren 970
    Replogle family, 1100
Greene Co., PA
    Brethren Church congregations, 1005
    Mason-Dixon Line extending to, 800
    place-names, Brethren, 1027
    Quiet Dell Brethren Church, PA, 1076
    Ryerson Station Church of the
      Brethren, PA, 1132
Greene Co., TN
    Mountain Valley Church of the
      Brethren, TN, 889
Greene Co., VA, 265, 413, 416, 462, 1317
    Industrial School (CB), *See* Church of
      the Brethren Industrial School,
      Greene Co., VA
    Mount Carmel Church of the Brethren,
      VA, 880
    Mountain Grove Fellowship Church of
      the Brethren, VA, 889
Greene congregation, IA, 1289
Greene, David Paul, Jr., 14, 1639
Greene, IA
    Church of the Brethren, **570**
    congregation
      Rock Grove German Baptist
      Brethren Church, IA, 1117
    "Dunkard's Church," *570*
Greene, Leroy, 1953
Greene, R. Dallas, 2280
Greene, Richard, 519
Greenhalgh, Jonathan, 1639
Greenhill Church of the Brethren, MD,
    570–571
Greenland
    Moravian Church missionaries to, 875
Greenland building, Windber, PA, Rummel
    Church of the Brethren, 1348
Greenland Church of the Brethren, WV,
    571, 1397
Greenland congregation, WV, 769
    Allegheny, WV, Church of the Breth-
      ren, 2125
    Harsh, Alva Carlton, 587
    Hays, Daniel, 590
    Jordan Run Church of the Brethren,
      WV, 676
Greenland, T. A., 45
Greenland, VA, congregation
    history of Brick Church, 1977
Greenloaf, Dorothy (later Steele), 2294
Greenlun, Amy, 64
Greenmount Church of the Brethren, VA,
    129, 165, **571**, 745, 1317
    Fairview-Mount Clinton Church of the
      Brethren, VA, 470
    Flat Rock Church of the Brethren, VA,
      493
    Grassroots, Concerns of the, 2193
    Harrisonburg, VA, First Church of the
      Brethren, 586
    Melbeth Grove Church of the Brethren,
      VA, 812
    Mount Zion-Linville Church of the
      Brethren, VA, 888
    North Mill Creek Church of the
      Brethren, WV, 949
    Pine Grove Church of the Brethren,

VA, 1024
South Fork Church of the Brethren, WV, 1205
Greenmount Council, 2036
Greenmount Meeting, *See* Grassroots, Concerns of the
Greensburg, PA, Church of the Brethren, 415, 214, **571**, 1891, 2072
Greenslade, Stanley L., 1953
Greentop German Baptist Brethren Church, MO, *See* Schuyler German Baptist Brethren Church, MO
Greentown territory, IN, 1348
Greenville Church of the Brethren, PA, **572**, Hostetler Church of the Brethren, PA
Rockton, PA, Church of the Brethren, preaching point of, 1118
Greenville College
Studebaker, Claud, 1229
Greenville Creek Church of the Brethren, IN/OH, *See* Union City, OH, Church of the Brethren
Greenville Creek (Union City) congregation, OH, 708
Greenville, MD
Piney Creek Church of the Brethren, MD, mission point, 1025
Greenville, OH, Church of the Brethren, *571*, **571–572**, 1288
Greenwalt, Janice Lee (later Largent), 1687
Greenwood, CA, Grace Brethren Church
Modesto, CA, Big Valley Grace Community Church (FGBC), former name of, 866
Modesto, CA, La Loma Grace Brethren Church, 867
Greenwood Church of the Brethren, MO, **572**
Greenwood Church of the Brethren, OH, **572**
Glenford, OH, Brethren Church, 553
Greenwood Church of the Brethren, WA, **572**
Greenwood Co., KS, 1213
Church of the Brethren, KS, **572**
Greenwood family
Greenwood Church of the Brethren, MO, 572
Greenwood, Grace, 1639
Greenwood Grace Brethren Church, Modesto, CA, *See* Modesto, CA, Big Valley Grace Community Church (FGBC)
Greenwood, IN
Christ Our Shepherd Church of the Brethren, **2193**
Winning the Race Ministries and, 2262
Greenwood, John W., 1639
Greenwood, MO, 237
Greenwood, MO, congregation, 244
Mountain Grove Church of the Brethren, MO, 888
Greenwood, OH, congregation
Olivet Church of the Brethren, OH, 973
Greenwood, WA, 1240
Greer Co., OK
Harrison, OK, Church of the Brethren, 586
Greeshilds family
Jenners, PA, Grace Brethren Church, 670
Gregersen, Joseph Paul, 2280

Gregg, Emma Jane Beery, 1953
Gregory, Brother, 357
Gregory, Constance
Winchester, VA, Blue Ridge Grace Brethren Church and, 2262
Gregory, Cora Garber (later Dunning), 1920
Gregory, Donald, 2280
Winchester, VA, Blue Ridge Grace Brethren Church and, 2262
Gregory, Edwin Stanley, 1639
Gregory, John Edward, 731, 1639
Gregory, O. B., 269, 502, 1212
Gregory of Nazianzus
oaths, taking of, 959
Gregory, Orrin B., 1639
Gregory, Steven W., 1639
Gregory, T. C., 553
Greider-Kreider family, 1990
Greider, Mel, 2180
Greiner, Alyson Lee
on Dunkers, 2334
Greiner, Beverly
Greiner, Robert G., 2194
Greiner, Donna
Greiner, Robert G., 2194
Greiner, Edna Mosemann
Greiner, Robert G., 2194
Greiner family, 2108
Greiner, J. Gerald, 247, 1639
Greiner, Mary, 256
Greiner, Robert G., 195, **2193–2194**, *2193*
Greiser, Terence E., 2280
Grenola, KS, Cana congregation, **572**
Mont Ida, KS, Church of the Brethren, 870
Gresh, Kenneth P., 2280
Gressley, Minor M., 1639
Gretna, VA
New Bethel Church of the Brethren, 925
Gretna, OH, Brethren Church, **572–573**, 693, 694
Greybill family, 2099
Greyer, Saylor G., 1639
Gribble, Florence Alma Newberry, 183, 268, 501, **573**, 1639, 1849, 1953
historical writing, 613
medical missions, 807
medical practice, 810
missions, 862
Noatemo, 938
Rollier, Antoine E. and Mary Ganshorn, in missionary party with, 1119
Sheldon, Chauncey Burt, missionary, 1175
Gribble, James S., 183, 268, 501, 527, 573, **573**, 588, 1639, 1849, *See also* Gribble, Florence Alma Newberry
biography, 1953
missions, 862
Rollier, Antoine E. and Mary Ganshorn, in missionary party with, 1119
Gribble, Jennie Grossman, 573
Gribble, Jim, 658
Gribble, Marguerite Edna, 1848
Gribble, Marguerite (later Dunning), 573
Moody Bible Institute, 873
Gribble Memorial High School, *See* James Gribble Memorial High School
Gribble, T. J., 573
grief

memorial services, 814
Grieve, Cheryl Ann Robinson, 1855
Grieve, Jerry Allen, 2194
Grieve, Dawn
Grieve, Jerry Allen, 2194
Grieve, Mrs. Dwight George, 377
Grieve, George, 377
Grieve, Mrs. George, 377
Grieve, Jerry Allen, 1639, 1855, **2194**
Grieve, John, 1321
Grieve, Marion
Grieve, Jerry Allen, 2194
Grieve, Mary Elizabeth Pierson
Grieve, Jerry Allen, 2194
Grieve, Nicole
Grieve, Jerry Allen, 2194
Grieve, Seth
Grieve, Jerry Allen, 2194
Griffin (Giffin) family, 752
Griffin, Kathi D., 2280
Griffin, W. LeRoy, 1639, 1838, 1953, 2280
Griffith, Charles Randy, 453, 2280
Petersons Chapel Church of the Brethren, NC, 1012
Griffith, Charles V., 1639
Griffith, Cora (later Prather), 1051
Griffith, David Robert, 1305, 1849
Griffith, Edith Diana, 1640
Griffith, Elias, 1640
Griffith family, 224
Peace Valley Church of the Brethren, MO, 1003
Pleasant Grove Church of the Brethren, NC, 1031
Griffith, George C., 1640
Griffith (Griffiths), D. C., 1639
Griffith, H. M., 1640
Griffith, Holt, E., 224, 453, 590, 1209, 1294, 1640,
Petersons Chapel Church of the Brethren, NC, 1012
Pigeon River Church of the Brethren, NC, minister, 1023
Griffith, J. H., 1294
Griffith, J. M., 1640
Griffith, Jim, 2280
Petersons Chapel Church of the Brethren, NC, 1012
Griffith, Joseph H., 1640
Griffith, Lee
on peace, theology of, 2334
on prison abolition, 2334
Griffith, Louis H., 1640
Griffith, Margaret, 1321
Griffith, Martha (later Fleming), 494
Griffith, Matison
Pigeon River Church of the Brethren, NC, 1023
Griffith, Patricia (later Kent)
Kent, Wendell E., 2211
Griffith, Robert, 566, 1251, 1640
Griffith, Samuel, 1640
Pigeon River Church of the Brethren, NC, minister, 1023
Griffith, Sonja Pauline, 2280
Lenexa, KS, Fellowship, 2214
Griffith, Susan Elaine Suter, 1849
Griffith, Vency Enos, 343, 1640
New Hope Church of the Brethren, TN, elder in, 929
Grigg, Anderson Irvin
family history, 1979
Griggs, OK, Bethel Church of the Brethren,

573

Grigsby family, 1914, 1917
Grim, Alton
    Old Order German Baptist Church
        minister, 972
Grim, David, Franklin, 1640, 2301
    Old Order German Baptist Church
        minister, 972
    Old Order German Baptist Church,
        2235
Grim, Ervin Glenn, 1640
Grim, John, 632
Grim, John Edwin, 1640, 2302
Grim, John Vernon, 1640
    genealogy and descendants, 1953
Grim, Kathryn R., 1953
Grim, Michael D.
    Old Order German Baptist Church,
        2235
Grim, Richard Ralph, 1640
    Pleasant View Church of the Brethren,
        PA, elder-in-charge, 1037
Grimes, David L., 2280
Grimes, Susan Alice (later Roop), 1122
Grimley, John
    historical writing, 613
    Pitsburg, OH, Church of the Brethren,
        sending to Africa, 1026
Grimley, John Bechtel, 1640, 1838, 1927,
    1953, 2302, **2383**
Grimley, Mildred May Hess, 748,
    1953–1954, 1838
Grimm, Melford H., 1640
Grindheim, Oscar J., 1640
Gripe, Anna Magdelena Kuns, 710
Gripe, Jacob, 273
Gripe, Joseph, 710
Gripe, Nicholas S., 157, 1640
Grise, Ida (later Moomaw)
    Moomaw, Ira Wilbur, mother of, 874
Grissinger family, 1958
Grisso, Adam
    Sidney, IN, Grace Brethren Church,
        1181
Grisso, Anna Kulp, 574
Grisso, Clarence C., 267, 318, 363,
    573–574, 1240, 1640
    New Enterprise Brethren Church, IN,
        elder in, 927
    Osceola, IN, Grace Brethren Church,
        interim pastor, 984
Grisso, Eli, 574
Grisso, Elnora Balsbaugh, 574
Grisso, Hawkins, 676
Grisso, Jacob, 1640
Grisso, Jane (later Henry), 598
Grisso, Lillian Etna, 381, **574,** 1838, 1893,
    2024
    mission schools, 854
    poetry, 1040
    prayer books, 1052
Grisso, Lydia Ohmart, 574
Grisso, Samuel Benton, 31, 130, 235, 360,
    362, 1285, 1640
Grisso, Vernon D., 54, 574, 1251, 1278,
    1640
Griswold, LeRoy, 1640
Grob, Rudolf Ernst, 1954
Große Versammlung, See Annual Meeting
Groesbeck, William, 1640
    New Virginia, IA, Brethren Church, as
        minister, 932
    Osceola, IA, Church of the Brethren,

minister, 983
Groff, Abraham, 574, 1870
Groff, Barbara (later Eby), 420
Groff, Benjamin, 2073
Groff, Carl R., 2280
Groff, Clyde L., 1954
    on Groff family, 2334
Groff, Daniel Groff, 1965
Groff, David, 269
Groff, Warren Frederick, 2194
Groff, Della, 1215
Groff, Earl D., 14
Groff, Edwin, 1640
Groff, Elias, family
    North Beatrice Church of the Brethren,
        NE, 945
    Hope Memorial, NE, congregation, 945
Groff, Elizabeth (later Eschelmann), 456
Groff, Elsa
    Hispanic Ministries (CB), 2199
Groff, Emma Patterson, 574
Groff, Everett R.
    on Christ, way of, 2334
Groff family, 2073, 2334
    Erbaugh family, 453
    Harley family, 583
    history of, 1954
    Hope Memorial Church (German
        Baptist Brethren), NE, 2375
    New Holland, PA, Church of the
        Brethren, 928
    sources on, 2314
Groff, Forrest Ray, 619, 1640
Groff, Forrest U., 51, 432, 574, 1215, 1640
    autobiography of, 2334
Groff, Francis, 2043
Groff (Grove) family, **574**
    Flat Rock Church of the Brethren, NC,
        493
Groff, Hans, 630
Groff, Hershey, 1640
Groff, Hettie (later Taylor), 1249
Groff, Jacob C., 42, 489, 1640
Groff, Johann Christoff, 574
Groff, Jonas G., 1640
Groff, Joseph, 574, 1640
Groff, Martha (later Royer), 1127
Groff, Mary Frick, 1883
Groff, Mary (later Horst), 630
Groff, May, 269
Groff, Mervin C., 2280
Groff, Nancy Dunkle, 574
Groff, Nathan D., 574, 1640
Groff, Paul LaVerne, 1640
Groff, Ruth Davidheiser
    Groff, Warren Frederick, 2194
Groff, Sadie N., 489
Groff, Samuel, 248, 1640
Groff, Walter B.
    on Groff family, 2334
Groff, Warren Frederick, 126–127, 335,
    470, 1640, 1954, 2136, **2194,** *2194*
    Annual Meeting and Brethren polity,
        1042
    Miller, Donald Eugene, 2223
    and neoorthodoxy, 923
    on prayer, 2334
Groff, Warren G., 574
Grogan, Truman Lee, 1640
Groh family
    family history, 2003
Gronewold family
    Placerville, CA, Sierra View Grace

Brethren Church, 1028
Groningen
    Collegiant community, 1241
Groom, Abram, 1640
Groote, Geert, 193
Großer family
    McFarland, CA, Church of the Breth-
        ren, 774
Grosh, A. B., 1293
Grosh, G., 1293
Grosh, Walter, 1640
Grosnickel, Johann, 574
Grosnickel, Peter, 574
Gross, Andreas, **574**
Gross, Edward M., 448, 1640, 2177
Gross, Jesse D., 1640
Gross, Maria Christina (later Sauer), *See*
    Sauer, Maria Christina Gross
Gross, Robert A.
    On Earth Peace Assembly, 2235
    Ministry of Reconciliation, 2224
Grossman, Jennie (later Gribble), 573
Grossman, Walter, 1954
Grossnickle, Barbara Grove, 593
Grossnickle, Charles Basil, 1584, 640
    Harmony, MD, congregation, 826, 906
Grossnickle, Christina Studebaker, 574
Grossnickle Church of the Brethren, MD,
    574
Grossnickle congregation, MD
    Harmony Church of the Brethren, MD,
        584
Grossnickle, Daniel, 1224, 1640
Grossnickle, David, 106, 1640
Grossnickle, Edwin
    on Grossnickle, Jonas, 2334
Grossnickle family, **574,** 1885
    Middletown Valley Church of the
        Brethren, MD, 826
    sources on, 2318
Grossnickle, George, 574, 1641
Grossnickle, Harold, 1641
Grossnickle, Hezekiah, 179
Grossnickle, Laura, *See* Hedrick, Laura
    Grossnickle
Grossnickle, Laura E. N. (later Hedrick),
    593, 1360, 1362, 1650
Grossnickle, Lawson, 593
Grossnickle, MD, congregation, 216
    Middletown Valley Church of the
        Brethren, MD, 826
    Myersville, MD, Church of the
        Brethren, 906
Grossnickle meetinghouse
    Grossnickle Church of the Brethren,
        MD, 574
    Harmony Church of the Brethren, MD,
        584
Grossnickle, Peter
    Middletown Valley Church of the
        Brethren, MD, 826
Grossnickle, Simon Peter, 1641
Groth, Harold J., 2280
Groth, John F., 527
Groth, John Francis, 1641
Grottoes, VA, Church of the Brethren,
    574–575
    Pleasant Hill Church of the Brethren,
        VA, 1033
    Pleasant Valley Church of the Brethren,
        VA, 1035
Ground Floor of Heaven (Pritchett and
    Aukerman)

excerpts from, 1061
Ground-Searching Questions, See Grund-forschende Fragen
group dynamics, **575**
Group, W. Grant, 1641
Grout, Paul Everett, 1641
Grout, Paul W., 1235
Grout Run Valley, WV, 1265
Grove, Barbara (later Grossnickle), 593
Grove, Boyd
    Myerstown, PA, Grace Brethren Church, pastor, 906
Grove, Boyd A., 1641
Grove, Charles, 2166, 2280
Grove, Elizabeth (later Hess), 601
Grove family, *See* Groff (Grove) family
    history of, 1954
Grove, George W., 1641
Grove, John William, 1838
Grove, Joseph, 1641
Grove, LaVonne, 1954
Grove, Leland F., 1641
    Salem Church of the Brethren, IA, 1137
Grove, Lois Marie Fruth, 1838
Grove, Martha Peightal, 222
Grove meetinghouse (PA), 121
    Fair-View (Georges Creek) Church of the Brethren, PA, 469
Grove, Oliver P., 1954
Grove (Plank Road), PA, congregation
    Pike Run Church of the Brethren, PA, 1023
Grove, Polly (later Ryan), *See* Ryan, Polly Grove
Grove schoolhouse
    La Place, IL, Church of the Brethren, 713
Grove, Solomon, 72, 1641
Grove, Terry L., 1641
Grove, William David, 1641
Grover family, 1280
    Hurricane Creek Old German Baptist Brethren Church, IL, 638
Grover Hill, OH, 142
Grover, Ira, 753
Grover, Jay, 753
Grover, John and Catherine
    Palouse Old German Baptist Brethren Church, 991
Grover, Mark, 1641
    Modesto, CA, Old German Baptist Brethren Church, minister, 867
Groves, C. M., 679, 1641
Groves family, 2077
Groves, John, 1641
Groves, S. T., 1641
GROW '73 (God Reaching Our World)
    nationwide evangelistic outreach (FGBC), **2194**
    program, 2134
Grow, Jacob B., 1641
Grubb, Charles Newton, 1641
    Meadow Mills Church of the Brethren, VA, 806
Grubb, Eldon, 2280
Grubb, Elizabeth (later Urner), 1298
Grubb family
    Orange, CA, Grace Brethren Church, 975
Grubb, Fred, Jr., 482
Grubb, Harlan Clifford, 1641, 2302
Grubb, Janice Swaney, 575

Grubb, Kenneth G., 1911
Grubb, Louie Blood, 575
Grubb, Luther L., 187, 188, 192, **575**, 578, 1641, 1954
    missions, 860
    Orange, CA, Grace Brethren Church, pastor, 975
    Rittman, OH, First Brethren Church, pastor, 1111
    San Bernardino, CA, Grace Brethren Church, pastor, 1141
Grubb, Michael R.
    on Anabaptists's perspective on warfare, 2334
Grubb, Pat, 482
Grubb, Paul M., 1641
Grubb, V. D., 1641
Grubb, Vernon D., 575
Grubbs, Emma, 720
Grubbs, Sherrill, 720
Gruber, Christian A., 1641
Gruber, Eberhard Ludwig, 68, 175, 288, 291, 330, 575, **575**, 697, 1954
    Basic Questions (Grundforschende Fragen), 2374
    mention of, 1943
    Rock, Johann Friedrich, 1116
    Grundforschende Fragen (Basic Questions), 575, 2374
        Meier, Marcus on answers by A. Mack, Sr. to, 2346
    Mack, Alexander, Sr., debating, 776
    possible father of Maria Christina Gross Sauer, 1148
Gruber, Johann Adam, 68, 330, 334, **575**, 1946, 1954–1955
    article about, 1921
    Skippack area, PA, 1189
Gruber, John
    article about, 1913
Gruber, Michael Alvin, 1955
Gruendler, Johannes, 1955
Grumbacker (Grumbacher) family, *See* Crumpacker family
Grumbacker, Ulrich (Uli, Wollery), 1641
Grumbine, Ezra, 1955
Grumbling, Alvin H., 1641
Grumbling, Glenn Wayne, 1641, 2280
    Greenwood, IN, Christ Our Shepherd Church of the Brethren, 2193
Grumbling, Jayne
    Greenwood, IN, Christ Our Shepherd Church of the Brethren, 2193
Grumbling, Richard A., 1641, 2302, **2383**
Grumrine family, *See* Krumrein family
    genealogy, 1955
Grundforschende Fragen (Basic Questions) (Grüber), 175, 288, 291, **575**, 2003, **2374**
    Brethren beliefs and practices, 1086
    Gruber, Eberhard Ludwig, 575
    Haug, Johann Friedrich, 589
    Mack, Alexander, Sr., debate with Gruber, 776
    Mack, Alexander, Sr., response to, 370
    Meier, Marcus on answers by A. Mack, Sr. to, 2346
    peace, 998–999
    publishing of, 1063
Grundy Center congregation, IA, 661
Grundy Center, IA, 218, *549*
    congregation, 661, 1229
Grundy Co., IA, 1219

Ivester Church of the Brethren, IA, 665
Grush, Jess, 248
Grutschnig-Kieser, Konstanze-Mirjam
    on Radical Pietist hymnal, 2334
Guamá River, Brazil, 173
Guatemala, **576**
    Church of the Brethren, 2157
    missions, 2225
    sources on, 2314
    Women's Conferences (CB) and, 2265
Guay, Paul T., 2280
Guengerich family, 1932
    first reunion, article about, 1955
Guengerich, J. D., 1955
Guengerich, Jacob, 1881
Guenther, Karen
    on Oley Valley, 2335
Güereña, Amy Laura Petter, 1849
    Mexico, missionary to, 820
Güereña, Felipe Araujo, 1849
Guerena, Kristy, 2157
Guerena, Martin Paul, 2157, 2173, 2280
Guerena, Phil, 1641
    Mexico, missionary to, 820
Guerena, Phillip, 114
Guernsey Church of the Brethren, IN, **576**
    Monticello/Pike Creek Church of the Brethren, IN, 872
Guerra, Francisco, 1955
Guessregen, Hans, 1955
Guetzkow, Harold S., 1955
Guggisberg, Kurt, 1955
Guhl, Thomas, 165
Guice, Christopher, 262
    Davidson Co., NC (later TN) (1780s), 946
Guice (Guist, Guß, Guss, Güß), Christopher, elder, **576**, 1641
    North Carolina Brethren settlement 946
Guice, Christopher, Jr., 576
Guice, Jonathan, 576
    "Guide Me, O Thou Great Jehovah" hymns, 643
A Guide to Biblical Studies, 1236, 2160
Guiles, Dave A. 2280
    on GBC, 2335
Guiles, Ronald A., 130, 439, 1641
Guimond, Anice Joseph
    biography of, 2335
Guinea Pigs, *See* Civilian Public Service; Control Patients; Minnesota Starvation Project
Guinn, Isaiah, 1641
Guinness World Records
    longest marriage, 2127
Guinther, Charles P., 1641
Guinther, John, 1641
Gujarat Bible
    translation, 139
Gujarat Christi Sammelan
    Solanki, Naranji V., officer, 1200
Gujarat Christian Council
    Bhagat, Premchand Ganeshji, 131
Gujarat United School of Theology, India, **576**, *See also* Bulsar Bible School
    Blough, Jacob M., 150
    India, Church of North, 2207
    mission schools, 853
    Satvedi, Govindji, 1145
Gujarati language, *See* Gram Sevaks
Gulak, Nigeria, 306
Gulfview (Port Richey) Grace Brethren

Church, FL
St. Petersburg, FL, Grace Brethren Church, 1136
Guli, Elizabeth
Guli, John, 139, 307, 1641, 2195
Nigerian church leader, minister, **2194–2195**, *2195*
Gulick family
Galion, OH, Grace Brethren Church, 527
Gully, Iris A. (later Soto)
McAllen, TX, Grace Brethren Church, 2218
Gumble, Herman F., 2280
Gumm, Max Douglas, 1641
Gummere, Henry V., 1955
Gump, Arlo K., 1641
on Gump family, 2335
Shultz and Paul families, related to, 1156
Gump, Charles Ora, 1641
Shultz and Paul families, related to, 1156
Gump, Edith Mae, (later Bosler) 1834, **2387**
Shultz and Paul families, related to, 1156
Gump family, 715
Irricana (First) Church of the Brethren, Alberta, Canada, 663
Gump, Henry, 1641
Gump, Jacob, 264, 265, 749, 1641
Gump, Jeremiah, 7, 153, 264, 326, 1641
Gump, Jesse, 504
Shultz and Paul families, related to, 1156
Gump, Jesse A., 1641
Gump, John B., 1641
Gump, Samuel S., 1641
Gumre (Gomri, Gomorry, Gomry), Anna, **576**
Gumre (Gomri, Gomorry, Gomry), Johann, 421, **576**, 684, 763
Gunderman, Harry M., 1641, 2302
Gunderman, Terry D., 2280
Gundiri, Audu B., 1641
Gunnell family, 753
Gunter, William W., 1641
Gunther family, 148
Gunzel, Mary Elizabeth Pletcher, 1641
Gustafson, J. Alfred, 1642
Gustav Otto, count of Sayn-Wittgenstein-Hohenstein, 1158
Gustin, David Walter, 1642
Gut, Bena
descendants, 1944, 1951
Gut, Christian
descendants, 1944, 1951
Gutek, Gerald
on Ephrata Cloister, 2335
Gutek, Patricia
on Ephrata Cloister, 2335
Gutelius, Fred W., 1642
Guth family, *See* Good (Guth) family
Guth, Hermann, 1955
on Schwarzenau Baptists, 2335
Guth, Jacob, 556
Guthrie, Aaron
May Hill Church of the Brethren, OH, minister, 804
Guthrie/Bethel, MN, congregation
Minnesota Brethren settlement, 848
Guthrie, Charley Wilbert, 758, 1330, 1642,

1955
Phoenix, AZ, First Church of the Brethren, pastor, 1019
Guthrie, Charles, 1642
Guthrie Church of the Brethren, MN, **576**
Guthrie Co., IA, 342, 661
Panora Church of the Brethren, 992
Guthrie, Donald Lee, 2280
Guthrie, Ellis Gerald, 109, 417, 1642, 1955, 2302
Guthrie, Grace (later Porte), 1047
Guthrie, J. A.
Ross Church of the Brethren, OH, leader, 1124
Guthrie, J. L., 373
Guthrie, James Allen, 6, 1243, 1642
Guthrie, Joseph, 1642
Guthrie, Joseph L., 380, 1642
Guthrie, Lulu Trout
Phoenix, AZ, First Church of the Brethren, pastor, 1019
Guthrie, OK
Church of the Brethren, **576**
German Baptist Brethren's Home Society, 541
Guthrie, William Richard, 347, 1642, 2053
Gutierrez, Clarence, 1642
Guyer, Albert, 670
Guyer, Carl Albert, 1642
Guyer, Charles O., 1642
Guyer family, 2081
Snider, Jacob, descendants of, 1154
Guyer, Herman S., 706, 1642
Guyer, Nelson Shaffer, 1642
Guyon, Jeanne Marie, 381
Guyon, Madame, *See* La Motte Guyon, Madame Jeanne-Marie de prayer, 1051
Guyton, Mary Magdalene, 1842–1843
Guzman, Fabricio Pimentel, 275, 1642
minorities, ethnic and racial, 850
South Bend, IN, Iglesia Evangelica Emanuel (CB) and, 2252
Gwari, Paul K., 306
Gwaski, Nigeria, 306
Gwin, Ethel A., 1955
Gwin, Jacob N., 1212
Gwin, Laura, 1788
Gwinn (Gwin), Jacob Noah, 1642
Gwinner, Bertha Edith, 1852
Gwong family, 201
Gwong, Moy, 201, *See also* Moy Gwong Han
Gwynn, Charles, 1642
gymnasiums, 2131

H., John, 424, **577**
Far Western Brethren, 475
Fraternity of Baptists, 511
Hendricks, John, 597
H., S. P., 1955
Ha, Jenny Me-Ai
Malaysia, missionary work in, 784
Haacke, John, 1642
Haag, Alys Anne Lickel, 1849
Mexico, missionary to, 820
Haag, Lloyd Delmar, 173, 745, 1642
Haag, Walter Eugene, 1642, 1849, 2302
Mexico, missionary to, 820
San Ysidro, CA, Grace Brethren Church, pastor, 1142
Haan, Perry
Cincinnati Grace Brethren Church,

Sharonville, OH, 1174
Haan, Sherri
Cincinnati Grace Brethren Church, Sharonville, OH, 1174
Haas, John, 1642
Haas, L. Frank, 1642
Habakkuk, 3:13, 39
Habecker, Phares M., 1642
Mechanic Grove Church of the Brethren, PA, free minister, 806
Habeger family, 2076
Habegger, David Luther, 1955
Habegger, Mary Ann Jeanette, 1849
Habegger, Peter
genealogy and descendants, 1955
Haber family
Erbaugh family, 453
Habitat for Humanity International, **2195**
homelessness, 2203
theology and, 2255
Hack, Elizabeth Jane Miller, 1955
Hackberry Hill Grace Brethren Church, CO, *See* Arvada, CO, Hackberry Hill Grace Brethren Church
Hacker, August "Gus," 1642
Häcker (Höcker), Eva op den Graef, 562, 577
Häcker (Höcker), Wilhelm, **577**
Häcker, J. T., 562
Hacker, Owen, 155
Hackett, Lucile Eleanor
on Beissel, Johann Conrad/Konrad, 2335
Hackman, Charles M., 721, 1642, 2302, **2383**
Hackman, Dorothy Elaine (later Grace), 1952
Hackman, Emma, 1013
Hackman family, 721
Snavely family, related to, 1193
Hackman, Galen R.
on Brethren beliefs and practices, 2335
on James 2:14–26, and influence on Brethren theology, 2335
on peace and nonresistance in Bible, 2335
Hackman, Jacob, 1642
Hackman, Jacob L., 721
Hackman, Johannes, 161
Hackman, Magdalena Shallenberger, 161
Hackman, Marya, 161
Hackman, Richard Hess, 1642, 2302
Hackman, Samuel J., 1650
Hackman, Violet G. (later Pfaltzgraff), **1013**, 1843, **2377**
Pfaltzgraff, Roy E., Sr., (CB) and, 2250
Hackman, Walter N., Jr.
on Mohler CB, PA, 2335
Hackman, Willis B., 1013
Hadadiyar Ekklesiyar Kristi a Nigeria (HEKAN), *See* Fellowship of Churches of Christ in Nigeria
Haddix family, 318
Haddix, KY, Brethren Church, 405, **577**, 689
Riverside Christian Training School, 1111
Hade, Les
Pentecostal Brethren, 1008
Hade meetinghouse
Falling Spring Church of the Brethren, PA, 471
Hades, See Hell, doctrine of

Hades, PA, Church of the Brethren, *See*
    Falling Spring Church of the
    Brethren, PA
Hadley Creek, IL, congregations, **577**, 740
Hadorn, Wilhelm, 1955
    historical writing, 611
Hadsell, B. A., 54, 275, **577**
Hady, E. S., 1642
Haeberle, Daniel, 1955
Haendiges, Emil, 1955
Haeusser, H. S., 2098
Hafner, Agnes L. (later Sollenberger), *See*
    Sollenberger, Agnes L. Hafner
Hagan, Charles
    San Jose, CA, South Bay community
        Church (FGBC), 142
Hagan family, 1958
Hagen, Victor Wolfgang von, 1955
Hagenbach, K. H., 1955–1956
Hagenberger, Gene M., Jr., 2280
Hagenbuck, George, 1642
Hagerman, George Gray, 1642
Hagerman, NM, 719
Hagerstown, IN, 752, 1250, 1339
    Church of God (New Dunkers), 297
    Nettle Creek Church of the Brethren,
        923–924
Hagerstown, MD, 136, 144, 155, 210, 256,
        343, 398, *446*, 733, 756, 1230,
        1329, 2072, 2105
    Broadfording (Bible) Brethren congre-
        gation elementary and high
        schools, 1163
    Calvary Grace Brethren Church, **578**
    Church of the Brethren, 42, *50*, 104,
        578, **578**, *1168*, 1920, 2042, 2338
    First Brethren Church, 32, **577–578**,
        1267
    Gateway Brethren Fellowship, **2195**
    Grace Brethren Church, 406, **578–579**
    Home for Orphan and Friendless
        Children, 625
    Maranatha Brethren Church, **579**
    Maryland Brethren, 799
    Maryland Grace Brethren activity, 799
    Maryland Progressive Brethren
        activity, 799
    St. James Brethren Church, near, 1134
    Valley Grace Brethren Church, **579**
Hagerstown, PA, as example of place name,
    911
Hagerstown Select School, *See* Linden
    Seminary
Haggai
    Ramirez, Frank on advent/Christmas
        sermons from, 2351
Hagle, Cornelius, 1642
Hagler, Eve Heier, 602
Hagler, Sebastian, 602
The Hague
    Fulk, George, 521
Hague family
    Fremont, OH, Grace Brethren Church,
        515
Hague, Isaac L., 142, 1642
Hahiawa, HI, 1312
Hahn family, 228, *See also* Höhn, Heinrich;
    Hon, Peter
    Farmington, DE, Bethany Church of
        the Brethren, 479
    Guthrie Church of the Brethren, MN,
        576
Hahn, George W., 1642

Hahn, H. C., 1642
Hahn, Hubert, 1642
Hahn, Jeremiah, 1642
Hahn, Margaret, 1883
Hahn, Martin Luther, 576, 114, 1642, **2383**
Hahn, Mathias William, 514, 1642
Hahnewalt family records, 1957
Haight, Dorothy Elizabeth, 1850
Haight, Floyd L., 1956
Haight, Mary Dietrich, 1956
Haines Acres area, York, PA, 1388
Haines, Amos Hoppock, 28, 335, **579**,
        1642, 1956
Haines, DeWitt, 746
Haines, Ella Wister, 2058
Haines, Homer G. (C.), 1642
Haines, Isaac
    Sergeantsville, NJ, Brethren Church,
        1167
Haines, J. Harry, 1956
Haines, John, 1642
Haines, Joseph, 579
Haines, Leland Milburn, 1956
Haines, Mabel Lambert, 579
Haines, Margaret Hoppock, 579
Haines, Mrs. Isaac
    Sergeantsville, NJ, Brethren Church,
        1167
Haines, Orion P., 688, 1642
Haines, W. F., 1642
hair and hairstyles, 400, **579**, *See also*
        beards
    Dunkard Brethren, 409
    Dunkard Brethren and nonconformity,
        940
    East Fairview Church of the Brethren,
        PA, 415
    prayer veil, 1053
Hair, Cletus D., 1642
Haist family, 2111
Haiti, **579–580**
    Brethren Charity Fund (BCF) and,
        2259
    Hagerstown, MD, Church of the
        Brethren, 578
    mission tours, 855
    missions, 2225
    orphan care, 276
    relief and service efforts, 1097
Haitian Church of the Brethren
    Miami, FL, Eglise des Frères Haitians,
        2222
Halberg, Roy, 1642
    River City Grace Community Church,
        pastor, 1134
Halberg, Roy D., 2280
Haldeman, Alice (later Hamilton), 580
Haldeman, Benjamin I., *618*
Haldeman, Daniel Cleophas, 1642
Haldeman family, 721, *See* Holderman
        family
Haldeman, Floyd, 1216, 1268
Haldeman, Hans, 618
Haldeman, Harriet Horning, 619
Haldeman, Jacob S., *618*
Haldeman, James Hosler, 1642
Haldeman, John, 1899
Haldeman, Michael S., 618, 721, 1642
Haldeman, Millard Sidney, 1643, 2302
    missions, 862
Haldeman, Minnie
    missions, 862
Haldeman, Myrtle Long

autobiography of, 2335
    on Civil War era, 2335
    on Long, David and family, 2335
Haldeman, Nicholas, 618
Haldeman, Olive, 1268
Haldeman, Peter, 618
Haldeman, Sally Ulrich, *618*
Haldeman, Samuel, 619, 1643
Haldeman-Scarr, Sara, 2280
Haldeman-Scarr, William L., 2280
Haldeman, William C., 2280
Haldemann, Daniel C., 441
Haldemann, Heinrich, 618
Halderman family
    Reinhardt family, 1094
Hale, Arthur Chester, Jr., 2280
Hale, Darlin, 1643
Hale family, 2077
    Gospel Grace Brethren Church, VA,
        559
Hale, John H., 1643
Hale, John P., 1956
Hale, Thomas, 2077
Haley, M. J., 1956
Halfhill, Ellie, *2144*
Halifax Co., VA, 1243
Haliru, Dzugwahi, 1643
Hall, Alvin, 296, 297
Hall, Charles
    Riner Grace Brethren Church, VA,
        pastor, 1110
Hall, Charles C., 1643
    Radford, VA, Fairlawn Grace Brethren
        Church, pastor, 1079
Hall, Charles M., 1956
Hall, Charles W., 2280
Hall, Claude, 1643
Hall, Claude B., 357, 1643
Hall, Claude E., 2302
Hall, Dorothy, 377
Hall, Elmer Cassidy, 1643, 2302
Hall, Elsie Marie Kindley, 1838
Hall, F. M., 1643
Hall family, 1243, 1302
    Garwin, IA, Carlton Brethren Church,
        532
    Roanoke, VA, Garden City Grace
        Brethren Church, 1113
Hall, Fetter, 211, 532, 662, 1643
Hall, George, 586
Hall, George W., 1346, 1643, 2302
Hall, J. Frank, 1643
Hall, J. I., 1305, 1643
    Martinsburg, PA, Grace Brethren
        Church, pastor, 798
    Pineville, VA, Mount Olive Brethren
        Church, pastor, 1025
Hall, J. Lincoln, 560
    hymns, 643
Hall, Jacob A., 586
Hall, James A., 1643
Hall, Jesse Keeney, 115, 349–350, 562,
        585, 1212, 1643, 2302, **2383**
Hall, Jonathan N., 16, 2280
Hall, Joseph I., 1643
Hall, Larkin, 1643
Hall, Leonard G., 1956
Hall, Lois Virginia, 1850–1851
Hall, Mary Lou Traugh, 1643, 2280
Hall, Myrtle, 503
Hall, Nelson Elam, 14, 626, 1267, 1270,
        1351, 1643
Hall, Paul, Sr.

Pulaski, VA, Church of the Brethren, minister, 1071
Hall, Ralph, 366, 2139
Hall, Ralph C., 180, 188, 674, 1643
    Meyersdale, PA, Grace Brethren Church, pastor, 822
Hall, Richard Joseph, 2280
Hall, S. D., 1643
Hall schoolhouse
    Liberty Church of the Brethren, TN, 740
Hall, Von Lee, 1838, **2387**
Hall, Warren, 2302
Hall, Warren E., 1643, 2302
Hall, Wayne A., 2280
Hall, William I., 1243, 1643
Halladay, Paul Karlton, 580
Halladay, Paul W., 580, 1643
Halladay, Ruth Mary, 580, 1838
Halladay, Sara Heebner, **580,** 1359
Halle circle, Württemburg, 1209
Halle, Germany, 545, **580**
    Camisards, 242
    Francke, August Hermann, 506
    Moravian Church, 875
    Muhlenberg, Henry Melchior, 892
    Muhlenberg, Henry Melchior reports to, 925
Halle Luther Bible, 138
Halle Orphanage, 5–6
    Neumann, Gottfried as teacher at, 924
Halle Pietists
    German Bibles, 1149
    printing press sought from, 1147
Halle, University of
    Miller, Daniel Long, 836
    Zinzendorf, Nikolaus Sudwig, Count von, 1399
Haller, Charles R.
    on German-Americans, distinguished, 2335
Haller, F. L., 1643
Haller family
    Gibbel (Gibble) family, 547
Haller, Friedrich Conrad, 147, **580,** 584, 1643
Haller, George, 2087
Haller, H. L., 1643
Haller, Jacob, 1643
Haller, John, 1643
Haller, Wesley, 673, 721, 1643, 1956, **2195,** 2302
    Milroy, PA, Grace Brethren Church, pastor, 843
    Minerva, OH, Grace Brethren Church, 843,
Hallesche Nachrichten, 1956
historical writing, 611
Hallett, George E., 1643
    Pampa, TX, Church of the Brethren, as minister, 991
Halliday family, 165
Halliday (Hollyday, Holliday) families
    bibliography, 1890
Hallowell, Marvin E.
    on Duché, Jacob, 2335
Hallowell-Paul family
    family history, 1974
Hally, George, 1643
Halpin, Meredith Milo, 1643
Halterman, Ernest B., 1643
Halterman family, *See* Holderman (Haldeman) family

Halterman, Harvey A., 1643
Halterman, M. Ward, 1643
Halterman, R. C., 1643
Halverson, Dorothy, 2280
Halvorson, Peter L., 1956
Ham, Gertrude, 708
Ham, John, **580,** 1643
    Far Western Brethren, 475
    H., John, 577
Ham, Mr. and Mrs. J. E., 503
Hamaker, Adam
    family history, 1956
Hamaker, John Irwin, 1956
Hambers, Theodore F., 1902
Hambrick, Polly, 157
Hamburg
    Driedger, Michael D. on populations of, 2325
    Fischer, Johann, 491
Hamburg-Altona, Germany, 157, 174, 545, **580,** 1223
    Brethren remnants in Europe, 1099
    Dompelaars in, 395
    Mehrning, Jacob, 811
    Petersen, Barthold Jurgen, 1012
Hamel, Janet (later Solomon)
    Hamel, Joseph Donat, 2196
    Sarasota, FL, Iglesia de los Hermanos (BC) and, 2246
Hamel, Jean Rowsey
    Hamel, Joseph Donat, 2196
Hamel, JoAnne
    Hamel, Joseph Donat, 2196
Hamel, John
    Hamel, Joseph Donat, 2196
Hamel, Joseph Donat, 1643, 2148
    minister, **2195–2196**
    Sarasota, FL, Brethren Church, pastor, 1145
Hämer, Anna, 159
Hamer, Eliza Blough, 580
Hamer, Esther Louise Rinehart, 924, 1838
    missionary sponsored by Salamonie Church of the Brethren, IN, 1136
Hamer family, 1956
Hamer, Gertrude Sharp, 580
Hamer, Harry M., 1956
Hamer, John Hicks, 1971
Hamer, John Leland, 727, 1643, 1838
    medical missions, 807
    missionary sponsored by Salamonie Church of the Brethren, IN, 1136
Hamer, Maryanna, 1956
Hamer, Oliver Stuart, **580,** 1643
Hamer, Oscar Wellington, 1323, 1643
Hamer, Thomas P., 580
Hamers, James, 670
Hamerson, Eva Ethyl, 1643
Hamilton, Alice Haldeman, 580, 1643
Hamilton, Alice (later Merrill), 1706
Hamilton, Beatrice M. (later Ludwick), 1643, 1697
Hamilton, Benjamin Arthur, 1849, 1956, 2302, 2335
    on FGBC missionary in Central Africa, 2335
Hamilton, Benjamin, Jr., 1643
Hamilton Co., KS
    Prairie View Church of the Brethren, KS, members living in, 1050
Hamilton Co., OH, 1281
    Cincinnati Grace Brethren Church, Sharonville, OH, 1172, 1174

Hamilton congregation, MO, 752
Hamilton, Cora Leah Goodwin, 580
Hamilton family, 1958
    Howard, IN, Church of the Brethren, 633
    Musselman family related to by marriage, 901
Hamilton, Hiel, 297, 464, **580,** 1643
    Howard, IN, Church of the Brethren, 633
Hamilton, Jacob, 1643
Hamilton, James, 1643
Hamilton, John Taylor, 1956
Hamilton, Kenneth G., 1956
Hamilton, Mabel C., 1956
Hamilton, Mabel Jeannette Crawford, 1849
Hamilton, Marvin, 1643
Hamilton, Mary, 217
Hamilton, Mary Croll, 580
Hamilton, Merle R., 1956
Hamilton, Miles, 580
Hamilton, MO, 692
    Church of the Brethren, *See* Kidder Church of the Brethren, MO
Hamilton, Nancy Kingery, 580
Hamilton, OH, First Church of the Brethren, **581**
Hamilton, Opal Horner, *See* Prisoners of War program
Hamilton, Sarah Ellen (later Whisler), 1338
Hamilton, Sinclair, 1956
Hamilton, Stanley
    Rural Life Association (RLA), 1130–1131
Hamilton, Walter J., 244, 453, **580–581,** 1643, 1918, 1956–1957
Hyndman, PA, Church of the Brethren, 643
    Monroeville, PA, Church of the Brethren, 870
    Rockwood Church of the Brethren, PA, pastor, 1118
Hamilton, William Edward, 1243, 1643
Hamilton, William H., 121, 1643
Hamler, OH
    Sand Ridge Church of the Brethren, OH, near, 1143
Hamlim, KS, congregation
    Morrill, KS, (First) Brethren Church, 32, 98, **581,** 773, 876
Hamm, David V., 1643
Hamm family, 145, 1345
Hamm, Johann Jacob, 1957
Hamm, Joseph J., 1644
Hamm, L. Katherine, 1836
Hamm, Peter, 1644
Hamm, Rachel (later Frantz), 1941
Hamm, Solomon, 1644
    Mud Valley Old German Baptist Brethren Church, IL, minister, 892
Hamm, Thomas D.
    on Quakers, 2335
Hamma family, 233
Hammaker, Adam, 1644
Hammaker, Mary (later Strickler), *See* Strickler family
Hammarskjöld, Dag, *344*
Hammel, Daniel A., 2280
Hammer, Annie Viola, 581
Hammer, Earl William, 1644
Hammer family, 1880
Hammer Fellowship
    Smith Creek Fellowship Church of the Brethren, WV, 1191

Hammer, Isaac, 672, 2093
Hammer, James, 503
Hammer, James D., 2302
Hammer, Mary Elizabeth (later Newcomer), 933
Hammer, Myles I., 581
Hammers, Daniel Lee, 1380, 1644, 1849
Hammers family, 688
Hammers, Harold, 674
Hammers, Mary Louise Ashman, 581
Hammers, Sharolyn Lucille Ulrich, 1849
Hammers, Thomas E., 515, **581**, 688, 768, 1270, 1644, 2302
    South Pasadena, CA, Grace Brethren Church, pastor, 1206
Hammon, Peter, 243, 1644
Hammond, Barbara K., 2280
Hammond, Herbert C., **2383**
Hammond, Hubert C., 1644
Hammond, Theresa M., 1957
Hammond, Todd R., 2280
Hampshire, 163
Hampshire Co., VA (later WV), 318, 171, 1339, 2053
Hampshire Co., WV, 254, 1249, 1336, 1339, 1341
    Harness Run Church of the Brethren, WV, 585
    migration of Brethren, 829
    Oak Grove Church of the Brethren, WV, 956
Hampton, Carrie, 239
Hampton congregation, PA, 1294
Hampton, IA, Church of the Brethren, *See* Union Ridge Church of the Brethren, IA
Hampton, Margaret Woods, 1957
Hampton, Marshall D., 1644
Hamstead, Joy, 1957
Hamstead, Obed, 1644
    Shiloh Church of the Brethren, WV, elder in, 1177
Han, Chang Yin, *See* Yin, Han Chang
Han, Moy Gwong, *See* Moy Gwong Han
Hanawalt, Barbara Replogle, 581
Hanawalt, Caroline McKee, 581
Hanawalt, Catherine Elizabeth Laman, 582
Hanawalt, D. W.
    Raisin City, CA, Church of the Brethren, 1083
Hanawalt, David Kirk, 249, **581**, 1644
    Oaks, PA, Green Tree Church of the Brethren, pastor, 958
Hanawalt, Dwight Lewis, 249, 1957
Hanawalt, Dwight Moody, 1957
Hanawalt, Eloise Clapper, 581
Hanawalt, Eve Kauffman, 581, 582
Hanawalt family, **582**, 1289, 1750, 1972, 1957
    Snowberger family, related to, 1154
Hanawalt, George L., 581, 582
Hanawalt, George S., 581, **581**, 582, 1644
    Robinson, PA, Church of the Brethren, 1116
Hanawalt, H. William, 232, 1644
Hanawalt, Harvey M., 1644
Hanawalt, Heinrich Georg, 582
Hanawalt, Henry W., 581
Hanawalt, Isaac, 1644
Hanawalt, J. S., 1644
Hanawalt, John, 582
Hanawalt, Joseph M., 1289, 1644
Hanawalt, Joseph Rothrock, **581**, 582,

1644, *See* language shift
Hanawalt, Lucinda Stutzman, 581
Hanawalt, Lucy May Pressel, 581
Hanawalt, Marjorie L. (later Morse)
    Morse, Kenneth Ivan, wife of, 878
Hanawalt, Mary Rothrock, 581, 582
Hanawalt, Mary Swigart, 581, 582
Hanawalt, Pearl Etta Turner, 581, 1957
Hanawalt, Phoebe Kirk, 581
Hanawalt, Susannah Rothrock, 582
Hanawalt, William Cyrus Replogle, 79, **581–582,** 1644
    McFarland, CA, Church of the Brethren, free minister, 774
Hanbold family
    Orange City, FL, Calvary Grace Brethren Church, 976
Hancock Co., IA, 162
Hancock Co., IL, 238, 1357, 1358
Hancock Co., OH, 364, 413, 734, 1235
    Rome Old German Baptist Brethren Church, OH, 956, 1121
Hancock, MD, 1224
Hancock, MN, Church of the Brethren, **582**
Hand, J. H., 1644
hand of fellowship, right, *See* right hand of fellowship
handbell choirs
    Palmyra, PA, Church of the Brethren, 991
Handbook on Christian Unity, 2167
handclasp, **582**, 698, *698*
    degrees of ministry, 374
    love feast, during, 763
handcrafts, *See* crafts
handicapped, *See* disabled
Handley, John William, 1644
Handlin, Oscar, 2019
Handwerk, Frank G., 1644
Handy, William Hardin, 749, 1644
    Mount Carmel Church of the Brethren, NC, minister, 880
    Mountain View Church of the Brethren, VA, 889
    New Bethel Church of the Brethren, NC, leadership in, 925
    New Haven Church of the Brethren, NC, elder in, 928
Haner, Karl, 19
Hanes, Iris Euvonne Neff, 1838
Haney, Irva Kendrick, 1957
Haney, Lurty, 1644
Haney, Robert, 141
Haney, Robert Ashbury, 273, 1644, 1957, 2302
    Peace Valley Church of the Brethren, MO, 1003
Hang, L. S. (S. L.), 1644
Hanger, Flora, 362
Hanger, William, 362
Hanikian, Milkron, 1644
Hankel, J. M., 672
Hankins, Roxie (later Weaver), 1324
Hankins, Steve A., 2280
Hanks family, 2046
Hanks, Thomas Patrick-Joseph, 2280
Hanle, Robert V., 1957
    historical writing, 613
Hanley, Richard Morgan, 2280
Hanley, Thomas O'Brien, 1957
Hanlin, Delbert Omer, 1243, 1644
Hanlin, Joseph, 106, 1644
Hann, Julia, 239

Hann, Melissa, 239
Hanna, Esther, 496
Hanna, G. Bright, 1644
    Marion, IN, Brethren Church, pastor, 793
Hanna, Homer M., 1644, 2302
Hanna, Joseph E., 1644
Hanna, Josephine, 752
Hanna, Raymond C., 2280
Hannah, Wayne Lee, 2280
    Richmond, VA, Grace Brethren Church, pastor, 1108
Hannan, W. J. H., 211
    Pleasant View Brethren Church, KS, pastor, 1036
Hannan, W. L., 1644
Hannan, William J., 503
Hanover Church of the Brethren, 2335
Hanover, PA, 136, 145, 2087
    Church of the Brethren, **582**
Hanover Twp., York Co., PA, 1350
Hanoverdale, PA, congregation, 142
Hansel, John, 1644
Hansel, Strother, 1644
Hansel, Todd, 529, 1644
Hansell, Allen T., Sr., 1644
    Korean Mission, 2211
Hansen, Christian, 361, 375, 1644
    missions, 860
Hansen, E. J. P., *See* Thalitzer, Johannes
Hansen, George, 52
Hansen, Harvey H., 1212
Hansen, Harvey J., 1644
Hansen, Johanna, 362
Hansen, Johannes, *See* Thalitzer, Johannes (Hansen)
Hansen, Kirsten Kathrine, 362
Hansen, Niels, Jr., 362
Hanson, Edward M., 1644
Hanson, Erlene Pritchett, 1060
Hanson, J. H., Jr., 1060
Hanson, Larry, 2280
Hanson, Phyllis Brechbiel
    on Brechbiel, Harry K., 2335
Hanson, Willetta Marie, 1848
Hantsch, (Brother), 2106
Hantz, John F., 1644
Hantzsch, Viktor, 1957
Hapner, George E., 1644
happiness
    Biblical lessons, 1968
Happy Corner, OH, 319, 366, 367, 696, 1276, 1355
    Church of the Brethren, *See* Clayton, OH, Happy Corner Church of the Brethren
    Flory, Abraham, 497
    meetinghouse, 696
    Nead family in cemetery of, 919
Happy Hill Church of the Brethren, MO, **582**
Hapsburg dynasty
    Evangelical Church in Austria, 459
Harada, Tomin
    World Friendship Center, 1369
Harader, Ammi, 1644
    Mount Etna, IA, Church of the Brethren, 881
Harader, Christian, 468, 1644
    Mount Etna, IA, Church of the Brethren, elder, 881
Harader, Daniel, 1645
    Mount Etna, IA, Church of the

Brethren, 881
Mulvane, KS, Brethren Church, pastor, 895
Harader, Edwin, 1645
Harader family
    Mount Etna, IA, Church of the Brethren, 881
    Payette Valley Church of the Brethren, ID, 996
Harader, I. S., 1645
Harader, Lee, 1645
Haradon, Virginia Ingles Maes, 1957
Harbach, Robert Cyrus, 1645
Harbaugh family
    history, 1957
Harbaugh, Henry, 1957
Harbor Springs, MI, 750
Harch, Samuel, 733
Harden, Elizabeth Burkett, 643
Harden (Hardin), Thomas, 1645
Harden, James, 643
Harden, John Thomas, 643
Hardesty, Bradley A., 2280
Hardin family, 318
Hardin, J. Lloyd, 1645
Harding, Catherine C. (later Snyder), See Snyder, Catherine C. Harding
Harding, Roger Lee, 1645
Hardman, Agnes (later Hostetler), 631
Hardman, Anthony (Anton Hartman), 582, See also Hartman, Anthony
    Shelby Co. German Baptist Brethren Church, KY, possibly preacher in, 1175
Hardman, D. C., 1645
Hardman, Daniel B., 1645
Hardman, Daniel R., 1645
Hardman, David, 923, 1645
Hardman, Elizabeth (later Hostetler), 631
Hardman, Elizabeth (later Miller)
    Müller (Miller) family, 894
Hardman family, 14, 384, 752, See also Hardtmann family
    Greene, IA, Church of the Brethren, 570
    Jasper, MO, Church of the Brethren, 669
    Shelby Co. German Baptist Brethren Church, KY, 1175
Hardman, Hannah (later Hostetler), 631
Hardman, John Henry, 1645
Hardman, Joseph, 1234, 1645
Hardman, Martin, 1645
Hardman, Olin, 1645
Hardman, Sarah (later Miller)
    Müller (Miller) family, 894
Hardon, John A., 1957
Hardtman family
    Shelby Co. German Baptist Brethren Church, KY, 1175
Hardtmann (Hardman, Hartman) family, 582–583
Hardy Co., VA
    Dunkard Brethren Church, 2106
Hardy Co., WV, 350, 694, 766, 1276, 1295, 1315, 1336
    Flat Rock Church of the Brethren, VA, 493
    history, 1980
    Mathias, WV, Church of the Brethren, 803
    Milam, WV, Mount Carmel Church of the Brethren, 2222

Moorefield, WV, Church of the Brethren, 874
Mount View Church of the Brethren, WV, 887
New Dale Church of the Brethren, WV, 926–927
Hardy, James H., 91, 1645
Hardy, Tracy, 1645
Hardy, VA
    Ninevah Church of the Brethren, VA, 938
Hare, Barbara J., 2280
Hare, Betty Arnett, 1838
Hare, Jack Denis, 2302
Hargett, K(ermit) Dewight, 1645
Hargleroad, Christian P., 1645
Haribhai, Jivanji, 1645
Haride, J. L., 1645
Hark, Ann, 1957
Hark, J. Max, 291, 1957
Harkins, Joseph L., 2280
Harkleroad, Christ, 1645
Harlacher, D. Bucher, 1645
Harlacher family, 320
Harlacher, Galen, 1645, 2302
    Newberg, OR, Dunkard Brethren Congregation, elder in, 933
Harlacher, George Washington, 1645, 1927–1928
Harlacher, John A., 1645
Harlacher, John B., 1645
Harlacher, Mary (later Fahnestock), 465
Harlan Church of the Brethren, IA, 583, 992
    Homestead Church of the Brethren, MI, 626
    Maxwell, IA, Church of the Brethren, 803
Harlan, MI, Church of the Brethren, 179, 583
    Marilla Church of the Brethren, MI, 793
    Michigan Brethren settlement, 824
Harlan, Rolvix, 1957
Harle (ship)
    Hochstaedter, Michael, 1950
    Lang, (Anna) Marie Studebaker, 724
    Lang, (John) Nicholas, 724
    Long, John, 724
    Shideler, Johann Georg, voyage on, to America, 1177
    Studebaker family, 1230
Harlem Park Urban Renewal Project, 2133
Harley, Abram, 1219
Harley, Alice, 662, 1361, 1645
    missions, 861
Harley, Benjamin, 583, 1645
Harley, Bessie M. Rider, 1838
Harley burying grounds, Indian Creek, PA, 267
Harley, Chester I., 1218, 1645, 1859, 1957, 2302
    New Carlisle, OH, Church of the Brethren, elder in, 926
Harley, David, 1645
    Philadelphia, PA, First Church of the Brethren, minister, 1015
Harley, Edith (later Donovan), 1918–1919
Harley, Elsie Vint Hollen, 583
Harley family, 260, 583, 2090, 2102
    Cassel, Abram H. letter about, 2102
    genealogy, 1918–1919, 1958
    Preiß (Price) family related to, 1055

Reinhardt family, 1094
Harley, George, 1645
Harley, H. M., 363, 1346
Harley, Hannah Stover, 1219
Harley, Harvey M., 1645
Harley, Henry Price, 320, 1645
Harley, Herbert, 1957–1958
Harley (Herli, Harli), Hans Rudolf, 27, 583, 583, 1645, 2024
    article about, 1958
    biography, 1957
Harley, Jacob K., 1219
Harley, John, 1645
Harley, Jonas, 583, 1645
Harley, Magdalena, 383
Harley, Margaret (later Randall)
    works by, 2322
Harley, Mary, 258
Harley, Mary Becker, 108, 583
Harley, Mary F., 583
Harley, Owen L., 173, 243, 1645
Harley, Rudolph II (1719–1809), 108
Harley, Samuel Abraham, 583, 1287, 1645
    Pipe Creek Church of the Brethren, MD, minister, 1026
Harley, Samuel C., 583
Harley, Sarah (later Reiff), 1094
Harley, Sarah Stover, 1219
Harley, William P., 1645
Harleysville congregation
    Pine Run German Baptist Brethren, 2377
Harleysville, PA, 175, 477, 524, 747, 1216, 1960, 2071
    Peter Becker Community, 1010
    young people, 1393
Harleysville, PA, Indian Creek Church of the Brethren, 49, 583–584, 682, See also language shift
    Mingo Church of the Brethren, PA, 843
Harling, Stephen, 1645
Harly, Rudolph, II, 583
Harman, Alvin T., 1645, 2302
Harman, Ananias, 727, 1645
Harman, Asa, 584, 1645
    Seneca Church of the Brethren, WV, elder, 1166
Harman, B. T., 1645
Harman Church of the Brethren, WV, 584
Harman, Culver M., 1645
Harman, E. Price, 1645
Harman, Ellsworth Samson, 584, 1645
Harman family, 1958
    Hylton family, 641
Harman, George, 1645
Harman, H. Clay, 1645
Harman (Harmon) family, 584
Harman, Hylton, 1645, 2196, 2196
Harman, J. W., 1958
Harman, Jackson, 1645
Harman, Maxine
Harman, Hylton, 2196
Harman, Oscar Price, 1646
Harman, Simon P., 1646
Harman, W. A., 20
Harman, Wayne Pershing, 1646
Harman, WV, congregation
    Red Creek Church of the Brethren, WV, 1088
Harmon Dick family
    sources on, 2312
Harmon family, 148, 731, 1326, 1958
    Fleming Co., KY, German Baptist

Brethren Church, 494

Harmon, Florence
Modesto, CA, South Modesto Community Church of the Brethren, 867
Harmon, Glenn M., 14, 59, 246, 663, 1646, 1958
Modesto, CA, South Modesto Community Church of the Brethren, 867
Harmon, Gordon A., 2280
Mount Vernon, OH, Conservative Grace Brethren Church, 2227
Harmon, H. J., 1646
Harmon, Jackson, 1646
Harmon, W. A., 1646
Harmon, Wendel, 584
Harmon, William, 676, 1646
Portage Church of the Brethren, OH, minister, 1047
harmony
Old German Baptist Brethren, 2233
Harmony Church of the Brethren, MD, **584**
Grossnickle Church of the Brethren, MD, 574
Middletown Valley Church of the Brethren, MD, 826
Myersville, MD, Church of the Brethren, 906
Harmony Society, **584**, 1866
communitarianism, 329
Concordia, 331
Haller, Friedrich Conrad, 580
New Harmony, IN, 928
Ohio, 329
Pennsylvania, 329
Harmonyville, PA, Church of the Brethren, **584**
Pottstown, PA, Coventry Church of the Brethren, 1049
Harms, H. H., 1921
Harner, Denton Daniel, 738, 1646
Harner, W. J., 1646
Harness, Charles B., 2280
Harness, Leah Oxley, 2280
Harness Run Church of the Brethren, WV, 106, **585**, 703, 1240
Harnish, Clarence H., 1958
Harnish, Esther Miller, 1958
Harnish, Jacob, 1646
Harnish, Maria E. (later Overholtzer), 986
Harnish, Samuel
descendants, 1940
Harnley, Elizabeth Hoerner, 585
Harnley, Henry H., 585
Harnley, Henry Jacob, **585**, 781
Harnley, Sarah Witmore, 585
Harnly, Eliz. Hoerner, 1958
Harnly family
history of, 1958
Harp, Catherine (later Leatherman), 733
Harp, George, 733
Harp, George Silas, 1646
Harp, James, 152, 470, 687–688, 1646
Newberg, OR, Church of the Brethren, pastor in, 933
Pilot Knob Church of the Brethren, AR, minister, 1024
Harp, Susanna (later Leatherman), 733
Harpel, A. P., *661*
Harper, Addison, 1313, 1646
Harper, Chase, 244
Harper, Clara Belle, 67, *248*, **585**, 1838,

2374, 2387
Harper Co., OK, 1287
Indian Creek Church of the Brethren, OK, 651
Harper, Douglas
on Witman incident, 2335
Harper, Earl, 1646
Harper, Elizabeth, 585
Harper, F. L., 585
Harper family, 1866
Harper, Glenn
on German Baptists and Ohio meeting houses, 2335
Harper, Hannah, 2081
Harper, J. Russell, 1958
Harper, William Rainey
Young, Emanuel Sprankle, 1389
Harper Woods, MI, Detroit First Church of the Brethren, **585**
Redford, MI, Trinity Church of the Brethren, 1090
Harpers Chapel
Smith Creek Fellowship Church of the Brethren, WV, preaching point, 1191
Harpers Chapel meetinghouse, WV, 1315
Harpers Chapel preaching point
Highland Co. Mission Church of the Brethren, VA, 605
Harpers Ferry, **585**, 2128, *See also* literature
Harpers Ferry, VA, 2091
Shenandoah Valley, VA, 1176
Harper's Magazine, 61
Harper's New Monthly Magazine
Pfautz, John Eby, 1014
Harpine, J. William, 1276, 1646
Harpine, Jacob William, 1958
Harpine, Jonathan
Pleasant View Church of the Brethren, VA, 1037
Harpold, John A., 1646
Harrader, D.
South Haven Brethren Church, KS, elder, 1205
Harrah, WA, Grace Brethren Church, **585**, 1383
Harrell, E. B., 1646
Harrell family
Pleasant Grove Church of the Brethren, NC, 1031
Harrell, Fred, 1294, 1646
Harrell, G. Richard, 270, 1646, 1849
Harriet, Howard, 209
Harriman, Allen P., family
Rosepine, LA, Church of the Brethren, 1123
Harriman, E. H., 1289
Harrington family
Niota, TN, Church of the Brethren, 938
Harris, Alexander, 1958
Harris, Charles J., 1646
Harris, C[larence] D.
memoirs, 2335
Harris Co., TX
Pleasant Grove Church of the Brethren, TX, 1031
Harris Creek Church of the Brethren, OH, 171, 237, **585**. 349,
Mohler, Samuel Sayler, 868
Oakland Church of the Brethren, OH, 957
Harris, Dorothy G., 1859
Harris, E. J., 1646

Harris, Earl Lafayette, 2280
Harris, Edgar Robert, 1646
Mountain Grove Church of the Brethren, MO, minister, 889
Harris, Ella Neher
Mountain Grove Church of the Brethren, MO, 889
Harris, Ethel Sherfy, 1958
Harris family, 16, 360, 1391, 1865, 1958
Mabton, WA, Grace Brethren Church, 771
Meadow Branch Church of the Brethen, TN, 805
Neher family, related to, 922
Harris, Glenn Newton, 1646, 2302
Rosepine, LA, Church of the Brethren, elder, 1123
Harris, Hazel, 2093
Harris, Isaac L., 1646
Mountain Grove Church of the Brethren, MO, minister, 889
Harris, Isham G., 1646
Harris, James P., 572, 1646
Harris, John P., 1391, 1646
Riddlesburg, PA, Church of the Brethren, minister, 1108
Harris, John T., 315
Harris, Kevin B., 2173
Harris, M. F., 1646
Harris, Mary Ann (later Stein), 1220
Harris, Mary Edith, 1849
Harris, Otto, 211, 1646
Harris, Ray, 688, 1213, 1646
Minot, ND, Church of the Brethren, elder, 851
Poplar Valley Church of the Brethren, MT, elder, 1047
Harris, Ray F., 1646
Harris, Ray T., 1646
Harris, Robert M., 1646
Harris-Ulrich family, 2093
Harris, Vance, 1215
Harris, Vernon J., 13, 319, 721, 1646
Roanoke, VA, Washington Heights Grace Brethren Church, pastor, 1114
Southern Lancaster Grace Brethren Church, PA, pastor, 1207
Harris, Virginia, 1215
Harris, W. F., 1646
Harris, William, 1646
Harris, William David, 1646
McClave, CO, Church of the Brethren, minister, 773
Harrisburg, OH
Nimishillen Church of the Brethren, 937
Harrisburg, PA, 1911
First Church of the Brethren, 142, 456, **586**, 1401, 2203
fellowship houses, 484
Ridgeway Community Church of the Brethren, PA, 142, 1109
Melrose Gardens Grace Brethren Church, **586**, 1388
Harrison Co., IA
Missouri Valley German Baptist Brethren, IA, 865
Soldier River German Baptist Brethren, IA, 1201
Harrison Co., IN
migration of Brethren, 829
Harrison Co., Indiana Territory

Pfautz family, 1014
Harrison Co., MO, 755
Harrison, David, 1303
Harrison, Emma, 380
Harrison, Ernest E., 157, 1646
Harrison family, 740, 1240, 2084
Harrison, Jimmie, 755
Harrison, John C., 1646
Harrison, Marguerite Balph, 1958
Harrison, OK, Church of the Brethren, **586**
    Red River Church of the Brethren, OK, 1089
Harrison, S. J., 282, 472, 1240, 1319, 1321, 1400
    Iowa, 661
Harrison, Sarah Watters, 586
Harrison, Stephen J., 186, 195, 398, **586,** 1646
    railroads and Brethren settlement, 1082
Harrison, Terri, 1303
Harrison, Thomas, 586
Harrison Twp., Darke Co., OH, 147
Harrison, William J., 1958
Harrisonburg, Abraham, 2106
Harrisonburg, VA, 165, 168, 745, 751, 1308, 2091
    Bethlehem Brethren Church, **586**
    Educational Association of the Schools (CB), 429
    First Church of the Brethren, 342, **586,** 2081
    Greenmount Church of the Brethren, VA, 571
Harrisonville, MO, 6
Harroff, Stephen Bowers, 1958
Harrold, Albert W., 1400, 1646, 2020
Harry, Ramsumair K., 1646
Harry, Romulus, 1646
    Red Oak Ridge German Baptist Brethren Church, WV, 1089
Harsh, Alva Carlton, 430, **586–587,** 922, 1646, 1838, *See also* China; Harsh, Mary Lou Hykes
    Petersburg, WV, Memorial Church of the Brethren, pastor and missionary, 1012
Harsh, Effie Fike, 587
Harsh, Jesse, 587, 1646
Harsh, Mary Lou Hykes, 587, **587,** 922, 1838, 1958, *See* China
    Petersburg, WV, Memorial Church of the Brethren, pastor and missionary, 1012
Harsh, Norman Luther, 585, 1647, 2138
Harshbarger, Albert Edward, 1647, 2302
Harshbarger, Anna Elizabeth Casner, 587
Harshbarger, Anna (later Glick), 553
Harshbarger, Blair Caleb, 1647
Harshbarger, Bud, *599*
Harshbarger, C. W., 599, 1647
Harshbarger, Charles H., 626, 1647
Harshbarger, Daniel, 1647
Harshbarger, Elisabeth (later Filbrun), 490
Harshbarger, Elizabeth, 161
Harshbarger, Elizabeth Rinehart, 490
Harshbarger, Ethel, 2093
    on Pleasant Hill CB Congregation, IL, 2362
Harshbarger, Ethel (later Henderson), *599*
Harshbarger, Ethel (later Weddle), 748
Harshbarger family, 415, 1326, 1930, 1958, *See also* Hershberger family
    Hertzler (Hartzler) family, 601

Salem Church of the Brethren, OH, 1138
Harshbarger, Florence (later Myers)
    Myers, Tobias Timothy, wife of, 905
Harshbarger (Harshberger), John M., 1647
Harshbarger, Henry, 490, 1647
Harshbarger, Hugh Priestley, 1958
Harshbarger, Isaac J., 550, 1647
Harshbarger, J., 1647
Harshbarger, J. H., 638
Harshbarger, J. J., 1647
Harshbarger, Jacob, 1865
Harshbarger, James, 72
Harshbarger, John, 490, **587,** 1958
    Mill Creek Church of the Brethren, VA, elder, 832
Harshbarger, John J., 587
Harshbarger, John M., 599
Harshbarger, John, Sr., 1647
Harshbarger, John W., 626, 740
Harshbarger, John William, 1647
Harshbarger, Joseph W., 1647
Harshbarger, Joshua Potter, 8, 599, 1647
Harshbarger, L. B., 673
Harshbarger, Lori B., 599, 674
Harshbarger, Luther H., 113, 545, **587,** 1647, 1958, **2374, 2383,** *See* prisoners of war
    War Prisoner's Aid program, 1058
    Young Men's Christian Association (YMCA), 1390
Harshbarger, Lydia Frantz, 490
Harshbarger, Margaret Ann Long, 587
Harshbarger, Margaret Early, 587
Harshbarger, Maria Eva, 1865
Harshbarger, Marian, *See* Prisoners of War program
Harshbarger, Martha Curwin, *599*
Harshbarger, Mary Van Dyke, 8
Harshbarger, Rebecca (later Gibson), 592
Harshbarger, Richard Benjamin, 1647
    North Manchester, IN, Church of the Brethren, elder (moderator), 949
Harshbarger, Samuel, 1647
Harshbarger, Samuel A., 587
Harshbarger, Sarah C. (later Miller)
    Miller, Robert Henry, wife of, 841
Harshbarger, Susannah, 161
Harshbarger, Vinna C. (later Rarick), 2041
Harshbarger, William, 750
Harshbarger, William R., 1647
Harshberger, Cornelius W., 1647
    Maple Grove Church of the Brethren, PA, 791
Harshberger, Estelle, 2107
Harshberger family, 752
Harshberger (Harshbarger), John J., Sr., 1647
Harshberger, I. A. B., 1647
Harshberger, Ira
    Maple Grove Church of the Brethren, PA, 791
Harshberger, J. S., 1647
Harshberger, Jennie
    Maple Grove Church of the Brethren, PA, 791
Harshberger, John William, 1958
Harshberger, L. B., 752
Harshberger, Lori B., 1647
Harshberger, Rebecca
    Maple Grove Church of the Brethren, PA, 791
Harshey, John, 1315, 1647

Mohler, Samuel Sayler, 868
Harshey, Susanah (later Long), 753
Harshman, Christian, 216, 1647
Harshman family
    Grossnickle family, 574
    Rotruck (Rothrock, Roderick) family, related to, 1124
Harshman, Michael
    Middletown Valley Church of the Brethren, MD, 826
Harshman, Nancy
    Santa Ana, CA, Church of the Brethren, 1144
Harshman, Ora B., 42, 1647
Harshman, Samson, 1647
Harstein, Richard, 1305
Harstine, Anna, 355
Harstine, Richard F., 1647
    Milroy, PA, Grace Brethren Church, 843
Harstine, Richard G.
    Roanoke, VA, Garden City Grace Brethren Church, pastor, 1113
Hart, Catherine Shoup, 587
Hart congregation, 1235
Hart, David M., 1647
Hart, Doris Virginia (later Shultz), 2249
Hart, Elizabeth Sellen, 587
Hart family, 215, 2053
Hart, Freeman Hansford, 1958
Hart, Henry S., *See* Hart family
Hart, Ira M., 1647
Hart, J. A., 1647
Hart, James, 1647
Hart, John, 297, 464, 505, **587,** 1281, 1295, 1647, 2126
Hart, MI, 410
    Dunkard Brethren Congregation, **2196**
    Church of the Brethren, 265, **587**
    Michigan Brethren settlement, 824
    Pleasant Ridge Dunkard Brethren Congregation, OH, mission point, 1034
Hart, Phoebe (later Murray)
    Murray, Samuel, wife of, 897
Hart, Russell, 1647
Hart, Susannah Smith, *See* Hart family
Hart, Virginia Faye (later Saner), 2053
Hartenburg, castle of, 1059
Harter, A. L., 1647
Harter, David, 1647
Harter, Dixie, 1215
Harter, Eli, 429
Harter family, 708, 1326, 1383, 2060
    Greene, IA, Church of the Brethren, 570
    Howard Co. Old German Baptist Brethren Church, IN, 633
Harter, Goldie Flora, 1958
Harter, Harold, 1215
Harter, Israel, 1647
    North Manchester, IN, Church of the Brethren, elder, 949
Harter, Joseph, 429, 1647
    North Manchester, IN, Church of the Brethren, 949
Harter, Lawrence, 384
Hartford City, IN
    Church of the Brethren, 128, **587**
    Grace Brethren Church, **587**
Hartford School of Missions
    Swartz, Goldie Elizabeth, 1243
Hartford Theological Seminary

Kulp, Harold Stover, 709
Pickett, Clarence Evan, 1021
Widdowson, Sadie Olive, 1343
Hartley, Anna, 245
Hartley Church of the Brethren, TX,
587–588
Hartley, Emanuel, 245
Hartley, Mrs. Thomas
Muncie, IN, Brethren Church, 896
Hartley, Thomas
Muncie, IN, Brethren Church, 896
Hartman, A. G., 1647
Hartman, Abraham, 583
Hartman, Adam, 583, 1959
Hartman, Anthony, 106, *See also* Hartmann,
Anthony, 1648, **2383**
Hartman, Asa (Amos) A., 1647
Hartman Association Historians, 1959
Hartman, Cecil Lee, 1647
Hartman, Charles, L., Jr., 2281
Hartman, Christian, 1647
Hartman, CO
mission point for Wiley, CO, Church of
the Brethren, 1345
Hartman, Daniel, 1647
descendants, 1959
Hartman, Elaine (later McGann), 2286
Hartman family, 686, 750, *See* Hardtmann
family
1761–1975, 1959
family history, 2008
Hyattsville, MD, University Park
Church of the Brethren, 641
Hartman, Gertrude Delores, 1844
Hartman, Grover L., 1958
Hartman, Guy N., 1647
Hartman, Henry
will, excerpt from, 1917
Hartman, J., 1647
Hartman, John, 768, 1351
Hartman, John E., 570, 1647
Hartman, John H., 1998
Hartman, John Obed, 1647
Hartman, Kenneth Irving, 365, 717, 1648
Hartman, Martin M., 1648
Pleasant View Church of the Brethren,
PA, elder-in-charge, 1037
Hartman, Mrs. Peter, 264
Hartman, P. S., Sr., 1648
Hartman, Peter, 264
Hartman, Peter S., 1958–1959
Hartman, R. G., 1648
Hartman, Regina, 2094
Hartman, Ruth Leanna Burkholder, 1959
Hartman, Samuel, 2063
Hartman, Susannah Long, 583
Hartman, Walter Webb, 1648
Hartman, Wayne, 2281
Hartman, William
Monroe Co. Church of the Brethren,
IA, 870
Hartman, W(illiam) H., 1648
Hartmann, Conrad, 1941
Hartnack, K.
historical writing, 611
Hartnack, Karl, 1959
Hartnack, Wilhelm, 1959
Hartong, Dana, 1311, 1648, **2383**
Hartough family, 1959
Hartranft, Kathryn Stone, 1959
Hartranft, Ralph M., 1961
Hartranft, Samuel David, 1648
Hart's Run, PA

Ryerson Station Church of the
Brethren, PA, preaching point,
1132
Hartsell, Jacob, 514
Hartsell, Mary, 514
Hartsell, Robert Allen, 274, 514, 1648
Hartsoch, Alfred, 1648
Hartsock, Daniel, family
Pipe Creek Church of the Brethren,
MD, 1026
Hartsock family, 1959
Hartsough, Clara Culler, 588, 1996
Hartsough, Daniel, 1648
Hartsough, Daniel F., 588, 1648
Hartsough, Daniel Max, 588
Hartsough, Dorothy (later Bolyard), 588
Hartsough, Edwin, 1648
Hartsough, Elizabeth (later Rosenberger)
Rosenberger family, 1123
Hartsough family, **588,** 1281, 1959, **2374**
Hartsough, George, 1281
Hartsough, Harvey L., 538, 588, 1648,
2140
Ministry and Home Mission Commis-
sion (CB), 848
North Manchester, IN, Church of the
Brethren, pastor, 949
Hartsough, Isaac, 424
Seneca Church of the Brethren, OH,
minister, 1166
Hartsough, John W., 124, 588, 1281, 1648
Hartsough, Joseph, 588, 1648
Hartsough, Lois (later Leasure), 588
Hartsough, Mary (later Miller), 588
Hartsough, Mary Mae, 1959
Hartsough, Max Daniel (Daniel Max), 1648
Hartsough, Roberta (later Berkebile), 588
Hartsough, Vera (later Finnell), 588
Harttmann, Johan(n) Christoph
organ builder, 900
Hartville, OH
Nimishillen Church of the Brethren,
annual meeting meetinghouse, 937
Hartville, OH, Calvary Chapel
Free Brethren, 513
Hartville, OH, Church of the Brethren, 416,
588
Hartwell, Jerry Lee, 1343, 1648
Hartz, Paul, 1648
Hartzel family, 1878
Hartzel, Gwendolyn Price (Nyce)
on Goshall, Leanna and descendants,
2346
on Nyce, Abraham and descendants,
2346
on Nyce, Susan (Goshall) and descen-
dants, 2346
Hartzell family, 2077
Hartzell, Michael, 1878
Hartzell, Nancy, 1878
Hartzler, Abram Lincoln, 588
Hartzler family, 1959, *See* Hertzler family
Hartzler, H. Harold, 1959, 1335
on King family, 2335
Hartzler, Lydia Schrock, 588
Hartzler, Martha Jones, 1959
Hartzler, Merle D., 1959
Hartzler, Naomi Schrock, 588
Hartzler, R. Z., 1959
Hartzler, Russell M., 242, **588**
harvesting machines
Houser, Daniel, 633
Harvey, Amos M., 1648

Harvey Co., KS, 1316
Royer Community Church of the
Brethren, KS, 1128
Harvey, Earl, 1959
Harvey family
English River Church of the Brethren,
IA, 447
Jasper, MO, Church of the Brethren,
669
Harvey, Frank H., 1648
Harvey, George W., 249, 1648
Newton, KS, Church of the Brethren,
pastor in, 934
Harvey, Gregory G., 2166
Harvey, H. W., 1648
Harvey, Henry M., 1648
Harvey, John Wesley, Jr., 468, 1648, 2302
Harvey, Orin, 1648
Harvey, Timothy Paul, 2281
Harvey, William M., 469, 572, 669, 1648
Hask, Edna Gretchen, 1849
Haskell, Harvey P., 1648
Haskins, Edward Erastus, 72, 673, 675,
1648
Portis, KS, Grace Brethren Church,
pastor, 1048
Haskins, R. R., 662
Hassan, Hazel Nice, 1959
Hassert, Arrent, Jr.
account of Dunker meetinghouse, 1919
Hassinger, Glenn Otho, 1648
Hassinger, Otho John, 157, 1648
Hassock family, 170
Hastings, MI
Grace Brethren Church, **588**
Hope Church of the Brethren, MI, 629
Hastings Street Mission, Chicago, IL, 171,
1296, See also Urban Ministry;
urban ministry
Bethany Brethren Hospital, 810
Hoff, Emanuel Buechley, 616
Van Dyke, Catherine Beery, 1302
White, Roy Irvin, 1339
Hatboro, PA, Suburban Grace Brethren
Church, **588,** 1220
Hatch, Burton G., 688, 1648
Hatch, Frost
Myrtle Point, OR, Church of the
Brethren, pastor, 906
Hatcher, William Landon, 1648
Rossville, IN, Church of the Brethren,
minister, 1124
Hatfield Church of the Brethren, PA, **588,**
1251, *See* Telford, PA, Penn Valley
Grace Brethren Church
Pine Run German Baptist Brethren,
2377
Harleysville, PA, Indian Creek Church
of the Brethren, 584
Hatfield, Harvey, 913
Hatfield, Mary (later Beery), 1302
Hatfield, PA, congregation
Nyce, William Godshall, 952
Hatfield, Terry, 1648, 1959, 2179
on Evangel 21. Vol., No. 1, 2336
Peoria IL, (First) Church of the
Brethren, pastor, 1009
Hathaway, Carrie E., **588–589,** 1849
Hathaway, Clerissa Ann, 2080
Hathaway, John Wesley, **588–589,** 913,
1648, 1849
Hatmark School mission point
Oakton, VA, Church of the Brethren,

958

hats, 400, *589, 589, See also* bonnets; caps; prayer veils
    Church of the Brethren, 254, 300, 301
    Dunkard Brethren, 254
    Dunkard Brethren and nonconformity, 940
    Nead, Peter, 404
    Old German Baptist Brethren men, 967
    plain people, 1029
    Plymouth Brethren, 1038
Hatt, Ralph R., 1648
Hattinger, Silas, 1243, 1648
Hatton, Ralph Russell, 1648
    Newberg, OR, Church of the Brethren, pastor in, 933
    Omaha, NE, Church of the Brethren, minister, 974
Haubert, Anna Mae Rowe, 1959
Hauch, Margaret (later Naas), 909
Hauer family
    Myerstown, PA, Grace Brethren Church, 906
Haug, Johann Friedrich, 19, 120, **589,** 1228, 1959, **2374**
Haug, Johann Jakob, 120, 589, 1959–1960
Haug, William, 1648
Haugendaugler, William, 373
Hauger, Belinda (later Livengood), 750
Hauger family
    Rockwood Church of the Brethren, PA, 1118
Hauger, Jacob S., 1323, 1648
    Middle Creek Church of the Brethren, PA, minister, 825
Haugh, Laura Esther, 1960
Haugh, Samuel, 1648
Haughendoughler, John, 1648
Haughman family, 1958
Haught, Albert M., 1648, 2302, **2383**
Haughtelin, Eliza Diehl, 589
Haughtelin, Jacob Diehl, **589,** 1648, 1960
    Panora, IA, Church of the Brethren 992
Haughtelin, James Irving, 1649
Haughtelin, John C., 589
Haughtelin, Maggie D. Chamberlain, 589
Haughtelin, N. Jennie Howell, 589
    Haulk, Randy Lee, 2281
Haun, C. C., 1649
Haun, Peter, *See* Hon, Peter
Haus, Catharine, 2070
Hausa language
    Fellowship of Churches of Christ in Nigeria, 484
Hausenfluck family
    Mount Pleasant Brethren Church, VA, 886
Hauser, Barbara (later Wolfe), 1358, 1359
Hauser family
    Dutch Bethel, German Baptist Brethren Church, 2373
Hauser, Frederick
    Dutch Bethel, German Baptist Brethren Church, 2373
Hauser, Stanley F., 332, 564, 1649
    Martinsburg, PA, Grace Brethren Church, pastor, 798
Haussmann, William A., 1960
Hautline family
    Roanoke, LA, Church of the Brethren, 1112
Haverford College Library (Haverford, PA),

52

Havice, Jack Lamar, 1649
Hawaii, **589–590**
    Foreign Missionary Society (BC, FGBC), 501
Hawbaker, Abram W., 179, 1649
Hawbaker, Annie Robins, 1128
Hawbaker, Claude C., 1960
Hawbaker, Duane L., 2281
Hawbaker, Emmert C., 1128
Hawbaker, Gladys Violet, 1843
Hawbaker, Gladys Violet (later Royer), **1128, 2378, 2388**
Hawbaker, John, 2302
Hawbaker, Roy Brechbill, 1649
Hawbaker, Samuel B., 1649
Hawbaker, Susie (later Royer), 1128
Hawbecker, Merle R., 582, 1649
Hawbecker, P. M., 1649
Hawk, Sarah A. (later Lauver), 728
Hawk, Terry, 1649
Hawke, Martin R., 1649
Hawke, Walter E., 581
Hawker, Catherine Putterbach (later Wolff), 1070
Hawker, Jacob, 1070
Hawkins Co., TN, 264, 1253, 1340
    Midway Church of the Brethren, TN, 827
Hawkins, Gilbert, 104, 122, 1649
Hawkins, Sally (later Wine), 1349
Hawkins, Stanley Harold, 2281
Hawkley, Louise
    on peace movement, 2336
Hawks, W. H.
    Mount Airy, NC, First Church of the Brethren, 880
Hawn, Jacob W., 1649
Hawn, Peter, *See* Hon, Peter
Hawood, Nathan, 1649
Haworth, Paul B., 1649
Hawpatch congregation , IN, 1267
Hawpatch, IN, Church of the Brethren, *See* Topeka, IN, Church of the Brethren
Haws, Gwen Hunsaker, 1976
Hawser, Joseph, 1649
Hawthorne, Anna Mary, 1839
Hawthorne, Bess L., 1960
Hawthorne Church of the Brethren, TN, **590**
Hawthorne, FL, Pine Grove Mission, 691
Hawthorne, Leroy M., 1649
Haxtun, CO, Church of the Brethren, 324, **590,** 1221
Hay, Christopher A., 2175, 2281
Hay, David R., 1998
Hay, Dorothy Ethel, 1849
Hay family
    Montclair, CA, Grace Brethren Church, 870
Hay, Frank E., 1649
Hay, James A., 1649
The Hay Loft Reporters
    publishing reports of Annual Meeting, 1069
Hay, William Newton, 1649, 2302
    Rockwood Church of the Brethren, PA, supply pastor, 1118
Haycock, Cecil Lee, 1276, 1649
    Meadow Mills Church of the Brethren, VA, minister, 806
Haycock Twp., PA

Lutheran Church, 2088
Hayden, James R., 1649
Hayer (Hyer) family
    family history, 1983
Hayes, Durward
    Romine Church of the Brethren, IL, providing leadership, 1121
Hayes family, 332
Hayes, Lynn (later Miller), 2287
Hayes, Rutherford B., 515, 912
Hayes Twp., McPherson Co., KS, 1387
Hayes, William A., 80, 1649, 2163, **2196–2197,** *2196,* 2302, **2383**
Haymaker, Jason
    Macedonia, OH, Western Reserve Grace Brethren Church, 2216
Haymaker, Jason Craig, 2281
Haynes family
    Mountain View Church of the Brethren, VA, 889
Haynes, Nathaniel S., 1960
Haynes, Peter Lawrence, 2281
Haynes, W. F. and Etta
    Patterson, CA, Church of the Brethren, 995
Haynes, William Franklin, 1649
Hays, Daniel, 288, 315, *590, 590,* 1649, 1960, 2053, 2082
    on Linville Creek CB, VA, 2354
    New Testament, 133
    on Shenandoah District CB, 2354
    World War I, 1370
Hays, Durward Eugene, 1649
Hays family, 1313, 2079
Hays, H. M., 1960
Hays, I. Minis, 1960
Hays, J. S., 1649
Hays, Jesse, 1649
Hays, John G.
    Shelby Co. Church of the Brethren, MO, leadership in, 1175
Hays, Kidder, 590
Hays, Lilian (later Oliver), 2033
Hays, Polly Lyon, 590
Hays, Sarah Hannah Catherine Meyers, 590
Haywood, (Jonathan) Nathan, 1649
Haywood, Nathan, 1295
A Hazard of New Fortunes (Howells), 747, 1975
Hazard, Samuel, 1960
Hazel, Jacob (Mr. and Mrs.), 558
Hazelton Union
    Sandy Creek Church of the Brethren, WV meetinghouse, 1143
Hazen, Lisa Lynn, 2281
Hazle Creek, KY, Baptist, congregation, 165
Hazlett (Haslett), James L., 1649
Hazlett, Lor(r)in Augustus, 121, 326, 347, 425, 746, 914, 1289, 1649
head coverings, *See* caps; hats; prayer veils
Head Start programs, 22
    Flower Hill Church of the Brethren, MD, 500
Headington, J. A., 1940
Headlee, IN
    Church of God (New Dunkers), 297
Headlee New Dunkard meetinghouse, IN
    Patton, Uriah, and, 996
headveiling
    Martin, Harold S. on, 2345
Heady, Hiram, 750

Heagley, Ferne (later Coffman), 1835, 2102
  Wetonka, SD, Willow Creek Church of
    the Brethren, 2379
Heagley, George A., 1649
  Wetonka, SD, Willow Creek Church of
    the Brethren, 2379
Heagley, John Homer, 1649
Heagy, Elizabeth (later Nye), 953
Heald, Edward Thornton, 1960
healing, **591**, 2021, 2027, *See also*
    Balsbaugh, C. H.; Dowie, J. A.;
    medical projects; medicine; patent
    medicine
  anointing for, 39–40, 591, 980, *See
    also* anointing the sick
  bibliography, 1871, 1885, 1904
  Cassel, Jacob C., 259
  faith healing, 2180
  Flory, Jacob S., 498
  Harrison, Stephen J., 586
  Holy Spirit, doctrine of, 624
  Holy Spirit Renewal Group, 625
  and hospitals, 123
  laying on of hands, 730–731
  ministry, 846
  nursing, 952
  Weiand, Albert Cassel, 1344
  worship and, 2266
Healing Home and Bible College
    Pentecostalism, 1008
health and medicine, **809–811**, 1887, *See
    also* Committee on Health and
    Welfare (CB); hospitals; wellness
  AIDS, **2129–2130**
  Association of Brethren Caregivers
    (ABC), 2129–2130, **2132**
  banning of, Faith Assembly, 2180
  Brethren Benefit Trust, insurance plans,
    2140
  death and dying issues, 370
  enteric fever, Landour, India, 217
  Fahrney, Peter, 466
  farming, 477
  fobidding of, Faith Assembly, 2180
  folk medicine, **2145–2146**
  Gribble, Florence Alma Newberry, 573
  healing of sick, 185
  Herring, Friedrich, 598
  Hospital Committee (CB), 630
  Hostetler, Joseph, 631
  India, 651
  The Inglenook Doctor Book, 656, 1978
  institutions, 19
  Interchurch Medical Assistance, Inc.
    (IMA), 657–658
  James Gribble Memorial High School,
    668
  list of institutions
    international, 1831
    USA, 1827
  medical projects, 808, 809
  Nigeria mission work, 936, 937
  patent medicines, 995
  Poling, James on, 2350
  pseumonic plague epidemics, Liao
    Chou, China, 217
  Snyder, Graydon F. on Anabaptists and,
    2357
  value of spiritual care in, 2157
Heaney, Howell J., 2094
Hearst press, 24
The Heart of the Crimson Cross (Henry),
    748

Heastand (Heistand, Histand), Jacob,
    1649
Heastand (Hiestand, Heestand), Abraham,
    1649
Heaston, Christian, 602
Heaston family, *See* Hiestand family
Heaston, Ollie (later Eberly), 417
Heater, Noah B., 1649
Heater, Wesley, 172
Heath family
  Hancock, MN, Church of the Brethren, 582
  Heatherdowns Church of the Brethren,
    Toledo, OH, 1266–1267
Heatherdowns, OH, Church of the Brethren,
    720, *See also* Toledo, OH,
    Heatherdowns Church of the
    Brethren
Heatwole, Daniel R., 1960
Heatwole family, 2095
  Eagle River, AK, Grace Brethren
    Church, 2175
Heatwole, Fannie, 2095
Heatwole, John L.
  on Civil War, impact of, 2336
Heatwole, Magdalena (later Showalter),
    753
Heatwole, Merle E., 1649, 2302
Heaven, **591**, *See also* eschatology; Hell;
    millennialism; resurrection
  doctrine on, 185
  eschatology, 453
  preaching about, 1053
Heavener, Ulysses S. A., 1960
Heavenly Recipes from Dunker Kitchens,
    340–341
Hebrew language, 160
Hebrew Old Testament, 43
Hebrews
  2:9, 55
  3:6, 14, 55
  6:2, 85
  10:22, 84
  book of, 1975
  Kent, Homer Austin, Jr., 2211, 2340
  McCann, Samuel N. on study of, 2344
Hebron, **591**
  Ephrata Community, 448
Hebron, ND, 164
Hebron School, preaching point maintained
    by Kansas Center Church of the
    Brethren, KS, at, 683
Hebron Seminary, 208, **591**, *See also* edu-
    cation; elementary education; sec-
    ondary education
  Bowman, Paul Haynes, 168
  Graybill, Alice Minora Hoffer, 567
  Graybill, Jacob Franklin, 567
  Mow, Anna Beahm and Baxter Merrill,
    890
  Nokesville, VA, Church of the
    Brethren, meetings at, 939
  Strayer, Ord Lee, 1228
Hebron, VA, meetinghouse, 164
Hebron, VA, mission point, Botetourt Co.,
    VA, Church of the Brethren, 164
Heck, Catherine Jean (later Shank), 1855,
    2247–2248
Heck family, 396
Heck, Finley, 102, 1649
Heck, Joel C., 1214, 1649
Heck, P. William, 264
Heck, Peter, Jr., 264, 1649
  North Hampton, OH, Donnels Creek

Old German Baptist Brethren
    Church, minister, 948
Heck, Roberta
  Shank, Catherine Jean (BC) and, 2247
Heck, S. M.
  Raystown Brethren Church, PA, pastor,
    1084
Heck, Vernon
  Shank, Catherine Jean (BC) and, 2247
Heck, William Peter, 1315, 1649
Heckel, Jeanne Wagoner, 1960
Heckert, Clinton I., 1960
Heckert, Mildred Mae Etter, 2197
Heckert family
  Orange City, FL, Calvary Grace
    Brethren Church, 975
Heckert, Mildred Mae Etter, 191, **2197**
Heckewelder, John, 2089
Heckler, James Y., 1960
  on Jarleysville and lower Salford
    Township, 2336
  poetry, 1039
Heckler, Jesse Y., 21, 1649
Heckler, Joseph, 1960
Heckler, Mary, 150
Heckman, Aaron
  Sidney, IN, Grace Brethren Church,
    1181
Heckman, Benjamin Franklin, 591, 592,
    912, 1385, 1649, 1838, 1960, *See
    also* Heckman, Minna Mote
  hospitals, 630
  medical missions, 807
Heckman, Barbara Ellen, 1837
Heckman, C. K., 1649
Heckman, C. L., 1649
Heckman, C. T., 1649
Heckman, Clarence C., 592, **592,** 1649,
    1838, 2076
Heckman, Creed, 115
Heckman, D. R., 1960
Heckman, David, 591, 592, 593
Heckman, David Harvey, 1650
Heckman, Elizabeth Miller, 591, 592
Heckman, Ellen (later Wagoner), 1961
Heckman family, 270, **593,** 750, 1960
Heckman, Galen Andrew, 1330, 1650,
    2030. 2302, **2383**
Heckman, Galen R., 1650
Heckman, Glenn Albert, 650, 1330, 1650,
    2302
Heckman, Hannah, 2353
Heckman, Hannah Brumbaugh, 593
Heckman, Harriet Price, 592
Heckman, Hattie Price, 592
Heckman, Irvin (Irwin) Daniel, 1650
Heckman, Jacob, 593, 713
Heckman, Jacob Hugh, **592,** 1650,
    1960–1961
Heckman, James Arthur, 1650
Heckman, Jennie A. Sellers, 592, 1961
Heckman, Johann Peter, 593
Heckman, John, 394, 438, 498, 592, **592,**
    1650, 1961
  Polo, IL, Church of the Brethren, elder,
    1045
Heckman, Kaylor (Kaylon, Keylon), 1650
Heckman, Lavina Moyer, 592
Heckman, Lucile Gibson, 550, **592,** 754,
    1838, 1961, **2387**
Heckman, Marlin L., 1650, 1859, 1961
  on Lordsburg Hotel/College building,
    2336

Heckman, Minna Mote, 591, **592**, 1838, 1961
Heckman, Olive (later Smeltzer), *See* Smeltzer, Olive Heckman
Heckman, Paul Hugh, 1650
Heckman, Peter, 1650
Heckman, S. K., 1650
Heckman, Samuel Brumbaugh, **593**, 1961
Heckman, Shirley J., 1327, 1961
    on congregational planning, 2336
    on covenant people, 2336
    on peace movement, 2336
    People of the Covenant (POC) (BC) and, 2237
Heckman, Vernon LeRoy, 1650
Heckman, William T., 270, 1215, 1650
Heckman, Winifred Adelaide, 593
Hector, Charles, 1274
Hedding, L. J.
    Golden Spring German Baptist Brethren Church, NE, 2374
Hedges, James A., 1961
Hedrick, George W., 593
Hedrick, J. A., 1650
    Maple Grove Church of the Brethren, NC, minister, 790
Hedrick, J. H., 1650
Hedrick, Jacob, 1264, 1650
    Nokesville, VA, Church of the Brethren, leadership in, 939
Hedrick, John, 1264
Hedrick, Laura E. N. Grossnickle, **593**, 1360, 1362, 1650, *See also* women ("Ministering Sisters")
    South Bend, IN, Ardmore Brethren Church, pastor, 1203
Hedrick, Sarah (later Flory), 498
Hedrick, William
    Rockford, IL, First Church of the Brethren, 1117
Hedricks, S. F., 1650
Hedwig Sophie, regent of Berleberg, 1354
Heebner, Sara (later Halladay), **580**, 1359
Heefner family
    Robins, IA, Church of the Brethren, 1115
Heestand, Aaron I., 1650
Heestand, Abraham, 602
Heestand, Eli L., 1650
Heestand family, *See* Hiestand family
Heestand, June Emelyne, 1846
Heestand, Marion
    North Georgetown, OH, Brethren Church, 948
Heestand, Warren, 1650
Heeter family, **593**, 1877
Heeter, Gorman B., 232, 593, 785, 1650
Heeter, Ken J., 1961
Heeter, Lydia (later Garber), 529
Heeter, Noah, 106
Heeter, Norman Bruce, 1650
Heeter, Robert Lynn, 1650, 2302
Heeter, Tessie M. (later Hoffman), 2202
Heeter, Wesley, 1650
Heffelfinger, Anna (later Zug), 1401
Heffley, Nathan L., 271, 448, 1650
Heffley, Robert Lee, 1650
Heffner, Joseph S., 1650
Heffner, Richard Allen, 1650, 2281
Hefner, Carl, 366
Hege, Christian, 1961
Hege, George, 1650
Hege, Marlin D., 106

Heidelberg, **593**
    confiscation of property, 334
    Frankenthal, 506
    Frenkendorf, 516
    Judaism, 677
    radical pietist dissension in, 990
    Wine family, 1350
Heidelberg Catechism, 241, **593**, 1258, 1563
    noncreedalism, 942
    Reformed Church and Brethren movement, 1092
    Sauer, Christopher, II, published by, 1146
Heidelberg house, Tulpehocken Church of the Brethren, PA, 1278
Heidelberg meetinghouse, PA, *762*
Heidelberg, PA, Church of the Brethren, *See* Reistville, PA, Heidelberg Church of the Brethren
Heier, Anna Barbara (later Shobe), 602
Heier, Clara Lutzler, 602, *See* Heier (Hire, Hyre, Hyer) family
Heier, Elizabeth (later Shobe), 602
Heier, Eve (later Hagler), 602
Heier family, *See* Heyer family
Heier (Hire, Hyre, Hyer) family, 2041
Heier, Lienert, 602, *See* Heier (Hire, Hyre, Hyer) family
Heier, Madaline (later Homan), 602
Heifer Project International, 9, 12, 54, 73, 113, **593–594**, 1331, 1373, 2090
    bibliography, 1871, 1897
    Brethren Church, 423
    Brethren Service Commission and, 198
    Brubaker, Leland Stanford, 218
    Bushong, Benjamin G., 233
    Church of the Brethren Emergency Disaster Fund, 2172
    Committee, 1097
    East Chippewa Church of the Brethren, OH, 415
    East Fairview Church of the Brethren, PA, 415
    Eberly, John H., 417
    Elizabethtown, PA, Church of the Brethren, 436
    Ethiopia, 458
    France, 506
    Germany, 200, 546
    Hartzler, Russell M., 588
    Helman, Alfred Blair, 2197
    Hershey, Milton C. on, 2336
    Holmesville Church of the Brethren, NE, 620
    Hoover, Susan Bame on, 2338
    Indiana, 653
    Italy, 665
    Japan, 669
    Larchmont Community Brethren Church, CA, 726
    livestock distribution, 684, 685
    material aid, 802
    McFarland, CA, Church of the Brethren, 774
    Metzger, Thurl D., 2222
    Middlebury, IN, Church of the Brethren, initiating, 826
    Mount Joy, PA, Florin Church of the Brethren, 882
    Nebraska Brethren contributions to, 921
    North Dakota, 2045

Pennsylvania Dutch, 1986
Petersime, Ray, 1012
Poages Mill Church of the Brethren, VA, 1039
Poland, 1040–1041
Polish Agricultural Exchange, 1041
Pritchett, Reuel Bowman, 1060
Puerto Rico, 1070
relief and social work, 301, 303, 312
Rolston, Frances Fitz Simon and William Wendell, 1120
Rural Life Association (RLA), giving funds to, 1131
Russia, 1288
Salem Church of the Brethren, OH, 1138
seagoing cowboys, 1161, *1161*
    sources on, 2313
Spain, relief work in, as basis for, 1207
Springfield, OH, First Church of the Brethren, 1215
United Nations Korean Reconstruction Agency (UNKRA), 1291
United Nations Relief and Rehabilitation Administration (UNRRA), 1291
west coast, 1979
West, Daniel, 1330, *1331*
world hunger issues (CB) and, 2266
youth story about, 1944
Zigler, Michael Robert, 1398
heifers
    Hagerstown, MD, Church of the Brethren, 578
Heifers for Relief program, 594, 1098
Heifner family
    Orange, CA, Grace Brethren Church
Heiges, George L.
    on colonial military hospitals in Lancaster County, 2336
Heikes, Mary, 343
Heil, Walter G., 1650
Heiland, William
    Pittsburg, IN, Church of the Brethren, 1027
Heiligh family, 2102
Heilman, Edwin C., 2281
Heilman, Magdalena (later Scherffig), *See* Scherffig, Magdalena Heilman
heilsgeschichte
    definition of, 386
Heim, Christian "Christly," 148
Heim, Elmer N., 1650
Heim family, 148, 1995
Heim, Gottlieb, 148
Heim, Jeffrey D., 742, 2281
Hein, Cleo, 173
Hein, Cleonise, 1850
Hein family, 265
Hein, George, 265
Hein, Gerhard, 1961
Hein, Herman H., Jr., 558, 687, 705, 1277, 1650
Hein, Luella, 558, 687
Hein, Rolland Neil, 496, 1650, 1961
Heinemann, Barbara, 330
Heiner, R. F., 1650
Heiney, D. B., 463
Heiney (Heinly), Daniel, 1650
Heiney (Heiny), Daniel B., 1650
Heinhold, Laura Kauffman, 1961
Heinicke, Milton H., 1961
Heinrich, Harry, 1335

Heinrich Roth (Rhoades) House, 214
Heinrich, Walter, 360, 1335
    Olive Grove Old German Baptist
        Brethren Church, CA, minister and
        presiding elder, 973
Heinrich, Walter A., 1651, 2302, **2383**
Heinrici, Max, 1961
Heinsman, William G., 1651
Heinstand, Elizabeth, 208
Heintz, Merril S,
    St. Petersburg, FL, First Church of the
        Brethren, pastor, 1135
Heiny, Anna (later Smeltzer), 1191
Heiny, Lena, 217
Heinz, H. J.
    Brumbaugh, Martin Grove and, 223
Heinz, Merril Samuel, 1651
Heiple family
    Freeling Settlement Old German
        Baptist Brethren Church, WV, 514
Heiple, Theodore, 1651
Heise, Johannes, *See* Heisey, John
Heisel, Grace, 364
Heisel John C., 198
Heiser, Escil
    Medford, OR, Church of the Brethren,
        pastor, 806
Heisey, Aaron S., 1651
Heisey, Amos S., 1651
    Mohler Church of the Brethren, PA,
        free minister, 868
Heisey Building
    Elizabethtown College, 437
Heisey, Chester Ray, 1961
Heisey, Enos B., 1651
Heisey family, 231, **595**, 1961
Heisey, Grace Nedrow, 1838, 1961
Heisey, Henry, 1878
Heisey, Herman Biever, 1651, 1838–1839,
    1961
Heisey, Herman E.
    Riddlesburg, PA, Church of the
        Brethren, minister, 1108
Heisey, Irwin W., 1651
Heisey, Isaac T., 1961
Heisey, Jan L., 2281
Heisey, Jeremiah, 1651
Heisey, John, 595
Heisey, John W., 1961
Heisey, Lester, 595
    Rock House Church of the Brethren,
        KY, pastor, 1117
Heisey, Marthan N. (later Stauffer), 1219
Heisey, Martin Luther, 1961
Heisey, Martin N., 1651
Heisey, Nancy (later Hess), 2281
Heisey, Orville Lester, 1651
Heisey, Paul Eugene, 1330, 1651
Heisey, Peter S., 1651
Heisey, Ralph B., 1651
Heisey, Sue Catheryn Rinehart, 1839, 1919
Heisey, Susannna Bucher, 1878
Heisey, Walter Jeremiah, 595, 1651, 1839,
    1936
Heisey, Walter Kline, 1651, 2281
Heisey, William, 1651
Heishman, Charles, 1276
Heishman family, 1958
Heishman, George W., 1276
Heishman, Irvin Russell, 2281
Heishman, Nancy S., 2281
Heisler, Arthur Gustav, 1651
Heisler, John, 1651

Philadelphia, PA, First Church of the
    Brethren, minister, 1015
Heiss, Heide-Inge
    on Evangelischen Schule am Karl-
        splatz, 2336
Heiss, Willard C., 1971
Heist family, 233
Heistand, A. I., 1651
Heistand, Barbara (later Moore), 2021
Heistand, Eli L., 504
Heistand family, 256, *See* Hiestand family
Heistand (Hastant, Hystandt) family, 2021
Heistand, Isaiah, 424
Heistand, Jacob, 152, 424, 602, 1651
Heistand, Jesse R., 1651
Heistand, Mary Eby, 602
Heitinger family
    Mesa, AZ, Community Church of the
        Brethren, 2222
Heitler, Andrew, 595
Heitler, Hannah Martin, 595
Heitler, Maria Susanna, 595
Heitler, Richard R., **595**
Heitler, P. Martin, **595**
Heitz, Sophia, 116, 1651
    Milmine Church of the Brethren, IL,
        elder, 843
Helbert, Minnie
    Mulvane, KS, Brethren Church, 895
Helbig, Richard E., 1859
Heldt, James, 749
Helen, Margaret, 1850
Helfer, Peter, 1651
Helfer, Phil, 2281
Helfert, Mary (later Waltz), 1316
Helft, 1651
    early minister at Ten Mile Church of
        the Brethren, PA, 1253
Helft family, 1253
hell
    doctrine on, 185
    eschatology, 453, 454
    Martin, David, doubts about eternal
        punishment, 797
    preaching about, 1053
Hell, doctrine of, **595**, *See also* eternity;
    universalism
Hell-for-Certain, KY, 689
Heller, Christopher, 1961
Heller family, 1961
    Ellison Church of the Brethren, ND,
        442
Heller, Jack B., 2281
Heller, Jacob, 1651
Heller, W. J., 1961
Hellevoetsluis
    historic sites, 609
Helm, C. Martin, 1651
Helm, Charles Allen, 1651
Helm family
    Mack family, 778
Helm, Martin, 1651
Helm, O. H., 1651
Helm, Otto F., 1651, 1961
Helman, Alfred Blair, 1651, 1961, **2197**,
    2197
    Helman, Patricia Kennedy, 2197
    Manchester College, President, 786
    Newton, KS, Church of the Brethren,
        pastor in, 934
    North Manchester, IN, Church of the
        Brethren, elder (moderator), 949
Helman, Adam, 1651

Helman, Cora Wise, 1961
Helman, Etta (later Flory), 1620
Helman, H. H.
    New Carlisle, OH, Church of the
        Brethren, elder in, 926
    Onekama, MI, Church of the Brethren,
        minister, 975
Helman, Harley Harrison, 1651, 1962
Helman, Harriet Ann, 2197
Helman Henry E., 2197
Helman, Howard Holmes, 1651
    Peru, IN, Church of the Brethren,
        pastor, 1010
Helman, James Q.
    Poplar Grove, OH, Church of the
        Brethren, 1046
Helman, James Quinter, 1651
Helman, Leslie, 579
Helman, Luie Pritt, 2197
Helman, Patricia Dawn Kennedy, 1651,
    1962, 2142, 2281, **2197**, *2197*
    on CB signs and symbols, 2336
Helmershausen, Adella, 1962
Helmick, Raymond Allen, 1315, 1651
Helms, Claxton, 1962
Helms, T., 1962
Helmuth, Wilma (later Schlabach), 2031,
    2057
HELP, *See* Homeless European Land
    Program;
Help for the Homeless
    repatriated prisoners of war, aid for,
        1058
The Helping Hand, **595**
    Missionary Reading Circle, 856
Helping Hands, **595**
    Emmert, David, 444
    Home for Orphan and Friendless
        Children, 625
    Vol. 1, 1882, 1962
Helse, Lewis J., 1651
Helsel, Charles, 1651
Helsel, Samuel A., 1651
Helsel, Samuel L., 1651
Helser, Albert David, 305, 306, *595,*
    595–596, 596, 709, 1651, 1839,
    1962, 2062
    mission schools, 854
    medical missions, 807
    Nigeria mission work, 936
Helser, Carl, 1651
Helser, David M., 595
Helser, Emma S. Zartman, 595
Helser family, 731
Helser, Lola Bechtel, 305, 596, **596,** 709,
    1839, 1871, **2374**
Helsey, Lawrence M., 330
Helsley family, 1868
Helsley (Helsey), Lawrence M., 1651
Helsley, Lawrence
    St. Luke, VA, Brethren Church, pastor,
        1135
Helstern, Bessie Erbaugh, 596
Helstern, George, 596
Helstern, Harold E., 1651
Helstern, Mary Sue (later Rosenberger),
    2049, 2291
    on Bethany Hospital, 2353
    on Brethren Health and Welfare
        Association, 2353
    on Brethren Homes, 2353
    on indigenization of missions, 2353
    on the Lord's Prayer, 2353

on peace in Vietnam, witnessing for, 2353

on Puerto Rico, Brethren in, 2353

on wellness from Biblical perspective, 2353

Helstern, Russell Fred, 247, 249, **596**, 1651, 1962

Helstern, Vina Bowers, 596

Helton, Austin, 1651

Helton, Hardin P., 1652

Heltzel, Charles Henry, 513, 1652

Riddlesburg, PA, Church of the Brethren, minister, 1108

Helwig, George, 1937

Helwys, Thomas, 87

Hemet, CA

Grace Brethren Church, **596**

Church of the Brethren, **596**

Hemming, A. L., 1652

Hempfield Church of the Brethren, PA, 416, **596**

Salunga, PA, Church of the Brethren merging with East Petersburg, 1140

Hempstead, Joshua, 1962

hen-medics

medical practice by women, 810

Henard, David Lafayette, 1652

Henckels, Eng(?) Everts, 596

Henckels, Johann Frederich, **596**, 923, **2374**

Solingen Brethren, 1201

Henckels, Matthias, 596

Hendershot, Regina Ruth, 1855

Henderson, Archibald, 1962

Henderson Co., TN, 353, 1253

Henderson, Ethel Harshbarger, *599*

Henderson family, 715

Henderson, S. C., 211, 318, 532, 581, 738

Morrill, KS, (First) Brethren Church, pastor, 876

Henderson, S. E., 515

Henderson, Samuel Chadbourne, 1652

Henderson, Sarah Miller

Müller (Miller) family, 894

Hendrick, John

Rowland, Joseph, 1126

Hendricks, Catherine

Rome Old German Baptist Brethren Church, OH, 1121

Hendricks, Clark, Sr., 1652

Hendricks, Daniel, 334, 476, 596, 597, 1292, 1342, 1652

Mount Zion Brethren Church, OH, minister, 888

Hendricks, David Keith, 1380, 1652, 2281

Hendricks, F. A., 335, 410, 561

Hendricks family, 752, 1342, 1863, 1907

Jasper, MO, Church of the Brethren, 669

Snider, Jacob, descendants of, 1154

sources on, 2315

Hendricks, family

Dutchman's Creek German Baptist Brethren Church, NC, 411

Hendricks, Frances(?), 597

Hendricks, Francis, Jr., 1652

Hendricks, Franklin A., 334, 476, **596–597**, 1652

Hendricks, H, H., 741, 1243

Silver Creek Church of the Brethren, OH, salaried pastor, 1182

Hendricks, Harold Henry, 6, 1652

Hendricks (Henricks) family, **597**

Hendricks, Isaac, 596

Hendricks, J., 1652

Hendricks, J. R.

North Star Church of the Brethren, OK, 950

Hendricks, Jacob, 1652

Hendricks, James, 321, 475–476, 597, **597**, 690, 1292, 1342, 1357, 1383, 1652

Roland, Gasper, related to, 1126

Hendricks, James, elder, *See* Hendricks, John, elder

Hendricks, Jean Lichty, 1652, 1962, 2320

Hendricks, John, 165, 398, 596, 597, **597**, 689, 1288, 1292, 1342, 1357, 1652

Far Western Brethren, 475

H., John, 577

Hendricks, John, elder

North Carolina Brethren, 946

Hendricks, Joseph, 1652

Hendricks, Joseph C., 2281

Hendricks, Leah (later Sell), *See* Sell, Leah Hendricks

Hendricks, Lovina, 321

Hendricks, Mary (later Arnold), 741

Hendricks, Mary Pike, 596

Hendricks, Noah, 1652

Rome Old German Baptist Brethren Church, OH, 1121

Hendricks, Stanley, 244

Hendricks, Z., 752

Hendrickson, Andrew C., 1652

Hendrickson, Daniel C., 1652

Hendrickson, Fred Dale, 1652

Hendrickson schoolhouse, WV, 2125

Hendrix, Charles, 231

Hendrix, Wright, 231

Hengst, Victor A., 1652

Hengstenberg, W. H. Alfred, 1962

Henkel, Paul, 1962

Henkels Stan[islaus] V., 1859

Henkle family, 2079

Henley family

Jackson Co. German Baptist Brethren, IN, 667

Olive Branch German Baptist Brethren Church, IN, 973

Henline family, 16

Henline, Joseph, 16

Henman, Kirk L., 2281

Hennighausen, L. P., 1962

Henning, Elma, 1962

Henning, Elma Snyder

on Rinehart, Ulrich and descendants, 2336

Henning family

Minerva, OH, Grace Brethren Church, 843

Henning, G. Mark, 16

Mission Viejo, CA, Saddleback Valley Grace Brethren Church, associate pastor, 855

Henning, Henry Yost, 1962

Henning, Naomi, 1849

Henning, Ted, 1849

Henninger family, 1962

Henny (Henney), Clint L., 1652

Henrich Albrecht, Count of Sayn-Wittgenstein-Hohenstein, 72, 82, 120, 174, **597–598**, 683, 716, 1158, 1354, 1355, 1951

antinomianism communes and, 236

Hüttental, 639

Mack, Alexander, Sr., and New

Baptists of Schwarzenau, 776

Henrick, James, 597, 1652

Henricks, A., 633

Henricks, Daniel, 597

Henricks, David, 1652

Henricks, Eldo R., 1652

Henricks, Elizabeth Snider, 597

descendants, 1918

Henricks family, *See* Hendricks (Henricks) family

Henricks, George

descendants, 1918

Henricks (Hendricks), Zaccheus, 1652

Henricks, Jacob, 597, 1652

Henricks, John, 597, 1918

Henricks, Margaret, 597

Henricks, S. F., 1652

Henrickson, A. C., 467

Henrico Co., VA, 1335

Henrikson, Robert (Mr. and Mrs.), 439

Henry, Arthur, 1652

Henry, Barry Kenneth, 264, 2281

Henry, Carl F. H., 2179

Henry Co., IN, 226, 297, 1294, 1339, 2099

Church of God (New Dunkers), 297

migration of Brethren, 829

Patton, George, move to, 996

Paul family in, 996

Shultz and Paul families, 1156

Henry Co., MO, 373

Osceola Church of the Brethren, MO, 984

Henry Co., OH, 411, 1235

Sand Ridge Church of the Brethren, OH, 1143

Henry Co., VA, 324

Jones Chapel Church of the Brethren, VA, 676

Henry Creek meetinghouse

Loudonville Church of the Brethren, OH, 760

Henry, Dale R., 1652

Henry, Dean L., 1962

Henry, Evelyn (later Fiscel), 491

Henry family, 1274, 1865

Henry Fork Church of the Brethren, VA, 43, **598**

Henry, George, 79

Henry, Jane Grisso, 598

Henry, Jerry Maurice, **598**, 748, 1652, 1962–1963, 2188

Leatherman, Jacob, statement about, 733

Selma, VA, Church of the Brethren, minister, 1166

Henry, John Francis, 673, 1652

Henry, John Thomas, 598

Henry K. Ober Hall

Elizabethtown College, 438

Henry, Kenneth E., 2281

Henry Kurtz

Sala, Johann, printer for, 1136

Henry Kurtz organ

Rarick, Ron on, 2351

Henry, Kurvin D., 1652

Henry, Martin S., 1652

Henry, Patrick, 1652

Henry, Paul, 1652

Henry, Samuel, 1652

Henry, Thomas L., 1963

Henry, Tobias Forney (Francis), 613, 637, 674, 1652, 1963

Roaring Spring, PA, First Church of

the Brethren, pastor, 1114
Hensel, Ananias, 1652
    Roberts, Warren E. on cabinetmaking
        of, 2352
Hensel, George, 461
Hensel, L. W., 1963
Hensley, Forney, 1652
Hensley, Joel, 1652
Hensley, Raymond Keith, 2281
Hensley, Tony, 1652
Henson, Hardy Divers, 1652
Hepburn Twp, PA, 2085
Hepler, Ralph W., 1652
Hepner, B. F., 1652
Hepner family
    French Broad Church of the Brethren,
        TN, 516
Hepner, Walter, 1652
Heppe, Heinrich, 1963
    Reformed Church and Pietism, 1021
Hepton Union Church, Nappanee, IN
    Male, E. William, 2217
Herald Magazine (FGBC), 2256
The Herald of a Better Time (*Der Herold
    einer bessern Zeit*), 1255
herbal cures, 2145–2146
    Weaver, William Woys on Sauer,
        Christoph, II and, 2362
    Wilmann, Christa M. on Sauer,
        Christoph, II and, 2363
    Wilson, Renate on Sauer, Christoph
        and, 2364
Herbers, Gottfried, 1963
Herbert, Frank William, 2281
herbs
    "Saur's Kleines Kräuterbuch," 1990
Herbst, Jacob
    Pleasant View Church of the Brethren,
        PA, 1037
Herbst, Julia
    Pleasant View Church of the Brethren,
        PA, 1037
Herder, Barbara, 593
Herder, Elizabeth Dilts, 593
Herder, Elizabeth Rarick, 593
Herder, George, 593
Herder, John, 593
Herder, Margaret, 593
Herder, Sebastian, 593
Herdlijcka, Joyce
    Omaha, NE, Grace Brethren Bible
        Church, 974
"Here in Our Upper Room"
    hymns, 643
    Robinson, Paul Minnich, author, 1115
heresy
    historical church and heretic encyclo-
        pedia (trans), 2009
    Hostetler, Joseph, 631
    manuals for preaching, 2003
Herington, KS
    Holland Church of the Brethren, KS,
        619
Herington, KS, Church of the Brethren, 1,
    598, *See also* Danish mission
        ("Full Circle")
*Heritage and Promise/Church of the
    Brethren Past and Present*
    study guide for, 1916
Heritage of Devotion (Grisso), 574
    poetry, 1040
heritage tours, *See* Brethren Heritage Tours
Herli, Barbara Reetly, 583

Herli, Hans Rudolf, 583, *See also* Harley
    (Herli, Harli), Hans Rudolf
Herman, Daniel, 1963
Herman family, 211
Herman, Michael, 1652
Herman, Stewart Winfield, 1963
Hermandszoon, Jacob (James/Jacob
    Arminius), 55, 56
hermeneutics, *See* Bible
    definition of, 386
hermitage, Mack, Alexander, Jr.
    Weber, Philipp, 1325
Hermitage Presbyterian Church, VA, 2100
hermits
    Society of the Woman in the
        Wilderness members living as, 687
    Wohlfahrt (Welfare), Michael, 1355
Hermon Church
    Flat Rock Church of the Brethren, VA,
        494
Hermosa Beach, CA, Church of the
    Brethren, *See* Redondo Beach, CA,
        South Bay Community Church of
        the Brethren
Hermosa, CA, 255
Herndon, Edward Robbins, 1263, 1653
Herndon, VA, Chandon Brethren Church,
    2197
Hernley family, 1229, 1964
Herr, Allan Hershey, 374, 406, 1653
    Modesto, CA, Big Valley Grace
        Community Church (FGBC),
        pastor, 866
    Montclair, CA, Grace Brethren Church,
        pastor, 871
Herr, Alma, 406
Herr, Ames, 1653
Herr, Anna Zug, 598
Herr, Charles, 1653
Herr, Donald M.
    on pewterware, PA German, 2336
Herr family, 2079, *See also* Pursel, Vida
    Miller
Herr, Hans, 1963
Herr, John, **598**, 1653, 2111, *See also* law
    enforcement ("How to Handle a
        Thief")
    Mohrsville Church of the Brethren, PA,
        elder, 869
    Myerstown, PA, Church of the
        Brethren, elder-in-charge, 905–906
    Reading, PA, First Church of the
        Brethren, elder-in-charge, 1084
    Reistville, PA, Heidelberg Church of
        the Brethren, elder, 1095
    Richland, PA, Church of the Brethren,
        elder-in-charge, 1107
    treatment of thieves, 730
Herr, John Henry, 1839
Herr, Judy Zimmerman
    on peace movement, 2336
Herr, Mark V., 2165
Herr, Robert
    on peace movement, 2336
Herr, Theodore Witmer, 1963
Herr, Theresa Jane Mohler, 1839
Herr, Tobias H., 1653
Herrell family
    Pleasant Grove Church of the Brethren,
        NC, 1031
Herring, Charles R.
    Pine Ridge Church of the Brethren, VA
        and, 2238

Herring, Etha K.
    Pine Ridge Church of the Brethren, VA
        and, 2238
Herring, Friedrich, 545, **598**, **2375**
Herring Papers, Elkhart County Historical
    Society, 2375
    Kurtz, H., and aid for German group,
        1198
Herrington, Bruce, 1653
Herrington, Chester, 1653
Herrington, William, 720
Herrnhaag
    Marienborn Moravian Church center,
        330, 792
Herrnhut
    Moravian Church, 875
Herrnhuter, 2351
Herrnhuters, *See* Moravian Church
Herron, Isaac L., 45
Hersch, Elmer Myron, 195, **598**
Hersch family, 1963
Hersch, Lauree (later Meyer), 2133, 2286
Hersch, Minnie Mae Eshelman, 598
Hersch, Nevin B., 598
Hersch, Orville Robert, 462, 1653, 1963
Hersch, Paul S., 1653, 1963
    Modesto, CA, Church of the Brethren,
        866
Hersch, Sudie Swartz, 598
Herschberger, Barbara B. Chastain and Eli
    P., 1963
Herschberger, Benjamin S., 2078
Herschberger, Catharine Berlincourt, 2078
Herschberger family, 2078
    Snider, Jacob, descendants of, 1154
Herschberger, Jonathan, 2078
Herschberger, Joseph Coblentz, 1963
Herschberger, Lydia Schmucker, 2078
Herschberger, Orpha P. Cooperider, 2088
Herscher Community Brethren Church, IN,
    1319
Hersey, Isaac, 513
Hershberger
    Snake Spring Valley Church of the
        Brethren, PA, free minister, 1192
Hershberger, Absolom P., 1963, 2088
Hershberger, Ada Menno, 2079
Hershberger, Amanda Neil, 1963, 2106
Hershberger, Amy Janzen, 2088
Hershberger, Anne Lorene Krabill, 1963
Hershberger, Betty Lou, 1835
Hershberger, Catherine E. (later Miller)
    family record, 1931
Hershberger, D. L., 1653
Hershberger, Dorothy Verle, 2088
Hershberger, Drusilla Yoder, 1963
Hershberger, Eli Daniel, 1963
Hershberger, Eli P. H., 1963
Hershberger, Eli V., 1963
Hershberger, Eli W., 2041
Hershberger, Emanuel, 2018
Hershberger, Emanuel Joseph, 1963
Hershberger, Emma N. Oah, 1963
Hershberger, Esther Miller, 1963
Hershberger family, 1881, 2028, 2088, 2107
    genealogy, 1963
    Page Co., VA, 1963
    Somerset Co., PA, 1964
Hershberger, Gabriel, 2015
Hershberger, George, 599
Hershberger, George Washington, 1963
Hershberger, Guy F., 1963–1964
Hershberger, H. S., 1653

Hershberger (Harshbarger) family, **598–599**
Hershberger, Henry, 599, 1653
Hershberger, Henry and Elizabeth Bender
genealogy, 1988
Hershberger, Howard S., 1653
Hershberger, I. A. B., 1653
Hershberger, Iona (later Nale), 2028
Hershberger, Isaac, 1653
Hershberger, Isaac J., 1881, 2106
Hershberger, Isaac J. and Fannie J. Miller
genealogy, 1963
Hershberger, Jean H., 1964
Hershberger, Jesse, 760
Hershberger, John, 599, 2107
Hershberger, John Steele, 1653
Hershberger, Ketie Ann Gingerich
Schmucker, 1963
Hershberger, Leo Daniel, 1964
Hershberger, Maria Studebaker, 599
Hershberger, Mary E., 1898
Hershberger, Peter and Elizabeth Yoder
genealogy, 1963
Hershberger, Peter P. and Leah Hochstetler
genealogy, 1964
Hershberger, Philip, 1653
Hershberger, Ronald Duane, 695, 1653,
2281
Hershberger, S. (J.) A. B., 1653
Hershberger, Sarah (later Schrock), 2059
Hershberger, Solomon, 1653
Hershberger, Verda Elizabeth, 1838
Hershberger, William R., 1653
Hershey, Abraham, 599
Hershey, Andrew, 600, 2062
Hershey, Benjamin, 600
Hershey, Christian, 600
Hershey, Daniel, 1653
Hershey, Effie Bowman, 599
Hershey, Elizabeth (later Forney), 502
Hershey, Emmanuel, 1653
Hershey, Esther (later Hess), 601
Hershey family, **600**, 1214, 1958, 1964
Moscow, ID, Church of the Brethren,
878
Hershey Freindschaft, 1964
Hershey, Graybill, 1340, 1653, **2383**
Hershey (Harshey) family, 735
Hershey, Henry, 1964
Hershey, Hosie Eyster, 599
Hershey, Isaac, 345, 572, 600, 923, 1653
Moscow, ID, Church of the Brethren,
presiding elder, 878
Hershey, J. Eby, 1964
Hershey, Jacob, 600, 1964
Hershey, Jacob L., 1964
Hershey, Joel Nye, 1653
Hershey, John, 600, 735, 1653
Hershey, John G., 1653
Hershey, John W. G., 235, 1653
Hershey, John Willard, **599**, 660
Hershey, Joseph, 600
Hershey, Joseph and Fannie H., 1964
Hershey, Kenneth H., 1340, 1653
Hershey, Laura (later Barwick), 912
Hershey, Lewis Blaine (General), **599**, 707
Hershey, Mary Jan Lederach
on Salford Mennonite Meetinghouse
Schools, fraktur from, 2336
Skippack Mennonite Meetinghouse
Schools, fraktur from, 2336
Hershey, Milton C., 1340
on free ministry, 2336
on Heifer Project, 2336

memoirs, 2336
Hershey, Milton L., 1653
Hershey, PA, 36, 142
as Annual Meeting location, 36
Middletown, PA, Swatara Hill Church
of the Brethren, 826
Palmyra, PA, Church of the Brethren,
991
Spring Creek Church of the Brethren,
39, 332, **599–600**, *600*, 756, 1316,
1351, 2318
Hershey, Ruth W., 1964
Hershey, Scott Funk, 1964
Hershman family, 1908
Hershman, John R., 1653
Hershy family
New Holland, PA, Church of the
Brethren, 928
Hertz, Daniel Rhine, 1964, *See* Ephrata
Community, Patriot's Day at
Hertzer family
Maryville, TN, Oakland German
Baptist Brethren Church, 799
Hertzler, Annie Shank, 600 or Hertzler,
Mary Ziegler, *600*
Hertzler, Catherine Myers, 601
Hertzler, Dean A., 1309
Hertzler, Elizabeth Royer, 601
Hertzler, Ephraim M., 1264, 1653
Rockton, PA, Church of the Brethren,
pastor, 1118
Hertzler family, 1916, 1927, 2026
Royer family related to, 1128
Hertzler (Hartzler) family, **601**, 1964
Hertzler, Jacob, 601, 1964
Hertzler, John, 601, 1653
Hertzler, John, Sr., 1964
Hertzler, Jonas, 1653
Hertzler, Jonathan, 601
Hertzler, Mary Ann Hoffer, 600, 601
Hertzler, Mary Ziegler, 600
Hertzler, Samuel Hoffer, *600*, **600–601**,
1653, 1964
Elizabethtown College, 437
Hertzler, Silas, 1964
Hertzler, William, 600, **601**, 1653
Philadelphia, PA, North Philadelphia
Church of the Brethren, providing
leadership, 1016
Shamokin, PA, Church of the Brethren,
1171
Hertzog family
Hertzler (Hartzler) family, 601
Hertzog, J. Paul, 1653
Hertzog, P. H., 572, 1653
Herzog, W. E., 1653
Hesketh, Clarence M., 1653
Hesketh, Raymond C., 2281
Hesketh, William (Billy) Alan, 2281
Hess, Aaron, 1653
Hess, Abram, 601
Hess, Abram C., 471, 1653
Hess, Abram M., 737, 1653, 2302
Hess, Alan W., 2281
Hess, Andrew, 2067
Hess, Anna Mary Hawthorne, 1839
Hess, Arthur H., 1653, 1964
Painesville, OH, Church of the
Brethren, 989
Hess, Arthur R., 1653
Hess, Asher Laubach, 1964
Hess, Asher S., 1964
Hess, Balzer, 1964

Hess, Caroline Myer, 601
Hess, Cecil David, 1654
Hess churchhouse
Lititz, PA, Dunkard Brethren
Congregation, 749
Hess, Cora B. (later Ober), 960
Hess, Daniel, 496, 601
Hess, Daniel M., 1654, 2302, **2383**
Hess, David
medical practice, 810
Hess, David Roy, 1964
Hess, Donald L., 471, 1654
Hess, Dora (later Roupp), 2049
Hess, Earl, 1160
Hess, Eldon H., 2153, 2281
Hess, Elias, 2047
Hess, Elizabeth Grove, 601
Hess, Elizabeth Miller
Hess, James Arthur, 2198
Hess, Esther Hershey, 601
Hess, Esther Miller, 601
Hess, Evelyn (later Benedict), 2135
Hess family, **601**, 1219, 2067, 1964, 1965
history of, 1940
New Holland, PA, Church of the
Brethren, 928
Royer family related to, 1128
Hess, Frank Ezra, 1964
Hess, George, 1964
Hess, George Balser, 601
Hess, Hans, 1965
Hess, Hans Jakob, 601
Hess, Harvey J., III, 1654
Hess, Hattie Hazel, 2067
Hess, Henry, 1654
Hess, Hettie K. Horst, 1964
Hess-Higbee families, 1867
Hess, Homer Clifton, 673, 1654, 2302
Penn Run Church of the Brethren, PA,
pastor, 1004
Rockton, PA, Church of the Brethren,
pastor, 1118
Hess, Howard Robert, 2281
Hess, Israel, 601
Hess, J. Daniel, 1964
Hess, J. W., 1654
Hess, James Arthur, 42, 1654, 2302
farmer, church leader, **2198**
Pigg River Old German Baptist
Brethren Church, VA, elder-in-
charge, 1023
Hess, Jeremiah
medical practice, 810
Hess, John, 601
North Fork Old German Baptist
Brethren Church, IN, minister, 948
Hess, John A., 1654
Hess, John F., 1654, 2281
Hess, John Huber, 1964–1965
Hess, John M., 2281
Hess, John R., 2049
Hess, John Reinhart, Sr., 1965
Hess, Kathryn (later Nye), 952–953
Hess, Kathy
church governance and, 2264
Hess, Lois V. Benshoff
Hess, James Arthur, 2198
Hess, Lucinda Wright, 2047
Hess, Lydia Ruth, 1964
Hess, Margaret (later Eby), 1925
Hess, Martha (later Bechtel), 596
Hess, Martha (later Rensberger), 601
Hess, Mary Beckner, 601

Hess, Mary (later Weybright), 601
Hess, Matthew, 2153
Hess, Matthew Henry, 2281
Hess, Maurice Abram, **601,** 1864, 1875
  McPherson College, teaching, 781
  on OGBB conscientious objectors, 2336
  prisons, 1060
  sources on, 2314
  World War I, 1370, 1371
Hess, Mildred May (later Grimley), 748, 1838
Hess, Miles Stoner, 1965
Hess, Milton, 1654
Hess, Moses, 601, 1654
Hess, Nancy Heisey, 2281
Hess, Nannie Oyler, 601
Hess, Nicholas, 1964
Hess, Ray B., *See* Old German Baptist Brethren
Hess, Richard, 1654, 2153
Hess, Richard E., 471
Hess, Robert A., 307, 1654, 1839
  on Lafiya program, 2336
  on missionary activities of CB in Nigeria, 2336
Hess, Robert Haldeman, 1654
Hess, Robert O., 1654, 2302, **2383**
Hess, Roland R., 2281
Hess, Rosa Cripe, 601
Hess, Samuel, 601, 1964–1965
Hess, Samuel H., 1654
Hess, Stephen R., 2281
Hess, Susanna (later Eberly), 417
Hess, William, 558, 1654
Hess, William T., 471, 1654
Hess, Willis A., 42, 1654, **2383,** *See also* Old German Baptist Brethren
  Hess, James Arthur, 2198
Hess, Willis C., 42, 1654
Hesse, 545, **601–602**
  Community of True Inspiration, 330
  Grebe (Grebi), Georg, 569
  Kassel, 684
  Pennsylvania Germans from, 1006
Hesse, Clarence George, 1654
  Somerset, PA, Church of the Brethren, pastor, 1202
Hesse, D. G., 206
Hess(e) family, 1994
Hesse (Germany)
  Vetter (Fetter), Lucas, 1304
Hesta, L., 1965
Het Bloedig Toneel (Braght, ed.), 171
heterodoxy
  Johnson City, TN, Knob Creek Church of the Brethren, 672
heterosexuality
  homosexuality, 2204
Hetland, Arthur, 688
Hetric, Arthur, 1654
Hetric (Hedrick), Jesse P., 1654
  Philadelphia, PA, First Church of the Brethren, providing leadership, 1015
Hetrich (Hetterich, Hetrick), Jacob, 1974
Hetrick, Arthur D., 1654
  Oakland Brethren Church, New Bethlehem, PA, elder in, 925
Hetrick, Daniel J., 1654
  Oakland Brethren Church, New

Bethlehem, PA, elder in, 925
Hetrick, David A., 1654
Hetrick, Effie, 918
Hetrick (Heterick) Daniel, 1654
Hetrick (Hetterich, Hetrich), Jacob, 1974
Hetrick, J. P., 1654
Hetrick, Joseph, 1654
Hetrick, Martha Louise, 1937, 2085
Hetterich (Hetrick, Hetrich), Jacob, 1974
Das Heutige Signal (Hesta), 1965
Hevener, Charles William, 1654
  Mechanic Grove Church of the Brethren, PA, free minister and pastor, 806
Hevener Church of the Brethren, WV, **602,** 2125
  Hevener, Adam, 602
  Hevener Mission, 602
  Pocahontas Church of the Brethren, WV, 1039
Hevener, John W., 1654
Hevener, Ollie C., 1340, 1654
Hewitt, Alva L., 1654
Hewitt, Nancy Marie, 2281
Hey, Edward, 629
Hey, Grace, 629
Heyer (Hyer, Heier, Hire) family, **602**
Heyer, Robert, 1965
Heyner, John W., 1654
Heyser, Emanuel, 1654
  Philadelphia, PA, First Church of the Brethren, minister, 1015
Hiatt, Ashby
  Shelton Church of the Brethren, NC, deacon in, 1176
Hiatt, Elihu, 1654
Hiatt, Howard
  Shelton Church of the Brethren, NC, secretary-treasurer in, 1176
Hiatt, Ira T., 1654
Hiatt, Jacob, 1654
Hiatt, M., 1654
Hiatt, Nathan C., 1654
Hiatt, Paul W., 1654
Hibert, W. T., 16
Hickman, Eugene, 1654
Hickman family, 1863, 2099
Hickman, James Wortha, 1654
Hickory Grove, AR
  New Hope Church of the Brethren, 929
Hickory Grove Church of the Brethren, IL, 59, **602,** 1111
  Hope, Christian, 628
Hickory Grove Church of the Brethren, IN, **602,** 1316
Hickory Grove congregation, OH, 261, 343, 1265
  Flory, Abraham, 497
  Maple Grove Old German Baptist Brethren Church, OH, 791
Hickory Grove German Baptist Brethren Church, OH, 130
  historic sites, 609
Hickory Grove, OH, Church of the Brethren, 396, 1295, *See also* Tipp City, OH, West Charleston Church of the Brethren
Hicks-Byerly family, 1965
Hicks, C. T., 1654
Hicks, Cadmus Metz, 579, 1654
Hicks, Clyde O., 1654
Hicks, Elias Elbert, 676, 1654
Hicks, Mark M., 676, 1654

Hicks, Mary Elizabeth (later Price), 1056
Hicks, Oliver Zeller, 1654
Hicks, Viola Byerly, 1965
Hicks, Wiliam F., 2281
Hicksville, OH, Church of the Brethren, **602,** 749
  Maumee Church of the Brethren, OH, 803
HICOG, *See* High Commissioner for the Occupation of Germany
Hidalgo, Edmundo (CB)
  Santa Ana, CA, Principe de Paz Fellowship (CB) and, 2246
Hidden Seed
  Moravian Church, 875
Hieber, Albrecht, 2336
Hiebert, Clarence, 1965
Hiel Hamilton Memorial Hospital (China)
  medical missions, 807
Hiel Hamilton Memorial Hospital, Liao Chao, China, 630
Hiers (Heyer, Hyer, Hier, Hire, Hires) family, 1965
Hiers Research Committee, 1965
Hieshman, George, 1654
Hiestand family, 2084
Hiestand (Heistand, Heestand, Heaston) family, **602**
Hiestand, John, 602
Hiester (Hüster) family
  Elsoff, 443
Higelmire, L. Howard, 1654
Higginbotham, Sam Robert, 1654
Higgins, Robert Kenneth, 758, 1654, 2302
Higgs, C. J., 1655
High Commissioner for the Occupation of Germany (HICOG), **603**
The High German American Almanac, 17, 18, See Der Hoch-Deutsch Americanische Calendar
  cover page (1773), 17
The High German Pennsylvanian Recorder of Events, See Der Hoch-Deutsche Pennsylvanische Geschichts-Schreiber
High, Josephine Burkholder, 1965
High Line Canal Company
  land purchased from for Wenatchee, WA, East Wenatchee Church of the Brethren, 1330
High, Mary Elizabeth (later Bieber), 706, 1834, 2137
High, Orion, 1655
High school age children, *See* youth
high schools, *See* secondary education
  Miami Valley Petition, 823
Highbarger, Jacob, 1655
Highbarger, Luella Mae (later Zeller), 1395
Highbarger, Otho Smith, 1655
Highberger, Jacob, 1655
higher education, *See* colleges and universities
Highland Avenue, Elgin, IL, Church of the Brethren, *See* Elgin, IL, Highland Avenue Church of the Brethren
  Lange, Andrea on, 2342
Highland Brethren Church, PA, **605**
Highland Church of the Brethren, NE, *See* Highline Church of the Brethren, NE
Highland Church, Windber, PA, Rummel Church of the Brethren, 1348
Highland Co., FL, 758

Highland Co., OH, 237, 240, 347, 364, 739, 1227, 1327, 1340
  Brush Creek German Baptist Brethren congregation, 237
  Honites, 628
  Ohio settlement, 961
  Ridge Church of the Brethren, OH, 1108
Highland Co., VA, 277, 1301
  Mission Church of the Brethren, VA, **605**
    Hiner Church of the Brethren, VA, 607
  Sangerville Church of the Brethren mission points, 1144
Highland congregation, IN (CB), *See* Akron, IN, Church of the Brethren
Highland congregation, NE, *See* Highline Church of the Brethren, NE
Highland congregation, PA, 1253
Highland, OH, 739
Highland Park, OK, Church of the Brethren, *See* Bartlesville, OK, First Church of the Brethren
Highlights
  Myers, Garry Cleveland, editor, 903
Highlights and Heartaches of Brethren Pioneers (Shuman)
  Shuman, L. Herman (OGBB) and, 2249
Highline Church of the Brethren, NE, **605–606**
Highpoint, WA, Church of the Brethren, *See* Seattle, WA, Highpoint Church of the Brethren
Higi people, 306
Higi people of Nigeria
  Ekklesiyar 'Yan'uwa a Nigeria (EYN), service to, 937
Higley family, 165
Hilary, Charles S., 250, 1380, 1655
  Quebec, 1075
Hilary, Lizzie, 250
Hilary, Mrs. S. C.
  Quebec, 1075
Hilbert, Carl Benoy, 923, 1339, 1655
Hilbert family
  Ozark Grace Brethren Church, MI, 987
Hilbert, James, 1655
Hilbert, John B., 269, 676, 1655
  New Hope Church of the Brethren, TN, elder in, 929
  Pleasant Valley Church of the Brethren, TN, 1035
Hilbert, Lloyd, 1655
Hilbert, Matthias F., 1655
Hilbert, Niles
  New Hope Church of the Brethren, TN, elder in, 929
  Pleasant Valley Church of the Brethren, TN, 1035
Hilbert, Robert A., 269, 590, 676, 1655
  Piney Flats, TN, Church of the Brethren, providing leadership, 1025
  Pleasant Valley Church of the Brethren, TN, 1035
Hilbert, W. T.
  Quiet Dell Brethren Church, PA, pastor, 1076
Hildbranch family, 1385
Hildebrand, Brian C., 2281
Hildebrand, Christian, 1655

Hildebrand, David, 331, 1655
Hildebrand, E. L., 211, 635
Hildebrand, Ed L., 114, 496, 1655
Hildebrand family
  Glück (Glick, Click) family, 553
  North Bethel Church of the Brethren, MO, 945
  South Bethel German Baptist Brethren, MO, 1204
Hildebrand, J. D., 1655
Hildebrand, Jacob, 1655
Hildebrand, Jacob R., 2336
Hildebrand, Johannes, 606, **606**, 1965
Hildebrand, John, 1655
Hildebrand, Lloyd Burton, 1655
Hildebrand, Maria (later Mack), 606, **606**
  Mack, Alexander, Sr., daughter-in-law, 777
  Mack, Johann Valentin, 778
Hildebrand, Stephen, 674, 676, 746, 1305, 1655
  Mineral Point, PA, Vinco Brethren Church, pastor, 843
Hildeburn, Charles R., 140, 1860
Hildreth, George Gayle, 1839, 1965
Hildreth, Janet, 2281
Hildreth, Lavona, 1965
Hile, Martha, 1243
Hileman, Carl
  Meadow Branch Church of the Brethen, TN, 806
Hileman family, 1874
Hileman, Mary C. Delozier
  Miller, Mary Grace Hileman, mother of, 841
Hileman, Mary Grace (later Miller)
  church and community worker, **841**
Hileman, Raymond Eugene, 654, 1655
Hileman, Thomas T.
  Miller, Mary Grace Hileman, father of, 841
Hilkey, Adam
  Overbrook, KS, Church of the Brethren, 986
Hilkey, James Edward, 345, 1655
  Overbrook, KS, Church of the Brethren, elder, 986
  Pleasant Grove Church of the Brethren, KS, 1031
Hill, Brenda, 2084
Hill Co., MT
  Milk River Valley Church of the Brethren, MT, 832
  Montana Brethren settlement, 870
Hill, Elizabeth, 1850
Hill family, 1224, 1866
Hill, Haven, 1655
Hill, J. Calvin
  Mesa, AZ, Community Church of the Brethren, 2222
Hill, J. K., family
  Selma, VA, Church of the Brethren, 1166
Hill, James H., 1655
Hill, James J., 568
  Northern Pacific Railroad, 951
Hill, Leonard Uzal, 1965
Hill, Mary Edith Harris, 1849
Hill, Matie Marie (later White), 1339
Hill meetinghouse, PA, 1323
Hill, R. H., 530
Hill, Robert, 1655
Hill, Robert L., 1655

Hill, Robert William, 755, 1849, 2302
  Osceola, IN, Grace Brethren Church, pastor, 984
  South Pasadena, CA, Grace Brethren Church, pastor, 1206
Hill, Samuel S.
  on CB in South, 2336
Hill, Verneta Elreta, 1965
Hillary, William H.
  Grundy Co. and Mercer Co., MO, 1202
Hillcrest Brethren Church, 687
Hillcrest Home (CB), *See* Brethren Hillcrest Homes, Inc.
  Walker, Galen Knepper, 1314
Hillcrest School, Jos, Nigeria
  Bieber, Charles M., 2137
  mission schools, 854
  Nigeria mission school, 936
  Shank, Glenn H. ("Doc") and Catherine Jean Heck (BC) at, 2248
  Shankster, Owen L., Jr., (CB) and, 2248
Hillcrest schoolhouse, NE, 1349
Hillegas, Charlotte Ellen (later Jobson), **671**, 139, 1361, 1850
  Riverside Christian Training School, teacher and missionary, 1111
Hiller, C(letus) M., 1655
Hiller, Philip Friedrich
  hymnals, 641
Hillery, Charles S., 1655
  Middle Creek Church of the Brethren, IA, minister, 825
Hillery, Elder, 1655
Hillery family
  Peace Valley Church of the Brethren, MO, 1003
Hillery, Howard, 1655
  Monrovia, MD, Bush Creek Church of the Brethren, minister, 870
Hillery, Jeremiah, 1655
Hillery, Lemuel, 115, 558, *606*, **606**, 1655, *See* salaried ministry ("Balaam's Saddle")
  extemporaneous preaching, 1137
  Middle Creek Church of the Brethren, IA, minister, 825
  Oak Grove Church of the Brethren, IL, 955
  Peace Valley Church of the Brethren, MO, elder, 1003
  Shannon, IL, Church of the Brethren, minister, 1172
Hillery, William H., 1655
Hilliker, Barbara Trudeau
  Island Pond, VT, Grace Brethren Church, 2209
Hilliker, William, 664
  Island Pond, VT, Grace Brethren Church, 2209
Hillinger, Charles, 1965
Hills
  on church life, early, 2336
Hillsborough Co., FL
  North Tampa, FL, Zion Church of the Brethren, 950
Hillsdale Co., MI
  Silver Creek Church of the Brethren, OH, 1182
Hilson, Cleaveland, 1965
Hiltabidel family, 1345
Hilton, Blanche Cover, 277, 606, **606**, 1839
Hilton, Donald H., 2281

Hilton, Elijah, 641
Hilton, George William, 277, 278, 606, **606–607**, 1655, 1839
    Minot, ND, Church of the Brethren, elder, 851
    orphans, care for, 982
Hilty family
    Rittman, OH, First Brethren Church, 1111
Himbach, Germany, **607**
    Community of the True Inspiration, 330
    Gruber, Eberhard Ludwig, 575
    Hoffmann, Eva Elizabeth, 617
    Liebe, Christian, 741
    Marienborn, village belonging to, 792
    Rock, Johann Friedrich, activity in Community of True Inspiration, 1116
Himelright family
    Reliance, VA, Mount Zion Brethren Church, 1096
Himes, George, 396
Himes, J. A., 1965
Himes, J. F., 1655
Himes, John
    Oak Grove Church of the Brethren, IA, district meeting delegate, 955
Himes, Levi, 226, 396, 1655
Himes, Margaret Alice (later DeLozier), 375
    Solomon, Jeannette Ruth DeLozier (BC) and, 2251
Himes, William B., 1655
Himmelsbaugh, Ida, 1839, 1965
Hinberger, S. H.
    Nishney Valley German Baptist Brethren, IA, elder in, 938
Hinds, Virginia Horner, 1965–1966
Hinds, William Alfred, 1965
Hindson, Ed, 1935
Hinduism, 226, **607**
Hinegardner, Benjamin D., 1285, 1655, 2302
Hinegardner, C. H., 1655, 2302
Hinegardner, Chelsie H., 1655
Hinegardner, G. A., 1655
Hinegardner, John A., 1655
    Midland, VA, Church of the Brethren, free minister, 827
Hinegardner, Weslie John, 1655
Hiner, C., 1655
Hiner Church of the Brethren, VA, **607**
    recipes from, 2336–2337
Hiner, Robert F., 1212, 1655
Hiner, VA
    Highland Co. Mission Church of the Brethren, VA, 605
Hines, Dostor F., 124, 1655
Hines family, 1213
Hines, J. W., 1655, 2302
    Pleasant View Church of the Brethren, TN, 1037
Hinke, William John, 1966, 2077, 2375
Hinkle
    South Fork Church of the Brethren, WV, preaching point, 1205
Hinkle, Alice, 406
Hinkle, Almeda (later Yoder), *1387*
Hinkle, James, 1655
Hinks, Donald R., 1655, 1860, 1966
    on hymnbooks and hymnals, 2337
    Spohn, Clarence E. on Brethren books

    from collection of, 2358
Hinkston Creek German Baptist Brethren Church, KY, *See* Nicholas Co. German Baptist Brethren Church, KY
Hinkston River, Kentucky, 688
Hinsberg, G., 1966
Hinson, E. Glenn
    on Steere, Douglas V., 2337
Hinson, Shelton Laverne, 1655
Hinson, Tana (later Durnbaugh)
    National Older Adult Conferences, 2229
Hintler, Joseph
    Golden Spring German Baptist Brethren Church, NE, 2374
Hinton, George David, 2281
Hinton, Grove VA, congregation, 342
Hintz, O., 2057
Hipel, Theophilus, 1656
Hipes, W. C., 692
    Rock Grove German Baptist Brethren Church, IA, minister, 1117
Hipes, William C., 1656
Hippensteel, Joan, 2097
hippie attire, 403
Hipple family
    Snake Valley Old German Baptist Brethren Church, PA, 1193
Hippolytus
    premillennialism, 833
Hipskind, Gene Frederick, 1656
Hira, Jivabhai, 1656
Hirabhai, Jethalal, 1656
Hire, Jacob
    Poplar Ridge Church of the Brethren, OH, 1047
Hire, Leonard, 602
Hire, William M., 1656
Hironimus, Bertha Marie, 2281
Hironimus, Leon F(rancis), 1656
Hiroshima, Japan
    World Friendship Center, 1369
Hirsch, Charles B., 1966
Hirsch, Emanuel, 1966
    Pietism subdivisions, 1021
Hirschler, Olga Anna Krebill, 1966
Hirschy, Kathryn Ruth, 1850
Hirst, Margaret E., 1966
Hirt, Anna M. (later Beeghley), 2134
Hirt, Benjamin Daniel, 757, 1656
Hirt, Catherine F. (later Ikenberry), 646
Hirt, Clyde Eugene, 264, 1656, 2134
Hirt, Daniel
    North Hampton, OH, Donnels Creek Old German Baptist Brethren Church, deacon, 948
Hirt, David, 264, 1656
Hirt, Elizabeth (later Landes), 722
Hirt, Ezra, 264, 1656
    Old Order German Baptist Church minister, 972
Hirt family, 228
    Olathe Old German Baptist Brethren Church, KS, 964
Hirt, Ira, 264, 1656
Hirt, Jesse, 1346, 1656
Hirt, Weldon, 264, 1656
Hirtzler, Cathrina, 225
His Pen in Her Hand (Mow)
    poetry, 1040
Hiser, Escil I., 1282, 1342, 1656, **2383**

Hisey Pierson, Anna Lee, 2281
Hisle/Hysell family
    sources on, 2318
Hispanic congregations
    in New Mexico, 931
Hispanic ministries, 1904
    Fellowship of Grace Brethren Churches 485
    minorities, ethnic and racial, 850
    missions, 860
Hispanic Ministries (BC), **2198,** *2199*
    Brethren Church in Peru and, 2237
    Hispanic Radio Ministry, **2199–2200,** *2200*
    The Missionary Board, 856
Hispanic Ministries (CB), **2198–2199**
    identities and liberation for, 304
    Lancaster, PA, Alfa y Omega (Alpha and Omega) Church of the Brethren, 2213
    mission work at Garden City, KS, 2011
    National Council of Churches of Christ in the USA and World Council of Churches, 2228
    relief and rehabilitation work, 186, 190
Histand, Ruth L. (later Mosemann), 2023
Histand, Samuel Swartz, 2023
Historic Ephrata, 1966
historic peace churches, 199, **607–610,** *608, 1966,* 2059, 2085, 2106, **2200,** *See also* nonresistance; pacifism; peace
    America, 1739–1789, 2005
    American Revolution and, 312
    article about, 1922
    Brockwell, Charles W., Jr. on history of, 2327
    Church of the Brethren, 316
    church-state relationship, 1982
    Churches of God (GC), 309
    conference of, 1990
    Conference of Historic Peace Churches, 333
    conscientious objectors, 301, 336, 1165, 1169
    Durnbaugh, Donald F.
        on history of, 2326, 2327
        on pacifism and, 2326
    Egan, Eileen on, 2329
    EIRENE, 432
    Enns, Fernando on, 2330
    hats, 589
    Hershey, Lewis Blaine, 599
    Historic Peace Church/Fellowship of Reconciliation (FOR) Consultative Committee, 2200
    historical writing, 611
    Holland, Scott on, 2330
    International Voluntary Services Agency (IVS), 660
    Keim, Albert N. on history of, 2340
    laws affecting, 2007
    Lord, Charles R. on Japanese American internment and, 2344
    Louis, Jeanne Henriette on, 2344
    Mennonite Church, 316
    Mennonites, 815
    military duty and conscientious objectors, 917–918
    military service, 831, 832
    Miller, Donald E. on, 2347
    Morocco, 876
    Muste, Abraham Johannes, 901
        and New Call to Peacemaking, 926

Nolt, Stephen M. on U. S. interaction with, 2348
non-associators in, 939
nonresistance, 944
nuclear weapons, 1001
Old German Baptist Brethren peace position, 1000
peace education, 1002
Pennsylvania government, 2006
Prague Conferences and, 2239
Puidoux Conferences, 1071
Re-imagining Conference and, 2240
reference to, 1958
Riggs, Ann K. on, 2330
Roop, Eugene F. on historical, 2353
Roosevelt, Franklin Delano, 1122
Rural Life Association (RLA), 1131
Schmoe, Floyd on relocation of Japanese and, 2355
Selective Service System and conscientious objectors, 1165
Seventh-Day Adventists, 1169–1170
Sittser, Gerald L. on World War II and, 2357
Society of Friends (Quakers), 316, 1199
sources on, 2319
Stoltzfus, Grant M. on history of, 2340
violence and, 2265
Historic Peace Churches Committee, 2163
historic sites, 609, See also King, Frank; museums; place-names, Brethren; Pricetown
Germantown Trust, 2188
Philadelphia, PA, Germantown Church of the Brethren, 1016
Historical Commission, See Historical Committee
Historical Committee, 610, See also Cassel Library
Cooper, Herbert Austin, 342
on Everett CB, PA, 2337
on GBC, 2337
organ owned by Henry Kurtz, 900
Pritchett, Reuel Bowman, 1060
Shultz, Lawrence W., 1180
on Stone Bridge CB, 2337
historical libraries, 610, 2030, See also Brethren Historical Library and Archives (BHLA); Cassel Library
Historical Review of North America, 1966
historical societies, 610, See also archives; Historical Committee (CB); Historical Records Committee (FGBC)
Historical Society of Pennsylvania, 52, 1966
Ephrata Press, 452
historical libraries, 610
Historical Society of York Co., PA, 1966–1967
historical writing, 610–613, See also descriptions of the Brethren
Brethren bodies, chart of, 1403–1405
Brethren history, teaching, and practice, 2200–2202
chronology, 1407–1436
"Church of the Brethren 1851–1976," 1997
divisions, list of, 1403–1405
Flying Eagle, The, 500
historiography, 2200
Holsinger's History of the Tunkers and

the Brethren Church, 623
Howe, Roland Levi, 633
Ivester, IA, Year Book, 1978
Mack, Alexander, Jr., 774
maps, historical, 1437–1464
Materials Towards a History of the Baptists, 803
Mehrning, Jacob, 811
Miller, Clara Worst, 834
Moore, John Henry, 874
Morris, James Henry, 877
Muir, Gladdys Esther, 893
non-Brethren sources of Brethren history, 18th and 19th centuries, 2054
Old Order Notes, 973
publishing books about, 1069
Renkewitz, Heinz Gottfried, 1099
Sachse, Julius F., 1133, 1170
Schwarzenau, 1158
Seidensticker, Oswald, 1165
Sell, James Arnold, 1166
Smith, Samuel, 1191
Tunkers and the Brethren Church, 1970
Historie der Wiedergeborenen (Reitz) (History of the Reborn) (Reitz), 1095
historiography, See historical writing
The History, Adventures, and Pilgrimage of John Engelsinger of Brotherstone Road (Lehman), 1997
History of Bedford, Somerset, and Fulton Counties, Pennsylvania, 1967
The History of Carroll Co., Illinois, 1967
A History of Christianity (Petry), 1013
History of Knox Co., Ohio, 1967
History of Montgomery Co., Ohio, 1967
History of the Brethren Church (Ronk), 180, 183
History of the Brethren in Virginia (Zigler, David H.), 1397
History of the Brethren Missionary Movements, 180
History of the Church of the Brethren in Western Pennsylvania (Blough), 151
A History of the Concept of Planning in the United States (Clayton), 319
History of the Early Settlement of the Juniata Valley (Jones)
excerpt from, 877
History of the German Baptist Brethren historical writing, 611
History of the German Baptist Brethren (Brumbaugh), 258, 259, 300
poetry, 1039
The History of the German Baptist Brethren in Europe and America, 613, See also historical writing
History of the German Baptist Brethren in Europe and America (Brumbaugh), 223
History of the Ohio Falls Cities and Their Counties, 1967
History of the Persecutions of the Anabaptists
Miller, John Peter, translating, 840
History of the Tunkers and the Brethren Church, See Holsinger's History of the Tunkers and the Brethren Church
History of Universalism (Eddy), 424
History: Southern District, 1967
Hitchman, David R., 672

Hitler, Adolph
Germany, 545
Hutterian Society of Brothers, 640
HIV/AIDS, 2129–2130, 2178
Hively, Anna M., 1967
Hiwasse, VA, Church of the Brethren, 613
Pulaski, VA, Church of the Brethren, 1071
Hixon, Armanus Jefferson, 613–614, 715, 1656
Reconstruction Committee, 1086
Pleasant View Brethren Church, KS, elder, 1036
Hixson, G. R.
Mount Hope Church of the Brethren, WA, 882
Hixson, Mary
Mount Hope Church of the Brethren, WA, 882
Hjorring congregation, Vendsyssel county, Denmark, 361
Eskildsen, Christen (?) Christensen, 456
Hoagland, John C., 1656
Hoak, Henry S., 1221
Hoak, Leah, 2074
Hoalder, Daniel, 1656
Hob, Margarette, 352
Hoback, James A., 1224, 1656
Hobart, Fritz
Simi Valley, CA, Grace Brethren Church, 1182
Hobart, Joyce
Simi Valley, CA, Grace Brethren Church, 1182
Hobbs, Charles L., 614, 1656
Pipe Creek Church of the Brethren, MD, 1026
Hobbs, W. William, 266
Hobert, David Kraig, 1849
Hobert, Susan Louise Thompson, 1849
Hobert, Tad K., 367, 1365, 1656
Hoblit, Bart L., 2281
Hoblit, Bruce, 350, 1656
Hobson, Melvin, 1656
Parkersburg, WV, Grace Brethren Church, pastor serving, 994
Hoby, James, 1911
Hoch, Beverly Repass
on fraktur art, 2328
Der Hoch-Deutsch Americanische Calendar (The High German American Almanac), 17, 18
cover page (1773), 17
Der Hoch-Deutsch Pennsylvanische Geschichts-Schreiber, 614, 1967
Hoch family, 1916
Hochetler, Jacob, 1973
Hochhuth, C. W. H., 1967
Hochman, John, 1656
Hochman, Philip Stein, 1656
Romney, WV, Church of the Brethren and, 2244
Hochmann von Hochenau, Ernst Christoph, 57, 120, 379, 386, 421, 481, 569, 589, 614–615, 751, 990, 1874, 1967, 2029, 2043, 2058, See also Rouse, Ruth
as a source for Beissel's ideas, 113
antinomianism communes and, 236
associaton with Samuel König, 706
Brethren beliefs and Radical Pietism, 1080

Brethren movement and, 174
Brethren sect, 1079
"Confession of Faith," 2337
description, 1980
Erb, Christian, 453
historical writing, 611
historiography, 2202
Hüttental, 639
Judaism, 677
Jung-Stilling, Heinrich, 678
Mack, Alexander, Sr., 775
mentoring, 2221
missions, 857
Moravian Church, 876
noncreedalism, 942
Reitz, Johann Heinrich, 1095
Renkewitz, Heinz Gottfried, wrote
    about, 1099
Schwarzenau residence, 1158
separatism, 1166–1167
sexuality, human, 1170
Simons, Menno, 814
sources on, 2315
theology of love, 761
universal restoration, 1292
Hochmann von Hochenau, Georg
    Christoph, 614
Hochmann von Hochenau, Heinrich
    Christoph, 614
Hochmann von Hochenau (Renkewitz),
    2143
Hochstaedter, Michael, descendants of,
    1950
Hochstedler, Christian
    Shelby Co. German Baptist Brethren
        Church, KY, minister in, 1175
Hochstedler, David, 1656
Hochstedler family, 1927
Hochstedler, Susanna (later Yoder), 1949
Hochstedtler, *See* Hochstetler; Hostetler
Hochstedtler, Annie Mae Yoder, 1967
Hochstedtler, Barbara. *See* Hochstetler,
    Barbara, 1973–1974
Hochstedtler, Samuel A. and Anna J. Miller
    family history and genealogy, 1967
Hochstedtler, Sue Mast, 1967
Hochstetler, *See* Hochstedtler; Hostetler
Hochstetler, Abraham H. and Susanna J.
    Yoder, 1974
Hochstetler, Andrew and Elizabeth Lehman
    family history, 1967
Hochstetler, Barbara, 2079, *See also*
    Hochstedtler, Barbara
Hochstetler, Barbara (later Fry), 1949
Hochstetler, Barbara Rupp, 615
Hostetler, Adam, 631
Hochstetler, Christian, 615, **615**, 1656
    captivity by Indians, 1974
Hostetler, Adam, 631
Hochstetler, Daniel E., 1967
Hochstetler, Daniel J., 1882
Hochstetler, David J., 1967
Hochstetler, Drusilla Yoder, 1967
Hochstetler, Elizabeth (later Lint), 744
Hochstetler, Elmer Levi, 1967
Hochstetler, Ervin L., 1967
Hochstetler family, 149, 1865, 1881, 2071
    Native Americans, 2229
    Royer family related to, 1128
Hochstetler, Frank, 1656
Hochstetler, Gideon J., 1867
Hochstetler (Hochstettler), Abram B., 1656
Hochstetler (Hochstettler), Edward K., 1656

Hochstetler (Hochstettler), Josiah, 1656
Hochstetler (Hostetler) family, 26, **615**
Hochstetler, Jacob, 615
Hochstetler, Jacob Emanuel, 1967
Hochstetler, John, 615
Hochstetler, John D. and Jemima Detweiler
    family history, 1967
Hochstetler, Joseph, 615
Hochstetler, Mary Mahlon Hochstetler,
    1967
Hochstetler, Melvin P., 1867
Hochstetler, Moses I., 1656, 1973
Hochstetler, Noah H. and Barbara Schrock
    family history, 2015
Hochstetler, Samuel, 2071
Hochstetler, Susanna Hochstetler, 1867
Hochstettler, D., 1656
Hochstettler, H. P., 1656
Hockelby, George, 1656
Hockenberry family, 695
Hockenberry, James H., 1656
Hockenberry, Roy, 1656
Höcker, Chris., 1865
Hocker, Edward W., 1967–1968
    historical writing, 611
    on PA Germans, 2337
Höcker, Heinrich, **615**
Höcker, J., 407
Hocker, John K., 1656
Hocker, Ludwig, 1968
Höcker (Hoecker), Ludwig, 451, **615–616**,
    1867, 1968, 2337, *See also* Sunday
    school movement
Höcker, Margaretha, 615
Höcker, Maria, 616
Hocking, Betty Ruth Reeves, 1849–1850
Hocking Co., OH, 364
    Mount Zion Brethren Church, 888
Hocking, David L., 563, 754–755, 755,
    1380, 1656, 1968
Hocking, Donald George, 1656, 1850
Hocking, Thomas G., 2281
Hockley, Albert E., 362, 2281
Hockman, India Lee, 1656
Hockman, Noah A., 766, 1656, 2302, **2383**
    Nimishillen Old German Baptist
        Brethren Church, OH, elder in,
        937–938
    North Hampton, OH, Donnels Creek
        Old German Baptist Brethren
        Church, elder-in-charge, 948
Hockman, P. Stein, 1315
Hockstetler (Hochstettler), Benjamin
    Franklin, 1656
Hodgden, Dorsey, 320, 1656, **2383**
Hodgden, Merrill O., 1656
Hodgden, Ralph Mark, 1656
Hodgden, Sidney, 649, 716, 923, 1656,
    2383
    Osage Church of the Brethren, KS,
        elder, 983
Hodgden, Dorothy Elizabeth Haight, 1850
Hodgdon, Earle C., 1850, 2302
Hodgdon, Ralph
    Paint Creek Church of the Brethren,
        KS, 990
Hodge, Bert, 1656
Hodge, Josiah, 1656
Hodge, Nathan E., 1656
Hodgen, M. O., 270
Hodgenville, KY, congregation, 689
Hodges family
    Faiview-Rocky Mount Church of the

Brethren, VA, 470
Hodges, Kathleen L., 2281
Hodges, Lester, 162
Hodges, Sarah, 157
Hodgkin, Henry, 659
Hodgon, Earle C., 1656
Hodson, Michael Lee, 367, 1656, 1968
Hoecker, Ludwig, *See also* Höcker, Ludwig
    See Ephrata Community, tumb-
        stone desctiptions,
    on Ephrata Cloister, 2337
Hoeff, Henry, 617
Hoefle, Dean Cleo, 1656
Hoefle, Ulysses H., 531, 1657
Hoefs, Albert, 1968
Hoening, Johann Georg, **616**
Hoensaker, Jacob, *See* Hunsaker, Jacob
Hoenstine, Floyd G., 2010
Hoerner, Eliz. (later Harnly), 1958
Hoerner, Elizabeth (later Harnley), 585
Hoerner family, 1958
Hoernerstown house, Big Swatara Church
    of the Brethren, PA, 142
Hoestetler family, 2100
Hofacker, Ludwig, 148
Hofecker, Kathryn (later Kinsey), 696
Hofecker, Terry A., 2173, 2281
Hoff, Amos, 1657
Hoff, Anna Gockley, 616, 617
    Mothers and Daughters' Association,
        879
Hoff, Christian Smith, 1657
Hoff, David, 617
Hoff, Effie Schrock, 617
Hoff, Emanuel Buechley, 46, 125, 127, 300,
    377, *616*, **616**, 617, 1215, 1344,
    1657, 1968
    Palestine, 990
    spelling changed to Buechly, **2375**
Hoff, Ernest Gockley, 201, 285, 381, *425,
    558*, 616, *616*, **617**, *632*, *1657*,
    1930, 1968, **2375**, 2388
    on CB (film), 2337
    photography as art, 1020
Hoff, Ernestine (later Emrick), 617, 1930
Hoff family, 1322
    Neher family, related to, 922
Hoff, Henry, 617, 1657
Hoff (Huff) family, *616*, **617**
Hoff, Ida Wagner, 616, 1361
Hoff, John, 617
Hoff, John B., 616
Hoff, John Luke, 1657
Hoff, John W., 1657
Hoff, Levi, 1657
Hoff, Lloyd Moses, 617, 1657, 1968
Hoff, Lottie F., 1968
Hoff, Lottie Neher, 617
Hoff, Mary Buechley, 616
Hoff, Peter, 617
Hoff, Peter, Jr., 279
Hoff, Peter, Sr., 279
Hoff, Ruthanna, 1968
Hoff, Samuel, 617
Hoff, Sarah Blocher, 617
Hoffard, R. Jeffrey, 2281
Hoffart (Hufford), Christian, 1968
Hoffer, Aaron H., 1657
Hoffer, Alice Minora (later Graybill), **567,**
    1838
Hoffer, Edgar M., 1968
Hoffer, Floy Souder Crouthamel, 617
Hoffer, George, 1657

Hoffer, Gertrude Schafer, 1968
Hoffer, Irwin Seymour, **617**, 1657
Hoffer, Jacob Franklin, **567**
Hoffer, John, 567
Hoffer, John H., 617
Hoffer, Magdalena Hostetler, 567
Hoffer, Mary Ann (later Hertzler), 600, 601
Hoffer, Mary (later Rarick), 2041
Hoffer, Mattias
    Risser, Audrey Gates on descendants
      of, 2352
Hoffer, Susan H. Bucher, 617
Hoffert, Andrew T., 128, 1657, 1839, 1968,
    2049
Hoffert, Casper, 597
Hoffert, Catherine Stihli, 597
Hoffert family
    Allen, passengers on, 2126
Hoffert, Franklin Pierce, 1968
Hoffert, Gordon R., 2281
Hoffert, Henry A., 606, 1657
Hoffert, Ruth (later Dowdy), 1919
Hoffman, Aaron, 618, 1657
Hoffman, Barbara Miller, 617
Hoffman, Bonnie
    Cincinnati Grace Brethren Church,
      Sharonville, OH, 1174
Hoffman, Catherine, 2107
Hoffman, Daniel
    Hoffman, Paul W., 2202
Hoffman, Mrs. David
Hoffman, Deborah, 2202
Hoffman, Elisha A., 560
Hoffman, Elizabeth Wertz, 618
Hoffman, Elsie, 2133
Hoffman, Eva Elizabeth, 683
Hoffman family, 375, 1281, 1891, 1927,
    1968, 2105
    Holtzapfel (Holsapple, Holsopple)
      family, 624
    Rio Linda, CA, congregation, 1134
Hoffman, Mrs. Freeman
Hoffman, Galen, 1367
Hoffman (Huffman) family, **617–618**
Hoffman, J. P., 1657
Hoffman, Jacob, 1657
Hoffman, Jacob A., 1968
Hoffman, James, 2202
Hoffman, Jesse K., 1657
    Skippack Church of the Brethren, PA,
      elder and moderator, 1189
Hoffman, Jim,
    Cincinnati Grace Brethren Church,
      Sharonville, OH, 1174
Hoffman, Joanna Begerow, 2202
Hoffman, John, 2202
Hoffman, John Charles, 1657
Hoffman, John E., 1657
Hoffman, John Michael, 2282
Hoffman, Joseph R., 1657
Hoffman, Josephine (later Steffler), 1220
Hoffman, Lovina (later Weaver), 1324
Hoffman, M. J., 1657
Hoffman, Martin, 1657
Hoffman, Matthias, 618
Hoffman, Matthias and Mary Hoover, 1968
Hoffman, Milton R., 1657
Hoffman, Myralene (later Van Dyke), 1302
Hoffman, Nancy, 618
Hoffman, Paul William, 1657, 1968, **2202,**
    2202
      McPherson College, president, 781
      Michigan City, IN, Church of the

Brethren, part-time pastor, 825
    North Manchester, IN, Church of the
      Brethren, elder (moderator), 949
    Redford, MI, Trinity Church of the
      Brethren, pastoral leadership, 1090
    Roann, IN, Church of the Brethren,
      1112
Hoffman, Peter, 1657
Hoffman, Philip, 617
Hoffman, Philip family
    Shade Creek Church of the Brethren,
      PA, 1170
Hoffman, Ralph W., 749, 1657, 2202
Hoffman, Robert C., 1657
Hoffman, Robert L.
    Rayman Fellowship Church of the
      Brethren, PA, pastor, 1084
Hoffman, Sylvester B., 1657
Hoffman, Tessie M. Heeter, 2202
Hoffman, Vern, 2133
    on Tarvin, George, 2337
Hoffman, Will
    Sand Creek Old German Baptist
      Brethren Church, KS, elder-in-
      charge, 1143
Hoffman, Willem Johan, 1968–1969
Hoffman, William H. C., 1657
Hoffmann, Barbara
    on Radical Pietists, 2337
Hoffmann, Eva Elizabeth, **617**
    expulsion of, from Ysenburg-Büdingen,
      1196
Hoffmann, Rudolph, 1969
Hoffmann, Wilhelm, 2049
Hoffmeyer family, 164
    Mill Run Grace Brethren Church, MD,
      833
Hoffmeyer, James F., 164, 670, 1320, 1657
    Mill Run Grace Brethren Church, MD,
      pastor, 833
Hoffsinger, Gletha Mae (later Eikenberry),
    431
Hofmann, Christena Gochenour, 617
Hofmann, Christian, 617
Hofmann, Erich, *See* Prisoners of War
Hofmann, John, 617
Hofmann, Martin, 1969
Hofmann, William H. C., 470
Hogan-Albach, Susan
    on women, Brethren, 2337
Hogan, Herbert W., 2, 1969, 2377
    historical writing, 612
    on Muir, Gladdys E., 2337
Hogan, Jan
    on Muir, Gladdys E., 2337
Hogan, Ruth S., 2183
Hogan, Samuel E., 1657
Hohenstein, Lewis C., 1322, 1343, 1657
Hohf, Adaline (later Beery), 566, 1361,
    1951, *See also* Beery, Adaline
    Hohf; Beery, Adaline (Hohf)
    hymns, 643
Hohf, David B., 1657
    Pleasant Hill Church of the Brethren,
      PA, presiding elder, 1032
Hohf, Elizabeth (later Utz), 1299
Hohf, Henry, 1657
Höhn, Christina, 618
Höhn, Eberhard, 2337
Höhn, Heinrich, **618**
Hoke, Christina Mellinger, 618
Hoke, Elizabeth, 382, 383
Hoke family, 1969, 2010, 2079

Shoemaker, David, related to, 1157
Hoke, George, 267, 295, 382, 383, 419,
    460, **618,** 711, 1657
    Brethren settlement in Ohio, 961
    Mahoning Church of the Brethren, OH,
      elder, 782
Hoke, George Washington, 1969
Hoke, Georgiana, 1969
Hoke, Henry, 1657
Hoke (Hoock), George
    Landes, David, 1993
Hoke, J. Frank
    Rosepine, LA, Church of the Brethren,
      elder, 1123
Hoke, Jonas, 1657
Hoke, Joseph Franklin, 1657
Hoke, Levi, 1657
Holaday, C. H., 297, 1969
Holbrook, Marjorie Arleen Ladd, 1969
Holbrook, Mark
    Orange, CA, Grace Brethren Church,
      elder, 975
Holcomb, Galen L., 1657
Holdcraft, Jacob M., 1969
Holdeman, Christian, 619, 733, 1214, 1657,
    1969, 2091
Holdeman, David S., 1979
Holdeman, Ella Gleta, 1969
Holdeman family, 1214, 2052, 2091
Holdeman, John, **618**, 1969
Holdeman People
    Brethren, relationship with, 1965
Holdeman, Susannah Martin, 619
"Holdeman's Church," MO, 1214
Holder, Daniel, 1657
Holder, James, 2302
Holder, Joseph, 1657
Holder, Thomas, 366
Holderman (Haldeman) family, **618–619**
Holderman, Jacob, 1657
Holderman, Samuel, 1657
Holderread (Holderreed), Andrew H., 1247,
    1658, 1839, 1969
Holderread, Arno Max, 264, 1657
Holderread, Elsie Lucore
    Sudan (CB) and, 2253
Holderread family, 141
Holderread, Henry
    Moyer, Naomi Ann Holderread, father
      of, 892
Holderread, Kenneth O., 445, 1658
    Sudan (CB) and, 2253
Holderread, Louis, 91, 142, 1658
Holderread, Minnie B.
    Moyer, Naomi Ann Holderread, mother
      of, 892
Holderread, Naomi Ann (later Moyer),
    1722
    home missionary, **892**
    Moyer, Elgin Sylvester, wife of, 892
Holderreed, Louise Virginia Garber, 1839
Hole, Elizabeth Kirk, 1839
Hole, William Thomas, 1839
Holfinger, Elizabeth (later Bowman), 2138
Holgate family
    Modesto, CA, La Loma Grace Brethren
      Church, 867
Holgerson family
    Redstone Valley Old German Baptist
      Brethren Church, WI and, 2240
holidays, *See* specific holidays
    observation of, 2147–2148
    worship services, 1378

holiness
beauty of, 2013
Brethren Church doctrine on, 183–184
Brethren in Christ and Weslyan, 189
Christian and Missionary Alliance, 259
Church of God, Anderson, IN, 296
Holiness Brethren, **619**
Holiness Churches
Pentecostalism, 1009
Holiness Movement
American, 56, **619**
Arminianism and, 56
Brethren Doctrine of Salvation, 1140
Pentecostalism, 1008
Holl, Carl Waldo, **619**
Holl, David Laverne, 1658
on Holl family, 2337
Roanoke, VA, Ninth Street Church of
the Brethren, pastor, 1113
Holl, Emma Swartz, 619
Holl, Ephriam, 1969
Holl family, 1390
Holl, Henry C., 1969
Holl, Samuel J., 619, 1658
Holland, *See* Netherlands
Holland Church of the Brethren, KS, 1, **619**
Holland Elementary School, Toledo, OH,
1267
Holland family, 731
Holland house, 1, 598
Holland, Scott
on historic peace churches, 2330
Holland, William, 251
Hollander, Else von, 639
Hollander, Emmy von (later Arnold), 639
Hollar, E. Cleveland, 1658
Hollar, Jacob, 1658
Hollar, M. P., 1658
Hollar, Sallie (later Will), 1345
Hollen, Elsie Vint (later Harley), 583
Hollenbach, Phyllis F., 1969
Hollenbaugh, L. R., 1969
Hollenberg, Ada Viola Dunning, 1839
Hollenberg family, 1926
Sharon Church of the Brethren,
Alberta, Canada, 1172
Hollenberg, Frederick M., 1969
Okeechobee, FL, Gace Brethren
Church, pastor, 963
Hollenberg, Frederick Mitchel, 244, 1658,
1839, **2383, 2387**
Modesto, CA, Church of the Brethren,
866
Peru, IN, Church of the Brethren, pas-
tor, 1010
Hollenberg, Grace, 209, 1969
Hollenberg, Keith Earl, 2282
Hollenberg, Naomi H., 1969
Hollenberg, Nora Loft Reber, 1839, 2024
India, missionary to, 1085
Hollenburg, Edward Lowell, 1658
Holler, Christian, 1658
Holler, Frederick, 366, 1658
Holler, George, 366, 1658
Holler, Harry Walter, 1658
Holler, Jacob, 1658
Holler, John, 1658
Holler, OH, congregation, 366
Holler, Walter H., 1658
Holliday, Carrie, 356
Holliday, Dennis I., 115, 1324, 1658
Holliday, Jack, 356
Hollidaysburg, PA, Brethren Church, *See*

Vickburg, PA, Grace Brethren
Church
Hollidaysburg, PA, Church of the Brethren,
619
Holling, Joseph, 1658
Hollinger, A. B.
Salem Church of the Brethren, ND,
1138
Hollinger, A. M., 1658
Hollinger, Abraham, 1658
Oak Grove Old German Baptist
Brethren Church, OH, minister,
956
Hollinger, Abraham K., 1658
Hollinger, Abram
Shippensburg, PA, Church of the
Brethren, minister in, 1177
Hollinger, Adam, 1658
Hollinger, Adam M., 1658
Hollinger, Albert, 1658, 1969
Merrington Church of the Brethren,
Sask., elder, 817
Hollinger, Allen B., 1658, 2302
Hollinger, Andrew B., 1658
Hollinger, Archie R., 1658
Hollinger, Catharine Risser, 1658
Hollinger, Catharine Shumaker, 620
Hollinger, Christian, 620
Hollinger, Clayton G. and Fianna B., 1969
Hollinger, Daniel, 620, 1658
Hollinger, David, 15, 250, 470, 572, 1658
Manchester College, acquisition of and
trustee, 785
Merrington Church of the Brethren,
Sask., elder, 817
Pleasant Valley Church of the Brethren,
Alberta, Canada, providing pas-
toral care, 1034
Hollinger, Donald E., 2282
Hollinger, Eli, 1658
Pleasant View Church of the Brethren,
OH, minister, 1032
Hollinger, Elizabeth Graybill, 620
Hollinger, Evelyn, 1969
Hollinger, Even Sylvester, 109, 1658
Hollinger family, **620**
Royer family related to, 1128
Hollinger, G. W., 1658
Hollinger, Gene, 1322
Hollinger, Gene Ray, 1658, 2156
Hollinger, George, 1658
Hollinger, H. H., 1658
Hollinger, Hans Jörg, 620
Hollinger, Harold
National Fellowship of Grace Brethren
Men, leadership in, 916
Hollinger, Henry B., 1658
Hollinger, Henry Kline, 1969
Hollinger (Hullinger, Holliger, Holiger,
Hollingerus) family, 1969
Hollinger, Isaac S., 1969
Hollinger, Jacob, 620, 757, 1658
Hollinger, J(acob), 1658
Hollinger, Jacob Harold, 1658
Hollinger, James E.
on service, world, 2337
Hollinger, James Lee, 1658
Hollinger, Jay, 596
Hollinger, Jesse, 1658
Hollinger, John, 620, 1659
Russell Co. Church of the Brethren,
KS, elder-in-charge, 1132
Sand Creek Church of the Brethren,

KS, elder, 1142–1143
Hollinger, John A., 1659
Hollinger, John and Esther Horst, 1969
Hollinger, John Harold, 2138
Hollinger, Joseph, 620, 1659
Hollinger, Kenneth Wandle, 1659, 1969,
2302
Hollinger, Lizzie Balsbaugh, 620
Hollinger, Lucy (later Basler), 2272
Hollinger, Magdalena (later Longenecker),
756
Hollinger, Moses, 109, 1659
Hollinger, Paul R., 1969
Hollinger, Peter, 1969
Hollinger, Samuel, 71
Hollinger, Shannon I., 2173
Hollinger, Walter Reitz, 1969
Hollinger, William H., 1659
Hollinger, William M., 1659
Hollingshead, Frederick Curie, 1659,
1969–1970,
Mount Morris, IL, Church of the
Brethren, pastor, 883
Redford, MI, Trinity Church of the
Brethren, pastoral leadership, 1090
Hollingshead, Mary Ellen Horst, 630
Hollins Road Church of the Brethren, VA,
See Roanoke, VA, Hollins Road
Church of the Brethren
Roanoke, VA, First Church of the
Brethren, 1113
Hollins, VA, Patterson Memorial Grace
Brethren Church, **620**
Hollis, A. B., 1659
Hollis, H. R., 72, 1659
Hollis, James, 1970
Hollis, NC, 1209
Hollman, John, 1659
Hollopeter, Jason Beer, 1659.
Rockton, PA, Church of the Brethren,
pastor, 1118
Hollow Church of the Brethren, OK,
620
Hollow Poplar Church of the Brethren,
NC, 78, 224, **620**
Petersons Chapel Church of the
Brethren, NC, 1012
Holloway, Abijah, 340
Holloway, Mrs. Abijah, 340
Holloway, Cecil, 1643
Holloway, Jacob H., 1659
Holloway, James T., 1659
Holloway, Lucinda (later Metzler)
Metzler, Burton and John D., Sr.,
mother of, 820
Holloway, Mark, 1970
Holloway, Vernon Howard, 1970
Hollowbush, Peter, 1659
Hollowtown, OH, 1340
Church of the Brethren, *See* White Oak
Church of the Brethren, OH
Hollsopple, PA
Holtzapfel (Holsapple, Holsopple) family,
624
Hollyday, Guy Tilghman, 1970
Hollywood Church of the Brethren, VA,
620, 2014
Holm family
Rittman, OH, First Brethren Church,
1111
Holman's Creek, VA, 2101
Church of the Brethren, *See* Flat Rock
Church of the Brethren, VA

Holmes, Benjamin, 540, 1946
Holmes, Burton Eugene, 1659
Holmes, C. E., 442, 1212
    Omak, WA, Church of the Brethren,
        elder, 974
Holmes, Carl T., 1970
    Beissel, Conrad, music of, 2337
Holmes, Cletus E., 1342, 1659
Holmes Co., OH, 242
Hochstetler, David J., descendants, 1967
    Nicholson, John, minister in, 935
Holmes, Eli, 1659
Holmes family, 1214, 1365
    Guthrie Church of the Brethren, MN,
        576
Holmes, G. W.
    Red River Church of the Brethren, OK,
        minister, 1089
Holmes, Garrett Arden, 1970
Holmes, George W., 1659
Holmes, Robert F., 626, 1659
Holmes, Shirley F.
    on Switzer family, 2337
Holmes, William Harvey, 1970
Holmesville, NE
    Church of the Brethren, 104, **620**
    Filley German Baptist Brethren
        Church, NE, 2374
    North Beatrice Church of the Brethren,
        NE, 945
    Old German Baptist Brethren Center-
        view, 921
    South Beatrice congregation, 384
Holsapple family, *See* Holtzapfel family
Holsberry, James K., 1659
Holsbury family
    Mount Zion Church of the Brethren,
        WV, 888
Holsbury, James
    Mount Zion Church of the Brethren,
        WV, 888
Holsinger, Amos Stover Alva, 1659
Holsinger, Christian A., 1659
Holsinger, Christian S., 110, 1659
    Raisin City, CA, Church of the
        Brethren, elder, 1083
Holsinger Church of the Brethren, PA, **623**
Holsinger, Clyde K., 621
Holsinger congregation, PA, 1364
Holsinger, Daniel, 406, 531, 1659
Holsinger, Daniel Mack, 170, 621, **621,**
    1659
Holsinger, David, 623, 1970
Holsinger, David R., 1659
Holsinger, Dennis Venard, 357
Holsinger, Elizabeth (later Fahrney), 465
Holsinger, Elizabeth Mack, 621, 623
Holsinger family, 405, 700, 1970
    Robins, IA, Church of the Brethren,
        1115
    Snider, Jacob, descendants of, 1154
    Snowberger family, related to, 1153
Holsinger, George Blackburn, 560, *621,*
    621, 623, 1970
    Brethren music, 899
    composition of hymns, 1279
    hymnals, 642
    hymns, 643
    singing schools, 1185
Holsinger, George M., 1659
Holsinger, George Mack, 410
Holsinger, H. L.
    Ridgely, MD, Brethren Church, pastor,

1109
Holsinger, Henry Ritz, 18, 67, 93, 99, 110,
    121, 178, *182,* 183, 186, 187, 195,
    197, 221, 235, 237, 285, 298, 388,
    466, 525, 559, 561, 619, **621–622,**
    622, 623, 682, 688, 712, 715, 720,
    734, 1213, 1394, 1659, 1908,
    1914, 1929, 1970, 2026, 2039,
    2052, **2375,** *See also* historical
    writing
    advocacy of German language, 725
    Annual Meeting and Brethren polity,
        1042, 1043
    article about, 1922
    Ashland Convention schisms, 368
    on baptism, doctrine of, 2089
    Christian Family Companion, 1283
    *The Christian Family Companion and
        Gospel Visitor,* 1058
    church trial, 1274
    critical of authority of Standing
        Committee, 1217
    departure from 1882 Annual Meeting,
        1151
    description of Dunkard worship serv-
        ice, 1375–1376
    Grossnickle, Laura (Hedrick), 1362
    historical writing, 611
    hymnals, 642
    Indiana, 652
    Iowa, 661
    investigation of, 1354
    length of prayers, 1378
    McClain, Alva J., 772
    Meyersdale, PA, 822
        Main Street Brethren Church,
            preaching, 823
    Miller, Howard, 837–838
    Moomaw, Daniel Crouse, 873
    Myers, Graybill, 903
    organ owned by Kurtz, Henry, 900
    Pennsylvania Brethren and schism,
        1005
    photography of Brethren, 1019
    The Pilgrim (published 1870–1880),
        1023
    The Pious Youth, 1025
    Progressive Brethren, 1061
    The Progressive Christian, 372, 1061
    "Progressive Principles," 372
    publishing, 1068, 1069
    publishing reports of Annual Meeting,
        1069
    Quinter, James, 1077
    railroad committees and agents, 1080
    sermons, on, 1168
    Sharp, S. Z., acceptance of baptism,
        1174
    Sontag, Jakob, 1203
    South Bend, IN, First Brethren Church,
        pastor, 1203
    Standing committee of Annual Meeting
        compared to secret society, 1164
    Stony Creek Brethren Church, PA,
        1225
    Sunday school literature, 1236, 1237
    temperance, 1359
    Tiosa, IN, Brethren Church, 1265
    The Youth's Teacher, 1394
Holsinger (Holtzinger) family, 58, **623**
Holsinger House, 623
Holsinger House, PA, 410
Holsinger, I. Edward, 1659

Holsinger, Isaac
    Oakville, IN, Brethren Church, 959
Holsinger, J. L., 1659
Holsinger, Jacob, 623, 1659
    Oakville, IN, Brethren Church, 959
Holsinger, John, 621, 623, 1659
Holsinger, John F., 623
Holsinger, John L., 1659
Holsinger, John M., 1659
Holsinger, John Snyder, 1659
    Manassas, VA, Church of the Brethren,
        elder, 785
Holsinger, Joseph, 1659
Holsinger, Joseph H., 621
Holsinger, L. T., 370, 399
Holsinger, Leonard L.
    Roaring Spring, PA, First Church of
        the Brethren, pastor, 1114
Holsinger, Leonard Replogle, 1659
    Riddlesburg, PA, Church of the
        Brethren, minister, 1108
Holsinger, Levi F., 1660
Holsinger, Levi Teeter, **623,** 1660
    Manchester College, acquisition of and
        trustee, 785
Holsinger, Lucille, 357
Holsinger, Lydia Mack, 623
Holsinger, Mary Jane
    Oakville, IN, Brethren Church, 959
Holsinger, Mary (Polly) Ritz, 621
Holsinger meetinghouse, Woodbury, PA,
    Church of the Brethren, 1364
Holsinger, Merton J., 1660
Holsinger, Nora E., 1970
Holsinger, Orville, 1660
Holsinger, PA
    New Enterprise, PA, Church of the
        Brethren, 927
Holsinger, PA, congregation, 318
Holsinger, Paul G., 1970
Holsinger, Polly Mack, 623
Holsinger, Ralph S., 1660
Holsinger, Rebecca Blackburn, 621
Holsinger, Robert, 2282
Holsinger, Rudolph, 623, 1970
Holsinger, S. R., 1660
Holsinger, Sallie A. Kagey, 621
Holsinger, Sally Knagey
    hymns, 643
Holsinger, Sarah
    Oakville, IN, Brethren Church, 959
Holsinger, Sarah Teeter, 623
Holsinger, Susanna Shoup, 621, *622*
Holsinger, T. L., 1660
Holsinger, Virgil Clair, 115, 1660
Holsinger, William H., 1346, 1660
    Smithfield Church of the Brethren, PA,
        pastor, 1192
Holsinger, William Henry, 1660
*Holsinger's History of the Tunkers and the
    Brethren Church,* 611, 622, **623**
Holsopple, Catherine Lehman, 623
Holsopple, Chester F., 1660
Holsopple, Clarence F., 1660
Holsopple, Daniel, 1660
Holsopple, Donald Galen, 1660, 1970
Holsopple, Edwin C., 1660
Holsopple, Edwin Erasmus, 1660
Holsopple, F. F., 578
Holsopple family, *See* Holtzapfel family
    family history, 1970
    Hoffman (Huffman) family, 618
Holsopple, Frank Ferry, **623,** 1660

Parker Ford, PA, Church of the
Brethren, pastor of, 994
Holsopple, Grace Quinter, 623, 1970
Holsopple, Hiram L., 1660
Prairie View Church of the Brethren,
MO, 1051
Holsopple, Ira A., 1970
Holsopple, Ira Calvin, 274, 1660
Holsopple, Jacob, 274, 1660
Holsopple, James Quinter, 912
Holsopple, Joseph, 623
Robinson, PA, Church of the Brethren,
elder, 1116
Holsopple, Kathren M. Royer, 1839, 1970,
2387
missionary to India, 1127
Holsopple, Quincy Adams, 912, 1660,
1839, 1970
Holsopple, Raymond, 1660
Holsopple, Rufus C., 1660
Holsopple, William W., 1660
Prairie View Church of the Brethren,
MO, 1051
Holsworth, Magdalena
Rodney Church of the Brethren, MI,
1119
Holsworth, Matthew
Rodney Church of the Brethren, MI,
1119
Holt Co., MO
North Bethel Church of the Brethren,
MO, 945
South Bethel German Baptist Brethren,
MO, 1204
Holt, Simma, 1970
Holtz, Catherina Ledermann, 733
Holtz, John, 733
Holtzapfel, Anna Barbara, 624
Holtzapfel, Erasmus, 624
Holtzapfel, Hans Leonard, 624
Holtzapfel (Holsapple, Holsopple) family,
624
Holtzapfel (Holsapple, Holsopple), Johann
Heinrich, **623,** 624
Holtzapfel, Lena, 623, 624
Holtzapfel, Sara Garber, 624
Holtzinger family, See Holsinger family
Holtzinger, Jacob, 623
Holtzinger, Nancy A. (later Warstler), 1319
Holtzmüller, Lewis, 1660
Prices Creek Old German Baptist
Brethren Church, OH, minister,
1057
holy days, See holidays
holy kiss, 698, **698–699,** 1379, See also
entries at kiss
avoidance, 292
Christian Brethren, 281
community, 329
deacons, 369
debates, 371
Declaration of Principles, 372
discipline, 387
doctrine on, 188
early 20th century sermon, 1168
election of church officers, 434
ethics, 457
exclusion from, 75
Far Western Brethren, 475
feetwashing, 481
God's Means of Grace (Yoder), 555
handclasp, 582
installation of ministers, 656

love feast, during, 763, 764
Mack, Alexander, Sr., and New
Baptists of Schwarzenau, 776
minorities, ethnic and racial, 849
Old German Baptist Brethren, 967
ordinances, 976, 979, 979–980
in other religious groups, 68, 69
Pennsylvania, 310
Primitivism, 1058
public worship ritual, 1375
Radical Pietists, 293
restitution, 1100
Restoration Movement, 1101
single mode feetwashing, 1186
Social Gospel Movement, 1197
worship and, 2267
Holy Land, See Bible lands, travel to;
Palestine
holy love, Brethren Church doctrine on,
183–184
Holy Roman Empire, 544, 1091
Holy Spirit, 1892
anointing by, 39
baptism of, 85, **86**
Brethren Church doctrine on, 184
Brethren Church ministry, 847
Brethren Doctrine of Salvation, 1140
Church of the Brethren, 304
coming of at Pentecost, 695
directing preaching by ministers, 845
doctrine of, **624,** 2048
and early Anabaptist identity, 29
Fourman, Larry D. on New Testament
and, 2331
grace, doctrine of, 562
human nature, doctrine of, 635
inner Word and outer Word, 656
invocation of, 333–334
last days, 2002
Pentecost, 1008
Priesthood of All Believers, 1057
prophecy, 1062
Rechte und Ordungen, 1086
repentance, doctrine of, 1100
Rosenberger, Isaac J., writing about,
1123
as source of authority for the Church,
73
sources on, 2316
symbolized by laying on of hands, 730,
731
theology and, 2254
wedding ceremonies, in, 1325
Holy Spirit Conference (CB), **2202–2203**
Holy Spirit movement, See revivalism
Holy Spirit Renewal Group, **625**
charismatic movement, 272
name change, 2150
Holzberry, J. H., 1660
Holzingen
Holsinger (Holtzinger) family, 623
Homan, Gerlof D.
on Mennonites and World War I, 2337
Homan, Madaline Heier, 602
Homan, Sigmund, 602
home building, 2032
home education
Old German Baptist Brethren, **2203,**
2235
Home for Orphan and Friendless Children,
595, **625**
The Home, Girard, IL, See Pleasant Hill
Village

Home Helper, 1236
The Home Helper, **625,** 1970
The Home Mirror, 1970–1971
Hygiene, CO, Church of the Brethren,
641
The Home Mirror and Our Flag, 1971
The Home Mirror and The Home Mirror
and Our Flag, **625**
Home Mission Board
The Missionary Board (BC), 855
Home Mission Board (BC), See Missionary
Board (BC)
Home Mission Board of Northeastern
District of OH
Mount Zion congregation, aid to, 931
Home Mission Council (GBC), PA
Ephrata Area Grace Brethren Church,
PA, 448
Home Mission Revolving Loan Fund
The Missionary Board (BC), 856
Home Mission Society, 165
home missions, 1904, 1905, 2022, See also
missions and missionaries
Early, Henry Clay, 413
Farmington, DE, Bethany Church of
the Brethren, 479
Fellowship of Grace Brethren Churches
(FGBC), 485–486
Forney, Daniel L., 502
Fruitdale Community Church of the
Brethren, OR, 520
GBC Christian Education (Depart-
ment), 533
General Board (CB), 535
General Mission Board (CB), 538
Gish, Barbara Kindig and James Rufus,
550
Goshen, IN, West Goshen Church of
the Brethren, 558
Grandview, WA, Grace Brethren
Church, 566
Grubb, Luther L., 575
Hadsell, B. A., 577
Hamilton, Walter J., 580
Hamlin, KS, Brethren Church, 581
Harrisburg, PA, First Church of the
Brethren, 586
Highland Co. Mission Church of the
Brethren, VA, 605
Hillery, Lemuel, 606
Hoxie, George W., 633
Indiana, 652
Kempton, Ida, 1333
Lahman, Joseph Christian, 718
Landis, Martha, 1333
Los Angeles, Ca, First Church of the
Brethren, 759
migrant labor, 827
Minot, ND, Church of the Brethren,
851
missions, 857–858, 858
Torreon Navajo Mission, NM, 1268
Tropico, CA, Church of the Brethren,
1275
urban ministry, 1295–1297
Williams, John Henry Bashor, 1345
Wine, David Glick, 1349
women, roles in, 1361, 1363
Woods, Mannesseh Frederick, 1364
Zigler, David H., 1397
Zigler, Michael Robert, 1398
Zug, Samuel Ruhl, 1401
Home Missions Advisory Committee

Zigler, Michael Robert, 1398
Home Missions and Evangelism (BC)
Black, James R., 2138
Home Missions Board
Hagerstown, MD, Church of the
Brethren, 578
Lake Shore Church of the Brethren,
OH, 719
Home Missions Commission
Leatherman, Irvin D., 732
Leatherman, Orpha Workman Keever,
732
Home Missions Council, 188
ecumenism, 422
evangelism, 460
FBGC, *See* Brethren Home
Missions Council
Goshen, IN, Grace Brethren Church,
558
Kokomo, IN, Indian Heights Grace
Brethren Church, 705
McAllen, TX, Grace Brethren Church,
2218
Native Americans, 2230
and New Troy, MI, Grace Brethren
Church, 932
Home Missions Council of North America
migrant laborers, service to, 827
Home of the Child Rescue Work, **625**, *See
also* orphanages
Home of the Children's Aid Society, **625**
The Home Pulpit, **625,** 1971
home remedies, folk medicine,
2145–2146
Mason, Edward, editor, 799
home schooling
Dunkard Brethren Church, 2175
Meador, Michael L. on, 2346
Old German Baptist Brethren, 2160,
2161
trend toward, 2145, 2159, 2160
women and, 2263
home visitation, 406, 460
Homebuilders of Tomorrow (Bowman), 169
The Homeless, 626
Homeless Children Committee, *See*
Children's Aid Societies
Child Rescue Work (pamphlet), 276
General Welfare Board (CB), 540
Homeless European Land Program
Row, W. Harold, 1126
Homeless European Land Program (HELP),
625
Murray, Don, 626
homeless ministries
Ramsey, Duane H. and, 2239
homelessness and social action, **2203**
Homer, AK, Kachemak Bay Grace Brethren
Church, 14, **626**
Jackson, Edward A., 2209
Homer family, 695
Homer, Louise
Winona Lake Auditorium, IN, 1353
Homer Township, OH, 144
Homerville, OH, Grace Brethren Church,
626
Homes, Alesia Beth (later Nonemaker),
1731
homes for the elderly, *See* retirement homes
and communities
homes used as meetinghouses, 811
Homeschool Legal Defense Fund
home education, 2203

Homestead Act (1862) and Nebraska
Brethren, 920
Homestead Church of the Brethren, MI,
626
Homestead, FL
Church of the Brethren, 305
Community of True Inspiration, 330
Old German Baptist Brethren Church,
497, **626**
Pine Grove Old German Baptist
Brethren Church, FL, 1025
Homestead, MI, 179, 1235
Harlan, MI, Church of the Brethren,
583
Michigan Brethren settlement, 824
homesteading, **626**
Kansas, 396
Pratt Co., KS, *146*
Homey, Samuel I., 1663
homiletics, 2040
Hommel, Rudolph, 1971
homosexuality, **2203–2204**
Brethren Church, 2178
Brethren/Mennonite Council for
Lesbian and Gay Concerns,
2151–2152
Church of the Brethren, 2163
Dunkard Brethren Church, 2174
ethics issues, 2177–2178
Fellowship of Grace Brethren Churches
(FGBC), 486, 487
Grassroots, Concerns of the, 2193
Miller, Donald Eugene, 2223
theology and, 2255
Hon, Elizabeth Clark, 626
Hon family, 1971, 2100
Nicholas Co. German Baptist Brethren
Church, 935
Hon, George H., 129
Hon (Hahn?), Daniel, 626
Hon (Hahn?), Jonas, 626
Hon (Hahn?), Joseph, 626
Hon (Hahn?), Mary Keithly, 626
Hon, Mary Wright, 626
Hon, Peter Keithly, 129, 177, 347, 494,
626–627, 689, 1340, 1357, 1660
Nicholas Co. German Baptist Brethren
Church, minister in, 935
Restoration Movement, 1101
Restoration movement, leadership in,
935
Ridge Church of the Brethren, OH,
preacher, 1108
writings about, 1928
Honites, 628
Hostetler, Adam, 631
Hostetler Brethren, 631
Hona Libu, Nigeria, 306
Honberger, S. A., 416, 469, 479, 572
Roanoke, LA, Church of the Brethren,
elder, 1112
San Diego, CA, First Church of the
Brethren, 1141
Honberger, Samuel A., 1660
Honberger, Samuel S., 760
Honberger, Sarah, 760
Honduras, **627**
Comisión Cristiana de Desarrollo
(Christian Development Commis-
sion), 2157
Guatemala, 576
Honey Creek Church of the Brethren, MO,
627

Honey Creek Home, *See* Orphans and Old
Folks Home (CB), Sulphur
Springs, IN
Honeycutt (Honeycut), J. W., 620, 1660
Petersons Chapel Church of the
Brethren, NC, 1012
Honeyman, B. F., 1660
Honeyman, Gale Edwin Spitler. 1971
on Deeter, John and descendants, 2337
on Deeter, Susanna (Ulrich) and
descendants, 2337
Honeyman, Lucy (later Klepinger), 700
Honeyman, Roy Francis, 109, 1660
Painter Creek Church of the Brethren,
OH, 990
Hönig, Hennrietha Wilhelmine von, 1880
Honites, 177, **628,** 2096
chart of Brethren bodies, place on,
1403–1405
Honn family, 142
honorific titles, opposition to, 1266
Honsaker, Bessie, 482
Honsaker, Clifford, Jr., 482
Hoober, Isaac B.
descendants, 1914
Hoock (Hoke), George
Landes, David, 1993
Hood, John, 1660
Mexico, IN, Brethren Church, 821
Hood, John H., 2302
Hood, Mrs. John
Mexico, IN, Brethren Church, 821
Hood, William H., 1660
The Hoodlum Priest, 626
Hoogenboom, Ari, 1986
Hook, James William, 1971
Hook, John L., 1660
Hooke, Lewis J., 490
Hooker, E. O., 1900
Hooker, Flora Janie Hamer, 1971
Hooker, I. C., 1660
Hooker, Isaac T., 1660
Hooker, Richard J., 1971
hooks and eyes, *See* dress
Hooks, Eric Lee, 2282
Hooks, Robert V., 1660
Hooley, Bessie Pearl Miller, 1971
Hooley family, 2026
Hooley, Gertrude Yoder, *See* Hooley family
Hooley, J. Y., *See* Hooley family
Hooley, Lester, *See* Hooley family
Hooley, Marietta, *See* Hooley family
Hooley, Martha, 1871
Hoonen, Katrina (later Shideler), *See*
Shideler, Katrina Hoonen
Hoop Scheffer, Jacob G., 1971
Hoopaugh, George, 1956
Hooper, C. J., 1660
Hooper, J. E., 1660
Hoopert, Daniel Arthur, III, 1660
hoops, **628**
Hoopwood (Hopwood), G. W., 1661
Hoover, Adam, 634
Hoover, Amos Burkholder, 1971
Hoover, Andrew, 1907
Hoover, Andrew and Elizabeth, 1971
Hoover, Andrew and Margaret Foutz, 1972
Hoover, Anna Amy (later Brown), *See*
Brown family
Hoover, Anna W., 1971
Hoover, Anna Weaver, 1971
Hoover, Blair, 1661
Hoover, Buryl Edwin, 1661

Hoover, Carrie May Yundt, 628
Hoover, Catherine, 155
Hoover, Catherine Bashore, 628
Hoover, Christian, 513, 634
Hoover, Clarence H., 1661
Hoover, Cyrus, 345, 634, 1661
Hoover, D. P., 674
    Maple Grove Church of the Brethren,
        PA, minister, 791
Hoover, Dale
    Markle, IN, Church of the Brethren,
        trustee, 794
Hoover, Daniel
    immigration to Canada from Pennsyl-
        vania, 1971
Hoover, David, 1338
Hoover, David E., 1661
Hoover, David F., 1661
Hoover, David M., 1971
Hoover, David M. and Verena A. Mercer-
    Hoover, 1971
Hoover, David Paul, 1661
Hoover, Donald Franklin, Jr., 1661
Hoover, Edna Weaver Shirk, 1972
Hoover, Eli, 532, 1321
Hoover, Elias B., 1971
Hoover, Elizabeth, 2042
Hoover, Elizabeth Cripe, 628, 1661
Hoover, Elmer B., 1661
Hoover, , 585, 1661
    Oak Grove Old German Baptist
        Brethren Church, OH,
            minister, 956, elder, 957
Hoover, Ernest V., 1971
Hoover, Esther Weaver, 1971
Hoover family, 216, 384, 700, 731, 1299,
    1320, 1330, 1885, 1896–1897
    1911, 1914, 1927, 1972, 1983,
    2044, 2047, 2073, *See also* Hüber
    family
    Ellison Church of the Brethren, ND,
        442
    Jasper, MO, Church of the Brethren,
        669
    Paul family joined in marriage, 996
    Rittenhouse family related to, 1111
    Robins, IA, Church of the Brethren,
        1115
    Schultz, Martin, related to, 1156
    South Haven Old German Baptist
        Brethren Church, MI, 1205
Hoover, Flora Etta, 168
Hoover, Frederic, 1661
Hoover, Galen Eugene, 1661
Hoover, George, 634, 1295, 1661
Hoover, George Augustus, 1661
    Rocky Ridge, MD, Monocacy Church
        of the Brethren, elder, 1119
Hoover, Gulah Velma (later Daron), 1914
Hoover, H. Allan
    Roanoke, VA, Ninth Street Church of
        the Brethren, preaching, 1113
Hoover, Harry M., 1661, 1971
Hoover, Henry Allan, 1661, 1971
Hoover, Henry Isaiah, 1971
Hoover, Herbert C., 634, 2005
Hoover, Herbert C. (President), 23
Hoover, Homer Franklin, 752, 1661
Hoover (Huber) family, 262
Hoover (Huber), John (Johannes) and Mary
    Watson, 1972
Hoover, Ida, 373
Hoover, IN, Corinth Brethren Church, *See*

Corinth Brethren Church, IN
Hoover, Isaac L., 730, 1661
Hoover, J. A.
    Roanoke, VA, Hollins Road Church of
        the Brethren, 1113
    Roanoke, VA, Ninth Street Church of
        the Brethren, 1113
Hoover, J. Minor, 1661
Hoover, Jacob, 628, 634, 1661
Hoover, Jacob William, 1661
Hoover, James L., 1388, 2282
Hoover, Joan Rosalie (later Aeby), 2127
Hoover, John, 634, 1661
    immigration to Canada from Pennsyl-
        vania, 1971
Hoover, John B., Jr., 248, 1661
    Oak Grove Old German Baptist Breth-
        ren Church, OH, minister, 956
Hoover, John B., Sr., 1661
    Oak Grove Old German Baptist Breth-
        ren Church, OH, minister, 956
Hoover, John H., 1661
Hoover, John J., 128, 1661
    Rocky Ford, CO, Church of the
        Brethren, 1118
Hoover, John L., 1661
Hoover, Jonathan, 1661
Hoover, Joseph, 416, 1661
    Pleasant Valley Church of the Brethren,
        IN, minister, 1034
Hoover, Joseph Johnson, 1661
Hoover, K. S., 1971
Hoover, Kathryn Schmucker, 1971
Hoover, Keith Kindell, 1661
Hoover, Lawrence, 1661
Hoover, Leonard W., 1661
Hoover, Levi Burget, 1661
Hoover, Lydia Weaver Martin, 1972
Hoover, M. M.
    Miamisburg, OH, Brethren Church,
        pastor, 823
Hoover, Margaret, 1360
Hoover, Marie (later Willoughby), 2297
Hoover, Martin, 634, 923, 1883
    immigration to Canada from
        Pennsylvania, 1971
    Richmond, IN, Church of the Brethren,
        holding revival meetings at, 1108
Hoover, Martin M., 1661
Hoover, Mary, 1360, 2092
Hoover, Mary Catherine Ruthrauff, 1972
Hoover, Mary Elizabeth Wentsler, 1839
Hoover, Mary J(eannette), 1661
Hoover, Mary L., 1944
Hoover, Mary Landis, 1972
Hoover, Mary (later Ulery), 1285
Hoover, Mina, 355
Hoover, Morse M., 1661
Hoover, Mrs. Amos B., 1971
Hoover, Mrs. George E., 1971
Hoover, Oliver Perry, 634, 1661
Hoover, Opal C., 748, 1972
Hoover, Paul, *191*
    on conscientious objectors, 2337
Hoover, Paul Milton, 1661
Hoover, Paul Stayer, 1661, 1839
Hoover, Pearl (later Wampler), 1316
Hoover, Perry R., 1235, 1333, 1661
    Michigan City, IN, Church of the
        Brethren, pastor, 825
Hoover, Peter, 1972
Hoover, Ralph W., 1662
Hoover, Raymond A., 242, 1662

Hoover, Robert David, 399, 424, 1662,
    1972
Hoover, Roy M., 1972
Hoover, Ruth Ruthrauff, 1972
Hoover, Samuel, 297, 634
Hoover, Samuel Blair, 1662
Hoover, Samuel W., 155, 205, 628, **628,**
    634, 1662, 1946
Hoover, Sarah (later Lichty), 741
Hoover, Silas, 273, 1225, 1662, 1972
Hoover, Stewart M., 1972
Hoover, Susan Bame
    on Heifer Project, 2338
Hoover, Susanna Weybright, 1338
Hoover, Tilman, 1662
Hoover, Tobias, 1662
Hoover, Walter A., 1662
Hoover, Warren William, 1662
    Mount Morris, IL, Church of the
        Brethren, pastor, 883
    Root River Church of the Brethren,
        MN, pastor, 1122
Hoover, Wilbur Replogle, 7, 446, 1662,
    1972
Hoover, William, 2302
Hoover, William A., 1971
Hoover, William C., 1662
Hoover, William E(llis), 1662
Hoover, William I. T., 118, **628,** 1662, 1972
    Hüber (Hoover) family, 634
Hoover, William N., 257, 619, 1214, 1662
Hooversville, PA, store in, *151*
Hooversville, PA, Church of the Brethren,
    151, **628**
    Geiger Church of the Brethren, PA,
        533
Hope, 355
    Langnecker, Ulrich, 756
Hope Beyond Healing: A Cancer Journal
    (Aukerman), 2133
Hope Brethren Fellowship, **2204**
Hope, Christian, 46, 273, 361, *361,* 362,
    370, 375, 598, 602, **628,** 629, *629,*
    682, 1243, 1296, 1662, *See also*
    Danish Mission
    Brooklyn, NY, urban ministry in, 933
    Eskildsen, Christen (?) Christensen,
        456
    Hope Memorial Church (German
        Baptist Brethren), NE, 2375
    missions and missionaries, 1839
Hope Church
    Brethren Church in Paraguay and, 2237
Hope Church of the Brethren, MI, **629**
    Elmdale, MI, Church of the Brethren,
        442
Hope Grace Brethren Church, PA, *See*
    Dillsburg, PA, Hope Grace
    Brethren Church
Hope, Mary Katherine Nielson, 628, **629,**
    629, 1839
Hope Memorial Church (German Baptist
    Brethren), NE, **2375**
    North Beatrice Church of the Brethren,
        NE, 945
Hope, Neva (later Day), *629*
Hope, NJ, Grace Brethren Church, **629,**
    929–930
Hope (ship), 456
    Flora, (Flory) family, 495
    Garber (Garver, Gerber) family, 529
    Reinhart, Ulrich, voyage to America
        on, 1094

Hopewell Grace Brethren Church, PA, **629**

Hopewell, PA, Church of the Brethren, *See* Yellow Creek Church of the Brethren, PA

Hopewell schoolhouse
Fly Creek Church of the Brethren, KS, 500

Hopewell Twp., Bedford Co., PA, 1384

Hopewell, VA, Church of the Brethren, **629**
Hopfinger, Frank, 1662

Hopkins, D. A., 231, 318
Sidney, IN, Grace Brethren Church, pastor, 1181

Hopkins, D. H., 1265
New Enterprise Brethren Church, IN, elder in, 927

Hopkins, Daniel A., 121, 758, 1662

Hopkins, Ernest, 1662

Hopkins family, 270
Genesee Old German Baptist Brethren Church, MI, 540
Germantown Old German Baptist Brethren Church, VA, 544

Hopkins, George, 1662

Hopkins, Kenneth F., 431, 1662

Hopkins, Luther Noel, 1662

Hopkins, Paul, 1662

Hopkins, Richard, 1662

Hopkinson, Francis, 1972

Hoppes, Arthur, 363, 417

Hoppes family, 233

Hopping, Carol Flora, 1972
on Flora, Henry Franklin, 2338

Hopping, Joseph, 334

Hopping, Joseph W., 630

Hoppingite group, 334

Hoppingite Schism, **630**
Pleasant Grove Church of the Brethren, KS, 1031

Hoppis, Arthur, 1662

Hopple, C. Lee, 1972

Hoppock, John D., 129, 1662

Hoppock, Margaret (later Haines), 579

Hopson, N. F., 1662

Hopson, Noah, 1662

Hopwood, G. H., 372–373

Hopwood, George W., 1662

Horche, Heinrich, 57
Philadelphia community (trans), 1967

Hordum, Denmark
Eskildsen, Christen (?) Christensen, 456

Horizons (CB), 1236
Our Young People (CB), 985

Horlacher, Hans Michael and Maria Veronica
family history, 1972

Horlacher, John Perry, 1324, 1662

Horlacher, Levi Jackson, 1972

Horlacher, Vanea Thomas, 1972

Horn, Carl von, 1972

Horn, Donald R.
Vega Baja, PR, Iglesia de los Hermanos Cristo El Señor (CB) and, 2258

Horn, Edward T., III, 1972

Horn, Elijah, 1340, 1662

Horn, Evelyn J., 1340, 1346, 1839

Horn, Gabriel, 1662

Horn, Glendon, 1662

Horn, Jacob, 1662

Horn, Linda Kay, 1852

Horn, Margaretha (later Wine), 1350

Horn, Samuel, 1662

Horn School, preaching point maintained by Kansas Center Church of the Brethren, KS, at, 683

Horn, Verda Krehbiel, 1972

Hornbacker, Tara Lea, 2282

Hornbaker, Melvin, 1913

Hornbaker, Vernon W., 1972

Hornbeck, J. H. (W.), 1662

Horne, Cora Beaver, 1972

Horne, Elijah, 1662

Horne, Henry T., 28, 1662

Horner, Abraham, 418

Horner, Anetta Wicks, 418

Horner, David D., 347, 1662

Horner, Dwight B., 1662
War Prisoner's Aid program, 1058
Young Men's Christian Associations (YMCA), 1390

Horner, Emma Ada, 1836

Horner, Emma E. (later Horst), 630

Horner, Emma (later Eby), **418**

Horner family, 1965–1966

Horner, Francis, 494

Horner, J. Richard, 21, 2282
Milroy, PA, Grace Brethren Church, pastor, 843

Horner, Jacob and Elizabeth Neff, 1972

Horner, John, 676

Horner, Joshua, 395–396, 1662

Horner, Lydia (later Myers), 2027

Horner, Meyers B., 1662

Horner, Richard, 320

Horner, Susan (later Schrock), *See* Schrock, Susan Horner

Horner, Viola Gates, 1972

Horner, Wilbert (Wilburt) J., 1662, 1972–1973

Horner, William, 1662

Hornerites, 688, *See also* Kentucky
Fleming Co., KY, German Baptist Brethren Church, 494

Horney, Samuel, 1248

Horney, Samuel Iradell, 1267, 1973
mass media, 801

Horning, A. Wilhelm, 1973

Horning, Daniel L., 1663, 1839, 1908
medical missionary, 807
Wetonka, SD, Willow Creek Church of the Brethren, 2379

Horning, Emma, 277, 1973

Horning, Emma Martin Martin, 1972

Horning, Estelle Ruth Boggs, 1839, 1973, 2133, 2172, 2282
Hispanic Ministries (CB), 2199

Horning, Esther (later Shirk), 2064

Horning family, 713
Preiß (Price) family related to, 1055

Horning, Franklin Musser, 1973

Horning, Hannah, 630

Horning, Hannah (later Ziegler), 1395, *1396*

Horning, Harriet (later Haldeman), 619

Horning, Jesse P., 1663

Horning, John S., 718, 1839
medical missions, 807

Horning, Jonas, 272, 1663

Horning, Lois (later Snyder)
National Older Adult Conferences, 2229

Horning, Martha A. Daggett, 1839

Horning, Mary Emma, **630**, 1973, 2387
Wetonka, SD, Willow Creek Church of

the Brethren, 2379

Horning, Mary (later Gilbert), 548

Horning, Moses and Lavina Gehman, 1973

Horning, Moses Musser, 1973

Horning, Samuel H., 462, 630, 1663
Wetonka, SD, Willow Creek Church of the Brethren, 2379

Horning, William W., 1663
Wetonka, SD, Willow Creek Church of the Brethren, 2379

Horning, W. W., family
Willow Creek, SD, congregation, 1205

Horning, William
Rock Creek Church of the Brethren, IL, 1116

Horning, William E., 1663

Hornish, J. F., 1243

Hornish, Jay F., 6, 602, 1663
Poplar Ridge Church of the Brethren, OH, free minister, 1047

Hornish, John, 1663

Hornish, John, Jr.
Poplar Ridge Church of the Brethren, OH, 1047

Hornish, John, Sr.
Poplar Ridge Church of the Brethren, OH, 1047

Hornor, W. M., Jr., 1973

Horring, Denmark
Hope, Christian, 361

Horsch, John, 1973

horse and buggy, *See* buggies, horsedrawn

horse training, Jesse Beery's works on, **111**, 1553, 1873

Horst, Abraham B., 115, 630, 1663

Horst, Abraham E., 2077

Horst, Abram Sauder, 1973

Horst, Anna Martin, 1973

Horst, Barbara, 630

Horst, C. B., 630, 1663

Horst, Christian, 630

Horst, Clarence W., 630, 1663

Horst, Clyde M., 630

Horst, Cora (later Sollenberger), 630, 2071

Horst, Curly Jacob H., *See* Horst family

Horst, David, 630, 1663

Horst, David H.
family history, 1973

Horst, Edith Mary (later Ramer), 2041

Horst, Edwin, 1973

Horst, Elizabeth Longenecker, 2097, *See* Horst family

Horst, Evelyn (later Borst), 630

Horst family, **630**, 2031, 2044, 2077
Heisey family, 595

Horst, George and Eva, 1973

Horst, Hazel (later Kurtz), 630

Horst, Hursch, 2071

Horst, Irvin B., 1860, 1973

Horst, Ivan, 630

Horst, Jacob, *See* Horst family

Horst, Jacob M., 1976

Horst, John, 1964

Horst, John E., 1973

Horst, John Good, 1973

Horst, Jonas, 630, 1391, 1400, 1663

Horst, Joseph, 630

Horst, Lizzie W., 2091

Horst, Mary Ellen (later Hollingshead), 630

Horst, Mary Groff, 630

Horst, Mathias M., 1973

Horst, Melvin Clyde, **630**, 1663, 1973

Horst, Michael, 630

Horst, Mildred W. (later Nolt), 2031
Horst, Myron C., 630, 1663
    Rockton, PA, Church of the Brethren,
        pastor, 1118
Horst, Naomi Martin, 630
Horst, Paul D., 1336
    on Brethren Mutual Fire Insurance
        Company, 2338
Horst, Peter, 630
Horst, Rebecca Miller, *See* Horst family
Horst, Samuel L., 1973, 2005
    works by, 2320
Horst, W. C., 1973
Horst, William Weber, 1973
Horton, H. O.
    Pulaski, VA, Church of the Brethren,
        minister, 1071
Horton, Joyce Gayle (later Spangler), 2294
Horton, Paul, Sr.
    Pulaski, VA, Church of the Brethren,
        minister, 1071
Horton, W(illie) Owen, Sr., 208, 515, 1663
Hosfeldt (Hosfield), Casper Frederick, 1663
Hosfield, Caspar
    Shippensburg, PA, Church of the
        Brethren, minister in, 1177
Hosfield family
    Ridge Church of the Brethren, PA,
        1108
Hosking, Archie C., 1663
Hosler, Paul White, 1663
Hosler, Wilbur H., 2282
hospices
    chaplaincy, 2157, 2158
    Hospital Committee (CB), **630**
    hospitality, women and, 2263
    hospitals, **630–631**, *See also* Bethany
        Brethren Hospital; healing; med-
        ical missions; medicine; nursing
    Adamawa Provincial Leprosarium, 306
    Association of Brethren Caregivers
        (ABC), 2132
    Bethany Brethren Hospital (CB), 275
    Boguila, Africa, 268
    Bremen, IN, 173
    Brethren Hospital and Sanitarium
        (CB), 188
    chaplains, 2072, 2157, 2158
    Civil War, 314
    Ephrata, 2006
    Garver, Earl S., 532
    hospital administration, article about,
        1928
    India, 1078
    Brethren Mission Hospital (CB), 191
    Interchurch Medical Assistance, Inc.
        (IMA), 658
    Lassa General Hospital, Nigeria,
        726–727
Liao Chou, 217
    list of institutions
        international, 1831
        USA, 1827
    medical missions, 807
    medical practice, 810
    medical projects, 808
    mergers of, article about, 1919
    mission schools, 853
    Nigeria, 306
    Pietism, 1022
    Puerto Rico
        Castañer Hospital, 230
    Quinter Memorial Hospital, 1078

relief training units, use of outside the
    USA, 1097
Revolutionary War, 1980
Showalter, Michael S. on American
    Revolution and Ephrata Cloister's,
    2356
Sudan Interior Mission hospital, 727
Hostedler family
    Farmington, DE, Bethany Church of
        the Brethren, 479
Hostetler, *See* Hochstedtler; Hochstetler
Hostetler, Abraham, 631
Hostetler, Adam, 615, 631, **631,** 689, 1357,
    1663
    Hon, Peter Keithly, 627
    Hostetler Brethren, 631
    Indiana, 652
    Olive Branch German Baptist Brethren
        Church, IN, 973
    Shelby Co. German Baptist Brethren
        Church, KY, minister in, 1175
Hostetler, Agnes Hardman, 631
Hostetler, Alice Elizabeth, 2078
Hostetler, Beulah Stauffer, 1912, 1973
    on Mennonite sect, 2338
    on Protestant movement, 2338
Hostetler Brethren, 58, 129, **631–632,** 689
    chart of Brethren bodies, place on,
        1403–1405
    Dutch Bethel, German Baptist Brethren
        Church, 2373
    Far Western Brethren, 475, 476
    frontier, 519
    Garber (Gerber), Daniel, 528
    Hendricks, James, 597
    Hon, Peter Keithly, 627
    Honites, 628
    Hostetler, Adam, 631
    Hostetler, Joseph, 631
    Jackson Co. German Baptist Brethren,
        IN, 667
    merger with Blue River Baptist
        Church, IN, 1380
    Olive Branch German Baptist Brethren
        Church, IN, 973
    Restoration Movement, 1101
    schism and migration of Brethren to
        Indiana, 829
    White River German Baptist Brethren
        Church, 1341
Hostetler, Bruce, 2282
Hostetler, C. K., 1973
Hostetler, Chauncey A., 1973
Hostetler, Christian, 582, 740, 2079
Hostetler Church of the Brethren, PA, **632**
Hostetler, D. W., 1920
Hostetler, Dale C., 1383, 1663
Hostetler, Daniel Webster, **631,** 1663
    Hostetler, Quincy Vern, 631
    Plevna, IN, Church of the Brethren,
        minister, 1037
Hostetler, David, 1663
Hostetler, David A., 1973
Hostetler, David and Alice Kenagy, 1974
Hostetler, Doran
    Riverside Christian Training School,
        1111
Hostetler, Dortha Tate, 631
Hostetler, Drusilla, 1973
Hostetler, Earl, 632, 1663
Hostetler, Elizabeth Hardman, 631
Hostetler, Elizabeth Schrock, 1867
Hostetler, Ella M. Doggett, 1973

Hostetler, Esther, 382
Hostetler family, 1974, 2079, *See also*
    Hochstetler (Hostetler) family
    Jackson Co. German Baptist Brethren,
        IN, 667
    Olive Branch German Baptist Brethren
        Church, IN, 973
Hostetler, Forest P., 1663
Hostetler, Hannah Hardman, 631
Hostetler, Harvey Roy, 534, 1663,
    1973–1974, **2388**
    Reedley, CA, Church of the Brethren,
        pastor, 1091
    on Stutzman Barbara, Hochstedler and
        descendants, 2338
    on Stutzman, Christian and descen-
        dants, 2338
Hostetler, Helene Maurine (later Schaffer),
    See Schaffer, Helene Maurine
    Hostetler
Hostetler, Henry P., 615
Hostetler, J. R. C., 1663
Hostetler, Jeptha S., 1974
Hostetler, John A., 1974
    plain people, 1029
    The Young Center and, 2267
Hostetler, Joseph, 177, 281, 548, 615, **631,**
    689, 740, 1663, 1858, 1974
    Hostetler Brethren, 632
    Indiana, 652
    references to, 1933, 1960
    Restoration Movement, 1101
Hostetler, Josiah, 80
Hostetler, Levi, 447
Hostetler, Lizzieann J., 1974
Hostetler, Magdalena (later Hoffer), 567
Hostetler, Menno J.
    genealogy and family history, 1974
Hostetler, Nancy
    Riverside Christian Training School,
        1111
Hostetler, Nettie, 2079
Hostetler, Norman, 669
Hostetler, PA, congregation
    Meyersdale, PA, Church of the
        Brethren, 822
Hostetler, Paul V., 1974
Hostetler, Pius, 1974
Hostetler, Quincy Vern, **631,** 1663
Hostetler, Rethan, 1974
Hostetler, Richard, 923
Hostetler, Samuel B., 1974
Hostetler, Sarah B. Frey, 1974
Hostetler, Solomon
    Mount Zion German Baptist Brethren,
        KY, minister in, 935
Hostetler, Susan Wissinger, 631
Hostetler, Susie Jane, 1974
Hostetler, Tom Richard, 1663
Hostetter, Albert K., 1974
Hostetter, C. Nelson
    on Brethren bodies, information about,
        2342
Hostetter, Christian N., Jr., 1974
Hostetter family, 1974
Hostetter (Hofstetter/Hochstetter) families
    bibliography, 1887
Hostetter, Hugh Bingley, 1974
Hostetter, J. Earl, 1663
Hostetter, Jacob, 2338
Hostetter, John D., 2282
Hostetter, John M., 1663
Hostetter, Julie Mader, 2165, 2282

Hostetter, Margaret, 1840
Hostetter, Maria, 2338
Hostetter, Oscar L., 1974
Hostetter, Oswald, 2338
Hostetter, Richard L., 2338
Hostetter, Rick E., 2282
Hostetter, Susannah (later Schrock), *See*
    Schrock, Susannah Hostetter
Hostettler, Sam, 347
Hostettler, Mrs. Sam, 347
Hostotler, Cora E. (later Keller), 1675
Hotchkin, Samuel Fitch, 1974
Hotchkiss, Jed, 2088
Hotel Radetsky (Hinterbühl, Austria), 73
Hotler, John, 1663
Hotsinpiller, Elizabeth Brumback, 2087
Hotsinpiller family, 2087
Hotsinpiller, Stephen, 2087
Hottel, Althea, 1361
Hottel, Benjamin K., 1663
Hottel, J. W. Holt
    Meadow Mills Church of the Brethren,
        VA, 806
Hottenstein, A(mos) S(tehman), 416, 1663
Hottenstein, Cora M. (later Moyer), *See*
    Moyer family
Hottinger, Silas J., 1663
Hottle, Ken, 1974
Houch, Diana, 231
Houchnour, F., 1663
Houck, Elizabeth S., 1974
Houff, James Lee, 424, 1663
Houff, Marlin Dean, 247, 2282
Houff, Robert Earle, 1324, 1663–1664,
    1974, 2302
Hougendougler (Hugendoughler), John,
    1664
Hough (Huff) family, 1885
    history in U. S., 1974
Hough, Granville W., 1974
Hough, Mary Paul Hallowell, 1974
Hougham, 1664
Hought, Albert, *See* Haught, Albert
Houghtelin, Hezekiah
    condensed record, 1960
Houghton family, 1383
Houghton, James E., 2282
Houk, Peter, 1664
    Pipe Creek Church of the Brethren, IN,
        elder, 1025
    Plevna, IN, Church of the Brethren,
        minister, 1037
house churches, 632, *632,* **632,** *See also*
    worship, in homes
    District of Columbia, 391
    Fellowship of Hope, 488
    Manos de Cristo fellowship (CB), 2252
House Committee on Military Affairs, 312
House of Clay (Statler), 748
House of the Church of the Brethren, 194,
    See also Brethren Press
House of Truth (Bet Emet), 191
housefathers
    ministry, terminology, 847, 848
householders
    ministry, terminology, 847, 848
housekeepers
    ministry, terminology, 847, 848
housekeeping, *See* church, doctrine of; dis-
    cipline; ministry, terminology
Housel, William, 1664
Houser, Catherine Swigart, 633
Houser, Daniel, 235, 348, **632–633**

inventions and scientific discoveries,
    660
Houser, Elizabeth Swigart, 633
Houser, Friedrick, 1664
Houser, Jacob, 632, 2080
Houser, Joseph, 1664
Houser, Loreeta, 1833
Houser, Magdalena Schrecongost, 632
Houser, Orville E., 1664
Houser, Rhorer, Dillman, and Hoover
    families, 1974
Houser, Salome Crull, 2080
Houser, Stanley
    Parkersburg, WV, Grace Brethren
        Church, 994
    Raystown Brethren Church, PA, pastor,
        1084
Houser, Susannah Royer Stoner, 633
Houser, Sylvia Rieman
    Rieman, Timothy Wayne (CB) and,
        2243
Houser, William Wesley, 1974
Houser's Church (Mennonite), MD, 467
housing
    Habitat for Humanity International,
        2195
    homelessness, 2203
    Kentucky Mountain Housing Develop-
        ment Corporation (KMHDC),
        2130–2131
housing cooperatives
    York Center Community Cooperative,
        Lombard, IL, 1389
Houston family
    Jackson Co. German Baptist Brethren,
        IN, 667
Houston, Tracy, 1664
Houston, TX, congregation, 1255
Hovatter, David
    Shiloh Church of the Brethren, WV,
        1177
Hovatter family
    Mount Cassell Old German Baptist
        Brethren Church, WV, 880
Hovatter, John, 1664
Hovatter, Obed, 1277, 1664
How Brethren Understand God's World,
    2141, 2148, 2172
How to Use Business Machines (Fasnacht),
    480
Howard, Antone Leroy, 1664, 1850
Howard, Bonnie (later Pifer)
    Pifer, Lester Elden and, 2238
Howard, Clifford, 379, 1974
Howard Co., IN, 217, 705, 1312
    Church of the Brethren, 77, **633**
    Howard, IN, Church of the Brethren,
        633
    North Kokomo Grace Brethren Church,
        IN, 948
    Old German Baptist Brethren Church,
        633, **633**
    Plevna, IN, Church of the Brethren,
        1037
Howard Co., MD
    Ellicot City, MD, Pine Orchard Church
        of the Brethren, 441
Howard, Courland David, 2282
Howard, Craig Alan, 2282
Howard, Dorothy Eileen Yerian, 1850
Howard, Harriet, 1834
Howard, Isaiah L., 1664
Howard, John Eager, 80

Howard, Kenneth, Ray, 1664
Howard, Lewis C., 1664
Howard, Roy, 1664
Howard, Samuel B., 1664
Howard, Wayne Edward, 320, 1664
Howard, William D., 319, 1664
Howard, William E., 579, 2302
Howe, Anna Gertrude Kearns, 633
Howe, Carl E., 1664
Howe, D. R., 1975
Howe, David N., *1351*
    Manchester College, President, 786
Howe, Edith R. Newcomer, 633
Howe, Edward Mohler, 1664
    Maitland Church of the Brethren, PA,
        minister, 783
Howe, Elizabeth, *See* Brubaker, Elizabeth
    Howe
    Pittsburgh, PA, Church of the Brethren,
        1027
Howe, Elizabeth (later Brubaker), 1296,
    1344, 1361
    Italian Sunday School (CB), 664–665
    Moody Bible Institute, 872
Howe, Elizabeth Wertz, 633
Howe, Hettie (later Eby), 419
Howe, IN, Brighton Chapel Brethren
    Church, *See* Brighton, IN,
        Brighton Chapel Brethren Church
Howe, Julia Ward
    Mothers' Day, 879
Howe, Mary Elizabeth (later Robinson),
    1115
Howe, Minnie E. (later Kinsey), 696
Howe, Roland Levi, **633,** 1975
    historical writing, 612
Howe, Sarah Mohler, 633
Howe-Singer sewing machines
    business beliefs and, 234
Howe, William Mohler, **633,** 1287, 1664,
    1975
    Johnstown, PA, Walnut Grove Church
        of the Brethren, 675
    Maitland Church of the Brethren, PA,
        minister, 783
    Meyersdale, PA, Church of the
        Brethren, pastor, 822
    Norristown, PA, Church of the
        Brethren, pastor, 945
Howell Co., MO
    Peace Valley Church of the Brethren,
        MO, 1003
Howell family, 1277
Howell, Frank D., 758, 1664
    Pomona, CA, Fellowship Church of the
        Brethren, 1045
Howell, Gilbert Lee, 1664
Howell, Gregory M., 556, 2282
Howell, Ida Shockley, 1975
    Pomona, CA, Fellowship Church of the
        Brethren, 1045
Howell, Isaac, 65
Howell, Jesse Paul, 1664
Howell, John, 1975
Howell, John D., 1664
Howell, Jonathan Stutsman, 1975
Howell, N. Jennie (later Haughtelin), 589
Howell, Steve, 1664
Howell, Thomas F., 564, 1664
    McLouth, KS, Brethren Church, pastor,
        779
Howells, William Dean, 747, 1975
    minorities, ethnic and racial, 851

Howes, Floyd Verlin, 1975
Howie Terry, 1664
Howitt, E., 378
Howitt, Emanuel, 1975
Howman family
    Homerville, OH, Grace Brethren
        Church, 626
Hoxie, George A., 1346
Hoxie, George W., 65, 520, **633,** 1664
    Oregon, 980
Hoxie, Sarah, 633
Hoy, Ira D., 262, 1664
    Red Hill Church of the Brethren, VA,
        pastoral leadership, 1088
Hoy, Virginia Senseman
    on Studebaker, Nancy and descendants,
        2338
    on Studebaker, Samuel and descen-
        dants, 2338
Hoye, Charles E., 1975
Hoyle Creek Church of the Brethren, OK,
    633–634
Hoyt, Aldo Elwyn, 53, 1664, 1850
Hoyt, Alice Luetta Russell, 1850
Hoyt, Anna Leola Dorsey, 634
Hoyt, C. Lowell, 1664, 1975
Hoyt, Clarence Lyman, 634
Hoyt, Dolores J.
    works by, 2309
Hoyt, Edwin Max, 634
Hoyt, Garner, 1664
Hoyt, Giles R.
    works by, 2309
Hoyt, Harriet L. Fitz, 634, 1353
Hoyt, Herman A., 136, 485, 563, 564, **634,**
    705, 1353, 1664, 1975, 2302
    The Brethren Minister's Handbook,
        788
    bibliography of, 2309
    on Boyer, James I., 2338
    End Times, The, 2338
    Grace Schools, 2192
    on Hoyt, Herman S., 2338
    Iowa, 661
    on McClain, Alva J., 2338
    prophecy conferences, 1062
    on prophetic word, 2338
    secret societies, Brethren opposition to,
        1164
    on 2 Peter, 2338
Hoyt, Herman A.
    sources on, 2322
Hoyt, Joseph Paul, 634
Hoyt, Kathryn Ruth Hirschy, 1850
Hoyt, Lowell, 377, 439, 731
Hoyt, Lynn Arthur, 53, 1664, 1850
Hoyt, Mary Eileen Knepper, 1850
Hoyt, Solon Waverly, 53, 360, 1664, 1850
Hromadka, Josef L., 286
Hsin, Chang Tzu, 1664
The Hub of the Tulpehocken (Ibach), 1977
Hubbard Co., MN
    Guthrie Church of the Brethren, 576
Hubbard, E. M.
    Newberg, OR, Church of the Brethren,
        pastor in, 933
Hubbard, Elbert, 1975
Hubbard family, 143
Hubbard, Floyd Bryce, 1664, 2302
Hubbard, Lawrence O., 267, 332, 439, 467,
    725, 1664
Hubbard, Leonard, 1664
    Peters Creek Old German Baptist

Brethren Church, VA, minister,
    1012
Hubbard, Marilyn
    on Washington Creek CB, KS, 2338
Hubbard, Oscar, 231
Hubbard, Will
    Peters Creek Old German Baptist
        Brethren Church, VA, minister,
        1012
Hubbard, William Miller, 1664
Hubbard, William Robert, 1664
Hubbart, Inez, 503
Hubbell, Donald George, 1664, 2282
Hubble, James W., 2282
Hubble, William, 1664
Huber, Andreas, 634
Huber, Anna (later Wenger), 1330
Huber, Calvin A., 1664
Huber family, 1975–1976, 2064
Huber, Ferdinand, 1664
Huber, Harold Eugene, 1975
Huber, Harry I., 1975
Huber Heights (Emmanuel), OH, congrega-
    tion, 365
Huber Heights, OH, 365
    Brethren Church, 366
Huber, Heinrich, 1897
Huber-Hoover family, **634,** 1299, 2073
    bibliography, 1894
    family history and genealogy, 1971
    sources on, 2320
Huber (Hoover), Johannes (John) and Mary
    Watson, 1972
Huber, Jacob Frederick, 1975
Huber, Johannes, 634
Huber, John Lewis, 1664–1665
Huber, Landis and Ellen, 1975
Huber, Leona, 352
Huber, Leonard, 205
Huber, Lester, 1665
Huber, Lewis, 121, 152
Huber, Margaret Pfautz, 634
Huber, Wilmer Books, 1975
Huch, C. F., 1976
Huckaby, G. W., 1665
huckster wagon, *234*
Huddleson, Anthony
    Pierce Co. Church of the Brethren, WI,
        1021
Hudson, Elizabeth Hill, 1850
Hudson, Elliott Anderson, 1665, 1850, 2282
Hudson, Harrison, 1665
Hudson, IA
    congregation, 155
    First Brethren Church, **635,** 661
Hudson, IL, 732
    Church of the Brethren, **635**
Hudson, John L., 104, 1665
Huelsbergen, Helmut L.
    on Koch, Stephen, 2338
Huelsman, Larry, 325
Huelsman, Sue, 325
Huesmann, Louis M., II, 2173, 2282
    London, OH, Grace Brethren Church,
        2215
Huetten, Ulric[h] von, 1977
Huff, Bernard Wilbur, 733, 1665
Huff, Charles, 1665
Huff family, 153, *See also* Hoff (Huff) fami-
    ly; Hough (Huff) family
    Freeling Settlement Old German
        Baptist Brethren Church, WV, 514
Huff, John, 1665

Huff, Lula B. (later Dove), 397
Huff, Peter
    Maumee Church of the Brethren, OH,
        minister, 803
Huffaker, Alice L. Thompkins, 635
Huffaker, Annette (later Beam), 1335
Huffaker, Catherine, *See* Huffaker family
Huffaker family, 2031
Huffaker, Harrison L., 635
Huffaker, John L., 1665
    on monologues on calls of Old Testa-
        ment leaders, 2338
Huffaker, Josephine Costello
    on Gish, Christian, 2338
Huffaker, Michael, *See* Huffaker family
Huffaker, Perry Lee, 242, **635,** 1215, 1335,
    1665
    hymns, 643
Huffard, D. D.
    Patterson, CA, Church of the Brethren,
        995
Huffer, Eliza (later Garst), 531
Huffer, John, 531
Huffer, Rachel Keen, 531
Huffert, John, 1665
Huffman, A. N., 1212, 1250
Huffman, Alva, 1213
Huffman, Bertha Barbara Thomas, 2205
Huffman, Bruce Edward, 2282
Huffman, Cathy Simmons
    on Hagerstown CB, MD, 2338
Huffman, Christian, 1976
Huffman, Clifford B., 1976
Huffman, David W., 1665
Huffman, Edward N., 1976
    South Saint Joseph Church of the
        Brethren, MO, pastor, 1135
Huffman, Edward Newton, 1665
Huffman, Eleanor Christine (later Myers),
    2205
Huffman, Ella Mae Sours, 1389, 2205
Huffman family, *See* Hoffman (Huffman)
    family
    Nevada, MO, Church of the Brethren,
        924
Huffman, Glenn
    on Wampler, Ben and descendants,
        2338
    on Wampler, Elizabeth Beery and
        descendants, 2338
Huffman, J. B. F., 1665
    Rileyville, VA, Church of the Brethren,
        1109
Huffman, Jacob S., 1665
Huffman, James W., 1665
Huffman, Jasper A., 1944
Huffman, John, 617, 1665
Huffman, John D., 1665
Huffman, John P., 1665
Huffman, Lester W., 236, 1665
Huffman, Lewis, 1665
Huffman, Lucy (later Sides), 1213
Huffman, Mason L., 494, 1276, 1665
Huffman, Mattie Deardorff
    South Saint Joseph Church of the
        Brethren, MO, 1135
Huffman, Milo G., 1665
    Pipe Creek Church of the Brethren, IN,
        elder, 1025
Huffman, Nancy Lionberger, 617
Huffman, Nelson Thomas, *2204, 2205*
    The Rockingham Male Chorus,
        2204–2205

Huffman, Nelson Thomas (son)
  Huffman, Nelson Thomas (father),
    2205
Huffman, R. G., 1976
Huffman, Reuben Ephriam, 2282
Huffman, Simon Peter, 1665
Huffman, Vernon Lowell, 1665
Huffman, William, 264
Huffman, William H., 2205
Huffman, Zola (later Wampler), 2259
Huffmann, Lou M., 2282
Hufford, Craig D., 2282
Hufford, David A., 605, 1665
  Salem Church of the Brethren, ND,
    elder, 1137
Hufford, Doris
  on Hufford, Frances, 2358
Hufford, Elizabeth (later Wagoner)
  Wagoner, Raymond K. (OGBB) and,
    2259
Hufford family, 232, 317
  Genesee Old German Baptist Brethren
    Church, MI, 540
  South Haven Old German Baptist
    Brethren Church, MI, 1205
Hufford, Frances
  Clark, Doris Hufford on, 2358
  Stall, Velma Hufford on, 2358
Hufford (Hoffart), Christian, 1968
Hufford, Isaac, 317, 1665
Hufford, Israel, 1665
Hufford, Lisa M., 2282
Hufford, Velma
  on Hufford, Frances, 2358
Hufford, William Edward, 1665
Hufstedler family, history of, 1950
Huftalen, Sarah Gillespie, 1976
"Hugenot-Dunkard-Mennonite Discipline,"
  1976
Huggett, John B., 2282
Huggins, Maloy A., 1976
Hugh, I. H.
  Peach Blossom Colored Church of
    Rising Light (CB), MD, deacon,
    1003
Hughes, Gerald, 1665
Hughes, John R., 1665
Hughes, Myrtle, 1665
Hughes, Thomas D., 1267, 1342, 1665
Hughes, William
  Mountain Valley Church of the
    Brethren, TN, part-time pastor, 889
Hughey, Bertha Ellen Robinson, 1976
Hughey, Hobert, 1665
Hughson, CA
  Empire, CA, Church of the Brethren,
    445
Hugo, C., 1976
Huguenots, 2050
  Community of True Inspiration,
    330–331
  Flora (Flory) family, 495
  Pennsylvania, 2072
Henrich Albrecht, 597
Huh, Ben Un, 2282
Huhns, Arlene, 366
Huinca Renancó, Argentina, 53
Huizinga (Huisinga), Jacob Dircks, 635
Huizinga, Jacob D., 1976
Hull, Abraham, 1665
Hull, George W., 1665
Hull, Judith Maxine Yarger
  on Jurger/Yarger, George and descen-

dants, 2349
Hull, Margaret Helen, 1850
  missionary to Central African
    Republic, 1019
Hull, Mildred
  on CB name index, Ohio, 2350
Hull, Robert Thompson, 571, 1665
Hull, William J., 1976
Hulse, Barbara Lee, 173, 1278, 1850
Hulse, F. M, 1665
Hulse, Lewis James, 590, 1665
Hulst, E. Merritt, Jr., 264, 1665
Hultgren, O., 1665
Hulvey, Glen Leroy, 1665
Hulvey, Velma June Good, 1976
human nature
  doctrine of, 29, 635
  nonconformity, 941
  original sin, 981
The Human Problem (Kurtz), 1992
human rights commission, Elgin, IL,
    Highland Avenue Church of the
    Brethren, 436
human sexuality, See sexuality
humanistic values, 695
humanitarianism, 635–636, See also funda-
    mentalism; social gospel
humanity, redemption of, 1090
Humbarger, John, 1, 1665
Humbarger, Lauren (Loren), 1665
Humbarger, S., 1665
Humberd, John Mahlon, 636
Humberd, Larry T., 579, 2186, 2282
Humberd, Russell I., 241, 318, 636, 748,
    1269, 1305, 1665, 1976
  Jews, 671
  Martinsburg, PA, Grace Brethren
    Church, pastor, 798
  Moody Bible Institute, 873
  prophecy conferences, 1062
Humbert family, 1391
Humbert, William Kinzie, 1665
A Humble Gleam
  Mack, Alexander, Jr., 774
A Humble Gleam of the Despised Little
    Light of Truth, See Geringer
    Schein, Ein (A Humble Gleam)
Humboldt Co., CA, congregation
  Myers, Jonathan, 904
Hume, Edgar Erskine, 1976
Humes family
  Osceola, IN, Grace Brethren Church,
    983
humility, 636, See also discipline; human
    nature, doctrine of; titles, honorific
  and art, 59
  Brethren Doctrine of Salvation, 1140
  dress and, 402
  Dunkard Brethren, 409
  feetwashing, 481
  incorporation, 649
  raised pulpits, 48
  redemption, 1090
  Sermon on the Mount, 1169
Humlong family
  Fleming Co., KY, German Baptist
    Brethren Church, 494
Hummel, Charles F.
  on PA Germans, arts of, 2333
Hummer, Catherine (later Keller), 636–637,
    732, 1233, 1309
  prophecy, 1062
  statement regarding, and Georg

Schreiber, 1156
  visions of, 132
Hummer, David A., 1665
Hummer, Elizabeth (later Gibbel), 547
Hummer family, 1312
Hummer, Frederick, 1665
Hummer, Lewis O., 513, 1941
Hummer, Peter, 636–637, 1665
Hummer, Samuel S., 1665–1666
humor
  Beahm, William M., 2135
  jokes, cultural expression, 2147
  manifestations, 1985
Humphrey, A. O., 1666
Humphrey, Bessie (later King), 694
Humphreys, Elwood F., 749, 1666, 2302
  autobiography of, 2338
Humphreys, Homer, 1666
Humphreys, Lewis G., 1324, 1666
Humphreys, Mrs. Isaac, 672
Humsberger, Clarence, 1666
Hundley, George, 1666
Hungarian Reformed Church and APC, 286
Hungary
  AFSC aid for, 23
  Hungarian Revolution and refugee resettle-
    ment, 1093
  Reformation, Protestant, 1091
  refugees from, 198, 200
hunger, 2021, 2265–2266, See also famine
  Mennonite Church (MC), 815
  Ridgeway Community Church of the
    Brethren, PA, concern of, 1109
Hunger of the Heart (Miller), 1052
Hungerford, A. N., 1929
Hungerford, Rae (later Mason), 1841
  biography, 2201
  Mason, George Edward, 2218
Hunkins, Margaret Glick ?, 554
Hunn, David LeRoy, 1666
Hunn, George Arthur, 1666
Hunn, Ivan
  Mishawaka, IN, Brethren Church, 852
Hunn, Kenneth D., 1666
Hunn, Mrs. Ivan
  Mishawaka, IN, Brethren Church, 852
Hunsaker, Abraham, 298, 1976
Hunsaker, Abraham (?), 1357
Hunsaker, Abram, See Union Co., IL
Hunsaker, Adam, 1288
Hunsaker, Anna, 637
Hunsaker, Anna (later Wolfe), 637, 1356
Hunsaker, Caleb, 62, 142, 1666
Hunsaker family, 298, See Hunsiker family
  Jackson Co. German Baptist Brethren,
    IN, 667
  Muhlenberg Co., KY, German Baptist
    Brethren, 893
Hunsaker, Hartmann, 637
Hunsaker (Hunsicker), John, 1666
Hunsaker, Jacob, 171
Hunsaker, John, 637
  medical practice, 810
Hunsaker, Jonathan, 1666
Hunsaker, Magdalena Beery, 637
Hunsaker, Mary (later Rowland), 637
Hunsaker, Q. Maurice, 1976
Hunsbarger, S. A., 1666
Hunsberger, Mary (later Ziegler), 1395,
    1396
Hunsberger, William H., 1666
Hunsecker, John, 1908
Hunsicker, Clifton Swenk, 1976

Hunsicker, Clinton P., 1666, 2126
Hunsicker family, 1976
Hunsicker, Harry, 1976
Hunsicker, Harry A., 1976
Hunsicker, Horace M., 1976
Hunsiker family, 2075
Hunsiker (Hunsaker) family, **637**
Hunsiker, Margaret Moyer
    Meyer family, 822
Hunsiker, Rudolph
    Meyer family, 822
Hunt, Cecil, 1976
Hunt family, 2105
Hunt, James
    Island Pond, VT, Grace Brethren
      Church, 2209
Hunt, James E., Jr., 662, 664, 1666
Hunt, James Franklin, Jr., 1850
Hunt, Mary Margaret Foley, 1850
Hunt, Mattie Lorea (later Kesler), 690
Hunt, True L., 349, 360, 1289, 1666, 2302
Hunter family
    Grandview, MO, Dunkard Brethren
      Congregation, 565
    Modesto, CA, La Loma Grace Brethren
      Church, 867
Hunter, Gayle (later Sheller), 2293
Hunter, James R., 1666
Hunter, John, 726
Hunter, John Wilbur, 1666
    Modesto, CA, Church of the Brethren,
      866
Hunter, Jonathan Cady, 1314, 1666
    Ridgeway Community Church of the
      Brethren, PA, pastor, 1109
Hunter, Thomas E., 1666
Hunter, William A., 1211
    on PA Germans, 2338
Hunterdon Co., NJ, 239, 383, 1287, 2070
    Calvary Brethren Church in, 929
    history and legends, 1998
    Naas, Johannes in, 929
    Sand Brook Church of the Brethren,
      NJ, 1142
    Sargeantville Progressive Brethren, 929
    tombstone inscriptions, 1976
Huntingdon Co., PA, 18, 144, 165, 219,
    222, 300, 317, 352, *678*, 724, 767,
    827, 1213, 1245, 1312, 1327,
    1389, 1400, 1863, 2051, 2075
    Brethren publishing, 1004
    Golden Dawn, The, 556
    Helping Hands, 595
    history, 1976, 2002
    Home for Orphan and Friendless
      Children, 625
    Sisters' Aid Society, 1187
Huntingdon Normal School and Collegiate
    Institute, *See* Juniata College
Huntingdon, PA, Kishacoquillas Valley
    Church of the Brethren, *See* Dry
      Run Church of the Brethren, PA
Huntingdon, PA, Stone Church of the
    Brethren, 52, **637**, 710, 1314, 1343
    Marklesburg, PA, James Creek Church
      of the Brethren, 794
Huntington City Church, OH, 320
Huntington (Co.) Church of the Brethren,
    IN, **637–638**, *See also* Huntington,
      IN, City Church of the Brethren
Huntington Co., IN, 319, 2111
    Paul family in, 996
    Shoemaker, David, 1157

Shultz and Paul families, 1156
Shultz, Lawrence W., 1180
Huntington Co., OH, congregation, 320
Huntington, IN, 736, 757, 1896
    City Church of the Brethren, **637**
      Flory, Ezra, 498
    First Brethren Church, 394, **637**
    Salamonie Church of the Brethren near,
      1136
Huntley, K. Dean, 1666
Huntsdale Church of the Brethren, PA, 394,
    638, 934, 1294
    Hollinger family, 620
Huntsman, E. T., 1666
Huntzinger, Israel, 109, 1666
Hunziker, Emanuel and Margaret, 1976
Hunziker, John, 1976
Hupp family
    Prosperity Brethren Church, WV, 1062
Huratado, Aubrelo, 1248
Huratiak, Dennis D., 2138
Hurd, Fred
    Beissel, Conrad, creed of, 2338
Hurd, G. Emery, 2282
Hurd, Michael L., 1666
Hurd, Mike, 274
Hurlbut, Marjorie Jean, 1848
Hurlbut, Phil, 2282
Hurley, Thomas E., 1666
Hurlock, Virgil, 705
Huron Co., Ontario
    Waterloo River, Ontario, Brethren con-
      gregation, 975
Hurricane Creek Church of the Brethren,
    IL, **638,** 646, 1232
    Mulberry Grove, IL, Church of the
      Brethren, 893
Hurricane Creek Old German Baptist
    Brethren Church, IL, **638**
Hurricane Floyd
    Barnes, Jay on Brethren disaster aid
      and, 2348
    Moore, Richard on Brethren disaster
      aid and, 2348
Hurricane of 1900, Galveston
    Manvel, TX, Church of the Brethren,
      destroying meetinghouse, 789
hurricanes
    Hanoverdale, PA, churchhouse
      destroyed, 142
Hursh, Donald Franklin, 268, 503, 674,
    1666
    Shippensburg, PA, Church of the
      Brethren, pastor in, 1177
Hurst, Frances Weaver Martin, 1976–1977
Hurst, John Calvin, 109, 1666
Hurst, Thomas A.
    On Earth Peace Assembly, 2235
Hurst, Wilmer R., 324, 1666, 2302
Hurt, Frank B.
    on German pioneers, 2338
Hus, Jan
    Reformation, Protestant, 1091
Huse, Horace Elmer, 1666
Huse, Robert Lester, 1666
Huskins, James C., 2282
Hussites (Czech Brethren)
    pacifism in Christian church history,
      998
Huston, Albert William, 1666
    Silver Springs, MD, Good Shepherd
      Church of the Brethren, pastor,
      1182

Huston, Barbara Baughman, 638
Huston, Ervin Leroy, 1666
    Jackpot Church, NV, 2212
Huston family
    Four Mile Church of the Brethren, IN,
      505
Huston, Mary (later Leedy), 734
Huston Memorial Peace Lectures, **638**
    Huston, Ora Ivan, 638
Huston, Nancy (later Miller)
    Müller (Miller) family, 894
Huston, Ora Ivan, 576, **638,** 1666, 1977
    Newberg, OR, Church of the Brethren,
      pastor in, 933
    Huston Memorial Peace Lectures, 638
Hut, Hans, 28
Hutchens, James M., 1666, 1977
Hutchins, Albert G., 1977
Hutchinson, Anna M.
    Sanger, Conrad, descendant of, and
      missionary, 1144
Hutchinson, Anna Martha, 417
Hutchinson, Cynthia Jane (later Kahle), *See*
    Kahle, Cynthia Jane Hutchinson
Hutchinson, George, 1666
Hutchinson, James Alexander, 1666
Hutchinson, Joseph, 1666
Hutchinson, KS, Community Church of the
    Brethren, **638**
    Pleasant View Church of the Brethren,
      KS, 1036
Hutchinson, Leslie I., 1666
    Portis, KS, Grace Brethren Church,
      pastor, 1048
    San Jose, CA, South Bay community
      Church (FGBC), pastor, 1142
Hutchinson, Martin Earl, 2282
Hutchinson, Samuel W., 744, 1666
Hutchinson, Samuel J., 1666, **2383**
Hutchinson, Sharon Cobb, 2282
Hutchinson, Wilson, 1666
Hutchison, Andrew M., 268, 438, 461,
    638–639, *639,* 1315, 1318, 1666,
    1977
    Missouri Brethren settlement, 864
Hutchison, Anna Martha, **639,** 1839, 1977
Hutchison, Cynthia, 638
Hutchison, Dona, 1840
Hutchison family, 1224
    Howard Co. Old German Baptist
      Brethren Church, IN, 633
Hutchison, G. W., 1666
Hutchison, Henry
    Peach Blossom Colored Church of
      Rising Light (CB), MD, 1003
Hutchison, James A., 639
Hutchison, James R., 1666–1667
Hutchison, Leslie I., 104
Hutchison, Mary Crumpacker, 639
Hutchison, Modena (later Miller)
    Miller, Samuel J., wife of, 842
Hutchison, Samuel, 638
Hutchison, Susanna Sanger, 639
Hüttenal
    Alexander Mack Museum, **2130,** 2143
    historic sites, 609
    Hüttental, 639, 640
    Old German Bible, *139*
    Schwarzenau, 1158
    Schwarzenau Brethren worship in, 911
Hutter, Jacob, 29
Hutterian Society of Brothers, 28, 29, 56,
    292–293, 329, **639–641,** 2025,

2098
Bowman, Carl F. on, 2341
founder of, 56
Jordan, Clarence, contact with, 705
Kraybill, Donald B. on, 2341
Mow, D. Merrill on struggle for renewal of, 2348
and New Covenant Fellowship, 926
nonconformity, 940
oaths, taking of, 959
plain people, 1029
Plow Creek Fellowship, 1038
Wagoner, Bob on Paraguay and, 2361
Wagoner, Shirley on Paraguay and, 2361
Huttle, Benjamin, 1667
Hutton, Albert, 1667
Hutton, Albert N., 1667
Hutton, Inez (later Ernzen), 1932
Hutton, Perry, 1667
Hyattsville, MD, University Park Church of the Brethren, **641**
Monrovia, MD, Bush Creek Church of the Brethren, 870
Hyde, Lambert
Sergeantsville, NJ, Brethren Church, 1167
Hyde, Lewis A., 90, 738, 1217, 1365, 1667
Maple Grove Church of the Brethren, WI, pastor, 791
Hyde, Robinson (Robeson), 129, 1667
Hydèhn, P., 1667
Hyden, KY, 689
Hyer, Enoch, 602, 1667
Hyer family, 2079, See also Heyer (Hyer, Heier, Hire) family
Hyer, Hans Rudolph, 602
Hyer (Hayer) familyhistory, 1983
Hyer (Hyre, Hier), Isaac, 1667
Hyer, Wesley, 1667
Hyera, Nigeria, 306
Hygiene, CO, 2071
Church of the Brethren, **641**
Flory, Jacob S., 498
migration of Brethren, 830
St. Vrain congregation, 324
Hykes, Charles, 587
Hykes, David K., 31, 1667
Hykes, Effie, 587
Hykes family, 721
Hykes, Mary Lou (later Harsh), 587, **587**, 1838, 1958, 1977, See also China
Petersburg, WV, Memorial Church of the Brethren, pastor and missionary, 1012
Hylkema-Cassel-Taylor correspondence
Durnbaugh, Donald F. on, 2326
Hylkema, Cornelius B., 1977
Hylton, A., 672
Hylton, A. H., 1667
Hylton, Abraham Neff, 515, 1267, 1667
Pleasant Hill Church of the Brethren, VA, elder, 1033
Hylton, Anna, 166
Hylton, Archelaus, 641
Hylton, Austin, 500, 1667
Parkway Church of the Brethren, VA, 994
Hylton, Benjamin B., 469, 1667
Hylton, C. D., 629, 1275
Protection Church of the Brethren, KS, elder, 1062
Selma, VA, Church of the Brethren,

minister, 1166
Hylton, Charles C., 1667
Hylton, Christian (Chrisley) D., 1667
Hylton, Clyde E., 1667
Grossnickle, MD, congregation, 826
Hylton, Dale
Meadow Branch Church of the Brethren, MD. pastor, 805
Hylton, Daniel Price, 1667
Hylton, Elbert, 1667
Hylton, Ethelbert E., 1667
Hylton family, **641**, 750, 1326, 2078
Hylton, George
missionary, 1144
Hylton, George W., 1977
Hylton, Gilbert W., 1667
Hylton, H. B., 1667
Hylton, Harden P., 500, 1667
St. Paul Church of the Brethren, VA, providing leadership, 1135
Smith River Church of the Brethren, VA, presiding elder, 1192
Hylton, Isaac L., 469, 1667
Hylton, J. B., 231
Peace Valley Church of the Brethren, MO, 1003
Hylton, Jacob, 1667
Hylton, John Bryant, 1667
Hylton, John W., 1667
Hylton, John W. B., 469, 1667
Hylton, Joseph B., 469
Hylton, Joseph Byerly, 1667
Hylton, Lester Dale, 1667
Hylton, Mrs. Blanche, 1977
Hylton, P. N., 1667
Hylton, R. N.
Shelton Church of the Brethren, NC, 1176
Hylton, Ralph, 1667
Hylton, Roy P. (T.), 1667
Hylton, S. A., 1667
Hylton, S. E., 1667
Parkway Church of the Brethren, VA, 994
Hylton, S. Elbert, 1667
Hylton, Solomon P., 1667
Hymer, Sophia, 91
"A Hymn of Feet-Washing"
humility, 636
Hymnal: A Worship Book (1992), 2162, **2205–2206**
language, inclusive, 2214
music, 2227
musical instruments, 2228
sources on, 2317
worship and, 2266
Hymnal: Accompaniment Handbook (1993)
Hymnal: A Worship Book, 2206
music, 2227
musical instruments, 2228
Hymnal, Church of the Brethren, 1977
Hymnal Companion (1996)
Hymnal: A Worship Book, 2206
hymnals, 3, 72, 111–112, **641–642**, 1970, 2027, 2029–2030, 2030, 2039, 2061, See also singing; tunes
Die Kleine Lieder Sammlung, 1987
Die Kleine Perlen-Sammlung, 1987
Beery, William, 1873
Beissel, Conrad, 1874
bibliography, 1858, 1859, 1860, 1867, 1889
Brethren, and Sauer press, 1149

Brethren movement and, 175, 176
Brethren music, 898
Brethren Press, 2149
The Brethren Songbook, 223
Brightbill, Alvin Francis, 209
choristers and, 279
Christian Education Commission (CB), 285
Christian education movement, 283
The Christian's Duty, 288
Das Davidische Psalterspiel, 330
debates, 371
Durnbaugh, Hedwig T. on, 2327
education, 426
Ephrata, 1947
Ephrata Community, 1147, 2088
Zionitischer Weyrauchs-Hügel, 2110
Ephrata hymnal, 2013
Ephrata Press, 452
Ewing, John Cook, 463
first Brethren hymnal, 1946
Frantz, Aaron, 508
Funk, Benjamin, 525
Geistreiches Gesang-Buch, 700
Geistreiches Gesang-Buch (Spiritual Songbook), 534
German, 700
in German, 2053
German hymnody, monograph on, 1922
German Reformed Church, 1966
Gesäng der einsamen und verlassenen Turtel-Taube, Das (The Songs of the Lonely and Forsaken Turtledove), 546
gilt edges discouraged, 1376
Glad Songs, 642, 1950
gospel songs, 560–561
Grutschnig-Kieser, Konstanze-Mirjam on Radical Pietist, 2334
Hinks, Donald R. on hymnbooks and, 2337
historical writing, 612
history of, 1922, 1937
Holsinger, Daniel Mack, 621
Holsinger, George Blackburn, 621
Holy Spirit, doctrine of, 624
humility, 636
Hymnal: A Worship Book, 2205–2206, 2227, 2228
hymns, 642
hymns composed by J. C. Beissel, 1952
influence of American music on, 1941
Kingdom Songs, 1985
Das Kleine Davidische Psalterspiel, 330, 1987
Das Kleine Davidische Psalterspiel der Kinder Zions, 700
Die Kleine Harfe, 700, 1987
Die Kleine Lieder-Sammlung, 700, 711
Kurtz, Henry, article about, 1924
language, inclusive, 2214
language shift traced in, 724
Main, Kari M. on Ephrata Cloister, 2345
Music Committee (CB), 899
Paradisisches Wunder-Spiel, 2034
poetry, 1039
printed by Christoph Konert, 706
publication of by J. C. Sauer, I, 1919
published by Henry Kurtz, 711, 712

published by Peter Leibert, 736
publishing of, 1063, 1067, 1068
Revival Songs and Best Hymns, 2044
schism, 1152
Showalter, Anthony J., 2064–2065
Showalter, Anthony Johnson, compositions, 1179
Showalter, J. Henry, 2065
Showalter, John Henry, compositions and editing, 1179
singing, 1184, 1185
"singings," 1186
sources on, 2311
Vorspiel der Neuen-Welt, 2088
Yoder, Eli Lorenzo, 1386
Zionitischer Weyrauchs Hügel (*Zionitic Hill of Incense*), 1400
hymns, 60, 148, **642–643,** 1211, 2020, 2058, *See also* lining; tunes
A Small Collection of Pearls, 1211
Amische Lieder, 1387
anniversary hymn and anthem, 1283
authored and composed by Brethren, 2073
background and interpretation of, 2098
baptismal, 1992
Beery's works on, 1873
Bible School Echoes and Sacred Hymns, 1924
bibliography, 1858, 1877, 1886–1887, 1888, 1909
black spirituals, 1211, 1279
Boyle, Philip, 171
Brethren movement and, 175
Brethren music, 898–899
camp-meetings, 1211, 1279
Chicago, IL, 2096
choirs and, 279
Church of the Brethren, 300, 301
collections of, 2068, 2104, 2111
composers of, 2068
debates, 371
Die Geistliche Viole, 1211
Die Kleine Perlen-Sammlung, 1211, 1279
Dock, Christopher, 394
Dunkard Brethren Church, 2098
Durnbaugh, Hedwig T. on Brethren, 2327
Durnbaugh, Hedwig T. on CB and, 2327
eighteenth-century Pennsylvania church music, 1914
Ephrata community, 1931, 2085, 2087
Fisher, Nevin Wishard, 492
Frantz, Ira Henry, 508
funerals, 523
Garrett, Marguerite Arthelda Bixler, 531
German-American, 1683–1800, 1960
German Evangelische church, history of, 1988
gospel music, 559, 560
handbook of, 2073
history of, 1945
Holy Spirit, doctrine of, 624
Huffaker, Perry Lee, 635
hymnal compiled by Stahly, Cora Miller, 1216
Kinsey, Samuel, 696, 1985
Der Kleine Kempis, 1987
Knepper, Wilhelm, 703
Kulp, Christina Masterton, 709

Landert, Maria, 722
lining of, **744**
Lint, Conrad Gillian, 744
Mack, Alexander, Jr., 2004
meditation on hymn texts, encouraged by Quinter, James, 1210
Mohler, John Saylor, writing, 868
Morse, Kenneth Ivan, 878
Naas, Johannes, composed, 909
Neumann, Gottfried composition of, 924
Pennsylvania Seventh-day Baptists, 1915
Pfautz, John Eby, publisher, 1014
Pietism, 1022
Pilger-Lied, 1872
poetry, 1039
prayer, 1051
prayer books, 1052
preparatory service for communion, 1056
Price, William Weidner, 1057
Shenandoah Valley, thesis on, 1933
singing, 1184, 1185
Southwood, John W., 1207
Tersteegen, Gerhard, 1254
Trout, Isaiah Bennett, compiled volume of gospel songs, 1276
tunes used for, 1278–1279
in verse, 2075
Von Der Liebe JESU, 1872
worship services, 1376, 1378, 2098
Hymns of Praise for the Church and Sunday School, 1977
Hymns of Worship
hymnals, 642
Hymns of Worship and Songs of the Gospel, 1977
gospel songs, 560
Hyndman, PA, Church of the Brethren, **643**
Hyre, Absalom, 356, 1667
Hyre, Amos, 350, 1223
Hyre, Edgar, 696
Hyre, Edward E., 1223, 1667
Palestine Old German Baptist Brethren Church, OH, 991
Hyre family, 2079
Hyre, Floyd L., 1667, *See also* Old German Baptist Brethren
Hyre, Greg Allen, 2282
Hyre (Hyer), Amos, 1667
Hyre, Leonard, 326, 1667
Hyre, Mary Denlinger, 1870
Hyre, Sarah Kinsey, 696
Hyre, Wesley, 153, 602

"I Have Made My Choice," Men's Work (CB) official hymn, 816
I Lift My Lamp (Myers), 747
I Was a Stranger (Statler), 748
Ibach, Earl W., 1977
Ibach, Robert D., Jr.
works by, 2309
Ice, Martha Anne, 1851
ice-skating
disapproved of by Brethren, 1241
Ickes, Wayne Frederick, 1667
Icoraci, Brazil, 172
ICYE, *See* International Christian Youth Exchange
Ida Grove, VA, congregation
Mount Zion Church of the Brethren,

VA, 888
Idaho, 157, 177, *645,* **645–646,** 913, *See also* Camp Wilbur Stover; colonization
Brethren movement, and migration to, 320
camping movement, 300
colonization, 299
conscientious objectors, 337
Dunkard Brethren Church, 320
Dunkers of, article about, 1961
farming, 477
frontier, 519
Graybill (Grabill, Krehbiel) family, 567
irrigation, 663
migration of Brethren, 830
Old German Baptist Brethren, 967
railroads and Brethren settlement, 1082
Snake River Brethren, history of, 2054
Idaho District (CB)
Jackpot Church, NV, 2212
Idaville, IN
Church of God (New Dunkers), 297, 464, 700
New Dunkard first meetinghouse, 996
identity, *See* Brethren identity
Idleman, Ollie, 1977
Idleman, Russell Thoburg, 1253, 1668
IFOR, *See* International Fellowship of Reconciliation
Iglesia Bautista de Emmanuel (Emmanuel Baptist Church), El Salvador, 2157
Iglesia Cristiana Pentecosal de Cuba (Christian Pentecostal Church of Cuba), 2157
Iglesia Cristiana Pentecostal (Christian Pentecostal Church), Cuba, 355
Iglesia Cristiana Pentecostal (Cuba)
Misión Mutua en las Américas, 852
Iglesia Cristiana Pentecostal de Cuba
Church of the Brethren partner denomination, **2207**
missions, 2225
Iglesia de Esperanza, *See* Hope Church
La Iglesia de los Hermanos, Dominican Republic
Hispanic Ministries (CB), 2198
Iglesia de los Hermanos en la Argentina (Argentine Brethren Church), 54
Iglesia de los Hermanos, FL
Hamel, Joseph Donat, 2196
Iglesia Evangélica del Pacto en el Ecuador (Evangelical Covenant Church of the Brethren)
ministry education, 268
Iglesia Evangélica Unida del Ecuador (United Evangelical Church of Ecuador)
missions, 861
Igreja da Irmandade, Communidade Pacificista Christa (Brazil), 2139
"Ihr jungen Helden, aufgewacht" (*"Awake, Ye Young Heroes"*)
hymns, 643
Ihrig, George, 1212
Ihrig, Irvin H., 1212, 1668
Ihrig, Irvin I., 1668
Ihrig, Lessie V., 1212, 1668
Ihrig, Levi Benton, 1212, 1668, 1977
Ihrig, Wealthy (later Fleming), 494
Ijpey, Annaeus, 1977
Ikenberry, Benjamin, 115

Quinter, KS, Church of the Brethren, 1077–1078

Ikenberry, Bertha, 1977

Ikenberry, C. L., 1668

Ikenberry, Catherine F. Hirt, 646

Ikenberry, Cecil C., 672, 1668, 1977

Ikenberry, Charles Samuel, 242, 359, **646,** 1668, 1977

Ikenberry, Christian, 1668

Ikenberry, Elizabeth Bucher, 646

Ikenberry, Elizabeth (later Peters), 1011

Ikenberry, Ernest LeRoy, **646,** 1668, 1839, 1977

Ikenberry family, 157, *See also* Eichenberg (Eikenberry, Ikenberry) family Jamison family, 668

Ikenberry, Frances, 214

Ikenberry, George S., 646

Ikenberry, Henry, 646, 1243, 1668
    Mount Hermon Church of the Brethren, VA, minister, 881

Ikenberry, Isaac
    Monticello/Pike Creek Church of the Brethren, IN, elder, 872

Ikenberry, John, 115, 1668
    Quinter, KS, Church of the Brethren, 1077–1078

Ikenberry, John W., 1668

Ikenberry, Levi Daniel, **646,** 1668
    Manchester College, acting President, 786

Ikenberry, Margaret Esterling, 646

Ikenberry, Minnie Layman, 646

Ikenberry, Olivia Dickens, **646,** 1839, 1977, *See also* Ikenberry, Ernest Leroy and Olivia Dickens

Ikenberry, Saloma Susan Wine, 646

Ikenberry, Samuel M., 1668

Ikenberry, William, 1668

Ikenberry, Wilsie Clayton, 1978

Iler family, 1927

Ilish Schpiegel (folk figure), 2147

"I'll Kill Him"
    Stories, from (J. E. Miller), 944

Iler (?), Valentine, 432

Iler, Conrad, 432

Iler, Jacob, 432

Iler, Margaret, 432

Illinois, 146, 176, *646,* **646–647,** 2061, *See also* Americans of Japanese ancestry; Bethany Brethren Hospital, Chicago, IL; *Brethren at Work;* child rescue work, S. Illinois; Chinese Sunday school; Christian Catholic Apostolic Church; Congregational Brethren; Eshelman, M. M.; Gish, James R.; Heckman, John; Livengood, Z. T.; migration; Miller, D. L.; Moore, J. H.; Paine, Adam; Pinecrest Manor; Pleasant Hill Village; Plow Creek Fellowship; Reba Place Fellowship; tracts; urban ministry; Vaniman, Daniel
    Amish settlers in, 26
    bibliography, 1860, 1883, 1906, 1910
    Brethren from, and Oregon, 980
    Brethren movement, and migration from, 320
    colleges, Christian, 2069
    Daily Vacation Bible Schools, 359
    Dairy Farm Assignments, 359
    Dairy Testing Assignments, 359

debatess, 370

district history, 1948, 1961

Far Western Brethren, 30, 321, 475, 910

Flickinger family, 1937

genealogy, 2188

Gibson, Isham, 548

history, Church of the Brethren, 1932

Maryland Brethren immigrating to, 798

Mennonite Church, 2069

Michigan Brethren settlement, 823

migration of Brethren, 829, 830

Mount Morris College, 883

North Dakota Brethren relocating to, 946

Old German Baptist Brethren, 967, 970

Pennsylvania Brethren and settlement, 1004

place-names, Brethren, 1027–1028

territorial records, 1978

Universalists, 1292

Illinois Council of Churches
    Zigler, Michael Robert, 1398

Illiokota District Conference, 695

illuminated writing, *See Fraktur*

illustration, *See* art

Ilyes, Charles Edward, 1668, 2302

Ilyes, Charles L., 2282

Ilyus family, 1958

IMA, *See* Interchurch Medical Assistance

Iman, *See* Eyman, Peter

Imboden, H. R., 1668

Imboden, Scott (Buzz), 551, 1380
    New Albany, OH, Rocky Ridge Grace Brethren Church, 2231

Imhof, Olive R., 1978

The Imitation of Christ (Kempis), 57, 193, 381

Imler, Charles, 1668

Imler, Conrad H., 647, 1668
    Ridgely, MD, Church of the Brethren, minister, 1109

Imler, Joseph
    Golden Spring German Baptist Brethren Church, NE, 2374

Imler, Sarah Catherine Kauffman, 647

Imler, Susanna Fluck, 647

Imler, Tobias Fluck, **647–648,** *648,* 720–721, 1668
    Elizabethtown College, 437

Imler, Tobias Fluck, 1668

Immanuel Baptist Church (ABC) of Wenatchee, WA, 1330

Immanuel congregations
    example of biblically inspired name, 911

Immanuel, MD, Church of the Brethren, *See* Elkton, MD, Immanuel Church of the Brethren

Immel, June Carol Berry, 1850

Immel, K. Howard, 1668, 1850

Immel, Mary, 348

Immel, Woodrow A., 1668

immersion, 87, 910, *See also* baptism
    Basic Questions (Grundforschende Fragen), 2374
    Mehrning, Jacob, writings on, 811
    Mennonite Brethren Churches, General Conference of, 814
    Mennonites at Leeuwarden, immersionist movement amongst, 1241
    "Message of the Brethren Ministry," 818

Old German Baptist Brethren baptism, 967

Orthodox Church baptism, 983

Petersen, Barthold Jurgen, of, 1012

Polish Brethren, 1041

rebaptism, 1085

Reitz, Johann Heinrich, 1095

response to attack on, 2001

Restoration Movement, 1101

Rothenberger, George Philip, 1124

Simons, Menno, 814

single, *See* single immersion

trine, *See* trine immersion

immigration, *See* emigrants and emigration; migration
    bibliography of ship passenger lists on voyages to North America, 1993
    Brethren, **443**
    Chinese, 278
    dress, 400
    East Maple Grove Church of the Brethren, KS, 415
    East Nodaway Church of the Brethren, IA, 416
    Elm Creek Church of the Brethren, KS, 442
    folklore, 2147–2148
    Fredonia, KS, Church of the Brethren, 513
    geographic history of Brethren, 1972
    German sources on, 2320
    Germanic peoples, 26
    Germans becoming citizens, 2000
    Germans in Pennsylvania, 2077
    index of names, 1989
    Know-Nothing party, 704
    Mack, Alexander, Sr., and New Baptists of Schwarzenau, 776, 777, 778
    minorities, ethnic and racial, 850
    naturalization, 918
    Neher family, 922
    oaths, taking of, 2126
    Paradise Prairie Church of the Brethren, OK, membership depletion by, 993
    Pietism, 1022
    Protestants in American and West Indian colonies, naturalization of, 1950
    Puterbaugh (Butterbaugh) brothers, 1752, 1998–1999
    relief and service efforts, 1096–1097
    Sarafian's personal history of, 2055
    Schwenkfelders to America, 1159
    Swiss sources on, 2311

Immigration Act of 1980
    Sanctuary Movement and, 2245

immigration agents, 250
    Bass, Max, 251
    Bock, Samuel, 155
    Brethren movement, 250
    chartered trains, 273
    Great Northern Railway, 251
    Mennonites, 250

immortality, *See* eschatology; universalism

Impartial History of the Church and Heretics (Arnold), *See Unparteyische Historie*

Imperial Co., CA, 1354

Imperial Heights, CA, Church of the Brethren, *See* Los Angeles, CA,

Imperial Heights Church of the
Brethren
Imperial Valley, CA
Gillett, Charles Edwin, 549
Imperial Valley, CA, Church of the
Brethren, *See* El Centro Church of
the Brethren, CA
Imperial Valley Dunker Bretheren Colony
(proposed), *See* El Centro Church
of the Brethren, CA
imperialism
Kostlevy, William on, 2341
imposition of hands, *See* laying on of
hands
imposters among the Brethren, **648**
Iran (Persia), 662
imprisonment, 1222, *See also* persecution;
prisons
Cérésole, Pierre, 1365, 1367
consientious objectors
World War I, 1370
World War II, 1372
Kline, John, 701–702
Knepper, Wilhelm, 703
Leopold, Nathan, 738
Liebe, Christian, 741
Lobach, Johann, 751
Spickler, Henry M., 1274
Stetius, Gottfried Luther, 1222
Traut, Johann Henrich, 1270–1271
Treytorrens, Nicolas Samuel de, 1274
Zaug, Hans, 1401
improvement and noncreedalism, 943
In catabaptistarum strophas elenchus
(Exposé of the Tricks of the
Anabaptists) (Zwingli), 348
In Love with Nature (Jacobs), 667
in order, *See* order of dress
In Our Own Strength (Eller), 748
In Sunny Nigeria (Helser), 596
"In the Beginning" (Kuroiwa), 2342
*In the Boyhood of Lincoln: A tale of the
Dunker Schoolmaster and the
Times of Black Hawk* (Butter-
worth), 747
in the order, *See* order of dress
Inboden, Buzz
Norton, OH, Grace Brethren Church,
pastor-in-training, 951
Inbody congregation, IN
Goshen, IN, Grace Brethren Church,
558
Inbody family, 1385
Incarnation of Christ, *See* Christology
inclusive language, *See* language, inclusive
income tax, *See* taxes
incorporation, **649**, *See also* Brethren
Church Properties, Inc.; Brethren
Press; higher education; names;
trustees of the General Conference
(GBB, CB)
indentured servants
redemptioners, 1090
Independence Day, **649**, *See also* church-
state relations
peace position, and festivities for, 999
Independence, KS, Church of the Brethren,
649
"Independence of the Local Church," 187
Independent Brethren, **649**
chart of Brethren bodies, place on,
1403–1405
congregational polity, 1041

Glendora, CA, Church of the Brethren,
553
Indiana, 326
Rowland Creek Church of the Breth-
ren, VA, 1127
Independent Brethren Church, CA, 239
Independent Colleges of Southern Califor-
nia
Fasnacht, Harold Dale, 480
*Index of Church of the Brethren Annual
Conference and General Board
Statements and Resolutions* (CB)
Washington Office (CB) and, 2260
Index: Record of the Faithful, 1881 (Miller)
Eby, Lela on, 2328
India, **649–651**, *650*, 1906, 2021, 2024,
2049, *See also* Agricultural
Missions, Incorporated; Bhagat,
Premchand G.; Brethren Mission
Hospital, Dahanu, India; Bulsari,
Theophil G.; Gandhi, Mohandas
Karamchand; Gram Sevaks;
Gujarat United School of
Theology; mission schools;
Quinter Memorial Hospital,
Bulsar, India; Satvedi, Govindji
H.; Solanki, Naranji V.
AFSC aid for, 23
agricultural missions, 9, 12
ALM involvement in, 24
Anklesvar, 1175, 1176–1177
baptism, 176
Bible translations, 139
Bombay, 146, 191
Brethren hospitals, 1078
Brethren in Christ, 189
Brethren Mission Hospital at Dahanu,
1078
Brethren movement, 2110
Bulsar Bible School, 229
Butterbaugh, Andrew G., 1333
Church of the Brethren, 2162, 2314
Church World Service, 146
community development in, 2066
Cottrell, Asher Raymond, 345
Cottrell, Laura Murphy, 345
Crowell, Larry, 1335
Crowell, Ruth, 1335
Early, Henry Clay, 413
Ebbert, Ella, 417
Ebey, Adam, 418, 706
Ebey, Alice King, 418, 706, 1307
Ebey, Leah Ruth, 1307
Eby, Emma Ada Horner and Enoch
Howe, 418
education in, 229
education of girls, article about, 1954
Ellis, Calvert Nice, 441
Emmert, Gertrude Elvina Rowland and
Jesse Benedict, 444
evangelism, 150, 182
famine, 23
famine relief, 475
Fasnacht, Everett, 1345
Fasnacht, Everett Merlin and Joy
Cullen, 480
Fasnacht, Joy Cullen, 1345
Flory, Marie Sarah Mason, 2185
Flory, Wendell Phillips, 2185
Forney, Anna Marie Shull and Daniel
L., 502
Freeburg Church of the Brethren, OH,
514

Friends Ambulance Unit, 23
Gandhi, Mohandas Karamchand, 528
Garner family, 531
General Conference Mennonite
Church, 536
Gibson family, 548
Global Women's Project, 2190
Goshen, IN, West Goshen Church of
the Brethren, 558
Gram Sevaks, 564–565
Gratis, OH, Church of the Brethren,
566
Grisso, Lillian Etna, 574
Gujarat United School of Theology
(GUST), 576
Heifer Project International, 594
Hinduism, 607
history of the mission, 1930
Hoff, Emanuel Buechley, 616
Holsinger (Holtzinger) family, 623
Holsopple, Kathren Royer, missionary
to, 1127
hospitals, 191, 630
India, Church of North, 2207
Ingraham, M. Virgil, 2208
Islam, 664
Juniata Church of the Brethren, NE,
678
Kiracofe, Anna Kathryn, 697, 1333,
2341
Lichty, Anna Eby, 741
Lichty, Daniel John, 741
Lichty, Nora S. Arnold, 741
literature, church, 150
Long, Effie Virginia Showalter, 753
Long, Isaac Samuel, 753
Mackey, John Crawford, endorsed for
missionary service to, 779
Mason, George Edward, 2218, *2218*
McCann, Elizabeth Gibbel, missionary
to, 771
McCann, Samuel Napoleon, missionary
to, 772
medical care, 810
medical missionaries to, 807, *807,* 808
Mennonite Brethren Churches, General
Conference of, 814
Mennonite Church (MC), 815
Mill Creek Church of the Brethren,
VA, sending missionaries to, 832
Miller, Beulah Woods, 145
Miller, Daniel Long and Elizabeth
Talley, travel to, *835*
Miller, Eliza Belle, missionary to, 837
Miller, Sadie Jane, missionary to, 842
Minnich, Herbert Spenser and Eva
Shepfer, missionaries to, 848
mission schools, 853, 854
mission tours, 855
missionaries to, 42
missionaries to, and Reber family, 1085
The Missionary Board (BC), 856
missionary conferences, 856
missions, 860, 861, 862, 2224, 2225
missions and missionaries, 267, 280,
299, 2077
Blickenstaff, Lynn A., 146
Blickenstaff, Mary D., 146
Blough, Anna Z. Detweiler, 149,
150
Blough, Jacob M., 150
Bollinger, Amsey Floyd, 158
Bollinger, Florence Moyer, 158

Bonsack, Charles Daniel, 160
Brooks, Harlan Jesse, 212
Brooks, Ruth elizabeth Forney, 212
Brubaker, Charles Henry, 217
Brubaker, Ella Miller, 217
Church of the Brethren, 2066
Warstler, Anna M., 2090
missions and missionaries in Church of Brethren, 250
missions, book about, 1939
missions education, 863
missions, short-term, 2226
Moomaw, Ira Wilbur, missionary to, 874
Mow, Anetta Cordula, missionary to, 890, 891
Mow, Anna Beahm and Baxter Merrill, missionaries to, 890, 891
Nickey, Barbara Marie, as physician missionary, 936
nurse missionaries, 952
order of dress in, 403
orphanages, 651, **651**
orphans, care for, 982
Peace Studies Institute, 1003
Pittenger, Florence Baker, 1026
Pittenger, John Milton, missionary, 1026
Pleasant Hill, OH, Church of the Brethren, missionaries sent to, 1032
Presbyterian relationships with Brethren, 1056
Quinter, Mary, missionary to, 1077, 1078
Quinter Memorial Hospital, 1078
relief and rehabilitation work in, 146, 149, 158, 200
relief and service efforts, 1097
relief from New Paris, IN, Church of the Brethren, 931
rioting, 23
Ross, Amos W., missionary to, 1213, 1193
Ross, Amos Walter and Flora Mae Nickey (Bjorklund), missionaries to, 1213
rural areas, mission work in, 1130
Rural Service Center (CB), 9, 158, 1131, *1131*
Satvedi, Anet Daniel on CB missions in, 2354
Satvedi, Govindji, 1145
Sewell, Laura A. (CB) in, 1346, 2247
Shirk, Bertha Ryan, missionary, 1177
Shull, Chalmer, 1307
Shull, Chalmer, Mary, and Susan, missionaries, 1180
Shull, Lois Netzley on CB missions in, 2356
Shumaker, Ida Cora, missionary, 1180
social issues, 2076
Solanki, Naranji V., 1200
sources on, 2319
Stover, Wilbur Brenner, opens foreign mission office, 912
student volunteer movement, 1231
Swartz, Goldie Elizabeth, 1243
travel to by Brethren, 1273
unity, 2065
Vaniman, Daniel, 1303
Vocational Training College, 1309

Vocational Training School at Anklesvar, 158
Warstler, Anna Margaret, 1319
Waterloo, IA, South Waterloo Church of the Brethren, 1323
Widdowson, Sadie Olive, 1343
Woman's Missionary Societies, 1363
Women's Conferences (CB) and, 2265
world hunger issues (CB) and, 2266
Yeremian (Yereman), O. H., 1385
Ziegler, Edward Krusen, 1395, 1397
Ziegler, Emma K., 1397
Ziegler, Ilda M. Bittinger, 1395, 1397
Ziegler, Kathryn, 1397
Zigler, Earl Myers, 1397
Zigler, Rachel E. Myers, 1397
Indian Americans
Smeltzer, Ralph Emerson, 1191
Indian Camp congregation, WV, *See also* Beans Chapel Church of the Brethren, WV
McCann, Samuel Napoleon, 771
Indian Creek, IA, Church of the Brethren, 661, 992
Maxwell, IA, Church of the Brethren, previous name of, 803
Indian Creek, IN, 1341
Pleasant View Brethren Church, 2377, *See also* Pleasant View Brethren Church, IN
Indian Creek, NC
Pfautz family, 1014
Indian Creek, OK, Church of the Brethren, **651**
Indian Creek, PA, Church of the Brethren, 335, 347, *524,* 1216, 2364, *See also,* Co. Line Church of the Brethren, PA; Elbethel Church of the Brethren, PA; Harleysville, PA
Indian Creek Church of the Brethren
Great Swamp Church of the Brethren, PA, 569
Harley burying grounds, 267
Harley family, 583
Harley (Herli, Harli), Hans Rudolf, 583
Hatfield Church of the Brethren, PA, 588
love feast preparation, *761*
Pennsylvania settlement, 1004
Price burying grounds, 267
The Thunderstorm (Rhoades), 747
young people, *1393*
Indian Eve, *See* Earnest family
Indian Head, Saskatchewan, Canada, 250
Indian Heights, IN, Grace Brethren Church, *See* Kokomo, IN, Indian Heights Grace Brethren Church
Indian Territory, OK, 241
Church of the Brethren, *See* Cameron Church of the Brethren, OK
Indian Village, Grant Co., IN, 1350
Indiana, 146, 163, 169, 176, 181, **652–653,** 689, 690, 2026, 2037, 2063, *See also* Boy's Camp, Plymouth; Brethren Care, South Bend; Brethren's Home; Burnetts Creek Normal School; Camp Living Waters; Christ's Assembly; Congregational Brethren; Goshen Conference; Grace Village, Winona Lake; Hostetler Brethren; Miller, R. H.; murals; Murray, Samuel; New Harmony; Old Folks

and Orphans Home, Mexico; Orphans and Old Folks Home, Sulphur Springs; Salem College; Shultz, L. W.; Timbercrest; Winger, O.
1866 meeting of congregations in, 30
Amish in, 26
bibliography, 1858, 1904–1905
bibliography of authors and works concerning, 1857
Brethren from, and Oregon, 980
Brethren in, 15
Brethren movement, 317, 2084
camping movement, 300
Christian pioneers, 2001
Christ's Assembly and, 280
colleges, Christian, 2069
conscientious objectors, 1966
debates, 370
descendants of Sanger family helping to build congregations, 1144
fiction, references in, 2097
Frances Slocum Trail, history of, 2101
genealogy, 2188
Germans in, history of, 1943
Henninger family, 1962
historiography
district histories, 2201
history of, 1933
Hostetler Brethren, 631
Michigan Brethren settlement, 823
migration of Brethren, 829, 830
missions and missionaries
Stinebaugh, J. Gilbert, 2074
North Carolina Brethren relocating to, 946
North Dakota Brethren relocating to, 946
northern Indiana families, 1911
Old Brethren, 971
Old German Baptist Brethren, 967
Old German Baptist Brethren and Amish in, 1958
Old Order German Baptists, 970, 972
Pennsylvania Brethren and settlement, 1004
pioneer boyhood in, 2097
place-names, Brethren, 1028
Rural Life Association, 12
Scholl family, 2058
Schowalter family migration to, 1155
Scott Co., genealogical records, 1911
Shultz and Paul families moving to, 1156
Smeltzer family, 1191
Universalists, 1292
Indiana Brethren Action Movement (little bam), 179
Indiana Brethren Retreat (BC), 249, 653, **654,** 1354,
Duker, William Irvin, 407
Rench, George W., 1099
Indiana, Church of the Brethren in
sources on, 2317
Indiana Co., PA, 273
Montgomery Church of the Brethren, PA, 872
Neuenschwander family in, 924
Penn Run Church of the Brethren, PA, 1004
Purchase Line Church of the Brethren, PA, 1072
Robinson, PA, Church of the Brethren,

1116
Indiana Cookbook, 340
Indiana Council of Churches
  Peters, Raymond Russell, 1011
  Schwalm, Florence Roselind
    Studebaker, 1157
Indiana District Board of Trustees
  Shively, Nora Early, 1178
Indiana District Fellowship of Grace
    Brethren Churches
  Clarkesville, IN, New Albany Grace
    Brethren Church, mission point of,
    318
Indiana Mission Board
  New Paris, IN, Brethren Church, sup-
    port to, 931
Indiana Missions Ministry
  Winning the Race Ministries and,
    2262–2263
Indiana, PA, Brethren Church, *See* Cherry
    Hill Brethren Church, PA
Indiana, PA, Church of the Brethren,
    693, **653–654**
Indiana Prohibition Party
  Finnell, Virgil Carl, 490
Indiana, religion in
  sources on, 2310
Indiana University
  Kintner, Edward, 697
Indianapolis, IN, 1349, 1395
  Eagle Creek Grace
    Brethren Church, **654**
  First Church of the Brethren, *See*
    Indianapolis, IN, Northview
    Church of the Brethren
  Northview Church of the Brethren,
    654, **654–655**
  Stutz, Harry Clayton, automobile
    industry, 1232–1233
  theological study conference (1981),
    1258
  urban mission, 1297
Indians, *See* American Indians; India;
    Native Americans
  interactions with Yellow Creek, PA,
    congregation members, 927
Indians, American
  minorities, ethnic and racial, 849, 850
  Paine, Adam, 989
Indians, North American, *See* Native
    Americans
indigenization
  mission schools, 853
  missions, 861
indigenous churches
  Ellis, Calvert Nice, 441
indigenous peoples
  Andean, 2052
  missions to, 2046
  North American, *See* Native Americans
individualism
  Brethren movement, 311
  Old German Baptist Brethren, 2234
Indochina
  refugees, 733
  relief organizations developed during
    Vietnamese War, 1305
Indochinese refugees, 198
Indonesia, **655**
  Fancher, Donald, missionary, 1136
  medical missions, 807
  Mennonite missionaries, 815
  missionary sponsored by Salamonie

Church of the Brethren, IN, 1136
  missions, 861
  missions in, congregations supporting,
    28
  Thompson, Joel Kent and, 2255
Indonesian Council of Churches, 655
industrial chaplaincy, 2158
Industrial Revolution, **655,** *See also* accul-
    turation; labor unions; sociological
    studies
  Brethren movement, 355
  family, 474
  impact on Brethren, 3, 74–75
industrial schools, *See* Brethren Industrial
    School for Mexicans, Falfurrias,
    TX; Church of the Brethren
    Industrial School, Greene Co., VA
  minorities, ethnic and racial, 850
  mission schools, 853
industrialism
industrialization
  discipline, doctrine of, 388
  publishing, 1067
industry, *See* business
inerrancy of Scripture
  Evangelistic and Bible Study League
    (BC), 461
  Fellowship of Grace Brethren Churches
    (FGBC), 487
  Whitcomb, John Clement, Jr. (FGBC,
    CGBCI) and, 2262
infant baptism, 5, 28, 83, 288, 308, 309,
    348, 407, **655,** 1972, *See also* bap-
    tismal instruction; church parents;
    dedication of infants
  Brethren movement doctrine on, 174
  church-state relations and, 309
  confirmation, 333–334
  Covenant Theology, 348
  Frenkendorf, 516
  Heidelberg Catechism, 593
  Hochmann von Hochenau, Ernst
    Christoph, 615
  human nature, doctrine of, 635
  Kunze, Johann Christoph, as defender
    of, 710
  Mehrning, Jacob, writings on, 811
  religious liberty, 1098
  Roman Catholic Church, 1120
  Sauer, Christopher II, as defender of,
    146
  and the Pennsylvania Synods, 33
  and the primitive church, 57
  Solingen Brethren, 1258
  as unbiblical and sacremental, 83
infants, dedication of
  Prather, John Perry, 1051
infares, *See* wedding customs
Influenza Pandemic, **655,** *See also* Bennett,
    Allen L.; Lichty, Nora Arnold
  Lichty, Nora S. Arnold, 741
  orphans, care for, 982
informal Christian communities
  Elkhart, IN, Southside Fellowship
    (CB/Menn), 439
information technology, 2188, *See* comput-
    ers; Internet use
  church computer use since 1980,
    2207–2208
  mass media, uses of, 2218
The Inglenook, 91, 194, 656, **656,** 748,
    1236, 1978
  Church of the Brethren, 300

Mahan, Grant, editor, 782
Miller, Howard, editor, 838
Miller, Sebastian Christian, editor, 842
The Pilot, 1024
publishing, 1069
railroads and Brethren settlement, 1082
Spickler, Henry M., 1273
Underhill, Nancy D. Blain, 1286
The Inglenook Cookbook, 194. 340, 656,
    656, 1978
The Inglenook Doctor Book, **656,** 1160,
    1978, 2146
Inglenook Nature Study Club (CB), **656**
Ingleright, A. H., 1668
Ingleright, A. J., 1668
Ingles, Casper, 1668
Ingles, Virginia (later Haradon), 1957
Inglewood, CA, Church of the Brethren,
    See Los Angeles, CA, Imperial
    Heights Church of the Brethren
Inglewood congregation, CA, 759
Ingold, Barbara (later Snowberger), *See*
    Snowberger, Barbara Ingold
Ingold, Roger Lynne, 306, 1668, 1839
Ingold, Virginia Mae Johnson, *1313,* 1839
Ingraham, Alice Larsen
Ingraham, M. Virgil, 1668, **2208, 2383**
  The Missionary Board (BC), 856
Ingstrom family
  South Bend, IN, Ireland Road Grace
    Brethren Church, 1203
Ingwaldson, Llewellyn D., 1668
  missionaries (family), home, 1019
  pastor, San Jose, CA, South Bay com-
    munity Church (FGBC), 1142
Inhauser, Marcos R., 2139, 2172, 2282,
    2338
  I Corintians, and community struggles,
    2338
Inhauser, Suely, 2282
Inken, Barro, 225
Inland Grace Brethren Church, 1270
Inland Northern regional dialect, 911
Inlow family
  Riverside, CA, Grace Community
    Church (FGBC) and, 2244
Inlow, Mary
  Riverside, CA, Grace Brethren Church,
    1111
Inlow, Tim
  Riverside, CA, Grace Brethren Church,
    and death of, 1111
Inman, Charles
  Dutch Bethel, German Baptist Brethren
    Church, 2373
Inman, Dorothy M., 349, 1839–1840
Inman, F. Thomas, 62, 325, 377, 1668
Inman family
  Dutch Bethel, German Baptist Brethren
    Church, 2373
Inman, Ivy, 684–685
Inman, Jesse Calvert, 251, 1215, 1668,
    1978
Inman, Roscoe, 684–685
Inman, Thomas F., 377
inner word and outer word, 73, 184, **656,**
    See also spiritual life
  Holy Spirit, doctrine of, 624
  salvation, Brethren doctrine of, 1140
Innocent III, Pope, 15
innovations
  Philadelphia, PA, First Church of the
    Brethren, 1015–1016

inspiration
  Fellowship of Grace Brethren Churches
    (FGBC), 487
inspiration of the Scriptures, *See* Bible
Inspirational Brethren
  Christ's Assembly and, 280
inspirational writings
  Take Heart (Hoff), 1968
Inspirationism
  congregation competing with New
    Baptists of Schwarzenau, 776
Inspirationists, 2030, *See also* Community
    of True Inspiration
  books about, 1951
  Brethren as forerunners, 1992
  Mack, Alexander, 2011
  Mack's attempt to discredit, account of,
    1955
installation into office, 698
  of ministers, 432, **656**, *See also* laying
    on of hands; ordination
  of officials
    laying on of hands, 730–731
  of pastors, **656–657**, *See also* free min-
    istry; ministry; ordination; salaried
    ministry
  services, 2056
Institute for Inter-American Affairs field
    mission
  Wampler, Frederick Jacob, 1316
Institute of Church Growth
  evangelism, 461
institutional histories
  historiography, 2201–2201
institutional homes
  orphans, care for, 982
insurance, **657**, 2048, *See also* business;
    lightning rods
  Dunkard Brethren, 409, 941
  Hersch, Elmer Myron, 598
  life insurance
    Brethren of Christ, 189
  mutual aid, 902–903
  nonconformity, 941
  Old Brethren German Baptists, 965
  Old German Baptist Brethren, 2233,
    2234
  Old Order German Baptists, 972
  Philadelphia, PA, First Church of the
    Brethren, 1015
  property insurance
    Annual Meeting, 192
insurance plans
  Brethren Benefit Trust, 2140
  Dunkard Brethren Church, 2174
insurance societies
  Kansas, 682
integrity, 1964
"Intemperance, Like a Raging Flood"
  gospel music, 559
intentional Christian fellowship
  New Covenant Fellowship, 926
intentional communities
  Fellowship of Hope, 488
inter-Brethren relations, *See* fraternal rela-
    tions
Inter-Church Aid and Service to Refugees,
    657, *See also* relief and rehabilita-
    tion work
  Zigler, Michael Robert, 1398
inter-racial exchange programs
  CHAMP, 1218
Inter-Religion Symposium on Peace

Bittinger, Desmond Wright, 143
Interchurch Medical Assistance, Inc. (IMA),
    197, 198, 200, **657–658**
  Church of the Brethren Emergency
    Disaster Fund, 2172
  medical projects, 809
  relief and service efforts, 1097
Interchurch Relations, *See* Committee on
    Interchurch Relations (CB)
  Fraternal Relations Committee (CB),
    510
  Fraternal Relations Committees (BC),
    511
Interchurch Relations Committee (Evangel-
    ical Covenant), 460
Interchurch Service to Greek Villages, **658**
  Greece, 569
  Greek Orthodox Church, 569
  Inter-Church Aid and Service to
    Refugees, 657
  Zigler, Michael Robert, 1398
Interchurch World Movement (IWM), **658**,
    See also ecumenism
Interchurch World Movement (IWWM)
  Church of the Brethren, 303
  Forward Movement, 504
  Kolb, William, Jr., 706
  Leckrone, Quincy, 733
  "Message of the Brethren Ministry,"
    817
  Williams, John Henry Bashor, 1345
Intercourse meetinghouse
  Leola, PA, Conestoga Church of the
    Brethren, 737
interdenominational missions organizations
  missions, 861
interest-taking, **658**
Interfaith Council for the Homeless
  homelessness, 2203
Interfaith Draft Counseling Center
  Redford, MI, Trinity Church of the
    Brethren, 1090
Interlachen, FL, 691
intern program
  East Chippewa Church of the Brethren,
    OH, 415
International Bible Students, *See* Jehovah's
    Witnesses
International Christian Youth Exchange
    (ICYE), 201, **658–659**
  relief and social work, 303
  Row, W. Harold, 1126
International Council of Christian Education
  Petersime, Ray, 1012
International Council of Religious Educa-
    tion, 284, **659**, *See also* Inter-
    national Sunday School
    Convention; International Sunday
    School Lessons
  Daily Vacation Bible Schools, 359
  ecumenism, 422
international exchanges
  International Christian Youth
    Exchange, 1231
  Russia, 1288
International Fellowship of Grace Brethren
    Churches
  beliefs and membership, **2208–2209**
International Fellowship of Reconciliation,
    659, *See also* Fellowship of
    Reconciliation (USA)
  EIRENE, 432
  Historic Peace Churches, 610

Morocco, 876
International Lesson Series (BC), 182
International Livestock Center
  Heifer Project International, 594
International Ministries Council (BC), 2141
  missions, short-term, 2226
International Missionary Conference
  Bhagat, Premchand Ganeshji, 131
International Missionary Council
  ecumenism, 422
  Foreign Missions Conference of North
    America, 501
International Refugee Organization (IRO),
    659
international relations
  Midwest Institute of International
    Relations, 2011
international resources
  geographical listings of congregations
    by denomination, nation, and state,
    1479–1503
  maps, historical, 1437–1464
International Sunday School Association
    (formerly International Sunday
    School Convention), **659**, *See also*
    American Sunday School Union
    (ASSU)
  Daily Vacation Bible Schools, 359
  graded lessons, 564
  Kurtz, Daniel Webster, 711
  Uniform Lessons, 283, **659–660**, 1236
    Church of the Brethren, 300
    Hoff, Ernest Gockley, 617
International Voluntary Services Agency
    (IVS), 20, 158, **660**, 693, 1367
  Edwards, Chandler S., 429
  foreign travel, 1273
  Gilbert, Martha Rupel, 2190
  Kimmel, Theodore Acroyd, 693
  Laos, 726
  Noffsinger, John Samuel, director in,
    939
  Peace Corps, 1002
  relief and service efforts, 1097
  relief and social work, 303
  Rolston, Frances Fitz Simon and
    William Wendell, 1120
  Row, W. Harold, 1126
  Vietnam, 1305
internationalists
  biographical dictionary, 1991
Internet use, 2188
  Dunkard Brethren Church, 2174
information technology, church use of,
    2207–2208
  mass media, uses of, 2218
  Old German Baptist Brethren, 2178
interracial programs, 201
interviews
  E. W. Stoner, D. C. Moomaw, and S. C.
    Crumpacker, 1978
inventions and inventors, **660**
  bibliographical sources, 2101
  Fahnestock, Adam G., 465
  Fahrney, Samuel, 466
  Houser, Daniel, 632–633
The Investigator, **660**, 1978
  Mason, Edward, editor, 799–800
investments
  Hostetler, Joseph, 631
Ionia Co., MI, 248, 753, 1263
  Hope Church of the Brethren, MI, 629
  migration of Brethren, 829

Ionia, KS, 743
Iowa, **660–662,** 690, 2046, *See also* Camp
　　Pine Lake; Child Rescue Home,
　　Ankeny, IA; Community of True
　　Inspiration; Far Western Brethren;
　　Old Folks Home, Marshalltown,
　　IA; Spurgeon Manor
　Amana Church Society, 330
　Brethren from, and Oregon, 980
　Brethren movement, 2080
　debates, 370
　Far Western Brethren, 475
　Illinois, 646, 647
　migration of Brethren, 830
　Minnesota Brethren settlement, 848
　missions and missionaries
　　　South Ottumwa Mission, 2103
　Nicholson, John, organization of con-
　　　gregations, 935
　Old German Baptist Brethren influence
　　　in, 967
　Ottawa, KS, Church of the Brethren,
　　　members moving from, 985
　place-names, Brethren, 1028
Iowa Brethren Action Movement (Iowa
　　BAM), 179
Iowa Center, IA, Church of the Brethren,
　　See Maxwell, IA, Church of the
　　Brethren
Iowa City, Iowa
　Community of True Inspiration, meet-
　　　ings in, 330
Iowa Co., IA
　North English, IA, Church of the
　　　Brethren, 947
　Pleasant Grove Grace Brethren Church,
　　　IA, 1031
Iowa River Church of the Brethren, IA,
　　661, **662**
Iran, 55
　BC mission efforts in, 52
　missions, 861
　Yoder, Charles Francis, 1385–1386
Iran (Persia), **662**
Iraq
　Kimmel, Theodore Acroyd, 693
Irasburg Grace Brethren Church, VT, **662,**
　　1304
Iredale, Edith, 748, 1978
Ireland, **662**
　missions, short-term, 2226
　relief and service efforts, 1097
Ireland, WV, 172
Irenaeus, 296
　premillennialism, 833
Irick, Simon Henry, 1978
Irish Grove, IA
　Brethren Church, 932
　Church of the Brethren, *See* Osceola,
　　　IA, Church of the Brethren
IRO, *See* International Refugee Organiza-
　　tion (IRO)
"Iron Curtain" countries, 23
Ironside, H. A., 390
Iroquois Indians, 2093
Irricana, Alberta, Canada
　(First) Church of the Brethren, 15, 59,
　　663, **663,** *663*
　　revival meetings, *1104*
　Second Church of the Brethren, 15, 59,
　　663
　　　Irricana (First) Church of the
　　　　Brethren, Alberta, Canada, 663

irrigation, **663–664,** *See also* colonization;
　　farming; migration
　Idaho, 645
irrigation projects
　land companies, 722
　Nampa, ID, 170
irrigation systems
　migration of Brethren, 830
Irvin Creek Church of the Brethren, WI, 90,
　　279, **664**
　Menomonie, WI, Church of the
　　　Brethren, 816
Irvin, David Floyd McFadden, 1668
Irvin, David M., 1668
Irvin family, 2103
Irvin, Floyd M., 1668
Irvin, George, 279
Irvin (Irwin), George, 1668
Irvin, Pliny (Pliny, Irvin?), 1668
Irvin, Trude Mishler, 1668
Irving family, 1274
Irwin, Charlotte
　Universalism, American, Pietist origins
　　　of, 1978
Irwin, Floyd
　Modesto, CA, South Modesto Com-
　　　munity Church of the Brethren,
　　　867
Irwin, Isabel
　Modesto, CA, South Modesto Com-
　　　munity Church of the Brethren,
　　　867
Irwin, L. J., 1978
Irwin, Lou
　family history, 1978
Irwin, Richard, 1978
Irwin, Samuel Dale, 1978
Irwin, Thedore, 1978
Irwin, William S., 1668
Is Any Among You Suffering?, 2130
Isaac (ship)
　Garst family, 532
Isabella Co., MI
　Shepherd Church of the Brethren, MI,
　　　1176
Isaiah
　42:1, 56
　42:6, 56
　45:1, 39
　49:1, 8, 56
　49:7, 56
　53: 36
　58:6, 1
　61:1, 39
Isenberg, David, 1668
Isenberg family, 740
　Meadow Branch Church of the
　　　Brethen, TN, 805
Isenberg, Foy, 1668
Isenberg, Frank Wesley, 673, 1668
　Midway Church of the Brethren, TN,
　　　providing leadership, 827
　New Hope Church of the Brethren, TN,
　　　elder in, 929
　Pleasant Hill Church of the Brethren,
　　　TN, pastor/elder, 1032
Isenberg, Gentry, 1668
Isenberg, John Y., 1668
Isenberg, Simon, 264
Isenburg, Clarence
　Meadow Branch Church of the Breth-
　　　ren, TN, 806
Isenburg, Frank W., 264

Pleasant Valley Church of the Brethren,
　　TN, 1035
Isenburg, George, 1668
Isenburg (Isenberg), Jasper K., 1668
Isenburg (Isenberg), Simeon, 1668
Isenburg, Robert
　Meadow Branch Church of the
　　　Brethren, TN, 806
Isenburg, W. D., 1668
Isett, John, 1668
Isett, John (2), 1668
Isherwood, Christopher
　diaries of, 2338
Islam, 55, **664,** *See also* Indonesia
　competition with Christianity, 2164
Indonesia, 655
　missions, 861
　Morocco, 876
　Muslim-Christian Convocation, 1116
　Nigeria, 305
Island Pond, VT, Grace Brethren Church,
　　664, 1304, **2209**
Isle of Pines, 355
isolation
　schism and, 1152
isolationism, 1222, 1297
Israel, **664,** *See* Bible lands, travel to;
　　Middle East; Palestine
　Brethren attitudes, 990–991
　Davis, John J., Jr. on Joshua-2 Kings
　　　and history of, 2363
　Jews, 671
　relief and rehabilitation work, 200
　relief and service efforts, 1097
　Whitcomb, John C., Jr. on Joshua-2
　　　Kings and history of, 2363
Israel: A Commentary on Joshua to 2 Kings
　Whitcomb, John Clement, Jr. (FGBC,
　　　CGBCI) and, 2262
Israel Creek, MD, Church of the Brethren,
　　362, *See* Beaver Dam Church of
　　the Brethren, MD
Istanbul
　refugee project, 1280
Istokpoga Mission, FL, Church of the
　　Brethren, 758, *See also* Lorida,
　　FL, Church of the Brethren
Istueta, Juan, 54
"It is the Hand of Christ!", 1978
Italian congregation, Brooklyn, NY, 1296
Italian immigrants
　missions, 859
Italian Sunday School (CB), **664–665,** *See*
　　Calvary Church of the Brethren,
　　Brooklyn, NY; Chinese Sunday
　　school; minorities, ethnic and
　　racial
Italian Sunday schoool
　Brooklyn, NY, First Church of the
　　　Brethren, 933
Italy, **665**
　Carrara, 200
　Homeless European Land Program
　　　(HELP), 625
　Kruger, Helena, 708
　relief and rehabilitation work, 200
　relief and service efforts, 1097
　relief and social work, 303
　United Nations Relief and
　　　Rehabilitation Administration
　　　(UNRRA), 1291
　University of La Verne degree pro-
　　　grams on military bases, 715–716

itinerant ministries
    Chapman, Giles, 271
    North Carolina, 271
    South Carolina, 271
Ives, Alender (Allen), 232, 269, **665**, 682,
    1223, 1319, 1668
    Sand Creek Church of the Brethren,
        KS, elder, 1142–1143
Ives, Alline, *See* Ives, Allen
Ives family, 1223
Ives, Mary Deeter, 665
Ivester Church of the Brethren, IA, 16, **665**,
    1229
IVS, *See* International Voluntary Services
    Agency (IVS); relief work
Ivy Farms Church of the Brethren, Newport
    News, VA, 934
Iwanicki, Edwin, 1978
Izer, Mary Ann, 425

J. H. Moore Memorial Church of the
        Brethren, *See* Sebring, FL, J. H.
        Moore Memorial Church of the
        Brethren
J. H. Moore Memorial Library, 187
J. Omar Good Visiting Distinguished
        Professorship of Evangelical
        Christianity, Juniata College
    Good, J. Omar, 556
Jack, David Russell, 1978
Jackpot Church, NV, **2212**, *2212*
Jackson, Alfred E., 676
Jackson, Anne (later Fremantle), 1941
Jackson Bible Brethren Church, OH, *See*
    Massillon, OH, Jackson Bible
    Church (BC)
Jackson Bible congregations, OH
    example of place name, 911
Jackson Co., AR
    Mount Hope Church of the Brethren,
        AR, 881
    Pennington, AR, Bethel Brethren
        Church, 1004
Jackson Co. German Baptist Brethren, IN,
    667
Jackson Co., IN
    migration of Brethren, 829
    revival and New Hope Church of the
        Brethren, 929
Jackson Co., KS
    Soldier Creek Church of the Brethren,
        KS, 1201
Jackson Co., MO, 298
Jackson Co., OK, 1213
Jackson Co., OR, 1346
    Hoxie, George W., 633
Jackson Co., WV, 2079
Jackson, Daniel J., 2282
Jackson, Dave, 1978
    on Reba Place Fellowship, 2339
    on violence, urban, 2338
Jackson, Dorothy, 927
Jackson, Edward A., 562, 626, 687, 1668
    Lakeland, FL, Grace Brethren Church,
        2213
    missionary, pastor, **2209**
    National Fellowship of Grace Brethren
        Men, leadership in, 916
    Orlando, FL, Grace Brethren Church,
        pastor, 982
Jackson family, 1380
Jackson, Forrest, 360
Jackson, G. Forrest, 366, 1668–1669

Jackson, George Pullen, 1211
Jackson, J. R., 555, 740
    Mount Airy, NC, First Church of the
        Brethren, pastor, 880
    Mountain View Church of the Breth-
        ren, VA, 889
    Pleasant Valley Church of the Brethren,
        TN, 1035
    Pleasant View Church of the Brethren,
        TN, 1037
Jackson, James E., 2282
    Lakeland, FL, Grace Brethren Church,
        2213
Jackson, John Julian, 1264, 2021, 2282
Jackson, John R., 78, 79, 1209, 1669
    Petersons Chapel Church of the Breth-
        ren, NC, 1012
    Pigeon River Church of the Brethren,
        NC, minister, 1023
Jackson, Joseph, 1978
Jackson, Mrs. Sumner
    South Bend, IN, First Brethren Church,
        1203
Jackson, Neta, 1978
    on Reba Place Fellowship, 2339
Jackson, Nettie Mary Beery, 1953
Jackson Park, TN, Church of the Brethren,
    See Jonesboro, TN, Jackson Park
    Church of the Brethren
Jackson, Pauline Shook
    Jackson, Edward A., 2209
Jackson, Pearl, 1669
    Richmond, IN, Church of the Brethren,
        preacher, 1108
Jackson, Peggy Oswald, 2049
Jackson, Richard J., Jr., 1276, 2302
Jackson, Rosaylind Royall, 1852
Jackson, S. M., 2022
Jackson, Thomas Jonathan "Stonewall," *41,*
    667, *See also* Civil War; Confed-
    erate States of America
Jackson Township, IN
    Patton, Uriah, 996
Jackson, W. J., 1209
Jackson, William M., 1209, 1669
Jacksonville congregation, PA, 1294
Jacksonville, FL, Church of the Brethren,
    667
Jacob A. Cline, 239
Jacob, Christian, 171
Jacob, Phillip E., 2067
Jacob, Rebekah Leigh
    on PA German iconography, 2339
Jacob Snyder
Jacobe, D. F.
    Peru, IN, Grace Brethren Church,
        pastor, 1010
Jacobi, Friedrich
    Modernism, 866
Jacobs, Cassel H., 667
Jacobs Creek Church of the Brethren, PA,
    See Mount Joy Church of the
    Brethren, PA
Jacobs Creek (Mount Joy), PA, congrega-
    tion, 189, 335
Jacobs Creek, PA, congregation
    Mount Joy Church of the Brethren, PA,
        previous name of, 882
Jacobs, Delmer F., 1669
Jacobs, Edwin Elmore, 66, 67, **667–668,**
    1978
Jacobs, Elisha J., 1275, 1669
    Ninevah Church of the Brethren, VA,

    pastor in, 938
    Red Hill Church of the Brethren, VA,
        pastoral leadership, 1088
Jacobs, Elizabeth Lindsey, 667
Jacobs family, 1389, 2105
    Fremont, OH, Grace Brethren Church,
        515
Jacobs, Gabriel, 1669
Jacobs, Henry E., 1978
Jacobs, Henry S., 467, 626, 667, 1669
Jacobs, J. Melvin, 1669
Jacobs, John Brown, 667
Jacobs, Leah, 215
Jacobs, M. A., 625
Jacobs, Mary Brown Cassel, 667
Jacobs, Melvin A., 1388, 1669
    Rouzerville Church of the Brethren,
        PA, minister, 1125
Jacobs, Samuel K., 1669
Jacobs, Susan (later Graybill), and family,
    1029
Jacobsen, Bruce A., 2282
Jacobsen, Richard, 1247, 1669
Jacobson, Jon R., 1669
Jacoby, John E., 1978
Jacoby, Rufus, 61
Jacot, Ben, *1238*
Jaebes, Brother, *See* Miller, John Peter
Jaebez, Brother
    Miller, John Peter, monastic name of,
        840
Jaffray, G. R., Jr.
    GROW '73, 2194
Jagger, Bruce A.
    on Wiggle family, 2339
    on Wolf family, 2339
Jahn family
    Riverside, CA, Grace Community
        Church (FGBC) and, 2244
Jalalpor, India, 649
    Miller, Eliza Belle, missionary, 837
    missions and missionaries, 212
    orphanages, 651
Jalem, Lellu, 1669
Jamagin, Isaac W., 1669
Jamaica
    Bible Brethren, support of missionary,
        136
James, See Epistle of James
    5:12, 7
    5:13–16, 39
    book of, symposium on, 1975
    Hackman, Galen R. on James 2:14–26,
        and influence on Brethren
        theology, 2335
    Kent, Homer Austin, Jr., 2211, 2340
    Martin, Harold S. on James 3: 1–12,
        2345
    Young, David S. on, 2365
James Creek Church of the Brethren, PA,
    See Marklesburg, PA, James Creek
    Church of the Brethren
James Creek congregation, PA
    Huntingdon, PA, Stone Church of the
        Brethren, 637
James, Edmund, 1978
James, Edna, 913
James family, *See* Rinehart family
James Goodwill (ship)
    Groff (Grove) family, 574
    Zug, Ulrich, and family, 1401
James Gribble Memorial High School, **668,**
    1246

mission schools, 854
James I, King of England, 87
James, Margaret Mayo, 1843
James River Church of the Brethren, ND, 256, **668**
James, William
   Modernism, 865
Jameson, J. Franklin, 1978
Jameson, Mary Jane (later Reed), 1091
   Reed, Kyle Thayer (DB) and, 2240
Jameson, Newton
   Reed, Kyle Thayer (DB) and, 2240
Jamestown, VA
   slaves, 2128
Jamieson, B. F., 1669
Jamison, Benjamin F., 1669
Jamison, C. E., 676
Jamison, Calvin D., 142, 1669
Jamison, Catherine Boone, 668
Jamison, Christian Emery, 1216, 1669
   Peters Creek Old German Baptist
      Brethren Church, VA, elder-in-
      charge, 1012
Jamison, Dale A., 2128
Jamison, Dale E., 1669
   Quinter, KS, Dunkard Brethren Con-
      gregation, presiding elder, 1078
Jamison, Dennis R., 2282
Jamison, Doris Pease, 2128
Jamison, Elmer W., 1669
   Peters Creek Old German Baptist
      Brethren Church, VA, minister,
      1012
   Pine Grove Old German Baptist
      Brethren Church, FL, elder-in-
      charge, 1025
Jamison, Emory T., 2282
   Peters Creek Old German Baptist
      Brethren Church, VA, minister,
      1012
Jamison, Ethel R., 1979
   on Gascho, John, Sr. and descendants,
      2339
Jamison, Eugene W., 2282
   Mountain View Old German Baptist
      Brethren, VA, 2227
Jamison family, 142, 157, 162, 216, **668,**
   2039, 2046, 2077, 2099
Jamison, George M., 1669
Jamison, Gordon, 1669
Jamison, Herman, 1669
Jamison, James, 668, 2099
Jamison, Jane Dickey, 668
Jamison, Joel H., 1669
   Pigg River Old German Baptist
      Brethren Church, VA, minister,
      1023
Jamison, John, 668, 1216, 1669
   Peters Creek Old German Baptist
      Brethren Church, VA, elder-in-
      charge, 1012
Jamison, John W., 1669, 2125
Jamison, Lloyd, 1669
   Pigg River Old German Baptist
      Brethren Church, VA, minister,
      1023
Jamison, Malissa Flora, 668
Jamison, Mary Elizabeth Bowman, *See*
   Jamison family
Jamison, Owen Thomas, **668,** 1669
   Quinter, KS, Dunkard Brethren Con-
      gregation, elder, 1078
Jamison, R. Glen, 2282

Jamison, Robert E.
   Old Order German Baptist Church,
      2235
Jamison, Samuel Henry, *See* Jamison
   family
Jamison, Sarah (later Flora), 2185
Jamison, Thomas, 668
Jamison, Virgil E., 626, 1669
   Peters Creek Old German Baptist
      Brethren Church, VA, minister,
      1012
Jane Street (United) Presbyterian Church,
   New York, NY
   Mackey, John Crawford, pastor, 779
Janet (ship)
   Simmons, Leonard, voyage on, to
      America, 1182
Janney, Samuel M.
   memoirs, 1979
Jans, John, 1389
Jans, Margaret Tesch, 1389
Janson, Reynier, 2045
Janzen, Amy, 2088
Janzen, David
   on Plow Creek Community, 2339
   on Reba Place Fellowship, 2339
Japan, **669**, *See also* Americans of Japanese
   Ancestry
   agricultural exchange program
      Wenatchee, WA, Brethren-Baptist
         Church United, 1330
   education programs, 185
   General Conference Mennonite
      Church, 536
   Grace Brethren International Missions,
      2191
   invasion of China, 23
   Mennonite Brethren Churches, General
      Conference of, 814
   Miller, Daniel Long and Elizabeth
      Talley, travel to, *835*
   missions, 2225
   missions and missionaries in, 189
      Brubaker, Leland Stanford, 218
   missions, short-term, 2226
   reconstruction after the war, 23
   relief and social work, 287
   World Friendship Center, Hiroshima,
      1369
Japanese-Americans, 23, 24, **24–25,** 200,
   230, 2025, 2047, 2250, *See also*
   Americans of Japanese Ancestry;
   Americans of Japanese ancestry;
   relocation centers and hostels
   detention camps, 2093
   internment of, 2324
   Lord, Charles R. on historic peace
      churches and internment, 2344
   Manzanar Relocation Center, 789
   minorities, ethnic and racial, 850
   relief and service efforts, 1097
   relocation camps, 419
   relocation, from Lindsay, CA, 2068
   resettlement, 1093
   Schmoe, Floyd on peace churches and
      relocation of, 2355
   Smeltzer, Ralph Emerson, 1190
   World War II relief work, 1373
   WWII, 302
Japanese immigrants
   minorities, ethnic and racial, 850
   missions, 859
   Smeltzer, Ralph Emerson, 1190

Japanese Sunday schools, 850
Jarboe, Anna Sweat, 669
Jarboe, Earl Elmer, 1215, 1669
   Salem Church of the Brethren, IA,
      1137
Jarboe, Edith Thomas, 669
Jarboe family, 142
Jarboe, Floyd T., 1669
   Peace Valley Church of the Brethren,
      MO, 1003
Jarboe, Henry, 1669
Jarboe, J. Edwin, *8, 87,* 461, *552*
   church membership, *812*
   Merrington Church of the Brethren,
      Sask., leading revival, 817
   railway travel by Brethren, *1082*
   revival meetings, *1103, 1104*
Jarboe, James William, 669, **669,** 1669
   Ottumwa, IA, Church of the Brethren,
      pastor, 985
   Pleasant View Church of the Brethren,
      KS, minister, 1036
Jarboe, John Edwin, *669, **669,** 1246, 1669
   Red Cloud, NE, Church of the Breth-
      ren, providing leadership, 1088
Jarboe, Joshua, 669
Jarboe, Mary E. Plaugher, 669
Jarboe, Mrs. J. Edwin
   revival meetings, *1104*
Jarboe, Russell Elmer, *446,* 1669
Jarboe, Sarah E. (later Roesch), 1119
Jarman, Ray Charles
   works by, 2316
Jarrell, Stephen M., 272, 2282
   Lexington, KY, Grace Bible Church,
      2215
Jarrell, Steven, 2180
Jarrett, David
   Palouse Old German Baptist Brethren
      Church, 991
Jarvis family, 342
Jarvis, Ronzil L., 1669
   New Troy, MI, Grace Brethren Church,
      pastor in, 932
   Parkersburg, WV, Grace Brethren
      Church, pastor serving, 994
Jasonville, IN, 690
Jasper Co., IA
   Prairie City Church of the Brethren,
      IA, 1050
Jasper Co., IN
   Mount Pleasant Old German Baptist
      Brethren, IN, 887
Jasper Co., MO, 1214
   Old German Baptist Brethren Church,
      IN, *See* Mount Pleasant Old
      German Baptist Brethren Church,
      IN
Jasper, MO, Church of the Brethren,
   669–670
   Nevada, MO, Church of the Brethren,
      visiting ministers to, 924
Javie Peraza
   Santa Ana, CA, Maranatha Grace
      Brethren Church, pastor, 1144
Jay Co., IN, 233, 1288, 1316
   Hickory Grove Church of the Brethren,
      IN, 602
Jay, Jonathan, 1669
Jayne, Horace, H. F., 1979
Jayne, Tony
   Romine Church of the Brethren, IL,
      providing leadership, 1121

J.B.S. (anonymous German scholar), 1223
Jecker, Hanspeter
    on Bohni/Boni family, 2339
Jeff Davis Co., GA, 540
Jefferson Brethren Church, IN, **670**
    Goshen, IN, First Brethren Church, 558
Jefferson Co., IA, 216, 661, 740, 1357,
    1358
    migration of Brethren, 830
    Pleasant Hill Church of the Brethren,
        IA, 1032
Jefferson Co., IL
    Pleasant Grove Church of the Brethren,
        IL, 1031
Jefferson Co., KS, 192
    Ozawkie, KS, Church of the Brethren,
        987
Jefferson Co., NE, 384
Jefferson Co., PA
    Shemokin Church of the Brethren, PA,
        1176
Jefferson Co., TN, 1340
    French Broad Church of the Brethren,
        TN, 516
Jefferson Co., WV, 735
    Jefferson Davis Parish
        Roanoke, LA, Church of the Brethren,
            1112
Jefferson (Goshen, IN) congregation
    Munson, Charles Robert, 2227
Jefferson (now Shelby) Co., KY, 734
    Jefferson, Thomas, 88
Jefferson Township, IN
    Patton, George and Magdaline, 996
Jeffersonville, OH, congregation
    minorities, ethnic and racial, 849
Jeffrey, George H., 692, 1669
Jeffries, Duke, 2186
Jefries (ship), 260
Jehnsen, Ernest R., 1669, 1979, 2302
Jehnzen, John C., 1669
Jehoiada, Brother, *See* Nägele, Hans
    Rudolph
Jehovah's Witnesses, **670**
    influences on, 157
Jellett, Edwin C., 1979
Jellison, Adam E., 1979
Jellison, James Hale, 1669
Jenkins, Alice K., 244
Jenkins, Charles F., 1979
Jenkins, Charles Lee, 1669, **2209**, 2302
Jenkins family, 1979, 2060
Jenkins, Fredric March, 1669
Jenkins, Harold, 667
Jenkins, Howard M., 1979
Jenkins, Janis Pleasant
    Jenkins, Charles Lee, 2209
Jenkins, Jesse Owen, 1669–1670
Jenkins, Karen, 2142
Jenkins, Lee, 318
Jenkins, Mabel, 667
Jenkins, Pleasant Tyra, 1670
Jenkins, Ross, 1670
Jenkins, Warren Y., 1979
Jenkins, William Ellis, 2031
Jenks, Dale D., 664, 2282
    Island Pond, VT, Grace Brethren
        Church, 2209
Jenners, PA, Grace Brethren Church, **670,**
    746
Jennersville, PA, Church of the Brethren,
    670
    Mechanic Grove Church of the

Brethren, PA, 806
Jennings family, 2087
Jennings, J. W., 1670
Jennings, Jean Maxwell Longanecker, 1979
Jennings, Joseph Ressler, 1670
    McFarland, CA, Church of the Breth-
        ren, pastor, 774
    Medford, OR, Church of the Brethren,
        pastor, 806
    World Friendship Center, 1369
Jennings, Lee, 1670
Jennings, Lizzie (Mrs. P. J.), 1670, 2125
    Oriskany, VA, Brethren Church, pastor,
        981
Jennings, N. W., 227, 235, 759, 1670
    Roanoke, VA, First Brethren Church,
        pastor, 1113
Jennings, OK, Bethany Church of the
    Brethren, **670**
Jennings, P. J., 1305, 1670
    Martinsburg, PA, Grace Brethren
        Church, pastor, 798
Jennings, Roy Franklin, 1670
Jennings, W. L., 1670
Jennings, W. W., 1281
Jenny Lind Brethren Church, CA, *See*
    Chapparal, CA, Jenny Lind
    Brethren Church
Jensen, Douglas S., 2282
Jensen, Richard, 192
    Mansfield, OH, Woodville Grace
        Brethren Church, pastor (youth or
        associate), 787
Jensen, Russell James, 2282
Jensen, W. Stanley, 1670
Jenson family, 192
Jenson, Per, 1670
Jentes, Donald, 532, 1670
Jentes, Michael A., 2282
Jephune, Brother, *See* Eckerlin, Samuel
Jeremiah
    8:22, 39
    31:31–34, 84
    Kinzie, Thomas A. on, 2341
Jerico Springs, MO, congregation, 263
Jerome, 296
Jerome, Trikamial B., 1670
Jerrold, E. M., 1670
Jerusalem Bible, 138
Jerusalem Gate of Büdingen
    Marienborn, 792
Jessamine Co., KY, 688
Jessup, Mary Elizabeth, 1670, 2339
Jesucristo Es La Verdad congregation
    Los Angeles, CA, Hermanos Unidos en
        Cristo, 2215
Jesus Christ, 2025, *See also* Christology
    and adultery, 6
    and anointing, 39
    baptism of, 84, 85
    Brethren Doctrine of Salvation, 1140
    crucifixion of, 2082
    divinity of, 448
    doctrine of, 2021
    dress of, 403
    Eller, Vernard on Christian anarchy of,
        2329
    as head of the faith community, 5
    his healing ministry, 39
    life of, 2027, 2098, 2108
    as the living Word, 29
    as the Messiah, 39
    millennial (thousand-year) rule of, 695

as savior, in confession of faith, 5
    Second Coming, documentation for,
        2082
    second coming of, 6, 29, 43, 695
    Sollenberger, David on work of, 2357
    as source of authority for the Church,
        73
Jesus movement, 1903, *See also* charismat-
    ic movements
    Lancaster Co., PA, 2001
Jeters Chapel Church of the Brethren, VA,
    164, **670**
    Cloverdale, VA, Church of the Breth-
        ren, preaching point for, 321
Jethro, Brother, *See* Gass, Jakob
Jewel[l] Co., KS, 742, 743, 2049
Jewell, Fern Irene Watkins, 2209
Jewell, Franklin A., 2209
Jewell, Jesse Paul, **2209**
Jewell, Maude E. Taylor, 2209
jewelry, 59, 400, 403–404, **670–671,** *See
    also* dress (plain)
    Dunkard Brethren, 409, 940
    gold, and Old Brethren German Baptist
        Church, 965
    missions, 862
    objections to Dunkard Brethren
        requirements regarding, 69
    Old German Baptist Brethren, 941
    simple life, 1183
Jewett, Mary (later Landis), 723
Jewett, Robert L., 638
Jewitt, George W., 1670
Jews and Judaism, **671, 677,** 2002, 2030,
    See also Assemblies of Yahweh;
    dispensationalism; love feasts;
    Palestine; sabbatarianism
    aid for, 23
    American Association for Jewish
        Evangelism, 634, 772
    attempts to evangelize, 1296
    Fellowship of Grace Brethren Churches
        (FGBC), 485, 486
    Fellowship of Reconciliation (USA),
        488
    Hochmann von Hochenau, Ernst
        Christoph, 614
    Islam, 664
    Jewish Christians, 147
    Jewish evangelism, **671,** *See also*
        Bauman, Louis S.; urban ministry
    *The Jewish Passover and the Lord's
        Supper,* Beer, 1873
    Judaism, 677
    millennialism, 834
    minorities, ethnic and racial, 850
    missions, 860
    missions and missionaries
        California, 188, 191
    National Interreligious Service Board
        for Conscientious Objectors
        (NISBCO) representation, 917
    Neumann, Friedrich and, 924
    persecution of, 23
    relief and rehabilitation work, 203
Jhibhai, Bhuribai, 2018
Jiangsu Academy of Sciences
    Chinese Agricultural Exchange, 2129
Jiddel, Nigeria, 306
Jilka, Wanda Ione Zirkle, 1979
Jillet, C. Z., *See* Gillett, C. E.
Jillet, Charles Edwin, *See* Gillett, Charles
    Edwin

Jillet, W. F., *See* Gillett, W. F.
"Jim Crow" discrimination, 2128
Jimenez, Danilo
    Los Toros, DR, Nuevo Renacer, 2216
Jimenez, Jose
    Los Angeles, CA, Hermanos Unidos en Cristo, 2215
Jiménez, Roy
    Hispanic Ministries (CB), 2199
Jimmink, Glenda Fasnacht, 480
Jinks, James Paul, 2283
Job
    19:25–27, 120
    31:1, 6, 7
Jobes, Hershel M., 1670
Jobson, Charlotte Hillegas, 139, **671**, 1361, 1850
    Riverside Christian Training School, teacher and missionary, 1111
Jobson, Orville Deville, 139, 381, **671**, 1670, 1850, 1979
    historical writing, 613
    Jobson, Charlotte Ellen Hillegas, 671
Jocob, Henry, 87
Joder family, *See* Yoder family; Yoder (Joder) family
    family history (trans), 1979
Joder, Jacob, 1670
Joder, John, 1670
Joder, Karl, 1979
Jodon, Rachel Edith, 221
Jodry, David L., 2283
Joel, Brother, *See* Bucher, Peter
Johann, Carl, (fl.), **255**
Johann Wilhelm (Roman Catholic Elector)
    interdenominational relations, 1183
Johannes Schwalm Historical Association, 1979
Johansen, Martin, **671**, 1670, **2375**
Johansen, Robert C., 638, 1979
    nuclear arms race, 2232
Johansen, Ruthann Knechel, 638, 1979
    on brain injuries of teenage son of, 2339
    Women's Conferences (CB) and, 2264
Johansen, William, 485
Johanson, Olof (Olaf), 1670
Johansson, Ola, 1670
1 John
    2:2, 55
    2:20, 27, 39
    5:6–8, 85
    5:11–12, 55
John, C., 1670
John, Catherine E. Miller, 671
John Chrysostom
    oaths, taking of, 959
John, Crissman, 1670
John, Eleazar Edward, 410, 1670
John Engelsinger (Lehman), 748
John F. Cuneo Company of Chicago, 194
John family
    Johnstown, PA, Geistown Grace Brethren Church, 674
John, First Epistle of
    Gingrich, Raymond Eugene, 2190
John, Frank P., 1670
John (Gospel)
    1:29–31, 84
    1:33, 86
    3:5, 85
    3:16, 55
    8:5, 6

9:6, 11, 39
10:28, 55
15:5, 55
19:40, 39
    Eller, Vernard on, 2329
    Fry, Dorotha Wenger on, 2345
    Kent, Homer Austin, Jr., 2211
    Kent, Homer Austin, Jr. on, 2340
    Mason, Dorotha Wenger Fry on, 2345
    Wenger, Dorotha on, 2345
John, Griffith, 675
John III
    book of, 1975
John, John A., 224
John, John Jay, **671**, 912, 1670
    Pipe Creek Church of the Brethren, MD, minister, 1026
John Kline (Dupler), 748
John M. Reed Home, **672**
John, Mary Jane McDonald, 671
John, Olin O., 1670
John, Sadie Bucher, 671
John Stauffer Memorial Assoc., 2073
John the Baptist, 84, 85
John, W. F., 1670
Johns, B. Frank, 1670
Johns, Christian M., 749
Johns, Ida Wechtenhiser
    Gahagen, Zella Johns, 2187
Johns, J. Bitzer, 1670
    Mohler Church of the Brethren, PA, free minister, 868
Johns, Loren
    on Believers Church, eschatology of, 2339
Johns, Louis, 1670
Johns, Magdalena J. (later Schrock), 2059
Johns, Mary, 1979
Johns, Ord
    Gahagen, Zella Johns, 2187
Johns, Zella (later Gahagen)
    teacher, bookkeeper, philanthropist, **2187**, *2187*
Johnson (ship)
    Mumma (Moomaw) family, voyage to America on, 896
Johnson, Albert, 1670
Johnson, Andy, 1294, 1670
    Petersons Chapel Church of the Brethren, NC, 1012
Johnson, Arthur, 1221, 1670
Johnson, Bonnie Marie Showalter, 1979, 1980
Johnson, Carman Cover, **672**, 1670, 1979
Johnson, Carolyn Elizabeth, 1850
Johnson, Cecil, 235, 629, 1224, 1670, **2383**
    Raystown Brethren Church, PA, pastor, 1084
Johnson, Cecil H., 248, 1285
Johnson, Charles Emil, 1224, 1670
    Matteson, MI, Brethren Church, 803
Johnson, Christopher, 1294, 1670
Johnson City, TN, 740, 742, 1253, 1339
    Niota, TN, migration to, 938
    First Church of the Brethren, **672**
    Grace Brethren Church, **672**
    Jackson Park Church of the Brethren
    Pleasant View Church of the Brethren, TN, daughter congregation of, 1037
    Knob Creek Church of the Brethren, *672*, **672–673**

early records, 2005
    migration of Brethren, 829
    Pleasant Hill Church of the Brethren, TN, 1032
Johnson, Clara T., 1979
    on Greek Team, 2339
Johnson, Cleo Grigg, 1979
Johnson, Cleonise Hein, 173, 1850
Johnson, Clifford F., 2175
Johnson Co., IA, 353
    Oak Grove Church of the Brethren, IA, 955
Johnson Co., KS, 415, 1311
    Olathe Old German Baptist Brethren Church, KS, 964
Johnson Co., MO, 268, 735, 1315, 1318
    migration of Brethren, 830
    Missouri Brethren settlement, 864
Johnson Co., NE
    Elk Creek Church of the Brethren, NE, 438
Johnson, Corliss, 1670
Johnson, Curt H., 1670
Johnson, Daniel M., 2283
Johnson, David A., 1670, 1979
Johnson, Diana, 1303
Johnson, Dona Hutchison, 1840
Johnson, Douglas, 1979
Johnson, E. C., home
    San Diego, CA, First Church of the Brethren, 1141
Johnson, E. O., 1670
Johnson, Edwin Dale, 1840, 1850
Johnson, Ella J. (later Moherman)
    Moherman, Tully S., wife of, 867
Johnson, Elmer Franklin, 1670
Johnson, Elwood (Woody) O., 2283
Johnson, Evelyn Ann Vnasdale, 1850
Johnson family, 731, 1214, 1365, 1900
    Mount Cassell Old German Baptist Brethren Church, WV, 880
    Nezperce, ID, Church of the Brethren, 935
    Ocala, FL, Grace Brethren Church, 2232
Johnson, Frank, 1670
Johnson, Fred A., 2283
Johnson, George Alan, 1365, 1670, 1850
    Millersburg, OH, Grace Brethren Church, 2224
    Peru, IN, Grace Brethren Church, pastor, 1010
Johnson, Guy, 2283
Johnson, H. Edward, **672**, 1670
Johnson, Herbert, 1670
Johnson, Howard P., 2283
Johnson, I(saiah), 1670
Johnson, J., 472
Johnson, J. C., 1670
Johnson, James B.
    Mud Valley Old German Baptist Brethren Church, IL, deacon, 892
Johnson, Jay J., 576, 1670, 1979
    Monticello/Pike Creek Church of the Brethren, IN, pastor, 872
    Omaha, NE, Church of the Brethren, minister, 974
Johnson, Jeffrey Howard, 1670
Johnson, Jeremiah Lee, 137, 1289, 2283
    Hart, MI, Dunkard Brethren Congregation, 2196
Johnson, John, 1235
    Massillon, OH, Trinity Church of the

Brethren, 802
Johnson, John Byron, 1670–1671
Johnson, John Cover, 672, 1671
Johnson, John J., 1671
Johnson, John L., **672**, 1671
Johnson, John Wesley, 514, 1671, 2302
Johnson, Joseph, 1671
Johnson, Linda Carol, 1671
Johnson, Mary Saylor Miller, 672
Johnson, Norman Lee, 173, 1671, 1850
Johnson, Obed, 1979
Johnson, Otis Wesley, 1671
Johnson, Patricia Givens, 587, 1979–1980
Johnson, Paul D., 2283
Johnson, Pauletta Eby, 672
Johnson, R. Norman, 1671
Johnson, R. S., 1980
Johnson, Ralph William, 1671, 2302
    Rossville, IN, Church of the Brethren,
      minister, 1124
Johnson, Raymond L., 1242, 1277, 1671,
    2283
Johnson, Ressie Baker, 1980
Johnson, Rhea Duryea, 1927
Johnson, Robert Clyde, 2283
Johnson, Ron, 587
Johnson, Ross, 1671
Johnson, Roy Arthur, 1671
    "Whither the Brethren?", 1980
Johnson, Ruby Ruth Krehbiel, 1972
Johnson, S. Jane, 1852
Johnson, Stephen, 531, 1212, 1671
    Nezperce, ID, Church of the Brethren,
      minister in, 935
Johnson, Thomas C., 1315, 1671
Johnson, Tom, 1303
Johnson, Virginia Mae, 1839
Johnson, W. F., 121, 377, 1671
    New Enterprise Brethren Church, IN,
      elder in, 927
Johnson, W. H., 1671
Johnson, Walfred (F.), 1671
Johnson, Wallace, 1671
Johnson, Walter L., 1881
Johnson, William, 1343, 1671
Johnson, William E., 239, 1671
    Reading Grace Brethren Church, PA,
      pastor, 1084
Johnson, William Thomas, 1980
Johnson, Wolford, 1671
Johnsontown Church of the Brethren, WV,
    119, **675**, 2126, **2375**
Jöhnsson, Per, 1671
Johnston, Frank A., 1980
Johnston, Helen Rohrer, 1980
Johnston, J. Edward (Edward J.), 1671
Johnston, Jim
    Modesto, CA, Big Valley Grace
      Community Church (FGBC), 866
Johnston, John, 1671
Johnston, Laura Wilhide, 1980
Johnston, Shirley
    Modesto, CA, Big Valley Grace
      Community Church (FGBC), 866
Johnstone, Mary Ann
    on Brethren village, 2339
Johnstown flood, **673**
    Mack Religious Bookstore and, 161
Johnstown, OH, Licking Co. Grace
    Brethren Church, See Pataskala, OH,
      Grace Brethren Church of Licking
      Co.
Johnstown, PA, 161, 696, 1233, 1265, 1314

Arbutus Church of the Brethren, **673,**
    675, 752
First Brethren Church, **673–674**, 703,
    733, 768, 2132
    Rench, George W., pastor, 1099
    Riverside Grace Brethren Church,
      674
    Second Brethren Church (Mox-
      ham), 675
    Third Brethren Church (Morrell-
      ville), 675
flood relief, 385
floods, 673
Geistown Grace Brethren Church, **674**
Hanawalt, George S., 581
Howe, William Mohler, 633
Johnstown Church of the Brethren, See
    Johnstown, PA, Roxbury Church
      of the Brethren; Johnstown,
      PA,
    Walnut Grove Church of the
      Brethren
Morrellville Church of the Brethren,
    674
Roxbury Church of the Brethren, 675
    Pleasant Hill Church of the
      Brethren, PA, 1032
Moxham Church of the Brethren, **674**
Pike Grace Brethren Church, **674**,
    (Conemaugh, Mundy's Corner), 68
Riverside Grace Brethren Church, 55,
    674
    First Brethren Church, 674
Rosedale Brethren Church, See
    Rosedale, PA, Brethren Church
Roxbury Church of the Brethren, 151,
    674–675
    Pleasant Hill Church of the
      Brethren, PA, 1032
Second Brethren Church (Moxham),
    675
Third Brethren Church, **675**
    Rosedale, PA, Brethren Church,
      1122
    Riddle, Earl M., pastor, 911, 1108
Walnut Grove Church of the Brethren,
    331, 332, **675**, 696, 1314,
    2009
    Arbutus Church of the Brethren,
      673
    Moxham Church of the Brethren,
      674
    Westmont Church of the Brethren,
      675
    Maple Grove Church of the
      Brethren, PA, 790–791
West Johnstown Church of the
    Brethren, See Johnstown, PA,
      Roxbury Church of the
      Brethren
    Pleasant Hill Church of the
      Brethren, PA, 1032
Westmont Church of the Brethren, **675**
Johnsville Church of the Brethren, VA,
    675–676
Johnsville mission point
    Peters Creek Church of the Brethren,
      VA, 1011
Johnsville Old German Baptist Brethren
    Church, VA, **676**
Joint Boards, See Council of Promotion
    (CB); Forward Movement (CB)
    Interchurch World Movement (IWM),

658
Joint Council
    Bhagat, Premchand Ganeshji, 131
Joint Educational Development, 284
Jojoda (Jehoiada), Brother, See Nägele,
      Hans Rudolph
jokes
    cultural expression, 2147
Joliet, IL
    as mission point from Naperville, IL,
      Church of the Brethren, 913
Jolley, Dick, 754
Jolliff family, 1365
Jonah
    Roop, Eugene F. on, 2353
Jonassen family, 731
Jonathan Creek, OH, Church of the
      Brethren, 733, 1221, 1339
    Leckrone, Quincy, 1192
    Olivet Church of the Brethren, OH,
      973
Jones, A. Duane, 70, 1671
Jones, Agnes, 731
Jones, Allen (Alan), 757, 1671
    New Troy, MI, Grace Brethren Church,
      pastor in, 932
Jones, Aubrey, 731
Jones, Baptist minister, Union Co., IL,
    1358
Jones, Barbara Blocher, 147
Jones, Bevel, 2135
Jones Chapel Church of the Brethren, VA,
    162, 360, **676**
    Germantown Brick Church of the
      Brethren, VA, 544
Jones, D. H., 1671
Jones, Daniel F., 676
Jones, Daren, 2283
Jones, Dean A., 1671
    Oak Grove Old German Baptist
      Brethren Church, OH, minister,
      956
Jones, Donald E., 1980
Jones, E. S., 1671
Jones, E. Stanley, 382
Jones, Elizabeth Miller
    descendants, 1959
Jones, Emeral(d) B., 1671
    New Salem Church of the Brethren,
      Milford, IN, as minister, 932
Jones, Emlyn H., 114, 1671
    San Bernardino, CA, Grace Brethren
      Church, pastor, 1141
Jones, Ernst (Ernest, Emmert), 1212, 1671
Jones, Eugene W., 2283
Jones, Evan (Chip) Luther, 2283
Jones family, 731
    Faiview-Rocky Mount Church of the
      Brethren, VA, 470
    family history and genealogy, 1980
    Mount Carmel Church of the Brethren,
      NC, 880
Jones, Gail Laverne, 1850
Jones, Galen, 1671
Jones, George E., 1671
Jones, George H., 332, 476, 674, **676**, 1348,
    1671
    Muncie, IN, Brethren Church, pastor,
      896
    Rosedale, PA, Brethren Church, pastor,
      1122
Jones, Glen Lee, 1671
Jones, Gregory L., 2283

Jones, Harold, 1251, 1671
Jones, Harold G., 1671
Jones, Harry Daniel, 695, 1671
Jones, Hazel, 1980
Jones, Henry (2 listed), 1671
Jones, Herman, 1212
Jones, Hiram, 1671
Jones, J. Edwin, 726, 1343
Jones, J. Estel, 1671
Jones, J. Ewing, 632, 1671, *See* Jones
  family
Jones, J. Herman, 1671
Jones, Janet, 587
Jones, Jesse C., 1671
Jones, Jesse Edwin, 1671
Jones, John E., 1672
Jones, John W., 2283
  Marion, OH, Grace Brethren Church,
  2218
Jones, Joseph, 1672, 1959
Jones, Keith M., 1672
Jones, Kenneth Woodrow, 1672
Jones, Kermit Lamoure, 1672
Jones, Laura S., 2053
Jones, Laurence Robert, 1672
Jones, Lewis (Louis), 1672
  Ewing Church of the Brethren, VA,
  2373
Jones, Marian Susanna Frey, 1980
Jones, Martha (later Hartzler), 1959
Jones, Mary Sellers, *See* Jones family
Jones Mills, PA, Valley Brethren Church,
  676
Jones, Minne Lee
  Reichel, Joseph J. on descendants of,
  2351
Jones, Nancy M., 2283
Jones, Norman E., 1980
Jones, Oliver F., 1672
Jones, Ollie P., 106, 244, 1672
Jones, Phil, 587
Jones, Phillip L., 2283
Jones, Ralph Douglas, 2283
Jones, Ralph Hunsberger, 588, 1672
Jones, Robert Raymond, 1672, 2302
Jones, Samuel P., 570, 1672
Jones, Thomas
  North Solomon Old German Baptist
  Brethren Church, KS, deacon, 949
Jones, Thomas Firth, 1980
Jones, Timothy K(ent), 1672
  on Manchester College, 2339
Jones, Uriah J., 1980
Jones, William M., 1672
Jonesboro, IL, 1288, 1359
Jonesboro, TN, 397
  New Hope Church of the Brethren, 929
  Jackson Park Church of the Brethren,
  676
Jonesboro Twp., Union Co., IL, 1356–1357
Jonestown, PA, 409, 1212
Jonison, Benjamin F., 172
Jönsson, Nils, 1672
Joo, Andre, 2283
Joplin, MO, Church of the Brethren, **676**
  Carthage, MO, Church of the Brethren,
  and organization of, 257
Jordan
  relief and service efforts in, 1097
Jordan, Clarence, 705
  Habitat for Humanity International,
  2195
Jordan, Donald Ray, 503, 1672

Jordan family, 1224
  Fruitdale, AL, Church of the Brethren,
  520
  Oak Grove Church of the Brethren,
  MO, 956
Jordan, Floyd, 1672
Jordan, Fred A., Sr., 1672, 2302
Jordan, Joseph Lewis, 1212, 1672
  Oak Grove Church of the Brethren,
  MO, elder, 956
  Pleasant Ridge Church of the Brethren,
  Alberta, Canada, elder, 1034
Jordan, John (2 listed), 1672
Jordan, John W., 1917, 1980
Jordan, Mildred, 1980
Jordan Mines, VA, Rich Patch Brethren
  Church (Arritt Brethren Church),
  676, 2375
Jordan Run Church of the Brethren, WV,
  676–677
Jordan, Samuel, 1672
Jordin, John N., family of, 1347
Jorgens, Duane S., 1212, 1240, 1672
Jorgensen family
  Prosser, WA, Community Grace
  Brethren Church, 1062
Jos, Nigeria, 727
Jose Marmol, Argentina, congregation
  Maconaghy, Dorothy Helen Lewis and
  Hill, 779
Joseph, Amanda
  Onekama, MI, Church of the Brethren,
  975
Joseph, Clyde E., 1672
Joseph, David, 1672
Joseph, Elysee, 2283
Joseph family, 1341
Joseph, John Elisha, 1341, 1672
  Marilla Church of the Brethren, MI,
  elder, 793
  Onekama, MI, Church of the Brethren,
  free minister, 975
Josephine Co., OR
  Fruitdale Community Church of the
  Brethren, OR, 520
Josephus' History among Dunkers
  comments about, 1917
Joshua
  Davis, John J., Jr. on history of Israel
  in, 2363
  Ramirez, Frank on faithfulness in, 2351
  Whitcomb, John C., Jr. on history of
  Israel in, 2363
Jotham, Brother, *See* Eckerlin, Gabriel
Jourdan, Nelson Roby, 1672
Journeys, 1236
  Our Boys and Girls, 985
"Joy to the World"
  hymns, 643
Joyce, Elisha Edward, 19, 410, 415, 1672
Joyce family
  Peace Valley Church of the Brethren,
  MO, 1003
The Joyful Scribes Corporation
  Helman, Patricia Kennedy, 2197
Joys of Cooking, 340
Juarez, Vidal
  Hispanic Ministries (BC), 2198
  Pasadena, CA, Centro Cristiano para la
  amilia (BC) and, 2237
Jubilee Church of the Brethren, VA, *See*
  Calvary Church of the Brethren,
  VA

Jubilee Church, VA, 239
Jubilee: God's Good News, 2149, 2160,
  2162
Jubilee: God's Good News Curriculum
  published 1994–1997, **2209–2210**
Jubilee Journey
  Beahm, I. N. H., 1168
Judaism, *See* Jews and Judaism
Juday, Brenda Joyce, 1850
Juday, Robert, 2283
Juday, Robert Hugh, 1850
Judd, Joseph Wayne, 206, 1324, 1672
Jude
  Martin, Harold S. on, 2345
judgment, 2021
judgment, doctrine of, *See* eschatology
Judith (ship)
  Heckman family, 593
Judy, Arthur M., 1672
Judy, Charles Edward, 1672
Judy, Ed, 1980
Judy family
  Garrett, PA, Church of the Brethren,
  531
  Glück (Glick, Click) family, 553
  Judy, Roy E., Jr., 1672
  Ridgely, MD, Church of the Brethren,
  pastor, 1109
Juhnke, James C.
  on Mennonites in 20th century, 2339
  on peace movement, 2336
Julian, Don W., 2283
Jülich, Germany, fortress at, 71, **677**, *677*
  Brethren movement, 241
  Goyen, Gossen, 562
  Grahe, Jakob, 564
  Grahe, Wilhelm, 564
  historic sites, 609
  radical pietist dissension in, 990
  Stetius, Gottfried Luther, 1222
  Solingen Brethren, 174, 421, 909, 1059
Julien, Doris Mardella Briner, 505, 1850
  Julien, Thomas, 504, 1980, 2210
  on Brethren creeds, 2339
  on GBC missions and missionaries,
  2339
Julien, Thomas Theodore, 1672, 1850,
  2149, 2182, 2183
  France, 505
  Grace Brethren International Missions,
  2191
  missionary, administrator, **2210**
Julius, Aaron, 1217, 1672
Julius, Glenn, 1672, **2375**
July Fourth, *See* Independence Day
Junction schoolhouse preaching point of
  Blue Creek, OH, congregation, 152
Jund, Rudolph, 1391
Juneteenth, 2128
Jung family, *See* Young entries; Young
  family
Jung, Paula Moyer, 1980
Jung-Stilling, Johann Heinrich, **677–678**,
  1980, 2105
Jüngst-Stetten, Johannes, 1980
Juniata Co., PA, 760, 1263, 1281
  Farmers Grove Fellowship (BC), PA,
  476
  history of, 1929
Juniata College, 61, 178, *426,* 428, 535,
  603, 678, **678–679**, *679,* 693, 696,
  1863, 1980–1981, 2035, *See also*
  Brethren's Normal College; educa-

tion; higher education
architecture of, 51
athletics programs at, 69
Bieber, Charles M., 2137
Blough, Anna Z. Detweiler, 149
Blough, Elizabeth Delp Rosenberger, 150
Blough, Jacob M., 150
Blough, Perry J., 149
Blough, Silas S., 149
Bonsack, Charles Daniel, 160
Book, William Ira, 161
Bowman, Paul Haynes, 168
Bowman, Warren Daniel, 169
Brethren archives at, 52
Brethren movement and, 2339
Bright, Jacob Homer, 208
Brougher, Mahlon J., 214
Brubaker, Elizabeth Howe, 217
Brumbaugh, Andrew Boelus, 219, 810
Brumbaugh, G. Edwin, 220
Brumbaugh, Gaius Marcus, 220
Brumbaugh, Henry Boyer, 220
Brumbaugh, Isaac Harvey, 220, 221
Brumbaugh, Jacob H., 221
Brumbaugh, John Boyer, 222, 698
Brumbaugh, Martin Grove, 222, 223, 300
Burkholder, Wealthy Agnes Clark(e), 231
Cassel, A. H., collection, 1942
Cassel Library, PA, 260
centennial history, 1982
Church of the Brethren, 300
competition with Plum Creek Normal School, 693
Culler, Arthur Jerome, 355
Dadisman, Mary Nancy, 359
Detweiler, George Lowell, 380
Durnbaugh, Donald F. on Correll, Ernst H. and, 2326
Elderton, PA, Plum Creek Church of the Brethren, 433
Ellis, Calvert Nice, 303, 441
Ellis, Charles Calvert, 441
Emmert, David, 444
Emmert, Gertrude Elvina Rowland and Jesse Benedict, 444
Ewing, John Cook, 463
Falkenstein, George Ness, 471
Fike, Earle William, Jr., 2184
Flory, Daniel Christian, 497
Fogelsanger, John Mervin, 500
fundamentalism, 522
Gahagen, Zella Johns, 2187
Geiger, Mary Schwenk, 533, 1361
Gibbel, Florence Baker, 547
Gibbel, Henry Royer, 547
Good, J. Omar, 556
Groff, Warren Frederick, 2194
Haines, Amos Hoppock, 579
Hanawalt, David Kirk, 581
Hanawalt, William Cyrus Replogle, 581–582
Heckman, Samuel Brumbaugh, 593
higher education, 605
historical libraries, 610
history, 1976
history of, 1914, 1929, 1930
The History of the German Baptist Brethren in Europe and America, 613
Holsopple, Frank Ferry, 623

Home for Orphan and Friendless Children, 625
Horst, Melvin Clyde, 630
Howe, William Mohler, 633
Huntingdon, PA, Stone Church of the Brethren, 637
inventions and scientific discoveries, 660
The Investigator, 660
Johnson, Carman Cover, 672
Kaylor, Earl C., Jr. on history of, 2340
Kimmel, Theodore Acroyd, 693
Kinsey, William, 696
Kulp, Harold Stover, 709
Kulp, Neta Ruth Royer, 709
Kurtz, Daniel Webster, 710, 711
Long, John Daniel, 2215
Long, W. Newton, 754
Marklesburg, PA, James Creek Church of the Brethren, 794
Mays, Morley Josiah, 804
McCann, Elizabeth Gibbel, 771
McCann, Samuel Napoleon, 771
Miller, Mary Grace Hileman, 841
missions and missionaries, lectures on, 2076
Moherman, Tully S., 867
Morse, Kenneth Ivan, 878
Murphy, Ross Dale, 896
Murphy, Sara Florence Fogelsanger, 897
museum photo, *477*
Myers, Garry Cleveland, 903
Myers, Oscar Reiff, 904
Myers, Tobias Timothy, 905
Neff, Robert Wilbur, 2230, 2231
Nyce, William Godshall, 952
Nye, Harry Hess, 953
Oller, Jacob Franklin, trustee and benefactor, 974
peace education, 1002
Pennsylvania, 1005
Pittenger, Florence Baker, 1026
Pittenger, John Milton, 1026
Plum Creek Normal School, 1038
Quinter, James, supporter and president, 1077
Quinter, Mary, 1077
Reber, Daniel Conrad, educator, 1085
refugee resettlement and, 2240–2241
Robinson, Paul Minnich, 1115
Ronk, Willis E., 1121
Rowland, Charles Luther, educator, 1126
Royer, Galen Brown, 1127
Saxton, PA, Stonertown Church of the Brethren, ministers provided for, 1150
Scholten, Marian Aetna Rinehart, 1154
School of Theology, 137, 303, 1155
School Visiting Committees, 1155
Shively, Charles S., 2144
Siegel, Nancy on, 2356
single mode feetwashing, 1186
Snider, Donald Mitchell, 1193
Statler, Foster Boyd, 1219
Stauffer, John N., 1219
students from as local preachers, 52
Swigart, Milton Clarke, 1245
Swigart, William Joseph, 1245
Taylor, Madolin Boorse, 1249
Walker, Galen Knepper, 1314
Waltz, Benjamin Franklin, 1316

Weaver, Mahlon J., 1324
Weiand, Albert Cassel, 1344
Widdowson, Sadie Olive, 1343
Wieand, David John, 1344
Yoder, Joseph Warren, 1387
Ziegler, Levi King, 1397
Zuck, Jacob Martin, 1400, 1401
Juniata Fundamental Brethren Church, PA, *See* Altoona, PA, Juniata Grace Brethren Church
Juniata Ladies Aid Society, *1187*
Juniata, NE, Church of the Brethren, **678**
Highline Church of the Brethren, 606
Juniata, PA, 21
Church of the Brethren, 1347, *See also* Altoona, PA, Juniata Church of the Brethren
Grace Brethren Church, *See* Altoona, PA, Grace Brethren Church
building from New Enterprise Church of God, 927
Juniata Park congregation, PA (CB), 1347, *See also* Altoona, PA, Juniata Church of the Brethren
Juniata Valley
early settlement, 1980
Junior Quarterly, 933
Junior, WV, Valley River Church of the Brethren, **679**
Junkins, Benton, 1672
Jurger/Yarger, George
Hull, Judith Maxine Yarger on descendants of, 2349
Peer, Marie Jean Smith on descendants of, 2349
Yarger, Judith Maxine on descendants of, 2349
juridical procedures, *See* law
juries
Church of God (New Dunkers), 297
Jurisson, Cynthia Ann
on Livermore, Harriet, 2339
Jurke, Ron, 1672
Jury, Mark, 504
jury service, *679, See also* law
Brethren movement, 310
Cartwright, Peter, 258
Just, Cyrus A., 1672
justice
O'Diam, Eva on, 2349
justice, economic
SERRV International (CB) and, 2247
Justice family, 1216
Justice, Harold, 1672
Justice, Samuel M., 1672
justice, social, *See* social justice
justification, doctrine of, 42, **679–680**, *See also* eternal security
and the Brethren, 71
Brethren Church doctrine on, 184
Brethren Doctrine of Salvation, 1140
Heidelberg Catechism, 593
sanctification and, 1142
sin, 1184
Solingen Brethren, 1258
Justin Martyr, 296, 698
peace in Christian church history, 998
premillennialism, 833
report of use of holy kiss, 698
Juvenali, Father
Russian Orthodox Church, *1132*
Juvenile Quarterly, 933

Kabba dialect, translation of scripture into, 688

Kabel, Saloma (later Scholl), *See* Scholl, Saloma Kabel

Kable, Harry G., 1981

Kable, Harvey J., 1981

Kable, Walter, 1277

Kachemak Bay, AK congregation, 687

Kachler family, 1958

Kadmie, Prasanth, 1855

Kaeppel, W. Dorian, 1672, 1673

Kaercher, N. A., 1391

Kagarise, Dean Allen, 1672, 673
  Pipe Creek Church of the Brethren, MD, minister, 1026

Kagarise, Nancy
  Snake Valley Old German Baptist Brethren Church, PA, death of, 1193

Kagarise, Samuel R., 1672
  Snake Valley Old German Baptist Brethren Church, PA, minister, 1192, 1193

Kagey, Abraham Neff, 2090

Kagey, Abram J., 1672

Kagey, Anna (later Wayland), 1323

Kagey, Elizabeth, 2079

Kagey family, 1391, 1981

Kagey, Franklin, 1981

Kagey, Henry, 2079

Kagey, Jacob
  Pleasant View Church of the Brethren, VA, 1037

Kagey, John (Johannes), 494, 1672

Kagey, Sallie A. (later Holsinger), 621

Kagi, John Henry, 585, 2091

Kagi (Kagey) family
  Harpers Ferry, 585

Kagora Bible School
  Mshelia, Madu B., 892

Kagy, Anna (later Fleure), 495

Kägy family
  family history, 1982

Kagy, Henry, 209

Kagy, Sarah (later Fleure), 495

Kahl, Amanda (later Kilhefner), 693

Kahle, Cynthia Jane Hutchinson
  Smith Chapel Church of the Brethren, WV, 1191

Kahle, Eugene H., 1672
  Oakvale Church of the Brethren, WV, pastor, 958

Kahle, Walter McDonald, 1672–1673

Kahler, Allen R., 2283

Kahler, Conrad, 251, 1673

Kahler family, 2092

Kahler, John F., 251, 1673

Kain, Dorothy Rosenberg, 2048

Kainadkar, D. P., 1673

Kaiser, C. H., 1673

Kakumiro, Uganda, 2128

Kalamazoo, MI, Shyridge Church of the Brethren, 681

Kalb, Ernst, 1981

Kalckglaeser, Jacob, 1959

Kalckgläser (Kalcklöser, Klacklößer, Kalckglasser), 506, 681, 1673
  Johann Heinrich
  Durnbaugh, Donald F. on, 2327

Kalcklöser family
  Allen, passengers on, 2126

Kaley, Merrel, 553

Kalidas, Lellubhai, 1673

Kalispell, MT, Church of the Brethren, 1342, *See also* Whitefish, MT, Church of the Brethren

Kallberg, Ethan, 2283

Kalm, Pehr, 1981

Kalmuck people, Buddhist, 198, 227

Kalmuck refugees, 681
  International Refugee Organization (IRO), 659
  minorities, ethnic and racial, 850
  refugee resettlement, 1093

Kaltenbaugh, Peter Charles, Jr., 1265, 1673

Kaltenstein, Germany
  Castle, 200, 681–682
  Royer, Byron P., model youth village consultant, 1127

Kaltglesser family, 1959

Kamerer, David, 1673
  Maquoketa German Baptist Brethren, IA, 791

Kammler, Nelly Zbinden, 1850

Kammler, Werner, 1850

Kampala, Uganda, 2128

Kämpfer, Johannes, 682

Kamwe language, Bible translation, 2137

Kanagy, Ezra Jacob, 1981

Kanagy family, 1981

Kanagy, Harvey A., 1981

Kanagy, John H., 1981

Kanawha Co., WV, 272

Kane, Joseph Nathan, 1981

Kaneshiro family, 1312

Kanitz, Hans, 1981

Kansas, 163, 682–683, 2020, 2046, *See also* specific towns, counties, and congregations
  Brethren from, organizing in Mississippi, 864
  Brethren movement, 217, 2107
  church colleges, 1922
  Church of the Brethren, 324
  Church of the Brethren, history of, 1911
  colonization, 324
  debates, 370
  Frantz family, 1941
  homesteading, 626
  migration of Brethren, 830
  Old German Baptist Brethren, 238, 967, 970
  Old Order German Baptists, 970, 972
  Paradise Prairie, OK, congregation, 964
  pioneer boyhood in, 2097
  place-names, Brethren, 1028
  railroads and Brethren settlement, 1082
  work camps
    Brethren Service Committee, 2103

Kansas Brethren Action Movement (K-BAM), 179

Kansas Center Church of the Brethren, KS, 683, 1062

Kansas City, KS, 682, 683
  Calvary Church of the Brethren (Armourdale Mission Church of the Brethren), 683
  history of, 1902
  urban ministry, 1296
  First Central Church of the Brethren, 683, 964
    Lenexa, KS, Fellowship, 2214
  Grandview, MO, Dunkard Brethren Congregation, 565

history of church in, 1902
  urban ministry, 1296

Kansas City, MO, 683
  Grace Brethren Church Missouri, 683, 864–865
  Grandview, MO, Dunkard Brethren Congregation, 565
    Yeremian (Yereman), O. H., 1385
  Messiah Church of the Brethren, 683, 2105
  urban ministry, 299

Kansas Council of Churches
  Bomberger, Harold Zug, 2138

Kansas-Nebraska Act (1854)
  Nebraska Brethren and, 920

Kant, Immanuel
  Modernism, 866
  Pietist background, 1022

Kanter, Rosabeth Moss, 1981

Kanthak, Robert, 1673

Kantner, Claude, 1673

Kao, Guy, 142, 1673

Kapenguri, Kenya, 2128

Kapp, Friedrich, 1981

Karchner, Byan G., 2283

Karck, Samuel, 1673

Karicofe, E. S., *See* Karicofe, Edgar Stuart

Karl August, count of Ysenburg-Büdingen-Marienborn, 175, 227, 683
  Hoffmann, Eva Elizabeth, 617
  Mack, Alexander, Sr., protesting expulsion, 1196
  religious freedom, 792
  Ronneburg Castle, use of, granted to Moravian Church, 1121–1122

Karl Ludwig, count of Sayn-Wittgenstein-Sayn, 683–684

Karl Philipp, Elector Platintate, 990

Karl, Wilhelm, Prinz von Isenburg, 2099

Karlsschule (Vienna, Austria), 73, 200, *684,* 684

Karlstadt, Andreas Bodenstein von
  Reformation, Protestant, and radical reformers, 1091–1092

Karn family
  Genesee Old German Baptist Brethren Church, MI, 540

Karn, Jacob
  North Manchester, IN, Church of the Brethren, elder, 949
  North Manchester Old German Baptist Brethren Church, IN, elder-in-charge, 949

Karn, Lora E., 1981

Karn, Oma, 748, 1981

Karney family
  South Solomon Old German Baptist Brethren Church, KS, 1206

Karns family
  Salem Church of the Brethren, OH, 1138

Karn(s), Gabriel, 1673

Karns, George
  Pleasant Center Church of the Brethren, OH, minister, 1030

Karns, Isaac, 1265, 1673
  Salem Church of the Brethren, OH, minister, 1138

Karn(s), Jacob B., 1673

Karns, Lon, 447, 1673, 2302

Karns, Roy, 1277, 1673

Karper, Barbara (later Snowberger), *See* Snowberger, Barbara Karper

Karre people
in French Equatorial Africa, 938

Karre tribe, Oubangui-Chari
Bickel, Florence Marguerite, 141

Karrer, Eva Margaret (later Schlosser), *See* Schlosser family

Karsandas, Jivanji, 1673

Karst, Theodor, 1981
on Beissel, Johann Conrad/Konrad, 2339

Karstetter, Daniel, 1673

Kasdorf, Julia
on Yoder, Joseph W., 2339

Käsebier, Johann Georg, 576, 684
letters from, translated, 1921
medicine, 809

Kaser, Alsada, 1266

Kaser, James D., 2302

Kaser, Warren, 1266

Kashischian, Pearl, 1922

Kashishian, Gracia Anne, 1851

Kasimir, Count, *See* Ernst Casimir, count of Ysenburg-Büdingen

Kaskaskia Church of the Brethren, IL, **684**

Kassel, Germany, 200, 239, 545, 546, **684–685**
Grebe (Grebi), Georg, 569
Hesse, 602
Murray, Don, 625
relief and service efforts, 1097
work camp coordination in Europe, 1367

Kassel House, 685, *685*
Rolston, Frances Fitz Simon and William Wendell, 1120

Kassel/Cassel, family
Fraktur artistry, 2186

Kassel/Milde house, 2130

Kässmann, Margot
violence and, 2265

Kasza, Timothy Eugene
Hart, MI, Dunkard Brethren Congregation, 2196

Kates, Alberta
on Stutzman, Danuel U. and descendants, 2339

Katherman, Jeremiah, 1673

Katherman, S. B., 1673

Katonah, Janine (later Thompson), 2255

Katonah, John C., 1673

Katy of Catoctin: Or, the Chain-Breakers (Townsend), 747

Kauai, HI
Medina, OH, Shepherd's Grace Church, 2219

Kaub, Jacob, 1673
Maple Grove Church of the Brethren, IN (Lick Creek), elder, 789

Kaucher, David J., 2030
News and Views from Speak for the Lord, 934

Kaucher, Howard Leroy, 733, 1673
Mountain Valley Church of the Brethren, TN, pastor, 889
New Hope Church of the Brethren, TN, elder in, 929

Kauerts, Amelia (later Stetius), 1222

Kauffman, Abraham and Susanna Keck
family history, 1982

Kauffman, Absalom, 1882

Kauffman, Andrew, 685

Kauffman, Andrew J., 685, 1673

Kauffman, Anna B. (later Reber), 1085, 2074

Kauffman, Annie, 151

Kauffman, Barbara Landis, 1937

Kauffman, Cary, 1981

Kauffman, Charles Fahs, 1981

Kauffman, Clarabel (later Weimer), 1327

Kauffman-Coffman families, 1981

Kauffman, David, 1981

Kauffman, Elizabeth (later Garver), 1923

Kauffman, Ella Beth (later Male)
Male, E. William, 2216

Kauffman, Eugene, 368, 1673

Kauffman, Eve (later Hanawalt), 581, 582

Kauffman family, 323, **685**, 1229, 1982, 2078
Harrisburg, PA, Melrose Gardens Grace Brethren Church, 586
Poplar Valley Church of the Brethren, MT, 1047
Scherffig family, related to, 1152

Kauffman, Frank, 239

Kauffman, Mrs. Frank, 239

Kauffman, Frank T., 1981

Kauffman, George, family
Rainey, Nellie Morgan, 1083

Kauffman, Harvey A., 685, 1346, 1673

Kauffman, Henry J.
on Dunkers, 2339

Kauffman, Herman D., 1673

Kauffman, Isaac, 685

Kauffman, Jacob, 1981, 1949

Kauffman, Jacob M., 1982

Kauffman, Jeremiah
on GBC, 2340

Kauffman, John, 424

Kauffman, John D.
life of, 1974

Kauffman, John S., 173, 1673

Kauffman, Joseph, 1363, 2046

Kauffman, Joseph Nelson, 1673

Kauffman, Julia A. Wood, 1361, **1363**

Kauffman, Katy, 1871

Kauffman, Laura (later Heinhold), 1961

Kauffman, Lloyd Charles, Sr., 1982

Kauffman, Lois (later Brown), 2152

Kauffman, Luke E., 106, 487, 1673, 2177
Myerstown, PA, Grace Brethren Church, pastor, 906

Kauffman, Mannoah A., 1982

Kauffman, Marie (later Miller), 2017

Kauffman, Mary, 1882

Kauffman, Moses, 1871, 2078

Kauffman, Nancy, 2079

Kauffman, Nelson E., 1982

Kauffman, Peter B., 1673

Kauffman, Rhoda Esther, 1982

Kauffman, Samuel, 1937

Kauffman, Sandra
on Merkey family, 2340

Kauffman, Sarah Catherine (later Imler), 647

Kauffman, Sarah (later Gingerich), 1949

Kauffman, Solomon W., 1673

Kauffman, Stewart Bruce, 637, 1673
on Gahagen, Zella John, 2340

Kauffman, William, 1673

Kauffmann, Michael, Jr.
Musselman, Christian, 901

Kauffmann, Michael, Sr.
Musselman, Christian, 901

Kaufman, Alma Elsie, 1982

Kaufman, Amanda (later Fahnestock), 465

Kaufman, Casper Joseph, 1982

Kaufman, Cheryl, 1850

Kaufman, Edmund George, 1982

Kaufman family, 1982, *See* Kaufman family

Kaufman-Frey, Cameron Blake, 2283

Kaufman, Gordon D., 638

Kaufman, John S., 1265

Kaufman, Katherine, 384

Kaufman, Michael
North Liberty, IN, Brethren Church, 948

Kaufman, N. R. and Fannie, 1982

Kaufman, Peter, 1255

Kaufman, Peter and Freni Strauz, 1982

Kaufman, Rebecca
North Liberty, IN, Brethren Church, 948

Kaufman, Stanley A.
on German Baptist Brethren, OH, 2340

Kaufmann, Peter, 1673, 1982

Kaurwatikari, Nigeria, 306

Kävlinge congregation, 1243

Kay Co., OK, 1280

Kay, John, 626

Kayler family
Grand River German Baptist Brethren Church, MO, 565

Kaylor, Earl C., Jr., 1673, 1982, 2201
on Brumbaugh, Martin Grove, 2340
on CB, Penn's history of, 2340
district histories, 2201
on Juniata College, history of, 2340
on Morrison's Cove, 2340

Kaylor family, 384

Kaylor, Harriet Beahm
on Morrison's Cove, 2340

Kaylor, Hiram E., 1673

Kaylor, Ina Marshburn, 1840, 1917

Kaylor, John I., 1840

Kaylor, John I. (2 listed), 1673

Kaylor, Peter C., 1982

Kaylor, Rosa Belie Wagoner, 1840, 2087

Kayser, R., 1982

Keagy, Abraham, 1673

Keagy, Franklin, 1982

Keagy, John, **685**, 1673, *See also* Lutherans

Keane, Timothy, 1673

Keane, William, 1380

Kearn, *See* Kern

Kearney, NE
mission work in, 920
Frantz, Hattie Netzley, home mission work, 945

Kearney, NE, Church of the Brethren, **685**

Kearns, Anna Gertrude (later Howe), 633

Kechi, KS, 1343

Keck, Elmer, M., 1673

Keck, Joseph, 664

Keck, Lorie, 2283

Kedar, **685–686**
Ephrata Community, 448
Ephrata Community meeting hall, 1004

Keebaugh, Alfred C., Jr., 1673

Keedy, Beulah (later Russell), 1132

Keedy, Clarence, 467

Keedy family
Hertzler (Hartzler) family, 601

Keedy, G. Wilmer, 1673

Keedy, Mary Ann, 685

Keefer, Christian, 1673

Keefer, Daniel

Müller (Miller) family, 894
Keefer, David, 1673
    Mexico Old German Baptist Brethren
        Church, IN, minister, 821
Keefer, Eve Miller
    Müller (Miller) family, 894
Keefer family, 2310
Keefer, Jacob, 1673
Keefer, William, 1673
Keegan, Gerald P., 2283
Keehn, Mary (Mollie) J. (later Stump),
    1232
Keeler, George, 1982
Keeling, John Calvin Montgomery
        (Monty), 79, 1673, 2283
Keeling, William D., 1673
Keen, Jacob, 367
Keen, Rachel (later Huffer), 531
Keener, Frederick Mark, 2283
Keener, Ronald, 1982
Keeney, Anita Sophia I. Soderstrom, 1840
Keeney, Delmas L., 1674
Keeney, Eli Samuel, 232, 1674
Keeney, Esther Shively, 1982
Keeney family, 1898
Keeney, Gwen Brumbaugh
    Sudan (CB) and, 2253
Keeney, John, 1013, 1674
Keeney (Keeny), D. Edward, 1674
Keeney/Keeny family, **686**
Keeney (Keeny), George H., 1674
Keeney (Keeny), Jacob H., 1674
Keeney (Keeny), Mark Ray, 1674
Keeney, Laverne E., 1674, 2167, 2302
Keeney, Magdalena Petry, 1013
Keeney, Mark Ray, 1840
Keeney, Mervin B.
    on CB, history of, 2340
    Sudan (CB) and, 2253
Keeney, Sarah (later Myers)
    Myers, Jacob L., wife of, 904
Keeney, Susan (later Pfaltzgraff), 2250
Keens, George D., 1674
Keeny, Earl C., 1674
Keeny, Eli S., 1674, 2302
    Penn Run Church of the Brethren, PA,
        pastor, 1004
Keeny, Ervin J., 338, 1674, 1982
Keeny family, 1391
Keeny, George H., 1674
    Pleasant View Church of the Brethren,
        PA, elder-in-charge, 1037
Keeny, George Wilmer, 1674
    Pleasant View Church of the Brethren,
        PA, elder-in-charge, 1037
Keeny, Henry, 1674
Keeny (Keeney), Walter A., 1674
*Keeping the Embers Aglow: 100 Years of
    the Ephrata Church of the
    Brethren* (Bieber), 2137
Keever, Josephine, 1837
Keever, Martha (later Snider), *See* Snider,
    Martha Keever
Keever, Orpha Workman (later Leather-
    man), 732
Keffer, Archie, 1674
Kegarise, Percy R., 1674, **2383**
Kegerreis, David H., 1674, 2167
Kegerreis, Henry, 409, **686,** 721, 1679
    Mechanicsburg, PA, Dunkard Brethren
        Congregation, 806
Kegerreis, Henry, 1674
Kegerreis, James M., **686,** 749, 1674, 2303

Kegley, Frederick B., 1982
Kegley, Lurty, 1674
Kehr, Iva Markey, 1982
Keifer, Jacob, 1674
Keifer, William, 467, 760, 1674
    Miamisburg, OH, Brethren Church,
        pastor, 823
Keihl, Samuel, **2383**
Keihler, J. B., 1674
Keil, Florence (later Kinsey), 696
Keil, Samuel, 1674, **2383**
    Miamisburg, OH, Brethren Church,
        pastor, 823
Keim, Albert N.
    on Bender, Harold S., 2340
    on CPS, 2340
    on peace churches, history of, 2340
    peace, 2201
Keim, Alexander S., 1674
Keim, Annie, 686
Keim, Arthur C., 367, 1674, 1982
    Pomona, CA, Church of the Brethren,
        pastor, 1045
Keim, Catherine Snyder, 686
Keim, Clarence Ray, **686,** 1674
    World War II, 1372
Keim, David, 339, 584, 686, 1674, 1880
Keim, DeBenneville Randoph, 1982
Keim, Elizabeth, 686
Keim family, 152, 2074, 1982, 1983
Keim, George N., 1674
Keim, Henry May, 1982
Keim, Howard, Jr., 1333, 1982, 2303
    Peoria IL, (First) Church of the
        Brethren, pastor, 1009
    Peru, IN, Church of the Brethren,
        pastor, 1010
Keim, Howard Henry, 1674, 1982, 2303
    Newberg, OR, Church of the Brethren,
        pastor in, 933
Keim, Jacob S., 44, 431, 686, 1674
    Ottawa, KS, Church of the Brethren,
        984
Keim, Johannes (John), 686
    family history and genealogy, 1982
Keim, Jonas, 686
Keim, Joseph, 1994
Keim, Josiah, 251, 760, 1333, 1674
Keim (Kime) family, 686
Keim, Lewis M., 686, 1674
Keim, Moses, 760
Keim, N. George, 1674
Keim, Richard Victor, 1674
Keim, Robert Edgecomb, 726, 1282, 1674
    Mesa, AZ, Community Church of the
        Brethren, 2222
Keim, Silas C., 1674
Keintz, Otto, 1674
Keiny (Keeney/Keeny) family, 686
Keiper, D. Howard, 674, 1674, 2303
    Philadelphia, PA, Calvary Church of
        the Brethren, pastor, 1015
Keiper, John David, 670, 1674
Keirn, Carol
    Placerville, CA, Sierra View Grace
        Brethren Church, 1028
Keirn, Daryll
    Placerville, CA, Sierra View Grace
        Brethren Church, 1028
Keirn family
    Placerville, CA, Sierra View Grace
        Brethren Church, 1028
Keiser, A. C., 1674

Keiser, Benjamin, 1674
Keiser, Cecil, 1983
Keiser, E. T., 1674
    Pomona, CA, Church of the Brethren,
        pastor, 1045
Keiser family
    Mortonhouse (ship), 2373, 2376
Keiser, Jacob W., 129, 152, 1674
    Pleasant Ridge Dunkard Brethren
        Congregation, OH, presiding elder,
        1034
    Silver Creek Church of the Brethren,
        OH, 1182
Keiser, William Thomas, 1674
Keister, Russell, 1338
Keith, Charles P., 1983
Keith, Charles W., 179, 347, 1674
    Pleasant View Church of the Brethren,
        OH, minister, 1032
Keith, Columbus, 1675
Keith family
    Roanoke, VA, Washington Heights
        Grace Brethren Church, 1114
Keith, George, 88, 113, 1305
Keith, Jacob F., 1675
Keith, Jean E., 2283
Keith, Leonard C., 469, 1675
Keith, Michael
    Richland Church of the Brethren, OH,
        1107
Keith, Zebrum (Zebrew), 1675
Keithian Baptists (Christian Quakers), 88,
    88, 113
    *Materials Towards a History of the
        Baptists,* 803
    Seventh-Day Baptist Church, 1170
Keithly, Mary Hon (Hahn?), 626
Kelford, Trevor, 349, 1675
Kelford, V. V., 1675
Kelhefner, Isaac, 235
Kellar, Mary S., 1944
Kellenburger, Joseph, 576
Keller, Ammon B., 1675
Keller, Anna
    Mount Hope Church Home (DB), nurs-
        ing administrator, 881
Keller, Barbara
    Keller, Paul W., 2210
Keller, Bettie, *687*
Keller, Carol
    Keller, Paul W., 2210
Keller, Catherine Hummer, 636–637, *See
        also* Hummer, Catherine
Keller, Cora E. Hostotler, 1675
Keller, Daniel, 1675
Keller, Daniel Henry, 738, 1380, 1675
Keller, David H., 367
Keller, Dorothy
    National Older Adult Conferences,
        2229
Keller, E. F., 1983
Keller, Eli, 1983
Keller, Elizabeth
    Spease, Rachel Keller on, 2357
Keller family, 158, 396, *686,* **686,** *687*
    Dutchman's Creek German Baptist
        Brethren Church, NC, 411
    family history, 1983
    Flat Rock Church of the Brethren, NC,
        493
    genealogy, 2003
Hardtmann (Hardman, Hartman) family,
    583

Pleasant Valley German Baptist
Brethren, IA, 1036
Keller, Franklin Elroy, 1675
Keller, Gottlieb (Godlove), 1675
Pipe Creek Church of the Brethren, IN,
elder, 1025
Keller, Hans Jacob
Spease, Rachel Keller on, 2357
Keller, Harvey E., 123, 686
Keller, Hazel Wright
Keller, Paul W., 2210
Keller, Henry, 211, 1675
Keller, Isaac B., 1675
Keller, J. Edwin, 123, 142, 686, 1675
Milk River Valley Church of the
Brethren, MT, elder, 832
Keller, Paul W., 2210
Keller, J. Hershey, 1675
Keller, J. Mervin, 1340, 1675
Lewiston, ME, Church of the Brethren,
2214
Keller, J. R., 1675
Martinsburg, PA, Grace Brethren
Church, pastor, 798
South Bethel German Baptist Brethren,
MO, minister, 1204
Keller, J. Roy, *687*
Keller, Jacob, 686
Shelby Co. Church of the Brethren,
MO, leadership in, 1175
Keller, Jacob B., *687*
Keller, Jacob Edwin, 1675
Keller, Jacob H., 686, 1675
Keller, Jacob R., 104, 1675
Keller, Jacob S. (2 listed), 1675
Keller, Jake H., 1675
Keller, James, 1940
Keller, John, 2072
Keller, John H., 1675
Keller, John Hershey, 1675
Keller, Judith
Keller, Paul W., 2210
Keller, Karen
Lewiston, ME, Church of the Brethren,
2214
Keller, Kevin Lee, 1675
Keller, Lanah, 2375
Keller, Levi, 686
Keller, Lottie M. (later Wine), 1349
Keller, Ludwig, 608
Keller, Martha E.
Monticello, MN, Church of the
Brethren, minister, 872
Keller, Martha Hilary, 367, 1675
Keller, Mary, 2072
Keller, Michael, *687,* 1675
Keller, Myrtle Watson, 2210
Keller, Paul W., 1983, **2210,** *2210,* 2183
Keller, Rachel
on Keller, Elizabeth, 2357
on Keller, Hans Jacob, 2357
Keller, Rosemary (later Skinner), 2051
Keller, Samuel S., 445, 1675
Marion, IN, Church of the Brethren,
pastoral leadership, 793
Keller, Samuel E., 1245, 1675, 2303
Keller, Sarah, *687*
Keller, Sarah (younger and elder), *687*
Keller, Sebastian, 636, 686
Keller, Stanley Grodon, 1675
Medford, OR, Church of the Brethren,
pastor, 806
Newberg, OR, Church of the Brethren,

pastor in, 933
Keller, Stanley C., 1983
Keller, T. D., 1675
Keller, Virginia, 2210
Keller, Walter Denton, 64, 578, 1675
Keller, William J., 1675
Kelley, Bradley A., 2283
Kelley Chapel congregation, WV, 1341
Kelley family
Prosser, WA, Community Grace
Brethren Church, 1062
South Loup Church of the Brethren,
NE, 1206
Kelley, Gerald L., 1324
Kelley, H. N., 1341
Kelley, Joseph J. Jr., 1983
Kellogg, Walter Guest, 1983
Kelly, Dick, 758
Kelly family, 1213, 1863
Kelly, Gerald
New Troy, MI, Grace Brethren Church,
pastor in, 932
Kelly, Hazel, 758
Kelly, John Perkins, 1675
Kelly, Josephine, 566
Kelly (Kelley), Hiram Nelson, 1675
Kelly, Lucinda (later Utz), 1299
Kelly, Martha A. (later Arnold), 57
Kelly, N. H., 1675
Kelly, Peter, 257
Kelly, Robert Lincoln, 1983
Kelly schoolhouse
Laurel Glen Brethren Church, WV, 728
Kelly, Susan
Saxton, PA, Stonertown Church of the
Brethren, 1150
Kelly, Thomas R.
Testament of Devotion, 382
Kelpianites, *See* Society of the Woman in
the Wilderness
Kelpius (Kelp), Johannes, 156, 686–687,
1354
articles about, 1942, 1955
prayer, 1051
reference to, 1943
Society of the Woman in the
Wilderness, 1199–1200
sources on, 2319
Woman in the Wilderness, 1995
works published by Peter Leibert, 736
Kelser, Laura, 690
Kelser, Lulu Thurman, 690
Kelser, Mattie Lorea Hunt, 690
Kelser, Sophiah Sink, 690
Kelso, Jacob, 433, 1675
Kelso, James, 1675
Kelso, Jonathan, 273, 274, 430, 1675
Kelso, Joseph
Pleasant Hill, OH, Church of the
Brethren, 1031
Keltner, Alexander
Portis, KS, Grace Brethren Church,
1047
Keltner, Charles H., 1675
Keltner, Della B., 515
Keltner family, 1936
Keltner, Levi Elmer, 1281, 1282, 1675
Phoenix, AZ, First Church of the
Brethren, pastor, 1019
Keltner, Lewis E., 1675–1676
Keltner, Margaret, 1215
Keltner, Peter R., 515, 1221, 1676, 1983
Rockford, IL, First Church of the

Brethren, pastor, 1117
Keltner, W. W., 1213, 1301, 1346, 1676
Keltner, Wayne, 1215
Kelton, David F.
works by, 2316
Kem, Frederick W., 687
Kem, George Frederick, **687**
Kem, Myron S., **687**
Kem, Sophia Eichoff, 687
Kemp, Annie Eliza Hyer, 1983
Kemp, Ed, 738
Kemp, Elizabeth (later Kintzy), 697
Kemp, Larry, 1676
Kemp, Marilyn
on Ephrata Cloister wall charts, 2362
Kemp, Roy Z., 1983
Kemp, W. E., 1285, 1676
Kemper, *See* Kämpfer, Johannes
Kemper, C. E., 1966
Kemper Church of the Brethren, PA
Ephrata Area Grace Brethren Church,
PA, 448
Kemper, David, 1676
Kemper, Heinrich, 1983
Kemper, Joseph David, 1348, 1676
Morrill, KS, (First) Brethren Church,
pastor, 876
Kemper, John, 1936
Kemper meetinghouse, New Ephrata, PA,
1213
Kemper, Willis Miller, 1983
Kempf, Lydia (later Baker), 1026
Kempfer, *See* Kämpfer, Johannes
Kempfer (Kemper) family, 1936
Kempis, Thomas á, 57, 193, 382
Imitation of Christ, 381
Kempton, Ida, 1333
Kenai, AK, Grace Brethren Church, 14, 30,
687
Soldotna, AK, Peninsula Grace
Brethren Church and, 2250
Jackson, Edward A., 2209
Kendall, Albert Lee, 1676
Kendall, Bayliss Frederick, 1676
Kendall Co., IL
Montgomery, IL, Boulder Hill
Neighborhood Church of the
Brethren, 872
Kendall, Fred, 1676
Kendall, J. Paul, 1676
Kendall, John
Richland Church of the Brethren, OH,
1107
Kendall, Lee, 237
Newton, KS, Church of the Brethren,
pastor in, 934
Kendall, Sherman, 1676
Kendall, William, 1676
Kendig brothers
Ritter, David R. on, 2352
Kendig, E. David, 1676
Kendig, Maudlin (later Weber), 1325
Kendrick, Irva (later Haney), 1957
Kenepp, Harold Milton, 1676
Kenepp, Samuel Jeremiah, 1676
Kenmare, ND, Church of the Brethren,
687–688, 1242
Kennan Massacre, WV, 2078
Kennedy, Dale, 2283
Kennedy, David W., 2283
Lakeland, FL, Grace Brethren Church,
2213
Marion, OH, Grace Brethren Church,

2218
Kennedy family, 1213
Harrah, WA, Grace Brethren Church, 585
Kennedy, Glenn, 1676
Sand Creek Old German Baptist Brethren Church, KS, minister, 1143
Kennedy, Hazel M., 1983
Kennedy, James B., 1676
Kennedy, James M., 12, 13, 558, 562, 1676
Kennedy, Julia Plum, 2197
Kennedy, Lester Washington, Sr., **688,** 1676, 1850
Kennedy, Lester Washington, Jr., 139, 1850. 2283
Kennedy, Lois Virginia Hall, 1850–1851
Kennedy, Matilda Wilhelmina Schwab, 139, **688,** 1851
Kennedy, Patricia (later Helman), 1651, 2142, **2197,** *2197,* 2281
Helman, Alfred Blair, 2197, *2197*
Kennedy, Robert, 1676
Kennedy, Robert J., 530,
Kennedy, Roy, 2197
Kennedy School of Missions, 697
Blough, Jacob M., 150
Bowman, James Brubaker, 167
Brubaker, Leland Stanford, 218
Kiracofe, Anna Kathryn, 697
Zigler, Earl Myers, 1397
Zigler, Rachel E. Myers, 1397
Kennedy, Stephen J., 1983
on Lehr, Albina Johnson (Hoover), 2340
Kennedy, W., 227
Kennel, J. G., 1676
Kennel, LeRoy E., 1676
Kenney, Addie, 482
Kenney, Eldridge, 482
Kensinger, Donna, 2165
Kensinger family, 384, 2323
Kensinger, Isaac B., 1676, 2105
Kensinger, Marvin, 1676
Kensinger, Wilmer
Roaring Spring, PA, First Church of the Brethren, interim pastor, 1114
Kensinger, Wilmer Roy, 415, 1676, 1983
Kent, Alice Wogaman, 688, 1353
Kent, Arthur H., 688
Kent, Beverly Page
Kent, Homer Austin, Jr., 2210
Kent Co., DE
Farmington, DE, Bethany Church of the Brethren, 479
Kent Co., MI, 239
Elmdale, MI, Church of the Brethren, 442
Hope Church of the Brethren, MI, 629
Kent, Elizabeth (later Kintzy), 697
Kent, Homer Austin, Jr., 564, 1676, 1983, **2210–2211,** *2211*
on Book of Acts, 2340
on Colossians, 2340
on 2 Corinthians, 2340
on early Church, history of, 2340
on Ephesians, 2340
on Epistle of James, 2340
on Epistle to the Hebrews, 2340
on Galatians, 2340
on Gospel of John, 2340
on Gospel of Mark, 2340
on Gospel of Matthew, 2340

Grace Schools, 2192
Meadors, Gary T. on, 2346
on Philemon, 2340
on Philippians, 2340
sources on, 2322
on 1 and 2 Timothy, 2340
on Titus, 2340
Kent, Homer Austin, Sr., 46, 97, 137, 391, 485, 563, 564, **688,** 725, 1353, 1676, 1983, 2303
Bible Institute of Los Angeles (BIOLA), 136
The Brethren Minister's Handbook, 788
historical writing, 612
Kent, Wendell E., 2211
Presbyterian seminary, attending, 1056
Kent, Leona Van Epps, 688
Kent, OH, Church of the Brethren, 13, **688**
Kent, Patricia Griffith, 2211
Kent, Ruth Marie, 1851
Kent State University
Beaver, Samuel Wayne, 2134
student demonstrations, 1306
Kent, VA, congregation, 210
Kent, W. David, 2283
Kent, WA, Grace Brethren Church, 115, **688**
Maple Valley, WA, Grace Brethren Church, 2218
Kent, Wendell E., 1324, 1353, 1676
pastor, missions executive, **2211**
Roanoke, VA, Washington Heights Grace Brethren Church, pastor, 1114
Kenton, Ben, 1285
Kentucky, 162, 176, **688–689, 2188,** *See also* specific towns, counties, and congregations
Appalachian ministries, 2130
Baptist movement, 2072
Far Western Brethren, 30, 475
Fellowship of Grace Brethren Churches (FGBC), 485
Illinois, 646
Indiana, 652
Lowery, Margaret E., 2216
migration of Brethren, 829
mission schools, 853
The Missionary Board (BC), 855, 856
missions in 44, congregations supporting, 28
North Carolina, and Brethren settlement, 946
Ohio, settlement of, 961
Shoemaker family, 2100
Williams family, 2100
Kentucky Dunkards, *See* Hostetler Brethren
Kentucky-Indiana Brethren
Disciples of Christ, 1014
Kentucky Mountain Housing Development Corporation (KMHDC), *1173* 2130–2131
Kenya
Africa Mission Project, **2127–2128**
evangelism in, 2180
Gribble, Florence Alma Newberry, 573
missions, 2225
Keokuk Co., IA, 661
English River Church of the Brethren, IA, 447
North English, IA, Church of the

Brethren, 947
South Keokuk Church of the Brethren, IA, 1205
Keokuk Co., OH, 214
Kephart, Calvin, 1983
Kepley family, 2049
Keplinger, Edgar, 1676
Keplinger family, 1345
Keplinger, Robert L., 1676, 2047
Kepner, Benjamin H., 1676
Kepner, Jacob, 1676
Kepner, Lillus Emma (later Mahan)
Mahan, Grant, wife of, 782
Keppel, Frederick P., 559
Keppel, Paul, 1311
Kepper, Harold Frederick, 1676
Kepple Hill, PA, Pleasant View Brethren Church, **689**
Kercheval, Samuel, 1983
Keresztesi, Michael, 1860
Kerkove, David, 2283
Kerlin, B. D., 738, 1676
Kerlin-Fahnestock-Worley families
family history, 1983–1984
Kerlin, William Worley, 1983–1984
Kerman, CA, Church of the Brethren, **689**
Fresno, CA, First Church of the Brethren, 516
Kern (Kearn), Abraham (Abram), **689,** 690, 1341, 1676
Dutch Bethel, German Baptist Brethren Church, 2373
Hostetler Brethren, 631
Restoration Movement, 1101
Kern, Adam, 689, 690, 2042
Kern Co., CA, 244
McFarland, CA, Church of the Brethren, 774
Kern (Kearn), Conrad, **689–690,** 1383, 1676, 1945
North Carolina Brethren, 946
Kern family, **690,** 1945, 1984, 2077
Nicholas Co. German Baptist Brethren Church, 935
Kern, George, 1676
Kern, J. D., 1984
Kern, John, 689
North Carolina Brethren, 946
Kern, Katharine Riblin, 689
Kern (Kearn), Hans, 1676
Kern, M. H., 1984
Kern, Margret (Margaret) (later Garrard), 1945
Kern, Maria Barbara Michaels, 689
Kern, Nicholas
family history, 2011
Kern, Robert D., 439, 1676, 2177, 2283
Mansfield, OH, Woodville Grace Brethren Church, pastor, 787
Myerstown, PA, Grace Brethren Church, pastor, 906
Kern, Simeon, 690
Kern, Stanley, 1945
Kern, Steve B., 2283
Kern, Susan Wilson, 689
Kerner, Charlotte, 2211
Kerner, David Christian, 2211, 2283
Kerner, Frank, 2211
Kerner, Gertrude Mary Boardman, 155, 2211
Kerner, Maude, 2211
Kerner, Trudy Boardman, 2137
Kerner, Virginia

Kerner, William Hoff, Sr., 1676, 2137, **2211**
Kerner, William, Jr., 2211
Kerns family
   Reliance, VA, Mount Zion Brethren Church, 1096
Kerns, Wilmer L., 1984
Kerr, Bertha, 275
Kerr Chapel, WV
   Pocahontas Church of the Brethren, WV, mission point of, 1039
Kerr, Janis (later Arnold), 1866
Kerr, Melvin D., 204
Kerr, Nellie, 275
Kerschensteiner, Edward, 157, 1333, 1676
Kerschner family
   Pleasant Valley German Baptist Brethren, IA, 1036
Kersting, Elsie Clam, 1847
Kesler, Benjamin Elias, 72, 124, 137, 211, 301, 370, 408–409, 461, 479, 558, **690**, 1289, 1984
   Dunkard Brethren member, 910
   Dunkard Brethren polity, 1045
   Eshelman, Matthew Mays, 455
   Maple Grove Church of the Brethren, WI, holding debate at, 791
   Missouri, 865
   Mount Hope Church of the Brethren, AR, 881
   Plattsburg Church of the Brethren, MO, pastor, 1030
Kesler, Dennis Wilbur, 565, 1676–1677
   Newton, KS, Church of the Brethren, pastor in, 934
Kesler family
   Jamison family, 668
Kesler, Jeremiah D., 124, 430, 1677
   Salem Church of the Brethren, ND, 1138
Kesler, Joseph, 1677
Kesler, Mary Whitmer, 1984
Kesler, Stephen, 690
Kesner, James
   South Mill Creek Church of the Brethren, WV, 1206
Kessel, Elizabeth Augusta, 1984
Kessler, See Kesler
Kessler, Agnes C., 1984
Kessler, B. E., See Kesler, B. E.
Kessler, Clinton Earl, 1677, 2283
Kessler, D. Marion, 2303, **2383**
Kessler, David E., 268, 753, 1677
   North Fork Old German Baptist Brethren Church, IN, minister, 947
   Sand Creek Old German Baptist Brethren Church, KS, minister, 1143
Kessler, Ellen (later Moore)
Moore, James Milton, wife of, 874
Kessler family, 162, 2087
   Flat Rock Church of the Brethren, NC, 493
Kessler, Frank E., 1677, 2303, **2383**
Kessler, James O., 1677
Kessler, Joseph, 1677
Kessler, Joshua, 638, 753, 1234, 1677
Kessler, Kevin L., 2283
Kessler, Leonard, 1984
Kessler, Lydia
   Myrtle Point Old German Baptist Brethren Church, OR, 906
Kessler, Marion, 1677

North Fork Old German Baptist Brethren Church, IN, minister, 948
Kessler, Philip L.
   Myrtle Point Old German Baptist Brethren Church, OR, 906
Kessler, Phillip Gene, 1333, 1677
Kessler, Raymond, 1677
   Sand Creek Old German Baptist Brethren Church, KS, minister, 1143
Kessler, Ruby, 1984
Kessler, Ulrich, elder, 2383
   North Carolina Brethren, 946
Keswick conferences
   Hoyt, Herman Arthur, 634
Keswick Convention, **691**
   Holy Spirit, doctrine of, 624
   influence on Brethren theology, 1261
   sanctification theory, 1210
Keswick movement
   Brethren Doctrine of Salvation, 1140
   devotional literature, 381
   Holiness Movement, American, 619
Keswick-related spirituality
   prayer, 1051
Ketler, Adam, 1677
Ketrow, Cal
   Sidney, IN, Grace Brethren Church, 1181
Kettell, Raymond Henry, 2, 320, 532, 579, 738, 1677, 2303
   Pleasant Grove Grace Brethren Church, IA, pastor, 1031
   Portis, KS, Grace Brethren Church, pastor, 1048
Kettering, Allen, 691
Kettering, Delbert Warring, 1677
   Lake Breeze Church of the Brethren, Sheffield Village, OH, 1174
Kettering family, 226
Kettering, George
   Mount Wilson Church of the Brethren, PA, 887
Kettering, Harold Engle, 1677
Kettering, Joseph W., **691**
Kettering, Mary
   Mount Wilson Church of the Brethren, PA, 887
Kettering, Merlyn
   Sudan (CB) and, 2253
Kettering, OH, 365
   Calvary Grace Brethren Church, **691**
   Prince of Peace congregation, 365
Kettering, Robert D., 1677, 2130
   Mount Joy, PA, Florin Church of the Brethren, pastor, 882
Kettering, Verda Wilhelm, 691
Ketterman, Curtis G., 2283
   Laughlin Church of the Brethren, MD, 2214
Ketterman, Richard Eugene, 2283
Kettinger, B. F., 1677
Keuka Church of the Brethren, FL, **691, 718**
   migration of Brethren, 831
Keuka, FL
   Family Companion, The, 474
Keussen, Hermann, 1984
Kevaldas, Laxmandas, 1677
Kewanna, IN, Church of the Brethren, 691
   Mexico, IN, Church of the Brethren, 821
"Key '73" program

Church of the Brethren, 305
Key, Carl B., 363, 739, 1677
Key, Carson Miller, 1308, 1677
   Olean Church of the Brethren, VA, leadership by, 973
   Roanoke, VA, Hollins Road Church of the Brethren, pastor, 1113
   Roanoke, VA, Williamson Road Church of the Brethren, pastor, 1114
Key, Isaac, 1677
Keyes, Romayne (later Flora), 495
Keymont Chapel, Mineral Co., WV, 1337
Keys, Ancel B., 1984
Keyser, Alan G., 1984
Keyser, Catharine Clemens, 691, 692
Keyser, Charles S., 1984
Keyser, Dirck, 1984
Keyser, E. Grant, 1984
Keyser family, **692,** 1984
   Mortonhouse (ship), 2373, 2376
   Mount Cassell Old German Baptist Brethren Church, WV, 880
Keyser, Hannah, 692
Keyser-Keysor family, 2011
Keyser, Lottie, 345
Keyser, Naaman H., 1984
Keyser, Peter D., 1984
Keyser, Peter Dirck, 692,
Keyser, Peter, Jr., 81, 175, 397, 477, **691–692,** 1292, 1677, 1900, 2012
   historic sites, 609
   Major, Sarah Righter, 783
   Philadelphia, PA, First Church of the Brethren, elder and minister, 1015
   Revolutionary War, 1106, 1974
Keyser, Peter, Sr., 692
Keyser, Philip Luther, 1984
Keyser, WV, Church of the Brethren, 106, **692,** 703
   mission point for Sunnyside Church of the Brethren, 1240
Keysor-Keyser family, 2011
Keyton, J. W.
   Pineville, VA, Mount Olive Brethren Church, 1025
K(G)reider, Michael and Elizabeth, 1990
Khengar, Govindji, 1677
Khergam, India, congregation
   Shumaker, Ida Cora, 1180
   Solanki, Naranji V., pastor and founder, 1200
Khmer refugees
   Lincoln, NE, Antelope Park Community Church of the Brethren, 743
Kiawe family, 153
Kiblinger, G. W.
   Mulvane, KS, Brethren Church, 895
Kiblinger, Salie
   Mulvane, KS, Brethren Church, 895
Kibukuland
   Musa, J. L. on missions in, 2348
Kickasola, Joseph N., 1984
Kidd, Sarah (later Early), 413
Kidder Church of the Brethren, MO, **692**
Kidder congregation, MO, 752
Kidder, Shawn, 2283
Kidder, Thomas Coleman, Jr., 1677
Kidwell, Ezra M., 504, 1255, 1677
Kidwell, Richard Wilson, 1677
Kidwell, W. M., 1677, **2383**
Kidwell, William R., 1677, **2383**
   New Carlisle, OH, Church of the

Brethren, elder in, 926
Kiefer, Archie, 1320
Kiefer, Donald L., 1677
Kiefer family
  Funck (Funk) family, 521
Kiefer (Keefer), Christian, 1677
Kiefer, Moses, 21
Kiefer, William, *See* Keifer, William
Kieffaber, Alan, 1679, 1840, 1984
Kieffaber, George W., 688, 1679
Kieffaber, Nancy Jo Royer, 1840
Kieffer, David, 1677
Kieffer, Elizabeth C., 1984
Kieffer, Jacob, 1677
Kieffer, William
  Smithville, OH, First Brethren Church, pastor, 1192
Kiehl, Samuel, 365, 366, **692**, 1677
Kierkegaard and Radical Discipleship
  (Eller), 2176
Kierkegaard, Soren
  historical writing, 612
  noncreedalism, 943
Kiess family, 61, 148
Kiess, Johannes, 1863
Kiester, Edith Mae, 2283
  Lybrook, NM, Tók'ahookaadí Church of the Brethren, 2216
Kiester, Russell Warren, 1677
  Lybrook, NM, Tók'ahookaadí Church of the Brethren, 2216
Kiev, Russia
  Russian Orthodox Church, peace seminar with, 1132
Kiger, Edward Clark, 1677
Kiggins, J. T., 670, 1677
Kilba, Haman Kwala, 1677
Kilba people, 306
Kilbert, John R., 1677
Kile schoolhouse, PA, 406
Kilhefner, Amanda Kahl, 693
Kilhefner, Catherine Gerstenlauer, 693
Kilhefner, David K., 1677
Kilhefner, E. L., 64
Kilhefner, Elsie Ziegler, 693
Kilhefner, Galen Cleophas, 247, **693**, 1677, 1984
  Ridgeway Community Church of the Brethren, PA, moderator, 1109
Kilhefner, Isaac, 64, 505, 572, **693**
  Mansfield, OH, Walcrest Brethren Church, preaching, 787
Kilhefner (Killhefner), Henry, 1677–1678
Kilhefner (Killhefner), Isaac, 1678
Kilhefner, Nathan, 1678
Kilhefner, William G., 693
Kilian, Oskar
  on Beissel, Konrad, 2340
Killbuck, IN, Church of the Brethren, *See* Antioch Church of the Brethren, IN
"Killed by the Word of God," 1984
Killian, George H., 602, 1678
Killian, John W., 1678
Killian, William, 1678
Killingsworth, Abel W., 263, 1678
  Oak Grove Church of the Brethren, MO, leadership by, 956
  Osceola Church of the Brethren, MO, minister and elder, 984
Killingsworth, David, 1213
Killingsworth family
  Oak Grove Church of the Brethren,

MO, 956
Killingsworth, Sarah, 224
Killingsworth, Wesley A., 2138, 2283
Killingsworth, William, 224
Killion, Goldie, 1678
Kilmer, Orvil R., 1678, 2303
Kilmer, Orvin Jay, 1678
Kilmore, Carolyn Joyce, 1852
Kilpatrick, J. W., 1678
Kim, Dan (Kwang Suk), 2283
  Korean Mission, 2211
Kim, Ick Won
  Korean Mission, 2211
Kimball, Ella, 520
Kime, *See* Keim
Kime, Carl Eugene, 157, 758, 1678
Kime family, *See* Keim family
Kime, Jeanne, 157
Kimmel, *See* Kimmell
Kimmel, Ada (later Rolston), 1120
Kimmel, Barbara Breniser, 693
Kimmel, Bertha, 25
Kimmel, Catherine Wenrick, 693
Kimmel, Charles E., 25, 1678
  Sheldon Church of the Brethren, IA, free minister in, 1175
Kimmel, David, 1234
  McLouth, KS, Church of the Brethren, 779
Kimmel, Elizabeth Wells, 693
Kimmel family, **693**
  Fahnestock family, 465
  Falls City Church of the Brethren, NE, 472
  Hunsiker (Hunsaker) family, 637
  Muhlenberg Co., KY, German Baptist Brethren, 893
  Pennsylvania farmhouse, *694*
  Reading Grace Brethren Church, PA, 1084
  Spohn, Clarence E. on, 2358
Kimmel farmhouse in PA, *694*
Kimmel, Fran, 693
Kimmel, Harry, 693
Kimmel, Harvey Centennial, 913
Kimmel, Harvey H., 1678
Kimmel, Homer D., 1678
Kimmel, Homer E.
  South Red Cloud Church of the Brethren, NE, minister, 1206
Kimmel House, Stony Creek Brethren Church, PA, 1225
Kimmel, Irene (later Shroyer), *See* Shroyer, Irene Kimmel
Kimmel, J. L., 235, 362, 366, 558, 760, 1225
  North Georgetown, OH, Brethren Church, pastor, 948
Kimmel, J. R.
  McLouth, KS, Brethren Church, pastor, 779
Kimmel, J. T., 1678
Kimmel, Joan Stuckey, 693, 1052, 1984–1985, 2283
Kimmel, Johann Michael, 693
Kimmel, John A., 1678
Kimmel, John M., 290, 417, **693**, 913, 1678, 1985, *See* Old German Baptist Brethren
  Chronicles of the Brethren, 788
  historical writing, 612
Kimmel, John M., Jr., 1356
Kimmel, John M., Sr., 1306–1307, 1356

Kimmel, Joseph, 588
Kimmel, Joseph L., 31, **693**, 1678
  Muncie, IN, Brethren Church, pastor
Kimmel, Josiah K., 693
Kimmel, Josiah Regal, 1678
Kimmel, Kay, 693
Kimmel (Kimmell), David, 1678
Kimmel, Lewis, 433, 693, **693**, 1678
  Miller, Howard, 837
  Pennsylvania Brethren secondary schools, 1004–1005
  Plum Creek Normal School, 1038
Kimmel, Lois E., 2283
Kimmel, Maria, 1302
Kimmel, Mary Miller, 693
Kimmel, Michael, 1678, **2383**
Kimmel, Milton L., 1678
Kimmel, Myers P., 1678, 2283
Kimmel (Old Dunkard) cemetery, 1359
Kimmel, PA, congregation
  Pike Run Church of the Brethren, PA, 1023
Kimmel, Susan, 693
Kimmel, T. L., family
  Sheldon Church of the Brethren, IA, 1175
Kimmel, Theodore Acroyd, **693**, 1678
Kimmel, Tobias, 693
Kimmel Twp., Bedford Co., PA, 1294
Kimmel, W. C., family
  Sheldon Church of the Brethren, IA, 1175
Kimmel, Walter, 242
Kimmel, Mrs. Walter, 242
Kimmell, Arthur Vance, 53, **693–694**, 715, 759, 861, 1343, 1678
Kimmer, Harry, 693
Kimsey Run Brethren Church, WV, **694**
Kincade (Kincaid), Nathaniel, 1678
Kincade, Nathaniel, 105
Kincaid family, 2087
Kincaid, Robert L., 1985
Kindall, John K., 1678
  Rappahannock Church of the Brethren, VA, pastor, 1083
Kindell, Donald Edward, 1678
Kinder, George D., 1985
kindergartens
  Kruger, Helena, 708
Kindig, Barbara (later Gish), *550, 1361*
Kindig, E. D., 1678
Kindig family
  Osceola, IN, Grace Brethren Church, 983
Kindig, Ira Nelson, 1678
Kindig, J. R., 331
Kindig, Jacob J., 1678
  Sappa Creek Church of the Brethren, NE, elder, 1145
  Silver Lake Church of the Brethren, NE, elder, 1182
Kindig (Kendig), James Rufus, 1678
Kindig, Rebecca Garber, 1985
Kindle, B. F., 1678
Kindley, Clarence R., 1678, **2383**
Kindley, Elsie Marie, 1838
Kindy, A. C., 439
Kindy, Clement Claypool, 1678
  Pasadena, CA, Church of the Brethren, pastor in, 994
Kindy, Dean Robert, 1678
Kindy, Sylva (later Ulery), 1285
Kindy, Virgil Ross, 1678

King, Albert, 1985
King, Alice (later Ebey), 137, 418, 706, 1836
King, Alvin R., 1678, 2283
King, Arthur
  Shady Grove Old German Baptist Brethren Church, OH, elder, 1171
King, Arthur C.
  Palestine Old German Baptist Brethren Church, OH, 991
King, Arthur Rufus, 1678, See Old German Baptist Brethren
  Palestine Old German Baptist Brethren Church, OH, 991
King, Barbara, 2111
King, Beatrice Mae, 1854
King, Bernard Nathan, 206, 1678
  autobiography of, 2341
King, Bessie Humphrey, 694
King, Bessie Marie (later Fox), 1838
King, Bill L., 244
King, Christian and Elizabeth, 1985
King, Christian L., 694
King, D. L.
  Smithville, OH, First Brethren Church, 1192
King, Dale Eugene, 1678
King, Daniel J., 418
King, Emma (later Ziegler), 1846, **2388**
King, Esther, 2093
King, Eugene, 343, 1678–1679
King family, 226, 319, 323, 1390, 1927, 1958, 2087, See König family
  bibliography, 1893, 1902
  Idaho, 645
  Moscow, ID, Church of the Brethren, 878
  South Haven Old German Baptist Brethren Church, MI, 1205
King Ferry, NY, Lake Ridge Church of the Brethren, **695,** 933, 2028
King, Florence, 706
King, Frank R., **694,** 2110
King, George J., 1679
King, H. B., 1679
King, Henry F., 1679
King, Israel, 1679
King, James A., 1679
King James version (KJV) of the Bible, 138
King, Jane Eileen (later Byler), 1854–1855, 2153, **2388**
King, Joe M., 1985
King, John H., Sr., 1679
  Palestine Old German Baptist Brethren Church, OH, 991
  Shady Grove Old German Baptist Brethren Church, OH, elder, 1171
King, Jonathan F., 1679
  Skippack Church of the Brethren, PA, minister, 1189
King, Katherine (later Ziegler), 1397
King, Keith O., 2283
King, Kevin Daniel, 2284
King (Koenig), Jacob, 1985
King (Koenig), Joshua Y., 1679
King (König), Matheus. 1985
King, Larry, 1985, 1985
King, Lavern O., 2284
King, LeRoy (Mr. and Mrs.), 579
King, Lester Vernon, **694–695,** 1679, **2375, 2384**
  New Lebanon, OH, First Brethren Church, pastor in, 930

King, Lewis W., 1679
  Shady Grove Old German Baptist Brethren Church, OH, elder, 1171
King, Lola Isabella, 2107
King, Lou, 323
King, Mrs. Lou, 323
King, Margaret, 215
King, Martin Luther, Jr., 313, **695**
  historic peace churches, 2200
  International Fellowship of Reconciliation, 659
King, Mary Grisso, 418
King, Mattie, 2106
King, Mrs. D. L.
  Smithville, OH, First Brethren Church, 1192
King, Philip J., 1679
King, Reuben Frantz, 1940
King, Rufus Bucher, 1679, 1985, 2020, 2303
  Rural Life Association (RLA), 1131
King, Russell C., 2284
King, Samuel S. and Elizabeth Zook, 1985
King, Sanford Jesse, 1985
King, Solomon, 992
King, Thomas, 1679
King, W. Bertram, 318, 1679
King, W. H., 1679
King, Wilbur Lewis, 1985
Kingdom of God, **695,** See also adventism; dispensationalism; eschatology; God, Kingdom of; social gospel
  citizenship and, 313
  eschatology, 454
  Modernism, 866
  and New Covenant Fellowship, 926
kingdom of heaven, 695
Kingdom Songs [Number One], 1985
  hymnals, 642
Kingdom Songs Number Two, 1985
  hymnals, 642
Kingery, C(hristian) H., 549, 1679
Kingery, Christopher
  Pleasant View Brethren Church, KS, 1036
Kingery, Eva Miller
  Müller (Miller) family, 894
Kingery family, 165, 320, See Gingerich family
  Four Mile Church of the Brethren, IN, 505
  Greene, IA, Church of the Brethren, 570
  Howard, IN, Church of the Brethren, 633
  Jamison family, 668
Kingery, John F., 496, 1679
Kingery, Joseph
  Müller (Miller) family, 894
Kingery, Leah Mae Standafer, 1840
Kingery, Nancy (later Hamilton), 580
Kingery, Steven A., 62, 1679
Kingfisher Co., OK
  Pleasant Home Church of the Brethren, OK, 1033
  Kingman Church, KS, Church of the Brethren, See Murdock Church of the Brethren, KS
Kingman, KS, Church of the Brethren
  Murdock Church of the Brethren, KS, previous name of, 896
2 Kings, 11:12, 39
  Davis, John J., Jr. on history of Israel

in, 2363
  Whitcomb, John C., Jr. on history of Israel in, 2363
King's Children Society, 285, **695**
  Yoder, Charles Francis, 1385
Kingsbury, Robert D., 2284
Kingsley, IA, Church of the Brethren, 110, **695**
Kingsport, TN, Church of the Brethren, **695–696**
Kinney family, 377
Kinney, George, 1679
Kinsel, Anna Kuns, 710
Kinsel, Glenn Eugene, 415, 1679, 2172
  Roanoke, VA, Hollins Road Church of the Brethren, pastor, 1113
  Shippensburg, PA, Church of the Brethren, pastor in, 1177
Kinsel, Jacob, 1679
  Maitland Church of the Brethren, PA, minister, 783
Kinsel, John, 710
Kinsel, Paul Wilbur, *199,* 511, 1276, 1679, 2129, 2303, **2384**
Kinsel, Waldo Everett, 6, 1679
Kinsel, William Z., 1679
Kinsey, Abraham, 697, 1679
  Oak Hill Old German Baptist Brethren Church, VA, elder-in-charge, 957
Kinsey, Allen V., 696
Kinsey, Almira (later Basore), 696
Kinsey, Alvey Lee, 1679
Kinsey, Barbara Ellen (later Fifer), 488
Kinsey, Barbara Nead, 488, 696, 919
Kinsey, Carrie Swan, 696
Kinsey, Catharina, 697
Kinsey, Charles P., 696
Kinsey, Christian, 697
Kinsey, Clarinda J. (later Miller), 696
Kinsey, Cynthia A. (later Lambert), 696
Kinsey, Daniel, 164
Kinsey, David, 696, 697
Kinsey, David, Jr., 1013
Kinsey, Elizabeth Brumbaugh, 696
Kinsey, Elizabeth Reed, 696
Kinsey, Ella (later Fifer), 696
Kinsey, Emma Taylor, 696
Kinsey, Essie O. Stoner, 696
Kinsey, Esther (later Fry), 517
Kinsey family, 170, 700, See Kintzi family history, 1985
Kinsey, Florence H., 2085
Kinsey, Florence Keil, 696
Kinsey, Hannah (later Wolfe), 1359
Kinsey, Henry, 697
Kinsey, Ida M., 696
Kinsey, Jacob, 696, 697
Kinsey, James L., 1679
Kinsey, Jesse, 1679
Kinsey, Jesse E., 696
Kinsey, Joel, 696
Kinsey, Johannes, 697
Kinsey, Kathryn Hofecker, 696
Kinsey (Kintzi), Abraham, 697
Kinsey (Kintzi), Catharina, 697
Kinsey (Kintzi), Christian, 697
Kinsey (Kintzi), David, 697
Kinsey (Kintzi), Henry, 697
Kinsey (Kintzi), Jacob, 697
Kinsey (Kintzi), Johannes, 697
Kinsey (Kintzi), Magdalena, 697
Kinsey (Kintzi), Maria, 697
Kinsey (Kintzy), Jacob1985

Kinsey, Levi, 696
Kinsey, Lewis, 1679
Kinsey, Lucretia, 696
Kinsey, Lydia L. (later Shoup), 696
Kinsey, Lydia (later Brandt), 696
Kinsey, M. J. H., 1985
Kinsey, Magdalena, 697
Kinsey, Margaret Jane Biser
    "U. S. According to US," 1985
Kinsey, Maria, 697
Kinsey, Marjorie Blocker
    on Blough family, 2341
Kinsey, Mary E. (later Yount), 696
Kinsey, Mary Petry, 1013
Kinsey, Minnie E. Howe, 696
Kinsey, N., 1679
Kinsey, Nettie Seiber, 696
Kinsey, Noah, 696
Kinsey, Samuel, 178, 205, 348, 488, 497,
    696, 919, 1223, 1306, 1679, 1985
    editor, *The Vindicator,* 2087
    perfectionism, 1009
    publishing, 1068
    The Vindicator, published in Ohio, 961
    writings of, 2341
Kinsey, Samuel, wife of, 1391
Kinsey, Sarah (later Hyre), 696
Kinsey, Susannah Boyer, 170
Kinsey, William Nead, 696, 1679, *See also*
    Old German Baptist Brethren
Kinsey, William, 516, **696,** 704, 1223,
    1679, 1985
Kinsinger, Ada Menno Hershberger, 2079
Kinsinger, Emile, 1986
Kinsinger, Ray S., 1986
Kinsley, Bob
    on Mack, Alexander, 2341
Kinsley, Charles F., 1679
Kinsley, Dean R., 2284
Kinsley family
    Nimishillen Old German Baptist
        Brethren Church, OH, 937–938
Kinsley, John, 1679
Kinsley, John M., 431, 1679
Kinsley, Myron J., 350, 1399, 1679
    Oak Grove Old German Baptist
        Brethren Church, OH, minister,
        956
    Old Brethren minister, 965
Kinsley, Raymond, 431, 1679
Kinsly, D. S., 1679
Kinsolving, Wythe Leigh, 1986
Kintner, Alvin Lavon, 6, 1679
    Root River Church of the Brethren,
        MN, pastor, 1122
    Rossville, IN, Church of the Brethren,
        minister, 1124
Kintner, B. F., *478,* 696
Kintner, Charles L., 373, 1679
Kintner, Dana, *1391*
Kintner, E. P., 1060
Kintner, Edith, 373
Kintner, Edw. or Owen, *483*
Kintner, Edward, 152, **696–697,** 741, 742,
    1333, 1679
Kintner, Elgin Perry, *478, 483, 557*
    autobiography of, 2341
    on descendants of, 2341
    on Kintner, Edward and descendants,
        2341
    on Kintner, Glada Snyder and descen-
        dants, 2341
    on Pritchett, Ella Poff, 2341

on Pritchett, Reuel B., 2341
North Manchester, IN, Church of the
    Brethren, elder (moderator), 949
Roann, IN, Church of the Brethren,
    elder and part-time pastor, 1112
scientist, 1160
Kintner, Elizabeth, 1840, 2062
Kintner, Emery Berton, 1679
Kintner, Ethel Pritchett, 1060
Kintner family, *11,* 373, *478*
    Rupp (Roop) family, related to, 1130
Kintner, Glada O. Snyder, 697
    Kintner, Elgin Perry on, 2341
Kintner, Jacob, Jr., 1679–1680
    Maumee Church of the Brethren, OH,
        minister, 803
Kintner, John
    and his woodpile, *697*
Kintner, Mary Walker, 697
Kintner, Nannie Wagner, 1986
Kintner, Owen, *483,* 1680
Kintner, Robert, 1986
Kintner, S. M., 1680
Kintner, W. I., 152, 1680
Kintzel, William
    Schuykill Church of the Brethren, PA,
        1157
Kintzel, William Z., 1680
Kintzi family, **697**
Kintzy, Elizabeth Kemp, 697
Kintzy, Elizabeth Kent, 697
Kintzy, Jacob, 697
Kinzer, Elizabeth (later Roop), 1130
Kinzie, Alice (later Gooden), 1637
Kinzie, Allan Fellers, 1680
Kinzie, Christian T., 153, 2068
    Mexico Old German Baptist Brethren
        Church, IN, 821
Kinzie, Ethel (later Beeghley), 2134
Kinzie family, 1267, 1277, 2068, *See also*
    Kintzi family
    family history and genealogy, 1981
    Graybill (Grabill, Krehbiel) family, 567
Kinzie, Fred V., 585, 708, 1680, 2303
Kinzie, Geneva, 1680
Kinzie, George W., 318, 699, 1680
    New Enterprise Brethren Church, IN,
        elder in, 927
    New Lebanon, OH, First Brethren
        Church, pastor in, 930
    Ripon, CA, Brethren Church, pastor,
        1110
Kinzie, J(oe) L., 1680
Kinzie, Joel H., 590, 1680
Kinzie, Joseph, 1680
Kinzie, Kenneth S., 1680
Kinzie, L. N., 570
Kinzie, Lester R., 1333, 1680, 2376
    Mexico Old German Baptist Brethren
        Church, IN, minister, 821
    North Fork Old German Baptist
        Brethren Church, IN, minister, 948
Kinzie, Letcher N., 1680
Kinzie, Levi
    North Manchester Old German Baptist
        Brethren Church, IN, 949
Kinzie, Paul, 1315
Kinzie, Paul W., 1680
Kinzie, Pauline Elizabeth Garst, 1840
Kinzie, Ronald C., 2138
Kinzie, Thomas A.
    on Book of Jeremiah, 2341
Kinzie, Thomas D(ale), 1680

Kinzie, William Amos, 1680
Kinzie, William Gerhard, 1680
Kinzie, William Henry, 1315, 1680
Kinzie, Wilma Lucille (later Filbrun), 2184
Kinzle, George, 1249
Kiowa Co., CO, 324
    Sheridan Lake Old German Baptist
        Brethren Church, CO, 1176
Kiowa congregation, OK, *See* Harrison,
    OK, Church of the Brethren
Kiowa, OK, Church of the Brethren, *See*
    Harrison, OK, Church of the
    Brethren
Kipe, Anna E. (later Flohr), 494
Kipp, Earl S., 1680, 2303
Kipp, James, 2129
Kipp, John Snyder, 2284
    Mount Olivet Church of the Brethren,
        PA, assistant pastor, 886
Kipp, Keith, 1680
Kipphan, Klaus, 1903
Kipping, Anna, 697
Kipping family
    Allen, passengers on, 2126
Kipping, J., 1943
Kipping, Johanna, 174, 616, 697, **697**
Kipping, Johannes, 174, 616, **697**
Kipping, Sivilla (Sybille), 697
Kippings family, 1920
Kipple family, *See* Gibbel (Gibbel) family
Kiracofe, Anna Kathryn, **697**
Kiracofe, B. A., 1680
Kiracofe (Karicofe), Edgar Stuart, 1673,
    1680
Kiracofe, Ellis L., 1986
Kiracofe family, 1950
Kiracofe, Homer Newton, 1235, 1312,
    1680, 2303
Kiracofe, James U., 697
Kiracofe, Kathryn A., 566, 1333, 1870
    Eaton, OH, Church of the Brethren,
        417
    memoirs in India, 2341
Kiracofe, Vinnie Eby, 697
Kirby, Daniel G., 740
Kirby, Harry, 755
Kirby, Jacob Henry, 1680
Kirby, Virden (later Taber), 1247
Kirche
    Gemeinde, Gemeinschaft, 534
Kircher, Jacob
    Mound Valley Church of the Brethren,
        MO, 879
Kiriadjidis, Athanasius, 1680
Kirk, Daniel W., 124, 1680
    Mount Hebron Church of the Brethren,
        WV, 881
    Pleasant Hill Church of the Brethren,
        WV, 1033
Kirk, Edwin, 1680
Kirk, Elizabeth, 1839
Kirk, Phoebe (later Hanawalt), 581
Kirk, Silas H., 1680
    Mount Zion Church of the Brethren,
        WV, 888
Kirkendall, James E., 2284
Kirkham, Omra O., 1680
Kirkland, Snowden, 321
Kirklin (Kirrlin), John R., 1680
Kirkman, Roland
    Shelton Church of the Brethren, NC,
        deacon in, 1176
Kirkpatrick, E. L.

Rural Life Association (RLA), 1131
Kirkpatrick family, 2064
Kirkpatrick, Larry
    Omaha, NE, Grace Brethren Bible
      Church, 974
Kirkpatrick, Marjorie
    Omaha, NE, Grace Brethren Bible
      Church, 974
Kirkpatrick, Truman
    on York Center Cooperative, IL, 2341
Kirks, John, 323
Kirks, Mrs. John, 323
Kirnbauer, Ted J., 2284
Kirschner, Ann
    on Ephrata Cloister, 2341
Kirschner, Elwood August, 1680
    Philadelphia, PA, Calvary Church of
      the Brethren, pastor, 1015
Kiser, Benjamin
    Sidney, OH, Trinity Church of the
      Brethren, 1181
Kiser, C. H., 265
Kiser, Cleveland, 626
Kiser family, 161, 265
Kiser, Jacob, 1680
Kiser, Jean F., 2184
Kishacoquillas, PA, congregation, 406, *See*
    also Aughwick, PA, congregation;
    Dry Valley Church of the Brethren,
    PA
Kishacoquillas Seminary, PA, 2, **697–698**
    Brubaker, Elizabeth Howe, 217
    Pennsylvania Brethren secondary
      schools, 1004
    Sharp, Solomon Zook, principal of,
      1174
    sources on, 2319
Kishacoquillas Valley, PA, Church of the
    Brethren, 1215, *See also* Dry
    Valley Church of the Brethren, PA
    Maitland Church of the Brethren, PA,
      783
Kisner, Mary Ann (later Rarig), *See* Rarig
    family
kiss, 396, *See also* holy kiss
    Dunkard Brethren, 409
    as greeting; personal appearance and
      beards, 1010
    Old German Baptist Brethren, 2233
kiss of charity, Pennsylvania Brethren
    Church and Grace Brethren, 1005
kiss of peace, *698*, *See also* holy kiss
    degrees of ministry, 374
    doctrine on, 185
    Dunkard Brethren Church, 2173
    illustration by Pyle, Howard, *1374*
    symbolism of, 2147
Kissinger, Warren Stauffer, 1680, 1986
Kistner, Roy, 565, 1680
Kitch, Nancy, 637
Kitchen, A. R., 1680
Kitchen, Amelia, 274
Kitchen, Charlotte, 274
Kiteley family, 1956
Kitson, John W., 540, 557, 1246, 1680,
    1986
Kittanning, PA, North Buffalo Grace
    Brethren Church, *See* North
    Buffalo Grace Brethren Church,
    PA
Kittanning, PA, West Kittanning Grace
    Brethren Church, **699**
    Glade Run Brethren Church, PA, 551

Kitterman, Gabriel, 1680
Kitterman, Jennie (later Petry), 1013
Kittinger, Benjamin F., 21, 1680
Kittinger, Levi, 1680
Kitzel, Sandra R., 2284
Kiwanis Clubs
    student exchange program, 1231
Kizer, Henry, 1680
Kizer, Sarah, 263
Kizer, William, 263
Klaasen, Walter, 2108
Klaber family, 317
Klahr Valley, PA, 1294
Klamath Falls Church of the Brethren, OR,
    699
Klappert family, 317
Klassen A. J., 1861
Klassen, Frank Henry, 1986
Klaus, Gerald E., 2284
Klees, Frederic, 1986
Klein, Abraham, 699, 700
Klein, Barbara Moyer
    Meyer family, 822
Klein, Clifford Frederick, 1680
Klein, David E., 699, 700,| 752, 1680
Klein, Dorothy Rebman, 699
    Mason, Floyd R. on descendants of,
      2346
    Mason, Kathryn Garst on descendants
      of, 2346
Klein, Eitel, 1986
Klein, Elizabeth Altaffer, 699
Klein, Elizabeth Breneiser, 700
Klein, Elizabeth (later Miller)
    Müller (Miller) family, 894
Klein, Elsa (later Schneider), *See*
    Schneider, Elsa Klein
Klein family, 267, **699–700**, 1956
Klein, George
    Müller (Miller) family, 894
Klein, George, Jr., 699
Klein, George, Sr., 1987
    Mason, Floyd R. on descendants of,
      2346
    Mason, Kathryn Garst on descendants
      of, 2346
Klein, Harry M. J., 1986
Klein, Jacob, 699
    Meyer family, 822
Klein, Jesse Roop, 106, 1680
Klein, Johann Friedrich, 1228, 1986
Klein, Joseph, 699
Klein, Karl Kurt, 1986
Klein, Mary Dornback, 700
Klein meetinghouse, *524*
    "The Klein Meetinghouse," 1978
    Klein meetinghouse (Vernfield, PA), 48,
      49
    Peter Becker Community, 1010
Klein-Nicolai, Georg, 1986–1987
Klein, Philip, 699, 700
Klein, Philip S., 1986
Klein, Samuel, 583
Klein, Sarah (later Sollenberger), 699
Klein, Walter C., 1986
Das Kleine Davidische Psalterspiel der
    Kinder Zions, **700**
Das Kleine Davidische Psalterspiel (The
    Small Davidic Psaltery), 176, 330,
    641, 1279, 1987
    publishing, and spiritual nurture, 1063
    singing, 1184
Klein(e), Georg(e), **699**, 750, 1680, 1916,

2375
Heckman family, 593
Mohrsville Church of the Brethren, PA,
    elder, 869
Die Kleine Harfe, 641, **700,** 1987
Der Kleine Kempis, 1987
    hymns by Alexander Mack, Jr., 2004
Die Kleine Lieder Sammlung, 171, **700,**
    711, 1057, 1987
    hymnals, 641
Die Kleine Perlen-Sammlung, 1014, 1987
    hymnals, 641
Kleiner, John W.
    on Mühlenberg, Heinrich Melchior,
      correspondence of, 2341
Kleiver, John F., 701
Klepinger, Aaron
    Peru, IN, Church of the Brethren, 1010
Klepinger, Aldeba (later Bright)
    sources on, 2318
Klepinger, Alfred L., 366, 1680
Klepinger, Benjamin S., **700**
Klepinger-Clippinger-Kleppinger family
    family history, 1987
Klepinger, Davis P.
    Pipe Creek Church of the Brethren, IN,
      elder, 1025
Klepinger, Della Rike, 700, *See also*
    Kleplinger, Della
Klepinger, Elmer, 700
Klepinger family, **701**
Klepinger, Henry, 297, **700**
Klepinger, John, *See* Kleppinger, John
Klepinger (Kleppinger), William, 1681
Klepinger, Lucy Honeyman, 700
Kleplinger, Benjamin S., 1680
Kleplinger, Davis P., 1680, *See also*
    Klepinger, Davis P.
Kleplinger, Della (later Ebling), 418, *See*
    also Klepinger, Della Rike
Klepper, D. B., 1681
Klepper, D. V., 742
Klepper family
    Maryville, TN, Oakland German
      Baptist Brethren Church, 799
Klepper, J. E., 570, 1681
Klepper, Jacob S., 1340, 1681
    Midway Church of the Brethren, TN,
      providing leadership, 827
Klepper, Peter, 1681
Klepper, Starks, 1340
Kleppinger, Carl Theodore, 1987
Kleppinger, Elizabeth Boyer, 170
Kleppinger family, 170
Kleppinger (Clippinger, Klepinger) family,
    701, 1987
Kleppinger, Henry, 701
Kleppinger, John, 701
Kleppinger, Ludwig, 701
Kleppinger, Stanley J., 1987
Klickitat Church of the Brethren, WA, *See*
    Stiverson Brethren Church, WA;
    Stiverson Church of the Brethren,
    WA
Klickitat Co., WA, 1223
Klickitat Valley, WA, 1319
Kliever, Freda Neufeld, 136, 270, **701,**
    1851
Kliever, Jacob Paul, 136, 270, **701,** 1681,
    1851, 2303
Kliever, Katherina Kliewer, 701
Kliever, Pastor
    Mennonite Brethren Churches, General

Conference of, 814
Kliewer, Albert, 1248
Kliewer, Albert W., 758, 1681
Kliewer, Katharina (later Kliever), 701
Kliewer, Robert C., 348, 758, 1337, 1681
   Mennonite Brethren Churches, General
      Conference of, 814
   Modesto, CA, Big Valley Grace
      Community Church (FGBC),
      pastor, 866
   Seal Beach, CA, Grace Brethren
      Church, pastor, 1161
Kline, Agnes, 1987
Kline, Alvin T., 1681
Kline, Amos, 263
Kline, Anna Wampler, 701
Kline, B. Franklin, 1681
Kline, Benjamin, 1681
Kline, Bonnie (later Smeltzer), 2293
Kline, Daniel R., 1681
   Murdock Church of the Brethren, KS,
      896
Kline, Donald Leslie, 1323, 1681
   Peoria IL, (First) Church of the
      Brethren, pastor, 1009
Kline, Elizabeth
   Mason, Floyd R. on, 2345
Kline, Elizabeth (later Putterbach), 1070
Kline, Elizabeth (later Ziegler/Zigler),
      1397, 1399
Kline family, 1318, *See also* Klein family
   Fahrney (Forney) family, 466
   Graybill (Grabill, Krehbiel) family, 567
   Hertzler (Hartzler) family, 601
   Hope Memorial Church (German
      Baptist Brethren), NE, 2375
   Sanger family, related to, 1144
Kline, Floyd R.
   on Zigler, Elizabeth Mason, 2345
Kline, Frank, 1681
Kline, George, 93, 701, 1340
Kline, Harmon S., 1987
Kline, Harvey Swope., 187, 327, 378, 1337,
      1681, 1987
   National Older Adult Conferences,
      2229
Kline, Helen, 1987
Kline, Henry S., 1681
Kline, Israel and Barbara Notestine, 1996
Kline, J. M., Jr., 1681
Kline, Jack, 1333, 1681
Kline, Jacob, 1681
Kline, Joel David, 1681
Kline, John, 61, 105, 129, 177, 211, 265,
      271, 274, 295, 310, 315, 380, 460,
      525, 584, *590*, 599, 602, 699–700,
      701–702, 918, 923, 1248, 1262,
      1295, 1308, 1349, 1391, 1681,
      1883, 1895, 1920, 1987, 1995,
      2028, 2068, 2104, 2110
   Annual Meeting moderator, 1151
   biography, 1938, 1943, 2054
   congregations visited by, 106
   conscientious objection, 2177
   criticism of Methodist public worship,
      1375
   divine inspiration of scripture, 132
   Durnbaugh, Donald F. on, 2327
   Eberly, William R. on Elder John Kline
      Bicentennial Celebration, 2328
   folk medicine, 2146
   Fraktur bookplate in hymnal, *2186*
   Funk, Joseph, 525

   graveclothes, 566
   historic sites, 609
   historiography
      biography of, 2201
   hymnal bookplate, 2105
   John Kline (Dupler), 748
   Kostlevy, William on, 2341
   Linville Creek Church of the Brethren,
      VA, 745, 746
   Longenecker, Stephen L. on preachings
      of, 2344
   Lower Lost River Church of the
      Brethren, WV, visit to, 766
   medical practice, 809
   memoir, 1987
   The Middle Man (Davis family), 748
   minorities, ethnic and racial, 849
   mission work, Seneca Church of the
      Brethren, WV, 1166
   missions, 857
   Mount Zion Church of the Brethren,
      VA, 888
   Mountain Grove Church of the Breth-
      ren, VA, 889
   Neff, Ray A. on, 2348
   perfectionism, 1009
   person baptized by, 92
   Petersburg, WV, Memorial Church of
      the Brethren, 1012
   picture book about, 1915
   preaching, 1053
   prisons, 1059
   relationship with John Letcher, 738
   Sappington, Roger E. (CB) and, 2246
   sources on, 2315, 2317, 2319
   Stoffer, Dale R. on, 2359
   Stone, Philip C. on, 2359
   travels on horseback, 1271
Kline, John H. (2 listed), 1681
Kline, John L., **702**, 1681
Kline, John M.
   Rappahannock Church of the Brethren,
      VA, moderator, 1083
Kline, John M., Sr., 1681
Kline, John Samuel, 1681, 1987
Kline, John W., family
   Mansfield, OH, First Church of the
      Brethren, 787
Kline, Kathryn, 2109
Kline, L. B., *678*
Kline, Mary, 263
Kline, Michael B. E., 1681
Kline, Paul G., 1987
   on Cline-Kline family, 2341
Kline, Paul Rufus, 1681
Kline, Permilla Battorf, 702
Kline, Roy, 1681
Kline, Theodore T., 1681
Kline, William, 1345
Kline, William and Maria Musselman, 1993
Kline, Wilmer, 1681
Klinedienst, Steve Lee, 2138
Klinefelter, Walter, 1987
Kling, Anna Margaretha(e) (later Mack),
      702, 703, **777–778**, *See also* Mack,
      Anna Margaretha Kling
   Mack, Alexander, Sr., 775
   Mack, Johann Valentin, 778
   Mack, Johannes, 778
Kling family, *702*, **703**
   inn in Schriesheim, *702*, 703
Kling, Johann Peter
   Mack, Anna Margaretha(e) Kling, 777

Kling, Johann Valentin, **702**, 703
   Mack, Alexander, Sr., leaving inheri-
      tance to, 777
   Mack, Anna Margaretha(e) Kling, 777
Kling, Valentin Johann, 383
Klingaman, George, 632
Klingaman, George, Sr., 632
Klingel, Robinson W., 1916
Klingensmith, Barney Ford, 703
Klingensmith, Christine Witter, 703
Klingensmith, Harriet, 703
Klingensmith, J. Raymond, 54, 64, **703,**
      1681, **2375, 2384**
   mass media, 801
   The Missionary Board (BC), 856
Klingensmith, Janet Lee, 703
"Klinger," 1987
Klinger, Donald E., 1681
Klinger family, 319, 1884, 1987
Klinger, Gene A., 754, 1681, 2284
Klinger, John Philip, 1987–1988
Klinger, Maywood Robert Boekeloo, 1987
Klinger, R. A., 1987
Klingspor, Karl, 1988
Klinzman, L. C., 463
KLM crash
   Brethren victims, **703**
   Disciples of Christ consolation, 1918
Kloepfer, H. W., 1988
Klopper, John, 1681
Klöppinger, Anna Margaretta Schreiner,
      701
Klöppinger, Johann Georg, 701, 1987
Kloss, Heinz, 1988
das Kloster (the cloister), *See* Ephrata
      Community
Kloths, Ed, 1278
Klotsche, Ernest H., 1988
Klotz, Alvin Frederick, 1312, 1383, 1681,
      1988, 2303
Klotz, Gladys Beeghly, 1681
Klotz, Lyle Milne, 1681, 2303
Klucker, Jospeh A., 1681
Klugh, Pat
   Southern Lancaster Grace Brethren
      Church, PA, 1207
Klus, Ben
   San Jose, CA, South Bay community
      Church (FGBC), 1142
Klus, Bernath McCrea, Jr., 1851
Klus, Martha Anne Ice, 1851
   San Jose, CA, South Bay community
      Church (FGBC), 1142
Knabel, Peter, 1681
Knagey, Sally (later Holsinger)
   hymns, 643
Knapp family, 2087
Knappenberger, Margaret Hostetter, 1840
Knappenberger, Robert Rollin, 1681, 1840
Knarr, Richard Henry, 1681
Knaus, Donald, 1315, 1681
Knaus family, 142
   Redstone Valley Old German Baptist
      Brethren Church, WI and, 2239
Knaus, Harley, 626
Knaus, Jess, 626, 1315, 2303
Knaus, Jesse A., 1681, **2384**
   Shoal Creek Old German Baptist
      Brethren Church, Newton Co.,
      MO, elder-in-charge, 1178
Knaus, Merl W., 2284
Knaus, Ray, 626, 1681
Knaus, Roger D., 2284

Knaus, Russell D., 626, 1681, 2138
Knauss, David C.
    on Midway CB, PA, 2341
Knauss, James O., 1988
Knavel, Berkey Earl, 1681
    Roaring Spring, PA, First Church of
        the Brethren, pastor, 1114
Knavel, Caroline
    Maple Grove Church of the Brethren,
        PA, 791
Knavel, Charles S., 1348, 1681
    Scalp Level, PA, Church of the
        Brethren, minister, 1151
Knavel, Maurice, 1681–1682
Knavel, Peter, 1682
    Scalp Level, PA, Church of the
        Brethren, elder, 1151
Knavel, Samuel
    Maple Grove Church of the Brethren,
        PA, 791
Knechel, Robert W., Jr., 1682
Knechel, Robert W., Sr., 7, 1682, **2384**
Knechel, Ruthann (later Johansen), 638
    Women's Conferences (CB) and, 2264
Knecht, William L., 1988
    kneeling, *See* prayer, posture in
        prayer, 1052, *1052*
Kneff, Robert Clinton, 1682
Kneisly family, 1988
Kneisly, Harry Loren, 1988
Kneisly, John A., 1277, 1682
Knep, Samuel W., 1682
Knepp family
    Fairview Church of the Brethren, MD,
        468
Knepp, Mary Ann Rhodes, 1988
Knepper, Clemens, **703**
Knepper, David Emerson, 1840
Knepper, Elizabeth, 1988
Knepper, Emma J. Brubaker, 703
Knepper, Eve Schrock, 703
Knepper family
    Allen, passengers on, 2126
    family history in United States, 1988
    Grand River German Baptist Brethren
        Church, MO, 565
Knepper, Glenn, 1319
Knepper, Harry, 1236
Knepper, Harry M., 1388
Knepper, Ida Iola Rathfelder, 1988
Knepper, Joel
    Gotha, FL, New Covenent Church of
        the Brethren, 2190
Knepper, John Henry, 20, 121, 215, 438,
        476, **703**, 720, 746, 1225, 1682
    Johnstown, PA, First Brethren Church,
        673
    Meyersdale, PA, Main Street Brethren
        Church, pastor, 823
Knepper, L. M., 1988
Knepper, Lewis Schrock, 214, 533, 1682
    Rockton, PA, Church of the Brethren,
        pastor, 1118
Knepper/Martin discoveries
    Durnbaugh, Donald F. on, 2326
Knepper, Mary Eileen, 1850
Knepper, Mary (later Martin)
    Martin family, 797
    Martin, George Adam, wife of, 797
Knepper, Mary (later Walker), 1314
Knepper, Nancy F., 243, 1932, 2284
    Gotha, FL, New Covenent Church of
        the Brethren, 2190

Knepper, R. Joel, 243
Knepper, Richard
    Gotha, FL, New Covenent Church of
        the Brethren, 2190
Knepper, Roger, 1682
Knepper, Solomon, 703, 1682
Knepper, Veronica Bloom, **703**
Knepper, Wayne F.
    on Knepper, Wilhelm, 2341
Knepper, Wilhelm, **703, 2375**
    Knepper, Wayne F. on, 2341
    Solingen Brethren, 1201
    testament of, 1988
Knicely, Allen Gene, 1682
Knieriem, Samuel Ray, 1682
Knierim, Stephen D., 319
Kniesley, Daniel S., 1682
Knife family, 1389
Knife, Wayne D., 2303
Knight, David William, 2284
Knight, Henry S., 416, 462, 1682
    Madison Church of the Brethren, VA,
        moderator, 781
    Pine Ridge Church of the Brethren, VA
        and, 2238
Knight, M. F., 1988
Knight, Mollie M.
    Pine Ridge Church of the Brethren, VA
        and, 2238
Knight, Nathaniel T.
    Pine Ridge Church of the Brethren, VA
        and, 2238
Knight's Chapel meetinghouse, VA, 416
Knight's Chapel, VA, congregation
    Mount Carmel Church of the Brethren,
        VA, 880
Knights of Pythias, Warsaw, IN,
        meetingouse purchased from, 1319
Knipfer, G. W., 1682
Knisely, Christopher, 1682
Knisely, George H., 1682
Knisley family, 2019
Knisley, J. C., 1988
Knisley, John, 1682
Knisley-Wolf family, 1873, 1988
Knittel, Walter A., 1988
Knob Creek community, TN
    Bowman anniversary (photo), 2379
Knob Creek congregation, 742, 1253
    Bowman Brethren, 364
    Garst, Henry, 531
    Hawthorne Church of the Brethren,
        TN, 590
    Solenberger, David, 1202
Knob Creek, TN, Church of the Brethren,
        167, 168, *See also* Johnson City,
        TN, Knob Creek Church of the
        Brethren
    to Niota, TN, Church of the Brethren,
        938
    Pritchett, Reuel Bowman, 1060
Knob Creek, TN, congregation (OGBB),
        264
Knob Fork, WV
    Ryerson Station Church of the
        Brethren, PA, preaching point,
        1132
Knobley Church of the Brethren, WV, 57,
        106, **703–704**, 1240
    Harness Run Church of the Brethren,
        WV, 585
Knobnoster, MO, 1315
Knobsville, PA, Church of the Brethren,

704
    Markey family, 794
Knodt, Hermann, 1988
Knoepfle, Charles, 313
Knoepfle, Mabel, 313
Knopsnider (Knopsnyder), William M.,
        1682
Knopsnyder, William M., 432
Knorr, Hannah (later Sauer), *See* Sauer,
        Hannah Knorr
Knotts, Donald Raymond, 2284
Knouff, Hannah Pfouts, **704, 2375**
Knouff, Henry, 704
Knouse, John Edwin, 1682
Know Nothing Party, **704**
    influence on Brethren, and Roman
        Catholic Church, 1120
Knox Co., OH, 364
Knox Co., MO
    Shelby Co. Church of the Brethren,
        MO, 1174
Knox Co., OH, 363, 374, 724, 734, 1367
    bibliography, 1877
    Brethren settlement, 961
    history, 1967, 2099
    Nicholson, John, minister in, 935
    Owl Creek Old German Baptist
        Brethren Church, OH, 986
Knox family, 2087
Knox, Ronald A., 1988
Knoxville, TN, Church of the Brethren,
        105, **704**
Knupp, Abraham, 1682
Knupp, Adam, 531, 1682
    New River Old German Baptist
        Brethren Church, ministers for,
        931
Knupp, Mary (later Zigler), 1398
Knuttel, Willem P. C., 1860
Knyphausen, Baron von
    Philadelphian Society, 1019
Kob, Lewis M., 507, 1682
Kobb, T. (Y.) J., 1682
Kober, Dieterich, 322
Kober, Mahala, 322
Kober, Margaretta, 322
Kober, Peter, 322
Koby, Keith, 1343
Kobzeff, Bill, 713
Kobzeff, Luba, 713
Koch, Anna Elizabeth, 704
Koch, Catharina, 704
Koch (Cook) family, **704–705**
Koch, D. P., 705
Koch, Daniel
    Silver Creek Church of the Brethren,
        OH, 1182
Koch, Daniel P., 1682
Koch, Eduard Emil, 1988
Koch, Euroia A. Lutz, 1988
Koch family, **704–705**, 1988
    Allen, passengers on, 2126
Koch, Hanna M., 1988
Koch, Hezekiah, 704
Koch, J. Albert, 704
Koch, Johann Jakob, **704**
Koch, Margretha Bosserman, 163
Koch, Oliver, 704
Koch, Oliver W., 704
Koch, Peter, 163
Koch, Richard A., 2284
Koch, Richard Henry, 1988
Koch, Roy D., 704

Koch, Stephan (Brother Agabus), **704,** 1682
  bibliography, 1988–1989
  Geistliche Fama, 533
  Kalcklöser, Johann Heinrich, 681
  Krefeld, Germany, 707
  Mack, Alexander, Jr., 774
  mysticism, 907
  Traut, Johann Henrich, 1270
Kochel family, New Holland, PA, Church
  of the Brethren, 928
Kochheiser, Gary Melvin, 2284
  on GBC, nonresistance in, 2341
Kocis, Jacob P.
  Island Pond, VT, Grace Brethren
    Church, 2209
Kocker (Koker), Gilles, **705**
Kocker (Koker), Jan, **705**
Kocker (Koker), Michael, **705**
Kocker (Koker), Pieter de, **705**
Kodear, Carolyn Louise, 1851
Koehler, Henry, 1989
Koehn, Elise M., 2284
Koenig (King), Jacob, 1985
Koenig (König), Simon, 706
Koenigswald, Harold von, 1989
Koger, M. V., 1989
Kohl, Tringen (later Lobach), 751
Kohler, Fred
  Filley German Baptist Brethren
    Church, NE, 2374
Kohler, Paul S., 2284
Kohlmeyer, James, 1682
Kohne, Joseph Casper, 1682
Kohne, L. W., 1682
Kohne, William Erasmus, 1682
Kohr family, 1274
koinonia, 291
  community, 329
Koinonia, CO, Church of the Brethren, *See*
    Grand Junction, CO, Koinonia
    Brethren-Baptist Church
Koinonia Farms, **705**
  Habitat for Humanity International,
    2195
Koker, de, family, 324, 923
  Rotterdam, of, giving aid to emigrants,
    1125
  "De Rotterdamsse Familie De Koker",
    2323
Koker, Gilles, **705**
Koker, Jan, **705**
Koker (Kocker) Gilles de, **705**
Koker (Kocker), Jan de, **705**
Koker (Kocker), Michael de, **705**
Koker (Kocker), Pieter de, **705**
Koker, Michael, **705**
Koker, Pieter de, **705**
Kokomo, IN
  Brethren Church, **705**
  Church of the Brethren, **705**
  Indian Heights Grace Brethren Church,
    705
  North Grace Church of the Brethren,
    See North Kokomo Grace Brethren
    Church, IN
  North Kokomo Grace Brethren Church,
    IN, 948
Kolb, Christian, 1989
Kolb, Clarence, 1346
Kolb, Clarence E., 130, 467, 1682
Kolb (Culp, Kulp, Kolp) family, **706**
Kolb, Dielman, 394, 706, 2057, 2071
  Mack family, 778

Kolb, Elizabeth, 706
Kolb family, **706,** 1989, 2075
Kolb (Kulp/Culp) families, 1901
Kolb/Kulp/Culp family
  sources on, 2321
Kolb (Kulp), Samuel and Catherine, 1991
Kolb, Lydia Mack (later Lentz), 706
  Mack family, 778
Kolb, Thomas J., 1682
  Rocky Ridge, MD, Monocacy Church
    of the Brethren, presiding elder,
    1119
Kolb, William, Jr., **706**
  Interchurch World Movement (IWM),
    658
Kolb, William M., 64, 65, 705, 1682, 2303
Kollar, George V., 1682
  Mount Zion Church of the Brethren,
    OH, resident elder, 888
Kollar, Peter, 1682
Kollnig, Karl, 1989
Kolp family, *See* Kolb family
Kolp (Kulp/Culp/Kalb/Colp) families, 1887
Konert, Christoph, 120, **706,** 1063
Konig, Christina (later Weiss), 1328
König family, **706**
König (King) family, **706**
König (King), Matheus, 1985
König, Samuel, 57, 239, **706**
König, Simon, 706, 1989
Konigmacher, Anna, 220, 223
Konigmacher family, 1961
  Spohn, Clarence E. on, 2357
Konigmacher, Jacob, 1989
Konkel, William, 1895
Konolfingen Co., Switzerland
  Gingerich (Kingery) family, 549
Kontra, Peter Joseph, 2284
Konves family
  Phoenix, AZ, Northwest Grace
    Brethren Church, 1019
Konves, Russell E., 318, 746, 1682
  Phoenix, AZ, Grace Brethren Church,
    pastor, 1019
Koolhof, Jerrett, 1682
Koones (Koontz), Emanuel G., 1682
Koons family
  Orange City, FL, Calvary Grace
    Brethren Church, 976
Koons, Ruth, 213
Koons, Ulysses Sidney, 747, 1989
Koontz Church of the Brethren, PA,
  706–707
  Snake Spring Valley Church of the
    Brethren, PA, churchhouse, 1192
Koontz, Claude R., 746, 1682
Koontz congregation, PA, 1323
Koontz, Cornelius, 1682
Koontz family, *See* Kuns family
  Fahrney (Forney) family, 466
  Orange City, FL, Calvary Grace
    Brethren Church, 976
Koontz, Frank, 332
Koontz, H. W.
  Roanoke, VA, First Brethren Church,
    pastor, 1113
Koontz, Henry, 170, **706,** 1682
Koontz, Henry S., 1682
Koontz, Herman W., 213, 349, 1353, 1388,
    1682, 2303
  Maitland, FL, Grace Brethren Church,
    pastor, 783
  Orange City, FL, Calvary Grace

Brethren Church, pastor, 976
  Orlando, FL, Grace Brethren Church,
    interim pastor, 982
  Ormond Beach, FL, Grace Brethren
    Church, pastor, 982
  St. Petersburg, FL, Grace Brethren
    Church, pastor, 1135
Koontz, Jacob, 706
Koontz, Jacob F., 674, 710, 725, 927, 1305,
    1682
  Martinsburg, PA, Grace Brethren
    Church, pastor, 798
  Mount Pleasant Brethren Church, VA,
    minister, 886
  Pineville, VA, Mount Olive Brethren
    Church, pastor, 1025
  Reliance, VA, Mount Zion Brethren
    Church, pastor, 1096
Koontz, James C., 2284
Koontz, John, Sr., 706
Koontz, Julia Whisman, 706
Koontz, Kenneth David, 674, 2284
  Orange City, FL, Calvary Grace
    Brethren Church, pastor, 976
Koontz (Koons), Jacob, 1682
Koontz, Leanna Fay, 1833
Koontz, Louis K., 1989
Koontz, Myra
  Maitland, FL, Grace Brethren Church,
    783
  Orlando, FL, Grace Brethren Church,
    982
  Ormond Beach, FL, Grace Brethren
    Church, 982
Koontz, Paul, 213
Koontz, Steve L., 2284
Koontz, Will
  Pineville, VA, Mount Olive Brethren
    Church, 1025
Koontz, William, 1264
Koontz, William C., 1682
Koontz, William H., 1989
Koontz, William Kenneth, 1682
Kope, Victor Homer, 1682
Kopenhaver, William D., 1683
Koplin, Matthew
  Pennsylvania Hospital, 1007
Koppenol, Antonius van, 1935
Koppes, Charles W., 1989
Koppes family, 1989
Koppock, J. D., 1683
Korea, **707**
Korean Mission, 2211–2212
  missions (CB), 2225
  United Nations Korean Reconstruction
    Agency (UNKRA), 1291
Korea, AFSC aid for, 23
Korean Evangelical Church
  Los Angeles, CA, Central Evangelical
    Church of the Brethren (Korean),
    2215
Korean Mission (CB)
  established 1984, **2211–2212**
  Korean War, 19, **707**
  Heifer Project International, 594
  incarceration of Brethren, 1060
  military service, 301
  missions and missionaries, 277
Kornhaus, Eva Nancy Steiner, 1989
Korson, George G., 1989
Kortwolde, **707**
  baptisms in, *1241*
  historic sites, 609

Kosch, Lewis F., **707**
Kosciusko Co., IN, 153, 352, 411, 1246,
    1280, 1333, 1877
    Eel River Old German Baptist Brethren
        Church, IN, 430
    North Winona Church of the Brethren,
        IN, 951
    Pleasant Hill College, 1033
    Snell, John and Magdalena, 1193
Köslin (Koszalin)
    Felbinger, Jeremias, 482
Köster, Heinrich Bernhard
    Society of the Woman in the Wilder-
        ness, 1200
Kostlevy, William C., 2284
    on Anabaptists, 2341
    on imperialism, 2341
    on Kline, John, 2341
    on Quinter, James, 2341
Kouchnour family, *See* Gochenour
        (Goughnour) family
Kough, Catherine, 1989
Kover, Virgil K., 2284
Krabill, Christian, 1683
Krabill, David, 1683
Krabill, John, 1683
    Portage Church of the Brethren, OH,
        minister, 1047
Krabill, John P., 1683
Krabill, John William, 1683, **2384**
Krabill, Lucile, 1989
Krabill, Peter, 1989
Kraemer, David M., 1989
Kraemer, Fritz, 1989
Kraemer, Gustav, 1989
Kraft, Charles H., 139, 335, 1683, 1855,
    1989–1990
    Readings in Dynamic Indigeneity, 1990
Kraft, Johann Heinrich, 421, 1228
Kraft, John L., 1990
    on Ephrata Cloister, 2341
Kraft, Marguerite Elaine Gerhart, 139, 1855
Krähenbühl family, *See* Graybill (Grabill,
        Krehbiel) family
Krahenbuhll family, 1994
Krahn, Cornelius, 1990
Krall, Clarence Nathan, 1683, 2303
Krall, Cyrus Bomberger, 1683
Krall, Frank, 1683
Kramer, Marilyn M., 1859
Kramer, Paulyne Mickley, 1990
Krane, Heribert, 1990
Kraning, Robert Lee, 1683
Krape family, 1389
Krape, J. David, 2284
    free ministry to New Fairview Church
        of the Brethren, PA, 927
Krape, John Edgar, 1337, 1683
    free ministry to New Fairview Church
        of the Brethren, PA, 927
Kratz, Amanda R. Reiff, 22
Kratz, Charles, 516
Kratz, Mr., *1055*
Kratz, William D., 1683
Kraus, Hertha, 1990
Krause family, 1990
Krause, Gerhard, 1922
Kraybill, Donald B.
    on Amish, 2341
    on Anabaptists, 2341
    on Brethren bodies, information about,
        2342
    on Brethren, compared to Hutterites,

Mennonites and Amish, 2341
    on Hutterites, 2341
    on Mennonites, 2325, 2341
    nuclear arms race, 2232
    on September 11, 2001 attacks, 2342
    works by, 2317
    The Young Center and, 2267
Kraybill family, 1990
Kraybill, Mary Jean, 1990
Kraybill, S. L., 1990
Kraybill, Spencer L., 1990
Kreamer, Myrna
    Omaha, NE, Grace Brethren Bible
        Church, 974
Kreamer, Tom
    Omaha, NE, Grace Brethren Bible
        Church, 974
Krebill, Agnes, 2025
Krebill family, 1966
Krebs, Friedrich, 1990
Kree, William H., 1683
Krefeld, 48, 107–108, 407, 421, **707**, 2027,
    2030, 2043, 2057, *See also*
        Schultz, Stephen
    asylum and Brethren movement, 174,
        175
    Brethren from, immigrating to Pennsyl-
        vania, 776
    Brethren in, history of, 1984
    Brethren, lineage of, 613
    Brethren movement, 157, 241, 376
    Brethren remnants in Europe, 1099
    Dompelaars in, 395
    emigration, Brethren, 443
    Germantown, 542
    Germany, 545
    Goyen, Gossen, 562
    Goyen, Maria Margaret (later Naas),
        909
    Grahe, Jakob, 564
    Häcker (Höcker), Wilhelm, 577
    Henckels, Johann Friedrich, 596
    Historic Peace Churches, 607
    historic sites, 609
    historical writing, 611
    Hochmann von Hochenau, Ernst
        Christoph, 615
    Holtzapfel (Holsapple, Holsopple),
        Johann Heinrich, 623
    Holy Spirit, doctrine of, 624
    Judaism, 677
    Jülich, 677
    Knepper, Clemens, **703**
    Koch, Johann Jakob, 704
    Koch, Stephan, 704
    Laschet (Laaschet, Laasche, Lausche,
        Laushe), Abraham van, 726
    Liebe, Christian, 527, 741
    Lobach, Johann, 751, 1222
    Lobach, Johann, nephew of, 1325
    Lucas, Martin, 766
    Marienborn Brethren moving to, 792
    Marienborn Brethren relocated in, 407
    Marienborn, migration from, 683
    Mennonite Church (MC) members
        from, 815
    migration from Ysenburg-Büdingen,
        1394
    missions, 857
    Naas, Johannes, family relocation to,
        909
    Netherlands connections, 923
    Petersen, Barthold Jurgen, 1012

Preiß, Johannes Jakob, 1055
Prussia, Brethren in, 1063
Rhine River Valley, Brethren origins in,
    1106
Ritter, Daniel, 1111
route to United States and, 159
sources on, 2316
Stetius, Gottfried Luther, 1222
Traut, Georg Balthasar "Balser," 1270
Vetter (Fetter), Lucas, 1304
Kreff, Robert C., 1683
Krehbiel, Edward H., 1990
Krehbiel family, 2077, *See also* Graybill
        family
    family history, 1990
    Mortonhouse (ship), 2373, 2376
Krehbiel, Henry P., 608, 1990
Krehbiel, Howard E., 1990
Krehbiel, Jacob, 1990
Krehbiel, Jacob P., 2077
Krehbiel, Johannes, 1953, 1998
Krehbiel, Johannes and Elizabeth Gella
    family history, 1990
Krehbiel, Jost, 1990
Krehbiel, Susanna Ruth, 1955
Krehbiel, Tobias J., 1972
Krehbiel, Valentine, 1955
Krehmeyer, Kathryn Carol, 1843
Kreider, Bard E., 1683
Kreider, Beulah (later Shank), *See* Shank,
        Beulah Kreider
Kreider, Caleb Aaron, 1340, 1683, 2303
    Mount Wilson Church of the Brethren,
        PA, minister, 887
Kreider, Daniel K., 1683
Kreider, David Bruce, 1234, 1683, 2134
Kreider, Elizabeth, 2092
Kreider, Esta E., 1683
Kreider family, 1990
Kreider, Frank, 1683
Kreider, Golda (later Flory), 499
Kreider-Greider family, 1990
    Jacob Kreider family, 1872
Kreider, Henry, 1940
Kreider House, White Oak Church of the
        Brethren, PA, 1340
Kreider, Howard Joseph, 740, 1333, 1683
Kreider, I. J., 1335
Kreider, Ira J., 1333, 1683
Kreider, Isaac J., 1683
Kreider, J. Kenneth, 193
    on BSC, 2342
Kreider, Jacob, 1683, 1872, 2035
Kreider (Krider), David, 1683
Kreider (Kryder, Cryder, Crider, Grider)
        family, 1990
Kreider (Krider), Landa U., 355, 1235,
    1683
Kreider, Lawrence, **707–708**, 1683
Kreider, Lydia Welbaum, 707
Kreider, Paul Eugene, 1990
Kreider, Robert, 1990
Kreider, Robert S.
    memoirs, 2342
Kreider, Rose Armina Shafer, 707
Kreider, Samuel, 430, 1683
Kreider, Samuel E., 1683
Kreider, Tobias, 585, 707, 1683
Kreider, Verona M. (later Smith), 1844,
    2019
Kreider, Willis C., 1683
Kreigh family, 1235
Kreighbaum, Aaron H., 1683

Kreighbaum, Hiram W., 1683
Kreighbaum, W. H., 1683
Kreimes, Roy E., 1683, 2303
  North Buffalo Grace Brethren Church, PA, pastor, 945
Kreiner (Kriner), Emma Young, 708
Kreiner (Kriner), Samuel A., **708,** 1683
Kreiter, Esta
  New River Old German Baptist Brethren Church, ministers for, 931
Kreiter, Esta Ellis, 1683
Kreiter, Samuel
  New River Old German Baptist Brethren Church, ministers for, 931
Kremlin, MT, Milk River congregation
  Montana Brethren settlement, 870
Kreps, Alfred, 668, 1683
  New Rockford, ND, Church of the Brethren, elder in, 932
Kreps, Esther E., 1840, 1990
  Pottstown, PA, Coventry Church of the Brethren, missionary, 1049
Kreps, George Milton, 1683, 1840
Kreps, J. A., 1990
Kreps, John P., 1683
Kreps, Noah, 1683
Kreps, Wilma Studebaker, 1840
Krewson family
  Pleasant Valley German Baptist Brethren, IA, 1036
Krewson, William A., 1683
Krider, Eldon Lynn, 1683
Krider, Marion, 345
Kriebel, E. S.
  Manchester College, President, 786
Kriebel, Howard Wiegner, 1990–1991
Kriebel, Reuben, 1991
Krieder, Lawrence, 109
Kriegbaum (Kreigbaum), Arnold R., 192, 265, 490, **708,** 758, 1322, 1683
  Lakeland, FL, Grace Brethren Church, 2213
  Mansfield, OH, Conservative Grace Brethren Church, 2217
  Ocala, FL, Grace Brethren Church, 2232
Kriegbaum, Ethel Shank, 708
Kriegbaum family, 265
  Ocala, FL, Grace Brethren Church, 2232
Kriegbaum, George N., 708
Kriegbaum, Laura Miller, 708
Kriegbaum, Salome, 716
Krieger, Albert, 1683
Krieger, Corda L. Wertz, 145, 1840
Krieger, Martin, 94, 1683
  Onekama, MI, Church of the Brethren, minister part-time, 975
Kriegh, W. H., 1683
Krieghbaum, Hiram William, 1991, 2050
  Osceola Church of the Brethren, IN, elder, 984
Kriner, *See* Kreiner, Samuel A.
Kristelig Tidende (Christian Times), **708**
Kritikakis, Herakles, 1683–1684
Kroh, Andreas
  on Radical Pietists in biographies of Wittgenstein, 2342
Kroll, Magdalena, 230
Krommes, Henry A., 1684
Krommes, Moses D., 1684
Kron, Gretchen, 1991
Kropf, Marlene, 2321

Krous family
  Johnson City, TN, Knob Creek Church of the Brethren, 672
Krous, Michael, 672
Krouse, Robert W., 1684
  Meadow Branch Church of the Brethren, MD. pastor, 805
Krouse, Susannah (later Wine), 1349
Krousz, Michael
  Miller, James F. on descendants of, 2347
Krout, Robert S., 1684
  free ministry to New Fairview Church of the Brethren, PA, 927
Krueger, Marianne Georgia, 1841
Kruger, Helena Braun, 200, **708,** 1255
  refugee resettlement, 1093
Kruger, Peter, 708
Krumrein, Catherine Brenner, 708
Krumrein (Crumrine, Grumrine) family, **708, 2384**
Krumrein, Georg Lenhart, 708
Krumrein, Jacob (elder), 708
Krumrein, Jacob (younger), 708
Krumrein, John, 708
Krumrein, Noah, 708
Krumrein, Peter, 708
Krupenbach, Jane (later Ramsey), 2239
Kruppp, Abraham
  "Watchman of the Night and Millennial Morning" (attributed to A. H. Cassel), 2342
Krynock, Roger, 1684
  Marysville, OH, Watkins Road Community Grace Brethren Church, pastor, 799
  New Troy, MI, Grace Brethren Church, pastor in, 932
Krypton, KY, Brethren Church, **708**
  Krypton Bible Center, **2212**
  Lowery, Margaret E., 2216
Ku Klux Klan, 2128
Kuburshosho, Nigeria, 306
Kuckenbaker family, 727
Kuehl, Warren, 1991
Kuepfer, Jacob and Marie Lichti, 1991
Kuepfer, Mrs. Menno W., 1991
Kuhl, Joseph, 1991
Kuhl(e)man, August, 1684
Kühlwein, Kathaina (later Baumann), 925
Kühlwein, Philipp, 925
Kuhn (Coon) family, 1878, 1898
Kuhn family, 2063
Kuhn, Gertrud
  on Beissel, Conrad, 2342
Kuhns, Amos M., 1684
Kuhns, C. M., 1991
Kuhns, Debby, 366
Kuhns, Ezra McFall, 1991
Kuhns family, 1991
Kuhns, Harold, 366
Kuhns, Harry Raifsnider, 1991
Kuhns, L. Oscar, 1991
Kuhny (Keeney/Keeny) family, 686
Kulp, Aaron, 709
Kulp, Anna (later Grisso), 574
Kulp, Bennett
  Shelby Co. Church of the Brethren, MO, leadership in, 1175
Kulp Bible College, Nigeria, 2164
  Shankster, Owen L., Jr., (CB) and, 2248
Kulp Bible School, Nigeria, 9, 92, 307,

709–710, 936
Guli, John, 2194, 2195
Mai Sule Biu, Board of Governors, 782
Mamza, Ngamariju Keliri, Board of Governors, 784
mission schools, 854
Kulp, Christina Masterton, **708–709,** 1684. 1840
Kulp, Clarence, Jr., *648*
Kulp family, 260, 2077, *See also* Kolb family
Kulp, H. F., 729
Kulp, Harold Stover, 305, 306, 596, 706, 708, **709,** *709,* 912, 1684, 1840
  Nigeria mission work, 936
  Philadelphia, PA, First Church of the Brethren, providing leadership, 1015
  Pottstown, PA, Coventry Church of the Brethren, missionary, 1049
Kulp, Henry B., 709
Kulp, Henry F., 21, **709,** 1684
Kulp, Hettie S., 260
Kulp, Isaac Clarence, Jr., *477,* 1684, 1922, 1991, 2109, 2186
  on Plain People, traditions of, 2342
Kulp, Janice (later Long), 2138, 2285
Kulp (Kolb), Samuel and Catherine, 1991
Kulp, Lizzie, *1393*
Kulp, Mable Fretz, 709
Kulp, Mary Ann Moyer, 1840, 1991
Kulp, Mary Jane, 1991
Kulp, Melvin, 1684
Kulp, Naomi Tyson, 709
Kulp, Neta Ruth Royer, **709,** 1840
Kulp, Philip Masterson, 709, 1684, 1840, **2387**
  on CB missions, 2342
  Ridge Church of the Brethren, PA, pastor, 1108
Kulp, Phyllis (later Eller), 706, 2176
Kulp, Robert
  Island Pond, VT, Grace Brethren Church, 2209
Kulp, Roy C., 1991
Kulp, Ruth Royer, 305, 596
  missionary to Nigeria, 1127
Kulp, S. K.
  Pottstown, PA, First Church of the Brethren, 1049
Kulp, Samuel W., 1684
Kulp, Susan B. (later Ober), 960
Kulp, William Kurtz, 628, 1684, 1918
  Rockwood Church of the Brethren, PA, pastor, 1118
Kult, G. D.
  on seminaries, merger of, 2342
Kumar, K. Prasantha, 651, 1684
Kumar, K. Vijaya, 1684
Kumar, Nirmala Roy, 1855
Kumar, Prasanth Kadmie, 1855
Kumar, Sujate, 1855
Kumar, Vijaya Radmiel, 1855
Kumm, Dr., 296
Kumps Station, MD, 1315
Kumptown, MD
  Piney Creek Church of the Brethren, MD, mission point, 1025
K'ung-Fu-Tzu (Master K'ung), 334
Kunkel family, 1927
Kunkle-Mack/Mock family, 2005
Kuns, Anna (later Kinsel), 710

Kuns, Anna Magdelena (later Gripe), 710
Kuns, David, 710
  Milmine Church of the Brethren, IL, 843
Kuns, Elizabeth (later Markey), 710
Kuns family, **710**, 1234, 1883
  family history and genealogy, 1991
  Musselman family related to by marriage, 901
Kuns, George Dilling, 1684
  McLouth, KS, Brethren Church, pastor, 779
  McLouth, KS, Church of the Brethren, pastor, 779
Kuns, George, Jr., 710
Kuns, George, Sr., 710
Kuns, Gladys, 204
Kuns, Henry, 710, 1684
  Milmine Church of the Brethren, IL, 843
Kuns, Henry L., 1991
Kuns, J., 1684
Kuns, J. S.
  Raisin City, CA, Church of the Brethren, 1083
Kuns, Jacob, Sr., 710
Kuns (Koontz, Kuntz) family, **710**
Kuns, Lewis
  Milmine Church of the Brethren, IL, 843
Kuns, Marlin E., 1684, 2284
Kuns, Merle Eugene, 1684
Kuns, Rachel E. (later Gillett), 549
Kuns, Raymond, 1278
Kuns, Richard R., 1684
  Herndon, VA, Chandon Brethren Church, 2197
Kuns, Russell, 204
Kuns, Stephen, 1343
Kunselman, Dorothy, 2284
Kuntz, Christian
  Smith, Catherine E. on, 2357
Kuntz family, 1991, See also Kuns family
  bibliography, 1870
Kuntz, George Michael, 1991
Kuntz, Jacob, 1684
Kuntz, James, 1684
Kuntz, Joyce, 1929
Kuntze, David, 1684
Küntzi, Christen, 697
Küntzi, Christian, 697
Küntzi family, See Kintzi family
Küny, Heinrich, 686
Küny, Johannes, 686
Küny (Keeney/Keeny) family, 686
Kunze, Johann Christoph, 31, 43, **710**, 767, 1991
Kuomintang (Nationalist Party, China), 23
Kurdish refugees, 198
Kuroiwa, Wallace Ryan
  on Brethren history, 2342
Kurpfalz, See Palatinate
Kurpfalz
  Pennsylvania Germans from, 1006
Kurt, Victor A., 2284
Kurta-Erb family, 2081
Kurta, Mr. & Mrs. John H., 1963
Kurtaneck, Nickolas, 1684
  Norwalk, CA, Grace Brethren Church, pastor, 951
Kurtz, Amanda, 355
Kurtz, Anna Catherine Loehr, 711, 712, 752
Kurtz, Calvin C., 1684

Kurtz, Catherine (later Miller)
  Miller, Jacob Kurtz, mother of, 838
Kurtz, Charles, 1684
Kurtz, Daniel Webster, 126, 242, 303, 335, 344, *537,* 545, *710,* **710–711,** 712, 714, 754, 912, 1274, 1684, 1991–1992, 1960, **2375**
  in Bethany Biblical Seminary, *710*
  divine inspiration of scripture, 132
  historical writing, 612
  McPherson College, president, 781
  Philadelphia, PA, First Church of the Brethren, providing leadership, 1015
  resurrection, and Brethren teachings about, 1102
  secret societies, Brethren opposition to, 1164
  Social Gospel Movement, 1197
Kurtz, Earl H., 195, 670, 1684
Kurtz, Elsie Mary, 2105
Kurtz, Emma, 220
Kurtz, Ethel Leonora Wheeler, 710
Kurtz family, 148, 158, 228, **712,** 1390, 1927, 2042, 2105
  family history, 2007, 2008
  Preiß (Price) family related to, 1055
Kurtz, Georg Jakob, 711
Kurtz, Hannah Harper, 2081
Kurtz, Harold G., 1684
Kurtz, Hazel Horst, 630
Kurtz, Henry, 3, 43, 148, 178, 204, 236, 277, 329, 331, 387, 426, 517, 518, 545, 561, 580, 584, **711–712,** 752, 1236, 1246, 1255, 1684, 1859, 1886, 1896, 1898, 1901, 1933, 1952, 2032, 2051, 2080, 2342, *See also* Rohrer, Alice LaVern Rupel
  aid for German group, 1198
  Alexander Mack's Bible, 777
  Annual Meetings and Pentecost, 1008
  and architecture, renewal, 2326
  articles about, 1921, 1922, 1924
  authority of scripture, 133
  biography, 2063
  Brethren Encyclopedia, 294
  Brethren Encyclopedia and Old Brethren German Baptist Church, 965
  Brethren settlement in Ohio, 961
  The Christian Family Companion and Gospel Visitor, 1058
  church government, 1044
  correspondence with Wolfe, George, II, 1357
  description of order of worship service, 1375
  Durnbaugh, Donald F. on, 2326
  early career, 2000
  Evangelische Besuch, Der, 460
  fictional stories about, 748
  The Gospel Visitor, 267, 281, 285, 288
  historic sites, 609
  historical writing, 611
  Hoke, George, 618
  Holsinger, Henry Ritz, 621
  hymnals, 641, 642
  hymnals, printing of, 700
  imposters among the Brethren, 648
  Juniata College, 678
  Mahoning Church of the Brethren, OH, elder, 782
  manuals, 788

  medical book publisher, 1160
  medicine, 809
  Menno Simons, 819
  mentoring, 2221
  Messenger, 818
  minorities, ethnic and racial, 849
  minutes, 852
  New Vienna Academy, OH, 932
  opposition to decline of German language, 725
  organ owned by, 899, *899, 900*
  pensions, military, 1008
  on polity, 294
  publication of pamphlet by John Kline, 701
  publishing, 1067, 1068
  Quinter, James, 1077
  railroads, 1081
  Rothenberger, George Philip, baptism of, 1124
  theological education, 1256
  Das Wochenblatt, 1355
  Zeugnisse der Wahrheit (*Testimonies of Truth*), 1355, 1395
Kurtz, Henry Clay, 2081
Kurtz, Henry (Heinrich), 1992
Kurtz, Henry J., 18, 712, **712,** 1992
Kurtz, Jacob, 279, 471, 712
Kurtz, Jacob (2 listed), 1684
Kurtz, Jacob Eberly, 1684
Kurtz, Jacob H., 1684
Kurtz, Jacob S., *See* Kurtz family
Kurtz, John, 1684
Kurtz, John (father of Daniel Webster Kurtz), 710
Kurtz, John Franklin, 1992
Kurtz, John H., 2105, 1986
Kurtz, John (son of Jacob), 712
Kurtz, Joseph, 1902
Kurtz, Joseph Enos, 2105
Kurtz, Leander P., 557, 558, 712, 1684
Kurtz, Leon, 2379
Kurtz, Lydia Mast, *See* Kurtz family
Kurtz, Mary Bollinger, 710
Kurtz, Mary Wheeler, 1992
Kurtz, Michael, 712, 1684
  Richland, PA, Church of the Brethren, elder-in-charge, 1107
Kurtz, Ray A., 1684, 2303
  Richland, PA, Church of the Brethren, elder-in-charge, 1107
Kurtz, Regina Henrietta, 711
Kurtz, Robert W., 1684
Kurtz, Ruth Mast Redcay, 2042
Kurtz, S. E. B., 1992
Kurtz, Thelma E.
  Lest We Forget, 1992
Kurtz, Willis E., 630, 1684
Kurtze Historie, 1992
Kurtze Nachricht, 1992–1993
  Eine Kurze un Aufrichtige Erklaerung, 1993
Kuster[s] family, *See* Custer family
Kuszmaul, Clarence Eugene, 1684
Kuszmaul, William
  Michigan City, IN, Church of the Brethren, 824
Kuszmaul, William, family
  Michigan City, IN, Church of the Brethren, 825
Kutz, Daniel C., 1684
Kutz, Sara K.
  works by, 2309

Kutztown, PA
  Dietrich family, 1917
Kwaga, Bitrus K. T., 1684
Kwagurwhulatu, Nigeria, 306
Kwaha, Daniel M., 1684–1685
Kwaha, Zira Dia, 1685
Kwambla, Ishaku S., 1684
Kwan, Tsun-Hsien, 1833
Kyerematen, Richard, 2284
  Philadelphia, PA, Germantown Church
    of the Brethren, *2189*
Kyger, M. Ellsworth, 2068
Kyle, Catherine Wertz, 712
Kyle, Harold, 712
Kyle, Joseph
  McClain, Alva J., 773
Kyle, Melvin Grove, 688
  McClain, Alva J., 773
  Winona Lake Auditorium, IN, 1353
Kyle, W. Ray, 197, **712**
  Sales Exchange for Refugee
    Rehabilitation Vocations (SERRV),
    1139
Kyodan of Japan
  ecumenism, 423
Kyrgyzstan
  Julien, Thomas T., 2210
  missions, short-term, 2226
Kyser, Gerald P., 1221, 2303
Kyser, J. Dale, 1380, 1685, 1993

L., D. G., 1993
L., M. W., 1993
La Brea fossil beds
  Gilbert, James Zacchaeus, 548
La Cabrera, Argentina, 53
  La Carlota, Argentina, congregation
  Maconaghy, Dorothy Helen Lewis and
    Hill, 779
La Forge, MO, Church of the Brethren, *See*
    Farrenburg Church of the Breth-
    ren, MO
La Grange Co., IN, 1246
La Habra, CA, Brethren Church, 1343
La Loma, CA, Grace Brethren Church
  Modesto, CA, Big Valley Grace
    Community Church (FGBC), 866
La Mirada, CA, 136, 1342
  Grace Brethren Fellowship Church,
    CA, **713**, 1342
La Motte, Elizabeth (later Sauer), *See*
    Sauer, Elizabeth La Motte
La Motte Guyon, Madame Jeanne-Marie
    de, 120, 1120
La Motte Prairie Federated Church of the
    Brethren, IL, **713**
La Place, IL, 270, 371
  Church of the Brethren, **713**
  Eikenberry, Amos R., 431
  Milmine Church of the Brethren, IL,
    843
  Oakley Brick Church of the Brethren,
    IL, 958
La Plata, P.R., 261
La Porte Co., IN, 713
  Portage Prairie, IN, Church of the
    Brethren, 1047
La Porte, IN, Church of the Brethren, **713**
  Michigan City, IN, Church of the
    Brethren, 824
  Portage Prairie, IN, Church of the
    Brethren, 1047
La Rochefoucauld-Liancourt, Francois A.

F., Duc de, 1995
La Rue, Raymond R., 1687
  New Haven Church of the Brethren,
    NC, pastor in, 928
La Vale Fire Hall
  La Vale, MD, Community Church of
    the Brethren, 714
La Vale, MD, Community Church of the
    Brethren, 363, **713–714**
La Verne, CA, 169, 362, 732, 1329, 1395,
    2071
  Brethren colonization of southern
    California, 1145
  England, William Ferdinand, 446
  Fasnacht, Harold Dale, 480
  Hixson, Armanus Jefferson, 613–614
  Hutchison, Andrew, 639
  minorities, ethnic and racial, 850
  Patterson, CA, Church of the Brethren,
    migration to, 995
La Verne, CA, Church of the Brethren, 711,
    714, **714**, 1314
  75 year anniversary, 1969
  Fellowship Church of the Brethren,
    714, 1045
  General Christian Workers' Board
    (CB), 536
  Pomona, CA, Church of the Brethren,
    mission point of, 1045
  Smeltzer, Mary Blocher (CB) and,
    2250
La Verne, CA, Grace Brethren Church, **715,**
    768
La Verne College, 535, 694, 1860, 2026,
    See also La Verne, University of
  article about, 1930
  Blickenstaff, Lynn A., 146
  Bowman, James Brubaker, 167
  Bowman, Merle Allen, 167
  Brandt, Lucile Long Strayer, 172
  Brubaker, Leland Stanford, 217
  Camp Greenhorn Mountain Park, CA,
    staff from, 244
  Carl family, 255
  Crouch, Eugene Morgan, 353
  Davis, Charles Ernest, 364
  Dickey, J. P., 383
  Eller, Vernard M., 2176
  Emmert, Jesse Benedict, 444
  England, William Ferdinand, 446
  Eshelman, Matthew Mays, 455
  Fasnacht, Harold Dale, 480
  Fasnacht, Joy Cullen, 480
  Faw, Chalmer Ernest, 480
  Fitzwater, Perry Braxton, 492
  Frantz, Edward, 508
  Funderburg, Isaac Vaughn, 523
  Garst, Samuel Sherfy, 531
  Hanawalt family, 582
  Hanawalt, William Cyrus Replogle,
    582
  higher education, 605
  historical libraries, 610
  history, 1932, 1993
  Hoff, Ernest Gockley, 617
  Hoover, William I. T., 628
  Houser, Daniel, 633
  Nininger, Harvey Harlow, teacher at,
    938
  Overholtzer, Samuel A., 986
  Pomona, CA, Fellowship Church of the
    Brethren, 1045
  Sanger, Samuel F., trustee of, 1143

School Visiting Committees, 1155
  Shively, Charles S., 2144
  Shull, Susan Lavinia Stoner, 1180
  Sickel, Clarence Leroy, 1181
  Smeltzer, Ralph Emerson, 1190
  Studebaker, Ellis M., 1230
  Tully, Robert W., 1278
  Vaniman, Susie Cordelia Neher, 1303
  Weiss, Edgar Lorell, 1328
La Verne, University of, 118, 238, *715,*
    715–716, 753, *See also* La Verne
    College
  Church of the Brethren, 300
  Kimmell, Arthur Vance, 694
  Kuns, David, 710
  Kuns, Henry, 710
  Kurtz, Daniel Webster, 711
  Larchmont Community Brethren
    Church, CA, 726
  McFarland, CA, Church of the
    Brethren, 774
  Miller, Mary Grace Hileman, 841
  Miller, Samuel J., 842
  Minnich, Herbert Spenser, 849
  Moy Wing Lum, 891
  Muir, Gladdys Esther, 893
  Murphy, Sara Florence Fogelsanger,
    897
  Pomona, CA, Fellowship Church of the
    Brethren, 1045
  Summer Service project
    Sunnyslope Church of the
      Brethren, WA, 1240
  Women's Conferences (CB) and, 2265
Laasphe, **716**
  castle, 1354
Labadie, Jean de
  influence on Brethren, and Roman
    Catholic Church, 1120
  prayer, 1051
  Saxby, Trevor J. on, 2354
Labadist colony, Bohemia Manor, MD
  monasticism, 869
Labodists
  Penn, William, and settlement of Penn-
    sylvania, 1004
  Saxby, Trevor J. on, 2354
Labanca, Hector
  South America Theological Seminary
    (BC) and, 2252
Labaree, L. W., 1940
Labette Church of the Brethren, KS, 19,
    716
  Neosho territory organized as, 923
Labette Co., KS, 716
  Fairview Church of the Brethren, KS,
    468
  in Neosho Valley Old German Baptist
    Brethren Church near, 923
  Parsons Old German Baptist Brethren
    Church, KS, 994
labor, **716**
  Protestant work ethic, 716
  laws
    Brumbaugh, Martin Grove and,
      223
  unions, **716**, *717*
    capitalism, 253
    Church of the Brethren, 301
    Dunkard Brethren, 409
    Eby, Kermit, 419
    ethics, 458
    Old German Baptist Brethren and

nonconformity, 941
Old Order Fellowships, 972
opposition to, 716
secret societies, Brethren opposition to, 1164
train conductors, *717*
Laboulaye, Argentina, 53
Lacey, WA, Community Church, **716–717**
Lackey, Cain
start of Goodwill, VA, congregation, 929
Lackey, Clarence, 2303
Lackey, Clarence H., 318, 1685
Pleasant Grove Grace Brethren Church, IA, pastor, 1031
Portis, KS, Grace Brethren Church, pastor, 1048
Lackey, William Elcaniah, 1685, 2027
Smith River Church of the Brethren, VA, minister, 1192
Laclede Co., MO, 733
Lactantius
peace in Christian church history, 998
premillennialism, 833
Lacy, IN
Sampson Hill Church of the Brethren, IN, 1141
Ladd, George Eldon, 2179
Ladd, Ruth Kline, 1993
Ladenburg
historic sites, 609
Ladera, CA, Church of the Brethren, 726, *See also* Los Angeles, CA, Ladera Church of the Brethren
Ladies Aid
Freeport, IL, Church of the Brethren, 515
Hartsough family, 588
Ladies Aid Society, 60, *See also* Sisters' Aid Society
Juniata, *1187*
Maple Grove Church of the Brethren, MD, 790
Lindsay Church of the Brethren, CA, 744
Piqua, OH, Church of the Brethren, 1026
Williamsburg, PA, Church of the Brethren, 1346
Ladies' Aid (Women's Fellowship)
Hopewell, VA, Church of the Brethren, 629
Ladies Bible Class, *578*
Ladoga, IN, 1221
Church of the Brethren, 652, **717**, 750, 1339
Mount Pleasant Church of the Brethren, IN, 886
Lady, Milford, 1993
Lafayette Aurora (Pottstown, PA)
Price, Isaac, copublisher, 1056
Lafayette, IN, Church of the Brethren, **717–718**, 1565
Lafayette, Marquis de
guest at Landis house, 723
Lafayette, OH, Church of the Brethren, *See* Baker Church of the Brethren, OH
Lafiya program, 92, *718*, **718**
Africa, nursing program, 952
Association of Brethren Caregivers (ABC), 2132
Church of the Brethren in Nigeria, 2164

Garkida General Hospital, 530
medical care, 810
medical missions, 807
Nigeria mission work in health care, 936, 937
relief and service efforts, 1097
Shankster, Owen L., Jr., and Celia Smith (CB) and, 2248
sources on, 2311
wellness and, 2261
LaFollette, A. C., 1685
Lafong, farm used for meetings
Zimmerman, OH, Beaver Creek Old German Baptist Brethren Church, 1399
LaForge Church of the Brethren, MO, *See* Farrenburg Church of the Brethren, MO
Lager der Einsamen (The Settlement of the Solitary), *See* Ephrata Community
LaGrange Co., IN, 753
Shipshewana, IN, Church of the Brethren, 1177
Lagrange Co., IN
English Prairie Church of the Brethren, IN, 447
Lagro, IN
soil conservation units, 1200
Lahman, Carroll P., 1993
Lahman, Christian, 718
Lahman, Clarence W., 1685, 1993
Lahman, Elizabeth Emmert, 718
Lahman family, *See* Lehman family
Lahman, J. T., 1685
Lahman, Joseph Christian, **718**, 1685
Palestine, AR, Ministry to Blacks, 991
Lahman, Lorena C. Diehl, 718
Lahman, Martin A.
family history, 1996
Lahman, Samuel, 1685
Lahman, Susan B. Gill, 718
Lahn River, 716
Laidler, George, 1993
Lair, Bonnie Layman
on Lair family, 2342
Lair, Daniel J., 1224, 1685
Salem Old German Baptist Brethren Church, OH, minister, 1139
Lair, Donald Gayle, 1685
Maple Grove Old German Baptist Brethren Church, OH, minister, 791
Lair, ___
Osceola Church of the Brethren, MO, elder, 984
Lair family, 1324
Johnson City, TN, Knob Creek Church of the Brethren, 672
Lair, Bonnie Layman on, 2342
Lair, Henry T., 1224, 1685
Lair, John (2 listed), 1685
Lair, John M., 1235, 1685
Riverside Church of the Brethren, MI, elder, 1112
Lair, Joseph B., 468, 1685, *See also The Prophetic Age*
Laird, James S., Sr., 2284
laity, **718–719**
distinction between clergy and laity, 718–719
New Testament use of term, 718, 719
Priesthood of All Believers, 1057
Lake Arthur, NM, Pecos Valley Church of

the Brethren, **719**
migration of Brethren, 830
Lake Branch German Baptist Brethren Church, MN, **719**
Minnesota Brethren settlement, 848
Lake Breeze Church of the Brethren, Sheffield Village, Lorain Co., OH, 1175
Lake Co., FL
Seneca Church of the Brethren, FL, 1166
Lake Co., OH
Painesville Church of the Brethren, 989
Lake, Daniel B., 1685
Lake Emily, MN
Hancock, MN, Church of the Brethren, 582
Lake, Leslie, 2284
Lake meetinghouse
Hartville, OH, Church of the Brethren, 588
Lake meetinghouse, OH, 416
Lake Michigan
Zion City, IL, 1400
Lake, Nancy
Pleasant View Brethren Church, IN, 2377
Lake Odessa, MI, 323, 719, 1263
Campbell, Old German Baptist Church, MI, 248, 824
Long, George, 753
Clarksville, MI, Grace Brethren Church, 318
Humberd, Russell I., 636
Jenkins, Charles Lee, 2209
Hastings, MI, Grace Brethren Church, 588
Hope Church of the Brethren, MI, 629
Thornapple Church of the Brethren, MI, 1263
Lake Park congregation, IA
Gillett Grove, IA, German Baptist Brethren, 549
Lake, Richard
Pleasant View Brethren Church, IN, 2377
Lake Ridge Church of the Brethren, NY, *See* King Ferry, NY, Lake Ridge Church of the Brethren
Lake Ridge Mission, 2028
Lake Ridge, NY, 1397
Mission work in, 933
Lake Shore Church of the Brethren, OH, **719**
Lake Twp., Wood Co., OH, 720
Lake View, MI, congregation
place-names, Brethren, 1028
Lakeland, FL
Church of the Brethren, **719**
congregation (OGBB)
Wagoner, Raymond K. and, 2259
Grace Brethren Church, **719–720**
established 1980, **2213**
Orlando, FL, Grace Brethren Church, 982
Laketon, TX
Pampa Church of the Brethren, 991
Lakeview Church of the Brethren, MI, 583, 824, 1235, *See also* Brethren, MI, Lakeview Church of the Brethren
Harlan, MI, Church of the Brethren, 583
Michigan Brethren settlement, 824

Lakeville, IN, Brethren Church, *See* Co. Line, IN, Brethren Church
Lakewood Brethren Church, CA, 754
Lakewood, CA, Grace Brethren Church (Artesia, CA, Carson Avenue Grace Brethren Church), **720**
Lakewood Community Church of the Brethren, WA, *See* Seattle, WA, Lakewood Community Church
Lakewood, OH, Church of the Brethren, **720**
Lalji, Timothy, 1685
Lam, Fels, 1685
Lam, Howard Orville, 1685
Lam, Lizzie Bucher, 1993
Laman, Catherine Elizabeth (later Hanawalt), 582
lamb, *See* Lord's supper, food at
Lord's supper, food at, 757–758
love feast, food at, 763
Lamb, Ardis Krieg
　on Gorgas, Christin (Mack), 2342
Lamb family
　Hyattsville, MD, University Park Church of the Brethren, 641
Lamber, Henry
　North Liberty, IN, Brethren Church, 948
Lamber, Nancy
　North Liberty, IN, Brethren Church, 948
Lambert, Amley, 1685
Lambert, Anderson, 1685
Lambert, Claudia Marie, 1853
Lambert, Cynthia A. Kinsey, 696
Lambert, Eli Akim, Jr., 1685
Lambert, Frank A., 411, 696, 1685
Lambert, George, 1685
Lambert, I., 6
Lambert, Jack B., 102, 1685
　Miamisburg, OH, Brethren Church, pastor, 823
Lambert, Linda Rae, 2284
Lambert, Mabel (later Haines), 579
Lambert, Merton, 533, 1685
Lambert, Terry, 1685
Lambright, Brad Lee, 2138
Lambsheim, **720**
　Germany, 545
　radical pietist dissension in, 990
　Traut, Johannes, 1270
Lamech, *See* Gass, Jakob, 1957
Lamech and Agrippa, *See* Chronicon Ephratense
Lamia, Nancy J. (later Peters), 2183
LaMoure Co., ND, 321
Lampeter Fellowship, PA
　Mechanic Grove Church of the Brethren, PA, 806
Lampeter, PA
　Schultz, Andreas, 1156
Lamphere, Edward Everett, 1993
Lampin, John C., 1685
Lampin, William Henry, 1685
Lan(a)ham, Ocia C., 1685
Lanark, IL, 647, 1337, 1339, 1389, 1394
　annual meeting of 1880, *721*
　Brethren Church, **720**, 750
　　Milledgeville, IL, Brethren Church, 833
　Church of the Brethren, 232, 273, **720**, 1276
　　Eshelman, Matthew Mays, 455

Family Companion, The, 474
Gospel Tract Association, 561
Lancaster Co., PA, 142, 144, 279, 309, 332, 375, 380, 383, 415, 535, 685, 686, 692, 693, 697, 721, 724, 734, 737, 756, 767, 1213, 1219, 1229, 1249, 1263, 1298, 1318, 1326, 1327, 1340, 1356, 1390, 1401, 1933, 2009, 2020, 2027, 2074, 2077
　Becker family, 1937
　bibliography, 1858, 1864, 1897
　biographical history of, 1958
　Blough family, 151
　Bollinger (Bolinger) family, 158
　Bowser family, 170
　Brethren movement, 175
　Bucher family, 226
　Bucher, Rufus Pfautz, minister to, 225
　Conestoga Crosswoods, PA, 2103
　Dunkers, 2060
　Earl Twp., PA, 2102
　Eby family, 1937
　Engle family history, 1930
　Ephrata Area Grace Brethren Church, PA, 448
　Ephrata Community, 451, 2052
　Frantz family, 509
　Frantz, Michael, 508
　Frey (Fry) family, 517
　Garb Law, 528
　Garst family, 532
　German Seventh-Day Baptists, 542
　Gibbel (Gibble) family, 547
　Gingerich (Kingery) family, 549
　Gish family, 551
　Gnagey (Gnaegi) family, 554
　Grace Brethren congregations, 1005
　Graybill (Grabill, Krehbiel) family, 567
　Groff (Grove) family, 574
　Heifer Project International, 594
　Heisey family, 595
　Heitler, Martin P., 595
　Hempfield Church of the Brethren, PA, 596
　Herr, John, 598
　Hershey family, 600
　Hess family, 601
　Hispanic Ministries (CB), 2199
　history 1929, 1993, 2090, 2099, 2104
　Höhn, Heinrich, 618
　Holderman (Haldeman) family, 618
　Holsinger (Holtzinger) family, 623
　homelessness, 2203
　Hunsiker (Hunsaker) family, 637
　index, will books and intestate records, 1943
　Mechanic Grove Church of the Brethren, PA, 806
　Mennonite Church, 2090
　Middle Creek Church of the Brethren, PA, 825
　migration of Brethren, 827
　Miller family, 2099
　Mohler Church of the Brethren, PA, 868
　Mohler family, 869
　Näff family settlement, 909
　Oberholtzer, Martin, 960
　Pennsylvania Brethren settlement, 1004
　Pennsylvania Dunkard Brethren, 1005
　Pennsylvania Old German Baptist Brethren, 1005
　Pennsylvania settlement, 1004

　Peters family, 1012
　Pfautz, Johann (Hans) Michael, 1013
　Pfautz, John, 1013
　Rineer, A(mos) Hunter, Jr. on churches and cemeteries of, 2352
　Sauer, Johann Christoph, I, 1147
　Sauer, Maria Christina Gross, 1148
　Scheublein, Christian and Esther Neff, 1178
　Schnebeli, Johann/Jakob, 1193
　Schultz, Andreas, 1156
　Shank family, 1172
　Sollenberger, John, 1202
　Sontag, Jakob, 1202
　Southern Lancaster Grace Brethren Church, PA, 1207
　Stevens, Thaddeus, 912
　Three Mile Island emergency evacuation, 952
　universalism, 2106
　Wright, E. Edward on, 2364
Lancaster Co., SC
　Eckerlin, Emmanuel, 1204
Lancaster family
　Mill Run Grace Brethren Church, MD, 833
Lancaster Grace Brethren Church, PA, 749
Lancaster, IN
　Salamonie Church of the Brethren, 1136
Lancaster, John W., 2, 1685
　Mill Run Grace Brethren Church, MD, pastor, 833
　Ozark Grace Brethren Church, MI, pastor, 987
Lancaster Mennonite Historical Society
　genealogy, 535
　historical libraries, 610
Lancaster Old German Baptist Brethren Church, PA, **721**
Lancaster, PA, Acts Covenant Fellowship (ACTS) (CB), **2213**
Lancaster, PA, Alfa y Omega (Alpha and Omega) Church of the Brethren, **2213–2214**
Lancaster, PA, Church of the Brethren, *648,* **720–721**, 1401, **2375**
　Allentown, PA, Church of the Brethren, 2126
　chronological history, 1911
　history, 1993
　Middle Creek Church of the Brethren, PA, 825
Lancaster, PA, Grace Brethren Church, **721**, 1380
　Elizabethtown, PA, Grace Brethren Church, 436
　Harrisburg, PA, Melrose Gardens Grace Brethren Church, 586
　New Holland, PA, Grace Brethren Church, as branch of, 928
　Southern Lancaster Grace Brethren Church, PA, mission point of, 1207
Lance, Alice Boone, 479
Lance, Forest F., 29, 115, 715, 1221, 1685, 2303, **2384**
　Montclair, CA, Grace Brethren Church, pastor, 871
Lance, H. J.
　Ormond Beach, FL, Grace Brethren Church, 982
Lance, Naomi

Ormond Beach, FL, Grace Brethren
Church, 982

Lance, Robert, 2303

Lancour, Harold, 1993

Land, *See* property

land agents
Miller, Daniel Long, 836

land companies, 54, **721–722**
Church of the Brethren, 299
colonization, 324
Cooperative Colonization Company, 342
frontier, 519
homesteading, 626
irrigation, 664
migration of Brethren, 830
railroads and Brethren settlement, 1082

land grant universities, 12

land grants to Mennonites and Dunkards, 1993

land opportunities
migration of Brethren, 829, 831
Pennsylvania, 1004, 1006

Lander, Edward H., Jr., 699, 1685, 2379
Columbus, OH, Church of the
Brethren, 2372

Landers, Ed, 552

Landert, Maria (*Sister Rafel*), 722

Landert, Sigmund, 686, **722**

Landes, Abraham
descendants, 1911

Landes, Alva D., 350, 1685
on Landes, Lucinda and descendants, 2342
on Landes, William and descendants, 2342

Landes, Angelika Trumper, 722

Landes, Benjamin, 1280

Landes, Benjamin Samuel, 1685

Landes, Bruce E., 2284

Landes, Catharine Glick, 553

Landes, Catherine Graff, 722

Landes, Christian, 553

Landes, Daniel E., 1356, 1685, 2303, **2384**
Maple Grove Old German Baptist
Brethren Church, OH, minister, 791

Landes, Daryl W., 1685

Landes, David, 373, 1993

Landes, Dennis D., 1685
Maple Grove Old German Baptist
Brethren Church, OH, elder-in-
charge, 791

Landes, Eldon D., 1685
Salem Old German Baptist Brethren
Church, OH, minister, 1139

Landes, Elisabetha, 1993

Landes, Elizabeth Hirt, 722

Landes family
Hiestand (Heistand, Heestand,
Heaston) family, 602
Royer family related to, 1128

Landes, Fritz, 1993

Landes, Glen L., 1685
Salem Old German Baptist Brethren
Church, OH, minister, 1139

Landes, Hans, 722

Landes, Heinrich Hirt, **722,** 723

Landes, Henry S., 1993–1994

Landes, Herbert P., 1685

Landes, Hiester L., 1685

Landes, Jacob, 1993–1994

Landes, Johann Heinrich, **722**

Landes, Johannes, **722**

Landes, John Webster, 1685

Landes, Katharina Schinz, 722

Landes, Kenneth E., 1685
Prices Creek Old German Baptist
Brethren Church, OH, elder or
minister, 1057

Landes/Landis/Landess family, 1994

Landes (Landis, Lantes, Lantis) family,
722–723, *723*

Landes, Lucinda

Landes, Alva D. on descendants of, 2342

Landes, Magdalena Oberholtzer
descendants, 1911

Landes, Mary (later Sontag), *See* Sontag,
Mary Landes

Landes, Melvin Bowman, 1685

Landes, Mrs. Raymond, 248

Landes, Nancy, 214

Landes, Olen Benjamin, 1685
Pine Ridge Church of the Brethren, VA
and, 2238

Landes, Rudolph, 722

Landes, Russell, 1356, 1685

Landes, Samuel, 1223, 1685

Landes, Wallace Bell, Jr., 1685
on Radical Pietism, contemporary,
2342

Landes, Walter D., 1685
Pleasant View Church of the Brethren,
OH, minister, 1037

Landes, Webster, 102, 1223
Painter Creek Old German Baptist
Brethren Church, OH, 990

Landes, William, 1223, 1685
Salem Old German Baptist Brethren
Church, OH, elder-in-charge, 1139

Landes, Alva D. on descendants of, 2342

Landesites
Salem Church of the Brethren, OH,
1138

Landess/Landes/Landis family, 1994

Landesville congregation
Somerset, IN, Church of the Brethren,
1202

Landesville (Landess), IN, Church of the
Brethren, **723**
Marion, IN, Church of the Brethren,
organized from, 793

Landing, James E., 1994

Landis, Abraham, 722, 2026, 2107
Salem Old German Baptist Brethren
Church, OH, deacon, 1139

Landis, Arella A. Miller, 723

Landis, Augustus S., 2063

Landis, B. Harrison, 1994

Landis, Barbara (later Kauffman), 1937

Landis, Barbara (later West), 1330, 1332

Landis, Bartley, 1685

Landis, Benjamin, 1994

Landis, Benjamin L., 2073

Landis, Benson Y., 1994

Landis, Betty Aleda Rowe, 1959, 1994

Landis Brethren, *See* Christian Brethren

Landis, Catherine Naomi, 2074

Landis, Claude, 1685

Landis, Cora (later Funk), 525

Landis, D. F., 377, 688, 738, 1685
Minot, ND, Church of the Brethren,
elder, 851

Landis, Daniel, 756, 1685

Landis, David, 1897

Landis, David (2 listed), 1685–1686

Landis, David Bachman, 1994

Landis, David Raymond, 1686

Landis, David, Sr., 2074

Landis, Edgar, 1686

Landis, Edwin C., Jr., 1994

Landis, Elias, 1686

Landis, Elizabeth, 430

Landis, Elizabeth Fishbourn, 722

Landis, Emma (later Eby), 741

Landis, Erma, 1994

Landis family, 236, 1219, 1325, 1390,
1927, 1972, 1994, 2073, 2074,
2077, *See also* Landes family
Fahnestock family, 465
family history, 1993, 1994
Greene, IA, Church of the Brethren,
570
Harley family, 583
Lancaster Co., PA, history and
directory, 1994
Muhlenberg Co., KY, German Baptist
Brethren, 893
Nicholas Co. German Baptist Brethren
Church, 935

Landis family Reunion, 1994

Landis, Frank B., 1686

Landis, George William, 28, **723,** 1686,
2303
Mount Hope Church of the Brethren,
OK, resident minister, 882, 964

Landis, H., 1686, 2057, *See also* Landis,
Augustus S.

Landis, Hannah (later Lauver), 728

Landis, Hannah Stober
Stover, William, 2379

Landis, Hans, 567, 1993

Landis, Harvey Moseman, 244, 1247, 1686

Landis, Harvey S., 1686

Landis, Hazel Minnich, 1840, **2387**

Landis, Henry, 439, 1686, 2024, 2284

Landis, Henry Franklin and Magdalena
Ebersole, 1994

Landis, Henry Naas, Jr., 722

Landis, Henry W., 1686
South Solomon Old German Baptist
Brethren Church, KS, minister and
elder, 1206

Landis, Herman Benjamin, 1686, 1840,
1994, **2384, 2388**
missionary, 1144
San Francisco, CA, Church of the
Brethren, 1141

Landis, Ira David, 1994

Landis, Jacob, 1686

Landis, Jacob Wissler, 1899

Landis, James E.
on Landis/Landes, John and descendants, 234-2

Landis, Jenny, 204

Landis, Jess H., 1994

Landis, John, 1958

Landis, John A., 1686

Landis, John H., 1686, 1994

Landis, John S.
Quakertown, PA, First Church of the
Brethren, moderator, 1075

Landis, John Samuel, 1686

Landis, Johnny, 722

Landis, Joseph, 281, 1686

Landis/Landes families
sources on, 2315

Landis (Landes), John, 1686

Landis/Landes, John

Landis, James E. on descendants of, 2342
Landis/Landes/Landess family, 1994
Landis, Martha, 1333
Landis, Mary, 430, 2107
Landis, Mary Carver, 722
Landis, Mary Jewett, 723
Landis, Michael, 281, 722, 757, 1355, 1686
Landis, Monroe, 204
Landis, Moyne, 326, 1213, 1686
Landis, Norman A., 1994
Landis, Otis I., 1686
Landis, Patricia, 1994
Landis, Rolla, 231
Landis, Ruth (later Metzger)
    Metzger, Thurl D., 2222
Landis, Sarah (later Sauer), *See* Sauer,
    Sarah Landis
Landis, Susan Overholt, 2023–2024
Landis, Velma (later Mohler)
    Mohler, Robert Ellsworth, wife of, 868
Landis, William H., 1994
Landsites, *See* Christian Brethren
The Landmark, **724,** 1995
    Miller, Howard, 838
Landon, Alfred M., 344
Landrum, Clyde Kermit, 155, 192, 318,
    724, 739, 1289, 1319, 1686. 2303
    Bible Institute of Los Angeles
        (BIOLA), 136
    Lexington, KY, Grace Bible Church,
        2214
    mission tours, 855
Landrum, David, 739
    Lexington, KY, Grace Bible Church,
        2214
Landrum family, 318
Landrum, Oldham Mize, 724
Landrum, Phil, 1319
Landrum, Richard Lee, 637, 1686
    Pomona, CA, Fellowship Church of the
        Brethren, pastor, 1045
Landrum, Ruby, 739, 1319
Landrum, Sandy, 739
    Lexington, KY, Grace Bible Church,
        2214
Landrum, Serena Belle Combs, 724
Landrum, Sewell S., 187–188, 318, 1686,
    2303
Landsites (Christian Brethren)
    Stony Creek Church of the Brethren,
        OH, 1225
Lane, Barbara (later Root), 1122
Lane Co., KS
    Prairie View Church of the Brethren,
        KS, members living in, 1050
Lane, Daniel, 1686
Lane, Elizabeth Miller, 1995
    on Weybright, Martin, III, 2342
Lane, James Richardson, 1686
Lane, Susannah Buckwalter (later Spitler),
    1212
Lang, (Anna) Marie Studebaker, 724
Lang, Christian, 2000
Lang family
    Royer family related to, 1128
Lang, (John) Nicholas, 724
Lang (Long) family, 58, **724**
Langacre, Hans, 756
Langaker, A. B., 1995
Langdon, Ida, 738
    minorities, ethnic and racial, 851
Langdon, Julia
    minorities, ethnic and racial, 851

Langdon, Kenneth J., 2284
Langdon, William C., 1995
Lange, Andrea, 2342
Lange, Burton, 398, 1686
Lange family
    San Diego, CA, Grace Brethren
        Church, 1141
Langenecker family
    Mortonhouse (ship), 2373, 2376
Langeneker/Longenecker, family
    Fraktur artistry, 2186
Langguth, Otto, 1995
Langhorne, Mrs. Orra, 1995
Langley, Ronald J., 1686
Langneker, Ulrich, 756
Langstrath, 1686
Langstroth family, 405
Langstroth, Hannah Jane (later Drexel), 405
language barriers
    social action, 1196
language, inclusive
    Bible translations, use of, 2137
    ethics and, 2178
    Hymnal: A Worship Book, 2205
    recent changes, **2214**
    Womaen's Caucus, advocation of, 2184
language of worship
    Donnels Creek Church of the Brethren,
        OH, 396
language shift (German to English), 175,
    724–725, 2045
    frontier, 519
    Germantown Academy, 544
    gravestones, 567
    Grundforschende Fragen (Basic
        Questions), 575
    Harleysville, PA, Indian Creek Church
        of the Brethren, 584
    Hatfield Church of the Brethren, PA,
        588
    Holsinger, Daniel Mack, 621
    hymnals, 642
    hymns, 642–643
    Nead, Peter, and transition from
        German to English, 918–919
languages
    bilingualism, 471
    Dayton, OH, Lower Miami Church of
        the Brethren, 367
    dialect of plain sects, Montgomery Co.,
        PA, 1991
    Hausa, in Nigeria, 937
    Miller, John Allen, proficiency in, 839
    Mow, Baxter Merrill, proficiency in,
        891
Lanham family, 164
Lanham, MD, Grace Brethren Church, 391,
    725
Lanham, Ralph, 1686
Lanier, Augustus Evans, Sr., 1686
Lansdale congregation, PA
    Harleysville, PA, Indian Creek Church
        of the Brethren, 584
Lansdale mission point
    Hatfield Church of the Brethren, PA,
        588
Lansing, MI
    First Church of the Brethren, **725,** 1239
    Grace Brethren Church, 240, **725**
    Michigan Brethren settlement, 824
Lanter, George M., 1686
lantern slides, *See* amusements, worldly
Lantes family, *See* Landes family

Lantis family, *See* Landes family, 1865
Lantis, Paul Carson, 1333, 1686, 1995
Lantis, Raymond M., 1686
    New Salem Church of the Brethren,
        Milford, IN, as minister, 932
Lantz, Abraham, 725
Lantz, Albert L., 332, 1212, 1686, **2384**
Lantz, Alice Boone, 438
Lantz, B. E., 1686
Lantz, Benjamin and Lydia Fisher, 1995
Lantz, Benjamin Lapp, 1995
Lantz, Christian, 725, 1995
Lantz family, 1927, 2087, 1995
Lantz, Gladys
    Okeechobee, FL, Grace Brethren
        Church, 963
Lantz, Henry, 1686
Lantz, Jacob Wissler, 1686, 1995
Lantz, Lawrence L., 1995
Lantz (Lentz) family, **725–726,** 1994
Lantz, Olen (Olin) B., 1686
Lantz, Philip, 2034
Lantz, Ray E., 1686
    Okeechobee, FL, Grace Brethren
        Church, 963
Lantz, S. E., 1686
Lanver, J. E., 1686
Laos, **726**
    Live Oak, CA, Church of the Brethren,
        750
    relief and rehabilitation work in, 158
    relief and service efforts, 1097
    Rolston, Frances Fitz Simon and
        William Wendell, working in, 1120
LaPaz, IN, Brethren Church, 347, *See* Co.
    Line Brethren Church, IN
Lapp, Christian, 1686
    Shelby Co. Church of the Brethren,
        MO, leadership in, 1175
Lapp, Dorothy B., 1865
    Maitland, FL, Grace Brethren Church,
        783
Lapp family, 715, 721, 2078
    New Holland, PA, Church of the
        Brethren, 928
Lapp, Ira J., 1330, 1686, 1995
    Miami, NM, Church of the Brethren,
        pastor, 823
Lapp, John
    Maitland, FL, Grace Brethren Church,
        783
Lapp, Joseph
    Pleasant Valley German Baptist
        Brethren Church, NE, 2377
Lapp, Oliver J., 463, 1686
Lapp, Robert, 436, 1686–1687
Lapp, Stephen Boyd, 2078
Laprad, John Andrew, 1687
Laprod family
    Germantown Old German Baptist
        Brethren Church, VA, 544
Larcher, David Matthias, 1687
    Shoal Creek Old German Baptist
        Brethren Church, Newton Co.,
        MO, elder-in-charge, 1178
Larchmont Community Church of the
    Brethren, WA, **726,** 1247
Lardin Gabas, 307, 1935, 1995, 2005, *See
    also* Church of the Brethren in
    Nigeria (*Ekklesiyar 'Yan'ura a
    Nigeria* (EYN))
Lardin Gabas (Morse, ed.), 878
Lare, Dawn Larue, 2284

Larew family, 1914
Large, Earl, 1687
Largent, Janice Lee Greenwalt, 1687
Largo family
  Lybrook, NM, Tók'ahookaadí Church of the
    Brethren, 2216
Larick, Ellen Louise, 714
  on La Verne Evergreen Cemetery
    tombstone inscriptions, 2329
Larick, Henry, 1687
  Rock Creek Church of the Brethren,
    CO, minister, *1116*
Larick, J. H., 1687
Larimer, John, 1687
Larimore, Christian, 590
Larimore, David, 1687, **2384**
Larimore, Elma Heim, 1995
Larison, Cornelius Wilson, 1995
Larkins, James, 1687
Larkins, S. J., 1687
Larkins, S. M., 1687
Larkins, S. O., 1687
Larkins, Samuel, 1687
Larmer, David, 1687
Larmon family
  Jenners, PA, Grace Brethren Church,
    670
Larned Church of the Brethren, KS, 424,
  726, 1316
Larrabee, W. H., 1995
Larsen, Alice (later Ingraham)
  Ingraham, M. Virgil, 2208
Larsen family, 164
Larsen, Otto, 1687
Larson family
  Harrisburg, PA, Melrose Gardens
    Grace Brethren Church, 586
  Modesto, CA, La Loma Grace Brethren
    Church, 867
Larson, Jon A. Knute, 64, 533, 1365, 1687,
  1995
Larson, Laura Evangeline (later Wagner),
  1312, 1687, 1851, 1854
Larson, Zelle Andrews, 1995
Larue Co., KY, 689
LaRue family, 2087
Larue, Raymond, 590
  Mountain Valley Church of the
    Brethren, TN, pastor, 889
Las Delicias, Ecuador, 1290
  missions, *860*
Las Perdices congregation, Argentina
  Siccardi, Luis, pastor, 1181
Laschet, Catrina van, 726
Laschet, Christian van, 1687
Laschet (Laaschet, Laasche, Lausche,
    Laushe), Abraham, van, **726**
Laschet (Laaschet, Laasche, Lausche,
    Laushe), Johannes Peter, van, 27,
  726
  minorities, ethnic and racial, 849
Laschet (Laaschet, Lashet, Lausche,
    Laushe), Abraham van, 1687
Laschet, Margaret Bechtelsheimer
    (Bechleshammer), 726
Lasell schoolhouse
Long Lake Church of the Brethren, MI, 756
Lash, Gene, 275
Lash, Lois, 275
Lashlee, Ernest L., 1995
Lasley, Minnie Ulery (later Green), 1953
Laslo, Andrew, 731, 1687
Lassa fever, **727**

nurse missionaries, 952
  Wine, Laura M., 1349
Lassa General Hospital, Nigeria, **726–727**
  medical missions, 807
Lassa, Nigeria, 306, 630, 718
  missions and missionaries
    Brumbaugh, Grayce, 220
last judgment, *See* eschatology
Last Supper, 2053
  Eucharist, 459
last things, *See* eschatology
Latham, Elizabeth, 679
Latham family
  Orange City, FL, Calvary Grace
    Brethren Church, 976
Latham, Ruth
  Maitland, FL, Grace Brethren Church,
    783
  Orlando, FL, Grace Brethren Church,
    982
Latham, Samuel A., 679
Latham, Vernon
  Maitland, FL, Grace Brethren Church,
    783
  Orlando, FL, Grace Brethren Church,
    981–982
Lathrop, CA, 1358, 1359
  Holsinger, Henry Ritz, 622
Lathrop, CA, (Wolfe Memorial) Brethren
    Church, **727**
  Manteca, CA, Northgate Community
    Brethren Church, members from,
    788
Latimer, Hugh, 56
Latimore congregation, PA, 1294
Latin America, *See* specific countries
  ALM involvement in, 24
  Board of Missions of the Methodist
    Churches of Latin America, 1290
  community development, 23
  credit unions, 351
  education programs, 185
  Heifer Project International, 594
  Mennonite Brethren Churches, General
    Conference of, 814
  Mennonite Church (MC), 815
  Mennonites, 815
  Mexico City, Mexico, Brethren
    Mission, 2222
  Misión Mutua en las Américas, 852
  mission schools, 854
  mission tours, 855
  The Missionary Board (BC), 856
  missions and missionaries, 161
  missions, short-term, 2226
  relief and rehabilitation work in, 200
  travel to by Brethren, 1273
Laton, CA, Church of the Brethren, 244,
  727
  Raisin City, CA, Church of the
    Brethren, 1083
  Reedley, CA, Church of the Brethren,
    1091
Latourette, Kenneth S., 114
Latsche, Frantz
  land contract, 1988
Latshaw, Isaac (2 listed), 1687
Latshaw, Robert M., 1687
Latter-day Saints
  North Spokane Church of the Brethren,
    building sold to, 1212
Latty, OH, 152, 1302
Latvia

Petersime, Ray, 1012
Latzenhiser, Sara, 683
Lau, John Harry, 1687
  Meadow Mills Church of the Brethren,
    VA, minister, 806
Laubach
  Hochmann von Hochenau, Ernst
    Christoph, 614
Laudeman, Joan Hippensteel, 2097
Laudenschlager, Ronald Lee, 1687
Lauderdale, Kerby, 1394, 1687, 1995
  historical writing, 612
Lauer, Carl N., 232, 1280, 1687
Lauer, Edna Viola Nancy Howl, 1996
Lauer, George M., 743
Lauer, Martha (later Geisert), 2187
Laughlin Church of the Brethren, MD,
  2214
Laughlin family
  Genesee Old German Baptist Brethren
    Church, MI, 540
Laughlin, Frank H., 1687
Laughlin, James
  North Hampton, OH, Donnels Creek
    Old German Baptist Brethren
    Church, elder-in-charge, 948
Laughlin, James R., 233, 1687
Laughlin, MD, congregation
  Maple Grove Church of the Brethren,
    MD, mission point of, 790
Laughrum, Marion, 1687
Laughrun, Augustus Marion, 269, 590, 673,
  740, 1687
  Meadow Branch Church of the
    Brethen, TN, 806
  Midway Church of the Brethren, TN,
    providing leadership, 827
  New Hope Church of the Brethren, TN,
    elder in, 929
  Petersons Chapel Church of the
    Brethren, NC, 1012
  Piney Flats, TN, Church of the
    Brethren, minister, 1025
Laughrun, Samuel M., 1687
Launder, Earl, 1687
Launtz family
  Johnstown, PA, Geistown Grace
    Brethren Church, 674
Laur, Carl N., 1687
Laurel Avenue, PA, Brethren Church, *See*
    Johnstown, PA, Third Brethren
    Church
Laurel Branch Church of the Brethren, VA,
  727, 1267
Laurel congregation, WA, 1364
Laurel Fork German Baptist Brethren
    Church, VA, **727–728**
Laurel Gap preaching point
  Highland Co. Mission Church of the
    Brethren, VA, 605
Laurel Glen Church of the Brethren, WV,
  728
  example of place name, 911
  Laurel Glen schoolhouse, 728
Laurel Hill Brethren Church, VA, *See*
    Wheatfield, VA, Laurel Hill
    Brethren Church
Laurel Hill Creek (Kimmel), PA, congrega-
    tion
  Pike Run Church of the Brethren, PA,
    1023
Laurel Mountain Grace Brethren Church,
    PA, *See* Boswell, PA, Laurel

Mountain Grace Brethren Church
Laurel, WA, 1223
    Church of the Brethren, *See* Stiverson
        Church of the Brethren, WA
Laurens, IA, Church of the Brethren,
        See Curlew Church of the Breth-
        ren, IA
Laursen, Ida, 1687
Laursen, Otto, 1687
Lausanne, Switzerland, 470
Lausch family
    Ephrata Area Grace Brethren Church,
        PA, 448
Lausche, *See* Laschet
Lausche, Abraham, 107
Lausche, Margaret (Bechtelsheimer), 107
Laushe, *See* Laschet
Lauver, George Myers, **728**, 1687
Lauver, H. N., 1687
    Pleasant Home Church of the Brethren,
        OK, minister, 1033
Lauver, Hannah Landis, 728
Lauver, Henry, 728
Lauver (Lawyer), John Emory, 1687
    Pleasant Home Church of the Brethren,
        OK, minister, 1033
Lauver, John, 1384
Lauver, John H., 1687
Lauver, Mary, 244
Lauver, Philip H., 244, 1687, 1996
Lauver, Sarah A. Hawk, 728
Lavington, George, 1996
Lavy, Benjamin
    Old Brethren German Baptist Church,
        minister, 965
Lavy, Clarence John, 1687
    Painter Creek Old German Baptist
        Brethren Church, OH, 990
    Salem Old German Baptist Brethren
        Church, OH, minister, 1139
Lavy, Dallas W., 1687
    Maple Grove Old German Baptist
        Brethren Church, OH, minister,
        791
Lavy, David
    Old Order German Baptist Church
        minister, 972
Lavy, Isaac, 1687
    Oak Grove Old German Baptist
        Brethren Church, OH, minister,
        956
Lavy, Jacob N., 1687
    North Hampton, OH, Donnels Creek
        Old German Baptist Brethren
        Church, elder-in-charge, 948
Lavy, Joseph Calvin, 2303
    Old Order German Baptist Church
        minister, 972
    Old Order German Baptist Church,
        2235
Lavy, Solomon
    Old Brethren German Baptist Church,
        minister, 965
law, **728–729**, *See also* lawsuits; legalism;
        litigation
    annual meeting decisions, 728–729
    attitudes toward litigation, 728–729
    civil lawsuits, 728–729
    doctrinal statements, 942
    Doctrine of, 42
    Dunkard Brethren, 409
    Dunkard Brethren and nonconformity,
        941

ecclesiastical law, 729
Fellowship of Grace Brethren Churches
        (FGBC), 486
Glick's *The Laws of Men and the Laws
        of God,* 1950
Harman, Hylton, 2196
home education, 2203
India, Church of North, 2207
lawsuits resulting from schisms, 729
occupation as lawyer, 728
Old German Baptist Brethren, 2233
"Order of the Brethren," 976
Progressive Brethren and fundamental-
        ism, 2006
study of, 841
suing, other religious groups opposed
        to, 69
Law and Grace (McClain), 486
*Law and the Christian Believer in
        Relation to the Doctrine of Grace*
        (McClain), 773
law, doctrine of, **729**
    Covenant Theology, 348
    Montgomery, Michael, 872
law enforcement, 729–730, **729–730**, *See
        also* bail
    Brethren, careers in, 1041
Law, John, 1687
Law, William, 381
Lawhorn family
    Sinking Spring, OH, Grace Brethren
        Church, 1186
Lawlor, G. Lawrence, 121, 1687, 2303
Lawon, Thomas, 1907
Lawrence Co., IL
    Allison Prairie Church of the Brethren,
        2126
Lawrence Co., IN, 689, 690, 1341
    Dutch Bethel, German Baptist Brethren
        Church, 2373
    migration of Brethren, 829
Lawrence Co., PA, 317
Lawrence Co., TN, 354, 753, 1253
Lawrence family, 1345
Lawrence, Joan (later Daggett), 2276
Lawrence, Joseph Wilson, 1996
Lawrence, KS, 682, 1346
    Church of the Brethren, **730**
Lawrence, Louisa
    Oak Grove Church of the Brethren, IA,
        district meeting delegate, 955
Lawrence, Marion, 659
Lawrence, Ruth, 2379
Lawrenceburg, TN, 753
Lawrenceville, PA, Church of the Brethren,
        See Parker Ford, PA, Church of the
        Brethren
Lawrenz, David, 1265
Lawshe, Isaac, 1687
    Somerset, IN, Church of the Brethren,
        elder, 1202
Lawson, Charles E., 122, 1276, 1687
Lawson, Dan L., 2284
Lawson, David Ronald, 2284
Lawson, Delmer G., 1687
Lawson, F. Wayne, 567, 1687
Lawson family
    Pleasant Hill Church of the Brethren,
        IA, 1032
Lawson, Janet, 662
Lawson, Onas, 755
lawsuits
    Brethren peace position, 999

Meyersdale, PA, Main Street Brethren
        Church, 823
Peru, IN, Brethren Churches, 1010
Plattsburg College, 1030
Lawter, William, 1687
Lawver, Michael, 1687–1688
Lawyer, Calvin Lee, 1688. 1996
Lay, H. D., 1240
lay members
    changing role of, 408
    participation in worship services, 1377
lay ministry
    Springfield, OR, Church of the
        Brethren, 1216
lay preachers, **730**
lay speakers, **730**
    ministry, terminology, 848
Laycook, Catherine L., 2284
Layen, Anna Flys, 681
    laying on of hands, 166, 185, **730–731**
    anointing the sick, 730–731
    baptism, 85
    confirmation, 333–334
    consecration at Missionary Convoca-
        tion, 856
    deacons, 369
    degrees of ministry, 374
    elder, 432
    God's Means of Grace (Yoder), 555
    healing, 591
    Holsinger, Henry Ritz, 621
    Holy Spirit, doctrine of, 624
    installation of pastors, 657
    missionaries, 327
    ordinances, 976, 979
    ordination, 980
    prayer, 1052
    public worship ritual, 1375
    worship and, 2266
Layman, D., 1688
Layman, D. C., 1688
Layman, Ezra, 1688, 2303
    Oak Hill Old German Baptist Brethren
        Church, VA, minister, 957
Layman family, 164, 1277, 1280, *See also*
        Lehman family
Layman, Frank Benjamin, Jr., 1688
    Monte Vista Church of the Brethren,
        VA, pastor, 871
Layman, Frank Benjamin, Sr., 1688
Layman, George G., 360
Layman, Harvey, 1688
Layman, Helen Frances Wenger, 1996
Layman, Henry B., 1688
Layman, J. Kline, 1688
Layman, J. T., 1688
    Pleasant Dale Church of the Brethren,
        VA, providing pastoral leadership,
        1031
    Selma, VA, Church of the Brethren,
        minister and elder, 1166
Layman, John D., 350, 496, 544, 1688
    Salem Old German Baptist Brethren
        Church, OH, elder-in-charge, 1139
Layman, John P., 760, 1688
Layman, John R., 1688
Layman, L. Ray, 1688
Layman, Minnie (later Ikenberry), 646
Layman, Norman R., 2284
Laymantown, VA
    Cloverdale, VA, Church of the Breth-
        ren, preaching point for, 321
Laymantown Valley, VA, 164

laymen, *See* men's fellowship; men's work;
National Fellowship of Grace
Brethren Men; National Laymen's
Organization
Layser family
Myerstown, PA, Church of the
Brethren, 906
Layser, Frank H., 1688
Layton, William Allison, 288, 1688
Leach family
Snake Valley Old German Baptist
Brethren Church, PA, 1193
Lead(e), Jane, 120
Hochmann von Hochenau, Ernst
Christoph, 614
Philadelphian Society, 1019
*The Leader, See The Church of the Brethren
Leader*
Leader, George, 1391
leadership
articles on, 1923
biographies, 2012
Brethren rural churches, organization
of, 1130
denominational naming based on, 910
from Church of the Brethren, Nampa,
ID, 913
of New Dunkards by Patton, George,
996
providing effective, 1968
study of 1850–1943, 1963
training in, Christian Education
Commission, 155
Young, David S. on church renewal
and, 2365
Young, Jerry R. on GBC and, 2365
Leadwell, R. B., 1688
Leady, A.H., 1688
Leaf River Old German Baptist Brethren
Church, MS, **731**
Mississippi Brethren settlement, 864
League of Nations, 1370
Leake, John W., 731
Leake, Sarah, 731
Leake's Chapel Church of the Brethren, VA,
731
Mount Zion Church of the Brethren,
VA, 888
Newport Church of the Brethren, VA,
joined with, 934
Leakesville, NC, *See* Eden, NC, Church of
the Brethren
Leaman, William Henry, 1688
Leamersville Church of the Brethren, PA,
257, 318, 407, 731, **731–732**
Leamersville house, 407
Fredericksburg, PA, Brethren Church,
512
Leamersville, PA, Grace Brethren Church,
731
"Leaning on the Everlasting Arms," 560
Lear family
Shull family, related to, 1156
Lear, Hannah Stutzman, 1233
Lear, John Wallace, 242, 270, 553, 638,
732, 1688, 1911, 1948, 1996
San Francisco, CA, Church of the
Brethren, 1141–1142
Lear, Jacob, 1285
Lear, John, 732
Lear (Leer), Abraham S., 1688
Lear, Lydia Ulrich, 1285
Lear, Martha E. Shull, 732, 1996

Lear, Mattie A., **732**, 1298, 1361, 1688
Hudson, IL, Church of the Brethren,
635
Lear, Philip, 1233
Learn, Levi, 1688
learning-disabled children
camping movement, 247
"Learning the Brethren Way" (Miller), 2013
Leas, Joseph Allen, 1996, 2105
Leas, L. Elmer, 1688
Lease, Anna Leiter, 2284
Leasure, Lois Hartsough, 588
Leasure, Melvin, 588
Leasure, Nettie Norris, 1996
Leatherman, Anna Maria (later Moser)
Middletown Valley Church of the
Brethren, MD, 826
Leatherman, Benjamin, 1688
Leatherman, Betsy (later Taylor), 1249
Leatherman, Catherine (daughter of
Daniel), 734
Leatherman, Catherine Harp, 733
Leatherman, Catherine (wife of Daniel),
732
Leatherman, Charles Lowell, 571, 1688,
2303
Leatherman, Christian (elder), 734
Leatherman, Christian (younger), 734
Leatherman, Daniel (Letterman), 58, 78,
145, 1688
Martin, David, ordaining, 797
Maryland Brethren activity, 798
Middletown Valley Church of the
Brethren, MD, elder, 826
Pipe Creek Church of the Brethren,
MD, presiding elder, 1026
Leatherman, Daniel (son of Daniel), 734
Leatherman, Daniel (son of Nicholas), 734
Leatherman, David, 272, 1688
New Carlisle, OH, Church of the
Brethren, elder in, 926
Leatherman, Detrick, 1688
Leatherman, Elias K., 1688
Leatherman, Elizabeth, 364
Leatherman, Ernest B., 1688
Leatherman family, 364, 740, 1253, 1336,
See also Arnold family; Leder-
mann family
family history, 1998
Grossnickle family, 574
Middletown Valley Church of the
Brethren, MD, 826
Rotruck (Rothrock, Roderick) family,
related to, 1124
Shelby Co. German Baptist Brethren
Church, KY, 1175
Leatherman, George, 584, 692, 1688
Leatherman, George W., 1240, 1688
Leatherman German Baptist Church, 1240
Leatherman, Godfrey, 734
Leatherman, Hannah, 734
Leatherman, Irvin Dresher, 461, 713, **732**,
1688
Leatherman, Isaac, 1688
Leatherman, Isaac W., 1688
Leatherman, J. N., 1688
Leatherman, J. W., 45
Leatherman, Jacob, 177, 216, **732–733**,
1688
missions, 857
Leatherman, Jacob (son of Christian), 734
Leatherman, John, 364, 558, 1280, 1688,
2384

Mount Pleasant Church of the
Brethren, IN, 886
Leatherman, John (1776–1867), 124
Leatherman, John Benjamin, 1688
Leatherman, John M., 129, 1688
Leatherman, John R., 1688
Leatherman, John (son of Christian), 734
Leatherman, John (son of Daniel), 734
Leatherman, John (son of Nicholas), 734
Leatherman, John Theobald (Hans Depelt
Lederman), 733
Leatherman, John William, 732
Leatherman, Jonas, 734
Leatherman, Joseph, 734
Leatherman, Laya, 734
Leatherman (Letterman), Daniel (son of
Hans Depelt Lederman), **732**, 733,
734
Leatherman, Lucy, 1841
Leatherman, Magdalena, 734
Leatherman, Martha, 734
Leatherman, Mary (daughter of Daniel),
734
Leatherman, Mary (later Spohn), 1253
Leatherman, Mary Martin, 1688
Leatherman, Mary Swigert, 732
Leatherman, Michael, 734
Leatherman, Minor Ellsworth, 211, 1688
Ridge Dunkard Brethren Congregation,
WV, elder and minister, 1109
Leatherman, Mollie Dresher, 732
Leatherman, N. Victor, 318, **733**, 1323
"Message of the Brethren Ministry,"
818
Ripon, CA, Brethren Church, pastor,
1110
Leatherman, Nicholas, 58, 106, 129, 734,
1383, 1688
Leatherman, Nicholas, elder
North Carolina Brethren settlement,
946
Leatherman, Nicholas (son of Christian),
734
Leatherman, Noble Victor, 318, 1323,
1688–1689
Leatherman, Orpha Workman Keever, 732
Leatherman, Paul Nelson, Jr., 1689, 2284
Leatherman, Paul Nelson, Sr., 1689
Leatherman, Peter, 732
Leatherman, Peter (son of Christian), 734
Leatherman, Peter (son of Daniel), 734
Leatherman, R. N., 417
Leatherman, Rachel, 734
Leatherman, Raphael Byron, 1689
Leatherman, Ray A.
Ridge Dunkard Brethren Congregation,
WV, 1109
Leatherman, Roger D., 2284
Leatherman, Roland N., 270, 313, 551,
1333, 1689, 1996
Leatherman, Sarah M. (later Young), 2298
Leatherman settlement, KY, 734
Leatherman, Susanna (daughter of
Nicholas), 734
Leatherman, Susanna Harp, 733
Leatherman, Virgil, 1689, 2303
Leavell, Benjamin W., 468, 1689
Leavell, O. W., 445, 1689
Leavenworth, KS
Ozawkie Church of the Brethren,
preaching points established by,
987
Leavenworth, Marie B., 2303

Leaverton, Landon W., 1689
Lebanon
  work camps, 1367
Lebanon Church of the Brethren, VA, 45, **733**
Lebanon Co., PA, 135–136, 158, 225, 226, 409, 712, 733, 737, 1278, 1318, 1330, 2077
  Grace Brethren congregations, 1005
  history of, 1927, 1940
  Lebanon Twp., 151
  Lebanon, PA, Church of the Brethren, **733**
    20 year anniversary, 1996
    Midway Church of the Brethren, PA, 827
    Midway Church of the Brethren, PA, 827
    Mount Wilson Church of the Brethren, PA, 887
    Mount Zion Road Church of the Brethren, PA, 888
    Snabali/Snavely, John, 1193
Lebanon Co., PA, congregation, 309
Lebanon German Baptist Brethren Church, MO, **733**
Lebanon (later Albany), OR, congregation, 1138
Lebanon, OH
  Bear Creek Brethren Church, 930
Lebanon, VA, congregation, 1236
  Pleasant Valley Church of the Brethren, VA, 1035
Lebanon Valley Brethren Home, **733**
Lebanon Valley, PA,
  historic landmarks, 1912
Lebo, Benjamin F., 1689
Lechliter, Emmon, 1689
Leckey, Howard R., 1996
Leckrone, Benjamin F., 733
Leckrone, Clifton (Clifford) J., 1689
Leckrone, Edith Fickel, 733
Leckrone, Elizabeth Boyer, 733
Leckrone, Elmer Franklin, 1689, 2303
Leckrone, Emanuel, 1333, 1689
Leckrone, Howard, 733
Leckrone, Iva (later Metzger)
  Metzger, Thurl D., 2222
Leckrone, Kenneth Merl, 1689
Leckrone, Quincy, 64, 572, **733**, 1340, 1689, 1996
  Smithville Collegiate Institute, 1192
Leckrone, Samuel, 1333, 1689
Leckrone, Walter, 733
LeCount, Eugene, 558
LeCount, Ronald Dean, 79, 1689
  Newton, KS, Church of the Brethren, pastor in, 934
Lectiones, See confession, Ephrata Community
Ledbetter, James, 1689
Ledbetter, W. S., 1689
Leddy, Peter J., 1689
Lederach family, 2077
Lederman, Hans Depelt (Leatherman, John Theobald), 733
Ledermann, Catherina (later Holtz), 733
Ledermann, Christian, 733
Ledermann, Daniel, 733
Ledermann, Godfrey (Gottfried), 733
Ledermann (Letterman, Leatherman) family, 58, **733–734**
Ledermann, Magdalena (later

Spohn/Spoon), 733
Ledermann, Michael, 733
Ledermann, Nicholas, 733
Ledington, John D., 2284
Ledwell, R. B., 1689
Lee, Barbara, 1850
Lee Bell, WV
  Elkins, WV, Church of the Brethren, 440
  meetinghouse, 164
Lee, Carl Q., 282
Lee Co., FL, 252
Lee Co., IA, 1358
Lee Co., IL, 384, 718
  Franklin Grove, IL, Church of the Brethren, 507
  Naperville Church of the Brethren, 913
Lee Co., VA, 145, 463
Lee, Daniel, 1689
Lee, Debra
  on ministry, 2357
Lee, Douglas Montgomery, 2284
Lee family, 1865
  Garrett, PA, Church of the Brethren, 531
  South Bend, IN, Ireland Road Grace Brethren Church, 1203
Lee, J., 1996
Lee, M. Louise (later Stauffer), 1219
Lee, Patricia, 1843
Lee, Robert E. (General), 1126
  Rowland, Ann Gilbert, 1126
Lee, Ruth Kline, 1996
Leech, Edmund M., 12, 553, 1689
Leech, H., 1689
Leech, Lida Shivers
  Men's Work (CB), 816
Leedy, Abraham, 31, 637, 734, 1689
  Ogan's Creek, IN, Church of the Brethren, elder, 960
Leedy, Amos
  place-names, Brethren, 1028
Leedy Brethren, 31, 32, 67, 177, 334, **734**, 1877, 2045
  chart of Brethren bodies, place on, 1403–1405
  feetwashing mode, 1186
  Fraternal Relations Committees (BC), 511
  Garber, Aaron Leedy, 528
  Garber, Levi Leedy, 529
  named after leader, 910
  Old German Baptist Brethren, 364, 368
Leedy, Daniel, 14, **734**, 1689
  migration of Brethren, 830
  Oregon, 980
Leedy, E. F., 286
Leedy, Elizabeth, 214
Leedy, Elizabeth Blocher, 147
Leedy, Elizabeth Bostater, 734
Leedy, Elizabeth Zook, 734
Leedy family, 14, 1944, 2032, 2099
  Salem Church of the Brethren, OH, 1138
Leedy, Harry E., 1689
Leedy, Isaac, 31, **734**, 1689
Leedy, Isabella Love, 734
Leedy, J. H.
  Old Brethren, 964
Leedy, J. K., 1689
Leedy, J. W., 1209
  Maurertown, VA, Brethren Church, 803
Leedy, Jacob A., 734

Leedy, John, 30, 1689
  Old Brethren German Baptist Church, minister, 965
  Old Order German Baptist Church minister, 972
Leedy, John H., 373
  Old Brethren minister, 965
Leedy, John H. (2 listed), 1689
Leedy, John W., 1689
Leedy, Joseph, 30, 637, 1689
Leedy (Leedey), Amos, 1689
Leedy, Lovina Wolf, 734
Leedy, Mary Huston, 734
Leedy, Mr. and Mrs. Ezra
  New Paris, IN, Brethren Church, 931
Leedy, Nancy Bostater, 734
Leedy, OK
  place-names, Brethren, 1028
Leedy, Samuel A., 31, 350, **734**, 1295, 1689
Leedy, Samuel F., 1295
Leedy, Samuel F., Jr., 1689, *See also* Old German Baptist Brethren
Leedy, Samuel F., Sr., 1689
Leedy, Sarah (later Frantz), 508
Leedy, Simon B., 734, 1689
Leedyites, *See* Leedy Brethren
  Old Brethren, 964
Leeper, Floyd E., 1689
Leer, Abraham S., 102, 732
Leer, Annie Mary (later Miller)
  Miller, Jacob A., wife of, 838
Leer, Benjamin, 1689
Leer, Daniel, 1385
Leer, Elizabeth (later Ulery)
  descendants, 1953
Leer, Elizabeth Studebaker, 732
Leer, Jacob, 1385, 1689
Leer, John, 1385, 1689
Leer, Samuel, 1384, 1385, 1689
Lees family
  Pipe Creek Old German Baptist Brethren Church, IN, 1026
Leesburg, IN, Grace Brethren Church, **735**
Leesburg mission
  Seneca Church of the Brethren, FL, 1166
Leese family, 1996
Leese, Lawrence, 1996
Leeton, MO, 1318
  Clearfork Church of the Brethren, **735**
  Mineral Creek Brethren Church, **735**
    Missouri, 865
    Missouri Brethren settlement, 864
    Mohler, Samuel Sayler, elder-in-charge, 868
Leetown, WV, Church of the Brethren, 119, **735**
  Martinsburg, WV, Moler Avenue Church of the Brethren, 798
  Mountain View Church of the Brethren, WV, 889
Lefeber, Isaac, 2025
Lefever, D. Welty, 1689
Lefever, Elias B., 1689
Lefever, Ernest W., 335, 1689, 1996
  and neoorthodoxy, 923
  War Prisoner's Aid program, 1058
  Young Men's Christian Associations (YMCA), 1390
LeFevre family, 1996–1997, 2079
LeFevre, Franklin D., 1996–1997
LeFevre, George Newton, 1996–1997
LeFevre, Ralph, 1997

Lefevre, William Hess, 2025
Lefler, Hugh T., 1996
Leftwich, Danny Robert, 2284
Leftwich, Joseph P., 1689
Leftwich, William P., 1689
Leftwich, Willie M., 1690
Legal issues, See law
    denominational naming, 910–911
legal services
    Mack, Alexander, Jr., 775
legalism, **735**, See also law; law, doctrine of
        Brethren avoidance of, 729
    interpretation of the Bible, 134
    Montgomery, Michael, 872
    simple life, 1183
legalistic bodies
    Church of the Brethren, 1957
Legato mission point
    Oakton, VA, Church of the Brethren,
        958
legends and myths
    Ruth, John L. on PA Mennonites and,
        2354
legislation
    relief training units, use of outside the
        USA, 1097
Legue, Gary, 145
Leher, Silas W., 736
Lehigh, Amos, 136
    Pleasant Hill Church of the Brethren,
        PA, tract ministry, 1032
Lehigh, Daniel Grant, 2284
Lehigh, David Weaver, 1690
Lehigh, Robert S., 2143, 2284
Lehigh, Samuel M., 136, 1690
Lehigh Valley, Bethlehem, PA, Grace
        Brethren Church, See Bethelehem,
        PA, Lehigh Valley Grace Brethren
        Church
Lehman, Anna, 2074
Lehman, B. H., 1911
Lehman, Benjamin, 544, 736
Lehman, Benjamin and Susan, 1997
Lehman, Bertha Belle, 236, 1835
Lehman, Birdie (later Morris)
    Morris, James Henry, wife of, 877
Lehman, Boyd Newton, 151, 1690
Lehman, Carl B., 1277, 1690
Lehman, Catherine (later Holsopple), 623
Lehman, Chris S., 1690
Lehman, Christian, **735–736**, 736, 1690
Lehman, Clifford David, 2074
Lehman, Clyde Beryl, 1690
    Red Hill Church of the Brethren, VA,
        pastor, 1088
Lehman, Dallas Dohner, 765, 1690
Lehman, Daniel M., 1383, 1690
    family history, 1997
Lehman, Daniel Richard, 1997
Lehman, David B. and Sarah L. Hege, 1997
Lehman, David J., 2074
Lehman, David S.
    family history, 1997
Lehman, Earl Modest, 1997
Lehman, Earl S., 557, 1690
    Richland, PA, Church of the Brethren,
        pastor, 1107
Lehman, Elizabeth, 735
Lehman family, 373, 1391, 1881, 1997,
        2010, 2072, 2074, 2106
    Heisey family, 595
    Holtzapfel (Holsapple, Holsopple)
        family, 624

McFarland, CA, Church of the
    Brethren, 774
Lehman, Fannie Vera (later Good), 1951
Lehman, Franklin B., 1690
Lehman, Galen A., 1690
Lehman, Galen T., **736**, 1690, 1997
Lehman, Gladys Mary, 2074
Lehman, Glen Otto, 2074
Lehman, Gottfried, 735, 736
Lehman, H. B., 1690
Lehman, Harvey C., 743, 1690
    Newton, KS, Church of the Brethren,
        pastor in, 934
Lehman, Helen Meyers, 2010–2011
Lehman, Henry, 531, 736, 1690
Lehman, Herman and Christena
        Hershberger, 2008
Lehman, Hiram, 1690
Lehman, Homer Feather, 1997
Lehman, Ira, 1690
Lehman, Ira M., 736
Lehman, Irene Mae, 2074
Lehman, J. B., 1690
Lehman, J. L., 1690
Lehman, Jacob, 736, 749
Lehman, Jacob, Jr., 1690
Lehman, James H., 748, 1997
    on Brethren, early, 2343, 2372
    historical writing, 612, 613
    "Season of Good Favor [Centennial
        Issue]", 1997
Lehman, James O., 1895, 1990, 1997
Lehman, James P., 1690
Lehman, John, 142, 736, 1690
Lehman, John Daniel, 2063
Lehman, John E., 1690
Lehman, John H., 1690
Lehman, John Hardman, 2106
Lehman, Joseph C., 1690
Lehman, Josiah R., 40, 1690
Lehman, Judith, 2023
Lehman, June Puterbaugh, 736
Lehman, Katie L., 1997
Lehman (Lahman) family, 1276
Lehman, Lawrence E., 619, 1312, 1690,
        1997
Lehman (Layman, Lahman) family, **736**
Lehman, Lorenzo J., 1690
Lehman (Luginbuhl), Abraham P., 1878
Lehman (Luginbuhl), Elizabeth, 1878
Lehman, Magdalena Emmert, 736
Lehman, Martin, 1997
Lehman, Mary Lehman, 2106
Lehman, Mary Trostle, 236, 736
Lehman, Murray Pius, 1690
    New Fairview Church of the Brethren,
        PA, elder in, 927
Lehman, Peter, **736**, 2072
    Miller, John Peter, 840
    monastic congregation, 1195
    reference to, 1939
Lehman, Peter S., 270, 1690, 1997
Lehman, Ralph B., 1690
Lehman, Randall S. M., 2284
Lehman, Samuel, 172, **736**, 1883
Lehman, Samuel Augustus, 1997
Lehman, Samuel C., Jr., 1690
Lehman, Samuel C. (son of Samuel), 736
Lehman, Samuel, Sr., 1690
Lehman, Sharlene Anne (later Morrison),
        2023
Lehman, Ulrich, 2023
Lehman, Ulrich and Judith, 1997

Lehman, W. C., 1212, 1690
Lehman, Wilbur Good, 1690
Lehman, William, 1690
Lehman, William Isaac, 1997
Lehman, Wilmer Mohler, 446, 1690, 2303
Lehmann, Hartmut
    on Dunkers, 2343
    on Franklin, B. compared with Sauer,
        Christoph, I, 2343
    on Sauer family, 2343
Lehmann-Haupt, Hellmut, 1997
Lehmann, Helmut T.
    on Mühlenberg, Heinrich Melchior,
        correspondence of, 2341
Lehmer, Clarence, 278
Lehmer, Della Snider, 736
Lehmer, G. G., 759
Lehmer, George C., 1690
Lehmer, Ida Frantz, 736
Lehmer, John R., 736
Lehmer, Lydia Gentzler, 736
Lehmer, Silas G., See Lehmer, Solomon G.
Lehmer, Silas W., 1690
Lehmer, Solomon Gentzler, 118, 278, 432,
        520, 727, 759, **736**, 1275, 1690
    Monitor Church of the Brethren, KS,
        minister, 869
    San Diego, CA, First Church of the
        Brethren, 1141
Lehner (Lehmer), John, 1690
Lehr, Albina Johnson Hoover, 1983
    Kennedy, Stephen J. on, 2340
Lehr, Edward Chester, 1997
Leibert, John
    publishing, 1067
Leibert, Mary Neiß (Nice), 736
Leibert, Peter, 18, 77, 288, *541*, 544,
        736–737, 1690
    hymnals, 642
    medicine, 809
    publishing, 1067
    Scharpnack, Heinrich, family, related
        to, 1152
Leibert Press, 139
    historical libraries, 610
Leibungutt, Peter, 2343
Leicht, Roy, 1690
Leichty, Carolee, 1842
Leid, John G., 1690
Leid, Noah Weaver, 1997
Leidy, Dorothy A., 2132
Leidy, Edward, 1691
Leidy, George C., 1691
Leidy, J. Brant, 2284
Leidy (Lidy), Samuel, 1691
Leidy, Richard D., 2132
Leigh, Tom, 664
    Island Pond, VT, Grace Brethren
        Church, 2209
Leigh, Trudy Lyon
    Island Pond, VT, Grace Brethren
        Church, 2209
Leight, LeRoy, 1691
Leighton family, 753
Leighton, Foster B., 1691
Leighton, Tenna, 672
Lein, Arnold Alfred, 1691
Leinbach, Aaron Barton, 1997
Leinbach, Ada Graybill Wanner, 1997
Leinbach, Paul S., 1997
Leinbach, William
    coverlets woven by, article about, 1915
Leinback, Mary (later Van Dyke), 1301

Leinhard, John G., 755, 1691, *See also*
 Lienhard, John G.
Leininger family, 1867
Leininger, John and Margaret Goss, 1998
Leininger, Mark, 1691
Leininger, Robert LeRoy, 1998
Leininger, Verne Henry, 1691
Leistner, Lowell J., 1691, 2303
leisure
 Christian theology, 1972
 recreation, 1086–1088
Leiter, Anna (later Lease), 2284
Leiter, Bert, 504
Leiter, David A., 2285
Leiter, Donald Eugene, 1691, 1998, 2155
Leiter, E. Donald, 122
Leiter family
 Orange, CA, Grace Brethren Church
Leiter, Laban Wingert, 1691
Leiter, Mamie Keller (later Ziegler), 1397
Leiton, Gerardo, 2285
Lemert, Ora C., 1691
Lemmon, Paul Allison, 1691
Lemon, C. Edward, 1691
Lemon, Dell G., 1691
Lemon family, 2105
Lemon, Homer, 1691
Lemon, J. D., 1691
Lemon, James T., 1998
Lemon, John H., 514
 Ruckers German Baptist Brethren
 Church, VA, elder, 1129
Lemon, John Harvey, **737,** 1691
Lemon, Walter D., 1691
Lemonites, *See* Free Will Dunkers
 (Lemonites)
Lena, IL, 1384
 Church of the Brethren, 419, **737,**
 1384, 2002, 2088
Lenawee, MI, 1334
Lenexa, KS, Fellowship, **2214**
Lengel, Dean Michael, 2285
Lenhart, John, 1998
Leninger, Kenneth G., 2285
Leninger, M. C., 236
Lenker, Charles Eugene, 262, 1691
 Rocky Mount, VA, Church of the
 Brethren, part-time pastor, 1119
Lenker, Joan L. Stickelman, 1840
Lenker, Robert Kenneth, 1691, 1840
Lenox, IA
 Salem Church of the Brethren, near,
 1137
Lent, **737**
Lentz, Blanche, 656
Lentz, Charles A., 735, 1691
Lentz family, *See* Lantz family
Lentz, George William, 268, 582, 683, 692,
 1691
 Mound Valley Church of the Brethren,
 MO, elder, 879
Lentz, Ira J., 1691
Lentz, Jacob, 725
 Mack family, 778
Lentz, Johannes, 725
Lentz/Lantz family, 1994
Lentz, Lydia Mack Kolb, 725
 Mack family, 778
Lenz, Michael, 1255
Leola, PA, 1213, 1278, 1340
 Conestoga Church of the Brethren,
 112, **737**
Leon, IA, 1247

Brethren Church, **737–738**
 Fellowship of Grace Brethren
 Churches (FGBC), 485
 Ronk, George Teller, pastor, 1121
Leonard, Bruce D., 1691
Leonard, David, 439, 1691
Leonard, Elias, 1691
Leonard family
 Myerstown, PA, Grace Brethren
 Church, 906
 Parsons Old German Baptist Brethren
 Church, KS, 994
Leonard, Mary, 741
Leonard, Rosalita Jean, 1359, 1840
 on CB women's writings, 2343
 on Gospel Messenger Obituary Index,
 2343
Leong Bow Jon
 Moy Way, wife of, 891
Leopold, Nathan F., 738, 1998
LePage, Richard, 2285
Leping Hsien, China, 278
Lepley, Daniel F., 137, 467, 1691, 1289
 "Echoes of 1916," 1998
Lepp, Pastor
 Mennonite Brethren Churches, General
 Conference of, 814
Lepp, Walter Alexander, 578, 768, 1691
Leppke, Harold, 1691, 2303
leprosy
 Adamawa Provincial Leprosarium, *See*
 Adamawa Provincial Leprosarium,
 Garkida, Nigeria
 ALM (American Leprosy Missions), 4,
 24, 432, 807
 Gribble, Florence Alma Newberry, *See*
 Gribble, Florence Alma Newberry
 Helser, Albert David, 596
 hospitals, 630
 medical missions, 807
 Nigerian State Leprosy Control
 Service, 4
 relief efforts, 24
 treatment of, 4
Leprosy Training Unit, 4
Lequear, John E., 1998
Lerch, James M., 1691
Lerch, Marilyn E., 2138, 2285
Lerew family, 145
Lerew, Isaac S., 1691
Lerew, Jacob P., 1691
Lerew, Lewis, 1691
 North Solomon Old German Baptist
 Brethren Church, KS, minister and
 elder, 949
 Portis, KS, Grace Brethren Church,
 deacon, 1047
Lerew, Samuel A., 1691
Lerg, Winfried B.
 on Müller, J. H., 2343
 on Sauer, J. C., 2343
Lernley family, 2087
Lers, Phil, 188
Lersch, E. Phillip, Jr., 1691, **2214**
Lersch, Jean, 188
Lersch, Jean Lindower, 744, 2214
lesbian and gay issues, *See* gay and les-
 bian issues; homosexuality
Lescer family, 2074
Lesh, Anna Moyer
 Meyer family, 822
Lesh, Christian, 1691
Lesh, Jacob

Meyer family, 822
Lesh, John, 1691
Lesher, Dana K., 2285
Lesher family, *See* Pursel, Vida Miller
Lesher, Harry A., 471, 1691, 2303, **2384**
Lesher, Henry E., 471, 1691
Lesher, John B., 471, 1691
Lesher, Mary (later Stover), 1225
Lesko, Phillip, 1691
Leslie, Alonzo G., 1691
Leslie, Claude Heckman, 1691
Leslie Co., KY, 689
Leslie, Guilford (Mr. and Mrs.), 558
Leslie (Lesley), Eli L., 1691
Leslie, Libbie, 1389
Leslie, Mr. and Mrs. Guilford, 914
Lessing, Gotthold E.
 Pietist background, 1022
Lessly, Ann (later Martin), *See* Martin, Ann
 Lessly
 Martin family, 797
Lesso, Carol, 1394
Lesso, James, 1394
Lester Altermatt, Jr., 275
Lester, E., 227
Letcher, John, 315, **738**
Letherman, I. John, 1998
Letherman, Lydia (later Tombaugh), 1267
Letherman Settlement
 Shelby Co. German Baptist Brethren
 Church, KY, 1175
Let's Stay Married (Rohrer), 1119
Lett, Annie, 246
Lett, Will, 246
"Letter Concerning Feetwashing"
 Mack, Alexander, Jr., 774
Letterman, Daniel, *See* Leatherman, Daniel
Letterman family, *See* Ledermann family
Letterman, Nicholas, 1691
Letters, Biblical, *See* specific titles, e.g.
 James
Letters from Europe and Bible Lands
 (Miller), 836
letters of membership, 5, **738**
 church membership, 813
 German Baptist Brethren, 540
 Highline Church of the Brethren, NE,
 606
 Sappington, Roger E. on VA and, 2354
letters of submission
 Far Western Brethren, 476
Letters of the Young from the Old World
 (Miller), 2013
letters of transfer
 Hoyle Creek Church of the Brethren,
 OK, 633
 Irricana (First) Church of the Brethren,
 Alberta, Canada, 663
 Joplin, MO, Church of the Brethren,
 676
 Juniata Church of the Brethren, NE,
 678
Letters to the Young from the Old Country
 (Miller), 837
Levefer, Ernest W., 1689
Levergood family
 Johnstown, PA, Geistown Grace
 Brethren Church, 674
Levering, Joseph M., 1998
Levers, C. G., 1691
Leviticus
 8:12, 30, 39
 14:15–18, 39

18:20, 6
20:10, 6
translation of, 2137
Leviton, Chuck, 1691
Levits, William, 1691
Levittown, PA, Brethren Church, *See*
Fairless Hills-Levittown, PA,
Brethren Church
Lewallen, J. Wilburn, 1691
Lewellen, Clifford Peters
on Peters-Lewellen families, 2343
Lewellen, Duane Austin, 674, 1691–1692,
2303
Lewig, Philip, 1692
Lewin, Kurt, 575
Lewis, Abram Herbert, 1998
Lewis, Albert, 1692
Lewis, Andrew J., 1315
Lewis, Andrew Jackson, 1692
Lewis, Arthur, 738, 1692
Lewis, Betty, 356
Lewis, Carrie Belle, 1833
Lewis, Charles A., 270, 274
Lewis, Charles Albert, 1692
Lewis, Clyde, 1692
Lewis Co., WA
Richland Valley Church of the
Brethren, WA, 1108
Lewis Co., WV, 172
Lewis, D. Edward, Sr., 227
Lewis, Daniel, 356
Lewis, David H., 1692
Lewis, David S., 740
Lewis, Debbie, 356
Lewis, Dorothy Helen (later Maconaghy),
779, 1851
Lewis, Edward A., 318, 357, 533, 1309,
1692, 2156, 2183
on GBC doctrine, 2343
North Lauderdale, FL, Grace Brethren
Church, pastor, 948
Lewis, Elizabeth
on Weiser, Conrad, 2349
Lewis family, 731, 738, 2087
Lewis, Howard B., 106, 1692, 2303, **2384**
Lewis, J. Frank, 1315, 1692
Lewis, J. Gideon, 1692
Lewis, J. I., 1692
Lewis, J. W., 1692
Lewis, James G., 1315
Lewis, Jesse E., 1315
Lewis, John T., **738**, 2128
minorities, ethnic and racial, 851, *851*
Lewis, Joseph Arthur, 1692, 2136, 2303
Laughlin Church of the Brethren, MD,
2214
Lewis, Lorren Burdette, 1692
Lewis, O. G., 1694
Lewis, Paul S., 1315, 1692
Lewis, Robert, 1998
Lewis, Solomon E., 1315, 1692
Lewis, W., 1692
Lewis, Walter James, 1251, 1692
Lewis, Warren K., 2285
Lewis, William R., 1692
Lewiston Church of the Brethren, MN,
738–739, 2041
Mathis, Jefferson H., pastor, 803
Minnesota Brethren settlement, 848
Lewiston, ME, Church of the Brethren
2214
Lewistown, PA, 697, 994, 1215, 1390
Church of the Brethren, 82, 303, 406,

739, *See also* Dry Valley Church
of the Brethren, PA
conservative theology and schism,
1005
Gospel Trumpet, The, 561
Maitland Church of the Brethren, PA,
783
split of 1948, 1948
Snider, Harold, 1194
Lexikon (Schem), 379
Lexington, KY,
Grace Bible Church, **2214–2215**
Grace Brethren Church, 689, **739**
Lexington, OH
Church of the Brethren, OH, **739**
Fairview Church of the Brethren, 469
Grace Brethren Church, **739**
West Alexandria, OH, Brethren
Church, 1333
Munson, Charles Robert, 2227
Leycuras, Alain, 1851
Leyh, Eduard F., 1998
Liao Chou, China, 209, 278
Cripe, Winifred E., 352
hospitals, 630
Hilton, George William, 607
Hutchison, Anna Martha, 639
mission schools, 853
Libby, Scott M., 2285
Libe, Christian, *See* Liebe, Christian
liberal Christianity
"Message of the Brethren Ministry,"
817
liberal theology
Church of the Brethren, 303
dispensationalism, 390
Haines, Amos Hoppock, 579
Historic Peace Churches, 608
Holiness Movement, American, 619
McClain, Alva J., 773
Mennonites' alternative to, 816
neoorthodox rejection of, 922
noncreedalism, 942, 943
vs. fundamentalism and neoorthodoxy,
923
Liberal United Brethren
Pleasant Ridge Dunkard Brethren
Congregation, OH, 1034
liberalism, 74, 695, **739–740**, *See also* mod-
ernism
Brethren Church and, 183
education, 428
Fellowship of Grace Brethren Churches
(FGBC), 484
impact on the Brethren, 73–74
influence on Brethren theology, 1261,
1262
kingdom of God, position on, 695
Kurtz, Daniel Webster, accused of, 711
Modernism, 866
*News and Views from Speak for the
Lord,* as critical of, 934
protest of, 68
Social Gospel Movement, 1197
liberation theology
Peace Studies Institute, 1003
Liberia, American Coloniztion Society, 22
liberty bonds, *See* war bonds
Liberty Brethren Church, PA, 229, **740**
Raystown Brethren Church, PA, 1084
Liberty Brethren Church, VA, **740**, 2101
Liberty Church of the Brethren, TN, **740**,
695, 696

Liberty German Baptist Brethren Church,
IN, **740**, 1141
Liberty, IL, 1356, 1357, *1357*
Church of the Brethren, 646, **740**, 757
Concord, IL, Church of the
Brethren, preaching point for,
331
Hadley Creek Church of the
Brethren, IL, 577
Liberty Meetinghouse congregation, SC,
1292
Liberty Mills, IN, Church of the Brethren,
429, **740**
Long, John Daniel, 2215
Liberty mission
Sandy German Baptist Brethren
Church, OH, 1143
Liberty, TN, congregation
Pleasant Valley Church of the Brethren,
TN, 1035
Libertyville, IA
Church of the Brethren, IA, **740**
migration of Brethren, 830
South Keokuk Church of the
Brethren, IA, 1205
German Baptist congregation, IA,
660–661
Pleasant Hill Church of the
Brethren, IA, 1032
libraries, *See* historical libraries
Alexander Mack Museum, **2130**
Brethren Historical Library and
Archives, 2134
Brethren hsitorical library and archives,
2002
Brethren loan library
Christian Education Commission, 155
genealogy, 2188
George Solomon Memorial Library,
2131
Sino-Brethren Library, 2129
Library of Congress
historical libraries, 610
library symbols, 1857
licensed ministers
Brethren Church ministry, 846
Church of the Brethren, 846
licensing, *See* degrees of ministry; elders;
election of church officers; instal-
lation of ministers; ordination
election of church officers, 434
placement of pastors, 1028
women, 304
Lichliter, Emra, 1692
Lichten, Frances, 1998
Lichtenberger, Lyle Irven, 1692, 2016
Sarasota, FL, Brethren Church, pastor,
1145
Lichtenberger, Walter, 1692
Lichtenwalter, A. B.
New Hope Church of the Brethren, KS,
as minister, 929
Lichtenwalter, Alonzo B., 1692
Lichti (Lichty) family, **740–741**
Lichty, Abraham, family
Milledgeville, IL, Brethren Church,
833
Lichty, Albert Henry, 1692
Lichty, Amanda (later Shull), *See* Speicher,
Amanda Lichty
Lichty, Anna, 1998
Lichty, Anna Eby, 102, **741**, 1840, **2375,
2388**

Lichty, Barbara Myers, 741
Lichty, C. J., 1692
Lichty, Christian, 741
Lichty, D. S., 720
Lichty, Dale Eugene, 1692
    Mountain Grove Church of the
        Brethren, MO, pastor, 889
Lichty, Daniel, 741
Lichty, Daniel John, **741**, 1692, 1840, 1998
Lichty, David, 741
Lichty, Dora, 2078
Lichty, Elizabeth Fike, 741
Lichty, Eloise, 1998
Lichty family, 231, 1240, 1322, 2078, *See
        also* Lichti family
    Falls City Church of the Brethren, NE,
        472
    Fike family, 490
Lichty, Fannie, 2078
Lichty, H. M., 255
Lichty, Mrs. H. M., 255
Lichty, J., 1692
Lichty, J. J.
    Morrill, KS, Church of the Brethren,
        elder, 876
Lichty, J. R., 255
Lichty, Jacob, 741, 1692
    Elk Lick, PA, congregation, elder, 1139
Lichty, Jacob Peter, 741, 1321
Lichty, Jean (later Hendricks)
    works by, 2320
Lichty, John A., 741
Lichty, John C., 741
Lichty, John R., 1692
Lichty, Jonas, 741, 1236, 1692
Lichty, Jonathan, 2078
Lichty, Jonathan J., 741, 1692
Lichty, Mary (later Miller), 741
    Miller, John Ezra, mother of, 839
Lichty, Michael, 741, 1692
    Rockwell City, KS, Maple Grove
        Brethren Church, pastor, 944
Lichty, Nora Susannah Arnold, **741**, 1840
Lichty, Rachel Miller, 741
Lichty, Sarah Hoover, 741
Lichty, Solomon, 1692, **2384**
Lichty, William H., 741, 1323, 1692
Lick Creek Church of the Brethren, IN,
        318, 355
    Maple Grove Church of the Brethren,
        IN, 789
Lick Creek district, OH
    Silver Creek Church of the Brethren,
        OH, 1182
Lick Creek meetinghouse (OH), *74*
Lick Creek, OH, Church of the Brethren,
        696, **741**
    Maumee Church of the Brethren, OH,
        803
    Poplar Ridge Church of the Brethren,
        OH, 1047
    Williams Co., OH, 961
    young people, *1392*
Lick, David Elsworth, 1998
Lickel, Alys Anne, 1849
Licking Co., OH, Pataskala Grace Brethren
        Church of, 995
Licking Creek, MD, Church of the
        Brethren, *See* Pleasant Ridge
        Church of the Brethren, PA
Licking Creek, PA, congregation
    Pleasant Ridge Church of the Brethren,
        PA, 1034, 1224

Liddicoat, Chester, 1692
Lidle, David, 1692
Lidy, Samuel, 1692
Liebau, J. M., 1692
Liebe, Christian, 121, 159, 174, 253, 545,
        562, 577, 707, **741–742**, 1246,
        1274, 1298, 1998, 2025, 2029,
        2096
    church discipline dispute, 909
    Dutch influence in release of, 923
    Eppstein, 452
    Estates General or States General, 456
    galleys, 527
    Historic Peace Churches, 607
    historic sites, 609
    Mennonites securing release of, 815
    persecution, 1009
    preaching, 1053
    prisons, 1058–1059
Liebe (Libe), Arnold, 741
Liebe (Libe), Christian, 121, **741–742**
Liebe (Libe), Christian, Jr., 741
Liebegott, George H., 1998
Lieby, S. C., 1692
Liechtenstein
    work camp, 1367
Liefmann, Robert, 1998
Lienert family, 2079
Lienhard, John G., 1692, *See also* Leinhard,
        John G.
Lierly, William R., 740, 1692
life
    memorial services honoring, 814
Life and Labors of Elder John Kline
        (B. F. Funk), 525
    On Earth Peace, 974
Life and Sermons of Elder James Quinter
        (Quinter), 1077
Life and Work movement
    faith and order, 470
life and work movement, **742**
Life Conferences
    Seneca Church of the Brethren, FL,
        1166
life insurance, *See* insurance
    Dunkard Brethren, 2174
"L.I.F.E." ("Living in Faithful Evangel-
        ism"), 2180
Life magazine
    Aukerman, Dale H., 2133
    Jacobs, Edwin Elmore, 667
The Life of D. L. Miller (Bates), 836
life of Jesus Christ
    Brethren Doctrine of Salvation, 1140
life, right to, 2127, *See also* abortion; fetal
        tissue, use of
Life-Stewardship report
    funerals, 524
lifelong process of salvation, 1140, 1142
Lifer, James E., 2285
lifestlyes
    simplification of, 1142
lifestyles, *See also* simple life
    Brethren in Christ, 189
    Brethren movement, 178, 2083
    Christian, 2070
    Christian Education Commission, 155
    Dunker Brethren movement, 148
    economic issues and, 2066
    frontier, 176
    frontier, and Brethren movement, 2085
    German-Americans
        simple life, 2106

head coverings, 160
marriage and family, 169
Mennonite Church (MC), 815
monastic life, 193
pastoral, 2078
pastors, country, 2079
Pietism, 1022
plain people, 1029
simple living, 155
urban, and congregational life, 175
Lifford, Louis, 586
Liggett, Julie, 2285
Light, C.
    Golden Spring German Baptist
        Brethren Church, NE, 2374
Light, Caleb, 1692
Light, Charles A., 1692
Light family
    Roanoke, VA, Washington Heights
        Grace Brethren Church, 1114
Light, Fannie
    Pasadena, CA, Church of the Brethren,
        994
Light from a Hillside (Metzler), 820
Light, George H., 1692
Light, H. E., 250
Light, Henry E., 1340, 1692
    Mountville, PA, Church of the
        Brethren, 890
Light, Horace D., Jr., 1692
    Mount Union (Airpoint) Church of the
        Brethren, VA, pastor, 887
    Oakvale Church of the Brethren, WV,
        leadership by, 958
Light, Joseph B., 1692
    Pleasant Center Church of the
        Brethren, OH, minister, 1030
Light, Mary Naomi (later Reed)
    photo of, *2240*
    Reed, Kyle Thayer (DB) and, 2240
"Light on Henry Kurtz's Early Career,"
        2000
Light, Roy, 1692
Lightcap, J. C., 1692
Lightner, B. F., 157, 1692, 1998
Lightner family, 161
lightning rods, 3, **742**
    opposition to, 742
Ligonier, PA
    Hanawalt, George S., 581
Ligonier, PA, Church of the Brethren, *See*
    Waterford, PA, Ligonier Church of
    the Brethren
Ligonier Valley, PA, 1321
Ligutti, Luigi G.
    biography of, 2108
    book about, 1953
Like a Living Stone (Statler), 214
likenesses, *See* photography
Liller, Henry, 16, 274, 1692
    Old Order German Baptist Church
        minister, 972
    Palestine Old German Baptist Brethren
        Church, OH, 991
Liller, James, 16, 274, 1693
Liller, Mark Wesley, 2285
Lillicoat, Lester, 1224
Lillies family
    Patterson, CA, Church of the Brethren,
        995
Lilligh, Henry, 638, 1693
    Santa Ana, CA, Church of the
        Brethren, elder, 1144

Lilligh, J. P.
  Mulberry Grove, IL, Church of the
    Brethren, 893
Lilly, Andrew J., 1693
Lilly Foundation
  Education for a Shared Ministry
    (EFSM), 429
  Parish Ministries Commission, grant to,
    993
Lilly, H. J., 72, 211, 255, 1693
  St. Francis Church of the Brethren, AR,
    minister, 1134
Lilly, Thomas, 1693
Lima, OH
  Elm Street Church of the Brethren,
    143, 410, **742,** 1235
  Grace Brethren Church, **742,** 1380
Limestone Church of the Brethren, KS, **742**
Limestone Church of the Brethren, TN,
  742, **742–743**
  migration of Brethren, 829
Limestone congregation, TN, 1253
Limestone (OGBB) congregation, KS
  Bashore, Jacob H., 997
Limestone Old German Baptist Brethren
  Church, KS, **743**
Limestone schoolhouse
  mission point for Wiley, CO, Church of
    the Brethren, 1345
Limestone, TN, 742, 1380
  John M. Reed Home, 672
Limestone, TN, Brethren Church, 1251, *See
  also* Telford, TN, Grace Brethren
  Church
Limestone, TN, congregation
  Johnson City, TN, Knob Creek Church
    of the Brethren, 673
Lin, Maya
  Neff, Robert Wilbur, 2231
Lin, Mow Choung, 1693
Linbaugh family, 1340
Linck, Martha (later Eckerlin), 421
Lincoln, Abraham, 41, 258, 314, 475, 912,
  2128
  baptism of, 743
  books about written by Brethren, 747
  Christianity, conversion to, 2084
  Friendship Train, 286
  Sayler, Daniel P., as advisor during
    Presidency, 1151
  secession, 1162
Lincoln Co., KS
  Saline Valley church of the Brethren,
    KS
Lincoln Co., MO, 1277
Lincoln Co., NC, 262
  Brethren settlement, 946
  Pfautz family, 1014
Lincoln, Co. ND, 321
Lincoln Co., OK
  Oak Grove Church of the Brethren,
    OK, 956
Lincoln Co., WV, 743
Lincoln family, 1979, 2046
Lincoln German Baptist Brethren Church,
  WV, **743**
Lincoln Heights Mission, OH, Church of
  the Brethren, *See* Mansfield, OH,
  First Church of the Brethren
  Mansfield, OH, First Church of the
    Brethren, former name of, 787
Lincoln, NE
  Annual Conference in, 920

Antelope Park Community Church of
  the Brethren, **743**
First Church of the Brethren, 743
Hattie Netzley Frantz, home mission
  work, 945
Lincoln, PA, 721
  Old German Baptist Brethren Church,
    See Lancaster Old German Baptist
    Brethren Church, PA
Lincolnshire congregation, IN
  Fort Wayne, IN, Beacon Heights
    Church of the Brethren, 503
Lincolnshire Elementary School, Toledo,
  OH, 1267
Lincolnshire, IN, Church of the Brethren,
  See Fort Wayne, IN, Lincolnshire
  Church of the Brethren
Lincolnway Fire Hall, York, PA, 1388
Lind, Abraham H., 1693
  Reed, William Sherman, baptism of,
    1091
  South Fulton Dunkard Brethren
    Congregation, IL, 1205
Lind, Paul A., 1693
Lindberg, George R., 1693
Lindberg, Paul, 1693
Lindblad family, 688
Lindblad, Frank, 65
Lindelef, Garth, 754
Lindell, B. H., 1693
Lindell, Emil, 1693
Lindeman, Freda, 1998
Lindemann, Carl
  Southern Lancaster Grace Brethren
    Church, PA, 1207
Lindemann, Jackie
  Southern Lancaster Grace Brethren
    Church, PA, 1207
Linden Seminary, **743**
  Maryland Brethren, 799
Linder, Wilbur, 1998–1999
  on Adams, Christina and descendants,
    2343
  on Butterbaugh, John Peter and descen-
    dants, 2343
  on Puterbaugh, Christina Adams and
    descendants, 2343
  on Puterbaugh, George and descen-
    dants, 2343
Lindley, William, 1693
Lindley, William B., 1999
Lindner, Hans-George, *See* Prisoners of
  War program
Lindner, Ingeborg, *See* Prisoners of War
  program
Lindower, Ann (later Eagle), 744
Lindower, Frank B., 743
Lindower, Ida Oliver, 744
Lindower, Jean (later Lersch), 744
  Lersch, E. Phillip, Jr., 2214
Lindower, John I., 744, 1266
Lindower, Leslie E., 252, 564, **743–744,**
  1693, 2047, **2375, 2384**
Lindower, Pearl Schrantz, 743
Lindower, Samuel W., 1693
  Nimishillen Old German Baptist
    Brethren Church, OH, minister in,
    937–938
  Rome Old German Baptist Brethren
    Church, OH, minister, 1121
Lindsay, CA
  Japanese-Americans relocation from,
    2068

Lindsay Church of the Brethren, CA, 244,
  744
Lindsay, Maude Lowry, 744
Lindsay, Pauline Anna Miller, 744, 1279
Lindsay, Rebecca (later Shank), *See* Shank,
  Rebecca Lindsay
Lindsay, Robert B., 744
Lindsay, Samuel David, 494, **744,** 1279,
  1693, **2375, 2384**
Lindsell, Harold, 487
Lindsey, Elizabeth (later Jacobs), 667
Lindsey, Irene, 170
Lindsey, OH, 720
Lindside, WV, Spruce Run Church of the
  Brethren, **744,** 1336
Lindstrom, D. E., 1932
Line, Jacob S.
  Polo, IL, Church of the Brethren, 1045
line out
  Holsinger, Daniel Mack, 621
  hymnals, 642
Line schoolhouse, KS, 1304
Lineback, Donald J., 1999
lined by a songleader (*Vorsänger*), 148
lined hymns
  singing, 1185
Lines, Jack, 1999
Lineville Creek, VA, congregation
  Ritchey (Ritchie) family, 1110
Linford, Enid
  Ripon, CA, Grace Brethren Church,
    1110
Linford, Perc
  Ripon, CA, Grace Brethren Church,
    1110
Ling family, 384
Lingehell, Anna Sabina E. von
  Hochmann von Hochenau, Ernst
    Christoph, 614
Lingenfelter family, 461, 731
Lingenfelter, Galen, 227
Lingenfelter, Galen M., 443, 503, 578, 1693
Lingenfelter, Homer, 462, 1693
Lingenfelter, Mathias, 1693
Lingenfelter, Rodney, 2285
Lingenfelter, Sherwood G., 1693
lining of hymns, **744**
Lininger, Lewis Lloyd, 1693
  Okeechobee, FL, Grace Brethren
    Church, pastor, 963
Lininger, Milton Charles, 65, 520, 1693
Link, Donald M.
  on Wine, Daniel and descendants, 2343
Link, Donald Norman, 733, 1840
Link, James D., 2138
Link, Nancy Moore, 733, 1840
Linkenhofer, Lydia (later Spitler), 1212
Linn Co., IA, 406, 661
  Robins, IA, Church of the Brethren,
    1115
Linn Co., OR
  Brethren settlement, 980
  migration of Brethren, 830
Linn Co., Oregon Territory, 734
Linn, Jo White, 1999
Linscheid, Katherine A. (later Weaver)
  Weaver, Clyde E. (CB) and, 2260
Lint, Catherine Flickinger, 744
Lint, Conrad Gillian, 273, **744,** *745,* 1693
  hymns, 643
  Hyndman, PA, Church of the Brethren,
    643
  Meyersdale, PA, Church of the

Brethren, elder, 822
Lint, Elizabeth Hochstetler, 744
Lint family, 1359
Lint, Gillian C., 744
Lint, Lydia (later Shumaker), *See* Shumaker, Lydia Lint
Lint, Mary (later Miller), 1216
Lint, Solomon, 531
Linthicum Heights, MD, Friendship Church of the Brethren, **745**
Linton, James Dale, 1693
Linville Creek Church of the Brethren, VA, 129, 211, 265, 350, 351, *745,* **745–746,** 766, 1265, 1279, 1291, 1295, 1318, 1391, 1397, 1398, 1399
   Cedar Run, VA, Church of the Brethren, preaching point for, 265, **265**
   Crab Run, WV, Church of the Brethren, mission point of, 350
   Fairview-Endless Caverns Church of the Brethren, VA, 470
   Flat Rock Church of the Brethren, VA, 493
   Germantown Old German Baptist Brethren Church, VA, 544
   Greenmount Church of the Brethren, VA, 571
   Hays, Daniel, 590
   Hays, D[aniel] on, 2354
   Mathias, WV, Church of the Brethren, 803
   Mount Olivet Church of the Brethren, VA, 886
   Mount View Church of the Brethren, WV, 887
   Mountain Grove Church of the Brethren, VA, 89
   North Mill Creek Church of the Brethren, WV, 949
   Sanger, S[amuel] F. on, 2354
   South Fork Church of the Brethren, WV, 1205
Linville Creek Congregation, WV
   Allegheny, WV, Church of the Brethren (Durbin, Pocahontas Co.), 2125
   Hevener Church of the Brethren, WV, 602
   historic sites, 609
Linville Creek, VA, 165, 699–700, 701
   Lower Lost River Valley as mission territory, 926–927
Linwood, MD, Brethren Church, **746**
   Riddle, Earl M., pastor, 1108
Linz, Austria, 200, **746**
   Brethren Haus, Linz/Donau, *746*
   medical projects, 809
Lion, Floyd, 1693
Lionberger, Nancy (later Huffman), 617
Lippincott, Joseph W., 1999
Lippy, Charles H.
   works by, 2309
Lipscomb, Dennis, 1693
Lipscomb, Kreston R., 1693
Lipscomb, William C., 2303
liquor, *See* alcohol; brewing and distilling
   Bowman, David, and Prairie View Church of the Brethren, MO, 1050
   mass media concerns, 801
   opposition to, and murder of Joseph Easter, 1135
Lischy, Jacob, 370

Lish, John, 1693
Liskey, A. Q., 586
Liskey, Perry B., 257, 1693, 2303
   Mount Wilson Church of the Brethren, PA, 887
   Shamokin, PA, Church of the Brethren, 1171
Liskey, Veda Celestine, 183, 1855
Liskey, Wilbur Isaac, 1394, 1693
   Raisin City, CA, Church of the Brethren, pastor, 1083
Lissner, James, 1338
List, Paul Henry, 1693, 1999
Listen
   Kulp, Harold Stover, 709
Lister, Dan, 145
Listie, PA, Grace Brethren Church, **746**
   Jenners, PA, Grace Brethren Church, 670
   Reading Grace Brethren Church, PA, 1084
Liston, Lloyd, 1693
lists, *See under* specific subjects, and in volume 3
Litchfield, IL, congregation
   Macoupin Creek Church of the Brethren, IL, mission point, 779
literacy, *See* education
   mass media, uses of, 2218
   mission schools, 853, 854
literal interpretation of Bible
   State of Israel, 990–991
Literary Activity of the German Baptist Brethren (Flory), 300
literary societies, 398, **746**
   debates, 371
lyceums, 768
literature, **747–748, 2375,** *See also* devotional literature; fiction; tracts
   Bible Helps, 136
   Blough, Elizabeth Delp Rosenberger, 150
   Blough, Jacob M., 150
   Brethren Book and Pamphlet Commission, 1269
   Brethren characters in, 1999
   Brethren's Book and Tract Committee, 1268, 1269
   children's, *See* children's literature
   confiscation of, 156
   The Divorce of Russell Hershey (Lehman), 1997
   eighteenth century, 1938
   "Fianna, The Dunkard" (Meade), 2009
   Germans in America, 1986
   Gujarati Bible, revision of, 150
   Henry, Jerry Maurice, 598
   News and Views from Speak for the Lord, 934
   nineteenth century, 1938
   novels, 747–748
   novels about plain people, 2001
   Pennsylvania Dutch in fiction, 2007
   Pennsylvania German, 2046
   Pennsylvania Germans, of, 2007
   plays, 748
   poems, 747
   Radical Pietism, 149
   short stories, 747
   Sunday school, 1236–1237, 1276
      Newcomer, Mauld Odessa and Brethren Publishing House, 933
   tracts, 1269

   twentieth century, 1938
   World War I peace literature, 1370
literature ministries
   Maconaghy, Dorothy Helen Lewis and Hill, 779
Litfin, Galen, 1693
   Newberg, OR, Dunkard Brethren Congregation, as minister, 933
Litfin, Lillian Deshnod, 1268
litigation, *See* law; lawsuits
   definition of doctrine and noncreedalism, 943
   Falling Spring Old German Baptist Brethren Church, PA, 471
   Fellowship of Grace Brethren Churches (FGBC), 485
   Meyersdale, PA, Main Street Brethren Church, 823
   Peru, IN, Brethren Churches, 1010
   sanctification, 1142
"Lititz and Ephrata in 1852," 1999
Lititz congregation, PA
   Gibbel, Florence Baker, 547
   Gibbel, Henry Royer, 547
Lititz Moravian Settlement
   Robinson, Yvonne on, 2352
Lititz, PA, 158
   Netzley, Jacob, 913
   Church of the Brethren, **748**
      Middle Creek Church of the Brethren, PA, 825
      Sawa, Bitrus Pilasar (CB) and, 2246
   Dunkard Brethren Church, 280, 465, **749**
   Grace Brethren congregations, 1005
   Grace Brethren Church, **749**
Littell, Franklin H., 114, 1921, 1999
   "Thoughts on the Church, for Brethren," 1999
Litten, John P., 1315, 1693, 2303
The Little Brother Magazine, **749,** 1999
Little Brown Church, CA, 1321
Little Brown Church, IN
   Peru, IN, First Brethren Church, 1010
Little Brush Church of the Brethren, MO, *See* Poplar Bluff, MO, Church of the Brethren
Little Brushy, MO, congregation
   Poplar Bluff, MO, Church of the Brethren, 1046
Little Capon congregation, WV (CB), *See* Capon Chapel Church of the Brethren, WV
Little Conestoga, PA, congregation, 685, 686
Little Conewago Church of the Brethren, PA, *See* Black Rock Church of the Brethren, PA
   Müller (Miller) family, 895
Little Conewago (Digges' Choice), PA, 733
Little Conewago, PA, congregation, 145, 352, 361, 1233, 1285, 1350
   Hendricks (Henricks) family, 597
   Hoff (Huff) family, 617
   Peters family, 1012
   Petri family, 1013
   Rowland, Gasper, minister, 1126
Little Country Chapel, Myersville, MD, 69
Little, David L., 1693
Little, Douglas, 2285
"Little Dunker Church," *See* Mumma meetinghouse ("Little Dunker Church,"

Antietam, MD)
Little family, 360
Little Flower Garden (Tersteegen), 1051
Little Garden of Paradise (Arndt), 1051, 1052
Little, J. E.
    "Dunkers," 1999
Little, John, 1693
Little Leatherwood, KY, preaching point, 405
The Little Man (Davis family), 748
Little Pine Church of the Brethren, IN, **749**
    Goshen, IN, West Goshen Church of the Brethren, 558
Little Pine Church of the Brethren, NC, **749**
Little River Church of the Brethren, VA, **749**
    Elk Run Church of the Brethren, VA, 439
Little Rock, AR, 54, 320
    Heifer Project International, 594
Little Round Top Church on the Eastern Shore
    Fairview Church of the Brethren, MD, 469
Little Round Top meetinghouse, MD, 416
Little Saint Joe, IN, Church of the Brethren, 96, **749–750**, 1135
Little Swatara Church of the Brethren, PA, 68, 93, 142, 383, 699, 700, 725, 737, **750**, 1278, 1397
    Markey family, 793
    Mohrsville Church of the Brethren, PA, 869
    Mount Zion Road Church of the Brethren, PA, 888
    twenty-fifth anniversary of, 2343
Little Traverse Church of the Brethren, MI, 317, **750**
The Little Visitor, 296
Little Walnut Church of the Brethren, IN, **750**
    Ladoga, IN, Church of the Brethren, 717
Little Washington Congregational Church, Mansfield, OH
    Kerner, William Hoff, Sr., 2211
Littleton, Virgil, 1693
Littletown, PA
    Ryerson Station Church of the Brethren, PA, meetinghouse site, 1132
Littman, Elsa Carter, 2285
Litton, Francis P., 1693
liturgy, *See* worship; worship, public
    bibliography, 1905
liturgy, rejection of, 1373, 1375
Litwiller, Veronica (later Gingerich), 1949
Live Oak, CA, Church of the Brethren, 323, **750**
Live Oak, TX, Church of the Brethren, *See* Weatherford, TX, Live Oak Church of the Brethren
Livengood, Abraham, 750
Livengood, Abraham, family
    Milledgeville, IL, Brethren Church, 833
Livengood, Belinda Hauger, 750
Livengood, David, 1693, **2384**
Livengood, Eliza (later Gnagey), *554*
Livengood, Fannie Meyers, 750
Livengood, John Arthur, 750
Livengood, Peter, 1693

Livengood, Samuel L., 438
Livengood, William, 1693
Livengood, Zachariah T., 366, 461, 720, **750**, 1693
    Milledgeville, IL, Brethren Church, pastor, 833
Livermore, Edward St. Loe, 750
Livermore, George, 1999
Livermore, Harriet, 81, **750–751**, 1373, 1915, 1979, 1999, 2000
    Jurisson, Cynthia Ann on, 2339
    Major, Sarah Righter, 783
    sources on, 2318
    Sweet, Leonard I. on, 2360
Livermore, Samuel T., 751, 1999
Lives of the Fathers, 57
Livesay family, 2087
livestock distribution
    Heifer Project, 684, 685
Living Bible, 138
Living Stone, MD, Church of the Brethren, 356, 713, *See also* Cumberland, MD, Living Stone Church of the Brethren
    35 year anniversary, 1999
Living Stone, PA, Church of the Brethren, 2046
Living the Word Sunday school materials, 1236
Livingood, Christiana (later Fike), 489
Livingston, Harvey R., 445, 1693
Livingston, June, 204
Livingston, William, 204, 1693
Livingstone, E. A., 1912
Livingstone, Fred, 1693
Livingstonia Mission, Zambia
    Kulp, Christina Masterton, 708
Livonia Ministerial Association
    Redford, MI, Trinity Church of the Brethren, 1090
Llano Grande, 1248
Lloyd, Mary (later Puterbaugh), 1072
Lloyd, Nelson M., 747, 1999
Lloyd, Robert H., 343, 1693
"Lo, a Gleam from Yonder Heaven", 643
loans, mission church, 188, 190
Lobach, Abraham, 2025
Lobach, Anna Catrina (later Weck), 1325
Lobach, Johann(es), 324, 545, **751**, 1222, 1254, 1865, 1867, 2009, 2029
    Apocrypha, citation of, 133
    correspondence with Stephan Koch, 704
    letter from Stephan Koch, 1989
    letters to nephew, Johann Weck, 1325
    Marsay, Charles Hector de St. Georges, Marquis de, 796
    medicine, 809
    Netherland visits of, 923
    reference to, 1911
    Smith, Samuel, quote from, 1191
    Solingen Brethren, 1201
    sources on, 2315
Lobach, Peter, 751, 2009
Lobach, Tringen Kohl, 751
Lobban, Zora, 1693
lobbying, **751**
    consciencious objectors, 391
lobbying, church, 1924
Lobwasser, Ambrosius, 700
Lochner, Electa I. Baltzell, 1999
Lochorn, 1693
Locke, Donald, 1693

Locke, Frances Virginia Funkhouser, 751
Locke, John Funk, **751**, 1693, 1999
Locke, Richard, 2034
Locke, Thomas Glenn, 751
Locker, William F., 62, 1693, 2303, **2384**
Lockhart family
    Parkersburg, WV, Grace Brethren Church, 994
Lockman, Miriam McNelly, 1999
Lockport, IN
    Church of God (New Dunkers), 297
Lockwood, MO, 1386
Locussol, Chantal S., 1855
Locust Grove chapel, IN
    organized from Nettle Creek Church of Brethren, 923
Locust Grove Chapel, PA, 136
Locust Grove Church of the Brethren, IN, **752**
Locust Grove Church of the Brethren, MD, **752**
    Monrovia, MD, Bush Creek Church of the Brethren, 870
    sources on, 2323
Locust Grove Church of the Brethren, PA, **752**
    Johnstown, PA, Walnut Grove Church of the Brethren, 675
Locust Grove Church of the Brethren, VA, *See* Free Union Church of the Brethren, VA
    Free Union, VA, Church of the Brethren, 513
Locust Grove, WV, Church of the Brethren, *See* Allegheny Church of the Brethren, WV
Lodge, Martin E., 1999
lodges, *See* secret societies
Lodico, Terry L., 1693
    Medina, OH, Brethren Church, 2219
Loehr, Anna Catherine (later Kurtz), 711, 712, 752
Loehr, Frederick Peter, 124, 711, **752,** 1693–1694, 1999
    imposters among the Brethren, 648
Loehr, Johann Heinrich, 711, 1997
Loehr, Judith Baer, 752
Log Creek, MO, Church of the Brethren, **752,** 1118, 1313
Log Union, *See* Fleming Co., KY, German Baptist Brethren Church
Logan, Chantal S. Locussol, 1855
Logan Co., KY, 177, 1356
Logan Co., OH, 281, 734, 1225, 1341
    Annual Meetings, *962*
    Christian Brethren and, 281
Logan Co., OK
    Guthrie, OK, Church of the Brethren, 576
    Mount Hope Church of the Brethren, OK, 881
    Paradise Prairie Church of the Brethren, 992
Logan family, 324
Logan Grove, NE, congregation
    migration of Brethren, *828*
Logan, Hays K., 1694
Logan, Linda, 1999
    on education of children, Christian, 2343
    "Fruit of the Vine," 2343
Logan, Mark Alexander, 324, 1855, 2285
Logan, OH

Church of the Brethren, *See* Stony Creek Church of the Brethren, OH
Pleasant View Church of the Brethren, OH, 1032
Humberd, Russell I., 636
Mount Zion Brethren Church, *See* Mount Zion Brethren Church, OH
Logansport, IN, 4
Church of God (New Dunkers), 297
Church of the Brethren, 4, 691, **752**
Mexico, IN, Church of the Brethren, 821
meetinghouse
Oak Grove, IN, Church of the Brethren, money from used to build, 955
Loganton, PA, 1235
Loganville, PA, 145
logos, *See* Brethren logos
Logsdon, Jeffrey, 1694
Loh, Philip, 1694
Lohe, Mrs. Jessie, 2000
Loher, Franz von, 1999
Lohman (Lowman), Henry, 121
Lohmann, Martin, 1999–2000
Lohmeyer, Karl, 2000
Lohnes, Maria
Medina, OH, Shepherd's Grace Church, 2219
Lohnes, William E., Jr., 2285
Medina, OH, Shepherd's Grace Church, 2219
Loho, China
missions, 2225
Lohr, Dennis Michael, 2285
Lohr, Samuel R., 1694
Loi, David, Lee-Hoot
Malaysia, missionary work in, 784
Loi, Jennie, 1694
Lol, David (Lot Lee-Iloot), 1694, 1855
Lol, Jenny Mee Al Ha, 1855
Lollic family
Barberton Bible Church, OH, 951
Loman, Jacob, 1694
Lombard, IL, 1388, 1389
York Center Church of the Brethren, *See* York Center, IL, Church of the Brethren
Lonanecker, Benjamin, 756
Lonanecker, Rebecca Wellbaum, 756
London, OH
meetinghouse, 396
Grace Brethren Church, **2215**
London Sunday School Union, 283
Lone Star Church of the Brethren, KS, **753,** 1321
Pleasant Grove Church of the Brethren, KS, 1031
Lone Star, KS, Fairview Brethren Church, **752–753**
Lone Star Church of the Brethren, TN, **753**
Lone Star Old German Baptist Brethren Church, KS, **753**
Lone Star schoolhouse, WV, 2125
Lone Star, TN, congregation, 354
Long, A. W.
Midland, VA, Church of the Brethren, free minister, 827
Long, Adam
family history, 1995
Long, Agnes Young, 2000
Long, Alva

McFarland, CA, Church of the Brethren, pastor, 774
Long, Amos, Jr., 2000
Long, Arthur Whitfield, 1694
Long, Arvil W.
Roaring Spring, PA, Albright Church of the Brethren, pastor, 1114
Long, B. Frank, 1694
Long, Barbara (later Miller), 754
Sanger family, related to, 1144
Long Beach Brethren Manor, 754, **755**
Long Beach, CA, 238, 362
Community Grace Brethren Church, **754**
First Brethren Church, 232, *See also* Long Beach, CA, Grace Brethren Church
missions, 862
First Church of the Brethren, 232, 348, 688, 710, **754,** 1939
Foreign Missionary Society (BC, FGBC), 501
Grace Brethren Church, 23. 97, **754–755,** 1303
Grace Brethren International Missions, 2191
Grace Graduate School and Bible Institute, 563
Menifee, CA, New Hope Community Church of the Valley, 2220
Mission Viejo, CA, Saddleback Valley Grace Brethren Church, 855
missions, 2225
Riverside, CA, Grace Community Church (FGBC) and, 2244
Seal Beach, CA, Grace Brethren Church mission point, 1161
Grace Brethren secondary school, 1163
Los Altos Brethren Church, **755**
North Long Beach Brethren Church (FGBC) (Second Brethren Church), 53, 115, **755**
Long Beach congregation, CA
example of place name, 911
Long, Benjamin, 1694
Long Branch German Baptist Brethren Church, MO, **755**
Long, C. E.
Mill Creek Church of the Brethren, VA, moderator, 832
Long, Caleb, 1694
Long, Catherine, 142, 1327
Long, Catherine (later Lutz), 767
Long, Catherine (later Miller)
Miller, Daniel Long, mother of, 836
Miller, David Alfred, mother of, 836
Long, Charles
Ross Church of the Brethren, OH, minister, 1124
Long, Charles E., 724
Long, Charles Edward, 1694
Long, Christian (1813–95), 170, 724, **753,** 1694
Panther Creek, IA, Church of the Brethren, 992
Long, Christian (1771–1848), 71, 724, 753
Long, Christian, Jr., 71
Long Creek, AR, congregation
Mount Hope Church of the Brethren, AR, 881
Long, Curtis, 318

Long, D. Melvin, 743, 754
Long, D. P., 1694
Long, D. W.
Long, John Daniel, 2215
Long, Dale, 1694
Middlefork Old German Baptist Brethren Church, IN, minister, 826
Long, Dale J., 1694
The Missionary Board (BC), 856
Long, Dan, 2285
Long, Dan L.
Mountain View Old German Baptist Brethren, VA, 2227
Long, Daniel, 1694
Long, Daniel H., 1694
Long, Daniel M., 2000
Long, Daniel Malcolm, 1694
Long, Daniel P., 1694
Long, Daniel W., 1694
Long, David
Long, John Daniel and Inez Goughnour, 2215
Pipe Creek Church of the Brethren, MD, minister, 1026
Long, David (3 listed), 1694
Long, David (1774–1848), 724
Long, David (1820–97), 724, 743, **753,** 754, 1694
Long, David Victor, 1694
Long, David W., 555
Long, Duane C., 2285
Long, E. F., 1694
Long, Effie Virginia Showalter, **753,** 1840
Long, Elias, 162
Long, Eliza Carpenter, 753
Long, Eliza Sanfley, 754
Long, Elizabeth, 161
Long, Elizabeth Baker, 753
Long, Elizabeth (later Snabali), *See* Snabali, Elizabeth Long
Long, Elizabeth (later Snavely), *See* Snavely, Elizabeth Long
Long, Elsie, 352
Long, Emmanuel (2 listed), 1694
Long, Etta Moore
Moore, John Henry, daughter of, 874
Long family, 142, 165, 1318, 1333, 1359, 1391, 2000, 2032, 2060, *See also* Lang family
cemetery inscriptions, 2000
family history, 2000
Garrett, PA, Church of the Brethren, 531
Hiestand (Heistand, Heestand, Heaston) family, 602
history of, 1933
Irricana (First) Church of the Brethren, Alberta, Canada, 663
Meadow Branch Church of the Brethen, TN, 805
Long, Francis Arthur, 1694
Long Friday, *See* Good Friday
Long, Gale, 2000
Long, George, 248, 442, **753–754,** 1263, 1694
Long, George C., 1694
Long, George Ernest, 2000
Long Green Valley Church of the Brethren, MD, **755,** 2042
Meadow Branch Church of the Brethren, MD, 805
Long, Harvey Lawrence, 484, 724, **754,** 2000

Long, Hazel Miller, 754
Long, Henry G., 2000
Long Hope Church of the Brethren, NC, **755–756**
  Flat Rock Church of the Brethren, NC, 493
Long, Howard C., 1694
Long, Huldah, 318
Long, I. S., 229, 692
Long, Inez Goughnour, 555, 765, 2000, 2201, 2343, **2215**
  on Long, John D., sermons of, 2343
Long, Ira Elmer, 505, 1694
Long, Isaac, 1391, 1694
  Madison Church of the Brethren, VA, 781
Long, Isaac (elder; d. 1787), 724
Long, Isaac, family of, 1333
Long, Isaac (father of Isaac, Jr.), 754
Long, Isaac, Jr., 724, 753, **754,** 1694
  Midland, VA, Church of the Brethren, overseer, 827
  Mill Creek Church of the Brethren, VA, elder, 832
Long, Isaac Samuel, 724, **753,** 1694, 1840
  Moody Bible Institute, 873
Long, Isaac (son of Jacob), 724
Long, Isaac (son of John), 724
Long, Isaac, Sr., 1694
  Mill Creek Church of the Brethren, VA, elder, 832
Long, J. Emery, 1333
Long, J. Henry, 1694, 1879, 2000
  "A Study in Compliance in a Complex Normative Organization," 2000
Long, Jacob, 724
  Maquoketa German Baptist Brethren, IA, minister, 791
Long, Jacob (3 listed), 1694
Long, Jacob F., 1694
Long, Jacob, family of, 1333
Long, Jacob M., 1694
Long, James, 1694
Long, Janice Kulp, 2138, 2285
Long, Jennie (later Miller), 1316
Long, Jesse (2 listed), 1694
Long, John, 1694, 2000
Long, John (1693–1767), 724
Long, John (1728–1791), 724
Long, John (1761–1838), 724
Long, John D., 555, 720–721, 1694, 2000, **2215,** 2303
  Long, Inez Goughnour on sermons of, 2343
Long, John L., 109, 1694
Long, John Richard, 2285
Long, Joseph, 704, 1694
Long, Joseph A., **2384**
Long, Joseph A., 255
Long, Joseph A. (2 listed), 1694
Long, Joseph Daniel, 1694–1695
Long, Joseph M., 1695
Long, Joseph R. (2 listed), 1695
Long, Joseph (son of Isaac), 753
Long, Joseph (son of John), 724
Long, Joseph William, 1695
Long, Joshua, 674, 1695
  St. James Brethren Church, MD, pastor, 1134
Long, Kathy (later Missildine)
  Long, John Daniel and Inez Goughnour, 2215
Long, Kenneth Guy, 692, 1695, 2000

"From Among Them," 2000
Long Lake Church of the Brethren, MI, **756**
  Michigan Brethren settlement, 824
Long Lake congregation, 1235
Long, Lucile, 748, 1834, See also Brandt, Lucile Long Strayer
Long, Lucinda Row(e), 753
Long, M. Alva, 1695
  Raisin City, CA, Church of the Brethren, pastor, 1083
Long, Margaret Ann (later Harshbarger), 587
Long, Margaret W., 2000
Long, Mary (later Garber), 529
Long, Mary (later Reavis)
  Shuman, L. Herman (OGBB) and, 2249
Long, Mary Reichard, 753
Long, McClellan, 912
Long Meadow Church of the Brethren, MD, 42
Long, Mollie Cross, 754
Long, Nancy Rowland, 753
Long, Norman Dale, 1695
Long, Omer
  on Fahrney, Peter and descendants, 2330
Long, Orville Valentine, 1695, **2384**
  Roaring Spring, PA, First Church of the Brethren, pastor, 1114
Long, Peter, 447, 724, 1263
Long, Peter (2 listed), 1695
Long, Philip, 1917
Long, Reuben S., 1234, 1348
Long, Richard, 2138
Long, Roy S., 239, 578, 674, 1348, 1695
  Sergeantsville, NJ, Brethren Church, pastor, 1167
Long Run Church of the Brethren, PA, **756**
Long, S. I., 1695
Long, Samuel, 142, 1695
Long, Samuel C., 2000
Long, Samuel D., 1695
Long, Sarah, 565
Long, Simon, 912, 1695
Long, Susannah Harshey, 753
Long, Susannah (later Hartman), 583
Long, Susie Gnagy
  Long, John Daniel, 2215
long-term care facilities
  chaplaincy, 2157–2158
Long, W. H.
  North English, IA, Church of the Brethren, elder, 947
Long, W. Joseph, 1695
Long, W. Newton, *199,* 510, 724, 745, **754,** 2143
Long, Walter Scott, 20, 1283, 1695
  "Our King and His Kingdom," 2000
Long, William, 531
Long, William Gabriel, 2000
Long, William H., 753, 1695
Long, Wilmer, 731
Long, Winnie, 735
Longacre-Longaker-Longenecker Family Reunion Association, 2000
Longanecker, Arlen Elwood, 1695
Longanecker, Daniel, 1695, 2000
Longanecker, Esther (later Eschelmann), 456
Longanecker family, 1229, 1916, 2089
Longanecker, Henry C., 122, 756, 1212, 1250, 1346, 1695

Longanecker, Henry, 1695
  North Star, OH, Church of the Brethren, 950
  Sidney, OH, Trinity Church of the Brethren, minister, 1181
Longanecker house
  Lititz, PA, Dunkard Brethren Congregation, 749
Longanecker, J., 2000
Longanecker, J. H., 1948
Longanecker, Joe, 264
Longanecker, Joseph, 262, 756, 1695
Longanecker-Longaker-Longacre family family history, 2000
Longanecker, Maria (later Gibbel), 547
Longanecker, Martha (later Garver), 532
Longanecker, Noah, 719, 756, 1695
Longanecker, Paul, 1323, 1695
Longanecker, Ralph W., 1695
Longanecker, Ulrich, Jr., 1979
Longenecker, Bertha, 1695
Longenecker, C. D., 411
Longenecker, Carl Melvin, 1695
Longenecker, Christian, 482, 1340, 1401, 1695, 2001, 2375
  Conestoga, performing baptisms at, 1177
Longenecker, Christian L., **756,** 1695
  publishing works of, 1067
Longenecker, Christian (son of John), 756
Longenecker, Daniel, 1695, 1995, 2375
Longenecker, Daniel (H.), 1695
Longenecker, David, 756
Longenecker, David L., 2285
Longenecker, Elizabeth (later Horst), *See* Horst family
Longenecker family, **756,** 2344, **2375**
  Mortonhouse (ship), 2373, 2376
  Royer family related to, 1128
Longenecker, family
  Fraktur artistry, 2186
Longenecker, George, 756
Longenecker, George T., Jr., 2167
Longenecker, Harry, 756
Longenecker, Henry, 348
Longenecker, H(enry) C., 1695
Longenecker House, White Oak Church of the Brethren, PA, 1340
Longenecker, J. H., 1351
  Palmyra, PA, Church of the Brethren, 991
Longenecker, Jacob Hollinger, **756,** 1695
Longenecker, Jason U., 721, 1695
Longenecker, Jerre L., 1695, 2285
Longenecker, John, 756, 2001
Longenecker, Linn B., 1340, 1695
Longenecker, Magdalene Hollinger, 756
Longenecker, Martha (later Garver)
  Garver, Earl Simeon, 2187
Longenecker, Mary Ann Gibble, 756
Longenecker, Mary Moore
  Moore, James Milton, daughter of, 874
Longenecker, Nancy, 61
Longenecker, Paul E., 1383
Longenecker, Paul Samuel, 273, 1695
  Paradise, CA, Church of the Brethren, 992
Longenecker, Peter, 756
Longenecker, Samuel, 670, 673, 676, 1293, 1695–1696
Longenecker, Samuel W., 1696, 2303
Longenecker, Solomon, 756
Longenecker, Stephen L., 2001, 2201

on Anabaptists, and community, 2344
on Annabaptists, emotionalism among, 2343
on Brethren, and the end times, 2344
on Brethren in Shenandoah Valley, 2344
on CB, history of Washington office of, 2343
on CB, urbanism and, 2343
on civil rights mediation, 2343
on Dunkers, history of, 2343
Forum for Religious Studies, 2202
on Kline, John, preachings of, 2344
on PA German diversity and tolerance, 2343
on PA German egalitarianism, 2343
on PA German piety and tolerance, 2343
on Pietism among Brethren, 2343
on slavery in Virginia and Shenandoah Valley, 2344
on Smeltzer, Ralph, 2343
works by, 2317
Longenecker, Thomas William, 2285
Longenecker, Ulrich, 1995, 2375
Longenecker, Walter Way, 1696
Longenecker, William Walgemuth, 1696, 2001
Mount Joy, PA, Florin Church of the Brethren, free minister, 882
Mount Wilson Church of the Brethren, PA, part-time pastor, 887
longevity
Shively, Lou Anna River, 2144
Longfellow, J. H., 1696
Longmeadow Church of the Brethren, MD, 104, **756–757**
Rowland, Jonas and Ann Gilbert, 1126
Longmont, CO
The Home Mirror and The Home Mirror and Our Flag, 625
Longnecker, Conrad, 153
Longsdorf, Kenneth D., 2001
Longstreet, Stephen, 2001
Longview, TX, 1255
Grace Brethren Church, **757**
Gingrich, Raymond Eugene, 2190
Longwell, Eric Matthew, 2285
Lonrd, Charles R.
on historic peace churches, and Japanese American internment, 2344
Lontz, Mary Belle, 2001
Loofbourow family, 375
Look to the Light (Emrick), 617
Lookingbill, Carmon E., 488, 1696
Lookingbill, D. A., 1696
Loomis Church of the Brethren, WA, *See* Ellisforde Church of the Brethren, WA
Loomis, Edward, 1696
Mount Zion congregation, New Philadelphia, OH, pastor in, 931
Loomis, Elisha Scott, 2001
Loon Creek Church of the Brethren, IN, **757**
Salamonie Church of the Brethren, IN, organized from, 1136
Loose, Darla, 2001
Loose, Jack Ward Wilson, 2001
Loose, Samuel M., 515, 1696
Pleasant Center Church of the Brethren, OH, minister, 1030

Loper, Carl V., 1696
Lopez, Maclovio, Jr., 1696
Lopez, Meliton Lind, 594
LoPrinzi, Charles, 1696
Lorah, Daniel, 479
Lorah family
Grand River German Baptist Brethren Church, MO, 565
Lorah, Paul, 1696
Loraine, IL, Church of the Brethren, 740, **757**
Loramie Church of the Brethren, OH, **757**
Mohler, Samuel, 868
Sidney, OH, Trinity Church of the Brethren, members transferring to, 1181
Lord, George, 504
Lord, Margaret Alta, 1851
The Lord, Our Righteousness (McCann), 2002
Lord's Acre Plan
Men's Work (CB), 816
Lord's day, *See* sabbatarianism
Lord's Prayer, **757**
Brethren practices regarding, 1051, 1052
preparatory service for communion, 1056
Rosenberger, Mary Sue Helstern on, 2353
use of in anointing, 39
worship and, 2266
The Lord's Prayer, 2017
Lord's Prayer (Miller), 1052
Lord's Supper, 189, 698, **757**, 763–764, 2037, 2048, *See also* communion; feetwashing; love feast; love feasts
as apart of the Schleitheim Confession, 29
Christian Brethren and, 281
Church of God, Anderson, IN, 296
Church of God (New Dunkers), 297
Church of the Brethren, 328
Churches of God (GC), 309
cooking, traditional, 341
Declaration of Principles, 372
Durnbaugh, Donald F. on Believers Church's perspectives on, 2325, 2326
Far Western Brethren, 475
feetwashing, 481
Fellowship of Grace Brethren Churches (FGBC), 486
food at, **757–758**
Frantz, Nadine Pence on, 2332
German Seventh-Day Baptists, 542
Honites, 628
Hutterian Society of Brothers, 640
memorial view of, 1246
"Message of the Brethren Ministry," 818
ordinances, 976, 978–979, *979*
Pleasant Dale Church of the Brethren, IN, debate over, 1030
preaching about, 1053
Rechte und Ordungen, 1086
Reformation, Protestant, and Brethren doctrine, 1092
relevance for faith and worship, 2004
sources on, 2312
Stoffer, Dale R. on, 2359
The Lord's Supper (Gibson), 547

Lordsburg, CA, 694, 714, 715, 732, *See also* La Verne, CA
Brethren Church, 238, *See also* La Verne, CA, Grace Brethren Church
Brethren colonization of southern California, 1145
Church of the Brethren, 348, *See also* La Verne, CA, Church of the Brethren
England, William Ferdinand, 446
weekly publication, 1932
Lordsburg (La Verne) College, 398, 694, *See* La Verne College; La Verne, University of
Chinese immigrants, 278
Crouch, Eugene Morgan, 353
Dickey, J. P., 383
Overholtzer, Samuel A., 986
School Visiting Committees, 1155
Lordship of Christ
Church of the Brethren, 2163
Loree, IN, 1338
Brethren Church, **758**
Lorenz, Henry, *234*
Lorenz, Lloyd, 2285
Lorenz, Orville A., 366, 715, 1696, 2303, **2384**
Lorenz, Peter, 1696
Lorida Brethren Retirement Homes, Inc., 991, *See also* The Palms
Lorida Church of the Brethren, FL, **758**
mission of Sebring, FL, J. H. Moore Memorial Church of the Brethren, 1162
The Palms retirement community, 991
Loroh, Daniel
Maumee Church of the Brethren, OH, minister, 803
Loroh (Lorah), Daniel, 1696
Lorsong, Gernot G., 2344
Lortz, E. C., 1696
Los Alamitos, CA, Rossmoor Grace Brethren Church, **758**, 2134
Los Angeles, CA, 191, 238, 694, 726, 733
Bella Vista Church of the Brethren, **758**
Belvedere Church of the Brethren, *See* Los Angeles, CA, Bella Vista
Calvary Church of the Brethren, *See* Los Angeles, CA, Ladera Church of the Brethren
Central Evangelical Church of the Brethren (Korean)
Church of the Brethren affiliation 1989, **2215**
Church of the Brethren, 994
Community Brethren Church, **758–759**
Compton Avenue Grace Brethren Church, *See* Bellflower, CA, Brethren Church
East Church of the Brethren, *See* Los Angeles, CA, First Church of the Brethren
First Brethren Church, 694, **759**
First Brethren Church (FGBC), 101
First Church of the Brethren, 118, **759**
Hermanos Unidos en Cristo reorganized 1995, **2215**
Imperial Heights Church of the Brethren, **759**
Redondo Beach, CA, South Bay Community Church of the Brethren, 109
Ladera Church of the Brethren, **759**

minorities, ethnic and racial, 850
missions, 860
Panorama City Church of the Brethren, **759**
Second Brethren Church, 694, *See* Bellflower, CA, Brethren Church
South Los Angeles Church of the Brethren, *See* Los Angeles, CA, Ladera Church of the Brethren
Third Brethren Church, *See* Los Angeles, CA, Community Brethren Church (FGBC)
urban ministry
Church of the Brethren, 299
urban mission, 1296–1297
Los Angeles Co., CA, 714, 754, 1275, 1343
Glendale, CA, Church of the Brethren, 552
Glendora, CA, Church of the Brethren, 553
New River Old German Baptist Brethren Church, 931–932, *932*
Pasadena, CA, Church of the Brethren, 994–995, *995*
Pomona, CA, Church of the Brethren, 1045
Redondo Beach, CA, South Bay Community Church of the Brethren, 1090
Los Guaricanos, DR, Fuente de Vida, **2215**
Los Toros, DR, Nuevo Renacer
Church of the Brethren affiliation 1990, **2215–2216**
Loser, Linda D.
Zeigler, Carl Wenger (CB) and, 2269
Losh, Barnett, 1696
Loshbaugh, D. E., 1696
Loshbaugh, O. E., 620, 1696
Loshbaugh, Ralph Edwin, 513, 567, 620, 1696, 2303
The Lost Children of the Alleghenies (McCarthy), 2002
Lost Creek, Breathitt Co., KY (BC mission program), 44
Lost Creek Brethren Church, KY, 187, 405, 689, 708, 724
Drushal Memorial Brethren Church, **759–760**
Haddix, KY, Brethren Church, 577
Riverside Christian Training School, 1111
Rowdy, KY, Brethren Church, 1126
Lost Creek Church of the Brethren, PA, 261, **760**, 1281
Scholten, Marian and Martin, pastors, 1155
sources on, 2314
Lost Creek, OH, Church of the Brethren, 261, 350, 363, 364, 365, 1127, *See also* Casstown, OH, Church of the Brethren
Lost Creek, OH, congregation, 261, 350, 364, 365
Lost Nation, IA
Maquoketa German Baptist Brethren, IA, mission point, 791
Lost River congregation, IN, 740
Lost River (later Old Liberty) congregation, IN
Hostetler, Joseph, 631
Lost River meetinghouse, WV, 1295
Lost River Valley, WV, 1295
Lost River, WV, 694

Lost River, WV, Kimsey Run Brethren Church, *See* Kimsey Run Brethren Church, WV
lost tribes of Israel, *See* British-Israelism; Eshelman, Matthew Mays
lot, casting of, 82, **760**
election of church officers, 434
Moravian Church use of, 876
Lott, Werner, *See* Prisoners of War program
lotteries, *See* gambling
Lotzenhizer, *See* Latzenhiser, Sara
Loucks, Garry Lynn, 1696
Loucks (Louks), William H., 1696
Loucks, Mary (later Weldy)
Weldy, Allen (CB) and, 2261
Loucks, William H., 2303
Louder, Cyril Clifford, 1696
Loudermilk family
Meyer family related by marriage, 822
Loudonville Church of the Brethren, OH, 67, **760**
Loudonville, OH, 1367
Parker, Isaac Dillon, born in, 993
Loudonville, OH, congregation
Rosenberger, Isaac J., minister, 1123
Lough, Glenn D., 2001
Lough, Morris L., 1346, 1696
Loughlin, James R.
Plum Creek Old German Baptist Brethren Church, KS, elder, 1038
Louis, Count Charles, *See* Ludwig, Count Karl
Louis, Jeanne Henriette
on peace churches, 2344
Louis, William, 1696
Louisa Co., VA, 1274
Louisa meetinghouse
Lena, IL, Church of the Brethren, 737
Louisa, VA, 1305, 1308
Dunkard Brethren congregation, 367
Louisiana, 190, **760**
migration of Brethren, 831
S. Plains district, 964
Louisville, KY
peace vigil following 1969 annual conference, 1305
Louisville, OH
Brethren Bible Church, **760**, 7
First Brethren Church, 77, 155, 166, 694, **760–761**, 769
love
Brethren Church doctrine on holy love, 183–184
Brethren Doctrine of Salvation, 1140
Holy Spirit, doctrine of, 624
human nature, doctrine of, 635
humility, 636
Mack, Alexander, Jr., 774
nonresistance, 944
O'Diam, Eva on, 2349
Reba Place Fellowship, 1084
redemption, 1090
Schwarzenau Brethren sectarian practices, 1079
theology of, **761**
Love-Feast of the Manheim Dunkers (Stephens), *299*
love feast, 15, 396, 698, *761, 762, 762–763,* **762–765**, 2000, 2001, 2047, **2375,** *See also* communion; Lord's Supper
accomodations for, 48, 51
Annual Meetings at Pentecost, 1008

Antietam area, 1195
avoidance and, 292
Barry Co., MO, Congregation, 334
bibliography, 1871, 1875, 1897
Big Creek Old German Baptist Brethren Church, KS, 142
Big Run Old German Baptist Brethren Church, OH, 142
Big Swatara Church of the Brethren, PA, 142
Black River Church of the Brethren, MI, 144
Black Rock Church of the Brethren, PA, 145
Bowbells Church of the Brethren, ND, 164
Bowman, John A., 169
Brazil, 173
Brethren, 1996
Brethren Church doctrine on, 183
Brethren in Christ doctrine on, 189
Brethren movement, 291
Brethren polity, 1042
Broadwater, MO, Church of the Brethren, 211
camp meetings, 246
Canada, 250
Cerro Gordo, IL, 270
Cheyenne, KS, Church of the Brethren, 274
children at, 2159, 2160
Chippewa Valley, WI, Church of the Brethren, 279
Christian Brethren and, 281
Christliches Hand-Büchlein (Christian Handbook), 288
Christmas, celebration of, 288
Christ's Assembly, 280
church membership, 813
Church of God (New Dunkers), 297
Church of the Brethren, 304
Cimarron River, CO, Old German Baptist Brethren Church, 313
closed to non-Brethren, 763, 764
Clouds Creek, SC, German Baptist Brethren Church, 321
Colorado Springs, CO, Church of the Brethren, 325
communion, 328
communion table, 328
community, 329
Community of the True Inspiration, 330
Conejo, CA, Church of the Brethren, preaching point for, 331
Conestoga congregation, PA, 722
cooking, traditional, 341
Cordier, Andrew W., comments about, 765
Crystal, MI, Church of the Brethren, 355
Cumberland Co., IL, Church of the Brethren, 356
Dayton, VA, Dunkard Brethren Congregation, 368
deacons, 369
debates, 371
description of, 1375, 2071
disagreement about in Oregon Territory, 1327
disorderly observers, 729
Duisburg, scrutinized by church authorities in, 407

Dunkard Brethren, 233, 409, 2093, 2100
Dunker, 1991
Dutch Bethel, German Baptist Brethren Church, 2373
early 20th century sermon, 1168
Easter, 416
Ebey home, 399
elders presiding at, 432
Elk City, OK, Church of the Brethren, 438
Ephrata Community, 448
essay on, 1948
Eucharist, 459
Everett, PA, Church of the Brethren, 461
Evergreen, VA, Church of the Brethren, 2372
exclusion from, 75
Fairview Church of the Brethren, KS, 468
Falling Springs, PA, congregation, 1256
Far Western Brethren, 475, 476, 829, 1357
feetwashing, 481
first among Brethren in North America, 108
first in America, 175, 704, 1270
first in Germantown, PA, 704
Flat Creek, KY, Church of the Brethren, *254*
food at, 1210
Frankfort, OH, Church of the Brethren, 506
Gantz (Gans), Georg Balthasar, 528
Genesee Old German Baptist Brethren Church, MI, 540
German Baptist Brethren, and Patton, George, disagreement with, 996
German influence, 2147
Germantown, first love feast, 1270–1271
Germantown Historical Museum, 2189
Germantown, PA, 2079
Germantown, PA, congregation, two-hundred-fiftieth anniversary, 1282
Gettysburg, PA, Marsh Creek Church of the Brethren, 547
Gibson, Daniel B., 547
Gibson, Isham, 548
God's Means of Grace (Yoder), 555
Grace Brethren and creeds, 943
grape juice, 566
Great Swamp Church of the Brethren, PA, 569
Grenola Church of the Brethren, KS, 572
Gumre (Gomri, Gomorry, Gomry), Anna and Johann, 576
handclasp, 582
Harlan Church of the Brethren, IA, 583
Hart, MI, Dunkard Brethren Congregation, 2196
Hemet Church of the Brethren, CA, 596
Hildebrand, Johannes, 606
history, 762–763, 1983
Hochmann von Hochenau, Ernst Christoph, 615
Höhn, Heinrich, 618
Holtzapfel (Holsapple, Holsopple), Johann Heinrich, 623

holy kiss in, 698–699
Honites, 628
Hopewell, VA, Church of the Brethren, 629
house churches, 632
Hurricane Creek Old German Baptist Brethren Church, IL, 638
Hymnal: A Worship Book, 2205
hymns, 643
illustration by Pyle, Howard, *1374*
imposters among the Brethren, 648
Indian Creek Church of the Brethren, OK, 651
Indian Creek Church of the Brethren, PA, *761*
Indianapolis, IN, Northview Church of the Brethren, 654
Influenza Pandemic, 655
Ivester Church of the Brethren, IA, 665
Johnsville Church of the Brethren, VA, 675
Kampala, Uganda, 2128
Kämpfer, Johannes, attendee at first love feast in Germantown, 682
Keagy, John, organizer of first love feast west of Allegheny Mountains, 685
Kearney, NE, Church of the Brethren early love feasts held in barn, 685
Kedar at Ephrata Community, 686
La Place, IL, Church of the Brethren, 713
La Porte, IN, Church of the Brethren, 713
Labette Church of the Brethren, KS, 716
Lancaster Old German Baptist Brethren Church, PA, 721
length of, 176
Leola, PA, Conestoga Church of the Brethren, 737
letter by William M. Fahnestock, 1934
Limestone Church of the Brethren, TN, 742
Loraine, IL Church of the Brethren, 757
Lord's supper, 189, 757
Lower Conewago Church of the Brethren, PA, 765
Lower Stillwater, OH, congregation, 232, 233
Lower Twin Old German Baptist Brethren Church, OH, 766
Mack, Alexander, Jr., letter on sermons about, 1168
Mack, Alexander, Sr., and New Baptists of Schwarzenau, 776
Mallott, Floyd Ellwood, 784
Mannhardt, Jacob on annual meeting in West Virginia and, 2345
manuals for, 788
Maple Spring Church of the Brethren, PA, 791
Maundy Thursday, 737, 764
Mexico, IN, Church of the Brethren, 821
Meyer Church of the Brethren, 2106
Middlebury, IN, Church of the Brethren, 826
Middletown Valley Church of the Brethren, MD, 826
Midland, VA, Church of the Brethren, 827

Mill Creek Old German Baptist Brethren Church, VA, 833
ministry, 845
missions, 857
Mont Ida, KS, Church of the Brethren, 870
Mount Joy Church of the Brethren, PA, 882
Mud Valley Old German Baptist Brethren Church, IL, 892
Myerstown, PA, Church of the Brethren, 906
Naas, Johannes, holding of, 909
Naperville, IL, Church of the Brethren, 913
Nebraska, 268
New Enterprise, PA, Brethren Church, 927
Ninescah congregation, KS, 1138
at Niswanger, Joseph home, 924
Oak Grove, OH, congregation (OGBB), 350
offerings, 960
Ogan's Creek, IN, Church of the Brethren, 961
Old Brethren Church, 2232
Old Furnace Church of the Brethren, WV, 966
Old German Baptist Brethren, 967, 969, 2233, 2234
Ontario Brethren, 975
"Order of the Brethren," 976
ordinances, 976, *977,* 978, 979
as the origin of Annual Meeting, 33
Owl Creek Old German Baptist Brethren Church, OH, 986
Ozark Church of the Brethren, MI, 986
Peabody Church of the Brethren, KS, 997
Peach Blossom Colored Church of Rising Light (CB), MD, 1003
Peniel, 1003
Pennsylvania Brethren settlement, 1004
Philadelphia, PA, Germantown Church of the Brethren, first held in America, 1016
Pine Creek Church of the Brethren, IL, 1024
Pine Creek Church of the Brethren, IN, 1024
Pine Grove Old German Baptist Brethren Church, FL, 1024–1025
Pine Ridge Dunkard Brethren Congregation, MS and, 2238
Plattsburg Church of the Brethren, MO, 1030
Pleasant Grove house, PA, 214
Pleasant Ridge Dunkard Brethren Congregation, OH, 1034
Pleasant Valley Church of the Brethren, NC, 1035
Pleasant Valley German Baptist Brethren, IA, 1036
Poplar Grove, OH, Church of the Brethren, 1046
Portland, TX, Bayview Church of the Brethren, 1048
Prairie Creek, IN, Church of the Brethren, 1050
prayer, posture in, 1052
Preiß, Johannes Jakob, present at first in America, 1055
preparatory service for communion,

1056

Pricetown Meetinghouse, 1057

Primitivism, 1058

public worship ritual, 1375, 1378

Ramirez, Frank on, 2351

Reedley, CA, Church of the Brethren, 1091

Reformation, Protestant, and Brethren doctrine, 1092

Reistville, PA, Heidelberg Church of the Brethren, 1095

restitution, 1100

Restoration Movement, 1101

Rice Lake, WI, Church of the Brethren, 1107

Richland Church of the Brethren, OH, 1107

Ridge Dunkard Brethren Congregation, WV, 1109

Ritter, Daniel, participating in first in America, 1111

Rocky Ford, CO, Church of the Brethren, 1118

Rome Old German Baptist Brethren Church, OH, 1121

Royer Community Church of the Brethren, KS, 1128

Salem Church of the Brethren, IL, 1137

Salem (Community) Church of the Brethren, 936

scheduling, 764

Schuykill Church of the Brethren, PA, 1157

Schwarzenau Brethren, 1079

Scottville Old German Baptist Brethren Church, MI, 1161

Selma, VA, Church of the Brethren, 1166

Seventh Day Baptists, 321

Shiloh Church of the Brethren, WV, 1177

Shoal Creek Old German Baptist Brethren Church, Newton Co., MO, 1178

Shrewsbury, PA, Dunkard Brethren Congregation, 1180

single mode feetwashing, 1186

Smith Chapel Church of the Brethren, WV, 1191

Social Gospel Movement, 1197

Soldier Creek Church of the Brethren, KS, 1201

Somerset German Baptist Brethren Church, MO, 1202

sources on, 2311

Spring Creek, PA, congregation, irregularities in, 334

Spring Creek, WY, Old German Baptist Brethren Church, 1213

Stayer, Johnathan R. on, 2358

Stillwater Old German BaptistBrethren Church, OH, 1223

Stone Bridge Church of the Brethren, MD, 1224

structure, 762–763

Sugar Creek Church of the Brethren, IN, 1234

Sunfield Church of the Brethren, MI, 1239

Surrey Old German Baptist Brethren Church, ND, 1242

as symbol of commandments, 1260

symbols in, 1246

tents used for, 1254

Texas, 1255

theological basis, 1261

theology of, 293

thesis about, 1938

Tire Hill Church of the Brethren, PA, 1265

tracts about, 1269

Urbana Church of the Brethren, IL, 1298

Walnut Church of the Brethren, IN, 1315

Walnut Grove Church of the Brethren, IL, 1315

Waynesboro, PA, Dunkard Brethren Congregation, 1324

West Branch Church of the Brethren, IL, 1333

West, Edmund Landon, argued that only members attend, 1332

Wetonka, SD, Willow Creek Church of the Brethren, 2379

White Water German Baptist Brethren Church, MO, 1342

Wildcat Territory, IN, 1345

Williams Creek Church of the Brethren, TX, 1346

Wolf River Church of the Brethren, KS, 1356

women, roles in, 1362

Women's Conferences (CB) and, 2265

Worden Church of the Brethren, WI, 1365

World Communion Day, 764

worship and, 2266

Wyeth, N. C., 379

youth and, 2268

youth participation in, 1392, 1394

Love, Isabella (later Leedy), 734

Love, Leonard Francis, 376, 463, 1696

Love, Stephen H., 766, 1696

Lovegrove family
Ozark Grace Brethren Church, MI, 987

Lovegrove, Helen, 725

Lovegrove, Herschel, 725
Ozark Grace Brethren Church, MI, 987

Lovegrove, J. W., 1696
Mound Valley Church of the Brethren, MO, 879

Lovegrove, L. F.
Ozark Church of the Brethren, MI, 986

Lovegrove, Rollin C., 1696
Ozark Church of the Brethren, MI, minister, 986

Lovegrove, W. Paul, 1696
Ozark Grace Brethren Church, MI, pastor, 987

Lovejoy, D. H., 1696

Lovejoy, David S.
on Ephrata Cloister, history of, 2344

Lovelace, Charles, 1342

Lovell family
St. Albany Old German Baptist Brethren Church, WV, 1134

Love's Crowning Jewel (Noffsinger), 747

Lovett, Diana L., 2285

Lovewell, KS, White Rock Church of the Brethren, 742, **765**

Loving Hands Gifts International (CB)
San Marcos, CA, North Country Church of the Brethren and, 2245

Lowdermilk, Donald Lee, 1696, 2001,

2303, **2384**

Lowe, E. Troy, 749, 1696

Lowe family, 1383

Lowe, John William, Jr., 1696, 2001
on Native Americans, and Brethren, 2344

Lowe, Leonard M., 1696, 2001

Lowe, Pamela Brubaker, 2001

Lowell, James, 912

Lowell, KS, congregation, 232

Lowell, MI
Hope Church of the Brethren, MI, 629

Lowell School building, Waterloo, IA, 1322

Lower, Bernice, 687

Lower Brummetts Creek Church of the Brethren, NC, *See* Brummetts Creek Church of the Brethren, NC

Lower Cheat, WV
Elkins, WV, Church of the Brethren, 440

Lower Claar Church of the Brethren, PA, **765**, 1294, 1364

Lower Conewago Church of the Brethren, PA, 141, 704, **765**, 1294, **2375**
Gochenour (Goughnour) family, 555
Hollinger family, 620

Lower Cumberland Church of the Brethren, PA, 19, 135, 157, 255, **765**, 1294
Huntsdale Church of the Brethren, PA, 638
Mechanicsburg, PA, Church of the Brethren, 806
Mount Olivet Church of the Brethren, PA, 886
New Testament Brethren, 932

Lower Deer Creek Church of the Brethren, IN, 77, 375, 463, **766**, 1294

Lower Four Mile Church of the Brethren, IN, **766**

Lower House of Lower Stillwater, OH, congregation, 349, 366

Lower Linville Church of the Brethren, VA, 745, *See also* Linville Creek Church of the Brethren, VA

Lower Lost River Church of the Brethren, WV, **766**
Mount View Church of the Brethren, WV, 887
subsequently New Dale Church of the Brethren, WV, 926–927

Lower Miami, OH, Church of the Brethren, 213, 319, 365, 366, 1281, 1355, 2031, *See also* Dayton, OH, Lower Miami Church of the Brethren
Meyer family, 822

Lower Rhine area
historical writing, 611
Hochmann von Hochenau, Ernst Christoph, 615

Lower Rhine Reformed Church
Dompelaar as term of use, 395

Lower Salford, PA, congregation
cemeteries, 2090
history of, 1960
Preiß (Price) family, 1055

Lower Stillwater, OH, Church of the Brethren, *See* Clayton, OH, Happy Corner Church of the Brethren
Miller, Jacob, organizing, 838
Salem Church of the Brethren organized from, 1138

Lower Stillwater, OH, congregation, 161,

231, 232, 237, 319, *319,* 366, 367, 696, 700, 701, 1223, 1276, 1302, 1306, 1355,
Nead, Peter, service to, 919
Lower Stillwater, OH, Old German Baptist Brethren Church, 1255
Flory, Abraham, 497
Lower Stillwater, PA, congregation, 375
Lower Twin, OH, Church of the Brethren, 1235, 1281, 1295, 1389, *See also* Sugar Hill Church of the Brethren, OH
Garver, Daniel M., 532
Lower Twin Creek congregation, OH
example of descriptive or grammatical place name, 911
Lower Twin Old German Baptist Brethren Church, OH, **766,** 1295
Lower Union Church of the Brethren, VA, *See* Free Union Church of the Brethren, VA
Lower York Co., PA, Dunkard Brethren congregation, *See* Shrewsbury, PA, Dunkard Brethren congregation
Lowery, Dixie, 406
Lowery, James W.
on *Martys' Mirror,* translation of, 2344
Lowery, Margaret, 708, **2216**
Krypton, KY, Brethren Church, 2212
Lowery, Marvin E., 406, 1696
Lowery, Richard H.
"Revelation: Hope for the World in Troubled Times," 2344
Lowman, David, family of, 1332
Lowman, Henry, 1696
Lowman, Jacob, 766, 1696
Lowman, Sylvester L., 241, 490, 553, 1696
Portis, KS, Grace Brethren Church, pastor, 1048
Lowman Valley Church of the Brethren, VA, **766**
Peak Creek Church of the Brethren, NC, 1003
Lowmaster, Charles, 439, 504, 760, 1696
Lowrey (Lowry), William L., 1696
Lowry, Alys Joan, 2285
Lowry, George W(ashington), 1696
Lowry, James L., 2285
Lowry, Maude (later Lindsay), 744
Lowry, Robert, 560
Lowther (ship)
Holsinger (Holtzinger) family, 623
Lehman family, 736
Loy, Leroy
Ridgeway Community Church of the Brethren, PA, moderator, 1109
Loyal Judith (ship)
Emmert family, 444
Weybrecht, Martin, 1338
Loyalists, 176, 177, 2067, 2072, 2074, 2089
American Revolution, 176, 2067, 2072, 2074, 2089
bibliography, 1892, 1898
Brethren involvement during Revolutionary War, American, 1105, 1106
Frederic Tory Plot, 2100
Maryland, 2074
migration of, 2089
Pennsylvania, 2067, 2108
Revolutionary War, and Sauer family, 1146
Virginia, 2105
loyalty, 5

Loysburg, PA, 706, 1323
López, Carmen M. (later Villanueva)
Villa Prades, PR, Iglesia Cristiana Getsemani (CB) and, 2258
Lucas, Anna Margaretha, 766
Lucas, D. R., 2001
Lucas family, 320
Lucas, Henry C., 1696
Lucas, Hester
Olean Church of the Brethren, VA, 973
Lucas, Martin, 334, **766**
Lucas, Mrs. Martin, 334
Lucas, Pauline Wenona, 1853
Lucas, Walter
Olean Church of the Brethren, VA, 973
Lucero, Rubel V., 1248, 1696, **2384**
Lückel, Ulf
on Radical Pietists in biographies of Wittgenstein, 2342
Lückert, W., 2096
Luckett, William T., 759, 1330, 1343, 1696–1697
Lucknow, India
publications, 2109
Lucore, Donald L., 2285
Lucore, Elsie (later Holderread)
Sudan (CB) and, 2253
Ludwig, Mary B. (later Arnold), 56, 58
Ludlow, OH, 1389
Church of the Brethren, 224
Pitsburg, OH, Church of the Brethren, 1026
Ludlow-Painter Creek, OH, congregation, 260
Old German Baptist Brethren, 967
Ludorff, A., 2001
Ludwick, Beatrice M. Hamilton, 1697
Ludwick, Berzy B., 347, 1347, 1364, 1697
Mount Pleasant, PA, Church of the Brethren, 886
Quakertown, PA, First Church of the Brethren, minister, 1075
Ludwick, G. Daniel, 2285
Ludwick, Ronald Elmer, 1697
Shippensburg, PA, Church of the Brethren, pastor in, 1177
Ludwig, Guy Ferguson, 714, 1697
Luebbecke, Friedrich, 2001
Luebke, Frederick C., 2001
Luecker, Erwin L., 2001
Lueckert, W., 2001
Lugenbeel, William, 1697
Luke, George, 1697
Luke (Gospel)
3:3–6, 84
3:16, 86
4:18, 39
7:29–30, 55
7:36–50, 39
12:33, 18
12:49–50, 85
22:22, 56
Lum, Moy Wing, *See* Moy Wing Lum
lumber business, 691
Lumberville meetinghouse (Coventry, PA), 22
Lumberville mission
Oaks, PA, Green Tree Church of the Brethren, 958
Lummis, Adair T.
on clergy women, 2365
Luna, Tony, Jr., 1697
Lunenburg, VA, Brethren Church, **766**

Lunkley, Charles Wesley, 345–346, 913, 1697, 1840
Lunkley, Rozella Mae Welsh, 1840–1841
Luray, VA, Church of the Brethren, **767**
Mount Zion Church of the Brethren, VA, 888
LuRon, Dale, 1247
Lute Valley Church of the Brethren, NE, **767**
Lutes, M. D., 2001–2002
Luther, Heinrich Ehrenfried, **767**
Luther, Martin, 266, *See also* Lutheran Church; reformation, protestant
Bible translations, 138
connection to Sauer, 1946
German translation of the Bible, 120, 1149, *1149*
Reformation, Protestant, 1091
salvation, and Priesthood of All Believers, 1057
Sauer family, relationship with, 2001
seed of, and peace, 998
Spener, Philipp Jakob, compared to, 1209
Lutheran Church, 28, **767,** 2023, 2057, *See also* American Lutheran Church
Augsburg Confession, 1368
Billmeyer, Michael, 736
Brethren movement and, 174, 280
Brethren music, 898
Bucks Co., PA, 2088
Church of the Brethren and, 148
On Earth Peace, 974
Easton, MD, Peach Blossom Church of the Brethren, 416
effect on Brethren, 71
egalitarian community, 293
Ephrata Community, 451
Ephrata Press, 452
episcopal polity, 1042
Ernst, Wilm, 1282
Established Churches, 456
Evangelical Church in Austria, 459
Evangelical Church in Germany, 459
Evangelical Covenant Church, 459
evangelicalism, 2178
excluded from National Council of Churches of Christ (NCCC), 915
Fairview Church of the Brethren, MD, 469
Falckner's Swamp, 470
Felbinger, Jeremias, 482
Fellowship of Reconciliation (USA), 488
Fort Scott, KS, Brethren Church, 503
Fraktur, 505
Francke, August Hermann, 506
Garner family, 531
Geiger, Mary Schwenk, 533
Germany, 241, 545
Gruber, Eberhard Ludwig, 575
Haycock Twp., PA, 2088
Heeter family, 593
higher education, 603
historical writing, 611
Hochmann von Hochenau, Ernst Christoph, 614
Holsinger (Holtzinger) family, 623
Hope, Christian, 628
interdenominational relations, 1183
International Fellowship of Reconciliation, 659
justification, doctrine of, 679

Kipping, Johannes, 697
Kunze, Johann Christoph, 710, 767
Kurtz, Henry, 711
Lutheran-Believers' Church dialogue, 71
migration from, 175
migration of Brethren, 829
Miller, John Peter, 2015
Moravian Church, 875
Muhlenberg, H. M., 767, 1292
Muhlenberg, Henry Melchior, 892
musical instruments, 900
North Dakota, 164
orthodoxy, 156
Peace of Westphalia, 1338
Pfautz family, 1014
Pfautz, Johann (Hans) Michael, 1013
Prague Conferences and, 2239
prisons and established churches, 1058
prophecy, 1062
Radical German Pietism, 1079
Reformation, Protestant, 1091
religious liberty, suppression of, 1098
reports of pastors, references to Brethren and Ephrata, 1956
sanctification and, 1142
Sauer, Johann Christoph, I, and controversies in, 1148
Seebach, Christoph, 1165
Splitter, Wolfgang on PA German, 2357
Stauffer, John N., 1219
Trostle, Michael, 1276
Union Chapel Church of the Brethren, PA, 1287
Wampfler, Hans Peter, 1318
Weiser, Johann Conrad, 1328
Lutheran Church of Christ in Nigeria (LCCN), 296, *See also* Fellowship of Churches of Christ in Nigeria
Lutheran communion
Pietism, 1021
Lutheran hymns, 1184
Lutheran leaders, Brethren children named for, 912
Lutheran Pietism
Francke, August Hermann, 506
Lutheran Theological Seminary
Bomberger, Harold Zug, 2138
Myers, Jacob Tobias, 904
Robinson, Paul Minnich, 1115
Lutheran World Relief, 197, 198, 286
material aid, 802
relief and service efforts, 1097
SERRV International (CB) and, 2247
Vietnam, 1305
Lutheranism
influence on Brethren theology, 1258, 1260
Reformed Church, 1092
Schmalkaldic Wars in Germany, 990
trinity, doctrine of, 1275
Luthi, Jesse L., 1697
Luthy, David
on German Bibles of North America, history of, 2344
on Sauer, C., imprints of, 2344
Lütjeharms, Wilhelm, 2002
Lutz, Abraham H., 767
Lutz, Abram H., 1697
Lutz, Catherine Long, 767
Lutz, Christian, 767
Lutz, D. Leonard, 1697
Lutz, Ezra, *767,* 2002

Lutz family, 740, **767,** 2002, 2108
Lutz, G. H., 1697
Lutz, George, 1697
Lutz, Howard J., 1697
Lutz, Isaac, family
Shannon, IL, Church of the Brethren, 1172
Lutz, Ivan Ray, 1697
Lutz, Jacob, 1697
Lutz, Jacob (1761–1826), 767
Lutz, Jacob (1761–1828), 71
Lutz, Jacob (arrived Philadelphia in 1752), 767
Lutz, Jacob Ludwig and Marie Cather Weidman, 1988
Lutz, John Ezra, 1697
Lutz, Leonard
Salem Church of the Brethren, IA, 1137
Lutz, Lydia Garver, 767
Lutz, Ohman (Orman) H., 1697
Lutz, Pearl (later Yoder), 183, 1385, 1386, 1854
Lutz, Peter, 740, 1054, 1697
Lutz, Ronald Gene, 1697
Lutz-Yountzy family, 2002
Lutzler, Clara (later Heier), 602, *See also* Heier (Hire, Hyre, Hyer) family
Lybrook, Anna Miller
Müller (Miller) family, 894
Lybrook, Baltzer, 766
Moss family, 878
Lybrook, Elizabeth (later Moss), 878
Lybrook family
Four Mile Church of the Brethren, IN, 505
Lybrook, Mary Eikenbery (later Moss), 878
Lybrook Navajo Community, Lybrook, NM, 931
Lybrook Navajo Community Ministry, **768**
minorities, ethnic and racial, 850
mission schools, 853
Native Americans, 2230
Lybrook Navajo Mission
Ikenberry, Ernest Leroy and Olivia Dickens, 646
Lybrook, NM, 768
Lybrook, NM, Tók'ahookaadí Church of the Brethren, **2216,** *2216*
Lybrook, Philip
Müller (Miller) family, 894
lyceums, 371, 398, **768**
Lycoming Co., PA, 147, 2085
Dunker settlement, 2005
Lydia (ship)
Simmons, Nicholas, voyage on, to America, 1182
Wampfler, Hans Peter, family of, 1318
Lydia, MD, Saint James Brethren Church, *See* Saint James Brethren Church, MD
Lydic, Ira Frank, 1697, 2002
Lykens family, 1876
Lyle, Jeanne
on Miller family, 2356
Lyle, WA, 1364
Lynard, Anna, 1234
Lynch, Danny W., 2138, 2285
Lynch, Elijah **768,** 1292, 1697
South Carolina minister, 1204
Lynch, James R., 2002
Lynch, Virginia Dare Boone, 912
Lynchburg, VA, 1254, 1308

Church of the Brethren, 129, **768**
Lynd, James, Sr., 81, 1697
Philadelphia, PA, First Church of the Brethren, minister, 1015
Lyndhurst, OH, Grace Brethren Church, **768**
Macedonia, OH, Western Reserve Grace Brethren Church, 2216
Lyndhurst, VA
National Park Service projects, 917
Lynn, Archibald Lee, 227, 235, 467, 532, 620, 715, **768,** 1697
Chestnut Grove German Baptist Brethren Church, pastor, 956
Roanoke, VA, First Brethren Church, pastor, 1113
Johnstown, PA, First Brethren Church, 673
Lynn, Arthur, 1697
Lynn, Artie Gillespie, 768
Lynn, Cora Lee Secrist, 768
Lynn, Ercell V., 308, 2002
Lynn family
Mission Viejo, CA, Saddleback Valley Grace Brethren Church, 855
Lynn, John, 768
Lynn Rock preaching point
Highland Co. Mission Church of the Brethren, VA, 605
Lynn, Thomas P., 2285
Lyon, ___ Stingly, 769
Lyon Co., KS, 345, 1304
migration of Brethren, 830
Lyon, Fannie Stover, 768, 769
Lyon, Floyd A., 1697
Lyon, France, 505
Lyon, Hiram
Lyon, William Marcellus, 2376
Moscow, ID, Church of the Brethren, 878
Lyon, Lillie M. Ritenour, 769
Lyon, Margaret Cassady
Lyon, William Marcellus, 2376
Lyon, Michael, 769, 1697
Lyon, Otis D., 1697
Lyon, Polly (later Hays), 590
Lyon, Quinter Marcellus, 912, **768,** 1237, 1697, **2375**
Lyon, Ruth Beekley, 768
Lyon, Thoburn C., **768–769,** 1319, 1697, 2002, **2376**
Lyon, Thomas D., 635, 1697
Pike Creek (Chenoa), IL, Church of the Brethren, elder-in-charge, 1023
Lyon, Trudy (later Leigh)
Island Pond, VT, Grace Brethren Church, 2209
Lyon, Violet, 1697
Lyon, W. E., 2002
Lyon, William A., 239, 725
Lyon, William H., 2002
Lyon, William Marcellus, 390, 768, 769, **769,** 1297, 1319, 1697, **2376**
missions, 860
North Georgetown, OH, Brethren Church, pastor, 948
Sergeantsville, NJ, Brethren Church, pastor, 1167
World War I, 1370
Lyon, William P., 1697
Lyons, Edward Eugene, 350, 1697, 2303
Michigan City, IN, Church of the Brethren, pastor, 825

Lyons, KS, 683
Lysell, Carl (Karl), 1697
Lytle, Carl, 1697
Lytle, David, 380, 1697
Lytle, Milton Scott, 2002
Lytle, W. F., 567
Lytle, W. T., 363, 637
Lytle, William T., 363, 637, 758, 1697

M. G. Brumbaugh CPS Unit
    medical projects, 808
Mabe, Clarence, 1697
Mount Airy, NC, First Church of the
    Brethren, supply pastor, 880
Mabel, OR, Church of the Brethren, **771**
Mabton, WA, Grace Brethren Church, **771**
    Grandview, WA, Grace Brethren
        Church, 566
Macapá, Brazil, 172, 173
MacArthur, Harry, 1697
McBride, Donna Kaye (later Elliott), 1836
Maccabees, 3, 120
McCann, Beryl Royce, 1841
McCann, Elizabeth Gibbel, 1841
McCann, Samuel Napoleon, 1841, 2076
McCann, Vivian Evelene Cherry, 1841
Macco, Herman Friedrich, 2002
McConnell, R. M., 2068
McConnick, Janice Marilyn, 1847
McCray, Jack Cameron, 1841
McCray, Lila Elizabeth Wright, 1841
McCutcheon family, 2087
McDairmant, Gracia Anne Kashishian,
    1851
McDairmant, Thomas John, 1851
Macdoel, CA, Church of the Brethren, *See*
    Butte Valley Church of the
        Brethren, CA
Macdonald, Samuel, 189
MacDonald, Susannah (later Eby), 2019
MacDowell, Betty, 2324
McDowell, Edythe Elizabeth Bowman,
    1841
McDowell, Kenneth Eugene, 1841
MacDowell, Marsha, 2324
Mace, David
    marriage counseling, 796
    marriage enrichment, 796
Mace, Vera
    marriage enrichment, 796
Macedon, OH
    Ross Church of the Brethren, OH, mis-
        sion point of, 1124
Macedonia, OH, Western Reserve Grace
    Brethren Church, **2216**
Macey, Louis, 1699
McFadden, Joyce Snyder, 1841
McFadden, Wilbur Dean, 1841
MacFarland, W. G., 2003
McGaffe, Ermal T., 1834
Machiavelli, Alexander [pseud.], 2003
    "Louisville: More Exciting Than
        Planned!", 2003
Machunga, A. W., 484
MacInturf, Jacob Arthur, 1699–1700
Mack, Agnes Gantz, 778
Mack, Alexander, Jr., 31, 43, 58, 98, 159,
    175, 176, 204, 262, 273, 324, 477,
    481, 491, 562, 580, 692, 697, 725,
    736, **774–775**, 996, 1397, 1700,
    2004
    Alexander Mack's Bible, inheriting,
        777

Apologia or Scriptural Vindication,
    290
baptism of Benjamin Lehman, 736
baptisms by, 692
    Kolb, Elizabeth, 706
close friend of Weber, Philipp, 1325
correspondance with Jacob Stutzman,
    1233
daughter of, in mixed marriage, 865
deaths noted
    Kipping, Johanna and Johannes,
        697
    Knepper, Wilhelm and Veronica
        Bloom, 703
    Landes, Johannes, 722
deaths of Lucas Fetter and wife noted
    by, 1304
discipline, ordinance of, 370, 381, 387
An Exercise for Youth, 283
feetwashing, 763
friend of Urner, Martin, 1298
Häcker (Höcker), Wilhelm, 577
Heckman, Samuel Brumbaugh, 593
historical writing, 611
Höcker, Heinrich, 615
Holsinger, Henry Ritz, 621
Holtzapfel (Holsapple, Holsopple),
    Johann Heinrich, 623
Huizinga (Huisinga), Jacob Dircks, 635
hymns, 642
interpretation of the Bible, 134
Kalcklöser, Johann Heinrich, death of,
    681
Kämpfer, Johannes, death of, 682
Keyser, Peter, as successor of, 691
Kunze, Johann Christoph, disagreement
    with, 710
love feast, 763
Mack, Alexander, Sr., 776
Mack, Anna Margaretha Kling, 778
Mack, Elizabeth Neiß (Nice), 778
Mack family immigrating to America,
    778
Manahaim colony, VA, 1307
Martin family members on list of
    deaths, 797
Mehrning, Jacob, 811
ministry, 844
missions, 857
naturalization of Stephen Ulrick report-
    ed to, 1285
oaths, on taking of, 2126
Petersen, Barthold Jurgen, 1012
Philadelphia, PA, Germantown Church
    of the Brethren, elder, 1016
poetry and hymns, 1039
poetry of, thesis on, 1961
Preiß (Price), Johannes (1751–1829),
    performed baptism of, 1055
publishing, 1063
publishing works of, 1067
references to, 1921
relationship with Daniel Leatherman
    (Letterman), 732
Rhode Island, visiting, 1107
Sauer, Christopher, II, friendship with,
    1145–1146
Scharpnack,Heinrich, family, related to,
    1152
Schlingluff, Heinrich, and wife, deaths
    of, 1153
Schreiber, Georg, death of, 1156
sermons, letter on, 1167–1168

theology of love, 761
"Theophilus" as writer for *The Gospel
    Visitor,* 258
Traut, Johann Henrich, 1270
widows, care for, 1344
Wissahickon Creek, 704
Wo bleiben meine Sinnen (poem), 700
writing on spiritual life, 1209
Mack, Alexander, Sr., 5, 9, 30, 82, 108,
    147, 174, 175, 184, 204, 242, 309,
    323, 324, 407, 421, 432, 481, 485,
    490, 589, 697, **775–777**, 1700,
    1866, 1895, 1899, 1900, 1936,
    2003–2004, 2026, 2040, **2373**
Allen, immigration on, 2126
Apocrypha, citation of, 133
article about, 1928
Aufrichtiges Mitglied (Artless
    Member=Alexander Mack, Sr.) in
    Grundforschende Fragen (*Basic
    Questions,* 1713, E. L. Gruber),
    575
on authority for the Church, 73
baptizer of chosen by lot, 760
Basic Questions (*Grundforschende
    Fragen*), 2374
Bible
    importance of, 131–132
    interpretation of, 134
    Luther translation, use of, 138
biography of, 1938, 2070, 2100
Brethren migration, 827
Brethren music, 898
Brethren organizer, **775–777**
on celibacy, 266
on Christology, 289, 290
church discipline, 2006
on church doctrine, 291
on church-state relations, 309
coffin for, construction of, 323
on continence and sexual relations, 338
debates, 370
descendants of, 32, 61
devotional literature, 381
Diehl family, 383
divorce issues, 393
emigration, Brethren, 443
Erb, Christian, 453
eschatology, 454
evangelism, 460
Falckner's Swamp, 470
Falkenstein, George Ness, 471
family, 472–474
Felbinger, Jeremias, 482
Geistreiches Gesang-Buch (*Spiritual
    Songbook*), 534
Grebe (Grebi), Georg, 569
Grund Forschende Fragen (Basic
    Questions), response to, 288, 575
Heaven, 591
Heidelberg, 593
Hildebrand, Maria (later Mack), 606
Himbach, 607
Historic Peace Churches, 607
historic sites, 609
historical society, *See* Alexander Mack
    Historical Society
historiography, 611, 2202
Hochmann von Hochenau, Ernst
    Christoph, 615
Hoffmann, Eva Elizabeth, 617
Holsinger (Holtzinger) family, 623
Holy Spirit, doctrine of, 624

human nature, doctrine of, 635
Hüttental, 639
hymnals, 641
hymns, 642
hymns by, 1933
immigration to Pennsylvania, 697
In Our Own Strength (Eller), 748
influence on theological development, 1260
inner Word and outer Word, 656
Inspirationists, attempt to discredit, account of, 1955
Judaism, 677
Kalcklöser, Johann Heinrich, as successor of, 681
Karl August, appeal of expulsion of baptized by, 683
Kinsley, Bob on, 2341
language, 1976
legalism, 735
life and work, 1983
love feast, 763
Mack, Alexander, Jr., 774
Mack, Anna Margaretha Kling, 777–778
Mack family, 778
Mack family immigrating to America, 778
Mack, Johann Philipp, 778
Mack, Johann Valentin, 778
Mack, Johannes, 778
Marienborn, baptisms performed in, 792, 2010
marriage, 702, 794–795
Meier, Marcus on, 2346
Melton, J. Gordon on, 2346
on Mennonites, 1258
Mennonites, contact with, 815
mentoring, 2221
ministry, 844
mocked by Wohlfahrt (Welfare), Michael, 1355
Mortonhouse (ship), 2376
mysticism, 906
Naas, Johannes, baptism of wife, 909
oaths, taking of, 959
on oathtaking, 309
ordained Urner, Martin, as elder, 1298
ordination, absence of evidence for, 719
peace position in *Grund Forschende Fragen,* 998–999
Pennsylvania settlement, 1004
personal seal, *2142*
Philadelphia, PA, Germantown Church of the Brethren, elder, 1016
Pietism, 375
place-names, Brethren, 1027
poetry and hymns, 1039
poor, caring for the, 1046
position on baptism, 83
prayer, 1051
preaching, 1053
preaching in Switzerland to radical pietists, 1246
primitive church and, 296
printing of early works, 706
public dispute with Georg Grebe, 703
publishing, 1063
publishing works of, 1067
Radical German Pietism, 1079
Rechte und Ordnungen (Rights and Ordinances), 132, 262, 283, 288,

289, 386–387, 1086, 1153
resurrection, 1102
Schneider, Hans on baptism and, 2355
school, *See* Alexander Mack School
Schriesheim, departure from, 1156
separatism and, 1166–1167
sexuality, human, 1170
social action, 1196
social welfare, 1197
Solingen Brethren, 1201
on spiritual life, metaphor of suffering pilgrim, 1209
stewardship, 1222
on "suffering community," 292
Surhuisterveen, settled in, 1241
theology of love, 761
thesis on, 1944
tradition, devaluation of, 133
translation of treatises by, 1920
travel to America with Schneider brothers, 1154
universalism, 1292
Universalism and sin, 1080
Willoughby, William G. on, 2363
Wissahickon hermits at funeral of, 1200
work published by Henry Kurtz, 712
works righteousness, 1368
writings of, 2344
writings of, and Sauer press, 1149
wrtings, 77, 120
Zeugnisse der Wahrheit (*Testimonies of Truth*), 1395
Mack, Anna (later Fox)
Mack family, 778
Mack, Anna Margaretha Kling, 174, 702, **777–778**
Mack, Alexander, Sr., 775
Mack, Johann Valentin, 778
Mack, Johannes, 778
Mack, Johannes, daughter of, 778
Mack, Anna Margarethe Südere
Mack, Alexander, Sr., daughter-in-law, 777
Mack, Johannes, 778
Mack, Christina, 776, 778
Mack, Christina Fillbrun, 775
Mack Creek, VA, 1027
Mack, Ebert, 778
Mack, Elizabeth, 606, 778
Mack, Elizabeth (later Holsinger), 621
Mack, Elizabeth Neiß (Nice), 774, **778**
Mack family, 159, 411, **778**, 1920, 2078, 2100
Mack, Hannah, 387
Mack, Hannah Englehart, 778
Mack, Hannah (later Weaver), 778, 1325
Mack, Hieronymus, 778
Mack, Jacob, 348, 469
Mack, Jacob (2 listed), 1700
Mack, Johann Georg, 778
Mack, Johann Philipp
Mack, Alexander, Sr., 775
Mack, Alexander, Sr., father of, **778**
Mack family, 778
Mack, Johann Valentin, 606, **778**, 1014, 2004
Mack, Alexander, Jr., 774
Mack, Alexander, Sr., 775, 777
Mack, Anna Margaretha Kling, 778
Mack family immigrating to America, 778
poetry and hymns, 1039

Schönes Lied, Ein, 1155
Mack, Johannes, **778**
Mack, Alexander, Jr., 774
Mack, Alexander, Sr., 775, 777
Mack, Anna Margaretha Kling, 778
Mack family immigrating to America, 778
Mack, Johann Valentin, 778
Mack, John
Mack family, 778
warning about Bermudian Seventh Day Baptist Brethren, 141
Mack, Lydia (later Holsinger), 623
Mack, Lydia (later Kolb, Lentz), 706, 725, 778
Mack, Magdalena (later Stetius), 1222
Mack, Margaretha, 606
Mack, Maria (later Hildebrand), *See* Hildebrand, Maria Mack
Mack, Mary (later Deffenbaugh), 553
Mack Memorial, OH, Church of the Brethren, 81, 102, 367, 1011, 2215, 2216
Mack, Phillipine, 778
Mack, Polly (later Holsinger), 623
Mack Religious Bookstore, 161, 673
Mack, Sara Neiß (later Scharpnack), 1152
Mack, Sarah (later Zeigler), 778, 1397
Mack seal, 774, 775, *2142,* **2142–2143,** 2146
Mack University, 500, **779,** 1939
Mack, Valentin Johann, 381
Mack, Valentine, 1942
Mack, William, 623, 778, 1027
Mackall, W. S., 1700
McKay, Charlotte Jane Swadley, 1841
Mackay, Dorothy (later Quynn), 2041
McKay, Robert Hicks, 1841
Mackey, John Crawford, 255, 332, 438, 578, **779,** 1289, 1324, 1700
India, 651
Meyersdale, PA, Main Street Brethren Church, pastor, 823
The Missionary Board (BC), 855
Morrill, KS, (First) Brethren Church, pastor, 876
Mackeysville (Hambleton, WV) meetinghouse
Eglon, WV, Church of the Brethren, 430
Mackinac Co., MI, Ozark Church of the Brethren, 986
Mackinet, Blasius Daniel, 1923
Macklin, Mrs. Charles F., 1920
Mack's Meadows, VA, 1027, *See also* Max Meadows
Mack's Mountain, VA, 1027
MacLee family, 1203
MacManes, Mary L., 1836, 1841
MacMaster, Richard K., 2005
on Brethren movement, 2345
on Elizabethtown CB, 2345
on Elizabethtown College, 2345
on Mennonite sect, 2345
MacMillan, David, and The Rockingham Male Chorus, 2205
MacMillan, Robert, Jr., 1303, 2285
Macomb, OK, New Hope Church of the Brethren, 929
Macon Co., IL, 270, 713, 1949
Milmine Church of the Brethren, IL, 843
Oakley Brick Church of the Brethren,

IL, 958
Mâcon, France, 505–506
Maconaghy, Dorothy Helen Lewis, 53, **779**, 1851, **779**
Maconaghy, Hill, 53, **779**, 1700, 1851, 2303, **2384,**
Macoupin Co., IL, 353, 1234, 1302, 1307
  Girard, IL, Church of the Brethren, 550
  Pleasant Hill Church of the Brethren, IL, 1032
  Pleasant Hill Old German Baptist Brethren Church, IL, 1033
  Snell family, 1193
Macoupin Creek Church of the Brethren, IL
    Montgomery Co., IL, 732, **779,** 1234,
MacPeck, Frederick, 1700
MacPherson, Beryl, 2005
Macy, Lewis, 1700
The Mad Morality (Eller), 2176
Madani, Galadima B., 1700
Madden family
  Fremont, OH, Grace Brethren Chapel, 515
Madden View, ID, Church of the Brethren, 170, *See also* Bowmont, ID, Church of the Brethren
Maddocks, Daniel Brumbaugh, 1700
Maddocks, Thomas Barnabas, 1700
Maddox, Rich, 1380
Madeira, Charles Calvin, 1700
Mader, Julie (later Hostetter), 2282
Madera Co., CA, 280
Maderia, Ronald Franklin, 1700
Madiera, Ronald
  Roaring Spring, PA, First Church of the Brethren, interim pastor, 1114
Madison Avenue Church of the Brethren, York, PA, *See* York, PA, Madison Avenue Church of the Brethren
Madison Church of the Brethren, VA
    Madison Co., VA, **781,** 1299
Madison Co., IA
  New Virginia, IA, Brethren Church, 932
  Osceola, IA, Church of the Brethren, 983
Madison Co., IN, 297
  Church of God (New Dunkers), 297
Madison Co., OH, 396
Madison Heights, MI, Bethany Church of the Brethren, *See* Detroit, MI, Bethany Church of the Brethren
Madison, James, 88
Madison, Kenneth J., 2285
Madison, KS, 1304
Madoski, Robert J., 1701
Madziga, Risku, 2005
Maes, Virginia Ingles (later Haradon), 1957
Maester, Jacobo, 1248, 1701
Magee, D. F., 2005
Magers, Martha, 362
Magers, Thomas, 362
magic lantern shows
  Miller, Daniel Long, 836
Magie, John E., 1701
Magill, Hugh S., 659
"Magnetic Healing," 287
Magnin, Jessie (later Young)
  The Young Center and, 2267
  Young, Galen S. and, 2268
Magnolia, AR
  soil conservation units, 1200

Mahadev (Madhav), Nathalal, 1701
MaHaffey, Thomas H., 1253, 2186, 2285
Mahan, Calvin L., 1701
Mahan, Catherine Miller
  Mahan, Grant, mother of, 781
Mahan, Daniel
  Mahan, Grant, father of, 781
Mahan, Grant, 137, 305, 355, **781–782,** 2005
  The Pilot, 1024
Mahan, Lillus Emma Kepner
Mahan, Grant, wife of, 782
Mahan, Walter Kepner, 571, 1701
Mahanaim, VA
  place-names, Brethren, 1027
Mahaska Co., IA
  Middle Creek Church of the Brethren, IA, 825
Mahatma (Great Soul) (Gandhi, M. K.), 528
Mahijibhai, Manilal, 1701
Mahle, Edward, 1701
Mahle, William
  Mulberry Grove, IL, Church of the Brethren, minister, 893
Mahler family, 1235
Mahler, George, 1701
Mahon, J. Grannum, 1701
  Philadelphia, PA, Calvary Church of the Brethren, pastor, 1015
Mahon, J. L., 1391, 1701, 2126
  Bethel Mahoning congregation, New Middleton, OH, pastor in, 931
Mahoney, Job, 1701
Mahoney, John, 1701
Mahoney (Mahorney), Jacob W., 1701
Mahoning Baptist Association, OH
  Restoration Movement, 1101
Mahoning Co., OH, 171, 711, 782, 1255, 1400
  Church of the Brethren, **782,** 931, 1400
  Quinter, James, elder, 1077
Mai Ada, 2216
Mai Ali Dogo I, 2216
Mai Arziki, 2216
Mai Bosler, 2216
Mai Gamaliya, 2216
Mai Gana, 2216
Mai Gideon, 2216
Mai Lahadi Yatchanum, 2216
Mai Maina Ari, 2216
Mai Ritkatu, 2216
Mai Sara Shisler, 2216
Mai Sule Biu, 307, 1701
  churchman, song writer, **2216,** *2217*
  elder, churchman, *782,* **782–783**
Maiden Creek congregation, PA, 699
  Gaube (Gaby), Martin, 532
Maiden Creek, PA
  Dunkard Brethren Church, 2078
Maiden Creek, PA, Church of the Brethren, *See* Mohrsville Church of the Brethren, PA
Maiden Creek, PA, congregation
  Mohrsville Church of the Brethren, PA, previous name of, 869
  Pricetown Meetinghouse, 1057
  Reading, PA, First Church of the Brethren, 1084
Maidha, Nathalal M., 1701
Mail, Edward, 1701
Mail-order business
  and *New Ideas,* 929

Maili (Mäyle, Meyle, Moyly), Johann (Jan) (Brother Amos), **804**
Main, Albert Leroy, 1701
Main, John Calvin, 106, 912, 1701
Main, Kari M.
  on hymnals of Ephrata Cloister, 2345
Main Mountain
  South Fork Church of the Brethren, WV, preaching point, 1205
  South Mill Creek Church of the Brethren, WV, mission point, 1206
Maina, Silaba, 1701
Maine, **783**
  prohibition, 1251
Mains, J. H., 1701
Maitland, PA
  Church of the Brethren, 81, 232, 406
  Grace Brethren Church, **783**
  Mifflin Co., PA, **783**
  Parkview Church of the Brethren, PA, leadership by Cox, Alvin S., 994
Major, Sarah Righter, 177, 242, 506, 706, 739, 750, *783,* **783–784,** 1334, 1360, 1701, 1922, 2183
  Amwell, NJ, congregation, preaching at, 1049
  Major, Thomas, wife of, 784
  Ohio ministry, 961
  Parker Ford, PA, Church of the Brethren, preaching at, 994
  Philadelphia, PA, First Church of the Brethren, minister, 1015
Major, Thomas, 257, 506, 739, 1701
  Major, Sarah Righter, husband of, 783, 784
  Ohio ministry, 961
  Philadelphia, PA, First Church of the Brethren, minister, 1015
Makakilo, HI, 1312
Makinster family, 265
Makofka, Stephen E., 2285
Malaimare, Evelyn, 1303
Malaimare, Ted, 490, 1303
Malaimare, Theodore, 2303
Malaysia
  evangelism, 182
  Ingraham, M. Virgil, 2208
  The Missionary Board (BC), 856
  missions, 862, 2224, 2225
Maldeis, A. B., 250, 1297, 1701, 1851
  Quebec, 1075
Maldeis, H. B., 1701
Male, E. William, 282, 1701, **2216–2217**
Male, Ella Beth Kauffman
  Male, E. William, 2216
Male, Sandra JoAnn
  Young, Galen S. and, 2268
Malenke, Elizabeth A., 2285
Males, Arthur
  North Buffalo Grace Brethren Church, PA, 945
Malgwi, Mari Y., 1701
Malick, Walker L., 2285
Malimare, Theodore, 1701
Maller, George, 1701
Mallery, L. S., 1701
Malles, Arthur N., 348, 349, 721, 1701
Malles, Larue, 1851
Malles, Mark, 1248, 1701
Malles, Mark Ellsworth, 21, 62, 496, 503, 1221, 1319, **2217,** 2303
  Phoenix, AZ, Grace Brethren Church, pastor, 1019

Mallet family, 2081
Mallet, H., 2005
Mallett, Manley W., 2005
    on MD families, 2345
Mallon, Henry Clemente, 2285
Mallory, Wilson
    Maple Grove Church of the Brethren,
      WI, holding debate at, 791
Mallott, Floyd Ellwood, 2, 153, 190, 242,
    248, 380, 388, 610, **784**, 1701,
    1841, 1892, 2005
    historical writing, 612
    mysticism, 907
    sources on, 2314
    Schwarzenau editor, 1157
Mallott, George
    Mallott, Floyd Ellwood, father of, 784
Mallott, Ira Floyd
    Mallott, Floyd Ellwood, son of, 784
Mallott, John, 1701
Mallott, Nettie
    Mallott, Floyd Ellwood, mother of, 784
Mallott, R. F., 235, 1701
    Milford, IN, Brethren Church, pastor,
      831
Mallott, Riley S., 1701
Mallott, Ruth Blocher, 1841, 2089
    Mallott, Floyd Ellwood, wife of, 784
Mallott, Sylvia Edith Kendall (later Parker),
    993
Mallow, Eldon, 1701
Mallow, Owen, 1701
Mallow, Terrell Wesley, 1701
Mallow, William D., 469, 1701
Malmö congregation, 1243
malnutrition
    medicine, 809
Malone, Sarah Quinter, 2285
Malony, J. L., 1701
Maltzbaugh, John, 31, 1701
Mambula, Jabani, 307, 2005
Mamza, Ibrahim U., 1701
Mamza, Karbam, 307
Mamza, Ngamariju Keliri, 307, 1701
    minister, nurse, church leader, **784**
man, doctrine of, *See* human nature,
    doctrine of
Mana, 31
Manahaim colony, VA, 1307
Manahan, Ronald E.
    Grace Schools, 2192
Manassa union church, 1263
Manassas, VA, 1308
    Church of the Brethren, 150, **784–785**
      bibliography, 1910
      history, 1945, 2005
      Oakton, VA, Church of the
        Brethren, 958
Manatee Co., FL
    Good Shepherd Church of the
      Brethren, FL, 556
Manatí, PR, Pueblo de Dios
    Church of the Brethren affiliation 1990,
      2217
Manchester Academy
    Ross, Amos Walter, 1123
    Shultz, Lawrence W., 1180
Manchester Church of the Brethren, IN
    Eberly, William R. on, 2328
Manchester College, 14, 137, 535, 697, *785,*
    785–786, *786,* 1860
    Aeby, John Milton, 2127
    Bixler, Edward Clinton, 144

Blickenstaff, David Emerson, 146
Blough, Carman George, 149
Blough, Jacob Roy, 150
Blough, Silas S., 149
Bollinger, Amsey Floyd, 158
Bollinger, Russell V., 158
Bookwalter, Levi Asbury, 161
Bosler, Billy M., 2161
Brandt, Lucile Long Strayer, 172
Bright, Jacob Homer, 208
Bright, John Calvin, 209
Bright, Minnie Flory, 209
Brooks, Harlan, 212
Brown, Kenneth L., 179
Brubaker, Ella Miller, 217
Brumbaugh, Grayce, 220
Buckingham, Minnie Susan, 226
Burke, Eldon R., 230
Cable, William Arthur, 237
Cable, William H., 2155
Church of the Brethren, 300
Cook, Mary L., 340
Coppock, Jacob, 343
Cordier, Andrew Wellington, 302, 344
Crouch, Eugene Morgan, 353
Deeter, Manly Huggins, 373
DeLauter, Ora Dale, 374
Dolby, Martha Cunningham, 395
Eberly, John H., 417
Ebey, Adam, 418
Eby, Kermit, 419
Eel River Church of the Brethren, IN,
    ministry to, 430
Eikenberry, Amos R., 431
Eikenberry, Ivan Leon and Mary
    Elizabeth Flora, 431
Fike, Paul Henry, 2184
Fitzwater, Perry Braxton, 492
Flory, Ezra, 498
Flory, Paul John, 499
Flory, Rolland F., 499
Forney, Anna Marie, 502
Frantz, Ira Henry, 508
Funderburg, Drue Dresher, 523
Garber, David Benjamin, 529
Garber, Ora W., 529
Garrett, Marguerite Arthelda Bixler,
    531
Garver, Earl Simeon, 532, 1391, 2187
Geisert, Wayne F., 2187, 2188
Gilbert, Martha Rupel, 2189, 2190
Grisso, Clarence C., 574
Grisso, Lillian Etna, 574
Halladay, Sara Heebner, 580
Hamer, Oliver Stuart, 580
Harper, Clara Belle, 585
Heckert, Mildred Mae Etter, 2197
Heeter family, 593
Helman, Alfred Blair, 2197
Helser, Albert David, 595
Helser, Lola Bechtel, 596
Helstern, Russell Fred, 596
higher education, 605
historical libraries, 610
history of, 1941
Hoff, Emanuel Buechley, 616
Hoff (Huff) family, 617
Hoffman, Paul W., 2202
Holl, Carl Waldo, 619
Holsinger, Levi Teeter, 623
Hoover, William I. T., 628
Howe, David, *1351*
Huffaker, Perry Lee, 635

Ikenberry, Charles Samuel, 646
Ikenberry, Levi Daniel, 646
Indiana, 653
John, John Jay, 671
Keim, Clarence Ray, 686
Keller, Paul W., 2210
Kintner, Edward, 696, 697
Kiracofe, Anna Kathryn, 697
Lichty, Anna Eby, 741
Lichty, Nora S. Arnold, 741
Long, Inez Goughnour, 2215
Mallott, Floyd Ellwood, 784
Markle, IN, Church of the Brethren,
    loan made to, 794
memories of, 2101
Metzger, Thurl D., 2222
Metzler, Burton, 820
Metzler, John D., Sr., 820
Meyer, Jacob Gibble, 821
Miller, Donald Eugene, 2222
Miller, Ella, 217
Miller, Robert Henry, 842
Minnich, Herbert Spenser, 848
Moherman, Tully S., 867
Moomaw, Ira Wilbur, 874
Morris, Charles Stephen, 877
Morris, James Henry, 877
Mount Morris College, 884, 885
Mow, Anna Beahm, 890
Moy Gwong Han, 891
Moyer, Elgin Sylvester, 892
Moyer, Emma Tyson, 158
Muir, Gladdys Esther, 893
Neff, Robert Wilbur, 2230
Neher, Medford D. at, 922
North Manchester, IN, Church of the
    Brethren, 949
Parker, Isaac Dillon, fund raising by,
    993
peace education, 1002
Peace Studies Institute, 1002
Perry, William, 1009
Peters, Woodford W., 1011
Petersime, Ray, trustee, 1012
Petry, Ray C., 1013
Puterbaugh, Amsey Hascall, instructor,
    1072
Reber, Daniel Conrad, educator, 1085
recreation laboratories, 248
relief training units, 1097
Roann, IN, Church of the Brethren,
    students as part-time pastors, 1112
Rohrer, Perry Lawrence, 1119
Ronk, George Teller, 1121
Royer, Byron P., 1127
Rural Life Association (RLA),
    1130–1131
Sanger, Samuel F., trustee of, 1143
School Visiting Committees, 1155
Schrock, Mark Y., 1156
Schwalm, Florence Roselind
    Studebaker, 1157
Schwalm, Vernon Franklin, 1157
Shamberger, Chauncey, 1171
Sherrick, Marvin Manam, 1176
Shisler, Sara Cassel, 1177
Shriver, Ruth Marie, 1180
Shultz, Lawrence W., librarian, 1180
Stahly, Cora Miller as head of music
    department, 1216
Steele, Lafayette, 1220
Stinebaugh, Vernon H., professor, 1207
Studebaker, Ted Allen, 1230

students of as local pastors and speakers, 12, 71
Swartz, Goldie Elizabeth, 1243
Teeter, Lewis Wallace, 1250
theological study conference (1960), 1258
Tully, Robert W., 1278
Ulery, Joseph Edson, 1285
Ulrey, Calvin, 1285
Ulrey, Miriam Buck, 1285
United Brethren in Christ, 1290
Wampler, Elizabeth Baker, 1316
Wampler, Sadie Irene Stutsman, 1317
Warstler, Anna Margaret, 1319
Weiand, Albert Cassel, 1344
Weimer, Glen Emerson, 1327
West, Daniel, 1330
Whisler, William on, 2363
White, Ralph Emerson, 1339
White, Roy Irvin, 1339
Wine, Mary Stoner, 1349
Winger, Ida Miller, 1350
Winger, Otho, 257, 344, 1350–1351, *1351*, 2101
Women's Conferences (CB) and, 2264–2265
Yoder, Charles Francis, 1385
Young, Andrew (J.) on, 2365
Young, Emanuel Sprankle, 1389
Young, Jean Childs, 1367
Zigler, Michael Robert, 1399
Zunkel, Charles Edward, 1402
Zunkel, Cleda Pearl Shull, 1402
Manchester, IN, Church of the Brethren, *See* North Manchester, IN, Church of the Brethren
Manchester, IN, congregation, 354
Manchester, MD
history of, 1934
Manchester, Milt, 738
Manchester Peace Commission, 2017
Manchester, S. D., 2068
mandatory decisions, 33, **786–787, 2376**
Brethren Church, 368
Declaration of Principles, 372
Progressive Brethren, rejection by, 67, 368, 786–787
Mandrillon, Joseph, 2005
Manduka, David William, 1380, 1701, 1851
Manduka, Kathleen Diane Shirley, 1851
Manges, Craig D., 2285
Manges, Edgar Lynn, 1701
Manges, John, 752, 1701
Mangum, Alan, 1701
Philadelphia, PA, Third Brethren Church, pastor, 1019
Mangus, Amy, 150
Manheim House, White Oak Church of the Brethren, PA, 1340
Manheim, PA, 747, 912, 1340
Manheim, PA, Grace Brethren Church, **787**
Manheim Twp., Lancaster Co., PA, 724
Manis family, 246
Manistee Co., MI, 1285
Marilla Church of the Brethren, MI, 793
Onekama, MI, Church of the Brethren, 975
place-names, Brethren, 1028
Manistee, MI, 756
Mankamyer, Raymond, 632, 1701
Mankey, Francis Henry, 1701
Mankey, Henry, 141, 1701
Mann, Margaret E. (later Bomberger), 2138

Mann, Thomas, 747, 1891, 2006
Mann, William J., 2006
Manners, C. May
South Bend, IN, City Church of the Brethren, home missionary, 1203
Mannhardt, Jacob
on love feast at annual meeting in WV, 2345
Mannheim
Erb, Christian, 453
Frankenthal, 506
Hochmann von Hochenau, Ernst Christoph, 615
radical pietist dissension in, 990
Manning, Chuck, 70
Manning, David S., 1285, 1701
Manning, Gerald R., 1701
Mannon, J. Flemming, 1701
Mannon, Noah Samuel, 1701
Manon, George, 619, 1701
Manor Brethren Church, PA, *See* Cherry Hill Brethren Church, PA
Manor church
Emmert family, 444
Manor Church of the Brethren, MD, 41, 42, 104, 119
meetinghouse as field hospital, 810
Reichard, John Rowland, free minister, 1094
Washington Co., MD, **787**
Manor Church of the Brethren, PA, *See* Purchase Line Church of the Brethren, PA
Manor, MD, Church of the Brethren, 398, 2006
Fahrney-Keedy Chapel Fellowship Church of the Brethren, MD, 467
Hagerstown, MD, Church of the Brethren, 578
Sharpsburg, MD, Church of the Brethren, 1174
Manor, MD, congregation, 1359
Manor, PA, congregation, 274
Neuenschwander family in, 924
Penn Run Church of the Brethren, PA, 1004
Purchase Line Church of the Brethren, PA, 1072
Manor schoolhouse, WV, 1254
Manos de Cristo fellowship (CB)
South Bend, IN, Iglesia Evangelica Emanuel (CB) and, 2252
Mansbridge, Robert, 395, 1701
Manschreck, Clyde L., 2006
Mansfield family
Mount Etna, IA, Church of the Brethren, 881
Mansfield, John Morgan, 1701
Morrill Church of the Brethren, MN, 877
Wetonka, SD, Willow Creek Church of the Brethren, 2379
Mansfield, MO, Church of the Brethren, *See* Fairview Church of the Brethren, MO
Mansfield, OH,
Conservative Grace Brethren Church, **2217–2218**
First Brethren Church, *See* Mansfield, OH, Walcrest Brethren Church
First Church of the Brethren, **787**
Richland Church of the Brethren, OH, 1107

Grace Brethren Church, **787**, 2168
Grant, Richard E., 2193
Mount Vernon, OH, Conservative Grace Brethren Church, 2226
Theological Practorium, The (CBBCI) and, 2254
Woodville Grace Brethren Church, 787
Marion Avenue Grace Brethren Church, 739
Walcrest Brethren Church, **787**
Miller, Edward Lewis, pastor, 837
Woodville Grace Brethren Church, **787**
Manteca, CA, Northgate Community Brethren Church, **787–788,** 2208
Manthos, Michael Charles, 2285
Mantis, S., 1701
Mantz, Felix, 28
Mantz, Shelvie J., 2285
manual arts schools
mission schools, 853
Manual of Church Expediency
Progressive Brethren church government, 1044
"Manual of Church Expediency" (BC), *See* "The Manual of Procedure for the Brethren Church"
"A Manual of Church Organization and Administration"
Moomaw, B. C., 873
Manual of Organization and Polity (CB)
manuals, 788, 1043, 1369
Manual of Procedure
Progressive Brethren church government, 1044
Theological Practorium, The (CBBCI) and, 2254
Manual of Procedure for the Brethren Church (BC), 37, 182, **788**
manuals, **788**
General Board (CB), 536
noncreedalism, 942
worship (CB), 300
manumission of slaves, *See* emancipation
manuscript illumination (decoration), *See Fraktur* Manvel, TX, Church of the Brethren, 1213
Brazoria Co., TX, **788–789**
Pleasant Grove, 1031
previous name of, 788–789
Manville, Helen Ronk, 1121
Manzanar Relocation Center
Brethren activity, 789
Smeltzer, Mary Blocher (CB) at, 2250
Smeltzer, Ralph Emerson, 1190
Mao Tse-tung, 278
Maphis, Omer Benjamin, 1215, 1701–1702
Maple Avenue, OH, Church of the Brethren, *See* Canton, OH, Maple Avenue Church of the Brethren
Maple Glen Church of the Brethren, PA
Elk Lick, PA, congregation, organized from, 1139
Somerset Co., PA, **789,** 1317
Maple Grove Brethren Church, Eaton, IN, *See* Eaton, IN, Maple Grove Brethren Church
Rench, George W., pastor, 1099
Maple Grove Brethren Church, Norcatur, KS, *See* Norcatur, KS, Brethren Church
Maple Grove Brethren Church, PA, *See*

Berlin, PA, Brethren Church
Maple Grove Child Rescue Home (CB)
  Eglon, WV, **789**
Maple Grove Church of the Brethren, IN,
  789, 923, 1280, 1287
Maple Grove Church of the Brethren, KS,
  741, **789**, *790*
  Jarboe, James William, 669
  Jarboe, John Edwin, 669
  Pleasant View Church of the Brethren,
    KS, 1036
Maple Grove Church of the Brethren, MD
  Garrett Co., MD, **790**
Maple Grove Church of the Brethren, NC
  790
  Fraternity Church of the Brethren, NC,
    511
Maple Grove Church of the Brethren, OH,
  7, 63, 64, 67, 760, **790**
Maple Grove Church of the Brethren, PA,
  790–791
  Johnstown, PA, Walnut Grove Church
    of the Brethren, 675
Maple Grove Church of the Brethren, WI,
  791, 1217, 1365
Maple Grove congregation, IN, 1280
  Goshen, IN, West Goshen Church of
    the Brethren, 558
Maple Grove German Baptist Brethren con-
  gregation, KS, 944
Maple Grove, IN, German Baptist Brethren,
  318
Maple Grove Old German Baptist Brethren
  Church, OH, **791**, 1379
Maple, Ontario, congregation
  Old Brethren, 970
Maple Press Company
  Ephrata Cloister, 2345
Maple Spring Church of the Brethren, PA
  Somerset Co., PA, **791**
Maple Spring meetinghouse
  Eglon, WV, Church of the Brethren,
    430
Maple Spring, PA, 1265, 1321
Maple Spring, PA, congregation, 149, 214
Maple Spring (Quemahoning) congregation,
  PA, 1139
  Geiger Church of the Brethren, PA,
    533
Maple Spring, WV, congregation
  Oak Park Church of the Brethren, MD,
    957
Maple Valley (Aurelia, IA) Mount Zion
  Brethren Church, **72**, 661, 773
Maple Valley Church of the Brethren, MN,
  2376
Maple Valley German Baptist Brethren
  Church, IA, 72
Maple Valley, WA, Grace Brethren Church
  2218
Mapleville, MD, 1362
  Brethren Church, **791**
  maps, historical, 1437–1464
Maquoketa German Baptist Brethren, IA,
  791
Marama, Nigeria, 306
  Utz, Ruth Earl, 1299
Maranatha Bible Institute
  Hispanic Ministries (BC), 2198
Marble Furnace Church of the Brethren
  Sinking Spring, OH, Grace Brethren
    Church, 1186
Marble Furnace, KY, congregation

Rock House Church of the Brethren,
  KY, yoked with, 1117
Marble Furnace, OH, Church of the
  Brethren, **791**
  Ridge Church of the Brethren, OH,
    1108
Marble, Verona Merribel, 2006
Marburg/Lahn
  Hesse, 602
Marburger, Walter, 1702
March, Catherine, 994
March, Margaret Mary, 384
Marchall Co., IN, 2089
Marchall, Dick A., 2285
Marchand, Frank Emile, 1702
  Red River Church of the Brethren, OK,
    minister, 1089
Marcinkowski, John P., 2006
Marconett, Andrew, 99
  Old Brethren German Baptist Church,
    minister, 965
  Old Brethren minister, 965
  Plum Creek Old German Baptist
    Brethren Church, KS, minister,
    1038
Marconett family, 1224
Marconett, John, 99
Marconette, Andrew, 1702
Marcoux, Claude, 662, 664
  Island Pond, VT, Grace Brethren
    Church, 2209
Marcoux, Mary Jane, 662
  Island Pond, VT, Grace Brethren
    Church, 2209
Marcy, General Randolph B., 475
Mares, Belisandro, 1248
Margaret (ship)*,* 147
  Harman (Harmon) family, 584
Margate Brethren Church, FL, *See* North
  Lauderdale, FL, Grace Brethren
  Church
Margate Grace Brethren Church, FL, *See*
  North Lauderdale, FL, Grace
  Brethren Church
Margi people, 306
Margush, Joseph J., 1702
Margush, Philip Edwin, 1702
Margush, Stephen G., 1702, 2303
  Maitland Church of the Brethren, PA,
    salaried minister, 783
Maria, Sister (Mother), *See* Eicher, Maria
Mariana, PA, Brethren Church, *See*
  Highland Brethren Church, PA
Marianna, PA, 1253
Marienborn area (Germany), 2030, 2043
  Brethren movement in, 354
  Eckartshausen, 421
  Eppstein, 453
  Frankenthal, 506
  Germany, 545
  Gruber, Eberhard Ludwig, 575
  historic sites, 609
  Holtzapfel (Holsapple, Holsopple),
    Johann Heinrich, 623
  Radical Pietism, 330–331
Marienborn Brethren, 174, 407
  Camisards, 242
Marienborn congregation
  Edict of 1712, 425
  Hoffmann, Eva Elizabeth, 617
Marienborn, Germany, 407, 720, *792,*
  792–793, 1394, 1399
  Brethren places of worhip at, 48

Community of True Inspiration, 132
Kalcklöser, Johann Heinrich, 681
Karl August, count of Ysenburg-
  Büdingen-Marienborn, 683
Koch, Johann Jakob, 704
König, Samuel, 706
Liebe, Christian, 741
Lucas, Martin, 766
Mack, Alexander, Sr.,
  performing baptisms, 776
  preaching and teaching, 775
  migration to Krefeld and Schwarzenau
    from, 683
  missions, 857
  Moravian Church contact with
    Brethren, 875
  Naas, Johannes as minister in, 909
  Neumann, Gottfried in, 924
  part of Wetterau region, 1338
  Preiß, Johannes Jakob, 1055
  public baptisms not permitted in, 683
  refuge for nonconformists, 990
  Ritter, Daniel, expulsion of, from, 1111
  Rock, Johann Friedrich and Brethren
    in, 1116
  sources on, 2313
  Traut family, 1270
  Traut, Georg Balthasar "Balser," 1270
Marietta, GA, Grace Brethren Church of
  Greater Atlanta, 540, **793**
Marietta meetinghouse, West Green Tree
  Church of the Brethren, PA, 1334
Marilla Church of the Brethren, MI, 179,
  793, 1235
  Harlan, MI, Church of the Brethren,
    583
  Michigan Brethren settlement, 824
Marindale family, 192
Marindale, Ray, 192
Marini, Stephen A., 2006
  spelling changed from Marani, **2388**
Marion Co., IA
  German Baptist Brethren, IA, **793**
Marion Co., IL
  Romine Church of the Brethren, IL,
    1121
  Salem Church of the Brethren, 1137
Marion Co., KS
  Peabody Church of the Brethren, KS,
    997
  Peabody Old German Baptist Brethren
    Church, KS, 997
  Ramona Church of the Brethren, KS,
    1083
Marion Co., OH, 374
  Marion, OH, First Church of the
    Brethren, 793
  Sciota Church of the Brethen, OH,
    1160
Marion Co., WV, 228
  Pleasant Hill Church of the Brethren,
    WV, 1033
Marion congregation
  Somerset, IN, Church of the Brethren,
    1202
Marion family, 228, 265
Marion, IA, 406
Marion, IN
  Brethren Church, **793**
  Church of the Brethren, 723, **793**, 1245
Marion, OH,
  First Church of the Brethren, **793**
  Grace Brethren Church, **2218**

Marion, OH, mission point
    Eden Church of the Brethren, OH, 424
Marion, VA, 766
marital avoidance, **793**
    discipline, 387
Mark
    1:4, 84
    1:8, 85, 86
    1:10, 85
    1:14, 84
    6:13, 39
    7:33–35, 39
    10:39, 85
Mark (Gospel)
    Kent, Homer Austin, Jr., 2211, 2340
    Ramirez, Frank on, 2351
Mark, John, 1702
Marken, Donald M., 342, 1702
Marken family, 342
Marker, Ernest A., 1702
Marker, Zimri, 750
Markesburg (James Creek), PA, congregation
    Fredericksburg, PA, Clover Creek Church of the Brethren, 513
Markey, A. E., 1318
Markey, Anna Miller
Markey family, 794
Markey, Dale E., 2285
Markey, David H., 710, 760, 1702
    Reading, PA, First Church of the Brethren, minister, 1084
Markey, David Jonathan, 1702, 2006
Markey, Edward A., 268, 1702
Markey, Elizabeth Kuns, 710
Markey, Ella
    Miller, Arlene Thomas on, 2347
    Miller Jacob L., Jr. on, 2347
    Thomas, Arlene on, 2347
Markey, Elsie V. (later Reber), 1085
Markey, Hans David
    Markey family, 794
Markey, Jacob
    family history and genealogy, 1982
    Markey family, 793–794
Markey, Jennie (later Stoner), *See* Stoner, Jennie Markey
Markey, Katherine, 363
Markey, Lester Michael, 1702
    free ministry to New Fairview Church of the Brethren, PA, 927
Markey, Magdalena Stump
    Markey family, 794
Markey (Merkey) family, **793–794**
Markey, Michael M., 1702
    New Fairview Church of the Brethren, PA, as minister, 927
Markey, Roger, 794
    free ministry to New Fairview Church of the Brethren, PA, 927
Markey, Roger Eugene, 704, 1702
Markey, Sarah, 793
Markle family, 1885
Markle, IN, Church of the Brethren, 30, **794**
    Huntington, IN, City Church of the Brethren, 637
    Salamonie Church of the Brethren, IN, 1136
Markle, Richard E.
    Barberton Bible Church, OH, 951
Marklesburg, PA, James Creek Church of the Brethren, 52, **794**

Markley, Anna (later Pfautz), 1014
Markley, David, 1702
Markley family, 141, 164, 1936, 2077
    Freeling Settlement Old German Baptist Brethren Church, WV, 514
Markley, Harvey B., 1702
Markley, James M., 442, 1702
Markley, John M., 147, 1702
Markley, Robert W., 342, 768
    Norton, OH, Grace Brethren Church, pastor, 951
Markley, Robert William, 1702
Markley, Stella Buffenmyer, 1702
Markleysburg, PA, Church of the Brethren (Asher Glade), **794**
    Farmington, PA, Bethel Church of the Brethren, 479
    Sandy Creek, WV, congregation, 215, 1143
    Thomas, Jacob M., 1262
    Thomas, Michael and Alexander, 1263
    Union Chapel Church of the Brethren, PA, 1287
Marks, C. H., 567, 1702
Marks, Dan K., 1702
Marks-Eller family, 1928
Marks, Evelyn Louise, 1851
Marks, J. F., 347
Marks, Mrs. J. F., 347
Marks, John, 2106
Marks, Marlin D., 2285
Marks, Ronald Lee, 1702
    Hart, MI, Dunkard Brethren Congregation, 2196
Marksbury, David E., 115, 688, 1702
    Maple Valley, WA, Grace Brethren Church, 2218
Marlborough, 162
Marlin, Hugh Crist, 349, **794,** 1702
Marling, William H., 2285
    New Albany, OH, Rocky Ridge Grace Brethren Church, 2231
Marquardt family, 1277
Marquet, Cynthia
    on Ephrata Cloister, 2345, 2358
Marquis (Marquies), William K., Jr., 1702
Marquis, William K., Sr., 1288, 1702
Marr, Ken
    Omaha, NE, Grace Brethren Bible Church, interim pastor, 974
Marriage
    New Born sect, discouragment of, 925
marriage, *599,* 1885, 2047, 2048, 2049, *See also* divorce; engagements; remarriage; wedding customs
    Brethren practices, **794–796,** *795*
    camping movement and enrichment of, 249
    caps and, 254
    counseling, 2013
    Cumberland Co., PA, 2005
    degrees of ministry, 374
    demographic trends, 2144
    discipline, 388–389
    divorce issues, 393
    Doctrinal Treatise, 394
    doctrine on family and, 169
    Dunkard Brethren, 410
    Ephrata Community, 448, 451, 452
    family, 474
    God's Means of Grace (Yoder), 555
    Hochmann von Hochenau, Ernst Christoph, 614

jewelry, 671
    Mack, Alexander, Sr., New Baptists, and sexual continence in, 776
    marriage enrichment, 796
    mixed marriages, 388
    Native Americans, 2229, 2230
    nonconformity, 940, 941
    Old German Baptist Brethren, 941, 967
    Plow Creek Fellowship, 1038
    Radical German Pietism, 1080
    Reba Place Fellowship, 1084
    Rechte und Ordungen, 1086
    remarriage, 2145
    remarriage after divorce, 1099
    sexuality and, 266, 1170
    sources on, 2313
    women and, 2263
    world's longest, 2127
    youthful, 2010
Marriage Consultation Center, 796
Marriage Council of Philedelphia, 796
marriage counseling, **796**
Marriage Encounter, 796
marriage enrichment, **796**
marriage, groups rejecting, 30
marriage practices
    Miller, Marcus on OGBB and, 2347
marriages
    Franklin Co., VA, 2102
    Mooreites, 875
    records of, 2104
    Rockingham Co., VA, 2077
Marsay, Charles Hector de St. Georges, Marquis de, **796**
Marsay, Marquis de, 1274, 2050
Marsden, Parker G.
    on CB vocations, 2345
Marsh Creek Church of the Brethren, PA, *See* Gettysburg, PA, Marsh Creek Church of the Brethren
Marsh Creek congregation, PA, 1295
    Hershey, John Willard, 599
    Pfoutz, David, elder, 1015
Marsh Creek Independent Brethren Church, *See* Gettysburg, PA, Marsh Creek Church of the Brethren
Marsh Creek Independent Brethren Church, PA, 1295
Marsh Creek, PA, Church of the Brethren history, 1998
Marsh Creek, PA, congregation, 383, 738
    Hoff (Huff) family, 617
Marsh, Daniel, 396
Marsh family
    Garwin, IA, Carlton Brethren Church, 532
Marsh, Gary, 1702
Marsh, MD
    Manor Church of the Brethren, MD, mission point of, 787
Marshall, C., 1702
Marshall, Christopher, 291, 2006
Marshall Co., IA, 661, 695, 1217
    Iowa River Church of the Brethren, IA, 662
Marshall Co., IN, 147, 173, 347, 1315, 1385
    Mount Pleasant Church of the Brethren, IN, 886
    Salem Church of the Brethren, IN, 1137
    Union Church of the Brethren, IN, 1038

Marshall Co., KS, 1230
Richland Center Church of the
Brethren, KS, 1107
Marshall Co., WV, 1336
Ryerson Station Church of the
Brethren, PA, members from, 1132
Marshall, Darius Hampton, 613, 1702
Marshall, Dick, 1235
Marshall, E., 1702
Marshall family
Phoenix, AZ, Northwest Grace
Brethren Church, 1019
Marshall, Jack
Salkum, WA, Community Church of
the Brethren, pastor, part-time,
1139
Marshall, James Boal, 53, 360, 1702, 1851
Peru, IN, Grace Brethren Church,
pastor, 1010
Marshall Plan
Kassel headquarters, funds for build-
ing, 684
Marshall, Ralph, 264
Marshall, Robert Ezra, 1702
Marshall, Ted
Phoenix, AZ, Grace Brethren Church,
1019
Marshalltown, IA, 1216
Church of the Brethren, *See* Iowa
River Church of the Brethren, IA
Hillery, Lemuel, 606
migration of Brethren, 830
Marshburn, Ina (later Kaylor), 1917
Marshe, Witham, 2006
Marston, Bruce S., 2285
Marston family
Montclair, CA, Grace Brethren Church,
871
Martens, Elmer A., 2134
Martha, Rebecca "Becky" Eller
Eller, Henry C. on, 2329
Martin, Aaron L., Jr., 2286
Martin, Abraham, 2007, 2045
Martin, Abraham Lincoln Brinser, 912,
1702
Martin, Adam Eugene, 1702
Martin, Adam Reecher, 2006
Martin-Adkins, Alice, 1703
Martin-Adkins, Ronald Ray, 1703, 2008
Martin, Allen H., 2007
Martin, Amos Burkholder, 2006
Martin, Amos M., 1702
Martin, Ann Lessley
Martin family, 797
South Carolina, 1204
Martin, Anna B. (later Gingrich), 1951
Martin, Archie, 1702
Martin, Barbara Neibert, 798
Martin, Betty Jean, 2006
historical writing, 611
Martin, Brenda, 2006
Martin, C. H., 2006
Martin, Calvin E., 1702
Martin, Cassie Weddle, 147
Martin, Catherine (later Vaniman), 1303
Martin, Catherine Newcomer, 798
Martin, Charles M., 65, 673, 1702, 2303
River City Grace Community Church,
pastor, 1134
Martin, Charles Raymond, 1702
Martin, Charles Walter, 1702
Martin, Christian, 797, 2008, 2090
Martin, Christian and Magdalena, 2008

Martin, Christian B., 2007
Martin, Christian F., 1702
Martin, Clifford, 1702
Martin Co., KY, 689, 1355
Martin Creek Church of the Brethren, IL,
797
example of place name, 911
Martin, Cripe Hannah, 352
Martin, D., 1702
Martin, D. B., 1217, 1702
Martin, Daniel, 1702, 2006
Martin family, 798
Martin, Daniel W., 2007
Martin, David, 210, 271, 321, 381, 425,
475, 511, 597, 732, 1249, 1292,
1702, 2095
Martin family, **797–798**
South Carolina, 1204
Martin, David B., 1972
Martin, David (SC), 30, 105
Martin, Delton, 2006
Martin, Dennis D., 2006
historical writing, 612
Mennonite Encyclopedia, Vol. 5 entry
by, 2328
Martin, Devon C., 1702
Martin, Donald I., 1702
Shamokin, PA, Church of the Brethren,
1171
Martin, Donna Ritchey, 2286
on Ephesians, 2345
Martin, Edgar Showalter, 125, 288,
1702–1703, 2006
St. Petersburg, FL, First Church of the
Brethren, pastor, 1135
Martin, Edward Francis, 2006
Martin, Eli M., 2006
Martin, Eli W., 2093, 2099
Martin, Elisha M., 2007
Martin, Elisha M. and Mary R. Heller, 1971
Martin, Elizabeth (later Roland), 1127
Martin, Emma (later Early), 212, 413, 2093,
2099
Martin, Emry, 147
Martin, Eva May Boyd, 2006
Martin, Evelyn Horst, 2007
Martin, Evelyn Zuck, 1841
Martin, F. Mervin, 1703
Martin family, 251, 713, 743, **797–798,**
1325, 1365, 1961, 2008, 2031,
2060, 2082, 2090, 2095, 2099
family history and genealogy, 2007
Fredericksburg, IA, Hillcrest Baptist
and Brethren Church, 512
genealogy, 1951
New Holland, PA, Church of the
Brethren, 928
Paul family relations, 996
Prosser, WA, Community Grace
Brethren Church, 1062
Royer family related to, 1128
Martin G. Brumbaugh Reconstruction
Unit (Civilian Public Service
Camp No. 43)
Castañer, PR, Church of the Brethren,
261
Martin, George, 2095
Martin, George Adam, 33, 42, 121, 141,
446, 732, **797**, 1232, 1298, 1703,
2006–2007
South Carolina, 1204
Antietam (Conococheague), PA/MD,
German Seventh-Day Baptist con-

gregation, pastor, 1194
Martin family, 797
Martin, Nicholas, 797
Pennsylvania Synods and Brethren
yearly meetings, 1007
publishing works of, 1067
Steiner family, 2378
Martin, George Castor, 2007
Martin, George M., 2095
Martin, George H., 2286
Martin, Glenn R., 1703
Martin, H. S.
divine inspiration of scripture, 132
Martin, H. Stanley, 2286
Martin, Hannah (later Heitler), 352, 595
Martin, Harold S., 1703, 2007
on Biblical inerrancy, 2345
on Biblical reliability, 2345
on Book of James, 2345
on Book of Jude, 2345
on Book of Revelation, 2345
on Brethren heritage, 2345
on Colossians, 2345
on headveiling, 2345
on James 3: 1–12, 2345
on new Christians, information for,
2345
on New Testament beliefs and prac-
tices, 2345
on Philemon, 2345
Pleasant Hill Church of the Brethren,
PA, presiding elder, 1032
*What Happened to the Church of the
Brethren,* 2007
Martin, Harvey J., 1703
Martin, Hazel (later Neff)
Neff, Robert Wilbur, 2230
Martin, Helen L., 2286
Martin, Helen Reimensnyder, 747, 2007
Martin, Henry
Shannon, IL, Church of the Brethren,
1172
Martin, Henry K., 2093, 2099
Martin, Henry M., 273, 1703
Martin, Horace Kurtz, 2007
Martin, Howard B., 1703
Martin, I. C., 1703
Martin, Irene Landis, 2007
Martin, Irvin S., 2007
Martin, Isaac, 2007
Martin, Isaac D., 1951
Martin, J. B., 1703
Martin, J. F., 1703
Martin, J. P., 102, 1703
Martin, Jacob, 797, 2007
Martin, Jacob M., 2006
Martin, Jacob W. and Mary Martin, 1972
Martin, Janice M., 2007
Martin, Jesse B., 2007
Martin, Johann, 922
Martin, John, 516, 552, 1703, 1867
Mohican Church of the Brethren, OH,
preacher, 867
Romine Church of the Brethren, IL,
providing leadership, 1121
Martin, John C., 1703
Oak Grove Old German Baptist
Brethren Church, OH, deacon, 956
Martin, John Jacob, 1997
Martin, John (Johannes), 513
Martin, John, Sr., 1883
Martin, John W., 1893, 1997
Martin, Jonathan R.

Old Brethren Church, 2232
Martin, Joseph H., 2007
Martin, Joseph S., 2095
Martin, Josiah, 1897
Martin, Kenneth, 417
Old Brethren minister, 965
Martin, Kenneth Charles, Jr., 1703
Martin, Kenneth Earl, 206
Martin, Kenneth L., 2286
Martin, Laura Mae, 2007
Martin, Levi E., 2007
Martin, Lois
on early Brethren movement, fictionalized account of, 2365
Martin, Louise A., 2007
Martin, Lydia Horst, 1867, 2007
Martin, Lyle W.
San Jose, CA, South Bay community Church (FGBC), pastor, 1142
Martin, Magdalena C., 2092
Martin, Manuel, 279
Martin, Margaret (later Paulus), 996
Martin, Margaret (later Stover), 1219
Martin, Margaret (later Worst), 1379
Martin, Martha, 1361
Martin, Mary, 1703
Martin, Mary Katherine (later Reichard), 1094
Martin, Mary Knepper
Martin family, 797
Martin, George Adam, wife of, 797
Martin, Mary (later Leatherman), 1688
Martin, Mary N., 2092
Martin, Menno, 2007
Martin, Moses W. and Anna Hoover, 2006
Martin, Naomi (later Horst), 630
Martin, Nathan, 733, 1703
Martin, Nathanial Z., 2007
Martin, Neil D., 2286
Old Brethren Church, 2232
Martin, Nicholas, 216, 732, **797**, 798, 1233, 1285, 1703
Martin, Nicholas (2 listed), 1703
Martin, Noah B., 2006
Martin, Noah Sensenig, 674, 1703, 2007
Martin, Noah W., 1213, 1703, 2303
Martin, Nora Ada, 2006
Martin, P. B., 1316
Martin, Paul Albert, 1703
Martin, Paul M., 2286
Martin, Perry O., 1703
Martin, Peter G., 1893
Martin, Peter P., 2051
Martin, Phares Weaver, 2007
Martin, Ralph Blaine, 1603
Pasadena, CA, Church of the Brethren, pastor in, 994
Martin, Raymond E., 1703
Martin, Reuben B., 2006
Martin, Richard Brubaker, 2007
Martin, Robert Allen, 6, 1841
Martin, Robert Edward, 629, 1703
Martin, Rodney C., 502, 1703
Martin, Roger, 1929
Martin, Ross D., 357, 1703
Martin, Russell S., 1703
Martin, Samuel, 1874, 2007
Martin, Sarah (later Faw), 481
Martin, Scott, 1703
Martin, Silas, 1703
Martin, Simeon Eby, 2007
Martin, Simon, 99, 373, 1703
North Fork Old German Baptist

Brethren Church, IN, minister, 947
Martin, Susannah (later Holdeman), 619
Martin, Susannah (later Zuck), 1400, 1401
Martin, Suzanne DeMoss
on compassion, 2331
Martin, Sylvia Yoder, 2007
Martin, Talmadge, 2007
Martin, Tim Ritchey, 2286
Martin Township, Lancaster Co., PA, 1933
Martin, Valentine B., 1703
Oak Grove Old German Baptist Brethren Church, OH, minister, 956
Martin, Wilbur A., 1703, 1841
Martin, Willard M., 2007
Martindale, Charles Tracy, 1703
Martindale, Ray M., 1268
Native Americans, 2230
Martineau, Harriet, 653, 2008
Martinez, De Figueroa Isabel, 2286
Martinez, Isabel (later Figueroa)
Rio Piedras, PR, Segunda Iglesia Cristo Misionera Fellowship (CB) and, 2243
Martinsburg, PA
Brethren Church
Hopewell Grace Brethren Church, PA, 629
Fredericksburg, PA
Brethren Church, 512
Clover Creek Church of the Brethren, 513
Grace Brethren Church, **798,** 1343
Home of the Child Rescue Work, 625
Memorial Church of the Brethren, **798**
Forney, Roy S., 503
Martinsburg, WV, 1337
Moler Avenue Church of the Brethren, 119, 735, **798**, 2376, **2376**
Fellowship Church of the Brethren, WV, 482
Rosemont Grace Brethren Church
Moler Avenue Church of the Brethren, originating from, **798**
Vanclevesville Church of the Brethren, See Martinsburg, WV, Moler Avenue Church of the Brethren
Martinson, Jacob Christian, 1703
Marty, Martin E.
"A Denomination in Trouble," 2008
Martyrer-Spiegel
reference to, 1911
martyrology, anabaptist
Blutige Schau-Platz oder Martyrer Spiegel der Tauffs Gesinnten, Der, 171
martyrs, See religious persecution of Anabaptists, 28
Blutige Schau-Platz oder Martyrer Spiegel der Tauffs Gesinnten, Der, 154
China, 1977
Kline, John, 701–702
Mantz, Felix, 28
Mennonite martyr literature as used by Brethren, 815
Müntzer, Thomas, 28
Der Pirmasenser Märtyrerspiegel, 1950, 1872
Martyr's Mirror, 2035, See also *Der Blutige Schau-Platz oder Martyrer Spiegel der Tauffs Gesinnten (The Bloody*

Theater or Martyrs' Mirror of the Baptist-Minded) (J. Böhme)
Lowery, James W., and translation of, 2344
Marvin, Lyle, Jr.
National Fellowship of Grace Brethren Men, leadership in, 916
Marvin, Lyle W., Sr., 553, 1703, 2303
Rittman, OH, First Brethren Church, pastor, 1111
San Bernardino, CA, Grace Brethren Church, pastor, 1141
Marx, Karl T., 747, 2008
Marxism
Church of the Brethren, 303
view of Anabaptism, 28
Mary Ann (ship)
Fischer (Fisher) family, 491
Marya, Anduwi J., 1703
Maryland, 162, 175, 2028, 2041, 2188, *See also* specific congregations
Baptists of, history by Morgan Edwards, 1926
bibliography, 1858, 1860, 1861, 1866, 1869
Brethren activity in, **798–799**, *799*
Church of the Brethren history, 1962–1963
Civil War battles, 1964
Committee of Observation, 327
cultural change in, 2
Dairy Farm Assignments, 359
Dairy Testing Assignments, 359
Delaware settlements, 374
Dunkard Brethren Church, 2083, 2105
early settlers in, list of, 2068
German culture, 2147
Germans of, history, 1913
historiography
district histories, 2201
history, 1920
Illinois, 647
Indiana, 652
Loyalists, 2074
Mallett, Manley W. on families in, 2345
Mason-Dixon Line, 800
Materials Towards a History of the Baptists, 803
Miami, OH, congregation, 961
migration of Brethren, 827
ministers, 2105
minorities, ethnic and racial, 849–850
North Carolina Brethren settlement, 946
Old German Baptist Brethren, 967
Old Order German Baptists, 970, 972
Pennsylvania Brethren and settlement, 1004
Pennsylvania Germans, 1006
printing industry
bilingual printers, 2105
Schildknecht, C. E. on history and genealogy of, 2355
slavery, 1189, 2128
Society for the History of Germans in Maryland, 1962
Stone Bridge, 2086
Western (Brethren in), 2
youth in the 1920's, memories of, 2079
Rosenstock Chapel, 1314
Maryland Collegiate Institute, *See* Blue Ridge College

Wampler, Sadie Irene Stutsman, 1317
Maryland Collegiate Institute/Blue Ridge
    College
    John, John Jay, 671
Maryland congregation (OGBB), 1243
Maryland Grace Brethren congregation, 391
Maryland Historical Society (Baltimore), 52
Maryland, IL, 724
Marysville, OH, Watkins Road Community
    Grace Brethren Church, **799**, 1380
Maryville, TN, Oakland German Baptist
    Brethren Church
    Blount Co., TN, **799**
Masillon Grace Brethren Mission
    Grant, Richard E., 2193
Mason, A. Hughlett, 2008
Mason, Carol E. O., 2165
Mason, Charles
    Mason-Dixon Line surveyor, 800
Mason Co., KY (later Fleming Co.), 171,
    688
Mason Co., MI, 756, 1235
    Scottville Old German Baptist Brethren
        Church, MI, 1161
Mason, Cynthia Gail, 2286
Mason-Dixon Line, **800**
    Danner (Tanner, Donner), Michael, 362
    Dunkard's Creek, 2008
    place-names, Brethren, 1027
    slavery, 1189
Mason, Dorotha Wenger Fry, 2286
    on Gospel of John, 2345
    on Winder, J. O., 2345
Mason, Edward Glenn, 46, 102, *182,* 186,
    195, 235, 368, 566, **799–800,**
    1332, 1703, 2008, 2012
    educator, **800**
    family of, 1400
    Homerville, OH, Grace Brethren
        Church, 626
    The Investigator, 660, 1978
    Mason, Edward Glenn, father of, 800
    Miamisburg, OH, Brethren Church,
        pastor, 823
    The Progressive Christian, 1061
    The Home Pulpit, 625, 1971
    Palestine, 990
Mason, Edward W., 124, 1703
Mason (EYN) Technical School, Nigeria,
    2165
Mason, Floyd R.
    on Garber, Barber Miller and descen-
        dants, 2346
    on Garber, Elizabeth and descendants,
        2346
    on Garber, John H. and descendants,
        2346
    on Garber, Niclous and descendants,
        2346
    on Klein, Dorothy Rebman and descen-
        dants, 2346
    on Mason, George, 2346
    on Mason, John and descendants, 2345
    on Mason, Mary Ann Miller and
        descendants, 2345
    on Miller, Mathias and descendants,
        2346
    on Miller, Michael and descendants,
        2345
    on Miller, Susannah Bechtl and descen-
        dants, 2345
    on Shank, Michael and descendants,
        2345

on Wampler, Hans Peter and descen-
    dants, 2346
on Ziegler, Philip and descendants,
    2345
on Ziegler, Regina Requel and descen-
    dants, 2345
on Zigler, Elizabeth Kline, 2345
on Zigler, John, 2345
Mason, George, 1703
    Mason, Floyd R. on, 2346
Mason, George Edward, 1841, 2201, **2218,**
    2218, 2286
Mason, Harold Albert, 1851
    medical missions, 807
Mason, Howard E., 1703
Mason, J. T., 469, 572
Mason, Jesse (Stair)
    South Saint Joseph Church of the
        Brethren, MO, 1135
Mason, John
    Mason, Floyd R. on descendants of,
        2345
    Mason, Kathryn Garst on descendants
        of, 2345
Mason, John H. (M.), 1703
Mason, John Stafford, 1399, 1703–1704
Mason, John Tipton, 1704
Mason, John W., 124
Mason, Joseph Michael, 109, 1704
    "A Brethren View of the Church," 2008
    "The Church and Planning: American
        Baptist and Church of the Brethren
        Perspectives," 2008
Mason, Kathryn Garst
    on Garber, Barber Miller and descen-
        dants, 2346
    on Garber, Elizabeth and descendants,
        2346
    on Garber, John H. and descendants,
        2346
    on Garber, Niclous and descendants,
        2346
    on Klein, Dorothy Rebman and descen-
        dants, 2346
    on Mason, John and descendants, 2345
    on Mason, Mary Ann Miller and
        descendants, 2345
    on Miller, Mathias and descendants,
        2346
    on Miller, Michael and descendants,
        2345
    on Miller, Susannah Bechtl and descen-
        dants, 2345
    on Shank, Michael and descendants,
        2345
    on Wampler, Hans Peter and descen-
        dants, 2346
    on Ziegler, Philip and descendants,
        2345
    on Ziegler, Regina Requel and descen
        dants, 2345
    on Zigler, Elizabeth Kline, 2345
Mason, Louis B., 2008
Mason, Lowell, 560, 643, 1185
Mason, Luther L., 1704
Mason, Margaret Alta Lord, 1851
Mason, Marie Sarah (later Flory), 1837,
    2185, *2185*
Mason, Mary Ann Miller
    Mason, Floyd R. on descendants of,
        2345
    Mason, Kathryn Garst on descendants
        of, 2345

Mason, Mary Zigler, 2185
Mason, Nathan, 2286
Mason, Norris, 2286
Mason, Olin James, 1704
    Gotha, FL, New Covenant Church of
        the Brethren, 2190
Mason, Oliver, 448
Mason, Paul, 1704
    Shelby Co. Church of the Brethren,
        MO, leadership in, 1175
Mason, Rae Hungerford, 1841, 2201, 2346
    Mason, George Edward, 2218
Mason, Ralph I., 2165
Mason, Rebecca Garver
    Mason, Edward Glenn, mother of, 800
    Mason, Edward, wife of, 799
Mason, Russell, 2185
Mason, Steven Watts, 2286
Mason, Walter W., 45, 1704
Mason, William, 1704
Masonic Order, *See* Freemasonry
Masons Cove Church of the Brethren, VA
    Peters Creek Church of the Brethren,
        VA, daughter congregation, 1011
    Roanoke Co., VA, **800**
Masontown, PA, 1356, 1360
    Brethren Church, 77, 495, 550, **800,**
        1178
masquerades, *See* drama
    costumes for, 401
mass media, **800–801,** *See also* radio; tele-
    vision
    ethics, 458
    Hagerstown, MD, Church of the
        Brethren, 578
    Hagerstown, MD, Grace Brethren
        Church, 579
    Medina, OH, Church of the Brethren,
        2219
    radio evangelism for missions, 862
    technology, **2218**
mass media, views of
    Dunkard Brethren Church, 2174
    Old German Baptist Brethren, 2145
Mass, William, 1704
Massachusettes
    Brethren activity, **801**
    conscientious objectors, 336
Massena, A., 1704
Massillon, OH,
    Jackson Bible Church (BC), 395, **801**
    Trinity Church of the Brethren,
        801–802
Mast, Amanda D. Byler, 2008
Mast, Amanda Yoder, 2008
Mast, Amelia Lehman, 2008
Mast, Amos, 1285, 1704
Mast, Andrew Lehman, 2008
Mast, Barbara Yost, 2079
Mast, Catherine (later Schlabach), 2057
Mast, Christian Z., 2008
Mast, D. D., 1704
Mast, Daniel, 345, 1315, 1704
Mast, David J., 2008
Mast, Eli Damas and Rebecca Miller, 2008
    family history, 2009
Mast family, 1299
Mast, Fannie E., 2009
Mast, Henry D., 1881
Mast, J. D., 1704
Mast, Jacob, 2008
Mast, Joseph J. and Mary Miller, 2009
Mast, Levi D., 2008

Mast, Lydia (later Kurtz), *See* Kurtz family
Mast, Malinda Yost, 2079
Mast, Moses C., 2008–2009
Mast, Moses E., 2009
Mast, Rachel (later Miller)
  descendants, 1961
Mast, Susie, 2009
Mast, Wayne W., 1704
Master, Charlotte J.
  Oak Hill Old German Baptist Brethren
    Church, WV, 957
Masters, Charles H., 1704
Masters family, 739
  Pleasant Grove Church of the Brethren,
    NC, 1031
Masters, Grady, 1294, 1704
  Pigeon River Church of the Brethren,
    NC, minister, 1023
Masters, Henry, 1384, 1704
Masters, Hoke H., 118, 1704
Masters, Lizzie, 1704
Masters, M., 424
Masters, Peter, Jr.
  on charismatic movement, 2363
Masterson, Anna Stauffer
  Masterson, Benjamin Franklin, mother
    of, 802
Masterson, Benjamin Franklin, 754, **802,**
  912, 1704
Masterson, Christina (later Kulp), 1684
Masterson, E. K., 1704
Masterson, Elizabeth Engle
  Masterson, Benjamin Franklin, wife of,
    802
Masterson, James Monroe, 912, 1704
Masterson, John Isaac, 1704
Masterson, Joseph
  Masterson, Benjamin Franklin, father
    of, 802
Masterson, Joseph A.
  McPherson, KS, First Church of the
    Brethren, 779
Masterson, Joseph S., 266, 586, 1280–1281,
  1704
Masterton, Christina (later Kulp), **708–709,**
  1840
The Mastery of the Master (Miller), 2013
materia medica, 809
material aid, **802**
  in Austria, 73
  in Belgium, 113
  Church of the Brethren, 303
  Evangelical Church in Austria, 459
  Germany, 545
  Germany, 546
  hospitals, 631
  Indiana, 653
  Japan, 669
  Kassel as distribution center, 684
  Maryland Brethren activity, 799
  medical projects, 808, 809
  Mennonite Church (MC), 815
  Metzler, John D., Sr., administrator,
    820
  Murphy, Sara Florence Fogelsanger,
    897
  Poland, 1041
  Spain, relief work in, 1207, *1208*
material aid programs, *See* relief and
  rehabilitation work
  Brethren Service Centers, 198
  Bushong, Benjamin G., 233
  Christian Rural Overseas Program

(CROP), 198
cut garment program, 198
Europe, 199
Puerto Rico, 199
Sales Exchange for Refugee
  Rehabilitation Vocations (SERRV),
  1139
seagoing cowboys, 198, 199
soap production program, 198
work camps and, 202
*Materials towards a History of the
  American Baptists* (Edwards),
  379, 429, **803**
  historical writing, 611
Matheny family, 768
Matheson family
  Grandview, WA, Grace Brethren
    Church, 566
Mathew 18 Project
  Fairchild, Janice on, 2361
  Ulrich, Daniel on, 2361
Mathews, Edward, 2009
Mathews, Shailer
  Social Gospel Movement, 1197
Mathhews, Robert, 1704
Mathias, Bob, *See* athletics
Mathias, Oscar, 1704
Mathias, Samuel, 803, 1704
Mathias, Wendell C., 1704
Mathias, WV,
  Brethren Church, 694, **803**
  Church of the Brethren, 350, **803**
    preaching point for Upper Lost
      River congregation, 1295
Mathis, Abraham and Susan
  Palouse Old German Baptist Brethren
    Church, 991
Mathis, Amanda
  Mathis, Jefferson H., mother of, 803
Mathis, Andrew G., 1704
Mathis, Cordelia Burton
  Mathis, Jefferson H., wife of, 803
Mathis, Jefferson, Sr., 1704, 2303
  autobiograhy of, 2346
  Mathis, Jefferson H., father of, 803
Mathis, Jefferson Hall, 738, **803,** 1704
  Shelby Co. Church of the Brethren,
    MO, leadership in, 1175
Mathis, Mary (later Goughnour), 555
Mathis, Terry Richard, 2286
matrimony, *See* marriage
Matson, Nehemiah, 2009
Matsuoka, Charlotte Metzler, 1841
Matsuoka, Fumitaka, 1704, 1841, **2384**
  Bethany Theological Seminary, 2136
Mattawana, PA, 1215
Matteau, Judy (later Phoenix)
  Island Pond, VT, Grace Brethren
    Church, 2209
Mattes, Solomon, 1704
Matteson, MI, Brethren Church, **803**
  Michigan Brethren settlement, 824
Matteson, Russell Leon, 2286
Matthai, Conrad
  Society of the Woman in the Wilder-
    ness, 1200
Matthes family, 326
Matthes, Quentin L., 326, 504, 1351, 1704
Matthew
  3:1–6, 84
  3:11, 86
  4:11, 85
  5:28, 6

5:33–37, 7
6:1–4, 18
6:33, 29
7:11, 55
16:13–20, 33
18, 68
18:15–18, 29, 33
19, 6
23:37, 55
26:12, 39
Matthew (Gospel)
  Kent, Homer Austin, Jr., 2211, 2340
Matthews, Donald Dewayne, 1277, 1704
Matthews family
  Orange City, FL, Calvary Grace
    Brethren Church, 975–976
Matthews, Robert, Jr., 721, 1704
Matthews, W. Eugene, 486, 1704, 2286,
  2303
Mattice, Howard LeRoy, 212, 1704
Matula, Elsie Berg, 1704
Matz, J. W., 411
Mau, John Samuel, 1864
Maudlin, Magdalene (later Stutzman), 1233
Maugan family, 1224
Maugans, Joseph
  Sciota Church of the Brethen, OH,
    minister, 1160
Maugans, Reason, 1704
  Sciota Church of the Brethen, OH,
    minister, 1160
Maugans, Willis W., 576, 1704
  Monticello/Pike Creek Church of the
    Brethren, IN, pastor, 872
  Pipe Creek Church of the Brethren, IN,
    elder, 1025
Maugen (Morgan), Peter, 332
Maumee Church of the Brethren, OH, 373,
  741, **803**
  Hicksville, OH, Church of the
    Brethren, 602
Maumee Valley Grace Brethren Church,
  OH, 1380
Maumee Valley Grace Brethren Church,
  Toledo, OH, 1267
Maundy Thursday, 416, 2147
Maupin, George A., 462, 1704
Maurer, B. B., 2009
Maurer, Charles L., 2009
Maurer, Kenneth R., 2009
Maurer, Marguerite, 2009
Maurertown Brethren Church, VA
  Harrisonburg, VA, Bethlehem Brethren
    Church, 586
Maurertown, VA, 1364
  Brethren Church, **803,** 837, 2248
    Waterbrook, VA, Brethren Church
      and, 2260
Maurery, John, 1704
Maurik, Wilhelm van, 2009
Mauritsson, Andras, 1704
Maus, Augustus, 377
Maus, Mrs. Augustus, 377
Maus, Gilbert L., 360, 1704
Mauss, Frank Raymond, 1705
Maust, Charles H., 269, 1705
  Seattle, WA, Olympic View
    Community Church of the
    Brethren, 1162
Maust family, 236
  Root River Church of the Brethren,
    MN, 1122
Maust, H. F. (V.), 236, 1705

Maust, John, 1705
Maust, M. J., 1705
Maust, Magdalena (later Thomas), 1262, 1263
Maust, Roland R., 443, 2286
Millersburg, OH, Grace Brethren Church, 2224
Maust, Samuel P., 1705
Mauzy, Carl, 1705, 2303
Mawery, H. R., 1705
Max (Mack's) Meadows, VA
place-names, Brethren, 1027
Maxey, Fred Edward, 1340, 1705
Maxey, Vankirk, 1705
Maxley, F. E., 264
Maxson family
Ocala, FL, Grace Brethren Church, 2232
Maxwell Co., IA, 157
Maxwell, IA, Church of the Brethren, 803–804
Fernald, IA, Church of the Brethren, 488
Maxwell, Jane Snay
Island Pond, VT, Grace Brethren Church, 2209
Maxwell, Mr., 296
Maxwell, Ronald B., 664
Island Pond, VT, Grace Brethren Church, 2209
May, Charles, 1705
May, James, 804
May, Clarence E., 2009
May Day programs, See drama
May, Donald L., 114, 1705
May, Edward A., 1705
May, Elzabeth Wilson
May, James, mother of, 804
May family, 313, 348
May, Henry
May, James, father of, 804
May Hill Church of the Brethren, OH, 804
Ridge Church of the Brethren, OH, 1108
May, James H., 313, 395, 804, 1705
minorities, ethnic and racial, 849, 850
Palestine, AR, Ministry to Blacks, 991
May, John B., 1705
May, Joseph R., 31, 672
May, Joseph Raymond, 1705
May, Melanie A., 2133
on Brethren movement in 20th century, 2346
Program for Women (CB) and, 2264
Women's Conferences (CB) and, 2265
May, Myrtle, 687
May, OK, 1287
May, Rebecca (later Garst), 531
May, Samuel, 1705
May, Sharon Nearhoof, 2286
May, Siram, 1705
May, Susan Dade, 395
May, James, wife of, 804
minorities, ethnic and racial, 850
"May the Grace of Christ Our Savior", 643
May, Viola M., 244, 1247
Maycumber, Evelyn Louise Marks, 1851
Maycumber, Randall Eugene, 349, 366, 1276, 1705, 1851
Okeechobee, FL, Grace Brethren Church, pastor, 963
Mayer, Brantz, 2009
Mayer, Elisabeth (later Eby), 420

Mayer family, 2009
Mayer, Frederick E., 2009
Mayer, Harold, 21
Mayer, Harold A., 725
Mayer, Harold Otto, 1705
Mayer, Israel, 1705
Mayer, J. Norman, 578, 2286
Mayer, Robin Wentworth
on guidance for "stumbing saints," 2346
Mayes, Charles W., 64, 101, 186, 192, 282, 357, 754, 755, 804, 11342, 1343, 1365, 1394, 1705, 2009
The Brethren Minister's Handbook, 788
"If I Wash Thee Not", 2009
Jews, 671
prophecy conferences, 1062
South Pasadena, CA, Grace Brethren Church, pastor, 1206
Mayes, Howard W., 366, 533, 1383, 1705
Ripon, CA, Grace Brethren Church, pastor, 1110
Mayes, Ina Garver
Mayes, Charles W., mother of, 804
Mayes, John H., 1240
Mayes, John Wallace, 713, 754, 757, 1342, 1705
Mayes, Marjorie G. Stone
Mayes, Charles W., wife of, 804
Mayes, Roger D., 343, 1394, 1705
Myerstown, PA, Grace Brethren Church, pastor, 906
Mayes, Wallace E.
Mayes, Charles W., father of, 804
Mayfair School
Lyndhurst, OH, Grace Brethren Church, 768
Mayhill Dora Thomas, 2009
Mayhill, R. Thomas, 2009
Mayhue, Richard L., 1380, 1705
Maylasia
Brethren activity, 784
Mäyle, Barbara (Catharina), 804
Mäyle (Meyle, Maili, Moyly), Johann (Jan) (Brother Amos), 804
Mayom, 1234
Mays, Essie Oaks
Mays, Morley Josiah, mother of, 804
Mays, Essie Oaks (later Rowland), 1126
Mays, John C., 1705
Mays, Lucinda Miller
Mays, Morley Josiah, wife of, 804
Mays, Morley Josiah, 804, 1705, 2009, 2376
Elizabethtown College, 438
Mays, Robert G., 1705, 2303
Seattle, WA, Olympic View Community Church of the Brethren, pastor, 1162
Mays, William Oscar
Mays, Morley Josiah, father of, 804
Mayville, ND, congregation
North Dakota Brethren settlement, 946
Red River Valley Church of the Brethren, 804–805
Mbaya, Anjili A., 1705
MBI (Moody Bible Institute), 872–873
Mbororo, Nigeria, 306
Mbya, Isheku P. K., 1705
Mbya, Kuthli K., 1705
MC (Mennonite Church), 815
McAdams, Ronald Lee, 2286

McAlevys Fort, PA, 1215
McAllaster, B. A., 1289
McAllen, TX, Grace Brethren Church, 2218–2219
McAuley, Mark, 373
McAuley, Roy E., 373, 1697
Elizabethtown College, 438
Omaha, NE, Church of the Brethren, minister, 974
McAvoy, E. C., 1698
McAvoy, E. W., 1698
McAvoy, Esther (later Ankrum), 32
McAvoy, James Otto, 357, 1343, 1698
Okeechobee, FL, Grace Brethren Church, pastor, 963
McBaffey, Edith, 209
McBernie, Robert S., 563, 1698, 2303
McBride, Paul Edwin, Sr., 1698
MCC, See Mennonite Central Committee
McCabe, Anne (later Ousterhout), 2034
McCabe Baptist Church, 142
McCabe, MT, 142
McCain, Wilbur A., 1698, 2303
McCall family
Montclair, CA, Grace Brethren Church, 871
McCallough, F. B., 605
McCaman, Samuel J., 565, 1698
McCann, Albert, 1698
McCann, Beryl Royce, 1698, 1841
medical missions, 807
McCann, Douvin J., 141, 1698
McCann, E. B., 1698
McCann, Elizabeth Gibbel, 771, 771, 1841
McCann family
at New Rockford, ND, Church of the Brethren, 932
McCann, J. W., 1698
McCann, Marlin Lee, 1698
McCann, Roxanne Gould, 771
McCann, S. B., 771
McCann, S. N., 140
publishing, 1069
St. Francis Church of the Brethren, AR, minister, 1134
McCann, Samuel Napoleon, 102, 771, 771–772, 1698, 1841, 2002, 2076
on Hebrews, study of, 2344
McCann, Vivian Evelene Cherry, 1841
McCann, William J., 102, 165, 1698
McCart, Arlie, 1698
McCarthy, Charles R., 2002
McCarthy, Richard D., 21, 564, 1698
New Holland, PA, Church of the Brethren, pastor in, 928
McCartney, Bill
men's movements, 2221
McCartney family, 332, 1305
McCartneysmith, L. O., 1698
McCartt, Arlie L., 1698, 2303
McCarty, G. Wayman, 2002
McCarty, Jake, 1698
McCarty, John S., 1698
McCarty, Joseph, 45, 1698
McCauley, I. H., 2002
McCauley, Mark, 1280
McCauliff, Linda L., 2286
McCaulley, Matthew G., 1698
McClain, Alva J., 67, 97, 102, 136, 137, 139, 183, 259, 319, 390, 484, 485, 486, 564, 688, 1261, 1297, 1353, 1365, 1698, 2002, 2146, 2181, See separatism

Bible Institute of Los Angeles (BIOLA), 136
Bible interpretation, 134
biographical information, 1918
biography of, 2201
The Brethren Minister's Handbook, 788
divine inspiration of scripture, 132
Grace Brethren sermons, 1168
Grace Schools (Grace Theological Seminary, Grace College), 563, 2192
Hoyt, Herman Arthur, 634
Iowa, 661
Mansfield, OH, Conservative Grace Brethren Church, 2217
"Message of the Brethren Ministry," 817
Miamisburg, OH, Brethren Church, pastor, 823
missions, 860, 861
Philadelphia, PA, First Brethren Church, pastor, 1015
Progressive Brethren church government, 1044–1045
Presbyterian seminary, attending, 1056
prophecy conferences, 1062
Rohrer, Norman B. on, 2353
Scofield Bible revised edition, 1160
statement of faith and noncreedalism, 943
theologian, educator, *772,* **772–773**
Theological Practorium, The (CBBCI) and, 2254
Was Christ Punished for Our Diseases?, 2002
McClain, Daryl, 42
McClain family
    Prosperity Brethren Church, WV, 1062
McClain Hall
    Grace Schools (Grace Theological Seminary, Grace College), 563
McClain, Josephine Gingrich, 772, 1353
McClain, Mary Ellen Gnagey
    McClain, Alva J., 772
McClain, Walter Scott, , **773,** 1319, 1698
    Holsinger, H. R., ordained by, 772
McClaines, Granville, 705
McClanahan, Elizabeth (later Royer), *132*
McClanahan, George, 1698
McClane (Maclean), John, 1698
McClave, CO, Church of the Brethren, **773**
McClave, CO, Dunkard Brethren congregation, *See* Cloverleaf Dunkard Brethren congregation, CO
McClave congregation, OH, 1345
McClellan family, 233
McClellan, George B. (General), 41, 475, 912
McClellan, James S., 192, 754, 688
    South Pasadena, CA, Grace Brethren Church, pastor, 1206
    San Bernardino, CA, Grace Brethren Church, pastor, 1141
McClellan, Thomas D., 1698
McClellan, Vivian, 192
McClellan, W. P., 1698
McClellan, Walter, 1698
McClellan, William P., 45
    South Loup Church of the Brethren, NE, minister, 1206
McClendon, James William
    on theology, systematic, 2344

theology and, 2255
McClintock, G. W., 334
McClintock, Isaac, 1698
McClintock, John, 1698
McClintock, W. Glascow, 1698
McCloskey, Chester Arthur, 1698
McCloskey, Mabel McFatridge, 2002
McCloy, John J., 603
McClung, Kevin, 2286
McClung, Raymond E., 1698
McClure, Andrew, 1327, 1698
McClure, Dennis H., 2286
McClure family, *See Out of the Melting Pot*
McClure, J. W., 1698
McClure, Katherine Louise (later Roehl), 2047
McClure, Martin J., 1698
McClure, Pheobe (later Miller)
    Müller (Miller) family, 894
McClurg, John, 1698
McComb, OH, 1235
McCombs, Earl W., 2286
McConaghy, Hill
    Homerville, OH, Grace Brethren Church, 626
McConahay, Rex William, 1698
McConaughy, E. P., 1698
McConkey, Clarence M., 567, 1698
McConkey, Eli
    Prairie Creek, IN, Church of the Brethren, 1050
McConnell, Charles H., 1698
McConnell, Charles S., 1698
McConnell, Guy, 2002–2003
McConnell, N. A., 2040
    Robins, IA, Church of the Brethren, site of debate, 1115
McCorkindale, Jeffrey, 1254
McCorkle, Uriah R., 1698
McCorkle, William, 297
McCormack (McCormick), John Arthur, 1698
McCormick, Cyrus Hall, 466
McCormick family, 1216
McCormick, Janice Marilyn (Ball), 1847
McCormick, Robert D., 758, 1698
McCormick, Ruth G. C., 2003
McCort, Dennis P., 2003
McCoy, Frank E., 1698
McCoy-Norris family, 1988
McCoy, Ray, 2286
McCracken, David, 1698
McCracken, PA, Sugar Grove Brethren Church, *See* Aleppo, PA, Grace Brethren Church
McCray Chapel Church of the Brethren, VA, 605, *See also* Highland Co. Mission Church of the Brethren, VA
McCray, Lila Elizabeth Wright, 1394, 1698, 1841
McCray, Jack Cameron, 1841
McCrea, James, 45, 1698
McCrickard, Glenn Anthony, 2286
McCrum, Arthur E., 1698
    Pleasant Grove Grace Brethren Church, IA, pastor, 1031
    South Pasadena, CA, Grace Brethren Church, pastor, 1206
McCue, B. M., 1698
McCulloch, Paul, 626
McCulloch, William, 2003
McCullough, Estle L., 1698

McCullough, Frank Bradbury, 1698
McCullough, John D., 142, 1698
McCullough, Larry, 579
McCune, F. E.
    Mount Morris, IL, Church of the Brethren, pastor, 883
McCune family
    Irricana (First) Church of the Brethren, Alberta, Canada, 663
McCune, Frank Eldon, 505, 1698–1699
McCune, Glen Isaac, 79, 1699
McCune, Isaac Mell, 15, 142, 663, 1699
McCune, Oleta, 1699
McCune, Orin R., 1699
McCune, Robert Franklin, 415, 1699
McCurry family
    Golden Church of the Brethren, NC, 555
McCurry (McKinney?), Abbie (later Flory), 498
McCutcheon family
    Hollins, VA, Patterson Memorial Grace Brethren Church, 620, 2087
McCutcheon, Mary (later Gillin), 549
McDarimant, Gracia Anne Kashishian, 1851
McDairmant, Thomas John, 1851
McDaneld, William Wallace, 1699
McDaniel, Alton Leigh, 1699
McDaniel, Charles, 204
McDaniel family, 280, 1216
McDaniel, Jewel N. on, 2344
McDaniel, Grace Courntney Beam
    McDaniel, Jewel N. on descendants of, 2344
McDaniel, Jack, 1699
McDaniel, Jewel N.
    on McDaniel family, 2344
    on McDaniel, Grace Courntney Beam and descendants, 2344
McDaniel, Linda Kay Stephens
    on Deeter, John and descendants, 2337
    on Deeter, Susanna (Ulrich) and descendants, 2337
McDaniel, Lucille, 204
McDaniel, Willard Beam, 59, 280, 1242, 1699
McDaniel, William A., 479, 1699
    Mount Olivet Brethren Church, DE, pastor, 886
McDaniels, D., 1699
McDaniels, Hardey Irving, 1699
McDannel, D. S., 1699
McDannel, Rufus B., 1699
McDonald, A. C., 1699
McDonald, Cecil D., Jr., 2003
McDonald, George, 564, 1699
McDonald, Grant, 12, 562, 1699, 2303
McDonald, H. Fenton, 1699
    San Jose, CA, South Bay community Church (FGBC), pastor, 1142
McDonald, Homer M., 1699
McDonald, Mary Jane (later John), 671
McDonald, Richard A., 2286
McDonald, Wallace, 1699
McDonaugh, George L., 1289, 2003
    Brethren colonization of southern California, 1145
    railroad immigration agent, 773, 1082
McDonnell, Michael
    Ormond Beach, FL, Grace Brethren Church, 982
McDonnell, Sally

Ormond Beach, FL, Grace Brethren Church, 982

McDonough Co, IL, 243

McDowell, Cloyd A., 1699
Sipesville, PA, Church of the Brethren, pastor, 1187

McDowell, Edythe Elizabeth Bowman, 1841

McDowell, Eugene Floyd, 1699

McDowell, Kenneth Eugene, 1699, 1841

McDowell, Kimberly Anne, 2286

McDowell, L. A. C., 2003
McElhaney, A., 1699

McElroy, Philip, 362

McElroy, Mrs. Philip, 362

McElwee, Francis, 356

McElwee, Marie, 356

McElwee, Vicki, 356

McFadden, Barbara Peters, 1011

McFadden, D. R., 415

McFadden, Dan, 627
on Brethren Volunteer Service, 2344

McFadden, David Robert, 1699

McFadden family, 1214

McFadden, Joyce Snyder, 1841
on CB, and stance on alcohol, tobacco, drugs and recovery, 2344

McFadden, Ralph Glenn, 1699, 2003, 2130
Parish Ministries Commission, executive secretary in, 993

McFadden, Wendy Chamberlain, 2149–2150
Brethren Press and, 2264
on Welch, Myra Brooks, poems of, 2345

McFadden, Wilbur Dean, 1841

McFadden, William Glenn, 1277, 1699, 1860, 2003
Michigan City, IN, Church of the Brethren, part-time pastor, 825
Pasadena, CA, Church of the Brethren, pastor in, 994

McFadden, William Robert, 191, 1277, 1699, 2003

McFaden, John Duke, 121, 205, 255, 598, **773–774,** 1225, 1297, 1699, 2003
Philadelphia, PA, First Brethren Church, pastor, 1015
Pittsburgh, PA, First Brethren Church, pastor, 1027
Portis, KS, Grace Brethren Church, pastor, 1048
St. James Brethren Church, MD, pastor, 1134

McFalls meetinghouse
Loudonville Church of the Brethren, OH, 760

McFarland, CA, Church of the Brethren, 79, 244, **774,** 1314

McFarland, Earl, 1699

McFarland, H. G.
Newark, OH, Brethren Church, as minister, 933

McFarland, John H., 1699

McFarland, Thomas
Oakvale Church of the Brethren, WV, pastor, 958

McFarland, William Earl, 1699

McGaffey, Ermal T. (Blickenstaff), 1834

McGaheysville, VA, Brethren Church, See Pineville, VA, Mount Olive Brethren Church

McGann, Elaine Hartman, 2286

McGee, Summerfield, 1699

McGehan, King, 1699

McGhan family
Prosser, WA, Community Grace Brethren Church, 1062

McGhee, Oliver, 758

McGlothlin, Diane, 587

McGlothlin, Floyd, 587

McGlothlin, Judith Mohler, 2286
Gotha, FL, New Covenent Church of the Brethren, 2190

McGonegal, Rosanna (later Yoder), 1387

McGreen family
Pleasant Valley Church of the Brethren, TN, 1035

McGrew family, 1885

McGuckin, Charles J., 2286

McGuffey readers
elementary education, 434

McGuffin, John, 277

McGuffin, Lois S., 152

McGuire family
Roanoke, VA, Garden City Grace Brethren Church, 1113

McGuire, Floyd, 1699

McGuire, Grant T., 758, 1699
Pasadena, CA, Church of the Brethren, pastor in, 994

McGuire, Kathryn
Pueblo, CO, Church of the Brethren, 1070

McGuire, Rell, 1699

McGuire, Rev. F. W., 1896

McHadden, Robert, 1699

McHarg family, 2003

McHarg, W. N., 2003

McHenry Co., ND, 1341

McIlhenny family, 1892

McIlhenny-King families
Adams Co., PA, 1965

McIlnay, Ronald F., 1699
Monticello, MN, Church of the Brethren, minister, 872

McInnis, Russell, 1245, 1339

McInnis, Russell Leonard, 1245, 1339, 1699

McIntire, Carl, 281, 2003
Bible Presbyterian Church, **774**

McIntire, James, 1699

McIntosh, John R., 1240, 1699
Mabton, WA, Grace Brethren Church, pastor, 771
Simi Valley, CA, Grace Brethren Church, pastor, 1182

McIntosh, R. E., 502

McIntosh, Richard T., 1277, 1699

McIntosh, Rufus E., 1699
Mount Hope Church of the Brethren, WA, 882

McInturff, J. A., 239, 586, 675

McKay, Charlotte, 306

McKay, John M., 165, 1700

McKay, Robert Hicks, 306, 1700, 1811

McKee Brethren Church, PA, See Vicksburg, PA, Grace Brethren Church

McKee, Caroline (later Hanawalt), 581

McKee, Charles Forney, 1700
Oaks, PA, Green Tree Church of the Brethren, pastor, 958

McKee, Donna (later Rhodes), 2165, 2290
on children, worship for, 2352

McKee Mountain Home Brethren

Church, PA, 1304

McKee, PA
Humberd, Russell I., 636

McKee schoolhouse, PA, 406

McKee, Wilbur Kaylor, 1700

McKeehan, E. K., 1700

McKeehan, King
Pleasant View Church of the Brethren, TN, 1037

McKeesport, PA, See East McKeesport, PA, Church of the Brethren

McKellar, Madge Hale, 2004

McKellip, David Charles, 1700

McKenzie, Dorothy, 758

McKenzie, Melvin, 758

McKibbens, Thomas R., Jr., 2004

McKibbins family, See Indiana

McKillen, Edna, 1278

McKillen, J. C. "Bill," 54, 62, 1278, 1700, 2303
Phoenix, AZ, Grace Brethren Church, pastor, 1019
San Jose, CA, South Bay community Church (FGBC), pastor, 1142

McKim, Stanley, 1700

McKimmy, James William, 1700
Midland, MI, Church of the Brethren, minister, 826

McKimmy, John A., 1700

McKimmy, Nathan(iel), 1266–1267, 1700

McKinley, Jay Gordon, 2173, 2286

McKinley, William, 261, 912
assassination of, 442
Brumbaugh, Martin Grove and, 222

McKinnell, James Charles, 1380, 2004–2005, 2177, 1700

McKinnell, Letha M., 2177, 2286

McKinney family, 430

McKinney, (McKimmy), Perry, 1700

McKinney, William, 1700

McKinnon, William, 2005

McKinsey, Charles D., 1700

McKinsey, Folger, 2100

McKnight, Parmelia A. (later Wolfe), 1356

McKnight School, MI, 179
McLaughlin, Thomas John, 2286

McLean Co., IL
Hudson, IL, Church of the Brethren, 635
Pike Creek (Chenoa), IL, Church of the Brethren, 1023

McLean, Hulda Brooke Hoover, 2005

McLean, Robert B.
Markle, IN, Church of the Brethren, trustee, 794

McLearn-Montz, Alan Lee, 2286

McLellan, Alfred E., 1700

McLellan, H. W., 1341

McLellan, W., 1700

McLellan, Walter, 1341

McLochlan, Winifred Morse, 2023

McLouth, KS
Brethren Church, **779**
Church of the Brethren, **779**
Ozawkie Church of the Brethren, preaching points established by, 987

McMahon, John, 1700

McManus, George H., 2005

McMaster, Thomas G., 1700

McMillan, Mary G. (later Green), 569

McMinn Co., TN
Niota, TN, Church of the Brethren, 938

McMinn, Edwin, 2005
McMinn, Joseph H., 2005
McMullen, James, 1700
McMurray, Francis, 2005
McMurtrie, Douglas C., 1860
McNabb, Matilda Bollinger, 256
McNalley, Calvin, 1700
McNealy (Mineely) family, 752
McNeely, John, 1700
McNeely, Richard I., 1700
McNeil, Cathy Brown
    works by, 2319
McNelly, Elsie Anna Denlinger, 2005
McNelly, Phyllis Filbrun, 2005
McNemar, William, 1700
McNett, George, 1923
McNett, Susan Armentrout, 1923
McNutt, Charles S., 1700
McPhail, Minnie, 754
McPhail, Pat, 754
McPherson Academy
    Miller, Sebastian Christian, 842
    Mohler, Robert Ellsworth, 868
McPherson Co., KS, 1386, 1387
    McPherson, KS, First Church of the
      Brethren, 779
    Monitor Church of the Brethren, KS,
      869
McPherson College, 535, 682, *780,*
    780–781, 2058, 2059
    agricultural education at, 12
    Bittinger, Desmond Wright, 143, 818
    Bowman, Curtis Buford, 165
    Bowman, Earl McKinley, 165
    Brown, Dale Weaver, 2152
    Burnworth, Benjamin Taylor, 232
    Church of the Brethren, 300
    Clement, John Addison (son), 320
    Crumpacker, Anna L. Newland, 354
    Crumpacker, Franklin Henry, 354
    Culler, Arthur Jerome, 355
    Davis, Charles Ernest, 364
    Ebbert, Ella, 417
    Eby, Emma Ada Horner, 418
    Eby, Enoch Howe, 418
    Educator and Companion, The, 429
    Eller, Jay Vernard, 440
    Elrod, James H., 442
    Enders, NE, Church of the Brethren,
      446
    Eshelman, Matthew Mays, 455
    evolution, 463
    Fahnestock, Samual Bigler, 465
    Fasnacht, Everett Merlin, 480
    Fasnacht, Harold Dale, 480
    Fasnacht, Joy Cullen, 480
    Fisher, Nevin Wishard, 492
    Fleming, Lenoir Avery, 494
    Flory, Lizzie Mae Neher and Raymond
      Chester, 499
    Frantz, Edward, 508
    Frantz, Ira Henry, 508
    Funk, Jacob, 525
    Geisert, Wayne F., 2187
    Gilbert, James Zacchaeus, 548
    Harman, Hylton, 2196
    Harnley, Henry Jacob, 585
    Harshbarger, Luther H., 587
    Heckman, Jacob Hugh, 592
    Helman, Alfred Blair, 2197
    Helman, Patricia Kennedy, 2197
    Hersch, Elmer Myron, 598
    Hershey, John Willard, 599

    Hess, Maurice Abram, 601
    higher education, 605
    Hilton, George William, 607
    historical libraries, 610
    Hoff, Emanuel Buechley, 616
    Hoffman, Paul W., president, 1112,
      2202
    Horning, Mary Emma, 630
    Huston, Ora Ivan, 638
    Ikenberry, Ernest Leroy and Olivia
      Dickens, 646
    Ikenberry, Levi Daniel, 646
    inventions and scientific discoveries,
      660
    Jarboe, John Edwin, 669
    Jewell, Jesse Paul, 2209
    Keim, Clarence Ray, 686
    Kurtz, Daniel Webster, 710
    Lauver, George Myers, 728
    Lehmer, Solomon G., 736
    McPherson, KS, First Church of the
      Brethren, 779, 780
    Mennonite Brethren Churches, General
      Conference of, 814
    Metzler, Burton, 820
    Miller, Howard, 838
    Miller, Samuel J., 842
    Miller, Sebastian Christian, 842
    Mines, Cynthia on, 2347
    Mohler, John Saylor, helping to estab-
      lish, 868
    Mohler, Robert Ellsworth, 868
    Morrill, KS, Church of the Brethren,
      876
    Morris, Charles Stephen, 877
    Mount Morris College, 885
    Moyer, Naomi Ann Holderread, 892
    Naylor, Kurtis Friend, graduation from,
      918
    Nininger, Harvey Harlow, degree from,
      938
    Ogden, Galen Brown, 961
    Peters, Woodford W., president, 1011
    Petry, Ray C., 1013
    Prather, John Perry, 1051
    Ramona Church of the Brethren, KS,
      sending young people to, 1083
    Rowland, Charles Luther, educator,
      1126
    School Visiting Committees, 1155
    Schwalm, Vernon Franklin, 1157
    Sharp, Solomon Zook, president of,
      1174
    Snyder, John Martin, newspaper editor,
      1196
    Vaniman, Daniel, 1303
    Vaniman, Ernest David, 1303
    Vaniman, Susie Cordelia Neher, 1303
    Weiand, Albert Cassel, 1344
    Weiss, Edgar Lorell, 1328
    Williams, John Henry Bashor, 1345
    Wine, David Glick, 1349
    Yoder, Joseph J., 1386
McPherson, KS, 8, 218, 682, 1344, 1395
    Church of the Brethren, 355, 415,
      779–780
      75 year anniversary, 2005
    Ebbert, Ella, 417
McPherson Co., SD
    Willow Creek, SD, congregation, 1205
McPherson, Steven Robert, 2286
McQuirty, 1700
McRoberts, Roy Jennings, 1700

McRostie, Garnette, 1700
McVay, F. F., 1700
McVey, Roy Allen, 1700
McVeytown, PA, 1215, 1302
    Hanawalt, George S., 581
McWhiney, Grady, 1939
McWhorter, Lloyd L., 565, 1700
McWhorter, William, 1700
McWilliams, Jay R.
    Pleasant View Church of the Brethren,
      PA, 1037
McWilliams, Richard LeGrande, 1700
    Pleasant View Church of the Brethren,
      PA, 1037
Mdurvwa, Audu D., 1705
Mead, Frank S., 379, 2009
Meade, Alma B., 747, 2009
Meador, Charley J.
    Olathe Old German Baptist Brethren
      Church, KS, deacon, 964
Meador family
    Gospel Grace Brethren Church, VA,
      559
Meador, Michael L.
    on home schooling, 2346
Meadors, Gary T.
    on Kent, Homer A., 2346
Meadow Branch, MD
    Church of the Brethren, 80, 81, 160,
      755, **805**
    cemetery, 161
    Rupp (Roop) family, 1130
    mission point for Westminster
      Church of the Brethren, MD,
      1337
    Pipe Creek Church of the
      Brethren, MD, 1026
    Reistertown-Evergreen Church of
      the Brethren, MD, 1095
Meadow Branch Church of the Brethren,
    TN, *805,* **805–806**
Meadow family
    Roanoke, VA, Garden City Grace
      Brethren Church, 1113
Meadow Mills Church of the Brethren, VA
    806
    Salem Church of the Brethren, VA,
      1138
Meadowcrest, Fort Wayne, IN, Brethren
    Church, *See* Fort Wayne, IN,
      Meadowcrest Brethren Church
Meadows of Dan, VA
    Parkway Church of the Brethren, VA,
      994
Meadows, Sally
    Sand Creek Old German Baptist
      Brethren Church, KS, 1143
Meadowview, CA, Church of the Brethren,
    See Sacramento, CA, Prince of
      Peace Church of the Brethren
    Rio Linda, CA, congregation, 1134
Mease, Gerald Ralph Henry, 1705, 2304
Mease, Gladys Price (Nyce)
    on Nyce, Abraham and descendants,
      2346
    on Nyce, Leanna (Goshall) and descen-
      dants, 2346
    on Price, Abraham and descendants,
      2346
    on Price, Susan (Alderfer) and descen-
      dants, 2346
Mease, Wilbur Dwain, 1705
meat

Lord's supper food, 757–758, 763–764
Mechanic Grove congregation, PA, 737
Mechanic Grove, PA, 461
  Church of the Brethren, 225, 226, **806**, 1920, 2109
    example of place name, 911
    sources on, 2320
    Jennersville, PA, Church of the Brethren, 670
Mechanicsburg, PA, 765
  Church of the Brethren, 322, **806**
  Dunkard Brethren, 322, **806**, 1172
    Johnson, John L., 672
    Ness, Jacob C., 2231
    Miller, Jacob A., 838
Mechanicstown (later Thurmont), MD, 1264
  Blue Ridge congregation, founding, 1996
Mechling, Sue E. T., 1937
Mechter, Charles K., 2009
Meck, Levi L., 115, 1705
  Omaha, NE, Church of the Brethren, elder, 974
Meck, William, 1705
Meckel, Anna Christina Stichs (later Sauer)
  See Sauer, Anna Christina Stichs Meckel
Mecosta Co., MI, 242
  Rodney Church of the Brethren, MI, 1119
medicine, folk, 31
Medford, OR, Church of the Brethren, **806**
media, See mass media
media issues
  Church of the Brethren, 2099
Media Research Bureau, Washington, DC, 2009
medical care
  missions, 2224
  Native Americans, 2230
medical decisions
  Snyder, Graydon F. on, 2357
medical experiments
  medical projects, 808
medical missions, **806–808**, *807, See also* missions, medical
medicine, 810
  missions, 861
  relief and service efforts, 1096–1097
medical personnel, training of
  Lafiya program, 718, *718*
medical profession
  Cover, Joseph Immel, 348
medical projects
  Puerto Rico, 1070
medical projects (BSC and CPS), **808–809**
  Castañer Hospital, 810
  research experiments, 810
Medical Projects (BSC and CPS), in Austria, 73
medical research
  burial customs and, 230
medical science
  funerals, 524
medical services
  China, 277
  hospitals, 630
  Nigeria, 306
medical work, See relief and rehabilitation work
  Brethren Navajo Mission and boarding School and, 193

Huntingdon, PA
  Brumbaugh, Andrew Boelus, 219
medicine, See health and medicine
Medicine Hat, Alberta, Canada, 15
Medicine Lake Church of the Brethren, MT, 142, 1301, See also Big Sky
  Church of the Brethren/American Baptist Church, MT
  Montana Brethren settlement, 870
medicines, See patent medicines
medicines, patent
  advertisements for, 1918
  "Sala's German Vegetable Elixir," 1136
Medina Co., OH, 145
Medina, OH
  Brethren Church, **2219**
  Church of the Brethren, **2219**
  Living Hope Brethren Church, **2219**
  Shepherd's Grace Church, **2219–2220**
meditations, 2017, 2025
  in verse, 2075
Meditations on Brethren Life
  Miller, DeWitt and Mary, 1282–1283
meditative writings
  daily meditations, 2013
  Glimpses of God, 1968
Mediterranean countries
  Near East Foundation service for, 920
Meek, Donna Smith, 447
Meek family
  Meadow Branch Church of the Brethen, TN, 805
Meek, L. L.
  Octavia, NE, Church of the Brethren, minister and elder, 960
Meek, Verley Kestler, 141, 447, 1705
  Monitor Church of the Brethren, OK, minister, 869
Meeker, Marvin E., 1285, 1705
  Milroy, PA, Grace Brethren Church, 843
Meeks, Gary M., 2286
Meer, Abraham ter, 2009
Meet the Brethren, 2143
meethelper
  ministry, terminology, 848
meetinghouses, 48–51, *47, 49,* 135, *811,* **811**
  architecture, **2131**
  barns, use of as, 90
  Brethren congregations as rural churches, 1130
  Brethren movement, 291
  Browns Mill meetinghouse, 2153
  Church of the Brethren, 300
  communion table, 328
  cooking, traditional, 341
  financial assistance for building, 295
  first built in American (1770), 48
  Fort Seybert, WV, Bethlehem Fellowship, 2185
  Franklin Grove, IL, Church of the Brethren, 1993
  furnishings, 1071, *1072, 1095*
  furnishings of, 48, 59
  gender separation, 2160
  General Church Erection and Missionary Committee (CB), 536
  Gibson family, 548
  Greenland Church of the Brethren, WV, 571
  Grossnickle Church of the Brethren, MD, 574

Hanawalt, Joseph Rothrock, 581
Historic Peace Churches, 608
historical societies, 610
Holsinger Church of the Brethren, PA, 623
house churches, 632
Iglesia Cristiana Pentecostal de Cuba, 2207
Indiana, 652
lofts, 48
Milam, WV, Mount Carmel Church of the Brethren, 2222
ministry, 845
museums in, 898
musical instruments, 900
Old German Baptist Brethren, 967, 969
origins of, 48
Pennsylvania settlement, 1004
plain people, 1029
Pleasant Grove Church of the Brethren, KS, first built in KS, 1031
of Puritans in New England, 48
raised pulpits, 48
of the Society of Friends, 48
sources on, 2313
use of in the 20th century, 51
Megenhardt, Anna, 318
Megenhardt, Mary, 318
Meginness, John Franklin, 2009
Mehlig, Johann Michael, 2009
Mehrning, Jakob, 296
  historian, **811**
Meidung
  Graybill (Grabill, Krehbiel) family, 567
Meier family, *See* Meyer family
Meier, Marcus
  on eschatology of early Brethren, 2346
  writings of, 2346
Meily, Elizabeth (later Spitler), 1212, 1249
Meinecke, Elka, 2346
Meiner, Anna Maria, 2009–2010
Meinke, Mrs. William
  Mishawaka, IN, Brethren Church, 852
Meinke, William
  Mishawaka, IN, Brethren Church, 852
Mekeel, Arthur J., 2010
Melanchthon, Phillip, 56
Melbeth Grove Church of the Brethren, VA, **811–812**
  Greenmount Church of the Brethren, VA, 571
  Pine Grove Church of the Brethren, VA, 1024
Melbourne, FL, Grace Brethren Church, **812**
  Orlando, FL, Grace Brethren Church, 982
Melbourne, IA, 1217
Melcher family, 1930
Melchers, Anna Catherine (later Studebaker), 1230
Melchoir family, 2010
Melchor-Weaver family, 2091
Melhorn, J. Jack, 1705, 2010
  McPherson College, president, 781
Mellen, Chuck, 2286
Mellenbruch, Laura Lehman, 2010
Mellick, Flo (later Collitt), 2166
Mellinger, Christina (later Hoke), 618
Mellinger family, 1212, 2010

Mellinger, John, 1705
Mellinger, Ruth N., 2010
Mellott, Absalom, 1705
Mellott, Alpheus
    Pleasant Ridge Church of the Brethren,
        PA, baptism of, 1034
Mellott, Dorothy A., 2286
Mellott family, 270
Mellott, Homer, 1705, 2304
Mellott, Isaiah, 1705
Mellott, John, 1705
Mellott, Laura, 566
Mellott, Patrick L., 2286
Mellott, Samuel Brethred, 1705, 2304
Mellott, Zenas L., 1705
Melrose Gardens Grace Brethren Church,
        PA, 1388, See also Harrisburg, PA,
        Melrose Gardens Grace Brethren
        Church
    example of place name, 911
Melrose meetinghouse
    Greenmount Church of the Brethren,
        VA, 571
Melser, Gene, 247
Melton, J. Gordon, 379, 2010
    on Beissel, Johann Conrad/Konrad,
        2346
    on doctrine of Brethren, 2346
    on Free Church, doctrine of, 2326
    on Mack, Alexander, Sr., 2346
Melvin Hill Church of the Brethren, NC
    Mill Creek Church of the Brethren,
        NC, 832
    Polk Co., NC, 812
membership, 400, 812, 812–814, 2028
    Brethren groups, and Pennsylvania,
        1005
    camp meetings, 245
    church, 5, 85, 812–814
    church and the individual, 2013
    church, interdependence of, and
        Priesthood of All Believers, 1057
    Church of the Brethren, basis of, 1997
    Church of the Brethren guidebook,
        2002
    Church of the Brethren instruction,
        1986
    classes, 86
    classes for, 2042
    confirmation, 333–334
    covenant of church membership, 2012
    discipline, 386
    dress symbol of, 401–404
    election of church officers, 434
    geographic distribution of, 1465–1478,
        1466–1478
    God's Means of Grace (Yoder), 555
    growth, 2004–2005
    Holy Spirit, doctrine of, 624
    inactive, 2001
    Influenza Pandemic, 655
    letters of, See letters of membership
    manuals, 2013, 2014
    Miami, NM, Church of the Brethren,
        associate status provision, 823
    minorities, ethnic and racial, 849, 851
    nature of church and, 812–813
    Progressive Brethren handbook, 2003
    Roman Catholic Church, 1120
    sources on, 2317, 2321
    U. S. churches, 1979
    voting for ministers, 844
Membership Committee, See Credential

Committee
membership records
    Old German Baptist Brethren, 970
membership statistics, 1218–1219
membership trends
    1980 to 2000, 2220
memoirs
    Mishler, John Diefenbach, 2019
Memorial Chapel (BC), 183
Memorial Church of the Brethren, PA, See
        Martinsburg, PA, Memorial
        Church of the Brethren
memorial service, 230, 814
    funerals, 524
men, See men's work; National Fellowship
        of Grace Brethren Men; National
        Laymen's Organization
    Brethren Church doctrine on role of,
        184
    ministries and, 177
    role of, 155
Men in Missions (Yokefellows)
    Jackson, Edward A., 2209
Menaugh, Albert S., 758, 914, 1705
    New Enterprise Brethren Church, IN,
        elder in, 927
    New Paris, IN, Brethren Church, pastor
        in, 931
    North Liberty, IN, Brethren Church,
        pastor, 948
    Sidney, IN, Grace Brethren Church,
        pastor, 1181
Mendenhall, George Eugene, 1705
Mendenz, Eliodora
    Los Toros, DR, Nuevo Renacer, 2215
Mendez, Miliciades, 2172–2173, 2286
Mendon School, preaching point main-
        tained by Kansas Center Church of
        the Brethren, KS, at, 683
Mendon, T. M., 757
Meneese family
    Fort Lauderdale, FL, Grace Brethren
        Church, 503
Menifee, CA, New Hope Community
        Church of the Valley, 2220
Menker, Harmon Remmel, 2286
Menker, Melvin
Medina, OH, Church of the Brethren, 2219
Menlo Church of the Brethren, KS, 814
Menn, Wilhelm, 2010
Menno, Ada, 2079
Menno Simons, 28, 292, 293, 711, 814,
        1092, 1860
    baptism, on, 1992
    baptisms by, 1973
    Holdeman, John, 618
    letter to Reformed critic Gellius Faber,
        29
Mennonites, 815
The Mennonite
    General Conference Mennonite
        Church, 536
    Mennonites, 2220
Mennonite Biblical Seminary, 126
Mennonite Brethren
    Believers Church Commentary Series,
        2134
    Christian education curricular materi-
        als, 2160
    Christ's Assembly and, 280
    Foundation series publications, 1237
    Hymnal: A Worship Book, 2205
    Jubilee: God's Good News Curriculum,

2209
Mennonite Brethren Churches, General
        Conference of, 814
Mennonites, 815, 2220
    Raisin City, CA, Church of the
        Brethren, pastor, 1083
Mennonite Brethren Churches, General
        Conference of, 814
Mennonite Central Committee (MCC),
116,
189, 814–815
    Canada, 815
    conscientious objectors, 337
    Fast Henry A., 480
    Friends Committee on Spain, 518
    Heifer Project International, 594
    Historic Peace Churches, 609
    Honduras, 627
    Karsschule rebuilding project, 684
    Mennonites, 815, 2221
    Miller, Orie O., 841
    Morocco, 876
    sponsorship of relief service in
        Vietnam, 1305
    violence and, 2265
Mennonite Central Council
    Reed, Kyle and Mary and, 2240
Mennonite Church, 815
Mennonite Church USA, 2220
Mennonite Encyclopedia, 116
    Dyck, C[ornelius] J. on, 2328
    Martin, Dennis D. entry in, 2328
Mennonite Family History, 535, 2188
Mennonite Historical Society Library, 610
    genealogy, 2188
Mennonite PAX (Alternative Service), 200
Mennonite Publishing House
    Jubilee: God's Good News Curriculum,
        2209
Mennonite-Quakers
    Germantown, 542
Mennonite World Conference, 815
Mennonites, 692, 815–816, 2021, 2029,
        2042, 2045, 2048, 2056,
        2220–2211
    "A Short and Sincere Declaration,"
        1178
    affiliation with Amish, 26, See also
        Amish Mennonites
    Allen Co., OH, 2086
    and alternative service, 19, 73
    Anabaptism and, 814, 815, 816
    The Andrew Center, 2130
    and Arminianism, 56
    baptism and, See baptism
    baptism, disagreement with John
        Kline, 701
    baptism doctrine, 168, 231
    Baptist attempt to unite with, 87
    BCA and, 185
    and beards, 103
    Believers Church Commentary Series,
        2134
    Bern, Switzerland
        suppression of, 2084
        Bernese Mennonites, 2025
    bibliography, 1858, 1874, 1883, 1887,
        1893, 1895, 1897, 1910
    bishops
        Burkholder, Peter, 231
        Bixler family, 144
        Boehm, Martin, 1289
        Bowman, Carl F. on, 2341

Brethren in Christ and, 188
Brethren/Mennonite Council for Lesbian and Gay Concerns, 2151–2152
Brethren movement, 174, 175, 280
Brethren neutrality and Revolutionary War, American, 1106
Brethren peace position, influence on, 999
Brethren remnants in Europe, 1099
Bristol Twp., OH, 2079
Brower, Daniel and Francis, 1286
Brubaker family (PA), 216
Bucks Co., PA, 2088
Byler, J. I., 1391
Cassel (Kassel) family, 260
Castañer Hospital, P.R., 261
Christian Day School movement, 282
Christian education curricular materials, 2160
Christian Peacemaker Teams (CPT), 2161
Church of the Brethren, 304
Civil War
    fugitives, 2086
colleges, 1973
Collegiants, 324
colonial era, 2085
Colorado Springs, CO, Church of the Brethren, 325
Columbia, MO, Fellowship, 2166
Committee of Observation, 327
Committee on Interchurch Relations, 2167
commutation tax, 331
Conference of Historic Peace Churches, 333
conscientious objection, 269, 316, 336
    World War II, 1371–1372
Continuation Committee of the Historic Peace Churches, 339
conversion, doctrine of, 339
CPS and, 315
criticism of, 16
CROP, 286
Danner (Tanner, Donner), Michael, 362
Delaware, settlements in, 374
delegations to FDR, 169
dissension about Peace of Westphalia, 1338
Dompelaars' withdrawal of from, 395
dress of, 401, 1949
Driedger, Leo on peacemaking and, 2325
Driver family, 405
Dunkard Brethren Church, 2106
Dutch, 1998
Eberle (Eberly) family, 417
economy and culture for Krefeld (trans), 1989
educational materials, 284
eighteenth century Pennsylvania church music, 1914
Elkhart, IN, Southside Fellowship (CB/Menn), 439
emigration to Pennsylvania, 1971
Ephrata Press, 452
Eschelbronn, Baden, Germany, 158
Eshelman (Eshleman) family, 455–456
Eternal Security, 456
evangelism, 2180
Fairfield Co., OH, 2086
Falfurrias, TX, Church of the Brethren, 471

family histories, 2070
Fast Henry A., 480
Felbinger, Jeremias, 482
fire fighting, 491
Fischer (Fisher) family, 491
Foundation series publications, 1237
Fraktur, 505
and *Fraktur* type, 60
fraternal relations, 510
Frederic Co., MD, 2100
Frey, Andreas, 517
Funck (Funk) family, 521, 2090
Funk, Benjamin, 525
Funk family, 2090
Funk, Joseph, 525
galleys (sidebar), 527
Garb Law, 528
Garber (Garver, Gerber) family, 529
Geistliche Fama (Spiritual Report), 533
genealogy, 534, 535, 2188
General Conference, *See* General Conference Mennonite Church
General Conference Mennonite Church, 536
German and hymnals, 72
German Baptist Brethren ordinances, 1969
Germantown, Battle of, 544
Germantown, PA, 2085
Gingerich (Kingery) family, 549
Gnagey (Gnaegi) family, 554
Good (Guth) family, 556
Gospel of Nicodemus, 296
Goyen family, 909
Goyen, Gossen, 562
Grahe, Wilhelm, 564
Grant Co., WV, 2079
Graybill (Grabill, Krehbiel) family, 567
Groff (Grove) family, 574
Häcker (Höcker), Wilhelm, 577
Hardtmann (Hardman, Hartman) family, 583
Hartzler, Russell M., 588
Heisey family, 595
Hershberger (Harshbarger) family, 598
Hershey family, 600
Hershey, Lewis Blaine, 599
Hiestand (Heistand, Heestand, Heaston) family, 602
Historic Peace Churches, 607, 608, 610
historic peace churches, 1981, 2200
historic sites, 609
historiography, 2201
    Forum for Religious Studies, 2202
history, 1942, 1953, , 2010, 2068
Hochmann von Hochenau, Ernst Christoph, 615
Holdeman, John, 618
Holtzapfel (Holsapple, Holsopple) family, 624
Holy Spirit, doctrine of, 624
Horst family, 630
Hostetler, Beulah Stauffer on, 2338
Hüber (Hoover) family, 634
Huizinga (Huisinga), Jacob Dircks, 635
Hutchinson, KS, Community Church of the Brethren, 638
Hymnal: A Worship Book, 2205
hymns, 643
Illinois, 2069
immigration agents, 250

Indiana, 2095
influence on Brethren, 43–44, 73
inner Word and outer Word, 656
joint ventures with Brethren Press, 2149
Jordan, Clarence, contact with, 705
Jubilee: God's Good News Curriculum, 2209
Kauerts, Amelia, 1222
Kauffman family, 685
Keyser family, 691
Keyser, Peter Dirck, 692
Kolb, Dielman, 706
Kraybill, Donald B. on, 2341, 2325
Krefeld, 707, 2058
Kruger, Peter, 708
Lancaster Co., PA, 2090
Lancaster, PA, Acts Covenant Fellowship, 2213
Landes, Johannes, 722
Lantz (Lentz) family, 725
Larned Church of the Brethren, KS, 726
Ledermann family, 733–734
Lehman family, 736
letter to, from Alexander Mack, Jr., 2004
Licht(y), Jacob Peter, 741
life style, 1974
lobbying for commutation fees for exemption during Civil War, 1233
Longenecker family, 756
Mack, Alexander, Sr., on, 776, 1258
MacMaster, Richard K. on, 2345
Maryland, 1920
mass media cooperative efforts, 801
Massachusetts Brethren activity, 801
Mast family, 1299
Materials Towards a History of the Baptists, 803
medicine, 809
meetinghouses, and Ontario Brethren, 975
Mehrning, Jacob, writings of, 811
membership, beliefs, and institutions early 21st century, 2220–2221
membership in 2000, 2220
Mennonite Brethren Churches, General Conference of, 814
Mennonite-Brethren heritage, plea for reappropriation of, 1925
Mennonite Central Committee (MCC), 814
Mennonite family histories, 2070
Mennonites, 815
Metzler family, 820
Meyer family, 821
migration of Brethren, 829
Milford Twp., PA, 2088
military service, 942
Miller, John Peter, 840
Miller, Samuel J., parents of, 842
Miller, Sebastian Christian, parents of, 842
Miller, Susan Fisher on revivalism and, 2347
minorities, ethnic and racial, 849
missions, 857, 2224
musical instruments, 900, 2228
Musselman, Christian, 901
Myerstown, PA, Church of the Brethren, 906
Nägele, Hans Rudolph, 910

National Institute of Health, volunteers, 2067
National Interreligious Service Board for Conscientious Objectors (NISBCO), 916–917
naturalization and refusal of loyalty oath to state, 918
Neiff (Neff) family, 909
Neuenschwander family associated with, 924
New Call to Peacemaking, 925–926
Nolt, Stephen M. on, 2349
and non-associators in Revolutionary War, 939
non-immersionists, 154
nonconformity, 940
oaths, taking of, 959
Oberholtzer family, 960
Old Brethren Christian Schools, 2232
Old German Baptist Brethren, 2235
Pennsylvania, 154, 158, 243, 1004, 2068, 2095
persecution of, 175
plain people, 1029
plea for tolerance, 2038
Plow Creek Fellowship, 1038
Prague Conferences and, 2239
prisoners of war, aid to, 1058
prisons, 1059
publications of, 154
Puidoux Conferences, 304
purchase of meetinghouse, Sugarcreek, OH, 1235
Reba Place Fellowship, 1084
Redford, MI, Trinity Church of the Brethren, 1090
Reformation, Protestant, and Brethren doctrine, 1092
relationship of the Brethren with, article about, 1921
relationship with early Brethren, 107
relief and service efforts, 1097
religious liberty and military service, 1098
religious toleration for, 407
restitution, 1100
Revolutionary War, in Maryland, 1997
Rittinghuysen, William, preacher, 1110
Roher (Rohrer) family, 1119
roots of, 28–29, 121–122
Rosenberger family, 1123
Rowland, Gasper, 1126
Rupp (Roop) family, 1130
Rural Life Association (RLA), 12, 1130
Ruth, John L. on PA, 2354
Schlabach, Theron F. on, 2355
Schwarzenau Brethren practices, 1079–1080
Selective Service System and conscientious objectors, 1165
Seneca Co., OH, 2086
Shank common family name, 1172
Simons, Menno, founder, 814
Skippack area, PA, 1189
Skyridge Church of the Brethren, Kalamazoo, MI, 681
sources on, 2313, 2320
South Bend, IN, Iglesia Evangelica Emanuel (CB) and, 2252
Spitler, Elizabeth Meily, 1212
Stauffer, Christian, 1219
Steiner family, 1221, 2378

Stetius, Gottfried Luther, 1222
Stouffer, Matthias, 1219
Strickler family, 1229
Stutzman, Christian and Magdalene (Maudlin), 1233
Stutzman, Jacob, 1233
Surhuisterveen colonized by, 1241
Swiss, 2056
textile industry and, 174
union Sunday school aided by, 157
Valley Brethren-Mennonite Heritage Center and, 2257–2258
Varner family, 1299
views on Brethren and Friends, 1990
violence and, 2265
Virginia, 168
Waterlander congregation, 1241
Weber (Weaver family), 1325
Welty, John, 1329
Wenger family, 1330
work camps, 1365
Yoder, Eli Lorenzo, 1386
Yoder, Joseph Warren, 1386–1387
Zug, Johannes and ___ Bachman, 1401
Zug, Ulrich, 1401
Mennonitischen Geschichtsvereins, 2010
Menomonie, WI, 1354
Church of the Brethren, **816**
Irvin Creek Church of the Brethren, 664
men's fellowships
1980–2000, **2221**
CB, *See* Men's Work
Indiana, 652
manuals for, 788
Men's Work, **816**, 2020, **2376**
General Board (CB), 535
Kettering, Joseph W., 691
Mohler, Robert Ellsworth, 868
Potsdam, OH, Church of the Brethren, 1049
Russell, Harl L., 1132
Mensch, Mervyn W., 1705
Mensching, Wilhelm, 517
Mensinger, Carol Jean, 1851, 2010
Mensinger, Edward Benjamin, 62, 1705, 1851
Mensinger, Linda Ann Paden, 1851
Mensinger, Wayne P.
Mill Run Grace Brethren Church, MD, pastor, 833
mental hospital service, 301, 316, **816–817**, *817,* 2354, 290
mentoring
ministerial leadership and personal faith, for, **2221–2222**
women and, 2263
Mentzer, D. Byron, 42, 1705
Mentzer, Daniel B., 1705–1706
Mentzer family
Robins, IA, Church of the Brethren, 1115
Mentzer, Maurice M., 1706
Mentzer, Samuel, 1706
Merced Co., CA, 246
Mercer Co., MO
Somerset German Baptist Brethren Church, MO, 1202
Mercer Co., OH, 1231, 1288
Pleasant Valley Church of the Brethren, OH, 1035
Ross Church of the Brethren, OH, 1124
Mercer Co., PA, 317

Mercer Co., WV, 154
Oakvale Church of the Brethren, WV, 958
Red Oak Ridge German Baptist Brethren Church, WV, 1089
Smith Chapel Church of the Brethren, WV, 1191
Mercer, Henry C., 61, 2010
Mercer, John W., 1706
Mercer, Lynn W., 2286
Mercer, OH, congregation
Ross Church of the Brethren, OH, 1124
Mercersburg, PA, *132,* 1329
Merchant, Agnes, 713
Merchant, Thomas L., 2010
Merci Train
Friendship Trains, 518
Meredith, Harry, 432, 1706
Meredith, John, 2010
mergers, *See* ecumenism
Mericle Church of the Brethren, OH, *See* Bremen, OH, Rush Creek Church of the Brethren
Meridan, KS
Ozawkie Church of the Brethren, preaching points established by, 987
Merington, Marguerite, 2010
Merkey, Ammon L., 1706
Merkey, David, 1706
Merkey, David R., 1706
Merkey family, 144, 700, 2010, *See also* Markey family
Kauffman, Sandra on, 2340
Merkey, George A., 1706
Merkey house
Little Swatara Church of the Brethren, PA, 750
Merkey, Howard A., 1706
Merkey, Jacob, 794, 1320, 1706
Merkey, Jacob P., 1706
Merkey, John, 793
Merkey, Joseph, 1706
Merkey, Kate (later Ziegler), 1397
Merkey, Nancy Moyer, 794
Merkey, Nellie V., 1706, 2010
Merkey, Paul, 1380
Merkey, Ruth, 1380
Merkey, Samuel M., 794
Merkey, Samuel R., 1706
Merkey, Vernon F., 1706
Merkle family, 1929
Merriam, IN, 153
Merrick, Francis A.
"The Reimer Ghost," 2010
Merrifield, Dan
Romine Church of the Brethren, IL, providing leadership, 1121
Merrifield, James Dale, 1706
Merrill, Alice Hamilton, 1706
Merrill, David M., 273, 1706
Merrill, Eleanor Weitzell, 273
Merrill, John, 273
Merrill, Nathaniel, 273, 1706
Merriman, Keith Andrew, 2167, 2286
Merrington Church of the Brethren, Sask., **817**
Merritt, Didra
on Studebaker family, 2360
Merritt, Russell E., 1706
Merton, Thomas, 659
Mertz family, 232
Mertz, Jacob H., 14

Mesa, AZ, Community Church of the Brethren, **2222**

The Message of Faith (Flora), 2141, 2148, 2156

The Message of the Book of Revelation (Hoff), 616

"Message of the Brethren Ministry", 68, 77, 183, 185, **817–818**
    authority of scripture, 133
    Burnworth, Benjamin Taylor and formulation of, 232
    Fellowship of Grace Brethren Churches (FGBC), 484, 486
    Fundamental Brethren Church, 522
    fundamentalism, 522
    Gearhart, William A., 533
    Gillin, John Lewis, 549
    Liberal theology and noncreedalism, 943
    Liberalism waning after, 1261
    McClain, Alva J., 772
    Miller, John Allen, 839
    reaffirmation by National Fellowship of Brethren Ministers, 916
    replaced by statement of faith, 1218
    Social Gospel Movement, 1197

Messamer, Ethel, 2010

Messamer, Orlo Elvin, 1706, 2010
    Modesto, CA, Church of the Brethren, pastor, 866

Messamer, Ruth Darlene (later Garwick), 1631

The Messenger, **818–819**, *See also The Gospel Messenger*
    Brethren identity, issue of, 2149
    Brethren profile study, 2150
    controversies over use of modern art, 61
    Frantz, Ruby June (later Rhoades) and, 2242
    General Services Commission (CB), 539
    Gospel Messenger Advisory Committee, 559
    Hays, Daniel, 590
    Helman, Patricia Kennedy, 2197
    Long, Inez Goughnour, 2215
    Mai Sule Biu, 782
    Morse, Kenneth Ivan, editor, 878
    motion pictures, 879
    name change discussion (CB), 2228
    Parish Ministries Commission involvement in, 993
    photographs and visual art, 1020
    poetry, 1039
    publication of, 2149, 2162
    Shamberger, Chauncey, 1171
    women and, 2264
    Zeigler, Carl Wenger (CB) and, 2269

Messenger family, 1312

messengers, *See* Credential(s) Committee
    delegates to Annual Meeting, 1044
    election of church officers, 434
    Receiving Committee membership, 1085

messengers (OGBB)
    delegates, 375
    women and, 2263

messengers to Annual Meetings, **819**

Messer, Hazel Elvina (later Moss), 1842, **2388**

Messerli, Jonathan, 2010

Messiah Church of the Brethren, MO, *See*

Kansas City, MO, Messiah Church of the Brethren

Messiah College, Grantham, PA, 189

Messiah congregations
    example of biblically inspired name, 911

messianic community
    Brethren movement, 293

Messick, David M., 1706

Messick, R. Wilson, 1706

Messina, Salvatore M., 2010

Messler, L., 1706

Messmore family, 1365

Messmore, Jesse, 581

Messner, Devraux, 1706

Messner, Peter B., 1706, 2010

Messner, Richard G., 1706, 2304

Metal stocks used on prisoners at Büdingen, *1009*

Metcalf family
    Mount Hope Church of the Brethren, WA, 882

Metcalf, H. P., 1706

meteorites
    Nininger, Harvey H., 781, 938

Metger family, 1883

Methacton congregation, PA
    Harleysville, PA, Indian Creek Church of the Brethren, 584

A Method of Prayer (Johannes Kelpius), 1051, 1200

Methodism
    Arminianism and, 56
    Brethren children named for leaders of, 912–913
    Evangelical Association, 459
    Holiness Movement, American, 619
    influence of, 16

Methodist Church, *See* United Methodist Church
    Bible classes and prayer meetings, 1053
    Board of Missions of the Methodist Churches of Latin America, 1290
    camp meetings, 245
    Cartwright, Peter, 257–258
    China, 296
    Church of God (New Dunkers), 297
    Church of North India, 298
    church shared with Brethren, 407
    Dolby, Martha Cunningham, 395
    Easton, MD, Peach Blossom Church of the Brethren, 416
    Ecuador, 1291
    Fairview Church of the Brethren, MD, 469
    Fellowship of Reconciliation (USA), 488
    Fleming Co., KY, German Baptist Brethren Church, 494
    Flower Hill Church of the Brethren, MD, 500
    frontier, 519
    Fry, Julia Ann Elder, 521
    higher education, 603
    Holsinger, Levi Teeter, 623
    Illinois, 647
    influence on United Brethren in Christ, 1289–1290
    Mason, George Edward, 2218
    Mount Morris College, 883
    New Troy, MI, Grace Brethren Church, pastor sharing with, 932

nonconformity, 940

Pentecostalism, 1008

Pietism, 1022

plain people, 1029

public worship criticized, 1375

slavery, 2128

Stiverson, James Ulysses Grant, 1223

Sunday school movement, 283

Sunnyside, WA, Grace Brethren Church, 1240

Trout, Philip, 1271

Union Chapel Church of the Brethren, PA, 1287

Union Co., IL, 1357

United, episcopal polity, 1042

United Methodist Church, 1291

United Methodist congregation, Wawaka, IN, 1323

Methodist Episcopal Church, 1962
    Nead, Peter, leadership in, 918

Methodist Theological School, OH
    consortium with Ashland Theological Seminary, 1291

Methodius of Olympus
    premillennialism, 833

Metropolitan Christian Council of Washington D.C., 2239

Metropolitan Detroit Council of Churches
    Redford, MI, Trinity Church of the Brethren, 1090

Metropolitan Nikodim, 2239

Metsgar family, *See* Metzger family

Metsker, Ellah Ruhannah (later Milligan), 2018

Metsker family, *See* Metzger family

Metsker, Gary, 2346

Metsker, John C., 820, 1914

Metsker, Phillip, 1914

Metsker, Samuel Wells, 1914

Metsker, Shirley, 2346

Metz, C. C., 1706

Metz, Christian, 330

Metz, Daniel O., 106, 1706

Metz, Eli, 1313, 1706
    Maumee Church of the Brethren, OH, minister, 803

Metz, Elizabeth (later Swihart), 1245

Metz, Jacob, 1234

Metz, Mary Catherine
    Mount Pleasant, PA, Church of the Brethren, 886

Metz, O., 1706

Metz, Peter G., 1706

Metz, W. Ray, 2010

Metzer family, 2093–2094

Metzgar family, *See* Metzger family
    Reading Grace Brethren Church, PA, 1084

Metzger, Aaron, 1385

Metzger, Minerva, father of, 819

Metzger, Aaron P., 1706
    Middlefork Old German Baptist Brethren Church, IN, presiding elder, 826
    Pipe Creek Old German Baptist Brethren Church, IN, minister, 1026
    Scottville Old German Baptist Brethren Church, MI, elder-in-charge, 1161

Metzger, Barbara, 2222

Metzger, Barbara Anderson, 1944

Metzger, Carl, 430, 1706

Metzger, Catherine

Metzger, Minerva, mother of, 819
Metzger, Christian, 2018
Metzger, Daniel
  North Fork Old German Baptist
    Brethren Church, IN, 947
Metzger, Dennis, 193
Metzger, Dennis O., 766, 1295, 1706
Metzger, Emily (later Mumma), 2288
Metzger, Ethel, 1860
Metzger family
  Genesee Old German Baptist Brethren
    Church, MI, 540
  Shively family, related to, 1178
  Shoemaker, David, related to, 1157
  South Haven Old German Baptist
    Brethren Church, MI, 1205
Metzger, Glen L., 1706, 2304, **2384**
  Mexico Old German Baptist Brethren
    Church, IN, 2376
  North Manchester Old German Baptist
    Brethren Church, IN, minister, 949
  Pine Grove Old German Baptist
    Brethren Church, FL, elder-in-
    charge, 1025
Metzger, Hannah Ulery
Metzger, John, wife of, 819
Metzger, Henry P., 373, 1294, 1706
  Pine Creek Old German Baptist
    Brethren Church, IN, minister,
    1026
Metzger, Homer E., 320
Metzger, Howard M.
Metzger, Thurl D., 2222
Metzger, Ida, 1841
  medical missions, 807
Metzger, Ira, 62, 1706
Metzger, Isaac, 430, 512, 1706
Metzger, Iva Leckrone
  Metzger, Thurl D., 2222
Metzger, Jacob, 429, 430, 637, **819**
  Metzger family, 820
  Metzger, John, father of, 819, 1706
  Middlefork Old German Baptist
    Brethren Church, IN, minister, 826
  North Manchester Old German Baptist
    Brethren Church, IN, elder, 949
Metzger, Jacob H., 1706
Metzger, Johann, Sr.
  Metzger family, 820
Metzger, John, 170, 270, 295, 714, **819,**
  1296, 1298, 1339, 1706, 1932
  biography by Eshelman, Matthew
    Mays, 455
  Hurricane Creek Church of the Breth-
    ren, IL, 638
  Metzger family, 820
  Milmine Church of the Brethren, IL,
    elder, 843
  Oakley Brick Church of the Brethren,
    IL, elder, 958
  Pleasant Dale Church of the Brethren,
    IN, 1030
  Rossville, IN, Church of the Brethren,
    elder, 1124
Metzger, Joseph S., 1706
  Middlefork Old German Baptist
    Brethren Church, IN, minister, 826
  North Manchester Old German Baptist
    Brethren Church, IN, minister, 949
Metzger, Joseph C., 1706
Metzger, Kathleen
  Metzger, Thurl D., 2222
Metzger, Lester C., 2304

Metzger, Mary Butterbaugh
  Metzger, John, mother of, 819
Metzger, Mary (later Morris)
  Morris, Charles Stephen, mother of,
    877
Metzger, Mary (later Skiles), See Skiles,
  Mary Metzger
Metzger, Melvin Lynn, 2286, 2304
Metzger (Metsgar), John, 1706
Metzger (Metsgar, Metzgar, Metzker)
  family, **820**
Metzger (Metzgar), John W., 1706
Metzger (Metzgar), Samuel, 1706
Metzger (Metzgar), Stephen, **819–820**
Metzger (Metzgar), Steven, 1706
Metzger, Minerva, **819**, 1841
Metzger, Orlin Ira, 62, 1706
Metzger, Permelia Wolfe
  Metzger, John, wife of, 819
Metzger, Richard, 2222
Metzger, Robert, 2222
Metzger, Robert D., 1706, 2286
Metzger, Ruth Landis, 2222
Metzger, Samuel, 1213, 1706
Metzger, Samuel (1841–99), 62
Metzger, Stephen
  Middlefork Old German Baptist
    Brethren Church, IN, presiding
    elder, 826
Metzger, Thurl D., 594, **2222**
  Polish Agricultural Exchange, 1041
Metzker, Andrew, 820
Metzker, Henry, 820
Metzker, Jacob, 820
Metzker, Jacob Ira, 1706–1707
Metzker, John, 820
Metzler, Alma Stump, 2376
Metzler, Ann (later Albright), 2376
Metzler, Anna Nissley, 820
Metzler, Burton, 619, **820**, 1707, 2010, **2376**
Metzler, Charlotte, 1841
Metzler, Christian, 1313, 1707
Metzler, David G., 820, 1707, 2376
  Rossville, IN, Church of the Brethren,
    minister, 1124
Metzler family, **820**
Metzler, Gertrude, 343
Metzler, John D., Jr., 539, 1707
Metzler, John D., Sr., 233, 286, **820**, 858,
  1707, 2304
Metzler, Karen Glick
  Sudan (CB) and, 2253
Metzler, Lucinda Holloway
  Metzler, Burton and John D., Sr.,
    mother of, 820
Metzler, Margaret Eldridge, 2376
  Metzler, John D., Sr., wife of, 820
Metzler, Mary (later Wagoner), 2376
Metzler, Steven P.
  Sudan (CB) and, 2253
Metzler, Valentine, 820
Metzler, Yost, 820
Mexican-Americans
  Outlook, WA, Church of the Brethren,
    986
Mexican Sunday schools
  minorities, ethnic and racial, 850
Mexican War, **820**
Mexicans, 2025
  Garden City, KS, Church of the
    Brethren, 530
Mexico, **820–821**
  Foreign Missionary Society (BC,

FGBC), 501
General Conference Mennonite
  Church, 536
Grace Brethren International Missions,
  2191
Hispanic Ministries (BC), 2198
Ingraham, M. Virgil, 2208
Mennonites migrating to, 815
Mexico City, Mexico, Brethren
  Mission, 2222
migration of Brethren, 827
Miller, Howard, land commissioner for,
  838
mission work in, 2157
The Missionary Board (BC), 856
missions, 862, 2224, 2225
missions and missionaries in, 182
missions, short-term, 2226
relief and rehabilitation work in, 186
Weaver, Scott L. (FGBC, CGBCI) and,
  2261
work camps, 1367
Mexico, AFSC aid for, 23
Mexico City, Mexico, Brethren Mission
  Brethren Church administration in
    Mexico, **2222**
Mexico congregation, IN, 652
Mexico, IN
  Brethren Church, 97, 377, 385, 694,
    821
  Corinth, IN, Brethren Church,
    branch of, 345
  Peru, IN, First Brethren Church,
    1010
  Church of the Brethren, 4, 30, 491,
    821, 1952, **2376**
    history, 2010
    Moss family, 878
  Peru, IN, Church of the Brethren,
    1010
  Roann, IN, Church of the Breth-
    ren, 1112
  Old German Baptist Brethren Church,
    4, **821**, **2376**
  Pipe Creek Old German Baptist
    Brethren Church, IN, 1026
Mexico Welfare Home, See Old Folks and
  Orphans Home, Mexico, IN
  Old Folks and Orphans Home (CB),
    Mexico, IN, 965, 1264–1265
Meyer, See Myer
Meyer, A. O., 1707
Meyer, Ammon B., 1707
Meyer, Ann, 821
Meyer, Anna, 821
Meyer, Anna Burkholder, 216
Meyer, Anna J. Royer
  Meyer, Jacob Gibble, wife of, 821
Meyer, Barbara, 821
Meyer, Christian, 821
  descendants, 1941
  Mason-Dixon Line, 800
Meyer, Christian Friedrich, 2010
Meyer, Christian, Jr., 821
Meyer, Christopher, 822
Meyer Church of the Brethren
  love feasts, 2106
Meyer, Dorothy, 405
Meyer, Elizabeth, 821
Meyer, Elizabeth (later Shank), See Shank,
  Elizabeth Meyer
Meyer, Emma, 2095
Meyer, Ernest L., 2010

Meyer family, 226, 534, 1380, 2011, 2023
  Harrisburg, PA, Melrose Gardens Grace Brethren Church, 586
  Royer family, related to, 1128
Meyer Family Historical Committee, 2011
Meyer, Frank, 1707
Meyer Genealogy, 2011
Meyer, H., 2023
Meyer, Hans, 821, 2011
  descendants, 1941
Meyer, Helen M. Brechbill, 2010–2011
Meyer, Henry, 821–822, 2011, 2025
Meyer, Hester, 821
Meyer, Ira C., 1707
Meyer, Jacob, 216, 821, 822
Meyer, Jacob (2 listed), 1707
Meyer, Jacob G., **821,** 1707, 2011
  Elizabethtown College, 437
Meyer, Jacob O., 68
Meyer, Jacob W., Jr., 1707
  Mount Zion Road Church of the Brethren, PA, minister, 888
Meyer, Jacob W., Sr., 1707
  Meyer, Jacob Gibble, father of, 821
Meyer, John, 821, 822
Meyer, Lauree Hersch, 2133, 2286
  on CB, liturgy, tradition and ministry of, 2347
  on CB pneumatology, 2347
  on fencerow theology, 2347
  Prague Conferences and, 2239
  on women, 2332
Meyer, Leah Gibble
  Meyer, Jacob Gibble, mother of, 821
Meyer, Maggie, 365
Meyer, Marie Nelson
  Meyer, Jacob Gibble, wife of, 821
Meyer, Martin (2 listed), 1707
Meyer, Mary Keysor, 2011
Meyer, Matthew M., 552, 1707, 2011, 2111
Meyer (Meier, Meyers, Moyer, Moyers, Myer, Myers) family, 26
Meyer, Michael
  Meyer family, 822
Meyer (Moyer, Myer, Meier, Meyers, Moyers, Myers) family, **821–822**
Meyer, Nathan M., 1707, 2304
Meyer, Norman, 1707
Meyer, Ora, 1707
Meyer, Rudolph I., 2011
Meyer, Samuel, 821, 1707
Meyer, Samuel G., 756, 1707
  Mount Zion Road Church of the Brethren, PA, minister, 888
Meyer, Ursula, 2011
Meyer, Virgil E., 1707
Meyer, Waldermer, 1707
Meyer, Walton, 193
Meyerding, Esther Smith, 2350
Meyers, *See* Myers
Meyers, A., 1707
Meyers, Andrew, 2074
Meyers, Anna Kauffman, 2074
Meyers, Anne Alverta (later Miller)
  Miller, Robert Paul, wife of, 842
Meyers, C. A., 227
Meyers, Daniel L., 676
Meyers, Darlene C., 2286
Meyers, David, 1707
Meyers, Elias
  Miller, Robert Paul, related by marriage, 842
Meyers, Estella, 183

Meyers family, 700, 1236, 1276, 1322, 2074, *See also* Meyer family
  Chambersburg, PA, 2011
  Farmers Grove Fellowship (BC), PA, 476
Meyers, Fannie (later Livengood), 750
Meyers, Frank F., 1707
Meyers, H. S., 746
Meyers, Harold R.
  Poplar Ridge Church of the Brethren, OH, pastor, 1047
Meyers, Henry, 472
Meyers, Henry, family
  Milledgeville, IL, Brethren Church, 833
Meyers, I. Austin, 2011
Meyers, Isaac (2 listed), 1707
Meyers, J. Frank, 1707
Meyers, J. L., 1707
Meyers, Jacob, **822**
Meyers, Jacob M., 1707
Meyers, Jacob T., 180, 561, 720, 1707, *See also* Myers, Jacob T.
  publishing, 1068
Meyers, James W., 2286
Meyers, John, 246, 1323, 1389, 1707
M(e)yers, John A.
  Pleasant Grove Grace Brethren Church, IA, pastor, 1031
Meyers, John G., 1707
Meyers, John W., 1707
Meyers, Joseph, **2384**
Meyers, Josiah P.
  Sipesville, PA, Church of the Brethren, Sunday School superintendent, 1187
Meyers, Leon E., 2287
Meyers, Lovina Ellen Young, 1707
Meyers, M., 746
Meyers, Maggie, 214
Meyers, Michael
  Ryerson Station Church of the Brethren, PA, preaching, 1132
Meyers, Michael Conway, 1225, 1707
  Muncie, IN, Brethren Church, pastor, 896
Meyers Mills meetinghouse
  Meyersdale, PA, 1139
Meyers (Moyer) family, 2011
Meyers (Myer), Jacob W., 1707
Meyers (Myer), Joseph, 1707
Meyers (Myers), Ananias, 1707
Meyers (Myers), Jacob, 518, 1293
Meyers (Myers), John L., 1707
Meyers (Myers), Jonathan David, 1707
Meyers (Myers), Martin, 1707
Meyers (Myers), S. S., 1707
Meyers (Myers), Samuel A., 1707
Meyers (Myers), Tobias, 1707
Meyers, P. S., 1215
Meyers, Philip, 472
Meyers, S. T., 1707
Meyers, Sarah Hannah Catherine (later Hays), 590
Meyers, Tobias, family
  Sheldon Church of the Brethren, IA, 1175
Meyers, Victor H., 715
Meyers, William Horace, 1707, 2011
Meyers, William S., 1707–1708
Meyers, Zola, 380, 1708
Meyersdale, PA
  Church of the Brethren, **822**

Elk Lick congregation, 1139
  history, 1998
  Hyndman, PA, Church of the Brethren, 643
Grace Brethren Church, **822**
Main Street Brethren Church, 68, 703, 485, **822–823,** 1236
  Meyersdale, PA, German Baptist Brethren congregation, 823
Second Brethren Church, *See* Summit Mills Grace Brethren Church, PA
Summit Mills Brethren Church, *See* Summit Mills Grace Brethren Church, PA
Meyle, Hans, 804
Meyle (Mäyle, Maili, Moyly), Johann (Jan) (Brother Amos), **804**
Meylin, Anna (later Eby), 420
Meynen, Emil, 140, 1860, 2011
Mhya, Samuel B., 1708
Mi-Wuk Village
  Sierra Pines Old German Baptist Brethren Church, CA, 1181
Miami Co., IN, 267, 758
  Mexico, IN, Church of the Brethren, 821
  Midway Dunkard Berthren Congregation, IN, 827
  New Enterprise Brethren Church, 927
  Pipe Creek Church of the Brethren, IN, 1025
  Pipe Creek Old German Baptist Brethren Church, IN, 1026
  Santa Fe Church of the Brethren, IN, 1144
Miami Co., KS, 682, 1311
Miami Co., OH, 157, 170, 237, 261, 281, 335, 343, 350, 363, 364, 365, 373, 1231, 1277, 1332, 1335, 1389
  history, 1965, 2013
  Maple Grove Old German Baptist Brethren Church, OH, 791
  Old German Baptist Brethren, 970, 2016
  Old Order German Baptist Brethren, 970
  place-names, Brethren, 1028
  Pleasant Hill, OH, Church of the Brethren, 1031
  Pleasant Hill, OH, First Brethren Church, 1032
  Potsdam, OH, Church of the Brethren, 1048
Miami, FL, Eglise des Frères Haitians, **2222**
Miami, NM, Church of the Brethren, **823,** 1995
Miami, OH
  congregation
    Miller, Jacob, 961
  secret societies, debate over, 1164
Miami, TX, 190, 1332
Miami Valley Elders, **823**
  Miami Valley Petition, 823
Miami Valley, OH, 178, 1890–1891
  migration of Brethren, 829
  Old German Baptist Brethren influence in, 967
  Royer family, 1128
  Shideler family, 1177
  Sollenberger family, 1202
Miami Valley Petition, 205, **823**
  Murray, Samuel M., 897

"Reconsidered Petition," 1086
    Siler, George V., signer of, 1181
Miamisburg, OH, Brethren Church, **823,**
    1267, 1320
    Mason, Edward, 799
Miatke, Ronald G., 1708
Michael, Conrad, 689
Michael, David
    Sidney, IN, Grace Brethren Church,
        1181
Michael, Elfred J., 1708
Michael, Elsie, 190
    Mexico, missionary to, 821
Michael family, 241
    Grand River German Baptist Brethren
        Church, MO, 565
    Howard Co. Old German Baptist
        Brethren Church, IN, 633
    Salem Church of the Brethren, OH,
        1138
Michael, G. I., 470, 688, 1213, 1708
    Minot, ND, Church of the Brethren,
        elder, 851
Michael, H. D.
    Edison German Baptist Brethren
        Church, NE, 2373
    Silver Lake Church of the Brethren,
        NE, elder and minister, 1182
Michael, Harold K., 663, 717, 1708
Michael, Henry, 2099
Michael, Herbert Delton, 1841
Michael, Howard Dalton, 190, 530, 1708,
    2011
    Myrtle Point, OR, Church of the
        Brethren, pastor, 906
    life and ministry, 2011
    Mexico, missionary to, 821
Michael, Marianne Georgia Krueger, 1841
Michael, Mary Christine Good, 1708
Michael, Michael Lynn, 2287
Michael (Michaels), Joseph F., 1708
Michael, N. D., 2011
Michael, Peter, *483, 589,* 1708, 1958
Michael, Thomas, 1708
Michael, William, 1708
Michael, William N., 1708
Michaels, Maria Barbara (later Kern), 689
Michaels, Paul H.
    Lexington, KY, Grace Bible Church,
        2215
Michaels, William, 1708
Michaelson, Don, 246
Michaelson, Phyllis, 246
Michigan, 163
    Brethren settlement, **823–824,** *824*
    Church of the Brethren congregational
        life, 1999
    church work, 2010
    colonization, 324
    Grace Brethren Church, 303
    history of Brethren in, 1924
    migration of Brethren, 829
    Ohio Dunkard Brethren, 963
    Old German Baptist Brethren, 967, 970
    place-names, Brethren, 1028
    southern Michigan families, 1911
Michigan City, IN
    Church of the Brethren, **824–825**
    Dunkers, 2008
Michigan State College, 9
Michigan Valley, KS, congregation
    Plum Creek Old German Baptist
        Brethren Church, KS, 1038

Mickle, Raymond, 1708
Mickle, Thomas B., 1708
Mickley, Anna May Sell, 2011
Mickley, Minnie F., 2011
Mid-Atlantic district office
    Ellicot City, MD, Pine Orchard Church
        of the Brethren, 441
mid-Western America
    social idealism, 2069
Middle Ages
    family worship, 474
Middle Creek Church of the Brethren, IA
    825
Middle Creek Church of the Brethren, MD,
    See Beaver Dam, MD, Church of
    the Brethren
Middle Creek Church of the Brethren, PA
    (Lancaster Co.), **825,** 720,
    737, 748
    Middle Creek Church of the Brethren,
        PA (West Conestoga), 14,
Middle Creek Church of the Brethren, PA
    (Somerset Co.), 211, 267, **825,**
    1139, 1202
    Fairview Church of the Brethren, PA,
        469
    Geiger Church of the Brethren, PA,
        533
    Greensburg, PA, Church of the
        Brethren, 571
    Maple Spring Church of the Brethren,
        PA, 791
    Mohler Church of the Brethren, PA,
        868
    Pike Run Church of the Brethren, PA,
        1023
    Rockwood Church of the Brethren, PA,
        1118
Middle District, OH, Church of the
    Brethren, *See* Tipp City, OH,
    Middle District Church of the
    Brethren
    100 year anniversary, 2011
Middle East, *See* specific countries
    missions, short-term, 2226
    peace efforts in, 23
    relief and rehabilitation work in, 199
Middle Flat Creek mission point
    Flat Creek Church of the Brethren, KY,
        493
Middle Fork congregation, IN, 1312, 1345
Middle House (Eel River), IN
    Eel River Church of the Brethren, IN,
        429
Middle Indiana district
    Shultz, Lawrence W., 1180
The Middle Man (Davis family), 748
Middle Pennsylvania district, Church of the
    Brethren
    affiliation wtih University Baptist
        Church, 1218
    Parkview Church of the Brethren, PA,
        organized by, 994
Middle River Church of the Brethren, IA
    English River Church of the Brethren,
        IA, 447
Middle River Church of the Brethren, VA,
    90, 413, 498, 528, 530, **825,** 1391
    bibliography, 1909
    Flat Rock Church of the Brethren, VA,
        493
    Forest Chapel Church of the Brethren,
        VA, 502

Grottoes, VA, Church of the Brethren,
    574
    Pleasant Hill Church of the Brethren,
        VA, preaching point of, 1033
    Pleasant Valley Church of the Brethren,
        VA, 1035
Middle States Association of Colleges and
    Secondary Schools
    Ellis, Calvert Nice, 441
Middle Taylor Twp., PA, 1944
Middlebranch, OH, congregation (BC), 761
    Shively, Martin, pastor, 1178
Middlebranch, OH, Grace Brethren Church,
    825, 2195
Minerva, OH, Grace Brethren Church, 843
Middlebury, IN, Church of the Brethren,
    825–826, 588, 1156, **2376**
    example of place name, 911
    Pleasant Valley Church of the Brethren,
        IN, 1034
Middlefork, IN, Church of the Brethren,
    See Rossville, IN, Church of the
    Brethren
Middlefork Old German Baptist Brethren
    Church, IN, **826,** 1188
Middlekauf family, 1359
Middlekauff, John Claude, 637, 1708, **2384**
    New Carlisle, OH, Church of the
        Brethren, elder in, 926
Middleton, MI
    New Haven Church of the Brethren,
        928
Middletown congregation
    Elizabethtown, PA, Church of the
        Brethren, 436
    Harrisburg, PA, First Church of the
        Brethren, 586
Middletown house, mission point of
    Southern Ohio District, 1235
Middletown, IN, 1294
    Church of the Brethren, **826,** 1295
Middletown, OH, 1235
    Church of the Brethren, **826**
    Hamilton, OH, First Church of the
        Brethren, 581
Middletown, PA, Swatara Hill Church of
    the Brethren, **826**
Middletown Valley Church of the Brethren,
    MD, 106, **826**
    Grossnickle Church of the Brethren,
        574
    Harmony Church of the Brethren, 584
    Myersville, MD, Church of the Breth-
        ren, 906
    Pleasant View Church of the Brethren,
        MD, 1037
Middletown Valley settlement, 732
Middleville, MI
    Hope Church of the Brethren, MI, 629
Midland Co., MI, 323
    Church of the Brethren, **826,** **2376**
Midland congregation, VA, 1301
Midland regional dialect, 911
Midland, VA, Church of the Brethren, 150,
    826–827, 939
    Madison Church of the Brethren, VA,
        781
    Manassas, VA, Church of the Brethren,
        785
    Mine Run Church of the Brethren, VA,
        843
Midlu, Nigeria, 306
Midway Church of the Brethren, PA, 733,

827, 1278, 2341
Midway Church of the Brethren, TN, **827**
Midway Dunkard Brethren Congregation, IN, **827**
Midway house, Tulpehocken Church of the Brethren, PA, 1278
midweek prayer meetings, 1053
Midwest
  on choice of legal name for denomination, 910
Midwest Institute of International Relations, 2011
Miekley, Walter H., 1708
Mielecki, Robert, 244
Mifflin Co., PA, 406, 697, 1215, 1245, 1929
  Hanawalt, Joseph Rothrock, 581
Maitland Church of the Brethren, PA, 783
  Pine Glen Church of the Brethren, PA, 1024
Mifflin, OH, 155
migrant labor, **827,** *828*
migrant labor camps, 201
migrant workers, outreach ministries to
  Sunnyslope Church of the Brethren, WA, 1240
migrant workers programs
  Church of the Brethren, 252
migration, 2057, *See also* frontier; pioneers
  of Brethren, **827–831,** *828*
    and art, 59
    effect on church, 3
    and farming, 9–12
      Mayville, ND, Red River Valley Church of the Brethren, 805
    Pennsylvania, 707
      Zinzendorf, Nikolaus Sudwig, count von, 1399
  Brethren after Revolutionary War, 1106
  Brethren congregations as rural churches, 1130
  Brethren, lineage of, 613
  colonization, 324
  evangelism, 295, 460
  farming, 477
  Farnhamville, IA, Church of the Brethren, 479
  Faw, Isaac, 480
  frontier, 518–519
  genealogy, 534, 2188
  General Conference Mennonite Church, 536
  Germany, 545
  gospel songs, 560
  Graybill (Grabill, Krehbiel) family, 567
  Great Northern Railroad, 568–569
  Griggs, OK, Bethel Church of the Brethren, 573
  Hevener Church of the Brethren, WV, 602
  Holderman (Haldeman) family, 618
  Holmesville Church of the Brethren, NE, 620
  Holtzapfel (Holsapple, Holsopple) family, 624
  Holy Spirit, doctrine of, 624
  homesteading, 626
  Honey Creek Church of the Brethren, MO, 627
  Hoyle Creek Church of the Brethren, OK, 633
  Hunsiker (Hunsaker) family, 637
  Idaho, 645
  Illinois, 646

Independence, KS, Church of the Brethren, 649
Indian Creek Church of the Brethren, OK, 651
The Inglenook, influence of, 1978
Jasper, MO, Church of the Brethren, 669–670
land grants to Mennonites and Dunkards, 1993
missions, 857
mural paintings at Camp Mack portraying, 896
Pennsylvania Germans, 1006
place-names, Brethren, 1027–1028
railroads, 1082
Rotterdam, Brethren sailing from, 1125
sources on Brethren regarding, 2323
to U.S.
  religious reasons for, 990
  westward, 1994, 2006
migration and settlement, 176, **2376**
  Revolutionary War, 426
migrations
  of Bernese Anabaptists, 121
  Mennonites, 815
  of Mennonites, 121
Mikesell, Simon, 366, 1708
Mikesell, Vinnie (later Flory), 499
Mikula, Donald Max, 1708
Mikula, Evelyn Rhodes, 2011
Milam, WV, Mount Carmel Church of the Brethren
  organized as a fellowship 1983, **2222**
Milbach house, Tulpehocken Church of the Brethren, PA, 1278
Miles, Austin
  hymns, 643
Miles, George I., 2011
Miles, Lois Elaine Fasnacht, 480
Miles, Minta, 2011
Miley, Wilbert Harley, 1708, 2011
Milford, IN, 67, 407, 1223
  Bethel Church of the Brethren, **831,** 835, 1036, 1099
  Brethren Church, **831**
  New Salem Church of the Brethren, 932
Milford Twp., PA
  Mennonite Church, 2088
Milham, W. H., 1708
militarism and taxes, 1248–1249
military chaplaincy, 100, 832, 1305, 1372–1373, 2157
military clothing, *See* uniform, military
military conscription, lobbying regarding, 751
military court martials, 1370, 1371
military exemptions, *See* alternative service; conscientious objection
  Civil War, 1308, 1380
  Kline, John, 701
  ministerial, 844
  World War I, 1370
military pensions, **1008,** 1304
military personages, Brethren children named for, 912
military recruitment, **831**
military service, 19–20, **56, 831–832,** 1864, *See also* National Interreligious Service Board for Conscientious Objectors (NISBCO); nonresistance; peace
  American Revolution, 387

Bible sanctions for, 2070
Brethren attitudes in World War I training camps, 2000
Brethren movement, 2090
Cartwright, Peter, 258
chaplaincy, 271
Christianity, and relationship to, 2073, 2087
Church of the Brethren, 301–302, 316, 387, 2162–2163
Civil War, 148–149, 167, 311, 314
Committee of Observation, 327
conscientious objectors, 1165, 1169
Czech Brethren, beliefs and, 357
discipline, ordinance of, 387
doctrine on, 159
Dunkard Brethren Church, 317
On Earth Peace Assembly, 2235
exemption tax, 333
exemptions, and Old German Baptist Brethren peace position, 1000
Fellowship of Grace Brethren Churches (FGBC), 486
fraternal relations, 510
Historic Peace Churches, 607
Hutchison, Andrew, 639
Hutterian Society of Brothers, 640
Jackson, Thomas Jonathan "Stonewall," 667
Kline, John, opposition of, 701
Korean War, 301
medical projects as alternative, 808
medicine as alternative, 810
Mennonite Church, 310, 312, 316, 815
Mennonite PAX (Alternative Service), 200
Men's Work (CB), 816
military recruitment, 831
ministerial exemption, 844
ministry to church members in, 1123, 1372
mustering, military, 901
New Left draft resistance, 930
noncombatant role in, other religious groups supporting, 69
noncreedalism, 942
oaths, taking of, 959
Old German Baptist Brethren Church, 387, 388, 1000
opposition to, and social action, 1196
"Order of the Brethren," 976
peace, 997
peace education, 1002
Pennsylvania, 310
Pennsylvania Brethren and Revolutionary War, 1004
pensions, military, 1008
Pleasant Ridge Church of the Brethren, Alberta, Canada, 1034
Powers, Valentine, 1050
protest demonstrations, and incarceration of Brethren, 1060
religious liberty, 1098
Revolutionary War, 176, 177
Rosepine, LA, Church of the Brethren, ministering to, 1123
Selective Service System, 316
Seventh-Day Adventists, 1169–1170
taxes, in lieu of, 149, 176
veterans, 24
World War I, 269, 301, 311–312, 387–388
World War II, 301, 388

military substitutes, 1233–1234, 1248
militia, 403, **832**
militias, organization and development of American Revolution, 2097
Milk River Valley Church of the Brethren, MT, **832**, 1897
Mill Church Church of the Brethren, WV, 1341, *See also* White Pine Church of the Brethren, WV
Mill Creek Church of the Brethren, IL, 740, 757, *See also* Liberty, IL, Church of the Brethren
  Concord, IL, Church of the Brethren, preaching point for, 331
  Far Western Brethren, 476
  migration of Brethren, 829
Mill Creek Church of the Brethren, NC, 212
  Melvin Hill Church of the Brethren, NC, 812, **832**
Mill Creek Church of the Brethren, VA, 462, **832–833**
  Madison Church of the Brethren, VA, 781
  Mine Run Church of the Brethren, VA, 843
  Mount Carmel Church of the Brethren, VA, 880
  Mount Pleasant Church of the Brethren, VA, 887
Mill Creek congregation, OH, Henry Kurtz, 711
Mill Creek (Liberty) congregation, IL, 331, 1356, 1357
Mill Creek, OH, Church of the Brethren, *See* Mahoning Church of the Brethren, OH
  Mahoning Church of the Brethren, OH, previous name of, 782
  New Middleton, OH, Bethel Church of the Brethren, 931
Mill Creek Old German Baptist Brethren Church, VA, **833**, 967
Mill Creek, VA, Church of the Brethren, 144, 328, 341, 413, 724, 754, 1391
  bibliography, 1878
  Committee on Saving our Children to the Church (CB), 328
  Free Union, VA, Church of the Brethren, 513
  Hardtmann (Hardman, Hartman) family, 583
  Harrisonburg, VA, First Church of the Brethren, 586
  Hershberger (Harshbarger) family, 599
  Midland, VA, Church of the Brethren, 827
Mill Rock, IA
  Maquoketa German Baptist Brethren, IA, mission point, 791
Mill Run Grace Brethren Church, MD, **833**
Mille Lacs Co., MN
  Minnesota Brethren settlement, 848
Milledgeville Church of the Brethren, IL **833**
Mathis, Jefferson H., pastor, **803**
Milledgeville, IL, 695, 750, 1339
  Brethren Church, 695, **833**
  Church of the Brethren (Dutchtown), 59, 695, 803, 905, **833**, 1250
    Fitzwater, Perry Braxton, 492
    Rock Creek Church of the Brethren, IL, 1116

Millennial Dawnists, *See* Jehovah's Witnesses
The Millennial Harbinger, 247, 281
millennialism, *See* eschatology/millennialism
Miller, ___, 2278
Miller, ___ Crumpacker, 842
Miller, Arthur Bruce (A. B.), 206, 578, *1168,* 2011
Miller, A. Brown, 1708
Miller, Abraham C., 1708
Miller, A. E., 1708
Miller, A. F., 1708
Miller, A. H., 210
Miller, A. J., 1225
Miller, A. L., 573
Miller, A. Luther, 1708
Miller, A. M. T., 1708
Miller, A. M. T., family
  Hope Memorial, NE, congregation, 945
  North Beatrice Church of the Brethren, NE, 945
Miller, A. P., 255
Miller, Mrs. A. P., 255
Miller, A. S., 1708
Miller, A. T., 1708
Miller, A. W., 1708
Miller, Aaron, 1708
  Miller, Harold Clayton, father of, 834
  Modesto, CA, Old German Baptist Brethren Church, minister, 867
  Müller (Miller) family, 894
  Oak Grove Old German Baptist Brethren Church, OH, minister, 956
Miller, Aaron B., 1708
Miller, Aaron K., 1708
Miller, Abednego W., 1708
Miller, Abigail (later Arnold), 58
Miller, Abraham, 1234, 1708; Miller, Abraham, 1249, 1708; Miller, Abraham (OGBB), 1347, 1708
  Maitland Church of the Brethren, PA, minister, 783
  Mount Pleasant Old German Baptist Brethren, IN, elder, 887
  Müller (Miller) family, 894, 895
  Plainview Dunkard Brethren Congregation, OH, presiding elder, 1029
  Poplar Ridge Church of the Brethren, OH, 1047
  Santa Fe Church of the Brethren, IN, minister, 1144
Miller, Abraham C., 1708
Miller, Abraham I., 1708
Miller, Abraham, III
  Miller, Daniel Long, 836
Miller, Abraham J., 540, 1708
Miller, Abram, 1333, **2384**
  Miller, Daniel Long, father of, 836
  Miller, David Alfred, father of, 836
  Oak Grove, IN, Church of the Brethren, elder, 955
Miller, Abram (3 listed), 1708
Miller, Abram J., 1708
Miller, Abram S., 2011
Miller, Ada Glick, 2014
Miller, Adam Henry, 1708
Miller, Adam Homer, 1708
Miller, Addie, 1335
Miller, Addison E., 1242, 1363, 1708
Miller, Alan E., 588, 1708

Miller, Alan George, 1708
Miller, Albert
  Pleasant Grove Grace Brethren Church, IA, pastor, 1031
Miller, Albert Wellington, 1708
Miller, Alexander, 1708–1709
Miller, Alfred, 1709
Miller, Alice G., 191
Miller, Allen C., 1897
Miller, Allen H., 2012
Miller, Allie Everhart, 2012
Miller, Alma Schmucker, 2015
Miller, Almer
  Ormond Beach, FL, Grace Brethren Church, 982
Miller, Althea, 2012
Miller, Amanda Weaver, 2016
Miller, Amos, 1350
Miller, Amos B., 1223
Miller, Amos Philander, 2012
Miller, Amzi R., 1709
  Scottville Old German Baptist Brethren Church, MI, elder-in-charge, 1161
Miller, Andrew, 264, 476, 1342, 1347, 2072
  Mud Valley Old German Baptist Brethren Church, IL, presiding elder, 892
  New River Old German Baptist Brethren Church, ministers for, 931
Miller, Andrew (4 listed), 1709
Miller, Andrew B., 1316, 1709
Miller, Andrew Bollinger, 2011–2012
Miller, Andrew F., 1709
Miller, Andrew G., 1709
Miller, Andrew, Jr., 1709
Miller, Andrew Luther, 1709
Miller, Andrew, Sr., 1709
Miller, Andrew Valentine, 2018
Miller, Anna, 1883, 2012, 2018
  South Saint Joseph Church of the Brethren, MO, 1135
Miller, Anna Bashore
  Müller (Miller) family, *895*
Miller, Anna (later Lybrook)
  Müller (Miller) family, 894
Miller, Anna (later Markey)
  Markey family, 794
Miller, Anna (later Zigler), 1399
Miller, Anna Martha (later Royer), 1127
Miller, Daniel Long, 836
Miller, Anna R., 231
Miller, Anna Yoder, 2017
Miller, Anne Alverta Meyers
  Miller, Robert Paul, wife of, 842
Miller, Anthony, 1709
Miller, Anthony (1851–1935), 62
Miller, Anthony A., 277, 605, 607, 1301, 1709
Miller, Arella A. (later Landis), 723
Miller, Arlene Thomas
  on Freindschaft, David, 2347
  on Freindschaft, Ella Markey, 2347
Miller, Arthur Bruce, 206, 578, *1168,* 1709, 2011, 2012
Miller, Arthur C., 1709
  Roaring Spring, PA, First Church of the Brethren, pastor, 1114
Miller, Arthur G., 1709
Miller, Arthur M. (2 listed), 1709
Miller, Arthur Simon B., 1709, 1841, 1880
Miller, B. B., 1709
Miller, B. F.

Newton, KS, Church of the Brethren, pastor in, 934
Miller, B. F. (2 listed), 1709
Miller, B. R., 1709
Miller, B. W., 1709
Miller, Barbara, 1881, 2017
Müller (Miller) family, 895
Miller, Barbara B.
Miller, Jacob, wife of, 838
Miller, Barbara Jane Bowman, 169
Miller, Barbara (later Garber), 529, 530
Müller (Miller) family, 895
Miller, Barbara (later Hoffman), 617
Miller, Barbara (later Long), 754
Miller, Barbara (later Schrock), 2017
Miller, Barbara (later Smith)
Müller (Miller) family, 894
Miller, Barbara (later Yoder), 2016
Miller, Barbara Long
Sanger family, related to, 1144
Miller, Barbara Saylor, 348
Miller, Barbara Yoder
Miller, Samuel J., mother of, 842
Miller, Sebastian Christian, mother of, 842
Miller, Barber
Mason, Floyd R. on descendants of, 2346
Mason, Kathryn Garst on descendants of, 2346
Miller, Barnabas, 1709
Miller, Beauford F., 1709
Miller, Benedict
descendants, 1961
Miller, Benjamin, 696, 1709
Miller, Benjamin A., 2017, 2018
Miller, Benjamin F. (3 listed), 1709
Miller, Benjamin Franklin, 1709
Miller, Benjamin O., 1709
Miller, Bertha
memoirs, 2348
Miller, Bertha Cline
Miller, DeWitt L., mother of, 836
Miller, Bertha (later Neher), 1361
Miller, Bertha (later Neher, Stine), 1223
Miller, Bette (later Radewald), 2041
Miller, Betty G., 482, 2181
Miller, Betty Louise, 2104
Miller, Beulah Mae Woods, 145, 1841
Miller-Beyer family, 2012
Miller, Bishop, 2082
Miller, Blanche Bonsack
physician, **834**
Miller, Bonnie Jean (later Winters)
Miller, Blanche Bonsack and Harold Clayton, 834
Miller-Bowman, OH, congregations, 838
Miller, Bruce, 2223
Miller, Bruce A., 1235, 1709
Miller, Bruce Alan, 2287
Miller, Bruce W., 1235
Miller, Bryan, 2223
Miller, Byron L., 923, 1709
Miller, C., 1709
Miller, C. C., 1709
Miller, C. L.
Martinsburg, WV, Moler Avenue Church of the Brethren, 798
Miller, C. William, 1860
Miller, Carl, 504, 585
Roanoke, VA, Washington Heights Grace Brethren Church, pastor, 1114

Miller, Carrie Mattern (later Swigart), 1245
Miller, Casper Lee, 1709
Miller, Catharine K. (later Schrock), 1952
Miller, Catharine (later Minnich)
Müller (Miller) family, 894
Miller, Catherine, 226, 1347, 2107
Miller, Catherine Brenneman, 2059
Miller, Catherine E. Hershberger, 1931
Miller, Catherine E. (later John), 671
Miller, Catherine Hoffman, 2107
Miller, Catherine J., 1881
Miller, Catherine Kurtz
Miller, Jacob Kurtz, mother of, 838
Miller, Catherine (later Mahan)
Mahan, Grant, mother of, 781
Miller, Catherine (later Moyer)
Meyer family, 822
Miller, Catherine (later Wampler), 2259
Miller, Catherine Long
Miller, Daniel Long, mother of, 836
Miller, David Alfred, mother of, 836
Miller, Charles, 1709
Miller, Charles A., 567, 1709
Miller, Charles Christian, 2012
Miller, Charley C., 1709
Miller, Christen A., 2287
Miller, Christian, 2012
Miller, Christian C., 1943
Miller, Christian J., 2068
Miller, Christian J. and Barbara A. Bontrager, 2013–2014
Miller, Clair E., 1709
Miller, Clara Worst, **834,** 1361, 2012
Miller, John Allen, wife of, 839
Miller, Clarence, 1709
Miller, Clarence D., 1216
Miller, Clarinda J. Kinsey, 696
Miller, Clark Wrenice, 53, 1319, 1709, 1851
Miller, Clayton B., 152, 493, 749, 2012
Pleasant Valley Church of the Brethren, NC, providing leadership, 1035
Miller, Clayton Basehore (Bashore?), 1709
Miller, Clessie Alvin, 1709
Miller, Cletus M., 1709
Miller, Clyde J., 1709
Miller, Cora (later Stahly), 1216
Miller, Curtis, 1709
merged with Miller, John Curtis, **2384**
Miller, D., 1709
Miller, D. A., 668, 692, 1213, 1709
Miller, D. B., 590, 1221
Miller, D. E. (2 listed), 1709
Miller, D. Elmer, 1709
Miller, D. F., 1709
Miller, D. J. A., 2012
Miller, D. L., 140, 193–194, 197, 205, 235, 299, 300, 348, 371, 400, 413, 488, *538,* 545, 628, 718, 724, 1226, 1258, 1273, 1709, 1870, 1911, 1923, 1938, 1946
bicentennial celebration, 1282
biographical notes, 2000
David's Children (Bates), 748
historical writing, 612
hymnals, 642
Maryland Brethren immigrating to Illinois, 798
McDonough, George L., 773
Messenger, 818
New Testament, 133
Palestine, 990
photographic slide shows, 1020

publications, official, 1068
publishing, 1069
railroad committees and agents, 1080, 1081
Royer, Galen Brown, 1127
Turkey, travel to, 1280
Woman's Christian Temperance Union 1359, 1359
Miller, D. M., 1354
Miller, D. P., 1709
Monroe Co. Church of the Brethren, IA, elder, 870
North English, IA, Church of the Brethren, elder-in-charge, 947
Miller, D. W.
North English, IA, Church of the Brethren, elder, 947
Miller, Dale Roland, 1345, 1709–1710
Miller, Daniel, 505, 766, 1285, 1295, 1385, 1860, 1877, 2018, 2087
Miller, Daniel (11 listed), 1710
Miller, Daniel B., 1710, 2015
Miller, Daniel C., 1931
Miller, Daniel (CB)
Monroe Co. Church of the Brethren, IA, elder, 870
Miller, Daniel D. (OGBB), 102, 1710, 2017
Miller, Daniel (descendent of Michael Miller)
Müller (Miller) family, 895
Miller, Daniel E., 2012, 2287
Miller, Daniel Edgar, 1710
Miller, Daniel (FGBC)
Myerstown, PA, Grace Brethren Church, pastor, 906
Miller, Daniel G., 1710
Miller, Daniel J. and Barbara Bontrager, genealogy, 1963
Miller, Daniel, Jr., 1710
Miller, Daniel Long (D. L.), 25, 46, 94, *103,* **834–836,** *835,* 1710, 2012
Miller, Elizabeth Talley, husband of, 837
missions, 861, 863
Mount Morris College, president, 884
Mount Morris, IL, Church of the Brethren, elder, 883
Miller, Daniel M., 1710
Miller, John Ezra, father of, 839
Miller, Daniel P., 1710, 1971
Miller, Daniel S., 1710
Miller, Daniel (son of Jacob Miller)
Müller (Miller) family, 894
Miller, Daniel (son of Lodowich Miller)
Müller (Miller) family, 895
Miller, Daniel, Sr., 375
Miller, Daniel Walter, 2012
Miller, Darrell E., 2287
Miller, Dave, 1710
Miller, David, 246, 652, 923, 1013, 1385, 2018, 2035, 2101
Miller, Jacob Kurtz, father of, 838
Mud Valley Old German Baptist Brethren Church, IL, presiding elder, 892
Miller, David (8 listed), 1710
Miller, David Aaron, 2012–2013
Miller, David Alfred, **836,** 1710
South Saint Joseph Church of the Brethren, MO, elder, 1135
Miller, David E., 2287
Miller, David (family of Michael Miller)
Müller (Miller) family, 895

Miller, David J., 1710
Miller, David L., 2287
Miller, David LeRoy, 1710
Miller, David Lloyd, 2287
Miller, David P., 1710
Miller, David Racy, 2287
Miller, David (son of Jacob Miller)
    Müller (Miller) family, 894
Miller, David (son of Lodowich Miller)
    Müller (Miller) family, 895
Miller, David, Sr., 1710, **2384**
    Portage Prairie, IN, Church of the
        Brethren, minister, 1047
Miller, David W., 755, 1319, 1710
Miller, David W., 1710
Miller, David W., 2287
Miller, David Y., 1710
    Middlefork Old German Baptist
        Brethren Church, IN, minister, 826
    Miller, Gene Edwin on, 2347
    Oak Grove Old German Baptist
        Brethren Church, OH, minister,
        956
Miller, Dean M., 417, 578, 1710, 2013,
    2155
Miller, DeLane F., 2287
Miller, Dessie Rebecca, 285, 2013
Miller, DeWitt and Mary
    Meditations on Brethren Life,
    1282–1283
Miller, DeWitt Henry, 588, 1277, 1710
    Philadelphia, PA, Calvary Church of
        the Brethren, pastor, 1015
Miller, DeWitt L., 381, 578, 588, **836–837,**
    1710, 2013, 2304
Miller, Donald E., 169, 1388, 1710
    North Manchester Old German Baptist
        Brethren Church, IN, minister, 949
Miller, Donald Eugene, 42, 102, 612, 2013,
    2111, 2153, 2161, **2222–2223,**
    2223, **2384**
    on Arnold, Gottfried, 2347
    on peace, 2347, 2349
    on Peachey, Paul, 2349
    violence and, 2265
    World Council of Churches, 2228
Miller, Donald E. (3 listed), 1710
Miller, Donald Frederick, 1851, 2304
Miller, Dora Evelyn Stoner
    Miller, John William, 2223, 2224
Miller, Douglas, 2134
Miller, Dove, 2184
Miller, Doyle, 188, 191, 1710
Miller, Duane L., 1710, 2287
Miller, Dwight L., 469, 1710
Miller, E. A., 1710
Miller, E. C. (2 listed), 1710
Miller, E. Irene, 1899, 2013
Miller, E. J., 2013
Miller, E. Jane, 2013
Miller, E. K., 2013
Miller, E. L., 567, 1289, 1297
    Meadow Mills Church of the Brethren,
        VA, 806
Miller, E. S.
    Pleasant Hill Church of the Brethren,
        PA, presiding elder, 1032
Miller, Earl J., 2014
Miller, Eddie
    Modesto, CA, Big Valley Grace
        Community Church (FGBC), 866
Miller, Edward, 1710
Miller, Edward A., 1710

Moomaw, Daniel Crouse, 873
Mountain Normal School, 889
Miller, Edward C., 1710–1711
    Mount Pleasant Old German Baptist
        Brethren, IN, minister, 887
    North Fork Old German Baptist
        Brethren Church, IN, overseer
Miller, Edward (CB), *2245*
Miller, Edward Douglas, 172, 1711, 1851
Miller, Edward Lewis, 356, **837,** 1711
    Mansfield, OH, Walcrest Brethren
        Church, pastor, 787
    Maurertown, VA, Brethren Church,
        pastor, 803
Miller, Edward S., 102, 1711
Miller, Edward Sweitzer, 1711
Miller, Edwin Daniel, 2013
Miller, Eileen Goodman, 1851
    Modesto, CA, Big Valley Grace
        Community Church (FGBC), 866
Miller, Eli J., 2015
Miller, Eli J. and Veronica Weaver, 2014
Miller, Eli S., 2017
Miller, Elias S., 1875
Miller, Eliza Belle, **837,** 1841, 1909–1910,
    2024, 2076
Miller, Eliza Coning, 2222
Miller, Eliza Saylor, 348
Miller, Elizabeth, 217, 1881, 2035
    Mount Pleasant Old German Baptist
        Brethren, IN, 887
Miller, Elizabeth Hardman
    Müller (Miller) family, 894
Miller, Elizabeth J. (later Erb), 1931
Miller, Elizabeth Jane (later Hack), 1955
Miller, Elizabeth Klein
    Müller (Miller) family, 894
Miller, Elizabeth (later Balsbaugh)
    Müller (Miller) family, 894
Miller, Elizabeth (later Glick), 553
Miller, Elizabeth (later Heckman), 591, 592
Miller, Elizabeth (later Hess)
    Hess, James Arthur, 2198
Miller, Elizabeth (later Jones), 1959
Miller, Elizabeth Petry, 1013
Miller, Elizabeth Shideler
    Müller (Miller) family, 894
Miller, Elizabeth Talley, *835, 837,* **837,**
    1273, 1936, 2013, 2018
    Miller, Daniel Long, wife of, *835,* 836
Miller, Elizabeth Ulrich, 1285
Miller, Elizabeth Virginia, 2069
Miller, Elizabeth Wise, 2035
Miller, Ella, 217, 1835
Miller, Elmer Lloyd, 2017
Miller, Elmer Sam, 2013
Miller, Elta Sensenig
    Miller, Orie O., wife of, 841
Miller, Elta Wolf
    Miller, Orie O., wife of, 841
Miller, Elva R., 351
Miller, Elvert Franklin, 1711
Miller, Emanuel
    Palestine Old German Baptist Brethren
        Church, OH, 991
Miller, Emanuel (2 listed), 1711
Miller, Emanuel J., 1711, 2013
Miller, Emanuel J. and Magdelena Weaver
    family history, 2008
Miller, Emma, 688
Miller, Emma A. (later Replogle), 2044
Miller, Emma Norris
    Miller, Robert Henry, mother of, 842

Miller, Robert Henry, wife of, 842
Mount Pleasant Church of the
    Brethren, IN, 886–887
Miller, Enos Harvey, 2013–2014
Miller, Ernest L., 1711
Miller, Ervin, 2287
Miller, Esther (later Harnish), 1958
Miller, Esther (later Hess), 601
Miller, Esther (later Roop), 1130
Miller, Ethel
    Oak Grove Church of the Brethren,
        LA, district meeting delegate, 955
Miller, Eugene, 257, 1711
Miller, Eunice Marie Bearinger, 1319, 1851
Miller, Eva Etta (later Smeltzer), *See*
    Smeltzer, Eva Etta Miller
Miller, Eva (later Kingery)
    Müller (Miller) family, 894
Miller, Eve (later Keefer)
    Müller (Miller) family, 894
Miller, Everett Wayne, 2014
Miller-Everhart family, 2012
Miller, F. E., 280, 1711
    Muscatine, IA, First Church of the
        Brethren, pastor, 898
Miller, F. H., 1711
Miller family, 145, 164, 172, 211, 215, 216,
    241, 262, 270, 332, 384, 430, 700,
    721, 1221, 1224, 1236, 1280,
    1281, 1322, 1342, 1385, 1389,
    1914, 1917, 1920, 1929, 2016,
    2017, 2018, 2040, 2072, 2079,
    2087, 2099, 2101, 2106, 2107, *See*
    also Arnold family; Müller family;
    Out of the Melting Pot; individual
    Millers
    bibliography, 1865, 1876, 1893, 1907
    Dutchman's Creek German Baptist
        Brethren Church, NC, 411
    Erbaugh family, 453
    family history, 2008, 2011, 2014
    Fike family, 490
    Flat Rock Church of the Brethren, VA,
        493
    Fredericksburg, IA, Hillcrest Baptist
        and Brethren Church, 512
    Fruitdale, AL, Church of the Brethren,
        520
    Garrett, PA, Church of the Brethren,
        531
    Gentry German Baptist Brethren
        Church, MO, 540
    Glück (Glick, Click) family, 553
    Good (Guth) family, 556
    Guthrie Church of the Brethren, MN,
        576
    Harrisburg, PA, Melrose Gardens
        Grace Brethren Church, 586
    Hope Memorial Church (German
        Baptist Brethren), NE, 2375
    Howard Co. Old German Baptist
        Brethren Church, IN, 633
    index, 2041
    Jasper, MO, Church of the Brethren,
        669
    Johnson City, TN, Knob Creek Church
        of the Brethren, 672
    Lyle, Jeanne on, 2356
    Mack family, 778
    Maple Valley, WA, Grace Brethren
        Church, 2218
    Mill Creek Old German Baptist
        Brethren Church, VA, 833

Mishler family, related to, 852

Mount Cassell Old German Baptist Brethren Church, WV, 880

Myerstown, PA, Grace Brethren Church, 906

Neher family, related to, 922

Nevada, MO, Church of the Brethren, 924

Niota, TN, Church of the Brethren, 938

North English, IA, Church of the Brethren, 947

Paul family joined in marriage, 996

Peabody Old German Baptist Brethren Church, KS, 997

Pleasant View Church of the Brethren, TN, 1037

Redstone Valley Old German Baptist Brethren Church, WI and, 2240

Reiff family, 1094

reunion, 1958

Robins, IA, Church of the Brethren, 1115

Rockingham and Shenandoah Counties Old German Baptist Brethren Church, VA, 1118

Rotruck (Rothrock, Roderick) family, related to, 1124

Salem Church of the Brethren, OH, 1138

Scherffig family, related to, 1152

Sell, Jeanne Lyle on, 2356

Sharpsburg, MD, Church of the Brethren, 1174

Snider, Jacob, descendants of, 1154

Miller, Fannie Erb, 2017

Miller, Fannie J., 1881

Miller, Fannie N. (later Schrock), 1959, 2059

Miller, Fanny, 2106, 2107
  Müller (Miller) family, 894

Miller, Fern (later Wagoner), 2259

Miller, Florence (later Shuman), 2249

Miller, Florence Shearer, 1843

Miller, Floyd, family, *1082*

Miller, Franklin Elroy, 445, 1711, 2014

Miller, Fred J., 1711

Miller, Frederick, 1711

Miller, Frederick and Mary Elizabeth Peery genealogy, 2015

Miller, Frederick Charles, 2012–2013

Miller, Fredric Geary, 2287

Miller, G. W., 1711

Miller, Galen Leroy, 1240, 1711, 2014

Miller, Gary, 1711
  Omaha, NE, Grace Brethren Bible Church, pastor, 974

Miller, Gene Edwin, 2014
  on Miller, David Y., 2347

Miller, George, 211, **837, 894,** 1711, 2099
  elder, 1968
  ox stolen, 458

Miller, George (1831–1902), 102, 1711

Miller, George H., 1711

Miller, George K., 1711

Miller, George Michael, 438

Miller, George Samuel, 2015

Miller, George (son of George Miller), 894

Miller, George (son of Michael Miller)
  Müller (Miller) family, 895

Miller, George W., 371, 394, 1711, 2014

Miller, George W., 1711

Miller, George, Sr., and Catherine, family history, 2011–2012

Miller, Glenn Alva, 2014

Miller-Graber family, 1989

Miller, Grace Hileman, *See* Miller, (Mary) Grace Hileman

Miller, Hannah, 214

Miller, Hannah Webb, 894

Miller, Hans Michael, **837,** 894, 895

Miller, Harold Clayton, 1711, 2014, **834**

Miller, Harold E., 1280, 1711

Miller, Harold W. (A.), 745, 1711
  Piqua, OH, Church of the Brethren, pastor, 1026

Miller, Harry D., 2014

Miller, Hartsough Mary, 381

Miller, Harvey, 1711

Miller, Harvey M., 2057

Miller, Hattie Zelma, 1833

Miller, Hazel (later Long), 754

Miller, Heinrich, 2014

Miller, Henderson, 1711

Miller, Henry, 153, 894, 1711

Miller, Henry B., 2013

Miller, Henry David, 2014

Miller, Henry Edward, 1711

Miller, Henry L., 1711

Miller, Henry R., 1711

Miller, Hiram G., 1711

Miller, Homer, 65

Miller, Homer J., 424, 1711
  Mill Creek Church of the Brethren, VA, pastor, 832

Miller, Howard, 139, 186, 204, 267, 288, 332, 433, 656, 693, 724, 742, **837–838,** 1218, 1281, 1347, 1711, 1860, 2014
  census and, 267
  historical writing, 611
  Holsinger, Henry Ritz, 622
  The Landmark, editor, 1995
  on Newton Grove Church of the Brethren, 934
  Philadelphia, PA, First Church of the Brethren, providing leadership, 1015
  Plum Creek Normal School, 1038
  The Progressive Christian, 1061
  The Record of the Faithful, 267
  The Record of the Faithful, 267, 1086

Miller, Howard Abram, 325, 1711

Miller, Hugh, 1277, 1333, 1711
  Oakland Church of the Brethren, OH, pastor, 957

Miller, I. A., 1711, 2014

Miller, I. M., 1711

Miller, I. N. (2 listed), 1711

Miller, I. William, 1711

Miller, Ida, 2101

Miller, Ida E. Blu(e)baugh

Miller, Jacob Kurtz, wife of, 839

Miller, Ira (2 listed), 1712

Miller, Irvin, 1286, 1712

Miller, Irvin B., 121, 239, 1712, 2304
  Martinsburg, WV, Rosemont Grace Brethren Church, pastor, 798
  Norton, OH, Grace Brethren Church, pastor, 951

Miller, Irvin R., 447

Miller, Isaac (1810–1895), 443, 1216, 1239, 1712

Miller, Isaac (1813–1882), 713, 1712

Miller, Isaac (1849–1923), 496, 1712

Miller, Isaac, 1712, 2014, 2107

Miller, Isaac Allen
  Miller, Robert Paul, father of, 842

Miller, Isaac Arnold, 1712

Miller, Isaac D. and descendants, history of, 2016

Miller, Isaac H., 1712

Miller, Isaac M.
  Pipe Creek Old German Baptist Brethren Church, IN, deacon, 1026

Miller, Isaac N., 124

Miller, Isaac N. (2 listed), 1712

Miller, Isaac S., 2017

Miller, Israel B., 1712

Miller, Ivan J., 2014

Miller, J. A., 1236, 1255
  Santa Ana, CA, Church of the Brethren, ministerial leadership, 1144

Miller, J. A. (3 listed), 1712

Miller, J. B.
  Quiet Dell Brethren Church, PA, 1076

Miller, J. Carson, 207, 406, 494, 1265, 1712

Miller, J. D., 1712, 2014
  Newberg, OR, Church of the Brethren, pastor in, 933

Miller, John Ezra, 140, 201, 536, 612, 1226
  Stories, 944

Miller, J. G., 236, 1212, 1712

Miller, J. H., 439, 755, 1292, 1712
  Ontario German Baptist Brethren, 975
  South Bethel German Baptist Brethren, MO, minister, 1204

Miller, J. Henderson, 1712

Miller, J. Herbert, 600, 2014

Miller, J. Kurtz, 212, 1296, 1712
  Brooklyn, NY, urban ministry in, 933
  Italian Sunday School (CB), 664

Miller, J. M., 1712

Miller, J. N., 347
  North Liberty, IN, Brethren Church, pastor, 948

Miller, J. Paul, 1712
  Modesto, CA, La Loma Grace Brethren Church, pastor, 867
  Ripon, CA, Grace Brethren Church, interim pastor, 1110

Miller, J. Peter, 154, 291, 381, 1328, 2039, *See also* Miller, John Peter
  Ephrata publishing, 1067
  Martin, George Adam, 797
  Miller, Hans Michael, 837
  Reformed Church and Brethren movement, 1092
  Rhode Island, visiting, 1107

Miller, J. Quinter, 335, 1326, 1901, *See also* Miller, Joseph Quinter
  "The Church and the Churches," 2014
  "Thinking With Sober Judgement," 2014

Miller, J. R., 251

Miller, J. W., 1256, 1712

Miller, J. William, 1712

Miller, Jacob, 224, 363, 366, 507, 544, 582, 587, 713, 722, **838,** 1294, 1307, 2016
  biography, 1938
  family history and genealogy, 1955, 1979–1980, 2014, 2015
  Miami, OH, congregation, minister, 961
  migration of Brethren, 829
  missions, 857
  Moss family, 878
  Mud Valley Old German Baptist Breth-

ren Church, IL, presiding elder, 892
Müller (Miller) family, 894–895
Santa Fe Church of the Brethren, IN 1144
Smith, William, 1191
Miller, Jacob, (CB) (1828–1853), 1712
Pennsylvania Brethren secondary schools, 1004
Select School, 1165
Miller, Jacob (1812–1871), 170, 505, 1265
Portage Prairie, IN, Church of the Brethren, minister, 1047
Miller, Jacob (4 listed), 1712
Miller, Jacob A. (1808–1901), 1712
Palestine Old German Baptist Brethren Church, OH, 991
Miller, Jacob A. (CB) (1859–1939), 190, 1712
Manvel, TX, Church of the Brethren, preaching, 789
Pleasant Grove Church of the Brethren, TX, 1031
Portland, TX, Bayview Church of the Brethren, 1048
San Antonio, TX, Church of the Brethren, 1141
Miller, Jacob A. (1871–1941), **838**, 1712
Lititz, PA, Dunkard Brethren Congregation, 749
Mechanicsburg, PA, Dunkard Brethren Congregation, presiding elder, 806
Miller, Jacob Andrew (CB) (1873–1962), 1712
Miller, Jacob B. (OGBB) (1815–1890), 270, 373, 1712
Miller, Jacob D., (CB) (1809–1893), 1322, 1712
Miller, Jacob D., (OGBB) (1855–1954), 270, 348, 373, 1712
Miller, Jacob D., (CB) (1886–___), 1712
Mabel, OR, Church of the Brethren, deacon, 771
Miller, Jacob Eli, 2015
Miller, Jacob J., 2015, 2072
Miller, Jacob, Jr., 2015
Miller, Jacob Kurtz, 160, **838–839**
Miller Jacob L., Jr.
on Freindschaft, David, 2347
on Freindschaft, Ella Markey, 2347
Miller, Jacob Leander, 1712
New Fairview Church of the Brethren, PA, elder in, 927
North Fort Myers, FL, First Church of the Brethren, 948
Miller, Jacob M., 2017
Miller, Jacob (son of Jacob Miller)
Müller (Miller) family, 894
Miller, Jacob (son of Lodowich Miller)
Müller (Miller) family, 895
Miller, Jacob Thomas, 629, 1712
Miller, Jacob W.
Royer Community Church of the Brethren, KS, 1128
Miller, James
South Haven Old German Baptist Brethren Church, MI, deacon, 1205
Miller, James Carson, 2015
Miller, James Emery, 1712
Miller, James F.
on Krousz, Michael and descendants, 2347

Miller, James Galen, 1712
Miller, James H., 1712
Miller, James Virgil, 2015
Miller, Jane Alexander, 837
Miller, Jaynie, 191
Miller, Jeannette E. Blough, 1841, 1942
Miller, John Ezra, wife of, 839
Miller, Jennie Long, 1316
Miller, Jeremiah, 1712, 2018, 2079
Müller (Miller) family, 895
Miller, Jeremiah and Lydia Troyer, 2013
Miller, Jerry D., 2106, 2107
Miller, Jerry Lee, 2287
Miller, Jesse E., 1712
North Fork Old German Baptist Brethren Church, IN, overseer, 947
Miller, Jesse Herbert, 1712–1713
Miller, Joel, 1713
Miller, Joel B., 2059
Miller, John, 1384, 2035
free ministry to New Fairview Church of the Brethren, PA, 927
Mont Ida, KS, Church of the Brethren, 870
South Bethel German Baptist Brethren, MO, leadership, 1204
Miller, John (5 listed), 1713
Miller, John A., 501, 2011–2012
Miller, John A. (6 listed), 1713
Miller, John Allen, 64, 66, 67, 133, 182, 204, 209, 362, 425, 439, 501, 558, 695, **839**, 1261, 1713, 1865, 2014, **2376**
The Brethren Pastor's Handbook, 788
human nature, doctrine of, 635
"Message of the Brethren Ministry," 817
Miller, Clara Worst, husband of, 834
prayer, writings on, 1051
Ronk, Albert Teller, ordination of, 1121
sin, on, 1183–1184
Miller, John B., 1713
Riddlesburg, PA, Church of the Brethren, minister, 1108
Miller, John Bowser, 1713
Miller, John C., 1713, 2014
Oak Grove Old German Baptist Brethren Church, OH, deacon, 956
Miller, John Curtis, 1713
merged with Miller, Curtis, **2384**
Miller, John D., 1713
Miller, DeWitt L., father of, 836
Miller, John Ezra, 27, 55, **839–840**, 1713, 1860, 1961, 2015, 2066
Mount Morris College, president, 884–885
Miller, John F. and Magdalena, 2013
Miller, John G., 1713
Miller, John H., 1342
Miller, John H. (4 listed), 1713
Miller, John Henry, 1914
Miller, John J., 766, 1882, 1887, 2012
Miller, John L.
Miller, Mary Grace Hileman, husband of, 841
Miller, John P., 1713
Miller, Howard, father of, 837
Miller, John Perry, 2015
Miller, John William, 2223
Miller, John Peter (Brother Agrippa), 31, 43, 98, 121, 123, 1713, 1910, 2015, *See* Moravian Brethren
historical materials regarding, 1950

Benjamin Franklin, reference to, 1940
bibliographical sources, 1912, 1946
Chroniccon Ephratense, 290
Eastern Synod of the Reformed Church, records about, 1923
Ephrata leader, *840,* **840**
Müller (Miller) family, 894
references to, 1919, 1939, 1957
Schelbert, Leo on letter of 1743 written by, 2355
Miller, John R., 217, 1713
Miller, John Samuel, 2015
Miller, John (son of Jacob Miller), 894
Miller, John (son of Michael Miller), 895
Miller, John Stufft, 2018
Miller, John W. (3 listed), 1713
Miller, John William, 102, 1713, 1936, 2014–2015, 2130, 2201, **2223–2224**, 2304, 2347, **2384**
on Brethren early doctrine, 2347
museums, 898
writings of, 2347
Miller, Jonas D., 2015
Miller, Jonas D. and Elmina, 2014, 2015
Miller, Jonas E., 2016
Miller, Jonas F., 1881
Miller, Jonas W., 1713
Miller, Jonathan, 493
Miller, Jonathan (2 listed), 1713
Miller, Jonathan J., 1898
Miller, Jonathan S., 2016
Miller, Joni and Susanna Hostetler, 2013
Miller, Joni J., 2059
Miller, Joseph, 2016, 2184, *See also* Müller (Miller), Joseph
Müller (Miller) family, *894*
Miller, Joseph (2 listed), 1713
Miller, Joseph A., 1713
Miller, Joseph C., 2057
Miller, Samuel J., father of, 842
Miller, Sebastian Christian, father of, 842
Miller, Joseph, descendants of, 1950
Miller, Joseph Henderson, 1713
Miller, Joseph M., 1713
Miller, Joseph Quinter, **840–841,** 912, 1713
Miller, Joseph (Reverend), 2016
Miller, Joseph William, 1713
Miller, Jost B., 2017
Miller, Joyce, 2023
Miller, Julie Sausser, 2181
Miller, June Adams, 2016, 2133
Miller, Karen Peterson, 2287
church governance and, 2264
on disciplines for spiritual growth, 2347
Miller, Kathleen Ann, 588, 1713
Miller, Katie Jacob, 2016
Miller, Katie (later Nisly), 2031
Miller, Kenneth E., 102, 1713
Miller, Kenneth Lee, 1713, 2287
Miller, Kurt A., 462, 629, 1713
Richmond, VA, Grace Brethren Church, pastor, 1108
Miller, Kurtz, 511, 1713
Miller, L. E., 445
Miller, L. H., 1713
Miller, L. William, 1713
Miller, Laura A. (later Plate), 1030
Miller, Laura (later Kriegbaum), 708
Miller, Lawrence A., 1713
Miller, L(awrence) Byron, 1713–1714
Miller, Leah, 246

Miller, Leah Blocher, 147
Miller, Leah Francis, 165
Miller, Leander, 396, 1385, 1714
    Old Order German Baptist Church
      minister, 972
Miller, Leighton, 482
Miller, Leo Homer, 59, 445, 504, 1714
    Myrtle Point, OR, Church of the
      Brethren, pastor, 906
Miller, Leona Fern, 2016
Miller Leslie
    on conscription during World War II,
      2347
Miller, Leslie A., 2016
Miller, Letitia J. Sanders
    Miller, Howard, wife of, 837
Miller, Levi
    North Fork Old German Baptist
      Brethren Church, IN, overseer, 947
    Old Folks and Orphans Home, donat-
      ing land for, 821
Miller, Levi (OGBB) (1863–1933), 270,
    1714
Miller, Levi, 1714
Miller, Levi A., 270
Miller, Levi D., 2018
Miller, Levi E., 1714
Miller, Levi P., 965
Miller, Lewis, 1714, 2106
Miller, Lewis H.
    Miller, Edward Lewis, father of, 837
Miller, Linneaus, 912, 1714
Miller, Lisa, 2223
Miller, Lloyd Orian, 1280, 1714
    Modesto, CA, Old German Baptist
      Brethren Church, minister, 867
    New River Old German Baptist
      Brethren Church, ministers for,
      931–932
Miller, Lodowich, 895
Miller, Lois Brown, 1943
Miller, Lois Elizabeth, 1851
Miller, Lois Elizabeth Miller, 1851
Miller, Lomax, 438, 1714
Miller, Lorenzo H., 1714
Miller, Louise, 2016
Miller, Lovina D., 1963
Miller, Lowell Edward, 2287
Miller, Lucinda (later Mays)
    Mays, Morley Josiah, wife of, 804
Miller, Lulu Netzley, 1909
Miller, Luther Samuel, 1714
Miller, Lydia, 214, 1883
Miller, Lydia B. Troyer, 2017
Miller, Lydia Eichholtz, 870
Miller, Lydia Fike
    Miller, Eliza Belle, mother of, 837
    Miller, Sadie Jane, mother of, 842
Miller, Lydia Garver, 2059
Miller, Lydia Smith
    Poling, Newton L. on descendants of,
      2350
    Poling, Virginia on letters of, 2350
Miller, Lydia Werner
Miller, Harold Clayton, mother of, 834
Miller, Lyle, 1714
Miller, Lynn Hayes, 2287
Miller, M. A., 2016
Miller, M. C., 1714
Miller, M. H.
    Reedley, CA, Church of the Brethren,
      elder, 1091
Miller, M. M. H., 2016

Miller, M. P., 1714
Miller, Mae Louise Wolf, 1841
Miller, Magdalena, 352, 1882, 1887, 2084
Miller, Magdalene (later Cripe), 895
Miller, Magdelena (later Schrock), 2059
Miller, Magdelena (later Snyder), 894
Miller, Malcolm E.
    Miller, Clara Worst, son of, 834
Miller, Malinda Yost Mast, 1909–1910,
    2079
Miller, Marcus, 2016
    Annual Meeting decisions, 1044
    on Brethren movement, development
      and operation of, 2347
    historical writing, 612
    on OGBB, 2347
    Old Order Notes, 973
    poetry, 1039
Miller, Margaret A. Roberts
    Miller, Edward Lewis, mother of, 837
Miller, Margaret (later Garver), 532
Miller, Marguerite Lucile, 2016
Miller, Maria Catherine
    Miller, Hans Michael, wife of, 837
Miller, Maria (later Fackler), 894
Miller, Marie Agnes Beachy, 2016
Miller, Marie Kauffman, 2017
Miller, Marion H., 2016
Miller, Marion M., 747, 1314
Miller, Martha, 45
Miller, Martha (CB), *2245*
Miller, Martha (later Schrock), 2059
Miller, Martha Troyer, 2017, 2018
Miller, Martin (3 listed), 1714
Miller, Martin (1800–1872), 105
Miller, Martin Baker, 1714
Miller, Martin H., 1714
Miller, Martin M., 1714
Miller, Martin P., 1714
Miller, Mary, 149, 169, 363
Miller, Mary Agnes Shipman
    Miller, Minor Cline, wife of, 841
Miller, Mary Ann
    Mason, Floyd R. on descendants of,
      2345
    Mason, Kathryn Garst on descendants
      of, 2345
Miller, Mary Ann Gearhart
    Miller, John William, 2223
Miller, Mary Blades
    Miller, Robert Henry, mother of, 841
Miller, Mary Dillman, 2101
Miller, Mary E. , 168
Miller, Mary Flory, 2016
    Miller, Sebastian Christian, wife of,
      842
Miller, Mary Grace Hileman, 278, **841,**
    1141
Miller, Mary Hartsough, 588, 2013
Miller, Mary Jane French, 2018
Miller, Mary (later Darst), 894
Miller, Mary (later Garber), 528
Miller, Mary (later Kimmel), 693
Miller, Mary Lichty, 741
    Miller, John Ezra, mother of, 839
Miller, Mary Lint, 1216
Miller, Mary Lois, 1851
Miller, Mary Louise Schrock, 2016
Miller, Mary (Minnie) E. Rowland
    Miller, David Alfred, wife of, 836
Miller, Mary P., 2018
Miller, Mary Saylor 672
Miller, Mathias, 1714

Miller, Floyd R. on descendants of,
    2346
Mason, Kathryn Garst on descendants
    of, 2346
Miller, Mattie Gingerich, 2015, 2016
Miller, Mattie (later Early), *414*
Miller, Maude Reiff
    Miller, Robert Henry, wife of, 842
Miller, May (later Frost), 1943
Miller, Merlin Gibson, 1714, 2016
Miller, Mervin A., 2016
Miller, Michael, 383, 2072, 2287
    Mason, Floyd R. on descendants of,
      2345
    Mason, Kathryn Garst on descendants
      of, 2345
    Müller (Miller) family, 895
    South Carolina, 1204
Miller, Michael (2 listed), 1714
Miller, Michael
    Beaver Creek congregation, SC, 105
Miller, Michael C., 1714
Miller, Michael, II, 2018
Miller, Michael, Sr., 2101
    Nimishillen Church of the Brethren,
      minister in, 937
Miller, Mildred, 1860
Miller, Milo H., 2016
Miller, Mima Lu Ella, 2107
Miller, Minnie L. Cline
    Miller, Joseph Quinter, mother of,
      840–841
    Miller, Minor Cline, mother of, 841
Miller, Minor Cline, **841,** 1326, 1714, 2016,
    2017
Miller, Modena Hutchison
    Miller, Samuel J., wife of, 842
Miller, Monroe B., 1714
Miller, Moses, 765, 1714, 2017, 2018
Miller, Moses Benjamin, 2017
Miller, Moses D., 2015
Miller, Moses I. and Elizabeth I., 2015
Miller, (Mrs.) Jones, 2016
Miller, (Mrs.) Levi L., Jr., 2016
Miller, Myron S., 1326
Miller, N. J., 494, 570, 571, 939
Miller, Nancy E. (later Shickel), *See*
    Shickel, Nancy E. Miller
Miller, Nancy Huston
    Müller (Miller) family, 894
Miller, Nancy (later Sanger), *See* Sanger,
    Nancy Miller
    Müller (Miller) family, 895
Miller, Naomi E. (later West), 1332, 2262
Miller, Nathan J., 1714
    Marion Co. German Baptist Brethren,
      IA, minister, 793
Miller, Nellie Shanholtz, 1345
Miller, Newton Jasper, 1714
Miller, Noah H., 1714
Miller, Norma Jean, 2287
Miller, Norman J., 1714
Miller, O. W.
    Pleasant Hill College, 1033
    Salem College president, 1138
Miller, Olan J., 2017
Miller, Olen L., 2059
Miller, Olive, 2017
Miller, Oliver W., **841**
Miller, Orie Allen, 2017
Miller, Orie O., 339, 608, **841**
Miller, Orla E., 2287
Miller, Oscar Ray, 2017

Miller, Oscar S., 1714, **2384**
Miller, Ovid, 239
Miller, Mrs. Ovid, 239
Miller, P. M., 1714
Miller, Paul, 1342, 1714, 1851
Miller, Mrs. Paul, 1851
Miller, Paul A., 1714
Miller, Paul E., 1714, 2017
Miller, Paul Eugene, 1714
Miller, Pauline Anna (later Lindsay), 744
Miller, Pearl Ann Fruth, 1841
Miller, Percy C., 553, 691, 1714
Miller, Perry U., 1714
Miller, Pete V., 2017
Miller, Peter, 290, 451, 736, 2016, 2053,
    2074, 2104, *See also* Miller, John
    Peter
    letters to, from Benjamin Franklin,
        1960
    monastic congregation, 1195
    poem about, 1972
    reference to, 1917, 1951
    Revolutionary War, American, 1106
    Wangman, Andrew on letter to Peter
        Lehman by, 2362
Miller, Peter (1785–1854), 825, 1714
    Middle River Church of the Brethren,
        VA, elder, 825
Miller, Peter J., 381
Miller, Peter S., 1714, 2017
    General Railway Transportation Agent,
        1080
    Roanoke, VA, First Church of the
        Brethren, elder, 1113
    Roanoke, VA, Hollins Road Church of
        the Brethren, elder, 1113
Miller, Peter, 1865
Miller, Pheobe McClure, 894
Miller, Philip, 2018
Miller, Philip (2 listed), 1714
Miller, Philip Jacob. 895
Miller, Philip Lee, 1841
Miller, Phillip, 102, 2012
Miller, Phillip D. and Fannie I., 1971
Miller, Phillip W., 2287
Miller, Phyllis Gibbel, 2223
Miller, Polly Plank, 1943
Miller, Polly Weirich, 2057
Miller, Preston, J., 1714, 2136
    Laughlin Church of the Brethren, MD,
        2214
Miller, Prudence, 683
Miller, R. E. A., 553, 1715
    Roanoke, VA, First Brethren Church,
        pastor, 1113
Miller, R. Eugene, 1714, 2287, 2304
Miller, R. Paul, 97, 137,155, 187, 192,
    203, 259, 274, 349, 460, 461, 485,
    503, 558, 694, 708, 1212, 1297,
    1714–1715
    Mansfield, OH, Conservative Grace
        Brethren Church, 2217
    Roanoke, VA, Washington Heights
        Grace Brethren Church, holding
        evangelistic meetings, 1114
Miller, R. Paul, Jr., 1289, 1715
    Maitland, FL, Grace Brethren Church,
        pastor, 783
Miller, Rachel, 217
Miller, Rachel (later Lichty), 741
Miller, Rachel Mast, 1961
Miller, Rachel Troyer, 2017
Miller, Ralph E., 1715

Miller, Ralph F., 349, 377, 1345, 1715
    Parkersburg, WV, Grace Brethren
        Church, pastor serving, 994
Miller, Ralph W., 1936
Miller, Randall M.
    on PA Brethren, 2347
Miller, Ray, 1715
Miller, Raymond W., 2017
Miller, Rebecca J.
    New Paris, IN, Brethren Church, 931
Miller, Rebecca (later Horst), *See* Horst
    family
Miller, Rex M.
    Shepherd's Spring Outdoor Ministries
        Center (CB) and, 2248
Miller, Rhea, 165
Miller, Richard Norris, 308, 367, 1715,
    2017
Miller, Robert A., 1715
Miller, Robert E., 629, 1270
    Martinsburg, PA, Grace Brethren
        Church, pastor, 798
Miller, Robert Elias Allen, 1715
Miller, Robert Henry, Jr., 714, 717, 745,
    842, 1052, 1330, 1715, 2017
    North Manchester, IN, Church of the
        Brethren, pastor, 949
Miller, Robert Henry, Sr., 242, 370, 371,
    468, 550, *841,* **841–842,** 1313,
    1354, 1714, 1715, 1952, 2023
    biography of, 2101
    North Manchester, IN, Church of the
        Brethren, elder and pastor, 949
    Ogan's Creek, IN, Church of the
        Brethren, 961
    Pipe Creek Church of the Brethren, IN,
        1025
    publishing, 1069
    Rockingham Church of the Brethren,
        MO, debated Daniel Sommer at,
        1118
Miller, Robert J., 2099
Miller, Robert M., *512*
Miller, Robert Paul, 1715, **842**
Maconaghy, Dorothy Helen Lewis and Hill,
    779
    The Missionary Board (BC), 855
    missions, 860, 861
Miller, Robert R., 2287
    on community, 2347
Miller, Rodney W., 2287
Miller, Ronald E., 1715
    Sierra Pines Old German Baptist
        Brethren Church, CA, minister,
        1181
Miller, Ronald Eugene, Sr., 2287
Miller, Roy E., 1715
    Marilla Church of the Brethren, MI,
        minister, 793
Miller, Roy Eugene, 1715, **2384**
Miller, Roy Keeny, 547, 692, 1715
Miller, Ruby (later Wagoner)
    Wagoner, Gerald C., Sr. (OGBB) and,
        2259
Miller, Russell E., 2018
Miller, Ruth (later Moore), 2022
Miller, Royal, 2018
Miller, S. G., 1715
Miller, S. J., 1715
    San Bernardino, CA, Church of the
        Brethren, pastor, 1141
Miller, S. P., 372
    Middle Creek Church of the Brethren,

IA, minister, 825
Miller, Sadie Jane, **842,** 1841, 2018
Miller, Samuel, 1715
Miller, Samuel, (BC), 572, 573
Miller, Samuel, 572, 573, 894, 1715, 2069
    family history and genealogy, 2014
Miller, Samuel A., 1715
Miller, Samuel and Barbara, 2014
Miller, Samuel and Elizabeth Kirkwood
    genealogy, 2012
Miller, Samuel B., 276, 1715, 2059
Miller, Samuel C., 1715, 2065
Miller, Samuel D., 1715
    Miller, Joseph Quinter, father of,
        840–841
    Miller, Minor Cline, father of, 841
Miller, Samuel Daniel, 733, 1236, 1715
    family history, 2012
Miller, Samuel E., 1715
Miller, Samuel G., 1321, 1715
Miller, Samuel H., 1240, 1323, 1715
Miller, Samuel J., **842,** 1141, 1715, 1891
    McPherson College, acting president,
        781
Miller, S[amuel] J., 2018
Miller, Samuel M., 1247
Miller, Samuel M. (2 listed), 1715
Miller, Samuel S., 2018
Miller, Samuel Sweitzer, 1715
Miller, Samuel T., 1214, 1715
Miller, Sarah, 236
Miller, Sarah C. Harshbarger
    Miller, Robert Henry, wife of, 841
Miller, Sarah Cupp, 1223, 1350
Miller, Sarah Hardman, 894
Miller, Sarah Henderson, 894
Miller, Sarah J., 2078
Miller, Sarah J. Shelter, 2018
Miller, Sarah (later Etter), 459
Miller, Sarah Schlabach, 2018
Miller, Sebastian Christian, **842,** 1217,
    1345, 1715
    The Inglenook, 656
Miller, Shem, 264
Miller, Simon Berkley
    Miller, Eliza Belle, father of, 837
    Miller, Sadie Jane, father of, 842
Miller, Sol (Mr. and Mrs.), 586
Miller, Solomon, 1356, 1715, 2013
    Old Order German Baptist Church
        minister, 972
    Painter Creek Old German Baptist
        Brethren Church, OH, 990
    Poling, Newton L. on descendants of,
        2350
    Poling, Virginia on descendants and
        letters of, 2350
Miller, Solomon S., 1715
Miller, Stephen, 1715
Miller, Stephen A., Sr., 2287
Miller, Stephen Petry, 1715
Miller, Steve, 739
Miller, Susan Fisher
    on Coffman, John S. and Mennonite
        revivalism, 2347
Miller, Susan (later Etter), 459
Miller, Susan (later Flory), 497
Miller, Susan (later Rowland), 1126
Miller, Susannah (later Thomas), 1262,
    1263
Miller, Susanna (later Showalter), *See*
    Showalter, Susanna Miller
Miller, Susanna (later Wine), 895

Miller, Susannah, 214
Miller, Susannah Bechtl
    Mason, Floyd R. on descendants of, 2345
    Mason, Kathryn Garst on descendants of, 2345
    Müller (Miller) family, 895
Miller, Susannah Bowman
    Worstner, Betty Miller on descendants of, 2364
Miller, Susannah (later Wine), 1350
Miller, Swigart F., 1715
Miller, Theodore, 275
Miller, Theodore E., 1715
Miller, Thomas, 1365
    Okeechobee, FL, Grace Brethren Church, pastor, 963
Miller, Thomas (2 listed), 1715
Miller, Thomas H., 1715
Miller, Thomas J., 1715
Miller, Thurston, 1715
Miller, Timothy
    Durnbaugh, D. F. and Anabaptists, 2347
Miller, V. R., 417, 1715
    New Paris, IN, Brethren Church, pastor in, 931
Miller, Valentine E., 2018
Miller, Valentine Joseph, 2018
Miller, Valley Virginia (later Diehl, Myers), 724, 913, 2011,
    Myers, Minor Morton, wife of, 904
Miller, Velma (later Shearer), 2293
Miller, Vernon Ferrell, 557, 1343, 1716, 2018
Miller, Veronica I., 2106
Miller, Vida Eunice (later Wampler), 724, 1316, 1846
Miller, W. Carl, 31, 350, 588, 1716
Miller, W. H.
    Filley German Baptist Brethren Church, NE, 2374
    Somerset, IN, Poplar Grove Brethren Church, pastor, 1202
Miller, W. R., 1296, 1716, 1936
    Onekama, MI, Church of the Brethren, minister, 975
    Palestine, 1272
Miller, Wade, 2018
Miller, Walter, 1242
    Palestine Old German Baptist Brethren Church, OH, 991
Miller, Walter A., 1716, 2384
    Maple Grove Church of the Brethren, WI, pastor, 791
Miller, Walter R., 1716, 2304
Miller, Walter S., 1716
Miller, Ward A., 1342, 1716
    Modesto, CA, Big Valley Grace Community Church (FGBC), pastor, 866
    Osceola, IN, Grace Brethren Church, pastor, 984
Miller, Warren E., 1716, 2133
Miller, Wayne, 2018
Miller, Wayne L., 1716, 2136
Miller, Welty G., 1716
Miller, Wesley L., 2287
Miller, Wilbert Ray, 2287
Miller, Will, 105
    Old Brethren German Baptist Church, minister, 965
Miller, William, 1385, 2384

Miller, William (2 listed), 1716
Miller, William A. (2 listed), 1716
Miller, William Andrew, 1716, 2012
    Mud Valley Old German Baptist Brethren Church, IL, presiding elder, 892
Miller, William (Berne, IN, cong. FGBC), 121
Miller, William C., 1716
Miller, William D., 2018
Miller, William H., 1716, 2018
    Pleasant Grove Grace Brethren Church, IA, pastor, 1031
Miller, William Harold, 2018
Miller, William Henry, 269, 345, 503, 1716
Miller, William J.
    San Antonio, TX, Church of the Brethren, called to ministry, 1141
Miller, William Josiah, 2018
Miller, William K. and Anna Brenneman family history, 1967
Miller, William L., 2018
Miller, William R., 275, 1716, 2018
Miller, Willis Harry, 2018
Miller, Winfield Taylor, 752, 1716
Miller-Wright-Orr genealogies, 2016
Miller, Yost D., 2017
Miller, Yost Henry, 2018
Miller, Yost (Joseph), 2018
Millers Grove, OH, Old German Baptist Brethren Church, See Painter Creek Old German Baptist Brethren Church, OH
Miller's meetinghouse
    Lower Cumberland Church of the Brethren, PA, 135, 765
Miller's schoolhouse, York Co., PA, 425
Millersburg, IA, Pleasant Grove Brethren Church, See Pleasant Grove Grace Brethren Church, IA
Millersburg, OH, Grace Brethren Church 2224
milliennialism, See theology
millenium predictions by Thurman, William C., 1264
    statement of faith, 1218
Milligan, Ellah Ruhannah Metsker, 2018
Milligan's Cove Valley, PA, 1347
Millikan, Judith Lynne, 1854
Million, F. Blake, 1107, 1716
Million, Floyd Blake, 2304
Million, Marie Jane Alkire, 843
Million, Robert, 297, 843
mills
    grain, 161, 206
    inventions for, 168
    woolen, 161
Mills, Calvert, 240
Mills, John B., 1716
Mills, John W., 1716
Mills, Joseph, 240
Mills, Judy (later Reimer), 2290
    church governance and, 2264
Mills, Lizzie, 365
Mills, Maynard, 1716
Mills, Noah, 240
Mills, Ralph E., 1716
Mills, W. Quintet, 240
Mills, Wanda (later Clark), 2275
Millspaugh, H. E., 1716
Milly and Mie Kwie (Karn), 748
Milmine Church of the Brethren, IL, 843
    Oakley Brick Church of the Brethren,

    IL, 958
Milne family
    Fredericksburg, IA, Hillcrest Baptist and Brethren Church, 512
Milner, Vincent L., 2019
Milroy, PA, 462
    Grace Brethren Church, 843
Milton, Jacob, 1716
Milton, John
    religious liberty, 1098
Milyard, Charles Luther, 1356, 1716
Milyard, Hettie (later Skiles)
    Skiles, Clement S. (OGBB) and, 2249
Min, Young Son, 2287
mind of Christ
    ethics, 457
Minderhout, Mary Alice, 1860
Minderman, Daniel L., 269, 1716, 2384
Mindikutaki, Nigeria, 306
Mine Run Church of the Brethren, VA, 115 843, 1274
    Hollywood Church of the Brethren, VA, 620
Minear, Lorenzo D., 1716
Mineely, John, 1716
Minegar, Ernest, 1716
Miner, Blaine Allan, 2287
Miner, Calvin (Mr. and Mrs.), 579
Mineral Co., WV, 703, 1240, 1337
    Old Furnace Church of the Brethren, WV, 966
    Ridge Dunkard Brethren Congregation, WV, 1109
Mineral Creek congregation, MO, 1318
Mineral Creek, MO, Church of the Brethren, See Leeton, MO, Mineral Creek Church of the Brethren
Mineral Point, PA, Vinco Brethren Church, 843
Minerva, OH, Grace Brethren Church, 843
Mines, Cynthia
    on McPherson College, 2347
Mingo Church of the Brethren, PA, 260, 843, 1395
    Skippack Church of the Brethren, PA, 1189
    Harleysville, PA, Indian Creek Church of the Brethren, 584
    Norristown, PA, Church of the Brethren, 945
Mingona Church of the Brethren, KS, See Elm Creek Church of the Brethren, KS
Minick, A. Rachel, 843–844, 1860
Ministerial and Missionary Relief Fund (CB), 844
    pension funds, 1007
Ministerial and Missionary Service Fund
    Pension Board, administration by, 1007
Ministerial Association (BC), See National Ministerial Association
    women and, 2264
Ministerial Association (CB)
    mentoring, 2221
Ministerial Board (CB), See General Ministerial Board (CB)
ministerial exemption
    from military service, 844
"Ministerial Memories"
    Early, Henry Clay, in The Gospel Messenger, 413
Ministerial Pension and Annuity Plan

Retirement Board (BC), 1102
Ministerial Relief and Retirement Board
    (GBC)
    Poland, Frank Jacob and, 2238
Ministerial Relief Board (FGBC), *See*
        Board of Ministerial Emergency
        and Retirement Benefits (FGBC)
ministers, *See* pastors
    biographies of, Antioch Church of the
        Brethren, 1873–1973, 1938
    Brethren Church ministry, 846
    Church of the Brethren
        divorce, doctrines of, 2109
    colonial era
        New Jersey, 2093
        New York, 2093
        Pennsylvania, 2093
    divorce, doctrines of
        Church of the Brethren, 2109
    dress, 402, 404
    Dunkard Brethren, 409–410
        Maryland, 2105
    education of, *See* educated ministry
    Erste Liebe, Die (*The First Love*), 453
    farming, 477
    free, *See* free ministry
    hats, 589
    lifestyles of country, 2079
    manuals for, 788, 2066
    missions, ordained ministers in, 9
    necrology, 1981–2000, 2309–2317
    Old German Baptist Brethren, 2016
    ordination, *See* ordination
    polity issues
        manuals for, 2066
    published lists of
        The Vindicator, 1306
    railroad fares, 1081
    recreational activities
        Church of the Brethren, 2097
    role in worship services, 1377
    rural issues, 2109
    salaried, 408
    self-perceptions of
        Church of the Brethren, 2096
    spouses of, 657
    survey of, 2034
    universalism, 2106
    wives of, 1361–1362
    worship services
        manuals for, 2066
Ministers' Association of the Church of the
        Brethren, **844**
Ministers, Brethren Church
    National Fellowship of Grace Brethren
        Ministers membership, 916
Minister's Manual (CB), 51, 840
    communion table, 328
    funerals, 524
ministers, published lists of, 1539–1823,
        2281–2317, *See also* yearbooks
    The Bible Monitor (Dunkard Brethren),
        1218
    Brethren's (*Family*) *Almanac,* 1218
    Directory of Officials (Old German
        Baptist Brethren), 1218
ministers, women as
    Sterling, Mary Malinda, 1221
    Stine, Bertha Miller Neher, 1221
ministry, 4, **844–847,** 2017, 2019, 2048,
        2050, **2224,** *See also* bus ministry;
        educated ministry; elders; free
        ministry; salaried ministry; youth

ministry
    advancement in, 4, **6,** 432, **656,** *See
        also* ordination
    Baptism, Eucharist, and Ministry
        (BEM) text, 2133–2134
    Biblical order, 1998
    Brethren Church and, 184
    Christ, of, 2002
    church membership, 813
    Church of the Brethren, 1969–1970,
        2164
    clergy crisis, 2014
    degrees of, 4, 6, 177, **374**
    among Amish, 26
    and beards, 103
    Dunker ancestry, 1996
    Durnbaugh, Donald F. on mutual aid
        in, 2325
    Early, Henry Clay, 414
    education, 428, 429
    Eisenbise, Debra Lee on, 2357
    election of church officers, 434
    ethical issues, 2178
    free, 3, 513, 956, 957, 975, 984, 2109
    from free to salaried, 2036
    future of Brethren ministry, 1998
    General Board (CB), 535
    German Reformed Churches, 1966
    higher education, 603
    history of Church of the Brethren, 2094
    Holtzapfel (Holsapple, Holsopple)
        family, 624
    Holy Spirit, doctrine of, 624
    house churches, 632
    interest-taking, 658
    James Gribble Memorial High School,
        668
    mentoring (CB), 2221
    messages and meditations, 1986
    messenger selection, 819
    minister's wife, 1992
    misconduct, 2178
    National Ordination Council (BC),
        2229
    new forms, 2011
    office of Bishop, 201
    ordination, *See* ordination
    Parish Ministries Commission involve-
        ment in, 993
    parsonage life, 2012
    placement of pastors, 1028
    prophecy, 1062
    redemptive, and Priesthood of All
        Believers, 1057
    Roman Catholic Church, 1120
    salaried, 3
    effects of on the church, 86
    sickness, dying and death, 2050
    Sider, E. Morris on Anabaptists and,
        2356
    Slough, Rebecca on, 2357
    Thurian, Max on CB and, 2361
    to African Americans, 417
    women, 2024, 2263
    youth, *See* youth ministry
Ministry and Home Mission Commission,
        848, 2017
    evangelism, 461
    Foreign Mission Commission (CB),
        500
    General Ministerial Board (CB), 538
    missions, 859
    Parish Ministries Commission, reorga-

nization by, 993
    Ziegler, Edward Krusen, 1395
    Zunkel, Charles Edward, 1402
ministry education
    Brethren Academy for Ministerial
        Leadership, **2139–2140**
ministry, entering
    Daniel P. Sayler, 1150
The Ministry of Music
    Music Committee (CB), 899
Ministry of Reconciliation (CB), 2163,
        2224
    *Discipleship and Reconciliation
        Committee Handbook,* 2172
    newsletter of, 2347
    On Earth Peace Assembly, 2235
ministry, terminology, **847–848**
ministry to blacks
    Dolby, Martha Cunningham and Dolby,
        Wiley (check this), 395
ministry, women in
    Sisters' Society of Christian Endeavor
        (BC), 1188
Minneapolis, MN
    First Church of the Brethren, *See*
        Minneapolis, MN, Golden Valley
        Community Church of the
        Brethren
    urban mission, 1297
Minnesota Brethren settlement, 848
    Monticello, MN, Church of the
        Brethren, 872
Minneapolis/St. Paul, MN
    Dunkard Brethren Church, 2082
Minnesota
    Brethren movement, 2080
    Brethren settlement, **848**
    Iowa, 661
    migration of Brethren, 830
Minnesota Starvation Project, **848,** *849*
    detached programs, 380
Minnich, Abraham, 849
Minnich, Adam, 849
Minnich, Catharine Miller, 894
Minnich, Dale E.
    Hispanic Ministries (CB), 2199
Minnich, David, 849, 1716
Minnich, Effie Eugenia Eby, 2019
Minnich, Elmer, 1716
Minnich, Eva Shepfer
    Minnich, Herbert Spenser, wife of, 848
Minnich family, **849,** 1929, 2019
Minnich, George, 849
    Müller (Miller) family, 894
Minnich, Granville W., 849, 1716
Minnich, Hazel (later Landis), 1840, **2387**
Minnich, Herbert Spenser, Jr., *435,* 912,
        1345, 1716, **848–849,** 2019, 2140
    Minnich family, 849
    Painter Creek Church of the Brethren,
        OH, 990
Minnich, Jacob S., 748
Minnich, James H.
    Lewiston, ME, Church of the Brethren,
        2214
Minnich, James Lowell, 1716
Minnich, Levi, 2019
Minnich family, 849
    Painter Creek Church of the Brethren,
        OH, 990
Minnich, L(evi) Jay, 1716
Minnich, Lois Ann
    Lewiston, ME, Church of the Brethren,

2214
Minnich, Mary (later Eshelman, Stude-
baker), 455, 748, 1845, **2388**
Minnich, Michael, 849, 1716
Minnich, Nancy Shoemaker
Minnich family, 849
Minnich, Nora (later Robinson), 1115
Minnich, Otto L., 596, 1348, 1716
Pomona, CA, Church of the Brethren,
pastor, 1045
Minnich, Patricia, 2019
Minnich, William 1868–1940), 1716
Minnick, William (1807–1882), 1716
Minnix family
Howard Co. Old German Baptist
Brethren Church, IN, 633
Minnix, Fleming H., 743
Minnix, Joseph C., 1716
Minor, Floyd Earl, 2287
minorities, *See* African Americans
Church of the Brethren, 2163, 2178
cultural disintegration, 1994
minorities, ethnic and racial, **849–851**
civil rights demonstrations, and incar-
ceration of Brethren, 1060
language, inclusive, 2214
Miller, Mary Grace Hileman, 841
ministry, 2224
Ministry and Home Mission
Commission (CB), 848
missions, 859
National Council of Churches of Christ
in the USA and World Council of
Churches, 2228
Peach Blossom Colored Church of
Rising Light (CB), MD, 1003
Philadelphia, PA, Germantown Church
of the Brethren, 1016
minorities, racial and ethnic
Major, Sarah Righter, ministry to, 783
Major, Thomas and Sarah Righter, 784
minority children, *See* children, underprivi-
leged
Minot, ND, 1242
Church of the Brethren, **851–852**, 1242
Minser, Mark, 274, 1716
Montgomery Church of the Brethren,
PA, minister, 872
Mintern, Michael J., 282
"Minute-Man" campaign, 188, 192
Minutes of Annual Conference of Church
of the Brethren, 1980–1984
Ruff, Phyllis Kingery and, 2353
minutes of Annual Meeting, **852**
1822, Article 17, 6
1827, Article 1, anointing, 39
1850, Article 12, 6
1868, Article 1, 6
basis for decisions, as, 36
first reference to anointing in, 39
index of, 204
publishing of, 1067
Miracle, Billie, 2373
Miranda, Juan Carlos, 1716–1717, 1855,
2157
Hispanic Ministries (BC), 2198
Hispanic Radio Ministry (BC), 2199
Mexico, missionary to, 820
minorities, ethnic and racial, 850
Pasadena, CA, Centro Cristiano para la
Familia (BC) and, 2237
Miranda, María Fiorenza, 1852, 2157
Hispanic Ministries (BC), 2198

Hispanic Radio Ministry (BC), 2199,
2200, *2200*
Mexico, missionary to, 820
missions and, 2264
Mire family, 2073
The Mirror, 535
Mischke, Bertha
Phoenix, AZ, Grace Brethren Church,
1019
Mischler, Ullrich
Mishler family, 852
misconduct
ministerial, 2164, 2178
Mishawaka, IN, Brethren Church, **852**
Misher, Joseph
Mishler family, 852
Mishier, John
Peru, IN, Church of the Brethren,
pastor, 1010
Mishler, Adam, 430
Mishler, Anna Marie, 1851–1852
Mishler family, **852,** 1390, 2019
Monitor Church of the Brethren, KS,
869
Salem Church of the Brethren, OH,
1138
Mishler, Floyd Ernest, 1717
Mishler, George, 7, 446, 1333, 1717
Sappa Creek Church of the Brethren,
NE, 1145
South Whitley, IN, Church of the
Brethren, minister, 1207
Mishler, Iverson E., 1717
Mishler, J. C., 1717
Mishler, J. E., 1717
Mishler, Jacob G., 1717
Mishler, Jacob S., 949, 1717
North Manchester Old German Baptist
Brethren Church, IN, elder-in-
charge, 949
Mishler, Jacob, Sr., 852
Mishler, John, 852, 1234, 1333
Mishler, John B., 13, 1717
Mishler, John D. (CB) (1864–1914), 1717
Rossville, IN, Church of the Brethren,
minister, 1124
Mishler, John D. (CB) (1916–1952), 1010,
1717
Mishler, John Diefenbach, 2019
Mishler, John L., 565, 1717
Pleasant Valley Church of the Brethren,
IN, presiding elder, 1034
Mishler, John M., 1881
Mishler, John Milton, 2019
Mishler, Joseph, 1385, 1717
Mishler, Joseph, Sr., 13, 1717
Mishler, M. J.
Newton, KS, Church of the Brethren,
pastor in, 934
Mishler, Martha Ellen Ropp, 2019
Mishler, Michael, 356
Mishler, Moses J., 1717
Mishler, Myrtle, 2019
Mishler, Roy Smith, 740, 1717
Mishoff, Willard O., 2019
Misión Mutua en las Américas, 300, 355,
852, 2157
Iglesia Cristiana Pentecostal de Cuba,
2207
missions, 861, 2225
Misner, Mary, 318
Misner, Rick, 318
Missar, Charles D., 2019

Missaukee Co., MI
Good (Guth) family, 556
Riverside Church of the Brethren, MI,
1111
Missildine, Kathy Long, 2215
Mission and Ministries Planning
Council (CB)
missions, 2225
Mission Board
Newberg, OR, Church of the Brethren,
organization of, 933
Stiverson Church of the Brethren, WA,
1223
Mission Board (BC), 53
Mission Board (DB), *See* General Mission
Board (DB)
Mission Board of Middle Iowa, *661*
Mission Board of Southeastern Kansas
Fort Scott, KS, Church of the Brethren,
503
Mission Board of the Eastern Maryland
district
Flower Hill Church of the Brethren,
MD, 500
mission boards, *See* Brethren Home
Missions Council (FGBC);
Foreign and Domestic Mission
Board; Foreign Missionary Society
(BC/FGBC); General Church
Erection and Missionary Commit-
tee; General Mission Board (CB);
General Mission Board (DB);
General Missionary and Tract
Committee; The Mission Board
(BC), **2376**
Homestead Church of the Brethren,
MI, 626
Old Order movement, 206
Mission Chapel, WV, 254
Mission Christiana de Nicaragua, 2225
mission guidelines (CB), **852–853**
mission schools, 853
Mission Hospital, Lassa, Nigeria (CB), *See*
Lassa General Hospital, Nigeria
(CB)
Mission in Mutuality in the Americas
Misión Mutua en las Américas, 852
Mission One (CB), **853**
mission points
Elizabethtown, PA, Church of the
Brethren, 436
Elkins, WV, Church of the Brethren,
440
Elkton Immanuel Church of the
Brethren, MD, 440
Elsie Church of the Brethren, MI, 443
Emmett Church of the Brethren, ID,
445
Empire, CA, Church of the Brethren,
445
established by at Naperville, IL,
Church of the Brethren, 913
Everett, PA, Grace Brethren Church,
462
Fairchance, PA, Church of the
Brethren, 467
Fairview Church of the Brethren, MD,
468
Farmington, DE, Bethany Church of
the Brethren, 479
Fellowship of Grace Brethren Churches
(FGBC), 485
Ferrum, VA, First Church of the

Brethren, 488
Flat Creek Church of the Brethren, KY, 493
Flat Rock Church of the Brethren, NC, 493
Fort Worth, TX, Church of the Brethren, 504
Fredericksburg, IA, Hillcrest Baptist and Brethren Church, 512
Freeburg Church of the Brethren, OH, 514
Freeport, IL, Church of the Brethren, 515
Front Royal, VA, Church of the Brethren, 518
Fruitland, ID, Church of the Brethren, 996
Germantown Brick Church of the Brethren, VA, 544
Glade Park, CO, Community Church of the Brethren, 551
Glady, WV, Church of the Brethren, 551
Grand Junction, CO, Church of the Brethren, 565
Grand Junction, CO, Koinonia Brethren-Baptist Church, 565
Greene, IA, Church of the Brethren, 570
Greenville, OH, Church of the Brethren, 572
Grottoes, VA, Church of the Brethren, 574
Hagerstown, MD, Grace Brethren Church, 579
Hagerstown, MD, Valley Grace Brethren Church, 579
Hanover, PA, Church of the Brethren, 582
Harlan Church of the Brethren, IA, 583
Harleysville, PA, Indian Creek Church of the Brethren, 584
Harness Run Church of the Brethren, WV, 585
Hartford City, IN, Grace Brethren Church, 587
Hatfield Church of the Brethren, PA, 588
Highland Co. Mission Church of the Brethren, VA, 605
Highline Church of the Brethren, NE, 606
Hiner Church of the Brethren, VA, 607
Hollywood Church of the Brethren, VA, 620
Hopewell, VA, Church of the Brethren, 629
Huntington, IN, First Brethren Church, 637
Indianapolis, IN, Eagle Creek Grace Brethren Church, 654
Irasburg Grace Brethren Church, VT, 662
Island Pond, VT, Grace Brethren Church, 664
Jenners, PA, Grace Brethren Church, 670
Jeters Chapel Church of the Brethren, VA, 670
Joplin, MO, Church of the Brethren, 676
Neosho Church of the Brethren, KS, as, 923

Newberg, OR, Church of the Brethren, 933
Patterson, CA, Church of the Brethren, as, 995
Peters Creek Church of the Brethren, VA, 1011
mission programs
Brethren congregations as rural churches, 1130
Brethren contact with Roman Catholic Church, 1120
Nokesville, VA, Church of the Brethren, support of overseas, 939
Pleasant Chapel Church of the Brethren, IN, 1030
Pleasant Valley Church of the Brethren, VA, 1035
St. Joseph, MO, 1134, 1135
mission schools, 853–855, *See also* Bulsar Bible School
boarding at, 1177
India, 229
India orphanages, 651
Shirk, Bertha Ryan, missionary to India, 1177
Sisterhood of Mary and Martha, 1187
mission statements
Brethren Church, 2141, 2148
Conservative Baptist Brethren Church, 2148
Dunkard Brethren, 2148
Fellowship of Grace Brethren Churches, 2148–2149
mission tours, **855**
Mission Twelve (CB), 169, **855**
Christian Education Commission, 285
Church of the Brethren, 304
group dynamics, 575
Warstler, Anna Margaret, 1319
West, Daniel, 1331
Mission Viejo, CA, Saddleback Valley Grace Brethren Church, 16, **855**
The Missionary Advocate, **855**, 2019
Missionary Assistance Programs
Relief Agency Brethren (FGBC), 1096
Missionary Aviation Fellowship, 268
Missionary Board (BC), 182, 187, 405, **855–856**, 2019
Berkshire, W. Clayton, 1251
Black, James R., 2138
Ekklesiyar 'Yan'uwa a Nigeria (EYN), cooperation with, 937
evangelism, 460
Florida, 497
Foreign Missionary Society (BC, FGBC), 501
Gearhart, William A., 533
Gillin, John Lewis, 549
Hispanic Ministries (BC), 2198
Hispanic Radio Ministry (BC), 2199, 2200
India, 651
Ingraham, M. Virgil, 2208
Kem, George Frederick, 687
Kerner, William Hoff, Sr., 2211
Klingensmith, J. Ray, 703
Locke, John Funk, 751
Malaysia, missionary work in, 784
McFaden, John Duke, 773
missions, 860
National Associaton of Evangelicals (NAE), 2179
Rench, George W., president, 1099

Riddle, Earl M., president, 1108
Riverside Christian Training School, 1111
shift of focus away from inner-city missions, 1297
Studebaker, Claud, 1229
Yoder, Charles Francis, 1385
missionary conferences, **856**
Missionary Convocation, **856**
Missionary Helpers Clubs (FGBC) missions education, 864
Missionary Hymns, 2019
Missionary Ministries Council (BC), 2141 missions, 2224
Missionary Reading Circle, **856–857**
Helping Hand, The, 595
missions education, 863
Stover, Wilbur Brenner, 1226
Missionary Training Institute, Nyack, NY
Tyson, Elizabeth Stauffer, 1284
The Missionary Visitor, 194, 205, 535, *See also The Brethren's Missionary Visitor (CB)*
Church of the Brethren, 300
Crumpacker, Franklin Henry, 354
Minnich, Herbert Spenser, editor, 848
Mow, Anetta Cordula, 891
Royer, Galen Brown, editor, 1128
Temperance Bulletin, 1252
The Missionary Worker, **857**, 2019
missions and missionaries, *857,* **857–863,** *858, 859, 860,* 2019, 2024, 2025, **2224–2226,** *2225, See also* foreign missions
Africa, 160, 501, 504, 506, 573, 1962, 2091, 2261
Africa Mission Project, **2127–2128**
African Americans, 2128
Agadez, Niger, 220
agricultural, *See* agricultural missions
Amazon River, at mouth of, 172
American Indians, *See* American Indians
among the Baptists, 88
and animism, 31
Anklesvar, India, 212
in Appalachia, 44
Appalachian ministries, **2130–2131**
Argentina, *See* Argentina
Argentina (BC), 2251–2252
Argentine Brethren Church, 2141
Arkansas, African American mission, 2128
Arkansas as mission field, 395
Armourdale Mission Church of the Brethren, 683
article about, 1935
Aurora, MO, 1214
and the automobile, 74
Bear Meadow, PA, 1215
Bethany Bible School, 859
Bible translations, 139
bibliography, 1868, 1871, 1875, 1877, 1878, 1888, 1891, 1893, 1896, 1904, 1905–1906, 2050, 2310
Blue Creek congregation, OH, mission point of Van Wert, OH, congregation, 152
Blue River, IN, Church of the Brethren, 153
book for children about, 1928
Boston Mountain, 1215
Brazil, 172, 501, 2269–2270

Breathitt Co., KY, 405
Brethren Church, 183, 2141
Brethren Church ministry, 846–847
Brethren Home Missions Council (FGBC), 187
Brethren homes and hospitals, 1993
Brethren movement, 2101, 2109
Brethren of Christ, 189
Brethren Youth Crusader Program, 2151
Brooklyn, NY, urban ministry in, 933
Brush Ridge, PA, 1215
Canada, 188
 Brethren Church, 250
Canton, OH
 First Church of the Brethren, 251
Caruso, John G., 258
Cassel, Henry C., 259
Cassel, Jacob C., 259–260
Castañer, PR, 202
 Church of the Brethren, 261
Central African Republic, 501, 527
 Fellowship of Grace Brethren Churches, 250
Central America, 2157
Chad, 270
Chad Republic, 501
changes in attitudes about, 1376
character formation by mission schools, 1969
Chateau of Saint Albain, 2158, 2159
Chibuk, Nigeria, 220
Chicago, IL, 2103
 Hastings Street Mission, 2103
children, stories about
 Church of the Brethren, 2078
China, 160, 201–202, 209, 217, 277, 296, 299–300, 499, 606, 607, 630, 1973
 Senger, Nettie, 2077
 Sino-Japanese War, 2089
Chinese immigrants, 278
Church of God (New Dunkers), 297
Church of Jesus Christ of Latter-day Saints, 298
Church of the Brethren, 2100, 2162, 2178, 2314
children stories about missions, 2078
Colombia (BC), 2251
comity agreements, 326
consecration at Missionary Convocation, 856
Cottrell, Asher Raymond, 345
Cottrell, Laura Murphy, 345
Covington, OH, Church of the Brethren, 349
Cripe, Winifred E., 352
Crumpacker, Anna L. Newland, 354
Crumpacker, Franklin Henry, 354, 779
Cuba
 Brethren in Christ, 189
Cuba, Iglesia Cristiana Pentecosal de Cuba (Christian Pentecostal Church of Cuba), 2157
Dadisman, Mary Nancy, 359
David Loi Lee-Hoot and Jenny Me-Ai Ha (Loi family), 784
Declaration of Principles, 372
decline of, 202
Deeter, Minnie, 373
Del Rey, 1249
Delaware, 374
Denmark, 160, 178, 273, 280, 361, 375

Detwiler, Vianna, 381
development of, 1222
devotional literature, 381
Dilling family, 384
dispensation issues, 2110
Doctrinal Treatise, 394
Dominican Republic, 2172
Douglas Park Missions of the Brethren, Chicago, IL, 171, 275
Dove family, 397–398
Dowdy, Dortha Mae Frank and James Paul, 398
dress for, 402
Dry Run, PA Church of the Brethren, 406
Duncans Chapel Church of the Brethren, VA, 407
Dunkard Brethren Church, 2175
Dunkard Brethren mission points, 410
Durnbaugh, Donald F. on Brethren, 2327
East Fairview Church of the Brethren, PA, support of, 415
East McKeesport, PA, Church of the Brethren, support of, 415
East Tampa, FL, 1247
Easton, MD, Peach Blossom Church of the Brethren, 417
Eaton, OH, Church of the Brethren, 417
Ebey, Adam and Alice King, 418
Eby, Enoch, 419
Eby, Kermit, 419
Ecuador, 187, 422, 1290
 Church of Brethren, 250
Eddy, [George] Sherwood, 424
education, 167, 209
Eglon, WV, Church of the Brethren, 430
Eikenberry, Ivan Leon and Mary Elizabeth Flora, 431
Elgin, IL, 435
Ellis, Calvert Nice, 441
Encyclopedia of Modern Christian Missions, 1950
England
 Brethren in Christ, 189
English Prairie Church of the Brethren, IN, 447
Eshelman, Matthew Mays, 455
ethical issues, 2178
ethics, 458
Europe, 218, 2015
Evangelical Association, 459
Evangelical Covenant Church, 460
evangelism, 178, 182, 2180
Fairchance mission, PA, 1289
Fairview Church of the Brethren, IA, 468
famine relief, 475
Fargo Valley, ID, mission, 157
farm machinery, 476
fellowship houses, 484
Fellowship of Grace Brethren Churches (FGBC), 484, 485–486, 2313
films portraying, 98
Fort Scott, KS, 990
Forward Movement, 504
France, 160, 488, 501, 2262
 Fellowship of Grace Brethren Churches, 250
Francke, August Hermann, 506
fraternal relations, 510

Freeburg Church of the Brethren, OH, 514
French Equatorial Africa, 268, 270, 501, 985, 985
Frey (Fry) family, 517
frontier, 519
Fruitdale Community Church of the Brethren, OR, 520
Gandhi, Mohandas Karamchand, 528
Garkida General Hospital, 220, 530
Garner family, 531
Garrison, IA, Church of the Brethren, 531
GBC Christian Education (Department), 533
Geiger, Mary Schwenk, 533
General Church Erection and Missionary Committee (CB), 536
General Conference Mennonite Church, 536
General Mission Board (CB), 538
geographic location of, 1458–1463
German Baptist Brethren missionaries, 690
German Reformed Churches, 1966
Germany, 501, 545
Gibson family, 548
Girard, IL, Church of the Brethren, 550
Gish Fund Books, 551
Goshen, IN, West Goshen Church of the Brethren, 558
Gospel Visitor, The, 561
Grace Brethren International Missions, 2191
Grace Schools (Grace Theological Seminary, Grace College), 563
Gratis, OH, Church of the Brethren, 566
Graybill, Alice Minora Hoffer and Jacob Franklin, 567
Graybill (Grabill, Krehbiel) family, 567
Great Commission, 568
Gujarat United School of Theology (GUST), 576
Hagerstown, MD, Church of the Brethren, 578
Halle on the Saale River, 580
Harleysville, PA, Indian Creek Church of the Brethren, 584
Harsh, Alva, and Mary Lou Hykes, 1012
Hartville, OH, Church of the Brethren, 588
Hastings Street Missions of the Brethren, Chicago, IL, 171
Hatfield Church of the Brethren, PA, 588
Hawaii, 501
Heisey family, 595
Hell-for-Certain, KY, 406
Helping Hand, The, 595
Helstern, Mary Sue on indigenization of, 2353
Hickory Grove Church of the Brethren, IL, 602
Hinduism, 607
historic sites, 609
history, 613, 2047
Hollins, VA, Patterson Memorial Grace Brethren Church, 620
Holsinger, Henry Ritz, 621
Holsinger (Holtzinger) family, 623
Holsopple, Kathren Royer, to India,

1127
Holtzapfel (Holsapple, Holsopple)
    family, 624
home, and Lenox, IA, 1137
Home Mission Society, 165
Honduras, Comisión Cristiana de
    Desarrollo (Christian Development
    Commission), 2157
Hoover, Samuel W., 628
hospitals, 630
Hull, Margaret, 1019
humanitarianism, 636
Huntsdale Church of the Brethren, PA,
    638
Illinois, 165
imposters among the Brethren, 648
India, 146, 149, 150, 158, 160, 189,
    217, 267, 280, 299, 502, 616,
    649–651, *650,* 2049, 2077,
    2247
    Church of the Brethren, 250. 2066
        Warstler, Anna M., 2090
Indiana
    Stinebaugh, J. Gilbert, 2074
Indonesia (CB), 2255
Ingwaldson, Lew, family, 1019
Inman, Dorothy, 349
Iowa, 2103
    South Ottumwa Mission, 2103
Islam, 664
Ivester Church of the Brethren, IA, 665
Jalalpor, India, 212
James Gribble Memorial High School,
    668
Japan, 218
    Brethren in Christ, 189
Jewish evangelism, 671
Juniata Church of the Brethren, NE,
    678
Kansas, 214
Kearney, NE, Church of the Brethren,
    685
Kentucky as mission field, interest fol-
    lowing Civil War in, 689
Kettering, OH, Calvary Grace Brethren
    Church, 691
Keyser, WV, 1240
Kulp, Philip M., 1108, 2342
Kulp, Ruth Royer, to Nigeria, 1127
Landis, Herman, 1141
Lassa, Nigeria, 220
Latin American
    Grace Brethren missionaries, 161
laying on of hands, 327, 731
lectures on, 2076
Lima, OH, 1235
list of, 1833–1855
and L.S. Bauman, 97
Mackey, John Crawford, endorsed for
    service, 779
Maconaghy, Dorothy Helen Lewis and
    Hill, to Argentina, 779
Madziga, Risku, life story, 2005
Mahan, Grant, proponent of, among
    Hispanics, 782
maintenance of statistics, 1219
Mallott, Floyd and Ruth, 784
Manor Hill, PA, 1215
manuals for, 788
Maple Spring Church of the Brethren,
    PA, supporting, 791
Mattawana, PA, 1215
McAlevys Fort, PA, 1215

medical, 24
medical care, 810
medicine, 810
Mennonite Brethren Churches, General
    Conference of, 814
Mennonites, 815
men's movements, 2221
Messiah Church of the Brethren,
    Kansas City, MO originally organ-
    ized as, 683
Messiah College, Gratham, PA
    Brethren in Christ, 189
methods of, 9
Metzger, Minerva, to China, 819
Mexico, 501, 2157, 2261
Mexico, and San Ysidro, CA, Grace
    Brethren Church, 1142
Mexico, to, 820–821
Middletown, OH, 1235
Mill Creek Church of the Brethren,
    VA, sending, 832
Miller, Daniel Long, supporting, 834
Miller, Eliza Belle, to India, 837
Miller, Jacob Kurtz, 839
Miller, Marcus on OGBB, 2347
Miller, Sadie Jane, to India, 842
*Milly and Mie Kwie: Servants of the
    Master* (Karn), 1981
Ministry and Home Mission
    Commission (CB), 848
Minnich, Herbert Spenser and Eva
    Shepfer, to India, 848
minorities, ethnic and racial, 850
Minot congregation, 1242
mission guidelines (CB), 852
mission schools, 853
missionary conferences, 856
Missionary Reading Circle, 856
missions, *859*
missions education, 863
Missouri, 165, 214
Mohler, Samuel Sayler, favoring, 868
Moomaw, Ira Wilbur, to India, 874
Moore, John Henry, 874
Moravian Church, 875
motion pictures publicizing, 879
Mount Joy, PA, Florin Church of the
    Brethren, 882
Mount Zion, MO, 1212
Mow, Anetta Cordula, to India, 890,
    891
Mow, Anna Beahm and Baxter Merrill,
    to India, 890, 891
Moy brothers, to China, 850
mural paintings at Camp Mack portray-
    ing, 896
Musa, J. L. on Kibukuland, 2348
Muscatine, Iowa, 2069
Myers, Estella Catherine, to Oubangui-
    Chari, 903
Myers, Minor Morton, to China, 904
Myers, Paul R., to Denmark, 904
Myerstown, PA, Church of the
    Brethren supporting, 906
Nampa, ID congregation mission in
    Boise Valley Church of the
    Brethren, ID, 157
Native Americans, 188, 2230
    Church of the Brethren, 2067
    Navajo Indians, 2072
Nebraska, 214, 920
Neher, Minneva Josephine in China,
    922

New York
    Fellowship of Grace Brethren
        Churches, 250
Niagara Christian College, Fort Erie,
    Ontario, 189
Nicaragua
    Brethren in Christ, 189
        Misión Cristiana (Christian Mis-
            sion), 2157
Nickey, Barbara Marie, physician, 936
Nielson, Johanna, 362, 936
in Niger, 936
Nigeria, 153, 160, 167, 183, 230, 306,
    307, 480, 511, *595,* 2073
    Brethren Church, 250
    Carlisle, PA, First Church of the
        Brethren, 255
    Church of the Brethren, 250, 2081
        in Nigeria, 936–937,
            2246–2247, 2248
Noatemo, Jean in French Equatorial
    Africa, 938
North Manchester, IN, (First) Brethren
    Church, supporting, 949
North Winona Church of the Brethren,
    IN, supporting, 951
in northern NY, 933
nurse missionaries, 220
nursing, 952
Oakley Brick Church of the
    Brethren, IL, from, 958
Ober, Mary Velma on China and CB,
    2349
offerings for, 960
Oiness, Sylvia Marie, 963
Old German Baptist Brethren, 2234
Omaha, NE, 2092
order of dress for, 403
ordination, 980
Oregon, 295, 981
orphans, care for, 982
Orrville, OH, 1221
Osage Church of the Brethren, KS,
    from, 983
Oubangui-Chari, 183
Panora, IA, Church of the Brethren,
    involvement in, 992
Paradise Church of the Brethren, OH,
    992
Paraguay, 2141
Peace Valley Church of the Brethren,
    MO, members from, 1003
Persia, 501
Pfaltzgraff, Roy Edward and Violet
    Hackman, 1013
Philadelphia, PA, 166
Pietism, 1022
Piney Creek Church of the Brethren,
    MD, 1025
pioneer (CB), 9
Pittenger, John Milton, 1026
Pittsburgh, PA, Church of the Brethren,
    supporting, 149, 1027
Pleasant Grove Grace Brethren Church,
    IA, 1031
Pleasant Hill, OH, Church of the
    Brethren, 1032
Pleasant View Church of the Brethren,
    OH, supporting, 1037
Plymouth Brethren, 1039
Pollock, Myrtle Ferris, to China, 869
Polo, IL, Church of the Brethren, 1045
Pottstown, PA, Coventry Church of the

Brethren, 1049
Presbyterian relationships with Brethren, 1056
Progressive Brethren, 298, 1061
publication of statistics, 1218, 1219
publications, 191, 192, 1069
Puerto Rico, 501, 1070, 2262
Quebec, to, 1075
Quinter, Mary, to India, 1077, 1078
Reed, Kyle, to China, 1091
rescue missions, 2069
Rhoades, J. Benton and, 2242
Roanoke, VA, First Church of the Brethren, supporting, 1113
Rollier, Antoine E. and Mary Ganshorn, 1119
Rosenberger, Mary Sue Helstern on indigenization of, 2353
Ross, Amos W., 1193
Ross, Amos Walter and Flora Mae Nickey (Bjorklund), to India, 1123
Royer, Galen Brown, inspecting, 1127
Royer, Gladys Violet Hawbaker and Harold Albertus ("Red"), to Nigeria, 1128
rural, 2242
Russell, Harl L., 1132
Salamonie Church of the Brethren, IN, 1136
Salem Church of the Brethren, OH, 1138
Santa Ana, CA, Church of the Brethren, 1144
Sayler, Daniel P., promotion by, 1151
Schaeffer, Mary Ann, 1135, 1152
Seattle, WA, Olympic View Community Church of the Brethren, assisting, 1162
Sebring, FL, J. H. Moore Memorial Church of the Brethren, 1162
Shansi, China, 218
Sheely, Lila, 1019
Shenk, Wilbert R. on Anabaptists and outreach and, 2356
Shirk, Bertha Ryan, 1177
Shisler, Sara Cassel, 1177
Short Mountain, 1249
short-term missions, **2226**
Shull, Chalmer, Mary, and Susan, 1180
Shumaker, Ida Cora, 1180
Sickel, Clarence Leroy, 1181
Sickel, Loree Cutright, 1181
Sino-Japanese War China, 2089
Sipesville, PA, Church of the Brethren, supporting, 1187
Snyder, Myrtle Mae, 1196
Sollenberger, O. C., 1202
sources on, 2312, 2313, 2317, 2319, 2321
South Ottumwa Mission, IA, 2103
Spain, 501
Spring Creek, IN Church of the Brethren, 1213
Spring Run, IL, 1214
Springfield, IL, 1215
Stilwell, Nyleta, to Nigeria, 1203
Stone Valley, PA, 1215
Stover, Wilbur Brenner, 1227
Stump, Paul on African Dunkard, 2360
Sudan (CB), 2253
supporters of, 149
Swan Creek Church of the Brethren,

VA, 1243
Sweden, 160
Switzerland, 160, 488
textbook on, 1956–1957
theology of, 9
Thomas, OK, Church of the Brethren, 1263
Thorny Bottom Church of the Brethren, WV, 1263
Toledo, OH, 1266
Torreon Navajo Mission, 2160, 2174, 2175
Training in Missionary Endeavor (TIME), 1231, 1270
trinity Church of the Brethren, VA, 1275
Turkey, 488
United Andean Indian Mission (UAIM), 1289
United Brethren in Christ, 1290
United States, 188
National Christian Mission, 169
urban ministry, 1295–1297
urban missions
Omaha, NE, 2092
USA, 2076
Utah, 1298–1299
Vaniman, Alice and Albert, 1035
Venezuela
Brethren in Christ, 189
Vermont
Fellowship of Grace Brethren Churches, 250
versus ecumenical approach, 2178
Vyara, India, 212
Waldorf, MD, 1253
Washington, 269
Carl, George Clinton, 255
Washington, DC, City Church, 2081
Wells, Amos R., 2094
Whitcomb, John Clement, Jr. (FGBC, CGBCI) and, 2262
Wilson, Homer, 349
within USA, and social welfare, 1198
Wolfe, Claude E., 1145
women and, 2264
women in, 1361, 1363
World Council of Churches, 1368
World Ministries Commission, 1369
Yoder, Charles Francis, 1385–1386
York, PA, Second Church of the Brethren, 1388
Young Men's Christian Association, prisoner-of-war camps, England, 1290
Zambia
Brethren in Christ, 189
Zimbabwe
Brethren in Christ, 189
missions education, **863–864**
missionary conferences, 856
Mow, Anetta Cordula, secretary, 890
Mississinewa Church of the Brethren, IN, 373, 1288, 1354, 1390, 2041, See also Union Grove Church of the Brethren, IN
Hickory Grove Church of the Brethren, IN, 602
Elkhart Co., IN, 1389
Mississippi
Brethren settlement, **864**
Old Brethren, 970
Old German Baptist Brethren, 967, 970

Old Order German Baptist Church, 2235
Mississippi Co., MO, 416
Mississippi Valley, 165
Missoula, MT
conscientious objectors, 337
fire fighting, 491
Missouri, 54, 163, 177, 217
Brethren movement, 2087
Brethren settlement, **864–865,** *865*
Church of the Brethren, 2068
debates, 370
Far Western Brethren, 321, 795
migration of Brethren, 830
North Carolina Brethren relocating to, 946
Old German Baptist Brethren, 967, 970
Old Order German Baptist Church, 972
Replogle family, 1100
Shoemaker family, 2100
southeastern Missouri mission work, 1924
Universalists, 1292
Williams family, 2100
Missouri Synod Lutheran Church
Jackpot Church, NV, 2212
Missouri Valley German Baptist Brethren, IA
Harrison Co., IA, **865**
Mitchel family, 1926
Mitchel, John Albert, 1717
Mitchel (Mitchell), John C., 1717
Mitchele, Charles, Sr., 1717
Mitchell, A. David, 1251, 1717
Mitchell Co., NC, 224, 1294
Brethren congregations, 946
Fundamental Brethren Church, 522
Hollow Poplar Church of the Brethren, NC, 620
Petersons Chapel Church of the Brethren, NC, 1012
Pigeon River Church of the Brethren, NC, 1023
Pleasant Grove Church of the Brethren, NC, 1031
Mitchell, Curtis C., 115, 1717
Seal Beach, CA, Grace Brethren Church, pastor, 1161
Mitchell, David A., 2287
Mitchell family, 2060
Poplar Valley Church of the Brethren, MT, 1047
Mitchell, Floyd H., 417, 1717, 2019
Mitchell, Glenn Hershberger, 1717
Mitchell, James S., Jr., 1717
Mitchell, Kathryn Rinehart
ordained ministry and, 2264
Mitchell, Lawrence, 6
Mitchell, Melvin S., 14
Mitchell, Michael T., 2019
Mitchell Mountain
South Fork Church of the Brethren, WV, preaching point, 1205
South Mill Creek Church of the Brethren, WV, mission point, 1206
Mitchell, Olden Davis, 504, 557, 1717, 2019, 2155
on Brethren evangelism, 2347
on Brethren preaching, 2347
Shippensburg, PA, Church of the Brethren, pastor in, 1177
Mitchell, Patrick, 1717
Mitchell, Robert, 1243, 1717

Mitchell, S. Earl, 130, 1717
Mitchell schoolhouse
    Fly Creek Church of the Brethren, KS, 500
Mitchell, SD, Brethren Church congregation
    Nicholson, John, 1205
Mitchell, Vernon D., 1330, 1717
Mitchell, Zion E., 598, 1717
Mittelberger, Gottlieb, 2019, 2347
Mitterling family, 153
Mitz, Peter, 1717
mixed marriage, **865**
    discipline, doctrine of, 388
mixed multitude, *See* love feast
Mize, Warren B., 1717
Moats, Alice
    St. James Brethren Church, 1134
Moats, John W., 1717
    Mount Morris, IL, Church of the Brethren, minister, 883
Mobile, AL, 14
Mock, *See* Mack
Mock, Clayton Joseph, 1717
Mock, Dorcas Elaine (later Sollenberger), 1717, 2163, **2251**, 2264
Mock, Edward, 1717
Mock family, 1944
Mock, Harry C., 1717
Mock, Kenneth C., 1717
Mock (Mack), Alexander
    Mack family, 778
Mock (Mack) House
    place-names, Brethren, 1027
Mock meetinghouse (Pleasantville, PA), 47
Mock, Robert G., 637, 913, 1717
Mock, Virgil E., 594, 1717
Mock, Wayne, 1270
Mode, Peter G., 519, 612, 2020
A Model Life (Eshelman), 455
moderates, *See* German Baptist Brethren
moderators, Annual Meeting, **865–866**
    authority of, 866
    Brethren Church General Conference,
        See Brethren Church General
        Conference
    Church of the Brethren Annual
        Conference, *See* Church of the
        Brethren Annual Conference
    congregational, 4
    Davy, Henry D, 1151
    Dunkard Brethren General Conference,
        See Dunkard Brethren General
        Conference
    election of church officers, 434
    foreman in OGBB, 502, 865
    Frantz, Aaron, 508
    Grace Brethren National Conference,
        See Grace Brethren National
        Conference
    Kline, John, 1151
    list of, 1505–1511
    Old German Baptist Brethren Annual
        Meeting, *See* Old German Baptist
        Brethren Annual Meeting
    ordination, 980
    organizational restructuring and, 2242
    polity, 866
        Sayler, Daniel P., 1151
moderators, local
    elders as, 433
    Madison Church of the Brethren, VA,
        781

Maple Grove Church of the Brethren,
    NC, 790
Mill Creek Church of the Brethren,
    VA, 832
Montebello Church of the Brethren,
    VA, 871
North Manchester, IN, Church of the
    Brethren, 949
Pulaski, VA, Church of the Brethren,
    1071
Quakertown, PA, First Church of the
    Brethren, 1075
Rappahannock Church of the Brethren,
    VA, 1083
Ridgeway Community Church of the
    Brethren, PA, 1109
Roanoke, VA, Williamson Road
    Church of the Brethren, 1114
Roaring Spring, PA, First Church of
    the Brethren, 1114
Saunders Grove Church of the
    Brethren, VA, 1150
Skippack Church of the Brethren, PA,
    1189
modern Brethren
    admission into the church, 5
modern Christian thought
    Miller, Donald Eugene, 2223
modernism, 73–74, 183, 187, **866**, *See also*
        liberalism
    Church of the Brethren, 303, 2070
    education, 428
    fundamentalism, 522
    Grace Schools (Grace Theological
        Seminary, Grace College), 563
    Humberd, Russell I., 636
    Marlin, High Crist, 794
    Mennonites, 816
    *News and Views from Speak for the
        Lord,* as critical of, 934
    noncreedalism, 942
    Social Gospel Movement, 1197
"Modernism's International Organization,"
        187
Modesto, CA, 1280, 1363, *See also*
        Brethren Service Center, Modesto,
        CA
    Big Valley Grace Community Church
        (FGBC), **866**
    Church of the Brethren, **866–867**
        Empire, CA, Church of the Breth-
            ren, 445
        South Modesto Community
            Church of the Brethren, 867
    Dunkard Brethren, 239
    First Brethren Church, *See* Modesto,
        CA, La Loma Grace Brethren
        Church
    La Loma Grace Brethren Church, **867**
        Ripon, CA, Grace Brethren
            Church, 1110
    Old German Baptist Brethren, 238–239
        867, 1335, 1363
    Pleasant Home Dunkard Brethren
        Congregation, 30, **867**
    South Modesto Community Church of
        the Brethren, **867**
Modaski, Robert, 1717, **2384**
Moe, Nils, 1717
Moeller, Daniel Paul, 2287
    Mill Run Grace Brethren Church, MD,
        pastor, 833
Moeller, Donna, 204

Moeller, Kenneth G., 1717
Moeller, Robert C., 239, 496, 674, 1717
Moellering, Christopher Paul, 2287
Moffit family, 256
Mogadore, OH, 708
Mogoba, Stanley
    violence and, 2265
Mohanial, Amritlal, 1717
Mohawk Valley, OR, congregation
    Mabel, OR, Church of the Brethren, 771
Moherman, Austin
    Moherman, Tully S., father of, 867
Moherman, Ella J. Johnson
    Moherman, Tully S., wife of, 867
Moherman, Hettie Wagner
    Moherman, Tully S., mother of, 867
Moherman, Jemima (later Parker), 993
Moherman, Mary Amanda (later Muir)
    Muir, Gladdys Esther, mother of, 893
Moherman, Tully S., 115, 360, **867**, 1717,
        2020
Mohican Church of the Brethren, OH
        144, 145, **867–868**
Mohican German Baptist Brethren congre-
        gation, OH
    Fair Haven Brethren Church, OH, 467
Mohlenbrock, Robert H., 2020
Mohler, Allen, 1346, 1717–1718
    Nimishillen Old German Baptist
        Brethren Church, OH, minister in,
        937–938
Mohler, Amos S., 1718
    Nimishillen Old German Baptist
        Brethren Church, OH, elder in,
        937–938
Mohler, Andrew, 1718
Mohler (Brethren) cemetery
    Heitler, Martin P., 595
    Heitler, Richard R., 595
Mohler, Carl
    Sarasota, FL, Brethren Church, 1145
Mohler, Catherine Sayler
    Mohler, John Saylor, mother of, 868
    Mohler, Samuel Sayler, mother of, 868
    Mohler, Samuel, wife of, 868
Mohler, Christian
    Mohler family, 869
Mohler Church of the Brethren, PA, 14,
        322, 448, **868**, 2335
Mohler, Clara E., 322
Mohler, Daniel L., 1718, 2020
    Mound Valley Church of the Brethren,
        MO, 879
Mohler, Daniel M., 565, 1315, 1718
Mohler, Daniel W., 1718, 2304, **2385**
    Mohler family, 869
    Olive Grove Old German Baptist
        Brethren Church, CA, presiding
        elder and minister, 973
Mohler, David, 1039, 1223, 1255, 1718,
        2020, 2080
Mohler, E. M., 2020
Mohler, Edwin
    Mohler, Robert Ellsworth, father of,
        868
Mohler family, 158, 735, 740, **868–869,**
        1917, 2020
    Nimishillen Old German Baptist
        Brethren Church, OH, 937–938
Mohler, Fern Shoemaker
    Mohler, Robert Ellsworth, wife of, 868
Mohler, Frank, 1718
Mohler, George W., 1718

Mohler, Glenn I., 1356, 1718
Mohler, Harold, 1718
Mohler, Harry Beelman, 1718
Mohler, Harvey Hershey, 1718
Mohler, Henry, 1920
Mohler, Hermos O., 1718
    Modesto, CA, Old German Baptist
        Brethren Church, minister, 867
Mohler, Horace H., 553, 1718, 1916, 2020,
    2304
Mohler, Humphrey, 1718
    Nimishillen Old German Baptist
        Brethren Church, OH, elder in,
        937–938
Mohler, Ira D., 633, 1718
    North Fork Old German Baptist
        Brethren Church, IN, minister, 947
Mohler, Ira Leroy, 1718
    New Hope Church of the Brethren, TN,
        elder in, 929
Mohler, Isaac W., 1718
    Nimishillen Old German Baptist
        Brethren Church, OH, elder in,
        937–938
Mohler, J. D., 1718
Mohler, J. M., 1718
Mohler, J. S., 1267, 1718
    Rock Creek Church of the Brethren,
        KS, elder, 1117
Mohler, Jacob, 1718, 1920, See also Mohler
    family
Mohler family, 869
Mohler, Samuel, father of, 868
    Painter Creek Church of the Brethren,
        OH, 990
Mohler, Jacob M., 350, 1718
Mohler, James E., 582
Mohler, James M., 735, 1280, 1718
    Prairie View Church of the Brethren,
        MO, 1051
Mohler, Jennie E., 1841, 1866
Mohler, Jesse D., 268, 1718
Mohler, John, 869, 1920
Mohler, John (2 listed), 1718
Mohler, John E., 724, 2020
    The Landmark, editor, 1995
Mohler, John E. (2 listed), 1718
Mohler, John, Jr.
    Mohler family, 868
Mohler, John L., 1718
Mohler, John M., 735
Mohler, John M. (2 listed), 1718
Mohler, John S., 2020
    hymns, 643
    Osceola Church of the Brethren, MO,
        984
Mohler, John Saylor, **868,** 1718
Mohler, Samuel Sayler, brother of, 868
Mohler, Joseph Deeter, 350, 1718
Mohler, Judith (later McGlothlin), 2286
Mohler, Levi, 442, 1718
Mohler, Levi D., 1718
Mohler, Levi S., 1718
Mohler, Louise Martin, 2020
Mohler, Lucy Leatherman, 1841, 2020
Mohler, Ludwig, 1920, See also Mohler
    family
    Mohler family, 868
Mohler, M. S., 1315
Mohler, Magdaline (later Garber), 1920
Mohler, Marlan Ray, 2287
Mohler, Martin, 698
Mohler, Martin S., 1718

Mohler, Mary Ann Deeter
    Mohler, Samuel Sayler, wife of, 868
Mohler, Mary H. Risser
    Mohler, John Saylor, wife of, 868
Mohler, Melvin, 1718
    Middlefork Old German Baptist
        Brethren Church, IN, minister, 826
Mohler, Merlin E., 1295, 1718
    Mohler-Moler genealogy, 2020
Mohler, Mrs. Carl
    Sarasota, FL, Brethren Church, 1145
Mohler-Murray genealogy, 2020
Mohler, Paul, 1718, 1841, See also Mohler
    family
    Rossville, IN, Church of the Brethren,
        minister, 1124
Mohler, Paul L., 350, 564, 746, 1718, 2304
Mohler, Rebecca (later Studebaker), 1230
Mohler, Reuben S., 1718
Mohler, Robert Ellsworth, 285, **868,** 1160,
    1718, 2020
Mohler, Roy H., 1718
Mohler, Rudolph, 348, 869, 1718
Mohler, Samuel, 349, 757, 869, 1718
    Mohler, John Saylor, father of, 868
    Mohler, Samuel Sayler, father of, 868
    Sidney, OH, Trinity Church of the
        Brethren, 1181
Mohler, Samuel R., 1718
Mohler, Samuel S., 2020
Mohler, Samuel Sayler, 735, 864, **868,**
    1313, 1318, 1324, 1718–1719
Mohler, Sarah (later Howe), 217, 633
Mohler, Sarah Wagoner
    Mohler, Robert Ellsworth, mother of,
        868
Mohler, Susanna, 226
Mohler, Theresa Jane, 1839
Mohler, Velma Landis
    Mohler, Robert Ellsworth, wife of, 868
Mohler, William, 1719
    Omak, WA, Church of the Brethren,
        leadership, 974
Mohler, William, 1719
Mohlers congregation (GBB), 2084
Mohlers meetinghouse
    Lower Cumberland Church of the
        Brethren, PA, 765
Mohlin, Gertrude, 2109
Mohn, Kerry
    on Ephrata Cloister, 2347
Mohney, Herman W., 190
Mohr, Anna, 2019
Mohr, Dan, 573
Mohr, Esther (later Dole), 1918
Mohr family
    Mortonhouse (ship), 2373, 2376
Mohr, Ferdinand Heltzel, 1719
Mohr, Johann
    Mohr, Jacob, Sr., 869
Mohr (Moore), Jacob, Sr., 1719
Mohr (More, Moor, Moore), Jacob, 27
Mohr (More, Moor, Moore), Jacob, Sr., **869**
Mohr, Peter, 2019
Mohrsville Church of the Brethren, PA, **869**
    Pricetown Meetinghouse, 1057
    Reading, PA, First Church of the
        Brethren, 1084
Moine family, 1221
Moist family
    Hertzler (Hartzler) family, 601
Moler Avenue Church of the Brethren, WV,
    See Martinsburg, WV, Moler

    Avenue Church of the Brethren
Moler Avenue congregation, WV, 735
Moler, Charles Clyde, 2020
Moler, Eve, See Mohler-Moler genealogy
Moler, George Adam, See Mohler-Moler
    genealogy
Moler, John, 1719
Moler, Lydia A. Stouffer, 2020
Moll, John Thomas, 338, 1719
Moll, Sarah Selvidge, 338
Molland, Einar, 2020
Molly (ship)
    Oberholtzer, Samuel, voyage to
        America on, 960
    Wenger, Christian, 1330
Molsbaugh, John, 1719
Molsbee, Abraham, 264, 504, 1255, 1719
    Ewing Church of the Brethern, VA,
        2373
    Meadow Branch Church of the
        Brethen, TN, 805
    Nocona Church of the Brethren, TX,
        elder in, 938–939
Molsbee, Absalom, 1719
Molsbee, J. O., 1719
Molsbee, Samuel, 264, 1719
Molyneux, Ralph, 2287
Mombert, Jacob I., 2020
Momeyer, Rebecca, 1319
Mon-Dak (CB), ND, **246**
monasticism, 28, 193, **869**
    Eckerlin family, 421
    Ephrata Community, 448, 451–452
    Gass (Gast), Jakob, 532
    Hildebrand, Maria (later Mack), 606
    marriage, 291
    Moravian Church, 875
    mysticism, 907
    "Order of the Brethren," 976
Moncrief, Bill, 1343
Mondavi, WI, 1354
money, See taxes
    printing of, and Ephrata Press, 452
    stewardship of, 1223
Moneysmith, David, 1719
Mongan family, 1342
Mongold, Charles, 1345
Mongold family, 1345
Mongtomery Co., PA, 1286
Monitor Church of the Brethren, KS
    McPherson Co., KS, **869**
Monitor Church of the Brethren, OK
    Grant Co., OK, **869–870**
Monitor family, See The Bible Monitor
Monitor, KS, congregation, 1386, 1387
Monitor, OK, Church of the Brethren
    Enid, OK, Church of the Brethren, 447
Monmouth., KS
    Parsons Old German Baptist Brethren
        Church, KS, 994
Monn, Emma C., 2020
Monn family
    Ridge Church of the Brethren, PA,
        1108
Monn, John, 1719
Monn, Timothy Lynn, 1719
Monnette, Jack D., 1719
    Mill Run Grace Brethren Church, MD,
        pastor, 833
Monnier, Charles M., 2020
Monocacy Church of the Brethren, MD,
    See Rocky Ridge, MD, Monocacy

Church of the Brethren

Monocacy congregation, MD, 1264, 1298, 1338

Monongahela Co., VA, *See* Preston Co., WV

Monongahela River Settlement (Cheat River), VA, Church of the Brethren, *See* Terra Alta, WV, Cooperative Brethren Church (CB/BC)

Monroe Church of the Brethren, WV, *See* Lindside, WV, Spruce Run Church of the Brethren

Monroe Co. Church of the Brethren, IA, **870**

Middle Creek Church of the Brethren, IA, 825

Ottumwa, IA, Church of the Brethren, 985

Monroe Co., IL, 1357

Monroe Co., WV, 744, 1216, 1336, 2023

Monroe, Fern (later Sandy), *See* Sandy, Fern Monroe

Monroe, Kenneth M., 136, 715, 1212, 1719, 2304

Monroeville, PA, Church of the Brethren, **870**

Pittsburgh, PA, Church of the Brethren, 1027

Monrovia (Bush Creek) congregation, MD

Frederick, MD, Church of the Brethren, 511

Hyattsville, MD, University Park Church of the Brethren, 641

Monrovia, CA, Brethren Church

Hispanic Ministries (BC), 2198

Monrovia, MD, Bush Creek Church of the Brethren, 106. **870**

Mont Ida, KS, Church of the Brethren, **870, 1161**

Montague Co., TX

Nocona Church of the Brethren, 938–939

Montague, Robbie, 754

Montana, 177, 913

Brethren churches and property in, 1943

Brethren settlement, **870–871**

colonization, 324

conscientious objectors, 337

Great Northern Railroad, 569

Iowa, 661

migration of Brethren, 830

North Dakota Brethren relocating to, 946

railroads and Brethren settlement, 1082

Snake River Brethren, history of, 2054

Montana, Brethren in, 2322

Montanus, Herman

Mehrning, Jacob, 811

Montauban, Verel, 2287

Montcalm Co., MI, 256, 355

Montclair, CA, Grace Brethren Church, **871**

Monte family, 353

Monte Vista Church of the Brethren, VA, 130, **871**

Montebello Church of the Brethren, VA, **871**

Montecello, IN

Church of God (New Dunkers), 297

Montecello, IN, congregation, 232

Montel, Gary

Pinecrest Manor (CB), administrator,

1025

Monteverde movement, 2098

Montezuma Church of the Brethren, VA, 105, **871**

Montgomery, Abraham S., 1719

Montgomery, Andrew

Montgomery, Michael, father of, 871

Montgomery, B. F., 1719

Montgomery, Benjamin, 1719

Montgomery, Calvin L., 2287

Montgomery, Charles

Peters Creek Old German Baptist Brethren Church, VA, elder-in-charge, 1012

Montgomery, Charles O., 1719, 2304, **2385**

Oak Hill Old German Baptist Brethren Church, VA, minister, 957

Montgomery, Charles S., 1719

Montgomery, Chris

Pine Grove Old German Baptist Brethren Church, FL, elder-in-charge, 1025

Montgomery, Christian A., 1719

Oak Hill Old German Baptist Brethren Church, VA, minister, 957

Montgomery Church of the Brethren, PA **872**

Rockton, PA, Church of the Brethren, 1118

Montgomery Co., IL

Macoupin Creek Church of the Brethren, IL, 779

Montgomery Co., IN, 717, 1339

census, 2089

deaths in, 2089

Mount Pleasant Church of the Brethren, IN, 886

Montgomery Co., KS

Fredonia, KS, Church of the Brethren, 513

Independence, KS, Church of the Brethren, 649

Montgomery Co., KY, 688

Nicholas Co. German Baptist Brethren Church, 935

Montgomery Co., MD

Flower Hill Church of the Brethren, MD, 500

Montgomery Co., OH, 319, 352, 363, 365, 380, 462, 696, 701, 710, 722, 756, 1212, 1223, 1225, 1231, 1246, 1276, 1281, 1303, 1318, 1327, 1335, 1338, 1355, 1356, 1359, 2021, 2074

Bear Creek, OH, congregation, 165

Blickenstaff family, 146

Boyer family, 170

Brandt family, 172

Brethren movement, 177

Bright family, 209

Brookville, OH, Church of the Brethren, 213

history, 1967

Kinsey family, 170

Kleppinger family, 170

Lower Stillwater, OH, congregation, 231

migration of Brethren, 829

Nafzger, John, settled in, 939

Nead, Daniel, in, 919

North Carolina Brethren relocating to, 946

Old German Baptist Brethren, 967, 970

Patton, George, move to, 996

Paulus, John, family in, 996

Pfautz family, 1014

Plainview Dunkard Brethren Congregation, OH, 1029

Replogle family, 1100

Salem Church of the Brethren, 1138

Salem Old German Baptist Brethren Church, OH, 1139

Montgomery Co., OH., 281

Montgomery Co., OH, Bear Creek congregation

Scheublein, Isaac and Christian, 1178

Montgomery Co., PA, 170, 259, 375, 701, 734, *1272,* 1312, 1968, 1976, 2051

cemeteries, 2090

Eshelman, Walter Witmer, 455

Flora, (Flory) family, 495

Funck (Funk) family, 521

Harleysville, PA, Indian Creek Church of the Brethren, 583

Hatfield Church of the Brethren, PA, 588

Mingo Church of the Brethren, PA, 843

Pennsylvania settlement, 1004

Sauer, David, 1147

Skippack area, 1189

Skippack Brethren, 383

Skippack Church of the Brethren, PA, 1189

Montgomery Co., VA, 288, 1255

Elliot's Creek Church of the Brethren, VA, 441

Johnsville Old German Baptist Brethren Church, VA, 676

Mount Jackson Church of the Brethren, VA, 882

Pulaski, VA, Church of the Brethren, 1071

Riner Grace Brethren Church, VA, 1110

Montgomery, David A., 1719

Oak Hill Old German Baptist Brethren Church, VA, elder-in-charge, 957

Montgomery, Elizabeth Peters

Montgomery, Michael, wife of, 872

Montgomery family

Shoal Creek Old German Baptist Brethren Church, Newton Co., MO, 1178

Montgomery, George, 431, 743, 1719

Montgomery, Hattie P. Bashor

Montgomery, Michael, wife of, 872

Montgomery, Howard

Shady Grove Old German Baptist Brethren Church, OH, minister, 1171

Montgomery, IL, Boulder Hill Neighborhood Church of the Brethren, **872,** 911

Montgomery, Isaac Lemuel, 1346, 1719

Montgomery, J. Howard, 1719

Montgomery, Joel A., 1719, 2304, **2385**

Oak Hill Old German Baptist Brethren Church, VA, elder-in-charge, 957

Shoal Creek Old German Baptist Brethren Church, Newton Co., MO, minister, 1178

Montgomery, Joel A., 1719

Montgomery, John, 1719

Milford, IN, Brethren Church, 831

Oak Hill Old German Baptist Brethren Church, VA, elder-in-charge, 957

Montgomery, John Lee, 1719
Montgomery, Joseph A., 2287
Montgomery, Martha A., 1883
Montgomery, Mary Catherine Turner
  Montgomery, Michael, wife of, 872
Montgomery, Michael, 468, **871–872,** 1315,
    1719, 2020
  Jews, 671
  Middlefork Old German Baptist
      Brethren Church, IN, presiding
      elder, 826
  Shoal Creek Old German Baptist
      Brethren Church, Newton Co.,
      MO, elder-in-charge, 1178
Montgomery, Owen, 1223
Montgomery, PA, congregation, 274, 350
Montgomery, Ray, 1925
Montgomery, Riley, 1719
Montgomery, Robert, 1719
  Oak Hill Old German Baptist Brethren
      Church, VA, minister, 957
Montgomery, Sallie Peters
  Montgomery, Michael, mother of, 871
Montgomery Twp., Franklin Co., PA, 1231
A Month of Sundays (Fike), 2184
The Monthly Gospel Visiter, 178, *See The
    Gospel Visitor*
Monticello, MN, Church of the Brethren,
    872
  Minneapolis, MN, Golden Valley
      Community Church of the
      Brethren, 848
  Minnesota Brethren settlement, 848
Monticello/Pike Creek Church of the
    Brethren, IN, 25, 77, 232, **872,**
    1128
  Guernsey Church of the Brethren, IN,
      576
  Oak Grove, IN, Church of the Breth-
      ren, preachers for, 955
Montis, Samuel, 374, 1719
Montoya, Colleen, 713
Montoya, Tony, 713
Montreal, Canada
  German Baptist Brethren, 250
Montreal, Canada, Brethren Church, *See*
    Quebec
Montreal, Canada, mission congregation,
    259
Montreal, France, 505
Montreal, Quebec
  Detwiler, Vianna, 381
  Foreign Missionary Society (BC,
      FGBC), 501
  missions, 860
Montville Church of the Brethren
  Wittman, Bruce C. on, 2364
Montz, Glen R., 79, 759, 1719
  Morrill Church of the Brethren, MN,
      pastor, 877
  Myrtle Point, OR, Church of the
      Brethren, pastor, 906
  Paradise, CA, Church of the Brethren,
      992
Montz, Roy Alman, 1719
Moody Bible Institute, **872–873**
  Brubaker, Elizabeth Howe, 217, 1344
  Byler, Robert Oliver, 2153
  Ebey, Alice King, 418
  Fellowship of Grace Brethren Churches
      (FGBC), 488
  Fitzwater, Perry Braxton, 492
  Humberd, Russell I., 636

Jobson, Charlotte Ellen Hillegas, 671
Long, Isaac Samuel, 753
Moyer, Elgin Sylvester, 892
Moyer, Laura Emma, 892
Moody, Dwight L., 283, 390, 460, 560,
    1273
  American revivalism, 1104
  Moody Bible Institute, founder, 872
  success of, and revival meetings, 1103
Moody-Sankey revivals, 691
Moog family, *11*
Moomaw, Amos, 1719
Moomaw, B. C., 205, 211, **873,** 1225, 1293,
    1719, 2021
  Rockbridge German Baptist Brethren
      Church, VA, 1117
Moomaw, Benjamin Franklin, 167, 227,
    315, 370, 567, **873,** 912, 1308,
    1327, 1719, 1946, 2012
  Alleghany Co., VA, Church of the
      Brethren, 2125
  Hoxie, George W., 633
  Jeters Chapel Church of the Brethren,
      VA, 670
  Moomaw, Daniel Crouse, father of,
      873
  Mumma (Moomaw) family, 896
Moomaw, Catherine Graybill
  Moomaw, John Crouse, wife of, 874
Moomaw, Catherine Snyder
  Moomaw, Benjamin Franklin, mother
      of, 873
Moomaw, Christian
  Moomaw, Benjamin Franklin, father
      of, 873
Moomaw, Daniel Crouse, 227, 320, 766,
    873, **873–874,** 1296, 1308, 2021,
    See Bridgewater College
  Bridgewater College difficulties, 1978
  Moomaw, Benjamin Franklin, son of,
      873
  Progressive Brethren church govern-
      ment, 1044
  Roanoke, VA, First Brethren Church,
      1113
  Mumma (Moomaw) family, 896
Moomaw, Elizabeth Bowman
Moomaw, John Crouse, wife of, 874
Moomaw family, 355, 1277, 2094, *See also*
    Mumma family
  Hollins, VA, Patterson Memorial Grace
      Brethren Church, 620
  Roanoke, VA, First Brethren Church,
      1113
Moomaw, Ida Grise
  Moomaw, Ira Wilbur, mother of, 874
Moomaw, Ira Wilbur, 9, 267, 568, 874,
    1305, 1719, 1841, 2021, 2024,
    2376, 2385, 2388
  Agricultural Missions, Inc. and, 2242
  Japan, 669
  memoirs, 2348
  mission schools, 853
  Rhoades, J. Benton and, 2242
  Rural Life Association (RLA), 1131
  Rural Missions Cooperating Committee
      (RMCC), secretary, 1131
  World Friendship Center, 1369
Moomaw, Jacob, 638, 1719
Moomaw, Jacob P., 115, 1719
  Platte Valley German Baptist Brethren
      Church, NE, elder, 1030
Moomaw, John (2 listed), 1719

Moomaw, John Crouse, **874,** 1719
Moomaw, Kenton B., 1719
Moomaw, Lenhart, 1909
Moomaw, Mabel
Moomaw, Mabel Ellen Winger, 669,
    1841–1842, 1984, **2388**
  memoirs, 2348
  Moomaw, Ira Wilbur, wife of, 874
  World Friendship Center, 1369
Moomaw, Mary Ann Crouse
  Moomaw, Benjamin Franklin, wife of,
      873
  Moomaw, Daniel Crouse, mother of,
      873
  Moomaw, John Crouse, mother of, 874
Moomaw-Mumma family, 1988
Moomaw, Mumma, Mumaw, Mumaugh
    genealogy
  Moomaw, Robert A. on, 2348
Moomaw, P. P.
  Moomaw, Ira Wilbur, father of, 874
Moomaw, Rebecca Ann Crumpacker
  Moomaw, Daniel Crouse, wife of, 873
Mumma (Moomaw) family, 896
Moomaw, Richard W., 1719
Moomaw, Robert A.
  on Moomaw, Mumma, Mumaw,
      Mumaugh genealogy, 2348
Moomaw, Robert M., 1719
Moomaw, W. P., 1719
  moon, creation, form and significance
      of, 2097
Moon, David C., 468, 728, 1719–1720
Moon family, 1281
*The Moon: Its Creation, Form and
    Significance* (Whitcomb)
  Whitcomb, John Clement, Jr. (FGBC,
      CGBCI) and, 2262
Moon Lake, AR, preaching point
  St. Francis Church of the Brethren,
      1134
Moon, R. R., 1720
Mooney, James E., 2021
Moor, Jacob, Sr., *See* Mohr (More, Moor,
    Moore), Jacob, Sr.
Moore, Albert Burton, 2021
Moore, Alfred B., 766, 924, 1720
  Palestine Old German Baptist Brethren
      Church, OH, 991
Moore, Alice (later Suter), 1845
  Moore, John Henry, daughter of, 874
Moore, Alice (later Vaniman), 1303, 1324
Moore, Ann Aukerman, 660
Moore, Annie Lula, 237
Moore, Barbara Heistand, 2021
Moore, Brian H., 377, 1720, 2021, 2156
Moore, Calvin Cooper, 2022
Moore, Charles W., 1720
  Sand Brook Church of the Brethren,
      NJ, minister, 1142
Moore, D. C., 1315
Moore, David C.
  Moore, John Henry, father of, 874
Moore, Dillard, 1720
Moore, Earl D.
  Melbourne, FL, Grace Brethren
      Church, pastor, 812
Moore, Edwin E., Jr., 2136
Moore, Elihu, 1720
Moore, Elizabeth, 383
Moore, Ellen Kessler
  Moore, James Milton, wife of, 874
Moore, Etta (later Long)

Moore, John Henry, daughter of, 874
Moore family, 142, 319, 1253, 2060
  Farmington, DE, Bethany Church of
    the Brethren, 479
  Johnstown, PA, Geistown Grace
    Brethren Church, 674
  Roanoke, VA, First Brethren Church,
    1113
  Salem Church of the Brethren, ND,
    1137
Moore, George, 281
  Moore, John Henry, son of, 874
Moore, George L., 2022
Moore, Gerald L., 1720
Moore, Gideon, 739
Moore, Glenn E., 239, 1720
  Southern Lancaster Grace Brethren
    Church, PA, associate pastor, 1207
Moore, H. Leslie, *497,* 1240, 1720
  Meyersdale, PA, Grace Brethren
    Church, pastor, 822
Moore, J. B., 7, 105, 1720
  Edison German Baptist Brethren
    Church, NE, 2373
  Sappa Creek Church of the Brethren,
    NE, 1145
Moore, J. E., 1720
Moore, J. H., 180, 187, 218, 276, 277, 300,
    371, *455,* 496, *530,* 550, *550,* 561,
    590, 606, 639, 691, 719, 720,
    1298, 1911, 1935, 1946, 1952, *See
    also Our Children at Work*
  advisement against mixed marriages,
    1325
  divine inspiration of scripture, 132
  historical writing, 612
  Holsinger (Holtzinger) family, 623
  Messenger, 818
  migration of Brethren, 831
  missions, 858
  Mount Morris College, 884
  Native Americans, 2230
  New Testament, 133
  Our Children at Work, 985
  prayer, writings on, 1051
  publishing, 1067, 1068
Moore, Jack R., 629
Moore, Jacob, *See* Mohr, Jacob
Moore, Jacob, Sr., *See* Mohr (More, Moor,
    Moore), Jacob, Sr.
Moore, James Milton, **874,** 1323, 1720
  Maple Grove Church of the Brethren,
    WI, pastor, 791
  Moore, John Henry, son of, 874
Moore, Jean Sarah, 2022
Moore, John
  Moore, James Milton, son of, 874
  Wetonka, SD, Willow Creek Church of
    the Brethren, 2379
Moore, John Henry, 474, **874,** 1720, 2022
  Sebring, FL, J. H. Moore Memorial
    Church of the Brethren, pastor and
    elder, 1162
  Moore, James Milton, father of, 874
Moore, John P., 1720, *See also* Mooreites
Moore, Joseph, 1720
  Silver Creek Church of the Brethren,
    OH, minister, 1182
Moore, Joseph B., 1720
Moore, Joy Hofacker
  on Studebaker, Ted, 2348
Moore, Lause (later Badgeley), 1919
Moore, Leslie

New Troy, MI, Grace Brethren Church,
    pastor in, 932
Moore, Lewis A.
  Mount Cassell Old German Baptist
    Brethren Church, WV, minister,
    880
Moore, Lewis Marshal, 1720
Moore, Lorene A., 1720
Moore, Martha, 1340
Moore, Mary, 167
Moore, Mary (later Longenecker)
  Moore, James Milton, daughter of, 874
Moore, Mary S. Bishop, 691
  Moore, James Milton, mother of, 874
  Moore, John Henry, wife of, 874
Moore, Matison, family
  Ramey Flats Church of the Brethren,
    VA, 1083
Moore, Meyers, 571
Moore, Michael, 1720
Moore, N. Hudson, 2022
Moore, Nancy (later Link), 733, 1840
Moore, Philip A., 1720
Moore, Phoebe Brower
  Moore, John Henry, wife of, 874
Moore, Richard Allen, 2022
  on Hurricane Floyd and Brethren disas-
    ter aid, 2348
Moore, Robert Allan, 2022
Moore, Rodney, 2287
Moore, Roland J., 142, 1720, 2304, **2385**
  North Manchester Old German Baptist
    Brethren Church, IN, minister, 949
Moore, Rommie E. (Frank), 1720
Moore, Ruth Miller, 2022
Moore, S. R., 1340
Moore, Samuel, 1720
Moore, Samuel A., 1720
Moore, Sarah Will
  Moore, John Henry, mother of, 874
Moore, William, 605, 1720
Moore, William K., 1720
Moore, William P.
  Sand Brook Church of the Brethren,
    NJ, 1142
Mooree, George, 1720
Moorefield, Julia S.
  Midway Church of the Brethren, TN,
    providing leadership, 827
Moorefield, WV, 1315
  Church of the Brethren, **874–875**
Moorehead, Michael, 1213, 1316, 1720
  Peabody Old German Baptist Brethren
    Church, KS, baptisms performed,
    997
  Sand Creek Old German Baptist
    Brethren Church, KS, elder, 1143
Moorehead, William G.
  McClain, Alva J., 773
Mooreites, **875,** 1142
  Amwell, NJ, congregation and, 929
  chart of Brethren bodies, place on,
    1403–1405
  Poulson, Israel, Jr., 1049
  Sand Brook Church of the Brethren,
    NJ, 1142
  Wise, John, 1354
Moorman family, 1865
Moot, D. C., 1720
Moothart, David M., 142
moral issues
  youth issues, 2100
Morales, Kevin E., 1720

morality, *See* ethics; works, doctrine of
  reproduction of lectures on, 1937
Moravia, 29
  Hutterian Brethren, 639
Moravian Brethren, 875, 2022, 2029
  Guice (Geist Guß, Guss, Güß),
    Christopher, 576
  Hildebrand, Johannes, 606
  historical writing, 611
  Mennonite Brethren Churches, General
    Conference of, 814
  Müller, Johann Heinrich, 893
  Neisser, George, 2060
  nonconformity, 940
  oaths, taking of, 959
  pietism, 2062
  Unitas Fratram, 357, 875, 1311
Moravian cause, Dutch attracted to, 923
Moravian Church, 176, 357, **875–876,** 1965
  Andreas Frey, statement about, 1942
    association with Surrey, ND,
    Church of the Brethren, 1242
  bishops
    Burkhart, Jehu, 231
  Brethren movement, descriptions of,
    378
  Brethren polity, 1042
  Christ's Assembly, 375
  comparison and detection, 1996
  controversies in, and Johann
    Christophe Sauer I, 1148
  Czech Brethren, 357
  de Koker, Jan, involved with, 705
  Dunkard Brethren Church and, 2093
  Durnbaugh, Donald F. on colonial
    America and, 2325
  Endt, Johann Theobald, 446
  Ephrata Community, 451
  Fraternity Church of the Brethren, NC,
    511
  French and Indian War, 516
  Frey, Andreas, 517
  Frey (Fry) family, 517
  Frey, Wilhelm, 517
  frontier, 519
  history of, 1933, 1956
  leaders in, 40
  Marienborn, 792
  Martin, George Adam, representing
    Brethren at Pennsylvania Synods,
    797
  migration of Brethren, 829
  Müller, Joseph, 893, 894
  Neumann, Gottfried at, 924
  and non-associators in Revolutionary
    War, 939
  North Carolina, 1942
  oaths, taking of, 959
  Parsons, Johanna Christina Zeidig, 994
  Pennsylvania Synods, 1007
  public worship criticized, 1375
  references to, 1941
  religion in the seventeenth and eigh-
    teenth centuries, 1988
  Renkewitz, Heinz Gottfried, seminary
    instructor, 1099
  Ronneburg Castle, use of, 1121–1122
  Rotruck (Rothrock, Roderick) family,
    1124
  social and economic organization of,
    1918
  Spangenberg, Augustus Gottlieb,
    1207–1208

Zinzendorf, Nikolaus Sudwig, Count von, 1399
Moravian Historical Society, 2042
Moravian Society Brethren, 1311
Moravian Tract
North Carolina Brethren settlement, 946
Moray (Murray), John
Murray, Samuel M., descended from, 897
More, Jacob, Sr., *See* Mohr (More, Moor, Moore), Jacob, Sr.
More, John W., 413, 1720
Moreash, R. C., 1720
Moreau, D. H., 1998
Morehouse, Eldon L., 1720, 2183
Moreland, Ora, 1720
Moreno, Raul R., 2022
Morey family, 768
Morgan, A. L., 633, 1720
Morgan Co., IL, 1234
migration of Brethren, 829
Rowland, Joseph, helping to establish congregations, 1126
Morgan Co., MO
Prairie View Church of the Brethren, MO, 1050
Morgan, Elias A., 1720
Morgan family, 233, 1234, 1267
Modesto, CA, La Loma Grace Brethren Church, 867
Morgan, G. Campbell
Winona Lake Auditorium, IN, 1353
Morgan, J. P., 253, 405, 568
Northern Pacific Railroad, 951
Morgan, James
South Haven Old German Baptist Brethren Church, MI, deacon, 1205
Morgan, John, 1945
Morgan Library
Grace Schools (Grace Theological Seminary, Grace College), 563–564
Morgan, Margaret Rittenhouse, 1901
Morgan (Maugen), Peter, 1720
Morgan, Nancy, 1083
Morgan, Nellie (later Rainey)
orphanage administrator, 1083
Morgan, Ralph E., 1277
Morgan, Ronald Keith, 1720
Morgan, Sarah, 161
Morgan, Terry, 1720, **2385**
Morgan Valley Christian (Disciples of Christ) Church
Prairie City Church of the Brethren, IA, 1050
Morgan, W. H., 1720
Morgan, William, 1083
Morgantown, WV
Fair-View (Georges Creek) Church of the Brethren, PA, 469
Morgantown, WV, Church of the Brethren, **876**
Mori, Gustav, 2022
Mormonism
Quinn, D. Michael on, 2351
sources on, 2319
Mormons, *See* Church of Jesus Christ of Latter-day Saints
Morning Star, 203
Morning Star mission point
Quinter, KS, Church of the Brethren,

1078
morning watch, *See* spiritual life
family worship, 475
The Morning Watch, **876,** 2023
Morningstar, Cecil L., 147, 1720
Morningstar, Clyde W., 425, 1720
Morningstar, M. Albert, 2287
Morocco, **876**
EIRENE, 432
relief and service efforts, 1097
Morphew, John Emory, 1720
Rice Lake, WI, Church of the Brethren, minister, 1107
Morphew, Paul L., 1720
Morphew, Timothy Sollenberger, 2155, 2287
Morr family, 2023
Morr, Harold F., 1720
Morr, Ralph B., 2023
Morrellville Church of the Brethren, PA, *See* Johnstown, PA,
Morrellville Church of the Brethren, PA, 503, 2050
centenial of, 2348
Morrill, Bertha Edith Gwinner, 1852
ship sinking en route to Africa, 863
Morrill Church of the Brethren, MN
Minnesota Brethren settlement, 848, **877**
Morrill, Curtis Glenn, 585, 1720, 1852
ship sinking en route to Africa, 863
Morrill, Elaine
ship sinking en route to Africa, 863
Morrill, Ethel Hubbard (later Dickens), 646
Morrill, KS, 1122, 1385, 1386
Brethren Church, 682, **876**
Hamlin, KS, Brethren Church, 581
Mackey, John Crawford, pastor, 779
McFaden, John Duke, 773
Pony Creek Brethren Church, KS, 98
Church of the Brethren, **876–877,** 1356, 2100
Mohler, John Saylor, elder, 868
Pony Creek, Church of the Brethren, KS, 1133
Rock Creek Church of the Brethren, KS, 1117
Soldier Creek Church of the Brethren, KS, 1201
Morrill, Stephen
ship sinking en route to Africa, 863
Morris, Arthur F., 1720
South Whitley, IN, Church of the Brethren, minister and elder, 1207
Morris, Barry
on Evergreen, VA, 2348
Morris, Birdie Lehman, 2023
Morris, James Henry, wife of, 877
Morris, Charles Stephen, **877,** 1720
Morris, David Junior, 1721
Morris, Elizabeth Ritchey
Morris, James Henry, mother of, 877
Morris family
Peace Valley Church of the Brethren, MO, 1003
Morris, Frank
Morris, Charles Stephen, father of, 877
Morris, Grace, 318
Morris, Henry M., 2097
Whitcomb, John Clement, Jr. (FGBC, CGBCI) and, 2262

Morris, James Henry, 40, 244, 719, **877,** 1247, 1287, 1721, 1938, 2023
Oklahoma, home missionary in, 964
Morris, John Gottlieb, 2023
Morris, Mary Metzger
Morris, Charles Stephen, mother of, 877
Morris, Mary Winey, 2023
Morris, Michael, 755
Morris, Paul R., 357, 558, 1721
Morris, Richard, 565, 1721
Morris, Robert Eugene, 1330, 1721
Morris, Robert Lee, III, 2287
Morris, William Johnson
Morris, James Henry, father of, 877
Morrison, Charles
Powell, OH, Grace Brethren Church and, 2238
Morrison Co., MN
Minnesota Brethren settlement, 848
Morrill Church of the Brethren, MN, 877
Morrison, David E., 2287
Morrison, Frank, 1721
Morrison, Hugh Alexander, 1860
Morrison, Matthew C., 2023
Morrison, Sharlene Anne Lehman, 2023
Morrisons Cove Home, **877**
Home of the Child Rescue Work, 625
Wilt, Joseph Wampler, 1347
Ziegler, Levi King, 1397
Morrisons Cove, PA, 317, **877,** 1323
Dutch writers of, 2105
French and Indian War, 516
Fredericksburg, PA, Brethren Church, 512
frontier, 519
Holsinger, Henry Ritz, 621
Kaylor, Earl C., Jr. on, 2340
Kaylor, Harriet Beahm on, 2340
Martin family, 797
Martinsburg, PA, Memorial Church of the Brethren, 798
massacre and peace position, 999
Metzger, John, 455
migration of Brethren, 827
minorities, ethnic and racial, 849
Native Americans, 2229
Neuenschwander family in, 924
New Enterprise Church of the Brethren, 927
Pennsylvania Brethren settlement, 1004
Pennsylvania Old Order Brethren, 1005
Snake Spring Valley Church of the Brethren, PA, 1192
Wentz, James E. on members of, 2363
Morrow Co., OH, 374
Sciota Church of the Brethen, OH, 1160
Morrow, James M., 1721
Morrow, Joseph, 1721
Portis, KS, Grace Brethren Church, 1047
South Solomon Old German Baptist Brethren Church, KS, minister, 1206
Morrow, Michael R., 2287
Morse, Alice (later Earle), 1923
Morse, Elinor, 1394
Morse, Emily Swope, 2023
Morse, Herman V.
Morse, Kenneth Ivan, father of, 878
Morse, Jedidiah, 379, 2023

Morse, Kenneth Ivan, 191, 285, **878**, 2023, 1721, 2304, **2376**
    "Are You Saved?", 2373
    hymns, 643
    Messenger, editor, 818–819
    poetry, 1039
    on preaching, 2348
Morse, Marjorie L. Hanawalt
    Morse, Kenneth Ivan, wife of, 878
Morse, Sadie Bennett
    Morse, Kenneth Ivan, mother of, 878
Morse, Wayne, 1394
Morse, Winifred (later McLochlan), 2023
Morsey, David, 1721
Mort, Sarah, 365
Morton family
    Mount Etna, IA, Church of the
        Brethren, 881
Morton, J. J., 468
Morton, Nell, 2183
Morton, Oren F., 2023
Morton, Robert, 2023, 2304
    Mansfield, OH, Woodville Grace
        Brethren Church, pastor (youth or
        associate), 787
Morton, Silas, 1721
Morton, Simon C., 62, 1721
    Nimishillen Old German Baptist
        Brethren Church, OH, elder in,
        937–938
    Old Brethren minister, 965
Morton, W. Owen, Sr., 613
Mortonhouse (ship), 456, **2376**
    emigration, 2373
Mosbaugh, Walter, 1721
Mosbee family
    Pleasant Valley Church of the Brethren,
        TN, 1035
Moscow Church of the Brethren, VA, **878**
    Elk Run Church of the Brethren, VA,
        439
Moscow, ID, 1223
    Palouse Old German Baptist Brethren
        Church, 991
    Church of the Brethren, **878**
Moscow, Russia
    Brethren movement, 2091
Mose, O. C., 172
Mosely, T. B., 2065
Mosemann, Edna (later Greiner), 2194
Mosemann, Ruth L. Histand, 2023
Moser, Anna Maria Leatherman, 584
    Middletown Valley Church of the
        Brethren, MD, 826
Moser, Gregg A., 2287
Moser, Mary Ann (later Quinter), 1077
Moser, Samuel, 1721
    "Moses of the Valley," *See* Shaver,
        Emanuel Bydler (GBB, BC)
Mosgrove, Glenna James, 2024
Moslem refugees, 198
Mosorjak, Gary Nicholas, 2287
Mosquito Creek, OH, Church of the Breth-
    ren, See Sidney, OH, Trinity
    Church of the Brethren, 1181
Moss, Aaron, 1333, 1721
Moss, Abraham, 1721
Moss, David C., 1721
Moss, Edmund, Sr.
    Moss family, 878
Moss, Elizabeth Lybrook
    Moss family, 878
Moss family, **878**

Four Mile Church of the Brethren, IN,
    505
Genesee Old German Baptist Brethren
    Church, MI, 540
Greene, IA, Church of the Brethren,
    570
Howard Co. Old German Baptist
    Brethren Church, IN, 633
Moss, Hazel Elvina Messer, 1842, **2388**
Moss, Heinz, 2105
Moss, John, 1721
Moss, Lorin L.
    Old Brethren minister, 965
Moss, Loring (Loren) Isaac, 137, 338, 433,
    878, 1289, 1334, 1721
    Mechanicsburg, PA, Dunkard Brethren
        Congregation, 806
Moss, Mary Eikenberry Lybrook, 878
Moss, Owen C., 1721
Moss, Philip, 297, 464, 570, 1721
    Mexico, IN, Church of the Brethren,
        elder, 821
Moss, William, 30, 1721
Moss family, 878
Mosser, Henry, 1721
Mosser (Moser/Musser/Muser) families
    bibliography, 1887
Mossey, Don (Mr. and Mrs.), 439
Mota, Santos
    Los Toros, DR, Nuevo Renacer, 2215,
        2216
Mote, Arthur O., 585, 1721, 2024
Mote, Esther Niswonger, 592
Mote, Harvey, 592, 1721
Mote, Minna (later Heckman), 591, 1838
    article about, 1961
Motes family
    Marietta, GA, Grace Brethren Church
        of Greater Atlanta, 793
Mother Katharine, *See* Drexel, Mary
    Katharine
motherhood
    sources on, 2320
Mothers and Daughters' Association,
    878–879, 1361
    request for Temperance and Purity
        Committee, 1252
    Van Dyke, Catherine Beery, 1302
Mothers and Daughters' Meetings
    Conference Program Committee (CB),
        333
Mothers' Day, **879**
motion pictures, 398–399, **879**
    Church of the Brethren, 2099
    doctrine on, 189
    Dunkard Brethren and nonconformity,
        941
    ethics, 458
    mass media, 800, 801
    Murray, Don, 625–626
    photography and movie cameras, 1020
    motor vehicles, *See* automobiles
    Mott, Charles W.
        Northern Pacific Railroad, 951
        railroad immigration agent, **879,**
        1082
Mott, Frank L., 2024
Mott, George S., 2024
Mott, John R., 422, 424, 989, 1231,
    1345, 1368
    American Methodist layman, **879**
Mouk, Curtiss Dean, 2287
Moulton, I. J., 713, 758

Moulton, Lucille, 713, 758
Mound Church of the Brethren, MO, *See*
    Adrian Church of the Brethren,
    MO
Mound City, MO, congregation
    North Bethel Church of the Brethren,
        MO, 945
Mound Valley Church of the Brethren, MO,
    6, **879**
    Cass Co., MO, **879**
mounds, archeological
    Bible stories supported by
        Adams Co., OH, 2096
Mounds congregation, OK, 723
Mount Airy, NC
    First Church of the Brethren, **880**
    St. Paul Church of the Brethren, VA,
        near, 1135
Mount Airy, PA, 2081
Mount Bethel Church of the Brethren,
    VA (Botetourt Co., VA), **880**
    Mount Joy Church of the Brethren, VA,
        882
Mount Bethel Church of the Brethren, VA
    (Rockingham Co.), **880,** 105
Mount Carmel Church of the Brethren, NC
    880
    Flat Rock Church of the Brethren, NC,
        493
Mount Carmel Church of the Brethren, VA,
    265, 413, 416, **880**
Mount Carmel congregations
    example of biblically inspired name,
        911
Mountain Grove Fellowship Church of the
    Brethren, VA, 889
Mount Carmel schoolhouse, WV, 1254
Mount Carroll, IL, Church of the Brethren,
    59, **880**
    Shady Grove Church of the Brethren,
        880
Mount Cassell (OGBB) congregation
    Shiloh Church of the Brethren, WV,
        880–881
        members leaving to form, 1177
Mount Eden German Baptist Brethren
    Church, KY, *See* Shelby Co.
    German Baptist Brethren Church,
    KY
Mount Etna, IA, Church of the Brethren,
    416, **881**
    Salem Church of the Brethren, IA,
        1137
Mount Garfield, CO, Church of the Breth-
    ren, **881**
    Grand Junction, CO, Koinonia
        Brethren-Baptist Church, 565
Mount Grove
    Sandy Creek Church of the Brethren,
        WV preaching point, 1143
Mount Healthy meetinghouse (Ragersville,
    OH), 80
Mount Hebron Church of the Brethren, WV
    881
Mount Herman Church of the Brethren,
    MO, **881**
    Fairview Church of the Brethren, MO,
        469
Mount Hermon Church of the Brethren,
    VA, 94, **881**, 1317
    Mount Carmel Church of the Brethren,
        VA, 880
    Germantown Brick Church of the

Brethren, VA, 544
Mount Hope Church Home (DB), PA, **881**
Mount Hope Church of the Brethren, AR, 929, **881,** *See also* New Hope Church of the Brethren, AR
Mount Hope Church of the Brethren, OK 723, **881–882,** 964
Mount Hope Church of the Brethren, WA **882,** 1212, 2077
Mount Hope Dunkard Brethren Church Home Board of Trustees
Ness, Jacob C., 2231
Mount Hope mission point
Quinter, KS, Church of the Brethren, 1078
Mount Horeb Church of the Brethren, VA **882**
Mount Jackson, VA, 1276, 1314
Church of the Brethren, VA, 21, **882**
Mount Joy Church of the Brethren, PA, **882,** 1364
Greensburg, PA, Church of the Brethren, 571
Mount Pleasant, PA, Church of the Brethren, 886
Mount Joy Church of the Brethren, VA, **882**
Mount Bethel Church of the Brethren, VA, 880
Mount Joy, PA, Florin Church of the Brethren, **882**
Mount Joy schoolhouse
Scott Valley Church of the Brethren, KS, 1161
Mount Joy, VA, meetinghouse, 164
Mount Joy, VA mission point, Botetourt Co., VA, Church of the Brethren, 164
Mount Laurel, NJ, Grace Brethren Church, **883,** 930
Mount Lebanon meetinghouse, VA, 416
Mount Lebanon, VA, congregation
Mount Carmel Church of the Brethren, VA, 880
Mount Morris Academy, *See* Mount Morris College
Mount Morris College, *603, 883,* **883–885,** *884, 885,* 1913, 2024, 2050
agricultural education at, 12
bibliography, 139, 1860
Blickenstaff, Lynn A., 146
Blough, Anna Viola, 149
Brandt, Lucile Long Strayer, 172
Brubaker, Ora George, 217
Brumbaugh, Aaron John, 219, 344
Burkhart, Samuel W., 231
Butterbaugh, Andrew G., 236
Butterbaugh, Bertha Belle Lehman, 236
Cassel Library, PA, 260
Clair, Aaron L., 317, 1345
Culler, David, 355
David's Children (Bates), 748
Early, John B., 414
Ebey, Alice King, 418
Eikenberry, Amos R., 431
Eikenberry, William Lewis, 431
Eisenbise, Forest Sard, 432
Emmert, Michael Wolf, 444
Falkenstein, George Ness, 471
Flory, John Samuel, 498
Flory, Martha Belle Shick, 499
Forney, Anna Marie, 502
Forney, Daniel L., 502

Frantz, Ira Henry, 508
Fruitdale Academy, 520
Garrett, Marguerite Arthelda Bixler, 531
Gilbert, James Zacchaeus, 548
Haines, Amos Hoppock, 579
Hamer, Oliver Stuart, 580
Harnley, Henry Jacob, 585
Heckman, Benjamin Franklin, 591
Heckman, Clarence C., 592
Heckman, Jacob Hugh, 592
Heckman, John, 592
Heckman, Lucile Gibson, 592
Heckman, Minna Mote, 592
Hersch, Elmer Myron, 598
Hoff, Emanuel Buechley, 616
Hoover, William I. T., 628
Horning, Mary Emma, 630
Illinois, 647
Iran (Persia), 662
Lahman, Joseph Christian, 718
Lear, John Wallace, 732
Lear, Mattie A., 732
Leckrone, Quincy, 733, 1192
Lehman, Galen T., 736
Lichty, Daniel John, 741
Lichty, Nora S. Arnold, 741
Long, Harvey Lawrence, 754
Mahan, Grant, 782
Manchester College, merger with, 785
Mathis, Jefferson H., 803
Metzger, Minerva, 819
Miller, Daniel Long, 836
Miller, Eliza Belle, 837
Miller, Jacob Kurtz, 839
Miller, Sadie Jane, 842
missions and missionaries, lectures on, 2076
Moherman, Tully S., 867
Mohler, Robert Ellsworth, 868
Moore, James Milton, 874
Morris, Charles Stephen, 877
Mount Morris, IL, Church of the Brethren, 883
Myers, Oscar Reiff, 904
Myers, Salome Stoner, 904
Myers, Tobias Timothy, 905
Neff, Earl, 313
Neff, James Monroe at, 922
Newcomer, Maud Odessa as student at, 933
Newcomer, Melchor Snively, as benefactor, 933
Nickey, Barbara Marie, as student in, 936
Noffsinger, John Samuel, president of, 939
Peters, Woodford W., president, 1011
Pittenger, John Milton, 1026
Robertson, Russell L., 1114
Rockford, IL, First Church of the Brethren, 1117
Rolston, Frances Fitz Simon and William Wendell, 1120
Ross, Amos Walter, 1123
Ross, Flora Mae Nickey (Bjorklund), 1123
Rothrock, Edgar Eli, 1124
Royer, Gladys Violet Hawbaker, 1128
Royer, Harold Albertus ("Red"), 1128
Royer, John Grove, 1128
School Visiting Committees, 1155
Sharp, Solomon Zook, educator at,

1174
Sherrick, Marvin Manam, 1176
Shively, Levi Stephen, president, 1177, 1178
Shull, Chalmer George, 1180
Shull, Mary Ruth Speicher, 1180
Spickler, Henry M., 1273
Stein, John William, 1220
Stine, Bertha Miller Neher, 1223
Stover, Mary Emmert, 1225
Stover, Wilbur Brenner, 1226
Swartz, Goldie Elizabeth, 1243
Taylor, Lydia E., 1249
Trostle, Eva Alora, 1276
Van Dyke, Catherine Beery, 1302
Vaniman, Chester Melvin, 1303
Wallick, Cyrus B., 1314
White, Amy Naomi Trout, 1339
Yeremian (Yereman), O. H., 1385
Young, Emanuel Sprankle, 1389
Mount Morris, IL, 243, 647, 1220, 1333
bibliography, 1860
Elgin, IL, Highland Avenue Church of the Brethren, 435, 436
Helping Hand, The, 595
history, 1981
The Home Helper, 625
hymnals, 642
Messenger, 818
The Pilot, 1024
publishing at, 25
Sisters' Aid Society, 1187
Mount Morris, IL, Church of the Brethren, 444, 488, 877, **883,** 1056, 2024
Pine Creek Church of the Brethren, IL, 1024
Rockford, IL, First Church of the Brethren, 1117
Mount Morris Index
Spickler, Henry M., 1273
Mount Morris Seminary
Miller, John Ezra, 839
Mount Olive Brethren Church, VA, 751, *See also* Pineville, VA, Mount Olive Brethren Church
Mount Olive Brethren Church, WV, *See* Racket, WV, Mount Olive Brethren Church
Mount Olive congregations
example of biblically inspired name, 911
Mount Olive, MS, 731
Mount Olive, VA, congregation, 166
Mount Olivet Brethren Church, DE, 374, **886**
Mount Olivet Church of the Brethren, PA **886**
Mount Olivet Church of the Brethren, VA **886,** 1265, 2348
Mount Olivet congregations
example of biblically inspired name, 911
Mount Pisgah, MO
Dunkard and Mennonite use of church, 1982
Mount Pleasant Brethren Church, IN, *See* Cambria, IN, Mount Pleasant Brethren Church
Mount Pleasant Brethren Church, VA
Reliance, VA, Mount Zion Brethren Church, 1096, **886**
Mount Pleasant Church of the Brethren, IN **886–887**

Mount Pleasant Church of the Brethren, VA **887**

Mount Pleasant College, 692

Mount Pleasant house
Ladoga, IN, Church of the Brethren, 717

Mount Pleasant, IN, congregation, 173, 1315
Teeter, Roy R., 1250

Mount Pleasant, MT, congregation
Montana Brethren settlement, 870

Mount Pleasant, OH
Church of the Brethren, 937, *See also* North Canton, OH, Mount Pleasant Church of the Brethren
Nimishillen Old German Baptist Brethren Church, OH, 937–938

Mount Pleasant Old German Baptist Brethren, IN, **887**

Mount Pleasant, PA
Brethren Church, **886,** 1339
Church of the Brethren, 335, **886**
Mount Joy Church of the Brethren, PA, 882

Mount Pleasant, VA, congregation, 335
Shaver, Emanuel Bydler (GBB, BC) and, 2248

Mount Sidney, VA, 733

Mount Solon, VA
Sangerville Church of the Brethren, VA, near, 1144

Mount Storm, Grant Co., WV
Allegheny, WV, Church of the Brethren, 2125

Mount Union (Airpoint) Church of the Brethren, VA, **887**

Mount Union Brethren Church, IN
Goshen, IN, First Brethren Church, 558

Mount Union Church of the Brethren, WV, 226, *See also* Morgantown, WV, Church of the Brethren
Fair-View (Georges Creek) Church of the Brethren, PA, 469
Morgantown, WV, Church of the Brethren, previous name of, 876

Mount Vernon Church of the Brethren, VA, 90, 228, 331, **887,** 904, 1340
Concord, VA, Church of the Brethren, preaching point for, **331**
Montebello Church of the Brethren, VA, 871
Oronoco Church of the Brethren, VA, 982

Mount Vernon congregation, WV, 1276

Mount Vernon, IL, Church of the Brethren, Pleasant Grove Church of the Brethren, IL, 1031

Mount Vernon, OH, Conservative Grace Brethren Church, 2168, **2226–2227**

Mount View Church of the Brethren, WV 350, **887,** 350, 927
Lower Lost River Church of the Brethren, WV, 766
Mathias, WV, Church of the Brethren, 803

Mount Wilson Church of the Brethren, PA, 39, **887**

Mount Zion
mission supported by Spring Branch Church of the Brethren, MO, 1212

Mount Zion Brethren Church, IA, *See* Aurelia, IA, Mount Zion Brethren Church

Mount Zion Brethren Church, IN, 347

Mount Zion Brethren Church, KS, *See* Norcatur, KS, Maple Grove Brethren Church

Mount Zion Brethren Church, OH, **887–888**

Mount Zion Brethren Church, VA, 343, *See also* Dayton, VA, Mount Zion Brethren Church; Reliance, VA, Mount Zion Brethren Church
Mount Pleasant Brethren Church, VA, 886

Mount Zion Church of the Brethren, KS, **888**

Mount Zion Church of the Brethren, OH, 424, **888**

Mount Zion Church of the Brethren, VA, 767
Fairview-Mount Clinton Church of the Brethren, VA, 470, **888**
Front Royal, VA, Church of the Brethren, 518
Greenmount Church of the Brethren, VA, 571
Newport Church of the Brethren, VA, joined with, 934
Rappahannock Church of the Brethren, VA, 1083
Rileyville, VA, Church of the Brethren, 1109

Mount Zion Church of the Brethren, WV, **888**

Mount Zion congregation, MD, 467

Mount Zion, KY
Nicholas Co. German Baptist Brethren Church preaching point, 935

Mount Zion-Linville Church of the Brethren, VA, **888**

Mount Zion meetinghouse
Greenmount Church of the Brethren, VA, 571

Mount Zion, OH, congregation
becomes New Philadelphia First Church of the Brethren, 931

Mount Zion (Reliance, VA) congregation
Shaver, Emanuel Bydler (GBB, BC) and, 2248

Mount Zion Road Church of the Brethren, PA, **888**

Mount Zion union house
Falling Spring Church of the Brethren, PA, 471

Mount Zion United Brethren meetinghouse
Gettysburg, PA, Marsh Creek Church of the Brethren, 547

Mountain Creek Church of the Brethren, NC, *See* Spindale, NC, Church of the Brethren

Mountain Creek congregation, 1209

Mountain Dale, WV, 254
Sandy Creek Church of the Brethren, WV, 1143

Mountain Day excursion, *603*

Mountain Grove chapel, VA, 2089

Mountain Grove Church of the Brethren, MO, **888–889**
example of place name, 911
Greenwood Church of the Brethren, MO, 572

Mountain Grove Church of the Brethren, VA, **889**
example of place name, 911

Mountain Grove Fellowship Church of the Brethren, VA, **889**

Mount Carmel Church of the Brethren, VA, 880

Mountain Grove meetinghouse
Eglon, WV, Church of the Brethren, 430

Mountain Grove, MO, 237

Mountain Grove, VA, congregation, 211

Mountain Normal School
Floyd Co. Church of the Brethren, VA, 500, **889**

Mountain Valley Church of the Brethren, TN, **889**

Mountain View Brethren Church, Hollins, VA, 398

Mountain View Church of the Brethren, Alberta, Canada, **889**

Mountain View Church of the Brethren, ID, *See* Boise, ID, Mountain View Church of the Brethren

Mountain View Church of the Brethren, VA **889**
Rowland Creek Church of the Brethren, VA, 1126

Mountain View Church of the Brethren, WV, **889–890**

Mountain View, CO, Church of the Brethren, 376, *See* Denver, CO, Prince of Peace Church of the Brethren

Mountain View congregation, VA, 43, *See also* Hollins, VA, Patterson Memorial Grace Brethren Church

Mountain View congregation, WV, 735

Mountain View Grace Brethren Church, VA, *See* Hollins, VA, Patterson Memorial Grace Brethren Church

Mountain View, OK, 693

Mountain View Old German Baptist Brethren, VA
new district 1994, **2227**

Mountain View, VA mission point, Botetourt Co., VA, Church of the Brethren, 164

Mountaindale Dunkard Brethren Congregation, MD, **890,** 1264, **2376**

Mountaindale, MD
example of place name, 911
Rocky Ridge, MD, Monocacy Church of the Brethren, 1119

Mountville congregation, PA, 1340
Hempfield Church of the Brethren, PA, 596

Mountville, PA
baptisms in, 2100
Church of the Brethren, 416, **890**

Mourer, George, 1, 1721

Mourer, John H., 1721

Mourners set
Finney, Charles G.'s "New Measures" revivialism, 930–931
mourning benches, *See* "New Measures"
evangelism, 460

Move in Our Midst (Morse), 878, 643

Mover, Ronald R. M.
Peter Becker Community, 1010

movies, *See* drama; motion pictures

Mow, Aaron I., 243, 1328, 1721, 2024
family home, *1329*
Mow, Anetta Cordula, father of, 890, 891
Mow, Baxter Merrill, father of, 891
St. Francis Church of the Brethren, AR,

pastor, 1134

Mow, Anetta Cordula, 1361, 1842, 2024, **2376, 2388**
family home, *1329*
mission schools, 854
missionary, educator, **890,** 891
missions education, 864
poetry, 1040

Mow, Anna Beahm, 381, 528, *890,* **890,**
1210, 1361, 1721, 1842, 1936,
2024–2025, 2026, 2079, 2201,
2376, 2388, **2376–2377, 2388**
missionary to India, 1984
Murray, Dorothy Garst on, 2348
mysticism, 907
prayer, writings on, 1051

Mow, Baxter Merrill, **890-891,** 1721, 1842,
2025, 2053, 2304, **2377, 2388**
family home, *1329*
Mow, Anna Beahm, husband of, 890

Mow, David Merrill, 2025
on Bruderhof's struggle for renewal,
2348
Mow, Anna Beahm, son of, 890

Mow family, 142, 226

Mow, Joseph B., 1721, 2025
Mow, Anna Beahm, son of, 890
refugee resettlement and, 2241

Mow, Lois Annette
Mow, Anna Beahm, daughter of, 890

Mow, Mary L. Baxter
Mow, Anetta Cordula, mother of, 890
Mow, Baxter Merrill, mother of, 891

Mower, Arnold, 1346

Mowery, Hugh R., 1721

Mowery, John, 406, 1721

Mowrer, Dick
Southern Lancaster Grace Brethren
Church, PA, 1207

Mowrer, Mary Lou
Southern Lancaster Grace Brethren
Church, PA, 1207

Mowrey, J. B., 45

Mowry, Ramsey, 1721

Moxham, PA
Brethren Church, *See* Johnstown, PA,
Second Brethren Church
Church of the Brethren, *See* Johnstown,
PA, Moxham Church of the
Brethren

Moxley family
Mount Carmel Church of the Brethren,
NC, 880

Moy A. Wing, 1721
San Bernardino, CA, Church of the
Brethren, 1141

Moy Gwong Han, 277, 278, **891,** 1721,
1842, 2025
minorities, ethnic and racial, 850
Moy Gwong, Mrs., 2025

Moy Way, 278, *891,* **891,** 1721
minorities, ethnic and racial, 850

Moy Wing Lum, 278, 850, **891–892**

Moyer, A. L., 1285

Moyer, Abraham, 822, 1721, 2025

Moyer, Alvin L., 532, 1721

Moyer, Anna, 380

Moyer, Anna Barbara (later Wolff), 821

Moyer, Anna (later Lesh), 822

Moyer, Anna Maria, 821

Moyer, Anna Maria (later Baugher), 822

Moyer, Barbara Ann (later Alder), 822

Moyer, Barbara Bloss, 822

Moyer, Barbara (later Klein), 822

Moyer, C. F., 2023

Moyer, Catherine Angle (?)
Engle/Angle family, 446

Moyer, Catherine Bloss, 822

Moyer, Catherine (later Deissinger), 821

Moyer, Catherine Miller, 822

Moyer, Catherine Shuey, 822

Moyer, Christena Ebert, 822
Meyer family, daughter of George
Jacob, 822

Moyer, Christian, 822

Moyer, Cora M. Hottenstein, *See* Moyer
family

Moyer, Daniel, family
Pipe Creek Church of the Brethren,
MD, 1026

Moyer, Delmar Harrison, 1721

Moyer, Dennis K.
on PA German fraktur writings and
folk art of, 2348

Moyer, Edna Faye, 1842

Moyer, Edwin
Penn Run Church of the Brethren, PA,
pastor, 1004

Moyer, Edwin F., 1721

Moyer, Elgin Sylvester, 137, 201, 335, **892,**
1721, 1842, 2025
historical writing, 613
missions education, 864
Moody Bible Institute, 872
Moyer, Naomi Ann Holderread, husband of, 892
Schwarzenau assistant editor, 1158

Moyer, Elizabeth, 157

Moyer, Elizabeth (later Frantz), 822

Moyer, Elmer M., 1721

Moyer, Emma Rittenhouse
Moyer, Elgin Sylvester, mother of, 892

Moyer, Emma Tyson, 158

Moyer, Eve Catherine (later Stetler), 821

Moyer family, 384, 534, 1882, 1942, 2025,
See also Meyer family
Four Mile Church of the Brethren, IN,
505
Preiß (Price) family, related to, 1055

Moyer, Florence T. (later Bollinger), 157,
1834, **2371**

Moyer, Frances (later Swigart), 1245

Moyer, George, 821

Moyer, George Jacob, 822

Moyer, George Jacob, Jr., 822

Moyer, Gideon, 821

Moyer, Glen A., 1721

Moyer, H. H.
Silver Creek Church of the Brethren,
OH, 1182

Moyer, Harold Swanson, 1364, 1721–1722,
2025
Roanoke, VA, Williamson Road
Church of the Brethren, pastor,
1114

Moyer, Henry
Moyer, Laura Emma, father of, 892

Moyer, Henry ("George")
Meyer family, 822

Moyer, Henry Harrison, 1722, 2025
Philadelphia, PA, Calvary Church of
the Brethren, pastor, 1015

Moyer, Henry (son of George Jacob), 822

Moyer, Henry (son of Johannes), 821

Moyer, J., 263

Moyer, Jacob, 1722, 822

Moyer, Jacob and Christina, 1980

Moyer, Jean, 2165

Moyer, Johannes, 821

Moyer, John, 505, 766, 822

Moyer, John B., 1722

Moyer, John Martin, 2288

Moyer, John W., 1722

Moyer, Joseph Gehman, 1722

Moyer, Laura Cassel
Moyer, Laura Emma, mother of, 892

Moyer, Laura E., 212, **2377**
Brooklyn, NY, urban ministry in, 933
Moody Bible Institute, 873
urban mission worker, **892**

Moyer, Lavina (later Heckman), 592

Moyer, Lela F. Sellers, 1842, 2025
Moyer, Elgin Sylvester, wife of, 892

Moyer, Mabel I., 2025

Moyer, Mahlon
Moyer, Elgin Sylvester, father of, 892

Moyer, Margaret (later Hunsiker), 822

Moyer, Margaret Shuey, 822

Moyer, Mary Ann, 1840

Moyer, Mary Earrey/Arey, 822

Moyer, Mary Margaret (later Conrad), 822

Moyer, Matthias, 1722

Moyer (Meyer) family, 262

Moyer (Meyers) family, 2011

Moyer, Michael, 1722, 822

Moyer/Myers, David, 822

Moyer-Myers families
Montgomery Co., OH, 1980

Moyer/Myers, Nicholas, 822

Moyer, Nancy (later Merkey)
Markey family, 794

Moyer, Nancy Lou (later Saddler), 2053

Moyer, Naomi Ann Holderread, **892,** 1722
Moyer, Elgin Sylvester, wife of, 892

Moyer, Peter, 822

Moyer, Phares H., 2025

Moyer, Philip, 822

Moyer, Ralph Ziegler, 1722

Moyer, Richard A., 1722

Moyer, Rudolph, 822

Moyer, Samuel C., 158

Moyer, Valentine, 821

Moyer, Walton Z., 247
on Beissel, Conrad, 2348

Moyer, William Q., 2025

Moyers, Clarence Marshall, 1277, 1722

Moyers family, *See* Meyer family

Moyers, Henry, 1722

Moyers, John R., 1722

Moyers, Moses, 1722

Moyers, Susanna
Rentmeister, Jean R. on, 2352
Wine, Clyde C. on, 2352

Moyly (Mäyle, Meyle, Maili), Johann (Jan)
(Brother Amos), **804**

Mr. Sunday School, *See* Etling, Harold
Hartz

Mshelbila, Mamadu K., 307, 709, 1256,
1722

Mshelbwala, Didu, 307, *1257*

Mshelia, Bilama Bata
Mshelia, Madu B., father of, 892

Mshelia, Madu B., 307, **892,** 1722

Mshelia, Mwajim D. Y., 1722

Mshelia, Wasinda B., 307, 1722

Mshelmbula, Dawuda Y., 1722

Mshelmizhili, Joshua K., 1722

Mubi, Nigeria, 306

Muck, Harry

Rouzerville Church of the Brethren, PA, minister, 1125
Muck, Harry Clifford, 1722
Mud Lake, IN, congregation
    Mexico, IN, Church of the Brethren, 821
Mud Lick Church of the Brethren, KY, *See* Flat Creek Church of the Brethren, KY
Mud Lick fellowship, 2130
    Flat Creek Church of the Brethren, KY, 493
Mud Valley Old German Baptist Brethren Church, IL, **2377**
    Fulton Co., IL, **892**
Mudd, Emily, 796
Muddy Valley Church of the Brethren, NE (Arcadia), **45–46,** *46*
Muehlenberg, Heinrich Melchior, *See* Mühlenberg, Heinrich Melchior
Muehlenhauser, Ursula (later Pfautz), 1013
Mueller, Bernhard, 2025
Mueller, D. L., 2025
Mueller, Edna Ruth, 2025
Mueller, Ernst, 2025
Muhleman, Keith A., 2009
Muhlenberg, Anna Maria Weiser
    Muhlenberg, Henry Melchior, wife of, 892
Muhlenberg Co., KY, 165, 398, 685, 688, 689, 2049
    Far Western Brethren, 476
    German Baptist Brethren, **893**
    Hostetler Brethren, 631
    migration of Brethren, 829
    Noffsinger, Peter, and Brethren settlement in, 939
Muhlenberg, Frederick A.
    Muhlenberg, John Peter Gabriel, brother of, 893
Muhlenberg, Henry Melchior, 378, 767, **892,** 925, 1292, 1952, 2006, 2025, 2045, 2080
    historical writing, 611
    Kleiner, John W. on correspondence of, 2341
    Muhlenberg, John Peter Gabriel, father of, 893
    Pietism, 1022
Muhlenberg, John Peter Gabriel
    Lutheran pastor, general, **892–893**
Muhlenberg, KY, 1232
    Muhlenberg, Peter (General)
    Sauer, Christopher, II, arrest of, during Revolutionary war, 1146
Mühlheim
    Tersteegen, Gerhard, 1254
Muhundkar, B. R., 1722
Muir, Freeman I.
    Muir, Gladdys Esther, father of, 893
Muir, Gladdys Esther, 190, **893,** 1361, 2026, **2377**
    Durnbaugh, Donald F. on, 2325
    historical writing, 612
    Hogan, Herbert on, 2337
    Hogan, Jan on, 2337
    Peace Studies Institute, 1002
Muir, Mary Amanda Moherman
    Muir, Gladdys Esther, mother of, 893
Mulberry Grove, IL, Church of the Brethren, **893**
Mule Lick, KY
    New Covenant Fellowship, 926

Mullen, J. F.
    St. James Brethren Church, 1134
Mullen, Lena Belle Ohlwin
    on Ohlwein, Johann Werner and descendants, 2348
Mullen, Wilbur Eugene, 204, 1722, 1917, 2026, 2379
    family of, 685
Mullennex, Linda, 1875
Mullens, J. P., 1722
Müller [-Bahlke], Thomas
    on Sauers, 2348
Müller, Ernest
    historical writing, 611
Müller family, 1927
    Royer family, related to, 1128
Müller, George
    Plymouth Brethren, 1039
Müller, Gerhard, 1922
Müller, Heinrich
    Sattler, Gary R. on Pietists view of individual in writings of, 2354
Müller, J. H.
    Lerg, Winfried B. on, 2343
Müller, Joh Peter, *See* Miller, John Peter
Müller, Johann Heinrich, 1999
Müller, Johann Michael
Müller (Miller) family, 895
Müller, Johann Peter, 2056
Müller, Joseph, 176, 517, 576, 923, 1399
    Marienborn Moravian Church center, staying in, 792
Moravian Church, 876
    Physician, Brethren and Moravian church leader, **893–894,** *894*
Müller (Miller) family, *894,* **894–895,** *895*
Müller (Miller), Johann Heinrich
    printer, **893**
Müller (Miller), Johann Peter, *See* Miller, John Peter
Müller/Miller, Michael
    Spohn, Clarence E. on, 2358
Müller, Veronica Frey, 517
    Müller, Joseph, wife of, 894
Mulligan, Clyde, 6, 1722
Mulligan, Frank, 1722
Mulligan, Glenn Franklin, 1722
Mullins, Alex, family
    Ramey Flats Church of the Brethren, VA, 1083
Mullins, Benjamin Harrison, 1722
Mullins, David, family
    Ramey Flats Church of the Brethren, VA, 1083
Mullins, Eulis, family
    Ramey Flats Church of the Brethren, VA, 1083
Mullins, J. H., 1722
Mullins, L. Myers, 1722
Mulsbaugh, John, 1722
    multi-cultural fellowship
    Hope Brethren Fellowship, 2204
Mulvane, KS, Brethren Church, 2, 682, 377, **895–896,** 1321, 2194
Muma, George, 1976
Mumaw, C. B. Z., 2026
Mumaw-Moomaw family, 2094
Mumert, John, 1722
Mumma, Beulah F., 2026
Mumma, Emily Metzger, 2288
Mumma family, 313, 701, 1359
Mumma, John, 896
Mumma, Juliana, 896

Mumma, Lenhart, 896
Mumma meetinghouse ("Little Dunker Church," Antietam, MD), *41,* 48
    Bible taken from, 738
    Manor Church of the Brethren, MD, mission point of, 787
    Maryland Brethren activity, *799*
Mumma (Moomaw), Christian, 896
Mumma (Moomaw) family, **896**
Mumma-Moomaw family, 1988
Mumma, S. H., 2026
Mumma, Samuel, family
    Sharpsburg, MD, Church of the Brethren, 1174
Mummert congregation, PA, 1294
Mummert, Daniel W., 1722
    Mummert family, 145
Mummert, Harlan Dale, 1722
Mummert, Harry, 406
Mummert, John D., 141, 1722
Mummert, John Ronald, 1722, 2288
    New Enterprise, PA, Church of the Brethren, as minister, 927
    on refugee ministries, 2348
Mummert, Meda, 406
Mummert, Moses M., 1722
    Pleasant Hill Church of the Brethren, PA, presiding elder, 1032
Munch, Gertraut
    Minnich family, 849
Munch, Magdalena, 2105
Munch, Wendel
    Minnich family, 849
Muncie, IN, 693, 1288
    Brethren Church, 495, **896**
    Church of the Brethren, 42, **896**
    Cornerstone Brethren Church and Ministries, **2227**
    missions, 860
Muncy, Raymond Lee, 2026
Mundel, Hedwig, 2026
Munder, A., 2052
Mundey, Paul Eston Risser, 745, 1722, 2111, 2026, 2130
Mundy, Mildred F., 1326
Mundy's Corner Brethren Church, *See* Johnstown, PA, Pike Grace Brethren Church
Munholland family, 683
Munholland, LeRoy, 683, 1722
Munn, Mary Elizabeth, 1852
Munoz, Jesus G., 2288
Munro, Harry C., 659
Munroe, William, 1722
Munson, A. A., 1722
    Newton Grove Church of the Brethren, minister in, 934
Munson, Bonnie, 188
Munson, Charles Robert, 203, 1722, 2026, 2169, **2227**
    Brethren Youth national director, 915
Münster, Germany, 28
Muntz, Lewis, 1722
Müntzer, Thomas, 28
    Reformation, Protestant, and radical reformers, 1092
Muntzing, Ernest E., 1722
    Roanoke, VA, Hollins Road Church of the Brethren, pastor, 1113
A Mural History of the Church of the Brethren (Schultz), 896
    mural paintings, Camp Mack, 61, **896**
    Shultz, Lawrence W. on history of CB

in, 2356
Murang, Timothy Ryan, 2285
Murch, James De Forest, 2026
murder
    Joseph Easter, 1135
    Bosler, Billy M., 2161
Murdock Church of the Brethren, KS, 128,
    896
Murdock, Martha Dorris (later Blough),
    748, 1834
Murfin, James V., 2026
Murphy, A. J., 345
Murphy, Diane, 1265
Murphy, Florence Fogelsanger, *199, 500,*
    1362
Murphy, George, 1722
Murphy, George W., 1722
Murphy, Helen Amanda, 2026
Murphy, J. L., 1722
Murphy, James E., 1722, 2026
Murphy, Kenneth Ward, 1722
Murphy, Laura M. (later Cottroll), 345,
    1836
Murphy, Mary E. Coates, 345
Murphy, Mary Jane Rummel
    Murphy, Ross Dale, mother of, 896
Murphy, Mary (later Frantz), 508
Murphy, Miles L, 1722
Murphy, Nancey Claire, 2288
Murphy, Norma
    Northhaven Retirement Residence, 951
Murphy, Ross Dale, **896–897,** 1348, 1722
    Murphy, Sara Florence Fogelsanger,
        husband of, 897
    Philadelphia, PA, First Church of the
        Brethren, providing leadership,
        1015
    Roaring Spring, PA, First Church of
        the Brethren, pastor, 1114
    Shippensburg, PA, Church of the
        Brethren, pastor in, 1177
Murphy, Sara Florence Fogelsanger,
    897, 1722–1723, **2377**
    Murphy, Ross Dale, wife of, 897
    Spain, relief work in, 1207, 1208
Murphy, Scott
    Murphy, Ross Dale, father of, 896
Murphy, W. R., 1723
Murphy, William (2 listed), 1723
Murphy, William R., 564, 679, 1723
Murr, Henry, 1723
Murray, Andrew, 158, 381, 691
    prayer, 1051
Murray, Catharine Rhodehamel, 2026
Murray, Catharine Saur
    Murray family, 898
Murray, Claude Hess, 1723
Murray, D. G., 2201
Murray, Darrell Richard, 326, 366, 1723,
    2026
Murray, David, 898, 1723
    Murray, Samuel M., father of, 897
Murray, Don, 20, 625–626
    motion pictures, 879
Murray, Dorothy Garst, 2026
    on Mow, Anna Beahm, 2348
Murray, Edward Lee, 141, 1215, 1723
Murray, Elizabeth Wellbaum
    Murray family, 898
Murray, F. F., 1723
Murray family, **898,** 1927, *See also* Indiana
Murray, Frederick, 1723
Murray, Jacob A., 898, 1323, 1723

Ryerson Station Church of the
    Brethren, PA, preaching, 1132
Murray, James, 13, 1723
Murray, James A., 16
    Ryerson Station Church of the
        Brethren, PA, minister, 1132
Murray, James C., 1723
    South Whitley, IN, Church of the
        Brethren, minister, 1207
Murray, James M., 16, 605, 1723
    Quiet Dell Brethren Church, PA,
        pastor, 1076
Murray, Jeremiah, 898
Murray, John, 662, 898, 1292, 1723
    Murray, Samuel, father of, 897
Murray, John Blair, 1723
Murray, John Clinton, 638, 914, 1723
Murray, John F., 2026
    on Neff familes and descendants, 2348
Murray, John S., 347
Murray, Joseph H., 154, 1723
    Roanoke, VA, Ninth Street Church of
        the Brethren, preaching, 1113
Murray, Julian, 1723
Murray, M. Roy, 683
Murray, Marilyn Jean (later Aspinall), 1854,
    2026
Murray, Martin Roy, 1723
    North Saint Joseph Church of the
        Brethren, MO, pastor, 1134
Murray, Max Andrew, 1723, 2026, 2108
    On Earth Peace Assembly, *2236*
Murray (Moray), John
    Murray, Samuel M., descended from,
        897
Murray, Oscar, 1723
Murray, Phoebe Hart
    Murray, Samuel, wife of, 897
Murray, Samuel, *897,* **897,** 1723, 2026
    Murray family, 898
    Murray, Samuel M., uncle of, 897
    Pipe Creek Church of the Brethren, IN,
        1025
Murray, Samuel M., 205, 350, **897–898,**
    1723
    Murray family, 898
    New River Old German Baptist
        Brethren Church, ministers for,
        931
    Nimishillen Old German Baptist
        Brethren Church, OH, elder in,
        937–938
Murray, Thomas, 1213
Murray, William, 16
Murray, William A., 898, 1723
Murray, William F., 1723
Murrey, Pearl Crumpacker, 2052
Murrow Creek, MO, Church of the
    Brethren, *See* Prairie View Church
    of the Brethren, MO
Prairie View Church of the Brethren,
    MO, 1050
Murtaugh, ID, 1282
Musa, J. L.
    on Kibukuland missionary activities,
        2348
Musa, Nigeria, 306
Muscatine, IA, First Church of the
    Brethren, **898**
missions and missionaries, 2069
museums, 149
    Brethren memorabilia, **898**
    Pennsylvania Brethren settlement, 1004

music, 60, **898–899,** *899,* 2044, 2049, 2050,
    See also hymnals; hymns; singing
    Amana Society, 1935
    Beissel, Conrad, 1874, 1970, 1974
    bibliography, 1862, 1874, 1879, 1880,
        1891
    Brethren music, 898
    changes since 1980, **2227–2228**
    choirs and instruments, 279–280
    Christian Brethren, 281
    Christian Education Commission (CB),
        285
    classes, 149, 155, 209
    Codorus, PA, Church of the Brethren,
        323
    colonial era
        Ephrata Community, 2098
    Columbia, MD, Oakland Mills Uniting
        Church (CB, UCC) and, 326
    Disciples of Christ, 385
    Downsville Church of the Brethren,
        MD, 398
    Dunkard Brethren Church, 2106
    Ephrata Community, 452, 1948, 2045,
        2053, 2006, 2090
    Glendale, CA, Church of the Brethren,
        552
    gospel songs, 560
    gospels, *See* gospel music
    Hagerstown, MD, Church of the
        Brethren, 578
    helpful hints, book about, 1945
    historiography, 2202
    Holsinger, George Blackburn, 621
    Holsinger (Holtzinger) family, 623
    Huffaker, Perry Lee, 635
    Huffman, Nelson Thomas, *2204,* 2205
    Hymnal: A Worship Book, 2205–2206
    hymns in worship services, 1376, 1378
    Ikenberry, Olivia Dickens, 646
    instrumental, 60
    Mai Sule Biu, 782, 2216
    McAllen, TX, Grace Brethren Church,
        2219
    McPherson, KS, First Church of the
        Brethren, 780
    Miller, Sadie Jane, 842
    Mohler, John Saylor, writing hyms, 868
    Morse, Kenneth Ivan, 878
    musical instruments in worship servic-
        es, 1376, 1378
    Potsdam, OH, Church of the Brethren,
        talent of members, 1049
    Protestant Church, 2074
    recorded music in worship services,
        1378
    recreational activities, 2084
    The Rockingham Male Chorus,
        2204–2205
    Rowland, Charles Luther, educator,
        1126
    singing in worship services, 1376, 1378
    Seachrist, Denise Ann on Snow Hill
        Nunnery and, 2355
    songs for recreational activities, 2084
    sources on, 2316, 2321
    in Sunday School, 22
    Virginia
        Funk, Joseph, 2090
    worship, use in, 2327
Music Committee (CB), 155, **899**
    General Sunday School Board, 540
    General Welfare Board, 540

Music and Worship Commission, 899
Stahly, Cora Miller, 1216
Music Committee (DB), **899–900**
music ministry, *See* choir
Palmyra, PA, Church of the Brethren, 991
Panther Creek, IA, Church of the Brethren, 992
musical drama, *See* drama
musical instruments, 189, 206, *899,* **900**
changes since 1980, **2228**
criticism of use in public worship, 1375
as divisive in Naperville, IL, Church of the Brethren, 913
Dunkard Brethren, 409
Hymnal: A Worship Book, 2206
missions, 862
music, 2227, 2228
Old German Baptist Brethren, 2233
and nonconformity, 941
organ owned by Kurtz, Henry, 899, *899,* 900
Philadelphia, PA, First Church of the Brethren, 1015
Plymouth Brethren, 1038
Progressive Brethren, 1061
recreation, 1087
simple life, 1183
singing, 1184
Muskegon, MI, Church of the Brethren, **900–901**
Muskingum Co., OH, 1339
Muslim-Christian Convocation
Robinson, Paul Minnich, 1116
Muslims, *See* Islam
Musselman, Addison P., 45, 246, 496, 505, 1723
Musselman, Christian
Musselman family, 901
Pennsylvania Mennonite, **901**
Musselman, Eliza Saylor
Saylor family ancestry, 2008
Musselman family, 260, 384, **901**
Schultz, Martin, related to, 1156
Musselman, Frances Yoder, 901
Musselman, Hiram, 901, 1723
Musselman, Jacob, 901
Musselman, Jacob (2 listed), 1723
Musselman, John
Old Order German Baptist Church minister, 972
Musselman, John D., 373, 965, 1723
Middlefork Old German Baptist Brethren Church, IN, presiding elder, 826
Musselman family, 901
Musselman, M. P., 21
Musselman (Muselman/Mussleman/Musleman) families, 1887
Musselman, Samuel, 263, 268, **901,** 1723
Musselman, Sara B., *449, 450, 543*
Musselman, Susanna Shively, 901
Musser, Benjamin Engle, 2026
Musser family, 1229, 2026
Fike family, 490
Musser, Isaiah N., 1723
Musser, Laura G., 2092
Musser, Leah (later Zuck)
National Older Adult Conferences, 2229
Musser, Mrs. Viona, *645*
Musser, Norman K., 1723

Musser, P. C., 1723
Musser, Samuel, 1723
Musser, Sarah Ann (later Stump), 1232
Musser, Tobias, 1723
mustache, 579, *See also* beard
Muste, Abraham Johannes, **901,** 2046
musterground
peace position, 999
mustering, military, **901**
Musto, John H., 212, 1723
Mutchler, J. Paul, 503, 1380, 1723
Osceola, IN, Grace Brethren Church, music and youth pastor, 984
Mutschler family, 1274
mutton, *See* lamb; Lord's Supper, food at
mutual aid, **901–903,** *902, 903,* 1222, *See also* credit unions
community, 329
debts, repaying of, 728
ethics, 457, 458
funerals, 523
insurance, 657
interest-taking, 658
Mack, Alexander, Sr., participant in at Schwarzenau, 776
Pleasant Valley German Baptist Brethren Church, NE, 2377
poor, caring for the, 1046
social welfare, 1197
as symbol of community, 1260
widows, care for, 1343–1344
mutual aid and insurance, property, 192
Mutual Aid Association of the Church of the Brethren, 192
mutual aid, barn raising, 89
Mutual Benefit Association, *See* German Baptist Brethren Mutual Protective Association of Western Maryland
Mwagim, Saki, 1961
My Favorite Reflections (Turner), 2256
Myer, *See* Meyer
Myer, Amanda Evans
Myer, Elizabeth, mother of, 903
Myer, Anna (later Flora)
Skiles, Clement S. (OGBB) and, 2249
Myer, Caroline (later Hess), 601
Myer, Clara B., 1842, **2388**
Myer, Clara D., 2026
Myer, Cyrus, 204
Myer, Dalta, 496
Myer, Dennis J.
Lewiston, ME, Church of the Brethren, 2214
Myer, Elam, 2073
Myer, Elizabeth, **903,** 1361, 2026
Myer, Everett, 496
Myer, Exie, 496
Myer family, 2073, *See also* Meyer family
Mount Pleasant, PA, Brethren Church, 886
Myer, I. A., 1724
Myer, Israel, 1724
Myer, James F., 1340, 1724, 2027
Myer, John (2 listed), 1724
Myer, John L., 1724
Mohler Church of the Brethren, PA, free minister, 868
Myer, John W., Sr., 1724
Myer, Mary Jane, 2288
Lewiston, ME, Church of the Brethren, 2214
Myer (Meyer), Diller S., 1723–1724
Myer (Meyer), John W., 1724

Myer, Ora A., 447, 668, 1213, 1346, 1724
Minot, ND, Church of the Brethren, elder, 851
New Rockford, ND, Church of the Brethren, elder in, 932
Myer, P. B., 1724
Myer, Paul R., 862
Myer, Reuben C., 1724
Myer, Samuel, 1724
Myer, Samuel R., 1724
Myer, Elizabeth, father of, 903
Myer, Verdi, 204
Myers, *See* Meyers
Myers, A. E., 1724
Myers, Abraham (2 listed), 1724
Myers, Abram, 1724
Mount Joy Church of the Brethren, PA, 882
Myers, Alice, 520
Myers, Amanda Elizabeth (later Robbins), 1114
Myers, Ananias W., 1724
Myers, Andrew, 1724
Myers, Anna, 216
Myers, Anna Stoner
Myers, Estella Catherine, mother of, 903
Myers, Anne, 2140
Myers, Barbara (later Lichty), 741
Myers, Benjamin F. A.
Myers, Minor Morton, father of, 904
Myers, Benton, 520, 1724
Myers, Carl E., 2027
Mount Morris, IL, Church of the Brethren, pastor, 883
Roaring Spring, PA, First Church of the Brethren, pastor, 1114
Myers, Carl Edsel, 1724
Myers, Caroline E. Clark
Myers, Garry Cleveland, wife of, 903
Myers, Catharine Elizabeth, 2092
Myers, Catherine (later Hertzler), 601
Myers, Catherine (later Spanogle), *See* Spanogle, Catherine Myers
Myers, Cevilla Widder
Myers, Paul R., mother of, 904
Myers, Theodore, wife of, 904
Myers, Charles, 1724
Myers, Charles R., 2288
Myers, Charles S., 1724
Myers, Christian, 1724
Myers, Clara (later Flora), **495,** 1360, 1619
Myers, Clark C., 1724
Myers, Cletus S., 1724, 2304
New Enterprise, PA, Church of the Brethren, as minister, 927
Myers, Craig Alan, 2288
Myers Creek Church of the Brethren, WA **905**
Omak, WA, Church of the Brethren, 974
Myers, Cyrus E., 1724
Myers, Daniel, 1724
Myers, Daniel family
Valley Brethren-Mennonite Heritage Center and, 2258
Myers, David, 1724
Myers, David R., 1724
Myers, Della Strike, 2027
Myers, Dennis D., 2288
Myers, Donald E., 2288
free ministry to New Fairview Church of the Brethren, PA, 927

Myers, Earl Rufus, 576, 1724
Myers, Edith Rutt, 2027
Myers, Eleanor Christine Huffman, 2205
Myers, Eliza Berkeley
    Myers, Tobias Timothy, mother of, 905
Myers, Elizabeth Garber
    Myers, Minor Morton, mother of, 904
Myers, Elizabeth (later Brubaker), *See*
    Brubaker family
Myers, Elizabeth (later Zigler), 1397
Myers, Elizabeth Z., 2110
Myers, Ernest, 1724
Myers (Eschelman), Henry, 1869
Myers (Eschelman), Maria, 1869
Myers, Estella Catherine, 139, 268, 501,
    573, **903**, 1852
    medical missions, 807
    and Noatemo, Jean in French
        Equatorial Africa, 938
    Pleasant Grove Grace Brethren Church,
        IA, missionary, 1031
    Rollier, Antoine E. and Mary
        Ganshorn, in missionary party
        with, 1119
    Snyder, Ruth on, 2357
Myers, F. C., 2027
Myers family, 683, 700, 1224, 1309, 1391,
    1869, 1953, 2023, 2027, 2100, *See
    also* Meyer family
    Fike family, 490
    Flat Rock Church of the Brethren, VA,
        493
    Hardtmann (Hardman, Hartman)
        family, 583
    Homerville, OH, Grace Brethren
        Church, 626
    Mount Cassell Old German Baptist
        Brethren Church, WV, 880
    North English, IA, Church of the
        Brethren, 947
    Prosser, WA, Community Grace
        Brethren Church, 1062
Myers, Florence Harshbarger
    Myers, Tobias Timothy, wife of, 905
Myers, Forrest, 558
Myers, Foster Leroy, 1724
Myers, Francis, 1724
    Monroe Co. Church of the Brethren,
        IA, elder, 870
Myers, Frank Andrew, 557, 1724
Myers, Frank Blaine, 1724, 2027
Myers, Frank L., 1724
Myers, Franklin A., 1724
Myers, Fred P., 2027
Myers, Galene Josephine, 2027
Myers, Garnet Hawbaker, 1724
Myers, Garry Cleveland, **903**, 1069, 1724
Myers, Gary, 1724
Myers, George, *See* Royer, Galen B.
    Myers, Graybill, father of, 903
Myers, George, 1724
Myers, George, elder, 1724
    Ottawa, KS, Church of the Brethren,
        984–985
Myers, George S., 1724
    Myers, Oscar Reiff, father of, 904
Myers, George W., 1724
Myers, Grabill, 1724
Myers, Graybill (1808-1887), 20, 71, **903**,
    1724
Myers, Guy L., 2288
Myers, H. S., 605, 1724
Myers, Hannah (later Fike), 2184

Myers, Harley Roberts, 1724
Myers, Harold R., 1724
Myers, Henry, 1725, **2385**
    Middle Creek Church of the Brethren,
        PA, elder, 825
    Milledgeville Church of the Brethren,
        IL, 833
Myers, Henry Smith, 605, 1725
    Mount Pleasant, PA, Brethren Church,
        pastor, 886
Myers, Horner, 1725
Myers, Howard, 1725, 2304
Myers, I. L., 269, 1725
Myers, Isaac, 1725
    Myers, Theodore, father of, 904
Myers, Isaac (CB), 1725
Myers, Isaac Christian, 1725
Myers, J., 2047, 2106
Myers, J. Allen, 1725
Myers, J. D., 1725
Myers, J. Frank
    Peoria, IL, (First) Church of the
        Brethren, 1009
Myers, J. H., 1725
Myers, J. M., 430
Myers, J. T., 1725
Myers, J. W., 1725
Myers, J. Weldon, 672, 676, 1277
    Roanoke, VA, Hollins Road Church of
        the Brethren, pastor, 1113
Myers, Jacob, 347, 1725, *See* Meyers,
    Jacob
Myers, Jacob E., 1725
Myers, Jacob L., 521, **903–904**, 1725
    Shrewsbury, PA, Dunkard Brethren
        Congregation, presiding elder,
        1180
Myers, Jacob L. (CB), 1725
Myers, Jacob Lincoln, 2288
Myers, Jacob M., 1725
Myers, Jacob Medford, 1725
Myers, Jacob T., 180, 218
Myers, Jacob Tobias, **904**, 1725
Myers, Jacob Y.
Myers, Jacob L., father of, 903
Myers, Jay G., 1240, 1725, 2304
Myers, Jesse, 1725
Myers, Johannes, 430
Myers, John, 495, 540, 1960
Myers John A., 1725
Myers, John Abner, 661, 1725
    Myers, Estella Catherine, father of, 903
    Myers, Garry Cleveland, father of, 903
Myers, John B., 1725, **2385**
    Maple Grove Church of the Brethren,
        OH, minister, 790
Myers, John C., 68, 1397
Myers John (CB) (Backcreek, PA), 1725
Myers, John (CB) (Lincoln, PA), 1725
Myers, John (CB) (Stone Bridge, PA), 1725
Myers, John Clarence, 1725
Myers, John H., 1725
Myers, John L., 243
Myers, John Melvin, 1725
Myers, John Royer, 1725
Myers, John Weldon, 1725
Myers, Jonathan, Jr., 1725
Myers, Jonathan, Sr., 561, **904**, 1281, 1725
    Myers, Jonathan, father of, 904
Myers, Joseph, 765, 924
    spelling changed to Myer, **2384**
Myers, Joseph (CB), 1725
Myers, Joseph (CB) (Sterling, IL), 1725

Myers, Joseph H., 1725
Myers, Joseph L., 1725
Myers, L., 269
Myers, L. A., 635, 1725
Myers, Lee, 503
Myers, Leonard, 106, 1725
Myers, Lester E., 1725
Myers, Lydia Belle Quinter
    Myers, Jacob Tobias, wife of, 904
Myers, Lydia Horner, 2027
Myers, M., 1725
Myers, M. C., 1725
Myers, M. Lee, 12, 360, 363, 447
    Mansfield, OH, Woodville Grace
        Brethren Church, pastor, 787
    Martinsburg, WV, Rosemont Grace
        Brethren Church, pastor, 798
    Roanoke, VA, First Brethren Church,
        pastor, 1113
Myers M. Leon, 1725, 2304
Myers, M. M., 1725, 1938
Myers, Mabel Dooley
    Myers, Oscar Reiff, wife of, 904
Myers, Magdalena Weidler
    Myers, Graybill, wife of, 903
Myers, Margaret, 862
Myers, Margaret E. Burkey
    Myers, Paul R., wife of, 904
Myers, Martin
    Sabetha, KS, congregation, elder-in-
        charge, 1133
Myers, Mary E. (later Waltz), 1316
Myers, Mary Elizabeth (later Emmert), 444
Myers, Matthias
    Roann, IN, Church of the Brethren,
        minister, 1112
Myers (Meyers), Andrew, 1724
Myers (Meyers), F. A., 1724
Myers (Meyers), John, 1725
Myers (Meyers), Joseph (CB) (Jacobs
    Creek, PA), 1725
Myers, (Meyers), Smith H., 1726
Myers, (Meyers), Walter N., 1726
Myers, Michael, 347, 416, 1725, **2385**
    New Virginia, IA, Brethren Church, as
        minister, 932
    Osceola, IA, Church of the Brethren,
        minister, 983
Myers, Millard R., 1725, 1936, 2018
Myers, Minor Morton, 206, **904**, 1725,
    1842, 2027
    Pleasant Valley Church of the Brethren,
        VA, pastor, 1035
Myers/Moyer, David, 822
Myers/Moyer, Nicholas, 822
Myers, Nancy
    Myers, Jacob L., mother of, 903
Myers, Oscar Reiff, **904**, 1726
Myers, Ottie Showalter, 1397
Myers, P. S., 1275
Myers, Patrick H.
    Pleasant View Church of the Brethren,
        PA, 1037
Myers, Patrick Henry, 2288
Myers, Paul E., 1726
Myers, Paul R., **904**, 1726, 2027, 2304
Myers, Peter S., 714, 759, 1726
Myers, Rachel E. (later Zigler), **1397, 2388**
Myers, Ralph W., 2018
Myers, Rebecca
    Myers, Theodore, mother of, 904
Myers, Rebecca M.
    Myers, Graybill, mother of, 903

Myers, Reuben, 25, 1726
Myers, Reuben E., 1726
Myers, Reuben T., 1726
Myers, Roger K., 2288
Myers, Roy C., 52
Myers, Roy Calvin, 1726
Myers, Royer, 1726
Myers, Ruth Ebersole, 2102
Myers, S. Blair, 1308
Myers, Salome Stoner, 2044
    Myers, Tobias Timothy, wife of, **904,**
      905
Myers, Samuel, 2027
Myers, Samuel (Adamsboro, IN), 1726
Myers, Samuel B., 1726
Myers, Samuel (Fredericksburg, PA), 1726
Myers, Samuel H., 1726
Myers, Samuel Lincoln, 1726
Myers, Samuel (Mexico, IN), 1726
Myers, Samuel R., 1726
Myers, Sara Christine Zigler, 1842
    Myers, Minor Morton, wife of, 904
Myers, Sarah Beshore
    Myers, Garry Cleveland, mother of,
      903
Myers, Sarah Elizabeth (later Trout), 1339
Myers, Sarah Keeney
    Myers, Jacob L., wife of, 904
Myers, Sarah (later Bixler), 144
Myers, Saylor Blair, 1726
Myers, Seth F., 1726
Myers, Susan Reiff
    Myers, Oscar Reiff, mother of, 904
Myers, Susannah Eichenberg, 430
Myers, Susannah (later Royer), 1128
Myers, Theodore, **904,** 1726
    Myers, Paul R., father of, 904
    Orion Dunkard Brethren Congregation,
      OH, presiding elder, 981
Myers, Thomas Miller, 2027
Myers, Tobias, 1226, 1726
    Myers, Tobias Timothy, father of, 905
    Palestine, 990
    Philadelphia, PA, First Church of the
      Brethren, providing leadership,
      1015
Myers, Tobias Timothy, 79, 212, **904–905,**
    905, 1726, 2027
    Juniata College School of Theology
      dean, 1155
    Myers, Jacob Tobias, brother of, 904
    Myers, Salome Stoner, husband of, 904
Myers, Valley Virginia Miller Diehl, 724,
    913, 1842, 2027
    Myers, Minor Morton, wife of, 904
Myers, Vera Fishburn, 2092
Myers, Victor
    Montclair, CA, Grace Brethren Church,
      pastor, 871
Myers, Viola (later Ankrum), 32
Myers, W. D., 1726
Myers, W. M., 1726
Myers, Waldemar, 271
Myers, Walter, 1726
Myers, Walter A., 1726
Myers, William Scott, 1726, 2027
    Myersdale Bible Conference
    missions and missionaries, lectures on,
      2076
Myersdale Church, PA, 2071
Myersdale, PA, congregation
    Long, John Daniel, 2215
Myerstown, PA

Church of the Brethren, **905–906,** 1278
    Reistville, PA, Heidelberg Church
      of the Brethren, 1095
Grace Brethren Church, **906,** 1274
Grace Brethren congregations, 1005
Myerstown (Little Kutztown), PA, con-
    gregation, 280
Myerstown house, Tulpehocken
    Church of the Brethren, PA, 1278
Myersville, MD
    Church of the Brethren, **906**
    Grossnickle Church of the Brethren,
      MD, 574
    Harmony Church of the Brethren, MD,
      584
    Little Country Chapel Free Brethren,
      513
    Middletown Valley Church of the
      Brethren, MD, 826
Myler, J. W., 1726
Mylin, Barbara K., 1943
Mylin, Doris E. (later Biechler), 2314
Mylin family, 2314
Mylin, Hans, 1954
Mylin, Martin, 1954
Myres, David R., 1726
Myrtle Point, OR, 255, 295
    Church of the Brethren, 81, 88, **906**
      Coquille Valley as previous name
      of, 906
    Coos Co., OR, 980, 981
    Old German Baptist Brethren Church,
      906
Mysterium Magnum (Boehme), 156
mysticism, 156, 193, **906–907,** 2046
    American mystic communities, 1978
    Beissel, Johann Conrad, works of,
      1873–1874
    Bernard of Clairvaux, 1259
    book about, 1941
    colonial era
      Pennsylvania, 2074
    devotional literature, 381
    English, 2082
    Francis of Assisi, 1259
    historical writing, 612
    Hochmann von Hochenau, Ernst
      Christoph, 614
    Holy Spirit, doctrine of, 624
    Kelpius or Kelp, Johannes, 686–687
    Koch, Stephan, 704
    medieval, 28
    Mow, Anna, writings of, 1210
    persons espousing, 56, 57
    prayer, 1051
    Radical German Pietism, 1079
    Rechte und Ordungen, 1086
    Spener, Philipp Jakob, defense of, 1209
    Tersteegen, Gerhard, 1254–1255
    theological treatise on, 2054
    theology and, 1259
    treatise on, 2054
    Virginia, 2104
    Zimmerman, Johann Jakob, 686

N., D. J., 2027
Naas, Anna Margaretha (later Grahe), 564
Naas, Elizabeth, 722, 909
Naas, Jakob Wilhelm, **909**
Naas, Johannes, 27, 107, 175, 383, 407,
    421, 491, 528, 551, 562, 564, 569,
    577, 583, 699, 701, 707, 722, 726,
    741, **909,** 990, 1222, 1270, 1726,

    1900, 1938, 2027, 2059, 2177
    articles about, 1921, 1958
    emigration, Brethren, 443
    founding, New Jersey congregations,
      929
    hymns, 643
    Mack, Alexander, Sr., welcoming to
      America, 777
    Marienborn, baptisms performed in,
      792
    medicine, 809
    Mohr, Jacob, Sr., 869
    Neumann, Gottfried baptism, 924
    picture book about, 1915
    poetry and hymns, 1039
    Preiß (Price) family, 1055
    prisons, 1059
    Quakertown, PA, First Church of the
      Brethren, 1075
    Prussia, 1063
    Rhine River, performed baptism in,
      1106
    Ritter, Daniel, letter written to Krefeld,
      1111
    Solingen Brethren, 1201
    The Tall Man (Davis family), 748
    voyage of, 1991
Naas, Margaret Hauch, 722, 909
Naas, Maria Margaret Goyen, 446, 562, 909
NAC, *See* National Achievement
    Competition (NAC); Nurturing
    Abilities for Christ (NAC)
Nace, Ward, 1726
Nachatelo, Ferrell D. family
    Redstone Valley Old German Baptist
      Brethren Church, WI and, 2239
Nachfolge, 289
    definition of, 386
Nachklang Zum Gesäng der einsamen
    Turtel Taube, 2027
NAE, *See* National Association of
    Evangelicals; National Association
    of Evangelicals (NAE)
Naff, A. T., 1726
Naff, Abraham, 163, 1726
Naff, Archie P., 1726
Naff, Arnold, 516
    Midway Church of the Brethren, TN,
      providing leadership, 827
Naff, Beatrice Ethel, 2027
    Monte Vista Church of the Brethren,
      VA, 871
Naff, Benjamin Thomas, 1726
Naff, C. D., 1726
Naff, D. Arnold, 262, 1726
    Mountain Valley Church of the
      Brethren, TN, pastor, 889
Naff, D. T., 1726
Naff, Daniel A., 163, 1726
Naff, Daniel Christian, 1726
Naff, David, 1726
Naff, David Arnold, 1726
Naff, Elbert Lee, Jr., 1726, 2288
Naff family, *See* Näff family, 1880
Naff, Isaac, 1726
Naff, Jacob, 910
Naff, James L., 1726
Naff, Joel, 43, 1727
Naff, Joel B., 2027
Naff, Joel Bowman, 1727
Naff, John Abraham, 1727
Naff, John B., 1727
Naff, Katherina Flure, 910

Naff, Mary Seilor, 910
Naff, Melissa M., 2027
Näff (Naff/Neff) family, **909–910**
Naff, Oscar, 1727
Naff, Paul M., 130, 1727
Naff, Robin Collins, 2288
Naff, Rudolph, 910
Naff, Sebastian, 910
Naff, William H., 30, 288, 1727
Naffsinger family, *See* Noffsinger family
Naffziger, Berneice Barbara Birkey, 2028
Naffziger, Charles William, 2028
Nafzger, Eli
    Lower Miami, OH, congregation, land
      donated by, 939
Nafzger family, 2031, *See also* Noffsinger
    family
Nafzger, John
    Montgomery Co., OH, settled in, 939
Nafzger, Matthias
    immigration to America, 939
Nafzger (Naftzger, Noffziger, Nofziger,
    Noftsinger, Noffsinger, Nofsinger)
    family, 2045
Nafzger, Peter, 939
Nafzger, Rudolph, 939
Nafzger, Samuel
    Lower Miami, OH, congregation, land
      donated by, 939
Nafziger, Christian, 2031
Nafziger, Ezra Andrew, 2028
Nafziger family, 2028, *See also* Noffsinger
    family
    reference to, 1915
Nafziger, John and Anna Garber, 1986
Nafziger-Nofziger, Christian, 2027
Nagao family, 1312
Nägele, Elizabeth, 910
Nägele, Hans Rudolph, 910
Nägele, Rudolph, **910**
Nageli, Hans Rudolph, 567
Nagle, John, 566
Nagpur, India
    Church of North India, 298
    India orphanages, 651
Naill, Arthur, 1727
Nair, Charles Edward, 129, 1727, 2028
Nair, Thomas J., 722, 1727
Nairn, Stanley D., 1727
    Middlebranch, OH, Grace Brethren
      Church, pastor, 825
Nairobi, Kenya, *1368,* 2128
Nale, Iona Hershberger, 2028
Nall, Joseph, 1727
Nalley, John A., 2288
name change discussion
    Church of the Brethren, **2228**
Names
    of Brethren, **910–911**
    congregational in North America,
      911–912
names (religious)
    Baptist, 82
    Brethren, *Taufgesinnten,* 82
Nampa Church of the Brethren
    centennial of, 2348
Nampa congregation, ID, 645
Nampa, ID, 155, 157, 170
    Church of the Brethren, 157, 645, 913,
      1314
    Schrock, Mark Y., 1156
Nance, Robert Ward, 280, 565, 567, 1727,
    2304

Nancy (ship)
    Grossnickle family, 574
Nanjing English Language Institute
    Chinese Agricultural Exchange, 2129
Nansel, Marion Eugene, 1727
Nantmeal
    French Creek, 516
Nanty Glo, PA, Church of the Brethren, **913**
    Johnstown, PA, Walnut Grove Church
      of the Brethren, 675
Nanty Glo, PA, Brethren Church, *See* Pike
    Grace Brethren Church, Johnston,
    PA
Nantz, John, 571
Napa Valley congregation, CA, 1358
Naperville, IL, Church of the Brethren, 517,
    736, 913, 1339, 1867, 2036
Napier, Mr.
    Rowdy, KY, Brethren Church, 1126
Napoleonic Wars
    Ephrata Community, 451
    Germany, 545
    Mennonite Church (MC), 815
Napp, John M., 2288
Nappanee, IN, 1280, 1287, 1338
    Brethren Service Center, 495
    Church of the Brethren, **914,** 1280
    First Brethren Church, 914
    Ingraham, M. Virgil, 837, 1250, 2208
    Old Brethren Christian Schools, 2232
    SERRV international gift shop, 1139
    Union Center congregation, 1232
Narsibhai, Icchabhai, 1727
Nash family, 1863
Nash, Francis, 2042
Nash, J. F., 1727
Nash, Ray, 2028
Nashville, IA
    Maquoketa German Baptist Brethren,
      IA, mission point, 791
Nashville, MI
    Hope Church of the Brethren, MI, 629
Nashville, OH, 1389
    Humbert, Russell I., 636
Nashville, TN, 1253
Nason, Charles Dickens, 2028
Nass, *See* Naas
Nass, Joe, 739
Nass, John B., 1727
Nass, Joseph E., 2288
    Lexington, KY, Grace Bible Church,
      2214–2215
Natal, Arcadio, 2288
    Manatí, PR, Pueblo de Dios, 2217
Natal, Millie
    Manatí, PR, Pueblo de Dios, 2217
Nathaniel, Brother, *See* Eicher, Nathaniel
National Achievement Competition (NAC),
    203, 533, **917**
National Association for the Advancement
    of Colored People (NAACP), 2133
National Association of Brethren Church
    Elders
    National Ordination Council, 2229
National Association of Evangelicals
    Brethren association with broadcasting,
      801
    contributions to World Relief Board,
      1369
    material aid, 802
    refugee resettlement, 1093
    Relief Agency Brethren (FGBC), 1096
    relief and service efforts, 1097

    Shultz, Joseph R. (BC) and, 2249
National Association of Evangelicals (BC),
    182, 189
National Association of Evangelicals (CB),
    197, 198
National Association of Evangelicals
    (NAE), 23, 914
    and the Brethren Church, 38
    Committee on Interchurch Relations,
      2167
    ecumenism, 422
    founding of, 2179
National Association of the Brethren
    Church Elders (NABCE)
    ordination of divorced persons, 2141
National Benevolent Board (BC), *See*
    Benevolent Board (BC)
National Board of Christian Education,
    1237
National Board of Evangelism
    Fetterhoff, Dean, 2184
    Miller, Robert Paul, 842
National Boys Brotherhood, *See* Young
    Men and Boys Brotherhood
National Brethren Bible Conference, **914**
    Fellowship of Grace Brethren Churches
      (FGBC), 485
    Hoyt, Herman Arthur, 634
    organization by Grace Brethren move-
      ment, 911
National Brethren Young People's Depart-
    ment Cabinet, 203, 917, *See also*
    National Youth Cabinet
National Brethren Youth, 285, **915**
National Brethren Youth Board, 203, *See*
    also Board of Christian Education
National Brethren Youth camp (conference)
    Polman, Leo, 1045
National Brethren Youth programs
    Dodds, Gilbert, 394
National Cabinet of Children's Work, 915
    as advisory body, **915**
    Christian Education Commission, 285,
      537
    General Council of Children's Work,
      537
National Cabinet of Women's Work
    Schwalm, Florence Roselind
      Studebaker, 1157
National Camp-meeting for the Promotion
    of Christian Holiness
    Holiness Movement, American, 619
National Catholic Rural Life Conference
    (NCRLC)
    CROP, 286
National Chrisitan Endeavor, *See* Brethren
    National Christian Endeavor
    Union
National Christian Council
    Bhagat, Premchand Ganeshji, 131
National Christian Council of China
    Ikenberry, Ernest Leroy, 646
National Christian Endeavor Board, *See*
    Board of Christian Education
National Christian Mission, 169
National Christian Teaching Missions
    evangelism, 461
National Church of the Brethren Youth
    Fellowship Cabinet, *See* National
    Youth Cabinet
National Conference (FGBC), *See* Grace
    Brethren National Conference
    Turner, Charles W. (FGBC) and, 2256

National Conference of Women, 1363

National Council of Boards, *See* Council of Boards

National Council of Christian Churches
mass media cooperative efforts, 801
Ziegler, Edward Krusen, 1395

National Council of Christian Churches (NCCC), 2165

National Council of Churches, 187, 209, 210, 308
Association of Council Secretaries, 1218
The Christian Beacon and, 281
Church of the Brethren, 303, 305
Church World Service, 303
Commission on Regional and Local Ecumenism, 1218
Committee on Interchurch Relations, 2167
Committee on Understanding and Reconciliation (CB) , 328
Communication Commission
mass media, uses of, 2218
conservative Brethren theology and schism, 1005
Davis, Charles Ernest, 364
disagreement with affiliation, Upper Marsh Creek Church of the Brethren, PA, 1295
Division of Home Missions
Ogden, Galen Brown, 961
Englewood, OH, Grace Brethren Church, 447
evangelism, 461
Free Brethren, 513
Friends Committee on Spain, 518
Fundamental Brethren Church, 522
fundamentalism, 522
Garver, Earl Simeon, 2187
Independent Brethren, 649
McIntire, Carl, 774
Miller, Donald Eugene, 2223
Miller, Joseph Quinter, 841
Miller, Minor Cline, 841
national statistics, 1218
Naylor, Kurtis Friend as staff member in, 918
Petersime, Ray, 1012
Row, W. Harold, 1126
Rural Missions Cooperating Committee (RMCC), 1131
Russell, Harl L., stewardship leader, 1132
Russian Agricultural Exchange Program, 2129
Sales Exchange for Refugee Rehabilitation Vocations (SERRV), 1139
Smeltzer, Ralph Emerson, 1191
Snider, Harold, opponent, 1194
state councils, 1218
Thompson, Joel Kent and, 2255
Yearbook of American Churches, 1218
Zunkel, Cleda Pearl Shull, 1402

National Council of Churches of Christ
Fellowship of Grace Brethren Churches (FGBC), 486
Helman, Patricia Kennedy, 2197
Neff, Robert Wilbur, 2231
Peters, Raymond Russell, 1011

National Council of Churches of Christ in the U.S.A., 915, 2028
Church of the Brethren ties with,

2228–2229

National Council of Churches of Christ in the USA (NCCC), 9, 23
ecumenism, 422, 423
groups opposed to participation in, 69

National Council of Churches of Christ in the USA (NCCCUSA)
Foreign Missions Conference of North America, 501
International Council of Religious Education, 659
International Sunday School Convention, 659
International Sunday School Lessons (Uniform Lessons), 659

National Council of Churches of Christ (NCCC) in the USA, **915**

National Council of Men's Work
Men's Work (CB), 816

The National Council of the Brethren Church of Argentina (*Consejo Nacional de La Iglesia de Los Hermanos de la Argentina*), 53

National Council of Women's Work, *See* Council of Women's Work
Halladay, Sara Heebner, 580

National Education Association
Eshelman, Walter Witmer, 455
Hoyt, Herman Arthur, 634
minorities, ethnic and racial, 850

National Education Association (NEA)
group dynamics, 575

National Farm Worker Ministry, Puerto Rico
Hispanic Ministries (CB), 2199

National Fellowship of Brethren Churches (NFBC), 2028, *See also* Fellowship of Grace Brethren Churches

National Fellowship of Brethren Laymen, 915, *See also* National Fellowship of Grace Brethren Men
description, 1954
history of, 1948

National Fellowship of Brethren Ministers, 916

National Fellowship of Brethren Retirement Homes, *See* Grace Village Retirement Complex

National Fellowship of Grace Brethren Churches, 183, 187, 251, *See also* Grace Brethren

National Fellowship of Grace Brethren Men, **915–916**
Grace Brethren Boys, 562
Jackson, Edward A., 2209

National Fellowship of Grace Brethren Men and Boys, 38, 916, *See also* Fellowship of Grace Brethren Churches (FGBC); National Fellowship of Grace Brethren Men
Grace Brethren Boys, 562

National Fellowship of Grace Brethren Ministers, 38, **916**, *See also* Fellowship of Grace Brethren Churches (FGBC)
divorce issues, 393

National Genealogical Research Institute, 2028

National Grange
student exchange program, 1231

National Guard Armory
San Diego, CA, Grace Brethren

Church, 1141

National Home Mission Board (Home Missions Council)
Fort Wayne, IN, First Brethren Church, 503

National Home Missions Council, *See* Brethren Home Missions Council

National Home Study Council
Noffsinger, John Samuel, director in, 939

National Institute for the Development of Ministries to Youth
CE National, Inc., 2156

National Institute for Christian Education
Male, E. William, 2217

National Institute of Health, 2067

National Interfaith Cable Coalition
mass media, uses of, 2218

National Interreligious Service Board for Conscientious Objectors (NISBCO), 19, 301, 316, 317, **916–917**, 1290, 1291, 1372, 2028, *See also* Brethren Advisory Committee For Conscientious Objectors (CB); Conscientious Objectors (conscientious objectors); peace issues; Service Committee (OGBB)
Continuation Committee of the Historic Peace Churches, 339
Evangelical Covenant Church, 459–460
French, Paul Comly, 515
Hershey, Lewis Blaine, 599
Historic Peace Churches, 608
Huston, Ora Ivan, 638
Kosch, Lewis F., 707
Seventh-Day Adventists, 1170
Spain, relief work in, as basis for, 1207
Wilson, Edward Raymond, 1347
Zigler, Michael Robert, 1398

National Kindergarten College
Swartz, Goldie Elizabeth, 1243

National Layman's Organization (FGBC), 2149, *See also* Brethren Men of Mission
Jackson, Edward A., 2209

National Laymen Organization (BC), 182, 190, 917, 1390
men's movements, 2221
mass media, 801
reorganization of, 915

National Laymen's Association, 155

National Men's and Women's organizations
ecumenism, 422

National Men's Work cabinet
Weldy, Allen (CB) and, 2261

National Mental Health Foundation
medical projects, 808
mental hospital service, 816

National Ministerial Association, *See* Fellowship of Grace Brethren Churches (FGBC); National Fellowship of Grace Brethren Ministers
Grace Brethren reorganization of, 916
Knepper, John Henry, 703

National Ministerial Association (BC), 183
Christner, David C., 289
"Message of the Brethren Ministry," 817
pension funds, 1007, 1008
Rench, George W., president, 1099

Rowsey, Herbert H., president, 1127
National Ministry Board (CB)
    Winning the Race Ministries and, 2262–2263
National Mission Board, *See* The Missionary Board
    Columbus, OH, Smoky Row Brethren Church, 2166
    The Missionary Board (BC), 855
National Missionary Board of The Brethren Church
    Medina, OH, Living Hope Brethren Church, 2219
National Older Adult Conferences (NOAC) (CB), 2163
    first held 1992, **2229**
National Ordination Council, **2229**
    Brethren Church ministry, 846
    Director of Pastoral Ministries, 2171
    women, ordination of, 2141
    ministry, 2224
National Park Service, **917**
    Sharpsburg, MD, Church of the Brethren meetinghouse, 1174
national parks
    chaplaincy, 2158
National Peace Committee, *See* Peace Committee
National Peace Committee, Church of the Brethren, 2028
National Recreational Fellowship, *See* Recreational Fellowship
National Register of Historic Places
    Pine Run German Baptist Brethren, 2377
National Religious Broadcasters
    Brethren association with, 801
National Service Board for Religious Objectors, 301, 316, 916, 1372, 2028, *See also* National Interreligious Service Board for Conscientious Objectors; National Interreligious Service Board for Consientious Objectors
    Continuation Committee of the Historic Peace Churches, 339
    French, Paul Comly, 515
    Hershey, Lewis Blaine, 599
    Row, W. Harold, 1126
    Seventh-Day Adventists, 1170
    Spain, relief work in, as basis for, 1207
National Socialism
    Judaism, 677
National Sunday School Association (BC), 154, **917**, 1239, 1392
    Duker, William Irvin, 407
    Jones, George H., 676
    Leatherman, N. Victor, 733
    Miller, Edward Lewis, 837
    Rowsey, Herbert H., 1127
    Stuckey, Melvin Atwood, 1229
National Sunday School Board (FGBC), 155, **917**, 1239
    Etling, Harold Hartz, 458
    GBC Christian Education (Department), 533
National Youth Board, 1239
    National Sunday School Board merger, 917
National Youth Cabinet, 203, **917**
    Christian Education Commission (CB), 285
National Youth Conference (FGBC), 250

National Youth Conference (NYC) (CB), **917–918**, 1929, 2162, 2268
    youth and, 2269
national youth conferences, 1391, 1392
National Youth Council (BC)
    youth and, 2269
Native American New Life Center
    McAllen, TX, Grace Brethren Church, 2219
Native Americans, 201, **2229–2230**, *See also* specific tribes
    AIM (American Indian Movement), 2230
    Andean Indians, service to, 1289
    colonial era Indian policies, 2089
    education for, 405
    Ephrata Community and Indian policy in Pennsylvania, 2089
    French and Indian War, 2091
    frontier, 519
    Grace Brethren North American Missions, 2191
    Grassroots, Concerns of the, 2193
    Great Serpent Mound, Adams Co., OH, 1332
    Heifer Project International, 594
    Historic Peace Churches, 607
    Hostetler family, 1973
    identities and liberation for, 304
    Indian Territory, church meetings in, 201
    Lowe, John W., Jr. on Brethren and, 2344
    McAllen, TX, Grace Brethren Church, 2219
    minorities, ethnic and racial, 849, 850
    missions and missionaries
        Arizona, 188
        Church of the Brethren, 2067
        Navajo Indians, 860, 2072
        New Mexico, 188
    missions, short-term, 2226
    Pennsylvania, Indian policies in, 2089
    raids on Brethren by, 42
    relief and rehabilitation work for, 24, 186, 188
    reservations, Brown family claims to, 1346
    SHARE program, 1172
    Virgina, battles in, 2102, 2105
    Weiser, Johann Conrad, 1328
nativity pageants
    Oakton, VA, Church of the Brethren, 958
nativity scenes (live)
    Chico, CA, Grace Brethren Church, 275
Natrona Heights, PA, Church of the Brethren, 415, **918**, 1027
natural law, 2013
Natural Law in the Spiritual World (Drummond), 1051
Naturalization, **918**
naturalization issues
    colonial era, 2105
The Nature of Biblical Creation (Whitcomb)
    Whitcomb, John Clement, Jr. (FGBC, CGBCI) and, 2262
Nauman, Norman W., 2028
Navajo
    missions to, 2240
Navajo Indians, 188, 192–193, *See also* Lybrook Navajo Community,

Lybrook, NM; minorities, ethnic and racial; Torreon Navajo Church, Sandoval Co., NM; Torreon Navajo Mission
    Brethren Navajo Mission, *See* Brethren Navajo Mission
    Fellowship of Grace Brethren Churches (FGBC), 485
    medical missions to, 808
    minorities, ethnic and racial, 850
    missions and missionaries, 860, 2072
    Torreon, *See* Torreon Navajo Mission
Navarre Church of the Brethren, Navarre, KS, 1, **918**
Nave, Margaret (later Shideler), *See* Shideler, Margaret Nave
Nave, Rodney, 1727
    Riner Grace Brethren Church, VA, pastor, 1110
Navy, *See* military service
Naylor, Kent Eldon, 237, 733, 1323, 1727
Naylor, Kurtis F., 286, 377, **918**, 1330, 1727, 2028
    Pomona, CA, Church of the Brethren, pastor, 1045
    Spain, mission to, 1207
Naylor, Lewis E., 124, 918, 1727
    South Red Cloud Church of the Brethren, NE, minister, 1206
Naylor, Virginia Friend, 918
Nazarene Church
    Hope Brethren Fellowship, 2204
Nazarene Dunkards
    Pleasant Valley Church of the Brethren, OH, 1035
Nazarenes, *See* Apostolic Christian Church
Nazareth Hospital, Israel
    Eisenbise, Forest Sard, 432
Nazi Regime, *See* World War II
    Germany, 545
    Jews, 671
NCCC, *See* National Council of Churches of Christ in the USA; National Council of Churches of Christ (NCCC)
Ndahi, Elijah, 1727
Ndirgaminyi, Yakub, 1727
Ndiriza, Ibrahim, 1727
Nead, A. E., 264, 1340, 1727
Nead, Abraham
    Pleasant Valley Church of the Brethren, TN, 1035
Nead, Barbara (later Kinsey), 488, 696, 919
Nead, Benjamin Matthias, 2028
Nead, Birdie (later Faw), 480
Nead, D. C. R., 1335, 1727
Nead, D. P., 919
Nead, Daniel, 918, 919
Nead, Daniel P., 1727
    Midway Dunkard Berthren Congregation, IN, presiding elder, 827
    Pipe Creek Church of the Brethren, IN, elder, 1025
Nead, Daniel W., 2028
Nead, Elizabeth Yount, 696, 918–920, *919*
Nead family, 2104
    Johnson City, TN, Knob Creek Church of the Brethren, 672
Nead, Jacob, 742
Nead, John, 672, 1727
Nead, M., 1727
Nead, Mary, 919

Nead, Matthias, 2104
Nead, OH
    place-names, Brethren, 1028
Nead, Peter, 58, 165, 178, 232, 233, 339,
    489, 510, 696, 746, **918–920**, *919,*
    1261, 1727, 1884, 1875, 1921,
    1928, 2028, 2087, 2091, 2104
    attack on writings, 1958
    Bible, interpretation of, 134
    Brethren music, 899
    Cassell, William, and marriage of, 260
    character and beliefs of, 2091
    Christology, 289, 290
    church-state relations, 310
    "community suffering," 292
    covenantal community, 291
    English language, shift to, 724–725
    eschatology, 293
    hat, 404
    historic sites, 609
    humility, 636
    as interpreter of doctrine, 1210, 1261
    length of prayers, 1378
    "Life of" by Samuel Kinsey, 696
    mentoring, 2221
    Miami, OH, and Brethren settlement,
    961
    ministry, and egalitarian community,
    294
    Mohler, Samuel Sayler, 868
    nonconformity, 941
    oaths, taking of, 959
    Old Order Movement, 970, 973
    perfectionism, 1009
    photography of Brethren, 1020
    place-names, Brethren, 1028
    prayer, 1051
    prayer, posture in, 1052
    Primitive Christianity, 310, 371
    on primitive Christianity, restoration of,
    2348
    publications of, 2100
    publishing, 1068, 1069
    publishing works of, 1067
    Seilhamer, Larry on, 2356
    spiritual life, 1210
    Stoffer, Dale R. on, 2359
    theological writings of, 2348
    *Theological Writings on Various
    Subjects,* 1258
    Tipp City, OH, West Charleston
    Church of the Brethren, 1265
    Tunker House, 1279
    The Vindicator, 1306
    works righteousness, 1368
Nead, Reed Hixon, 743, 1727
    Old Brethren German Baptist Church,
    minister, 965
    Old Brethren minister, 965
    Old Order German Baptist Church
    minister, 972
Nead, Samuel, 919, 1727
    place-names, Brethren, 1028
(*Neads Theology*) *Theological Writings on
    Various Subjects* (Nead, P.), 919,
    *See also Theological Writings on
    Various Subjects*
Neal family, 1267, 2087
Neal, George, 1727
    Mountain Grove Church of the
    Brethren, MO, minister, 889
Neal, Henry, 1727
Neal, Pearl (later Rohrer), 1119

Neal, William F., 1727
Nealis, Harry, 356
Nealis, Louise Maxine, 2288
Neander, Joachim, 700
Near East, *See* specific countries
    American Committee for Relief in,
    22–23, 55, 1096
Near East Foundation, **920**
Near East Relief, 920
Nearhoff, Susan (later Patton), 996
Nearhoof, Henry, 406
Nearhoof, Sharon (later May), 2286
Nebraska, 682
    Cassel (Kassel) family, 260
    Church of the Brethren, 324
    homesteading, 626
    migration of Brethren, *828,* 830
    Old German Baptist Brethren, 967
    overview of Brethren in, *920,* **920–921**
    Rotruck (Rothrock, Roderick) family,
    1124
    settlement, by Pennsylvanians, 1995
    Welch, Gladys Snavely on wines of,
    2362
Neckcloths, 921
neckerchief, 400, 401, 921
neckties, 403, **921, 2377,** *See also* dress
    (plain)
    Dunkard Brethren and nonconformity,
    940
    Mow, Baxter Merrill, 891
    objections to Dunkard Brethren
    requirements regarding, 69
Nediger, Johanna, 159
Nedrow, Elmer F., 695, 1727, 2028
Nedrow, Grace (later Heisey), 1838, 1961
Nedrow, Harold, 755
Nedrow, J. Lloyd, 432, 752, 1727, 2028
Nedrow, Robert A., 511, 695, 1727
    Rockton, PA, Church of the Brethren,
    elder and minister, 1118
Needmore, PA
    New Testament Brethren, 932
Needmore, WV
    New Dale Church of the Brethren, WV,
    926–927
Needy Ministers' Fund
    pension funds, 1007
needy, relief of
    South Saint Joseph Church of the
    Brethren, MO, 1135
Neely, John S., 130, 191, 332, 1277, 1727
    Mansfield, OH, Woodville Grace
    Brethren Church, pastor, 787
Neely, Sarah, 191
Neer, Jewell Josephine (later Gammon),
    1944
Nees, Opal Eileen Pence, 740, 1727
Neff, _____ Fisher, 922
Neff, Abraham, 1727
Neff, Abraham L., 1246, 1727
Neff, Albert A., 323, 540, 1727
    Oak Grove Old German Baptist
    Brethren Church, OH, minister,
    956
    Scottville Old German Baptist Brethren
    Church, MI, minister, 1161
Neff, Allen, 1727
    Painter Creek Old German Baptist
    Brethren Church, OH, 990
Neff, Barbara, 420
Neff, Benjamin, 922, 1727
Neff, Benjamin W., 1276, 1313, 1728

Neff brothers settlement, 910
Neff, Catherine (later Wine), 1349
Neff, Charles, 1728
Neff, Charles Scott
    Neff, Robert Wilbur, 2230
Neff, Christian, 1961, 2029
Neff, Daniel, 1728
Neff, David, 1728
Neff, Dorothy M. Rosewarne, 706
    Neff, Robert Wilbur, 2230
Neff, Earl Chester, 313, 1728
Neff, Edward E., 1728
Neff, Eleanor Marguerite, 357
Neff, Elizabeth Clifford, 910, 2029
Neff, Elmer Ellsworth, 1728, 2029
Neff, Esther (later Scheublein), *See*
    Scheublein, Esther Neff
Neff familes
    Murray, John F. on descendants of,
    2348
Neff family, 384, 731, 1229, 1897, 2062,
    2069, 2077, *See also* Näff family
    genealogy, 1994
    Glück (Glick, Click) family, 553
    Jamison family, 668
    Shady Grove Old German Baptist
    Brethren Church, OH, 1171
Neff, Florence, 2029
Neff, Francis, 909, 2029
Neff, Gabriel, Sr., 1728
Neff, George, 1728
    Pleasant View Brethren Church, IN,
    2377
Neff, H. J.
    South Whitley, IN, Church of the
    Brethren, minister, 1207
Neff, Harry C., 1728
Neff, Hazel Martin
    Neff, Robert Wilbur, 2230
Neff, Heather
    Neff, Robert Wilbur, 2230
Neff, Henry (Codorus, PA), 1728
Neff, Henry H., 1728
Neff, Henry H., Jr., 1728
Neff, Henry J., 173, 558, 1728
    Mount Pleasant Church of the
    Brethren, IN, 886
    Rockford, IL, First Church of the
    Brethren, pastor, 1117
Neff, Henry, Sr., 1287, 1728
Neff, Henry, Sr. (1798–1868), 124
Neff, Herman, 731
Neff, Hilda, 2068
Neff, Iris Euvonne, 1838
Neff, Isaac M., 1234, 1728
Neff, J. M.
    NM congregation, leadership in, 931
Neff, Jacob, 242, 495, 910
    descendants, 1933
    Native Americans, 2229
Neff, James Monroe, 14, 313, 322, 520,
    595, 683, 912, 922, 1728, 2029,
    2036
    and family, on a mission, *858*
    Home Helper, The, publisher, 625
    The Petitioner, 1012
    migration of Brethren, 830
    missions, 858
Neff, James N., 205, 2080
Neff, Johann, 909
Neff, John, 1728
Neff, John Allen, 1728
Neff, John B., 1728

Neff, John Henry, 909, 910
Neff, John, Jr.
Shady Grove Old German Baptist
Brethren Church, OH, minister,
1171
Neff, John S., 1246
Neff, John W., 1728
Shady Grove Old German Baptist
Brethren Church, OH, elder, 1171
Neff, Katherine Fleure, 495
Neff, Larry M., 1984
Neff, Michael H., 2069
Neff (Naff), Isaac, 1728
Neff, Noble W., 1728
Neff, Raleigh R., 1728
Neff, Ray A., 2201
on Kline, John, 2348
Neff, Robert W., 305, 335, 706, 1728, 2108,
2133, **2230–2231**, *2230*
National Council of Churches of Christ
in the USA, 2228
Neff, Rudolph, 910
Neff, Wilbur H., 415, 1728, 2029
Neff, Robert Wilbur, 2230
Neff, William B., 1728
Neff, Willis Olin, 1728
Neffs family, *See* Indiana
Neffsville meetinghouse, PA, 416
Neffsville, PA
Ecker, Thomas C., 421
Home for Orphan and Friendless
Children (CB), 625
Brethren Home, *See* Brethren Village,
Lancaster, PA
Taylor, Isaac W. and Catherine
Shirk, 1249
Nefzger, Ray, 142
Negley, Betty Jane
on divine legacy, 2348
Negley family, 251, 715
Negley, Jacob, 1728
Ottawa, KS, Church of the Brethren,
984
Negley, Marian
Lewiston, ME, Church of the Brethren,
2214
Negley, Shannon
Lewiston, ME, Church of the Brethren,
2214
Negro Missions, *See* Minorities, Ethnic and
Racial
Negroes, *See* African Americans; Minor-
ities, Ethnic and Racial
Nehama Co., NE
Pleasant Valley German Baptist
Brethren Church, NE, 2377
Nehemiah, Brother, *See* Hageman, Heinrich
Neher, A. P., 1728
Neher, Abraham S., 1728
Neher, Ada Shank, 922
Neher, Amos A., 1728
Neher, Ananias, 1728
Neher, Andrew, 273, 442, 1728
Salem Church of the Brethren, ND,
elder, 1137
Neher, Asa P., 1728
Neher, Bertha Miller (later Stine), 748,
1223, 1361, 1728, 2029, *See also*
Stine, Bertha Miller Neher
memoirs, 2348
Milford, IN, Bethel Church of the
Brethren, 831
Neher, Daniel, 1728

Neher, Daniel P., 1728
Neher, David, 237, 1728
Neher, Dean, 658
Neher, Elizabeth (later Shively), *See*
Shively, Elizabeth Neher
Neher, Ella (later Harris)
Mountain Grove Church of the
Brethren, MO, 889
Neher, Emma Fike, 2029
Neher, Ezra J., 691, 913, 1728
Neher family, 353, **922**, 1893
Shull family, related to, 1156
Neher, George W., 922
Neher, Gerald Alvin, 1842
Neher, I. F.
Romine Church of the Brethren, IL,
minister, 1121
Neher, J. C., 1728
Oak Grove Church of the Brethren,
OK, minister, 956
Neher, J. G., 1728
Neher, J. P., 1728
Neher, Jacob, 1728
Neher, James H., 1728
Neh(e)r, John
Middle Creek Church of the Brethren,
IA, minister, 825
Neher, John F., 438, 504, 541, 1728
Neher, John H., 503, 1728
St. Francis Church of the Brethren, AR,
pastor, 1134
Neher, Joseph D., 1729
Neher, L. H., 1729
Neher, L. M., 1729
Neher, Leila (later Polman), 1045
Neher, Leon C., 1729, 2029
Rural Life Association (RLA), 1131
Neher, Levi M., 1223, 1729
Milford, IN, Bethel Church of the
Brethren, 831
Neher, Lizzie Mae (later Flory), **499, 1837**
Neher, Lois Ruth Yoder, 1842
Neher, Lottie Flory, 922
Neher, Lottie (later Hoff), 617
Neher, M., 1729
Neher, Martin, 1729
Neher, Mary, 2029
Neher, Mary F., 499, 1303
Neher, Medford D., 12, 61, 374, **922**, 1729
Michigan City, IN, Church of the
Brethren, pastor, 825
mural paintings at Camp Mack, 896
Peoria IL, (First) Church of the
Brethren, pastor, 1009
Neher, Minneva Josephine, 587, 922, 1842,
1969, *See also* China
Neher, Noah G., 499, 1303
Neher, Oscar Warner, 237, 1729
Neher, Priscilla Cripe, 922
Neher, Robert Trostle, 1729
Neher, Roy H., 1729
Osage Church of the Brethren, KS,
elder, 983
Neher, S. J., 257
Neher, S. S., 1282, 2029
Neher, Samuel F.
Pleasant Hill Old German Baptist
Brethren Church, IL, deacon, 1033
Neher, Samuel S., 1316, 1729
Pleasant Dale Church of the Brethren,
IN, elder, 1030
Neher, Sara Blocher, 147
Neher, Saylor J., 1729

Neher, Susie Cordelia (later Vaniman),
1303, 1845
Neher, Ursula Jetter, 922
Neher, Vernita Jane (later Davis), 2276
Neher, W. H., 1729
Neher, William, 922
Neher, William D., 1729
Nehr, Ezra J., 1729
Nehr, John F., 1729
Nehr, John H., 1729
Nehrenberg, Edna Willard, 2029
Neibert, Barbara (later Martin), 798
Neibert, Flavius Josephus, 1729
Neida, R. D. von, 2029
Neiderhiser, Emanuel, 1729
Neiderhiser, Martha (later Parker), 2034,
1842, **2388**
Neiff family, *See* Neff family
Neiff, Francis, 909, *See also* Neff, Francis
Neiff, Heinrich, *See* Neff, Francis
Neiff, Johann, 909
Neikirk, Daniel H., 1729
Neikirk family
Sharpsburg, MD, Church of the
Brethren, 1174
Neil, Amanda, 2106
Neill, Stephen C., 2049
Neilsen, J. C., 629
Neilsen, Johanna, 629
Neilsen, N. C., 1729
Neilson, Gilbert, 1729
Neimeyer, Rufus A., 1729, 2126
Neinstadt, H. C.
printers, and publishing, 1067
hymnals, 642
Neiß, Elizabeth (later Mack), **778**
Mack, Alexander, Jr., 774
Neiß (Nice), Mary (later Leibert), 736
Neiß (Nice), William
Mack, Elizabeth Neiß (Nice), 778
Neisser, George, 2029
Neiswander family, 2029
Neiswander, Harry A., 2029
Neiswander, Lois Marian, 2029
Neiswanger, Ann, 924
Neiswanger family, 1923
Neiswanger, Jacob, 924
Neiswanger, Joseph, 924
Neiswonger (Niswonger), Everett, 1729
Nell, Allen L., 2288
Nell, Harry B., 1729
Nell, Kenneth Eugene, 2288
Nell, Paul L., 2288
Nell, Vernon E., 1729
Nelson Co., VA, 768
Montebello Church of the Brethren,
VA, 871
Nelson family, 2080
Nelson, John E., 2288
Nelson, Leland Alvin, 1215, 1729, 2304
Modesto, CA, Church of the Brethren,
866
Nelson, Marie (later Meyer)
Meyer, Jacob Gibble, wife of, 821
Nelson, Nels B. (N. B.), 90, 266, 1729
Nelson, Nels Peter, 1729
Nelson, Norman A., 115, 1729
Nelson, Robert James, Jr., 1729, 2029
Nelson, Russell Sage, Jr., 2029
Nemadji Church of the Brethren, MN, *See*
Barnum Church of the Brethren,
MN
Nemaha Co. KS

Granada Church of the Brethren, KS, 565

Rock Creek Church of the Brethren, KS, 1117

Sabetha, KS, Church of the Brethren, 1133

neo-Pentecostal Church
charismatic movement, 272

Neoorthodoxy, 73–74, **922–923**
Christian education movement, 284

Neosho Co., KS
Church of the Brethren, KS, 270, 716, 923
Fairview Church of the Brethren, KS, 468
Parsons, KS, Church of the Brethren, divided from, 994
Galesburg Church of the Brethren, KS, 527
Neosho Valley Old German Baptist Brethren Church near, 270, **923**
Pleasant View Brethren Church, KS, 1036

Neptune (ship)
Grossnickle family, 574
Stoner family, 1221

Nérée, Luc R., 276, 579

Nesbitt, Leslie B., 2288

Nesler, Charles (CB), 1729

Ness, Charles H. (DB), 1729

Ness, Christian, 1729

Ness family, 1389

Ness, Fern Fahnestock, 2231, *2231*

Ness, Jacob C., 1324, 1729, 2143, **2231,** *2231,* 2304

Ness, John, 2231

Ness, John G., 1729

Ness, Mabel, 2231

Ness, Mary (later Falkenstein), 471

Nesselrodt, Charles, *84,* 1729, 2312

Nester, C. L., 1729

Nester family
Mount Cassell Old German Baptist Brethren Church, WV, 880

Nestlé Company, boycott of, 2139

Nestor, Worthy, 1729

Nestorians
Iran (Persia), 662

Netherclift family, 2081

Netherlands, 28, 55, **923,** *See also* Estates General, Dutch
Amsterdam, 30, 55
Brethren in, in eighteenth century, 2002
Community of the True Inspiration, 330
CROP, 286
Dompelaars in, 395
Felbinger, Jeremias, 482
Germany, 545
historic sites, 609
history of Pietists and Mystics in, 1963
Huizinga (Huisinga), Jacob Dircks, 635
immigration from and the Society of the Woman in the Wilderness, 1199
immigration of Brethren to, 776–777, 778
Leiden, 30
Lobach, Johann, 1325
Mack, Johannes, migrating to, 778
Mennonites providing refuge for Brethren, 815
missions and missionaries in, 174

prisoner of war camps, 199
Reformation, Protestant, and radical reformers, 1091, 1092
Reformed Church, 1092
relief and rehabilitation work in, 200
Rotterdam, 1125
work camps, 1367

Nethigeim, Widow, *See* Boni, Johanna Neothinger

Nettie Memorial
Smith Creek Fellowship Church of the Brethren, WV, preaching point, 1191

Nettle Creek Church of the Brethren, IN, 206, 226, 752, **923–924,** 1294, 1339, 2096
migration of Brethren, 829
Müller (Miller) family, 894
Jasper, MO, Church of the Brethren, 669
Kansas, settlement of Brethren in, 682
Teeter, Lewis Wallace and Nancy Ellen Bowman, 1250

Nettle Creek meetinghouse, 432

Nettle Creek Old German Baptist Brethren Church, IN, 924

Nettleton, Charles H., 1729
Slifer, IA, church of the Brethren, pastor, 1190

Nettleton, G. Stephen, 2288

Netzley family, 1341, 1909
Hope Memorial Church (German Baptist Brethren), NE, 2375
Shull family, related to, 1156

Netzley, Hattie (later Frantz), 685, 945

Netzley, Jacob, 913

Netzley, John W., 1729
Hope Memorial, NE, congregation, 945
North Beatrice Church of the Brethren, NE, 945

Netzley, Lois Irene, 1844

Netzley, William, 1729

Neu, Heinrich, 2029

Neu-Täufer, See Apostolic Christian Church

Neu-Täufer Brethren
criticism of, 1954

Neu-vermehrtes Gesäng der einsamen Turtel-Taube, zur gemein-schaftlichen Erbauung gesammelt und ans Licht gegeben, 2029

Neubauer, Frank R., III, 2288

Neue Sammlung von Psalmen, Lobgesängen und Geistlichen Liedern, zum Gebrauch für den Privat-, Familien-, und öffenlichen Gottesdienst der Alten Brüder und allerinnigen, heilsuchenden Seelen, 2029–2030

Neue Sammlung von Psalmen (New Collection of Psalms)
hymnals, 641

Neue Täufer ("New [Ana]Baptists"), *See* Names
Brethren movement, 292
chart of Brethren bodies, 1403–1405
Mack, Alexander, Sr., 775
names of Brethren fellowships, 910

Neuegold family
San Diego, CA, Grace Brethren Church, 1141

Neuenschwander, Albert, 2029

Neuenschwander, Christian, 2029

Neuenschwander family, **924,** 2030

Neuenschwander, John, 2029

Neuenschwander, Willis L., 2029

Neuenschwandger (Nighswander, Niswanger) family, 1993

Neuer Nachklang des Gesängs der ein samen Turtel-Taube, 2030

Neues (De Nyce, Newes, Nice, Neiss, Nyce), Hans, 2032

Neufeld, Freda (later Kliever), 136, **701,** 1851

Neufeld, Herbert
Raisin City, CA, Church of the Brethren, pastor, 1083

Neufeld, John H., 701

Neufeld, Justina Wiens, 701

Neuhof family, 164

Neuman-Lee, Jeff, 2288

Neumann, Elinor Brecht, 924

Neumann, Friedrich C., **924,** 2030
Judaism, 677

Neumann, Gottfried, 330, **924,** 2030
Moravian Church, 875

Neusbaum, Frank, 748, 2030

Neutral, KS
New Hope Church of the Brethren, KS, 929

neutrality
Revolutionary War, American, 1105

Neuwied
Community of the True Inspiration, 330

Neuwirth, Richard K., 2288

Nevada, 924

Nevada, MO, Church of the Brethren, 354, **924**

Nevada, OH, Church of the Brethren, *See* Eden Church of the Brethren, OH

Nevinger, Granville, 587, 1729
Onekama, MI, Church of the Brethren, free minister, 975

Nevins, Archie L., Jr., 1729
Northview, OH, Brethren Life Church/Vineyard Community Church, 2232

New Age pantheism
Grassroots, Concerns of the, 2193

New Albany Grace Brethren Church, IN, 927, *See also* Clarksville, IN, New Albany Grace Brethren Church

New Albany, OH, Rocky Ridge Grace Brethren Church, **2231**

New American Standard Bible, 138

New Anabaptists, *See* Names

New Baptists, *See* Names
Brethren movement, 292
Grundforschende Fragen (Basic Questions), 575

New Beginnings, 2130

New Bethel Church of the Brethren, NC, 925
New Haven Church of the Brethren, NC, as mission point, **928**

New Bethel Church of the Brethren, VA, **925,** 1277
Germantown Brick Church of the Brethren, VA, 544

New Bethel, IN, Church of the Brethren, 924–925

New Bethel, VA, congregation
Ruckers German Baptist Brethren Church, VA, 1129

New Bethlehem, PA

Oakland Brethren Church in, **925**
New Birth, *See* Conversion
new-birth experience
  Evangelical Association, 459
The New Birth (Hoyt), 634
New Born (German-American sect), 98,
  720, **925**
New Brunswick, Canada, 176, **925,**
  bibliography, 1858, 2003
  early journalism, 1978
  Sauer, Christopher, III, 1147, 1996
New Call to Peacemaking, **925–926,** *926*
  Brown, Dale Weaver, 2152
  Church of the Brethren, 304
  Historic Peace Churches, 610
  peace caravans, 1001
New Carlisle congregation, OH, 396, 1265
  Church of the Brethren, **926**
New Castle, IN
  Church of God (New Dunkers), 297
New Co-Operation, 2030
New Covenant Fellowship, **926**
  Church of the Brethren, 329
New Creation Fellowship
  Shalom Covenant, 926, 1084
New Creation Fellowship (Newton, KS)
  Fellowship of Hope, 488
New Creek Church of the Brethren, WV,
  See Sunnyside Church of the
  Brethren, WV
New Creek congregation, WV, 692, 1240
New Dale Church of the Brethren, VA
  Fairview-Endless Caverns Church of
  the Brethren, VA, 470
New Dale Church of the Brethren, WV,
  350, **926–927,** 1291
  Lower Lost River Church of the
  Brethren, WV, 766
  Mathias, WV, Church of the Brethren,
  803
  Mount View Church of the Brethren,
  WV, 887
New Day Incorporated of Johnstown
  Gahagen Charitable Foundation, 2187
New Dunkard Church of God, 2030,
  2038
New Dunkard News, **927**
New Dunkers, *See* Church of God (New
  Dunkers)
New English Bible, 138
New Enterprise Brethren Church, IN, **927,**
  929
  Hopewell Grace Brethren Church, PA,
  629
  Roann, IN, (First) Brethren Church,
  1112
New Enterprise, PA, 694, 1294, 1323, 1364
  Brethren Church, **927**
  Church of the Brethren, 709, **927**
  Snake Spring Valley Church of the
  Brethren, PA, 1192
New Fairview Church of the Brethren, PA,
  323, **927**
  Holiness Brethren, 619
  Markey family, 794
  Reber, Norman Franklin, minister,
  1085
New Freedom, PA, 1388
  Church of the Brethren, **927**
  Shrewsbury, PA, Church of the
  Brethren, 1179
New Hampshire, 928
New Harmony colony

Harmony Society, 584
New Harmony, IN, communitarian colony,
  928
New Haven Church of the Brethren, MI,
  355, **928,** 1304
  Shepherd Church of the Brethren, MI,
  ministers sent to, 1176
New Haven Church of the Brethren, NC,
  928
  Sexton family founded, 925
New Haven, CN, Congregational church,
  710
New Highland Brethren Church, IN, *See*
  Akron, IN, Church of the Brethren
New Holland Grace Brethren Church, PA,
  928–929
  Trappe, PA, Tri-County Grace Brethren
  Church and, 2256
New Hope Church of the Brethren, AR, 54,
  929
  Mount Hope Church of the Brethren,
  AR, 883
New Hope Church of the Brethren, IN, **929**
  Rossville, IN, Church of the Brethren,
  1124
New Hope Church of the Brethren, KS,
  273, **929**
  Osage Church of the Brethren, KS, 983
New Hope Church of the Brethren, OK,
  723, **929**
New Hope Church of the Brethren, VA,
  472, **929,** 1267
New Hope meetinghouse, Udell, IA, 1285
New Hope, WV
  Pocahontas Church of the Brethren,
  WV, mission point of, 1039
New Ideas, **929**
  Fogelsanger, John Mervin, 500
New International Version of the Bible,
  138, 139
New Jersey, 175, 1866, 2057
  Brethren Church, article about, 1958
  colonial era
  ministers, 2093
  Dairy Farm Assignments, 359
  Dairy Testing Assignments, 359
  history of, by Morgan Edwards, 1926
  *Materials Towards a History of the
  Baptists,* 803
  Pennsylvania district (BC), congrega-
  tions in, 1005
  place-names, Brethren, 1027
New Jersey congregations, **929–930**
New Jersey Historical Records Survey,
  2030
New Lebanon, OH, First Brethren Church,
  694, **930,** 962, 1178
  Munson, Charles Robert, 2227
New Left protest movement, **930**
New Liberty mission point
  Grand Junction, CO, Koinonia
  Brethren-Baptist Church, 565
New Liberty preaching point
  Fruita, CO, Church of the Brethren,
  520
New Life Christian Center
  Pleasant Valley Church of the Brethren,
  IN, 1034
New Life Ministries (CB), 2130, 2180, *See
  also* Andrew Center, The
New Light Christians
  Disciples of Christ, 385
  "New Lights" revivalism, **930**

Restoration Movement, 1101
New Living Learning Center (Founder's
  Hall)
  Elizabethtown College, 438
New Madison, OH, 338
New Madrid Co., MO
  Farrenburg Church of the Brethren,
  MO, 479
New Madrid, MO
  earthquakes, 1357
New Market, MD, 1299
New Market, VA, 1291
  Brethren Church, *See* Arkton, VA,
  Brethren Church
New Meadow Run (Farmington, PA)
  Hutterian Society of Brothers, 640
"New Measures," **930–931**
  prayer, 1051
  protracted meetings, 1063
  revival meetings, 1103
  Winebrenner, John, 309
New Mexico, **931**
  Church of the Brethren, 322
  irrigation, 663
  medical missions, 808
  migration of Brethren, 830–831
  minorities, ethnic and racial, 850
  mission schools, 853
  missions, 860
  Oklahoma district, 964
  pioneer boyhood in, 2097
  Torreon Navajo Mission (NM), 1268
New Middleton, OH, Bethel Church of the
  Brethren, 782, **931**
New Paltz, NY
  colonial settlers, 1997
New Paris, IN, 693
  Brethren Church, 407, **931,** 1089, 1108
  Church of the Brethren, 124, **931,** 1280
  Solomon's Creek Church of the
  Brethren, 1202
New Philadelphia, OH, First Church of the
  Brethren, **931**
  Mount Zion Church of the Brethren,
  OH, 888
New Plymouth, ID
  mission activity in, 996
New Prophets, *See* Community of True
  Inspiration
New Prospect Church of the Brethren, VA,
  See Allegheny Church of the
  Brethren, VA
"New Reformation Theology," 922
New Revised Standard Version of the Bible
  language, inclusive, 2214
New River, *See* Monroe Co., WV
New River Old German Baptist Brethren
  Church, CA, **931–932,** *932*
New River settlement, VA, 1307, 1311,
  1325
  early settlement, 1980
New Rockford, ND, Church of the
  Brethren, 256, **932**
New Salem Church of the Brethren, IN,
  124, 373, **932,** 1280
New Stark, OH, 413
New Sudan Council of Churches (NSCC)
  Sudan (CB) and, 2253
New Sweden, 1863
New Testament, *See* Bible; Old Testament;
  specific books
  basis for love feast, 763–764
  basis of order of worship, 1377, 1378

Believers Church Commentary Series, 2134
book about, 1937
Brethren canon, 133
Brethren Church doctrine on, 183
Brethren movement, 289, 2070
Brethren peace position, influence on, 999
and church discipline, 3, 75
Church of the Brethren, 2111
commentaries and revised texts, 2080
dietary rules, 147
disagreement about details as basis for schism, 1210
doctrine, 2022
ecclesia/church, 2131
Fourman, Larry D. on Holy Spirit and, 2331
as guide for the Brethren, 39
importance of, as creed, 1258, 1259
interpretation of the Bible, 134
kingdom of God, 695
laity, use of term, 718, 719
Luther translation published by Henry Kurtz, 711
Martin, Harold S. on beliefs and practices of, 2345
oaths, taking of, 959
obedience to, 1209
ordinances, outline study of, 1936
polity, 368
restitution, 1100
role of in Anabaptist thought, 29
as source of authority for the Church, 73
survey of, 1960
and swearing, 7
taxes addressed in, 1248
Teeter, Lewis Wallace, commentary on, 1250
translations, 138
trine immersions, 2080
trinity, doctrine of, 1275
New Testament Baptist Church, CA, 726
New Testament Brethren, **932**
chart of Brethren bodies, place on, 1403–1405
New Testament Christianity
Hope, Christian, 362
New Testament church, *See* apostolic church
"The New Testament Church at Winona," 2180
New Troy, MI, Grace Brethren Church, 68, 260, 932
Michigan Brethren settlement, 824
New Vienna Academy, OH, 2, 739, **932**
early Brethren school, 961
Miller, Oliver W., principal, 841, 1138
Quinter, James, 1077
West, Edmund Landon, 1332
New Virginia, IA, Brethren Church, **932**
New Windsor Center (Morse), 878
New Windsor College, 152
New Windsor, MD, 152, 161, 200, 712, 755, 1399, 2023
Brethren Service Center, 385, 685, 1956
center for Civilian Public Service camps, 1373
On Earth Peace, 974
Murray, Don, 625
relief and social work, 303

Sams Creek Church of the Brethren, MD, near, 1141
seagoing cowboys based at, 1161, *1161*
SERRV (Sales Exchange for Refugee Rehabilitation Vocations), 1139
soil conservation units, 1200
New York, **932–933**
colonial era
ministers, 2093
Dairy Farm Assignments, 359
Dunkard Brethren Church, 2100
missions and missionaries in
Fellowship of Grace Brethren Churches, 250
religious movements in, 2085
universalism, history of, 2081
New York, Amish settlers in, 26
The New York Evening Post
Sauer, Christopher, III, 1147
New York, NY, 2, 22, 137
Foreign Missions Conference of North America, 501
relocation of Japanese-Americans to, 1373
urban mission, 1297
New York (state)
Old German Baptist Brethren, 2235
Quebec, missionary efforts toward, 1075
New York Theological Seminary, *See* Bible Teacher Training School
Newark, DE, Grace Brethren Church, 374, **933**
Newark, OH, Brethren Church, **933**
Newberg, OR, 1302, 1364
mission point established, 933
Church of the Brethren, **933**
Dunkard Brethren, **933**, 981
Newberry Co., SC, 210, 2078
Newberry, Florence Alma (later Gribble), 183, 501, 1639, 1849, 1953
medical missions, 807
missions, 862
Newberry, Joseph C., 573
Newberry, Saphronea, 573
Newberry, SC, 768, 2033
"The Newborn," 2030
Newcastle congregation, IN, 464
Newcomb, Lewis S., 1729
Mount Bethel Church of the Brethren, VA, pastor, 880
Newcomer, Aaron, 1729
Rouzerville Church of the Brethren, PA, minister, 1125
Newcomer, Alexander, 2030
Newcomer, Alice
National Older Adult Conferences, 2229
Newcomer, Catherine (later Martin)
Martin family, 798
Newcomer, Charles Daniel, 1729, 2076
Newcomer, Christian, 2030
Newcomer, Edith
Missionary Reading Circle, 856–857
Newcomer, Edith R. (later Howe), 633
Newcomer, Edna A., 748, 2030
Newcomer, Elizabeth Emmert, 933
Newcomer, Elizabeth (later Fogelsanger), 500
Murphy, Sara Florence Fogelsanger, mother of, 897
Newcomer, Emanuel, 516, 1729
Newcomer, Emma Phillips, 933

Newcomer family, 1892, 2030
Fahrney (Forney) family, 466
Fahrney-Keedy Chapel Fellowship Church of the Brethren, MD, 467
Ridge Church of the Brethren, PA, 1108
Newcomer, Henry, *See* Newcomer family
Newcomer, Hubert
National Older Adult Conferences, 2229
Newcomer, Hubert Rex, 1729
North Manchester, IN, Church of the Brethren, pastor, 949
The Palms, FL, retirement community, 991
Newcomer, Isaac, 933
Newcomer, John
Sand Creek Church of the Brethren, KS, elder, 1143
Newcomer, John S. (Dorrance, KS), 1729
Newcomer, John S. (White Oak, PA), 1340, 1729
Mountville, PA, Church of the Brethren, 890
Newcomer, Jolene, 2030
Newcomer, Maud, 1361
Newcomer, Maud Odessa, **933**
Newcomer, Melchior S., 2030
Newcomer, Melchor Snively, **933**, 1729
Maryland Brethren immigrating to Illinois, 798
Mount Morris College, 884, 885
Newcomer, P. S., 1730
Newcomer, Paul K., 1730
Pleasant Hill Church of the Brethren, PA, presiding elder, 1032
Newcomer, Peter, *See* Newcomer family
Newcomer, Randy, 2030
Newcomer, Samuel Isaac, 933, 1730
Newcomer, Stephen, 627, 2139
Hispanic Ministries (CB), 2199
Newell, James, 754
Newland, Anna L., 354, 1836
Newland, Anna (later Crumpacker), 1912
Newland, Emily Thomas, 354
Newland, Joseph, 354
Newlanders, **934**
Newlands Reclamation Act
irrigation, 663
Newlin, Stuart, 720
Newlin, Stuart Gordon, 2288
Newman, George Frederick, 1954, 2030
Newman P. B., 1730
Newman, Parsons, 2030
Newman, William M., 1956
Newman, Woodrow W., 1730
Newport, Anne (later Royall), 2050
Newport Church of the Brethren, VA, **934**
Mount Zion Church of the Brethren, VA, 731, 888
Mount Olivet Church of the Brethren, VA, 886
Newport News, VA, 1308
Ivy Farms Church of the Brethren, 904, **934**
Newport, VA, 1265
Newport, VT, 1304
News and Views from Speak for the Lord, **934**
Newsletter, 179
Fellowship of Brethren Genealogists (FOBG), 484
Newsome, Albert R., 1996

Newspaper Enterprise Association, 149
newspapers, 1861
    early German-American, 1860
    Sauer, C., 1858
Newton, C. H., 1730
Newton Co., MO, 1214
    Fairview, MO, Shoal Creek Church of the Brethren, 468
    Shoal Creek Old German Baptist Brethren Church, MO, 1178
Newton Country, KS Church of the Brethren, 1316, *See also* Royer Community Church of the Brethren, KS
Newton, Earle W., 2030
Newton Grove Church of the Brethren, MI, 288, **934**
Newton, KS
    Church of the Brethren, **934**, 2197
    Royer Community Church of the Brethren, 1128
    General Conference Mennonite Church, 536
    Historic Peace Churches, 608
Newton, OH, Church of the Brethren, *See* Pleasant Hill Church of the Brethren, OH
Newton (Pleasant Hill), OH, congregation, 237, 335, 349
Newtonia, MO
    Fairview, MO, Shoal Creek Church of the Brethren, 468
Newtonville, OH, 1224
Newton, William A., 1730
Newville congregation, PA
    Huntsdale Church of the Brethren, PA, 638
Newville, ND
    Salem Church of the Brethren, ND, near, 251, 1137
Newville, PA, 1294, 1331
    Church of the Brethren, **934–935**
Nez Perce Co., ID
    Palouse Old German Baptist Brethren Church, 991
Nezperce, ID, Church of the Brethren, 935, *935,* 1348
Nez Perce Indian reservation, 935
Ngamariju, K. Mamza
    Ekklesiyar 'Yan'uwa a Nigeria (EYN), general secretary of, 937
Ngganjiwa, Hamnu, 1730
Ngganjiwa, Hamza, 307
Nggwa, Yaro B. B., 1730
Ngurthlavu, Nigeria, 306
Niagara Christian College, Fort Erie, Ontario, 189
Nicaea, decisions of, 289
Nicaragua
    Church of the Brethren, 2157
    Misión Cristiana (Christian Mission), 2157
    Misión Mutua en las Américas, 852
    missions and missionaries in, 189
Nicarry, Frances Oberholzer
    Nicarry, Wayne A., 2231
Nicarry, Ronald, 2231
Nicarry, Wayne A., 1730, **2231**
Nicary, Snively Omar, 1730
Niccum, David Henry, 447, 668, 1730
Nice, Emma Reed (later Ellis), 441
Nice family, 1959
Nice, Hazel (later Hassan), 1959

Nice, Henry Clemmer, 1959
Nice, Mary Catherine, 1959
Nice (Neiß), Elizabeth (later Mack), **778**
Nice (Neiß), William
    Mack, Elizabeth Neiß (Nice), 778
Nice (Nyce), William P., 1730
Nice, Rachel, 1916
Nicene Creed
    Brethren Church and, 184
Nicewonger, George Beers, 2030
Nicholas Church, WV, 1341
Nicholas Co., KY, 688, 690
    migration of Brethren, 829
    German Baptist Brethren Church, **935**
Nicholas Gardens Community Church, OR, 1215–1216, *See also* Springfield, OR, Church of the Brethren
Nicholas (Nichols), Edna, 1730
Nichols, Charles L., 2030
Nichols family, 2087
    Pipe Creek Old German Baptist Brethren Church, IN, 1026
Nichols, Mark Wayne, 2288
Nicholson, C. C., 1730
Nicholson family
    Hancock, MN, Church of the Brethren, 582
Nicholson, J., 1730
Nicholson, John, 72, 211, 347, **935–936**, 1321, 1730,
    Iowa, 661
    Mitchell, SD, Brethren Church congregation, 1205
    North Manchester, IN, (First) Brethren Church, leadership by, 949
Nicholson, John (Danville, OH), 1730
Nicholson, Kenneth J., 2030
Nickel, Arthur T., 1730, 2304
Nickels, D. C.
    Newberg, OR, Church of the Brethren, pastor in, 933
Nickerson, KS
    Brethren Church, **936**
    Church of the Brethren, **936**
        Salem Community Church of the Brethren, located near, 1138
Nickerson, Lois, 2099
Nickey, Amos Joseph, 678, 936, 1123, 1730
    Monticello, MN, Church of the Brethren, elder-in-charge, 872
    Omaha, NE, Church of the Brethren, 974
Nickey, Argus, 1730
Nickey, Barbara Marie, 191, 678, 807, **936**, 1967, 2388
Nickey, Benjamin F., 1730
Nickey family, 2018
Nickey, Flora Mae (later Ross; Bjorklund), 678, **1123–1124**, 1834
Nickey, G. S., 1730
Nickey, Mary Heckman, 936
Nickey, Paul A., 1730
    Monticello, MN, Church of the Brethren, minister, 872
Nickey, Samuel George, 590, 606, 1730
Nickler, Arthur Loyal, 1842
Nickler, Forrest, 1730
Nickler, Hildegard Barbara Welsch, 1842
Nicknames, *See* Names, Brethren
Nicodemus, Albert D., 695, 1730
Nicodemus family, 695, 1243
Nicodemus, Larry, 1730
    North Hampton, OH, Donnels Creek

Old German Baptist Brethren Church, minister, 948
Nicodemus, Rutherford Herman, 912, 1227, 1730
Nicola, C. G., 564, 1730
Nicolas Church Church of the Brethren, WV, *See* White Pine Church of the Brethren, WV
Nicolson, John, 715
Niebuhr, Reinhold
    on neoorthodoxy, 922
Niebuhr, Richard
    on neoorthodoxy, 922
Niederhiser, John, 406
Nieff, Johann Heinrich, *See* Neff, Francis
Nielsen, Johanna, 53, 362
Nielsen, Kirsten K. Hansen, 936
Nielsen, Mary (later Hope), 628, *629*
Nielsen, Niels C. "Daddy," 361, 362
Nielsen, Johanna, **936**, 1852, 2304
Nielson, Mary Katherine, 1839
Nielson, Niels C., 936
Nielson, Niels C., Jr., 1730
Nielsson, S. C., 1730
Niemoeller, Martin, 659
Nieper, Friedrich, 379, 611, 2030
Niepoth, Wilhelm, 2031
Nies, Curt D., 2288
Nies, Frank Emory, 1730
Niesley, David, 1730
Nieter, Dorothy, 318
Nieter, Fred, 318
Nieter, Rod, 318
Nietigheydt can de Kinderdoop (Mehrning), 811
Niger, **936**
    missions and missionaries, 220
    missions, short-term, 2226
Nigeria, *595,* **936–937**, 1234, 2026, *See also* Adamawa Provincial Leprosarium, Garkida, Nigeria; Church of the Brethren in Nigeria; Fellowship of Churches of Christ in Nigeria
    ALM involvement in, 24
    article about, 1953
    Baldwin, Elmer and Ferne, 1213
    Basel Mission work in, 92
    Bible translations, 139, 2137
    bibliography, 1868, 1904
    Bieber, Charles M., 2137
    Bittinger, Desmond Wright, 143
    Bittinger, Irene Frantz, 143
    books about, 1953, 1954, 1961
    Brethren Church, 250, 306
    Brethren in, history of, 1995
    Carlisle, PA, First Church of the Brethren, 255
    Church of the Brethren mission in, 3–4, 9, 92
    Covington, OH, Church of the Brethren, 349
    Dadisman, Mary Nancy, 359
    Dick, Velva Jane, missionary to, 1049
    Eikenberry, Ivan Leon and Mary Elizabeth Flora, 431
    Ellis, Calvert Nice, 441
    evangelism, 461
    EYN, 305–308
    Faw, Chalmer Ernest, 480
    Fellowship of Grace Brethren Churches, 250
    fraternal relations, 510

Fraternity Church of the Brethren, NC, 511

Freeburg Church of the Brethren, OH, 514

Garkida General Hospital, 530–531

Garkida Leper Colony, 1917

Gibbel, Paul, 1307

Gibson family, 548

Girard, IL, Church of the Brethren, 550

Global Women's Project, 2190

Good, Ada Ziegler, 1397

Grieve, Jerry Allen, 2194

Guli, John, 2194, 2195

Harleysville, PA, Indian Creek Church of the Brethren, 584

Harper, Clara Belle, 585

Hartville, OH, Church of the Brethren, 588

Heckman, Clarence C. and Lucile Gibson, 592

Heckman, John, 592

Helser, Albert David, 596

Helser, Lola Bechtel, 596

historic sites, 609

Horn, Evelyn, 1340, 1346

hospitals, 630

imposters among the Brethren, 648

Inman, Dorothy, 349

Islam, 664

Kulp Bible School, 9, 92, 709–710

Kulp, Christina Masterton, 708

Kulp, H. Stover, 709, *709*, 912, 1049

Kulp, Neta Ruth Royer, 709

Kulp, Philip M., missionary to, 1108

Kulp, Ruth Royer, missionary to, 1127

Lafiya program, 718, *718*

Lardin Gabas, 300

Lassa fever, 727

Lassa General Hospital, 726–727

Link, Donald N., 733

Link, Nancy Moore, 733

Mai Sule Biu, 782, 2216

Mallott, Floyd and Ruth, missionaries to, 784

Mamza, Ngamariju Keliri, church leadership in, 784

medical missions, 807, 810

mission, founding of, 1962

mission schools, 853, 854

mission tours, 855

mission work in, 305, 306

missionaries to, 7, 12, 13, 1136, 1141, 1144

missionaries voyaging to, 863

The Missionary Board (BC), 856

missionary conferences, 856

missions, 861, 862, 2225

missions and missionaries, 2073
  Church of the Brethren, 2081

missions and missionaries in, 153, 160, 167, 183

missions in, agricultural, 9, 12

missions, short-term, 2226

Morse, Kenneth Ivan, 878

Mshelia, Madu B., 892

nurse missionaries, 952

Oiness, Sylvia Marie, appointed as misssionary to, 963

order of dress in, 403

Pfaltzgraff, Roy Edward and Violet Hackman, 1013, 1388

Pleasant Hill, OH, Church of the Brethren, missionaries sent to, 1032

Ragnijiya, T. H. on continuing education program for Ekklesiyar 'Yan'uwa a Nigeria, 2351

refugee relief, 23

relief and rehabilitation work in, 200

relief and service efforts, 1097

Robertson, Russell L., missionary to, 1115

Royer, Gladys Violet Hawbaker and Harold Albertus ("Red"), missionaries to, 1128

Rupel, Naomi Zigler, 1397

rural areas, mission work in, 1130

Shisler, Sara Cassel, missionary, 1177

Stilwell, Nyleta, missionary, 1203

student volunteer movement, 1231

Sudan Interior Mission hospital, 727

Theological College of Northern Nigeria, *1256, 1257*

Thomasson, Kermon on CB and, 2360

Thompson, Jan, 1335

travelogues
  Thomas(s)on, Kermon, 2081

Utz, Ruth Earl, 1299

Waka Teachers' Training College and Secondary School, 1312–1313

wellness and, 2261

Williams, John Henry Bashor, 1346

Wilson, Homer, 349

Wine, Laura M., 733, 1349

Women's Conferences (CB) and, 2265

Nigerian Council of Churches
  Kulp, Harold Stover, 709

Nighswander (Neuenschwandger, Niswanger) family, 1993

Night of Broken Glass (Nov. 9–10, 1938), 23

Nightingale, Florence
  nursing careers, 952

Nihart, Clyde E., 1730

Nihiser, John, 1730

Nikodim, Metropolitan (Russian Orthodox Church), 286, 304, **937**, 2239
  McIntire, Carl, 774

Nikolaus Ludwig, Count von Zinzendorf, *See* Zinzendorf, Nikolaus Ludwig, Count von

Nill, Joseph, 1089, 1730
  McFarland, CA, Church of the Brethren, free minister, 774
  Red River Church of the Brethren, OK,

Nillson, Johann, 1730

Nimishillen, OH
  migration of Brethren, 829
  Stark Co., OH, 961

Nimishillen, OH
  Church of the Brethren, 13, 267, 416, 520, 600, 852, **937**
    Hartville, OH, Church of the Brethren, 588
    North Canton, OH, Mount Pleasant Church of the Brethren, 945–946
    Old German Baptist Brethren Church, 145, **937–938**

Nine family
  Fairview Church of the Brethren, MD, 468

Nine, Garfield, 1730

Nine, William F., 236, 1730

Ninescah Church of the Brethren congregation, KS

Salem Community Church of the Brethren, KS, 1138

Ninescah, KS, Church of the Brethren, *See* Salem Community Church of the Brethren, KS

1958 General Conference as the Committee on Indoctrination Materials, 180

1905 *Almanac,* 172

nineteenth century
  Brethren territories, 44–45
  education in the, 2
  German characteristics of the Brethren, 3
  history of Brethren during, 2055
  immigration of Germanic peoples, 26
  late
    advertising, 7
    dress, example of, *45*
  Oxford movement (England), 51
  poor, care for the, 18
  preaching, 8
  westward migration of Brethren, 3

Ninevah Church of the Brethren, VA, **938**
  Brick congregation, 938

Ninger family
  Hollins, VA, Patterson Memorial Grace Brethren Church, 620

Nininger, Benjamin F., 360

Nininger, Charles E., 65, 1730

Nininger, Christian, 1730

Nininger, Harvey Harlow, 781, **938**, 1160, 1730, **2377**
  inventions and scientific discoveries, 660
  McPherson College, 781
  Paradise Prairie Church of the Brethren, OK, 993

Nininger, Jacob C., 1730
  St. Francis Church of the Brethren, AR, 1134

Nininger, James B., 938

Nininger, Mary Ann Bower, 938

Nininger, Peter, 1730, 2125

Nininger, R. W., 1730

Ninninger, Roy, 1730

Ninth Street Church of the Brethren, VA, *See* Roanoke, VA, Ninth Street Church of the Brethren

Niota, TN, Church of the Brethren, **938**

NISBCO, 2163, *See also* National Interreligious Service Board for Conscientious Objectors (NISBCO); National Interreligious Service Board for Consientious Objectors

Nishney Valley German Baptist Brethren, IA, **938**

Nisley, Elizabeth Delila, 2031

Nisley family, 1881

Nisly, Abraham C., 2031

Nisly, Clara, 2031

Nisly, Katie Miller, 2031

Nissley, Anna (later Metzler), 820

Nissley family, 2043, 2079

Nissley, Jacob, 1730

Niswander, Albert M., 1730

Niswander, Alpha (later Stumph), 1845

Niswander family, 211, 2031, *See also* Neuenschwander family

Niswander, Isaac Burner, 1731

Niswander, Samuel Franklin, 1731

Niswander, W. Earl, 2031

Niswanger (Nighswander, Neuenschwand-

ger) family, 1342, 1993
Niswender family, 1932
Niswikawa, Joseph Y., 1731
Niswinger family, *See* Neuenschwander family
Niswonger, E. B., 562
Niswonger, Esther (later Mote), 592
Niswonger, Everett B., 319, 527, 1731
　Rittman, OH, First Brethren Church, pastor, 1111
Niswonger family, *See* Neuenschwander family
Nix, Dayne E., 62, 2288
Nix, Leonard, 516
Nixon, Richard M., 599
Nixon, Tim, 2288
Nixon, William, 1731
No Creed: The Bible and Biblical Interpretation (Haines), 579
Noah's Ark of Safety
　Frostburg, MD, First Church of the Brethren, 519
Noatemo, Jean, **938**
Nobel, David, 1731
Nobel Peace Prize
　American Friends Service Committee and the Friends Service Council of London, 23
　Cordier, Andrew Wellington, 344
Nobel Prizes
　Flory, Paul John, 499, 660
　Urey, Harold C., for chemistry, 1298
Noble, Abel, 88
　Seventh-Day Baptists, 1170
Noble Co., IN, 153, 264, 1323
Noble, David, 1380
Noble, David and Nancy,
　Pataskala, OH, Grace Brethren Church of Licking Co., 995
Noble family, 318, 2324
　Pataskala, OH, Grace Brethren Church of Licking Co., 995
Nobles Co., MN, 1380
Noblesville, IN, Church of the Brethren, 109, **938**
Nocona Church of the Brethren, TX, **938–939**, 1255
　Fort Worth, TX, Church of the Brethren, 504
Nodaway Co., MO, 1342
　Honey Creek Church of the Brethren, MO, 627
Nodle, Abraham, 1328
Nodle, Sarah, 1328
Noe family, 1234, 1340
Noe, W. P., 1340
Noe, W. Sterling, 516
　Pleasant Hill Old German Baptist Brethren Church, IL, providing leadership, 1033
Noe, William Sterling, 270, 1731
　Mud Valley Old German Baptist Brethren Church, IL, minister, 892
Noecker, Helen (later Reber), 1085
Noethiger, Johanna (later Boni), 159, *See also* Boni, Johanna Noethiger
Noffsinger, Amos, 939
Noffsinger, Bruce Adams, 1731, 2288
Noffsinger, C. T., 674
Noffsinger, Charles, 23
Noffsinger, Daniel, 1731
　Lower Miami, OH, congregation, elder in, 939

Noffsinger, Dorothy (later Brown)
　works by, 2319
Noffsinger, Ezra, 1731
Noffsinger family, 162, 373, **939**
　Muhlenberg Co., KY, German Baptist Brethren, 893
Noffsinger, Fianna Neidich, 939
Noffsinger, Florence M. Wieand, 939
Noffsinger, Hannah, 685
Noffsinger, Harley, 2031
Noffsinger, Jacob
　Poplar Ridge Church of the Brethren, OH, 1047
Noffsinger, Jesse, 1731
Noffsinger, John
　Poplar Ridge Church of the Brethren, OH, 1047
Noffsinger John Samuel, **939**, 1731, 2031
　International Voluntary Services Agency (IVS), 660
Noffsinger, Orville R. C., 1731, 1939
Noffsinger, Paul, 1731
　Michigan City, IN, Church of the Brethren, pastor, 825
Noffsinger, Peter, 939
Noffsinger, Ross Lawrence, 31, 1731, 2031
Noffsinger, Rudolph, 2031
Noffsinger, Sadie Brallier, 747, 2031, 2319
Noffsinger, Stanley Brallier, 913, 1731
Noffsinger, Susan, 214
Noffsinger, William P., 1731
Noffzinger family, 2087
Nofsinger, Mary (later Roop), 1130
Nofsinger, Orville, 505
Nofziger, Christ R., 2031
Nofziger family, *See* Noffsinger family
Nofziger, Jacob P., 1731
Nofziger, Marcile Elizabeth Rupp, 2031
Nofziger, Thurlow H., 2031
Nofzinger family, *See* Noffsinger family
Nofzinger, Rouse, 1731
Nogle, Joel F., 2288
Nokesville congregation, VA
　Hollywood Church of the Brethren, VA, 620
Nokesville, VA, *414,* 1301
　Church of the Brethren, **939**
Nokesville, VA, congregation
　Flory, George W., 498
Nolan, Gary, 19, 1731
Nolan, Ione Adamson, 2031
Nolan, Phyllis (later Carter), 2264
　Rio Prieto, PR, Iglesia de los Hermanos (CB) and, 2244
Nold, Jacob, Jr., 2080
Nolen, Lula, 168
Nolen, P. L.
　Mount Hermon Church of the Brethren, VA, minister, 881
Nolen, Posey Lester, 1731
Nolen, Wilfred E., 2140, 2288
　SHARE program, 1172
Noll, Margaret, 2031
Noll, Mark A., 2031
Noll, Samuel P., 1731
Nolley, Davis, 1731
Nolley, Eugene D., 1731
Nolley, William Davis, 1731
Nolt, Enos Dale, 1731
Nolt, Mildred W. Horst, 2031
Nolt, Paul M., 2031
Nolt, Richard Lloyd, 1731
Nolt, Stephen M.

on Brethren movement, 2349
　on Mennonite sect, 2349
　on OGBB, 2349
　on peace churches, 2348
Nolte, Phil, 467
non-associators, American Revolution, 939
non-Catholic Christian denominations, 2097
non-immersionist Mennonites
　publications, 154
Non-Military Service Committee, 1372
A Non-Partisan History of the Church and Heresy, See Unparteiische Kirchen- und Ketzer-Historie
Non-profit organization, *See* tax exempt status
nonassociators
　Brethren neutrality and Revolutionary War, American, 1106
　Revolutionary War, 310, 312
noncombatant denominations
　Miller, Howard, 838
noncombatant military service, 831–832
　Civilian Public Service, 1372
　World War I, 1370
　World War II, 1372
noncombatant service, *See* military service
noncombatant services
　Guice (Geist Gub, Guss, Güb), Christopher, 576
nonconformity, 3, 29, 399, **939–942**, 1373
　alcohol abstinence, 1251–1252
　and art, 59, 60
　bibliography, **950–952**, 1910
　book about, 1932
　Brethren doctrine, 939–942
　Brethren in Christ, 189
　Brethren movement, 314, 378, 2073
　Brethren music, 898
　church membership, 813
　Church of God, Anderson, IN, 296
　Church of the Brethren, 300
　confession of faith, 333
　and Conrad Beissel, 113
　converts, and oaths, taking of, 959
　Declaration of Principles, 372
　discipleship, 386
　Doctrinal Treatise, 394
　doctrine on, 185
　dress as symbol of, 401
　Dunkard Brethren Church, 2173
　electricity, 434
　Elsoff, 443
　Ernst Casimir, 453
　eschatology, 454
　ethics, 457, 458
　Eyman, Peter, 464
　family, 474
　Fast Element, 480
　fellowship, 482
　Fellowship of Grace Brethren Churches (FGBC), 484, 486
　fundamentalism, 522
　funerals, 523
　furniture, 525
　German Baptist movement, 2073
　God's Means of Grace (Yoder), 555
　higher education, 603
　hoops, 628
　humility, 636
　hymns, 643

Independence Day, 649
Industrial Revolution, 655
informal rituals as acknowledgment of, 1378–1379
instruction about, 5
Miami Valley Petition, 823
ministry, 845
motion pictures, 879
New Left movements attractiveness, 930
noncreedalism, 942
Old Brethren, 964
Old Brethren German Baptist Church, 965
Old German Baptist Brethren, 967, 2233
Old Order Fellowships, 971
Old Order Movement, 973
"Order of the Brethren," 976
Pennsylvania Dunkard and Old Order Brethren, 1005
Plymouth Brethren, 1038–1039
preaching about, 1053
Rechte und Ordungen, 1086
Reformation, Protestant, and Brethren doctrine, 1092
religious liberty, 1098
sanctification, 1142
Sermon on the Mount, 1169
simple life, 1183
sources on, 2313
Stein, John William, 1220
Stoffer, Dale R. on, 2359
theological basis, 1210, 1261
theology and, 2255
tobacco use, 1266
trinity, doctrine of, 1275
wallpaper advised against at annual meeting, 1314
Wittgenstein territory, 1354–1355
noncreedalism, 133, 409, 1258–1259
Brethren movement, **942–944**
Church of God (New Dunkers), 297
Ephrata Community, 448
ethics, 457
Franklin, Benjamin, 506
fundamentalism, 522, 1155
Haines, Amos Hoppock, 579
Mack, Alexander, Sr., and New Baptists of Schwarzenau, 776
McClain, Alva J., 773
"Message of the Brethren Ministry," 817, 818
"Order of the Brethren," 976
theology and, 2254
Willoughby, William G., description of, 1375
Wohlfahrt (Welfare), Michael, 1355
Nonemaker, Alesia Beth Homes, 1731
Nonemaker, Beth (CB)
Rio Prieto, PR, Iglesia de los Hermanos (CB) and, 2243
Nonemaker, Keith Andrew, 1731, 2031
Rio Prieto, PR, Iglesia de los Hermanos (CB) and, 2243
Nongo u Kristu Ken Sudan Hen Tiv (NKST), 296
Nongo u Kristu ken Sudan hen Tiv (NKST), *See* Fellowship of Churches of Christ in Nigeria
nonlitigant (law) religious groups
census and, 267
nonlitigation, *See* Law

nonliturgical nature of worship, 1373, 1375
Nonnemacher, Harry, 164, 1731
A Nonpartisan History of Church and Heresy (Unparteiische Kirchen und Ketzer-Historie, 1699–1700), 57
nonprofit organizations, 19
nonresistance, 28, 29, **944**, 2021, *See also* conscientious objection; military service
American Revolution and, 2018
articles about, 1928, 1956
biblical doctrine, 1975
bibliography, 1874
Blooming Grove Dunkers, 148–149
Brethren in Christ, 188
Brethren movement, descriptions of, 378
Bromback (Brumbach), Jacob, 516
Catawba, NC, German Baptist Brethren Church, and effects of, 262
Christian Brethren and, 281
Church of God (New Dunkers), 297
Civil War, 148–149, 314, 2082, 2107
Community of the True Inspiration, 330
confession of faith, 333
converts, and oaths, taking of, 959
CPS, 199
Davy, Henry Dorsey, 364–365
Declaration of Principles, 372
Doctrinal Treatise, 394
doctrine on, 185
dress symbol of, 401
Dunkard Brethren, 148, 409
Dunkard Brethren Church, 2077, 2173
Durnbaugh, Donald F. on Brethren movement and, 2326
Early, Henry Clay, 414
elections, electioneering, 434
eschatology, 454
Fast Henry A., 480
Fischer, Johann, 491
fraternal relations, 510
Frenkendorf, 516
frontier, 283, 519
fundamentalism, 522
Gandhi, Mohandas Karamchand, 528
Germantown, 542
God's Means of Grace (Yoder), 555
Graybill, Jonas, 567
Historic Peace Churches, 607–610, 944
historical materials, 1872
historiography, 2201
Illinois, 647
Jackson, Thomas Jonathan "Stonewall," 667
Mallott, Floyd Ellwood, 784
martyrology, anabaptist, 171
Mennonites, 816
migration of Brethren, 829
military service, 831, 832
militia nonparticipation, 832
Montgomery, Michael, 872
Moomaw, Benjamin Franklin, 873
nonconformity, 940
noncreedalism, 942
North Carolina Brethren and Revolutionary War, 946
Old German Baptist Brethren, 967, 2233
opposition to litigation, 728–729
"Order of the Brethren," 976

peace, 997, 999, 1000
Pennsylvania Brethren and Revolutionary War, 1004
Plow Creek Fellowship, 1038
Powers, Valentine, 1050
preaching about, 1053
principle of, and Indian interactions, 927
Reformation, Protestant, and Brethren doctrine, 1092
religious liberty, 1098
Revolutionary War, American, 176, 1105
sanctification, 1142
Sauer, Johann Christoph, I, urged by, 1147
Schwarzenau Brethren and Anabaptism, 1079
sources on, 2312, 2313, 2319, 2322, 2323
thesis about, 1961
Thurman, William C., 1264, 2082
vs. pacifism, 989
War, Peace, and Nonresistance (Hershberger), 1963
Weaver, J. Denny on, 2362
Wolfe, George, II, 1357
World War I, 301, *336,* 1370
World War II, 1372
nonviolence, 1262, 1973, 1979, *See* nonresistance; pacifism; peacemaking
article about, 1945
Christian Peacemaker Teams (CPT), 2161
Egan, Eileen on, 2329
Kahler, Dean, 1306
peace, 997
Peace Studies Institute, 1003
play about, 1941
sources on, 2319
Nora Springs mission point
Greene, IA, Church of the Brethren, 570
Norcatur, KS
Maple Grove Brethren Church, **944–945**
Mount Zion Church, 944–945
Norcross, David A., 348, 552, 553, 1731
Nord, Chris, 115
Nordheim, 545
radical pietist dissension in, 990
Nordhoff, Charles, 2031
Nördlingen, Germany, 193
Norfolk Church of the Brethren, VA, *See* Virginia Beach, VA, Christian Church Uniting (CB/UCC)
Norfolk, VA, 1308
Normal Department, Juniata College
Brumbaugh, Martin Grove, 223
normal schools, 150, 408, **945,** *See also* Brethren's Normal College; Juniata College
athletics, 49
education, 426
emergence of, and relation to secondary education, 1163
higher education, 605
Mount Morris College, 884
Mountain Normal School, 889
Showalter, John Henry, 1179
Spring Creek Normal School, 1213
Virginia Normal School, 1213
Normal term, 697

Kishacoquillas Seminary, 697
Norman family, 1289
Norman, Shirley, 2288
Norras, S. A., 1731
Norris, Ada, 2031
Norris, Donald C., 1731
Norris, Edward O., 1731
Norris, Emma (later Miller)
    Miller, Robert Henry, mother of, 842
    Miller, Robert Henry, wife of, 842
    Mount Pleasant Church of the
        Brethren, IN, 886–887
Norris, Esther L., 2288
Norris family, 1345
Norris, Floyd L., 1731
Norris, Glen Elvin, 21, 1243, 1731, 1842,
    2094, 2304, **2385**
Norris, Isabelle Price, *1020*
Norris, James W., 723, 1731
    Marion, IN, Church of the Brethren,
        elder, 793
    Plevna, IN, Church of the Brethren,
        minister, 1037
Norris, Jane, 1339
Norris, Lina (later Stoner), 1349
Norris, Lisa, 2075
Norris, Lois Anna Detwiler, 244, 1243,
    1731, 1842
Norris, Lona Beabes
    National Older Adult Conference, 2229
Norris, Marion M., 1731
Norris, Mark M., 2288
Norris-McCoy family
    family history, 1988
Norris, Philip E., 1731
Norris, S. L., 1731
Norris, Samuel A., 1731
Norris, Victor S., 1731
Norris, Wilbur J., 1731
Norriss, J. H., 257
Norristown congregation, PA
    Harleysville, PA, Indian Creek Church
        of the Brethren, 584
Norristown, PA, Church of the Brethren,
    633, 648, **945**
    Mingo Church of the Brethren, PA, 843
Norsworthy, Rolan, 2288
North America
    Mennonites, 815
North American Baptist Conference, *See*
    German Baptists
North American Great Plains
    farm machinery, 476
    farming, 477
The North American Review
    Native Americans, 2229
North Atlantic district, Church of the
    Brethren, 404, 1950
    Eshelman, Walter Witmer, 455
North Atlantic District Fellowship
    New Jersey congregations, 930
North Avenue Community Center
    Fresno, CA, First Church of the
        Brethren, 517
North Baltimore, MD, Church of the
    Brethren, *See* Baltimore, MD,
    Trinity Church of the Brethren
North Beatrice Church of the Brethren, NE,
    945
North Bend, OH, Church of the Brethren,
    See Danville Church of the
    Brethren, OH
North Bethel, MO

Church of the Brethren, **945**
North Buffalo Grace Brethren Church, PA,
    699, **945**
North Canton, OH
    Church of the Brethren, 937
    Mount Pleasant Church of the Breth-
        ren, 13, **945–946**
    Nimishillen Old German Baptist
        Brethren Church, OH, 937–938
North Carolina, 162, 175, 689
    American Revolution
    militias, organization and development
        of, 2097
    Baptists, 1976
    Baptists of, history by Morgan
        Edwards, 1926
    Brethren, 2012
    Brethren settlement, **946**
    Brethren Universalists, 177
    Dunkers, 1914–1915, 1923, 1996
    German settlement in, 2069
    Graybill (Grabill, Krehbiel) family, 567
    historical works on Brethren in, 2054
    Indiana, 652
    itinerant ministries, 271
    *Materials Towards a History of the
        Baptists,* 803
    migration of Brethren, 829, 830
    Moravian Church, 875, 876, 1942
    Native Americans, 2229
    Old German Baptist Brethren, 967, 970
    Pennsylvania Brethren and settlement,
        1004
    Pennsylvania Germans, 1006, 2104
    preacher circuits in, 164, 167, 169
    universalism, history of, 2099
    Universalists, 1292
North Dakota, 177, *568*
    Brethren churches and property in,
        1943
    Brethren settlement, 946–947, *947*
    Catholics, 164
    colonization, 251, 299, 324
    congregations
    free ministry and, 251
    Dunkard Brethren Church, 2077, 2082
    first Dunker colony, article about, 1937
    frontier, 519
    Great Northern Railroad, 569
    homesteading, 626
    Lutherans, 164
    migration of Brethren, 830
    Minnesota Brethren settlement, 848
    Montana Brethren settlement, 870
    Old German Baptist Brethren congre-
        gations, 967
    Peters, Amos B., assisting colonization,
        1011
    pioneer boyhood in, 2097
    place-names, Brethren, 1028
    railroads and Brethren settlement, 1082
    Worst, John H., 1379
North Dakota, Brethren in, 15, 94
North English Church of the Brethren, IA
    English River Church of the Brethren,
        IA, 236, 447, **947**
    Pleasant Grove Grace Brethren Church,
        IA, 1031
North Fork Church of the Brethren, WV,
    947, *See also* Jordan Run Church
    of the Brethren, WV
    Flintstone, MD, Glendale Church of
        the Brethren, 494

North Fork, IN, Church of the Brethren,
    652, 1345, *See also* Pyrmont, IN,
    Church of the Brethren
North Fork Old German Baptist Brethren
    Church, IN, **947–948**, 1312
North Fork Church of the Brethren, WV,
    947
    Jordan Run Church of the Brethren,
        WV, 676
    Pocahontas Church of the Brethren,
        WV, mission point of, 1039
North Fort Myers, FL, First Church of the
    Brethren, **948**
North Georgetown, OH, Brethren Church,
    744, 761, **948**
    Reading Church of the Brethren, OH,
        1084
North Hampton, OH, Donnels Creek Old
    German Baptist Brethren Church
    Donnels Creek congregation, **948**
North House
    West Goshen congregation, IN, 749
North Indiana District Meeting
    Salem College, 1138
North Kill Church of the Brethren, PA, *See*
    Falckners Swamp, PA
North Kokomo Grace Brethren Church, IN,
    948
North Lauderdale, FL, Grace Brethren
    Church, **948**
    Fort Lauderdale, FL, Grace Brethren
        Church, 503
North Liberty Brethren Church, OH, 734,
    See Butler, OH, North Liberty
    Brethren Church
North Liberty, IN, 1963
    Brethren Church, **948**
    Church of the Brethren, 749, **948**, 1864
        Oak Grove, IN, Church of the
            Brethren, 955
        Pine Creek Church of the
            Brethren, IN, 1024
        Schrock, Mark Y., 1156
North Long Beach, CA
    Brethren Church, **238**
    Grace Brethren Church
        Riverside, CA, Grace Community
            Church (FGBC) and, 2244
North Manchester College, *See* Manchester
    College
North Manchester, IN, *652*, 740, 1285,
    1334, 1350, 2101
    Bible school, 137
    Church of the Brethren, 344, 357, 429,
        842, **949**, 1011, 2031, 2101
        Ogan's Creek, IN, Church of the
            Brethren, 960
    First Brethren Church, 949, 1250, 1121
    historic sites, 609
    Timbercrest, 1264–1265
    Old German Baptist Brethren Church,
        357, 430, **949**
        Annual Meeting in (1977), *966,
            968*
    West Manchester meetinghouse, 1334
North Mill Creek Church of the Brethren,
    WV, 129, 171, 949
North Morrill, KS, Church of the Brethren,
    See Morrill, KS, Church of the
    Brethren
North Mountain, Berkeley Co., WV
    Allensville, WV, Church of the
        Brethren, 2126

North Park seminary, Chicago, IL
  Evangelical Covenant Church, 460
  North Plains District
    sponsor of Spurgeon Manor, 1216
North Pole
  attempt to reach by dirigible by Chester
    Melvin Vaniman, 1303
North Pole, AK, congregation
  Jackson, Edward A., 2209
North Poplar Ridge, OH, congregation, 373
North Riverdale Grace Brethren Church,
  OH, 367, *See also* Dayton, OH,
  North Riverdale Grace Brethren
  Church
North Sacramento, CA
  Rio Linda, CA, congregation, 1134
North Saint Joseph, MO, Church of the
  Brethren, 1134, 1135, *See also*
  Saint Joseph, MO, North Saint
  Joseph Church of the Brethren
North Santaam River (OR), 14
North, Shelby Orland, 338, 1732, 2304
North Solomon, KS, Brethren Church,
  Portis, KS, Grace Brethren
  Church, 1047–1048
North Solomon Old German Baptist
  Brethren Church, KS, **949–950**
North Spokane Church of the Brethren,
  Spokane, WA, 1212
North Star Church of the Brethren, OK, 62,
  950
North Star, OH, Church of the Brethren, 62,
  574, **950**
  Oakland Church of the Brethren, OH,
    957
North Tampa, FL, Zion Church of the
  Brethren, 212, 1247
  Hillsborough and Pinella Counties, FL,
    950
North Topeka, KS
  Free Discussion, 513
North Valley Christian Center Church of
  the Brethren, CA, 275
North Vandergrift, PA, Brethren Church,
  689, *See also* Kepple Hill, PA,
  Pleasant View Brethren Church
North Wales Twp., PA, 701
North Webster, IN, 690
  Church of the Brethren organized from
    Tippecanoe, IN, congregation, *950,*
    950–951
North Winona Church of the Brethren, IN,
  124, **951,** 1280, 1895
  Puterbaugh, Amsey Hascall, elder,
    1072
North Yakima, WA, 1383
  Church of the Brethren, *See* Yakima,
    WA, Church of the Brethren
Northampton Co. (now Lehigh Co.), PA
  Flickinger family, 1937
Northampton Co., PA, 701, 711, 1864
Northampton Co., VA
  Jacob Schowalder, 1155
Northeastern District of OH
  Alliance, OH, Church of the Brethren,
    2126
  Mount Zion congregation, aid to, 931
Northeastern Kansas District Mission Board
  East Maple Grove Church of the
    Brethren, KS, 415–416
Northern Advisory Council of Protestant
  Churches and Misisons
  Eikenberry, Ivan Leon and Mary

Elizabeth Flora, 431
Northern Baptist Convention, *See* American
  Baptist Churches USA
Northern California Brethren Conference
  purchase of land for Stockton, CA,
    Brethren Church, 1224
Northern Colorado, CO, Church of the
  Brethren, *See* Windsor, CO,
  Northern Colorado Church of the
  Brethren
Northern District of Virginia, 2031
Northern Illinois district (CB), 419
Northern Indiana Brethren Men's Group
  Heifer Project International, 594
Northern Indiana District, Church of the
  Brethren, 2056
  Bieber, Charles M., 2137
  Florence, MI, Church of the Brethren,
    496
  Schrock family, 1155–1156
Northern Indiana mission board
  Flat Rock Church of the Brethren, IN,
    493
  Salem Church of the Brethren, IN,
    1137
Northern Missions Council
  Bieber, Charles M., 2137
Northern Ohio District Mission Board
  Eden Church of the Brethren, OH, 424
Northern Pacific Railroad
  Brethren colonization, **951**
  Brethren settlement, 1082
  Carrington, ND, Church of the
    Brethren, 256
  chartered trains, 273
  colonization of Yakima Valley, WA,
    1319
  Great Northern Railroad, 568
  migration of Brethren, 830
  Montana Brethren settlement, 870
  Mott, Charles W., 879
  North Dakota Brethren settlement, 946
  role in western migration, 1240
Northern Plains District Church of the
  Brethren, 1956
Northgate Community Brethren Church,
  CA, *See* Manteca, CA, Northgate
  Community Brethren Church
Northhaven Retirement Residence, Seattle,
  WA, **951**
Northkill
  Nass, Johannes, congregational devel-
    opment, 909
Northkill congregation, PA, 699, 1233
  Mohrsville Church of the Brethren, PA,
    869
  Solenberger, Sarah, 1202
Northrup, R. Truman, 663, 1732,
  2031–2032, **2385**
  Michigan City, IN, Church of the
    Brethren, part-time pastor, 825
  Modesto, CA, Church of the Brethren,
    866
Northumberland Co., PA, 369, 752, 2031
Northview, IN, Church of the Brethren, *See*
  Indianapolis, IN, Northview
  Church of the Brethren
Northview, OH, Brethren Life
  Church/Vineyard Community
  Church, **2232**
Northwest Center for Racial Justice
  Redford, MI, Trinity Church of the
    Brethren, 1090

Northwest Chapel, AZ, Brethren Church,
  1278, *See also* Tucson, AZ,
  Northwest Brethren Chapel
Northwest Territory
  migration of Brethren, 829
Northwestern Ohio District
  Fostoria, OH, Church of the Brethren,
    505
Northwestern University
  Brooks, Harlan, 212
Norton Co., KS, 682
  Maple Grove, KS, German Baptist
    Brethren congregation, 944
Norton, Mary Beth, 2032
Norton, OH, Grace Brethren Church
  Barberton Bible Church, **951**
Norton, WV
  Elkins, WV, Church of the Brethren,
    440
Norwalk, CA, Grace Brethren Church, **951**
Norway, 157
  Assembly of Christ, 376
Norwich, Stanley, 1732
Norwood, Frederick A., 2032
Nosam
  Mason, Edward, pseudonym of, 799
Nottingham Chapel, WV
  Pocahontas Church of the Brethren,
    WV, mission point of, 1039
Nottoway Co., VA
  Mill Creek Old German Baptist
    Brethren Church, VA, 833
Nova Scotia, 1858
Novak, Michael, 2032
novels, *See* fiction, references in; litera-
  ture, Brethren and
Novelty congregation, MO
  Shelby Co. Church of the Brethren,
    MO, 1175
noviolence
  Christian Peacemaker Teams (CPT),
    2161
Nowag, Bernard, 1732
Nowag, George B., 715
Nowag, H. Walter, 746, 1732, **2385**
Noyes, John Humphrey, 2032
NSBRO, *See* National Interreligious
  Service Board for Conscientious
  Objectors (NSBRO); Robinson, Jo
  Ann Ooiman
NSCC, *See* New Sudan Council of
  Churches (NSCC)
Näf, Jacob, 2029
Näf, Rudolf, 2029
nuclear energy
  Brethren and, **951–952**
  Peace Seminars, 1002
nuclear family
  Brethren movement, 294
nuclear weapons, *See* disarmament
  arms race, Brethren views on, **2232**
  bibliography, 1867
  disarmament, 1965
  peace position, 1001
  Russia, 1288
  sources on, 2311
  Urey, Harold C., 1298
Nuer Bible translations, 2137
  Sudan (CB) and, 2253
Numer, Adam C., 1732
Numer, J. H., 1732
  numerical place name, 911
Numrich, Paul David, 2288

Nun, Mary (later Edwards), 429
Nunez, Argentina, 54
Nunnemacher family, 2031
nunneries
Pennsylvania, 2070
Nürnberg
Hochmann von Hochenau, Ernst
Christoph, 615
nursery schools
Leola, PA, Conestoga Church of the
Brethren, 737
nurses
mission schools, 853
nursing, 123, 2048
Brethren interest in, **952**
Brumbaugh, Grayce, 220
Hospital Committee (CB), 630
medical missions providing training,
807
Oiness, Sylvia Marie, missionary, 963
Nursing Education Fund, 952
nursing homes, *See* retirement homes and
communities
Nurturing Abilities for Christ (NAC)
CE National, Inc., 2156
youth and, 2268
Nusbaum, Earl, 1732
Nusbaum, John, 1384, 1732
Nutter, Leslie D., 1380, 1732
Nutts, Elizabeth (later Booher), *See* Booher
family
Nuzum, Albert
Pleasant Hill Church of the Brethren,
WV, 1033
Nuzum, Frederick M., 2288
Nyack, NY
Fellowship of Reconciliation (USA),
488
Nyce, Abraham
Hartzel, Gwendolyn Price (Nyce) on
descendants of, 2346
Mease, Gladys Price (Nyce) on descen-
dants of, 2346
Nyce, Abraham H., 952
Nyce, Alfred Price, 1732
Nyce, Anna, *761*
Nyce, Catherine M., 260
Nyce, Ellsworth, *1393*
Nyce family
Preiß (Price) family, related to, 1055
Nyce, Frances Clemens, 2032
Nyce, Gladys Price
on Nyce, Abraham and descendants,
2346
on Nyce, Leanna (Goshall) and descen-
dants, 2346
on Price, Abraham and descendants,
2346
on Price, Susan (Alderfer) and descendants, 2346
Nyce, Gwendolyn Price
on Nyce, Abraham and descendants,
2346
on Nyce, Leanna (Goshall) and descendants, 2346
Nyce, Jonas, *27, 477, 1393*
Nyce, Leanna Godshall, 952
Hartzel, Gwendolyn Price (Nyce) on
descendants of, 2346
Mease, Gladys Price (Nyce) on descendants of, 2346
Nyce, Gwendolyn Price on descendants
of, 2346

Nyce, Mamie Shelley, *27*
Nyce, Mary Price, 952
Nyce, William G., 1732
Nyce, William Godshall, **952**
Nyce, William P., 1732, 2032, 2304
Sales Exchange for Refugee
Rehabilitation Vocations (SERRV),
director, 1139
Nyce Manufacturing Co., Vernfield, PA,
235
Nye, Elizabeth Heagy, 953
Nye, Harry Hess, 952–953, 1732, 2032
Elizabethtown College, 437
Nye, Joe (Mr. and Mrs.), 579
Nye, John K., 952–953
Nye, Kathryn Hess, 952–953
Nye, Paul E., 2288
Nyswaner, Susannah (later Crumrine), 708

"O God, Our Help in Ages Past," 643
"O Happy Day," 559
Oahu, HI, 1312
Oak Brook, IL, 613
Oak Creek Church of the Brethren, OK, *See*
Elk City, OK, Church of the
Brethren
Oak Forest, MO, congregation
Mount Hermon Church of the
Brethren, MO, previous name of,
881
Oak Grove Brethren Church, VA, *See*
Gillaspie, VA, Oak Grove Brethren
Church
Oak Grove, CA, congregation, 727
Reedley, CA, Church of the Brethren,
1091
Oak Grove Church of the Brethren, IA, **955**
English River Church of the Brethren,
IA, 353, 447
Oak Grove Church of the Brethren, IL, **955**
Oak Grove Church of the Brethren, LA,
760, **955–956**
Oak Grove Church of the Brethren, MD,
956
Pine Grove Church of the Brethren,
MD, 1024
Oak Grove Church of the Brethren, MO,
956, *See also* Log Creek Church of
the Brethren, MO
Oak Grove Church of the Brethren, OH,
418, **956,** 1235
Oak Grove Church of the Brethren, OK,
956
Portage Church of the Brethren, OK,
1047
Oak Grove Church of the Brethren, VA, *See*
Roanoke, VA, Oak Grove Church of
the Brethren
Oak Grove Church of the Brethren, WV,
254, **956**
Oak Grove congregation, TN, 1340
Oak Grove Congregational Christian
Church, IL, 713
Oak Grove, IN
Church of God (New Dunkers), 297
Million, Robert, elder, 843
Church of the Brethren, 297, **955**
North Liberty, IN, Church of the
Brethren, 948
Oak Grove Old German Baptist Brethren
Church, OH, 350, **956,** 957, *See
also* (Big) Oak Grove Old German
Baptist Brethren Church, OH

Oak Grove-South Church of the Brethren,
VA, 43, 103, **956**
Oak Grove, TN, congregation, 1340
Church of the Brethren, VA, **957**
Oak Hill congregation, VA, 1364
example of place name, 911
Germantown Old German Baptist
Brethren Church, VA, 544
Oak Hill congregation, WV
example of place name, 911
Oak Hill Old German Baptist Brethren
Church, VA, **957**
Oak Hill Old German Baptist Brethren
Church, WV, **957**
Oak Hill, WV, Brethren Church
Chestnut Grove German Baptist
Brethren Church, originated from,
956–957
Gatewood Brethren Church, WV, 532
"Leaning on the Everlasting Arms,"
560
Oak Park Church of the Brethren, MD, **957**
Oak Park German Baptist Brethren Church,
See Elkhart, IN, City Church of
the Brethren
Oak Ridge schoolhouse, VA, 1313
Oakdale, CA
Modesto, CA, Big Valley Grace
Community Church (FGBC), mis-
sion point of, 866
SERRV international gift shop, 1139
Oakdale Church of the Brethren, PA, 350,
957
Oakland Brethren Church, PA, *See* New
Bethlehem, PA, Oakland Brethren
Church
Oakland, CA, Church of the Brethren, **957**
Empire, CA, Church of the Brethren,
445
Oakland Church of the Brethren, OH, 62,
950, **957–958,** 963
Harris Creek Church of the Brethren,
OH, 585
Petersime, Ray, 1012
Oakland Church of the Brethren, TN, *See*
Maryville, TN, Oakland German
Baptist Brethren Church
Oakland, MD, 1243
Church of the Brethren, *See* Pine
Grove Church of the Brethren, MD
Oakland Mills Uniting, MD, Church of the
Brethren, *See* Columbia, MD,
Oakland Mills Uniting Church
(CB/UCC)
example of verbal inflections and plu-
rals in place name, 911
Oakley, Annie
Brethren, relationships with, **958**
Oakley Brick Church of the Brethren, IL,
226, 270, 713, **958**
Milmine Church of the Brethren, IL,
843
Oaks, Essie (later Mays)
Mays, Morley Josiah, mother of, 804
Oaks, Ethel, 343
Oaks family, 1341
Oaks, Lewis C., 1732
Oaks, PA, Green Tree Church of the
Brethren
100 year anniversary, 1984
Coventry, PA, congregation, 958
Oaks, Peter R., 1732
Oaks, Phoebe, 467

Oakton, VA, Church of the Brethren, 399, **958,** 1228
Oakvale Church of the Brethren, WV, **958–959**
  Olean Church of the Brethren, VA, 973
Oakville, IN, 1338
  Brethren Church, 694, **959,** 703
  Muncie, IN, Brethren Church, 896
    Cornerstone Brethren Church and Ministries, 2227
Oakwood, OH, 142
oaths, 7, 29, **959–960, 2126**
  Brethren and Revolutionary War, American, 1106, 2126
  Brethren, as criminal acts, 1058
  Brethren in Christ, 188
  Brethren opposition to secret societies, 1164
  Brethren peace position, 999
  Christian Brethren and, 281
  Christliches Hand-Büchlein (Christian Handbook), 288
  church-state relations, 309
  citizenship, refusal to swear oath of, 720
  Declaration of Principles, 372
  doctrine on, 159, 185
  Dunkard Brethren, 409, 941
  Eller family, 440
  England, allegiance to, 2078
  ethics, 457
  Eyman, Peter, 464
  Frenkendorf, 516
  governor oath of office, 222
  Heidelberg Catechism, 593
  Hutterian Society of Brothers, 640
  "Message of the Brethren Ministry," 818
  nonswearing, 959–960
  Old German Baptist Brethren, 967, 2233
  in other religious groups, 69
  Pennsylvania, 310
  police, Brethren as, 1041
  Powers, Valentine, questioning, 1050
  refusal to swear, and sanctification, 1142
  refusal to swear, and Sermon on the Mount, 1169
  Revolutionary War, 176, 1059
  Rowland, Gasper, taking, 1126
  Sauer, Christopher, II, defense of, 1146
  Solingen Brethren, 1258
  Stutzman, Jacob, 1233
  Traut, Johann Henrich, imprisoned for refusal to take oath, 1270
  Uwharrie German Baptist Brethren Church, NC, 1299
Obadiah School of the Bible at Bethel (Assemblies of Yahweh, PA), 68
O'Bannon Baptist Church, OH, Church of the Brethren, *See* Stonelick Church of the Brethren, OH
Obannon Creek, OH, congregation migration of Brethren, 829
Obannon German Baptist Church, 1224
Obed, Brother, *See* Höcker, Ludwig
Obededom, Brother, *See* Mack, Alexander, Jr.
obedience, *See* discipleship
  Brethren Doctrine of Salvation, 1140
  church membership, 813
  ethics, 457

law, doctrine of, 729
  legalism and, 735
  love, relationship to, 761
  redemption, 1090
  sanctification, 1142
Ober, Barbara F., 2288
Ober, Cora B. Hess, 960
Ober, David, 1732
Ober, Henry Kulp, 658, **960,** 1732, 2032
  Elizabethtown College, 437
  Interchurch World Movement (IWM), 658
Ober, James Allen, 1732
Ober, Janet Lee, 2288
Ober, Mary Velma, 1842, **2388**
  on CB missions to China, 2349
Ober, Michael R., 960
Ober-Miller, David (Skip) Charles, 2288
Ober, Stanley H., 1732
Ober, Susan B. Kulp, 960
Ober, Susan (later Widdowson), 1343
Oberbrunner, Kary, 2288
Oberholser family, *See* Oberholtzer family
Oberholser, J. E., 1732
Oberholtzer, D. V., 318
Oberholtzer family, **960,** 1338, 2010, 2032
  genealogy, 534
Oberholtzer, H. M., 318, 362, 505, 515, 562
  Mansfield, OH, Walcrest Brethren Church, preaching, 787
  Quiet Dell Brethren Church, PA, pastor, 1076
  Roanoke, VA, First Brethren Church, pastor, 1113
Oberholtzer, Harvey Melvin, 16, 130, 1732
  Brethren Church minister, 960
Oberholtzer, Isaiah Ebersole, 1732, 1842, 2032
Oberholtzer, Jacob, 960, 2001
Oberholtzer, Levi Nolt, 2032
Oberholtzer, Lizzie Burkholder Weaver, 2032
Oberholtzer, Magdalena (later Landes) descendants, 1911
Oberholtzer, Martin, 960, 1941–1942
Oberholtzer [Overholtzer?], Margeret Elizabeth Weybright, 1276, 1732, 1842, 1942, **2388**
Oberholtzer, Samuel
  Terre Hill branch of family, 960
Oberholtzer, Samuel Andrew, 1732
Oberholtzer, (Terre Hill) family, 2034
Oberholtzer, W. E., 1732
Oberholtzer, William H., 1732
Oberholzer, Clarence
  McFarland, CA, Church of the Brethren, free minister, 774
Oberholzer, Frances (later Nicarry)
  Nicarry, Wayne A., 2231
Oberland region, Canton Bern, Switzerland, 697
Oberlausitz
  Zinzendorf, Nikolaus Sudwig, Count von, 1399
Oberlin, Allen A., 4, 752, 1732
Oberlin, Charles Royer, 576, 752, 1732
  Monticello/Pike Creek Church of the Brethren, IN, pastor, 872
  Peru, IN, Church of the Brethren, pastor, 1010
Oberlin School of Theology
  Boyer, James L., 2139
  Weimer, Glen Emerson, 1327

Oberstenfeld, 697
  Germany, 545
obituaries, 2188
  Fort Wayne, Co., IN, records, 2099
Oblinger, Samuel (L. Olinger?), 719, 1732
O'Brien, Charles Willis, 1732
O'Brien family, 1345
O'Brien, Grace (later Surbey), 1241
O'Brien, Jacob, 467
Oburn, L. E., 2288
Oburn, Vanessa, 2137
Ocala, FL, Grace Brethren Church, **2232**
O'Callaghan, Edmund B., 1860
occupations of Old German Baptist Brethren, 2234
Ocealis, Michael A., 2288
Ocean Grove, NJ, 197
  as Annual Meeting location, 36
Ocean, NJ, 1351
Oceana Co., MI, 265
oceans
  lessons from, 2012
Ochiltree Co., TX, 1312
Ochocki, John Carl, 1852
Ochocki, Kathleen Elizabeth, 1852
Ochs, Elizabeth, 146
Ockenga, Harold John, 2179
Ockerman, Daniel, 961, 1340, 1732
  Ridge Church of the Brethren, OH, minister, 1108
Ockerman, David Allen, 1732
Ockerman, David Earl, 109, 1732, 2304
Ockerman family
  Nicholas Co. German Baptist Brethren Church, 935
Ockerman, J. E., 1732
Ockerman, Joseph, 2032
Ockerman, Leslie Elwood, 705, 1732
Ocmulgee (Armudgee) congregation, GA, 540
Octavia, NE, Church of the Brethren, 115, **960,** 1349
Oda, Wilbur H., 1860–1861, 2032
Odd Fellows, *See* secret societies
  Brethren opposition to secret societies, 1163
Odd Fellows Hall
  Staunton, VA, 1219
  Waynesboro, VA, 1324
  use of, and division of congregations, 1135
  Westernport, MD, 1337
O'Deens, Daniel P., 2288
O'Dell, Cecil G., II, 2288
O'Dell family, 241
O'Dell, Roger, 1345, 1732
Ogden, W. A., 673
O'Diam, Eva
  on love and justice, 2349
O'Donnell, Gerald Francis, 1732
Oehler, Robert Georg, 2032
Oehrle family, 2032
Oehrle, Johannes, 1923
Oehrlin, Thomas, 1923
Oellig, Catherine Nicodemus, *159*
Oellig, Charles Rush, 1732
Oellig family, 1876
Oellig, Ruby K. (later Wampler), 1317
OEPC, *See* On Earth Peace
Oesch, Jeffrey, 1732
Oessenich, Frank, 2288
offerings, **960,** 1379
Office of Personnel Administration (CB)

placement of pastors, 1028
offices, civil, *See* elections
overseer of the poor, 986
offices of the church, *See* ministers; ministry
dress for, 402
Dunkard Brethren, 409–410
Offord, Ralph E., 1732
Ogando, Luis, 2173
Ogan's Creek, IN, Church of the Brethren, 30
North Manchester, IN, Church of the Brethren, 949, 960–961
Ogburn, Carolee Leichty, 1842
Ogburn, Howard L., 740, 1732, 1842
Ogden, David Edward, 2288
Ogden family, 1359
Ogden, Frances C. Coffman, 961
Ogden, Galen Brown, 139, 195, 216, 539, 714, **961**, 1732, 1861, 2032, 2140, 2304
San Bernardino, CA, Church of the Brethren, pastor, 1141
Ministry and Home Mission Commission (CB), 848
Ogden, John, 2032
Ogden, John, family
genealogy of, and Ogden, Galen Brown, 961
Ogden, Oma Marie Abuhl, 961
Ogden, Orlando, 468, 961, 1733
Ogden, Russell W., 12, 377
Ogden, Ruth Brown, 961
Ogden, UT, 1299
Ogden, W. L., 1733
Ogden, W. Russell, 377, 725
South Bend, IN, Ireland Road Grace Brethren Church, pastor, 1203
Ogden, Wilbur Lee, 1733
Ogden, William, 1285
Ogden, William Augustus, 490, 560, 673, 725, 759, **961,** 1733
Ogden, William Russell, 1733
Ogemaw Co., MI, 1400
Ogg family, 1322
Root River Church of the Brethren, MN, 1122
Ogg, Joel, 273
Ogg, John, 1733
Root River Church of the Brethren, MN, minister, 1122
Ogg, Joseph, 719, 1322, 1323, 1733
Root River Church of the Brethren, MN, minister, 1122
Ogier, Lois McNeil, 2032
Ogle, Alfred, 1733
Middle Creek Church of the Brethren, IA, minister, 825
Ogle Co., IL, 724, 1219, 1333, 2032
Garber, Samuel, 529
Maryland Brethren immigrating to, 798
Naperville Church of the Brethren, 913
Pine Creek Church of the Brethren, IL, 1024
Polo, IL, Church of the Brethren, 1045
Preiß (Price) family, 1055
Rowland (Roland) family, 1127
Ogletown, PA, 1348
Ohio, 163, 176, 181, 1883, 2038–2039
Amish in, 26
Brethren in, 15
Brethren movement, 317
Brethren settlement, 961–963

Cassel (Kassel) family, 260
Church of the Brethren
Middle District, 1876–1976, 1915
northeastern Ohio, history of, 1917
northwestern Ohio, history of, 1924
southern Ohio, history of, 1945
communitarianism, 329
Fellowship of Brethren Churches, southern Ohio district, history of, 1916
genealogy, 2188
Grace Brethren Church, 303
Grace Schools (Grace Theological Seminary, Grace College), 563
history of northeast, 2111
history of northwest, 2102
Indiana, 652
Michigan Brethren settlement, 823
migrant labor camps, 827
migration of Brethren, 829
minorities, ethnic and racial, 849
North Carolina Brethren, 946
North Dakota Brethren, 946
northwestern, Brethren in, 1993
Ohio Falls Cities, 1967
Old Brethren, 971
Old German Baptist Brethren, 967, 970, 2234
Old Order German Baptist Church, 972
Pennsylvania Brethren and settlement, 1004
religious movements in, 2085
Rural Life Association, 12
Scheublein, Christian and Esther Neff, children of, 1178
Southern, Church of the Brethren in, 1962
Southern District name index, 2324
Ohio Brethren Action Movement (NO-BAM), 179
Ohio Conference (BC), 12
Ohio State University, 696
Ohio Valley, *See* frontier; Migration
German Baptist settlement, 1928
Ohler, Barbara
autobiography of, 2362
Ohlsson, Hans, 1733
Ohlwein, Johann Werner
Mullen, Lena Belle Ohlwin on descendants of, 2348
Ohlwin, Lena Belle on descendants of, 2348
Ohlwin, Lena Belle
on Ohlwein, Johann Werner and descendants, 2348
Ohmart, Catherine, 352
Ohmart family
Neher family, related to, 922
Parsons Old German Baptist Brethren Church, KS, 994
Ohmart, Lydia (later Grisso), 574
Ohmart (Omert), Noah, 224, 1733
Ohmart, S. M., 1733
Ohmart, Sophia (later Frantz), *509*
Ohmert family, 396
oikoumene, See ecumenism
Oiman, Peter, *See* Eyman, Peter
Oimanites, *See* New Dunkard Church of God
Oiness, Sylvia Marie, 963, 1842, 2032, **2388**
ship sinking en route to Africa, 863

Okanogan Co., WA, 1342, 1364
Ellisforde, Church of the Brethren, WA, 442
Myers Creek Church of the Brethren, WA, 905
Okanogan Valley Church of the Brethren, WA, *See* Ellisforde Church of the Brethren, WA
Okaw, IL, 371
Church of the Brethren, 270, 713, *See* La Place, IL, Church of the Brethren
Osage Church of the Brethren, KS, 983
Oke, Festus E., 2289
Okeechobee, FL
Sebring, FL, J. H. Moore Memorial Church of the Brethren mission, 1162
Grace Brethren Church Sebring, FL, Church of the Brethren, **963–964**
Okello, Theresa, 2127–2128
Oklahoma, 163, 1906
Brethren movement, 217, 273
Brethren settlement, **964**
District of, and orphans, care for, 982
Dunkard Brethren Church
fiction, references in, 2099
frontier, 519
land rush, and Osage Church of the Brethren, KS, 983
migration of Brethren, 830
missions, *858*
Old German Baptist Brethren, 967
orphans, care for, 276
place-names, Brethren, 1028
Oklahoma City, OK, 2023
Church of the Brethren
Clark, C. C., **964**
Oklahoma district
Texas and Louisiana district, merger with, 939
Oklahoma Dust Bowl
Griggs, OK, Bethel Church of the Brethren, 573
Oklahoma Live Wire Union, 992
Guthrie, OK, Church of the Brethren, 576
Okley, John H., 1733
Olathe, KS, Church of the Brethren, 415, 683, 1311
Wade Branch, KS, congregation, **964**
Olathe Old German Baptist Brethren Church, KS, **964**
old black book
hymnals, 642
Old Brethren, **964–965**, 2032, *See also* Old German Baptist Brethren
automobile, reaction to, 75
chart of Brethren bodies, place on, 1403–1405
Cripe, Owen C., 1255
description of, 2095
developed from Old German Baptist Brethren, 1250
guide to, 1997
membership in 2232
Moss, Loring Isaac, 878
Old Brethren Christian Schools, 2232
Old Brethren German Baptist Church, 965
Old Brethren's Reasons, 965
Old German Baptist Brethren divisions,

964–965, 969–970
Old Order Fellowships, 971, 972
Old Order German Baptist Church, 972, 1403–1405
Ontario, 975
Pilgrim, The, 1023
The Old Brethren
historical writing, 612
Old Brethren Christian Schools, **2232**
Old Brethren Church, Salida, CA, 1363
Old Brethren German Baptist Church, OH, **965**
The Old Brethren's Reasons
Old Brethren, 964, **965**
Old Brick Church
Franklin Co. Church of the Brethren, VA, 507
Old Brick schoolhouse
Wood Grove Brethren-Christian Parish, MI, 1363
Old Conemaugh congregation, PA, 752
"Old Evangelical" movement
Historic Peace Churches, 608
Old Fairview Church
George's Creek Old German Baptist Brethren Church, PA, 540
Old Fellows Lodges used as meeting houses, 683
Old Fields, WV, 1341
Old Folks and Orphans Home (CB), Mexico, IN, **965–966**
old folks homes, *See* Brethren Homes for the Aged; retirement homes and communities
Old Furnace Church of the Brethren, WV, 106, **966**
Old Furnace congregation, WV, 1339, 1345
Old German Baptist Brethren (OGBB), 75, *483, 509, 589, 966,* **966–970,** *968,* 2020, 2032–2033, 2033, 2052, **2233–2235,** *2234, See also* Old Order movement
abortion, 2127
admission into the church, 5
aid for Appalachia, 44
alcohol, use of, 16
Annual Meeting, *See* Old German Baptist Brethren Annual Meeting
and anointing, 39
archival policy, 52
authority of scripture, 133
automobiles, 1271
automobiles and, 228
baptism accepted by Dunkard Brethren, 409
and beards, 103
Bible translations and versions, 138
Bible translations, response to, **2137**
bibliography, 1871
books about, 747
Bowman Brethren, 364
Brethren Encyclopedia, Inc., **2143**
Brethren Heritage Center, **2148**
Brethren identity, **2149**
Brethren music, 899
burial customs and, 230
business doctrine, 235
California, 238, 239, 2313
camping movement, 250
Canada, 250
capital punishment, 253
caps, 254
carpets, use of, 256

chaplaincy, 271
charismatic movement, 272
chart of Brethren bodies, place on, 1403–1405
children, teaching, 2159–2160
Christian day school movement, 282, **2160**
Christian education, 283, 284
Christ's Assembly and, 280
church extensions, 295
Cimarron River, CO, Old German Baptist Brethren Church, 313
communion, 328
Conference of Historic Peace Churches, 333
confession of faith, 333
Conscientious Objector Committee of, 2349
conscientious objectors, 336
religious issues, statements on, 2107
conscientious objectors and, 2336, 2349
consensus, 337
Conservative German Baptist Brethren, 338
controversy over Sunday school literature, 1236
cookbooks, traditional, 340
courts of law, attitudes toward use of, 728
Credential(s) Committee, 351
Crist family, 353
Davy, Henry Dorsey, 364
deacons, 369
dedication of infants, 372
degrees of ministry, 374
delegates, role of, 375
description of, 2095
devotional literature, 381
discipline, 389
disfellowship, 388
disputes of 1870s and 1880s, 1151
district organization, 391
division of congregations, 392
divisions, 970
divisions of, *See* divisions
divorce and remarriage, 1099, 2145
divorce issues, 389, 393
Doctrinal Treatise, 394, 2149
drama, position on, 399
dress, *146*
dress, order of, 402, 404
Driver family, 405
Easter, 416
ecumenism, 423
education, 428
Edwards, Lorraine Frantz on, 2328, 2329
elder, 433
elder's table, 2131
election of church officers, 434
electricity, 434
elementary education, 435
environmental issues, **2177**
eschatology, 454
ethics, 457
evangelicalism, **2179**
evangelism, 460, **2180**
evolution, 463
expelled members, 7
Fairview, MO, Shoal Creek Church of the Brethren, 468

family, 474, 2145
farm machinery, 476
farming, 477, **2181**
Faw, Jacob, 481
feetwashing, 364, 396, 481, 1186
fellowship, 482
Filbrun family, 490
flags, 493
Flora, (Flory) family, 495
Florida, 497
foreman, 502
fraternal relations, 510
Fraternity, NC, congregation, 946
Fraternity Old German Baptist Brethren Church, NC, 511
free ministry, 513, 1137
Free Will Dunkers, 514
frock coats, 1029
fundamentalism, 522
funerals, 524
furniture, 525
Garber (Garver, Gerber) family, 529, 530
genealogy, 535
generation of congregation near Salem Church of the Brethren, OH, 1138
German Baptist Brethren, 540, 973
German Baptists, 542
Germantown Trust, 2189
Germany, 546
Gingerich (Kingery) family, 549
Good (Guth) family, 556
gospel music, 559, 561
grape juice, 566
group name modifications, 910
hairstyle, 579
hats, 589
Hess family, 601
Hess, James Arthur, 2198
Hess, Maurice Abram, 601, 2336
historical libraries, 610
historical writing, 612
history, 290, 1985
holy kiss and handclasp, 698
home education, 2203
home schooling, 2160, 2161
homestead of, *146*
homosexuality, 2204
honorific titles, 1266
Howard, IN, Church of the Brethren, 633
humanitarianism, 636
humility, 636
hymnals, 642, 696
ice-skating and roler-skating, use of, 26
Idaho, 645
Illinois, 647
Indiana, 147, 652
information technology, church use of, 2208
insurance, 657
Internet use, 2178
isolationism, 1297
Jamison family, 668
jewelry, 671
Jews, 671
Johnsville Church of the Brethren, VA, 675
Kansas, 682
language, inclusive, 2214
lay preachers, 730
laying on of hands, 731
Leedy Brethren, 364, 368

Lemon, John H., 1129
lining of hymns, 744
Lord's prayer, 757
love feast, 763, 764
maintenance of statistics, 1219
Mallott, Floyd Ellwood, 784, 2005
marriage, 389, 796, 2145
mass media, 800, 2145, 2218
medical missions, 810
membership trends 1980 to 2000, 2220
military service, 311, 388, 832
Miller, Marcus on marriage practices and, 2347
ministry, 845
minorities, ethnic and racial, 850, 851
Mishler family, 852
missions, 9, 860
missions, short-term, 2226
Missouri congregations, 865
Mohler, David, 1255
motion pictures, 879
Murray family, 898
music, 2227
musical instruments, 900, 2228
Musselman family, 901
mutual aid, 902–903
National Service Board for Religious Objectors (NSBRO) cooperation, 917
neckties, avoidance of, 921
neoorthodox influence, 923
Nolt, Stephen M. on, 2349
nonconformity, 3, 941, 967
noncreedalism, 943
North Dakota congregations, 946, *947*, 967
Oak Grove Old German Baptist Brethren Church, OH, 350, 956
oaths, taking of, 959, 967
Ohio, 349
Ohio membership, 961, 967
Old Brethren, 964, 970
Old Brethren German Baptist Church, 965
The Old Brethren's Reasons, 965
Old German Baptist Brethren, 970, 972
Old Order Fellowships, **970–972**, 972
Old Order German Baptist Church, **972**, 2235,
Old Order Notes, 973
Ontario, 975
opposition to innovations, 73, 75
opposition to labor unions, 716
opposition to radio and television, 1251
opposition to secret societies, 1164
opposition to telephone use, 1250
ordination, 980
Oregon, 981
origins of, 178–179
parochial schools, 1163
peace education, 1002
peace position, 1000
Pennsylvania membership, 1005
pension system, lack of, 1008
Peters Creek Church of the Brethren, VA, 1011
Peters family, 1012
Pfoutz, Isaac, 1015
photographs, 1020
placement of pastors, 1028
Portis, KS, North Solomon Church of the Brethren, 1048
position on alcoholic beverages, 1252

practices of, 698, 2067
prayer meetings, acceptance by Annual Meeting, 1051
prayer, posture in, 1052
prayer veil, 1053
Price, Jacob, 1056–1057
principles and practices, 1989
prohibition, 1061
publications of, 2087–2088
publishing, 1068
Puderbaugh family, 1070
pulpits, 1071
queries, 1076
reaction to the automobile, 75
rebaptism, 1085
Reinhardt family, 1094
reprinting of *The Wisdom and Power of God* (Nead, P.), 919
Resolutions Passed at the Special Conference, 1100
restoration of disciplined members, 1102
Roberson, Holly on, 2352
Root family, 1122
sermons, 1168
Service Committee, 1169
Shoup, William J., minister, 1179
Shuman, L. Herman on ordinances and, 2356
simple life, 1183
singing, unaccompanied, 1185
"singings," 1186
sources on, 2313, 2317, 2319
Spruce Run, WV, Old German Baptist Brethren Church, 1216
stand on Vietnamese War, 1305
Standing Committee, 1217
symbols and logos, attitudes about, 2147
television viewing prohibited, 1251
temperance movement, 388
tents used by, 1254
theological education, 1256
theology of, 1259, 1261, 2254
Thompson, Charles Dillard on, 2360–2361
tobacco use, 1266
urban ministry and, 2257
use of English language, 725
The Vindicator, 1306–1307
Virginia, 1308
wedding customs, 1326
West Virginia, 1336
Willoughby, William G. on, 2363
wine, in communion services, 1349
Wisconsin, 1354
women, roles of, 1361, 1362, 2263
World War I, 1370
World War II, 1372
worship and, 1376, 1378, 2266–2267
Wyoming, 1380
Yoder, Rosa L. on obituaries, 2364
youth and, 1392, 2268
Old German Baptist Brethren Annual Meeting, **36–37**, 75, *966, 968,* 969, 972, 2198, 2203, 2233, *2234,* 2263, 2268
accomodations at, 36
Flory, Abraham, 497
location of, 36
messengers (delegates) to, 36
messengers to, 819
Mexico Old German Baptist Brethren

Church, IN, held at, 821
moderators
Metzger, Jacob, 819
Musselman, Samuel, 901
office of, 865–866
Skiles, Jacob W., 1188
opposition to labor unions, 716
Pentecost, held at, 1008
polity, 1042, 1044
Prices Creek Old German Baptist Brethren Church, OH, hosting, 1057
queries, process for, 36, 37
Receiving Committee, 36, 1085
schedule of, 36
sense of community fostered by, 37
at Wolf Creek Congregation, Montgomery Co., OH, (1908, 1972), *34*
Old German Baptist Brethren Centerview, Holmsville, NE, 921
Old German Baptist Brethren congregation, CA, 238, 239
Old German Baptist Brethren Hymnal, 1039
Old German Baptist Brethren of Greene Co., OH
Old German Baptist Brethren, division of, 970
Old German Baptist Brethren Old Folks and Orphans Home (CB), 276
Old German Baptist Brethren Service Committee
Skiles, Jacob W., 1189
Old German Bible, *139*
Old Mennonite Church
Mennonite Church (MC), 815
Old Order Amish, *See* Amish
Old Order Annual Meetings, *See* Old German Baptist Brethren Annual Meetings
Peters Creek Church of the Brethren, VA, 1011
Old Order German Baptist Church, 972
Old Order Fellowships, **970–972**
automobile, impact of, 74, 75
bibliography, 1877, 1883
farming, 479
nonconformity, 940
offerings, 960
Ohio membership, 961
Old German Baptist Brethren, 965
Ontario, 975
"Order of the Brethren," 976
traditionalist branches, 970–972, *971*
Old Order hymnal of 1882, 1185, 1186
Old Order movement, 8, 75, 102, 106, 178, 206, 396, 406, 696, **972–973,** 2016, *See also* Old German Baptist Brethren
and Annual Meeting authority, 33
automobiles and, 228
Big Run Old German Baptist Brethren Church, OH, 142
Black River Church of the Brethren, OH, 144
Black River Old German Baptist Brethren Church, OH, 145
Brethren movement, 178
Brush Creek, MO, Old German Baptist Brethren Church, 224
Buckeye, KS, Church of the Brethren,

226

Carson City, MI, Old German Baptist Brethren Church, 256
Cedar Co., IA, Old German Baptist Brethren Church, 263
Cedar Grove, TN, Church of the Brethren, 264
Cedar, IA, Church of the Brethren, 263
Chestnut Grove, WV, Old German Baptist Brethren Church, 274
choirs and, 279
church membership, 813
conservation movement, 337
cookbooks, traditional, 340–341
Cover, Joseph Immel, 348
Davy, Henry Dorsey, 365
discipline, 388
disciplined community, 292
disfellowship, 365
division of 1881, 410
dress, order of, 402
Eel River Church of the Brethren, IN, 429
Eight Mile Old German Baptist Brethren Church, KS, 431
Fairview Church of the Brethren, IA, 468
Fairview Church of the Brethren, IN, 468
Falling Spring Church of the Brethren, PA, 471
Falling Spring Old German Baptist Brethren Church, PA, 471
Fast Element opinion of, 480
first love feast held in FL, 1024–1025
First Petition, 491
Flat Rock Old German Baptist Brethren Church, OH, 494
foreman, 502
Frantz, Aaron, 508
Fraternity Church of the Brethren, NC, 511
Freeling Settlement Old German Baptist Brethren Church, WV, 514
fundamentalism, 523
furniture, 525
Garrison Old German Baptist Brethren Church, IA, 531
generation of congregation near Salem Church of the Brethren, OH, 1138
George's Creek Old German Baptist Brethren Church, PA, 540
Germantown Old German Baptist Brethren Church, VA, 544
group name modifications, 910
Harris Creek Church of the Brethren, OH, 585
historical writing, 612
history of, 290
Indiana, 652
Industrial Revolution, 655
interest-taking, 658
Iowa, 662
Johnson City, TN, Knob Creek Church of the Brethren, 672
Kinsey, Samuel, support for, 919
    mandatory decisions, 787
Maple Grove Old German Baptist Brethren Church, OH, 791
Maryland Brethren, 798
Metzger, Jacob, 819
Miami Valley Elders, 823
Miami Valley, OH, 961

Miami Valley Petition, 823
Middlefork Old German Baptist Brethren Church, IN, 826
millennialism, 834
Miller, Abram, 955
missions, 858, 860
Mohler, Samuel, 868
Moorehead, Michael, minister, 997
Mount Cassell Old German Baptist Brethren Church, WV, 880
Murray, Samuel M., establishing congregations, 898
Myrtle Point Old German Baptist Brethren Church, OR, 906
Nettle Creek Old Baptist Brethren Church memebers, 924
noncreedalism, 942
North Fork Old German Baptist Brethren Church, IN, 947
Oak Grove, OH, congregation (OGBB), 350
Ohio, 261
Olathe Old German Baptist Brethren Church, KS, 964
Old Brethren's Reasons, 965
Old German Baptist Brethren, 966, 969
Old Order Fellowships, 970
Old Order German Baptist Church, 972
"Order of the Brethren," 976
Osceola Church of the Brethren, MO, 984
Owl Creek Old German Baptist Brethren Church, OH, 986
Parsons, KS, Church of the Brethren, 994
Peabody Church of the Brethren, KS, 997
Pennsylvania Brethren and schism, 1005
Pennsylvania congregations, 1005
Peters Creek Old German Baptist Brethren Church, VA, 1012
photography of Brethren, 1020
Pigg River Old German Baptist Brethren Church, VA, 1023
Pipe Creek Church of the Brethren, MD, 1026
Plain People, *See* Robertson, Archibald T.
plain people, 1029
Pleasant Grove Church of the Brethren, KS, 1031
poetry, 1039
polity, 294
Prices Creek Church of the Brethren, OH, 1057
publishing, 1068
Pyrmont, IN, Church of the Brethren, 1073
radio, 1080
Red Oak Ridge German Baptist Brethren Church, WV, 1089
Resolutions Passed at the Special Conference, 1100
revival meetings, opposition to, 1103
Robins, IA, Church of the Brethren, 1115
Rockingham and Shenandoah Counties Old German Baptist Brethren Church, VA, 1118
Rome Old German Baptist Brethren Church, OH, 1121
Rouzerville Church of the Brethren,

PA, 1125
salaried ministry, 206, 845
Sandy Creek Old German Baptist Brethren Church, WV, 1143
schism, 298
Shiloh Church of the Brethren, WV, members leaving to join, 1177
Shoal Creek Old German Baptist Brethren Church, Newton Co., MO, members of, 1178
Sidney, OH, Trinity Church of the Brethren, losing members, 1181
Siler, George V., 1181
singing, 1185
Skiles, Jacob W., 1188
State Center, IA, Old German Baptist Brethren Church, 1217
Stonelick Church of the Brethren, OH, 1224
Stony Creek Church of the Brethren, OH, 1225
Sunday school, opposition to, 1239
Sunday schools, 427
Swedeland Valley Old German Baptist Brethren Church, WV, 1243
Tennessee, 1253
Theological Writings on Various Subjects (Nead, P.), 1258
Thornapple, MI, congregation (GBB, CB), 248
Tipp City, OH, West Charleston Church of the Brethren, 1265
traditionalists, 972–973
West Branch Church of the Brethren, IL, 1333
West Nimishillen, OH, congregation, 946
White Oak Grove Old German Baptist Brethren Church, OH, 1341
wine, in communion services, 1349
Wolf Creek Church of the Brethren, OH, 1355
Yellow Creek Church of the Brethren, IN, 1384
York Co. Old German Baptist Brethren Church, 1389
Old Order Notes
    genealogy, 535, 2188
    historical writing, 612
    Old German Baptist Brethren, 973
    publishing, 1069
    Wagoner, Gerald C., Sr. (OGBB) and, 2259
Old Order Resolutions
    Oak Hill Old German Baptist Brethren Church, VA, 957
Old Order River Brethren, *See* Brethren in Christ (River Brethren)
Old Peoples and Orphans Home, Church of the Brethren
    Pinecrest Manor (CB), 1025
Old Peoples and Orphans Home of the German Baptist and Brethren Church of the District of Northern Illinois
    Pinecrest Manor (CB), 1025
Old Pine Church of the Brethren, WV, *See* White Pine Church of the Brethren, WV
Old Pine Church, WV, 1341
    Old Spring Creek meetinghouse, Hershey, PA, *600*
Old Stony Creek meetinghouse

(Noblesville, PA), 109

Old Testament, *See* Bible; New Testament; specific books
  Anabaptist thought, role in, 29
  Believers Church Commentary Series, 2134
  Brethren canon, 133
  dietary rules, 147
  Huffaker, John L. on monologues on calls of leaders in, 2338
  interpretation of the Bible, 134
  oaths, taking of, 959
  survey of, 1960
  textbook on, 1961
  translations, 138

Old Union congregation, IN, 1341

Old Union meetinghouse, Tipp City, OH, 1265

Old Valley Church of the Brethren, VA, *See* Botetourt Co. Church of the Brethren, VA

Old Vlamingen Mennonites
  Huizinga (Huisinga), Jacob Dircks, 635

older persons, *See* aged persons

Oldham, Joseph H., 422, 1368

Olds, Dan W., 2033

Olds, Doris R., 2033
  on Walnut Grove CB Cemetery, 2349

Oldwine, C., 1733

Olean Church of the Brethren, VA, **973**
  Oakvale Church of the Brethren, WV, 958–959

Olevianus, Caspar, 593

Oley congregation, PA, 697, 699, 1387

Oley, John
  Salkum, WA, Community Church of the Brethren, minister, 1139

Oley meetinghouse, Pricetown, PA, 1237

Oley, PA, 175
  Baumann, Mattheis, residence, 925

Oley, PA, congregation
  Mohrsville Church of the Brethren, PA, 869
  Pennsylvania settlement, 1004
  Pricetown Meetinghouse, 1057
  Ritter, Daniel, helping to establish, 1111

Oley section, Philadelphia (now Berks) Co., PA, 697

Oley Valley, Berks Co., PA
  annals, 1912

Oligee, David S., 2289

Olin, O. P., 1733

Olinger, Antone Tony, 1733

Olinger, Emma (later Shank), *See* Shank, Emma Olinger

Olivares family
  Sanctuary Movement and, *2245*

Olive Branch chapel, IN
  organized from Nettle Creek Church of Brethren, 923

Olive Branch congregation, NC, 1233

Olive Branch German Baptist Brethren Church, IN, **973**
  migration of Brethren, 829

Olive Branch of Peace
  Holsinger, Henry Ritz, 622

The Olive Branch of Peace
  Hays, Daniel, 590
  Sanger, Samuel F., coeditor, 1143

Olive Branch school, near Port Royal, PA, 1281

Olive Grove Old German Baptist Brethren

Church, CA, 360, **973**, 981, 1335, **2377**
  example of place name, 911

Olive, Sadie, 1846

Oliver, Claude
  Matteson, MI, Brethren Church, 803

Oliver, David, 1733

Oliver, F. A(be), 142, 1733

Oliver family, 164

Oliver, Gordon V., 2289

Oliver, Ida (later Lindower), 744

Oliver, J. Lincoln, 1733

Oliver, Lilian Hays, 2033

Oliver, Mrs. Claude
  Matteson, MI, Brethren Church, 803

Olivet, OH, 1339
  Church of the Brethren, **973–974**
    history and directory, 1969
  Jonathan Creek congregation
    Greenwood Church of the Brethren, 572

Olivieri, Michael, 1733

Oller, Anna Kathryn, 611, 2033

Oller, Elizabeth Bonebrake, 974

Oller, Jacob Franklin, 235, 441, **974**, 1323, 1733
  Steiner family, 2378

Oller, Joseph, 974

Oller, Myrtle F., 625

Oller, Rebecca Stoner, 974

Olovsson, M. Victor, 1733

Olsen, John, 1733

Olseröd congregation, 1243

Olson, May E., 140, 1857

Olsson (Olesen), Christian, 1733

Olszewski, Bud, 357, 1365, 2289

Olt, Madelaine (later Rummel), 1842, 2051

Oltiser, Elias, 1733

Oltman, Berwyn Lee, 378, 1956, 1733, 2172
  Gotha, FL, New Covenent Church of the Brethren, 2190

Olustie, OK, 1213

Olympia, WA, 717, 1227
  Church of the Brethren, 269
    Schrock, Mark Y., 1156
  Lacey Community Church, *See* Lacey, WA, Community Church
  urban mission, 1297

Olympic View Community Church of the Brethren, WA, 1247, 1940, *See also* Seattle, WA, Olympic View
  Northhaven Retirement Residence, 951

Olympics, 70 (sidebar)

Omaha, NE
  Grace Brethren Bible Church, **974**
  mission work in, 920
  missions and missionaries in, 2092
  urban mission, 1297
  Peace Church of the Brethren, 346, **974**

Omaja, Cuba, congregation, 355

Omak, WA, Church of the Brethren
  Myers Creek Church of the Brethren, WA, 905, **974**

O'Malley, J. Steven
  on Radical Pietists, 2349

Omdorf, Nancy Sue, 1852

Omman, Abraham, 2289
  Lenexa, KS, Fellowship, 2214

Omstott family
  Scherffig family, related to, 1152

On Earth Peace (OEP) (CB), On Earth

Peace Assembly (OEPA), On Earth Peace Conference (OEPC)
  Brown, Dale Weaver, 2152
  Church of the Brethren, 301
  developed mid-1970s, **2235–2236**
  Gilbert, Martha Rupel, 2190
  history of conference, 1975
  Maryland Brethren activity, 799
  On Earth Peace Conference (OEPC), **974**
  Harman, Hylton, 2196
  Ministry of Reconciliation, 2224
  organizational restructuring and, 2242
  program, 161
  Shank, Glenn H. ("Doc") (BC) and, 2248
  governance, 2163
  youth participation, 2160

On Earth Peace
  Durnbaugh, D. F., editor, 974, 1966

On Election to Grace (Boehme), 156

on-line accounting and financial packages
  Brethren Benefit Trust (BBT), 2140

On the Threefold Life of Man (Boehme), 156

Onas, Effie J., 2106

Ondra, J. N., 286

One Great Hour of Sharing
  Lent, observance of, 737

One Hundred Dunkers for Peace, 179, 301, **974–975**
  West, Daniel, 1331

1-W Service, 2059, *See also* alternative service

O'Neal family
  Outlook, WA, Church of the Brethren, 986

O'Neal, Glenn F., 30, 64, 136, 562, **2236**, 2304

O'Neal, Russell
  Oakvale Church of the Brethren, WV, leadership by, 958

O'Neal, Russell R., 1733

O'Neall, John Belton, 2033

Onega, WV
  Seneca Church of the Brethren, WV, 1166

Oneida, NY, 1397

O'Neill family, 332

Onekama congregation, 1235

Onekama, MI, 179
  Church of the Brethren, 179, 1285
    history of, 1961
  Manistee Co., MI, **975**
  Michigan Brethren settlement, 824

Oneonta, AL, Church of the Brethren, 415, **975**

Onesimus, Brother, *See* Eckerlin, Israel

Onesimus, the Runaway Slave (Brumbaugh), 220, 747

Onkst, D. A., *See* Old German Baptist Brethren

Ontario, Canada, 1870
  Amish in, 26
  Brethren in, mentions of, 1931
  Brethren settlement, **975**
  Old German Baptist Brethren, 967, 970
  Pennsylvania Germans, 1006
  Tunkers (BC), 189

Ontario, OH, Maranatha Grace Brethren Church
  Mansfield, OH, Woodville Grace Brethren Church, 787

opera houses used as meeting houses, 683
Operation Barnabas (FGBC), 533, 2269
　CE National, Inc., 2156
Opocenský, Milan
　on First and Second Reformations,
　　2349
Opperman, Owen, 2033
Opportunity Grace Brethren Church,
　　Spokane, WA, 1212, *See* Spokane
　　Valley Grace Brethren Church,
　　WA
oppression, *See* persecution
　emigration, Brethren, 443
Orange, CA, Grace Brethren Church, **975**
Orange Center, IA, 1321
Orange City, FL, Calvary Grace Brethren
　　Church
Orlando, FL, Grace Brethren Church,
　　975–976, 982
Orange Co., CA
　Santa Ana, CA, Church of the
　　Brethren, 1144
Orange Co., FL, 1353
Orange Co., IN, 740
　Hostetler, Joseph, 631
　migration of Brethren, 829
Orange Co., VA, Church of the Brethren,
　　See Mine Run Church of the
　　Brethren, VA
　Mine Run Church of the Brethren, VA,
　　previous name of, 843
Orange Twp., Black Hawk Co., IA, 1322
oratory, *See* drama
ordained elders
　Brethren Church ministry, 846
ordained ministers, *See* ministers
order of dress, 401
Order of Spiritual Virgins (later the Roses
　　of Sharon)
　Ephrata, 1172
　Hildebrand, Maria (later Mack), 606
"Order of the Brethren", **976**
Old Order Movement, 973
order of the church, 2047, 2064
　Dunkard Brethren delegates, 410
　Hostetler, Daniel W., 631
　Old Order Fellowships, 971
ordinances, 15, 176, **976–980**, 2036, 2040,
　　See also sacraments; specific ordi-
　　nances
　anointing, **39–49**
　baptism and Lord's Supper, 1962
　basic, **184–185**
　Brethren, and Roman Catholic Church,
　　1120
　Brethren Church and, 184
　Brethren movement, 291
　Brethren music, 898
　Brethren, practiced by Adventists in
　　Maine, 782
　Christ's Assembly and, 280
　church membership, 813
　Church of God (New Dunkers), 297
　Dayton, OH, Patterson Park Grace
　　Brethren Church, 367
　debates, 370
　Declaration of Principles, 372
　defense of baptism, 1987
　devotional literature, 381
　discipleship, 386
　Doctrinal Treatise, 394
　dress, 399
　Dunkard Brethren, 409

Ephrata Community, 448
ethics, 457
Far Western Brethren, 475
feetwashing, 396, 481, 482
German Baptist Brethren ordinances,
　　Nead, Peter, impressed by, 918
Gish, Barbara Kindig and James Rufus,
　　550
of God, 698
God's Means of Grace (Yoder), 555
Grace Brethren Church, 1975
Grace Schools (Grace Theological
　　Seminary, Grace College), 563
Herring, Friedrich, 598
highlighted on Brethren's Card, 2152
Historic Peace Churches, 608
historical writing, 612
Hoke, George, 618
holy kiss, 698
Hoyt, Herman Arthur, 634
humility, 636
love feasts, 2001
Mallott, Floyd Ellwood, 784
Mason, Edward, writing about, 799
Menno Simons, 814
"Message of the Brethren Ministry,"
　　818
missions, 857
Mooreites, 875
noncreedalism, 942
observance of
as basis for spirituality, 1209
practiced by followers of Thurman,
　　William C., 1264
Progressive Brethren, 1259
tracts about, 1269
Old Brethren, 964
Old Brethren German Baptist Church,
　　965
Old German Baptist Brethren, 967
Old Order Fellowships, 971
"Order of the Brethren," 976
ordination, 980
outline of practices, National
　　Fellowship of Brethren Churches,
　　1954
Patton, George, disagreement with, 996
plain coat, 1029
Plaster, David R. on, 2350
Pleasant Valley Church of the Brethren,
　　NC, 1035
prayer, 1052
preaching about, 1053
Priesthood of All Believers, 1057
Progressive Brethren, 2008
public worship, 1375
publishing books about, 1069
Reformation, Protestant, and Brethren
　　doctrine, 1092
restitution, 1100
robes, 1115
sacred acts, 976–980, *977, 978, 979*
Schwarzenau Brethren, 1079
Shultz, Joseph R. on Brethren move-
　　ment and, 2356
Shuman, L. Herman on OGBB and,
　　2356
Yoder, Charles Francis, 1386
ordination, 6, **980**, *See also* ministers; min-
　　istry
　baptism and, 719
　chaplaincy positions, 2157–2158
　Church of the Brethren, 846, 2163

commissioning for service, 980
distinction between clergy and laity,
　　718–719
divorced persons, 2141
education, 428
elder, 4, 185, 432
election of church officers, 434
ethics and, 2178
God's Means of Grace (Yoder), 555
Grace Brethren Church ministry, 847
Grassroots, Concerns of the, 2193
Holy Spirit, doctrine of, 624
Hymnal: A Worship Book, 2205
laying on of hands, 730
Mack, Alexander, Jr., 1146
Miller, Donald Eugene, 2223
ministry in the Brethren Church, 2224
National Ordination Council (BC),
　　2229
nonsacramental, and Priesthood of All
　　Believers, 1057
Ordination Study Committee (BC),
　　2141–2142
placement of pastors, 1028
revocation of, 729
Sauer, Christopher, II, 1146
Scholten, Marian, 1155
theology, and 2255
through baptism and annointing, 85
uniformity of for Grace Brethren, 1045
　of women, 1360–1361, 1362,
　　2141, 2157, 2184, 2264, *See also*
　　women as ministers
　women, and Sisters' Society of
　　Christian Endeavor (BC), 1188
Ordway family, 1944
O'Rear, Godfrey, 1733
Oregon
　Brethren in, 14, 88
　Brethren movement in, 217
　Brethren settlement, **980–981**
　Church of the Brethren history, 1983
　conscientious objectors, 337
　Dairy Farm Assignments, 359
　Far Western Brethren, 476
　frontier, 519
　migration of Brethren, 830
　missions and missionaries, 295
　Old German Baptist Brethren, 239,
　　967, 970
　Universalists, 1292, 1293
Oregon, IL, 1333
Oregon School for the Deaf
　Early, John B., 414
Oregon Short Line Railroad, 155, 1289
　Brethren colonization, **981**
　Idaho, 645
　migration of Brethren, 830
Oregon Territory, 177
　Weigle family, 1327
Oren, Alva Warren, 1733
Oren, Ira Aaron, 264, 1733
Oren, Kenneth W., 2289
Oren, Noah, 257, 1733
organ
　Rarick, Ron on Henry Kurtz, 2351
organ transplants
　burial customs and, 230
organization, *See* polity
organs, *See* musical instruments
　Kurtz, Henry, *800,* 899, 900
Orient, *See* Asia
Oriental meetinghouse

Lost Creek Church of the Brethren, PA, 760

Origen of Alexandria, 296
  agape meals, 757
  oaths, taking of, 959
  peace in Christian church history, 998
original sin, **981**
  human nature, doctrine of, 635
Orion congregation (DB), North Canton, OH, 708, 981, 1241
  Myers, Paul R., deacon, minister, elder, 904
  Shroyer, Reuben, 1180
Oriskany, VA, Brethren Church, 981
Orlando Community Church of the Brethren, FL, 1353
Orlando, FL
  Church of the Brethren, *See* Winter Park, FL, Church of the Brethren
  Community Church of the Brethren, **981**
  Grace Brethren Church, 719, **981–982**
    Calvary Grace Brethren Church, 975
    Jackson, Edward A., 2209
  Highland Community Church
    Community Church of the Brethren, 981
  STAKE (BC) and, 2252
Orleans Co., VT, 1304
  Irasburg Grace Brethren Church, VT, 662
Orme, Lawrence S., 2289
Ormond Beach congregation, CA
  example of place name, 911
Ormond Beach, FL, Grace Brethren Church, **982**
Orndorff, Jan M. R., 2289
Orner (Urner), Martin, *See* Urner, Martin
Oronoco Church of the Brethren, VA
  Amherst Co., VA, **982**
  Mount Vernon Church of the Brethren, VA, 887
Oronoque, KS, Maple Grove Brethren Church
  Norcatur, KS, Maple Grove Brethren Church, 944
Oroville, WA
  Shamberger, George A., 1171
orphans and orphanages
  Aged, Infirm and Orphans' Home, Darlow KS
    Wise, John, 1354
  American Advisory Committee for China Relief, 277
  Bhagat, Premchand Ganeshji, 131
  Brethren's Orphan Home (CB), 276
    Bulsar, India, 131
  care for, 5–6, 8, 18, 982–983
  Carlisle, PA, 1388
  Child Rescue Home (CB), 275
  Child Rescue Services (Aide-aux-Enfants), 276
  Child Rescue Work (CB), 276
  The Children's Society of the Church of the Brethren, 276
  Church of the Brethren, 305
  Collegiants, 324
  Eglon, WV, *See* Maple Grove Child Rescue Home
  Emmert, David, 235, 444
  famine relief, 475

Forward Movement (five-year plan), 276
Geiger, Mary Schwenk, 533
General Child Rescue Committee, 276
German Baptist Brethren's Home Society, 276, 540–541, 964
  girls' home, Linz, Austria, 746
  Greece, 569
  Helping Hands, 1962
  Hilton, George William, 607
  Home for Orphan and Friendless Children, 625
  Home of the Children's Aid Society, 625
  homes for, 25, 204
  humanitarianism, 636
  Imler, Tobias F., 648
  India, 649, 651
  India orphanages, 651
  Indiana, 652
  Italy, 200
  Kansas, 410, 682
  list of institutions
    international, 1831
    USA, 1827
  Maple Grove Child Rescue Home (CB), 789
  medical care, 810
  Miller, Eliza Belle, missionary, 837
  minorities, ethnic and racial, 850
  mission schools, 853
  missions, 861, 2224
  Near East Foundation care for, 920
  Old Folks and Orphans Home (Girard, IL) (CB), 276
  Old Folks and Orphans Home (Mexico Welfare Home, Mexico, IN), 1264–1265, 1295
  Old Folks Home (CB), Timberville, VA, 966
  Orphans' and Old Folks' Home, Sulphur Springs, IN, **983**, 1295
  Pennsylvania Church of the Brethren, 1005
  Pietism, 1022
  Ping Ting Chou boys' school, China, 1303
  Pleasant Hill Village, 1033
  Plymouth Brethren, 1039
  post-WWII aid to Netherlands, 923
  retirement homes and, 1102
  Rhodes, William, administrator, 377, 1107
  Sheridan House, Denver, CO, 1209
  Shirk, Bertha Ryan, missionary to India, 1177
  Smyrna, 1280
  social welfare, 1198
  Stover, Wilbur Brenner, 1226
  Sulphur Springs, IN, 983, 1295
  Texas, 276
Orphans' Home, Timberville, VA, **983**
Orr, Alphonse E., 1733
Orr family, *See Out of the Melting Pot*
Orr, Samuel M., 572, 1733
Orrison, Lillie, 342
Orrville, OH, 1221
  Church of the Brethren
    Paradise Church of the Brethren, divided from, 992
    congregation, 279
      West Nimishillen, OH, congregation, 945

Ort, David Allen, 2289
Ortega, Frank, 2289
Orth family, 1927
Orthodox Churches, *See* Eastern Orthodox Churches
Orthodoxy
  holy kiss used in, 698
Osage Church of the Brethren, KS, **983**
Osage Co., KS, 682
  Plum Creek Old German Baptist Brethren Church, KS, 1038
Osage, KS, congregation, 173, 226, 273
Osage, Sasketchewan, Canada, 15
Osborn, John, 1733
Osborne, Beldon, 518
Osborne, Betty
  Simi Valley, CA, Grace Brethren Church, 1182
Osborne, Bristoe
  Shelton Church of the Brethren, NC, pastor in, 1176
Osborne Co., KS
  North Solomon Old German Baptist Brethren Church, KS, 949
  South Solomon Old German Baptist Brethren Church, KS, 1206
Osborne, D. B.
  Mount Airy, NC, First Church of the Brethren, pastor, 880
Osborne, Ed
  Simi Valley, CA, Grace Brethren Church, 1182
Osborne family
  in New Bethel Church of the Brethren, NC, 925
Osborne, Gilbert
  New Haven Church of the Brethren, NC, pastor in, 928
  Reddies River, NC, Riverside Church of the Brethren, minister, 1089
Osborne, Helen L., 2289
Osborne, John D., 728, 1733
Osborne, T., 2086
Osborne's Ford, VA, 728
Osbourne, Gilbert, 1733
Osbourne (Osborne), David Bristoe, 1733
Osceola Church of the Brethren, MO
  Oak Grove Church of the Brethren, MO, 956
  St. Clair Co., MO, **984**
Osceola, IA, Church of the Brethren, **983**
  Marion Co. German Baptist Brethren, IA, 793
Osceola, IN
  Bethel Brethren Church
    Elkhart Grace Brethren Church, 439
  Church of the Brethren, 96, **984**
  Grace Brethren Church, 948, **983–984**, 2134
  Grace Brethren secondary school, 1163
  St. Joseph Co., **984**
Osceola mission point
  Gladys, WV, Church of the Brethren, 551
Osgood
  Neher family immigration, 922
Oshiro family, 1312
Oskin, Michael D., 2289
Osnaburg, OH, 1355, 1395
Osterwise, John G., 1733
Ostrander
  Sciota Church of the Brethen, OH

preaching point, 1160
Ostrander, Michael, 496, 562, 585, 1212, 1733
O'Sullivan, John
  conscientious objectors in World War II, 2332
Osuna, Juan Jose, 2033
Oswald, Ann (later Ross), 2049
Oswald family, 2049
Oswald, Magdalene Esch, *See* Oswald family
Oswald, Peggy (later Jackson), 2049
Oswald, Peter, Sr., *See* Oswald family
Oswalt, Dallas Leon, 1842
Oswalt, Glen Dale, 1733
  Old Brethren German Baptist Church, 2232
  Old Brethren German Baptist Church, minister, 965
  Old Order German Baptist Church minister, 972
Oswalt, Sylvia Jean Eidemiller, 1842
Oswinski, Thomas E.
  on musical document of Ephrata Cloister, 2349
Otho Winger (Vernon Schwalm), 1157
Ott, Clarice Jean, 1842
Ott, Clifford W., 2289
Ott, Dale Leroy, 662, 758, 1733, 2033
Ott, James Howard, 1733
Ott, Luther Ernest, 1733
Ott, Richard E., 1733
Ottaviano, Frand, 1733
Ottawa Co., KS
  Saline Valley Church of the Brethren, KS, 1139
Ottawa, KS, 1331
  Church of the Brethren, *984*, **984–985**, 1311
  Helman, Alfred Blair, 2197
Otter Creek congregation, IL, 1234, 750
  Gibson, Daniel B., 547
  Gibson, Isham, 548
Otter Creek, IL, Church of the Brethren, *See* Sugar Creek Church of the Brethren, IL
Otterbeck, *Pilgerhütte* (Pilgrim's Hut), 1255
Otterbein College, 692
Otterbein, Philip W., 188, 1289
Otto, Anna, 503
Otto, Earl E., 1733
Otto, Eugene, 503
Otto, John E., 1733
  Sharpsburg, MD, Church of the Brethren, elder, 1174
Otto, Lester, 1733
Otto, Walter, 2136
Ottoman Turks, 55
Ottoni-Wilhelm, Dawn, 2297
  on sin, understandings of, 2349
Ottumwa, IA, Church of the Brethren, **985**
Oubangui-Chari, French Equatorial Africa, 268, 270, 688, **985**, *985*
  Bible translations, 139
  Bickel, Florence Marguerite, 141
  Deeter, Minnie, 373
  Emmert, Mary Le(n)ora, 444
  Foster, Joseph Henry and Rose Alverda Brosius, 504
  Gaiwaka, Noel, 527
  Gribble, Florence Alma Newberry, 573
  Hathaway, Carrie E. and John Wesley, 588

historic sites, 609
hospitals, 630
Jobson, Charlotte Ellen Hillegas, 671
Jobson, Orville Deville, 671
Kliever, Freda Neufeld, 701
medical care, 810
medical missions, 807
Sheldon, Chauncey Burt, missionary, 1175
mission schools, 853, 854
missions and missionaries in, 183, 867, 1979
Myers, Estella Catherine, missionary to, 903
Noatemo, Jean, 938
relief and rehabilitation work, 236
Rollier, Antoine E. and Mary Ganshorn, missionaries to, 1119
Sheldon, Hattie Louise Cope, missionary, 1175
Taber, Ada Zellner, 1247
Tyson, Elizabeth Stauffer, 1284
Voloungou, Marc, 1309
Our Almanac and Annual Register for the Year of our Lord 1880, 18, 2033
Our Boys and Girls, 933, 1236, 1390, 1394, 2033, 2108
  Church of the Brethren, **985**
Our Brethren Heritage: Student Manual for Adults (Zeigler)
  Zeigler, Carl Wenger (CB) and, 2269
Our Children, 933, 1236, 2034
  Mount Morris, IL, 276
Our Children at Work, 2034
  German Baptist Brethren, **985**
Our Church Guidebook (Ronk), 180, 788
Our Faith, 180
Our Field, Opportunity and Need (Ross), 1123
Our Little Folks, 1237
Our Sunday School, 1236, 1389, 1394, 2078
  Our Children at Work, 985
  The Young Disciple, 985
Our Sunday School (Solomon Zook Sharp), 1174
Our Young People, 194, 203, 1236, 2034
  Church of the Brethren, 985
  Van Dyke, Joe, 1302
Ours, Randall D., 2289
Ousterhout, Anne McCabe, 2034
Out of the Melting Pot, Being a Search into the History of Some Early American Families, 2016
Outdoor Ministries
  On Earth Peace Assembly, 2235
outdoor ministries
  pamphlet for, 1932
Outdoor Ministries Association, 249, *See also* Brethren Camps Committee (CB)
  organizational restructuring and, 2242
outer aspects of faith
  Brethren Doctrine of Salvation, 1140
Outer Word, *See* Inner Word and Outer Word
Outline and Argument of Romans (McClain), 773
Outlook, WA, 1240
  Church of the Brethren, **985–986**
outreach
  Hamel, Joseph Donat, 2196
  sources on, 2324

outreach programs
  Salamonie Church of the Brethren, IN, 1136
  Mission One (CB), 853
  Montgomery, IL, Boulder Hill Neighborhood Church of the Brethren, 872
Oved, Yaacov
  on communes, first, 2349
  on Ephrata Cloister, 2349
Overbrook, KS, 1321
  Church of the Brethren, 1321
  Washington Creek, KS, congregation, **986**
Overdorf, Timothy, 759
Overfelt, Samuel A., 1733
Overfield, Richard A., 2034
Overholser, Barbara Brubaker, 217
Overholser, Daniel, 960
Overholser family, 158, *See also* Oberholtzer family
  Howard, IN, Church of the Brethren, 633
  Salem Church of the Brethren, OH, 1138
Overholser, J. E., 171, 1734
Overholser, J. Spencer, 2034
Overholser, John, 960
Overholser, Lewis B., 65, 1734
  Indiana congregations, elder, 960
Overholser, William E., 1734
Overholt, Bliss, 1734
Overholt family, 2034, *See* Oberholtzer family
  Rittman, OH, First Brethren Church, 1111
Overholt, James J., 923, 1734
  From Tiny Beginnings, 2349
Overholt, Jonas C., 1734
Overholt, Lawrence Quinten, 2034
Overholt, Susan (later Landis), 2023–2024
Overholtz, J.
  Pleasant Valley Church of the Brethren, ND, elder, 1035
Overholtz, John N., 1734
Overholtzer, Anna (later Wolfe), 1359
Overholtzer, Darius, 1734
Overholtzer, David J., 1734
Overholtzer, Durand, 1734
  on Brethren history lectures, 2349
  Olive Grove Old German Baptist Brethren Church, CA, minister, 973
Overholtzer, E. C., 1734
Overholtzer family, 323, 752, 1227, *See also* Oberholtzer family
Overholtzer, I. E., 1734
Overholtzer, J., 438
Overholtzer, Jesse Irvin, 136, 275, 1734,
  biographical information, 1918
  Overholtzer, Samuel A., 2377
Overholtzer, Maria E. Harnish, 986
Overholtzer, Peter, 348, 692, 752, 1734
Overholtzer, Samuel A., 348, **986**, 1734, **2377**
Overholtzer, William
  Mohrsville Church of the Brethren, PA, elder, 869
Overholtzer, William E., 1734
Overhultz, J. N., 1734
  Pleasant Valley Church of the Brethren, Alberta, Canada, elder, 1034
Overhultz, John N., 1734

Overley family
    Fleming Co., KY, German Baptist
        Brethren Church, 494
Overley, Jacob, 494
Overly, Richard Coulter, Sr., 1734, 2304
Overly, Ronald H., 2289
Overpeck family, 396
Overpeck, Michael J., 2289
overseer, *See* elder; ministry, terminology
overseer of the poor
    Germantown, PA, congregation, **986**
overseers
    ministry, terminology, 847
overseers of the poor
    deacons, role as, 369
Overton, B. F., 1734
Owen, Benj[amin], 2034
Owen Co., IN, 753, 2373
    Maple Grove Church of the Brethren,
        IN, 789
    migration of Brethren, 829
Owen Co., KY, 689
Owen, Dan, 1270
Owen, R. M., 1734
Owen, Robert, 248, 331, 438, 584, 711
Owens, Arnold L., 2289
Owens, Benjamin F., 553, 1734
Owens, Billie Louise, 2034
Owens, Martin
    Peak Creek Church of the Brethren,
        NC, minister, 1003
Owens, Martin G., 1734
Owens, Robert James, 2034
Owings Mills Prayer Circle
    Reistertown-Evergreen Church of the
        Brethren, MD, 1095
Owl Creek Church of the Brethren, OH,
    See Ankenytown, OH, Owl Creek
    Church of the Brethren
Owl Creek, OH, Old German Baptist
    Brethren Church, **986**
ownership
    common, and New Baptists of
        Schwarzenau, 776
Oxenrider, Jack L., 670, 1734, 2034
Oxford movement (England), 51
Oxford Resolution
    similar to Twenty Thousand Dunkers
    for Peace movement, 1281
Oxley, Charles F., 1734
Oxley family
    Greenwood Church of the Brethren,
        MO, 572
Oxley, Howard W., 1734
Oxley, John H., 565, 567, 1734
Oxley, Leah (later Harness), 2280
Oxley, Ora I., 1734
Oxley, Thomas P., 1734
Oxnard Hilton Inn, meetingplace for
    Ventura, CA, Grace Brethren
    Church, 1303
Oyer, Margaret Birkey, 2034
Oyer, Verle Christian, 2034
Oyler, David, 766, 1734
Oyler family, 1927, *See* also Eiler family
Oyler, Floretta Rinehart, 601
Oyler, Howard M., 1280, 1335
    Sierra Pines Old German Baptist
        Brethren Church, CA, elder-in-
        charge, 1181
Oyler, James Lloyd, 264, 431, 470, 496,
    601, 1734
Oyler, John O., 373, 431, 1734

Oyler, Joseph L., 1734, 2304, **2385**
    Modesto, CA, Old German Baptist
        Brethren Church, presiding elder,
        867
Oyler, Nannie (later Hess), 601
Oyonnax, France, 505
Oysterville, WA, German Baptist Brethren
    Church, **986**
Ozark Church of the Brethren, MI, **986–987**
    Michigan Brethren settlement, 824
Ozark Grace Brethren Church, MI, **987**
Ozark, MI, congregation, 373
Ozark villages
    Dunkard Brethren Church
        sociological study of, 2102
Ozawkie, KS, 192, 682
    Church of the Brethren, **987,** 1267,
        1356
    McLouth, KS, Church of the Brethren,
        779
    Root family, 1122
    Soldier Creek Church of the Brethren,
        1201

Pacheco, Eloy, 357, 1734
Pacheco, Jose, 1248
Pacific Highway, 14
Pacific Northwest
    colonization, 324
    history of, 1928
    migration of Brethren, 830
Pacific School of Religion
    Eller, Vernard M., 2176
"Pacific Slope Number," 2034
pacifism, *See* conscientious objection;
        historic peace churches; nonvio-
        lence; peace
    Albigensian, 15
    Biblical basis, 2013
    bibliography, 1874, 1875, 1877, 1885,
        1891, 1892, 1895, 1902
    Bittinger, Desmond Wright, 143
    Church of the Brethren, 2162–2163
    Civil War, 1973
    colonial Pennsylvania, 1963
    Conference of Pacifist Churches, 1973,
        1990
    defined, 989
    development during war time, 1968
    doctrine of, 2074, 2094, 2100
    Durnbaugh, Donald F. on peace
        churches and, 2326
    Dyck, Harvey L. on, 2328
    Eller, Cynthia Lorraine on, 2329
    Fellowship of Reconciliation (USA),
        488
    Historic Peace Churches, 607–610
    historical writing, 613
    Hochmann von Hochenau, Ernst
        Christoph, 614
    nonresistance, 944
    peace in Christian church history, 998
    perspectives in, 2003
    Puidoux Conferences, 1071
    religious liberty, 1098
    Snider, Harold, opponent, 1194
    sources on, 2318, 2320
    U. S., 1919–1941, 1970
    World War II, 2057
Packwood, M. E. M., 2034
Paden, Anita Sundquist, 1852
Paden, Bruce, 1734
Paden, Linda Ann, 1851

Paden, Robert Bruce, 1852
Padget, Elijah
    South Carolina minister, 1204
Page, Beverly (later Kent)
    Kent, Homer Austin, Jr., 2210
Page Co., IA, 416
Page Co., VA, 767, 1229, 2077
    Hiestand family, 2084
    Madison Church of the Brethren, VA,
        ministers from, 781
    Mount Zion Church of the Brethren,
        VA, 888
    Newport Church of the Brethren, 934
    Shenandoah Valley, VA, 1176
Page Co., WV
    Flat Rock Church of the Brethren, VA,
        493
Page, Jack, 754
Page, Kirby, 253, **989,** 2034
Page, Ronald E., 2289
pageantry, *See* drama
paid ministry, *See* ministry, salaried;
        salaried ministry
Paine (Payne), Aaron, 989
Paine (Payne), Adam, 747, **989,** 1914,
        2044, 2074, 2083, 2229
    Bureau Co., IL, 2009
    Native Americans, 2229
Painesville, OH, Church of the Brethren,
    989
Paint Creek Church of the Brethren, KS,
    354, **989–990**
    Mount Zion Church of the Brethren,
        KS, 888
Paint Creek Church of the Brethren, OH,
    990
    minorities, ethnic and racial, 849
Painter, Charles, 1734
Painter Creek, OH, 349
    Church of the Brethren, 224, **990,**
        1327, 1389, 2019
    Pitsburg, OH, Church of the
        Brethren, 1026
    Potsdam, OH, Church of the
        Brethren, 1048
Painter Creek Old German Baptist Brethren
    Church, OH, **990**
Painter, D. Franklin, 1734
Painter, Eleanor, 1734
Painter, George W. (Newport, VA), 1734
    Newport Church of the Brethren, VA,
        leadership in, 934
Painter, George W. (Henry Co., IN), 1734
Painter, Harold D., 566, 1240, 1278, 1734
    Modesto, CA, La Loma Grace Brethren
        Church, pastor, 867
    Montclair, CA, Grace Brethren Church,
        pastor, 871
    South Pasadena, CA, Grace Brethren
        Church, pastor, 1206
Painter, Luther, 1734
Painter, M. L., 1734
Painters Chapel, VA, mission point,
        Botetourt Co., VA, Church of the
        Brethren, 164
Pajaro Valley, CA, 1358
Palaci, June Byler, 1855
Palatinate, 407, **990,** 2043
    Anabaptists and, 146, 159
    Bollingen, 158
    Brethren movement and, 174
    Brethren remnants in Europe, 1099
    Danner (Tanner, Donner), Michael, 362

description, 990
Eberbach, 417
Eller family, 440
emigrants from, to American colonies, 1990
emigration, early eighteenth century, 1988
emigration from, 425
Eppstein, 452–453
Flora, (Flory) family, 495
Frankenthal, 506
Funck (Funk) family, 521
Garber (Garver, Gerber) family, 529
Germany, 545
Gish family, 551
Graybill (Grabill, Krehbiel) family, 567
Guice (Geist Guß, Guss, Güß), Christopher, 576
Heidelberg, 593
Himbach, 607
Hochmann von Hochenau, Ernst Christoph, 615
Holsinger (Holtzinger) family, 623
Hoover families, 2073
Hunsiker (Hunsaker) family, 637
Hutterian Brethren, 639
interdenominational relations, 1183
Kauffman family, 685
Kling family inn, *702, 703*
Lambsheim, 720
later settlement in Wetterau, 1338
Liebe, Christian, 741
Longenecker family, 756
Mack, Alexander, Sr., 775
Marienborn, Palatine dissenters finding refuge in, 683
Martin, Nicholas, 797
migration from, 1221
missions for religious refugees, 857
movement to Ysenburg-Büdingen, 1394
Mumma (Moomaw) family, 896
Naas family, 909
Newlanders and immigration to New World, 934
Pennsylvania Germans from, 1005
Pfautz, Johann (Hans) Michael, 1013
Pietism and, 159
Reformed Church, 1092
refugees from, 421
Reitz, Johann Heinrich, expelled from by French troops, 1095
Rhine River Valley, Brethren origins in, 1106
Ritter, Daniel, native of, 1111
Rosenberger family, 1123
Rowland, Gasper, emigrated from, 1126
Royer family, 1128
schoolmasters in, 156
Solingen Brethren, 147
Steiner family, 2378
Stutzman, Jacob, 1233
Traut, Georg Balthasar, 1270
Palatinate (Electoral, Rhenish), 9, 29
Palatinate, Upper, 990
Palatine
    sources on, 2320
Palatine
    defined, 990
Palau, T. P. Bitrus Y., 1734
Palestine, **990–991**, 2027, *See also* Bible lands, travel to; Israel; Middle East

aid to refugees, 23
Crist, Daniel Albert, and lectures on, 352
debates, and historical, 371
Eisenbise, Forest Sard, 432
excavation sites in, Brethren visiting, 46
Hoff, Emanuel Buechley, 616
Jewish evangelism, 671
millennialism, 834
tours of, 202
travel to by Brethren, *1272,* 1274
Palestine, AR
    ministry to Blacks, **991**
        minorities, ethnic and racial, 850
    mission field, 395
    St. Francis Church of the Brethren, 1134
Palestine, IL, 713
Palestine, IN, Church of the Brethren, *See* Oak Grove, IN, Church of the Brethren
Palestine, OH, 693, 1325, 1333
    Church of the Brethren, *See* West Branch Church of the Brethren, Old German Baptist Brethren Church, **991**
Palghar, India, 649
    Ebbert, Ella, 417
Palisade, CO, Church of the Brethren, *See* Mount Garfield, CO, Church of the Brethren
    Mount Garfield, CO, Church of the Brethren, previous name of, 881
Palmer, Charles William, 1734
    Rockton, PA, Church of the Brethren, pastor, 1118
Palmer family, 1365
    Mayville, ND, Red River Valley Church of the Brethren, 805
Palmer, Harrison, 1734
    Somerset German Baptist Brethren Church, MO, 1202
Palmer, J. H., 130, 1734
    New Troy, MI, Grace Brethren Church, pastor in, 932
    Oakville, IN, Brethren Church, pastor, 959
Palmer, John H., 1319
    Roanoke, IN, Brethren Church, pastor, 1112
Palmer, Melvin C., 1734
Palmer, N. M., 1734
Palmer, Robert, 1734
Palmer, Stuart, 1734
Palmer, William H., 1734
The Palms, FL, retirement community, 758, **991**
    Sebring, FL, J. H. Moore Memorial Church of the Brethren, 1162
Palms Manor and Health Care Center
    Weimer, Glen Emerson, 1327
Palmyra, PA, Church of the Brethren, 256, **991**, 1005, 1899
    Hershey, PA, Spring Creek Church of the Brethren, 599, *600,* 756
Palmyra, PA, Grace Brethren Church, **991**
    Harrisburg, PA, Melrose Gardens Grace Brethren Church, 586
Palouse Old German Baptist Brethren Church, ID, 645, **991**
    migration of Brethren, 830
Palouse, WA, 1319

Palsgrove, Eugene, 1277, 1734
    Modesto, CA, South Modesto Community Church of the Brethren, 867
Palsgrove, Lenore
    Modesto, CA, South Modesto Community Church of the Brethren, 867
Pampa, TX, Church of the Brethren, **991,** 1255
A Pamphlet of Hymns, 696
pamphlets, 2021
    Bible Helps, 136
    Harshbarger, John, 587
    Kurtz, Daniel Webster, 711
Pamphlin, James, 1734
    Racket, WV, Mount Olive Brethren Church, pastor, 1079
Panama
    route to California, 177
Pandya, James A., 2304
Pangle family
    Reliance, VA, Mount Zion Brethren Church, 1096
Panhandle, TX, Church of the Brethren, *See* Pampa, TX, Church of the Brethren.
Pannebaker family
    Farmers Grove Fellowship (BC), PA, 476
Pannebaker, William, 1734
Pannell, William T., 1734
Panora, IA, Church of the Brethren (Coon River), 342, 661, 662, 992, 1960
    Farnhamville, IA, Church of the Brethren, 479
    Harlan Church of the Brethren, IA, 583
    Soldier River German Baptist Brethren, IA, 1201
Panora, IA, Dunkard Brethren Church, 491
Panorama City, CA, Church of the Brethren, *See* Los Angeles, CA, Panorama City Church of the Brethren
    Glendale, CA, Church of the Brethren, 552
Panther Creek Church of the Brethren, IA, 360, 378, 661–662, 753, 803, **992**
    100 year anniversary, 2010
    Emmert, Michael Wolf, 444
Panther Creek, IL, Church of the Brethren, **992**
    Gish, Barbara Kindig and James Rufus, 550
    Gish family, 551
Paola, KS, 728, 1311
Paoli Immanuel Church of the Brethren, PA, *See* Berwyn, PA, Paoli Immanuel Church of the Brethren
Papago Park, AZ, Brethren Church, 1251, *See* Tempe, AZ, Papago Park Brethren Church
paper manufacturing industry, 1093
Papias of Hierapolis
    premillennialism, 833
Pappas, John C., 1380, 1734, 1852
Pappas, Rebecca Lee Fabbro, 1852
Pará River, Brazil, 172
Parable of the "Supper," 696
parables
    bibliography and history of interpretation, 1986
    Great Gospel Feast, 1985
    in verse, 1992

Paracelsus, 156
Paradies-Gärtlein (Little Garden of Paradise) (Arndt), 1051, 1052
Paradise, CA, Church of the Brethren, **992**
Paradise Church of the Brethren, OH, 945–946, 992
Paradise Prairie Church of the Brethren, OH, 992
Paradise Prairie Church of the Brethren, OK, 44, 992, 993
  migration of Brethren, 830
Paradise Prairie, OK, congregation
  Appleman, Jacob, 964
Paradise Prarie (Williams, C. B.), 748, 993
Paradise schoolhouse
  Longmeadow Church of the Brethren, MD, 756–757
Paradoxes of Democracy (Eby), 420
Paragon, See Ausbund
Paraguay
  Brethren Church missions, 2141
  General Conference Mennonite Church, 536
  Hutterian Society of Brothers, 640
  Institute for Inter-American Affairs field mission
    Wampler, Frederick Jacob, 1316
  Julien, Thomas T., 2210
  Mennonites migrating to, 815
  missions, 2224, 2225
  Wagoner, Bob on Society of Brothers (Bruderhof) in, 2361
  Wagoner, Shirley on Society of Brothers (Bruderhof) in, 2361
Paraguay, Brethren Church in, **2237**
Paramount Brethren Church, *See* Long Beach, CA, Community Grace Brethren Church
Pardoe, Elizabeth Lewis
  on Weiser, Conrad, 2349
parents
  training children, 2159
Parham, Charles
Pentecostalism, 1008
Paris, France, 24
Parish, J. A., 1734
Parish Ministries Commission (CB), 285, 993, 1906
  Brethren profile study, 2150
  Brethren Renewal Service (BRS), 2150
  Church of the Brethren, 305
  Committee on Health and Welfare (CB), 327
  Education for a Shared Ministry (EFSM), 429
  General Board (CB), 535
  General Services Commission (CB), 539
  Good Shepherd Church of the Brethren, FL, 557
  Hayes, William (Bill) A., 2197
  homosexuality, 2204
  language, inclusive, 2214
  marriage enrichment, 796
  missions, 859
  on National Youth Conferences, 918
  origin of, 36
  Women's Conferences (CB) and, 2264
Parish Volunteer Service (CB), 993
  commissioning services, for members of, 327
Park, Jang-Kyun (John), 2289
  Los Angeles, CA, Central Evangelical

Church of the Brethren (Korean), 2215
Park, Kwang Ja, 173, 1852
Park, Mildred White, 2097
Park Street Brethren Church, OH, *See* Ashland, OH, First Brethren Church
Parker, Alice (later Gray), 1953
Parker, Andrew J., 1315
Parker, Benjamin S., 2034
Parker, Betty (later Weaver)
  Weaver, Scott L. (FGBC, CGBCI) and, 2261
Parker, Carl
  Romine Church of the Brethren, IL, providing leadership, 1121
Parker, Catherine, 1735
Parker, Cephas, 993
Parker Co., TX, 1324
Parker, Dale, 673
Parker, Daryl M., 261, 1842, **2388**
  medical missionary, 807
  medical projects, 808
  Rural Life Association (RLA), 1131
Parker, Don
  on Studebaker, Ted, 2349
Parker Ford, PA, Church of the Brethren, **994**
  Myers, Jacob Tobias, pastor, 904
Pottstown, PA, Coventry Church of the Brethren, 1049
Parker, Helen
  Okeechobee, FL, Grace Brethren Church, 963
Parker, Isaac Dillon, 439, 993, 1735
  train travel, 1271
Parker, Jemima Moherman, 993
Parker, Jonathan Fred, 2289
Parker, Maggie Aumbrum, 993
Parker, M. Margaret, 2034
  Okeechobee, FL, Grace Brethren Church, 963
Parker, Martha Neiderhiser, 1842, 2034, **2388**
Parker, Mary Hummel, 994
Parker, Nondas
  Okeechobee, FL, Grace Brethren Church, 963
Parker, Perry S., 7, 1735
Parker, Sarah Priest, 993
Parker, William Herbert, 993, 1735
Parkerford Baptist Church, 1298
Parkerford, PA, 994
Parkersburg, IL, 1315
Parkersburg, WV, 1337
Parkersburg, WV, Grace Brethren Church, **994**
Parkerson family, 170
Parks family, 1215
  Johnstown, PA, Geistown Grace Brethren Church, 674
  Prosperity Brethren Church, WV, 1062
Parks, Flora Belle (later Brumbaugh), 223
Parks, Harold, 532, 1735
Parks, James Kenneth, 1215, 1735
parks, state and national
  chaplaincy, 2158
Parks, Talmage, 1735
Parkview Church of the Brethren, PA, **994**
Parkway Church of the Brethren, VA, 231, **994**, 1267
Parmer, John A.
  on Ephrata Cloister, geography of low

mill tract of, 2349
Parmer, Samuel G., 1735
Parmer, William, 211
Parochial Schools, *See* Christian Day School Movement
Parr, Alvery Bowman, 2304
Parr, John M., 121, 1735
Parrett, Sara Blocher, 147
Parris Island Marine Corps base, SC
  Zigler, Michael Robert, 1398
Parris, Melba Marie Burger, 1842
Parris, Wayne Lavern, 1735, 1842
Parrish Court Grace Brethren Church, VA, *See* Covington, VA, Grace Brethren Church
Parrish family, 1885
Parrot, Mary Anne
  on hymns and songs of Bible, 2349
Parry, Absalom C., 1735
  parsonages
    Germantown, *543*
parsons, *See* ministers
Parsons, Carl
  Rowland Creek Church of the Brethren, VA, 1126–1127
Parsons family, 1865
Parsons, Johann Julius, 994
Parsons, Johanna Christina Zeidig, **994**
Parsons, KS
  Church of the Brethren, 923, **994**
    Galesburg Church of the Brethren, 527
    Neosho Church of the Brethren, 923
Parson's Music Hall, used as meetingplace
  Waterloo, IA, (First) Brethren Church, 1321
Parsons Old German Baptist Brethren Church, KS, **994**
Parsons, William, 994
  Alexander Mack, 1980
  family and Moravian Church, 1998
Parsons, William T., 2034
  on witness, effects of, 2349
Parsons, WV, 1287
Partch, A. Homer, 1735
  Powelis Valley Church of the Brethren, OR, 1050
Partch family
  Outlook, WA, Church of the Brethren, 986
P[arthemore], E. Winfield Scott, 2034
Parthenopolis, See Ephrata Community
partitions, moveable, *632*
Partmann, Anna Dorothea, *See* Becker, Anna Dorothea (Partmann)
Parton family, 1267
Pasadena, CA
  Centro Cristiano para la Familia (BC), 238, **2237**
  Church of the Brethren, 759, **994–995**, *995*, 2087
    Funderburg, Isaac Vaughn, 523
  East Pasadena Grace Brethren Church, *See* Temple City, CA, Grace Brethren Church
  Hispanic Ministries (BC), **2198**, *2199*
  Hispanic Radio Ministry (BC), **2199**, *2200*
  urban ministry and, 2257
Paschal Day, *See* Good Friday
Passau, Bavaria, early Anabaptists imprisoned at, 72
Passing on the Promise (PotP), 2160, 2162

Brethren Church, 2180
Church of the Brethren, 2180
Durbin, WV, Church of the Brethren, 2175
passion play
Christian Catholic (Apostolic) Church, 282
Passover
Honites, 628
The Passover, The Lord's Supper, The Communion (Shuman)
Shuman, L. Herman (OGBB) and, 2249
Pastor, *See* Ministry
pastoral duties
Pietism, 1022
pastoral placement work
Parish Ministries Commission involvement in, 993
Pastorius, Francis Daniel, 542
pastors, *See* ministers; ministry
Brethren Church ministry, 846
emergency and retirement benefits, 155
finding, and congregational polity, 1044
Grace Brethren Church ministry, 847
manuals for, 788
marriage counseling, 796
records and reports, study of, 1982
salaried, 189
summer pastorates, 2006
work of, 1983
Pastors' Association (CB), 1906
Ministers' Association of the Church of the Brethren, 844
The Pastor's Manual, 39, 2184
laying on of hands, 731
marriage ceremonies, 1326
order of worship, 1377
Yoder, Joseph J., 1386
Pastor's Training School (Chibuk, Nigeria)
Mai Sule Biu, 782
Pataskala, OH, Grace Brethren Church of Licking Co., **995**, 1380
Patches, Luther Ralph, 1340, 1735
Patchet, Elijah, 425, 1735
Patching, Albert, 754
Patch's Church
Greenland Church of the Brethren, WV, 571
Patchwork (Myers), 747
Patel, Aytaram, 1735
Patel, Chimanlal M., 1735
Patel, Lois Jean Gibble, 1842
Patel, Maganlal M., 1735
Patel, Makan, 1735
Patel, Makanbhai S., 1735
Patel, Philemon P., 229, 1735
patent medicines, 7, 18, 809, **995**
business beliefs and, 234
Fahrney, Peter, 466
Flory, Jacob S., 498
"Sala's German Vegetable Elixir," 1136
scientific activities, 1160
Paterson, Harry James, 1735
"Pathfinder," 2017, *See also* Fike, Earl, Jr.
Pathway Publishers (Larange, IN and Aylmer, Ontario), 26
Pathways of Peace (Eisan), 316
Paticular Baptists, 87
Patience (ship)
Garst family, 532
Patras, Doreen, 2035

patriarchy
family, 472
Patrick, Archie Loren, 530, 540, 1735
Patrick, C. L., 1735
Patrick Co., VA
New Hope Church of the Brethren, 929
Smith River Church of the Brethren, VA, 1191–1192
Patrick, John A., 1735, 2304
Patrick, John Aungst, 1735, 2289
Patrick, Lohman, 1735
Patrick, Norman W., 1735, 2304
Patrick Springs, VA
Church of the Brethren
West, Murray Guy (CB) and, 2261
Smith River Church of the Brethren, VA, preaching point, 1192
Patrick, Thomas, 1735
Patriotism, *See* Church-State Relations
patriotism
church-state relations, 310–311
military recruitment, 831
Patristics, *See* Church Fathers
Patten (Patton), John, 1365, 1735
Patten, Thomas, 1735
Patterson, **2380**
Patterson, CA, Church of the Brethren, **995–996**
Empire, CA, Church of the Brethren, 445
Patterson, Edna, 1852
Patterson, Emma (later Groff), 574
Patterson, George, 1735
Patterson, Henry, 297
Patterson, John E., 320, 620, 1735
Patterson Memorial Grace Brethren Church, VA., *See* Hollins, VA, Patterson Memorial Grace Brethren Church
Patterson Park Church, OH, 365
Patterson Ranch Company, 995
Patterson, Roy A., **995**
Patterson, Sheryl Lynn, 1848
Patton Brethren, *See* Church of God (New Dunkers).
Patton family, *See* Out of the Melting Pot
Patton, George, 297, 464, 700, **996,** 1735
Indiana, 652
Patton, Leroy T. (Lee), 1735
Patton, Levi, 996
Patton, Magdaline Whistler, 996
Patton, Norma, 996
Patton, Susan Nearhoff, 996
Patton, Thomas, 996
Patton, Uriah, 297, **996**
Paul, Apostle, on baptism, 85, 2023
Paul, Clifford, 1735
Paul, Daniel W., 1735
Paul, Doris (later Reed), 2304
Paul, E. Clifford, 1735
Paul, Eileen (later Rutherford), 2052
Paul family, **996,** 1304, 2052, 2080
Maple Valley, WA, Grace Brethren Church, 2218
Snowberger family, related to, 1154
Paul-Hallowell family, 1974
Paul, Henry, 1735, 2080
Schultz, Martin, related to by marriage, 1156
Paul, Ira Clifford, 1735
Pleasant View Church of the Brethren, OH, pastor, 1037
Paul, Jerry, 1286
Paul, Lewis, 1735

Paul, Mrs. Noah
Muncie, IN, Brethren Church, 896
Paul, Mrs. Ora
Muncie, IN, Brethren Church, 896
Paul, Noah J., 1735
Muncie, IN, Brethren Church, 896
Paul, Ora
Muncie, IN, Brethren Church, 896
Paul (Paulus), Daniel, 513
Paul-Ritchie families, 1986
Paul, Susannah, 2080
Paul, William, 1735
Paulding Co., OH, 142, 152, 410, 1302
Flat Rock Old German Baptist Brethren Church, OH, 494
Grover Hill, Latty, and Washington townships, 1966
Rome Old German Baptist Brethren Church, OH, 1121
Paullin, Norman W., 1735
Philadelphia, PA, Geiger Memorial Church of the Brethren, minister, 1016
Paulmer, Frank, 439
Paul's Chapel, IN
Church of God (New Dunkers), 297
Paulsboro, NJ, 161
Paulson, Israel, Sr., *See* Poulson, Israel, Sr.
Paulus, Daniel, 996, 1735
Paulus, Johann Henrich, Jr., 996
Paulus, Johann Henrich, Sr., 996
Paulus, John, 996
Paulus, Margaret Martin, 996
Pauw (Pfau), Adrian, 324, **996**
Collegiant society and caring for the poor, 1046
Paw Paw, MI, 18
Pawnee Co., KS, 424
Pawnee Co., NB
Turkey Creek congregation in, 920
Pawnee Co., NE, 1280
Pawnee Co., OK
Jennings, OK, Bethany Church of the Brethren, 670
Paxton, James, 1735
Paxton, MT, 142
Paxton, PA, congregation, 142
Payette congregation, ID
Fruitland, ID, Church of the Brethren, 520
Payette Valley Church of the Brethren, ID, **996,** 1328
Payne, Adam, 1914, 2074, 2083, *See also* Paine (Payne) Adam
The Prairie Schooner (Barton), 747
Payne Co., OK, 141
Payne, E. G., 1735
Payne, Elizabeth S., 2035
Payne, John Collins, 2035
Payne, Robert M., Jr., 1735
Payne, William Jackson, 1735
Payton, Samuel W., 1735
New Bethel, IN, Church of the Brethren, elder in, 924–925
PCOM, *See* Philadelphia College of Osteopathic Medicine (PCOM)
Peabody Church of the Brethren, KS, **997**
Ramona Church of the Brethren, KS, 1083
Royer Community Church of the Brethren, KS, 1128
disbandment of, 934
Peabody Old German Baptist Brethren

Church, KS, **997**
peace, **997–1001**, 2022, 2026, 2028, 2034, 2047, 2050, *See also* historic peace churches; pacifism; non-violence
American Legion, Brethren and, 24
American Revolution, 999, 2005, 2074
belief in, 15, 20
bibliography, 1864, 1866, 1867, 1868, 1880, 1884, 1886, 1892, 1906, 1910, 2309
Brethren, and prisons, 1058
Brethren movement, 311
Brethren Peace Witness, 2327
Christian Education Commission (CB), 285
Christian education movement, 284
Church of the Brethren, 316
Civil War, 2053
Congo crisis, 1972
conscientious objectors, 1169
Continuation Committee of the Historic Peace Churches, 339
On Earth Peace Assembly, 2235
On Earth Peace Conference (OEPC), 974
education, 23–24, 284
EIRENE, 432
Elgin, IL, Highland Avenue Church of the Brethren, 436
Eller, Vernard on stewardship of, 2329
Envoys of Peace: The Peace Witness in Christian World Mission (Beaver), 1872
ethics, 458
evangelism, 461
Freundschaftsheim (Friendship House), 517
Fulk, George, 521
Gandhi, Mahatma (Mohandas Karamchand), 313, **528**
Garver, Earl S., 532
General Board (CB), 535
General Conference Mennonite Church, 536
Glendale, CA, Church of the Brethren, 552
Goshen Conference, 559
Griffith, Lee on theology of, 2334
Guthrie, OK, Church of the Brethren, 576
Harman, Hylton, 2196
hats, 589
Hays, Daniel, 590
Heifer Project International, 593–594
Hershey, Lewis Blaine, 599
Hess, Maurice Abram, 601
historic peace churches, 607, 1966, 2200
historical writing, 612, 2201
Howe, William Mohler, 633
Huston Memorial Peace Lectures, 638
Huston, Ora Ivan, 638
International Fellowship of Reconciliation, 659
Ireland, 662
Israel, 664
Jacksonville, FL, Church of the Brethren, 667
kiss of, *698*
Mallott, Floyd Ellwood, 784
mass communication, 1972
mass media messages concerning, 801
Mennonite Church, 316, 815

Mexican War, 820
mid 20th century sermon, 1168
military recruitment, 831
Ministry of Reconciliation, 2224
Mothers' Day, 879
Murray, Don, 625–626
Muste, Abraham Johannes, 901
Native Americans, 2229
Neff, Robert Wilbur, 2231
Ness, Jacob C., 2231
nuclear arms race, 2232
Old German Baptist Brethren, 2233
One Hundred Dunkers for Peace, 974–975
Page, Kirby, 989
Paradise Church of the Brethren, OH, 992
peace education seminars, 391
peace-loving people, 1974
Peachey, Paul, ed., *Peace Politics and the People,* 2349
Pickett, Clarence Evan, 1021
position, instruction about, 5
preaching about, 1053
preservation, 2015
programs for, American Friends Service Committee, 23–24
recreation, 1088
Reidy, Miriam on volunteers for, 2351
religious freedom and persecution, 1009
Revolutionary War, 426, 1994
Rogers, Ingrid, and dramas on, 2353
Roosevelt, Franklin Delano, sympathetic to concerns about, 1122
Rosenberger, Mary Sue Helstern on Vietnam and witnessing for, 2353
Russia, anti-nuclear sentiment against, 1288
Russian Orthodox Church, seminars with, 1132
Schwenkfelder Church, 1159
seminar, 2013
Sermon on the Mount, 1169
Seventh-Day Adventists, 1169–1170
Snider, Harold, opponent, 1194
Society of Friends, 316
sources on, 2312, 2319, 2324
United Nations, 1291
West, Daniel, 1331
witness, key persons leading, 81
work camps, 1365, 1367
World War I, 1371
World War II, 1372
youth involvement, 1391–1392
Zigler, Michael Robert, 1398–1399
peace advocacy
Board of Christian Education (CB), 155
Bowman, Rufus David, 168
Brethren in Christ, 189
Civil War and, 228
Fellowship of Reconcilliation, 233
Peace and World Relief Committee, 1001
peace caravans, 23, 201, 975, **1001**
Peace Church of the Brethren, IA, *See* Council Bluffs, IA, Peace Church of the Brethren
Peace Church of the Brethren, NE, 346
peace circles, Sisters' Aid Society, 1187
Peace Committees, 686, **1001, 1002,** 1252, 1372
General Welfare Board (CB), 540

Hays, Daniel, 590
peace education, 1001, 1002
peace position, 1000
report, chaplaincy, 271
World Relief Board, 1369
World War I, 1370
Peace Community Church of the Brethren, OR, *See* Portland, OR, Peace Church of the Brethren
Peace Corps, 20, 303, **1002,** 1942
Crowell, Larry, 1335
Crowell, Ruth, 1335
foreign travel, 1273
Heifer Project International, 594
International Voluntary Services Agency (IVS), 660
inventions and scientific discoveries, 660
Noffsinger, John Samuel, senior counselor in, 939
Rolston, Frances Fitz Simon and William Wendell, 1120
Smeltzer, Mary Blocher (CB) and, 2250
Sunnyslope Church of the Brethren, WA, 1240
peace education, **1002**
AFSC, 23
Camp Mount Hermon, KS, peace education institute, 246
missions, 859
Peace Committee (BC), 1001
theology and, 2255
peace, kiss of, *See* kiss, holy
peace literature
Peace Committee (BC), 1000
Peace Committee (CB), 1002
Peace Messenger of Concordia
Sala, Johann, printer, 1136
peace ministry
dissertation on, 1040
mission guidelines (CB), 853
peace movement, *See* Brethren Peace Witness; conscientious objectors; reconciliation, doctrine of
American Revolution, 2074
Baker, John C. on, 2326
Bible sanctions for war, 2070
Brethren movement, 2090
chests, peace, 2087
Christianity doctrine of, 2068
Christocentricism, 2098
Church of God (New Dunkers), 297
Church of the Brethren, 1911, 2097, 2108
churches, historic peace, 2085, 2106
Committee of Observation, 327
Committee on Counsel for Conscientious Objectors (CB), 327
convictions on, 2096
Durnbaugh, Donald F. on, 2325, 2326
education, peace
in homes, 2096
Kline, John, 2104
Miller Leslie on conscription during World War II and, 2347
New Call to, 2106
peace chests, 2087
publications about, 2066
Rogers, Ingrid, and songs on, 2353
Thompson, Joel K., 2081
Vietnam War, 286, 1305
Wang, Tung, 2089

war and peace, 2100
witnesses, peace
World War II, 2108
World War II, 2074
Church of the Brethren, 2094
writings about, 1921, 1927
youth issues, 2066, 2107
Peace of Westphalia, *See* Westphalia, Peace of
Established Churches, 456
Germany, 545
Prussia, 1063
peace oratory competition, 601
Peace Pledge Union
similar to Twenty Thousand Dunkers for Peace movement, 1281
peace position
required by Civil War veterans, 1304
peace rally
Washington, D. C., *997*
peace reform, 1916
peace seminars
Geneva, Switzerland, ecumenism, *423*
Germany, 546
peace institutes, **1002**
peace studies
Bethany Theological Seminary, 1984
Peace Studies Institute, **1002–1003**
Manchester College, 785–786
Muir, Gladdys Esther, 93
peace studies program, 1002
peace symbol, 403
Peace to the City campaign
violence and, 2265
peace treaties
Peace of Westphalia, 1338
Peace Valley Church of the Brethren, MO, **1003**
Peace With Justice Center, CA
Smeltzer, Mary Blocher (CB) and, 2250
peace witness
and New Covenant Fellowship, 926
war and, 253
peacemaking, *See* nonviolence; pacifism
Brethren Church, 2178
Christian Peacemaker Teams (CPT), 2161–2162, 2163
Eddy, [George] Sherwood, 424
sources on, 2311, 2321
Peach Blossom Colored Church of Rising Light (CB), MD, 417, **1003**
minorities, ethnic and racial, 849–850
Peach Blossom, MD, Church of the Brethren, 48, 416, *See also* Easton, MD, historic sites, 609
Peach Grove Church, VA, 239
Peach Grove meetinghouse, VA
Calvary (formerly Jubilee) congregation, 1138
Peachey, Linda Gehman
on September 11, 2001 attacks, 2342
Peachey, Paul L., 2035
Miller, Donald E. essays on peace, 2349
Peacock, A. J., 1735
Peacock, Alice Marie, 1852
Peacock, Martin Lloyd, 417, 1735
Peak Creek Church of the Brethren, NC, 152, **1003**
example of dative case in place name, 912
Flat Rock Church of the Brethren, NC,

493
Peak family
Mountain View Church of the Brethren, VA, 889
Peak, J. M., 1341
Pearce, Alan S., 725, 1735
Pearce, Elmer
Okeechobee, FL, Grace Brethren Church, 963
Pearce, Lula
Okeechobee, FL, Grace Brethren Church, 963
Pearce, Samuel W., 331, 674, 1735
Pearl City, IL, 1384
Pearl Creek mission point
Fredericksburg, IA, Hillcrest Baptist and Brethren Church, 512
Pearl Harbor
attack on, 24
Hawaii, 589
Pearl of Christian Counsel for the Broken-hearted (Eller), 2329
Pearsall, A. L., 1735
Pearse, William, 1736
Pearson, A., 1736
Pearson, Claude Herbert, 1736
Pearson, Drew, 286, 518
Pearson, H. James, 1736
Rouzerville Church of the Brethren, PA, part-time pastor, 1125
Pearson, John, 105, 1736
South Carolina minister, 1204
Pearson, John O., 1736
Pearson, Olive, 343
Pearson, Robert J.
Philadelphia, PA, Crossroads Grace Brethren Church and, 2238
Pearson, Sharon
Philadelphia, PA, Crossroads Grace Brethren Church and, 2238
Pearson, Walter V., 204
Pease, Doris (later Jamison), 2128
Pease, Walter C., 1736, 2304
Peck Church of the Brethren, PA, *See* Maple Glen Church of the Brethren, PA
Peck, Daniel J., 1736
Peck family
Falls City Church of the Brethren, NE, 472
South Haven Old German Baptist Brethren Church, MI, 1205
Peck, J. H., 1736
Peck, Jacob, 760
Peck, Jacob C., 1736
Peck, Jacob W., 1736
Peck, John H., 1736
Peck, Lewis A., 1736
Maple Glen Church of the Brethren, PA, minister, 789
Peck, PA, congregation
Maple Glen Church of the Brethren, PA, previous name of, 789
Peck, Samuel J., 1736
Peckham, Howard H., 1858
Peckover, Walter Edward, 1736
Salkum, WA, Community Church of the Brethren, pastor, 1139
Pecos River Valley, NM, 931
Pecos Valley, NM, Church of the Brethren, *See* Lake Arthur, NM, Pecos Valley Church of the Brethren
Peden, Howard Richard, 1736

Menomonie, WI, Church of the Brethren, elder and pastor, 816
pedilavium, *See* feetwashing
Peebler, Albert James, 275, 520, 1736
Peebler family, 14, 740
Peebler, Roy, 1736
Peek, Francis Marion, 6, 1736
Peek, George O., 755, 1736, 2304
Seal Beach, CA, Grace Brethren Church, pastor, 1161
Peek, O. M., 1736
Peel, Cynthia Ann, 2289
Peeler, Jeffrey Kyle, 2180, 2289
Peep, F., *See* Peek, Francis M.
Peer, Earle Edwin, 121, 586, 1736, 2304
Martinsburg, WV, Rosemont Grace Brethren Church, pastor, 798
Peer, Marie Jean Smith
on Garman, Mary and ancestors and descendants, 2349
on Jurger/Yarger, George and descendants, 2349
on Rudy, John and ancestors and descendants, 2349
on Rudy, Mary Garman and ancestors and descendants, 2349
Peer, Peter Paul, 1736, 1852, 2289
Peery, Auzie Lorenza, Jr., 1736
Mount Bethel Church of the Brethren, VA, pastor, 880
Pleasant Dale Church of the Brethren, VA, pastor, part-time, 1031
Peffer, John, 1736
Peffley, Barbara (later Bicksler), 144
Peffley (Peffly, Pefley) family, 1943
Garst family, 532
Mortonhouse (ship), 2373, 2376
Pegg, Wyatt E., 2289
Pegler, Westbrook
on Dunkers, 2349
Peifer, Lewis R., 1736
Peightal, Martha, 222
Peightal, Susan (later Brumbaugh), 220
Pekarek, Arthur L., 275, 754, 1736
Pekarek, Betty, 754
Peking
Yin, Han Chang, 1385
Peking, China
Neher, Minneva Josephine in, 922
Pelambirni, Nigeria, 306
Pell, George P., 2035
Pellet, A., 1736
Pellett, Elizabeth, 1842
Pemberton, John, 2035
Penang, Malaysia
missions, 2225
Pencak, William
on PA history of Brethren in, 2347
Pence, Daniel, 1736
Pence, Esther (later Garber), 748, 1944
Pence family
Pleasant Valley Church of the Brethren, TN, 1035
Pence, George F., 1736
Pence, J. B., 742, 1736
Pence, Joseph, *207,* 1736
Pence, J(oseph) Wayne, 1736
Pence, Mary, 1251, 1360, 1736
Pence, Nadine (later Frantz), 1327, 2133, 2278
Pence, Opal Eileen (later Nees), 1727
Pence, Samuel, *207,* 1736
Pendleton Co., WV, 264, 354, 1243

North Fork Church of the Brethren,
  WV, 947
Seneca Church of the Brethren, WV,
  1166
Simmons, Nicholas and Leonard, 1182
Smith Creek Fellowship Church of the
  Brethren, WV, 1191
South Fork Church of the Brethren,
  WV, 1205
South Mill Creek Church of the
  Brethren, WV, 1206
Pendleton, Philip E.
  on OGBB, 2350
Pendleton, IN, 1225
Peniel, **1003–1004**
  Ephrata Community, 448
  Hebron, 591
  women's meeting hall at Ephrata, 1172
Penn family
  correspondence with Dunkers, 2015
Penn, John, 2035
Penn, Lady Juliana
  Miller, John Peter, 2015
Penn Laird, VA, Brethren Church, *See*
  Pineville, VA, Mont Olive
  Brethren Church
Penn Run Church of the Brethren, PA, 236,
  1004
  Purchase Line Church of the Brethren,
    PA, 1072
Penn Valley Grace Brethren Church, PA,
  See Telford, PA, Penn Valley
  Grace Brethren Church
  Trappe, PA, Tri-County Grace Brethren
    Church and, 2256
Penn View Christian School, Souderton,
  PA, 1251
Penn, William, 158, **1004**
  Graybill (Grabill, Krehbiel) family, 567
  Society of Friends (Quakers), 1199
Pennington, AR, Bethel Brethren Church,
  54, **1004**
Pennock, Mary (later Sellers), 2062
Pennonites, *See* Schultz, Stephen
Pennsburg, PA
  Schwenkfelder Church, 1160
Pennsylvania, **1004–1006**, 2019, 2029,
    2035–2036, 2048, 2049, *See also*
    Ephrata Community; specific city;
    specific county
  Aesch, Switzerland, emigration from,
    2073
  American Revolution, 2067, 2106
  Amish in, 26
  arts and crafts, 2076
  bibliography, 1866
  Boone (Bohne) family, 162
  Bosserman family, 163
  Brethren Church, 181
  Brethren in, mentions of, 1931
  Brethren movement, 175
  Brethren peace position, 999
  BRF (Brethren Revival Fellowship),
    303
  Bucklew, Solomon, oversight of con-
    gregations in, 226
  camping movement, 300
  Cassel (Kassel) family, 260
  Church of the Brethren
  history of, 2111
  Church of the Brethren, history of,
    1921, 1927–1928
  Church of the Brethren, western

Pennsylvania, history of, 1918
church-state relations, 309
churches, 2037
colonial era, 1950
  brotherhood issues, 2074, 2076
  charity school movement,
    2092–2093
  devotional literature, 2074
  ministers, 2093
  mysticism, 2074
  Native Americans, 2089
colonial times, church people in, 1986
Committee of Observation, 327
communitarianism, 329
Congregation of God in the Spirit, 309,
  334
congregations, members living in
  Maryland, 799
Dairy Farm Assignments, 359
debates, 370
Delaware, status of, 374
district histories, 2188
Dunkard Brethren Church, 2069, 2103
Dunkers and colonial government,
  1966, 1980
Durnbaugh, Donald F. on Radical
  Pietism and German emigration to,
  2326
education issues, 2098
emigration to, 2080
Ephrata, 1992–1993, 2008
Ephrata Community, 448–452, 451,
  2040
established churches, 309
farming in, 12
First Day Baptist Church, 2077
Flickinger family, 1937
folk art, 2094, 2097
frontier, 519
Garb Law, 528
genealogical data, 2060
geographic history of Brethren, 1972
Georgia, 540
German Baptist Brethren Church, 2097
German culture, 2147
German Evangelische-Lutherans
  (trans), 2006
German language newspapers, 2088
German pietiests in, 2053
German Reformed Church, 1966
German Reformed congregations in,
  156
Germans of
  bibliographical sources, 1857
  history of, 1873
  immigrant settlement by, 1006
Germantown, Mount Airy, and
  Chestnut Hill, 1974
Germany, 545
Grace Brethren Church, 303
Graybill (Grabill, Krehbiel) family, 567
historical records, 1927, 1949
historical writing, 611
historiography
  district histories, 2201
history, 1950, 1952, 1986, 2076, 2078
  1608–1903, 1979
  1683–1776, 1983
  1688–1748, 1983
Huffman, Nelson Thomas, 2205
Huguenot movement, 2072
Illinois, 647
imigration from Germany, 2077

Indiana, 652
Kentucky, settlements in, 689
Loyalists, 2067, 2108
Maryland Brethren from, 798
Mason-Dixon Line, 800
*Materials Towards a History of the
  Baptists,* 803
Mennonite Church, 2068, 2095
Miami, OH, congregation, 961
Middle District, history of, 1982
migration of Brethren, 827, 830
Miller, Randall M. on history of
  Brethren in, 2347
ministers, 2093
minutes of district meetings, Eastern
  District, 1867–1896, 1946
Moravian Church, 40, 875, 876
Morrisons Cove, 877
Mount Hope Church Home (DB), 881
mysticism, 2074
Naas family immigration to, 909
Näff family immigration to, 909
names of immigrants, 2052
Native Americans, 2089, 2229
naturalization in, 918
North Carolina Brethren settlement,
  946
notes on third Pennsylvania synod,
  1912
notices by German and Swiss settlers
  seeking information about family
  members, 1934
nunneries, 2070
Old German Baptist Brethren, 967,
  970, 2234
Ontario, 975
Pencak, William on history of Brethren
  in, 2347
place names, 1027, 1933
poems, 2076
preacher circuits in, 169
quilting
  sociological aspects of, 2074
religious movements, 2076, 2085
Ruth, John L. on Mennonites of, 2354
Sauer's description of, 2055
settlement of by religious dissenters,
  1004
Seventh Day Baptist Church, 2077
Shenandoah Valley, PA, 2068
Shoemaker family, 2100
songs and legends, 1989
southeastern, geographical study, 1998
Switzerland, emigration from, 2070
Three Mile Island emergency evacuation, 952
travelogues, 2103
Trippstadt, Palatinate, migrations from,
  2073
Underground Railway, 2069, 2072
Universalists, 1292–1293
western, history and genealogy, 1980
Williams family, 2100
Zizendorf visit, and religious condi-
  tions in, 2071
Pennsylvania Abolition Society, 1
Pennsylvania Archives
  naturalization lists, 918
Pennsylvania Assembly
  "A Short and Sincere Declaration,"
    1178
  naturalization and conscientious refusal
    of oath, 918

Pennsylvania Association of Colleges and Universities
    Ellis, Calvert Nice, 441
Pennsylvania Bible Institute
    Moyer, Laura Emma, 892
Pennsylvania Council of Churches
    Hanawalt, David Kirk, 581
Pennsylvania district
    Church of The Brethren in New Jersey, 929
Pennsylvania Dutch, *See* Pennsylvania Germans
Pennsylvania Farmer
    Reber, Norman Franklin, editor, 1085
Pennsylvania Folklife, 1859
Pennsylvania German Folklore Society, 1858, 2074
Pennsylvania German Society, 1006
Pennsylvania Germans, 1007
Pennsylvania German Magazine
    index of, 2309
Pennsylvania German sectarians
    prayer, 1051
Pennsylvania German Society, **1006**
    Bucher, William Pfautz, Sr., 226
Pennsylvania Germans, 1007
The Pennsylvania Germania: A Popular Journal of German History and Ideals in the United States, 1990
Pennsylvania Germans, 16, 188, 724, **1006–1007,** 2049
    American Revolution, 2106
    astrology, 2102
    astronomy, 2102
    bibliography, 1857, 1860, 1861
    books about, 747
    cooking style, 340–341
    culture, 60, 61
    barnraising, 89
    barns, 89
    Distelfink Country, 1980
    Durnbaugh, Donald F. on emigration of, 2326
    Evangelical Association, 459
    Evangelical United Brethren Church, 460
    family farms, 2000
    folk art, 2094
    folk medicine, 2145–2146
    folklore and art forms, 2147
    Fraktur, 505, 2094
    Franklin, Benjamin, 2091
    Frysinger, Anne on, 2355
    furniture makers, 1984
    German and Swiss settlements, 1991
    German dialect (Pennsylvania Dutch), 26
    German hero in colonial era, 2005
    German settlement, importance of 1999
    Jacob, Rebekah Leigh on iconography of, 2339
    language of, 725
    Longenecker, Stephen L.
        on diversity and tolerance among, 2343
        on egalitarianism among, 2343
        on piety and tolerance among, 2343
    Moyer, Dennis K. on fraktur art of, 2348
    musical instruments, 900
    North Carolina, 2104

Pennsylvania German Folklore Society, 2074
    pioneers from Wertheim Co., 1995
    poems, 2076
    prayer books, 1052
    Schifflet, Anne Frysinger on, 2355
    Shenandoah Valley, PA, 2068
    social conditions in 18th century, 1988
Pennsylvania history
    bibliography of, 2310
Pennsylvania Hospital
    medicine, 809
    Philadelphia, PA, **1007**
    Sauer, Johann Christoph, I, philanthropy of, 1148
Pennsylvania Mennonite Heritage, 535
Pennsylvania Merchant (ship)
    Gish family, 551
    Hunsiker (Hunsaker) family, 637
    Schweinhart, Georg Michael and Margaret, 1246
Pennsylvania, migration to
    Kalcklöser, Johann Heinrich, 681
    Sauer, Johann Christoph, I, family of, 1147
Pennsylvania (Moravian) Synods
    Laschet, Johannes Peter van, 726
Pennsylvania Old German Baptist Brethren
    Chestnut Grove, WV, Old German Baptist Brethren Church, 274
Pennsylvania Packet (ship), 452
Pennsylvania Petition, *See* Short and Sincere Declaration, A
"The Pennsylvania Pilgrim" (Whittier), 259
Pennsylvania State University, 693
    Chinese Agricultural Exchange, 2129
    University Baptist Church, 1218
Pennsylvania Synods, 33, 40, 68, 176, **1007**
    ecumenism, 423
    fraternal relations, 510
    Frey, Andreas, 517
    Great Awakening, 568
    Historic Peace Churches, 607
    Kalcklöser, Johann Heinrich, representing Ephrata Community at, 681
    Martin, George Adam, representing Brethren, 797
    Moravian Church, 875
    Müller, Joseph, 894
    Pietism, 1022
    Vogt, Peter on Zinzendorf and first, 2361
    Zinzendorf, Nikolaus Sudwig, Count von, 1399
Pennsylvania Town and Country-Man's Almanack (1754–59), 18
Penny, Orville Clyde, 373, 2304, 1736
Pennypacker, Samuel W., 259, 1859, 2035
    historical writing, 611
penology
    Gillin, John Lewis, 549
Penrod, J. B., 1736
Penrod, Robert R., 2289
Penrose, Harold B., 136, 755, 1736
    South Gate, CA, First Brethren Church, pastor, 1205
Pension Board (CB), 2241
    Brethren Benefit Trust, 2140
    Cable, William H., 2155
    Geisert, Wayne F., 2188
    Greiner, Robert G., 2194
Pension Plan (CB)
    Brethren Benefit Trust, 2140

pensions, **1007–1008**
    Finance Commission (CB), 490
    General Board (CB), 535
    military, **1008,** 1304
    nonconformity, 941
    Old Order German Baptist Church, 972
    Pension Board, General Board (CB), 535, 536, **1007**
    retirement benefits, 155
Pensylvanische Berichte
    Pennsylvania Hospital, support for, 1007
Pentecost, 695
    as the date for Annual Meeting, 33, 36
    Brethren observances, **1008**
    Knepper, Elizabeth, 1988
Pentecostal Brethren, **1008**
Pentecostalism, **1008–1009,** 1893
    charismatic movement, 272
    Christ's Assembly and, 280
    Fellowship of Grace Brethren Churches (FGBC), 487
    Full Gospel Business Men's Fellowship International, 521
    Glady, WV, Church of the Brethren, 551
    Idaho, 157
    statement of faith as counter to, 1218
Pentz, Dorothy Saylor, 2036
Pentz family, 1912
Pentz, John Angelo, 2036
People of the Covenant (POC), 2160, **2237**
Peoria, IL, (First) Church of the Brethren, **1009,** 1915
Pepin Co., WI, 279
Pepperdine University (Malibu, CA), 114
Pepple, Dorsey I., 1736
    Roaring Spring, PA, Albright Church of the Brethren, pastor, 1114
Pepple, Elmer, 1736
Pepple family
    Snider, Jacob, descendants of, 1154
Pepple, Russell E., 1736
    Shultz and Paul families, related to, 1156
Pequea Publishers (Gordonville, PA), 26
Peraza, F. Javier, 1736
Perdieu, Charles P., 1736, 2304, **2385**
    Oak Hill Old German Baptist Brethren Church, VA, minister, 957
Perdue, Charles W., 1736
Perdue, John, 424
Pereira, Onaldo Alves, 2139
Perfection, attainment of
    New Born sect, 925
perfectionism, **1009**
    among the Angel Brethren, 30
    sanctification, 1142
performances, *See* drama
periodicals, 7, 17–18, 25, 63, 120, 186, 190, 191–192, 205, *See also* publishers and publishing; Sauer (Sower), Christopher; specific periodicals
    Amish, 6
    as art, 60
    art and illustration, use of, 61, 62
    bibliography, 1860, 1861
    bibliography of German-American newspapers and periodicals, 1857
    Brethren, list of, 1924
    circulation of, 24
    German language newspapers and periodicals, 1918
    languages of, 203–204

Mahan, Grant, contributor, 782
newspapers, weekly, 180
pietist movement, 1946
The Primitive Christian, **1058**
The Primitive Christian and the Pilgrim, **1058**
publishing of, 1067, 1068
Quinter, James, 1077
Rolston, Frances Fitz Simon writing for, 1120
Rosenberger, Isaac J. writing for, 1123
Royer, John Grove writing for, 1128
Sauer newspapers, 1990–1991
Perkepile, *See* entries at Berkebile
Perkins, Margaret, 2036
Perkins, Robert R., 1736
    Pleasant Chapel Church of the Brethren, IN, called to ministry, 1030
Perkins, Scott Eugene, 2289
The Perkiomen Region, 1990–1991
Perkiomen region, Palatinate, 2091
Perkomen Valley, PA, 2077
Perrin, Bertha (later Atkins), 1847
Perrin, Charles, 1736
Perrin, William H., 2036
Perrine, Sheldon, 596, 1736
Perrott, George A., 1736
Perry, Bessie Warvel, 1009
Perry Church of the Brethren, PA, *See* Three Springs Church of the Brethren, PA; Three Springs, PA, Church of the Brethren
Perry Co., KY, 689
Perry Co., OH, 1221
    Glenford, OH, Brethren Church, 553
    Olivet Church of the Brethren, OH, 973
Perry Co., PA, 161, 1263, 1929
    Mount Olivet Church of the Brethren, PA, 886
Perry family, 1885
Perry, I. Newton, 1736
Perry, Jasper N., 1736
Perry, W. C., 345, 1319
    Mexico, IN, Brethren Church, pastor, 821
    North Manchester, IN, (First) Brethren Church, pastor, 949
    Oakville, IN, Brethren Church, pastor, 959
    Roann, IN, (First) Brethren Church, pastor, 1112
Perry, William C., 64, **1009**, 1736
persecution, 400, **1009–1010**, *See also* Diehl, Johann Georg; religious persecution
    of Baptists, 87
    Basil, Switzerland, 159
    of Bernese Anabaptists, 121
    Brethren, lineage of, 613
    Brethren movement, 289
    of the early Brethren, 9, 107
    ethics, 458
    Fischer, Johann, 491
    galley servitude and, 159
    Germantown, 542
    Hoffmann, Eva Elizabeth, 617
    Holland and, 147
    Hope, Christian, 628
    Mack, Anna Margaretha Kling, and family fleeing to Schwarzenau/Eder, 778

Mennonites, 815
migration of Brethren, 829
militia nonparticipation, 832
Mumma (Moomaw) family, 896
mural paintings at Camp Mack portraying, 896
nonresistance, 944
peace and Anabaptists, 998
pillories, use of, 159
Radical German Pietism, 1079
religious liberty, 1098
Rosenberger family fleeing in Palatinate, 1123
Royer family, 1128
Smith, Samuel on, of Brethren, 1191
Solingen Brethren, 147, 990
Persia, *See* Iran
    Foreign Missionary Society (BC, FGBC), 501
    imposters among the Brethren, 648
    missions, 861
Persinger, George
    St. Albany Old German Baptist Brethren Church, WV, deacon, 1134
Person, Frances Joyce, 2289
personal appearance, **1010**
personal ownership of land, congregational names derived from, 911
Persons, Helen E., 2304
Persson, N., 1736
Perth, ND, 1281
    Church of the Brethren, 251, *See* Turtle Mountain Church of the Brethren, ND
Pertle Springs, MD
    General Education Board (CB), 537
Peru
    Brethren Church, 2141, **2237**
    Institute for Inter-American Affairs field mission
        Wampler, Frederick Jacob, 1316
    missions, 2224, 2225, 2226
Peru, IN, 256, 758
    Center Chapel Brethren Church, *See* Center Chapel Brethren Church, IN
    Church of the Brethren, **1010**
        Mexico, IN, Church of the Brethren, 821
    First Brethren Church, 485, **1010**
    Grace Brethren Church, **1010**
Petcher, Dorothy
    memoirs and poetry of, 2350
Petcher, Edith, 263
Petcher, Esther Mae Wilson, 1842
Petcher family
    Fruitdale, AL, Church of the Brethren, 520
Petcher, Glenn William, 143, 263, 516, 520, 1736
Petcher, Paul Walter, 1737, 1842
Petcher, Rhett Ralph, 695, 1737, **2385**
    Red Hill Church of the Brethren, VA, pastor, 1088
    memoirs and poetry of, 2350
Petcher, Richard L., 2289
Petcher, Steven P., 2289
Peter Becker Community, 108, **1010**
Peter Becker Memorial Home (CB), *See* Peter Becker Community
Peter, George

Little Conewago, PA, congregation, 1012
Peter, Jack K., Jr.
    North Lauderdale, FL, Grace Brethren Church, pastor, 948
Peter Lehman
    Wangman, Andrew on letter by Miller, Peter to, 2362
"Peter Miller's Scheme of Floating Firewood on Creeks" (Sachse), 2015
Peter of Bruys
    oaths, taking of, 959
Peter, Stephen
    Little Conewago, PA, congregation, 1012
Peter, Timothy H., 2289
Peterman family, 738
Peterman, Henry
    Mud Valley Old German Baptist Brethren Church, IL, deacon, 892
1 Peter
    1:1–2, 55
    1:20, 56
    2:4, 6, 9, 55, 56
    3:20–21, 85
2 Peter
    1:10, 55
    3:9, 55
Peters, Aaron Newton, 1737
Peters, Abraham C., 268, 1737
    Filley German Baptist Brethren Church, NE, 2374
Peters, Alice Kathryn Eller, 1011
Peters, Amos Ben, 94, 124, 251, 299, 569, 572, **1011**, 1240, 1319, 1330, 1737
    migration of Brethren, 830
    Mount Hope Church of the Brethren, WA, elder, 882
    North Dakota Brethren settlement, 946
    railroads and Brethren settlement, 1082
Peters, Barbara Blocker, 1011
Peters, Barbara (later McFadden), 1011
Peters, Charles W., 350, 1737, 2304, **2385**
Peters, Chester A., 2036
Peters, Christena Brubaker, 217
Peters Creek Church of the Brethren, VA, 343, **1011**, 2081
    example of place name, 911
    Green Hill Church of the Brethren, VA, 570
    Johnsville Church of the Brethren, VA, 675
    Masons Cove Church of the Brethren, VA, origin as mission point of, 800
    Poages Mill Church of the Brethren, VA, 1039
    Roanoke, VA, Oak Grove Church of the Brethren, 1113
Peters Creek Old German Baptist Brethren Church, VA, 164, **1012**
    Mill Creek Old German Baptist Brethren Church, VA, 833
Peters, Daisy, 2036
Peters, Daniel, 1243, 1737, *See also* Peters family
Peters, Daniel A., 470, 1737
Peters, David, 496, 1737
Peters, David A., 1737
Peters, David B., 1737
Peters, Denton, 62
Peters, Donald, 496, 1737
Peters, Donald B., 2289
Peters, Donald E., Jr., 2289

Peters, E. Rowena Stoner, 1011
Peters, Edward L.
    on Peters, Michael, descendants of, 2350
Peters, Elizabeth Ikenberry, 1011
Peters, Elizabeth (later Montgomery)
    Montgomery, Michael, wife of, 872
Peters family, 355, 717, **1012**, 1280, 1389, 1956, 2040
    Graybill (Grabill, Krehbiel) family, 567
    Hanawalt family, 582
Peters, Fred George, 1737, 1852, 2304
Peters, Gary L., 2289
Peters, George W., "Dunker Barn," *90, 1361*
    mutual aid, 903
Peters, Harvey Wilford, 424, 1737
Peters, Hazel M.
    On Earth Peace Assembly, 2235
    National Older Adult Conferences, 2229
Peters, Hiram W., 725, 1737
Peters, Isaac B., 1011
Peters, J. Bentley, 1011, 1737
Peters, J. Bunyan, 1737
    Pulaski, VA, Church of the Brethren, moderator, 1071
    Roanoke, VA, Williamson Road Church of the Brethren, moderator, 1114
Peters, J. H., 626
Peters, J. H., Jr., 1216
Peters, Jack K., Jr., 503, 1302, 1737
Peters, Jack K., Sr., 579
    Lakeland, FL, Grace Brethren Church, 2213
Peters, Jacob, 1737
Peters, Jesse, 1737
Peters, Joel H., Sr., 1737
    Oak Hill Old German Baptist Brethren Church, VA, elder-in-charge, 957
Peters, Joel B., 1737
Peters, Joel Howard, Jr., 1737
    Oak Hill Old German Baptist Brethren Church, VA, minister, 957
    Peters Creek Old German Baptist Brethren Church, VA, minister, 1012
Peters, John Bunyan, 912, 1011
Peters, John R., 226, 1321, 1737
Peters, Jonas J., 1737
Peters, Joseph J., 2036
Peters, Keith A., 2289
Peters-Lewellen families
    Lewellen, Clifford Peters on, 2343
Peters, Lloyd W., 62, 1737
Peters, Loren, family
    Sheridan Lake Old German Baptist Brethren Church, CO, ministers travelling to, 1176
Peters, Maria Epp, *See* Peters family
Peters, Marjorie Herlache, 2036
Peters, Mary C. Eller, 1011
Peters, Merrill Roosevelt, 1737
Peters, Michael
    immigration to America, 1012
Peters, Edward L. on descendants of, 2350
Peters, Mildred Hull
    on CB name index of Southern District of Ohio, 2350
Peters, Morton Hook, 1737
    Manvel, TX, Church of the Brethren, elder, 789
Peters, N. A., 1295
Peters, Nancy, 1359

Peters, Nancy J. Lamia, 2183
Peters, Nathan, Mr. and Mrs.
    at New Lebanon, OH, First Brethren Church, 930
Peters, Newton, 62
Peters, Owen, 743, 1737
    Pleasant Valley German Baptist Brethren Church, NE, 2377
Peters, Preston, 1737
Peters, Raymond Russell, 242, 248, 304, 327, 912, *1011*, **1011**, 1368, 1737, 2036, 2201, 2350
    National Older Adult Conferences, 2229
    North Manchester, IN, Church of the Brethren, pastor, 949
Peters, Richard, 1878
Peters, Riley L., 1737
Peters, Robert, 1737
    Peters Creek Old German Baptist Brethren Church, VA, minister, 1012
Peters, S. Jane Johnson, 1852
Peters, Sallie (later Montgomery)
    Montgomery, Michael, mother of, 871
Peters, Stephen Paul, 579, 2289
Peters, Thomas A., 2289
Peters, Victor, 2036
Peters, Wilfred, 1737
Peters, William
    Rileyville, VA, Church of the Brethren, preacher, 1109
Peters, William Denton, 1737
    Oak Hill Old German Baptist Brethren Church, VA, minister, 957
Peters, William H., 1737
    Oak Hill Old German Baptist Brethren Church, VA, elder-in-charge, 957
Peters, William J., 1737, 2304, **2385**
    Mexico Old German Baptist Brethren Church, IN, minister, 821
    Pipe Creek Old German Baptist Brethren Church, IN, minister, 1026
Peters, Woodford W., **1011**, 1737
    McPherson College, president, 781
Petersburg Co., WV, 171
Petersburg, WV, 1336
    Memorial Church of the Brethren, 1397, **2377**
    Grant Co., WV, **1012**
Petersen, Barthold Jügen, 580, **1012**
Petersen, Johanna Eleanore, 120
Petersens
    Philadelphian Society and Universalism, 1080
Petersheim, Anna Yoder, *See* Petersheim family
Petersheim family, 2036
Petersheim, Jacob J., *See* Petersheim family
Petersheim, Tobie E., 2036
Petersime, Ira, 1012
Petersime, Mary Anna, 1842, 1846
Petersime, Ray, 246, **1012**, *1331*
Peterson, A. M., 244
    Mountain Grove Church of the Brethren, MO, minister, 889
Peterson, Amos M., 105, 1737
Peterson, Andrew P., 1737
Peterson, B. M., 1737
Peterson Chapel, *See* Hollow Poplar Church of the Brethren, NC
Peterson, Charles, 1737

Peterson, Deborah D., 2289
Peterson, Dick, 676
Peterson, Elhanan, 620, 1737
Peterson, Eugene, 2137
Peterson family
    Hollow Poplar Church of the Brethren, NC, 620
    Maryville, TN, Oakland German Baptist Brethren Church, 799
    Mount Etna, IA, Church of the Brethren, 881
Peterson, Gertrude (later Ensor), 1610
Peterson, Glenn R., 1737
Peterson, Henry H., 1737
    Petersons Chapel Church of the Brethren, NC, 1012
Peterson, Hiram, 1737
Peterson, J. D., 1737
    Petersons Chapel Church of the Brethren, NC, 1012
    Pigeon River Church of the Brethren, NC, minister, 1023
Peterson, Jerry
    on disciples of new church development, 2350
Peterson (Petersen), Johann
    Philadelphian Society, 1019, 1080
Peterson, John Henry, 79, 105, 1737
Peterson, Joseph, 79
Peterson, Karen (later Miller), 2287
    church governance and, 2264
Peterson-Karlan, Cheryl Lynn, 2289
Peterson, Lynell, 1737
    Pigeon River Church of the Brethren, NC, minister, 1023
Peterson, Merenius, 1738
Peterson, Peter, 1384
Peterson, Peter C., 598, 1738
Peterson, Richard, 1738
Peterson, Solomon, 1738
Peterson, Sue, *2144*
Peterson-Synan, Carl, 243
Peterson-Synan, Kristina, 243
Peterson, T. C., 1738
Petersons Chapel Church of the Brethren, NC, **1012**
Pethel family
    Osceola, IN, Grace Brethren Church, 983
Petit family
    Rittman, OH, First Brethren Church, 1111
Petitioner, The, **1012**, 2036
"Petitioners," *See* Old Order German Baptists
    Old Order German Baptist Church, 972
petitions, *See Short and Sincere Declaration, A; Wrightsman, Peter R.*
    Old Order Movement and noncreedalism, 942
    to annual meetings by Old German Baptist Brethren, 967
petitions, land advertising, opposing (1897), 7
petitions to Annual Meeting
    conservative elders and deacons, 1985
Petre, David R., 210, 1738
Petre family, *See* Petri family
Petre, Ira Samuel, 307, 1738, 1842
Petre, Mary Magdalene Guyton, 1842–1843
Petri (Petry, Petre) family, **1013**
Petrie family
    Sanger family, related to, 1144

Petrobrusians
  oaths, taking of, 959
Petroleum, IN, 1316
Petry, Andrew A., 1738
Petry, Anna Danner, 1013
Petry, Benjamin Franklin, 417, 1013, 1738
Petry, C. C., 262
Petry, C. H., 1213
Petry, Carl G., 1738
Petry, Carroll Marvin, 1738, 1843
Petry, Catherine (later Bucher), 1013, 2036
Petry, Charles E., 1738
Petry, Chester H., 1738
  Richmond, IN, Church of the Brethren,
    holding revival meetings at, 1108
Petry, Cornelius C., 1738
Petry, Daniel Franklin, Sr., 1738
  Mill Creek Old German Baptist
    Brethren Church, VA, minister,
    833
Petry, Daniel Mark, 2289
Petry, Edgar G., 246, 264, 1738, 2036
Petry, Edwin C., 1738
Petry, Elden M., 1738, 2304
  Muncie, IN, Church of the Brethren,
    minister, 896
Petry, Elizabeth (later Miller), 1013
Petry, Elizabeth (later Schlothaur), 1013
Petry, Elizabeth Wehrly, 1013
Petry, Elmer S., 1738
Petry family, See Petri family
  Genesee Old German Baptist
    Brethren Church, MI, 540
Petry, Francis Michael, 2011–2012
Petry, Frank
  Prices Creek Old German Baptist
    Brethren Church, OH, presiding
    elder, 1057
Petry, George (Mineral Springs, MO), 1738
Petry, George (Upper Codorus, PA), 1738
  Little Conewago, PA, congregation,
    minister, 1013
Petry, Harry H., 1738
Petry, Henry, 1013
Petry, Jacob, 1013
  Twin Creek, OH, congregation, 1013
Petry, James F., 1738
Petry, Jennie Kitterman, 1013
Petry, John, 415
Petry, John R., 65
Petry, Joyce E., 2289
Petry, Luther, 1738
  Richmond, IN, Church of the Brethren,
    1108
Petry, Magdalena, 686, 1013
Petry, Margaret Mayo James, 1843
Petry, Marion Lester, 1738
Petry, Mary, 166
Petry, Mary Elizabeth, 2036
Petry, Mary (later Garber;Kinsey), 1013
Petry, Michael, 1738, 2036
  Pipe Creek, MD, congregation, elder,
    1013
Petry, Michael W., 1738
Petry, Ralph Roosevelt, 1242, 1738, 2036
Petry, Ray C., **1013**
Petry, Ronald Dean, 1738, 2036
Petry, Samuel (Mill Creek, VA), 1738
Petry, Samuel (Prices Creek, OH), 1738
Petry, Stephen (Steffan), 1013, 2051
Petry, Stephen S., 122, 1738
Petry, Wilmer A., 1738
Pett, Mark, 1738

Petter, Amy Laura, 1849
Pettersson, John, 1738
petticoats, quilted, See hoops
Pettikofer family
  Allen (ship), passengers on, 2126
Pettikoffer, Anna Elizabeth, 2377
Pettikoffer, Gertrud, 2377
Pettikoffer house, Germantown, PA, 1344
Pettikoffer, John, 2377
Pettikoffer, Martha Lina, 2377
Pettikoffer (Pettighofer, Pethkoffer) family,
  2377
Petty, Donald B.
  on Ephrata Cloister, printing at, 2350
Petty, Richard, 165
Peugh, Nancy Sue Orndorf, 1852
Peugh, Roger Dennis, 439, 1738, 1852
pews, 2131
pewterware
  Herr, Donald M. on PA German, 2336
Peyton, James Madison, 2289
Peyton, Samuel, 1738
Pfäffli family
  Mortonhouse (ship), 2373, 2376
Pfahler, Larry, 1738
  medical missions, 807
Pfaltzbach family, See Balsbaugh family
Pfaltzgraff, Roy E.
  medical missions, 807
Pfaltzgraff Eller, Enten Vernard, 2289
Pfaltzgraff Eller, Kathryn Joyce, 2289
Pfaltzgraff family, 686
  Pfaltzgraff pottery and, 2250
Pfaltzgraff, G. Nevin, 1013
Pfaltzgraff, George B.
  Pfaltzgraff pottery and, 2250
Pfaltzgraff, Henry B.
  Pfaltzgraff pottery and, 2250
Pfaltzgraff, Johann George, 2250
Pfaltzgraff, John B., 2250
Pfaltzgraff, Kathryn Carol Krehmeyer, 1843
  Pfaltzgraff, Roy E., Sr., (CB) and, 2250
Pfaltzgraff, Mary Roth, 1013
Pfaltzgraff pottery
  Pfaltzgraff family and, 2250
Pfaltzgraff, Roy E., Jr., 2289
Pfaltzgraff, Roy E., Sr., (CB), 4, 24, 1388
  Pfaltzgraff, John B. and, 2250
Pfaltzgraff, Roy Edward, Sr., **1013**, 1738,
  1843, 2250, **2377**
Pfaltzgraff, Roy Edward, Jr., 1738, 1843
  Pfaltzgraff, Roy E., Sr., (CB) and, 2250
Pfaltzgraff, Roy Edward and Violet
  Hackman, **1013**
Pfaltzgraff, Susan Keeney, 2250
Pfaltzgraff, Violet G. Hackman, **1013**, 1843,
  2377
  Pfaltzgraff, Roy E., Sr., (CB) and, 2250
Pfarr, Adam, 720
Pfau, Adrian, See Pauw, Adrian
Pfau, Anna Magdalena Yount, 1013
Pfau, Catherine Disslin, 481
Pfau (Faw) family, **1013**
Pfau, Gregory, 715, 1738
Pfau, Jacob, See Faw, Jacob
  immigration from Switzerland, 1013
Pfau (Pauw) family, 324
Pfauts family, See Pfautz family
Pfautz, Anna, 225
Pfautz, Anna Markley, 1014
Pfautz, Catherine Doyle, 1015
Pfautz, Catherine (later Crumpacker), 1013
Pfautz, Catherine Slough (Schlauch), 1013

Pfautz, Daniel M., 2036
Pfautz, Elizabeth Eby, 1014
Pfautz family, 298, 1299, See also Fouts
  (Foutz, Pfoutz, Pfautz) family
  article about, 1914
Pfautz, Fianna, 225
Pfautz (Fouts) family
  Fahnestock family, 465
    Flat Rock Church of the Brethren, NC,
    493
  Pfautz (Fouts, Foutz) family, 2037
Pfautz, J. E., 611, 613, 1211, 1862
  hymnals, 641
  publishing German language poetry
    and hymns, 1057
Pfautz, Jacob, 1014, 1738
  Pfautz, Johann (Hans) Michael, son of,
    1013
Pfautz, Jacob F.
  Pfautz, John Eby, father of, 1014
Pfautz, Jacob K., 1738
Pfautz, Johann (Hans) Michael, Jr., 1014
Pfautz, Johann (Hans) Michael, Sr., **1013**
  Pfoutz, Johann Michael, 1014–1015
Pfautz, Johann Michael, 1738
Pfautz, John, 1013
Pfautz, John Bauer, *1014*
Pfautz, John David, 1014
Pfautz, John Eby, 331, **1014**, 2036–2037
  Schönes Lied, Ein, 1155
Pfautz, John Michael, 2037
Pfautz, Laura Susan Frantz, 1940
Pfautz, Margaret (later Huber), 634
Pfautz, Michael, 547, 1739, 1900
  Pipe Creek, MD, congregation, 1013
Pfautz (Pfouts, Fouts) family, **1014**
  Pfautz, Johann (Hans) Michael, 1013
Pfautz, Theobald, 1014
Pfautz, Ursula Muehlenhauser, 1013
Pfeffer, Mary Lou, 2304
Pfeiffer, Caroll Marie Stiverson, 2289
Pfeiffer, Robert A., 2289
Pfister, Andrew, 1292
Pfleiderer, Florizel A., 1739
Pflug, Günther
  on Ephrata Cloister, 2350
Pfouts family, See Pfautz family
Pfouts, Hannah (later Knouff), **704**
Pfoutz, Abraham, 1739
Pfoutz, Catherine, 1015
Pfoutz, Catherine Beard, 1015
Pfoutz, Christian Lahman, 1739
Pfoutz, Daniel, 1739
Pfoutz, David (father), 546, **1014–1015**,
  1739
Pfoutz, David (son), 1015
Pfoutz, Donald W., 1739
Pfoutz, Elizabeth, 160, 1015
Pfoutz, Esther (later Stoner), 1225
Pfoutz family, See Fouts (Foutz, Pfoutz,
  Pfautz) family; Pfautz family;
  Rinehart family
Pfoutz, George, 1739
Pfoutz, Hannah, 1015
Pfoutz, Isaac, 106, **1015**, 1739
Pfoutz, Jacob, 1015
Pfoutz, Johann Michael
  Pfautz, Johann (Hans) Michael,
    1014–1015
Pfoutz, John, 1015
Pfoutz, John, family
  Pipe Creek Church of the Brethren,
    MD, 1026

Pfoutz, Mary, 1015
Pfoutz, Mary Bosserman, 163
Pfoutz, Mary Diehl, 1015
Pfoutz meetinghouse
    Gettysburg, PA, Marsh Creek Church
        of the Brethren, 546
Pfoutz, Michael, 163
Pfoutz (Pfautz), Jacob, 1739
Pfoutz, Samuel, 1739
Pfoutz, Sarah (later Trostle), 1276
Pfoutz, Sydney Ann, 1276
Phabler, Larry Lee, 1852
Phabler, Linda Kay Horn, 1852
Phares (Pharis), Boyd H., 551, 558–559,
    1287, 1739
Pharisburg
    Sciota Church of the Brethen, OH
        preaching point, 1160
Pheasant, Clayton, N., 1739
Pheasant, Paul Ernest, 109, 1739
Phelps Co., MO, 1324
Phelps, Louis C., 157, 1739
Phelps, William Henry, 1739
Phennicie, William Franklin, 1739, 2304
Phibbs, Dawn Glick, 554
Phibbs, Garnett Ersiel, 552, 1739, 2037
    Pulaski, VA, Church of the Brethren,
        minister, 1071
Phibbs, Raymond C.
    and neoorthodoxy, 923
    Pulaski, VA, Church of the Brethren,
        minister, 1071
Phiel, Abram, 1739
Phiel, Adam, 1739
Phiels (Phields), Samuel W., 1739
Philadelphia Centennial Exposition, 913
Philadelphia Co. (now Montgomery Co.),
    PA
    Skippack area, PA, 1189
Philadelphia College of Medicine, 809
Philadelphia College of Osteopathic
    Medicine (PCOM)
    Young, Galen S. and, 2268
Philadelphia, PA, 18, 22, 166, 175, 191,
    1284, 1890, 2039, 2056
    Allen's (ship) arrival at, 2126
    Behmenism, 2082
    Bethany Church of the Brethren, 91,
        1015
    Brethren fundamentalism, 1005
    Brethren movement in, 2067
    Durnbaugh, Donald F. on, 2326
    Calvary Church of the
        Brethren, 1015
    congregations, 248, 255, 283, 692,
        1401, 1373
        insurance, 657
        Sunday school movement, 1239
        universalism, 1292
    Crossroads Grace Brethren Church,
        2238
    First Brethren Church
        missions, 861
    First Brethren Church (BC), 239, 259,
        694, 706
        charters/charter membership, 273
    First Church of the Brethren, 81, 694,
        706, 709, 710, 1015–1016,
        1016, 1245, 1373
        historical writing, 612
        Howe, Roland Levi, 633
        minorities, ethnic and racial, 850

Philadelphia, PA, Bethany Church
    of the Brethren, 1015
    study of congregation, 1975
First Grace Brethren Church, 96, 97,
    1015
    Crossroads Grace Brethren Church
        and, 2238
    Hatboro, PA, Suburban Grace
        Brethren Church, 588
Geiger Memorial Church of the
    Brethren, 355, 1016
German Baptist Brethren congregation,
    259, 697
German Reformed Church, 1221
Grace Brethren congregations, 1005
history and development of
    Philadelphia community, 1967
Kalmyks in, 1923
Keyser, Peter, 691
The Missionary Board (BC), 855
missions, 860
North Philadelphia Church of the
    Brethren, 1016–1019
Pennsylvania Germans' preferred point
    of entry to America, 1006
publishing, 1063
Sauer family printing business,
    1146–1147, 1148–1149
Sisterhood of Mary and Martha, 1187
Stutzman, Jacob, 1233
Sunday school movement, 283
Swigart, William Joseph, 1245
Third Brethren Church (FGBC), 1019
    Hatboro, PA, Suburban Grace
        Brethren Church, 588
universalism, history of, 2081
urban ministry, 1296, 1297
Whisler family, 2097
Yeremian (Yereman), O. H., 1385
Zimmerman mystics, 686
Philadelphia, PA, Germantown Church of
    the Brethren, 21, 122, 175, 1016,
    1017, 1018, 1226, 1227, 1316,
    1325, 2081, 2188, 2189, 2189
    Alexander Mack's Bible, 777
    anniversary love feast, two-hundred-
        fiftieth anniversary, 1282
    bibliography, 1859
    cemetery, 405
    German Baptist Brethren Historical
        Association, 540
    Germantown Trust, 2188, 2189
    Heidelberg Catechism, 593
    Heinrich Scharpnack, 1152
    historical writing, 611
    Höhn, Heinrich, 618
    library catalogue, Dunker Sunday
        school, 1947
    Mack, Alexander, Jr., elder and pastor,
        774, 775
    Mack, Elizabeth Neiß (Nice), 778
        ministry, 844
    Myers, Jacob Tobias, 904
    Myers, Tobias Timothy, pastor, 905
    Oak Hill Old German Baptist Brethren
        Church, VA, 957
    overseer of the poor, 986
    Parsons, Johanna Christina Zeidig, 994
    Pennsylvania settlement, 1004
    Philadelphia, PA, First Church of the
        Brethren, 1015
    Philipp Weber family property sold for
        meetinghouse, 1325

poor box, 1046
Preiß (Price) family, 1055
Pricetown Meetinghouse, 1057
publications, 1947
Sauer, Christopher, II, elder and pastor,
    774
Skippack area, PA, 1189
Sunday school movement, 1237
Sunday schools, 427
Swigart, Milton Clarke, 1245
Traut family, 1270–1271
universalism, 1292
urban ministry in Philadelphia, 1296
widows, care for, 1344
Philadelphia Record
    French, Paul Comly, 515
Philadelphian movement
    Marsay, Charles Hector de St. Georges,
        Marquis de, 796
    Reformation, Protestant, and Brethren
        doctrine, 1092
    Reitz, Johann Heinrich, 1095
Philadelphian Society, 30, 1019
    Universalism, 1080
philanthropy
    Collegiants, 324
    Sauer, Johann Christoph, I, 1148
Philathea Hall
    Grace Schools (Grace Theological
        Seminary, Grace College), 563
Philemon
    Kent, Homer Austin, Jr., 2211, 2340
    Martin, Harold S. on, 2345
Philemon, Brother, See Reisman, Johann
Philippi, Albert J., 1739
Philippians
    2:12–13, 56
    Kent, Homer Austin, Jr. on, 2340
The Philippines
    missions, 2225
    missions, short-term, 2226
    Noffsinger, John Samuel, educator in,
        939
    University of La Verne degree pro-
        grams on military bases, 715–716
Philipps University, Marburg Germany
    Brethren Colleges Abroad (BCA) pro-
        gram, 2142
Philippy, Fianna Pfautz, 225
Philips, Dirk, 29
Philips, Obbe
    Menno Simons, 814
Phillippi, William R., 1739
Phillips, Bobby L., 1739
Phillips, C. L.
    Mount Zion Church of the Brethren,
        WV, 888
Phillips, Carl H., 1739
Phillips, Carl M., 2289
Phillips Co., KS
    Pleasant View Church of the Brethren,
        KS, 1036
Phillips, David, 1739
Phillips, Edna (later Sutton), 768
Phillips family, 143
    Mount Cassell Old German Baptist
        Brethren Church, WV, 880
Phillips, George A., 1324, 1739
Phillips, George W., 439, 1316, 1739, 2385
    Rock Run Church of the Brethren, IN,
        summer pastor, 1117
Phillips, H. Ison, 1739
Phillips, Howard B., 1739

Phillips, Joanne (later Dolnikowski), 2241
Phillips, Joyce, 566
Phillips, Keeley, 566
Phillips, Marvin Conard, 1739
Phillips, Mary Palmer, 2037
Phillips, Nora Almira (later Flory), 1837, 1923, 2185
Phillips, W., 1739
Phillips, William B., 1739
Phillips, William R., 1739
The Philorhetorian, 2024
philosophers, Brethren children named for, 912
philosophy
    Martin, Jacob, 2007
Phnom Penh, Vietnam
    missions, 2225
Phoenix, AZ
    First Church of the Brethren, **1019,** 1314
        Lynnhaven Community Church of the Brethren, **1019**
        Mesa, AZ, Community Church of the Brethren, 2222
    Grace Brethren Church, **1019**
        Malles, Mark Ellsworth, 2217
    Tempe, AZ, Papago Park Brethren Church, 1251
    Northwest Grace Brethren Church, **1019,** 2132
Phoenix Brethren Christian School, 2132
Phoenix, Judy Matteau
    Island Pond, VT, Grace Brethren Church, 2209
Phoenix, Michael
    Island Pond, VT, Grace Brethren Church, 2209
Phoenix (ship)
    Erbaugh family, 453
    Etter family, 459
    Garber (Garver, Gerber) family, 530
    Noffsinger family, 939
photographs and photography, **1019–1021**
    doctrine on, 189
    dress in, 402
    Fahrney, Jacob, 465
    historical libraries, 610
    historical writing, 611
    Hoff, Ernest Gockley, 617
    Holsinger's History of the Tunkers and the Brethren Church, 623
    mass media, 800
    movie cameras, 1020
    Sachse, Julius F., 1133
Phouts family, *See* Pfautz family
Phoutz family, *See* Pfautz family
physically handicapped, *See* disabled
physicians
    Africa
        volunteer service, 2073
    on family, 2082
    Sauer, Peter, 1149
    Wrightsman, Peter R., 1380
    Yeremian (Yereman), O. H., 1385
Pia desideria (Spener), 1209, *See also* Spener, Philipp Jakob
Pietism, 1021
pianos, *See* musical instruments
Piatt Co., IL, 152, 270, 713
    Osage Church of the Brethren, KS, 983
Picard, Fred A., 1876
Picard, John Steward, 2289
    Mansfield, OH, Conservative Grace

Brethren Church, 2218
Picard, Paul, 1979
Picard, Paula (later Bowser), 2273
Picard, Ronald J., 1286, 1739
Pickaway Co., OH, 313
Pickels, W. Herman, 319, 746, 1739
Pickering, Ernest, 2037
Pickett, Clarence Evan, 608, **1021,** 1207, 2037
Pickrell, NE
    Hope Memorial, NE, congregation, 945
Piedmont
    Brethren, lineage of, 613
Piedmont mission point
    Germantown Brick Church of the Brethren, VA, 544
Piel, William T., 1224, 1739
Pieniazek, S. A., 2129
    Poland and relief efforts, 1041
Piepkorn, Arthur Carl, 379, 2037
Pierard, Richard V., 2037
Pieratt, Carolyn Ann (later Schrock), 1844
    Sudan (CB) and, 2253
Pierce, C. M., 635, 1739
Pierce, Cindy Wright
    Island Pond, VT, Grace Brethren Church, 2209
Pierce Co. Church of the Brethren, WI, **1021**
Pierce, Daniel
    Island Pond, VT, Grace Brethren Church, 2209
Pierce, William, 1739
Pierson, Augustus B., 1739
Pierson, IA, congregation, 695
Pierson, Mary Elizabeth (later Grieve)
    Grieve, Jerry Allen, 2194
Piesen, Joseph F., 1739
Pieters, John, 2157
Pieters, Tracey, 2157
Pietism, 407, **1021–1022,** 1022, 1986, 2005, 2043, 2045, 2046, 2051, 2059, *See also* Radical German Pietism
    as a source for Beissel's ideas, 113
    in Alsace, France, 19
    antinomian communes and, 236
    Apocrypha, use of in, 43
    and Arminianism, 56
    art, attitude toward in, 59
    Bedächtliches Antwortschreiben, 1872
    Berleburg Bible, 138
    in Berleburg, Germany, 120
    Bible, study of, 131–132
    bibliography, 1892
    Boehmists and, 156
    books about, 1951
    Brethren doctrine of salvation, 1140
    Brethren movement, 174, 379
    Brethren movement, influences of, 355
    Brown, Dale Weaver, 2152
    Camisards, 242
    Christian education movement, 283
    church membership, 813
    Churches of God (GC), 309
    collegia pietatis, 323
    communitarianism, 328
    contributions to Brethren beliefs, 2075
    conversion, doctrine of, 16, 339
    covenant theology, 348
    Denmark and, 157
    devotional literature, 381
    dissertation on, 1916

Dueck, A. on community and, 2325
Durnbaugh, Donald F., 2325, 2326, 2327
Eckartshausen, 421
Eckerlin, Michael, 421, 2053
Eller, David B. on, 2329
Eppstein, 452
Eternal security, 456
Evangelical Association, 459
Evangelical Covenant Church, 459
family, 472, 474
Francke, August Hermann, 506, 1258
fundamentalism, 522
Geistreiches Gesang-Buch (Spiritual Songbook), 534
German Sectarians of Pennsylvania, The, 542
Goebel, Max, 555
grace, doctrine of, 562
Grahe, Wilhelm, 564
Great Awakening, 568
Grebe (Grebi), Georg, 569
Gruber, Eberhard Ludwig, 575
Halle pietists, 580, 1209
    Bibles, 1149
    printing press sought from, 1147
Haug, Johann Friedrich, 589
Heidelberg, 593
Henckels, Johann Friedrich, 596
Henrich Albrecht, 597
Hesse, 602
history, 611, 612, 2201, 2074, 2088
Holy Spirit, doctrine of, 624
honorific titles, 1266
human nature, doctrine of, 635
humanitarianism, 635
Hymnal: A Worship Book, 2206
hymns, 642
influence of, 5
influence of Gottfried Arnold on, 57
influence on Brethren theology, 1258–1260
influences, 294
interdenominational relations, 1183
International Fellowship of Grace Brethren Churches, 2208
Jung-Stilling, Heinrich, 677, 1980
Kämpfer, Johannes, listed as member of pietest group leaving for Pennsylvania, 683
Karl Ludwig, count of Sayn-Wittgenstein-Sayn, denunciation of pietists by, 683
Kling, Johann Valentin, 702
König, Samuel, 706
Lambsheim, 720
Liebe, Christian, 741
Lobach, Johann, 751
Longenecker, Stephen L. on Brethren among, 2343
love, theology of, 761
Lucas, Martin, 766
Lutheran Church, 767
Mack, Alexander, Sr., 375, 775, 776
Mack, Anna Margaretha Kling, 778
Mack, Johann Philipp, distressed by son's activities in, 778
Mallott, Floyd Ellwood, 784
Mennonite Brethren Churches, General Conference of, 814
Mennonites, 816
millennialism, 833
missions, 857

Moravian Brethren, 875, 2062
noncreedalism, 942
Palatinate and, 159
peace position of Brethren, 999
periodicals, 1946
pietist conventicles, 1223, 1227–1228
prayer, 1051
priesthood of all believers, 1057
Raabe, Paul on, 2351
radial pietism, 1921
Radical German Pietism, 1079
radical pietism, thesis on, 1930
redemption, 1090
Reformation, Protestant, and Brethren
    doctrine, 1092
reformation, thesis on, 1948
research trends, 1921
Rock, Johann Friedrich, 1116
role in development of Brethren theolo-
    gy, 1258–1260
roots of adoption in, 5–6
Roth, John D. on, 2353
salvation, 1142
Scheublein, Christian, 1178
separatism and, 1166–1167
sexuality, human, 1170
Sider, E. Morris on conversion narra-
    tives for, 2356
sin, 1184
singing, 1184
Social Gospel Movement, 1197
Solingen Brethren, 1201
sources on, 2310, 2312, 2313, 2315,
    2319, 2321, 2324
Spener, Philipp Jakob, 1209, 1258,
    1259
spiritual life, 1209
Stoffer, Dale R. on, 2359
Stumpf, Julian, 1232
suppression of
    Bern, Switzerland, 2084
theology, 303
theology and, 2255
Treytorrens, Nicolas Samuel de, 1274
trinity, doctrine of, 1275
visions, 1309
Weck, Wilhelm, 1325
Wetterau region, 1338
Wittgenstein, Countesses, 2074
Wittgenstein territory, 1354–1355
works righteousness, 1368
worldliness, nonconformity to, 1373
worship, nonliturgical nature of, 1373
The Young Center and, 2267
Zinzendorf, Nikolaus Sudwig, Count
    von, 1399
pietist conventicles
    house churches, 632
pietistic awaker, 188
pietistic revivals
    Evangelical United Brethren Church,
        460
piety
    appearance of, 1985
    definition of, 386
Pifer, Bonnie
    Pifer, Lester Elden and, 2238
Pifer, Fred, 1739
Pifer, Genevene Edna
    Pifer, Lester Elden and, 2238
Pifer, Lester Elden, 188, 443, 515, 1739,
    2037, 2139, **2238**
    South Bend, IN, Ireland Road Grace

Brethren Church, pastor, 1203
Pifer, Samuel, 1739
Pigeon Creek Church of the Brethren, IL
    Oak Grove Church of the Brethren, IL,
        955
Pigeon Creek churchhouse, Ten Mile
    Church of the Brethren, PA, 1253
Pigeon River Church of the Brethren, IN,
    1022–1023, See also English
        Prairie Church of the Brethren, IN
Pigeon River Church of the Brethren, NC,
    224, **1023**
    Fundamental Brethren Church, 522
Pigg River Old German Baptist Brethren
    Church, VA, 43, **1023**
    Hess, James Arthur, 2198
    Mountain View Old German Baptist
        Brethren, VA, 2227
Pike Brethren Church, PA, See Johnstown,
    PA, Pike Grace Brethren Church
Pike Co., IL, 321
    Hadley Creek Church of the Brethren,
        IL, 577
Pike Co., KY, 689
    Rock House Church of the Brethren,
        KY, 1117
Pike Creek (Chenoa), IL, Church of the
    Brethren, 345, **1023**
Pike Creek Church of the Brethren, IN, See
    Monticello/Pike Creek Church of
    the Brethren, IN
Pike Grace Brethren Church, PA, See
    Johnstown, PA, Pike Grace
    Brethren Church
Pike, James A., 338
Pike, Mary (later Hendricks), 596
Pike (Mundy's Corner) Brethren Church,
    PA, See Johnstown, PA, Pike
    Grace Brethren Church
Pike, Nedra, 2037
Pike Run Church of the Brethren, PA, **1023**
Pilgerhütte (Pilgrim's Hut), 1255
The Pilgrim, **1023,** 2037, 2093, 2103
    Brumbaugh, Henry B., 219
    Brumbaugh, John Boyer, 219, 220, 221
    Burkholder, Wealthy Agnes Clark(e),
        231
    Huntingdon, PA, Stone Church of the
        Brethren, 637
    Messenger, 818
    Old Brethren, 965, 970
    Old Brethren Church, 2232
    patent medicine advertisements in, 995
    The Primitive Christian, 1058
    publishing, 1068
    Quinter, James, 1077
    renamed The Weekly-Pilgrim, 1327
    united with *The Primitive Christian,*
        1327
The Pilgrim Almanac, 18, 2037
Pilgrim Congregational UCC
    linked with Larchmont Community
        Church, Tacoma, WA, 1247
*Pilgrimage of Faith: The Witness of the
    Brethren Church* (video), 2148,
    2172
Pilgrim's Progress
    Ephrata Press, 452
pilgrimage of pillories, use of, 159
The Pilot, **1023–1024,** 1236, 2037
    The Inglenook, 656
    Mahan, Grant, editor, 782
    Miller, Howard, editor, 838

Native Americans, 2229
Pilot House, *See* Baltimore, MD, Pilot
    House Project
Pilot Knob Church of the Brethren, AR,
    1024
Pindar, Miti
    Mshelia, Madu B., mother of, 892
Pine Creek Church of the Brethren, IL,
    394, **1024,** 1333
    Forney, Daniel L., 502
Polo, IL, Church of the Brethren, 1045
Pine Creek Church of the Brethren, IN,
    147, **1024,** 1220, 1287
    125 year anniversary, 1974
    family histories, 1983
    Peters, Amos B., minister and elder,
        1011
    West Goshen congregation, IN, 749
Pine, E(a)rnest F., 21, 1739
Pine Glen Church of the Brethren, PA,
    1024, 1215
Pine Grove Church of the Brethren, MD,
    1024
Pine Grove Church of the Brethren, VA,
    1024
    Greenmount Church of the Brethren,
        VA, 571
    Melbeth Grove Church of the Brethren,
        VA, 812
Pine Grove congregation, FL
    Homestead Old German Baptist
        Brethren Church, FL, 626
Pine Grove Grace Brethren Church, PA, *See*
    Tremont, PA, Pine Grove Grace
    Brethren Church
Pine Grove, MD, Church of the Brethren,
    430, 728
    Oak Grove Church of the Brethren,
        MD, 956
Pine Grove, MI, Church of the Brethren,
    See Homestead Church of the
    Brethren, MI
Pine Grove Mission, Hawthorne, FL, 691
Pine Grove, MO, Old German Baptist
    Brethren Church, *See* Bay Creek
    Old German Baptist Brethren
    Church, MO
Pine Grove Old German Baptist Brethren
    Church, FL, 497, **1024–1025**
Pine Grove, PA, 1274
    Schuykill Church of the Brethren,
        PA, near, 1157
Pine Grove, PA, Grace Brethren Church
    Myerstown, PA, Grace Brethren
        Church, 906
Pine Grove schoolhouse
    Laurel Glen Brethren Church, WV, 728
Pine Grove, WV
    Allegheny Church of the Brethren,
        WV, 2125
    Pocahontas Church of the Brethren,
        WV, mission point of, 1039
Pine Hill congregation, TN, 1349
Pine Hill, PA, 144
Pine Orchard, MD, Church of the Brethren,
    See Ellicott City, MD, Pine
    Orchard Church of the Brethren
Pine Ridge Church of the Brethren, VA,
    2238
Pine Ridge Dunkard Brethren congregation,
    MS, **2238**
Pine Ridge meetinghouse, VA, 416
Pine Ridge, VA, congregation

Mount Carmel Church of the Brethren, VA, 880

Pine Run congregation, PA
Harleysville, PA, Indian Creek Church of the Brethren, 584
Pine Run German Baptist Brethren, **2377**
Pine Run mission point
Hatfield Church of the Brethren, PA, 588
Pinecrest Manor, Mount Morris, IL, **1025**
Newcomer, Melchor Snively, as benefactor, 933
Statler, Foster Boyd, 1219
Pinella Co., FL
North Tampa, FL, Zion Church of the Brethren, 950
Pineville, VA, Mount Olive Brethren Church, **1025**
Piney Creek Church of the Brethren, MD, **1025**
Piney Creek, PA, Church of the Brethren, 2087
Piney Flats, TN
Church of the Brethren, **1025**, 1339, 1907
Ping, Soo, 201
Ping Ting Chou, China, 209, 277, 278
boys' school, 1303
Horning, Mary Emma, 630
hospital, 630, 1316
mission schools, 853
Pink Eye schoolhouse
mission point for Wiley, CO, Church of the Brethren, 1345
Pinkerton, Adolph, 279
Pinkerton family, 1885
Pinkerton, Kevin W., 2289
Pinkerton, P., 1739
Pinkham, David W., 2289
Pinkstaff, Lawrence Co., IL
Allison Prairie Church of the Brethren, 2126
Pinney, Sandra, 2037
Pioneer Boys Club, See scouting programs
Pioneer Church of the Brethren, NE, See Enders, NE, Church of the Brethren
Pioneer, OH, Bethesda Brethren Church, See Bethesda Brethren Church, OH
Pioneer schoolhouse, NE, 1349
pioneers, 2034, See also frontier; migration
Franklin Co., VA, 2067, 2102
Indiana, 2105
sources on, 2318
western USA, 2103
Pious Chapel, IN
Church of God (New Dunkers), 297
New Dunkard meetinghouse, IN
Patton, Uriah, and, 996
The Pious Companion (Kinsey), 696, 1985
The Pious Youth, **1025**, 1236
German language column, 725
publishing, 1068
Pipe Creek Church of the Brethren, IN, 701, **1025**
Midway Dunkard Berthren Congregation, IN, 827
Nead, D. P., elder in, 919
Peru, IN, Church of the Brethren, 1010
Pipe Creek Church of the Brethren, MD, 80, 106, 425, **1025–1026**
Annual Meeting and Brethren polity, 1042
Maryland Brethren activity, 798
Meadow Branch Church of the Brethren, MD, 805
migration of Brethren, 829
minorities, ethnic and racial, 851
Pipe Creek congregation, MD, 1221, 1225, 1287, 1298
Pipe Creek, MD, 147, 1233, 2075
congregation, 169, 170, 738, 1141, 1152, 2047
mission point for Westminster Church of the Brethren, MD, 1337
Old German Baptist Brethren, 967
Pipe Creek Old German Baptist Brethren Church, IN, **1026**
Mexico Old German Baptist Brethren Church, IN, 821
pipe organ
Ellisforde, Church of the Brethren, WA, 442
Piper family, 1956
Piper, W. H., 1739
Pippen, Everett, 1739
Pippen, Fred
Matteson, MI, Brethren Church, 803
Pippenger, Wesley E.
on Pippenger, William and descendants, 2350
Pippenger, William
Pippenger, Wesley E. on descendants of, 2350
Pippinger family, 153, 1214
Pippinger, Frank, 1356
Salem Old German Baptist Brethren Church, OH, minister, 1139
Pippinger, John, 664, 1739
Piqua, OH, Church of the Brethren, 349, **1026**
Pisel family, 2066
Pisgah, WV, preaching point at, 2125
Pister, Grace Rodabaugh
on Rodabaugh family, 2350
pistology, 386
Piszczon-Czaja, Anna, 2069
Pitcairn, PA, See East McKeesport, PA, Church of the Brethren
Pitman family, 1868
Pitman, Harold Minot, 2037
Pitsburg, OH, Church of the Brethren, 224, **1026,** 2127
Painter Creek Church of the Brethren, OH, 990
Potsdam, OH, Church of the Brethren, 1048
Pittenger, Florence Baker, **1026,** 1843
Pittenger, John Milton, 912, **1026–1027,** 1739, 1843
Pittenger, Joshua W., 1026
Pittenger, Mary Ann Sensemann, 1026
Pittenger (Pittinger), John S., 1740
Pittinger, C. Frank, 2385
Pittman, Henry E., 1740
Pittman, Jesse C., 1740
Pittman, Marianne Rhoades, 2138, 2289
Pittsburg, IN, Church of the Brethren, 375, **1027**
Pittsburgh, PA, 462, 711, 1867
Church of the Brethren, 415, **1027**
congregation, 768
example of place name, 911
First Brethren Church, **1027**
McFaden, John Duke, pastor, 773
Grace Brethren Church, See Corapolis, PA, Bon Meade Grace Brethren Church
Greensburg, PA, Church of the Brethren, 571
Mission Church, 1880
urban ministry, 299
Pittstown, NJ, Calvary Brethren Church, See Calvary Brethren Church, NJ
Pittsylvania Co., VA, 362, 363
New Bethel Church of the Brethren, 925
Ruckers German Baptist Brethren Church, VA, 1129
Pitzer, Donald E.
on communes, 2350
Pitzer, John Riley, 40, 573, 1312, 1321, 1740
Place names
Brethren, **1027–1028**
pronunciation of, 911
placement of pastors, **1028**
General Ministerial Board (CB), 538
Ministry and Home Mission Commission (CB), 848
Placerville, CA, Sierra View Grace Brethren Church, **1028**
Placeway, Richard, 239, 443, 1740
Manheim, PA, Grace Brethren Church, pastor, 787
Parkersburg, WV, Grace Brethren Church, pastor serving, 994
Placeway, Timothy, 2289
Plagge, Andreas
on Beissel, Johann Conrad/Konrad, 2350
plagiarism, 2017
Plain congregation, 1240
plain dress, See dress
plain people, 59, 60, 61, **1029,** 1967, 2046
Amish Mennonites and other sects, 1988
Kulp, Isaac Clarence, Jr. on traditions of, 2342
Lancaster Co., PA, 1986
Pennsylvania, 2002–2003
Plain Remarks on Light-Mindedness . . ., 696
Plain, WA, Church of the Brethren, See Greenwood Church of the Brethren, WA
Plaine, D. H., 164
Plaine, David H., 1740
Peters Creek Old German Baptist Brethren Church, VA, elder-in-charge, 1012
Plaine family, 161
Plainfield congregation, PA, 711
Plainfield, NJ
Seventh-Day Baptist Historical Society, 1133, 1170
Plains meetinghouse
Linville Creek Church of the Brethren, VA, 746
Plains, VA, 1265
Plainview Dunkard Brethren Congregation, OH, **1029**
Englewood, OH, Dunkard Brethren Congregation, 447
plane crashes
Kimmel, Theodore Acroyd, 693
KLM crash, 703
Plank family, 323, 2087

Plank, Jacob Donald, 232, 1740
Plank, John M., 1740
Plank, Polly (later Miller)
    genealogy and descendants, 1943
Plank Road, PA, congregation
    Pike Run Church of the Brethren, PA,
        1023
Planks family, See Indiana
Planning Coordinating Committee (CB)
    organizational restructuring and, 2242
plant life, congregational names derived
    from, 911
Plaster, David R., 55, 1319, 1740, 2149
    on conscientious objectors, 2350
    on GBC, 2350
    on ordinances, 2350
Plate, F. W., 1030
Plate, Laura A. Miller, 1030
Plate, Lewis (Ludwig) A., 180, 218, **1030,**
    2038
Platou, Arnold S.
    on Sharpsburg Church of Brethren,
        MD, 2350
Platt, Emma Funk, 758
Platt family, 323
Platt, Harriet M.
    Ripon, CA, Grace Brethren Church,
        1110
Platt, John Wesley, 332, 913, 1224, 1740
    Manteca, CA, Northgate Community
        Brethren Church, pastor, 788
    Ripon, CA, Grace Brethren Church,
        1110
Platt, Mary (later Faw), 480, 1837
Platt, William Melvan, 758, 1740
    San Bernardino, CA, Church of the
        Brethren, pastor, 1141
Platte Valley German Baptist Brethren
    Church, NE, **1030**
Platter, David Edwin, 2038
Platter family, 2038
Platter, Fenton Henry, 1740
Plattsburg College, **1030**
    Plattsburg Church of the Brethren,
        MO, 1030
    Sharp, Solomon Zook, president of,
        1174
Plattsburg, MO, 690
    Church of the Brethren, **1030,** 2038
    Harman, Hylton, 2196
Plauger, A. J., 1740
Plaugher, Mary E. (later Jarboe), 669
plays, See drama
    Van Dyke, Joe, author of, 2087
Pleß, Viktor, 2038
    Pleasant Center Church of the
        Brethren, OH, **1030**
Pleasant Chapel Church of the Brethren,
    IN, 265, **1030**
Pleasant Dale Church of the Brethren, IN,
    1030–1031, 1316
Pleasant Dale Church of the Brethren, VA,
    360, **1031**
Pleasant Gap, MO
    Gibson, Isham, 548
Pleasant Grove Church of the Brethren, IL,
    1031
Pleasant Grove Church of the Brethren, KS,
    730, **1031,** 1311, 1321, 1346
    Hoppingite Schism, 630
Pleasant Grove Church of the Brethren,
    NC, 224, **1031**
Pleasant Grove Church of the Brethren, TX,
    1031
Pleasant Grove Grace Brethren Church, IA,
    1031
Pleasant Grove, IA, Brethren Church, 236,
    661
Pleasant Hill Church of the Brethren, IA,
    1032
Pleasant Hill Church of the Brethren, IL,
    352, 353, 360, **1032,** 1234, 1303,
    1307, 2093
    Gibson family, 548
    Girard, IL, Church of the Brethren, 550
    Harshbarger, Ethel on, 2362
    Weddle, Ethel Harshbarger on, 2362
Pleasant Hill Church of the Brethren, PA,
    136, 145, **1032**
    Pleasant View Church of the Brethren,
        PA, 1037
Pleasant Hill Church of the Brethren, PA
    (Cambria Co.), 118
Pleasant Hill Church of the Brethren, PA
    (York Co.), 44
Pleasant Hill Church of the Brethren, TN,
    209, **1032**
    Johnson City, TN, Knob Creek Church
        of the Brethren, 673
Pleasant Hill Church of the Brethren, VA,
    231, **1033,** 1267
    Grottoes, VA, Church of the Brethren,
        574
    Middle River Church of the Brethren,
        VA, 825
Pleasant Hill Church of the Brethren, WV,
    125, **1033**
    Mount Hebron Church of the Brethren,
        WV, 881
Pleasant Hill College, **1033**
    Miller, Oliver W., 841
Pleasant Hill congregation, PA
    Gochenour (Goughnour) family, 555
    Johnstown, PA, Roxbury Church of the
        Brethren, 675
Pleasant Hill house, Pleasant View congre-
    gation, MO, 1314
Pleasant Hill, IA, 1217
Pleasant Hill, IN, Church of the Brethren,
    See Agape Church of the Brethren,
    IN
Pleasant Hill meetinghouse, near Virden,
    IL, 1234
Pleasant Hill mission point, IA, 740
Pleasant Hill (Newton) German Baptist
    Brethren, OH
Pleasant Hill, OH, 694, 1332
    Church of the Brethren, **1031–1032**
    Congregational Brethren, 237, **335**
    First Brethren Church, 77, 335, **1032**
Pleasant Hill Old German Baptist Brethren
    Church, IL, **1033**
Pleasant Hill schoolhouse
    meeting place for State Center Old
        German Baptist Brethren Church,
        IA, 1217–1218
Pleasant Hill, TN, congregation, 167
Pleasant Hill Village, **1033**
Pleasant Hill (Weddle), 647, 748
Pleasant Home Church of the Brethren,
    OK, **1033,** See Monitor Church of
    the Brethren, OK
    Monitor Church of the Brethren, OK,
        previous name of, 869
Pleasant Home Dunkard Brethren congre-
    gation, CA, 239, See Modesto,
CA, Pleasant Home Dunkard
    Brethren congregation
Pleasant, Janis (later Jenkins)
    Jenkins, Charles Lee, 2209
Pleasant Mound Church of the Brethren,
    TN, **1033**
Pleasant Mound, IL
    Hurricane Creek Church of the
        Brethren, IL, 638
Pleasant Mound, IN, Church of the
    Brethren, 1323, See also Wawaka,
    IN, Church of the Brethren
Pleasant Plains Church of the Brethren,
    OK, **1034**
Pleasant Prairie, MO, Church of the
    Brethren, 263
Pleasant Ridge Church of the Brethren,
    Alberta, Canada, 59, **1034**
    Sharon Church of the Brethren, 1172
Pleasant Ridge Church of the Brethren, NC,
    See Pleasant Valley Church of the
    Brethren, NC
Pleasant Ridge Church of the Brethren, PA,
    1034
Pleasant Ridge Dunkard Brethren Congre-
    gation, OH, **1034,** 1268
    Pine Ridge Dunkard Brethren Congre-
        gation, MS and, 2238
    Hart, MI, Dunkard Brethren Congrega-
        tion, 2196
    Michigan Brethren settlement, 824
Pleasant Ridge, IN
    Church of God (New Dunkers), 297
Pleasant Ridge, NC, congregation
    Pleasant Valley Church of the Brethren,
        NC, 1035
Pleasant Ridge, OH, Church of the Breth-
    ren, 413
Pleasant Ridge, PA, 1224
Pleasant Ridge (Valley) congregation, NC
    Flat Rock Church of the Brethren, NC,
        493
Pleasant Run, VA, congregation, 342
Pleasant Valley Bible School
    Enders, NE, Church of the Brethren,
        445–446
Pleasant Valley Brethren Church, MD, See
    Accident Grace Brethren Church,
    MD
Pleasant Valley Brethren Church, MI, 260,
    See Cassopolis, MI, Brethren
    Church
Pleasant Valley Church of the Brethren,
    Alberta, Canada, 250, **1034**
Pleasant Valley Church of the Brethren, IN,
    1034
    Middlebury, IN, Church of the
        Brethren, 825
Pleasant Valley Church of the Brethren,
    NC, **1035**
Pleasant Valley Church of the Brethren,
    ND, 251, 322, **1035**
Pleasant Valley Church of the Brethren,
    OH, 151, **1035,** 1288
Pleasant Valley Church of the Brethren, TN,
    397, **1035**
Pleasant Valley Church of the Brethren, TX,
    1035
Pleasant Valley Church of the Brethren, VA
    1035
    Alum Ridge, **21,** 413, 1267, 1341
    Duncans Chapel Church of the
        Brethren, VA, 407

Early, Henry Clay, 413
Free Union, VA, Church of the Brethren, 513
Fremont Church of the Brethren, VA, 515
Grottoes, VA, Church of the Brethren, 574
Hardtmann (Hardman, Hartman) family, 583
Weyers Cave, 45, 733, 824, **1035–1036,** 1235–1236, 1317, 2017
Pleasant Valley Church of the Brethren, WV, **1036**
Pleasant Valley congregation, ND
Flora Church of the Brethren, ND, 496
Pleasant Valley congregation, TN, 740
Plesant Valley German Baptist Brethren Church, NE, **2377**
Pleasant Valley German Baptist Brethren, IA, **1036**
Pleasant Valley, KS, congregation
Pleasant View Brethren Church, KS, 1036
Pleasant Valley, MD, Brethren Church, *See* Accident, MD, Grace Brehtren Church
Pleasant Valley, MI, congregation
Michigan Brethren settlement, 824
Pleasant Valley, ND, congregation, 251
Pleasant Valley, OH, 151
congregation, 1288
Pleasant Valley, TN, congregation, 397
Pleasant View Brethren Church, IN, **1036, 2377**
Goshen, IN, First Brethren Church, 558
Pleasant View Brethren Church, Kepple Hill, PA, 689
Pleasant View Brethren Church, KS, **1036**
Pleasant View Chapel Church of the Brethren, IN, **1036**
Pleasant View Church of the Brethren, IN, **1036**
Sugar Creek, IN, congregation, 1036
Pleasant View Church of the Brethren, KS, **1036–1037**
Pleasant View Church of the Brethren, MD, **1037**
sources on, 2323
Pleasant View Church of the Brethren, MO, *See* Bethany Church of the Brethren, MO
Pleasant View Church of the Brethren, OH, **1037**
Pleasant View Church of the Brethren, PA, **1037**
Pleasant View Church of the Brethren, TN, **1037**
Pleasant View Church of the Brethren, VA, **1037**
Flat Rock Church of the Brethren, VA, 493
Pleasant View Church of the Brethren, WV, 125, **1037**
Pleasant View congregation, 323, 1234
South Whitley, IN, Church of the Brethren, 1207
Pleasant View congregation, MO, 1314
Pleasant View congregation, VA, 1313, 1314
Pleasant View, IN, congregation
Rossville, IN, Church of the Brethren, 1124

Pleasant View Mennonite Church
Pleasant View Brethren Church, IN, 2377
Pleasant View, MO, Church of the Brethren, *See* Bethany Church of the Brethren, MO
Pleasant View, PA, Brethren Church, *See* Kepple Hill, PA, Pleasant View Brethren Church
Pleasant View (Reno Co.) congregation, KS
Hutchinson, KS, Community Church of the Brethren, 638
Pleasant View, TN, congregation, 269
Pleasant View, WV, congregation
Chestnut Grove German Baptist Brethren Church, WV, 956
Please Pray With Me (Fike), 2184
Pleickersdorffer, Christian, 146
Pleickersdorffer, Hans Jacob, 146
Pleickersdorffer, Johannes, 146
Pleickersdorffer, Ulrich, *See* Blickenstaff, Ulrich
Pleickersdorffer, Yost, *See* Blickenstaff, Yost
Plenk, Peter, 1740
Pletcher, Calvin, 1740
Pletcher, Henry
Ryerson Station Church of the Brethren, PA, minister, 1132
Pletcher, Irvin R., 1740
Okeechobee, FL, Grace Brethren Church, pastor, 963
Pleasant Hill Church of the Brethren, PA, pastor, 1032
Pletcher, Jeremiah, 1740
Pletcher, Mary Elizabeth (later Gunzel), 1641
Pletcher, Ordo Myers, 752, 1740
Ridge Church of the Brethren, PA, pastor, 1108
Pletcher, Remo, 1740
Pletcher, W. D., 241
Plevna, IN, Church of the Brethren, 653, **1037–1038**
Plevna, IN, Dunkard Brethren, *408,* 409, 705, **1038**
Plew, Daniel, 411
Plew, Thomas H., 411, 567, 1740
Somerset, IN, Poplar Grove Brethren Church, pastor, 1202
Plock family
at New Rockford, ND, Church of the Brethren, 932
Plough Publishing House
Hutterian Society of Brothers, 641
Plow Creek Fellowship, **1038,** *See also* Shalom Covenant of Communities
Shalom Covenant, 1084
Plow Creek Fellowship, PA, 2069
Plow Creek (Tiskilwa, IL)
Brethren movement, 329
Fellowship of Hope, 488
Pluck, David W., 1740, 2304
Plue, Thomas, *See* Plew, Thomas
Plum Creek Church of the Brethren, PA, *See* Elderton, PA, Plum Creek Church of the Brethren
Plum Creek Normal School, 693, **1038**
Elderton, PA, Plum Creek Church of the Brethren, 433
Miller, Howard, teaching school, 837
Plum Creek Old German Baptist Brethren Church, KS, **1038**

Plum, Julia (later Kennedy), 2197
Plum, L. Edward, 2038
Plum, LeRoy E.
Rouzerville Church of the Brethren, PA, pastor, 1125
Plum Run meetinghouse, 1367
Loudonville Church of the Brethren, OH, 760
Plum, Samuel Stover, 1740
Plummer family, 2044
Jenners, PA, Grace Brethren Church, 670
Plummer, Richard, 1740
Plunge Creek (Chapel) congregation, IN, 740
Plunge Creek, IN, Church of the Brethren, *See* Liberty Mills, IN, Church of the Brethren
Plunkett family
Filbrun family, 490
Pleasant Hill Old German Baptist Brethren Church, IL, 1033
Plunkett, Moses, 264, 268, 1740
Plunkett, Mrs. Moses, 264
Plunkett, N. Geraldine
on Brethren in Civil War, 2350
pluralism, 1310
pluralism in religions
membership trends 1980 to 2000, 2220
plurals in place name, 911–912
Plymouth Brethren, **1038–1039**
Córdoba, Argentina and Reina, Domingo, 1094
dispensationalism, 390
millennialism, 834
nonconformity, 940
Plymouth Co., IA, 695
Plymouth, IN, 161, 1287, 1385
Church of the Brethren, **1038,** 1287
pneumonic plague, 277
Poage Lane, WV
Pocahontas Church of the Brethren, WV, mission point of, 1039
Poages Chapel Church of the Brethren, VA, *See* Poages Mill Church of the Brethren, VA
Poages, Elijah
Poages Mill Church of the Brethren, VA, 1039
Poages Mill Church of the Brethren, VA, **1039,** 2038
Peters Creek Church of the Brethren, VA, daughter congregation, 1011
Roanoke, VA, Oak Grove Church of the Brethren, 1113
Pobst family, 164, 165
Prosperity congregation, Oak Hill Old German Baptist Brethren Church, WV, 957
Pobst, Frank Edward, 164, 1740
Pobst, Henry G.
Oak Hill Old German Baptist Brethren Church, WV, 957
Pobst, Marie Elizabeth, 1843
Pobst, Sarah B.
Oak Hill Old German Baptist Brethren Church, WV, 957
POC, *See* People of the Covenant (POC) (BC)
Pocahontas Co., IA, 356
Pocahontas Co., WV, 602
Allegheny, WV, Church of the Brethren, 2125

Pocahontas Church of the Brethren, WV, **1039**
Pocahontas Mission, *See* Pocahontas Church of the Brethren, WV
Hevener Church of the Brethren, WV, 602
Pocatello, ID, *645*
Pochmann, Henry A., 1861, 2038
Podraza, Joseph R., 443, 629, 1740
Poe family, 270
Poe, Rodney, 448
Poehlmann, Gunda (later Gray)
Island Pond, VT, Grace Brethren Church, 2209
poetry, 172, 191, **1039–1040**, 1962, *See also* literature
By a Quiet Stream (Jehnsen), 1979
Beahm, Anna (later Mow), 1361
Beery, Adaline Hohf, 1873
biblical, 2020
bibliography, 1861, 1868, 1869, 1886, 1891, 1906
Brand, Millen, 747
Cripe, Edith S., 1911
Danner (Donner), Henry, 361
Danner (Donner), Jacob, 362
debates, 371
devotional, 2049
dialect, 2042
Diehl, Elias Henry, 1917
Doernberg, Emil, 747
Ein Schoen Lied, 2058
Ephrata, 2008, 2046
Garber, Ora W., 529
Geib, Amos P., 1945
German-American, 2085, 2087
Gesäng der einsamen und verlassenen Turtel-Taube, Das (*The Songs of the Lonely and Forsaken Turtle-dove*), 546
giving, doctrine of, 2105
Heckler, James Y., 1960
Heckman, Samuel Brumbaugh, 593
hymns, 642
inspirational, 1983
Kinsey, Samuel, 696
Mack, Alexander, Jr., 774, 1961
Miller, Peter, 1972
Mohler, David, 1255
Myers, Frank B., 2027
mysticism, 907
Pennsylvania German, 2076
photography as art, 1020
"Pilgrim Stranger" by Whittier, about Harriet Livermore, 1373
prayer books, 1052
Price, William Weidner, 1057
publishing, 1069
religious, 2094
The Religious Poetry of Alexander Mack, Jr., 2004
Robinson, Mary N., 747
Sell, James A., 2061
Sherrick, Marvin M., 2064
Stafford, William Edgar, 1216, 2358
Statler, Ruth Beeghly, 1219
Stoner, Lina Norris, 2075
Stories That Could Be True (Stafford), 1216
Tersteegen, Gerhard, 1222, 1254–1255
Teufel, Delores E., 2080–2081
Thomas, Daniel D., 2081
Traveling Through the Dark (Stafford),

1216
Watermarks, 1970
Welch, Myra Brooks, 1329
Whittier, John Greenleaf, 747
Wine, Mary Stoner, 1350, 2101
by women, 2024
Ziegler, Edward Krusen on readings and, 2365
Zollers, George DeHaven, 1400
Zunkel, Cleda Pearl Shull, 1402, 2111
Poff, Chester W., 1740
Poff, Elizabeth Chandler, 1060
Poff, Ella (later Pritchett), 1060
Kintner, Elgin Perry on, 2341
Poff, John W., 1060
Poff, Roy Alvin, 1740, 2304
Poff, Theobald, 262
Pohahontas Co., WV, 1263
Pohl, Marsilla Elizabeth Seilhamer, Chester Whitmore on, 2356
Pohlhaus, Karl (Charlie) A., 2289
Point Church of the Brethren, PA, 410, **1040**
Poirer, Robert, 122, 1740
Pokogan, MI, Church of the Brethren, 260, **1040**
spelling changed to Pokagon, **2378**
Pokogan, MI, congregation
Portage Prairie, IN, Church of the Brethren, 1047
Poland, 23, 29, **1040–1041**
agricultural exchange, 198, **2129**
agricultural exchange program
Wenatchee, WA, Brethren-Baptist Church United, 1330
Metzger, Thurl D., 2222
Petersime, Ray, 1740
Reformation, Protestant, and radical reformers, 1091, 1092
relief and rehabilitation work, 200
relief and service efforts, 1097
relief and social work, 303
United Nations Relief and Rehabilitation Administration (UNRRA), 1291
work camps, 1367
Poland, Alta Elizabeth Dawson
Poland, Frank Jacob (FGBC, CGBC), **2238**
Poland, Larry, 1740
Poland, OH, 711
Evangelische Besuch, Der, 460
historic sites, 609
The Monthly Gospel Visiter (later *Visitor*), 961
Poley, Benjamin, 1740
police, **1041**, *See also* law enforcement
police departments
chaplaincy, 2158
Poling, Arley V., 1287, 1740
Poling, Edward Lee, 247, 1740, 2038
Poling family, 1908, 2080
Mount Cassell Old German Baptist Brethren Church, WV, 880
Poling, Godfrey J., 1740
Poling, Henry O., 1287, 1740
Poling, Ida Belle
Mount Cassell Old German Baptist Brethren Church, WV, 880–881
Poling, Ira, 1740
Poling, J. K. R., 1740
Poling, James Newton, 193, 1337, 1740, 2038
on health and welfare, 2350

Poling, Larry R., 2290
Poling, Nancy Werking, 2038
Poling, Newton L., 733, 1740, 2304, **2385**
on Crumbacker, Hans and descendants, 2350
on Crumpacker, Ulrich and descendants, 2350
on Miller, Lydia Smith and descen-0 dants, 2350
on Miller, Solomon and descendants, 2350
Poling, Russell Lewis, 1740
Poling, Stingley E., 1287, 1740
Poling, Thomas W., 1740
Mount Cassell Old German Baptist Brethren Church, WV, minister, 880
Old Order German Baptist Church minister, 972
Poling, Virginia
on Crumbacker, Hans and descendants, 2350
on Crumpacker, Ulrich and descendants, 2350
memoirs, 2350
on Miller, Lydia Smith and descendants and letters of, 2350
on Miller, Solomon, letters of, 2350
Polish Agricultural Exchange, 357, **1041**
Rolston, Frances Fitz Simon and William Wendell, 1120
Metzger, Thurl D., 2222
Polish Brethren, **1041**
Christliches Hand-Büchlein (Christian Handbook), 288
Felbinger, Jeremias, 482, 1259
Reformation, Protestant, and radical reformers, 1092
role in development of Brethren theology, 1259
Socinus, Faustus, 1041
Stritzka, 1229
Polish Minor Church
Polish Brethren, 1041
political activism
Dunkard Brethren, 2174
political issues, *See* polity
Calvinism and, 240
Church of the Brethren, 2094
governor of Pennsylvania, 222
historical relation of Brethren to state, treatise on, 2054
world-wide, Brethren movement relationship to, 2106
politics, *See* electioneering; elections
Brethren movement, 311
Christian education and, 283
church, in, 2003
Goshen Conference, 559
oaths, taking of, 959
prohibition, 1061–1062
youth in New Left movements, 930
polity, **1041–1045**, *1042*, *1043*, 1906, *See also* authority; delegates; district organization; schisms
article about, 1954
Brethren Church, 37–38, 182, 294
Brethren general, 32
Brethren movement, 176
Christ's Assembly and, 280
church membership, 813
Church of God, Anderson, IN, 296
Church of God (New Dunkers), 297

Church of the Brethren, 36, 294, 305, 1973
Churches of God (GC), 309
Congregational Brethren, 335
congregational, of Mack, Alexander, Sr., and New Baptists of Schwarzenau, 776
consensus, changes from, 178
conservative German Baptist Brethren, 1982
Conservative Grace Brethren Churches International, 2217
Davy, Henry Dorsey, 365
definition of, 294
denominational naming based on, 910–911
Disciples of Christ, 385
divorce issues, 393
doctrines and, 2105
Dunkard Brethren, 37, 294, 409–410, 2174
Dunkers and, 2325
episcopal
    government of church, 1041, 1042
    Roman Catholic Church, 1120
Fellowship of Grace Brethren Churches, 38, 284, 484, 485
Flory, John, 498
frontier, 519
General Board (CB), 536
government of church, 1041, 1042–1043
Hertzler, Samuel Hoffer, 600
Historic Peace Churches, 608
historiography, 2202
Hochmann von Hochenau, Ernst Christoph, 615
humility, 636
language, inclusive, 2214
majority rule *vs.* concensus, 372
manual for, 2109
Manual of Procedure for the Brethren Church (BC), 788
manuals for, 788
manuals of, for ministers, 2066
Mennonites, 815–816
minutes, 852
moderators, 866
Moomaw, B. C., 873
National Ordination Council (BC), 2229
New Testament, 368
Old German Baptist Brethren, 36–37
Old Order movement, 294
"Order of the Brethren," 976
organizational restructuring and, 2241
pension funds, 1007
Progressive Brethren, 942–943, 1044–1045
The Record of the Faithful, 1086
Restoration Movement, 1101
Roman Catholic Church, 1120
schism over, 1152
Polity Committee (BC), 2169
church membership, study of, 2142
Polk Co., FL, 719
    Pine Grove Old German Baptist Brethren Church, FL, 1024
Polk Co., IA
    Gochenour (Goughnour) family, 555
Polk Co., NC, 353
    Brethren congregations, 946
    Golden Church of the Brethren, NC, 555
    Green River Cove Church of the Brethren, NC, 570
    Melvin Hill Church of the Brethren, NC, 812
    Mill Creek Church of the Brethren, NC, 832
Polk Co., NE
    Platte Valley German Baptist Brethren Church, NE, 1030
Polk Co., OR, 360
Polk, Edna, 1847
Polk, Mary (later Ellenberger), 1608
Polk, Willis, 231
Poll, John, Jr., 1740
Pollak, Michael, 2038
Pollard family
    Garrett, PA, Church of the Brethren, 531
Pollard, Lee W., 1740
Pollard, Richard Thomas, 531, 1740
    Pollock family, 2087
Pollock, L. Alvin (L. A.), 94, 1740
Pollock, [Mrs.] Mark, 2038
Pollock, Myrtle Ferris, 1843, 2107
    Monitor Church of the Brethren, KS, 869
Polman, Elaine (later Brenneman), 1353
Polman, Gerald Bernard, 447, 725, 1388, 1740
    Meyersdale, PA, Grace Brethren Church, pastor, 822
Polman, Leila Neher, 1045, 1353
Polman, Leo, 192, 250, 503, 504, **1045,** 1353, 1741
    South Gate, CA, First Brethren Church, pastor, 1205
Polman, Roy, 443, 1277, 1741
Polo, Francine Andrae, 1847
Polo, IL, Church of the Brethren, **1045**
    Pine Creek Church of the Brethren, IL, 1024
Polo, Marco, 334
Polo, MO, 752
Polos, Nicholas C.
    on Brandt, Jesse Christian, 2350
polygamy
    Church of Jesus Christ of Latter-day Saints, 298
Pomona, CA, Fellowship Church of the Brethren, 714, **1045**
Pomona College
    Nininger, Harvey Harlow, degree from, 938
Pompano Beach congregation, FL
    example of place name, 911
Pompano Beach, FL, Grace Brethren Church, **1045–1046**
    Fort Lauderdale, FL, Grace Brethren Church, 503
Ponca City, OK, 1280
Poncebaker, Gertrude I. (later Shafer), 2038
Poncebaker, Lottie, 2038
Pond Bank, PA, Grace Brethren Church, *See* Chambersburg, PA, Grace Brethren church
Ponn, William Edward, Jr., 1741
Pontiac, MI, 399
    Church of the Brethren, 340, 1924, *See also* Drayton Plains, MI, First Church of the Brethren
Pontius, Abraham, 153
Pontius, Bert, 1741
Pontius, George C., 319, 626, 1741
Pontius, Peter, 1741
Pony Creek Brethren Church, KS, 362, 1133, *See also* Hamlin, KS, Brethren Church, 581; Morrill, KS, Brethren Church, 876
Pooderback, George, 2040
Pool, David, 1263, 1741
Pool, Ezra, 246
Pool family, 251
Pool, John, Jr., 1214, 1741
Poole, Daniel Lee, 2290
poor box, **1046**
    Germantown, PA, social welfare, 1197–1198
poor, care of, 18, **1046,** 1991, *See also* poverty
    Global Women's Project, 2190
    Habitat for Humanity International, 2195
    homelessness, 2203
    ministry, 845
    mutual aid, 902
    nursing, 952
    overseer of the poor, 986
    Pauw, Adrian, gifts from, 996
    Philadelphia, PA, congregation, 692
    Pietism, 1022
    relief and service efforts, 1096, 1097
    Relief Board (DB), 1097
    Philadelphia, PA, congregation, 692
Pope, Jonathan W., 1741
Pope, Roman Catholic, 1120
    considered as Antichrist by Spener, Philipp Jakob, 1209
Popejay, Emanuel, 1741
Popejay, William A., 1741
Popenoe, Paul
    marriage counseling, 796
Poplar Bluff Church of the Brethren, AR, **1046**
Poplar Bluff, MO, 137, 211, 409, 690
    Church of the Brethren, **1046**
Poplar Grove Brethren Church, IN, 1288, *See also* Somerset, IN, Poplar Grove Brethren Church
Poplar Grove, OH, Church of the Brethren, **1046**
    Pleasant Valley Church of the Brethren, OH, 1035
Poplar Grove, AR
    St. Francis Church of the Brethren preaching point, 1134
Poplar Ridge Church of the Brethren, OH, 373, 374, 736, 741, 939, **1047**
Poplar Valley, MT, 142, 1301
    Church of the Brethren, MT, **1047**
    Montana Brethren settlement, 870
Popp, Kathryn M., 748, 2030
Popp, Stephan, 2038
population, *See* statistics
Pordage, John
    Philadelphian Society, 1019
pork, *See* dietary laws
    eating of, **1047**
pornography
    Fellowship of Grace Brethren Churches (FGBC), 487
Porst, Johann, 57
Port-au-Prince, Haiti
    Child Rescue Services (Aide-aux-Enfants), 276
Port Providence, PA

Oaks, PA, Green Tree Church of the Brethren, 958

Port Republic, VA
Miller, Valley Virginia (later Myers) in, 913

Port Richey, FL, Gulfview Grace Brethren Church, **1047**
St. Petersburg, FL, Grace Brethren Church, 1136

Portage Church of the Brethren, OH, **1047**
Rome, OH, congregation, 956

Portage, IN, congregation, 260, 652
Pokogan, MI, Church of the Brethren, 1040

Portage, MI, congregation, 224

Portage Prairie, IN, Church of the Brethren, 713, **1047**, 2105

Porte, Clara Fowler, 1047

Porte, Grace Guthrie, 1047

Porte, John W., 269, 1047, 1741

Porte, Robert Fowler, 130, 239, 360, **1047**, 1741
Mount Zion Brethren Church, OH, minister, 888
Sergeantsville, NJ, Brethren Church, pastor, 1167

Porter, Evalena (later Blocher)
Smeltzer, Mary Blocher (CB) and, 2250

Porter family, 1917

Porter, Myrtle Crist, 748, 2038

Porter, Nolan F(rederick), 759, 1741, 2304

Porter, P. D., 1741

Porter, Paul, 1741

Porter, Powell B., 1741

Porter, Samuel E., 171, 1741

Porter, Terry Nolan, 1741

Porter, Thomas Conrad, 2038

Portis, KS, 1305
Grace Brethren Church, 682, **1047–1048**
North Solomon Church of the Brethren, 232, **1048**, 1305

Portland, IN, 1288
Church of the Brethren, **1048**

Portland, OR
Grace Brethren Church, **1048**, 1276–1277
Peace Church of the Brethren, **1048**
Powelis Valley Church of the Brethren, OR, 1050
urban mission, 1297

Portland, TX, Bayview Church of the Brethren, **1048**

portraits, *See* photography
photographs of Brethren, 1019–1020
prohibited by Annual Meeting, 402
recreation, 1087

The Portraiture of Primitive Christians, See Erste Liebe, Die

Portugal
Julien, Thomas T., 2210
missions, short-term, 2226

Portugal, Joe T., 1741

possessives in place name, 911

Post-American magazine
Sojourners Fellowship, 1200

Post, Johann Christoph, 2063

Postma, Sarah Elizabeth, 1843, 2038

postmillennialism
millennialism, 833–834

The Postscript, See Marlin, H. C.
Marlin, High Crist, publisher, 794

potatoes
introduced to Surhuisterveen area by Brethren, 1241

Pote, Edwina C., 2290

Potomac, MD, Church of the Brethren, *See* Downsville, MD, Church of the Brethren

Potomac River, 1336
Nead, Peter, baptism in, 918

Potsdam, OH, Church of the Brethren, **1048–1049**
Pitsburg, OH, Church of the Brethren, 1026
Salem Church of the Brethren, OH, 1138

Pott brothers
Camisards, 242

Pottawatomie Co., OK
New Hope Church of the Brethren, OK, 929

Potter, Hazel, 2038

Potter, John E., 2038

Potter, Martha Jean, 1836

Pottinger, A. Leander, 54, 1741

Potts, Catherine A. (later Sower), *See* Sower, Catherine A.Potts

Potts Creek Church of the Brethren, VA, *See* Alleghany Church of the Brethren, VA

Potts Creek, VA, mission point, Botetourt Co., VA, Church of the Brethren, 164

Potts, W[illiam] John, 2038

Pottstown, PA, 709, 1056, 1286, 2375
Coventry Church of the Brethren, 22, 175, 994, **1049**
Harmonyville, PA, Church of the Brethren, 584
First Church of the Brethren, **1049**, 1314, 2038
Parker Ford, PA, and, 994

Poulsen, C., 1741

Poulson, Isaac, Sr.
Mooreites, 875

Poulson, Israel, Jr., 28, 1741
Mooreite division, 1049

Mooreites, 875

Poulson, Israel, Sr., 28, 129, **1049**, 1741, 2070
Major, Sarah Righter, 783

Poulson, P. C., 1741
Pound River Church of the Brethren, VA, **1049**

Pound River, VA, congregation, 356

POV, *See* Program to Overcome Violence (POV)

poverty, *See* poor, care of
Dunkard Brethren, 410
Elgin, IL, Highland Avenue Church of the Brethren, 436
medicine, 809

Powell, Alice (later Sewell)
Sewell, Laura A. (CB) and, 2247

Powell, C. A., 613, 1741
Pulaski, VA, Church of the Brethren, minister, 1071

Powell, David L., 1741

Powell, E. M., 1741

Powell, Esther Weygandt, 2038

Powell family, 2087
Mount Etna, IA, Church of the Brethren, 881

Powell, George, 271

Powell, Jim A., 1741

Powell, Josephine, 1843

Powell, Josie, 683

Powell, Lewis Eugene, 2290

Powell, OH, Grace Brethren Church, **2238**
Jackson, Edward A., 2209

Powell, Robert, 1741

Powell, Vernon Showalter, 496, 1741, 2304

Powell, William, 1741
Singer Hill Grace Brethren Church, PA, pastor, 1184

Powell, William Ellis, 1741

Powell's Fort congregation, VA, 1364
Oak Hill Church of the Brethren, 957

Powells Valley Church of the Brethren, OR, **1049–1050**
Portland, OR, Peace Church of the Brethren, 1048

power
schism and, 1153

Power, Carrie Rodeffer, 2039

Power family, 2105

Power, Martin, 1336

Powers, Avery, 1741

Powers, Edward, 125

Powers family
sources on, 2315

Powers, Felty, 2078

Powers, Gladys, 2039

Powers, James J., 2290

Powers, Martin, 732, 1050, 1741
South Branch Church of the Brethren, WV, 1204

Powers, Mary, 1050

Powers, Thomas Samuel, 2290

Powers, Valentine, 732, **1050**, 1336, 1341, 1741, 2105
Brethren peace position, 999
South Branch Church of the Brethren, WV, and disfellowship of, 1204

Powers, Valentine, Jr., 1050

Poweshiek Co., IA, 372

Pownall, Thomas, 2039

powwowing, folk medicine, 2145–2146

Poyner, James L., 366, 1741
Port Richey, FL, Gulfview Grace Brethren Church, 1047

Poyner, Randall E., 579, 674, 725, 1741

Pérez, Luis (Luiche) (CB)
Rio Prieto, PR, Iglesia de los Hermanos (CB) and, 2243–2244

practical Christianity
Social Gospel Movement, 1197

practice
queries about, 1076

The Practice of Mental and Vocal Prayer (de Labadie), 1051

Prague, Czechoslovakia
conferences, history of, **2239**
CPC and, 286
Christian Peace Conference, 357

Prairie City Church of the Brethren, IA, **1050**
Marion Co. German Baptist Brethren, IA, 793
Maxwell, IA, Church of the Brethren, 803
Miller, David Alfred, 836

Prairie Creek, IN, Church of the Brethren, **1050**
Salamonie Church of the Brethren, IN, 1136

Prairie Grove, IA, congregation

Osceola, IA, Church of the Brethren, 983

Prairie Hall Schoolhouse
Salem Community Church of the Brethren, KS, 1138

Prairie Lake Church of the Brethren, OK, **1050**

Prairie Longue, AR, Church of the Brethren, *See* Carlisle, AR, Church of the Brethren

Prairie Presbyterian Chapel
Fremont, OH, Grace Brethren Church, 515

The Prairie Schooner (Barton), 747

Prairie View Church of the Brethren, KS, **1050**

Prairie View Church of the Brethren, MO, **1050–1051**

praise bands, 2228

praise choruses, 2227

Prali, Italy, 1365

Prather, A. T., 1741

Prather, Cora Griffith, 1051

Prather, Elvis, 1741

Prather, Enoch L., 1741

Prather, H. M., 1741

Prather, Hendrick, 493

Prather, Hope L. Deardorff, 1051

Prather, John Perry, 64, 381, **1051**, 1741, 2039

Prather, Marion, 363, 755, 1741

Prather, Martin, 1741

Prather, Mary, 1741

Prather, O. J., 1741

Prather, Thomas, 1051

Pratt, C., 1741

Pratt Co., KS, *146,* 682
Sand Creek Old German Baptist Brethren Church, KS, 1143

Pratt, Edwin W., 1741

Pratt, Eugene W., **1051**, 1741

Pratt family
Hancock, MN, Church of the Brethren, 582
Outlook, WA, Church of the Brethren, 986

Pratt, Martha Anne Glick, 1051

Pratt, Ward Emanuel, 65, 726, 738, 1383, 1394, 1741

Pratt, William, 1742

prayer, **1051–1052**, 2018, 2036
Brethren movement, 291
Brethren rural churches, 1130
corporate prayer in worship services, 1376, 1378
family worship, 474
funerals, 524
God's Means of Grace (Yoder), 555
gospel songs, 560
Harleysville, PA, Indian Creek Church of the Brethren, 584
healing, 591
Humberd, Russell I., 636
hymns, 643
laying on of hands, 730
Lord's prayer, 757
New Testament practices, 2013
Patton, George, on, 996
posture in, **1052**
power of, steps to, 1984–1985
preparatory service for communion, 1056
schisms and, 167

Sermon on the Mount, 1169
sources on, 2311
worship and, 2266–2267

prayer books, **1052–1053**

prayer coverings, *See* prayer veils

Prayer Life and Teachings of Jesus (Wieand), 1051

prayer meetings, **1053**
Annual Meeting, acceptance by, 1051
Dallas Center, IA, Church of the Brethren, **360**
Declaration of Principles, 372
discouragement of, 1376
Eby, Kermit, 420
Holiness Brethren, 619
Old Order movement, 206
Pleasant Ridge Dunkard Brethren Congregation, OH, 1034
Progressive Brethren movement, 972

prayer services, midweek, 1052

prayer veils, 254, **1053**, 1373, 1376, 2023, *See also* caps
Christian Brethren and, 281
Church of the Brethren, 300
Declaration of Principles, 372
Dunkard Brethren Church, 2173
graveclothes, 567
hairstyle, 579
Miller, Elizabeth Talley, 837
objections to Dunkard Brethren requirements regarding, 69
Old German Baptist Brethren, 967, 2233
Pennsylvania Brethren Church and Grace Brethren, 1005
prophecy, 1062
symbolism of, 2147
use of in other religious groups, 68
women and, 2263

prayers
book containing, 1936
Groff, Warren Frederick, 2194
Roop, Eugene F. on, 2353
Ziegler, Edward Krusen on, 2365

prayers, doctrine of, 2098

preaching, *530,* **1053–1055**, *1054,* 1871, 1886, *See also* sermons
"Arrested for Preaching the Gospel," 1–2
Church of the Brethren, 300
debates, 371
dynamic indigeneity, 1990
Ephrata Community, 448
Fairview Church of the Brethren, MD, 468
Far Western Brethren, 475
Fike, Samuel A., 490
Garrett, Marguerite Arthelda Bixler, 531
General Church Erection and Missionary Committee (CB), 536
Golden Church of the Brethren, NC, 555
Hedrick, Laura E. N. Grossnickle, 593
"heretic's" manuals for, 2003
Hertzler, Samuel Hoffer, 600
Hillery, Lemuel, 606
Hochmann von Hochenau, Ernst Christoph, 614
Hon, Peter Keithly, 627
Hostetler, Adam, 631
Hostetler, Joseph, 631
humanitarianism, 636

Hyndman, PA, Church of the Brethren, 643
ministry, 845, 846
Mitchell, Olden D. on Brethren and, 2347
Morse, Kenneth I. on, 2348
Naas, Johannes, performance of, 909
plain coat, 1029
pre-Civil War period, treatise on, 2055
"Preaching in a Tavern," 27 box
respecting age, 8

Preaching in a Tavern (Morse)
"Are You Saved?", 2373

preaching points
Breathitt Co., KY, 405
Elkins, WV, Church of the Brethren, 440
Ellisforde, Church of the Brethren, WA, 442
Elm Creek Church of the Brethren, KS, 442
Fairview Church of the Brethren, MO, 469
Fairview-Mount Clinton Church of the Brethren, VA, 470
Flint, MI, Church of the Brethren, 494
Fruita, CO, Church of the Brethren, 519–520
Grand Junction, CO, Koinonia Brethren-Baptist Church, 565
Greenbrier Church of the Brethren, WV, 570
Greenville Church of the Brethren, PA, 572
Independence, KS, Church of the Brethren, 649
Indian Creek Church of the Brethren, OK, 651
Johnstown, PA, Walnut Grove Church of the Brethren, 675
Kansas Center, maintained by, 683
Mifflin Co., PA, 406
by Nampa, ID, Church of the Brethren, 913
and Nicholas Co. German Baptist Brethren Church, 935
Ozawkie Church, KS, of the Brethren, established by, 987
Panora, IA, Church of the Brethren, 992

preaching skills
extemporaneous, 1137

Preble Co., OH, 766, 1231, 1235, 1281, 1295, 1332, 1355, 1389
Eldorado Dunkard Brethren Congregation, OH, 433
Petri family, 1013
Prices Creek Church of the Brethren, OH, 1057
Prices Creek Old German Baptist Brethren Church, OH, 1057
Snell, John and Magdalena, 1193

predestination, 55–56, **1055**
Calvinism, 1091
human nature, doctrine of, 635
justification, doctrine of, 680
predictions, weather, 17

Preiß, *See* Price

Preiß, Daniel, 1055

Preiß, Elizabeth Weidner, 1055, 1057

Preiß family
Skippack area, PA, 1189

Preiß, George, 1742

Price, Isaac, descendant, 1056
Preiß, John, 1055
Preiß (Price) family, **1055–1056**
Preiß (Price), Johannes
    poet, son of Preiß, Johannes Jakob, **1055**
Preiß (Price), Johannes (1751–1829), **1055**
Preiß (Price), Johannes Jakob, 381, 387, 583, 1057, 1055, 1742, 2039, 2090
    immigrant to America, patriarch of Price family, 1055
    Native Americans, 2229
    publishing, 1063
Preiß (Price), Johannes (John), 42
Preist, Marvin, 42
Preiston Co., WV, 2099
Premchand Raichand Teachers' Training College, Ahmedabad, India, 229
premillennialism, *See* millennialism
    Cassel, Jacob C., 259
    Jews, 671
Premonstratensian canons, 28
Prentice, George Warren, 1742
preparatory service for communion, **1056**
    deacons' visits, 369
    Old German Baptist Brethren love feast, 967
presbyterial polity
    Reformed Church, 1092
    government of church, 1041–1042
Presbyterians, **1056**, 2039
    Calvinism and, 240
    camp meetings, 245
    in Canada, 15
    Fellowship of Reconciliation (USA), 488
    Fitzwater, P. B., 136
    higher education, 603
    Iran (Persia), 662
    Jackpot Church, NV, 2212
    Kulp, Christina Masterton, 708
    meetinghouses in, 152
    missions and missionaries, 296
    New Sudan Council of Churches, 2162
    pastors and, 155
    Reformation, Protestant, 1091
    Reformed Church, 1092
    Rio Prieto, PR, Iglesia de los Hermanos (CB) and, 2243
    SERRV International (CB) and, 2247
    slavery, 2128
    Stone, Barton Warren, 1224
    Stuckey, Melvin Atwood, 1229
    Sunday school lessons, 1237
    Sunnyside, WA, Grace Brethren Church, 1240
    United Andean Indian Mission (UAIM), 1289
    Van Dyke, Archibald and Mary Leinback, 1301
    Whitefish, MT, Church of the Brethren, 1342
    Wilson, Edward Raymond, 1347
preschools
    Orange, CA, Grace Brethren Church, 975
prescribed dress, *See* dress
presiding elders, *See* elders
    ministry, terminology, 847
Presley, Glen, 1742
Presley, Guy C., 264, 1742, 2304
    Meadow Branch Church of the Brethen, TN, 806

New Hope Church of the Brethren, TN, elder in, 929
Pleasant View Church of the Brethren, TN, 1037
Presnell, Thomas F., 16, 241, 1742
Pressel, Lucy May (later Hanawalt), 581
Pressel, Valentine, 1742
Preston Co., WV, 157, 274, 728, 1254, 1336, 2023
    Freeling Settlement Old German Baptist Brethren Church, WV, 514
    Salem Church of the Brethren, WV, 1138, 1143
    Sandy Creek Church of the Brethren, WV, 1143
    Sandy Creek Old German Baptist Brethren Church, WV, 1143
Preston, MN, Church of the Brethren, *See* Root River Church of the Brethren, MN
Preston, Owen H., 1742
Preston, Thomas William, 2290
Price, *See* Preiß
Price, Abraham, *See* Price family
    Mease, Gladys Price (Nyce) on descendants of, 2346
Price, Abram A., 1742
Price, Alec, 1285
Price, Amanda, *761*
Price, Anthony M., 2290
Price, Benjamin E., 1742
Price burying grounds, Indian Creek, PA, 267
Price, Caesar Augustine, 1742
Price, Charles Henry Frederick, 2039
    North Beatrice Church of the Brethren, NE, 945
Price Co., WI
    Elk River Church of the Brethren, WI, 438
Price, Collin C., 1341, 1742
Price, Cora R., 2039
Price, D. E.
    Shannon, IL, Church of the Brethren, elder, 1172
Price, Daniel G.
    Pine Creek Church of the Brethren, IL, 1024
Price, Daniel R., 2039
    Stitzel, Iva May on, 2358
    Stitzel, Quinter on, 2358
Price, David E., 912, **1056**, 1742
    Mount Morris, IL, Church of the Brethren, elder, 883
Price, Douglas E., 2290
Price, E. Joe, 1742
Price, E. W., 1742
Price, Edward H., 1742
Price, Emmett P., 1742
Price family, 165, 256, 1219, 1281, 2032, *See also* Preiß family
    Harley family, 583
    Marietta, GA, Grace Brethren Church of Greater Atlanta, 793
    Reinhardt family, 1094
Price, G. Arthur, 2039
Price, George, 27 (sidebar), 1742
    Oaks, PA, Green Tree Church of the Brethren, preacher, 958
Price, George D., 1742
Price, Gladys
    on Nyce, Abraham and descendants, 2346

on Nyce, Leanna (Goshall) and descendants, 2346
on Price, Abraham and descendants, 2346
on Price, Susan (Alderfer) and descendants, 2346
Price, Glen
    Manzanar Relocation Center, teaching at, 789
Price, Gwendolyn
    on Nyce, Abraham and descendants, 2346
    on Nyce, Leanna (Goshall) and descendants, 2346
Price, Hannah Umstad, 1056, 1286
Price, Harriet (later Heckman), 592
Price, Helen E. Rowland, 1056
Price, Henry (A.), *1056,* 1742
Price, Isaac, 460, **1056**, 1286
    minorities, ethnic and racial, 849
    Oaks, PA, Green Tree Church of the Brethren, minister, 958
    Parker Ford, PA, Church of the Brethren, preaching at, 994
Price, Isaac (Green Tree, PA), 1742
Price, Isaac (Pleasant Hill, OH), 1742
Price Isaac (Schuykill, PA), 1742
Price, Isabelle
    Stitzel, Iva May on, 2358
    Stitzel, Quinter on, 2358
Price, J. H., 1742
Price, Jacob, 42, 1056, **1056–1057**, 1742, 2090, *See also* Preiß, John Jacob
Price, Jacob M., 1742
Price, James Quinter, 912
Price, Jasper, 1251
Price, Joe, 115
    recreation, *1086*
Price, John B. (1829–1879), 1742
Price, John Everett, 1742
Price, John H. (1891–1963), 1742
    Modesto, CA, Church of the Brethren, 866, 867
Price, John Jacob, *See* Preiß (Price), Johannes Jakob (John Jacob)
Price, John R., 1056
Price, John R., Jr., 958, 1742
Price, John R., Sr., 958, 1742
Price, John W., 21
    Pine Creek Church of the Brethren, IL, 1024
Price, Jonas, 1742
Price, Joseph (Lineboro, MD), 1742
Price, Joseph (Upper Codorus, PA), 1742
Price, Marcia
    Manzanar Relocation Center, teaching at, 789
Price, Mary Ann Stoner
    Steiner family, 2378
Price, Mary Elizabeth Hicks, 1056
Price, Mary (later Nyce), 952
Price, Mary (later Strickler), 1228
Price, Mary Reiff, 1057
Price, Maurice E., 2290
Price, Melton V., 1742
    Pilot Knob Church of the Brethren, AR, minister, 1024
Price-Miller family, 2038
Price, Phoebe, 338
Price (Preis), William, 1742
Price (Preisz, Preiß), John (Johannes)
    Native Americans, 2229
Price schoolhouse, PA, 406

Price, Sophia Swartly, *1055*
Price, Susan, *See* Price family
Price, Susan (Alderfer)
  Mease, Gladys Price (Nyce) on descendants of, 2346
Price, Susan Emmert, 1056
Price, Theodore B., 1742
Price, W. A., 2039
Price, William B., 384, 1742
Price, William Weidner, **1057**, 1742
Price, Wilson T., 211, 1742
  Mount Hope Church of the Brethren, AR, 881
  Poplar Bluff Church of the Brethren, AR, pastor/elder, 1046
Prices Church, 1227
Prices Creek Church of the Brethren, OH, 262, 264, 756, **1057**
  Siler, George V., 1181
Prices Creek Old German Baptist Brethren Church, OH, **1057**
Prices meetinghouse (PA), 42, 1227
  Gaube (Gaby), Martin, 532
Pricetown, PA, 1237
  Church of the Brethren, 2039
  German Baptist Brethren, 2039
  meetinghouse, 48, 176, *811, 1004,* **1057**
  Mohrsville Church of the Brethren, PA, 869
Prichard, George, 1742
Pricket, L. E., 1742
Prickett, Edward, 1742
Prickett family
  Mount Etna, IA, Church of the Brethren, 881
Priddy, Anson C., 1742
Priddy, David, 1742
Priddy, Jacob, 1742
Priddy, Jacob W., 1742
Priddy, Louise, 275
Priddy, Mollie, 2039
Priddy, Paul M., 1742
  Shelton Church of the Brethren, NC, pastor in, 1176
Priddy, Ronald, 275
Pridemore family
  South Haven Old German Baptist Brethren Church, MI, 1205
Pridgen family, 1863
Priebe, Mrs. Berl, 2076
Priebe family, 2076
Priest, Nancy, 382
Priest, Sarah (later Parker), 993
priesthood of all believers, 401, **1057–1058**
  Brethren movement, 293–294
  ministry, 845
  ordination, 980
  Pietism, 1022
  prophecy, 1062
  Reformation, Protestant, 1091
priesthood of believers
  distinction between clergy and laity, 718–719
  Lutheran Church, 767
Pietist movement, 1258
  Spener, Philipp Jakob, 1209
Prigel, John Matthias, 755, 1742
Primitive Baptists
  Gibson, Isham, 547
  Log Creek Church of the Brethren, MO, 752
The Primitive Christian, 180, 193,
  1058, 1327, 2039, 2093
Children at Work and, 276
Christian Family Companion and Gospel Visitor, 286, 2188
  Church of the Brethren, 300
  Gospel Visitor, The, 561
  Messenger, 818
  Ontario, 975
The Pilgrim (published 1870–1880), 1023
The Primitive Christian and The Pilgrim, 25, **1058,** 1327
  anxious-bench denounciation, 930
  Messenger, 818
  The Pilgrim (published 1870–1880), 1023
  Pleasant Grove Church of the Brethren, IL, 1031
  publishing, 1068
  Quinter, James, 285, 1077
  Swigart, William Joseph, 1245
Primitive Christianity, Or a Vindication of the Word of God (Nead, P.), 310, 371, 919, 1279, 2028
Primitive Dunkard Brethren, *See* Conservative German Baptist Brethren
  chart of Brethren bodies, place on, 1403–1405
  Moss, Loring Isaac, organizer, 878
primitivism, 43–44, 48, 296, *See also* apostolic church; restitutionist community
  Anabaptism and, 1058
  apostolic church, patterning after, 1058
  Brethren, lineage of, 613
  Brethren movement, 292–293, 1080
  Campbell, Alexander, 247
    church membership, 813
  debates, 371
  devotional literature, 381
  dietary rules and, 147
  Erste Liebe, Die (*The First Love*), 453
  eschatology, 454
  ethics, 457
  Herring, Friedrich, 598
  higher education, 603
  house churches, 632
  Miller, Daniel Long, practicing, 834
  ministry, 845
  ordination, 980
  Plymouth Brethren, 1038
  Reformation, Protestant, and Brethren doctrine, 1092
Prince Edward Island, 1858
Prince George Co., VA
  Hopewell, VA, Church of the Brethren, 629
Prince George's Co., MD, 1246
Prince of Peace Church of the Brethren, CA, *See* Sacramento, CA, Prince of Peace Church of the Brethren
Prince of Peace Church of the Brethren, CO, *See* Denver, CO, Prince of Peace Church of the Brethren
Prince of Peace Church of the Brethren, IN *See* South Bend, IN, Prince of Peace Church of the Brethren
Prince of Peace Church of the Brethren, OH, *See* Dayton, OH, Prince of Peace Church of the Brethren
Prince of Peace Church of the Brethren, OR, *See* Portland, OR, Peace Church of the Brethren
Prince of Peace congregations
  example of biblically inspired name, 911
Prince of Peace Trust Fund, 185
Prince William Co., VA, 1301, 1308, 1363–1364
  Beahm, I. N. H., and Jubilee Journey, 1168
  Manassas, VA, Church of the Brethren, 784–785
  Nokesville, VA, Church of the Brethren, 939
Prince William Normal School (Brentsville Academy), *592, See also* Hebron Seminary
Princell, Pamela Sue, 2290
Princess Augusta (ship)
  Markey, Hans David, voyage to America on, 793
  Scheublein, Christian, and family, voyage to America on, 1178
  Spitler, Johannes and Catharina Schaffner, 1212
Princeton Theological Seminary
  Lyon, Quinter Marcellus, 768
  Metzler, Burton, 820
  Porte, Robert Fowler, 1047
  Robinson, Paul Minnich, 1115
  Statler, Foster Boyd, 1219
  Stuckey, Melvin Atwood, 1229
Pringle, John L., 1224
Pringle, Joseph, 1742
Pringle, Roscoe Emmert, 1742
printers, 2070
  Brethren movement, 2080
  colonial era, 2104
  Goeb, Frederick, 2078
  Pfautz, John Eby, 1014
  publishing, 1063, *1065, 1066*
  Sala family, 1136
  Sauer, Christopher, 2071, 2073
  Sauer family, 1145, 1146–1150
  Schäffer, Eduard, 1136
  Sower, Charles G., 1207
  Wartmann, Laurentz, 2104
printing industry
  American Revolution, 2088
  bilingual printers, 2105
  Ephrata Community, 2081, 2090, 2110
  history of, 2081
  Roeber, A. G[regg] on German and Dutch books and, 2352
  Sauer press, 2067, 2069, 2074, 2081, 2086
  types, history of, 2086
  Virginia
    bilingual printers, 2105
    German-Americans, 2104
printing ministry
  Boguila, Africa, 268
printing presses
  German language, use of, 724
  King, Frank, 694
Priscilla (ship)
  Naff brothers immigration, 910
Priser, Clarence G., 1383, 1742
Priser, David E., 1742
Priser family
  Mishler family, related to, 852
Priser, Harvey Allen, 1743
Priser, J. N., 1743
Priser, J. W., 1743
Priser, Yvonne Renee (later Riege), 2291
prison chaplaincy, 2157, 2158

prison ministry, 78, *1059*, 1060
    Lancaster, PA, Alfa y Omega (Alpha
       and Omega) Church of the
       Brethren, 2213
    Mennonite Church (MC), 815
    Michigan City, IN, Church of the
       Brethren, 825
prison reform
    call for, Annual Conference (CB), 1060
prisoners
    American Revolution, 2074
    prisoners of war programs
       Brethren Service Committee
          World War II, 2110
prisoners of war, 199, **1058**, 2039
    aid for, 91
    and Belgian YMCA camps, 113
    Cassel, Henry C., 259
    chaplains, 343
    Civil War, 261
    Germany, 545
    Grace Schools, 2192
    Griffith, Lee on abolition of, 2334
    Hochmann von Hochenau, Ernst
       Christoph, letter regarding arrest,
       1967
    medicine, 809
    prisons, **1058–1060**
    relief and service efforts, 1097
    Visser 't Hooft, Willem Adolph, 1309
    Young Men's Christian Associations
       (YMCA), 1290, 1390
    "The Prisoner's Hymn," 1987
Pritchett, Daniel J., 691, 2290
Pritchett, Ella Poff, 1060
    Kintner, Elgin Perry on, 2341
Pritchett, Erlene (later Hanson), 1060
Pritchett, Ethel (later Kintner), 1060
Pritchett, Evelyn (later Watkins), 1060
Pritchett, Gomer, 1060
Pritchett, James A., 1060, *1060*
Pritchett, John Alfred, Jr., 1743
Pritchett, John Alfred, Sr.
    changed from Pritchett, John R., **2385**
Pritchett, John R., 1743
    changed to Pritchett, John Alfred, Sr.,
       2385
Pritchett, Mary Chilton, 1060
Pritchett, Rebecca A. Bowman, 1060, *1060*
Pritchett, Reuel Bowman, *36*, 209, 516,
    590, 704, **1060–1061**, 1743, 2039
    biography of, 2054
    Kintner, Elgin Perry on, 2341
    Meadow Branch Church of the
       Brethren, TN, *805*, 806
    museums, 898
    Ramey Flats Church of the Brethren,
       VA, minister and elder, 1083
    recreation at the home of, *1087*
    Rock House Church of the Brethren,
       KY, elder-in-charge, 1117
    sayings of, 1061
Pritt, Luie (later Helman)
    Helman, Alfred Blair, 2197
private Brethren
    ministry, terminology, 848
Prjapati, Jethalal Hiralal, 1741
Proclaim Good Tidings, 2180
professional ministry, *See* ministry, salaried;
    salaried ministry
    honorific titles, 1266
    seen as encouraged by Sunday schools,
       1239

theological education and, 1256–1257
Program for Women (CB)
    ministry and, 2264
Program to Overcome Violence
    World Council of Churches, 2228,
       2265
Progressive Brethren, 693, **1061**, 2021,
    2047, *See also* Brethren Church
    Annual Meeting and Brethren polity,
       1042–1043
    Ashland College, 1192
    Ashland Convention, *See* Ashland
       Convention (1882)
    Ashland Convention, support for, 368
    authority of scripture, 133
    baptism, 2089
    Beer, Joseph W. in, 936
    Bethel, MI, congregation, 288
    Black Log, Valley Point Church of the
       Brethren, PA, 144
    Black River Church of the Brethren,
       OH, 144
    Blue Creek, IN., congregation, 152
    Brethren Church, 181, 298, *See also*
       Brethren Church
    Brethren Church, orgins of, 166
    Brethren movement, 178
    Brown, Phillip J., 215
    Brush Valley Brethren Church, PA, 224
    Cadwallader, John, 237
    California, 238
    Calrion German Baptist Brethren as,
       925
    Center Church of the Brethren, IN, 267
    Center Hill Church of the Brethren,
       PA, 268
    Chanute, KS, Church of the Brethren,
       270
    Cherry Hill, PA, Brethren Church, 274
    Christian education movement, 283
    The Christian Guide, 286
    Christiania, MI, German Baptist
       Brethren (CB), 288
    church government, 1044–1045
    Clarion, PA, Church of the Brethren,
       317
    Clay City, IN, First Brethren Church
       (FGBC), 318
    Conemaugh, PA, Church of the
       Brethren , 332
    confession of faith, 333
    Congregational Brethren, 186, 335
    conservatism, 2104
    control of Ashland College, 66
    criticism of Standing Committee, 1217
    Dallas Center, IA, Church of the
       Brethren, 360
    Danville, OH, Church of the Brethren,
       363
    Dayton Convention, 335, 368
    debts, and attitude of, 371
    Declaration of Principles, 133, 372
    denominational name, 910
    discipline, doctrine of, 388
    dispensationalism, 390
    dissension in New Enterprise, PA,
       Church of the Brethren, 927
    Doctrinal Points, 1918
    doctrines of, 2075
    dress, 388, 402
    Duncansville, PA, 256
    Dunlap(s), IN, Brethren Church, 410
    elections, electioneering, 434

    eschatology, 454
    ethics, 457
    Far Western Brethren, 476
    favorable view of education, 67–68
    feetwashing, 481, 1186
    first, unofficial convention of, *See*
       Ashland Convention
    Franklin, IA, Church of the Brethren,
       507
    Fraternal Relations Committees, 511
    Fredericksburg, PA, Brethren Church,
       512
    Fredonia, KS, Church of the Brethren,
       513
    frontier, 519
    fundamentalism, 522, 523
    Garber, IA, Church of the Brethren,
       529
    George's Creek Old German Baptist
       Brethren Church, PA, 540
    Glade Run Brethren Church, PA, 551
    Gnagey, A. D., 1236
    Good (Guth) family, 556
    Gospel Messenger, The (1881–1883),
       559
    Gretna, OH, Brethren Church, 572
    Hamlin, KS, Brethren Church, 581
    Harrison, Stephen J., 586
    Heckman family, 593
    Hendricks, Franklin A., 597
    higher education, 283
    Highland congregation, PA, 1253
    history, 1983
    Holsinger, Henry Ritz, 621, 1217
    *Holsinger's History of the Tunkers and
       the Brethren Church,* 623
    Hudson, IA, First Brethren Church,
       635
    Huntington (Co.) Church of the
       Brethren, IN, 637
    Illinois, 647
    Indiana, 652
    Industrial Revolution, 655
    Iowa, 661
    Iowa River Church of the Brethren, IA,
       662
    issues
    alchohol, use of, 16
    Annual Meeting authority, 33, 37
    leadership, taking, 8
    Jacob Tyson and Joseph Easter uniting
       with, 1135
    Jasper, MO, Church of the Brethren,
       669
    Johnstown, PA, First Brethren Church,
       673
    Johnstown, PA, Pike Grace Brethren
       Church, 674
    Johnstown, PA, Walnut Grove Church
       of the Brethren, 675
    Jones Mills, PA, Valley Brethren
       Church, 676
    Kansas, 682
    Kinsey, Samuel, opposition to, 919
    Lyon, William Marcellus, 769
    mandatory decisions, 786–787
    Maple Grove Church of the Brethren,
       IN, 789
    Maple Grove Church of the Brethren,
       KS, members leaving to start con-
       gregations, 789
    Maple Grove, IN, German Baptist
       Brethren, 318

Maryland Brethren activity, 799
Mason, Edward, active in movement, 799
Masontown, PA, Brethren Church, 800
Maurertown, VA, Brethren Church, 803
McClain, Walter Scott, 773
McLouth, KS, Church of the Brethren, sharing meetinghouse with, 779
merger with Leedy Brethren, 31, 67
Meyersdale, PA, Church of the Brethren, 822
Michigan Brethren settlement, 824
Milledgeville Church of the Brethren, IL, 833
millennialism, 834
Miller, Robert Henry, 842
Mineral Point, PA, Vinco Brethren Church, 843
missions and missionaries, 283, 860
Missouri, 864
Moomaw, B. C., 873
Moomaw, Daniel Crouse, 873
Morrill, KS, Church of the Brethren, 876
Mount Etna, IA, Church of the Brethren, 881
Mount Zion Brethren Church, OH, 888
movement, 3, 63, 67
Mumma (Moomaw) family, 896
Neher, E. J., 913
New Bethel Church of the Brethren, VA, split, 925
Nicholson, John, minister in, 935
nonconformity, 940
noncreedalism, 942
Oakdale Church of the Brethren, PA, 957
Ohio membership, 961
Old German Baptist Brethren, 298, 966
openness of, 73
opposition to labor unions, 716
"Order of the Brethren," 976
Osceola, IA, Church of the Brethren, 983
Pennsylvania, 1005
Pleasant Hill, OH, First Brethren Church, 1032
Pleasant Valley, MI, formation, 934
polity, 1044–1045
Portis, KS, Grace Brethren Church, 1047–1048
Portis, KS, North Solomon Church of the Brethren, 1048
Prosperity Brethren Church, WV, 1062
Protestantism, 291
publishing, 1068
Reading Church of the Brethren, OH, 1084
Reconstruction Committee, 1086
restitution, 1100
revivalism, 1210
Ryerson Station Church of the Brethren, PA, 1132
St. Luke, VA, Brethren Church and schism of 1881–1883, 1135
salaried, trained ministers, 1136–1137
sanctification theology, 1210
Sargeantville, NJ, 929
schisms, 348, 350
singing, accompanied, 1185
Skiles, Jacob W., 1188
Smeltzer family, 1191
Stony Creek Brethren Church, PA,

1225
Stony Creek Church of the Brethren, OH, 1225
Strasburg, VA, Round Hill Brethren Church, 1228
Swihart, Jonathan H., 1245
Swihart, Jonathan H., sympathetic to, 1245
temperance, 1359
theological education, 1256
theology, 1259, 1261
as true Church of the Brethren, 2003
urban ministry, 1297
Virginia, 1308
Wampler, John B., 1318
White Dale congregation, 1254
White Oak Church of the Brethren, OH, 1340
Wolf River Church of the Brethren, KS, 1356
Wolfe, George, III, 1358, *1358*, **1358–1359**
Wolfe, John P., 1359
women, roles of, 1360
Woodstock Church of the Brethren, VA, 1364
worship, public, 1376
Worst, John H., 1379
Progressive Brethren congregation, KS, 270
Progressive Brethren congregations, NB emergence of, 921
Progressive Brethren, PA, congregation, 259
The Progressive Christian, 63, 178, 186, 195, **1061**, 2039
Bashor, S. H., 372
Declaration of Principles, 372
Gospel Messenger, The (1881–1883), 559
Gospel Preacher, The, 560
Holsinger, Henry Ritz, 286, 372, 622, 1164
Miller, Howard, 838
minorities, ethnic and racial, 849
publishing, 1068
Progressive/Conservative schism of 1883
Maple Valley Church of the Brethren, MN, 2376
Progressive Convention
Gratis, OH, Brethren Church, 566
Progressive movement, 195
Altoona, PA, 407
Cadwallader, John, 1031
definition of progressivism, 2075
Fair Haven Brethren Church, OH, 467
Fairview Church of the Brethren, IA, 468
Fairview Church of the Brethren, KS, 468
Fairview Church of the Brethren, OH, 469
Falls City, NE, Brethren Church, 472
Fast Element, 480
Fellowship of Grace Brethren Churches (FGBC), 484
Kansas, 232
Maple Valley Church of the Brethren, MN, 2376
Mohican Church of the Brethren, OH, 867
Ninescah congregation, KS, 1138
Old German Baptist Brethren, 969
Old Order Fellowships, 970

Old Order Movement, 972, 973
Olivet Church of the Brethren, OH, 973
Parsons, KS, Church of the Brethren, 994
Pipe Creek Church of the Brethren, MD, 1026
Pleasant Ridge, OH, Church of the Brethren, 413
Portage Prairie, IN, Church of the Brethren, 1047
Sandy German Baptist Brethren Church, OH, loss of members, 1143
Shaver, Emanuel Bydler (GBB, BC) and, 2248
Silver Creek Church of the Brethren, OH, 1182
Social Gospel Movement, 1197
Progressive National Baptist Convention
Committee on Interchurch Relations, 2167
Prohibition, **1061–1062**, *See also* temperance movement
Brethren movement, 311
Church of the Brethren, 301
social action, 1196
Prohibition Party, 1251
Finnell, Virgil Carl, 490
projectors
motion-picture or slide, *See* drama
A Promise Fulfilled (Iredale), 748
Promise Keepers, 2221
Promising Always to Love and Serve (PALS) program
CE National, Inc., 2156
property, *See* church property; confiscation of goods
prophecy, 166, **1062**, 1885
Brethren Church ministry, 846
Community of the True Inspiration, 330
dispensationalism, 390
Humberd, Russell I., 636
millennialism, 834
prayer, 1051
Rock, Johann Friedrich, having gift for, 1116
Rosenberger, Isaac J., writing about, 1123
The Trumpet Call, 1277–1278
Wittschiebe, Charles E. on, 2364
prophecy conferences, 68, 97, **1062**
development of Bible conferences from, 136
evangelism, 460
McClain, Alva J., 772
missionary conferences, 856
The Prophetic Age, 2039–2040
proprietary medicines, 995, *See also* medicines; patent medicines
proselytization
Ephrata Community, 451
Historic Peace Churches, 608
Prosperity Brethren Church, WV, **1062**
Prosperity, WV, congregation
Oak Hill Old German Baptist Brethren Church, WV, 957
Prosser, WA, Community Grace Brethren Church, **1062**
Grandview, WA, Grace Brethren Church, 566
Protection Church of the Brethren, KS,

1062–1063

Protestantism, 2026, 2042, 2047, *See also* specific groups, e.g. Lutheran Church
amillennialism, 833
Brethren of Christ, 189
Brethren theology traced to, 1259
capital punishment, 292
Christian Catholic (Apostolic) Church, 282
Christian education movement, 284
Christ's Assembly and, 280
Church Committee for China Relief, 295
church membership, 812–813
church music, 2074
church parents, 308
communion table, 328
concordances, 331
conservative theology and Brethren Doctrine of Salvation, 1140
educational materials, 284
Evangelical Church in Germany, 459
Great Awakening, 568
Lord's day observances, Brethren general acceptance of interpretation of, 1133
millennialism, 834
Modernism, 866
monastic institutions and Ephrata Community, 175
Moravian Church, 875
ordinances, 976
original sin, 981
Pentecostalism, 1009
Progressive Brethren (BC, FGBC), 291
reformation, *See* Reformation (Protestant)
religious liberty, 1098
styles of churches, 300
trinity, doctrine of, 1275
view of sanctification, 1259
Ward W. R[eginald] on evangelical movement, 2362
Zeiser, Samuel R. on mission of colonial German, 2365
Protests of an Ex-organization Man (Eby), 420
The Protocols
Conservative Grace Brethren Churches International, 2217
Protocols of the Conservative Grace Brethren Churches International, 2168
protracted (evangelistic) meetings
Holsinger, Henry Ritz, 621
protracted meetings, **1063,** *See also* revival meetings
Brethren of Christ, 189
camp meetings, 245
Declaration of Principles, 372
disagreements over, 1053, 1054
evangelism, 460
evangelistic work, 178
Fast Element, 480
Miami Valley Petition, 823
Mohler, Samuel Sayler, 868
"New Measures" revivalism, 930–931
Old Order movement, 206
Quinter, James, 349
revival meetings, 1103
Rock Run Church of the Brethren, IN, 1117

Spanogle, W. L., 353
tradition of, 134
Proud, Robert, 310, 378, 2040
historical writing, 611
Smith, Samuel, 1191
Prough, ___, 1743
Prough, Daniel, 1743
Prounce, D., 1743
Provance family
Prosperity Brethren Church, WV, 1062
Provance, John W., 228, 1743
Provance (Province), David, 320, 1743
Provant, Joseph
Mount Pleasant Old German Baptist Brethren, IN, minister, 887
Provant, William, 1743
proverbs, studies in, 2085
providence
sources on, 2316
Prowant, Christian, 410
Prowant, Daniel, 410, 1743
Prowant, David, 142, 430, 540, 1743
Prowant, Elmer E., 1743
Prowant, Erma (later Etter), 1612
Prowant family, 2083
Prowant, Henry, 142, 410, 1743
Prowant, John, 410, 1743
Prowant, Lawrence Henry, 443, 1235, 1743
Prowers Co., CO, 1345
Prowers congregation, CO, 1345
Prue, Fred, 662
Prue, Marge, 662
Prue, Patricia, 662
Prue, Terrill, 662
Pruit, James, 572
Prupacher family, *See* Brubaker family
Prussia, **1063**
Prussian Army
Nass, Johannes, capture of, 909
Prymont, IN
Sunday school, *1238*
Pryor family
Montclair, CA, Grace Brethren Church, 871
Psalms
45:7, 39
104:15, 39
Psalterspiel, See Davidische Psalterspiel; Kleine Davidische Psalterspiel
Pseudo-Macarius, 57
pseumatology, 386
psychotherapy
Christian vocations, 2110
public auctions, prohibition of alcoholic beverages at, 1251
public confession, *See* confession, public
public health
Japanese civilian internment camp, thesis on, 1913
public offenses, *See* discipline
public office holding
Brethren movement, 310
Church of the Brethren, 312
public policy advocacy and CB Washington Office, 2260
public schools, *See* education, 426
public shows, *See* fairs and public shows
Publication Board
Shively, Nora Early, 1178
Surbey, Howard J., 1241
Publication Board (BC), *See* Brethren Publishing Company (BC)
Publication Board (DB), **1063**

Ness, Jacob C., 2231
publications, *See* entries at print; periodicals; publishers and publishing
almanacs, *See* almanacs
broadside, first genealogy, 158
changes in attitudes about, 1376
denominational, 193, 195, 196
Ephrata Community and, 154, 171
European, 175
languages of, 180, 203–204
Miller, Daniel Long, supporting, 834
missions and missionaries, 191
mural paintings at Camp Mack portraying, 896
1958 General Conference as the Committee on Indoctrination Materials, 180
official, 1068
out-of-print books, 161
schisms caused by, 178
Publications Board
Gillin, John Lewis, 549
Rowsey, Herbert H., 1127
publishers and publishing, 7, 17–18, 25, 77, **1063–1070,** *1064, 1065, 1066,* 2043, 2062, *See also* publications; publishers
almanacs, 712, 1063
Amish, 26
art and illustration, use of, 62
in Ashland, OH, 63
Baltimore, MD, 2067
Bible Monitor Publishing Co., 1289
Bible Monitor Publishing Company, 137
bibliography, 1858, 1860, 1861, 1862, 1863, 1866, 1867, 1876, 1877, 1886, 1890, 1899, 1900, 1901, 1906, 1907
Brethren, lineage of, 613
Brethren Missionary Herald Company, 192, 1237
Brethren Press, 161, 193–195
Brethren Publishing Company (BC), 180, 182, 186, **195–197,** *197*
Brethren Publishing House, 1276
church, history of, 2012
Church of the Brethren, 2162
David C. Cook (publisher), 1237
denominational, 193, 195, 196
Dunkers as publishers, 2003
early American, 2000
education, 426–427
Ephrata Community, 154, 171, 451, 1067, 1970
Ephrata publications, 260
Evangelical Association, 459
Forward Movement, 504
Franklin publications, 260
Frey, Andreas, 517
Funk, Benjamin, 525
Funk, Joseph, 525
Garber, Aaron Leedy, 528
Gass (Gast), Jakob, 532
Geistliches Magazien, Ein (A Spiritual Storehouse), 534
genealogy, 534–535
General Mission Board (CB), 538
General Services Commission (CB), 539
Germantown, PA, 544, 1968
Gish, Barbara Kindig and James Rufus, 550

Gospel Light (publisher), 1237
Gospel Messenger, The (1881–1883), 559
Gospel Preacher, The, 559–560
Gospel Tract Association, 561
Gospel Trumpet, The, 561
Gospel Visitor, The, 561
Grundforschende Fragen (*Basic Questions*), 575
Halle on the Saale River, 580
Hamilton, Walter J., 581
Haug, Johann Friedrich, 589
Heitler, Martin P., 595
Heitler, Richard R., 595
Helping Hand, The, 595
Hersch, Elmer Myron, 598
historiography
    Radical Pietism, 2201
Hoff, Ernest Gockley, 617
Holsinger, Henry Ritz, 621, 622
Holsinger's History of the Tunkers and the Brethren Church, 623
Hoyt, Herman Arthur, 634
Humberd, Russell I., 636
Huntingdon, PA, Stone Church of the Brethren, 637
Hutterian Society of Brothers, 641
Illinois, 647
Kinsey, Samuel, 696
Kurtz, Henry J., 711–712
mass media, 800
missions, 407, 859
Moore, John Henry, 874
Native Americans, 2229
Nyce, William Godshall, 952
Old German Baptist Brethren, 969
Old Order movement, 206
peace policies of Quakers supported, 999
Pennsylvania Brethren settlement, 1004
Pennsylvania Germans, 1987
periodicals, *See* periodicals
Pfautz, John Eby, 1014
photographs, 1020
place-names, Brethren, 1028
printers, 2070
Sauer family, 2003, 2015
Sauer press, 260, 2104, *See also* Sauer press
Scripture Press (publisher), 1237
Sunday school literature, 1236–1237
tracts, 1269
translations, 1997
type-founding, 2067, 2104
U. S., first in, 1976
United Brethren in Christ, 1290
Zur Geschichte der deutschen Presse in Amerika (Becker), 1872
Puckett family, 1866
Puckett, R. Scott
    Grace Village Retirement Complex, 2193
Pudding Springs territory
    Elk Run Church of the Brethren, VA, 439
Puderbaugh, Aaron, 1743
    Puderbaugh family, 1951
Puderbaugh, Jamb
    Puderbaugh family, 1070
Puderbaugh (Puterbaugh, Butterbaugh) family, **1070**
Puderbaugh, Susannah Ulrich, 1070
Pueblo, CO, Church of the Brethren, **1070**

Rocky Ford, CO, Church of the Brethren, 1118
Puerto Rican Council of Churches
    Hispanic Ministries (CB), 2199
Puerto Rico, **1070–1071,** 2025
    Castañer Hospital, 230, 344
    Church of the Brethren in, 2243–2244, 2258, 2267
    Civilian Service project, book about, 1945
    Cordier, Andrew Wellington, 344
    Florida, 496
    Foreign Missionary Society (BC, FGBC), 501
    Garver, Earl Simeon, 532, 2187
    Gilbert, Martha Rupel, 2190
    Heifer Project International, 594
    Heifers for Relief, 1331
    Hispanic Ministries (CB), 2198, 2199
    hospitals, 630
    Lancaster, PA, Alfa y Omega (Alpha and Omega) Church of the Brethren, 2213
    Leopold, Nathan, 738
    Manatí, PR, Pueblo de Dios, 2217
    Mason, George Edward, 2218
    medical projects, 808
    missions, 862
    relief and service efforts, 1097
    Rosenberger, Mary Sue Helstern on Brethren of, 2353
    Serrano, Olga on Brethren of, 2356
    sources on, 2324
    Whitcomb, John Clement, Jr. (FGBC, CGBCI) and, 2262
    Women's Conferences (CB) and, 2265
Puerto Rico Church of the Brethren
    Dominican Republic, mission in, 2172
Puffenbarger, Amos, 1743
Puffenbarger, George M., 1743
Puffenberger, William Vernon, 1743
Pugh, Allen D., 1743
Pugh, Anna Eloise, 2040
Pugh, John William, 1743
Pugh, Lucinda Alice (later Finnell), 490
Pugh, Michael Lynn, 2290
Pugh, Russell, 163
Pugh, William M., III, 1743
Pugh, Wilma DeEtt Prowant Benson, 2040
Puidoux conferences, 610, *1071,* 1071, 1867, 1921, 1922, *See also* Robinson, Jo Ann Ooiman
    Aukerman, Dale H., 2133
    Church of the Brethren, 304
    Zigler, Michael Robert, 1398
Pulaski Club Hall, Phoenix, AZ, 1251
Pulaski Co., IN, 228, 297, 1347
    Church of God (New Dunkers), 297
Pulaski Co., MO, 1324
Pulaski Co., VA
    Church of the Brethren, **1071, 2378**
    Red Oak Grove Church of the Brethren, VA, 1089
    Hiwasse, VA, Church of the Brethren, 613
    place-names, Brethren, 1027
Pullan, Leighton, 2040
Pullen, elder in Cincinnati, NE, 1280
Pullen, Elizabeth
    on Beissel, Georg Conrad, Eros and androgeny in mysticism of , 2351
    on Conrad, Georg, eros and androgeny in mysticism of, 2351

Pullen family, 750
Pullen, William, 1743
Pullen, William H., 1743
Pullen, William Henry, 1743
Pulley, William L., 1743
Pulpit Words for Pew People (Turner), 2256
pulpits, 48, 59, 2131
    advised against at annual meeting, 1376
    chancel designs, pulpit-centered *vs.* alter-centered, 51
    elders' table, 1071, *1072*
    free ministry, 1071
    house churches, 632
    meetinghouses, **1071–1072,** *1072*
    ministry, 845
    Old German Baptist Brethren, 1071
    placement of, 301
    raised pulpits, 48, 51
punishment, *See* persecution
    eschatology, 454
    eternity, 457
    Far Western Brethren, 475
    Fellowship of Grace Brethren Churches (FGBC), 486
    galleys, 527
    Hell, doctrine of, 595
    Martin, David, doubts about, 797
    unbelievers, **1072**
Purcell, John, 248
Purchase Line Church of the Brethren, PA, **1072**
Pure Food and Drug Act (1906), 995
Purefoy, George W., 2040
Purgitsville, WV, 1341
Puritan Revolution (England), and religious liberty, 1098
Puritanism
    Brethren Church and, 184
    Christmas, celebration of, 288
    congregational polity, 1041
    meetinghouses, 48
    nonconformity, 940
    Pietism, 1022
    premillennialism, 833
    Radical German Pietism, 1079
    Reformation, Protestant, 1091
    Sabbatarianism, 1133
Pursel family, 2040
Pursel, Vida Miller, 2040
Pursley, Augustine Franklin, 1743
    Mount Bethel Church of the Brethren, VA, pastor, 880
    Mount Joy Church of the Brethren, VA, minister, 882
    Rockbridge German Baptist Brethren Church, VA, 1117
Pursley, Cyrus Mason
    Mount Bethel Church of the Brethren, VA, 880
Pursley, Glenn, 1743
Pursley, John W., 227, 1743
    Rockbridge German Baptist Brethren Church, VA, elder, 1117
Pursley, William T., 1743
    Rockbridge German Baptist Brethren Church, VA, 1117
Puterbaugh, A. B., 430
Puterbaugh, Amsey Hascall, 440, **1072,** 1743, 2040
    Osceola Church of the Brethren, IN, elder, 984
Puterbaugh (Butterbaugh) family, 2040

Puterbaugh, Christina Adams, 384
    on Linder, Wilbur on descendants of,
        2343
Puterbaugh, Collin Porter, 2040
Puterbaugh, David B., 415, 1743
Puterbaugh, Earl, 1743
Puterbaugh, Edwin Milton, 1743
Puterbaugh family, 1338, 1951, *See also*
        Puderbaugh family
Puterbaugh, Georg, 1998
Puterbaugh, George, 1285
    descendants, 1943
    Linder, Wilbur on descendants of, 2343
Puterbaugh, George and Christina Adams
        family history, 1999
Puterbaugh, Hannah Ulrich, 1285
Puterbaugh, Henry, 1072, 1285
Puterbaugh, Jesse Porter, 1743
Puterbaugh, John Clarence, 1971, 2040
Puterbaugh, June (later Lehman), 736
Puterbaugh, Levi, 1743
Puterbaugh, Lois Arnold, *58,* 1072
Puterbaugh, Martin, 1743
Puterbaugh, Mary Lloyd, 1072
Puterbaugh, Mary Ulrich, 1285
Puterbaugh, Milton P., 1072–1073, **2378,**
Puterbaugh, Rilla Clem, 1072
Puterbaugh, Samuel, 1743
        Shady Grove Old German Baptist
            Brethren Church, OH, elder, 1171
Putman, Andrew, 2105
Putman Co., FL, 691
    migration of Brethren, 831
    Putman family, 2105
Putnam Co., IN, 717, 750
Putnam Co., OH, 142, 410
Putnam Co., WV
    St. Albany Old German Baptist
        Brethren Church, 1134
Putney, VT, Genesis Church of the Breth-
    ren, **2239**
Putnum family
    Mount Pleasant Brethren Church, VA,
        886
Putterbach, Catherine (later Hawker;Wolff),
        1070
Putterbach, Christina Adams, 1070, 2343
Putterbach, Christina (later Dilling), 1070
Putterbach, Elizabeth Kline, 1070
Putterbach family, *See* Puderbaugh family
Putterbach, George
    Puderbaugh family, 1070
Putterbach, George, Jr., 1070
Putterbach, Johann Peter
    Puderbaugh family, 1070
Putterbach, John, 1070
Putterbach, Mary (later Burkett), 1070
Putterbach, Mary Ulrich, 1070
Putzier, Eldon, 1351
Puzier, Grace, 1351
PVS, *See* Parish Volunteer Service
Pyle, Emerson O., 1743
Pyle family, 1289
Pyle, Howard, 61, 379, 1862, 2040, 2093
    Pfautz, John Bauer, portrait of, 1014,
        1014
    public worship, illustrations of, *1374*
Pyle, William Harrison, 1743
Pyles, Claudius D., 1295, 1743
Pyramid Publications, 656
Pyrmont congregation, IN, 717
Pyrmont, IN, 1312, 1345
    Church of the Brethren, 345, *1073,*

1073
    Fairview Church of the Brethren,
        IN, 468
    Rossville, IN, Church of the
        Brethren, 1124
Pysel family
    Sandy Creek Old German Baptist
        Brethren Church, WV, 1143
Pysell, Jacob, 1743

Quaint Old Germantown in Pennsylvania
    (Sachse), *543*
Quakenbush, Ralph Waldo, 1743
Quakers (Society of Friends), 23, 24, 88,
    1199, 2068, *See also* entries at
        Friends
    American Friends Service Committee,
        23–24
    American Revolution, 1190, 1916,
        2010
    attitude toward art, 59
    and baptism, 83
    beliefs, 24
    Boone, Squire, Sr., 161
    Brethren Church, 255
    Brethren loyalism and Revolutionary
        War, American, 1105
    Brethren movement, descriptions of,
        378
    Brethren origins and, 176
    Brethren peace position, influence on,
        999
    Castañer Hospital, P.R., 261
    Christian Peacemaker Teams (CPT),
        2161
    Church of the Brethren, 304
    church-state relations, 309
    Civil War, 331
    Collegiants, 324
    conscientious objection, 269, 316,
        335–336, 337
        World War II, 1371–1372
    Continuation Committee of the Historic
        Peace Churches, 339
    CPS and, 315
    delegations to FDR, 169
    Dove family, 398
    dress of, 401
    Durnbaugh, Donald F. on Brethren and,
        2326
    emigration, Brethren, 443
    Ephrata Press, 452
    fraternal relations, 510
    French, Paul Comly, 515
    Freundschaftsheim (Friendship House),
        517
    Friends Committee on Spain, 518
    frontier, 519
    Geringer Schein, Ein (*A Humble
        Gleam*), 540
    Germantown Academy, 544
    Hendricks (Henricks) family, 597
    Hendricks, John, 597
    historic peace churches, 316, 607, 608,
        611, 2085, 2200
    historical writing, 611
    Hochmann von Hochenau, Ernst
        Christoph, 614
    International Fellowship of
        Reconciliation, 659
    Italy, 665
    Janney, Samuel M., minister, 1979
    Japan, 669

    Judaism, 677
    Keithians, *See* Keithian Baptists
    lobbying for commutation fees for
        exemption during Civil War, 1233
    marriage enrichment, 796
    meetinghouse of, 48
    Mennonites, 815
    Mexico, missionaries to, 821
    migration of Brethren, 829
    migration to Pennsylvania, 1976
    minorities, ethnic and racial, 849
    Muir, Gladdys Esther, 893
    National Interreligious Service Board
        for Conscientious Objectors
        (NISBCO), 916–917
    naturalization and refusal of loyalty
        oath to state, 918
    New Call to Peacemaking, 925–926,
        926
    Newberg, OR, established by, 933
    and non-associators in Revolutionary
        War, 939
    nonconformity, 940
    oaths, taking of, 959
    partnership with Bethany Theological
        Seminary, 2136
    peace principles, 1966
    Penn, William, 1004
    in Pennsylvania, 309
    plain people, 1029
    Plow Creek Fellowship, 1038
    Plymouth Brethren, 1038
    Puidoux Conferences, 304
    Quaker Party
        Franklin, Benjamin, 2110
    queries, 1076
    relationship of the Brethren with, 1921
    relief and service efforts, 1097
    religious liberty and military service,
        1098
    Reynolds, Barbara, 1369
    Rural Life Association (RLA), 12,
        1130
    Selective Service System and conscien-
        tious objectors, 1165
    slavery, 1189–1190
    slavery issues, 2093
    Smith, Samuel, 133, 1191
    Society of Friends, 1199
    Sollenberger, Howard Edwin, 1202
    Spener, Philipp Jakob, defense of, 1209
    style of worhip, 48
    underground railroad, 1286
    Venice, FL, Church of the Brethren
        and, 2258
    violence and, 2265
    visit to the Gestapo, 23
    Wilson, Edward Raymond, 1347
    Wohlfahrt (Welfare), Michael, 1355
    work camps, 1365, 1367
    World Council of Churches, 2228
    Wright, John, 1380
Quakertown, NJ, Brethren Church, *See*
    Calvary Brethren Church, NJ
Quakertown, PA, 1216
    First Church of the Brethren, **1075**
        Harleysville, PA, Indian Creek
            Church of the Brethren, 584
Quann, Daniel P., 620, 1743
Quann, G. Melvin, 1743
Quantrill, William C.
    Rothrock, Abraham, 1124
Quantrill's raiders

burned home of Jacob Ulrich, Breckrenridge Co., KS, 1286
Quarles, Doris, 2165
Quarryville, PA, 461, 2109
Quatipuru River, Brazil, 173
Quay, Clarence E., 232
Quay, Clarence E., Jr., 1743
Quear, Fannie (Darrow), 72
Quear, Hazel (later Austin), **72**, 461
Quear, Jacob E., 72
Quebec, Canada, **1075**
    Brethren, and Roman Catholic Church, 1120
    German Baptist Brethren, 250
Quedlinburg, Germany, 57
Queen meetinghouse, Woodbury, PA, Church of the Brethren, 1364
Queen of Denmark (ship)
    Snowberger, Hans, family voyage from Switzerland, 1153
Queen, PA, Church of the Brethren, **1075**, 1294
Queen's Avenue Community Church of the Brethren, CA, *See* Yuba City, CA, Queen's Avenue Community Church of the Brethren
Queensland, Alberta, Canada
    Pleasant Ridge Church of the Brethren, Alberta, Canada, 1034
Quelch, William, 1743
Quellhorst, J. H., 21
Quemanhoning Creek, PA, 151
Quemanhoning, PA, congregation, 151, 1265, 1321, *See also* Maple Spring, PA, congregation
    Hochstetler (Hostetler) family, 615
    Hooversville, PA, Church of the Brethren, 628
    Sipesville, PA, Church of the Brethren, 1186, 1187
Quensberry, Hensel
    Mount Union (Airpoint) Church of the Brethren, VA, deacon, 887
Quensberry, Mary Lee
    Mount Union (Airpoint) Church of the Brethren, VA, deaconess, 887
queries, **1076**
    Brethren music, 899
    Brethren polity, 1042, 1044
    card playing and, 254
    definition of, 33, 176
    funerals, 524
    General Board (CB), 535
    General Sunday School Board (CB), 539
    German Baptist Brethren Historical Association, 540
    German Baptist Brethren's Home Society, 541
    insurance, 657
    Korean Mission, 2211
    messengers carrying to Annual Meetings, 819
    Milledgeville Church of the Brethren, IL, on dress, 833
    Old German Baptist Brethren, process for, 36, 37
    recreation, 1087
    Standing Committee
        processing of, 1216, 1217
    uniform pattern for Sunday schools, 1239
Quesenberry, James Hebron, 2290

Quesenberry, Joseph M., 1743, 2040
Quesinberry family
    Outlook, WA, Church of the Brethren, 986
Questers' Bible Series, 173
Quick, Charles L., 1744
Quicksburg, VA, 740
    Liberty Brethren Church, *See* Liberty Brethren Church, VA
Quiet Dell Brethren Church, PA, 16, **1076**
quiet hour
    family worship, 475
quietists
    Hochmann von Hochenau, Ernst Christoph, 614
quilting, *60*
    at Annual Conference (CB), 61–62
    Brethren art form, *2144*, 2147
    at General Conference (BC), 62
    sociological aspects of, in Pennsylvania, 2074
Quimby, Dorothy Petcher
    memoirs and poetry of, 2350
Quimby, Phineas P., 287
Quincy, PA, 694
    Snow Hill Community, 1195
Quinlan, Ellen Dailey, 1076
Quinlan, James T., 441, **1076**, 1296, 2040
    biography, 1929
Quinlan, Michael, 1076
Quinn, Bernard, 1979
Quinn, D. Michael
    on Mormonism, 2351
Quinn, Jack W., 2290
Quinn, William H., 1744
Quinter and Brumbaugh (publishers)
    Ewing, John Cook, 463
Quinter Dunkard Brethren
    Root, Isaac William, 2378
Quinter family
    Holtzapfel (Holsapple, Holsopple) family, 624
Quinter, Fannie Studebaker, *1076*, 1077
Quinter, Grace (later Holsopple), 623
Quinter, James, 18, 48, 102, 110, 178, 180, 242, 273, 274, 285–286, 348, 349, 364, 370, 371, 381, 430, 460, 469, 480, 561, 712, 739, 932, 1004, *1076*, **1076–1077**, 1020, 1068, 1210, 1236, 1320, 1332, 1744, 1952, 2030, 2039, 2040, **2378**, *See also Our Children at Work*
    biography, 1938
    Brethren and science, 1160
    Brethren children named for, 912
    The Christian Family Companion, 822
    debate over secret societies, 1164
    historic sites, 609
    historical writing, 611
    Holsinger, Henry Ritz, 621
    Holsopple, Frank Ferry, 623
    Huntingdon, PA, Stone Church of the Brethren, 637
    hymnals, 642
    hymns, 643
    imposters among the Brethren, 648
    Juniata College, 678
    Kostlevy, William on, 2341
    Mack, Alexander, Sr., describing, 777
    Mahoning Church of the Brethren, OH, 782
    Messenger, 818
    Miller, Howard, 837

minorities, ethnic and racial, 849
    minutes, 852
    Myers, Jacob Tobias, father-in-law of, 904
    New Vienna Academy, OH, 961
    Our Children at Work, 985
    Parker Ford, PA, Church of the Brethren, preaching at, 994
    The Pilgrim (published 1870–1880), 1023
    place-names, Brethren, 1028
    poetry, 1039
    The Primitive Christian, 1058
    The Primitive Christian and the Pilgrim, 1058
    publishing, 1069
    Robins, IA, Church of the Brethren, site of debate, 1115
    Shiloh Church of the Brethren, WV, missionary to, 1177
    on single immersion, origin of, 2351
Quinter, John, 1076
Quinter, KS, 142, 682, 1289
    Church of the Brethren, 115, 352, **1077–1078**, *1078*
        Menlo Church of the Brethren, KS, 814
        Olathe, KS, Church of the Brethren, 964
    Dunkard Brethren Congregation, **1078**
    place-names, Brethren, 1028
Quinter, Lydia Belle (later Myers)
    Myers, Jacob Tobias, wife of, 904
Quinter, Mary Ann Moser, 1077
Quinter, Mary N., **1077**, 1078, 1843, 2040
    Quinter Memorial Hospital, 1078
Quinter, Mary Smith, 1076, 1361
Quinter Memorial Hospital, **1078**
    medical missions, 807
Quinter Memorial Hospital, Bulsar, India
    hospitals, 630
Quinter, Sarah (later Malone), 2285
Quinton, G. W., 1744
Quintrell, Gregory Scott, 2290
Quiring, Esther Mae Thieszen, 2040
Quitmeyer, MT, 142
Quito, Ecuador, 200
    Naylor, Kurtis Friend Brethren Service work in, 918
Quynn, Dorothy Mackay, 2041

Raabe, Paul
    on Pietists, 2351
    on Separatists, 2351
Raber, Daniel J., 2041
Raber, David M., 2041
Raber family, 2041, *See also* Reber family; Reber (Raber) family
Raber, Jacob, 2041
Raber, Johann, 2041
Raber, John A., 2041
Raber, Menno Jacob, 2041
Raber, Nellie M., 2041
Raccoon Church District, IN, 717
Raccoon Creek, IN, congregation
    Miller, Robert Henry, minister and elder, 841
Raccoon, IN, Church of the Brethren, *See* Ladoga, IN, Church of the Brethren
race, 2037
Race, Ella, 239
race relations, *See* minorities, ethnic and

racial
SHARE program, 1172
slavery, 1189–1190, 1199
Racer, John A., Sr., 1744
Racer, John Abram, 1744
Racey, Patrick
St. Luke, VA, Brethren Church, 1135
Racey, W. H.
Meadow Mills Church of the Brethren, VA, 806
racial justice
Elgin, IL, Highland Avenue Church of the Brethren, 436
racial minorities, *See* ethnic and racial minorities
racial prejudice
Dolby, Martha Cunningham, 395
Reid, Kathy Goering on, 2351
Reid, Stephen Breck on, 2351
Racket, WV, Mount Olive Brethren Church, **1079**
Rada, WV, 1341
Radabaugh family
Prosperity Brethren Church, WV, 1062
Radatz, Charles, Jr., 2041
Radcliff, David Richard, 152, 1744
Korean Mission, 2211
Radcliff, Grace (later Evans), 1933
Radcliff, Jerald D., 1744
Radcliffe, Carl D., 2304
Radcliffe family
Hyattsville, MD, University Park Church of the Brethren, 641
Raddatz, D. B., 2041
Radebach, Gwen (later Rieman)
Rieman, Timothy Wayne (CB) and, 2243
Radewald, Bette Miller, 2041
Radford family
Roanoke, VA, Garden City Grace Brethren Church, 1113
Radford, Henry L., 1345, 1744, 2304
Roanoke, VA, Garden City Grace Brethren Church, pastor, 1113
Radford, Rosemary (later Ruether), 1928, 2051
Radford, VA, Fairlawn Grace Brethren Church, **1079**
Radical German Pietism, 57, 120, **1079–1080**, 2058, *See also* Pietism
American history, 1999
"Angel Brethren" (*Engel-Brüder*), 30
anointing, 293
Arnold, Gottfried, as historian, 994
baptism, 293
and baptism, 82, 83
Berleburg Bible, 138
Bible, study of, 131–132
bibliography, 1899
Boehmists and, 156
Brethren movement and, 174
Brethren remnants in Europe, 1099
celibacy and, 266
Christliches Hand-Büchlein (Christian Handbook), 288
church membership, 813
Community of True Inspiration, 330–331
confiscation of property, 334
description of Brethren worship by, 1375
Diehl, Johann Georg, 383
Diehl, Nicolaus, 383

Dippel, Johann Konrad, 385
discipline, doctrine of, 386
Durnbaugh, Donald F. on German emigration to PA and, 2326
Eller family, 440
Erb, Christian, 453
eschatology, 454
feetwashing, 293
Frankenthal, 506
Frenkendorf, 516
Geistliche Fama (*Spritiual Report*), 533
Gichtel, Johann Georg, 548
Harmony Society, 584
Haug, Johann Friedrich, 589
Historic Peace Churches, 607
historical writing, 611, 612, 2201
Hochmann von Hochenau, Ernst Christoph, 614
Holy Spirit, doctrine of, 624
house churches, 632
influence on Brethren, 29, 43, 73, 1120
influences, 294
inner Word and outer Word, 656
interest-taking, 658
kiss (holy), 293
König, Samuel, 706
Kroh, Andreas on in biographies of Wittgenstein and, 2342
Landes, Wallace B. on contemporary, 2342
law, participation in courts of, 293
literature of, 149
Lückel, Ulf on biographies of Wittgenstein and, 2342
Mack, Alexander, Sr., 775, 1246
missions, 857
move to Indiana, 928
mysticism, 906–907
Neumann, Gottfried, 924
nonconformity, 940
noncreedalism, 942
O'Malley, J. Steven on, 2349
Palatinate supporters, 990
Pietism movement, 1021
prayer, 1051
priesthood of all believers, 1057
primitivism, 1058
Reformation, Protestant, and Brethren doctrine, 1092
refusal to swear oath of citizenship, 720
restitution, 1100
resurrection, and Brethren teachings about, 1102
Sauer German Bibles, 1149
Schneider, Hans on, 2355
Schrader, Hans-Jürgen on publications of, 2355
Seebach, Christoph, 1165
separatism and, 1167
sexuality, human, 1170
sin, 1184
Society of the Woman in the Wilderness, 1199
Stillen im Lande, Die, 1223
theology of love, 761
universal restoration, 1292
visions, 1309
radical movement, Brethren heritage as, 1986
radical Protestantism, Brethren participation in, 1921

Radical Puritanism
Historic Peace Churches, 607
Radical Reformation, *See* Protestantism; Reformation
historic peace churches, 607
historiography, 2201
role in development of Brethren theology, 1259
radio, 399, 1080
Adelante Juventud (Onward Youth), 2153
The Brethren Hour, **2148**
Brethren of Christ doctrine on, 189
Church of the Brethren on use of, 2099
Covington, OH, First Brethren Church (FGBC), 350
Daily Radio Broadcast, Taos, NM, 1248
Darst, John Charles, 363
ethics, 458
forbidding of, 1251
Gems of Grace, 2127
Grace Brethren International Missions, 2191
Hamel, Joseph Donat, 2196
Hispanic Ministries (BC), 2198
Hispanic Radio Ministry (BC), 2199–2200
influence of on Dunkard Brethren, 2174
Lancaster, PA, Alfa y Omega (Alpha and Omega) Church of the Brethren, 2213
Marlin, High Crist, conducting Bible school programs, 794
mass media, 800–801, 2218
ministry by Mennonite Church (MC), 815
The Missionary Board (BC), 856
missions, 862, 2225
Myerstown, PA, Grace Brethren Church, 906
Old German Baptist Brethren, 941, 969, 2233
ownership and use, 1080, *1080*
Platicas Cristianas (Christian Chats), 2153
Sarasota, FL, Brethren Church, 1145
Sarasota, FL, Iglesia de los Hermanos (BC) and, 2246
Skiles, Jacob W., 1189
Think About It, 2184
Wenatchee, WA, Brethren-Baptist Church United, 1330
women and, 2264
York, PA, Second Church of the Brethren, 1388
Radmiel, Vijaya, 1855
Radway, Wilson O., *385*
Raffensberger, Ella (Webster), 30
Raffensberger, John H., 1744
Raffensberger, Levi, 1744
Ragen, Alfred, 1315
Rager, Adam H., 14, 720, 1744, 2304
Rager, Don K., 332, 674, 1744
Singer Hill Grace Brethren Church, PA, supply pastor, 1184
Raghevji, Naomibai, 229
Ragnijiya, T. H.
on Nigeria, continuing education program for Ekklesiyar 'Yan'uwa a, 2351
Rahn, Barbara Elizabeth Shearer, 2041

Rahn, Charles J., 2041
Rahn, Josephine (later Boorse), 1249
Raikes, Robert, 283, 427, 1237
    Sunday school movement, 283
Railroad Committee, 1271
railroad committees and agents, **1080**
    Annual Meeting attendance, for, 1080,
        1081
    Annual Meeting, provisions by, 178
    Bass, Max, 94
    Brumbaugh, Jacob H., 221
    colonization and, 155, 177, 238
    colonization of Brethren in California,
        1143
    McDonough, George L., 773
    Mott, Charles W., 879
    Peters, Amos B., 1011
railroads, *1081*, **1081–1083**, *1082*, 2020,
        See also individual railroads
    Brethren colonization, 1145
    Canadian Pacific Railway,
        250–251
    Central Pacific Railroad, 1289
    chartered trains, 273
    Church of the Brethren, 299
    colonization, 324
    colonizing, use in, 7, 14
    Cooperative Colonization Company,
        342
    evangelists and missionaries, travel by,
        1271, *1272*
    frontier, 519
    Great Northern, 946, 951, 974, 1342
    homesteading, 626
    irrigation, 664
    land companies, 722
    migration of Brethren, 830
    Miller, Howard, 838
    Northern Pacific, 946, 951, 1240
    Oregon Short Line Railroad, 981, 1289
    photographs taken of travellers, 1020
    Railroad Committee, 1271
    role in western migration, 1240,
        1281–1282, 1288–1289
    Santa Fe Railroad, 238, 715
    Southern Pacific Railroad, 238, 1289
    stocks, and capitalism, 253
    Taylor, Isaac W., secured special serv-
        ices from, 1249
    Union Pacific Railroad, 238, 1282,
        1288–1289
Rainbow Grace Brethren Church, HI, *See*
    Ewa Beach, HI, Rainbow Grace
    Brethren Church
Rainey, Andrew Lee, 1083, 1744
Rainey, Nellie Morgan, 395, **1083**
Rairigh, George, Jr.
    Montgomery Church of the Brethren,
        PA, 872
Rairigh, George S. (1814–1915), 212, 350,
    376, 1744
    Montgomery Church of the Brethren,
        PA, minister, 872
Rairigh, Isaac F., 248, 1744
Rairigh, Isaiah F., 355, 1304, 1744
Rairigh, S. F., 1744
Rairigh, Samuel, 997, 1343, 1744
    Oakland Church of the Brethren, OH,
        leadership by, 957
Raiser, Konrad
    violence and, 2265
Raish, John B., 1744
Raisin City, CA, Church of the Brethren,

244, **1083**
Mennonite Brethren Churches, General
    Conference of, 814
Rajahmundry, India, 651
Rajvadi, Amersing N., 1744
Rajvadi, Shantilal B., 1744
Rajwadi, Chunilal L., 1744
Rajwadi, Damodarbhai P., 1744
Rakes, Malinda
    Snuffer, Thomas Earl on descendants
        of, 2357
Raleigh Church of the Brethren, WV, *See*
    Crab Orchard, WV
Raleigh Co., WV, 350
    Prosperity congregation, Oak Hill Old
        German Baptist Brethren Church,
        WV, 957
Ralph W. Schlosser Residence for women
    Elizabethtown College, 438
Ralster, Jesse, 1744
Ralston, J. E., 1744
Rambo, Ralph E., 585, 1270, 1744
    Modesto, CA, La Loma Grace Brethren
        Church, pastor, 867
Rambow, George, 1744
Rambsel, David L., 1744
    Massillon, OH, Jackson Bible Church
        (BC), pastor, 801
Ramer, Edith Mary Horst, 2041
Ramer family, 738
Ramer, Philip, 738, 1744
Ramey Flats Church of the Brethren, VA,
    1083
    Cumberland, VA, Church of the
        Brethren, preaching point of, 356
Ramirez, Frank Robert, 1744
    on Apocalypse, 2351
    on Book of Daniel, 2351
    on Book of Haggai, Advent/Christmas
        sermons from, 2351
    on Book of Joshua, faithfulness in,
        2351
    on Gospel of Mark, 2351
    on love feast, 2351
    on Snyder, Graydon F., 2351
    on Universal Restoration, 2351
Ramirez, Tomas M., 2290
Ramji, Devji, 1744
Ramona Church of the Brethren, KS, **1083**
Ramsay family, 1956
Ramsbaugh family
    Martinsburg, WV, Rosemont Grace
        Brethren Church, 798
Ramsey, A. J., 1744
Ramsey, Avis Beatrice Wise, 2041
Ramsey, Barbara
    Ramsey, Duane H. and, 2239
Ramsey, Brian
    Ramsey, Duane H. and, 2239
Ramsey Co., ND
    Salem Church of the Brethren, ND,
        1137
Ramsey, D. F., 332, 1744
Ramsey, Dicen F., 1744
Ramsey, Duane H., 1320, 1343, 1744,
    2183, **2239**
Ramsey, Jane, 2239
Ramsey, Kathy, 2239
Ramsey, M. H., 25, 227, 1744, 2125
    Oriskany, VA, Brethren Church, pastor,
        981
Ramsey, Michael, 2239
Ramsey, Nancy, 2239

Ranck, Annie (later Tombaugh), *473*
Ranck, Benjamin F., 1744
Randall, Margaret Harley
    sources on, 2322
Randeve, Satwikrao, 1744
Randive, P. S., 1744
Randolph Co.
    Brethren settlement, 946
Randolph Co., IN, 281, 1288
    Pleasant Valley Church of the Brethren,
        OH, 1035
Randolph Co., NC, 1299
Randolph Co., OH, 233
Randolph Co., WV, 164
    Elkins, WV, Church of the Brethren,
        440
    Glady, WV, Church of the Brethren,
        551
    Harman Church of the Brethren, WV,
        584
Randolph, Corliss F., 2041
Randolph, Henry Sherfey, 1744, 2041
Randolph, T. G., 1744
Raney, William, 270
Range, Sarah, 672
Ranjiya, Toma, 307
Rans-berger family, 2087
Ransom Co., ND
    Englevale Church of the Brethren, ND,
        447
Rants, Jack V., 2290
    Maple Valley, WA, Grace Brethren
        Church, 2218
Rapp, Jesse
    Old Order German Baptist Church
        minister, 972
Rapp, Johann Georg, 147, 545, 584, 711,
    928
Rapp, Roger K., 350, 1744
    Sugar Grove Old German Baptist
        Brethren Church, OH and, 2254
    Rappahannock Church of the Brethren,
        VA, **1083**
    Mount Zion Church of the Brethren,
        VA, 888
Rappahannock, VA, 1209
    Church of the Brethren, VA, 1083
    Copps Chapel Brethren Church, *See*
        Sperryville, VA, Copps Chapel
        Brethren Church
Rappite movement, division within, 148
    communitarianism, 329
Rappolt, Hedwig, 2355
rapture, **1083**
Rarich, George, 1744
Rarick, Alden J., 2041
Rarick, Conrad, *See* Rarick family
Rarick, Elizabeth (later Herder), 593
Rarick family, 2041
    Snider, Jacob, descendants of, 1154
Rarick, Harold J., 1744
Rarick, Henry, *See* Rarick family
Rarick, John G.
    Pleasant Valley Church of the Brethren,
        OH, pastor, 1035
Rarick, Mary Hoffer, 2041
Rarick (Rairigh), Jacob W., 1744
Rarick (Rairigh), John Glenn, 1744, 2041
Rarick, Ralph Glen, 1744, 2041
    Michigan City, IN, Church of the
        Brethren, pastor, 825
Rarick, Ron
    on Henry Kurtz organ, 2351

Rarick, Vinna C. Harshbarger, 2041, 2351
Rarick, W. Carl, 436, 1745
    Rarig family, 2044
Rarig, John, *See* Rarig family
Rarig, Mary Ann Kisner, *See* Rarig family
Rarigh, George R.
    Peabody Old German Baptist Brethren
        Church, KS, deacon, 997
Rarigh, Samuel
    Peabody Old German Baptist Brethren
        Church, KS, elder, 997
Rascher, Harry Herman, 1745
Rash, John, 494
Rash, W. Richard, 1212
Rasor, Daniel, 1338
Rasor, Elizabeth Weybright, 1338
Rasp, Conrad D., 21, 1745
A Raspberry Seed Under God's Dentures
    (Fike), 2184
Ratchford, Michael, 1745
Ratekin, Sarah D. (later Funderburg), 523
Rath, A. B., 1745
Rath, Michael J., 2290
Rathbun, Betty
    minorities, ethnic and racial, 850
    Native Americans, 2230
Rathke family
    Modesto, CA, La Loma Grace Brethren
        Church, 867
Ratlief, Walter, 1745
Ratliff, Paul, 2290
Ratliffe, Carl D.
    Riner Grace Brethren Church, VA, pastor,
        1110
Ratterman, Heinrich A., 2041, 2061
Rau, Elma R., 1745
Rau family, 2098
Rau, Jonathan
    printers, and publishing, 1067
Raudenbusch, Henry, 1745
Raumer, Frederick L. G. von, 2041
Rauschenbusch, August, 379, 542, 2042
Rauschenbusch, Walter
    "Message of the Brethren Ministry,"
        817
    Social Gospel Movement, 1197
Rauser, George, 1745
Raush, Charles, 366
Rausser, Gideon, 1745
Raval, Chhaganlal V., 1745
Raven Run Church of the Brethren, PA,
    1083–1084
    example of dative case in place name,
        912
    Riddlesburg, PA, Church of the
        Brethren, 1108
    Saxton, PA, Stonertown Church of the
        Brethren, worship services with,
        1150
Rawlinson, F. H., 72, 1745
    Rockwell City, KS, Maple Grove
        Brethren Church, minister, 944
Ray Church of the Brethren, ND, *See*
    Spring, Brook ND, Ray Church of
    the Brethren
Ray Co., MO, 752, 1313
    Rockingham Church of the Brethren,
        MO, 1118
Ray, David Burcham, 468, 1220, 2074
Ray family
    Grand River German Baptist Brethren
        Church, MO, 565
Ray, J. E., 229, 629, 740, 927

Martinsburg, PA, Grace Brethren
    Church, pastor, 798
Ray, James A., 1745, 2290
Ray, Jennifer Kathryn, 2264, 2290
Ray, Mark A., 2290
Ray, Sherman, 672
Ray, Timothy, 2157
    Rayman Fellowship Church of the
        Brethren, PA, **1084**
Rayman, Jacob
    Rayman Fellowship Church of the
        Brethren, PA, 1084
Raymon, Samuel, 1745
Raymond, Edith Madeline Replogle
    on Replogle, Replogle genealogy, 2351
Raymond family
    Prosser, WA, Community Grace
        Brethren Church, 1062
Raymond, Harold, 343, 1745
Raymond, John, 1745
Raymond, William O., 2042
Raymor, William Elwood, Jr., 1745, 2290
Raynal, Guillaume T. F., 2042
Raystown Brethren Church, PA, **1084**
Razor, Mary, 170
Re-Imagining Conference, **2240**
    Grassroots, Concerns of the, 2193
Rea, John, 1745
Read, John A., 1745
Reade, Maynard, 558
Reading, OH, Church of the Brethren, **1084**
    Alliance, OH, Church of the Brethren,
        2126
    bibliography, 1881
    Freeburg Church of the Brethren, OH,
        514
    Reading House
        Sandy German Baptist Brethren
            Church, OH, 1143
Reading, OH, Grace Brethren Church, **1084**
Reading, PA, 176
    Flying Eagle, The, 500
    Hispanic Ministries (CB), 2199
Reading, PA, First Church of the Brethren,
    746, **1084**
Reading Twp., York (Adams) Co., Pa., 163
readings
    Ziegler, Edward Krusen on poetry and,
        2365
reaffirmations of faith, annual, 5
Reagan, Della (later Fischer), 1937
Reagan, J. Francis, 319, 715, 1281, 1745
real estate, *See* church property; property
realized eschatology, *See* eschatology
Ream family, 752
    Holtzapfel (Holsapple, Holsopple)
        family, 624
Ream (Reahm), James F., 1745
Ream, Susan (later Yoder), 1953
Reaman, G. Elmore, 2042
Réamonn, Pàraic
    on First and Second Reformations,
        2349
Reamstown, PA, East Cocalico Church of
    the Brethren, **2239**
Reasons of the Petitioners for Not Accept-
    ing the Work of the Committee
    Sent From Annual Meeting to the
    Covington Church, 1920 and 1921
    Old Order German Baptist Church, 972
Reaugh, Lilian (later Gray), 1953
Reavis, Clarence, 1745
    North Manchester Old German Baptist

Brethren Church, IN, minister, 949
Reavis, Henry
    Shuman, L. Herman (OGBB) and,
        2249
Reavis, Mary Long
    Shuman, L. Herman (OGBB) and,
        2249
Reavis, Richard, 1745
    Mexico Old German Baptist Brethren
        Church, IN, minister, 821
Reavis, Ruby (later Shuman)
    Shuman, L. Herman (OGBB) and,
        2249
Reba Place Fellowship, **1084–1085,** *1085,*
    2069, *See also* Shalom Covenant
    of Communities
    Church of the Brethren, 329
    Fellowship of Hope, 488
    and New Covenant Fellowship, 926
    Plow Creek Fellowship, 1038
    religious communities, 1978
rebaptism, 5, 302, **1085,** 2141, 2181, 2182,
    See also baptisms
    Brethren Church doctrine on, 183
    Brethren movement doctrine on, 174
    capital punishment, 292
    Carl, Johann (fl.), 255
    Church of God (New Dunkers), 297
    defellowship, reversal of
        Bowman, John A., 170
    Dunkard Brethren, 409
    Fellowship of Grace Brethren Churches
        (FGBC), 487
    Kalcklöser, Johann Heinrich, not asked
        to undergo, 681
    letters of membership in lieu of, 738
    persecution, 1009
    Solingen Brethren, 255
Reber, Aaron C., 1745
Reber, Anna B. Kauffman, 1085
Reber, Barbara (later Deardorff), 1085
Reber, Clara (later Schaeffer), 2042,
    See also Schaeffer, Clara Reber
Reber, Clara Snyder, 1085
Reber, D. C., *537,* 912, 2111
    Elizabethtown College, 437
    Interchurch World Movement (IWM),
        658
Reber, Daniel Conrad, **1085,** 1745
    Reber family, 1085
Reber, Daniel Herbert, 1085, 2042
Reber, Dean, 1085
Reber, Elizabeth Smith (Schmidt), 1085
Reber, Elsie V. Markey, 1085
Reber, Helen Noecker
    Long Run, PA, congregation, 1085
Reber, Henry H., 1745
    Mohrsville Church of the Brethren, PA,
        elder, 869
Reber, Howard
    Long Run, PA, congregation, 1085
Reber, J. G., 235
Reber, James Quinter, 912
Reber, Jesse Daniel, 1745, 2042
    Pennsylvania Council of Churches,
        1085
    Philadelphia, PA, First Church of the
        Brethren, providing leadership,
        1015
    Shippensburg, PA, Church of the
        Brethren, pastor in, 1177
Reber, Johann Bernhart (Leonhardt), 2042,
    Reber family, 1085

Reber, Jonathan G., 1085, 1745, 2042
  India missions, supporter of, 1085
  Mohrsville Church of the Brethren, PA,
    elder, 869
Reber, Morris B., 2042
Reber, Nora (later Hollenberg)
  missionary to India, 1085
Reber, Nora Loft, 1839
Reber, Norman
  free ministry to New Fairview Church
    of the Brethren, PA, 927
Reber, Norman Franklin, **1085**, 1745, 2042,
  2304
Reber, Patricia Ann (later Belida), 1085
Reber (Raber) family, **1085**
rebirth, *See* conversion
Rebman, Dorothy (later Klein), 699
  Mason, Floyd R. on descendants of,
    2346
  Mason, Kathryn Garst on descendants
    of, 2346
Receiving Committee (OGBB), **1085**
Rechte und Ordnungen (Rights and
    Ordinances) (Alexander Mack,
    Sr.), 132, 147, 175, 262, 283, 288,
    289, 386–387, 472–474, 776,
    1085–1086, 1153, 2003–2004
  feetwashing, 481
  Heaven, 591
  oaths, taking of, 2126
  publishing of, 1063
recipes, *See* cooking Brethren
recitals, *See* drama
Reck, Philipp Georg Friedrich von, 2042
Recknor, Joseph, 1745
*Reckoning with Apocalypse: Terminal
    Politics and Christian Hope*
    (Aukerman), 2133
reconciliation, *See* peace movement
  Bittinger, Desmond Wright, 143
  Church of the Brethren, 2108
  Holsinger, Henry Ritz, 622
  remarriage after divorce, 1099
  sources on, 2311
Reconciliation Committee
  Ministry of Reconciliation, 2224
"Reconsidered Petition," 205, **1086**
Reconstruction Committee (BC), **1086**
Reconstruction Era, **1086**, 1308, 2128
  The Record of the Faithful, 139, 172,
    228, 267, **1086**, 1218, 2014
  historical writing, 611
  Miller, Howard, 838
recreation, *1086*, **1086–1088**, *1087*, 1907,
    2047, 2084, *See also* amusements,
    worldly
  athletics, **69–70**, *70*, 557, 1087, 2045,
    2232
  Christian Education Commission (CB),
    285
  family fun in Southeastern Region,
    1977
  Miami, NM, Church of the Brethren,
    1995
  Sabbatarianism and Sunday recreation,
    1133
  songs for, 2084
Recreation Fellowship
  Helstern, Russell Fred, 596
  Recreation in the Local Church, 1088,
    1278
Recreation in Theory and Practice
    (Rohrer), 1088, 1119

recreation laboratories
  Church of the Brethren, 248
  Manchester College, 248
Recreation Quarterly
  Recreational Fellowship (CB), **1088**
recruitment
  Ephrata Community, 451
  Rector family, 2087
recycling
  Elgin, IL, Highland Avenue Church of
    the Brethren, 436
Red Bank, PA, Church of the Brethren,
    See Oakdale Church of the
    Brethren, PA
  Red Bank, PA, congregation, 350
  Oakdale Church of the Brethren, PA,
    957
Red Bird Development Co.
  Flat Creek Church of the Brethren, KY,
    493
red book
  hymnals, 642
Red Cliff, Alberta, Canada
  Pleasant Valley Church of the Brethren,
    Alberta, Canada, mission point,
    1034
Red Cloud, NE, Church of the Brethren,
    535, **1088**
  Webster Co. Museum, 1312
Red Creek Church of the Brethren, WV,
    1088
Red Cross, 1962
  Child Care in Aviation Incident
    Response (CAIR), 2171, 2172
  Disaster Child Care, 2171
  Relief and Reconstruction Committee,
    aided by, 1096
  works by, 2310
Red Elm schoolhouse
  Fairview Church of the Brethren, KS,
    468
Red Hill Church of the Brethren, VA, 130,
    163, **1088–1089**, *See* Clearbrook
    Grace Brethren Church, VA
Red Lake Community Grace Brethren
    Church, Tonalea, AZ, 1267
Red Oak Grove Church of the Brethren,
    VA, 288, *1089*, **1089**, 1224, 1255,
    2027
  Elliot's Creek Church of the Brethren,
    VA, 441
  Floyd Co. Church of the Brethren, VA,
    500
Red Oak Grove, VA, Old German Baptist
    Brethren Church, *See* Stonewall
    Old German Baptist Brethren
    Church, VA
Red Oak, MD, *See* Fairview Church of the
    Brethren, MD
Red Oak Ridge German Baptist Brethren
    Church, WV, **1089**
Red River Church of the Brethren, OK,
    1089
Red River Valley Church of the Brethren,
    ND, *See* Mayville, ND, Red River
    Valley Church of the Brethren
Redcay, Ruth Kurtz Mast, 2042
Redcliff, Alberta, Canada, 250
Reddick family
  Honey Creek Church of the Brethren,
    MO, 627
Reddick, Lily (later Shamberger), *See*
    Shamberger, Lily Reddick

Reddick, Ruth, 1852
Reddies River, NC, Riverside Church of the
    Brethren, **1089–1090**
Redding, B. F., 1745
Redding, Lewis J., 1745
redeemed community
  ethics, 458
Redekop, Calvin W.
  on BSC/PAX reconstruction of
    Karlsschule, 2351
  plain people, 1029
  Valley Brethren-Mennonite Heritage
    Center and, 2257–2258
Redekopp, Orlando, 2290
redemption
  doctrine of, **1090**
  Nead, Peter, writings on, 919
  Priesthood of All Believers, 1057
  remarriage after divorce, 1099
redemptioners, **1090**
Redenbo, Oscar Benton, 1745
Redford, MI, Trinity Church of the
    Brethren, **1090**
Redmon, S. S., 1745
  Oak Grove Church of the Brethren,
    OK, minister, 956
Redondo Beach, CA, South Bay
    Community Church of the
    Brethren, **1090**
Redrow, Wesfield J., 268
Redstone Baptist Association, PA
  Restoration Movement, 1101
Redstone Valley Old German Baptist
    Brethren Church, WI, **2239–2240**
Reece, C. L., 1216
Reece, Elmer
  Olive Grove Old German Baptist
    Brethren Church, CA, deacon, 973
Reece, Enos J., 1745
Reece family, 153
Reece, John M., 1745
  Sand Creek Old German Baptist
    Brethren Church, KS, elder-in-
    charge, 1143
Reece, Richard L., 2290
Reece, Wiley, 1216
Reed, A. J., 755
Reed, A. P.
  Miller, Robert Paul, 842
  Ronk, Albert Teller, ordination of, 1121
Reed, Albert Price, 1745
Reed, Amos A., 1348, 1745
Reed, Andrew, 21, 1745
  Oakvale Church of the Brethren, WV,
    leadership by, 958
Reed, Andrew G., 1745
Reed, Andrew J., 1745
  Mount Carmel Church of the Brethren,
    NC, minister, 880
Reed, Anna B. Weaver, 2042
Reed, Bertie W. Altizer, 1090
Reed, C. W., 1240
Reed, Cansada Darnell, 1091, 1745
Reed, Cecil C. (G.), 1745
Reed, Charley, 1745
Reed, Connie
  Olean Church of the Brethren, VA, 973
Reed, Cornelius, 21, 1745
Reed, Creed, 1091
Reed, D. Paul, 1745
Reed, Darius, 1341
Reed, Doris Paul, 2304
Reed, Douglas E., 2290

Reed, Earl W. N., 243, 1212, 1240, 1745
Reed, Elias Madison, 527, 1745
Reed, Elizabeth (later Kinsey), 696
Reed, Elta B. Scheaffer, 1745
Reed, Enoch, 1745
Reed, Everett, 515, 1745
Reed, F. D., 1745
Reed, F. W., 1745
Reed family, 265, **1091**, 1224, 1289, 1341,
    1389, 2060
    Hanawalt family, 582
    Hiestand (Heistand, Heestand,
        Heaston) family, 602
    Mountain View Church of the Breth-
        ren, VA, 889
    in New Bethel Church of the Brethren,
        NC, 925
    Prosperity congregation, Oak Hill Old
        German Baptist Brethren Church,
        WV, 957
    Redstone Valley Old German Baptist
        Brethren Church, WI and, 2239,
        2240
Reed, Frank, 496
Reed, Frank L.
    on Eckerlin, Israel, 2351
Reed, G. D., 1745
Reed, G. Oliver, 1745
Reed, Griffith, 1746
Reed, H. C., 345
Reed, Mrs. H. C., 345
Reed, Harvey Lee, 1341, 1746
Reed, Hayes, 1746
    Modesto, CA, Pleasant Home Dunkard
        Brethren Congregation, presiding
        elder, 867
Reed, Henry, 1746
Reed, Herbert P., 2042
Reed Hill
    Sharon Church of the Brethren,
        Alberta, Canada, mission point,
        1172
Reed, Ira
    Olean Church of the Brethren, VA, 973
Reed, Isaac A., 1746
Reed, Isaac, Sr., 21, 1746
Reed, J. W., 1746
Reed, James, 2290
Reed, Jason L., 2290
Reed, John Alfred, 749, 1746
    Mountain View Church of the Breth-
        ren, VA, 889
    New Bethel Church of the Brethren,
        NC, elder in, 925
    New Haven Church of the Brethren,
        NC, pastor in, 928
    Newberg, OR, Church of the Brethren,
        pastor in, 933
Reed, John Amos, 1746
Reed, John Ford, 2042
    on Ephrata Cloister and American
        Revolution, 2351
Reed, John M., 672
Reed, Kyle Thayer (DB), 2225, *2225,* **2240,**
    2240
    China, missionary to, 1091
Reed, Lester Galen, 2290
Reed, Lester W., 1746
Reed, Lillian Freeman, 496
Reed, Margaret, 1394
Reed, Marion, 265
Reed, Martha Breidenbaugh, 2042
Reed, Mary, 2225, *2225,* **2240,** *2240*

Reed, Mary Jane Jameson, 1091
Reed, Michael, 407, 1746
Reed, Nancy, 1341
Reed, Noah, 1341, 1746
Reed, Noel, Jr., 1746
Reed, Norm C., 749, 1746
    Mountain View Church of the Breth-
        ren, VA, 889
Reed, Norman C.,
    New Bethel Church of the Brethren,
        NC, elder in, 925
    New Haven Church of the Brethren,
        NC, pastor in, 928
    Shelton Church of the Brethren, NC,
        pastor in, 1176
Reed, O. D., 1746
Reed, Ora E. Dulaney, 1090
Reed, Paul, Jr., 2304
Reed, Peter Duncan, 1340, 1746
    Midway Church of the Brethren, TN,
        providing leadership, 827
    Pleasant Valley Church of the Brethren,
        TN, 1035
Reed, Phlem
    Olean Church of the Brethren, VA, 973
Reed, Quincy D., 527, 620, 1746
Reed, Ray C., 1746
    Dallas Center, IA, congregation, minis-
        ter and elder, 1091
Reed, Ray Rolland, 1746, 2305
Reed, Richard, 705, 1746
Reed, Robert, 12, 1746
    Ramey Flats Church of the Brethren,
        VA, minister, 1083
Reed, Robert William, 2290
Reed, Roscoe Quinter Evans, **1090,** 1746
Reed, Ross E., 1746
Reed, Samuel, 1746
Reed, Samuel P., 407, 1341, 1746
Reed, Samuel Sylvester, 1746
Reed, Sarah, 373
    Olean Church of the Brethren, VA, 973
Reed, Susan, 1304
Reed, T. S., 2042
Reed, Thomas, 1746
Reed, Tiberias Ulysses, 1746
    Poplar Valley Church of the Brethren,
        MT, elder, 1047
Reed, Tom, 1394
Reed, Will A., 363, 555, 749
    Melvin Hill Church of the Brethren,
        NC, pastor and elder, 812
    Mountain View Church of the
        Brethren, VA, 889
Reed, William A., 212, 1209, 1274, 1746
Reed, William E., 1746
Reed, William (Etna Green, IN), 1746
Reed, William Sherman, **1090–1091,** 1746,
    2240, 2305
Reed, William (Topeco, VA), 1746
Reed, Willoughby Henry, 2042
Reed, Wyatt, 1341, 1746
Reede, E. J., 1746
Reeder family, 1302
Reedley, CA, Church of the Brethren, 244,
    727, 744, **1091**
Reeds Creek
    Smith Creek Fellowship Church of the
        Brethren, WV, preaching point,
        1191
Reedsville congregation, VA (CB), 21
Reedy Creek congregation, NC, 734, 1311,
    1383

    nonresistance and Revolutionary War,
        946
Reedy, George
    Maitland Church of the Brethren, PA,
        salaried minister, 783
Reely, Martin, 1746
Reese, A. W., 268, 1318, 1746
Reese family, 267, 727
Reese, J. M., 1746
Reese, John W., 1746
    Portage Church of the Brethren, OH,
        minister, 1047
Reese, Karl
    Olean Church of the Brethren, VA,
        pastor, 973
Reese, Polly, 365
Reese, Sherry (later Vaught), 2296
Reese, Whildin Ancon, 1746
Reesor, [Mrs.] Barkis, 2042
Reetly, Barbara (later Herli), 583
Reeves, Alfred (Alford) H., 90, 1746
Reeves, Betty Ruth, 1849–1850
Reeves, Bonnie Joanne, 1853
Reeves, C. D., 90, 1746
Reeves-Graybill, Edward E., 2042
Reeves, Harry I., 1746
Reeves, Marvin G., 1746
reform, 2022, *See* Dunkard Brethren
    The Bible Monitor, role in, 137
    religious, 1977
Reformation, 28–29, 56, **1091–1092**
    attitude toward art, 59
    Brethren doctrine of salvation and,
        1140
    Brethren, lineage of, 613
    Brethren noncreedalism, 942
    Brethren roots in, and Roman Catholic
        Church, 1120
    concordances, 331
    Covenant Theology, 347
    Danner (Donner), Jacob, 362
    distinction between clergy and laity,
        718–719
    Evangelical Church in Austria, 459
    Evangelical Church in Germany, 459
    Geneva, 540
    Germany, 545
    Germany, 546
    infant baptism, 655
    left wing of, 28
    Lutheran Church, 767
    monasticism, 869
    musical instruments, 900
    oaths, taking of, and state churches,
        959
    peace, 998
    Peace of Westphalia, 1338
    polity, 1041
    Protestant, and Priesthood of All
        Believers, 1057
    Radical German Pietism, 1079
    Radical Reformation, 28–29, 1092
    religious liberty, suppression of, 1098
    sin, 1184
reformation of doctrine, 1258
reformation of heart and life
    Spener, Philipp Jakob, 1209
reformations, *See* First and Radical
    Reformations
    church, 2096
    family worship, 474
    Second Reformation, Opocensky on,
        2349

Reformed (Calvinist) Church, 28, 29, 107, 1092, **1092**, *See also* Calvinism
  Arminian party, 324
  Baumann, Mattheis, and, 925
  Bittinger family, 144
  Boehm, Johann Philip, 156
  Boni (Bohni, Boney), Andreas and, 158
  Brethren inroads into, 156
  Brethren movement and, 174
  Brethren music, 898
  Calvinism and, 240
  China mission, 296
  consistory, 407
  Easter Synod in U. S., history of, 1986
  education and ministers, 293
  Ephrata Community, 451
  Erb, Christian, 453
  Established Churches, 456
  established churches and prisons, 1058
  Evangelical Church in Austria, 459
  Evangelical Church in Germany, 459
  father of Johann Christoph Sauer I, pastor in, 1147
  in German Palatinate, 990
  Germany, 241, 545
  Grahe, Wilhelm, 564
  Grebe (Grebi), Georg, 569
  Heidelberg Catechism, 593
  Henckels, Johann Friedrich, 596
  history of, 1951
  immigration from, 175
  Indonesia, 655
  interdenominational relations, 1183
  International Christian Youth Exchange (ICYE), 659
  justification, doctrine of, 679
  Kling, Johann Valentin, 702
  Krefeld, 707
  Lucas, Martin, 766
  Mack, Alexander, Sr., baptized in, 775
  Mack, Johann Philipp, elder, 778
  Martin, George Adam, 797
  migration of Brethren, 829
  Miller, John Peter, minister, 840
  Moravian Church, 875
  musical instruments, 900
  New Sudan Council of Churches, 2162
  Otterbein, Phlip W., 1289
  Pauw, Adrian, support from, 996
  persecution by, 159
  Prague Conferences and, 2239
  presbyterial polity, 1041–1042
  Presbyterians, 1056
  prophecy, 1062
  Radical German Pietism, 1079
  Reitz, Johann Heinrich, pastor, 1095
  religious liberty, suppression of, 1098
  Rothenberger, George Philip, 1124
  Rummel, George, 1129
  sanctification and, 1142
  Sauer, Johann Christoph, I, and controversies in, 1148
  Schlatter, Michael, pastor, 1153
  Schwarzenau, 1158
  singing, 1184
  Solingen Brethren, 1201
  Sunday school lessons, 1237
  Tersteegen, Gerhard, 1254–1255
  Tulpehocken, PA, 1328
  Winebrenner, John, 309
refuge
  Mennonites providing for Brethren, 815

refugee resettlement, 197, 198, 202, **1092–1093, 2240**
  Aukerman, Dale H., 2133
  Bach, Jeffrey A. on, 2348
  Carlisle, PA, First Church of the Brethren, 255
  Dolnikowski, George and, 2240–2241
  Kokomo, IN, Church of the Brethren, 705
  Lebanon, PA, Church of the Brethren, 733
  Lincoln, NE, Antelope Park Community Church of the Brethren, 743
  Linz, Austria, 746
  Live Oak, CA, Church of the Brethren, 750
  Lone Star Church of the Brethren, KS, 753
  minorities, ethnic and racial, 850
  Montgomery, IL, Boulder Hill
  Mummert, J. Ronald on, 2348
  Neighborhood Church of the Brethren, 872
  Mount Joy, PA, Florin Church of the Brethren, 882
  Myersville, MD, Church of the Brethren, 906
  Oakland Church of the Brethren, OH, 957
  relief and service efforts, 1097
  Roanoke, VA, Central Church of the Brethren, 1112
  social welfare, 1198
  sources on, 2321
  world hunger issues (CB) and, 2266
refugee sponsorship
  Kalmuck refugees, 681
  Skyridge Church of the Brethren, Kalamazoo, MI, 681
  State College, PA, University Baptist and Brethren Church, 1218
  Sugar Ridge Church of the Brethren, MI, 1235
  Sunnyslope Church of the Brethren, WA, 1240
  Topeka, KS, Church of the Brethren, 1267
  World Council of Churches, Turkey, 1280
refugees, *See* displaced persons
  alternative service assignees and, 19, 23
  Americans of Japanese ancestry, 200
  Boise, ID, Mountain View Church of the Brethren, 157
  Brethren as, and caring for the poor, 1046
  Bushong, Benjamin G., 233
  Civil War, 314
  congregations sponsoring, 30
  Crumpacker, Franklin Henry, 354
  East Fairview Church of the Brethren, PA, 415
  Elgin, IL, Highland Avenue Church of the Brethren, 436
  Elizabethtown, PA, Church of the Brethren, 436
  Enders, NE, Church of the Brethren, 446
  France, post-Spanish Civil War, 146
  Germans, ethnic, 201
  Germany, 545

  Greece, 569
  Hagerstown, MD, Church of the Brethren, 578
  Homeless European Land Program (HELP), 625
  Honduras, 627
  humanitarianism, 636
  Hungarian, 73, 200
  Huntsdale Church of the Brethren, PA, 638
  Hüttental, 639
  Inter-Church Aid and Service to Refugees, 657
  International Refugee Organization (IRO), 659
  Judaism, 677
  Korean refugees, camps for, 707
  Kruger, Helena, 708
  Maple Grove Church of the Brethren, IN, helping, 789
  Marienborn, and religious freedom, 792
  Maryland Brethren activity, 799
  medical projects, 809
  medicine, 809
  Moravian, 1399
  Murray, Don, 626
  Palestinian, 23
  Polo, IL, Church of the Brethren, sponsoring, 1045
  post-WWII, 198, 200
  Prairie City Church of the Brethren, IA, sponsorship of, 1050
  Reading, PA, First Church of the Brethren, sponsorship of, 1084
  relief and service efforts, 1096–1097
  relief for (AFSC), 23
  resettling of, 1912
  Salamonie Church of the Brethren, IN, 1136
  student exchange program, 1231
  "The Roads to Everywhere" (Hoover), 1972
  Visser 't Hooft, Willem Adolph, 1309
  Volksdeutsche, 1309
  Volksdeutsche, 201
  Wittgenstein, 1959
  work camps as assistance, 1367
  World War I, 23
  World War II, 17, 73
  WWII, 146
  Young Men's Christian Associations (YMCA), 1390
  Zigler, Michael Robert, 1398
Regel, Bessie Belle, 2042
regeneration
  Brethren Doctrine of Salvation, 1140
Der Reggeboge
  Pennsylvania German Society, 1006
Regina, Sasketchewan, Canada, 15
regions, *See* district organization
  camping movement, 249
  Church of the Brethren, 304–305, **1093–1094**
  Forney, Roy S., 503
  list of districts and regions by denomination, 1513–1538
Regoonath, Ancil, 2290
Reguel, Regina (later Ziegler), 1397
Regular Baptists of Redstone Association
  Campbell, Alexander, 247
Rehm, Frank R., 1746
Rehobeth, MD

Church of the Brethren, 305
Rehobeth meetinghouse, Allegheny Church of the Brethren, WV, 2125
Rehrersburg, PA, 750, 1397
Reiber, Russell, 1746
Reice family, 735
Reichard, Catherine Balsbaugh, 753
Reichard, Daniel, 753, 1746
    Manor Church of the Brethren, MD, starting temperance society, 787
Reichard, Harry Hess, 2042
Reichard, John Rowland, **1094,** 1746
    Manor Church of the Brethren, MD, minister, pastor, elder, 787
    Sharpsburg, MD, Church of the Brethren, elder, 1174
Reichard, Mary Katherine Martin, 1094
Reichard, Mary (later Long), 753
Reichard, Otelia H. Rowland, 1094
Reichard, Robert H., 1094
Reichard, V. M., 1746
    St. James Brethren Church, 1134
Reichard, W. Scott, *578*
Reichard, Winfield Scott, 912, 1746, 2042
Reichel, Johann Friedrich, 2042
Reichel, John Frederick
    military service, lack of, by Dunkers and Quakers, 999
Reichel, Joseph J.
    on Jones, Minne Lee and descendants, 2351
Reichel, Levin T., 378, 2042
Reichelderfer, Laura Alice Buchman, 2042
Reichly, Ruth Berkey, 2314
Reichmann, Eberhard
    on Radical Pietists, 2351
Reichmann, Felix, 140, 611, 1861, 1918, 2043, **2388**
    Sangmeister, Heinrich (Ezechiel), diary, 1144
Reid, A. P., 1746
Reid, Alexander, 297
Reid, Daniel G.
    on Christianity in America, 2351
Reid, Kathryn Goering, 2290
    on racism, 2351
Reid, Lester R., 377, 1746
Reid, Lester W., 1747
    Maple Grove Church of the Brethren, NC, minister, 790
Reid, Stephen Breck, 2290
    on racism, 2351
Reidenbach, Rudolph S., 1747
Reidy, Miriam
    on volunteers for peace, 2351
Reiff, Christian, 1094
Reiff, Conrad, 2099
Reiff, Elizabeth (later Amick), 58
Reiff, Elizabeth (later Royer), 1094, 1128
Reiff, Elizabeth Titlow, 1094
Reiff family, 164, 232, 260, 2099
Reiff, Hannah (later Amick), 25
Reiff, John B., 1747
Reiff, John Cassel, 1747
Reiff, John George, 2045
Reiff, Joseph, 1094
Reiff, Lillie (later Fisher), 491
Reiff, Mary (later Price), 1057
Reiff, Maude (later Miller)
    Miller, Robert Henry, wife of, 842
Reiff, Opal G., 2290
Reiff (Rife) family, **1094**
Reiff, Sarah Harley, 1094

Reiff, Susan (later Myers)
    Myers, Oscar Reiff, mother of, 904
Reigard, John M., 1747
Reigart, Anna, 1899
Reigart, Richard K., 1747
Reighard, Joseph, 674, 1747
Reiley, Erastus C., 1747
Reilly, Elizabeth Carroll, 2043
Reiman, Elizabeth G. (later Glick-Reiman), 1636
Reiman family
    Fike family, 490
Reiman, Ralph W., 1747
Reimensnyder, Helen (later Martin), 747
Reimer, Judy Mills, 2163, 2290
    church governance and, 2264
Reimers, Dagmar, 2043
Rein, Kurt, 2043
Reina, Domingo, 53, **1094**
Reiner, Jacob, 588
Reiner, Joel K., 1747
    Philadelphia, PA, North Philadelphia Church of the Brethren, minister, 1016
Reiner, Lenore, 2043
Reinhard, Eliza Margretha, 2024
Reinhard family, *See* Reinhardt (Reinhard, Rinehart, Rhinehart) family
Reinhard, Johann Georg, 2024
Reinhardt (Reinhard, Rinehart, Rhinehart) family, 262, 505, 2024
Reinhardt (Rinehart, Rhinehart) family, *1094,* **1094–1095**
Reinhardt, Martin, 1094
Reinhart, Abraham, 1094, 1747
Reinhart, Andrew, minister, 1094
Reinhart, David
    Monrovia, MD, Bush Creek Church of the Brethren, minister, 870
Reinhart, David, minister, 1094
Reinhart, Martin, 1747
Reinhart, Peter, 1094, *1094,* 1747
Reinhart (Rhinehart), David, family
    Pipe Creek Church of the Brethren, MD, 1026
Reinhart, Ulrich
    immigrant to America, 1094
Reinhold, Benjamin, 1747
Reinhold, Jacob, 1747, 2043
Reininger, Linda L., 2290
Reinke, J. Herman, 1747
    Rheinland/Pfalz
        reference to in thematic atlas, 1956
Reinoehl, C. Truman, 1747
Reinoehl, Cheryl Elaine Scheib, 1843
Reinoehl, Clara (later Urey), 1298
Reinoehl, P. Graydon, 1843
Reisch, Christian, 148
Reisen, Gideon, 1747
Reiser, Esther M. (later Garber), 1944
Reish, Charles W., 1747
Reish, Joseph D., 758
    Pleasant Valley Church of the Brethren, Alberta, Canada, providing pastoral care, 1034
Reish, Joseph Daniel, 1747, 2043
Reisinger, Ernest L., 1747
Reiss, Elizabeth Clark, 1927
Reist, Catherine (later Urner), 1298
Reist, H. F., 471
Reist, J. Clarence, 2043
Reist, Mabel E. Brubaker, 2043
Reist, S. B., 72

Reistertown-Evergreen Church of the Brethren, MD, **1095**
    Ellicot City, MD, Pine Orchard Church of the Brethren, 441
    Meadow Branch Church of the Brethren, MD, 805
Reistville, PA, 1278
    Heidelberg Church of the Brethren, *1095,* **1095**
Reiswitz, Georg L. von, 2043
Reiter, A. O., 2043
Reitz, H. H., 1747
Reitz, Johann Heinrich, 57, 133, 138, **1095,** 2043
Reliance, VA
    Mount Zion Brethren Church, 368, **1095–1096**
relief, *See* Brethren service; service
Relief Agency Brethren (FGBC), **1096**
    social welfare, 1198
relief aid societies
    Kansas settlers, 682
    World Relief Corporation, 914
Relief and Reconstruction Committee (CB), **1096**
    General Mission Board (CB), 539
    Miller, John Ezra, 840
    Williams, John Henry Bashor, 1345
relief and rehabilitation work, 19, 113, *1096,* **1096–1097,** 1222, 2017, 2029
    Abraham Lincoln Friendship Train, 286
    administrators
        Bushong, Benjamin G., 233
    Africa, 186, 236
    agencies, 1990
    agriculture projects, 167, 186, 198, 200, 1097
    alternative to military service, 1331
    animal husbandry projects, 200
    Arizona, 186
    Armenians, 302
    Austria, 23, **73,** 200, 1097
    Belgium, 200
    Bhutan, 186
    Bilboa, Spain, 146
    blacks, 186
    Bremen, 173, 230
    Brethren Food Preservation Systems (CB), 186
    Brethren of Christ, 189
    Brethren view of Roman Catholic Church, 1120
    Brethren war relief policy, formation of, 218
    CARE, 342
    Castañer Hospital, 344
    Castañer, PR, 146, 199, 316
    China, 200, 209, 218, 227, 277, 278, 295
    China Suffers (Wampler, Ernest Michael), 1316
    Christopher Sauer Workshops, 173
    Church of the Brethren, 2162–2163
    Church of the Brethren peace position, 1000
    Church of the Brethren programs, 303
    Church World Service (CWS), **2165**
    Cleveland, OH, Brookpark Community Church of the Brethren, 320
    Codorus, PA, Church of the Brethren, 323

Colorado, 186
Conemaugh, PA, Church of the
  Brethren, 332
consecration at Missionary
  Convocation, 856
Cordier, Andrew Wellington, 344
Council of Relief Agencies Licensed
  for Operation in Germany, 173
Covington, OH, Church of the
  Brethren, 349
CRALOG, 346
Crumpacker, Franklin Henry, 354
Culler, Arthur Jerome, 355
cut-garment program, 198
Cyprus, 357
Dallas Center, IA, Church of the
  Brethren, 360
Dayton, OH, Emmanuael Church of the
  Brethren, 365
detached programs, 380
Disaster Child Care, 2171
disaster relief, 198
Disaster Response Program,
  2171–2172
displaced person resettlement, 200
Dominican Republic, 186
Ecuador, 200
educational materials, 284
Elderton, PA, Plum Creek Church of
  the Brethren, 433
Enders, NE, Church of the Brethren,
  446
ethics, 458
Europe, 230
Europe, shipments to, 1180
Evangelical Church in Austria, 459
Evangelical Church in Germany, 459
evangelism, 461
Falfurrias, TX, 202
Florida, 186
Forney, Anna Marie Shull and Daniel
  L., 502
Forney, John, 502
France, 146, 200, 506
fraternal relations, 510
Friends Committee on Spain, 518
Friendship Trains, 518
General Board (CB), 535
General Mission Board (CB), 538
Geneva, 540
Germany, 545, 546
Germany, post-World War II
  Kaltenstein Castle, 681–682
  Karlsschule, 684
  Kassel as headquarters of, 684
Greece, 200, 569
Greek Orthodox Church, 569
Guatemala, 576
handicapped, vocational training for,
  173
Harlan Co., KY, 209
Hartzler, Russell M., 588
Heifer Project International, 233,
  593–594
Hispanics, 186, 190
Historic Peace Churches, 607
Holland, 200
Homeless European Land Program
  (HELP), 625
hospitals, 630–631
humanitarianism, 636
Ikenberry, Ernest Leroy, 646
India, 146, 149, 158, 200

Indiana, 653
Interchurch Service to Greek Villages,
  658
interdenominational, 198, 202–203
International Christian Youth Exchange
  (ICYE), 659
Italy, 665
Ives, Allen, 665
Japan, 287, 669
Kalmuck people, Buddhist, 198, 227
Kansas, grasshopper invasion, 232
Kassel, 200
Korea, 707
La Place, IL, Church of the Brethren,
  713
Laos, 158
Latin America, 200
Lebanon, PA, Church of the Brethren,
  733
low-income communities, 186
Maryland Brethren activity, 799
material aid, 198, 199, 802
medical projects, 808
medical work, 193
Mennonite Central Committee (MCC),
  814–815
Mexico, 186
Mexico, missionaries to, 820
migrant labor camps, 201
Miller, Orie O., in Russia, 841
missions, 859, 861
Mississippi, 864
Modesto, CA, 197
Moomaw, John Crouse, 874
Morocco, 876
motion pictures publicizing, 879
Mount Joy, PA, Florin Church of the
  Brethren, 882
mural paintings at Camp Mack portray-
  ing, 896
Murphy, Sara Florence Fogelsanger,
  897
mutual aid, 903
Nappanee, IN, 198
Native Americans, 188
Nebraska, 186
New Windsor, MD, 198–199, 230, 233,
  309
Nigeria, 200
Norristown, PA, Church of the
  Brethren, 945
North Carolina, 186
ordination of workers, 980
Oubangui-Chari, 236
Palestine, 990
Paradise Church of the Brethren, OH,
  992
Peace Committee (BC), 1001
Peters, Woodford W., 1011
Poland, 200, 1040–1041
post-WWII Germany, 200
Puerto Rico, 199, 1070
Root River Church of the Brethren,
  MN, 1122
rural areas, 1130
Russia, 1288
seagoing cowboys, 198, 199
Sebring, FL, J. H. Moore Memorial
  Church of the Brethren, 1162
senior citizens, 186
South Saint Joseph Church of the
  Brethren, MO, 1135
Spain, 146, 1331

Spanish Civil War, 155
Sri Lanka, 186
study of effects of hunger, University
  of Minnesota, 1955
Texas, 190
Thalham, 200
United Nations, 186
United Nations Relief and
  Rehabilitation Administration
  (UNRRA), 1291
Vietnam, 1305
Walcheren, the Netherlands, 230
Wampler, Nelie Florence, 1317
West Milton, OH, Church of the
  Brethren, 1335
World Friendship Center, 1369
World Health Organization (WHO),
  1369
World Relief Board, 1369
World War I, 1371
World War II, 286, 308, 312, 1373
WWII, 199
Yeremian (Yereman), O. H., 1385
Young Men's Christian Associations
  (YMCA), 1390
Zigler, Michael Robert, 1398
Relief Board (DB), **1097**
  Torreon Navajo Mission, 1268
relief training units, **1097–1098**
Die Religion in Geschichte und Gegenwart
  (Schmidt)
  Pietism subdivisions, 1021
Religion, southern United States, 2309
religions
  Christianity, 1972
  conversions, handbook of religious,
    2071
  ethnic issues, 2069
  history of, 2066
  influence of Brethren on other
    Christian denominations, 2055
  suppression of, 2084
The Religious Bodies of America
  (Mayer), 2009
religious diversity
  Pennsylvania Germans, 1006
religious liberty, suppression of, 1098
religious doctrines
  death, 2079
  resurrection, 2079
  soul, immortality of, 2079
religious education, *See* Christian education; Sunday school
  Parish Ministries Commission involve-
    ment in, 993
  United Ministries in Education, 1327
  US Supreme Court decisions
    released-time programs on public
      school property, 1326–1327
  Virginia Council of Churches, 1326
  Virginia Council of Religious
    Education, 1326
  Virginia Sunday School Association,
    1326
  weekday religious education,
    1326–1327
Religious Education, 399
Religious Education Association, 283–284
religious freedom, *See* religious liberty
religious issues
  conscientious objectors, statements on,
    2107
  conversions, handbook of, 2071

education
    Sunday school movement, 2084
German church groups, 2108
South Carolina, 2088
world-wide, Brethren movement relationship to, 2106
religious liberty, 28, 87, 88, 107, 113, 400, **1098–1099**
    Brethren movement, 292
    Bromback (Brumbach), Jacob, 516
    capital punishment, 253
    Christopher Sauers, 2001
    Edict of 1712, 425
    Ernst Casimir, 453
    Established Churches, 456
    ethics, 457, 458
    Garb Law, 528
    German nobility, 1982
    Germany, 545
    Hamburg-Altona, 580
    Henckels, Johann Friedrich, 596
    Henrich Albrecht, 597
    Hochmann von Hochenau, Ernst Christoph, 615
    loyalism and Revolutionary War, American, 1105
    Marienborn, 792
    North American Brethren, 1009
    Penn, William, and settlement of Pennsylvania, 1004
religious movements
    New York, 2085
    Ohio, 2085
    Pennsylvania, 2076, 2085
religious objector, 917, See also conscientious objector
religious persecution, See persecution
The Religious Poetry of Alexander Mack, Jr. (Heckman), 593
religious services, See entries at worship
religious tolerance, 19, 28–29, 72, 82
    at Berleburg, 120
    Krefeld, 421
    Prussia, 1063
    Radical German Pietism, 1079
    religious liberty, 1098
religious wars and religious liberty, 1098
Relly, James, 1292
relocation
    frequency of free ministers *vs.* salaried, 1137
relocation centers and hostels for Japanese
    Bethany Seminary at Chicago, IL, *24,* 24–25
    Brooklyn, NY, 25
    Manzanar in CA, 24
relocation centers, World War II, 2079
remarriage, 6, **1099**
    Brethren Church, 389, 2145
    Church of the Brethren, 389, 2145
    discipline, doctrine of, 388–389
    divorce issues, 393
    Dunkard Brethren Church, 2173, 2174
    family, 474
    Fellowship of Grace Brethren Churches, 389, 2145
    marriage, after divorce, 795
    marriage concerns, 795
    Old German Baptist Brethren, 2145
    Rosenberger, Isaac J., writing about, 1123
Rembe, Heinrich, 2043

Rembert, Karl, 2043
Remburger, M. M.
    Milk River Valley Church of the Brethren, MT, elder, 832
Reminiscences of Juniata College (Emmert), 444
remnants in Europe of Brethren, **1099**
Remonstrance (1610), 55
Remonstrant (Arminian) party
    Collegiants, 324
Rempel, Henry G., 496, 1289, 1383, 1747
Rempel, Pastor
    Mennonite Brethren Churches, General Conference of, 814
Remple, Henry, 1289
Remple (Rempel), John, 1747
Remsey, Dwight K., 2290
Renau, David W., 2096
Renau, Delores, 2096
Rench, Abraham, 1099
Rench family, 384
Rench, George W., 166, 417, 500, 558, **1099,** 1747
    The Brethren Pastor's Handbook, 788
    Johnstown, PA, First Brethren Church, 673
    Milford, IN, Brethren Church, pastor, 831
    North Manchester, IN, (First) Brethren Church, pastor, 949
    Oakville, IN, Brethren Church, pastor, 959
Rench, Joseph, Sr., 1747
Rench, Mrs. George
    South Bend, IN, First Brethren Church, 1203
Rench, William, 1224
Rendt, Gloria Jean Woods, 2043
    renewal, 2007
    religious and moral, and Pietism, 1021
    Young, David S. on, 2365
Renewed Moravian Church, See Moravian Church
Renfree family, 739
Renfro, J. W., 1747
Renick, James Russell, 1747, 1852
Renick, Joyce Wilma Baker, 1852
Renicker Cemetery
    sources on, 2313
Renicker family
    Genesee Old German Baptist Brethren Church, MI, 540
Renicker, Ida (later Wagoner), See Wagoner, Ida Renicker
Renicker, Rodney Duane, 2290
Renicker, Samuel
    Ogan's Creek, IN, Church of the Brethren, 960–961
Renicker, Virgil
    Sierra Pines Old German Baptist Brethren Church, CA, 1181
Renken, Charles George, 2290
Renkewitz, Heinz Gottfried, 379, **1099,** 2043, 2143, 2202
    historical writing, 611
    Moravian Church, 876
    noncreedalism, 942
    Pietism subdivisions, 1021
    on von Hochenau, Hochmann, 2351–2352
Renn, Henry, 1747
Renner, Eli (Levi), 1747
Renner, F. C.

patent medicine remedy business, 995
Renner family, 1341
Renner, Francis, 1747
Renner, Isaac, 1747
Rennick, Percival G., 2044
Renno, John R.
    on Eckerlin, Israel, 2351
Reno Co., KS
    Pleasant View Church of the Brethren, KS, 1036
    Salem Community Church of the Brethren, KS, 1138
Reno, J. Paul, 579, 1747
    Sinking Spring, OH, Grace Brethren Church, pastor, 1186
Rensberger, Martha Hess, 601
Rensberger, Melvin N., 470, 1747
    Pleasant Valley Church of the Brethren, Alberta, Canada, providing pastoral care, 1034
Rensberger, Samuel, 601
Rentmeister, Jean R.
    on Moyers, Susanna, 2352
    on Wine, Christian, 2352
    on Wine, Susanna Moyers, 2352
Renz, James Eugene, 1747
reorganization plans
    Commission of Fifteen, 165
repentance
    Brethren Church and, 184
    Brethren Doctrine of Salvation, 1140
    conversion, 339
    doctrine of, **1099–1100**
    Finney, Charles G.'s "New Measures" revivalism, 930–931
    grace, doctrine of, 562
    Lent, 737
    life of, 5
    Old German Baptist Brethren, 967
    preaching about, 1053
    redemption, 1090
"Repentance" (Bowman), 166
Repert, J. J., 1747
Replogal family, See Replogle family
Replogal, Rynard, 1100
Replogle
    Raymond, Edith Madeline Replogle on, 2351
    Replogle, Paul Hudson on, 2351
Replogle, Abraham, 468, 1747
Replogle, Abram Brown, 1747
Replogle, Alfred, 1747
    New Carlisle, OH, Church of the Brethren, elder in, 926
Replogle, Andrew Jay, 1747
Replogle, Balzer, 1100
Replogle, Barbara, 1100
Replogle, Barbara (later Hanawalt), 581
Replogle, Catherine Brown, 216
Replogle, Chauncey L., 1747
Replogle, D. Alfred, 926, 1323–1324, 1747, 2044
Replogle, David H., 1747
Replogle, Edith Madeline
    on Replogle, Replogle genealogy, 2351, 2352
Replogle, Emma A. Miller, 2044
Replogle family, 216, **1100,** 1224
    Fruitdale, AL, Church of the Brethren, 520
    Greene, IA, Church of the Brethren, 570
    Hanawalt family, 582

Jasper, MO, Church of the Brethren, 669
Musselman family, related to, 901
Shively family, related to, 1178
Snowberger family, related to, 1153
Replogle, Frank G., 1747
Replogle, Fred A., 1747
Replogle, George, 1747, 2305
South Fulton Dunkard Brethren Congregation, IL, presiding elder, 1205
Replogle, George Brown, 1747
Replogle, Harvey Snowberger, 674, 1747
Oaks, PA, Green Tree Church of the Brethren, pastor, 958
Scalp Level, PA, Church of the Brethren, pastor, 1151
Replogle, J. C., 1747
Replogle, Jacob Frederick, 713, 1747, 2044
memoirs, 2352
Mount Joy, PA, Florin Church of the Brethren, pastor, 882
Replogle, Jacob H., 1748
Replogle, James S., 195, 2149
Replogle, John, 1100
Replogle, John B., 1748
Replogle, John Philip, 1100
Replogle, John Rinehart, 1100
Replogle, Joseph E., 1748
Replogle, Joseph Z., 1748
Replogle, Justin, 2352
Replogle, Martin, 1748
Replogle meetinghouse, Woodbury, PA, Church of the Brethren, 1364
Replogle, Neva M., 2044
Replogle, Norman L., 174, 2290
Replogle, Oliver C., 1748
Replogle, Paul Hudson, 2044
on Replogle-Replogle genealogy, 2351
Replogle, Peter, 77, 297, 463, 766, **1100,** 1748
Replogle, Rinehart, Jr., 216
Replogle, Rinehart Zook, 566, 642, 673, 927, 1748, 2044
Replogle, Sara G., 1843, 1916
Replogle, Shawn Flory, 2290
Replogle, Walter R., 1748
Okeechobee, FL, Grace Brethren Church, pastor, 963
Rossville, IN, Church of the Brethren, minister, 1124
The Reporter for Conscience' Sake, 917
Repp, Samuel F., 106, 1748
Reppart, J. J., 438, 1748
Reppert family, 280
repression
Sedition Act, 1165
reproductive issues, 2127
Reprogle family, *See* Replogle family
Republic of Chad
mission schools, 854
missions, 862
Republican Party
Church of the Brethren, 301
"Request to President Wilson," 2028
rescue missions, *See* urban ministry
Brethren movement, 2069
Reser, William Marven, 2044
resettlement, displaced person, 200
Resh, Timothy E., 2290
residential church communities
Reba Place Fellowship, 1084
residential communities, 181

resolutions
Old Order Movement and noncreedalism, 942
Resolutions Passed at the Special Conference, 206, **1100**
Flory, Abraham, 497
Metzger, Jacob, signer, 819
Metzger, Stephen, signer, 819
Murray, Samuel M., 897–898
Musselman, Samuel, 901
Old German Baptist Brethren, 967, 969, 2234
Old Order Movement, 973
Siler, George V., signer of, 1181
responsibility
Brethren doctrine of salvation and, 1140
sin, 1183–1184
Transformationist strategy, 2000
Resser, Charles E., 1748
Resser, George M., 1748
Ressler, Harvey William, 683, 1748
Ressler, Marlin C., 1748
Ressler, Martin E., 2044
Ressler, Willard David, 2290
restitutionism and restitutionist community, **1100,** *See also* primitivism
Anabaptism, 293
Brethren movement, 292
debates, 370
Disciples of Christ, 385
noncreedalism, 942
"Order of the Brethren," 976
ordination, 980
Plymouth Brethren, 1038
Restoration congregation, Danville, OH, 1340
Restoration movement, 43, 171, 177, 185, 247, 689, **1100–1101,** 1291–1292, *See also* Disciples of Christ; universal restoration
Brethren movement, 247
Campbell, Alexander, 247
The Christian Baptist and, 281
Davy, Henry Dorsey, 365
Disciples of Christ, 385
Dutch Bethel, German Baptist Brethren Church, 2373
Fleming Co., KY, German Baptist Brethren Church, 494
Hon, Peter Keithly, 627, 935
Honites, 628
Hostetler Brethren, 631
Hostetler, Joseph, 631
Indiana, 652
noncreedalism, 942
origins of, 1928
Ridge Church of the Brethren, OH, 1108
Shelby Co. German Baptist Brethren Church, KY, members leaving to join, 1175
Stone, Barton Warren, 1224
restoration of membership/fellowship, 698
Church of God (New Dunkers), 297
confession and repentance, 402
confession, public, 333
disciplined members, **1101–1102**
Flory, John, 498
handclasp, 582
Restoration, Universal
Ramirez, Frank on, 2351
Restorationism, *See* Universalism

restructuring, discussions of
Miller, Donald Eugene, 2223
restructuring, organizational (CB), **2241–2242**
resurrection, 695, **1102**
Brethren Church and, 184
Brethren doctrine of salvation, 1140
burial customs and, 230
conversion, 339
doctrine, 2020, 2079
Easter, 416
eschatology, 453
ethics, 457
Fellowship of Grace Brethren Churches (FGBC), 486
funerals, 523
memorial services, 814
preaching about, 1053
The Resurrection (Mohler), 868
retail merchants
Johann Sala, 1136
Retherford, Audrey L., 2044
Retigers, Frank
Roanoke, IN, Brethren Church, pastor, 1112
retirement benefits, 155, *See also* pensions
Retirement Board (BC), **1102**
retirement homes and communities, 7, 8, 18, 25, 116–117, 276, 810, **1102,** *See also* Brethren Homes for the Aged
Agape Acres, Inc., 790
Aged, Infirm and Orphans' Home, Darlow, KS, 266
Wise, John, 1354
Brethren Hillcrest Homes, 714
Brethren Manor, Long Beach, CA First Church of the Brethren, 754
Brethren Old Folks' Home, Timberville, VA, 1265
Bridgewater Home
West, Murray Guy, 1332
The Cedars, 265–266
chaplaincy, 2157–2158
Church of the Brethren, 305
Casa de Modesto Retirement Center, CA, 258
Church of the Brethren Home, 305
Crist, Daniel Albert, 352
Cross Keys retirement home, PA, 1388
Fahrney-Keedy Memorial Home, 467, 1299, 1361
Fostoria, OH, *See* Good Shepherd Home
Friendship Manor, 518
Garden Terrace retirement home, Wenatchee, WA, 530, 1330
Good Shepherd Home (CB), 557, *557*
Grace Brethren, Dayton, OH, 963
Grace Village Retirement Complex, 563, 564
Greenville, OH, *See* Brethren's Home, Inc.
Indiana, 182, 204
John M. Reed Home, 672
Kansas, 266, 682
Lebanon Valley Brethren Home, 733
list of institutions in USA, 1827
Long Beach Manor, 754, 755
Marshalltown, IA, 966, 1216
medical care, 810
Mexico, IN, 965–966
Mexico, IN, Church of the Brethren, 821

Mexico Welfare Home, Mexico, IN, 1264–1265, 1295
Missouri, 266
Morrisons Cove Home, 877, 1347, 1397
Mount Hope Church Home (DB), 881
Mount Hope, PA, and Ray Shank, 1172
Mount Morris, IL, *See* Pinecrest Manor
Neffsville, PA, Brethren Home
    Taylor, Isaac W. and Catherine Shirk, 1249
Ohio, 180, 182, 204
Ohio Church of the Brethren, 963
opposition to television viewing, 1251
Orphans' and Old Folks' Home, Sulphur Springs, IN, 1295
The Palms, FL, 758, 991
Pennsylvania, 187, 202, 231, 270
Pennsylvania Church of the Brethren, 1005
Pennsylvania Dunkard Brethren, 1005
Peter Becker Community, 1010
Pinecrest Manor, Mount Morris, IL, 1219
Pleasant Hill Village, 1033
polity, 1043
Rhodes, William, 377, 1107
Scalp Level, PA, *See* Church of the Brethren Home, Windber, PA
Seattle, WA, Olympic View Community Church of the Brethren, 1162
social welfare, 1198
sources on, 2314
Spurgeon Manor, Dallas Center, IA, 360, 1216
television viewing prohibited, 1251
Timbercrest (IN), 1264–1265
Timberville, VA, 966, 983
trend toward, 2145
Virginia, 208
W. Pennsylvania district, 305
West View Manor, Wooster, OH, 1336, 1365
widows, care for, 1344
retreats
    Indiana Brethren Retreat at Shipshewana Lake, 1354
    Mission Twelve (CB), 855
    Shepherd's Spring Outdoor Ministries Center (CB), 2248
Rettinger, John C., 1748
Rettinger, John R., 1748
return of Jesus Christ, *See* Second Coming
Reuel B. Pritchett Museum, *See* Pritchett, Reuel B.
    museums, 898
reunions, family
    Hershey family, 1964
Reuß count of Vogtland, 684
Reuss, Henry
    Peace Corps, 1002
Reusser, Mary (later Wittmer), 1948
Reutsch, Joseph, 1748
revelation
    Boehme, Jakob, 156
    direct special revelation and doctrine of Holy Spirit, 624
Revelation, 2023
    1:5–6, 84
    7:13–14, 84
    21:2, 26
    21:3, 85

21:4, 85
    book of, 1968, 1975
    Martin, Harold S. on, 2345
"Revelation: Hope for the World in Troubled Times" (Lowery), 2344
Revised Minutes, *See* Classified Minutes
Revised Standard Version (RSV) of the Bible, 138
    Fundamental Brethren Church, 522
revival meetings, *8, 1103,* **1103–1104,** *1104, See also* evangelism
    Ashland convention support for, 67
    Brethren music, 899
    Dunkard Brethren Church, 2175
    Henry, J. M., at Selma, VA, Church of the Brethren, 1166
    Mount Zion Church of the Brethren, KS, 888
    Myers, Paul R., 904
    Ness, Jacob C., 2231
    Ozark Church of the Brethren, MI, 986
    Price, Isaac, preacher, 1056
    Progressive Brethren movement, 972
    prophecy conferences, 1062
    protracted meetings, 1063
    publishing, 1069
    Ridge Dunkard Brethren Congregation, WV, held at, 1109
    Rileyville, VA, Church of the Brethren, 1109
    Robbins, Joseph P., elder, 1114
    Rockingham Church of the Brethren, MO, 1118
    Sand Ridge Church of the Brethren, OH, 1143
    Shrewsbury, PA, Dunkard Brethren Congregation, 1180
    Shroyer, Reuben, 1180
    similarity of Bible conferences to, 136
revivalism, **1104–1105**
    Ashland Convention, 368
    Brethren Revival Fellowship, 1262
    camp meetings, 245
    Church of the Brethren, 299
    Carl, George Clinton, 255
    confession of faith, 333
    Dayton, VA, Dunkard Brethren Congregation, 368
    debates, 371
    DeBolt, George, 255
    Dunkard Brethren, 1210
    early opposition to, 1210
    Eby, Kermit, 420
    effects of on church architecture, 51
    Ephrata Community, 451
    Evangelical Association, 459
    evangelism, 460
    Fairview Brethren Church, PA, 468
    Flory, George W., 498
    Fostoria, OH, West Independence Brethren Church, 505
    Frey, Andreas, 517
    frontier, 16, 519
    Frostburg, MD, First Church of the Brethren, 519
    Gatewood Brethren Church, WV, 532
    German Baptist Brethren, 1210
    Goshen, IN, Dunkard Brethren Congregation, 558
    gospel music, 559, 560
    grace, doctrine of, 562
    Gravel Hill Church of the Brethren, KS, 567

Hickory Grove Church of the Brethren, IN, 602
Holy Spirit, doctrine of, 624
Hostetler Brethren, 631
Hummer, Catherine, 636
Huntington, IN, City Church of the Brethren, 637
Hutchison, Andrew, 639
hymnals, 641
hymns, 642
influence of Pietists and Anabaptists, 1260–1261
Jarboe, John Edwin, 669, *669*
Johnson, H. Edward, 672
Juniata Church of the Brethren, NE, 678
Kalcklöser, Johann Heinrich, 681
"New Lights" in, 930
"New Measures," 930–931
Pennsylvania German churches in nineteenth century, 2009
Pietism, 1022
Progressive Brethren, 1210
services, 166
techniques, 177, 178
United Brethren in Christ, 1290
revivals
    changes in attitudes about, 1376
    church membership, 813
    discouraged by annual meeting, 1376
    Drayton Plains, MI, 399
    Great Kentucky Revival, 1224
    informed observation of, 1916
    Lanark, IL, Brethren Church, 720
    Mechanicsburg, PA, Dunkard Brethren Congregation, 806
    Mennonite Brethren Churches, General Conference of, 814
    Mennonites, 816
    migration of Brethren, impetus for, 827
    millennialism, 834
    seen as encouraged by Sunday schools, 1239
    tents used for, 1254
    Umstad, John, converted, 1286
    visions in, 1309
    Walnut Grove Dunkard Brethren Congregation, MD, 1315–1316
    West Fulton Dunkard Brethren Congregation, OH, 1334
    White Church of the Brethren, IN, 1339
    Wolfe, George, II, 1358
revocation of ministerial status
    Kulp, Henry F., 709
Revolutionary War, *See* American Revolution
Rex, Barbara, 760
Rexrode, Carl N., 1748
Reyer, Johannes, 61
Reyer (Reier, Reiher, Royer), John Michael, 2051
Reyes, David
    Los Toros, DR, Nuevo Renacer, 2216
Reyes, Olga
    Los Angeles, CA, Hermanos Unidos en Cristo, 2215
Reyher, Mildred, 1345
Reynolds, Barbara
    World Friendship Center, 1369
Reynolds, Charles, 1748
Reynolds, Charles B., 1748
Reynolds, Clarence L.

on Rothenberger, George Philip and
descendants, 2352
Reynolds, John, 258, 1748
Reynolds, Margaret C.
on Plain Women in River Brethren,
2352
Reynolds, Philip B., 2290
Reynolds, W. W., 1748
Rheems meetinghouse, West Green Tree
Church of the Brethren, PA, 1334
Rheinderken
refuge for nonconformists, 990
Rheinland/Pfalz, 1596
Rhem, Frank, 1748
Rhen, James H., 2290
Reamstown, PA, East Cocalico Church
of the Brethren and, 2239
Rhenish Palatinate, *See* Palatinate
Rhine, Pearl Eugene, 1312, 1748
Rhine River, 19, 174, 609, **1106–1107**
Rhinehart family, 211, 1359, *See* Reinhardt
family
Rhinehart, Henry, 264
Rhinehart, John, 264
Rhoades, David B., 1748
Rhoades, Doris, 2039
Rhoades, J. Benton, 422, 1290, 2242
Rhoades, Elizabeth, 258
Rhoades family
Shull family, related to, 1156
Rhoades, Gerald Lee, 1748
Rhoades, H. Q., 674
Rhoades, Henry, 1124
Rhoades, James Benton, 25, 669, 1748,
1843, 2044, **2242**, *2242*
Rhoades, John Rutter, 1748
Rhoades, Marianne (later Pittman), 2138,
2289
Rhoades, Nelda Irene, 1748
Rhoades, Orpha Benton, 2242
Rhoades, Paul J., 2242
Rhoades, Ruby June Frantz, 422, 508,
1843, 2044, 2108, **2242**, *2243*
church governance and, 2264
Washington Office (CB) and, 2260
Rhoads family, 1299, 1912, 2044
Hunsiker (Hunsaker) family, 637
Muhlenberg Co., KY, German Baptist
Brethren, 893
Rhoads, Henry, *See* Roth, Heinrich, Sr.
Rhoads, Henry L., 2044
Rhoads, Henry, Sr., *See* Roth, Heinrich
(Rhoads, Henry, Sr.)
Rhoads, Jacob, 740
Rhoads, John N., 747, 2044
Rhoads, Nettie Forry, *See* Rhoads family
Rhoads, Willard R., 2044
Rhoads, William H., *See* Rhoads family
Rhode, Anna (later Strickler), 1228
Rhode, Elizabeth (later Young), 1390
Rhode Island, **1107**
*Materials Towards a History of the
Baptists,* 803
Rhodehamel, Catharine (later Murray),
2026
Rhodes, David B., 1313, 1748
Rhodes, Donna McKee, 2165, 2290, 2352
Rhodes family, 262, 700, 1313, 1330, 1876
Salem Church of the Brethren, ND,
1137
Rhodes, Floyd F., 1927
Rhodes, Grace Edith Snyder, 2044
Rhodes, Haddon Quinter, 1748

Maitland Church of the Brethren, PA,
salaried minister, 783
Roaring Spring, PA, First Church of
the Brethren, pastor, 1114
Rhodes, Henry
family history, 2011
Rhodes, John T.
Oak Hill Old German Baptist Brethren
Church, WV, 957
Rhodes, Mark, 629
Rhodes, Mary S.
Oak Hill Old German Baptist Brethren
Church, WV, 957
Rhodes, P. S., 1958
Rhodes, Rebecca O., 2290
Rhodes Scholarships
Mow, Baxter Merrill, 891
Rhodes schoolhouse, WV, 1254
Rhodes, Sidney, 1748
Rhodes, Thomas, 1748
Rhodes, William, 377, 1209, **1107,** 1748
minorities, ethnic and racial, 850
Rhön Bruderhof
Hutterian Society of Brothers, 639
Rhondda Valley, South Wales
work camp, 1367
Rhone mission point
Grand Junction, CO, Koinonia
Brethren-Baptist Church, 565
Rhone preaching point
Fruita, CO, Church of the Brethren,
520
Rhudy, C. Curtis, 1748
Rhule, Walter, 1748
Rhyne, Margaret Whitehead, 2044
Rialto, CA, Grace Community Church
(FGBC), **1107**
Ribble, John, 740
Ribblett, David C., 1748
Ribblett family, 752
Ribelin family, 1341
Riblin, Katharine (later Kern), 689
Ricard, Ronald J., 2305
Riccius, Daniel E., 2290
Rice, Arthur B., 1264, 1748
Mountaindale Dunkard Brethren
Congregation, MD, presiding
elder, 890
Rice Co., KS, 683
Rice Co., MN, 719
Minnesota Brethren settlement, 848
Rice, David L., 2290
Rice, Edman
Pleasant Hill Church of the Brethren,
WV, pastor, 1033
Rice, Edman Eugene, 1748
Rice family
Jasper, MO, Church of the Brethren,
669
Reading Grace Brethren Church, PA,
1084
Rice, Frank, 496
Rice, Fred, 2044
Rice, H. Lawrence, 518, 1748, 2044
Roanoke, VA, Ninth Street Church of
the Brethren, pastor, 1113
Roanoke, VA, Oak Grove Church of
the Brethren, minister, 1113
Rice, Hazel, 496
Rice, Joshua, 1748
Mountaindale Dunkard Brethren Con-
gregation, MD, 2376
Rice Lake, WI, Church of the Brethren,

90, **1107**
Menomonie, WI, Church of the
Brethren, 816
Rice, Mary, 2044
Rice, Nathan C., 669, 1748
Rice, Otis K., 2044
Rice, Robert E., Jr., 2290
Rice, Willis Hartman, 42, 1748
Rice, Willis M., 42
Rouzerville Church of the Brethren,
PA, minister, 1125
Rice, Willis Miller, 1748
Rich Hill, MO, Church of the Brethren,
See Happy Hill Church of the
Brethren, MO
Rich, Jesse, 1748
Rich, Norville J., Sr., 1748, 2305
San Diego, CA, Grace Brethren
Church, pastor, 1141
Rich Patch Brethren Church, VA, *See*
Jordan Mines, VA, Rich Patch
Brethren Church
Richard, Abraham, 1748, 1749
Richard and Elizabeth (ship), 170, 352
Richard and Mary
Stuber, Johann Wilhelm (William
Stover), 1219
Richard, Jacob
Maitland Church of the Brethren, PA,
minister, 783
Richard, Jacob H., 1748
Richard, Mrs. J. B., 1748
Richard, Sue C., 2290
Richard, W. Scott, 1748
Richard, Wesley D., 2291
Richard, Wolford, 1748
Richards, Alva, 1748
Richards, Anne, 2044
Richards, Clifford H., 2045
Richards, David R., 109, 1748
Richards, Don M., 1749
Richards family, 405
Richards, Frank
Oakvale Church of the Brethren, WV,
pastor, 958
Richards, Herbert F., 1749, 2045
North Manchester, IN, Church of the
Brethren, pastor, 949
Rossville, IN, Church of the Brethren,
minister, 1124
Richards, Henry M. M., 2045
Richards, James A., 1749
Richards, Joel E., 2291
Modesto, CA, La Loma Grace Brethren
Church, pastor, 867
Richards, John, *543*
Richards, Mary Cline, 714
Richards, Mrs. T. E., 1749
Richards, Robert E. (Bob, "Pole-vaulting
Parson"), *70,* 70, 714, 1749, 2045
Richards, T. E., 1749
Richardson, Bert Guy, 555, 696, 740, 749,
1749, **2385**
Falls City congregation (formerly
Silver Creek German Baptist
Brethren), 921
Richardson Co., NE
Falls City Church of the Brethren, NE,
472
Richardson family, 342
Mount Carmel Church of the Brethren,
NC, 880
Richardson, George, 1223, 1270, 1749

Richardson, J., 1749
Richardson, J. F., 1749
Richardson, James Allen, 1749
Richardson, James C., 1749
Richardson, Kesler Elmer, 115, 320, 564,
     1749, 2305
     Radford, VA, Fairlawn Grace Brethren
          Church, pastor, 1079
     Riner Grace Brethren Church, VA,
          pastor, 1110
Richardson, Lonnie L., 2291
Richardson, Lyon N., 2045
Richardson, Mary Jane Stauffer, 2073
Richardson Park, DE, Church of the
     Brethren, See Wilmington, DE,
     Church of the Brethren
Richardson, R. F., 1749
     Mountain View Church of the
          Brethren, VA, 889
Richardson, R. J. R., 1749
Richardson, Rex. W., 2291
Richardson, S. P., 1749
Richardson, T. Simon, 1749
Richardson, W. H., 747, 2045
Richardson, William, 1749
Richcreek, F. O., 1749
Richer, Glea Brown, 2045
Richer, Maria
     Stuckey, Clara Mabel on descendants
          of, 2360
     Svejda, Ellen on, 2360
Richeson, Larry, 1351, 2291
Richey, Abraham, 1749
Richey, Henry, 1749
Richey, I. S., 1749
Richey, Paul W., 1749
Richey, Roy S., 345, 1749
Richey, William, 1749
Richfield meetinghouse
     Lost Creek Church of the Brethren, PA,
          760
Richland Center Church of the Brethren,
     KS, 1107
Richland Church of the Brethren, OH,
     1107–1108
     Mansfield, OH, First Church of the
          Brethren, 787
Richland, Co. congregation, WI (CB), 63
Richland Co., IL, 1315
Richland Co., OH
     Richland Church of the Brethren, OH,
          1107
Richland Co., OH.
     The Christian Guide, 286
Richland Co., WI, 1354
     migration of Brethren, 829
Richland congregation, WA
     Grandview, WA, Grace Brethren
          Church, 566
Richland house, Tulpehocken Church of the
     Brethren, PA, 1278
Richland, OH, Church of the Brethren,
     2043
Richland, PA, Church of the Brethren, 1107
     Allentown, PA, Church of the Brethren,
          2126
     Reistville, PA, Heidelberg Church of
          the Brethren, 1095
Richland Valley Church of the Brethren,
     WA (Ajlune, WA), 1108, 1139,
     1338, 2097
Richman, Irwin
     on Beissel, Johann Conrad/Konrad,

2352
Richmann, Felix, 1861
Richmond, Elizabeth Boardman, 155
Richmond, IN, Church of the Brethren,
     1108
     Four Mile Church of the Brethren, IN,
          505
Richmond (ship), 996
Richmond, VA
     Grace Brethren Church, 228, 1108,
          1308, 1335
     West Richmond Church of the
          Brethren, 1395, See also West
          Richmond Church of the Brethren,
          VA
Richter, Conrad M., 747, 2045
Richter, Gregor, 156
Richter, Helmut, 2352
Richty, Henry T., 1749
Richwine, Albert
     Ridgeway Community Church of the
          Brethren, PA, moderator, 1109
Rickard, Abraham
     Rockingham and Shenandoah Counties
          Old German Baptist Brethren
          Church, VA, minister, 1118
Rickel, Harrison, 716
Rickert, Edna (later Gehman), 1945
Riddle, Andrew Jackson, 1108
Riddle, Earl M., 761, 1108, 1749
     The Missionary Board (BC), 856
Riddle, George W., 1749
Riddle, Inez Camerer, 1108
Riddle, N. A., 1749
Racket, WV, Mount Olive Brethren Church,
     pastor, 1079
Riddle, Samuel, 1749
Riddlebarger, William W., 1749
Riddlesberger, Isaac, 1749
Riddlesberger, John, 1749
Riddlesburg, PA, Church of the Brethren,
     1108
     Raven Run Church of the Brethren,
          PA, 1084
Ridenhour, Henry Isely, 2045
Ridenour, A. M., 130, 211, 505
Ridenour, Adam, 2105
Ridenour, Annie Marie, 347
Ridenour family, 2045, 2105
Ridenour, J. A., 1265
     Milford, IN, Brethren Church, pastor,
          831
Ridenour, James, 496
Ridenour, James A., 1749
Ridenour, John, 531, 1749
Ridenour, Magdalena Munch, 2105
Ridenour, Peter Darcuss, 2045
Ridenour, Reta, 2045
Rider, Bessie M., 1838, 1964
Rider, Jacob, 279, 1749
     revival and New Hope Church of the
          Brethren, IN, 929
Rider Memorial Hall
     Elizabethtown College, 437
Rider, Sherman, 1749
     revival and New Hope Church of the
          Brethren, IN, 929
Ridge, Arthur, 448
Ridge Church of the Brethren, OH, 1108,
     1227
     Marble Furnace, OH, Church of the
          Brethren, 791
     May Hill Church of the Brethren, OH,

804
Ridge Church of the Brethren, PA, 42, 270,
     1220
     Cumberland Co., PA, 1108
Ridge Dunkard Brethren Congregation,
     WV, 211, 1109
Ridge schoolhouse
     La Place, IL, Church of the Brethren,
          713
Ridgely, Dow A., 1749
Ridgely, MD, Brethren Church, 1109
Ridgely, MD, Church of the Brethren, 376,
     1109, 1397, 1401
Ridgely, Robert J., 1749
Ridgeway Community Church of the
     Brethren, PA, 142, 1109
     Harrisburg, PA, First Church of the
          Brethren, 586
Ridgeway family, 233
Ridinger family, 1383
Ried, Johann Philib, See Reed family
Riedemann, Peter, 292, 293
Riedt, Johann Philib, See Reed family
Riegart, Richard, 1749
Riege, Yvonne Renee Priser, 2291
Riegle, Daniel, 1749
Riehl family, 721
Riehl, Naomi Irene (later Shaum), 2063
Rieley, George D., 152, 1749
Rieman, Emma Walker
     Rieman, Timothy Wayne (CB) and,
          2243
Rieman, George S.
     Rieman, Timothy Wayne (CB) and,
          2243
Rieman, Gwen Radebach
     Rieman, Timothy Wayne (CB) and,
          2243
Rieman, Kenneth Martin, 2291
Rieman, Louise Baldwin, 1749, 2291
     missions, short-term, 2226
     Sudan (CB) and, 2253
Rieman, Philip Wayne, 2243, 2291
     missions, short-term, 2226
     Sudan (CB) and, 2253
Rieman, Samuel, 1749
Rieman, Sylvia (later Houser), 2243
Rieman, Timothy Wayne (CB), 1324, 1388,
     1749, 2045, 2243, 2243, 2305,
     2385
     North Manchester, IN, Church of the
          Brethren, elder (moderator), 949
Riemer, Shirley J., 2309
Riest, S. B., 1749
Rieth, Johann Philib, See Reed family
Riewald, J. G., 2045
Rife, David, 1094
Rife, Ennis, 275
Rife, Esther Stanley, 1094
Rife family, See Reiff family
Rife, Frances, 1094
Rife, Jacob, 505, 1749
     Four Mile, IN, congregation, minister,
          and Reiff family, 1094
Rife, John, 1094
Rife, John D., 1749
Rife, John Merle, 2045
Rife, Joseph D., 1749
Rife, Lee Erasmus, 2045
Rife, Leota, 275
Rife, Mary, 355
Rife, Obed C., 1749–1750
Rife, Ruth, 275

Rife, Sara, 208
Rife, Sarah, 275
Riffe, Joel, 744
Riffe, John, Jr., 2175
Riffee, Levi, 1750
Riffey, Alva C., 264, 731, 1750
Riffey, Edward, 2291
Riffey family
    Pleasant Hill Old German Baptist
        Brethren Church, IL, 1033
    Redstone Valley Old German Baptist
        Brethren Church, WI and, 2239
Riffey, Frederick Lee, 1750
Riffey, Harold, 109, 431, 1750
Riffey, James
    Sand Creek Old German Baptist
        Brethren Church, KS, 1143
Riffey, John W., 1750
Riffey, Mark A., 2291
Riffey, Tima
    Sand Creek Old German Baptist
        Brethren Church, KS, 1143
Riffle, Conrad
    on GBB, 2352
Rifles for Washington (Singmaster), 747
Rigby family
    Fremont, OH, Grace Brethren Chapel,
        515
Rigdon, Sidney, 298
Riggle, Daniel, 1750
Riggle, H. M., 1984
Riggleman, John, 1750
Riggleman, Marion L., 1750
Riggleman, William Luther, 1276, 1750
Riggles Gap congregation, PA, 20, 21, 1347
Riggs, Ann K.
    on historic peace churches, 2330
right fellowship, 698
    Ruth, John L. on Mennonites and, 2354
right hand of fellowship
    installation of ministers, 656
    installation of pastors, 657
Righter, John, 1750
    Major, Sarah Righter, father of, 783
    Philadelphia, PA, First Church of the
        Brethren, minister, 1015
Righter, Sarah, 177, Righter, Sarah (later
        Major), 177, 506, 706, 739, 750,
        783, **783–784**, 1360, 1701, 2183,
        See also Major, Sarah Righter
    article about, 1922
    Major, Thomas, wife of, 784
Rights and Ordinances (Mack)*, See Rechte
        und Ordnungen*, 2004
    Mack, Alexander, Sr., 776
    mystery, involvement in, 1968
    publishing of, 1063
Rigorigato, Leonard R., 2045
Rijnsburg
    Collegiants, 324
Rikard, Larry, 55
Rike, Della (later Klepinger), 700
Rike, Emmett, 1276
Rilea, E. E., 1750
Riley, Aloysius C.
    Lexington, KY, Grace Bible Church,
        2215
Riley, Belinda, 1275
Riley, Bobby A., Sr., 2291
Riley, Christine, 739
Riley, E. C., 1750
Riley, Forrest, 1750
Riley, J. H., 1750, **2385**

Riley, James Whitcomb
    Winona Lake Auditorium, IN, 1353
Riley, Jobie E., 2045, 2385
    on Sisters of Saron, 2352
    works by, 2310
Riley, Levi, 1275
Riley, Ralph, 1750
Riley, Richard David, 2291
Rileyville, VA, Church of the Brethren,
    1109
    Mount Zion Church of the Brethren,
        VA, 888
Riling, Mildred, 2045
Rill, Jeffrey B., 2291
Rineer, A(mos) Hunter, Jr.
    on Lancaster County, churches and
        cemeteries of, 2352
Rinehart, A. H., 1750
Rinehart, Abraham, 1094, 1750
Rinehart, Charles Francis, 209, 673, 1209,
        1750
    Mountain Valley Church of the
        Brethren, TN, pastor, 889
    Pleasant Hill Church of the Brethren,
        TN, pastor/elder, 1032
Rinehart, David, 1750
Rinehart, David, elder, 1094
Rinehart, Donald R., 1750
Rinehart, Elizabeth (later Harshbarger), 490
Rinehart, Esther Louise, 1838
Rinehart family, *See* Reinhardt (Reinhard,
        Rinehart, Rhinehart) family
Rinehart, Floretta (later Oyler), 601
Rinehart, Henry, 204, 496, 1335, 1346,
        1363, 1750
    New River Old German Baptist
        Brethren Church, ministers for,
        931–932
Rinehart, J. B., 633
Rinehart, John (CB), 1750
Rinehart, John (OGBB), 431, 1094, 1750
Rinehart, Joseph Paul, 1209, 1750, **2385**
Rinehart, Josiah B., 1346, 1750
Rinehart, Kathryn M. (later Mitchell), 2045
    ordained ministry and, 2264
Rinehart, Marian Aetna (later Scholten),
    See Scholten, Marian Aetna
        Rinehart
Rinehart, Mary, 161
Rinehart, Mary Ann (later Stouffer), 1219
Rinehart, Mary Snader, *1109*, 1110
Rinehart, Mrs. R. L., 2019
    The Missionary Advocate, president
        and editor, 855
Rinehart, Sue Catheryn, 1839
Rinehart, William Henry, 61, *1109,*
        1109–1110, 2052
Riner Grace Brethren Church, VA, **1110**
Riner, J. A., 1750
Riner (Reiner), Jacob K., 1750
Riner, Samuel Wellington, 1750
Riner, W., 1750
Rines, Dorothy (later Dingfelder), 1918
Ringeisen, Garold Delose, 1750
Ringer, Harry, 1750
Ringgold, Carroll S., 1750
Ringgold, Cora, 228
Ringgold, Daniel S., 2181
Ringler family
    Johnstown, PA, Geistown Grace
        Brethren Church, 674
Ringler, H. D., 1750
Ringler, Lois Jane, 1852, 1853

Ringlet, Aline, 356
Ringlet, Charles, 356
Ringlet, Ronald, 356
Ringlet, William, 356
Ringoes, NJ, 722, 723
rings, *See* jewelry
Rininger, Glenn W., Jr., 2291
Rink, Mary Frances, 351
Rinker, Esther, 318, 1907
Rinker family
    Fairview Church of the Brethren, MD,
        468
    Reliance, VA, Mount Zion Brethren
        Church, 1096
Rinker, George S., 1750
    Mount Pleasant Brethren Church, VA,
        minister, 886
    Reliance, VA, Mount Zion Brethren
        Church, elder and pastor, 1095
Rinker, Joseph, 1750
Rinker, Nicholas (CB-1), 1750
Rinker, Nicholas (CB-2), 1750
Rinks, Lloyd D., 1750
Rio Cuarto, Argentina, 52, 53, 180, 1386
    mission schools, 854
Rio Cuarto, Brazil, 155
Rio Grande Co., CO
    Rock Creek Church of the Brethren,
        CO, 1116
Rio Linda, CA, *See* Sacramento, CA,
    Prince of Peace Church of the
        Brethren
Rio Linda, CA, congregation, 323
Rio Piedras, PR, Segunda Iglesia Cristo
        Misionera Fellowship (CB), **2243**
Río Prieto, PR, congregation
    Manatí, PR, Pueblo de Dios, 2217
Rio Prieto, PR, Iglesia de los Hermanos
        (CB), **2243–2244**
Rio Tercero, Argentina, 53
Rio Verde, Goias State, Brazil, Church of
        the Brethren, 2139
Ripley congregation, CA, 727
Ripon, CA
    Brethren Church, **1110**
    Grace Brethren Church, **1110**
        Modesto, CA, La Loma Grace
            Brethren Church, 867
        Old German Baptist Brethren, 967
Rippley, La Vern J., 2045
Risberg, Jans M., 1750
Risden, Raymond, 505, 1750
    Maitland Church of the Brethren, PA,
        salaried minister, 783
    Salem Church of the Brethren, IA,
        1137
Risk, Lawrence, 1750
Risler, Jeremias, 2045
Risler, Walther, 2045
Risser, Audrey Gates
    on Hoffer, Mattias and descendants,
        2352
Risser, C. Dean, 343, 739, 1750
    Marion, OH, Grace Brethren Church,
        2218
    North Lauderdale, FL, Grace Brethren
        Church, pastor, 948
Risser, Catharine (later Hollinger), 1658
Risser, John D., 2045
Risser, Joseph, 585, 1750
Risser, Mary H. (later Mohler)
    Mohler, John Saylor, wife of, 868
Risser, Mary Wenrick (later Royer), 1094

Rist, Henry Hartner, III, 1750
Rit, Johann Philip, *See* Reed family
Ritchey
    Snake Spring Valley Church of the
      Brethren, PA, free minister, 1192
Ritchey, Adam (great-grandson of patri-
    arch), 1110
Ritchey, Adam (patriarch), 1110
Ritchey, Arthur Wenner, 1750, 2305
    Martin Creek Church of the Brethren,
      IL, pastor, 797
    Romine Church of the Brethren, IL,
      providing leadership, 1121
Ritchey, Catherine Snyder, 1110
Ritchey, Debra, 2137
Ritchey, Dolar Carlos, 109, 633, 713, 1750
Ritchey, Donald Eugene, 1750
    Mexico, IN, Church of the Brethren,
      paid minister, 821
Ritchey, Donna (later Martin), 2286
Ritchey, Eliza, 1907
Ritchey, Elizabeth (later Morris)
    Morris, James Henry, mother of, 877
Ritchey family, 1281
    Snider, Jacob, descendants of, 1154
    Snowberger family, related to, 1153
Ritchey, Fanny (later Weaver), 1324
Ritchey, Francis, 1110
Ritchey, George S., 241, 1750
    Milroy, PA, Grace Brethren Church,
      843
    Sinking Spring, OH, Grace Brethren
      Church, pastor, 186
Ritchey, George H., 2305
Ritchey, Henry K.
    Snake Valley Old German Baptist
      Brethren Church, PA, deacon,
      1192, 1193
Ritchey, I. S., 1750
Ritchey, Isaac, Sr., 1110, 1750
Ritchey, James, 1907
Ritchey, John W., 1110, 1750, 2067, 2305
Ritchey, Lucretia M., 2291, 2305
Ritchey, Mary Whetstone, 1110
Ritchey, Melvin S., 1750–1751
Ritchey, Moore, Dorothy L., 2291
Ritchey, Paul Edward, 1751
Ritchey (Ritchie) family, **1110**
Ritchey, Ronald B., 1751
Ritchey, Rosannah Snowberger, 1110
Ritchey, Samuel, 1751
Ritchey, Sarah Snowberger, 1110
Ritchey, William, 1245
Ritchey, William S., *See* Royer, Galen B.
Ritchey, William Snyder, 1110, 1751
Ritchie, Amy S. Gall, 2291
Ritchie, C. W., 1751
Ritchie Co., WV, 1336
    Racket, WV, Mount Olive Brethren
      Church, 1079
    Rock Camp German Baptist Bethren
      Church, WV, 1116
Ritchie, David, 1751
Ritchie family, *See* Ritchey family
Ritchie, Kurt R., 2291
    Rio Prieto, PR, Iglesia de los
      Hermanos (CB) and, 2244
Ritchie, Lowell E., 468, 1751
Ritchie-Paul families, 1986
Ritchie, Ricky Lee, 2291
Ritchie, VA, schoolhouse, 211
Ritenour, Lillie M. (later Lyon), 769
rites, *See* ordinances

Rites and Ordinances, See Rechte und
    Ordnungen
Ritgers, J. M., 260
Ritschl, Albrecht B., 2046
    historical writing, 611
    Reformed Pietism, 1021
Ritt, Johann Philib, *See* Reed family
Rittenhouse, Anna, 1901
Rittenhouse, Benjamin, 1901
Rittenhouse, Catherine Cassel, 1111
Rittenhouse, D. Julian, 2291
Rittenhouse, David, 353, 602, **1110**, 1111,
    1751, 1901, 2046
    Hispanic Ministries (CB), 2199
    Rock Creek Church of the Brethren,
      IL, elder, 1116
Rittenhouse, David A., 129, 1751
    Norcatur, KS, Mount Zion Church, 945
Rittenhouse, David Beahm, 1751, 1843
    Yahuecas, PR, Iglesia de los Hermanos
      Cristo Nuestra Paz (CB) and, 2267
Rittenhouse, David M., 1751
Rittenhouse, Davis
    Silver Creek Church of the Brethren,
      OH, minister, 1182
Rittenhouse, Eli M., 1751
Rittenhouse, Emma (later Moyer)
    Moyer, Elgin Sylvester, mother of, 892
Rittenhouse, Esther, 1901
Rittenhouse family, **1110–1111**
Rittenhouse, Frank C., 2133
Rittenhouse, Joseph, 144, 145, 417, 1111,
    1751
Rittenhouse, Joseph Samuel, 1751
Rittenhouse, Laura Jean Stone, 1843
    Hispanic Ministries (CB), 2199
Rittenhouse, Mary Smith, 1110
Rittenhouse, Nathaniel, 1111
Rittenhouse, Nelson H., 1751
Rittenhouse, Ruth R., 2046
Rittenhouse, Samuel, 1111
Rittenhouse, Sarah Smith, 1110
Rittenhouse, William, 2051
Ritter, Daniel, **1111**
Ritter, David R.
    on Kendig brothers, 2352
Ritter family, 14, 1870
Ritter, Herman H., 347, 1751
    Newberg, OR, Church of the Brethren,
      pastor in, 933
Ritter, Warren W., 1751
Ritterman, Gabriel, 1751
Rittgers, J. B., 332, 673, 1751
    Sidney, IN, Grace Brethren Church,
      pastor, 1181
Rittgers, J. M., 1751
    South Bend, IN, Ardmore Brethren
      Church, pastor, 1203
Rittgers, John B.
    Philadelphia, PA, First Brethren
      Church, pastor, 1015
Rittinger, John R., 1751
Rittinghuysen, David, 1110
Rittinghuysen, Mathias, 1110–1111
Rittinghuysen, William
    Rittenhouse, David, 1110
Rittle, John David, 600, 1751, 2305
Rittman, OH
    First Brethren Church (FGBC), **1111**
    Grace Brethren Church, 251, 2132
rituals, *See* ordinances
Ritz, Mary (later Holsinger), 621
Ritzens family, 1281

Ritzens, Henry, 1751
Ritzens, Noah, 1751
Ritzius, Henry, 2385
Rive, Sarah, 209
Rivell, William Henry, 1751
River Brethren, *See* Brethren in Christ
River City Grace Community Church, CA,
    1134
River, Lou Anna (later Shively), **2144**
River View preaching point
    Highland Co. Mission Church of the
      Brethren, VA, 605
River View, VA, 1301
River Wupper, baptisms in, 1222
Rivera, Doris (later Gonzblez)
    Yahuecas, PR, Iglesia de los Hermanos
      Cristo Nuestra Paz (CB) and, 2267
Rivera, Ignacio, 261, 1751
Rivera, Jaime Luis, 2291
    Hispanic Ministries (CB), 2199
    Vega Baja, PR, Iglesia de los
      Hermanos Cristo El Señor (CB)
      and, 2258
Rivera, Jorge, 2172
    Hispanic Ministries (CB), 2199
Rivera, Jorge A., 2291
Rivero, José
    South America Theological Seminary
      (BC) and, 2252
Rivero, Malva de
    South America Theological Seminary
      (BC) and, 2252
Rivero, Marcela
    South America Theological Seminary
      (BC) and, 2252
Rivers, congregational names derived from,
    911
Riverside, CA
    Chinese Sunday Schools (CB), 278
    minorities, ethnic and racial, 850
    San Bernardino, CA, Church of the
      Brethren, 1141
Riverside, CA, Grace Community Church
    (FGBC), 115, 755, **1111, 2244**
Riverside Christian Training School, 44,
    187, 405, 760, **1111**
    Christian Day School movement, 282
    mission schools, 853
    The Missionary Board (BC), 855
    missions, 860
    Riverside Institute, 689
Riverside Church of the Brethren, MI,
    1111–1112
Riverside Church of the Brethren, NC, *See*
    Reddies River, NC, Riverside
    Church of the Brethren
Riverside Co., CA
    Hemet Church of the Brethren, CA,
      596
    San Bernardino, CA, Church of the
      Brethren, 1141
Riverside Evangelical United Brethren
    Church, 211
Riverside Grace Brethren Church, PA, *See*
    Johnstown, PA, Riverside Grace
    Brethren Church
Riverside Institute, Lost Creek, KY, 183,
    See also Riverside Christian
    Training School
    Christian Day School movement, 282
    Emmert, Mary Le(n)ora, 444
    Humberd, Russell I., 636
    Jobson, Charlotte Ellen Hillegas, 671

Landrum, Clyde Kermit, 724
relief and service efforts, 1096
Sheldon, Hattie Louise Cope, missionary, 1175
Rivinus, Marion W. M., 2046
Roach, Hannah Benner, 2046
Road Ridge, WV, 254
Roadcap, Martin
Newport Church of the Brethren, VA, leadership in, 934
Roann, IN, *473*, 1245, 1338
Brethren Church, 96, 97, 267, 354, 394, 1108, 927, 1108, **1112**, 1311
Kerner, William Hoff, Sr., 2211
Church of the Brethren, 103, 340, **1112**, 1937, 2019
New Enterprise Brethren Church, 927, *929*
Humbred, Russell I., 636
Mexico, IN, Church of the Brethren, 821
Roann, IN, New Enterprise Brethren Church, *See* New Enterprise Brethren Church, IN
Roanoke City Church of the Brethren, VA, *See* Roanoke, VA, First Church of the Brethren
Roanoke Classical Seminary
Manchester College, origins in, 785
Roanoke Co., VA, 162, **162**, 216, 320, 1307, 1345
Gospel Grace Brethren Church, VA, 559
Green Hill Church of the Brethren, VA, 569
Johnsville Church of the Brethren, VA, 675
Masons Cove Church of the Brethren, VA, 800
migration of Brethren, 829
Mount Union (Airpoint) Church of the Brethren, VA, 887
Peters Creek Church of the Brethren, VA, 1011
Peters Creek Old German Baptist Brethren Church, VA, 1012
Poages Mill Church of the Brethren, VA, 1039
Roanoke, VA, Summerdean Church of the Brethren, 1113
Roanoke, IN
Brethren Church, 394, **1112**
Roanoke, LA, 1897
Church of the Brethren, 760, **1112**
Rosepine, LA, Church of the Brethren, 1123
Roanoke, VA, 168, 1275, 1308, 1339
Boones Chapel Brethren Church, *See* Boones Mill Grace Brethren Church, VA
Central Church of the Brethren, **1112**, 1113
Flory, George W., 498
history, 1978
Clearbrook Grace Brethren Church, *See* Clearbrook Grace Brethren Church, VA
First Brethren Church, *See* Roanoke, VA, Ghent Grace Brethren Church
Friendship Manor, 518
First Church of the Brethren, **1113**

Central Church of the Brethren, 1112
Hollins Road Church of the Brethren, 1113
Peters Creek Church of the Brethren, VA, daughter congregation, 1011
Garden City Grace Brethren Church, **1113**, 1345
Ghent Grace Brethren Church, **1113**
Gospel Grace Brethren Church, *See* Gospel Grace Brethren Church, VA
Hollins Road Church of the Brethren, **1113**
Ninth Street Church of the Brethren, **1113**
Oak Grove Church of the Brethren, 957, **1113**, 1364, 2072
Peters Creek Church of the Brethren, VA, daughter congregation, 1011
Poages Mill Church of the Brethren, VA, 1039
Patterson Memorial Grace Brethren Church, 768, *See also* Hollins, VA, Patterson Memorial Grace Brethren Church
Summerdean Church of the Brethren, **1113–1114**
Washington Heights Grace Brethren Church, **1114**
Williamson Road Church of the Brethren, 1113, **1114**
Roaring Spring, PA
Albright Church of the Brethren, 513, **1114**
First Church of the Brethren, 896, **1114**
Native Americans of, 2229
Robacker, Earl F., 2046
Robbins, Amanda Elizabeth Myers, 1114
Robbins, Austin, 1751, 1852
Robbins, Betty Lou Eby, 2046
Robbins, Carolyn Joyce Kilmore, 1852
Robbins, D. Richard, 691
Robbins, Joseph P., **1114**, 1751
Midway Dunkard Brethren Congregation, IN, holding revival, 827
Robbins, Shirley Whitehead, 1852
Robbins, Thomas, 2046
Robbins, Walter L., 2046
Robbins, Wilford M., 1751
Robenett family
Plum Creek Old German Baptist Brethren Church, KS, 1038
Roberson, Holly
on OGBB, 2352
Roberson (Robertson), James Benjamin, 1751
Roberson, William, 1751
Robert family
Ocala, FL, Grace Brethren Church, 2232
Robert Huston Smith collection of archaeological artifacts, 46
Roberts, Agnes Seabrooks, 1114
Roberts, Clarence Vernon, 2046
Roberts, Conrad, 147
Roberts, D. W., 1751
Roberts, Deborah K., 2291
Roberts, Donald Eugene, 923, 1751
Roberts, Edward, 2065
Roberts, Elizabeth Goughnour (Gochnour),

147, 1114
Roberts, Elwood E., 1751
Roberts family, 739
Montclair, CA, Grace Brethren Church, 871
Roberts, Frank, 1751
Roberts, I. F., 1751
Roberts, J. H., 1751
Roberts, Jill, 2323
Roberts, John, 1751
Roberts, Joseph, 1114
Roberts, Levi, **1114**, 1294, 1751
Roberts, M. D., 1751
Pleasant Valley Church of the Brethren, OH, 1035
Roberts, Margaret A. (later Miller)
Miller, Edward Lewis, mother of, 837
Roberts, Mark William, 2175, 2291
Roberts, Mrs., 1247
Roberts, Nancy L.
on Brethren leaders in peace, 2352
Roberts, Oral
American revivalism, 1104
Roberts, Roy R., 348, 1751
Seal Beach, CA, Grace Brethren Church, pastor, 1161
Roberts, Sarah Ellen "Nellie," 255
Roberts, Warren E.
on Hensel, Ananias, cabinetmaking of, 2352
Robertson, A. D., 1751
Robertson, Archibald T., 2046
Winona Lake Auditorium, IN, 1353
Robertson, Bertha Idell Cecil, 511, 1114, 1843
Robertson, Billy
Mount Hermon Church of the Brethren, VA, minister, 881
Robertson, Clara H., 2046
Robertson, Dick, 277
Robertson family
Jenners, PA, Grace Brethren Church, 670
Robertson, George R., 1751
Robertson, J. Frank, 1751
Maple Grove Church of the Brethren, NC, co-moderator, 790
Robertson, Jesse David, 733, 1751
Robertson, Jesse P., 1114, 1751
Robertson, Kim G., 2291
Robertson, Lew, 246
Robertson, Mary Crouch, 1114
Robertson, McComb, 1751
Robertson, Price, 1751
Robertson, Russell L., 3, 511, **1114–1115**, 1843
medical missions, 807
Robertson, Vernice, 246
robes, 403, **1115**
choir, 279, 1377
pastors', 1377
Robeson, Jesse J. (I.), 273, 1751
Robey, William H., 1751
Pierce Co. Church of the Brethren, WI, 1021
Robins, Annie (later Hawbaker), 1128
Robins, IA, 406
Church of the Brethren, **1115**
Robinson, Addaline Gish, 1115, *1115*
Robinson, Bud
Seattle, WA, Lakewood Community Church, pastor, 1162
Robinson, Cheryl Ann, 1855

Orlando, FL, Grace Brethren Church, 982

Robinson, Cheryl (later Grieve)
Grieve, Jerry Allen, 2194
Robinson, Delmer T., 1751–1752
Robinson, Donald Lee, 1115, 1752, 2046
Robinson, Dorothy M., 2046
Robinson, Dorothy Muriel, 1852
Robinson, Elizabeth (later Swigart), 1245
Robinson, Elmo Arnold, 2046
Robinson, Elwyn Burns, 2046
Robinson family, 1111, 1341
Robinson, Felix G., 2046
Robinson, Gordon E., 1953
Robinson, H. E., 2046
Robinson, J. R., 1752
Robinson, James, 2079
Robinson, Jimmy R., 1752
Robinson, Jo Ann Ooiman, 2046
Robinson, John A., 377
Robinson, John Amos, 247, 356, **1115,** 1370–1371, 1752
Johnstown, PA, Arbutus Church of the Brethren, 673
Robinson, Paul Minnich, 1115
Robinson Junior High School, Wichita, KS, 1343
Robinson, M. J., 1752
Robinson, Mary Elizabeth Howe, 1115
Robinson, Mary N., 747, 2046
Robinson, Milton Mahlon, 683, 1752
Robinson, Mitchell
on conscientious objectors in World War II, 2352
Robinson, Nora Minnich, 1115
Robinson, PA, 1321
Church of the Brethren, **1116**
Robinson, Patricia Roop, 2291
Robinson, Paul Minnich, 126, 578, **1115–1116,** 1752, 2046
hymns, 643
Robinson, John Amos, 1115
Robinson, Ralph Avery, 1752, 1852
Orlando, FL, Grace Brethren Church, 982
Robinson, Rebecca (later Gibson), 548
Robinson, Robert, 2046
Robinson, Ronald, 738, 1752
Robinson, Roy, 1752
Robinson, Thomas A., 152, 173, 1115, *1115,* 1752
Muscatine, IA, First Church of the Brethren, pastor, 898
Peace Valley Church of the Brethren, MO, 1003
Plainview Dunkard Brethren Congregation, OH, presiding elder, 1029
Robinson, William, 1752
Robinson, Yvonne
on Ephrata Cloister, 2352
on Lititz Moravian Settlement, 2352
Robison, G. R., 1752
Robison, Joseph Stewart, 1752
Roby, Benjamin, 1752
Roby, James M., 2046
Roby, William, 1752
Rochester Community Church of the Brethren, KS, *See* Topeka, KS, Church of the Brethren
Rochester, IN, Brethren Church, *See* Tioss, IN, Brethren Church
Rock Camp German Baptist Bethren Church, WV, **1116**

Rock Creek Church of the Brethren, CO, *1116,* **1116**
Rock Creek Church of the Brethren, IL, **1116–1117,** 1221, 1395
materials used for White Rapids Church of the Brethren, WI, 1341
Rock Creek Church of the Brethren, KS, **1117**
Sabetha, KS, congregation, 1133
Rock Grove German Baptist Brethren Church, IA, **1117**
Rock House Church of the Brethren, KY, **1117,** 1280, 1355
Rock, James Oliver, 1752
Rock, Johann Friedrich, **1116,** 330
as a source for Beissel's ideas, 113
Rock Lake Church of the Brethren, ND, *See* Ellison Church of the Brethren, ND
Rock, Martin R., 2151
"Rock of Ages"
gospel songs, 560
Rock River Church of the Brethren, IL, *See* Franklin Grove, IL, Church of the Brethren
migration of Brethren, 829
Rock River congregation, IL, 736
Rock River Seminary
Mount Morris College, 883–884
Rock Run Church of the Brethren, IN, **1117,** 1338, 1929, **2378**
Goshen, IN, City Church of the Brethren, 557
Goshen, IN, West Goshen Church of the Brethren, 558
Heifer Project International, 594
Pleasant Valley Church of the Brethren, IN, 1034
Shipshewana, IN, Church of the Brethren organized from, 1177
Solomon's Creek Church of the Brethren, IN, 1202
Rock, Woodrow (Mr. and Mrs.), 579
Rockafellow, Michael J., 436, 496, 1319, 1752, 2138
Rockbridge, Co., VA, 228, 331
Rockbridge German Baptist Brethren Church, VA, **1117**
Rockefeller, John D.
Sand Brook Church of the Brethren, NJ, 1142
Rockford, IL, 1243
First Church of the Brethren, **1117,**1865
Mount Morris, IL, Church of the Brethren, 883
Funderburg, Drue Dresher, 523
urban mission, 1297
Rockhill Furnace, PA, Rockhill Church of the Brethren, 144, **1117–1118**
Rockingham Academy
Hüber (Hoover) family, 634
Rockingham and Shenandoah Counties Old German Baptist Brethren Church, VA, **1118**
Rockingham Church of the Brethren, MO, 124, **1118,** 1813–1814
Rockingham Co., VA, 149, 206, 208, 209, 211, 265, 334, 341, 351, 367, 380, 383, 493, 701, 740, 1243, 1253, 1291, 1292, 1330, 1345, 1391, 1397, 2077, 2091
Bowman, Benjamin, as minister in, 918
Briery Branch congregation, 1144

census, 2077
slavery issues, 2077
Daniel Schowalder, 1155
Fairview-Endless Caverns Church of the Brethren, VA, 470
Fairview-Mount Clinton Church of the Brethren, VA, 470
Funck (Funk) family, 521
Garbers Church of the Brethren, VA, 530
Greenmount Church of the Brethren, VA, 571
Harrisonburg, VA, First Church of the Brethren, 586
history of, 2090
marriages, 2077
Melbeth Grove Church of the Brethren, VA, 812
migration of Brethren, 829
Mill Creek Church of the Brethren, VA, 832
Montezuma Church of the Brethren, VA, 871
Mount Bethel Church of the Brethren, VA, 880
Mount Olivet Church of the Brethren, VA, 886
Mount Pleasant Church of the Brethren, VA, 887
Mount Zion-Linville Church of the Brethren, VA, 888
Mountain Grove Church of the Brethren, VA, 889
Pine Grove Church of the Brethren, VA, 1024
Rockingham and Shenandoah Counties Old German Baptist Brethren Church, VA, 1118
Shenandoah Valley, VA, 1176
Snell, John and Mary, 1193
sources on, 2318
Swope family, 2080
Thurmanites, 1264
Timberville Church of the Brethren, 1265
Valley Brethren-Mennonite Heritage Center and, 2257–2258
The Rockingham Male Chorus, **2204–2205**
Huffman, Nelson Thomas, 2205
The Rockingham [VA] *Register*
article by Thurmanites, 1264
Rockton, PA
Church of the Brethren, 129, **1118**
Greenville Church of the Brethren, PA, 572
preaching point of, 1118
Rockview Old Folks Home
Morrisons Cove Home, previous name of, 877
Rockwell City, KS, Brethren Church, *See* Norcatur, KS, Maple Grove Brethren Church
Rockwell, Edna, 540
Rockwell family
Genesee Old German Baptist Brethren Church, MI, 540
Rockwell, Sharon, 540
Rockwood Church of the Brethren, PA, **1118**
Middle Creek Church of the Brethren, PA, 825
Rocky Ford, CO, 1316
Church of the Brethren, **1118,** 1940

Pueblo, CO, Church of the
Brethren, 1070
minorities, ethnic and racial, 850
Rocky Mount, VA, 162, 163
Church of the Brethren, **1118–1119**
Rocky Ridge, MD, Monocacy Church of
the Brethren, 106, **1119**
Mountaindale Dunkard Brethren
Congregation, MD, 890
Rocky Springs (Full Gospel)
Frederick, MD, Church of the
Brethren, 511
Rodabaugh, Abraham, 1752
Rodabaugh, Arthur, 1752
Rodabaugh, D. Edwin, 1380, 1752
Rodabaugh, Edwin G., 1752
Pleasant Hill Church of the Brethren,
IA, 1032
Rodabaugh, Elisabeth J., 163
Rodabaugh family, 740, 1324
Oak Grove Church of the Brethren,
MO, 956
Pister, Grace Rodabaugh on, 2350
Pleasant Hill Church of the Brethren,
IA, 1032
Rodabaugh, Grace on, 2350
Rodabaugh, Grace
on Rodabaugh family, 2350
Rodabaugh, Stanley E., 1752, 2291
Rodabaugh, Willis P., 1752, 2046
Rodahaver, J. J., 1752
Rodamer, Lawrence, 1752
Roddis, Charles, 1752
Rodebaugh (Rodabaugh), Adam, 319
Rodecap family
Sanger family, related to, 1144
Rodecap, Martin, 1752
Rodecker, Thomas, 1752
Rodeffer, Carrie (later Power), 2039
Rodeffer, Charles, 1752
Rodeffer, Conrad, *See* Rodeffer family
Rodeffer family, 2039
Rodeffer, Nancy Showalter, *See* Rodeffer
family
Rodeffer, William H., 731, 1752
Mount Pleasant Church of the Breth-
ren, VA, part-time pastor, 887
Rodenbough, Theo Francis, 2046
Roderick family, 1920, *See* Rotruck family
Roderick, James, 1752
Roderick, Lewis, 1752
Rodes, Aldine Jackson, 1752
Rodes family, 1866
Rodes, Richard R., 325
Rodgers family
Martinsburg, WV, Rosemont Grace
Brethren Church, 798
Rodgers, John C., 128, 1752
Rodgers, Thomas, 1348
Rodgers, Zeta O., 1877
Rodkey family. 1876
Rodney Church of the Brethren, MI, **1119**
Rodrigeuz, Eduardo
South America Theological Seminary
(BC) and, 2251–2252
Rodrigeuz, Mariela
South America Theological Seminary
(BC) and, 2251–2252
Rodriguiz, Janice E., 2046
Roe, Weily, 1752
Roeber, A. G[regg]
on Brethren in colonial America, 2352
on Ephrata Cloister, 2352

on printing German and Dutch books,
2352
on Sauer family, 2352
on Sauer press, 2352
Roediger, Stephen R., 16
Roehl, Katherine Louise McClure, 2047
Roensch, L. H., 2047
Roesch, Dale, 1752
Roesch, John H., 1119
Roesch, Katie Finkenbinder, 1119
Roesch, LaRue, 1752
Roesch, Marion Arthur, 322, 1752
Roesch, Mary Ellen, 352
Roesch, Melvin C., 322, **1119**, 1752, 2305
South Fulton Dunkard Brethren
Congregation, IL, 1205
Roesch, Sarah E. Jarboe, 1119
Rogers, Albert N., 2047
Rogers, Albert Porter, 1752
Rogers Church of the Brethren, AR, *See*
Springdale, AR, Church of the
Brethren
Rogers, Clifford B., 105, 363, 2291
Rogers congregation, AR, 1215
Rogers, David L., 1752
North Manchester, IN, Church of the
Brethren, pastor, 949
Rogers, Donald, 482
Rogers, Elia Elizabeth, 1834
Rogers, Ellis, 629, 1320
Rogers family, 153
Rogers, G. Leslie, 1752
Rogers, George, 2047, 2106
Rogers, George W., 731, 1752
Rogers, Gerald H., 345, 1752
Salem Church of the Brethren, IA,
1137
Rogers, Gideon, 1752
Rogers, H. Kendall, 2291
Rogers, Harry K., 1752
Mount Etna, IA, Church of the
Brethren, pastor, 881
Rogers, Ingrid
and peace, dramas on, 2353
and peacemaking, songs on, 2353
Rogers, Irene, 482
Rogers, James White, 719, 1753
Rogers, John C., 1753
Rogers, L. Ellis, 1753
Rogers, Levi, 1753
Rogers, Meredith V., 1333, 1753
Panora, IA, Church of the Brethren, as
minister, 992
Rogers, Moses, 1753
Rogers, Samuel R., 1753
Rogers, Thomas, 1753
Rogers, VA
Elliot's Creek Church of the Brethren,
VA, 441
Rogers, Victor S., 16, 275, 670, 731, 1753
Pleasant Grove Grace Brethren Church,
IA, pastor, 1031
Rogers, W. F., 1753
Rogue River German Baptist Brethren
Church, OR, *See* Williams Church
of the Brethren, OR
Rogue River Valley, OR, 1346
Hoxie, George W., 633
Oregon settlement, 981
Rohart, Dale E., 1753
Rohart, Emerson J., 1348, 1753
Meadow Mills Church of the Brethren,

VA, 806
Rohart, Harry W., 1753
Rohart, Joseph F., 1753
Rohart, Paul, 1753
Rohebaugh, Lynn Edward, 1753
Roher (Rohrer) family, **1119**
Rohr, John von, 2047
Rohrbach family, 2047
Erbaugh family, 453
Rohrbach, Germany
Marienborn, village belonging to, 792
Rohrbaugh, Lewis Bunker, 2047
Rohrer, Abram (Abraham), 1753
Rohrer, Alice LaVern Rupel, 2047
Rohrer, Barbara (later Spitler), 1212
Rohrer, Bruce L., 1753
Rohrer, David Russell, 1119, 2047
Norton, OH, Grace Brethren Church,
pastor-in-training, 951
Rohrer, Dean Clifford, 1119, 1753
Peace Valley Church of the Brethren,
MO, 1003
Rohrer, F. C., 1119
Meadow Branch Church of the
Brethen, TN, 806
Midway Church of the Brethren, TN,
providing leadership, 827
Mount Carmel Church of the Brethren,
NC, minister, 880
New Bethel Church of the Brethren,
NC, elder in, 925
Peak Creek Church of the Brethren,
NC, 1003
Rohrer family, 721, 1980, 2079, 2094, *See
also* Roher (Rohrer) family
Farmers Grove Fellowship (BC), PA,
476
Rohrer, Ferdie Clifford, 105, 493, 1119,
1753, 2305
Okeechobee, FL, Grace Brethren
Church, pastor, 963
Rohrer, Glen Neal, 505, 740, 1119, 1753
Rohrer, H. W., 1753
Rohrer, Jacob, 1119
Rohrer, Johanne, 2094
Rohrer, John, 1119
Rohrer, Joseph, 1753
Rohrer, Levi, 2079
Rohrer, Norman B., 2201, 2377
on McClain, Alva J., 2353
Rohrer, Pearl Emma Neal, 1119, 1753
Rohrer, Perry Lawrence, 171, 190–191,
242, 248, **1119**, 1331, 1753, 1996,
2047
recreation, 1088
Rohrer, Richard A., 596, 755, 1753
Ripon, CA, Grace Brethren Church,
pastor, 1110
Rohrer (Rorer) family, 2007
Rohrer, Ruth Alspaugh, 1119
Rohrer, Samuel, 1119
Rohrer, Sarah (later Sayler), *See* Sayler,
Sarah Rohrer
Rohrer, Wilbur G., 2291
Rohrerstown, PA, Grace Brethren Church
Haller, Wesley, 2195
Rojas, Guillermo
South America Theological Seminary
(BC) and, 2252
Rojas, Manuel
Hispanic Ministries (BC), 2198
Pasadena, CA, Centro Cristiano para la
Familia (BC) and, 2237

Rokeby, NE, 743
Roland, David, 1753
Roland, Elizabeth Martin, 1127
Roland family, *See* Rowland family
Roland, Gasper, Sr., *See* Rowland (Roland), Gasper, Sr.
Roland, Hannes
    immigrant to America, 1127
Roland, Jacob, 1127
Roland, Jimm A., 2291
Rolette Co., ND, 1281
The Roll of Drums (Wallower), 747
Rolland, W. B., 1753
Roller, Anna Wampler, 470, 2047
Roller family, 1318
Roller, Goldie, 2135
Roller, J. S., 1291
Roller, John Michael, 1753, 2305
Roller, John Samuel, 1753
Roller, M. G., 1753
Roller, Mark S., 518, 1753
    Meadow Mills Church of the Brethren, VA, minister, 806
Roller, Michael J., 470, 1753
Roller, Naomi, 1833
Roller, Robert Samuel, 1753, 2135
Roller, Samuel, 470
Rollier, Antoine E., **1119–1120**, 1753, 1852
Rollier, Antoine E. and Mary Ganshorn, **1119–1120**
Rollier, Mary Ganshorn, **1119–1120,** 1852
Rollins, Bernard McClain, 519, 692, 1753
    Petersburg, WV, Memorial Church of the Brethren, 1012
Rollins, Eva V. Martin, 1753
Rolston, Ada Kimmel, 1120
Rolston, Frances Fitz Simon, 685, 726, 748, **1120,** 2047
Rolston, Frances Fitz Simon and William Wendell, **1120**
Rolston, Jesse Edward, 1120, 1753
    Sheldon Church of the Brethren, IA, free minister in, 1175
Rolston, Rodrick R., 1120, 1753
Rolston, William Wendell, 685, **1120**
Roman Catholic Church, 28, **1120**, *See also* Counter-Reformation
    on beards, 102
    canonical scripture, 43
    capital punishment, 292
    Catholic Relief Services and SERRV International (CB), 2247
    charismatic movement and, 272
    church parents, 308
    communion table, 328
    CROP, 286
    episcopal polity, 1042
    established churches, 456
    established churches and prisons, 1058
    Evangelical Church in Austria, 459
    evangelicalism and, 2178
    excluded from National Council of Churches of Christ (NCCC), 915
    Fellowship of Reconciliation (USA), 488
    France, 506
    Germany, 241, 545
    higher education, 603
    Hochmann von Hochenau, Ernst Christoph, 614
    Honduras, 627
    interdenominational relations, 1183
    Jackpot Church, NV, 2212

Know-Nothing party opposed to, 704
    married monastics, 291
    mass compared to love feast, 762–763
    Menno Simons on, 29
    missionaries to in Argentina, 1386
    Modernism, 866
    Moravian Church, 875
    National Interreligious Service Board for Conscientious Objectors (NISBCO) representation, 917
    North Dakota, 164
    "Order of the Brethren," 976
    ordinances, 979
    Orthodox Church, 983
    peace, 998
    Peace of Westphalia, 1338
    Pentecostalism, 1009
    Quebec, 1075
    Reformation, Protestant, 1091
    Reformation, Protestant, and Brethren doctrine, 1092
    and religious conflict in Palatinate, 990
    religious liberty, suppression of, 1098
    role in development of Brethren theology, 1259
    Thirty Years' War, 1262
    trinity, doctrine of, 1275
Romanengui, Billy
    South America Theological Seminary (BC) and, 2252
Romanenghi, Egydio, 53, 1753, 1852
Romanenghi, Robert, 53
Romanenghl, Eleanor Yoder, 1852
Romanofsky, Peter, 2047
Romans
    3:9–20, 55
    6:3–11, 85
    8:28–29, 55
    10:11–13, 55
    10:21, 55
    book of, 1975, 2007
    book of, outline and summary, 2002
    scriptural exposition of, 55
Rome, OH, Church of the Brethren, *See* Oak Grove Church of the Brethren, OH
Rome, OH Old German Baptist Brethren Church, **1121**
Romero, Gilbert, Jr., 2291
Romine Church of the Brethren, IL, **1121**
    Salem Church of the Brethren, IL, 1137
Romney, WV, Church of the Brethren, **2244**
Rondthaler, Edward, 2047
Ronk, Albert Teller, 93, 130, 180, 183, 326, 377, 461, **1121,** 1210, 1753, 2047
    historical writing, 612, 613
    inventions and scientific discoveries, 660
    mysticism, 907
    Our Church Guidebook, 788
    Sidney, IN, Grace Brethren Church, pastor, 1181
Ronk, Charles Walter, 552, 1753
Ronk, Columbus G., 1753
Ronk, D. E., 1281
Ronk, David William, 1121, 1753
Ronk, Dorman, 204
Ronk, G. T., 1281, 1285
Ronk, George Teller, 737, 738, **1121,** 1281, 1285, 1753
    missions, 860
Ronk, Goldie Fouts, 1121

Ronk, Helen Brandenburg, 1121
Ronk, Helen (later Manville), 1121
Ronk, Isaac, 1753
Ronk, Ivan, 1121
Ronk, Jesse D., 445, 1753–1754
Ronk Joan, 2137
Ronk, John, 1754
Ronk, Kenneth R. (CB), 1754
    New Enterprise Brethren Church, IN, elder in, 927
Ronk, Kenneth R. (FGBC), 121, 1754
Ronk, Mary Louise (later Bohr), 1121
Ronk, Robert, 1121
Ronk, Rua Olivette Wolfe, 1121
Ronk, Susan Elizabeth Teller, 1121
Ronk, Willis E., 67, 319, 195, **1121,** 1754
Ronneburg Castle, **1121–1122,** *1122*
    Community of the True Inspiration, 330
    Germany, 545
Ronsdorfer sect
    Eller family, 440
Rood family, 1320
Roof, Alfred Benjamin, 1754
    Middletown, IN, Church of the Brethren, elder, 826
Rooks Co., KS
    Sand Creek Church of the Brethren, KS, 1142
Roop, Anna (later Royer), 1130
Roop, Calvin Mark, 2291
Roop, Catherine Royer, 1130
Roop, Christian C., 752
Roop, Christian (father) (1733–1810), 1754
    descendants, 1930
    immigrant to America, 1130
Roop, Christian (son), 1130
Roop, David, **1122,** 1130, 1754
    Meadow Branch Church of the Brethren, MD, 805
    Seneca Church of the Brethren, OH, elder, 1166
Roop, Earl William, 1754, 2047
Roop, Elizabeth Kinzer, 1130
Roop, Esther Miller, 1130
Roop, Ethel Amelia, 1843
Roop, Eugene F., 1130, 1754, 2047, 2136
    on Book of Esther, 2353
    on Book of Jonah, 2353
    on Book of Ruth, 2353
    on Genesis, 2353
    on peace churches, historical, 2353
    on prayers, 2353
    on stewardship and the Biblical story, 2353
Roop, Ezra, family of, 1318
Roop family, 161, *See also* Rupp family genealogy, 1930
    South Keokuk Church of the Brethren, IA, 1205
Roop, George Edward, 1754
Roop, Isaac, 2048
Roop, Israel, 1754
    Seneca Church of the Brethren, OH, elder, 1166
Roop, Jacob, 2034
Roop, Jesse (CB-1), 752, 1754
    Monrovia, MD, Bush Creek Church of the Brethren, elder, 870
Roop, Jesse (CB-2), 1754
Roop, Joel, 1754
Roop, John David, Jr., 1130, 1754, 2047
Roop, Jonas E.

The Missionary Board (BC), 855
Roop, Joseph, 1130
Roop, Joseph, family
    Pipe Creek Church of the Brethren,
        MD, 1026
Roop, Joseph, Jr., See Roop, Wendell
Roop, Joseph N., See Roop, Wendell
Roop, Mary Nofsinger, 1130
Roop, Patricia Lee (later Robinson), 1843,
    2291
Roop (Rupp, etc.) family, 2048
Roop, Rupp family
    Roop, Wendell on descendants of, 2353
Roop, Susan Alice Grimes, 1122
Roop, Wendell, 2048
    on Roop, Rupp family and descen-
        dants, 2353
Roop, William Ezra, 1754
    Reistertown-Evergreen Church of the
        Brethren, MD, elder, 1095
Roop, William Keith, 1754
    Roaring Spring, PA, First Church of
        the Brethren, pastor, 1114
Roose, Eli, 1754
    Michigan City, IN, Church of the
        Brethren, 824
    Weldy, Allen (CB) and, 2261
Roose, Ellen Culp
    Weldy, Allen (CB) and, 2261
Roose, Hiram, 1754
Roose, Nina (later Weldy), 1805, 2261
Roose, Randall E., 1754
Roose, Reuben O., 1754
Roosen, Berend Carl, 2048
Roosevelt Co., MT, 142
    Montana Brethren settlement, 870
    Poplar Valley Church of the Brethren,
        MT, 1047
Roosevelt, Eleanor, 1122
Roosevelt, Franklin Delano, 169, 316, 599,
    1122
    historic peace church meeting on con-
        scientious objector status, 917
    World War II, 1371, 1372
Roosevelt, Theodore, 343, 912
    Copp, Zed H., 343
Root, A. C., 40, 278, 325, 377, 633, 1754
    Rhodes, William, 1107
Root, Andrew, 1122
Root, Andrew (CB), 1754
Root, Andrew (OGBB), 1754
Root, Barbara Lane, 1122
Root, Benjamin E., 1280, 1754, 2156
Root, C. C., 2385
Root, Dayton Evred, 758, 1754
Root, Eli David, 410, 1122, 1754
Root, Emma
    Root, Isaac William, 2378
Root, Emmert H., 1315, 1754
    Mexico Old German Baptist Brethren
        Church, IN, minister, 821
Root, Ernest L., 1754
Root, Ethel L. Booze
Root, Isaac William, 2378
Root, F. C., 1754
Root family, 280, 1122, 1221, 1280
    McFarland, CA, Church of the
        Brethren, 774
Root, Gerald H., 349, 366, 1754
    Okeechobee, FL, Grace Brethren
        Church, pastor, 963
    Peru, IN, Grace Brethren Church,
        pastor, 1010

Root, Herbert A., 738, 1312, 1754
Root, Hezekiah, 1754
Root, Isaac William, 2305, 2378
Root, Jacob B., 430, 638, 1754, 2048
    Mount Pleasant Old German Baptist
        Brethren, IN, minister, 887
Root, Jacob H., 1356
Root, John, 1122, 1754
Root, John A., 1122, 1754
Root, John H., 1754
Root, John S., 1754
Root, John William, 1754
Root, Joseph, 322
Root, Isaac William, 2378
Root, Joseph A., 1754, 2156, 2291
Root, Leonard Henry, 325, 730, 1754
    Mount Morris, IL, Church of the
        Brethren, pastor, 883
Root, Lester, 1754
Root, Louis, 1754
    Myrtle Point, OR, Church of the
        Brethren, pastor, 906
Root, Louisa Barbara Fess, 1122
Root, Mary, 313
Root, Noah W., 313, 1755
    South Haven Old German Baptist
        Brethren Church, MI, minister,
        1205
Root River, MN, 2071
    Church of the Brethren, 1122
        migration of Brethren, 830
        Minnesota Brethren settlement,
            848
Root, Susan Noffsinger, 214
Root, T. C., 633, 1755
Root, William, 1755
Root, Willis E., 1755
    Ropp, Maria (later Everhart), 1934
    Ropp, Martha Ellen (later Mishler),
        2019
Rorer (Rohrer) family, 2007
Rorie, Tinnie, 1755
Rosa, Philipp S., 2048
Rosales, Daniel, 2291
    Sarasota, FL, Iglesia de los Hermanos
        (BC) and, 2246
Rosales, Salvador
    Los Angeles, CA, Hermanos Unidos en
        Cristo, 2215
Rosanna of the Amish (Yoder, Joseph
    Warren), 1387
Rosario, Argentina, 53, 54
Rose Bud, PA, congregation, 274
Rose, Calvin J., 1755
    Middle Creek Church of the Brethren,
        PA, pastor, 825
    Rockwood Church of the Brethren, PA,
        pastor, 1118
Rose, Charles (BC)
    Rose, Smith Fuller (BC) and, 2244
Rose, Charles Lindbergh, 432, 912, 1755
Rose, Florence Vincent (BC)
    Rose, Smith Fuller (BC) and, 2244
Rose, Harold Enlow, 1755
Rose, Harold Wickliffe, 2048, 2291
Rose, Jacob, 1348
Rose, James K., 2291
Rose, Jefferson Davis, 1755
Rose, Lewis Day, 1755, 2048
    Schwarzenau contributing editor, 1158
Rose, Martha (BC), 2244
Rose, Mary Ferguson, 565, 2244
Rose Point, VA

Madison Church of the Brethren, VA,
    mission point, 781
Rose, Rosemary Block, 1255–1256, 2048
Rose, Smith F., 269, 1755, 2047, 2244
Rose, William A., 1755
    Mount Garfield, CO, Church of the
        Brethren, elder-in-charge, 881
Rosedale, PA, Brethren Church, 1122
    Johnstown, PA, Third Brethren Church
        (Morrellville), 675
Roseland, NE
    Silver Lake Church of the Brethren,
        NE, near, 1182
Rosemead Boulevard Brethren Church, East
    Pasadena, CA
    South Pasadena, CA, Grace Brethren
        Church, 1206
Rosemont, IL
    New Call to Peacemaking, 926
Rosemont, WV, Grace Brethren Church,
    See Martinsburg, WV, Rosemont
        Grace Brethren Church
Rosena, CA, 715
    Nicholson, John, colonization by, 935
Rosenbach, Johann Georg, 697
Rosenberg, Dorothy (later Kain), 2048
Rosenberg, Ephraim, 531
Rosenberg family, 2048
Rosenberg, Frank J., 2048
Rosenberg, Jacob H., 2048
Rosenberg, John, 531
Rosenberger, Abram Seidell, 150, 1123,
    1755
Rosenberger, Bruce Elmer, 1123, 1755
Rosenberger, Clarence Haines, 1123, 1755,
    2048, 2305
Rosenberger, Daniel R., 1123, 1235, 1755
Rosenberger, Edward H., 1123, 1235, 1755
Rosenberger, Elizabeth, 1123
    Rosenberger, Isaac J., mother of, 1123
Rosenberger, Elizabeth Delp, 150, 1123,
    2048, See also Blough, Elizabeth
        Delp Rosenberger
Rosenberger, Elizabeth Hartsough, 1123
Rosenberger, Ella, 1123
Rosenberger, Elmer, 1123
Rosenberger, Erasmus, 2048
Rosenberger family, 534, 1123, 1868, 2009,
    2048, 2049
Rosenberger, Francis Coleman, 2048
Rosenberger, Gordon Earle, 1123, 1755
Rosenberger, Henry, 1942
Rosenberger, Henry, Sr.
    immigrant to America, 1123
Rosenberger, Homer Tope, 1861, 2048
Rosenberger, Isaac J. (I. J.), 77, 299, 461,
    1123, 1123, 1211–1212, 1235,
    1755, 1945, 1946, 2048
    Oak Grove Church of the Brethren,
        OH, 956
    Ontario German Baptist Brethren, 975
    Sand Ridge Church of the Brethren,
        OH, revival meeting, 1143
    train travel, 1271
Rosenberger, Israel, 1123
Rosenberger, James Henry, 1999
Rosenberger, Jesse Leonard, 2048–2049
Rosenberger, Joseph Detweiler, 1990
Rosenberger, Joyce Marie, 1843
Rosenberger, Lester, 1123
Rosenberger, Margaret Ebersole, 1123
Rosenberger, Mary Sue Helstern, 2049,
    2291

on Bethany Hospital, 2353
on Brethren Health and Welfare
Association, 2353
on Brethren Homes, 2353
on indigenization of missions, 2353
institutional histories, 2201
on the Lord's Prayer, 2353
on peace in Vietnam, witnessing for,
2353
on Puerto Rico, Brethren of, 2353
on wellness from Biblical perspective,
2353
Rosenberger, Mary Workman, 1123
Rosenberger, Melissa C. Young, 1123
Rosenberger, Mrs. H. G., 1999
Rosenberger, Nancy (later Faus), 1613,
1935, 2277
Rosenberger, Sabrina Workman, 1123
Rosenberger, Wellington Clemens, 714,
1123, 1755
Rosenberry, Morris Claude, 2049
Rosenmiller, Mary A. (later Eylar)
descendants, 1934
Rosenstock Chapel, Maryland Baptist
College
used by Walkersville, MD, Glade
Valley Church of the Brethren,
1314
Rosepine, LA, Church of the Brethren,
760, **1123**
Roanoke, LA, Church of the Brethren, 1112
Roser family, 1389
Roses of Sharon (originally the Order of
Spiritual Virgins)
Ephrata, 1172
Rosewarne, Dorothy M. (later Neff), 706
Neff, Robert Wilbur, 2230
Rosicrucians, **1123**
as a source for Beissel's ideas, 113
Ross, Amos Walter, **1123–1124,** 1213,
1755, 1843, 2049
missionary to India, 1193
Ross, Amos Walter and Flora Mae Nickey
(Bjorklund), **1123–1124**
Ross Church of the Brethren, OH, 71, **1124**
Ross Co., OH, 272, 1327
Fairview Church of the Brethren, OH,
469
Paint Creek Church of the Brethren,
OH
Shoemaker, Martin, descendants, 1157
Ross, D. M., 45
Ross, Elizabeth E., 2049
Ross, Faith, 654
Ross family
Mill Run Grace Brethren Church, MD,
833
Ross, Flora Mae Nickey (later Bjorklund),
678, **1123–1124,** 1834
Ross, George
Ross, Keith E. on, 2353
Ross, George Henry, 1755
Ross, Gilbert, 152
Ross, Hannah Heckman
Ross, Keith E. on, 2353
Ross, Harry E., 2049
Ross, Helen M. Ross
on Eikenberry, John, 2353
on Eikenberry, Mary Clingenpeel, 2353
Ross, Henry H., 1755
Ross, Isaac, 241, 362, 505, 1755
Ross, J. F., 1755
Ross, J. T., 1755

Ross, Jimmy Randall, 398, 1755, 2014,
2049
Ross, Keith E.
on Eikenberry, John, 2353
on Eikenberry, Mary Clingenpeel, 2353
on Heckman, Hannah, 2353
on Ross, George, 2353
on Ross, Hannah Heckman, 2353
Ross, Ken, 654
Ross, Robert, 1123
Ross, Roy G., 659
Ross, S. L., 1755
Ross, Samuel, 1755
Ross, Susan Snell, 1123
Ross, W. L., 1755
New Hope Church of the Brethren, IN,
building of, 929
Ross, William, 1755
Rossburg House
La Porte, IN, Church of the Brethren,
713
Rossburg, IN, congregation
Portage Prairie, IN, Church of the
Brethren, 1047
Rosser, James, 12
Rossman, Donald W., 1755
Rossman, Randall L., 20–21, 241, 318, 564,
731, 1755
Rossville, IN, 1345
Church of the Brethren, 717, **1124**
Middlefork Old German Baptist
Brethren Church, IN, 826
Pyrmont, IN, Church of the Brethren,
sharing pastor with, 1073
Rotenberger, Linford James, 1388, 1755,
2305
Roth, Alvin N., 1991
Roth, Ann Oswald, 2049
Roth, David, 1755
Roth, Elmer, 2049
Roth family, 319
Roth, G. W., 1755
Roth, George, 1755
Roth, Heinrich (Rhoads, Henry, Sr.), **1124**
Roth, Henry, 2049
Roth, Henry (Rhoades), Jr.
Roth, Heinrich (Rhoads, Henry, Sr.),
1124
Roth, Jacob, 2049
Roth, Janice, 2049
Roth, John D.
on Anabaptist hermeneutics, 2353
on Pietists, 2353
Roth, Lorraine, 1991
Roth, Lyle D., 1755
Roth, Mary (later Pfaltzgraff), 1013
Roth, Paul W., 738, 1755
Roth, Reuben E., 2049
Roth (Rhoads), Catherine
Roth, Heinrich (Rhoads, Henry, Sr.), 1124
Roth, Vida, 1351
Roth, William, 1351
Roth, Zelma (later Studebaker), 1230
Rothenberger, Daniel, 1755
Tippecanoe, IN, congregation, leader-
ship by, 951
North Webster, IN, *950*
Rothenberger, Daniel and Mary Jane Nock,
family of, *10*
Rothenberger, George Phillip, **1124,** 1755
Reynolds, Clarence L. on descendants
of, 2352
Tippecanoe, IN, congregation, bishop,

951
Rothenberger, Jacob, 1755
Rothenberger, Mary Jane, family
North Webster, IN, *950*
Rothenberger, Philip
Alexander Mack's Bible, 777
Rothermel, Jeremiah, 1755
Mohrsville Church of the Brethren, PA,
minister and elder, 869
Rothermund, Dietmar, 2049
Rothert, Otto A., 2049
Rothgeb, Martin, 1755
Rothgebs family, 2077
Rothrock, Abraham, 682, **1124,** 1356, 1755
Rothrock, Bertha Sweitzer, 1124
Rothrock, Dale L., 2049
Rothrock, David, 1755
Rothrock, Edgar Eli, 128, 244, 248, 463,
620, 714, **1124,** 1755, 2049
Pomona, CA, Church of the Brethren,
pastor, 1045
Silver Lake Church of the Brethren,
NE, elder and minister, 1182
Rothrock, Edgar Paul, 2049
Rothrock, Eli S., 128, 1124
Rothrock, Eli Sanford, 1755–1756
Rothrock family, 413, 1223, 1338, 2036,
See also Rotruck family
Fahrney (Forney) family, 466
Rothrock, George, *See* Rothrock (Rodrock,
Rotruck, Roderick, Roadrock)
family
Rothrock, Hazel Marie, 1843
Rothrock, Henry Shirley, 2049
Rothrock, Horace Mann, 912, 1756
Rothrock, Johann Georg, 2049
Rothrock, John, 1756
Rothrock, Joseph
Maitland Church of the Brethren, PA,
minister, 783
Rothrock, Lottie Viola (later Studebaker),
1230
Rothrock, Mary Beashor, 1124
Rothrock, Mary (later Hanawalt), 581, 582
Rothrock, Peter, *See* Rothrock (Rodrock,
Rotruck, Roderick, Roadrock)
family
Rothrock, Philip, *See* Rothrock (Rodrock,
Rotruck, Roderick, Roadrock) family
Rothrock (Rodrock, Rotruck, Roderick,
Roadrock) family, 2049
Rothrock, Samuel, 1756
Rothrock, Samuel D., 1756
Rothrock, Susan Forney, 1124
Rothrock, Susannah (later Hanawalt), 582
Rothrock, Elizabeth (later Amick), 25
Rothscheidt, W., 2049
Rotov, Boris, *See* Nikodim, Metropolitan
Rotruck, Andrew
immigrant to America, 1124
Rotruck, Dorsey Edward, 1265, 1756, 2305
Rotruck family, 16
Rotruck, Gregory A., 2291
Rotruck, Johann Georg, 1124
Rotruck, Johannes (father), 1124
Rotruck, Johannes (son), 1124
Rotruck, Ludwig, 1124
Rotruck, Margaretha (later Schultz), 1124
Rotruck, Noah M., 1756
Rotruck, Philip Jacob, 1124
Rotruck (Rothrock, Roderick) family,
1124–1125
Rotruck, William D., 1756

Rotterdam, Netherlands, 159, **1125**
  Brethren migration to America through,
    923
  emigration, Brethren, 443
  Koker family, 705
Rottier, Frank, 1756
Rottler, Carson Ellsworth, 1756, 1852
Rottler, Rosaylind Royall Jackson, 1852
Rotzien family, 1277
Rouch family
  Poplar Valley Church of the Brethren,
    MT, 1047
Roudebush family, 1304
Rough, H. Don, 674, 1756
Round Hill Brethren Church, VA, *See*
    Strasburg, VA, Round Hill
    Brethren Church
Round Hill Church of the Brethren, VA,
    1125, 1301, 1364
Round Mountain Church of the Brethren,
    AR, 241, **1125**, 1215
Round Top schoolhouse
  Little Pine Church of the Brethren, NC,
    749
Roupp, Dora Hess, 2049
Roupp, Frank, 2049
Rouse, Ruth, 2049
Rouserville, *See* Rouzerville
Roush, Tirlla
  Pleasant Valley German Baptist
    Brethren Church, NE, 2377
Roussaki, Peter E., 1756
[Rousselot] De S[urgy, Jacques] P., 2050
Routh, Joseph D., 2291
  Medina, OH, Church of the Brethren,
    2219
Rouzerville Church of the Brethren, PA, 42,
    1125
Row, Erma Yaple, 1125
Row family, 2098
Row, George, 1756
Row, Golden Frank, 1125
Row, Leona (later Eller), 638, 1125, 2378
  World Friendship Center, 1369
Row, W. Harold, 199, 288, 316, 738, *1125,*
    1125–1126, 1331, 1756, 1867,
    2050, *2129,* **2378**
  Bible interpretation, 134
  International Voluntary Services
    Agency (IVS), 660
  Junior, WV, Valley River Church of the
    Brethren, 679
  museums, 898
  Peace Corps, 1002
  Poland and relief efforts, 1041
  Russian Orthodox Church, 1132
  Washington Office (CB) and, 2260
Row, W. J., 679, 1756
Rowan Co., NC, 230, 689–690, 1383, 1871,
    2051, *See also* Davies Co., NC
  Brethren settlement, 946
  Ham, John, 580
  Pfautz family, 1014
Rowan (later Randolph) Co., NC, 1233
Rowan (now Davidson) Co., NC, 734
Rowand (ship), 146
Rowdabaugh, J. W.
  "Annual Conference of 1882" and,
    2353
Rowdy, KY, Brethren Church, 405, 689,
    1126
  Riverside Christian Training School,
    1111

Rowe, Anna Mae (later Haubert), 1959,
    1994
Rowe, Barry L., 2291
Rowe, Betty (later Landis), 1959
Rowe, Charles Benton, 360, 1756
Rowe, Dewey E., 1247, 1394, 1756
  Salkum, WA, Community Church of
    the Brethren, pastor, part-time,
    1139
  Seattle, WA, Olympic View Commun-
    ity Church of the Brethren, pastor,
    1162
Rowe, Donald Eldon, 1756, 2050
  Pasadena, CA, Church of the Brethren,
    pastor in, 994
Rowe, E. B., 1756
Rowe, Earnie J., 590, 676, 740, 1756
  Midway Church of the Brethren, TN,
    providing leadership, 827
  Pleasant View Church of the Brethren,
    TN, 1037
Rowe family, 1221, 1959, 2098
Rowe, Gary, 748, 2050
  Martinsburg, PA, Memorial Church of
    the Brethren commissioning play
    by, 798
Rowe, Landon Luther, 1756
Row(e), Lucinda (later Long), 753
Rowe, Mary Mae, 1959
Rowe, Ray Noble, 1756
Rowe, Robert L., 695, 1756
Rowe, Twyla D., 2291
Rowell, Geoffrey, 2050
Rowell, W. R., 1756
Rowland, A. E., 2050
Rowland, Aaron, 2093
Rowland, Abraham S., 444, 1756
Rowland, Ann Gilbert, **1126**
Rowland, Casper H., 1756
  Hunsiker (Hunsaker) family, 637
Rowland, Charles Luther, **1126**
Rowland, Collin P., 438, 1756
Rowland Creek Church of the Brethren,
    VA, **1126–1127**
Rowland, Curtis Glenn, 2291
Rowland, D. W., 1756
Rowland, David Abner, 438, 1756
  Polo, IL, Church of the Brethren,
    pastor, 1045
Rowland, David (CB-1), 1756
Rowland, David (CB-2), 1756
Rowland, Earl Dwight, 1756
  Mount Wilson Church of the Brethren,
    PA, part-time pastor, 887
Rowland, Edward K., 2050
Rowland, Elmer Scott, 757, 1756
Rowland, Essie Oaks Mays, 1126
Rowland family, 153, 1359, 2081, 2093
  Dutchman's Creek German Baptist
    Brethren Church, NC, 411
  Hunsiker (Hunsaker) family, 637
  Jackson Co. German Baptist
    Brethren, IN, 667
Rowland (Roland), Gasper, Sr., 30, 475,
    493, 597, **1126**, 1292, 1383, 1756
  immigrant to America, 1127
  North Carolina Brethren settlement,
    946
Rowland, Gasper, Jr., 1126, 1756
Rowland, Gertrude Elvina (later Emmert),
    444, 1361, 1837
Rowland, Harold R., 757, 1756
Rowland, Helen E. (later Price), 1056

Rowland, Henry J., 2050
Rowland, Jacob, 1126, 1219
Rowland, John, 580, 1126, 2050
Rowland, John E., 760, 1330, 1756
  Rouzerville Church of the Brethren,
    PA, part-time pastor, 1125
Rowland, John H., 1756
Rowland, John M., 623
Rowland, Jonas, 757, 1126
Rowland, Joseph, 398, 475, 688, **1126,**
    1234, 1756, 2050
  immigrant to America, 1127
Rowland, Joseph Emmert, 1756
Rowland, Julia (later Colborn), 2166
Rowland, Katie (later Trostle), 1276
Rowland, Levi, 2093
Rowland, Mary Hunsaker, 637
Rowland, Mary (Minnie) E. (later Miller)
  Miller, David Alfred, wife of, 836
Rowland, Nancy (later Long), 753
Rowland, Nancy (later Stouffer), 1219
Rowland, Otelia H. (later Reichard), 1094
Rowland, Philip, 1127
Rowland (Roland) family, **1127**
Rowland, Susan Friedly, 444
Rowland, Susan Miller, 1126
Rowland, W. B., 1756
Rowlins Co., KS, 274
Rowser, Donald E., 1756, 2047
Rowsey, Elwood A., 1756–1757
  Mansfield, OH, Walcrest Brethren
    Church, pastor, 787
Rowsey, Harriett E. Becknell, 1127
Rowsey, Henry J., 1127
Rowsey, Herbert H., 64, **1127,** 1757
Rowsey, James, 1757
Rowsey, Jean (later Hamel)
  Hamel, Joseph Donat, 2196
Rowsey, John David, 1855
  The Missionary Board (BC), 856
Rowsey, Lucy B., 1127
Rowsey, Regina Ruth Hendershot, 1855
Rowsey, W. H.
  Roanoke, VA, First Brethren Church,
    pastor, 1113
Roxborough, PA, 1298
Roxbury Church of the Brethren, PA, *See*
    Johnstown, PA, Roxbury Church
    of the Brethren
Roy, Nirmala, 1855
Roy school
  Saline Valley church of the Brethren,
    KS, 1139
Royall, Anne Newport, 2050
Royall, Rosaylind, 1852
Royce, Peter
  Steiner family, 2378
Royer, A. J.
  Powelis Valley Church of the Brethren,
    OR, deacon and minister, 1049,
    1050
Royer, Abram H., 1757
Royer, Albert A., 1128
Royer, Allen, 1757, 2291
Royer, Anna J. (later Meyer)
  Meyer, Jacob Gibble, wife of, 821
Royer, Anna Martha Miller, 1127
  Miller, Daniel Long, 836
Royer, Anna (Miller), 94
Royer, Anna Roop, 1130
Royer, Anne Neiderhiser (later Fleming),
    494
Royer, Annie M., 709

Royer, B. Franklin, 2050
Royer, B. Mary, 1843, 1973, 1977
Royer, Bertha Wolgamuth, 1128
Royer, Bess (later Bates), 748
    Miller, Daniel Long, 836
Royer, Brother
    Pipe Creek Church of the Brethren,
        MD, 1026
Royer, Byron Paul, 681, **1127**, 1757, **2378,**
    2385
Royer, Catherine (later Roop), 160, 1130
Royer, Charles, 1757
Royer, Charles F., 2050
Royer, Chester H., 1757
Royer, Christian, 1128, 1757
    Meadow Branch Church of the
        Brethren, MD, 805
Royer, Christian (OGBB), 471, 1757
Royer, Clyde D., 1757
    Maple Grove Old German Baptist
        Brethren Church, OH, elder-in-
        charge, 791
Royer Community Church of the Brethren,
    KS, **1128**
    Newton, KS, Church of the Brethren,
        as mission of, 934
Royer, David H., 228, 1757
    Nimishillen Old German Baptist
        Brethren Church, OH, minister in,
        937–938
Royer, David W.
    Old Brethren Church, 2232
Royer, Donald M., 2, 2050
    historical writing, 612
    Rural Life Association (RLA), 1131
Royer, Donald Mark, 518, 1757
Royer, Edward, 1757, 2305
    Nimishillen Old German Baptist
        Brethren Church, OH, minister in,
        937–938
    Old Brethren minister, 965
Royer, Elizabeth, 228
Royer, Elizabeth "Bess," See Bates,
    Elizabeth "Bess" (Royer)
Royer, Elizabeth (later Gibbel), 547, 771
Royer, Elizabeth (later Hertzler), 601
Royer, Elizabeth McClanahan, *132*
Royer, Elizabeth Reiff, 1094, 1128
Royer, Elizabeth Smith, 1094
Royer, Emig, 1128
Royer, Evelyn, 246
Royer family, 153, 158, 161, 228, 232, 721,
    1128–1129, *1129,* 1219, 1221,
    1338, 1359, 1390, 2050–2051
    children named for Bible personages,
        912
    family history, 2010
    genealogy, 1940
    Hertzler (Hartzler) family, 601
    history of, 1948
    Mack family, 778
    in Neosho Valley Old German Baptist
        Brethren Church near, 923
    Nimishillen Old German Baptist
        Brethren Church, OH, 937–938
    reference to, 1956
    Royer, Harry K. on descendants of,
        2353
    Snavely family, related to, 1193
The Royer Family in America (Francis),
    534
Royer, Florence Shearer Miller, 1843
Royer, Galen Brown, 94, 160, 205, 413,

538, 709, *1127,* **1127–1128,** 1273,
    1345, 1757, 1936, 2018, 2050
    historical writing, 613
    hymns, 643
    imposters among the Brethren, 648
    Iran (Persia), 662
    Johnstown, PA, Morrellville Church of
        the Brethren, 674
    Miller, Daniel Long, 836
    missions, 861
    Royer, John Grove, 1128
    The School and Home, publisher of,
        1155
Royer, Galen Brown, Sr., 1757
    Natrona Heights Church of the
        Brethren, elder in, 918
Royer, Galen Brown, Jr., 1757
Royer, George, 246, 1128
Royer, Gladys Irene Cool, 2050
Royer, Gladys Violet Hawbaker, **1128,**
    1843, **2378, 2388**
Royer, Harold Albertus ("Red"), 9, **1128,**
    1843
    relief workers from New Paris, IN,
        Church of the Brethren, 931
Royer, Harold G.
    Old Brethren Church, 2232
Royer, Harry K.
    on Royer family and descendants, 2353
Royer, Harvey L., 1757
Royer, Henry, 1757
    Jefferson Co., KS, arrival in, 987
    Ozawkie, KS, Church of the Brethren,
        987
Royer, Henry D., 721, 1757
Royer, Howard E., 2050
    Messenger, editor, 819
Royer, Ira Roscho, **1128,** 1757
Royer, J. W. (OGBB-1), 1757
Royer, J. W. (OGBB-2), 1757
Royer, Jacob, 1128
Royer, Jacob E., 228, 1757
    Nimishillen Old German Baptist
        Brethren Church, OH, minister in,
        937–938
Royer, Jerry, 669
Royer, Jesse, 1757
    Nimishillen Old German Baptist
        Brethren Church, OH, minister in,
        937–938
Royer, Jesse E., 1757
Royer, Jesse W., 1757
Royer, Joe L., 2291
    Old Brethren Church, 2232
Royer, John, 1757
Royer, John and Elizabeth McClanahan,
    family, *1129*
Royer, John Calvin, 912
Royer, John Fleck, 2050
Royer, John G., 1127, 1345, 2050
Royer, John Grove, 231, 232, 275, 1094,
    1128, 1757, 2027, 2058
    military recruitment, 831
    Miller, John Ezra, 839
    Monticello/Pike Creek Church of the
        Brethren, IN, minister, 872
    Mount Carroll, IL, Church of the
        Brethren, elder, 880
    Mount Morris College, president, 884
    The School and Home, publisher, 1155
    The Sick, the Dying and the Dead, 788
Royer, John L., 1757
Royer, John M., 1757

Royer, John Reiff, 1094
Royer, John W., 106, 1389, 1757
Royer, Jonas, 1757
Royer, Josiah Abraham, 1757
Royer, Kathren (later Holsopple)
    missionary to India, 1127
Royer, Kathren M. (later Holsopple), 338,
    1757, 1839, **2387**
Royer, L. E., 1757
Royer, Lester W., 733, 1757
Royer, Madison
    Peach Blossom Colored Church of
        Rising Light (CB), MD, 1003
Royer, Martha Groff, 1127
Royer, Mary Ann Culp, 1128
Royer, Mary Wenrick Risser, 1094
Royer, Milton D., 1757
Royer, Naomi (later Will), 1345
Royer, Nora Faye (later Wagoner), 1312
Royer, Oliver, 1757
Royer, Orville, 1757
Royer, Peter, 1130
Royer, Ralph Austin, 1843
Royer, Ruth, 305
Royer, Neta Ruth (later Kulp), 596, **709,**
    1312, 1840
    missionary to Nigeria, 1127
Royer, Samuel, 1757
Royer, Sebastian, 1940, 2050, 2051
    immigrant to America, 1128
Royer, Stephen L.
    Old Brethren German Baptist Church,
        965, 2232
Royer, Susannah Myers, 1128
Royer, Susie Hawbaker, 1128
Royer, Thomas L., 2291
    Old Brethren Church, 2232
Royer, U. S., 1757
Royer, William, 1127, 1757
    Painter Creek Church of the Brethren,
        OH, 990
Royer, William Elsewere, 1757
Royer's house, Tulpehocken Church of the
    Brethren, PA, 1278, 1969
Royersford, PA, Church of the Brethren,
    1129
    Mingo Church of the Brethren, PA, 843
Royle family
    South Loup Church of the Brethren,
        NE, 1206
Royman Fellowship, 214
Roynon, Helen (later Stephens), 714
Royse, Earl, 713
Royse, Marian, 713
Rozell, Melancthon F., 1757
Rubincam, Milton, 1990, 2051
Ruble, Lawrence D., 1757
Rubsom (Ruebsome), Henry, 1757
Rucker, Kenneth A.
    Grace Village Retirement Complex,
        2193
Ruckers German Baptist Brethren Church,
    VA, **1129**
Rudolph, L[avere] C., 2310
Rudolph, Robert, 29
Rudolph, Sophia (later Fike), 144
    family reunion (photo caption), 2373
Rudoph family, 2087
Rudy, Elizabeth Brubacher Martin, 2051
Rudy, Isaac L., 1757–1758
Rudy, John
    Peer, Marie Jean Smith on ancestors
        and descendants of, 2349

Rudy, Mary Garman
  Peer, Marie Jean Smith on ancestors
    and descendants of, 2349
Ruebush family
  Funck (Funk) family, 521
Ruebush, Joseph K., 1860
Rues, Simon Friedrich, 2051
Ruesch, Timothy J., 2173
  London, OH, Grace Brethren Church,
    2215
Ruetenik, Hermann J., 2051
Ruether, Rosemary Radford, 1928, 2051
Ruff, Clifford Raymond, 445, 1240, 1758
Ruff, Edward, 1758
Ruff, G. A.
  North Georgetown, OH, Brethren
    Church, 948
Ruff, Jerry Wayne, 1758, 2051
Ruff, Phyllis Kingery
  Minutes of Annual Conference of CB,
    1980–1984, 2353
Ruffner family, 2077
Ruffner, George, 1758
Ruggles, Todd Wiliam, 2157
  Mexico City, Mexico, Brethren
    Mission, 2222
Ruggles, Tracy Ann Clawson, 2157
  Mexico City, Mexico, Brethren
    Mission, 2222
Ruhl, Allen B., 1758
Ruhl, Audrey, 654
Ruhl, Donald E., 1758, 2305
Ruhl, Elizabeth (later Zug), 1401
Ruhl family, 749
Ruhl, John, 654
Ruhlman, Edwin, 1758
Ruiz, Cirilo
  Hispanic Ministries (BC), 2198
Rule, Eli, 1758
Rule, Harrison, 1758
  Middlefork Old German Baptist
    Brethren Church, IN, minister, 826
Rule, Harrison G., 1758
Rule, Lawrence J., 1758
Rulon, Dale Paul, 1758, **2385**
Rumball-Petre, Edwin A. R., 2051
Rumble, C. Joseph, 2305, **2385**
  Modesto, CA, Old German Baptist
    Brethren Church, presiding elder,
    867
Rumble, Charles B., 1363, 1758
  Modesto, CA, Old German Baptist
    Brethren Church, minister, 867
  Mud Valley Old German Baptist
    Brethren Church, IL, presiding
    elder, 892
Rumble, David L., 2291
Rumble family, 405
Rumble, Gordon, 1758
  Modesto, CA, Old German Baptist
    Brethren Church, minister, 867
Rumble, Hubert L., 1758
  Miller, John William, 2224
  Modesto, CA, Old German Baptist
    Brethren Church, presiding elder,
    867
Rumble, John, 1758, 2156, 2291
  Modesto, CA, Old German Baptist
    Brethren Church, minister, 867
Rumble, Joseph
  Miller, John William, 2224
Rumble, Joseph Mark, 2291
Rumble, Paul

Modesto, CA, Old German Baptist
  Brethren Church, 867
Rumble, Russell Lee, 2291
Rummel, Arthur, 752, 1321, 1758
Rummel, Arthur LeRoy, 1265, 1758, 2305
Rummel Church of the Brethren, PA, *See*
  Windber, PA, Rummel Church of
  the Brethren
Rummel congregation
  Shade Creek Church of the Brethren,
    PA, 1170
Rummel, Dale Eugene, 1758
Rummel, Donald Wayne, 1758
  Palmyra, PA, Church of the Brethren,
    991
Rummel family, **1129–1130,** 1346, 2051
Rummel, George (father)
  immigrant to America, 1129
Rummel, George (son), 1129
Rummel, Glenn Irvin, 1758
Rummel, Isaiah, 1129–1130
Rummel, Jacob, 2051
Rummel, John, 1129
Rummel, Madelaine Olt, 2051
Rummel, Mariah Strycker, 1130
Rummel, Mary Jane (later Murphy)
  Murphy, Ross Dale, mother of, 896
Rummel, Merle Clifford, 1758, 1962, 2051
  on Four Mile Community, IN, 2353
Rummel, Valentin, 1934
Rummel, William David, 628, 1758
Rummel, William H., 675, 1758
Rummell, Paul Zimmerman, 1758, 2305
Rumor of Innocence (Rowe), 748
  Martinsburg, PA, Memorial Church of
    the Brethren, 798
Rumple, Jethro, 2051
Rundell family
  Garwin, IA, Carlton Brethren Church,
    532
Rung, Albert M., 2051
Runion, Ira F., 1758
Runkel family, 1937
Runkle, Dwayne A., 2291
Runner family
  Mount Cassell Old German Baptist
    Brethren Church, WV, 880
Runyan, Melvin
  South Bend, IN, Ardmore Brethren
    Church, 1203
Ruoff, Fr[iedrich], 2051
Ruoff, Henry Wordmar, 2051
Rupel, Alice LaVern (later Rohrer), 2047
Rupel, Andrew M., 1758
Rupel, Charles David, 1758
Rupel, Charles Franklin, 572, 1758
Rupel, Claude Merrill, 1843
Rupel, David, 1758
  Pine Creek Church of the Brethren, IN,
    1024
Rupel, Diantha
  South Bend, IN, First Brethren Church,
    1203
Rupel, Esther Fern, *444, 599, 600,* 2051,
    2143, 2202
  on dress of members of CB,
    2353–2354
  historical writing, 612
Rupel, Jesse C., 1758
Rupel, Marie Elizabeth Pobst, 1843
Rupel, Martha (later Gilbert), 518,
    2189–2190, *2189*
  Spain, relief work in, 1207, 1208

Rupel, Mary Ellen, 352
Rupel, Naomi Zigler, 1397, 1843
Rupel, Paul Whitmer, 1758, 1843
Rupel, Samuel G., 1758
Rupert, Adam
  family of, 1926
Rupert, Edward Jack, 2292
Rupley, Freda
  South Bend, IN, Prince of Peace
    Church of the Brethren, 1204
Rupley, George
  South Bend, IN, Prince of Peace
    Church of the Brethren, 1204
Rupp, Allen Eugene, 2051
Rupp, Barbara (later Hochstetler), 615
  Hostetler, Adam, 631
Rupp, Christian, 1130
Rupp family, 373
Rupp, Henry, 2005
Rupp, Israel Daniel, 2051
Rupp, Johann Jonas, 2052
Rupp, Johannes, 2051
Rupp, Marcile Elizabeth (later Nofziger),
    2031
Rupp (Roop) family, **1130**
Rupp (Rupe/Roop/Roup) families, 1887
Rup(p)ert, Jacob and Rebecca (Peggy)
    Oyster, 1969
Ruppert, Kundichunda, 1243
Ruppert, Wolfgang, 1243
rural congregations, **1130**
  Education for Shared Ministry (EFSM),
    2162
  farming, 477
  farming and, 2181
  Holmesville Church of the Brethren,
    NE, 620
  Iowa, 661
  ministers, 2109
  worship services, 2109
rural development
  agricultural, *See* agriculture and farm-
    ing
  Edwards, Chandler S., 429
rural life
  cooking, traditional, 341
  higher education, 603
  minorities, ethnic and racial, 851
Rural Life Association (RLA), 12,
    1130–1131
The Rural Mailbox
  Rural Life Association (RLA), 1131
rural missions and ministry, 1130–1131,
    2017, 2021, *See also* agricultural
    missions; Agricultural Missions,
    Inc.
Rural Missions Cooperating Committee
    (RMCC), **1131**
Rural Service Center, Anklesvar, India, 9,
    158, 651, *1131*
  Gram Sevaks, 565
  India, Church of North, 2207
  Mason, George Edward, 2218, *2218*
Rusch, Elizabeth, 430
Ruschenburg, Anna, 258
Ruse, Hiram, 1758
Rush, Anna (later Shank), *See* Shank, Anna
  Rush
Rush, Benjamin, 89, 379, 1292, 2052
  oaths, taking of, and 18th-century
    Pennsylvania Brethren, 959
Rush, Capt. Peter, 1863
Rush, Charles W., 1758

Portis, KS, Grace Brethren Church, pastor, 1048
Rush Co., WI, 322
Rush Creek Church of the Brethren, OH, *See* Bremen, OH, Rush Creek Church of the Brethren
Rush, David, 2292
Rush, Harley, 1758
Rush, Jacob B., 1758
Rush, John S., 1758
Rush, Mrs. S. M., 1758
Rushby, William F., 2052
Rusk, William S., 2052
Rusmisel, Dan David, 2292
Russel, Charles Taze, 670
Russel, Robert, 21
Russel, William A., 2052
Russell, Alice Luetta, 1850
Russell, Beulah Keedy, 1132
Russell, Charles T., 157
Russell Co., KS, 215, 396
    Church of the Brethren, **1132**
Russell, Galen (CB-1), 1758
Russell, Galen (CB-2), 1758
Russell, Harl L., **1131–1132**, 2140, **2378**
Russell, Hazel Weimer, 1132
Russell, Helen H., 2052
Russell, Kenneth E., 121, 1758
    New Holland, PA, Church of the Brethren, pastor in, 929
Russell, Ota Lee, 748, 2052
Russell, Robert
    Rittman, OH, First Brethren Church, pastor, 1111
Russell, Robert A., 2292
Russellites, *See* Jehovah's Witnesses
Russellville, IL
    Allison Prairie Church of the Brethren, 2126
Russia, 55, 1288
    Agricultural Exchange Program, **2129**
    aid for, 23
    Julien, Thomas T., 2210
    Mennonite Brethren Churches, General Conference of, 814
    Mennonite Central Committee (MCC) providing relief, 814
    Mennonites migrating to, 815
    Miller, Orie O., relief worker, 841
    missions, short-term, 2226
Russian immigrants, missions to, 859
Russian Orthodox Church, 201, **1132**, *1132*, 2033
    Agricultural Exchange Program, 2129
    Brethren contact, and Roman Catholic Church, 1120
    Brown, Dale Weaver, 2152
    Church of the Brethren, 304
    McIntire, Carl, 774
    Nikodim, Metropolitan, priest in, 937
    Orthodox Church, 983
    Ramsey, Duane H. and, 2239
    Row, W. Harold, 1126
    Vietnam War, 286
Russian refugees, aided by Maple Grove Church of the Brethren, IN, 789
Russiaville, IN, Mount Pleasant Brethren Church, *See* Cambria, IN, Mount Pleasant Brethren Church
Rust, Arthur G., 1758
Rust, C. Timothy, 1758, 2292
Rust, Glenn C., 109, 262, 1758
Rust, Rayburn Stedman, 1212, 1758

Rust, Robinson S., 1758–1759
Ruth, 3:3, 39
Ruth
    Roop, Eugene F. on, 2353
Ruth, Brian Curtis, 2292
Ruth, John L., 2052
    on Dunkers, 2354
    on Mennonites, 2354
Ruth Royer Kulp Memorial Hospital, *See* Garkida General Hospital
Ruth Royer Kulp Memorial Hospital, ne. Nigeria, *See* Garkida General Hospital
Ruth, Susanna (later Krehbiel), 1955
Rutherford Co., NC, 1209
    Brethren congregations, 946
Rutherford Co., TN
    Gibson, Isham, 547
Rutherford, Eileen Paul, 2052
Rutherford Heights, PA, 142
Ruthrauff, Grace Crumpacker, 2052
Ruthrauff, Herbert L., 714, 759, 1759, 2305
Ruthruff, John B., 1759
Rutledge, Hallie, 1345
Rutrough, C. Abram, 1759
    Mountain View Old German Baptist Brethren, VA, 2227
    Pigg River Old German Baptist Brethren Church, VA, minister, 1023
Rutrough, Ezra W., 1759
    Pigg River Old German Baptist Brethren Church, VA, elder-in-charge, 1023
Rutrough, I. Stephen
    Mountain View Old German Baptist Brethren, VA, 2227
Rutrough, J. H.
    Mountain Normal School, 889
Rutrough, John
    Pigg River Old German Baptist Brethren Church, VA, minister, 1023
Rutrough, John T., 1759
Rutrough, Lester, 1216, 1759
Rutrough, Stephen, 2292
Rutt, Aaron B., 2052
Rutt, Anna Ebersole, 2086
Rutt, Anna Mae Weaver, 2052
Rutt, Edith (later Myers), 2027
Rutt family, 2027
Rutt, Harvey S., 2052
Rutt, Phares W., 2052
Rutter, Thomas, 88, 113
    Seventh-Day Baptists, 1170
Ruusbroeck, Jan, 57
Ruyts, F. Robert, 695, 1759
Ryan, Bertha (later Shirk), 1226, 1296, 1361, 1844, *See also* Shirk, Bertha Ryan
    India, 649
    India orphanages, 651
Ryan family
    Mount Cassell Old German Baptist Brethren Church, WV, 880
Ryan, Jacob S., 1177, 1759
Ryan, Janet, 1303
Ryan, Marilyn
    SERRV International (CB) and, *2247*
Ryan, Michael, 1759
    Seal Beach, CA, Grace Brethren Church, pastor, 1161
Ryan, Polly Grove, 1177

Ryan, Tom, 1303
    SERRV International (CB) and, *2247*
Rycroft, William Stanley, 2052
Ryerson, Greg A., 1212, 1267, 1759
Ryerson, Milton M., 130, 377, 532, 1759
Ryerson Station Church of the Brethren, PA, 16, **1132**
Ryman, Christena (later Wine), 1349
Ryman family, 396
Ryman, John M., 1759
Ryman, Mary (later Frantz), 508

"S," 2052
S., H. J., 2052
S., J. B., 2052
Saal, Ephrata Community, *449, 450*, 1003, 1004
Sabbatarian Dunkers, 1311
    North Carolina Brethren settlement, 946
Sabbatarian Ephrata Community
    fellowship naming to distinguish from, 910
Sabbatarianism, 68, 88, 113, 1863, *See also* Ephrata Community
    Brethren, *1133*
    Copp, Zed H., 343
    doctrine on, 175
    Eckerlin, Samuel, 422
    Edisto German Baptist Brethren Church, SC, 425
    Eicher, Daniel, 431
    French Creek, 516
    Georgia, 540
    German Seventh-Day Baptists, 542
    Martin, George Adam, 1194
    Martin, George Adam, giving leadership to, 797
    pork, eating of, 1047
    publishing, 1067
    Rhode Island, in and Brethren visiting, 1107
    Seventh-Day Adventists, 1169
    Seventh-Day Baptist Church, 1170
    Snowberger, Andrew and Barbara, 1195
    South Carolina, 1204
    Virginia, 2104
    Wohlfahrt (Welfare), Michael, 1355
Sabbath, 2048
    doctrine of, 2082
    Illinois, 647
    origin and observance, 1984
    seventh day, 2010
Sabbath Recorder
    Fahnestock, William M., 465
Sabbath school, *See* Sunday school
Sabbath-school, Ephrata Community, 451
Sabbath services, Ephrata Community, 448
Sabetha, KS, Church of the Brethren
    Morrill, KS, Church of the Brethren, 876
    Pony Creek, KS, congregation, **1133**
    Rock Creek Church of the Brethren, KS, 1117
Sabin, Douglas Dean, 2292
Sabin, Emma J. Schlosser, 2053
Sabin, Joseph, 1861
Sabine, Lorenzo, 2053
Sachs, Elmer Bernhardt, 1759, 2305
Sachse, Eugen, 2053
Sachse, Julius F., 290, 379, 381, 452, 542, *543*, **1133**, 1170, 1861, 1960,

2053, 2142, *See also* Ephrata
Community, Patriot's Day
historical writing, 611
history of Germantown, 1935
Rosicrucian influence, writing about,
1123
Wissahickon hermits at funeral of
Alexander Mack, Sr., 1200
Sack, Saul, 2053
Sacks, Herbert, 1759
sacramentalism, 28, 83, 84
Sacramento, CA, 1133–1134
Gillett, Charles Edwin, 549
Prince of Peace Church of the
Brethren, **1134**
River City Grace Community Church,
70, **1134**
Sacramento Valley, CA, Church of the
Brethren, 322, *See also* Codora,
CA, Church of the Brethren
sacraments, *See* ordinances
Brethren definition of, 83
Brethren movement, 291
Brethren polity, 1042
Donatist view of, 396
ordinances, 976
Orthodox Church, 983
Reformation, Protestant, 1091
Roman Catholic Church, 1120
Sanger's treatise on, 2054
Schwenkfelder Church, 1159
The Sacred Name Broadcaster (Assemblies
of Yahweh), 68
Sacred Name movement, 68, *See also*
Assemblies of Yahweh
The Sacred Scriptures, Bethel Edition
(Assemblies of Yahweh), 68
Sadd, Tracy Wenger, 2292
Saddleback Valley, CA, Mission Viejo
Grace Brethren Church, *See*
Mission Viejo, CA, Saddleback
Valley Grace Brethren Church
Saddler, Donald Dean, 2053
Saddler, Nancy Lou Moyer, 2053
Saddler, William, 1759
Sadler, John W., Jr., 1759
Sadler, John W., Sr., 1759
Sage, Clara McC., 2053
Sage, Glen Harrison, 1759
Red Hill Church of the Brethren, VA,
pastor, 1089
Saginaw, MI, Church of the Brethren, *See*
Elsie Church of the Brethren, MI
Saginaw, TX, Church of the Brethren, *See*
Fort Worth, TX, Church of the
Brethren
Sagot, Francois, 2053
Sagrada Scholarship Bible Camp, 2175
Sahuda, Nigeria, 306
St. Joseph Co., IN, 2105
Saint Paul Church of the Brethren, NC,
1135
St. John, Clyde, 1759
St. John, Dean, 1759
St. John, Dennis, 1759
St. John, William R., 1759
saints and sainthood generally, *See* canon-
ization; specific names (e.g.,
Augustine of Hippo)
St. Alban's Episcopal Church
Windsor, CO, Northern Colorado
Church of the Brethren, 1348
St. Albany Old German Baptist Brethren

Church, WV
Putnam Co., WV, **1134**
St. Andrew (ship), 146, 225, 693
Hertzler (Hartzler) family, 601
Kimmel family, 693
Klöppinger, Anna Margaretta
Schreiner, 701
Klöppinger, Johann Georg, 701
Lutz, Christian, 767
Lutz, Jacob, 767
voyage on, to America, by J. and U.
Sollenberger, 1202
St. Clair Co., MO, 224
Oak Grove Church of the Brethren,
MO, 956
Osceola Church of the Brethren, MO,
984
St. Clair, Ronald J., 2294
St. Fleur, Ludovic, 2294
Miami, FL, Eglise des Frères Haitians,
2222
St. Francis Church of the Brethren, AR
Palestine, AR, near, 1134
St. Francis Co., AR
St. Francis Church of the Brethren,
1134
St. Georgen
Thalham Tubercular Sanitorium,
1255–1256
St. Jacob, Switzerland
Frantz family, 509
St. James, MD, 1339
Brethren Church, **1134,** 694
Lowery, Margaret E., 2216
sources on, 2318
St. James Station
St. James Brethren Church Sunday
school near, 1134
St. Jo, TX, 1255
St. John, W. Dean, 2167
Englewood, OH, Dunkard Brethren
Congregation, 447
St. John, New Brunswick, Canada, 18
St. John School, preaching point maintained
by Kansas Center Church of the
Brethren, KS, at, 683
St. John, Thomas M., 2294
St. Joseph Co., IN, 318, 347, 352
North Liberty, IN, Church of the
Brethren, 948
Oak Grove, IN, Church of the
Brethren, 955
Osceola Church of the Brethren, IN,
984
Pine Creek Church of the Brethren, IN,
1024
Portage Prairie, IN, Church of the
Brethren, 1047
Replogle family, 1100
South Bend, IN, Crest Manor Church
of the Brethren, 1203
St. Joseph, IN, Church of the Brethren, *See*
South Bend, IN, Crest Manor
Church of the Brethren
St. Joseph, MO, 1134–1135, 1342
mission, 1976, 1987
North Saint Joseph Church of the
Brethren, **1134–1135**
South Saint Joseph Church of the
Brethren
Miller, David Alfred, 836
St. Joseph (South Bend, Crest Manor), IN
congregation, **1135**

St. Joseph Valley Church of the Brethren,
IN, **1135**
St. Joseph's Co., MI, 1246
St. Louis, MO, 161, 1277
missions, 859
Universalist society, 1277
urban ministry, 299
urban mission, 1296
St. Luke Union Church
St. Luke, VA, Brethren Church, **1135**, 1164
Mathias, WV, Brethren Church, 803
St. Marys, KS
Ozawkie, KS, Church of the Brethren,
preaching point, 987
St. Matthew's Church of Christ, Wabash,
IN, 1311
St. Paul Brethren Church, Roanoke, IN, *See*
Roanoke, IN, Brethren Church
St. Paul Church of the Brethren, NC, **1135**
St. Paul Church of the Brethren, VA, **1135,**
1267
St. Paul, MN, *568*
St. Petersburg, FL, Brethren House (BC),
See Brethren House Ministries
St. Petersburg, FL, First Church of the
Brethren, **1135**
Lersch, E. Phillip, Jr., 2214
St. Petersburg, FL, Grace Brethren Church,
1135–1136
St. Vrain, CO, Church of the Brethren,
See Hygiene, CO, Church of the
Brethren
Flory, Jacob S., 498
Sala family, 1914, 2036
reference to, 1960
Fraktur artistry, 2186
Sala, G. W., 1759
Sala, Jacob, **1136,** 2041
printers, and publishing, 1067
Sala, Johann, 517, **1136**
Sala, Joseph W., 237, 141, 173, 1759
Sala printers, 2019
Sala, Solomon, 700, **1136,** 1255
printers, and publishing, 1067
Salamonie Church of the Brethren, IN, 30,
757, **1136,** 2053
Huntington, IN, City Church of the
Brethren, 637
Markle, IN, Church of the Brethren,
organized from, 794
Murray, Samuel, presiding elder, 897
Prairie Creek, IN, Church of the
Brethren, 1050
Salamonie Reservoir
relocation of congregation, 1136
salaried ministry, 157, 182, 189, 204, 206
Ashland Convention, support for, 368
Brethren movement, 294
Brethren rural churches, 1130
changes in attitudes about, 1376
Church of the Brethren, 300, 846
Codorus, PA, Church of the Brethren,
323
Declaration of Principles, 372
disagreements over, 1053–1054
Dunkard Brethren, 408
education, 427
elder, functions of, assumed, 433
election of church officers, 434
Ellison Church of the Brethren, ND,
442
Fast Element, 480
Flat Rock Church of the Brethren, VA,

494
Fraternity Church of the Brethren, NC,
511
Fredericksburg, PA, Clover Creek
Church of the Brethren, 513
free ministry, 513
Garrison, IA, Church of the Brethren,
531
Geiger Church of the Brethren, PA,
533
Girard, IL, Church of the Brethren, 550
Goshen, IN, City Church of the
Brethren, 557
Goshen, IN, West Goshen Church of
the Brethren, 558
Grossnickle Church of the Brethren,
MD, 574
Hanover, PA, Church of the Brethren,
582
Harman Church of the Brethren, WV,
584
Hatfield Church of the Brethren, PA,
588
Heisey family, 595
Hershey, PA, Spring Creek Church of
the Brethren, 599
Holmesville Church of the Brethren,
NE, 620
Holsinger Church of the Brethren, PA,
623
Holsinger, Henry Ritz, 621
Horst family, 630
house churches, 632
Imler, Tobias F., 647
installation of pastors, 656
Iowa River Church of the Brethren, IA,
662
Irricana (First) Church of the Brethren,
Alberta, Canada, 663
Ivester Church of the Brethren, IA, 665
Miami Valley Petition, 823
missions, 858
Myers, Tobias Timothy, 905
Old German Baptist Brethren, 845
opposition to in *The Landmark,* 724
pension funds, 1007
Philadelphia, PA, First Church of the
Brethren, 1015
Priesthood of All Believers, 1057
Progressive Brethren movement, 972
prophecy, 1062
Rosenberger, Isaac J., opposition to,
1123
schism, 1152
vs. free, 1136–1137
"Sala's German Vegetable Elixir"
patent medicine, 1136
Salazar, Amado, 1248
Salazar, Robert, 1248, 1759
Salem Brethren Church, IN, 231
Salem Brethren Church, OH, 319, *See also*
Clayton, OH, Grace Brethren
Church
Salem Brethren Church, WV, *See*
Fayetteville, WV, Salem Brethren
Church
Salem Church, IN, *See* Burlington, IN,
Brethren Church
Salem Church of the Brethren, IA, 226,
1137
Salem Church of the Brethren, IL, **1137**
Romine Church of the Brethren, IL,
1121

Salem Church of the Brethren, IN, 1287,
2048
Union congregation, **1137,** 1364
Salem Church of the Brethren, ND,
1137–1138
Salem Church of the Brethren, OH, 208,
144, 963, **1138,** 1265, 1335
Pitsburg, OH, Church of the Brethren,
1026
Potsdam, OH, Church of the Brethren,
1048
Salem Church of the Brethren, VA, 239,
1138
Peters Creek Church of the Brethren,
VA, 1011
Salem Church of the Brethren, WV
Sandy Creek, WV, congregation, 1138,
1143
Salem College, Bourbon, IN, **1138**
Eby, David Bowman, 418
literary societies, 746
Miller, Oliver W., president, 841
Mount Pleasant Church of the Brethren,
IN, 886
Murray, Samuel, 897
Pleasant Hill College, 1033
Parker, Isaac Dillon, as teacher in, 993
Salem Community Church of the Brethren,
KS, 683
Nickerson, KS, Brethren Church, start-
ed by, 936, **1138**
Ninescah congregation, 1138
Salem congregation, KS
Pleasant View Church of the Brethren,
KS, 1036
Salem congregation, OH, 224, 380, 1355
Root family, 1122
Salem congregations
example of biblically inspired name,
911
Salem German Baptist Brethren
Church, OR, 14
Willamette Valley (originally South
Santaam) congregation, **1138–1139**
Salem Grace Brethren Chruch, VA, *See*
Wildwood Grace Brethren Church,
VA
Roanoke, VA, Garden City Grace
Brethren Church, 1113
Salem House, West Branch Church of the
Brethren, IL, 1333
Salem Old German Baptist Brethren
Church, OH, 967, 1139, 1224
Salem, PA, Church of the Brethren, 2076
Salem (Willamette Valley), OR, congrega-
tion
Powelis Valley Church of the Brethren,
OR, 1049
Salemville, PA, 694
German Seventh-Day Baptists, 542
Sales Exchange for Refugee Rehabilitation
Vocations, See SERRV Inter-
national
Salford Mennonite Meetinghouse Schools
Hershey, Mary Jan Lederach on *fraktur*
from, 2336
Salford Station, Montgomery Co., PA, *1272*
Salgiver, Robert, 2292
Salida, CA, 1363
Old Brethren, 964
Old Brethren Church, 2232
"Salida Brethren," *See* Old Order Fel-
lowship

Salinas, Margarita (CB)
Santa Ana, CA, Principe de Paz Fel-
lowship (CB) and, 2246
Saline Co., MO, 145, 320, 683
Saline Co., NE, 396
Saline Valley Church of the Brethren,
KS, 1, **1139**
Abilene, KS, congregation, 1139
Salisbury Brethren Church, PA, *See* Elk
Lick, PA,
Salisbury-Garrett-Beachdale congregation,
PA, 1316
Salisbury meetinghouse
West Salisbury, PA, 1139
Salisbury, PA, Church of the Brethren, 214,
380, **1139**
Maple Glen Church of the Brethren,
PA, 789
Maple Spring Church of the Brethren,
PA, 791
Markleysburg, PA, Church of the
Brethren, 794
Meyersdale, PA, Church of the
Brethren, 822
Salisbury, Ruth, 1861
Salkum, WA, 1338
Community Church of the Brethren,
1139
Richland Valley congregation,
1139–1140
Salmon, George
Manteca, CA, Northgate Community
Brethren Church, 788
Salmon, Mrs. George
Manteca, CA, Northgate Community
Brethren Church, 788
Salmon(s), A. O., 1759
Salomon, Ronald W., 2053
Salsbury, Charles Lewis, 1759
Salt Lake City, UT, 1298
Salt Plains, OK, Church of the Brethren,
See Monitor Church of the
Brethren, OK
Monitor Church of the Brethren, OK,
previous name of, 869
Salter, Elizabeth
violence and, 2265
Salter family
Sharon Church of the Brethren, Alberta,
Canada, 1172
Saltillo, PA, Baptist congregation
Rockhill Furnace, PA, Rockhill Church
of the Brethren, ecumenical federa-
tion with, 1118
Salunga, PA, Church of the Brethren, 416
East Petersburg congregation, **1140**
Hempfield Church of the Brethren, PA,
596
salutation, *See* kiss, holy
Salvadoran coffee, boycott of, 2139
salvation, 2022, 2029
Beery's tract on, 1873
Brethren Church and, 184
Brethren movement, 291
Bucher, Rufus P., 461
conversion, 339
doctrine of, 409, **1140–1141**
in Anabaptist thought, 29
in Antinomianism, 42
in Arminianism, 55–56
in Fellowship of Grace Brethren
Churches, 42
free will, 514

Grace Brethren Church ministry, 847
grace, doctrine of, 562
Holy Spirit, doctrine of, 624
human nature, doctrine of, 635
hymns, 643
justification, doctrine of, 680
ministry, 844
Old German Baptist Brethren, 967
ordinances, 978
predestination, 1055
Priesthood of All Believers, 1057
reality and symbol, 2009
redemption, 1090
Reformation, Protestant, 1091
relation to baptism, 85
resurrection, and Brethren teachings
about, 1102
sanctification, 1142
singing, 1185
Social Gospel Movement, 1197
through works, 1368
Wiles, Virginia on, 2363
Salvation Army
Modesto, CA, South Modesto Comm-
unity Church of the Brethren
money given to, 867
Salvi, A. F., 1759
Salyards, Harry H., 2292
Salyards, Joseph, 265
Samarin, Ruth Marie, 1852
Samarin, William John, 1759, 1852
Eine Sammlung von Psalmen (*A Collection
of Psalms*)
hymnals, 641
Samokin, PA, 1232
Sampey, John R.
Winona Lake Auditorium, IN, 1353
Sampleville Brethren Mission, *See*
Glenwood, OH, Grace Brethren
Community Church
Sampson Hill Church of the Brehren, IN,
1141, 2071
Sampson, Lloyd, 2305
Sams Creek Church of the Brethren, MD
Pipe Creek Church of the Brethren,
MD, 1026
Pipe Creek congregation, **1141**
Samsel, Charles, 704
Samsel family
Erbaugh family, 453
Samtee, CA
San Diego, CA, First Church of the
Brethren, original location, 1141
1 Samuel
10:1, 39
16:1–13, 39
Samuel R. Zug Memorial Library
Elizabethtown College, 438
San Antonio, TX
homelessness, 2203
Church of the Brethren,
Bethel congregation, **1141**, 1255
San Bernardino, CA
Church of the Brethren, 432, **1141**
San Marcos, CA, North Country
Church of the Brethren and,
2245
Grace Brethren Church, **1141**
San Diego, CA, Grace Brethren Church, 88,
1141
San Fernando Valley, CA, *See* Los Angeles,
CA, Panorama City Church of the
Brethren

San Francisco, CA
Church of the Brethren, **1141–1142**
conscientious objectors, 2089
missions, 860
urban mission, 1297
San Joaquin Co., CA, 1359
Olive Grove Old German Baptist
Brethren Church, CA, 973
San Joaquin Valley, CA, 744, 1281, 1358
German Baptist Brethren congregation,
245
San Jose, CA, South Bay community
Church (FGBC), **1142**
San Juan, PR
Martin G. Brumbaugh Reconstruction
Unit (Civilian Public Service
Camp No. 43), 261
Rio Piedras, PR, Segunda Iglesia Cristo
Misionera Fellowship (CB) and,
2243
San Luis, DR, Principe de Paz (Prince of
Peace, CB), **2245**
San Mar
Fahrney, Peter, 466
San Marcos, CA, North Country Church of
the Brethren, **2245**
San Patricio Co., TX
Portland, TX, Bayview Church of the
Brethren, 1048
San Ysidro, CA, Grace Brethren Church,
1142
Sanchez family
Maple Valley, WA, Grace Brethren
Church, 2218
sanctification, **1142**
Brethren Church and, 184
Brethren doctrine of salvation, 1140
Cassel, Jacob C., 259
Church of God (New Dunkers), 297
conversion, 340
Dunkard Brethren, 1210
early opposition to, 1210
entire, 691
ethical-moral state, 1142
German Baptist Brethren, 1210
Holiness Movement, American, 619
Holy Spirit, doctrine of, 624
humility, 636
hymns, 643
justification, doctrine of, 679
Keswick Convention, 691, 1210
perfectionism, 1009
Progressive Brethren, 1210
Protestant reformation view of, 1259
sin, 1184
Sanctity of Life Committee
Fellowship of Grace Brethren Churches
(FGBC), 486–487
Sanctuary Movement, **2245**
Sand Brook Church of the Brethren, NJ, 28,
129, 929, **1142**, 1287
Mooreites, 875
Sand Brook Historical Society
meetinghouse of Sand Brook Church of
the Brethren, NJ, 1142
Sand Creek Church of the Brethren, KS,
1142–1143
Sand Creek congregation, KS
example of place name, 911
Sand Creek Old German Baptist Brethren
Church, KS, 682, **1143**
Fairview Old German Baptist Brethren
Church, KS, 470

Footprints of the Sand Creek Church
(Kesler and Kesler), 1984
Sand Ridge, OH, 1235
Church of the Brethren
Sugar Ridge congregation, 340,
411, **1143**
Sandberg, Emanuel W., 2141, 2166, 2170
South America Theological Seminary
(BC) and, 2252
Sander, Larry D., 1843
Sander, Sandra, 1843–1844
Sanders, Alfred William, 1759
Sanders, Cynthia Sue, 2292
Sanders family, 1315
Phoenix, AZ, Northwest Grace Breth-
ren Church, 1019
Sanders, Henry C., 102, 124, 1287, 1759
Mount Zion Church of the Brethren,
WV, 888
Pleasant Hill Church of the Brethren,
WV, 1033
Pleasant Valley Church of the Brethren,
WV, free minister, 1036
Sanders, John L., 1759
Sanders, Letitia J. (later Miller)
Miller, Howard, wife of, 837
Sandoval, Grace (later Trujillo), 1277
Sands, E. E., 515
Sands, Morton L., 20, 130, 250, 467, 1759,
1852
Quebec, 1075
Sandusky Co., OH, 720
Rome Old German Baptist Brethren
Church, OH, 1121
Sandusky family, 1213
Sandy, A. Rollin, 1759, 2305
Sidney, IN, Grace Brethren Church,
pastor, 1181
Sandy, Conard K., 715, 738, 755, 759,
1143, 1759
River City Grace Community Church,
pastor, 1134
South Gate, CA, First Brethren Church,
pastor, 1205
Sandy congregation, OH
Freeburg Church of the Brethren, OH,
514
Hiestand (Heistand, Heestand,
Heaston) family, 602
Sandy, Conrad A., 586
Sandy Creek Baptist Association, 2040
Sandy Creek Church of the Brethen, WV,
1263, 1336
Farmington, PA, Bethel Church of the
Brethren, 479
Fike family, 489
First District of WV, 2081
Markleysburg, PA, Church of the
Brethren, 794
Salem Church of the Brethren, WV,
began as preaching point of, 1138,
1143
Sandy Creek, WV, congregation, 157, 215,
1262
Sandy Creek, NC
Pfautz family, 1014
Sandy Creek Old German Baptist Brethren
Church, WV
Sandy Creek Church of the Brethren,
1143
Sandy, D. Brent, 2292
Sandy family
Harrisburg, PA, Melrose Gardens

Grace Brethren Church, 586
Sandy, Fern Monroe, 1134, 1143
Sandy, Florence, 1143
Sandy German Baptist Brethren Church, OH, **1143**
    Mahoning Church of the Brethren, OH, 782
    Reading Church of the Brethren, OH, 1084
Sandy, Jacob D., 272, 1759
Sandy, Reuben, 1143
Sandy Ridge mission point
    Germantown Brick Church of the Brethren, VA, 544
Sandy Ridge, WV, Fellowship
    North Fork Church of the Brethren, WV, 947
Saner, Virginia Faye Hart, 2053
Sanfley, Eliza (later Long), 754
Sanford, Don A.
    on Seventh Day Baptists, 2354
Sanford, NC, Grace Brethren congregation, 946
Sanford, Seth, 1759
Sangamon Co., IL, 258, 1234
    Far Western Brethren, 475
    migration of Brethren, 829
    Pleasant Hill Old German Baptist Brethren Church, IL, 1033
    Rowland, Joseph, helping to establish congregations, 1126
Sangamon Valley, IL, congregation
    Oakley Brick Church of the Brethren, IL, 958
Sanger, Anna Brillinger, 1144
Sanger, Conrad, 1144, *See* Miller, Michael, II; Sanger family
Sanger, Elizabeth Flory, 1143
Sanger family, 355, 415, **1144**, 1950, 2062
Sanger, Frank P., 1759
Sanger, H. E.
    Peach Blossom Colored Church of Rising Light (CB), MD, 1003
Sanger, Homer F., 1898, 1938
Sanger, Isaac J., 61
    "Feetwashing," *59*
Sanger, John, 1143
Sanger, Kate, 540
    Oak Hill Old German Baptist Brethren Church, WV, 957
Sanger, Martin, 1759
Sanger, Nancy Miller, 1144
    Müller (Miller) family, 895
Sanger, Paul Bowman, Jr., 1759
Sanger, Paul Bowman, Sr., 1759
Sanger, Perry H., 1759
Sanger, Samuel A., 115, 462,
    Mill Creek Church of the Brethren, VA, elder, 832
Sanger, Samuel Abraham, 416, 462, 513, 1759
    Madison Church of the Brethren, VA, 781
    Mount Carmel Church of the Brethren, VA, presiding elder, 880
Sanger, Samuel F., 205, 315, 342, 445, 590, 722, **1143–1144,** 1759, 1946, 2053, 2082
    on Linville Creek CB, VA, 2354
    medicine, 810
    on Shenandoah District CB, 2354
    South Bend, IN, City Church of the Brethren, elder, 1203

Sanger (Senger), Martin Garbert, 1759
Sanger-Stewart family, 1980
Sanger, Susan V., 354
Sanger, Susanna (later Hutchison), 639
Sanger, Susanna (later Thomas), 1263
Sanger, William Elmer, 417, 1759, 2054
Sanger, William Henry, 1759–1760, 2053
Sangerville Church of the Brethren, VA, 105, 208, 1263, 1301, 1939
    Beaver Creek congregation, 1144
    Highland Co. Mission Church of the Brethren, VA, 605
    Hiner Church of the Brethren, VA, 607
Sangmeister, Heinrich Ezechiel, 98, 291, 452, 704, **1144**, 2043, 2054, 2354
    Ephrata chronicler, 1990
    historical writing, 611
    Spohn, Clarence E. on writings of, 2357
Sango language, Bible translation, 2134
sanitariums
    Hygiene, CO, 2071
    Thalham Tubercular Sanitarium, 708. 1255–1256
    tuberculosis, 200
sanitation
    medical projects, 808
Sankey, Ira D., 560
Sanmeister, E., 379
Sanner, Jacob, 1760
Sansom, John E., 1760, 2305
Santa Ana, CA
    Church of the Brethren, 348, **1144**
    Maranatha Grace Brethren Church
        minorities, ethnic and racial, 850
        Spanish-speaking congregation, **1144**
    Principe de Paz Fellowship (CB) and, **2245–2246**
Santa Barbara, CA
    O'Neal, Glenn, 2236
Santa Clara Co., CA
    migration of Brethren, 830
Santa Claus
    Brethren movement on, 288
Santa Fe Ave. Mission, CA, 758
Santa Fe Church of the Brethren CA, *See*
    Los Angeles, CA, Bella Vista Church of the Brethren
Santa Fe Church of the Brethren, IN
    Peru, IN, Church of the Brethren, 1010
    Pipe Creek Church of the Brethren, IN, 1025, **1144–1145**
    Plevna, IN, Church of the Brethren, 1037
Santa Fe, KS, Church of the Brethren, **1144**
Santa Fe Railroad (Atchison, Topeka, and Santa Fe)
    Brethren colonization, **1145**
    Brethren settlement, 1082
    chartered trains, 273
    colonization and, 238
    Eshelman, Matthew Mays, 455
    McDonough, George L., 773
    migration of Brethren, 830
Santa Fe School, preaching point maintained by Kansas Center Church of the Brethren, KS, at, 683
Santa Maria, CA, Grace Brethren Church, **1145**
Santa Rosa, CA
    Swallow, James F., 1243
Sante Fe Railroad

La Verne, University of, 715
Santee Church of the Brethren, CA, *See*
    San Diego, CA, First Church of the Brethren
Santiago, Monica
    South America Theological Seminary (BC) and, 2252
Santo Domingo, Ecuador, 1290
Sappa Creek Church of the Brethren, NE, **1145**
    Edison German Baptist Brethren Church, NE, 2373
Sappington, Beulah Snader (CB)
    Sappington, Roger E. (CB) and, 2246
Sappington, George Klein, 106, 1760
Sappington, Mrs. L.
    The Missionary Advocate, treasurer, 855
Sappington, Roger Edwin, 140, 535, 1760, 1861, 2054–2055, 2100, 2188, **2246**, *2246,* **2385**
    on Alabama Brethren, 2354
    Brethren history, 2201
    on certificates of membership from VA, 2354
    on family life, Brethren, 2354
    historical writing, 612
    on industrial America, Brethren in, 2354
    on Tennessee Brethren, 2354
Sappington, Ross F. (CB), 2246
Sarafian, Kevork, 2055
Sarasota, FL, 171, 497
    Brethren Church, **1145**
    Brethren Church in Peru and, 2237
    Hamel, Joseph Donat, 2196
    Iglesia de los Hermanos (BC), **2246**
    urban ministry and, 2257
Saratoga, IL, 1288
Saratoga, NY, Grace Brethren Church, 1251
Saratoga, WY, 1213
Sardinia, *See* Homeless European Land Program
    relief and service efforts, 1097
Sargeantville, NJ
    Progressive Brethren in, 929
Sargent, Curtis H., 1760
Sargent, Frank N., 123, 1760
Sargent, Galen B., 1760
Sargis, E. Y., 1760
Sarris, G.
    home education, 2203
Sartoris, Ann (later Fahrney), 466
Sarver, Alberta, 588
Sarver, Daniel, 239
Sarver, Mrs. Daniel, 239
Sarver, David, 2292
Sarver, Kay Carol, 1855
Sarver, Mrs. Russell, 239
Sarver, Russell A., 239, 588, 1760
Saskatchewan, Canada, **15**
    Brethren Church in, 250
    Brethren of Christ, 189
    Fairview Church of the Brethren, 250, 469
    Glen Mary, 15
    Indian Head, 250
    migration of Brethren to, 830
Sassafrass Hill churchhouse, MD, 1329
Sasse, Bernhard Heinrich, 1211
Satan (Devil), 462, 486, 1103
Satover, Noah Webster, 2076
Satsangi, Jivanji H., 1760

Satterfield, Benjamin F., 1760
Satterfield family
    French Broad Church of the Brethren,
        TN, 516
Satterfield, John R., 516, 1760
Sattler, Gary R.
    on Francke, August Hermann, 2354
    on Müller, Heinrich and Pietists view
        of individual, 2354
Sattler, Michael, 28, 291
Saturation of the Target Area for Kingdom
    Expansion (STAKE) (BC), See
    STAKE (BC)
Saturday, See Sabbatarianism; Sabbath
Sabbath observance, 1133
    Ephrata Community, 1133
Satvedi, Anet Daniel, 2292
    on India, CB in, 2354
Satvedi, Govindji Khengariji (CB), 229,
    650, **1145**, 1760
    mission schools, 853
Satvedi, Kankubai
    Bible teacher, 1145
Satvedi, Valentina F., 2292
satyagraha
    Gandhi, Mohandas Karamchand, 528
Satygrahi, Timothi, 1760
Sauble, Tempe
    Rockford, IL, First Church of the
        Brethren, mission worker, 1117
Sauder, Barbara G. Good, 2092
Sauder, Christian M., 2092
Sauder, Elizabeth, 1951
Sauder, Lizzie B. Weaver, 2092
Sauder, Magdalena C. Martin, 2092
Sauder, Steven E., 2292
Sauer almanacs, See almanacs
Sauer, Andrew, 2056
Sauer, Anna Christina Stichs Meckel, 1147
Sauer Bible, 120, *1149*, 1953, 1973, 1981,
    2067, 2071, 2104, 2106
    New Testaments, 2052
    owners, list of, 2104
    publishing, and spiritual nurture, 1063
    Russian Orthodox Church, presented
        to, *1132*
Sauer, Catharine (later Murray), 898
Sauer, Catherine Scharpnack, 774, 775,
    1146, 1152
Sauer, Christopher I, See Sauer, Johann
    Christoph (Christopher I)
Sauer, Christopher (Christopher II), *17,* 18,
    61, 77, 176, 334, 477, 509, 521,
    532, 544, 716, 736, **1145–1146,**
    1248, 1298, 1760, 1861, 1886,
    1895, 1901, 2034, 2035, 2084
    acquaintances of, 117
    admonition to, 1325
    Apocrypha, citation of, 133
    arrest of, 999
    bibliography, 1860
    biographical materials, 1868, 2038,
        2051, 2055, 2093, 2312, 2318,
    Christopher Sauer Workshops, 290
    church-state relations and, 309–310
    Durnbaugh, Donald F. on, 2327
    Franklin, Benjamin and, 2010
    friend of Georg Schreiber, 1156
    funeral, hymn sung at, 2004
    Geistliches Magazien, Ein (*A Spiritual
        Storehouse*)*,* 534
    Heidelberg Catechism, 593
    historic sites, 609

historiography, 2201
hymns by, 1933
Kalcklöser, Johann Heinrich, death of,
    681
Mack, Alexander, Jr., 774, 775
Mack, Elizabeth Neiß (Nice), 778
medicine, 809
Miller, George, 837
Muhlenberg, Henry Melchior, 892
Muhlenberg, John Peter Gabriel, secur-
    ing release of, 892
Müller, Johann Heinrich, 893
New England Primer, printing of, 1764,
    1999
peace policies of Quakers, 999
persons ordained by, 123
Philadelphia, PA, Germantown Church
    of the Brethren, elder, 1016
poetry and hymns, 1039
prayer books, printing of, 1051, 1052
printer and Loyalist, 1145–1146, 1152
publishing, 1063, 1067, 1167
references to, 1955
Revolutionary War, 2009
Revolutionary War, American, arrest
    during, 1106
Revolutionary War, refusal to partici-
    pate in, 1059
Sauer Press, 50, 1149
slavery, 1190
Weaver, William Woys on herbal cures
    of, 2362
wife of, 1959
Wilmann, Christa M. on herbal cures
    of, 2363
Wilson, Renate on herbal cures of,
    2364
Womelsdorf, Josef on, 2364
Sauer, Christopher (Christopher III), 18,
    544, 925, **1146–1147,** 1858, 1861,
    1898, 1914, 1988, 2019, 2022,
    2023, 2033, 2034, 2042,
    2055–2056, 2073, 2087
    account of Canadian experience, 1958
    biography of, 2081, 2093
    Durnbaugh, Donald F. on, 2327
    grave of, 2090
    letter from on New York loyalists,
        March 1, 1779, 1915
    letters of, 2055–2056
    loyalism and arrest during
    Revolutionary War, American, 1106
        Müller, Johann Heinrich, 2014
    Musselman, Christian, 901
    New Brunswick, 1996
    printer and Loyalist, 1146–1147,
        1148–1149
    publishing, 1067
    references to, 1911, 1913, 1915
Sauer, David
    publishing, 1067
    son of Christopher Sauer, II, **1147,**
        1152
Sauer, Elizabeth La Motte, 1149
Sauer family, 394, 1927, 2045, 2056, 2060,
    2061, 2071, 2078, 2080, 2086
    American Revolution, 925, 1067, 1146,
        1147, 1149, 2055
    Benjamin Franklin, reference to, 1940
    clockmaking, 1926
    fictional stories about, 748
    historical materials regarding, 1950,
        2055

Müller [-Bahlke], Thomas on, 2348
Pennsylvania settlement and Brethren
    publishing, 1004
references to, 1912, 1940, 1943, 1961
Roeber, A. G[regg] on, 2352
social action, 1196
sources on, 2320
Sauer, H. F., 1760
Sauer, Hannah Schlosser, 1149
Sauer, Johann Christoph (Christopher I),
    17–18, 40, 60, 68, 120, 176, 258,
    259, 394, 521, 533, 574, 575, 684,
    767, 918, **1147–1148,** 1861, 1874,
    1877, 1886, 1895, 1946, 1994,
    2009–2010, 2025, 2029, 2031,
    2034, 2035, 2043, 2046, 2049,
    2055, 2057, 2069, 2070, 2073,
    2081, 2090, 2093, 2095,
    2098–2099, 2102, 2103, 2104
    anecdotes about, 1942
    articles about, 1913, 1920, 1921, 1943,
        1946
    associates of, 117
    Bible publishing of, 1865
    bibliographical sources, 140, 1859
    bibliography, 1858, 1860
    biographical notes, 140, 1958, 2051,
        2038
    biography, 1868, 1938, 1957, 1959,
        2093, 2098, 2105
    Brethren beliefs and Radical Pietism,
        1080
    Christopher Sauer Workshops, 290
    defense of in "An Answer to an
        Invidious Pamphlet," 1912
    on education, 2098
    encyclopedia references, 2071
    ethics, 457
    eulogy for, 1150
    family, 2038
    father of Christopher Sauer II, 1145
    German votes in 1755, 2110
    historic sites, 609
    historical writing, 611, 2201
    *Der Hoch-Deutsch Pennsylvanische
        Geschicht-Schreiber,* editor, 1967
    hymnal publication, 1919
    immigration, 1917
    on J. Conrad Beissel, 113
    Koker, Pieter de, as intermediary for,
        705
    Lehmann, Hartmut on Franklin, B.
        compared with, 2343
    Leibert, Peter, apprentice to, 736
    Lerg, Winfried B. on, 2343
    letter to C. Weiser, 1952
    letters from, 1942, 1959–1960
    letters from, translated, 1921
    letters from Weiser, Conrad, 2093
    letters of, 2055, 2098
    literary landmarks of Philadelphia,
        1978
    Luther translation of Bible, use of, 138
    medicine, 809
    Muhlenberg, Henry Melchior, 892
    museum containing clock case made
        by, 898
    mysticism, 907
    naturalization of, 1932
    Newlander exposure, 934
    optometry training, 1981
    peace policies of Quakers, 999
    Pennsylvania Hospital, 1007

Preiß, Johannes, poems of, published by, 1055
publications by, article about, 1912
publisher, 1063, 1999
redemptioners, 1090
references to, 1914, 1933, 1934, 1935, 1941, 1947, 1951, 1955, 1939, 1956
research paper about, 1936
Sauer Press, 50, 1149
separatism and formation of sectarian groups, 1167
Wellenreuther, Hermann on, 2362
work in Laasphe, 716
writings about, 1919
Sauer, Maria Christina Gross
Ephrata Community, 1145, 1147, **1148**
mother of Christopher Sauer II, 1145
wife of Johann Christoph Sauer I, 1147, 1148
Sauer, Peter, 18, 176, **1148–1149,** 1955
loyalism during Revolutionary War, American, 1106
printing business, 1146
publishing, 1067
son of Christopher Sauer, II, 1148–1149
Sauer Press, 56, 60, 72, 139, 425, 426, 427, 451, **1149–1150,** 1211, 1292, 2023, 2024, 2028, 2041, 2061, 2067, 2069, 2074, 2081, 2086, 2094, 2104
American Revolution, 925, 1067, 1146, 1147, 1149, 2055
Berleberg Bible, advertisements for, 138
bookbinding, essays about, 1941
elementary education, 434
Franklin, Benjamin, 506
Geringer Schein, Ein (*A Humble Gleam*), 540
German language, use of, 724
Germantown, 544
Hildebrand, Johannes, 606
Historic Peace Churches, 608
historic sites, 609
historical libraries, 610
history, 1967–1968
hymnals, 700
legacy, **1150**
letter describing, 2055
minorities, ethnic and racial, 849
Müller, Johann Heinrich, rival of, 893
Native Americans, 2229
peace policies of Quakers, 999
poetry, 1039
publishing, 1063, 1067
Roeber, A. G[regg] on, 2352
spiritualism, 1211
universalism, 1292
Zionitischer Weyrauchs Hügel (*Zionitic Hill of Incense*), 1400
Zur Geschichte der deutschen Presse in Amerika (Becker), 1872
Sauer, Samuel, 175, 700, **1149,** 1760, 1861
Baltimore, MD, 1998
Durnbaugh, Donald F. on, 2326
planned partnership with brother Christopher Sauer III, 1147
publications of, 260, 288
publisher of letter on sermons, 1167–1168
publishing, 1067

son of Christopher Sauer II, 1149
Sauer, Sarah Landis, 1149
Sauer, Wilbur Waterman, 2056
Sauer, William Henry and Mary Schaup, 2006
Sauer Workshops, 173, **290,** 809
Saul (cantata), 399
Saul, Emily, 2103
Sauls, Albert Lee, 1330, 1760
Saunders family
South Loup Church of the Brethren, NE, 1206
Saunders Grove Church of the Brethren, VA, 164, 1150
Saunders, James C., 2292
Saunders, Mark E., 448, 2177, 2292
Saunders, Mary (later Whitten), *See* Whitten, Mary Saunders
Saunders, Phillip
Saunders Grove Church of the Brethren, VA, 1150
Saunders, Samuel (Lemuel), 262, 1760
Saunders, Samuel R., 1760
moderator, Saunders Grove Church of the Brethren, 1150
Saunders, Thomas James, 2157
Saur, *See* entries at Sauer
Saur *Almanac, See* Riewald, J. G.
Saurer, Roger Lee, 1365, 1760, 1852
Sausser, Julie (later Miller), 2181
Sautzman, Eliza, 2107
Savage, Clarence, 1760
Savage, Donald E., 2292
Savannah, OH, congregation
Munson, Charles Robert, 2227
Savannah, VA, congregation
Moomaw, B. C., pastor, 873
Saville, Isaac J., 1760
Saville, Richard Russell, 129, 714, 1315, 1760
"Saving our Children"
marriage concerns, 795
Savings Bonds, *See* War Bonds
"Savior of My Soul"
hymns, 643
Sawa, Bitrus Pilasar (CB), 306, 2056, *2246,* **2246–2247**
Sawa, Joshua, 2247
Sawa, Markus, 2247
Sawa, Nkwarfaku, 2247
Sawa, Olive, 2247
Sawa, Pilasar K. (CB), 2246
Sawa, Sunday, 2247
Sawatsky, Rodney J., 2056
Sawyer, Albert (Allie), 1760
Sawyer family, 153
Sawyer, KS
Sand Creek Old German Baptist Brethren Church, KS, near, 1143
Sawyer, William Henry Harrison, 1760
Morrill, KS, Church of the Brethren, elder, 876
Saxby, Trevor J.
on Ephrata Cloister, 2354
on Labadie, Jean de, 2354
on Labadists, 2354
Saxton, PA, 740
Bunker Hill Brethren Church, *See* Bunker Hill Brethren Church, PA
Liberty Brethren Church, *See* Liberty Brethren Church, PA
Raystown Brethren Church, *See* Rays-

town Brethren Church, PA
Stonerstown Church of the Brethren, **1150**
Raven Run Church of the Brethren, PA, 1084
Sayer, Hazel Hannah
Von Flue, Eleanor Grace on ancestors of, 2361
Sayler, Anna (later Weybright), 1338
Sayler, Barbara
On Earth Peace Assembly, 2235
Sayler, Catherine (later Mohler)
Mohler, Samuel Sayler, mother of, 868
Mohler, Samuel, wife of, 868
Sayler (Saylor), Daniel P., 48, 106, 170, 460, 491, 580, 1211, **1150–1151,** *1151,* 1875, 1920, 2056
baptism of Abraham Lincoln, 743
biography of, 2055
elder, ordination as, 1150–1151
German Baptist Installation Service, 788
mandatory decisions, 787
Maryland Brethren, 798
minorities, ethnic and racial, 849
Rocky Ridge, MD, Monocacy Church of the Brethren, presiding elder, 1119
Seiler, Daniel, grandson of, 1165
Sayler family, 1221, 2056
Sayler, James Lanning, 2056
Sayler, Sanford, 1760
Sayler, Sara Root Smith
wife of Daniel P. Sayler, 1150
Sayler (Saylor), Daniel K., 160, 1760
Sayler (Saylor), Daniel P., 1760
Steiner family, 2378
Sayler (Saylor), Henry P., 1760
Sayler (Saylor), Jacob, 1760
Saylor, Barbara, 348
Saylor, Catherine (later Sauer), 1147
Saylor, D. R.
Rocky Ridge, MD, Monocacy Church of the Brethren, presiding elder, 1119
Saylor, Daniel, family
Pipe Creek Church of the Brethren, MD, 1026
Saylor, Daniel Richard, 1264, 1760
Saylor, Dorothy (later Pentz), 2036
Saylor, F. D., 1760
Saylor family, 152, 262, 267
Rotruck (Rothrock, Roderick) family, related to, 1124
Saylor, Guy R., 2056
Saylor, H. S., 1760
Saylor, Harry, 106
Saylor, John M., 1760
Saylor, Levi, 1760
Saylor, Lydia (later Schrock), *See* Schrock, Lydia Saylor
Saylor, Mary, *See* Seilor, Mary (later Naff)
Saylor, Mary Ann, 1835, 1844
Saylor, Rudy A., 1760
Saylor (Sayler), Catherine (later Mohler)
Mohler, John Saylor, mother of, 868
Sayn-Wittgenstein-Berleburg, 120, 1354
Sayn-Wittgenstein-Hohenstein, 120, 174, 1354
economic and social conditions, 1986
Elsoff, 443
Laasphe, 716
Sayn-Wittgenstein-Hohenstein

count of, 597–598
Gustav Otto, count of, 1158
Henrich Albrecht, count of, 683, 1158
Karl Ludwig, count of, 683–684
Sayre, John Earl, 1760
Sayre, Louise Miller, RN, 1845
missionary to India, *807*
Sayre, Ralph Hall, 2056
Saywell Hall, Topeka, KS, Church of the Brethren, 1267
Scaggs, Lewis C., 1760
Scaggs, Maynard, 1760
Scalf, James E., 1760
Scalp Level, PA, Church of the Brethren
Shade Creek congregation, **1151–1152,** 1170, 1348
Scarbro, Roger L., 2292
scarf, 401, 404
Scary, WV
St. Albany Old German Baptist Brethren Church near, 1134
"Scene of Judgement" (Mack), 2004
Scenery Hill, PA, Highland Brethren Church, *See* Highland Brethren Church, PA
Schaadt-Patterson, J. Michael, 2292
Schaal, Rockne, 1760
Schacht family, 1267
Schaefer, Elizabeth, 2157
Schaefer, James, 2157
Schaefer, James E., 2157, 2292
Schaeffer, Clara Reber, 1152
Schaeffer, Georg, 1174
Schaeffer, Isaac, 1152
Schaeffer, Judith (later Stover), 1227
Schaeffer, Mary, 2039
Schaeffer, Mary A., 720–721
Schaeffer, Mary Ann, **1152,** 1844, **2388**
St. Petersburg, FL, First Church of the Brethren, leadership, 1135, 1152
Schaefferin, Johanna (later Senger), 2062
Schaff (Scheff), David, 1760–1761
Schaff, Philip, 379, 2056
American Encyclopedia, 379
Schaffer, Alyce Ann, 1152
Schaffer, Helene Maurine Hostetler, 1152
Schaffer, Herbert Paul, 1152
Schaffer, Robert P., 2292
Schaffer, William H., 106, 121, 332, 699, **1152,** 1212, 1277, 1760
Portland, OR, Grace Brethren Church, 1048
Schaffer, William Lewis, 1152
Schaffner, Catharina (later Spitler), 1212
Schäfter family, 148
Schantol, Ollie
River City Grace Community Church, associate pastor, 1134
Schantz, Mary (later Eichelberger), 2028
Schanz family, 1383
Harrah, WA, Grace Brethren Church, 585
Schaper, Fred
Mulvane, KS, Brethren Church, 895
Schaper, Mrs. Fred
Mulvane, KS, Brethren Church, 895
Scharf, John Thomas, 2056
Scharpnack, Catherine (later Sauer), *See* Sauer, Catherine Scharpnack
Mack, Alexander, Jr., 774, 775
Scharpnack (Sharpnack), Heinrich, **1152**
Schatz family
Johnstown, PA, Geistown Grace

Brethren Church, 674
Schaub, James Richard, 1760
Schäuben (Shively) family, 1865
Schaublin, Christian and Barbara Spitler genealogy, 1980
Scheaffer, Elta B. (later Reed)?, 1745
Schechter, David Oliver, 1760, 2056
Michigan City, IN, Church of the Brethren, pastor, 824–825
Redford, MI, Trinity Church of the Brethren, pastoral leadership, 1090
on Yordy, Amos, 2354
on Yordy, Jessie, 2354
Schechter, David Pearl, 1760
Schechter, Elnora, 1835
Schechter family
Hancock, MN, Church of the Brethren, 582
Schechter, Joshua J., Jr., 211, 1380, 1760, 1844
Schechter, Joshua J., Sr., 1380
Schechter, Samuel H., 1760
Schechter, Virginia Moyer Bollinger, 1844
Schechter, Walter, 1340
Scheff, David, *See* Schaff, David
Scheffer, Johann Adam, 120
Scheffler, Johannes, 700
Scheib, Cheryl Elaine, 1843
Scheidegger, Hans, 1852
Scheidler family, *See* Shideler family
Scheidler, Jacob
Longenecker, Christian, elder, baptized by, at Conestoga, 1177
Scheidler, Susanna
Longenecker, Christian, elder, baptized by, at Conestoga, 1177
Schelbert, Leo, 2056
on CB dress, 2355
on Ephrata Cloister, 2355
on Miller, John Peter and letter of 1743, 2355
on Müller, Johann Peter, 2354–2355
on Thommens family, 2355
writings of, 2354, 2355
Schelhorn, J. W., 2056
Schell, O., 2057
Scheller, Catherine (later Emmert), 444
Schem, Alexander J.
Lexikon, 379, 2042
Schemmer, Ronald A., 2157, 2292
Schemmer, Sue, 2157
Schempp, Hermann, 2057
Schenck family, *See* Shank family
Schenck, Lorain
Pompano Beach, FL, Grace Brethren Church, 1046
Schenck, Stan
Pompano Beach, FL, Grace Brethren Church, 1046
Scheppard, Carol A., 2292
Scherffig family, 1152
Scherffig, Kaspar, *See* Sherfey family
Scherffig, Magdalena Heilman, 1152
Scherffig/Sherfy family
Sherfy, Robert Livingston (CB) and, **1152,** 2248–2249
Schermerhorn, Charles M., 1761
Scherr, WV
Greenland Church of the Brethren, 571
Scheublein, Barbara Spiteller
immigrant, 1736, 1178
Scheublein, Catherine (later Zook), 1178
Scheublein, Christian

Montgomery Co., OH, Bear Creek congregation, 1178
Scheublein, Christian (immigrant, 1736), son of, 1178
Scheublein, Christian (immigrant, 1736)
Shively family as descendants, 1178
Scheublein, Elizabeth, 1178
Scheublein, Esther Neff, 1178
Scheublein family
Shively family, related to, 1178
Scheublein, Isaac
Montgomery Co., OH, Bear Creek congregation, 1178
Scheublein, Jacob
Stark Co., OH, 1178
Scheublein, Uhli, 1178
Scheuner, Gottlieb, 2057
Scheytt, W. O., 307
Schick, Martha Flory, 278
Schick, Urias (Uriah), 1761
Schickle, Joseph, 1761
Schiefer, Thomas E., 2166, 2292
Schiet family, 148
Schifflet, Anne Frysinger
on PA German families, 2355
Schilbert (Schilpert), Peter, 267, 407
Schildknecht, C. E.
on MD history and genealogy, 2355
Schildt, Dwane E., 2292
Schildt, Elmer P., 1761
Rocky Ridge, MD, Monocacy Church of the Brethren, presiding elder, 1119
Schildt, Paul E., 2292
Schildt, Ralph E., 1761
Rocky Ridge, MD, Monocacy Church of the Brethren, 1119
Schillinger, Mary (later Swihart), 1245
Schilperoort, Bonnie Green, 1852–1853
Schilperoort, Richard, 1853
Schimmels, Ed
Simi Valley, CA, Grace Brethren Church, 1182
Schimmels, Eileen
Simi Valley, CA, Grace Brethren Church, 1182
Schimpf, Herbert, 1761
Schindler, Ethel (later Fast), 480
Schinz, Katharina (later Landes), 722
Schisler, Benjamin F., 715, 1761
schism(s), **1151–1153,** 1857, 1875, *See also* entries at division; polity
1848, and Brethren opposition to secret societies, 1164
acculturation issues, 298
Ashland Convention, 372
Brethren Church, 183, 366, 963, 2006
Brethren in Christ, 189
Brethren movement, 179, 355
The Brethren's Reasons, 696
Calvary Independent Church of the Brethren, PA, 240
celibacy, doctrine on, 175
charismatic figures and, 175, 177
colonization caused by, 238
consensus decision making, 337
Cowanshannock, PA, Brethren Church, 350
Crist family, 353
division between Church of the Brethren and Dunkard Brethren, 134
division of 1880s, 134

division of 1882–1883, and salary for ministers, 1136
division of Wagner family, 1312
doctrinal conflicts, 157, 175
Dunkard Brethren Church, 303
Dunkards, article about, 1918
evangelism, 298
First Church of the Brethren of Lewistown, PA, 240
fundamentalism, 303
Funk, Benjamin, 525
German Baptist Brethren, 1152–1153, 1995
German Baptist Brethren in Ohio, 349
Grace Brethren, 251, 366
higher education, 298
historical writing, 611, 613
Holsinger, H. R., and Annual Meeting of 1882, 368, 1151
Holsinger's History of the Tunkers and the Brethren Church, 623
Hostetler Brethren, 740, 829
incorporation, 649
jury service, 679
Kansas congregations affected by 1881 schisms, 682
Keithian Baptists (Christian Quakers), 1170
Kentucky, divisions in, 688–689
Lanham, MD, Grace Brethren Church, 725
lawsuits resulting from, 729
Lewistown, PA, Church of the Brethren, 739
Liberty German Baptisit Brethren Church, IN, 740
Maryland congregation founded after 1881–1883 schism, 1134
Mennonites, 816
Miami Valley Elders, 823
Milledgeville Church of the Brethren, IL, 833
missions, 298, 858, 861
Mooreites, 875
musical instruments as an issue, 900
naming of Brethren fellowships, 910
nonconformity, 941
Northwest district, 1319
Oak Grove, OH, congregation (OGBB), and membership reduction, 350
Ohio congregations, 961
Old Order Fellowships, 970–972
Old German Baptist Brethren Church separation in 1881, 2075
Pennsylvania Brethren, 1005
Peru, IN, First Brethren Church, 1010
Peters Creek Church of the Brethren, VA, 1011
Peters Creek Old German Baptist Brethren Church, VA, 1012
Pfoutz, Isaac, 1015
Philadelphia, PA, First Brethren Church, 1015
Philadelphia, PA, First Church of the Brethren, lack of effect on, 1016
Piney Creek Church of the Brethren, MD, 1025
plan of ministry, 845
Pleasant Grove Church of the Brethren, KS, 1031
Pleasant Valley Church of the Brethren, IN, 1034

Pleasant Valley Church of the Brethren, OH, 1035
preaching, and agreements about, 1053
Price, Isaac, 1056
Progressive Brethren church government, 1044–1045
Progressive movement, 348
protracted meetings, 1063
publications
    Brethren Church, 186
    Church of Brethren, 187
    German Baptist Brethren, 205–206
    Old German Baptist Brethren, 205–206
publishing, 1068
reasons for, 1210
Resolutions Passed at the Special Conference, 1100
Ryerson Station Church of the Brethren, PA, 1132
St. Luke, VA, Brethren Church and schism of 1881–1883, 1135
Shaver, Emanuel Bydler (GBB, BC) and, 2248
Shroyer, Reuben, and Dunkard Brethren, 1926, 1180
Silver Creek Church of the Brethren, OH, 1182
Skiles, Jacob W., 1188
Sunday school movement, 298
theological controversies, 1261
traditions, status of, 134
Universalism and, 231
Wayne Heights, PA, Brethren Church, 1323
Winger, Otho, 1351
youth programs, 285
Schlabach, Catherine Mast, 2057
Schlabach, Christian D., 2018
Schlabach, Daniel, 2057
Schlabach, Daniel and Sally Kaufman, 2013
Schlabach, Daniel D., 1898
Schlabach, Eli J., 2084
Schlabach, Elias, 2057
Schlabach family, 2084
Schlabach, Jacob Christian, 2057
Schlabach, John, 2057
Schlabach, John G., 2057
Schlabach, Magdalena Miller, 2084
Schlabach, Sarah (later Miller), 2018
Schlabach, Theron F.
    on Mennonites, 2355
Schlabach, Wilma Helmuth, 2057
Schlaback family, 2068
Schlabaugh, Catharine (later Gingerich) descendants, 1946
Schlabaugh, Mahlon Christian, 2057
Schlabaugh, Samuel John, 2057
Schlatter, Michael, 1153, 2058
    Charity Schools and Sauer's opposition to, 1957
    Charity School proposal, 1148
Schlauch (Slough), Catherine (later Pfautz), 1013
Schlechter, Edward W., 2057
Schlechter, Walter, 1761
Schlegel, John M., 1761
Schleiermacher, Friedrich
    Modernism, 866
    Pietist background, 1022
Schleifer, John, Jr., 1761
    Pleasant View Church of the Brethren, MD, minister, 1037

Schleitheim Confession (1527), 29, 816
    Mennonites, 816
Schleitheim, Germany, 29
Schlichtig, Ralph, 1761
Schlingluff, Heinrich
    Germantown, PA, congregation, deacon, 1153
Schload, Jess L., 2292
Schlosser, Emma J. (later Sabin), 2053
Schlosser, Emma Wiest, 1152
Schlosser, Eva Margaret Karrer, See Schlosser family
Schlosser family, 2053
Schlosser, Hannah (later Sauer), See Sauer, Hannah Schlosser
Schlosser, Jacob, See Schlosser family
Schlosser, John W., 1152, 1761
    Mohler Church of the Brethren, PA, free minister, 868
Schlosser, Manfred, 2057
Schlosser, Ralph Wiest, 1153, 1761, 2042, 2057
    Elizabethtown College, 437
Schlothaur, Elizabeth Petry, 1013
Schlothaur, Michael, 1013
Schlotman, Samuel, 1761
Schlotter family, 715
Schlotterer, Warren K., 2057
Schmalkaldic Wars, Germany, 990
Schmauk, Theodore E., 2057
Schmick, John Jacob (Brother), 2106
Schmidt, August, 2057
Schmidt, Charles C., 1761
Schmidt, Hubert G., 2057
Schmidt, John G., 1761
Schmidt, John Henry, 1761
Schmidt, Jonathan D., 1761
    Newton, KS, Church of the Brethren, pastor in, 934
Schmidt, Martin, 2057
    Pietism subdivisions, 1021
Schmidt, Michael and Margaret, 1973
Schmiedt, Lester Alan, 1761
Schmitt, Jakob, 2057
Schmitt, Martin E., 2057
Schmoe, Floyd
    on peace churches and relocation of Japanese, 2355
Schmoller, G., 2057
Schmoyer, Melville B., 2057
Schmucker, Alvin (Oscar), 1761
Schmucker, Christian, 1761
Schmucker, Isaac, 1761
Schmucker, Joseph
    Mansfield, OH, Walcrest Brethren Church, 787
Schmucker, Lydia, 2078
Schmucker, Mrs. Joseph
    Mansfield, OH, Walcrest Brethren Church, 787
Schmucker, Samuel M., 2057
Schnaithman, Paul, 1761
Schnebele family, 2070, See also Snavely (Snively) family
Schnebeli, Johann Jakob, 2070
    Lancaster Co., PA, 1193
Schnebli, John Ulrich, See Snavely family
Schneder family, 2057
Schneeberger, Andreas, 2058
Schneeberger, Barbara, 2058
Schneeberger, Catherine, 1195
Schneeberger family, 1153–1154, 1195, See also Snowberger family

Schneeberger, Johannes (Hans), 1153, 1195
Schneider, Bernard N., 16, 137, 155, 349, 503, 725, **1154**, 1761, 2305
    Mansfield, OH, Conservative Grace Brethren Church, 2217
Schneider, Catharine Haus, 2070
Schneider, Christian, 1154, 2070
Schneider, Christy
    Cincinnati Grace Brethren Church, Sharonville, OH, 1174
Schneider, Elsa Klein, 1154
Schneider family, **1154**, 2058, 2070, 2105
    bibliography, 1865
    Royer family, related to, 1128
Schneider, Frances Rose, 1855
Schneider, Hannes, 2070
Schneider, Hans, 2058
    on Beissel, Georg Conrad, 2355
    historiography
        Radical Pietism, 2201
    on Mack, Alexander and baptism, 2355
    on Radical Pietists, 2355
    on water baptism, 2355
Schneider, Jacob, 1154, 2058
Schneider, Jakob, wife of, 1360
Schneider, Johannes, 2058
Schneider, Madgalena, 1154, 2058
Schneider, Mary, 503
Schneider, Rick
    Cincinnati Grace Brethren Church, Sharonville, OH, 1174
Schneider, Robert Isaac, 1891
Schneider (Snider), Hans Adam, 262
Schneider (Snider, Snyder) family, 1154, *1154*
Schneider, Susanna, 1154
Schneider, Ulf-Michael
    on Community of True Inspiration, 2355
Schneiders, Francis A., II, 2292
Schnieders, Richard G., 2292
Schnurr, Mrs. W. L., 1761
Schock family, 1936
Schock, Grace
    on Shock, Bessie, 2361
    on Shock, Elmer, 2361
Schock, Joseph H., 1936
Schock, Mary (later Flory), 499
Schoeff, George
    Roanoke, IN, Brethren Church, 1112
Schoen, Th., 2058
Schoeneck, PA, congregation, 322
Schoff, Kit, 2058
Schofield, Elijah, 1761
    Olivet Church of the Brethren, OH, 973
    Ridge Church of the Brethren, OH, minister, 1108
scholarship
    sources on, 2313
scholarship funds
    Maryland students and, 153
Scholarships
    from National Laymen's Organization, 917
Scholl, A. G., 2058
Scholl, Anna Susanna Dorothea, *See* Scholl family
Scholl, Emory F., 2292
Scholl family, 2058, *See also* Schull family
    bibliography, 1885
Scholl, Frederick, 1156, 1942
Scholl, John Peter, *See* Scholl family

Scholl, John William, 2058
Scholl, Jonas Edgar, 2058
Scholl, Peter
    Macoupin Co., IL, 1156
Scholl, Philip, *See* Scholl family
Scholl, Saloma Kabel
    Bermudian, PA, congregation, 1156
Scholl (Shull) family, 2065
Scholten, Marian Aetna Rinehart, **1154–1155**, 1761
    Pottstown, PA, Coventry Church of the Brethren, preacher, 1049
Scholten, Martin, 760, 1155, 1761
Scholtz family, 2058
Scholtze, Christoph, 2058
Schomer, Howard, 638
Spain, mission to, 1207
Schönes Lied, Ein (Johann Valentin Mack), **1155**
Schoofs, Connie
    Cincinnati Grace Brethren Church, Sharonville, OH, 1174
Schoofs, Tom
    Cincinnati Grace Brethren Church, Sharonville, OH, 1174
The School and Home
    Mount Morris, IL, **1155**
school bus, horse-drawn, *1163*
School of Practical Arts (Anklesvar, India)
    mission schools, 853
School of Theology, Juniata College, **1155**
    fundamentalism, 522
    Juniata College, and conservative theology, 1005
    School Visiting Committee
        General Education Board (CB), 537
    school visiting committees, 428, **1155**
Schooley, Edgar Ellsworth, 1761
Schooley's Station, 313
Schoolfield Church of the Brethren, VA, 363, *See also* Danville, VA, First Church of the Brethren
Schoolhouse No. 7, *180*
schoolhouses
    Acme schoolhouse, North Manchester, IN, 1334
    Allegheny Church of the Brethren, WV, 2125
    Allison Prairie Church of the Brethren, IL, 2126
    Black Valley Federated Church of the Brethren and Christian Church, PA, 145
    Brake, WV, 171
    meetinghouses, use as, 152, 811
    Burnett schoolhouse, White Rock Church of the Brethren, VA, 1341
    Enterprise schoolhouse, Whitestone Church of the Brethren, WA, 1342
    Flat Rock congregation, VA, 1313
    Greenville Creek congregation, OH, 1288
    Hillcrest schoolhouse, NE, 1349
    Kidder Church of the Brethren, MO, 692
    Knobsville, PA, Church of the Brethren, 704
    La Motte Prairie Federated Church of the Brethren, IL, 713
    Labette Church of the Brethren, KS, 716
    Lakeland, FL, Grace Brethren Church,

720
    Lansing, MI, Grace Brethren Church, 725
    Larned Brethren Church, KS, 726
    Laurel Glen Brethren Church, WV, 728
    Lawrence, KS, Church of the Brethren, 730
    Leetown, WV, Church of the Brethren, 735
    Lewistown, PA, Church of the Brethren, 739
    Liberty Brethren Church, VA, 740
    Liberty Church of the Brethren, TN, 740
    Liberty Mills, IN, Church of the Brethren, 740
    Libertyville Church of the Brethren, IA, 740
    Limestone Church of the Brethren, TN, 742
    Little Pine Church of the Brethren, NC, 749
    Little Traverse Church of the Brethren, MI, 750
    Locust Grove Church of the Brethren, PA, 752
    Lone Star Church of the Brethren, KS, 753
    Long Lake Church of the Brethren, MI, 756
    Longmeadow Church of the Brethren, MD, 756–757
    Loon Creek Church of the Brethren, IN, 757
    Loramie Church of the Brethren, OH, 757
    Louisville, OH, Brethren Bible Church, 760
    Lovewell, KS, White Rock Church of the Brethren, 765
    Lyndhurst, OH, Grace Brethren Church, 768
    Pioneer schoolhouse, NE, 1349
    Robinson Junior High School, Wichita, KS, 1343
    Spring Brook, ND, Ray Church of the Brethren, 1212–1213
    Spring Creek Old German Baptist Brethren Church, WY, 1213
    State Center Old German Baptist Brethren Church, IA, 1217–1218
    Stevens Hill Church of the Brethren, PA, 1222
    Stone Bridge Church of the Brethren, MD, 1224
    Stony Creek Church of the Brethren, OH, 1225
    Summit Church of the Brethren, VA, 1235
    Summit Mills Grace Brethren Church, PA, 1236
    Tear Coat Church of the Brethren, 1249
    Telford, PA, Penn Valley Grace Brethren Church, 1251
    Temple Hills, MD, Grace Brethren Church of Greater Washington, 1253
    Terra Alta, WV, Cooperative Brethren Church, 1254
    Thomas OK, Church of the Brethren, 1263
    Thornapple Church of the Brethren, MI, 1263

Three Springs Church of the Brethren, PA, 1263
Tiosa, IN, Brethren Church, 1265
Toledo, OH, Maumee Valley Grace Brethren Church, 1267
Trotwood, OH, Grace Brethren Church, 1276
Troy, OH, Church of the Brethren, 1277
Tucson, AZ, Northwest Brethren Chapel, 1278
Turkey Creek Church of the Brethren, OK, 1280
Turnmore Church of the Brethren, AR, 1281
Tuscarora Brethren Church, PA, 1281
Upper Deer CreekChurch of the Brethren, IN, 1294
Upper Twin Church of the Brethren, OH, 1295
Valley Church of the Brethren, VA, 1301
Verdigris Church of the Brethren, KS, 1304
Victor Church of the Brethren, KS, 1305
Wade Branch Church of the Brethren, KS, 1311
Wakeman's Grove Church of the Brethren, VA, 1313
Walnut Church of the Brethren, IN, 1315
Walton Church of the Brethren, KS, 1316
Washington Creek Church of the Brethren, KS, 1321
Washington, PA, Grace Brethren Church, 1320
Washita Church of the Brethren, OK, 1321
Waterloo, IA, Grace Brethren Church, 1322
Welty Church of the Brethren, MD, 1329
West Branch Church of the Brethren, IL, 1333
Wiley, CO, Church of the Brethren, 1345
Willow Grove schoolhouse, VA, 1314
Wolf Creek Church of the Brethren, KY, 1355
Wolf Creek Old German Baptist Brethren Church, OH, 1356
Wood Colony Old German Baptist Brethren Church, CA, 1363
Wood Grove Brethren-Christian Parish, MI, 1363
Worden Church of the Brethren, WI, 1365
Yakima, WA, Grace Brethren Church, 1383
Yellow Creek Church of the Brethren, IL, 1384
Yellow Creek Church of the Brethren, PA, 1384
Youngstown, OH, Woodworth Church of the Brethren, 1390–1391
Zion Church of the Brethren, MI, 1400
schooling, home, *See* home schooling
schools, *See* Christian education; education; elementary education; higher education; normal schools; secondary education; singing schools; Sunday schools; specific institutions; specific schools
Alexander Mack Schule, 1158
bibliography, 1906
Brethren children in parochial schools, 2145
Brethren Way of Christ, 2150
Dunkard Brethren Church, 2159, 2160, 2174–2175
meeting houses, used as, 683, 685, 687, 691
mission, *See* mission schools
mural paintings at Camp Mack portraying, 896
Nigeria, 2164, 2165
Old Brethren, 965
Osceola, IN, Grace Brethren Church, 984
prayer in, 1052
public schools, 2159, 2160
Quinter, James, supporting, 1077
Salem College, 1138
Simi Valley, CA, Grace Brethren Church, preschool and day school, 1182
statements of doctrine, 942
used as Sunday schools, 1134
Woodstock School, India, 1180
Schoop, John C., 2058
Schöpf, Johann David, 2058
Schottstadt, Bruno, 546
Schowalder, Christian
    Rockingham Co., VA, 1155
    Schowalters, possible ancestor of, 1155
Schowalder, Daniel
    Rockingham Co., VA, 1155
Schowalder, Jacob
    possible ancestor of Schowalters, 1155
Schowalder, Ulrich
    Fayette Co., PA, 1155
Schowalder, Valentine
    Rockingham Co., VA, 1155
Schowalter, A. R.
    Brethren minister, 1155
Schowalter, C. J.
    Progressive movement, 1155
Schowalter, Cecil O.
    Brethren minister, 1155
Schowalter family, **1155**, 2058
Schowalter, J. Henry, 1155
Schowalter, Jacob, 2058
Schowalter, Jacob M., 1155
Schowalter, John A., 1155
Schowalter, O[tto], 2058
Schowalter, Russell K.
    Brethren minister, 1155
Schowfield, Jesse
Sciota Church of the Brethen, OH, minister, 1160
Schrab, Lawrence, 1761
Schrader, Hans-Juergen, 2058
    Radical Pietist publishing, 2201, 2355
Schrader, Ken
    Ripon, CA, Grace Brethren Church, 1110
Schrag, Casper, 1155
Schrag, Christian, 1155
Schrag family, **1155–1156**
Schrag, Franie Good, 1155
Schrag, Martin H., 2059
Schrag, Mary Stuckey, 1155
Schrag (Schrock) family, 26
Schrag, Wilma Cathrine, 1844
Schrantz, Pearl (later Lindower), 743
Schrecongost, Magdalena (later Houser), 632
Schreiber, Anna
    death of, wife of Georg Schreiber, 1156
Schreiber, Georg, 1761
    Germantown, PA, congregation, minister, **1156**
Schreiber, Nathaniel, 1761
Schreiber, Robert A., 1761
Schreiber, V. Lester, 1761
    Mechanic Grove Church of the Brethren, PA, free minister, 806
Schreiner, Anna Margaretta (later Klöppinger), 701
Schreiner family, 749
Schriber, Andrew, 2065
Schriber family
    Scherffig family, related to, 1152
Schriesheim, Germany, 9, **1156**, *1156*
    Erb, Christian, 453
    Germany, 545
    historic sites, 609
    history, 611, 1989
    Hochmann von Hochenau, Ernst Christoph, 615
    inn at, belonging to Kling family, *702*
    Kling family inn, *702, 703*
    Mack, Alexander, Sr., 775
    Mack family, 778
    Mack, Johann Philipp, mayor, 778
    radical pietist dissension in, 990
Schrock, Alta Elizabeth, 2059
Schrock, Anna, 2072
Schrock, Anna Bontrager, 2059
Schrock, Anna J. Yoder, 2059
Schrock, Arlene, 654
Schrock, Barbara (later Brenneman), 2016
    Newton, KS, Church of the Brethren, pastor in, 934
Schrock, Carolyn Ann Pieratt, 1844
    Sudan (CB) and, 2253
Schrock, Catharine K. Miller, 1952
Schrock, Catherine, 2107
Schrock, Charles Irwin, *554*
Schrock, Christian, 1761
    Pleasant Valley, IN, congregation, elder, 1155
Schrock, Clarence E., 7, 345, 1761
Schrock, Claudia Marie Lambert, 1853
Schrock, David D., 1952
Schrock, Edith Gephart, 230, 1156
Schrock, Effie (later Hoff), 617
Schrock, Elias, 1761
Schrock, Elizabeth, 2095
Schrock, Emma Yutzy, 2059
Schrock, Eve (later Knepper), 703
Schrock family, 1243, 1881, 2042, 2059, *See also* Schrag family; Schrag (Schrock) family
    Fike family, 490
    Hancock, MN, Church of the Brethren, 582
Schrock, Fannie N. Miller, 2059
Schrock, George, 214, 1761
    Brothersvalley congregation, minister, 1155
Schrock, Gladden, 2059
Schrock, Harvey, 1761
Schrock, Henry, 2017
Schrock, Homer, 399
Schrock, Homer A., 1761
Schrock, J. Harvey, 230, 1156, 1761

Schrock, James Roger, 718, 738, 1844, 2292
  Sudan (CB) and, 2253
Schrock, Janet West
  on Brethren Volunteer Service, 2355
Schrock, John, 1956
Schrock, John C., 1761
  Middle Creek congregation, 1155
Schrock, John J., 2059
Schrock, Joseph D., 1871, 2059
Schrock, Karl, 1761
Schrock, Levi Joni, 2059
Schrock, Lloyd, 654
Schrock, Lois Evelyn Buikema, 1853
Schrock, Lydia (later Hartzler), 588
Schrock, Lydia Saylor, 1155
Schrock, Lynn, 53, 1761, 2139
Schrock, Lynn Daniel, 1853
  San Diego, CA, Grace Brethren
    Church, pastor, 1141
Schrock, Mabel Frederick, 1156
Schrock, Magdalena J. Johns, 2059
Schrock, Magdalena Miller, 2059
Schrock, Marguerite (later Burke), 230,
    306, 530, 726, 1835, 2372
Schrock, Mark Y., 717, 1156, 1761
Schrock, Martha A. H., 2059
Schrock, Martha Miller, 2059
Schrock, Menno Joseph, 2059
Schrock, Moses S., 1882
Schrock, Naomi (later Hartzler), 588
Schrock, Noah J., 2059
Schrock, Norman Edward, 114, 1761, 1853
Schrock, Peter, 2107
Schrock, Peter C., 2059
Schrock, Ralph L., 1761
Schrock, Rebecca Walker, 1155
Schrock, Sam Reuben, 2013, 2016, 2059
Schrock, Samuel J., 2013
  descendants of, 2016, 2059
Schrock, Sarah Hershberger, 2059
Schrock, Susan Horner, 1155
Schrock, Susannah Hostetter, 1155
Schrock, Tobias, 2059
Schrock, Vernon, 1761
Schrock, William G., 1761, 2059
  Brothersvalley congregation, minister,
    1155
Schroeder, Vella K., 2088
Schroyer, Adam, 1235, 1761
Schroyer, Chester F., 1761
Schroyer, Daniel, 1761
Schroyer, David, 1235
Schubert house
  Little Swatara Church of the Brethren,
    PA, 750
Schuder, Floyd A., 1761
Schue, Albert Clayton, 1761
Schuhle, William, 1945
Schul, Grace, 410
Schuler, Lydia (Allen), 671, 990
Schuler, Rodney, 2292
Schuler (Shuler), Moses, 1761
Schulkill Co., PA, 1274
Schull family, 1156
Schultz, Andreas
  Lampeter, Lancaster Co., PA, 1156
Schultz, Andrew, 1156
Schultz, Arthur, 1861
Schultz, Arthur L., 67
Schultz, B. F.
  Mathias, WV, Brethren Church, 803
Schultz, Benjamin, 1876

Schultz, Caspar, 1156
Schultz, Christoph, 2059
Schültz, Christoph, 149
Schultz, Clyde E., 1761
Schultz, David, 318
Schultz family, 1156–1157, 2059
Schultz, Gary L., 2292
Schultz, George, 2059
Schultz, Jacob S., 2059
Schultz, John
  Rotruck family, related by marriage,
    1124
Schultz, Joseph R., 67
Schultz, Joshua, 1761
  Maquoketa German Baptist Brethren,
    IA, elder, 791
Schultz, Margaretha Rotruck
  immigrant to America, 1124
Schultz, Martin
  Huntingdon Co., PA, 1156
Schultz, Melchior, See Schultz, Christoph
Schultz, Raymond
  Peoria IL, (First) Church of the
    Brethren, 1009
Schultz, Stephen, 2059
Schultz, Susanna, See Schultz, Christoph
Schultz, Thomas Arnold, 1761
Schultze, David, 2059
Schulz, Lorenz, 1761
Schumacher, Daniel
  Annual Meeting, 1827, held in home
    of, 1157
Schumacher family, 1157
  Osceola, IN, Grace Brethren Church,
    983
Schumacher, John, 325
Schumacher, John and Barbara Steiner
  family history, 1996
Schumacher, Lois Jane Ringler, 1853
Schumaker, John, 1761
Schumann-Heink, Ernestine
  Winona Lake Auditorium, IN, 1353
Schuricht, Hermann, 2059
Schuster, George, 186
Schuster, Jerome, 1380, 1761
Schutz, J. Raymond, 1761
Schutz, Jacob, 511
Schutze family
  Hatboro, PA, Suburban Grace Brethren
    Church, 588
Schuykill Church of the Brethren, PA, 1157
Schuyler German Baptist Brethren Church,
    MO, 1157
Schuylkill Co., PA, 737, 1929
Schuylkill River, 175
Schwab and related families, 1887
Schwab, Barbara
  Blocher family, 2371
Schwab, Matilda Wilhelmina (later
    Kennedy), 688, 1851
Schwalm, E. J.
  on conscientious objectors and World
    War I and II, 2355
Schwalm family, 1929
Schwalm, Florence Roselind Studebaker,
    1157
Schwalm, Harrison Monroe, 1157, 1761
Schwalm, Harvey W., 1761
Schwalm, Johannes, 2060
  Historical Association, 1979
Schwalm, Margaret Spohn, 1157
Schwalm, Vernon F., 96, 781, 786, 1157,
    1344, 1351, 1761, 2059

Schwartz (Black) family, 1299
Schwartz, Clara Evelyn, 1853
Schwartz, Edward S., 1761
Schwartz family
  Pleasant Hill Church of the Brethren,
    IA, 1032
Schwartz, Martha Marie Frady, 1853
Schwartz, Ralph Roy, 1761, 1853
Schwartz, T. D., 1761
Schwartz, Walter, 191, 1761
Schwarz, Hillel, 2060
Schwarze, Robert M., 2292
Schwarze, W. N., 2060
Schwarzenau, Germany, 5, 16, 17, 72, 82,
    640, 697, 1158–1159, 1159, 1228,
    1354–1355, 2001, 2012
  Alexander Mack Museum, 2130, 2143
  Alexander Mack school, 1283
  antinomianism communes and, 236
  article about, 1957
  baptism of women, 1360
  baptisms, 697
  Bolle, Simon, 157
  Bolle, Soren, 157
  Boni, Andreas, 159, 1246
  Brethren congregations as rural church-
    es, 1130
  Brethren, lineage of, 613
  Brethren prayer, 1051
  Christ's Assembly, 280, 375
  church membership, 813
  Community of True Inspiration, 132,
    330
  description of, 1926
  description of public worship, 1375
  documents, 716
  Eckerlin family, 421
  Elsoff, 443
  Erb, Christian, 453
  example of place name, 911
  Flora, Delbert Benjamin, 495
  Gantz (Gans), Georg Balthasar, 528
  Geistreiches Gesang-Buch (Spiritual
    Songbook), 534
  Germany, 545, 546
  Grebe, George, 239
  Grebe (Grebi), Georg, 569
  Gruber, Eberhard Ludwig, 575
  Gruber, Johann Adam, 575
  Henrich Albrecht, count of Sayn-
    Wittgenstein-Hohenstein, provid-
    ing refuge for Brethren in, 597,
    683
  Hesse, 602
  historic sites, 609
  historical writing, 611
  Hochmann von Hochenau, Ernst
    Christoph, 615
  Hoening, Johann Georg, 616
  Hüttental, 639
  International Fellowship of Grace
    Brethren Churches, 2208
  Kalcklöser, Johann Heinrich, 681
  Käsebier, Johann Georg, 684
  Kipping, Johanna and Johannes, 697
  Mack, Alexander, Jr., 774
  Mack, Alexander, Sr.,
    family, fleeing to, 776, 778
    freedom of religious expression,
      1156
  Marienborn, migration from, 683
  Miller, John William, 2224
  missions, 857, 862

musical instruments, 900
mutual aid, 902
Old German Bible, *139*
peace position, 998
publishing, 1063
records, early 1700's, 1959
Reformation, Protestant, and Brethren
    doctrine, 1092
Seebach, Christoph, 1165
simple life, 1182–1183
survey of groups and individuals, 1959
two-hundred-fiftieth anniversary cele-
    bration, 1274, *1282, 1283,* 1355
Vetter (Fetter), Lucas, 1304
work camp, 1365
Schwarzenau, 139, 190, 1158, 2060
historical societies, 610
historical writing, 612
Mallott, Floyd Ellwood, editor, 784
Schwarzenau Baptists, *See* names, Brethren
Schwarzenau Brethren, 5, 15, 82, 113, 120,
    193
aid from Collegiants, 923
Anabaptism, 292
bicentennial, 298
Brethren remnants in Europe, 1099
Camisards, 242
celibacy and, 266
Christliches Hand-Büchlein (Christian
    Handbook), and inspiration for,
    288
Christ's Assembly and, 280
Church of the Brethren, 305
community, 329
on education, and ministers, 293
founding of, 1079
Holiness Movement, American, 619
nonconformity, 940
Petersen, Barthold Jurgen, visiting,
    1012
places of worship, 48
Plymouth Brethren, 1039
Polish Brethren, 1041
poor, caring for the, 1046
prisons, 1058
sources on, 2312
Schwarzenau movement
Durnbaugh, Donald F. on Brethren
    bodies and, 2327
fraternal relations, 510
Schwarzenau Täufer ("[Ana]Baptists")
    names of Brethren fellowships, 910
Schwartz, Ralph
Santa Maria, CA, Grace Brethren
    Church, pastor, 1145
Schweinhart, Georg Michael, 1246
Schweinhart, Margaret, 1246
Schweinitz, Edmund A. De, 2060
Schweitzer, Albert, **1159**
eschatology, 454
Schweitzer, Barbara (later Urner), 1298
Schweitzer, Christoph E., 1970
Schweitzer, Matthew, 1761
Schweizer, Lorentz
Durnbaugh, Donald F. on, 2327
Schwenckfeld von Ossig, Caspar, 156
Schwenk, Charles A. (CB-1), 1762
Schwenk, Charles A. (CB-2), 1762
Schwenk family, 2077
Schwenk, Jacob, 533
Schwenk, Mary G., 533
Schwenk, Mary (later Geiger), 533, **533,**
    1361

Schwenkfelder Church, **1159–1160**
Historic Peace Churches, 608
Schwenkfelder Church, and *Fraktur* type,
    60
Schwenkfelder, 1887, 1991
dissertation on, 1918
Moravian Church, 875
naturalization and refusal of loyalty
    oath to state, 918
and non-associators in Revolutionary
    War, 939
Pennsylvania, in, 1990
Schwenkfelder Library, 2039
historical libraries, 610
science, **1160**
Brethren attitudes toward, article about,
    1924
creationism and, 2097
ethics and, 2178
Harnley, Henry Jacob, 585
Inglenook Nature Study Club (CB),
    656
*Science and Health with Key to the
    Scriptures* (Eddy), 287
Science Center
Grace Schools (Grace Theological
    Seminary, Grace College), 564
Science Hill Congregation
Alliance, OH, Church of the Brethren,
    2126
Freeburg Church of the Brethren, OH,
    514
scientists, Brethren children named for, 912
Sciota Church of the Brethen, OH, 374,
    1160
Scioto Valley, OH, 1327
Scioto Church of the Brethren, OH, **1160**
SCLC, Southern Christian Leadership
    Conference
Scobey, MT, 142
Scofield Reference Bible, 390, 486, **1160**
McClain, Alva J., 773
revision, 139
Scofield, Cyrus I., 390
Scofield, Edward B., 1762
Scofield, Edward G., 165
Scofield, Jesse, 1762
Scofield, Matthew, 2128
Scofield, Terry L., 2128
Scofield, Tim E., 2128
Scofield, William, 2128
Scoggs family
Riner Grace Brethren Church, VA,
    1110
Scoles, Todd Stephen, 2292
Scothorn family, 1927
Scotland
Kulp, Christina Masterton, 708
Reformation, Protestant, 1091
Scott, Clinton Lee, 2060
Scott Co., IL, 165
Scott Co., IN
genealogical records, 1911
Scott Co., KS
Prairie View Church of the Brethren,
    KS, members living in, 1050
Scott Co., KY, 689, 1243
Scott Co., VA, 727, 1349
Scott family
Jackson Co. German Baptist Brethren,
    IN, 667
Scott, James Earl, 204
Scott, Jesse, 204

Scott, Kenneth, 2060
Scott, Kerry
STAKE (BC) and, 2252
Scott, L. Kenneth, 2060
Scott, Robert, 1762
Scott, Stephen, 2060
on dress of conservative Brethren,
    2355
Scott Valley Church of the Brethren, KS,
    42, 1161
Mont Ida, KS, Church of the Brethren,
    870, **1160–1161**
Scott, Walter
Restoration Movement, 1101
Scott, Winfield, 912
Scottsdale, AZ
Tempe, AZ, Papago Park Brethren
    Church, 1251
Scottsdale Community Center, meeting-
    place for Papago Park Brethren
    Church, Tempe, AZ, 1251
Scottville, MI, 323
Scottville Old German Baptist Brethren
    Church, MI, near, **1161,** 1235
Michigan Brethren settlement, 824
scouting programs, **1161,** 190, *See also*
    camping programs
Boy Scouts, 190, 439
Dunkard Brethren peace position on,
    1001
Flower Hill Church of the Brethren,
    MD, 500
Hanawalt, David Kirk, 581
traditional opposition to, 1161
Windber, PA, Church of the Brethren,
    1348
Xenia, OH, Beavercreek Church of the
    Brethren, 1383
Scow, Oliver, 755
Scripture
Rechte und Ordungen, 1086
Swartley, Willard on Anabaptists and
    use of, 2360
Scripture Press (publisher), 1237
Scriptures, *See* Bible
Scriveners
Earnest, Corrine Pattie on, 2328
Earnest, Russell on, 2328
Scrogin, Michael C., 1218, 1762
Scrogum, Ada, 440, 1762
Scrogum, Arthur, 2, 1337, 1762
Pasadena, CA, Church of the Brethren,
    pastor in, 994
Scrogum, Ira D., 1762, 2060
Scrogum, John Jacob, 164, 440, 1762
Scuffletown schoolhouse, meetingplace for
    Upper Twin Church of the
    Brethren, OH, 1295
Scully, William
Hope Memorial Church (German
    Baptist Brethren), NE, 2375
Sculton Church of the Brethren, PA, *See*
    Fairview Church of the Brethren,
    PA
Sculton meetinghouse
Fairview Church of the Brethren, PA,
    469
SDS, *See* Student for Democratic Society
seagoing cowboys, 198, 199, 202, 312, 316,
    1161, *1161*
Heifers for Relief, 1331
Heifer Project International, 594
United Nations Relief and

Rehabilitation Administration (UNRRA), 1291

Seabourn, Alan
Sinking Spring, OH, Grace Brethren Church, pastor, 1186

Seabrooks, Agnes (later Roberts), 1114

Seachrist, Denise Ann
on baptism at Snow Hill Nunnery, 2355
on musical tradition at Snow Hill Nunnery, 2355
on Seventh Day Baptists, 2355
on Sisters of Saron, 2356
on Snow Hill Nunnery, 2355

Seadley, William H., 2060

Seal Beach, CA
Brethren Church, CA, 755
example of place name, 911
Grace Brethren Church, **1161**
Hawaii, 590

Sealed Book of Daniel Opened (Thurman, W. C.), 1264

Sealthiel, Brother, *See* Landert, Sigmund

Seaman family, 700

Seaman, Joann, 2137

Seaman, Lenny, 181

Sears, A. L., 1762

Sears family, 740, 1299, 1341
Nicholas Co. German Baptist Brethren Church, 935
Prosperity Brethren Church, WV, 1062

Sears, Mollie, 738

Sears, Oliver, 1762

Sears, S. F., 738

Sears, Stephen W., 2060

Seattle, WA, 350, 1227, 1247
Chinese Sunday Schools (CB), 278
Kent, WA, Grace Brethren Church, 688
Lakewood Community Church, **1161–1162**
minorities, ethnic and racial, 850
missions and missionaries in, 269
Northhaven Retirement Residence, 951
Olympic View Community Church of the Brethren, **1162**
urban mission, 1297

Seaver, Jesse Montgomery, 2060

Seawright, Sant W., 1762

Sebert, Dorotha Mae Karns, 1762

Sebert, Robert H., 1762

Sebring, FL, 496, 758
Church of the Brethren, 1399
Grace Brethren Church, **1162**
J. H. Moore Memorial Church of the Brethren, **1162**
migration of Brethren, 831
Okeechobee, FL, Grace Brethren Church, 963
The Palms retirement community, 991

Sebring, George
Sebring, FL, J. H. Moore Memorial Church of the Brethren, 1162

Secaur family
Ocala, FL, Grace Brethren Church, 2232

Secaur, Jeff, 439

secession
opposition to, **1162**

Second Brethren Church, CA, 362

Second Brethren Church, IN, *See* Fort Wayne, IN, Grace Brethren Church

Second Brethren Church, Philadelphia, PA, 259

Second Cedar Co. Church of the Brethren, MO, *See* Cedar Co. Church of the Brethren, MO

Second Church of the Brethren, Denver, CO
Rainey, Nellie Morgan, 1083
Rhodes, William, minister, 1107

Second Church of the Brethren, PA, 2072

Second Coming, 6, 695, *See also* eschatology/millennialism
Brethren doctrine of salvation, 1140
Fellowship of Grace Brethren Churches (FGBC), 486
God's Means of Grace (Yoder), 555
Hochmann von Hochenau, Ernst Christoph, 614
rapture, **1083**

Second German Baptists
Mooreites, 1142

Second Grace Brethren Church of Mansfield, OH
Mansfield, OH, Woodville Grace Brethren Church, previous name of, 787

Second Great Awakening
gospel songs, 560
"New Lights" revivalism, 930

Second Irricana Church of the Brethren, Alberta, Canada, 15, 59, *See also* Irricana, Alberta, Canada, Second Irricana Church of the Brethren

Second Reformation, 2349

Second Vatican Council, 422–423

second work of grace, Keswick movement
avoiding doctrine of, 691

secondary education, 2, **1162–1163**, *See also* education, secondary
education, 426
Holsinger, Henry Ritz, 621
Jacob Miller's Select School, 1165
McPherson College offering, 781
Mennonite Church (MC), 815
Miami Valley Petition, 823
New Vienna Academy, OH, 932
Old German Baptist Brethren, 969
Osceola, IN, Grace Brethren Church, 984
Pennsylvania, 1004–1005
schism, 1152

Secor family
Osceola, IN, Grace Brethren Church, 983

The Secret of Married Love (Mow), 890

secret societies, 2020, 2048
Church of God (New Dunkers), 297
Declaration of Principles, 372
Dunkard Brethren, 408, 409, 941, 2173
Evangelical Association, 459
Eyman, Peter, 464
Freemasonry, 514
God's Means of Grace (Yoder), 555
Holsinger, Henry Ritz, 622
Know-Nothing party, 704
oaths, taking of, 959
Odd Fellows, 1135
opposition to, **1163–1164**
United Brethren in Christ, 1290

Secrist, Caleb, 417, 1762

Secrist, Cora Lee (later Lynn), 768

Secrist, David, 1762

Secrist, Isaac, 1762

Secrist, Jacob S., 717, 2061, 2385
millennialism, 834

Oak Grove Church of the Brethren, IA, elder, 955
Portland, OR, Peace Church of the Brethren, 1048

Secrist, Nancy (later Yoder), 1385, 1386

sect-church typology, 1164–1165, **1164–1165,**
ethical characteristics, 1996
plain people, 1029
sociological studies of Brethren, 1200

sectarianism, 2053, 2058
book about, 1937
Ephrata Community, 451
Geistliche Fama (Spritiual Report), 533
German Sectarians of Pennsylvania, The, 542
Germantown Academy, 544
Great Awakening, 568
Gruber, Eberhard Ludwig, 575
Herring, Friedrich, 598
Historic Peace Churches, 608
historical writing, 611
Hochmann von Hochenau, Ernst Christoph, 615
Mack, Alexander, Sr., and New Baptists of Schwarzenau, 776
musical instruments, 900
nonconformity, 940
Old Order Movement, 972

sects, 5
Albigenses, **15**
becoming churches, 1987
Eby, Kermit, 420
psychology of, 2002
Radical German Pietism, 1079

secular humanism
Old German Baptist Brethren, 2233, 2234

sedition
Goshen Conference, 559, 1165
social action, 1196

See, E. A., 1762

"See Him in the Garden Lone"
hymns, 643

See, S. W., 1762

Seebach, Christoph, 120, **1165,** 2061, 2086
Basic Questions (Grundforschende Fragen), 2374

Seebass, Ruth (later Aukerman), 2133

The Seed Packet, 2165

Seeger case, US Supreme Court, 917

Seehorn, J. E., 1762

"seeker" congregations, 2131

seekers service structure
worship and, 2266

Seelig, Johann G.
Society of the Woman in the Wilderness, 1200

Seeme Brook
historic sites, 609

Seems family, 743

Sees, N. A., 244

Seese, Anna Bowman, 1844, 1884

Seese, Dorsey G., 1762

Seese, Florence, 25

Seese, Frederick Henry, 1762

Seese, Herald Victor, 1762, 2305

Seese, Leland D., 2180, 2292

Seese, Mary Ann (later Statler), 1219

Seese, Nelson M., 2356

Seese, Norman Alexander, 679, 1762, 1844, 2027

Mount Zion Church of the Brethren, WV, 888
Seese, Susanna (later Thomas), 1263
Seiber, Nettie (later Kinsey), 696
Seiber, Solomon, 1762
Seibert, Floyd, 12
Seibert, John C., 251, 1217, 1762
　Oak Grove Church of the Brethren, IA, elder and district meeting delegate, 955
Seibert, John, 1217
Seibert, O. E., 1762
Seibert, W. A., 1762
Seidensticker, Oswald, 140, 259, 379, **1165,** 1861, 1927, 2041, 2061
　historical writing, 611
Seider, Jacob, 1762
Seidler, Carl, 683, 1762
Seifert, David, 1380, 1762
　Modesto, CA, Big Valley Grace Community Church (FGBC), pastor, 866
Seifert, Wilbur H., 2088
Seiler, Daniel, 1165, 1763
Seiler, Kenneth, 1278
Seiler, Sarah Anna Buechley, 1165
Seilhamer, Chester Whitmore
　on Seilhamer, Marsilla Elizabeth Pohl, 2356
　on Seilhamer, Nicholas Johann, 2356
Seilhamer, Larry, 2061
　on Nead, Peter, 2356
Seilhamer, Marsilla Elizabeth Pohl
　Seilhamer, Chester Whitmore on, 2356
Seilhamer, Nicholas Johann
　Seilhamer, Chester Whitmore on, 2356
Seilor, Mary (later Naff), 910
Seitz, May Albright, 2061
Seitz, Rosa Brown, 2061
Selby, Curtis
　Sierra Pines Old German Baptist Brethren Church, CA, minister, 1181
Selby, Curtis E., 1763
Selby, Lloyd
　Sierra Pines Old German Baptist Brethren Church, CA, 1181
Selby, Paul, 1870
Select School, Jacob Miller's, 1165
A Selection of Hymns
　hymnals, 642
Selective Service System, 20, 316, 1165
　detached programs, 380
　Emergency Farm Labor, 443
　Hershey, Lewis Blaine, 599
　Kosch, Lewis F., 707
Selective Training and Service Act (1940), 19, 917, 1370, 1371
Self, Charles Victor, 1763
Self, Don Stuart, 2292
self-esteem
　membership trends 1980 to 2000, 2220
self examination
　preparatory service for communion, 1056
Self-Help Well-Digging Project, Nigeria
　Shankster, Owen L., Jr., (CB) and, 2248
Selisia, 156
Sell, Abraham
　Plattsburg Church of the Brethren, MO, 1030
Sell, Ada, *See* Plattsburg, MO, Church of the Brethren

Sell, Albert K., 1763
Sell, Alice Dorothy Lehman, 1763
Sell, Anna (later Gish), 550
Sell, Arthur
　Old Order German Baptist Church minister, 972
Sell, Arthur K., 1763
Sell, Brice, 1763
Sell, Byron, 628, 1763
Sell, Cecil L., 1763
Sell, Daniel
　father of Daniel and James Sell, 1165
Sell, Daniel D., 1763
　Plattsburg Church of the Brethren, MO, free minister, 1030
Sell, Daniel, elder, 1165
Sell, David B., 732
Sell, David D. (CB-1), 1763
Sell, David D. (CB-2), 1763
Sell, David Elmer, 1763, 2061
Sell, Donna-Christine, 1861
Sell, Esther B. Stiffler, 1165
Sell family, 1878, 2061, 2099
　Gentry German Baptist Brethren Church, MO, 540
Sell, Felix, 2099
Sell, J. S., 1763
Sell, James A., 256, 407, 619, **1165–1166,** *1166,* 1213, 1283, 1294, 1763, 2061, *See also* Royer, Galen B.
　article about, 1930
　Queen, PA, Church of the Brethren, 1075
　Roaring Spring, PA, First Church of the Brethren, moderator, 1114
Sell, Jeanne Lyle
　on Miller family, 2356
Sell, Joseph B., 1763
Sell, Leah Hendricks, 1165
Sell, Leroy, 1763
Sell, Matthew W., 619
Sell, Rachel Detwiler, 1165
Sell, Ruth, 432, 1763
Sell, W. C.
　Rockton, PA, Church of the Brethren, pastor, 1118
Sell, Walter Cecil, 1763, 2061
Sell, William B., 20, 513, 540, 755, 1280, 1342, 1763
Sell, William K., 1763
Sellen, Elizabeth (later Hart), 587
Seller family, 2061–2062
Seller, John, 2062
Sellers, Ancil
　Sidney, IN, Grace Brethren Church, 1181
Sellers, Arthur Lee, 1763, 2062
Sellers, David, 2062
Sellers, David Randolph, 2062
Sellers, David Wampole, *See* Sellers family
Sellers, E. G., 1763
Sellers, Edwin Jacquett, 2062
Sellers, Esther Bair (later Bittinger), 143–144
Sellers family, 2062
　Filbrun family, 490
Sellers Family Association, 2062
Sellers, George W., 1763
Sellers, Harry Edward, 1763
Sellers, Hattie W. (later Frantz), 508
　Frantz, Ruby June (later Rhoades) and, 2242
Sellers, James C., 1763

Sellers, Jennie A. (later Heckman), 592
Sellers, Jesse, 424
Sellers, John W., 476
Sellers, John William, 476, 1763
Sellers, Lela F. (later Moyer), 1842, 2025
　Moyer, Elgin Sylvester, wife of, 892
Sellers, Mary (later Jones), *See* Jones family
Sellers, Mary Pennock, 2062
Sellers, Nada B., 2292
Sellers, Noah S., 145, 1763
Sellers, Philip Henry, *See* Sellers family
Sellers, Richard D., 145, 239, 319, 377, 705, 725, 1319, 1763
Sellers, Samuel, 2062
Sellers, Sarah Pennock, 2062
Selma, AL
　Brethren participants in Martin Luther King, Jr., campaign, 695
　Smeltzer, Ralph Emerson, 1190, 1191
Selma mission point, IA, 740
Selma, VA, Church of the Brethren, 350, **1166**
Selmanson family
　Riverside, CA, Grace Community Church (FGBC) and, 2244
Selmanson, Karen
　Riverside, CA, Grace Brethren Church, 1111
Selmanson, Marvin
　Riverside, CA, Grace Brethren Church, 1111
Selvidge, Sarah, 338
seminarians, self-perceptions of, 2096
seminaries
　Kult, G. D. on merger of, 2342
　marriage counseling, 796
　ministers, and salary, 1136–1137
Semmelroth, Bonnie
　Medina, OH, Shepherd's Grace Church, 2219, 2220
Semmelroth, John
　Medina, OH, Shepherd's Grace Church, 2219, 2220
Semones, James A., 1763
Seneca Church of the Brethren, FL, **1166**
Seneca Church of the Brethren, OH, **1166, 2378, 2380**
Seneca Church of the Brethren, WV, **1166**
　Flintstone, MD, Glendale Church of the Brethren, 494
Seneca Co., OH
　Dunkard Brethren Church, 2086
　Fostoria, OH, Church of the Brethren, 505
　Mennonite Church, 2086
　Pleasant Center Church of the Brethren, OH, 1030
　Rome Old German Baptist Brethren Church, OH, 1121
　Scipio Church of the Brethren, OH, 1160
　Seneca Church of the Brethren, OH, 1166
Seneca Indian reservation
　Community of True Inspiration, meetings in, 330
Sener, S. M., 2062
Senften, Lester, 1763
Senger, Anthony, 1763
Senger, Daniel, 406
Senger, David B., 1763
Senger, D[avid] B., 2062

Senger family, *See* Sanger family
  North English, IA, Church of the
    Brethren, 947
Senger, Felix
  Maquoketa German Baptist Brethren,
    IA, minister, 791
Senger, I. C., 1763
Senger, Isaac E., 1763
Senger, Johanna Schaefferin, 2062
Senger, Michael, 2062
Senger, Nellie M., *See* Miller, Michael, II
Senger, Nettie Mabelle, 127, 277, 503,
    1763, 1844, 1864, 2062, 2077
  article about, 1960
  Sanger, Conrad, descendant of, and
    missionary, 1144
Senger, Paul D., 272
Senger, Rachel (later Bowen), *See* Sanger
    family
Senger, Ray W.
Sanger, Conrad, descendant of, 1144
Senger, Samuel J., 1763
senior citizens, ministry to
  Elizabethtown, PA, Church of the
    Brethren, 436
senior ministry
  Pifer, Lester Elden and, 2238
  Ramsey, Duane H. and, 2239
Senior, Randolph V., 1763
Sensemann, Mary Ann (later Pittenger),
    1026
Sensenbaugh, Charles Russel, 1763
Senseney, A. H.
  Pipe Creek Church of the Brethren,
    MD, minister, 1026
Senseney, A. Hanson, 106
Senseney, Ezra M., 106, 1763
Senseney (Senseny), A. Hanson, 1763
Sensenig, E. Elmer, 2062
Sensenig, Elta (later Miller)
  Miller, Orie O., wife of, 841
Seoul, Korea
  Korean Mission, 2211
Separate Baptists, 87
  Catawba, NC, German Baptist Brethren
    Church, membership with, 262
separation (marital)
  allowance of, 795
  Old German Baptist Brethren and non-
    conformity, 941
separation meeting, 406
separation of church and state, *See* church
    and state
separation of Old German Baptist Brethren,
    from the world, 969
Separatism, 15, 28–29, 87, 120, 407, 2037
  antinomianism communes and, 236
  Bohni family, 2083
  Brethren and, 1166–1167
  Christmas, celebration of, 288
  Church of the Brethren, 2094
  Congregation of God in the Spirit, 334
    conventicles, 1989
  Diehl, Johann Georg, 383
  Diehl, Nicolaus, 383
  Edict of 1712, 425
  Elsoff, 443
  Ephrata Community, 451
  Ephratism and Shakerism, 1983
  Established Churches, 456
  established churches, and nonconformi-
    ty, 940
  flags, 492

Frey, Andreas, 517
Gass (Gast), Jakob, 532
Geringer Schein, Ein (*A Humble
  Gleam*), 540
Germany, 545
Gross, Andreas, 574
Grundforschende Fragen (*Basic
  Questions*), 575
Haller, Friedrich Conrad, 580
Henning, 1989
historical writing, 611
Hochmann von Hochenau, Ernst
  Christoph, 614
honorific titles and, 1266
Mack, Alexander, Sr., 775
Marienborn, and religious freedom,
  792
Marsay, Charles Hector de St. Georges,
Marquis de, 796
  migration of, 147
  missions, 857, 860
  Moravian Church, 875
  Muhlenberg, Henry Melchior, 892
  Neumann, Gottfried, 924
  oaths, taking of, 959
  Raabe, Paul on, 2351
  Radical Pietist movement, 1079, 1222
  refuge for, and Schwarzenau, 1158
  Wittgenstein territory, 1354–1355
September 11, 2001 attacks
  Disaster Child Care, *2171*
  Kraybill, Donald B. on, 2342
  Peachey, Linda Gehman on, 2342
Septuagint, 43
Serampore University Licentiate in
    Theology standard
  Gujarat United School of Theology
    (GUST), 576
Sergeantsville, NJ, Brethren Church, 769,
    1167, 1220, 1347
Sergon, Stephen, 1763
Seriff, Edith (later Bieber), 2137
Sermon on the Mount, **1169**, 2017
  bibliography and history of interpreta-
    tion, 1986
  Brethren Church ethics, 183
  ethics, 457
  Hutterian Society of Brothers, 639
  lessons from, 2010, 2011
  Metzler, Burton, writing study of, 820
  ministry according to, 845
  peace, 998
  theology and, 2255
sermons, *1167*, 1167–1169, *1168*, 2020,
    2048, *See also* preaching
  Columbia, MD, Oakland Mills Uniting
    Church (CB, UCC) and, 326
  eternal themes, 2007
  extemporaneous, 1137
  Fahnestock, Adam G., 465
  Fike, Samuel A., 490
  first, 160, 162
  frontier lifestyles, 283
  funerals, 524
  Hertzler, Samuel Hoffer, 600
  Hoff, Emanuel Buechley, 617
  Sherrick, Marvin M., 2064
  Virginia Council of Churches, and CB
    pastors' sermons, 2361
  worship and, 2266
Serrano, Mario Edwardo E., 2292
  Hispanic Ministries (CB), 2199
Serrano, Olga

Hispanic Ministries (CB), 2199
  on Puerto Rico, Brethren of, 2356
  Rio Prieto, PR, Iglesia de los
    Hermanos (CB) and, 2243–2244
SERRV International (Sales Exchange
    for Refugee Rehabilitation
    Vocations), 197, 198, 1139, 2163,
    2247, *2247*
  General Offices (CB), 539
  Kyle, W. Ray, 712
  Maryland Brethren activity, 799
  organizational restructuring and, 2242
  relief and service efforts, 1097
  relief and social work, 303
San Marcos, CA, North Country Church of
    the Brethren and, 2245
servanthood, *See* discipleship
Servia, 23
service, *See* entries at Brethren service;
    relief
Service Civil Volontaire International, 1367
Service Committee (OGBB), **1169**
  peace education, 1002
  Skiles, Jacob W., 1189
service, doctrine of
  Austria, 2100
  Brethren Service Committee, 2086
  Church of the Brethren, 2086
  Mennonite Church, 2086
  volunteers, training of, 2070
service programs and projects, *See* specific
    groups
  ordination, 980
  Pleasant Valley Church of the Brethren,
    VA, 1035
  Sojourners Fellowship, 1200
  Springfield, OH, First Church of the
    Brethren, 1215
services, *See* entries at worship
Serving My Master
  formerly Sisterhood of Mary and
    Martha, **1169**
  GBC Christian Education (Depart-
    ment), 533
  missions education, 864
Sessler, Jacob John, 2062
Setinsek family
  Harrisburg, PA, Melrose Gardens
    Grace Brethren Church, 586
settlement and settlers, *See* frontier; migra-
    tion; pioneers
Setty, Christina, 347
Setty family, 1227
Setty, Sanford, 1763
Seven Falls, CO, *1271*
Seven Fountains, VA, Trinity Brethren
    Church, **1169**
Seven Years' War, *See* French and Indian
    War
Seventeen (Long), 748
seventeenth century
  Alsace, France, 19, 25
  Ammann group (Amish), 25
  "Angel Brethren" (*Engel-Brüder*), 30
  Swiss Brethren, 25
Seventh-Day Adventists, **1169–1170**, 2068
  building used by Temple Hills, MD,
    Grace Brethren Church of Great
    Washington, 1253
  Church buildings used as meeting
    houses, 683
  debates, 371
  Flower Hill Church of the Brethren,

MD, 500
millennialism, 834
Stein, John William, settled with, 1220
wellness and, 2261
Worthington, OH, Columbus Grace
Brethren Church, 1380
Seventh-Day Baptists, 87, 210, **1170**, 2047,
See also Milner, Vincent L.; Potter,
John E.
bibliography, 1867
books about, 747
English, *See* English Seventh-Day
Baptists
Ephrata Community, 2041
letter to, about Ephrata, 1989
Fahnestock, William M., 465
fellowship naming to distinguish from,
910
German Baptist Church, *See* German
Seventh-Day Baptists
German Seventh-Day Baptists, 542
Library (Plainfield, NJ), 52
love feasts, 321
*Materials Towards a History of the
Baptists,* 803
in Pennsylvania, 2077
Plainfield, NJ, headquarters, 1133
Rhode Island, in and Brethren visiting,
1107
Sanford, Don A. on, 2354
Saturday Sabbath observance, 1133
Seachrist, Denise Ann on, 2355
Snow Hill (Nunnery), 1911, 2062
Wohlfahrt (Welfare), Michael, 1355
Seventh-Day Dunkers, 210
Seventh-Day German Baptist Church, *See*
German Seventh-Day Baptists
Seventh-Dayers
Ephrata Community, 1133
fellowship naming to distinguish from,
910
Severn, Pearl E. Peterson, 1763
Sevits, William, 214, 1763
revival meetings, 1103–1104
Seward, Stafford Co., KS
Moorehead, Michael, minister, 997
Sewart, Susan, 2074
Sewell, Alice Powell (CB)
Sewell, Laura A. (CB) and, 2247
Sewell, Charles H. (CB)
Sewell, Laura A. (CB) and, 2247
Sewell, Laura, 1346, 1844, **2247, 2388**
Sexton family
New Haven Church of the Brethren,
NC, 928
Sexton, John R.
New Haven Church of the Brethren,
NC, elder in, 928
sexuality, **1170,** *See also* celibacy; conti-
nence; fornication; homosexuality
in Boehmist thought, 113
Egge, Doris Cline on, 2329
Grassroots, Concerns of the, 2193
homosexuality, 2203–2204
marriage and, 266, 794, 795, 1170
Miller, Donald Eugene, 2223
theology and, 2255
Seyfert, Kenneth A.
Grace Brethren Investment Foundation,
2191
Seyler, Daniel, 106
Seymour, IN
New Hope Church of the Brethren, 929

Seymour, Israel, 210, 516
Seymour, J. L.
Miller, Donald Eugene, 2223
Shackleton, Donald, 1763
Hochstetler (Hostetler) family, 615
Shade Creek Church of the Brethren, PA,
119, 149, 150, **1170**, 1348, 2062
Shade, George Russell, 65, 1763–1764
Shade, Ralph, 1764
Shady Grove Old German Baptist Brethren
Church (formerly Union City),
Darke Co., OH, **1170–1171**
Shaeffer, John F., 1764
Shaeffer, Leah, 1838
Shafa
Utz, Ruth Earl, 1299
Shafa, Nigeria, 306
Shafer family, 2083
Shafer, Gertrude I. Poncebaker, 2038
Shafer, Joseph, *See* Schäfer, Joseph, **2378**
Shafer, Joseph J.
Shade Creek Church of the Brethren,
PA, pastor, 1170
Shafer, LeRoy W., 399, 443, 1764
Muskegon, MI, Church of the
Brethren, elder and pastor, 901
Shafer, Rose Armina (later Kreider), 707
Shafer, T. (L.) W., 1764
Shaffer, Andrew, 2062
Shaffer, Bradford
Mount Zion Church of the Brethren,
WV, 888
Shaffer, Charles K., 1764
Shaffer, D. David, 1764
Shaffer, D. J., 1764
Shaffer, Daniel D., 1764
Shaffer, Daniel E., 1764
Shaffer, Dean E., 2292
Shaffer, Dewey, 1764
Shaffer, Dorothy Lee (later Franks), *See*
Franks, Dorothy Lee Shaffer
Shaffer, Ellen, 2062
Shaffer family
Homerville, OH, Grace Brethren
Church, 626
Minerva, OH, Grace Brethren Church,
843
Mount Cassell Old German Baptist
Brethren Church, WV, 880
Rockingham and Shenandoah Counties
Old German Baptist Brethren Church,
VA, 1118
Shaffer-Faust, Harvia Coates, 2062
Shaffer, Foster, 1764, 2305
Shaffer, Francis, 472
Shaffer, Frank E., 1764, 2292
Shaffer, Godfrey H., 1764
Shaffer, J. B., 564, 1764
Shaffer, J. S.
Osceola Church of the Brethren, MO,
district representative, 984
Shaffer, Jacob B., 1764
Shaffer, John B., 2292
Prices Creek Old German Baptist
Brethren Church, OH, presiding
elder, 1057
Shaffer, Joseph J., 619, 1764
Shaffer, Kenneth Merril, Jr., 1764, 2070
on Brethren history and beliefs, 2333
on Brethren Volunteer Service, 2356
historical writing, 612
on texts in Transit II, 2357
works by, 2310

Shaffer, Lewis Gains, 1764
Good Samaritan Church of the
Brethren, PA, 2190
Scalp Level, PA, Church of the
Brethren, pastor, 1151
Shaffer, Levi, 1764
Shaffer, Mary, 244
Shaffer, R. J., 1764
Shaffer, Rudy A., 2292
Shaffer, Rudy E., 2128
Shaffer, Samuel, 1764
Shaffer, W. H.
Shiloh Church of the Brethren, WV,
elder in, 1177
Shaffer, William H. H., 1764
Mill Run Grace Brethren Church, MD,
pastor, 833
Shaffner, Etta (later Gillin), 549
Shafford, John W., 1764
Shahan, Emory, 564
Shiloh Church of the Brethren, WV,
elder in, 1177
Shahan, G. E., 1287
Shahan (Shakan), Emory George, 1764
Shakarian, Demos, 521
Shaker Church, 2098
Shakespeare, William, 398
Shalangwa, Usman L., 1764
Shalenberger, David, 1764
Shalkross, Herbert, 213
Shallabarger, John
Ross Church of the Brethren, OH, min-
ister, 1124
Shallcross, Betty, 213
Shallenberger, John Bugher, 2062
Shallenberger, Clyde R., 745, 1764
Shallenberger, Magdalena, 161
Shallenberger (Schellenberg, Schellenberg-
er, Schallenberger, Schallenbruger,
Schullenberger, Schellberger,
Schellabarger, Scheneberger, et al.)
family, 2062
Shallenberger, Ulrich, 2004
shalom
peace, 997–998
Shalom Covenant Communities, 2062
and New Covenant Fellowship, 926
Plow Creek Fellowship, 1038
Reba Place Fellowship, 1084
Shalom Publishers
Fellowship of Hope, 488
Shalom Teams, 2172
Shalom Tracts, 193
Shamback family
Mortonhouse (ship), 2373, 2376
Shambarger, George A., 1764
Shambaugh, Bertha M. Horack, 2062
Shambaugh family
Mortonhouse (ship), 2373, 2376
Shamberger, C. A., 1764
Shamberger, Chauncey Howard, 203, 242,
248, *248,* 520, 536, **1171**, 1331,
1764, 2062, **2378, 2385**
Shamberger family, 1391
Sharon Church of the Brethren,
Alberta, Canada, 1172
Shamberger, George A., 59, **1171**, 1764
Mountain View Church of the
Brethren, Alberta, Canada, nonres-
ident elder, 889
Sharon Church of the Brethren,
Alberta, Canada, elder, 1172
Shamberger, Henry, 1764

Shamberger, J. E., 1171
Shamberger, Jacob, 1764
Shamberger, Jesse E., 627, 1134, 1764
Shamberger, John H., 128, 1764
Shamberger, Lily Reddick, 1171
Shamberger, Susan Catherine Silvuse, 1171
Shamokin, PA, 1397
    Church of the Brethren, 1157, *1171,*
    1171–1172
Shanadore congregation, VA
    Funck (Funk) family, 521
Shanaman, Frederick L., Jr., 2305
    Pleasant View Church of the Brethren,
    PA, 1037
Shanan, George E., 1764
Shaneour, David
    Silver Creek Church of the Brethren,
    OH, minister, 1182
Shaneour, Jacob, 1764
Shanghai, China, 277
Shanhan, George, 1764
Shanhan, James, 1764
Shanholtz, Bruce C., 1764
Shanholtz, James Luther, 1764
Shanholtz, Nellie (later Miller), 1345
Shanholtz, Vernon N., 1345, 1764
Shanholtzer family
    family history and genealogy, 1984
Shank, Abram, 1172
Shank, Ada (later Neher), 922
Shank, Adam, 2001
Shank, Alice Caylor, 1172
Shank, Amos, 2062
Shank, Anna Rush, 1172
Shank, Annie (later Hertzler), 600
Shank, Beulah Kreider, 1172
Shank, Catherine Jean Heck, 1855,
    2247–2248
Shank, Charles A., 1345, 1764
Shank, Charles P., 619
Shank, Christian, 334, 561, 630, 1764
Shank, D. Glenn Harding, 1764
Shank, Daniel P., 2063
Shank, Donald Hoffman, 252, 405, 1172,
    1764
Shank, Eileen Smith, 1172
Shank, Elizabeth Meyer, 1172
Shank, Elizabeth Smith, 1172
Shank, Emanuel, 1172, 1764
Shank, Emma Olinger, 1172
Shank, Ethel (later Kriegbaum), 708
Shank family, 241, 360, **1172,** 1214, 1345,
    2062–2063, 2072, 2100
    Mill Creek Old German Baptist
    Brethren Church, VA, 833
    Royer family, related to, 1128
Shank, Frank O., 1172, 1764, 2063
Shank, George, 1172
Shank, Gladys Mae, 2062
Shank, Glenn Harding ("Doc"), 1855,
    2247–2248
    Herndon, VA, Chandon Brethren
    Church, 2197
Shank, Glenn H. ("Doc") and Catherine
    Jean Heck, **2247–2248**
Shank, Harvey (BC), 2247
Shank, Henry Mercer, III, 2063
Shank, Herschel G., 170, 247, 520,
    1764–1765, 2063
Shank House meetinghouse (PA), 77
Shank house, Upton, PA, Church of the
    Brethren, 1295
Shank, I. David, 2292

Shank, J. B., 1765
Shank, Jacob, 271, 1765
Shank, James Taft, 2063
Shank, John, 1765, 2063, 2072
Shank, John (BC), 18, 1765
Shank, John Clayton, 2063
Shank, John
    Back Creek congregation, Franklin
    Co., PA, elder, 1172
Shank, Lena Fay Cocklin, 1172
Shank, Merna Ruth Brenneman, 2063
Shank, Michael
    Mason, Floyd R. on descendants of,
    2345
    Mason, Kathryn Garst on descendants
    of, 2345
Shank, Ray O., 496, **1172,** 1765
Shank, Ray S., 1765, 2305
    Dunkard Brethren, elder, 1172
Shank, Rebecca Lindsay, 1172
Shank, Rose (BC), 2247
Shank, Sanford Lee, 2063
Shank, Sara (later Zigler), 1397
Shank (Schenck), John, 2062
Shank, Virginia, 2100
Shank, Walter Eshleman, 1765
Shankel family
    Minerva, OH, Grace Brethren Church,
    843
Shanks (Back Creek), PA, congregation
    Holderman (Haldeman) family, 619
Shanks, D. C., 2063
Shanks, Daniel, 152
Shanks, James, 1878
Shankster, Carl
Shankster, Owen L., Jr., and Celia Smith
    (CB) and, 2248
Shankster, Celia Marion Smith, 1844, **2248,**
    2248
Shankster, Donald O., 696, 1765, 2248
    New Haven Church of the Brethren,
    NC, pastor in, 928
Shankster, Edwin, 2248
Shankster family
    Redstone Valley Old German Baptist
    Brethren Church, WI and, 2240
Shankster, James Philip, 1323, 1765
Shankster, Janice, 2248
Shankster, Owen L., Jr., and Celia Smith
    2248, *2248*
Shankster, Owen LaRue, Jr., 1765, 1844,
    2248, *2248,* 2305
Shankster, Owen Silvan, 1765
Shankster, Susan, 2248
Shanksville, PA, Downey Brethren Church,
    See Stone Creek Brethren Church,
    PA
Shannholtz, Ola W., 2063
Shannon, Emory, 1765
Shannon, IL, Church of the Brethren, 273,
    1172
    meetinghouse, Stanley, WI, 1217
Shannon, Thomas A., 1765
Shanour, Jacob, 1765
Shansi, China, 295
    mission schools, 853
    missions, 861
Shansi province, China
    Neher, Minneva Josephine in, 922
    Shantz, Mary Rinehart, 994
SHARE, 44, **1172**
    Church of the Brethren, 304
    minorities, ethnic and racial, 850

relief and service efforts, 1097
Shared Ministry
    State College, PA, University Baptist
    and Brethren Church, 1218
Shargel, Cheryl Ann Weirbach, 1853
Shargel, David William, 1765, 1853
sharing
    Reba Place Fellowship, 1084
Sharing Observations with the Home
    Church (Bonsack), 160
S(h)aron sisterhouse'(originally Hebron) at
    Ephrata, 1172, *1173*
    Ephrata Community, 448, *449,* 1980
    Hebron, 591
    Peniel as chapel for, 1003–1004
Sharon Church of the Brethren, Alberta,
    Canada, 59
origins of, 1172
    Pleasant Ridge Church of the Brethren,
    Alberta, Canada, 1034
Sharon Memorial Hall, Worthington, OH,
    Columbus Grace Brethren Church,
    1380
Sharonville, OH, Cincinnati Grace Brethren
    Church, **1172, 1174**
Sharp, Albert Morgan, 14, 430, 442, 1281,
    1765
    Salem Church of the Brethren, ND,
    1138
Sharp, Benjamin Franklin, 572, 1765
    Poplar Grove, OH, Church of the
    Brethren, elder, 1046
Sharp, C. H.
    Pleasant Valley German Baptist
    Brethren Church, NE, 2377
Sharp, Christian, 2063
Sharp, Eli, 2063
Sharp family, 2087
Sharp, George H., 1765
Sharp, Gertrude (later Hamer), 580
Sharp, John E., 2063
Sharp, Joseph E., 2063
Sharp, Leo, 1765
Sharp, Magdalena Zook
    mother of Sharp, Solomon Zook, 1174
Sharp mission point
    Quinter, KS, Church of the Brethren,
    1078
Sharp, Peter, 2063
Sharp, Solomon Zook, 63, 64, 66, 186, 187,
    205, 520, 559, 603, 682, 697, 780,
    781, 884, 885, 1030, **1174,** *1174,*
    1236, 1389, 1765, 1952, 2063
    historical writing, 613
    Maryville, TN, Oakland German
    Baptist Brethren Church, elder,
    799
    McPherson College, president, 780,
    781
    Our Children at Work, 985
    Plattsburg Church of the Brethren, MO,
    1030
Sharp, Salome Zook
    wife of Sharp, Solomon Zook, 1174
Sharp, Solomon
    father of Sharp, Solomon Zook, 1174
Sharp, Suzy, 2157
Sharp, Thomas L., 2157, 2305
Sharpe family
    Mabton, WA, Grace Brethren Church,
    771
Sharpnack, Henry, *See* Scharpnack, Henry
Sharpsburg, Battle of, *See* Antietam, Battle

of
Sharpsburg, MD, Church of the Brethren
Manor Church of the Brethren, MD,
daughter congregation of, 787,
1174
Pleasant View Church of the Brethren,
MD, 1037
Sharpsville, IN, 705, 1348
Shatto, Ambrose, 1341, 1765
Shatto, Lora, 1836
Shatto, Luther S., 59, 1341, 1765
Omak, WA, Church of the Brethren,
leadership by, 974
Sharon Church of the Brethren,
Alberta, Canada, minister, 1172
Shattuck, Lois Marie, 2292
Shattuck, William Everett, 2292
Shaub, Elizabeth W., 2063
Shaub, Phillip Harmon, 2063
Shaum family, 2052
Shaum, Naomi Irene Riehl, 2063
Shave, E. B., 1228
Shaver, Alfred J., 679, 1765
Shaver, Byrl Eugene, 674, 1765
Shaver, Daniel Harvey, 343, 765
Shaver, Emanuel Bydler (GBB, BC), 54,
368, 578, 586, 675, 740, 751, 760,
1254, 1364, 1765, **2248**
Maurertown, VA, Brethren Church,
pastor, 803
Mount Pleasant Brethren Church, VA,
minister, 886
Pineville, VA, Mount Olive Brethren
Church, pastor, 1025
Reliance, VA, Mount Zion Brethren
Church, pastor, 1095
Saint James Brethren Church, pastor,
MD, 1134
Seven Fountains, VA, Trinity Brethren
Church, 1169
Shaver family, 233, 1216, 1277, 1308
Muhlenberg Co., KY, German Baptist
Brethren, 893
Shaver, George, H., 751, **1174–1175**, 1364,
1765
Shaver, Emanuel Bydler and, 2248
Shaver, Isaac Henry, 343, 1765
Shaver, Jacob E., 745
Shaver, John, 343
Shaver, R. Mae, 745
Shaver, Samuel A., 1765
Shaver, Emanuel Bydler (GBB, BC)
and, 2248
Shaver, W. D., 1765
Shavers, E. B.
St. Luke, VA, Brethren Church, pastor,
1135
Shavers family, 2077
Shavers, George
St. Luke, VA, Brethren Church, pastor,
1135
Shaw, Bruce, 1765
Shaw, Charlotte, 727
Shaw, Florence (later Eikenberry), 431
Shaw, Henry K., 2063
Shaw, James H., 1765
Shaw, James Russell, 2292
Shaw, John, 1765
Shaw, Olin F., 1765
Shaw, Oliver, 1765
Shaw, Ralph R., 140, 1861
shawls, 401
personal appearance, 1010

Shawler, Charles, Jr., 1765
shawls and capes
dress for sisters, **1175**
Shawn family
Barberton Bible Church, OH, 951
Shawsville, TX, 1255
Sheaffer, Charles A., 2292
Sheaffer (Shaffer), D. J., 1765
Sheaffer, Timothy E., 2292
Sheaffer, William Ira, 1765
Shearer, Barbara Elizabeth (later Rahn),
2041
Shearer, Charles Raymond, 2063
Shearer, Clark C., 2292
Shearer family, 2063
Shearer, Keith A., 2293
Shearer, Samuel S., 1765
Shearer, Velma Miller, 2293
Shearer, Wilbert R., 1765
Shedd, Dan, 1342, 1765
Shedd, Doris, 713
Sheely, Lila, 1853
missionary to Central African Republic,
1019
Sheenaberry, E. P., 1765
Sheets, Adam, 1765
Peak Creek Church of the Brethren,
NC, minister, 1003
Sheets, Andrew, 1765
Peak Creek Church of the Brethren,
NC, minister, 1003
Sheets, Annie, 1928
Sheets, Antoinette H., 1765–1766, 2305
Richland Church of the Brethren, OH,
pastor, 1107
Sheets, Clay, 243
Sheets, Emmanuel M., 1766
Sheets family, 152, 165, 1299
Prosperity Brethren Church, WV, 1062
Sheets, George Hosler, 1766
Sheets, Greer R., 1766
Sheets, Henry, 493, 755, 1341, 1766
Mount Carmel Church of the Brethren,
NC, minister, 880
Sheets, J. P., 1766
Sheets, Jesse, 1766
Sheets, John Kintner, 1766
Sheets, ND, 164
Sheets, Rex, 518, 1766
Sheets, T. A., 152, 1766
Sheffer, Rebecca Lynn, 1849
Sheffer, Salmon S., 1766
Sheffield Village, OH, Lake Breeze Church
of the Brethren, **1175**
Sheidler family, *See* Shideler family
Shelar, Roy, 1766
Shelby, Cass K., 2063
Shelby Co. Church of the Brethren, MO,
1175, 2011
Shelby Co., IA
Harlan Church of the Brethren, IA, 583
Shelby Co., KY, 688, 734, 1249, 2100
German Baptist Brethren Church, **1175**
Hostetler Brethren, 631
migration of Brethren, 829
Shelby Co., OH, 261, 757
Pleasant View Church of the Brethren,
OH, 1032
Sidney, OH, Trinity Church of the Brethren,
1181
Shelby family
Prosser, WA, Community Grace
Brethren Church, 1062

Shelby, William L., 275, 566, 1766
Prosser, WA, Community Grace
Brethren Church, pastor, 1062
Sheldon, Chauncey Burt, 136, 1766, 1853
missionary, **1175**
Sheldon Church of the Brethren, Sioux Co.,
IA, **1175**
Gillett Grove, IA, German Baptist
Brethren (Church), 549
Sheldon, Hattie Louise Cope, 136, 1853
missionary, **1175**
Shell, Lorena (later Eaker), 1923
Shell products, boycott of, 2139
Shellabarger, David, 1766
Shellabarger, Isaac
North Hampton, OH, Donnels Creek
Old German Baptist Brethren
Church, deacon, 948
Shellabarger, Jacob, 1766, *See also* Old
German Baptist Brethren
Shellabarger, John, 1766
Shellabarger, Samuel, 1766
Shellaberger, Jacob
Painter Creek Old German Baptist
Brethren Church, OH, 990
Shellenberger, A. A., 1766
Shellenberger, David, 1766
Shellenberger, David (CB), 1766
Shellenberger, Enoch, 81
Shellenberger, Eva (later Falkenstein), 471
Shellenberger family, 1953, 2098
Shellenberger, H. S., 1766
Shellenberger, Helen, 1766
Shellenberger, J. H., 1766
Shellenberger, John, 1896
Shellenberger, John B., 232, 1766
Shellenberger, Maggie, 81, 232
Shellenberger, Peter, 406
Shellenberger (Shellabarger) families, 1896
Sheller, Catherine Strickler, *646*
Sheller, Daniel, *646*
photography of Brethren, 1019
Sheller, E. M., 2063
Sheller family, 164
Sheller, Francis Jane, 1844
Sheller, Gayle Hunter, 2293
Sheller, Harry Lynn, 1216, 1766
Shelley, Donald A., 2063
Shelley, Fannie W. (later Zug), 1401
Shelley, P. G., 1766
Shellhaas, Mark, 247, 1766
Shellhaas, Thelma, 247
Shellhorn, Balser
family history, 1999
Shellman family, 241
Shelly, David Franklin, 1766
South Keokuk Church of the Brethren,
IA, minister, 1205
Shelly, Edwin, 1766
Shelly, Elwood Spickler, 1766
Shelly, Emmert, 1766
Shelly, Emmert O., 1766
Shelly, Galen Scott, 2293
Shelly, John A., 2293
Shelly, Maynard, 2063
Shelor, Roy L., 1766
Shelor schoolhouse
Faiview-Rocky Mount Church of the
Brethren, VA, 470
Shelter, Sarah J. (later Miller), 2018
Shelton
St. Paul Church of the Brethren, VA,
meetinghouse, 1135

Shelton Church of the Brethren, NC, **1175–1176**
   Mount Airy, NC, First Church of the Brethren, 880
   St. Paul congregation, 1175
Shelton family
   Garwin, IA, Carlton Brethren Church, 532
Shelton, Gilbert Luther, 1766
Shelton, Harry W., 2293
Shelton, Joel, 1766
Shelton, NC, congregation, 1267
Shelton, Susan Jane, 2305
Shelton, Thomas, 1766
Shemokin Church of the Brethren, Jefferson Co., PA, **1176**
Shenadoah National Park
   Montebello Church of the Brethren, VA, 871
Shenandoah Co., VA, 330, *493,* 1301, 1313, 1314, 1350, 1364
   Flat Rock Church of the Brethren, VA, 493
   Garber, Aaron Leedy, 528
   history of, 2077, 2090, 2091, 2101
   Neiff bothers settlement, 909
   Oak Hill Church of the Brethren, VA, 957
   Pleasant View Church of the Brethren, VA, 1037
   Rileyville, VA, Church of the Brethren, 1109
   Rockingham and Shenandoah Counties Old German Baptist Brethren Church, VA, 1118
   Round Hill Church of the Brethren, VA, 1125
   Salem Church of the Brethren, 1138
   Shenandoah Valley, VA, 1176
Shenandoah congregation, VA
   example of place name, 911
Shenandoah District, Church of the Brethren
   Hays, D[aniel] on, 2354
   Sanger, S[amuel] F. on, 2354
Shenandoah National Park
   Mount Vernon Church of the Brethren, VA, 887
Shenandoah Valley Normal School, *See* Bridgewater College
Shenandoah Valley, PA
   Pennsylvania Germans, 2068
Shenandoah Valley, VA, 175, 206, 617, **1176,** 1219, 1292, 1295, 1307–1308, 1329, 2076
   Burkholder-Bowman controversy, dissertation on, 1918
   Coffmans settling in, 685
   Engle family history, 1930
   Fairview Church of the Brethren, MD, 468
   family, 474
   farming, 477
   Flat Rock Church of the Brethren, VA, 493, 494
   Funck (Funk) family, 521
   Garber (Garver, Gerber) family, 530
   Garber (Gerber), John H., 529
   The Gift of the Morningstar (Gordon), 747
   Glück (Glick, Click) family, 553
   Greenhill Church of the Brethren, MD, 570

Hays, Daniel, 590
Holsinger (Holtzinger) family, 623
Jackson, Thomas Jonathan "Stonewall," 667
Johnson City, TN, Knob Creek Church of the Brethren, 672
Longenecker, Stephen L. on slavery in, 2344
migration of Brethren, 829
Miller, Valley Virginia (later Myers) in, 913
minorities, ethnic and racial, 849
Newport Church of the Brethren, 934
North Fork Church of the Brethren, WV, 947
Pennsylvania Germans, 1006
Pleasant View Church of the Brethren, WV, 1037
Reconstruction Era, 1086
The Rockingham Male Chorus, 2204
Shaver, Emanuel Bydler (GBB, BC) and, 2248
Shaver, George H., 1174
Shoemaker, Martin, descendants, 1157
Smith Creek Fellowship Church of the Brethren, WV, 1191
Valley Brethren-Mennonite Heritage Center and, 2257–2258
Shenandoah/Virgina Brethren Action Movement (SH-BAM), 179
Shendi, Anand K., 1766
Shenefelt, Dale Eugene, 565, 1766
Shenefelt, Ernest M., 633, 1766
Shenefelt, Francis Lee, 1766
Shenefield, Hale T., 2063
Shener family, 1223
Shenk, Daniel M., 1766
Shenk family, *See* Shank family
   Heisey family, 595
Shenk, Gary, minister, 1172
Shenk, Gerald, 2356
Shenk, J. Marvin, 1340, 2293
Shenk, John Richard, 1172, 1766
   Mount Olivet Church of the Brethren, PA, pastor, 886
Shenk, Pamela
   works by, 2323
Shenk, Wilbert R.
   on Anabaptists and mission and outreach, 2356
Shenton, Stacy Leigh, 377, 1766
Sheol, See Hell, doctrine of
Shepfer, Edward, 80, 572, 1766
Shepfer, Eva (later Minnich)
   Minnich, Herbert Spenser, wife of, 848
Shepherd Church of the Brethren, Isabella Co., MI, **1176**
Shepherd family, 1340
Shepherd, Henry D., 1766
Shepherd, John, 1766
Shepherd, Joseph M., 1766
The Shepherd of the Valley (Blair), 748
Shepherd, William, 1766
Shepherd's Spring Outdoor Ministries Center (CB), **2248**
Shepherdstown, PA, 765
Shephler, Earl, 564
Shepler, Abraham, 1766
   Pipe Creek Church of the Brethren, IN, elder, 1025
Shepler, Earl, 1766
Shepler family
   Pipe Creek Old German Baptist

Brethren Church, IN, 1026
Shepler, Isaac, 1766
Shepler, Joseph, 1766
Shepp, Benjamin
   Pasadena, CA, Church of the Brethren, 994
Shepp, E. B.
   Pasadena, CA, Church of the Brethren, 994
Sheppard, Daniel J., Jr., 2293
Sheppard, Winifred (later Garver)
   Garver, Earl Simeon, 2187
Sherbinin, Michael Andrew de, 1296, 1766
Sherbrook, Quebec
   missionary appointees to Vermont, 1304
Sherck, Abraham B., 2064
Sherck, George Samuel, 496, 1766
Sherck, Lucille (later West), 1331
Sherck, Ronald G., II, 2293
Sherfey family, 1943, 2063
Sherfey, William Emory, 2063
Sherffig family, *See* Scherffig family
Sherfig, Catharine Bosserman, 163
Sherfig, Jacob, 163
Sherfy, Abram, 553
Sherfy, Anna Glick, 553
Sherfy, Casper, 1766
Sherfy, Effie Strohm (CB), 2249
Sherfy, Ernest Francis, 672, 1766–1767, 2249
   Ramona Church of the Brethren, KS, pastor, 1083
   Roanoke, VA, Williamson Road Church of the Brethren, pastor, 1114
Sherfy, Ethel (later Harris), 1958
Sherfy family, *See* Scherffig family; Scherffig/Sherfy family
   Good (Guth) family, 556
Sherfy, Frederick, 44, 1767
Sherfy, Jacob, 546
Sherfy, Joel, 570, 1767 (CB-1), **2386**
   Pleasant View Church of the Brethren, TN, 1037
Sherfy, Joel (CB-2), 1767
Sherfy, John, 1767
Sherfy, John (CB), 2249
Sherfy, John Samuel, 147, 1767
Sherfy, Joseph, 546, 2386
Sherfy, Mary (later Snell), *See* Snell, Mary Sherfy
Sherfy, N. B.
   Pleasant Hill Church of the Brethren, TN, free minister, 1032
Sherfy, Robert
   New Carlisle, OH, Church of the Brethren, elder in, 926
Sherfy, Robert D., 2305
Sherfy, Robert Livingston, 206, 511, *1283,* 1767, 2064, 2305, **2248–2249**
Sherfy, S. L., 672
Sherfy, Samuel S., 1767
Sherfy, Sonja (later Griffith)
   Lenexa, KS, Fellowship, 2214
Sheridan Home
   Rhodes, William, administrator, 1107
Sheridan Home, Denver, CO, 1209
Sheridan Lake Old German Baptist Brethren Church, Kiowa Co., CO, 324, **1176**
Sheridan, Philip, 314
Sherk family, 144

Sherland, Fred W., 1767
Sherley, N. B., 1767
Sherlock, Douglas D., Jr., 2293
Sherlock, Harvey, 1767
Sherman Co., KS, 274
    Fairview Church of the Brethren, KS, 468
Sherman Co., NE
    South Loup Church of the Brethren, NE, 1206
Sherman family
    Mount Cassell Old German Baptist Brethren Church, WV, 880
Sherman (Hamilton), Catherine, *84*
Sherman, John R., 1767
Sherman, Margaret May (later Thompson), 2295
Sherman, Orville and Lois
    relief workers from New Paris, IN, Church of the Brethren, 931
Sherman, Russell A., 1767
Sherred, Lyall Ross, 1767
Sherrick family
    Sharpsburg, MD, Church of the Brethren, 1174
Sherrick, Jesse, 1176
Sherrick, Joseph Francis, 1767
Sherrick, M. M., 265
Sherrick, Marvin Manam, 1176, **1767**, 2064
Sherrick, Minnie Mae Buck, 1176
Sherrick, Rebecca Brandal, 1176
Sheterom, J. A., 1767
Shetler, Amanda (later Van Dyke), 1302
Shetler, David Dean, 1767
Shetler, Dean R., 1767
Shetler, Nettie Beachy (later Gingerich), 1949
Shetter, Jacob Huber, 2064
Shick, Catherine Forney, 499
Shick family
    McFarland, CA, Church of the Brethren, 774
Shick, Jesse Norman, 499, 1767
Shick, Martha Belle (later Flory), 201, 277, **499**, 1621, 1767, 1837
Shick, Uriah, 103
Shick, Urias, 384, 1767
    North Beatrice Church of the Brethren, NE, elder, 945
Shickel, Elsie Naomi, **1176–1177**, 1844, 1977
Shickel family, 1950
Shickel, Joseph, 1176, 1767
Shickel (later Woodlawn) schoolhouse, WV, 1249
Shickel, Nancy E. Miller, 1176
Shickler, B. F., 1767
Shideler, Daniel W., 1177, 1767
Shideler, Elizabeth (later Miller)
    Müller (Miller) family, 894
Shideler, Emerson W., 1767
Shideler family, **1177**, 1253
Shideler, George, 1177
Shideler, Harry Wilson, 2064
Shideler, Henry, 273, 1177, 1767
Shideler, Jacob, 1177
Shideler, Johann Georg, 1177
Shideler, John, 1177, 1894, *See* Shidler family
Shideler, Katharine Wise, 1177
Shideler, Katrina Hoonen, 1177
Shideler, Margaret Barkley, 1177
Shideler, Margaret Nave, 1177

Shideler, Noah M., 1767
    Roanoke, VA, Ninth Street Church of the Brethren, pastor, 1113
Shideler, Noah, 1177
    Rossville, IN, Church of the Brethren, minister, 1124
Shideler, Peter, 1177
Shideler, William, 1177
Shidler Church, Washington Co., PA, 1177
Shidler, Elizabeth Wise, 1177
Shidler family, 2064, *See also* Shideler family
    Snowberger family, related to, 1154
Shidler, Jacob, 1177
Shidler, William H., 1767
Shields family
    Minerva, OH, Grace Brethren Church, 843
    Parkersburg, WV, Grace Brethren Church, 994
Shiery, Flory, 626
Shiery, Floyd William, 715, 1767, 2305
Shiffler, C. C., 1767
Shifflet, Gilmer
    feetwashing (photo caption), 2378
Shifflett, Alvin M., 1767
Shiflet, Anfield, 1767
Shillings family, 1224
Shilo, AR, preaching point
    St. Francis Church of the Brethren, 1134
Shiloh Church of the Brethren, WV, **1177**
Shiloh Church of the Brethren, VA, *See*
    Evergreen Church of the Brethren, VA
    Eastern Mount Carmel Church of the Brethren, VA, 416
    Mount Carmel Church of the Brethren, VA, 880
Shiloh, VA, Brethren Church, *See*
    Mauertown, VA, Brethren Church
Shimer family, 280
Shimer, Rebecca
    Reedley, CA, Church of the Brethren, 1091
Shimer, William C., 1315, 1767
    Reedley, CA, Church of the Brethren, 1091
Shimp, Charlotte Stauffer, 2064
Shimp family, 721
Shinaberry, Emby (Emory) P., 1767
Shindel, Benjamin (Mr. and Mrs.), 578
Shindler, Henry, 1767
Shingleton, Edon Gale, 1767
Shingleton, Leonard (Mr. and Mrs.), 579
Shipley, Clete, 758
Shipley, Greg, 2293
Shipley, Herbert, 725
Shipley, Mary, 758
Shipley, Steve, 213
Shipley, Steven, 1767
Shipley, Violet, 725
Shipman, James R., 206–207
Shipman, Mary Agnes (later Miller)
    Miller, Minor Cline, wife of, 841
Shipman, William (Bill) J., 2293
Shippee (Sheppee), G. W., 1767
Shippen, Joseph, 2064
Shippensburg, PA, Church of the Brethren, 42, **1177**
    Ridge Church of the Brethren, PA, 1108
Shipping interests

    Newlanders, 934
ships
    Adventurer, 595
    Allen, See Allen
    Betsy, 741
    Britannia, See Britannia
    Brotherhood, 151, 1155
    Brothers, 380, 2371
    Charming Nancy, 615, 1229
    diet on shipboard, 2364
    Fame, 617
    Fortune, 641
    Francis and Elizabeth, 554
    Friendship, 112, 260, 1127
    Hope, See Hope
    Isaac, 532
    James Goodwill, 574, 1401
    Jefries, 260
    Judith, 593
    Lowther, 623
    Loyal Judith, 444
    Margaret, 584
    Mary Ann, 491
    Mortonhouse, 456, 2373, 2376
    Nancy, 574
    Neptune, 574
    passenger lists for emigration to USA, 2080
    Patience, 532
    Pennsylvania Merchant, See Pennsylvania Merchant
    Phoenix, See Phoenix
    Princess Augusta, See Princess Augusta
    Rawley, 96
    Richard and Elizabeth, 352
    Richmond, 996
    St. Andrew, 601
    Shirley, 79
    Thamesis, 863
    Thistle, 523, 868
    Two Brothers, 1070
    Two Sisters, 1085
    Virtuous Grace, 602
    William & Sarah, 1013
    William Johnston, 118
    Zam Zam, See Zam Zam
Shipshewana congregation, IN, 1267
Shipshewana, IN, 654
    Church of the Brethren
        Florence, MI, Church of the Brethren, 496, 1177
Shipshewana Lake
    Indiana Brethren Retreat, 1354
Shipshewana Retreat Center, *See* Indiana Brethren Retreat
Shirely, Nora Early, 183
Shireman, Wayne, 265
Shirery, John E., 1767
Shirey, Roy (Mr. and Mrs.), 579
Shirey, Vicki Anne, 1848
Shirk, Anna Mary, 2095
Shirk, Bertha Ryan, 42, **1177**, 1226, 1296, 1361, 1844, 2076
Shirk, Catherine (later Taylor), 1249
Shirk, D. W., 1767
Shirk, Dan A., 752, 1767
Shirk, Esther Horning, 2064
Shirk, Glen W., 2293
    Ripon, CA, Grace Brethren Church, pastor, 1110
Shirk, Harvey F., 1177
Shirk, Isaac W., 1767

Shirk, Jacob B., 1767
    Ramona Church of the Brethren, KS,
        1083
Shirk, John, 1876
Shirk, Joseph, 2064
Shirk, L., 1767
Shirk, Martin Sauder, 2064
Shirk, Nelson E., 1767–1768
Shirk, Noah Martin, 2064
Shirk, Oliver, 1768
    Octavia, NE, Church of the Brethren,
        960
Shirk, Willis L., Jr.
    on Ephrata Cloister, 2356
Shirkey, Inez, 1388
Shirkey, John H., 1768
Shirkey, Louis R., 1388, 1389
Shirkey, Samuel Bowman, 1313, 1768
    Rockingham Church of the Brethren,
        MO, elder, 1118
Shirkle, Joseph, 1768
Shirky, Earl Wayne, 1768
Shirky family, 1313
Shirley (ship)
    Minnich family voyage to America on,
        849
Shirley, Kathleen Diane, 1851
Shirleysburg, PA, 144
Shisler, Hannah Cassel, 1177
Shisler, James B., 1768
Shisler, John B., 1177
Shisler, Sara Cassel, 584, 1177, 1844
Shive, Arthur, 2133
Shive, Janet, 2133
Shively, Aaron, 1768
Shively, Arthur W., 1768
Shively, Benjamin F., 1869
Shively, Calvin, 1768
Shively, Catherine Ehresman, 1178
Shively, Charles S., 2144
Shively, Christian, 1878
Shively, Daniel, 691, 1768
Shively, Daniel P., 1768
    Pipe Creek Church of the Brethren, IN,
        elder, 1025
Shively, David B., 243, 1178, 1768
Shively, Donald E., 2293
Shively, Earl O., 1178
Shively, Edna Wolf, 1178
Shively, Elizabeth, 384
Shively, Elizabeth Neher, 1178
Shively, Emma Whisler, 1178
Shively, Emmanuel E., 1768
Shively, Ernest, 1768
Shively family, 108, 146, 215, 323, 753
    family history, 1980, 1982
    Howard Co. Old German Baptist
        Brethren Church, IN, 633
    Musselman family related to by mar-
        riage, 901
    Salem Church of the Brethren, ND,
        1137
    Scheublein family, related to, 1178
Shively, G., 1768
Shively, G. W., 317, 1768
Shively, George, 267, 571, 1768
    Penn Run Church of the Brethren, PA,
        pastor, 1004
Shively, George B. (CB-1), 243, 1768
Shively, George B. (CB-2), 1768
Shively, George Jacob, 654, 1768
Shively, Glen M., 319, 1768
Shively, Greene, 1768, 2064

Shively, Henry and Mary Banta
    family history, 2003
Shively, Herbert T., 1768
Shively, Howard M., 31
Shively, Isaac A.
    Pipe Creek Old German Baptist
        Brethren Church, IN, deacon, 1026
Shively, J. C., 753, 1768
Shively, John William, 1213, 1768
    Salem Church of the Brethren, ND,
        1138
Shively, Jacob, 1355
Shively, Jacob B., 1768
    Mount Pleasant Church of the
        Brethren, IN, minister, 886
    Salem Church of the Brethren, IN,
        elder, 1137
Shively, Joel, 96, 1768
    Osceola Church of the Brethren, IN,
        elder, 984
Shively, John B., 468, 1345
    Middlefork Old German Baptist
        Brethren Church, IN, minister, 826
    Pipe Creek Church of the Brethren, IN,
        elder, 1025
    Pyrmont, IN, Church of the Brethren,
        elder-in-charge, 1073
Shively, John E., 1768
    Santa Fe Church of the Brethren, IN,
        elder, 1144
Shively, John J., 1177
Shively, John K., 1768
Shively, John P., 1768
Shively, John S., 1768
Shively, John W., 1768
Shively, Jonathan Adin, 2293
Shively, Leah Blickenstaff, 1177
Shively, Levi Stephen, 1768, 1177–1178
Shively, Lou Anna River, 2144
Shively, Loyal L., 1178
Shively, Martin, 102, 130, 211, 319, 366,
        425, 505, 715, 1178, 1281, 1333,
        1768
    Miamisburg, OH, Brethren Church,
        pastor, 823
    New Lebanon, OH, First Brethren
        Church, pastor in, 930
    revivalist from Bear Creek Brethren
        Church, OH, 930
    Ronk, Albert Teller, baptism of, 1121
Shively, Nora Early, 1178
Shively, Roger F., 1768
Shively, Susanna (later Musselman)
    Musselman family, 901
Shively, Susannah, 352
Shively, Susannah Cripe, 352
Shively, Thomas A., 1768
    Pipe Creek Church of the Brethren, IN,
        elder, 1025
Shively, Thomas R., 1768
Shively, Ulery J., 1178
Shively, Ulrich
    Nimishillen Church of the Brethren,
        minister in, 937
Shively, W. R., 1768
Shively, Walter, 1768
Shively, Willard W., 1768
Shivers, Lida (later Leech)
    Men's Work (CB), 816
Shoaf family
    Snake Valley Old German Baptist
        Brethren Church, PA, 1193
Shoal Creek, MO, Church of the Brethren,

    See Fairview, Mo, Shoal Creek
        Church of the Brethren
Shoal Creek Old German Baptist Brethren
    Church, Newton Co., MO, 1178,
        1220
Shoals, IN
    Sampson Hill Church of the Brehren,
        IN, near, 1141
Shobe, Anna Barbara Heier, 602
Shobe, Elizabeth Heier, 602
Shobe family, 2064
    Mayville, ND, Red River Valley
        Church of the Brethren, 805
Shobe(?) family, 171
Shobe, Franklin Dilling, 2064
Shobe, Jacob, 602
Shobe, Martin, 602
Shober, Emil Edgar, 1768, 2305
Shober, Ralph E., 511, 1768
    Roanoke, VA, Ninth Street Church of
        the Brethren, pastor, 1113
Shober, Samuel U., 1768
Shober, Seline Roberdean (later Fercken),
        488
Shock, Adam, 2064
Shock, Bessie
    Voorheis, Grace Schock on, 2361
Shock, Catherine Ann, 161
Shock, Clarence I., 1768
Shock, D. Warren, 550, 1212, 1768–1769,
        2064
    Minneapolis, MN, Golden Valley
        Community Church of the
        Brethren, minister, 848
    Minot, ND, Church of the Brethren,
        851
    Pleasant Valley Church of the Brethren,
        ND, elder, 1035
    Raisin City, CA, Church of the
        Brethren, pastor, 1083
Shock, Elmer
    Voorheis, Grace Schock on, 2361
Shock family
    Howard Co. Old German Baptist
        Brethren Church, IN, 633
    South Haven Old German Baptist
        Brethren Church, MI, 1205
Shock, Garret, Mr. and Mrs.
    at New Lebanon, OH, First Brethren
        Church, 930
Shock, Irene (later Ferverda), 1936
Shock, Joseph H., 2064
Shock, Laura J., 1844, 2101
Shock, Pauline (later White), 1936
Shock, R. M., 1769
Shockley, Clarence D., 1769
Shockley family
    Outlook, WA, Church of the Brethren,
        986
Shockley, Roby B., 1769
Shoe, Abram, 1769
Shoeberger, A., 1769
Shoel family, 148
Shoemaker, Adam, 1157
Shoemaker, Alfred L., 1861, 2064
Shoemaker, Benjamin H., III, 2064
    on Shoemaker family, 2356
Shoemaker, Charles Wesley, 1769
Shoemaker, David, 320, 1234, 1769
    Clear Creek, IN, congregation, minister
        and elder, 1157
Shoemaker, Donald Paul, 439, 755, 1769
Shoemaker, Dottie, 1215

Shoemaker, Edwin, 1769
Shoemaker, Eli, 1769
Shoemaker family, 1221, 2064, 2077, 2100, *See also* Schumacher family
    Plattsburg Church of the Brethren, MO, 1030
Shoemaker, Benjamin H., III on, 2356
Shoemaker, Fern (later Mohler)
    Mohler, Robert Ellsworth, wife of, 868
Shoemaker, George, 189
    Mount Joy Church of the Brethren, PA, minister, 882
    Oakdale Church of the Brethren, PA, 957
Shoemaker, George (immigrant ca.1770), 1157
Shoemaker, George (immigrant of 1728), 1157
Shoemaker, George L.
    Manchester College, trustee, 785
Shoemaker, Hayes, 1311
Shoemaker, Isaac, 189, 347, 1769
Shoemaker, Isaac, Sr., 1769
    Plattsburg Church of the Brethren, MO, minister, 1030
Shoemaker, John B., 1157, 1769
    Mohican Church of the Brethren, OH, preacher, 867
Shoemaker, Joseph, 1769
Shoemaker, Peter
    Oakdale Church of the Brethren, PA, 957
Shoemaker, Philip
    Conestoga church member, 1157
    Musselman, Christian, 901
Shoemaker, Richard, H., 140, 1861
Shoemaker, Raymond, 1769
Shoemaker, Sarah (later Swartz), 1243
Shoemaker, Sherman Henry, 1769
Shoemaker (Shumaker), John, 1769
Shoemaker, Silas Henry, 1769
Shoemaker, Simon A., 1769
Shoemaker, Solomon S., 588, 1769
Shoemaker, Thomas Everett, 1769
Shoemaker, Thomas H., 2064
Shoemaker, W. Warren, 1215, 1769
Shoemakerites, *See* Brethren in Christ (Shoemakerites)
Shoffer, J. B., 1769
Sholl family, *See* Scholl family; Schull family
Sholley, Lanta Asa, Jr., 1769
Sholly, Duane, 1769
Sholly, Jennie, 406
Sholly, John J., 377, 406, 532, 1769
Sholty, B. F., 1769
Shomber, H., 1769
Shomber, Henry, 1769
Shomber, M. D., 1769
Shonberger, Jesse E., 1769
Shong, Daniel, 1769
    Maumee Church of the Brethren, OH, minister, 803
Shong, David, 1769
Shonk, John, 245
Shontz, John, 211, 1769
    Seneca Church of the Brethren, OH, minister, 1166
Shook, Alice
    Portis, KS, Grace Brethren Church, 1048
Shook, D. B.
    Portis, KS, Grace Brethren Church,

1047, 1048
Shook family
    Root River Church of the Brethren, MN, 1122
Shook, Gregory Paul, 2293
Shook, Pauline (later Jackson)
    Jackson, Edward A., 2209
Shook, R. M., 1769
Shook, S. Barton, 1769
Shook, Silas E., 1769
Shoop, Carl
    River City Grace Community Church, 1134
Shoop, John Sidney, 2103
Shoop, Nellie
    River City Grace Community Church, 1134
Shope, Adam J., 1769
Shope, Albert, 1302
Shope, David, 1769
Shope family, 1302
Shope, Jacob E., 746, 1769
Shope, John E., Jr., 110, 144, 1769
Shope William, 749
Shopshire, James M., 2064
Shorb, David M., 447, 469, 668, 688, 1242, 1769
    Pleasant Valley Church of the Brethren, ND, elder, 1035
Shorb family
    South Bend, IN, Ireland Road Grace Brethren Church, 1203
A Short and Sincere Declaration, 176, 310, 312, **1178–1179,** 1993, 2064
Short and Very Easy Method of Prayer (Guyon), 1051
Short family, 1340
Short Mountain, WV, 1249
"Short Sketch of the Far Western Brethren of the so-called Dunkard Church (Clingingsmith 155, 321
Shorter College
    Furry, William Davies, 526
Shorter family
    Meadow Branch Church of the Brethen, TN, 805
Shorter, P. B., 1769
Shortt, James Sylvester, 1340, 1769
Shotts, Michael C., 1769
    Pigeon River Church of the Brethren, IN, elder, 1023
Shou Yang, Shansi province, China, 209
    hospitals, 630
    mission schools, 853
    Neher, Minneva Josephine in, 922
Shoulders, Anna Belle (later Fisher), 1617
Shoultz, Abraham (?)
    East Union German Baptist Brethren, KY, minister in, 935
Shoup, Catherine (later Hart), 587
Shoup, Daniel Edward, 696, 1399, 1769
Shoup, Daniel Miller, 1179, 1399, 1769
Shoup family, 1214, 1383
Shoup family (OGBB), *1179*
Shoup, Irvin (Irvan) B., 1769
    North Hampton, OH, Donnels Creek Old German Baptist Brethren Church, elder-in-charge, 948
Shoup, Jacob
    North Hampton, OH, Donnels Creek Old German Baptist Brethren Church, deacon, 948
Shoup, Jesse J., 1769

Maple Grove Old German Baptist Brethren Church, OH, minister, 791
Shoup, John, 1769
Shoup, Lela M., 2064
Shoup, Lydia L. Kinsey, 696
Shoup, Maria Wampler, 1179
Shoup, Marvin L., 1769
    North Hampton, OH, Donnels Creek Old German Baptist Brethren Church, minister, 948
Shoup, Mary A. Flory, **1179**
Shoup, Moses W., 1769
    North Hampton, OH, Donnels Creek Old German Baptist Brethren Church, minister, 948
Shoup, Rebecca, 363
Shoup, Susanna (later Holsinger), 621, *622*
Shoup, William J., 396, 766, **1179,** 1293, 1769, 2020, 2064
Shouty, Jacob, 1769
    Seneca Church of the Brethren, OH, minister, 1166
Show, James Ray, 1769, 2305
Showalter, A. Ray, 343, 692
Showalter, Aaron, 1769
Showalter, Addie Bell, 166
Showalter, Albert H., 1769
    Masons Cove Church of the Brethren, VA, pastor, 800
Showalter, Anthony J., **1179,** 1185, 2064–2065
Showalter, Arnold Ray, 1769–1770
Showalter, B. H., 1770
    Prosperity Brethren Church, WV, pastor, 1062
Showalter, Carl Eugene, 1770
    Peru, IN, Church of the Brethren, pastor, 1010
Showalter, Cecil Oliver, 692, 1770
Showalter, Christian
    Prosperity Brethren Church, WV, minister, 1062
Showalter, Christian J., 16, 1770
Showalter, Clarence H., 1770
Showalter, Daniel
    Roann, IN, Church of the Brethren, minister, 1112
Showalter, David Henry
    family history, 1979
Showalter, Dora Belle Tooker, 1844
Showalter, Effie Virginia (later Long), 753, 1840
Showalter, Elijah, 1321, 1770
Showalter, Elizabeth Anna, 2065
Showalter, Elizabeth Ellen Blosser, *See* Showalter family
Showalter, Emma Brumbaugh, 1179
Showalter family, 211, 232, 1277, 2065, *See also* Schowalter family
    Funck (Funk) family, 521
    history of, 1934
    Pennsylvania, 1975
    Prosperity Brethren Church, WV, 1062
    Sanger family, related to, 1144
Showalter, George Branner, 2065
Showalter, Grace Deal, 1770
Showalter, Hazel, 1770
Showalter, J., 42
Showalter, J. D., 1263
Showalter, John Henry, 560, **1179,** 1335, 1770, 2065
    singing schools, 1185

Brethren music, 899
hymnals, 642
hymns, 643
Showalter, J. Lester, 1770
Showalter, Jacob, 570
Peters Creek Old German Baptist
Brethren Church, VA, elder-in-
charge, 1012
Showalter, Jacob (CB), 1770
Showalter, Jacob (OGBB), 1770
Showalter, Jacob T., 2065
Showalter, Jacob W., 1893
Showalter, John, 228, 1770
Showalter, John J.
Olean Church of the Brethren, VA,
leadership by, 973
Showalter, John S., 1770
Olean Church of the Brethren, VA,
leadership by, 973
Red Hill Church of the Brethren, VA,
pastoral leadership, 1088
Showalter, John W., 1770
Nimishillen Old German Baptist
Brethren Church, OH, elder in,
937–938
Showalter, Joseph, 1770
Showalter, L. A., 1770
Showalter, L. W., 492
Showalter, Magdalena Heatwole, 753
Showalter, Margaret Heatwole, 1893
Showalter, Marion F., 1844
Showalter, Mary Ann (later Early), 413
Showalter, Michael S.
on American Revolution and Ephrata
Cloister hospital, 2356
on Ephrata Cloister, 2356
on tombstones in Cocalico Valley, IL,
2356
Showalter, Nancy (later Rodeffer), See
Rodeffer family
Showalter, Ottie (later Myers), 1397
Showalter, Peter, 1770
Showalter, Peter H., 753, 1770
Showalter, Portia (later Everett), 1934
Showalter, Preston M., 2065
Showalter, Quinter, 1770
Showalter-Rodeffer, David Henry, 2065
Showalter, Roland L., 1770
Showalter, Russell Kemper, 733, 1308,
1770, 2065, 2305
Roanoke, VA, Ninth Street Church of
the Brethren, pastor, 1113
Showalter, Russell L., 1770
Showalter, Simon, 1770
Showalter, Simon Andrew, 1770
Showalter, Susanna Miller, 1179
Showalter, Thomas, 1770
Showalter, Vada Elizabeth, 2065
Showalter, Virginia (later Fisher), 492, **492,**
2374
Showalter, Willie Swartz, 492
Shower family, 1934
Mill Creek Old German Baptist
Brethren Church, VA, 833
Shower, R. B., 1770
Showmaker, Z. B.
Ontario Brethren, 975
shows, See drama
Shrader, Hazel, 2038
Shrader, J. E., 1770
Shrantz, Michael, 1770
Shreckhise, Richard Fulton, 1770
Shreiner family, 721

Shreve family, 2080
Shreve, Richard J., 1770
Shrewsbury , PA, 338
New Freedom congregation, 323, 927
Church of the Brethren, **1179–1180**
Dunkard Brethren Congregation, **1180**
Hart, MI, Dunkard Brethren
Congregation, 2196
Shrider, Paul Franklin, 1770
Shriner, Birnie (Bernie), 1770
Shriner, Susie C. (later Anthony), 40
Shriver, Aaron F., 13, 1180, 1770
Shriver family, 2065, 2079
Shriver, H. C., 2065
Shriver, Jacob, 2065
Shriver, Jennie, 1180
Shriver, Ruth Marie, 285, **1180**
Shriver, Samuel Smith, 2065
Shriver (Schreiber), Lewis, 2065
Shriver, Thomas, 2065
Shriver, William Payne, 2065
Shrock, Benjamin, 2016
Shrock, Elizabeth Ann Yoder, 2016
Shrock, Enos, 171
Shrock, Mrs. Enos, 171
Shrock, H. J. (Mr. and Mrs.), 558
Shrock, Jacob, 1319
Shrock, Katie J. (later Yoder)
genealogy and descendants, 1943
Shrock, Mary Louise (later Miller), 2016
Shrock, Owen Benjamin, 2016
Shrope, Francis, 2293
shrouds, See burial customs; graveclothes
Shrove Tuesday, 2147
Shroyer, Daniel, 1770
Shroyer, Irene Kimmel, 1180
Shroyer, Reuben, **1180,** 1770
Orion Dunkard Brethren Congregation,
OH, presiding elder, 981
Shrum, Alonzo E.
Pennington, AR, Bethel Brethren
Church, elder, 1004
Shuck, Darrell, 1346, 1770
Shuck, Ephraim, 1770
Shuck, J. F., 1770
Shuck, Karl, 145
Shuck, Millard LeRoy, 1770
Shuck, Samuel A., 1770
Shue, Philip, 1770
Shuey, Catherine (later Moyer)
Meyer family, 822
Shuey, Daniel
Meyer family related by marriage, 822
Shuey, Margaret (later Moyer)
Meyer family, 822
Shuey, Martin
Meyer family related by marriage, 822
Shuler, Elizabeth (later Van Meter), 743
Shuler, Jacob, 431, 743, 753, 1346, 1770
Shuler, Moses, 1770
Shull, Albert M., 2066
Shull, Anna Marie (later Forney), **502,** 1837
Shull, Annie, 2076
Shull, Arthur, 1977
Shull, Arthur E., 2065
Shull, Arthur G., 1770
on Shull, Clara Elizabeth Gibson and
descendants, 2356
on Shull, William Harrison and descen-
dants, 2356
Shull, Chalmer George, **1180,** 1307, 1770,
1844, 1996, 2065
relief workers from New Paris, IN,

Church of the Brethren, 931
Shull, Clara Elizabeth Gibson
Shull, Arthur G. on descendants of,
2356
Shull, Clara Gibson, 1180, 1402
Zunkel, Cleda Shull on descendants of,
2365
Shull, Cleda Pearl (later Zunkel), **1402,**
2111
on Shull, Clara Gibson and descen-
dants, 2365
Shull, Elizabeth Brubaker, 502
on Shull, William H. and descendants,
2365
Shull, Ernest Melvin, 1770, 1844, 2066,
2305
Shull family, See Scholl family; Schull
family
Snider, Jacob, descendants of, 1154
Shull, George, 502, 1156
Shull, Gordon, 1770, 2066
and neoorthodoxy, 923
Shull, Harrison, 1770
North Hampton, OH, Donnels Creek
Old German Baptist Brethren
Church, minister, 948
Shull, Horatio Gates, 2058
Shull, Jesse Charles, 1215, 1770–1771
Shull, Lois Irene Netzley, 1844, 2066
on CB missions in India, 2356
Shull, Martha E. (later Lear), 732
Shull, Mary Grace, 1844
Shull, Mary Ruth Speicher, 1180, 1844
Shull, Merlin C., 672, 1771, 2066
Church of the Brethren military service
during World War II, 1000
Midway Church of the Brethren, TN,
providing leadership, 827
Shull, Merlin Grosh, Jr., 1771, 1844, 2066
Shull, Susan Lavinia Stoner, 1180, 1844,
2388
Shull, William H., 550, 1771
on Shull, William H. and descendants,
2365
Virden and Girard, IL, congregations,
elder, 1156
Zunkel, Cleda Shull on descendants of,
2365
Shull, William Harrison, 1180, 1402
Shull, Arthur G. on descendants of,
2356
Shull, William Russell, 738, 1771, 2066
socialism, 1198–1199
Shultz, Arthur V., 1771
Shultz, B. F., 1235, 1771
Shultz, C. R., 2066
Shultz, Carl, 1180
Shultz, Carole, 1180
Shultz, Christena, 1884
Shultz, Clyde, 2305
Shultz, Cora Winger, 1180
Shultz, Doris Virginia, 2249
Shultz, Elizabeth Ulrich, 1180
Shultz family, 1341, 2066, 2067, See also
Schultz family
Columbus, OH, Smoky Row Brethren
Church, 2166
Paul family joined in marriage, 996
Shultz, Harry, 2249
Shultz, Isaac L., 1180
Shultz, John C., 1771
Shultz, John F., 1771
Shultz, Joseph R., 68, 183, 1771, 2066,

2131, 2141, 2143, **2249,** *2249,*
2305
on Ashland Brethren, 2356
on Brethren ordinances, 2356
historical writing, 612
Shultz, Joshua, 1341, 1771
Shultz, Lawrence W., 139, 191, *199,* 202,
242, *248,* 317, *608,* 484, **1180,**
1271, 1274, 1771, 2066, 2101
historical writing, 612
on murals of history of CB, 896, 2356
Native Americans, 2230
Paul family, related to, 1157
Poland, 1041
World War II, 1372
Shultz, Martin, 1884
Shultz, Ruth, 2249
Shultz, Ruthanne, 1180
Shultz, Sarah (later Teeter), 1250
Shultz, Wilbur LeRoy, 2067
Shultzman, Bonnie Joanne Reeves, 1853
Shultzman, Terrence Dee, 1853
Shumake, Lawrence A., 1771, 2305
Shumake, Priscilla Garber, 1274
Shumaker, Alexander E., 1180
Shumaker, Catharine (later Hollinger), 620
Shumaker, David F., 674, 1771
Shumaker, Edwin F., 1771
Shumaker, Ida Cora, **1180–1181,** 1771,
1844, 2024, **2378**
Shumaker, John B.
Paradise Church of the Brethren, OH,
992
Shumaker, Lydia Lint, 1180
Shumaker, Sheila D., 2293
Shuman, Anna
Mount Wilson Church of the Brethren,
PA, 887
Shuman, David E., 2293
Shuman, Florence Miller
Shuman, L. Herman (OGBB) and,
2249
Shuman, John A., 1771, 2305
Mount Wilson Church of the Brethren,
PA, minister, 887
Shuman, L. Herman, 109, 396, 990, 1771,
2067, **2249**
on OGBB ordinances, 2356
Shuman, Luther, 109, 1771
Shuman, L. Herman (OGBB) and,
2249
Shuman, Nimrod E., 109, 1771
Shuman, Ruby Reavis
Shuman, L. Herman (OGBB) and,
2249
Shumate, David K., 2293
shunning, *See* avoidance; ban
Shuplin, John, 531
Shuplin, Mary, 531
Shuss
Snake Spring Valley Church of the
Brethren, PA, free minister, 1192
Shuss, Alva Robert, 1771
Shuss family, 1348
Shuss, John, 1771
Shutt, Barry L., 2293
Shutt, Michael H., 80, 1771
Shutt (Shott), Noah H., 1771
Shutz, Betty Marie, 1180
Shyder-Brown family, 2037
Sibert, Floyd, 1771
Rittman, OH, First Brethren Church,
pastor, 1111

Sibert, O. E., 532
Sibley, MO, 683
Sibley, Mulford Q., 2067
Siccardi, Herminia Zanetti
Tanacha Brethren church congregation,
1181
Siccardi, Luis, 53
pastor, Argentina, 1181
Sichele, Christina Regina (later Early),
1923
Sicily, *See* galleys; Liebe, Christian
galleys, 527
sick, anointing, *See* anointing the sick
The Sick, the Dying and the Dead (Royer),
788, 1128
Sickel, Clarence LeRoy, 53, 136, 172, 755,
1181, 1343, 1771, 1853
Sickel, Lois Loree Cutright, 1853
Sickel, Loraine (later Yocky), *See* Yocky,
Loraine Sickel
Sickel, Loree Cutright, 53, 136, **1181**
Sickel, Miriam (later Churchill), 1848, *See
also* Churchill, Miriam Sickel
Mexico, missionary to, 820
side camps, *See* Civilian Public Service
Forest Service, 502
Sider, E. Morris, 2067
on Anabaptists, conversion narratives
for, 2356
on Anabaptists ministry, 2356
on Pietists, conversion narratives for,
2356
Sider, Ronald J., 638, 1949, 2161
New Call to Peacemaking conference,
926
Siders, Donald O., 2293
Siders, John H., 69
Siders, Philip, 1771
Sides, Levi Harman, 511, 1771
Sides, Lucy Huffman, 1213
Sides, Owen Josiah, 109, 1771
Painter Creek Old German Baptist
Brethren Church, OH, 990
Sides, William, 511
Maple Grove Church of the Brethren,
NC, minister, 790
Sidney congregation, OH, 757
Sidney, IN, 636, 1213
Grace Brethren Church, **1181**
Sidney, OH, 151
Trinity Church of the Brethren, **1181**
Siebentäger, *See* Seventh-Day Baptists;
Risler, Jeremias
Siebert, Alvin V., 2293
Siebert, Wilbur Henry, 2067
Siegel, Mrs. Clarissa
South Bend, IN, First Brethren Church,
1203
Siegel, Nancy
on Juniata College, 2356
Siegmund-Schultze, Friedrich, 659
Siegrist family, 749
Sieman family, *See* Simmons family
Sierra Pines Old German Baptist Brethren
Church, CA, 1181, 1335
example of place name, 911
Sierra View Grace Brethren Church, *See*
Placerville, CA, Sierra View Grace
Brethren Church
Sievers, Alma, 1915
Sifrit, Lynn Curtis, 1771
Sifrit, Robert L., 141, 1312, **2386**
Sifrit, Robert LaVerne, Jr., 1771

Sifting Time
Frey, Andreas, 517
Moravian Church, 875, 876
Sigerfoos, Andrew
Pleasant View Brethren Church, IN,
2377
Sigerfoos, Emma, 561
Sigle, Dennis E., 2293
Sigler family, 1383, *See also* Ziegler family
bibliography, 1874
Signau, Switzerland, 1401
Signs of the Times, 2161
Sikes, David E., 2067
Siler, George, 205
Siler, George V., **1181–1182,** 1771
Prices Creek Old German Baptist
Brethren Church, OH, presiding
elder, 1057
Sill, D. Elmer, 1771
Silver, Albert Peter, 2067
Silver City
Wilson, Leland on, 2363
Silver Creek Brethren Church, NE, *See*
Falls City, NE, Brethren Church
Silver Creek Church of the Brethren, OH,
129, 741, **1182**
Silver Creek German Baptist Brethren, NE,
921
Silver Creek, IL, Church of the Brethren,
355, 1220, 1226, 1333
Mount Morris College, 884
Mount Morris, IL, Church of the
Brethren, 883
Silver Creek, KS Church of the Brethren
(Arkansas City), **54**
Silver Creek, NE, Church of the Brethren,
See Falls City Church of the
Brethren, NE
Silver, Elmer G., 438, 1771
The Silver Feather (Coffman), 748
Silver Lake Church of the Brethren,
NE, **1182**
Silver Lake, IN, 1333
Silver Leaf, VA, congregation
Red Oak Grove Church of the
Brethren, VA, 1089
Silver, Rollo Gabriel, 1861, 2067
Silver Springs, MD, Good Shepherd
Church of the Brethren, **1182**
Silver Springs, PA, 2099
Silverbell Grace Brethren Church, Tucson,
AZ, 1278
Silvers, Arthur, 1223
New River Old German Baptist
Brethren Church, ministers for,
931–932
Silvers family, 142
Silvers, James Garson, 1771
Silvuse, Susan Catherine (later Shamber-
ger), *See* Shamberger, Susan
Catherine Silvuse
Simafranca, Cyndi, 463
Simafranca, Rick, 463
Simi Valley, CA, Grace Brethren Church,
1182
Simm, Ed, 731
Simmons, Alfred T., 1771
Simmons, Alonzo L., 1771
Simmons, Andrew L., 1771
Shady Grove Old German Baptist
Brethren Church, OH, minister,
1171
Simmons, Benjamin Forest, 1771, 2067

Simmons, Bernard, 749, 1221, 1380, 1771
Simmons, Brian, 2293
Simmons, C. R., 246
Simmons, Carl, Jr., 1383. 1771, 2305, **2386**
Simmons, Charles Hamilton, 514, 1771
Simmons, Christian, 1771
Simmons, Claude Reynolds, Jr., 424, 1771, **2386**
Simmons, Evelyn W., 1771
Simmons family, 224, 717, **1182**
   North English, IA, Church of the Brethren, 947
   Shady Grove Old German Baptist Brethren Church, OH, 1171
Simmons, Glennis (later Walker), 2296
Simmons, Grant DeWayne, 1772
Simmons, J. T.
   Osceola Church of the Brethren, MO, district representative, 984
Simmons, James Woodrow, 1772, 2305
Simmons, John B., 1223, 1772
Simmons, John M., 1772
   Shady Grove Old German Baptist Brethren Church, OH, minister, 1171
Simmons, Keith Walter, 2293
Simmons, Nicholas, 1182
Simmons, Omar N., 1772
Simmons, Phillip J., 21, 275, 515, 586, 688, 746, 1772, 2305
   Southern Lancaster Grace Brethren Church, PA, associate pastor, 1207
Simmons, Randall V., 679, 2293
Simmons, Reynolds C., 1287
Simmons, Reynold
   Pipe Creek Church of the Brethren, MD, minister, 1026
Simmons, Richard James, 714, 745, 1333, 1772
Simmons, Roger Norman, 1772
Simmons, Rolandus Velton, 129, 912, 1772
Simmons, Samuel, 263
Simmons, Sarah, 263
Simmons, Thomas Jefferson, 373, 1772
Simmons, W. B., 1772
Simmons, W. P., 1772
Simmons, William K., 1772
   Pleasant Valley Church of the Brethren, OH, 1035
Simms, P. Marion, 2067
Simms, William
   Quiet Dell Brethren Church, PA, 1076
Simon, Claude E., 1120
Simon, Elizabeth Fitz, 1120
Simon family, *See* Simmons family genealogy, 1956
Simon, Frances Fitz (later Rolston) relief and service volunteer, 1120
Simon, Grant M., 2083
Simon, J. Edwin, 265
Simon, (Supt.), 2067
Simond family
   at New Rockford, ND, Church of the Brethren, 932
Simone, Margareta, 209
Simons, Howard, 2067
Simons, Menno, *See* Menno Simons
simple life, 155, 1142, **1182–1183**, 2099, 2101, 2109, *See also* lifestyles
   alcohol and, 16
   bibliography, 1884
   Brethren concern and doctrine, 1182–1183

Church of the Brethren, 300
Community of the True Inspiration, 330
   dress in, 403, *See also* dress
   ethics, 458
   funerals, 523, 524
   furniture, 525
   General Welfare Board (CB), 540
   Grace Schools (Grace Theological Seminary, Grace College), 563
   hoops, 628
   Lancaster Co., PA, 2060
   Nead, Peter as spokesman for, 918–920, *919*
   Nigeria, 307
   nonconformity, 940, 941
   Old German Baptist Brethren, 969, 2178
   Old Order, 973, 1965
   sanctification, 1142
   Sermon on the Mount, 1169
   theology and, 2255
Simpson, A. B., 259
Simpson, A. P., 1772
Simpson Co., KY (originally Warren Co.), 398, 688, 689
Simpson family
   Osceola, IN, Grace Brethren Church, 983
Simpson, Hannah Catherine (later Arnold), 1397
Simpson, Harry
   Osceola, IN, Grace Brethren Church, lay pastor, 984
Simpson, Harry G., 1772
Simpson, Henry, 2067
Simpson, Joanne, 318
Simpson, John
   Island Pond, VT, Grace Brethren Church, 2209
Simpson, O. P., 1772
Simpson, Russell Edwards, 164, 318, 2293
Simpson, Sandra Carlene, 173, 1848
Simrishamn congregation, 1243
Sims, James L., 1772
Simultaneum
   Roman Catholic edict on interdenominational relations, **1183**
sin, **1183–1184**, 1868, 1874, 2024
   acknowledgment of, and restoration of disciplined members, 1102
   Brethren doctrine of salvation, 1140
   Christian Brethren and, 281
   Eternal Security, 457
   free will, 514
   human nature, doctrine of, 635
   humility, 636
   original sin, 981
   Ottoni-Wilhelm, Dawn on understandings of, 2349
   repentance, doctrine of, 1099
   sanctification, 1142
   sources on, 2319
   wellness and, 2261
"Sincere Account," *See* "Aufrichtige Nachricht"
Sinckler family
   at New Rockford, ND, Church of the Brethren, 932
Sincock, David, 2293
Sine, C., 2067
Sines, Abraham Lincoln, 558, 1772
Sines, Albert J., 558, 1772

Sines, C. B., 1772
Sines, Emmanuel, 1772
Sines family, 2019
Sines, Henry B., 1772
Sines, Jonas W., 124, 728, 1772, 2305
   Pleasant Hill Church of the Brethren, WV, pastor, 1033
Sines, Lum, 1772
Sines, S. J., 1772
Sines, Sell, 1772
Sines, U. Grant, 558, 1772
Sines, W. F., 1772
Sines, William T., 1772
Singer, Anna, 2105, 2186
Singer, Barbara, 1144
Singer family, 708, 1144, *See also* Sanger family
Singer, Hanna, 2067
Singer Hill Grace Brethren Church, PA, **1184**
Singer, John, 1144, *See* Sanger family
Singer, Ralph L., 1772
Singers Glen, VA
   Gospel Trumpet, The, 561
   Funk, Joseph, 525
   Mount Zion congregation
   Flory, John, 498
singing, 60, **1184–1185**
   Brethren music, 898–899
   choristers and, 279
   Christian Brethren and, 281
   debates, 371
   family worship, 474
   funerals, 524
   gospel songs, 561
   hymnody in religious communal societies, 2006
   hymns, 643
   Kingdom Songs, 1985
   Music Committee (CB), 899
   Music Committee (DB), 899–900
   musical instruments, 900
   Plymouth Brethren, 1038
   worship services, 1375, 1376, 1378
singing schools, 151, 171, **1185–1186**
   Brethren music, 899
   Ephrata Cloister, 1963
   hymnals, 642
   masters of, and gospel songs, 560
   Showalter, Anthony Johnson, 1179
   Showalter, John Henry, 1179
"singings," 899, **1186**
single immersion, 2040
   backward, 68
   Plymouth Brethren, 1038
   Quinter, James on origin of, 2351
single mode of feetwashing, 237, 334, 335, 763, **1186**, *1186*
   Brethren Church, 185
   Congregational Brethren, 335
   Daniel Vaniman, 1303
   Declaration of Principles, 372
   disfellowship, 334, 734
   Eyman, Peter, 464
   Far Western Brethren, 475, 476
   feetwashing, 481, 1186, *1186*
   Flory, John, 498
   Gibson, Daniel B., 547
   Greenmount Church of the Brethren, VA, 571
   Hendricks, Franklin A., 597
   Hendricks, John, 597
   Hoppingite Schism, 630

Hostetler Brethren, 631
Leedy Brethren, 734
Miami Valley Petition, 823
Old Order movement, 206
Oregon, 980
Thurman, W. C., 1308
Wolfe, George, III, 1358
"Single Mode" Brethren, **1186**
single persons
    fellowship houses, 482
    Kedar community house at Ephrata
        Community for, 685–686
    outreach to, Skyridge Church of the
        Brethren, Kalamazoo, MI, 681
Singmaster, Elsie, 747, 2067
Singo, Tom, 2293
Sink, Ammon, 1338
Sink, Barry Dean, 2293
Sink, Clarence David, 439, 1323, 1772
Sink, David F., 1772
    Reedley, CA, Church of the Brethren,
        elder, 1091
    Salem Church of the Brethren, IA,
        pastor, 1137
Sink, David (FGBC), 1772
Sink, Doris Onalee Beougher, 2067
Sink family
    Germantown Old German Baptist
        Brethren Church, VA, 544
    Greenwood Church of the Brethren,
        MO, 572
    Salem Church of the Brethren, IA,
        1137
Sink, Henry A., 1772
Sink, Julia, 157
Sink, Robert L., 31, 46, 1772
    Mexico, IN, Church of the Brethren,
        paid minister, 821
    Myrtle Point, OR, Church of the
        Brethren, pastor, 906
    Rossville, IN, Church of the Brethren,
        minister, 1124
Sink, Sophiah (later Kesler), 690
Sinking Spring, OH, 1227
    Grace Brethren Church, **1186**
        Marble Furnace Church of the
        Brethren
Sinking Springs congregation, PA
    Frystown, PA, Bethel Dunkard
        Brethren Congregation, 521
Sinks family, 2044
Sinnett, C. N., 2067–2068
Sino-Brethren Library, 2129
Sino-Japanese War
    missions and missionaries during
        China, 2089
Sinteff, Michael David, 2293
Sinu, Dandi O., 306
Sioux Co., IA
    Sheldon Church of the Brethren, IA,
        1175
Sipe, Aaron, 1772
Sipe, Robert C., 1772
Sipes, Sarah, 373
Sipesville, PA, Church of the Brethren,
    1186–1187
    Geiger Church of the Brethren, PA,
        533
    Maple Spring Church of the Brethren,
        PA, 791
Siple, George Lee, 1772
Sircle, W. R., 1772
Sirk family, 1912

Sisco, Richard, 2293
Siskiyou Co., CA, 236
Sisler, Michael, 360, 1772
Sisler, Sam L., 1772
Sisler, Samuel A., 1772
Sisler schoolhouse, WV, 1254
Sisson, Carl E., 114, 1772
Sister Abigail, See Hildebrand, Maria (later
    Mack)
Sister Albina, See Höcker, Margaretha
Sister Lucia (Roses of Sharon), 1172
Sister Marcella, See Sauer, Maria Christina
    Gross
Sister Maria, *See,* Eicher, Maria
Sister Petronella, See Höcker, Maria
Sister Rahel, See Landert, Maria, 722
Sister Sarah Buried, 2068
Sisterhood of Mary and Martha, 97–98,
    182, 1161, **1187,** *See also* Serving
    My Master
    Miller, Clara Worst, 834, 864
    Missions education, 864
    Serving My Master, 1169
    Sisters' Society of Christian Endeavor
        (BC), 1188
    Women's Missionary Society, 1187
Sisters' Aid Sewing Society
    Harrisburg, PA, First Church of the
        Brethren, 586
Sisters' Aid Societies, 179, 220, 308, **1187,**
    1361, 1363, *See also The Mission-
    ary Advocate*
    Big Sky Brethren Church/American
        Baptist Church, MT, 142
    Church of the Brethren
        Council of Women's Work, 1187,
        1188
    The Missionary Advocate, 855
    missions education, 864
    Murphy, Sara Florence Fogelsanger,
        president, 897
    first statistical reports, 1218
    relief and service efforts, 1097
    Rock Creek Church of the Brethren,
        KS, 1117
    Swigart, Anna Swigart, 1245
    White Branch Church of the Brethren,
        IN, 1339
Sisters and Brother, Inc.
    on conscientious objectors and World
        War II, 2356–2357
Sisters of Saron, *See* Snow Hill Nunnery
    Riley, Jobie E. on women of, 2352
    Seachrist, Denise Ann on, 2356
Sisters of the Common Life, *See* Brethren
    (Sisters) of the Common Life
Sisters' Society of Christian Endeavor
    (SSCE), 116, 381, **1187–1188,**
    1359, 1361, 1362
    Hedrick, Laura E. N. Grossnickle, 593
    pension funds, 1007
    revivals at Nappanee, IN, (First)
        Brethren Church, 914
    Shively, Nora Early, 1178
    Sterling, Mary Malinda, 1221
    Women's Missionary Society,
        1187–1188
Sites, Barbara (later Flory), *495*
Sites, I. William, 1772
Sites, S. G., 1772
    North Mill Creek Church of the
        Brethren, WV, elder, 949
Sitka, IN

Church of God (New Dunkers), 297
    Patton, Uriah, 996
Sittler, Joseph
    address on environmental ethics, 1916
Sittser, Gerald L.
    on historic peace churches and World
        War II, 2357
Sivit, William, 1772
Six, Joseph, 1318
Six Mystical Points (Boehme), 156
Six-Principle Baptists, 87
sixteenth century
    Anabaptism, 5
    Reformation, 28–29
    revolutionary peasant movements, 28
    Strasbourg (Straßburg), France, 19
*The Sixtieth Anniversary of the Brethren
    Publishing Interest,* 2068
Sizemore, A. Butler, 209, 1772, 2068
Sizemore, Joseph I., 264, 1772, **2386**
Sizemore, Joseph J., 1772
Sizemore, Monroe, 1772
Skaggs, Ralph E., 582, 1280, 1772, 2305
Skean family, 326
Skeels, W. N., 1772
Skeen, Denise Elaine Adair, 1853
Skeen, Robert Allan, 1772, 1853, 2293
Skeggs, Annie Foutz, 1316
Skeggs, Frank W., 1316
Skeggs, Rebeccca C. (later Wampler), **1316,**
    1846, 2017
Skeldon, William R., 1772
    Mishawaka, IN, Brethren Church,
        pastor, 852
Skidmore schoolhouse, MI, 1304
Skiles, Amanda, 2068
Skiles, Barbara
    Ripon, CA, Grace Brethren Church,
        1110
Skiles, Beth
    Ripon, CA, Grace Brethren Church,
        1110
Skiles, Brad
    Modesto, CA, Big Valley Grace
        Community Church (FGBC), 866
Skiles, Clement, 109, 431, 496, 1772–1773,
    2249–2250
    Mud Valley Old German Baptist
        Brethren Church, IL, presiding
        elder, 892
    Pigg River Old German Baptist
        Brethren Church, VA, elder-in-
        charge, 1023
Skiles, Daniel C., 1773
Skiles, Daniel V., 965, 2305
Skiles, David A., 965, 2249–2250, 2305
Skiles, Esther (Hettie) Marie, 2249
Skiles family, 405, 1213
    Genesee Old German Baptist Brethren
        Church, MI, 540
Skiles, Frances
    Modesto, CA, Big Valley Grace
        Community Church (FGBC), 866
Skiles, Gary
    Skiles, Clement S. and, 2250
Skiles, Henry A., 373, 1773
Skiles, Hettie Milyard, 2249
Skiles, Jacob W., 373, **1188–1189,** 1333,
    1773, 2068
    Middlefork Old German Baptist
        Brethren Church, IN, presiding
        elder, 826
    Service Committee for Conscientious

Objectors, 1372
Skiles, Jesse E., 1335, 1773
Skiles, John, 2068
Skiles, John J., 105, 1188, 1773,
Skiles, Joseph D., Jr., 109, 1773, 2305
Skiles, Joseph D., Sr., 105, 109, 1773, **2386**
Skiles, Leland, 2293
Skiles, Lonnie
    Modesto, CA, Big Valley Grace Com-
        munity Church (FGBC), 866
Skiles, M. Keith, 1773, 2305, **2386**
    Shady Grove Old German Baptist
        Brethren Church, OH, minister,
        1171
Skiles, Marvin Edward, 1773
    Shady Grove Old German Baptist
        Brethren Church, OH, minister,
        1171
Skiles, Mary Metzger, 1189
Skiles, Noah H., 1773
    Middlefork Old German Baptist
        Brethren Church, IN, minister, 826
Skiles, Ora Samuel, 1354, 1773, 2305
    Modesto, CA, Big Valley Grace
        Community Church (FGBC), 866
Skiles, Paul David, 2293
Skiles, Richard, 496, 1773
    Ripon, CA, Grace Brethren Church, lay
        pastor, 1110
Skiles, Roy D., 1773, 2305
    Oak Grove Old German Baptist
        Brethren Church, OH, minister,
        956
Skiles, Sara Malinda Wolf, 1188
Skiles, Sherry
    Modesto, CA, Big Valley Grace
        Community Church (FGBC), 866
Skiles, Virginia Frantz
    Skiles, Clement S. (OGBB) and, 2250
Skinner, Charles M., 2068
    on Ephrata Cloister, 2357
Skinner, Harry, 2305
Skinner, L. Beecher
    Mexico, IN, Brethren Church, 821
Skinner, Rosemary Keller, 2051
Skinner, Virginia (later Cullen), 480
Skippack, Associated Brethren of, *See*
    Associated Brethren of the
    Skippack
Skippack Mennonite Meetinghouse
    Schools, 2336
Skippack, PA, 175, 394, 1055, **1189**, 2036
    Church of the Brethren, PA, 584, 843,
        1189
Skippack Valley, PA, 2036
skirt extenders, *See* hoops
skits, *See* drama
Skordas, Gust, 2068
Skyridge Church of the Brethren,
    Kalamazoo, MI, 681
Slabaugh, Dennis L., 2378
    on Dompelaars, 2357
    on Dunkers, 2357
    on First and Radical Reformations,
        2357
    historiography, 2201
    Prague Conferences and, 2239
Slabaugh, Emma Gensinger, 1189
Slabaugh family, 1330, **2378**, *See also*
    Schlabach family
Slabaugh, James Warren, 1380, 1773
Slabaugh, Mary Beckner, 1189
Slabaugh, Warren William, 126, 381, **1189,**

1341, 1388, 1773, 2068, **2378**
Onekama, MI, Church of the Brethren,
    minister, 975
Slabaugh, William H., 1189
Slaggs, Slone, 1773
Slagle, George W., 264, 453, 590, 1773
    Midway Church of the Brethren, TN,
        providing leadership, 827
    Petersons Chapel Church of the
        Brethren, NC, 1012
    Pleasant View Church of the Brethren,
        TN, 1037
Slagle, Henry Oscar, 2068
Slagle, Maude Brenneman, 2068
Slate Creek, KS, Church of the Brethren,
    340, *See also* Conway Springs,
    KS, Church of the Brethren
Slater, Edgar O., 1773
    Rockingham Church of the Brethren,
        MO, pastor, 1118
Slater, Lloyd A., 1773
Slater, P. E., 1773
slavery, 1, *See also* abolition of slavery;
    galley slaves
    African Americans, 2128
    American Colonization Society, 22
    ASSU, 283
    Brethren forbidden to own, 838
    Brethren opposition to, **1189–1190**
    Cartwright, Peter, 258
    census, Rockingham Co., VA, 2077
    Civil War, 314
    doctrine on, 175, 179
    emancipation, 443
    Evangelical Association, 459
    Fisher, Elias, 491
    galley slaves, 253
    Georgia, 540
    Harpers Ferry, 585
    Hon, Peter Keithly, 627
    Hostetler Brethren, 631
    Hylton family, 641
    Longenecker, Stephen L. on Virginia
        and Shenandoah Valley and, 2344
    minorities, ethnic and racial, 849
    Moomaw, Benjamin Franklin, 873
    opposition to
        Kline, John, 701
        Knouff, Hannah Pfouts, 704
        Virginia, 1307–1308
        Wolfe, George, II, 1357
        Yount, Daniel, 1391
    opposition to, and social action, 1196
    preaching against, 1–2
    Price, Isaac, advocating abolition, 1056
    Sauer, Johann Christoph, I, opposition
        to, 1147
    Shaver, George H., opposition to, 1174
    Social Gospel Movement, 1197
    Society of Friends, 1199, 2093
    sources on, 2324
    Virginia, 2110
    Weir, Samuel, 1327–1328
Slawter, H. Vernon, 1773
Slayback, George Pendleton, Jr., 2068
Slease, O. C., 1773
Slee, Jacobus C. van, 2068
sleighbells, *See* bells
Slider, James R., 1773
Slife, Malinda (later Appleman), 44
Slifer, ___ (son-in-law of Jacob Long), 724
Slifer, Charles H., 45, 1773
Slifer, Emanuel, 1773

Slifer, Esrom, 274
Slifer family, 216, 1359, 1920
Slifer, IA, Church of the Brethren
    (Farnhamville), 479, **1190**
Slifer, John (Schleifer), 216
Slifer, O. C., 1773
Slifer, Oscar Raymond, Jr., 1773
Slifer, Sarah (later Gilbert), 548
Slifer, Walter Lloyd, 1773, 2068
Sligar, Sam J., 1773
Sligloff family
    Mortonhouse (ship), 2373, 2376
Slingluff, *See* Schlingluff
Slingluff, A. Henry
    translated *Rechte und Ordnungen*
        (*Rights and Ordinances*), 1152
Slingluff family
    Mortonhouse (ship), 2373, 2376
    Scherffig family, related to, 1152
Slingluff, John H., 1773
Slingluff, John U., 565
Sloan, Amy
    Okeechobee, FL, Grace Brethren
        Church, 963
Sloan, Jacob, 317
Sloatman, Samuel, 1773
Slocum, Frances
    Native Americans, 2230
Sloniker, Aaron
    St. Francis Church of the Brethren, AR,
        1134
Sloniker (Slonaker), Jacob, 1773
Slothour, Harold, 471, 1773, 2153
Slothour, Wilbur M., 2293
Slothower, George W.
    South Solomon Old German Baptist
        Brethren Church, KS, deacon, and
        Eight Mile (OGBB) congregation,
        1206
Slothower, Sarah
    South Solomon Old German Baptist
        Brethren Church, KS, 1206
Slough, Jacob, 1013
Slough, Rebecca
    on ministry, 2357
Slough (Schlauch), Catherine (later Pfautz),
    1013
Sloughfy, JuliAnne Bowser, 2293
Slusher, C. D., 1773
Slusher family, 1345
Slusher, Henry, 231
Slusher, Jerry H., 727, 1773
Sluss, Charlie J., 1773
    Pound River Church of the Brethren,
        VA, elder, 1049
Sluss, Cline, 1773
Sluss, Earle, 1773
Sluss, Elijah, 1773
Sluss, General W., 1773
Sluss, James Paul, 1773
    Krypton, KY, Brethren Church, 2212
Sluss, Johnny, 1773
Sluss, Paul Timothy, 2293
Sluss, S. C., 1773
Slusser family, 153
    Musselman family related to, 901
Slyder, James, 1773
Small, Charles E., 2068
A Small Collection of Pearls (hymnal),
    1211
    Pfautz, John Eby, 1014
Small, Edward, 1773
small-group ministries

People of the Covenant (POC) (BC), 2237
Small, James Edwin, 1773
Small, Jane, 1773
Smalley, David
    Gotha, FL, New Covenent Church of the Brethren, 2190
Smalley, David L., 2293
Smalley, Marjorie Mae, 2293
Smalley, Paul, 1773
Smals, James Russel, 227, 1773
Smals, Ronald Alvin, 1309, 2293
    Ocala, FL, Grace Brethren Church, 2232
Smawley family
    Golden Church of the Brethren, NC, 555
Smead, Elizabeth, 274
Smell, Donald G., 1773, **2386**
Smelser family, 2038
Smeltzer, Abraham, 1191
Smeltzer, Amos
    Cando, ND, 1191
Smeltzer, Anna Heiny, 1191
Smeltzer, Bonnie Kline, 2293
Smeltzer, Delbert, 1191
Smeltzer, Elias, 1191
Smeltzer, Eva Etta Miller
    Cando, ND, 1191
Smeltzer family, **1191**, 2068
Smeltzer, Henry, 1191
Smeltzer, J. E., 1773
Smeltzer, J. W., 1773
Smeltzer, Jesse, 1191
Smeltzer, Jesse Adam, 1773, 2068
Smeltzer, John E., 505, 1191, 1773
Smeltzer, Kenneth Kline, 2293
Smeltzer, Maria Gascho, 1191
Smeltzer, Mary Blocher, *24,* 24–25, 200–201, 1190, 1359, 2183, **2250**
    Manzanar Relocation Center, teaching at, 789
    World Friendship Center, 1369
    World War II relief work, 1373
Smeltzer, Mary E. Klinzman, 1773
Smeltzer, Maurice R., 187, 1191
Smeltzer, Moses, 1191, 1773
Smeltzer, Olive Heckman, 1191
Smeltzer, Philip, 1191
Smeltzer, R. E., 695
Smeltzer, Ralph Emerson, *24,* 24–25, 73, 200–201, 302, **1190–1191**, 1191, 1773, 2068, 2079, 2093
    biography of, 2201
    Japan, 669
    Longenecker, Stephen L. on, 2343
    minorities, ethnic and racial, 850
    and neoorthodoxy, 923
    Selma, AL, 1191
    Smeltzer, Mary Blocher (CB) and, 2250
    social justice leader, 1190–1191
    Washington Office (CB) and, 2260
    World War II relief work, 1373
Smeltzer, Willard Wesley, 1773
Smigh, William, 2069
Smiley, David, 1774
Smiley, H. M., 2068
Smiley, Nathan, 2105
Smitely, Lester O., 1774
Smitely, William H., 1774
Smith, A. Harrison, 1774
Smith, A. J., 576, 633

North Star Church of the Brethren, OK, elder, 950
Smith, Aaron, 1243, 1774
Smith, Adam Herbert, 1774
Smith, Adam R., 1774
Smith, Albert J., 40, 1774
Smith, Albert Ray, 1774, 1844, 2047
Smith, Anna Margaret (later Early), 414
Smith, Anna Piszczon-Czaja, 2069
Smith, Anne (later Forney)
    descendants, 1939
Smith, Arthur Eugene, 2293
Smith, Arthur Morris, 1774, 2305
Smith, B. W., 692
Smith, Barbara Miller
    Müller (Miller) family, 894
Smith, Bartley, 1774
Smith, Beatrice P. (later Gingrich), 550
Smith, Belinda, 540
Smith, Benjamin W., 1774
    Old Furnace Church of the Brethren, WV, presiding elder, 966
Smith, Berton E., 1774
Smith, Beverly Albert, 228, 246, 676, 1774, **2386**
    Mountain Valley Church of the Brethren, TN, pastor, 889
    Pleasant Hill Church of the Brethren, TN, pastor/elder, 1032
Smith, Bill
    Lakeland, FL, Grace Brethren Church, 2213
Smith, Bonnie Carol Throne, 1844
Smith, Branson, 362
Smith, Brian, 1774
    Riverside, CA, Grace Brethren Church, pastor, 1111
Smith, C. Henry, 2068
Smith, Caleb H., 1774
Smith, Carl Franklin, 752, 1774
    Manassas, VA, Church of the Brethren, minister, 785
Smith, Catherine E., 2068
    on Kuntz, Christian, 2357
Smith, Cecil, 1774
Smith, Celia (later Shankster), 1844, **2248**
Smith Chapel Church of the Brethren, WV, 1191
    Red Oak Ridge German Baptist Brethren Church, WV, **1089**
Smith, Charles Bragg, 1774
    Morrill, KS, Church of the Brethren, pastor, 876
    North Beatrice Church of the Brethren, NE, elder, 945
    Red Cloud, NE, Church of the Brethren, providing leadership, 1088
Smith, Charles Russell, 1774, 2069, 2305
Smith, Charles W., 1774
Smith, Christian, 2293
Smith, Clara, 155, 362
Smith, Clara A. Walker, 104, 1774
Smith, Clarence L., 1774
Smith, Clifford, family
    San Ysidro, CA, Grace Brethren Church, 1142
Smith, Clifford Neal, 2069
Smith Co., KS
    North Solomon Old German Baptist Brethren Church, KS, 949
Smith, Colleen
    Gotha, FL, New Covenent Church of

the Brethren, 2190
Smith, Craig H., 2293
Smith Creek Fellowship Church of the Brethren, WV, 342, **1191**
    example of place name, 911
Smith, Curtis, 356
Smith, D. D., 40, 1774
Smith, D. M., 1774
Smith, Daniel, 1774
Smith, David (CB-1), 1774
Smith, David (CB-2), 1774
Smith, Delbert Le Roy, 1774
    Newton, KS, Church of the Brethren, pastor in, 934
Smith, Dwight, 740
Smith, E., 1774
Smith, E. H., 229, 239, 484, 562, 629
    Mansfield, OH, Walcrest Brethren Church, pastor, 787
    Raystown Brethren Church, PA, pastor, 1084
Smith, E. I., 1774
Smith, E. J., 447, 633, 651
    Martinsburg, PA, Grace Brethren Church, pastor, 798
Smith, E. Lee, 1774
Smith, Edward S., 2069
Smith, Edward Sanger, 2069
Smith, Edward Stanley, 1774
Smith, Edwin W., 1774, 2305
Smith, Eileen (later Shank), *See* Shank, Eileen Smith
Smith, Elizabeth (later Royer), 1094
Smith, Elizabeth (later Shank), *See* Shank, Elizabeth Smith
Smith, Elizabeth (later Ziegler), 1397
Smith, Elmer L., 2068
Smith, Elmer S., 2068
Smith, Emmanuel J., 1774
Smith, Emory Clayton, 1774, 2305
Smith, Esther
    memoirs, 2350
Smith, Eugene E., 1774
Smith, Eugene Heckman, 350, 551, 674, 927, 1774
    Sergeantsville, NJ, Brethren Church, pastor, 1167
Smith, Eugene McHugh, 1774
Smith, Ezra, 1774
Smith family, 164, 165, 332, 461, 733, 1304, 2084, 2094, *See* Indiana
    Fremont, OH, Grace Brethren Chapel, 515
    history of, 1957
    Minerva, OH, Grace Brethren Church, 843
    Mishler family, related to, 852
    Phoenix, AZ, Northwest Grace Brethren Church, 1019
    Reliance, VA, Mount Zion Brethren Church, 1096
    Royer family, related to, 1128
Smith Fork Church of the Brethren, MO, *See* Plattsburg Church of the Brethren, MO
    example of place name, 911
Smith Fork congregation, CO
    example of place name, 911
Smith, Francis Jane Sheller, 1844
Smith, Frank R., 1774
Smith, Fred William, 1774
Smith, George, 1774
    Phoenix, AZ, Northwest Grace

Brethren Church, pastor, 1019
Schuykill Church of the Brethren, PA, elder, 1157
Smith, George C., 1774
Smith, George S., 1774
Smith George V., 2305
Smith, H. Berlin, 1774
Smith, H. J., 1774
Smith, Hannah W., 691
prayer, 1051
Smith, Harlan, 504
Smith, Harold D., 1160, 1774
On Earth Peace Assembly, 2235
Smith, Harold E., 1774–1775
Smith, Harry C., 1775
Smith, Harry L., 1775, 2068
Smith, Henry W., 1775
Smith, Henry Z., 1775
Smith, Herbert, 733
Ridgeway Community Church of the Brethren, PA, pastor, 1109
Smith, Hilda Neff, 2068
Smith, Hiram, 14, 65, 1775
Smith, Horace W., 2069
Smith, Isaac, 1363, 1775
Smith, J. D., 1775
Smith, J. E., 1775
Smith, J. Edward, 1775
Smith, J. Harry, 1775
Smith, J. W., 1775
Smith, Jacob, 500, 1775
Müller (Miller) family, 894
Smith, Jacob O., 1775
Smith, James B., 1775
Smith, James R., 21, 447, 743, 1775
Silver Lake Church of the Brethren, NE, elder and minister, 1182
Smith, Jasper Emory, 1775, 2305
Smith, Jeffrey
Theological Practorium, The (CBBCI) and, 2254
Smith, John Asa, 1775
Smith, John (CB-1), 404, 1275, 1775, 2075
Smith, John (CB-2), 1775
Smith, John F., 588, 2293
Smith, John Henry, 1775
Smith, John M., 1363, 1775
Smith, John W., 1224
Smith, John W. (OGBB-1), 1775
Smith, John W. (OGBB-2), 1775
Smith, Joseph, 248
Smith, Joseph H., 2069
Smith, Joseph Jr., 298
Smith, Kenneth L., 2004
Smith, L. C., 399
Smith, L. Garvin, 332, 417, 720, 1775
Smith, L. R., 1775
Smith, L. S., 1775
Smith, L. W., 141, 1775
Paradise, CA, Church of the Brethren, 992
Smith, Larry
on Blair County Brethren, 2357
Smith, Laurean
Moorefield, WV, Church of the Brethren, pastor, 874
Smith, Laurean R., 1315, 1775
Smith, Leander, 447, **1191**, 1215, 1775, 2069
Minot, ND, Church of the Brethren, elder, 851
Muscatine, IA, First Church of the Brethren, pastor, 898

Myrtle Point, OR, Church of the Brethren, pastor, 906
Newberg, OR, Church of the Brethren, pastor in, 933
Smith, Lee R., 1775
Smith, Lem, 1775
Smith, Lenn Wesley, 1775
Smith, Leonard William, 1775, 2293
Smith, LeRoy, 1775
Smith, Levi F., *550*
Smith, Lydia
Poling, Newton L. on descendants of, 2350
Poling, Virginia on descendants of, 2350
Poling, Virginia on letters of, 2350
Smith, Mariah, 540
Smith, Marie Jean
on Rudy, John, ancestors and descendants of, 2349
on Rudy, Mary Garman and ancestors and descendants of, 2349
Smith, Marion W., 1775
Smith, Mary (later Quinter), 1076
Smith, Mary (later Rittenhouse), 1110
Smith, Mary (later Winger), 1350
Smith, Mattie, 672
Smith, Michael David, 590, 1775
Smith, Michael E., 2293
Smith, Michelle
Gotha, FL, New Covenent Church of the Brethren, 2190
Smith, Mikal
Menifee, CA, New Hope Community Church of the Valley, 2220
Smith, Nevin L., 1775
Smith, Olive Murann, 169
Smith, Paul, 1775
Smith, Paul H., 1775
Smith, Peter, 2293
Smith, Peter A., 1775
Smith, "Racoon" John, 627
Smith, Randall Lee, 1775
Smith, Raymond R., 1775, 2305
Smith, Reilly Richard, 2166, 2170, 2293
South America Theological Seminary (BC) and, 2252
Smith, Richard Allen, 670, 1775
Smith, Richard M., 1775
Smith River Church of the Brethren, VA, **1191–1192,** 1267
start of other congregations, 929
Smith River congregation, WV
example of place name, 911
Smith, Robert E.
Ridgeway Community Church of the Brethren, PA, moderator, 1109
Gotha, FL, New Covenent Church of the Brethren, 2190
Smith, Rolland Perry, 1844
Smith, Rolland Wallace, 1775
Smith, Rufus E., 1775
Pound River Church of the Brethren, VA, pastor, 1049
Smith, S. D., 345
Smith, S. S., 1775
Smith, Samuel, 378, 491, 608, **1191,** 2069
historical writing, 611
New Testament as Brethren canon, 133
Smith, Samuel M., 442, 1400, 1775
Smith, Samuel Z., 1775
Sidney, OH, Trinity Church of the Brethren, minister, 1181

Smith, Sara Root (later Sayler), *See* Sayler, Sara Root Smith
Smith, Sarah Ann (later Stein), 1220
Smith, Sarah (later Rittenhouse), 1110
Smith (Schmidt), Elizabeth (later Reber), 1085
Smith (Schmidt), Peter, 1383
Smith-Shuman, Ken, 662
Smith-Shuman, Nancy, 662
Smith, Shyrl R., 2293
Smith, Sue
Ripon, CA, Grace Brethren Church, 1110
Smith, Susan (Bechtel), 107
Smith, Susannah (later Hart), *See* Hart family
Smith, T. M., 1775
Smith Thomas, H., 2293
Smith, Timothy L., 2069
on evangelism and Brethren, 2357
Smith, Verona M. Kreider, 1844, 2019
Smith, W. S., 1775
Smith, Warren, 322
Smith, Warren C., 1775
Smith, Welty G., 1775
Smith, Wilbur Isaac, 1775–1776
Myrtle Point, OR, Church of the Brethren, pastor, 906
Ripon, CA, Grace Brethren Church, 1110
Smith, Willard H., 2069
Smith, William (fl. 1800), 500, 544, **1191**
Smith, William, 1945, 1980, 2069
A Brief State. . ., 1914
answer to *A Brief State of the Province of Pensylvania* [*sic*], 1912
Smith, William (1), 1776
Smith, William (2), 1776
Smith, William (3), 1776
Smith, William (4), 1776
Smith, William A., 1776
Smith, William (CB-1), 1776
Smith, William (CB-2), 1776
Smith, William Dwight, 1776
Smith, William Franklin, 1776
Smith, William Harlan, 1776, 1844, 2063
Smith, William R., 717
Smith, William W., 115, 188, 725, 1776
North Kokomo Grace Brethren Church, IN, pastor, 948
Smith, Willie Dee, Sr., 1776, 2305
Smithfield Brethren Church, 1221
Smithfield, PA, Church of the Brethren, **1192**
Fairview Church of the Brethren, PA, 469
Smithley family
Parkersburg, WV, Grace Brethren Church, 994
Smithley, Lester O., 588
Smithville Collegiate Institute, **1192**
Leckrone, Quincy, 733
Smithville, OH, 256
First Brethren Church, 395, **1192**
Flora, Delbert Benjamin, 495
Paradise Church of the Brethren, 992
Zion Hill Brethren Church
Rittman, OH, First Brethren Church, 1111
Smithwick, Larry, 30, 1776
Ripon, CA, Grace Brethren Church, pastor, 1110
Smitley, Elsie

Mount Laurel, NJ, Grace Brethren
Church, 883
Smitley, Lester Olin, 2294
Mount Laurel, NJ, Grace Brethren
Church, 883
Parkersburg, WV, Grace Brethren
Church, pastor serving, 994
Smitley, W. M., 1776
smokejumpers
conscientious objectors, 337
fire fighting, 491
Smoker, Joseph, 1776
smoking, See tobacco
Smouse, Jacob W., 350, 674, 927, 1776
Martinsburg, PA, Grace Brethren
Church, pastor, 798
Mineral Point, PA, Vinco Brethren
Church, pastor, 843
Smucker, Carl Simon, 1776, 2069
Smucker, Christian, 1776
Smucker, Donovan E., 29, 2110
Smucker, Frank, 1879
Smyrna, 1280
orphans, care for, 982
Smyth Co., VA, 766
Rowland Creek Church of the
Brethren, VA, 1126
Smyth, John, 87
Snabali, Elizabeth Long, 1193
Snabali, John, 1193
Snader, Abram Philip, 752, 1776
Snader, Beulah (later Sappington), 2246
Snader, David, 1776
Snader, David H., Jr., 14, 1776
Snader, David P., 14, 1776
Snader, Earl Engler, Jr., 1776, 1844
Snader, Edward A., 1776
Snader, Edwin A., 1776
Snader family, 749
Snader, Gertrude Delores Hartman, 1844
Snader, Mary (later Rinehart), *1109, 11110*
Snake River Brethren (Idaho and Montana),
history of, 2054
Snake Spring Valley Church of the
Brethren, PA, 21, 62, 274, 461,
1192, See also, Artemas, PA,
Church of the Brethren
Snake Spring Valley congregation, PA, 706,
710
from Yellow Creek, PA, congregation,
927
Snake Valley Old German Baptist Brethren
Church, PA, **1192–1193**
Snare, Lois Eleanor, 1846
Snavely, Barbara (later Graybill), 567
Snavely, Chester Charles, 2040
Snavely, Conrad L., 242, 1776, 1844–1845
Snavely, Elizabeth Long
Lebanon Co., PA, 1193
Snavely, Esther, 2094
Snavely family, 231, 236, **1193,** 2034,
2040, 2069–2070, See also Pursel,
Vida Miller
Fahrney (Forney) family, 466
Ocala, FL, Grace Brethren Church,
2232
Snavely, George Harry, Jr., 1776
Snavely, Gladys
memoirs, 2362
on Nebraska wines, 2362
Snavely, Harper M., 641, 1776
Snavely, Henry C., 1955
Snavely, I. G., 496

Snavely, Ida B., 2069
Snavely, Ira Calvert, 7, 144, 446, 685, 1776
Snavely, Irma Fisher, 1845
Snavely, J. Welton, 1776
Snavely, James E., 749, 2294
Snavely, John, 1193
Snavely, John L., 21, 1776
Snavely, John Y., 1776
Snavely, Maria (later Good), 556
Snavely, Moses Y., 685
Reedley, CA, Church of the Brethren,
1091
Snavely, Olan David, 2069
Snavely, Russell
Ocala, FL, Grace Brethren Church,
2232
Snavely, S. U., 1776
Pleasant Center Church of the Breth-
ren, OH, minister, 1030
Snavely, Sally
Reedley, CA, Church of the Brethren,
1091
Snavely, Viola
Ocala, FL, Grace Brethren Church,
2232
Snay, Jane (later Maxwell)
Island Pond, VT, Grace Brethren
Church, 2209
SNCC, See Student Nonviolent Coordinat-
ing Committee
Sneider family, 1958
Sneider, Sara, 685
Snell, Daniel, 1333, 1776, 1193, *1193*
Snell, David, 1193
Snell, Donald, 1776
Snell, Elizabeth Beery, 1193
Snell, Elizabeth (later Snyder), *See* Snyder,
Elizabeth Snell
Snell, Ella, 374
Snell family, 215, 1193, *1193,* 1224, 2069
McFarland, CA, Church of the Breth-
ren, 774
Sanger family, related to, 1144
Snell, Galen Robert, 781, 1776
Snell, George W., 355, 1776
Snell, Harvey, 345, 348, 1776
Modesto, CA, Church of the Brethren,
866
Raisin City, CA, Church of the
Brethren, pastor, 1083
Snell, Helen Jean
Snell, William Harrison (FGBC) and, 2250
Snell, J. F., 1776
Snell, J. H., 1776
Sappa Creek Church of the Brethren,
NE, leadership provided, 1145
Snell, Jacob Henry, 7, 1193, 1776
Snell, Jacob S., 1776
Snell, James P., 2070
Snell, John H., 233, 1776, 2069
Maple Grove Old German Baptist
Brethren Church, OH, minister,
791
Preble Co., OH, and Kosciusko Co.,
IN, 1193
Rockingham Co., VA, 1193
Sidney, IN, Grace Brethren Church,
1181
Snell, John Amsa, 1776
Snell, Joseph, 1193
Snell, Judy, 380
Snell, Judy (later Detrick), 380, *See also*
Detrick, Judy Snell

Snell, Levi, 1193, 1776
Sappa Creek Church of the Brethren,
NE, leadership provided, 1145
Snell, Magdalena Brower
Preble Co., OH, and Kosciusko Co.,
IN, 1193
Snell, Mary, 1193, 2069
Snell, Mary Sherfy, 1193
Snell, Myrtle, 233
Snell, Philip
Conewago, PA, congregation, 1193
Stover, William, 2379
Snell, Rebecca
Swartz, George on, 2360
Swartz, Joseph on, 2360
Snell, Samuel, 1193, 1776–1777
Snell, Solomon G., 1777
Midland, VA, Church of the Brethren,
minister, 827
Snell, Susan (later Ross), 1123
Snell, Timothy A., 2294
Snell, William Harrison, 1777, **2250**
Martinsburg, PA, Grace Brethren
Church, pastor, 798
Meyersdale, PA, Grace Brethren
Church, pastor, 822
Snelling, William James, 520, 1777, 2305
Snider
Snake Spring Valley Church of the
Brethren, PA, free minister, 1192
Snider, Aaron B., 1777
Snider, Arthur, 1777
Mathias, WV, Brethren Church, 803
Snider, Catherine (later Graybill), 567
Snider, Charles D., 1194
Snider, Chester, 1777
Snider, D. C., 1380, 1777
Newberg, OR, Church of the Brethren,
pastor in, 933
Snider, Daniel J., 1777, 2305
Olivet Church of the Brethren, OH,
973
Snider, Della (later Lehmer), 736
Snider, Donald Mitchell, 248, 285,
1193–1194, 1777, 2070
family of, 685
Snider, Elias Weber Bingeman, 2070
Snider, Elizabeth (later Henricks), 597
descendants, 1918
Snider family, 236, 2067, 2070, See also
Schneider family
Snider, George A., 1777
Snider, Hannah Bingeman, 2070
Snider, Harold, 187, 240, 281, 561, 739,
1194, 1777, 1952, 2070, **2378,**
2386
Snider, Howard S., 1193
Snider, Jacob, 597, 1154
Snider, Jacob C., 2070
Snider, John Bricker, 2070
Snider, John G., 1304
Pittsburgh, PA, First Brethren Church,
pastor, 1027
Snider, Mamie, 1194
Snider, Margaret Studebaker, 597, 1154
Snider, Martha Keever
Brethren Service Commission, 1194
Snider, PA
New Enterprise, PA, Church of the
Brethren, 927
Snider, Paul Scott, 479, 1777
Snider, R. Wayne, 1777, 2294
Snider, Ruth Stover, 1193

Snider (Snyder), David, 1777
Snider (Snyder), David C., 1777
Snider (Snyder), Jacob, 1777
Snider (Snyder), Jacob (CB), 1777
Snider (Snyder), John G., 1777
Snider, Susanna
    Eiler (Eilar, Oyler) family, 432
Snider, W. W., 2070
Snively, Catherine Stouffer, 2070
Snively family, 2034, 2070, *See also*
    Snavely family
Snively, Howard M., 687, 1777
    Mabton, WA, Grace Brethren Church,
        pastor, 771
Snively, J., 2070
Snively, J. Scott, 1777
    The Missionary Board (BC), 855
Snively, Jacob, 1777
Snively, Kate S., 2070
Snively, William Andres, 2070
Snoberger, Harvey, 1777
Snoderly family, 2085
Snoeberger, A. L.
    Newton, KS, Church of the Brethren,
        pastor in, 934
Snoeberger, A. S., 1777
Snow, ___, 2070
Snow Creek Church of the Brethren, VA,
    See Boones Chapel Church of the
    Brethren, VA
Snow Creek, VA, congregation, 162
Snow Hill Cloister, *See* Snow Hill Nunnery
    commitment in communes and utopias,
        1981
    Franklin Co., PA, 2002
    history of, 1918
    nunnery, reference to, 1939
    paper on, 1911
    sources on, 2314, 2320
Snow Hill Community, 215, 694, 736,
    1194, **1194–1195**, 2090
    chart of Brethren bodies, place on,
        1403–1405
    Durnbaugh, Donald F. on, 2326
    Ephrata Community, 451
    Fahnestock family, 465
    Fraktur type at, 60
    German Seventh-Day Baptists, 542
    Katy of Catoctin: Or, the Chain-
        Breakers (Townsend), 747
    King, Frank, 694
    Miller, John Peter, 840
    Pennsylvania Brethren settlement, 1004
    seventh-day observance of Sabbath,
        1133
    singing, 1184
    Snowberger family, 1153, 1195
Snow Hill Nunnery, 2020, 2028, 2058,
    2070, 2075, 2084, 2094, 2167, *See*
    also Seventh-Day Baptists; Sisters
    of Saron
    artifacts from, 2326
    fiction, references in, 2083
    notes about, 2326
    Seachrist, Denise Ann on, 2355
        on baptism and, 2355
        on musical tradition at, 2355–2356
    Spohn, Clarence E. on, 2358
    Thomasson, Kermon on, 2360
Snow, R. John, 436, 662, 674, 1777
Snowberger
    Snake Spring Valley Church of the
        Brethren, PA, free minister, 1192

Snowberger, Andrew (Andreas), 1777
    Snow Hill Community, 1153, **1195**
Snowberger, Andrew C., 1777
    Rock Creek Church of the Brethren,
        CO, minister, 1116
Snowberger, Barbara Ingold
    German Seventh Day Baptists, 1153
Snowberger, Barbara Karper
    Ephrata and Snow Hill Communities,
        1195
    Snow Hill Community, 1153, 1195
Snowberger, Daniel, 1777
Snowberger, Elizabeth
    Snow Hill Community, 1195
Snowberger, Ella M., 2070
Snowberger family, 2357, *See also*
    Schneeberger family
    Paul family joined in marriage, 996
Snider, Jacob related to, 1154
    Snow Hill Community, 1153, 1195
    Wells, (Mrs.) Cecil F. on, 2362
Snowberger, Harvey, 1777
Snowberger, Isaac Newton, 1777
    Pigeon River Church of the Brethren,
        IN, minister, 1023
Snowberger, Johannes, *See* Schneeberger,
    Johannes (Hans)
Snowberger, John, 1777
    Monticello/Pike Creek Church of the
        Brethren, IN, minister, 872
Snowberger, John (grandson of Johannes)
    Snow Hill Community, 1195
Snowberger, John (great-grandson of
    Johannes), 1153
Snowberger, John S., 105, 590, 1777
Snowberger, John W., 469
Snowberger, Joseph S., 1777
Snowberger, Levi, 406, 1777
Snowberger, Levi A., 1777
Snowberger, Obed, 2070
    Snow Hill Community, 1195
Snowberger, PA, *See* New Enterprise, PA
Snowberger, Rosannah (later Ritchey), 1110
Snowberger, Samuel
    Snow Hill Community, prior, 1195
Snowberger, Sarah (later Ritchey), 1110
Snowberger (Snoeberger), Abraham
    Lincoln, 1777
Snowberger, Ulrich
    German Seventh Day Baptists, 1153
Snowden, Armon Carl, 1777
Snufer, Isaac
    Snuffer, Thomas Earl on descendants of,
        2357
Snufer, Malinda (Rakes)
    Snuffer, Thomas Earl on descendants of,
        2357
snuff, *See* tobacco use
Snuffer family
    Prosperity congregation, Oak Hill Old
        German Baptist Brethren Church,
        WV, 957
Snuffer, Matthew P., 1777
Snuffer, Peter, 350
Snuffer, Thomas Earl
    on Snufer, Isaac and descendants, 2357
    on Snufer, Malinda (Rakes) and
        descendants, 2357
Snyder, Aaron B., 1777
Snyder, Abraham, 2089
    Müller (Miller) family, 894
Snyder, Adam Armstrong, 1777, 2105
Snyder, Adam F., 1777

Snyder, Arthur, 694
Snyder, Barbara
    Mansfield, OH, Walcrest Brethren
        Church, 787
Snyder, Benjamin Franklin, 115, 1777
Snyder, Blaine, 318, 1777, 2305
Snyder, Blair G., 1863
Snyder, Byard Frank, 448, 1777
    Milk River Valley Church of the
        Brethren, MT, elder, 832
Snyder, C. Arnold
    Anabaptism, 2201
Snyder, Charles Russell, 257, 1777
    Okeechobee, FL, Grace Brethren
        Church, pastor, 963
Snyder, Carl Harrison, 2294
Snyder, Catherine C. Harding, 1196
Snyder, Catherine (later Keim), 686
Snyder, Catherine (later Moomaw)
    Moomaw, Benjamin Franklin, mother
        of, 873
Snyder, Catherine (later Ritchey), 1110
Snyder, Charles Russell, 1777
Snyder, Clara (later Reber), 1085
Snyder, Clarence, 1777
    South Bend, IN, Ireland Road Grace
        Brethren Church, pastor, 1203
Snyder Co., PA
    Brubaker family, 2111
    history of, 1929
Snyder Cross Roads meetinghouse,
    Woodbury, PA, Church of the
    Brethren, 1364
Snyder, D. R., 1777
Snyder, Daniel, 274, 1777, 1907
Snyder, David, 727
Snyder, David James, 2294
Snyder, David R., 1777
    Snake Valley Old German Baptist
        Brethren Church, PA, elder, 1192,
        1193
Snyder, Elizabeth Finfrock, 1196
Snyder, Elizabeth (later Stutz), 1232
Snyder, Elizabeth Snell, 1192
Snyder, Elsie Ruth Croker, 1853
Snyder, Emmaline Kline, 1891
Snyder, Ernest M., 2294
Snyder family, 153, 211, 430, 727, 1277,
    1359, 2044, 2070, 2089, 2105, *See*
    also Schneider family
    descendants of Johannes Snyder of
        Berne, Switzerland, 1872
    family history, 1973
    Fort Lauderdale, FL, Grace Brethren
        Church, 503
    Grace Brethren Church of Canton, OH,
        562
    history of, 1957
    Robins, IA, Church of the Brethren,
        1115
    Snavely family, related to, 1193
    Snowberger family, related to, 1154
Snyder, Frederick T., 1777
    Marion, IN, Brethren Church, pastor,
        793
Snyder, G. A., 505
Snyder, Gail Alvin, 565, 1777
Snyder, George
    Pleasant View Brethren Church, IN,
        2377
Snyder, George D., 1777
Snyder, George Henry, 1777–1778
Snyder, Gerald, 213, 1778

Snyder, Glada O. (later Kintner), 697
  Kintner, Elgin Perry on, 2341
Snyder, Grace Edith (later Rhodes), 2044
Snyder, Graydon Fisher, 139, 191, 1778,
    2070, 2136
  historical writing, 612
  on health and medicine, 2357
  on medical decisions, 2357
  Ramirez, Frank on, 2351
  on texts in Transit II, 2357
Snyder, Ida Grabill, 1865, 2070
Snyder, Jack L., 1778, 2167, 2306
Snyder, Jacob, 267, 1778, 2070
Snyder, Jacob, III
  Ritchey (Ritchie) family, related to,
    1110
Snyder, Jacob, Jr.
  Snake Spring Valley Church of the
    Brethren, PA, 1192
Snyder, Jacob S., **1195–1196,** 1778
Snyder, Johannes, 1872
Snyder, John G., 676, 687
  Martinsburg, PA, Grace Brethren
    Church, pastor, 798
  Pineville, VA, Mount Olive Brethren
    Church, pastor, 1025
  St. James Brethren Church, MD,
    pastor, 1134
Snyder, John Martin, 218, **1196,** 1778, 1926
  Educator and Companion, The, 429
Snyder, John Romeo, 399, 1778
Snyder, John William, 1196
Snyder, Joseph B., 1924
Snyder, Joseph F., 1778
Snyder, Joyce, 1841
Snyder, Lewis S., 1778
  Missouri Valley German Baptist
    Brethren, IA, 865
Snyder Lake Church of the Brethren, ND,
    223, *See also* Brumbaugh Church
    of the Brethren, ND
  place-names, Brethren, 1028
Snyder, Laura Frances, *See* Snyder family
Snyder, Lois Horning
  National Older Adult Conferences,
    2229
Snyder, Lyman H., 1778
Snyder, Myrtle Mae, 501, 573, **1196,** 1853
  medical missions, 807
  Rollier, Antoine E. and Mary
    Ganshorn, in missionary party
    with, 1119
Snyder, Magdelena Miller
  Müller (Miller) family, 894
Snyder, Marlene, 687
Snyder, Mary (later Baker), 1882
Snyder, Miles J., 1778
  Mapleville, MD, Brethren Church,
    pastor, 791
Snyder, Miriam Helen, 2070
Snyder, Nathaniel Z., 2070
Snyder, Noah, 274, 1778
  Old Order German Baptist Church
    minister, 972
Snyder, Oliver, 1891
Snyder, Orville A., 2070
Snyder, Peter B., 1865, 2070
Snyder, Phineas, 1778
Snyder, Rachael (later Fike), 489
Snyder, Rebecca, 80
Snyder, Roy Bernard, 1778, 1853
Snyder, Ruth, 1853
  on Myers, Estella, 2357

ship sinking en route to Africa, 863
Snyder, S. P., 2040
Snyder, Sheldon W., 629, 1778
Snyder, Sue Cushen, 2294
Snyder, Thomas G., 1778
  Robins, IA, Church of the Brethren,
    minister, 1115
Snyder, Walter, 1778
Snyder, Wilbur Oscar, 1778
Snyder, William Henry, *See* Snyder family
So Who's Afraid of Birthdays (Mow), 890
soap production program, 198
social action, **1196–1197**
  General Board (CB), 535
  historic peace churches, 2200
  history of Brethren social policy, trea-
    tises on, 2054
  homelessness, 2203
  mass media concerns, 801
  missions, 861
  nonconformity, 940
  Peace Studies Institute, 1003
  religious liberty, 1098
  sources on, 2316, 2320
social change, 6
social class
  dress, 400
social concerns
  definition of, 386
  simple life, 1183
Social Concerns Committee
  Brethren Church peace position, 1000
  Peace Committee (BC), 1001
  peace education, 1002
social customs, *See* lifestyles
Social Darwinism, 534
Social Education, Church of the Brethren
  Weiss, Edgar Lorell, 1328
Social Gospel movement, **1197**
  Brethren Church, 183
  Church of the Brethren, 187
  dispensationalism, doctrine of, 390
  fundamentalism, 522, 523
  Goughenour, Herbert L., 562
  influence on peace witness, 1262
  McClain, Alva J., 773
  "Message of the Brethren Ministry,"
    817
  Modernism, 866
  noncreedalism, 942
social justice, 1197
social group theology
  Church of the Brethren, 303
social issues
  Brethren movement, 2096–2097
  Church of the Brethren, social develop-
    ment of, 2094
  churches and, 2084
  Civil War, 2085
  colonial era, 2085
  dress, effect on, 402
  General Conference Mennonite
    Church, 536
  India, 2076
  leadership issues, 176
  oaths, taking of, 959
  Old German Baptist Brethren, 969
  plain people, 1029
  quilting and, in Pennsylvania, 2074
  recreation activities, 2084
  social idealism, 2069
  social service, 2069
    Seattle, WA, Olympic View Com-

munity Church of the Brethren,
    1162
socialism, 2068
values
  urban communities and, 175
  world-wide, Brethren movement rela-
    tionship to, 2106
social justice
  Eddy, [George] Sherwood, 424
  One Hundred Dunkers for Peace, 974
  Page, Kirby, 989
  Peace Studies Institute, 1003
  Smeltzer, Ralph Emerson, 1190–1191
social meetings
  prayer meetings, 1053
"The Social Message of Christianity"
  fundamentalism, 522
social protest movements
  premillennialism, 833
Social Recreation Primer (Tully), 1088,
    1278
Social Security
  Amish exemption from, 26
  nonconformity, 941
  Old German Baptist Brethren, 2233,
    2234
social service
  Christian, 2069
  missions, 861
  Montgomery, IL, Boulder Hill
    Neighborhood Church of the
    Brethren, 872
  SHARE program, 1172
  Woodbridge, VA, Church of the
    Brethren, 1364
Social Service Commission
  Goughenour, Herbert L., 562
Social Service Committee
  Gillin, John Lewis, 549
social welfare, **1197–1198,** 2050, 2056
  alternative service, 20
  Church of the Brethren, 301
socialism, **1198–1199,** 2032, 2068
Society for the Scientific Study of Religion
  Brethren profile study, 2150
Society of Brothers, *See* Hutterian Society
    of Brothers
Society of Friends, *See* Quakers
Society of the Woman in the Wilderness,
    1199–2000, 112
  as a source for Beissel's ideas, 113
  ascetic regimen of, 686
  celibacy and, 266
  Germantown, 544
  hermits, living as, 687
  Kelpius or Kelp, Johannes, 686–687
  Radical Pietists, 1199–1200
  Rosicrucian influence on, 1123
  settlement on Wissihickon Creek, 1354
  Seventh-Day Baptists, 1170
  Socinians, *See* Polish Brethren
Socinus, Faustus, 1041
sociological studies, **1200,** *See also* cultural
    considerations; descriptions of the
    Brethren
  alternative service
    Church of the Brethren, 2100
  Dunkard Brethren Church
    Ozark village, 2102
  Gillin, John Lewis, 549
  historical writing, 612
  quilting
    Pennsylvania, 2074

sect-church typology, 1200
Socknat, Thomas P.
    works by, 2318
sod house, *627*
Sod House, Enders, NE, *920*
Söderblom, Nathan, 422, 742
Soderstrom, Anita Sophia I., 1840
software
    on-line accounting packages, Brethren
        Benefit Trust (BBT), 2140
soil conservation
    detached programs, 380
    World War II units, **1200**
Sojourners Fellowship, **1200**
Sokvitne, Miriam Helen Snyder, 2070
Sol Lavy Union, *See* old Brethren German
        Baptists
sola fide, 29
sola gratia, 29
sola Scriptura, 29
Solanki, Benabai, 1200
Solanki, Naranji V., *650,* **1200–1201,** 1778
Solano, Abner Aldero, 2294
Soldier Creek Church of the Brethren, KS,
        1201
Soldier River German Baptist Brethren, IA
    Harrison Co., IA, **1201**
Soldotna, AK, 687
    Peninsula Grace Brethren Church,
        2250–2251
Solenberger, David, 1202
Solenberger, Sarah
    Northkill, PA, congregation, 1202
Soler, Edna Marie Switzer, 1845
Solingen Brethren, 71, 421, 545, *677,* **1201,**
        2057
    article about, 1921
    Calvinism and, 241
    capital punishment, 253
    Carl, Johann (fl.), 255
    chaplaincy, 271
    Collegiants, and release of, 324
    doctrine of, 1258–1259
    Dutch influence in release of, 923
    Estates General or States General, 456
    Fischer, Johann, 491
    freedom of, securing, 1196
    Geistreiches Gesang-Buch (*Spiritual
        Songbook*), 534
    Goyen, Gossen, 562
    Grahe, Jakob, 564
    Grahe, Wilhelm, 132, 564
    Heidelberg Catechism, 593
    Henckels, Johann Friedrich, 596
    Historic Peace Churches, 607
    historic sites, 609
    history, 611, 1962
    hymn-prayers, 1051
    hymnals, 641
    imprisonment of, 147, 174
    Jülich, 677, 1991
    Koker family involvement in release,
        705
    Lobach, Johann, 751, 1325
    missions, 857
    music, 898
    Naas, Jakob Wilhelm, visited during
        Jülich imprisonment, 909
    oaths, taking of, 959, 2126
    persecution, 990, 1009
    prisons, 1059
    references to, 1911, 1948
    Smith, Samuel, quote from, 1191

Stetius, Gottfried Luther, 1222
Studebaker family, 1230
    tradition, devaluation of, 133
    visited by Clemens Knepper, 703
Solitary Brethren and Sisters
    *Gesäng der einsamen und verlassenen
        Turtel-Taube, Das* (*The Songs of
        the Lonely and Forsaken
        Turtledove*), 546
Sölle brothers, 2087
Sollenberger, Aaron D., 103, 424, *687,*
        1202, 1778
    North Beatrice Church of the Brethren,
        NE, elder, 945
    Hope Memorial Church (German
        Baptist Brethren), NE, 2375
Sollenberger, Agnes L. Hafner, 1201
Sollenberger, Benjamin Trimmer, 1845
Sollenberger, Beth (later Sollenberger
        Morphew)
    Sollenberger, Dorcas Elaine Mock
        (CB) and, 2251
Sollenberger, Carmon Ellis, 228, 232, 1778
Sollenberger, Clarence Benjamin, 1289,
        1778
Sollenberger, Clarence C., 630, 674, 1778
    Salem Church of the Brethren, OH,
        minister, 1138
Sollenberger, Cora Horst, 630, 2071
Sollenberger, D. Raymond, 1346, 1778
Sollenberger, David
    on Brethren heritage tour of Europe,
        2357
    on Brethren movement, early history
        of, 2357
    on BSC, MD (video), 2357
    on Jesus, work of, 2357
    on Zigler, M. R., 2357
Sollenberger, David Peffley, 1778
Sollenberger, Dennis L., 2294
Sollenberger, Donald Dale, 1778
Sollenberger, Dorcas Elaine Mock (CB),
        2251
    church governance and, 2264
Sollenberger family, **1202**
    related to Snowberger family, 1154
    Snider, Jacob, descendants of, 1154
Sollenberger, Hazel Coppock Delany, 1201,
        1265, 1845, 1927
Sollenberger, Howard Edwin, 277, 278,
        1201–1202, 1939, 2071
    tractor unit, 1268
    World War II relief work, 1373
Sollenberger, Ira J., 1778, 2071
Sollenberger, Jacob, 1778
Sollenberger, John, 2031
    Franklin Co., PA, and Montgomery
        Co., OH, 1202
    Lancaster Co. and Cumberland Co.,
        PA, 1202
Sollenberger, John W., 1778
Sollenberger, Joseph, 699, 1202, 1778
Sollenberger, Leon, 2251
Sollenberger, Lori, 2251
Sollenberger, M. E., 1927–1928
Sollenberger-Morphew, Beth Eileen, 2251,
        2294
Sollenberger-Morphew, Timothy, 2294
Sollenberger, Nelda Weaver, 1845
Sollenberger, Oliver Clark, 277, 1201,
        1265, 1778, 1845, **2386, 2388**
    missionary to China, 1202
Sollenberger, Olive Clark, 2071

Sollenberger, Ray A., 2251
Sollenberger, Sarah Klein, 699
Sollenberger, Ulrich, 1202
Solomon, Carolyn Elaine
    Solomon, Kenneth LeRoy and, 2251
Solomon family, 324, 2071
Solomon, George Walton, 1778, **2251**
Solomon, Grace Marie Bryson, 2251
Solomon, I. J., 1778
Solomon, Janet Hamel (BC)
    Sarasota, FL, Iglesia de los Hermanos
        and, 2246
Solomon, Jeannette Ruth DeLozier (BC),
        1855, **2251**
Solomon, Jesse E., 1778
Solomon, Jessie Mae, 2251
Solomon, Joel
    Solomon, Kenneth LeRoy and
        Jeannette Ruth DeLozier Solomon
        (BC) and, 2251
Solomon, Kenneth LeRoy, 324, 1778, 1855,
        2251
    Sarasota, FL, Iglesia de los Hermanos
        (BC) and, 2246
Solomon, Kenneth LeRoy and Jeannette
        Ruth DeLozier Solomon (BC),
        2251
Solomon, Leroy A., 1778, 2132
Solomon, LeRoy Quinter
    Solomon, Kenneth LeRoy (BC) and,
        2251
Solomon, Margaret (later Dodds), 2251
Solomon, Paul J., 2071
Solomon, Rebecca (later Abbott), 2251
Solomon, Roger, 695, 1240, 1778
Solomon, Timothy, 2251
*Solomon to the Exile: Studies in Kings and
        Chronicles*
    Whitcomb, John Clement, Jr. (FGBC,
        CGBCI) and, 2262
Solomon Valley, KS, Church of the
        Brethren, 232
    Portis, KS, North Solomon Church of
        the Brethren, 1048
Solomon Valley, KS, German Baptist
        Brethren
    Portis, KS, Grace Brethren Church,
        1047
Solomon, Victor, 2071
Solomon, William, 1778
Solomon's Creek Church of the Brethren,
        IN, 124, **1202,** 1246, 1280
    Pleasant View Chapel Church of the
        Brethren, IN, 1036
    Milford, IN, Bethel Church of the
        Brethren, 831
Somabhai, Jayanand, 1778
Some Brethren Pathfinders
    historical writing, 612
Some Who Led (Miller), 836
Somerset Brethren Church, NE, *See* Beaver
        City, NE, Grace Brethren Church
Somerset Church of the Brethren
    seventy-fifth anniversary of, 2357
Somerset Co., MD
    Greenhill Church of the Brethren, MD,
        570
Somerset Co., NJ, 1367, 2070
Somerset Co., PA, 150, 151, 214, 215, 225,
        267, 322, 332, 348, 383, 685, 686,
        693, 736, 741, 746, 1225, 1232,
        1236, 1263, 1265, 1322, 1878,
        1935, 2071

Brethren Church congregations, 1005
death records, 2104
Fairview Church of the Brethren, PA, 469
history, 1967
history and genealogy, 1989
Holtzapfel (Holsapple, Holsopple) family, 624
Hostetler Church of the Brethren, PA, 632
Maple Glen Church of the Brethren, PA, 789
Maple Spring Church of the Brethren, PA, 791
Middle Creek Church of the Brethren, PA, 825
migration of Brethren, 827
Pike Run Church of the Brethren, PA, 1023
place-names, Brethren, 1027
Rayman Fellowship Church of the Brethren, PA, 1084
Reading Grace Brethren Church, PA, 1084
Rockwood Church of the Brethren, PA, 1118
Sipesville, PA, Church of the Brethren, 1186
Somerset German Baptist Brethren Church, MO, **1202**
Somerset, IN
Church of the Brethren, 257, 723, **1202,** 1311
Poplar Grove Brethren Church, **1202**
Somerset, PA, 746
Church of the Brethren, 118, 121, **1202**
Middle Creek congregation, 1202
Grace Brethren Church, **1202**
Sommer, Daniel, 1313, 2017, 2023
Rockingham Church of the Brethren, MO, debated R. H. Miller at, 1118
Sommer, Jon
Medina, OH, Shepherd's Grace Church, 2219
Sommer, Karen
Medina, OH, Shepherd's Grace Church, 2219
Sommerfeld, Jan, 2142
Sommers, Harvey A., 1778
Sommers, Jacob, 318, 1778
Sommers, John, 1778
Sommers, Paul, 1778
Sommers, Quinter, 318
Sommers, W. W., 758
Son of Thunder, See Fike, Samuel A.
Sonafrank, George D., 1778
Sonafrank, Harold Elson, 1778
The Song Leader
Music Committee (CB), 899
Song of the Susquehanna (Stover), 747
Song Praises
hymnals, 642
songs, See hymns; music
Sonnenberg
migrations from, 2074
Sonoma Lighthouse Mission
Swallow, James F., 1243
Sonon, Henry S., 416, 1778
Sons of Temperance
Brethren opposition to secret societies, 1163
Sontag, Jacob, **1202–1203,** 1778–1779, 1900

Sontag, Mary Landes, 1203
Sooby, Robert Lee, 373, 1779
Sophie, Hedwig, regent of Berleberg, 1354
Sorensen, C. H., 1779
Sorge, Virgil Paul, 320, 1779
Sorrells, Bernice, 2071
soteriological belief
Brethren movement, 291
Soteriology, See salvation, doctrine of soteriology
Brethren Church and, 184
definition of, 386
Soto, Iris A. Gully
McAllen, TX, Grace Brethren Church, 2218
Soto, Robert A., 2294
McAllen, TX, Grace Brethren Church, 2218
Sotola, Federico, 53
Souder, J. F., 1779
Souder, John D., 2071
Souder, P., 1779
Souder, Sue, *1055*
Souders, J. F., 2071
Root River Church of the Brethren, MN, pastor, 1122
Souderton mission point
Hatfield Church of the Brethren, PA, 588
Souderton, PA, 1251
soul, immortality of
doctrine on, 2079
The Soul of Symbols (Shultz)
Shultz, Joseph R. (BC) and, 2249
Soule, Donald James, 2294
souls, reality of, See Animism
Sounds of Grace Radio Ministry, CA, 755
soup kitchens
Ramsey, Duane H. and, 2239
Source
General Services Commission (CB), 539
source books on Brethren history, See historical writing
Sources and Documents
Pennsylvania German Society, 1006
Sours, Ella Mae (later Huffman)
Huffman, Nelson Thomas, 2205
Sours, Hubert F., 1779
Sousley, Treva H., 2071
Souter, John C., 1779
South Africa
World Council of Churches, 2228
South America, See Latin America
South America Theological Seminary (BC), **2251–2252,** *2251*
missions, 2224–2225
South Annville meetinghouse, (Long's tent) (Annville, PA), 39
South Bay Community Church of the Brethren, CA, See Redondo Beach, CA, South Bay Community Church of the Brethren
South Bay Grace Brethren Church, Torrance, CA, 1267–1268
South Beatrice congregation, NE, 217, 830, 920, See also Holmesville Church of the Brethren, NE
Filley German Baptist Brethren Church, NE, 2374
South Beatrice, NE, Church of the Brethren, 2071, See also Holmesville Church of the

Brethren, NE
South Bend, IN, 1345
minorities, ethnic and racial, 850
St. Joseph Valley Church of the Brethren, IN, 1135
Studebaker family, 1231
Sturgis, Daniel B., 1232
Sunday schools, 278
urban mission, 1297
Young Men and Boys' Brotherhood, 1390
South Bend, IN
Ardmore Brethren Church, **1203**
Fairview Brethren Church, 1203
Mishawaka, IN, Brethren Church, 852
Church of the Brethren, See North Liberty, IN, Church of the Brethren; Oak Grove, IN, Church of the Brethren; Pine Creek Church of the Brethren
City Church of the Brethren, **1203**
Portage Prairie, IN, Church of the Brethren, 1047
Second South Bend Church of the Brethren, formerly, 1203
Crest Manor Church of the Brethren, **1203**
North Liberty, IN, Church of the Brethren, 749, 948
Oak Grove, IN, Church of the Brethren, 955
St. Joseph Co., IN, 1203
Fair View Brethren Church, See South Bend, IN, Ardmore Brethren Church
First Brethren Church, **1203**
First Church of the Brethren, See South Bend, IN, Crest Manor Church of the Brethren
Iglesia Evangelica Emanuel (CB), **2252**
Ireland Road Grace Brethren Church, **1203–1204**
Sunnymede Grace Brethren Church, 1203–1204
North Liberty congregation, 267
Prince of Peace Church of the Brethren, **1204**
Second Church of the Brethren, See South Bend, IN, City Church of the Brethren
Sunnymede Grace Brethren Church, See South Bend, IN, Ireland Road Grace Brethren Church
South Bethel German Baptist Brethren, MO, **1204**
South Bethel, MO, congregation
North Bethel Church of the Brethren, MO, **945**
South Branch Church of the Brethren, WV
Grant (formerly Hampshire) county, WV, 1204
South Carolina, **1204–1205**
Baptist Church, 2083
Baptists of, history by Morgan Edwards, 1926
Brethren movement, 2083
Brethren Universalists, 177
Dunkers, 210
Georgia, 540
German settlement in, 2069
itinerant ministries, 271
Kentucky, settlements in, 689

Materials Towards a History of the Baptists, 803
migration of Brethren, 829
Naas, Jakob Wilhelm, arrival, 909
Old German Brethren, 175
Pennsylvania Brethren and settlement, 1004
religious issues, 2088
Universalists, 1292
South Carolina Almanack (1755–1758), 18
South Co., FL, Youth and Family Recreation Center, 171
South Dakota, **1205**, 1973
Brethren movement, 2080
homesteading, 626
Iowa, 661
minorities, ethnic and racial, 850
South English, IA, Church of the Brethren, *See* English River Church of the Brethren, IA
migration of Brethren, 830
South English, IA, congregaton, 1263
South Fork Church of the Brethren, WV, **1205, 2378**
Milam, WV, Mount Carmel Church of the Brethren, 2222
South Fork congregation
South Mill Creek Church of the Brethren, WV, 1206
South Fork Valley, NC, 2106
South Fulton Dunkard Brethren congregation, IL, 69, 911, **1205**, 1364
South Garkida , Nigeria, 306
South Gate, CA, First Brethren Church, **1205**
South Grove, IA
Maquoketa German Baptist Brethren, IA, mission point, 791
South Hampton Branch meetinghouse (PA), 62
South Haven Brethren Church, KS, **1205**
South Haven Old German Baptist Brethren Church, MI, **1205**
Michigan Brethren settlement, 824
South Indiana Mission Board
Sampson Hill Church of the Brehren, IN, 1141
South Keokuk Church of the Brethren, IA, **1205–1206**
English River Church of the Brethren, IA, 447
South Korea
Church of the Brethren, 2162
missions, short-term, 2226
United Nations Korean Reconstruction Agency (UNKRA), 1291
South Los Angeles, CA, Church of the Brethren, 1955, 2071
South Loup Church of the Brethren, NE, *812*, **1206**
South Margi Uba, Nigeria, 306
South Mill Creek Church of the Brethren, WV, **1206**
South Fork Church of the Brethren, WV, preaching point, 1205
South Modesto Community Church of the Brethren, CA, *See* Modesto, CA, South Modesto Community Church of the Brethren
South Morrill, KS, Church of the Brethren, *See* Morrill, KS, Church of the Brethren
South Ottumwa, IA, Church of the

Brethren, *See* Ottumwa, IA, Church of the Brethren
South Ottumwa Mission, IA
missions and missionaries, 2103
South Paca Street Church of the Brethren, MD, *See* Baltimore, MD, South Paca Street Church of the Brethren
South Pasadena, CA, Grace Brethren Church
Fremont Avenue Brethren Church, **1206**
Mayes, Charles W., 804
South Red Cloud Church of the Brethren, NE, **1206**
Red Cloud, NE, Church of the Brethren, 1088
South River, IA, Church of the Brethren, *See* Osceola, IA, Church of the Brethren
South Saint Joseph Church of the Brethren, MO, **1135**
South Santaam German Baptist Brethren Church, OR, *See* Albany, OR, Sunrise Community Church (CB)
South Santaam (later Willamette Valley), OR, congregation, 980, 1138
South Solomon Old German Baptist Brethren Church, KS, **1206**
North Solomon Old German Baptist Brethren Church, KS, 950
Portis, KS, Grace Brethren Church, 1047
Portis, KS, North Solomon Church of the Brethren, 1048
South Warrensburg Church of the Brethren, MO, 1318, *See also* Warrensburg, MO, Church of the Brethren
South Waterloo, IA, Church of the Brethren, *See* Waterloo, IA, South Waterloo Church of the Brethren
South Whitley, IN, 1213, 1234
Church of the Brethren, **1206–1207**
Southampton Church, Snake Spring Valley, PA, Church of the Brethren, *See* Artemas, PA, Church of the Brethren
Southampton Co., VA, 216
Southern Association of Schools and Colleges, 168
Southern Baptists
Convention, 22
excluded from National Council of Churches of Christ (NCCC), 915
Theological Seminary (Louisville, KY), 114
McCann, Samuel Napoleon, 772
Metzler, Burton, 820
Morris, James Henry, 877
Southern California Immigration Agency, 722
Southern California-Nevada Council of Churches
Fasnacht, Harold Dale, 480
Southern Californian, 2071
Southern Christian Leadership Conference (SCLC), 695
Southern District
history, 1967
Southern District Fellowship of Grace Brethren Churches
Georgia, 540
Southern District of Pennsylvania (CB)
Elizabethtown College, 437

history of, 1950
Southern Indiana District, Church of the Brethren
Fairview Church of the Brethren, IN, 468
Southern Kansas Mission Board
Independence, KS, Church of the Brethren, 649
Southern Kansas Railroad
McDonough, George L., 773
Southern Lancaster Grace Brethren Church, PA, **1207**
Southern Missouri and Arkansas District
district history, 1959
Southern Missouri and Arkansas District, Church of the Brethren
Farrenburg Church of the Brethren, MO, 479
Southern Morrisons Cove Towns, 1863
Southern Ohio district
Grace Brethren Village, 563
Southern Ohio District (CB)
Flat Creek Church of the Brethren, KY, 493
Southern Ohio Mission Board
Cincinnati, OH, Church of the Brethren, 313
Greenville, OH, Church of the Brethren, 572
Southern Pacific Railroad, 1289
California, 238
colonization and, 238
Roanoke, LA, Church of the Brethren, 1112
Southern Pennsylvania District
Putney, VT, Genesis Church of the Brethren and, 2239
Southern Plains District
Brethren movement and, 2357
history of, 1958
Southern regional dialect, 911
Southside Fellowship, IN (CB), *See* Elkhart, IN, Southside Fellowship (CB/Menn.)
Southwest District Fellowship, NM, 931
Southwood, John W., 430, **1207,** 1779, 2071
poetry, 1039
Southwood, Joseph, 1207
Southwood, Lydia, 1207
Southwood, William, 1779
Souza family, 1312
Sove, Michael F.
Northview, OH, Brethren Life Church/Vineyard Community Church, 2232
Sove, Mike, 2294
Soviet Union
Dull, Christine on visits to, 2325
Dull, Ralph on visits to, 2325
Mennonites, 815
Nikodim, Metropolitan, priest in Russian Orthodox Church, 937
religious liberty, suppression of, 1098
Sower, *See* entries at Sauer
Sower, Albert M., 2071
Sower, Allen M., 2071
Sower Bible, *See* Sauer Bible
Sower, Bishop Christopher, 1894
Sower, Christopher, III
loyalist, 2053
loyalist letters, 2056
Sower, Catherine A. Potts, 1207

Sower, Cecilia Chollet, 1207
Sower, Charles G., 1861, 1900, 2071, **2388**
  Sauer, Christopher, II, great-grandson of, 1207
Sower, David Elias, 756, 1779
Sower, David, Jr., 1147, 1207
Sower, Edson, 658
Sower family, 686, 2071, *See also* Sauer family
  Bibles, 1930
  bicentenary, greetings for, 1940
  Harley family, 583
Sower Press, *See* Sauer Press
Sower, Samuel, 1149, 1858, 2056, 2061
  reference to, 1913
Sowers, Charles E., 1216, 1779, 2306
Sowers, D. E., 210
Sowers, Daniel B., 1779, 2294
Sowers, Graham B., 613, 1779, 2306
  Maple Grove Church of the Brethren, NC, minister, 790
Sowers, Hubert F., 1779
Sowers, Hubert Ray, 1779
Sowers, Jeddie Burnice, 515, 1779
Sowers, Joe, 2294
Sowers, Larry B., 579, 768, 1779
Sowers, Leslie, 1216
Sowers, Maston (Marton) Harmon, 1779
Sowers, William, 689
Sowerwine family, *See Out of the Melting Pot*
Sox, Alvin
  Maitland Church of the Brethren, PA, salaried minister, 783
Spach, Jacob, 511
Spacht, John Rapha, 1779
Spacht, Mark B., 1779
Spacht, Mark M., 318
Spaeth, Harry, 1779
Spahr, Jacob, 2071
Spaid, A. R., 1779
Spaid, Daniel B., 1779
Spaid, Darrel Robert, 2294
Spain, **1207**, *1208*
  Civil War relief work, 1331
  education programs, 185
  Foreign Missionary Society (BC, FGBC), 501
  Heifers for Relief, 1331
  Loyalists and Nationalists, 23
  missions, short-term, 2226
  relief and rehabilitation work, 200
  relief and service efforts, 1097
  relief and social work, 303
  West, Daniel, 1331
  work camp, 1367
  World War I, 23
  World War II relief work, 1373
Spain, Alfred
  Pleasant Grove Grace Brethren Church, IA, pastor, 1031
Spalding family
  Roanoke, LA, Church of the Brethren, 1112
Spalen Gate
  prison of Andreas Boni, *1059*
Spall, James J., 1779
  New Hope Church of the Brethren, IN, building of, 929
Spangenberg, Augustus Gottlieb, 378, 2071
  recommended Koker family to emigrants, 705

Moravian bishop, **1207–1208**
Moravian Church, 875
Spangle, Jacob, 1779
Spangler, Alice (later Wallick), 1314
Spangler, Carl Dempster, 1779
  Ninevah Church of the Brethren, VA, pastor in, 938
  Red Hill Church of the Brethren, VA, pastoral leadership, 1088
Spangler, Carol Compton, 1845
Spangler, Charles L., 1779
  Pulaski, VA, Church of the Brethren, minister, 1071
Spangler, Clarence W., 1779
Spangler, D. W., 2071
Spangler family, 2079
Spangler, Harman W., 1779
Spangler, Horace C., 1779, 2072
Spangler, Isabella (later Trostler), 1276
Spangler, John, 1779
Spangler, Joyce Gayle Horton, 2294
Spangler, Keith Allen, 2294
Spangler, Ruth Josephine, 1846
Spangler, Samuel G., 1779
Spangler, W. B., 1779
Spangler, Wayne Eller, 1845
Spanish-American War
  relief for victims, **1208**
  Swallow, James F., 1243
Spanish center
  Elgin, IL, Highland Avenue Church of the Brethren, 436
Spanish Civil War
  Gilbert, Martha Rupel, 2189
  Heifer Project International, 593
  Murphy, Sara Florence Fogelsanger, 897
  relief and rehabilitation work in, 146, 199
  relief program, 1331
  Spain, relief work in, **1207**, 1208, *1208*
  work camp, 1367
Spanish Fellowship
  Chicago, IL, First Church of the Brethren, 275
Spanish language ministry
  McAllen, TX, Grace Brethren Church, 2219
  Santa Ana, CA, Maranatha Grace Brethren Church, 1144
  Sarasota, FL, Brethren Church, 1145
Spanish language-speaking congregations in New Mexico, 931
Spanogle, Andrew, Jr., 1779
Spanogle, Andrew, Sr., 317, 1779
Spanogle, Catherine Myers, 1208
Spanogle, Elizabeth (later Cox)
  family history, 1911
Spanogle, Harry
  Maitland Church of the Brethren, PA, minister, 783
Spanogle, Harry A., 1779
Spanogle, J. L., 332
Spanogle, Jacob, 1263, 1779
  Philadelphia, PA, First Church of the Brethren, minister, 1015
Spanogle, John, 1208, 1779
Spanogle, William L., 20, 215, 353, 512, 927, **1208–1209**, 1304, 1779
  Martinsburg, PA, Grace Brethren Church, pastor, 798
  Pittsburgh, PA, First Brethren Church, pastor, 1027

Sparks, Andrew J., 1779
Sparks, Mary, 1779
Sparling, Gary and Barbara, 70
Sparling, Philip J., 2294
Sparta, NC, 749
  New Bethel Church of the Brethren, NC, 925
  New Haven Church of the Brethren, NC, 928
Spartanburg Co., SC, 212
Spartansburg, SC, congregation
  Melvin Hill Church of the Brethren, NC, 812
Sparzak, Chet J., 2294
Spaugh, Levi, 511
  Maple Grove Church of the Brethren, NC, minister, 790
Speak For the Lord (organization)
  News and Views from Speak for the Lord, publication for, 934
Speaker, Donovan Earl, 1779
speakers
  ministry, terminology, 848
speaking in tongues
  charismatic movement, 272
Spear family, 1885
Spearhead
  Mexico City, Mexico, Brethren Mission, 2222
Spears, Gene
  Pompano Beach, FL, Grace Brethren Church, 1046
Spears, Marg
  Pompano Beach, FL, Grace Brethren Church, 1046
Spears, Richard, 2139
Speas, Esther J. Yoder, 2072
Speas, Walter R., 2072
Spease, Rachel Keller
  on Keller, Elizabeth, 2357
  on Keller, Hans Jacob, 2357
Specht, Alva J., 1779
  Royersford, PA, Church of the Brethren, pastor, 1129
speech, *See* drama
Speer, Robert E., 989, 1231, 1345
Speicher, Abraham, 2072
Speicher, Amanda Lichty, 1180
Speicher, Barbara Weaver, 2072
Speicher, David, 2072
Speicher, E. E., 1779
Speicher family, 1322, 2072
  Fredericksburg, IA, Hillcrest Baptist and Brethren Church, 512
Speicher, H., 244
Speicher, Henry, 2
Speicher, Jacob, 1180, 1779
Speicher, Jacob B., 1779
Speicher, John, 1323, 1779
Speicher, Mary Grace, 1844
Speicher, Mary Ruth (later Shull), 1844, *See also* Shull, Mary Ruth Speicher
Speicher, Paul Ira, 2072
Speicher, Richard Dwayne, 1779–1780
Speicher, Ross, 468, 632, 1780
Speicher, Sara
  Durnbaugh, Donald F. and, 2327
  violence and, 2265
Speicher, Timothy D., 2294
Spence, Phillip E., 2294
Spencer, C. C., 377, **1209**, 1780
  minorities, ethnic and racial, 850

Spencer, Charles Amos, 1780
    Shepherd Church of the Brethren, MI, minister and elder in, 1176
Spencer Co., IN
    Replogle family, 1100
Spencer, Dean, 436
Spencer, Elliott
    Oak Hill Old German Baptist Brethren Church, WV, 957
Spencer, Herbert, 912
Spencer, John H., 1780, 2072
Spencer, Robert, 674, 1780
Spener, P. J., 506
Spener, Philipp Jakob, 19, 57, 283, 323, **1209**, 1258, 1259
    dissertation on, 1916
    noncreedalism, 942
    Pietism, 1021
    Radical German Pietism, 1079
    Stein, K. James on, 2358
Sperryville, VA, Copps Chapel congregation, **1209**
Spessard, Howard Lehman, 2072
Speyer, Germany
    Reformation, Protestant, 1091
Spicer family
    Mount Laurel, NJ, Grace Brethren Church, 883
Spicer, Robert M., 1780
    Mount Laurel, NJ, Grace Brethren Church, pastor, 883
Spicer, Ruth, 13
Spicher, Dan, 1780
Spicher family, 2072
Spicher, George W., 1780
Spicher, Jacob W., 274, 1780
    Montgomery Church of the Brethren, PA, minister, 872
Spicher, John W., 1780
Spicher, M. H.
    Montgomery Church of the Brethren, PA, minister, 872
Spicher, M. W., 1780
Spicher, Milan H., 376, 1780
Spicher, Samuel
    Montgomery Church of the Brethren, PA, 872
Spickerman, J. S., 1780
Spickerman, J. S. C., 1780
Spickler, Henry M., 1273, 2072
Spidle, David, 1780
Spidle (Spidel), William Franklin, 1780
Spigel, Rex, 1780
Spiggle, William H., 1780
    Maurertown, VA, Brethren Church, 803
    Meadow Mills Church of the Brethren, VA, minister, 806
Spiggle, William P.
    Meadow Mills Church of the Brethren, VA, 806
Spigle family, 1277
Spiker, Milan H., 1780
Spiker, Walter Scott, 1780
Spillers, Daniel C., 1780
    South Haven Old German Baptist Brethren Church, MI, minister, 1205
Spillers, Estal
    South Haven Old German Baptist Brethren Church, MI, 1205
Spillers, Mary
    South Haven Old German Baptist Brethren Church, MI, 1205

Spillman, Rebecca
    Peabody Old German Baptist Brethren Church, KS, 997
    Sand Creek Old German Baptist Brethren Church, KS, 1143
Spillman, Vern, 1780
Spindale, NC, 1339
    Church of the Brethren, **1209**
Spire, Catherine Brill, 2294
Spire, Ronald Duane, 516, 672, 696, 1780
Spire, Samuel Glenn, 2294
Spire, Steven Ronald, 2294
Spirit, *See* Holy Spirit
spiritual growth
    Miller, Karen Peterson on disciplines for, 2347
    Parish Ministries Commission involvement in, 993
spiritual life, **1209–1211**
    Bechtold's writings on, 1872
    Church of the Brethren, 304
    fasting, 480
    publishing, 1063, 1067
    theology and, 2254
    Yoder, Charles Francis, 1386
spiritual songs, **1211**, *See also* hymns
Spiritual Storehouse
    Mack, Alexander, Jr., 774
    religious periodical, 1146
spiritual union
    marriage, 794–795
spiritual uplift
    National Youth Conference, 917–918
spiritualism, **1211–1212**
spiritualists, in Silesia, 156
spirituality
    dress and, 402
    Wuthnow, Robert on, 2364
Spirituality, God's Order of Being (Rieman)
    Rieman, Timothy Wayne (CB) and, 2243
spirituals, *See* gospel music
Spiteller, Barbara (later Scheublein), *See* Scheublein, Barbara Spiteller
Spitler, Anna (later Whistler), 1212
Spitler, Barbara Rohrer, 1212
Spitler, Catharina Schaffner, 1212
Spitler, D. N., 1780
Spitler, Elizabeth Meily, 1212
Spitler family, **1212**, 1989
Spitler, Jacob, 1212
Spitler, Jacob, II, 1212
Spitler, Johannes, 1212
Spitler, Johannes, II, 1212
Spitler, John, 1212
Spitler, Joseph, 1212
Spitler, Lydia Linkenhofer, 1212
Spitler, Nathan, 1212
    Newport Church of the Brethren, VA, leadership in, 934
Spitler, Noah E., 1780
    New River Old German Baptist Brethren Church, ministers for, 931
    Salem Old German Baptist Brethren Church, OH, elder, 1139
Spitler, Samuel, 1780
    Newport Church of the Brethren, VA, leadership in, 934
Spitler, Susan, 170
Spitler, Susannah Buckwalter Lane, 1212
Spitler, Susannah Wise, 1212
Spittler, Johannes and Catharina Schaffner

genealogy, 1971
Spitzer family, 1313, 1345
Spitzer, G. C., 1780
Spitzer, J. F., 1348, 1780
Spitzer, Jacob, 561, 1264, 1780
Spitzer, Joseph F., 1780
Spitzer, Lee Franklin, 1780
Spitzer, Syram Fred, 1780
Splitter, Wolfgang
    on German Lutherans in PA, 2357
    writings of, 2357
Spohn, ___, early minister at Ten Mile Church of the Brethren, PA, 1253
Spohn, Clarence E., 2072
    writings of, 2357–2358
Spohn family, 1253
Spohn, John, 1780
Spohn, Margaret (later Schwalm), *See* Schwalm, Margaret Spohn
Spohn, Mary Leatherman, 1253
Spohn (Spoon), Magdalena Ledermann, 733
Spohn (Spoon), Martin, 733, 1253
Spohr, Karen (later Carter), 2274
Spokane Valley Grace Brethren Church, WA, 101, **1212**
    Miller, Robert Paul, pastor, 842
Spokane, WA
    Church of the Brethren, **1212**
    congregation, 1250
    First Brethren Church of Spokane, *See* Spokane Valley Grace Brethren Church, WA
    North Spokane Church of the Brethren, **1212**
    missions, 860
    urban mission, 1297
Sponcellar, John, 602
Sponseller, Elmer S., 1780
Sponseller, John L., 1780
sports, **69–70**, *70*, 557, 1087, 2045, 2232, *See also* amusements, wordly; recreation
Spotts, Charles D., 2072
Spradling, Homer S., 1780
Spradling, Ralph
    Red Hill Church of the Brethren, VA, pastor, 1088
Spradling, Ralph M., 1780
Sprague, Byron C., 1780
Spraker, Ella Hazel Atterbury, 2072
Sprang, Godfry, 1780
Sprankel, Samuel, 1780
Spranker, Samuel, 719
Sprankle, Catherine (later Young), 1389
Sprankle, Samuel, *1390*
    Spray Church of the Brethren, NC, *See* Eden, NC, Church of the Brethren
Spray, NC, *See* Eden, NC, Church of the Brethren
Sprecher, Robert, 242
Sprenkel, John F., 2072
Sprenkel, Rodney D., 2294
    Sugar Grove Old German Baptist Brethren Church, OH and, 2254
Sprenkle, Barbara, 405
Sprigg family, 1345
    Spring Branch Church of the Brethren, MO, **1212**
    history, 1977
Spring Brook, ND, Ray Church of the Brethren, 1212–1213
Spring Creek Church of the Brethren, IA,

See Fredericksburg, IA, Hillcrest
Baptist and Brethren Church
history, 1988
Spring Creek Church of the Brethren, IN,
429, **1213,** 1367
Spring Creek Church of the Brethren, KS,
1213, 1304
Spring Creek Church of the Brethren, PA,
See Hershey, PA, Spring Creek
Church of the Brethren
100 year anniversary, 2014
Palmyra, PA, Church of the Brethren,
separated from, 991
Spring Creek congregation, *See*
Fredericksburg, IA, Hillcrest
Baptist and Brethren Church
South Whitley, IN, Church of the
Brethren, 1207
Spring Creek congregation, PA, 142
Hertzler (Hartzler) family, 601
Spring Creek mission point
Flat Creek Church of the Brethren, KY,
493
Spring Creek Normal School, 206–207
Flory, Daniel Christian, 497
Spring Creek Normal School, Spring Creek,
VA, **1213**
Spring Creek Old German Baptist Brethren
Church, OK, **1213**
Spring Creek Old German Baptist Brethren
Church, WY, **1213,** 1380
Spring Grove Church of the Brethren, PA,
1213
Spring Grove congregation, PA, 737
Spring Mount, PA, 1283
Church of the Brethren, PA,
115, **1213–1214,** 1283, 1347,
Spring River Church of the Brethren, MO,
257, 334, **1214**
Spring River Old German Baptist Brethren
Church, MO, **1214**
Spring Run Church of the Brethren, IL,
233, **1214**
Spring Run Church of the Brethren, PA,
406, *1214,* **1215,** 2358
Maitland Church of the Brethren, PA,
783
Sharp, Solomon Zook, baptism of,
1174, 1245
Pine Glen Church of the Brethren, PA,
1024
Springdale, AR, Church of the Brethren,
1215
Round Mountain Church of the
Brethren, 1125
Springer family
South Solomon Old German Baptist
Brethren Church, KS, 1206
Springer, Nelson P., 1861
Springfield Center, OH, Brethren Church,
See Akron, OH, Ellet Grace
Brethren Church
Springfield Church of the Brethren, PA,
1216
Harleysville, PA, Indian Creek Church
of the Brethren, 584
Quakertown, PA, First Church of the
Brethren, 1075
Scholten, Marian and Martin, pastors,
1155
Springfield congregation (GBB), MO, 733
Springfield, IL, 736
Church of the Brethren, **1215**

Springfield, IN, Church of the Brethren, *See*
Wawaka, IN, Church of the
Brethren
Springfield meetinghouse, IN, 1323
Springfield, MO, Good Shepherd Church of
the Brethren, **1215**
Springfield, OH
city mission, 1978
First Church of the Brethren, 395, 396,
1215
Sisters' Aid Society, *1188*
Springfield Church of the Brethren, OH,
688, 937, *See also* Akron, OH,
Springfield Church of the Brethren
Springfield, OR, Church of the Brethren,
1215–1216
homelessness, 2203
Nicholas Gardens Church of the
Brethren, *See* Springfield, OR,
Church of the Brethren
Springfield Presbytery
Restoration Movement, 1101
Springfield Township, OH, 13
Springville congregation, PA, 322, 686
Ephrata, PA, Church of the Brethren,
448
Mohler Church of the Brethren, PA,
868
Sprinke, Jonathan, 637
Sprinkle family
Hiestand (Heistand, Heestand,
Heaston) family, 602
Sprinkle, John, 2072
Sproat, James, 2072
Sprogel, Salome Margaret (later Zeidig),
994
Sprogle, John, 1780
Sprogle, Samuel H., 1780
Sprouse family, 768
Sprout, Oliver S., 2072
Sprowls, Thomas E., Jr., 2294
Medina, OH, Living Hope Brethren
Church, **2219**
Spruce Run Church of the Brethren, WV,
See Lindside, WV, Spruce Run
Church of the Brethren
Spruce Run Old German Baptist Brethren
Church, WV, **1216**
Red Oak Ridge German Baptist
Brethren Church, WV, 1089
Sprunger, Arthur, 439, 1221, 1780
Manheim, PA, Grace Brethren Church,
pastor, 787
Sprunger, Arthur L., 241
Spry, Charles G., 2294
Spurgeon, J. B., 1780
Panther Creek, IA, Church of the
Brethren, 992
Spurgeon Manor, 360, **1216**
Dallas Center, IA, Church of the
Brethren, 360
Old Folks Home (CB), Marshalltown,
IA, 966
Spurlock family
Haddix, KY, Brethren Church, 577
Spurlock, Harvey, 507
Spyker, Edward Henry, 1780
Spyker family, 2072
Squaw Creek Church of the Brethren, MO,
North Bethel Church of the Brethren,
MO, 945
Squires family, 1365
Squires, John H., 755, 1221, 1365, 1780

Squirrel, 383
Squirrel Creek, IN congregation, 1245
Roann, IN, Church of the Brethren,
1112
Srack (Schrack), Grace Prudence, 1361,
1780
St., *See* entries at Saint
Sta____, Susanna Angle
Engle/Angle family, 446
Staatsbote (State Messenger)
Müller, Johann Heinrich, 893
Stabler, Dorothy Witwer, 2072
Stabler family, 148
Stacht, Mark B.
Pleasant Grove Grace Brethren Church,
IA, pastor, 1031
Stacy, Harold, 2153
Staffen (Stepfen), Conrad, 1780
Stafford Co., KS, 424
Moorehead, Michael, minister, 997
Stafford Co., VA
Hollywood Church of the Brethren,
VA, 620
Stafford, John, 1780
Stafford, Robert, 2294
Stafford, William Edgar, **1216, 2378**
memoirs, 2358
poetry of, 2358
stage, *See* drama
Stage, John Lewis, 1943, 2072
stages of ministry
Brethren Church ministry, 846
Stagg, Charles W., 2040
Staggs, Slone T., 1780
Stahl, Charles, 239
Stahl, Mrs. Charles, 239
Stahl, Dorothy, 588
Stahl, Herman A., 1780
Stahl, Kenneth, 239, 588
Stahl, Mrs. Kenneth, 239
Stahl, R. N., 1780
Stahl, W. L., 1780
Stahlschmidt, Johann Christian, 2072
Stahly, Clayton, 1216
Stahly, Cora Miller, 1216
Staiger family, 148
Stainer family, 1385
Stair family, 1365
Stair, Jesse, *See* Mason, Jesse (Stair)
Stair, Jesse (Mason)
South Saint Joseph Church of the
Brethren, MO, 1135
Stair, Marion Ellsworth, 21, 345, 1780
STAKE (BC), **2252**
Staley, Austin R., 332, 360, 532, 626, 1285,
1780–1781
Staley, Robert T., 2072
Stall, Velma Hufford
on Hufford, Frances, 2358
Stallsmith, Susan (later Butterbaugh), 1070
Stallter, Sharon Ann Terrell, 1853
Stallter, Thomas Marshall, 1853, 2294
Stalnaker, Andrew J., 1781
Stalnaker family
Prosperity Brethren Church, WV, 1062
Staly (Straley), D. M., 1781
Staman, C. H., 1781
Stambaugh, Albert, 1781
Stambaugh, George W., 463, 606, 743,
1781
Golden Spring German Baptist
Brethren Church, NE, 2374
Nishney Valley German Baptist

Brethren, IA, elder in, 938
Platte Valley German Baptist Brethren
Church, NE, elder, 1030
Stambaugh, Jacob, 268, 1217, 1781
Stamburg, John, 1781
Stamm, Gregory Alan, 2294
Stamp, Francis, 1232
Stamy, Abraham, 1781
Stamy, Daniel W., 1335, 1781, 2306, **2386**
New River Old German Baptist
Brethren Church, ministers for,
931–932
Stamy family
Robins, IA, Church of the Brethren,
1115
Stamy, Hubert, 360
Stamy, John H., 406, 1781
Stamy, Kenneth, 360, 1335, 1781
New River Old German Baptist
Brethren Church, ministers for,
931–932
Stamy, Solomon, 105, 406, 1234, 1781
New River Old German Baptist
Brethren Church, ministers for,
931
Stamy (Stamey), John F., 1781
Standafer family
Hancock, MN, Church of the Brethren,
582
Standafer, Leah Mae, 1840
Standard Readers (Brumbaugh), 223
Standing Committee, 402, **1216–1217**
Beeghley, John W., 2134
Benedict, Harry G., 2135
Bowman, Carl W., 2138
Brethren polity, 1042, 1043, 1044
Brubaker, Harold A., 2153
Church of the Brethren Annual
Conference, *See* Church of the
Brethren Annual Conference
Committee on Resolutions (CB), 328
Committee on Understanding and
Reconciliation (CB) , 328
Congregational Brethren, 334
in the Dunkard Brethren, 37
On Earth Peace Assembly, 2235
election of church officers, 434
expanded role in the Church of the
Brethren, 36
Filbrun, Stanley Clarence, 2184
Flora, John F., 495
formation and function of (before
1880), 33
Garber, Henry, 529
George's Creek Old German Baptist
Brethren Church, PA, 540
Harshbarger, John, 587
Hart, John, 587
Hays, Daniel, 590
Helstern, Russell Fred, 596
Herr, John, 598
Hertzler, William, 601
Hess, James Arthur, 2198
Hoke, George, 618
Holsinger, Henry Ritz, 622
Hutchison, Andrew, 639
Kilhefner, Galen C., 693
Laschet (Laaschet, Laasche, Lausche,
Laushe), Abraham van, 726
Lear, John Wallace, 732
Lindsay, Samuel David, 744
Long, David, 753
Long, George, 753

Long, W. Newton, 754
Longenecker, Jacob Hollinger, 756
manual for, 788
members, 178
name change discussion, 2228
Old German Baptist Brethren, 969
in the Old German Baptist Brethren,
36, 37
organizational restructuring and, 2242
Price, David E., serving on, 1056
Price, Jacob, serving on, 1056–1057
queries, 1076
Quinter, James, 1077
Receiving Committee, 1085
Skiles, Jacob W., 1188
Stoner, Ephraim Winfield, 1225
Swigart, William Joseph, 1245
Taylor, Isaac W., 1249
Teeter, Lewis Wallace, 1250
Thomas, Daniel, 1262
Thomas, Jacob M., 1263
Umstad, John Horning, 1286
Wagoner, Morris B., 1312
Winger, Otho, 1351
Wise, John, 1354
Wolfe, David, 1356
Zollers, George DeHaven, 1400
Zunkel, Cleda Pearl Shull, 1402
Stanford, Glenn R., 157, 516, 1240, 1781
McFarland, CA, Church of the
Brethren, pastor, 774
San Marcos, CA, North Country
Church of the Brethren and, 2245
Stanislaus Church of the Brethren, CA,
1217
Stanislaus Co., CA, 1217, 1280, 1321,
1335, 1363, 2083
Empire, CA, Church of the Brethren,
445
Modesto, CA, Church of the Brethren,
866
Modesto, CA, South Modesto
Community Church of the
Brethren, 867
Old Brethren, 964
Patterson, CA, Church of the Brethren,
995
Stanley, Charles, family
Ramey Flats Church of the Brethren,
VA, 1083
Stanley, Esther (later Rife), 1094
Stanley, Joseph, family
Ramey Flats Church of the Brethren,
VA, 1083
Stanley, Maston S., 515
Stanley, Noah, family
Ramey Flats Church of the Brethren,
VA, 1083
Stanley, VA, 731
Stanley, WI, 1354, 1365
Church of the Brethren, **1217**
Maple Grove Church of the
Brethren, WI, 791
Stanley, WI, congregation
proceeds to, from sale of Shannon, IL,
Church of the Brethren, 1172
Stansbury, George, 106, 1781
Stanton, Levi, 1781
Stanturf, Judson C., 1781
Staples, M. L., 43
Stapleton, Ammon, 1861, 2072
Star of Cathay, 2072
Star schoolhouse, Wiley, CO, Church of the

Brethren, 1345
Starbard, Earl M., 1781
Stark Co., OH, 267, 318, 382, 383, 413,
424, 711, 712, 752, 1231, 1287,
1355, 1395
Brethren settlement, 961
Freeburg Church of the Brethren, OH,
514
Grace Brethren Church of Canton, OH,
562
Hartville, OH, Church of the Brethren,
588
history of, 1960
landmarks, 1914
Massillon, OH, Trinity Church of the
Brethren, 801
migration of Brethren, 829
Nicholson, John, minister in, 935
Nimishillen Church of the Brethren,
937
Nimishillen Old German Baptist
Brethren Church, OH, 937–938
Ontario Brethren, 975
Orion Dunkard Brethren Congregation,
OH, 981
Replogle family, 1100
Rome Old German Baptist Brethren
Church, OH, 1121
Sandy German Baptist Brethren
Church, OH, 1143
Scheublein, Jacob, and family, 1178
Shideler family, 1177
Stark Co., OH, congregation
migration of Brethren, 829
Stark, Darlington, 1781
Stark, G. H., 1781
Stark, Henry, 1315
Starke Co., IN
Salem Church of the Brethren, IN,
1137
Starke Co., OH, 1246
Starkey, J. H., 743, 1781
Starkey, VA, Gospel Grace Brethren
Church, 163
Starlings family
Patterson, CA, Church of the Brethren,
995
Starn, O. C., 1781
Rittman, OH, First Brethren Church,
pastor, 1111
Starook, Samuel S., 1781
Starr, Edward C., 1861
starvation experiment, *See* Minnesota
Starvation project (CPS)
starvation project
CPS volunteers in World War II, 1984
state
allegiance to and oathtaking, 959
Brethren attitude toward, *See* church-
state relations
historical relation of Brethren to, trea-
tise on, 2054
welfare of and religious liberty, 1098
State Center German Baptist Brethren, IA,
1217
State Center Old German Baptist Brethren
Church, IA, **1217–1218**
state churches, *See* established churches
Radical German Pietism, 1079
State College, PA, University Baptist and
Brethren Church, **1218**
State Councils of Churches
Miller, Joseph Quinter, 841

state Councils of Churches, **1218**
State Messenger (Staatsbote)
Müller, Johann Heinrich, 893
state parks
chaplaincy, 2158
State Sabbath School Association
Tuscarora Brethren Church, PA, 1281
"Statement of Faith," **1218**, *See also* confession, of faith
Fellowship of Grace Brethren
Churches, 133
Grace Brethren and creeds, 943
International Fellowship of Grace
Brethren Churches, 2209
membership in National Association of
Evangelicals (NAE), 914
"Message of the Brethren Ministry,"
818
Message of the Brethren Ministry
adopted as, 916
National Fellowship of Brethren
Churches, 486
replacing "Message of the Brethren
Ministry," 1218, 1261
theological basis, 1261
Staten, Leonard, 275
States, Etta Mae, 375
States General, *See* Estates General
states, geographical listings of, 1479–1503
statistics, 2041
Brethren groups, 1911
Brethren, history and geography of the
Mississippi, 1937
Brethren movement, 267
compilation of, 1465–1478
General Services Commission (CB),
539
recording of, **1218–1219**
U. S. churches and church membership, 1956
Statler, Catherine (later Good), *See* Good
family
Statler, Christian
Pleasant Dale Church of the Brethren,
IN, 1030
Statler, Dana Eugene, 2294
Statler, Ephraim, 1219
Statler, Ernest S., 161, 1219
Statler family
Holtzapfel (Holsapple, Holsopple)
family, 624
Statler, Foster Boyd, 439, 1219, 1348,
1781, 1784
Huntingdon, PA, Stone Church of the
Brethren, 637
Mount Morris, IL, Church of the
Brethren, pastor, 883
Statler, Grace B. Stayer, 1219
Statler, Harold Boyd, **1219**, 1781, 2072
Statler, Mary Ann Seese, 1219
Statler, Ruth Beeghly, 161, 190, 214, 748,
1219, 1918, 2072, 2073
Staton, Charles
Richmond, VA, Grace Brethren
Church, 1108
Staton, Loretta
Richmond, VA, Grace Brethren
Church, 1108
Staton (Stratton), W. L., 1781
Stauber, Jacob, 2076
Staudt family, 1929, 2073
Staudt, Richard W., 2073
Stauffer, Abram, 1220

Stauffer, Albert A., 1781
Stauffer, Amos K., 1924, 2073
Stauffer, Anna (later Masterson)
Masterson, Benjamin Franklin, mother
of, 802
Stauffer, Annie, 356–357
Stauffer, Benjamin, 42
Stauffer, Benjamin G., 1781
Stauffer, Beulah (later Hostetler), 1912
Stauffer-Bolanderhof family, 2073
Stauffer, Charles Albert, 2073
Stauffer, Charlotte (later Shimp), 2064
Stauffer, Christian, 1219, 1220
Stauffer, Clinton W., 1781
Stauffer, Daniel, 1882
Stauffer, David Clay, 1312, 1781
Stauffer, Edgar, 244, 565, 749, 1781
Silver Lake Church of the Brethren,
NE, elder and minister, 1182
Stauffer, Elizabeth (later Tyson), 1284,
1854
Stauffer, Elmer J., 1781
Stauffer, Ezra Nelson, 2073
on Stauffer, Jacob and descendants,
2358
Stauffer family, 319, 534, **1219–1220**, 2073
Fahrney (Forney) family, 466
Harley family, 583
Hatboro, PA, Suburban Grace Brethren
Church, 588
Stauffer, Fannie, 256
Stauffer, Frederic, 1781
Stauffer, George, 1781
Stauffer, Glenn Eugene, 1781
Stauffer, H., 1781
Stauffer, H. Cecilia Stauffer, 2073
Stauffer, Harry M., 1219
Stauffer, Harvey, 1781
Shepherd Church of the Brethren, MI,
pastor and elder in, 1176
Stauffer, Hellmut, 2073
Stauffer, Henry, 2073, 2076
genealogy and descendants, 1941
Stauffer, Jacob, 1883, 2073
Stauffer, Ezra Nelson on descendants of,
2358
Stauffer, Johannes Hans, 2073, 2076
Stauffer, John, 2051, 2064
Stauffer, John L.
Lewiston, ME, Church of the Brethren,
2214
Stauffer, John N., 678, **1219, 2378**
Stauffer, John Wesley, 2073
Stauffer, June
Lewiston, ME, Church of the Brethren,
2214
Stauffer, Lloyd B., 513, 1781
Stauffer, M. Louise Lee, 1219
Stauffer, Martha (later Eberly), 2175
Stauffer, Marthan N. Heisey, 1219
Stauffer, Mary Jane, 2073
Stauffer, Menno, 116, 1781
Romine Church of the Brethren, IL,
elder, 1121
Stauffer, Oliver B., Sr., 1781
Stauffer, Otis, family
North Beatrice Church of the Brethren,
NE, 945
Stauffer, Paul, 338
Stauffer, Paul Wilbur, 1781
Stauffer, Pearl Charlotte, 54, 1834, 2084
Stauffer, Richard Eugene, 2073
Stauffer, S. C., 2073

Stauffer-Sauder family, 1969
Stauffer (Stouffer), Jacob M., 1781
Stauffer (Stouffer/Stover) families, 1909
Stauffer (Stouffer, Stover) family,
1219–1220
Stauffer, Wilfred Noble, 1781, **2386**
New Enterprise, PA, Church of the
Brethren, as minister, 927
Staufier, Peter, 1781
Staunton, VA, 1308
Church of the Brethren, 45, 90, **1220**
Stayer, David A., 1781
Stayer, Esther, 1384
Stayer, Grace B. (later Statler), 1219
Stayer, Irene Moszkowska, 2073
Stayer, Jacob Clyde, 1781
Stayer, Jesse Lee, 1781
Stayer, John R.
Roaring Spring, PA, Albright Church
of the Brethren, minister, 1114
Stayer, John Replogle, 1781
on love feast, 2358
Stayer, John S., 1781
Stayer, Raymond, 1845, **2388**
Stayer, Samuel, 1384
Stearn, Roy E., 1782
Stearns Street Brethren Church, CA, 755
Stebbins, Alice (later Garber), 529
Stebbins, George C., 560
Stech, Opal
Poland, 1041
Stecher family, 2091
Steckel, William R., 2073
historical writing, 611
Steckley, Henry, 1782
Steckman family
Reading Grace Brethren Church, PA,
1084
Steel, Elias, 1782
Steel family
history of, 1912
Snake Valley Old German Baptist Brethren
Church, PA, 1193
Steele, ___
Snake Spring Valley Church of the
Brethren, PA, free minister, 1192
Steele Co., ND, 321
Steele, Cyrus, 1782
Steele, D. Bert, 1782
Steele, D. E., 1782
Steele, Daniel
North Liberty, IN, Brethren Church,
948
Steele, David A., 2294
Steele, Dorothy Greenloaf, 2294
Steele, Eli, 632
Steele family, 165, 1289, 2094
Reliance, VA, Mount Zion Brethren
Church, 1096
Steele, George, 1220
Steele, Jacob, 1384, 1782
Pleasant Ridge Church of the Brethren,
PA, 1034
Steele, Jay H., 2294
Steele, John Walter, 1782
Steele, Lafayette, 912, **1220,** 1782
Steele, Mary, 1220
Steele, Phillip C., 365, 1302
Steele, Randy L., 765, 2306
Steele, Sarah
North Liberty, IN, Brethren Church,
948
Steele, Una Cripe, 1220

Steele, William McClellan, 913, 1782
Steely family, 721
Steeman, Abraham, 1782
Steeman, Charles H., 1782
steeples, *See* architecture (church), furnishings
Steere, Douglas V.
    Hinson, E. Glenn on, 2337
Steerman, Charles H.
    Mechanicsburg, PA, Church of the
        Brethren, pastor/elder, 806
Stees, Israel, 1782
Steffan, Nicklous and Elizabeth Pfister
    family history, 1999
Steffen, Conrad, 1782
Steffler, Alva, 673
Steffler, Herman, 1220
Steffler, Josephine Hoffman, 1220
Steffler, William Arno, 366, 588, 1220,
    1782
    Philadelphia, PA, Third Brethren
        Church, pastor, 1019
Steffy, Ella Elizabeth, 173
Stehman family, *See* Pursel, Vida Miller
Stehman, Harry Robert, 1782
Stehman, Willis B., 1782
StehmanKeagy, Jacob, 685
StehmanKeagy, Veronica, 685
Stein and Ray Debate, 371, 2074
    *The Stein and Ray Debate: A Church
        Discussion Between the Brethren
        and Baptists,* 1220
Stein, John Henry, 1220
Stein, John W., 884, 2073–2074
    Mount Morris College, 2380
Stein, John William, 370, 468, **1220–1221,**
    1782, 2074
    True Evangelical Obedience, 381
Stein, K. James
    on Spener, Philipp Jakob, 2358
Stein, Mary Ann Harris, 1220
Stein, Sarah Ann Smith, 1220
Steinbarger, S. J., 1782
Steinberger, Albert C., 1782
Steinberger, Samuel J., 1782
    Maitland Church of the Brethren, PA,
        minister, 783
Steinberger, Samuel, Jr. (BC), 1782
Steinberger, Samuel, Jr. (CB), 1782
Steiner, Abraham, 1221
Steiner, Anna, 2051
Steiner, Bernard C., 2074
Steiner, Christian, 1221
Steiner, Daniel, 1945
Steiner, Daniel and Magdalena Basinger
    genealogy, 1989
Steiner, Donna Forbes, 193, 1287, 1782,
    2165, 2183
Steiner, E. L.
    Smithville, OH, First Brethren Church,
        1192
Steiner family, **1221,** 2074, 2099
    Rittman, OH, First Brethren Church,
        1111
    Royer family, related to, 1128
Steiner, Florence S., 2074
Steiner, Henry, 1221
Steiner, Irene Mae Lehman, 2074
Steiner, Jacob, 1221, 2074
Steiner, John, 1221, 2099
Steiner, John Conrad, 1221
Steiner, Lewis Henry, 2074
Steiner, Mary Louise, 2074

Steiner, Mrs. E. L.
    Smithville, OH, First Brethren Church,
        1192
Steiner, Paul, 1287
Steiner, Paul David, 1287, 1782
Steiner, Rudolph, 1221
Steiner, Steiner Anna, 2099
Steiner (Stoner) family, **2378**
Steiner, Ulrich
    descendants, 1916
Steinmetz, C. M., 2074
Steinmetz, Hiram E., 2074
Steinmetz, Mary Owen, 2074
Steinmetz meetinghouse (Akron, PA), 14
Steinmetz, PA, congregation, 322
Steinmetz, Rollin C., 2074
Steinour family, 1281
Steinour, J. E., 758, 1282, 1782
Steirer, William F., 2074
Stem, Patricia L. Bittinger, 1845
Steman, Sylvan, 447, 1782
Stemm family
    Mayville, ND, Red River Valley
        Church of the Brethren, 805
Stemmler family, 164
Stemple, Samuel J., 274, 1782
Stenning, R. E.
    on Brethren service, 2358
stenographic report of business, *See* verbatim report of business
Stentz, Howard W.
    on Brethren movement, history of,
        2358
    on Frey, Andreas, 2358
Stephen family
    Parsons Old German Baptist Brethren
        Church, KS, 994
Stephens, A., 1782
Stephens, Alice Barber, *299*
Stephens City, VA
    Salem Church of the Brethren located
        near, 1138
Stephens, George, 1782
Stephens, Helen Roynon, 714
Stephens, J. S., 1782
Stephens, Rezin (Resin), 1782
Stephens, Samuel
    Meadow Mills Church of the Brethren,
        VA, 806
Stephens, William Mogrady, 1782
Stephenson Co., IL, 419, 1384
    Freeport, IL, Church of the Brethren,
        515
    Naperville Church of the Brethren, 913
    Waddams Grove, IL, Church of the
        Brethren, 2002
Stephenson, Mrs. R. E., 1782
Steps to Prayer Power (Kimmell), 1052
stereopticon slides
Stover, Wilbur Brenner, 1226
Sterling, Andrew Jackson, 605, 673, 1782
    Masontown, PA, Brethren Church,
        pastor, 800
Sterling, CO
    Church of the Brethren, 324, **1221**
        Ross, Amos Walter, pastor, 1123
    Haxtun, CO, Church of the Brethren,
        590
Sterling congregation, OH
    Smithville, OH, First Brethren Church,
        1192
Sterling, Elizabeth De Bolt, 1221
Sterling family, 2089

Sterling, IL, 151
    Church of the Brethren, **1221**
    Lutheran Church, 1221
Sterling, John, 1221
Sterling, Mary A.
    Masontown, PA, Brethren Church,
        pastor, 800
Sterling, Mary B., 1360
Sterling, Mary Malinda, **1221,** 1782
Sterling, OH, Brethren Church, *See*
    Smithville, OH, Brethren Church
Sterling, OH, Grace Brethren Church, 768,
    1221
    Gingrich, Joseph L., 550
    Malles, Mark Ellsworth, 2217
Stern, Charles Vernon, 45, 1782
    Omak, WA, Church of the Brethren,
        leadership by, 974
Stern, D. M., 45, 463
Stern, Donald L., 1782
Stern, Ella Mae, 1846
Stern family
    Guthrie Church of the Brethren, MN,
        576
    Irricana (First) Church of the Brethren,
        Alberta, Canada, 663
Stern, George Earl, 1782
Stern, Irven Fike, 307, 709, 1782, 1845,
    2111
Stern, Jacqueline, 2133
Stern, Marion Madison, 1782
    Myrtle Point, OR, Church of the
        Brethren, pastor, 906
Stern, Mary Ellen, 2358
Stern, Michael S., 2294
Stern, Oscar Evert, 46, 90, 1782, **2386**
    Wetonka, SD, Willow Creek Church of
        the Brethren, 2379
Stern, Pattie L., 2294
Stern, Roy E., 529, 1782
Stern, Roy Louis, 378, 399, 1782
Stern, Susan (later Boyer), 2273
Stern, Vernon, 2133
Stet, MO, Church of the Brethren, *See*
    Bethany Church of the Brethren
Stetius, Amelia Kauerts, 1222
Stetius, Gottfried Luther, 751, **1222,** 1254,
    1867, 2059, **2379**
    Solingen Brethren, 1201
Stetius, Johann Wilhelm, 1222
Stetius, Magdalena Mack, 1222
Stetler, Eva Catherine Moyer
    Meyer family, 821
Stetler family
    family history and genealogy, 1984
Steuben Co., IN
    English Prairie Church of the Brethren,
        IN, 447
    Pigeon River Church of the Brethren,
        IN, 1023
Steudier, Jean-Louis, 1853
Steudler, Giovannoni Colette, 1853
Steury, Mark Flory, 2294
Stevens, Anna
    Sampson Hill Church of the Brehren,
        IN, 1141
Stevens, Barbara, 245
Stevens, Bill, 1782
Stevens, C. Dick, 208
Stevens, Carson Berkley, 2294
Stevens Co., MN
    Hancock, MN, Church of the Brethren,
        582

Stevens Co., WA
  Forest Center Church of the Brethren, WA, 502
  Mount Hope Church of the Brethren, WA, 882
Stevens, Dan
  Sidney, IN, Grace Brethren Church, 1181
Stevens, Frank E., 2074
Stevens, George, 1783
Stevens, Glenn Douglas, 2294
  on Saunders Grove CB, VA, 2358
Stevens Hill (Community) Church of the Brethren, PA, **1222, 2252**
  Elizabethtown, PA, Church of the Brethren, 436
Stevens, J. S., 1783
Stevens, James F., 1783
Stevens, Larry, 579
Stevens, Leonard
  Sampson Hill Church of the Brehren, IN, 1141
Stevens, Nicholas, 1783
Stevens, PA
  Eby family, 1937
Stevens, Robert
  address on environmental ethics, 1916
  medical projects, 808
Stevens, S. M., 1783
Stevens, S. P., 1783
Stevens, Samuel S., 1783
Stevens, Thaddeus, 314
  Pennsylvania Brethren and military service, 1004
Stevens, William, 318, 1212, 1248
Stevenson family, 241
Stevenson, Richard Henry, 406, 1783
Stevenson, Robert Murrell, 2074
Steward (Stewart), E. M. (D.), 1783
stewardship, **1222–1223**, 2036, 2046
  Brethren and, **2252–2253**
  church membership, 813
  courses on, 1960
  Four-Year Program, 505
  funerals, 524
  funerals and, 230
  Grubb, Luther L., 575
  literature on, Council of Promotion (CB), distribution of, 346
  Men's Work (CB), 816
  Minnich, Herbert Spenser, 848
  The Missionary Board (BC), 856
  money offerings, 1379
  Neff, Robert Wilbur, 2231
  Roop, Eugene F. on Bible and, 2353
Stewardship Council
  ecumenism, 422
Stewart, Catherine Naomi Landis, 2074
Stewart, Clarence A., 758, 1249, 1783
  Mishawaka, IN, Brethren Church, pastor, 852
  New Enterprise Brethren Church, IN, elder in, 927
Stewart, Elbert, 1783
Stewart family
  Idaho, 645
  Moscow, ID, Church of the Brethren, 878
  Mount Cassell Old German Baptist Brethren Church, WV, 880
Stewart, H. H., 1783, 2306
  Portis, KS, Grace Brethren Church, pastor, 1048

Stewart, John G., 2068
Stewart, Lyman, 136
Stewart, Roger, 1783
Stewart, Russell, 1215
Stewart, Thomas, 1783
  Moscow, ID, Church of the Brethren, minister, 878
Stewart, William B., Jr., 2294
Stewart, Wilma, 1215
Stichs, Anna Christina (later Meckel, and Sauer), *See* Sauer, Anna Christina Stichs Meckel
Stickelman, Joan L., 1840
Sticker, Sarah, 2074
Stickler family
  Pleasant Valley German Baptist Brethren, IA, 1036
Stickler, Howard, Sr. (Mr. and Mrs.), 579
Stickler, William E., 1783
  Pleasant Valley German Baptist Brethren, IA, elder, 1036
Stiehl family, 1956
Stieneke, Frederick Simon, 1783
Stietzel family, 1281
Stiff, S. B., 1783
Stiff, Samuel, 1783
Stiffler, Esther B. (later Sell), *See* Sell, Esther B. Stiffler
Stiffler, Roy, 1783
Stiffler, Vernon, 1251
Stihli, Catherine (later Hoffert), 597
Still, David, 1783
Still, J. Walter, 1783
  Midway Church of the Brethren, TN, providing leadership, 827
"Stillen im Lande, Die," **1223**
Stillwater (Covington), OH, Old German Baptist Brethren Church, **1223**
  Fifer, Jesse C., 488
Stillwater, OH, congregation, 237, 348, 349
Stillwater, OK
  German Baptist Brethren's Home Society, 541
Stillwater Old German Baptist Brethren Church, OH, 1223, **2379**
Stilwell, Nyleta
  missionary to Nigeria, 1203
Stine, Arthur Myers, 1223, 1783
  Panther Creek, IA, Church of the Brethren, 992
Stine, Bertha Miller Neher, **1223,** 1783
Stine, Claire, 594
Stinebarger, Adam, 1783
Stinebarger (Steinbarger), S. J., 1783
Stinebaugh family
  Reiff family, 1094
Stinebaugh, James Gilbert, 375, 1783, 2074
  Rossville, IN, Church of the Brethren, minister, 1124
Stinebaugh, Vernon Howard, 1783
  South Whitley, IN, Church of the Brethren, pastor, and Manchester College, music professor, 1207
Stinebaugh, Walter C., 1316, 1783
  Pipe Creek Church of the Brethren, IN, elder, 1025
Stingly, ___ (later Lyon), 769
Stingly, William, 571
Stinnette, Robert Lee, 1783
Stinson, Ed, 714
Stinson, June, 714
Stinson, N. E., 1783
Stinson, Samuel Gene, 1783

Stirling (Sterling), Andrew J., 1783
Stirup Grove, IL, 1234
Stitely, David R., 106, 1783
Stitely, David W., 106, 1783
Stitely, Isaac P., 106, 1783
Stitely, Mary, 365
Stitzel, Alice Mae, 217
Stitzel, David Henry, 2074
Stitzel family, 2074
Stitzel, Iva May
  on Price, Daniel R., 2358
  on Price, Isabelle, 2358
Stitzel, Joseph, 1783
Stitzel, Quinter, 2074
  on Price, Daniel R., 2358
  on Price, Isabelle, 2358
Stitzel, Sara Sticker, 2074
Stiverson, Caroline Fehl, 1223
Stiverson, Caroll Marie (later Pfeiffer), 2289
Stiverson Church of the Brethren, WA, **1223**
  Outlook, WA, Church of the Brethren, 985–986
Stiverson family
  What's in a Name?, 2377
Stiverson, James Ulysses Grant, 912, **1223,** 1247, 1319, 1383, 1783
  Moscow, ID, Church of the Brethren, minister, 878
  Oakland, CA, Church of the Brethren, elder and pastor, 957
  Omak, WA, Church of the Brethren, leadership by, 974
  Oysterville, WA, German Baptist Brethren Church, 986
Stiverson, William, 1223
Stober, Catherine (later Gish), 2379
Stober, Daniel, 2379
Stober, Elizabeth (later Stoner), 2379
Stober, Elizabeth Süss, 2379
Stober, Emanuel, 2379
Stober, Esther (later Feaster), 2379
Stober, George, 2379
Stober, Hannah (later Landis), 2374
Stober, Jacob, 2379
Stober, Johann Wilhelm, 2379, *See also* Stover, William (Johann Wilhelm Stober)
Stober, Judith End, 2379
Stober, Margaret (later Britz), 2379
Stober, Margaret Süss, 2379
Stober, Michael, 2379
Stober, Susannah (later Gish), 2397
Stober, Valentine, 2379
Stober, Wilbur B., 2379
Stober, Willem, *See* Stuber, Johan Wilhelm
Stober, William, 2379, *See also* Stover, William; Stover, William (Johann Wilhelm Stober)
Stocker, Jerry, 482
Stocker, Louise, 482
Stockheim, Germany
  Marienborn, village belonging to, 792
Stockman, George, 741
Stockman, Isaac, 1783
  Maumee Church of the Brethren, OH, minister, 803
Stockmyer, William, 1783
Stocksdale (Stockdale), Charles, 1783
Stockton, CA
  Brethren Church, **1223–1224**
  Hope Brethren Fellowship, 2204

Inland Grace Brethren Church, **1224,** 1270

Stockwell, Foster
on communes, early, 2358

Stoddard Co., MO, 211

Stoeffler, F. Ernest, 1922, 2074

Stoever, Greg E. C., 2294

Stoff, Jacob, 2075

Stoffer, Bryan Sewall, 1320, 1783, 2074

Stoffer, Dale Rupert, 919, 1783, 2075
1988 reorganization, 2170
on Anabaptists, Swiss, 2359
Background and Development of Brethren Doctrines, 2143
Beulah Beach II, 2137
on Brethren doctrines, 2359
Brethren Encyclopedia, Inc., 2143
The Brethren Evangelist, 2141
on Brethren missions, 2359
on Brethren movement, past and future of, 2359
on Brethren pilgrimage in discipleship, 2359
Brethren World Assembly, 2151
on Brethren World Assembly, 1998, 2359
A Centennial Statement, 2156
Columbus, OH, Smoky Row Brethren Church, 2166
on dress, 2358
Hispanic Ministries (BC), 2198
historical writing, 612
historiography, 2202
on Kline, John, 2359
on the Lord's Supper, 2359
on Nead, Peter, 2359
on nonconformity, 2359
on Pietists, 2359
theology and, 2255

Stoffer family
Columbus, OH, Smoky Row Brethren Church, 2166
Fahrney-Keedy Chapel Fellowship Church of the Brethren, MD, 467

Stoffer, R. W., 626

Stogsdill, Clarence A., 1783, **2386**

Stogsdill, Claude, 1783

Stogsdill, Roger O., 2294

Stohl, Pat (later Fortna), 1959

Stohner family, 1221

Stokes, Ruth, 2359

Stoll, Jacob (Jakob), 266, 381, **1224,** 1248, 1340, 1783
mysticism, 907
poetry and hymns, 1039
publishing works of, 1067
spiritual life, metaphor of suffering pilgrim, 1209

Stoll, Kenneth J., 588, 1783

Stoll, Mrs. Henry, 1987

Stolle family, 148

Stoltzfus, Elizabeth (later Fisher), 1937

Stoltzfus, Grant M., 2075
peace, 2201
on peace churches, history of, 2340

Stoltzfus, John, 2107

Stoltzfus, Joyce Ann, 1783

Stone, Abraham
marriage counseling, 796

Stone, Barton Warren, 177, 248, 385, **1224**
in "New Lights" revivalism, 930
Restoration Movement, 1101

Stone Bridge Church of the Brethren, MD, **1224,** 2086

Stone, Carolyn (later Elmore), 2277

Stone, Charles H., 1783

Stone Church of the Brethren, PA, 2075, *See* Huntingdon, PA, Stone Church of the Brethren

Stone, David Edgar, 2075

Stone, David L., 2148, 2294

Stone, Edwin Martin, 2075

Stone family, 224
Oak Grove Church of the Brethren, MO, 956
Peabody Old German Baptist Brethren Church, KS, 997
Rittenhouse family, related to, 1111

Stone, George Ethan, 323, 355, 602, 1783–1784

Stone, Hannah
marriage counseling, 796

Stone, Henry, 1784

Stone, Jacob S., 2075

Stone, Kathryn (later Hartranft), 1959

Stone, Laura Jean, 1843

Stone Lick, OH, 165, 177

Stone, Marjorie G. (later Mayes)
Mayes, Charles W., wife of, 804

Stone movement
Restoration Movement, 1101

Stone, Philip C.
on Kline, John, 2359

Stone, Steve, 505

Stone, Steven Frederick, 505, 1784, 2075

Stone Valley, PA, 1215
Stone Wall Old German Baptist Brethren Church, VA, **1224**

Stoneback, J. William, 1784

Stonebraker, William J., 2177, 2294
Island Pond, VT, Grace Brethren Church, 2209

Stoneburner, E. A., 1784
Sidney, IN, Grace Brethren Church, 1181

Stoneburner, Israel
Pleasant Dale Church of the Brethren, IN, 1030

Stoneburner, Jesse W., 1784

Stoneburner, John, 1784

Stoneburner, Levi, 1784

Stoneburner, Phillip, 1784

stonecutting mill, meetings held in, 1209

Stonelick Church of the Brethren, OH, **1224,** 1225, 1325
Müller (Miller) family, 895
Ohio settlement by Brethren, 961

Stonelick Lake, OH, 1224

Stonelick Old German Baptist Brethren Church, OH, **1224**

Stoner, Abraham, 2378

Stoner, Agnes (later Arnold), 2378

Stoner, Andrew, 1915, 2075

Stoner, Ann Dierdorff
Myers, Salome Stoner, mother of, 904

Stoner, Anna (later Myers)
Myers, Estella Catherine, mother of, 903

Stoner, Autrain Ferguson, 1221

Stoner, Barbara Garst, 1221

Stoner, Belinda Engel, 1225

Stoner, Benjamin O., 1784

Stoner, Calvin C., 2075

Stoner, Catharine Albaugh, 1221

Stoner, Catherine (later Arnold)

Steiner family, 2378

Stoner, D. W., 1784

Stoner, David, 1225, 1784
Myers, Salome Stoner, father of, 904
Steiner family, 2378

Stoner, David L., 1784

Stoner, Dora Evelyn (later Miller)
Miller, John William, 2223, 2224

Stoner, E. Rowena (later Peters), 1011
Stoner, Eli, 1221, 1784

Stoner, Elizabeth Stober

Stoner, Ephraim Winfield, **1225,** 1784, 2075, 2379, *See also* Bridgewater College
Bridgewater College difficulties, 1978
Pipe Creek Church of the Brethren, MD, minister, 1026
Steiner family, 2378

Stoner, Essie O. (later Kinsey), 696

Stoner, Esther Pfoutz, 1225

Stoner family, 384, 713, 731, 1219, 1221, 2074, 2075, 2088, *See also* Steiner family
Genesee Old German Baptist Brethren Church, MI, 540
Harrisburg, PA, Melrose Gardens Grace Brethren Church, 586
Mack family, 778

Stoner, H. K., 1994

Stoner, J. E., 1784

Stoner, Jacob
Steiner family, 2378

Stoner, Jacob H., 2075

Stoner, Jacob, II, 1221, 2075

Stoner, Norris Eugene on descendants of, 2359

Stoner, Jacob S., 1915

Stoner, Jennie Markey, 1180

Stoner, Jesse C., 1784

Stoner, John, 1784
Steiner family, 2378
Weber, Richard R. on descendants of, 2362

Stoner, John B., 109, 1225, 1295, 1784
Pipe Creek Old German Baptist Brethren Church, IN, minister, 1026

Stoner, John E., 1784

Stoner (Land) Company of Ohio, 15

Stoner, Leroy, 1180

Stoner, Levi, 1784

Stoner, Lina Norris, 1349, 2075

Stoner, Lucy C., 2075

Stoner, Margaret (later Stouffer), 1219

Stoner, Marillis Flory, 1225

Stoner, Mary Ann (later Price)
Steiner family, 2378

Stoner, Mary (later Wine), 1221, **1349–1350,** 2039

Stoner, Milton S., 1213, 1784

Stoner, Norris Eugene
on Stoner, Jacob, II and descendants, 2359

Stoner, Peggy J., 2294

Stoner, Philip, 1233

Stoner, Plantina Stutzman, 1233

Stoner, R. R., 250

Stoner, Rebecca (later Oller), 974

Stoner, Reuben, Mr. and Mrs.
at New Lebanon, OH, First Brethren Church, 930

Stoner, Robert Douthat, 2075

Stoner, Robert Titus, 2075

Stoner, Salome (later Myers), **904**, 2044
  Myers, Tobias Timothy, wife of, 905
Stoner, Samuel D., 1349, 1784
  Mount Pleasant Church of the
    Brethren, IN, presiding elder, 886
Stoner, Solomon, 106, 396, **1225**, 1784
  Meadow Branch Church of the
    Brethren, MD, presiding elder, 805
  Piney Creek Church of the Brethren,
    MD, 1025
  Pipe Creek Church of the Brethren,
    MD, minister, 1026
  Steiner family, 2378
Stoner, Solomon (OGBB, 1873–1953), 105,
  109, 1784
Stoner, Susan Lavinia (later Shull), 1844,
  See also Shull, Susan Lavinia
    Stoner
Stoner, Susannah Royer (later Houser), 633
Stoner, Vera Barnhart, 2075
Stoneroad, Samuel, 102, 1356, 1784
Stonerock family, 2019
Stonerstown, PA, Church of the Brethren,
  See Saxton, PA, Stonerstown
    Church of the Brethren
Stonerstown, PA, congregation, 161
Stonesifer, Helen S., 2171
Stonewall, VA, congregation
  Red Oak Grove Church of the Brethren,
    VA, 1089
Stong, George Washington, 1784
Stong, Lorenzo W., 1784
Stony Creek Brethren Church, PA, 121,
  1225
Stony Creek Church of the Brethren, OH,
  115, 118, **1225**
  Pleasant View Church of the Brethren,
    OH, 1032
Stony Creek Church of the Brethren, VA,
  See Flat Rock Church of the
    Brethren, VA
Stony Creek congregation, Somerset Co.,
  PA
  Martin, George Adam, 1194
Stony Creek, IN, Church of the Brethren,
  See Beech Grove Church of the
    Brethren, IN
Stony Creek, IN, congregation
  Noblesville, IN, Church of the Breth-
    ren, support of, 938
Stony Creek, PA, 151
Stony Creek, PA, congregation, 214
  Martin, George Adam, 797
  Roth, Henry (Rhoades), Jr., 1124
Stony Creek (VA), *84*
Stony Creek, WV
  Pocahontas Church of the Brethren,
    WV, mission point of, 1039
Stookey family, 320
Stookey, Sherman, 1784
Stoops, Clara, 489
Stopp, Klaus
  on *fraktur* certificates, 2359
Storaci, David, 2294
Storer, Agnes Williamson, 2075
Stories From Brethren Life (Miller), 840
Stories, (J. E. Miller)
  "I'll Kill Him," 944
Stories That Could Be True (Stafford), 1216
Storm, Jacob, 1784
Storm, Levi, 1784
Stormer family, 332
Story Co., IA, 661

Maxwell, IA, Church of the Brethren,
  803
The Story of Jesus
  Mason, Edward, using pseudonym
    Nosam, 799
The Story of Our Church (Miller), 840
Story, Thomas, 2075
Stotelmyer, Irving R., 1784
Stotler, F. B., 1784
Stotler, Ronald Wayne, 1784
Stottlemyer family
  Grossnickle family, 574
Stottler, Peter, 1784
Stouder, Charles Frank, 558, 1784
Stouder, Christian, 1225
Stouder, David W., 42, 1224, **1225**, 1784
  early Ohio minister, 961
Stouder family, 1224
Stouder, James Ambrose, 1784
  Shelby Co. Church of the Brethren,
    MO, leadership in, 1175
  Oak Grove Church of the Brethren,
    OK, minister, 956
Stouder, John, 1225
Stouder, John, Sr., 1225
Stouder, Samuel, 1225
Stouder, William, 1225
Stoudt family, 2073
Stoudt, John Baer, 2073
Stoudt, John Joseph, 1861, 2075–2076
  historical writing, 611
Stouffer, Abraham, 42, 142, 1225
Stouffer, Abraham D., 1784
Stouffer, Abram, 1784
Stouffer, Albert, 1784
Stouffer, Benjamin F. (CB), 1784
Stouffer, Benjamin F. (OGBB), 1784
Stouffer, C. S., 2070
Stouffer, Catherine, 2070
Stouffer, Christian, 1219, 2076
Stouffer, Clarence D., 2294
Stouffer, Daniel, 1219
Stouffer, Daniel Emmert, 1784
Stouffer, Daniel F., 461, **1225**, 1784
Stouffer, Darlene W., 2295
Stouffer, David, 2076
Stouffer, Drusilla Chaney, 1225
Stouffer, Edgar H., 619, 1784
Stouffer, Elizabeth (later Rowland), 1219
Stouffer, Elizabeth Welty, 1219
Stouffer, Elsie Mae, 2076
Stouffer, Emmanuel, 1219
Stouffer, Ephraim, 1784
Stouffer family, 686, 1219–1220, 2070,
  2073, 2076, *See also* Stauffer
    family
Stouffer, George, 1219
Stouffer, Glenn N., 2076
Stouffer, Jacob, 1219, 2070
Stouffer, John L., 62, 142, 1784
Stouffer, Lydia A. (later Moler), 2020
Stouffer, Margaret Martin, 1219
Stouffer, Margaret Stoner, 1219
Stouffer, Mary Ann Rinehart, 1219
Stouffer, Mary Zarger, 2076
Stouffer, Matthias, 1219, 2076
Stouffer, Nancy Rowland, 1219
Stouffer, Samuel M., 1784
  Newville, PA, Church of the Brethren,
    pastor in, 934–935
Stouffer, Susan Fahrney, 1225
Stouffer, Waldo (Mr. and Mrs.), 579
Stout, Alexander McKillip, 1784

Stout family, 313, 1912, 2073, 2077
  Mount Pleasant, PA, Brethren Church,
    886
Stout, Jerry, 1784
  Middle Creek Church of the Brethren,
    IA, minister, 825
Stout, John C., 1246, 1784
  New Salem Church of the Brethren,
    Milford, IN, as minister, 932
Stout, Kurtis Allen, 2295
Stout, Russell H., 1784
Stout, Thomas J., 1348, 1784
Stout, William T., 507, 1784
Stout, William J., 1784
Stovall, Earl F., 2295
  Shelton Church of the Brethren, NC,
    pastor in, 1176
Stovall, William Carl, 1784–1785
  Roanoke, VA, Hollins Road Church of
    the Brethren, pastor, 1113
Stover, Arthur Reece, Sr., 2076
Stover, Catherine (later Stouffer), 1219
Stover, Charles A., 1785
  Rocky Ridge, MD, Monocacy Church
    of the Brethren, presiding elder,
    1119
Stover, Christopher, 2076
Stover, D. E., 1785
Stover, Daniel, 1219, 1785
Stover, Daniel C., 1219
Stover family, 384, 1219, 1229, 1333,
  2067–2068, 2073, 2076, 2084,
  2087, *See also* Stauffer family
  Harrah, WA, Grace Brethren Church,
    585
  Schultz, Martin, related to, 1156
Stover, Fannie (later Lyon), 768
Stover, George, 1219
Stover, Mrs. Gordon, 2100
Stover, Hannah (later Harley), 1219
Stover, Henry Roy, 1785
  Salem Church of the Brethren, IA,
    1137
Stover, Herbert E., 747, 2076
Stover, Hugh Mitchell, 1785
  Rouzerville Church of the Brethren,
    PA, minister, 1125
Stover, J. Emmert, 2076
Stover, J. Harman, 236, 1212, 1785
  Myers Creek Church of the Brethren,
    WA, elder, 905
Stover, Jacob, 566, 1219
Stover, Jacob A., 1225, 1785
Stover, Jacob K., 1219
Stover, John Emmert, 1785
Stover, John M., 171, 1785, 2076
Stover, Joseph, 1785, 2084
Stover, Judith Schaeffer, 1227
Stover, Margaret H., 2076
Stover, Mary, 378
Stover, Mary Emmert, 42, 378, 444, 1144,
  1225–1227, *1226,* 1845, 2077
  India, 649
Stover, Mary (Mollie) Lesher, 1225
Stover, Mary S., 355
Stover Memorial Church, Des Moines, IA,
  See Des Moines, IA, Stover
    Memorial Church of the Brethren
  Gochenour (Goughnour) family, 555
Stover, Miriam, *418*
Stover, Noah Webster, 2076
Stover, Peter J., 1785
Stover, Robert, 1785

Stover, Ruth (later Snider), *See* Snider,
　　Ruth Stover
Stover, Sarah (later Harley), 1219
Stover, Wilbur Brenner, 42, 247, 299, 320,
　　378, 381, 444, 595, 747, 749,
　　912, 1219, **1225–1227**, *1226,*
　　1227, 1273, 1296, 1785, 1854,
　　2076–2077
　　biography, 1938, 2015
　　historic sites, 609
　　India, 649
　　India orphanages, 651
　　The Little Brother Magazine, editor,
　　　　1999
　　Missionary Reading Circle, 856
　　missions education, 863, 864
　　Philadelphia, PA, Germantown Church
　　　　of the Brethren, 1016
　　Royer, John Grove, 1128
　　Wilbur B. Stover, Pioneer Missionary
　　　　(Miller), 840
Stover, Wilbur J., 717
Stover, William 1219, 1225, 1227
Stover, William, (Johann Wilhelm Stuber
　　[Stober]), 42, 1219, **1225,** 1227,
　　1785, 1941, 1976, **2379**
　　Miller, Jacob, 838
　　Weber, Richard R. on descendants of,
　　　　2362
Stover wind engine, 1219
Stowe, David
　　on Ephrata Cloister music, 2359
Stoystown, PA, 150
　　Reading Grace Brethren Church, *See*
　　　　Reading Grace Brethren Church,
　　　　PA
Strait Creek Church of the Brethren, OH,
　　1227
Strait Creek, KY, congregation
　　Rock House Church of the Brethren,
　　　　KY, yoked with, 1117
Strait Creek Valley, OH, congregation, 1227
　　Ridge Church of the Brethren, OH,
　　　　1108
Straley, Anna Louisa (later Gillin), 549
strange Brethren
　　ministry, terminology, 848
Strasbourg, *See* Straßburg, France, 19,
　　1227–1228, *1228*
　　church history, 1973
　　Eckerlin, Michael, 421
　　Eckerlin, Samuel, 422
　　France, 505
　　Germany, 545
　　Gross, Andreas, 574
　　Haug, Johann Friedrich, 589
　　Reformation, Protestant, and radical
　　　　reformers, 1092
　　Rhine River Valley, Brethren origins in,
　　　　1106
　　Spener, Philipp Jakob, 1209
Strasbourg University, France
　　Brethren Colleges Abroad (BCA) pro-
　　　　gram, **2142**
Strasburg, VA, 2087
　　Round Hill Brethren Church, **1228**
Strassburger family, 2077
Strassburger, Jacob Andrew, 2077
Strassburger, Ralph Beaver, 2077, 2375
Strate, Martin, 669
　　Stratford, NJ, Grace Brethren Church,
　　　　See Mount Laurel, NJ, Grace
　　　　Brethren Church

Straub, Jean S., 2077
Strausbaugh, George S., 1400, 1785
Strausbaugh, Maurice, 105, 1785
　　Red Hill Church of the Brethren, VA,
　　　　pastor, 1088
Strausburg, John, 1785
Strauser, Earle W., 1785
Strauser, Hazel (later Yetter)
　　Parkview Church of the Brethren, PA,
　　　　leadership by, 994
Strawsburg, Kent, 1785
Strawser, Elizabeth, 226
Strawser, George, 1785
Strayer, C., 1785
Strayer, Chester, 2133
Strayer, Clarence, 673
Strayer, Earl Waldo, 1785
Strayer, Ephraim, 1228
Strayer family
　　Hanawalt family, 582
Strayer, Hannah Brallier, 1228
Strayer, Hilda Flohr, 1228
Strayer, Lucile Long (later Brandt), 748,
　　2372, 2387
Strayer meetinghouse
　　Hudson, IA, First Brethren Church,
　　　　635
Strayer, Nannie Hanawalt, 673
Strayer, Ord Lee, 368, **1228,** 1785, 2077
Strayer, Peter C., 1785
Strayley, David, 1785
Strecker family
　　Erbaugh family, 453
Streeter, John O., 502, 1212, 1785, 2077
　　Mount Hope Church of the Brethren,
　　　　WA, minister, 882
　　Octavia, NE, Church of the Brethren,
　　　　minister, 960
Streeter, W. H., 1785
Streets, Thomas Hale, 2077
Strege, Merle D.
　　on baptism, 2359
Strehlow, Shirli, 2077
Stremmel family, 145
Stretch, John, 18, 1785
　　Newton Grove Church of the Brethren,
　　　　minister in, 934
Stretch, Sarah, 240
Strickler, Abigail M. Hull, 2077
Strickler, Abraham, 1229
Strickler, Anna Rhode, 1228
Strickler, Baptist H., 1785
Strickler, Carol Brake, 2181, 2295
Strickler, Catherine (later Sheller), *646*
　　photography of Brethren, 1019
Strickler, D. H., 1785
Strickler, D. Walter, 1785
Strickler, Daniel, *See* Strickler family
Strickler, Duanne Lee, 1785, 2181
Strickler, Ellis S., 1785
Strickler family, 149, 228, **1229,** 2030,
　　2077
　　old Studebaker house, *1231*
　　Preiß (Price) family, related to, 1055
Strickler, Harry Miller, 2077
Strickler, Heinrich, 1229
Strickler, Henry, 587
　　Illinois, 647
Strickler, Henry P., 665, 1229, 1785
Strickler, Henry W., 59, **1228–1229,** *1229,*
　　1785
Strickler, J. P., family
　　Ramona Church of the Brethren, KS,

1083
Strickler, Jacob, 228, 1229
Strickler, John, 1229
Strickler, Mary Hammaker, *See* Strickler
　　family
Strickler, Mary Price, 59, 1228
Strickler, Robert Lee, 1785, 2077
Strickler, Ronald A., 2295
Strickler, S. S., 1785
Strickler, Ulrich, 1229
Strickler, Walter D., 1785
　　Newport Church of the Brethren, VA,
　　　　leadership in, 934
Strickler, William
　　debates with member of Disciples of
　　　　Christ, 1157
Strietzel, Arlen, 1912
Strietzel, Paul Herbert, 1785, 2077, 2306
Strike, Carl J., 1785
　　North Manchester Old German Baptist
　　　　Brethren Church, IN, minister, 949
Strike, Della (later Myers), 2027
Strike, Ray L., 471, 1785, 2153, 2306, **2386**
Strite, Cyrus L., 1785
Strite, Harry E., 2295
Strite, James Carl, 42, 1330, 1785
Strite, Kenneth, 1785
Strite, Kermit Henry, 42, 1785
Strite, Laban Chester, 1785
Strite, Rachel Elaine, 2077
Strite, Stephen C., 2295
Stritzka, 1229
Strock, Julius
　　Mount Bethel Church of the Brethren,
　　　　VA, pastor, 880
Stroede, Oscar F., 2295
Strohm, Alma Ferne, 1833
Strohm, Effie (later Sherfy), 2249
Strohm, Fred Edwin, 1785–1786
Strohm, John A., 1786
　　San Antonio, TX, Church of the
　　　　Brethren, minister, 1141
　　Shelby Co. Church of the Brethren,
　　　　MO, leadership in, 1175
Strohm, Sadie (later Yoder), 1386
Strohm, T. E.
　　San Antonio, TX, Church of the
　　　　Brethren, minister, 1141
Strole, M. L., 1786
Strole, Park W., 1786
Strollo, Anthony, 213
Strollo, Barbara, 213
Strollo, Kathy, 213
Strom, Jonathan, 2310
Stroman, Curtis W., 114, 578, 1786, 2306
Strong family
　　Garwin, IA, Carlton Brethren Church,
　　　　532
　　Haddix, KY, Brethren Church, 577
Strong, Marge, 739
Strouder, Charles, Jr., 1786
Stroup, Donald W., 2295
Stroup, Eli, 1786
Stroup family
　　South Bend, IN, Ireland Road Grace
　　　　Brethren Church, 1203
Stroupe family
　　Marietta, GA, Grace Brethren Church
　　　　of Greater Atlanta, 793
Strouphauer meetinghouse
　　Schuykill Church of the Brethren, PA,
　　　　1157
Struble, ___ (Brother)

Sidney, OH, Trinity Church of the Brethren, 1181
Struble, Peter, 1786
    Mont Ida, KS, Church of the Brethren, 870
Strumpf family
    sources on, 2311
Strung, G. W., 1786
Struphaar, Joshua, 1786
Strutz, Edmund, 2077
Strycker, Esther Mary Gault, 1786
Strycker family, 165
    Mayville, ND, Red River Valley Church of the Brethren, 805
Strycker, James, 1786
Strycker, Mariah (later Rummel), 1130
Strycker (Stricker), George R., 1242, 1305, 1786
Stryz, Jan
    on Ephrata Cloister, 2360
Stuart Church of the Brethren, VA
    Parkway Church of the Brethren, VA, name changed into, 994
Stuart congregation, 1267
Stuart, Frances A., 2077
Stuart, J. E. B., General
    Monrovia, MD, Bush Creek Church of the Brethren meetinghouse used by, 870
Stuart, VA
    New Hope Church of the Brethren, 929
Stuarts Draft, VA, 1340
stubble mulch
    farm machinery, 476
Stuber, Carl, 1278
Stuber, Johann Wilhelm (William Stover), 1219, 2050
Stuber, John W., 1786
Stuber, Ray Lamar, 2295
Stuber, Verne, 241, 1786, 2306
Stuble family, 148
Stucker, William, 1786
Stuckey, Anna Barbara Brauer, 1229
Stuckey, Christian
    Stuckey, Clara Mabel on descendants of, 2360
    Svejda, Ellen on, 2360
Stuckey, Clara Mabel
    on Stuckey, Christian and descendants, 2360
    on Stuckey, Maria Richer and descendants, 2360
Stuckey, David F., 251, 514, 1786, 2126
Stuckey family, 1912
Stuckey, Fred, 693
Stuckey, Jacob A., 1786
Stuckey, Joan (later Kimmel), 693
Stuckey, Levi Teeter, 1786
Stuckey, Maria Richer
    Stuckey, Clara Mabel on descendants of, 2360
    Svejda, Ellen on, 2360
Stuckey, Mary (later Schrag), See Schrag, Mary Stuckey
Stuckey, Melvin Atwood, 68, 1229, 1786, 1861
Stuckey, Myrtle, 693
Stuckey, Sherman, 1786
Stuckey, Simon B., 1786
Stuckman, Ephraim, 1786
Stuckman family, 153
Stuckman, H. F.
    Morrill, KS, (First) Brethren Church,

pastor, 876
    Rosedale, PA, Brethren Church, pastor, 1122
Stuckman, Harley F., 1786
Stuckman, Isaac, 1786
Stuckman, James A., 1786
Stuckman, John, 567, 1786
Stuckman, Lawrence, 1251
Stuckman, Peter, 1786
Stuckrath, Anna, 365
Stuckrath, Justus, 365
Stucky, Harley J., 2077
Studebaker, Adam, 1786
Studebaker, Alexander, 1157
Studebaker, Anna Catherine Melchers, 1230
Studebaker, (Anna) Marie (later Lang), 724
Studebaker brothers, 1876
    history, 2001
    inventions and scientific discoveries, 660
Studebaker Brothers Company, 75, 1230, 1231
    history of, 1932
    South Bend, IN, City Church of the Brethren, 1203
Studebaker, Charlotte Etter, 1230
Studebaker, Christina, 2094, 2095
Studebaker, Christina (later Grossnickle), 574
Studebaker, Claud, 167, 241, 581, 738, 758, **1229–1230,** 1786
Studebaker, Clement, 75, 574, 1230, 1865
Studebaker, D. B., 1786
Studebaker, D. W., 1786
Studebaker, Daniel, 1786
    Macoupin Creek Church of the Brethren, IL, minister, 779
Studebaker, David (1), 1786
Studebaker, David (2), 1786
Studebaker, David Emmet
    on Studebaker family, 2360
Studebaker, David Herbert, 1142, 1288, 1786
    biography of, 2099
    Reedley, CA, Church of the Brethren, pastor, 1091
    San Francisco, CA, Church of the Brethren, minister, 1142
    on Studebaker, Paul Basinger, 2360
Studebaker, Earl B., 1281, 1786
    Modesto, CA, La Loma Grace Brethren Church, pastor, 867
Studebaker, Elizabeth, 1231
Studebaker, Elizabeth (later Leer), 732
Studebaker, Ellis, 1930
Studebaker, Ellis M., 1230, 1786
Studebaker, Ephraim, 1786
Studebaker family, 235, 535, 1389, 1899, 1912, 2077, 2078, 2094, 2099
    Engle/Angle family, 446
    Epler, Ruth on, 2360
    Fahnestock family, 465
    Merritt, Didra on, 2360
    Modesto, CA, La Loma Grace Brethren Church, 867
    Salem Church of the Brethren, OH, 1138
    Snider, Jacob, descendants of, 1154
    Studebaker, David Emmert on, 2360
Studebaker Family National Association
    genealogy, 535
Studebaker, Fannie (later Quinter), *1076,* 1077

Studebaker, Florence Roselind (later Schwalm), See Schwalm, Florence Roselind Studebaker
Studebaker, Florence S., 748, 2077
    autobiography of, 2360
Studebaker, G. W., 682, 1354
Studebaker, George
    baptism by, at Sampson Hill Church of the Brethren, IN, 1141
    Muncie, IN, Church of the Brethren, 896
Studebaker, George E., 1786
    Monitor Church of the Brethren, KS, minister, 869
    Pleasant Plains Church of the Brethren, OK, elder, 1034
    Prairie Lake Church of the Brethren, OK, elder, 1050
    Rocky Ford, CO, Church of the Brethren, elder-in-charge, 1118
    Santa Fe, KS, Church of the Brethren, elder-in-charge, 1144
Studebaker, George L., 320, 1351, 1786
Studebaker, George W., 42, 63, 233, 273, 513, 1288, 1316, 1786
    Cherokee, KS, congregation, organization of, 929
    Pleasant Dale Church of the Brethren, IN, 1030
    Prairie Creek, IN, Church of the Brethren, elder, 1050
Studebaker, Gertrude May Blankenship, 1229
Studebaker, Henry, 2077
Studebaker, Henry (1826–1895), 75
Studebaker, Henry (Heinrich), 1230–1231
Studebaker, Henry (son of John Clement), 1230
Studebaker, Herbert A., 1786
Studebaker, Isaac, 1786
    Olathe Old German Baptist Brethren Church, KS, minister and elder, 964
    Sand Creek Church of the Brethren, KS, elder, 1143
    Sheridan Lake Old German Baptist Brethren Church, CO, minister in, 1176
Studebaker, Isaac S., 1786
Studebaker, J., 373
Studebaker, Jacob, 558, 1230, 1347, 1786
    Rock Run Church of the Brethren, IN, elder, 1117
    Snake Spring Valley Church of the Brethren, PA, 1192
Studebaker, Jesse, 1304, 1786
    Scott Valley Church of the Brethren, KS, elder-in-charge, 1160–1161
Studebaker, Jesse (CB), 1786
Studebaker, John, 281, 1327, 1786, 1787
    historic sites, 609
    Salem Church of the Brethren, OH, minister, 1138
Studebaker, John (CB), 1786–1787
Studebaker, John Clement, 1230
Studebaker, John Mohler, 1230, 1353, 2077
Studebaker, John P., 1229, 1230, 1787
Studebaker, John S., 1288
Studebaker, John U., 1288, 1787
    Prairie Creek, IN, Church of the Brethren, elder and bishop, 1050
Studebaker, Joseph, 1231

Studebaker, Joseph E., 1787
Studebaker, Lloyd Raymond, 1787, 1845
   medical missions, 807
Studebaker, Lottie Viola Rothrock, 1230
Studebaker, Lovina Baisinger, 1157
Studebaker, Margaret (later Snider), 597,
   See Snider, Margaret Studebaker
Studebaker, Maria (later Hershberger), 599
Studebaker, Marietta Brown, 1229
Studebaker, Mary Jane Stull, 2077
Studebaker, Modena Elizabeth Minnich,
   748, 1845, 2077–2078, **2388**
Studebaker National Association, 1231
Studebaker, Paul Basinger, 246, 432, 1787
   Modesto, CA, Church of the Brethren,
      866
   Pasadena, CA, Church of the Brethren,
      pastor in, 994
   San Francisco, CA, Church of the
      Brethren, 1141–1142
   Studebaker, David H. on, 2360
Studebaker, Peter (son of John Clement),
   1230–1231
Studebaker, Philip, 1231
Studebaker, Rebecca Mohler, 1230
Studebaker, Ruth Epler
   on Studebaker family, 2360
Studebaker, Samuel, 1787
Studebaker, Simon, 1230, 1787
Studebaker, Stanley, 1230
Studebaker, Stephen, 1321
Studebaker (Studybaker, Stutenbecker)
   family, 1230–1231
Studebaker, Susan, 343
Studebaker, Ted Allen, 302, **1230**, 1335,
   2177
   death in Vietnam, 1305
   Moore, Joy Hofacker on, 2348
   Parker, Don on, 2349
Studebaker, Ven Pak Lee, 1230
Studebaker, W. George, 264
Studebaker Wagon Manufacturing
   Company
   Mount Morris College, 884, 885
Studebaker, Wilma, 1840
Studebaker, Zelma Roth, 1230
Studemaker, Guy Mack, 2295
Studeman, Jacob, *See* Stutzman, Jacob
student exchange programs, 12, 198, 200,
   1231, **1231**, 1273–1274
   article about, 1925
   Church of the Brethren, 303
   East Fairview Church of the Brethren,
      PA, 415
   Elgin, IL, Highland Avenue Church of
      the Brethren, 436
   Germany (Federal Republic of
      Germany), 546
   International Christian Youth Exchange
      (ICYE), 659
   Japan, 669
Students for Democratic Society (SDS),
   930
Student Nonviolent Coordinating
   Committee (SNCC), 930
Student Volunteer Movement, 1871
   Church of the Brethren, 299
   Crumpacker, Franklin Henry, 354
   devotional literature, 381
   Eby, Enoch Howe, 418
   Emmert, Jesse Benedict, 444
   Harper, Clara Belle, 585
   Kurtz, Daniel Webster, 710

Pittenger, Florence Baker, 1026
Pittenger, John Milton, 1026
Student Volunteer Movement for
   Foreign Missions, **1231–1232**
   ecumenism, 422
   missions, 861
   missions education, 864
   Mott, John Raleigh, 879
   Weaver, Mahlon J., 1324
   Williams, John Henry Bashor, 1345
students
   Juniata College directories and alumni,
      1981
   Mount Morris College, *883,* 885
Studer, Gerald, 2078
Studies in Brethren History (Mallott), 2005
Studies in Doctrine and Devotion (Blough),
   151
   noncreedalism, 942
Studies in the Book of Acts (Hoff), 616
Study family, 1939
*A Study in the Physical Vigor of American
   Women* (Jacobs), 667
Studybaker family, *See* Studebaker family
Stufflebeam, L. C., 1787, 2306
Stull, Brian K., 2295
   Sugar Grove Old German Baptist
      Brethren Church, OH and, 2254
Stull family, 153
Stull, George R., 1787
Stull, Gerald G., 1787
   Sugar Grove Old German Baptist
      Brethren Church, OH and, 2254
Stull, Harry E., 1385, 1787
Stull, Joseph W., 1385, 1787
   Mud Valley Old German Baptist
      Brethren Church, IL, minister, 892
   Scottville Old German Baptist Brethren
      Church, MI, minister, 1161
Stull, Mary Jane, 2077
Stull, Paul H., 153, 1385, 1787
   Scottville Old German Baptist Brethren
      Church, MI, elder-in-charge, 1161
Stultz, Owen Glennard, 585, 1787, 2078
Stultz, R. L., 1787
Stump, Abraham, 1232
Stump, Alma (later Metzler)
   Metzler, Burton, 2376
Stump, Alpha Niswander, 1845, 2031
Stump, B. C., 1787
Stump, B. F., 255, 1787
Stump, Mrs. B. F., 255
Stump, Caspar, 1232
Stump, Catherine (later Burkholder), 1232
Stump, Christopher, 2078
Stump, Clarence, M., 1787
Stump, Cleophas P., 343, 1787
Stump, Daniel, 1232
Stump, Edward, 1787
Stump, Elizabeth Becker, 1232
Stump family, 153, 686, 1312, 2067, 2078,
   See also, Stumpff family
Stump, Floyd V., 1787
Stump, Francis, 689, 1232, 1787
   Muhlenberg Co., KY, German Baptist
      Brethren, 893
Stump, Frederick, 1955
Stump, George C., 109, 1787
Stump, George T., 1787
Stump, Guy K., 1787
Stump, Harley Harold, 247, 445, 1312,
   1787
Stump, J. M., 2078

Stump, Jacob, 1232
Stump, John (1855–1925), 190, 471, **1232,**
   1255, 1312, 1324, 1787
   missions, 858
Stump, John (1890–1924), 1787
Stump, Joseph, 2078
Stump, Levi Albert, 1232, 1845
   article about, 1916
Stump, Louisa Weaver, 1232
Stump, Magdalena (later Markey)
   Markey family, 794
Stump, Mary Beery, 2127–2128
Stump, Mary J. Keehn, 1232
Stump, Maud, 582, 1787
Stump, Michael, Sr., 2078
Stump, Paul L., 1787, 2127–2128
   on Dunkard mission in Africa, 2360
Stump, Rachael, 1232
Stump, Samuel, 472, 1316
   Peabody Church of the Brethren, KS,
      997
   Pleasant Dale Church of the Brethren,
      IN, 1030
Stump, Samuel C., 1787
Stump, Sarah Ann Musser, 1232
Stump, Solomon, 733, 1324, 1787
Stump, Thomas, 343
Stump, Thurman, 2078
Stump, William, 1232
Stumpf and related families, 1887
Stumpf, Julian, 1232
Stumpff family
   Royer family, related to, 1128
Stumpff (Stump) family, **1232**
Stunden
   Lutherans and Radical German
      Pietism, 1079
Sturgill, Betty
   Orlando, FL, Grace Brethren Church,
      981
Sturgill, Ray
   Lakeland, FL, Grace Brethren Church,
      2213
   Orlando, FL, Grace Brethren Church,
      981
Sturgis, Anna (later Gibson), 547
Sturgis, Daniel B., 30, 298, 370, 476, 511,
   547, **1232**, 1787
   Hurricane Creek Church of the
      Brethren, IL, 638
   Illinois, 646
Sturgis, Hannah Bartlett, 1232
Sturgis, James, 1232
Sturgis, John, 1787
Sturley, John, 1787
   South Pasadena, CA, Grace Brethren
      Church, pastor, 1206
Sturz family
   San Diego, CA, Grace Brethren
      Church, 1141
Sturz, Harry A., 114, 115, 585, 755, 1787,
   2306
Stutesman, Alice Elizabeth Hostetler, 2078
Stutesman family, 2078, *See also* Stutzman
   family
Stutesman, Ferdinand Franklin, 2078
Stutesman, John Hale
   on Dunkers and American Revolution,
      2360
   on Stutzman, Jacob and descendants,
      2360
Stutesman, John Jacob, 2078
Stutler, Boyd B., 2078

Stutsman, Allie (later Eisenbise), 1608
Stutsman, Arnold, 1787
Stutsman, Benjamin Franklin, 1317, 1787
Stutsman, Bennett T., 377, 1787
Stutsman, Charles H., 1787
Stutsman, Charles Noble, 65, 1787
Stutsman, Daniel B., 558, 1787
Stutsman, David C., 1787
Stutsman, Dewey L., 1787
Stutsman family, *See* Stutzman family
Stutsman, George Otis, 445, 740,
   1787–1788
Stutsman, J. S., 1788
Stutsman, Jesse, 1788
Stutsman, John R., 1788
Stutsman, Joseph, 1788
Stutsman, Mary Imogene Dewey, 1317
Stutsman, Melvin D., 558
Stutsman, Noble, 520
Stutsman, Sadie Irene, 1317, *See also*
   Wampler, Sadie Stutsman
Stutsman (Stutzman), Melvin D., 1788
Stutsman, William Manford, 1788
Stuttgart, AR, German Baptist Brethren
   Church, **1232**
Stuttgart congregation, Germany (Federal
   Republic of Germany), 546
Stutz, Blanche Clarke, 1233
Stutz, Clara Dietz, 1232
Stutz, Elizabeth Snyder, 1232
Stutz, Harry Clayton, 75, 235, **1232–1233**
   inventions and scientific discoveries,
   660
   Stutz Motor Car Co., 75, 1233
Stutz, Henry J., 1232
Stutz, Janet, 319
Stutzman, Abraham, 674, 1233, 1243, 1788
Stutzman, Alma, 2078
Stutzman, Anna Bontrager, 2078
Stutzman, Anna Stoltzfus, 2078
Stutzman, Barbara, 1914
Stutzman, Charles Wilson, 469, 1788
Stutzman, Christian, 1233, 1973–1974
Stutzman, Christina Ulrich, 1285
Stutzman, D. D., 2078
Stutzman, Daniel, 1233
Stutzman, Daniel Levi, 2078
Stutzman, David, 1233
Stutzman, David S., 2078
Stutzman, Eliza (later Yoder), *See* Yoder
   family
Stutzman, Elizabeth, 2107
Stutzman, Elizabeth (later Vaniman), 1302
Stutzman family, 142, 149, 280, 377, **1233,**
   1243, 1389, 1865, 2087
   Hanawalt family, 582
   Jackson Co. German Baptist Brethren,
   IN, 667
Stutzman, Fannie Lichty, 2078
Stutzman, Floyd Levi, 1952
Stutzman, Hannah (later Lear), 1233
Stutzman, Hannah (later Ulrich), 1233
Stutzman, Jacob, **1233,** 1285, 1299, 1915
   family history and genealogy, 1975
Stutesman, John Hale on descendants of,
   2360
Stutzman, Jacob (1727–1813), 1237, 1788
Stutzman, Jacob (1777–1859), 1788
Stutzman, Jacob C., 2078
Stutzman, Jacob, Jr., 1285
Stutzman, Jacob, Sr.
   family history, 1914
Stutzman, Jesse, 1788

Ontario German Baptist Brethren, 975
Stutzman, Johan Jacob, 1233
Stutzman, John, 2078
Stutzman, John S.
   Filley German Baptist Brethren
   Church, NE, 2374
Stutzman, John W., 1788
Stutzman, Joseph, 2078
Stutzman, Joseph J. and Rachel Yoder
   family history, 2008
Stutzman, Lucinda (later Hanawalt), 581
Stutzman, Magdalene (Maudlin), 1233
Stutzman, Mary Ann Beckler, 2078
Stutzman, Perry A., 2078
Stutzman, Plantina Stoner, 1233
Stutzman, Sarah J. Miller, 2078
Stutzman (Stutsman, Stutesman) family,
   1233
Stutzman, Susannah Ulery, 1233
Stutzman, W. Henry, 2078
Stutzman, William, 280
Stutzman, Wilma, 2078
Stutzman, Wilson, 1788
Stuver, Richard L., 1788
Stycker family, 1305
Styers, Henry H., 1788
Style of Brethren life
   Nead, Peter as spokesman for,
   918–920, *919*
Suartz, Elias J., 1788
subsidies, crop
   nonconformity, 941
substitutes
   conscientious objectors and, 149
   military service, and peace position,
   999, **1233–1234**
   Revolutionary War, 176
Suburban, Sacramento, CA, Church of
   the Brethren, *See* Sacramento, CA,
Prince of Peace Church of the Brethren
Sudan, **1034,** 1877, *See also* Nigeria; specif-
   ic cities, missions stations, and
   congregations
   Bible translation into Nuer, 2137
   Church of Christ in the Sudan, 296
   Church of the Brethren, 2162
   mission to, *2253*
   missions, 1962, 2225
   Neff, Robert Wilbur, 2231
   relief and service efforts, 1097
   Schrock, J. Roger, 738–739
   Schrock, Roger and Carolyn, 1234
Sudan Interior Mission hospital, 727
Sudan United Mission (SUM), 296
Sudan Interior Mission (SIM)
   Helser, Albert David, 596
Sudan United Mission (SUM), 296
   Fellowship of Churches of Christ in
   Nigeria, 484
Südere, Anna Margarethe (later Mack)
   Mack, Alexander, Sr., daughter-in-law,
   777
   Mack, Johannes, 778
"suffering community"
   Brethren movement, 292
Sugar Creek Church of the Brethren, IL,
   102, 646, **1234,** 1302, 1335
   Far Western Brethren, 475
   Macoupin Creek Church of the
   Brethren, IL, 779
   migration of Brethren, 829
   Oakley Brick Church of the Brethren,
   IL, 958

Pleasant Hill Church of the Brethren,
   IL, 1032
Sugar Creek Church of the Brethren,
   IN, 109, **1234**
   Mishler family, 852
   South Whitley, IN, Church of the
   Brethren, 1207
Sugar Creek congregation, IA, 661
Sugar Creek congregation, IN
   place-names, Brethren, 1028
   Pleasant View Church of the Brethren,
   IN, 1036
Sugar Creek congregation, OH, 214, 236,
   345, 742
   Allen Co., OH, 961
Sugar Creek mission point
   Flat Creek Church of the Brethren, KY,
   493
Sugar Creek Old German Baptist Brethren
   Church, IL, **1234**
Sugar Creek West Church of the Brethren,
   OH, 71, **1234–1235**
   Pleasant View Church of the Brethren,
   OH, 1037
Sugar Grove Brethren Church, PA, *See*
   Aleppo, PA Grace Brethren
   Church; Aleppo, PA, Grace
   Brethren Church
Sugar Grove cemetery
   Lexington, OH, 1333
   shared community church, Upper Twin
   Old German Baptist Brethren
   Church, OH, 1295
Sugar Grove Church of the Brethren, OH,
   See Camp Sugar Grove;
   Covington, OH, Church of the
   Brethren
Sugar Grove Church of the Brethren, PA,
   See Blough, PA, Sugar Grove
   Church of the Brethren
Sugar Grove Church of the Brethren, WV,
   See Trout Run Valley Church of
   the Brethren
Sugar Grove congregation, OH, 1330
Sugar Grove congregation, WV, 1276
Sugar Grove house, *See* Blough, PA, Sugar
   Grove Church of the Brethren
Sugar Grove, OH, congregation, 348, 349,
   384
   Mohler family, 869
   Mohler, Samuel, minister, 868
Sugar Grove Old German Baptist Brethren
   Church, OH, **2253–2254**
   Wagoner, Gerald C., Sr. (OGBB) and,
   2259
Sugar Hill Church of the Brethren, OH,
   1235, 1281, 1295
   Deshler Church of the Brethren, OH,
   380
   Middletown, OH, Church of the
   Brethren, 826
   Sugar Ridge Church of the Brethren,
   MI, **1235**
   West Alexandria, OH, Church of the
   Brethren, 1333
Sugar Ridge Church of the Brethren, MI,
   1235
   Hart, MI, Church of the Brethren, 587
   Riverside Church of the Brethren, MI,
   1111–1112
Sugar Ridge Church of the Brethren, OH,
   1235
   Rome, OH, congregation, 956

Rosenberger, Isaac J., minister, 1123
Sugar Run meetinghouse (Hill Valley, PA), 71
Sugar Valley Church of the Brethren, PA, 228, **1235**
Sugarcreek, OH
    Church of the Brethren, *See* Baltic, OH, Church of the Brethren
    Sugarcreek East Church of the Brethren, 80, **1235**
Sugarland meetinghouse
    Eglon, WV, Church of the Brethren, 430
Suggs, E. G. B., 2078
suing, *See* law
Suit family
    Mountain View Church of the Brethren, VA, 889
Suit, R. L., 1788
Suitt, Chris, 2295
    Menifee, CA, New Hope Community Church of the Valley, 2220
Sule, Biu Mai, *See* Mai Sule Biu
Sullabarger, John, 1788
Sullivan Co., TN, 167
    Piney Flats, TN, Church of the Brethren, 1025
    Pleasant Hill Church of the Brethren, TN, 1032
    Pleasant Mound Church of the Brethren, TN, 1033
Sullivan, Kenneth L., 1788, 2136, 2172
Sulser, Lola, 1345
Suman, Edward, 204
Sumarin, Ruth Marie, 1852
Sumey, Charles Robert, 1320, 1788, 1853
Sumey, Pauline Wenona Lucas, 1853
Summa doctrinae de foedere et testamento Dei (*Comprehensive Theology of the Covenant and Testament of God*) (Cocceius), 347
Summer, Albert E., 1788
Summer, Benjamin Franklin, 1788, 1845
    article about, 1930
Summer Crusader program (BC)
    youth and, 2269
Summer Crusader programs, 1392
Summer, Daniel, 1788
Summer, David, 1788
Summer, George Leland, 2078
Summer Ministry Program (BC)
    youth and, 2269
Summer, Nettie Peal Brown, 226, 1845
Summer, W. H., 345
Summerdean Church of the Brethren, VA, *See* Roanoke, VA, Summerdean Church of the Brethren
    Roanoke, VA, First Church of the Brethren, 1113
Summerford, OH, congregation, 396
Summerly, William, 1788
Summers, Earl L., 270, 1788
Summers family, 165
Summers, Harmon, 1788
Summers, Joseph W., 1292, 2078
    South Carolina minister, 1204
Summers, Lewis P., 2078
Summers, Marvin P., 1788
Summers, William W., 121, 231, 323, 347, 363, 496, 637, 1788
    North Manchester, IN, (First) Brethren Church, pastor, 949
    Roann, IN, (First) Brethren Church,

pastor, 1112
Somerset, IN, Poplar Grove Brethren Church, pastor, 1202
Summersgill, Herbert
    Mishawaka, IN, Brethren Church, 852
Summersgill, Mrs. Herbert
    Mishawaka, IN, Brethren Church, 852
Summit Church of the Brethren, VA, **1235–1236**, 2051
    Pleasant Valley Church of the Brethren, VA, 1035
Summit Co., OH, 1390
Summit Mills Church of the Brethren, PA, **1236**
    Elk Lick congregation, 1139
    Geiger Church of the Brethren, PA, 533
    Gnagey, Abraham Daniel, 554
Summit Mills Grace Brethren Church, PA, 68, **1236**
Summy, Abraham, 1788
Sumner, Claude, 129, 1788
Sumner Co., KS, 340
    South Haven Brethren Church, KS, 1205
Sumner Co., TN, 1253
Sumner, J. W., 1788
Sumner, Roy, 1788
Sumpter, Lynette Marie, 2295
Sun Valley Church of the Brethren, AL, *See* Birmingham, AL, Sun Valley Church of the Brethren
Sunday
    observance of, 1133
    work, omission of, 1133
Sunday Baptists
    names of Brethren fellowships, 910
Sunday, Billy
    American revivalism, 1104
    Winona Lake Auditorium, IN, 1353
Sunday, observance of, *See* entries at Sabbath
Sunday school, *13,* 149, *492, 507,* 2034, 2084, *See also* union Sunday schools
    advocated by Daniel Vaniman, 1303
    anniversary curricula and resources, 1283
    Annual Meeting and Brethren polity, 1042
    Ashland Convention, support for, 368
    Ashland Convention support of, 67
    bibliography, 1865, 1867, 1880, 1895, 1904
    Big Sky Brethren Church/American Baptist Church, MT, 142
    Black River Church of the Brethren, MI, 144
    Breathitt Co., KY, 405
    Brethren of Christ, 189
    BRF, 303
    changes in attitudes about, 1376
    Chicago extension, 2018
    children in, 2158, 2159
    Chinese, 2025
    Chinese immigrants, *See* Chinese Sunday School
    Chinese Sunday school mission, Chicago, IL, 1296
    Christian Education Commission (CB), 285
    Christian education movement, 283
    Church of the Brethren, 300

Clement, John Addison (son), 320
Coppock, Jacob, 343
curriculum, 1236–1237
    BRF, 303
    Daily Vacation Bible Schools, 359
    Declaration of Principles, 372
    decline in attendance, 2160, 2162
    Detroit Chinese Sunday School, 2100
    devotional literature, 381
    Disciples of Christ, 385
    Doctrinal Treatise, 394
    doctrine on, 178
    Dolby, Martha Cunningham, 395
    dress for teacher or officer, 402
    Early, Henry Clay, 413
    East Nodaway Church of the Brethren, IA, 416
    Ebersole, John P., 418
    education, 427
    Eel River Church of the Brethren, IN, 429
    Elderton, PA, Plum Creek Church of the Brethren, 433
    Elkhart Valley Church of the Brethren, IN, 440
    Ellison Church of the Brethren, ND, 442
    Elmdale, MI, Church of the Brethren, 442
    Emmert, Gertrude Elvina Rowland and Jesse Benedict, 444
    Emmert, Michael Wolf, 444
    Empire, CA, Church of the Brethren, 445
    Englewood, OH, Dunkard Brethren Congregation, 447
    Enid, OK, Church of the Brethren, 448
    Ephrata, PA, Church of the Brethren, 448
    Evangelical Association, 459
    evangelism, 461
    Everett, PA, Church of the Brethren, 461
    Evergreen, 462
    Fairchance, PA, Church of the Brethren, 467
    fairs and public shows, 467
    Fairview Church of the Brethren, IA, 468
    Fairview-Mount Clinton Church of the Brethren, VA, 470
    Farmers Grove Fellowship (BC), PA, 476
    Farmington, DE, Bethany Church of the Brethren, 479
    Fast Element, 480
    Flat Creek Church of the Brethren, KY, 493
    Flat Rock Church of the Brethren, VA, 494
    Flint, MI, Church of the Brethren, 494
    Flintstone, MD, Glendale Church of the Brethren, 494
    Flora, IN, Grace Brethren Church, 496
    Flory, Ezra, 498
    for Italian immigrants, Brooklyn, NY, 1296
    Forest Chapel Church of the Brethren, VA, 502
    Fort Worth, TX, Church of the Brethren, *1238*
    Forward Movement, 504
    Franklin Grove, IL, Church of the

Brethren, 507
Frantz, Christian and Jacob Ebersole, 396
Fremont Church of the Brethren, VA, 515
Front Royal, VA, Church of the Brethren, 518
Fruitvale Church of the Brethren, CA, 520
Garden City, KS, Church of the Brethren, 530
Garrett, PA, Church of the Brethren, 531
GBC Christian Education (Department), 533
Geiger, Henry, 533
General Board (CB), 535
General Sunday School Board (CB), 539
Glad Songs hymnal for, 642, 1950
Glendale, AZ, Church of the Brethren, 552
Glendale, CA, First Brethren Church, 552
Golden Dawn, The, 556
gospel music, 559, 560
Gospel Visitor, The, 561
Grace Brethren Sunday School of the Year, Saint Petersburg, FL, 1136
graded lessons, 564
Grand Rapids, MI, Church of the Brethren, 565
Grandview, MO, Dunkard Brethren Congregation, 566
Gratis, OH, Church of the Brethren, 566
Greenville, OH, Church of the Brethren, 572
Guthrie Church of the Brethren, MN, 576
Hadley Creek Church of the Brethren, IL, 577
Hamilton, Walter J., 581
Hancock, MN, Church of the Brethren, 582
handbook for parents and teachers, 2098
Harmonyville, PA, Church of the Brethren, 584
Harnley, Henry Jacob, 585
Harper Woods, MI, Detroit First Church of the Brethren, 585
Harris Creek Church of the Brethren, OH, 585
Herr, John, 598
Hertzler, Samuel Hoffer, 601
Hertzler, William, 601
Hilton, Blanche Cover, 606
history of
 Church of the Brethren, 2082
Höcker, Ludwig, 616
Hoff, Ernest Gockley, 617
Hollidaysburg, PA, Church of the Brethren, 619
Hollywood Church of the Brethren, VA, 620
Holsinger, Henry Ritz, 621
Homestead Church of the Brethren, MI, 626
Hoover, Samuel W., 628
Hostetler Church of the Brethren, PA, 632
house churches, 632

Howe, Roland Levi, 633
Huntingdon, PA, congregation, 220
Huntington, IN, City Church of the Brethren, 637
hymnals, 1970
Hyndman, PA, Church of the Brethren, 643
Ikenberry, Charles Samuel, 646
Imler, Tobias F., *648*
Indian Creek Church of the Brethren, OK, 651
Indiana, 652
Indianapolis, IN, Northview Church of the Brethren, 654
Influenza Pandemic, 655
instruction, and catechism, 262
internation Sunday school conventions, 1273
International Council of Religious Education, 659
International Sunday School Lessons, 1236
Iowa, 2039
Italian Sunday School (CB), 664–665
Jamison, Owen Thomas, 668
Johnson, John L., 672
Johnstown, PA, Moxham Church of the Brethren, 674
Johnstown, PA, Westmont Church of the Brethren, 675
Jones Chapel Church of the Brethren, VA, 676
Jones, George H., 676
Keyser, WV, Church of the Brethren, 692
Knouff, Hannah Pfouts, 704
Knoxville, TN, Church of the Brethren, 704
Krypton, KY, Brethren Church, 708
La Verne, CA, Church of the Brethren, *714*
Larchmont Community Church of the Brethren, CA, 726
Leamersville Church of the Brethren, PA, 732
Lebanon Church of the Brethren, VA, 733
Leon, IA, Brethren Church, 737
lesson commentary, 1919
lessons in *The Bible Student,* 137
Lewistown, PA, Church of the Brethren, 739
literature, 155, 193, 195, 205, 284, 554, **1236–1237**
 International Sunday School Association Uniform Lessons, *See* International Sunday School Association (formerly International Sunday School Convention)
Lyon, Quinter Marcellus, 768
Miller, John Ezra, 839–840
missions education, 864
Lititz, PA, Church of the Brethren, 748
Little Pine Church of the Brethren, IN, 749
Little Swatara Church of the Brethren, PA, 750
Locust Grove Church of the Brethren, IN, 752
Logansport, IN, Church of the Brethren, 752
Lone Star Church of the Brethren, KS,

753
Long Beach, CA, Community Grace Brethren Church, 754
Long Green Valley Church of the Brethren, MD, 755
Long Lake Church of the Brethren, MI, 756
Loraine, IL, Church of the Brethren, 757
Lorida Church of the Brethren, FL, 758
Los Angeles, CA, Bella Vista Church of the Brethren, 758
Los Angeles, CA, Ladera Church of the Brethren, 759
Miami Valley Petition, 823
Miller, Daniel Long, supporting, 834
ministry, 845
minorities, ethnic and racial, 850
Mohler, Samuel Sayler, 868
Moore, John Henry, 874
movement, 24, **1237–1239**
music in, 22
Myer, Elizabeth, 903
Myers, Tobias Timothy, 905
Neher, Medford D. illustrated, 922
Old Order movement, 206
ordination of leaders, 980
organization and supervision, outline of, 1938
Parish Ministries Commission involvement in literature and curriculum of, 993
Philadelphia, PA, 1296
 First Church of the Brethren, 1015
photographs taken of, 1020
Plum Creek congregation, 693
Price, Isaac, advocate, 1056
Progressive Brethren, 298, 1061
Progressive Brethren movement, 180, 972
Prymont, IN, *1238*
publications about Sunday schools, 2078
publications for, 1068–1069
Raikes, Robert, 283
rejection of, 68
religious education, 2084
resources, 2161, 2179
Sharp, Solomon Zook, advocate and author, 1174
Spokane Valley Grace Brethren Church, WA, 1212
Spring Creek, IN, Church of the Brethren, 1213
Spring Mount, PA, Church of the Brethren, 1213
Springfield Church of the Brethren, PA, 1216
Springfield, IL, Church of the Brethren, 1215
Stanley, WI, Church of the Brethren, 1217
statistics, 1218
Summit Mills Grace Brethren Church, PA, 1236
Sunday school movement, 1237
Sweden, *1244*
Swigart, Milton Clarke, 1245
Tampa, FL, Church of the Brethren, 1247
teacher training, 1239
tents used for, 1254

Thomas, OK, Church of the Brethren, 1263

Toledo, OH, Heatherdowns Church of the Brethren, 1266

Topeka, IN, Church of the Brethren, 1267

training of teachers at Bible conferences, 136

Trevilian Church of the Brethren, VA, 1274

Tropico, CA, Church of the Brethren, 1275

Union Center Church of the Brethren, IN, 1287

Union Grove Church of the Brethren, IN, 1288

United Brethren in Christ, 1290

Upper Deer Creek Church of the Brethren, IN, 1294

Upper Twin Church of the Brethren, OH, 1295

Upton, PA, Church of the Brethren, 1295

Vinton, VA, Church of the Brethren, 1307

Virginia Beach, VA, Christian Church Uniting, 1308

Virginia Second District, 2013

Wabash Country Church of the Brethren, IN, 1311

Walnut Church of the Brethren, IN, 1315

Walnut Grove Church of the Brethren, IL, 1315

Waterloo, IA, City Church of the Brethren, *1322*

Waterside, PA, Church of the Brethren, 1323

Wawaka, IN, Church of the Brethren, 1323

Waynesboro, PA, Church of the Brethren, 1323

West, Edmund Landon, 1332

West Otter Creek Church of the Brethren, IL, 1335

Westernport, MD, Church of the Brethren, 1337

Westminster Church of the Brethren, MD, 1337

White Branch Church of the Brethren, IN, 1339

White Cottage, OH, Church of the Brethren, 1340

White Rapids Church of the Brethren, WI, 1341

Whitefish, MT, Church of the Brethren, 1342

Winter Park, FL, First Church of the Brethren, 1353

Wolf Creek Church of the Brethren, OH, 1355

Wolfe, John P., 1359

women, roles in, 1361

Wood Grove Brethren-Christian Parish, MI, 1363

Wooddale Church of the Brethren, PA, 1364

Worden Church of the Brethren, WI, 1365

Yellow Creek Church of the Brethren, IL, 1384

Yellow Creek Church of the Brethren, IN, 1384

Yoder, Eli Lorenzo, 1386

Youngstown, OH, Woodworth Church of the Brethren, 1390–1391

Sunday School Advisory Board, Church of the Brethren, 300, *See also* General Sunday School Board

Sunday School Boards, *See* Board of Christian Education; General Sunday School Board; National Sunday School Board

Sunday School Times
Ellis, Charles Calvert, 441

Sunderland, Henry, 669

Sunderland, Sara Taylor, 2080

Sunderland, William Henry DeHart, 1788

Sundin, Carl, 1788

Sundquist, Anita, 1852

Sunfield Church of the Brethren, MI, 725, 1239
Schrock, Mark Y., 1156

Sunny Hill-Charity
Smith River Church of the Brethren, VA, preaching point, 1192

Sunnyland Church of the Brethren, FL, 758, *See also* Lorida, FL, Church of the Brethren

Sunnymede Grace Brethren Church, South Bend, IN
South Bend, IN, Ireland Road Grace Brethren Church, 1203

Sunnyside Church of the Brethren, WV, **1240**
Harness Run Church of the Brethren, WV, 585
Sunnyside Chapel, 1240

Sunnyside First Brethren Church, WA
Grandview, WA, Grace Brethren Church, 566

Sunnyside Grace Brethren Church, WA, 1383

Sunnyside, KS, 1304

Sunnyside, PA
Rockton, PA, Church of the Brethren, preaching point of, 1118

Sunnyside, WA,
Brethren Church
Sickel, Loree Cutright, 1181
Church of the Brethren, **1240**
Outlook, WA, Church of the Brethren, 986
First Brethren Church
McClain, Walter Scott, 773
Grace Brethren Church, 101
formerly First Brethren Church, **1240**

Sunnyslope Church of the Brethren, WA, **1240**

Sunrise Community, OR, Church of the Brethren, *See* Albany, OR, Sunrise Community Church

Sunrise Grace Brethren Church, *See* Powell, OH, Grace Brethren Church

Sunshine Church of the Brethren, NM, 931, **1240**

Superannuated Ministers' Fund
pension funds, 1007
Retirement Board (BC), 1102

superstition
Brethren view of Roman Catholic Church, 1120

support
non-monetary, for ministers, 1136

support agencies
Church of the Brethren ministry, 846

supported ministry, *See* salaried ministry

Supportive Congregations Network, 2151

Supreme Court, US
capital punishment rulings, 253
conscientious objectors, 336
Fellowship of Grace Brethren Churches (FGBC), 487
released-time religious education on public school property, 1326–1327
Schemp decision, 1327
Seeger case and National Service Board for Religious Objectors (NSBRO), 917
Wisconsin vs. Yoder (1972), 26

Surbaugh family, 2087

Surbey, Arlene (later Flora), 2185

Surbey, Charles C., 1241

Surbey, Clarence, 1788

Surbey, Grace O'Brien, 1241

Surbey, Howard J., 137, 408, 1240, **1241,** 1788, 2143, 2306

Surbey, Minnie Young, 1241

Surhuisterveen, 159, *1241,* **1241–1242**
Brethren remnants in Europe, 1099
emigration from, Brethren, 443
Germany, 545
Historic Peace Churches, 607
historic sites, 609
Huizinga (Huisinga), Jacob Dircks, 635
Koker family, 705
Kortwolde, 707
Petersen, Barthold Jurgen, 1012
publishing, 1063
Schwarzenau Brethren in, 923

Surhuisterveen, in Friesland
Brethren moving to, 1158

Surhuisterveen, Netherlands
Brethren places of worhip at, 48
immigration of Brethren to, 776–777, 778
Mack, Alexander, Jr., 774
Mennonites providing refuge for Brethren, 815
missions, 857

Surhuisterveen, 2078
Surin, Joseph Philip, 2295

The Surprise, 2078

Surrey, ND, Church of the Brethren, *1242,* **1242**
Minot, ND, Church of the Brethren, 851, 852

Surrey, ND, congregation
Ward Co., ND, 946

Surrey, ND, congregation (OGBB), 321

Surrey Old German Baptist Brethren Church, ND, **1242,** *1242*

Surrey Ward Co., ND
homes in, *147*

Survey of the India Mission Field (Ross), 1123

Susquehanna Grace Brethren Church, PA, *See* Wrightsville, PA,

Susquehannah Grace Brethren Church
Süss, Elizabeth (later Stober)
Stover, William, 2379
Süss, Margaret (later Stober)

Stover, William, 2379

Sutcliffe, Robert, 378, 2078

Suter, Alice Moore
Moore, John Henry, daughter of, 874

Suter, Cyrus M., 1788

Suter, John Rudolph, 1788
  Monticello, MN, Church of the
    Brethren, minister, 872
Suter, Susan Elaine, 1849
Suter (Sutter), Rudy, 1788
Suterville Old German Baptist Brethren
  Church, KY, **1243**
Sutherland, TN, 1315
Sutief family
  Maple Valley, WA, Grace Brethren
    Church, 2218
Sutphin, Dora (later Woods), 1364
Sutphin, Elmon, 1788
Sutphin family, 1224
  Outlook, WA, Church of the Brethren,
    986
  Radford, VA, Fairlawn Grace Brethren
    Church, 1079
Sutphin, Hazel James, 2078
Sutphin, L., 21
Sutphin, Stanley T., 520, 1788
Sutter, Albert A., 1788
Sutter Co., CA, 750
Sutter family, 1289
  Roanoke, LA, Church of the Brethren,
    1112
Sutter, Hannah DeHaven, 760
Sutter, Mabel, 2078
Sutter, Percival J., 356, 1788
Sutter, Sem C., 2078
Sutter, Simon A., 760
Suttle, Bernard H., 350, 1788, 2306
Sutton, Bishop, 1788
Sutton, David Corliss, 2295
Sutton, Edna Phillips, 768
Sutton, Hilde E., 1788
Sutton, Robert P.
  on Ephrata Cloister, 2360
Sutton, Thomas, 1788
Suzuki, Lester E., 2079
Svejda, Ellen
  on Stuckey, Christin, 2360
  on Stuckey, Maria Richer, 2360
Swab family, 1281
Swab, John, 1788
Swadberg, Ole A., 1788
Swadburg, Glen Mary, 1788
Swadley, Charlotte Jane, 1841
Swadley, Henry, 264, 672, 1788
Swadley, Laura Gwin, 1788
Swadley, William Henry, 78, 673, 1788
Swaim family, 2105
Swallen, Helen Jean (later Snell)
  Snell, William Harrison (FGBC) and,
    2250
Swallow, Carl C., 1788
Swallow, Earl L., 1788
  Omak, WA, Church of the Brethren,
    leadership by, 974
Swallow Falls Dunkard Brethren Congrega-
  tion, MD, **1243**
  Ness, Jacob C., 2231
Swallow, James F., **1243**, 1289, 1354,
  1788–1789
Swamp Creek mission point
  Oakland Church of the Brethren, OH,
    957
Swamp Creek, OH, Church of the Brethren,
  See North Star, OH, Church of the
  Brethren
Swan, Carrie (later Kinsey), 696
Swan Creek Church of the Brethren, MI
  Fairview Church of the Brethren, MI,

469
Swan Creek Church of the Brethren, OH,
  118, 741, **1243**
Swan Creek Church of the Brethren, VA,
  1243
Swan, John H., 1789
Swane, P. L., 1789
Swaney, Janice (later Grubb), 575
Swank, Betty, 1285
Swank, Christian, 2026
Swank family, 142, 353, 2079
Swank, Harry K., 142, 1789
Swank, Harry M., 1789
Swank, Ira, 2079
Swank, James M., 2079
Swank, John, 189
Swank, Mary Louise Gorden, 1845
Swank, Robert Ray, 173, 399, 1789, 1845
  South Bend, IN, Prince of Peace
    Church of the Brethren, minister,
    1204
Swank, Scott T.
  on arts of PA Germans, 2360
Swann, Thomas, 2063
Swanner, William, 1789
Swarr, Ellen (later Forney), 502
Swarr, Howard, 2079
Swarr, Phillip Cassel, 2079
Swart Piebe, 2095
Swart, S., 1789
Swartley, Willard M., 2134
  on Anabaptists and use of scripture,
    2360
Swartz, Benjamin F., 1243
Swartz, Elias J., 1789
Swartz, Emma (later Holl), 619
Swartz, Fred Wilson, 191, 1113, 1789,
  2079, 2333
Swartz, George
  on Swartz, George William, 2360
  on Swartz, Rebecca Snell, 2360
Swartz, George William, 2079
  Swartz, George on, 2360
  Swartz, Joseph on, 2360
Swartz, Goldie Elizabeth, 67, **1243**, 1955
Swartz, Harvey P., 1789
Swartz, John, 1789
Swartz, Joseph
  on Swartz, George William, 2360
  on Swartz, Rebecca Snell, 2360
Swartz, Rebecca Snell
  Swartz, George on, 2360
  Swartz, Joseph on, 2360
Swartz, Sarah Shoemaker, 1243
Swartz, Sudie (later Hersch), 598
Swartz, Timothy Daniel, 1789
Swartz, Willie (later Showalter), 492
Swartzendruber, Edna Annie Yoder, 2105
Swartzentruber, Ada Menno Hershberger
  Kinsinger, 2079
Swartzentruber, Barbara Yost Mast, 2008,
  2079
Swartzentruber, Daniel, 2079
Swartzentruber, Dora Lichty, 2078
Swartzentruber, Esther C. Yoder, 2079
Swartzentruber, Lucy Ann, 2079
Swartzentruber, Peter, 2079
Swartzwelder, Cecil Clair, 1789
Swatara Hill congregation, *See* Middletown
  congregation
Swatara Hill, PA, Church of the Brethren,
  See Middletown, PA, Swatara Hill
  Church of the Brethren

Swatara, PA, congregation
  Pfautz, Johann (Hans) Michael, 1013
Swatara Twp., Lebanon (later Lancaster)
  Co., PA, 1318
Swayne, George W. (H.), 1789
Swaziland
  Oiness, Sylvia Marie, misssionary to,
    963
swearing, *See* oaths
Swearingen, Dale, 360, 1789
Sweat, Anna (later Jarboe), 669
Swedeland Valley Old German Baptist
  Brethren Church, WV, **1243**
Sweden, *See* specific cities, missions
  stations, and congregations
  Assembly of Christ, 376
  Church of the Brethren deacons, *1244*
  conscientious objectors, 336, 337
  General Church Erection and
    Missionary Committee (CB), 536
  Graybill, Alice Minora Hoffer and
    Jacob Franklin, 567
  Graybill (Grabill, Krehbiel) family, 567
  Hope, Christian, 628
  Hope, Mary Katherine Neilsen, 629
  missions, 859
  missions and missionaries in, 160
  missions in, **1243, 1245**
  relief and rehabilitation work, 200
  Vaniman, Albert W., 1303
  Vaniman, Alice and Albert, missionar-
    ies to, 1035
  Vaniman, Alice Moore, 1303
Swedenborg, Emanuel, 1211
Swedenborgians
  Easton, MD, Peach Blossom Church of
    the Brethren, 416
  Fairview Church of the Brethren, MD,
    469
  Fercken, Gaston J., 1051
  Fercken, Gaston John, 488
Swedish Evangelical Free Church China,
  296
Swedish Evangelical Mission Covenant
  Church, *See* Evangelical Covenant
  Church
Swedish immigrants, Brooklyn, NY, 1296
Swedlin Valley schoolhouse
  South Fork Church of the Brethren,
    WV, preaching point, 1205
Sweet Co., MT
  Montana Brethren settlement, 870
Sweet, Leonard I.
  on Livermore, Harriet, 2360
Sweet Water Lake congregation
  Salem Church of the Brethren, ND,
    1137
Sweet, William Warren, 2079
  historical writing, 612
Sweeton, James C., 673, 1789, 2079
Sweetser, IN, Church of the Brethren
  Cart Creek, IN, Church of the
    Brethren, 257
  Marion, IN, Church of the Brethren,
    793
Sweetser, IN, Church of the Brethren, **1245**
Sweetwater Valley Church of the Brethren,
  TN, *See* Niota, TN, Church of the
  Brethren
Sweitzer, Bertha (later Rothrock), 1124
Sweitzer, Henry Z., 1789
Sweitzer, Merle, 1789
Sweitzer, Samuel K., 1789

Sweitzer, Wendell Henry, 1789
Sweitzer, William C., 363, 1789
    Mount Horeb Church of the Brethren,
        VA, pastor, 882
    Shelton Church of the Brethren, NC,
        pastor in, 1176
Swell, Jacob, 1789
Swendsen, Theodor, 1789
Swerdeger, Don, 1789
Swibart, Jacob, 1789–1790
Swick, Michael R., 2295
Swick, Rebecca
    Midway Church of the Brethren, TN,
        providing leadership, 827
Swift, Cheri
    Riverside, CA, Grace Brethren Church,
        1111
Swift, David
    Riverside, CA, Grace Brethren Church,
        1111
Swift family
    Riverside, CA, Grace Community
        Church (FGBC) and, 2244
Swift, W. C., 1789
Swigart, Anna Swigart, 1245
Swigart, Carrie Mattern Miller, 1245
Swigart, Catherine (later Houser), 633
Swigart, Christian, 1245
Swigart, Elizabeth (later Houser), 633
Swigart, Elizabeth Robinson, 1245
Swigart, Esther (later Van Dyke), 220,
        1301, 1302
Swigart family, 2079
Swigart, Frances Moyer, 1245
Swigart, George Hanawalt, 1245, 1789
Swigart, J. William, 1789
Swigart, Jay Leon, 765, 1789
Swigart, John, 406, 1215, 1245, 1789
    Maitland Church of the Brethren, PA,
        minister, 783
Swigart, John C., 1789
Swigart, John W., 2079
Swigart, Jonathan H., 1952
Swigart, M. C.
    Philadelphia, PA, Germantown Church
        of the Brethren, 1016
Swigart, Mary (later Hanawalt), 581, 582
Swigart, Milton Clarke, 1245, 1347, 1789,
        2079
Swigart, N. C., 1789
Swigart, Paul E., 1789, 2306
Swigart, Rebecca Dunmire, 1245
Swigart, Rettie, 720
Swigart, Samuel, 720
Swigart, Samuel J., 739, 1789
Swigart, Wilbur C., 232, 1789
Swigart, William Joseph, 52, 728, **1245,**
        2079
    War Relief and Reconstruction
        Committee, 1370
Swigert, Mary (later Leatherman), 732
Swihart, Aaron, 1246, 1789
Swihart, Aaron M., 1301, 1789
    Poplar Valley Church of the Brethren,
        MT, elder, 1047
Swihart, Adam, 1246
Swihart, Ananias, 1789
Swihart, Clarence B., 1789
Swihart, Daniel, 2079
Swihart, David, 1246, 1789
Swihart, Elias C., 1789
Swihart, Elizabeth Metz, 1245, 1246
Swihart, Ellen Marie, 2295

Swihart family, 153, **1246,** 1253, 1305,
        2079, 2085
    Mayville, ND, Red River Valley
        Church of the Brethren, 805
    Osceola, IN, Grace Brethren Church,
        983
Swihart, Floyd, 1789
Swihart, Gabriel, II, 1246
Swihart, George (1842–1908), 558, 1246,
        1315, 1333, 1789
    Mayville, ND, Red River Valley
        Church of the Brethren, elder, 805
    Poplar Valley Church of the Brethren,
        MT, elder, 1047
    Sidney, IN, Grace Brethren Church,
        pastor, 1181
Swihart, George (1866–1949), 1789
Swihart, George E., 267, 1789
Swihart, George T., 1789
Swihart, Harvey E., 1234, 1789, 2079
Swihart, Jacob, 1246
    Pleasant View Brethren Church, IN,
        2377
Swihart, John K. L., 1790
Swihart, Jonathan, 1790
Swihart, Jonathan H., 121, 130, *182,* 186,
        211, 231, 323, 335, 345, 425, 439
        559, 758, 1245, 1246, 1321, 1790,
        2079
    Miller, John Allen, 839
    missions, 860
    Pennington, AR, Bethel Brethren
        Church, elder, 1004
    Pleasant Grove Grace Brethren Church,
        IA, 1031
    Roanoke, IN, Brethren Church, pastor,
        1112
Swihart, Joseph, 1246
Swihart, Joseph C., 1246, 1790
Swihart, Lucinda Beam, 1245
Swihart, Mary Schillinger, 1245
Swihart, Merle W., 1790, 2306
Swihart, Neri, 1790
Swihart, Peter, 1246
Swihart, Roy J., 1790, 2306
Swihart, Samuel Thomas, 1246, 1790
    Pennington, AR, Bethel Brethren
        Church, elder, 1004
Swihart, Stephen, 1790
Swihart, Walter, 1790
Swihart, Wayne E., 1790
Swihart, Wilson, 1790
Swihart, Zelma, 2079
Swindler, William, 2008
Swinehart, Ephraim, 144
Swinehart, Gabriel, 1246
Swinehart, Joseph, 144
Swinehart, Philip Meek, 211, 1790
Swinger, Ausby, 251, 638
    Romine Church of the Brethren, IL,
        providing leadership, 1121
Swinger, Ausby Ward, 1790
    Martin Creek Church of the Brethren,
        IL, pastor, 797
    Swinger family, 713, 2019
Swinger, Glenn Calvin, 2327, 1790
    Roanoke, LA, Church of the Brethren,
        pastor, 1112
Swinger, Jacob, 1790
Swinger, Walter R., 1790
Swinger, William, 1790
Swinney family
    Pleasant View Church of the Brethren,

TN, 1037
Swisher family
    Howard Co. Old German Baptist
        Brethren Church, IN, 633
Swisher, George J., 373, 1790
    Pipe Creek Old German Baptist
        Brethren Church, IN, minister,
        1026
Swiss
    emigrants to the American Colonies,
        1935
Swiss Brethren, 25, 28, 43, *See also*
        Anabaptism; Anabaptists
    Mennonite Church (MC), 815
    oaths, taking of, 959
Switzer, Charles
    Modesto, CA, Pleasant Home Dunkard
        Brethren Congregation, 867
Switzer, Edna Marie, 1845
Switzer, F. O., 1790
Switzer family
    history of, 1912
    Reinhardt family, 1094
Switzer, Harry, 482
Switzer, James Lebbaeus, 232, 765, 1790
    medicine, 810
Switzer, John William, 1790
Switzer, Mr. and Mrs. H. A.
    North Manchester, IN, (First) Brethren
        Church, 949
Switzer, Owen, 1319
Switzer, Perna
    Modesto, CA, Pleasant Home Dunkard
        Brethren Congregation, 867
Switzerland, 25, 28, 29, 1246, *See also* spe-
        cific city, missions station, or
        congregation
    Boni, Andreas, persecution of, 1010
    Brethren movement and, 174
    Brethren remnants in Europe, 1099
    church movements, 2096
    Community of the True Inspiration,
        330
    Fercken, Gaston John and Seline
        (Phebe), 488
    Garber (Garver, Gerber) family, 529
    General Church Erection and
        Missionary Committee (CB), 536
    Germany, 545
    historic sites, 609
    Keller family immigrating from, 686
    migration from, 1221
    migrations from, 2070, 2074
    missions, 861
    missions and missionaries in, 160
    Naas, Johannes, ministering through,
        909
    Näff family, 909
    Pennsylvania, and emigrations from,
        2070
    Pennsylvania Germans from, 1006
    Puidoux Conferences, 1071, *1071*
    Reformation, Protestant, 1091
    religious movements in, 43, 121–122
    Russian Orthodox Church, peace semi-
        nar with, 1132
Swomley, John M., Jr., 638
Swonger (Swonguer), Michael, 1790
Swope, Emanuel J., 2080
Swope, Emily (later Morse), 2023
Swope family, 2079, 2080
Swope Family Historical Committee,
        2080

Swope, Gilbert Ernest, 2079
Swope, Harper E., 2079
Swope, John, 71, 2295
Swope, Maggie Burkholder, 2080
Swope (Schwab, Schwob) family, 2023
Swope, Wilmer D., 2079–2080
Swope's Valley meetinghouse
    Schuykill Church of the Brethren, PA,
        1157
Swoveland, Jacob S., 1790
Swyer, Christine, 383
Sycamore Brethren Church, VA, See
    Sperryville, VA, Copps Chapel
        Brethren Church
Sycamore congregation, 1209
Syford, Alfred, 1790
Sykes, Clarence, 2295
Sylvan , IL, congregation
    Rockford, IL, First Church of the
        Brethren, 1117
Sylvester, Hubert, 1790
symbolism
    Christian denominations and sects,
        1988
    feetwashing, 481–482
    Helman, Patricia Kennedy, 2197
    worship services, 1377
symbols, 59, **1246**
    love feast as, 1254, 1260
    teaching of, 1992
    tents as symbol of movable tabernacle,
        1254
Symensma, Guy Lavon, 1790
sympathy, folk medicine, 2145–2146
Symphony Grace Brethren Church,
    Arvada, CO, See Arvada, CO,
        Hackberry Hill Grace Brethren
        Church
The Symphony of Life, 1992
Synod of Dort, Dutch Reformed Church
    (1619), 55
    Congregation of God in the Spirit, 334
    Reformed Church, 1153
    Zinzendorf, Count, 334
Syracuse, IN, Church of the Brethren, 124,
    1246, 1280
    Solomon's Creek Church of the
        Brethren, IN, 1202
Syria, 23, See also Turkey
    Miller, John Ezra, surveying relief
        needs, 840
    Relief and Reconstruction Committee,
        aided by, 1096
    relief from Near East Foundation, 920
systematic theology
    McClendon, James William on, 2344
Systematic Theology (McClendon)
    theology and, 2255
Syster, John, 1790

Taber, Ada Delores Zellner, **1247,** 1853
Taber, Bettie (later Cashman), 2156
Taber, Betty, 1853
Taber, Charles Russell, 1319, 1853
Taber, Floyd William, 139, **1247,** 1790,
    1853
    medical missions, 807
Taber, Miles H., 64, 65, 490, 738, **1247,**
    1790, 2156
Taber, Virden Kirby, 1247
Tabler, James D., 1790
Tabor College
    Mennonite Brethren Churches, General

        Conference of, 814
Tabor, Emily (later Flory), 499
Tachai, China, 278
Tacoma, VA, 728
Tacoma, WA
    Church of the Brethren, 269
    Larchmont Community Church of the
        Brethren, **1247**
    urban mission, 1297
Taft, William H.
    Brumbaugh, Martin Grove and, 223
T'ai Yuan Fu, China
    Horning, Mary Emma, 630
Taiwan
    General Conference Mennonite
        Church, 536
Takami, Rio
    Rocky Ford, CO, Church of the
        Brethren, 1118
Takanii (Takemaye), Rio, 1790
Take Heart (Hoff), 617
"Take My Hand and Lead Me, Father"
    hymns, 643
Talbot Co., MD
    Peach Blossom Colored Church of
        Rising Light (CB), MD, 1003
Talbot, Louis T., 98
Talbot Theological Institute, See Bible
    Institute of Los Angeles
Talbot Theological Seminary, 136
    McClain, Alva J., lecturer, 772
Talcott, James Eugene, 1790
A Tale of the Kloster (Koons/Brother
    Jabez), 747
Talent Church of the Brethren, OR, See
    Williams Church of the Brethren,
        OR
Talent, OR, 1346
Talheim, Byron, 1790
Talheim, Humphrey, 1790
The Tall Man (Davis family), 748
Talley, Elizabeth (later Miller), 1936, 2018
    Miller, Daniel Long, wife of, *835, 836*
Talley, J. O., 500, 695
    Milledgeville, IL, Brethren Church,
        pastor, 833
    missions, 861
Talley, John O., 1790
Talley, John D., Jr., 350, 367, 1790
Tama Co., IA, 661
Tamesis (ship)
    sinking missionaries' ship, 863
Tamkin, Warren E., 436, 578–579, 579,
    588, 664, 1319, 1790, 2186
    Island Pond, VT, Grace Brethren
        Church, 2209
    Martinsburg, PA, Grace Brethren
        Church, pastor, 798
Tampa, FL
    Church of the Brethren, 1247
    Town and Country Brethren Church,
        1247
    Zion Church of the Brethren, See North
        Tampa, FL, Zion Church of
        the Brethren
Tana Co., IA
    Garwin, IA, Carlton Brethren Church,
        532
Tanacha Brethren Church congregation,
    Argentina
    Siccardi, Luis, pastor, 1181
Tancacha, AR, Brethren Church congrega-
    tion, 382

Tancacha, Argentina, 53
    Brethren Church, 382
Tandel, Lailubbai P., 1790
Taney, Roger B.
    statue of, by Rinehart, William Henry,
        1109
Taneytown, MD, 1315
Tanger, Esther Snavely Bergyold, 2094
Tanger, Jacob, 2094
Tanger-Metzer family, 2093–2094
Tanner, See Danner
Tanner (Danner) family, 1900
Tanner (Danner), John
    Madison Church of the Brethren, VA,
        781
Tanner, George, 511
Tanner, John, 1790
    tanning business, 691
Tannreuther, William O., 1323, 1790, 2080
Tanselle, G. Thomas, 2080
Taos, NM
    First Brethren Church (FGBC), **1248**
        minorities, ethnic and racial, 850
    Hispanic congregations in, 931
Tappan, Arthur, 22
Tappan, Lewis, 22
Tappert, Theodore G., 1209, 2080
Tarayyar Ekklesiyoyin Kristi a Nigeria, See
    Fellowship of the Churches of
        Christ in Nigeria
Tarfa, Gwanu, 307
Tarfa, Mwapu I., 306
Tarman, H. James, 1939
Tarr, Dorothy, 629
Tarr, Earl, 629
Tarr family
    at New Rockford, ND, Church of the
        Brethren, 932
Tarrant Co., TX
    Fort Worth, TX, Church of the
        Brethren, 504
tartaros, See Hell, doctrine of
Tarvin, George, 171, 1790
Tasiguano, Raul, 1248
Tasker, A. Cecil, 1790
Tate, Dortha (later Hostetler), 631
Tatesville, PA, **1384**
Tatian
    peace in Christian church history, 998
Tatterson, Clerissa Ann Hathaway, 2080
Taucher community
    history of, 2072
Täufer ("[Ana]Baptists")
    names of Brethren fellowships, 910
Täufer Brethren
    Wittgenstein, 1955
Taufers
    history of, 1917
Taufgesinnten ("Baptist-minded")
    names of Brethren fellowships, 910
Taufgesinnten (Tauffs-gesinnte), See names,
    Brethren
Taufschein
    Fraktur, 505
Tauler, Johann, 381
Tavel, C., 1790
Tawzer, J. J., 45, 1790
    Silver Lake Church of the Brethren,
        NE, elder and minister, 1182
taxation
    in lieu of military service, See exemp-
        tion tax
    Civil War, 149

Revolutionary War, 176
National Service Board for Religious
 Objectors (NSBRO) and tax
 exempt status, 917
non-associators in Revolutionary War,
 939
refusal to pay, **1248–1249**
religious freedom and persecution,
 1009
Shelby Co., KY, tax lists, 2100
Tay, Herbert H., 715, 1790–1791, 2306,
 2386
Tayler, Charles Guy, 1791
Tayler, Steve, 503
Taylor, Alfred, 1791
Taylor, Alice, 365
Taylor, Allen, 1791
Taylor, Arthur E., 1791
Taylor, Barnard C., 2080
Taylor, Betsy Leatherman, 1249
Taylor, Catherine Shirk, 1249
Taylor, Charles V., 1791
Taylor, Christina Bashor, 1249
Taylor Co., IA, 416
Taylor Co., KY, 689
Taylor, Cynthia B., 2295
Taylor, Darrel Glen, 2295
 Sidney, IN, Grace Brethren Church,
  pastor, 1181
Taylor, Donald R., 496, 1791
 Ozark Grace Brethren Church, MI,
  pastor, 987
Taylor, Emma (later Kinsey), 696
Taylor, Eugene
 on Beissel, Conrad, 2360
Taylor family, 1249, 2044
 Mabton, WA, Grace Brethren Church,
  771
Taylor, Florence Neff, 2080
Taylor, Frank T., 320, 1791, 2306
Taylor, George, 1249
Taylor, Glen Franklin, 1791, 1985
 Redford, MI, Trinity Church of the
  Brethren, pastoral leadership, 1090
Taylor, Harley, 1267
Taylor, Herman E., 2080
Taylor, Hettie Groff, 1249
Taylor, Hewett R., 373, 520, 1791
Taylor, I. N., 1249
Taylor, Isaac W., 14, 721, 1213, **1249**, 1791
Taylor, J. E., 1959, *See also* urban ministry
Taylor, Jabez, 282
Taylor, Jack, 2295
Taylor, James O., 2295
 Lakeland, FL, Grace Brethren Church,
  2213
Taylor, John, 1249
Taylor, Joseph E., 1249
Taylor, Kenneth, 705
 Minerva, OH, Grace Brethren Church,
  843
Taylor, Lawrence Russell, 738, 1791
Taylor, Lydia E., **1249**, 2080
Taylor, Madolin Boorse, **1249**, 1791
 Pottstown, PA, Coventry Church of the
  Brethren, preacher, 1049
Taylor, Maude E. (later Jewell)
 Jewell, Jesse Paul, 2209
Taylor, Melvin J., 14, 1240
Taylor, Michael C., 2295
Taylor, Milton Miller, 1791
Taylor, Olive I., 2080
Taylor, Samuel C., 1791

Taylor, Samuel David, 1791
 Pleasant View Church of the Brethren,
  TN, 1037
Taylor, Samuel W., 1791
Taylor, Sara, 2080
Taylor, Scott B.
 Lexington, KY, Grace Bible Church,
  2215
Taylor, Sophia Weaver, 1249
Taylor, Steve W., 12, 2295
Taylor, Terrance T., 562, 629, 739, 1791
 Manheim, PA, Grace Brethren Church,
  pastor, 787
 Pompano Beach, FL, Grace Brethren
  Church, pastor, 1046
Taylor, Thomas, 425, 1249
Taylor, William
 Pompano Beach, FL, Grace Brethren
  Church, pastor, 1046
Taylor, William Addison, 1791
Taylor, William C., 1791
Taylor, William L., 2306
Taylor, WV, 254
Taylors Valley, VA, 1315
TCNN, *See* Theological School of Northern
 Nigeria
Teach, Carolyn (later Denlinger), 1916,
 1945
 works by, 2324
Teach, Roy B., 1791, 1880
 teacher training
  Bridgewater College, 2089
  Kishacoquillas Seminary, 697
  La Verne, University of, 715–716
teachers, *See* faculty
 Mount Morris College faculty, 884,
  885
 normal schools, 945
 women as, 1361
 Woods, Mannesseh Frederick, 1364
teaching ministry, 846
Teague, Elijah, 2063
Teague, Kenneth L., 1791
 Roanoke, VA, First Brethren Church,
  pastor, 1113
Teal, Mark A., 2295
 Medina, OH, Church of the Brethren,
  2219
Teal, Samuel, 1281
Tear Coat Church of the Brethren, WV, 106,
 254, **1249**
Teasdale, Calvin T., 1791
Teater, Catherine (later Glick), 553
technology, *See* computers; information
 technology
 Old German Baptist Brethren, 941,
  2233, 2234
Teegarden, IN, 1338
 Brethren Church, **1249–1250**
Teegarden, Robert Aaron, 1791, 2306
Teel family, 743
teenagers
 church membership, 813
 McAllen, TX, Grace Brethren Church,
  2219
Teeter, Abraham, 384
Teeter, Allene Mae, 2295
Teeter, B. Y. S., 1791
Teeter, Benjamin Franklin, 2080
Teeter, Chester Frank, 2295
Teeter, Christina
 Oakville, IN, Brethren Church, 959
Teeter, D. A. C., 269, 318, 637, 699, 758,

1791
 New Enterprise Brethren Church, IN,
  elder in, 927
Teeter, Daniel K., 1791
Teeter, Daniel V., 1250
Teeter, Daniel W., 669, 1791
Teeter, David, 1791
 Oakville, IN, Brethren Church, 959
Teeter, E.
 Pleasant Valley German Baptist
  Brethren, IA, 1036
Teeter, Edward Clayton, 1791
Teeter, Elias Kaylor, 335, 384, 694, 1250,
 1719
 Pleasant Hill, OH, First Brethren
  Church, 1032
Teeter family, 2080
 Jasper, MO, Church of the Brethren,
  669
 Mount Hope Church of the Brethren,
  WA, 882
 Paul family relations, 996
Teeter, Gerald W., 12, 349, 579, 1791, 2306
 Martinsburg, PA, Grace Brethren
  Church, pastor, 798
Teeter, I. C., 1791
Teeter, John L., 670, 1791
Teeter, John R., 1270
Teeter, Lewis Wallace, 138, 205, 923, **1250,
 1250**, *1791*, 1946, 2080
 New Testament, 133
 prayer, posture in, 1052
 publishing, 1069
 Shultz and Paul families, related to,
  1156–1157
Teeter, Martha Bowman Ulrich, 1250, *1250*
Teeter, Mary E. Flory, 1791
Teeter, Melvin, 1791
Teeter, Mona Lou, 1845
Teeter, Mrs. J. D., *639*
Teeter, Nancy Ellen Bowman, 1250
Teeter, Roy Russell, 186, 231, 363, 562,
 694, 758, **1250,** 1791
 Milledgeville, IL, Brethren Church,
  pastor, 833
 Oakville, IN, Brethren Church, pastor,
  959
Teeter, Samuel John, 1791
Teeter, Sarah (later Holsinger), 623
Teeter, Sarah Shultz, 1250
Teeter, Susannah, 1250
Teeter, W. C., 1791
Teeter, William Constant, 1791
Teetor, Zola Houser, 2080
Teets family
 Fremont, OH, Grace Brethren Church,
  515
Teets, Laban W., 1791
Teets, William Lindsey, 1791
Teevan, John, 1791
 on GBC, 2335
TEKAN (Fellowship of Churches of Christ
 in Nigeria)
 mission schools, 854
 missions, 861
 Mai Sule Biu, vice-chairman, 782
Tekoa, WA, Church of the Brethren, 1212,
 1250
telecommunications
 Christian perspective, 1972
telephones
 Old Brethren, 964, 970
 Old Brethren German Baptist Church,

965

Old Brethren's Reasons, 965

Old German Baptist Brethren, 969

Old Order German Baptist Church,
2235

Old Order German Baptists, 972
Skiles, Jacob W., 1189

use, opposition to, **1250**

television, 399, **1251**

Brethren of Christ doctrine on, 189

Church of the Brethren on use of, 2099

Dunkard Brethren, 409, 941

Dunkard Brethren Church, 2174

ethics, 458

forbidding of, 1251

mass media, 800, 801

mass media, uses of, 2218

ministry by Mennonite Church (MC),
815

Murray, Don, 626

Old German Baptist Brethren, 941,
969, 2160, 2233

recreation, 1087

Television Awareness Training

mass media cooperative effort, 801

Telford, PA, Penn Valley Grace Brethren
Church, **1251**

Telford, TN, Grace Brethren Church, **1251**

Telgenhoff, Leonard A., 1791

Tell Me, 1236

Teller, Susan Elizabeth (later Ronk), 1121

Temme, Willi
writings of, 2360

Tempe, AZ, Papago Park Brethren Church,
1251

Temperance, 2080

Temperance and Purity Committee (CB),
1252

General Welfare Board, 540

Peace Committee, 1002

Temperance Bulletin, **1252**

Temperance Committee (CB), 1252

Lear, John Wallace, 732

prohibition, 1061–1062

temperance movement, 16, **1251–1252,**
2037, *See also* alcoholic beverages

on alcohol, 2091

annual conference decisions, 1939

article about, 1928

Baptists, 167

bibliography, 1883, 1906

brewing and distilling industry and,
206

Christian Education Commission, 155

Church of God (New Dunkers), 297

Church of the Brethren, 301

circles, and Sisters' Aid Society, 1187

Coppock, Jacob, 343

Culler, David, 355

Ebersole, John P., 418

Evangelical Association, 459

Finnell, Virgil Carl, 490

General Welfare Board (CB), 540

gospel music, 559

grape juice, 566, 1349

Harnley, Henry Jacob, 585

Herndon, Ed R., 1263

leaders in, 149, 161, 163

Major, Sarah Righter, 783

Manor Church of the Brethren, MD,
starting society for, 787

Men's Work (CB), 816

Minnich, Levi, 990

murder of Joseph Easter, 1135

nonconformity, 940

Old German Baptist Brethren Church,
388

play about, 1941

Price, Isaac, advocating, 1056

prohibition, 1061

publications for, 1069

Rowland, Ann Gilbert, 1126

sermon on, 1168

social action, 1196

Social Gospel Movement, 1197

Studebaker, Florence S., 2077

Sunday school movement, 283

Swigart, Milton Clarke, 1245

thesis on, 1957

Thomas, OK, Church of the Brethren,
1263

United Brethren in Christ, 1290

The Voice of Thy Brother's Blood
(Studebaker), 748

wine, use in communion services, 1349

Woman's Christian Temperance Union,
1359

Women's Christian Temperance Union
Stahly, Cora Miller, 1216

Yoder, Charles Francis, 1385

Temple City, CA, Grace Brethren Church,
1252

Rosemead Boulevard Brethren Church,
East Pasadena, CA, 1206

Temple, Henry W., 2080

Temple Hills, MD, Grace Brethren Church
of Greater Washington, **1252–1253**

Temple, Thomas, 24

Temple University, 693

Temple, William, 422

Templeton, Leland George, 1791–1792

Templeton, Thomas T., 1792

Ten Dollar/Growth Partner Club
The Missionary Board (BC), 856

Ten Mile Brethren Church, PA, *See* Odell,
PA, Ten Mile Brethren Church,
2379

Ten Mile Church of the Brethren, PA, 48,
58, 1177, **1253**, 1354, 1936

Highland Brethren Church, PA, 605

Tennent, Gilbert
Great Awakening and American
revivalism, 1104

Tennent, William
Great Awakening and American
revivalism, 1104

Tennessee, 689, **1253–1254**, 2063, *See also*
specific towns, counties, and congregations

Brethren settlement and North
Carolina, 946

Far Western Brethren, 30

history of Brethren in, 168

Illinois, 646

Indiana, 652

migration of Brethren, 829

Old German Baptist Brethren, 967

preacher circuits in, 164, 167

Sappington, Roger E. on Brethren in,
2354

Simmons family, 1182

Tennessee, Brethren in, 54

Tennessee, Etta, 165

Tennessee Rural Minister of the Year
(1956)

Pritchett, Reuel Bowman, 1060

Tennis, Samuel, 1792

Tennison, K. G., 1255, 1324, 1792

Tennstadt
Seebach, Christoph, 1165

tent meetings

Champaign, IL, Church of the
Brethren, 270

Cheyenne, KS, Church of the Brethren,
274

First Brethren Church, CA, 362

Goshen, IN, City Church of the
Brethren, 557

Juniata Church of the Brethren, NE,
678

New Jersey, 239

tents, as meeting places, **1254,** *See also*
board buildings

annual meeting of 1913, Winona Lake,
IN, *1352*

council tents, 1254

dining tents, 1254

Enders, NE district meeting, *1254*

Leaf River Old German Baptist
Brethren Church, 731

Little Traverse Church of the Brethren,
MI, 750

Long Beach, CA, North Long Beach
Brethren Church, 755

Los Angeles, CA, Bella Vista Church
of the Brethren, 758

Los Angeles, CA, Community Brethren
Church, 759

Old German Baptist Brethren Annual
Meetings, 969

Spring Creek Old German Baptist
Brethren Church, 1213

Springfield, IL, Church of the
Brethren, 1215

symbolic of movable tabernacle, 1254

Thomas OK, Church of the Brethren,
1263

Turkey Creek Church of the Brethren,
OK, 1280

use of for Annual Meetings, *34, 35,* 36

use of for love feast, 1

Whittier, CA, Grace Brethren Church,
1343

Tepper, Michael, 2080

Teran, Philip M., 348, 1792

Terra Alta congregation, WV, 744

Elkins, WV, Church of the Brethren,
440

Terra Alta, WV

Cooperative Brethren Church, 155,
1254

White Dale Brethren Church, 164,
1254

Terrace View Church of the Brethren, VA,
1254

Terrell, John R., 367, 674, 1240, 1792

Martinsburg, PA, Grace Brethren
Church, pastor, 798

Terrell, Sharon Ann, 1853

Terror in the Name of God (Holt), 1070

Terry family

Radford, VA, Fairlawn Grace Brethren
Church, 1079

Tersteegen, Gerhard, 57, 381, 751, 1222,
1254–1255, 1867, 2080

correspondence with Stephan Koch,
704

Hochmann von Hochenau, Ernst
Christoph, 615

Pauw, Adrian, support from, 996
prayer, 1051
sources on, 2315
Tertullian, 296
agape meals, 757
oaths, taking of, 959
peace in Christian church history, 998
premillennialism, 833
theological resource, 1261
Terwilleger, Samuel, 1792
Tesch, Margaret (later Jans), 1389
Testament of Devotion (Kelly), 382
Testigo Fiel (Faithful Witness), 53–54, **1255**
The Testimony of Truth, **1255**, 2080
Tetlow, Ellen
Portis, KS, Grace Brethren Church, 1048
Teufel, Delores E., 2080–2081
Teutonia (communitarian society), 331, **1255**
Freidensbote von Concordia, Der (The Peace Messenger of Concordia), 517
Sala, Solomon, 1136
Texas, **1255**, *See also* specific towns, counties, and congregations
Brethren movement in, 217
Church of the Brethren, 322
migration of Brethren, 830
mission schools, 853
orphans, care for, 27
Panhandle
Oklahoma district, 964
railroads and Brethren settlement, 1082
relief and rehabilitation work in, 190
Texas and Louisiana district
Oklahoma district, merger with, 939
Texas Chapel Church of the Brethren, VA, **1255**
Red Oak Grove Church of the Brethren, VA, 1089
Texas Co., MO
Greenwood Church of the Brethren, MO, 572
Mountain Grove Church of the Brethren, MO, 888
textile industry
Mennonites and, 17
Texts in Transit, 139
Thacker, Robert M., 2295
Thailand
Julien, Thomas T., 2210
missions, 2225
missions, short-term, 2226
Thakor, Joseph K., 1792
Thakor, Madhavlal N., 1792
Thakor, Peter J., 1792
Thalham (Austria) Tubercular Sanitorium, 73, **1255–1256**, 1792
hospitals, 631
Kruger, Helena, 708
medical projects, 809
relief and rehabilitation work in, 200
Thalitzer, Johannes Hansen, 280, **1256**
on history of Brethren movement, 2360
Old German Baptist Brethren, 970
Thanksgiving Day
Indianapolis, IN, Northview Church of the Brethren, 654
Tharrington, Bruce Allen, 157, 1792
That Colony of Brethren, 2081
That Unknown Country
Moomaw, B. C., 873

Thayer Co., NB
Carleton congregation, 921
Thayer Co., NE
migration of Brethren, 830
Thayer, J Hudson, 1792, 2167, 2168
Mansfield, OH, Conservative Grace Brethren Church, 2217, 2218
Mansfield, OH, Grace Brethren Church, pastor, 787
Theological Practorium, The (CBBCI) and, 2254
theater, *See* drama
theatrical shows
musical instruments, 900
Then Would My Servants Fight (Hoyt), 634
Theobald, oder die Schwärmer (Jung-Stilling), 678
theodicy, question of, 156
"Theological Basis of Personal Ethics"
marriage concerns, 795
Theological College of Bangalore, India
Warstler, Anna Margaret, 1319
Theological College of Northern Nigeria, 307, 702, 936, *1256, 1257,* 2164
Fellowship of Churches of Christ in Nigeria, 484
Guli, John, 2194
Mai Sule Biu, Board of Governors, 782
mission schools, 854
sources on, 2316
theological education, 67–68, **1256–1257,** *1256, 1257*
developing countries, 1980
disagreements over, 1053, *1054, 1054–1055*
mission schools, 853, 854
sharing of facilities, 22
Theological Practorium, The (CBBCI), 2254
Theological Practorium, **2254**
Conservative Grace Brethren Churches International Fellowship, 2168
Mansfield, OH, Conservative Grace Brethren Church, 2217, 2218
Mount Vernon, OH, Conservative Grace Brethren Church, 2226, 2227
theological principles, denominational naming based on, 910
"Theological Realism," 922
theological study conferences, 304. **1257–1258**
church membership, 813
Theological Writings (Nead), 724–725, 919, 1185, 1258–1259
theology, 55, 1258–1262, 1972, **2254–2255,** *See also* Bible; Christology; evangelism; Holy Spirit; liberalism; neo-orthodoxy; premillennialism
Anabaptist, 29
antiintellectualism, 1258–1259
antitheological beliefs, 1258–1259
authority of the Bible, *See* authority of the Bible
of baptism, **82–86**
believers' church concept, book about, 1945
Brethren movement, 289
Brethren thought, development of, 2014
church attitude towards, 2093
Church of the Brethren, 303
concept of church, 1260

definition of, 386
discipleship, *See* discipleship
Doctrinal Treatise, 1261
Dunkard Brethren Church Polity, 1261
eternity, journey to, 2004
false Anti-Christ, 1967
fencerow theology, Meyer, Lauree Hersch on, 2347
German Baptist Brethren movement, in Europe, 2074
God's Means of Grace (Yoder), 555
God's spirit, 1965
Grace Brethren, 55, 303
Groff, Warren Frederick, 2194
history, 1983
incarnation, commentary on, 1937
India, 651
James Gribble Memorial High School, 668
liberalism, 739
love and obedience, 761
McClain, Alva J., systematic theology, 773
Miller, John Allen, teaching, 839
milliennialism, 1261
modern Tunkers, 1977
Moravian Church, 875
mystical, *See* mysticism
narrative for children, 1954
New Protestant, 1966
New Testament as creed, 1259, 1260
non Brethren, warning about, 1983
noncreedalism, 942, 1258–1259
peace, 1966
pluralism and voluntaryism, 1310
recurrent questions, 1986
role in division of churches, 1261
sanctification, *See* sanctification
souls, 1965
statement of faith, 1218
summarized on Brethren's Card, 2152
systematic, 2344
trinity, doctrine of, 1275
unity and diversity, 1968
universalism, 1260
vision of Stephan Koch, 1988
works-righteousness, 1259
Theology of Anabaptism (Friedmann, R.), 1259
Theophilus, *See* Mack, Alexander, Jr.
Theosophia Practica, See Theosophische Sendschreiben (*Theosophical Epistles*) (Gichtel)
Theosophical Letters (Boehme), 156
Theosophische Sendschreiben (*Theosophical Epistles*) (Gichtel), 548
Therapeutic Homes, Inc.
Modesto, CA, Church of the Brethren, 866–867
Thiessen, Emil A., 2081
Thieszen, Esther Mae (later Quiring), 2040
Thill, Marvin W., 1240, 1792
Think About It, 2184
mass media, 801
Third Brethren Church, Philadelphia, PA, 259
The Third Day, 2177
1300 Select Sayings (Fahnestock, Adam G.), 465
Thirteenth Amendment, 1
Thirty Years' War, 29, 990, **1262**
Brethren beginnings, and Roman Catholic Church, 1120

Halle on the Saale River, 580
Mack family losing mill, 778
Mack, Johann Philipp, 778
Peace of Westphalia, 1338
religious liberty, 1098
Ronneburg Castle, 1121
This Do in Remembrance of Me (Hoyt), 634
Thistle (ship)
    Funderburgh family, 523
    Mohler, Ludwig, family, voyage to
        America on, 868
Thoma, Anastasia(?), 2081
Thomas, A. E., 235, 1249
Thomas, A. S., 354
Thomas, Abel C., 2081
Thomas, Abram Sager, 1792
Thomas, Albert E., 1792
Thomas, Alexander, 1792
Thomas, Alexander, Jr., 1263
Thomas, Alexander, Sr., 1263
Thomas, Allen O., 1792, 2081
Thomas, Andrew, 1263
Thomas, Archibald, 1792
Thomas, Arlene
    on Freindschaft, David, 2347
    on Freindschaft, Ella Markey, 2347
Thomas, Augusta Annie Dillman, 2081
Thomas, Barbara Boger, 1263
Thomas, Bertha Barbara (later Huffman)
    Huffman, Nelson Thomas, 2205
Thomas, Bertha F., 2081
Thomas, Carl D., 1322, 1792
Thomas, Charles C., 1792
Thomas, Chester, 1792
Thomas Co., KS
    Menlo Church of the Brethren, KS, 814
    Thomas Co., KS, Church of the
        Brethren, *See* Menlo Church of the
        Brethren
Thomas, D. D.
    Phoenix, AZ, First Church of the
        Brethren, pastor, 1019
Thomas, Daniel, 105, 170, **1262**, 1263,
    1792
    Pleasant View Church of the Brethren,
        WV, 1037
Thomas, Daniel Driver, 1792, 2081
Thomas, David, 1792
Thomas, Dorothy
    Redondo Beach, CA, South Bay
        Community Church of the
        Brethren, 1090
Thomas, Dorothy Kurtz Erb, 2081
Thomas, Edith (later Jarboe), 669
Thomas, Elizabeth, 1950, 2016
Thomas, Elizabeth Bowman, 1262
Thomas, Elizabeth (later Arnold), 58
Thomas, Elliott B., 1792
Thomas, Emily, 354
Thomas, Ernest, 1792
Thomas family, 1253, **1263**, 1336, 2060
    Fike family, 490
    Garwin, IA, Carlton Brethren Church,
        532
    genealogy, 1927, 2009
    Markleysburg, PA, Church of the
        Brethren, 794
Thomas, George, 163
Thomas, George W., 1792
    Nezperce, ID, Church of the Brethren,
        organization by, 935
    Peabody Church of the Brethren, KS,
        997

Thomas, Harry Eldon, 1792, 2306
    Pomona, CA, Church of the Brethren,
        pastor, 1045
Thomas, Harvey V., 1792
    Pleasant Center Church of the
        Brethren, OH, minister, 1030
Thomas, Herbert Roland, 1380, 1792, 2306
Thomas, Irvin, 1792
Thomas, Isaac, 424, 759
Thomas, Isaac J., 1792
    New Virginia, IA, Brethren Church, as
        minister, 932
    Osceola, IA, Church of the Brethren,
        minister, 983
Thomas, Isaac W., 1792
Thomas, Isaiah, 2081
Thomas, J. Irvin, 1330
Thomas, J. L., 430, 442
Thomas, J. Walter, 1792
Thomas, J. William, 1223, 1792
    Salem Old German Baptist Brethren
        Church, OH, elder-in-charge, 1139
Thomas, Jacob (Bangor, MI), 1792
Thomas, Jacob M., 101, 272, 273,
    1262–1263, 1792
    Salem Church of the Brethren, WV,
        1138
Thomas, Jacob (Mount Etna, IA), 1792
Thomas, Jacob (Pleasant Valley, VA), 1792
Thomas, Jacob (Spring Creek, VA), 1792
Thomas, James A., 1792
Thomas, James L., 124, 1792, 2295
    Prairie City Church of the Brethren,
        IA, elder, 1050
Thomas, Jennifer Ellen, 2157
    Mexico City, Mexico, Brethren
        Mission, 2222
Thomas, Jeremiah, 1263, 1287, 1792
Thomas, Jesse Irwin, 1792
Thomas, Jim, 275
Thomas, John, 1262, 1263, 1792
Thomas, John, (1826–1891), 353
Thomas, John Andrew, 1792
Thomas, John E., 237, 565, 1792–1793
Thomas, John L., 72
Thomas, Lawrence Eugene, 1793
Thomas, Lewis Edward, 105, 704, 1793,
    2081
    South Keokuk Church of the Brethren,
        IA, part-time pastor, 1205
Thomas, Magdalena Maust, 1262, 1263
Thomas, Margaret, 275
Thomas, Margretha Bosserman Koch, 163
Thomas, Marion, 165
Thomas, Marion R., 30, 320, 515, 1793
Thomas, Mary Fike, 1262
Thomas, Michael, 1262, 1263
Thomas, Michael J., 1793
    New Virginia, IA, Brethren Church, as
        minister, 932
    Osceola, IA, Church of the Brethren,
        minister, 983
Thomas, Michael M., 1793
Thomas, OK, Church of the Brethren, **1263**
Thomas, Oscar Reeves, 1793
Thomas, Paul, Jr.
    Pleasant Chapel Church of the
        Brethren, IN, called to ministry,
        1030
Thomas, Peter Swope, 276, 1793
Thomas, Philip, 1793
Thomas, Phyllis Knapp, 2081
Thomas, Ralph Franklin, 1793, 2081

Romine Church of the Brethren, IL,
    providing leadership, 1121
Thomas, Raymond L., 673, 1793
Thomas, Richard Wood, Sr., 2295
    on faith questions and answers, 2360
Thomas, Ricky Lane, 2295
Thomas Road Baptist Church of Lynch-
    burg, VA, 232
Thomas, Rodger Jay, 2295
Thomas, Rodney A., 1793
Thomas, S. Marguerite, 2081
Thomas, Samuel B., 1793
Thomas, Silas, 1793, 2081
Thomas, Susanah Miller, 1262, 1263
Thomas, Susanna Sanger, 1263
Thomas, Susanna Seese, 1263
Thomas, Susannah, 163
Thomas, Susie Mae, 1845, 2081, 2360
Thomas, V., 1793
Thomas, Walter S., 1793
Thomas, Wilbur, 248
Thomas, Wilbur L., 1793
Thomas, William Ernest, 204, 269, 758,
    1793
Thomas, William J., 759, 1793
Thomas, William (Ontario), 1793
Thomas, William (Pleasant View, PA), 1793
Thomasius, Christian, 614
Thomasson, Kermon Robert, 1845, 2081
    on CB in Nigeria, 2360
    Messenger, editor, 819
    Thomasson, Margaret Wampler, 1845
    on Snow Hill Nunnery, 2360
Thommens family
    Schelbert, Leo on, 2355
Thompkins, Alice L. (later Huffaker), 635
Thompson, Alby, Elmer, 1793
Thompson, Betty Carter
    Thompson, Robert W. (FGBC) and, 2256
Thompson, Carrie, 720
Thompson, Charles Dillard
    on OGBB, 2360–2361
Thompson, Christine
    Mount Union (Airpoint) Church of the
        Brethren, VA, deaconess, 887
Thompson, Daniel W., 2081, 2295
Thompson, Dave E., 1793
Thompson, David, 16, 1212, 1793
    Pleasant Grove Grace Brethren Church,
        IA, pastor, 1031
Thompson, Donald, 239
Thompson, Mrs. Donald, 239
Thompson, Doris Elizabeth, 1837
Thompson, Ezekiel Gerald, 1793
    Pleasant View Church of the Brethren,
        PA, 1037
    Pleasant View Church of the Brethren,
        PA, elder-in-charge, 1037
Thompson, F. J., 2082
Thompson family
    Hardtmann (Hardman, Hartman)
        family, 583
    Lybrook, NM, Tók'ahookaadí Church
        of the Brethren, 2216
    Orange, CA, Grace Brethren Church,
        975
Thompson, G. C., 1793
    Thompson, Joel Kent and, 2255
Thompson, Goldianne, 2081
Thompson, Howard
    Mount Union (Airpoint) Church of the
        Brethren, VA, deacon, 887
Thompson, I. O., 1793

Thompson, J. O., 1793
Thompson, Janine Katonah
    Thompson, Joel Kent and, 2255
Thompson, Joel Kent, 195, 539, 1335,
    1793, 1845, 2081, 2140,
    2255–2256, *2256,* 2306, **2386,**
    2388
    Roann, IN, Church of the Brethren,
        pastor, 1112
Thompson, John W., 368, 1793
Thompson, Joshua (1838–1871), 1793
Thompson, Joshua (Carter Depot, TN),
    1793
Thompson, Kevin
    Thompson, Joel Kent and, 2255
Thompson, Kraig
    Thompson, Joel Kent and, 2255
Thompson, Lester, 239
Thompson, Mrs. Lester, 239
Thompson, Lois
    Thompson, Joel Kent and, 2255
Thompson, Margaret May Sherman, 2295
Thompson, Paul Evans, 1793
Thompson, Phyllis Darlene Yount, 1845
    Thompson, Joel Kent and, 2255
Thompson, Raymond W., 115, 2306
Thompson, Renee
    Thompson, Joel Kent and, 2255
Thompson, Robert E. S., 2082
Thompson, Robert W. (FGBC), 188, 1337,
    2256, 2306
Thompson, Rollin Jan, 1335, 1845, 2082,
    2171, *2171,* 2295
    Sudan (CB) and, 2253
Thompson, Roma Jo Mickey, 1845, 2171
    Sudan (CB) and, 2253
Thompson, Ron E., 620, 1793, 2295
    Richmond, VA, Grace Brethren
        Church, pastor, 1108
Thompson, Roy, 2082
Thompson, S. E., 21, 530, 743
Thompson, S. H., 1793
Thompson, Samuel, 701
Thompson, Samuel P., 1793
Thompson, Silas Claben, 1793
Thompson, Stephen F., 1793
Thompson, Susan Louise, 1849
Thompson, Vera Brubaker, 2082
Thompson, Wendell S., 1793
Thompson, William Edward, 1793
Thompson, William H., 1793
Thompstown, PA, 1281
Thomsonian System of Medical Practice,
    2146
Thoreau, Henry David, 313
Thorn Chapel, VA
    Simmons family, 1182
Thornapple Church of the Brethren, MI,
    248, 753, **1263**
    Elmdale, MI, Church of the Brethren,
        442
    Hope Church of the Brethren, MI, 629
    Michigan Brethren settlement, 824
    migration of Brethren, 829
    Rodney Church of the Brethren, MI,
        1119
Thornapple, MI, German Baptist Brethren,
    248, 318, *See also* Campbell Old
    German Baptist Brethren Church
Thorne, Dorothy Golbert, 2082
Thorne family, 171
Thornley, Jeffrey Mark, 1253, 2186, 2295
Thornton, CA, Brethren Church

Ingraham, M. Virgil, 2208
Thornton, Charles G., 227, 725, 1240
    Millersburg, OH, Grace Brethren
        Church, 2224
Thornton, Daniel E., 2295
Thornton, Wile Frank, 2295
Thorny Bottom Church of the Brethren,
    WV, **1263**
Thorny Bottom congregation, VA
    Highland Co. Mission Church of the
        Brethren, VA, 605
Thornydale Elementary School, Tucson,
    AZ, meetingplace for Northwest
    Brethren Chapel, 1278
Thorpe family
    Howard Co. Old German Baptist
        Brethren Church, IN, 633
Thorton, Charles G., 527, 1793
Thralls, Don J. W., 1793
Thralls, Kenneth O., 40, 141, 1793
three estates, *See* Estates General or States
    General
Three Mile Island
    emergency evacuation, 952
Three Springs Church of the Brethren, PA,
    161, **1263–1264**
    Farmers Grove Fellowship (BC), PA,
        476
Three Springs, PA, Baptist congregation
    Rockhill Furnace, PA, Rockhill Church
        of the Brethren, ecumenical feder-
        ation with, 1118
Three Top congregation, NC
    Flat Rock Church of the Brethren, NC,
        493
Thrilling Echoes from the Wild Frontier
    (Flory), 747
Throne, Alfred A., 1793
Throne, Bonnie Carol, 1844
Throne, George Samuel, 1794
    Silver Creek Church of the Brethren,
        OH, 1182
Throne, George M., 1793–1794
Throne, John E., 1794
The Thunderstorm (Rhoades), 747
Thune, Nils, 2082
Thurian, Max
    on CB and baptism, eucharist and
        ministry, 2361
Thurley Homes, Winona, MN, Church of
    the Brethren, 1351
Thurman, Lulu (later Kesler), 690
Thurman, William C., 43, 177, 315, 334,
    364, 498, 561, 571, **1264,** 1308,
    1373, 2023, 2082–2083, *See also*
    Greenmount Council
    Brethren minister, and Seventh-Day
        Adventist followers, 1169
    eschatology, 454
    followers of, and feetwashing mode,
        1186
    Maine, debate held in, 783
    Massachusetts Brethren activity, 801
    millennialism, 834
    The Morning Watch, publisher, 876
Thurmanites, 334, **1264**
    chart of Brethren bodies, place on,
        1403–1405
    feetwashing dispute, 1186
    Mount Zion-Linville Church of the
        Brethren, VA, 888
    named after leader, 910
Thurmont, MD, Church of the Brethren,

1264
Thurneysen, Eduard, 2083
Thurston, Marian Doris, 1853–1854
Tibbens family, *See* Rinehart family
Tice, Effie J. Onas, 2106
Tice family
    Peabody Old German Baptist Brethren
        Church, KS, 997
Tice, James Gardner, 1794
Ticknor, Bessie, 2083
Tidrick, F. M.
    debate with Owen C. Cripe, 1912
Tiffin, OH
    Church of the Brethren, **1264**
    Seneca Church of the Brethren, OH,
        mission point, 1166
Tigner family
    Sharon Church of the Brethren,
        Alberta, Canada, 1172
Tigner, William H., 502, 1194, 1212, 1305
    Sharon Church of the Brethren,
        Alberta, Canada, 1172
    Mount Hope Church of the Brethren,
        WA, 882
Tijuana, Mexcio
    Buen Pastor Church, 1142
    missions, 862
Til Eulenspiegel (folk figure), 2147
Tilberg, Frederick, 2083
Tiller, Garnett, 1794
Tiller, Mrs. Garnett
    Oakvale Church of the Brethren, WV,
        leadership by, 958
    Olean Church of the Brethren, VA,
        leadership by, 973
Tilley, James
    Maple Grove Church of the Brethren,
        NC, minister, 790
Tilley, James Clarence, 209, 1794
    Pleasant Hill Church of the Brethren,
        TN, pastor/elder, 1032
Tilley, Jay
    New Haven Church of the Brethren,
        NC, pastor in, 928
    Shelton Church of the Brethren, NC,
        pastor in, 1176
Tillman family
    Meyer family related by marriage, 822
Tilman Co., OK
    Red River Church of the Brethren, OK,
        1089
Tilsman, A. L., 1794
Tilton, Edward
    Huntingdon, PA, Stone Church of the
        Brethren, 637
1 and 2 Timothy
    Kent, Homer Austin, Jr. on, 2340
Timber Creek Church of the Brethren, VA,
    See Roanoke, VA, Hollins Road
    Church of the Brethren
Timbercrest
    Mexico, IN, Church of the Brethren,
        821
Timbercrest (retirement home), **1264–1265**
    Cable, William H., 2155
    Helman, Patricia Kennedy, 2197
    Old Folks and Orphans Home (CB),
        Mexico, IN, 966
Timberlake, Lewis, 246
Timberville, VA, Church of the Brethren,
    746, **1265,** 1291
    Mount Olivet Church of the Brethren,
        VA, 886

Brethren Old Folks' Home, 1265
Fairview-Endless Caverns Church of the Brethren, VA, 470
Flat Rock Church of the Brethren, VA, 493
Pleasant View Church of the Brethren, VA, 1037
TIME, 203, *See* Training in Ministry Experiences (TIME); Training in Missionary Endeavor
Time
Murray, Don, 626
Timmons, Bennie W., 1794
Timmons, Glenn Frank, 758, 1276, 1794
Timmons, W. Ben, 264
Timotheus, Brother, *See* Mack, Alexander, Jr.
1 Timothy
1:19, 55
2:4–6, 55
"Timothy Teams"
GBC Christian Education (Department), 533
Tingley, Henry, 263, 1794
Tingley, J., 1794
Tinkcom, Harry M., 2083
Tinkcom, Margaret B., 2083
Tinkel, Della (later Garber), 528, 529
Tinkel, Jacob C., 723, 1794
Tinkel, John W., 1794
Tinkel, Paul D., 1794
Retirement Board (BC), 1102
Tinker Creek, VA, Church of the Brethren
Roanoke, VA, Hollins Road Church of the Brethren, 1113
Tinkham, George H., 2083
Tinkle, Arthur H., 1794, **2386**
Marion, IN, Brethren Church, pastor, 793
Sidney, IN, Grace Brethren Church, pastor, 1181
Tinkle, Arthur J., Jr., 1794
Tinkle, William J., 1794, 2083
Tinkling Spring, VA, 2100
Tinsman, George H., Jr., 1794
Tiosa, IN, 1338
Brethren Church, **1265**
Riddle, Earl M., minister, 1108
Tipp City (Middle District), OH, congregation
Salem Church of the Brethren, OH, 1138
Tipp City, OH, 535
Middle District Church of the Brethren, **1265**
Mohler, Samuel, 868
West Charleston Church of the Brethren, **1265**
Tippecanoe and Blue Ridge College River, IN, congregation, 153
Tippecanoe, IN, 1345
German Baptist Brethren Church, *See* Blue River Old German Baptist Brethren Church, IN
Fairview Church of the Brethren, IN, 468
North Webster, IN, Church of the Brethren, 951
Tippecanoe, MO, congregation, *See* Schuyler German Baptist Brethren Church, MO
Tippecanoe Old German Baptist Brethren Church, IN, *See* Tipton, R. Vance,

1794
Tipton, R. Vance, 1294, 1794
Petersons Chapel Church of the Brethren, NC, 1012
Pigeon River Church of the Brethren, NC, minister, 1023
Tiraku, Nigeria, 306
Tire Hill Church of the Brethren, PA, **1265**
Maple Spring Church of the Brethren, PA, 791
100 year anniversary, 1979
Tisdale, William, 1323, 1794
Tiskilwa, IL
Plow Creek Fellowship, 1038
Tissel family
history of, 1912
Titer (Teeter), John, 1794
tithe system
Rockingham Co., VA, 2077
Titler, George, 1794
Titler, John (1805–1865), 1794
Titler, John (1823–1868), 1794
Titles, Honorific, **1266**
Titlow, Elizabeth (later Reiff), 1094
Tittle, Maynard G., 527, 1794
Titus, 3:5, 84
Kent, Homer Austin, Jr. on, 2340
Titus, Albert, 1794
Titus, Michael R., 2295
Tjoelker, A., 2083
To Save a Soul from Death (Miller), 842
To Serve the Present Age, Durnbaugh, D. F., editor, 974
tobacco, 7, 203, 398, **1266**
article about, 1936
Brethren views on growing and use of, 2089
discipline, doctrine of, 388
Dunkard Brethren, 409
Evangelical Association, 459
Fellowship of Grace Brethren Churches (FGBC), 486
Hess, Maurice Abram, 601
McFadden, Joyce on stance of CB on, 2344
nonconformity, 940
Old Brethren German Baptist Church, 965
Old German Baptist Brethren, 941
Old Order German Baptist Church, 972
publications on, 7
United Brethren in Christ, 1290
Walnut Creek Old German Baptist Brethren Church, MO, controversy over, 1315
Tobias family, 319, 2080
Tobias, Francis Henry, 1794
Tobias, Mary Ann, 2080
Tobias, Wendell Hanna, 1794
Tobin's Business College, used as meeting place
Waterloo, IA, (First) Brethren Church, 1321
Tobler, John, 2046
Todd, Aubrey, 1794
Todd, George, 241
Todd, Richard E., 2295
Tok'ahookaadi' Church, *See* Lybrook, NM, Tok'ahookaadi' Church of the Brethren
Native Americans, 2230
Tokyo
Christian education world convention,

364
Toledo, Jorge, 2172
Hispanic Ministries (CB), 2198
Vega Baja, PR, Iglesia de los Hermanos Cristo El Señor (CB) and, 2258
Toledo, OH, 720
congregation, 1932
Heatherdowns Church of the Brethren, **1266–1267**
Maumee Valley Grace Brethren Church, **1267,** 1380
Toler, Harry E., 1794
tolerance, *See* religious tolerance
Toleration Act of 1689
Society of Friends (Quakers), 1199
toleration (religious), *See* religious tolerance
Toll Gate schoolhouse, 406
Lewistown, PA, Church of the Brethren, 739
Tollardo, David, 1794
Tolleson, W. S. H., 1794
Tolley, S. C., 1794
Tolstoy, Leo
Gandhi, Mohandas Karamchand, 528
Tolzmann, Don Heinrich, 1861–1862
Tombaugh, Anna Bauman, 1267
Tombaugh, Annie Ranck, *473*
Tombaugh, Delilah, 1220
Tombaugh, Etta, 1360, 1794
Tombaugh family, 413, 2083
Tombaugh, George C. (family), *473*
Tombaugh, Hez, 1794
Tombaugh, Jacob, 1794
Rodney Church of the Brethren, MI, minister, 1119
Tombaugh, James M., 102, 578, 746, **1267,** 1320, 1324, 1794, 2083
Mapleville, MD, Brethren Church, pastor, 791
Miamisburg, OH, Brethren Church, pastor, 823
Tombaugh, Lydia Letherman, 1267
Tombaugh, Reno, 2083
Tombaugh, Solomon, 1267
Tombaugh, Verlin Carl, 1794
Tombaugh, William E., 1794
tombstones
Brethren movement, 267
cemeteries, 2090
inscriptions
Bermudian Church of the Brethren Cemetery, 2084
Keim family, 2084
Stump family, 2084
Showalter, Michael S. on Cocalico Valley, IL, 2356
Tomlonson, James Eugene, 1794, 2083
Root River Church of the Brethren, MN, pastor, 1122
Tomlonson, John Dean, 681, 1794
Tompkins Co., NY
Mission work in, 933
Tompkins, Dock, 749
Tompkins, Jonathan, 2295
Tom's Branch, KY, preaching point, 405
Tom's Run meetinghouse, West Alexandria, OH, 1235, 1333
Tonalea, AZ, Red Lake Community Grace Brethren Church, 1267
Tonasket, WA, 1342, 1364
Toney, Carey, 1794

Toney family
family history, 1962
Four Mile Church of the Brethren, IN, 505
Toney, N. S., 1794
Toney, William S., 1794
Tönnies, Ferdinand, on plain people, 1029
Tooker, Dora Belle, 1844
Tooker, Grant, 445, 1794
Wetonka, SD, Willow Creek Church of the Brethren, 2379
Tooker, Lester, 246
Toon, Joene, 1848
Topeco Church of the Brethren, VA, 21, 231, 345, 727, **1267**, 1308, 1326
Floyd Co. Church of the Brethren, VA, 500
Mount Jackson Church of the Brethren, VA, 882
Pleasant Hill Church of the Brethren, VA, 1033
Rock Hill Church of the Brethren, 1267
Smith River Church of the Brethren, VA, 1192
West Arm, 1267
Topeka, IN, Church of the Brethren, **1267**
Shipshewana, IN, Church of the Brethren, organized from, 1177
Topeka, KS, 682
Church of the Brethren, **1267**
Toppenish, WA, Grace Brethren Church, **1267**
Topsfield Terrace, 181, *See also* Brethren Care, Inc., South Bend, IN
Torah, D., 1794
Torbert, Robert G., 2083
Tories, *See* Loyalists; Loyalists in American Revolution
tornado damage
Kokomo, IN, Church of the Brethren, 705
Wabash Country Church of the Brethren, IN, 1311
Worden Church of the Brethren, WI, 1365
Toroian, J. Simon, 265
Toroian, Simon, 318
Toroian, Simon T., 21, 2306
Torolan, Simon, 1794
Toronto, Canada, 250
Toronto, Ontario
international Sunday school convention addressed by Brumbaugh, M. G., 1273
Stump, Abraham, family of, 1232
Torrance, CA South Bay Grace Brethren Church, **1267–1268**
Torre[j]on Navaho Mission, Sandoval Co., NM, 322, 410, 539, 931, **1268**, 2160, 2174, 2175, 2230
Christian Day School movement, 282
Daily Vacation Bible Schools, 359
Dallas Center, IA, Church of the Brethren, and volunteers for, 360
medical care, 810
medical missions, 808
mission schools, 853
missions, 860, 2225
Reed, Kyle Thayer (DB) and, 2240
Reed, William Sherman, minister, 1091
Torrey, Reuben A., 136
McClain, Alva J., 772

Winona Lake Auditorium, IN, 1353
Total Mobilization
missions, 2225
totalitarian government
socialism, 1198
Toth, Karoly, 286
Totzauer (Totzaurer), Michael, 738, 1794–1795
"The Touch of the Master's Hand"
poetry, 1040
Touring the Holy Land (Myers), 904
tourism, *See* Brethren Heritage Tours
Ephrata Community, 451
Towe, William H., 1795
St. Paul Church of the Brethren, NC, minister, 1135
Tower City, PA, Church of the Brethren, *See* Shamokin, PA, Church of the Brethren
Town and Country Brethren Church, Tampa, FL, 1247
town hall, services held in, 689
Towner, Co., ND, 223, 321
Cando, ND, congregation, 946
Egeland, ND, Church of the Brethren, 430
Ellison Church of the Brethren, ND, 442
migration of Brethren, 830
Towns, Harmon, 1795
Townsend, Charles, 760
Townsend, France R., 2295
Townsend, George Alfred, 747, 2083
Townsend, George D., 2295
Townsend, Harley V., 94, 1795
Townsend, Kenneth G., 2295
Townsend, Leah, 2083
Townsend, Ralph H., 1845
medical projects, 808
Townview congregation, OH, 1276
Toy, James, 268
Tracey family
Oak Grove Church of the Brethren, MO, 956
Tracey, James H., 1795
Mount Pleasant Church of the Brethren, IN, 886
Tract Examining Committee, 1268
Gospel Messenger Advisory Committee, 559
Rosenberger, Isaac J., member, 1123
tract ministry
missions, 858
Old Brethren Church, 2232
Pleasant Hill Church of the Brethren, PA, 1032
Tract Society, *See* Gospel Tract Association
tractor projects/tractor unit
China, **1268,** *1269*
Ethiopia, 458
Peace Corps, 1002
Russia, 1288
United Nations Relief and Rehabilitation Administration (UNRRA), 1291
tractors
Old Order German Baptists and use of, 972
Tract Examining Committee, **1268**
tracts, **1269–1270,** 1946
biography of Weir, Samuel, 1332
Brethren Church, 167, 195, 196
Brethren Publishing House, 300

Brethren rejoinder to Quaker tract, 1946
Church of the Brethren, 179, 203
Eshelman, Matthew Mays, 455
General Church Erection and Missionary Committee (CB), 536
General Mission Board (CB), 538
Ein geringer Schein (*A Humble Gleam*)*,* 132
Gospel Tract Association, 561
Gross, Andreas, 574
Grubb, Luther L., 575
Hoover, Samuel W., 628
Hoxie, George W., 633
Humberd, Russell I., 636, 1976
India, 651
"It is the Hand of Christ!", 1978
Landes, David, 1993
mass media, 800
missions, 860
noncreedalism, 942
publication of, 192, 195, 196, 204, 205
Quinlan, James T., 1076
World War I peace literature, 1370
Tracy, CA, 1223
Grace Brethren Church, **1270**
Tracy, Pauline Shafer, 2083
tradition
devaluation of, 133–134
Trafford, PA, *See* East McKeesport, PA, Church of the Brethren
Trageser, Lillian Fances (later Brumbaugh), 2274
Trahair, Richard C. S.
on Ephrata Cloister, 2361
Trail Co., ND, 321
training
lay speakers, 730
Training in Ministry Experience (TIME)
youth and, 2269
Training in Ministry (TRIM), 2140, 2164
Miller, Donald Eugene, 2223
Training in Missionary Endeavor (TIME), **1270**
developed from Brethren Student Life Volunteers, 1231
GBC Christian Education (Department), 533
Training the Sunday School Teacher (Hoff), 616
trains, *See* railroads
Transactions, 2083
transatlantic passage, **1270,** *See also* emigrants and emigration; ships
Boni, Andreas, letter with best route to America, 159
emigration, Brethren, 443
Kalcklöser, Johann Heinrich; signor of open letter warning of dangers of, 681
Käsebier, Johann Georg; letter to Count Ernst Casimir giving impressions of, 684
Krefeld to Pennsylvania, 1270
luggage and dress for, *150*
medicine, 809
Naas, Johannes, description by, 1270
published reports warning immigrants, 1270
redemptioners, 1090
Rhine River, reaching European ports by way of, 1106–1107
Transit II

Shaffer, Kenneth M., Jr. on texts in, 2357
Snyder, Graydon F. on texts in, 2357
translations, *See* Bible translations
Grieve, Jerry Allen, 2194
Guli, John, 2195
Hispanic Ministries (BC), 2198
Kulp, Harold Stover, 709
Luther translation published by Henry Kurtz, 711
Miller, John William, 2224
transportation, *See* transatlantic passage; travel
automobiles, 228
buggies, 228
horse-drawn buggies, 1994
Trapp, Nicholas, 570, 1795
Trappe, PA, Tri-County Grace Brethren Church, **2256**
Traub, George, 2295
Traugh, Mary Lou (later Hall), 1643
Traughber, Earl Hiram, 520, 1795
Traup, Henry, 1795
Traut family
Dutchman's Creek German Baptist Brethren Church, NC, 411
Traut, Georg Balthasar "Balser," 1270
Traut, Henrich Johann, 392, 704
Traut, Jeremiah, 1270
Traut, Johann Henrich or Heinrich, 506, 720, **1270**
Traut, Philip, 1271
Traut (Trout) family, **1270–1271**
travel and travelogues
Asia, 2101
by bicycle, around the world, 2072
Canada, 2103
domestic, **1271,** *1272*
Europe, 2101
foreign, **1271–1274,** *1272, 1273*
Wieand, Albert Cassel, 1344
Winger, Otho and Ida Miller Winger, 1351
Yoder, Joseph J., 1386
Holy Land, 2101
Illinois, 2103
Indiana, 2103
Michigan, 2103
Miller, Daniel Long, 2012
Miller, Daniel Long and Elizabeth Talley, 836, 837
missionary conferences, 856
New York, 2103
Ohio, 2103
Old German Baptist Brethren, 969, 2233, 2234
Pennsylvania, 2103
publishing books about, 1069
railroads, on, by Brethren, 1081
world, and photographic slide shows, 1020
Zigler, M. Robert, 2111
Travelers Rest, SC, Church of the Brethren, 1205, **1274**
Traveling Through the Dark (Stafford), 1216
Traver, R. Glen, 1795, 2130
Travis, Daniel D., 2295
Travis, William, 2083–2084
Treadway, William Eugene, 2084
treason
Sauer, Christopher, II, charged with, 1146

A Treatise on Trine Immersion (Teeter, L. W.), 1250
Treaty of Rijswick, 990
Treaty of Westphalia, *See* Westphalia, Peace of
Trechsel, R., 2084
Trefry, Robert A., 2295
Treher, Charles W., 2084
Treiber, Ludwig, 405
Tremaine, Marie, 1862
Tremont, PA, Pine Grove Grace Brethren Church, **1274**
Trenner, Edward A., 1795, 2295
Orange, CA, Grace Brethren Church, elder, 975
Trent, Council of, 1120
Trent, Sarah (later Flora), 494
Tresise, Foster, 590, 1312, 1795
Tresise, Marguerite, 590
Tressier, J. Ward, 1795
Tressier, Osmer, 1795
Tressler, J. Ward, 21, 275, 318, 515, 705, 725
Trevilian Church of the Brethren, VA, 1274
Mine Run Church of the Brethren, VA, 843
Trevino family
Mabton, WA, Grace Brethren Church, 771
Treytorrens, Nicolas Samuel de, **1274,** 2084, 2088
prisons, 1059
trials, **1274–1275**
Eller, Enten, 2176–2177
Triandiflou, George, 1795
Tridle, Mary Jane (later Ulrey), 1285
Trimble, David B., 2084
Trimble, Glenn W., 2098
Trimmer, Chauncey E. (Franklin?), 1795
Trimmer, D. K., 1795
Trimmer, Emory P., 270
Trimmer family, 1389
Trimmer, Jacob E., 1795
Trimmer, Peter, 765, 1795
Trimmer, Rodney W., 2084
Trimmer, William, 765, 1795
Trin Valley meetinghouse, near West Alexandrie, OH, 1235
Trindale, Ivanildo C., 2295
trine, 82
Trine, E. L. S., 2084
trine immersion, 43, 82, 83, 85, 1250, 1275, 1872, 1975, 2021, 2022, 2039, 2040, *See also* baptism
article about, 1918
Brethren Church doctrine on, 183
Dowie, John Alexander, 1400
Dutch Bethel, German Baptist Brethren Church, 2373
Fahnestock, William M., on, 1934
Fellowship of Grace Brethren Churches, 2178, 2181, 2182
Holdeman, John, 618
Hon, Peter Keithly, 627
Honites, 628
Hostetler Brethren, 631
Mack, Alexander, Sr., receiving and performing, 776
"Message of the Brethren Ministry," 818
Primitivism, 1058
rebaptism, 1085
restitution, 1100

Teeter, Lewis Wallace, 1250
Triune Immersion (Quinter), 1077
Wolfe, George, II, 1357
trine immersions, *See under* baptism, doctrine of
Trinidade, Eulalio, 173
Trinity
abandoned by Universalists, 1292
Brethren movement, 289
Christian Brethren, 281
debates, 371
doctrine of, 409, **1275**
Ephrata Community, 448
Islam, 664
reference to in anointing, 39
Reformation, Protestant, and Brethren doctrine, 1092
rejection of, 68
in statement of faith, 1218
Trinity Church of the Brethren, MD, *See* Baltimore, MD, Trinity Church of the Brethren
Trinity Church of the Brethren, MI, *See* Redford, MI, Trinity Church of the Brethren
Trinity Church of the Brethren, OH, *See* Sidney, OH, Trinity Church of the Brethren
Trinity Church of the Brethren, VA, **1275,** 1277
Mount Zion Church of the Brethren, VA, 888
Trinity congregations
example of biblically inspired name, 911
Trinity, MI, Church of the Brethren, 2084
Trinity United Methodist congregation
Scalp Level, PA, Church of the Brethren, sharing building, 1151–1152
Trinity University
Stuckey, Melvin Atwood, 1229
Trinity, VA, 164
Trinity, VA, Church of the Brethren, 2084
Trinus Immersio (Beaver), 1872
Triplehorn, Bruce W., 2296
Tripp school
Saline Valley church of the Brethren, KS, 1139
Trippstadt, Palatinate
Huber-Hoover family, 2073
Tritt, June Replogle, 417, 1845
Tritt, Ray L., 417, 1845
Triune Immersion (Quinter), 1077
Trobaugh, Alexander
Pineville, VA, Mount Olive Brethren Church, 1025
Trobaugh, H. L., 1795
Trochelmann, William, 1795
Trocmé, André, 432
Troeltsch, Ernst, **1275,** 2084
plain people, 1029
sect-church typology, 1164–1165
Trolinger family, 1914
Trombley, Claude E., 399, 1795
Tropico, CA, Church of the Brethren, 348, 759, **1275**
Trostle, Alice (later Gingrich), 550
Trostle, Alice Wingert, 1276
Trostle congregation, PA, 1294
Trostle, Elizabeth Pfoutz, 160
Trostle, Ephraim P., 1276, 1795
Trostle, Ernest Ciffford, 1795

Trostle, Eva Alora, 137, 394, **1276**
    Moody Bible Institute, 873
Trostle family, 161, 695, **1276**
Trostle, Ida (later Bonsack), 160, 2134
    Miller, Blanche Bonsack, mother of,
        834
Trostle, Isabella Spangler, 1276
Trostle, J. P., 1795
Trostle, J. W., 348, 695, 1217, 1795
Trostle, Jacob Diehl, 415, 752, 1276, 1795
    McPherson, KS, First Church of the
        Brethren, elder, 779
    Monitor Church of the Brethren, KS,
        elder, 869
    Monrovia, MD, Bush Creek Church of
        the Brethren, elder, 870
Trostle, John, 160, 1276, 1795
Trostle, Joseph, 1276
Trostle, Katie Rowland, 1276
Trostle, Levi, 1276, 1795
Trostle, Mary, 236
Trostle, Mary (later Lehman), 736
Trostle, Michael, 1276
Trostle, Percival J., 1795
Trostle, Sarah Pfoutz, 1276
Trostle, Sarah Van Orsdal, 1276
Trostle, Susan Diehl, 1276
Trostle, William E., 432, 754, 1276, 1795
    Pasadena, CA, Church of the Brethren,
        pastor in, 994
Trotwood congregation, OH, 1355
Trotwood, OH
    Church of the Brethren, 102, 963, **1276**
    Grace Brethren Church, 366, 447, **1276**
Troublesome Creek, Kentucky, 689
Troup, Ella, 407
Troup, H. H.
    Maxwell, IA, Church of the Brethren,
        minister, 803
Troup, Henry, 1795
Troup, Jeanette, 727
Trousdale, Joseph, 1795
Trout, Amy Naomi (later White), 1339
Trout, Andrew, 1276
Trout, Charles E., 1795
    Roanoke, VA, Ninth Street Church of
        the Brethren, preaching, 1113
Trout, David, 1271, 1795
Trout, Eliza Bennett, 1276
Trout family, 2084, *See also Out of the
    Melting Pot;* Traut family
    Oak Grove Church of the Brethren,
        MO, 956
Trout, Henry F., 1795
Trout, Henry T.
    Sand Brook Church of the Brethren,
        NJ, minister, 1142
Trout, Isaiah Bennett, 205, 1271, **1276,**
    1339, 1795, 2084
    Brethren Publishing House, 1276
    National Normal University, 1276
    Our Young People, 985
Trout, J. B., 1795
Trout Lake, MI
    Ozark Grace Brethren Church, MI, 987
Trout, Mary Dannehower, 2084
Trout, Philip, 1271
Trout Run,, PA, congregation, 347
Trout Run Valley Church of the Brethren,
    WV, **1276**
Trout, Sarah Elizabeth Myers, 1339
Trout, Thomas James, 2084
Trout, William Henry, 2084

Troutdale, OR, Grace Brethren Church,
    1276–1277
Troutville, VA, Church of the Brethren,
    164, 262, 1275, **1277**
Troutville, VA, Grace Bible Brethren
    Church, **1277**
Trowbridge, Glen Ellsworth, 1795
Troxel, David, 1795, 2296
    Milmine Church of the Brethren, IL,
        elder, 843
Troxel, Elias, 1795
Troxel family, 2007
Troxel, Henry, 1795
    Pleasant Valley Church of the Brethren,
        TX, minister, 1035
Troxel, Jacob, 1795
Troxel, Jacob (d. 1905), 54
Troxel, Jacob J., 340, 572, 1795
Troxel, Joseph, 1795
Troxel, Joseph J., 1795
Troxel, Levi W., 531, 1795
Troxel, Minnie B., 2084
Troxell, Derwood Leroy, 1346, 1795
Troy Co., MO, 1292
Troy German Baptist Brethren Church,
    MO, **1277**
Troy, OH, Church of the Brethren, 261,
    1277
    sources on, 2311
Troy, OH, congregation, 261
Troy, OH, Grace Brethren Church, 319,
    1277
Troyer, Donna Jean, 1854
Troyer family, 1881
    North Solomon Old German Baptist
        Brethren Church, KS, 950
Troyer, John
    history, 1993
Troyer, Lester, 2084
Troyer, Levi Eli, 2084
Troyer, Luella, *See* Hooley family
Troyer, Lydia B. (later Miller), 2017
Troyer, Martha (later Miller), 2017, 2018
Troyer, Mary J.
    history of, 2016
Troyer, Nathaniel O., 1795
Troyer, Paul, *See* Hooley family
Troyer, Rachel (later Miller), 2017
Troyer, Sarah E. Weaver, 2084
Troyer, Zachariah, 268
Truax, Floyd A., 2306
Truax, Roger, 1795
Truax, William Ross, 1795
Truby, D. M., 1795
Truby, David
    Shipshewana, IN, Church of the
        Brethren, minister in, 1177
Trudeau, Barbara (later Hilliker)
    Island Pond, VT, Grace Brethren
        Church, 2209
True Christianity (Arndt), 1051
True Evangelical Obedience (Stein), 381
True Vital Piety (Eshelman), 381
Truit, J. B., 1795
Trujillo, Grace Sandoval, **1277**
Trujillo, John, 1267, 1277, 1795
Trujillo, Lee, **1277,** 1795–1796, 2306
Truman, Harry S. (President), 19
    CRALOG, 346
Trumbull Co., OH
    Mennonite Church, 2079
Trumbull Co., VA, 209
Trump, Charles L., 1796

Trump, Daniel, 1796
Trumper, Angelika (later Landes), 722
Trumpet and Universalist Magazine, 1292
The Trumpet Call, **1277–1278**
Trundle family, 1917
Trussell, John B. B., Jr., 1862
    works by, 2310
Trustee Board (Dunkard Brethren Church),
    1278
Trustees of the General Conference, **1278**
Trusty, H. Clay, 2084
The Truth About Tobacco (Finnell), 490
Tryon's war against the Regulators, 87
Tschetter, Evelyn Ruth, 1854
Tschetter, John, 2296
Tshudy, James A., 2084
Tuazon, Bernie
    Hope Brethren Fellowship, 2204
Tubbs, John L., 2296
tuberculosis sanitoriums
    Thalham Tubercular Sanitorium,
        Austria, 1255–1256
Tuchosokin (Tuckaseeking) Sabbatarian
    community
    Georgia, 540
Tucker, A. Granville, 515, 1796
Tucker Co., WV, 1287
    Mount Cassell Old German Baptist
        Brethren Church, WV, 880
    Red Creek Church of the Brethren,
        WV, 1088
Tucker, E. E., 1338, 1796
Tucker family
    in Neosho Valley Old German Baptist
        Brethren Church near, 923
Tucker, George W., 749, 1796
    Reddies River, NC, Riverside Church
        of the Brethren, minister, 1089
Tucker, Glenn, 2084
Tucker, Helen, 2084
Tucker, John (1831–1942), 1796
    Mud Valley Old German Baptist
        Brethren Church, IL, minister, 892
Tucker, John (Hagers Grove, MO), 1796
Tuckers, F. P., 2084
Tuckwiller family, 2087
Tucson, AZ
    urban ministry and, 2257
    Church of the Brethren, 237, **1278**
    (First) Brethren Church, 1251, **1278**
    Northwest Brethren Chapel, **1278**
    Silverbell Grace Brethren Church,
        1278
Tuigly, William, 1796
Tulare Co., CA, 744
Tuller, Edwin H., 22
Tully, Jesse, 1278
Tully, Richard B., 1278
Tully, Robert C., 1278
Tully, Robert W., 245, 248, 249, 1278,
    1796, 1907, 2084
    Newton, KS, Church of the Brethren,
        pastor in, 934
    recreation and youth, 1088
Tully, Ruth Weaver, **1278,** 2084
Tully, Winnie T., 1278
Tulpehocken, PA, 421, 1232, 1328
    Church of the Brethren, 712, **1278**
        Midway Church of the Brethren,
            PA, 827
        Myerstown, PA, Church of the
            Brethren, 905
        Reistville, PA, Heidelberg Church

of the Brethren, PA, 1095
Richland, PA, Church of the Brethren, 1107
congregation, 158, 225, 226, 733, 1340
German Baptist Brethren congregation, register of regular meetings, *844*
German Reformed congregation
Miller, Hans Michael, 837
Tumblers
as nickname of Brethren fellowships, 910
Tumplers
Georgia, 540
as nickname of Brethren fellowships, 910
Tunck-Täufer
as nickname of Brethren fellowships, 910
Tunckers
Materials Towards a History of the Baptists, 803
Tunes, **1278–1279**
Tuninys, ___, 1796
Tunker, 2084
Tunker-Baptists as name for Brethren, 429, 653, *See also* Brethren
Tunker House, Broadway, VA, 744, 745–746, 918, **1279,** *1279,* 1391
fraternal relations, 510
historic sites, 609
museums, 898
theology and, 2255
Yount, Joseph B., III on, 2365
Tunker, IN
place-names, Brethren, 1028
Tunker Society of Hampshire Co., VA, 106
Tunker Society, OH, congregation
Richland Church of the Brethren, OH, 1107
Tunkers, *See* Dunkard Brethren
as name for Brethren, 910
Tunkers, 2084–2085
Tunkers, Engl. Dunkers, 2085
Tuntland, Mrs. John, 2085
Tuolumne, CA
Old Brethren Christian Schools, 2232
Old Brethren Church, 2232
Tuolumne Co., CA
Sierra Pines Old German Baptist Brethren Church, CA, 1181
Tuolumne Old German Baptist Brethren Church, CA, 1280
Modesto, CA, Old German Baptist Brethren Church, 867
Turkey, 55, **1280,** *See also* specific cities, mission stations, and congregations
excavation sites in, Brethren visiting, 46
Fercken, Gaston John and Seline (Phebe), 488
Julien, Thomas T., 2210
Miller, D. L., travel to, 1280
mission schools, 853
missions, 860
missions, short-term, 2226
relief and rehabilitation work, 200
Turkey Creek Church of the Brethren, IN, 124, 914, **1280,** 1287
Maple Grove Church of the Brethren, IN, 789
Turkey Creek Church of the Brethren, KY, **1280**

Rock House Church of the Brethren, KY, 1117
Turkey Creek Church of the Brethren, MO, **1280**
Turkey Creek Church of the Brethren, NE, 920, **1280**
Turkey Creek Church of the Brethren, OK, **1280–1281**
Turkish empire, 22
Turley, Charles Eugene, 2296
Turley, John R., 1796, 2296
Turlock, CA, 733
Brethren Church, **1281**
Turman, Frank K., 1796, 2306
Turner, Alvah, 1796, 2306, **2386**
Sand Creek Old German Baptist Brethren Church, KS, elder-in-charge, 1143
Turner, Barbara, 1941
Turner, Charles Russell, 2296
Turner, Charles Whitaker, 192, 496, 1796, 2085, 2143, **2256,** *2256,* 2306
Rittman, OH, First Brethren Church, pastor, 1111
Turner, D. T., 1796
Turner, Daniel, 1796
Turner family
Shoal Creek Old German Baptist Brethren Church, Newton Co., MO, 1178
Turner, Frederick Jackson, 2085
historical writing, 612
Turner, Gale L., 2296
Turner, George A., 345, 1796
Turner, H. O., 1796
Turner, Hazel Frantz, 1941
Turner, Herman B., 257, 740, 1796
Turner, John (Rock Ridge, WI), 1796
Turner, John (Tomahawk, WV), 1796
Turner, Leonard Fernando, 1796
Turner, Mary Catherine (later Montgomery)
Montgomery, Michael, wife of, 872
Turner, Mildred E. (later Grant)
Grant, Richard E., 2193
Turner Mill
Valley Brethren-Mennonite Heritage Center and, 2258
Turner, Nat, 2128
Turner, Pearl Etta (later Hanawalt), 581, 1957
Turner, Robert R., 1796, 2306
Salunga, PA, Church of the Brethren, pastor, 1140
Turner, Samuel, 1796
Turner, Trenton, 641, 1796
Turner, Washington
Shoal Creek Old German Baptist Brethren Church, Newton Co., MO, deacon, 1178
Turner, Will, 323
Turner, Mrs. Will, 323
Turnmore Church of the Brethren, AR, **1281**
Turnridge, Ralph Edwin, 79, 1796
Seattle, WA, Lakewood Community Church, pastor, 1162
Turpin, M. B. A., 2085
Turpin, Roy Uriah, 407, 2296
Turtle Creek, PA, *See* East McKeesport, PA, Church of the Brethren
Turtle Mountain Church of the Brethren, ND, 251, **1281**
Ellison Church of the Brethren, ND,

442
Turtle Rock, VA, 1224
Tuscarawas Co, OH, 364
Brethren settlement, 961
Leatherman, John, 2384
New Philadelphia First Church of the Brethren, 931
Nicholson, John, minister in, 935
Tuscarawas, OH, Church of the Brethren, *See* Eden Church of the Brethren, OH
Tuscarora Church of the Brethren, PA, **1281**
Farmers Grove Fellowship (BC), PA, 476
Tuscola, IL, 713
Tusing, David Wellington, 1345, 1796
Tussing, Ann K. U.
on Beissel, Conrad, 2361
Tussley, J. W., 1796
Tuttle, Effie, 637
Tuttle, Steven Lynn, 1796
Twain, Mark, 2128, *See also* Clemens, Samuel
minorities, ethnic and racial, 851, *851*
Tweeddale, William F., 721, 1251, 1796
St. Petersburg, FL, Grace Brethren Church, pastor, 1135
Tweedie, Stephen William, 2085
Twelve Mile, IN, Brethren Church, *See* Corinth Brethren Church, IN
Twelve Mile school
Saline Valley church of the Brethren, KS, 1139
12th century, 15
20th century
admission into the church, 5
agriculture, Brethren and, 9, 12
Church of the Brethren, intellectual impact on, 1969
dancing, 26
degrees of ministry, 4
early, advertising, 7
education in the, 2
impact on Brethren intellectual life, 2
late
young brethren, 3
theological movements of, 73–74
Twenty-Eighth Street Church of the Brethren, Altoona, PA, 328
Committee on Understanding and Reconciliation (CB) , 328
Twenty Thousand Dunkers for Peace, **1281**
West, Daniel, 1331
Twin Church of the Brethren, OH, 1235, **1281,** 1295
Twin Creek, OH, congregation
Petry, Jacob, 1013
Twin Falls, ID, 1345
Church of the Brethren, **1281–1282**
Jackpot Church, NV, 2212
Twin Valley, OH, Church of the Brethren, *See* Lexington Church of the Brethren, OH
Two Brothers (ship)
voyage to America on, by Putterbach brothers, 1070
Two Centuries of Brothersvalley (Cooper), 342
Two Centuries of the Church of the Brethren, 140
conference, **1282**
(Falkenstein), 471
historical writing, 612

(Miller), 2012
Two-hundred-fiftieth Anniversary, founding
    of the Brethren, 17, 168, 2075,
    1282–1283, 2085, *See also* bicen-
    tennial celebration
    Flora, Delbert Benjamin, 495
    Germany (Federal Republic of
        Germany), 546
    KLM crash, 703
    Mack seal, 775
    Harrisonburg, VA, Church of the
        Brethren, *1283*
    Schwarzenau, 1274, *1282, 1283*
    Sherfy, Robert L., *1283*
Two Sisters (ship)
    Reber, Johann Bernhart (Leonhardt),
        voyage to America on, 1085
*Two Sticks: Or, the Lost Tribes of Israel
    Discovered* (Eshelman), 209
Tye, Vincent, 2156, 2296
Tyler, Alice Felt, 2085
Tyler, Delton, 239
Tyler, Mrs. Delton, 239
Tyler, Edward B., 259
Tyler, Gretchen Beatrice, 2016
Tyler, James Wayne, 1277, 1796
Tyler, Wilbur, 239
Tyler, Mrs. Wilbur, 239
Tyneck family
    Grandview, WA, Grace Brethren
        Church, 566
Tyner, Ira L., 2296
type, moveable
    origins of, 2104
    made in America, 1146
    publishing industry, 2067
typhus
    Ephrata Community, 451
Tyrone, PA, 18
    Church of the Brethren, 1214, **1283**
The Tyrone [PA] *Herald*
    Holsinger, Henry Ritz, 621
Tyson, A. S., 1796
Tyson, Abram J., 1796
Tyson, Conway, 1796
Tyson, Elizabeth Stauffer, 1284, 1854
    medical missions, 807
Tyson, Emma, 158
Tyson, George, 1796
    Portage Church of the Brethren, OH,
        minister, 1047
Tyson, Jacob
    St. Paul Church of the Brethren, NC,
        minister, 1135
Tyson, Naomi (later Kulp), 709
Tyson, William, family
    St. Paul Church of the Brethren, VA,
        1135

U Thant, 344, *344*
Uba, Nigeria, 306
Uberlândia, Brazil, 173
"Überschlag die Kost" ("Count Well the
    Cost")
    hymnals, 641
    hymns, 642
Udell, IA
    Church of the Brethren, *See* Fairview
        Church of the Brethren, IA
    Grace Brethren Church, 661, **1285**
Uganda
    Dunkard Brethren congregation, 2128
    evangelism in, 2180

missions, 2225
Montgomery, IL, Boulder Hill
    Neighborhood Church of the
    Brethren, resettling refugees from,
    872
Uhl family, 211
Uhlendorf, B. A., 2085
Uhnruh, John P., 2086
Ukadbhai, Somchand, 1796
Ukena, Richard Alvin, 1796
Ukleja, Mike, 758
Ulery, Carlyle J., 1796
Ulery, Daniel, 1796
Ulery, David, 429, 1796
    family of, 1345
Ulery, Elizabeth Leer, 2085
    descendants, 1953
Ulery family, *See* Ulrich family
Ulery, H. G., 1796
Ulery, Hannah (later Metzger)
    Metzger, John, wife of, 819
Ulery House
    St. Joseph Valley Church of the
        Brethren, IN, 1135
Ulery, IN, Church of the Brethren, *See*
        Saint Joseph Valley Church of the
        Brethren, IN
Ulery, J. Edson, 179, 212, 1296
    family history, 1961
    Marilla Church of the Brethren, MI,
        elder, 793
    North Manchester, IN, Church of the
        Brethren, elder (moderator), 949
    Onekama, MI, Church of the Brethren,
        pastor, 975
Ulery, Jacob, 1796
Ulery, Jacob C., 1796
Ulery, John C., 1796, 2085, **2386**
Ulery, John P., 1796
Ulery, Joseph Edson, 1285, 1796
Ulery, Levi, 439
Ulery, Mary Hoover, 1285
Ulery, Minnie (later Green), 1953
Ulery, Miriam Buck, 1937
Ulery Reunion Association, 2085
Ulery, Samuel, 1345, 1796
Ulery, Solomon, 1285
Ulery, Susannah Stutzman, 1233
Ulery, Sylva Kindy, 1285
Ulery, Yohannis (John)
    descendants, 1953
Ulle, Robert F., 2005, 2085
Ullery, Claude D., 1796
Ullery, D. C., 1796
    South Bend, IN, First Brethren Church,
        1203
Ullery, Daniel (1852–1919), 1796
Ullery, Daniel (ca. 1818), 1796
Ullery family, *See* Ulrich family
Ullery, Fred E., 2085
Ullery, Howard E., Jr., 2296
Ullery, J. Forest, 1796
Ullery, Jacob
    Osceola Church of the Brethren, MO,
        elder, 984
Ullery, John
    Osceola Church of the Brethren, MO,
        elder, 984
Ullery, Mose, 1223
Ullery, Samuel, 1796
Ullery, Victoria Lynn, 2296
Ullmann, Richard K., 2085
Ullom family, 1320, 1345

Fredericksburg, IA, Hillcrest Baptist
    and Brethren Church, 512
Ullom, Homer, 1345, 1796
Ullom, Lulu Pearl (later Coffman), 1345,
    1836
Ullom, Orville D., 1796
Ullom, Rosalie, 1345
Ullrey, Carlton, 2085
Ullrey, Catherine, 2085
Ullrey, Dana, 2085
Ullrey, Ebon, 2085
Ullrey family, 2085
Ullrey, Jacob, 2085
Ullrey, Jennie, 2085
Ullrey Kinsfolk Association, 2085
Ullrick, C. L., 1796
Ulman, W. J., 267
Ulman, Mrs. W. J., 267
Ulmer, David C., 2085
Ulmer family, 148
Ulmer, Grace (later Ziegler), 1397
Ulrey, Calvin, **1285**
Ulrey, Daniel
    Romine Church of the Brethren, IL,
        minister, 1121
Ulrey family, 1246, 2042
    Mill Creek Old German Baptist
        Brethren Church, VA, 833
    Mishler family, related to, 852
Ulrey, Gabriel, 1877
Ulrey, Isaac
    Eel River congregation, IN, 949
    North Fork Old German Baptist
        Brethren Church, IN, overseer, 947
Ulrey, J. C., 415
Ulrey, Jacob C., 54, 572, 1796, 2085
Ulrey, John, 1796
Ulrey, John C., 1796
Ulrey, Mary Jane Tridle, 1285
Ulrey, Miriam Buck, 1285, 2085
Ulrey, Ruth F., 1845
Ulrey, Samuel, 430, 1796
    Ritchey (Ritchie) family, related to,
        1110
Ulrey, Stephen S., 1285, 1796–1797
Ulrey (Ulery), Gabriel, 1796
Ulrey/Ulrich family, 1312
Ulrich, Bartow Adolphus, 2085
Ulrich, Christina (later Stutzman), 1285
Ulrich, Claire Gilbert, 2133
Ulrich, D., 1355
Ulrich, Dale V., 1160, 2133, 2143
Ulrich, Daniel Warren, 1285, 2296
    information technology, church use of,
        2208
    on Mathew 18 Project, 2361
Ulrich, David, 1285
Ulrich, Elizabeth, 216, 352
Ulrich, Elizabeth Cripe, 1285
Ulrich, Elizabeth (later Miller), 1285
Ulrich, Elizabeth (later Shultz), *See* Shultz,
    Elizabeth Ulrich
Ulrich (Ullery, Ulery) family, 146, 262,
    708, **1285–1286,** 1911, 1953,
    2085, 2093, **2379**
    Engle/Angle family, 446
    Jackson Co. German Baptist Brethren,
        IN, 667
    Musselman family related to by mar-
        riage, 901
    Shively family, related to, 1178
Ulrich, Frederick, 1797
Ulrich, George, 1285

Ulrich, Hannah (later Butterbaugh), 1070
Ulrich, Hannah (later Puterbaugh), 1285
Ulrich, Hannah Stutzman, 1233
Ulrich, Jacob, 345, 682, 1286, 1321, 2134
    Metzger family, related to, 820
    migration of Brethren, 830
Ulrich, John, 1797
Ulrich, Larry Kenneth, 1797, 2086
Ulrich, Lewis Elmer, 1797
Ulrich, Lydia (later Lear), 1285
Ulrich, Martha Bowman (later Teeter), *1250*
Ulrich, Mary (later Puterbaugh), 1070, 1285
Ulrich, Matthew, 1285
Ulrich, Michael, 424
Ulrich, Sally (later Haldeman), *618*
Ulrich, Samuel, 424, 1285, 1797
    Yellow Creek, PA, elder in, 927
Ulrich schoolhouse, KS, 1321
Ulrich, Sharolyn Lucille, 1849
Ulrich, Stephen, 1233, 1285, 1797
    Martin, Nicholas, 797
Ulrich, Susannah (later Puderbaugh), 384,
    1070
Ulrich, William Martin, 1797
Ulrick, *See* entries at Ulrich
Ulrick, C. A., 1285
Ulrick, Stephen, 1285
Ulsh family, *See* Rinehart family
ultimate destinies, doctrine on, 185
Umatilla Co., OR, 1338
Umbaugh, Emanuel, 431, 1797
    Plum Creek Old German Baptist
        Brethren Church, KS, minister,
        1038
Umbaugh, Jonas, 1797
Umbel, Andrew, 1797
Umbel, Samuel C., 1797
Umberhocker, Gladys (later Whetstone),
    1338
Umble, John S., 2086
Umphlet, J., 145, 1797
Umphlet, Price M., 668, 1797
Umstad, Ann Brower, 1286
Umstad, Hannah (later Price), 1056, 1286
Umstad, Isabella (later Fitzwater), 1286
Umstad, John, 295, 460
    single mode feetwashing, 1186
Umstad, John Horning, **1286,** 1797
    Norristown, PA, Church of the
        Brethren, 945
    Oaks, PA, Green Tree Church of the
        Brethren, minister, 958
    Parker Ford, PA, Church of the
        Brethren, preaching at, 994
    Price, Isaac, 1056
Umstad (Umstead), John Horning, *1286*
Umstead, *See* Umsted
unbelievers, punishment of, **1072**
"Uncle" John Metzger, *See* Metzger, John
underground railroad, **1286**
    Pennsylvania, 2069, 2072
Underhill, Nancy D. Blain, **1286,** 1797
Underhill, William D., 1286
Understanding Pietism (Brown), 2152
Underwood, Arnold Clarence, 2086
Underwood, Charles, 755
Underwood, Viola, 357
UNESCO, 78, 1365
Unger, Allen, 1797
Unger, Claude W., 1887
Unger, Ken
    Winchester, VA, Blue Ridge Grace
        Brethren Church and, 2262

Unger, Virginia
    Winchester, VA, Blue Ridge Grace
        Brethren Church and, 2262
Unicorn, PA, 461
uniformity
    nonconformity, 941
    Old German Baptist Brethren, 967, 969
uniforms
    civil service, 403
    military, 403
Union, OH, Community Grace Brethren
    Church, **1286**
Union Bridge, MD, 152, 1225
    Church of the Brethren, **1287**
        Pipe Creek Church of the
            Brethren, MD, 1026
Union Center
    Sandy Creek Church of the Brethren,
        WV, preaching point, 1143
Union Center Church of the Brethren, IN,
    231, 1232, 1280, **1287**
    Maple Grove Church of the Brethren,
        IN, 789
Union Center Church of the Brethren, OK,
    1287
Union Center, MT, 142
Union Central, WV
    Pocahontas Church of the Brethren,
        WV, mission point of, 1039
Union Chapel Church of the Brethren, PA,
    1287
Union Chapel Church of the Brethren, VA,
    21, 1291
    Fairview-Endless Caverns Church of
        the Brethren, VA, 470
Union Chapel Church of the Brethren, WV,
    1287
Union Church of New Jersey (CB), NJ,
    129, **1287**
Union Church of the Brethren, Elk Creek,
    CA, 438
Union Church of the Brethren, IN, 1287
    Plymouth, IN, Church of the Brethren,
        1038
union churches, 48, **1287**
    Blue River Baptist Church, IN, 1380
        Glade Creek, VA, 152
    La Motte Prairie Federated Church of
        the Brethren, IL, 713
    Lacey, WA, Community Church,
        716–717
    Manassa union church, 1263
    Methodists and Brethren, 407
    State College, PA, University Baptist
        and Brethren Church, **1218**
    Sugarcreek, OH, 1235
    Texas, 1255
    Vinton, VA, 1307
    Virginia Beach, VA, Christian Church
        Uniting, 1308
    Wawaka, IN, Church of the Brethren,
        1323
    Welty Church of the Brethren, MD,
        1329
    Wenatchee, WA, Brethren-Baptist
        Church United, 1330
    Youngstown, OH, Woodworth Church
        of the Brethren, 1390–1391
    Yuba City, CA, Queens Avenue
        Community Church, 1394
Union Churchhouse, Gortner, MD, Eglon,
    WV, Church of the Brethren, 430
Union City, IN, Church of the Brethren,

1327, *See also* Union City, OH,
    Church of the Brethren
    Pleasant Valley Church of the Brethren,
        OH, 1035
Union City, OH
    Church of the Brethren, **1288**
    Greenville Creek congregation, 708
    Poplar Grove, OH, Church of the
        Brethren, 1046
Union Co., IA
    New Virginia, IA, Brethren Church,
        932
    Osceola, IA, Church of the Brethren,
        983
Union Co., IL, 177, 647, 1356–1357, 1358,
    1359, 2020
    Church of the Brethren, **1288**
    Clear Creek congregation, 597
    Far Western Brethren in Illinois
        Territory, 475
    migration of Brethren, 829
    place-names, Brethren, 1027–1028
    Union Co. Church, 740
Union Co., IN, 705
    Four Mile Church of the Brethren, IN,
        505
    Howard, IN, Church of the Brethren,
        633
    Miami, OH, Brethren settlement, 961
    migration of Brethren, 829
Union Co., OH, 374
    Sciota Church of the Brethen, OH,
        1160
Union Co., PA
    history of, 1929
    Pennsylvania Old Order Brethren, 1005
Union Grove Church of the Brethren, IN
    (Mississinewa), 42, 63, 171, **1288**
    Pine Creek Church of the Brethren, IN,
        1024
Union meetinghouse (Baltic, OH), 80
Union Minnie Wood Chapel, VA
    Salem Church of the Brethren, VA,
        preaching point, 1138
Union Mission Chapel
    Greensburg, PA, Church of the Breth-
        ren, 571
Union of Soviet Socialist Republics
    (USSR), **1288,** *See also* Russia
Union, OH, Community Grace Brethren
    Church, **1286**
Union, OH, congregation
    Ridge Church of the Brethren, OH,
        1108
Union Pacific/Central Pacific Railroad
    frontier settlement, 1082
Union Pacific Railroad, **1288–1289**
    Annual Meetings on property of, 1081
    colonization and, 238
    McDonough, George L., 773
    migration of Brethren, 830
    money donated for church building,
        Twin Falls, ID, Church of the
        Brethren, 1282
    Oregon Short Line Railroad, 981
Union Pacific Railroad, 2086
Union Ridge Church of the Brethren, IA,
    1289
union Sunday schools
    Boone River Church of the Brethren,
        IA, 162
    Larned Church of the Brethren, KS,
        726

Los Angeles, CA, Bella Vista Church of the Brethren, 758
Mennonites and, 157
Nampa, ID, 170
Shady Creek, PA, congregation, 151
Union Theological Seminary
Row, W. Harold, 1125
Union/West Milton, OH, Community Grace Brethren Church
Englewood, OH, Grace Brethren Church, 447
unions, labor, See labor unions
Uniontown, IN
revival and New Hope Church of the Brethren, 929
Uniontown, PA, 232, 409, 1356
Church of the Brethren, **1289**
Fair-View (Georges Creek) Church of the Brethren, PA, 469
Fairchance, PA, Church of the Brethren, 467
First Brethren Church, See Uniontown, PA, Grace Brethren Church
Grace Brethren Church, **1289**
Uniontown Meeting (1924), Church of the Brethren, **1289**
Unitarian-Universalist faiths, See Universalists and Universalism
Unitas Fratram, See Unity of Brethren
United Andean Indian Mission (UAIM), **1289**
Ecuador, 422
United Brethren in Christ, 158, 188, **1289–1290,** 1291
American revivalism, 1104
debates, 371
Elkhart, IN, Brethren Church, 439
Evangelical Association, 459
Evangelical United Brethren Church, 460
Fairview Church of the Brethren, OH, 469
Glendora, CA, Church of the Brethren, 553
Hart, MI, Church of the Brethren, meetinghouse at, 587
Julien, Thomas T., 2210
Manchester College, origins in, 785
Middletown, PA, Swatara Hill Church of the Brethren, 826
mission work in China, 296
Nappanee, IN congragation, 914
Pleasant View Brethren Church, IN, 1036, 2377
Sugar Valley Church of the Brethren, PA, meetinghouse at, 1235
United Brethren College
Perry, William, 1009
United Christian Brethren, See Mooreites
United Church of Canada, 15, 59
mission work in China, 296
Sunday school lessons, 1237
United Church of Christ, **1290**
Columbia, MD, Oakland Mills Uniting Church (CB, UCC), chartered by, 326
CROP, 286
ecumenism, 423
Erie, PA, Community United Church (CB/UCC), 453
Evangelical Church in Germany and, 459
Hayes, William (Bill) A., 2197
Heifer Project International, 594

International Christian Youth Exchange (ICYE), 659
Kingsley, IA, 695
Klamath Falls, OR, 699
Schwenkfelder Church, 1159
SERRV International (CB) and, 2247
Sunday school lessons, 1237
United Andean Indian Mission (UAIM), 1289
United Church of Christ formed from, 1290
Virginia Beach, VA, 1309
United Church of Genoa, NY, 695
United Church of New Jersey
Sand Brook Church of the Brethren, NJ, 1142
United Church of North India (Presbyterian, congregational)
Church of North India, 298
United Church of the Brethren of Canada
Church of the Brethren, 250
United Community Church, Yuba City, CA, 1394
United Evangelical Church of Ecuador, 187, 268, 422, 1289, **1290**
ministry education, 268
missions, 861
Pentecostalism, 1009
Presbyterian relationships with Brethren, 1056
United Methodist Church, 1291
United Foundation, Ecuador, 422
United Free Church (Presbyterian) of Scotland, 708
United Kingdom, **1290**
Baptists in, 803
emigration from, 2079
French and Indian War, 516
immigrants departing from, 1290
loyalty oaths to British crown, 918
missions, 1290
missions and missionaries in Brethren in Christ, 189
missions, short-term, 2226
Nigeria missions and British colonial administration, 305
oath-taking issues, and allegiance to, 2078
prisoner of war camps, 199
Quakers in, 23
Reformation, Protestant, 1091
Sunday school movement, 283
Sunday school movement in England, 1237
World War II relief work, 1373
Young Men's Christian Association in prisoner-of-war camps, 1290
Young Men's Christian Associations (YMCA), 1390
United Methodist Church, **1291**
in Canada, 15
church membership, 813
episcopal polity, 1042
International Christian Youth Exchange (ICYE), 659
Jackpot Church, NV, 2212
mass media cooperative efforts, 801
Red Bird Mission, 2130–2131
SERRV International (CB) and, 2247
Wawaka, IN, 1323
United Ministries in Education
Frantz, Dave and Dena Pence, 1327
Heckman, Shirley, 1327

"Peace Making, Militarism, and Education" program, 1327
United Nations, 23, **1291,** *2129*
Blickenstaff, David Emerson, 146
Cordier, Andrew Wellington, 344, *344,* 765
Davis, Charles Ernest, 364
Eby, Kermit, 302
Germany, 546
historic peace churches, 2200
Israel, 664
Neff, Robert Wilbur, 2231
Peace Seminars, 1002
Peace Studies Institute, 1003
World Health Organization (WHO), 1369
Young, Andrew, 1367
United Nations Civil Assistance Command
Cassel, Franklin J., 707
United Nations Department of Economic Affairs
Blough, Jacob Roy, 150
United Nations Food and Agriculture (FAO) office
student exchange program, 1231
United Nations Homeless European Land Program (HELP), 625
United Nations Korean Reconstruction Agency (UNKRA), **1291**
United Nations Relief and Rehabilitation Administration (UNRRA), 200, **1291**
Brethren Service Unit, 2071
Brethren Service Unit in China, history of, 1939
Bushong, Benjamin G., 233
China, 2071
displaced persons, 390
Ethiopia, 458
Heifer Project International, 594
Heifers for Relief, 1331
history of, 2103
International Refugee Organization (IRO), 659
Metzger, Thurl D., 2222
Poland, 1040
tractor unit, 1268, *1269*
United Presbyterian Church
United Andean Indian Mission (UAIM), 1289
United Press
French, Paul Comly, 515
United Society Called Shakers, 2086
United States, See American Revolution; colonial America
acculturation of Brethren to American society, See acculturation
AFSC involvement in, 23–24
ALM involvement in, 24
churches in, 2098
civil religion and, 314
colleges, Christian
mid-Western, 2069
colonial America, See colonial America
conscientious objectors, 336
demographic trends, 2144
eighteenth century observer, general remarks by, 2005
history of, 2072
Industrial America, Brethren in, 2354
missions and missionaries, 2076
naming Brethren children after, 912
Nolt, Stephen M. on peace churches

and government of, 2348
peace education in, 23–24
relief and rehabilitation work by youth
from, 200
religions, history of, 2066
religious liberty, 1098
Revolutionary War, *See* American
Revolution
tours of, 202
United States Agency for International
Development (USAID)
Laos, 726
United States Capitol Building
Rinehart, William Henry, artisan,
1109–1110
United States Census Department
Brethren movement, 2086
religious group statistics, 1218
United States Coast Guard
Lyon, Thoburn C., 768
United States Commissioner of Education
in Puerto Rico
Brumbaugh, M. G., 300
United States Congress
candidates, 14, 93
House Military Affairs Committee
Bowman, Paul H., testimony to,
1372
Letcher, John, 738
Livermore, Edward St. Loe, 750
Selective Service law, 19
United States Constitution, *See* Constitu-
tion, US
United States Department of Agriculture
Forest Service, 502
United States Department of State
Eby, Kermit, 302
student exchange program, 1231
United States Forest Service
CPS camps, 316
United States Government
and alternative service, 19, 20
employment in, 149, 150
evacuation of the Japanese, 24
United States Government, 2086
United States Ministries Council (BC),
2141
United States presidents, Brethren children
named for, 912
United States Soil Conservation Service
CPS camps, 316
United Zion Children, 189
unity
Christian, *See* entries at ecumenical,
ecumenism
church, *See* church unity
General Conference Mennonite
Church, 536
Gospel Visitor, The, 561
India, 2065
Unity Baptist Church, KY, 2049
Unity Church of the Brethren, VA, 129,
746, **1291**
Fairview-Endless Caverns Church of
the Brethren, VA, 470
Unity of Brethren (*Unitas Fratum*)
Moravian Church, 357, 875, 1311
Universal Christian Conference on Life and
Work
ecumenism, 422
universal church
church membership, 813
Universal Conference on Life and Work,

1368
A Universal History, 2086
universal restoration, 30, **1291–1293,** 2100,
2108, *See also* Universalism
differences on in Oregon Territory,
1327
Drakes Creek German Baptist Brethren
Church, KY, 398
Far Western Brethren, 829, 1357
Germantown, PA, 2087
Hendricks, John, 1357
Holdeman, John, 618
Hostetler Brethren, 631
love and, 761
Martin, David, 797
millennialism, 834
Olive Branch German Baptist Brethren
Church, IN, 973
Philadelphian Society, 1019
Ramirez, Frank on, 2351
Rechte und Ordungen, 1086
Reformation, Protestant, and Brethren
doctrine, 1092
resurrection, and Brethren teachings
about, 1102
Rowland, Joseph, 1126
Sauer, J. C., 2060
Troy German Baptist Brethren Church,
MO, noted for espousal of, 1277
Vidler, William, 2087
White Water German Baptist Brethren
Church, MO, 1342
Winchester, Elhanan, 1348
Wolfe, George, II, 1357
*The Universal Restoration: Exhibited in
Four Dialogues Between a
Minister and his Friend*
(Winchester, Elhanan), 1348
Universalist Brethren
development of denomination, 1292
North Carolina, 177
settlement in Nashville, TN, area, 1253
South Carolina, 177
Universalist Quarterly Review
Eddy, Richard, 424
Universalist Register
Eddy, Richard, 424
Universalists and Universalism, 1291–1293,
1292–1293, *See also* Unitarian-
Universalist faiths
Bower, Jacob, 165
Brethren Church, 185
Brethren movement, 177, 241, 2098
Chapman, Giles, 271
Christian Brethren and, 281
Church in America, 2018
Church of the Brethren, 1968
contrast with universal restoration,
1291
Dunker-Universalists, 2002
Dunkers and, 1926
Dutchman's Creek German Baptist
Brethren Church, NC, 411
Eddy, Richard, 424
Eller, David B. on sectarian, 2329
eschatology, 454
Far Western Brethren, 475, 476
first Universalist minister in America,
117
Fraternity of Baptists, 511
Fröhliche Botschafter, Der (*The
Cheerful Messenger*), 518
frontier, 519

Gaylord, N. M., 1277
German Baptists and, 1926
Gospel, preaching of, 1986–1987
H., John, 577
Ham, John, 580
Hendricks, John, 597
history of, 1915, 2081, 2098
North Carolina, 2099
Kentucky schisms related to, 689
Lynch, Elijah, 768
Mack, Alexander, Sr., and New
Baptists of Schwarzenau, 776
Martin, David, 210, 797
Meyers, Jacob, 822
migration to, 177
ministers, 2106
Missouri Brethren settlement, 864
North Carolina Brethren, 946
Polish Brethren, 1041
publications, 149
Radical German Pietism, 1080
relief and rehabilitation work, 203
restitution, 1100
Rowland, Gasper, 1126
schisms and, 231
Seebach, Christoph, 1165
Shoup, William J., 1179
sources on, 2310
South Carolina, 210, 1204
Spring Creek, PA, congregation, 334
Stutzman, Jacob, refusal of oath of
allegiance, 1233
theologians of, 79
Troy German Baptist Brethren Church,
MO, relationship to, 1277
White Water German Baptist Brethren
Church, MO, 1342
Winchester, Elhanan, 1347–1348
universities generally, *See* colleges and uni-
versities
University Baptist and Brethren Church,
State College, PA, 1218
University Microfilms, Ann Arbor, MI, 191
University of Chicago
Aukerman, Dale H., 2133
Newcomer, Maud Odessa as student at,
933
University of Chicago Divinity School
Mow, Baxter Merrill, 891
Smeltzer, Ralph Emerson, 1190
University of Illinois
Nickey, Barbara Marie, as student in,
936
University of La Verne, *See* La Verne,
University of
University of Pennsylvania, 693
University of Vienna, 924
University Park Church of the Brethren,
MD, 1320, 1395, 1397, 1894, *See
also* Hyattsville, MD, University
Park Church of the Brethren
Silver Springs, MD, Good Shepherd
Church of the Brethren, 1182
UNKRA, *See* United Nations Korean
Reconstruction Agency
unleavened bread, **1293**
communion, 328
Eucharist
Brethren Church, 185
love feast, 764
Old German Baptist Brethren love
feast, 967
Unparteiische Kirchen- und Ketzer-Historie

(*A Nonpartisan History of Church and Heresy,* 1699–1700), Gottfried Arnold, 57, 1275, **1294,** 1866, 2086

Unquillo, Argentina, 54

UNRRA, *See* United Nations Relief and Rehabilitation Administration

Unschuldige Nachrichten, 2086
historical writing, 611

Unterschiedliche Erfahrungsvolle Zeugnisse, 2086

Updegraff, Patricia (later Bonomi)
works by, 2316

Updike, Daniel B., 2086

Updike, Murl D., 1797
Riner Grace Brethren Church, VA, pastor, 1110

Uphouse, Norman H., 16, 367, 1277, 1348, 1797, 2306
Meadow Mills Church of the Brethren, VA, pastor, 806

Uplinger, Wilbur, 1797, 2306

Upole, Wreatha Winters, 1797, 2086

Upper and Lower Linville Creek Church of the Brethren, VA, *See* Linville Creek Church of the Brethren, VA

Upper Black Log house, Black Log, Valley Point Church of the Brethren, PA, 144

Upper Brummetts Creek Church of the Brethren, NC, 224, 522, 1294

Upper Claar Church of the Brethren, PA, 765, **1294**
Queen, PA, Church of the Brethren, 1075

Upper Codorus Church of the Brethren, PA, 145, *762,* 1220, *See also* Black Rock Church of the Brethren, PA
Pleasant Hill Church of the Brethren, PA, 1032

Upper Conwego Church of the Brethren, PA, 141, 215, 338, 406, 765, **1294**

Upper Cumberland Church of the Brethren, PA, 255, 765, **1294**
division of, 934
Huntsdale Church of the Brethren, PA, 638

Upper Deer Creek Church of the Brethren, IN, **1294**

Upper Dublin congregation, PA (CB), *See* Ambler, PA, Church of the Brethren

Upper Fall Creek Church of the Brethren, IN, 42, **1294–1295**
Middletown, IN, Church of the Brethren, 826

Upper Four Mile, IN, Church of the Brethren, *See* Four Mile Church of the Brethren, IN

Upper Fulton, IL, Church of the Brethren, *See* Canton, IL, Church of the Brethren

Upper Linville Creek congregation, VA, 745
Greenmount Church of the Brethren, VA, 571

Upper Lost River Church of the Brethren, WV, 350, **1295**
Mathias, WV, Church of the Brethren, preaching point of, 803

Upper Marsh Creek Church of the Brethren, PA, **1295**
Gettysburg, PA, Marsh Creek Church

of the Brethren, 547

Upper Room
feetwashing, 481

The Upper Room, Our Daily Bread (De-Haan), 382

Upper Spring Creek mission point
Flat Creek Church of the Brethren, KY, 493

Upper Stillwater, OH, Church of the Brethren, *See* Harris Creek Church of the Brethren, OH

Upper Twin Church of the Brethren, OH, 766, 1235, 1281, **1295**
Eaton, OH, Church of the Brethren, 417
example of descriptive or grammatical place name, 911
Gratis, OH, Church of the Brethren, 566

Upper Twin Old German Baptist Brethren Church, OH, **1295**

Upper Ward Fire Co., PA, 736

Upshur Co., WV, 2079
Goshen Church of the Brethren, WV, 558

Upton House meetinghouse (PA), 77

Upton, PA, Church of the Brethren, 77, 736, **1295**

urban congregations, 202
Dayton, OH, 693
Fort Wayne, IN, 693
Muncie, IN, 693

Urban, Louis Michael, 2296

Urban Ministries Consultation, *2257*

urban ministry, 845, **1295–1297, 2256–2257**
and Bethany Theological Seminary, 126
Brethren Volunteer Service, 1965
Brooklyn, NY, 932–933
Church of the Brethren, 299
cities and Church of the Brethren, 1999
Hastings Street Mission, 125
Hayes, William (Bill) A., 2197
Hispanic Ministries (CB), 2199
Lancaster, PA, Acts Covenant Fellowship, 2213
Lancaster, PA, Alfa y Omega (Alpha and Omega) Church of the Brethren, 2213–2214
Minnesota Brethren settlement, 848
The Missionary Board (BC), 855
missions, 859
missions, short-term, 2226
Missouri, 864
Native Americans, 2230
nursing, 952
Shisler, Sara Cassel, 1177
sources on, 2321
Stover, Wilbur Brenner, 1226

Urban Ministries Consultation, *2257*
Virginia, 1308
women, roles in, 1361
York, PA, Belvidere Church of the Brethren, 1388

urban missions
Brooklyn, NY, 217
Chicago, Illinois, 217
Flory, Lizzie Mae Neher and Raymond Chester, 499
hospitals, 630
Illinois, 217
Indiana, 217

Los Angeles, CA, Bella Vista Church of the Brethren, 758
Metzger, John, 819
missions, 860
Ohio, 217
Omaha, NE, 2092
Pennsylvania, 217

Urbana Church of the Brethren, IL, 1297–1298

Urey, Clara Reinoehl, 1298

Urey, Harold C., **1298**
inventions and scientific discoveries, 660

Urey, John H., 70, 1797

Urey, S. C., 1797

Urey, Samuel Clayton, 1298, 1797

Urlinger, Josef, 2086

Urner, Barbara Schweitzer, 1298

Urner, Catherine Reist, 1298

Urner, Elizabeth Grubb, 1298

Urner family, 215, 2086
Reinhardt family, 1094

Urner, Hans, 1298

Urner, Isaac Newton, 912, **1298,** 2086–2087

Urner, Jacob, 1298

Urner, John, 1298

Urner, Jonas, 1797
Pipe Creek Church of the Brethren, MD, minister, 1026

Urner, Martin (1725–1799), 33, 211, 446, 532, 569, **1298,** 1797, 2375
Martin, George Adam, 797
Maryland Brethren activity, 798
Miller, George, 837
Pipe Creek Church of the Brethren, MD, 1025, 1026
Pottstown, PA, Coventry Church of the Brethren, 1049
Quakertown, PA, First Church of the Brethren, 1075
Revolutionary War, American, 1106
Revolutionary War incident, 2005
Sams Creek Church of the Brethren, MD, elder, 1141
Sauer, David, baptism of, 1147
Steiner family, 2378

Urner, Martin (1695–1755), 1233, 1797

Urner, Ulrich, family of, 1298

Ursinus College, 1891

Ursinus, Zacharias, 593

Uruguay
General Conference Mennonite Church, 536
Julien, Thomas T., 2210
missions, 2225
missions, short-term, 2226

U.S. Supreme Court, *See* Supreme Court, U.S.

US vs. Enten V. Eller
Eller, Vernard on, 2330

USA, *See* entries at United States

USAID (United States Agency for International Development)
Laos, 726

Use Me
Recreational Fellowship, 1088

Usner, Edna Eby, 2087

USSR, *See* Russia; Unites Soviet Socialist Republic (USSR)

Utah, **1298–1299**
evangelism, 298
minorities, ethnic and racial, 850

utopianism, 1866
  reference to Ephrata, 1939
Utsman, A. T.
  Midway Church of the Brethren, TN,
    providing leadership, 827
Utt, Otte E., 515, 749, 1797
Utz, Elizabeth Hohf, 1299
Utz, Franklin N., 1797
Utz, Harley Dewey, 2127
Utz, Hontas, 1299
Utz, John H., 106, 1299, 1797
Utz, Joseph H., 1797
Utz, Lucinda Kelly, 1299
Utz, M. Ella (later Ecker), 421
Utz, Norman, 2087
Utz, Robert O., 1299
Utz, Ruth Earl, **1299**, 1845, **2379, 2388**,
  See also Oiness, Sylvia
  medical missions, 807
  ship sinking en route to Africa, 863
Utz, Ruth Utz, Samuel, 752
Utz, Samuel H(ohf), **1299**, 1797
  Piney Creek Church of the Brethren,
    MD, performing baptisms, 1025
Utz, Silas K., 752, 1797
Utz, Sylvia Booker, 2127
Uwharrie Colony
  Flat Rock Church of the Brethren, NC,
    493
Uwharrie (Ewarry) congregation, NC, 732,
  1233
  nonresistance and Revolutionary War,
    946
  Stutzman family history, 1914
Uwharrie German Baptist Brethren Church,
  NC, **1299**

Vacation Bible School
  children and, 2159
  daily, 192–193
  East Nodaway Church of the Brethren,
    IA, 416
  Enders, NE, Church of the Brethren,
    446
  Jackpot Church, NV, 2212
  Meadow Branch Church of the
    Brethren, MD, 805
  Ozark Church of the Brethren, MI, 986
Vada, India, 649
  Lichty, Anna Eby, 741
Vail, E. H., 1797
Vakil, Louise Miller Sayre, 1845
Valdes, Nydia
Vega Baja, PR, Iglesia de los Hermanos
  Cristo El Señor (CB) and, 2258
Valencourt, Carol Jean Dunlap, 1845
Valencourt, James Roy, 1797, 1845
Valentine, Albert George, II, 2296
Valentine, Carroll M., 1797
  Rouzerville Church of the Brethren,
    PA, minister, 1125
Valentine, Donald G., 1295, 1797, 2296
Valentine, J. Ford, 244, 1797
Valentine, Mrs. Ford, 244
Valentine, Michael Carroll, 1295, 1797
Valentine, T. S. (F.), 1797
Valez-Pirez, Ernesto, 261
Vali-Umalla, India, 649
  Eby, Emma Ada Horner and Enoch
    Howe, 418
  Miller, Eliza Belle, missionary, 837
Valji, Naranji, 1797
Vallentine, R. F., 679

Valley Bethel Church of the Brethren, VA,
  152, 277, **1301**
  Highland Co. Mission Church of the
    Brethren, VA, 605
Valley Brethren Church, PA, *See* Jones
  Mills, PA, Valley Brethren Church
Valley Brethren-Mennonite Heritage
  Center, **2257–2258**
Valley Church of the Brethren, MT, 1277,
  1301
Valley Church of the Brethren, VA, 939,
  1301
Valley congregation, VA, 1277
Valley of Huts, *See* Hüttental; *Hüttental*
Valley of Virginia, *See* Shenandoah Valley
Valley Pike Church of the Brethren, VA,
  1301, 1364
  Round Hill Church of the Brethren,
    VA, 1125
  Woodstock Church of the Brethren,
    VA, 1364
Valley Point meetinghouse, Black Log,
  Valley Point Church of the Breth-
    ren, PA, 144
Valley River Church of the Brethren, WV,
  See Junior, WV, Valley River
    Church of the Brethren
Valley Turnpike, 2090
Valley View Community Church of the
  Brethren, CA, *See* Whittier, CA,
    Valley View Community Church
    of the Brethren
Valley View meetinghouse, VA, 1301
Valton congregation, WI (CB), 63
Valton, Fridtjof, 2087
values, social
  urban communities and, 175
Vamgo, Audu W. U. U., 1797
Van Bebber, Matthias
  Skippack area, PA, 1189
Van Bibber, Mark Allen, 1797
Van Buren Co., MI, 144, 752
  migration of Brethren, 829
  South Haven Old German Baptist
    Brethren Church, MI, 1205
Van Buren family, 322
Van Buren, IN, congregation
  Shipshewana, IN, Church of the
    Brethren, organized from, 1177
Van Buren, J. L., 1797
Van Buren, Thomas D., 322, 1365,
  1797–1798
Van Burskirk family
  Maple Valley, WA, Grace Brethren
    Church, 2218
Van den Doel, Anthonie, 1798, **2386, 2388**
van der Aa, A. J., 1862
Van der Bent, Ans J., 2087
Van Doren, Carl, 2087
Van Duyne, Kenneth, 1798, **2386**
Van Dyck, Harry R.
  on conscientious objectors and World
    War II, 2361
Van Dyke, Amanda Shetler, 1302
Van Dyke, Archibald, 220, **1301–1302**
  North Beatrice Church of the Brethren,
    NE, elder, 945
Van Dyke, Archibald (father), 1301
Van Dyke, Catherine (Cassie) Beery, 952,
  1302, 1361, 1798
  hospitals, 630
  Mothers and Daughters' Association,
    879

Van Dyke, Chester N., 1798
Van Dyke Church of the Brethren Mission,
  PA, *See* Tuscarora Church of the
    Brethren, PA
Van Dyke, Eleanor J. (later Brumbaugh),
  220, 222, 1301
Van Dyke, Esther Swigart, 220, 1301, 1302
Van Dyke, George Henry, 123, 952, **1302,**
  1798
  hospitals, 630
  medicine, 810
Van Dyke, Irvin C., 1798
Van Dyke, J. G., 1798
Van Dyke, Joseph, *248,* **1302**, 1798, 2087,
  2379
Van Dyke, Mary Leinback, 1301
Van Dyke, Mina Crowel, 1302
Van Dyke, Mrs. S. P.
  Prairie Lake Church of the Brethren,
    OK, 1050
Van Dyke, Myralene Hoffman, 1302
Van Dyke, PA, 1281
Van Dyke, S. J., 1798
Van Dyke, S. Perry, **1302**, 1798
  Newberg, OR, Church of the Brethren,
    pastor in, 933
  Newberg, OR, Dunkard Brethren
    Congregation, elder in, 933
  Prairie Lake Church of the Brethren,
    OK, 1050
Van Epps, Leona (later Kent), 688
Van Hoose, Robert, 2296
Van Horn, Daniel Morgart, 1798
  Snake Spring Valley Church of the
    Brethren, PA, free minister, 1192
Van Horn family
  Snider, Jacob, descendants of, 1154
Van Horn, George Marshall, 1798
Van Horn, John, 923
Van Horn, L. M., 432
Van Horn, W. A., 432
Van Houten, Steven Wayne, 2296
Van Laschet, *See* Laschet, Van
van Laschet, Johann
  slavery, 1190
Van Meter, Elizabeth Shuler, 743
Van Meter, Isaac, 1798
Van Meter, John L., 1798
Van Norsdel, Isaac, 1217
Van Orman, Melvin D., 629
Van Orsdal, Sarah (later Trostler), 1276
Van Pelt, Bertha B., 1798
Van Pelt, Edward B., 1798
Van Pelt family
  Sinking Spring, OH, Grace Brethren
    Church, 1186
Van Pelt, John Franklin, 1798
Van Scoyk family, 228
Van Scoyk, Leo Archer, 1798
Van Sickle, George W., 1798
Van Sickle, Walter E., 1798
Van Trump family, 1313
Van Vleet, Daniel, 2296
Van Wert Brethren, *See* Flat Rock Old
  German Baptist Brethren Church,
    OH
Van Wert Church of the Brethren, OH, 152,
  1302
  Good family, 1945
Van Wert Old German Baptist Brethren
  Church, OH, *See* Big Run Old
    German Baptist Brethren Church,
    OH

Vanator, Fred, 195, 497, 562, 626, 1797
    Sarasota, FL, Brethren Church, 1145
Vanator, Helen Robbins, 1360
Vance family
    Phoenix, AZ, Northwest Grace Breth-
        ren Church, 1019
Vance, Harvey Jason, 2296
Vance, Paul R., 2296
Vancil, Daniel, 1798
Vancil, David Ephraim, 1798
Vancil, Joel Albert, 90, 1798
Vancouver, BC, 1220
Vandalia Elementary School, OH, 1302
Vandalia, OH, Grace Brethren Church, 367,
    1302
Vander Wiele, Dean
    Rockton, PA, Church of the Brethren,
        pastor, 1118
Vanderau, Ernest R., 1798, 2087
Vanderbilt family, 739
Vandergrift Heights, PA, Brethren Church,
    See Kepple Hill, PA, Pleasant
    View Brethren Church
Vandergrift Heights, PA, First Brethren
    Church of, 689
Vandermark, James Curtis, 2296
Vanderveer, Loyal Howard, 1798
Vandevender, Demer, 1798
Vaniman, Albert W., 504, 1243, 1255, 1267,
    1302, 1303, 1324, 1337, 1798,
    1845, 1946, 2087, 2097
    Raisin City, CA, Church of the
        Brethren, 1083
    Pleasant Valley Church of the Brethren,
        TX, 1035
Vaniman, Alice, 504, 1243
    Pleasant Valley Church of the Brethren,
        TX, 1035
Vaniman, Alice Moore, 1303, 1324, 1845
Vaniman, Calvin, 1303
Vaniman, Catherine Martin, 1303
Vaniman, Chester Melvin, 1303
Vaniman, Daniel, 299, 331, 682, 1296,
    1302–1303, 1798, 1946, 2087
    Hurricane Creek Church of the
        Brethren, IL, 638
    Macoupin Creek Church of the
        Brethren, IL, elder, 779
    missions, 861
    World War I, 1370
Vaniman, David, 1303, 2106
Vaniman, Diana Brubaker, 1303
Vaniman, Elizabeth Stutzman, 1302
Vaniman, Ernest David, **1303**, 1798
Vaniman family, **1303**
    Neher family, related to, 922
Vaniman, George, 1303
Vaniman, Jacob, 1302
Vaniman, Jacob P., 683, 1303
Vaniman, John, 1303
Vaniman, Mary Bowman, 1302
Vaniman, Susie Cordelia Neher, 1303,
    1845, 1968
Vanimen, Ernest David, 1845
Van Meter, Mike, 739
Vann, Elizabeth Chapman Denny, 2087
Vanneberga congregation, 1243
Vannoy, Bernice, 1278
Varela, José, 54
Various Records and Genealogical Notes of
    Families of Plank Yoder, Blough,
    Noffzinger, Stutzman, King, Lantz
    and Miller, 2087

Varner, Edith
    Maple Grove Church of the Brethren,
        PA, 791
Varner family, 752, 1299
Varner, James Michael, 2296
Varner, Janet, 1854
Varner, R. Dale, 1798
Varner, Samuel
    Maple Grove Church of the Brethren,
        PA, 791
Varner, William, 1798
Varnum, Edward, 448
Vasto, Lanza del, 659
Vatican Councils, 422–423, 1120
Vaughan, B. R., 1798
Vaughn, Leonard Edward, 663, 1798, 2306
Vaughn, Tracey (later Wolfe), 2297
Vaught, George, 1798
Vaught, Sherry Reese, 2296
Vaught, Terry L., 2296
Vawter, Dorothy Ann Byler, 2087
Veach family, 377, 2087
Veach, John D., 1798
Veach, Robert Spangler, 1798, 2087
Veal, Russell E., 2296
Veale, Melvin, 755
Vecchio, Joseph Vincent, 2296
Veech, James, 2087
Vega Baja, PR, Iglesia de los Hermanos
    Cristo El Señor (CB), **2258**
    Hispanic Ministries (CB), 2198
Velanzon, Patrick Richard, 2296
Ven Pak Lee (later Studebaker), 1230
Venable, C. L., 2087
Venango Co., PA, 317
Vendsyssel Brethren congregation
    Johansen, Martin, 671
Venema, F. W., 2087
Venezuela
    missions and missionaries in
        Brethren in Christ, 189
    relief from New Paris, IN, Church of
        the Brethren, 931
Venice, FL, Church of the Brethren, **2258**
Venkatsammy, Parsram, 1798
Ventura, CA, Grace Brethren Church, 1303
Vera Cruz, battle of (Spanish American
    War), 912
verbal inflections in place name, 911–912
verbatim report of business
    Annual Meetings, 1069
    dress in, 402
    minutes of annual meetings, **1303**
Verdigris Church of the Brethren, KS, 42,
    345, 1213, **1304**
    Mont Ida, KS, Church of the Brethren,
        870
    Gravel Hill Church of the Brethren,
        KS, 567
Verdun
    reconstruction of war-damaged homes,
        1367
Vermillion, IL, Church of the Brethren
    Cornell, IL, Church of the Brethren,
        345
    Pike Creek (Chenoa), IL, Church of the
        Brethren, 1023
Vermillion, KS, Church of the Brethren,
    1230
    Richland Center Church of the
        Brethren, KS, 1107
Vermont, **1304**
    missions and missionaries in

Fellowship of Grace Brethren
    Churches, 250
    Quebec, missionary efforts toward,
        1075
Vernard, Wilbur, 357
Vernon, CA, Church of the Brethren, *See*
    Los Angeles, CA, Ladera Church
    of the Brethren
Vernon Chapel Brethren Church, TN, *See*
    Telford, TN, Grace Brethren
    Church
Vernon Co., MO, 734
    Nevada, MO, Church of the Brethren,
        924
Vernon District congregation, CA, 759
Vernon, Mrs. R. H., 296
Vernon Parish, LA, 760
    Rosepine, LA, Church of the Brethren,
        1123
Vernon St. Mission
    Los Angeles, CA, Ladera Church of the
        Brethren, 759
Versailles, MO, Church of the Brethren, *See*
    Praire View Church of the Brethren,
    MO
Versluis, Arthur
    on Ephrata Cloister, 2361
Vertz family
    Ozark Grace Brethren Church, MI, 987
Vesey, Denmark, 2128
Vessler, James O., 1798
Vest, William F., 1798
Vestaburg, MI, Church of the Brethren,
    355, 725, **1304**
    New Haven Church of the Brethren,
        928
vestments
    worn by pastors and choirs, 1377
veterans (military), **1304**
    Brethren Church peace position, 1000
Vetter (Fetter), David, 1304
Vetter (Fetter), Lucas, 174, **1304**
    Hesse, 602
Vetter (Fetter), Margarita, 1304
Vetter (Fetter), Sophia, 1304
Vetter family, 1920
    Mortonhouse (ship), 2373, 2376
Vetter, J. W., 1798, 2087
Via, A. R., 513
Via, Fannie, 513
Via, Jacob W., 269, 1798
Via, Jennie Miller, 399
Viar family, 1224
Vickers, Daniel M., 1798
Vickery, Veda Zirkle, 1979
Vicksburg, PA
    Brethren Church, 2087
    Grace Brethren Church, **1304–1305**
Victor Church of the Brethren, KS, **1305**
Victor, Kurt A., 2296
Victoria School, preaching point maintained
    by Kansas Center Church of the
    Brethren, KS, at, 683
victorious life movement, 691, *See also*
    Keswick movement
Victory Mountain Grace Brethren Chapel,
    188, *See also* Dryhill, KY, Victory
    Mountain Grace Brethren Chapel
videos
    Dunkard Brethren Church, 2174
Vidler, William, 2087
Vidora, Sask., Battle Creek Church of the
    Brethren, **1305**

Viehmeyer, L. Allen, 2087
 on Ephrata Cloister, 2361
Vielbrunn, *See* Filbrun family
Vienna, Austria
 Karlsschule, 684
 work camps, 1367
Vienna, VA, Dunkard Brethren Congregation, 367, 1308, **1305**
Viers, John D., 268, 1798
Vietnam, **1305**
 congregations sponsoring refugees from, 30
 missions, 2225
 missions, short-term, 2226
 Montgomery, IL, Boulder Hill Neighborhood Church of the Brethren, resettling refugees from, 872
 Polo, IL, Church of the Brethren, sponsoring refugees, 1045
 refugee relief, 23
 refugees resettled by Sugar Ridge Church of the Brethren, MI, 1235
 relief and service efforts, 1097
 Rosenberger, Mary Sue Helstern on witnessing for peace in, 2353
Vietnam Christian Service, 1305, 2021
 Studebaker, Ted Allen, 1230
Vietnam Summons (Moomaw, Ira W.), 1305
Vietnam War, 6, **1305–1306**
 amnesty for conscientious objectors, 26
 BAM and, 179
 chaplaincy, 271
 Church of the Brethren anti-war movement involvement, 1000
 conscientious objectors, 336–337
 conscientious objectors and, 917
 Edwards, Chandler S., 429
 ethics, 458
 Grace Brethren chaplain, 1977
 incarceration of Brethren, 1060
 Messenger, 819
 military service, 301
 New Left opposition to, 930
 relief and service efforts, 1097
 Studebaker, Ted Allen, killed in, 1230
Vietnamese refugees
 Hagerstown, MD, Church of the Brethren, 578
 Maple Grove Church of the Brethren, IN, 789
Vieuble, Jean Claude, 1854
Vieuble, Martine, 1854
Viewpoint Church of the Brethren, PA, *See* Johnstown, PA, Westmont Church of the Brethren
 changed to Viewmont, **2379**
Vilegwa, Nigeria, 306
Villa Dolores, Argentina, 54
Villa Prades, PR, Iglesia Cristiana Getsemani (CB), **2258**
Villanueva, Carmen M. López
Villa Prades, PR, Iglesia Cristiana Getsemani (CB) and, 2258
Villanueva, Oscar
 Villa Prades, PR, Iglesia Cristiana Getsemani (CB) and, 2258
Villard, Henry
 Northern Pacific Railroad, 951
Vinay, Valdo, 2087
Vincent, Eugene, 366
Vincent, Florence (later Rose)
 Rose, Smith Fuller (BC) and, 2244

Vinco, PA, (First) Brethren Church, *See* Mineral Point, PA, Vinco Brethren Church
The Vindicator, 178, 205, **1306–1307**, 1384, 2087–2088, 2088–2088, 2099, *See also* Old German Baptist Brethren
 article on temperance, 1252
 articles referenced, 48
 Bible translations and versions, controversy about, 138
 bibliography of, 2310
 Brubaker, Harold A., 2153
 choirs, 1185
 Chronicles of the Brethren (Kimmel), 290
 Committee
  Cassell, William, 260
  Doctrinal Treatise, 1261
  Frantz, Aaron, 508
  Miller, John William, 2224
  official church publishing, 1069
 Cover, Joseph Immel, editor of, 348
 Davy, Henry Dorsey, 365
 Doctrinal Treatise, 394, 2149
 electricity, 434
 Fifer, Jesse C., 489
 Flory, Abraham, 497
 Garber, Henry, 529
 genealogy, 535, 2188
 historical libraries, 610
 humility, 636
 Kimmel, John M., 693
 Kinsey, Samuel, 693, 696
 ministry, 845
 Montgomery, Michael, writing for, 872
 Nead, Peter, as contributor to, 919
 Ohio, published in, 961
 Old German Baptist Brethren, 967, 2235
 Old Order Movement, 972
 poetry, 1039
 publishing, 1068
 Shuman, L. Herman (OGBB) and, 2249
 Southwood, John W., 1207
 Yoder, D. Willard (OGBB) and, 2267
Vines, Andrew J., 1798
Vines, Forest (Foster), 1798
Viney, Fred, 1799
Vineyard Fellowship of Franklin, OH
 Northview, OH, Brethren Life Church/Vineyard Community Church, 2232
Vinton, VA, Church of the Brethren, **1307**
 Roanoke, VA, First Church of the Brethren, 1113
Viola, Annie (later Hammer), 581
violence, *See* conscientious objectors; nonviolence; pacifism; peace
 Brethren and, 2265
 ethics and, 2178
 firearms control, 2000
 mass media concerns, 801
 sources on, 2318
Virden, IL, Church of the Brethren, 1234, **1307**
 Girard, IL, Church of the Brethren, 550
 Pleasant Hill Church of the Brethren, IL, 1032
 Shull, William H., elder, 1156
Virginia, **1307–1308**, 2016–2017, 2059, *See also* specific city; specific county

Brethren from, and Miami, OH, congregation, 961
Brethren movement, 175, 2110
Brethren settlements, 1307–1308
 on choice of legal name for denomination, 910
Civil War, 314, 2110
Committee of Observation, 327
court records, 2104
Daily Vacation Bible Schools, 359
Dairy Testing Assignments, 359
district organization, 1308
Dunkard Brethren Church, 2068, 2090
Eckerlin family, 2102
folk art, 2105
Fraktur
 penmanship, 2105
frontier, 519
frontier history, 1989
German-Americans, 2104, 2105
German culture, 2147
German settlement in, 2069, 2105
Graybill (Grabill, Krehbiel) family, 567
history of Baptists in by Morgan Edwards, 1926
history of Brethren in, 2055
Indiana, 652
Kentucky, settlements in, 688
land grant surveys, 1982
Longenecker, Stephen L. on slavery in, 2344
Loyalists, 2105
marriages, 1700–1799, 2003
Materials Towards a History of the Baptists, 803
migration of Brethren, 829
mission schools, 853
Moravian diaries of travel through, 1966
music
 Funk, Joseph, 2090
mysticism, 2104
Native Americans, 2229
 battles, Indian, 2102
North Carolina Brethren settlement, 946
Old German Baptist Brethren, 238, 967, 970, 2234
Pennsylvania Brethren and settlement, 1004
pioneers, 2075
place-names, Brethren, 1027
preacher circuits in, 164, 167, 169
printing industry, 2104, 2105
Sabbatarians, 2104
Sappington, Roger E. on certificates of membership and, 2354
Shoemaker family, 2100
slavery, 1189, 2110, 2128
Universalists, 1292
Valley of Virginia, 1983
 weekday religious education in public schools, 1326–1327
 Williams family, 2100
 Girard, IL, Church of the Brethren, 550
Virginia Beach, VA
 Christian Church Uniting, **1308–1309**
 German Brethren Church, 227–228
 Grace Brethren Church, **1309**
Virginia, Brethren in
 sources on, 2311
Virginia Council of Churches
 Locke, John Funk, 751

Miller, Minor Cline, 841, 1326
Miller, Myron S., 1326
Mundy, Mildred F., 1326
sermons by CB pastors, 2361
weekday religious education, 1326
Virginia Council of Religious Education
Miller, Minor C., 1326
weekday religious education, 1326
Virginia District Mission Board
Hevener Church of the Brethren, WV, 602
Virginia Military Tract
migration of Brethren, 829
Virginia Normal School, 207, *See also* Bridgewater College
Virginia Sunday School Association
Miller, Minor C., 1326
weekday religious education, 1326
Virlina district (CB)
Friendship Manor, 518
Virtuous Grace (ship)
Heyer (Hyer, Heier, Hire) family, 602
Visakhapatnam, India, 651
visions, **1309**, *See also* mysticism
of Baumann, Mattheis, 925
Hummer, Catherine, 132
Koch, Stephan, 704
mysticism, 906
visits and visiting
deacons' visit, *See* deacons' visit
home visitation, 406, 460
ministry of visit brothers, 845
recreation, visiting as, 1087
Visser 't Hooft, Willem Adolph, 422, 1282, **1309**, *1368*, *1368*, **2379**
participation in two-hundred-fiftieth anniversary convocation, Schwarzenau, 1282
VISTA (Volunteers in Service to America), **1310**
Vitringa, Campegius
Covenant Theology, 348
Viveros, Dan, 348, 1799
Vivolo, Mary (later Ziegler), 1395
Vliet, Claire Ackerman, 2088
Vnasdale, Evelyn Ann, 1850
Vnasdale, Lester Arl, 2168, 2296
Mansfield, OH, Conservative Grace Brethren Church, 2218
vocational education
minorities, ethnic and racial, 850
mission schools, 853, 854
missions, 861
Vocational Training College, Anklesvar, India, 9, 131, 158, 651, 853, **1309**
vocations
chaplaincy, 2091
Marsden, Parker G. on CB, 2345
psychotherapy, 2110
Vogel family, 2108
Vogt, Dorothy Verle Hershberger, 2088
Vogt, Esther Loewen, on Brethren woman during Civil War, 2361
Vogt, Peter
on PA Synod under Zinzendorf, 2361
writings of, 2361
Vogt, Vella K. Schroeder, 2088
Vogtland, Reuß count of, 684
Voice Newsletter, 2168
Voice of Calvary, Mendenhall, MS
minorities, ethnic and racial, 850
The Voice of Seven Thunders (Holsinger), 1970

The Voice of Thy Brother's Blood (Studebaker), 748
Voight family
Plum Creek Old German Baptist Brethren Church, KS, 1038
South Solomon Old German Baptist Brethren Church, KS, 1206
Voigt, Gilbert P., 2088
Voint family, 2105
Voliva, Wilbur Glenn, 281–282
Volksdeutsche refugees, 73, 201, 303, 746, 1093, **1309**
Volmer family, Prosser, WA, Community Grace Brethren Church, 1062
Voloungou, Marc, **1309**, 1310, 1799
Volovski, Michael J., 21, 1277, 1799
Voltaire, François Marie Arouet de, **1310**, 2088
voluntary belief, *See* religious liberty
voluntary churches
ethics, 458
religious liberty, 1098
voluntaryism, 813, **1310**
volunteers, 2096
Brethren Student Life Volunteers, 1231
church programs, 2001
Disaster Response Program, 2171–2172
physicians in Africa, 2073
student volunteer movement for foreign missions, 1231–1232
Training in Missionary Endeavor (TIME), 1231, 1270
United Student volunteers, 1969
Volunteers in Service to America (VISTA), **1310**
von Beckerath, Gerhard, 1872
Von Christi Testamenten (Boehme), 2142
von der Burg family, 1943
von Flue, Eleanor Grace
on Sayer, Hazel Hannah and ancestors, 2361
von Hansen, Theophil, 684
von Hochenau, Hochmann
Renkewitz, Heinz on, 2351–2352
von Hollander, Emmy (later Arnold), 56, 639
Von-Reisenkampff-Ulrich family, 2085
Vonderlack, Robert W., 1799
Voorhees, Dora Ellen, 1854
Voorhees, Isaac, 1799
Voorhees, William Duey, 1854
Voorheis, Grace Schock
on Shock, Bessie, 2361
on Shock, Elmer, 2361
Vorhees family
Mesa, AZ, Community Church of the Brethren, 2222
Vorsänger, See chorister
Vorschrift
Fraktur, 505
Vorspiel, 747, 748
Vorspiel der Neuen Welt (*Prelude to the New World),* 451, 2088
Voss family
Fremont, OH, Grace Brethren Church, 515
Votaw, John M.
works by, 2310
voting issues, *See* elections
German votes in 1755, 2110
Sauer, J. C., I, 2110
Vought, Charles Earl, 728, 1799

vows, *See* oaths
Vroman, Dorrance C., 1799
Vuilleumier, Henri, 2088
Vulgamore, Howard D., 1799, 2088
Vyara, India, 212, 229, 649
mission schools, 853

Waas, Benaiah Frank, 1799
autobiography of, 2361
Red Cloud, NE, Church of the Brethren, providing leadership, 1088
Silver Lake Church of the Brethren, NE, elder and minister, 1182
Waas, Bennie S., 1799
Waas, David Asher, 1799
Waas, Martha (later Gilbert), 2279
Wabash Co., IN, 170, 257, 323, 352, 708, 1223, 1246, 1278, 1334
history of, 2101
North Manchester, IN, Church of the Brethren, 949
North Manchester Old German Baptist Brethren Church, IN, 949
Roann, IN, Church of the Brethren, 1112
Somerset, IN, Church of the Brethren, 1202
Wabash Country Church of the Brethren, IN, 708, **1311**
Somerset, IN, Church of the Brethren, 1202
Wabash, IN
Brethren Church, **1311**
City Church of the Brethren, **1311**
College Corner Brethren Church, *See* College Corner Brethren Church, IN
Wabash Railroad
chartered trains, 273
Wachovia, NC
Fraternity Church of the Brethren, NC, 511
French and Indian War, 516
North Carolina Brethren settlement, 946
Wachovia (Wachau), NC, **1311**
Wacker, IL, 602
Wadarusa, IN, 2007
Waddams Grove, IL, Church of the Brethren, KS, *See* Lena, IL, Church of the Brethren
Waddell, Joseph A., 2088
Wadding, Robert, 1799
Wade Branch Brethren Church, KS, **1311**, 1321,
Olathe, KS, Church of the Brethren, 964
Ottawa, KS, Church of the Brethren, 985
Pleasant Grove Church of the Brethren, KS, 1031
Wade, Charles E., 1799
Mount Hebron Church of the Brethren, WV, 881
Wade, Daniel Lawrence, 1799
Mount Hebron Church of the Brethren, WV, 881
Wade, Daniel S., 1799
Wade, Dawson R., 1799
Wade, John L., 142, 1799
Oak Grove Old German Baptist Brethren Church, OH, minister,

956

Wade, Marvin D., 2296
Wade, William Franklin, 1799
Wademan, Silas, 1799
Wadia, John S., 1799
Wadsworth, William J., Jr., 1799
    Quakertown, PA, First Church of the
        Brethren, minister, 1075
Waenger, Anna Mary Shirk, 2095
Waer, Robert, 1799
Wagaman, Benjamin Franklin, 1799, 2306
Wagaman, Jonathan G., 1799
Wageman, J. G., 1346
Wageman, J. Lafayette, 97
Wageman, J. W., 1212
Wageman, Judith P., 97
Wageman, Mary (later Bauman), 1360
Wageman, Mary Melissa, See Bauman,
    Mary Melissa (Wageman)
Waggoner family, 146, 1960, 2088, See also
    Wagner family
    Fremont, OH, Grace Brethren Chapel,
        515
Waggoner, George, 1312
Waggoner, Hans, 1312
    South Carolina, 1204
Waggoner, John, 1338
Waggoner, John, Sr., 1312
Waggoner, Mary Weybright, 1338
Waggoner, Philip, 1312
Waggoner, Phillip, 1312
Waggoner, Timothy L., 515, 2296
Wagner, Abraham, 1876
Wagner, Charles Alonzo, 717, 1223, 1240,
    1799
Wagner, Clark R., 2088
Wagner, Daniel S.
    Old Brethren Church, 2232
Wagner, David Timothy, 684, 1799
Wagner, Edwin Reuben, 2088
Wagner family, 148, 1312, 1342, 1960,
    2045, 2088
    Outlook, WA, Church of the Brethren,
        986
Wagner, Frank Abraham, 1799
Wagner, Harold E., 1799
Wagner, Hettie (later Moherman)
    Moherman, Tully S., mother of, 867
Wagner, Ida (later Hoff), 616, 1361
Wagner, Isaac, 2088
Wagner, John, 1242
    history and genealogy, 1986
    Salem Church of the Brethren, IA,
        1137
Wagner, John Calvin, 1799
Wagner, John O., II, 1799
Wagner, John Otto, 1799, 2306
Wagner, Joseph E.
    Old Brethren Church, 2232
Wagner, Katherine (later Funk), 525
Wagner, Kenneth Charles, 2296
Wagner, Laura Evangeline Larson, 1312,
    1854
Wagner, Liane E., 2296
Wagner, Lloyd E., 2296
    Old Brethren Church, 2232
Wagner, Michael, 1240
Wagner, Murray Loray, Jr., 1799
    Prague Conferences and, 2239
    on First CB, PA, 2361
    on postmillennial views among
        Brethren, 2361
Wagner, Murray Loray, Sr., 1277, 1799,

2306

Mechanic Grove Church of the
    Brethren, PA, pastor, 806
Pleasant Valley Church of the Brethren,
    VA, pastor, 1035
writings of, 2361
Wagner, Oscar William, 1799
Wagner, Philip, 1933
Wagner, Ray, 338
Wagner, Ricardo, 53, 1312, 1799
Wagner, Robert W., 1799, 1253
Wagner, Samuel S., 1799
Wagner, Susan (later Fields), 2278
Wagner, W., 1799
Wagner, Walter H.
    on Ephrata Cloister, 2361
Wagner, Will, 323
Wagner, Mrs. Will, 323
Wagner, William H. (Mr. and Mrs.), 558
Wagner, William U., 1799
Wagner, A. Paul, 1799
Wagner, Abraham, 2107
Wagner, Abram
    North Fork Old German Baptist
        Brethren Church, IN, 947
Wagner, Andrew, 224, 1213, 1335
    Olive Grove Old German Baptist
        Brethren Church, CA, deacon, 973
Wagner, Barbara Ellen Heckman (later
    Forney), 502, 1837
Wagner, Benjamin, 1312
Wagner, Catherine, 345
Wagner, Cecil Denlinger, 2138
Wagner, Gerald C., Sr. (OGBB) and, 2259
Wagner, Charles, 71, 2386
Wagner, Cripe Esther, 352
Wagner, Curtis H., 2296
Wagner, David, 1799
    North Fork Old German Baptist
        Brethren Church, IN, 947
Wagner, Eldo, 1188, 1799, 2306, 2386
    North Manchester Old German Baptist
        Brethren Church, IN, elder-in-
        charge, 949
Wagner, Elizabeth, 2107
Wagner, Elizabeth Hufford
    Wagoner, Raymond K. (OGBB) and,
        2259
Wagner, Elizabeth (later Eikenberry), 431
Wagner, Ella Beery, 1312
Wagner, Ellen Heckman, 1961
Wagner, Ellis H., 1799
Wagner, Eric Floyd, 2296
Wagner, Esther, 352
Wagner, Esther (later Emmons), 1930
Wagner, Ezra, 1799
    Middlefork Old German Baptist
        Brethren Church, IN, presiding
        elder, 826
Wagoner family, 142, 164, 535, 727, 1960,
    2088, See Wagner family
    Genesee Old German Baptist Brethren
        Church, MI, 540
    Irricana (First) Church of the Brethren,
        Alberta, Canada, 663
    letters of, 1930
    Plum Creek Old German Baptist
        Brethren Church, KS, 1038
Wagoner Family Museum, 535
Wagoner, Fern Miller
    Wagoner, Raymond K. (OGBB) and,
        2259
Wagoner, Floyd, 2138, See also Old

German Baptist Brethren
Wagoner, Floyd R., 1223, 1799, 2088,
    2138, 2259, See also Old German
    Baptist Brethren
Wagoner, Gene, 1799, 2296
Wagoner, Gerald C., Sr. (OGBB), 2259
    Old Order Notes, 973
Wagoner, Glen, 1799
Wagoner, Gordon, 2259
Wagoner, Grant F., 1799
Wagoner, Harvey L., 496, 540, 1799, 2306,
    2386
    Middlefork Old German Baptist Breth-
        ren Church, IN, minister, 826
Wagoner, Ida Renicker
    Skiles, Jacob and Sara, foster daughter
        of, 1188
Wagoner, Ira B., 1799
    Red Cloud, NE, Church of the
        Brethren, providing leadership,
        1088
    Silver Lake Church of the Brethren,
        NE, elder and minister, 1182
    South Red Cloud Church of the Breth-
        ren, NE, minister, 1206
Wagoner, Isaac N., 1799
    Morrill Church of the Brethren, MN,
        elder, 877
Wagoner, J. Elmer, 1799, 2014
Wagoner, Jacob, 1213
Wagoner, Jacob Melvin, 1312, 1800
Wagoner, Jeanne (later Heckel), 1960
Wagoner, Jesse A., 373, 1242, 1800, 2259
Wagoner, John, 1800
Wagoner, John J., 1213
Wagoner, John Robert, 1800, 2306, 2386
Wagoner, Joseph, 1800, 1911
    North Fork Old German Baptist
        Brethren Church, IN, overseer, 947
Wagoner, Josiah Elmer, 1846
Wagoner, Leonard J., 1800
    North Fork Old German Baptist
        Brethren Church, IN, overseer, 947
Wagoner, Melvin E., 496, 1800
    North Fork Old German Baptist
        Brethren Church, IN, overseer, 947
Wagoner, Mildred (later Bowman), 2138,
    2139
Wagoner, Morris B., 1312, 1800, 2259
    Middlefork Old German Baptist
        Brethren Church, IN, presiding
        elder, 826
    Mud Valley Old German Baptist
        Brethren Church, IL, presiding
        elder, 892
    North Fork Old German Baptist
        Brethren Church, IN, minister, 948
Wagoner, Noah B., 1213, 1800
    Red Cloud, NE, Church of the
        Brethren, providing leadership,
        1088
    South Red Cloud Church of the
        Brethren, NE, elder, 1206
Wagoner, Nora Faye Royer, 1312
Wagoner, Paul, 1800
Wagoner, Philip, 1213
Wagoner, Ralph Wendell, 262, 923, 1800
Wagoner, Ray S., 576, 1800
Wagoner, Raymond K. (OGBB), 373, 1800,
    2259
Wagoner, Robert E., 2088, 2361
Wagoner, Robert Glen, 1800

Wagoner, Rosa Belie, 1840, 2087
Wagoner, Ruby Miller, 2259
Wagoner, Samuel, 1213
Wagoner, Sarah (later Mohler)
    Mohler, Robert Ellsworth, mother of,
        868
Wagoner, Shirley
    on Society of Brothers (Bruderhof) in
        Paraguay, 2361
Wagoner, Stephen Eugene, 2296
Wagoner, Susan, 226
Wagoner, W. William, 21
Wagoner (Waggoner), Jacob, 1800
Wagoner, Zandra Lynnae, 2296
Wagstaff, Donald E., 1800
Wahiawa, HI, Grace Brethren Church, See `
    Waipio Acres, HI, Grace Brethren
        Church
Wahite, Elizabeth Horst, 2097
Wahre Abbildung des inwendigen
    Christenthums (*True Portrayal of*
    Interior Christianity, 1709), 57
Wahres Christentum (*True Christianity*)
    (Arndt), 381, 1051
Waidele, Johann Michael, 1326
Waimalu, HI, Grace Brethren Church, See
    Aiea, HI, Waimalu Grace Brethren
        Church
Waipio Acres, HI, Grace Brethren Church,
    1312
Waiseman family, 2102
Waite, Frances Wise, 2088
Waite, John K., 1800
Waite, Norman Charles, 1800
Waits, Timothy O., 2296
Waka, Nigeria, 306
Waka School
    Mamza, Ngamariju Keliri, Board of
        Governors, 784
Waka Schools, Nigeria, 936–937
Waka Secondary School, 307
Waka Teachers College, 306–307
    Eikenberry, Ivan Leon, 431
    Sawa, Bitrus Pilasar (CB) and, 2246
    Shank, Glenn H. ("Doc") and Catherine
        Jean Heck (BC) at, 2248
    Shankster, Owen L., Jr., and Celia
        Smith (CB) at, 2248
Waka Teachers' Training College
    Royer, Harold Albertus ("Red"), 1128
Waka Teachers' Training College and
    Secondary School, Nigeria,
    1312–1313
    mission schools, 854
Waka, TX, Church of the Brethren, 1255,
    1312
Wakarusa, IN, 1384, 1385
    Old Brethren Church, 2232
    Church of the Brethren, 96, **1313**
    congregation
        Old Brethren, 970
Wakawa, Thiama, 307, 1800
Wakawa, Yerkawa, 1800
Wakefield, Robert M., 1800
Wakefield, William R., 1800
Wakeman, Charles H., 356, 1800
    Purchase Line Church of the Brethren,
        PA, 1072
Wakeman, Henry Early, 731, 1800
Wakeman, J. Ozias, 1313
Wakeman, Jonas W., 1800
Wakeman, Lemuel D., 1800
Wakeman's Grove Church of the Brethren,

VA, **1313**
Pleasant View Church of the Brethren,
    VA, 1037
Waken, Edward W., 2296
Wakenda Church of the Brethren, MO, 124,
    1313–1314
    Rockingham Church of the Brethren,
        MO, 1118
Walbridge, Doris, 2165
Walch Johann Georg, 2088
Walcheren, the Netherlands
    relief and rehabilitation work, 230
Waldenrath, Alexander, 2088
Waldenses/Waldensians, 15, **1314,** *See also*
    Waldo, Peter
    Agape retreat center, 1365
    apostolic church, as link to, 43
    Czech Brethren, similarities to, 357
    Czechoslovakia, 357
    Historic Peace Churches, 608
    Italy, 665
    Mehrning, Jacob, writings of, 811
    nonconformity, 940
    oaths, taking of, 959
    pacifism in Christian church history,
        998
    religious liberty, suppression of, 1098
    role in development of Brethren theolo-
        gy, 1259
Waldo, OH
    Sciota Church of the Brethen, OH,
        preaching point, 1160
Waldo, Peter, 1314
Waldorf, MD, 1253
Waldport, OR, 317
Wales, George E., 1800
    San Antonio, TX, Church of the
        Brethren, minister, 1141
Walgreen, Virginia Golden, 2088
Walhounding Brethren Church, OH, *See*
    Coshocton, OH, Church of the
        Brethren
Walizer, Gerald Elwood, 695, 1800
"Walk in the Light"
    gospel music, 559
Walk, William D., 1800
Walker, Aaron
    Pipe Creek Church of the Brethren, IN,
        1025
Walker, Antonia, 1800
Walker, Cort I., 2296
Walker, Daniel H., 1314, 1800
Walker, Dinah, 149
Walker, Donna Jean Troyer, 1854
Walker, Emma (later Rieman), 2243
Walker, Ernest Hartwell, 1800
Walker family, *11,* 743
    Grandview, WA, Grace Brethren
        Church, 566
    Parkersburg, WV, Grace Brethren
        Church, 994
Walker, Fern E. Coppock, 1314
Walker, Galen Knepper, 553, 714, **1314,**
    1394, 1800
    Huntingdon, PA, Stone Church of the
        Brethren, 637
    Pottstown, PA, First Church of the
        Brethren, pastor and elder-in-
        charge, 1049
Walker, Glennis Simmons, 2296
Walker, Henry, 1800
Walker, Ira D. S., 1800
Walker, Ivan B., 623, 670, 1800, 2306

Walker, Jesse, 1348
Walker, Jesse E., 1800
Walker, John Earl, 2296
Walker, Lawrence A., 1800
    Omaha, NE, Church of the Brethren,
        minister, 974
Walker, Lydia H., 2171
Walker, Mary Knepper, 1314
Walker, Mary (later Kintner), 696
Walker, Orrin and Melody, 16
Walker, Rebecca (later Schrock), *See*
    Schrock, Rebecca Walker
Walker, Robert C., 1800
Walker, Robert J., 1314
Walker, S. A.
    Seneca Church of the Brethren, OH,
        elder, 1166
Walker, Stephen S., 1800
Walker, Thomas, 1962, 2078, 2088
Walker, Wheeler D., 1800
Walker, William LeRoy, 1854
    medical missions, 807
Walker's Chapel Church of the Brethren,
    VA, **1314**
    Pleasant View Church of the Brethren,
        VA, 1037
Walkers Well Church of the Brethren, VA,
    See New Bethel Church of the
        Brethren, VA
Walkersville, MD, Glade Valley Church of
    the Brethren, **1314**
    Frederick, MD, Church of the
        Brethren, 511
Walkerton, IN, Brethren Church, *See*
    Teegarden, IN, Brethren Church
walking doctor, *See* Fahrney, Peter
Walkup, Lorena, 265
Wall, Carol, 1862
Wall family, 2088
Wall, H. V.
    Raisin City, CA, Church of the
        Brethren, 1083
Wall, Henry, 1217
Wall, Margareta, 2088
Wall, O. J., 2088
Wallace, Abner, 320, 1800
Wallace, Carl E., 1800
Wallace, Edith Clay, 2089
Wallace family, 461
Wallace, George Kirkwood, 1800, 1854
    Mansfield, OH, Woodville Grace
        Brethren Church, pastor, 787
    Pleasant Grove Grace Brethren Church,
        IA, pastor, 1031
Wallace, John, 438
Wallace, Judith Lynne Millikan, 1854
Wallace, Lewis, 1801
Wallace, Lucinda, 438
Wallace, Mike, 2296
Wallace, Paul A. W., 2089
Wallace, Robert B., 1218, 1801
Wallace, Stewart, 2089
Wallach, Glenn, 2089
Wallauer, Maralyn A., 2089
Walle, Dennis F., 1861
Walleck (Wallech), John S., 1801
Waller, Stephen, 1801
Wallick, Alexander Barnes, 1801
Wallick, Alice Spangler, 1314
Wallick, Cyrus F., 137, **1314,** 1801
Wallick, Franklin
    Peace Corps, 1002
Wallick, Galen, 1801

Wallick, Kathryn Blocher, 2089
Wallick, Walter, 2089
Walliford, Ralph, 1801
Wallmann, Johannes
  Pietism, 2201
  writings of, 2361
Wallower, Lucille, 747, 2089
  on Dunkers children's book, 2361
wallpaper, 59, **1314**
Walls, Irvin P., 1801
  Rockton, PA, Church of the Brethren,
    pastor, 1118
Walls, Jacob Edward, 1801
Walls, PA, *See* East McKeesport, PA,
    Church of the Brethren
Walnut Church of the Brethren, IN, **1315**
  Mount Pleasant Church of the
    Brethren, IN, 886
Walnut Creek Church of the Brethren, MO,
  1315
  Missouri, 865
Walnut Creek congregation, MO
  example of place name, 911
Walnut Creek Old German Baptist Brethren
    Church, MO, **1315**
Walnut Grove Church of the Brethren, IL,
  1315
  Big Creek congregation, 1315, 2126
  cemetery, 2349
  Martin Creek Church of the Brethren,
    IL, organized from, 797
Walnut Grove Church of the Brethren, PA,
    See Johnstown, PA, Walnut Grove
    Church of the Brethren
Walnut Grove Church of the Brethren, VA,
  1315
Walnut Grove Church of the Brethren, WV,
  1315
  Moorefield, WV, Church of the
    Brethren, 875
Walnut Grove Dunkard Brethren Congrega-
    tion, MD, 1241, **1315–1316**
Walnut Grove, MO, Church of the
    Brethren, *See* Plattsburg Church of
    the Brethren, MO
Walnut Grove, MO, congregation
  Plattsburg Church of the Brethren, MO,
    1030
Walnut Grove, OH, meetinghouse, 2025
Walnut Grove, PA, Church of the Brethren,
    2089
Walnut Grove, PA, congregation, 380
  Conewago, PA, Church of the
    Brethren, mission point for, 333
Walnut House meetinghouse (Fulton Co.,
    IL), 69
Walnut, IN, Church of the Brethren, 2047,
    2089
Walnut Level Church of the Brethren, IN,
    152, **1316**
  Hickory Grove Church of the Brethren,
    IN, 602
  Pleasant Dale Church of the Brethren,
    IN, 1030
Walnut meetinghouse
Woodland Church of the Brethren, IL, 1364
Walnut Ridge, IA, congregation
  Prairie City Church of the Brethren,
    IA, 1050
Walnut St. Church of the Brethren, IN, *See*
    North Manchester, IN, Church of
    the Brethren
Walnut Valley Church of the Brethren, KS,

726, **1316**
Walpusk family
  Jenners, PA, Grace Brethren Church,
    670
Walruff, Charles A., 1801
Walschmidt family
  Meyer family related by marriage, 822
Walser, Giles
  Maple Grove Church of the Brethren,
    NC, 790
Waltemyer, Christian, 1801
Walter, Charles H., 1801
Walter, Christina (later Claar), 1294
Walter, Dean I., 1253, 1305, 1801, 2306
Walter family, 2111
Walter, Fred M., 708
Walter, Fred William, 16, 746, 1801
  North Buffalo Grace Brethren Church,
    PA, pastor, 945
Walter, Genevene Edna (later Pifer), 2238
Walter, Hugo G.
  on Francke, August Hermann, 2362
Walter, Johannes, 1211
Walter, Johannes von
  Pietism subdivisions, 1021
Walter, KS, congregation, Royer Commu-
    nity
  disbandment, 934
Walter, Lloyd A., 1801
Walter, Melvin R., 1801
Walter, W. F., 1801
Walters, Clara Rae, 1846
Walters, Crystal Pauline Randel, 2089
Walters family, 1304, 2089
Walters, Fred C., 1801
Walters, Fred W., 585
Walters, Jacob O., 1801
Walters, John, 1801
Walters, Jonathan S., 2089
  on Fayette County PA Brethren, 2362
Walters, Matilda (later Zunkel), 1402
Walters, Robert E., 1801
Walters, Rolland, 1801
Walters, William Eugene, 1801
  Mount Joy, PA, Florin Church of the
    Brethren, free minister, 882
  Shippensburg, PA, Church of the
    Brethren, pastor in, 1177
Waltersdorff, Christy Jo, 2296
Walther, Richard, 2175
Waltman, J. K., 1801
  Oak Grove Church of the Brethren,
    OK, minister, 956
Waltner, Christian, 2088
Waltner, Freni, 2088
Waltner, Lena, 2088
Walton Church of the Brethren, KS, **1316**
Walton, Harold W., 1801
Walton, IN, Church of the Brethren, **1316**
Walton, Joseph Hester, 1801
Walton, Joseph S., 1895, 2089
Walton, KS, congregation
  Royer Community Church of the
    Brethren, KS, 1128
Waltz, Benjamin Franklin, 21, 599, 912,
    1316, 1801, 2089
Waltz, Brethred E., 1801
Waltz, Conrad B., 1316
Waltz, Daniel, 1801
Waltz family, 148
Waltz, Mary E. Myers, 1316
Waltz, Mary Helfert, 1316
Wambold, Roger L., 1801

Wampfler, Hans Peter, 1318
Wampler, Amos, 268, 1801
  Miami, NM, Church of the Brethren,
    elder, 823
Wampler, Anna Driver, 1316
Wampler, Anna (later Kline), 701
Wampler, Anna (later Roller), 470
Wampler, Barbara S., 2089
Wampler, Benjamin Franklin, *1317*
Wampler, Byron Joseph, Jr., 672, 676, 1801
Wampler, Catherine Miller, 2259
Wampler, Charles W., Sr. (CB), 1801, 2089,
    2259
Wampler, D. B., 1801
Wampler, Daniel, 1801
Wampler, Daniel J., 445, 1318, 1801
Wampler, Daniel Saylor, 273, 1801
Wampler, David, 1318
Wampler, David B., 1801, 2089, 2306
  Pulaski, VA, Church of the Brethren,
    pastor, 1071
Wampler, David, family of, 1332
Wampler, Edward, 1801
  Mud Valley Old German Baptist
    Brethren Church, IL, minister, 892
Wampler, Eliza Beer, 1317, 1318
Wampler, Elizabeth Baker, 1316, 1846,
    1866
Wampler, Ellen, 416
Wampler, Ernest Michael, 277, **1316**, 1801,
    1846, 2089
Wampler family, 173, 700, 1318, 1338,
    2089
  North Bethel Church of the Brethren,
    MO, 945
  South Bethel German Baptist Brethren,
    MO, 1204
Wampler, Frank, 1801
Wampler, Fred F., 2089
Wampler, Frederick Jacob, **1316**, 1801,
    1846, 1938
  medical missions, 807
Wampler, Frederick William, 1801, 1846
Wampler, Guy Edgar, Sr., 163, **1316–1317**,
    1801, 2089, **2386**
  Mount Hermon Church of the
    Brethren, VA, pastor, 881
Wampler, Guy Edgar, Jr., 503, 1317, 1801
Wampler, Hans Peter
  Mason, Floyd R. on descendants of,
    2346
  Mason, Kathryn Garst on descendants
    of, 2346
Wampler, J. D. (Lima, OH), 1801
Wampler, J. D. (Smith Creek), 1801
Wampler, J. Galen, 1801
Wampler, J. W., 173, 923
Wampler, James C., 2089
Wampler, Jessie Z., *578*
Wampler, John, 7, 746, 1214, 2259
  family of, 1938
Wampler, John B., 110, 224, 268, 274, 350,
    551, **1317**, 1318, 1801–1802, 2089
  Jones Mills, PA, Valley Brethren
    Church, 676
  Masontown, PA, Brethren Church,
    pastor, 800
  Oakland Brethren Church, New Bethle-
    hem, PA, elder in, 925
  Reconstruction Committee, 1086
Wampler, John F., 1802
Wampler, Joseph
  Pleasant View Church of the Brethren,

OH, minister, 1037
Wampler, Joseph (1831–1876), 1315, 1802
Wampler, Joseph (1833–1890), 1802
Wampler, Joseph Benjamin, 1317
Wampler, Joseph D.
    writings of, 2362
Wampler, Joseph (Knobnoster, VA), 1802
Wampler, Joseph W., 2089
Wampler, Joseph William, 1802
Wampler, Kenneth Franklin, 1802
Wampler, Mae Wine, 2259
Wampler, Magdalene Garber, 1318
Wampler, Margaret, 1845
Wampler, Maria (later Shoup), *See* Shoup,
    Maria Wampler
Wampler, Marilyn J., 2089
Wampler, Mark W., 1802
Wampler, Mary Garber, 1317
Wampler, Mary (later Wilt), 1347
Wampler, Mrs. Ernest M., 2011
Wampler, Nelie Florence, 416, 462, **1317,**
    2089
Wampler, Pearl Hoover, 1316
Wampler, Peter, Jr., 1318
Wampler, Philip, 1318, 1802
Wampler, Rebecca C. Skeggs, **1316,** 1846,
    2017
Wampler, Ruby K. Oellig, 1317
Wampler, Ruth Josephine Spangler, 1846
Wampler, S. J.
    New Hope Church of the Brethren, TN,
        elder in, 929
Wampler, S. L., 1316
Wampler, Sadie Irene Stutsman, *248,* **1317,**
    2101
Wampler, Sadie S., 1361
Wampler, Sadie Zigler, 2259
Wampler, Samuel, 1802
Wampler, Stanley R., 1802
Wampler, Susannah (later Flory), 498
Wampler, Susie (later Glick), 553
Wampler, Vernon E., 1802
Wampler, Vida Eunice Miller, 724, 1316,
    1846
Wampler, Zola Huffman, 2259
Wampole family, 2062
Wanamaker, John
    Brumbaugh, Martin Grove and, 223
    Sand Brook Church of the Brethren,
        NJ, 1142
Wandali, Nigeria, 306
*Wanderungen zwischen Hudson und
    Mississippi* (Busch), 232
Wang, Tung, 2089
Wanger family, 1936, 2095, *See also*
    Wenger family
    Heisey family, 595
Wanger, George F. Price, 2089–2090
Wangerd family, 2095
Wangman, Andrew
    on Miller, Peter and letter to Peter
        Lehman, 2362
Wanker, Antonia, 1802
Wanner, Abraham Groff, 2090
Wanner family
    family history, 2003
Wantz, Douglas Edward, 2296
war, *See* conscientious objection; mili-
    tary service; specific war
    conscientious objectors and, 916–917
    missions, 861
    mural paintings at Camp Mack portray-
        ing, 896

peace witnesses and, 253
    sources on, 2322
    in Sudan (CB), 2253
    taxes, *See* taxes
    validity and legality, 2004
War Between the States, *See* Civil War
war bonds
    recommendation not to purchase, **1318**
    World War I, 1370–1371
    World War II, 1373
War Department
    Swigart, William Joseph, meetings
        with, 1245
War of 1812, **1318**
    church-state relations, 310
    Müller (Miller) family, 894
    peace, 999
    Shelby Co. German Baptist Brethren
        Church, KY, members leaving
        after, 1175
War Prisoner's Aid program
    prisoners of war, Brethren service to,
        1058
War Problems Committee of the Friends
    General Conference
    French, Paul Comly, 515
War Relief and Reconstruction Committee,
    1370, *See also* Relief and Recon-
    struction Committee
War Versus Peace (Funk), 525
Ward, Asa, 752
Ward, Bernard, 1802
Ward, Calvin A., 753, 1802
Ward, Charles Monroe, 1802
Ward Co., ND, 164, 1242
    Surrey, ND, congregation, 946
Ward family
    Marietta, GA, Grace Brethren Church
        of Greater Atlanta, 793
    South Loup Church of the Brethren,
        NE, 1206
Ward, Henry E., 1802
Ward, J. P., 1802
Ward, James W., Jr., 1280, 1802
Ward, John Martin, 1802
Ward, Julia (later Howe)
    Mothers' Day, 879
Ward, Leo R., 2090
Ward, Richard Daniel, 1802
    Onekama, MI, Church of the Brethren,
        minister, 975
Ward, Robert Elmer, 1862, 2090
Ward, Russell M., 357, 365, 367, 768, 1802
Ward, Samuel, 1802
Ward, Sterling, 2170
Ward, Ted, 1896
Ward Townsend, 2090
Ward, W. R[eginald]
    historiography, 2201
    on Protestant evangelical movement,
        2362
Ward, Winifred Adelaide (later Heckman),
    593
Wardensville, WV, 1276
Wardlaw, Gretchen Diane Davis, 2296
Wards Church Dunkard Brethren congrega-
    tion, PA, *See* Waynesboro, PA,
    Dunkard Brethren congregation
Ware, L. G., 555, 1802
Wareham, Isaac, 1802
    Snake Spring Valley Church of the
        Brethren, PA, free minister, 1192
Wareham, C. Roscoe, 257, 1802, 2306

Wareham, J. Richard, 1802
warfare, *See* conscription; specific wars
    Grubb, Michael R. on Anabaptists's
        perspective on, 2334
Warfel family, 1885
Warfel, Stephen G.
    on Ephrata Cloister, 2362
Waridel, Lily, 1854
Waridel, Pierre-Andre, 1854
Warne, Thomas P.
    New River Old German Baptist
        Brethren Church, ministers for,
        931
Warner, Arthur L., 1802
Warner, D. S., 296
Warner, David, 2, 1802
Warner, David F., 1802
Warner, De Main, 2090
Warner family
    Hurricane Creek Old German Baptist
        Brethren Church, IL, 638
    Mishler family, related to, 852
    Osceola, IN, Grace Brethren Church,
        983
    Salem Church of the Brethren, OH,
        1138
Warner, Jonathan, 1802
Warner, Joseph, 1802
    Peach Blossom Colored Church of
        Rising Light (CB), MD, minister,
        1003
Warner, Noah
    Pleasant Hill Old German Baptist
        Brethren Church, IL, 1033
Warner, Norman Hart, 417, 1802
Warner, Paul Dean, 1846
Warner, Ruth Arlene, 1846
Warner, Schuyler
    Sand Creek Church of the Brethren,
        KS, minister, 1143
Warner, William Frederic, 2090
Warren, Charles, 1802
Warren Co., IA
    New Virginia, IA, Brethren Church,
        932
    Osceola, IA, Church of the Brethren,
        983
Warren Co., KY
    Ham, John, 580
    later Allen and Simpson Cos., 398,
        688, 689
    migration of Brethren, 829
    Rowland (Roland) family, 1127
Warren Co., NJ
    Hope Grace Brethren, 930
Warren Co., OH, 165, 1281
Warren Co., VA, 343, 368
    Front Royal, VA, Church of the
        Brethren, 518
    Mount Pleasant Brethren Church, VA,
        886
    Reliance, VA, Mount Zion Brethren
        Church, 1096
Warren County, IN
    Old Brethren Church, 2232
Warren family, 1885
    Prosser, WA, Community Grace
        Brethren Church, 1062
Warren, Isaac Edward, 1802
Warren, James, 321
    South Carolina minister, 1204
Warren (later Allen) Co., KY, 398
Warren (later Simpson) Co., KY

Far Western Brethren, 475
Warren (Warne), Thomas P., 1802
Warrenfeltz, Annettea, 2090
Warrensburg, MO, 735
    Church of the Brethren, **1318**
Warrenville, PA
    Netzley, Jacob, 913
Warrick, Ronald, 332, 1380, 1802
Warrington, James, 1862
Warriors Mark Church of the Brethren, PA,
    See Spring Mount Church of the
    Brethren, PA
wars, *See* Civil War; Revolutionary War;
    World War I; World War II
    dissertations on, 169
    material aid, 802
    Mennonites, 815
Warsaw Christian School, Warsaw, IN,
    1319
Warsaw, IN, 256
    Christner, David C., 289
    Community Grace Brethren Church,
        744, **1319**, 1353, 1385
        Riddle, Earl M., pastor, 1108
    Dutchtown Brethren Church, *See*
        Dutchtown Brethren Church, IN
    (First) Brethren Church, **1318–1319**
    Lakeland Conservative Grace Brethren
        Church, 2168
Warstler, Anna Margaret, 558, **1319**, 1846,
    2090
    Holsinger (Holtzinger) family, 623
Warstler, Calvin Walter, 70, 1802
    Natrona Heights Church of the Breth-
        ren, 918
    Penn Run Church of the Brethren, PA,
        elder, 1004
Warstler, Charles E., 1319
Warstler, Hugh T., 1802
Warstler, John Henry, 1802
Warstler, Nancy A. Holtzinger, 1319
Warstler, Otho H., 1246, 1802
Warstler, Walter, 1802
Wartman, J. H., 2090
Wartmann, Laurentz, 2104
Warvel, Bessie (later Perry), 1009
Warvel, Etta (later Bowman), 1360
Warwick Twp., PA, 158, 686, 1401
Wash, William Blaze, Jr., 1802
Washburn, Burl A., 1802
Washburn, David, 1862
Washburn, Mabel Thacher Rosemary, 2090
washing of feet, 698
Washington Bible College
    CE National, Inc., 2156
Washington Bible School, 688
Washington Brethren Action Movement
    (WASH-BAM), 179
Washington City congregation, 1363–1364
Washington City, MD, congregation
    Hyattsville, MD, University Park
        Church of the Brethren, 641
    Monrovia, MD, Bush Creek Church of
        the Brethren, 870
Washington Co., AL
    Fruitdale, AL, Church of the Brethren,
        520
Washington Co., AR
    Round Mountain Church of the
        Brethren, AR, 1125
Washington Co. Historical Society, MD
    Sharpsburg, MD, Church of the
        Brethren meetinghouse, 1174

Washington Co., IA, 353
Washington Co., IN, 1380
    Hostetler, Joseph, 631
Washington Co., MD, 166, 170, 216, 398,
        718, 724, 734, 756, 1224, 1225,
        1303, 1312, 1320, 2105
    Emmert family, 444
    Fahrney, Peter, 466
    Good (Guth) family, 556
    Manor Church of the Brethren, MD,
        787
    Pfautz family, 1014
    St. James Brethren Church, 1134
Washington Co., PA, 1246, 1253, 2091
    Brethren Church congregations, 1005
    Dunkard Brethren Church, 2106
    Highland Brethren Church, PA, 605
    Nafzger, Rudolph, settled in, 939
    Shideler family, 1177
Washington Co., TN, 167, 264, 269, 740,
        742, 1253, 1349
    Hawthorne Church of the Brethren,
        TN, 590
    New Hope Church of the Brethren, TN,
        929
    Pleasant Valley Church of the Brethren,
        TN, 1035
    Pleasant View Church of the Brethren,
        TN, 1037
        to Niota, TN, Church of the
            Brethren, 938
Washington Co., VA, 1315
Washington Court House, OH, Fairview
        Brethren Church, **1320–1321**
    Miamisburg, OH, Brethren Church,
        823
Washington Creek Church of the Brethren,
        KS, 682, 753, 1311, **1321**
    migration of Brethren, 830
    Overbrook, KS, Church of the
        Brethren, 986
    Pleasant Grove Church of the Brethren,
        KS, 1031
Washington, George, 211, 311, 516
    arrest of Christopher Sauer II during
        Revolutionary war, 1146
    Brethren children named for, 912
    Ephrata Community, 451
    Germantown, Battle of, 544
    guest at Landis house, 723
    protest against Sunday law trials, 1931
    remembered by Jacob Forrer's mother,
        1320
    Revolutionary War, American, 1105
Washington Heights Grace Brethren
        Church, VA, *See* Roanoke, VA,
        Washington Heights Grace
        Brethren Church
Washington, IN, Church of the Brethren,
        See North Winona Church of the
        Brethren, IN
Washington, KS, Church of the Brethren,
        1320
    Markey family, 794
Washington Office (CB), **2260**
    sources on, 2322
Washington, PA
    Bermudian Church of the Brethren
        Cemetery, 2084
    Grace Brethren Church, **1320**
Washington schoolhouse, WV, 1254
Washington (State), **1319**
    colonization, 299, 320

conscientious objectors, 337
Cooperative Colonization Company,
    342
Dairy Farm Assignments, 359
frontier, 519
Graybill (Grabill, Krehbiel) family, 567
Great Northern Railroad, 569
Idaho, 645
migration of Brethren, 830
missions and missionaries, 269
missions and missionaries in
    Carl, George Clinton, 255
North Dakota Brethren relocating to,
    946
Old German Baptist Brethren, 967,
    2235
Peters, Amos B., assisting colonization,
    1011
preacher circuits in, 169
railroads and Brethren settlement, 1082
Washita Church of the Brethren, OK, **1321**
Waskeys Mill, VA mission point, Botetourt
    Co., VA, Church of the Brethren,
    164
Wassam family
    Peace Valley Church of the Brethren,
        MO, 1003
Wassam, J. J., 237, 1213, 1802
Wastler, LeRoy Edwin, 1330, 1802, 2306
"Watchman of the Night and Millennial
    Morning" (attributed to A. H.
    Cassel)
    Kruppp, Abraham on, 2342
Waterbrook, VA, Brethren Church, **2260**
Waterford, CA
    Church of the Brethren, **1321**
    Empire, CA, Church of the Brethren,
        445
Waterford, CA, Dunkard Brethren congre-
    gation, 239, *See also* Modesto,
    CA, Pleasant Home Dunkard
    Brethren congregation; Modesto,
    CA, (Waterford) Pleasant Home
    Dunkard Brethren congregation
Waterford, PA, Ligonier First Church of the
    Brethren, **1321**
    Robinson, PA, Church of the Brethren,
        1116
Waterlander Mennonite congregation, 1241
Waterloo Co., Ontario, 1870
Waterloo, IA, 741
    Cedar Heights Community Brethren
        Church, **1321–1322**
    Church of the Brethren, 661
    City Church of the Brethren, 149,
        1322, **1322**
    (First) Brethren Church, 114, 155,
        1321, 1322
        Hudson, IA, First Brethren
            Church, **635**
    Grace Brethren Church, 101, **1322**
        Cedar Rapids, IA, Grace Brethren
            Church, mission point of, 265
    Hammond Avenue Brethren Church
        (BC, CB), **2260**
    South Waterloo Church of the Breth-
        ren, 661–662, 1321, 1028,
        1322–1323
Waterloo Township, Ont.
    biographical history of, 1924
Waters, Edith, 713
Waters family
    Golden Church of the Brethren, NC,

555
Robins, IA, Church of the Brethren,
1115
Waters, Jacob C., 1802
Waters, Mary Ellen (later Drushal)
Beulah Beach I and II, **2136–2137,**
2141, 2170
church governance and, 2264
founding member of Ashland, OH,
University Church, 2132
moderator of General Conference,
2141, 2170
Waters, Ronald L., 1802
Waterloo, IA, Hammond Avenue
Brethren Church and, 2260
Waters, Ronald Wayne, 186, 2137, 2170,
2296
Waters, Willard, 1862
Waterside, PA
Church of the Brethren, 706, **1323**
New Enterprise, PA, Church of the
Brethren, 927
Watkins, A. B., 1060
Watkins, Evelyn Pritchett, 1060
Watkins, Fern Irene (later Jewell), 2209
Watkins, Howard M., 1802
Watkins, Lafayette, 912, 1802
Watkins, Thomas J., 1802–1803
Watkins, Thomas, Jr., 674
Watkins, William C., 1803
Watson, George W., 1803
Watson, Isaac, 1224
Watson, J. F., 104, 673
Watson, J. Fremont, 1803
Watson, Jesse E., 1803
Watson John F., 2090
Watson, M. D., 1803
Mount Zion Church of the Brethren,
KS, 888
Watson, Myrtle (later Keller), 1215
Keller, Paul W., 2210
Watters, Jacob C., 1803
Watters, Sarah (later Harrison), 586
Watts family, 2087
Howard Co. Old German Baptist
Brethren Church, IN, 633
Minerva, OH, Grace Brethren Church,
843
Watts, Isaac, 1211
hymns, 643
Watts, John G., 1803
Watts, William S., 1215, 1803
Waugh, William Albert, 2296
Wauseon, OH, 409, 1334
Dunkard Brethren Church, 1243
wave
logo of Church of the Brethren, 2146,
2147
Waverly, WA, 1212
Wawaka family, 1312
Wawaka, IN, Church of the Brethren, **1323**
Wawaka, TX, Church of the Brethren, *See*
Waka, TX, Church of the Brethren
Way, Moy, *See* Moy Way
The Way of Christ (Boehme), 156
Waybright, Elizabeth (later Oberholtzer)
article about, 1942
Waybright, George W., 1803
Waybright, Stanley Milton, 1803, 2297
Waybright, Wilma Erma Bittinger, 1803
Waycross, GA, 691
Wayland, Anna Kagey, 1323
Wayland, Francis Fry, 2090

Bridgewater College, 2362, 2372
Wayland, John Walter, 534, **1323,** 1803,
2090–2091
historical writing, 611
hymns, 643
Wayland, John Wesley, 1323
Wayland, Mattie V. Fry, 1323
Wayman Valley congregation, IA
Garber, IA, Church of the Brethren,
529
Waymire family, 1299
Waymire, John Rudolph, 2044
Wayne Co., IL
Martin Creek Church of the Brethren,
IL, 797
Wayne Co., IN, 352, 384, 2107
Miami Valley, OH, 961
migration of Brethren, 829
Nettle Creek Church of the Brethren,
923–924
Nettle Creek Old Baptist Brethren
Church, 924
Reiff (Rife) family, 1094
Replogle family, 1100
Shultz and Paul families, 1156
Wayne Co., OH, 145, 215, 233, 279, 415,
2074
Fair Haven Brethren Church, OH, 467
migration of Brethren, 829
Mohican Church of the Brethren, OH,
867
Ontario Brethren, 975
Paradise Church of the Brethren, 992
Shoemaker, Martin, descendants, 1157
Smithville, OH, First Brethren Church,
1192
Wayne Co., WI
German Baptist Church
history, 1940
history of, 1940
Wayne Heights, PA, 733
Brethren Church, **1323**
(Waynesboro) Brethren Church, 32
Wayne, L. B., 518
Wayne Nicarry Social Science Building
Elizabethtown College, 438
Waynesboro congregation, PA
example of place name, 911
Waynesboro, PA, 203, 1302, 1329, 1397
Church of the Brethren, 42, **1323–1324**
Dunkard Brethren Congregation, **1324**
First Brethren Church, 1323
German Baptist congregatons
Grace Brethren Church, **1324**
Greencastle, PA, Conococheague Grace
Brethren Church, 2193
Wayne Heights Brethren Church, *See*
Wayne Heights, PA, Brethren
Church
Waynesboro, VA, 1308
Church of the Brethren, 90, 152, **1324**
Waynesville Church of the Brethren, MO,
1324
Wayside, WA, 1212
WCC, *See* World Council of Churches
WCTU, *See* Women's Christian Temperance
Union
We Care Fellowship
Elkhart, IN, City Church of the
Brethren, 439
Elkhart Valley Church of the Brethren,
IN, 440
example of Christian community place

name, 911
We Gather Together (CB) (1979), 39, 51
laying on of hands, 731
We Won't Murder (French), 515
Weakley, Phoebe, *679*
Wealy, Adam, 1803
Wean family, 164
Weand family, 2091, *See also* Wieand
family
weapons, use of, *See* arms, bearing of
Wear family
Grandview, WA, Grace Brethren
Church, 566
Weatherford, TX, Live Oak Church of the
Brethren, **1324**
Weatherholt, Otis S., Jr., 2297
Weatrock, O., 1803
"Weave"
People of the Covenant (POC) (BC)
and, 2237
Weaver, Aaron Detweiler, 1803, 2091
Weaver, Abram A., 1803
Weaver, Adam
Mack family, 778
Weaver, Alvin L., 2091
Weaver, Anna, 1951
Weaver, Anna B. (later Reed), 2042
Weaver, Anna Mae (later Rutt), 2052
Weaver, Barbara, 2072
Weaver, Benjamin, 2091, 2092
Weaver, Betty Parker
Weaver, Scott L. (FGBC, CGBCI) and,
2261
Weaver, Beverly G., 2297
Weaver, Bruce H., 1803
Weaver, Carpenter, 2087
Weaver, Charles E., 2091
Weaver, Christian, 1323, 1803
Weaver, Clayton, 1803
Weaver, Clayton F., 338, 721, 1803
free ministry to New Fairview Church
of the Brethren, PA, 927
Weaver, Clyde E., 190, 1803, 2091, 2306,
2260–2261, *2260,* **2386**
Weaver, Conrad, 1803
Weaver, Cora E. Z., 2091
Weaver, Cora (later Brown), 2152
Weaver, D. F., 1803
Weaver, Daniel, 235, 494, 1803
Weaver, David, 2091
Weaver, David Harry, 1803, 2091
Weaver, David W., 1803
Weaver, E. Paul, 1803, 1846, 2091
memoirs, 2362
Mexico, IN, Church of the Brethren,
paid minister, 821
Weaver, Earnest Frank, 1803
Weaver, Edward S., 1803
Weaver, Edwin Lemuel, 2091
Weaver, Elias A., 2018
Weaver, Elizabeth, 1325
Weaver, Elizabeth Kreider, 2092
Weaver, Elizabeth Schrock, 2095
Weaver, Elizabeth W. Burkholder, *See*
Weaver family
Weaver, Ella Mae Stern, 1846
Weaver, Elmer, 1803
Weaver, Emma
Weaver, Clyde E. (CB) and, 2260
Weaver, Emma Jean, 1846
Weaver, Ervin, 173, 269, 1212, 1803, 2091
Osceola Church of the Brethren, IN,
pastor, 984

Rock Run Church of the Brethren, IN, pastor, 1117
Weaver, Esther Susan, 2091
Weaver, Ethan Allen, 2091
Weaver family, 164, 233, 1224, 1227, 1907, 2052, 2062, 2073, 2087, 2091, 2092, *See also* Weber family
family history, 1964, 1978, 2009
Glück (Glick, Click) family, 553
history of, 1912
Hoffman (Huffman) family, 618
Irricana (First) Church of the Brethren, Alberta, Canada, 663
Mount Pleasant Brethren Church, VA, 886
New Holland, PA, Church of the Brethren, 928
Weaver, Fanny Ritchey, 1324
Weaver, Francis B., 2091
Weaver, Frederick, 1224, 1325
Weaver, Garnet E., 2297
Weaver, George E., 1803
Weaver, George W., 1803
Weaver, Glenn, 2091
Weaver, Grant Earl, 1803
Penn Run Church of the Brethren, PA, pastor, 1004
Weaver, Hannah Mack
Mack family, 778
Weaver, Hazel Weaver, 1959
Weaver, Henry, 1325
Weaver, Henry B., 2091, 2092
Weaver, Herbert G., 2297
Weaver, Herschel S., 1803
Weaver, Ira Eugene, 1803
Rural Life Association (RLA), 1131
Weaver, Irvin, 1803
Weaver, Irvin R., 2091
Weaver, Isaac M., *See* Weaver family
Weaver, J. A., 122, 164, 663, 687, 1803
Weaver, J. D.
Anabaptism, 2201
Weaver, J. Denny
on nonresistance, 2362
Weaver, Jacob A., 1324
Weaver, Jacob B., 2091–2092
Weaver, James Bruce, 1803
Weaver, James Edwin, 1803, 2092
Weaver, James Norman, 1803, 2306
Weaver, Jennie, 1290
Weaver, James P., 2092
Weaver, Joel Adam, 1803
Weaver, John, 1325, 2091, 2092
letters to Samuel Weaver, 2092
Weaver, John B., 2091, 2092
family history and genealogy, 1971
Weaver, John B. and Anna H. Oberholtzer
genealogy, 1971
Weaver, John E., 1803
Weaver, John L.
Potsdam, OH, Church of the Brethren, 1048
Weaver, John P., 2008–2009
Weaver, Jonathan R., 2091
Weaver, Joseph, 1803
Weaver, Josiah L., 115, 1803
Penn Run Church of the Brethren, PA, pastor, 1004
Weaver, Katherine A.
Weaver, Clyde E. (CB) and, 2260
Weaver, L. John, 2306, 2379
Midway Church of the Brethren, PA, pastor, 827

Weaver, Laura G. Musser, 2092
Weaver, Lee A., 357, 1803
Weaver, Leon John, 1803–1804
Weaver, Levi and Esther Sauder
family history, 1997
Weaver, Levi H., 1804
Weaver, Lizzie B., 2092
Weaver, Lizzie W. Horst, 2091
Weaver log house
Valley Brethren-Mennonite Heritage Center and, 2258
Weaver, Lois Eleanor Snare Carter, 1846
Weaver, Louisa (later Stump), 1232
Weaver, Lovina Hoffman, 1324
Weaver, M.
Johnstown, PA, Moxham Church of the Brethren, 674
Ontario Brethren, 975
Weaver, Mabel, 225–226
Weaver, Mahlon J., **1324**, 1804
Johnstown, PA, Arbutus Church of the Brethren, 673
Roaring Spring, PA, First Church of the Brethren, pastor, 1114
Weaver, Mary, 2092
Weaver, Mary Hoover, 2092
Weaver, Mary N. Martin, 2092
Weaver, Mary W., 2095
Weaver, Merrell G., 2092
Weaver, Millard H., 1804
Weaver, Milton R., 345, 1804, 2092
Omaha, NE, Church of the Brethren, leadership by, 974
Weaver, Monroe Atlee, 2092
Weaver, Moses, 1804
Weaver, Naomi (later Zeigler)
Zeigler, Carl Wenger (CB) and, 2269
Weaver, Nelda, 1845
Weaver, Nickolas, 2095
Weaver, Paul C., 1804
Weaver, Paul M., 247, 248, 249, 1846, **2388**
Weaver, Pauline E., 118
Weaver, Peter, 2092
Weaver, Philip, *See* Weber, Philipp
Weaver, Reuben and Lydia Shirk
family history and genealogy, 1976–1977
Weaver, Robert Kean, 2092
Weaver, Roxie Hankins, 1324
Weaver, Ruth (later Tully), 1278
Weaver, Samuel, 2092
Weaver, Samuel B., 2092
Weaver, Samuel Clyde, 1804, 2260
Weaver, Samuel Edward, 1804
Weaver, Samuel P., 633, 1804
Weaver, Sarah M., 2092
Weaver, Scott L., 155, 1804, **2261**
Osceola, IN, Grace Brethren Church, pastor, 984
South Bend, IN, Ireland Road Grace Brethren Church, pastor, 1203
Weaver, Sophia (later Taylor), 1249
Weaver, Stephen A., 629, 1804
Weaver, Susanna, 1325
Weaver, Theron G., 1245, 1333, 1804
Mexico, IN, Church of the Brethren, paid minister, 821
Middlebury, IN, Church of the Brethren, pastor, 826
Peru, IN, Church of the Brethren, pastor, 1010
Weaver, Vera Fishburn Myers, 2092
Weaver, Virgil Clement, 2092

Weaver (Weber) family
Flat Rock Church of the Brethren, NC, 493
Weaver, William Banks, 2092
Weaver, William F., 1804
Weaver, William Otis, 2092
Weaver, William Penn, 1959
Weaver, William Woys, 1092
on Sauer, Christoph, II and herbal cures, 2362
Weaver (Witwer), Catherine, 2092
Weaver (Witwer) family, 2092
Weaver (Witwer), Isaac, 2092
Weaver, Zalma Faw, 1846
Weaverland, PA, 2092
Webb, Dossie (Fewell), 752
Webb, George, 1804
Webb, Hannah (later Miller)
Müller (Miller) family, 894
Webb, Henry, 1804
Webb, Isaac E., 416, 1804
Webb, Jacob, Sr., 163
Webb, Leonard C., 53, 1325, 1804, 1854
Reina, Domingo, 1094
Webb, Mary Maude Cripe, 53, **1324–1325,** 1804, 1854
Reina, Domingo, 1094
Webb, Tony F., 2297
Webber, Everett, 2092
Weber (Weaver) family, **1325**
Weber (Weaver), Philipp, **1325**
Weber, Angus G., 2092
Weber, Anna Bowman, 1325
Weber, Arthur H.
Manheim, PA, Grace Brethren Church, pastor, 787
Weber, Barbara Buckwalter, 1325
Weber, Barbara Good, 1325
Weber, Barbara Ohler, 2362
Weber, Barry, 1804
Weber, Burton B., 663, 1804
Weber, Clinton Ira, 683, 1804
Omaha, NE, Church of the Brethren, minister, 974
Weber, Daniel, 1804
Weber, Daniel H., 1941
Weber, Daniel M., 2092
Weber family, 731, 2073, 2091, 2093
Harrisburg, PA, Melrose Gardens Grace Brethren Church, 586
Lancaster Co., PA, 1993
Weber, George, 1325, 2092
Weber-Han, Cynthia, 1804
Weber-Han, Samuel L., 1804
Weber, Hannah Mack, 1325
Weber, Hans, 2092
Weber, Henry, 1325, 2062, 2092
Weber, Irene S., 2092
Weber, J. Irwin, 2092
Weber, Jacob, 1325, 2062
Weber, Johann Anton, 1325
Weber, John, 360, 1325, 1804, 2062
Weber, John M., 2092
Weber, John T., 2092
Weber, Joseph S., 1897
Weber, Linda F., 2297
Weber, Maudlin Kendig, 1325
Weber, Max, 113
thesis of sect-church continuum, 1275
worldly asceticism, 716
Weber, Moses M., 1989
Weber, Peter S., Sr., and Katharine Schowalter, 1966

Weber, Philipp, 397
Weber, Richard R.
    on Stoner, John and descendants, 2362
    on Stover, William and descendants, 2362
Weber, Russell H., 320, 578, 586, 673, 1804, 2306
Weber, Susanna, 1325
Weber-Weaver family, 2092
Webster, Charles Franklin, 1804
Webster Co., IA
    Farnhamville, IA, Church of the Brethren, 479
Webster Co., NE
    Museum, 1312
    Red Cloud, NE, Church of the Brethren, 1088
    South Red Cloud Church of the Brethren, NE, 1206
Webster, David Kulp, 1804
Webster, Eugene, 662
Webster family, 2105
Webster, Hazel Harris, 2093
Webster, Lorraine, 662
Webster Mills Free Brethren Church, McConnellsburg, PA, 69
    Free Brethren, 513
Webster's New Biographical Dictionary
    on Beissel, J. C., 2093
    on Sower, Christopher, I, 2093
    on Sower, Christopher, II, 2093
    on Sower, Christopher, III, 2093
Wechtenhiser family, 164
Wechtenhiser, Ida (later Johns), 2187
Weck, Anna Catrina Lobach, 1325
Weck, Johann, 1325
Weck, Wilhelm, **1325**
wedding customs, 1325–1326, **1325–1326**
    bride's home as site of ceremony, 1325, 1326
    first wedding, 162
    Hymnal: A Worship Book, 2205
    marriage banns, 1325, 1326
    marriage to non-Brethren, 1325, 1326
    non-Brethren ministers, 1325
    pastors paid for ceremony, 1326
    payment of pastors for ceremony, 1326
    receptions, 1325, 1326
    sanctions against fornication, 1325–1326
Wedding, Doloris, 725
Weddle, A. G.
    Parkway Church of the Brethren, VA, 994
Weddle, Andrew J., 1236, 1804
Weddle, Anna Eller, 1326
Weddle, Benjamin, 1326
Weddle, Cassie, 147
Weddle, Christian, 1326
Weddle, E. H., 647
Weddle, Elijah, 1326
Weddle, Elizabeth Boone, 1326
Weddle, Elkanah, 2093
Weddle, Ethel Harshbarger, 535, 748, 2068, 2093
    on Pleasant Hill CB Congregation, IL, 2362
Weddle family, **1326, 2379**
    Hylton family, 641
    Mountain View Church of the Brethren, Alberta, Canada, 889
    Parkway Church of the Brethren, VA, 994

Weddle, George Curtis, 1804
Weddle, George Washington, 147, 345, 1804
Weddle, Harvey, 1804
Weddle, Joel, 1804
Weddle, John, 1804
Weddle, Joseph, 1326, 1804
Weddle, Joseph L., 1804
    Mountain View Church of the Brethren, Alberta, Canada, minister, 889
Weddle, L. C., 147
Weddle, LeRoy C., 1804
    Peoria IL, (First) Church of the Brethren, pastor, 1009
Weddle, LeRoy M., 1804
Weddle, Lonnie V., 515
Weddle, Michael, 1326
Weddle, Ora E., 236, 759, 1804
    San Bernardino, CA, Church of the Brethren, pastor, 1141
Weddle, Roley M., 1804
Wedel, Delmar, *See* Prisoners of War program
Wedel family
    Mortonhouse (ship), 2373, 2376
Wedertz, Johnnie Lou, 192
Wedertz, Larry, 1804–1805
Wedertz, Lou, 192
    weekday religious education, **1326–1327,** *See also* Christian Day School movement
Weekend activities
    love feasts at Naperville, IL, Church of the Brethren, 913
The Weekly-Pilgrim, 1327, 2093
Weekly, Rendal A., Jr., 720, 2297
    Lakeland, FL, Grace Brethren Church, 2213
    St. Petersburg, FL, Grace Brethren Church, interim pastor, 1135
Weeks family
    at New Rockford, ND, Church of the Brethren, 932
Weeks, Frank Edgar, 2093
Weeks, Stephen B., 2093
Weeping Water Church of the Brethren, NE, *See* Alvo, NE, Church of the Brethren
Weger family, 2089
Wegley, John W., 469, 533, 1805
Weglyn, Michi, 2093
Wegnast, Anna Catharine (later Blocher), 2371
Wegner family, 2095
Wehrly, Elizabeth (later Petry), 1013
Wehrly family, 686
Wehrly, Henry P., 1805
    Prices Creek Old German Baptist Brethren Church, OH, minister and presiding elder, 1057
Wehrly, Jonathan P., 1805
    Pigeon River Church of the Brethren, IN, minister, 1023
Weiant family, 2097
Weibert, J. C., 445
Weibly, Israel, 695, 1805
Weichers, Dick, 1321
Weideman, Silas, 1805
Weidenhamer, Bradley E., 1805
Weidler, David W., 1805
Weidler, Ira W., 1805
Weidler, Magdalena (later Myers)

    Myers, Graybill, wife of, 903
Weidman, Friedrich, 463, 1805
Weidman, Robert, 1253
Weidman, Silas, 1805
Weidner, C. E., 130, 635
Weidner, Charles A., 269, 1805
Weidner, Elizabeth, 1055
Weidner, Elizabeth (later Preiß), 1057
Weidner, Lazarus, 1055
Weidner, Marilyn Kemp
    on Ephrata Cloister wall charts, 2362
Weigand family, 2097
Weigand, Martha Creager Bonine, 2297
Weigel, Gustave, S. J., 2093
Weigel, Valentine, 156
Weigle (Wigle), Jacob W., **1327**
Weigle, Elizabeth, 484
Weigle family
    migration of Brethren, 830
Weigle, Jacob, 476
    Oregon, 980
Weigle, Larry, 1805
    Reading Grace Brethren Church, PA, pastor, 1084
Weigle, Luther A., 2093
Weiler, H. O., 1805
Weily (Weiley), William, 1805
Weimar, Germany, 1327
Weimer, Adam, 1327
Weimer, Allen H., 572, 1805
Weimer, Amzie, 1805
    Mount Pleasant Brethren Church, VA, minister, 886
Weimer, Asa H., 1805
Weimer, Blanche Fox, 1327
Weimer, C. C., 1805
    Somerset, IN, Poplar Grove Brethren Church, pastor, 1202
Weimer, Clarabel Kauffman, 1327
Weimer, Clarence, 281
Weimer, Dan
    Simi Valley, CA, Grace Brethren Church, 1182
Weimer, Daniel, 1805
Weimer, Dennis, 1805
    Mine Run Church of the Brethren, VA, 843
Weimer, Doris
    Simi Valley, CA, Grace Brethren Church, 1182
Weimer, Eathel, 365
Weimer, Elsworth, 180
    Plevna, IN, Church of the Brethren, minister, 1037
Weimer, F. N., 1805
Weimer family, 430, **1327,** 2076, 2093
    Fike family, 490
Weimer, Frank J., 1805
Weimer, Frederick Benjamin, 514, 1805
Weimer, George B., 1327
Weimer, Glen Emerson, 55, 247, **1327,** 1805, 2093
Weimer, Hazel (later Russell), 1132
Weimer, Israel, 676, 1805
Weimer, Jacob, 1805
Weimer, James (Moscow, ID), 1805
Weimer, James (Waynesboro, PA), 1805
Weimer, John, 16, 1327
Weimer, Lawrence A., 1805
Weimer, Mary, 1240
Weimer, Michael, 1327
Weimer, Morse, 365
Weimer, Pearl, 955

Weimer, Peter, 516, 1327
Weimer, R. E., 2093
Weimer, Ronald, 363, 1805
Weimer, Ruby E. (later Dilley), 1601, 1805
Weimer, Ruth, 1929, 1944, 1953
Weimer, Samuel, 263, 1215, 1240, 1805
Weimer, Valentine, 1327
Weimer, Virgil Dennis, 1805, 2093
Weimer, Wilbur M., 1805
Weimert, Mrs. F. E., 489
Weingart family, 233
Weinhold family, 721
Weinlick, John R., 2093
Weinman, Friedrich, 148
Weir, James, 1327
Weir, Lucy Bird, 1327
Weir, Samuel, 257, 313, 506, 990,
    1327–1328, 1332, 1805, 2096,
    2128
    May, James, 804
    minorities, ethnic and racial, 849
    Moomaw, Benjamin Franklin, 873
    Scioto Valley, OH, congregations, lead-
        ership by, 961
Weirbach, Cheryl Ann, 1853
Weirich, Jacob, 1805
Weirich, Polly (later Miller), 2057
Weirick family
    Grace Brethren Church of Canton, OH,
        562
Weirsing family
    Sandy Creek Old German Baptist
        Brethren Church, WV, 1143
Weis, Frederick, 2093
Weisel, Morris, 1805
Weiser, Anna Maria (later Muhlenberg)
    Muhlenberg, Henry Melchior, wife of,
        892
Weiser, Clement Zwingli, 2093
Weiser Community Church, *See* Weiser, ID,
    Church of the Brethren
Weiser, Frederick Sheely, 1984, 2093–2094
    on Ephrata Cloister, 2362
Weiser, ID
    Church of the Brethren, **1328**
    Mission House, *1328*
    Mow, Aaron I., family home, *1329*
Weiser, Johann Conrad, **1328**, 1890, 2089,
    2093
    letters from Saur, Christopher, 2093
    Lewis, Elizabeth on, 2349
    Miller, Daniel on, 2347
    Miller, Hans Michael, 837
    Miller, John Peter, 840
    minorities, ethnic and racial, 849
    Muhlenberg, Henry Melchior, son-in-
        law of, 892
    Native Americans, 2229
    Pardoe, Elizabeth Lewis on, 2349
Weiser, Reuben, 2094
Weiss, Christina Konig, 1328
Weiss, Emanuel, 1328
Weiss, Georg Michael, 925, 2094
Weiss, Jacob, 1354
Weiss, Lister Oliver, 2094
Weiss, Lorell Edgar, 445, **1328**, 1805, 2094
    historical writing, 612
    Pomona, CA, Church of the Brethren,
        pastor, 1045
Weiss, Sylvia Mae DeHart, 1328
Weissport, PA, 756
Weitzel, Elias, 1805
Weitzel, Louise A.

on Ephrata Cloister, 2362
Weitzell, Eleanor, 273
Weitzell, Elias, 273
Welbaum family
    Root family, related by marriage, 1122
Welbaum, Lydia (later Kreider), 707
Welborn, Beverly, 687
Welborn, Glen H., 14, 738, 1351, 1805,
    2306
Welch, Carl Henry, 1805
Welch, David P., 1805
Welch, Dwight O.
    poetry, 1040
Welch family, 1914
Welch, Gladys Snavely
    memoirs, 2362
    on Nebraska wines, 2362
Welch, Janice (later Dorsey), 2277
Welch, Myra Brooks, **1329**, 2094
    poem by, 2345
    poetry, 1040
Welch, Otis Melvin, 1329
Welday family, 1885
Weldy, Alice
Weldy, Allen (CB) and, 2261
Weldy, Allen, 1805
Weldy, Allen (CB), 1805, **2261**
Weldy, Edgar, 2261
Weldy, Gilbert, 2261
Weldy, Levi, 2261
Weldy, Mary Loucks, 2261
Weldy, Nina Roose, 1805, 2261
Weldy, Winfred, 2261
Welfare Board, *See* General Welfare Board
Welfare, Michael, *See* Wohlfahrt, Michael
welfare programs, *See* social welfare
Welfley, William H., 1878, 2094
well-drilling, 9
Wellbaum, Elizabeth (later Murray)
    Murray family, 898
Wellbaum, Rebecca (later Lonanecker), 756
Wellenreuther, Hermann
    on Sauer, Christoph, I, 2362
Weller, Can, 142
Weller, Daniel E., 1805
Weller, Delphos Petter, 411, 1805
Weller, Emma Martin, 2093
Weller family
    Ellison Church of the Brethren, ND,
        442
    Shull family, related to, 1156
Weller, Forrest L., 1805, 2094
Weller, Henry Albert, 1805
Weller, J., 1806
Weller, Jacob, 1224, 1806
Weller, M. J., 1806
Weller, Russell H., 1806
Welling, Brenda, 2157
Wellington, Mrs. Glen, 1806
Wellington, John R., 1806
Welliver, Ruth Glick ?, 554
Wellman, Walter, 1303
wellness, *See* health and medicine
    Bethany Hospital, 2136
    Brethren and, **2261**
    Helstern, Mary Sue on Biblical per-
        spective of, 2353
    Rosenberger, Mary Sue Helstern on
        Biblical perspective of, 2353
    sources on, 2311, 2321
Wells, Amos R., 2094
Wells, Charles, 676
Wells Co. Church of the Brethren, ND, *See*

    Bowden Valley Church of the
        Brethren, ND
Wells Co., IN, 1316
    Hickory Grove Church of the Brethren,
        IN, 602
    Markle, IN, Church of the Brethren,
        794
Wells Co., ND, 164
Wells, Elizabeth (later Kimmel), 693
Wells family, 721
    Mount Zion Church of the Brethren,
        WV, 888
Wells, Forest Orland, 1309, 1806
Wells, Gratton
    Peters Creek Old German Baptist
        Brethren Church, VA, minister,
        1012
Wells, Gratton E., 1806, 2306, **2386**
Wells, James M., 676, 1806
Wells, John Edward, 470, 1806
    Ozark Church of the Brethren, MI,
        minister, 986
Wells, Levi E., 1806
Wells, Maurice, 731
Wells, Monroe, 1806
    Mount Zion Church of the Brethren,
        WV, 888
Wells, (Mrs.) Cecil F.
    on Snowberger family, 2362
Wells, Nelson, 1806
Wells, Samuel Reed, 676, 1213, 1346, 1806
Wells (Welles), John, 1806
Wellsville, KS, 1311
Wels, Austria
    medical projects, 809
Welsch, Hildegard Barbara, 1842
Welsh, Marilyn C., 2094
Welsh, Ronald Nevin, 2297
Welsh, Rozella Mae, 1840–1841
Welsh Run Church of the Brethren, PA, 42,
    77, 119, **1329**
Welsh Run, MD congregation
    Martin family, 797–798
Welsh Run, PA, congregation, 1224
    Engle/Angle family, 446
    Pleasant Ridge Church of the Brethren,
        PA, 1034
    Welstead, Muriel (later Boardman),
        155, 1847
Weltkirchenlexikon
    Pietism subdivisions, 1021
Weltmer, R. Donald, 377, 1806
    Martinsburg, WV, Rosemont Grace
        Brethren Church, pastor, 798
Welty, Abraham
    Roland, Gasper, related to, 1126
Welty, Catherine (later Fahrney), 465
Welty Church of the Brethren, MD, 42,
    1329–1330
Welty, Elizabeth (later Stouffer), 1219
Welty family, 411, 1219
    Nicholas Co. German Baptist Brethren
        Church, 935
Welty, John, 1329
Welty, Ulrich, 1871
Welty, W. A., 130, 1806
    North Georgetown, OH, Brethren
        Church, pastor, 948
Welty's
    Hoffman (Huffman) family, 618
Wemyss, Stanley, 1862
Wenatchee Park, WA, Church of the
    Brethren, *See* Greenwood Church

of the Brethren, WA
Wenatchee Valley congregation, 1240
Wenatchee Valley, WA, 1319
  Church of the Brethren, 1319, *See also* Wenatchee, WA, Brethren-Baptist Church United
Wenatchee, WA, 1240, 1345
  Brethren-Baptist Church United, **1330**
  Church of the Brethren, *See* Sunnyslope Church of the Brethren, WA
  East Wenatchee Church of the Brethren, **1330**
  Garden Terrace Retirement Home, 530
Wencker family, 2095
Wendell, W., 726
Wengar family, 2095
Wenger, Aaron M., 2094
Wenger, Alvin P., 1806
Wenger, Ammon P., 1806
  Rossville, IN, Church of the Brethren, minister, 1124
Wenger, Anna Huber, 1330
Wenger Building, Elizabethtown College, 1330
Wenger Center for the Humanities, *See* Fairview Hall
Wenger, Christian, 1330, 1806, 1936
Wenger, Christian G., 2095
Wenger, Christian Martin, 2094, 2095
Wenger, Christina Studebaker, 2095
Wenger Clan Notes, 2095
Wenger, Daniel, 2095
Wenger, David, 2094
Wenger, Dorotha Fry (later Mason)
  on Gospel of John, 2345
  on Winger, J. O., 2345
Wenger, Earle Kermit, 2094
  on Wenger family, 2362
Wenger, Edna H. Fox, 2094
Wenger, Edward George, 745, 1806
  Oak Park Church of the Brethren, MD, 957
Wenger Edward Meyer, 1806, 2095
  Mount Zion Road Church of the Brethren, PA, minister, 888
Wenger, Eli D., 2095
Wenger, Elizabeth, 380
Wenger, Elsworth G., 14
Wenger, Emery, 2049
Wenger, Emma Meyer, 2095
Wenger, Eve Graybill, 1330
Wenger, Ezra, 1806, 2095
Wenger family, 701, 733, **1330,** 1338, 2028, 2049, 2092, 2094, 2095, 2101
  history of, 1936, 1940, 2363
  Royer family, related to, 1128
  Wenger, Earl K., Sr. on, 2362
  Wenger, Helen L. on, 2362
  Wenger, Samuel S. on, 2362
Wenger, Fannie Heatwokle, 2095
Wenger, Flossie, 2095
Wenger, Gene Ellis, 683, 1806
Wenger, H. C., 1806
Wenger, Hannah Brenneman, 1940
Wenger, Hans, 1330
Wenger, Harold P(aul), 1806
  Middletown, OH, Church of the Brethren, copastor, 826
Wenger, Harriet Jane (later Finney), 1616
Wenger, Helen L.
  on Wenger family, 2362
Wenger, Henry, 414, 1330
Wenger, Isaac D., 1806

Wenger, Israel W., 1806
Wenger, J. Calvin, 1806
Wenger, Jacob, 1940
Wenger, Jacob C., 2092
Wenger, Jacob F., 1806
Wenger, Jay, 2095
Wenger, John, 1330
Wenger, John C., 2095
Wenger, John N., 1806
  Philadelphia, PA, First Church of the Brethren, minister, 1015
Wenger, John S., 2095
Wenger, Jonas G., 2095
Wenger, Joseph, 1330
Wenger, Joseph H., 2095
Wenger, Kenneth Edward, 1806
Wenger, Levi A., 1220, 1806
Wenger, Lois
  Middletown, OH, Church of the Brethren, co-pastor, 826
Wenger, Magdelene (later Early), 414
Wenger, Martin Light, 2094, 2095
Wenger, Michael S., 2095
Wenger, Paul D., 737, 1806
Wenger, Perry J., 733, 1806
Wenger, Richard C., 513, 717, 726, 1806
Wenger Roy Harper, 2095
Wenger, Russell Cloppert, 317, 1806
Wenger, Samuel Bernis, 1806
Wenger, Samuel K., 1806
Wenger, Samuel Stoner, 2095
  on Wenger family, 2362
Wenger, Stanley C., 1806
Wenger, Tracy (later Sadd), 2292
Wenger, William Warren, 2297
Wengerd, Ben V., 2095
Wengerd, Elizabeth, 1898
Wengerd family, 2095, *See also* Wengert family
Wengerites (Pentecostal Brethren in Christ), 189
  Pentecostal Brethren, 1008
Wengert family, 2095
Wenrick, A. D., 1806
Wenrick, Catherine (later Kimmel), 693
Wenrick, Jonathan, 1806
  Palestine Old German Baptist Brethren Church, OH, 991
Wenrick, Thomas B., 1806
Wentsler, Mary Elizabeth, 1839
Wentz, Abdel Ross, 2095
Wentz, Donald Edwin, 1806
Wentz, Donald J.
  Rockton, PA, Church of the Brethren, pastor, 1118
Wentz, James E.
  on Morrison's Cove members, 2363
  Wentz, Richard E., 2095
  on Ephrata Cloister, texts of, 2363
Wenzek, Darrell E., 1270
Wenzel, Ronald L., 2297
Werking, Josie D., 2096
Werking, Oscar D., 923, 1806–1807
  Richmond, IN, Church of the Brethren, elder, 1108
Werner family, 211
Werner, Gerhart, 2096
Werner, Lydia (later Miller)
  Miller, Harold Clayton, mother of, 834
Werner, William L., 2096
Wernle, Paul, 2096
Wernman, Isaac, 1807
Werntz, Christian, 633

Somerset German Baptist Brethren Church, MO, love feast, 1202
Wersyer, Linnie, 354
Wertenbaker, William Harrison, 759, 1807
Wertenberger, Andrew J., 1807
Wertenberger family, 2314
Wertz, Catherine (later Kyle), 712
Wertz, Christian (Christley), 1807
Wertz, Corda L. (later Krieger), 145, 1840
Wertz, Daniel J., 142, 1807
Wertz, David L., 1807, 2306
Wertz, Elizabeth (later Hoffman), 618
Wertz, Elizabeth (later Howe), 633
Wertz, Elizabeth Oller (later Ellis), 441
Wertz, Emery, 322, 1807, 2306
Wertz family
  Hoffman (Huffman) family, 618
Wertz, John B. (1844–1915), 142, 431, 1807
Wertz, John B. (Prairie View, KS), 1807
Wertz, Leonard, 1807, 2174
  youth and, 2268
Wertz, Mary, 150
Wertz, Mary Alice, 151
Wertz, Mary Elizabeth (later Wieand), 1344
Wertz, W. Clay, 1807
Wesley Chapel preaching point
  Highland Co. Mission Church of the Brethren, VA, 605
Wesley Chapel, VA, 1301
Wesley, Charles
  hymns, 643
  influence of Spener, Philipp Jakob on, 1209
  Pietism, 1022
Wesley, John, 117, 2096
  Holiness Movement, American, 619
  hospitality of de Koker family to, 705
  hymns, 643
  influence of Spener, Philipp Jakob on, 1209
  Pietism, 1022
Wesleyanism
  Evangelical Association, 459
  Holy Spirit, doctrine of, 624
  nonconformity, 940
Wesson family, 170
West Alexandria, OH, 1235, 1295
  Brethren Church, **1332–1333**
  Church of the Brethren, 1235, **1333**
  Grace Brethren Church, *See* Glenwood, OH, Community Grace Brethren Church
West, Andrew Eldridge, 1332, 2261
West Arm of Floyd Co. Church of the Brethren, VA, *See* Topeco Church of the Brethren, VA
West, Barbara Landis, 1330, 1332
West Bethlehem Twp., Washington Co., PA, 1253
West, Beulah I., 2096
West Branch, *See* Flat Rock Church of the Brethren, VA
West Branch Church of the Brethren, IL, **1333**
  Mount Morris, IL, Church of the Brethren, 883
  Pine Creek Church of the Brethren, IL, 1024
West Branch Church of the Brethren, OH, 109, 345, **1333,** 1384,
West Branch, MI, 1400
West Branch Old German Baptist Brethren

Church, IL, **1333**

West Branch, VA, Church of the Brethren, *See* Flat Rock Church of the Brethren, VA

West, C. Edward, Jr., 1285, 1807, 2297

West, (Charles) Elmer, 1807, 2306
Salem Church of the Brethren, IA, 1137

West Charleston Church of the Brethren, Tipp City, OH, 1265

West Colony congregation, CA, 727

West Conestoga, PA, Church of the Brethren, 720, 737, 748, *See also* Middle Creek Church of the Brethren, PA
Middle Creek Church of the Brethren, PA, 825

West Covina, CA, Grace Brethren Church, 348, *See also* Covina, CA, New Life Grace Brethren Church

West Creek, KS, 1304

West, Daniel, 179, 203, 233, 242, 246, 247, 248, *248*, 301, 518, 1281, **1330–1332**, *1331*, 2096, **2379**, 2106
articles about, 1925
books by, 1331
fiction about, 748
Heifer Project, 1161
One Hundred Dunkers for Peace, 974
recreation and youth, 1088
Rural Life Association (RLA), 1131
Spain, relief work in, 1207, 1208
work camps, 1367
World War I, 1371
World War II, 1372

West, David, 2170
Hüber (Hoover) family, 634

West Dayton, OH, Church of the Brethren, *See* Dayton, OH, Mack Memorial Church of the Brethren

West, Delta L., *661*

West Earl Twp., PA
census, 2092

West, Edmund Landon, 313, 395, 739, 1227, 1330, **1332**, *1332*, 1807, 2096
May, James, 804
minorities, ethnic and racial, 849
Native Americans, 2230
Ohio ministry, 961
Ontario German Baptist Brethren, 975

West Eel River Church of the Brethren, IN, 429, **1333**

West, Ellis H., 1807

West, Exonie Elizabeth Akers, 1332, 2261

West family, 740, 1383, 2096
Engle/Angle family, 446
Golden Church of the Brethren, NC, 555
Harrah, WA, Grace Brethren Church, 585
Parkway Church of the Brethren, VA, 994
Prosperity Brethren Church, WV, 1062

West Friesland (Netherlands)
Germany, 545

West Fulton congregation, OH
example of descriptive or grammatical place name, 911

West Fulton Dunkard Brethren Congregation, OH, **1333–1334**

West, George (Clayton, IL), 1807

West, George M. (Cleveland Mills, NC), 1807

West, George (Hoyle Creek, OK), 633, 1807

West Germany
work camps, 1367

West Good Hope, CO, Church of the Brethren, 1221, *See also* Sterling, CO, Church of the Brethren; Haxtun, CO, Church of the Brethren

West Goshen, IN, Church of the Brethren, 352, 749, 1280, 1287, 1384, *See also* Goshen, IN, West Goshen Church of the Brethren
history, 1929, 1962
Maple Grove Church of the Brethren, IN, 789
Osceola Church of the Brethren, IN, 984

West Goshen, IN, Elkhart congregation
Rock Run Church of the Brethren, IN, 1117

West Green Tree Church of the Brethren, PA, 279, 456, **1334**, 1401
Mount Joy, PA, Florin Church of the Brethren, 882

West, Hazel, 377

West Homer Brethren Church, OH, *See* Homerville, OH, Grace Brethren Church

West Homer Grace Brethren Church, OH, *See* Homerville, OH, Grace Brethren Church

West House, Yellow Creek Old German Baptist Brethren Church, IN, 1385

West Independence Brethren Church, OH, *See* Fostoria, OH, West Independence Brethren Church
Shively, Martin, pastor, 1178

West Indies
Moravian Church missionaries to, 875
Rolston, Frances Fitz Simon and William Wendell, working in, 1120

West, James K., 1209, 1332, 1807, 2102

West, Janet
on Brethren Volunteer Service, 2355

West, Joel D., 2096

West Johnstown congregation, PA, 150, *See also* Johnstown, PA, Roxbury Church of the Brethren
Johnstown, PA, Morrellville Church of the Brethren, 674
Johnstown, PA, Walnut Grove Church of the Brethren, 675
Pleasant Hill Church of the Brethren, PA, 1032

West, Juanita, 1278

West Kittanning Grace Brethren Church, Kittanning, PA, **699**
North Buffalo Grace Brethren Church, PA, 945

West, L. B., 1807

West Liberty, OH, 1341

West, Lucille Sherck, 1331

West Manchester, IN
Acme school, 1940
Church of the Brethren, **1334–1335**
North Manchester, IN, Church of the Brethren, 949
meetinghouse, North Manchester, IN, *1334*
shelter for annual meeting of 1878,

1335

West, Margaret, 1332

West Marva District (CB)
sources on, 2315

West, Mel
works by, 2313

West Milgrove, OH, 1334
Church of the Brethren, **1335**

West Milton, OH, Church of the Brethren, **1335**
Salem Church of the Brethren, OH, 1138

West Modesto Old German Baptist Brethren Church, CA, **1335**
Olive Grove Old German Baptist Brethren Church, CA, 973
Modesto, CA, Old German Baptist Brethren Church, 867
Sierra Pines Old German Baptist Brethren Church, CA, 1181
Wood Colony Old German Baptist Brethren Church, CA, 1363

West, Murray Guy, 206, 461, **1332**, 1807, 2306, **2261–2262**, **2379**, **2386**

West, Naomi Elizabeth Miller, 1332, 2262

West Nimishillen Church of the Brethren, OH, 937
Nimishillen Old German Baptist Brethren Church, OH, members from, 937
North Canton, OH, Mount Pleasant Church of the Brethren, 945–946

West Otter Creek Church of the Brethren, IL, 1234, **1335**

West Pine congregation, WI (CB), 63

West Plains District
Nebraska District merger with, 921

West Point, IA
General Conference Mennonite Church, 536

West, Raymond Arthur, 2096

West, Richard T., 1807

West Richmond Church of the Brethren, VA, **1335–1336**

West Rock Church of the Brethren, ND, *See* Brumbaugh Church of the Brethren, ND

West Rock Lake Church of the Brethren, ND, *See* Brumbaugh Church of the Brethren, ND

West, Russell, 40, 247, 377

West, Russell Greene, Sr., 692, 1807, 2096

West, S. Phineas, 263, 406, 1807
New River Old German Baptist Brethren Church, ministers for, 931

West Salem, OH, Brethren Church, *See* Fair Haven Brethren Church, OH

West, Salome Garman, 1332

West Star, OH
Sala, Johann, physician, 1136

West Sugar Creek House, IN, 1234

West Tenth Street Brethren Church, Ashland, OH, *See* Ashland, OH, Grace Brethren Church

West Thorndale, MI, Church of the Brethren, *See* Elmdale, MI, Church of the Brethren

West View Manor, Wooster, OH, **1336**, 1365

West Virginia, *1336*, **1336–1337**, 2044
annual meeting and love feast in, 2345
Church of the Brethren, *1336*
Church of the Brethren in, 2009

congregations, members of living in
  Maryland, 799
Dairy Testing Assignments, 359
district histories, 2201
genealogy, 2188
German Settlement congregation,
  history of, 1936
Kennan Massacre, 2078
migration of Brethren, 829
missions and missionaries in, 206
Old German Baptist Brethren, 967, 970
Old Order German Baptist Church, 972
oversight of congregations in, 226
Pennsylvania district (BC), congrega-
  tions in, 1005
place-names, Brethren, 1027
preacher circuits in, 164, 177
Sanger family descendants helping to
  build congregations, 1144
schisms in 1880s, 1336–1337
West Virginia University (Morgantown,
  WV), Brethren historical collec-
  tions at, 52
West, W. K., 1209
West, Walter
  Rouzerville Church of the Brethren,
    PA, minister, 1125
West, Walter Aaron, 42, 1807
West Washington Street School, 210
West Whittier, CA, 1342
West Wichita, KS, Church of the Brethren,
  See Wichita, KS, West Church of
  the Brethren
West, William Ellis, 1807
West York Church of the Brethren, PA,
  1337, 1388
Westan, Roxie Imogene, 1847
Westcott, Thompson, 2056
Westdahl, A., 1807
Westen, W. Sanford, 1807
Westenport, MD, 462
Westergaard, Waldemar, 2096
Westermeyer, Paul, 2096
Western College Association
  Fasnacht, Harold Dale, 480
Western Conservative Baptist Seminary
  McClain, Alva J., lecturer, 772
Western Fayette Co., PA, 177
The Western Herald, **1337**, 2096–2097
Western Pennsylvania Christian Broad-
  casting Company
  Holy Spirit Renewal Group, 625
Western Pennsylvania District, Church of
  the Brethren, 1918
  Erie, PA, Community United Church
    (CB/UCC), 453
Western Plains District, Church of the
  Brethren, 2363
Western Region (CB) district board
  San Francisco, CA, Church of the
    Brethren, 1142
Western Reserve (Case)
  Stuckey, Melvin Atwood, 1229
Western Theological Seminary
  Weaver, Mahlon J., 1324
westernization
  mission schools, 853
Westernport, MD, Church of the Brethren,
  144, **1337**
Westernport, MD, Mill Run Grace Brethren
  Church, *See* Mill Run Grace
    Brethren Church, MD
The Western Observer

Sals, Johann and Solomon, printers,
  1136
Westervain, *See* Surhuisterveen
Westfall, Robert Dennis, 2297
Westfeldt, Mettha Katheryn (later Eshle-
  man), 1932
Westminster, CA, Grace Brethren Church,
  1337
  Thompson, Robert W. (FGBC) and,
    2256
Westminster Church of the Brethren, MD,
  1337
  Meadow Branch Cemetery, 161
  Meadow Branch Church of the
    Brethren, MD, 357, 805
Westmont College
  Ashman, Charles Henry, Jr., 2132
Westmoreland Co., PA, 189, 289, 347, 348,
  693
  Alverton and Tarr cemeteries, 1937
  Brethren Church congregations, 1005
  congregation, 693
  Mount Joy Church of the Brethren, PA,
    882
  work camp, 1367
Westmoreland, Donald A., 130, 1235, 1807
Weston, OR, Church of the Brethren, **1338**
Westphal, Milton C., 2097
Westphalia, Peace of, **1338**
  historical writing, 611
Westrich, Oliver, 1280, 1807
Westrom, Walter E., 1807
westward movement, *See* migration of
  Brethren
Wetonka, SD, Willow Creek Church of the
  Brethren, **2379**
Wetterau (Wetteravia) region, Germany,
  1338
  Camisards, 242
  Ernst Casimir, 453
  Ronneburg Castle, 1121
Wetzel, Charles J., 2097
Wetzel Co., WV
  Mount Hebron Church of the Brethren,
    WV, 881
  Ryerson Station Church of the
    Brethren, PA, members from, 1132
Wetzel, Paul, 218, 1807
Wexler, Joe
  Philadelphia, PA, Crossroads Grace
    Brethren Church and, 2238
Wexler, Theresa
  Philadelphia, PA, Crossroads Grace
    Brethren Church and, 2238
Weyand family, 2066
Weyand, Michael, 1807
Weyandt family, 2105
Weyant, E. Myrl, 1807, 2306
Weyant family, 2097
Weyant, John S., 2297
Weyant, Michael, 1807
Weyant, Samuel C., 1807
Weyant, Samuel G., 1807
Weybright, Anna Sayler, 1338
Weybright, Charles E., 123
Weybright, Charlotte (later Wise), 1338
Weybright, Elizabeth (later Oberholtzer),
  1732
Weybright, Elizabeth (later Rasor), 1338
Weybright family, **1338**
Weybright, Frederick, 1234, 1338
Weybright, George D., 2097
Weybright, Jacob, 601, 1338

Weybright, Jesse P., 2097
Weybright, John, 1338
Weybright, John D., 1807
Weybright, John S., 1807
Weybright, Margeret Elizabeth (later
  Oberholtzer [Overholtzer?]), 1842,
  2388
Weybright (Weybrecht), Martin, 124, 558,
  1338, 1807, 2097
Weybright (Weybricht), Martin, III, 1338
  Lane, Elizabeth Miller on, 2342
Weybright, Martin, IV, 1338
Weybright, Mary Hess, 601
Weybright, Mary (later Waggoner), 1338
Weybright, Miriam (later Cable), 2155
Weybright, Samuel Royer, 1807
Weybright, Sarah (later Cripe), 1338
Weybright, Susan Mary, 1846
Weybright, Susanna (later Hoover), 1338
Weybright, Victor
  publishing, 1069
Weybright, William Lee, 1807, 1846
  Overbrook, KS, Church of the
    Brethren, elder, 986
Weybright, Wilma Bittinger, 1807
Weyers Cove, VA, *1317*
Weygandt, Cornelius, 2097
Weygandt, Esther (later Powell), 2038
Weygandt family, 2091, 2097
Weygandt-Frase-Bechtel family, 2038
Weygant, Charles H., 2097
Weygant family, 2097
Weygindt family, 2105
*Weyrauchs Hügel, See Zionitischer
  Weyrauchs Hügel*
Whalen, William J., 2097
Whallon, C. V., 913
Whanger family, 2095
Wharton, ___, Colonel, 315
Wharton, G. Robert, 1807
Wharton, Paul K., 1807
What's in a Name?, **912–913**, **2377**
Wheatcroft, A. S., 1807
  Philadelphia, PA, Third Brethren
    Church, pastor, 1019
Wheatfield, VA, Laurel Hill Brethren
  Church, **1338**
Wheatland, MO, 1212
Wheatley, Phillis, 2128
Wheaton Area Fellowship, MD, Church of
  the Brethren, *See* Silver Spring,
  MD, Good Shepherd Church of the
  Brethren
Wheaton Christian Grammar School
  Fetterhoff, Dean, 2184
Wheaton College
  Fellowship of Grace Brethren Churches
    (FGBC), 488
Wheatville, OH
  Gratis, OH, Church of the Brethren,
    566
Wheatville, OH, 1295
Whedon, Nellie Woods, 2097
Wheeland family, 1365
Wheeland, Frank Elliott, 2297
Wheeler, Arthur G., 1807–1808, 2306
Wheeler, Clara C., 320
Wheeler, E. Milton, 2097
Wheeler, Elizabeth (later Anspach), 40
Wheeler, Elliot, 1808
Wheeler, Ethel Leonora (later Kurtz), 710
Wheeler family, 164
Wheeler, Frank M., 662, 1808

Wheeler, Lyle Glenn, 1808
Wheeler, Wayne E., 1808
  Massillon, OH, Trinity Church of the Brethren, 802
When We Walk with the Lord (Coffman), 748
"Where Is Holsinger?", 2020
Wherry, Neal M., 2097
Whetstone, David, 738, 1808
Whetstone family, 738
Whetstone, Gladys Umberhocker, 1338
Whetstone, Mary (later Ritchey), 1110
Whetstone, Sylvester Marion, **1338**, 1808
  New Enterprise Brethren Church, IN, elder in, 927
Whetzel, Bobby W., 2297
Whetzel, J. Diann, 2297
Whetzel, James C., 1808
  Rockingham and Shenandoah Counties Old German Baptist Brethren Church, VA, minister, 1118
Whetzel, L. J., 1808
Whipkey, J. C., 1808
Whipple, Charles David, 1808
Whipple, Darrel K., 2097
Whipple family
  Rio Linda, CA, congregation, 1134
Whipple, John, 2097
Whipple, Joseph, 2097
Whipple, Judith C., 2097
Whipple, Lee G., 275, 1216, 1343, 1394, 1808, 2306, 2097
Whippple family, 2097
Whisler, B. F., 1808
Whisler, Charles M., 471
Whisler, David, 2080
Whisler, Ezra LeRoy, 269, 1319, **1338–1339**, 1808, 2097
  Richland Valley Church of the Brethren, WA, preacher, 1108
  Salkum, WA, Community Church of the Brethren, 1139
Whisler, Emma (later Shively), *See* Shively, Emma Whisler
Whisler family, 1330, 2080, 2097
  Payette Valley Church of the Brethren, ID, 996
Whisler, Glen Dale, 1808
Whisler, H. A.
  McFarland, CA, Church of the Brethren, free minister, 774
Whisler, Harry Arthur, 1808
Whisler, Heinrich, 2097
Whisler, Henry Allen, 1808
Whisler, Isaac, 1808
Whisler, Israel, 1808
Whisler, Jonathan B., 431, 1808
  Rockingham and Shenandoah Counties Old German Baptist Brethren Church, VA, minister, 1118
Whisler, Levi, 1338, 1808
Whisler, Mrs. M. A., 2097
Whisler, Martha Jane, 1338
Whisler, Mary Ann Tobias, 2080
Whisler, Merton Albert, 1808
  Oak Grove Church of the Brethren, IL, preacher, 955
  Peoria, IL, (First) Church of the Brethren, elder-in-charge, 1009
Whisler, Samuel, 1808
Whisler, Sarah Ellen Hamilton, 1338
Whisler, William, 2097
  on Manchester College, 2363

memoirs, 2363
Whisler, William H., 153
Whisman, Julie (later Koontz), 706
Whistler, Anna Spitler, 1212
Whistler family, 727
Whistler, J. B., 1346
Whistler, James, 61
Whistler, John, 1212
Whistler, John Marquiss, 2097
Whistler, Levi
  Raisin City, CA, Church of the Brethren, 1083
Whistler, Magdaline (later Patton), 996
Whistler, William, 1808
Whitacre, A. J., 1345
Whitacre, A. Ruth, 1808
Whitacre, Alan L., 367, 1808, 2306
Whitacre, Alphaeus J., 1339, 1808
Whitacre, Annie Ruth Beahm, 1339
Whitacre, Bertha Fike, 1339
Whitacre, Charles Jerome, 1324, 1808
Whitacre, Christopher J., 2297
Whitacre, Cornelius, 1956
Whitacre, Daniel J., 1808
Whitacre family, **1339**, 1345, 2104
Whitacre, Howard Alphaeus, 339, 1808, 2306
Whitacre, Irvin William, 1339, 1808
Whitacre, James S., 1339, 1808
Whitacre, Jesse William, 570, 1339 1808, 2306
Whitacre, John William, family of, 1339
Whitacre, Joseph, 1808
Whitacre, Joseph Edward, 767, 1339, 1808
  Oak Grove Church of the Brethren, WV, elder, 956
Whitacre, Lacy Ann Abe, 1339
Whitacre, Linna Ades, 1956
Whitacre, Orpha Bennett, 1339
Whitacre, Robert, 1808
Whitacre, Ruth Beam, 1321, 2306
Whitacre, Theodore Emmanuel, 1808
Whitaker family
  South Bend, IN, Ireland Road Grace Brethren Church, 1203
Whitaker, J. K., 1808
Whitaker (Whitacre), Loring A., 738, 1808
Whitaker (Whitacre), Walter, 1808–1809
Whitcher, Forest, 471
Whitcher, Walter E., 72, 1809
Whitcomb, John Clement, Jr., 1809, 2097, **2262**
  on astronomy and Bible, 2363
  on Biblical creation, 2363
  Brethren Statement of Faith, 2167–2168
  The Conservative Grace Brethren Publications, 2168
  on charismatic movement, 2363
  on GB schism, 2363
  on Joshua-2 Kings and history of Israel, 2363
  suspension from duties, 2182
  Whitcomb Ministries, 2262
  writings of, 2363
Whitcraft, John Monroe, 1333, 1809
White, Mrs. J. K., 27
White, Alexander McCormic, 445, 1809
White, Amy Naomi Trout, **1339**
White Branch chapel, IN
  organized from Nettle Creek Church of Brethren, 923
White Branch Church of the Brethren, IN,

1339
White, Brian L., 365, 2297
White Church of the Brethren, IN, **1339**
White Co., IN, 228, 1390
  Church of God (New Dunkers), 297
  Guernsey Church of the Brethren, IN, 576
  Monticello/Pike Creek Church of the Brethren, IN, 872
  Oak Grove, IN, Church of the Brethren, 955
  Patton, Uriah, 996
White Cottage (Goshen) congregation, OH
  Greenwood Church of the Brethren, OH, 572
White Cottage, OH, Church of the Brethren, **1339–1340**
  Olivet Church of the Brethren, OH, 973
White, D. E., 556
White Dale Brethren Church, Terra Alta, WV, 774, 1254
White, Daniel, 227
White, Daniel A., 1277, 1809
White, David, 248, 256, 1809
  Old Order German Baptist Church minister, 972
White, David C. (younger), 1339
White, David Clark, 461, 1323, **1339**, 1809, **2379, 2386**
White, Delbert, 739
White, Don E.
  Good Shepherd Church of the Brethren, FL, 2190
White, E. William, 264
White, Elias O., 626, 1809
  South Gate, CA, First Brethren Church, pastor, 1205
White, Elias D., 715
White, Ellen Gould Harmon
  Seventh-Day Adventists, 1169
White, Evelyn, 1339
White family, 1917, 2097
  Fruitdale, AL, Church of the Brethren, 520
  Galion, OH, Grace Brethren Church, 527
  Shull family, related to, 1156
White, Forrest D., 406, 1809
White, Francis M., 1809
White, George D., 1339
White, George (Mr. and Mrs.), 439
White Hill Church of the Brethren, VA, **1340**
  Mount Vernon Church of the Brethren, VA, 887
White Horn Church of the Brethren, TN, 265, **1340**
White Horn Old German Baptist Brethren Church, TN, 264, **1340**
White, J. K., 274
White, Jacob A., 2097
White, Janet R.
  on Ephrata Cloister, architecture and culture of, 2363
White, John Bowman, 672, 1339, 1809
  Pleasant Valley Church of the Brethren, TN, 1035
White, John P., 1809
White, Lawrence, 1809
White, Mack S., 417, 505, 1809
White, Mary Anna Petersime, 1846
White, Mary Buckman, 1339

White, Matie Marie Hill, 1339
White, Melvin, 241
White, Mildred, 2097
White, Nancy Yost, 1339
White, Neva Lois, 2097
White Oak Church of the Brethren, OH, **1340**
White Oak Church of the Brethren, PA, 737, 748, 756, **1340**, 1401
  Hummer, Catherine, 636
  Lewiston, ME, Church of the Brethren, 2214
  Mountville, PA, Church of the Brethren, 890
White Oak Grove Old German Baptist Brethren Church, OH, **1341**
White Oak, PA, congregation, 279, 283, 1278
  Froelich (Fröhlich), Samuel Heinrich, 518
  Pennsylvania, large congregation, 1005
  Pennsylvania settlement, 1004
  Sunday school organized, 1237
White, Paul Robert, Sr., 516, 739, 1809
  Roanoke, VA, Ninth Street Church of the Brethren, pastor, 1113
  Somerset, PA, Church of the Brethren, pastor, 1202
White, Pauline Shock, 1936
White Pine Church of the Brethren, WV, 106, 129, **1341**
  South Branch Church of the Brethren, WV, 1204
White, Pleasant, 1809
White, Ralph Emerson, 511, 672, 912, **1339**, 1809
  Piney Flats, TN, Church of the Brethren, providing leadership, 1025
White Rapids Church of the Brethren, WI, **1341**
  Rock Creek Church of the Brethren, IL, 1117
White, Richard, 739
White River German Baptist Brethren Church, IN, 689, **1341**
White River Union Church (Dunkard), Lawrence, IN, 1863
White Rock Church of the Brethren, NC, **1341**
White Rock Church of the Brethren, ND, **1341**
White Rock Church of the Brethren, VA, 21, **1341**
White Rock, KS, Church of the Brethren, 232, 742, *See also* Lovewell, KS, White Rock Church of the Brethren
White, Roy Irvin, 209, 748, 1209, **1339**, 1809, 2097, **2379**, **2386**
White, S. W.
  Chestnut Grove German Baptist Brethren Church, pastor, 956
White Shoals, VA
  Ewing Church of the Brethern, VA, 2373
White, Stephen A., 758, 1809
  Pomona, CA, Fellowship Church of the Brethren, 1045
White, Thomas L., 2306
White, Vicie, 739
White Water German Baptist Brethren Church, MO, **1342**

Missouri Brethren settlement, 864
White, Wava Rowe, 2097–2098
White, Wilbert W., 137
  prayer, 1051
White, William Edward, 520, 1339, 1809
Whited family, 683
Whited (Whitted), Robert D., 104, 683, 1388, 1809
  Pleasant Grove Grace Brethren Church, IA, pastor, 1031
  San Jose, CA, South Bay community Church (FGBC), pastor, 1142
Whitefield, George
  Great Awakening and American revivalism, 1104
Whitefish (White Fish), MT, Church of the Brethren, **1342**
  Montana Brethren settlement, 870
Whitehair, S. K., 1254
Whitehair, Spencer K., 1809
Whitehead, Argus
  Eberly, Eloise Whitehead on, 2328
  Eberly, William R. on, 2328
Whitehead, Brad, 2297
Whitehead Church, IN, Church of the Brethren, *See* Maple Grove Church of the Brethren, IN
Whitehead, Clayton S., 1809
  Mount Joy Church of the Brethren, PA, salaried minister, 882
Whitehead family, 2044
  Maple Grove Church of the Brethren, IN, 789
Whitehead, Margaret (later Rhyne), 2044
Whitehead, Myrtle
  Eberly, Eloise Whitehead on, 2328
  Eberly, William R. on, 2328
Whitehead, Shirley, 1852
Whiteneck, John S., Jr., 1809, 2101
  Somerset, IN, Church of the Brethren, presiding elder, 1202
Whiteneck, Martin, 1809
Whitenight, M. P., 1987
White's Bible Teacher Training School, *See* Bible Teacher Training School
White's Store, Waynesboro, VA
  used as meetingplace, 1324
Whitesboro, TX, 1255
Whiteside Co., IL, 1221
Whiteside, Jeffrey L., 2166
Whiteside, Jeffrey Lynn, 2297
Whitestine family
  Gentry German Baptist Brethren Church, MO, 540
Whitestine, William, 1809
Whitestone Church of the Brethren, WA, 1342, 1364
  Ellisforde, Church of the Brethren, WA, 442
Whitesville German Baptist Brethren Church, MO, **1342**
Whitewater Creek congregation, MO
  Hendricks, James, 597
  Far Western Brethren, 475
Whitewater, IN, congregation
  later New Bethel, IN, Church of the Brethren, 924–925
Whitford, ___, 1809
Whither Thou Goest (Statler), 748
Whiting, Hiram, 1224
Whitlatch, C. Robert, 1809
Whitley Co., IN, 153, 696, 734, 1234
  German Baptist Brethren, 696

  place-names, Brethren, 1028
Whitley, Edythe Johns R., 2098
Whitley, IN, congregation (South), 340
Whitley, William Thomas, 1862, 2098
Whitman Co., WA, 1212, 1250
Whitman, Lauris B., 2098
Whitman, Slim, 1948
Whitmer, A. T., 1809
Whitmer, Abraham, 1287, 1809
  Oak Grove, IN, Church of the Brethren, elder, 955
  Pine Creek Church of the Brethren, IN, 1024
Whitmer, Benjamin B., 1809
  Menlo Church of the Brethren, KS, elder, 814
  Pleasant View Church of the Brethren, KS, elder, 1036
Whitmer, C. Delbert, 1809
Whitmer, Daniel, 1346, 1809
  Oak Grove, IN, Church of the Brethren, elder, 955
Whitmer, David, 1809
Whitmer family, 700
  Nimishillen Old German Baptist Brethren Church, OH, 937–938
Whitmer, George
  Plattsburg Church of the Brethren, MO, 1030
Whitmer, Henry
  North Liberty, IN, Brethren Church, 948
Whitmer, John, 1809
Whitmer, M. I., 1346
Whitmer, Mary
  North Liberty, IN, Brethren Church, 948
Whitmer, Merrill I., 1809
  Oak Grove, IN, Church of the Brethren, elder, 955
Whitmer, Peter E., 1809
  South Bethel German Baptist Brethren, MO, minister, 1204
Whitmer, Victor, 1809
Whitmer-Witmer family, 1984
Whitmer (Witmer), Sylvester, 1809
Whitmore, Albert, 740
Whitmore, Albert Lentz, 1809
Whitmore, Amanda Bosserman, 2098
Whitmore, Bruce C., 1809
Whitmore family, 161
Whitmore, Jacob C., 1809–1810
  Raisin City, CA, Church of the Brethren, 1083
Whitmore, Jacob, Jr., 1809
Whitmore, Jonathan, Jr.
  Portage Church of the Brethren, OH, minister, 1047
Whitmore, Kevin B., 2297
Whitmore, Salome, 505
Whitmore (Whitmer), Celestine, 1809
Whitmore (Witmore), Jonathan Cover, Sr., 1810
  Portage Church of the Brethren, OH, minister, 1047
Whitney, Mary E.
  on Gibbel family, 2363
Whitney, Norman, 2098
Whitson, I. C., 1810
Whitsuntide, *See* Pentecost
Whittaker family, *See* Whitacre family
Whittaker, Walter, 1810
Whitted, Albert E., 104, 1810

Morrill, KS, (First) Brethren Church, pastor, 876

Portis, KS, Grace Brethren Church, pastor, 1048

Whitted, W. E.

Norcatur, KS, Maple Grove Brethren Church, pastor, 944

Whitted, Wiley Francis, 1810

Whittemore, Thomas, 580, 1292, 2098

Whitten, B. S., 1810

Whitten, David A., 2297

Whitten, E. W., 1254

Whitten, Hubert Nathaniel, Sr., 43, 1254, 1810

Whitten, Mary Saunders

Saunders Grove Church of the Brethren, VA, 1150

Whittier, CA, 238, 694

New River Old German Baptist Brethren Church, 931–932, *932*

Community Grace Brethren Church, 713, **1342**

Simi Valley, CA, Grace Brethren Church, 1182

Grace Brethren Church, 20, 694, **1342–1343**

Old German Baptist Brethren Church, *See* New River Old German Baptist Brethren Church, CA

Valley View Community Church of the Brethren, **1343**

Whittier, John Greenleaf, 259, 747, 750–751, 2098

"Hymn of the Dunkers," description of, 1923

Whittle, Mark, 2097

WHO, *See* World Health Organization

Who Are These Brethren? (Deeter), 2149

Whole Gospel Mission, 52

Whole Gospel Mission Brethren Church, PA, 166

Whole Gospel Mission, PA, congregation (BC), **381**

"Why the Apostolic Church?" (Bowman), 166

Wichita Co., KS

Prairie View Church of the Brethren, KS, members living in, 1050

Wichita, KS, 682

Church of the Brethren

Peace Committee (CB), 1002

East Church of the Brethren, *See* Wichita, KS, First Church of the Brethren

First Church of the Brethren, **1343**

Grace Brethren Church, **1343**

Mission Church of the Brethren, *See* Wichita, KS, West Church of the Brethren

West Church of the Brethren, **1343**

Wick family, 1988

Wickard, Elias, 424

Wickel, Elmer, 1810

Wickersham, James P., 2098

Wickersham, Mary, 1907

Wickham, Calvin, 1810

Wickham, Dorothy, 213

Wickham, Harold, 213

Wickham, Jack, 588

Wickham, John, 670, 1810

Mechanic Grove Church of the Brethren, PA, free minister, 806

Wickham, Joy, 588

Wickham, L. C., 1810

Wickham, Samuel S. M., 1810

Wickline, Jerry L., 2181

Wicks, Clifford E., 1810

Somerset, PA, Grace Brethren Church, pastor, 1202

Widder, Cevilla (later Myers)

Myers, Paul R., mother of, 904

Myers, Theodore, wife of, 904

Widder, D. H., 1810

Widder, George, 1810

Widdowson, E. B., 1343

Widdowson, James, 1810

Widdowson, Sadie Olive, **1343,** 1846, 2098

Widdowson, Susan Ober, 1343

Wideman, Elizabeth Frey Diefenbacher, 2098

Wideman, Henry, 2042

Widener family, 1315

Widman incident, 2074

widows, *See* women

care of, **1343–1344**

emergency and retirement benefits, 155

mutual aid, 902

poor, caring for, 1046

Wie, H., 1810

Wieand, Albert Cassel, 46, 61, 123, 125, 127, 137, 138, 279, 284, 300, 381, 545, 616, 691, 1210, 1215, 1274, **1344,** 1386, 1810, 2060, 2098

hymns, 643

Palestine, 990

prayer, writings on, 1051

revival at Wakenda Church of the Brethren, MO, 1313

Rockingham Church of the Brethren, MO, held revival meeting at, 1118

Schwalm, Vernon; *Albert Cassell Wieand,* 1157

Wieand, David John, **1344–1345,** 1389, 1810, 2098, **2379, 2387**

Wieand, Elizabeth Cassel, 1344

Wieand, Ella, 1810

Wieand family

Rupp (Roop) family, related to, 1130

Wieand, Florence M. (later Noffsinger), 939

Wieand, John B., 237, 1810

Omaha, NE, Church of the Brethren, minister, 974

Peru, IN, Church of the Brethren, pastor, 1010

Wieand, Katherine G. Broadwater, 1344

Wieand, Mary Elizabeth Wertz, 1344, 2098

Wieand, Theodore Calvin, 1810

Wiebley, Israel L., 1810

Wied, Werner, 2098–2099

Das Wiedergefundene Paradies (The Rediscovered Paradise), 2099

Freidensbote von Concordia, Der (The Peace Messenger of Concordia), 517

Concordia, 331

Wiedertäufer, 2058

Wiedman family, 1359

Wiedman, Frederick W., 1810

Wiedman, Silas, 1810

Wiegand, Martha Steiner, 2099

Wiegner, Christoph, 540

Journal of, 1931

Wieler, Emma Martin, 2099

Wiens, David, 1929

Wiens, Justina (later Neufeld), 701

Wierback, Eugene S., 2099

Wiest, Donald Paul, 1810

Wiest, Emma (later Schlosser), *See* Schlosser, Emma Wiest

Wigandt family, 2091

Wiggers, Mrs. Orville E., 1979

Wiggers, Orville E., 1979

Wight, Willard E., 2099

Wigle, David, 740, 1810

Wigle family, 14

Wigle, Jacob W., *See* Weigle, Jacob W.

Wigle, Peter, 1810

Wike, Henry B., 757, 1810

Wike, I. B., 320

Wike, Isaac B., 1810

Wilbur B. Stover, Pioneer Missionary (Miller), 840

Wilcox, S. E. Y., 2099

Wilcox, Wayne A., 2099

Wild Cat Church of the Brethren, PA, 1321

Wild Horse, Cheyenne Co., CO

Sheridan Lake Old German Baptist Brethren Church, CO, ministers travelling to, 1176

Wildasin, Mark Arthur, 1810

Wildcat Territory, IN, **1345**

Pyrmont, IN, Church of the Brethren, 1073

Wildell mission point

Glady, WV, Church of the Brethren, 551

wilderness, 425

Brethren movement, 1983

education, 426

Wilderness, Society of the Woman in, *See* Society of the Woman in the Wilderness

Wildish, Curtis B., 1810

Wildwood Grace Brethren Church, **1345**

Wile family

Freeling Settlement Old German Baptist Brethren Church, WV, 514

Wiles, Truman Dale, 1810

Wiles, Virginia

on salvation, 2363

Wiles, William, 579, 1810

Wiley, CO, Church of the Brethren, **1345**

McClave, CO, Church of the Brethren, 773

Wiley Ford, WV, Church of the Brethren, 106, 1339, **1345**

Old Furnace Church of the Brethren, WV, 966

Wiley, Galen E., 1810

Minerva, OH, Grace Brethren Church, pastor, 843

Mansfield, OH, Woodville Grace Brethren Church, pastor (youth or associate), 787

Wiley, James Allen, 2306

Wiley, Ralph Emerson, 1810

Wiley, S. T., 2099

Wiley, W. A., 1810

Wiley, William, 1810

Wilfong, Asa, 2175

Wilfong, Benjamin, 1810

Wilhelm, Dawn Ottoni, 2297

Wilhelm family

Freeling Settlement Old German Baptist Brethren Church, WV, 514

Wilhelm, Frederick, 2099

Wilhelm, George, 2306

Wilhelm, George F., 1380, 1810, 2138, 2306

Wilhelm, J. L., 1810
Wilhelm, Jonathan, 274
Wilhelm, Lu, 1380
Wilhelm, Paul A.
    on conscientious objectors in World
        War II, 2363
Wilhelm, Verda (later Kettering), 691
Wilhelm, Vernon, 2099
Wilhelm, Victor Clinton, 1810
Wilhide, Lester
    Phoenix, AZ, Grace Brethren Church,
        1019
Wilkens, Cleo Goff, 2099
Wilkens, L. B.
    New Lebanon, OH, First Brethren
        Church, pastor in, 930
Wilkerson, Charles, 1810
Wilkerson, Kenneth Eugene, 2297
Wilkes-Barre, PA
    flood, disaster response to, 2171
Wilkes (later Ashe) Co., NC
    Brethren settlement, 946
    Friendship Church of the Brethren, NC,
        518
    Reddies River, NC, Riverside Church
        of the Brethren, 1089
Wilkes, O. Magee
    Mesa, AZ, Community Church of the
        Brethren, 2222
Wilkins, Arnold D., 1810
Wilkins, Charles L., 1810
Wilkins family
    Pataskala, OH, Grace Brethren Church
        of Licking Co., 995
Wilkins, George W., 1810
Wilkins, Kevin A., 2297
Wilkins, Lois Nickerson, 2099
Wilkins, Lyman B., 2, 467, 746, 1320, 1810
Wilkins, Mr. and Mrs. Vernon
    Newark, OH, Brethren Church, as min-
        ister, 933
Wilkins, Ruby Sawtell, 2099
Wilkins, Vernon Moyer, 1315, 1810
    Mountain Valley Church of the
        Brethren, TN, pastor, 889
    New Haven Church of the Brethren,
        NC, pastor in, 928
Wilkins, Walter, 1810
Wilkins, Charles L.
    Sand Ridge Church of the Brethren,
        OH, elder-in-charge, 1143
Wilkinson, Bruce Gerald, 2297
Wilkinson, Charles, 1810–1811
Wilkinson, Norman B., 1858, 1862
Wilkinson, William Lester, 1811
Wilkinson, William T., 1811
Wilkison, Charles D., 1811
Will family, 1338
Will, Harper Sailor, 399, 504, 740, 1282,
    1330, **1345**, 1811, 2099
Will, Mabel, 2099
Will, Naomi Royer, 1345
Will, Sallie Hollar, 1345
Will, Samuel G., 1345
Will, Sarah (later Moore)
    Moore, John Henry, mother of, 874
Willamette Valley German Baptist Brethren
    Church, OR, See Albany, OR,
        Sunrise Community Church
Willamette Valley, OR
    Oregon Brethren, 980, 981
Willamette Valley (originally South
    Santaam), OR, congregation

division of, 1138
Willard, O. H., 1811
Willard, Frances E., 1359
Willard, WI, Church of the Brethren, **1345**
Willard, William C., 213, 227, 1811
Willauer, David Raymond, 1811
Willet, John
    London, OH, Grace Brethren Church,
        2215
Willett, David L., 29, 1252, 1811
Willett, Donald, 1380
Willett, James A., 106, 1811
Willett, John, 375, 1380, 1811
Willey, Martin, 1811
William & Sarah (ship), 1013
William, Robison, 1811
Williams, Ada, 410
Williams, Albert B., 2099
Williams, Albert Lloyd, 1263, 1811
Williams, Alma Ball, 1345
Williams, Alonzo, 297
Williams, Alta (later Frantz), 508
Williams, Alvina, 2099
Williams, Anna Blough
    on Conner, Jesse and descendants,
        2363
Williams, Beulah, 163
Williams, Brian, L., 2297
Williams, Bruce S., 430, 1811
Williams, C. Ronald, II, 2165
Williams, Carmel A., 170, 1811
Williams, Caroline (later Bowser), *See*
    Bowser family
Williams, Catherine Deardorff, 1916
Williams, Cecil B., 748, 2099
    Paradise Prairie Church of the Breth-
        ren, OK, 993
Williams Center, OH, 741
Williams, Charles Emmett, 1811
Williams, Charles H., 343, 1811
Williams Church of the Brethren, OR, 65,
    1346
    Fruitdale Community Church of the
        Brethren, OR, 520
Williams Co., ND, 1346
Williams Co., OH, 224, 741
    Lick Creek, OH, congregation, 961
    Pleasant Ridge Dunkard Brethren
        Congregation, OH, 1034
    Silver Creek Church of the Brethren,
        OH, 1182
Williams Creek Church of the Brethren,
    OR, *See* Williams Church of the
    Brethren
Williams Creek Church of the Brethren,
    TX, 1255, **1346**
    migration of Brethren, 830
Williams, David L., 6, 145, 320, 1811, 2099
Williams, Don, 556
Williams, Dorman L., 2297
Williams, Dulcie Lovie, 1836
Williams, E. Thomas, 2297
Williams, Edwin Melvin, 2099
Williams family, 164, 170, 265, 1216, 1235,
    1274, 1305, 1383, 2087, 2100
    bibliography, 1885
    Goldendale, WA, Community Grace
        Brethren Church, 556
    Mabton, WA, Grace Brethren Church,
        771
    Prosser, WA, Community Grace
        Brethren Church, 1062
Williams, George H., 113, 114

Reformation, 2201
Williams, George L., 673, 1390, 1811
    Myrtle Point, OR, Church of the
        Brethren, pastor, 906
Williams, Glenn, 6
Williams, Herbert Hoover, 912, 1811
    Interchurch World Movement (IWM),
        658
    missions, 859
Williams, James, 565
Williams, John, 1916
Williams, John Enoch, 580, 2099
Williams, John Henry Bashor, 160, *537,
    538,* 585, 1273, **1345–1346,** 1386,
    1811, 1998, 2015
Williams, Larry E., 2297
Williams, Lenora
    ship sinking en route to Africa, 863
Williams, Louisa Bashor, 1345
Williams, Lysle, 1811
Williams, Margaret, 566
Williams, Max, 1811, 2306
Williams, Mervin B., 278, 2100
Williams, Milo D., 1811
Williams, Nathaniel K., 1345
Williams, Nelson A., 1811
Williams, Oliver Perry, 1811, 2100
    ship sinking en route to Africa, 863
Williams, Robert Francis, 564, 1811
Williams, Robert Stephen, 585, 1811, 1854
Williams, Roger, 2306
    religious liberty, 1098
Williams, Roscoe, 1811
Williams, Russell L., 275, 566, 914, 1383,
    1811, 2306
    New Troy, MI, Grace Brethren Church,
        pastor in, 932
Williams, Steven E., 2297
Williams, Susie Lenom Deisch, 1854
Williams, Thomas J. C., 2100
Williams, Ward, 1811
Williamsburg, IA, Pleasant Grove Brethren
    Church, *See* Pleasant Grove Grace
    Brethren Church, IA
Williamsburg, PA, 1397
    Church of the Brethren, **1346**
    Fairview Church of the Brethren, PA,
        469
Williamson, Agnes, 2075
Williamson, Chet
    on Elizabethtown College, 2363
Williamson, Eleanor, 2100
Williamson, John W., 1811
Williamson Road Church of the Brethren,
    VA, *See* Roanoke, VA, Williamson
    Road Church of the Brethren
Williamson, Thomas W., 2100
Williamsport, MD, 374
    soil conservation units, 1200
Williamsport, PA, 148
    Blooming Grove Colony, 1922
Williamstown, OH, Brethren Church, **1346**
    Munson, Charles Robert, 2227
Williar, Frank Ecker, 1277, 1308, 1811
Williar, Jacob O., 752, 1811
Williard, Robert L., 1811
Williford, David A., 1846
Williford, J. Ralph, 1811
Williford, William R., 516, 1811
Willis, David, 1811
Willis family, 313
Willis, George L., Sr., 2100
Willis, John, 128, 1811

Pigeon River Church of the Brethren, NC, minister, 1023
Willis, Robert N., 620, 1811
Willis, VA, Grace Brethren Church, **1346**
Williston Church of the Brethren, ND, **1346**
Williston, ND, congregation, 1213
    North Dakota Brethren settlement, 946
Willoughby, Carolyn S., 2297
Willoughby, Donald E., 1811
Willoughby, Lena, 2100
Willoughby, Marie Hoover, 2297
Willoughby, William George, 191, 357, 717, 1811, 2100, 2143, 2379
    on Brethren Church, 2363
    on Church of the Brethren, 2363
    description of public worship, 1375
    on Dunkers, 2363
    on Grace Brethren, 2363
    historical writing, 612
    historiography, 2202
    on Mack, Alexander, 2363
    on Old German Baptist Brethren, 2363
Willow Creek, SD, congregation, 1205
Willow Grove schoolhouse, VA, 1314
Willow Springs Old German Baptist Brethren Church, KS, 682, **1346–1347**, 2134
wills
    Hostetter family, 1974
    Miller family, 2018
    records of, 2104
Wills, Charles E., 1811
Will's Creek Church of the Brethren, PA, **1347**
Wills, Daniel T., 1811
    Palestine Old German Baptist Brethren Church, OH, 991
Wills family, 1865
    Snake Valley Old German Baptist Brethren Church, PA, 1193
Wills, W. A., 1811
Willson, Curtis
    San Jose, CA, South Bay community Church (FGBC), 1142
Wilm, Ernst
    participation in two-hundred-fiftieth anniversary convocation, Schwarzenau, 1282
Wilmann, Christa M.
    on Sauer, Christoph, II and herbal cures, 2363
Wilmerding, PA, *See* East McKeesport, PA, Church of the Brethren
Wilmington, DE, Church of the Brethren, 374, **1347**
Wilmoth, William L., 1811
Wilpen mission, near Waterford, PA, 1321
Wilsdorf, Heinz G. F., 2310
Wilsey family, 1348
Wilson, A. J., 1811
Wilson, Chuck, 1394
Wilson Co., KS
    Fredonia, KS, Church of the Brethren, 513
    Independence, KS, Church of the Brethren, 649
Wilson, David Cree, 323, 1811
Wilson, Edmund C., 1811
Wilson, Edward Raymond, **1347**
Wilson, Elizabeth (later May)
    May, James, mother of, 804
Wilson, Emmert R., **1347**
Wilson, Esther Mae, 1842

Wilson family, 1866
    Fairview Church of the Brethren, MD, 468
    Mount Cassell Old German Baptist Brethren Church, WV, 880
    Mount Zion Church of the Brethren, WV, 888
Wilson, Frances Fouts, 2030
Wilson, Frederick D., 1811
Wilson, Henry E., Sr., 2297
Wilson, Henry F., 558, 1811
    Shiloh Church of the Brethren, WV, elder in, 1177
Wilson, Homer, 349
Wilson, Howard McKnight, 2100
Wilson, J. H., 1811–1812
Wilson, James, 318, 1812
Wilson, Jeremiah D., 1812
Wilson, Jerrald John, 1812
Wilson, Jesse, 2100
Wilson, Joseph
    Sergeantsville, NJ, Brethren Church, 1167
Wilson, Josiah S., 679, 1812
Wilson, Keither, 1812
Wilson, Leland, 669, 714, 1812, 2100
    on Silver City, 2363
    World Friendship Center, 1369
    writings of, 2363
Wilson, Lois, 1854
Wilson, M. G.
    Red Hill Church of the Brethren, VA, pastor, 1088
Wilson, Merle, 2100
Wilson, Merna, 1394
Wilson, Millard George, 216, 511, 1812
Wilson, Mrs. Joseph
    Sergeantsville, NJ, Brethren Church, 1167
Wilson, Norman Albert, 1812
Wilson, Nute, 1812
Wilson, Ralph H., 2297
Wilson, Raymond, *608*
Wilson, Renate
    on Sauer, Christoph and herbal cures, 2364
Wilson, Robert L., 62, 104, 377, 566, 1812
Wilson, Robin Dawn, 2306
Wilson, Roy X., 1812
Wilson, Rufus Rockwell, 2100
Wilson schoolhouse
    Fairview Church of the Brethren, MD, 468
Wilson, Solomon Nimrod, 1812
Wilson, Susan (later Kern), 689
Wilson, Thomas (Barbour Co., WV), 1812
Wilson, Thomas (Chicago, IL), 80, 1812, 2100
Wilson, Virginia Shank, 2100
Wilson, W. H., 1958
Wilson, Woodrow (President), 78, 559
    Brumbaugh, Martin Grove and, 223
    military service, 269
    Swigart, William Joseph, meeting with, 1245, 1249
    Taylor, Isaac W., meeting with, 1249
    World War I, 1369–1370
Wilt, A. E., 1812
Wilt family, 1304
Wilt, J. R.
    Pine Grove Old German Baptist Brethren Church, FL, deacon, 1024

Wilt, John C., 1347
Wilt, Joseph Wampler, 21, 115, 274, 1213, **1347,** 1812
Wilt, Kenneth E., 384, 670, 731, 1388, 1812, 2307
Wilt, Lloyd T., 1812
    Pleasant Hill Church of the Brethren, WV, 1033
Wilt, Mary Wampler, 1347
Wilt, Samuel W., 121, 505, 1225, 1812
Wilt, Wilson, 1812
    Mill Creek Old German Baptist Brethren Church, VA, elder, 832
    Mount Cassell Old German Baptist Brethren Church, WV, 880
    Pine Grove Old German Baptist Brethren Church, FL, elder-in-charge, 1024, 1025
Wiltfong, F., 1812
Wiltrout, Charles, 1812
Wiltschek, Walter J., 2297
Wimer family, 1346, 2080
Wimer, Fred, 1812
Wimer, Wesley, 1812
Wimmer, Dave, 1812
Wimmer, Frank Hill, 343, 1812
Wimmer, I. N., 1812
    Oakvale Church of the Brethren, WV, leadership by, 958
Wimmer, Isaac, 343, 1224, 1812
Wimmer, Isaac K., 721
Wimmer, J. H., 154
    Montgomery Church of the Brethren, PA, pastor, 872
Wimmer, John H., 343, 654, 1812
    Selma, VA, Church of the Brethren, pastor and minister, 1166
Wimmer, Joseph E., 343, 1812
Wimmer, Madison, 1224
Wimmer, Newton Preston, 1812
Wimmer, Noah P., 343, 1812
Wimmer, S. D., 1812
    Oakvale Church of the Brethren, WV, minister, 958, 959
"Win Men to Christ"
    evangelism, 461
Winand, George, 1812
Winchester Co., VA, 2090
Winchester, Elhanan, 379, 1291, 1292, **1347–1348**, 2087, 2100
    biography of, 2075
    Choice Collection of Hymns, 288
    prayer, 1051
Winchester, ID, Church of the Brethren, **1348**
Winchester, OH, Brethren Church, *See* Gratis, OH, Brethren Church
    Winchester, VA, 566, 1308
Winchester, VA
    Blue Ridge Grace Brethren Church, **2262**
    Grace Brethren Church, 382, **1348**
Winckel, Friedrich Wilhelm, 2100
Windber, PA
    Brethren Church, **1348**
    Church of the Brethren, 1151, **1348**
    Church of the Brethren Home, 305
    Rummel Church of the Brethren, **1348**
Winder, J. O.
    Mason, Dorotha Wenger Fry on, 2345
Winder, Jessie Helene, 2101
Winder, William C., 1812
Windesheim, congregation, 193

Windfall Church of the Brethren, IN, **1348**
winding sheets
  graveclothes, 566
Winding Waters Brethren Church, IN, *See*
    Elkhart, IN, Winding Waters
    Brethren Church
Windsor, CO, Northern Colorado Church of
    the Brethren, **1348–1349**
wine, 16, *See also* alcoholic beverages;
    grape juice
  communion, 328
  love feast, 764, 967
  Old German Baptist Brethren, 328, 967
Wine, O., 1813
Wine, A. F., 361
Wine, A. J.
  Pleasant View Church of the Brethren,
    TN, 1037
Wine, Abraham Joseph, 1812
Wine, Adam, 553, 1350
Wine, Alonzo Franklin, 1812, 1846, 2029
Wine, Attie Cline, 361, 1846, 2029
Wine, Barbara Beahm, 1349
Wine, C., 331
Wine, Catherine Neff, 1349
Wine, Cecil J., 2101
Wine, Charles, 1349
Wine, Christena Ryman, 1349
Wine, Christian, 348, 759, 1349, 2101
  Rentmeister, Jean R. on, 2352
Wine, Clyde C. on, 2352
Wine, Christian (1810–1893), 1812
Wine, Christian (ca. 1846–1907), 1812
Wine, Clyde C.
  on Moyers, Susanna, 2352
  on Wine, Christian, 2352
  on Wine, Susanna Moyers, 2352
Wine, Dallas Glen, 446, 1812
Wine, Daniel, 1276, 1350
  Link, Donald M. on descendants of,
    2343
  Mount Pleasant Church of the
    Brethren, VA, 887
Wine, Daniel David, 1812, **2387**
Wine, Daniel P., 1812
Wine, David, 1812
Wine, David G., 7, 46, 446
  Edison German Baptist Brethren
    Church, NE, 2373
  Octavia, NE, Church of the Brethren,
    minister and elder, 960
  Red Cloud, NE, Church of the
    Brethren, providing leadership,
    1088
  South Red Cloud Church of the
    Brethren, NE, minister, 1206
Wine, David Glick, **1349**, 1812
Wine, David M., 1812
Wine, Effie (later Frantz), 508
Wine, Eliza Good, 1350
Wine, Elizabeth Garber, 1349
Wine, Elizabeth Glick, 553
Wine, Emma Jean Weaver, 1846
Wine, Ernest, 1812
Wine, Ernest J., 65, 1812
Wine family, 170, 700, 733, 740, 1318,
    1350, 1391, 1950, 2101
  English River Church of the Brethren,
    IA, 447
  Farmington, DE, Bethany Church of
    the Brethren, 479
  Flat Rock Church of the Brethren, VA,
    493

French Broad Church of the Brethren,
    TN, 516
Fruitdale, AL, Church of the Brethren,
    520
  Good (Guth) family, 556
  Jasper, MO, Church of the Brethren,
    669
  Rockingham and Shenandoah Counties
  Old German Baptist Brethren
    Church, VA, 1118
Wine, Frances, 45
Wine, Frank, 246
Wine, G. L., 2101
  Mount Morris, IL, Church of the
    Brethren, pastor, 883
  Rossville, IN, Church of the Brethren,
    minister, 1124
Wine, Galen M., 430, 1812
  Shelton Church of the Brethren, NC,
    pastor in, 1176
Wine, Galen D., 1812–1813
Wine, Galen L., *654*
Wine, George, 1813
  family history, 2014
  North English, IA, Church of the
    Brethren, minister, 947
Wine, George S., 598
Wine, George S. (1833–1907), 1813
Wine, George S. (1841–1924), 1813
Wine, George W., 1813
Wine, Glen(n) C., 1813
Wine, Grover Lorington, 206, 1350, 1813
  North Manchester, IN, Church of the
    Brethren, pastor, 949
Wine, H. William, 264
Wine, Hazel Barkdoll, 1869
Wine, Henry, 1814
Wine, J. B., 45
Wine, J. C., 590, 672
Wine, J. F., 1813
Wine, J. Floyd, 239, 518, 1813
  Meadow Mills Church of the Brethren,
    VA, 806, 1138
Wine, J. R., 438, 445, 447, 1343, 1813
Wine, Jacob, 516, 1340, **1349**, 1813
Wine, Jacob (1811–1880), 1813
Wine, Jacob (1837–1915), 1813
Wine, Jacob Calvin, 676, 1813
Wine, Jacob Calvin, Jr., 1846
Wine, Jacob D., 2101
Wine, Jacob William, 1813
Wine, James R., 1813
Wine, Joe A., 246
Wine, Johann Georg, 1350
Wine, Johann George, 2101
Wine, John, 1349, 1813
Wine, John M., 115, 1349, 1813, 2101
Wine, John Michael, 1813, 2297
Wine, Joseph, **1349**, 1813
  Pleasant Hill Church of the Brethren,
    TN, elder, 1032
Wine, Joseph Floyd, 2101
Wine, Laura, 727, *727,* 733, 1846
  nurse missionary, 952
Wine, Laura M., **1349**
Wine, Lottie M. Keller, 1349
Wine, M. N., 1813
  Reedley, CA, Church of the Brethren,
    elder, 1091
Wine, Madison, 1813
Wine, Mae (later Wampler), 2259
Wine, Margaret (later Etter), 459
Wine, Margaretha Horn, 1350

Wine, Mary Stoner, 1221, **1349–1350,**
    2039, 2101
Wine, Max, 1813
Wine, Michael, 45, 494, **1350**, 2101
  Octavia, NE, Church of the Brethren,
    minister, 960
Wine, Michael, II, 494, 1350
Wine, N. B., 417, 585
Wine, Norman B., 566, 1813
Wine, Ray, 209, 264, 590, 672, 1340
  Midway Church of the Brethren, TN,
    providing leadership, 827
  Mountain Valley Church of the
    Brethren, TN, free minister, 889
  Pleasant Hill Church of the Brethren,
    TN, pastor/elder, 1032
Wine, Ronald Keith, 209, 516, 676, 740,
    1813
Wine, Sally Hawkins, 1349
Wine, Saloma Susan (later Ikenberry), 646
Wine, Samuel (1837–1904), 1813
Wine, Samuel A., 740
Wine, Samuel (Mount Sidney, VA), 1813
Wine, Samuel Walter, 1813
Wine, Sara (later Fulk), 521
Wine, Stoner Mary, 381
Wine, Susanna Miller
  Müller (Miller) family, 895
Wine, Susanna Moyers
  Rentmeister, Jean R. on, 2352
  Wine, Clyde C. on, 2352
Wine, Susannah Krouse, 1349
Wine, Susannah Miller, 1350
wine, use in communion services, **1349**, *See*
    temperance
Wine, Virginia, 685
Wine, W. M., 571
Wine, William
  Mountain Valley Church of the
    Brethren, TN, free minister, 889
Wine, William H., 1340, 1813
Wine, William M., 479
Wine, William M., 239, 494, **1350,** 1813
Wine, William N., 1813
Wine, William Ray, 1813
Winebrennarian Churches of God, *See*
    Churches of God, General
    Conference
Winebrenner, John, 309
Wineland, Dale
  Maitland, FL, Grace Brethren Church,
    783
Wineland family, 1304
Wineland, Jacob L., 1813
Wineland, Lela
  Maitland, FL, Grace Brethren Church,
    783
Wineman, David Bock, 1813
Wineman family
  Ridge Church of the Brethren, PA,
    1108
Winey, Christian Graybill, 1813
Winey, J. G., 248
Winey, Josiah G., 318, 1813
Winey, Steve
  Macedonia, OH, Western Reserve
    Grace Brethren Church, 2216
Winey, Thomas, 1813
Winey, Thomas G., 1813
Wineyard, Joseph D., 1813
Winfield, Kay Carol Sarver, 1855
Winfield, Richard Clarence, 186, 1813,
    1855, 2137

Wingard, Blanche, 244, 2101
Wingard, Edward, 362
Wingard, Edward N., 1813
Wingard family, 2095
    Mayville, ND, Red River Valley
        Church of the Brethren, 805
Wingard, Joseph D., 417, 1813
Wingart family, 2095
Winger, Alvin Leroy, 2101
Winger, Anne (later Garber)
    National Older Adult Conferences,
        2229
Winger, Clarence, 2101
Winger, Cora (later Shultz), *See* Shultz,
    Cora Winger
Winger, David, 1813
Winger, Elizabeth Frantz, 2102
Winger family, 2089, 2095, 2101, 2102, *See
    also* Wenger family
    history of, 1936
Winger, H. H., 1813
    Mount Garfield, CO, Church of the
        Brethren, 881
Winger, Henry, 2101
Winger, Henry R., 1813
Winger, Ida Miller, **1350**, 2101
Winger, John Martin, 1350
Winger, Joseph Oscar, 1813
    Marion, IN, Church of the Brethren,
        elder, 793
    Peru, IN, Church of the Brethren, 1010
Winger, Mabel Ellen (later Moomaw), 669,
    1841–1842, **2388**
    Moomaw, Ira Wilbur, wife of, 874
Winger, Mary Smith, 1350
Winger, Otho, 6, 242, 257, 344, *538*, 610,
    786, *786*, 1330, 1350, **1350–1351**,
    1351, 1813–1814, 2059, 2101
    biography of, 2101
    books by, 1351
    historical writing, 612
    Michigan City, IN, Church of the
        Brethren, 824
    missions, 861
    Native Americans, 2230
    North Manchester, IN, Church of the
        Brethren, elder (moderator), 949
    prayer, posture in, 1052
Winger, Paul, 1350
Winger, Robert, 1350
Winger, Roger Daniel, 641, 1814, 2101
Winger, W. W., 1814
Wingerd (Winegard), Paul E., 263, 1814
Wingert, Alice (later Trostle), 1276
Wingert, Edward B., 1814
Wingert family, 1214, 2089, 2095, *See also*
    Wenger family
Wingert, Frank Edward, 1814
Wingert, Harry Hewitt, 695, 1814
Wingert, Lizzie (later Benedict), 2135
Wingert, Mrs. Peter N., 1311
Wingert, Sudie M., 625, 1928
Wingfield, D. Michael, 350, 443
Wingfield, James H., 559, 1814
    Roanoke, VA, Garden City Grace
        Brethren Church, pastor, 1113
Wingfield, Marshall, 2102
Wingfield, Michael, 1814
Wingler family, 152
Wingler, Green, 1814
Wingler, Spencer, 1814
Winimac, IN, Church of the Brethren, **1347**
Winklebleck, Levi, 128, 445, 587, 1321,

1814
Winkler, Golan James, 2297
Winkler, Louis, 2102
Winkler, Robert, 1814
Winning the Race Ministries, **2262–2263**
Winnipeg, Manitoba
    General Conference Mennonite
        Church, 536
Winona Co., MN, 738
    migration of Brethren, 830
    Minnesota Brethren settlement, 848
Winona Lake Annual Meeting (CB)
    Early, Henry Clay, 413–414
Winona Lake Bible Conference, 136
    Grace Schools (Grace Theological
        Seminary, Grace College), 564
    Hoyt, Herman Arthur, 634
Winona Lake Christian Assembly, 1351,
    1353
    Grace Schools (Grace Theological
        Seminary, Grace College), 564
    historic sites, 609
    Hoyt, Herman Arthur, 634
    McClain, Alva J., Board of Directors,
        772
    prophecy conferences, 1062
Winona Lake, IN, 13, 192, 250, 653, 1302,
    1351, *1352,* 1353
    as Annual Meeting location, 36
    Fellowship of Grace Brethren Churches
        (FGBC), 484
    Foreign Missionary Society (BC,
        FGBC), 500
    Fort Wayne, IN, First Brethren Church,
        504
    God's Means of Grace (Yoder), 555
    Grace Brethren retirement home, 1198
    Grace Village Retirement Complex,
        564
    Hammers, Thomas E., 581
    history of, 1944
    Kent, Homer Austin, Jr., 2210
    National Brethren Bible Conference,
        914
    as sight of General Conference (BC),
        37, 63
    Women's Missionary Council, 1363
Winona Lake, IN, Grace Brethren Church,
    1319, **1353**, 2132
Winona Lake School of Theology
    Flora, Delbert Benjamin, 495
    Grace Schools (Grace Theological
        Seminary, Grace College), 563
Winona, MN, Church of the Brethren, *See*
    Lewiston, MN, Church of the
    Brethren
Winona, MN, Grace Brethren Church, **1351**
    Minnesota Brethren settlement, 848
Winrich, John, 1814
Winter, Charles H., 585, 1814
Winter, Mrs. Dwight George Richard, 377
Winter family, 2082
Winter, Isaac
    Smithville, OH, First Brethren Church,
        1192
Winter, Mrs. Isaac
    Smithville, OH, First Brethren Church,
        1192
Winter, Nevin O., 2102
Winter Park, FL, First Church of the
    Brethren, **1353**
    Gotha, FL, New Covenent Church of
        the Brethren, 2190

Hispanic Ministries (CB), 2198–2199
Orlando, FL, Community Church of
    the Brethren, 981
Winter, Pearl Bowman, 165
winter residents
    St. Petersburg, FL, First Church of the
        Brethren, part of congregation,
        1135
Winter, Richard, 377
Winter, Mrs. Richard, 377
Winter, Roy, 2171
Winter, Sharon Ruth Felb, 1855
Winter, William Paul, 1855
Winterhaven Dunkard Brethren Congrega-
    tion, CA, 239, **1354**
Winterish, John T., 2102
Winters, Bonnie Jean Miller
    Miller, Blanche Bonsack and Harold
        Clayton, 834
Winters, Carrie, 1354
Winters, Glen Ranck, 1814
Winters, Nelson, 1354
Winters, Vernon, 1814
Winters, William Homer, 1814
Winters, Wreatha, 1797
Wire, Rachel, 396
Wirick, Arthur T., 377, 1249, **1354**, 1814
    North Liberty, IN, Brethren Church,
        pastor, 948
    South Bend, IN, Ardmore Brethren
        Church, pastor, 1203
Wirick, George, 1354
Wirick, Mary, 1354
Wirt, Andrew Lowell, 2297
Wirt, Christian Frederick, 738, 1814
Wirt Co., WV
    Parkersburg, WV, Grace Brethren
        Church, 994
    Prosperity Brethren Church, WV, 1062
Wirt family, 738
Wirt, Florence G., 2102
Wirt, Fulsom, 628
Wirt, Jacob, 738, 1814
Wirt, James, 1307, 1814
Wirt, John Henry, 738, 1814
Wirt, Sarah, 738
Wirth, Lena Marie, 1846
Wisconsin, 176, *646*, **1354**, 2061
    district history, 1961
    Illinois, 647
    Michigan Brethren settlement, 823
    migration of Brethren, 829
    Old German Baptist Brethren, 967,
        2235
    Wisconsin vs. Yoder (1972), 26
    The Wisdom and Power of God (Nead,
        P.), 919, 1257
Wise, Abraham, 1814, 2041
Wise, Abram A., 1814
Wise, Adam, 16, 1814
Wise, Avis Beatrice (later Ramsey), 2041
Wise, Carol A., 2297
Wise, Charlotte Weybright, 1338
Wise, Christian, 1814, 2102
Wise Co., VA, 356, 728
Wise, Cora (later Helman), 1961
Wise, D. W., 104, 1814
Wise, Daniel, 1338
Wise, David, 373, 1294
    Pleasant Center Church of the
        Brethren, OH, minister, 1030
Wise, David (1802–1881), 1814
Wise, David (1817–1900), 1814

Wise, Elizabeth (late Arnold), 58
Wise, Elizabeth (late Miller), 2035
Wise, Elizabeth (later Shidler), *See* Shidler, Elizabeth Wise
Wise family, 142, 1253, 1320, 2063
　Musselman family related to by marriage, 901
Wise, Fred
　Quiet Dell Brethren Church, PA, 1076
Wise, George
　Outlook, WA, Church of the Brethren, elder, 986
Wise, George Elgy, 1383, 1814
Wise, Henry, 241, 332, 1814
　Pittsburgh, PA, First Brethren Church, pastor, 1027
　Ryerson Station Church of the Brethren, PA, minister, 1132
Wise, Hugo Paul, 1814
Wise, Jacob, 1242, 1814
　Sand Creek Old German Baptist Brethren Church, KS, minister, 1143
Wise, Jacob Funck, 2102
Wise, John, 16, 72, 170, 211, 442, 682, 1253, 1324, **1354,** 1814
　Hurricane Creek Church of the Brethren, IL, 638
　Mount Hope Church of the Brethren, OK, elder, 882
　Murdock Church of the Brethren, KS, elder, 896
　Prosperity Brethren Church, WV, 1062
　Ryerson Station Church of the Brethren, PA, elder, 1132
Wise, John S., 2102
Wise, Joseph M.
　Piqua, OH, Church of the Brethren, 1026
Wise, Katharine (later Shideler), *See* Shideler, Katharine Wise
Wise, Mary
　Piqua, OH, Church of the Brethren, 1026
Wise, Nancy Grable, 1354
Wise, Olive Viona, 1846
Wise, Paul E.
　Mount Zion Church of the Brethren, OH, 888
Wise, Samuel, 766
　Replogle, Peter, 1100
Wise, Susannah (later Spitler), 1212
Wise, Vernon Laing, 2102
Wise, William M., 44, 1814
Wise Words in a Wicked World (Turner)
　Turner, Charles W. (FGBC) and, 2256
Wiseman, B. W. S., 2102
Wiseman, Marvin, 349
Wiser, Tracy Lee, 2297
Wisler, Claude H., 1814, 2307
　Skippack Church of the Brethren, PA, moderator and minister, 1189
Wisler, Jacob
　St. Paul Church of the Brethren, NC, 1135
Wisler, Jacob, family
　St. Paul Church of the Brethren, VA, 1135
Wisley, Thomas N.
　Readings in Dynamic Indigeneity, 1990
Wisman, G. W., 1814
Wisman, John Henry
　St. Luke, VA, Brethren Church, 1135

Wisman, P. W., 740, 1814
　St. Luke, VA, Brethren Church, 1135
Wisman, W. M.
　St. Luke, VA, Brethren Church, pastor, 1135
Wisner, John, 629
Wisner, Pearl, 629
Wissahickon
　Glen of, and the Monks-Monastery, 1962
Wissahickon Creek, 82, **1354,** 2061
　baptism of Urner family, 1298
　Germantown, 542
　historic sites, 609
　Höcker, Heinrich, 615
　Koch, Stephan, 704
　Mack, Alexander, Jr., 704, 774
　Philadelphia, PA, Germantown Church of the Brethren, baptisms performed in, 1016
　Society of the Woman in the Wilderness, 1170, 1199
　Zimmerman mystics, 686–687
Wissinger family
　Pipe Creek Old German Baptist Brethren Church, IN, 1026
Wissinger, John
　Midway Dunkard Berthren Congregation, IN, 827
Wissinger, Susan (later Hostetler), 631
Wissler, Aaron, 235
Wissler family, 1961
Wister, Charles J., 2090
Witacre, J. W., 1814
Witcraft, John R., 2102
With Christ in the School of Prayer and The Prayer-Life (Murray), 1051
With Williams Our Secretary (Miller), 840
Withers, Alexander Scott, 2102
Withers, Carl, 2102
Withers, E. L.
　Newberg, OR, Dunkard Brethren Congregation, elder in, 933
Withers, Edward, 1814
Withers, Robert G., 1218
Witkovsky, Lowell David, 2297
Witkovsky, Lowell H., 1814
　Meadow Branch Church of the Brethren, MD, pastor, 805
　Redford, MI, Trinity Church of the Brethren, pastoral leadership, 1090
　Silver Springs, MD, Good Shepherd Church of the Brethren, pastor, 1182
Witman, Michael, 2074
Witmer, Amos S., 2074
Witmer, Anna Lehman, 2074
Witmer family, 2041, 2074
　Heisey family, 595
　Redstone Valley Old German Baptist Brethren Church, WI and, 2240
Witmer, George, 692, 1814
Witmer, J. S., 1814
Witmer, Jacob, 1814
Witmer, Johannes (John), 2049
Witmer, John H., 1814
Witmer, Mary Brubaker, 2074
Witmer, Mary Marna, 2074
Witmer, Nelson H., 2297
Witmer, Nettie, 2074
Witmer, Richard Clark, 1814, 2155, 2307
　Mount Morris, IL, Church of the Brethren, pastor, 883

Witmer, Samuel M., 2074
Witmer, Samuel Zug, 333, 1814
Witmer-Whitmer family
　family history and genealogy, 1984
Witmer (Whitmer), Isaac S., 1814
Witmore, Amanda
　Portland, TX, Bayview Church of the Brethren, minister, 1048
Witmore, Anna Mae, 1835
Witmore, Ira, 582
　Mound Valley Church of the Brethren, MO, 879
Witmore, Jacob, 331, 1815
　Phoenix, AZ, First Church of the Brethren, 1019
　Portland, TX, Bayview Church of the Brethren, minister, 1048
　San Antonio, TX, Church of the Brethren, 1141
Witmore, Jonathan, 1815
Witmore, Jonathan C., 1815
Witmore, Nora, 582
Witmore, Sarah (later Harnley), 585
Witmore (Whitmore), Ira, 1814–1815
witness
　Parsons, William T. on effects of, 2349
　queries about, 1076
Witness in the Sky (Lyon), 2002
Witness to Washington (CB)
　Washington Office (CB) and, 2260
Witt, Charles W., 237
Witt, G. Douglas, 16, 1277, 1815
Witt, G. W., 1815
Witt, Jerry, 1285, 1815
Witten family, 1927
Wittenberg University
　Stauffer, John N., 1219
Witter, Alton, 1815
　Osceola, IN, Grace Brethren Church, pastor, 984
Witter, C. Orville, 562, 1815
Witter, Christine (later Klingensmith), 703
Witter, E. C., 1815
Witter, Elizabeth (later Wrightsman), 1380
Witter, F. C., 1815
Witter family, 1864
　Four Mile Church of the Brethren, IN, 505
　Hertzler (Hartzler) family, 601
Witter, Marcus A., 699, 746, 1324, 1815
　Philadelphia, PA, Third Brethren Church, pastor, 1019
Witters, Donald Rutt, 1815
Wittgenstein, 159, **1354–1355,** 2057
　Brethren in, 1989
　Dutch religious dissenters at, 923
　Edict of 1712, 425
　Elsoff, 443
　Germany, 545
　Grundforschende Fragen (Basic Questions), 575
　Haug, Johann Friedrich, 589
　Henrich Albrecht, 597
　historical writing, 611
　history, 1963
　Hochmann von Hochenau, Ernst Christoph, 615
　Hüttental, 639
　Käsebier, Johann Georg, 684
　Konert, Christoph, 706
　König, Samuel, 706
　Laasphe, 716
　letters to, from former residents, 2001

maps of, 2104
radical pietists, 1292
refuge for nonconformists, 990
Sayn-Wittgenstein-Hohenstein, Gustav
    Otto, count of, 1158
Sayn-Wittgenstein-Hohenstein, Henrich
    Albrecht, count of, 683, 1158
Sayn-Wittgenstein-Sayn, Karl Ludwig,
    count of, 682–684
Treytorrens, Nicolas Samuel de, 1274
Wittgenstein Brethren
    Camisards, 242
    Marsay, Charles Hector de St. Georges,
        Marquis de, 796
Wittgenstein, Countesses, 2074
Wittgenstein (Germany), 9
    Brethren in, Rock, Johann Friedrich
        known to, 1116
    Moravian Church contact with
        Brethren, 875
    Philadelphian Society, 1019
    Reitz, Johann Heinrich, 1095
Wittgenstein magazine (Fall, 1979)
    historiography, 2201
Wittgenstein village
    antinomianism communes and, 236
Wittke, Carl Frederick, 2074
Wittler, Catherine
    Bungalow, The, 2364
Wittlinger, Carlton O., 2102
Wittman, Bruce C.
    on Montville CB, 2364
Wittmer, Jacob, 1948
Wittmer, Mary Reusser, 1948
Wittner, Lawrence S., 2074
Wittrock, Bette, 713
Wittrock, Harold, 713
Wittrock, Lucille, 713
Witts, Will, 70
Wittschiebe, Charles E.
    on prophetism, 2364
Wittwer, John, Sr., 2017
Witwer, Ananias Cline, 2102
Witwer, Dorothy, 2072
Witwer family, 2072, 2092, 2102
Witwer, George, 1815, 2102
Witwer, Michael, 2102
Witzky family, 739
Witzky, Gene E., 504, 2297
    Mansfield, OH, Woodville Grace
        Brethren Church, pastor, 787
    Pompano Beach, FL, Grace Brethren
        Church, pastor, 1046
    South Bend, IN, Ireland Road Grace
        Brethren Church, pastor, 1203
Witzky, Willis, 1815
"*Wo bleiben meine Sinne*" ("My Senses Are
    Failing Me")
    hymns, 642
Woburn, IL, Brethren Church, **1355**
Das Wochenblatt (*The Weekly Newspaper*),
    1355, 2103
Woder, Sarah (later Blosser), 1879
Woertman, Derick Jans, 1367
Wogaman, Alice (later Kent), 688
Wogaman, Burkett, Holdery, 1991
Wogoman, Jesse, 1356
Wogoman, Joel, 1815
Wohlfahrt (Welfare), Michael (Brother
    Agonius), **1355**
    Franklin, Benjamin, 506, 1040
    noncreedalism, 943
    Seventh-Day Baptists, 1170

speeches by, 2103
Wohlford, John M., 1112
Wokeck, Marianne Sophia, 2364
Wolf, Abraham, 1359, 1815
    Pleasant Hill Church of the Brethren,
        IA, minister, 1032
Wolf, Albert Ambrose, 1815
Wolf, Anna, 375
Wolf, Anna Brovont, 1188
Wolf, Arlan, 2297
Wolf, C. Edward, 81, 2103
    Ottumwa, IA, Church of the Brethren,
        pastor, 985
Wolf, Calvin, 1815
Wolf, Catharine, 352
Wolf, Catharine Cripe, 352
Wolf Creek Church of the Brethren, KY,
    689, 1280, **1355**
    Rock House Church of the Brethren,
        KY, 1117
Wolf Creek Church of the Brethren, OH,
    102, 1276, 1302, 1327, 1338,
    1355–1356
    Salem Church of the Brethren organ-
        ized from, 1138
Wolf Creek district, OH, 462
Wolf Creek, OH, 208, 722
    congregation, 213, 281, 366, 757, 1306
Wolf Creek Old German Baptist Brethren
    Church, OH, *34,* 967, **1356**
    Yoder, D. Willard (OGBB) and, 2267
Wolf Creek, PA, congregation, 352
Wolf, D. Ernst
    Groff, Warren Frederick, *2194*
Wolf, D. L.
    Mexico Old German Baptist Brethren
        Church, IN, elder-in-charge, 821
Wolf, D. S., 1815
Wolf, D. W., 1815
Wolf, Daniel, 1815
Wolf, Daniel F., 2103, 2307
    Old Brethren minister, 965
    The Pilgrim, 965, 1023
Wolf, David Albert, 1815
Wolf, David B., 1815
Wolf, David Wesley, 1815
Wolf, Dorothy K.
    on Indian Creek CB Cemetery, 2364
Wolf, Dorothy Mae (later Beaver), 1847
Wolf, Edna (later Shively), *See* Shively,
    Edna Wolf
Wolf, Elizabeth, 142
Wolf, Elta (later Miller)
    Miller, Orie O., wife of, 841
Wolf (Wolfe), Ezra, 1815
    Quinter, KS, Dunkard Brethren
        Congregation, presiding elder,
        1078
Wolf family, 142, 2103, *See also* Wolfe
    family
    Mayville, ND, Red River Valley
        Church of the Brethren, 805
    Plum Creek Old German Baptist
        Brethren Church, KS, 1038
    Redstone Valley Old German Baptist
        Brethren Church, WI and, 2239
    sources on, 2312
Wolf, George, *See* Union Co., IL
Wolf, George B., 14, 1815
Wolf, Gregory, 2297
Wolf, Hannah Kinsey, 1907
Wolf, Harvey Leroy, 1815
Wolf, Hiram J., 1815

Wolf, Jacob, 1815, 1907
Wolf, John B., 142
Wolf, John F., 142, 1363. 1815
    Mud Valley Old German Baptist
        Brethren Church, IL, deacon, 892
    Old Brethren minister, 965
    Sand Creek Old German Baptist
        Brethren Church, KS, minister,
        1143
    Sheridan Lake Old German Baptist
        Brethren Church, CO, minister in,
        1176
Wolf, John I., 1815
Wolf, John P., 1815
Wolf, Joseph M., 1815
Wolf, Katie Fritz, 1359
Wolf-Knisley family, 1988
Wolf, L. D., 1815
Wolf, Lovina (later Leedy), 734
Wolf, Mae Louise, 1841
Wolf, Mahlon K., 42, 1815
Wolf, Mary, 142
Wolf, Michael, 2072
Wolf, Paul B., 142, 1815, 2307, **2387**
Wolf, Philip, 142, 496, 633, 1188,
    1815
    Nimishillen Old German Baptist
        Brethren Church, OH, minister in,
        937–938
    North Fork Old German Baptist
        Brethren Church, IN, minister, 947
Wolf, Philip Andrew, 1815
Wolf River Church of the Brethren, KS,
    682, **1356**
Wolf River, KS, congregation, 682
Wolf, Samuel D., 1815
Wolf, Samuel N., 14, 1815
Wolf, Sara Malinda (later Skiles), *See*
    Skiles, Sara Malinda Wolf
Wolf, Stephanie Grauman, 2103
Wolf, Steven D., 2297
Wolf, Susannah, 216
Wolf, William, 1265
Wolf (Wolfe), C. Edward, 1815
Wolf (Wolfe), Daniel A., 1815
Wolfe, Aaron K., 2177, 2186
Wolfe, Albert
    Pleasant Center Church of the
        Brethren, OH, minister, 1030
Wolfe, Alfred Paul, 1815
Wolfe, Andrew, family
    Pipe Creek Church of the Brethren,
        MD, 1026
Wolfe, Anna Hunsaker, 637, 1356, 1357
Wolfe, Anna Overholtzer, 1359
Wolfe, Ardelta Delores (later Baker)
    works by, 2312
Wolfe, Barbara Hauser, 1358, 1359
Wolfe, C. Edward, 638
Wolfe, Calvin R.
    Markleysburg, PA, Church of the
        Brethren, pastor, 794
Wolfe, Catherine, 1359
Wolfe, Charles E., 1815
Wolfe, Charles H.
    Sciota Church of the Brethen, OH,
        elder, 1160
Wolfe, Claude Elven, 1815, 1846
    Santa Fe Church of the Brethren, IN,
        1145
Wolfe, Daniel, 1815
Wolfe, David, **1356,** 1357, 1815
Wolfe, Donald Richard, 1815

Wolfe, Eli M., 236, 1815
Wolfe, Esther Hoff, 2103
Wolfe family, 144, 1299, 1338, **1359**, 2103
  Hunsiker (Hunsaker) family, 637
  migration of Brethren, 830
  Muhlenberg Co., KY, German Baptist
    Brethren, 893
  Neher family, related to, 922
Wolf(e) family, 146, 177, 236, 238
  English River Church of the Brethren,
    IA, 447
Wolfe, Frieda Mayme, 2103
Wolfe, Galen Weybright, 1815, 1846
Wolfe, George, I, 177, 215, 251, 271, 469,
    519, 561, 689, 727, 743, **1356,**
    1359, 1815–1816, 2046
  baptism of Abraham Lincoln, 743
  biography, 1938
  Hunsiker (Hunsaker) family, 637
  thesis on, 1923
Wolfe, George, II, 177, 258, 295, 370, 460,
    475–476, 519, 548, 597, 740,
    1234, 1288, 1292, 1327, 1356,
    1356, **1356–1357,** 1357, *1357,*
    1358, 1359, 1364, 1816
  Hendricks, John, 597
  Hon, Peter Keithly, 627
  Hostetler, Adam, 631
  Illinois, 646
  Iowa, 661
  migration of Brethren, 829
  minorities, ethnic and racial, 849
  photography of Brethren, 1020
  place-names, Brethren, 1027–1028
  travels on horseback, 1271
Wolfe, George, III, 177, 215, 238, 245, 334,
    335, 364, 476, 519, *1358,*
    1358–1359, 1816
  migration of Brethren, 830
  Myers, Jonathan, 904
Wolfe, Hannah Kinsey, 1359
Wolfe, Harold, 1224
Wolfe, Jacob, 271, 1288, 1356, 1357, 1358,
  1359
  Illinois, 646
Wolfe, John P., 1357, **1359**, 1816, 2103
  Santa Fe Church of the Brethren, IN,
    minister, 1144
Wolfe, Joseph H., 1816
Wolfe, June Emelyne Heestand, 1846
Wolfe, Kenneth, 1816
  Southern Lancaster Grace Brethren
    Church, PA, 1207
Wolfe, Leonard, 1816
  Romine Church of the Brethren, IL,
    minister, 1121
Wolfe, Mark W., 105, 343, 1816, 2307
  Oakvale Church of the Brethren, WV,
    leadership by, 958
Wolfe, Marshall R., 1816, 2103
Wolfe, Mirna Belle Flory, 1846
Wolfe, Permelia A. McKnight (later
    McKnight), 1356
  Metzger, John, wife of, 819
Wolfe, Rolland, 1816
Wolfe, Rua Faggart, 1358, *1358,* 1359
Wolfe, Rua Olivette (later Ronk), 1121
Wolfe, Ruth
  Southern Lancaster Grace Brethren
    Church, PA, 1207
Wolfe, S. N., 235
Wolfe, Tracey Vaughn, 2297
Wolfe, Verling H., 2297

Wolfe (Wolf), Calvin R., 1815
Wolfe (Wolf), Frank B., 1815
Wolff, Anna Barbara Moyer
  Meyer family, 821
Wolff, C. E.
  Myrtle Point, OR, Church of the
    Brethren, pastor, 906
Wolff, Catherine Putterbach Hawker, 1070
Wolff, Charles
  Milk River Valley Church of the
    Brethren, MT, elder, 832
Wolff, Christian, 2103
Wolff, Conrad, 1934
Wolff, David, Sr., 1070
Wolff family, 2103
Wolff, Georg Michael, 1934
Wolff, John Barnardt, 1934
Wolff, John George, 2062
Wolff, Marie (later Craig), 1911
Wolff, Raymond Alvin, 2103
Wolfinbarger, Charles W.
  Northview, OH, Brethren Life
    Church/Vineyard Community
    Church, 2232
Wolfkill, D. Ellis, 1816
Wolford, A. Klein, 1816
Wolford, Eva, 1816
Wolford, Harley H., 1281, 1816
  Ripon, CA, Brethren Church, pastor,
    1110
Wolford, Mary Kathryn, 214
Wolford, William Edward, 1321, 1816
Wolgamult, Anna, 384
Wolgamuth, Bertha (later Royer), 1128
Wolgamuth meetinghouse
  Lower Conewago Church of the
    Brethren, PA, 765
Wolgemuth, Harry O., 737, 1816
Wolgemuth, Herbert Ober, 1816, 2307
  Shamokin, PA, Church of the Brethren,
    1171
Wollenweber, Louis A., 2103
Wolters, Garrett John, 1816
  Portis, KS, Grace Brethren Church,
    pastor, 1048
Wolters, H. C. H.
  Portis, KS, Grace Brethren Church,
    1048
Wolters, J. H.
  Portis, KS, Grace Brethren Church,
    1048
Womaen's Caucus, **1359**, 1362, 2183–2184
  Smeltzer, Mary Blocher (CB) and,
    2250
  women and, 2264
Women's Conferences (CB) and, 2264
Woman in the Wilderness, Society of, *See*
    Society of the Woman in the
    Wilderness
Woman's Missionary Societies, **1359–1360,**
    1361, 1363
Woman's Missionary Society (BC)
  missions education, 864
The Woman's Outlook, 191–192, 203, 1360
Womelsdorf, Josef
  on Sauer, Christoph, 2364
women, *578, 1360,* **1360–1362,** *1361,* 2032,
    2263–2264, *See also* gender roles;
    Sisters of Saron; Snow Hill
    Nunnery; widows
  baptism
  roles in, 1361
  Schwarzenau, 1360

  Brethren Church, 184, 846–847
  Brown, Barbara on clergy women,
    2365
  BSC projects, 199
  Chang, Patricia M. on clergy, 2365
  Christian Education Commission (CB),
    155, 285
  Church of the Brethren, 304, 846,
    2109, 2163
  Church of the Brethren ministry, 846
  deacons, 2169
  doctrine on, 177
  Dominican Republic, 2172–2173
  Eller, Vernard on feminism grammar,
    2329
  Ephrata Community, 2051
  equality, striving for, in the Church of
    the Brethren, 2001
  ethics issues, 2177–2178
  evangelism and, 204
  faith, 1962
  Far Western Brethren, 475
  Fellowship of Grace Brethren Churches
    (FGBC), 487
  feminism, impact of, **2183–2184**
  Flora, Jerry on Women's Missionary
    Society presidents, 2331
  Flora, Julie on Women's Missionary
    Society presidents, 2331
  Frantz, Nadine Pence on, 2332
  Freeport, IL, Church of the Brethren,
    515
  General Board (CB) on women's work,
    535
  Gibson, Daniel B., 547
  Gilbert Julia A., 548
  Global Women's Project, 2190
  Goosen, Rachel Waltner on conscien-
    tious objectors and, 2334
  Grace Brethren Church ministry, 847
  graveclothes, 567
  hairstyle, 579
  Hedrick, Laura E. N. Grossnickle, 593
  Helman, Patricia Kennedy, 2197
  Hispanic Radio Ministry (BC),
    2199–2200
  Hogan-Albach, Susan on Brethren,
    2337
  homes of Dunkards, 1975
  Hutchison, Anna Martha, 639
  Iglesia Cristiana Pentecostal de Cuba,
    2207
  Ikenberry, Olivia Dickens, 646
  Inglenook Cook Book, The, 656
  Iowa, 661
  language, inclusive, 2214
  Leonard, Rosalita J. on CB writings of,
    2343
  Lummis, Adair T. on clergy, 2365
  marriage, equality in, 795
  mass media concerns about exploita-
    tion, 801
  meditations for, 2111
  mentoring, 2221
  Meyer, Lauree Hersch on, 2332
  name change discussion (CB), 2228
  Nigeria, 2165
  person awareness, 304
  physicians, 810
  prohibited from ministry by Dunkard
    Brethren, 845
  Reynolds, Margaret C. on Plain
    Women in River Brethren, 2352

role in worship services, 1377
role of, 177–178, 189
Smeltzer, Mary Blocher (CB) and, 2250
sources on, 2318, 2319
Vogt, Esther Loewen on Civil War experiences of Brethren, 2361
voting for ministers, 844
Zikmund, Barbara Brown on clergy, 2365
Women and Religion in America, 2051
women as ministers, 1362, 2322
article about, 1938
Brethren Church, 2141, 2224
Church of the Brethren, 2224
Dolby, Martha Cunningham, 395
ethics and, 2178
Kurtz, Daniel Webster, committee recommending licensing of, 711
Lear, Mattie A., 732
Major, Sarah Righter, 1334
ordination of women, 1360–1361, 1362, 2141, 2157, 2184, 2264
Pence, Mary, 1251
right to preach, 1360–1361
Sisters' Society of Christian Endeavor (BC), 1188
Sterling, Mary Malinda, 1221
Stine, Bertha Miller Neher, 1221
Taylor, Madolin Boorse, 1249
Underhill, Nancy D. Blain, 1286
urban missions, role in, 1296
Whitacre, Annie Ruth Beahm, 1339
Womaen's Caucus, 2184
women in leadership positions
Scalp Level, PA, Church of the Brethren, 1151
Schwalm, Florence Roselind Studebaker, 1157
Women's Aid Societies
Plattsburg Church of the Brethren, MO, 1030
Women's Bible School, China
Horning, Mary Emma, 630
Women's Caucus, 304
Global Women's Project, 2190
sexuality, human, 1170
Women's Christian Temperance Union, **1359**
Halladay, Sara Heebner, 580
Lowery, Margaret E., 2216
Stahly, Cora Miller, 1216
Women's Conferences (CB), *2263*
Women's Fellowship, 347, 1361, **1362**, *See also* Council of Women's Work (CB)
Indiana, 652
manuals for, 788
Maple Grove Church of the Brethren, MD, 790
missions education, 864
Nigeria (ZME), 2165
poetry, 1040
Sebring, FL, J. H. Moore Memorial Church of the Brethren, 1162
Williamsburg, PA, Church of the Brethren, 1346
women's liberation, *See* feminism
women's missionary circles
missions education, 863
Women's Missionary Council, 38, 1361, 1363, **1363**, *See also* Fellowship of Grace Brethren Churches (FGBC)

missions education, 864
women and, 2264
Women's Missionary Societies, **1363**
Women's Missionary Society, 181, 182
Black, Shirley Andrick, 2138
devotional literature, 382
Miller, Clara Worst, 834
Shively, Nora Early, 1178
Sisterhood of Mary and Martha, 1187
Sisters' Society of Christian Endeavor (BC), 1187–1188
women and, 2264
women's organizations
devotional literature, 381
women's rights, 22
Women's School and Girls' Senior Primary School, Nigeria, 1312, *1313*
Women's Work, **347,** 1362, 1996, 2000
Bible Department, devotional literature produced by, 381
Fairview Church of the Brethren, IA, 468
formation of, 1361, 1362
Gibbel, Florence Baker, 547
Halladay, Sara Heebner, 580
Hartsough family, 588
Mothers and Daughters' Association, 878
Mow, Anetta Cordula, secretary, 890
Murphy, Sara Florence Fogelsanger, 897
Sisters' Aid Society (CB), 1187, *1188*
Wine, Mary Stoner, 1350
Wondergem, Margaret F., 2103
Wonderlich, Charles, Jr., 1816
burial, 2000
South Keokuk Church of the Brethren, IA, elder, 1205
Wonderlich family
South Keokuk Church of the Brethren, IA, 1205
Wonso, Jacqueline Kuhn
on Kuhn, John, 2331
on Kuhn, Susannah Mock, 2331
Wood, Alfred
Quiet Dell Brethren Church, PA, 1076
Wood, Blanche Bowman, 2103
Wood, Bruce Kenneth, 1041, 1816, 2307
Wood, C. A., 1816
Wood, Charles H., 1816
Wood, Charles S., 1816
Wood, Clara Rebecca Chaloupka, 1041, 1816
Wood Co., OH, 380, 720, 1235
Portage Church of the Brethren, OH, 1047
Rome congregation, OH, 956
Wood Co., OK
Prairie Lake Church of the Brethren, OK, 1050
Wood Colony congregation, CA, 1335
Wood Colony Old German Baptist Brethren Church, CA, *1363,* 1363
Modesto, CA, Old German Baptist Brethren Church, 867
Wood family
Oak Grove Church of the Brethren, MO, 956
Wood, G. W., 1816
Wood, George, 317, 1816
Wood Grove Brethren-Christian Parish, MI, 94, 824, 1263, **1363**
Wood, J. B., 1816

Wood, J. J., 1816
Wood, Jerome H., 2103
Wood, Julia A. (later Kauffman), 204, 1361, **1363,** 2103
Wood, L., 377
Wood, L. A., 1816
Wood, Levi G., 377, 503, 1816
Roanoke, VA, First Brethren Church, pastor, 1113
South Haven Brethren Church, KS, elder, 1205
Mulvane, KS, Brethren Church, pastor, 896
Wood, Nancy, 2093
Wood, Ralph, 2103
Wood, Richard, 145
Wood River, NE, Church of the Brethren, *See* Kearney, NE, Church of the Brethren
Wood River, NE congregation, 685
Wood, Stacy B. C., Jr.
on Gorgas, Christin (Mack), 2364
Wood, Stephen, 1816
Wood, T. C., 925, 1816
Wood, Violet, 2103
Woodard family
Fruitdale, AL, Church of the Brethren, 520
Woodberry, MD, Church of the Brethren, 2099, *See also* Baltimore, MD, Woodberry Church of the Brethren
Woodbridge, George, 2103
Woodbridge, Joseph, 268, 1217, 1363, 1816
Woodbridge, VA, Church of the Brethren, 1320, **1363–1364**
Woodbury Co., IA, 695
Woodbury, PA, 1323
Church of the Brethren, 357, 765, **1364**
Holsinger Church of the Brethren, PA, 623
from Yellow Creek, PA, congregation, 927
Woodcrest (Rifton, NY)
Hutterian Society of Brothers, 640
Wooddale Church of the Brethren, PA, **1364**
Mount Joy Church of the Brethren, PA, 882
Woodcox, Josiah H., 1816
Woodford Co., IL
Oak Grove Church of the Brethren, IL, 955
Panther Creek Church of the Brethren, 992
Woodhatch, Maurice Leroy, 247, 1816
Rosepine, LA, Church of the Brethren, elder, 1123
Woodhead family
Harrisburg, PA, Melrose Gardens Grace Brethren Church, 586
Woodie, Elbert C., 424, 1277, 1816
Pleasant View Church of the Brethren, WV, pastor, 1037
Woodie, Fred E., 1816
Maple Grove Church of the Brethren, NC, pastor, 790
Woodie, Henry Jackson, 1816
Shelton Church of the Brethren, NC, pastor in, 1176
Woodie (Woody), John C., 755, 1816
Peak Creek Church of the Brethren, NC, minister, 1003
Woodie, Talton Lee, 72, 1816

Woodiel, Fayette, 72
  Mount Hope Church of the Brethren,
    AR, 881
Woodiel, W. L., 72, 1816
  Mount Hope Church of the Brethren,
    AR, 881
Woodiel, William, 558
Woodin, Ataloa Snell, 2298
Wooding, Susannah (later Byroads), 955
Woodland Church of the Brethren, IL, 69,
  1364
Woodland congregation, 1239, 1263
Woodland, MI, 1363
  Hope Church of the Brethren, MI, 629
Woodland, MI, Church of the Brethren, See
    Wood Grove Brethren-Christian
    Parish, MI
Woodland, MI, Woodland Village Church
    of the Brethren, 1363, **1364**
  Schrock, Mark Y., 1156
Woodland, VA mission point, Botetourt Co.,
    VA, Church of the Brethren, 164
Woodlawn schoolhouse, WV, 1249
Woodmansee, Euclid Jerome, 2103
Woodmason, Charles
  Carolina, 1971
Woodruff, Paul E., 319, 654
Woodruff, Paul Ed, 1816
Woods, Beulah Mae (later Miller), 145,
    1841, 1982
Woods, Charles M., 1816
Woods, Dora Sutphin, 1364
Woods, Ephriam
  Howard Co. Old German Baptist
    Brethren Church, IN, 633
Woods, Glen
  Matteson, MI, Brethren Church, 803
Woods, Gloria Jean (later Rendt), 2043
Woods, Jean, 2104
Woods, Manasseh Frederick, 269, 442,
    1223, 1342, **1364**, 1816
Woods, Margaret (later Hampton), 1957
Woods, Michael L., 2298
Woods, Mrs. Glen
  Matteson, MI, Brethren Church, 803
Woods, Otho C., 1816
Woodside family, 2105
Woodside, MD, 1350
Woodstock Brethren Church, VA, See Saint
    Luke, VA, Brethren Church
Woodstock Church of the Brethren, VA,
    330, **1364, 2372**
  Flat Rock Church of the Brethren, VA,
    493
  Oak Hill Church of the Brethren, VA,
    957
  Round Hill Church of the Brethren,
    VA, 1125
  Salem Church of the Brethren organ-
    ized from, 1138
Woodstock German Baptist Brethren
    (Church of the Brethren), 1228
  St. Luke, VA, Brethren Church, 1135
Woodstock School, India
  Shull, Susan Lavinia Stoner, 1180
Woodstock School, Landour, India
    mission schools, 854
Woodstock, VA, 1301
Woodward, A. B., 479, 1816
Woodward, Bernice, 1351
Woodward Co., OK
  Indian Creek Church of the Brethren,
    OK, 651

Woodward, David, 2103
Woodward, David Earl, 1846
Woodward, Eleanore Friederika Behrendt,
    1846
Woodward, Emma Jean, 2297
Woodward family, 2103
Woodward, Lewis, 1337
Woodward, Mary Boyd, 2103
Woodward, T. E., 2103–2104
Woodworth, OH, Church of the Brethren,
    See Youngstown, OH, Woodworth
    Church of the Brethren
Woody, J. C., 755
Woody, Marie Hannah (later Brubaker),
    218, 1835, **2387**
Woolery family
  Jackson Co. German Baptist Brethren,
    IN, 667
Wooley, Beverly Jean, 1849
Wooleytown, IN, congregation
  Mexico, IN, Church of the Brethren,
    821
Woolford family, 373
Woolley, Edwin Dilworth, 1907
Woolman family
  Grandview, WA, Grace Brethren
    Church, 566
Woolman, John, 117
  Society of Friends (Quakers), 1199
Woolman, Lloyd A., 275, 1343, 1816
Wooster, OH
  Christ Church of the Brethren, **1365**
  Sala, Johann, printer, 1136
  West View Manor, 1336
  Church of the Brethren, 279,
    Paradise Church of the Brethren,
      divided from, 992
      West Nimishillen, OH, con-
        gregation, 945–946
  Grace Brethren Church, 68, 467, 963,
    1365
  Johnson, George, 2224
Wooten, Eddie, 2298
word, external and internal, See inner word
    and outer word
Worden, WI, 1217, 1354
  Church of the Brethren, **1365**
  Maple Grove Church of the
    Brethren, WI, 791
wordly amusements, See amusements,
    worldly
Words, Jessie Mae (later Solomon), 2251
work camps, *1365*, **1365**, *1366*, **1367**, See
    also camping movement
  in Austria, 73
  Blough work camp, *1366*
  Europe, *1366, 1367*
  Flat Creek Church of the Brethren, KY,
    493
  Freundschaftsheim (Friendship House),
    517
  Germany, 546
  Historic Peace Churches, 608
  Kansas
    Brethren Service Committee, 2103
  Kassel as headquarters for international
    work camp program, 684
  Lersch, E. Phillip, Jr., 2214
  migrant labor, 827
  Nigeria, 2165
  One Hundred Dunkers for Peace, 975
  Poland, for international students, 1041
  post-WWII Germany, 200

  relief and rehabilitation work, 200, 202
  relief and service efforts, 1097
  relief and social work, 303
  Russia, 1288
  Schwarzenau, 1158, *1365*
  theology and, 2255
  West, Daniel, 1331
  Young, Andrew (J.) on BSC and, 2365
  youth and, 2269
Workman, Andrew J.
  Mabel, OR, Church of the Brethren,
    771
Workman, Arthur S., 1367, 1816–1817
Workman, Charles
  Mount Olivet Brethren Church, DE,
    886
Workman, Clifford Arthur, 1367, 1817
Workman, Columbus J., 1367, 1817
Workman, Dale, 2298
Workman, Daniel N., 719, 1817
Workman, David A., 326, 1367, 1817
Workman, David N., 383, 1367, 1817
  Mohican Church of the Brethren, OH,
    867–868
Workman, Elwood
  Mount Olivet Brethren Church, DE,
    886
Workman family, **1367**, 1865, 2056
Workman, George W., 1817
Workman, Isaac, 1367
Workman, James, 1367
Workman, James J., 1817
Workman, Jemima R.
  Rosenberger family, 1123
Workman, John J., 1367, 1817
Workman, Joseph C., 363, 1367
Workman, Joseph Thomas, 1817
Workman, Joshua J., 1367, 1817
Workman, Lavina Dickey, 1367
Workman, Levi, 1213, 1367, 1817
Workman, Lewis, 1367, 1817
Workman, Luella (later England), 446
Workman, Maria
  Mabel, OR, Church of the Brethren,
    771
Workman, Mary (later Rosenberger), 1123
Workman, Morgan, 760, 992, 1367, 1817
Workman, Mrs. Charles
  Mount Olivet Brethren Church, DE,
    886
Workman, Mrs. Elwood
  Mount Olivet Brethren Church, DE,
    886
Workman, N(orman) C., 1367, 1817
  Maple Grove Church of the Brethren,
    KS, 789
Workman, Orpha (later Keever; Leather-
    man), 732
Workman, Philip, 14, 1817
  Mabel, OR, Church of the Brethren,
    771
Workman, S. J., 1817
Workman, Sabrina (later Rosenberger),
    1123
Workman, Sylvester
  Pleasant View Church of the Brethren,
    KS, 1036
Workman, William P., 1367, 1817
Works (Böhme, J.), 923
works, doctrine of, 42
  Brethren Doctrine of Salvation, 1140
  Doctrinal Treatise, 394
  Reformation, 1091

sanctification, 1142
Works Progress Administration (WPA)
    Wilmington, DE, Church of the
        Brethren, 1347
works righteousness, 1259–1260
    Anabaptists accused of, 1368
    public worship seen as, 1373, 1375
World Alliance of Reformed Churches
    Reformed Church, 1092
World Campus Afloat
    Bittinger, Desmond Wright, 143
World Communion Day
    love feast on, 764
World Conference of Christian Youth
    Prather, John Perry, 1051
World Conference on Faith and Order, 470
World Council of Churches (WCC), 199,
        210, 308, 422, *423*, **1368–1369,**
        2028
    Baptism, Eucharist, and Ministry
        (BEM) text, 2133–2134
    The Christian Beacon and, 281
    Church of the Brethren, 303, 2087,
        2228–2229
    Committee on Interchurch Relations,
        2167
    Cordier, Andrew Wellington, 344
    ecumenism, 423
    environmental issues, 2177
    faith and order, 470
    fraternal relations, 510
    fundamentalism, 522
    Geneva, 540
    Germany, 546
    Greece, 569
    Greek Orthodox Church, 569
    Historic Peace Churches, 610
    Inter-Church Aid and Service to
        Refugees, 657
    Interchurch Service to Greek Villages,
        658
    international exchange with Russia,
        1288
    life and work movement, 742
    McIntire, Carl, 774
    Metzler, John D., Sr., 820
    Miller, Donald Eugene, 2223
    Nikodim, Metropolitan, president of,
        937
    Orthodox Churches, 983
        Peters, Raymond Russell, 1011
    Puidoux Conferences, 1071
    Re-imagining Conference and, 2240
    refugee resettlement, 1093, 2240
    religious liberty, 1098
    Renkewitz, Heinz Gottfried, 1099
    Row, W. Harold, 1126
    Russian Orthodox Church, 1132
    Spain, missions to, 1207
    Turkey, refugee project, 1280
    two-hundred-fiftieth anniversary,
        Schwarzenau, 1282, 1355
    violence and, 2265
    Visser 't Hooft, Willem Adolph, 1309
    work camps, 1365
    Ziegler, Edward Krusen, 1395
    Zigler, Michael Robert, 1246, 1397,
        1398
World Council of Churches (WCC) Uppsala
    Assembly (1968)
    historic peace churches, 2200
World Day of Prayer
    Lent, observance of, 737

World Friendship Center, Japan, **1369,** 2364
    Japan, 669
    Smeltzer, Mary Blocher (CB) and,
        2250
World Health Organization (WHO), **1369**
    Cassel, Franklin J., 707
    Korea, 1291
world hunger, *See* famine; hunger
World Ministries Commission, 201, **1369**
    bibliography, 1906
    Brazil, 2139
    Church of the Brethren, 303, 305
    Dominican Republic, 2172
    Ecuador, 422
    Ekklesiyar 'Yan'uwa a Nigeria (EYN),
        cooperation with, 937
    Frantz, Ruby June (later Rhoades) and,
        2242
    General Board (CB), 535–536
    General Services Commission (CB),
        539
    Honduras, 627
    Israel, 664
    mission tours, 855
    On Earth Peace, 974
    On Earth Peace Assembly, 2235
    origin of, 36
    refugee resettlement, 1093
    SERRV (Sales Exchange for Refugee
        Rehabilitation Vocations), 1139
    Sudan, 1234
    Thompson, Joel Kent and, 2255
World Missionary Conference
    ecumenism, 422
World Missionary Council, 1368
World Relief Board, 182, **1369**
    Peace Committee (BC), 1001
    relief and service efforts, 1097
    social welfare, 1198
World Relief Corporation, 182
    relief and service arm of National
        Association of Evangelicals
        (NAE), 914
    relief and service efforts, 1097
World Service Committee of the World
    Council of Churches, 308
World Student Christian Federation
    Visser 't Hooft, Willem Adolph, 1309
World Sunday School Association
    ecumenism, 422
    Kurtz, Daniel Webster, 711
The World That Perished (Whitcomb)
    Whitcomb, John Clement, Jr. (FGBC,
        CGBCI) and, 2262
World Trade Center, *See* September 11,
    2001 attacks
world travel, 2012
World view, Brethren life
    Nead, Peter as spokesman for,
        918–920, *919*
World War I, 78, **1369–1371,** 1862
    and Armenians, 55
    Armenians, relief and rehabilitation
        work, 199
    Brethren Church, 1370
    capitalism and, 253
    Central Service Committee, 1245
    chaplaincy, 271
    Church of the Brethren, 1370
    conscientious objection, 1370–1371
    conscientious objectors, 269, 336, 916,
        1249, 2068
        death of in Ohio military camp,

1327
    Wilson, Edward Raymond, 1347
    defense industry employment, 301
    dress reform during, 403
    Eglon, WV, Church of the Brethren,
        430
    ethics, 458
    Fast, Henry A., 480
    flags, 492
    Forward Movement, 504
    fraternal relations, 510
    fundamentalism, 522
    Germany, 545
    Goshen Conference, 559
    Greece, 569
    Heifer Project International, 593
    Henry, Jerry Maurice, 598
    Hess, Maurice Abram, 601
    higher education, 603
    Historic Peace Churches, 608
    Influenza Pandemic, 655
    Interchurch World Movement (IWM),
        658
    International Fellowship of Reconcilia-
        tion, 659
    Kruger, Helena, 708
    loyalty of German-Americans, 2001
    material aid, 802
    "Message of the Brethren Ministry,"
        817
    military service, 269, 301, 311,
        387–388, 831
    Moomaw, Daniel Crouse, 874
    nonresistance, 301
    Old German Baptist Brethren, 1370
    opposition to Nebraska Brethren, 921
    patriotism, 311
    Peace Committee (CB), 1002
    peace position, 1000
    Pennsylvania war supplies for, 223
    post-war neoorthodox rejection of theo-
        logical liberalism, 922
    prisons, 1060
    publications, effects on, 191–192
    relief for victims of, 22, 23
    religious freedom and persecution,
        1009
    religious liberty and military service,
        1098
    Schwalm, E. J. on conscientious objec-
        tors and, 2355
    Sedition Act, 1165
    social action, 1196
    sources on, 2322
    Swigart, William Joseph, 1245
    Syrians, relief and rehabilitation work,
        199
    Taylor, Isaac W., 1249
    Weimer family, 1327
    world hunger issues (CB) and, 2266
World War II, 23, 403, 1371–1373,
        1371–1373, *See also* Americans of
        Japanese Ancestry
    Allison Prairie Church of the Brethren,
        IL, moved to make room for air
        plane training field during, 2126
    alternative service program, 316
    American Legion, activities of, 24
    amnesty for conscientious objectors, 26
    Bremen, relief and rehabilitation work,
        173
    Brethren Church, 1372
    Brethren in Christ, 189

Brethren Service stamps, 201
BSC, 2110
building boom, 51
chaplaincy, 271
Church of the Brethren, 1372
    relief and service projects with the
    Waldensian Church, 1314
Conference of Historic Peace
    Churches, 333
conscientious objectors, 312, 317, 336,
    916–917, 1371–1372, 2068, 2089,
    2108, 2111
conservation movement, 338
CPS, 9, 19, 23, 315
CROP, 286
detention camps, 2093
displaced persons, 390
Dunkard Brethren, 1372
ecumenism, 422
Elderton, PA, Plum Creek Church of
    the Brethren, 433
elementary education, 434
Elgin, IL, 436
Elizabethtown College, 438
Emergency Farm Labor, 443
ethics, 458
Evangelical Church in Germany, 459
fact-finding tour of Europe, 1273
Fernald, IA, Church of the Brethren,
    488
Filbrun, Stanley Clarence, 2184
fire fighting, 491
fraternal relations, 510
Garver, Earl Simeon, 2187
Germany, 545, 546
Gilbert, Martha Rupel, 2190
Grace Brethren, 1372
Graybill, Alice Minora Hoffer and
    Jacob Franklin, 567
Greece, 569
Hamel, Joseph Donat, 2195
Harley family, 583
Harsh, Alva Carlton, 587
Harsh, Mary Lou Hykes, 587
Heifer Project International, 594
Hershey, Lewis Blaine, 599
Hesse, 602
High Commissioner for the Occupation
    of Germany (HICOG), 603
Homeless European Land Program
    (HELP), 625
Homestead Old German Baptist
    Brethren Church, FL, 626
hospitals, 631
Hutterian Society of Brothers, 640
incarceration of Brethren, 1060
India, 651
Indiana, 653
Indiana conscientious objectors, 1966
Ingraham, M. Virgil, 2208
Interchurch Service to Greek Villages,
    658
International Voluntary Services
    Agency (IVS), 660
Italy, 665
Japan, 669
Japanese-Americans, 302, 2093
Jenkins, Charles Lee, 2209
Jewell, Jesse Paul, 2209
Kaltenstein Castle used as detention
    center during, 681
Karlsschule, 684
Kosch, Lewis F., 707

Manzanar Relocation Center, 789
Mathis, Jefferson H., 803
medical projects, 808–809
mental hospital service, 816, *817*
Messenger, 818
military service, 388, 831
Minnesota Starvation Project, 848
minorities, ethnic and racial, 850
missionary ship sinking, 863
Myers, Minor Morton, 904
Nebraska contributions to post-war
    efforts, 921
Neumann, Friedrich and, 924
Old German Baptist Brethren, 1000,
    1372
pacifism, doctrine of
    Church of the Brethren, 2094
peace movement
    Church of the Brethren, 2074
peace witnesses, 2108
poetry, 1039–1040
post-war aid to Netherlands, 923
prisoners of war, Brethren service to,
    1058
prisoners of war programs, 2110
Puerto Rico, 1070
refugee resettlement, 1093, 2240–2241
refugees, *See* refugees, World War II
relief and service efforts, 1097
relief and service work
    United Nations Relief and Reha-
    bilitation Administration
    (UNRRA), 1291
relief and service work in Germany fol-
    lowing, *See* relief and service work
relief effort, 1927
relief training units, 1097
religious liberty and military service,
    1098
relocation centers
    Church of the Brethren, 2079
Robinson, Mitchell on conscienious
    objectors in, 2352
Schrock, Mark Y., 1156
Schwalm, E. J. on conscientious objec-
    tors and, 2355
Selective Training and Service Act of
    1940, 19
SERRV International (CB) and, 2247
Sisters and Brother, Inc. and conscien-
    tious objectors during, 2356–2357
Sittser, Gerald L. on historic peace
    churches and, 2357
Skiles, Jacob W., 1189
social action, 1196
soil conservation units, 1200
Spain, relief and rehabilitation work,
    146
starvation project, 1984
Van Dyck, Harry R. on conscientious
    objectors and, 2361
Washington Office (CB) and, 2260
Wilhelm, Paul A. on conscientious
    objectors and, 2363
world hunger issues (CB) and, 2266
Ziegler, Levi King, 1397
worldliness, **1373**
    The Bible Monitor, teachings about,
    137
worldly amusements, *See* amusements,
    worldly
Worldwide Church of God, 209
Worle family, 148

Worley-Fahnestock-Kerlin families
    family history, 1983–1984
Worley, Henry, 1817
Worley, Ken, 2298
Worline, James R., 2298
Wormsley family, 752
Worner, William F., 2104
Worrell, Anne Lowry, 2104
Worrell, Margaret F., **1373**
Wors, Iscia, 256
Worsell, Lillian
    Reading Grace Brethren Church, PA,
    1084
Worship and Praise for the Church and
    Sunday School, 2104
worship conferences, 209
worship points, *See* preaching points
worship, public, *632,* **1373-1379,** *1374,*
    2016, 2023, *See also* music
    among Society of Friends (Quakers),
    48
    annual meeting rulings, 1376
    architecture (church), influence on, 301
    Brethren and, **2266–2267**
    Brethren music, 898
    caps and, 254
    ceremonies of community, 1379
    Christian Education Commission (CB),
    285
    Christmas, celebration of, 288
    Columbia, MD, Oakland Mills Uniting
    Church (CB, UCC) and, 326
    communion table, 328
    community, 329
    cooking, traditional, 341
    criticism of other denominations, 1375
    deacons role, 369
    degrees of ministry, 374
    descriptions of, 1375–1376
    Disciples of Christ, 385
    drama in, 399
    EYN, *306*
    family, 474
    freedom of expression in
    Christ's Ambassadors, 280
    frontier family, 283
    funerals, 523
    Germantown Trust, 2188
    God's Means of Grace (Yoder), 555
    Good Friday, 556
    gospel music, 559
    in homes, 48
    house churches, 632
    Hymnal: A Worship Book, 2205–2206
    hymnals, 641
    illustrations by Pyle, Howard, *1374*
    Influenza Pandemic, 655
    leadership, 1376, 1377
    liturgical, Roman Catholic Church,
    1120
    Lord's prayer, 757
    manuals (CB), 300
    manuals for, 788
    ministry, 845
    Morse, Kenneth Ivan, 878
    music, 2227–2228
    Music Committee (CB), 899
    music in, 22
    musical instruments, 2228
    nonliturgical nature of, 1373, 1375
    offerings during services, 960
    Old Order Movement, 970, 972
    order of worship, 1375, 1377–1378

Pietism, 1022
prayer books, 1052
prayer meetings, 1053
Rechte und Ordungen, 1086
Reformation, Protestant, and Brethren
   doctrine, 1092
rituals, 1378–1379
robes, 1115
Sermon on the Mount, 1169
settings, 1377
sources on, 2319, 2322
styles of, 2266
symbolism, 1377
use of art in, 59, 60, 61
wellness and, 2261
worship resources
   Parish Ministries Commission involve-
      ment in, 993
worship services
   anthology of worship materials, 1954
   Blooming Grove congregation and, 148
   children in, 2158–2160
   Christian Education Commission, 155
   development, 1997
   doctrine of, 2093
   Dunkard Brethren Church, 2106
   Ephrata Community, 448
   family worship
      publication on, 2076, 2109
   hymns, 2098
   manual for, 2109
   manuals of, for ministers, 2066
   publications, and family, 2076
   resources for, 1935
   responsive readings, 2104
   rural issues, 2109
   singing, 1184–1185
Worst, Clara (later Miller), 1361
   Miller, John Allen, wife of, 839
   teacher, author, **834**
Worst, David R., 1817
Worst family
   Homerville, OH, Grace Brethren
      Church, 626
Worst, George (–1945/46?), 1817
Worst, George (1826–1898), 1817
Worst, George, 1379
Worst, Henry (1775–1858), 1817
Worst, Henry (1808–1881), 1817
Worst, John H., 186, 505, **1379–1380,**
   1817, 1952, 2104
   patent medicine remedy business, 995
   Reconstruction Committee, 1086
Worst, Margaret Martin, 1379
Worst, N. S., 566
Worster, Linna, 363–364
Worster, Morris, 1817
   Rowdy, KY, Brethren Church, pastor,
      1126
Worster, Sarah (later Bixler), 531
Worthington Church of the Brethren, MN,
   1380
   Minnesota Brethren settlement, 848
Worthington, Maria L., 167
Worthington, OH, Columbus Grace
      Brethren Church, 145, 375, **1380**
   Cincinnati Grace Brethren Church,
      Sharonville, OH, 1172, 1174
   Grant, Richard E., 2193
   London, OH, Grace Brethren Church,
      2215
   Pataskala, OH, Grace Brethren Church
      of Licking Co., organized from,

995
Powell, OH, Grace Brethren Church
   and, 2238
Wortinger, Albert, 1817
Wotschke, Theodor, 2104
Wounded Knee, SD
   Native Americans, 2230
"Woven Together in Love"
   People of the Covenant (POC) (BC)
      and, 2237
Wratchford, Eugene Philip, 1817
Wratchford, Mike, 1817
Wray, Benjamin (1824–1891), 1817
Wray, Benjamin (1852–1931), 544, 1817
Wray, Benjamin (Mount Etna, IA), 1817
Wray, Cecil, 313
Wray, Charles Herman, 1817
Wray, Chesley Daniel, 313, 544, 1817
   Mount Pleasant Old German Baptist
      Brethren, IN, elder, 887
   South Haven Old German Baptist
      Brethren Church, MI, minister,
      1205
Wray, Dennis L., 1817, 2156
   Sierra Pines Old German Baptist
      Brethren Church, CA, minister,
      1181
Wray, Eugene
   North Hampton, OH, Donnels Creek
      Old German Baptist Brethren
      Church, minister, 948
Wray, Everett Wayne, 2298
Wray family
   Pipe Creek Old German Baptist
      Brethren Church, IN, 1026
   Salem Church of the Brethren, IA,
      1137
Wray, Harry W., 2298
Wray, J. Eugene, 1817
Wray, J. P., 1817
Wray, Jesse A., 431, 1817, 2307, **2387**
Wray, Joel P., 1817
   Maple Grove Old German Baptist
      Brethren Church, OH, elder-in-
      charge, 791
Wray, John, 1817
Wray, John D., 313, 1817
Wray, John H., 1817, 2298
Wray, Lydia, 313
Wray, Marshall L., 2298
Wray, Mary Root, 313
Wray, Michael A., 1817, 2298
   Olive Grove Old German Baptist
      Brethren Church, CA, minister,
      973
Wray, Samuel Lee, 1335, 1817
   Sierra Pines Old German Baptist
      Brethren Church, CA, elder-in-
      charge, 1181
Wray, Wilmer C., 313, 430, 1242, 1333,
   1817
   North Manchester Old German Baptist
      Brethren Church, IN, minister, 949
Wrede, Günther, 2104
Wright, Abel, 1817
Wright, Albert L., 1817
   North Manchester, IN, Church of the
      Brethren, elder and pastor, 949
Wright, Andrew James Omar, 2298
Wright, Arnie, 1817
Wright, B. H., 1817
Wright, Boyd, 2175
Wright, Charles Aldus, 1817

Wright, Charles C., 208
Wright, Cindy (later Pierce)
   Island Pond, VT, Grace Brethren
      Church, 2209
Wright Co., MN
   Minnesota Brethren settlement, 848
Wright, D. B. (H.), 411, 1817
Wright, David, 263
Wright, E. Edward
   on Lancaster County, 2364
Wright, Edward Needles, 2104
Wright family, 165, 1950, *See Out of the
   Melting Pot*
   Roanoke, VA, Washington Heights
      Grace Brethren Church, 1114
Wright, Floyd, 1817
Wright, George Washington, 467, 1817
Wright, Hazel (later Keller)
   Keller, Paul W., 2210
Wright, I. B., 1817
Wright, J. E., 1817
Wright, J. K., 1817
Wright, J. T., 1817
Wright, John, 177, **1380,** 2104
   Hostetler Brethren, 632
   Restoration Movement, 1101
   Rossville, IN, Church of the Brethren,
      minister, 1124
Wright, John Charles, 1817
Wright, John H., 638, 1333, 1817
   North Manchester, IN, Church of the
      Brethren, elder (moderator), 949
   Pleasant View Church of the Brethren,
      IN, elder, 1036
   South Whitley, IN, Church of the
      Brethren, minister, 1207
Wright, John, Sr., 2104
Wright, John William, 1817
Wright, Lee-Lani, 2298
   on church unity and CB, 2364
   on hymns, poets and composers, 2332
Wright, Lewis Van Buren, 504, 552,
   1817–1818
   Marble Furnace, OH, Church of the
      Brethren, elder and minister, 791
Wright, Lila Elizabeth, 1841
Wright, Lucinda (later Hess), 2047
Wright, Mary (later Hon), 626
Wright, Maurice Elton, 1818
Wright, Milton B., 1818
Wright, N. D., 1818
   Racket, WV, Mount Olive Brethren
      Church, pastor, 1079
Wright, Nancy, 263
Wright, Paul J., 376, 1383, 1818
Wright, Peter
   Hostetler Brethren, 632
   Restoration Movement, 1101
Wright, Ronald Harold, 1818
Wright, William, 1818
Wrights' schoolhouse
   Leetown, WV, Church of the Brethren,
      735
Wrightsman, Anthony W., 264, 1818
Wrightsman, Catherine Bolton, 1380
Wrightsman, Daniel, 1380
Wrightsman, Dean, 2298
Wrightsman, Elizabeth Witter, 1380
Wrightsman, Everett, 1385, 1818
Wrightsman, F. B., 1818
Wrightsman family, 701
   Pleasant Hill Old German Baptist
      Brethren Church, IL, 1033

Pleasant Valley Church of the Brethren, TN, 1035

Redstone Valley Old German Baptist Brethren Church, WI, and, 2239

Wrightsman, John, 1818
St. Joseph Valley Church of the Brethren, IN, minister, 1135

Wrightsman, John B., 500
Mountain Normal School, 889

Wrightsman, Peter R., 170, 192, 315, 682, 918, 1213, **1380**, 1818
medical practice, 810

Wrightsman, Raymond E., 430, 1818

Wrightsman (Reichsmann) family, 2045

Wrightsman, Willard, 1385, 1818

Wrightsville, PA, Susquehanna Grace Brethren Church, **1380**

Wrigle family
at New Rockford, ND, Church of the Brethren, 932

wristwatches, *See* jewelry
Dunkard Brethren, 940
Dunkard Brethren Church, 2174
Old German Baptist Brethren, 941

Wroth, Lawrence C., 2104

Wu Feng (Bittinger), 748

Wunderlich, A. Mervyn, Jr., 1818

Wupper River, 174
historic sites, 609

Wurojam, Nigeria, 306

Wurstner, Betty Louise Miller, 2104, 2364

Würtemberg, 697, 1328
dissenters, 147
Germany, 545
Halle circle of theologians and pastors, 1209
Hofacker, Ludwig, 148
Pennsylvania Germans from, 1006

Wurz, Rudolf, 2104

Wurzburger, Kenneth D., 2298

Wust, Klaus G., 1862, 2104–2105
on Dunkers, 2364
on emigration of 1738, 2364
on shipboard diets, 2364

Wuthnow, Robert
on spirituality, 2364

Wyand, E. Clayton, 2105

Wyand family, 2105

Wyand, Florence L., 2105

Wyand, Jeffrey A., 2105

Wyandot Co., OH, 424
Oak Grove Church of the Brethren, OH, 956
Rome Old German Baptist Brethren Church, OH, 1121

Wyandot, OH, Church of the Brethren, *See* Eden Church of the Brethren, OH

Wyandotte Co., KS
Olathe, KS, Church of the Brethren, 964

Wyandotte, OH, congregation, 340

Wyandt, Christian, 2105

Wyandt family, 2105

Wyant, Frank, 1818

Wyatt, Archie, 1818
Pleasant Valley Church of the Brethren, NC, providing leadership, 1035

Wyatt, Boyd
Modesto, CA, Pleasant Home Dunkard Brethren Congregation, 867

Wyatt family, 280

Wyatt, J. Arthur, 683

Wyatt, Joseph Arthur, 1818, 2105

Wyatt, Lela
Modesto, CA, Pleasant Home Dunkard Brethren Congregation, 867

Wyatt, Rufus, 676, 1818
Prairie Lake Church of the Brethren, OK, elder, 1050
Santa Fe, KS, Church of the Brethren, minister, 1144

Wyatt, Wilson, 1818

Wycliffe Bible Commentary, 2262

Wycliffe Bible Translators
The Missionary Board (BC), 856

Wycliffe, John
Reformation, Protestant, 1091

Wyeth, N. C., 379

Wygal family, 1914

Wygant family, 2097

Wyland, Washington, 583, 1818

Wyman, Victor R., 2298

Wyman, Worth Forger, 1818

Wymer family
South Keokuk Church of the Brethren, IA, 1205

Wyne family, *See* Wine family

Wyne, Jacob, 1818

Wyne, John, 1818
Santa Ana, CA, Church of the Brethren, ministerial leadership, 1144

Wyne, John M., 1818

Wynne, AR
New Hope Church of the Brethren, 929
Wyoming, **1380–1381**
Old German Baptist Brethren congregations, 967

Wyrick, Ronald Eugene, 692, 1818

Wyse family, 1902

Wysong, Daniel, 1818

Wysong, Henry, 1818

Wysong, Rodney E., 366, 1818

Wysor family, 1914

Xavier University, New Orleans, LA, 405

Xenia, OH, Beavercreek Church of the Brethren, **1383**

Xenia Theological Seminary, 688
McClain, Alva J., 772, 773
Ronk, Willis E., 1121
Taber, Floyd W., 1247
Taber, Miles, 1247

Yabuki, Ken, 1818

Yadkin (Crane Creek), NC, congregation, 690

Yadkin German Baptist Brethren Church, NC, **1383**

Yadkin Valley, NC, 161

Yaeager, Arthur M., 2105

Yagel, Cameron G., 1818

Yagel, Herman Linwood, 1818

Yager, Charles
North Kokomo Grace Brethren Church, IN, 948

Yager, Marie Anna, 383

Yager, Sandy
North Kokomo Grace Brethren Church, IN, 948

Yahuecas, PR, Iglesia de los Hermanos Cristo Nuestra Paz (CB), **2267**

Yakima, WA, 1319
Church of the Brethren, **1383**
Grace Brethren Church, **1383**
migration to from Illinois and Iowa,

1240

Northern Pacific Railroad and Brethren colonists, 951

Yale Divinity School
Shamberger, Chauncey, 1171
Wampler, Ernest Michael, 1316
West, Murray Guy, 1332
Will, Harper S., 1345

Yaloke, Central African Republic
Tyson, Elizabeth Stauffer, 1284
mission schools, 807, 854
rebellion
Gribble, Florence Alma Newberry, 573

Yaloke station (Africa), 1309, 1310
Emmert, Mary Le(n)ora, 444

Yamasa, DR
Los Guaricanos, DR, Fuente de Vida, 2215

Yancey Co., NC, 1384
Brethren congregations, 946
German Baptist Brethren Church, NC, **1384**
Johnson City, TN, Knob Creek Church of the Brethren, 673

Yaney, Israel Franklin, 152, 1818

Yankey, F. A., 1818

Yant, Abraham, 424, 1818

Yants-Crills family, 1928

Yaoder, Anna Bontrager, 2106

Yaple, Erma (later Row), 1125

Yarbaha, J. A., 1818

Yarger, Judith Maxine
on Jurger/Yarger, George and descendants, 2349

Yarlick, Iva C., 2105

Yasak family, 1312

Yates, Harley A., 1818

Yaughar family
Peabody Old German Baptist Brethren Church, KS, 997

Yaussy Albright, Kim A., 2298

Yeager, Charles S., 2105

Yeager family, 700, 2077, 2105

Yeager, Harold E., 2298

Yeager, J. M., 2105

Yeager, Martha, 2102

Yeager, ___, Reverend, 145

Yeakley church building
Martinsburg, WV, Moler Avenue Church of the Brethren, 2376

Yearbook, Brethren Press, 2149

yearbooks, 18, **1384**
analysis, 1985
Church of the Brethren, 1218, 1219, 1985
Church of the Brethren, study of, 1957
Elsie Church of the Brethren, MI, 443
Fairview Church of the Brethren, IN, 468
Fairview Church of the Brethren, PA, 469
Glade Park, CO, Community Church of the Brethren, 551
Glen Rock (Glenrock), NE, Church of the Brethren, 551
Goshen Church of the Brethren, WV, 558
Grand Junction, CO, Church of the Brethren, 565
Gravel Hill Church of the Brethren, KS, 567
Green River Cove Church of the

Brethren, NC, 570
Homestead Church of the Brethren, MI, 626
Neosho Church of the Brethren, KS, in, 923
Yearly Meetings, *See* Annual Meeting
yearly visits, *See* deacons' visits
Yearout, Charles Madison, 42, 72, 461, 682, 1212, **1384**, 1818
Yearout, Floyd Alvin, 1818
Yearout, James A., 1384
Yearout, June, 1240, 1818
Yearout, Lydia Bauman, 1384
Yearout, William, 1818, **2387**
Yeater, D. L., 275
Yeater, Dorothy, 275
Yeater, Norman David, 2298
Yeatter, David Breneman, 1818
Yeazell, Carol L., 2298
Hispanic Ministries (CB), 2199
Yelinek, Prudence B., 179, 2298
Yellow Creek, IL
Church of the Brethren, IL, 63, **1384**
Eby, Enoch, 419
Freeport, IL, Church of the Brethren, 515
congregation, 737
Frey (Fry) family, 517
Fry, Daniel, 520
Yellow Creek, IN, 153
Church of the Brethren, **1384**
Elkhart Valley Church of the Brethren, IN, 440
Goshen, IN, West Goshen Church of the Brethren, 558
Old German Baptist Brethren Church, IN, **1385**
Yellow Creek, PA
Brethren Church, PA, *See* Hopewell Grace Brethren Church, PA
Church of the Brethren, PA, 461, 1294, 1323, 1364, **1384**
Holsinger Church of the Brethren, PA, 623
Raven Run Church of the Brethren, PA, 1083
Snake Spring Valley Church of the Brethren, PA, churchouse, 1192
Snowberger family, 1153
congregation, 216, 384, 407, 410, 927
Yellow Poplar Church of the Brethren, NC, *See* Hollow Poplar Church of the Brethren, NC; Petersons Chapel Church of the Brethren, NC
Yellow River, IN
Church of the Brethren, *See* Mount Pleasant Church of the Brethren, IN
Mount Pleasant, IN, congregation, 243, 1315
Old German Baptist Brethren Church, IN, **1385**
Yelton, Andrew L., 555, 1209, 1294, 1818
Yelton family
Golden Church of the Brethren, NC, 555
Yenser, Herald E., 2298
Yeomans, C. J., 1818
Yeremian (Yereman), O. H., **1385**, 1818, 1846
early convert at Smyrna, 1280
medical missions, 807

Yerian, Dorothy Eileen, 1850
Yerian, Jerry A., 1818
Yerkey, Berma, 2298
Yerkovich, Milan, 1818
Mission Viejo, CA, Saddleback Valley Grace Brethren Church, pastor, 855
Yeso, NM, 1240
Yett, Laura, 1854
Yett, Percy L., 1819, 1854
Yetter, Hazel Strauser
Parkview Church of the Brethren, PA, leadership by, 994
Yevtushenko, Yevgeny
Dolnikowski, George and, 2241
Yi, Tae Ho, 2298
Yiengst, Jeremiah
Murdock Church of the Brethren, KS, 896
Yimirshika, Nigeria, 306
Yin, Han Chang, **1385**, 1819
Yingling, David Addison, 1334, 1819
Shelby Co. Church of the Brethren, MO, leadership in, 1175
Yingling, Harvey Carroll, 1819
Yingst, Kenneth, 743
Yingst, Kenneth Harry, 1819
Montgomery, IL, Boulder Hill Neighborhood Church of the Brethren, pastor, 872
YMCA, *See* Young Men's Christian Association
Yocky, Loraine Sickel, 1181
Yocum, George C., 2298
Yoder, Aaron T., 1882
Yoder, Agnes Pauline, 2105
Yoder, Almeda Hinkle, 1387
Yoder, Andrew, 279
Yoder, Anna, 1871
Yoder, Anna J. (later Schrock), 2059
Yoder, Anna (later Miller), 2017
Yoder, Anna (later Petersheim), *See* Petersheim family
Yoder, Annie Forney, 1386
Yoder, Barbara Eash, 2016
Yoder, Barbara (later Engle), 1930
Yoder, Barbara (later Miller)
Miller, Samuel J., mother of, 842
Miller, Sebastian Christian, mother of, 842
Yoder, Barbara Miller, 2016
Yoder, Carl, 173
Yoder, Carl B., 1819
Yoder, Carl E., 733, 1819, 2105
Yoder, Caroline Yutzy, 2106
Yoder, Catherine Schrock, 2107
Yoder, Charles Francis, 52, 53,114, 132, 180, 183, 184, 186, 195, 250, 256, 381, 501, 555, 558, 691, 1210, 1297, 1319, 1349, **1385–1386,** 1819, 1854, 2105
Hispanic Ministries (BC), 2198
historical writing, 613
Iran (Persia), 662
prayer, posture in, 1052
prayer, writings on, 1051
Quebec, 1075
South Bend, IN, Ardmore Brethren Church, pastor, 1203
mission schools, 854
The Missionary Board (BC), 855
missions, 861, 862
Morrill, KS, (First) Brethren Church,

876
Testigo Fiel magazine, 1255
Yoder, Charles M., 1819, 2105
Yoder, Christian, 1387, 2107
Yoder, Christian C., 2105
Yoder, Christian H. and Barbara, 1963
Yoder, Christian Zook, 1387, 2105
Yoder, Clara J., 1949
Yoder, Clarence H., 1819
Yoder, Conrad, 2106
Yoder, D. Willard, 1819, 2307, **2267, 2387**
Yoder, Daniel, 373
descendants, 1949
family history, 1953
Yoder, D. Willard (OGBB) and, 2267
Yoder, Daniel D., 1819
Yoder, Daniel J., 1819, 2307, **2387**
Yoder, Daniel J. and Elizabeth Eash, 2008
Yoder, David C., 2107
Yoder, David S., 2107, *See also* Yoder family
Yoder, David T., 2105
Yoder, David V., 1819, 1943
Yoder, David Y., 1887
Yoder, Dean Lester, 1819
Yoder, Don, 1211, 2043, 2105–2106, 2106
on fractur art, 2364
Yoder, Dorothy Bowman
Yoder, D. Willard (OGBB) and, 2267
Yoder, Edison
Pompano Beach, FL, Grace Brethren Church, 1046
Yoder, Edna Annie, 2105
Yoder, Edna Mae, 2016
Yoder, Edna Yoder, 2106
Yoder, Edward, 2106
Yoder, Effie J. Onas Tice, 2106
Yoder, Eleanor, 1852
Yoder, Eli Lorenzo, 67, *182,* 186, 581, 1385, **1386**, 1387, 1819
Reconstruction Committee, 1086
Yoder, Eli V., 2016
Yoder, Elias A., 2106
Yoder, Elias J., 2078, 2079
Yoder, Eliza Stutzman, 2031, 2107; *See also* Yoder family
Yoder, Elizabeth Ann (later Shrock), 2016
Yoder, Elizabeth (later Beachy), 1923
Yoder, Elizabeth Stutzman, 2107
Yoder, Elizabeth T., 2106
Yoder, Mrs. Elmer E., 2106
Yoder, Elmina Yoder, 2106
Yoder, Elva Basinger Lehman, 2106
Yoder, Emanuel, 279
Yoder, Emma Vaniman, 2106
Yoder, Ephraim P., 1819
Yoder, Estelle Harshberger, 2107
Yoder, Esther C., 2079
Yoder, Esther J., 2072
Yoder family, 262, 1240, 1881, 1927, 2031, 2072, 2078, 2079, 2087, 2097, 2105, 2106, 2107
family history, 2008
Homerville, OH, Grace Brethren Church, 626
Monitor Church of the Brethren, KS, 869
Neher family, related to, 922
Yoder, Fannie Bender, 2107
Yoder, Frances (later Musselman), 901
Yoder, Franklin Bruce, 1819
Yoder, Mrs. Fred H., 2106
Yoder, Fred Roy, 2106

Yoder, G. M., 2106
Yoder, Gary Dean, 2298
Yoder, George E., 673, 1819
    New Carlisle, OH, Church of the
        Brethren, elder in, 926
    New Enterprise, PA, Church of the
        Brethren, as minister, 927
Yoder, Gertrude (later Hooley), *See* Hooley
        family
Yoder, Glee Goughnour, 555, 2106
Yoder, Gordon, 555
Yoder, Harold E., 2106
Yoder, Harriet (later Gilbert), 548
    Mothers and Daughters' Association,
        879
Yoder, Harry Benjamin, 235, 1819
Yoder, Henry J., 2106
Yoder Hill Church of the Brethren, PA, *See*
        Johnstown, PA, Westmont Church
        of the Brethren
Yoder, Ida, 2106, 2107
Yoder, Isabelle King, 2106
Yoder, Jacob, 1387, 2106
Yoder, Jacob (Bethel, NE), 1819
Yoder, Jacob C., 2106
Yoder, Jacob D., 281, 1386, 1387, 1819
    Monitor Church of the Brethren, KS,
        869
Yoder, Jacob J., 1974
Yoder, Jacob (Logan, IA), 1819
Yoder, Jacob (Mohrsville, PA), 1819
Yoder, Jane, 214
Yoder, Jeremiah, 2107
Yoder, Jerry, 1967
Yoder, Jim, *1387*
Yoder (Joder) family, 26, **1387**, *1387*
Yoder, Joe D., 2041
Yoder, John, 638, 664, 1387, 1819
Yoder, John D., 2097, 2105
Yoder, John Howard, 2106
    theology and, 2255
Yoder, John Isaac, 2106
Yoder, John, Jr., 1819
Yoder, John Otis, 2107
Yoder, John T., 2106
Yoder, Jonas, 2107
Yoder, Jonas D., 2031
Yoder, Joseph, 1949
Yoder, Joseph J., 160, *538, 585,* **1386,**
        1387, 1819
    McPherson, KS, First Church of the
        Brethren, pastor, 779
    Monitor Church of the Brethren, KS,
        elder, 869
Yoder, Joseph S., 1881
Yoder, Joseph Warren, **1386–1387,**
        2106–2107
    books by, 1387
Yoder, Kathryn, 2107
Yoder, Katie J. Shrock, 1943
Yoder, Keith B., 2107
Yoder, L. J., 1819
Yoder, Lena R., 2107
Yoder, Leo Menno, 2107
Yoder, Leon Ray, 2298
Yoder, Levi M., 2106
Yoder, Levi S., 1819
Yoder, Lizzie Garber, 2267
Yoder, Lois Ruth, 1842
Yoder, Lola Isabella King, 2107
Yoder, Magdalena Gingerich, 2105
Yoder, Malinda J. (later Gingerich), 1949
Yoder, Manasses, 1917

Yoder, Marcia A., 1837
Yoder, Margaret Kagarice, 1876
Yoder, Martha Anne, 1834
Yoder, Martin Matthias, 2107
Yoder, Mary Borkholder, 1881
Yoder, Mary Edna Yoder, 2107
Yoder, Mary Elizabeth, 2107
Yoder, Mary M., 2107
Yoder, Mattie (later Fry), 1943
Yoder, Mattie Sarah Kauffman, 2107
Yoder, Michael, 2009, 2105, 2107
Yoder, Michael L., 2107
Yoder, Mima Lu Ella Miller, 2107
Yoder, Moses, 2016
Yoder, Moses H., 2107
Yoder, Mrs. Roman E., 2041
Yoder, Nancy Secrist, 1385, 1386
Yoder, Nathaniel, 1819
Yoder, Noah D., 1874
Yoder, Paton, 2107
Yoder, Paul, 171, 1819
Yoder, Mrs. Paul, 171
Yoder, Paul Eli, 2107
Yoder, Paul R., 1819
Yoder, Pauline Alice Felts, 1917
Yoder, Pearl Lutz, 52, 183, 501, 1385,
        1386, 1854
Yoder, Peter, 2105
Yoder, Peter and Nancy, 2007
Yoder, Polly (later Early), 414
Yoder, Randall Lee, 1819
Yoder, Richard B., 2107
Yoder, Rosa L., 2107
    on OGBB obituaries, 2364
Yoder, Rosanna McGonegal, 1387
Yoder, Roy A., 2107
Yoder, Rufus Alexander, 1819
Yoder, Rufus R., 1280, 1819, 2307, **2387**
    Shady Grove Old German Baptist
        Brethren Church, OH, elder, 1171
Yoder, Russell
    on Beissel, Conrad and confidential
        writings, 2364
Yoder, Ruth (later Graybill), 1953
Yoder, Sadie Strohm, 1386
Yoder, Samuel, 2009
Yoder, Samuel E., 596, 1819
Yoder, Sarah, 1386, 1387, 1881
Yoder, Sarah F., 171
Yoder, Silvanus, 2107
Yoder, Simeon H., 2107
Yoder, Simon S., 2014
Yoder, Stephen E., 759, 1819
Yoder, Susan Ream, 1953
Yoder, Susanna Hochstedler, 1949
Yoder, Sylvan Moses, 2107
Yoder, Valentine and Elizabeth Coblentz
        family history and genealogy, 1967
Yoder, Valentine T., 2107
Yoder, Verda
    Pompano Beach, FL, Grace Brethren
        Church, 1046
Yoder, Willard, 1356, 1819
    Painter Creek Old German Baptist
        Brethren Church, OH, 990
Yoder, William Henry, 1323, 1387, 1819,
        2107
    Monitor Church of the Brethren, KS,
        pastor, 869
Yoder, William Jay, 2036
Yoder, Yost D., 1819, 2072
Yoder (Yothers/Yotter) families, 1887
Yohe family, 2091

Yohe, Milton William, 1819
Yohe, Robert G., 2298
Yohn, Clarence H., 1819
Yohn family
    Harrisburg, PA, Melrose Gardens
        Grace Brethren Church, 586
yoked congregations
    Cherry Lane and Snake Spring Valley
        Church of the Brethren, PA, 1192
    Four Mile, IN, congregation and
        Richmond, IN, Church of the
        Brethren, 1108
    Hiwassee, VA, congregation and
        Pulaski, VA, Church of the
        Brethren, 1071
    Octavia, NE, Church of the Brethren,
        960
    Outlook, WA, Church of the Brethren,
        986
    Pine Grove and Oak Grove Churches
        of the Brethren, MD, 956, 1024
    Pitsburg, OH, Church of the Brethren
        and Painter Creek, OH, congrega-
        tion, 1026
    Pleasant Valley Church of the Brethren,
        OH, and Poplar Grove, OH, con-
        gregation, 1035
    Plum Creek congregation and Oakdale
        Church of the Brethren, PA, 957
    Prairie City Church of the Brethren,
        IA, and Morgan Valley Christian
        (Disciples of Christ) Church, 1050
    Rock Creek Church of the Brethren,
        KS, 1117
    Rock House Church of the Brethren,
        KY, 1117
    Rockhill Furnace, PA, Rockhill Church
        of the Brethren, 1117
    Salem Church of the Brethren, IA, and
        Mount Etna congregation, 1137
    Sharpsburg, MD, congregation and
        Pleasant View Church of the
        Brethren, MD, 1037
    Slifer, IA, church of the Brethren, 1190
Yon, Hannah (later Garner), 531
Yontz, Andrew J., 1819
Yordy, Amos, 1819
    Schechter, D[avid] O. on, 2354
Yordy, Jessie
    Schechter, D[avid] O. on, 2354
Yordy, Joel, 1819
Yordy, Salome
    Phoenix, AZ, First Church of the
        Brethren, Sunday school worker,
        1019
York Center Church of the Brethren, IL,
        2365
York Center Community Cooperative,
        Lombard, IL, **1389,** 2341
York Center, IL, Church of the Brethren,
        1388–1389
York Center, IL, congregation, 275
York Co., ND,
    Church of the Brethren, *See* Pleasant
        Valley Church of the Brethren, ND
York Co., PA, 136, 141, 145, 147, 151, 163,
        170, 309, 323, 361, 362, 370, 383,
        425, 685, 686, 732, 733, 736,
        1229, 1233, 1285, 1337, 1350,
        1391, 1401, 1899, 2072, 2077
    Bermudian Church of the Brethren
        Cemetery, 2084
    biographical history, 1948

Brethren congregations, 147
family history and genealogy,
1966–1967
German-Americans in, 2095
Holiness Brethren, 619
migration of Brethren, 827
New Fairview Church of the Brethren,
927
Old German Baptist Brethren Church,
1389
Pennsylvania Dunkard Brethren, 1005
Pennsylvania Old Order Brethren, 1005
Pennsylvania settlement, 1004
Peters family, 1012
Pfautz family, 1014
Pleasant Hill Church of the Brethren,
PA, 1032
Pleasant View Church of the Brethren,
PA, 1037
Three Mile Island emergency evacua-
tion, 952
York, PA
Belvidere Church of the Brethren,
1387–1388
First Church of the Brethren, **1388**
First congregation, 323
Grace Brethren Church, **1388**
Harrisburg, PA, Melrose Gardens
Grace Brethren Church, 586
Madison Avenue Church of the
Brethren, **1388**
Second Church of the Brethren, **1388**
Pfaltzgraff, John B. and, 2250
West Church of the Brethren, *See* West
York Church of the Brethren, PA
York Springs, PA, 1294
Yorkana Church of the Brethren, PA, *See*
New Fairview Church of the Brethren,
PA
Yost, Abram L., 2107
Yost, Barbara, 2079
Yost, C. M.
Mill Creek Old German Baptist
Brethren Church, VA, deacon, 833
Yost, Cora Gingerich, 1978
Yost family, 224, 1962, 2107
Oak Grove Church of the Brethren,
MO, 956
Yost, George, 1819–1820
Yost, Geraldine
Winchester, VA, Blue Ridge Grace
Brethren Church and, 2262
Yost, Henry A., 1820
Mud Valley Old German Baptist
Brethren Church, IL, deacon, pre-
siding elder, 892
Yost, Herbert
Winchester, VA, Blue Ridge Grace
Brethren Church and, 2262
Yost, J. Irwin, 2107
Yost, Jacob A., 1820
Oak Grove Church of the Brethren,
MO, leadership by, 956
Osceola Church of the Brethren, MO,
minister and elder, 984
Yost, Lydia Bauermeister, 2107
Yost, M. Dwayne, 102, 1820
Yost, Malinda, 2079
Yost, Nancy (later White), 1339
Yost, Samuel
Modesto, CA, Old German Baptist
Brethren Church, minister, 867
Yost, Samuel D., 1820

Yost, Samuel W., 431, 496, 1213, 1820
Old Brethren minister, 964, 965
Yostites, *See* Old Order fellowships
Old Brethren, 964
Yothers, Esther, 720
Lakeland, FL, Grace Brethren Church,
2213
Yothers, Jacob
Yothers, Richard J., Jr. on descendants
of, 2365
Yothers, Richard J., Jr.
on Yothers, Jacob and descendants,
2365
Yothers, Willard, 720
Lakeland, FL, Grace Brethren Church,
2213
Younce, Abraham, 1389, 1820
Younce, Davis, 1389, 1820
Younce family, **1389**
Younce, George, 1389
Younce, John, 1288, 1389, 1820
Younce, Joseph W., 1389
Younce, Margaret Byrket, 1389
Younce, Millie (later Flory), 209, 498, 2099
Younce, Philip, 224, 348, **1389**, 1820
Pitsburg, OH, Church of the Brethren,
1026
Potsdam, OH, Church of the Brethren,
elder, 1048
Younce, Samuel, 1389, 1820
Younce's Church of teh Brethren, OH, *See*
Brush Creek Church of the
Brethren, OH
Young, A. Carlton, 1333, 1820
Young, A. R., 2108
Young, Abraham, 211, 1820
Young, Abraham C., 1390, 1820
Young, Adam, 1390, 1820
young adult ministries
fellowship houses, 482
Parish Ministries Commission involve-
ment in, 993
Young, Amos D.
Roanoke, IN, Brethren Church, 1112
Young, Andrew J., 1367
on BSC and workcamps, 2365
on Manchester College, 2365
Young, Andrew W., 2107
Young, Brigham, 298
Young, Carl, 1820
Young, Catherine Sprankle, 1389
The Young Center, **2267**, *2268*
Young, Charles L., 2298
Roanoke, VA, Washington Heights
Grace Brethren Church, associate
pastor, 1114
Young Companion, 26
Young, Daniel, 1390, 1820
Young, David, 13, 148, 1390, 1820
Nimishillen Old German Baptist
Brethren Church, OH, minister in,
937–938
Young, David G., 2307
Young, David Geiman, 1820
Young, David Samuel., 557, 1820,
2107–2108
on Book of James, 2365
on leadership and church renewal,
2365
The Young Disciple, 1236, **1389–1390,**
1394, 2108
Burkholder, Wealthy Agnes Clark(e),
231

Children at Work, 276
Miller, Elizabeth Talley, writing for,
837
Our Boys and Girls, 985
Our Children at Work, 985
Our Sunday School, 985
Young, Dole Ardys, 1820
Young, Doro, 1820
Young, E. A., 1390
Young, Edith, 356
Young, Elizabeth Rhode, 1390
Young, Elwin, Jr., 1820
Modesto, CA, Old German Baptist
Brethren Church, minister, 867
Young, Emanuel Sprankle, 14, 137, 251,
252, 418, 505, 1285, **1389**, *1390,*
1820, 2108
Manchester College, acquisition of and
trustee, 785
Manchester College, President, 786
Mount Morris College, 884
publishing, 1069
Young, Emma (later Kreiner), 708
Young, Ethel, *248*
Young, F. E., 2108
Young family, 148, 1326, *1390,* **1390,** 2060,
2108
Royer family related to, 1128
Young, Frederick, 1390, 2108
Young, Galen D.
Young, Galen S. and, 2268
Young, Galen S., 404, **2268**
The Young Center and, 2267
Young, George, 1820
Young, George W., 1820
Young, Guy B.
Orlando, FL, Community Church of
the Brethren, 981
Young, Harry, 1390, 1820
Young, Harvey, 1390
Young, Henry J., 2108
Young, Henry Simon, 1390, *1390,* 1820,
2108
Young, Isaac, 1390, 1820
Young, Israel R., 1390, 1820, 2108
Young, J. C., 1820
Young, J. H., 1820
Young, J. R., 1820
Young, James O., 1820
Young, James F.
Roanoke, IN, Brethren Church, 1112
Young, James O., 349, 1221
Young, Janice E., 2108
Young, Jean Childs, 1367
Young, Jeffrey R.
Young, Galen S. and, 2268
Young, Jerry R., 439, 579, 654, 749, 1820,
2298
on GBC and leadership, 2365
Young, Jessie Magnin
The Young Center and, 2267
Young, Galen S. and, 2268
Young, John Ezra, 103, 1820
North Beatrice Church of the Brethren,
NE, 945
Young, John Theodore, 1820
Young Ladies Sunday school class, *648*
Young, Leonard D., 1820
Young, Lester A., 1333, 1390, 1820
Young, Levi, 1820, 2083
Young, Loreen, 654
Young, Lovina Ellen (later Meyers), 1707
Young, Margaret C., 2108

Young, Mary E., 2307
Young, Melissa C. (later Rosenberger), 1123
Young Men and Boys' Brotherhood, 182, 733, **1390**
Young, Menno, 1820
Young, Menno S., 1390
Young Men's Christian Association, 113, 199, **1390,** 1914, *See also* YMCA, BSC, 2110
   camps, 1989
   ecumenism, 422
   Eddy, [George] Sherwood, 424
   German YMCA
   Kaltenstein Castle first model youth village of, 681–682
   Ikenberry, Ernest Leroy, 646
   Kaltenstein Castle first model youth village of German YMCA, 681–682
   Mott, John Raleigh, 879
   Myers, Minor Morton, 904
   prisoner-of-war camps, England, 1290
   prisoners of war, Brethren service to, 587, 1058
   relief and service efforts, 1097
   United Kingdom, 1290
   World War II, article about, 1958
   YMCA buildings, as meeting places
      Lexington, KY, Grace Brethren Church, 739
      Louisville, OH, Brethren Bible Church, 760
      Lyndhurst, OH, Grace Brethren Church, 768
      Washington, PA, Grace Brethren Church, 1320
      Wichita, KS, Grace Brethren Church, 1343
   YMCA War Prisoners Aid, 587, 1058
Young, Minnie (later Surbey), 1241
Young People's Society of Christian Endeavor, 192, 695, 1391–1392
Young, Richard Allen, 1820
Young, Robert, 331
Young, Robert John, 1820
Young, Robert S., 1820, 2307
Young, Samuel, 1390
Young, Samuel L., 1390, 1820
Young, Sandra JoAnn (later Male), 2268
Young, Sarah M. Leatherman, 2298
Young, Simon, 1389
Young, Simon S., *1390*
   Manchester College, acquisition of and trustee, 785
Young, Theodore B., 1820
Young, Victor Clay, 740, 1820, 2298
Young, W. B., 1820
Young, W. E., 1820
Young, Walter, 1235
Young, Walter Milton, 725, 1235, 1820–1821, 2108, 2307
Young, Will, 1821
Young, William Charles, 1821
Young, William, home
   San Francisco, CA, Church of the Brethren, 1141
Young Women's Christian Association, (YWCA)
   building used as meetingplace,
      Lafayette, IN, Church of the Brethren, 717
      Lansing, MI, Grace Brethren

Church, 725
   Springfield, MO, Good Shepherd Church of the Brethren, 1215
ecumenism, 422
Zigler, Rachel E. Myers, 1397
Younger, Dan C., 320
   Sebring, FL, Grace Brethren Church, pastor, 1162
Younger family, 1341
Younger, S. S., 1821
Younger, Walter, 1821
Youngstown, New Middleton, OH, 931
Youngstown, OH, Woodworth Church of the Brethren, 532, 931, **1390–1391**
Younker, Carol Constance (later Boyer)
   works by, 2317
Younker, Frank, 1821
Younkin family
   Jenners, PA, Grace Brethren Church, 670
Younkins, Gale Harley, 2298
Younkins, Morse A., 1821
Younkins, Virginia, 342
Yount, Anna Magdalena (later Faw), 480, 481
Yount, Anna Magdalena (later Pfau), 1013
Yount, Barbara Brillhart, 1391
Yount, Benjamin, 1279, 1391, 1821
Yount, Catherine Dagen, 1391
Yount, Daniel (1785–1861), **1391,** 1821, **2380**
   Mill Creek Church of the Brethren, VA, elder, 832
Yount, Daniel (1832–1885), 1821
Yount, Elizabeth Bowman, 1391
Yount, Elizabeth (later Nead), 696, 918, *919*
Yount family, 686, 1299, 1338, **1391,** 2044, 2108, **2380**
   history of, 1941
   Schowalter family, related to, 1155
Yount, George, 696
Yount, Jacob, 1391
Yount, Joseph, 1391
Yount, Joseph B., III, 2108
   on Tunker House, VA, 2365
   Yount, Daniel, 2380
Yount, Margaret Bowman, 1391
Yount, Mary E. Kinsey, 696
Yount, Oliver F., 1265, 1821, 2108
Yount, Oren (Oran) S., 1277, 1821
Yount, Phyllis Darlene (later Thompson), 1845, 2255
Yount, Rudolph, 2108
Yount, Walter Bowman, 207, **1391,** 1821
Yount, William Calvin, 2108
Yount, William M., 2108
Younts family, 2049
Younts, Samuel, 1821
Yourtee, Eli, 41, 475, 1821
Yourtee family, 216
Yourtee, George, 475
Yourtee, Mary, 475
Youstra, George Thomas, 2298
youth, 2024, 2028, 2033–2034, 2036, 2040, 2047
   Anderson, IN, conference, 989, 2050
   books for, 1953
   Boys' Clubs, **180,** 203, 915, 1251, 2032
   Brethren and, **2268–2269**
   Brethren Church, 37, 285
   Brethren college students' beliefs, 1977
   camping movement, 249

   camping programs, 171, 192, 202
   CE National, Inc., 2156
   choices, 1992
   Christian Education Commission (CB), 285
   Christian Workers' Meetings (CB), 287–288
   Christian Education Commission, 155
   church history, 2015
   church membership, 813
   Church of the Brethren, 300, 2162
   Church of the Brethren societies for, 1994
   college students, *27*
   Committee on Saving our Children to the Church (CB), 328
   comparative study of Brethren and non-Brethren young people, thesis on, 1913
   Covina, CA, Church of the Brethren, *349*
   CSB, 287
   delinquents, programs for, 201
   devotional literature, 381
   Dunkard Brethren, 408, 2173–2174
   On Earth Peace Assembly, 2235
   and ecumenical movement, 2059
   exchange programs, 201
   Fairview Church of the Brethren, IA, 468
   General Board (CB), 535
   General Christian Workers' Board (CB), 536
   Glendale, CA, Church of the Brethren, 552
   Greece, 569
   Guthrie, OK, Church of the Brethren, 576
   halfway houses, 246
   Hamilton, Walter J., 581
   handbook for young Christians, 2089
   Handbook for Young Christians (Julien), 1980
   Harleysville, PA, Indian Creek Church of the Brethren, 584
   healing arts vocation, article about, 1911
   historical writing, 612
   Hollins, VA, Patterson Memorial Grace Brethren Church, 620
   hospital administration vocation, article about, 1928
   Hospital Committee (CB), 630
   Hostetler Church of the Brethren, PA, 632
   humility, 636
   Ikenberry, Olivia Dickens, 646
   India, 651
   Indiana, 652
   Indianapolis, IN, Eagle Creek Grace Brethren Church, 654
   The Inglenook, 656
   Inglenook Nature Study Club (CB), 656
   International Council of Religious Education, 659
   international programs, 23
   international work experience, 200
   Jones, George H., 676
   manuals for, 788
   moral issues, 203, 2100
   National Youth Conference, 917–918, 1978, 1982

in New Left movements, 930

nursing vocation, article about, 1932

at Old German Baptist Brethren Annual Meeting, 36

peace movement, 2107

The Pious Youth, 2037

publications for, 1069

Quinlan, James T., working with, 1076

Ramona Church of the Brethren, KS, activities for, 1083

recreation, 1087, 1088

Recreational Fellowship, 1088

rehabilitation villages, 200

Roanoke, VA, Central Church of the Brethren, programs for, 1112

scouting programs, *See* scouting programs

sources on, 2320

stories for, 1944

teenage girls, sewing classes for, 250

work programs, 203

Youth and Young Adult Ministry (CB)

missions, short-term, 2226

Youth Board, 154, *See also* Board of Christian Education; National Brethren Youth

National Brethren Youth, guidance for, 915

youth conferences

Elizabethtown College, 247

Rice Lake, WI, Church of the Brethren, 1107

youth director

Shamberger, Chauncey, 1171

Youth Fellowship, 203

Youth for Christ

Collitt, Robert B., 2166

evangelism, 461

Youth Incentive program

National Achievement Competition (NAC), 914

youth ministry, 2017, *See also* ministry

Elgin, IL, Highland Avenue Church of the Brethren, 436

Fellowship of Grace Brethren Churches, 2183

Fellowship of Grace Brethren Churches (FGBC), 484

Garber, Julie on, 2332, 2333

GBC Christian Education (Department), 533

missions, 859

Parish Ministries Commission involvement in, 993

Ramsey, Duane H. and, 2239

youth movement

Hutterian Society of Brothers, 639

peace movement, 2066

youth programs and organizations, 695, 1161, **1391–1392,** *1393,* 1394, *See also* Sunday school

Brethren Student Life Volunteers, 1231

King's Children Society, 695

Linz, Austria, 746

National Brethren Youth, 915

Oklahoma Live Wire Union, 992

student exchange, 1231

Student Volunteer Movement, 1231

Training in Missionary Endeavor (TIME), 1231, 1270

United Evangelical Church of Ecuador, 1290

West, Daniel, 1331

youth fellowship, **1394**

Youth Retreats

Dunkard Brethren Church, 2174

Youth Summer Crusaders

Hispanic Ministries (BC), 2198

The Youth's Advance, 1236, 1389, **1394,** 2108

Children at Work, 276

Eshelman, Matthew Mays, 455

Youth's Quarterly, 1237

The Youth's Teacher, 1236, 1237, **1394,** 2108

Ysenberg-Büdingen, 407, 545, **1394,** 2043

Eckartshausen, 421

Edict of 1712, 425

Ernst Casimir, *See* Ernst Casimir, count of Ysenburg-Büdingen

Himbach, 607

Marienborn territory of, 792

refuge for nonconformists, 990

Ysenburg-Büdingen-Marienborn congregation, 174

count of, *See* Karl August, count of Ysenburg-Büdingen-Marienborn

Yuba City, CA

congregation, 750, 1314

Queens Avenue Community Church, **1394**

Yucca Valley, CA, Grace Brethren Church, **1394**

Yugoslavia

relief and rehabilitation work, 200

work camps, 1367

Yundt, Carrie May (later Hoover), 628

Yundt, Simon E., 1821

Pomona, CA, Church of the Brethren, elder, 1045

Yunker, Robert, 1821

Yutzey, A. W., 424

Yutzy, Caroline, 2106

Yutzy, Emma (later Schrock), 2059

YWCA, *See* Young Women's Christian Association

Yzermans, Vincent A., 2108

Zabaugh family

Root River Church of the Brethren, MN, 1122

Zacher family

Prosser, WA, Community Grace Brethren Church, 1062

Zachman, Lee F., 1821

Zagaja, Professor, 2129

Zahn, Gordon, 2108

Zahn, Joseph, 1821

Zaiger, James D., 1306, 1395, 1862

works by, 2310

Zaire

General Conference Mennonite Church, 536

Gribble, Florence Alma Newberry, 573

Mennonite Brethren Churches, General Conference of, 814

Zakahi, Nathan M., 2298

Zalduando, P.R., 261

Zam Zam (ship)

missionaries voyaging to Africa on, 863

Oiness, Sylvia Marie, voyage to Africa on, 963

sinking of, 2032

Zambia

Kulp, Christina Masterton, 708

missions and missionaries in Brethren in Christ, 189

Zane, Harry

Simi Valley, CA, Grace Brethren Church, 1182

Zane, Margaret

Simi Valley, CA, Grace Brethren Church, 1182

Zanesville, OH, 1339

Zanetti, Herminia (later Siccardi), *See* Siccardi, Herminia Zanetti

Zarger family, 2076

Zarger, Mary, 2076

Zarger, Ulrich, 2076

Zargker family, 2076

Zartman, Emma S. (later Helser), 595

Zaug, Hans, 1401, 1872

Zayas, Irma

Hispanic Ministries (CB), 2199

Zayas, Irma R. (CB)

Rio Prieto, PR, Iglesia de los Hermanos (CB) and, 2243–2244

Zbinden, Nelly, 1850

Zeche, Adolfo, 53, 1386

Zeidig, Johanna Christina, 2060

Zeidig, Salome Margaret Sprogel, 994

Zeigler, Ada, 1838

Zeigler, Carl Wenger, Jr., 1821

Zeigler, Carl Wenger (CB) and, 2269

Zeigler, Carl Wenger, Sr., 109, 733, 1821, 2109, **2269, 2387**

Zeigler, Carole Mae, 1359, 2109, 2183

Zeigler, Curtis, 1821

Zeigler family, *See* Ziegler family

Zeigler, George W., 2269

Zeigler, Henry C., 1821

Zeigler, Jacob, 1397

Mack family, 778

Zeigler, Joseph, 153, 1821

Zeigler, Linda D. (later Loser), 2269

Zeigler, Moses M., 1821

Zeigler, Naomi Weaver, 2269

Zeigler, Philip, 279

Zeigler, S. D., 415

Zeigler, S. M., 1821

Zeigler, Sarah Mack, 1397

Mack family, 778

Zeigler/Ziegler family, 1994

Zeilasko family, 172–173

Zeilasko, John W., 172–173

Zeller, Harry Knode, 1821

Zeiler, Herbert, 373

Zeiler, Herbert D., 1348

Zeiser, Samuel R.

on mission of colonial German Protestants, 2365

Zelinsky, William, 2108

Zell family

Ephrata Area Grace Brethren Church, PA, 448

Zeller, Harry Knode, Jr., 714, **1395,** 1821, 2108, **2380**

Zeller, Harry Knode, Sr., 1395

Zeller, Herbert Dale, 1821

Zeller, Luella Mae Highbarger, 1395

Zeller, Roseann Elizabeth (later Angle), *446*

Zellers family

Grace Brethren Church of Canton, OH, 562

Zellner, Ada Delores, 1853

Zellner, Ada (later Taber), 1247

Zem, Jacob, 1821

Zeman, Jarold K., 2108

Zen family, 1944
Zentgraf, Johann Joachim, 2108
    answer to *Evangelischen Kirchen-Convents . . .,* 1959
Zerbey, Ella (later Elliott), 1929
Zerbey family, 1929
Zerfass family
    Spohn, Clarence E. on, 2358
Zerfass, Samuel Grant, 2105, 2108
Zerkel (Zirkle), Ludwig
    family history, 1979
Zern, Jacob, 105
Das Zeugniß eines Wieder-Gebornen, 2109
Zeugnisse der Wahrheit (*Testimonies of Truth*), 1255, 1355, **1395**, 2109
Zhongyi, Liu, 2129
Ziegler, Ada (later Good), 1397
Ziegler, Charles H., 1821
Ziegler, Dale T., 2307
Ziegler, Daniel C., 1397
Ziegler, Daniel P., 1395, 1821, 2109
Ziegler, David E., 2109
Ziegler, Earl Keller, 145, 1821, 2109, 2172
    historical writing, 612
    Mechanic Grove Church of the Brethren, PA, pastor, 806
Ziegler, Earl M., 672, 2110
Ziegler, Edward Krusen, 79, 190, 191, 461, 528, 672, 1314, **1395**, 1397, 1821, 1846, **2380, 2387, 2388**
    autobiography of, 2109
    poetry, 1039, 2365
    on prayers, 2365
    Roanoke, VA, Williamson Road Church of the Brethren, pastor, 1114
Ziegler, Elizabeth Kline, 1397
Ziegler, Elizabeth Smith, 1397
Ziegler, Elsie, 693
Ziegler, Elsie (later Kilhefner), 693
Ziegler, Emma King, 250, 1397, 1846, **2388**
Ziegler family, 700, *1396,* 1397, **1397,** 2077, 2109
    history of, 1912
    Myerstown, PA, Grace Brethren Church, 906
    Ziegler, John L. on, 2365
Ziegler, Gertrude Mohlin, 2109
Ziegler, Glen
    Mount Hope Church Home (DB), administrator, 881
Ziegler, Grace Ulmer, 1397
Ziegler, H. N., 417
Ziegler, H. Z., 1821
Ziegler, Hannah Horning, 1395, *1396*
Ziegler, Harriet E. Curry, 1395
Ziegler, Harry Horning, 1395, *1396,* 1821, 2109
Ziegler, Henry C., 1821
Ziegler house
    Little Swatara Church of the Brethren, PA, 750
Ziegler, Ilda M. Bittinger, 430, 1395, 1397, 1846
Ziegler, Ira A., 1305
Ziegler, Ira M., 1821
Ziegler, J. A. M., 2109
Ziegler, Jesse Conner, **1395,** *1396,* 1821, 2109
    Elizabethtown College, 437
Ziegler, Jesse H., 2, 190, 1388, 1389, **1395, 1397,** 1821, 2109–2110, 2307

historical writing, 612
Ziegler, John, 1397, 2109
Ziegler, John L.
    on Ziegler family, 2365
Ziegler, Kate Merkey, 1397
Ziegler, Katherine King, 1397
Ziegler, Kathryn, 720–721, 1397, 1846–1847, 2110
Ziegler, Kathryn Kline, 2109
Ziegler, Levi C., 1821
Ziegler, Levi John, 1821
Ziegler, Levi King, 21, 376, 695, 1323, **1397,** 1821–1822
Ziegler, Mamie Keller Leiter, 1397
Ziegler, Mary Conner, 1395
Ziegler, Mary Hunsberger, 1395, *1396*
Ziegler, Mary (later Hertzler), 600
Ziegler, Mary Vivolo, 1395
Ziegler, Michael, 2109
Ziegler, Nicholas, 2109
Ziegler, Peter, 2109
Ziegler, Philip, 1397, 2109
    Mason, Floyd R. on descendants of, 2345
    Mason, Kathryn Garst on descendants of, 2345
Ziegler, Philip (1764–___), 1822
Ziegler, Philip (1804–1874), 1822
Ziegler, Rebecca, 2110
Ziegler, Regina Reguel, 1397
    Mason, Floyd R. on descendants of, 2345
    Mason, Kathryn Garst on descendants of, 2345
Ziegler, Samuel H., 1822, 2110
Ziegler, William, 1397
Ziegler/Zeigler family, 1994
Zielasko, Jean Beveridge, 1854
    Zielasko, John Warlow (FGBC, CGBCI) and, 2269
Zielasko, John Warlow (FGBC, CGBCI), 1822, 1854, 2110, 2167, 2168, 2182, **2269–2270**
    Grace Brethren International Missions, 2191
    South Bend, IN, Ireland Road Grace Brethren Church, pastor, 1203
Zigler, Amy Arnold, **1397,** *1398,* 1398–1399, 2110
Zigler, Anna Miller, 1399
Zigler, Carl Huffman, 1822
Zigler, Daniel H., 2110
Zigler, David C., 1822
Zigler, David H., **1397,** 1822, 2374
Zigler, Earl Myers, **1397,** 1822, 1847
Zigler, Elizabeth Kline, 1399
    Mason, Floyd R. on, 2345
    Mason, Kathryn Garst on, 2345
Zigler, Elizabeth Myers, 1397
Zigler family, 405, 700, *1279,* 1318, *See also* Ziegler family
    Tunker House, 1279
Zigler, Geraldine, 1398
Zigler Hall, Brethren Service Center, New Windsor, MD, 198, 685
Zigler, Isaac Newton, 115, 1822
Zigler, Jacob Daniel, 733, 1822
Zigler, Jacob S., 1822
Zigler, John, 356, 1265, *1279,* 1399
    Mason, Floyd R. on, 2345
Zigler, John P., 1822
Zigler, Leona (later Row), 1125
Zigler, Michael Robert, 198, 199, 200, 233,

284, 286, 301, 302, 303, 308, 316, *435,* 510, 538, 540, 545, 569, 608, *608,* 683, 708, 742, 746, *1125,* 1246, 1273, 1279, 1345, 1368, *1368,* 1369, 1397, *1398,* **1398–1399,** 1822, 1884, 1922, 2108, 2110, 2111, 2143, 2374, **2380, 2387,** *See also* relief work
    biography of, 2201, 2326
    Durnbaugh, Donald F. on, 2325, 2326, 2327
    On Earth Peace, 974
    fiction about, 748
    Historic Peace Churches, 610
    historic sites, 609
    Interchurch Service to Greek Villages, 658
    interview with, 2111
    missions, 859
    On Earth Peace Assembly, 2235
    peace, 2000
    recollection of Andrew W. Cordier, 765
    Sollenberger, David on, 2357
    theology and, 2255
    tribute to, 2326
    World War I, 1371, 1398
    World War II, 1372, 1398
    Young Men's Christian Associations (YMCA), 1390, 1398
Zigler, Mary Knupp, 1398
Zigler, Mary (later Mason), 2185
Zigler, Michael, 396, 1398
Zigler, Naomi (later Rupel), 1397, 1843
Zigler, Rachel E. Myers, **1397,** 1847, **2387**
Zigler, Robert
    Son of M. R. Zigler, 726, 1398
Zigler, S. David, 1397
Zigler, Sadie (later Wampler), 2259
Zigler, Samuel, **1399,** 1822
Zigler, Samuel D., 1822
Zigler, Sara Christine (later Myers), 1842
    Myers, Minor Morton, wife of, 904
Zigler, Sarah Shank, 1397
Zigler, William Homer, 749, 1822, 2110
Zijpp, N. van der, 2110
Zikmund, Barbara Brown
    on clergy women, 2365
Zimbabwe
    missions and missionaries in Brethren in Christ, 189
Zimmerly, Jan Elaine (later Eagle), 2157
Zimmerman, Amos M., 2110
Zimmerman, Anna Martin, 2110
Zimmerman, C. W., 1822
Zimmerman, Caleb S., 366, 367, 1324, 1822, 2307
Zimmerman-Carpenter family, 1974
Zimmerman, Charles H., 2110
Zimmerman, Chester, 1822
Zimmerman, Christian, 2110
Zimmerman, David N., 2110
Zimmerman, Earle C., 2110
Zimmerman, Edwin R., 1822
Zimmerman, Elias Edward, 2110
Zimmerman, Esther Bauman, 2110
Zimmerman family, 262, 752, 2044, 2110
Zimmerman, H. Dale, 268, 1822
Zimmerman, Hans, 2110
Zimmerman, Jacob, 170, 1822
Zimmerman, Jacob Samuel, 1323, 1822
    Modesto, CA, Church of the Brethren, 866
Zimmerman, Johann Jakob, 686

Zimmerman, John, 1822
Zimmerman, John J., 2110
Zimmerman, Jonathan, 1822
Zimmerman, Joseph, 1822, 2110
Zimmerman meetinghouse
    Long Run Church of the Brethren, PA,
        756
Zimmerman, Noah Lauver, 1990
Zimmerman, OH, 1255, 1277
    Beaver Creek Old German Baptist
        Brethren Church, **1399**
Zimmerman, Rachel, 170
Zimmerman, Roscoe Earl, 1822
Zimmerman, Ruth, 366
Zimmerman, Samuel Peter, 1822
Zimmerman, William B., 1822
Zimmermann, Frederick, 2110
Zimmermann, Johann Jakob
    mention of, 1943
    Society of the Woman in the Wilder-
        ness, 1199
Zink, David, 1822
Zinn, Anneliese, 1847
Zinn, Daniel Willard, 1847
Zinn family
    family history and genealogy, 2002
Zinn, Philip Noel, 518, 1822
    Pleasant Grove Church of the Brethren,
        NC, pastor, 1031
    San Bernardino, CA, Church of the
        Brethren, pastor, 1141
Zinzendorf, Nikolaus Ludwig, Count von,
        40, 120, 309, 330, 334, 378, 923,
        1399, 2093
    Annual Meetings and Brethren polity,
        1042
    challenges made to Brethren, 176
    ecumenism, 423
    fraternal relations, 510
    Frey, Andreas, 517
    Great Awakening, 568
    Gruber, Johann Adam, 575
    Henckels, Johann Friedrich, 596
    Hildebrand, Johannes, 606
    Historic Peace Churches, 607
    influence of Spener, Philipp Jakob on,
        1209
    Koker, Jan de, involved with, 705
    Moravian Church, 875, 876, 1207
    Müller, Joseph, 894
    Pennsylvania Synods, 1007
    Pietism, 1022
    Rock, Johann Friedrich, friend of, 1116
    Ronneburg Castle, 1122
    visits to the German sects of
        Pennsylvania, 33, 40, 68
    Vogt, Peter on PA Synod and, 2361
Zion Bethel, IN
    Church of God (New Dunkers), 297
    New Dunkard meetinghouse and Uriah
        Patton, 996
Zion Brotherhood, 1965
Zion building, Ephrata Community, 448,
        1004, **1399–1400**
Zion Church of the Brethren, FL, *See* North
        Tampa, FL, Zion Church of the
        Brethren
Zion Church of the Brethren, MI, **1400**
Zion Church of the Brethren, ND, See
        Cando, ND, Church of the
        Brethren
Zion City, IL, **1400,** 1910
    Christian Catholic (Apostolic) Church,

281
    Dowie, John Alexander, 398
Zion congregations
    example of biblically inspired name,
        911
Zion Hill Brethren Church, OH, *See*
        Smithville, OH, First Brethren
        Church
Zion Hill Church of the Brethren, Colum-
        biana, OH, *1167,* **1400**
    Mahoning Church of the Brethren, OH,
        782
Zion Hill Community Church
    Smithville, OH, First Brethren Church,
        1192
Zion Hill, OH, Brethren Church, 694, 931
Zion, IL
    Ellis, Calvert Nice, 441
    Ellis, Charles Calvert, 441
Zion meetinghouse
    Eden Church of the Brethren, OH, 424
Zion, MI, 179
Zion, ND, 251
Zionitic Brotherhood, See also Ephrata
        Community
    Eckerlin, Emmanuel, 421
    Miller, Hans Michael, 837
Zionitic passport
    Hochmann von Hochenau, Ernst
        Christoph, 615
Zionitischer Weyrauchs Hügel (Zionitic Hill
        of Incense), **1400,** 2110
    Sauer and Beissel, controversy bet-
        ween, 2055
    Sauer, Johann Christoph, I, publisher
        of, 1147
Zira, David T., 306
Zirk, William Leroy, 494, 1822
Zirkle family, 1229, 2110
    history of, 1958
Zirkle, Gordon K., 2110, 2134
Zirkle, Mary R., 740
Zirkle, Ora Hamilton, 1822
    Middletown, IN, Church of the
        Brethren, pastor, 826
Zirkle (Zerkel), Ludwig
    family history, 1979
Zirkles family, 2077
ZME women's center, Nigeria, 2165
Zoahts, Nick
    Phoenix, AZ, Grace Brethren Church,
        1019
Zoar Society
    Sala, Solomon, 1136
Zobler, William Nicholas, 416, 1822
zodiac, signs of, 17
Zollers, Catherine (later Emmert), 1225
Zollers, Edward, 1400
Zollers, G. D., 1354
Zollers, George DeHaven, 602, **1400,** 1822,
        2110–2111
    Hope, Christian, 628
    South Bend, IN, City Church of the
        Brethren, elder, 1203
Zollers, Maria, 1400
Zook, Anna, 1834
Zook, Barbara King, 2111
Zook, Barbra, 2026
Zook, Bastian Jesse, 2111
Zook, Carl E., 1822, 2307
Zook, Catherine Scheublein, 1178
Zook, Charles A., 1822
Zook, Daniel, 1822–1823

Pleasant Hill Church of the Brethren,
        IA, elder, 1032
Zook, David, 2111
Zook, Edward Charles, 733, 1240, 1823
Zook, Edward E., 350
Zook, Elizabeth (later Leedy), 734
Zook, Emeline Bailey, 2111
Zook, F. R.
    Shippensburg, PA, Church of the
        Brethren, pastor in, 1177
Zook family, 251, 2111, See Zug family
    Harrisburg, PA, Melrose Gardens
        Grace Brethren Church, 586
Zook, Gerald Dean, 1285, 1823
Zook, Gorman A., 31, 567, 1823
    Osage Church of the Brethren, KS,
        minister, 983
Zook, Harry D.
    on Zub/Zuck/Zook family and descen-
        dants, 2365
Zook, J. Herbert, 2307
Zook, Jacob, 2026, 2105
Zook, John, 1178
Zook, John L., 1823
Zook, Joseph (Fairview, IA), 1823
Zook, Joseph (Udell, IA), 1285, 1823
Zook, Keith L., 350, 1823, 2307
    Pleasant Grove Grace Brethren Church,
        IA, pastor, 1031
    Rialto, CA, Grace Community Church,
        pastor, 1107
Zook, Leslie L., 2111
Zook, Lester, 1823
Zook, Lois Martin
    on early Brethren movement, fictional-
        ized account of, 2365
Zook, Loren
    Sacramento, CA, River City Grace
        Community Church, 1134
Zook, Lydia, 1902
Zook, Magdalena (later Sharp), See Sharp,
        Magdalena Zook
Zook, Margaret
    Sacramento, CA, River City Grace
        Community Church, 1134
Zook, Martin L., 2111
Zook, Mervin D., 2111
Zook, Ray E., 31, 496, 1823, 2111
    Root River Church of the Brethren,
        MN, pastor, 1122
Zook, Salome (later Sharp), See Sharp,
        Salome Zook
Zook, Wallace M., 1823
Zook (Zuck), David, 1823
Zook (Zuck), Frederick R., 1823
Zook (Zug) family, 1974, 2008
Zubly, John Joachim, 2111
Zuck, Abram Willis, 1823
Zuck, Carl W., 1823
Zuck, David Martin, 1823
Zuck, Evelyn, 1841
Zuck, Jacob Martin, 222, *679,* **1400–1401**
    article about, 1959
    Juniata College, 678, 1077
Zuck, John, 263, 1401, 1823
Zuck, Leah Musser
    National Older Adult Conferences,
        2229
Zuck, Lowell Hubert, 1823
Zuck, Lydia J. Bohrer, 1401
Zuck, Nevin Harold, 557, 670, 733, 1823,
        2111
Zuck, Paul L., 1823

Zuck, Susannah Martin, 1400, 1401
Zuckschwerdt, Otto S(alvatore) (Peter), 1823
Zuercher family, 2074
Zuercher, Tom L., 2298
Zug, ___ Bachmann, 1401
Zug, Abraham, 1823
Zug, Anna Heffelfinger, 1401
Zug, Anna (later Herr), 598
Zug, Barbara, 225
Zug, Barbara Bachman, 509
Zug, Benjamin, 1401
Zug, Benjamin Fox, 1823
Zug, Charles Keller, III, 2111
Zug, Christian, 1401
Zug, Elizabeth Ruhl, 1401
Zug family, **1401–1402**, 1927, 2089, 2111
    genealogy, 1913
    Royer family, related to, 1128
Zug, Fannie W. Shelley, 1401
Zug, Glenn C., 1823
    Ridgeway Community Church of the
        Brethren, PA, pastor, 1109
Zug, Henry S., 1823
Zug, Johannes, 756, 1340, **1401**, 1823
    marriage, 796
Zug, John, 1823
    Mohrsville Church of the Brethren, PA,
        elder, 869
Zug, John Cletus, 1823
    singing schools, 1185

Zug, Magdalena (later Frantz), 509, 532
Zug, Michael, 1940, 2111
Zug, Moritz, 1401
Zug, Samuel Ruhl, *103,* 205, 279, 586,
    2111, **1401**, *1401,* 1823
    hymnals, 642
Zug, Ulrich, 509, 1401
    marriage, 796
Zug, Venona (later Bomberger), 2138
Zug/Zuck/Zook family, 1974
    family history, 2008
    Zook, Harry D. on descendants of,
        2365
Zugabe Einiger Auserlesenen Lieder, 2111
Zumbrun, Brent, 1823
Zumbrun, Christian K., 1823
Zumbrun family, 2051
Zumbrun, Melvin J., 2298
Zumbrunnen, Albert, C., 2111
Zunkel, Alvin Paul, 1823
Zunkel, Charles Edward, 1330, **1402**, 1823,
    2111, 2307, **2380, 2387, 2388**
    Michigan City, IN, Church of the
        Brethren, part-time pastor, 825
    Ministry and Home Mission
        Commission (CB), 848
Zunkel, Charles Wayne, 193, 552, 759,
    1823, 2111
on Brethren evangelism, 2365
    on Brethren movement, 2365
Zunkel, Cleda Pearl Shull, 381, **1402**, 2111

    on Shull, Clara Gibson and descen-
        dants, 2365
    on Shull, William H. and descendants,
        2365
Zunkel family
    Shull family, related to, 1156
Zunkel, John W., 1823
Zunkel, Matilda Walters, 1402
Zunkel-Walter family, 2111
Zunkel, Walter R., 1402
Zurfluh, Abraham, 1997
Zürich, Switzerland, 28, 216
    Froelich (Fröhlich), Samuel Heinrich,
        518
    international Sunday school convention
        addressed by Brumbaugh, M. G.,
        1273
Zuwa, Nigeria, 306
Zwingli, Huldrych (Ulrich), 28
    In catabaptistarum strophas elenchus
        (Exposé of the Tricks of the
        Anabaptists), 348
    De peccato originali (*On Original Sin*),
        348
    prophecy, 1062
    Reformation, Protestant, 1091, 1092
    Reformed Church, 1092
Zwingli United Church of Christ, building
    use by Telford, PA,